Civil Liberties and Human Rights

This fourth edition has been extensively re-written in order to consider the impact of the Human Rights Act 1998 over the first seven years of its existence. It considers recent key domestic decisions in the post-Human Rights Act era, including *Campbell, A and Others v Secretary of State for the Home Dept, Ghaidan v Mendoza* and *R (Gillan) v Commissioner of Police of the Metropolis*.

Particular attention is paid to recent Labour legislation, especially in the fields of criminal justice and terrorism, including the Terrorism Acts 2005 and 2006 and the Serious and Organised Crime and Police Act 2005. A new chapter on developments in counter-terrorism law has been included for this edition. Important recent developments in the sphere of media freedom are also covered, including the impact of the Communications Act 2003, and in the field of anti-discrimination law, including the Equality Act 2006.

This book is a detailed, thought-provoking and comprehensive text that is valuable, not only for students, but also for all those interested in the development of human rights and civil liberties in the early years of the twenty-first century. This is an era in which human rights are coming increasingly under pressure – one in which terrorism concerns are dominating the political and legal agenda, but also one that has seen the inception of the Human Rights Act.

Helen Fenwick is Professor of Law at the University of Durham and Director of the Human Rights Centre.

Civil Liberties and Human Rights

Fourth edition

Helen Fenwick

Routledge·Cavendish
Taylor & Francis Group

Fourth edition published 2007
by Routledge-Cavendish
2 Park Square, Milton Park, Abingdon, Oxon OX14 4RN

Simultaneously published in the USA and Canada
by Routledge-Cavendish
270 Madison Ave, New York, NY 10016

Routledge-Cavendish is an imprint of the Taylor & Francis Group, an informa business

© 1994, 1998, 2002, 2007 Helen Fenwick

Previous editions published by Cavendish Publishing Limited

First edition 1994
Second edition 1998
Third edition 2002

Typeset in Times New Roman and Gill Sans by
Florence Production Ltd, Stoodleigh, Devon

Printed and bound in Great Britain by
CPI Antony Rowe, Chippenham, Wiltshire

British Library Cataloguing in Publication Data
A catalogue record for this book is available from the British Library

Library of Congress Cataloging in Publication Data
A catalog record for this book has been requested

ISBN10: 1–85941–937–2 (pbk)

ISBN13: 978–1–85941–937–3 (pbk)

For Paul, Clare, Daniel and Patrick

Contents

Preface   xiii
Table of cases   xv
Table of UK statutes   lvii
Table of UK statutory instruments   lxxvii
Table of national legislation from other jurisdictions   lxxxi
Table of treaties and conventions   lxxxiii
Table of EC legislation   xci

PART I
**Theories of rights; legal protection for rights and liberties
in the UK**   I

1   The nature of rights and liberties   5

   1 Where do rights derive from? 6
   2 What is meant by a right? 10

2   The European Convention on Human Rights   17

   1 Introduction 17
   2 The supervisory procedure for the Convention 20
   3 The substantive rights and freedoms 39
   4 Additional guarantees to the primary rights 106
   5 Restriction of the rights and freedoms 110
   6 Conclusions 112

**3   Methods of protecting civil liberties in the UK; the Bill of
Rights debate foreshadowing the Human Rights Act**   115

   1 Introduction 115
   2 Methods of protecting civil liberties in the UK 116
   3 The 'Bill of Rights' debate 140
   4 Conclusions 156

4   The Human Rights Act   **157**

1 Introduction 157
2 The choice of rights 165
*3 The interpretative obligation under s 3; the remedial process
    and pre-legislative scrutiny 169*
4 The position of public authorities under the Human Rights Act 215
5 Private bodies and indirect horizontal effect 249
*6 The stance of the judiciary in adjudicating on the Human
    Rights Act 256*
7 Scrutiny of the workings of the HRA 291
8 Conclusions 295

PART II
Expression   **299**

5   Restraining freedom of expression under the law of contempt   **316**

1 Introduction 316
2 Publications prejudicing proceedings: the strict liability rule 319
3 Intentionally prejudicing proceedings: common law contempt 363
4 Prior restraints restricting reports of court proceedings 383
5 Protecting justice as a continuing process 394
6 Disclosure of jury deliberations 398
7 Protection of sources 408

6   Offensive speech   **451**

1 Introduction 451
2 Law and pornography: theoretical considerations 453
3 Legal responses to explicit expression 461
4 Blasphemy, seditious libel, religious and racial hatred 484
5 Regulating broadcasting 509
6 The internet, films and videos 550
7 Conclusions 587

7   Official secrecy; access to state information   **590**

1 Introduction 590
2 Official secrets 592
3 Breach of confidence 616
4 Defence Advisory notices 624
*5 Freedom of information: general principles and the position
    prior to the 2000 Act 625*
6 The Freedom of Information Act 2000 630

8   Freedom of protest and assembly   **659**

   1 Introduction 659
   2 Rights to assemble and to protest 678
   3 Legal regulation of meetings and marches: the statutory
      framework 701
   4 Criminalisation of trespass and obstruction of the highway 733
   5 Breach of the peace, binding over and bail conditions 750
   6 Criminalising public disorder and anti-social behaviour 780
   7 Riot, violent disorder and affray 799
   8 Conclusions 800

PART III
The protection of privacy   **803**

9   Protection for personal information   **809**

   1 Introduction 809
   2 Protection for personal information under the Human Rights
      Act 813
   3 Broadcasting regulation and press self-regulation 830
   4 Specific reporting restrictions 851
   5 Trespass, defamation, harassment; proposals for a new privacy
      tort 866
   6 Liability for disclosing personal information under the new privacy
      doctrine 876
   7 The Data Protection Act 1998 920
   8 Balancing speech and privacy claims under the HRA 937
   9 Remedies 981
   10 Conclusions 990

10   Powers of the security and intelligence services; state surveillance;
search and seizure of property   **993**

   1 Introduction 993
   2 Police powers of entry and search 995
   3 Powers of the security and intelligence services 1010
   4 The interception of communications 1032
   5 State surveillance 1053
   6 The single tribunal 1080
   7 The Anti-Terrrorism, Crime and Security Act:
      acquisition of information 1090
   8 Conclusions 1097

PART IV
Personal liberty   1099

**11   Freedom from arbitrary search, arrest and detention;
suspects' rights in criminal investigations**   1101

   1 Introduction 1101
   2 Stop and search powers 1111
   3 Powers of arrest 1139
   4 Detention in police custody 1163

12   Police questioning: safeguards for suspects   1186

   1 Introduction 1186
   2 Police interviews 1192
   3 The right of access to legal advice 1208
   4 The right to silence 1234

13   Redress for police malpractice   1255

   1 Introduction 1255
   2 The Human Rights Act and trial remedies 1259
   3 Exclusion of evidence 1262
   4 Tortious remedies 1303
   5 Complaints against the police and disciplinary action 1310
   6 Prosecution of the police 1321
   7 Conclusions 1323

14   Anti-terrorism law and human rights   1328

   1 Introduction 1328
   2 Terrorism and human rights 1335
   3 The Terrorism Acts 2000 and 2006 – extending the ambit of
      the counter-terrorism scheme 1363
   4 The Anti-Terrorism, Crime and Security Act 2001, Part IV –
      the detention without trial scheme 1421
   5 The Prevention of Terrorism Act 2005 – control orders 1438
   6 Conclusions 1462

PART V
Equality and theories of anti-discrimination laws   1469

15   Anti-discrimination legislation   1476

   1 Introduction 1476
   2 Sources of anti-discrimination law 1479

3 *Domestic anti-discrimination measures 1486*

4 *Direct discrimination on grounds of sex, marital status, gender reassignment, race, disability, sexual orientation 1526*

5 *Indirect discrimination on grounds of sex, race or sexual orientation; disability-related discrimination 1538*

6 *Victimisation and harassment: sex, race, disability, sexual orientation 1556*

7 *Lawful discrimination 1567*

8 *Positive action: sex, race, disability, sexual orientation 1572*

9 *Remedial action: efficacy of the individual method 1586*

10 *The Commission for Racial Equality; the Equal Opportunities Commission; the Disability Rights Commission; the new Commission for Equality and Human Rights 1593*

11 *Conclusions 1600*

Index   1604

Preface

This fourth edition was completed six years after the third. The delay was partly due to the great changes that have occurred in the legal landscape in this field over that period of time, which made completing the fourth edition a daunting task. In writing this fourth edition the contradictions surrounding the Human Rights Act (HRA) have been thrown into sharp relief. On the one hand, it is beginning to bed down, and there has been, since the *Belmarsh* case in 2004 in the House of Lords, a sea-change in the judicial attitude towards it. The judges have, for the last three years, quite often shown that they treat the duty under s 6 HRA with a seriousness that was not apparent in the first few years of the HRA's life. In a series of cases, often related to counter-terrorism law, the judges have departed from the government's view as to justifiable infringements of liberty. On the other hand, since 9/11, the HRA has come under threat. For almost the whole of its existence it has been under attack, from the government, parts of the media and the Conservative party, largely on the ground that it stands in the way of an effective counter-terrorist policy. The tensions between the HRA and the four main counter-terrorist statutes introduced over the life of the Blair Government are explored in a lengthy new chapter, Chapter 14.

The second and third editions of this book were written during the early stage of the Blair Government, when a new era seemed to be dawning in Britain in human rights terms. This edition was completed at the end of the Blair years, at a time at which the future of the HRA looks highly uncertain in Britain. The future of human rights in Britain clearly does not depend only on the HRA; Britain would, of course, remain bound to the Convention rights at the international level; moreover, this book charts a number of other positive developments under the Labour Government, such as the Equality Act 2006 and the Freedom of Information Act 2000. But in some contexts, such as public protest, police powers, counter-terrorist powers, the HRA has proved crucial in protecting rights. The case for the HRA has not been made to the British public, allowing the Conservative Party to pass off the plan to repeal the HRA as an aid to counter-terrorist strategy, and a return to 'British values', in the sense that the less responsible sections of the media can and will present it in that way, playing on the ignorance of the British people as to the relationship between the HRA and the *European* Convention on Human Rights. The inception of the Commission for Equality and Human Rights in 2007 might have some counteractive effect in explaining the HRA to the British public and selling it to them as the protector of vulnerable persons, such as old people in care homes.

Contradictions are also evident in the judicial attitude to the HRA. This book traces the signs of the judicial acceptance of a constitutional human rights jurisdiction, held back at present to an extent by the House of Lords' decisions in *Ullah* and in *Price*. As Chapter 4, in particular, seeks to suggest, *Ullah* can be circumvented and in any event is in tension, not only with *R v A, A and Others (No 2)* (the 2005 'foreign torture evidence' judgment) and with *Campbell*, but with the whole enterprise of the HRA and the general approach in Britain to constitutional instruments. The tension between the approach that sees the HRA merely as a vehicle for giving easier access to the Convention domestically and the one that sees it as a constitutional human rights instrument is reaching a head, and forms one of the main themes of this book. It is perhaps somewhat ironic that, just at the moment when the HRA seems ready to step forward as a Bill of Rights, plans to repeal it to replace it with a 'British Bill of Rights' have been put forward by the Conservative Party and are also being considered by Gordon Brown.

The decision was taken in writing this new edition to reach for depth rather than breadth, and to that end certain chapters were dropped, in particular the chapter on freedom of movement. If this discipline is to retain some coherence and to move forward in a way that continues to appeal to students, it needs to be selective and to recognise how far it overlaps with others, such as employment law or immigration law.

I must acknowledge the contribution of all the people who helped in formulating the ideas expressed in this book. In relation to this edition my thanks are due to Aaron Baker, Senior Lecturer at Durham University, for reading and commenting on Chapter 15 and to Professor Gavin Phillipson of Durham University who commented on Chapter 4. Professor Colin Warbrick offered helpful criticism of early drafts of Chapters 2 and 3 of the first edition. Daniel Fenwick gave invaluable help at the proof stage of the book. I have drawn on certain of my articles and books as indicated at various points.

The main body of the text was completed by January 2007, but it was possible to add some later material in May and June 2007.

The book is dedicated with love and affection to Paul, Clare, Daniel and Patrick.

Durham
July 2007

Table of cases

A and Byrne and Twenty-Twenty Television v United
Kingdom (1998) 25 EHRR CD 159...................................946–48, 960, 968, 980
A and Others v Secretary of State for the Home Dept
[2004] UKHL 56; [2004] QB 335; [2005] 2 AC 68;
[2005] 2 WLR 87; [2005] 3 All ER 169, HL; [2002]
EWCA Civ 1202, CA... 202, 205, 260,
266, 282, 283, 287, 288, 290,
297, 1066, 1099, 1328, 1332,
1336, 1337, 1338, 1341, 1345–47,
1362, 1363, 1430–38, 1442, 1443,
1454, 1465, 1467
A (Disclosure of Medical Records to the GMC), Re,
[1998] 2 FLR 641...433
A Health Authority v X [2001] 2 FLR 673..433
A v B plc [2003] QB 195 ....254, 438, 883, 911
A v Secretary of State for the Home Department (No 2)
[2004] EWCA Civ 1123; [2005] 1 WLR 414, CA;
[2005] UKHL 71, HL...1345, 1454–60
A v UK (1999) 27 EHRR 611...46, 47, 75
ADT v UK (2001) 31 EHRR 33 82
Abdulaziz, Cabales and Balkandali v UK (1985) 7
EHRR 471 ....89, 109, 135, 1432
Abrahamsson and Anderson v Fogelqvist Case C-407/98
[2000] IRLR 732..1584
Absolam (1989) 88 Cr App R 332, CA............................1193, 1196, 1197,
1281, 1282, 1284
ACAS v Taylor EAT/788/97...1574
Ackroyd v Mersey Care NHS Trust [2003] EMLR 820.....................426–30, 434, 435,
437, 438
Aerts v Belgium [1998] EHRR 777.. 63
Abu Qatada and Secretary of State for the Home Dept
File No SC15/2002 1428
Ahmed v UK (1998) 5 BHRC 111; [1999] IRLR 188................................93, 98
Airedale NHS Trust v Bland [1993] AC 789; [1993] 1
All ER 821, CA and HL...42, 77

Airey v Ireland (1979) 2 EHRR 305 .... 63, 72
Aitken and Others (1971) (unreported) 593, 595
Akdivar v Turkey (1997) 23 EHRR 143 30
Aksoy v Turkey (1996) 23 EHRR 553 .... 46, 47, 1176, 1435
Al Fayed v Commissioner of Police for the Metropolis
    [2004] EWCA Civ 1579 1156
Albert v Lavin [1982] AC 546; [1981] 3 All ER 878,
    HL 755, 760, 761, 1111,
                                                                                              1140, 1142
Alexander v Home Office [1988] 1 WLR 968 1509
Ali v Office for National Statistics (2005) (unreported) 1527
Ambard v Attorney General for Trinidad and Tobago
    [1936] AC 322; [1936] 1 AII ER 704 396
Ambrose (1973) 57 Cr App R 782
American Cyanamid Co v Ethicon Ltd [1975] AC 396;
    [1975] 1 All ER 504, HL 378, 618, 984, 986–88
AMICUS v Secretary of State for Trade and Industry
    [2004] EWHC 860 .... 1571, 1572
Amin [1983] 2 AC 818, HL 1505, 1508
Amin [2000] 1 WLR 1071; [2000] Crim LR 174 1324
Amministrazione delle Finanze dello Stato v Simmenthal
    Case 106/77; [1978] ECR 629 138
Amuur v France (1996) 22 EHRR 533 55
Anderson [1972] 1 QB 304; [1971] 3 WLR 939; [1971]
    3 All ER 1152, CA 470, 471, 472
Anderson v UK Case No 33689/96; (1998) 25 EHRR
    CD 172; [1998] EHRR 218 .... 99, 697, 699, 749
Andronicou and Constantinou v Cyprus (1996) 22 EHRR
    CD 18; (1998) 25 EHRR 491 .... 41, 63, 1163
Anisminic Ltd v Foreign Compensation Commission [1969]
    2 AC 147, HL 1030, 1085
Anton Piller KG v Manufacturing Processes Ltd [1976]
    Ch 55; [1976] 1 All ER 779, CA 791, 1006
Anufrijeva and Another v Southwark London Borough
    Council [2004] QB 1124; [2004] 2 WLR 603 ....241, 244
Appleby v UK 6 May 2003 ....682, 699
Archer v Williams [2003] EMLR 38 982
Archibald v Fife Council [2004] IRLR 651 1553
Arrowsmith v Jenkins [1963] 2 QB 561; [1963] 2 All
    ER 210 ....679, 734, 737
Arrowsmith v UK No 7050/75, 19 DR 5 (1978) 98
Asch v Austria (1990) Case 30/1990/221/283;(1991) 15
    EHRR 597 66
Ashworth Hospital Authority v MGN Ltd [2002] 1
    WLR 2033; [2002] 4 All ER 193, HL; [2001] 1
    WLR 515; 1 All ER 991, CA 420–38, 448–50

Associated Provincial Picture House v Wednesbury
  Corporation [1948] 1 KB 223; [1948] 2 All ER 680, CA...................127–29, 131,
133, 273, 276, 277, 285, 288,
300, 447, 564, 649, 692, 693,
768, 783, 839, 1087, 1156,
1157, 1305, 1432, 1520
Association X v UK (1978) Appl No 7154/75; 75, 14 DR 31................................41, 42
Aston Cantlow and Wilmcote with Billesley Parochial
  Church Council v Wallbank [2004] 1 AC 546......................195, 219, 225–31, 240
Attorney General v Antigua Times Ltd [1976] AC 16..151
Attorney General v Associated Newspapers and Others
  [1994] 1 All ER 556; (1994) 142 NLJ 1647...399
Attorney General v BBC [1981] AC 303; [1980] 3 WLR 109, HL............................349
Attorney General v BBC (1992) The Independent, 3 January...................................350
Attorney General v BBC 1 December 1995 (unreported)..346
Attorney General v BBC, Same v Hat Trick Productions
  Ltd (1996) The Times, 26 July..341, 345, 354
A-G v BBC [2001] EWHC Admin 1202...350
Attorney General v Birmingham Post and Mall Ltd [1998]
  4 All ER 49...340, 347
Attorney General v Blake [2001] 1 AC 268..611
Attorney General v English (Dr Arthur's case) [1983]
  1 AC 116; [1982] 2 All ER 903, HL...............................125, 351–55, 357–58, 360
Attorney General v Express [2005] EMLR 13...351
Attorney General v Guardian Newspapers Ltd (No 1)
  (Spycatcher litigation) [1987] 3 All ER 316; [1987]
  1 WLR 1248, CA and HL..618, 619, 951
Attorney General v Guardian Newspapers (No 2)
  (Spycatcher litigation) [1990] 1 AC 109; [1990] 3
  WLR 776; [1988] 3 All ER 545, HL.................................595, 597, 617–22,
810, 877, 887, 897, 900, 920
Attorney General v Guardian Newspapers (No 3)
  [1992] 1 WLR 874; [1992] 3 All ER 38, CA.....................350, 359, 388, 415
Attorney General v Guardian Newspapers [1999]
  EMLR 904...345, 347–48, 353–56
Attorney General v Guardian Newspapers [2001] EWCA
  Crim 1351...388, 389
Attorney General v Hislop and Pressdram [1991] 1 QB
  514; [1991] 1 All ER 911; [1991] 2 WLR 219, CA.........................338, 341, 342,
345, 350, 359, 368, 381
Attorney General v Independent TV News and Others
  [1995] 2 All ER 370...342, 343, 353
Attorney General v Jonathan Cape [1976] QB 752...616
Attorney General v Jones and BBC (1995) (unreported)...341
Attorney General v Leveller Magazine Ltd [1979] AC 440;
  [1979] 2 WLR 247, HL...384, 390

Attorney General v MGN [1997] 1 All ER 456..........................340, 342, 344, 353, 356
Attorney General v MGN (1997) EMLR 284 340
Attorney General v MGN [2002] EWHC 907 351
Attorney General v New Statesman [1981] QB I...405, 406
Attorney General v News Group Newspapers [1987] 1
   QB 1; [1986] 2 All ER 833; [1986] 3 WLR 365, CA 332, 340, 342
Attorney General v News Group Newspapers plc [1989]
   QB 110; [1988] 3 WLR 163; [1988] 2 All ER 906......................363–66, 368, 395
Attorney General v News Group Newspapers (1999)
   (unreported)..343
Attorney General v Newspaper Publishing plc (1990)
   The Times, 28 369
Attorney General v Newspaper Publishing plc (*Spycatcher*)
   [1988] Ch 333; [1987] 3 All ER 276; [1988] 3 WLR
   942, CA..124, 364
Attorney General v Newspaper Publishing plc (No 2)
   (*Spycatcher*) [1990] 1 AC 109; [1990] 3 WLR 776;
   [1988] 3 All ER 545, HL 381, 382
Attorney General v Newspaper Publishing plc and Others
   [1997] 3 All ER 159; (1997) The Times, 2 May, CA.................................369
Attorney General v Punch, 6 October 2000 (unreported), QB 371
Attorney General v Punch [2003] 1 AC 1046; [2003] 2
   WLR 49; [2003] 1 All ER 289 ....365, 370–82
Attorney General v Scotcher [2005] 1 WLR 1867 ....402, 403, 406, 408
Attorney General v Sport Newspapers Ltd [1991] 1
   WLR 1194..365, 366
Attorney General v Times Newspapers Ltd [1974] AC
   273; [1973] 3 All ER 54; [1973] 3 WLR 298, HL 335, 336, 339, 358, 395
Attorney General v Times Newspapers Ltd [1992] 1 AC
   191; [1991] 2 All ER 398; [1991] 2 WLR 994, HL.............................329, 333, 363,
   369, 370
Attorney General v Times Newspapers Ltd (*Tomlinson* case)
   (2001) EMLR 19...623, 895
Attorney General v Times Newspapers Ltd and Others
   (1983) The Times, 12 February, DC 340, 346, 353, 358
Attorney General v TVS Television, Attorney General v
   HW Southey & Sons (1989) The Times, 7 July....................................359, 360
Attorney General v Unger (1998) EMLR 280 ....342, 348, 353, 354
Attorney General ex rel McWhirter v IBA [1973] QB
   629, CA...477
Attorney General for New South Wales v Trethowan [1932]
   AC 526 155
Attorney General of Hong Kong v Lee Kwong-Kut [1993]
   AC 951 273
Attorney General's Reference (No 3 of 1999) [2001] 2
   WLR 56, HL 1077, 1290, 1291,
   1324, 1325

Attorney General's Reference (No 3 of 2000) [2001]
    Crim LR 645 1299
Attorney General's Reference (No 4 of 2002) [2003]
    EWCA Crim 762; [2003] 3 WLR 1153; [2004] 1
    All ER 1 .... 1390, 1391, 1394,
                                                                                                                      1409, 1464
Attorney General's Reference (No 1 of 2004) [2004] 1
    WLR 211 178
Attorney General's Reference (No 4 of 2004) [2004]
    UKHL 43; [2005] 1 AC 264; [2005] 1 All ER 237 .... 1337, 1354, 1355, 1356
Austin and Saxby v Commissioner of Police of the
    Metropolis [2005] HRLR 20; [2005] EWHC 480 .... 125, 703, 722,
                                                                                                                  723, 763–71, 801,
                                                                                                                      1157, 1308
Austria v Italy (1961) Appl No 788/60 4 YB 112 1278
Autronic AG v Switzerland (1990) 12 EHRR 485 36
Averill v UK (2001) 31 EHRR 36; (2000) The Times,
    20 June 65, 1209, 1211–15, 1221,
                                                                                                                  1234, 1240, 1277
Aydin v Turkey (1997) 25 EHRR 251 47
Aziz v Trinity St Taxis [1988] WLR 79; [1988] 2 All
    ER 860, CA 1563–65

B (A Minor), Re, [1981] 1 WLR 1421, CA 42
B v Chief Constable of Avon and Somerset Constabulary
    [2001] 1 WLR 340 .... 790, 792
B v France (1992) 16 EHRR 1; (1992) 13 HIRLJ 358 .... 70, 85, 86, 95
B v UK (1983) 34 D & R 68; (1983) 6 EHRR 354 81
BB v United Kingdom (2004) 39 EHRR 635 243
BBC Scotland v UK (1998) 25 EHRR CD 179 .... 234, 324, 325, 326,
                                                                                                                  329, 331, 354, 355
Badek and Others v Landesanwalt bein Staatgerichtshof
    des Landes Hessen (Case C-158/97) [2000] All ER
    (EC) 289 1584
Badham [1987] Crim LR 202 1005
Baggs v UK (1987) 52 DR 29 90
Bailey v Williamson (1873) LR 8 QB 118 678
Baldry v Director of Public Prosecutions of Mauritius
    [1983] 2 AC 297; [1982] 3 All ER 973 396
Balfour v Foreign and Commonwealth Office [1994] 2
    All ER 588 .... 1088, 1343
Barber and Others v NCR (Manufacturing) Ltd [1993]
    IRLR 95 1501
Barbéra, Messegué and Jabardo, Judgment of 6 December
    1988, A 14 6(2) (1989) 64, 65, 1188, 1263
Barclay v UK (1999) Appl No 35712/97 .... 816, 826, 945
Barreto v Portugal [1996] 26 EHRR 214 71

Barrett v Enfield LBC [1999] 3 All ER 193..62
Barry v Midland Bank [1999] 1 WLR 1465...1543
Barrymore v NGN Ltd [1997] FSR 600......................881, 887, 902, 903, 910, 916
Barton v Investec [2003] ICR 1205...1560
Bates v UK (Appl No 26280/95)...1351
Baynton v Saurus [1999] IRLR 604...1549
Beales [1991] Crim LR 118..1272
Beatty v Gillbanks (1882) 9 QBD 308   691, 723, 772, 773,
                                                                778, 779
Beckles v UK (2002) 36 EHRR 162...1246, 1249, 1327
Belgian Linguistic Case (No 2), Judgment of 23 July
  1968, A 6; (1968) 1 EHRR 252..62, 70, 105
Belilos v Switzerland (1988) EHRR 466...112
Bellinger v Bellinger [2001] EWCA Civ 1140; [2003]
  2 AC 467...86, 179, 182, 185, 186
Benham v UK (1996) 22 EHRR 293...789, 792, 1342, 1410
Bensaid v UK [2001] 33 EHRR 10..863, 961, 967
Bentham v UK, B 80 (1983)...61
Benthem v Netherlands (1985) 8 EHRR 1...63
Bentley v Brudzinski [1982] Crim LR 825; (1982) The
  Times, 3 and 11 March..1110
Benveniste v University of Southampton [1989] IRLR 122.................................1499
Berktay v Turkey (Application No 22493/93 March 1, 2001)......................766, 769
Bernstein v Skyviews & General Ltd [1978] QB 479;
  [1977] 2 All ER 902..994
Beycan [1990] Crim LR 185..1231
Bibby v Chief Constable of Essex (2000) The Times,
  24 April...779
Bilka-Kaufhaus GmbH v Weber von Hartz [1986] IRLR
  317; [1986] CMLR 701...1498, 1501–03, 1540,
                                                                1541, 1547, 1549
Birch v Director of Public Prosecutions [2000] Crim
  LR 301..735–37
Birmingham City Council ex p EOC [1989] AC 1155;
  [1989] 1 All ER 769, HL...1527, 1537
Birse v HM Advocate (2000) (unreported)...1009
Black v Director of Public Prosecutions (1995) (unreported)..............................1116
Blackledge and Others (Ordtech) [1996] 1 Cr App R 326, CA..............................370
Bladet-Tromsø v Norway (1999) 6 BHRC 599..623
Blair v Associated Newspapers (Case no HQ0001236)...............................889, 894
Blake [1989] 1 WLR 432, CA...1281
Blake [1991] All ER 481...1272
Bonnard v Perryman [1891] 2 Ch 269, CA..368
Borowski v AG of Canada (1987) 39 DLR (4th) 731..80
Botta v Italy (1998) 26 EHRR 241...71, 1483
Bouamar v Belgium, Judgment of 29 February, A 129
  (1988); [1988] 11 EHRR I...54

R v Bowden (1999) The Times, 25 February... 1245, 1249
Bowers v Hardwick [1986] 478 US 186 82
Bowman v UK (1998) 25 EHRR 1 93
Boyle v Rice, Judgment of 27 April 1988, A 131.. 90
Bozano v France (1986) 9 EHRR 297..55, 57
Brannigan and McBride v UK Series A 258-B (1993);
    (1993) 17 EHRR 539 and 594; (1993) The Times,
    28 May..37, 57, 111, 1168–70
Brennan v UK (2002) 34 EHRR 18 ....1209–14, 1225, 1240
Brickley and Kitson v Police (1988) Legal Action, July 706
Bridges v California (1941) 314 US 252..398
British Gas v Sharma [19911] ICR 19; [1991] IRLR 101 1588
British Steel Corporation v Granada Television [1981] AC
    1096; [1981] 1 All ER 417, HL..410, 419, 424, 916
Broadcasting Complaints Commission ex p Granada TV
    Ltd (1993) The Times, 31 May; affd [1995] EMLR
    163; (1994) The Times, 16 December, CA...839
Broadcasting Standards Commission ex p BBC [2000] 3
    WLR 1327..818, 839, 848, 849
Brogan, Coyle, McFadden and Tracey v UK, Judgment
    of 29 November 1988, A 145; (1989) 11 EHRR 117...................37, 57, 111, 135,
                                                                    1148, 1167–70
Brokdorf Case (1985) 69 BVerfGE 315...572, 665
Brown [1993] 2 WLR 556; [1993] 2 All ER 75, HL.. 83
Brown v Stott [2001] 2 WLR 817; [2001] 2 All ER 97,
    PC...176, 184, 190, 261, 268,
                                                    271, 693, 1252, 1253, 1261,
                                                                    1279, 1325
Brown v TNT Express Worldwide (UK) Ltd [2001]
    ICR 182...1563
Bruggemann and Scheuten v Federal Republic of Germany
    (1975) 10 DR 100 89
Brutus v Cozens [1973] AC 854; [1972] 2 All ER 1297;
    [1972] 3 WLR 521; (1973) 57 Cr App R 538, HL....................................782
Bryan v UK (1995) 21 EHRR 342.. 63
Bryce [1992] 4 All ER 567; (1992) 95 Cr App R 230;
    (1992) 142 NLJ 1161, CA..1297
Buchholz, Judgment of 6 May 1981, A 42 63
Buckley v UK (1997) 23 EHRR 101 89
Bugdaycay v Secretary of State for Home Affairs [1987]
    AC 514, HL 129
Burden v Rigler [1911] 1 KB 337...680
Burden v UK (2006) App no 93378/05 203
Burton v UK (1996) 22 EHRR 135 CD...90
Burton and Another v De Vere Hotels [1996] IRLR 596;
    (1996) The Times, 3 October.................................... 1517, 1558, 1561, 1562

C v UK (1989) 61 DR 285..324, 326
CRE ex p Westminster City Council [1984] IRLR 230,
    QBD...1535
Cable and Others v UK, Appl No 24436/94; (1999)
    The Times, 11 March...63
Caesar-Gordon ex p University of Liverpool [1990] 3
    All ER 821..679
Calder (John) Publishing v Powell [1965] 1 QB 159;
    [1965] 1 All ER 159...470
Calder and Boyars [1969] 1 QB 151; [1968] 3 WLR 974;
    [1968] 3 All ER 644; [1968] 52 Cr App R 706, CA............470, 471, 472
Cambridge Health Authority ex p B [1995] WLR 898;
    (1995) TLR 159, CA...131
Camelot Group Ltd v Centaur Communications [1998]
    EMLR 1; [1999] QB 124.............................272, 415–19, 450
Camenzind v Switzerland, RJD 1997-III 2880..............................72
Cameron v Network Rail [2006] EWHC 1133 QB........................218
Campbell v Frisbee [2002] EMLR 31...957
Cambell v MGN [2004] 2 WLR 1232; [2004] 2 AC 457..........253–55, 297, 430, 431,
                                                          438, 449, 701, 826, 863–65,
                                                          851, 867, 875, 878, 882, 884,
                                                          888, 889, 893, 895, 911–15,
                                                          919, 920, 932–35, 938, 957–59,
                                                          963, 965, 968, 969, 970, 972,
                                                          976, 977, 979, 982, 991,
                                                          1180, 1181
Campbell v UK (1992) 15 EHRR 137..91
Campbell and Cosans v UK, Judgment of 25 February
    1982, A 48; (1982) 4 EHRR 293.........................47, 74, 105
Campbell and Fell v UK, Judgment of 28 June 1984,
    A 80; (1985) 7 EHRR 165...61, 1400
Campbell and Hartley v United Kingdom (1990) 13
    EHRR 157.............................1152, 1143, 1160, 1164
Canale [1990] 91 Cr App R 1; [1990] All ER 187, CA.................1276
Capon v DPP Case CO/3496/97 Judgment 4 March
    1998, LEXIS transcript; [1998] Crim LR 870–75...........673, 740, 742, 743,
                                                          747, 748
Castells v Spain A 236; Judgment of 23 April 1992;
    (1992) 14 EHRR 445...94
Castorina v Chief Constable of Surrey (1988) 138 NLJ
    180, CA...1151–56
Caunt (1947) 64 LQR 203..487
Central Criminal Court ex p Crook [1995] 1 WLR 139;
    (1984) The Times, 8 November..............................391, 971
Central Criminal Court ex p Francis and Francis [1989]
    AC 346; [1988] 3 All ER 375; [1988] 3 WLR 989, HL..........1003, 1009

Central Independent Television plc and Others, Re, [1991]
1 All ER 347; [1991] 1 WLR 242...387
Chahal v UK (1997) 23 EHRR 413....................................49, 53, 55, 58, 1343,
1344, 1359, 1360, 1423,
1424, 1437, 1450, 1457
Chalkley and Jeffries [1998] 2 All ER 155; [1998] 3
WLR 146; [1998] 2 Cr App R 79, CA...................................126, 1157, 1266, 1286,
1290, 1291, 1324
Chamberlain and Emezie v Emokpae; Webster v Brunel
University 8 February 2004, (unreported)... 1528, 1586
Chandler v Director of Public Prosecutions [1964] AC 763;
[1962] 3 AII ER 142, HL...594
Chapman v Director of Public Prosecutions (1988) Cr App
R 190; [1988] Crim LR 843.. 1154, 1155
Chappel v UK (1990) 12 EHRR 1; No 1258/86 (1987);
(1988) 10 EHRR 510...90, 687, 688, 725
Chappell & Co Ltd v Columbia Gramophone Co [1914]
2 Ch 745..874
Chassagnou v France (1999) 7 BHRC 151, Judgment of
29 April 1999; (2000) 29 EHRR 615 ....230, 435, 737
Cheall v UK (1985) 8 EHRR 74..97
Chief Constable for Devon and Cornwall ex p CEGB
[1982] QB 458 753
Chief Constable of Avon ex p Robinson [1989] All ER
15; [1989] 1 WLR 793 1223
Chief Constable of Kent Constabulary ex p Kent Police
Federation Joint Branch Board and Another (1999)
The Times, 1 December 1164
Chief Constable of Lancashire ex p Parker and McGrath
[1993] 2 WLR 428; [1993] 1 All ER 56;(1992)142
NLJ 635 999, 1001, 1002
Chief Constable of North Wales Police ex p Thorpe [1999]
QB 396..917, 970
Chief Constable of Sussex ex p International Ferry Traders
Ltd [1999] 2 AC 418; [1999] 1 All ER 129 ....273, 692, 748
Chief Constable of West Midlands Police ex p Wiley,
Chief Constable of Nottinghamshire Police ex p
Sunderland [1995] 1 AC 274; [1994] 3 All ER 420;
(1995) 1 Cr App R 342, HL..1320
Chief Constable of West Yorkshire Police ex p Khan (2001)
The Times, 16 October, HL; [2000] IRLR 324; [2000]
ICR 1169, CA.. 1563, 1565
Chief Metropolitan Magistrates' Court ex p Choudhury
[1991] 1 QB 429; [1991] 1 All ER 306...................................137, 486, 487, 492, 493
Chorherr v Austria A 266-B (1993)...69, 97, 321, 681,
686, 697, 759

Christian Lawyers Assoc of South Africa v The Minister
    of Health 1998 (11) BCLR 1434 80
Christians Against Racism and Fascism v UK (1984)
    24 YB ECHR 178; No 8440/78; 21 DR 138 ....97, 709, 729
Christie v UK (1993) No 21482 / 93, 78-A DR E Com
    HR 119 ....1026, 1027, 1029, 1043,
                                                                          1044, 1046, 1061,
                                                                          1074, 1089
Christou [1992] QB 979; [1992] 4 All ER 559, CA 1296, 1297
Clarke v General Accident Fire and Life Assurance
    Corp plc [1998] 1 WLR 1647 174
Clarke v Eley IMI Kynoch Ltd [1983] ICR 703 1540
Clegg [1995] 2 WLR 80 45
Clerkenwell Metropolitan Stipendiary Magistrate ex p
    The Telegraph and Others [1993] 2 All ER 183;
    (1992) The Times, 22 October 386
Clymo v Wandsworth LBC [1989] ICR 250 1544
Coco v AN Clark (Engineers) Ltd [1969] RPC 41 ....877, 882, 899, 901, 920
Coffin v Smith (1980) Cr App R 221 1110
Cohen v California (1971) 403 US 15 ....307, 491
Colloza v Italy, Judgment of 12 February 1985, A 89;
    (1985) 7 EHRR 516 64
Commission v France (Case 318/86); [1989] 3 CMLR 663;
    [1988] ECR 3559 ....1579–81, 1583–85
Condron v UK [2001] 31 EHRR 1, Appl No 35718/97;
    [2000] Crim LR 679; Judgment of 2 May 189, 1246, 1247,
                                                                          1249, 1325
Condron and Another [1997] 1 Cr App R 185; (1997)
    161 JP 1; (1996) The Times, 4 November, CA 1244, 1245
Conegate Ltd v Customs and Excise Commissioners
    [1987] QB 254; [1986] 2 All ER 688 479
Confait Case Report of the Inquiry by the Hon Sir Henry
    Fisher, HC 90 (1977-78) 1103, 1230, 1267
Connors v UK [2006] 40 EHRR 189 197
Constantine v Imperial Hotels [1944] KB 693 1507
Corelli v Wall (1906) 22 TLR 532 873
Cosgrove v Caesar and Howie [2001] IRLR 653 1548
Cossey v UK, Judgment of 27 September 1990, A 184;
    (1990) 13 EHRR 622 ....38, 39, 85, 95, 103
Costello-Roberts v UK, Judgment of 25 March 1993,
    A 247-C; (1993) 19 EHRR 112; (1993) The Times,
    26 March 47, 75, 76
Council of Civil Service Unions v Minister for Civil Service
    (GCHQ) [1985] AC 374; [1985] 3 WLR 1174; [1984]
    3 All ER 935, HL 100, 127
Council of Civil Service Unions v UK (1987) No 11603/85,
    50 DR 228; (1988) 10 EHRR 269 ....37, 101

Cox [1993] Crim LR 382 1196
Coyne v UK, Judgment of 24 October 1997; RJD
  1997-V 1842..63
CRE ex p Prestige Group plc [1984] 1 WLR 335;
  [1984] ICR 473...1594-98
CRE v Dutton [1989] WLR 17; [1989] 1 All ER 306, CA...........................1508
Cream Holdings Ltd and others v Banerjee [2004] 3
  WLR 918... 355, 378, 379, 622,
  957, 988-91
Creation Records Ltd v News Group Newspapers Ltd
  [1997] EMLR 444...900
Crémieux v France (1993) 16 EHRR 357 91
Crown Court at Snaresbrook ex p Director of Public
  Prosecutions [1988] QB 532; [1988] 1 All ER 315...............................1003
Culnane v Morris [2006] 2 All ER 149...183
Cumming v Chief Constable of Northumbria Police
  [2003] EWCA Civ 1844 .... 1152, 1153
Cyprus v Turkey (1976) 4 EHRR 482 89

D v UK (1998) 24 EHRR 423.. 46, 194
Daily Express Case (1981) The Times, 19 December..............................359
Dallison v Caffrey [1965] 1 QB 348; [1964] 3 WLR
  385, CA 1151
Darbo v Director of Public Prosecutions [1992] Crim
  LR 56; (1992) The Times, 4 July...475
Dattani v Chief Constable of West Mercia Police (2005),
  (unreported)..1536
Davis, Rowe and Johnson [1993] 1 WLR 613 1076
Dawkins v Department of Environment [1993] ICR 517............1508
de Freitas v Permanent Secretary of Ministry of Agriculture,
  Fisheries, Lands and Housing [1999] 1 AC 69.................. 286, 287, 289, 406,
  407, 414, 416, 430, 434,
  439, 449
De Geouffre de la Pradelle v France (1993) HRLJ 276 106
De Haes and Gijsels v Belgium (1997) 25 EHRR 1 64
De Jong, Baljet and Van de Brink, Judgment of 22 May
  1984, A 77; (1984) 8 EHRR 20...59
De Souza v Automobile Association [1986] ICR 514.............. 1557, 1569
De Vargattirgah v France (1981) Appl 9559/81 30
De Wilde, Ooms and Versyp v Belgium (1971) EHRR 373.............91
Dekker v VJV Centrum [1991] IRLR 27; [1990] ECR I-3941 .... 1530, 1532
Dehal v Crown Prosecution Service [2005] EWHC 2154 .... 506, 507, 736,
  745, 783, 785, 797
Delaney (1989) 88 Cr App R 338; (1988) The Times,
  20 August, CA..1274, 1275, 1286
Derbyshire v St Helen's Metropolitan BC [2006] ICR 90 1566

Derbyshire County Council v Times Newspapers [1992]
3 All ER 65, CA; [1993] AC 534; [1993] 1
All ER 1011; [1992] 3 WLR 28, HL.....................................125, 126, 128, 130, 137,
152, 203, 303

Director of Public Prosecutions ex p Kebilene and Others
[1999] 4 All ER 801; [1999] 3 WLR 372, HL........................ 178, 204, 265, 271,
272, 273, 280, 690, 691, 693,
695, 817, 829, 830, 957, 1260,
1337, 1347–53, 1369, 1405,
1413, 1464

Director of Public Prosecutions ex p Treadaway (1997)
The Times, 18 November 1180, 1305, 1316

Director of Public Prosecutions v A and BC Chewing
Gum Ltd [1968] 1 QB 159..472

Director of Public Prosecutions v Bayer [2003] EWHC
2567 (Admin); 167 JP 666; [2003] All ER (D) 28
(Nov), High Court 744

Director of Public Prosecutions v Billington [1988] All
ER 435; (1988) Cr App R 68...1280

Director of Public Prosecutions v Blake [1989] 1 WLR
432, CA..1108, 1172, 1281

Director of Public Prosecutions v Capon: see Capon v DPP

Director of Public Prosecutions v Channel Four Television
Co Ltd and Another [1993] 2 All ER 517; (1992)
The Times, 14 September...443, 445, 446

Director of Public Prosecutions v Clarke [1992] Crim
LR 60 ....784, 788, 789, 796

Director of Public Prosecutions v Fidler [1992] 1 WLR 91 ....782, 783

Director of Public Prosecutions v Hawkins [1988] 1 WLR
1166; [1988] 3 All ER 673.. 1159, 1160

Director of Public Prosecutions v Jones and Lloyd [1997]
2 All ER 119, DC; [1999] 2 WLR 625; [1999] 2 All
ER 257; [1999] AC 240, HL...126, 692, 700, 711–21,
725, 730, 745

Director of Public Prosecutions v Jones [2002] EWHC 110.............723, 726, 727, 735

Director of Public Prosecutions v Jordan [1977] AC 699, HL..................473

DPP v Meaden [2003] EWHC 3005 (Admin); [2004] 1
WLR 945..724

Director of Public Prosecutions v Morgan [1976] AC 182...................869, 870

Director of Public Prosecutions v Moseley, Woodling and
Selvanayagam, Judgment of 9 June 1999; The Times
23 June 1999; [1999] J Civ Lib 390 ....126, 793, 795

Director of Public Prosecutions v Orum [1988] 3 All ER 449 782

Director of Public Prosecutions v Rouse; Same v Davis
(1992) Cr App R 1108

Director of Public Prosecutions v Whyte [1972] AC 849;
[1972] 3 All ER 12, HL...470, 471

Director of the Serious Fraud Office ex p Smith [1993]
   AC 1; [1992] 3 WLR 66..1250
Djeroud v France (1991) A 191-B..89
Doe v Bolton (1973) 410 US 179; (1973) 35 L E 2d 201.......................76
Donelly v Jackman (1970) Cr App R 229; [1970] 1 WLR 562 1110
Dornan v Belfast County Council [1990] IRLR 179...............1528, 1536
Douglas (Michael, Catherine Zeta-Jones, Northern and
   Shell plc) v Hello! Ltd [2001] 2 WLR 992; [2001]
   2 All ER 289; [2001] QB 967, CA................252, 254, 366, 378, 431,
                                              701, 838, 867, 875, 882, 883,
                                              890, 902–12, 970, 983, 985,
                                              986, 987, 1180, 1181
Douglas v Hello! Ltd (No 3) [2005] EWCA 595...........826, 894, 911, 982, 983
Driskel v Peninsula Business Services Ltd [2000]
   IRLR 151 1561
Dudgeon v UK, Judgment of 22 October 1981, A 45;
   (1982) 4 EHRR 149...70, 72, 76, 81, 82,
                                              98, 746, 803, 976, 1571
Duncan v Jones [1936] 1 KB 218..663, 772
Dunn (1990) 91 Cr App R 237; [1990] Crim LR 572, CA 1285
Durant v Financial Services Authority [2003] EWCA Civ
   1746; [2004] FSR 28..927

Ex p United States Tobacco [1992] 1 QB 353.................................131
East African Asians cases (1973) 3 EHRR 76 ....25, 48, 98, 108
Eckle A 51; (1982) 5 EHRR 1...60
Editor of New Statesman (1928) 44 TLR 301...............394, 396, 397
Edward Fennelly [1989] Crim LR 142........................1138, 1288, 1289
Edwards v Director of Public Prosecutions (1993) 97
   Cr App R 301; (1993) The Times, 29 March........................1144–46
Edwards v UK (1992) 15 EHRR 417; (1993) The Times,
   21 January..64
Effick (1992) 95 Cr App R 427; (1992) 142 MU 492, CA;
   [1994] 3 WLR 583; (1994) 99 Cr App R 312, HL.....................1050
Ekbatani v Sweden (1988) 13 EHRR 504.......................................64
Elias v Secretary of State for Defence (2005), (unreported)............1578
Ellen Street Estates Ltd v Minister of Health [1934] 1 KB
   590, CA..155
Elliniki Rasdio Phonia Tiles Rassi AE v Dimotiki Etaria
   (1991) ECR 1-2925 ....139, 140
Elsholz v Germany [2000] 2 FLR 486...944
Empower Scotland Ltd v Khan (2005), (unreported)....................1561
Enderby v Frenchay [1994] 1 All ER 495; [1993] ECR
   1-5535, ECJ; [1992] IRLR 15, CA and ECJ........ 1499, 1501, 1503, 1541
Engel v The Netherlands (No 1) (1976) 1 EHRR 647......................790, 792
Ensslin, Bader and Raspe v Germany (1978) 14 DR 64....................48
Entinck v Carrington (1765) 19 St Tr 1029...................................124

Erikson v Italy, Appl 37900 / 97; 26 October 1999 42
Esbester v UK (1993) 18 EHRR CD 72 ....1026, 1027, 1029
Ezelin v France (1991) A 202-A; (1991) 14 EHRR 362 .... 39, 662, 680,
683, 688, 696,
723–26, 730, 736,
737, 746–48

Fairnie (Decd) and Others v Reed and Another (1994)
20 May, Transcript from LEXIS, CA 896, 899
Falkirk Council v Whyte [1997] IRLR 560 1541
Farah v Commissioner of Police for the Metropolis [1997]
1 All ER 289, CA 1509
Fanell v Secretary of State for Defence [1980] 1 All ER
166, HL 791
Fayed v UK (1994) 18 EHRR 393 .... 61, 62
Federal Communications Commission v Pacifica Foundation
(1978) 438 US 726 510
Fell [1963] Crim LR 207 593
Fenelley [1989] Crim LR 142 .... 1288, 1289
Fernandez v Government of Singapore [1971] 2 All ER 691 936
Fey v Austria (1993) 16 EHRR 387 63
Findlay v UK (1997) 24 EHRR 221 63
Fitzpatrick v Sterling Housing Association [1998] 2 WLR
225, CA; [1999] 3 WLR 1113, HL 1525
Forbes [2001] 2 WLR 1; [2001] Crim LR 649 .... 1288, 1303, 1324
Foulkes v Chief Constable Merseyside Police [1998] 3
All ER 705 755
Fox, Campbell and Hartley v UK, Judgment of 30 August
1990, A 178; (1990) 13 EHRR 157 .... 54, 56, 765, 769, 1153,
1160, 1161
Francis (1992) LEXIS CO/1434/91 1115
Francome v Mirror Group Newspapers Ltd [1984] 1 WLR
892; [1984] 2 All ER 408 .... 311, 811, 898–900, 904,
909, 910, 915, 918, 984

Francovich v Italy [1992] 21 IRLR 84; [1991] ECR
1-5357; [1995] ICR 722 937
Fraser v Evans [1969] 1 QB 349 917
Fressoz and Roire v France (2001) EHRR 2 427
Friedl v Austria, No 15225 / 89; A 305B; (1995) 21
EHRR 83 97
R v Friend [1997] 1 WLR 1433; [1997] 2 All ER 1012 1239
Fulling [1987] QB 426; [1987] 2 WLR 923; [1987] 2
All ER 65, CA 1271
Funke v France (1993) 16 EHRR 297 .... 65, 72, 91

G v Director of Public Prosecutions [1989] Crim LR 150 1146
G v Federal Republic of Germany No 13079/87(1980)
21 DR 138 .... 683, 747

G, H and I v UK 15 EHRR CD 41 .... 1025, 1028
Gall (1990) 9O Cr App R 64,CA 1289
Garyfallou AEBE v Greece (1999) 28 EHRR 344 61
Gaskin v UK (1990) 12 EHRR 36 .... 73, 94, 135, 626,
   803, 924–25
Gay News v UK (1982) 5 EHRR 123 .... 310, 467, 485, 487,
   488, 496, 942, 966
Geillustreerde de Pers NV v the Netherlands [1977] D & R 8 109
Ghaidan v Godin-Mendoza [2002] 4 All ER 1162; [2003]
  2 WLR 478; [2004] 3 WLR 113; [2004] 2 AC 557
  (HL) 174, 180, 184–87, 190,
   200, 214, 281, 286, 297,
   729, 1525, 1526
Gibson [1990] 2 QB 619; [1991] 1 All ER 439; [1990]
  3 WLR 595, CA 474, 477, 482, 483,
   568, 587
Gill v Hearst Publishing Co 253 P 2d 441 (Cal 1953) 821
Gillick v West Norfolk and Wisbeach Area Health
  Authority [1986] AC 112; [1985] 3 WLR 830, HL 259, 557, 960, 961
Gillingham Borough Council v Medway Dock Co [1992]
  3 All ER 931 798
Gladstone Williams (1983) Cr App R 276 1111
Glasenapp v Federal Republic of Germany (1986) 9
  EHRR 25 .... 93, 97
Glasgow CC v Zafar [1998] ICR 120 .... 1527, 1538
Glimmerveen and Hagenbeek v Netherlands (1979) 18
  DR 187 500
Goldberg [1988] Crim LR 678 127
Golder v UK Judgment of 21 February 1975, A 18 .... 37, 62, 66, 135
Goldsmith and Another v Bhoyrul and Others [1997] 4
  All ER 268;(1997) The Times, 20 June 126
Goodwin v UK (1994) No 17488/90 Com Rep; (1996)
  22 EHRR 123, (1994) The Guardian, 26 May 126, 272, 286, 287,
   289, 379, 399, 407, 408,
   413–19, 421, 424, 425,
   427–32, 435–37, 439, 440,
   445, 446
Goodwin v UK [2002] ECHR 583 .... 85, 86,
Goswell v Commissioner of Metropolitan Police (1996)
  The Guardian, 27 April 1305
Gough v Chief Constable of the Derbyshire Constabulary
  [2002] QB 459 791
Govell v UK (1997) 4 EHRLR 438 1069
Graham-Kerr [198811 WLR 1098; 88 Cr App R 302, CA 478, 557
Graham Waddon (1999) Southwark Crown Court, 30
  June; appeal dismissed 6 April 2000 583

Granger v UK, Judgment of 28 March 1990, A 174 62
Grant v South West Trains Ltd (Case 249/96) [1998] IRLR 206 1516
Gray [1900] 2 QB 36; (1900) 69 LJ QB 502 396
Greek Case (1969) Report of 5 November; (1969) 12 YB 1 .... 46, 75, 76, 111, 1175
Greene v Home Secretary [1942] AC 284 1305
Gregory v UK (1997) 25 EHRR 577 406
Griggs v Duke Power Company 401 US 424 (1971) 1489
Griswold v Connecticut (1965) 381 US 479 624
Guerra v Baptiste (1995) The Times, 8 November 151
Guerra v Italy (1998) 26 EHRR 357 .... 42, 71, 90
Guildford Four Case, Final Report, 1993-94 HC 449 .... 1103, 1171
Guildhall Magistrates' Court ex p Primlacks Holdings
    Co (Panama) Ltd [1989] 2 WLR 841 .... 441, 1003
Gul v Switzerland (1996) 22 EHRR 93 70
Gulec v Turkey (1999) 28 EHRR 121 43
Gustaffson v Sweden (1996) 22 EHRR 409 98
Guzzardi v Italy (1980) 3 EHRR 333 .... 55, 765, 769, 1120, 1131,
                                                        1132, 1451, 1452

H v Norway (1992) 17004/90 (1992) 73 DR 155 .... 43, 80
H v UK (Appl No l5023/89) 1350
H, re, [1998] AC 72 192
HL v UK (Application No 45508/99) 763
H, W, P and K v Austria (1989) 62 DR 216 665
HRH Prince of Wales v Associated Newspapers Ltd [2006]
    EWCA Civ 1776, [2006] All ER (D) 335 .... 827, 878, 881, 882,
                                                        883, 893, 894, 970,
                                                        977–79, 981, 991

HRH Princess of Wales v MGN Newspapers Ltd and
    Others (1993) 8 November (unreported) 883–85, 891, 892,
                                                        898–901, 909, 910,
                                                        920, 1069
H v UK 33 D & R 247 (1983) 30
Haase (1977) Report of 12 July; DR 11(1978) 63
Habermann-Beltermann [1994] ECR 1-1657 1531
Hadjianastassiou v Greece (1992) 16 EHRR 219 64
Hagan (1987) The Times, 20 May 968
Hague v Committee for Industrial Organisation 307 US
    496 (1938) 661
Halford v UK [1997] IRLR 471; (1997) 24 EHRR 523;
    (1997) The Times, 3 July 775, 1034, 1038, 1042,
                                                        1043, 1055, 1074, 1083, 108
Hamer v UK (1979) Report of 13 December; 24 DR 5 103
Hampson v Department of Education and Science [1991]
    1 AC 171; [1990] 2 All ER 513, HL 1540, 1547
Hancock and Shankland [1986] AC 455; [1986] 1 All
    ER 641; [1986] 3 WLR 1014, HL 363

Handels-og Kontorfunktionaeremes Forbund i Danmark
v Dansk Arbejdsgiverforening (the *Danfoss* case)
(Case 109/88) [1989] ECR 3199; [1989] IRLR 532 .... 1501, 1502
Handyside v UK, Judgment of 7 December 1976, A 24;
(1976) 1 EHRR 737 .... 14, 36, 37, 69, 81, 94,
278, 310, 451, 464, 465, 467,
485, 532, 542, 543, 568, 588,
677, 729, 780, 942, 966
Hansen v Turkey (2004) 1 FLR 142, App no 36141/97 945
Harman and Hewitt v UK Appl 1211 75/86; (1992) 14
EHRR 657 .... 74, 1010, 1025, 1026,
1027, 1029, 1069, 1089
Harman and Hewitt v UK (no 2) Appl No 20317/92 (1993) (unreported) 1026
Harman v UK (1982) Appl 10038 / 82; (1984) Decision
of 11 May; [1984] 38 DR 53 67
Harris v Harris [2001] 2 FLR 895 962
Harris v Minister of the Interior (1952) (2) SA 428 155
Harrison v Duke of Rutland [1893] 1 QB 142 .... 714, 717
Harrow London Borough Council v Qazi [2004] 1 AC 983 197
Harvey [1988] Crim LR 241 1273
Hashman and Harrup v UK (1996) 22 EHRR CD 184;
(1999) 30 EHRR 241; (2000) 8 BHRC 104 .... 480, 668, 680, 683,
684, 686, 689, 691, 746, 751,
752, 759, 775, 777
Hautanemi v Sweden (1996) 22 EHRR CD 156 220
Hayes v Malleable WMC [1985] ICR 703 1530
Hayward v Cammell Laird [1988] 2 All ER 257, HL 1496, 1497, 1503
Heinz v Kendrick [2000] IRLR 141 1549
Hellewell v Chief Constable of Derbyshire [1995] 1
WLR 804; [1995] 4 All ER 473 .... 811, 811, 878, 888, 884,
898–901, 904, 915, 916,
984, 1078
Hendrickson and Tichner [1977] Crim LR 356 707
Herbage v The Times Newspapers and Others (1981)
The Times, 1 May 873
Herczegfalvy v Austria A 244; (1992) 14 HRLJ 84;
(1993) 15 EHRR 437 91
Hereford and Worcester County Council v Clayton
[1996] ICR 514 1557
Hicklin (1868) 3 QB 360 .... 469, 471
Hickman v Maisey [1900] 1 QB 752 .... 711, 714, 716, 717, 994
Hills v Ellis [1983] QB 680; [1983] 1 All ER 667 .... 1110, 1111
Hilton v UK No 5613/72, 4 DR 177 (1976) 98
Hirst and Agu v Chief Constable of West Yorkshire
(1987) 85 Cr App R 143 .... 679, 734–36
Hoare v UK [1997] EHRLR 678 .... 466, 569
Hoffman v Austria (1993) 17 EHRR 293 70

Hokkanen v Finland (1994) 19 EHRLR 139 .... 70, 71 945
Holden (Amanda) v The Star (2001) (unreported) see
    (2001) The Guardian, 2 July; (2001) The Observer,
    15 July 838
Holgate-Mohammed v Duke [1984] 1 AC 437; [1984] 1
    All ER 1054, HL 1156, 1305
Hollandia, The [1983] 1 AC 565 152
Holmes v Bournemouth Crown Court (1993) (unreported) 772, 777
Holy Monasteries v Greece (1995) 20 EHRR 1 220
Hood v UK (2000) 29 EHRR 365, Judgment of 25
    February 1997 63
Horseferry Road Metropolitan Stipendiary Magistrate
    ex p Siadatan [1991] 1 QB 260; [1991] 1 All ER
    324; [1990] 3 WLR 1006 ....786, 787
Horsham Justices ex p Farquharson [1982] 2 WLR 430;
    [198212 All ER 269, CA 385, 386
Howard v UK (1987) 52 DR 198 90
Howell [1982] 1 QB 416; [1981] 3 All ER 383, CA;
    [1981] 1 WLR 1468, HL 752, 753, 769,
                                                                                        780, 1141
Hubbard v Pitt [1976] QB 142; [1975] 3 All ER 1 .... 677, 691, 719,
                                                                                        798, 799
Huber v Austria (1973) Report of 8 February DR 2
    (1935) 91
Huber v Austria (1974) Appl 6821/74; 6 DR 65(1977) 59
Huddersfield (University of) v Wolff [2004] ICR 828 1528
Hughes [1988] Crim LR 519, CA 1222, 1223, 1271, 1279
Hughes v Holley (1988) 86 Cr App R 130 751
Hulbert (1999) (unreported) 397
Humphries v Connor (1864) 17 ICLR 1 ....755, 760
Hunter v Canary Wharf [1997] AC 655 994
Huntingdon Life Sciences Ltd and Another v Curtin and
    (1997) The Times, 11 December; (1998) 3(1) J Civ Lib 37 ....793, 794
Hurtado v Switzerland A 280-A (1994) Com Rep 75, 1175
Hussain and Singh v UK (1996) 21 EHRR 1 58
Hussein v Chong Fook Kam [1970] AC 942 1153
Hutchinson (1954) (unreported) 469
Huvig v France (1990) 12 EHRR 547 1026

Ibrahim [1914] AC 599 1273
Igen v Wong [2005] ICR 931 .... 1528, 1536, 1586, 1587
Ignaccolo-Zenide v Romania (2000) Reports of judgments
    and decisions 2000-I 945
Imbrioscia v Switzerland (1993) 17 EHRR 441; A 275
    (1993) 1210
Incal v Turkey (1999) 29 EHRR 449 .... 1355, 1395, 1413

Inquiry under the Companies Security (Insider Dealing)
    Act 1985, Re, [1988] 1 All ER 203 411
Interbrew SA v Financial Times Ltd [2002] EMLR 24.........................419–22, 426, 429,
                                                                          430, 434–39, 449
International Transport Roth GmbH v Secretary of State
    for the Home Department [2002] 3 WLR 344 ....184, 281
Ireland v UK (1978) 2 EHRR 25..46, 47, 98, 1432
Isequilla [1975] All ER 77...1267
Isgro v Italy (1991) Case 1/1990/192/252; [1993] Crim
    LR 261...66
Ismet Ala v Secretary of State for the Home Department
    [2003] EWHC 521...276

JS v UK App1 No 191173/91, 3 January 1993...71
James and Others v UK (1986), A 98; (1986) 8 EHRR 123 104
James v Eastleigh Borough Council [1990] AC 751;
    [1990] 2 All ER 607, HL 1527, 1534, 1537,
                                                                              1538, 1548
Jenkins v Kinsgate [1981] IRLR 388...1498
Jepson and Dyas-Elliott v The Labour Party [1996]
    IRLR 116 1574
Jersild v Denmark (1992) 14 HRLJ 74; (1994) 19
    EHRR 1.. 90, 93 310, 312, 500,
                                                            501, 515, 532, 533, 942,
                                                                      947, 966
JM v UK (2001) 2 EHRLR 215 187
Jockey Club ex p RAM Racecourses Ltd [1993] 2 All
    ER 225..233
Johansen v Norway (1996) 23 EHRR 33..945
John v Express Newspapers (2000) The Times 26 April.......417, 418, 429, 450
Johnson v HM Prison Service and Others (1996) The Times
    31 December 1589
Johnson v UK (1997) 27 EHRR 296...1309
Johnson v Whitehouse [1984] RTR 38...1511
Johnston v Chief Constable of the RUC (Case 222/84)
    [1986] ECR 1651..108, 1579, 1581–85
Johnstone v Ireland, Judgment of 18 December 1986,
    A 112; (1987) 9 EHRR 203...103
Jones and Lloyd v DPP see Director of Public Prosecutions
    v Jones and Lloyd
Jones v Chief Adjudication Officer (1990) EOR 1991 1542
Jones v Post Office [2001] IRLR 384; [2001] ICR 805 1549
Jordan v Burgoyne [1963] 2 QB 744; [1963] 2 All ER 225 ....772, 783
Jordan, Kelly, Arthurs, Donnelly and Others v UK (2001)
    The Times 18 May..40, 207
Joseph [1993] Crim LR 206, CA 1280

Judith Miller, Petitioner v US and M Cooper and Time
    inc, Petitioners v US, Supreme Court (2005) No 04–1508 409
Julie Bower v Cheapside (SSL) Ltd (formerly Schroder
    Securities Ltd) ET (2002), (unreported) 1590

K, F and P v UK (1984) 40 DR 298 30
Kalanke v Freie Hansestadt Bremen (Case 450/93)
    [1995] IRLR 660 ....1579, 1580, 1583–85
Kamasinski (1988) Report of 5 May; (1991) 13 EHRR 36 65
Katz v US (1967) 389 US 347 1071
Kay v Lambeth London Borough Council [2006] UKHL 10 .... 195, 197,
                                                                248, 267, 883
Kay v UK (1998) 40 BMLR 2O 55
Kaye v Robertson and Another [1991] FSR 62; (1991)
    The Times, 21 March, CA 832, 868, 873–77,
                                                                910, 955
Keenan [1990] 2 QB 54; [1989] 3 WLR 1193; [1989] 3
    All ER 598, CA 1280
Kelly v BBC [2000] 3 FCR 509; [2001] 1 All ER 323;
    [2001] 2 WLR 253; [2001] Fam 59 .... 858, 860, 864, 952,
                                                                960, 968, 973
Kelly v Chief Constable of Hampshire (1993) The Independent,
    25 March 772, 779
Kelly v UK (1990) Appl 17579/90; (1993) 16 EHRR CD
    20; [1993] 74 D & R 43, 44, 45
Kent v Metropolitan Police Commissioner (1981) The Times,
    15 May 288, 693, 708, 721
Khan [1993] Crim LR 54, CA 1279
Khan (Sultan) [1995] QB 27, CA; [1997] AC 558; [1996] 3
    All ER 289; [1996] 3 WLR 162; (1996) 146 NLJ
    1024, HL 126, 1056, 1077,
                                                                1289, 1324
Khan v UK (1999) 27 EHRR CD 58; (2000) 8 BFRC 310 ....1055, 1056, 1074,
                                                                1089, 1267, 1291–94,
                                                                1320
Khanna v MOD [1981] ICR 653 1528
Khorasandjian v Bush [1993] 3 All ER 669; [1993] QB 727;
    [1993] 3 WLR 476, CA 994
King v Hodges [1974] Crim LR 424 ....760, 1142
Kiszko (Stefan) (1992) The Times, 18 February 1103
Klass v Federal Republic of Germany, Judgment of
    6 September 1978, A 28; (1978) 2 EHRR 214 ....27, 73, 101, 107, 108,
                                                                1009, 1025, 1028, 1029, 1032,
                                                                1036, 1041, 1042, 1044, 1046,
                                                                1068, 1074, 1081, 1097
Knudsen v Norway, No 11045/84, 42 DR 247 (1985) 236

Knuller v Director of Public Prosecutions [1973] AC 435;
[1972] 3 WLR 143; (1972) 56 Cr App R 633, HL 310, 434, 470, 476,
477, 480, 482, 483,
587, 942, 966
Kokkinakis v Greece A 260-A, p18 (1993) 98
Kommunistische Partei Deutschland v Federal Republic
of Germany (1957) Appl 250/57; YB 1 (1955-57) 30, 167
Kopp v Switzerland (1999) 27 EHRR 91; [1998]
HRCD 6 .... 480, 814, 1008,
1009, 1042–44
Korematsu v United States 584 F Supp 1406 (1984) 289
Kosiek v FRG (1987) 9 EHRR 328 .... 93, 97
Kownacki v Commissioner of Metropolitan Police (1996)
The Guardian, 30 April 1306
Krause (1902) 18 TLR 238 707
Kröcher and Möller v Switzerland No 8463/78, (1983) 34 DR 25;
(1984) 6 EHRR 345 .... 37, 48
Kruslin v France (1990) 12 EHRR 528 .... 1023, 1043
Kuddus v Chief Constable of Leicester Constabulary
[2002] 2 AC 122 1590
Kuhnen v FRG (1988) 56 DR 205 500
Kuwait Airways Corporation v Iraqi Airways Co (Nos 4
and 5) [2002] UKHL 19, [2002] 2 AC 883 1456

LCB v UK (1998) 27 EHRR 212 .... 40, 42
Laker Airways v Department of Trade [1977] QB 643;
[1976] 3 WLR 537, CA 100
Lam v Koo and Chiu [1992] Civil Transcript No 116, CA 900
Lambert v France (1999) 1 EHRLR 123 1044
Lambeth BC v CRE [1990] IRLR 231, CA 1570, 1574
Lamy v Belgium (1989) 11 EHRR 529 59,
84
Latif [1996] 1 WLR 104; [1996] 1 All ER 353, HL 1266
Lauko v Slovakia [1999] EHRR 105 61
Lawless v Ireland (1959) Report of 19 December, B 1
(1960-61) p 64; Judgment of 1 July 1961, A 3
(1960-61); (1961) 1 EHRR 15 .... 32, 36, 53, 54, 765,
1133, 1425, 1435
Leander v Sweden, Judgment of 26 March 1987, A 116;
(1987) 9 EHRR 443 .... 37, 72, 73, 106,
1027, 1029
Leeds City Council v Price [2006] UKHL 10 .... 195, 197, 201, 248
Lehideux and Isornia v France (1998) 5 BHRC 540 500
Lemon (Gay News) [1979] QB 10; [1978] 3 WLR 404,
CA; [1979] AC 617; [1979] 2 WLR 281; [1979]
1 All ER 898, HL 485, 487, 496
Lennon v News Group Newspapers [1978] FSR 573 931

Letellier v France (1991) A 207; (1991) 14 EHRR 83...57
Leverton v Clwyd County Council [1989] 2 WLR 47;
    [1989] 1 All ER 78, CA and HL 1495, 1497
Lewis v Cox (1985) Cr App R I...1110
Lewis ex p (1888) 21 QBD 191..678
Li Shu-Ling [1989] Crim LR 58 1204
Li Yau-wai v Genesis Films Limited [1987] HKLR 711 900
Liberal Party v UK (1980) 21 DR 211 106
Lingens v Austria (No 2) (1986) 8 EHRR 103.............................. 90, 310, 966
Lion Laboratories v Evans and Express Newspapers [1985]
    QB 526; [1984] 2 All ER 417, CA..................................616, 917, 984
Lithgow v UK (1984) Report of 7 March, A 102; (1986)
    8 EHRR 335..64
Litster v Forth Dry Dock Engineering [1989] 1 All ER 1194........................174
Liverpool Juvenile Court ex p R [1987] All ER 688 1270
Loizidou v Turkey (1996) 23 EHRR 513...90
London Regional Transport v Mayor of London [2003]
    EMLR 4...963
London Underground v Edwards (No 2) [1998] IRLR 364.............. 1543, 1544
Lonhro plc and Observer plc, Re, [1990] AC 154; [1989]
    2 All ER 1100, HL 349
Lopez Ostra v Spain (1994) 20 EHRR 277....................................... 71, 90
Lord Advocate v Scotsman Publications Ltd [1990] 1
    AC 812; [1989] 2 All ER 852 ....599, 612, 620
Lord Chancellor ex p Lightfoot [2000] 2 WLR 318.............................130, 133
Lord Chancellor ex p Witham [1998] QB 575; [1997] 2
    All ER 779 ....130, 131, 152
Lord Saville of Newdigate ex p A [1999] 4 All ER 860;
    [2000] 1 WLR 1885...130, 132, 953
Ludi v Switzerland (1993) 15 EHER 173 1298
Lustig-Prean and Beckett v UK (1999) 29 EHRR 548;
    (1999) 7 BHRC 65..72, 76, 81, 1207, 1208,
                                                1514, 1516, 1518, 1520, 1521

M v Secretary of State for the Home Department
    [2004] EWCA Civ 324...1430
M v UK (1982) Appl 9907/82; [1983] 35 DR 130 48
M and N (Minors), Re, [1990] 1 AC 686; [1988] 3
    WLR 485, HL...136, 970
MCN Pension Trustees Ltd v Bank of America National
    Trust and Savings Association [1995] EMLR 99............................353, 387
MS v Sweden, RJD 1997-IV 1437; (1999) 28 EHRR 313 ....72, 1023
McCann v Manchester Crown Court [2002] 4 All ER 593......................791, 794
McCann, Farrell and Savage v UK, A 324; (1995) 21
    EHRR 97...37, 40, 44, 45, 207
Macdonald v Advocate General for Scotland; Pearce v
    Governing Body of Mayfield School [2003] UKHL 34 ....1517–19, 1558, 1564

McElduff v UK (Appl No 21322/92): see Tinnelly v UK
McFeeley v UK (1980) 20 DR 44 852
McGlinchey v UK (2003) 37 EHRR 41...1175
McGonnell v UK (2000) 8 BHRC 56..63
McCowan v Chief Constable of Kingston on Hull [1968]
    Crim LR 34..1000
McGinley and Egan v UK (1998) 27 EHRR 1..70
McIlkenny and Others (*Birmingham Six* Case); see
    R v McIlkenny and Others
McKennitt v Ash [2006] EWCA Civ 1714...................254, 255, 827, 878, 883,
                                                             890, 893, 913–15, 919,
                                                             933, 991
McKenzie [1993] 1 WLR 453; (1992) 142 NLJ 1162, CA 1301
McLeod v Commissioner of Police of the Metropolis
    [1994] 4 All ER 553 755
McLeod v UK (1998) 27 EHRR 493..761, 776, 777
McLorie v Oxford [1982] 1 QB 1290...993
McVeigh, O'Neill and Evans v UK (1981) Report of
    18 March; [1981] 25 D & R 15; (1981) 5 EHRR 71.................................53, 1133
Markt Intern Verlag v FRG A 165 (1989)..92
Maguire (1990) 90 Cr App R 115; [1989] Crim LR 815, CA 1194, 1195
Maguire (*Maguire Seven* Case), see R v Maguire
Mainstream Loudoun v Board of Trustees 2 F Supp 2d
    783 (EDVa 1998); 4 F Supp 2d 552 (1998)...581, 582
Malone v Commissioner of Police of the Metropolis (No 2)
    [1979] Ch 344... 115, 898, 982,
                                                             1033, 1054
Malone v UK (1982) Report of 17 December, A 82;
    (1984) 7 EHRR 14..73, 114, 775, 898, 1033,
                                                             1042, 1043, 1055, 1072,
                                                             1074, 1097
Mandla v Dowell Lee [1983] 2 AC 548; [1983] 2 WLR
    620; [1983] 1 All ER 1062, HL..1508
Mansfield Justices ex p Sharkey [1985] QB 613 774
Mantovanelli v France (1997) 24 EHRR 370 64
Mapp v Ohio 367 US 643 (1961)...1265
Marckx v Belgium (1979) 2 EHRR 330 .... 70, 87, 1525
Marschall v Land Nordrhein-Westfalen Case C-409/95,
    Judgment of 11 November 1997; [1998] IRLR 39.....................1584, 1585, 1576
Marsh [1991] Crim LR 455..1194–96
Marshall (1992) The Times, 28 December 1274
Marshall (No 2) [1993] 4 All ER 586...139, 1589
Martin Secker and Warburg [1954] 2 All ER 683; [1954]
    1 WLR 1138..469
Mary Quayson [1989] Crim LR 218 1282
Mason [1987] Crim LR 119; [1988] 1 WLR 139;
    [1987] 3 All ER 481, CA..1272, 1277, 1296

Mathias (1989) The Times 24 August; (1989) 139 NLJ
    1417, CA 1274, 1275
Mathieu-Mohin v Belgium (1987) 10 EHRR 1 106
Mats Jacobson v Sweden (1990) 13 EHRR 79 .... 60, 104, 113
Matthews (1990) Cr App R 43; [1990] Crim LR 190, CA 1193–97
Maudsley v Palumbo and Others (1995) The Times,
    19 December 899, 901
Medway Council v BBC [2002] 1 FLR 104 .... 860, 864
Meer v Tower Hamlets [1988] IRLR 399 1546
Metropolitan Police Commissioner ex p Blackburn [1968]
    2 All ER 319, CA 397, 477
Miailhe v France (1993) 16 EHRR 332 .... 69, 91
Michalak v Wandsworth LBC [2002] EWCA Civ 271 1525
Middleweek v Chief Constable of Merseyside [1992]
    AC 179; [1990] 3 WLR 481 1304
Miller v California (1973) 413 US 15 469
Mills (Heather) v News Group Newspapers Ltd [2001]
    EMLR 41; (2001) WL 720322; 879, ... 889, 893, 907–9, 911,
                                                                                    915, 919, 938, 951,
                                                                                    953–56, 970, 985,
                                                                                    987, 988
Minister of Home Affairs v Fisher [1980] AC 319 192
Ministry of Agriculture, Fisheries and Food ex p Hamble
    [1995] 2 All ER 714 129
Ministry of Defence ex p Smith and Others [1996] 2
    WLR 305; [1996] 1 All ER 257; [1996] ICR 740, CA 128, 129, 286,
                                                                                    1305, 1520
Minto v Police [1987] 1 NZLR 374 756
Miranda v Arizona 384 US 436 (1966) 1265
Mohammed (Allie) v State [1999] 2 WLR 552 (Trinidad
    and Tobago) 1284
Monnell and Morris v UK (1987) 10 EHRR 205 64
Morris v Duke-Cohen (1975) 120 SJ 826 1487
Montgomery v Lord Advocate [2003] 1 AC 641; [2001]
    2 WLR 779 1454
Moonsar v Fiveways Express Transport Ltd EAT (2004)
    27 September 1560
Moor [20001 J CIv Lib 155 77
Moran v Burbine 475 US 412 (1986) 1265
Morgans v Director of Public Prosecution [1999] 1 WLR
    968, CA; [2000] 2 WLR 386, HL 1050
Morgentaler v R [1988] 1 SCR 60 80
Morpeth Ward Justices ex p Ward (1992) 95 Cr App R 215 .... 772, 773
Morse v Wiltshire CC [1998] ICR 1023; [1998] IRLR 352 1551
Moss v McLachlan [1985] IRLR 76 .... 125, 756, 757,
                                                                                    760–62, 771
Moustaquim v Belgium (1991) 13 EHRR 802 89

Mullady v DPP [1997] COD 422; WL 1103678 1159
Mullen [1999] 2 Cr App R 143; [1999] 3 WLR 777 .... 1260, 1266
Müller v Switzerland (1991) 13 EHRR 212 .... 95, 465, 481, 483, 484,
488, 588, 684, 783
Murray v DPP [1994] 1 WLR 1; 99 Cr App R 396, HL 1239
Murray v UK (1994) 19 EHRR 193 .... 54, 56, 72, 74, 1152,
1160, 1161, 1208, 1221,
1232, 1234, 1235,
1249, 1327
Murray (John) v UK (1996) 22 EHRR 29; [1996]
Crim LR 370; (1996) The Times, 9 February 65, 1209, 1210–15,
1239, 1240, 1252

N v Portugal Appl No 20683/92, 20 February 1995 .... 71, 945
N v Secretary of State for the Home Department [2005]
2 WLR 1124 .... 194, 267
Nadir Choudhary v UK (1999) 1 EHRLR 522 .... 1044, 1050
Nagarajan v London Regional Transport [1999] 4 All ER
65; [1999] 3 WLR 425 .... 1564, 1565
Nagy v Weston [1966] 2 QB 561; [1965] 1 WLR 280 .... 734, 735
Napier v Scottish Ministers [2005] UKHRR 268 1176
Nebraska Press Association v Stuart 427 US 539 (1976) 320
Nedrick [1986] 3 All ER 1; [1986] 1 WLR 1025, CA 363
Neumeister v Austria, Judgment of 27 June 1968; (1979–80);
(1968) 1 EHRR 91 .... 57, 58, 64
New York Times Co v US (*Pentagon Papers* Case) 403
US 713 (1971) 445, 604
News Group Newspapers Ltd v SOGAT [1986] ICR 716;
[1986] IRLR 337 .... 705, 798
News Verlags v Austria (2001) 31 EHRR 8; (2000) 9
BHRC 625 .... 322, 326, 327, 333,
354, 355, 382
Nicol v Director of Public Prosecutions (1995) 160 JP
155; (1996) 1 J Civ Lib 75 .... 773, 774, 777–79
Nielsen v Denmark (1988) 1 EHRR 175; (1959) Appl
343/57, 2 YB 412; (1961) 1 DR 388 .... 29, 30
Niemietz v Germany, A 251-B; (1992) 16 EHRR 97 .... 72, 73, 74, 818,
1009, 1070
Nold v Commission [1974] ECR 481 138
Noone [1988] ICR 813; [1988] 83 IRLR 195 1589
Norris v Ireland (1991) 13 EHRR 186 72
Norwich Pharmacal Co v Customs and Excise
Commissioners [1974] AC 133 .... 410, 420, 426, 427, 436,
437, 439, 448, 449
Norwood v DPP (2003) WL 21491815 .... 506, 784
Norwood v DPP [2004] EWHC 69 797
Norwood v UK (2005) 40 EHRR SE 11 .... 506, 784

Nottingham CC v Mohammed Amin [2000] 1 WLR 1071;
    [2000] Crim LR 174, CA 1299
Nottinghamshire CC v Meikle [2004] IRLR 703 1552

O v UK (1987) 10 EHRR 82 61
O'Connor v Euromoney Publications Inc (1999) Guardian,
    6 June 1522
O'Hara v Chief Constable of the RUC [1997] WLR 1;
    [1997] 1 All ER 129, HL 1150, 1152, 1154, 1155
O'Kelly v Harvey (1883) 14 LR Ir 105 755
O'Leary [1988] 87 Cr App R 387; [1988] Crim LR 827, CA 1300
O'Neill (1996) The Times, 7 June 1531
Oberschlick v Austria (1997) 25 EHRR 357 90
Observer v UK; Observer and Guardian v UK A 216;
    (1992) 14 EHRR 153 .... 94, 96, 597, 620, 794,
                                                                                    946, 985, 1355, 1357
Ocalan v Turkey (1999) 30 November 113
Ojutiku v Manpower Services Commission [1982] IRLR 418 .... 1540, 1546
Oliver, Hartrey and Baldwin [2003] Cr App R 28 .... 478, 557
Olsson v Sweden, A 130; (1988) 11 EHRR 259 .... 69, 72
Olsson v Sweden (No 2), A250 (1992) 34
Open Door Counselling and Dublin Well Woman v Ireland
    (1992) 15 EHRR 244 .... 43, 80, 93, 95, 407
Oransaye [1993] Crim LR 772, CA 1194
Osman v Director of Public Prosecutions (1999) The Times,
    29 September 1126
Osman v UK (2000) 29 EHRR 245; [1999] 1 FLR 193;
    (1999) BHRC 293 .... 41, 61, 62, 246, 952
Otto-Preminger Institut v Austria (1994) 19 EHRR 34 .... 38, 95, 467, 486, 488–96,
    568, 570, 944, 946, 948
Owino [1995] Crim LR 743 45
Oxfordshire County Council [1997] 1 FLR 235 960
Oxfordshire Council v L and F [1997] 1 FLR 235 968
Ozgur Gundem v Turkey (2001) 31 EHRR 49 .... 422, 446, 447

P, Re, [2007] EWCA Civ 2 .... 242, 268, 269

P v S and Cornwall County Council, Judgment of 30
    April 1996; [1996] ECR 1-2143; [1996] 1 IRLR
    347; [1996] All ER (EC) 397; [1996] ICR 795 .... 139, 1504, 1516
Pakelli v Germany, Judgment of 25 April 1983, A 64;
    (1983) 6 EHRR 1 66
Paris, Abdullah and Miller (*Cardiff Three* Case) (1993)
    97 Cr App R 99; [1994] Crim LR 361, CA 1207, 1230, 1272
Parris [1989] Crim LR 214; [1989] 9 Cr App R 68, CA 1300
Pataki (1960) Appl 596/59; YB III 31
Paton v UK (1981) 3 EHRR 408 43

Paton v Procurator Fiscal (Alloa) (1999) Judgment of
  24 November 1215
Pearson (1998) The Times, 20 February 1261
Peck v United Kingdom (2003) 36 EHRR 41 .... 818, 819, 822, 884,
  885, 894, 946, 968
Pel Ltd v Modgifi [1980] IRLR 142 1535
Pendragon v UK No 31416/96 (1998) 687, 688, 725, 726, 736
Pepper v Hart [1993] 1 AC 593; [1993] 1 All ER 42;
  [1992] 3 WLR 1032, HL 241, 279
Percy v Director of Public Prosecutions [1995] 3 All
  ER 124 .... 772, 775, 779
Perera v Civil Service Commission [1983] IRLR 166;
  [1983] ICR 428, CA 1541, 1546
Peterkin v Chief Constable of Cheshire (1999) The Times,
  16 November 756, 761
Petrovic v Austria (2001) 33 EHRR 14 1525
Pharmaceuticals Ltd v Director of the SFO [2002] EWHC
  3023 .... 1007, 1010
Pickstone v Freemans [1989] AC 66; [1988] 2 All ER 803;
  [1988] 3 WLR 265, HL 174, 1494
Piddington v Bates [1961] 1 WLR 162 .... 752, 753
Ping Lin [1976] AC 574 1267
Plange v Chief Constable of South Humberside Police
  (1992) The Times 23 March 1154
Planned Parenthood of Southeastern Pennsylvania v Casey
  (1992) 505 US 833 80
Plattform 'Ärzte für das Leben' v Austria (1982) Appl
  1012/82; [1985] D & R 44; (1988) 13 EHRR 204 .... 37, 97, 107, 778
Plon (Société) v France (No 58148/00, 18 May 2004) 432
Poitrimol v France, A 277-A (1993); (1993) 18 EHRR 130 65
Ponting [1985] Crim LR 318 .... 117, 593, 594
Poplar Housing and Regeneration Community Associations
  Ltd and the Secretary of State for the Environment
  v Donoghue [2001] 3 WLR 183; [2001] EWCA
  Civ 595, CA 175, 184, 220–224, 226,
  230, 231, 607, 608
Powell v UK (1990) 12 EHRR 355 .... 72, 90
Pratt v Attorney General for Jamaica [1993] 3 WLR 995;
  [1993] 4 All ER 769 .... 151, 152
Preston (1992) 95 Cr App R 355, CA; [1994] 2 AC 130;
  [1993] 3 WLR 891; [1993] 4 All ER 638; (1994)
  98 Cr App R 405, HL 1049–51
Pretty v UK (2002) 35 EHRR 1 77
Price v Civil Service Commission [1977] 1 WLR 1417;
  [1978] 1 All ER 1228 1539
Price v Leeds City Council [2005] 1 WLR 1825 .... 197, 198, 199, 279
Pullar v UK (1996) 22 EHRR 391 63

Quinn [1990] Crim LR 581; (1990) The Times, 31 March, CA 1289

R [1992] Fam Law 108; [1991] 4 All ER 481; [1991]
    3 WLR 767; [1992] Crim LR 207, HL 67, 148
R v A [2002] 1 AC 45 (HL); [2001] 2 WLR 1546; [2001]
    2 Cr App R 21 .... 174, 178, 184, 185, 186,
                                                                                    187, 190, 202, 209, 214,
                                                                                                        408, 729
R v Alladice (1988) 87 Cr App R 380; [1988] Crim LR
    608, CA 1223, 1272, 1275,
                                                                                                        1282, 1286
R v Anderson [1993] Crim LR 447 1278
R v Argent [1997] 2 Crim App R 27; (1996) The Times,
    19 December, CA 1238, 1244
R v Bailey and Smith [1993] 3 All ER 513; (1993)
    The Times, 22 March, CA 1296
R v Beck ex p Daily Telegraph [1993] 2 All ER 177 388
R v Beckles [2004] EWCA Crim 2766 .... 1246, 1247, 1249, 1327
R v Bow Street Stipendiary Magistrate, ex p Pinochet
    Ugarte (No 3) [1999] 3 WLR 827 46
R v Bournewood Community and Mental Health NHS
    Trust ex p L [1999] 1 AC 458 764
R v Bowden [2000] 2 All ER 418 .... 478, 586
R v Bresa [2005] EWCA Crim 1414 .... 1247, 1248
R v Bristol Crown Court ex p Bristol Press and Picture
    Agency Ltd (1987) 85 Crim App R 190 .... 447, 448
R v Broadcasting Complaints Commission ex p Granada
    Television Ltd [1995] EMLR 163 849
R v Central Criminal Court ex p Bright [2001] 2 All ER 244 447
R v Central Criminal Court ex p Telegraph plc [1993] 1
    WLR 980 .... 385, 387
R v Central Independent Television [1994] Fam 192 .... 856, 970, 971
R v Chief Constable of Sussex ex p International Ferry
    Traders Ltd [1999] 1 All ER 129; [1999] 2 AC 418 .... 273, 748
R v Coney (1882) 8 QBD 534 766
R v Cowan [1996] 1 Cr App R 1 1238
R v Darrach (2000) 191 DLR (4th) 539 189
R v Director of Public Prosecutions [2006] All ER (D) 250 .... 782, 784
R v Director of Public Prosecutions, ex p Kebilene,
    see DPP ex p Kebilene and Others
R v El-Faisal [2004] EWCA Crim 456 1417
R v Friend [1997] 1 WLR 1433 1239
R v Governor of Durham Prison ex p Singh [1984] 1 WLR 704 1424
R v H [2004] UKHL 3; [2004] 2 AC 134 1344
R v Hammond [2004] EWHC 69 .... 783, 797
R v Hampshire Farmers Markets, ex p Beer [2003]
    EWCA Civ 1056 .... 226, 228–29

R v Holding [2006] 1 WLR 1040...183
R v HM Treasury, ex p Cambridge University [2000] 1
    WLR 2514 (ECJ)..223
R v Hundal (Avtar Singh); R v Dhaliwal (Kesar Singh)
    2004 WL 62035 (CA (Crim Div)), [2004] 2 Cr App
    R 19, [2004] 2 Cr App R (S) 64, (2004) Times
    February 13, [2004] EWCA Crim 389...1392
R v IBA ex p Whitehouse (1985) The Times 4 April...848
R v James (1996) Crim LR 650..1197
R v Johnstone (Robert Alexander) [2003] UKHL 28...178
R v Jones; R v Milling; R v Olditch; R v Pritchard;
    R v Richards; Ayliffe v Director of Public Prosecutions;
    Swain v Director of Public Prosecutions [2006] UKHL 16........................744, 745
R v Jones and Mirrless 65 Cr App R 250, CA..766
R v Kansal [2002] 2 AC 69...240
R v Keogh [2007] All ER (D) 105 (Mar); [2007] EWCA
    Crim 528.. 1337, 1354, 1355, 1356
R v Khan [1997] AC 558...270, 273, 828
R v Killen [1974] NI 220...1350
R v Lambert [2001] 3 All ER 577...177, 178, 185, 239
R v Lambert [2002] 2 AC 545..1390
R v Maguire [1992] 2 All ER...1103, 1171
R v McIlkenny and Others [1992] 2 All ER 417; (1991)
    The Times, 28 March...324, 332, 339, 1103,
                                                                    1104, 1171, 1315
R v Manchester Crown Court, ex p H and D [2000] 2
    All ER 166...394
R v Mirza, R v Connor [2004] 1 All ER 929; [2002] 2
    WLR 201...400–4, 406
R v Mushtaq [2005] 1 WLR 1513.. 1269, 1270
R v Offen [2001] 1 WLR 253..185, 186, 1362
R v Panel of Take-overs and Mergers ex p Datafin [1987]
    QB 815..231
R v Perrin [2002] EWCA Crim 747, CA...................................472, 584, 586
R v Shaheed [2002] 2 NZLR 377 (CA)...1266
R v Shayler [2002] 2 WLR 754.....................................375, 376, 599, 607–11, 615
R v Smith [2005] 1 WLR 704...401, 405
R v Spear [2003] 1 AC 734..267
R v Staines; R v Morrisey [1997] 2 Cr App R 426, CA.............................1251
R v Taylor (1993) 98 Cr App R 361, CA...345, 382
R v Ward (1992) 96 Cr App R 1.. 1103, 1171
R (A) v Partnerships in Care Ltd [2002] EWHC 529.................224–25, 231
R (Bernard) v Enfield LBC (2003) HRLR 111...247
R (Brehony) v Chief Constable of Greater Manchester
    [2005] EWHC 640..706, 722, 726
R (Burkett) v Hammersmith and Fulham LBC [2002]
    UKHL 23..241

R (D) v Secretary of State for the Home Department
[2003] 1 WLR 1315 202
R (European Roma Rights Centre) v Immigration Officer
at Prague Airport (United Nations High Commissioner
for Refugees intervening) [2005] 2 AC 1 .... 1135, 1136
R (Greenfield) v Secretary of State for the Home
Department [2005] 1 WLR 673 ....195, 242, 244, 247
R (H) v Mental Health Tribunal, North and East London
Region and Another (2001) The Times, 2 April.............192, 201, 202, 204
R (Haw) v Secretary of State for the Home Dept [2006]
EWCA Civ 352...732
R (Limbuella) v Secretary of State for the Home
Department [2005] UKHL 66; [2004] QB 1440 1360
R (Mambakasa) v Secretary of State for the Home Office
[2004] QB 1124; [2004] 2 WLR 603 241
R (MB) v Secretary of State for the Home Department
[2006] EWCA Civ 1140 179
R (N) v Secretary of State for the Home Office [2004]
QB 1124; [2004] 2 WLR 603..241
R (on the application of Alan Lord) and the Secretary
of State for the Home Department [2003] EWHC 2073........636
R (on the application of Alconbury Ltd) v Secretary of
State for the Environment, Transport and the
Regions [2001] 2 All ER 929; (2001)
NLJ 135, HL... 107, 183, 184, 192,
                                                         201, 202, 237, 276
R (on the application of Anderson) v Secretary of State
for the Home Department [2003] 1 AC 837.......177, 181, 185, 186, 360
R (on the application of B) v Mental Health Review
Tribunal [2002] EWHC 1553...243, 850
R (on the application of Ford) v Press Complaints
Commission [2002] EMLR 5..233
R (on the application of Gillan) v Commissioner of
Metropolitan Police [2006] UKHL 12..................269, 274, 277–78, 726,
                                                        1119–21, 1131–37,
                                                        1139, 1140, 1158,
                                                        1325, 1356, 1465
R (on the application of Heather and others) v Leonard
Cheshire Foundation [2002] EWCA Civ 336; [2002]
2 All ER 936...223–224, 226–32,
                                                                234, 247, 248
R (on the application of Johnson) v Havering London
Borough Council [2007]All ER 271..................222, 226–227, 231
R (on the application of KB and Others) v Mental Health
Review Tribunal and Another [2003] 2 All ER 209;
[2002] EWHC 639..243, 247

R (on the application of the Kurdistan Workers' Party
and others) v Secretary of State for the Home
Department [2002] EWHC Admin 644 ....1358, 1402, 1415
R (on the application of Laporte) v Chief Constable of
Gloucester [2004] EWCA Civ 1639.. 287, 288, 290, 297,
662, 690, 692, 693, 721, 730,
733, 751, 755, 757–63, 766,
767, 770, 771, 775, 777,
801, 1140
R (on the application of Laporte) (FC) v Chief Constable
of Gloucestershire [2006] UKHL 55...1140, 1142, 1143, 1251
R (on the application of Marper) v Chief Constable of
South Yorkshire [2004] 1 WLR 2196.................................... 187, 194, 267, 1339
R (on the application of Pretty) v DPP and Secretary of
State for the Home Department [2001] UKHL 61 ....77, 374
R (on the application of the Prolife Alliance) v BBC
[2002] 2 All ER 756; [2004] 1 AC 185 ....179, 234, 274–76, 280,
510, 530–45, 851
R (on the application of Rottnam) v Commissioner of
Police for the Metropolis [2002] 2 All ER 865...1000
R (on the application of Ullah) v Special Adjudicator
[2004] UKHL 26.. 188, 194, 196, 199,
267, 279, 1338, 1339
R (Quark Fishing Ltd) v Secretary of State for Foreign
and Commonwealth Affairs [2005] 3 WLR 837...195
R (S) v Chief Constable of the South Yorkshire Police
[2004] UKHL 39, [2004] 1 WLR 2196...1437
R (SB) v Denbigh High School [2006] 2 WLR 719 ....195, 275, 286
R (Uttley) v Secretary of State for the Home Department
[2003] 1 WLR 1590...202
Rai, Alimond and 'Negotiate Now' v UK (1995) 81-A
DR 46; (1995) 19 EHRR CD 93..68, 685
Rainey v Greater Glasgow Health Board [1987] AC 224;
[1986] WLR 1017; [1987] 1 All ER 65, HL.................... 1498, 1499, 1503, 1547
Ramsay and Foote (1883) 15 Cox CC 231 ....484, 485
Rasool [1997] 4 All ER 439; (1997) The Times, 17
February; CA..1050
Redmond-Bate v DPP [1999] All ER (D) 864; (1999)
Crim LR 998; (1999) The Times, 28 July.................................... 661, 662, 691, 701,
723, 778, 779, 801
Rees v UK, Judgment of 17 October 1986, A 106; (1986)
9 EHRR 56...38, 85, 103, 139
Reid [1987] Crim LR 702 ....125, 705
Remli v France (1996) 22 EHRR 253 63
Remmers and Hamer v The Netherlands (1999) 27
EHRR CD 168 1046
Rennie [1982] 1 WLR 64; [1982] 1 All ER 385, CA...1268

Re S and W, see: S (Children) (Care Order: Implementation
of Care Plan) Re
Reynolds (Albert) v Times Newspapers Ltd and Others
[1998] 3 WLR 862; [1999] 4 All ER 609; [1999]
3 WLR 1010, HL..126, 311, 376, 377, 715,
718, 917, 951, 954, 1358
Ribemont v France (1995) 20 EHRR 557..327, 357, 382
Ribbitsch v Austria (1992) 21 EHRR 573...48, 1175
Rice v Connolly [1966] 2 QB 414; [1966] All ER 649;
[1966] 3 WLR 17..1109
Ricketts v Cox (1981) Cr App R 298..1110
Riem v Sweden (1992) 16 EHRR 155...70, 88
Ringeisen v Austria, Judgment 16 July 1971, A 13; (1971)
1 EHRR 455...61, 1086, 1319, 1341
Roberts v Parole Board [2005] UKHL 45..1344
Rodriguez v British Columbia (1993) 85 CCC (3d) 15...................................78
Rowe and Davis v UK, Appl No 28901/95; [1999] Crim
LR 410; (2000) 30 EHRR 1.....................................64, 1259, 1320
Ruiz-Mateos v Spain (1993) 16 EHRR 505...64
Runa Begum v Tower Hamlets London [2002] 2 All ER 668.........................280
Rutherford v Sec of State for Trade and Industry (No 2)
[2006] UKHL 19..1542

S, (Children) (Care Plan: Implementation of Care Plan),
Re, [2002] 2 AC 291; [2002] UKHL 10..................184, 185, 186, 430, 1341
S, (A Child), Re, [2004] UKHL 47; [2005] 1 AC 593.......................826, 855, 861–85,
957, 959, 961, 963, 968–70,
972–75, 979–81
S v Miller 2001 SC 977..792
SW v UK; and C v UK (1995) 2I EHRR 404..67
Saidi v France (1994) 17 EHRR 251..1187, 1259
Salabiaku v France (1988) A 141-A; (1988) 13 EHRR 379......................64, 191, 794,
1350, 1351
Salgueiro da Silva Mouta v Portugal (1999) Judgment
of 21 December..1521
Salman v Turkey, Judgment of 27 June 2000..47
Saloman v Commissioners of Custom and Excise
[1967] 2 QB 116...136
Samuel [1988] QB 615; [1988] 2 All ER 135, [1988] 2
WLR 920, CA...1217, 1220, 1223, 1225,
1234, 1281, 1283, 1284,
1288, 1289
Samuel v Commissioner of Police for the Metropolis
(1999) (unreported)..1138
Sang [1980] AC 402; [1979] 3 WLR 263; [1979] 2
All ER 1222, HL..1268, 1277, 1289, 1290, 1295, 1297
Sat-Bhambra (1988) JP Rep 365; (1988) Cr App R 55, CA............................1300

Saunders v Punch Ltd [1998] 1 WLR 986..................................417, 418, 429, 450
Saunders v Richmond-upon-Thames London Borough
    Council [1978] IRLR 362..1528
Saunders v Scottish National Camps (1981) EAT 7/80.................................1522
Saunders v UK (1994) No 19187/91; (1997) 23 EHRR 313.........65, 271, 1239, 1240,
    1250–54, 1270, 1279
Savundranayagan and Walker [1968] 3 All ER 439; [1968]
    1 WLR 1761, CA...335, 365
Schabas (1994) 43 ICLQ 913..48
Schenk v Switzerland (1988) 13 EHRR 242...........................270, 1291, 1299
Scherer v Switzerland, A 287 (1993) Com Rep 281.............466, 467, 568, 569
Schering Chemicals v Falkman [1981] 2 WLR 848.......................915, 918
Schmidt and Dahlströhm v Sweden, Judgment of 6
    February 1976, A 21; (1976) 1 EHRR 632...102
Schwabe v Austria (1992) 14 HRLJ 26...94
Schuler-Zraggen v Switzerland (1993) 16 EHRR 405.................................1483
Scialacqua v Italy (1998) 26 EHRR CD 164..42
Scott [1991] Crim LR 56, CA...1194
Secretary of State for Defence v Guardian Newspapers
    [1985] AC 339; [1984] 3 All ER 601, HL...................411, 419, 420, 445
Secretary of State for the Home Department v Rehman
    [1999] INLR 517 (SIAC); [2000] 3 All ER 778;
    (2000) The Times, 31 May, CA; [2001] 3 WLR
    877, HL..1088, 1343, 1425, 1426
Secretary of State for Defence ex p Perkins [1997]
    IRLR 297...1516
Secretary of State for Employment ex p Equal
    Opportunities Commission (EOC) [1994] 2 WLR
    409; [1994] 2 WLR 409, HL.....................132, 152, 294, 1598
Secretary of State for Employment ex p Seymour-Smith
    and Perez (No 2) [2000] 1 WLR 435; [2000] IRLR
    263, HL..1542, 1543
Secretary of State for Foreign Affairs ex p The World
    Development Movement [1995] 1WLR 386; [1995]
    1 All ER 611...236
Secretary of State for Home
    Affairs ex p Chahal [1995] 1 WLR 526; [1995] 1
    All ER 658; (1993) The Times, 12 March, CA................1088, 1089
Secretary of State for Home Affairs ex p Ruddock [1987]
    1 WLR 1482; [1987] 2 All ER 518................................1023
Secretary of State for Home Affairs ex p Stitt (1987)
    The Times, 3 February...127
Secretary of State for the Home Department ex p Adams
    [1995] All ER (EC) 177..139
Secretary of State for the Home Dept ex p Brind [1991]
    1 AC 696; [1991] 1 All ER 720; [1991] 2 WLR
    588, HL.......................................127, 128, 129, 152, 237, 304

Secretary of State for the Home Department ex p Daly,
    [2001] 3 All ER 433; [2001] UKHL 26, HL.....................131, 285, 286, 374, 609
Secretary of State for the Home Department ex p
    Hosenball [1977] 1 WLR 766; [1977] 3 All ER
    452, CA...127
Secretary of State for the Home Department ex p McQuillan
    [1995] 3 All ER 400; (1994) The Independent, 23 September............................128
Secretary of State for the Home Department and Others
    ex p Norney and Others (1995) The Times, 6 October......................................132
Secretary of State for the Home Department ex p
    Northumbria Police Authority [1989] QB 26;
    [1988] 2 WLR 590; [1988] 1 All ER 556, CA...127
Secretary of State for the Home Department ex p Simms
    [2000] 2 AC 115; [1999] QB 349; [1999] 3 All ER
    400, CA; [1999] 3 WLR 328, HL 130, 152, 237, 300,
                                                            310, 311, 314, 377, 715, 855,
                                                            939–42, 950, 951, 954, 966,
                                                            979, 1458
Secretary of State for the Home Department v E [2007]
    EWHC 33 (Admin)...1342, 1346, 1452
Secretary of State for the Home Department v JJ and
    Others [2006] EWHC 1623 (Admin)..1451–54
Secretary of State for the Home Dept v Rideh and J [2007]
    EWHC 804 (Admin)...1346, 1453
Secretary of State for Social Security ex p Joint Council
    for the Welfare of Immigrants [1996] 4 All ER 385;
    (1996) 146 NLJ 985...130, 132
Secretary of State for Transport ex p Factortame [1990]
    2 AC 85; [1989] 2 WLR 997; [1989] 2 CMLR 353, HL 139, 154, 1599
Secretary of State v MB [2006] EWHC 1000; [2006]
    HRLR 29; [2006] 8 CL 108 ....1340, 1342, 1447,
                                                            1453, 1461
Selmouni v France (2000) 29 EHRR...46, 47, 1175
Shannon [2001] 1 WLR 51, CA 1296, 1299, 1303, 1325
Shafir ur Rehman see Secretary of State for the Home
    Department v Rehman
Sharpe v Director of Public Prosecutions (1993) JP 595 1289
Shaw v Director of Public Prosecutions [1962] AC 220;
    [1961] 2 WLR 897, HL..481, 482
Shayler (2001) 14 May Hearing..1030
Sheffield and Horsham v UK (1998) 27 EHRR 163;
    [1998] 2 FLR 928...85
Sheldrake v DPP [2004] UKHL 43; [2005] 1 AC 264;
    [2005] 1 All ER 237 ....178, 185, 1391, 1414
Shelley Films Limited v Rex Features Ltd [1994]
    EMLR 134..884, 898, 900,
                                                            901, 920

Shields v E Coomes [1978] WLR 1408; [1979] 1 All
    ER 456, CA 1497
Sibson v UK A 258; (1993) 17 EHRR 193; (1993)
    The Times, 17 May 99
Siddiqui v Swain [1979] RTR 454 1155
Sidhu v Aerospace Composite Technology Ltd [1999]
    IRLR 683 1558
Sidiropoulos v Greece (1998) (unreported) 98, 1359, 1401
Sidis v F-R Publishing Corporation 113 F 2d 806 (2d Cir)
    (1940) 885
Silcott (1991) The Times, 9 December 1236
Silver v UK, Judgment of 25 March 1983, A 61; (1983)
    5 EHRR 347 .... 66, 90
Simon-Herald v Austria (1969) App 430/69 CD 38; 14
    YB 352 41
British Railway Engineers [1986] ICR 22 1547
Skirving [1985] QB 819 .... 470, 472
Skoogstrom v Sweden (1981) 1 Dig Supp para 5.2.2.1;
    (1982) 5 EHRR 278 56
Slade (1996) LEXIS CO/1678/96 1115
Smith v Gardner Merchant [1996] ICR 790; [1996] IRLR
    342; [1998] 3 All ER 582; [1999] ICR 134 .... 1516, 1517
Smith and Grady v UK (2000) 29 EHRR 493 .... 72, 81, 107, 285,
                                                                        286, 1207, 1516, 1518,
                                                                                        1520, 1571
Smurthwaite [1994] 1 All ER 898; (1994) 98 Cr App
    R 437, CA 1295, 1296, 1299
Socialist Party and Others v Turkey, App No 20/1997/
    804/1007; (1999) 27 EHRR 51 .... 38, 97, 98, 681, 1358
Soering v UK, Judgment of 7 July 1989, A 161; (1989)
    11 EHRR 439 .... 37, 43, 48–50, 98,
                                                                                        113, 1359
Spencer (Earl) v UK (1998) 25 EHRR CD 105; [1998]
    EHRLR 348 .... 30, 71, 816, 817, 828,
                                                                                        831, 901, 945
Sporrong and Lonroth v Sweden (1982) 5 EHRR 35 104
Stedman v UK (1997) 23 EHRR CD 168 1483
Steel v The Post Office [1977] IRLR 288 1539
Steel, Lush, Needham, Polden and Cole v UK Appl
    No 24838 / 94; (1999) 28 EHRR 603 .... 68, 242, 683, 685–89,
                                                                        694, 695, 722, 725, 730,
                                                                        736, 741, 746, 747, 775,
                                                                                    777–80, 797, 800
Stephens v Avery [1988] Ch 449; [1988] 2 WLR 1280;
    [1988] 2 All ER 477 .... 881, 896, 899, 902
Stewart v Cleveland Guest Ltd [1996] ICR 535 1557

Stewart v UK (1982) Appl 10044/82; 39 DR 162 (1984);
   (1985) 7 EHRR 453 43
Stott v Brown 2000 SLT 379 1252
Straker [1965] Crim LR 239 .... 477, 479
Sunday Times v UK, Judgment of 26 April 1979, A 30;
   (1979) 2 EHRR 245 .... 36, 68, 94, 135, 150, 310,
                                   322, 324, 329, 333, 335–60,
                                         362, 395, 966
Sunday Times v UK (No 2) (1991) 14 EHRR 229 759
Sutherland v UK, Appl No 25186/94; (1996) 22 EHRR
   CD 182; (1997) EHRLR 117 .... 81, 82
Swanston v Director of Public Prosecutions (1997)
   The Times, 23 January 782

T v Malta (1999) 29 EHRR 185 57
Tammer v Estonia (2003) 37 EHRR 43; (2001) 10 BHRC
   543 .... 945, 946, 963, 972, 976
Taylor [1994] TLR 484 333
Taylor v Anderton [1995] 2 All ER 420, CA 1320
Taylor v Director of Public Prosecutions [1973] AC 964 799
Teixeira de Castro v Portugal (1998) 28 EHRR 101 .... 1214, 1259, 1267, 1291,
                                   1293, 1294, 1298, 1299
Tekin v Turkey (2001) 31 EHRR 4 1175
Theakston v MGN [2002] EMLR 22 .... 909, 911
Thomas [1990] Crim LR 269, DC 1289
Thomas (Esther) v News Group Newspapers (2001)
   WL 753464, Judgment of 18 July 871
Thomas v NUM [1985] 2 WLR 1081; [1985] 2 All ER 1 124
Thomas v Sawkins [1935] 2 KB 249 .... 676, 1000
Thompson v Commissioner of Police for the Metropolis
   [1997] 3 WLR 403; [1997] 2 All ER 762, CA 1306, 1310
Thompson and Venables v Associated Newspapers and
   Others: see Venables, Jon, Thompson, Robert v News
   Group Newspapers Ltd, Associated Newspapers Ltd, MGM Ltd
Thompson Newspapers Ltd ex p Attorney General [1968]
   1 All ER 268; [1968] 1 WLR 1 .... 253, 334, 367, 391
Thorgeir Thorgeirson v Iceland (1992) 14 EHRR 843 .... 93, 94, 310, 966
Thynne, Wilson and Gunnel v UK, Judgment of 25 October
   1990, A 190; (1990) 13 EHRR 666 .... 58, 113
Tilly v Director of Public Prosecutions (2001) The Times
   27 November 741, 743, 744
Tinnelly and McElduff v UK (1998) 27 EHRR 249 .... 61, 62, 1031, 1088,
                                   1320, 1343, 1344
Tisdall (1984) The Times, 26 March 96, 593
Tolstoy Miloslavsky v UK (1995) 20 EHRR 442; The
   Times, 19 July 96
Tomasi v France (1992) 15 EHRR 1 .... 46, 48, 1175, 1176

Tottenham Three case (1991) The Times, 9 December..1103
Tower Boot Co v Jones [1997] ICR 254; [1997] IRLR 168 .... 1561, 1564
Treadaway v Chief Constable of West Midlands (1994)
      The Times, 25 October 1305
Trussler [1988] Crim LR 446..1274
Turley v Allders [1980] ICR 66 1529
Tyrer v UK, Judgment of 25 April 1978, A 26; (1978)
      2 EHRR 1 ....32, 47

UDR Four Case [1988] 11 NIJB 1 1171
United Communist Party of Turkey v Turkey 1998 WL
      1043934 (ECHR); 4 BHRC 1; (1998) 26 EHRR 121;
      [1998] HRCD 247...1357

VGT v Switzerland (2000) 34 EHRR 159...209, 539, 542
Vagrancy Cases, Judgment of 18 June 1971, A 14 (1972)
      1 EHRR 373..55
Valenzuela v Spain (1998) 28 EHRR 483 1044
Van Colle v Chief Constable of Hertfordshire [2006]
      EWHC 360 QB..247
Van der Mussele v Belgium Judgment of 23 November
      1983, A 70; (1983) 6 EHRR 163...51
Van Mechelen v Netherlands (1998) 25 EHRR 647 1259
Van Oosterwijck v Belgium, Judgment of 6 November
      1980, A 40; (1980) 3 EHRR 557...**33**
Vel v Owen (1987) JP 510...1278
Venables, Jon, Thompson, Robert v News Group Newspapers
      Ltd, Associated Newspapers Ltd, MGM Ltd [2001]
      1 All ER 908; [2001] 2 WLR 1038.............................. 890, 905–7, 908, 909,
                                                       911, 912, 915, 938, 951,
                                                       956, 970, 985, 987, 988
Vernillo v France (1991) 13 EHRR 880...63
Vernon [1988] Crim LR 445...1222
Victoria Park Racing Co v Taylor (1937) 58 CLR 479..994
Video Appeals Committee of the BBFC ex p BBFC
      [2000] EMLR 850... 548, 554, 564, 565,
                                                       569, 570
Vijayanathan v France (1992) 15 EHRR 62 27
Vilvarajah and Four Others v UK (1991) Judgment of
      30 October 1991;(1991) 14 EHRR 248; A 215 (1991)....................30, 49, 107
Vince and Another v Chief Constable of Dorset (1992)
      The Times, 7 September 1171
Vogt v Germany (1995) 21 EHRR 205...98, 1359
Von Hannover v Germany (2006) 43 EHRR 7 ....195, 431, 818–24, 828,
                                                       830, 836–38, 845, 848, 880,
                                                       883–85, 893–95, 914, 915,
                                                       933, 948–50, 956, 968, 969,
                                                       979, 991, 1070

W, Re, [2002] 2 AC 291..184, 186, 968
W (A Minor) (Wardship: Freedom of Publication), Re,
    [1992] 1 All ER 794 CA.............................856, 859, 960, 961, 968
W (A Minor) (Wardship: Restriction on Publication),
    Re, (1995) 2 FLR 466...856, 968
W (Children), Re, [2005] EWHC 1564 ....972–5, 980
W v Egdell [1990] Ch 359; [1989] 2 WLR 689, CA;
    [1990] 1 WLR 1502, HL...916
W v UK (1983) Appl 9348/81; 32 DR 190 (1983)...........................41
W and B (Children) (Care Plan), Re, [2002] 2 WLR 720.........176, 177
W, B v UK (1987) Judgment of 8 July; A 121; (1987)
    10 EHRR 29..88
Waddington v Miah [1974] 1 WLR 683; [1974] 2 All ER
    377, CA and HL..123
Wahab [2003] 1 Cr App R 15..1274
Wainwright v Home Office [2004] 2 AC 406..............239, 240, 810, 825,
                                                        866, 991, 1107, 1136,
                                                        1176, 1177–81, 1326
Wales v Commissioner of Police for the Metropolis
    [1995] IRLR 531..1564
Walsh [1989] Crim LR 822; (1989) 19 Cr App R 161,
    CA...1280, 1283, 1287
Ward v Chief Constable of Somerset and Avon
    Constabulary (1986) The Times, 26 June, CA....................1151
Watkins (Respondent) v Home Office (Appellants) and
    Others [2006] UKHL 17...239
Watson v UK [1997] EHRR 181...58
Webb v Chief Constable of Merseyside Police [2000]
    1 All ER 209...1410
Webb v Emo Air Cargo (UK) Ltd (No 2) [1994] 3 WLR
    941; [1994] All ER 115; [1994] QB 718........................1531–33
Webb v Emo Air Cargo (UK) Ltd [1992] CMLR 793,
    CA; [1993] 1 WLR 49; [1992] 4 All ER 929, HL.........1530, 1533
Webber [2004] UKHL 1..1239
Webster v Southwark London Borough Council [1983]
    QB 698; [1983] 2 WLR 217..678
Weekes [1993] Crim LR 222; (1992) The Times, 15 May,
    CA..1195, 1196
Weeks v UK, Judgment of 5 October 1988, A 114; (1987)
    10 EHRR 293 ....53, 58, 234
Welch v UK (1995) 20 EHRR 247 67
Weldon v Home Office [1991] WLR 340; [1990] 3 All ER
    672, CA...1304, 1307
Wemhoff v Germany, Judgment of 27 June 1968; (1968)
    1 EHRR 58..58
West Midlands Passenger Transport Executive v
    Jaquant Singh [1988] WLR 730, CA...................................1536

Westminster City Council v Morris [2006] 1 WLR 505...203
Wheeler v Leicester City Council [1985] AC 1054;
    [1985] 2 All ER 1106, HL...125
Whelan v Director of Public Prosecutions [1975] QB 864..1394
White v Metropolitan Police Commissioner (1982)
    The Times, 24 April..1305
Whitehead v Brighton Marine Palace and Pier Company
    Ltd (2005) Case 3102595/04 18 April..1560
Whitfield v Cleanaway UK (2005) 4 February (unreported).....................................1560
Wickramsinghe v UK [1998] EHRLR 338...61
Widmer v Switzerland, No 20527/92(1993) (unreported)..42
Wiggins v Field [1968] Crim LR 50...477
Williams [198713 All ER 411; [1987] Crim LR 167..45
Williams [1989] Crim LR 66..1196
Williams and O'Hare v Director of Public Prosecutions
    [1993] Crim LR 775... 1296, 1299
Wilson v Chief Constable of Lancashire Constabulary
    (2000) 23 November (unreported)..1159
Wilson v The First County Trust Ltd [2001] 3 All ER 229;
    [2001] EWCA Civ 633... 175, 176, 186,
                                                                                                      200, 286
Winder v Director of Public Prosecutions (1996) The Times,
    14 August..739, 740, 743, 747
Windisch v Austria (1990) 13 EHRR 281...66
Winer v UK (1986) 48 DR 154.. 71, 815, 816, 828

Wingrove v UK, Judgment of 25 November 1996, (1994)
    18 EHRR CD 54; (1996) 24 EHRR 1..38, 490, 491,
                                                                                                      494, 496, 570
Winn v Director of Public Prosecutions (1992) 142 NLJ..786
Winterwerp v Netherlands, Judgment of 24 October 1979,
    A 33; (1979) 2 EHRR 387...52, 55
Wise v Dunning [1902] 1 KB 167..772, 773, 780
Wloch v Poland (2002) 34 EHRR 9...327
Woodward v Hutchins [1977] 1 WLR 760; [1977] 2
    All ER 751, CA...918–20, 931, 984
Woolgar v Chief Constable of Sussex [1999] 3 All ER 604...433
Woollin [1999] 1 AC 82, HL...363
Worm v Austria (1997) 25 EHRR 557; (1998) 25 EHRR
    454...321–26, 328, 329, 331,
                                                                                                      353–57, 362, 382
Wynne v UK (1994) 19 EHRR 333...58

X v Austria (1963) Appl 1852/63; (1965) YB VIII..91
X v Austria (1970) Appl 4428/70; (1972) YB XV..66, 67
X v Austria (1976) No 7045/75, 7 DR 87...236
X v Austria (1973) Appl 5362/72, Coll 42; 42 DR 145..64

X v Austria (1979) 18 DR 154..74
X (A Child), Re, [2001] 1 FCR 541...860, 864, 970, 971
X (Minors) v Bedfordshire CC [1995] 2 AC 633, CA;
    [1995] 3 WLR 152; [1995] 3 All ER 353, HL.....................................62
X v Belgium (1961) 4 YB 324...97
X v Denmark (1979) Appl 8828/79; 30 DR 93 (1982).............................48, 56
X v Federal Republic of Germany (1956) 1 YB 202...90
X v Federal Republic of Germany (1969) Appl 4045/69;
    (1970) YB XIII...109
X v Federal Republic of Germany (1970) Appl 4653/70;
    (1974) 46 CD 22; 17 YB 148...51
X v Federal Republic of Germany (1979) Appl 8410/78;
    (1979) 18 DR 216..51
X v Federal Republic of Germany (1980) DR 17...65
X v Ireland (1973) 16 YB 388..52
X v Morgan Grampian Publishers and Others [1991]
    AC 1, CA; [1990] 2 WLR 1000; [1990] 2 All ER
    1, HL...412–15, 418, 419, 420, 425
X v Netherlands (1974) 2 DR 118..70
X v Netherlands (Appl 2894/66); (1966) 9 YB 564..57
X v Norway (1961) Appl 867/60; 4 YB 270...**27**
X v Spain Appl 10227/82; DR 37(1984)...43
X v Sweden (Appl 7911/77) (1977) 12 DR 192...105
X v UK (1973) Appl 5877/72; 16 YBCHE 328...............................814, 1070
X v UK (1975) Appl 6564/74; 2 DR 105 (1975)..104
X v UK (1978) Appl 8324/78 (unpublished)..48
    (1978) Appl No 7154/75; 14 DR 31(1978)....................39, 41, 42, 70
X v UK (1980) Appl 8416/78; 19 DR 244 (1980).............................43, 80, 89
X v UK (1981) Appl 7990/77; 24 DR 57..30, 203
X v UK (1981) Appl 8306/78, 25 DR 147; (1981) 3
    EHRR 63...28, 30, 1521
X v UK (1982) 5 EHRR 273...60
X v UK (1998) 25 EHRR CD 88...61
X v UK and Ireland (1982) Appl 9829/82 (unpublished)...............................41
X v Y [1988] 2 All ER 648...916
X (A Minor) (Wardship: Injunction) (*The Mary Bell Case*)
    [1984] 1 WLR 1422..855, 961
X and the Church of Scientology v Sweden (1977) Appl
    7805/77; (1979) YB XXII; 16 DR 68...92
X and Y v Austria (1974) Appl 7909/77; 15 DR 160 (1978)..........................65
X and Y v Netherlands (1985) 8 EHRR 235...................................70, 74, 804
X, Y and Z v UK (1997) 24 EHRR 143...87
Young, James and Webster v UK, Judgment of 13 August
    1981, A 44; (1981) 4 EHRR 38....................................34, 99, 150
YL v Birmingham City Council and Others [2007]
    All ER 271, CA; [2007] UKHL 27, HL.............................222, 226, 227

Z (A Minor) (Identification: Restrictions on Publication),
  Re, [1995] 4 All ER 961, CA..855, 856–59, 862, 865,
                                                                    946, 957, 959, 960, 961,
                                                                    968, 969, 980
Z v Finland (1997) 25 EHRR 371..425, 430, 432, 438
Z and E v Austria (1986) 49 DR 67..88
Z and Others v UK Appl 28945/95; (2001) The Times
  31 May...62
Zamir v UK (1983) Report of 11 October, 40 DR 42
  (1983)...55
Zana v Turkey (1998) 4 BHRC 242; (1997) 27 EHRR
  667...64
Zand v Austria (1978) 15 DR 70..63
Zaveckas (1970) 54 Cr App R 202, CA...1268, 1273
Ziliberberg v Moldova App no 61821/00, 4 May 2004,
  (unreported)..680, 759
Zimmermann and Steiner v Switzerland (1983) 6 EHRR 17...............................90

Table of UK statutes

Abortion Act 1967..................284, 285

Access to Health Record Act 1990.....926

Access to Personal Files Act 1987.....923, 924, 926

Administration of Justice Act 1960
  s 12(1)..................................390, 853

Administration of Justice Act 1973
  Sched 5..................................570

Ancient Monuments and
  Archaeological Areas Act 1979.......687

Anti Social Behaviour Act
  2003..................................660, 672, 701, 706, 788, 854
  s 57..................................739

Anti-terrorism, Crime and
  Security Act 2001..................203, 211, 1090–94, 1329, 1332, 1334, 1335, 1374, 1407, 1408, 1421–26, 1458, 1466, 1468
  Pt 3..................1090, 1091, 1093
  Pt 4..................171, 228, 289, 1332, 1363, 1421–39, 1443, 1463, 1465, 1466
  Pt11..................1090, 1091, 1093
  s 17..................................1092
  s 17(2)..................................1092
  s 17(2)(a)..................1091, 1093
  s 17(2)(b)..................1091, 1093
  s 17(2)(c)..........1091, 1092, 1093, 1094
  s 17(2)(d)..........1091, 1092, 1093, 1094

s 17(3),(4)..................................1092
s 17(5)..................................1092, 1093
s 17(6)..................................1092
s 18..................................1093
ss 21–23..................................1429, 1432
s 21 288, 289, 1427, 1433, 1455, 1436
s 21(1)..................................1426, 1427
s 21(1)(a), (b)..................................1430
s 21(2)..................................1426
s 21(3)..................................1426
s 21(5)..................................1426
s 21(8)..................................1429
s 23..................................288, 289, 1427, 1433, 1438, 1455, 1436
s 23(1)..................................1427
s 23(2)..................................1427
s 25..................................1429, 1455
s 27(9)..................................1430
s 30..................................1431
s 39..................................781
s 94..................................1122
ss 102, 103..................................1093
s 116..................................1019
s 117..................................1412

Appellate Jurisdiction
  Act 1876..................................1019, 1398

Armed Forces Act 1996
  ss 21–28..................................1568

Army Act 1955..................................100
  s 66..................................1519

Atomic Energy Act 1946
  s 11..................................615

Bail Act 1976 774

Banking Act 1987 1249

Broadcasting Act 1981
  s 29(3) 302

Broadcasting Act 1990 .... 234, 274,
                                          512, 518,
                                          519, 537
  s (2) 550
  s 6(1)(a) 179, 516, 535
  s 43 546
  s 142 839
  s 162 .... 509, 520, 524
  s 164(2), (4) 498

Broadcasting Act 1996 .... 512, 516, 519,
                                          537, 546,
                                          842, 848
  s 89 546
  s 106 .... 528, 840
  s 107 841
  s 119 841

Carriage of Goods by Sea Act
  1971 s 1(2) 170

Children Act 1989
  s 1(1) 856, 972
  s 97 853

Children and Young Persons Act 1933
  s 39(1) 392, 394, 854, 906
  s 49 854
  s 53(1) 906

Cinemas Act 1985 .... 551, 561

Cinematograph Act 1909 .... 262, 551,
                                          561

Cinematograph (Amendment) Act 1982 ...
  587

Civil Aviation Act 1942
  s 40 994

Civic Government (Scotland) Act 1982 ....
  469, 583, 585
  s 57(1) 1215

Civil Partnerships Act 2004 1472

Civil Procedure Act 1997 168

Civil Service Reform Act 1978 591

Companies Act 1985 1251
  s 431(5) 1239
  s 432(2) 1250
  s 437 .... 271, 1239, 1249

Communications Act 2003 .... 206, 208,
                                          214, 296, 315,
                                          511–16, 518,
                                          519, 812, 840
  Pt3 516
  s 2(1), (2) 520
  s 198(1) 520
  s 198(2) 521
  s 198(5), (6) 521
  ss 232–40 .... 520, 546
  s 237 520
  s 296 511
  s 309 511
  s 319 .... 209, 514, 520, 521
  s 319(c) 511, 523, 524, 533
  s 319(1), (2) 522
  s 319(2)(a) 522
  s 319(2)(f) 522, 523
  s 319(2)(g) 209, 210, 518
  s 319(4) 522, 523
  s 319(4)(f) 523
  s 320 511
  s 321 .... 209, 210, 533
  s 321(2), (3) 209, 518
  s 392 520
  Sched1 841

Computer Misuse Act 1990 .... 923, 924

Conspiracy and Protection of Property
  Act 1875
  s 7 .... 669, 705

Constitutional Reform Act 2005 257

Consumer Credit Act 1974
  s 127(3) 175, 200

Contempt of Court
  Act 1981 .... 32, 94, 150 183, 330,
                                          334–363, 394, 398
  s 1 .... 337, 361

s 2...361
s 2(2)..................339, 340–357, 361, 362
s 2(3)..338
s 3...361
s 4(a)-(e) 338
s 5.............................. 124, 331, 337–361,
                                    362, 674
s 6(c)...363
s 8...402
s 10...420
ss 12, 13.......................................338
Sched 1...338

Courts and Legal Services Act 1990
  s 71 1080

Crime and Disorder Act 1998
  s 1......................673, 674, 780, 854, 872
  s 1(10)...674
  s 25....................................... 673, 1122
  s 28..781
  s 31..781

Crime (Sentences) Act 1997.................854
  s 28...58
  s 29..181
  s 45..392

Criminal Appeals Act 1968....................338
  s 2(1)..1260

Criminal Appeals Act 1995................. 1260

Criminal Attempts Act 1981.................739
  s 1(4)...739

Criminal Justice Act 1987 1250
  s 2...1249
  s 2(4)..999

Criminal Justice Act 1988
  ss 23, 25, 26................................. 1294
  s 93D(6) 1349
  s 99...1217
  s 139..1114
  s 160....................................476, 478, 481

Criminal Justice Act 1991
  s 33(2)..202
  s 34...58
  s 37(4)..202
  s 39..202

Criminal Justice and Police
  Act 2001......................673, 1090, 1099,
                              1129, 1255, 1256,
                                 1310, 1323
  Pt 2...442
  s 41...872
  s 42...780, 787
  s 50.....................441, 442, 1003, 1255
  s 50(1),(2)..................................... 1003
  s 51...1255
  s 51(1)–(2)......................................1129
  ss 52-61 442
  s 54..442
  s 55..442
  s 60..442
  s 61..442
  s 62..442
  s 62(4)..442
  s 73 ....1160, 1166, 1172
  s 76 1204
  Sched1..1003

Criminal Justice and Public
  Order Act 1994......118, 119, 123, 159,
                         669, 670, 701, 710,
                         738, 1101, 1104, 1111,
                         1113, 130, 1137, 1186,
                         1189–91, 1209, 1236,
                       1239, 1244, 1249, 1250,
                         1255, 1284, 1323,
                         1325, 1364, 1366
  s 34, 36, 37.....................1205, 1209,
                       1213, 1235, 1238, 1239,
                       1241–43, 1247, 1327
  s 34–37 ....1189, 1212, 1235
  s 34 ....1238, 1239, 1240, 1242,
                           1244, 1247, 1248
  s 34(1).. 1237
  s 34(1)(A)......................................1241
  s 34(2)(a) 1200
  s 34(2)(d) 1212
  s 34(2A)................. 1212–15, 1241, 1242
  s 36–37 ....1189, 1205, 1212,
                           1213, 1235, 1242
  s 38(3)..1238, 1241
  s 60 .... 758, 1104, 1122, 1124, 1126,
      1133, 1134

s 60(4), (5)...........................1138
s 60AA............................758, 1125
s 61......................................748, 749
s 68........................672, 697, 748,
780, 1057, 1327
s 68(1)......................................744
s 68(2)...............................744, 745
s 68(3)......................................744
s 69.............673, 688, 697, 748, 749
s 71...1327
s 80(5(b))...............................1184
s 81(1)....................................1118
s 82.............................1369, 1409
s 84...............................478, 556
s 90...562
s 142..........................393, 851
s 143...82
s 143–148.................................556
s 146..........................1513, 1520
s 154................................780, 785
s 163.........................1068, 1073
s 168.......................................583

Criminal Justice (Terrorism
and Conspiracy) Act 1998.............1250,
1365–69
s 5...1367
s 20(1)....................................1367

Criminal Law Act 1967...........1140, 1143
s 3...................735, 744, 745, 1162

Criminal Law Act 1977
s 1A.......................................1367
s 5(3)..482
s 53...472
s 62...............................1188, 1208

Criminal Procedure and
Investigations Act 1996....................1075
s 3(4)......................................1048
ss 37, 38 58(4)........................852

Customs and Excise Management Act
1979
s 49...479

Data Protection Act 1984..........139, 150,
627, 921, 922–923
s 5...922

ss 10, 11, 21, 22, 24............................923
Sched 1.......................................922

Data Protection Act 1998.......................624,
640, 804, 810, 812,
813, 824, 831, 847,
848, 867, 881, 888,
889, 890, 901, 911,
920–937, 1021,
1064, 1093
s 1(1)..........................927, 929
s 2..928
s 3..937
s 6(6)..936
s 7..930
s 10..............................930, 932, 933
s 13...935
s 17...929
s 17(1)...929
s 17(3)...929
s 21(1)...935
s 23(1)...929
s 32...935
s 32(1)-(4).............................932, 933
s 32(3)...834
s 40(1)...935
s 42...935
s 43...935
s 47...935
s 48...936
s 49...936
s 49(6)...936
Sched 1................................928, 929
Sched 2...................929, 930, 931
Sched 3...................929, 931, 934
Sched 8..934
Sched 9...93

Disability Discrimination
Act 1995..............1481, 1485, 1511–13,
1526, 1536, 1537,
1547–58, 1563–65,
1574, 1575, 1577, 1588,
1593, 1595, 1599
Pts 2–4....................................1597
s 1(1)......................................1512
s 2(1)......................................1512
s 3A(1)...........................1547, 1548

s 3A(2)........................1551
s 3A(3)........................1548
s 3A(5)........................1536
s 3A(6)........................1552
s 4...............................1563
s 4A(1)........................1551
s 4A(3)........................1552
s 5...............................1550
s 5(3)...........................1549
s 5(5)...........................1550
s 5A.............................1597
s 6.......................1550, 1551
s 6(3)...........................1551
s 17A(1)(c)..............1537, 1548
s 17A(3)........................1588
s 18B(1)........................1552
s 18B(2)........................1553
s 19...............1512, 1553, 1554
s 20(4)..........................1549
s 21.............................1554
s 21B............................1554
s 21F............................1553
s 22.............................1512
s 25(9)..........................1548
s 28A............................1513
s 28A(3)........................1513
s 28B(6), (7)...................1549
s 28C............................1554
s 28C(2), (3)...................1555
s 28R............................1513
s 28R(6)(c).....................1513
s 28T............................1554
s 28T(2)........................1555
s 53A.....................1555, 1595
s 55.............................1563
s 58.............................1561
s 71.............................1511

Disability Discrimination
  Act 2005.......................1536
  s 12...........................1553

Drug Trafficking Offences
  Act 1986....................67, 558

Education Act 1996..................75

Education (No 2) Act 1986...........74
  s 43......................679, 733

Employment Act 2002...............1492

Employment Appeals Tribunals Act 1996
  s 10...........................1031

Employment Rights Act
  1996.....................1484, 1521
  s 71...........................1506
  s 71(1)........................1506
  s 72(1)........................1506
  s 73...........................1506
  s 73(1)........................1506
  s 99.....................1491, 1529
  s 193..........................1031

Employment Rights Act 1999
  Sched 8........................1031

Equality Act 2006.................1482
  Pt 2...........................1482
  Pt 3.........293, 1482, 1515, 1596, 1602
  s 81...........................1522

European Communities Act 1972.....152
  s 2(4)...........153, 154, 1479, 1486

Financial Services Act 1968
  s 177..........................1249
  s 178..........................1249

Football Spectators Act 1989
  s 14A, 14B.....................791

Freedom of Information
  Act 2000.............217, 590, 591, 627,
                       628, 630–658, 921,
                       1021, 1385
  s 1(1)(b)..................634, 639
  s 1(3).........................650
  s 2........................637, 653
  ss 3-6.........................633
  s 3............................632
  s 3(1)(b)......................633
  s 4...........................1040
  s 4(1)-(3)................632, 633
  s 5.............................63
  s 7(1),(3).....................633
  s 8............................650
  s 9............................650
  s 10(1)........................650
  s 12...........................640

s 14..640
s 16..650
s 19..654
s 19(1)(a)..654
s 20..654
s 21..635
s 21(2)(a)..639
s 22..647
s 23(1)...................................639, 650
s 26..648
s 27..648
s 28...648, 649
s 29..648
s 30(1)................641, 643, 644, 649
s 31....................641, 642, 642, 649
s 31(2)....................................647, 648
s 32..649
s 33...648, 649
s 34..639
s 35............................635, 641, 646, 649
s 35(1)...644
s 35(2)...645
s 36...644, 649
s 37..647
s 37(1)(a)..649
s 37(1)(b)..649
s 38..648
s 40(1)...640
s 41..640
s 42...647, 649
s 43...648, 649
s 43(1)...647
s 50..652
s 50(1)...652
s 52(1)...652
s 52(2)...652
s 53(1)...653
s 56..652
s 57(2),(3)..653
s 58(1)...653
s 59..653
s 63(1)...649
s 64(1)...649
Sched 1...................................233, 632
Sched 2...652
Sched 3...652

Friendly Societies Act 1992................1249
Further and Higher Education
   Act 1992..................................1524
Gender Recognition Act
   2004...............................836, 1569
Government of Wales Act 1988
   s 107(1)......................................213
   Sched2.......................................213
Highways Act 1980.....................734, 735,
                                          736, 798
   s 137.................679, 734, 735, 798
   s 137(1).....................................716
   s 258...667
Human Rights Act 1998.....................1–4,
       15, 20, 40, 77, 114, 116,
       119, 122, 129, 131–34,
       136, 142, 145, 148, 156,
       157–298, 299, 306, 308,
       312, 314, 315, 318, 319,
       337, 350, 351, 352, 366,
       376, 377, 380, 395, 399,
       400, 415, 419, 422–24,
       437, 448, 450, 452, 462,
       464, 475, 480, 487, 492,
       493, 501, 505, 510, 517,
       531, 533, 538, 543, 545,
       549, 558, 566, 567, 568,
       569, 582, 588, 596, 600,
       606, 615, 617, 619, 632,
       661, 662, 671, 675, 678,
       692, 693, 695, 696, 702,
       708, 709, 712, 720, 721,
       726, 728, 730, 734, 735,
       743, 749, 752, 771, 774,
       778, 781, 790, 795, 799,
       800, 801, 804, 807, 810,
       812, 813, 817, 824, 827,
       828, 831, 832, 834, 846,
       847, 850, 858, 860, 863,
       865–67, 875, 876, 881,
       893, 896, 903, 904, 909,
       916, 918, 928, 935–37, 959,
       980, 984, 985, 99193, 995,
       1001, 1012, 1021, 1024, 1025,

1028, 1030, 1032, 1034,
1042, 1046, 1052, 1054,
1059, 1068, 1084, 1086,
    1087, 1093, 1097,
1098–1100, 1102, 1104,
1105, 1126, 1129, 1130,
1134, 1141, 1150, 1152,
    1155–57, 1164, 1168,
1169, 1177, 1180, 1181,
1190, 1207, 1208, 1210,
1234, 1249, 1252, 1256,
1261, 1263, 1265, 1267,
    1287–90, 1292, 1293,
1302, 1303, 1307, 1309,
1310, 1316, 1325–27, 1335,
1337, 1341, 1349, 1361,
1369, 1401, 1414, 1424,
1431, 1438, 1448, 1460–65,
1474, 1479, 1484–86, 1510,
1515, 1516, 1518–20, 1526,
    1566, 1569
s 1(2)...................................169, 170
s 1(4)...165
s 2................................165, 169, 191, 192,
    193, 207, 214, 257, 264,
    279, 330, 255, 356, 360,
    376, 492, 501, 682, 746,
    761, 762, 824, 829, 848,
    959, 990, 1046, 1179,
    1267, 1307, 1338, 1521
s 2(1).......................193, 829, 954, 1435
s 3...........................2, 130, 170, 171, 172,
    173, 174, 176, 180,
    191–199, 201, 202, 208,
    211, 213, 214, 216, 237,
    249, 251, 255, 257, 261,
    280, 281, 284, 285, 95,
    296, 297, 312, 330, 337,
    365, 360, 363, 400, 402,
    403, 404, 408, 420, 445,
    446, 501, 505, 543, 567,
    596, 603, 604, 607, 608,
    614, 617, 680, 702, 721,
    722, 727, 730, 733, 736,
    737, 741, 747, 750, 799,
    804, 847, 848, 871, 872,
    895, 935, 936, 037, 938,

986, 987, 1024, 1051, 1078,
    1085, 1088, 1128, 1129,
    1163, 1213, 1261, 1305,
    1307, 1336, 1337, 1340,
    1349, 1350, 1352, 1345,
    1370, 1390, 1394, 1396,
    1398, 1408, 1409, 1419,
    1443, 1448, 1461, 1484,
    1486, 1505, 1518–20,
    1525, 1526, 1571, 1572
s 3(1)................171, 176, 177, 178, 206,
    215, 224, 355, 360, 389,
    415, 420, 440, 444, 445,
    531, 537, 538, 541, 544,
    545, 568, 728, 747, 748,
    858, 860, 862, 864, 959,
    1094, 1256, 1571, 1432,
    1433
s 3(2)................164, 171, 199, 437, 1433
s 3(2)(a)...172
s 3(2)(b)...171
s 3(2)(c)............................ 171, 296, 1254
s 4...........................16, 171, 175, 185 186,
    187, 199–204, 214, 280,
    281, 284, 296, 400, 531,
    535, 537, 538, 959, 1051,
    1052, 1094, 1431, 1432
s 4(1)...199
s 4(2)............................ 199, 200, 1447
s 4(4)...199
s 4(5)..200, 202
s 4(6)...201
s 5(1)...200
s 5(2)..200, 204
s 6.....................164, 165, 170, 193, 198,
    212, 218, 221, 222, 224,
    226, 227, 231, 236, 237,
    238, 239, 248, 249, 250,
    251, 252, 253, 254, 255,
    264, 274, 275, 278, 281,
    283, 296, 297, 330, 332,
    333, 366, 378, 388, 420,
    437, 438, 445, 446, 448,
    480, 492, 501, 515, 516,
    531, 543, 567, 584, 607,
    617, 619, 622, 632, 633,
    661, 680, 700, 701, 706,

720, 722, 729, 730, 736,
749, 750, 752, 760, 762,
764, 797, 799, 808, 824,
825, 836, 837, 848, 849,
850, 864, 866, 867, 871,
872, 875, 878, 905, 937,
938, 958, 981, 989, 991,
1007, 1030, 1047, 1048,
1075, 1076, 1078, 1080,
1084, 1085, 1086, 1087,
1093, 1139, 1157, 1179,
1181, 1251, 1252, 1259–61,
1263, 1265, 1270, 1277,
1294, 1302, 1305–10,
1318, 1336, 1337, 1341,
1355, 1370, 1386, 1396,
1397, 1454, 1455, 1484,
1485, 1519, 1521, 1569
ss 6–9 229
s 6(1)........................... 15, 215, 216, 231,
237, 254, 281, 530, 567,
825, 858, 959, 963,
s 6(1)(a)....................................700
s 6(2)...........................164, 216, 296, 314,
581, 1094, 1259, 1307
s 6(2)(a)....................................216
s 6(2)(b).............216, 1088, 1261, 1352
s 6(3)(a)..............................217, 954
s 6(3)(b)....................217, 227, 228, 229,
233, 248, 530
s 6(5) 216
s 6(6) 215
s 7................................165, 237, 295, 867,
905, 982, 991, 1081,
1089, 1445, 1179, 1180,
1258, 1260, 1308,
1397, 1405
s 7(1).......................... 237, 237–239, 493,
1163, 1398
s 7(1)(a)..................234, 235, 236, 238,
239, 241, 531, 544, 567,
581, 700, 701, 749, 808,
825, 846, 847, 848, 849,
850, 876, 981, 1008, 1051,
1055, 1078, 1079, 1080,
1086, 1089, 1094, 1131,
1180, 1257, 1262, 1304,

1307–09, 1319, 1347,
1398, 1484, 1521, 1521,
1524, 1567, 1569,
s 7(1)(b)...........235, 237, 238, 493, 720,
1008, 1047, 1055, 1076,
1134, 1137, 1232, 1258,
1307, 1309
s 7(2).....................................238
s 7(3)...............................236, 493
s 7(5)...............................236, 240
s 7(7)....................235, 237, 295, 701
s 7(9).....................................238
s 8.............................165, 400, 401, 847,
849, 981, 991, 1007, 1089,
1131, 1137, 1179, 1180,
1257, 1258, 1260, 1306,
1309
s 8(1)......................241, 400, 401
s 8(2).....................................241
s 8(3)...............................241, 244
s 8(4)...............................242, 1309
s 9(3)......................................59
s 10 ....201, 202, 204–206,
214, 296, 1438
s 10(2).....................................204
s 11 .... 116, 1309
s 12 ....213, 237, 252, 253,
300, 475, 622, 623, 624,
674, 795, 834, 847, 865,
871, 872, 875, 890, 902,
910, 930, 938, 950, 952,
956, 958, 981, 985, 986,
987, 1096
s 12(1)............... 795, 895, 952, 985, 987
s 12(2)...........................212, 617, 795
s 12(3)......................212, 378, 379, 617,
622, 938, 952, 955, 985,
986, 987, 988, 989, 990
s 12(4)....................212, 213, 252, 253,
254, 378, 567, 617, 619,
624, 795, 860, 886, 892,
895, 905, 909, 938, 952,
957, 958, 959, 985, 987
s 12(4)(a)(i) 887, 895, 928,
s 12(4)(b).........833, 834, 848, 905, 938
s 12(5)..................................212
s 13 ....207, 220

s 14 1425
s 14(1)(a) 1168
s 15 1359
s 16 1425
s 19 .... 16, 171, 207, 214,
296, 505, 518,
545, 1250
s 19(1)(a) 206, 207, 210,
1337, 1369
s 19(1)(b) 206, 210, 214
s 19(a)
s 20 204
s 21 213
s 21(1) 199, 216
s 22(4)(b) 239
Sched 1 .... 165, 166, 169, 229,
558, 1119,
1187, 1400,
1448, 1486
Sched 2 205
Sched 3 ....???

Immigration Act 1971
ss 3–3B   1427
Sched 3 1424

Indecent Displays (Control) Act
1981 .... 478, 483, 587
s 1(1), (2) 478
s 1(4) 479

Insolvency Act 1986
s 236 1249
s 433 1249

Intelligence Services Act 1994 124,
159, 999,
1010, 1029,
1040, 1054,
1075, 1078,
1080, 1090,
1097, 1098
s 1(1), (2) 1013
s 3(2) 1013
s 5 .... 1016, 1059, 1061, 1066
s 5(2) 1016
s 6 1016
s 9 607
s 10 1014

Interception of Communications
Act 1985 .... 73, 114, 123,
615, 1010, 1017, 1022,
1032–1034, 1040, 1041,
1044, 1046, 1049, 1052,
1054, 1055, 1057, 1061,
1065, 1079, 1085, 1089
s 1 .... 1038, 1048, 1050
s 1(1) 1048, 1049
s 1(2) 1038
ss 2–5 1042
s 2(1) 1034
s 2(2) 1034, 1049
s 2(3), (5) 1035
s 4(5), (6) 1036
s 6(3) 1049
s 7 1040
s 7(3), (4) 1040
s 7(5) 1084
s 7(8) 1051
s 8 1036
s 8(1)(a) 1039
s 8(3) 1039
s 9 .... 1040, 1048,
1049, 1050,
1051, 1082,
1253
s 9(1) 1399
s 9(1)(a) 1050
s 11(7) 1048
s 19 1048

Justices of the Peace Act 1361 ... 686, 750

Justices of the Peace Act 1968 750

Knives Act 1997
s 7 1122

Local Government (Access to
Information) Act 1985 627

Local Government Act 1972 Pt VA 627

Local Government Act 1986
s 2A 1524

Local Government Act 1988
s 17 1576
s 28 1524

Local Government Act 2000
s 104... 1524

Local Government Act 2003
s 122... 1524

Local Government (Miscellaneous
Provisions) Act 1982................469, 587

Magistrates' Courts Act 1980
s 69(2).. 853

Medical Reports Act 1988...................... 925

Mental Health Act 1983...........................245
s 73....................................201, 202, 205
s 74..202
Pt VII..391

Metropolitan Police Act 1839
s 54(13) 1521

Misuse of Drugs Act 1971 178
s 23..996, 999
s 28...1349
s 33...1114

National Assistance Act 1948................224
s 21..223
s 26..226

National Heritage Act 1983 687

Northern Ireland Act 1998 ......1083, 1084
s 90 1031

Northern Ireland (Emergency Provisions)
Act 1978
s 7(1)...1350
s 11 1152

Northern Ireland (Emergency
Provisions) Act 1987...........................1240

Northern Ireland (Emergency Provisions)
Act 1991
s 28 1382

Northern Ireland (Emergency
Provisions) Act 1996............1117, 1331,
1364

Northern Ireland (Emergency
Provisions) Act 1998..........1364, 1366

Obscene Publications
Act 1959......................94, 464, 465, 469,
479, 481, 482, 483,
485, 509, 524, 526,
550, 552, 553, 560,
563, 583, 585, 586
s 1...509, 550
s 2...466
s 2(1)...469
s 2(5)..1349
s 4..............................124, 454, 674

Obscene Publications Act 1964
s 1(1),(2)..469
s 1(3)..1349

Offences Against the Person
Act 1861... 1415
s 4...1417, 1419
s 18...1415
s 23...1415
s 24...1415
s 28...1415
s 29...1415

Official Secrets Act 1889......................522
s 1...596

Official Secrets Act 1911 ...592, 602, 614
s 1.............................592, 602, 603, 615
s 2.....................592–595, 613, 614

Official Secrets Act 1989.............595–616
s 1–4..................................596, 603
s 1...1203
s 1(1)...............................596, 597, 600,
603, 605, 606, 607,
608, 610–616
s 1(3).............................598, 599, 600,
603, 604, 605,
613, 614
s 1(4)..599
s 1(4)(a)..599
s 1(5)...1349
s 1(9)..608
s 2.............................600, 601, 613
s 2(1)..603, 604
s 2(2)..600, 613
s 2(2)(b), (c)....................................601

s 2(3)............................1349, 1343
s 2(4)...............................600, 1353
s 3...........................603, 604, 613
s 3(1).....................................601
s 3(1)(a)................................601
s 3(1)(b)..................601, 603, 604,
605, 613, 614
s 3(2).....................................601
s 3(2)(b)................................601
s 3(3)..............................601, 602
s 3(5).....................................601
s 3(4)...................................1349
s 3(6).....................................601
s 4............................602, 603, 607,
608, 613
s 4(1)................603, 606, 607, 608,
611, 612
s 4(2)........................600, 602, 606
s 4(2)(a)................................606
s 4(2)(b)................................606
s 4(3)...............603, 605, 614, 615
s 4(4).............................606, 1349
s 4(5)...................................1349
s 4(6).....................................602
s 5...........................596, 604, 613
s 5(1)..............................596, 507
s 5(1)(a)(i), (iii)......................602
s 5(1)(b)(ii)............................602
s 5(6).....................................603
s 6..607
s 6(1).....................................603
s 6(2).....................................604
s 6(3).....................................604
s 6(4).....................................604
s 6(5).....................................604
s 7..................................604, 605
s 7(3).....................................607
s 12...............................607, 608

Parks Regulation (Amendment) Act
1926................................68, 686,

Parliament Act 1911............................82
s 2...120

Police Act 1964
s 47.......................................100
s 48......................................1309

s 51.......................................1108
s 51(3)......................1109, 1117

Police Act 1976................................1311

Police Act 1977................................1324

Police Act 1996................................1311
Pt III....................................1056
Pt IV.....................................1311
s 67(2)..................................1311
s 70.......................................1311
s 72.......................................1311
s 75(3)..................................1311
s 83.......................................1311
s 86.......................................1108
s 89.......................................1149
s 89(1)..............1109, 1117, 1137, 1139
s 89(2)....................1111, 1137, 1139

Police Act 1997........................118, 119,
120, 998, 1054
ss 17, 18...............................998
s 91(1)................998, 1057, 1058
s 93(2)................998, 1056, 1057
s 93(4)......................998, 1056
s 93(5)..................................1057
s 94.......................................1057
s 94(2)..................................998
s 95(1)..................................1057
s 97.......................................1058
s 97(2)..................................1057
s 97(2)(b).............................1058
s 97(3)..................................1058
s 98.......................................1058
s 99.......................................1058
s 102.....................................1040
Sched 5.................................1000
Sched 9 1013

Police and Criminal Evidence
Act 1984..................76, 119, 120, 194,
440–442, 762, 898,
996–997, 999, 1001,
1003, 1004, 1005,
1007, 1067, 1097,
1103–21, 1137–41, 1143,
1151, 1152, 1154, 1158,
1161, 1163, 1165–68, 1171,

1172, 1179, 1187,
1188–1210, 1215, 1216,
1220, 1226, 1232, 1234,
1236, 1254, 1255, 1256–58,
1262, 1263, 1265, 1267,
1268, 1279–1300, 1303,
1304, 1310, 1317, 1318,
1320, 1323–5
Pts I–IV 1107
Pt II 441
Pt IV 1165, 1171, 1303
Pt V 1166, 1171, 1188
s 1 .... 1113, 1117, 1119,
112, 1128, 1130, 1132
s 1(1) 1113, 1114
s 1(1)(a), (b) 1114
s 1(2) 1113, 1123
s 1(4) 1114
s 2 .... 1114, 1130, 1138
s 2(1) 1129
s 2(3) 1130
s 3 .... 1114, 1129, 1130, 1138
s 4 .... 1113, 1114
s 8 998
s 8(1) 441, 1002
s 8(1)(c) 998
s 8(1)(d) 441
s 8(2) 1001
s 9 .... 441, 447, 1002
s 9(2) 441
s 10 1003
s 10(2) 1003
s 11 .... 441, 1002
s 14 .... 441, 1002
s 15 998
s 15(5A) 998
s 15(3),(6) 998
s 16 .... 998, 999
s 16(5)(b), (c) 998, 999
s 16(8) 999
s 17 .... 996, 997, 1000, 1114
s 17(1)(c) 676
s 17(5),(6) 1000
s 18 .... 996, 997, 1114, 1138
s 18(4) 1005
s 19 .... 999, 1001
s 22(1) 1001, 1002

s 22(2)(a) 1002
s 24 (now repealed and 1256
replaced by new s 24)
s 24 .... 679, 1122, 1131, 1143–45,
1150, 1155, 1167, 1303
s 24(1)(a) 1131
s 24(1)(b) 1144
s 24(1)(c) 1131, 1144
s 24(1)(d) 1131, 1144
s 24(1)(e) 1131
s 24(2) 1144
s 24(3)(a) 1144
s 24(4)(a) 1155
s 24(5) 1144–46
s 24(5)(a) 1155
s 24(5)(e), (f) 1145
s 24(6) 1153
s 25(7)(a) 1155
s 24 .... 1217, 125
s 24A 1145
s 25 .... 1145, 1146
s 28 .... 1149, 1158, 1160, 1161
s 29 1162
s 30 .... 1197, 1200
s 30(1) 1200, 1201
s 32 997
s 32(1) 1181
s 32(2) 1181
s 32(2)(b) 997
s 36 1171
s 36(1) 1171
s 37 .... 1165, 1166, 1172
s 37(2) 1187
s 37(3) 1165
s 38 .... 1166, 1172
s 40 1166
s 40(1)(b) 1166, 1172
s 40A 1166
s 41 1165
s 42(1) 1165
s 43(1) 1166
s 44 1166
s 45A 1166, 1172
s 45A(4) 1166
s 51(d) 1167
s 54 1181
s 55 .... 1179, 1181

s 56 ....1189, 1192
s 58 ....1189, 1218, 1255,
1282, 1286, 1309
s 58(8) 1216–18
s 58(6)(b) 1217
s 58(8A)–(8B) 1217
s 60 ....1203, 1203
s 60A 1204
s 62 ....1183, 1184
s 63 ....1183, 1184
s 64 1290
s 65 1184
s 66 1103
s 67(8) 1187, 1311
s 67(10) 1107, 1304, 1308
s 67(11) 1108, 1138
s 76 ....1199, 1206, 1275–78,
1287, 1289, 1290, 1300
s 76(2) 1271, 1275, 1276
s 76(2)(a) 1204, 1206, 1269–75,
1346, 1462
s 76(2)(b) 1272–75, 1300
s 76(4) 1253, 1293
s 76(8) 1206, 1271
s 77 ....1300, 1301
s 78 ....120, 1049, 1051, 1077,
1089, 1107, 1138, 1199, 1214,
1251, 1272, 1275–1300
s 82(3) 1287, 1300
s 84(4), (5) 1311
s 87(4) (repealed and replaced ...1311
by new s 87(4))
s 94(2) 998
s 105(4) (repealed and replaced .1311
by new s 105(4))
s 116 1165
s 117 ......1128, 1158, 1162, 1163, 1179
Sched 1..441, 44, 446, 447, 448, 1002
Sched 7 1002

Police and Magistrates' Court Act 1994
s 37(f) 1189

Police Reform Act 2002 ....1172, 1311,
1313, 1123–1321
Pt 2 1314
Sched 3 1314
s 12 1321

Police (Scotland) Act 1967
s 1 1037

Post Office Act 1953 477
s 58 1033
s 58(1) 1033

Postal Services Act 2000
s 85 479

Prevention of Terrorism
Act 2005 ....3, 179, 205,
1099, 1100, 1329,
1332, 1335, 1354,
1362, 1374, 1422,
1438–52, 146,
ss 1–9 1438
s 1(1) 1440
s 1(3) 1441
s 1(9) 1441, 1442, 1449
s 2 1442
s 2(1)(a), (b) 1445
s 2(4) 1442
s 3 ....1447, 1448, 1449
s 3(1) 1445
s 3(1)(a) 145
s 3(2), (3) 1445
s 3(5), (6) 1445
s 3(10) 1445, 1447, 1449,
1450, 1452
s 3(11) 1445
s 3(12) 1452, 1453
s 3(13) 1447
s 4 ....1442, 1444
s 4(3) 1444
s 4(7) 1444
s 4(8) 1443
s 7 1442
s 8 1440
s 8(2) 1439
s 8(4) 1440
s 11(2) 179, 1445, 1448
s 13(2) 1439
s 25 1455
Sched 1451

Prevention of Terrorism (Additional
Powers) Act 1996 119

Prevention of Terrorism
(Temporary Provisions)
Act 1989..................443, 1118,
1122, 1219, 1334
s 12..57
s 13A(4)......................................1118
s 13B(3)......................................1118
s 14..................1121, 1146, 1167
s 14(1)..1121
s 14(1)(b)......................1147, 1148
s 14(4)..............................1167, 1169
s 14(5)..1167
s 15(3),(4).................................1121
s 16..1121
s 16A..272
s 16B..444
s 20..................................1148, 1149
s 51(1).......................................1000
Sched 5..........................1121, 1170
Sched 6A......................................997
Sched 7..............................442, 999

Protection from Harassment
Act 1997.......................234, 673, 691,
780, 813, 824, 863,
866, 869, 870–872
s 1..674, 870
s 1(1)(c)..87
s 2..870
s 3..871
s 7(3),(4).....................................871

Protection of Children
Act 1978.....................556, 557, 567,
568, 569, 586
s 1..447, 585, 586
s 7(6)..556

Public Interest Disclosure Act 1998..409,
591

Public Order Act 1936......497, 669, 701
s 1..676
s 2..399
s 2(1)(a)......................................400
s 2(1)(b)..............................399, 400
s 2(6)..677
s 3..........................669, 704, 707, 708
s 3(1)..661

s 3(3)..709
s 55..................710, 772, 783, 787

Public Order Act 1986........125, 502, 503,
669, 672, 673,
674, 701, 707,
708, 709, 1417
Pt I..676
Pt II...676
Pt III..................497, 502, 505, 573
s 1..676, 677
s 2..676, 677
s 3..676, 677
s 3A..502
s 4..676
s 4A......................................507, 676
s 4A(3)(c)....................................674
s 5..................507, 676, 1141, 1521
s 5(3)(c)......................................674
ss 11-14A....................................676
s 11..................................674, 702, 704,
709, 764, 1149
s 11(1),(2)...................................702
s 11(4)–(6)..................................702
s 11(7)...765
s 11(7)–(9)..................................703
s 12..................................673, 674, 702,
704–706, 707, 708,
720, 721, 722, 723,
724, 725, 728, 729,
764, 1149
ss 12-14A..................720, 722, 725
ss 12-14.......................................721
s 12(1)...723
s 12(1)(a)....................................704
s 12(1)(b)....................................705
s 12(4)...707
s 12(5)...707
s 12(6)...707
s 13..................................675, 692, 700, 702,
709, 710, 720, 725,
729, 730
s 13(1)..................................708, 729
s 13(5)...708
s 13(7)...708
s 13(8)...708
s 13(10).......................................708

s 14.................673, 674 679, 706–707, 720, 721, 722, 723, 724, 725, 726, 728, 729, 764, 1149
s 14(1)..706
s 14(4)..707
s 14(5)..707
s 14(6)..707
s 14(7)..707
s 14A.............................673, 697, 700, 709, 710–722, 725, 726, 727, 728, 729
s 14A(1)...................................710, 712
s 14A(4)..710
s 14A(5)..........710, 711, 712, 727, 728
s 14B..727
s 14B(5)...727
s 14B(7)...727
s 14C...............................673, 697, 710
s 16...676
s 18...503
s 18(4)..1349
s 19...503
s 19(2)..1349
s 20...503, 573
s 20(2)..1349
s 21...503, 573
s 21(3)..1349
s 22...503
s 22(3)–(5)..1349
s 23...573
s 29A-29G................................502–505
s 29B..505
s 29J..504, 505
s 54A..507

Public Records Act 1958............303, 627, 628, 632

Race Relations Act 1965.....................1562
s 6...497

Race Relations Act 1968.....................1562

Race Relations Act 1976.............224, 496, 502, 1126, 1134, 1136, 1137, 1208, 1312, 1316, 1481, 1484, 1507–11, 1521, 1527, 1547, 1548,

1556, 1562, 1563, 1565, 1657, 1569, 1574, 1577, 1588, 1593, 1600
s 1(1)(a)............1535, 1558, 1562, 1565
s 1(1)(b)..................................1545–7, 1549
s 1(1A)..1544, 1545
s 2...1563
s 3A..1559
s 4...1556, 1557
s 4A.......................................1570, 1586
s 17..1557
s 19B..1509
s 20..1508
s 32..1561
ss 35-38..1575
s 37..1575
s 41(1)...1569
s 42..1569
ss 48-50..1594
s 53..1509
s 54(a)–54ZA................................1536
s 56(1)(b).......................................1558
s 57(1), (3).....................................1586
s 69(2)(b)..1569
s 71D...1578
s 71(2)–(4)......................................1597
s 75..1505

Race Relations (Amendment) Act 2000....................1125, 1126, 1208, 1509, 1577, 1594
s 7..1569

Race Relations Remedies Act 1994..1589

Racial and Religious Hatred Act 2005.......................................502, 573

Regulation of Investigatory Powers Act 2000..............120, 124, 199, 207, 604, 810, 993, 995, 1010, 1012, 1034–1053, 1054, 1058, 1059, 1324, 1397, 1399
Pt I...................1034, 1042, 1044, 1046, 1050, 1052, 1055, 1061, 1072, 1075

Pt II................. 1038, 1054, 1055, 1056,
1057, 1058–1065, 1066,
1067, 1068, 1069, 1071,
1072, 1074, 1075, 1076,
1078, 1079, 1082
Pt IV.. 1078
s 1.................... 1038, 1039, 1047, 1076
s 1(1),(2)................................... 1044
s 1(3).. 1039
s 1(5)(c)...................................... 1048
s 1(6).. 1038
s 2.. 598
ss 2–5................................ 1039, 1084
s 2(1).. 1034
s 2(3).. 1035
s 3.................... 1037, 1038, 1044, 1050
s 3(2)................................. 1037, 1038
s 4..................................... 1037, 1038
s 4(1).. 1048
s 4(2).. 1038
s 5(2)-(5).................................... 1035
s 5(3)................................. 1034, 1044
s 5(3)(a), (c).............................. 1036
s 5(5).. 1034
s 6(2).. 1037
s 7(1), (2)................................... 1035
s 7(1)(a)...................................... 1051
s 8(1).. 1037
s 8(7).. 1035
s 9(6).. 1036
s 11(4), (5)................................. 1037
s 11(7)............................... 1037, 1052
s 11(8).. 1052
s 15.. 1038
s 15(4)(d).................................... 1048
s 16(1).. 1048
s 17.......................... 1047, 1050, 1052,
1075, 1081, 1085
s 17(1)............................... 1048, 1051
s 17(1)(b).................................... 1048
s 17(2)............................... 1047, 1048
s 17(4).. 1048
s 18.......................... 1048, 1050, 1051
s 18(1).. 1048
s 18(1)(f).................................... 1398
s 18(4)............................... 1048, 1050
s 18(6)–(8).................................. 1048

s 18(9)................................. 1048, 1052
s 18(9)(b).................................... 1051
s 18(10)...................................... 1051
s 19.. 1052
s 19(4).. 1081
s 19(4a)...................................... 1081
s 21(4).. 1039
s 26.. 1038
s 26(2).. 1062
s 26(3).. 1060
s 26(4)(b).................................... 1062
s 26(5).. 1062
s 27(2).. 1078
s 28.. 1063
s 28(2).. 1063
s 28(3).. 1073
s 30.. 1063
s 30(2).. 1063
s 32(2).. 1061
s 32(3)............................... 1060, 1073
s 32(3a)...................................... 1063
s 32(3)(c).................................... 1063
s 32(6).. 1061
s 33.. 1061
s 34.. 1061
s 34(4).. 1061
s 35.. 1061
s 36.. 1061
s 37................................... 1061, 1064
s 41.. 1061
s 42.. 1061
s 43................................... 1061, 1063
s 43(3)(a)............................ 1061, 1063
s 43(3)(b).................................... 1063
s 43(3)(c).................................... 1063
s 44(3).. 1061
s 44(5)(a).................................... 1063
s 47................................... 1062, 1064
s 47(1), (2)................................. 1062
s 48(1).. 1060
s 48(4).. 1062
s 48(7).. 1060
s 48(7)(b).................................... 1060
s 49.. 1039
s 57.. 1038
s 57(2).. 1039
s 57(2)(a).................................... 1039

s 57(8)...1036
s 58...1039
s 58(1)..1039
s 58(6), (7)..1040
s 58(7)..1040
s 62...1063, 1065
s 65.....................................607, 1040, 1051,
                            1068, 1076, 1079
s 65(2)...............238, 1051, 1079, 1080
s 65(2a)...........1078, 1083, 1084, 1085
s 65(2)(b)..1085
s 65(2c)....................................1082, 1085
s 65(2d).....................................1082, 1085
s 65(3).....................1079, 1081, 1082
s 65(4)..1082
s 65(5)......................................1079, 1081
s 65(6)......................................1079, 1082
s 65(7),(8)..1082
s 66(3)..1082
s 67(3)(b)..1082
s 67(5)..1081
s 67(7)..1084
s 67(8)......................................1051, 1085
s 67(9)..1085
s 68(4)..1083
s 68(6), (7)..1083
s 69...1085, 1088
s 69(2)(h)..1084
s 70(2)(c)..1079
s 71...1066, 1068
s 71(3)(a)...................................1062, 1077
s 72(2)..1067
s 78(1)..1037
s 81(2)..1060
s 81(3)............................1034, 1044, 1060
s 81(7)..1035
Sched 1...1063
Sched 4.......................................1065, 1081

Rehabilitation of Offenders
  Act 1974..889

Rent Act 1977...1525
  Sched1................................180, 282, 1525

Representation of the People Act 1983
  s 76..183
  ss 95, 96.......................................678, 733
  s 97..680

Road Traffic Act 1988.........................1122,
                                  1163, 1252
  s 163....................................1122, 1163
  s 172.........................271, 1249, 1252

School Standards and Framework
  Act 1998..47
  s 131...75

Scotland Act 1998..................................459
  s 29(2)(b)...213
  s 29(2)(d)...213
  s 57...213
  Sched 5..213

Security Services Act 1989......614, 1022,
                                 1028, 1080
  s 1...1013
  s 1(1)..1013
  s 1(3)..1013
  s 1(4)..1013
  s 5...607

Security Services Act 1996
  s 1...1013
  s 134(1)...1013

Seditious Meetings Act 1817
  s 3...679

Serious and Organised
  Crime Act 2005.....................3, 672, 702,
                                 996, 1099,
                                 1104, 1411
  s 110...................................1144, 1256
  s 111...1145
  s 113(4)..998
  ss 132–138.....................673, 701, 730
  Sched7...1217

Sex Discrimination
  Act 1975.....................982, 1481, 1484,
                          1488–93, 1497, 1498,
                          1504–06, 1508, 1510,
                          1511, 1514, 1515–19,
                          1521, 1529, 1535,
                          1545, 1548, 1556,
                          1558, 1563, 1565–67,
                          1569, 1574, 1575, 1588,
                          1589, 1593, 1600

s 1 1517
s 1(1) 1529
s 1(1)(a) 1565
s 1(1)(b) 1538–40, 1545, 1549
s 1(1)(1)(a) 1565
s 1(1A) 1545
s 1(2) 1538, 1541
s 1(2)(b) 1540, 1541–3
s 2A 1504, 1505, 1534
s 2A(1) 1534
s 3(1)(a) 1534
s 3A 1505, 1506, 1529
s 3A(1) 1505
s 3A(2) 1506
s 4 1563
s 4(1) 1561, 1562, 1564
s 4A 1559
s 5(3) 1518, 1529, 1534
s 6 1505
s 6(6)(b) 1556
s 7 1568
s 7(1)(a) 1518
s 7(2) 1568
s 7(2)(a), (b), (g) 1568
s 7A 1568, 1569
s 7B 1569
s 22 1505
s 29 1505
ss 41, 42 1586
s 42A 1574
s 48 1575
s 53(1) 1599
s 56A(10) 1587
s 63A 1528, 1586
s 65(1)(b) 1588
s 65(1B) 1589
s 66(1) 1588
s 66A 1528, 1586
s 74(2) 1587
s 74(2) 1587

Sex Disqualification
(Removal) Act 1919 1487

Sexual Offences Act 1956 479
s 13 480
s 30(2) 1349

Sexual Offences Act 1967
s 1 ....82, 556
s 1(5) 1519
s 2 1519
s 4(1)(a) 851

Sexual Offences Act 2003 477,
                                         555, 556
s 45(2) 556
s 51 556

Sexual Offences (Amendment) Act 1976
s 4(1)(a) 393

Sexual Offences (Amendment) Act 1992
s 1(1) 393, 851

Sexual Offences (Amendment) Act 2000
s 1 .... 81, 82, 556

Special Education Needs and
Disability Discrimination
Act 2001 1593

Special Immigration Appeals Act 1997
s 1 1083

Suicide Act 1961
s 2 78

Supreme Court Act 1981
s 31 329
s 69 1085

Terrorism Act 2000 .... 3, 120, 124,
                                199, 207, 208,
                           442–444, 446, 671,
                           672, 673, 698, 997,
                           1007, 1013, 1099,
                           1104, 1106, 1111,
                           1118, 1121, 1128,
                        1130–50, 1158, 1162,
                        1163, 1165, 1167–71,
                           1183, 1184, 1191,
                           1193, 1198, 1201,
                     1204, 1207, 1210, 1216,
                        1218–20, 1225, 1251,
                     1250–55, 1278, 1293–95,
                        1304, 1310, 1311, 1316,
                     1318, 1324, 1325, 1329–32,
                     1334, 1335–38, 1345–49,

1352–55, 1363, 1364, 1368–75,
1377–84, 1386–90, 1392,
1394, 1397, 1398–1402,
1404–15, 1420, 1422,
1426–29, 1439, 1442,
1463–65, 1467, 1468
s 1 ....671, 1117, 1148, 1149,
1204, 1334, 1347, 1357,
1370, 1377, 1378, 1381,
1382–87, 1389, 1392,
1395, 1405–8, 1411, 1414,
1420, 1439, 1442, 1465
s 1(1).....................671, 698, 1011, 1426
s 1(2)... 1420
s 1(3)(b)... 1420
s 1(5) 1396
s 2(1)(a) 1385
s 3.............................1383, 1385, 1386,
1388, 1392, 1395, 1404
s 3(1)... 1383
s 3(3)... 1383
s 3(3)(b).. 1397
s 3(4)..............................674, 1383, 1384
s 3(5)...................................... 674, 1384
s 4.. 1397
s 4(3)... 1397
s 5.. 1397
s 5(3)... 1397
s 5A-5C.. 1384
s 6.. 1399
s 7.. 1399
s 9...1397, 1398
s 10.. 1397
s 11 ....178, 1146, 1347,
1389, 1394
s 11(1), (2)..............178, 1353, 1389–92
s 11(3)... 178
s 12.............................1146, 1347, 1395,
s 12(1)... 1427
s 12(2)... 1393
s 12(2)(c) 1393
s 12(3)(a) 1393
s 12(4).......................................1393, 1394
s 13 .... 1347, 1393, 1394
s 13A.......................................1118, 1123
s 13A(8) 1118
s 14 1396

ss 15–18 ....1146, 1396,
1412, 1414
s 15 1396
s 16 1396
s 16A 1353
s 17 1396
s 18 ....1347, 1396
s 19 ....444, 1347, 1396,
1412–14
s 20 1378
s 21A 1413, 1414
s 21A(5) 1413
s 21B 1413
s 28 1410
ss 33-36 997
s 38B 1412, 1413
s 40(l)(a) 1146, 1147, 1149
s 40(1)(b).........................1146–48, 1149
s 41 ....1111, 1146, 1147–50,
1161, 1168–70, 1204,
1255, 1334, 1410
s 41(4)-(7) 1169
s 41(4)... 1170
s 41(5)... 1170
s 41(6)... 1170
ss 43–47 1117
s 43 ....1115, 1124, 1117,
1121, 1133
ss 44-47... 1119
ss 44-46... 1118
s 44 ....1104, 1113, 1117–21,
1123–26, 1133–35, 1407
s 44(3)... 1117
s 45(1)(a), (b) 1118
s 46(1)-(7) 1119
s 47 1119
s 54 .... 1411, 1146, 1411
ss 56-63 1146
s 56 ....1347, 1407, 1408, 1415
s 57 .... 1347, 1353, 1409
s 58 1347
s 58(1)......................... 444, 1347, 1415
s 59 ....1415, 1416
s 59(1)..1415, 1428
s 59(2)..1415, 1416
s 59(3)... 1415
s 60 ....1415, 1416

s 61 .... 1413, 1416
s 82 1146
s 83 1146
s 89 1254
s 89(2) 1251, 1254
s 96 1137
s 98 1137
s 99 1130
s 101 1130
s 114 .... 1158, 1162, 1163
s 114(2) 1128
s 116(2) 1117
s 117 1370
s 118 .... 1352–54, 1393,
                                           1394, 1414, 1415
s 118(1) 1352
s 118(2) 1352, 1352
Sched 2 .... 1383, 1386
Sched 3 .... 1397, 1398
Sched 5 .... 442, 443, 996, 997,
                                           1000, 1002, 1253
Sched 7 .... 1122, 1130,
                                           1169, 1171, 1204
Sched 8 .... 1169, 1170, 1183,
                                           1184, 1201, 1210,
                                           1218, 1219, 1225,
                                                               1255
Sched 12 .... 1304, 1305
Sched 14 .... 1130, 1137, 1138

Terrorism Act 2006 .... 3, 672, 1099,
                                           1104, 1168, 1327,
                                           1329, 1331, 1332,
                                           1335, 1338, 1354,
                                           1355, 1364, 1384,
                                           1392, 1393, 1406,
                                           1407, 1410, 1416,
                                                               1465,
s 1 .... 1149, 1347, 1460
s 5 .... 1149, 1460
s 6 1411

ss 8–12 1411
s 34 1377

Theatres Act 1968 .... 470, 503
  s 3 .... 472, 554

Theft Act 1968
  ss 12, ... 1114

Trade Union and Labour
  Relations Act 1974 99

Trade Union Reform and Employment
  Rights Act 1993
  ss 23–25 1529
  Scheds 2, 3 1529

Treason Act 1814 592

Video Recordings Act 1984 .... 233, 469,
                                                          551, 553,
                                                          562–566
  s 2(2) 562, 563
  s 4 .... 562, 566
  s 4(1) 490
  s 4(1)(a) 552
  s 4(3) 563
  s 4A 562, 566
  s 9–11 563

Work and Families Act
  2006 .... 1489, 1492

Youth Justice and Criminal
  Evidence Act 1999
  s 25 852
  s 34 188
  s 41 .... 260, 408
  s 41(3)(c) 175, 189
  s 44 .... 392, 854
  s 48 .... 393, 851
  s 58 .... 1212, 1213,
                                               1241, 1277
  Sched 2 .... 392, 854

Table of UK statutory instruments

Access to Health Records
(Control of Access)
Regulations 1993
(S1 1993/746) 925

Access to Personal Files (Social
Services) (Amendment) Regulations
1991
(S1 1991/1587) 925

Access to Personal Files
(Social Services) Regulations 1989
(SI 1989/206) 925

Civil Procedure Rules 239, 428
Pt 24 428
Pt 39 739

Community Charge
(Administration and
Enforcement) Regulations 789

Criminal Evidence (Northern
Ireland) Order 1988 (SI 1988/
1987/NI/20) 1235,

Data Protection (Subject Access
Modifications) Health Order
1987 (SI1987/1903) 921

Disability Discrimination Act 1995
(Commencement No 9) Order 2001
(SI 2001/2030)
Art 3a 1513, 1550

Disability Discrimination Act 1995
(Commencement No 1) Order
2005 (SI 2005.2676)
arts 3, 4 1577

Disability Discrimination Act 1995
(Commencement No 2) Order 2005
(SI 2005/2774) 1513
Art 3 1577
art 4 ....1554, 1577

Disability Discrimination (Guidance
and Code of Practice) (SI 1996/
1996) 1511

Disability Discrimination (Private
Clubs, etc) Regulations 2005
(SI 2005/3258) 1513

Disability Discrimination
(Questions and Replies)
Order (SI 1996/2793) 1511

Disability Discrimination
(Services and Premises)
Regulations (SI 1996/1836)......... 1511

Employment Equality (Sexual
Orientation) Regulations 2003
(SI 2003/1660) 1522, 1597
reg 2(1) 1522
regs 29, 32 1588

Equality Act 2006
(Commencement No 1)
Order 2006 (SI 2006/1082)............293
Art 4 1577

Human Rights Act (Amendment)
Order 2001 (SI 2001 / 1216) 111

Human Rights Act 1998
(Commencement)
Order 1998 (SI 1998/2882) 208

Human Rights Act 1998
(Designated Derogation)
Order 2001 (SI 2001/3644) 1425

Investigatory Powers Tribunal
Rules 2000 (S1 2000/2665)......... 1083
r2 1083
r9(2)...1083
r9(3)...1083
r9(4)...1083
r9(6)...1083

Local Government for England
(Community Charge and
Council Tax, Administration
and Enforcement)
Regulations 1995
(SI 1995/247)
reg 4l 789

Magistrates' Courts (Sex
Offender and Anti-Social
Behaviour Orders) Rules
1998 681

Official Secrets Act 1989
(Prescription)(Amendment)
Order 1993 (S11993/847).............. 607

Official Secrets Act 1989
(Prescription) Order 1990
(SI 1990/200) 607

Parental Leave and Maternity etc
Regulations 1999
(SI 1999/3312) 1491

Part-Time Workers (Prevention
of Less Favourable Treatment)
Regulations 2000
(SI 2000/1551) 1490

PACE Code of Practice A 1997
(SI1997/1159) 1116

Police (Conduct) Regulations
1999 1314

Police (Conduct) Regulations
2004 (SI 2004/845) 1314

Regulation of Investigatory
Powers Act 2000 (Prescription
of Offices, Ranks and
Positions) Order 2000
(SI 2000/2417) 1063

Rules of the Supreme
Court Ord 1085

Satellite Television Service
Regulations 1997
(SI 1997/1682)............................. 546

Serious Organised Crime
and Police Act 2005
(Designated Area)
Order 2005
(SI 2005/1537) 732

Sex Discrimination (Gender
Reassignment) Regulations
1999 (SI 1999/1102) 1505

Sex Discrimination (Indirect
Discrimination and
Burden of Proof)
Regulations 2001
(SI 2001/2660)................. 1482, 1538,
1542

Sex Discrimination and
Equal Pay (Remedies)
Regulations 1993
(SI 1993/2798) 1589

Sexual Orientation
  Regulations 2003
  (SI 2003/1661) 1477, 1482, 1514,
                              1515, 1517,
                              1522–24
  Reg 2(1) 1522
  Reg 6 1522–24
  Reg 30(2) 1589

Special Immigration Appeals
  Commission (Procedure)
  Rules 1998 (SI 1998/1881) 1430

Special Immigration Appeals
  Commission (Procedure)
  (Amendment) Rules 2000
  (SI 2000/1849)............................ 1430

Television Broadcasting
  Regulations 1998
  (SI 1998/3196) 546

Terrorism Act 2000 (Proscribed
  Organisations) (Amendment)
  Order 2001
  (SI 2001/1261) 1386, 1387

Terrorism Act 2000 (Proscribed
  Organisations) (Amendment)
  Order 2002
  (SI 2001/2724) 1387

Terrorism Act 2000 (Proscribed
  Organisations) (Amendment)
  Order 2001
  (SI 2005/2892) 1387

Trafalgar Square Regulations
  1952 (S1952/776) 68,676,686

Working Time Regulations
  1998 (SI 1998/1833) 1489

Table of national legislation from other jurisdictions

Austria

Austrian Criminal Code–
Arts 284, 285............................679

Australia

Security Service Intelligence
Organisation Amendment
Act 1986............................118

Canada

Access to Information Act 1982..........630

Bill of Rights 1960..............................170

Charter of Rights and
Freedoms 1982..................147, 190, 260,
261, 285, 320,
1438

Criminal Code......................189, 260, 285,
818, 1071

Freedom of Information
Act 1967......................................630

Protection of Privacy
Act 1974..............................803

Security Intelligence Service
Act 1984 s2............................1016

Denmark

Code of Criminal Procedure..............1036
Art 126l..............................1057
Art 126m..............................1063

France

Civil Code
Art 1382............................803

Germany

Basic Law..............................153, 161
Art 1..............................305
Art 8..............................665
Art 10..............................803

Civil Code
s823(1)..............................803

Criminal Code
s184(3)..............................471
s24(1)..............................683

New Zealand

Bill of Rights 1990..............120, 170, 182,
192, 625

s6 173
s14..............................462

South Africa

Bill of Rights..............................168
Art 34(1)..............................1235

USA

Bill of Rights..............................148, 149,
155, 162, 167
Art V..............................155

First Amendment..................300, 307, 309,
311, 320, 456,
462, 491, 493,

494, 511, 581, 582,
626, 660, 665, 682,
718, 874, 890,
956, 969

Fourth Amendment...........995, 1071, 1135

Foreign Intelligence
    Surveillance Act......................1016, 1018
Privacy Act 1974.............................803, 920

Table of Treaties and Conventions

EC Treaty 1957............... 1479, 1480, 1485
  Art 13 1480
  Art 34 1480
  Art 119... 1480
  Art 141............................ 1479, 1480, 1585
  Art 157...514

European Convention for the Prevention
  of Torture and Inhuman and
  Degrading Treatment or
  Punishment 1987 ....45, 1360,
                                          1458–60
  Art 15 ....1456, 1457

European Convention for the
  Protection of Individuals
  with regard to the
  Automatic Protection of
  Data 1980 .... 139, 151, 921

European Convention on the
  Protection of Human
  Rights and Fundamental
  Freedoms 1951.................1, 2, 7, 18, 19,
                        20, 21, 23, 24, 26,
                        30, 32–41, 43, 47–50,
                        52, 53, 55, 59–61,
                        68–71, 74, 75, 79,
                        81, 84–86, 88, 91,
                        97–103, 106–114, 116,
                        121, 122, 124–29, 132–57,
                        159–299, 311, 312, 314,
                        315, 318, 319, 322, 323,
                        328–30, 334, 336, 337, 352,
                        355, 360, 363, 372, 374,
                        376–78, 380, 381, 382, 383,
                        388, 389, 393, 400, 402, 403,
                        413, 419, 420, 423, 424, 426,
                        430, 431, 435, 438, 442, 454,
                        467, 486, 491–93, 500, 515,
                        517, 518, 531, 532, 536, 538,
                        5540, 541, 545, 548,
                        552, 567, 568, 588, 596,
                        601, 607, 608, 611, 619,
                        622, 623, 661, 678, 680,
                        682, 684, 688, 690–92,
                        694–97, 699, 701, 712,
                        714, 715, 718, 719, 721,
                        722, 726–30, 737, 744,
                        745–48, 750, 760, 761, 764,
                        7867, 770, 771, 777, 780,
                        784, 790, 795, 796, 801,
                        8893, 804, 808, 814, 815,
                        817, 824–31, 839, 846–50,
                        858, 860, 863–85, 875, 905,
                        906, 908, 915, 920, 936–39,
                        942–44, 946, 950–58, 962,
                        963, 970, 973, 977, 980,
                        981, 995, 986, 989–93, 995,
                        1006, 1009, 1010, 1015,
                        1024–27, 1029–31, 1035,
                        1038, 1042, 1044, 1046–48,
                        1052, 1054–56, 1059, 1060,
                        1068, 1070, 1074, 1078–82,
                        1085, 1086, 1090, 1096–99,
                        1100, 1105, 1107, 1126, 1129,
                        131, 1134, 1139, 1148, 1153,
                        1157, 1161, 1163, 1177,
                        1179, 1181, 1190, 1207, 1215,
                        1235, 1250, 1252, 1253,
                        1256–63, 1265, 1267, 1287,

1290, 1291, 1293,-95, 1302,
1303, 1306–10, 1316, 1319,
1322, 135, 1326, 1329, 1331,
1332, 1335–42, 1347, 1349–52,
1355–61, 1369, 1370, 1382,
1383, 1386, 1387, 1391,
1398–410, 1418, 1422, 1429,
1431, 1432, 1435, 1436, 1439,
1442, 1443, 1448, 1449, 1454–56,
1459, 1460, 1462, 1463, 145–68,
1472, 1478, 1479, 1482–47, 1511,
1514–19, 1572
Art 1 .... 134, 135, 165, 197, 905
Arts 2–18 167
Arts 2-14 .... 19, 29
Arts 2-12 165
Arts 2-7 .... 18, 273
Arts 2–4 27
Art 2 .... 27, 37, 39–45, 46, 48,
49, 77, 79, 80, 103,
110, 159, 207, 247,
253, 284, 285, 294,
295, 907, 912, 943,
952, 953, 970, 987, 989,
1163, 1175, 1302, 1307,
1322, 1424
Art 2(1) 79, 1581, 1582
Art 2(2) 1579, 1580, 1583
Art 2(3) 1579, 1580
Art 2(4) 1579, 1581–84
Art 3 .... 37, 43, 45–50, 74,
75, 76, 77, 79, 103,
108, 110, 162, 166,
168, 187, 194, 195,
253, 267, 284, 288,
295, 300, 408, 434,
907, 912, 943, 952,
953, 970, 987, 989,
1174–80, 1206, 1207,
1256, 1269, 1293–95,
1301, 1302, 1306–09,
1322, 1339, 1341,
1345–47, 1358–63,
1422–24, 1427, 1429,
1453, 1454, 1456, 1457,
1462, 1520, 1567
Art 4 .... 50–51, 295, 300, 943

Art 4(1) 51, 110, 1424
Art 4(2) 51
Art 5 .... 19, 50, 51–59, 68, 111,
201, 205, 208, 211,
214, 238, 246, 269,
290, 295, 680, 748,
752, 763, 764, 768,
769, 770, 771, 1009,
1107, 1121, 1128, 1131,
1132, 1134, 1135–37,
1139, 1146, 1149, 1153,
1155, 1157, 1164, 1166,
1187, 1256, 1295,
1306–08, 1332, 1337,
1362, 1363, 1407, 1422,
1425, 1431–33, 1435,
1437–39, 1441–43, 1449,
1451, 1453, 1460,
1466, 1484
Art 5(1) 52, 55, 202, 205,
269, 763, 765, 1120,
1121, 1131, 1133, 136,
1147, 1163, 1164, 1308,
1424, 1425, 1432,
1451, 1452
Art 5(1)(a) 1131, 132
Art 5(1)(b) 759, 771, 1120,
1121, 1132, 1133
Art 5(1)(c) 54, 57, 759, 765,
766, 768, 769, 771,
1132, 1148–50, 1152,
1153, 1155, 1157, 1308
Art 5(1)(d) 54
Art 5(1)(e) 764
Art 5(1)(f) 55, 1423, 1424
Art 5(2) 1160, 1161, 1163
Art 5(2) 56
Art 5(3) 57, 58, 59, 63, 1161, 1163,
1167–70
Art 5(4) 55, 58,
59, 202, 205, 243, 244, 1163, 1341,
1342, 1454–57, 1460
Art 5(5) 59, 1309
Art 6 .... 19, 50, 58, 59–66, 104,
166, 168, 170, 175–77,
179, 186–89, 192, 193,
196, 200, 204, 242, 244,

245, 246, 260, 261, 271,
274, 284, 316, 317, 319,
321, 322, 324, 327, 328–34,
355–57, 362, 382–84, 388,
393, 394, 400, 401, 408,
417, 475, 789–93, 795, 926,
943, 1030, 1031, 1050–52,
1077, 1085–88, 1090, 1100,
1131, 1139, 1187, 1188, 1193,
1200, 1202, 1210, 1212–15,
1219, 1221, 1225, 1232, 1235,
1239, 1240, 1243, 1244, 1246,
1248, 1249, 1251, 1252, 1256–62,
1267, 1278, 1279, 1291–95,
1298, 1302, 1303, 1307, 1309,
1318, 1319, 1321, 1337, 1339,
1340, 1344–46, 1348, 1354,
1363, 1381, 1399, 1400, 1407,
1410, 1430, 1448–51, 1455,
1457, 1461, 1462, 1484,
1486, 1521, 1567
Art 6(1).....................58, 59–62, 65, 176,
190, 245, 270, 272, 295,
323, 324, 326, 328, 392,
402, 406, 789, 790, 792,
970, 971, 972, 1050, 1051,
1076, 1086, 1087, 1135, 1210,
1211, 1226, 1235, 1239–41,
1249, 1252–54, 1259–61,
1270, 1271, 1277, 1291–94,
1309, 1319–21, 1338–43, 1345,
1347, 1400, 1410, 1447,
1461, 1462, 1464
Art 6(2)...........................64, 65, 110, 178,
272, 273, 295, 323,
326, 327, 790, 792,
794, 1235, 1239–41,
1252, 1254, 1259, 1260,
1281, 1341, 1342, 1347–54,
1390–92, 1409, 1410, 1413,
1414, 1454
Art 6(3)...........................63, 64, 295, 790,
792, 1087, 1259,
1278, 1319
Art 6(3)(a), (b)..65
Art 6(3)(c)............................ 62, 65, 1210,
1211, 1213, 1240,

1262, 1277,
1281, 1309
Art 6(3)(d)..................66, 791, 794, 1320
Art7......................19, 50, 66–68, 110,
202, 295, 300, 486,
493, 558, 943,
1359, 1424
Art 7(1)...66
Art 7(2)...67, 493
Arts 8-11.................. 18, 36, 62, 68, 110,
212, 272, 286, 300,
943, 944, 956
Arts 8-12.................................. 18, 44, 295
Art8..........................49, 69–91, 94, 103,
107, 108, 175, 177, 179,
180, 187, 188–90, 195–97,
221, 223, 224, 227–29,
234, 241, 242, 247, 249,
250, 252–55, 260, 261,
268, 270, 277, 282, 284,
285, 294, 317, 383, 393,
394, 408, 425, 430,
431–35, 437–40, 446, 447,
449, 493, 513, 598, 697,
698, 776, 788, 795, 802,
804, 806, 808, 812–14,
816–39, 845–51, 858, 860,
861, 863–67, 871, 872,
875, 876, 878, 879, 883,
884, 892, 895, 898, 902,
907–11, 914–18, 924, 925,
930, 932, 935, 936–39,
944–54, 957–92, 995,
1007–1010, 1021, 1025–31,
1033, 1036, 1042–45, 1047,
1052, 1054, 1055, 1056,
1058, 1059, 1060, 1064,
1067–78, 1079, 1086, 1090,
1093, 1094, 1096–98, 1108,
1131, 1160, 1176, 1177,
1179–81, 1207, 1208, 1289,
1290, 1292, 1294, 1295,
1301, 1302, 1306–08, 1324,
1326, 1342, 1363, 1399,
1401, 1431, 1454, 1483,
1484, 1514, 1518–21,
1524–26, 1569, 1571, 1572

Art 8(1)........................ 77, 194, 248, 269,
813, 834, 864, 905,
945, 955, 962, 963,
1025, 1026, 1027, 1042,
1043, 1069, 1071, 1073,
1178, 1339, 1341
Art 8(2)........................69, 72, 75, 78, 82,
194, 248, 277, 433, 437,
905, 925, 947, 948, 958,
963, 1008, 1009, 1025,
1028, 1029, 1033, 1035,
1044, 1073, 1075, 1076,
1088, 1092, 1093, 1094, 1136,
1160, 1178, 1181, 1207, 1339,
1351, 1571
Arts 9-11..72
Art 9...................................... 77, 91, 94, 95,
211, 212, 220, 275, 299,
312, 328, 486, 487, 488,
490, 492, 493, 494, 495,
496, 497, 505, 531,
865, 944
Art 9(1)..78, 486
Art 9(2)........................69, 91, 275, 1351
Art 10 ....14, 33, 36, 37, 70, 75,
91, 92–96, 111, 125, 126,
130, 137, 152, 179, 195,
203, 209–12, 234, 250,
252, 254, 255, 269, 274,
278, 284, 287, 288, 299,
300, 303, 310, 312, 314,
317–19, 321, 322, 324–34,
335–40, 347, 351–53, 357,
358, 360, 362, 363, 366,
368, 370, 372, 374, 377–84,
386–89, 391, 393–95, 398,
400, 402–15, 419, 420,
422–24, 427–31, 433–35,
437–40, 443, 444–48, 451,
453, 463, 464, 466, 467, 475,
476, 480, 483, 485–90, 494,
496, 497, 500, 501, 505–07,
513, 515, 531, 533, 535,
537–39, 541, 542, 544, 545,
548, 549, 564, 567–71, 581,
584, 590, 596–600, 603,

607–09, 612, 614, 617, 619–21,
623–26, 641, 661–63, 671,
677, 678, 680–750, 755, 757,
760, 761, 769, 770, 771,
775–79, 783–85, 787–89, 792,
794–801, 813, 816, 824, 830,
834, 837, 845, 851, 858–62,
864–66, 870, 872, 878, 883,
884, 890, 895, 905, 906, 909,
914, 916–18, 924, 925, 930,
932, 935–39, 942–51, 954,
957–92, 1338, 1342, 1355,
1357, 1382, 1386, 1389, 1391,
1395, 1396, 1401, 1402, 1404,
1405, 1407, 1413, 1414, 1419,
1420, 1441, 1454, 1484, 1521
Art 10(1)..................... 94, 269, 336, 347,
463, 464, 466, 467, 469,
500, 532, 541, 542, 907,
947, 952, 955, 958,
962, 987
Art 10(2).............69, 72, 252, 253, 277,
309, 310, 328, 329, 336,
353, 360, 366, 377, 378,
382, 387, 400, 408, 413,
414, 415, 418, 420, 421,
425, 433, 435, 437, 443,
452, 463–66, 475–484,
485, 486, 489–500, 531,
532, 535, 541–43, 548,
549, 569, 584, 588, 609,
611, 686, 760, 775, 776,
783, 858, 859, 905, 907,
909, 944, 947, 952, 954,
955, 958, 963, 977, 987,
1339, 1351, 1363
Art 11 ....94, 96–102, 111, 287,
288, 312, 661–63, 677,
678, 680–750, 753, 755,
757, 760, 761, 769, 770,
771, 775, 777, 779, 785,
788, 789, 792, 794–801,
1027, 1355–57, 1382, 1386,
1389, 1396, 1401, 1402,
1404, 1405, 1407, 1408,
1441, 1454, 1484

Art 11(2)............69, 99, 101, 102, 277,
                 686, 728, 760, 775, 776,
                 1339, 1352, 1357
Art 12........................18, 86, 87, 102–04
Arts 13-21 25
Art 13 ....30, 86, 101, 102, 106–09,
                 165, 197, 203, 819, 839,
                 936, 1007, 1029, 1031,
                 1087, 1088, 1089, 1090,
                 1094, 1134, 1179, 1180,
                 1319, 1320, 1343, 1400,
                 1451, 1486, 1520
Art 14......................48, 68, 77, 78, 82,
                 86, 87, 94, 108–10, 111,
                 165, 166, 167, 180, 190,
                 203, 205, 260, 268, 282,
                 284, 294, 295, 487, 492,
                 567, 784, 958, 1028,
                 1099, 1134–37, 1139,
                 1175, 1207, 1301, 1302,
                 1306, 1308, 1332, 1337,
                 1401, 1420, 1432–34,
                 1436–38, 1479, 1482–86,
                 1514, 1519, 1521, 1524–26,
                 1567, 1571, 1572
Art 14(1)............................... 1526
Art 15....................29, 110–11, 135, 190,
                 211, 1167, 1168, 1359,
                 1362, 1363, 1424, 1425,
                 1431–33, 1443, 1445
Art 15(1)............. 1095, 1431, 1434–37
Art 15(2)............................. 12, 40
Art 15(3)............................. 1424
Arts 16-18................................165
Art 16.................................111–112
Art 17..................30, 91, 110, 112, 167,
                 500, 506, 784, 1336,
                 1357, 1382, 1401
Arts 19-56...............................23
Arts 19-51...............................23
Arts 19-24...............................24
Art 19....................................21
Art 20....................................24
Alt 21....................................24
Art 22....................................23
Art 24 (old)............................26

Art 25 ....26, 1068
Art 25 (old)..............................26
Art 26 ....191, 254
Art 26 (old).................23, 26, 27, 30,
                 32, 219, 234,
                 235, 236
Art 27 25
Art 27(b) (old)..........................29
Art 27(2)..........................191, 254
Art 27(2) (old)......................28, 31
Art 27(3) (old)..........................30
Art 28 28
Art 29(old)..............................32
Art 29(1)................................28
Art 31 ....191, 254
Art 32 25
Art 32 (old)..............................25
Art 32(2)(b).............................29
Art 33 26
Art 34 ....23, 26, 27, 32,
                 219, 234, 235, 236
Art 34 (old)..............................23
Art 35 ....28, 30
Art 35(1)................................28
Art 35(1)(b).............................29
Art 35(3)............................28, 31
Art 36(1)................................30
Art 36 (old)..............................23
Art 37(1)................................32
Arts 38-43 (old).........................24
Art 38 (old)..............................24
Art 38(1)(a).............................32
Art38(1)(b).............................31
Art 40 ....25, 392
Art 41.................34, 242, 245, 246
Art 43 ....25, 34
Art 43 (old)..............................24
Art 44 34
Art 44 (old)..............................23
Art 45 (old)..............................25
Art 46 ....34, 191, 254
Art 48 (old)..........................23, 32
Art 50 59
Art 50 246
Art 52 (old)........................34, 242
Art 55 33

Art 57................................ 110, 112, 1359
Art 58.. 1359
Art 59..34
Art 64..29

Protocol 1 ....19, 27, 29,
104, 112, 167
Arts 1-3 165
Art 1...........................104, 107, 175, 176,
200, 295, 719, 1355,
1363, 1402
Art 2..................................75, 105, 1524
Art 3....................................105, 106, 295

Protocol 2 21

Protocol 3 21

Protocol 4 ....19, 104, 106, 165,
Art 2..................................52, 1120,

Protocol 5 21

Protocol 6 .... 19, 27, 29, 43,
104, 1427
Art 1....................................106, 165, 295
Art 2....................................106, 165, 295

Protocol 7 ....19, 104, 106, 165

Protocol 8 21

Protocol 9 ....21, 23

Protocol 10..21

Protocol 11................ 20–7, 32, 33, 35, 106

Protocol 12............................ 104, 106, 1486

Protocol 13....................................19, 104, 165

Protocol 12..104

Protocol 14..........................20, 21, 27, 35

European Court of Human
Rights Rules of Court
r4 24
r22(1)...25
r23..25
r25(1)...25
r42(2)...32

rr49(2), (3)(b)..28
r51..33
r53(2)..28
r53(3)..31

European Social Charter
1961...19, 138, 169

EU Charter of Fundamental
Rights...138, 169

EU Draft Convention on
Mutual Assistance in Criminal
Matters 1998
Art 16... 1035

Hague-Visby Rules................................152

ILO Freedom of Association
Convention 1947......................................37

International Covenant on
Civil and Political Rights............... 1235,
1359, 1425

International Covenant on
Economic Social and
Cultural Rights 1966........ 19, 100, 1511

International Covenant on Economic
Social and Cultural Rights.............. 1511

International Convention on the
Elimination of All Forms of
Racial Discrimination........................ 1511

Treaty of Amsterdam 1997
(see also EC Treaty)............... 138, 1486,
1585
Art 6a.. 1515

Treaty on European Union 1992
(Maastricht Treaty) 1992.....................138
Art F1...138
Art F2...138

Treaty of Nice 2000.................................138

Treaty of Rome (see EC Treaty)

United Nations Covenant on Civil and
Political Rights..29

United Nations Convention
Against Torture and Other
Cruel, Inhuman or Degrading
Treatment or Punishment
1984...45, 1359

United Nations Convention
on the Elimination of All
Forms of Discrimination
Against Women 1979
Art 4(1)... 1582

United Nations Convention on the
Rights of the Child.............................392

United Nations Convention
on the Status of Refugees 1951.........49
Art 32, 33... 1423

Universal Declaration of Human Rights..
17, 167
Art 10...94
Art 18...495

Table of EC legislation

Directive 75/117/EEC Equal Pay 151, 1480, 1494, 1502, 1516, 1531, 1018, 1026, 1054, 1055
Art 119 1019

Directive 76/207/ EEC Equal Treatment 139, 1480, 1482, 1486 1504, 1505, 1515, 1516, 1518, 1543, 1568, 1569, 1572, 1579, 1581, 1582, 1589
Art 1(1) 1585
Art 2(2) 1568, 1569, 1585
Art 2(4) 1585
Art 2(6) 1568
Art 2(7) 1568

Directive 86/378/EEC Social Security Schemes 1480

Directive 89/552/EEC Transfrontier Television 513, 526, 546–48
Art 2a 547
Art 2a(2)
Arts 2(1), (2), 3(2) 546
Art 22(1) 526, 547

Directive 92/85/EC Pregnancy and Maternity 1480, 1529, 1532

Directive 93/104/EC Working Time 1489

Directive 95/46/EC Data Protection 926, 936, 937, 1073
Art 6 926

Directive 96/34/EC Part-Time Workers 1490

Directive 96/97/EC Social Security Schemes (Amendment) 1480

Directive 97/80/EC Burden of Proof 1480, 1482, 1538, 1542, 1545, 1546, 1587

Directive 98/52/EC Burden of Proof (Amendment) 1480

Directive 2000/43/EC Race Discrimination 1480, 1486, 1510, 1511, 1544–47, 1559, 1570, 1583, 1589, 1599

Directive 2000/78/EC Framework Directive on Equal Opportunities 1480–82, 1486, 1505, 1514, 1522, 1526, 1536, 549, 1551, 1555, 1571, 1582, 1599

Directive 2002/73/EC
Equal Treatment
(Amendment).............................1480, 1538

Directive 2002/85/EC;
Directive 2006/24/EC
Communications......................1095, 1097

Directive 2004/113/EC
General Sex Equality.............1480, 1538

Directive 2006/54/EC
'Equality'..1480

Directive 96/34 Parental Leave..........1491

Part 1

Theories of rights; legal protection for rights and liberties in the UK

In many Western democracies, the rights of citizens are enshrined in a constitutional document usually known as a Bill or Charter of Rights. As Chapters 1 and 3 will explain, the rights protected under such a constitutional document are often given a special status; in a number of countries they are entrenched. Until the inception of the Human Rights Act 1998 (HRA), the UK had no similar charter of rights. In 2000, the HRA afforded further effect to the European Convention on Human Rights. But even under the HRA, the rights are not entrenched. Traditionally, in order to discover which freedoms are protected and the extent of that protection, it has been necessary to examine the common law, statutes and the influence of treaties to which the UK is a party, especially the European Convention on Human Rights. Civil liberties have traditionally been defined as residual, not entrenched as in other countries.

Traditional judicial reasoning in civil liberties cases quite often consisted merely of a mechanical application of the law deriving from statute and common law precedents; the negative liberty was simply what was left over after the scope of the restrictions had been determined. Often there was an application of common law precedents or a mechanistic approach to statutory interpretation, which was devoid of principle in the sense of recognising that any important issues were at stake requiring a departure from that normal judicial technique. This approach was very marked in freedom of assembly cases. In the first edition of this book it was necessary to confront a mass of common law and statutory restrictions on liberties to consider the width of these restrictions in order to determine the size of the residual area left within which liberty could be exercised.[1] This did not mean that civil liberties were without protection and in the late 1990s, the immediate pre-HRA era, certain common law 'rights' found recognition, as Chapter 3 explains. Thus, it was often said that civil liberties in the UK were in a more precarious position than they were in other democracies, although this did not necessarily mean that they were inevitably less well protected: some Bills of Rights offered only a theoretical protection to freedoms which was not reflected in practice.

Certain particular characteristics of the UK constitution have determined and, under the HRA, are continuing to determine – albeit with some modification – the means of protecting fundamental freedoms in the UK. The doctrine of the supremacy of Parliament means that constitutional law can be changed in the ordinary way – by Act

---

1   See: Gearty, C and Ewing, K *Freedom under Thatcher* (1990), OUP; Feldman, D *Civil Liberties* 1st edn, 1993, Clarendon; Gearty, C and Ewing, K *The Struggle for Civil Liberties*, 2000, Clarendon.

of Parliament. As every student of constitutional law knows, Parliament has the power to abridge freedoms that in other countries are seen as fundamental rights. It follows from this that, aside from EU law, all parts of the law are equal – there is no hierarchy of laws and therefore constitutional law cannot constrain other laws. In general there is no judicial review of Acts of Parliament. If, for example, a statute is passed containing a provision which in some way limits freedom of speech, a judge must apply it, whereas in a country with an entrenched Bill of Rights the provision might be struck down as unconstitutional. As Chapter 4 explains, s 3 HRA has placed pressure on this traditional position, but technically it still subsists. However, where fundamental rights are protected by EU law, which also reflects the principles of the European Convention on Human Rights, they take precedence over statutory provisions due to the supremacy of EU law. Thus if a domestic provision comes into conflict with an EU provision, the judge will decide to 'disapply' it, unless the conflict can be resolved. Thus, parliamentary sovereignty has suffered some limitation. Where EU law does have an impact on fundamental freedoms, it provides a protection which may broadly be said to remove certain freedoms, or aspects of them, from the reach of Parliament, at least while the UK is a member of the EU.

These constitutional arrangements have not been fundamentally changed by the HRA but, as Chapter 4 indicates, they have been placed under pressure. The HRA affected a difficult compromise between protecting parliamentary sovereignty and achieving effective rights protection. Under the HRA, a judge is not able to declare a statutory provision invalid because it conflicts with a Convention right protected by the Act. The Human Rights Act can be modified or repealed in the same way as any other statute.

That is the constitutional background to the HRA. It is still of great significance since it is crucial in the development of civil liberties in this country and because the HRA has been greatly influenced by the domestic constitutional traditions. This Part will seek to show that although the HRA is of immense constitutional significance, it has not brought about a fundamental constitutional transformation. It has afforded the European Convention on Human Rights further effect in domestic law; there are signs that the judiciary are prepared to give a domestic effect to the rights that affords them a broader scope than they are afforded at Strasbourg. Further, although judges cannot strike down legislation under the HRA, they can change it through interpretation, which includes implying 'missing' words into it, or declare the incompatibility. Where they take the latter course, the government, as Chapter 4 shows, normally tends to respond. Thus the HRA is on the way to becoming a Bill of Rights, despite its limitations, which were imposed on it in accordance with British constitutional traditions. This notion of transition from an instrument giving an international instrument domestic effect to something resembling a Bill of Rights forms a main theme in this Part, and indeed in this book as a whole.

Chapter 1 will offer an indication of the theoretical basis of rights and liberties and of the distinction between them, seeking to demonstrate that a shift from liberties to rights has occurred. Chapter 2 will undertake analysis of the Treaty which has been afforded further effect in domestic law and which is tending to act, in effect, as a UK Bill of Rights – the European Convention on Human Rights. Chapter 3 will consider the nature and adequacy of the traditional domestic arrangements which protected fundamental freedoms only as liberties and will consider the extent to which the Convention influenced the domestic protection of civil liberties in the pre-HRA era. Chapter 4 will consider the nature of the instrument that has, in a sense, received the Convention into domestic law – the HRA. It will examine the domestic HRA jurisprudence over the first six years of its life.

The HRA was introduced by the Labour Government in 1997 on the basis that the Convention rights were, finally, to be 'brought home'.[2] There were expectations at that time that the HRA would revive the civil liberties tradition – there was a sense of a break with the erosions of liberty of the past.[3] But in 2000 two major pieces of Labour legislation were passed that in a number of respects were in tension with the Convention rights – the Terrorism Act 2000 and the Regulation of Investigatory Powers Act 2000. Then before the HRA had had a chance to gain acceptance among politicians and the British people generally, the world was hit by the devastating 9/11 attacks. As a key aspect of the UK response to the heightened terrorist threat in 2001, only one year after the Act came into force, the Labour Government derogated from one of the most fundamental freedoms – the right to liberty. The derogation and the legislation it covered are discussed in Chapter 14. The legislation passed after the HRA, which is considered in this book, including the Terrorism Act 2000, the Regulation of Investigatory Powers Act 2000, the Serious and Organised Crime Act 2005 and the Terrorism Act 2006, is in some respects more authoritarian than legislation passed in the pre-HRA years.

Thus, a key aim of this book is to consider the impact which the HRA could have in enhancing the protection for liberty in the face of a range of statutes enhancing state power very significantly. At the same time it will examine the danger that the Convention rights can be minimised and undermined in Parliament and in the courts. There is the possibility that, in Parliament, the rights might become merely empty guarantees which cast a legitimising cloak over rights-abridging legislation and executive action.[4] This book will argue that since the Convention has been received into domestic law, it should be afforded a genuine efficacy, going beyond its interpretation at Strasbourg, since the alternative would be likely to lead to a *decrease* in state accountability and an obscuring of political discourse as to the nature of state power and countervailing civil rights. In other words, the fact that we now have a document that looks something like a Bill of Rights, in the tradition of other democracies, should not blind us to the traditional concerns of the executive which are especially pressing at the present time. Almost ten years after the introduction of the HRA the Labour Government frequently appears to be uneasy with its own creation. This is largely attributable to the reverses the government has experienced in relation to the anti-terrorism measures it has sought to introduce, some of which have been challenged successfully through the courts, relying on the HRA, as Chapter 14 explains. The perception that the HRA stands in

---

2   See *Bringing Rights Home: Labour's plans to incorporate the ECHR into UK Law: A Consultation Paper*, December 1996 (1997) and the White Paper, *Rights Brought Home*, Cm 3782, October 1997; see also Straw, J and Boateng, P (1997) 1 EHRR 71.

3   See Cooke, Lord, 'The British embracement of human rights' (1999) EHRLR 243; Feldman, D, 'The Human Rights Act and constitutional principles' (1999) 19(2) LS 165.

4   This danger was pointed out by Gearty, CA, in 'Terrorism and human rights: a case study in impending legal realities' (1999) 19(3) LS 367, p 379.

the way of adopting necessary security measures has been disingenuously promoted in the media. In disseminating this and other distorted views of the HRA, the media have not had to attack an instrument that is 'owned' by the British people in the way that Canadians appear to own their Charter or US citizens their Constitution. The idea that the HRA prevents the UK deporting terrorist suspects who risk torture abroad is the driving force behind the current plan of the Conservative Party to introduce a 'British Bill of Rights' – a plan that fails to confront the problem that Britain is bound by the Convention at the international level.[5] So the HRA is under immense pressure at the present time, a time when, ironically, in a number of respects it has shown its ability to change the face of rights-protection in the UK. This is an age in which counter-terrorist and organised crime concerns dominate the political agenda, and when the need for an instrument that can curb executive tendencies to introduce in response hasty, over-broad rights-abridging measures is especially pressing. These concerns are also currently encouraging the Prime Minister, Gordon Brown, to explore the idea of introducing a 'British Bill of Rights' and repealing the HRA.[6]

5   See Chap 14 pp 1358–61 for discussion of this point.
6   Gordon Brown indicated this in his inaugural speech as Prime Minister on 24 June 2007. See further below p 156.

Chapter 1

The nature of rights and liberties

This book is intended to provide an analysis of the legal protection given to civil liberties in the UK.[1] The term 'civil liberties' will be used to denote the broad class of rights often referred to as civil and political rights as they are recognised in the UK.[2] In order to provide a coherent analysis, a theoretical position will be outlined from which to mount an internally consistent critique of the state of civil liberties and human rights in the UK today. This chapter will therefore aim to outline such a position in order to provide an account of a method of deriving rights from more general political theory and criticisms of this derivation; consideration of the nature of these rights and of methods of resolving conflicts between individual rights and the claims of society; and analysis of what we may be requiring of others when we assert a right or liberty.[3] Broadly, the position adopted will tend to reflect the particular brand of political liberalism expounded by John Rawls and Ronald Dworkin, in so far as their theories converge. Perhaps it should be noted at this point that the liberal conception of rights which will be discussed differs significantly from the tradition

---

1   Texts referred to throughout this book: Bailey, SH, Harris, DJ and Jones, BL, *Civil Liberties: Cases and Materials*, 5th edn, 2002, OUP; Feldman, D, *Civil Liberties and Human Rights in England and Wales*, 2002, OUP; Whitty, N, Murphy, T and Livingstone, S, *Civil Liberties Law*, 2001, LexisNexis UK; Fenwick, H and Phillipson, G; *Media Freedom under the Human Rights Act*, 2006, OUP; Fenwick, H, *Civil Rights: New Labour, Freedom and the Human Rights Act*, 2000, Longman; Clayton, R and Tomlinson, H, *The Law of Human Rights*, 2nd edn 2006, OUP, Chapter 16; Robertson, G, *Freedom, the Individual and the Law*, 7th edn, 1993, Penguin (for background); Ewing, KD and Gearty, CA, *Freedom Under Thatcher*, 1990; Thornton, P, *Decade of Decline: Civil Liberties in the Thatcher Years*, 1989, Civil Liberties Trust (for background); Klug, F, Starmer, K and Weir, S, *The Three Pillars of Liberty: Political Rights and Freedoms in the UK*, 1996, Routledge; Gordon, R and Wilmot-Smith, R (eds), *Human Rights in the UK*, 1997, OUP; Lord Lester of Herne Hill and Pannick, D, *Human Rights Law and Practice*, 2000, Butterworths.

2   The term 'civil and political rights' is used in contradistinction to the term 'economic and social rights' to denote first generation rights – those which have long been recognised in the Western democracies from the time of the French and American Declarations of the 'Rights of Man' in the eighteenth century.

3   The literature is immense, but the following are of particular importance. Simmonds, NE, *Central Issues in Jurisprudence*, 1986, Sweet and Maxwell, provides a brief but extremely lucid introduction to relevant jurisprudential issues. Substantive texts: Rawls, J, *A Theory of Justice*, 1972, Clarendon; Dworkin, R, *Taking Rights Seriously*, 1977, Duckworth, and *A Matter of Principle*, 1985, Clarendon; Hart, HLA, *The Concept of Law*, 1961, Clarendon, and *Essays in Jurisprudence and Philosophy*, 1983, Clarendon; Waldron, J (ed), *Theories of Rights*, 1984, OUP.

which views rights as naturally inherent in the human person.[4] By contrast, as will be seen, liberals start by devising a general political theory from which they then seek to derive a series of rights.

1 Where do rights derive from?

The liberal conception of rights can be seen to owe its antecedents to the school of so-called social contractarians which found perhaps its earliest advocate in the writings of John Locke.[5] Locke imagined an actual social contract between individuals and the state at the setting up of civil society in which citizens, in order to secure the protection of their property, handed over certain powers (most importantly, a monopoly of coercive force) to the government in return for the guarantee of certain rights to 'lives, liberties and estates'. Locke thus introduced the idea, which is still central to liberalism today, that the overriding purpose of the state is the securing and protection of its citizens' basic liberties. The idea of the social contract is thus clearly an immensely potent one and it is John Rawls's revival and radical revision of the idea in his *A Theory of Justice* (1972) which has almost single-handedly transformed the face of political theory; as HLA Hart has commented, rights-based theories have replaced utilitarianism[6] as the primary focus of attention.[7] Robert Nozick, a right-wing critic of Rawls whose work *Anarchy, State and Utopia* (1974) mounts a sustained attack upon Rawls's theory, has written: 'Political philosophers now must either work within Rawls's theory or explain why not'.[8]

Rawls imagines not an actual, but a hypothetical, social contract taking place in what he terms 'the original position'. The essential feature of this position is that the contractors (Rawls's men) are devising amongst themselves the outlines of 'the foundation charter of their society' whilst behind 'the veil of ignorance'. The men are ignorant not only of what will be their positions in the future social hierarchy, but also of their skills, weaknesses, preferences and conceptions of the good life – whether, for example, they will be strict Muslims or humanist academics. Since none of the contractors knows what mode of life he will wish to pursue, he is bound (if he is rational) to choose a tolerant society and one which guarantees him the rights necessary to pursue any individual goals he may in future choose. In other words, the men will wish to put in place the means whereby they will, in future, be able to pursue their goals rather than adopting structures which might in future prevent them from doing so. Thus, almost any conception of the good life will require, for example, freedom from arbitrary arrest, the right to a fair trial and freedom from inhuman treatment. In addition, the man who will become the Muslim might *in future* wish to restrict freedom of speech on religious matters but, *at present*, self-interest dictates that he consider the possibility that his conception of the good life might necessarily include the exercise

---

4   For a modern exposition of the Natural Law School, see Finnis, J, *Natural Law and Natural Rights*, 1980, Clarendon.

5   Locke, J, *The Second Treatise of Government*, 1698.

6   See discussion below, pp 8–9.

7   See Hart's comments on this phenomenon generally in 'Between utility and rights' in Cohen, M (ed), *Ronald Dworkin and Contemporary Jurisprudence*, 1984, Duckworth.

8   Nozick, R, *Anarchy, State and Utopia*, 1974, Blackwell, p 183.

of freedom of speech. Thus Rawls's men adopt, *inter alia*, 'the first principle', stating that 'each person is to have an equal right to the most extensive, total system of equal basic liberties compatible with a similar system of liberty for all'.[9] These basic liberties are identical with any familiar list of civil and political rights.

Although similar to Rawls in political outlook, Ronald Dworkin offers a theoretical construct which derives rights in a different manner, and indeed has criticised Rawls's theory, arguing that a *hypothetical*, unlike an *actual*, contract provides no grounds for binding actual people to its terms.[10] Dworkin attempts to derive rights from the premise, to which he hopes all will agree, that the state owes a duty to treat all of its citizens with equal concern and respect – a premise which he argues persuasively is the deep assumption underlying Rawls's use of the contract device. Dworkin is not concerned with defending rights from despotic and repressive governments and indeed he sees no need to protect – by designating them as rights – those individual interests which the *majority* would like to see protected, since these will in any case be ensured by the democratic process which he assumes as a background to his theory. Dworkin's particular concern is to justify the protection of *unpopular* or minority rights – or those whose exercise may on occasion threaten the overall well-being of the community – because such rights would potentially be put at risk if their validity were to be determined through a democratic vote.

Clearly, the institution of democracy and most familiar sets of political policies, such as seeking the economic betterment of the majority, seem to be satisfactorily explained by an underpinning utilitarianism.[11] Dworkin hypothesises that the great appeal of utilitarianism is owed at least in part to its appearance of egalitarianism through its promise to 'treat the wishes of each member of the community on a par with the wishes of any other',[12] taking into account only the intensity of the preference and the number of people who hold it. This appeal is evinced in the utilitarian maxim: 'everybody to count for one, nobody for more than one.' Dworkin finds, however, that raw utilitarianism betrays this promise, since it fails to distinguish between what he denotes external and personal preferences. For example, if the question of whether homosexual acts should be permitted in private between adults were to be decided by a majority vote (*preference maximisation*), homosexuals would express their personal preference for freedom to perform those acts. Certain heterosexuals, however, would vote against allowing this freedom, because their external preference is that homosexuals should not be free to commit such acts.

Thus, resolution of the question could be affected by the fact that certain citizens think that the homosexual way of life is not deserving of equal respect; a decision would therefore have been made at least partly on the basis that the way of life of

9   For this reference and a brief summary of the theory, see Rawls, J, *A Theory of Justice*, 1972, pp 11–15.

10 Dworkin, *Taking Rights Seriously*, 1977, Chapter 6.

11 Utilitarianism is a major political philosophy. The original conception of utilitarianism espoused by Jeremy Bentham saw the aim of government as being to promote the greatest happiness of the greatest number of people (see Burns (ed), *Collected Works of Jeremy Bentham*, 1970). A more recent and fashionable version states that an ideal society is one in which there is the maximum amount of preference satisfaction (see, generally, Smart, C and Williams, B, *Utilitarianism: For and Against*, 1973, CUP). References in the text will be to this latter version, known as 'preference utilitarianism'.

12 Dworkin, *Taking Rights Seriously*, 1977, p 275.

certain citizens was in some way contemptible. If the government enforced this decision through the use of coercive force (the criminal law), it would clearly have failed in its central duty to treat its citizens with equal concern and respect. In other words, utilitarianism – and therefore democracy – has an in-built means of undermining its own promise of equality. Since for Dworkin protecting this promise of equality is the central postulate of political morality, he finds that homosexuals should be granted a right to moral autonomy which cannot be overridden even by a majority decision-making process.

Opposition to the liberal conception of human rights

Utilitarianism

Utilitarianism has historically been generally hostile to the idea of rights, most famously to the notion of natural and inalienable human rights as set out, for example, in the American Declaration of Independence, which was characterised by Jeremy Bentham as merely so much 'bawling upon paper'.[13] The opposition of utilitarians to the notion of *natural* rights sprang mainly from their legal positivism – their belief that a legal right only exists if there is a specific 'black letter' provision guaranteeing it. But in general, since utilitarianism sets out one supreme goal of happiness or, in its more modern version, preference maximisation, it would clearly follow that rights under utilitarianism can have only a contingent justification. In other words, they are to be respected if they help bring about the goal of maximum satisfaction of preferences, but not otherwise. It may seem odd to postulate an opposition between utilitarianism and human rights, bearing in mind that JS Mill combined utilitarianism with a passionate belief in the desirability of free expression and civil rights generally. It should be noted, however, that Mill's arguments for free speech depend essentially on a belief that allowing free speech will, in the long term, have good effects – such as increasing the likelihood that the truth will be discovered – rather than on a belief that free expression is a good in itself or something to which human beings are entitled without reference to its likely effects. A utilitarian, confronted with a situation in which infringing a right would undeniably benefit society as a whole, would have no reason to support the inviolability of the right; for example, he or she would find it hard to explain why criminal suspects should not be tortured if it were proved that reliable evidence would be derived thereby, leading to increased convictions, deterrence of crime and substantial consequential benefit to society.

A further variant of the theory which has sometimes been termed 'rule utilitarianism', however, states that the goals of utilitarianism can best be reached by constructing rules which it is thought will, in general, further the goal of happiness or 'preference maximisation' and then applying these rules to situations as absolutes rather than considering in each individual situation what can best further the goal (for discussion, see Smart and Williams).[14] Such rules could, of course, consist, at least in part, of a set of human rights. In relation to the example of torture given in the text, a rule utilitarian

---

13 Bentham, J, 'Anarchical fallacies', in Bowring, J (ed), *Collected Works of Jeremy Bentham*, 1843, p 494.
14 Smart, C and Williams, B, *Utilitarianism: For and Against*, 1973.

could plausibly maintain that a general rule of humane treatment of citizens is likely to lead to the greatest happiness. In deciding whether to torture an individual suspect, this would mean that instead of considering whether in this case overall utility would be increased thereby, the state should apply the rule of humane treatment, even if in the particular case it would lead to a decrease in utility. It can be seen that for rule utilitarians, the good (the goal of preference maximisation or greatest happiness) is prior to the right, in opposition to Rawls's clearly expressed conviction that the right (a system of just entitlements of citizens) is prior to any conceptions of the good – the substantive moral convictions by which individuals will live their lives.

Marxism

The former socialist bloc of states – the Soviet Union and Eastern Europe – was the driving force behind the international recognition of economic, social and cultural rights. This was at least partly due to the fact that there is a measure of hostility within Marxist thought to civil and political rights.[15] Such hostility exists mainly because Marxism advocates establishing a state which, far from being neutral amongst its citizens' varying conceptions of the good and guaranteeing them the liberties necessary to pursue their private goals, instead imposes a particular conception of the good upon society. Since it regards the protection of this conception (the achievements of the revolution) as the supreme value and duty of the state, the exercise of liberties which threaten this achievement can be justifiably curtailed; hence the consistently poor record of the former Soviet bloc states and Communist China on such civil rights as freedom of speech. A theoretically related, but more moderate, critique of the Western liberal conception of human rights can be found in the writings of the so-called communitarians.[16]

Critical Legal Studies

The Critical Legal Studies movement (CLS) attacks the whole liberal conception of law as neutral, objective and rational. It seeks to expose the value judgments, internal inconsistencies and ideological conflicts which it sees as concealed under law's benevolent exterior of impartial justice.[17] Since the whole structure of legally guaranteed human rights is a creature of the liberal conception of law, the CLS attack fastens by extension onto the liberal notion of rights. Mark Tushnet, for example, has made four main criticisms of the liberal theory of rights in what he calls 'a Schumpeterian act of creative destruction'. He asserts that rights are: first, unstable – that is, meaningful only in a particular social setting; secondly, they produce 'no determinate consequences if claimed'; thirdly, 'rights talk ... falsely converts into empty abstractions ... real experiences that we ought to value for their own sake'; and fourthly, if conceded a dominant position in contemporary discourse, rights threaten to 'impede advances by progressive social forces'.[18] It would be inappropriate to attempt a detailed refutation

---

15 See, e.g., Marx, K, *On the Jewish Question*, 1843.
16 See, e.g., Sandel, M, *Liberalism and the Limits of Justice*, 1982, CUP.
17 Unger, R, *The Critical Legal Studies Movement*, 1986, Harvard University Press.
18 Tushnet, M, 'An essay on rights' (1984) 62(18) Texas L Rev 1363.

of the CLS position here.[19] Perhaps the most important weakness in its critique of rights is that, as many writers have pointed out,[20] it offers no guidance whatsoever as to how the interests of vulnerable minorities are to be protected without the institution of legal rights.

2 What is meant by a right?

The preceding section has set out, in a very basic manner, some of the more influential liberal theories concerning the means of deriving a system of rights from a more general moral theory. In this section, two aims will be pursued. First, an attempt will be made to shed some light on what one can be taken to mean, in general terms, when one asserts a right; secondly, a brief explanation will be given of Hohfeld's exposition of a right as an umbrella term, covering a number of more precisely delineated claims.

Distinguishing moral and legal rights

The endeavour to distinguish legal from moral rights involves a central issue in jurisprudence, namely, the relationship between law and morality, on which there is a vast literature and a number of clearly defined schools of thought. Only the barest indications of the various positions on this tendentious issue are possible here.

Legal positivism

Clearly, from a common sense point of view, if X makes a claim that she has a right to Y and there is no clear, black letter law giving her such a right, she must be taken to be asserting that she has a strong *moral* claim to Y and (probably) that this claim ought to be given *legal* force through the enactment of a specific legal right. The above point of view is – very crudely – that put forward by the school of jurisprudence known as legal positivism, whose central insistence is that there is no *necessary* connection between law and morality.[21]

Natural law

To a member of the natural law school in its traditional form,[22] by contrast, the question of whether X's claim to Y was moral or legal would be decided not empirically, by consulting the statute book, but rather by examining the normative claim made by her. If her claim was supported by an abstract notion of justice, then a measure purporting to deny the claim would not be accepted as a valid law since it would be unjust. The approach sounds extreme, but was employed during the Nuremberg trials as the

---

19 For a general critique of the CLS attitude to rights, see, e.g., Price, DA, 'Taking rights cynically' [1989] CLJ 271.
20 Ibid See also, e.g., Rhodes, DL, 'Feminist critical theories' (1990) 42(3) Stanford L Rev 634–38.
21 For a full discussion of this issue, see Hart, HLA, 'Positivism and the separation of law and morals', in *Essays in Jurisprudence and Philosophy*, 1983.
22 For the classical exposition of this theory, see Aquinas, T, '*Summa theologica*', in d'Entreves, P (ed), *Selected Political Writings*, 1970, Blackwell.

underlying justification for what might otherwise have been seen as the retrospective criminalisation of those who committed their crimes under the Nazi laws thought valid at the time.

Dworkin's theory

The views of Ronald Dworkin[23] provide a middle ground between these two theories – a 'third theory of law'.[24] His theory is highly complex, but in essence is more inclusive than the positivist theory; recognising black letter legal rights,[25] it insists that the law may contain *further* rights which have never yet been recognised by a statute or in any judicial decision. Thus, X could correctly claim she had a right to Y, on Dworkin's account, if (a) the right would be consistent with the bulk of existing law and (b) it would figure in the best possible interpretation of the area of law concerned. By this, Dworkin means that the relevant past judicial decisions would be most satisfactorily justified by showing them all to have been concerned with protecting the right at issue, even if previous individual judgments did not explicitly recognise its existence. Such a claim might well, of course, be controversial, but it is precisely this that is at the root of Dworkin's disagreement with the positivists: finding out what the law is, he argues, will require not merely an empirical test of the law's *pedigree* (does it emanate from the right body?), but rather a complex inquiry which will, as he puts it, carry the lawyer 'very deep into moral and political theory'.[26]

If one is convinced by Dworkin's ingenious argument, the existence of a legal right can be adduced through interpretation (at least in common law jurisdictions). Alternatively, a right could, in any event, be given clear explicit protection so that its legal status was not a matter for controversy.

The strength of a right: conflicts with other claims

If a legal right is conceded to exist, it must next be asked what is and should be the nature and strength of the protection thereby given. The right may come into conflict with the claims of society, such as that a certain standard of morality should be upheld. Clearly, in resolving such a conflict, a judge will inevitably draw upon his or her background political theory. If, for example, a judge in the European Court of Human Rights, who is a utilitarian by conviction, has to consider a convincing demonstration by a defendant government that the particular application of the right to free speech

---

23 For an exposition of Dworkin's account of the relationship between law and morality, see his theory of judicial adjudication in Chapters 2–4 of *Taking Rights Seriously*, in which his theory is cast mainly in the form of a critique of legal positivism. For a fuller development of the theory, see *Law's Empire*, 1986, Fontana.

24 The term was coined by Mackie, J, 'The third theory of law', in Cohen, M (ed), *Ronald Dworkin and Contemporary Jurisprudence*, 1984.

25 Note that in *Law's Empire* Dworkin seems to discard any reliance on recognising 'black letter' law by some means reminiscent of Hart's rule of recognition and comes to a position in which law is entirely a matter of interpretation. For criticism of this position see, e.g., Simmonds, NE, 'Imperial visions and mundane practices' [1987] CLJ 465 and Cotterell, R, *The Politics of Jurisprudence*, 1989, pp 172–81.

26 Dworkin, *Taking Rights Seriously*, p 67.

claimed by the applicant will, on balance, make society worse off as a whole, he or she will be inclined to find for the government and allow the infringement of the right. Such infringement will, of course, be more readily allowable if the right is framed or has developed in such a way as to be open-ended in scope with in-built exceptions.

Both Dworkin and Rawls have argued persuasively against making rights vulnerable to utilitarian considerations in this way. The idea that '[e]ach person possesses an inviolability founded on justice that even the welfare of society as a whole cannot override'[27] lies at the centre of Rawls's political thought. The idea of such inviolable rights may seem extreme, but is in fact accepted by all civilised countries in the case, for example, of torture. It is not thought to be a sound argument for a government to assert that it is justified in torturing certain of its citizens on the grounds that it can increase the general welfare thereby. The acceptance of this principle is attested to by the non-derogability of the right to freedom from torture in all international human rights treaties, including the European Convention on Human Rights (Art 15(2)).

Dworkin has addressed the specific question as to the means of understanding a legal right in an adjudicative context in some detail. Earlier, the distinction between moral and legal rights was discussed. Here it should be noted that Dworkin also distinguishes between rights that have 'trump' status and those that do not. He gives as an example of the latter a legal right to drive either way on a two-way road: such a right is a 'weak' legal right, because it is not an important human interest which is likely to be denied to certain groups through the influence of external preferences. It follows that such a right could justifiably be overridden by the government (through making the road one-way) if it thought it in the general interest to do so. By contrast, his conception of the strength of 'trump' rights leads to his insistence that an assertion of (for example) a right to free speech held by citizens 'must imply that it would be wrong for the government to stop them from speaking, even when the government believes that what they say will cause more harm than good'.[28]

It can be seen, then, that Dworkin gives us a very clear prescription for the approach that a judge should take in weighing strong or 'trump' rights against the general welfare of society. He roundly condemns the idea that a judge, in adjudicating upon a right or a government in framing it, should carefully weigh up the right of the citizen against the possible adverse social consequences, accepting that it is sometimes preferable to err on the side of society, sometimes on the side of the individual, but on the whole getting the balance about right. 'It must be wrong', he argues, to consider that 'inflating rights is as serious as invading them'. For to *invade* a right is to affront human dignity or treat certain citizens as less worthy of respect than others, while to *inflate* a right is simply to pay 'a little more in social efficiency'[29] than the government *already* has to pay in allowing the right at all. Thus, for Dworkin, if one asserts a 'trump' right, ordinary counter-arguments about a decrease in the welfare of society as a whole are simply irrelevant.

---

27 Rawls, *A Theory of Justice*, 1972, p 3.
28 Dworkin, R, *Taking Rights Seriously*, p 191.
29 Ibid, p 199.

In what circumstances, then, may a strong individual right be overridden? Dworkin has argued[30] that there are three general justifications for infringement and these appear to be generally accepted by liberal thought.

Competing rights

First, there is the situation in which there is a clear competing individual claim, so that the exercise of the original right will directly infringe the competing right. The paradigmatic example of such a collision of individual rights arises where one individual uses his right of free speech to prejudice the fair trial of another. Another is where one incites violence against the other, thus infringing his right to security of the person. In such cases, since both rights are, as it were, from the same class of 'strong' rights, they will compete on equal terms, but it may nevertheless be possible to resolve the conflict by undertaking a balancing act between them based on proportionality.[31] In the case of prejudice to a trial, this could be done by physically removing the trial from the area affected by the speech in question. If such avoidance of conflict was impossible, a determination might be made as to the damage inflicted on each right if the other was allowed to prevail. In the case of incitement to violence, the damage inflicted if free speech was allowed to prevail might be almost irretrievable, since the group affected might be placed at great risk for a period of time. In contrast, the damage to free speech created by avoidance of the risk might be of a lesser nature, although undesirable: the speech could be uttered in another form or another forum, so that its meaning was not lost, but it was rendered less inflammatory. Alternatively, utterance of the speech could be delayed until the situation had become less volatile. The words advocating immediate violence might be perceived as outside the area of protected speech and so might be severed from the accompanying words which could be permitted.

The right is not really at stake

The second situation in which rights may be overridden is one where the values protected by the right are not at stake in this particular situation. In other words, it may be argued that most rights have a 'core', the invasion of which will constitute an actual overriding of the right, but they also have a 'penumbra' – an area in which the value the right protects is present only in a weaker form.[32] An invasion of the penumbra may be said to constitute only an *infringement* of the right and may therefore be more readily justified. The argument that commercial speech should not be afforded the same protection as other kinds of speech would appear to rest precisely on the argument

30 Ibid, p 200.
31 See Chapter 9, pp 962–79.
32 This view is not attributed to Dworkin, although he does accept that there will be situations in which the core value of the right will not be at stake. Dworkin has comprehensively rejected Hart's theory of statutory construction and application of the rules from past cases based around the notion of a core of certainty and a penumbra of uncertainty (for Hart's position, see *The Concept of Law*; for Dworkin's critique, op. cit., fn 3, Chapters 2–4). Dworkin argues that the areas of a rule which form the core and those which fall in the penumbra, can only be elucidated through a judge's interpretation, which will carry him or her far from the specific words of the statute.

that it is in the penumbra of free speech;[33] by contrast, political speech is clearly in the 'core' of free speech.[34]

A real risk to society

The third situation justifying infringement is one in which the exercise of a right may pose a real danger to society. In such instances, liberals are unwilling to take danger to mean danger to some abstract attribute to society, such as its moral health,[35] but rather insist that the danger must ultimately amount to a threat to some concrete aspect of its citizens' well-being. Thus, typically, liberals are hostile to characterising the likelihood of shocking or offending citizens as a concrete harm justifying the suppression of the right of free speech. Dworkin's own, perhaps rather unrealistically stringent, test is that the 'risk to society' justification for overriding rights is only made out if the state demonstrates 'a clear and substantial risk' that exercise of the right 'will do great damage to the person or property of others'.[36] It seems unlikely that governments would be prepared to accept such a test; the criterion laid down, for example, by the European Court of Human Rights for curtailing the right of free expression as set out in Art 10 does not even approach Dworkin's prescription in either stringency or clarity; instead, it has adopted the somewhat weak and uncertain phrase, 'a pressing social need'.[37] Dworkin's rights analysis should not, therefore, be taken as a description of the way rights and liberties are *actually* treated in the UK and under human rights treaties, but rather as an ideal against which the reality of such 'rights' protection can be measured.

Distinguishing rights and liberties

Having given an account of what may, in general terms, be meant by an assertion of a right in the liberal tradition, we may now turn to an analysis of the more specific claims that the assertion of a right may entail and employ this analysis to make a few general remarks about the nature of 'rights' protection in the UK.

Hohfeld's analysis

One of the more influential attempts to analyse closely the nature of a right was made by the American jurist Wesley Hohfeld.[38] Hohfeld attempted to demonstrate the way that claims of rights in everyday language can in fact be broken down into four more

---

33 Judgment of US Supreme Court, *Bolger v Youngs Drug Products Ltd* (1983) 103 Ct 2875, 2880–81.

34 The House of Lords appeared to recognise the central importance of free political speech in their pre-HRA decision that neither local nor central government could pursue an action in defamation: *Derbyshire CC v Times Newspapers* [1993] 1 All ER 1011.

35 Eg, see the attacks by Hart, 'Social solidarity and the enforcement of morality', in *Essays in Jurisprudence and Philosophy*, and Dworkin, 'Liberty and morality', in *Taking Rights Seriously*, on Lord Devlin's view that society may justifiably use the criminal law to enforce a shared morality.

36 Dworkin, R, *Taking Rights Seriously*, p 204.

37 See *Handyside v UK* (1976) 1 EHRR 737. For further discussion of this test, see Chapter 5, p 336–37.

38 Hohfeld, W, *Fundamental Legal Concepts as Applied in Judicial Reasoning*, 1920, particularly pp 35–41.

specific claims. First, if it is claimed that X has a right proper or 'claim right' to A, then this means that persons, generally or particularly, are under some specific corresponding duty to ensure that X has access to A. Secondly, X may be said to have an immunity as against a particular person or body; this means that they are disabled from interfering with the exercise by X of the interest (A) protected by the immunity. Thirdly, if X has only a liberty (what Hohfeld calls a privilege) to do A, this far weaker claim merely means that X does no wrong in exercising his liberty – the rights of others are not thereby infringed. However, no one has a duty to allow him to exercise A or to assist him to exercise it. Fourthly, X may have a power to do B, such as to sell his property. This last category is not particularly relevant to the subject of civil liberties.

Hohfeld applied to the reality of 'rights' protection

Hohfeld's explanation is a useful analytical tool; it can be seen by utilising it that Dworkin is advocating that rights be set out as a series of immunities – areas of entitlement which even democratically elected governments are disabled from interfering with. The US Constitution and its Amendments represent such a list of immunities. In applying Hohfeld's theory to 'rights' protection in the UK, it can be seen that it endows the commentator with the ability to distinguish between the different forms of protection offered towards different freedoms. The commentator must now apply these analytical tools to the Human Rights Act 1998 in order to find that a very significant break with the traditional findings as to rights protection in the UK has occurred.

If Dworkin's analysis is used, all rights in the UK are technically 'weak' since, even under the Human Rights Act 1998, all are at least theoretically subject to infringement by Parliament. Under Hohfeld's view, the picture is more mixed. It becomes clear that, traditionally, most freedoms in the UK were merely liberties; one did no wrong to exercise them, but there was no positive duty on any organ of the state to allow or facilitate them. For example, the Public Order Act 1986 nowhere placed upon chief constables a duty to ensure freedom of assembly and speech. Nevertheless, some of our entitlements clearly had and have the quality of Hohfeldian claim rights in that they are protected by a positive correlative duty. For example, arrested persons have the right of access to a solicitor while in police custody as guaranteed by S 58 of the Police and Criminal Evidence Act 1984. Equal treatment in certain contexts is provided for under domestic and EU instruments. However, even when a citizen holds a right, there were – under domestic law – no *legal* guarantees that the legislation providing the positive protection would not be repealed. Similarly, a citizen enjoying a liberty could not be certain that legislation would not be introduced into a previously unregulated area, thus destroying or limiting that liberty.

When the Human Rights Act 1998 came fully into force, however, in October 2000, many of our Hohfeldian liberties became rights in Hohfeldian terms since, as Chapter 4 explains, public authorities were laid under a positive duty to respect them and are acting unlawfully if they do not (s 6(1)), unless the only possible reading of contrary primary legislation is that the right must be infringed. Even in that instance, once the incompatibility is declared, the government will normally respond by introducing remedial legislation. It is now much less likely that legislation will be introduced which would have the effect of limiting the rights protected under the 1998 Act, since such legislation might eventually be declared incompatible with the guarantees of those rights (s 4). Further, when such legislation was introduced, the relevant Minister would have to declare that a statement of compatibility could not be made (s 19, HRA), which would be politically embarrassing. (It has only occurred once so far.)[39] Similarly, existing legislative protection for a right recognised under the HRA would be unlikely to be repealed, since the repealing legislation could not be accompanied by such a statement and, moreover, a citizen might bring an action at Strasbourg challenging the failure to make domestic provision to deliver the right. Thus, in Hohfeldian terms, the 1998 Act itself does not provide a set of immunities since it can be overridden by primary legislation, while in Dworkinian terms the rights remain 'weak'. As indicated, the guarantees of the rights are not absolute; the deterrents against infringing them at the parliamentary level are ultimately political ones. But the Act clearly represents a dramatic shift in rights protection in the UK, away from residual freedoms towards positive rights.

39 The Communications Act 2003 was not accompanied by a statement of compatibility; see Chapter 6, p 518.

Chapter 2

The European Convention on Human Rights

1 Introduction[1]

The European Convention on Human Rights was conceived after the Second World War as a means of preventing the kind of violation of human rights seen in Germany during and before the war. However, it has not generally been invoked in relation to large-scale violations of rights, but instead has addressed particular deficiencies in the legal systems of the Member states, who on the whole create regimes of human rights in conformity with it. Drafted in 1949 by the Council of Europe, it was based on the United Nations Declaration of Human Rights,[2] and partly for that reason and partly because it was only intended to provide basic protection for human rights, it appears today as quite a cautious document, less far reaching than the International Covenant on Civil and Political Rights.[3] Nevertheless, it has had far more effect on UK law than any other human rights treaty due to its machinery for enforcement, which includes the European Court of Human Rights, with the power to deliver a ruling adverse to the governments of Member states. Moreover, the Court insists upon the dynamic nature of the Convention and adopts a teleological or purpose-based approach to its interpretation which has allowed the substantive rights to develop until they may cover situations unthought of in 1949. Had it been a more radical document, the Convention might have been self-defeating because it might have failed to secure the necessary acceptance from Member states, both in terms of ratifying various parts of it, such as the right of individual petition, and in terms of responding to adverse judgments.

---

1 Texts referred to below: Clayton, R and Tomlinson, H, *The Law of Human Rights*, 2nd edn, 2006; Ovey, C and White, R, *Jacobs and White European Convention on Human Rights*, 4th edn, 2006, OUP; Bailey, SH, Harris, DJ and Jones, BL, *Civil Liberties: Cases and Materials*, 5th edn, 2002; Feldman, D, *Civil Liberties and Human Rights in England and Wales*, 2002; Van Dijk, P and Van Hoof, F, *Theory and Practice of the European Convention on Human Rights*, 3rd edn, 1998, Kluwer; Mowbray, A, *Cases and Materials on the European Convention on Human Rights*, 2001, LexisNexis UK; Janis, M, Kay, R and Bradley, A, *European Human Rights Law*, 2nd edn, 2000, OUP; Harris, D, O'Boyle, K and Warbrick, C, *Law of the European Convention on Human Rights*, 1995, Butterworths; Dickson, B (ed), and Connelly, A, *Human Rights and the European Convention*, 1996, Sweet and Maxwell; Farran, S, *The UK Before the European Court of Human Rights*, 1996, Blackstone. Background: Beddard, R, *Human Rights and Europe*, 3rd edn, 1980, CUP; Fawcett, JES, *The Application of the European Convention on Human Rights*, 2nd edn, 1987, Clarendon; Jacobs, F, *The European Convention on Human Rights*, 1975, OUP; Nedjati, ZM, *Human Rights under the European Convention*, 1978, Elsevier; Merrills, JG and Robertson, AH, *Human Rights in Europe*, 3rd edn, 1993, Manchester University Press.
2 The Declaration was adopted on 10 December 1948 by the General Assembly of the UN.
3 1966.

Although the European Court of Human Rights may rule against the governments of Member states, its approach – which is reflected throughout the machinery for the supervision of the Convention – is not ultimately coercive. A persuasive or consensus-based approach is evident at every stage through which an application may pass. A friendly settlement may well be reached before the case comes before the Court; even if it does not, and the case reaches the stage of a final ruling adverse to the government in question, the government is in effect free to determine the extent of the changes needed in order to respond, although the possibility of future adverse rulings at Strasbourg may exercise an influence on its decision. This approach is also reflected in the doctrine of the 'margin of appreciation' which has been developed by the Strasbourg authorities. This doctrine, to which we will return below,[4] involves allowing the domestic authorities a degree of discretion in deciding what is needed to protect various public interests in their own countries, even though such interests have an impact on protection for Convention rights. The use of this doctrine allows evasion of conflict over very sensitive issues between Strasbourg and the Member state. Clearly, its use may lead at times to an acceptance of a lower standard of human rights than some liberal critics would advocate,[5] but some commentators have suggested that it can be an appropriate influence on the dealings between Strasbourg and democracies with generally sound human rights records.[6]

When examining the substantive rights, they may be said to fall into two groups: Articles 2–7, covering the most fundamental human rights and containing, broadly, no express exceptions,[7] or narrow express exceptions; and Arts 8–12, which may be said to cover a more sophisticated or developed conception of human rights and which are subject to a broad range of express exceptions. Thus, under Arts 2–7, argument will tend to concentrate on the question of whether a particular situation falls within the compass of the right in question, whereas under Arts 8–11 it will largely concentrate on determining whether the interference with the guarantee can be justified (Art 12 contains only one exception, but of a very broad nature). There is an enormous amount of overlap between the Articles and it may be found that weaknesses or gaps in one can be remedied by another, although the Convention will be interpreted as a harmonious whole.[8] It will also be found that invocation of a substantive right in order to attack a decision in the national courts on its merits may sometimes fail, but that a challenge to the *procedure* may succeed under one of the Articles explicitly concerned with

---

4 See pp 36–39.
5 See: McDonald, RJ, 'The margin of appreciation in the jurisprudence of the European Court of Human Rights', *International Law and the Time of its Codification*, 1987, pp 187–208; Van Dijk and Van Hoof, op. cit., fn 1, p 82 *et seq*; O'Donell, 'The margin of appreciation doctrine: standards in the jurisprudence of the European Court of Human Rights' (1982) 4 Human Rights Q 474; Morrisson, C, 'Margin of appreciation in human rights law' (1973) 6 Human Rights J 263; Jones, T, 'The devaluation of human rights under the European Convention' [1995] PL 430; Mahoney, P, 'Marvellous richness or invidious cultural relativism?' (1998) 19 Human Rights LJ 1.
6 See Gearty, C, 'Democracy and human rights in the European Court of Human Rights: a critical appraisal' (2000) 51(3) NILQ 381, esp p 387.
7 Article 6 provides that trial judgments should be pronounced publicly except where, *inter alia*, the interest of morals, public order or national security demand otherwise but the primary right – to a fair hearing – is not subject to these exceptions.
8 Van Dijk and Van Hoof, op. cit., fn 1, Chapter II.

fairness in the adjudicative process – Arts 5, 6 and 7.[9] The rights and freedoms are largely concerned with civil and political rather than social and economic matters; the latter are governed by the 1961 European Social Charter and the 1966 International Covenant on Economic, Social and Cultural Rights.[10]

The Convention has grown by way of additional protocols so that it now creates a more advanced human rights regime based on Arts 2–14 with the First Protocol[11] in conjunction with the Fourth,[12] Sixth[13] and Seventh[14] Protocols. The very significant Protocol 12 was opened for ratification in November 2000.[15] The UK has not yet ratified the rights contained in the Fourth and Seventh Protocols, and at present does not intend to ratify the Twelfth Protocol, suggesting that although there is a measure of harmony between the basic Convention regime and the UK legal system, this is not the case as far as aspects of the more advanced regime is concerned. The UK has ratified Protocol 13 which abolishes the death penalty in all circumstances. The Joint Committee on Human Rights in 2005 recommended that the government should ratify the Fourth and Twelfth Protocols.[16]

In considering the operation of the Convention in practice, it should be remembered that it was not intended to mimic the working of a domestic legal system. Thus, individuals could not, until recently, take a case directly to the European Court of Human Rights in Strasbourg[17] and, in fact, it is a feature of the Court that it hears very few cases in comparison with the number of applications made.[18] However, its jurisprudence has had an enormous impact, not merely through the outcome of specific cases, but in a general symbolic, educative and preventive sense. Its function in raising

9   This point is developed below; see p 60. See Gearty, C, 'The European Court of Human Rights and the protection of civil liberties: an overview' [1993] CLJ 89 for argument that the Convention as a whole is largely concerned with *procedural* rights.

10   (1965) Cmnd 2643; see Harris, D, *The European Social Charter*, 1984, University of Virginia Press. The charter does not have a system of petitions. On an international level, the UK is also party to the 1966 International Covenant on Economic, Social and Cultural Rights, Cmnd 6702. It is not enforceable as regards the UK by individual petition.

11   Cmnd 9221. All the parties to the Convention except Switzerland are parties to this Protocol, which came into force in 1954.

12   Cmnd 2309. It came into force in 1968; the UK is not yet a party. It contains rights relating to the field of immigration law, which have raised governmental concerns regarding the nature of the obligations created and the government has indicated that it does not intend to ratify it at present: see the White Paper, *Rights Brought Home: the Human Rights Bill*, Cm 3782, 1997, paras 4.10–4.11. It has, however, considered the possibility of future ratification with reservations: the *Home Office Review of Human Rights Instruments* (amended), 26 August 1999. See below, p 165.

13   (1983) 5 EHRR 167. It came into force in 1985. The UK is now a party to it and it is included in the Human Rights Act, Sched 4. See below, Chapter 4, p 165.

14   (1984) 7 EHRR 1. It came into force in 1988. The UK is not a party but proposes to ratify imminently: see the White Paper, *Rights Brought Home: the Human Rights Bill*, Cm 3782, 1997, paras 4.14–4.15, and the *Home Office Review of Human Rights Instruments* (amended) 26 August 1999. Note that the other Protocols are concerned with the procedural machinery of the Convention.

15   See Chapter 4, p 165, and Chapter 15, p 1486 and see below, p 106.

16   Seventeenth Report of Session 2004–5 HL Paper 99, HC 264, paras 34 and 37.

17   Once the Eleventh Protocol came into force, individuals acquired the right to take a case directly to the Court; see below, pp 24 *et seq*.

18   Eg, in 1991, the Commission registered 1648 applications; it referred 93 cases to the Court, which gave judgment in 72. European Court of Human Rights, Survey of Activities 1959–91.

awareness of human rights was of particular significance in the UK since, until the enactment of the HRA, no equivalent domestic instrument had the role of doing so. Since the HRA has afforded the Convention further effect in UK law, its interpretation, the values it encapsulates and the development of the control machinery have become of even greater significance. An understanding of the workings of the Convention is now crucial since the jurisprudence is now being very frequently relied on in the domestic courts.

The enormous increase in the number of applications from the UK since the early days of the Convention suggests that before the HRA was enacted, it was seen as a guardian of human rights by UK citizens, although to an extent it held out a promise that it could not fulfil. The immensely slow and difficult route to Strasbourg discouraged applicants from using it. It is still a slow and cumbersome route owing to the number of applications, despite improvements in the mechanisms for considering them.[19] Further reforms were introduced under Protocol 11 intended to address the increasing backlog of cases. That aim does not appear to have been realised; Protocol 14 is also intended to speed up the process and deal with the backlog when it comes into force. The fact that an application may take, at present, five years to be heard is perhaps one of the main deficiencies of the Convention enforcement machinery.[20] This chapter therefore devotes some time to explaining that process and the highly significant part which was, until recently, played in it by the European Commission on Human Rights,[21] before going on to consider the substantive rights. This chapter provides an overview of the substantive rights; the more recent cases are referred to at relevant points in the succeeding chapters.

2 The supervisory procedure for the Convention

Introduction

The Convention's procedural machinery has been altered several times by Protocols. Reform of the procedure recently occurred, stemming from a recommendation of the Parliamentary Assembly of the Council of Europe that the Commission should be abolished and its function merged with that of the Court, so that there would only be one body – the single Court. It was proposed[22] that the new Court would come into operation in 1995 and that there would be a transitional period from 1995 to 2000 during which the old Commission and Court would hear cases already referred to them while new cases would be referred to the new Court. This established a fundamental change in the machinery of the Convention. The new arrangements governing the

---

19 Eg, procedures were introduced under the Eighth Protocol, including a summary procedure for rejecting straightforward cases.

20 The *average* time is a little over four years: see e.g. 'Reform of the control systems' 15 EHRR 321, p 360, para 7. See further below, pp 23–28.

21 See further Bratza, N and O'Boyle, M, 'Opinion: the legacy of the Commission to the new Court under the 11th Protocol' (1997) EHRLR 211.

22 Recommendation 1194 adopted on 6 October 1992 by the Parliamentary Assembly of the Council of Europe.

control mechanism[23] are contained Protocol 11[24] which has had a radical effect on the Convention procedure. Its most significant reform was to set up the single, restructured, Court,[25] which now sits full-time in place of the Court and Commission (under Art 19). Now that the Court and Commission have merged, it may be argued that the authority of the Convention has increased because its jurisprudence will no longer be influenced by the decisions of an administrative body; the control system has become, in this respect, more akin to that of a domestic legal system. Protocol 11 also abolished the judicial functions of the Committee of Ministers. Protocols 2, 3, 5, 8, 9 and 10 were superseded by Protocol 11.

Below, the original arrangements for the Convention are considered and compared with the current arrangements under Protocol 11. The further changes that will occur under Protocol 14 are also discussed. Although the Commission has been abolished, it had a considerable influence on the Strasbourg jurisprudence. Moreover, the admissibility role it carried out has now, in essentials, been taken over by the Court. Therefore, for both reasons, it is still of importance to understand the role and functioning of the Commission. Originally, under Art 19, the Convention set up the European Commission on Human Rights (here-after referred to as 'the Commission') and the European Court of Human Rights (hereafter referred to as 'the Court'). Thus, the machinery for the enforcement of the Convention is impressive compared to that used in respect of other human rights treaties, particularly the 1966 International Covenant on Civil and Political Rights, which, as far as the UK is concerned, has been enforceable only through a system of assessment of national reports.[26]

The role of the Commission evolved over time. It was conceived as an advisory body which provided assistance for the Committee of Ministers (see below), composed of the Foreign Affairs Ministers of each state, who had the key role in supervising the Convention. The idea of an independent body interfering in the use of governmental powers in relation to their own citizens gained gradual acceptance, and the Commission became less of an administrative and more of a judicial body, giving Opinions on the law, albeit without the ability to take binding decisions except in relation to inadmissibility (see below). Broadly, creation of the Commission represented a compromise: it was thought too controversial merely to allow citizens to take their governments before the Court. There was a feeling that an administrative body might be more sympathetic to Member states' cases and the Member state might feel less on trial than in the

---

23 See 'Reform of the control systems' (1993) 15 EHRR 321. For comment, see Mowbray, A [1993] PL 419.

24 Protocol 11 came into force on 1 November 1998 under Art 5 of the Protocol, which provides that it comes into force one year after it has been ratified by all the Member states. See (1994) 15 HRLJ 86. The merger procedure was completed in November 1998 when the Commission was abolished. For discussion see, e.g., Schermers, H, 'The Eleventh Protocol to the European Convention on Human Rights' (1994) 19 EL Rev 367, at p 378 and (1995) EL Rev 3; Lord Lester of Herne Hill QC, 'The European Convention in the new architecture of Europe' [1996] PL 5.

25 See 'Reform of the control systems' (1993) 15 EHRR 321.

26 The Optional Protocol to the Covenant governs the right of individual petition; but it has not been ratified by the UK. For comment on the general efficacy of the reporting system, see (1980) HRLJ 136–70.

Court.[27] Therefore, the Commission was created as an administrative barrier between the individual and the Court and was used as a means of filtering out a very high proportion of cases, thus considering far more cases than the Court. This might seem a strange device: European Community lawyers would be horrified at the idea of creating a European Commission to keep cases out of the European Court of Justice; they would feel that for justice to be done, the individual's case must be considered by the Court itself rather than by an administrative body reaching its decisions in secret.[28] Nevertheless, in human rights matters, the Commission was until recently viewed as an acceptable and useful device. That view recently underwent a change which led to the proposal for abolition of the Commission and the takeover of the Commission's role by the Court, which was carried out in Protocol 11; we will return to this matter below.

The previous role of the European Commission on Human Rights

The main role of the Commission was to filter out cases as inadmissible, thereby reducing the workload of the Court. However, it also had another role: it tried to reach a friendly settlement between the parties and could give its Opinion on the merits of the case if it was not intended that a final judgment should be given. It could also refer the case to the Court or the Committee of Ministers[29] for the final judgment. As explained below, parts of this role have been taken over by the Court. That judicial role of the Committee was abolished under the Protocol 11 reforms.

The Commission consisted of one member for every Member state.[30] The members were elected by the Committee of Ministers[31] and their period of service was managed with a view to ensuring that the membership would change constantly.[32] The members of the Commission (who were unsalaried) were not government representatives; Art 23 provided that they served 'in their individual capacity'.[33] In the UK, members tended to come from within the Civil Service, thus raising some doubt as to their neutrality. Apart from the criterion contained in Art 23, members of the Commission were, in practice, expected to display high moral integrity, have a recognised competence in

---

27 See Janis, Kay and Bradley, op. cit., fn 1, p 27.
28 The Commission's sessions were held *in camera* (old Art 33).
29 For the composition and functioning of this body see below, pp 25–26.
30 Under (old) Art 20, no two members of the Commission could be nationals of the same state.
31 Under (old) Art 21, the members of the Commission were elected by the Committee of Ministers by an absolute majority of votes, from a list of names drawn up by the Bureau of the Consultative Assembly and this procedure was followed as far as it was applicable when a state became a party to the Convention and when vacancies had to be filled.
32 Under (old) Art 22, the members of the Commission were elected for a period of six years and could be re-elected. However, of the members elected at the first election, the terms of seven members chosen by lot expired at the end of three years. In order to ensure that, as far as possible, one half of the membership of the Commission was renewed every three years, the Committee of Ministers could decide that the term of office of a member to be elected should be for a period other than six years but not more than nine and not less than three years.
33 The members usually held other posts in their own countries as university professors, legal advisers or judges. They were aided by the lawyers on the staff of the Commission.

human rights matters and have substantial legal experience.[34] The Commission decided by a majority of votes (old Art 34) and the President had the casting vote.[35] As it was a part-time body which usually only sat for about 14 weeks a year, it tended to build up a backlog of cases, thus contributing to the long delay in dealing with applications.

The role of the Commission came under review for a number of reasons. It was barely able to deal with the number of applications it received and, as states which used to be part of the Soviet Union or Yugoslavia became signatories to the Convention, this problem was exacerbated. Such countries do not have as developed a system for protection for human rights as the old Member states, and so tend to use the Convention as a means of developing such protection. Thus, although a two-tier system involving two part-time bodies may have been an acceptable control mechanism when the Convention was drawn up, it became much less appropriate. Moreover, although the notion of the involvement of an administrative body in dealing with cases may have been acceptable in 1950, it arguably detracted from the authority of the Convention.[36]

The European Court of Human Rights[37]

The Court has increased enormously in standing and efficacy over the last 30 years, partly due to its activism and creativity in interpreting the Convention and its willingness to find that Member states have violated the rights of individuals. It has been pointed out that an explosion in the number of cases it considered occurred in the 1980s as lawyers in the different European countries realised that it held out the possibility of a remedy for their clients and also of bringing about important legal change.[38] It may be considered the European constitutional court as far as human rights matters are concerned.

As originally set up, however, the Court did not bear a great resemblance to a domestic supreme or higher court in a number of respects. In particular, individuals could not take a case directly to it and its role was restricted because of the likelihood to the European Commission on Human Rights finding a case inadmissible. When Protocol 9 came into force,[39] the individual, or a group of individuals, was added to the bodies who could refer a case to the Court, under amendments to (old) Arts 44 and 48. The UK was not one of the consenting parties. Protocol 9 was repealed by Protocol 11, which now governs the ability of individuals to refer cases to the Court (Art 34).

---

34 Protocol 8 required that members 'must either possess the qualifications required for appointment to judicial office or be persons of recognised competence in national or international law'.
35 The Commission drew up its own rules of procedure (old) Art 36.
36 For discussion, see (1987) HRLJ 8.
37 For discussion of the role of the Court in interpreting the Convention, see Gearty, 'The European Court of Human Rights and the protection of civil liberties' [1993] CLJ 89. The Court's constitution and jurisdiction were governed by the Convention Arts 19–56, but under Protocol 11 these Articles were replaced by a revised Section II of the Convention (Arts 19–51).
38 See Harris, O'Boyle and Warbrick, op. cit., fn 1, p 648.
39 On 1 October 1994, for the 13 states which consented to it. Under Protocol 9, Art 48, as amended, an individual could refer a case to the Court only after it had been screened by a panel of three members of the Court. If it did not raise a 'serious question affecting the interpretation or application of the Convention' and did not for any other reason warrant consideration by the Court, the panel could decide that it should not be considered by the Court.

Under the previous arrangements, if an application was found inadmissible by the Commission, the case would not reach the Court, as explained below. If it was found admissible, but a friendly settlement was reached, the Court might not have been required to decide on the application of the Convention. Thus, the question of admissibility and the mechanism allowing for a friendly settlement were crucial within the system for enforcing the Convention. The possibility of avoiding the Court's involvement meant, it is argued, that a lower standard of human rights than that allowed by the Convention tended to be maintained, especially in the older decisions of the Commission. From November 1998, under Protocol 11, the admissibility and the examination of the merits with a view to reaching a friendly settlement were undertaken by the Court. This reform was generally seen as representing a more satisfactory arrangement, since a judicial as opposed to an administrative body is now making the key decisions. Nevertheless, since the admissibility criteria remain unchanged under Protocol 11, as indicated below, current criticism of them is still applicable.

The terms of membership of the Court, governed now by Arts 19–24 of the Convention (previously by Arts 38–43), are intended to ensure that the judges will act independently of their own governments. Under Art 20 (previously Art 38), each Member state will send to the Court[40] one judge, who must be 'of high moral character and must either possess the qualifications required for appointment to high judicial office or be jurisconsults of recognised competence' (Art 21). Rule 4 of the Rules of Court[41] provides that judges may not engage in 'any political or administrative activity or any professional activity which is incompatible with their independence or impartiality or with the demands of a full-time office'. However, this does not mean that a judge may not have served within the government and, in fact, UK judges have at times come from the Foreign and Commonwealth Office's Legal Advisers department which is responsible for defending the government in Strasbourg. The judges tend to serve for substantial periods of time, but under the Protocol 11 reforms, the initial period of office has been shortened, since they are initially elected for six rather than nine years. The Court will not have the same composition for all that time, because the terms of certain members expire earlier than those of others.[42]

The form of the Court was governed by (old) Art 43 which provided that it would consist of a Chamber composed of seven judges.[43] Like the Commission, it used to sit

---

40   A list of persons is nominated by the Members of the Council of Europe and they are then elected by the Consultative Assembly. Under Art 22 (previously 39), each member shall nominate three candidates, of whom two at least shall be its nationals. Countries which are not yet parties to the Convention may have judges on the Court as have Hungary, Czechoslovakia, Poland and Bulgaria with representatives from Estonia, Latvia and Lithuania expected.

41   The European Court of Human Rights Rules of Court (4 November 1998).

42   Under (old) Art 40, the members of the Court were elected for a period of nine years. The period is now six under Art 23(1). They may be re-elected. However, of the members elected at the first election, the terms of four members shall expire at the end of three years and the terms of four more members shall expire at the end of six years chosen by lot. The Consultative Assembly may decide, before proceeding to any subsequent election, that the term or terms of office of one or more members to be elected shall be for a period other than six years, but not more than nine and not less than three years.

43   The names of the judges are chosen by lot by the President before the opening of the case. The judge who is a national of any state Party concerned will sit as an *ex officio* member of the Chamber.

temporarily.[44] Its hearings will continue to be public,[45] although the Court deliberates in private.[46] Its decisions will continue to be taken on a majority vote.[47] The Court has jurisdiction under Art 32 (previously Art 45) of the Convention to consider all cases which raise issues as to the interpretation and application of the Convention.

Under the Protocol 11 reforms, the Court sits in Committees of three judges, Chambers of seven judges and in a Grand Chamber of 17 judges (Art 27). Chambers designate Judge Rapporteurs to examine applications. The Plenary Court does not perform a judicial function; it elects its President and Vice-President for three-year terms and sets up Chambers, constituted for three years.[48] Under Art 43, a party to a case may request that it be referred to the Grand Chamber within a period of three months from the date of the judgment of the Chamber. A panel of five judges from the Grand Chamber will accept the request if it raises a serious issue regarding the interpretation of the Convention or an issue of general importance. This procedure represents a further significant improvement brought about by the Eleventh Protocol since it seemed anomalous that a human rights Convention should make no provision for appeals. In general, adoption of the Eleventh Protocol has brought about quite radical changes in the role of the Court, changes that have not been welcomed wholeheartedly by some critics.[49]

The Committee of Ministers

The Committee was not set up by the Convention; its composition and functions are regulated in the statute of the Council of Europe (Arts 13–21). The Committee consists of one representative from the government of each Member state of the Council of Europe, usually the Minister for Foreign Affairs.[50] The Committee is, therefore, a political body which, as indicated below, was nevertheless performing a judicial role prior to the Protocol 11 reforms. Like the creation of the Commission, this was the result of a compromise; it was thought when the Convention was drafted that a Court of Human Rights with full compulsory jurisdiction would be too controversial and would therefore be unacceptable to all Member states.

Pre-Protocol 11 the Committee of Ministers used to have a judicial decision-making function. The Committee received a Report from the Commission giving its Opinion on the merits of an application. If there was no move by the Commission within three months to bring the case before the Court, the Committee would take the final decision (old Art 32). Oddly, the Convention was silent as to when a case should go to the Court and when to the Committee of Ministers; the matter appeared to be in the discretion of the Commission. In practice, non-contentious cases were usually referred to the Committee. They included those cases which did not raise significant Convention issues

---

44 It used to sit for about 80–90 days a year (see (1993) 15 EHRR 322, at p 327).
45 Under (current) Art 40.
46 Rule 22(1).
47 Rule 23 of the Rules of the Court.
48 Rule 25(1).
49 See, e.g., Schermers, H, 'The Eleventh Protocol to the European Convention on Human Rights' (1994) 19 EL Rev 367, p 378.
50 If an alternative is nominated, he or she should also be a member of the government (Art 14).

and/or those which raised issues which concerned established Convention case law. A sub-Committee would be appointed to examine the case which decided by a two-thirds majority.[51] If it decided that there had been a violation, it would make suggestions as to the measures to be taken by a certain period and if they were not taken, it published the report. This was a sanction: a degree of humiliation would be expected to flow from the declaration by all the Foreign Ministers of the other Member states that a certain state had violated international human rights norms. Also, ammunition would thereby be offered to the opposition parties in the particular state. In practice, if the Commission had given its opinion that a violation had occurred, the state in question usually took measures to address the violation and the Committee did not have to give judgment.

It may be noted that the position of the individual applicant before the Committee was very weak; he or she had no right to appear or to make representations. The individual was in an equally weak position before the Court, but the role of the Commission before the Court allowed the individual's interests to be represented in a way which did not occur before the Committee.

Like the role of the Commission, the decision-making role of the Committee was viewed with increasing dissatisfaction, and under the Protocol 11 reforms, the Committee's adjudicatory function was removed, although it continues to discharge a role, discussed below, in supervising the execution of the Court's judgments.

The right of complaint: inter-state applications

Under Art 33 (previously Art 24) any Contracting Party may refer to the Commission, through the Secretary General of the Council of Europe, any alleged breach of the provisions of the Convention by another Contracting Party. The violation in question may be against any person; it need not be a national of the complainant state. Further, it can be an abstract application: one that does not allege a violation against any specified person but concerns incompatibility of a state's legislation or administrative practices with the Convention. There have been 19 inter-state applications so far, but more than one complaint has sprung from the same situation; only six situations have, in fact, given rise to complaints.[52] Thus this right has not proved effective; generally, states prefer not to sour their relations with other states if no interest of their own is involved. Therefore, inter-state complaints have had a much less significant impact on human rights in the Member states than the individual's right of petition.

The right of complaint: individual applications

Article 25 (now Art 34), widely viewed as the most important article in the Convention since it governs the right of individual complaint, enables citizens of Member states to seek a remedy for a breach of Convention rights by petitioning the European Court. Under Art 34, the Court (previously the Commission) can receive petitions from any

---

51 In *Huber v Austria*, Report of 8 February 1973, D & R 2 (1935) and the *East African Asians* cases (1973) 3 EHRR 76, the Committee could not obtain a two-thirds majority as to the determination whether there had been a violation of the Convention; its resolution in both cases was to take no further action on the applications.

52 See Van Dijk and Van Hoof, op. cit., fn 1, p 43.

person, non-governmental organisation or group of individuals claiming to be the victim of a violation of one or more of the rights set forth in the Convention. Prior to the Protocol 11 reforms, the right of petition arose only if the state allegedly responsible for the violation had declared (as the UK had) that it recognised the competence of the Commission to receive such petitions (Art 25). Under the reforms, this qualification no longer appears in the relevant Article (Art 34).

The individual need not be a national of the state in question, but must be in some way subject to its jurisdiction. The Court has established that the applicant must have been personally affected by the particular violation; it is not possible to bring an abstract complaint.[53] Therefore, an application alleging that Norwegian abortion legislation conflicted with Art 2 (guaranteeing protection of life) failed because the applicant did not allege that he had been personally affected by it (*X v Norway*).[54] However, there are two exceptions to this principle. First, the application can have a mixed nature: it can be partly abstract so long as there has been some personal impact on the applicant. In *Donnelly v UK*[55] the complaint concerned the allegation that the applicants had been tortured during their detention in Northern Ireland. They also wanted a full investigation of the whole system of interrogation employed by the security forces. It was found that so long as the applicants had been *affected*, a more wide ranging review was possible in the public interest, and the complaint was admissible on that basis. Second, a potential victim may make a complaint if the circumstances are such that the complainant is unsure whether or not he or she is a victim of a violation of a Convention right. This was found to be the case in a complaint concerning the possibility that the applicants' telephones were being tapped (*Klass v Federal Republic of Germany*)[56] where, by virtue of the very nature of the action complained of, it was impossible for the applicants to be certain that they had been affected.

Individual applications – procedure

The process of making a complaint remained a long drawn out one and was extremely cumbersome despite some improvement to it undertaken in 1990 under the Eighth Protocol. At present, despite the Protocol 11 reforms, there are still a very large number of hurdles to be overcome which arise, in particular, from the question of admissibility. In essentials, the procedure remains the same, although the role of the Commission has been removed. (Under the Protocol 14 reforms, discussed below, the hurdles will be made more difficult to overcome.) A number of stages can be identified.

Pre-complaint

Before lodging the application, it must appear that:

(a) prima facie, a violation of one or more of the rights or freedoms contained in the Convention has taken place. This refers to Arts 2–14 and, as far as the UK is concerned, the First and Sixth Protocols;

---

53 *Klass v Federal Republic of Germany* (1978) 2 EHRR 214.
54 Appl 867/60, 4 YB 270, 276; see also *Vijayanathan v France* (1992) 15 EHRR 62.
55 Appl 5577–82/72, Yearbook XVI.
56 Judgment of 6 September 1978 A 28 (1979–80); 2 EHRR 214 (see (1980) 130 NLJ 999).

(b) the available domestic remedies have been exhausted (Art 35);
(c) the application has been made within six months of the final decision of the highest competent court or authority (Art 35(1)).

These questions will be considered at the stage of determination of admissibility, so they will not be discussed now, but chronologically, they arise before the question of admissibility and it should be borne in mind that prima facie they must be fulfilled before the complaint can be set in motion. Whether they are fulfilled will be determined by a Chamber of the Court.[57] It is worth noting that of 34,297 applications submitted to the Commission up to December 1996, only 3,458 were ultimately declared admissible.[58]

Registration of the complaint

Registration merely means that an application is pending before the Court; it has no bearing on admissibility. The Court Registry (previously the Secretary to the Commission) will open a provisional file on the complaint. The Court may indicate a preliminary view of admissibility to the complainant. This may imply that the complaint had better be withdrawn. This practice is open to criticism since it may appear to the applicant that the application is inadmissible although its admissibility has not been fully considered. It is an additional means of cutting down on the very large number of applications.

Determination of the admissibility of the complaint

Determining the question of admissibility was the Commission's main function and it is still the main method of filtering out applications. Under the current arrangements, when an application is made, it is assigned to a Chamber of the Court which designates a Judge Rapporteur to examine it.[59] Having given it consideration, the Judge refers it to a Committee or to a Chamber.[60] Under a new 'fast track' procedure the Committee can decide, by a unanimous vote only, that the application is inadmissible.[61] If so, the decision is not subject to appeal.[62] If it does not so decide, it refers the application to the Chamber for the decision on admissibility and the consideration of the merits.[63]

The complaint must satisfy the admissibility conditions as follows:

(a) The application must not constitute an abuse of the right of complaint.[64] This condition is not often used; it concerns either the aim of applicant – it may appear that the case is obviously being brought for political propaganda purposes – or his or her conduct.

---

57 Article 29(1).
58 Noted in Van Dijk and Van Hoof, *Theory and Practice of the ECHR*, 1998, p 45: figures from European Commission on HR Survey of Activities and Statistics, 1996.
59 Rule 49(2).
60 Rule 49(3)(b).
61 Article 28 and Rule 53(2).
62 Rule 53(2).
63 Article 29(1).
64 Article 35(3) (previously Art 27(2)).

(b) Under Art 35(1)(b), the matter must not be the same as a matter already examined.[65] This means that unless it contains relevant new information, the complaint must not concern a matter 'which is substantially the same as a matter which has already been examined by the Court or has already been submitted to another procedure or international investigation or settlement or contains no relevant new information'.[66] The limitation in respect of complaints submitted to another international organ has not, in practice, been of significance; no UK complaints have been rejected on this basis. This is mainly because the UK has not accepted the individual right of complaint to the UN Covenant on Civil and Political Rights. The limitation in respect of previous complaints made to the Court (previously the Commission) refers to substantially similar applications. If the same applicant makes a complaint, new *facts* are needed if it is not to be rejected.[67]

(c) The application must not be incompatible with the provisions of the Convention.[68] This provision encompasses a number of aspects. Incompatibility will occur if:

- the application claims violation of a right not guaranteed by the Convention. This includes the substantive rights of Section 1 (Arts 2–14) and, as far as the UK is concerned, the First and Sixth Protocols. However, it may be that the right in question does not appear in the Convention, but that if the claim is not granted, violation of one of the Convention rights might then occur; the right claimed may thereby acquire indirect protection;

- the application claims violation of a right which is the subject of a derogation (Art 15) or reservation (Art 64) by the relevant Member state.[69] Thus, the right does appear in the Convention, but the state in question is not, at present, bound to abide by it. A reservation is made when a state ratifies the Convention, while a derogation may be made if an emergency arises, thus suspending part of the state's Convention obligations. Some rights, as will be seen, are non-derogable, because they are viewed as particularly fundamental;

- the applicant or respondent are persons or states incompetent to appear before the Commission. An application from an individual can only be directed against those states which are Contracting Parties. Further, the complaint must be directed against an organ of government, not against individuals.[70] However, the violation of the Convention by an individual may involve the responsibility of the state. The state may have encouraged the acts in question or failed to prevent or remedy them. Thus, the condition will be fulfilled if the state is in some way responsible for the alleged violation. This is an aspect of the phenomenon known as *Drittwirkung*, which means that human rights provisions can affect the legal relations between private individuals, not only between individuals and the public authorities;[71]

---

65 Previously Art 27(b).
66 Article 32(2)(b).
67 *X v UK* (1981) 25 DR 147.
68 Article 27(2).
69 These provisions are discussed below, pp 110–12.
70 See, e.g., *Nielsen v Denmark* (1988) 11 EHRR 175.
71 See Van Dijk and Van Hoof, op. cit., fn 1, Chapter 1, Part 6. For commentary on *Drittwirkung*, see Alkema, E, 'The third party applicability or *Drittwirkung* of the ECHR in protecting human rights', in *The European Dimension*, 1988, pp 33–45.

- the application is aimed at the destruction or limitation of one of the rights or freedoms guaranteed by the Convention and therefore conflicts with Art 17. The intention is to prevent an applicant claiming a right which would enable him or her to carry out activities which ultimately would lead to the destruction of the guaranteed rights. Therefore, the Commission rejected the application of the banned German Communist Party due to its aims (*Kommunistische Partei Deutschland v Federal Republic of Germany*).[72] This provision suggests that the Convention adopts a teleological view of freedom; in other words, freedom is valued instrumentally as something which will lead to benefit for society as a whole, rather than as being a good in itself.

(d) Domestic remedies must have been exhausted.[73] In brief, this means that the applicant must provide prima facie evidence of exhaustion of remedies. The burden then shifts to the state to show that a remedy was reasonably ascertainable by the applicant, that the remedy does exist and has not been exhausted and that the remedy is effective. The requirement that domestic remedies must have been exhausted refers to: the 'legal remedies available under the local law which are in principle capable of providing an effective and sufficient means of redressing the wrongs for which the Respondent state is said to be responsible'.[74] If there is a doubt as to whether a remedy is available, Art 35 (previously Art 26) will not be satisfied unless the applicant has taken proceedings in which that doubt can be resolved.[75] This generally means that judicial procedures must be instituted up to the highest court which can affect the decision but also, if applicable, appeal must be made to administrative bodies. However, the applicant only needs to exhaust those possibilities which offer an *effective* remedy, so if part of the complaint is the lack of a remedy under Art 13, then the application is not likely to be ruled inadmissible on this ground.[76] A remedy will be ineffective if, according to established case law, there appears to be no chance of success,[77] and the Court will decide whether a remedy did in fact offer the applicant the possibility of sufficient redress. If there is a doubt as to whether a given remedy is able to offer a real chance of success, that doubt must be resolved in the national court itself.[78] Until recently, the Court viewed judicial review as a sufficient remedy,[79] but this is no longer necessarily the case, as explained below.[80] If it can be said that the state practice complained of is a repetition of one that is in breach of the Convention, but tolerated by the state authorities, it may be argued that taking the proceedings available would be ineffective.[81]

The application must have been submitted within a period of six months from the date on which the final national decision was taken (Art 36(1)). Time runs from

---

72 Appl 250/57, Yearbook I (1955–57), Vol 6, p 222.
73 Article 35(1) (previously Arts 26 and 27(3)).
74 *Nielsen v Denmark* Appl No 343/57; (1958–59) 2 YB 412, p 412.
75 *De Vargattirgah v France*, Appl 9559/81.
76 *X v UK* (1981) Appl 7990/77; 24 D & R 77.
77 Appl 5874/172, Yearbook XVII (1974). See *H v UK* 33 D & R 247(1983) (Counsel's opinion as to inefficacy sufficient). Cf *K, F and P v UK* 40 D & R 298 (1984).
78 *Spencer v UK* (1998) 25 EHRR CD 105.
79 See *Vilvarajah and Four Others v UK* (1991) Judgment of 30 October 1991; Appl 12 (1991).
80 See below, p 107.
81 *Akdivar v Turkey* (1997) 23 EHRR 143, paras 66–67.

the decision taken by the last national authority that had to be used and after the point when the decision has been notified to the applicant; ineffective remedies will not be taken into account in assessing the point from which time runs.

(e) The application must not be manifestly ill-founded (Art 35(3), previously Art 27(2)). Previously, this admissibility condition afforded a very significant power to the Commission. Formerly, the Commission was not empowered to act judicially and therefore it was not intended that it should come to a judgment on the merits of the application. Yet, when it made a determination as to manifest ill-foundedness, it was pronouncing on the merits because it was determining whether or not a prima facie violation had taken place. Thus, this condition created an extension of the role of the Commission behind the cloak of merely determining admissibility: it was, in fact, in a number of instances taking the *final* decision on the merits.

Under the current procedure, the Committee or a Chamber of the Court finds this condition unfulfilled if the facts obviously fail to disclose a violation. In theory, this ground should only operate if the ill-founded character of the application is clearly manifest. It has been said that 'the task of the Commission is not to determine whether an examination of the case submitted by the applicant discloses the actual violation of one of the rights and freedoms guaranteed by the Convention but only to determine whether it includes any possibility of the existence of such a determination'.[82] In practice, the Commission went further: the ill-founded character of the application was not always as manifest as this would imply. This was clear from the Commission's voting procedure: it was not necessary to have unanimity on this condition; a bare majority was sufficient. Under the current arrangements it is necessary to have unanimity if a Committee declares the application inadmissible,[83] but a majority if a Chamber does so. Although it is more satisfactory that the decision is being taken judicially, it is arguable that it should have been necessary to have unanimity or a two-thirds majority as to a finding of manifest ill-foundedness by a Chamber, even though a bare majority suffices in respect of the other conditions.

The examination of the application and friendly settlements under Art 38(1)(b)

If the application is declared admissible, the Court places itself at the disposal of the parties under Art 38(1)(b) with a view to securing a friendly settlement between the parties. If both parties are willing, they can reach a friendly settlement straight after the application has been declared admissible.[84] The settlement is a compromise; its danger is that it could aid in maintaining lower standards of human rights in particular states than the Convention allows, although, under Art 38(1)(b), the settlement should be on the basis of the respect for human rights accorded by the Convention. This may mean that, if the state Party in question is prepared to pay compensation and the victim

---

82 *Pataki*, Appl 596/59, Yearbook III (1960).
83 Rule 53(3).
84 If a friendly settlement is reached, the Commission will draw up a report stating the facts and solution reached. Up to the end of 1996, 324 friendly settlements had been reached.

is willing to receive it, the Court may nevertheless continue the examination of the application if the respect for human rights under the Convention demands that it should do so (Art 37(1)). In other words, the Court should have regard to its general purpose of improving human rights protection and not just the particular interest of the victim. By this means, it could prevent further applications from the same state alleging the same violation. In fact, this power is rarely invoked.[85] If the application is declared admissible and no friendly settlement is reached, it is examined under Art 38(1)(a).

Under the old procedure, if no settlement was reached, the Commission would state its Opinion as to the alleged violation in the Report to the Committee of Ministers.[86] The Report generally only went to individual applicants if the Court considered it. After having declared the application admissible, the Commission could still, after further examination, declare it inadmissible.[87]

The judgment of the Court

Prior to the Protocol 11 reforms, the Court could not hear a case unless it had gone through all the Commission's procedure and a Report had gone to the Committee of Ministers. The fact, as mentioned above, that the individual in question could not refer the case to Court[88] did not seem odd at the inception of the Convention, when the right of individual petition in itself seemed controversial. However, it came to seem increasingly anomalous, and provided part of the impetus for reform. The Commission was likely, however, to bring the case before the Court and did bring the vast majority of cases once it had found them admissible. In exercising its discretion as to bringing a case before the Committee of Ministers or the Court, the Commission, as indicated above, was influenced by its nature. In general, a difficult question would go to the Court while, if the Commission was unanimous that no breach had occurred, it would go to the Committee. The trend was to refer far more cases to the Court in relation to the number of cases declared admissible.

The Court was not bound by the Report of the Commission. The function of the Commission was 'to present to the Court the issues in the case and all the relevant information which we ourselves have obtained concerning the case'.[89] The Court could disagree with points of the Commission's decisions; it could consider admissibility again and then reject the application as inadmissible. In other words, the Court was no more bound by the Commission on admissibility than it was on Opinion. It was

---

85 *Tyrer v UK* (1978) 2 EHRR 1.
86 (Old) Art 31 provided that if a solution was not reached, the Commission would draw up a Report on the facts and state its Opinion as to whether the facts found disclosed a breach by the state concerned of its obligations under the Convention. The Opinions of all the members of the Commission on this point could be stated in the Report.
87 (Old) Art 29. At this stage, if it was to be rejected, it had to be rejected unanimously. In such a case, the decision could be communicated to the parties.
88 Under (old) Art 48, the following could bring a case before the Court: the Commission; a High Contracting Party whose national was alleged to be a victim; a High Contracting Party which referred the case to the Commission; a High Contracting Party against which the complaint had been lodged. But Protocol 11 gave the individual the right to seize the Court under Art 34.
89 *Lawless*, A 1 (1960–61), p 360; (1961) 1 EHRR 15.

arguable that this procedure did not maintain equality between the parties, because a negative decision on admissibility would never come before the Court, while a positive one would.[90] However, in practice, the Court tended to agree with the Commission on admissibility. Nevertheless, this and other aspects of the proceedings before the Court and Commission did involve a duplication of function which was time consuming and so supported the argument for abolition of the Commission.

Under the current procedure, the proceedings before the Chamber of seven judges will consist of a written stage, followed by a hearing.[91] The Chamber may appoint one or more of its members to conduct the initial examination. The arrangements are characterised by their flexibility: within the Rules, the Court is free to decide on a procedure which can be tailored to the nature of a particular application[92] and this may include visiting a particular place, such as a prison. An on-the-spot inquiry can be conducted by a delegate of the Court. The Court can also order a report from an expert on any matter. After this initial stage, the Chamber will normally conduct an oral hearing if there has been no oral admissibility hearing.

The applicant used to be in a weak position in the hearing. Previously, he or she did not have any right to take part in the proceedings; after a change in the rules of procedure in 1982, an applicant could be heard as a person providing clarification. Under the current Protocol 11 procedure, each of the parties can address the Court; in practice, hearings take half a day and each party is given 45 minutes to make oral submissions. If a violation appears to be established, the state must attempt to demonstrate that the case falls within an exception to the right in question. The Court is not bound by its own judgments.[93] Nevertheless, it usually follows and applies its own precedents unless departure from them is indicated in order to ensure that interpretation of the Convention reflects social change.

The procedure before the Court may conclude before the judgment on the merits if the state settles. However, the Court does not have to discontinue the procedure; it can proceed in the interests of the Convention and may give a declaratory judgment even though the state is now willing to settle. The judgment does not state what remedial measures should be taken; it is up to the state to amend its legislation or make other changes in order to conform with the judgment. Thus, a response may well be in doubtful conformity with the Convention.[94] The Court is not ultimately a coercive body and relies for acceptance of its judgments on the willingness of states to abide by the Convention. Under Art 45, reasons must be given for the judgment of the Court and if the judgment does not represent in whole or in part the unanimous opinion of the

90   See *Van Oosterwijck v Belgium*, Judgment of 6 November 1980, A 40; (1980) 3 EHRR 557. The Court disagreed with the Commission's decision that the application was admissible; the Court held that local remedies had not been exhausted; thus the Court's decision was not on the merits.

91   Under Art 55, the Court shall draw up its own rules and determine its own procedure.

92   See Rule 42(2).

93   Rule 51, para 1 of the Rules of the Court. See Feldman, D, 'Precedent and the European Court of Human Rights' Law Com Consultation Paper No 157 (1999), Appl C.

94   The Contempt of Court Act 1981 may be said to represent such a response to the ruling that UK contempt law violated Art 10 in that it preserved common law contempt, which appears, especially since the decision in *AG v Times Newspapers Ltd* (see Chapter 5, pp 335–37), to give insufficient weight to freedom of speech.

judges, any judge shall be entitled to deliver a separate opinion. Under (old) Art 52, the judgment of the Court was final,[95] but now under Art 43 it can be referred to the Grand Chamber 'in exceptional cases' for judgment. Under Art 44, the judgment of the Grand Chamber is final, while a judgment of a Chamber will become final: when the parties declare that they will not request referral to the Grand Chamber; or, where after three months no such request has been made; or where the panel of the Grand Chamber rejects the request. Under Art 46, the judgment of the Court is binding on the state Party involved.

The Court can award compensation under Art 41. The purpose of the reparation is to place the applicant in the position he would have been in had the violation not taken place. It will include costs unless the applicant has received legal aid. It can also include loss of earnings, travel costs, fines and costs unjustly awarded against the applicant. It can also include intangible or non-pecuniary losses which may be awarded due to unjust imprisonment or stress.[96]

Supervision of the judgment by the Committee of Ministers

Under Art 46, the Committee is charged with supervising the execution of the Court's judgment. This includes both the judgment on the merits and on compensation. The Committee notes the action taken to redress the violation on the basis of information given by the state in question. If the state fails to execute the judgment, the Committee decides what measures to take: it can bring political pressure to bear, including suspension or even, as a final sanction, expulsion from the Council of Europe. Doubts have been raised over the fitness of the Committee to oversee one of the key stages in the whole Convention process, namely the implementation of national law to bring it into line with the findings of the Court.[97] It is apparent that a rigorous analysis of the changes that the offending state has made in its law would be desirable, to ensure that the judgment is fully implemented and to make future similar breaches of the Convention by that state impossible. The Committee would not prima facie appear to be capable of carrying out such a quasi-judicial role and, indeed, it appears that in practice the Committee usually merely notes the receipt of the state's explanation of the changes it has made without any attempt to conduct the kind of analysis which it is suggested should be undertaken.

The question of the full implementation of a judgment of the Court arose in *Olsson v Sweden (No 2)*.[98] The applicants complained that despite a previous judgment of the Court to the effect that a violation of the Convention had occurred, the Swedish authorities had continued the practice, which was contrary to the Convention. However,

---

95 As noted above, this is no longer the case under Art 43 of the Convention.

96 Eg, in the *Young, James and Webster* case (1981) Judgment of 13 August 1981, Appl 44; (1981) 4 EHRR 38, pecuniary and non-pecuniary costs were awarded: the Court ordered £65,000 to be paid. See further Chapter 4, pp 242–43.

97 See Leuptracht, P, 'The protection of human rights by political bodies', in Nowak, M, Steurer, P and Tretter, H (eds) *Progress in the Spirit of Human Rights*, Strasbourg, 1988, pp 95–107.

98 A 250. Note that a similar issue arose in *Christie v UK* (No 21482/93, 78-A DR 119) which was, however, found inadmissible by the Commission.

the Court found that the fresh complaint raised a new issue and that therefore, the question as to whether the state had fulfilled its obligations under Art 53 by implementing the judgment did not arise. Thus, this judgment avoided addressing the Art 53 issue. However, it is suggested that the Court should be able to rule on the question whether measures introduced to implement its own judgment are sufficient. If it became clear that it could do so, one of the main concerns regarding the procedure for supervising its judgments would be addressed, although there seems to be a case for also requiring more of the Committee in terms of analysing the measures taken to implement the judgment. The role of the Committee in supervising judgments under (old) Art 53 was retained under Protocol 11, reflecting the view that its authority has played a part in persuading states to adopt measures implementing the judgment of the Court. Reforms under Protocol 14 will afford the Court a role in enforcing its judgments once Protocol 14 comes into force.

Protocol 14 reforms

Protocol 14 follows on from Protocol 11 in introducing changes designed to improve the efficiency of operation of the Court. The volume of cases remains a problem and the Court's case load is unacceptably high. Under Protocol 14 cases that have less chance of succeeding will be 'filtered' out, as will those that are broadly similar to cases brought previously against the same Member state. Moreover, a case will not be considered admissible where an applicant has not suffered a 'significant disadvantage'. This latter ground can only be used when an examination of the application on the merits is not considered necessary and where the subject-matter of the application had already been considered by a national court. The UK Joint Committee on Human Rights broadly welcomed the contents of Protocol 14, since it considered that it included many positive aspects which should improve the functioning of the control system of the Convention. But it found that the introduction of a new requirement that an applicant to the European Court of Human Rights must have suffered a 'significant disadvantage', was 'very controversial' because it restricts the right of individual petition.[99]

Significantly, a new mechanism is introduced with Protocol 14 to assist enforcement of judgments by the Committee of Ministers. The Committee can ask the Court for an interpretation of a judgment and can even bring a Member state before the Court for non-compliance with a previous judgment against that state. Thus although Protocol 14 could be viewed as a retrograde step in human rights terms, since a higher number of cases will be declared inadmissible under its reforms, adverse judgments against Member states that are given have a higher chance of being implemented.

Protocol 14 also amends Art 59 of the Convention, allowing for the European Union to accede to it. So far, Protocol 14 has been signed by every Council of Europe Member state. All forty five Member states have ratified the Protocol; only Russia has failed to do so. Protocol 14 will come into force only when it has been ratified by all Member states.

99 1st Report Session 2004–5.

The doctrine of the 'margin of appreciation'[100]

The European Court of Human Rights has stated that the role of the Convention in protecting human rights is subsidiary to the role of the national legal system[101] and that since the state is better placed than the international judge to balance individual rights against general societal interests, Strasbourg will operate a restrained review of the balance struck. Under this doctrine, a degree of discretion will be allowed to Member states as to legislative, administrative or judicial action in the area of a Convention right. However, Strasbourg will finally determine whether such action is reconcilable with the guarantee in question.

The doctrine of the margin of appreciation conceded to states was first adopted in respect of emergency situations,[102] but it was allowed to affect the application of all the Articles although it has a particular application with respect to para 2 of Arts 8–11. It has now reached the stage where it can be said that it permeates the Convention jurisprudence. In different instances, a wider or narrower margin of appreciation has been allowed. The width allowed depends on a number of factors including the aim of the interference in question and its necessity. If a broader margin is allowed, Strasbourg review will be highly circumscribed. For example, the minority in the *Sunday Times* case[103] (nine judges) wanted to confine the role of Strasbourg to asking only whether the discretion in question was exercised in good faith and carefully and whether the measure was reasonable in the circumstances. A narrow margin conceded to the state means that a rigorous or intensive review of the proportionality between the aim of an interference and the extent and nature of the interference will be undertaken. This occurred in the *Sunday Times* case; it was held that Strasbourg review was not limited to asking whether the state had exercised its discretion reasonably, carefully and in good faith; it was found that the state's conduct must also be examined in Strasbourg to see whether it was compatible with the Convention.

Although the doctrine is well established, it has not been applied very consistently. Therefore, it is not always easy to predict when each approach will be taken, but a number of relevant factors may be identified. The nature of the right in question may be relevant. The doctrine is particularly applicable to the Arts 8–11 group of rights since it is used in determining whether an interference with the right is justifiable on grounds of one of the exceptions contained in para 2 of these Articles. Within this group, Art 10 may be viewed as particularly fundamental.[104] Also, the particular instance will be considered: does it concern, for example, a very significant need for

---

100 For general discussion of the doctrine, see McDonald, RJ, 'The margin of appreciation in the jurisprudence of the European Court of Human Rights', *International Law and the Time of its Codification*, 1987, pp 187–208; Van Dijk and Van Hoof, op. cit., fn 1, p 82 *et seq*; O'Donell, 'The margin of appreciation doctrine: standards in the jurisprudence of the European Court of Human Rights' (1982) 4 Human Rights Q 474; Morrisson, 'Margin of appreciation in human rights law' (1973) 6 Human Rights J 263; Morrisson, 'Margin of appreciation in human rights law' (1973) 6 Human Rights J 263; Jones, T, 'The devaluation of human rights under the European Convention' [1995] PL 430; Mahoney, P, 'Marvellous richness or invidious cultural relativism?' (1998) 19 Human Rights LJ 1.

101 *Handyside v UK* A 24, para 48 (1976).

102 See the *Lawless* case, Publ ECHR B 1 (1960–61), p 408; (1961) 1 EHRR 15.

103 Series A 30 (1979); 2 EHRR 245.

104 See, e.g., the judgment of the Court in *Autronic AG v Switzerland* (1990) 12 EHRR 485.

free expression since there is a strong public interest in the subject matter? The presence of such factors may predispose the Strasbourg authorities to conduct a wide ranging review. Such review also tends to be applicable under Arts 2[105] and 3,[106] although it may be narrowed where the state claims that the demands of national security justify the measures sought to be challenged under these Articles.[107] On the other hand, in considering the imposition of positive obligations placed on the state, a broad margin will be allowed.[108]

The nature of the restriction is significant. Some restrictions are seen as more subjective than others. It is therefore thought more difficult to lay down a common European standard and the Court and Commission have, in such instances, shown a certain willingness to allow the exceptions a wide scope in curtailing the primary rights. For example, Art 10 contains an exception in respect of the protection of morals. This was invoked in the *Handyside* case[109] in respect of suppression of a booklet aimed at schoolchildren which was circulating freely in the rest of Europe. It was held that the UK Government was best placed to determine what was needed in its own country in order to protect morals and, therefore, it could make an initial assessment of those requirements, which would then be considered for compatibility with Art 10 by Strasbourg.

The Court and Commission consider that in certain sensitive matters, most notably national security,[110] states are best placed to determine what is needed within their own particular domestic situation. Thus, emergency situations and the invocation of threats to national security invite deference. In *Council of Civil Service Unions v UK*[111] the European Commission, in declaring the Unions' application inadmissible, found that national security interests should prevail over freedom of association even though the national security interest was weak while the infringement of the primary right was very clear: an absolute ban on joining a trade union had been imposed. It is worth noting that the International Labour Organisation (ILO) Committee on Freedom of Association had earlier found that the ban breached the 1947 ILO Freedom of Association Convention. However, in general, if a restriction is very far-reaching, the Strasbourg authorities may be prepared to make a determination as to the need to impose it which differs from that of the state Party in question.[112]

The high (or low) point of deference was perhaps reached in *Brannigan and McBride v UK*,[113] in which the European Court of Human Rights upheld a derogation entered by the UK after the decision in the case of *Brogan and Others v UK*.[114] The Court found 'a wide margin of appreciation [on the question] of the presence of an emergency . . . and on the nature and scope of derogations necessary to avert it [should be allowed]'.[115]

---

105 *McCann, Farrell and Savage v UK* (1995) 21 EHRR 97, A 324, Council of Europe Report.
106 *Soering v UK*, Judgment of 7 July 1989, A 161; (1989) 11 EHRR 439.
107 *Kröcher and Möller v Switzerland* No 8463/78, 34 DR 25.
108 See *Plattform 'Ärzte für Das Leben' v Austria* (1988) 13 EHRR 204.
109 (1976) 1 EHRR 737.
110 See *Leander v Sweden* Series A 116, para 67 (1987).
111 No 11603/85, 50 DR 228 (1987); 10 EHRR 269.
112 See, e.g., *Golder*, Judgment of 21 February 1975; A 18. Discussed p 62.
113 Series A, 258-B (1993).
114 Judgement of 29 November 1988 (1989) Series A 145-B (1988); 11 EHRR 117. See further Chapter 11, p 1168.
115 Para 207.

The Court is greatly influenced by general practice in the Member states as a body and will interpret the Convention to reflect such practice so that a state which is clearly out of conformity with the others may expect an adverse ruling. However, where practice is still in the process of changing and may be said to be at an inchoate stage as far as the Member states generally are concerned, the Court may not be prepared to place itself at the forefront of such changes, although it will weigh the lack of a consensus against the degree of detriment to the applicant.[116] Thus, the notion of common standards strongly influences the doctrine of the margin of appreciation. Where a common standard, or a trend towards such a standard, cannot be discerned among Member states, greater deference to particular state practice is shown.[117] For example, the lack of a uniform standard was the key factor in the ruling in *Otto-Preminger Institut v Austria*.[118] The decision concerned the seizure of film likely to offend religious feeling. The European Court of Human Rights found that the film would receive protection under Art 10, but that its seizure fell within the 'rights of others' exception. In considering whether its seizure and forfeiture was 'necessary in a democratic society' in order to protect the rights of others to respect for their religious views (under Art 9), the Court took into account the lack of a uniform conception within the Member states of the significance of religion in society and therefore considered that the national authorities should have a wide margin of appreciation in assessing what was necessary to protect religious feeling. In this instance, the national authorities had not overstepped that margin and therefore, the Court found that no breach of Art 10 had occurred. Similarly, in *Wingrove v UK*[119] the Court found that the English common law offence of blasphemy was sufficiently clear and precise. The Court further found: 'there is as yet not sufficient common ground in the legal and social orders of the Member states of the Council of Europe to conclude that a system whereby a state can impose restrictions on the propagation of material on the basis that it is blasphemous is in itself unnecessary in a democratic society and incompatible with the Convention.'[120]

On the other hand, where a principle has received general acceptance in the Member states and, in particular, where it is closely linked to the notion of democracy, the Court will afford a narrow margin only. For example, in *Socialist Party and Others v Turkey*,[121] the Court found that the dissolution of the Socialist Party of Turkey had breached Art 11 since: 'there can be no democracy without pluralism . . . It is of the essence of democracy to allow diverse political programmes to be proposed and debated . . . Taking these matters into account . . . In determining whether a necessity existed, the Contracting state was found to possess only a limited margin of appreciation.' The picture is more confused where a principle may be said to have received some general acceptance within the Contracting states and where the Court itself appears to have espoused it in the past, but where it cannot clearly be said that a common standard can be found. Such confusion appears to underlie the remarks in *Cossey v*

116   *Rees v UK* (1986) 9 EHRR 56, A 106.
117   See *Rees v UK*, ibid at para 37.
118   Series A 295-A; (1994) 19 EHRR 34.
119   (1996) 24 EHRR 1.
120   Paragraph 57.
121   Judgment of 25 May 1998 (Appl No 20/1997/804/1007), (1999) 27 EHRR 51, paras 41, 47 and 50.

UK[122] of Judge Martens in his dissenting Opinion: 'this caution [in allowing a wide margin of appreciation based on a strict application of the common standards doctrine] is in principle not consistent with the Court's mission to protect the individual against the collectivity[123] . . . in this context [of legal recognition of gender reassignment] there simply is no room for a margin of appreciation.' Thus, even within the Court there is disagreement as to the interferences which fall within the margin conceded to the state. In the only decision of the Court finding a violation of the freedom of assembly guarantee of Art 11, *Ezelin v France*,[124] two of the partly dissenting judges considered that the interference in question fell within that margin,[125] although the majority found that the state had exceeded it.

As the discussion suggests, the margin of appreciation doctrine may tend to undermine the Convention and its growth has therefore attracted criticism. Van Dijk and Van Hoof have written of it as: 'a spreading disease. Not only has the scope of its application been broadened to the point where in principle none of the Convention rights or freedoms are excluded, but also has the illness been intensified in that wider versions of the doctrine have been added to the original concept'.[126] As mentioned at the beginning of this chapter, the doctrine may sometimes be appropriate as part of a general consensus-based approach to the supervision of the Convention. However, an arbitrariness is evident in its application, a theme which is pursued below and at a number of points in this book.

3 The substantive rights and freedoms

In what follows, an outline will be given of the scope of the Articles covering the substantive rights and freedoms. In the case of Arts 3, 5, 6 and 8–11, much more detailed treatment of decisions which are relevant to particular areas of UK law will be undertaken when those areas of domestic law are considered.

Article 2: Protection of life

   (1) Everyone's right to life shall be protected by law. No one shall be deprived of his life intentionally save in the execution of a sentence of a court following his conviction of a crime for which this penalty is provided by law.

   (2) Deprivation of life shall not be regarded as inflicted in contravention of this article when it results from the use of force which is no more than absolutely necessary:

---

122 A 184 (1990).
123 Paragraph 5.6.3.
124 A 202-A (1991).
125 Judges Ryssdal and Pettiti, at pp 26 and 28–30.
126 Van Dijk, P and Van Hoof, F, *The Theory and Practice of the European Convention on Human Rights*, 1990, p 604. For further discussion of the doctrine see O'Donell, 'The margin of appreciation doctrine: standards in the jurisprudence of the European Court of Human Rights' (1982) 4 Human Rights Q 474; Morrisson, 'Margin of appreciation in human rights law' (1973) 6 Human Rights J 263; Jones, T, 'The devaluation of human rights under the European Convention' [1995] PL 430; Mahoney, P, 'Marvellous richness or invidious cultural relativism?' (1998) 19 Human Rights LJ 1.

      (a) in defence of any person from unlawful violence;

      (b) in order to effect a lawful arrest or to prevent the escape of a person lawfully detained;

      (c) in action lawfully taken for the purpose of quelling a riot or insurrection.

The right to life can be viewed as the most fundamental of all human rights. Its significance receives recognition under all human rights' instruments[127] and its vital importance is recognised under UK common law.[128]

Scope of the right

Article 2 provides non-derogable protection of the right to life.[129] This might seem straightforward – governments are enjoined to refrain from the wanton killing of their subjects – but aside from that instance, it is not a straightforward matter to determine what the guarantee under Art 2 encompasses. The Court has said: 'the first sentence of Art 2 enjoins the state not only to refrain from the intentional and unlawful taking of life, but also to take appropriate steps to safeguard the lives of those within its jurisdiction'.[130] Thus, while the state must not order or empower its agents to kill its subjects, except within the specified exceptions, it also has further responsibilities under Art 2 to protect the right to life by law. But clearly, it is difficult to pinpoint the stage at which it may be said that the responsibility of a state for a person's death is so clear, the causal potency between the state's action or omission and the death so strong, that it is possible to find that the right to life has been violated.[131]

    Decisions under Art 2 have not yet entirely clarified this issue, but they do suggest that two, usually distinct duties are placed on the national authorities, although their scope is unclear. First, as indicated, Art 2 places the public authorities under a duty not to take life except in certain specified circumstances. This duty covers intentional, officially-sanctioned killings (executions, deliberate killing to save life) and unintentional killings (where the risk of killing is taken by using lethal force in a riot situation). Where state agents do take life, the obligation to protect the right to life by law requires that 'there should be some form of effective official investigation'.[132] This requirement was found to be breached in *Jordan, Kelly, Arthurs, Donelly and Others v UK*[133] in respect of the killing of eight IRA members by the SAS in 1987. Second, Art 2 places a positive obligation on the state authorities to protect the right to life

---

127 Although in, e.g., the US and India, the right is protected only on a 'due process' basis. Deprivation of life can occur, but it must be in accordance with the due process of the law.

128 It is recognised in the crimes of murder, manslaughter and infanticide. The deliberate killing of another human being is viewed as requiring to be marked out from other crimes by means of the mandatory life sentence penalty. For an early response of the UK courts to Art 2 under the HRA see below, p 77. For a full discussion, see Clayton and Tomlinson, op. cit., fn 1, Chapter 7.

129 See Art 15(2). Derogation is not allowed in times of emergency or war; derogation is only possible in respect of death resulting from acts of war themselves.

130 *LCB v UK* (1998) 27 EHRR 212, para 36.

131 See further Sieghart, P, *The Lawful Rights of Mankind*, 1986, Clarendon, Chapter 11.

132 *McCann v UK* (1995) 21 EHRR 97, para 161.

133 (2001) *The Times*, 18 May.

by law. This positive obligation may take a number of forms. It requires that reasonable steps be taken in order to enforce the law in order to protect citizens (*X v UK and Ireland*).[134] It was held in *W v UK*[135] that these measures will not be scrutinised in detail. Clearly, the state may not be able to prevent every attack on an individual without an enormous expenditure of resources.[136] Therefore, the Convention will leave a wide margin of discretion to the national authorities in this regard, although the state will be under some duty to maintain reasonable public security.[137] Where state agents' actions are very closely linked to the preservation of a known individual's life as, for example, the actions of police officers are during a hostage situation, the state will be under a positive obligation not only to seek to preserve life, but also to act reasonably in so doing. The need to preserve life in the immediate situation would appear to override the general duty to maintain state security and prevent crime. These notions seem to underlie the findings of the Commission in *Andronicou and Constantinou v Cyprus*.[138] Article 2 was found to have been violated by Cypriot police when, in attempting to deal with a siege situation in which a hostage had been taken, they fired a number of times at the hostage taker, killing the hostage. The number of bullets fired reflected, it was found, a response which lacked caution.

Similarly, situations may arise in which, while state agents do not directly take life, the state is responsible for creating a life-threatening situation. Where the state has directly created such a situation, its responsibility will arguably be greater. In *LCB v UK*,[139] the applicant had contracted leukaemia; her father had been present during British nuclear tests on Christmas Island. She complained of a breach of Art 2 since the state had not advised her parents to monitor her health. In deciding that no breach had occurred, the Court found, taking into account the information that was available at the time, that the state had done all it was required to do to prevent an avoidable risk to her life. Had the information regarding the risk been available at the time, the decision might well have gone the other way, implying that the Court is prepared in principle to hold the state responsible in such instances.

Such an instance may be distinguished from a situation created by others, or by natural causes but in which it may be said that the state still has some responsibility. The positive obligation may entail the taking of appropriate steps to safeguard life[140] where state agents do not themselves unintentionally take life and/or the state itself has not created the life-threatening situation, but the breadth of this duty is unclear. It seems that it will include the provision of adequate medical care in prisons[141] since,

---

134 Appl 9829/82 (not published).
135 Appl 9348/81, 32 D & R (1983), p 190.
136 It was accepted in *Osman v UK* (1998) 29 EHRR 245 that the obligation to protect the right to life had to be interpreted 'in a way that does not impose an impossible or disproportionate burden on the authorities' (para 116). In that instance, the police had failed to take measures to prevent a murder taking place despite very strong indications that the victim was in imminent danger. See further below, on the Art 6 issue in the case, p 62.
137 Appl 7145/75, *Association X v UK* (1978) Appl 7154/75; 14 DR 31.
138 (1996) 22 EHRR CD 18.
139 (1998) 27 EHRR 212.
140 *X v UK*, No 7154/75, 14 D & R 31 (1978), p 32.
141 *Simon-Herald v Austria*, Appl 430/69 CD 38 (the application was declared admissible and a friendly settlement was later reached).

in this instance, the state is directly responsible for the welfare of citizens during their imprisonment. However, it is unclear how far the individual should have a right to secure the expenditure of resources so that the state can save or preserve his or her life. The state may bear some responsibility in a number of instances. For example, a person might die due to poor housing conditions after repeated pleas for re-housing, or due to deficiencies in health care such as a lack of a vaccination programme or poor implementation of the programme,[142] or to exposure to bacteria in certain parts of a hospital while suffering from a condition weakening the immune system. Road traffic regulations and their implementation engage the state's responsibility; life might be put at risk, for example, due to a failure to impose a particular speed limit in poor driving conditions.

The Court is proceeding cautiously in relation to the state's positive obligations under Art 2. It has shown some reluctance to read Art 2 so widely as to cover such situations, although there are indications that this stance may be changing. In *Guerra v Italy*,[143] it was said that the time may be ripe for 'the court's case law on Article 2 . . . to start evolving, to develop the respective implied rights, articulate situations of real and serious risk to life or different aspects of the right to life'.

In *LCB v UK*, the Christmas Island case mentioned above,[144] the state had a direct responsibility for the lives in question and the expenditure of resources to meet it would not have been burdensome, whereas in relation to the provision of housing of a certain standard, the responsibility is less direct and immediate, and the impact on resource allocation much greater. The issue of imposing a speed limit in particular conditions raises questions of the directness of the responsibility. Drivers would be expected to drive in accordance with the road conditions. Moreover, there would be no direct relationship between those state agents involved in traffic control and those affected. The obligation to provide health care in order to save life and to regulate hospitals in such a way as to protect life has, however, been recognised.[145]

It is unclear how far Art 2 places states under an obligation to seek to ensure the continuance of life where the individual involved, or those acting on his or her behalf, wish it to end. The Commission has found that passively allowing a person to die need not attract criminal liability in order to satisfy Art 2.[146] This might apply to allowing a handicapped baby or a patient in a persistent vegetative state to die.[147] However, a breach of Art 2 would probably be found where a positive act had occurred in order to end life.

The question has arisen in the context of national legislation on abortion whether the foetus can fall within the interpretation of 'everyone', but it has been determined that even if the foetus is protected, its right to life will be weighed against the mother's life

---

142 See *Association X v UK* (1978) Appl 7154/75; 14 DR 31.
143 (1998) 26 EHRR 357, p 387.
144 *LCB v UK* (1998) 27 EHRR 212, para 36.
145 *Scialacqua v Italy* (1998) 26 EHRR CD 164 and *Erikson v Italy*, Appl 37900/97, 26 October 1999.
146 *Widmer v Switzerland*, No 20527/92 (1993) unreported.
147 The position under British law seems to be that failing to intervene to save the life of a handicapped baby may be acceptable in some circumstances: see *Arthur* (unreported), discussed by Gunn, M, and Smith, JC [1985] Crim LR 705; *Re B (A Minor)* [1981] 1 WLR 1421, CA. Allowing a patient in a persistent vegetative state to die will be acceptable if it can be said, objectively, to be in his or her best interests because no improvement can be expected (*Airedale NHS Trust v Bland* [1993] AC 789, HL).

and physical and mental health.[148] In *Paton v UK*[149] it was found by the Commission that Art 2 applies only to persons who have been born. Had the Commission found otherwise, all national legislation in the Member states permitting abortion would have been in breach of Art 2, since abortion even to save the mother's life would not appear to be covered by any of the exceptions. *H v Norway*[150] clarified the position. The Commission found that the lawful abortion of a 14-week foetus on social grounds did not breach Art 2. It took this stance on the basis that since the state Parties' laws on abortion differ considerably from each other, a wide margin of discretion should be allowed. It appears that the abortion laws within the Member states probably comply with Art 2, although in *Open Door Counselling v Ireland* the Court left open the possibility that Art 2 might place some restrictions on abortion.[151]

Exceptions

A very significant express exception to Art 2, limiting the scope of para 1, is in respect of the death penalty, which also includes extradition to a country where the death penalty is in force.[152] Protocol 6 has now removed the death penalty exception and it was ratified by the UK on 27 January 1999. It may be possible to challenge use of the death penalty in countries which have not ratified Protocol 6 under other Convention rights, such as Art 3.[153]

Generally, the para 2 exceptions are reasonably straightforward and are aimed mainly at unintentional deprivation of life. This was explained in *Stewart v UK*,[154] which concerned the use of plastic bullets in a riot. It was found that para 2 is concerned with situations where the use of violence is allowed as necessary force and may, as an unintended consequence, result in loss of life. On this basis, the use of plastic bullets was found to fall within its terms. However, paras 2(a), (b) and (c) also cover instances where the force used was bound to endanger life and was intended to do so, but was necessary in the circumstances. Thus, national laws recognising the right to use self-defence are, in principle, in harmony with para 2(a). Clearly, the state can use lethal force where absolutely necessary in order to quell a riot. But, the necessity will be carefully scrutinised: state agents must act with caution in resorting to lethal force.[155]

Also, in certain circumstances, the state can sanction the use of force with the intention of killing. It can do so, however, only when such force is absolutely necessary

---

148 *X v UK*, Appl 8416/78; 19 D & R (1980), p 244.
149 (1981) 3 EHRR 408. It has been argued that a woman's right to an abortion must therefore have been impliedly accepted: Rendel, M (1991) 141 NLJ 1270.
150 No 17004/90 (1992) 73 DR 155.
151 Eur Ct HR, Judgment of 29 October 1992; (1992) 15 EHRR 244. For comment, see (1992) 142 NLJ 1696.
152 Appl 10227/82, *X v Spain* D & R 37 (1984), p 93.
153 See *Soering*, below, pp 46–47 (59–60) in relation to Art 3.
154 Appl 10044/82; D & R 39 (1985); (1985) 7 EHRR 453; see also *Kelly v UK* (1993) 16 EHRR 20, in which the European Commission found that the use of force to prevent future terrorist acts was allowable. For criticism of the decision in *Kelly*, see (1994) 144 NLJ 354.
155 A breach of Art 2 was found in *Gulec v Turkey* (1999) 28 EHRR 121: gendarmes had fired into a crowd to disperse it; less forceful means could have been used.

for the fulfilment of one of the para 2 purposes. This issue was considered by the Commission in *Kelly v UK*,[156] in which a young joyrider was shot dead by soldiers in Northern Ireland when he tried to evade an army checkpoint. It was found that the application was manifestly ill-founded, since the use of force was justified. However, it can be argued that this finding does not represent a strict application of a strict proportionality test. Kelly was apparently shot in order to prevent him escaping, but it would not appear that it was 'absolutely necessary' to shoot to kill in the circumstances, since it might well have been possible to arrest him later.

The Court addressed the question of the strictness of the 'absolutely necessary' test in *McCann, Farrell and Savage v UK*,[157] the first judgment of the Court to find a breach of Art 2. The case concerned the shooting by SAS soldiers of three IRA members on the street in Gibraltar. The UK argued that this was justified on the basis that they apparently had with them a remote control device which they might have used to detonate a bomb. The Court found that para 2 primarily describes situations 'where it is permitted to use force which may result, as an unintended outcome in the deprivation of life', but that para 2 would also cover the intentional deprivation of life. However, the use of force must be no more than absolutely necessary for the achievement of one of the para 2 purposes and the test of necessity to be used was stricter than that used in respect of the test under paragraph 2 of Arts 8–11. The main question for the Court was the extent to which the state's response to the perceived threat posed by the IRA members was proportionate to that threat. The Court found that the use of force could be justified where 'it is based on an honest belief which is perceived for good reason to be valid at the time but which subsequently turns out to be mistaken. To hold otherwise would be to impose an unrealistic burden on the state and its law enforcement personnel.' Following this finding, the Court found that the actions of the soldiers who carried out the shooting did not amount to a violation of Art 2.

However, the organisation and planning of the whole operation had to be considered in order to discover whether the requirements of Art 2 had been respected. The Court focused on the decision not to arrest the suspects when they entered Gibraltar. This decision was taken because it was thought that there might have been insufficient evidence against them to warrant their charge and trial. However, this decision subjected the population of Gibraltar to possible danger. The Court considered that taking this factor into account and bearing in mind that they had been shadowed by the SAS soldiers for some time, the suspects could have been arrested at that point. Further, there was quite a high probability that the suspects were on a reconnaissance mission at the time of the shootings and not a bombing mission. This possibility, the possibility that there was no car bomb or that the suspects had no detonator, was not conveyed to the soldiers and since they were trained to shoot to kill, the killings were rendered almost inevitable. All these factors were taken into account in finding that the killing of the three constituted a use of force which was more than absolutely necessary in defence of persons from unlawful violence within the meaning of para 2(a) of Art 2. The state had sanctioned killing by state agents in circumstances which gave rise to a breach of Art 2.

156 Appl 17579/90; (1993) 16 EHRR CD 20; 74 D & R 139 (1993).
157 (1995) 21 EHRR 97, A 324, Council of Europe Report.

This was a bold decision which departs from the stance taken in *Kelly*. It emphasises that a strict proportionality test must be used in determining issues under para 2 of Art 2. Applying this test, it would appear that where an alternative to the deliberate use of deadly force exists, it should always be taken. It would therefore seem that the use of such force to effect an arrest would never be justified except where, in the circumstances, there was near-certainty that the suspect would kill if allowed to escape. This might apply, for example, in situations where hostages had been taken and threats against them issued. It would also apply in circumstances similar to those arising in *McCann*, but where no opportunity for apprehension had previously arisen and where there was a stronger likelihood that a bomb might be about to be detonated. In such instances, of course, both sub-paras (a) and (b) of Art 2(2) would be in question and it therefore appears that the McCann judgment leaves little room for the operation of sub-para (b) independently of sub-para (a) *McCann* and *Kelly* make clear the partially subjective nature of the judgment as to when the use of deadly force is 'absolutely necessary'. Article 2 itself does not make it clear whether the phrase 'absolutely necessary' is to be treated objectively or subjectively. On its face it is unclear whether Art 2 would be breached where the person using such force honestly believed, due to a mistake, that it was necessary, although in actuality it was not. In such a case, Art 2 would not be breached if there were also reasonable grounds for believing that such force was necessary. It may be noted that this stance is not in accord with UK law, which allows the use of force, including deadly force, so long as an honest (not necessarily reasonable) belief is formed that force is required,[158] and the force used is in proportion to the circumstances as the defendant believed them to be.[159] Thus, an objective test is only used in relation to the question of the proportionality between the apparent circumstances and the force used.[160]

Article 3: Freedom from inhuman treatment

No one shall be subjected to torture or to inhuman or degrading treatment or punishment.

The right to freedom from torture or inhuman or degrading treatment or punishment is recognised in international human rights Treaties[161] and in many, although not all, domestic human rights instruments.[162] The right is also protected by specific Conventions, the United Nations Convention Against Torture and Other Cruel, Inhuman or Degrading Treatment or Punishment 1984[163] and the European Convention for the Prevention of Torture and Inhuman and Degrading Treatment or Punishment 1987.[164] Torture is a

---

158 *Williams* [1987] 3 All ER 411.
159 *Owino* [1995] Crim LR 743.
160 This seems to have been the basis of the decision of the House of Lords in *Clegg* [1995] 2 WLR 80, which concerned a killing of a joyrider by a soldier in Northern Ireland.
161 Article 5 of the Universal Declaration and Art 7 of the ICCPR.
162 For discussion of this right as recognised in other jurisdictions, see Clayton and Tomlinson, op. cit., fn 1, Chapter 8, esp pp 412–29.
163 Cmnd 9593, 1985; it came into force in 1987 and it was ratified by the UK in December 1988.
164 Cm 1634, 1991; it was ratified by the UK in June 1988. For discussion, see Evans, M, and Morgan, R, *Preventing Torture: A Study of the European Convention for the Prevention of Torture*, 1998, OUP.

crime under international law.[165] Thus, there is strong international recognition of the fundamental values enshrined in this right.

Article 3 contains no exceptions and it is also non-derogable. Thus, on the face of it, once a state has been found to have fallen within its terms, no justification is possible.[166] However, it has been suggested that the exceptions to Art 2 must be taken as applying also to Art 3 since, if the state in certain circumstances may justifiably take life, it must be justifiable *a fortiori* to inflict lesser harm on citizens in the same circumstances.[167] This may be correct, but clearly it is not intended to be taken to mean that all the exceptions to Art 2 apply to all forms of Art 3 treatment. The Art 2 exceptions suggest elements of immediacy which would be applicable to severe wounding but not usually to, for example, the form of torture, severe beating of all parts of the body to extract information, which occurred in the *Greek* case.[168] Similarly, state laws allowing wounding by private individuals in self-defence would not appear to be in breach of Art 3 so long as they were in accord with para 2 of Art 2. The Court has made it clear that the use of forms of Art 3 treatment in order to extract information, even in order to combat terrorism, is unjustifiable.[169] However, it might be argued that if life can be taken in order to save life (for example, in a hostage situation where no other course is available), or as a punishment in the form of execution, Art 3 treatment used in extreme circumstances in order to obtain information to save life (the classic ticking bomb in one of a large number of crowded shopping centres, or an atomic device placed somewhere in Central London) might be viewed as justifiable if effective where no other course was available and where it was otherwise inevitable that large numbers of people would be killed.

The responsibility of the state extends beyond prohibiting the use of Art 3 treatment by state agents. It includes a duty to ensure that individuals within their jurisdiction are not subjected to Art 3 treatment by other individuals.[170] It also includes an obligation not to deport a person who needs medical treatment to a country where he will not receive it.[171] The state also has a positive obligation to carry out an effective investigation into allegations of breaches of Art 3.[172]

In determining the standard of treatment applicable below which a state will be in breach of Art 3, a common European standard is applied, but also all the factors in the situation are taken into account.[173] The Court has found that such factors include: 'the nature and context of the treatment, its duration, its mental and physical effects and, in some instances, the sex, age and state of health of the victim.'[174] Thus, it does not connote an absolute standard and, in its application, it allows for a measure of discretion. It

---

165 See *R v Bow Street Stipendiary Magistrate ex p Pinochet Ugarte* (No 3) [1999] 2 WLR 827.
166 *Ireland v UK* (1978) 2 EHRR 25.
167 See Harris, O'Boyle and Warbrick, op. cit., fn 1, p 56.
168 (1969) Yearbook XII 1, p 504, Com Rep; CM Res DH (70) 1.
169 *Tomasi v France* (1992) 15 EHRR 1.
170 In *A v UK* (1999) 27 EHRR 611, a violation of Art 3 was found since the law had failed to protect a child from excessive chastisement by his stepfather.
171 In *D v UK* (1998) 24 EHRR 423, a violation of Art 3 was found since the UK proposed sending D back to the West Indies after he had contracted AIDS, where he would not receive appropriate treatment for his condition.
172 *Aksoy v Turkey* (1996) 23 EHRR 533; *Selmouni v France* (2000) 29 EHRR 403.
173 The *Greek* case (1969), Yearbook XII 186–510.
174 *A v UK* (1998) 27 EHRR 611, para 20.

is clear that, in order to determine this issue, *present* views must be considered rather than the views at the time when the Convention was drawn up. The three forms of treatment mentioned represent three different levels of seriousness. Thus, torture, unlike degrading treatment, has been quite narrowly defined to include 'deliberate inhuman treatment causing very serious and cruel suffering'.[175] In a number of cases, there has been a finding of torture against Turkey. In *Aksoy v Turkey*,[176] the applicant had been stripped naked, his arms had been tied behind his back and he had then been hung from his arms. In *Aydin v Turkey*,[177] the rape of a young girl by a military official was found to amount to torture; the other forms of ill treatment to which she was subjected, including beating for an hour, also amounted to torture. In *Selmouni v France*,[178] the Court found that beatings and humiliation in custody amounted to torture rather than inhuman or degrading treatment, bearing in mind the fact that 'the increasingly high standard being required in the area of protection of human rights and fundamental liberties correspondingly and inevitably requires greater firmness in assessing breaches of the fundamental values of democratic societies'.[179]

Clearly, treatment which could not come within the restricted definition of torture could still fall within one of the other two heads, especially the broad head – 'degrading treatment'. In order to characterise treatment as inhuman, it must reach a minimum level of severity.[180] Physical assault,[181] the immediate threat of torture,[182] and interrogation techniques causing psychological disorientation[183] have all been found to amount to inhuman treatment.

Treatment may be both inhuman and degrading, but degrading treatment may not also amount to inhuman treatment.[184] Degrading treatment is treatment that is grossly humiliating.[185] Degrading punishment does not inevitably include all forms of physical punishment, although it can include certain forms of corporal punishment, including caning,[186] which have been found not to amount to torture or inhuman punishment. Corporal punishment which could be said to be of a 'normal' type may be distinguished, it seems, from degrading corporal punishment.[187] Thus, the mere fact that physical punishment is administered will not, without more, necessarily involve a breach of Art 3 and nor will the mere threat of such punishment.[188]

175 *Ireland v UK* (1978) 2 EHRR 25.
176 (1996) 23 EHRR 553.
177 (1997) 25 EHRR 251. See also *Salman v Turkey*, Judgment of 27 June 2000 (beatings in custody with rifle butts and sticks amounted to torture).
178 (2000) 29 EHRR 403.
179 Ibid, para 101.
180 *A v UK* (1998) 27 EHRR 611, para 20.
181 *Ireland v UK* (1978) 2 EHRR 25.
182 *Campbell and Cosans v UK* (1982) 4 EHRR 293.
183 *Ireland v UK* (1978) 2 EHRR 25.
184 *Tyrer*, Judgment of 25 April 1978, A 26; (1978) 2 EHRR 1.
185 *Greek* case (1969) 12 YB 1.
186 *Tyrer*, Judgment of 25 April 1978, A 26; (1978) 2 EHRR 1. In *Warwick v UK*, Eur Comm HR Report of 15 June 1986, the Commission considered that corporal punishment in schools amounted to degrading treatment.
187 *Costello-Roberts v UK*, Judgment of 25 March 1993; A 247-C (1993). It may be noted that the School Standards and Framework Act 1998 has abolished corporal punishment in the independent sector; it had already been abolished in the state sector.
188 *Campbell and Cosans*, Judgment of 25 February 1982, A 48; (1982) 4 EHRR 293.

A number of cases have arisen concerning the position of detainees. It is now clear that if a person enters police custody in a sound physical condition but, on release, is found to have sustained injuries such as bruising, the state must provide a plausible explanation.[189] In determining whether a particular treatment, such as solitary confinement, amounts to a violation of Art 3, a number of factors must be taken into account. These will include the stringency and duration of the measure,[190] the objective pursued – such as the need for special security measures for the prisoner in question[191] or the fear of stirring up discontent among other prisoners[192] – and the effect on the person concerned. The applicant will need to submit medical evidence showing the causal relationship between the prison conditions complained of and his or her deterioration in mental and physical health. If the adverse treatment has been adopted as a result of the claimant's own unco-operative behaviour, it is probable that no breach will be found.[193]

Article 3 has been interpreted widely as to the forms of treatment it covers, which include some not readily associated with the terms it uses. It could probably be used, for example, in relation to involuntary medical intervention such as sterilisation or Caesarean section,[194] and, as indicated below, racial discrimination can amount to degrading treatment. Article 3 has been used to bring rights within the scope of the Convention which are not expressly included. Thus, Art 3 could be invoked in relation to discriminatory treatment on the basis of race and possibly on the basis of sex or sexual orientation, because such treatment can be termed degrading according to the Commission in the *East African Asians* cases.[195] This possibility could help to compensate for the weakness of the Art 14 guarantee against discrimination which does not create an independent right.[196]

Other rights which otherwise would not be recognised under the Convention include the right to remain in a certain country. Violation of Art 3 may occur because of the treatment a person may receive when returning to his or her own country having been expelled or refused admission. It will have to be clearly established that the danger of such treatment is really present. The question arose in *Soering v UK*[197] whether expulsion to a country (the US) where the applicant risked the death penalty would be compatible with Art 3 because it would subject him to conditions on Death Row likely to cause him acute mental anguish. Of course, since Art 2 specifically excludes the death penalty from its guarantee, the possibility of its use cannot in itself create a violation

---

189 *Tomasi v France* (1992) 15 EHRR 1; *Ribbitsch v Austria* (1992) 21 EHRR 573.
190 Complete sensory isolation is likely to amount to Art 3 treatment: *Ensslin, Bader and Raspe v Germany* (1978) 14 DR 64, p 109.
191 In *Kröcher and Möller v Switzerland* D & R 34 (1983); (1984) 6 EHRR 345 it was found that harsh conditions imposed to ensure security may not constitute a violation of Art 3.
192 Appl 8324/78, *X v UK* (not published) (the ability to encourage other prisoners to acts of indiscipline was taken into account).
193 Appl 9907/82, *M v UK* D & R 130 (1983) (dangerous behaviour of detainee taken into account in considering conditions).
194 See *X v Denmark* (1983) 32 DR 282.
195 (1973) 3 EHRR 76.
196 See below, pp 108–9.
197 Judgment of 7 July 1989, A 161; (1989) 11 EHRR 439. For discussion, see Schabas, W (1994) 43 ICLQ 913.

of Art 3 because that would render those words of Art 2 otiose (assuming that the state in question had not ratified Protocol 6). The Convention must be read as a whole. However, the Court found that the manner and circumstances of the implementation of the death penalty could give rise to an issue under Art 3. The Court held that it had to consider the length of detention prior to the execution, the conditions on Death Row, the applicant's age and his mental state. Bearing these factors in mind, especially the very long period of time spent on Death Row and the mounting anguish as execution was awaited, it was found that expulsion would constitute a breach of Art 3. (In response to this ruling, the UK and the US agreed to drop the charges to non-capital murder and then extradite the applicant.)

The principle laid down in *Soering* was followed in *Chahal v UK*.[198] Originally an illegal immigrant, Mr Chahal obtained leave to remain in Britain indefinitely in 1974. In 1984, he visited the Punjab for a family wedding and met the chief advocate of creating an independent Sikh state. Later, he was arrested by Indian police and allegedly tortured. He escaped from India and became the founder of the International Sikh Youth Federation in the UK. In 1990, he was arrested after a meeting at a Southall temple. The Home Office accused him of involvement in Sikh terrorism and decided to deport him on national security grounds. He sought asylum on the ground that he would be tortured if sent back to India and applied to the European Commission, alleging, *inter alia*, a breach of Art 3. The Court found that since there were strong grounds for believing that Mr Chahal would indeed have been tortured had he been returned to India, a breach of Art 3 had occurred.[199]

For a breach of Art 3 to be established in the context of deportation or extradition cases, there must be a clear risk of ill treatment; a 'mere possibility' will be insufficient. In *Vilvarajah and Four Others v UK*,[200] the applicants, Sri Lankan Tamils, arrived in the UK in 1987 and applied for political asylum under the UN Convention of 1951 Relating to the Status of Refugees, contending that they had a well-founded fear of persecution if returned to Sri Lanka. The Home Secretary rejected the applications and the applicants sought unsuccessfully to challenge the rejection by means of judicial review. The applicants were then returned to Sri Lanka where, they alleged, four of them were arrested and ill-treated. They claimed that their deportation constituted breaches of Arts 3 and 13 of the European Convention. The Court considered whether the situation in Sri Lanka at the time the applicants were deported provided substantial support for the view that they would be at risk of Art 3 treatment. The Court determined that the general unsettled situation in Sri Lanka at the time did not establish that they were at greater risk than other young male Tamils who were returning there; it established only a possibility rather than a clear risk of ill treatment. No breach of Art 3 could therefore be established.[201] Arguably, this decision suggests that although an Art 3 issue may arise in asylum cases, the Convention cannot be viewed as a substitute for an effective domestic means of determining refugee claims. (It should be noted that Art 8 issues may also arise in some immigration claims; this possibility will be discussed below.)

---

198 (1997) 23 EHRR 413.
199 The Art 5 issue is considered below, p 58.
200 (1991) 14 EHRR 248, A 215.
201 See further for comment on this case, Warbrick, C, *Yearbook of European Law*, 1991, OPU, pp 545–53.

Soering is a very broad decision. The approach taken in the judgment may mean that a state would infringe the Convention whenever it facilitated the breach of a Convention Article by another state. However, in general, liability arises under the Convention only where a breach has already occurred, not where it is merely probable. An exception was made to that rule in *Soering* in view of 'the serious and irreparable nature of the alleged suffering risked'.[202] Thus, the *Soering* facilitation principle may apply only where the state receiving the individual in question is likely to subject him or her to treatment amounting to serious and irreparable suffering. This would include treatment in breach of Arts 3 and 2 (such as state execution without trial) and probably 5 and 6 (imprisonment without trial). Possibly, it might also include deportation leading to the probability of treatment in breach of Arts 6[203] or 7 in the receiving state which would then be likely to result in the execution or imprisonment of the individual. For example, if an individual committed an act in his or her own state before leaving for another state – a Party to the Convention – and the act committed was then criminalised with retrospective effect, the second state might act in breach of Art 7 if it extradited the individual in order to face charges and the possibility of imprisonment under the new law.

Article 3 is considered further in relation to police powers and anti-terrorism law.[204] Relevant issues are also raised in Chapter 15, dealing with aspects of discrimination.

Article 4: Freedom from slavery, servitude and forced or compulsory labour

(1) No one shall be held in slavery or servitude.

(2) No one shall be required to perform forced or compulsory labour.

(3) For the purpose of this article the term 'forced or compulsory labour' shall not include:

    (a) any work required to be done in the ordinary course of detention imposed according to the provisions of Article 5 of this Convention or during conditional release from such detention;

    (b) any service of a military character or, in case of conscientious objectors in countries where they are recognised, service exacted instead of compulsory military service;

    (c) any service exacted in case of any emergency or calamity threatening the life or well-being of the community;

    (d) any work or service which forms part of normal civic obligations.

Article 4 provides a guarantee which is largely irrelevant in modern European democracies, although it is conceivable that as states with less developed human rights regimes become signatories to the Convention, it might prove to be of value. Owing to its restrictive wording, it has not proved possible to interpret Art 4 in such a way as to allow it to cover rights unthought of when it was conceived.

---

202 Judgment of 7 July 1989, A 161, para 90.
203 See *Soering*, A 161, para 113.
204 See Chapter 11, p 1174–77 and 1180–1 and Chapter 14, p 1358 and 1363.

It is necessary to distinguish between slavery and servitude under Art 4(1) and forced or compulsory labour under Art 4(2). Slavery denotes total ownership, whereas servitude denotes less far reaching restraints; it is concerned with the labour conditions and the inescapable nature of the service. Article 4(1) contains no express exceptions and is also non-derogable.

Article 4(1) has not generated much case law and the few cases which have been brought have failed. Article 4(2) is not concerned with the total situation of the claimant concerned; it covers the compulsory character of services which will usually be temporary and incidental to the claimant's main job or total situation. Forced or compulsory labour has been held to denote the following: 'first that the work or service is performed by the worker against his will and, secondly, that the requirement that the work or service be performed is unjust or oppressive or the work or service itself involves avoidable hardship.'[205] Most of the case law arises in the area of professional obligations arising from certain jobs. For example, a German lawyer complained of having to act as unpaid or poorly paid defence counsel. The Commission rejected the complaint on the basis that if a person voluntarily chooses the profession of lawyer, aware of this obligation, then he can be taken to have impliedly consented to fulfil the obligation.[206] This argument will apply if the obligations are a normal part of the profession. Less emphasis was placed on the implied consent of the applicant in *Van der Mussele*,[207] which also concerned compulsory legal aid work. The Court took the view that the mere fact that the applicant had impliedly consented to the obligation was only a factor to be considered; it was not decisive. It decided that looking at all the factors, including the small amount of time devoted to such work – only 18 hours – and the fact that such work enabled the obligation under Art 6(3)(c) (if necessary to have free legal advice) to be fulfilled, no breach had occurred.

Article 5: Right to liberty and security of person

(1) Everyone has the right to liberty and security of person. No one shall be deprived of his liberty save in the following cases and in accordance with a procedure prescribed by law:

(a) the lawful detention of a person after conviction by a competent court;

(b) the lawful arrest or detention of a person for non-compliance with the lawful order of a court or in order to secure the fulfilment of any obligation prescribed by law;

(c) the lawful arrest or detention of a person effected for the purpose of bringing him before the competent legal authority on reasonable suspicion of having committed an offence or when it is reasonably considered necessary to prevent his committing an offence or fleeing after having done so;

(d) the detention of a minor by lawful order for the purpose of educational supervision or his lawful detention for the purpose of bringing him before the competent legal authority;

---

205 *X v Federal Republic of Germany* Appl 8410/78 (1980); D & R 216, p 219.
206 *X v FRG*, Appl 4653/70; (1974) 46 CD 22.
207 Judgment of 23 November 1983, A 70.

(e) the lawful detention of persons for the prevention of the spreading of infectious diseases, of persons of unsound mind, alcoholics or drug addicts or vagrants;

(f) the lawful arrest or detention of a person to prevent his effecting an unauthorised entry into the country or of a person against whom action is being taken with a view to deportation or extradition.

(2) Everyone who is arrested shall be informed promptly, in a language which he understands, of the reasons for his arrest and of any charge against him.

(3) Everyone arrested or detained in accordance with the provisions of para 1(c) of this article shall be brought promptly before a judge or other officer authorised by law to exercise judicial power and shall be entitled to trial within a reasonable time or to release pending trial. Release may be conditioned by guarantees to appear for trial.

(4) Everyone who is deprived of his liberty by arrest or detention shall be entitled to take proceedings by which the lawfulness of his detention shall be decided speedily by a court and his release ordered if the detention is not lawful.

(5) Everyone who has been the victim of arrest or detention in contravention of the provisions of this article shall have an enforceable right to compensation.

Although Art 5 speaks of liberty *and* security as though they could be distinguished, they are not treated in the case law as though there is any significant distinction between them. The use of the term 'security' does not appear to add anything to the term 'liberty'. The guarantee refers to protection from deprivation of physical liberty, not to protection for physical safety.[208] The presumption embodied in the Article is that liberty and security must be maintained. However, it then sets out the two tests which must be satisfied if it is to be removed. First, exceptions are set out where liberty can be taken away; second, under paras 2–4, the procedure is set out which must be followed when a person is deprived of liberty. Thus, if the correct procedure is followed, but an exception does not apply, Art 5 will be breached, as, conversely, it will if an individual falls within an exception but, in detaining him or her, the correct procedure is not followed. It will be found that a number of successful applications have been brought under Art 5 with the result that the position of detainees in Europe has undergone improvement. It should be noted that Art 5 is concerned with total deprivation of liberty, not restriction of movement, which is covered by Art 2 of Protocol 4 (at the time of writing, the UK is not yet a party to Protocol 4).

In general, the case law of the Court discussed below suggests that the circumstances in which liberty can be taken away under para 5(1)(a)–(f) will be restrictively interpreted, although the instances included are potentially wide. Article 5(1) not only provides that deprivation of liberty is only permitted within these exceptions, it also requires that it should be 'in accordance with a procedure prescribed by law'. In *Winterwerp v Netherlands*,[209] the Court found that this meant that the procedure in question must be in accordance with national and Convention law, taking into account the general principles on which the Convention is based, and it must not be arbitrary. In *Chahal v*

---

208 *X v Ireland* (1973) 16 YB 388.
209 Judgment of 24 October 1979, A 33; (1979) 2 EHRR 387.

UK,[210] the applicant complained, *inter alia*, that he had been detained although there had been no court hearing. The Home Office decided to deport him on national security grounds, but he applied for asylum. He was then imprisoned for over six years. He applied to the European Commission on Human Rights, alleging, *inter alia*, a breach of Art 5, which guarantees judicial control over loss of liberty. The Court found that a breach of Art 5 had occurred, since his detention should have been subject to scrutiny in court. It had been considered by an advisory panel, but that did not provide sufficient procedural safeguards to qualify as a court.

5(1)(a): Detention after conviction

This exception covers lawful detention after conviction by a competent court. Thus, the detention must flow from the conviction. This calls into question the revocation of life licences because, in such instances, a person is being deprived of liberty without a fresh conviction. In *Weeks*[211] the Court considered the causal connection with the original sentence when a life licence was revoked after the applicant was released. The Court accepted a very loose link between the original sentence and the revocation of the life licence on the basis that the sentencing judge must be taken to have known and intended that it was inherent in the life sentence that the claimant's liberty would hereafter be at the mercy of the executive. The Court declined to review the appropriateness of the original sentence.

5(1)(b): Detention to fulfil an obligation

This exception refers to deprivation of liberty in order to 'secure fulfilment of an obligation prescribed by law'. This phrase raises difficulties of interpretation and is clearly not so straightforward as the first form of such deprivation permitted under para 5(1)(a). It is very wide and appears to allow deprivation of liberty in many instances without intervention by a court. It might even allow preventive action before violation of a legal obligation. However, it has been narrowed down; in *Lawless*[212] it was found that a specific and concrete obligation must be identified. Once it has been identified, detention can in principle be used to secure its fulfilment.

The obligation includes a requirement that specific circumstances, such as the possibility of danger to the public, must be present in order to warrant the use of detention. A requirement to submit to an examination on entering the UK has been found to be specific enough.[213] Moreover, it must be apparent why detention rather than some lesser measure is needed to secure compliance with the obligation. Thus, the width of Art 5(1)(b) has been narrowed down by the use of restrictive interpretation in line with furthering the aims of the Convention.

210 (1997) 23 EHRR 413.
211 Judgment of 5 October 1988, A 114; (1987) 10 EHRR 293.
212 Report of 19 December 1959, B 1 (1960–61) p 64; Judgment of 1 July 1961, A 3 (1960–61); (1961) 1 EHRR 15.
213 *McVeigh, O'Neill and Evans v UK* (1981) Report of 18 March 1981, D & R 25; (1981) 5 EHRR 71.

5(1)(c): Detention after arrest but before conviction

This provision refers to persons held on remand or detained after arrest. Article 5(3) requires that in such an instance, a person should be brought 'promptly' to trial; in other words, the trial should occur in *reasonable* time. The part of 5(1)(c) which causes concern is the ground – 'arrest or detention to prevent him committing an offence'. This is an alternative to the holding of the detainee under reasonable suspicion of committing an offence; arguably, the two should have been cumulative. This ground would permit internment of persons even if the facts which showed the intention to commit a crime did not, in themselves, constitute a criminal offence. In *Lawless*[214] the Court narrowed this ground down on the basis that internment in such circumstances might well not fulfil the other requirement in Art 5(1)(c) that the arrest or detention would be effected for the purpose of bringing the person before a competent legal authority. This interpretation was warranted because all of Art 5 must be read together.

A level of suspicion below 'reasonable suspicion' will not be sufficient; in *Fox, Campbell and Hartley*,[215] the Court found that Art 5(1)(c) had been violated on the basis that no reasonable suspicion of committing an offence had arisen, only an honest belief (which was all that was needed under s 11 of the Northern Ireland (Emergency Provisions) Act 1978). The only evidence put forward by the government for the presence of reasonable suspicion was that the applicants had convictions for terrorist offences and that when arrested, they were asked about particular terrorist acts. The government said that further evidence could not be disclosed for fear of endangering life. The Court said that reasonable suspicion arises from 'facts or information which would satisfy an objective observer that the person concerned may have committed the offence'. It went on to find that the government had not established that reasonable suspicion was present in justifying the arrests in question. The Court took into account the exigencies of the situation and the need to prevent terrorism; however, it found that the state Party in question must be able to provide some information which an objective observer would consider justified the arrest. It was found that the information provided was insufficient and therefore a breach of Art 5 had occurred. This ruling suggests that in terrorist cases, a low level of reasonable suspicion is required and this test was applied in *Murray v UK*.[216] The Court found that no breach of Art 5(1)(c) had occurred, even though the relevant legislation (s 14 of the Northern Ireland (Emergency Provisions) Act 1987) required only suspicion, not reasonable suspicion, since there was some evidence which provided a basis for the suspicion in question.

5(1)(d): Detention of minors

This provision confers far-reaching powers on national authorities with regard to those under 18 years of age. This has led the Court to interpret the term 'educational purpose' restrictively. In *Bouamar v Belgium*[217] it was found that mere detention without educational facilities would not fulfil Art 5(1)(d)); there had to be educational facilities in the institution, and trained staff.

---

214   (1961) 1 EHRR 15.
215   Judgment of 30 August 1990, A 178; (1990) 13 EHRR 157.
216   (1994) 19 EHRR 193.
217   Judgment of 29 February 1988, A 129; (1988) 11 EHRR 1.

5(1)(e): Detention of non-criminals for the protection of society

This sub-paragraph must, of course, be read in conjunction with para 5(4) – all the persons mentioned have the right to have the lawfulness of their detention determined by a Court. The width of para 5(1)(e) was narrowed down in the *Vagrancy* cases, in which the question arose of the current application of the term 'vagrant'.[218] The term had been applied to the applicants who had, therefore, been detained. The Court considered whether the applicant was correctly brought within the ambit of the term in the relevant Belgian legislation, but it refused to conduct a more than marginal review of municipal law; the question of the interpretation of national law was separated from the application of the Convention. However the Court did then turn to the Convention and conduct a far reaching review of the meaning of 'vagrant' in accordance with the Convention on the basis of a common European standard; it then found that the applicants had not been correctly brought within that term. Thus, ultimately, the margin of appreciation allowed was narrow. This stance prevents too wide an interpretation of the application of the categories of para 5(1)(e).

In *Winterwerp v Netherlands*[219] the Court found that the detention of the mentally disordered or handicapped could be justified only where there was reliable medical evidence of the mental disorder; it must be of a type justifying compulsory detention; and the condition in question must persist throughout the period of detention. In *Kay v UK*[220] a breach of Art 5(1)(e) was found since the first of these conditions had not been complied with; *current* medical information had not been considered.

5(1)(f): Detention of aliens and deportees

The importance of this provision is that the Convention does not grant aliens a right of admission or residence in contracting states, but para 5(1)(f) ensures that an alien who is detained pending deportation or admission has certain guarantees; there must be review of the detention by an independent body[221] and the arrest must be in accordance with national law.[222] The nature of the measures taken, including the period of detention before review, must ensure that the detention is not arbitrary.[223] Also, because the lawfulness of the detention may depend on the lawfulness of the deportation itself, the lawfulness of the deportation may often be in issue.[224]

Safeguards of paras 2–4: general

Paragraphs 2–4 reiterate the principle that the liberty of the person is the overriding concern; if one of the exceptions mentioned in para 5(1) applies, the safeguards of

---

218 *Vagrancy* cases, Judgment of 18 June 1971, A 14.
219 (1979) 2 EHRR 387.
220 (1998) 40 BMLR 20.
221 In *Chahal v UK* (1996) 23 EHRR 413 review by the immigration advisory panel procedure was found to be sufficient to guard against arbitrariness.
222 In *Bozano v France* (1986) 9 EHRR 297, a French deportation order was found to be invalid under national law since it was – in effect – a disguised extradition order. A violation of Art 5(1)(f) was found.
223 *Guzzardi v Italy* (1980) 3 EHRR 333; *Amuur v France* (1996) 22 EHRR 533.
224 *Zamir v UK*, Report of 11 October 1983; 40 D & R 42 (1983).

sub-paras 2–4 must still be complied with. If they are not, the deprivation of liberty will be unlawful even if it comes within the exceptions. Paragraphs 2–4 provide a minimum standard for arrest and detention.

Promptly informing of the reason for arrest

Paragraph 5(2) provides that a detainee or arrestee must be informed promptly of the reason for arrest. This information is needed so that it is possible to judge from the moment of its inception whether the arrest is in accordance with the law so that the detainee could theoretically take action straight away to be released. All the necessary information – the factual and legal grounds for the arrest – need not be given at the point of arrest; it can be conveyed over a period of time, depending on the circumstances. A period of two days between the arrest and the conveying of the information has been found not to breach Art 5(2).[225] The Commission's view is that this information need not be as detailed and specific as that guaranteed by para 6(3) in connection with the right to a fair trial.[226]

In *Fox, Campbell and Hartley v UK*[227] the applicants, who were arrested on suspicion of terrorist offences, were not informed of the reason for the arrest at the time of it, but were told that they were being arrested under a particular statutory provision. Clearly, this could not convey the reason to them at that time. At a later point, during interrogation, they were asked about specific criminal offences. The European Court of Human Rights found that Art 5(2) was not satisfied at the time of the arrest, but that this breach was healed by the later indications made during interrogation of the offences for which they had been arrested. Clayton and Tomlinson comment that this finding was 'an unacceptable dilution of a basic guarantee'.[228]

In *Murray v UK*[229] soldiers had occupied the applicant's house, thus clearly taking her into detention, but she was not informed of the fact of arrest for half an hour. The question arose whether she was falsely imprisoned during that half hour. The Court found that no breach of Art 5(2) had occurred in those circumstances. Mrs Murray was eventually informed during interrogation of the reason for the arrest and although an interval of a few hours had elapsed between the arrest and informing her of the reason for it, this could still be termed prompt.

Both these decisions were influenced by the terrorist context in which they occurred and provide examples of the Court's tenderness to claims of a threat to national security made by governments of Member states. In both, a very wide margin of appreciation was allowed. It would appear that both were influenced by the crime control consideration of allowing leeway to the police to resort to doubtful practices in relation to terrorist suspects and both exhibit, it is suggested, a lack of rigour in relation to due process. Such lack of rigour might be acceptable if there was a real connection between a failure to give information to suspects and an advantage to be gained in an emergency

---

225 *Skoogstrom v Sweden* (1981) 1 Dig Supp para 5.2.2.1.
226 It was determined in Appl 8828/79, *X v Denmark* D & R 30 (1983), p 93 that para 5(2) does not include a right to contact a lawyer.
227 Judgment of 30 August 1990, A 182; (1990) 13 EHRR 157.
228 Ibid, p 498.
229 (1994) 19 EHRR 193.

situation, since the principle of proportionality would then be satisfied. However, in Mrs Murray's case, for example, once she was in detention and her house in effect sealed off from the outside world, it is not clear that telling her of the fact of the arrest could have created or exacerbated the unsettled situation. Thus, the Court has allowed some departure from the principle that there should be a clear demarcation between the point at which the citizen is at liberty and the point at which her liberty is restrained.

Promptness of judicial hearing

Article 5(3) confers a right to be brought promptly before the judicial authorities; in other words, not to be held in detention for long periods without an independent hearing. It refers to persons detained in accordance with Art 5(1)(c) and therefore covers both arrest and detention, and detainees held on remand. The significance of Art 5(3) rests on its strong link to the purpose of Art 5 itself.[230] There will be some allowable delay in both situations; the question is, therefore, what is meant by 'promptly'. Its meaning was considered in *Brogan v UK*[231] in relation to an arrest and detention arising by virtue of the special powers under s 12 of the Prevention of Terrorism (Temporary Provisions) Act 1989. The UK had entered a derogation under Art 15 against the applicability of Art 5 to Northern Ireland, but withdrew that derogation in August 1984. Two months later, the *Brogan* case was filed. The applicants complained, *inter alia*, of the length of time they were held in detention without coming before a judge, on the basis that it could not be termed prompt. The Court took into account the need for special measures to combat terrorism; such measures had to be balanced against individual rights. However, it found that detention for four days and six hours was too long. The Court did not specify how long was acceptable; previously, the Commission had seen four days (in ordinary criminal cases) as the limit.[232] Following this decision, the UK Government ultimately chose to derogate from Art 5 and this decision was eventually found to be lawful by the European Court of Human Rights.[233]

The question whether detainees on remand have been brought to trial or released in a reasonable time has also been considered. The word 'reasonable' is not associated with the processing of the prosecution and trial, but with the detention itself. Obviously, if the trial takes a long time to prepare for, there will be a longer delay, but it does not follow that detention for all that time will be reasonable. In the *Neumeister* case,[234] the Court rejected an interpretation of 'reasonable' which associated it only with the preparation of the trial. Thus, continued detention on remand will be reasonable only so long as the reasonable suspicion of para 5(1)(c) continues to exist. But, grounds for continued detention other than those expressly mentioned in para 5(1)(c) could be considered, such as suppression of evidence or the possibility that the detainee will abscond. However, it is clear from *Letellier v France*[235] that such dangers must persist throughout the period

---

230 See *Bozano v France* (1986) 9 EHRR 297; *Assenov v Belgium* (1999) 28 EHRR 652; *T v Malta* (1999) 29 EHRR 185.
231 Judgment of 29 November 1988; (1989) 11 EHRR 117; A 145.
232 *X v Netherlands* (1966) 9 YB 564.
233 *Brannigan and McBride v UK* (1993) 17 EHRR 594.
234 Judgment of 27 June 1968; (1979–80) 1 EHRR 91.
235 A 207 (1991).

of detention; when they cease, specific reasons for continued detention which have been properly scrutinised must be apparent. Once the accused has been released on bail, Art 5(3) does not apply, but Art 6(1) does, as will be seen later. The question of a reasonable time for preparing for the trial can also be considered under Art 6(1).

There is no absolute right to bail under Art 5(3), but the authorities must consider whether bail can achieve the same purpose as detention on remand.[236] It is also clear that detention after demand of an excessively large sum for bail will be unreasonable if a lesser sum would have achieved the same objective.[237]

Review of detention

Article 5(4) provides a right to review of detention, whatever the basis of the detention. The detainee must be able to take court proceedings in order to determine whether a detention is unlawful. This is an independent provision: even if it is determined in a particular case by the Commission that the detention was lawful, there could still be a breach of Art 5(4) if no possibility of review of the lawfulness of the detention by the domestic courts arose. The review must be by a court and it must be adequate to test the lawfulness of the detention. This requirement was found not to have been satisfied by judicial review proceedings or by habeas corpus in *Chahal v UK*:[238] neither procedure provided a sufficient basis for challenging a deportation decision.

Article 5(4) was in issue in the a number of cases against the UK regarding discretionary life sentences, and it was found that there had to be an element in the sentence which, of its nature, was reviewable.[239] Thus, a mandatory life sentence arguably consisting wholly of a punitive element would be unreviewable since no relevant circumstance could have changed.[240] In the *Weeks* case,[241] the sentence contained a security element and therefore allowed review of the applicant's progress. In *Thynne, Wilson and Gunnel v UK*,[242] the sentence consisted of both a punitive and a security element. When the punitive element expired, a judicial procedure for review of the sentence should have been available because there was then something to review; if it had been purely punitive, there would not have been. Thus, in both cases, a breach of Art 5(4) was found. Section 34 of the Criminal Justice Act 1991 clarified the position of discretionary lifers,[243] but the secretive procedure for tariff fixing still raised issues under Art 5(4) and Art 6.[244] This is also the case in respect of the power of the Home Secretary to detain young offenders at her Majesty's pleasure.[245]

---

236 *Wemhoff*, Judgment of 27 June 1968; (1968) 1 EHRR 55.
237 *Neumeister*, Judgment of 27 June 1968; (1979–80) 1 EHRR 91.
238 (1997) 23 EHRR 413.
239 *Wynne v UK* (1994) 19 EHRR 333.
240 Ibid.
241 (1987) 10 EHRR 293.
242 Judgment of 25 October 1990, A 190; (1990) 13 EHRR 666. For comment, see Richardson, G, 'Discretionary life-sentences and the ECHR' [1991] PL 34.
243 On the UK response in the Criminal Justice Act 1991, s 34 (see Crime (Sentences) Act 1997, s 28) see: Fitzgerald, E, 'The Criminal Justice Act 1991: preventive detention of the dangerous offender' [1995] EHRLR 39.
244 See *Watson v UK* [1997] EHRLR 181.
245 *Hussain and Singh v UK* (1996) 21 EHRR 1.

Article 5(4) also applies to remand prisoners. It was found in *De Jong, Baljet and Van de Brink*[246] that it grants to a person on remand a right of access to a court after the decision (in accordance with Art 5(3)) to detain him or prolong detention has been taken. It also allows access to the files used in coming to the decision on remand.[247]

Compensation

Paragraph 5(5) provides for compensation if the arrest or detention contravenes the other provisions of Art 5.[248] This provision differs from the general right to compensation under Art 50[249] because it exists as an independent right: if a person is found to have been unlawfully arrested under domestic law in the domestic court, but no compensation is available, he or she can apply to the European Court of Human Rights on the basis of the lack of compensation. As far as other Convention rights are concerned, if a violation of a right occurs which is found unlawful by the national courts, but no compensation is granted, the applicant cannot allege breach of the right. Article 5(5) is considered at a number of points in this book, but most extensively in Chapter 12.

Article 6: Right to a fair and public hearing

(1) In the determination of his civil rights and obligations or of any criminal charge against him, everyone is entitled to a fair and public hearing within a reasonable time by an independent and impartial tribunal established by law. Judgment shall be pronounced publicly but the press and public may be excluded from all or part of the trial in the interest of morals, public order or national security in a democratic society, where the interest of juveniles or the protection of the private life of the parties so require, or to the extent strictly necessary in the opinion of the court in special circumstances where publicity would prejudice the interests of justice.

(2) Everyone charged with a criminal offence shall be presumed innocent until proved guilty according to law.

(3) Everyone charged with a criminal offence has the following minimum rights:

(a) to be informed promptly, in a language which he understands and in detail, of the nature and cause of the accusation against him;

(b) to have adequate time and facilities for the preparation of his defence;

(c) to defend himself in person or through legal assistance of his own choosing or, if he has not sufficient means to pay for legal assistance, to be given it free when the interests of justice so require;

(d) to examine or have examined witnesses against him and to obtain the attendance and examination of witnesses on his behalf under the same conditions as witnesses against him;

---

246 Judgment of 22 May 1984, A 77, pp 25–26; (1984) 8 EHRR 20.
247 *Lamy v Belgium* (1989) 11 EHRR 529.
248 See the reference to Art 5(5) in HRA, s 9(3).
249 Appl No 6821/74, *Huber v Austria* 6 D & R 65 (1977), p 65.

(e) to have the free assistance of an interpreter if he cannot understand or speak the language used in court.

Article 6 is one of the most significant Convention Articles and the one which is most frequently found to have been violated. This is partly due to the width of Art 6(1), which may cover numerous circumstances in which rights are affected in the absence of a judicial hearing. This may mean that even where a substantive claim under another Article fails, the Art 6(1) claim succeeds because the procedure used in making the determination affecting the applicant was defective.[250] In order to appreciate the way it operates, it is crucial to understand the relationship between paras 1 and 3. Paragraph 1 imports a general requirement of a fair hearing applying to criminal and civil hearings which covers all aspects of a fair hearing. Paragraph 3 lists minimum guarantees of a fair hearing in the criminal context only. If para 3 had been omitted, the guarantees contained in it could have arisen from para 1, but it was included on the basis that it is important to declare a minimum standard for a fair hearing. In practice, then, paras 1 and 3 may often both be in question in respect of a criminal charge.

Since para 3 contains *minimum* guarantees, the para 1 protection of a fair hearing goes beyond para 3. In investigating a fair hearing, the Commission is not confined to the para 3 guarantees; it can consider further requirements of fairness. Thus, if para 1 is not violated, it will be superfluous to consider para 3 and if one of the para 3 guarantees is violated, there will be no need to look at para 1. However, if para 3 is not violated, it will still be worth considering para 1. It follows that although civil hearings are expressly affected only by para 1, the minimum guarantees may also apply to such hearings too.

Article 6(1): Fair hearing

Field of application

The term 'criminal charge' has an autonomous Convention meaning. The question of what is meant by 'a criminal charge' has generated quite a lot of case law. 'Charge' has been described as 'the official notification given to an individual by the competent authority of an allegation that he has committed a criminal offence'.[251] The proceedings in question must be *determinative* of the charge. Therefore, proceedings *ancillary* to the determination of the charge do not fall within Art 6.[252]

Offences under criminal law must be distinguished from those arising only under *disciplinary law*. In order to determine whether, whatever the classification of an 'offence' in national law, it should be viewed as criminal in nature, the Court will consider the nature of the offence and the nature and severity of the penalty the person

---

250 Eg, in *Mats Jacobson v Sweden* (1990) 13 EHRR 79, the applicant was prevented from making changes to his property. His substantive claim under Art 1 of Protocol 1 failed, but his Art 6(1) claim succeeded, since he was allowed no adequate access to a court to challenge the prohibition.

251 Judgment of 15 July 1982, *Eckle* A 51; (1982) 5 EHRR 1, p 33.

252 See, e.g., *X v UK* (1982) 5 EHRR 273 (appointment of a legal aid lawyer was found to fall outside Art 6).

is threatened with.[253] In *Campbell and Fell v UK*,[254] the Court had to consider whether prison discipline could fall within Art 6(1) as the determination of a criminal charge. The applicants, prisoners, were sentenced to a substantial loss of remission. This was such a serious consequence that the procedure in question could be considered as of a criminal character, but the Court considered that not all disciplinary offences in prison which in fact had an equivalent in the ordinary criminal law would be treated as of a criminal character. In general, disciplinary offences will not be viewed as criminal since they are a matter of concern to the particular profession, not a matter regulated by the law in general.[255]

'Regulatory' offences are also, in general, viewed as matters that relate to a specific group rather than to persons in general.[256] But, classification of a petty offence as 'regulatory' rather than criminal will not be decisive for Art 6(1) purposes; Strasbourg may yet determine that the offence is of a criminal character.[257] Otherwise, by reclassifying offences, the state in question could minimise the application of the Convention.

The term 'civil rights and obligations' also has an autonomous Convention meaning and therefore cannot merely be assigned the meaning of 'private' as understood in UK administrative law. Thus, the meaning of 'civil rights and obligations' does not depend upon the legal classification afforded the right or obligation in question by the national legislator; the question is whether the content and effect of the right or obligation (taking into account the legal systems of all the contracting states) allows the meaning 'civil right' or 'civil obligation' to be assigned to it.[258] This wide provision allows challenge to decisions taken in the absence of legal procedures in a disparate range of circumstances.[259] The civil right must have some legal basis as established in the state in question, but assuming that there is such a basis, Art 6 may apply to immunities or procedural constraints preventing the bringing of claims to court.[260]

In *Tinnelly v UK*[261] the Court found that a clearly defined statutory right aimed at freedom from discrimination should be viewed as a civil right. Strasbourg may be moving towards a position in which 'all those rights which are individual rights under the national legal system and fall into the sphere of general freedom ... must be seen as civil rights'.[262] Clearly, this question remains a problematic one. It is clear that there must be a dispute between the parties, but the extent to which this is the case is not entirely settled. In *Fayed v UK*[263] it was found that although, strictly, there was no legal basis for the action and so no dispute to trigger Art 6, Art 6 applied to blanket immunities preventing access to a court.

---

253 *Campbell and Fell*, Judgment of 28 June 1984, A 80; (1985) 7 EHRR 165; *Garyfallou AEBE v Greece* (1999) 28 EHRR 344, para 33; *Lauko v Slovakia* [1999] EHRLR 105, para 56.
254 Ibid.
255 *Wickramsinghe v UK* [1998] EHRLR 338.
256 See *X v UK* (1998) 25 EHRR CD 88.
257 *Özturk*, Judgment of 21 February 1983, A 73; (1984) 6 EHRR 409.
258 Judgment of 16 July 1971, *Ringeisen v Austria*, A 13, p 39; (1971) 1 EHRR 455.
259 Eg, *O v UK* (1987) 10 EHRR 82 concerned a decision to terminate access to a child in care although no legal procedure was in place allowing consideration of its merits.
260 See *Osman v UK* (1998) 5 BHRC 293; *Fayed v UK* (1994) 18 EHRR 393.
261 (1998) 27 EHRR 249.
262 *Bentham v UK*, B 80, para 10 (1983), dissenting opinions of Mr Melchior and Mr Frowen.
263 (1994) 18 EHRR 393.

A right of access to a court

Besides the procedural guarantees, Art 6(1) has been found to provide, impliedly, a right of access to a court whether the domestic legal system allows access to a court in a particular case or not. The right is not absolute, but restrictions must not impair the essence of the right.[264] Restrictions must have a legitimate aim and be proportionate to the aim pursued. The test is, therefore, the same as that used in respect of that under para 2 of Arts 8–11.[265] In *Osman v UK*[266] the Court found, controversially, that the immunity of the police from actions in negligence breached this right of access to a court.[267] Other public policy based immunities have subsequently been found not to breach this right,[268] in pursuit of what may arguably be termed a retreat from *Osman*, and not all other constraints will do so.[269]

Once it has been determined that a particular instance falls within Art 6(1), it must be determined whether the claim in question is covered by the right of access to a court. It seems that, for example, Art 6(1) does not confer a right of appeal to a higher court.[270] It may include access to legal advice and, by implication, legal aid. These issues arise in relation both to access to a court hearing and the *fairness* of the hearing. In the very significant decision in *Golder*,[271] it was found that a refusal to allow a detainee to correspond with his legal advisor would be contrary to Art 6(1), since in preventing him even initiating proceedings, it hindered his right of access to a court. In other words, the right of access to a court must be an *effective* one.

Access to legal advice in order to obtain access to a court may not always imply a right to legal aid. The circumstances in which it will do so were considered in *Granger v UK*.[272] The applicant had been refused legal aid and so did not have counsel at appeal; he only had notes from his solicitor which he read out, but clearly did not understand. In particular, there was one especially complex ground of appeal which he was unable to deal with. In view of the complexity of the appeal and his inability to deal with it, legal aid should have been granted. It was found that paras 6(1) and 6(3)(c) should be read together and, if it would be apparent to an objective observer that a fair hearing could not take place without legal advice, then both would be violated. *Granger* was concerned with the fairness of the hearing rather than with the ability to obtain access to a court at all. However, in some instances, a person unable to obtain legal aid would

---

264 *Tinnelly and McElduff v UK* (1998) 27 EHRR 249; *Fayed v UK* (1994) 18 EHRR 393.

265 See *Fayed v UK* (1994) 18 EHRR 393, para 67. See also above, pp 61–62.

266 (1998) 5 BHRC 293.

267 The decision was severely criticised by Lord Browne-Wilkinson in *Barrett v Enfield London LBC* [1999] 3 All ER 193 on the ground that there was no immunity, but in fact no right to make a claim at all. See also the criticisms of Lord Hoffmann in 'Human rights and the House of Lords' (1999) 62 MLR 159.

268 See *Z and Others v UK*, App 28945/95 (2001) *The Times*, 31 May; the case resulted from a decision of the House of Lords in *X v Bedfordshire CC* [1995] 2 AC 633 that P could not bring an action in negligence against the local authority.

269 In *Fayed v UK* (1994) 18 EHRR 393, the Court found that a limitation on the ability of the applicants to take legal proceedings to challenge the findings of a governmental inquiry into the applicants' business affairs did not constitute an unjustified denial of access to a court.

270 *Belgian Linguistics* cases, Judgment of 23 July 1968, A 6; (1968) 1 EHRR 252.

271 Judgment of 21 February 1975, A 18.

272 Judgment of 28 March 1990, A 174.

be unable to obtain legal advice and therefore might be unable to initiate proceedings. In such instances, access to a court would be the main issue.[273] But, in civil proceedings, legal aid is not fully guaranteed, as it is in Art 6(3); circumstances have been accepted in which legal aid can be denied.[274]

An independent and impartial tribunal established by law

All courts and tribunals falling within Art 6 must meet this requirement. The tribunal must be established by law[275] and be independent of the executive.[276] Factors to be taken into account will include the appointment of its members, their terms of office, and guarantees against outside influence.[277] Impartiality is judged both subjectively and objectively.[278] In other words, actual bias must be shown, but also the existence of guarantees against bias.[279] The decision in *McGonnell v UK*[280] left open the question whether a judge having both legislative and executive functions could be viewed as independent and impartial. In a number of cases against the UK, military discipline as exercised by way of courts-martial has not been found to satisfy the requirement of impartiality.[281]

Hearing within a reasonable time

The hearing must take place within a reasonable time. These are the same words as are used in Art 5(3), but here, the point is to put an end to the insecurity of the applicant who is uncertain of the outcome of the civil action or charge against him or her rather than with the deprivation of liberty.[282] Thus, the ending point comes when the uncertainty is resolved either at the court of highest instance or by expiry of the time limit for appeal. In determining what is meant by 'reasonable', fairly wide time limits have been applied so that in some circumstances, as much as seven or eight[283] years may be reasonable. The Court has approved a period of nearly five years[284] and the Commission a period of seven and a half.[285] It will take into account the conduct of the accused (which may have contributed to the delay) and the need for proper

273 See *Airey v Ireland* (1979) 2 EHRR 305; *Aerts v Belgium* [1998] EHRLR 777.
274 In *Andronicou and Constantinou v Cyprus* (1998) 25 EHRR 491 it was found that *ex gratia* assistance was sufficient.
275 *Zand v Austria* (1978) 15 DR 70 (this means law emanating from Parliament, although aspects of the judicial organisation may be delegated to the executive).
276 *Benthem v Netherlands* (1985) 8 EHRR 1.
277 *Bryan v UK* (1995) 21 EHRR 342.
278 *Fey v Austria* (1993) 16 EHRR 387; *Pullar v UK* (1996) 22 EHRR 391.
279 *Remli v France* (1996) 22 EHRR 253.
280 (2000) 8 BHRC 56.
281 See *Findlay v UK* (1997) 24 EHRR 221; *Hood v UK* (2000) 29 EHRR 365, Judgment of 25.2.97; see also *Coyne v UK*, Judgment of 24.10.97, RJD 1997-V 1842; *Cable and Others v UK*, Appl. no 24436/94 (1999) *The Times*, 11 March.
282 See, generally, Van Dijk and Van Hoof, op. cit., fn 1, pp 446–47.
283 In *Vernillo v France* 12 HRLJ 199, seven and a half years in respect of civil proceedings was not found too long owing to the special responsibilities of the parties.
284 *Buchholz*, Judgment of 6 May 1981, A 42.
285 Report, 12 July 1977, in *Haase* D & R 11 (1978), p 78.

preparation of the case, bearing in mind any special circumstances such as those which might arise in child care cases. In order to determine how long the delay has been, the point from which time will run must be identified. In criminal cases, it will be 'the stage at which the situation of the person concerned has been substantially affected as a result of a suspicion against him'.[286] In civil cases, it will be the moment when the proceedings concerned are initiated, not including pre-trial negotiations.[287]

Other aspects of fairness

Apart from access to legal advice and the other minimal guarantees of Art 6(3), what other rights are implied by the term a 'fair hearing'? It has been found to connote equality between the parties,[288] and in principle, entails the right of the parties to be present in person,[289] although criminal trial in *absentia* does not automatically violate Art 6: the right can be waived[290] and does not normally extend to appeals.[291] The hearing should be adversarial[292] in the sense that both parties are given an opportunity to comment on all the evidence that is adduced.[293] A refusal to summon a witness may constitute unfairness,[294] as may a failure to disclose evidence.[295] The court must give a reasoned judgment.[296] These and further significant aspects of fairness are discussed further at relevant points in the following chapters, especially Chapter 13.[297]

Article 6(2): The presumption of innocence in criminal cases

Paragraph 2:

> requires *inter alia* that when carrying out their duties, members of a court should not start with the preconceived idea that the accused has committed the offence charged; the burden of proof is on the prosecution and any doubt should benefit the accused. It also follows that it is for the prosecution to inform the accused of the case that will be made against him so that he may prepare and present his defence accordingly and to adduce evidence sufficient to convict him.[298]

---

286 *Neumeister*, Judgment of 27 June 1968; (1979–80) 1 EHRR 91.
287 Report of 7 March 1984, *Lithgow v UK*, A 102 (1986) p 120; (1986) 8 EHRR 335.
288 *Neumeister*, Judgment of 27 June 1968; (1979–80) 1 EHRR 91; *De Haes and Gijsels v Belgium* (1997) 25 EHRR 1.
289 *Colloza v Italy*, Judgment of 12 February 1985, A 89 (1985); *Zana v Turkey* (1998) 4 BHRC 242.
290 *Colloza v Italy*, Judgment of 12 February 1985, A 89 (1985).
291 *Ekbatani v Sweden* (1988) 13 EHRR 504, cf *Monnell and Morris v UK* (1987) 10 EHRR 205.
292 *Ruiz-Mateos v Spain* (1993) 16 EHRR 505.
293 *Mantovanelli v France* (1997) 24 EHRR 370.
294 *X v Austria* Appl No 5362/72, Coll 42 (1973), p 145.
295 *Edwards v UK* (1992) 15 EHRR 417 (it was found that the hearing in the Court of Appeal remedied this failure). In *Rowe and Davis v UK* (2000) 30 EHRR 1, the failure of the prosecution to make an application to the trial judge to withhold material caused a breach of Art 6. Review of the material later by the Court of Appeal could not remedy the breach.
296 *Hadjianastassiou v Greece* (1992) 16 EHRR 219, para 33.
297 See pp 1259–62. Also, for further discussion, see Ashworth, A, 'Article 6 and the fairness of trials' [1999] Crim LR 261.
298 Judgment of 6 December 1988, *Barbéra, Messegué and Jabardo*, A 14 6(2) (1989) p 33. See also *Salabiaku v France* (1988) 13 EHRR 379.

It follows from the presumption of innocence that the court must base its conviction exclusively on evidence put forward at trial.[299] Thus, a conviction based on written statements which were inadmissible breached para 6(2).[300] This provision is very closely related to the impartiality provision of para 6(1).

The expectation that the state bears the burden of establishing guilt requires that the accused should not be expected to provide involuntary assistance by way of a confession. Thus, the presumption of innocence under para 6(2) is closely linked to the right to freedom from self-incrimination which the Court has found to be covered by the right to a fair hearing under para 6(1) (*Funke v France*).[301] In *Murray (John) v UK*,[302] on the other hand, the Commission did not find that para 6(1) had been breached where inferences had been drawn at trial from the applicant's refusal to give evidence. The Court also found no breach of Art 6 due to such drawing of inferences in the particular circumstances of the case, taking into account the fact that 'the right to silence' could not be treated as absolute, the degree of compulsion exerted on the applicant and the weight of the evidence against him.[303] However, the Court did find that Art 6(1) had been breached by the denial of access to a lawyer since such access was essential where there was a likelihood that adverse inferences would be drawn from silence. In *Saunders v UK*[304] the Commission found that the applicant's right to freedom from self-incrimination had been infringed in that he had been forced to answer questions put to him by inspectors investigating a company takeover or risk the imposition of a criminal sanction. The ruling of the Court was to the same effect, taking into account the special compulsive regime in question for Department of Trade and Industry inspections.[305]

Sub-paragraphs 6(3)(a), (b) and (c): time, facilities and legal representation in criminal cases

These sub-paragraphs are closely related due to the word 'facilities' used in sub-para (b). Sub-paragraphs (b) and (c) may often be invoked together: (c) in respect of the assignment of a lawyer, and (b) in respect of the time allowed for such assignment. It is not enough that a lawyer should be assigned; he or she should be appointed in good time in order to give time to prepare the defence and familiarise herself or himself with the case.[306] Both sub-paragraphs also arise in relation to notification of the right of access to legal advice and it has been held that an oral translation of the requisite information is insufficient.[307] As has already been noted in relation to *Granger*, the legal advice provisions must be read in conjunction with the right to a fair trial. A lawyer must be assigned if, otherwise, an objective observer would consider that a fair hearing

---

299 *X v Federal Republic of Germany* D & R 17 (1980), p 231.
300 *Barbéra* [1987] 3 All ER 411.
301 (1993) 16 EHRR 297.
302 (1996) 22 EHRR 29. For comment, see Munday, R [1996] Crim LR 370.
303 *Murray (John) v UK* (1996) 22 EHRR 29. See also *Averill v UK* (2001) 31 EHRR 36.
304 No 19187/91 Com Rep paras 69–75.
305 *Saunders v UK* (1997) 23 EHRR 313. See further Chapter 12, p 1239.
306 *X and Y v Austria* Appl 7909/74; 15 D & R 160 (1979).
307 *Kamasinski*, Report of 5 May 1988, para 138; (1991) 13 EHRR 36.

would not occur. In *Poitrimol v France*[308] the Court stated: 'Although not absolute, the right . . . to be effectively defended by a lawyer, assigned officially if need be, is one of the fundamental features of a fair trial.' In furtherance of the notion of providing effective legal representation, it has been found that para 6(3)(c) does not merely import a right to have legal assistance, but rather it includes three rights:[309]

(a) to have recourse, if desired, to legal assistance;
(b) to choose that assistance;
(c) if the defendant has insufficient means to pay, for that assistance to be given it free if the interest of justice so require.[310]

6(3)(d): Cross-examination in criminal cases

The Strasbourg case law has left a wide discretion to the national court[311] as to the interpretation of the first limb of para 6(3)(d) – the right to cross-examine witnesses – and so has deprived this right of some of its effect. This right would seem to be specific and unambiguous in its guarantee that witnesses against the defendant must be at the public hearing if their evidence is to be relied on. It would therefore seem to outlaw hearsay evidence. The Court has, however, shrunk at times from a straightforward assertion that this is the case.[312] The second limb – the right to call witnesses and have them examined under the same conditions as witnesses for the other side – obviously allows for a wide discretion as it only requires that the prosecution and defence should be treated equally as regards summoning witnesses.[313] So, conditions and restrictions can be set so long as they apply equally to both sides. This provision relates to the concept of creating equality between parties; it is closely related to the fair hearing principle and therefore, will apply in civil cases too.

Art 6 is considered at various points in this book, and extensively in Chapters 11–14, especially in relation to its impact on pre-trial procedures.

Article 7: Freedom from retrospective effect of penal legislation

(1) No one shall be held guilty of any criminal offence on account of any act or omission which did not constitute a criminal offence under national or international law at the time when it was committed. Nor shall a heavier penalty be imposed than the one that was applicable at the time the criminal offence was committed.

---

308 (1993) A 277-A; (1993) 18 EHRR 130.
309 From *Golder*, Judgment of 21 February 1975, A 18; see also *Silver v UK*, Judgment of 25 March 1983, A 61, (1983) 5 EHRR 347.
310 *Pakelli*, Judgment of 25 April 1983, A 64.
311 See, e.g., *Asch v Austria* (1991) 15 EHRR 597.
312 Such an assertion was made in *Kostovski v Netherlands* (1989) 12 EHRR 434 and *Windisch v Austria* (1990) 13 EHRR 281. However, these decisions were not followed in *Isgro v Italy* (1991) Case 1/1990/192/252. For further discussion of this right, see [1993] Crim LR 261–67.
313 Appl 4428/70, *X v Austria* (1972) Yearbook XV, p 264.

(2) This article shall not prejudice the trial and punishment of any person for any act or omission which, at the time when it was committed, was criminal according to the general principles of law recognised by civilised nations.

Article 7 contains an important principle and it is, therefore, non-derogable, although it is subject to the single exception contained in para 2. It divides into two separate principles:

(a) the law in question must have existed at the time of the act in question for the conviction to be based on it;

(b) no heavier penalty for the infringement of the law may be imposed than was in force at the time the act was committed.

As far as the first principle is concerned, this also means that an existing part of the criminal law cannot be applied by analogy to acts it was not intended for.[314] Allowing such extension would fall foul of the general principle that the law must be unambiguous, which is part of the principle that someone should not be convicted if he or she could not have known beforehand that the act in question was criminal. In order to determine whether these requirements have been met, the Strasbourg authorities are prepared to interpret domestic law,[315] although normally they would not be prepared to do so. Although it will be cautious in this respect, the Commission must take note of an allegedly false interpretation of domestic law. *Harman v UK*[316] concerned unforeseeable liability for contempt of court. It had not previously been considered to be contempt if confidential documents were shown to a journalist after being read out in court. The Commission declared the application admissible, but meanwhile a friendly settlement was reached.

Article 7 was found to have been breached in *Welch v UK*.[317] Before the trial of the applicant for drug offences, a new provision came into force under the Drug Trafficking Offences Act 1986, making provision for confiscation orders. This was imposed on the applicant, although the legislation was not in force at the time when he committed the offences in question. It clearly had retrospective effect and was found to constitute a 'penalty' within Art 7(1). In *SW v UK* and *C v UK*[318] the applicants claimed that marital rape had been retrospectively outlawed and that therefore, their criminalisation for forced sexual intercourse with their wives created a breach of Art 7. Their convictions were based on the ruling of the House of Lords in *R*,[319] which removed the marital exemption. The Court found that the anticipated reform of the law undertaken in R was almost inevitable and that therefore, the applicants should have foreseen that their conduct would be found to be criminal. Thus, no breach of Art 7 was found.

Paragraph 7(2) provides an exception which appears to arise if a person is convicted retrospectively for an offence recognised in other countries, but not the one in question at the material time. This exception is potentially quite wide; it is not restricted to war

314 Appl 1852/63, *X v Austria* (1965) Yearbook VIII.
315 This was determined in *X v Austria*, above, fn 314.
316 Appl 10038/82; Decision of 11 May 1984; 38 D & R 53 (1984).
317 A 307-A; (1995) 20 EHRR 247.
318 (1995) 21 EHRR 404. For comment on the ruling, see Osborne, C (1996) 4 EHRR 406.
319 [1991] 4 All ER 481; [1991] 3 WLR 767; [1992] Fam Law 108; [1992] Crim LR 207, HL.

crimes and could cover any deeply immoral conduct generally recognised as criminal in national laws.[320] The law in civilised countries which are not Member states can be taken into account in determining the applicability of the exception.

General restrictions on the rights and freedoms contained in Arts 8–11

These Articles have a second paragraph enumerating certain restrictions on the primary right. The interests covered by the restrictions are largely the same: national security, protection of morals, the rights of others, public safety. As indicated above, the state is allowed a 'margin of appreciation' – a degree of discretion – as to the measures needed to protect the particular interest.[321]

To be justified, state interference with Arts 8–11 guarantees must be prescribed by law, have a legitimate aim, be necessary in a democratic society and be applied in a non-discriminatory fashion. In most cases under these Articles, Strasbourg's main concern has been with the 'necessary in a democratic society' requirement; the notion of 'prescribed by law' has been focused upon to some extent, but always with the result that it has been found to be satisfied. The 'legitimate aim' requirement will normally be readily satisfied; as Harris, O'Boyle and Warbrick point out, the grounds for interference are so wide that 'the state can usually make a plausible case that it did have a good reason for interfering with the right'.[322] The provision against non-discrimination arises under Art 14 and it is potentially very significant.[323]

The 'prescribed by law' requirement means that the restriction must be in accordance with a rule of national law which satisfies the Convention meaning of 'law'. Also, the law on which the restriction is based is aimed at protecting one of the interests listed in para 2; in other words, the restriction falls within one of the exceptions. Interpreting 'prescribed by law' in *Sunday Times v UK*,[324] the European Court of Human Rights found that 'the law must be adequately accessible' and 'a norm cannot be regarded as a "law" unless it is formulated with sufficient precision to enable the citizen to regulate his conduct'. This finding has been flexibly applied; for example, in *Rai, Allmond and 'Negotiate Now' v UK*,[325] the Commission had to consider the ban on public demonstrations or meetings concerning Northern Ireland in Trafalgar Square. The ban was the subject of a statement in the House of Commons and many refusals of demonstrations had been made subsequent to it. The Commission found that the ban was sufficiently prescribed by law: 'It is compatible with the requirements of foreseeability that terms which are on their face general and unlimited are explained by executive or administrative statements, since it is the provision of sufficiently precise guidance to individuals . . . rather than the source of that guidance which is of relevance.'[326] In

---

320 See, generally, Beddard, R, 'The rights of the criminal under Article 7 ECHR' (1996) ELR 3.
321 See above, pp 36–39.
322 *Law of the European Convention on Human Rights*, 1995, p 290.
323 See below, pp 108–9.
324 A 30, para 49 (1979).
325 81-A D & R 46 (1995).
326 Ibid, p 152. The power in question arose from the Trafalgar Square Regulations 1952 SI 1952/776 para 3 made under the Parks Regulation (Amendment) Act 1926. The Act allowed the Secretary of State to 'make any regulations considered necessary . . . for the preservation of order . . .' in the parks.

Steel and Others v UK[327] the Commission introduced a very significant qualification: 'The level of precision required depends to a considerable degree on the content of the instrument, the field it is designed to cover, and the number and status of those to whom it is addressed.'[328] Although the term 'margin of appreciation' was not used, this finding appears to allow the Member state a certain leeway in relation to the 'prescribed by law' requirement.

The Court has interpreted 'necessary in a democratic society' as meaning that: 'an interference corresponds to a pressing social need and, in particular, that it is proportionate to the legitimate aim pursued'.[329] Thus, in the particular instance, it can be said that the interference is necessary in the sense that it is concerned with a particular restriction such as the protection of morals, and in the particular case, there is a real need to protect morals – a pressing social need – as opposed to an unclear or weak danger to morals. Further, the interference is in proportion to the aim pursued; in other words, it does not go further than is needed, bearing in mind the objective in question.

But, the doctrine of proportionality is strongly linked to the principle of the margin of appreciation: the Court has stated that the role of the Convention in protecting human rights is subsidiary to the role of the national legal system[330] and that since the state is better placed than the international judge to balance individual rights against general societal interests, Strasbourg will operate a restrained review of the balance struck. The notion of a margin of appreciation conceded to states permeates the Art 8(2), 9(2), 10(2) and 11(2) jurisprudence, although it has not influenced the interpretation of the substantive rights.

Art 8: Right to respect for 'privacy'

(1) Everyone has the right to respect for his private and family life, his home and his correspondence.

(2) There shall be no interference by a public authority with the exercise of this right except such as is in accordance with the law and is necessary in a democratic society in the interests of national security, public safety or the economic well-being of the country, for the prevention of disorder or crime, for the protection of health or morals, or for the protection of the rights and freedoms of others.

Article 8 seems to cover four different areas, suggesting that, for example, private life can be distinguished from family life. However, the case law suggests that these rights usually need not be clearly distinguished from each other.[331] There will tend to be a clear overlap between them; for example, it is often unnecessary to define 'family',

---

327 (1998) 28 EHRR 603.
328 Paragraph 145. The Commission based these findings on the judgments of the Court in *Chorherr v Austria* Series A 266-B, para 23 (1993) and in *Cantoni v France*, para 35 (1996) 96 ECHR 52.
329 *Olsson v Sweden*, A 130, para 67 (1988).
330 *Handyside v UK*, A 24, para 48 (1976).
331 In *Mialhe v France* (1993) 16 EHRR 332 it was made clear that the four aspects of private life tend to constitute overlapping concepts.

because the factual situation might so obviously fall within the term 'private'. The inclusion of the wide (and undefined) term 'private' means that rights other than those arising from the home, family life and correspondence may fall within Art 8.

It should be noted that Art 8 only provides right to respect for private life, etc. Thus, the extent of the respect required can vary to an extent in view of the various practices in the different states. In contrast to Art 10, finding that a claim is covered by para 1 is not a simple matter: attention cannot merely focus on the exceptions. The negative obligation – to refrain from interference – is central,[332] but a number of requirements to take positive action have been accommodated within Art 8. Clayton and Tomlinson posit a number of different forms of such positive action.[333] The first arises where the applicant suffers from state inaction.[334] In *McGinley and Egan v UK*[335] the government was engaging in activities inherently dangerous to the health of the applicant. It was found that Art 8 requires that effective procedures should be in place to ensure that all the relevant information was made available.

A wide range of issues may be accommodated within the right to respect for private life. Other Convention guarantees, particularly those of Art 3, may also be relevant. The right to respect for family life, as the discussion below indicates, is a narrower concept, with which the right to respect for private life overlaps. The European Court of Human Rights has clearly recognised that private life covers individual, personal choices: *Dudgeon v UK*.[336] Equally, respect for family life covers freedom of parental choice,[337] within limits created by the opposing interests of the child.[338] Thus, the interest of individuals in exercising freedom of choice in decisions as to the disposal of or control over the body may be protected. Usually the individual is, in effect, asking the state to leave him or her alone to make such decisions in order to preserve autonomy. This is a negative obligation which is clearly within the scope of Art 8 where the interference can be viewed as arbitrary.[339]

In some instances, however, the individual will be requiring the assistance of the authorities in ensuring that he or she is able to exercise autonomy. The scope for the acceptance of positive obligations as an aspect of respect for private or family life is less wide. But the European Court has characterised claims that the state is under an obligation to provide such assistance as necessary in order to demonstrate respect for private or family life.[340] In other words, the state may be obliged to provide

332   See, e.g., *Gul v Switzerland* (1996) 22 EHRR 93, para 38.
333   *The Law of Human Rights*, 2000, pp 822–24.
334   The transsexual cases in which applicants have argued that they should be allowed to have their birth certificates changed to indicate their current gender (discussed in Chapter 15, p 1515) provide an example; those against the UK failed until *Goodwin v UK* in 2002, discussed below. The finding of a breach in *B v France* (1992) 16 EHRR 1 occurred since the Court took into account the fact that the applicant was likely to be asked to reveal her birth certificate more often than in the UK.
335   (1998) 27 EHRR 1.
336   (1982) 4 EHRR 149.
337   See *Hoffman v Austria* (1993) 17 EHRR 293; *X v Netherlands* (1974) 2 DR 118.
338   See *Rieme v Sweden* (1992) 16 EHRR 155.
339   See *Belgian Linguistics (No 2)* (1968) 1 EHRR 252, para 7; *X and Y v Netherlands* (1985) 8 EHRR 235; *Hokkanen v Finland* (1994) 19 EHRR 139.
340   *X v UK* Appl No 7154/75; 14 D & R 31, p 32 (1978); *Marckx v Belgium* (1979) 2 EHRR 330, para 31. See also Chapter 9, pp 813 *et seq.*

legal protection for the individual even when the public authorities are not themselves responsible for an interference with the Art 8 right, although given that the state merely has to show 'respect', its discretion in determining the means of so doing tends to be increased.[341]

Where a positive obligation is claimed, Strasbourg will afford a wide margin of appreciation. The margin can widen or narrow depending on the circumstances of the case, resulting in a variation of the intensity of the Court's review of the state's actions. Two further factors may also be present in this context and may influence Strasbourg in conceding a particularly wide margin of appreciation where a complainant seeks to lay a positive obligation on the state. First, where the harm complained of flows from the action of a private party, rather than the state itself, so that the so-called 'horizontal effect' of the Convention is in issue and, second, where there is a potential conflict with another Convention right. Clearly, these factors may arise independently of each other. In a number of key decisions under Art 8 discussed in Chapter 9, all three were present,[342] which may explain the somewhat unsatisfactory and misleading nature of some of the judgments given, although as Chapter 9 makes clear, a change of stance is now evident.[343] These factors may also arise in this context and may explain the cautious nature of certain of the decisions.

Thus the state may be found to be under a duty to act positively to prevent an interference with the Art 8 guarantees by another private individual. The pollution cases mentioned below[344] provide examples in which it was found that the state had a duty to act to prevent or curb the pollution and to ensure that information regarding the dangers was available. Further, the positive obligation may require a positive act by private persons.[345]

The question of the extent to which positive obligations are recognised under Art 8 is pursued further in this book, especially in Chapter 9.[346] But clearly, there will be limitations. In *Botta v Italy*[347] it was found that although a positive obligation might arise in the circumstances, a fair balance had to be struck: the obligations did not extend to providing a disabled person with access to the beach and sea distant from a holiday residence. In *Barreto v Portugal*[348] no breach was found where each family was not provided with its own home or where a landlord could not recover the possession of rented accommodation.

---

341 See *JS v UK* Appl No 191173/91, 3 January 1993. The Commission rejected an application in which it was alleged that an insurance company had carried out a clandestine surveillance in investigating a claim.

342 All three were present in: *Winer v UK* (1986) 48 IR 154; *Spencer v UK* (1998) 25 EHRR CD 105, and *N v Portugal* Appl No 20683/92, 20 February 1995; however, the third was influential only in *Winer*.

343 See *Von Hannover*, pp 818–24.

344 See the cases of *Guerra v Italy* (1998) 26 EHRR 375 and Lopez Ostra, (1994) 20 EHRR.

345 In *Hokkanen v Finland* (1994) 19 EHRLR 139 it was found that a private data collection firm must grant access to its records.

346 See pp 814–18.

347 (1998) 26 EHRR 241.

348 (1996) 26 EHRLR 214.

Exceptions and justification under Art 8(2)

There must be an 'interference' by the public authorities. But, as the discussion above indicates, this can include the failure to carry out a positive obligation. In the absence of a positive obligation, however, a failure to act would not constitute an interference.[349] Where an interference occurs, proper safeguards must be in place to protect individuals from arbitrary interference; there must be a legal framework which satisfies the 'in accordance with the law' test and strict limits must be placed on the power conferred.[350] Where very intimate aspects of private life are involved, very particular reasons for the interference must be adduced.[351]

If the exception in respect of national security is invoked, the state may find that is relatively easy to justify the interference.[352] But where interferences, such as searches or surveillance, occur in respect of criminal activity, a higher standard will be required. Thus, judicial authorisation of searches or surveillance may be required.[353] Where a grave invasion of privacy has occurred, judicial authorisation and a warrant may not be enough.[354] This matter is pursued in Chapter 11.[355]

The head 'the economic well-being of the country' is unusual; it does not appear in para 2 of Art 8's companion Articles, Arts 9–11. A number of interferences have been found to be justified under this head.[356] In *MS v Sweden*[357] the obtaining of access to medical records in order to assess a social security claim was found to be justified.

Justification under the heads 'for the prevention of disorder or crime' depends on the seriousness of the crime or threat to disorder, the nature and extent of the interference and the question whether a judicial warrant has been obtained. In *Camenzind*[358] the limited scope of the search and the procedures in place meant that the search was proportionate to the aim of preventing crime. In *Murray v UK*[359] the entry and search of Mrs Murray's home was not disproportionate to that aim, bearing in mind her links to terrorism.

In contrast to the stance taken under Art 10(2),[360] the exception for the protection of morals has received a restrictive interpretation. The Court has required an especially significant justification in order to be satisfied as to proportionality.[361] This exception is sometimes also raised where the exception in respect of the rights of others is invoked especially in relation to family life, where the protection of health may also be in issue. For example, in *Olsson v Sweden*,[362] the decision to take three children into care was an interference with family life. However, it could be justified as being for the protection of the health and the rights of the child.

---

349 *Airey v Ireland* (1979) 2 EHRR 305.
350 *Camenzind v Switzerland*, RJD 1997-III 2880.
351 *Lustig-Prean v UK* (1999) 7 BHRC 65; *Smith and Grady v UK* (2000) 29 EHRLR 493.
352 See *Leander v Sweden* (1987) 9 EHRR 433.
353 *Funke v France* (1993) 16 EHRR 297.
354 *Niemietz v Germany* (1992) 16 EHRR 97.
355 See pp 1042–46.
356 Eg *Powell v UK* (1990) 12 EHRR 355.
357 RJD 1997-IV 1437.
358 See above, fn 350.
359 (1994) 19 EHRR 193.
360 See Chapter 6, pp 463–67.
361 See *Norris v Ireland* (1988) 13 EHRR 186 and *Dudgeon v UK* (1981) 4 EHRR 149.
362 (1988) 11 EHRR 259.

The concept of respect for private life

In *Niemietz v Germany*,[363] the Court said:

> 'It would be too restrictive to limit the notion [of private life] to an "inner circle" in which the individual may live his own personal life as he chooses and to exclude therefrom entirely the outside world not encompassed within that circle. Respect for private life must also comprise to a certain degree the right to establish and develop relationships with other human beings.'

As Harris, O'Boyle and Warbrick observe: 'this extends the concept of private life beyond the narrower confines of the Anglo-American idea of privacy, with its emphasis on the secrecy of personal information and seclusion.'[364] Thus, 'private life' appears to encompass a widening range of protected interests, but this development has been accompanied by a reluctance of the Court to insist on a narrow margin of appreciation when considering what is demanded of states by the notions of 'respect' for private life and by the necessity of interferences with privacy.

Privacy of personal information

Respect for the privacy of personal information clearly falls within the notion of private life, but the Court has approached this aspect cautiously, tending to be satisfied if a procedure is in place allowing the interest in such control to be weighed up against a competing interest. Thus, in *Gaskin v UK*,[365] the interest of the applicant in obtaining access to the files relating to his childhood in care had to be weighed up against the interest of the contributors to it in maintaining confidentiality, because this interference with privacy had a legitimate aim under the 'rights of others' exception. It was held that the responsible authority did not have a procedure available for weighing the two. Consequently, the procedure automatically preferred the contributors and that was disproportionate to the aim of protecting confidentiality and therefore could not be 'necessary in a democratic society'.

The opposite result was reached, but by a similar route, in *Klass v Federal Republic of Germany*,[366] brought in respect of telephone tapping. It was found that although telephone tapping constituted an interference with a person's private life, it could be justified as being in the interests of national security and there were sufficient controls in place (permission had to be given by a minister applying certain criteria including that of 'reasonable suspicion') to ensure that the power was not abused. In the similar *Malone* case,[367] however, there were no such controls in place and a breach of Art 8 was therefore found, which led to the introduction of the Interception of Communications Act 1985. A similar path was followed in *Leander v Sweden*[368] in respect of a complaint

---

363 (1992) 16 EHRR 97, A 251-B, para 29 (1992).
364 *Law of the European Convention on Human Rights*, 1995, p 304.
365 (1990) 12 EHRR 36.
366 (1978) 2 EHRR 214; see also *Ludi v Switzerland* (1993) 15 EHRR 173.
367 Report of 17 December 1982, A 82; (1984) 7 EHRR 14. See below, p 1033.
368 Judgment of 26 March 1987, A 116; (1987) 9 EHRR 443. See also to similar effect *Ebchester v UK* (1993) 18 EHRR CD 72.

that information about the applicant had been stored on a secret police register for national security purposes and released to the navy so that it could vet persons who might be subversive. The applicant complained that he had had no opportunity of challenging the information, but the Court found that as there were remedies in place, albeit of a limited nature, to address such grievances, Art 8 had not been breached because the national security exception could apply. Again, in *Harman and Hewitt v UK*[369] a breach of Art 8 was found as there was no means of challenging the secret directive which had allowed the storage of information on the applicants. In *Murray v UK*,[370] the taking of a photo of the applicant after arrest at an army centre was found to constitute an interference with her Art 8 right to respect for her private life. The notion that personal information should remain private even outside obviously private spaces was strongly indicated in *Niemietz v Germany*.[371]

Bodily integrity and automony

Under Art 8, bodily privacy has a number of aspects. The European Court of Human Rights adopted a broad definition of privacy in *X and Y v Netherlands*:[372]

> [the concept of] private life . . . covers the physical integrity . . . of the person . . . Art 8 does not merely compel the State to abstain from . . . interference [with the individual]: in addition to this primarily negative undertaking, there may be positive obligations inherent in effective respect for private . . . life.[373]

Thus, Art 8 recognises that individuals have an interest in preventing or controlling physical intrusions on the body and they may therefore lay claim to a negative right to be 'left alone' in a physical sense. Such a right might also encompass positive claims on the state to ensure that bodily integrity is not infringed. Thus, the state may fail to respect privacy if it fails to prevent infringement of it by others or if in itself it allows such infringement.

Interference with bodily integrity may breach the guarantee of freedom from degrading punishment under Art 3 of the European Convention on Human Rights and the guarantee of respect for privacy under Art 8. In general, any compulsory physical treatment of an individual will constitute an interference with respect for private life.[374] We will return below to the question as to the level of consensual bodily harm which will be forbidden.

Certain forms of physical punishment may be seen as an unjustified intrusion into bodily integrity. Corporal punishment was outlawed in UK state schools[375] after the decision of the European Court of Human Rights in *Campbell and Cosans v UK*,[376]

---

369 (1992) 14 EHRR 657.
370 (1994) 19 EHRR 193; cf *Friedl v Austria* (1995) 21 EHRR 83.
371 (1992) 16 EHRR 97. The case concerned a search of a lawyer's office.
372 (1985) 8 EHRR 235.
373 *Ibid*, paras 22 and 23.
374 *X v Austria* 18 D & R 154 (1979).
375 Under the Education (No 2) Act 1986.
376 (1984) 2 EHRR 293.

which was determined not on the basis of Arts 3 or 8 but under Art 2 of the First Protocol, which protects the right of parents to have their children educated according to their own philosophical convictions. However, corporal punishment in private schools was not outlawed, and in *Costello-Roberts v UK*[377] the European Court of Human Rights found that the UK had a responsibility to ensure that school discipline was compatible with the Convention even though the treatment in question was administered in an institution independent of the state. However, although the Court considered that there might be circumstances in which Art 8 could be regarded as affording protection to physical integrity, which would be broader than that afforded by Art 3, in the particular circumstances the adverse effect on the complainant was insufficient to amount to an invasion of privacy. The Court took into account the 'public' context in which the punishment had occurred and its relatively trivial nature. Corporal punishment in both private and public sector schools was abolished in the UK.[378]

Parents or persons with parental responsibility may also use force to discipline a child. In *A v UK*[379] the applicant was a nine year old who had been beaten by his stepfather with a garden cane. The stepfather was acquitted of assault causing bodily harm after the jury were instructed that the crime did not include reasonable chastisement by a parent. It was found that the beating fell within Art 3 and that it was incumbent on states to take measures to ensure that individuals within their jurisdiction are not subject to Art 3 treatment. Had the beating been less severe, a breach of Art 8 rather than Art 3 might have been found. It is clear that, by definition, beating amounting to Art 3 treatment cannot be viewed as reasonable and therefore, in future, the defence of reasonable chastisement could not cover the degree of force used in *A*.

Under Art 8, physical intrusions on the bodily integrity of individuals by state agents may be justified if the requirements of Art 8(2) are satisfied. Equally, UK law also recognises a need to create a balance between the interest of the state in allowing physical interference with individuals for various purposes, including the prevention of crime and the interest of the individual in preserving his or her bodily integrity. UK law determines that in certain circumstances, bodily privacy may give way to other interests. Articles 3 and 8 together provide substantive guarantees against certain types of custodial ill-treatment. But, clearly, Art 3 will cover only the grossest instances of ill-treatment. It is notable that the Convention contains no provision equivalent to that under Art 10 of the International Covenant on Civil and Political Rights which provides 'persons deprived of their liberty shall be treated with humanity and with respect for the inherent dignity of the human person'.

In the *Greek* case,[380] the conditions of detention were found to amount to inhuman treatment due to overcrowding, inadequate food, sleeping arrangements, heating, toilets and provision for external contacts. Failure to obtain medical treatment after a forcible arrest was found to infringe Art 3 in *Hurtado v Switzerland*.[381] Conduct which grossly

---

377 (1993) 19 EHRR 112; A 247-C.
378 Education Act 1996, s 548, as substituted by School Standards and Framework Act 1998, s 131.
379 (1999) 27 EHRR 611.
380 12 YB 1 (1969) Com Rep.
381 A 280-A (1994) Com Rep.

humiliates is degrading treatment contrary to Art 3.[382] Article 8 may be viewed as overlapping, to an extent, with Art 3, but it also covers some matters which would not be serious enough to amount to Art 3 treatment.[383] In order to bring Art 8 into play, it must be found that its protection extends to the matter in question – in this context, it would probably be that 'private or family life' is affected. [384] Certain conditions or incidents of detention may fall outside Art 8, such as a failure to provide an interpreter. But a failure to allow a juvenile or a mentally disturbed person to consult privately with a member of his or her family, acting as an appropriate adult, might be viewed as an interference with either private or family life.

Personal autonomy has been recognised for some time in the USA as strongly linked to privacy. In *Doe v Bolton*,[385] Douglas J said that 'the right to privacy means freedom of choice in the basic decisions of one's life respecting marriage, divorce, procreation, contraception, education and upbringing of children'. At Strasbourg, the value of personal autonomy has also received quite clear recognition.[386] Personal autonomy connotes an interest not only in preventing physical intrusion by others, but also with the extent to which the law allows an individual a degree of control over his or her own body.

But the choice of adults as to the disposal of their own bodies is highly circumscribed. In the Member states, although in general suicide is no longer a crime, in the vast majority of Member states aiding and abetting suicide has not been de-criminalised. Thus, for example, a relative of a person who is unable to commit suicide because she is incapacitated through illness cannot help her to die in order to avoid severe pain and suffering without risking prosecution for murder or manslaughter. Euthanasia is legal in Holland[387] and in Belgium. It is not recognised in UK law,[388] except in the very narrow sense that allowing a patient in a persistent vegetative state to die will be acceptable if it can be said, objectively speaking, to be in his or her best interests

---

382 The *Greek* case, 12 YB 1 (1969) Com Rep.
383 See the findings in the corporal punishment case of *Costello-Roberts v UK* (1993) 19 EHRR 112 (above). The Court found that the treatment was not severe enough to fall within Art 3; in the particular circumstances it did not fall within Art 8, but the Court considered that there might be circumstances in which Art 8 could be viewed as affording a wider protection to physical integrity than that which is afforded by Art 3.
384 Code of Practice A (2006) made under the Police and Criminal Evidence Act 1984 (PACE), provides safeguards for a search by police officers of more than outer clothing which appear to be coterminous with the right to respect for privacy under Art 8. There are also Code provisions protecting persons during intimate and strip searches. The domestic relationship between Code provisions and Art 8 is discussed in Chapter 11, pp 1107, 1131, 1176–80
385 (1973) 410 US 179; (1973) 35 L E 2d 201.
386 *Dudgeon v UK* (1982) 4 EHRR 149; *Lustig-Prean v UK* (1999) 7 BHRC 65. For discussion, see Feldman, op. cit., fn 1.
387 The law in The Netherlands has been severely criticised: see Keown, J, 'The law and practice of euthanasia in the Netherlands' [1992] 108 LQR 51–78. In 30 years Holland has moved from assisted suicide to euthanasia, from euthanasia of people who are terminally ill to euthanasia of those who are chronically ill, from euthanasia for physical illness to euthanasia for mental illness, from euthanasia for mental illness to euthanasia for psychological distress or mental suffering, and from voluntary euthanasia to involuntary euthanasia, termed in Holland 'termination of the patient without explicit request'. For discussion of the moral issues see Dworkin, R, *Life's Dominion*, 1993, HarperCollins.
388 For discussion, see Orst, S, 'Conceptions of the euthanasia phenomenon' [2000] JCIVLIB 155.

because no improvement can be expected.[389] Also, under the so called 'double effect' doctrine, a doctor will not be guilty of murder if he or she administers a very high level of a pain-killing drug which he or she knows is likely to cause death so long as the primary intention is to relieve pain.[390] A conflict with Art 2 might arise[391] if euthanasia was allowed in other situations; it has merely been found at Strasbourg that passively allowing a person to die need not attract criminal liability in order to satisfy Art 2.[392] The consent of the victim would be irrelevant; euthanasia is not covered by any of the Art 2 exceptions.

In 2001, an action was brought in the UK under the HRA against the Director of Public Prosecutions (DPP) in relation to his decision that a husband who wishes to help his wife to die once her terminal Motor Neurone Disease reaches a certain stage would be liable to the risk of prosecution.[393] The woman wanted a declaration that her husband would not be prosecuted and argued that the state has a responsibility to make such a declaration since otherwise Arts 3 and 8 would be breached. The claim was backed by the UK group *Liberty*. The claim was rejected by the House of Lords and Diane Pretty took the case to Strasbourg.[394] She complained under a number of Articles, including Art 8. She relied on Art 8 in arguing that the Article explicitly recognises the right to self-determination, and on Art 9, complaining that the failure to give the undertaking and provide a lawful scheme for allowing assisted suicide violated her right to manifest her beliefs. Under Art 14, she argued that the blanket prohibition on assisted suicide discriminates against those who are unable to commit suicide without assistance, whereas the able-bodied are able to exercise the right to die, under domestic law. She also complained, under Art 2 of the Convention, that it is for the individual to choose whether to live and that the right to die is the corollary of the right to live and also protected. Accordingly, she argued that there is a positive obligation on the state to provide a scheme in domestic law to enable her to exercise that right. She also complained under Art 3 that the UK Government is obliged not only to refrain from inflicting inhuman and degrading treatment itself, but also to take positive steps to protect persons within its jurisdiction from being subjected to such treatment. The only effective step available to protect her would be an undertaking not to prosecute her husband if he assisted her to commit suicide.

The Court found that the case fell within the ambit of para 1 of Art 8. The applicant was prevented by law from exercising her choice to avoid what she considered would be an undignified and distressing end to her life. The Court was not prepared to exclude that this constituted an interference with her right to respect for private life as guaranteed under Art 8(1), but reiterated that an interference with the exercise of

---

389 *Airedale NHS Trust v Bland* [1993] AC 789, HL.
390 *Cox* [1992] BMLR 38. In *Moor* (see [2000] J CIV LIB 155), a doctor who had administered a very high dose of diamorphine to an elderly patient who had pleaded with him for a speedy death was charged with murder. He was acquitted on the basis of evidence showing that the double effect doctrine applied, not on the basis of any right to be assisted to die.
391 See pp 42–43.
392 *Widmer v Switzerland*, No 20527/92 (1993), unreported. See also pp 42–43.
393 The claim was rejected on appeal to the HL: *R (on the application of Diane Pretty) v DPP and Secretary of State for the Home Dept* [2001] UKHL 61.
394 *Pretty v UK* (2002), 23 HRLJ 194.

an Art 8 right would not be compatible with Art 8(2) unless it was 'in accordance with the law'; had an aim or aims that was or were legitimate under that paragraph; and was 'necessary in a democratic society' to attain such aim or aims. The only issue arising from the arguments of the parties was the necessity of any interference and those arguments had focused on its proportionality. In this connection the applicant had attacked the blanket nature of the ban on assisted suicide. The Court found, in agreement with the House of Lords, that states were entitled to regulate through the operation of the general criminal law activities which were detrimental to the life and safety of other individuals. The law in issue in this case, S 2 of the Suicide Act 1961, was designed, it found, to safeguard life by protecting the weak and vulnerable and especially those who were not in a condition to take informed decisions against acts intended to end life or to assist in ending life.

The Court did not consider that the blanket nature of the ban on assisted suicide was disproportionate. The government had stated that flexibility was provided for in individual cases by the fact that consent was needed from the DPP to bring a prosecution and by the fact that a maximum sentence was provided, allowing lesser penalties to be imposed as appropriate. It did not, the Court found, appear to be arbitrary for the law to reflect the importance of the right to life by prohibiting assisted suicide while providing for a system of enforcement and adjudication which allowed due regard to be given in each particular case to the public interest in bringing a prosecution, as well as to the fair and proper requirements of retribution and deterrence. Further, in the circumstances the Court did not find anything disproportionate in the refusal of the DPP to give an advance undertaking that no prosecution would be brought against the applicant's husband. Strong arguments based on the rule of law could be raised against any claim by the executive to exempt individuals or classes of individuals from the operation of the law. In any event, the seriousness of the act for which immunity was claimed was such that the decision of the DPP to refuse the undertaking sought could not be said to be arbitrary or unreasonable. The Court concluded that the interference could be justified as 'necessary in a democratic society' for the protection of the rights of others, and that there had therefore been no violation of Art 8.

The Court observed that not all opinions or convictions constituted beliefs as protected by Art 9(1). The applicant's claims did not involve a form of manifestation of a religion or belief, through worship, teaching, practice or observance as described in the second sentence of the first paragraph. The term 'practice' did not cover each act which was motivated or influenced by a religion or belief. To the extent that the applicant's views reflected her commitment to the principle of personal autonomy, her claim was a restatement of the complaint raised under Art 8. The Court concluded that there had been no violation of Art 9 since the claim was not covered by para 1.

For the purposes of Art 14 the Court reiterated that a difference in treatment between persons in analogous or relevantly similar positions was discriminatory if it had no objective and reasonable justification, that is if it did not pursue a legitimate aim or if there was not a reasonable relationship of proportionality between the means employed and the aim sought to be realised. Discrimination could also arise where states, without an objective and reasonable justification, failed to treat differently persons whose situations were significantly different. There was, in the Court's view, objective and reasonable justification for not distinguishing in law between those who were and those who were not physically capable of committing suicide. Cogent reasons existed for not seeking to distinguish between those who were able and those who were unable to commit suicide unaided. The borderline between the two categories would often be a very fine one and to seek to build into the law an exemption for those judged to be incapable of committing suicide would seriously undermine the protection of life which the 1961 Act was intended to safeguard and greatly increase the risk of abuse. Thus it was found that there had been no violation of Art 14.

As regards Art 2 the Court reiterated that it safeguarded the right to life, without which enjoyment of any of the other rights and freedoms in the Convention was rendered nugatory. It covered not only intentional killing, but also the situations where it was permitted to use force which resulted, as an unintended outcome, in the deprivation of life. The Court stated that it had held that the first sentence of Art 2(1) enjoined states not only to refrain from the intentional and unlawful taking of life, but also to take appropriate steps to safeguard the lives of those within its jurisdiction. This obligation might also imply in certain well-defined circumstances a positive obligation on the authorities to take preventive operational measures to protect an individual whose life was at risk from the criminal acts of another individual.

In its case law in this area the Court stated that it had placed consistent emphasis on the obligation of the state to protect life. In these circumstances it was not persuaded that 'the right to life' guaranteed in Art 2 could be interpreted as involving a negative aspect. Article 2 could not, without a distortion of language, be interpreted as conferring the diametrically opposite right, namely a right to die; nor could it create a right to self-determination in the sense of conferring on an individual the entitlement to choose death rather than life. The Court accordingly found that no right to die, whether at the hands of a third person or with the assistance of a public authority, could be derived from Art 2. There had therefore been no violation of that provision.

As regards Art 3, it was, the Court noted, beyond dispute that the respondent government had not, themselves, inflicted any ill-treatment on the applicant. Nor was there any complaint that the applicant was not receiving adequate care from the state medical authorities. The applicant had claimed rather that the refusal of the DPP to give an undertaking not to prosecute her husband if he assisted her to commit suicide and the criminal law prohibition on assisted suicide disclosed inhuman and degrading treatment for which the state was responsible. This claim however placed a new and extended construction on the concept of treatment. While the Court reiterated that it had to take a dynamic and flexible approach to the interpretation of the Convention, any interpretation had also to accord with the fundamental objectives of the Convention and its coherence as a system of human rights protection. Article 3 had to be construed in harmony with Art 2. Article 2 was first and foremost a prohibition on the use of lethal force or other conduct which might lead to the death of a human being and did not confer any claim on an individual to require a state to permit or facilitate his or her death. The Court sympathised with the applicant's apprehension that without the possibility of ending her life she faced the prospect of a distressing death. Nonetheless, the positive obligation on the part of the state which had been invoked would require that the state sanction actions intended to terminate life, an obligation that could not be derived from Art 3. The Court therefore concluded that no positive obligation arose under Art 3 in this context and that there had, accordingly, been no violation of that provision.

It may be noted that a parallel action was brought in a Canadian case, *Rodriguez v British Columbia*.[395] A similar argument was received sympathetically; it was found that the Criminal Code prohibition on aiding and abetting suicide did infringe her right to security of the person. However, the application failed on the basis that it did not do so in breach of the principles of fundamental justice, the exception clause.

The European Court of Human Rights has so far avoided the question whether the foetus is protected by Art 2 – in other words, whether it would come within the term 'everyone'. In *Open Door Counselling v Ireland* the Court deliberately left open the possibility that Art 2 might place some restrictions on abortion.[396] If it was to find that the foetus is protected, the result, in terms of changes to almost all the state parties' laws on abortion, would be immense, since only abortion falling within the exceptions to Art 2 would be permitted. There would be an immense increase in dangerous illegal abortions and women would travel outside the Member states for abortions, leading to an increase in later terminations. It has been found in the context of national legislation on abortion that the woman seeking abortion can rely on Arts 2 and 8, since her life and physical and mental health are in question.[397]

The Commission has, however, committed itself to the view that the foetus is not protected under Art 2. In *H v Norway*[398] the Commission found that the lawful abortion of a 14-week foetus on social grounds did not breach Art 2. It took this stance partly on the basis that otherwise, a conflict with the mother's Art 8 rights might arise, and partly because, since the state Parties' laws on abortion differ considerably from each other, a wide margin of discretion should be allowed. There are strong reasons for considering that a question concerning an irreconcilable conflict of moral views should be left to the national legislatures.[399] The stance taken in a number of other jurisdictions suggests that where this human rights issue comes before the highest national courts, the woman's right to security of the person and to freedom of choice is viewed as paramount[400] and it has been found that the right to life does not extend to the foetus.[401]

Sexual autonomy

Protection for personal information may be regarded as part of the 'core' of the concept of respect for private life, but as the Court has made clear in a number of decisions, aspects of relations with others will also fall within the concept. The Court has made it clear that the choice to have sexual relations with others falls within Art 8. In this sphere, it is suggested that the Court has gradually abandoned its initially cautious approach.

---

395 (1993) 85 CCC (3d) 15.

396 ECtHR, Judgment of 29 October 1992; (1992) 15 EHRR 244. For comment, see (1992) 142 NLJ 1696.

397 *X v UK*, Appl No 8416/78; 19 D & R 244 (1980).

398 Appl No 17004/90 (1992) 73 DR 155.

399 See pp 280–85. For discussion, see Dworkin, R, *Life's Dominion*, 1993.

400 See the decision of the Canadian Supreme Court in *Morgentaler v R* [1988] 1 SCR 60; the decision of the US Supreme Court in *Planned Parenthood of Southeastern Pennsylvania v Casey* (1992) 505 US 833.

401 *Christian Lawyers Assoc of South Africa v The Minister of Health* 1998 (11) BCLR 1434; *Borowski v AG of Canada* (1987) 39 DLR (4th) 731.

In *Dudgeon*,[402] the Northern Ireland prohibition of homosexual intercourse was found to breach Art 8: however, this case concerned a gross interference with privacy since it allowed the applicant no means at all of expressing his sexual preference without committing a criminal offence. In 1984,[403] the Commission declared inadmissible an application challenging s 66 of the Army Act 1955, which governs conviction for homosexual practices in the armed forces, on the basis that it could be justified under the prevention of disorder or protection of morals clauses.[404] That stance has now been abandoned, and the Court has taken a much more interventionist stance in relation to the sexual autonomy of homosexuals.[405]

Dudgeon v UK[406] concerned the law in Northern Ireland (Offences Against the Person Act 1861), which made buggery between consenting males of any age a crime. Dudgeon, who was suspected of homosexual activities, was arrested on that basis and questioned, but the police decided not to prosecute. He applied to the European Commission on the grounds of a breach of the right of respect for private life under Art 8. The European Court of Human Rights held that the legislation in question constituted a continuing interference with his private life, which included his sexual life. He was forced either to abstain from sexual relations completely, or to commit a crime. Clearly, there had been an interference with his private life; the question was whether the interference was necessary in order to protect morals. The Court considered that some regulation of homosexual activity was acceptable; the question was what was necessary in a democratic society. The Court took into account the doctrine of the margin of appreciation, as considered in the *Handyside* case,[407] where it was held that state authorities were in the best position to judge the requirements of morals. However, the Court found that the instant case concerned a very intimate aspect of private life. A restriction on a Convention right cannot be regarded as necessary unless it is proportionate to the aim pursued. In the instant case, there was a grave detrimental interference with the applicant's private life while, on the other hand, there was little evidence of damage to morals. The law had not been enforced and no evidence had been adduced to show that this had been harmful to moral standards. So the aim of the restriction was not proportional to the damage done to the applicant's privacy and, therefore, the invasion of privacy went beyond what was needed. It was found unnecessary since the prohibition had not in fact been used in recent times and no detriment to morals had apparently resulted. Northern Ireland amended the relevant

---

402 Judgment of 22 October 1981, A 45; (1982) 4 EHRR 149.
403 *B v UK* 34 D & R 68 (1983); (1983) 6 EHRR 354; A 9237/81.
404 The charges had involved a soldier under 21. Note that the Select Committee on the Armed Forces Bill 1990–91 recommended that s 66 should be replaced (para 41, p xiv). See, now, *Smith and Grady v UK* (2000) 29 EHRR 493 in which it was found that the ban breached Art 8. The ban is no longer being applied; see Chapter 15, pp 1520.
405 See Chapter 15, p 1520 for discussion of *Lustig-Prean v UK* (1999) 29 EHRR 548 in which it was found that the army ban breached Art 8; see also Chapter 12, pp 1207–8, and *Sutherland v UK*, Appl. no 25186/94 [1997] EHRLR 117, in which an application regarding the age of consent for homosexual relations (8.9.1999) was postponed since the government assured the Commission that the Sexual Offences (Amendment) Bill would proceed equalising the age of consent (see, now, Sexual Offences (Amendment) Act 2000 s 1).
406 (1982) 4 EHRR 149.
407 (1976) 1 EHRR 737.

legislation in consequence,[408] allowing intercourse between consenting males over 21. *Dudgeon* demonstrates that the European Court of Human Rights is prepared to uphold the right of the individual to choose to indulge in homosexual practices[409] and suggests that the term 'private life' in Art 8 may be used to cover a wide range of situations where bodily or sexual privacy is in question.

In the UK s 143 of the Criminal Justice and Public Order Act 1994 amended s 1 of the Sexual Offences Act 1967 to lower the age of consent for homosexual intercourse to 18. The differential ages of consent under s 143 continued to allow discrimination between homosexuals and heterosexuals and between male and female homosexuals. In *Sutherland v UK*[410] s 143 of the 1994 Act was successfully challenged under Art 8 in conjunction with Art 14 on the basis that it allowed discrimination between male and female homosexuals, since the age of consent for female homosexual intercourse is 16 under the criminal law as it stands at present, as indicated above. The Commission found by 14 votes to four that the fixing of a minimum age of consent at 18 as opposed to 16 was a violation of Art 8 and was discriminatory treatment under Art 14. It took into account the fact that many other states have equalised the ages of consent for homosexual and heterosexual acts and further found that the interference could not be justified on the grounds, including that of protecting public morality, put forward under Art 8(2). It appeared that the European Court of Human Rights was prepared to reconsider its remarks on the point in *Dudgeon* since, as indicated above, it tends to take the view that in sensitive matters of this nature, it should hold back until a clear European standard seems to be emerging; at the stage when a trend is clear, but no such standard has emerged, it will tend to invoke the margin of appreciation.[411] Given the changes in the law on this matter in the different Member states, it seemed that such a standard was emerging regarding equalisation of the ages of consent. The decision was postponed when the government assured the Commission that the Sexual Offences (Amendment) Bill would proceed with equalising the age of consent.[412] This was eventually achieved under s 1 of the Sexual Offences (Amendment) Act 2000; the government had to use the Parliament Act 1911 (as amended) procedure in order to pass the Bill against the opposition of the House of Lords.

Despite these changes, the law governing the sexual freedom of homosexuals was still not in accord with Art 8 due to the restrictions on homosexual intercourse which did not apply to heterosexuals.[413] In particular, the law had to be changed so as to allow consenting homosexual intercourse in private between more than two men as a result of the '*Bolton Seven*' case brought against the UK.[414] The applicants were prosecuted in 1998 on the basis of a video which showed them engaging in consensual group sex. They were convicted of gross indecency. One of the men, Williams, and another,

---

408   Homosexual Offences (Northern Ireland) Order 1982. See also *Norris v Ireland* (1991) 13 EHRR 186 which followed *Dudgeon*.
409   Cf the stance of the US Supreme Court in *Bowers v Hardwick* (1986) 478 US 186; for comment see (1988) 138 NLJ 831.
410   Appl No 25186/94; [1997] EHRLR 117.
411   See discussion on this point in relation to transsexuals, below, pp 85–87
412   On 8 September 1999.
413   See further Chapter 6, pp 556–58. For discussion, see Wintemute, R, S*exual Orientation and Human Rights*, 1995, Clarendon, Chapter 4.
414   *ADT v UK* (2000) 2 FLR 697; see the *Guardian*, 27 July 2001.

Connell, admitted to having had sex with one of the other five who was, at the time, six months under 18, the then age of consent. Williams was convicted of buggery, although his suspended sentence was later revoked by the Court of Appeal. At the time of the convictions, the Court was warned that the prosecutions breached Art 8. Five of the men applied to the European Court of Human Rights and, in July 2001, in order to avoid defeat in the Court, the government offered each of them compensation in an out-of-court settlement. The Sexual Offence Act 2003 brought about equalisation of the position. By these incremental steps, legal acceptance of the sexual autonomy of homosexuals was brought about, in the sense of achieving equality with heterosexuals.

In the case of *Brown*,[415] the House of Lords found that a person cannot consent to the infliction of harm amounting to actual bodily harm. However, consent to such harm may negate liability if there is good reason for the harm to be caused. There are a number of activities involving the causing of, or the risk of, consensual harm which have been found to be justified as in the public interest. In *Brown*, a group of sado-masochistic homosexuals had regularly over a period of ten years willingly participated in acts of violence against each other for the sexual pleasure engendered in the giving and receiving of pain. They were charged with causing actual bodily harm contrary to s 47 and with wounding contrary to s 20 of the Offences Against the Person Act 1861 and were convicted. The convictions were upheld by the Court of Appeal which certified the following point of law of general public importance:

> Where A wounds or assaults B occasioning him actual bodily harm in the course of a sado-masochistic encounter, does the prosecution have to prove lack of consent on the part of B before they can establish A's guilt under s 20 and s 47 of the Offences Against the Person Act 1861.

The House of Lords, by a majority of three to two, answered this question in the negative, finding, therefore, that consent could operate only as a defence and would be allowed so to operate only where the public interest would thereby be served. It was found that in a sado-masochistic context, the inflicting of injuries amounting to actual bodily harm could not fall within the category of 'good reason' and therefore, despite the consent of all the participants, the convictions of the defendants were upheld.

The judgments of the majority in the House of Lords are couched in terms which suggest that distaste for the activities in question was a significant influencing factor. Lord Mustill, in the minority in the House of Lords, considered each of the grounds considered by the majority to be in favour of criminalising the activities in question and discounted each of them. These included fear of the spread of AIDS and the possibility that things might get out of hand if activities such as these were allowed. AIDS, as Lord Mustill pointed out, may be spread by consensual buggery, which is legal, rather than by the activities in question. If a person consents to a lesser harm than that which is actually inflicted, the existing law could be used to punish the perpetrator.

It is unclear that any public interest was served by bringing the prosecution: the activities in question were carried on privately, and there was no suggestion that any of

---

415 [1993] 2 WLR 556; [1993] 2 All ER 75; for comment, see (1993) 109 LQR 540; (1994) 20(3) JLS 356.

the 'victims' were coerced into consenting to them: all had apparently chosen freely to participate. No hospital treatment was needed and the police only discovered what had been occurring by chance. Thus, this decision may be criticised for its subjectivity; it is unclear why it is acceptable that boxing contests may be carried out which can result in serious permanent injury or even death, while activities such as those in *Brown* are criminalised although they may result in a lesser degree of harm.[416] An inference which may be drawn is that while boxing, rough horseplay or private heterosexual activities are regarded by some members of the judiciary as acceptable and perhaps 'manly', they have little or no sympathy with, or understanding of, the value of some aspects of sexual expression, especially the sexual expression of homosexuals. The majority in the House of Lords in *Brown* did not appear to regard the decision as allowing an interference with private sexual activity between adults, but rather as an application of the criminal law to offences of violence which had a sexual motive.

Three of the men who were convicted in *Brown* applied to the European Commission on Human Rights, arguing that their convictions were in breach of Art 8 of the Convention,[417] since they constituted an interference with their private life. The Commission found that no violation of Art 8 had occurred and referred the case to the Court, which came to the same conclusion: *Laskey, Jaggard and Brown v UK*.[418] The Court considered that the activities in question could be seen as occurring outside the private sphere: many persons were involved and videos had been taken. However, as the issue of privacy was not in dispute, the Court accepted that an interference with respect for the applicants' private life had occurred.

The question was whether the interference was necessary in a democratic society. It found that the harm was serious, since it concerned genital torture. The state is entitled to regulate the infliction of physical harm, and the level of harm to be tolerated by the state where the victim consents is in the first instance a matter for the state concerned. The activities had the potential to cause harm in the sense that if encouraged, harm, including the spread of AIDS, might occur in future. Was the interference proportionate to the aim pursued? Numerous charges could have been preferred, but only a few were selected. The level of sentencing reflected the perception that the activities were rendered less serious by the consent of the 'victims'. The Court, therefore, found that the state had not overstepped its margin of appreciation, taking into account the need for regulation of such harm and the proportionate response of the authorities. Thus, no violation of Art 8 was found. The partly dissenting judgment of Judge Pettiti is of interest. He reasoned that the case did not fall within Art 8 at all, since Art 8 provides protection for a person's intimacy and dignity, not for a person's baseness or criminal immorality. The wording of this judgment echoes the wording of parts of the majority judgments of the House of Lords in allowing distaste and lack of sympathy for the activities in question to have some bearing.

The judgment of the Court reflects, it is suggested, the tendency of the operation of the margin of appreciation to dilute the Convention standards. As suggested elsewhere

---

416   See further on this point Roberts's discussion of the Law Commission, Consultative Paper No 139, *Consent in the Criminal Law*, 1995; (1997) 17(3) OJLS 389.

417   *Laskey, Jaggard and Brown v UK* (1997) 24 EHRR 39 Appl No 21974/93. The case of *V, W, X, Y and Z v UK* Appl No 21627/93 raises the same issues.

418   (1997) 24 EHRR 39.

in this book,[419] a strong justification for trusting human rights and freedoms to the judicial as opposed to the democratic process is that the interests of minorities (including sexual minorities) may thereby be safeguarded, whereas, if they were at the mercy of majoritarianism, they might be at risk. However, this judgment lends credibility to the arguments of those who view the Convention as ineffective as a protector of minorities who stray too far from conventional forms of sexual expression, even where all involved are consenting adults. Clearly, if a similar prosecution is brought in future, Art 8 arguments might be raised with more success, bearing in mind the fact that the margin of appreciation doctrine has no application in domestic law.

Sexual identity

UK law did not give full expression to the fundamental interest of individuals in determining their own identity. This significant aspect of private life arose in a number of cases brought under the European Convention on Human Rights against the UK by transsexuals. In *Rees v UK*[420] the applicant, who was born a woman but had had a gender re-assignment operation, complained that he could not have his birth certificate altered to record his new sex, thereby causing him difficulty in applying for employment. However, the Court refused to find a breach of Art 8, because it was reluctant to accept the claim that the UK was under a positive obligation to change its procedures in order to recognise the applicant's identity for social purposes. It followed a similar route in *Cossey v UK*,[421] although it did consider whether it should depart from its judgment in *Rees* in order to ensure that the Convention might reflect societal changes. However, it decided not to do so because developments in this area in the Member states were not consistent and still reflected a diversity of practices. In *B v France*[422] it was found that although there had been development in the area, no broad consensus among Member states had emerged. Nevertheless, the civil position of the applicant in terms of her sexual identity was worse than that of transsexuals in the UK and on that basis, a breach of Art 8 could be found.

These decisions accepted that sexual identity is an aspect of private life, although they did not afford full recognition to a right of individuals to determine both their own identity and the public expression of it. However, the Court appears to be coming closer to recognising a breach of Art 8 in such circumstances.[423] In his dissenting Opinion in *Sheffield and Horsham v UK*, Judge Van Dijk said: 'there has been a steady development in the direction of fuller legal recognition [of the status of transsexuals] and there is no sign of any retreat in this respect.'[424] In *Goodwin v UK*[425] the Court finally took the step of affording that full recognition to the status of transsexuals under Article 8.

419 See Chapter 4, pp 263–65, 266, 270–77.
420 (1986) 9 EHRR 56.
421 A 184; (1990) 13 EHRR 622. A similar application also failed in *Sheffield and Horsham v UK* (1999) 27 EHRR 163.
422 (1992) 13 HRLJ 358; for comment, see [1992] PL 559.
423 *Sheffield and Horsham v UK* (1999) 27 EHRR 163, para 60.
424 Ibid, para 3.
425 [2002] ECHR 583.

In *Goodwin* the applicant complained about the lack of legal recognition of her post-operative sex and about the legal status of transsexuals in the United Kingdom. She complained, in particular, about her treatment in relation to employment, social security and pensions and her inability to marry. She relied on Arts 8, 12, 13 and 14 of the Convention. The Court found under Art 8 that although the applicant had undergone gender re-assignment surgery provided by the national health service and lived in society as a female, she remained for legal purposes a male. This had effects on her life where sex was of legal relevance, such as in the area of pensions, retirement age etc. A serious interference with private life also arose, it was found, from the conflict between social reality and law which placed the transsexuals in an anomalous position in which they could experience feelings of vulnerability, humiliation and anxiety. The Court noted that there was clear and uncontested evidence of a continuing international trend in favour of not only increased social acceptance of transsexuals but also of legal recognition of the new sexual identity of post-operative transsexuals. It was also noted that the UK Government were currently discussing proposals for reform of the registration system in order to allow ongoing amendment of civil status data.

The Court found that although the difficulties and anomalies of the applicant's situation as a post-operative transsexual did not attain the level of daily interference suffered by the applicant in *B v France*[426] the Court emphasised that the very essence of the Convention was respect for human dignity and human freedom. Under Art 8 of the Convention in particular, where the notion of personal autonomy was an important principle underlying the interpretation of its guarantees, protection was given to the personal sphere of each individual, including the right to establish details of their identity as individual human beings. In the twenty-first century, the Court found, the right of transsexuals to personal development and to physical and moral security in the full sense enjoyed by others in society could no longer be regarded as a matter of controversy requiring the lapse of time to cast clearer light on the issues involved.[427] Although the Court did not underestimate the important repercussions which any major change in the system would inevitably have, not only in the field of birth registration, but also for example in the areas of access to records, family law, affiliation, inheritance, social security and insurance, these problems were far from insuperable. The Court also considered that society might reasonably be expected to tolerate a certain inconvenience to enable individuals to live in dignity and worth in accordance with the sexual identity chosen by them at great personal cost.

The Court also noted that despite it's reiteration since 1986 and most recently in 1998 of the importance of keeping the need for appropriate legal measures under review having regard to scientific and societal developments, nothing had effectively been done by the respondent government. Having regard to the above considerations, the Court found that the respondent government could no longer claim that the matter fell within their margin of appreciation, save as regards the appropriate means of achieving recognition of the right protected under the Convention. It concluded that the fair balance that was inherent in the Convention now tilted decisively in favour of

---

426 (1992) 13 HRLJ 358.
427 Domestic recognition of this evaluation could be found, the Court noted, in the report of the Interdepartmental Working Group on Transsexual People and the Court of Appeal's judgment in *Bellinger v Bellinger* (EWCA Civ 1140 [2001]).

the applicant. There had, it found, accordingly, been a failure to respect her right to private life in breach of Art 8.

As regards Art 14 the Court considered that the lack of legal recognition of the change of gender of a post-operative transsexual lay at the heart of the applicant's complaints under Art 14 of the Convention. These issues had been examined under Art 8 and resulted in the finding of a violation of that provision. In the circumstances, the Court found that no separate issue arose under Art 14 and made no separate finding.

The Court found that while it was true that Art 12 referred in express terms to the right of a man and woman to marry, the Court was not persuaded that at the date of this case these terms restricted the determination of gender to purely biological criteria. The Court went on to consider whether the allocation of sex in national law to that registered at birth was a limitation impairing the very essence of the right to marry in this case. In that regard, it found that it was artificial to assert that post-operative transsexuals had not been deprived of the right to marry as, according to law, they remained able to marry a person of their former opposite sex. The applicant in this case lived as a woman and would only wish to marry a man. As she had no possibility of doing so, she could therefore claim that the very essence of her right to marry had been infringed. Though fewer countries permitted the marriage of transsexuals in their assigned gender than recognised the change of gender itself, the Court did not find that this supported an argument for leaving the matter entirely within the Contracting states' margin of appreciation. This would be tantamount to finding that the range of options open to a Contracting state included an effective bar on any exercise of the right to marry. The margin of appreciation could not extend so far. While it was for the Contracting state to determine, *inter alia*, the conditions under which a person claiming legal recognition as a transsexual established that gender re-assignment has been properly effected and the formalities applicable to future marriages (including, for example, the information to be furnished to intended spouses), the Court found no justification for barring the transsexual from enjoying the right to marry under any circumstances. It concluded that there had been a breach of Art 12.

Respect for family life

The concept of 'family life'

This concept under Art 8 may encompass many types of 'family' – formal or informal – but if the 'family' in question might not fall within the term as, for example, a foster parent might not do, there might still be an interference with private life.[428] Generally, a close relationship falling within the term will be presumed where close ties such as those between parent and child exist; for other relations, the presumption will be the other way. In *X, Y and Z v UK*[429] the Court considered that no breach of Art 8 had arisen where the UK refused to recognise a female to male transsexual as the father of a child born after artificial insemination by a donor. The father had lived with the mother in a stable relationship for ten years and acted as the child's father after the

---

428 See generally Liddy, J, 'The concept of family life under the ECHR' [1998] EHRLR 15; Kilkelly, U, *The Child and the ECHR*, 1999, Chapter 9.
429 (1997) 24 EHRR 143.

birth. Nevertheless, the Court did find that a family relationship existed between the 'father' and the child, taking into account his involvement with the child before and after the birth.

There are signs that Art 8 jurisprudence has rejected the notion that respect for family life, and perhaps for privacy generally, entails failure to interfere in the family when other rights or freedoms are in danger of abuse. In *Marckx v Belgium*,[430] the applicant complained under Art 8 in conjunction with Art 14 that an illegitimate child was not recognised as the child of his or her mother until the latter had formally recognised the child as such. Also, the child was treated under Belgian law as, in principle, a stranger to the parents' families. In finding that the state was under an obligation to ensure the child's integration in the family and therefore, that Art 8 applied, the Court impliedly rejected the view put forward by the UK judge, Sir Gerald Fitzmaurice:

> It is abundantly clear that the main if not indeed the sole object and intended sphere of application of Art 8 was that of what I will call the 'domiciliary protection' of the individual. He (*sic*) and his family were no longer to be subjected to domestic law. Such and not the internal regulation of family relationships was the object of Art 8.

It is reasonably clear that this notion of the meaning of respect for family life represents an impoverished view of the Convention requirements. Respect for family life means, negatively, that the state should abstain from interference except where to do so would mean failing to adhere to the requirements of respect for the private life of the child or to the requirements of another Convention Article.[431] The requirement of respect for family life also places positive obligations on the authorities to 'allow those concerned to lead a normal family life'.[432]

Various aspects of family life have been in issue in cases brought against the UK.[433] *W, B v UK*[434] concerned a claim that access should be allowed to children in the care of the local authority. The Court noted that Art 8 does not contain any explicit procedural requirements, but found that, in itself, that fact could not be conclusive. When the local authority made decisions on children in its care, the views and interests of parents should be taken into account and the decision-making process should allow for this. If parents' views were not taken into account, then family life was not being respected. Therefore, a breach of Art 8 was found on the basis that there was insufficient involvement of the applicants in the process. This decision thus avoided a judgment on the substantive merits of denying parents a right of access to children in care. Had the parents been involved in the decision-making process which had then led to the same conclusion, it would seem that no breach of Art 8 would have occurred.

Although the term 'family' may receive a broad interpretation, this has not consistently been the case with respect to the requirements arising from the need to respect family

---

430   (1979) 2 EHRR 330.
431   See *Riem v Sweden* (1992) 16 EHRR 155.
432   See Ovey, C and White Jacobs, R, *The European Convention on Human Rights*, 4th edn, 2006, Chapter 11; Bainham, A, 'Can we protect children and protect their rights?' [2002] Fam Law 279.
433   *Z and E v Austria* (1986) 49 DR 67.
434   Judgment of 8 July 1987, A 121; (1987) 10 EHRR 29.

life. In *X v UK*,[435] which was found inadmissible by the Commission, it was determined that 'family life' cannot be interpreted so broadly as to encompass a father's right to be consulted in respect of an abortion. The Commission could have rested the decision on para 2 – the 'rights of others' exception – by taking the rights of the woman in question into account, but it preferred to interpret the primary right restrictively. Had it not adopted such an interpretation, 'family life' might have come into conflict with 'private life' since pregnancy and its management has been accepted as an aspect of a mother's private life, although not to be divorced entirely from consideration of the life of the foetus.[436] Family life has also received a narrow interpretation in immigration cases in respect of a right to enter a country. In *Abdulaziz, Cabales and Balkandali v UK*[437] it was found that:

> The duty imposed by Art 8 cannot be considered as extending to a general obligation . . . to respect the choice by married couples of the country of their matrimonial residence and to accept the non-national spouses for settlement in that country.

However, in contrast, where an alien is faced with expulsion from a country in which he or she has lived for some time and where members of the family are established, the Court has recently shown itself willing to uphold the right to maintain family ties if satisfied that the ties are clearly in existence.[438]

Respect for the home

In this area, the Strasbourg authorities have adopted a cautious attitude and tend to practise only marginal review of the justification of restrictions. At the core of the right to respect for the home is the right to occupy the home and a right not to be expelled from it. Thus, a violation of Art 8 was established in *Cyprus v Turkey*[439] which concerned occupying forces expelling citizens and making their return to their homes impossible. This was a very clear violation of the right. A contrasting result was reached in *Buckley v UK*.[440] A gipsy, who had lived in her home for five years without planning permission, was still entitled to respect for her home – the concept was not found only to cover homes lawfully established. However, no violation of this right was found where planning permission for retaining the applicant's caravan on her own land was refused. The refusal was partly based on the planning authority's policy in controlling the sites on which gipsies could live. The Court found that a wide margin of appreciation should be allowed to the Member state and that such margin

---

435 Appl No 8416/78; 19 D & R 244 (1980).
436 *Brüggemann and Scheuten v Federal Republic of Germany* Appl No 6959/75, 10 D & R 100 (1975), Eur Comm HR, Report of 12 July 1977. See above, p 43 for possible conflict between Art 8 and Art 2 in respect of abortions. See above, p 88 for further discussion of the possible conflict between family life and private life.
437 Judgment of 28 May 1985, A 94; (1985) 7 EHRR 471. A breach of the Convention was found when Art 8 was read in conjunction with Art 14 (see above, p 109).
438 See *Moustaquim v Belgium*, A 193 (1991); (1991) 13 EHRR 802 and *Djeroud v France*, A 191-B, 1991; for comment, see (1991) YBEL 554–56.
439 (1976) 3 EHRR 482.
440 (1997) 23 EHRR 101.

had not been exceeded since procedural safeguards were in place which allowed for the weighing up of the interests involved: the interest of the applicant in her traditional lifestyle in a caravan and the interest of the planning authority in regulating the use of the land in the area for the benefit of the local community.

So, the concept of the home is quite broad, although it does not cover a future home which is not yet built.[441] Further, the right to respect for the home does not include a right to a home; nor does it extend to providing a decent home,[442] nor to providing alternative accommodation.[443] Interference can arise due to a direct interference such as a seizure order,[444] or to the use of a Compulsory Purchase Order threatening the actual home.[445]

The concept does not cover merely proprietorial rights; it includes the ability to live freely in the home and enjoy the home.[446] The peaceful enjoyment of the home is established as an aspect of respect of the home,[447] and this notion has been extended to cover various forms of interference with the enjoyment of the home, such as pollution by traffic fumes on the basis that the right implies that the home is private space to be enjoyed free from the covert or overt blight of pollution. A number of cases have concerned noise pollution. In *Powell v UK*,[448] a claim in respect of airport noise was rejected on the basis that a fair balance had to be struck between the interests of the individual and of the community. In *Lopez Ostra v Spain*,[449] a breach of Art 8 was found after considering the fair balance to be struck, in respect of a failure to prevent a waste treatment plant releasing fumes and smells. Failure to prevent the risk of serious pollution was also found to breach Art 8 in *Guerra v Italy*.[450] Where applications in such instances fail under Art 8 owing to the caution evinced in Strasbourg when dealing with this substantive right, they may succeed under Art 6(1) if the procedure allowing challenge to such interference is non-existent or defective.[451]

Correspondence

The case law in this area has concerned the right of a detainee to correspond with the outside world and, in the UK, has led to a steady relaxation of the rules relating to preventing, stopping and censoring of prisoners' correspondence.[452] In general, the supervision *per se* of prisoners' letters is not in breach of Art 8, but particular instances, such as stopping a purely personal letter, may be.[453] It does not have to be personal:

---

441 *Loizidou v Turkey* (1996) 23 EHRR 513.
442 *X v Germany* (1956) 1 YB 202.
443 *Burton v UK* (1996) 22 EHRR 135 CD.
444 *Chappel v UK* (1989) 12 EHRR 1.
445 *Howard v UK* (1987) 52 DR 198.
446 *Howard v UK* (1987) 52 DR 198.
447 *Arrondelle v UK*, No 7889/77; 26 D & R 5 (1982).
448 (1990) 12 EHRR 355. See also *Baggs v UK* (1987) 52 DR 29.
449 (1994) 20 EHRR; for comment, see Sands, P, 'Human rights, environment and the *Lopez Ostra* case' [1996] EHRLR 597.
450 (1998) 26 EHRR 375.
451 See, e.g., *Zimmermann and Steiner v Switzerland* (1983) 6 EHRR 17.
452 See, e.g., *Silver v UK*, Judgment of 25 March 1983, A 61; (1983) 5 EHRR 347.
453 *Boyle and Rice*, Judgment of 27 April 1988, A 131.

in *Campbell v UK*,[454] correspondence with the applicant's solicitor was read; that was a restriction on correspondence that amounted to a breach of Art 8. Supervision of correspondence during detention has also, to an extent, been found to breach Art 8.[455] It should be noted that an Art 10 issue may also arise in such circumstances since the detainee's right to receive or impart information is affected.[456] Searches and seizures fall within the head of 'correspondence' and, indeed, within all the rights except the right to respect for family life.[457]

Article 9: Freedom of thought, conscience and religion

(1) Everyone has the right to freedom of thought, conscience and religion; this right includes freedom to change his religion or belief and freedom, either alone or in community with others and in public or private, to manifest his religion or belief, worship, teaching, practice and observance.

(2) Freedom to manifest one's religion or beliefs shall be subject only to such limitations as are prescribed by law and are necessary in a democratic society in the interests of public safety, for the protection of public order, health or morals or for the protection of the rights and freedoms of others.

The right under Art 9 of possessing certain convictions is unrestricted. Restrictions are only placed on the *expression* of thought under Art 10, and the manifestation of religious belief in Art 9(2). Of course, in general, unless thoughts can be expressed, they cannot have much impact. However, Art 9 provides a valuable guarantee against using compulsion to change an opinion[458] or prohibiting someone from entering a profession due to their convictions. In the latter instance, Art 17 (which allows restrictions where a person's ultimate aim is the destruction of Convention rights)[459] might, however, come into play if someone of fascist or perhaps communist sympathies was debarred from a profession.

Freedom of religion will include the freedom not to take part in religious services, thus particularly affecting persons such as prisoners, but it may also include the opposite obligation – to provide prisoners with a means of practising their religion. However, in such instances, Strasbourg has been very ready to assume that restrictions are inherent in the detention of prisoners or are justified under para 2. For example, in *Huber v Austria*,[460] broad 'inherent limitations' on a prisoner's right to practise religion were accepted. Similarly, in *X v Austria*,[461] the Commission found no violation in respect of a refusal to allow a Buddhist prisoner to grow a beard. It is arguable, however, that inherent limitations should not be assumed in relation to a right which admits express exceptions.

454 (1992) 15 EHRR 137.
455 *De Wilde Ooms* (1971) 1 EHRR 373.
456 See *Herczegfalvy v Austria* (1992) 14 HRLJ 84; (1993) 15 EHRR 437.
457 *Funke v France* (1993) 16 EHRR 297; *Mialhe v France* (1993) 16 EHRR 332; *Crémieux v France* (1993) 16 EHRR 357. For further discussion, see Chapter 11.
458 Such action would normally also involve a violation of Art 3.
459 See below, p 112.
460 (1971) Yearbook XIV, p 548.
461 Appl No 1753/63 (1965) Yearbook VIII, p 174.

Article 10: Freedom of expression

(1) Everyone has the right to freedom of expression. This right shall include freedom to hold opinions and to receive and impart information and ideas without interference by public authority and regardless of frontiers. This article shall not prevent states from requiring the licensing of broadcasting, television or cinema enterprises.

(2) The exercise of these freedoms, since it carries with it duties and responsibilities, may be subject to such formalities, conditions, restrictions or penalties as are prescribed by law and are necessary in a democratic society, in the interests of national security, territorial integrity or public safety, for the prevention of disorder or crime, for the protection of health or morals, for the protection of the reputation or rights of others, for preventing the disclosure of information received in confidence or for maintaining the authority and impartiality of the judiciary.

Article 10 obviously overlaps with Art 9, but it is broader, since it protects the means of ensuring freedom of expression; even if the person who provides such means is not the holder of the opinion in question, she or he will be protected. The words 'freedom to hold opinion' used in Art 10 cannot be distinguished from the phrase 'freedom of thought' used in Art 9. There is also an obvious overlap with Art 11 which protects freedom of association and assembly.

Scope of the primary right

The stance taken under Art 10 is that while almost all forms of expression will fall within the primary right, all expression is not equally valuable. It was found in *X and Church of Scientology v Sweden*[462] that commercial speech is protected by Art 10, but that the level of protection should be less than that accorded to the expression of political ideas, thereby implying that political speech should receive special protection. In *Markt Intern Verlag v Federal Republic of Germany*,[463] the Court found: 'the European Court of Human Rights should not substitute its own evaluation for that of the national courts in the instant case, where those courts, on reasonable grounds, had considered the restrictions to be necessary,' an extreme statement of the extent to which Strasbourg should defer to the national decision. It appears to have been affected by the fact that the Court was dealing with commercial speech which it views as of much less significance than political speech.[464] As Harris, O'Boyle and Warbrick put it in *Law of the European Convention on Human Rights*:[465] 'The privileged position of political speech derives from the Court's conception of it as a central feature of a democratic society . . .'

---

462 Appl No 7805/77 (1979); YB XXII.
463 In *Markt Intern Verlag v FRG*, Series A 165, para 47 (1989).
464 See the statements regarding the significance of political speech in *Lingens v Austria* (1986) 8 EHRR 103; *Jersild v Denmark* (1994) 19 EHRR 1; *Oberschlick v Austria* (1997) 25 EHRR 357.
465 1995, p 397.

The motive of the speaker may be significant; if it is to stimulate debate on a particular subject, Art 10 will be more readily applicable.[466] The Court has stressed that Art 10 applies not only to speech which is favourably received, but also to speech which shocks and offends. In *Jersild v Denmark*,[467] the Commission accepted that this may include aiding in the dissemination of racist ideas. In this instance, the applicant had not himself expressed such views; his conviction had arisen due to his responsibility as a television interviewer for their dissemination. This factor was also taken into account by the Court in finding that the conviction constituted an interference with freedom of expression in breach of Art 10.[468] The television programme in question had included an interview with an extreme racist group, the Greenjackets; such interviews were found to constitute an important means whereby 'the press is able to play its vital role as public watchdog' and therefore strong reasons would have to be adduced for punishing a journalist who had assisted in the dissemination of racist statements by conducting the interview, bearing in mind that the feature taken as a whole was not found by the Court to have as its object the propagation of racist views. The Court pointed out that the racist remarks which led to the convictions of members of the Greenjackets did not have the protection of Art 10.

There is some evidence that the Court is reluctant to intervene in instances which may not be perceived as constituting a direct interference with freedom of expression by the domestic authorities. If, as in *Glasenapp v Federal Republic of Germany*,[469] the interference can be seen as in some way indirect or as largely concerned with another interest, it may find that the Art 10 guarantee is inapplicable. The case concerned a German schoolteacher who had written a letter to a newspaper indicating her sympathy with the German Communist Party. This was found to be contrary to legislation controlling the employment of people with extreme political views and her appointment as a teacher was revoked. Her claim that this constituted an interference with her freedom of expression failed since the Court characterised the claim as largely concerned with a right of access to the civil service rather than with freedom of speech. In *Bowman v UK*,[470] restrictions imposed on persons spending money in support of parliamentary candidates was found to be a disproportionate interference with freedom of expression. In *Ahmed v UK*,[471] the Court upheld restrictions preventing certain local government officers holding political office. The Court took into account the need to protect the rights of others to effective political democracy which was answered by seeking to ensure the neutrality of local government officers.

Article 10 includes an additional guarantee of the freedom to receive and impart information. However, the seeking of information does not appear to connote an obligation on the part of the government to make information available; the words 'without restriction by public authority' do not imply a positive obligation on the part of the authority to ensure that information can be received. So, the right is restricted in

466 See *Thorgeir Thorgeirson v Iceland* (1992) 14 EHRR 843.
467 (1992) 14 HRLJ 74; see also the *Open Door Counselling and Dublin Well Woman Centre Ltd* case (1992) 15 EHRR 244 (below, pp 95–96).
468 (1994) 19 EHRR 1.
469 (1986) 9 EHRR 25. See, to the same effect, *Kosiek v FRG* (1987) 9 EHRR 328.
470 (1998) 25 EHRR 1.
471 (1998) 5 BHRC 111.

situations where there is no willing speaker. Article 10 is not, therefore, a full freedom of information measure.[472] In fact, the freedom to seek information was deliberately omitted from Art 10 – although it appears in the Universal Declaration of Human Rights – in order to avoid placing a clear positive obligation on the Member states to communicate information.

A number of aspects of Art 10 and its impact on domestic law are discussed extensively in Part II.

Restrictions and exceptions

Mediums other than written publications can be subjected to a licensing system under Art 10(1) and because this restriction is mentioned in para 1, it appears that a licensing system can be imposed on grounds other than those outlined in para 2, thereby broadening the possible exceptions. This is discussed further in Chapter 6.[473] Any such exceptions must, of course, be considered in conjunction with the safeguard against discrimination under Art 14: for example, if the state has a monopoly on a medium, it must not discriminate in granting air time to different groups.

The restrictions of Art 10(2) are wide and two, 'maintaining the authority of the judiciary' and 'preventing the disclosure of information received in confidence', are not mentioned in Art 10's companion Articles, Arts 8, 9 and 11. The first of these exceptions was included bearing in mind the contempt law of the UK, but it was made clear, in the well known *Sunday Times* case,[474] that in relation to such law, the margin of appreciation should be narrow due to its 'objective' nature. In other words, what was needed to maintain the authority of the judiciary could be more readily evaluated by an objective observer than could measures needed to protect morals. The case in question concerned reporting on a matter of great public interest – the Thalidomide tragedy – and therefore, only very compelling reasons for preventing the information being imparted could be justified. It was held that because Art 10 is a particularly important right and the particular instance touched on its essence, a breach could be found; in response, the Contempt of Court Act 1981 was passed. The 'rights of others' exception may also receive a narrow interpretation – at least in cases of defamation against a public body or person where the applicant was acting in good faith and was attempting to stimulate debate on a matter of serious public concern.[475]

A very different approach was taken in the *Handyside* case[476] arising from a conviction under the Obscene Publications Act 1959 and concerning the more subjective nature of the 'protection of morals' exception. The applicant put forward certain special circumstances – that the prohibited material in question was circulating in most other countries and so suppression could not be very evidently necessary in a democratic society – but such circumstances were barely discussed. A wide margin of appreciation

---

472   This was supported in the *Gaskin* case (1990) 12 EHRR 36 (see above, p 73): the Art 10 claim failed on this basis.
473   See p 463.
474   Judgment of 26 April 1979, A 30; (1979) 2 EHRR 245 (discussed in full in Chapter 5, pp 336–37).
475   See *Thorgeir Thorgeirson v Iceland* (1992) 14 EHRR 843; *Castells v Spain* (1992) 14 EHRR 445; *Schwabe v Austria* (1992) 14 HRLJ 26.
476   Judgment of 7 December 1976, A 24; (1976) 1 EHRR 737. See further Chapter 6, pp 464–65.

was left to the national authorities as to what was 'necessary'. One possible reason for this was that the authority of the judiciary is a more objective notion than the protection of morals and this may have led to a variation of the necessity test. A similar approach was taken in *Müller v Switzerland*,[477] the Court stating:

> [I]t is not possible to find in the legal and social orders of the Contracting states a uniform European conception of morals. By reason of their direct and continuous contact with the vital forces of their countries state authorities are in a better position than the international judge to give an opinion on the exact content of these requirements.

The lack of a uniform standard was also the key factor in the ruling in *Otto-Preminger Institut v Austria*.[478] The decision concerned the showing of a satirical film depicting God as a senile old man and Jesus as a mental defective erotically attracted to the Virgin Mary. Criminal proceedings for the offence of disparaging religious doctrines were brought against the manager of the Institute which had scheduled the showings of the film. The film was seized by the Austrian authorities while criminal proceedings were pending. The European Court of Human Rights found that the seizure of the film could be seen as furthering the aims of Art 9 of the Convention and therefore it fell within the 'rights of others' exception. In considering whether the seizure and forfeiture of the film was 'necessary in a democratic society' in order to protect the rights of others to respect for their religious views, the Court took into account the lack of a discernible common conception within the Member states of the significance of religion, and therefore considered that the national authorities should have a wide margin of appreciation in assessing what was necessary to protect religious feeling. In ordering the seizure of the film, the Austrian authorities had taken its artistic value into account, but had not found that it outweighed its offensive features. The Court found that the national authorities had not overstepped their margin of appreciation and therefore decided that no breach of Art 10 had occurred. This decision left a very wide discretion to the Member state, a discretion which the dissenting judges considered to be too wide.

The stance taken in *Otto-Preminger* and in *Müller* echoes the view expressed in *Cossey v UK*[479] that where a clear European view does emerge, the Court may well be influenced by it, but it also suggests a particularly strong reluctance to intervene in this very contentious area. The margin of appreciation in respect of the protection of morals will not be unlimited, however, even in the absence of a broad consensus. The Court so held in *Open Door Counselling and Dublin Well Woman v Ireland*,[480] ruling that an injunction which prevented the dissemination of any information at all about abortion amounted to a breach of Art 10. This accords with the view expressed in *B v France*[481] that what can be termed the common standards principle is only one factor to be taken into account and must be weighed against the severity of the infringement of rights in question.

477 (1991) 13 EHRR 212.
478 (1994) 19 EHRR 34.
479 (1990) 13 EHRR 622.
480 (1992) 15 EHRR 244.
481 (1992) 13 HRLJ 358.

The exception in respect of confidential information overlaps with others, including national security and the rights of others, but a situation could be envisaged in which a disclosure of information did not fall within those categories and could therefore be caught only by this extra exception. This might arise in respect of a disclosure by a civil servant which did not threaten national security or any person's individual rights, such as that made in the *Tisdall* case.[482]

Actions in respect of both prior and subsequent restraints on freedom of expression may be brought under Art 10, but pre-publication sanctions will be regarded as more pernicious and thus harder to justify as necessary (*Observer and Guardian v UK*).[483] In relation to post-publication sanctions, criminal actions will be regarded as having a grave impact on freedom of expression, but civil actions which have severe consequences for the individual may also be hard to justify. In *Tolstoy Miloslavsky v UK*,[484] the European Court of Human Rights considered the level of libel damages which can be awarded in UK courts. Libel damages of £1.5 million had been awarded against Count Tolstoy Miloslavsky in the UK in respect of a pamphlet he had written which alleged that Lord Aldington, a high-ranking British army officer, had been responsible for handing over 70,000 people to the Soviet authorities without authorisation, knowing that they would meet a cruel fate. The Count argued that this very large award constituted a breach of Art 10. Was the award necessary in a democratic society as required by Art 10? The Court found that it was not, having regard to the fact that the scope of judicial control at the trial could not offer an adequate safeguard against a disproportionately large award. Thus, a violation of the applicant's rights under Art 10 was found.

Article 11: Freedom of association and assembly

(1) Everyone has the right to freedom of peaceful assembly and to freedom of association with others, including the right to form and to join trade unions for the protection of his interests.

(2) No restrictions shall be placed on the exercise of these rights other than such as are prescribed by law and are necessary in a democratic society in the interests of national security or public safety, for the prevention of disorder or crime, for the protection of health or morals or for the protection of the rights and freedoms of others. This article shall not prevent the imposition of lawful restrictions on the exercise of these rights by members of the armed forces, of the police or of the administration of the state.

Assembly

The addition of the word 'peaceful' has restricted the scope of para 1: there will be no need to invoke the para 2 exceptions if the authorities concerned could reasonably believe that a planned assembly would not be peaceful. Thus, assemblies can be subject to permits so long as the permits relate to the peacefulness of the assembly and not to

---

482 See Chapter 7, p 593.
483 (1991) 14 EHRR 153.
484 (1995) 20 EHRR 422.

the right of assembly itself. However, a restriction of a very wide character relating to peacefulness might affect the right to assemble itself and might therefore constitute a violation of Art 11 if it did not fall within one of the exceptions.

It should be noted that freedom of assembly may not merely be secured by a lack of interference by the public authorities; they may have positive obligations to intervene in order to prevent an interference with freedom of assembly by private individuals, although they will have a very wide margin of appreciation in this regard.[485] It has been held in respect of the guarantees of other Articles that states must secure to individuals the rights and freedoms of the Convention by preventing or remedying any breach thereof. If no duty was placed on the authorities to provide such protection, then some assemblies could not take place.

It will be argued in Chapter 8 that the freedom of assembly jurisprudence under Art 11 is cautious. In finding that applications are manifestly ill-founded, the Commission has been readily satisfied that decisions of the national authorities to adopt quite far reaching measures, including complete bans, in order to prevent disorder are within their margin of appreciation.[486] The Court has also found 'the margin of appreciation extends in particular to the choice of the reasonable and appropriate means to be used by the authority to ensure that lawful manifestations can take place peacefully'.[487]

Association

'Association' need not be assigned its national meaning. Even if a group such as a trade union is not an 'association' according to the definition of national law, it may fall within Art 11. The term connotes a voluntary association, not a professional organisation established by the government. It should be noted that it is only with respect to trade unions that the right to form an association is expressly mentioned, albeit non-exhaustively. Such a right in respect of other types of association is clearly implicit – a necessary part of freedom of association. The key rights protected by Art 11 include the basic right to form associations[488] and the right to autonomy of an association.[489] An association itself can exercise Convention rights, including freedom of expression (*Socialist Party and Others v Turkey*).[490]

Non-union associations

The earlier Strasbourg jurisprudence tended to be protective of state interests,[491] but the recent 'association' jurisprudence of the Court is more interventionist. In *Socialist Party*

485 Appl 1012/82, *Plattform 'Ärzte für das Leben' v Austria* D & R 44 (1985); (1988) 13 EHRR 204 (it was not arguable that Austria had failed in its obligation to prevent counter-demonstrators interfering with an anti-abortion demonstration).
486 See *Christians against Racism and Fascism v UK* No 8440/78, 21 DR 138; *Friedl v Austria* No 15225/89 (1995) 21 EHRR 83.
487 *Chorherr v Austria* Series A 266-B, para 31 (1993).
488 *X v Belgium* (1961) 4 YB 324.
489 *Cheall v UK* (1985) 8 EHRR 74.
490 Judgment of 25 May 1998, Appl No 20/1997/804/1007; (1999) 27 EHRR 51, paras 41, 47 and 50.
491 See *Glasenapp v FRG* A 104 (1986); *Kosiek v FRG* A 105 (1986); *CCSU v UK* (1988) 10 EHRR 269.

and Others v Turkey,[492] the Court allowed only a very narrow margin of appreciation in finding that the dissolution of the Socialist Party of Turkey had breached Art 11. The Court linked the three freedoms of expression, association and assembly together in finding that democracy demands that diverse political programmes should be debated, 'even those that call into question the way a state is currently organised'. The Court did not accept that the message of the group that a federal system should be put in place which would ensure that Kurds would be put on an equal footing with Turkish citizens generally, amounted to incitement to violence. The dissolution of the party was disproportionate to the aim in view – the preservation of national security. This stance is in accordance with the Convention jurisprudence, which has quite consistently recognised the need to protect the interests of minority and excluded groups.[493]

Similar findings were made in *Sidiropoulos v Greece*[494] in respect of an association formed to promote the interests of the Macedonian minority in Greece. The Court said that one of the most important aspects of freedom of association was that citizens should be able to form a legal group with the aim of acting collectively in their mutual interest. In *Vogt v Germany*[495] the Court held that a woman who was dismissed from her teaching post because of her membership of an extreme left wing group had suffered a violation of both Arts 10 and 11. These decisions suggest that where political associations are in question, the Court will take a strict stance, in accordance with its stance on political expression.[496] But these decisions may be contrasted with that in *Ahmed v UK*.[497] The applicants were local government officers who were active in local politics. Regulations were introduced with a view to ensuring local government impartiality; they restricted the political activities of certain categories of local government officers; thereupon the applicants had to resign from their political parties and cease canvassing for elections. The Court found that the interference with their Art 10 and 11 rights was proportionate to the aims in view since it was intended to ensure that the traditional political neutrality of council officers was maintained. Thus, unless a countervailing Convention value is also in issue, it may be assumed that political associations will receive particular protection.

Trade Unions[498]

Trade unions are expressly protected under para 1. But a wider margin may be conceded to the Member state in respect of interference with trade union membership, where the interest at issue cannot be viewed as political.[499] Apart from political associations and

492 Judgment of 25 May 1998 (Appl. no 20/1997/804/1007); (1999) 27 EHRR 51, paras 41, 47, and 50.
493 Such groups have included criminals: *Soering v UK* A 161 (1989); prisoners: *Ireland v UK* A 25 (1978), *Golder v UK* A 18 (1975); racial minorities: *East African Asians cases* (1973) 3 EHRR 76, *Hilton v UK* Appl No 5613/72, 4 DR 177 (1976) (no breach found on facts); sexual minorities: *Dudgeon v UK* A 45 (1982), *B v France* A 232-C (1992); political minorities: *Arrowsmith v UK* Appl No 7050/75, 19 DR 5 (1978); religious minorities: *Kokkinakis v Greece* A 260-A (1993).
494 (Chamber) (1998) available from the Court's website, www.dhcour.coe.fr.
495 (1995) 21 EHRR 205.
496 See the Introduction to Part II, pp 303–5, 309–11.
497 (1998) 5 BHRC 111; [1999] IRLR 188.
498 For general discussion, see Lightman, G and Bowers, J, 'Incorporation of the ECHR and its impact on employment law' [1998] EHRLR 560.
499 See *Gustaffson v Sweden* (1996) 22 EHRR 409.

trade unions, Art 11 protects, in general, groups set up in order to further the common interests of the members. But Strasbourg has taken a fairly narrow view of association; it excludes merely social groupings.[500] The question whether freedom of association implies protection against compulsory membership of an association was considered in *Young, James and Webster*.[501] In 1975, British Rail entered a closed shop agreement that made membership of a certain trade union a condition of employment. The three applicants, who were already employed by British Rail, disagreed with the political activities of trade unions; they therefore refused to join the union and were dismissed. They claimed that their dismissal on this ground constituted an infringement of Art 11 of the European Convention. The European Court of Human Rights found that the agreement between British Rail and the unions was lawful under the Trade Union and Labour Relations Act 1974, which allowed for dismissal for refusing to join a trade union unless the refusal was on grounds of religious belief.

In determining whether that provision infringed Art 11, the Court considered the 'negative aspect' of freedom of association, in other words, the right not to join a group. It was found that the negative aspect was not on the same footing as the positive aspects, but that when an individual's freedom of choice in association was so abridged – where there was only one ground on which it was possible to refuse to join a union – then an interference with freedom of association had occurred since it must necessarily include freedom of choice. This did not mean that all closed shop agreements would infringe Art 11; the Court was careful to confine its argument to the facts of the specific case. (The drafters of the Convention were aware of closed shop agreements operating in certain of the Member states in 1949 and therefore deliberately omitted a clause protecting an individual's right not to be compelled to join an association.) The Court did not find that the agreement was necessary under Art 11(2) but decided the case solely under para 1. It was found that a measure of freedom of choice is implicit in Art 11; this amounts to a negative aspect of the right to join a trade union and is not therefore on the same footing as the positive aspect, but it is still a part of freedom of association. The Court left open the question whether a closed shop agreement would always amount to a breach of Art 11; in this instance, the possibility of dismissal due to refusal to join the union was such a serious form of coercion that it affected the essence of the Art 11 guarantee. It seems that the closed shop practice may be a violation of Art 11 where there is legislation allowing it, even if the body enforcing it is not an emanation of the state (an example of *Drittwirkung*). It may be noted that the degree of freedom of choice under Art 11 is limited; it does not appear to include as a necessary component the freedom to choose between unions.[502]

The need to show a very clear curtailment of choice where the negative aspect of freedom of association is in question was affirmed by the decision of the European Court of Human Rights in *Sibson v UK*,[503] which concerned a choice between unions rather than a choice as to whether to join one at all. The applicant had resigned from his union, the TGWU, due to dissatisfaction with its decision in respect of a complaint he had made; he had then been ostracised by his workmates, who threatened to go

---

500 *Anderson v UK* [1998] EHRLR 218. For discussion, see Chapter 8, p 749.
501 Judgment of 13 August 1981, A 44; (1981) 4 EHRR 38.
502 *Sibson v UK*, A 258; (1993) 17 EHRR 193.
503 A 258; (1993) *The Times*, 17 May.

on strike unless he rejoined the union or was employed elsewhere. He joined another union and his employer then sought to employ him at a depot some distance away; he refused this offer, resigned and claimed constructive dismissal. When this claim failed in the domestic courts, he applied to the European Commission on Human Rights, alleging a breach of Art 11. The Court found that no breach had occurred: his treatment did not infringe the very substance of his freedom of association; he had not been subject to a closed shop agreement and had had the offer of continuing to work for the company without joining the union. Moreover, he had had no objection to union membership as such.

It may be argued that this decision should not be characterised as one entirely concerned with the negative aspect of freedom of association since, in order to rejoin the TGWU, the applicant would have had to resign from the second union. Therefore, the claim could be characterised as concerning the right of an employee to choose which particular union to join free from pressure from workmates or the employer. The applicant had been faced with the choice of working elsewhere or resigning from one union and joining another. It might appear that such a situation concerns a highly significant interest – the freedom to choose between associations – and that therefore, this decision is unfortunate in leaving such freedom unprotected so long as the employee retains the basic freedom not to join a union. It is instructive to note that the International Covenant on Economic, Social and Cultural Rights, unlike the European Convention, includes 'the right to join the trade union of *his choice*' (emphasis added).

In the UK, during the Conservative Government's period of office from 1979–97, no move was made to outlaw union membership *per se* or to prevent the formation of unions in general. Such a move would, of course, have constituted a clear breach of Art 11. However, certain measures were taken which curtailed choice of unions or which had the effect of reducing the size of the group that retains the right to union membership. Certain bodies, such as the army under the Army Act 1955, the police under s 47 of the Police Act 1964 and certain public officials have traditionally been debarred from union membership, but this group was enlarged when civil servants working at Government Communications Headquarters (GCHQ) were de-unionised. Their challenge to the ban on trade unions was considered in *Council of Civil Service Unions v Minister for the Civil Service*[504] (the *GCHQ* case). The Minister for the Civil Service, the Prime Minister, Margaret Thatcher, gave an instruction issued under Art 4 of the Civil Service Order in Council to vary the terms of service of the staff at GCHQ with the effect that staff would no longer be permitted to join national trade unions. Six members of staff and the union involved applied for judicial review of the minister's instruction on the ground that she had been under a duty to act fairly by consulting those concerned before issuing it. In the House of Lords it had first to be determined whether the decision was open to judicial review. In this instance, the Prime Minister was exercising powers under the royal prerogative, traditionally seen as unsusceptible to judicial review as they derive from the common law and not from statute. However, Lord Denning in *Laker Airways v Department of Trade*[505] seemed to have effected some erosion of that principle and, following his lead, the House of Lords

504 [1985] AC 374; [1985] 3 WLR 1174; [1985] 3 All ER 935; for comment, see [1985] PL 177, p 186.
505 [1977] QB 643.

determined that the mere fact of the power deriving from the prerogative as opposed to statute was not a sufficient reason why it should not be open to review.

Having made this determination, the House of Lords then found that the decision-making process had in fact been conducted unfairly. Usual practice had created a legitimate expectation that there would be prior consultation before the terms of service were altered; therefore, there was a legitimate expectation that that practice would be followed which had not been fulfilled. However, the Prime Minister argued that national security considerations had outweighed the duty to act fairly; had there been prior consultation, this would have led to strikes which would have affected operations at GCHQ – the very reason why union membership had been withdrawn. In her assessment, the requirements of national security outweighed those of fairness. The appellants argued, first, that this argument was an afterthought, and secondly, that national security had not been and would not be affected, in part because the unions were offering a no-strike agreement. However, the House of Lords held that the Prime Minister was better placed than the courts to determine what was needed by national security, although it was held that there must be some evidence of danger to national security; a mere assertion that such danger existed would be insufficient. As some evidence of such a danger had been put forward, the challenge to the union ban failed.

A group from GCHQ applied to the European Commission alleging a breach of both Art 11 and of the Art 13 provision that there must be an effective remedy for violation of a Convention right.[506] They were claiming that judicial review did not afford such a remedy. Accepting that the ban infringed the applicants' freedom of association, the government argued that it fell within Art 11(2) because it was adopted in furtherance of the interests of national security and that the margin of appreciation allowed to Member states in that respect should be wider than in respect of the other exceptions,[507] since it should be assumed that only the domestic authorities were competent to make a determination as to the needs of national security. Therefore, once it had made a determination that national security would be affected by industrial disruption and that a no-strike agreement would be inadequate, its decision could not be questioned by an outside body. It followed that the blanket ban imposed was not disproportionate to the end in view, which was to protect national security.

The applicants argued, on the other hand, that the exception under Art 11(2) in respect of the needs of national security could not apply because the ban was out of proportion to the aim pursued; there was no sufficiently pressing need to impose it. Only if such a need could be shown could such a grave infringement of freedom be justified. No such pressing need could be shown because there had been no recent action at GCHQ and when there had been such action, the government had not reacted to it for three years, thereby suggesting that it was not over-concerned about the effect on national security. Further, the government had stated in 1981 in Parliament that action at GCHQ had not affected national security. A no-strike agreement, it was argued, would be in proportion to the requirements of national security.

The government's second argument was that the applicants fell within the second sentence of Art 11(2) which allowed restrictions to be imposed on the police, armed

---

506 *Council of Civil Service Unions v UK* (1987) 20 DRE Com HR 228; (1988) 10 EHRR 269.
507 This had been accepted in other decisions including the *Klass* case (1978) A 28; 2 EHRR 214.

forces or the members of the administration of the state. It was argued that 'restriction' could include a total ban. The applicants, however, argued that the sentence should be narrowly construed; the word 'lawful' should mean that it should be interpreted in accordance with Convention limits and that, accordingly, it could not authorise a complete denial of trade union membership.

The Commission found that the ban amounted to a clear prima facie breach of Art 11; the question was whether it could be justified. The word 'lawful' was interpreted as meaning 'in accordance with national law'. The Civil Service Order in Council that had been made fulfilled that requirement. Could the term 'restriction' mean 'destruction'? It was found that the fact that the ban was complete did not mean that it would not be proportionate to the aim pursued, which was to protect national security, one of the exceptions contained in Art 11(2). The second sentence of Art 11 was considered. It was found that it allowed for restrictions which could not be justified under the first sentence; it was also applicable to the ban. The application was found to be manifestly ill-founded as far as Art 11 was concerned. The Commission further accepted the government's argument in relation to the alleged breach of Art 13 that judicial review afforded a sufficient remedy. Thus, the application was found to be inadmissible. Those who refused to give up their trade union membership were eventually sacked. The right to join a union was only reinstated at GCHQ in 1997 after the Labour Government came to power.

The right to join a trade union involves allowing members to have a union that can properly 'protect the interests of the members'. So, a union must have sufficient scope for this, although this need not mean a right to strike; this right can be subject to the restrictions of the national legislature.[508] Moreover, extra restrictions may be placed on certain groups of employees under the second sentence of para 2 and these do not expressly need to be 'necessary'. However, the purposes of the Convention imply that they should, indeed, be necessary.

Article 12: The right to marry and to found a family

> Men and women of marriageable age have the right to marry and to found a family, according to the national laws governing the exercise of this right.

Article 12 contains no second paragraph setting out restrictions, but it obviously does not confer an absolute right due to the words 'according to the national laws' which imply the reverse of an absolute right – that Art 12 may be subject to far reaching limitations in domestic law. The reference to national laws also accepts the possibility that legal systems may vary among Contracting states as to, for example, the legally marriageable age. However, this does not mean that the Convention has no role at all; it may not interfere with national law governing the exercise of the right, but may do so where it attacks or erodes its essence. If a person was denied the right to marry due to limited mental faculties or health or poverty, the essence of the right would be eroded assuming that he or she was capable of genuine consent. However, where erosion of the essence of the right arises from the national rule that only persons of the opposite

508 Judgment of 6 February 1976, *Schmidt and Dahlström v Sweden*, A 21 (1976); 1 EHRR 632.

sex can marry, it may be acceptable. In *Rees*,[509] a woman who had had a gender re-assignment operation complained that she was unable to marry. It was held that there was no violation of Art 12 because the state can impose restrictions on certain men and women due to the social purpose of Art 12 which is concerned with the ability to procreate; marriages which cannot result in procreation may, therefore, fall outside its ambit. This interpretation was supported on the ground that the wording of the Article suggests that marriage is protected as the basis of the family; thus, Art 12 is aimed at protecting the traditional biological marriage. In other words, what appeared to be a clear interference with the essence of the right could be found not to be so under this restricted interpretation. Therefore, preventing the marriage of persons not of the opposite biological sex was not found to breach Art 12. This ruling was followed in *Cossey*[510] on the ground that changes in social values did not indicate a need to depart from the decision in *Rees*.

The principle that the Convention will not interfere with national laws which only regulate the *exercise* of the right to marry is also subject to exceptions. If a person is, in general, free to marry, but in particular circumstances will suffer detriment flowing solely from the fact of being married, Art 12 may be breached. Thus, the right to marry may include placing no sanction on marriage, such as sacking a person when he or she marries. But if a priest is sacked when he ceases to be celibate, that would not seem to constitute a breach since he has, in a sense, chosen freely not to marry.

The right to divorce or dissolution of marriage is not included under Art 12[511] so that the state need not provide the means of dissolving a marriage although, in some circumstances, Art 8 may be relevant. It seems that the state need not provide such means as the right has been deliberately left out of the Convention, and although the Convention is subject to an evolutive interpretation (in other words, changes in social conditions can be taken into account), that will not apply to a right which has been totally omitted.

In accordance with the general Convention policy of reluctance to impose positive obligations on states, the right to found a family does not include an economic right to sufficient living accommodation for the family: it denotes an interference with the ability to found a family and thus prevents the non-voluntary use of sterilisation or abortion. Article 3 (and conceivably Art 2)[512] would probably also apply. The national laws are again allowed to regulate the enjoyment of this right, but they must not erode its essence. However, it might be argued that inherent limitations on the right in certain situations may be allowed because restrictions are not enumerated under Art 12, and therefore such limitations would not create a conflict with the general Convention doctrine governing inherent limitations which tends to reject such limitations where the restrictions are enumerated. However, it was found in *Hamer*[513] that prisoners do have the right to marry under Art 12; inherent restrictions are possible, but they must not affect the essence of the right. The applicant had two years to wait; that did affect the essence of the right and therefore led to a breach of Art 12. In contrast, in *X v*

509   Judgment of 17 October 1986, A 106; (1986) 9 EHRR 56.
510   Judgment of 27 September 1990, A 184; (1990) 13 EHRR 622.
511   *Johnstone*, Judgment of 18 December 1986, A 112; (1987) 9 EHRR 203.
512   See above, pp 43–45.
513   Report of 13 December 1979; D & R 24 (1981).

UK,[514] it was found that denial of conjugal visits to a detainee was not a violation of Art 12 since the Article grants the general right to found a family; it does not grant that that possibility should be available at any given moment.

The Protocols to the Convention

The First, Fourth, Sixth, Seventh, Thirteenth and Twelfth Protocols to the Convention add to it a number of substantive rights. Only the First, Sixth and Thirteenth Protocols have so far been ratified by the UK.

First Protocol

Article I

> Every natural or legal person is entitled to the peaceful enjoyment of his possessions. No one shall be deprived of his possessions except in the public interest and subject to the conditions provided for by law and by the general principles of international law.

> The preceding provisions shall not, however, in any way impair the right of a state to enforce such laws as it deems necessary to control the use of property in accordance with the general interest or to secure the payment of taxes or other contributions or penalties.

The property Article of the First Protocol echoes Art 12 in allowing the national authorities considerable freedom to regulate the exercise of the primary right. The case law has supported this; it was determined in *James and Others*[515] that the margin of appreciation open to the legislature in implementing social and economic policies should be a wide one.[516] Thus, in this area, the Strasbourg authorities have adopted a cautious attitude to this right and tend to practise only marginal review of the justification of restrictions. As mentioned above, claims of interference with property may fail under Protocol 1, Art 1, but succeed under Art 6, where a defective procedure has authorised the interference.[517]

In *Sporrong and Lonroth v Sweden*,[518] the Court found that while a wide margin of appreciation should be allowed to the Member state in respect of prohibitions affecting the applicants' properties due to planning regulations, that margin had been exceeded since procedural safeguards were not in place which allowed the applicants to seek a reduction of the time limits on the prohibitions. A fair balance between their interests and that of the community in general had not been struck. The fair balance is the key matter under Art 1. It must be clear that there has been a weighing up of the interests

---

514   Appl 6564/74; D & R 2 (1975).
515   A 98; (1986) 8 EHRR 123.
516   See further Harris, O'Boyle and Warbrick, op. cit., fn 1, p 516; Clayton and Tomlinson, op. cit., fn 1, pp 1301–20.
517   *Mats Jacobson v Sweden* (1990) 13 EHRR 79. See above, p 60.
518   (1982) 5 EHRR 35.

involved: the interest of the applicant in the peaceful enjoyment of possessions, and the interest of the community in regulating the use of the land or possessions for the benefit of the local community.

Article 2

No person shall be denied the right to education. In the exercise of any functions which it assumes in relation to education and to teaching, the state shall respect the right of parents to ensure such education and teaching in conformity with their own religious and philosophical convictions.

The UK is a party to the First Protocol, but has made the following reservation to Art 2:

[I]in view of certain provisions of the Education Acts in force in the United Kingdom, the principle affirmed in the second sentence of Article 2 is accepted by the United Kingdom only so far it is compatible with the provision of efficient instruction and training and the avoidance of unreasonable public expenditure.'

The right guaranteed under the first sentence of Art 2 can be exercised by the child or the parent;[519] if one parent loses custody to the other, that parent ceases to be able to exercise the right.[520] The right in question is expressed negatively; therefore, it guarantees an equal right of access to the educational facilities that are already available. However, this implies that some facilities should be available but leaves the state a wide margin of appreciation in respect of the provision.[521] In the *Belgian Linguistic* cases,[522] it was held that Art 2 does not require the Contracting states to provide a particular type of education: it implies the right of persons to 'avail themselves of the means of instruction existing at a given time'.

Article 3

The High Contracting Parties undertake to hold free elections at reasonable intervals by secret ballot, under conditions which will ensure the free expression of the opinion of the people in the choice of the legislature.

Article 3 provides an undertaking (not formally expressed as a right) which is clearly central to a democratic society.[523] However, it does refer to a right that individuals can

519   *Campbell and Cosans v UK* (1982) 4 EHRR 293, para 40.
520   *X v Sweden* (1977) 12 DR 192.
521   See further Wildhaber 'Right to education and parental rights', in Macdonald, R, Matscher, F, and Petzold, H (eds), *The European System for the Protection of Human Rights*, 1993, Kluwer; Clayton and Tomlinson, op. cit., 1st edn, fn 1, pp 1357–66.
522   Judgment of 23 July 1968, A 6; (1968) 1 EHRR 252.
523   For discussion, see Clayton and Tomlinson, op. cit., fn 1, Chapter 20.

invoke.[524] Article 3 does not imply an absolute right to vote, but that elections should be held at regular intervals, should be secret, free from pressure on the electorate and the choice between candidates should be genuine. It does not confer a right to a particular form of electoral system.[525]

Further Protocols

Articles 1 and 2 of the Sixth Protocol abolish the death penalty except in time of war or the threat of war. Protocol 13 abolishes it in all circumstances, including in war time. The Fourth and Seventh Protocols cover, broadly: freedom of movement (Protocol 4), the right of an alien lawfully resident in a state to full review of his or her case before expulsion, rights of appeal, compensation for miscarriages of justice, the right not to be subjected to double jeopardy and sexual equality between spouses as regards private law rights and responsibilities (Protocol 7). They are discussed in Chapter 4, as are the plans for their implementation in national law.[526] A Protocol on Minority Rights was recommended to the Committee of Ministers in 1993, but it has not been adopted.[527] Protocol 12 provides, very significantly, a free-standing right to equality which is discussed further in Chapter 15.[528] The Joint Committee on Human Rights in its review of International Human Rights legislation in 2005 recommended that the government should ratify the Fourth and Twelfth Protocols with appropriate reservations where necessary.[529]

The other Protocols, including Protocol 11, are concerned with the procedural machinery of the Convention. These other procedural Protocols were abolished when Protocol 11, discussed above,[530] came into force.

4 Additional guarantees to the primary rights

Article 13: The right to an effective remedy before a national authority

> Everyone whose rights and freedoms as set forth in this Convention are violated shall have an effective remedy before a national authority notwithstanding that the violation has been committed by persons acting in an official capacity.

In *Leander v Sweden*[531] it was found that 'the requirements of Art 13 will be satisfied if there exists domestic machinery whereby, subject to the inherent limitations of the

---

524 *Mathieu-Mohin v Belgium* (1987) 10 EHRR 1, para 50.
525 *Liberal Party v UK* (1980) 21 DR 211 (it could not be read with Art 14 to confer a right to a system of proportional representation on the basis that the lack of such a system discriminated against the Liberal Party).
526 See further p 165.
527 See 14 HRLJ 140.
528 See p 1486.
529 17th Report of Session 2004–5 HL Paper 99, HC 264, paras 34 and 37.
530 See pp 21 and 33.
531 Judgment of 26 March 1987, A 116; (1987) 9 EHRR 443. Note that if such machinery exists, but is of doubtful efficacy, a challenge under Art 6(1) may be most likely to succeed (*de Geouffre de la Pradelle v France* (1993) HRLJ 276).

context, the individual can secure compliance with the relevant laws'. This machinery may include a number of possible remedies. It has been held that judicial review proceedings will be sufficient. In *Vilvarajah and Four Others v UK*,[532] the applicants maintained that judicial review did not satisfy Art 13 since the English courts could not consider the merits of the Home Secretary's decision in this instance, merely the manner in which it was taken. In holding that the power of judicial review satisfied the Art 13 test, the Court took into account the power of the UK courts to quash an administrative decision for unreasonableness, and the fact that these powers were exercisable by the highest tribunal in the UK. Thus, no violation of Art 13 was found. However, more recently, in *Smith and Grady v UK*,[533] the Court said of the concept of Wednesbury unreasonableness: 'the threshold at which the ... Court of Appeal could find the Ministry of Defence policy irrational was placed so high that it effectively excluded any consideration by the domestic courts of the question whether the interference with the applicants' rights answered a pressing social need or was proportionate to the national security and public order aims pursued, principles which lie at the heart of the Court's analysis of complaints under Art 8 of the Convention.[534] This is not the last word on the matter. It is arguable that judicial review may provide a sufficient remedy in respect of breaches of Art 1, Protocol 1 especially where a large element of policy-making concerning social and economic matters is at issue.[535] This matter is pursued further at various points in this book.[536]

Article 13 does not contain a general guarantee that anyone who considers that his or her rights have been violated by the authorities should have an effective remedy; it can only be considered if one of the substantive rights or freedoms is in question. The words do not and cannot connote a requirement that there should be domestic machinery in place to address any possible grievance. The words 'are violated' of Art 13 do not mean that the violation must have been established before the national courts because clearly it could not have been – if it could, that would suggest that an effective remedy *did* exist. They mean that a person should have an arguable claim; there will be no breach of Art 13 if the complaint is unmeritorious – in other words, if it is clearly apparent that no violation of the Convention has taken place. Even if no violation of the other Article is eventually found, it can still be argued that the national courts should have provided an effective means of considering the possible violation. Moreover, a claim may eventually be held to be manifestly ill-founded and yet arguable. This is an odd result but, in principle, it is what the case law appears to disclose. In *Klass*[537] it was found that 'Art 13 must be interpreted as guaranteeing an effective remedy before a national authority to everyone who claims that his rights and freedoms under the Convention have been violated'. In *Plattform 'Ärzte für das Leben'*[538] it was found that

---

532 Judgment of 30 October 1991, A 215.

533 (2000) 29 EHRR 493.

534 *Ibid*, para 138.

535 See the decision of the House of Lords in *Alconbury* [2001] 2 All ER 929; (2001) 151 NLJ 135 (apart from the Art 1 issues, the matter concerned the application of Art 6 under the Human Rights Act).

536 See in particular Chapter 4, p 193.

537 Judgment of 6 September 1978 A 28; 2 EHRR 214.

538 (1988) 13 EHRR 204.

the claim must be arguable. Thus, Art 13 can be invoked only if no procedure is available which can begin to determine whether a violation has occurred. In theory, then, there could be a breach of Art 13 alone and in that sense, it protects an independent right. In practice, case law tends not to follow this purist approach, and if no violation of the substantive right is found, it is likely that no violation of Art 13 will be found either (as it may be argued occurred in the *Ärzte für das Leben* case).

In the *Klass* case, it was determined that phone tapping did not breach Art 8 since it was found to be in the interests of national security. The applicants claimed that Art 13 could be considered on the basis of their assertion that no effective domestic remedy existed for challenging the decision to tap. The Court accepted that the existing remedy was of limited efficacy: it consisted only of the possibility of review of the case by a parliamentary committee. Nevertheless, it found that in all the circumstances, no more effective remedy was possible. Thus, the Court allowed the doctrine of the margin of appreciation to resolve the difficulty which arose from the fact that the tapping was done in order to combat terrorism in its attack on democracy but the means employed, which included the suspension of judicial remedies, might well be termed undemocratic.

Article 14: Prohibition of discrimination

> The enjoyment of the rights and freedoms set forth in this Convention shall be secured without discrimination on any ground such as sex, race, colour, language, religion, political or other opinion, national or social origin, association with a national minority, property, birth or other status.

Article 14 does not provide a *general* right to freedom from discrimination, only that the rights and freedoms of the Convention must be secured without discrimination. Thus, if discrimination occurs in an area which is not covered by the Convention, such as most contractual aspects of employment, Art 14 will be irrelevant. Thus, Art 14 remains of limited value since it is not free standing and does not cover social and economic matters lying outside the protected rights. But, these weaknesses will eventually be addressed by Protocol 12, which will provide a free-standing right to freedom from discrimination in relation to rights protected by law.[539] The protection from discrimination under Protocol 12 will render Art 14 redundant. However, at present, the UK Government has not ratified it and, strangely for a Labour Government committed to anti-discrimination policies, it does not currently intend to do so.[540]

However, Art 14 is not the only Convention vehicle which may be used to challenge discriminatory practices. Not only may discrimination be attacked though the medium of one of the other Articles, most particularly Art 3,[541] but the Convention may be of particular value as a source of general principles in sex discrimination cases before the European Court of Justice.[542] An applicant may allege violation of a substantive

---

539 For further discussion of the draft Discrimination Protocol, see Moon, G (2000) 1 EHRLR 49.
540 See further Chapter 15, p 1486.
541 *East African Asians* cases (1973) 3 EHRR 76.
542 See, e.g., *Johnstone v Chief Constable of the RUC* [1986] ECR 1651.

right taken alone and also that he or she has been discriminated against in respect of that right. However, even if no violation of the substantive right taken alone is found and even if that claim is manifestly ill-founded, there could still be a violation of that Article and Art 14 taken together so long as the matter at issue is covered by the other Article. This was found in *X v Federal Republic of Germany:*[543] 'Article 14 of the Convention has no independent existence; nevertheless a measure which in itself is in conformity with the requirement of the Article enshrining the right or freedom in question, may however infringe this Article when read in conjunction with Article 14 for the reason that it is of a discriminatory nature.' In this sense, the Court has granted more autonomy to Art 14 than appeared to be intended originally.[544]

This ruling allowed more claims to be considered than the 'arguability' principle applying under Art 13. For example, in *Abdulaziz, Cabales and Balkandali*,[545] the female claimants wanted their non-national spouses to enter the UK and alleged a breach of Art 8, which protects family life. That claim was rejected. But a violation of Art 14 was found because the way the rule was applied made it easier for men to bring in their spouses. It was held that: 'Although the application of Art 14 does not necessarily presuppose a breach [of the substantive provisions of the Convention and the Protocols] – and to this extent it is autonomous – there can be no room for its application unless the facts at issue fall within the ambit of one or more of the rights and freedoms.' In response to this ruling, the UK Government 'equalised down', placing men and women in an equally disadvantageous position as regards their non-national spouses.

Under Art 14, discrimination connotes differential treatment which is unjustifiable. The differential treatment may be unjustifiable either in the sense that it relates to no objective and reasonable aim, or in the sense that there is no reasonable proportionality between the means employed and the aim sought to be realised.[546] In *Abdulaziz*, the aim was to protect the domestic labour market. It was held that this was not enough to justify the differential treatment because the difference in treatment was out of proportion to that aim. The outcome in this case illustrated the limitations of Art 14 which it shares with all anti-discrimination measures: it is concerned only with procedural fairness and can only ensure equal treatment which may be unjustifiable. Unjustifiable equal treatment is, however, unlikely to occur when the group in question is comparing itself with the dominant group since the dominant group will ensure, through the democratic process, that it does not experience a lower standard of treatment. However, where, as in *Abdulaziz*, the differentiation is occurring within a non-dominant group, the way is opened for equally poor treatment. This can be averted only by comparing the group as a whole with the dominant group. However, this argument was rejected by the European Court of Human Rights, which found that the treatment was not racially discriminatory.

---

543 Appl 4045/69 (1970) Yearbook XIII.
544 For comment on the increasing autonomy of Art 14, see Livingstone, S, 'Article 14 and the prevention of discrimination in the ECHR' (1997) 1 EHRR 25.
545 A 94; (1985) 7 EHRR 471.
546 *Geïllustreerde Pers NV v Netherlands* D & R 8 (1977).

5 Restriction of the rights and freedoms

The system of restrictions

As the discussion of the substantive rights demonstrated, all the Articles except Arts 3, 4(1) and 6(2) are subject to certain restrictions, either because certain limitations are inherent in the formulation of the right itself,[547] or because it is expressly stated that particular cases are not covered by the right in question, or because general restrictions on the primary right contained in the first paragraph are enumerated in a second paragraph (Arts 8–11). Certain further general restrictions are allowed under Arts 17, 15 and 57 (previously 64). In considering the restrictions, Art 18 must also be borne in mind. It provides that the motives of the national authority in creating the restrictions must be the same as the aims appearing behind the restrictions when the Convention was drafted.

Article 15: Derogation from the rights and freedoms in case of public emergency

(1) In time of war or other public emergency threatening the life of the nation any High Contracting Party may take measures derogating from its obligations under this Convention to the extent strictly required by the exigencies of the situation, provided that such measures are not inconsistent with its other obligations under international law.

(2) No derogation from Article 2, except in respect of deaths resulting from lawful acts of war or from Articles 3, 4 (para 1) and 7 shall be made under this provision.

(3) Any High Contracting Party availing itself of this right of derogation shall keep the Secretary General of the Council of Europe fully informed of the measures which it has taken and the reasons therefore. It shall also inform the Secretary General of the Council of Europe when such measures have ceased to operate and the provisions of the Convention are again being fully executed.

Article 15 allows derogation in respect of most, but not all of the Arts. Derogation from Art 2 is not allowed except in respect of death resulting from lawful acts of war, while Arts 3, 4(1) and 7 are entirely non-derogable. Apart from these exceptions, a valid derogation requires the state in question to show that there is a state of war or public emergency and, in order to determine the validity of this claim, two questions should be asked. First, is there an actual or imminent exceptional crisis threatening the organised life of the state? Second, is it really necessary to adopt measures requiring derogation from the Articles in question? A margin of discretion is allowed in answering these questions because it is thought that the state in question is best placed to determine the facts, but it is not unlimited; Strasbourg will review it if the state has acted unreasonably. However, the Court has not been very consistent as regards the margin allowed to the

---

547   Eg, Art 14, which prohibits discrimination, is inherently limited because it operates only in the context of the other Convention rights and freedoms.

state.[548] In general, if a derogation is entered, it must first be investigated and if found invalid, the claims in question will then be examined.

The UK entered a derogation in the case of *Brogan*[549] after the European Court of Human Rights had found that a violation of Art 5, which protects liberty, had occurred. At the time of the violation, there was no derogation in force in respect of Art 5 because the UK had withdrawn its derogation. This might suggest either that there was no need for it or that the UK had chosen not to derogate despite the gravity of the situation which would have justified derogation.[550]

However, after the decision in the European Court, the UK entered the derogation, stating that there was an emergency at the time. This was challenged as an invalid derogation,[551] but the claim failed on the basis that the exigencies of the situation did amount to a public emergency and the derogation could not be called into question merely because the government had decided to keep open the possibility of finding a means in the future of ensuring greater conformity with Convention obligations.[552] The fact that the emergency measures had been in place since 1974 did not mean that the emergency was not still in being. However, it may be argued that a state's failure to enter a derogation need not preclude the claim that a state of emergency did exist. If, whenever a state perceived the possibility that an emergency situation might exist, it felt it had to enter a derogation as an 'insurance measure' this would encourage a wider use of derogation, which would clearly be undesirable.

In the *Greek* case,[553] the Commission was prepared to hold an Art 15 derogation invalid. Greece had alleged that the derogation was necessary due to the exigencies of the situation: it was necessary to constrain the activities of communist agitators due to the disruption they were likely to cause. There had been past disruption which had verged on anarchy. Greece, therefore, claimed that it could not abide by the Articles in question: Arts 10 and 11. Apart from violations of those Articles, violations of Art 3, which is non-derogable, were also alleged. The Commission found that the derogation was not needed; the situation at the decisive moment did not contain all the elements necessary under Art 15.

Article 16: Restriction on the political activity of aliens

Nothing in Articles 10, 11 and 14 shall be regarded as preventing the High Contracting Parties from imposing restrictions on the political activity of aliens.

Since Art 16 applies to Arts 10 and 11, it implies that restrictions over and above those already imposed due to the second paragraphs of those Articles can be imposed on

---

548 See pp 36–39.
549 Judgment of 29 November 1988; (1989) 11 EHRR 117; A 145 (1989).
550 See Chapter 11, pp 1167–69.
551 *Brannigan and McBride v UK* (1993) 17 EHRR 539.
552 It may be noted that the derogation has now been withdrawn due to the inception of the Terrorism Act 2000, s 41 and an amendment was made to the Human Rights Act, Sched 3, Part 1, by order, accordingly: Human Rights Act (Amendment) Order (2001) SI 2001/1216; in force from 1 April 2001.
553 Report of 5 November 1969, Yearbook XII.

aliens in respect of their enjoyment of the freedoms guaranteed, as far as their political activity is concerned. This does not mean that aliens have *no* safeguard of freedom of expression, association or assembly; restrictions can be imposed only if they relate to political activities. Through its effect on Art 14, Art 16 affects all the rights in the Convention, since it means that the national authorities can discriminate in relation to aliens as far as any of the Convention rights are concerned. Article 16 has, therefore, been greatly criticised as creating consequences which 'hardly fit into the system of the Convention'.[554] The fact that discrimination as regards the protection afforded to Convention rights is allowable, would not, however, preclude claims that the substantive rights – other than those arising under Arts 10 and 11 – had been violated.

Article 17: Destruction of Convention rights

> Nothing in this Convention may be interpreted as implying for any State, group or person any right to engage in any activity or perform any act aimed at the destruction of any of the rights and freedoms set forth herein or at their limitation to a greater extent than is provided for in the Convention.

Article 17 prevents a person relying on a Convention right where his or her ultimate aim is the destruction or limitation of Convention rights. Article 17 is dealt with on the issue of admissibility, but it can be looked at a later stage too. Its 'restriction' applies to all the rights and freedoms. In general, if Art 17 is violated, this may well mean that one of the other restrictions on the freedom in question applies too; thus, Art 17 is of importance only when it appears that some measure allows evasion of a Convention guarantee in a manner not covered by the other restrictions. Thus, Art 17 must be read in conjunction with all the articles as allowing for a new exception. This is of particular importance where the guarantee in question is subject to few or no restrictions.

Making a reservation: Art 57

Article 57 provides that a state can declare when signing the Convention that it cannot abide by a particular provision because domestic law then in force is not in conformity with it. This may be done when the Convention or Protocol is ratified. The Court will review the reservation in order to see whether it is specific enough: it should not be of too general a nature.[555] The UK has only entered a reservation in respect of Protocol 1.[556]

6 Conclusions

It is clear that in one sense, the Convention has been astoundingly successful in creating a standard of human rights which is perceived by so many Europeans as relevant and

---

554 See Van Dijk and Van Hoof, op. cit., fn 1, p 410.
555 In *Belilos v Switzerland* (1988) EHRR 466 it was found that the reservation did not comply with Art 64 because it was too general.
556 See above, p 105.

valuable despite the fact that almost half a century has passed since it was created. The enormous and continuing increase in the number of petitions in the late 1980s, during the 1990s and post-2000 suggest that its potential has only recently been understood. Its influence is likely to increase now that a number of Eastern European states have become signatories to it. Although it was only intended to create a minimum standard of human rights, it has succeeded in revealing basic flaws in UK law in relation to, for example, the decision to maintain or renew the detention of life prisoners.[557]

At the same time, its ability to bring about change in the laws and practices of Member states must not be exaggerated. Arguably, the Convention may be termed a largely procedural charter in the sense that a challenge to a flawed procedure is more likely to succeed under it than a claim that a substantive right has been violated.[558] Further, it may be argued that the machinery for the enforcement of the Convention is wholly inadequate, particularly in the face of a government unashamedly prepared to breach it for long periods of time.[559] This chapter spent some time dwelling on the stages through which an application will pass if it is pursued all the way through the system. The process means that if an application which is ultimately successful takes five years before the final decision, the individual affected may have to suffer a violation of his or her rights for all that time, although an interim remedy may be available under Rule 39 where the Chamber or its President considers that it should be adopted in the interest of the parties or of the proper conduct of the proceedings. Usually, such a remedy would be granted where there is an immediate risk to life or health, in death penalty cases[560] or in deportation or extradition cases.[561] There is no formal mechanism available, such as an interim injunction, to prevent the continuing violation, but a Rule 39 request is normally complied with. Now that the Court and Commission have merged, some of the overlapping stages, such as the dual consideration of admissibility, have disappeared, although the question of admissibility itself still arises. If the admissibility stage were eliminated, the workload of the single Court would increase enormously, although the quality of decision making in some individual cases might be improved. The process is still likely to be lengthy, especially as it is expected that the number of petitions will increase enormously due to the accession of Eastern European Member states.

If a petition comes before the European Court of Human Rights, it may decide that no violation has occurred due to its invocation of the margin of appreciation. If, however, it declares that a breach has indeed occurred, the violation may well subsist for some years while the Member state concerned considers the extent to which it will respond. Eventually, a measure may be adopted which may still represent a violation

557 See, e.g., *Thynne, Wilson and Gunnel v UK*, Judgment of 25 October 1990; (1990) 13 EHRR 666, discussed above, p 58.
558 See, e.g., *Mats Jacobson v Sweden* (1990) 13 EHRR 79, above, p 60.
559 The UK Government is quite frequently slow to respond to an adverse ruling, and when the response comes, it may be inadequate. See Chapter 11, pp 1033–34.
560 *Ocalan v Turkey*, 30.11.99.
561 *Soering v UK* (1989) 11 EHRR 439.

of rights, but of a less pernicious nature.[562] A challenge to such a measure would have to go through the same lengthy process in order to bring about any improvement in the protection afforded in the Member state to the right in question.

Thus, it may be concluded that reliance on the Convention has tended to produce only erratic, flawed and weak protection of freedoms in the UK. However, as argued at the beginning of this chapter, the solution does not appear to be adoption of a more coercive process since that might lead to open conflict with Strasbourg and perhaps, ultimately, withdrawal of some state Parties from the Convention. It was intended that the twin problems of the slow procedure and inadequate enforcement would be addressed by the reception of the Convention into UK law under the HRA. The framework of the HRA, as the means of affording the needed further effect to the Convention in domestic law, is considered in Chapter 4. It will be asked whether, in terms of efficacy, it can fairly be said that the rights have now been 'brought home'.

---

562 The response of the UK Government to the ruling in *Malone v UK* (1984) 7 EHRR 14, which was to place telephone tapping on a statutory footing (under the Interception of Communications Act 1985), may be an example of an inadequate implementation of a ruling since the Act did not require independent authorisation of intercept warrants even in cases unconcerned with national security. The position under the legislation which replaced the 1985 Act – the Regulation of Investigatory Powers Act 2000, Part 1 – is, in essentials, the same. (See further Chapter 10, pp 1032–38.)

Chapter 3

Methods of protecting civil liberties in the UK; The Bill of Rights debate foreshadowing the Human Rights Act

1 Introduction

The premise behind the adoption of Bills of Rights all over the world is that citizens can never be fully assured of the safety of their fundamental civil and political rights unless those rights are afforded protection from state interference. It is thought that such protection can be achieved by enshrining a number of rights in a Bill of Rights, affording it some constitutional protection and entrusting it – in effect – to the judiciary on the basis that a government cannot be expected to keep a satisfactory check on itself; only a source of power independent of it can do so. Democracies across the world that have adopted a Bill or Charter of Rights have entrusted its application largely to the judiciary on the basis that among such sources of power, they are best placed to ensure the delivery of the rights to citizens. Dworkin has argued that under a Bill of Rights, a government is not free to treat liberty as a commodity of convenience or to ignore rights that the nation is under a moral duty to respect.[1]

In the UK, however, it was thought until relatively recently that the unwritten constitution recognising residual liberties, as maintained by Parliament and the judiciary, provided a sufficiently effective means of ensuring that power was not abused.[2] Residual liberties were, however, vulnerable to invasion: the doctrine of parliamentary sovereignty meant that Parliament could legislate in an area of fundamental rights, thereby restricting or even destroying them.[3] The judiciary could also invade liberties in developing the common law, while unless a right could be said to be recognised by the common law, public authorities could invade it without relying on statute, the prerogative or common law rules.[4]

The argument that residual liberties were ineffective and that the change to a rights-based approach should be brought about gathered momentum during the 1970s and 1980s and gained ascendancy in the 1990s. This change of view was clearly traceable to the development and influence of international human rights law,[5] especially the impact of the European Convention on Human Rights. The argument was further fuelled by the invasions of liberty that occurred under the Conservative Governments

---

1 Dworkin, R, *A Bill of Rights for Britain*, 1990, p 23, Chatto and Windus.
2 See Jennings, WI, *The Approach to Self-Governance*, 1958, CUP.
3 Thus, freedom of assembly was severely restricted in the 1990s and beyond; see Chapter 8, pp 710–12, 738–43.
4 See *Malone v MPC* [1979] Ch 344, p 372.
5 See further Hunt, M, *Using Human Rights Law in English Courts*, 1997, Hart.

from 1979 to 97. It was argued that the traditional checks on government power could now be seen as insufficiently effective. These two developments were, it is suggested, interlinked; as Hunt argues: 'no single factor has been more significant in exposing this gap between theory [the traditional account of domestic constitutional arrangements] and practice than the international dimension which [over the last 25 to 30 years] domestic constitutional practice has been forced to accommodate'.[6]

This view of the record of those Conservative Governments, viewed from the perspective offered by international human rights law, was used to support the introduction of the Human Rights Act 1998 (HRA),[7] which came fully into force on 2 October 2000. The HRA received the European Convention on Human Rights into UK law, thereby providing the UK with an instrument that, while arguably not amounting to a 'Bill of Rights' in the modern sense,[8] provided a new and very significant protection for human rights and freedoms. The HRA comes as close to creating a Bill of Rights as the UK has ever come.

This chapter begins by considering the traditional methods of protecting civil liberties in the UK: the changes that are being brought about under the Human Rights Act must be placed in that context. Clearly, while the inception of the Human Rights Act is intended to provide a new and effective means of protecting certain fundamental rights, it does not entail an abandonment of the *traditional* methods of protecting liberties; it may provide a means of strengthening them. Moreover, existing established rights and existing rights to bring proceedings are preserved by s 11 of the HRA; therefore, all the existing methods of protecting civil liberties already developed under the law are still highly relevant. Indeed, as explained below, they provide the usual forum in which arguments relating to civil liberties are being put forward in the post-HRA era, based either on the Convention and/or on established common law principle. The chapter goes on to consider some of the arguments that were put forward, especially in the 1990s, as to the need to enact a Bill of Rights, and as to the disadvantages of taking that step. Finally, it indicates the choices that had to be taken when the HRA was enacted, against the background of the preceding debate. Chapter 4 goes on to consider the HRA itself. The Bill of Rights issue remains pertinent, despite the inception of the HRA, since at the present time the Conservative Party plans, if it comes to power in 2009 or 2010, to introduce a Bill of Rights in order to replace the HRA. Gordon Brown is also interested in this possibility.

2 Methods of protecting civil liberties in the UK

The democratic process as the guardian of civil liberties

It has traditionally been thought that Parliament provides a means of allowing the will of the people to influence the government towards the maintenance of liberty[9] through free elections and secret ballots and aided by the operation of a free press. It can react to the needs of civil liberties by providing specific legislative safeguards and, in so

---

6   Ibid, p 1.
7   The HRA received Royal Assent on 9 November 1998.
8   See below, pp 147–51.
9   See, e.g., Dicey, AV, *The Law of the Constitution*, 1959, Macmillan, pp 189–90; Hume, D, *Political Discourses*, 1906, Walter Scott (first published 1752), p 203.

doing, can take into account the views and expertise of a range of groups. Moreover, it will govern according to the rule of law, which will include the notion that it will accept certain limits on its powers based on normative ideals.[10]

However, commentators such as Ewing and Gearty, evaluating governments in the 1980s, argued that these traditional checks were insufficiently effective as methods of curbing the power of a determined and illiberal governing party: 'Mrs Thatcher has merely utilised to the full the scope for untrammeled power latent in the British Constitution but obscured by the hesitancy and scruples of previous consensus-based political leaders.'[11] In particular, it is clear that when the government in power has a large majority, as the Thatcher Government had, it may more readily depart from traditional constitutional principles if it is minded to do so, because Parliament is likely to be ineffective as a check on its activities. Even where the governing party does not have a large majority, it can still introduce legislation abridging basic freedoms, especially where the main opposition party sympathises with its stance. As this book indicates at a number of points, the Major Government exemplified this tendency. The Thatcher and Major Governments introduced very little legislation protective of civil liberties except where they were forced to do so by a ruling of the European Court of Human Rights, an EC Directive or a ruling of the European Court of Justice. In short, the dangers of the doctrine of parliamentary sovereignty in terms of threatening fundamental liberties became more apparent during the Conservative years of 1979–97. While it is important not to allow the record of those Conservative Governments to distort debate as to the efficacy of the democratic process in protecting civil liberties, it is also important to bear in mind the lessons which have been learnt as to the constitutional weaknesses which those governments exposed.

Government secrecy and executive discretion

Parliament's ability to create a check on government has, as Birkinshaw points out,[12] been hampered by the lack of a Freedom of Information (FoI) Act in scrutinising the actions of Ministers. This lack meant that the government could choose what and how much to reveal in response to opposition questions and therefore – as the *Ponting* case[13] made clear – was able to present a selective picture of events. Until 2000, Britain did not have an FoI Act, unlike other democracies, and, following the tradition of secrecy, Parliament until recently saw no need to enact one.[14] Although FoI legislation is now in place, there are grounds for arguing that its impact in terms of enabling Parliament to play an effective role may be limited, as Chapter 7 argues.[15]

Moreover, as this book will indicate at a number of points,[16] decisions affecting civil liberties are frequently taken not under Parliamentary scrutiny, but by ministers and officials exercising discretionary powers. The exercise of such powers may receive more

10 See, e.g., Wade, W and Bradley, A, *Constitutional and Administrative Law*, 1985, Longman, pp 99–100.
11 Ewing, KD and Gearty, CA, *Freedom under Thatcher*, 1989, p 7.
12 See Birkinshaw, P, *Freedom of Information*, 1996, Butterworths, Chapter 3.
13 *Ponting* [1985] Crim LR 318. See further Chapter 7, pp 593–94.
14 See Chapter 7, p 630 *et seq*.
15 See p 645 *et seq*. for discussion of recent developments in this area.
16 See, in particular, Chapter 10.

scrutiny in other jurisdictions. For example, the Australian Government has accepted that there should be a parliamentary committee charged with scrutiny of the Australian Security Service.[17] In the UK, in contrast, when the Security Services Bill 1989 was debated, the government refused an amendment which would have subjected MI5 to scrutiny by a Select Committee.[18] It continues to be the case that questions about the operation of MI5 and MI6 will not be answered in Parliament. Clearly, matters which are hidden from the public and from opposition MPs may tend to evade the checks arising from the democratic process, such as they are.

Opposition complicity in curtailing liberties

Aside from these issues, which have become particularly pressing over the last two decades, it may also be questioned whether the Westminster Parliament by its nature provides an effective forum for taking the protection of civil liberties into account in passing legislation. A number of writers[19] have noted that Parliament at times displays a readiness to pass emergency legislation which may go further than necessary in curtailing civil liberties and which is apt to remain on the statute book long after the emergency is over. MPs, whether in government or out of it, tend to respond in an unconsidered fashion to emergencies, apparent or real. Governments wish to be perceived as acting quickly and decisively, while members of the opposition parties, mindful of their popularity, may not wish to oppose measures adopted in the face of scares whipped up by some sections of the media. Such reactions were seen in relation to the original Official Secrets Act 1911, passed in one day with all-party support in response to a spy scare. The far reaching s 2, which was never debated at all, remained on the statute book for 78 years. Similarly, the Birmingham pub bombings on 21 November 1974 led, four days later, to the announcement of the Prevention of Terrorism Bill,[20] which was passed by 29 November virtually without amendment or dissent.

In the 1990s, Parliament quite frequently showed a marked readiness to accept claims that a number of proposed statutory measures would lead to the curbing of terrorist or criminal activity. Although such measures were likely to represent an infringement of civil liberties, they did not in general encounter determined criticism from the opposition. During the last Conservative years, Labour in opposition under Blair took a stance that could hardly be viewed as civil liberties-oriented. A number of political scientists have observed that in the 1990s, there was a general policy convergence, with the front-benchers of the Labour and Conservative Parties closer on many issues than at any point since the 1970s.[21] In the civil liberties context, two key examples were provided by the opposition impact on the Criminal Justice and Public Order Act 1994 and the Police Act 1997. Many pressure groups protested against the 1994 Bill: it probably attracted more public opposition than any other measure during the Conservative

---

17 See the Australian Security Service Intelligence Organisation Amendment Act 1986.
18 That position remained unchanged despite the enactment of subsequent legislation relating to the accountability of the intelligence Services: see Chapter 10, pp 1014–15.
19 Eg, Robertson, G, *Freedom, the Individual and the Law*, 1993, p 506; Walker, C, *The Prevention of Terrorism in British Law*, 2nd edn, 1992, Manchester University Press, Chapter 4, p 32.
20 HC Debs Vol 882 Col 35.
21 Seldon, A, 'The consensus debate' (1994) 14 Parliamentary Affairs 512.

years in government from 1979 to 1997, apart from the 'Poll tax'. But, despite protests against the Bill and the far-reaching nature of many of the new provisions, it went through Parliament relatively intact. As ATH Smith observes: 'Presumably for fear of being seen to be soft on crime . . . the Labour Party declined to oppose the Bill on Second Reading, leaving the serious opposition to the Bill to the Peers. Given the target of [the public order aspects] of the Act and the social make-up of their Lordships' House . . . the prospects of serious opposition were negligible.'[22]

As Chapter 10 explains, the Liberal Democrats took the lead in proposing the more far-reaching amendments to the 1997 Police Bill.[23] The Labour Party initially supported the proposals in the Bill to allow the police self-authorising powers to place bugging devices on property. Their stance was modified only after a government defeat on this matter in the Lords and severe criticism from various quarters. Jack Straw, then Shadow Home Secretary, finally agreed with Michael Howard on a compromise which would ensure that in certain serious cases the police had to seek authorisation from a judicial committee.[24] This compromise was criticised in many quarters as providing only marginally more protection for civil liberties.

The debate in the House of Commons on the Prevention of Terrorism (Additional Powers) Act 1996, which was guillotined, failed to consider in depth either the efficacy of the measure in terms of curbing terrorist activity or its likely impact on civil liberties. The debate provided, in microcosm, a good instance of the debasement and impoverishment of Parliamentary criminal justice debate in the mid-1990s. The Labour Party supported the proposals partly on the narrow ground that they represented only a small increase on the extended police powers which were included in the Criminal Justice and Public Order Act 1994 and which were not challenged on grounds of principle at the Committee stage of that Bill.[25] Thus, issues as to the real value of these powers fell to be asked only by Labour backbenchers and, owing to pressure of time and the stance of the leadership, they could not be pressed home.

Examples can be found to support the other side in this debate. It is generally agreed that the democratic process worked well in creating the Police and Criminal Evidence Act 1984,[26] and it is fair to say that it had at least some impact, as suggested above, on the Police Act 1997. It might be argued that the 1994 Act was a product of special Parliamentary conditions which are unlikely to recur: a particularly illiberal Home Secretary piloted it through Parliament and the Shadow Home Secretary supported its key provisions. However, subsequent developments suggest that similar conditions continued throughout and beyond the late 1990s.

The change of government in 1997, when Labour came to power after 18 years of Conservative rule, heralded the introduction of two key pieces of liberal legislation – the HRA 1998 and the FoI Act 2000. Nevertheless, the prevailing stance on both government and opposition benches remained a largely anti-liberal one during the following ten years of Labour rule. For example, the first significant counter-terrorist measure passed under the

---

22 Smith, ATH [1995] Crim LR 19, p 27.
23 See p 1057.
24 See, now, s 91(1) of the Act.
25 Straw, J, HC Deb 2 April 1996 Col 221.
26 See Zander, M, *The Police and Criminal Evidence Act 1984*, 1995, Sweet and Maxwell, p xi: '. . . there can be no denying that the whole exercise was an example of the democratic process working.'

Labour Government, the Criminal Justice (Terrorism and Conspiracy) Bill 1998, strongly resembled the 1996 Act in terms both of its content and of the Parliamentary process it underwent. The Bill was rushed through both Houses in two days in the wake of the Omagh bombing on the basis that the powers were needed immediately for operational reasons. In fact, no immediate action occurred in reliance on the new powers. The two central measures enhancing state power introduced in the first term of the Blair Government – the Terrorism Act 2000 and the Regulation of Investigatory Powers Act 2000, showed, it is argued in this book, even less respect for human rights than measures such as the Police Act 1997. The stance of the Labour Government is indicated at various points in the following chapters. It will be contended that the consensus which some commentators viewed as 'shaping the politics of the 1990s'[27] continued post-2000. As Chapters 14 and 8 in particular point out, post 9/11, Labour criminal justice, anti-terrorism and public order legislation became markedly authoritarian. The Conservative opposition under Duncan-Smith adopted a stance which was arguably more authoritarian and even less civil rights-minded than that of the Labour Government. It seems clear that the Conservative approach has remained essentially unchanged after the General Elections in 2001 and 2005. It may be argued, then, that there has been little effective opposition in the Commons on human rights matters from the mid-1990s onwards and, at present, little prospect of any.

The House of Lords

The fact that the UK possesses a second chamber was sometimes used as an argument against the introduction of a Bill of Rights. The argument ran on these lines: other countries adopted Bills of Rights for a variety of reasons – either because they were at a stage in their development when human rights were particularly at risk, or because of a particular feature of their constitution, such as the lack of a second legislative chamber[28] to keep a check on the lower House;[29] their experience is not, therefore, analogous to that in the UK. But it must be questioned how far a second chamber can protect civil liberties. The House of Lords has had some successes, notably its influence on the incorporation into the Police and Criminal Evidence Act 1984 of a provision with clear potential to safeguard the liberty of the citizen – s 78.[30] As mentioned above, the Lords also passed amendments to Michael Howard's Police Bill in 1997 allowing for judicial authorisation of bugging warrants. Crucial amendments to the Terrorism Act 2000, which narrowed the definition of 'terrorism' in cl 1, were passed in the Lords.[31] However, the powers of the Lords to thwart the wishes of the Commons are limited. Section 2 of the Parliament Act 1911 makes various provisions for presenting a Bill for the royal assent against the opposition of the Lords. When a Bill has been passed by the Commons in two successive sessions and it is rejected for a second time by the Lords, it can be presented on its second rejection for the Royal Assent. The very existence of this power means that the need to invoke it is unlikely to arise because the Lords will wish to avoid the need for the Commons to use it.[32]

---

27 Dutton, D, *British Politics since 1945*, 2nd edn, 1997, Blackwell, p 155.
28 New Zealand, which adopted a Bill of Rights in 1990, has no second chamber.
29 This view was put forward by Lord McCluskey in his 1986 Reith Lectures.
30 House of Lords, *Hansard*, 31 July 1984, Cols 635–75. See Chapter 13, p 1277 *et seq*.
31 See Chapter 14, p 1378.
32 The House of Lords will, however, on occasion use its powers of suspension fully as it did in relation to the Trade Union and Labour Relations (Amendment) Bill 1974–75.

Prior to the reform of the House of Lords, begun in 1999, the Lords were generally circumspect in using their powers; when they opposed a Bill sent up by the Commons, they tended to propose amendments at the Committee stage rather than vote against the second reading, and they followed the convention that amendments at the Committee stage should not re-open matters of principle already accepted by the Commons. The Lords rarely insisted on their amendments to a government Bill. O Hood Phillips has observed[33] that there was almost a convention that the Lords would not return a government Bill to the Commons for reconsideration more than once.[34] Hereditary peers (over 750 of them) formed the majority of those entitled to sit in the Lords and ensured the continuance of a Conservative majority. Although many of them were not regular attenders, they were occasionally brought in to secure the passage of Conservative legislation which the regular attenders might be inclined to reject.[35] Their voting rights were abolished in 1999 as the first part of the Labour reform of the Lords.[36] The partially reformed House of Lords currently sees itself as having greater credibility than its predecessor and, as a result, is more interventionist.[37] Clearly, the fully reformed House may take the same or a more radical view.[38] The Lords may, therefore, become more effective in civil liberties terms. Their activism may be enhanced by the HRA since, as explained below, when Bills are introduced into the Lords, they are accompanied by a statement of compatibility with the Convention rights.[39] Thus, the Lords now have a set of standards by which to measure the impact of the legislation in question on human rights.

Conclusions

It may be concluded that Parliament has demonstrated that it is willing to move quickly to cut down freedoms, but it is, at the same time, slow to bring in measures to protect them, because civil liberties issues tend to be perceived as difficult to handle and as doubtful vote-winners. It may even be the case that the governing party would like

---

33 See Hood Phillips, O, *Constitutional and Administrative Law*, 7th edn, 1987, Sweet and Maxwell, p 148.
34 Lord Hailsham said in March 1976 in relation to the Trade Union and Labour Relations (Amendment) Bill that opposition had exhausted their powers in sending the Bill back once to the Commons and so had discharged their duty.
35 This occurred in May 1988 in relation to the introduction of the Community Charge (Poll tax).
36 The House of Lords Act 1999 removed the automatic right of hereditary Peers to sit in the House of Lords. An 'interim' House of Lords of 90 members, elected by the Peers, is currently sitting, until the reform is completed.
37 See Lord Cranborne, HL Deb 22 February 2000 Cols 151–52 and Cols 163–64. The Lord Privy Seal stated in the House Magazine on 27.9.99 that the new House of Lords will 'be more legitimate because its members have earned their places and therefore more effective . . .'. In the Committee stage of the Criminal Justice (Mode of Trial) Bill in the Lords, the first amendment put down was a 'wrecking' amendment which was carried by the Lords and resulted in the immediate withdrawal of the Bill (HL Deb 20 Jan 2000 Col 1246 et seq).
38 See the Wakeham Report of the Royal Commission published in January 2000, *A House for the Future*, Cm 3534 (available on the web: http://www.official-documents.co.uk/document/ cm45/4534/4534.htm). The report suggested a mainly appointed House of 550 with a minority of elected representatives; the Government is pledged to act on the proposals: HL Deb 7 March 2000 Col 912.
39 Human Rights Act, s 19; see Chapter 4, pp 206–11.

to bring forward legislation on a civil liberties issue, such as introducing legislation making discrimination on grounds of sexual orientation unlawful, but be hesitant to do so because of its controversial nature.[40] This received Parliamentary wisdom has meant that measures protecting civil liberties are vulnerable to under-funding,[41] and, this book will argue, in the case of the HRA, to the undermining impact of later legislation.

Under the HRA, the Westminster Parliament is still dominated by the executive and, aside from the impact of EU law, still has in theory an untrammelled power to introduce rights-abridging legislation throughout the UK.[42] In this context, it cannot yet be said that radical constitutional reform which would genuinely constrain the power of the Westminster executive has occurred. Thus, in so far as it can be said that Parliament has shown itself to be ineffective in protecting civil liberties, it may be argued that a need for a further means of protection has been demonstrated. But such protection, under the HRA, need not be sought wholly or mainly outside Parliament. The HRA creates mechanisms which would allow Parliament to be more proactive in protecting civil rights, as explained in Chapter 4. But, as indicated at a number of points in this book, an optimistic or complacent attitude towards the impact of the HRA, in terms of enhancing the traditional protection offered to such rights by Parliament, is misplaced. In the early years of the HRA, Parliament appeared to accept quite readily that when Bills were presented to it and were declared to be compatible with the Convention rights under s 19 of the HRA,[43] that meant that a process of human rights auditing had already occurred and that, therefore, concerns about the effect on human rights of the provisions in question could be allayed.[44]

It is clearly pertinent to ask whether the democratic process can be trusted to safeguard civil liberties in the context of the doctrine of parliamentary sovereignty. The further question that this book will address is whether the HRA is providing or could be expected to provide the effective protection for fundamental rights that has not been achieved through the operation of the democratic process, bearing in mind the fact that parliamentary sovereignty remains intact. As indicated, the influence of the HRA on that process in a direct sense is a significant theme.

Rules and judicial interpretation: current relevance of the traditional constitutional position

Residual liberties

The influential constitutional writer AV Dicey expressed the traditional view of rights as follows:

---

40 See for the current position, Chapter 15, p 1513 *et seq*.
41 Bodies such as the Equal Opportunities Commission may be under-funded, provision of legal aid may be cut without much (or any) public outcry.
42 See pp 170–73. The government can, of course, use the Parliament Act procedure in order to get its legislation through the Lords, as it did in respect of the Sexual Offences (Amendment) Bill 2000. The Lords have recently shown signs that they are tending to refuse to accept the conventional restraints in which they previously acquiesced.
43 See below, pp 207–8.
44 See further Chapter 14, p 1335 *et seq*.

[Most] foreign constitutions have begun by declarations of rights . . . On the other hand, there remains through the English constitution that inseparable connection between the means of enforcing a right and the right to be enforced which is the strength of judicial legislation . . . Englishmen whose labours . . . framed the completed set of laws and institutions we call the constitution, fixed their minds more intently on providing remedies for the enforcement of rights . . . than upon any declaration of the rights of man. . . .[45]

The Diceyan tradition holds that the absence of a written constitution in the UK is not a weakness, but a source of strength. This is because the protection of the citizen's liberties is not dependent on vaguely-worded constitutional documents but, rather, flows from specific judicial decisions which give the citizen specific remedies for infringement of his or her liberties. It follows from the Diceyan thesis that judges will be concerned to construe legislation strictly against the executive if it conflicts with fundamental liberties arising from the common law.[46]

Dicey regarded one of the great strengths of the British Constitution as lying in the lack of broad discretionary powers vested in the executive. Citizens could only be criminalised for clear breaches of clearly established laws and such laws also governed the extent to which individual freedoms could be infringed. Where there was no relevant law, citizens could know with absolute confidence that they could exercise their liberty as they pleased without fear of incurring any sanction.

Parliamentary sovereignty is central to the Diceyan thesis. One of its significant aspects is the position whereby, unless international treaties are incorporated into domestic law, they cannot have legal effect, domestically. This aspect derived from the supremacy of Parliament over the executive: since the making of a treaty is an executive act, any attempt by the courts to afford domestic effect to its provisions would mean undermining that supremacy. Thus, traditionally, the judiciary adopted a 'dualist' approach to such treaties; they represented a system of law external to the domestic one and not part of it. This approach entailed a resistance to any use of unincorporated international law before domestic courts.

Central aspects of Dicey's thesis are, however, unconvincing as an analysis of UK contemporary legal culture, for a number of reasons. The Diceyan view of the law as imposing only narrow and tightly defined areas of liability is no longer representative, given the prevalence of broadly drawn offences such as those arising under counter-terrorist legislation post-2000 or under the Criminal Justice and Public Order Act 1994. The view that the judges will construe rules strictly against the executive is also problematic, especially in relation to the use of quasi- and non-legislation authorising interference with civil liberties. Many such rules, including the Home Office Guidelines relied on by the police until 1997 in using surveillance devices, remain on a non-statutory basis for many years; they therefore receive no Parliamentary scrutiny and little or no judicial scrutiny either. When such rules are placed on a statutory basis, as they were under the Interception of Communications Act 1985, the Security Services

---

45 Dicey, AV, *Introduction to the Study of the Law of the Constitution*, 10th edn, 1987, Macmillan, p 198; see also p 190.
46 See, e.g., *Waddington v Miah* [1974] 2 All ER 377, HL.

Act 1989 and the Intelligence Services Act 1994, judicial scrutiny of their operation is, typically, largely ousted. This tradition was continued by the New Labour Government under the Terrorism Act 2000 and the Regulation of Investigatory Powers Act 2000, as this book will point out, and significant aspects of these schemes are found in Codes of Practice and statutory instruments. The result is that there have been and will continue to be a number of significant areas of executive action which are largely closed to judicial scrutiny.

The following discussion indicates the inadequacies of Dicey's account in a number of further respects. In particular, it indicates the extent to which the European Convention on Human Rights was used as an interpretative tool and became a source of values relied upon in the development of the common law in the 1990s.

Judicial protection for liberties outside administrative law

Under the traditional view of the constitution, the judges will interpret common law doctrines so that fundamental freedoms are protected.[47] Street, in *Freedom, the Individual and the Law*, argues: 'our judges may be relied on to defend strenuously some kinds of freedom. Their emotions will be aroused where personal freedom is menaced by some politically unimportant area of the executive.'[48] Ewing and Gearty have argued, however, that the first half of the twentieth century saw a marked judicial reluctance to protect such freedoms.[49] Consideration of key decisions in the latter half of the twentieth century also suggests that there did not seem to be a clear conception, shared by most members of the judiciary, of their role as protecting liberties. For example, during the miners' strike in 1984–85, striking miners shouted abuse at miners going in to work guarded by police; the working miners claimed that such action was unlawful, and it was found that although no obvious legal pigeon-hole, such as assault, could be found for it owing to the circumstances, it could be termed 'a species of private nuisance' and injunctions against the striking miners were, therefore, granted.[50] The use of common law contempt in the *Spycatcher* litigation provides a further example.[51]

On a number of occasions, the judiciary interpreted uncertain areas of the common law, such as breach of the peace, very broadly, to some extent undermining the safeguards for liberties provided by statutes covering equivalent areas. Where an attempt has been made in a statute to seek to ensure that a particular freedom is protected, as is the case in s 4 of the Obscene Publications Act 1959 and s 5 of the Contempt of Court Act 1981, it may be found that the common law begins to take on a role which undermines the statutory provisions. This can be said of the common law doctrines of breach of the peace, contempt, and conspiracy to corrupt public morals.[52] It is noticeable that when the judges are enjoined in a statute to take account of a value such as freedom of expression – as they are under s 5 of the Contempt of Court Act 1981 – they are

---

47 See *Entinck v Carrington* [1765] 19 state Tr 1029.
48 Street, H, *Freedom, the Individual and the Law*, 1982, Penguin, p 318.
49 See Ewing, KD and Gearty, CA, *The Struggle for Civil Liberties*, 1999.
50 *Thomas v NUM* [1985] 2 All ER 1.
51 *AG v Newspaper Publishing plc* [1988] Ch 333; [1987] 3 All ER 276; [1988] 3 WLR 942, CA. See further Chapter 5, pp 368–70.
52 See further Chapter 5, p 363 *et seq*, Chapter 6, pp 482–84, Chapter 8 p 750 *et seq*.

more likely to adopt a rigorous approach than when dealing with a wide and uncertain power arising at common law.[53] Ewing and Gearty have argued that, for this reason, a Bill of Rights would be undesirable since the people need Parliament to protect them from the judges, not merely the judges to protect them from Parliament.[54]

From the perspective of the 1980s, it can be said that when a commentator in the common law tradition, such as TRS Allan, sought to defend the record of the common law in protecting fundamental rights,[55] a rather ironic pattern emerged. Allan contended that the case law showed support for civil liberties; he quoted from cases which purportedly supported his contention – and then found himself apologising for the inadequacies of the Lords' approach. Having cited *Wheeler v Leicester CC*[56] as an instance of the sturdy defence of free speech, he conceded that Lord Roskill did not use free speech grounds at all, while Lord Templeman did, in general terms, but unfortunately 'failed to address the level of principle demanded by the freedoms at issue'.[57] When he turned to the *Spycatcher* litigation, he was forced to concede from the outset that the speeches are 'disappointing'. Having praised Lord Keith for affirming the general freedom to speak, he then went on to admit that his Lordship failed to injunct only because 'all possible damage to the interests of the Crown had already been done' and that he was 'unwilling to . . . base his decision on any considerations of freedom of the press'.[58]

As this book will indicate, a number of twentieth-century decisions showed similar characteristics. Judicial activism in the 1990s, however, led to a number of significant decisions protective of liberty. They were influenced by International Human Rights law, and more specifically by the European Convention on Human Rights, in the sense that the judiciary began to demonstrate a strong inclination to show that the common law had long recognised the values encapsulated in the Convention. By so doing, they avoided the difficulties, discussed below, of determining the precise status of the European Convention in domestic law, while allowing for the infusion of such values into the common law.

The decision of *Derbyshire v Times Newspapers*,[59] which has been acclaimed as 'a legal landmark',[60] provides an important example of this tendency. The House of Lords found, without referring to Art 10 of the European Convention, that the importance the common law attached to free speech was such that defamation could

---

53 Contrast the approach to freedom of speech taken in *AG v English* [1983] 1 AC 116 in relation to s 5 of the 1981 Act, with that taken in *AG v Newspaper Publishing plc* [1988] Ch 333 in relation to common law contempt; also the approach to the Public Order Act 1986 taken in *Reid* [1987] Crim LR 702 with that taken to breach of the peace in *Moss v McLachan* [1985] IRLR 76 and *Austin and Saxby* [2005] EWHC 480. See Chapter 5, pp 357–58 and 369 and Chapter 8, pp 705 and 756, 763–71 respectively.

54 Ewing and Gearty, *Freedom under Thatcher*, 1989, pp 270–71.

55 Allan, TRS, 'Constitutional rights and common law' (1991) OJLS 453–60.

56 [1985] AC 1054; [1985] 2 All ER 1106, HL.

57 Allan, ibid, p 459.

58 Allan, ibid, p 460.

59 [1993] AC 534; [1993] 1 All ER 1011; [1992] 3 WLR 28, HL.

60 See Laws, J (Sir), 'Is the High Court the guardian of fundamental constitutional rights?' [1993] PL 67.

not be available as an action to local (or central) government.[61] In the House of Lords, Lord Keith said: 'I find it satisfactory to be able to conclude that the common law of England is consistent with the [freedom of expression] obligations assumed under [the Convention].'[62] Butler-Sloss LJ said in the Court of Appeal: 'I can see no inconsistency between English law upon this subject and Article 10 . . . This is scarcely surprising, since we may pride ourselves on the fact that freedom of speech has existed in this country perhaps as long, if not longer than . . . in any other country in the world.'[63]

While it might be argued that the decision appears to support the Diceyan thesis, it could also be said, more convincingly, that this explanation does not account for the recognition of Convention values in the common law. Hunt argues that: 'the supposed identity of common law and ECHR is surely a modern manifestation of the ancient myth that judges are not law-makers . . . [it is hard to deny that the courts are] developing the common law, extending it to cover rights and interests not previously valued by a conservative common law which privileged above all property-based or personal liberty interests.'[64] In the later seminal decision in *Reynolds v Times Newspapers Ltd*,[65] also in the field of defamation, the influence of the Convention was more overt. The House of Lords found that qualified privilege could apply to a publication where the media could establish that the information promulgated was matter that the public had a right to know. Lord Nicholls of Birkenhead found that this conclusion was firmly based on established common law principle. Lord Steyn gave more weight to Convention-based arguments in finding that: 'it is necessary to recognise the "vital public watchdog role of the press" as a practical matter'. In support of this argument, he relied on *Goodwin v UK*.[66]

But, while an attachment to free speech values that is arguably consonant with the value it is accorded at Strasbourg, is clearly evident in these decisions, this book discusses a number of decisions taken in the mid- to late-1990s affecting equally fundamental rights, in the fields of public protest,[67] police powers and fair trial rights,[68] which took a very ungenerous approach to rights and liberties. The reasons for the adoption of such an approach are discussed further in the relevant chapters. But, it is suggested here that while the decisions on fair trial rights do reflect Convention values, to varying degrees, they also assert an allegiance to the dualist approach, which was not evident in *Derbyshire*. The public protest decisions, it is argued, go even further in that direction.

---

61 *Derbyshire* was followed and its principle extended in *Goldsmith and Another v Bhoyrul and Others* [1997] 4 All ER 268; (1997) *The Times*, 20 June. It was found that a political party cannot sue in libel, although individual candidates would be able to.

62 [1993] AC 534, p 551.

63 [1992] 3 WLR 28, p 60.

64 Hunt, M, *Using Human Rights Law in English Courts*, 1997, p 186.

65 [1999] 4 All ER 609.

66 (1996) 22 EHRR 123, p 143, para 39.

67 Examples of such decisions discussed in this book include: the Divisional Court and House of Lords decisions in *DPP v Jones* and *Lloyd v DPP* [1999] 2 AC 240; [1997] 2 All ER 119 (for comment, see Fenwick and Phillipson, 'Public protest, the Human Rights Act and judicial responses to political expression' [2000] PL 627) *DPP v Moseley, Woodling and Selvanayagam*, Judgment of 9 June 1999; reported [1999] J Civ Lib 390, (Chapter 9, p 711 *et seq.* and p 793, respectively).

68 *Khan* [1996] 3 WLR 162; *Chalkley* [1998] 2 Cr App R 79.

Thus, it can be said that over the last three decades, prior to the introduction of the HRA, the judiciary did not develop a coherent approach to the protection of civil rights and liberties, although the influence of the European Convention on Human Rights became very marked, especially in the field of freedom of expression, in the 1990s. The dualist approach became 'in reality a matter of degree'.[69] But the difference of degree was sometimes quite remarkable.

Judicial review

It may be said that, before the 1990s, when fundamental human rights became an increasingly significant factor in judicial review, the judiciary maintained the classic dualist position in judicial review despite the acceptance of Convention values in other areas of the law. This was on the basis that to do otherwise would be to break down the traditional divide between review and appeal. And even within a strict review jurisdiction, strong deference was shown to executive decision-making in the politically important areas of executive action. The reluctance of judges to intervene in such areas, including those of public security or deportation, was evident in a number of decisions. Those in *Secretary of State for the Home Department ex p Northumbria Police Authority*[70] and *Secretary of State for the Home Department ex p Hosenball*[71] showed this tendency to a particularly marked degree. Thus, traditionally, the doctrine remained fundamentally limited in that as long as a minister appeared to have followed a correct and fair procedure, to have acted within his or her powers and to have made a decision which was not clearly unreasonable under the traditional *Wednesbury* test, the decision had to stand regardless of its potentially harmful impact on civil liberties. The fact that basic liberties were curtailed in, for example, the *GCHQ*[72] case did not, in itself, provide a ground for review. In other words, the courts were confined to looking back at the method of arriving at the decision rather than forward to its likely effects. In cases which touched directly on national security, so sensitive were the judges to the executive's duty to uphold the safety of the realm, that they tended to define their powers even to look back on the decision as almost non-existent.[73]

A development in the stance the judiciary was prepared to take when an administrative decision infringed human rights was evident in *Secretary of State for the Home Department ex p Brind*.[74] The change was explained by Lord Bridge. He rejected the argument that state officials must take the European Convention on Human Rights into account in exercising discretionary power, and thus the possibility of extending the role of the Convention in domestic law by importing it into administrative law was rejected. He made it clear that although the courts would presume that ambiguity in domestic legislation should be resolved by arriving at an interpretation in conformity with the

---

69 Hunt, M, *Using Human Rights Law in English Courts*, 1997, p 41.
70 [1989] QB 26; [1988] 2 WLR 590; [1988] 1 All ER 556, CA.
71 [1977] 1 WLR 766.
72 *Council of Civil Service Unions v Minister for Civil Service* [1985] AC 374; [1985] 3 WLR 1174; [1984] 3 All ER 935, HL (the Prime Minister's decision struck directly at freedom of association).
73 See *Secretary of State for Home Affairs ex p Stitt* (1987) *The Times*, 3 February.
74 [1991] 1 AC 696; [1991] 1 All ER 720; [1991] 2 WLR 588, HL (political speech was directly curtailed); [1990] 1 All ER 469, CA.

Convention, it did not follow that where Parliament had conferred an administrative discretion on the executive without indicating the precise limits within which it had to be exercised, it could be presumed that it had to be exercised within Convention limits. It had been argued that to import such a principle must have been the legislature's intention, but the House of Lords considered that this would be an unwarranted step to take, bearing in mind that Parliament had chosen not to incorporate the Convention. Thus, the decision in *Brind* reaffirmed the accepted principle that the Convention should be taken into account where domestic legislation was ambiguous. It also determined that state officials were not bound by the Convention in exercising discretionary power.[75] Lord Bridge, reflecting the view of the majority, accepted nevertheless that where fundamental rights are in issue, they will affect the review of the exercise of such power. He said:

> we are entitled to start from the premise that any restriction of the right of freedom of expression requires to be justified and nothing less than an important competing public interest will be sufficient to justify it. The primary judgment as to whether the particular competing public interest justifies the particular restriction . . . falls to be exercised by the Secretary of State . . . But we are entitled to exercise a secondary judgment by asking whether a reasonable Secretary of State on the material before him could reasonably make that primary judgment.[76]

Thus, where fundamental human rights were in question, the *Wednesbury* test had to be refined. This argument was applied and taken further in *Ministry for Defence ex p Smith and Others*.[77] The case concerned the legality of the policy of the Ministry of Defence in maintaining a ban on homosexuals in the armed forces. The applicants, homosexuals who had been dismissed due to the existence of the ban, applied for review of the policy. Their application was dismissed at first instance in the Divisional Court and the applicants appealed. Rejecting the argument of the Ministry of Defence that it had no jurisdiction to review the legality of the policy in question, the court applied the usual *Wednesbury* principles. This meant that it could not interfere with the exercise of an administrative discretion on substantive grounds save where it was satisfied that the decision was unreasonable in the sense that it was beyond the range of responses open to a reasonable decision maker. But, in judging whether the decision maker had exceeded that margin of appreciation, the human rights context was important: 'the more substantial the interference with human rights, the more the court will require by way of justification before it will be satisfied that the decision

---

75   It may be noted that the then Conservative Government subsequently accepted that state officials exercising such powers should comply with the Convention: HL Deb 559 WA 7 December 1994 Col 84 and WA 9 January 1995 Vol 560 Col 1.

76   [1991] 1 All ER 720, p 723.

77   [1996] 1 All ER 257; [1996] ICR 740. See also *Secretary of State for the Home Department ex p McQuillan* [1995] 3 All ER 400; (1994) *Independent*, 23 September, in which Laws J's approach was expressly followed. Sedley J was unable to find for the applicant due to the particular statutory framework in question.

was reasonable.'[78] The Court rejected the argument of the Ministry of Defence that a less exacting test than applying *Wednesbury* principles of reasonableness was required. Applying such principles and taking into account the support of the policy in both Houses of Parliament, it could not be said that the policy crossed the threshold of irrationality. The concept of proportionality, as considered by the Master of the Rolls in this instance, was not viewed as a separate head of challenge, but merely as an aspect of *Wednesbury* unreasonableness.[79]

The significance of this decision lay in the meaning attributed to the word 'reasonable'; it denoted only a decision which was 'within the range of responses open to a reasonable decision-maker'.[80] But, the decision maker was required to take account of human rights in appropriate cases and she had to have a more convincing justification the more her decision was likely to trespass on those rights. That decision, however, remained primarily one for the decision maker. The courts would only intervene if the decider had come up with a justification which no reasonable person could consider trumped the human rights considerations – a position which was akin to classic *GCHQ* irrationality.[81] However, *Smith* did require a variable standard of review, depending on the human rights context.

A further, linked, factor of significance in *Smith* was the determination as to which policy considerations were to be allowed to override rights and which were not. It appeared that in making this determination, easily satisfied criteria were adopted. The policy factors were not required to satisfy the test of meeting a 'pressing social need',[82] since satisfying a lesser test nevertheless brought the decision within the range of responses open to a reasonable decision maker. This decision echoed that of Lord Bridge in *Brind* in relation to determinations as to overriding individual rights as guaranteed in the European Convention on Human Rights.[83]

In 1993, Sir John Laws, in an important article,[84] suggested a method of developing judicial review so that it could afford greater protection to liberties. His persuasive thesis is still of relevance in the post-HRA era since it can be used as a tool in order to measure the change brought about in judicial review in the pre-HRA era and by the HRA. He – in effect – anticipated the effect of the HRA, but, as indicated below, it appeared that, initially at least, most of his fellow judges were not prepared to do so. The main thrust of the thesis was, briefly, as follows. He proposed that review could develop such that in a case in which the exercise of discretion could have an adverse impact on fundamental rights, a two-stage test would be imposed by the courts. With respect to the first stage, the thesis noted that the courts have imposed an insistence

---

78 [1996] 1 All ER 257, p 263. See also *Bugdaycay v Secretary of State for the Home Dept* [1987] AC 514, p 531. For comment, see Fordham, M, 'What is anxious scrutiny?' [1996] JR 81.

79 For further argument as to the notion of proportionality, see Himsworth, C [1996] PL 46; his argument that the notion of proportionality as a separate head of review remains a possibility rests on an examination of *Ministry of Agriculture, Fisheries and Food ex p Hamble* [1995] 2 All ER 714.

80 Ibid.

81 Fenwick, H and Phillipson, G, *Sourcebook on Public Law*, 1997, Cavendish, (2nd edn, 2002), p 803.

82 See Chapter 2, pp 68–69.

83 See *Brind* case [1991] 1 AC 696.

84 Laws [1993] PL 59–79.

on decision makers that their power may be used only for the purpose for which it was granted to them, the courts being the final arbiter of the nature of that purpose. As part of this attribution of purpose, the courts have consistently imposed on decision makers the presumption that power is granted to be exercised in a rational, not a capricious manner. It was proposed that a rather more stringent presumption could be imposed – namely, that no statute's purpose could include interference with fundamental rights embedded in the common law and that such interference would only be allowed if it was demonstrated that reading the statute to permit such interference was the only interpretation possible.[85] This was the first stage of the test. This approach was uncontroversial in assuming that power is only granted on the understanding that it will be exercised rationally – indeed, this could be said to be a basic requirement of formal justice. By contrast, to assume that power is never granted to infringe basic liberties is to make a substantive claim – and until the late 1990s, the courts were not prepared to make it. Preparedness to impose such a presumption in all cases implied the kind of unified, purposeful determination to protect civil liberties which most commentators failed to perceive in the judiciary during most of the 1980s and 1990s.[86]

This aspect of the thesis, concerning statutory interpretation in relation to fundamental human rights, found expression in a number of decisions in the immediate pre-HRA era. In this sense, s 3 of the HRA (see Chapter 4 below) was prefigured in certain decisions that recognised common law rights which cannot be abrogated except by express words or necessary implication – where there is only one way of reading the legislation in question. They included the rights of access to the courts,[87] to free speech,[88] and to basic subsistence,[89] and these decisions are discussed further below.[90] The rule of construction in these instances was described in one of the most significant of these decisions, *Ex p Simms*,[91] by Lord Hoffmann, as follows:

85   Laws adverts to the fact that an argument very similar to his was rejected in the *Brind* case. However, he considers that this was because the submission made in that case was that their Lordships should make such a presumption (in this case that free speech would not be infringed) under Art 10 of the ECHR. He argues that this is a mistaken approach as it amounts to an attempt to incorporate the ECHR through the back door, which the courts rightly resist since it offends against constitutional principles. Instead, he urges that the correct approach would be to argue that the norms implicit in the ECHR are already reflected in the common law – an approach which gains some support from the House of Lords decision in the *Derbyshire* case [1993] AC 534; [1993] 1 All ER 1011; [1992] 3 WLR 28, HL – and that it is the importance consequently attached by the common law to fundamental rights which provides a justification for the presumption that statutes do not intend to override them.

86   See, e.g., Oliver, D, 'A Bill of Rights for the United Kingdom', pp 151, 163; Ewing and Gearty, *Freedom under Thatcher*, 1989, generally and pp 64, 111, 157–60, 270–71 for particular criticisms of anti-libertarian judicial decisions and attitudes; Lester, A, 'Fundamental rights: the United Kingdom isolated?' [1984] PL 46.

87   *R v Lord Chancellor ex p Witham* [1998] QB 575. But *cf R v Lord Chancellor ex p Lightfoot* [2000] 2 WLR 318. For comment on the first instance decision [1998] 4 All ER 764, see Elliott, M, 'Lightfoot: tracing the perimeter of constitutional rights' [1998] JR 217.

88   *R v Secretary of State for the Home Dept ex p Simms* [1999] 3 All ER 400, CA; [1999] 3 WLR 328, HL.

89   89 *R v Secretary of State for Social Security ex p Joint Council of Welfare of Immigrants* [1996] 4 All ER 835; *Lord Saville ex p A* [1999] 4 All ER 860.

90   See Part II, pp 310–11.

91   *R v Secretary of State for the Home Dept ex p Simms* [1999] 3 All ER 400, CA; [1999] 3 WLR 328, HL.

Parliamentary sovereignty means that Parliament can if it chooses legislate contrary to fundamental principles of human rights . . . But the principle of legality means that Parliament must squarely confront what it is doing and count the political cost. Fundamental rights cannot be overridden by general or ambiguous words . . . because there is too great a risk that the full implications of their unqualified meaning may have passed unnoticed in the democratic process . . . In this way the courts of the UK, though acknowledging the sovereignty of Parliament, apply principles of constitutionality little different from those which exist in countries where the power of the legislature is expressly limited by a constitutional document.[92]

In *Ex p Witham*,[93] Laws J found that the power of the Lord Chancellor to prescribe court fees was not based on sufficiently precise words to allow him to deny the right of access to a court by preventing an applicant on income support from issuing proceedings for defamation.

The second aspect of Sir John Laws' proposed thesis was as follows: in the pre-HRA era, the courts insisted that relevant considerations should be taken into account when making a decision, but held that the weight to be given to those considerations was entirely for the decision maker to determine. Laws argued that, on principle, while this might be a reasonable approach when the matter under consideration involved such issues as economic policy, this was far from the case where fundamental rights were at stake, since it meant that the decision maker would be free 'to accord a high or low importance to the right in question, as he chooses' which 'cannot be right'. He argued that the courts should therefore insist that the right could only be overridden if an 'objective, sufficient justification'[94] existed so that the infringement was limited to what was strictly required by the situation. While such a development would undoubtedly have been welcome, in terms of the protection afforded by judicial review to liberties in the pre-HRA era, two objections were inescapable. The first was simply that there appeared to be no compelling reason to suppose that such a concept of proportionality (as a separate head of challenge rather than as merely an aspect of *Wednesbury* unreasonableness)[95] would not remain waiting in the wings as merely a theoretical possibility prior to the introduction of the HRA.[96] The possibility of its development as a separate head of review was first floated in the *GCHQ* case. Variable enthusiasm by the judiciary to develop it was evident after that decision. The decision in *Smith* clearly failed to reflect Laws' thesis, although it gave an appearance of doing so. The Laws approach was applied in order to reach an outcome protective of individual rights in *Cambridge HA ex p B*[97] in which Laws J himself was presiding; his decision was immediately overturned by the Court of Appeal.[98] In contrast to that decision,

92   [1999] 3 All ER 400, p 412.
93   [1998] QB 575.
94   Laws [1993] PL 59–79, p 14.
95   See, e.g., the remarks of Taylor LJ in *Ex p United States Tobacco* [1992] 1 QB 353, p 366, to which Laws adverts.
96   For discussion of other proposals for the development of judicial review, see Jowell, J and Lester, A, 'Beyond *Wednesbury*: substantive principles of judicial review' [1987] PL 369.
97   [1995] TLR 159; [1995] WLR 898, CA.
98   [1995] 1 WLR 898.

the decision in *R v Lord Saville ex p A*[99] arguably prefigured the introduction of the proportionality test under the HRA and was consistent with that of Laws in *Ex p B*. The Court of Appeal subjected the decision not to afford anonymity to witnesses in the 'Bloody Sunday' inquiry to anxious scrutiny and went on to find that the inquiry had acted irrationally in so doing since it had failed to attach sufficient importance to the right to life.

It was a notable feature of the *Ex p B* case that the Court of Appeal took a wholly different approach from Laws J, a fact which led one commentator, Mallender, to question whether judicial review, which is of course supposed to represent the practical application of the rule of law, was in fact offending against the doctrine by virtue of its increasing uncertainty.[100] Mallender went on to find that in fact, on a more general jurisprudential level, both approaches 'reveal an intention to give effect to recognisably legal values' which restrain the discretion of both of them. Nevertheless, it was clear that since the two courts differed so markedly as to which (legal) matters were (a) relevant and (b) determinative of the matter in hand, it was apparent that the rapid development of this area of law was likely to entail a period of considerable uncertainty as to the content and scope of its core principles.

The second objection to Laws' thesis was that, even if such a head of challenge had been developed prior to the introduction of the HRA, the really crucial factor would have been the criteria the courts had decided to use to determine which policy considerations were to be allowed to override rights and which were not. If easily satisfied criteria had been adopted – a contingency which appeared likely – then the increased judicial protection offered to basic liberties might have turned out to consist rather more of theory than of substance. As indicated below, this will be a crucial issue under the HRA.

This discussion of judicial review in the immediate pre-HRA era indicates that it is possible to identify a common law tradition of upholding fundamental rights in certain limited, but central areas. That development is very clearly continuing in the HRA era[101] since the common law is being affected by the values of the Convention rights. The decisions considered, together with a number of others of a similar nature,[102] reaffirm, it is suggested, the value of judicial review as a means of ensuring that some harmony between UK executive practice and the standards laid down by the European Convention on Human Rights is achieved, and this was the case even in the pre-HRA era. Murray Hunt has argued that a common law tradition of developing human rights that reflected those enshrined in international human rights treaties was

---

99 [1999] 4 All ER 860.

100 Mallender, R, 'Judicial review and the rule of law' (1996) 112 LQR 182–86.

101 See *Secretary of State for the Home Dept ex p Daly* [2001] 3 All ER 433; [2001] UKHL 26, HL. The case concerned the examination of legal correspondence between a prisoner and his solicitor. The applicant claimed that he should be able to be present while his correspondence was being read. The House of Lords upheld his claim on the basis that the policy was disproportionate to the aim in view. Lord Steyn said: 'it is of great importance . . . that the common law itself is recognised as a sufficient source of the confidential right to confidential communication with a legal advisor for the purpose of obtaining legal advice' (para 30).

102 See, e.g., *Secretary of State for Social Security ex p Joint Council for the Welfare of Immigrants* [1996] 4 All ER 385; *Secretary of State for the Home Dept and Another ex p Norney and Others* (1995) *The Times*, 6 October.

well established.[103] Where, however, a statute uses specific words abrogating human rights,[104] and therefore it is necessary to argue that the decision was unreasonable, the limitations of the *Wednesbury* doctrine, albeit refined by reference to the human rights context, persisted. The decision in *Smith* may be said to demonstrate the limitations of judicial review in this respect. The reception of the European Convention on Human Rights into UK law under the HRA means that proportionality has been established as a separate head of review where the Convention guarantees are in issue, since the need for the administrative decision or measure in question has to be considered in relation to its impact in terms of the those guarantees.

Judicial review had already shown its potential to play a much greater part in the protection of human rights in the UK in the areas of activity affected by EU law.[105] In such areas, the merits of the decision were relevant and express words used in a statute could not overcome EU provisions.[106]

Conclusions

Two points seem to emerge from the above discussion. First, in the pre-HRA era, the judiciary did not seem to be united around a clear conception of their role. No compelling evidence emerged of a common understanding that they should form a bulwark to protect the citizens' liberties against the burgeoning power of the executive. While decisions in the field of free speech suggested an acceptance that Convention values were recognised as common law principles, decisions in the areas in which the common law had traditionally taken a non-rights-based stance, such as public order and exclusion of physical evidence unlawfully obtained, showed a persistence of that tradition. Second, even in the area in which a clear acceptance of the role of the common law in protecting fundamental human rights was present – judicial review – the courts seemed to lack the determination to continue pushing the limits of the doctrine outwards in order to ensure greater protection. They stopped short of introducing a full proportionality test.

It may be persuasively argued that since the judiciary had no 'textual anchor for their decisions' and had to 'rely on an appeal to normative ideals that lack any mooring in the common law',[107] it is unsurprising that common practice as regards fundamental freedoms did not emerge. Dawn Oliver points out that what has been termed the 'ethical aimlessness' of the common law – its lack of a sense of clear direction – means that because the judiciary as a body has no clear conception of the way the law should develop, they have not framed any set of 'guiding principles or priorities where civil and political rights clash with public interests'.[108] Thus, the judges in general showed,

---

103 Hunt, M, *Using Human Rights Law in English Courts*, 1997, p 5.
104 See *Lord Chancellor ex p Lightfoot* [2000] 2 WLR 318.
105 See *Secretary of State for Employment ex p EOC* [1994] 2 WLR 409, HL.
106 For the view that the direct influence of the Convention in the UK due to its significance as a source of general principles of EU law is not confined only to those areas of activity affected by EU law: see Beyleveld, D, 'The concept of a human right and incorporation of the ECHR' [1995] PL 577.
107 Justice William Brennan of the US Supreme Court in Hart, *Lectures on Jurisprudence and Moral Philosophy*, p 12, 24 May 1989.
108 Oliver, D, 'A Bill of Rights for the United Kingdom', p 151.

at times, uncertainty as to the weight to afford to a particular liberty, while the more executive-minded amongst them could take advantage of this uncertainty to grant it little or no weight. These tendencies meant that debate as to the principles underlying civil liberties was stifled and only the most obvious instances of their infringement received attention – where very basic rights were in question.

In the years immediately preceding the coming fully into force of the HRA, there was, as indicated, an emergence of common law rights going well beyond those rights, particularly to property, that the common law had traditionally recognised. However, it is arguable that without a constitutional document such as the ECHR, with its accumulated jurisprudence, to give them substance and depth, they might have remained at an uncertain and early stage of development, especially as there was some reluctance on the part of the judiciary to import ECHR principles and a preference for relying on a coincidence between such principles and those apparently already embedded in the common law.

Now that the judges have a 'textual anchor' in the form of the European Convention on Human Rights, applied domestically under the HRA, it is nevertheless unlikely that common practice among them will become rapidly evident; as this book will indicate, clear differences of approach were already emerging in the early years after the HRA came fully into force. This is unsurprising: judges in the US Supreme Court and in the European Court of Human Rights differ very widely as to their conceptions of liberty. However, it seems unarguable that the introduction of the Convention is achieving an increase in unity amongst domestic judges; while different judges will give different weights to rights and freedoms, at the very least all are certain about when they have to be taken into account. In particular, it is clear that the structure of judicial reasoning is changing under the HRA.[109]

In relation to both the key points indicated, it may plausibly be argued that in the last century, the judiciary as a body were not able to construct for themselves a clear justification for increasing their powers over government, although signs of judicial activism in the 1990s suggested that some of them considered that they should do so. The reception of the European Convention on Human Rights into domestic law, which may be viewed as a public statement from the nation as a whole of the importance that they attach to human rights, has given the judges a clearer mandate to develop a domestic human rights jurisprudence.

The influence of the European Convention on Human Rights in the pre-HRA era

Under Art 1 of the European Convention on Human Rights, the member states[110] must secure the rights and freedoms to their subjects, but they are free to decide

---

109 See Chapter 4, esp pp 267–91.

110 Currently, the Western European members include: Albania, Andorra, Austria, Belgium, Cyprus, Denmark, Finland, France, Germany, Greece, Iceland, Ireland, Italy, Liechtenstein, Luxembourg, Malta, The Netherlands, Norway, Portugal, San Marino, Spain, Sweden, Switzerland, Turkey, UK. Eastern European members include: Bulgaria, Croatia, the Czech Republic, Estonia, Georgia, Hungary, Latvia, Lithuania, Macedonia, Moldova, Poland, Romania, Russia, Slovakia and Slovenia and Ukraine. The numbers increased owing to the disintegration of the Soviet Union and Yugoslavia.

how this should be done.[111] Each state decides on the status the Convention enjoys in national law; there is no obligation under Art 1 to allow individuals to rely on it in national courts. In some states, it has the status of constitutional law;[112] in others, of ordinary law.[113]

In the pre-HRA era, rulings of the European Court of Human Rights led to better protection of human rights in such areas as prisoners' rights,[114] freedom of expression[115] and privacy.[116] But, as an external force, the influence of the Convention was limited. In contrast to the influence of European Union law, discussed below, the influence of the European Convention was, and is, procedurally rather than substantively limited. As pointed out in Chapter 2, the effect at the international level of a ruling of the European Court of Human Rights is dependent on the government in question making a change in the law. The UK government has been able to minimise the impact of an adverse judgment by interpreting defeat narrowly,[117] by avoiding implementation of a ruling,[118] or by obeying the letter of the Article in question, but ignoring its spirit.[119] The impact of the Convention at the international level was, and is, diminished since the process of invoking it, considered in Chapter 2, is extremely cumbersome, lengthy[120] and expensive.[121] It may not become less so despite the change which occurred under the Eleventh Protocol, including merger of the European Court and Commission of Human Rights[122] and the more recent changes discussed in Chapter 2.[123] Under the HRA, litigants may still take cases to Strasbourg as a last resort, but, as Chapter 2 demonstrated, while the system of the long trek to Strasbourg (starting with the exhaustion of domestic remedies) remains substantially, as at present, only the most exceptionally determined and resourceful litigants are likely to pursue it.[124]

In the UK, prior to the introduction of the HRA, the Convention had no domestic binding force. Until 1997, successive UK governments considered that it was not

---

111 This was affirmed by the Irish Supreme Court in *The State (Lawless) v O'Sullivan and the Minister for Justice*; see *Yearbook of the Convention on Human Rights Vol II* (1958–59), pp 608–22.

112 E.g., Austria.

113 This includes Belgium, France, Italy, Luxembourg and Germany.

114 E.g., *Golder*, Eur Court HR, A 18, Judgment of 21 February 1975.

115 *Sunday Times*, Judgment of 26 April 1979; (1979) 2 EHRR 245. See further Chapter 5, pp 336–37.

116 E.g., *Gaskin v UK* (1990) 12 EHRR 36. See further Chapter 9, p 924. See further Farren, S, *The UK before the European Court of Human Rights*, 1996.

117 As in *Golder*, Eur Court HR, A 18, Judgment of 21 February 1975.

118 *Brogan, Coyle, McFadden and Tracey v UK* (1988) 11 EHRR 117 (Case No 10/1987/133/184–7). The government refused to implement the ruling, entering a derogation under Art 15. See further Chapter 2, p 111.

119 *Abdulaziz, Cabales and Balkandali v UK* (1985) 7 EHRR 471. To implement the ruling, the UK 'equalised down'. See further Chapter 2, p 109.

120 The Commission used to make over 3,000 provisional files a year. The average petition took five years and nine months between 1982 and 1987 if it went all the way through the system – four years before the Commission, nearly two before the Court (15 EHRR 321, p 327). Petitions can take nine years. When the Commission was abolished admissibility was then determined by a Chamber of the Court, as Chapter 2 explains. The average time is around four years; for some years the Court has had 5,000 cases pending. See further Chapter 2, pp 23–29.

121 Legal aid is not available until after the complaint has been held admissible.

122 See Chapter 2, pp 25–29.

123 See pp 27–29.

124 See Chapter 2, pp 28–31.

necessary for the Convention to be part of UK law; they always maintained that the UK's unwritten constitution was in conformity with it. Thus, until 2000, a UK citizen could not go before a UK court and simply argue that a Convention right had been violated by a public authority. Nevertheless, before the HRA came fully into force, the influence of the Convention was rapidly becoming more significant in domestic law through rulings in UK courts and in the European Court of Human Rights. As indicated below, the Convention also had an increasing significance in human rights-related rulings of the European Court of Justice. It may be said that the Convention was encroaching steadily on UK law from every direction,[125] and that its direct domestic reception under the HRA was merely the culmination of that process.[126]

The discussion above regarding the influence of human rights values in the common law pre-HRA demonstrated that the courts in a number of significant decisions tended to prefer to refer to common law principle rather than explicitly to the Convention in respect both of statutory interpretation and the development of the common law. However, in both respects, a strand of thinking became very evident to the effect that the Convention itself should be explicitly relied upon. It had an impact through domestic courts in the pre-HRA era in the following ways.

The domestic impact of the ECHR in the pre-HRA era: statutory construction

It became a general principle of construction that statutes would be interpreted if possible so as to conform with international human rights treaties to which the UK is a party, on the basis that the government is aware of its international obligations and would not intend to legislate contrary to them.[127] A legal presumption developed that 'Parliament does not intend to act in breach of international law' (per Diplock LJ in *Saloman v Commissioners of Custom and Excise*),[128] so that a reading of the relevant legislation that did not create a breach of rights would be adopted by the courts if such a reading was possible. However, as Lord Brandon of Oakbrook made clear in *re M and H (Minors)*,[129] the English courts were under no duty to apply the Convention's provisions directly: 'While English courts may strive where they can to interpret statutes as conforming with the obligations of the UK under the Convention, they are nevertheless bound to give effect to statutes which are free from ambiguity even if those statutes may be in conflict with the Convention'. Thus, quite a strong protection against legislative encroachment on civil and political rights, especially those arising under the Convention, became increasingly available. Other international human rights treaties to which the UK is a party, including the International Covenant on Civil and Political Rights, had much less influence, as indicated below.[130]

---

125 For the argument that the extent of such encroachment has been exaggerated, see Klug, F and Starmer, K [1997] PL 223.
126 See esp pp 114 and 210.
127 See the judgment of Lord Brandon of Oakbrook in *re M and H (Minors)* [1990] 1 AC 686; [1988] 3 WLR 485, HL, p 498; [1990] 1 AC 686.
128 [1967] 2 QB 116, p 143.
129 [1988] 3 WLR 485, p 498; [1990] 1 AC 686, HL.
130 See also p 17. See further Clayton, R and Tomlinson, H, *The Law of Human Rights*, 2000, pp 89–103.

The interpretation of ambiguous provisions in conformity with the Convention thus left it great scope to influence domestic law even before the introduction of the HRA.

The domestic impact of the ECHR in the pre-HRA era: influence on the common law

Lord Scarman, in *AG v BBC*,[131] considered that the Convention could also influence the common law. He said that where there was some leeway to do so, a court which must adjudicate on the relative weight to be given to different public interests under the common law should try to strike a balance in a manner consistent with the treaty obligations accepted by the government: 'If the issue should ultimately be . . . a question of legal policy, we must have regard to the country's international obligation to observe the Convention as interpreted by the Court of Human Rights.' This approach was endorsed by the House of Lords in *AG v Guardian Newspapers (No 2)*,[132] Lord Goff stating that he considered it to be his duty, where free to do so, to interpret the law in accordance with Convention obligations. Similarly, in *Chief Metropolitan Magistrates' Court ex p Choudhury*,[133] Art 10 was taken into account in reviewing the decision of the magistrates' court not to grant summonses against Salman Rushdie and his publishers for the common law offence of blasphemous libel.

The need to take the Convention into account was emphasised even more strongly by the Court of Appeal in *Derbyshire CC v Times Newspapers Ltd*,[134] Ralph Gibson LJ ruling that where a matter 'was not clear [by reference to] established principles of our law . . . the court must . . . have regard to the principles stated in the Convention'. Butler-Sloss LJ put the matter even more strongly: 'where there is an ambiguity or the law is otherwise unclear or so far undeclared by an appellate court, the English court is not only entitled but . . . obliged to consider the implications of Article 10.' As indicated above, the House of Lords considered that in the particular instance, the common law could determine the issues in favour of freedom of speech[135] and that therefore, recourse to the Convention was unnecessary, but the guidance offered by the Court of Appeal was still of value where the common law was uncertain. That guidance suggested that judges had no choice as to whether to consider the Convention where the law was ambiguous[136] or – and this did appear to be a new development – where it was not yet settled in an appellate court. It may, therefore, have been the case that all areas of the common law which were not clearly settled in the House of Lords and which affected Convention rights, were expected to reflect Convention principles even before the HRA came into force. Thus, some disregard for the classic dualist stance became apparent in the common law.

---

131 [1981] AC 303, 354; [1980] 3 WLR 109, p 130, HL.
132 [1990] 1 AC 109, p 283.
133 [1991] 1 QB 429; [1991] 1 All ER 306.
134 [1993] AC 534; [1993] 1 All ER 1011; [1992] 3 WLR 28, HL.
135 [1993] 1 All ER 1011. For comment, see Barendt, E, 'Libel and freedom of speech in English law' [1993] PL 449.
136 See further on this point (1992) MLR 721.

The influence of European Union law

It is clear that membership of the European Community has had a dramatic impact on civil liberties in the UK in the last three decades. This is despite the fact that, clearly, EU law is concerned more with social and economic than civil rights. Where EU law protects civil rights, this may not be its primary purpose. Although Community law is intended to create social benefits in addition to economic benefits, social benefits may be conceived of as a by-product of, or adjunct to, economic integration.[137] Even without the HRA, the European Convention on Human Rights would have an impact via the EU, although the two systems of law are technically separate. EU provisions themselves also influence the protection of fundamental rights in the UK.

The influence of the Convention in EU law became increasingly important due to acceptance of the principle enunciated in *Amministrazione delle Finanze dello Stato v Simmenthal*[138] and *Nold v Commission*,[139] namely, that respect for fundamental rights should be ensured within the context of the EU. The Convention has come into a closer relationship with EU law as the process of European integration has continued. The influence of EU human rights law is increasing, especially after the Amsterdam Treaty came into force.[140] The doctrine of respect for fundamental rights, as guaranteed by the European Convention and as resulting from the constitutional traditions common to member states, is now embodied in Art F(2)(6)(2) of the Treaty on European Union.[141] But although Art F2 states that the EU will respect fundamental rights as recognised by the Convention, the European Court of Justice (ECJ), in Opinion 2/94 (28 March 1996),[142] held that the EU cannot accede to the Convention, on the ground that an amendment to the Treaty of Rome would be required in order to bring about this change, since it would go beyond the scope of Art 235. Under the Treaty of Amsterdam, Art F1, voting rights of member states who fail to observe the principle embodied by Art F(2)(6)(2) can be suspended. The EU Charter of Fundamental Rights, although not yet of binding force, aids in the interpretation of EU law.[143]

---

137   This is exemplified in the case of harmonisation of a minimal level of employment protection provisions in order to create a 'level playing field' of competition for employers in the Single Market. See, e.g., Nielsen and Szyszczak, *The Social Dimension of the European Community*, 2nd edn, 1993, Copenhagen Business School Press, pp 15–18; Hoskyns, 'Women, European law and transnational politics' (1986) 14 Int J Soc Law 299–315.

138   Case 106/77 [1978] ECR 629.

139   [1974] ECR 481.

140   The Treaty came into force in 1999. It extends a number of existing rights under EU law and amends the Social Charter, which lays down minimum rights for workers in the Community countries. The Conservative Government failed to ratify it, but in the Agreement annexed to the Protocol on Social Policy in the Treaty of Maastricht the other member states recorded their agreement to 'continue along the path' laid down in it. The Labour Government has withdrawn the opt-out.

141   For enforcement of the Convention by this means, see Craig, P and De Burca, G, *European Law: Text and Materials*, 2nd edn, 1998, OUP.

142   (1996) *The Times*, 16 April.

143   The Charter, published in May 2000 (available from the European Commission website and from the website of the House of Lords Select Committee on the European Parliament) contains those rights recognised under the European Convention on Human Rights together with a number of new social rights, including the right to strike, guarantees of maximum working hours, worker consultation and trade union membership. The rights could, potentially, bind the EU institutions. Certain member states and the European Commission proposed that the Charter should be included in the Treaty of

EU law has already had an important impact, as this book will demonstrate, in the areas of sex discrimination,[144] data protection[145] and race discrimination.[146] Where national measures come within the scope of Community law, they must comply with the human rights standards it maintains.[147] As this book indicates at a number of points, EU human rights law is increasingly becoming a powerful force both in terms of the protection offered by the ECJ, and of its domestic implications.[148]

The result of these developments is that, in all the member states, implementation of EU measures in national law is clearly subject to respect for the Convention rights, although an individual cannot make an application to Strasbourg against the Union alleging that the Union has violated the Convention. Even though formal accession of the Union to the Convention has not yet occurred, the Convention will control Union conduct. Thus, the decision of the ECHR in *Rees*[149] was relied upon by the ECJ in deciding, in *P v S and Cornwall CC*,[150] that transsexuals fall within the Equal Treatment Directive. This was found on the basis that the Directive is simply the expression of the principle of equality, which is one of the fundamental principles of European law.

It is therefore probable that, as the influence of the Convention on EU law becomes more significant and the impact of EU law becomes greater in the UK, the Convention may also have more influence, indirectly, aside from the HRA. If the HRA was repealed this influence would continue. EU law can, of course, have direct effect in UK courts and can even override a UK statute.[151] The ability of Parliament to infringe rights under the HRA, as discussed below, is therefore subject to the ability of the judiciary to disapply domestic law which is incompatible with EC law. The position is as set out in the leading case *Elliniki Rasdio Phonia Tiles Rassi AE v Dimotiki Etaria*:[152] 'as soon as any [national] legislation enters the field of application of Community law, the [ECJ] as the sole arbiter in this matter, must provide the national court with all the elements of interpretation which are necessary in order to enable it to assess the compatibility of that legislation with the fundamental rights – as laid down particularly in the European Convention on Human Rights – the observance of which the Court ensures.' Thus, any national law within the field of application of EU law can be assessed as to its compliance with the Convention rights. In particular, where a member state is seeking to carve out an exception to the general principles of EU law, the review of the European Court of Justice is most intensive. But, as a matter of EU

Nice in December 2000. Britain considers that the Charter should not become part of the Treaty, and therefore have binding effect, but should have a merely declaratory status. At present, in July 2007, this is still the position. See for discussion, Wicks, E [2001] PL 527.

144 See, e.g., *Marshall (No 2)* [1993] 4 All ER 586. See further Chapter 15, p 1589.

145 For example the Data Protection Act 1984 (now 1988) derived from the European Convention for the Protection of Individuals with regard to the Automatic Protection of Data, 17 September 1980. See further Chapter 9, p 921 *et seq.*

146 See Chapter 15, p 1480.

147 See, e.g., *R v Secretary of State for the Home Dept ex p Adams* [1995] All ER (EC) 177.

148 See further Betten, L and Grief, N, *EU Law and Human Rights*, 1998, Longman; Neuwahl, N and Rosas, A, *The EU and Human Rights*, 1995, Martinus Nijhoff; Jacobs, F, 'Human rights in the EU: the role of the ECJ' [2001] 26(4) ELR 331.

149 (1986) 9 EHRR 56.

150 [1996] ECR I-2143; [1996] 2 CMLR 247; [1996] All ER(EC) 397. See further Chapter 16, pp 988–89.

151 See *Factortame Ltd v Secretary of State for Transport* [1991] 1 All ER 70, HL.

152 [1991] ECR I-2925.

law, the Convention rights are not directly justifiable since they are not free standing rights. The position under *Elliniki* was not, therefore, changed by Art F(2)(6)(2). The domestic courts can disapply legislative provisions which appear to conflict with EU law as interpreted in reliance on those rights. Certain Convention principles may therefore come to be of limited binding force in the UK as forming part of EU law. However, the potential impact of the Convention in the UK by this means has not as yet been fully realised.[153]

3 The 'Bill of Rights' Debate

Introduction[154]

The question, canvassed over the last 30 years, whether the UK should incorporate the European Convention on Human Rights into domestic law in order to act – in effect – as a substitute for a Bill of Rights, initially gained impetus due to the UK's acceptance of the right of individual petition under the European Convention on Human Rights. It rapidly came to seem anomalous to some that the Strasbourg judges should have the power to rule on the compatibility of UK law with Convention rights, while domestic judges had no such power. The idea that a dissatisfied litigant could leave the House of Lords to seek 'better' justice abroad was obviously distasteful to many domestic judges.

In 1968, Anthony Lester QC proposed the incorporation of the European Convention on Human Rights into national law[155] and the Charter '88 Group,[156] among others,

153 See further on this issue, Van Dijk and Van Hoof, *Theory and Practice of the ECHR*, 3rd edn, 1998, Chapter 8; Clapham, *Human Rights and the European Community: A Critical Overview*, 1991, Clarendon; Schermers, HG (1990) 27 CMLR 249; Grief [1991] PL 555; Coppel, J and O'Neill, A [1992] 29 CMLR 669; Foster, N (1987) 8 HRLJ 245; Lenaerts (1991) 16 ELR 367; O'Leary, S, 'Accession by the EC to the ECHR' (1996) 4 EHRR 362.

154 Texts referred to below and background reading: Lord Scarman, *English Law – The New Dimension*, 1974, Scarman; Wallington, P and McBride, J, *Civil Liberties and a Bill of Rights*, 1976, Blackwell; Bailey, SH, Harris, DJ and Jones, BL, *Civil Liberties: Cases and Materials*, 5th edn, 2002, Chapter 1; Feldman, D, *Civil Liberties and Human Rights in England and Wales*, 2002, Chapter 2; Waddington, PAJ, *Liberty and Order*, 1994, Routledge; Clayton, R and Tomlinson, H, *The Law of Human Rights*, 2nd edn, 2006, Chapter 1; Jaconelli, J, *Enacting a Bill of Rights*, 1980, Clarendon; Zander, M, *A Bill of Rights*, 4th edn, 1997, Sweet and Maxwell; Dworkin, R, *A Bill of Rights for Britain*, 1990; Ewing, KD, *A Bill of Rights for Britain*, 1990; 'Do we need a Bill of Rights?' (1976) 39 MLR 121; 'Should we have a Bill of Rights?' (1977) 40 MLR 389; 'Britain's Bill of Rights' (1978) 94 LQR 512; 'Legislative supremacy and the rule of law' [1985] CLJ 111; 'Incorporating the Convention' (1990) 25 LAG, April; 'Fundamental rights: the UK isolated?' [1984] PL 46; Craig, PP, *Public Law and Democracy in the United Kingdom and the United States of America*, 1990, Clarendon; Waldron, J, 'A rights-based critique of constitutional rights' (1993) 13 OJLS 18; Adjei, C, 'Human rights theory and the Bill of Rights debate' (1995) 58 MLR 17; Oliver, D, 'A Bill of Rights for the United Kingdom', in *Government in the United Kingdom*, 1991, Open University Press; Lester, A, 'The judges as law-makers' [1993] PL 269.

155 Lester, A, *Democracy and Individual Rights*, 1968, Fabian Society, pp 13–15. For the view that the Convention did not need to be formally adopted into UK law since it was already part of it and could be directly relied upon in domestic courts, see Beyleveld, D, 'The concept of a human right and incorporation of the ECHR' [1995] PL 577.

156 Charter '88 advocated enshrining civil liberties by means of a Bill of Rights, but it did not put forward a text. See Stanger, N (1990) 8 Index on Censorship 14.

brought the issue into prominence during the late 1980s and the 1990s. But some judges[157] and academic writers remained opposed to the reception of the Convention into domestic law or unconvinced[158] of the value of so doing, as did a number of politicians, including most Conservative MPs and right-wing commentators generally.[159] Nevertheless, support for the adoption of a 'Bill of Rights' grew among lawyers, academics and politicians[160] during the 1980s and 1990s prior to the introduction of the Human Rights Act 1998 under the Labour Government.

The political history of the debate

Britain was the first member state to ratify the European Convention,[161] despite some strong feeling against it in Cabinet, particularly from Lord Chancellor Jowitt. The government at the time recognised that it was politically necessary to accept the Convention, but Jowitt described it as 'so vague and woolly that it may mean almost anything. Any student of our legal institutions must recoil from this document with a feeling of horror.'[162] However, the government did not, at that time, accept the right of individual petition or the jurisdiction of the European Court and there was no question of incorporation of the Convention into domestic law. When the government[163] eventually accepted the right of individual petition in 1966, there appears to have been little realisation of the significance of this move, but it was unsurprising that it should be followed by a call for enactment of the Convention into domestic law – though without being directly enforceable.[164] The call for a 'Bill of Rights' was taken up by Lord Lambton (Conservative) in 1969, who sought leave to introduce a 'ten-minute rule' Bill to preserve the rights of the individual – in other words, to curb the power of the Labour Government in such areas as freedom of speech and education. There was little support for the Bill and it was rejected.

From the 1970s onwards, growth of support for a UK Bill of Rights became apparent pre-HRA outside the ranks of the Conservative Party, although certain senior Conservatives displayed some such support when in opposition. Labour, which toyed with the notion in 1975, opposed it before and during the 1992 General Election, eventually decided to espouse it as official policy in 1993, while there was a long history

---

157 Eg, Lord McCluskey in his 1986 Reith Lectures.
158 See, e.g., Ewing, KD and Gearty, CA, *Freedom under Thatcher*, 1989, p 273 *et seq*; Waldron, J (1993) 13 OJLS 18, pp 49–51; Loughlin, M, *Public Law and Political Theory*, 1992, Clarendon, esp pp 220–27.
159 The official policy of the Conservative Party was opposed to a Bill of Rights before and at the time of the introduction of the HRA: see Conservative Research Department Brief, *Civil Liberties*, 1990. See below for full discussion, pp 142–43.
160 See Zander, M, *A Bill of Rights?*, 1997, Chapter 1; Lord Scarman, *English Law – The New Dimension*, 1974, Parts II and VII; see also Robertson, G, *Freedom, the Individual and the Law*, 1993, Chapter 12; Lester, A, 'Fundamental rights: the United Kingdom isolated?' [1984] PL 46; Lord Lester [1995] PL 198, fn 1; Barendt, E, *Freedom of Speech*, 1987, pp 329–32.
161 In March 1951.
162 CAB 130/64 xcA034022; for comment, see Lester, A, 'Fundamental rights: the United Kingdom isolated?' [1984] PL 46, pp 50–55.
163 The Labour Government headed by Harold Wilson.
164 In 1968, from Mr Anthony Lester QC. His suggestion was that a Constitutional Council should be set up with powers to preview legislation and advise Parliament of potential conflict with the Bill of Rights.

of Liberal and Liberal Democrat support for it. It is notable that the years of Thatcherism eventually led the main party of opposition to accept the need to receive the Convention into domestic law. The chequered history of the debate which follows suggests two things: first, that there was a general and increasing consensus for some time that the European Convention on Human Rights should be incorporated into domestic law, and that this course should be taken as opposed to enacting a UK Bill of Rights; second, that although support for 'a Bill of Rights' was concentrated in the centrist and centre-left parties, it was not confined to them. The first point is one that should, it is argued, give the Conservative and Labour parties pause in the years from 2007 onwards in the run up to the next General Election: there were cogent reasons why the HRA, incorporating the ECHR, rather than a British Bill of Rights, was introduced.

Conservative opposition to incorporation of the Convention

In 1969, Mr Quintin Hogg MP published a pamphlet, New Charter,[165] in which he stated: 'Parliament has become virtually an elective dictatorship. The party system makes the supremacy of a government like the present, automatic and almost unquestioned.' The solution, he thought, was to make the European Convention on Human Rights enforceable in domestic courts. Mr Hogg was opposition Front Bench Spokesman on Home Affairs and the pamphlet was published by the Conservative Political Centre, but the views were stated to be the author's own and not the Party's. However, in 1970, as Lord Chancellor, he spoke against a Bill of Rights proposed by Lord Arran,[166] although he did not state that he was against all Bills of Rights. In 1975, when Labour was in power, he wrote four letters to *The Times* advocating a written constitution entrenching individual rights.[167] Also in 1975, Sir Keith Joseph published a pamphlet entitled Freedom under the Law[168] giving his view that a Bill of Rights was needed to curb the power of Parliament.

In August 1976, Sir Michael Havers (Shadow Attorney General) gave an indication that the official view of the Conservative Party was tending towards incorporation of the European Convention when he advocated such a move in a letter to the *Daily Mail*, and, in a report entitled 'Another Bill of Rights?', the Society of Conservative Lawyers supported this proposition. In 1978, Mr Leon Brittan, opposition Front Bench Spokesman on Devolution, moved an amendment to the Scotland Bill at Committee stage which would have made the European Convention effective in Scotland. The move was opposed by the government on the ground that the question was too important to be decided in such a context, and the amendment was defeated by 251 votes to 227.[169]

When the Conservative Party came to power in 1979, it made no move to incorporate the Convention, despite some backbench interest.[170] In 1980, the government opposed Lord Wade's Bill of Rights Bill in the Commons, as it did Lord Scarman's Bill in 1988,

---

165   Conservative Political Centre, No 430.
166   House of Lords, *Hansard*, Vol 313 Col 243, 26 November 1970. Lord Arran had moved the Second Reading of his Bill.
167   In May 1975.
168   Published by Conservative Political Centre.
169   House of Commons, *Hansard*, Vol 943 Col 580.
170   107 Conservative MPs signed a motion in June 1984 calling for incorporation of the Convention.

which was passed in the Lords, and Sir Edward Gardner's 1989 Bill incorporating the European Convention. An indication of future official Conservative policy was given by Margaret Thatcher in a letter to Bernard Crick[171] on 26 May 1988:

> The government considers that our present Constitutional arrangements continue to serve us well and that the citizen in this country enjoys the greatest degree of liberty that is compatible with the rights of others and the vital interests of the State.

This view was reiterated in 1990[172] and remained the official view of the Conservative Party in the 1997 General Election. In debate on the Human Rights Bill in 1997, however, the Conservative opposition abstained on Second Reading. The Conservative Party website[173] greeted the coming into force of the Human Rights Act by attacking it; William Hague (then the leader of the Conservative Party) stated: 'I believe that to influence our law through our elected representatives is itself a right. It is threatened by this bad law.' The Conservative manifesto for the 2001 General Election did not, however, state that, if elected, a Bill would be introduced to repeal or amend the Human Rights Act. Therefore, although it is clear that if the Conservatives under Major had taken office in 1997 they would not have introduced a measure similar to the Human Rights Bill, they appeared to have accepted, reluctantly, that repeal of the HRA would be controversial and perhaps politically damaging. At the 2005 election, however, amendation of the HRA was a manifesto pledge. Under Duncan-Smith, and then under Cameron, however, they came to favour repeal, and that remains the current stance in the years leading up to the 2009 or 2010 General Election. As indicated above, the plan is to replace the HRA with a 'British Bill of Rights'. As Cameron said in an article in 2007: ". . . under my leadership, we have opposed ID cards and will replace the Human Rights Act with a British Bill of Rights that better protects both our security and our freedom."[174] However, this plan is problematic since Britain would remain bound at the international level by the European Convention.

The Liberals and the Liberal Democrats

The Liberal Party was strongly associated with the movement to introduce a Bill of Rights. The Liberal Peer, Lord Wade, who had in 1969 initiated a four-hour debate in the House of Lords on the question of the protection of human rights, moved a further debate in 1976 in the Lords on a new Bill designed to incorporate the European Convention into UK law. It provided that the Convention would prevail over subsequent legislation unless the legislation specifically provided otherwise. Lord Harris, the Secretary of State at the Home Office, said that the government could not form a view until there had been wide public discussion of the issue. The House gave the Bill an unopposed second reading. When Lord Wade's Bill was debated again in 1977[175] and referred to a Select

---

171 Founder member of Charter '88.
172 Conservative Research Department Brief, *Civil Liberties*, 1990.
173 www.conservatives.com.
174 *Daily Telegraph*, 15 January 2007.
175 House of Lords, *Hansard*, Vol 379 Col 973.

Committee, the Committee recommended that if a Bill of Rights were enacted, it should be the European Convention, but said that they had not reached agreement on the desirability of enacting such a Bill. Lord Wade moved an amendment, which was carried, to introduce a Bill of Rights to incorporate the Convention. He introduced his Bill again in 1978 and in 1981; each time it passed the Lords and was eventually debated in the Commons in 1981, although no second reading was secured. Lord Scarman, who has been one of the most influential supporters of adoption of a Bill of Rights, made a very significant contribution to the debate in his Hamlyn lecture in 1974 in which he concluded that certain human rights should be rendered inviolate by entrenched laws protected by a Bill of Rights. In 1988, he failed to get a Bill through the Commons – although it passed the Lords – which provided that no Minister, bureaucrat or public body should do any act which infringed the rights set out in the European Convention. In accordance with his long-standing support for the reception of the Convention into domestic law, Lord Scarman spoke in favour of the Human Rights Bill on Second Reading in the House of Lords in 1997.[176] The Liberal Democrats continued to favour adoption of the Convention before, during and after the 1992 and 1997 General Elections.[177]

The change in the Labour position

In a House of Commons Debate on the Bill of Rights question in 1975,[178] Dr Shirley Summerskill, Labour Minister of State at the Home Office, said that the government was not 'committed against a Bill of Rights', but that the question required further consideration. In 1976, the Labour Government published a discussion document which had been prepared by the Human Rights sub-Committee chaired by Mrs Shirley Williams, recommending the adoption of the European Convention on Human Rights into national law. Just before its publication, the Home Secretary, Mr Roy Jenkins, indicated that he was moving in the direction of favouring incorporation,[179] and in 1976, the Attorney General, Mr Sam Silkin, also gave such an indication.[180] That the government was taking this question very seriously was apparent from the composition of the Working Party which drew up the Discussion Document 'Legislation on Human Rights', published by the Home Office in 1976. Senior civil servants from a large number of different departments were involved. The document was intended only to be descriptive and explanatory: no firm conclusion on the issue was reached and official Labour Party policy did not change as a result.

In 1991 and 1992, however, Labour officially opposed adoption of a Bill of Rights on the ground that government reforms would be endangered if power were transferred from government to the judiciary. The then Shadow Home Secretary, Mr Roy Hattersley, disassociated his party from Charter '88. He wrote: 'the only method of restraining the excesses of a bad government is to replace it with a good one.'[181] However, in a speech to the Fabian Society Conference on 6 January 1990, he explained more fully

176 House of Lords, *Hansard*, Col 1256, 3 November 1997.
177 *Partners for Freedom and Justice*, Liberal Democrat Federal White Paper No 2 (1989).
178 The motion was put forward by Mr James Kilfedder (Ulster Unionist) House of Commons, *Hansard*, Vol 894 Col 32, 7 July 1975.
179 In a speech to the Birmingham Law Society on 12 February 1975. In 1976, at a conference organised by the British Institute of Human Rights, he left no doubt that he was in favour of incorporation.
180 In the MacDermott lecture at Queen's University, Belfast.
181 See the *Guardian*, 12 December 1988.

Labour's proposed alternative method of protecting civil rights: 'The commitment to a series of detailed and specific Acts of Parliament – each one of which establishes rights in a specific area – is a much more practical way of ensuring the freedoms we propose.' This view was encapsulated in the Labour Party Charter of Rights 1990.[182]

However, after Labour lost the General Election of 1992 and Mr Hattersley resigned as Shadow Home Secretary, John Smith, the new leader of the party, announced a change in policy in March 1993 after the Labour Party Conference and committed the party to incorporation of the European Convention using the device of a 'notwithstanding' clause for protection and with a view to the eventual adoption of a home-grown Bill of Rights. When Tony Blair took over the leadership of the party after John Smith's death, he supported the policy of incorporation, as did the new Shadow Home Secretary, Jack Straw.

On 11 January 1994, the Labour MP Mr Graham Allen introduced a Private Members' Bill, the Human Rights No 3 Bill, which proposed incorporation of the European Convention on Human Rights with the First Protocol and the creation of a Human Rights Commission. It embodied many of the previous Labour Party proposals. It received a first reading in the Commons but did not progress to a second reading. In December 1996, the Labour Party issued a Consultation Paper on the matter entitled *Bringing Rights Home: Labour's Plans to Incorporate the European Convention on Human Rights into UK Law.*[183] The paper proposed incorporation of the Convention with the First Protocol and the creation of a Human Rights Commission; it also promised review of the possibility of ratifying later Protocols. It left it unclear whether such ratification would also imply that later Protocols would subsequently be incorporated into UK domestic law. It also promised that, in future, consideration would be given to the possibility of introducing a tailor made UK Bill of Rights. After the 1997 General Election, the Labour Government committed itself in the Queen's Speech to introducing a Bill incorporating the 'main provisions' of the Convention. The Human Rights Bill, receiving the 'main provisions' of the Convention into domestic law, was introduced into Parliament in October 1997. During the ten years of Labour rule between 1997 and 2007, the Labour Government made no move to amend the HRA in any significant fashion (except in respect of derogations).[184] But as this book demonstrates at various points, the Labour Government does not always seem entirely happy with the HRA that it itself introduced. That was entirely predictable, which is why it was laudable to introduce it. At the present time, Gordon Brown, the current Prime Minister, is showing some interest in introducing a 'British Bill of Rights', which presumably would be based on the HRA.

Central arguments in the debate

Introduction

Broadly, rightists and leftists among academics and politicians tend to be opposed to Bills of Rights. As indicated in Chapter 1, certain groups on the left, in the UK and abroad, tend to view civil rights with hostility. Under the theory put forward by a number

---

182 *The Charter of Rights: Guaranteeing Individual Liberty in a Free Society*, Labour Party document, 1990.
183 Straw, J and Boateng, P, *A Consultation Paper*, 1997.
184 Chapter 14, p 1424 *et seq*.

of writers on the left, such instruments merely focus progressive attention on 'negative rights' which foster only formal equality since in practice, they may be used by the powerful to consolidate their power over the weak.[185] At the same time, this theory finds that such attention is directed away from 'positive rights' which would lead to substantive equality through the redistribution of economic resources.[186] The liberal view has been indicated in Chapter 1; it is generally sympathetic to the notion of civil rights,[187] and is now supportive of the HRA. The remarkable increase pre-HRA in liberal and centre-left support prior to 1997 for adoption of a UK 'Bill of Rights'[188] was – at least in part – attributable to the fact that one party was in power for 18 years and, in particular, to the effect on civil liberties of the Thatcher and Major Governments.

The 'Bill of Rights' debate will be considered here as a background to the discussion of the HRA itself, which follows. Clearly, the debate has now moved on; it is concerned less with the merits of receiving the Convention into domestic law, than with the response of public authorities, particularly the judiciary, to it. However, consideration of a key argument against reception of the Convention – the argument from democracy – is illustrative of the choices that were made when framing the HRA. The further questions as to the role of the HRA in providing improved protection for civil liberties and human rights concern the nature, status and enforcement of the Convention, and these questions are addressed in Chapter 4.

In the mid-1990s, there was a consensus among most academic commentators that the traditional methods of providing protection for civil liberties were insufficiently effective, but no clear agreement as to the means which should be adopted in order to provide further protection. A degree of suspicion and distrust was often aroused at the notion of effecting such protection by means of a Bill of Rights which may have found its roots in the traditional view that Bills of Rights are high-sounding documents which are ineffective in practice, but dangerous because they create complacency as to liberty and that, moreover, they are the marks of a primitive, undeveloped legal system. In 1776, Bentham described declarations of rights as merely so much 'bawling upon paper'. Dicey wrote that there is 'in the English constitution an absence of those declarations or definitions of rights so dear to foreign constitutionalists', but that this was a strength rather than a weakness because such rights may be constantly suspended, whereas the suspension of the English Constitution 'would mean with us nothing less than a revolution'. Lord Hailsham has said: 'show me a nation with a Bill of Rights and I will show you a nation with fewer actual human rights than Britain because the escape clauses are used, often quite ruthlessly.'[189] It has also been suggested that the notion of liberty and of the need to protect it must emanate from a source outside the Bill of Rights; Judge Learned Hand has written: 'Liberty lies in the hearts and minds of men and women; when it dies there no constitution, no law, no court can save it.'

---

185 See further McColgan, A, *Women under the Law: The False Promise of Human Rights*, 2000, Pearson.

186 See Tushnet, M, 'An essay on rights' (1984) 62 Texas L Rev 1363; Herman, D, 'Beyond the rights debate' (1993) 2 Social and Legal Studies 25.

187 This is not intended to imply that all liberals support the adoption of a Bill of Rights in the UK; as discussed below, a number of liberals are reluctant to trust the judges to give full weight to its provisions. For an attack on such adoption from a liberal point of view see Allan, J, 'Bills of Rights and judicial power – a Liberal's quandary' 16(2) OJLS 337–52.

188 For a full account, see Zander, M, *A Bill of Rights?*, 1997, Chapter 1.

189 House of Lords, *Hansard*, Vol 369 Cols 784–85.

Pre-HRA, the argument that Bills of Rights *per se* are ineffective or actually inimical to the protection of liberty, tended to give way to the argument that although some independent restraint on the excess or abuse of power was needed, it would be dangerous or pointless to enact a Bill of Rights because it would not be wise to trust UK judges with such a significant power:[190] they would invoke the exceptions in order to interpret it in an executive-minded manner, thus perhaps emasculating the freedoms it was supposed to protect. Commentators such as Lee, Ewing and Gearty argued that it would be dangerous to trust to a Bill of Rights and that there was too great a tendency to regard one as a panacea for all that was wrong with civil liberties in the UK.[191] Ewing and Gearty considered that genuine constraints on the power of the Prime Minister were needed and that a Bill of Rights would merely amount to a cosmetic change. It was further argued that whether or not UK judges could be trusted with a Bill of Rights, the whole notion of endowing an unelected group with a considerable area of power removed from the reach of the legislature is incompatible with democratic theory.[192] Allan, for example, argued that '[entrenched] Bills of Rights are singularly undemocratic'.[193]

Ceding power to unelected judges

Whether or not it is acceptable in a democracy that unelected judges should wield the power of a Bill of Rights partly depends on its authority and the availability of review of legislation. The most contentious possibility arises when, as in the US, judges are empowered to strike down legislation in conflict with the Bill of Rights, which is also given a higher authority than other statutes by being entrenched, so that no possibility of correction of judicial decisions by subsequent legislation arises, except in so far as provided for by the method of entrenchment. The argument from democracy has the greatest force only if a Bill of Rights can prevail over subsequent inconsistent legislation. It obviously has much less force if a form of Parliamentary override clause prevents it from so doing. This is the case in Canada where the Charter of Rights is protected by a so called 'notwithstanding clause' – subsequent legislation can only override it if the intention to do so is clearly stated in the legislation. The perpetrators of the argument against trusting the judges did not always make clear whether they opposed both of these possibilities or only the first. It is obviously a crucial distinction as, in the second, Parliament clearly still retains ultimate power over the law. Introduction of a notwithstanding clause merely requires candour if rights are to be interfered with, which, as Dworkin has commented, 'is hardly incompatible with democracy'.[194]

However, the argument that a fully entrenched Bill of Rights would be incompatible with democracy should not be too readily conceded. Such an argument seems to proceed from the premise that any restriction upon the freedom of legislative bodies

---

190 Eg, Ewing, KD and Gearty, CA, *Freedom under Thatcher*, 1989, pp 262–75; Lord McCluskey (the Solicitor General for Scotland under the Wilson Labour government) in his 1986 Reith Lectures, Lecture 5.
191 Lee, *Judging Judges*, p 166; Ewing and Gearty, ibid p 275.
192 Waldron, J, 'A rights-based critique of constitutional rights' (1993) 13 OJLS 18.
193 'Bills of rights and judicial power – a Liberal's quandary' [1996] 16(2) OJLS 337–52.
194 Dworkin, R, op. cit., fn 1.

– even those designed to protect fundamental rights – is undemocratic. A true partisan of democracy ought also to be opposed to UK membership of all international human rights treaties, since the basic premise of all of these is that certain rights of citizens should be placed beyond the power of the majority to infringe them. The contrary notion, that there should be no limits on the power of the majority, can be defended only by reference to a rather crude form of preference utilitarianism[195] and arguably amounts to an impoverished conception of democracy. Such a conception could provide no reason why, for example, the majority should not authorise the internment, torture and summary execution of all terrorist suspects if it was clear that this would end terrorist attacks and thus immeasurably benefit the mass of the people. Those who insist that Parliament's power should be untrammeled presumably do not think that it should use its powers in this way and their conviction that it should not do so can only be justified by a belief that there must be limits on what the majority can inflict on even profoundly anti-social individuals and minorities. Thus, it may be assumed that there is general acceptance of this fundamental conviction which lies behind every Bill of Rights. Those who remain opposed to entrenched rights usually profess not to be hostile to the idea of human rights *per se*, but to be concerned with other issues.

Thus, one respected commentator, Jeremy Waldron, in setting out what could be termed the 'argument from controversy',[196] was concerned not so much that the majority should have unlimited power, but that any particular formulation of rights would inevitably be controversial and that entrenching it would amount to a permanent disabling of those who hold a contrary view about which rights should be protected. Thus, he asked rhetorically: 'Are the formulations of one generation to be cast in stone and given precedence over all subsequent revisions?' Three objections to this position are apparent. First, to characterise a Bill of Rights as setting formulations 'in stone' seems to exhibit a failure to take cognizance of the immense diversity of interpretations which can be extracted from a broadly worded document such as the European Convention,[197] and the way in which such interpretations can develop to reflect changes in popular attitudes.[198] The fact that one document – the American Constitution – has been found

195 See Chapter 1, pp 8–9 for discussion of utilitarianism.
196 This term is used because the fact of controversy as to the favoured list of rights lies at the heart of Waldron's argument against entrenched rights. 'A rights-based critique of constitutional rights' (1993) 13 OJLS 18.
197 Waldron's objections seem all the more strange in that prima facie they do not seem to take account of those adjudicatory theories which explain the vital part that both the judges' moral and political convictions and the mass of shared assumptions and understanding in a particular society play in the interpretation of texts. (For an extremely lucid and accessible exposition of the above point, see Simmonds, N, 'Between positivism and idealism' [1991] CLJ 308.) However, Waldron does mention such theories in several places (e.g. pp 41–43) where he states that his objection is not so much that judges should be able to interpret and modify citizens' rights, but that democratic institutions should be disabled from doing so. But once Waldron has conceded the point that judges can radically amend the meaning of texts, his point about setting rights in stone is lost. The reason why democratic institutions should be disabled from interference with some fundamental rights is discussed in the text below: pp 149–51.
198 It is indeed arguable that judges can more readily respond to marked changes in the moral climate than politicians. e.g., the judiciary, in response to a growing consensus that the marital rape exemption was indefensible, abolished the immunity of husbands at a time when there were no indications that Parliament was prepared to make time for legislation (*R* [1991] 4 All ER 481).

at different times to support both black slavery and positive discrimination in favour of black people provides clear evidence to support this argument.

The second objection is that the 'controversy' thesis determinedly ignores the reasonable degree of consensus that exists around many basic rights. For example, when discussing the possibility of protecting the right to participate in democracy, Waldron argues that democratic procedures themselves cannot be entrenched, because 'People disagree about how participatory rights should be understood . . .'. Noticeably, however, he fails to mention the near-complete agreement on the fundamental right of universal adult suffrage. This point leads on to the third objection to the 'controversy' thesis, namely that, paradoxically enough, its own implications are contrary to democracy.[199] The refusal to disable the majority by entrenchment of rights includes, as just noted, a refusal to entrench democracy itself. This refusal in effect means that Waldron will not deny the right of the majority of the day to destroy democracy by disenfranchising a group such as all non-whites or even voting democracy itself out of existence, thereby denying it to future generations. Since, by contrast, a Bill of Rights is ultimately concerned with preserving a worthwhile democracy for the future, it can be persuasively argued that entrenched basic rights show more respect for democratic principles than do the advocates of retaining the untrammeled power of the majority of the day.[200] Entrenchment of the Convention under the HRA was not contemplated by the Labour Government and would probably be possible in the UK system only by means of a written constitution. Such a task would almost certainly not be undertaken without a referendum; if the people considered such a settlement desirable, they would in effect be expressing their will to be ruled by an unelected body within certain defined areas as the price of curbing elected power.

The argument against endowing the judges with power under an entrenched Bill of Rights should also be considered in the light of the experience of America. The most striking feature of the American system is the power of the Supreme Court to render inoperative acts of the elected representatives of the people (first asserted in *Marbury v Madison*).[201] This power seems alien to UK jurists, but the justification offered for it is that the legitimacy of judicial review of legislation derives not from electoral accountability, but from the particular positions of the judges within the constitution. The classic statement of this theory is that of Alexander Hamilton in *Federalist #78*:

> The executive not only dispenses the honours but holds the sword of the community. The legislature not only commands the purse but prescribes the rules by which the

---

199 A further paradox in Waldron's argument, the existence of which he concedes (p 46), is that if the majority vote in a referendum for an entrenched Bill of Rights they must, on his argument, be allowed to have one. Clearly, the only way to prevent the majority from entrenching a Bill of Rights would be to have an entrenched law forbidding the entrenchment of laws. This would obviously be impossible on its own terms. Since, as Dworkin notes (op. cit., fn 1, pp 36–37), opinion polls reveal that more than 71% of the population favour an entrenched Bill of Rights, Waldron's argument appears to be self-defeating.

200 Such a view is of course endorsed by a number of legal philosophers and civil libertarians. See Dworkin, op. cit., fn 1; the view also clearly underpins his general political philosophy: see, e.g., 'Liberalism', in *A Matter of Principle*, 1985. See also Hart, HLA, *Law, Liberty and Morality*, 1963 and Lester, *Democracy and Individual Rights* 1968.

201 (1803) 5 US (1 Cranch) 137.

duties and rights of every citizen are to be regulated. The judiciary, on the contrary, has no influence over either the sword or the purse; no direction either of the strength or of the wealth of society. [Thus it will be] the least dangerous to the political rights of the Constitution.[202]

It could also be noted in this context that the UK has a constitutional precedent in the shape of the House of Lords for allowing an unelected body to influence legislation. The notion was not therefore entirely foreign to the UK system. Of course, this is not a complete analogy: the House of Lords has a much more limited role in this respect than judges under an entrenched Bill of Rights would have had.

If a Bill of Rights is unentrenched, as in Canada, the argument from democracy loses some of its cogency but fastens instead on the question of policy making under the Bill of Rights. A Bill of Rights would inevitably contain open-textured provisions which would have to be interpreted and that interpretation would often involve political choices. An obvious example is the choice before the European Court in the *Young, James and Webster* case[203] concerning the question of the closed shop. Ought judges – although finally subject to Parliament under an unentrenched Bill of Rights – be given a much broader policy-making role or ought politicians to be the sole arbiters of such questions? Clearly, many questions which would have to be determined by the judges in applying the provisions of a Bill of Rights would lie rather in the moral than the political arena because civil rights are rights claimed against public authorities,[204] not against particular political parties. Nevertheless, it has been argued by such opponents of a Bill of Rights as Lord McCluskey that an Act of Parliament, arrived at after full consideration of the issues involved and the likely effects and covering specific areas, is a better way to protect, for example, the right to privacy than a Bill of Rights containing a provision such as 'Everyone has the right to privacy' followed by certain exceptions.

It was argued by the Labour Party in 1990[205] that rather than introducing a Bill of Rights, more certain protection would be assured by creating a number of statutes, each of which would cover one area of civil liberties. However, the introduction of such protection by this means would have been time-consuming and might therefore have been unlikely to find a place in a legislative programme mainly concerned with social and economic issues. The lack of legislation passed over the 18 years of the Conservative Governments from 1989 to 1997 with the sole or main intention of protecting a particular liberty supported this argument. The legislation that was passed – the Contempt of Court Act 1981; the Equal Pay (Amendment) Regulations; the Data Protection Act 1984 – was Europe-driven.[206] There was clearly a lack of legislation

202 Mentor (ed), *The Federalist Papers*, 1961, Muller, pp 464, 465. See also Bickel, AM, *The Least Dangerous Branch: The Supreme Court at the Bar of Politics*, 1962, Irvington.

203 Eur Court HR, A 44, Judgment of 13 August 1981; (1981) 4 EHRR 38.

204 Or against private individuals where a public authority bears some responsibility for failure to protect a right. See the discussion of *Drittwirkung* in Chapter 2, p 29.

205 See *The Charter of Rights: Guaranteeing Individual Liberty in a Free Society*, Labour Party document, 1990.

206 The Contempt of Court Act 1981 was passed in response to the judgment of the European Court of Human Rights in *Sunday Times*, Judgment of 26 April 1979, A 30; (1979) 2 EHRR 245. The Data Protection Act derived from the Convention for the Protection of Individuals with regard to the

passed to protect civil liberties which was enacted without such coercion; in particular, the UK, unlike other jurisdictions, has failed so far to enact a Privacy Act. If the party of government tends to abjure its policy-making role in these areas, it may be argued that the only alternative is enactment of a Bill of Rights which largely hands such a role to the judges. Even assuming that Parliament is prepared to legislate in these areas, it can still be argued that a Bill of Rights is of value as providing a remedy which is more flexible and comprehensive than a statute and which can adapt to changing social conditions more readily. Moreover, specific pieces of legislation can have the protection they offer to liberties eroded by subsequent legislation through the operation of the doctrine of implied repeal; the protection gained is therefore more precarious than that offered by a Bill of Rights enjoying greater constitutional protection, even if only due to a convention of respect for it.

Readiness of the domestic judiciary to use rights-based reasoning

It was also argued that the judges had already shown how they would acquit themselves under a Bill of Rights and that the results were not promising.[207] For example, the Privy Council, in considering questions arising from Commonwealth Bills of Rights, sometimes gave certain guarantees of rights a very restrictive interpretation. In *AG v Antigua Times Ltd*,[208] the Privy Council found that a constitutional guarantee of freedom of speech was not infringed by Antiguan legislation requiring a licence from the Cabinet and a large deposit as a surety against libel in order to publish a newspaper. However, in later decisions the Privy Council appeared to adopt a more liberal approach. In *Guerra v Baptiste*,[209] the Privy Council had to consider delay in carrying out an execution. Guerra was convicted of murder in the Republic of Trinidad and Tobago and sentenced to death. In 1989, he appealed against his sentence, but the appeal was not heard until October 1993. The Privy Council took into account the decision in *Pratt v AG for Jamaica*[210] in which it was found that where a state wishes to retain capital punishment, it must accept the responsibility of ensuring that execution follows as swiftly as possible after sentence, allowing a reasonable time for appeal and consideration of reprieve. If the appeal procedure allows the prisoner to prolong appellate proceedings over a period of years, the fault lies with the appeal procedure, not with the prisoner. In *Pratt*, it was found that a reasonable target would be to complete the hearings within approximately one year and to carry out the sentence of death within two years. In the present instance there had been substantial delay amounting to nearly five years between sentence and the point at which the sentence was to be carried out. The fact that problems were created by the shortage of court resources did not justify the delay. Such problems had also been a factor in the *Pratt* case. It was, therefore, found that the sentence must be commuted to one of life imprisonment. This decision and that in

Automatic Processing of Data (17 September 1980) and the Equal Pay (Amendment) Regulations from the Council Directive (75/117/EEC) of 10 February 1975.

207 Ewing, KD and Gearty, CA, *Freedom under Thatcher*, 1989, p 274.

208 [1976] AC 16.

209 (1995) *The Times*, 8 November.

210 [1993] 3 WLR 995. Bailey, SH, Harris, DJ and Jones, BL, (*Civil Liberties: Cases and Materials*, 4th edn, 1995) comment that this decision would not be open to the usual criticism that traditional methods of interpretation would be used in determinations under a Bill of Rights (p 18).

Pratt suggested that UK judges were quite capable of adopting a generous approach to a Bill of Rights.[211] Thus, there was some basis for the argument that the judges would take decisions applying the Convention under the HRA which would not emasculate it owing to adoption of a narrow and technical approach.

As indicated above, however, certain decisions of UK judges applying the Convention could be criticised as adopting traditional, limiting methods of interpretation. In *Brind* (in the Court of Appeal) and in *AG v Guardian Newspapers*,[212] judges applied the principles of the European Convention and then proceeded to uphold the restrictions in question. On the other hand, as discussed above, in *Derbyshire CC*[213] the Court of Appeal relied on Art 10 to produce a result protective of freedom of expression. The decisions in *Ex p Witham*[214] and *Ex p Simms*,[215] considered above, relied on fundamental human rights standards in, it is suggested, a creative and dynamic fashion.

Moreover, where an international treaty has been incorporated into domestic law, the English courts showed a willingness to adopt a broad teleological approach. In *The Hollandia* (concerning provisions of the Hague-Visby Rules, which have been incorporated into UK law) Lord Diplock said that such provisions 'should be given a purposive rather than a narrow literalistic construction, particularly wherever the adoption of a literalistic construction would enable the stated purpose of the international Convention . . . to be evaded . . .'[216] It should also be noted that UK judges adapted remarkably quickly to the demands of EU law as it affected fundamental rights and were prepared to take decisions and make pronouncements upholding such rights which were probably unthinkable when the European Communities Act 1972 was passed.[217] Lester made a forceful point in support of this proposition in his comments on the way that the courts dealt with the task of applying broadly worded EU directives on sex discrimination, provisions which a legal traditionalist would term 'so vague and woolly that they might mean almost anything'. He considered that: 'English judges have interpreted and applied these general principles in a manner which recognises their fundamental nature and which gives full effect to their underlying aims,' and from this he concluded that: 'Those sceptics who doubt the ability of British judges to protect the fundamental rights of the [European] Convention should consider their impressive record in translating the fundamental rights of Community law into practical reality.'[218]

Possible models for the protection of the Convention

As indicated above, the constitutional status of Bills or Charters of Rights varies from jurisdiction to jurisdiction. Such instruments may have no special status or they may be afforded (or may acquire) some special protection from express or implied repeal

---

211 Roberts considers that a purposive approach has continued to be evident in interpretations of Bills of Rights from Commonwealth jurisdictions: 'The Law Lords and human rights: the experience of the Privy Council in interpreting Bills of Rights' [2000] EHRLR 147.
212 [1987] 3 All ER 316. See also the *Brind* case [1991] 1 AC 696.
213 [1992] 3 WLR 28; see further above, p 114; HL ruling: [1993] 1 All ER 1011.
214 [1998] QB 575.
215 [1999] 3 All ER 400.
216 [1983] 1 AC 565, p 572.
217 Eg, *Secretary of State for Employment ex p EOC* [1994] 2 WLR 409, HL.
218 Lester, 'Fundamental rights' [1984] PL 70–71.

which may, at its highest, involve their entrenchment.[219] Thus, a variety of models was available to choose from in considering the model to be used in order to protect the Convention. The choice arrived at, which is discussed in Chapter 4, was extremely significant, in terms of the allocation of power between the judiciary, Parliament and the government.

The terms 'entrenchment' and 'protection' which will be used below require explanation because both may encompass a number of possibilities. 'Protection' will be used to refer to any means of giving a statute a special status without seeking to entrench it in any sense of that word. 'Entrenchment' refers to requirements of form or manner or restrictions as to substance. A requirement of form denotes the need to use a particular form of words if a subsequent enactment is to repeal a former one, rather than simply allowing the normal rules of implied repeal to operate. A requirement of manner refers to the manner in which legislation is passed if it is to repeal a previous enactment. Examples of such a requirement would include the use of a two-thirds majority in the Parliamentary body if a particular piece of legislation is to be repealed or amended. A restriction as to substance refers to the most stringent form of entrenchment: no method of repealing the legislation in question is provided in it. Parts of the German Basic Law are entrenched in this manner and, therefore, they can never be amended or repealed unless a break with the existing legal order occurs in Germany.

Thus, a requirement of 'form' may be termed weak entrenchment since it is the weakest possible form of entrenchment available. A requirement of manner may be referred to as semi or partial entrenchment, while a restriction as to substance may be referred to as full entrenchment. Bearing this in mind, it may be found that s 2(4) of the European Communities Act 1972 has been treated as imposing a requirement of form and possibly of manner. Unless Parliament declares in an Act of Parliament that it intends to override Community law, such law will prevail over subsequent inconsistent domestic legislation. However, since no means of overriding Community law is provided for in the 1972 Act, it may even be the case that if Parliament made such a declaration, the courts would not give effect to it. In that case, there would be no means of escaping from the impact of Community law except by withdrawing from the EU.

The most common requirements of manner – such as, that legislation repealing the Bill of Rights will not be valid unless passed by a 75 per cent majority – are incompatible with democracy if that concept is understood to connote simple majoritarianism. A Bill of Rights protected in this manner could be preserved against the wishes of the majority of the elected representatives in the legislature, so long as that majority was less than 75 per cent. A restriction as to substance is most obviously incompatible with democracy, unless one takes the view, which is based on a different argument,[220] that full entrenchment of Bills of Rights, or at least certain fundamental provisions in them, is essential in order to maintain a healthy democracy.

In many jurisdictions, Bills of Rights are afforded a higher status than other legislation. Owing to the operation of the doctrine of parliamentary sovereignty, this possibility would be constitutionally controversial in the UK. However, the status of

---

219 See Jaconelli, J, *Enacting a Bill of Rights*, 1980, for a full discussion of this issue.
220 See above, p 148.

EU law in the UK provided a precedent for adopting the course of partially entrenching the Convention. Section 2(4) of the European Communities Act 1972 provides: 'any enactment passed or to be passed ... shall be construed and have effect subject to the foregoing provisions of this section ...'. 'The foregoing' are those provisions referred to in s 2(1) giving the force of law to 'the enforceable Community rights' there defined. The words 'subject to' suggest that the courts must allow Community law to prevail over a subsequent Act of Parliament. This does not, of course, mean that the European Communities Act itself cannot be repealed. It may follow that Parliament has partially entrenched s 2(1) of the European Communities Act by means of s 2(4) imposing a requirement of form (express words) on future legislation designed to override Community law. In *Secretary of State for Transport ex p Factortame*[221] in the Court of Appeal, Bingham LJ said that where the law of the Community is clear:

> ... whether as a result of a ruling given on an Article 177 reference or as a result of previous jurisprudence or on a straightforward interpretation of Community instruments, the duty of the national court is to give effect to it in all circumstances ... To that extent a UK statute is not as inviolable as it once was.

This finding was confirmed in the House of Lords.[222]

There was also the possibility of using a so-called 'notwithstanding' clause. The Human Rights No 3 Bill introduced by the Labour MP Mr Graham Allen in January 1994 would have adopted this method of protection for the Bill of Rights. The civil rights group Liberty gave support to this possibility,[223] as did some other commentators at the time.[224] Based on the model of the Canadian Charter, the clause would state that subsequent legislation would only override the Convention if the intention of doing so were expressly stated in such legislation. Under a 'notwithstanding' clause, the judiciary would not be required to strike down legislation without a mandate from the democratically elected government. If that government did not include the clause in any legislative provision which subsequently was found to infringe the Convention, the government could impliedly be taken to be mandating the judiciary, by its omission, to strike down the offending legislation. Thus, although under such a model the judiciary are required to disapply provisions in Acts of Parliament, a role which the domestic judiciary might find constitutionally problematic, they are not required to act against the wishes of the democratically elected government. Dworkin has observed, in relation to such a clause, that: 'In practice this technically weaker version of incorporation would probably provide almost as much protection as [formal entrenchment].'[225] However, this model accepts the possibility which clearly arises that future governments might come to use the clause more frequently. A government might be uncertain whether a

---

221   [1989] 2 CMLR 353.
222   [1989] 2 WLR 997.
223   See Klug, F and Wadham, J [1993] PL 579.
224   See, e.g., Dworkin, *A Bill of Rights for Britain*, pp 24–29. The Labour Party supported this position at its conference in 1993, but had changed its position by 1996, as its 1996 consultative document reveals.
225   Dworkin, R, op. cit., fn 1.

particular measure would be in breach of the rights, but decide that a 'notwithstanding' clause should be used on insurance grounds. It is possible that use of such a clause might prove ultimately to be quite an ineffective protective device.

More effective protection for constitutional rights can be achieved by full entrenchment. Constitutions throughout the world adopt a number of different forms of entrenchment of codes of rights. The constitution of the US can be amended only by a proposal which has been agreed by two-thirds of each House of Congress or by a convention summoned by Congress at the request of two-thirds of the states. The proposed amendment must then be ratified by three-quarters of the states' legislatures. The amendment procedure itself – Art V of the Constitution – can be amended only by the same method. It was generally thought that if a Bill of Rights had been introduced containing a provision that it could not be repealed except in accordance with some such procedure, the courts would not have given effect to it. Parliament might have legislated expressly contrary to it and the possibility of unwitting implied repeal would have remained. If it had been found that a later provision would not admit of a construction in accordance with its guarantees, it was thought that judges would probably apply the later provision, thereby repealing the right in question to the extent of its inconsistency. Authority for this can be found in the dicta of Maughan LJ in *Ellen Street Estates Ltd v Minister of Health*[226] to the effect that Parliament cannot bind itself as to the form of future enactments.

However, De Smith suggests that Parliament could redefine itself so as to preclude itself as ordinarily constituted from legislating on a certain matter. The argument is based on the redefinition of Parliament under the Parliament Acts: if Parliament can make it easier for itself to legislate on certain matters, it could equally make it harder, thereby entrenching certain legislation. This analogy has, however, come under attack from Munro[227] on the ground that the Parliament Act procedure introduces no limitation on parliamentary sovereignty. The analogy of EC law would arguably support De Smith's proposition and authority is also available from other constitutions; in *AG for New South Wales v Trethowan*,[228] the Privy Council upheld the requirement of a referendum before a Bill to abolish the upper House could be presented for the royal assent. Although, as De Smith argues, this decision may be of limited application as involving a non-sovereign legislature, it does suggest that a class of legislation exists for which it may be appropriate to delineate the manner and form of any subsequent amendment or repeal. The South African case of *Harris v Minister of the Interior*[229] is to similar effect. Dicey has argued that the Bill of Rights could be entrenched within a written constitution since it would be untenable to espouse 'the strange dogma, sometimes put forward, that a sovereign power such as the Parliament of the United Kingdom, can never by its own act divest itself of authority'.[230] The point cannot be regarded as settled.

226 [1934] 1 KB 590, p 597.
227 Munro, C, *Studies in Constitutional Law*, 1999, Butterworths.
228 [1932] AC 526.
229 (1952) (2) SA 428.
230 Dicey, AV, *An Introduction to the Study of the Law of the Constitution*, 10th edn, 1987, p 68.

Thus, a proposal of the Labour Government that the Convention should be fully entrenched would have been constitutionally controversial and – possibly – impossible without a written constitution. However, the government did not put forward such a proposal and there was by no means agreement between supporters of the domestic incorporation of the Convention that it would have been desirable.

4 Conclusions

At the present time, it is Conservative party policy to repeal the Human Rights Act and replace it with a 'British Bill of Rights' It is possible that the Labour party, as part of its change of direction under Gordon Brown, may also espouse the idea of a 'British Bill of Rights'[231] as opposed to the HRA. The discussion in this chapter as to entrenchment of a Bill of Rights and the options before Parliament in introducing the HRA currently have pertinence, not only in relation to the background to the HRA, but also to the current Bill of Rights possibility. The problem that the HRA faces in terms of its image in the popular consciousness is two-fold. It was never really 'sold' to the people of the UK in 1998. Further, it is perceived as a European instrument, as something imposed from outside, and as associated with the EU and over-regulation. A 'British Bill of Rights' could fulfil the role played currently by the HRA, and could be based on it and on the European Convention, but could be sold to the British public as an instrument based more firmly on core British values. So long as the Bill of Rights did not deliver *less* than the Convention in terms of rights, it would still satisfy the goal of allowing British people to rely on the Convention rights in domestic courts. But it might also hold out the possibility of dealing with some of the gaps and inadequacies inherent in the HRA, which are explored in Chapter 2. They include the narrow definition of 'public function' that has been adopted[232] under s6HRA, the problems created by the doctrine of indirect horizontal effect and the inadequacies of the Convention itself.

Chapter 4 considers the model of protection that was chosen for the Convention, in the Human Rights Act.

---

231 Gordon Brown said in his inaugural speech as Prime Minister (on 24.6.07): "I want a new constitutional settlement for Britain. And the principles of my reforms are these . . . civil liberties safeguarded and enhanced . . .".

232 See Chapter 4, pp 223–29. This approach was confirmed by the House of Lords in *YL v Birmingham City Council* [2007] UKHL 27.

Chapter 4

The Human Rights Act

1 Introduction[1]

The Labour Government came to power in 1997 with a manifesto that promised a radical programme of constitutional change and, most significantly, the introduction of the Human Rights Act 1998 as the means of receiving the European Convention on Human Rights into domestic law, nearly 50 years after it was signed. Finally, rights were, in the government's words, to be 'brought home'.[2] It would not be too much of an exaggeration to say that the advent of the HRA appeared at the time to herald a new dawn for civil liberties. Relief seemed to be at hand, after many years of seeing the country condemned at Strasbourg and elsewhere, during the Conservative years, for its human rights' record. Ronald Dworkin said, famously, of the Thatcher years,

---

1 Texts referred to below and background: Clayton, R and Tomlinson, H, *The Law of Human Rights*, 2nd edn, 2006; Singh and Hunt, *Assessing the Impact of the Human Rights Act*, (2003), Hart; Jowell and Cooper (eds), *Delivering Rights? How the HRA is working and for whom*, 2003, Hart; Fenwick, Masterman, Phillipson (eds), *Judicial Reasoning under the HRA*, 2007, CUP; Hoffman and Rowe, *Human Rights in the UK*, 2006, Longman; Pannick, D and Lester of Herne Hill QC, Lord, *Human Rights Law and Practice*, 2nd edn, 2004, Butterworths; Gearty, C, *Principles of Human Rights Adjudication*, 2004, OUP; Wadham, J and Mountfield, H, *The Human Rights Act*, 1999, Blackstone (useful guide); Smith, R, *Textbook on International Human Rights*, 2nd edn, 2005, OUP; Steiner & Alston, *International Human Rights in Context: Law, Politics, Morals*, 2nd edn, 2000, OUP; Hunt, M, *Using Human Rights Law in English Courts*, 1997; Singh, R and Hunt, M, *A Practitioner's Guide to the Impact of the Human Rights Act*, 1999; Grosz, Beatson and Duffy, *Human Rights: The 1998 Act and the European Convention*, 2000, Sweet and Maxwell; Fenwick, H, *Civil Rights: New Labour, Freedom and the Human Rights Act, 2000*, Chapter 2; Clements and Thomas (eds), *The HRA: A Success Story?* 2005, Blackwell; Irvine, Lord, 'The impact of The Human Rights Act: Parliament, The Courts and The Executive' (2003) *Public Law*, Sum, 308–25; Klug, F, 'Judicial Deference Under the Human Rights Act 1998' (2003) EHRLR 2, 125–33; Klug F, 'Standing Back From The Human Rights Act: How Effective is it Five Years On' (2005) *Public Law*, Win, 716–28; Lester of Herne Hill, Lord 'The Human Rights Act – five years on' [2004] EHLR 259; Steyn, Lord, 'Deference: A Tangled Story' (2005) Public Law 346; Kavanagh, A, 'Statutory interpretation and human rights after Anderson: a more contextual approach' [2004] PL 537; Steyn, Lord, '2000–2005: Laying The Foundations Of Human Rights Law In The United Kingdom (2005) EHRLR, 4, 349–62; Sunkin, M, 'Pushing Forward the Frontiers of Human Rights Protection: the meaning of public authority under the HRA' [2004] PL 643; Leigh, I, 'Taking Rights Proportionately, Judicial Review, the HRA and Strasbourg' [2002] PL 265; Klug, F and Starmer, K [2001] PL 654; McGoldrick, D, 'The HRA in theory and practice' (2001) 50(4) ICLQ 901.

2 See: *Bringing Rights Home: Labour's plans to incorporate the ECHR into UK Law: A consultation Paper*, December 1996 (1997) and the White Paper: *Rights Brought Home*, October 1997 Cm 3782; see also Straw, J and Boateng, P (1997) 1 EHRR 71.

'Liberty is ill in Britain'.[3] Ewing and Gearty wrote in 1989: 'It should now be clear that civil liberties in Britain are in a state of crisis'.[4] There were expectations that the HRA would prove to be something akin to a panacea for all that was wrong with fundamental freedoms in Britain or, at the least, commentators perceived that civil liberties had been re-energised. With the creation of positive rights, there was a sense of a break with the erosions of liberty of the Conservative years.[5]

Under the Diceyan model of the constitution, discussed in Chapter 3, civil liberties are protected by individual judicial decisions; a document termed a Bill or Charter of Rights is both unnecessary and undesirable as a means of protecting them.[6] Under this model, citizens in a state in which everyone is free to do all which the law does not forbid, enjoy, Dicey argued, greater liberty than those whose liberty is protected by such a document because, by being delineated, rights would be more limited. The Diceyan model underpinned the view expressed in the post-war years that a constitution embodying a presumption of liberty provided a protection for rights that could not be achieved by basing them on a constitutional document such as a Bill of Rights. From the perspective of the post-war, pre-1979 era, there appeared to be some basis for that view. Although it would be problematic to argue that there was ever a 'golden age' of civil liberties in Britain,[7] the post-war years appeared to a number of commentators to come closer to one than the Thatcher and Major years,[8] in comparison with the records in other European countries.

It has been argued that there was a post-war understanding as to the use of Parliamentary power in British politics until the Thatcher Government 'dismantled much of the consensus'.[9] 'Old Tory statecraft based on patriotism, social cohesion, Union and Empire disintegrated in the face of . . . alternative visions of post-Imperial Conservative nationhood . . . . Enoch Powell's free economy . . . prevailed as the basis of Thatcherite strategy'.[10] Under this view of the consensus, high Tory values underpinned respect for political freedoms, but under Conservative rule since 1979 liberty suffered and Britain began to lag behind many other democracies in respect of her human rights' record. The Thatcher Government was said to have demonstrated a 'mundane

---

3   Dworkin, R, *Index on Censorship*, 1988, pp 7–8.
4   *Freedom under Thatcher*, 1989, p 255.
5   See Cooke 'The British Embracement of Human Rights' [1999] EHRLR 243; Feldman, D, 'The Human Rights Act and Constitutional Principles' 1999) 19 (2) LS 165.
6   Dicey, AV, *The Law of the Constitution*, 8th edn, 1959.
7   Ewing and Gearty argue that there is a misconception that the first half of the twentieth century constituted such an age in *The Struggle for Civil Liberties: Political Freedom and the Rule of Law in Britain 1914–1945*, 1999.
8   See Thornton, P, *Decade of Decline: Civil Liberties in the Thatcher Years* (1989). Ewing and Gearty, writing in 1989 found: 'In recent years there has been a marked decline in the level of political freedom enjoyed in Britain'. They found that the turning point and beginning of the decline might be said to have occurred in the 1970s but that 'the process of erosion became more pronounced' after the Conservative election victory in 1979 (Preface to *Freedom under Thatcher* 1989, OUP).
9   Fraser, D, 'Post-War Consensus: A debate not long enough' [2000] 53(2) Parliamentary Affairs 347.
10 Baker, D, in [2000] 6(2) Party Politics 250, commenting on Lynch, D, *The Politics of Nationhood, Sovereignty, Britishness and Conservative Politics* (1999).

and corrupting insensitivity to liberty'.[11] Although the Major Government showed in certain respects a greater awareness of the value of individual rights,[12] in its central criminal justice Act, the Criminal Justice and Public Order Act 1994, it demonstrated, as Chapter 8 argues, a similar insensitivity. The Conservative years from 1979–97 were marked by the attempts of outside bodies – the European Court of Justice and the European Court of Human Rights – to protect liberties in the UK, attempts that were met, increasingly, by hostility among sections of the Conservative party.[13]

Contrary to the Diceyan thesis, liberty was receiving a significant measure of protection as a result of the impact of the European Convention on Human Rights at the international level, rather than being the result of decisions of the judiciary applying the common law. In *Freedom under Thatcher*[14] Ewing and Gearty pointed out that Thatcher had exposed the precarious nature of the constitutional means of protecting liberty. Their central criticism was not that she had changed the constitutional structures to her advantage, but that she 'merely utilised to the full the scope for untrammelled power latent in the British constitution but obscured by the hesitancy and scruples of previous, consensus-based political leaders'.[15] In other words, she exposed and exploited the weaknesses of the British constitution. As David Feldman puts it:

> few of the values of our society find expression in constitutional form . . . This was not too serious a problem when politics was dominated by a high Tory willingness to restrain individualism in order to further communal goods . . . the belief that *noblesse oblige*. However that belief has been eroded. Thatcherite belief in the market as the supreme arbiter of human worth marginalised the values of traditional Toryism.[16]

In the context of fundamental rights, then, Thatcherism exposed the flawed nature of the Diceyan constitutional model.[17] Since under that model the Constitution provides no effective check to untrammelled parliamentary sovereignty, a government determined to push through a legislative programme extending the reach of state power which, perhaps almost incidentally, erodes the residual areas of liberty, is able to do so. Despite strong common law traditions of upholding certain fundamental rights, constitutional inadequacy became, inevitably, apparent. The civil liberties record of the Conservative Governments of 1979–97 revealed the difficulties of relying on the democratic process to protect civil liberties within the traditional British constitutional arrangements. A

11 Dworkin, R, *Index on Censorship*, 1988, pp 7–8. See also Thornton, P, *Decade of Decline: Civil Liberties in the Thatcher Years*, 1989.

12 The 'Open government' initiatives were introduced under the Major Government: see The White Paper: *Open Government*, Cm 2290 and the *Code of Practice on Access to Government Information*. The Intelligence Service was placed on a statutory basis under the Intelligence Services Act 1994 (see Chapter 10 pp 1010–13).

13 The reaction of Senior Cabinet members at the time, particularly Michael Heseltine, to the decision of the European Court of Human Rights in *McCann v UK* (1995) 21 EHRR 97 that the UK had breached Art 2 (right to life) was particularly hostile.

14 1989.

15 Ibid at p 7.

16 'The Human Rights Act 1998 and Constitutional Principles' [1999] 2 LS 165 at p 166.

17 Dicey, *The Law of the Constitution*, 8th edn.

constitution based on the twin notions of Parliamentary supremacy and negative liberties provides no reliable protection against the erosion of a liberty to the point where it exists largely as an exercise of police discretion.[18]

Thatcherism therefore influenced the long-running debate between those commentators and policy-makers who had always wanted to leave liberties to the protection of that process[19] and those in the liberal tradition who had wished to entrust them, for the most part, to the judiciary.[20] The Labour opposition of the time, now the Labour government, changed sides in that debate,[21] apparently in the main as a response to Thatcherism. The Labour Green Paper: *Bringing Rights Home*,[22] published in 1997, concluded: 'We aim to change the relationship between the state and the citizen, and to redress the dilution of individual rights by an over-centralising government that has taken place over the past two decades.' This aim was to be achieved through the introduction of the European Convention on Human Rights into domestic law. Once Labour came to power in 1997 the White Paper: *Rights Brought Home* was published[23] and the Human Rights Bill was introduced into Parliament. The Act came fully into force on 2 October 2000. The Labour Government deserves credit for accepting that check on its own power to introduce rights-abridging legislation into Parliament. Given its Parliamentary majority, the HRA provided a significant and self-imposed curb. The Convention thus received into domestic law created a constitutional transformation, not only in terms of rights-protection, but also in terms of judicial reasoning.[24] Since, traditionally, the constitution recognised only negative liberties as opposed to positive rights, the judicial focus of concern always tended to be on the content and nature of the restrictions in question rather than on the value and extent of the right.

While the Diceyan tradition demanded a basis in law for interference with liberties by public authorities, under the HRA this demand was clarified and confirmed in respect of interferences with the guarantees.[25] The Act obliges public authorities, in particular the police, not only to discharge duties such as the duty to keep the peace, but to uphold human rights. It asks the judiciary to consider matters such as the 'quality' of law, not merely its formal existence.[26] Most importantly it asks them to examine the necessity in a democracy of interfering with a right, the proportionality of the means used with the aim in question, and, if necessary, it asks them to inform Parliament that on one or more of these matters it has breached the Convention. Placing the judges in a position

---

18 Chapter 8 argues that freedom of expression by means of public protest provided an example of such a liberty pre-HRA: pp 661–63.
19 See, e.g., Griffith, JAG, 'The Political Constitution' [1979] MLR 1; Loughlin, Martin, *Public Law and Political Theory*, 1992.
20 Leading exponents of this position included: Zander, M, *A Bill of Rights?* 1996; Robertson, G, *Freedom, the Individual and the Law*, 1993; Lord Lester of Herne Hill QC, 'Fundamental Rights: the UK Isolated?' [1994] PL 70; Lord Scarman, *English Law. The New Dimension*, 1974.
21 See Chapter 3, pp 144–45.
22 Straw, J and Boateng, P, *Bringing Rights Home: Labour's Plans to Incorporate the ECHR into UK Law: A Consultation Paper*, 1997.
23 October 1997 CM 3782.
24 See Sir Stephen Sedley on this point (2005) 32 JLS 3, p 9.
25 See Chapter 2, esp p 68.
26 See Chapter 10, pp 1043–44.

where they need to consider the proportionality of a restriction on a Convention right with its aim changed the role of the judges; it brought them into the constitutional sphere previously occupied only by Parliament and covered by the doctrine of parliamentary sovereignty. For the first time the judges were invited to consider the compatibility of primary legislation with the Convention rights, and to take the responsibility for determining how far into the contracted-out sector the Convention rights should reach, and on what basis. The previous divergence of constitutional role between Parliament and the judiciary was narrowed down, and that doctrine itself came under very strong pressure. These were bold, imaginative constitutional changes. However, such boldness had apparent limits, which are reflected in the HRA.

A seminal constitutional decision involving a choice between judicial and Parliamentary checks on executive power, and therefore as to the allocation of power, had to be taken regarding the choice of model for the enforcement of the Convention. The choice made was to afford the HRA no special constitutional protection and to leave the ultimate task of curbing executive power to Parliament; so judicial rulings remain (at least as a matter of constitutional theory) subject to primary legislation. The HRA therefore sought to reconcile rights protection placed to a significant extent in the hands of the courts with parliamentary sovereignty. Although the Convention contains the familiar list of rights usually found in a number of Bills or Charters of Rights, the HRA was not intended to be a Bill of Rights in the way that the US Amendments to the Constitution or the Canadian Charter are Bills of Rights, in the sense that those rights have a higher status than other laws: laws that conflict with the rights can be struck down. Further, unlike the German Basic Law or the US Amendments, the HRA can simply be repealed or amended like any ordinary statute and it is, therefore, in a far more precarious position.

So although there was a significant transfer of power to the judiciary, the HRA imposed limitations on its use. On a face-value reading of the HRA, legislation incompatible with the Convention can be passed and legislation declared incompatible remains valid. It is readily apparent, then, that there is a contradiction between the liberal aim of affording the Convention rights efficacy in domestic law in order to aid in reversing the effects of the over-centralisation of power, and the aim of preserving the key feature of the constitution which gave rein to that power. The factors underlying this contradiction form one of the central themes explored throughout this book – the search for a means of giving efficacy to the rights in the face of hostile legislation, including Labour legislation.

But this chapter will argue that while the tension between government criminal justice and counter-terrorist policy and the Convention rights in 2000–7 is indeed a key theme of this book, the particular resolution of the contradiction created by the HRA has not been the determining factor in settling the rules of engagement. As explored in this chapter, and in the following ones, the particular constitutional choices reflected in the HRA have on the whole *not* been exploited to allow the government, as dominant within Parliament, to disregard or limit the Convention rights to an extent that the Convention itself does not allow. As Keith Ewing wrote in 1999, 'we should be careful about distinguishing form from substance, principle from practice. As a matter of constitutional legality, Parliament may well be sovereign, but as a matter of constitutional practice, it has transferred significant power to the judiciary [under the

HRA]'.[27] The nuclear option of repeal of the HRA is available and is the one favoured by the Conservative opposition at the present time; it would allow the doctrine of Parliamentary sovereignty to re-emerge as a source of power untrammeled except by EU law. But the lesser means of recognising that doctrine introduced in the HRA have not been the most significant factors in balancing governmental power and rights, as this chapter sets out to demonstrate. In other words, a doctrinal analysis of the status of the Convention in domestic law is inadequate to explain its impact, since such an analysis has been superceded by the political stance that the government has taken.

This chapter thus attempts a doctrinal analysis of the HRA mechanisms that takes account of a political reality in which overt disregard of the Convention has largely been avoided. But it also takes account of the status of the Convention in the popular consciousness since it poses a continuing problem for human rights advocates in the UK. The inception of the HRA was not accompanied by the kind of popular debate that preceded the US Bill of Rights in 1789, or that accompanied the adoption of the Canadian Charter of Fundamental Rights and Freedoms as part of the patriation of the Canadian constitution in 1982. Thus, although at the time the new Labour Government commanded widespread popular support, and the HRA was passed during its honeymoon period, it did not seek to make the case for the HRA to the British people. That proved eventually to create problems, when the HRA came under pressure in relation to counter-terrorist strategy, and the war in Iraq led to a rapid diminution of the Labour Government's popularity. It was possible for popular ignorance of and lack of adherence to the HRA to be exploited and manipulated by the Conservative Party and a hostile media. The then Prime Minister, Tony Blair, also criticized the ECHR and HRA in relation to control orders and to the problem of deporting terrorists where they could face Art 3 treatment in the receiving country;[28] for example, he attacked the judicial review decision concerning the deportation of Afghan refugees.[29]

Concern about the need to improve public confidence in the HRA and in its operation was one of the reasons given by the government for setting up the *Review of the Implementation of the Human Rights Act* conducted in 2006 by the Department of Constitutional Affairs.[30] As regards myths spread by the media it found:

> So far as the wider public are concerned . . . different types of myth [are] in play . . . there are those which derive from the reporting (and often partial reporting) of the launch of cases but not their ultimate outcomes. This leaves the impression in the public mind that a wide range of claims are successful when in fact they are not – and have often been effectively laughed out of court. The most notable example in this category is the application made by Denis Nilsen in 2001 to challenge a decision of the Prison Governor to deny him access to pornographic material. The case is now often cited as a leading example of a bad decision made as a result of the Human Rights Act. In fact it failed at the very first hurdle.[31]

---

27 'The HRA and Parliamentary Democracy' [1999] 62(1) MLR 79, p 92.
28 *Daily Telegraph*, 6 August 2005.
29 [2006] EWCA Civ 1157, affirming Sullivan J at [2006] EWHC 1111 (Admin); see also Chapter 14 pp 1451–54 for decisions adverse to the control orders regime. For Tony Blair's comments, see the *Observer*, 14 May 2006.
30 Published, DCA, July 2006. Available from DCA website.
31 DCA Review, *Myths and Misconceptions*, p 4.

The key question that the Review set out to answer was whether the HRA had impeded the achievement of the government's objectives on crime and terrorism and so led to the public being exposed to additional and unnecessary risk. The Review answered this question in the negative, finding that while the security agencies had stated that significant resource implications are involved in servicing the structures set up to deal with dangerous terrorist suspects, these result not from the HRA, but from the decisions of the Strasbourg Court in cases such as *Chahal*.[32] But the perception created by the media that the HRA is hindering counter-terrorist and crime control measures remains, and the appeal to the fear of terrorism, has been effective in creating a false image of the HRA. Perhaps this is a classic example of an *argumentum ad metum* or *argumentum in terrorem* as a logical fallacy in which parts of the media attempt to create support for opposition to the HRA by increasing fear and prejudice towards it. The appeal to emotion is being used to exploit existing fear of terrorism to create support for the speaker's proposal, namely that the HRA should be repealed. A false dilemma fallacy is involved, suggesting that the only alternatives are rights protection or security, so such repeal would destroy the main barrier to introducing effective counter-terrorist measures.[33]

There are other reasons why a narrow doctrinal legal analysis is at best incomplete and at worst, positively misleading. Critical analysis of, for example, the theoretical protection for individuals under the HRA is of little value without an awareness of the influence of wider societal factors. There should be an awareness of how much that theoretical protection is in reality available to the underprivileged individuals who are often in most need of asserting their rights (in particular, working class black men, the most likely target of police harassment or misuse of police powers, such as stop and search).

The main concern of this book is with the years 2000–7: the Human Rights Act years. It seeks to evaluate the impact the HRA has actually had in various areas of fundamental rights and asks how far the expectations it aroused in 1998 have been answered. It will be argued that at times the Convention rights have been minimised and undermined in Parliament and in the courts.[34] In Parliament, the rights have at times been treated as almost empty guarantees which cast a legitimising cloak over rights-abridging legislation and executive action.[35] Under the model termed 'minimalist', judges have at times been able to duck the hard issues, purporting to review government actions under the Convention standards, but adopting a deferential stance which fails to create any real accountability.[36] An appearance of human rights auditing has sometimes been created which is belied by the reality. But it will be argued throughout this book that there are signs that the HRA in 2007 is beginning to bed down; the senior judges are taking their role as the guardians of human rights seriously; a fusion between Strasbourg principles and common law ones is now successfully occurring.[37] It will

---

32 Ibid, p 34.
33 See further Chapter 14, pp 1462–68 on this point. Tony Blair has been quoted as 'demanding to know "why the fuck" it was so impossible to rewrite human rights legislation to allow decisive action against a terrorist threat' (*Observer* 7 August 2005).
34 See, e.g., Chapter 6 at pp 370 *et seq.* and Chapter 7, pp 606 *et seq.*
35 This danger was pointed out by Conor Gearty in 'Terrorism and human rights: a case study in impending legal realities' (1999) 19(3) LS 367, p 379.
36 See below pp 192–96.
37 See, e.g., Chapter 9 pp 829–30, 911 *et seq.*

further be argued that the HRA has indeed had an impact on executive power, and has had an effect in protecting the rights of vulnerable and minority groups. Possibly it is a victim of its own success in the sense that the Labour Government has found that its own creation has been used against it, and to an extent the government has either colluded with or acquiesced in the idea that the HRA stands in the way of the introduction of initiatives designed to tackle terrorism and organised crime.

The HRA has proved to be a more controversial piece of legislation than its sponsors can have predicted. After it had been in force only a year, terrorists flew planes into the Twin Towers in New York, triggering a global 'war on terrorism' that has placed the HRA under pressure during almost the whole of its existence. The years 2001 to 2007 saw increasing attempts by the right-wing press and by the Conservative Party to discredit the HRA on the basis that it is a bar to the use of effective counter-terrorist measures. In March 2005, for example, a *Daily Star* leader stated bluntly: 'Rights law is wrong'.[38] The HRA remains in a very precarious position. As Chapter 14 argues, the idea that the HRA bars the way to effective counter-terrorist action is misconceived. But it is obscuring, at least in the popular consciousness, the more general 'endeavour' of the HRA – to provide UK citizens with a guarantee of a range of fundamental rights, enforceable in their own courts, rather than at Strasbourg. The terrorist attacks of 9/11 and of 7/7 in London immediately placed the Labour Government's commitment to the HRA under pressure. It appeared probable that as an aspect of counter-terrorist policy they would exploit the leeway created by the HRA for introducing legislation incompatible with the Convention. That leeway is discussed below but, as Chapter 14 argues, the Labour Government did *not* take that route in introducing counter-terrorist measures.[39] In general the government has not sought to use the avenues the HRA itself provided which would have allowed Labour policies in relation to organised crime and terrorism a freer reign.

This chapter, which considers and analyses the HRA and certain very significant decisions taken under it in the first seven years of its life, is intended to provide a framework for the discussion of the impact of the Act, which pervades the whole book. The discussion embarks on a doctrinal analysis of the central aspects of the Act, but also argues that such an analysis is inadequate to explain the operation of the Act in practice. In certain respects, explored below, the deliberate choice was made in a number of the areas, especially the question of indirect horizontal effect in s 6, to leave options open, requiring political and moral choices to be made by the judiciary in adjudicating on the HRA. It will also be argued that certain choices were made in settling on the wording of the key sections of the Act, in particular ss 3(2) and 6(2), creating exceptions to Convention-adherence, which did not reflect the political reality of the involvement of Britain in the Convention system, or the acceptance of the implications of transferring power to the judiciary. That reality then became apparent over the early HRA years. The preference shown by the government and the judiciary for accepting the limitations on the rights afforded by the Convention, *not* those provided by the HRA, forms a key theme of this chapter, and of the book as a whole.

---

38 4 March 2005.
39 See in particular pp 1424–26, 1438–44.

2 The choice of rights

The rights protected under the HRA

As Chapter 2 demonstrated, the Convention continues to grow by means of additional Protocols, reflecting more developed conceptions of human rights. However the UK has not ratified all of them. Ratification decisions have affected the choice of rights received into domestic law under the HRA. But also the decision was taken to omit Art 13, requiring that an effective remedy should be available in national law for breach of the Convention rights,[40] and Art 1 which provides for the state to secure to everyone within its jurisdiction the Convention rights and freedoms. The rights received into domestic law are, under s 1(1) HRA, Arts 2–12 and 14 of the Convention, Arts 1–3 of the First Protocol and Arts 1 and 2 of the Sixth Protocol[41] as read with Arts 16–18 of the Convention. The rights are set out in Sched 1 of the HRA; further Protocols could be added by the Secretary of State, by order, under s 1(4). Equally, rights could be removed and any other amendments to the Act could be made, by the same route in order to 'reflect the effect, in relation to the UK, of a Protocol'. The UK has ratified Protocol 13, which abolishes the death penalty in all circumstances, but it is not included in Sched 1.

The omission of Art 13 is particularly significant. The idea behind it is that the function of that Article will be carried out by s 8 of the HRA (see below) and that its inclusion might have encouraged the judiciary to provide new remedies, going beyond those that could be provided under s 8. Possibly, Art 13 could have been utilised in an attempt to create new free-standing causes of action between private parties – direct horizontal effect. As indicated below, ss 6 and 7 seek to ensure that the creation of a new cause of action under the HRA confines it to use against public authorities. Arguably, the Art 13 jurisprudence can, however, be taken into account by the judiciary under s 2 of the HRA.[42]

This choice of rights in Sched 1 is significant and obviously in part reflects UK decisions as to ratification. It is clearly a deficiency of the international record of the UK in human rights matters that it has not ratified all the Protocols. The most satisfactory course would have been their ratification and then inclusion in the list of rights in Sched 1. As Chapter 2 indicated, the government has considered the question of ratifying the Fourth[43] and Seventh Protocols. It has declared an intention to ratify the Seventh Protocol,[44] but has not yet decided to ratify the Fourth, which would require changes to immigration legislation or the entry of a reservation.[45] The very significant

---

40 See Chapter 2, pp 106–7.
41 (1983) 5 EHRR 167. It came into force in 1985.
42 See Grosz, Beatson and Duffy, op. cit., fn 1, para 1–6; see also Feldman, D, 'Remedies for violation of Convention Rights under the HRA' [1998] EHRLR 691.
43 Cmnd 2309. It came into force in 1968; the UK is not yet a party.
44 (1984) 7 EHRR 1. It came into force in 1988. The UK is not a party but has proposed ratification: see the White Paper: *Rights Brought Home: the Human Rights Bill*, Cm 3782, 1997, paras 4.14–4.15, and the Home Office Review of Human Rights Instruments (amended) 26 August 1999.
45 It contains rights relating to the field of immigration law, which have raised governmental concerns regarding the nature of the obligations created and the government indicated in 1997 that it did not intend to ratify it at that time: see the White Paper: *Rights Brought Home: the Human Rights Bill*,

Anti-Discrimination Protocol, Protocol 12, was opened for ratification in November 2000.[46] As explained in Chapter 2 it provides a guarantee of freedom from discrimination extending beyond the civil rights' arena since, unlike Art 14, it does not depend on the engagement of another Convention right.[47] The UK at present does not intend to ratify the Twelfth Protocol. Clearly there are concerns that while there is reasonable harmony between the basic Convention regime and the UK legal system, that is not fully the case as far as aspects of the more advanced Protocol-based regime is concerned. The Joint Committee on Human Rights in 2005 recommended that the government should ratify the Fourth and Twelfth Protocols.[48] The question of extending the scope of the Convention in this way is of particular significance in relation to Protocol 12, but at the present time, the government has not yet ratified it[49] and clearly is not therefore at present minded to include it in Sched 1.

Deficiencies and limitations of the Convention

At the present time the Conservative Party has declared its intention, if it is elected in 2008, 9 or 10, to repeal the HRA and introduce a 'Modern Bill of Rights' for Britain.[50] It is possible that if repeal of the HRA occurred, there might be a reluctance to follow it by the introduction of a Bill of Rights. At present the seriousness with which the Bill of Rights plan is taken is not apparent. But the plan affords the following discussion a particular pertinence at the present time.

It must be asked why the decision was made in the HRA to provide protection for parts of the European Convention on Human Rights, as opposed to introducing a tailor-made UK Bill of Rights or incorporating the International Covenant on Civil and Political Rights. In taking this course, the Labour Government followed a long

---

Cm 3782, 1997, paras 4.10–4.11. It has, however, considered the possibility of future ratification with reservations: the Home Office Review of Human Rights Instruments (amended), 26 August 1999. In a written answer to the Commons 10 June 2002 it was stated that there were no plans to ratify it: 'To ask the Secretary of State for the Home Department what plans he has to introduce legislation to enable the UK to ratify the Fourth Protocol to the ECHR. [58371]. Beverley Hughes: None at the present time'. See further Chapter 2, p 106.

46 See Chapter 2, p 108.
47 See Chapter 2, p 106 and Chapter 15, pp 1482–86.
48 Seventeenth Report of Session 2004–5 HL Paper 99, HC 264, paras 34 and 37.
49 It was opened for signature in November 2000.
50 David Cameron in a speech to the Centre for Policy Studies, London, 26 June 2006: *Balancing freedom and security – A modern British Bill of Rights*, stated that the HRA should be repealed . . . 'The Human Rights Act has a damaging impact on our ability to protect our society against terrorism . . . I am today committing my Party to work towards the production of a Modern Bill of Rights'. He also stated that the new Bill of Rights should be entrenched. He accepted that the UK would remain bound by the decision in *Chahal v UK* (the decision preventing deportation of terrorist suspects if they would be at risk of Art 3 treatment in the receiving country – see Chapter 14, p 1359) but considered that repeal of the HRA would curb delays and cost in the criminal justice system. He did not explain what would occur if a person sought to rely on their Convention rights under the new Bill of Rights' fair trial article or what would occur if there was a successful application to Strasbourg under Art 6 which would also have succeeded domestically under the HRA but which failed under the new Bill of Rights due to the modifications to the fair trial right that Cameron presumably has in mind in speaking of the hindrance created by the HRA in terms of using criminal justice measures.

UK tradition of proposals for a Bill of Rights that favoured the Convention over other instruments. The overwhelming majority of human rights Bills considered by Parliament over the years have simply advocated incorporation of the European Convention on Human Rights[51] into UK law. The House of Lords Select Committee on a Bill of Rights was unanimous on the question of creating a tailor-made Bill of Rights: 'To attempt to formulate *de novo* a set of fundamental rights which would command the necessary general assent would be a fruitless exercise.'[52] Starting from scratch and developing a Bill of Rights for the UK would have been a burdensome task because the political parties (and the various pressure groups) would have had great difficulty in reaching agreement on it, while the process of hearing and considering all the representations made by interested parties would have been extremely lengthy.

Zander has argued that it was politically and psychologically easier to incorporate the Convention,[53] since it was already binding on the UK internationally, and both major parties when in power have accepted the jurisdiction of the European Court of Human Rights and the right of individual petition.[54] A key argument put forward by supporters of the Convention was that the advantage to be gained by adopting the course of creating a home-grown Bill of Rights would have had to be weighed up against the possible detriment caused if the jurisprudence of the European Court of Human Rights had been seen as less directly applicable. The British judiciary might have felt that they had lost the 'anchor' of the authority of the Court and the constraint of the need to apply a reasonably uniform European standard of human rights.

Arguments against relying on the Convention were based partly on its defects of both form and content, which have often been criticised.[55] It is a cautious document: it is not as open textured as the American Bill of Rights, and contains long lists of exceptions to the primary rights – exceptions which suggest a strong respect for the institutions of the state. Perhaps the most outstanding example of inadequacy is the limited scope of Art 14.[56] There is also the dangerous potential of Art 17.[57] From today's perspective, the nearly 60-year-old Convention looks very much like a creature of its period,[58] with its provision against slavery[59] and its long lists of exceptions to certain fundamental rights. Its out-of-date feel has led a number of commentators to echo the

---

51 This reference to incorporation of the Convention refers to Arts 2–18 and the First Protocol – the course advocated by the House of Lords Select Committee on Human Rights in 1978.

52 Report of Select Committee, HL Paper 176, June 1978.

53 Zander, M, *A Bill of Rights?*, p 83.

54 It may be noted that under the changes made by Protocol 11, the right of individual petition can no longer be withdrawn; see Chapter 2, p 27.

55 See, e.g., Hewitt, P, *The Abuse of Power*, 1982, Martin Robertson, pp 232–40; Gearty, C [1993] CLJ 89.

56 Article 14 provides a guarantee of freedom from discrimination, but only in the context of the substantive rights. See further Chapter 2, pp 108–9.

57 It was used by the Commission to allow the banning of the German Communist party: *Kommunistische Partei Deutschland v Federal Republic of Germany*, Application 250/57 Yearbook I (1955–57), Vol 6, p 222.

58 The Convention was drafted in 1949 and based on the United Nations Declaration of Human Rights. The Declaration was adopted on December 10 1948 by the General Assembly of the UN.

59 Although slavery in the sense of human trafficking is still a live issue in Europe. See 26th Report of the JCHR on human trafficking 2005–6, HL Paper 245–1, HC Paper 1127–1, published 13 October 2006. See also *Guardian*, March 23 2007.

plea put forward some years ago by Tomkins and Rix for 'a document of principle for the 1990s and not a document of exceptions from the 1950s'.[60]

It could be argued that at first glance in its present manifestation the Convention is simply not adequate to the task of bringing about far-reaching reforms, and thereby fulfilling the constitutional role which a number of commentators had enthusiastically mapped out for it pre-HRA.[61] As Feldman puts it, the Convention rights are 'by no means a comprehensive basis for a modern system of protection for [individualistic and public] values'.[62] The far more thorough South African Bill of Rights, which covers certain social, economic and environmental rights, provides an example of such a system. The pressure group Liberty's *Manifesto for Human Rights* proposed that a domestic Bill of Rights could be drawn up, based on the Convention, but using more up-to-date language and addressing certain of the inadequacies indicated in Chapter 2.[63] In particular, Liberty criticised the lack of minimum conditions for detention outside Art 3, and the lack of a right to jury trial. It has also often been pointed out that the Convention contains no specific rights for children.[64] The HRA can also be criticised on the basis that the opportunity was lost to include certain social and economic rights,[65] including some of those protected under the International Covenant on Social, Economic and Cultural Rights. The dynamic approach of the Strasbourg Court can only marginally address the failure to provide second or third generation rights under the HRA, although, as Chapter 2 pointed out, there are signs of a change of approach in this respect.[66]

The decisions of the European Court of Human Rights documented in this book make it clear, however, that the Convention is sufficiently open-textured to be able to cover circumstances not envisaged when it was created[67] and to adapt to changing social values. For example, although a right of access to legal advice in police custody is not expressly included, the Court has – in effect – read one into Art 6, arising in a number of circumstances.[68] The Convention, with its associated jurisprudence, comes close to comprising a modern 'document of principles' thanks largely to the enterprise of the Court, which has insisted upon the dynamic nature of the Convention and has adopted a teleological or purpose-based approach to interpretation which has allowed the substantive rights to develop.[69] Those principles cannot always be sought in the

---

60 'Unconventional use of the Convention' (1992) 55(5) MLR 721, p 725. See also Ashworth, A, 'The European Convention on Human Rights and English criminal justice: ships which pass in the night?', in Andenas, M (ed), *English Public Law and the Common Law of Europe*, 1998, Key Haven, p 215.

61 See, e.g., Feldman, D, 'The Human Rights Act 1998 and constitutional principles' (1999) 19(2) LS 165; Lord Lester of Herne Hill QC, 'First steps towards a Constitutional Bill of Rights' (1997) 2 EHRLR 124.

62 Op. cit., Feldman, (1999) p 170.

63 National Council for Civil Liberties 1997 (now *Liberty*). See also the Bill drawn up by the Institute for Public Policy Research: Constitution Paper No 1, 'A British Bill of Rights', 1990.

64 Fortin, J, 'Rights brought home for children' (1999) 62 MLR 350.

65 See Ewing, KD and Gearty, CA, 'Rocky foundations for Labour's new rights' (1997) 2 EHRLR 149.

66 See Chapter 2, p 42.

67 See, e.g., *Soering v UK*, Judgment of 7 July 1989, A 161; (1989) 11 EHRR 439.

68 See Chapter 12, p 1210.

69 See: Van Dijk, P and Van Hoof, F, Theory and Practice of the European Convention on Human Rights, 3rd edn, 1998.

outcomes of applications, especially in older Commission admissibility decisions.[70] But Strasbourg decisions are not binding on domestic courts. The traditional approach of the doctrine of precedent in UK courts has not been applied to Strasbourg decisions under s 2 HRA, giving the courts some leeway, as discussed below, in developing the domestic Convention jurisprudence.[71]

But it remains legitimate to attack the HRA as an instrument which has selected and elevated 'first generation' civil rights, ignoring the social and economic ones which would have aided in giving those civil rights some substantive rather than formal value.[72] That argument could possibly, however, be utilised in future to press for introducing second generation rights to future Protocols to the Convention,[73] for including Protocol 12 in Sched 1 and for giving consideration to the reception of other unincorporated treaties into domestic law. As Ewing has put it: 'the HRA provides a valuable template for other international treaties . . .'.[74] The inadequacies of the HRA also provide an argument for giving further effect to the European Social Charter 1961 in domestic law,[75] and for affording binding effect to elements of the EU Charter of Fundamental Rights, which includes a number of social and economic rights.[76] The Charter contains those rights recognised under the European Convention on Human Rights, together with a number of new social rights, including the right to strike, guarantees of maximum working hours, worker consultation and trade union membership, but, as Chapter 15 notes, the Charter is merely waiting in the wings at the moment and can only have an indirect influence on EU law.[77] At the present time, however, when the very existence of the HRA is under threat, there is little likelihood of persuading the government that further rights should be included in the list of those protected.

3 The interpretative obligation under s 3; the remedial process and pre-legislative scrutiny

Introduction

Once the decision had been taken that the European Convention should be given further status in domestic law, as opposed to seeking to create an entirely new Bill of Rights or incorporating the International Covenant on Civil and Political Rights, the question

---

70 See Chapter 2, p 22.
71 See pp 197–98.
72 See further Ewing, KD, 'Social rights and constitutional law' [1999] PL 104.
73 With a view to adding such Protocols to Sched 1 to the HRA 1998.
74 Ewing, 'Social rights and constitutional law' [1999] PL 104, p 110.
75 Liberty campaigned for this possibility at the time when the Human Rights Bill was proposed but at the present time, the Labour Government has shown no interest in it. See further Ewing, KD, 'Social rights and human rights: Britain and the Social Charter – the Conservative legacy' (2000) 2 EHRLR 91.
76 The Charter was published in May 2000 (available from the European Commission website and from the website of the House of Lords Select Committee on the European Parliament). The rights could, potentially, bind the EU institutions. Britain considers that the Charter should not become part of the Treaty, and therefore have binding effect, but should have a merely declaratory status and, at the present time, it merely has such a status.
77 See Chapter 15, p 1481.

arose as to the constitutional protection the Convention should be given under the HRA. One possible form of entrenchment for the Convention would have been by means of a so called 'notwithstanding clause', on the model employed by the Canadian Charter. That would have meant allowing Parliament to legislate contrary to the Convention, but only if the legislation contained a provision stating, for example, 'X provision is to be given effect notwithstanding Art 6 of the Convention'. As indicated in Chapter 3, this means entrenchment by means of a requirement of form.[78] In considering the constitutional model chosen for the protection of the Convention, it is worth bearing in mind that the need to introduce further forms of protection might become apparent in future, at least for key Convention rights. Pre-HRA, the pressure group Liberty suggested that certain rights may be viewed as more fundamental than others and, therefore, might be entrenched while others might be afforded less protection.[79] At the present time, when the HRA has been in force for nearly seven years, there is, however, no evidence of governmental interest in this possibility.

The Charter 'notwithstanding clause' model was not used for the HRA, although the constitutional protection it has received bears some similarities to the use of a 'notwithstanding clause'. The HRA is modelled to an extent on the New Zealand Bill of Rights which uses a rule of construction under s 6 to the effect that a court is obliged, wherever an enactment can be given a meaning that is consistent with the rights and freedoms contained in the Bill of Rights, to prefer that meaning to any other meaning.[80] In so far as one expects a Bill of Rights to demonstrate a strong commitment to human rights, demanding, if necessary, constitutional changes to provide such protection, the HRA, like the New Zealand Bill of Rights, does not have the characteristics of a Bill of Rights. The HRA does *not* 'incorporate' the Convention rights into substantive domestic law, since it does not provide that they are to have the 'force of law', the usual form of words used when international treaties are incorporated into domestic law.[81] Instead, under s 1(2) of the HRA, certain of the rights discussed in Chapter 2 are to 'have effect for the purposes of this Act'.[82] The rights are not directly enforceable between private parties. But the rights are in a sense incorporated into domestic law when asserted against public authorities.

The key mechanism affording the Convention under the HRA a higher status than other laws is s 3, which requires the judiciary to interpret legislative provisions compatibly with the Convention rights if at all possible. This means that although the judges cannot strike down a provision as incompatible with the rights, s 3 can be

---

78 See pp 153–55.
79 See Klug, F and Wadham, J, 'The democratic entrenchment of a Bill of Rights: Liberty's proposals' [1993] PL 579.
80 For discussion as to the use of this model, see Taggart, M., 'Tugging on Superman's cape: lessons from the experience with the New Zealand Bill of Rights' [1998] PL 266; Butler, A, 'Why the New Zealand Bill of Rights is a bad model for Britain' [1997] OJLS 332; Schwartz, H, 'The short and happy life and tragic death of the New Zealand Bill of Rights' [1998] NZLR 259. The New Zealand Bill of Rights 1990 was disabled from overriding pre-existing legislation and was subject to express or implied repeal by future enactments. This model was also adopted for the Canadian Bill of Rights 1960 which was replaced by the Charter.
81 See, e.g., the Carriage of Goods by Sea Act 1971, s 1(2).
82 According to the then Lord Chancellor, the rights are a form of common law and, in that sense, they are part of domestic law: HL, Third Reading, Col 840, 5 February 1998.

relied upon to bring the provision into conformity with them if possible. The judges, as will be seen below, have adopted a robust stance under s 3, coming very close to, or even crossing, the boundary between legislating and interpreting in so doing. If a provision cannot be rendered compatible with the Convention, the incompatibility can be declared, under s 4, leaving the government to introduce remedial legislation. In this way a delicate compromise was struck between creating greater rights protection and preserving Parliamentary sovereignty. The HRA also preserved the possibility that Parliament might deliberately introduce legislation that was incompatible with the Convention. This is implicit in s 19, as discussed below. If this occurred, and the legislation could not be rendered compatible through the use of s 3, it would remain valid and could be applied, under s 3(2). There is nothing in the HRA to prevent Parliament from including a 'notwithstanding' clause in legislation,[83] but so far the government has shown no inclination to do so. Indeed, as will become apparent, although Parliament could legislate contrary to the Convention rights, the government in introducing new Bills has not made a statement that this has occurred.[84] A derogation was adopted to protect Part 4 of the Anti-Terrorism Crime and Security Act 2001, but that allowed a s 19 statement of compatibility to be made.[85] So in *practice* the Convention under the HRA is not readily distinguishable from a Bill of Rights.

The interpretative obligation under s 3[86]

Introduction

Thus, under the Human Rights Act 1998, which largely reflects the proposals in Labour's Consultation paper on the matter,[87] the Convention[88] receives a subtle form of constitutional protection. The key provision in creating this form of protection for the Convention under the HRA is s 3(1), which reads: 'So far as it is possible to do so, primary and subordinate legislation must be read and given effect in a way which is compatible with the Convention rights . . .'. Section 3(2)(b) reads: 'this section does not affect the validity, continuing operation or enforcement of any incompatible primary legislation; and (c) does not affect the validity, continuing operation or enforcement of any incompatible subordinate legislation if . . . primary legislation prevents the removal

---

83 This possibility is considered further below, at p 190.

84 As discussed below, the Communications Bill 2003 was not accompanied by a statement of its compatibility with the Convention, under s 19(1)(1), but the government's stated position is that it is compatible – see pp 206, 210 below.

85 See Chapter 14, pp 1424–26.

86 For discussion in the very early post-HRA years see Elliott, MC, 'Fundamental rights as interpretative constructs: the constitutional logic of the HRA', in Forsyth, C (ed), *Judicial Review and the Constitution*, 2001, Hart; A. Lester, 'The Art of the Possible – Interpreting Statutes under the Human Rights Act' [2000] EHRLR 665; Bennion, 'What Interpretation is 'Possible' under Section 3(1) of the Human Rights Act' [2000] PL 77; Edwards,'Reading down Legislation under the Human Rights Act' (2000) 20 LS 353;

87 Bringing Rights Home: Labour's Plans to Incorporate the ECHR into UK Law. See Straw and Boateng (1997) 1 EHRR 71. For discussion, see Lyell, N (Sir) (1997) 2 EHRR 132; Wadham, J (1997) 2 EHRLR 141; Ewing, op. cit., fn 72.

88 The term 'the Convention' will be used to refer to the Convention rights currently included in Sched 1 to the HRA 1998.

of the incompatibility'. Significantly, s 3(2)(a) makes it clear that the obligation imposed by s 3 arises in relation to both previous and subsequent enactments.

It is clear from s 3 that the Convention has, in one sense, a lower status than ordinary statutes in that it cannot *automatically* override pre-existing law. But, more significantly, s 3 demands that all statutory provisions should be rendered, if possible, compatible with the Convention rights. Therefore, by imposing this interpretative obligation on the courts, the rights become capable of affecting subsequent legislation in a way that is not normally possible.[89] If legislation cannot be rendered compatible with the rights, a declaration of incompatibility can be made under s 4;[90] remedial legislation can then be introduced into Parliament to modify or repeal the offending provisions under s 10.[91] This subtle form of protection avoids entrenchment and therefore creates a compromise between leaving the protection of rights to the democratic process and entrusting them fully to the judiciary.

When the HRA was introduced it was apparent that some existing provisions were likely to be found to be prima facie incompatible with one or more of the Convention rights. Under s 3, the possibility of impliedly repealing such provisions was ruled out, but it was clear that unless they would admit of no interpretation compatible with the Convention right(s) in question they could be made to conform with it. So it was clear that the outcome would normally be the same as that which would have been achieved had implied repeal occurred. But the intention under the HRA was that if the courts could not achieve compatibility in relation to such a provision, the Convention right itself would cease to have effect to the extent of its incompatibility with that particular statutory provision, at least until and if amending legislation was passed, under s 10 (see below) – in effect, a reversal of the normal rules of implied repeal.

Use of this model for the Convention obviously places protection for human rights very much at the mercy of judicial interpretation of statutes. It means that a more liberal-minded judge can find that most, if not almost all statutory provisions, even if unambiguous, can be modified through interpretative techniques in order to achieve harmony with the Convention. The requirement to construe legislation 'so far as it is *possible* to do so' consistently with the Convention (emphasis added) makes it clear that such a stance best reflects the intention of Parliament, although it may also be pointed out that since Parliament has enacted s 4, it clearly contemplated *some* limits on what could be achieved by means of s 3. Lord Lester observed, on this point pre-HRA: 'Would [the courts use the incorporating measures] to go much further than the traditional position in which the courts seek to interpret ambiguous legislation so as to be in accordance with rather than breach treaty obligations undertaken by the UK? I hope and believe that they would indeed do so . . .'.[92] At the Committee stage of the Human Rights Bill Lord Irvine said:

> We want the courts to strive to find an interpretation of legislation which is consistent with Convention rights so far as the language of the legislation allows,

---

89 For extensive consideration of this point, see Clayton and Tomlinson, op. cit., fn 1, Chapter 4.
90 See below, pp 199–204.
91 See below, pp 204–6.
92 'First steps towards a constitutional Bill of Rights' (1997) 2 EHRR 124, p 127.

and only in the last resort to conclude that the legislation is so clearly incompatible with the Convention that it is impossible to do so.[93]

Clearly, however, a very bold approach to s 3, going well beyond use of an interpretative technique, would not have democratic legitimacy and would encroach on the role of Parliament. The question that faced the judges at the inception of the HRA was as to the line that should be drawn under s 3 between interpreting and legislating.

It was clear from the outset that the courts would not receive much assistance in deploying s 3 from the interpretation of the somewhat similar rule of construction in New Zealand – s 6 of the Bill of Rights, which provides that wherever an enactment can be given a meaning that is consistent with the rights and freedoms contained in the Bill of Rights, that meaning should be preferred. It was found as to s 6:

> a consistent meaning is to be preferred to any other meaning. The preference will come into play only when the enactment can be [given such a meaning]. This must mean, I think, 'can reasonably' be given such a meaning. A strained interpretation will not be enough.[94]

A similar approach was taken in subsequent cases,[95] prompting criticism from commentators.[96] This somewhat timid and uncreative approach arguably overlooked the fact that s 6 must apply to itself. Therefore, if a meaning of s 6 was adopted which curbed the impact of the right or freedom in question, there was an argument that there had been a failure to use the rule of construction correctly. The meaning could have been adopted which would have allowed s 6 to give the right full scope, which would have meant in the above instance, refusing to read the word 'reasonably' into the section.

In any event, it was always clear that the courts should not imply the word 'reasonably' into s 3.[97] They are expected to find a *possible*, not a reasonable, interpretation, according to its wording. An opposition amendment, which would have imported the word 'reasonably' into the section, was opposed by the government.[98] That was a clear starting point, which was opposed to the New Zealand approach. It allowed straining or distorting the meanings of words or 'reading down' statutory provisions in order to afford them a narrow construction, compatible with the right in question, since all those techniques were *possible* ones. At the outset it was also arguable that it would include reading certain words into the statute. As Lord Lester observed, 'the courts will need where possible to read provisions into ambiguous or incomplete legislation'.[99]

---

93   *Hansard*, HL Deb Col 535, 18 November 1997. The Lord Chancellor further observed that 'in 99 per cent of the cases that will arise, there will be no need for judicial declarations of incompatibility' and the Home Secretary said 'We expect that, in almost all cases, the courts will be able to interpret the legislation compatibly with the Convention': Hansard (HL Debates,) 5 February 1998, col 840 (3rd reading) and Hansard (HC Debates,) 16 February 1998, col 778 (2nd reading).

94   *Ministry of Transport v Noort* [1992] 3 NZLR 260, p 272.

95   See, e.g., *Quilter v AG of New Zealand* [1998] 1 NZLR 523.

96   See Taggart, M, 'Tugging on Superman's cape: lessons from the experience with the New Zealand Bill of Rights' [1998] PL 266; Butler, op. cit., fn 80; Schwartz, H, 'The short and happy life and tragic death of the New Zealand Bill of Rights' [1998] NZLR 259.

97   This was confirmed by the House of Lords in *R v A* [2001] 2 WLR 1546 by Lord Steyn, para 44.

98   Vol 313, HC Deb Col 421, 3 June 1998.

99   'Interpreting statutes under the HRA' 20(3) Statute L Rev 218, p 225.

In 2000 Clayton and Tomlinson suggested that the domestic courts would be able to obtain assistance in dealing with the new rule of construction by taking into account four interpretative techniques: the rule of construction;[100] the rules used to construe statutes in relation to EC law; the doctrines of reading in and reading down and the rule of construction in New Zealand.[101] Thus the response of the House of Lords in *Pickstone v Freemans*[102] to EU law provided a model to be used under s 3. The House of Lords had found that domestic legislation – the Equal Pay Amendment Regulations – made under s 2(2) of the European Communities Act appeared to be inconsistent with Art 119 of the Treaty of Rome. The Lords held that despite this apparent conflict, a purposive interpretation of the domestic legislation would be adopted; in other words, the plain meaning of the provision in question would be ignored and an interpretation would be imposed upon it which was not in conflict with Art 119. This was done on the basis that Parliament must have intended to fulfil its EU obligations in passing the amendment regulations once it had been forced to do so by the European Court of Justice. The House of Lords followed a similar approach in *Litster v Forth Dry Dock Engineering.*[103]

A 'purposive' approach in this context means, it is argued, first adopting the interpretation of the Convention right which gives effect to its core values as interpreted at Strasbourg. This point was considered in Chapter 2[104] and is returned to below. Then, second, it means using the relevant interpretative technique in relation to the statutory provision in question in order, if possible, to impose on it a meaning that achieves the purpose revealed by a consideration of those values, so long as they are in harmony with the underlying purpose of the statute.[105]

Interpretative techniques adopted under s 3[106]

The early signs were that the judiciary were prepared to take an extremely vigorous stance when interpreting existing law in the light of Convention provisions under s 3 since they took the view from the outset that their s 3 obligation allowed them to write words into statutes. The findings of the House of Lords in *R v A*[107] suggested that they were prepared to ensure that the outcome which allowed the Convention to prevail was achieved even if this involved a significant disregard for statutory language. Lord Steyn used an extremely bold interpretative technique – that of reading words

---

100 E.g., *Clarke v General Accident Fire and Life Assurance Corp plc* [1998] 1 WLR 1647.
101 Clayton and Tomlinson, op. cit., fn 1, p 156.
102 [1988] 3 WLR 265.
103 [1989] 1 All ER 1194.
104 At pp 38–39.
105 See *Ghaidan* [2004] 3 WLR 113 at para 35. *Ghaidan* is discussed below at pp 180–81.
106 For comment on s 3(1) generally in the first three years of the HRA, see further: Lester, A, 'The Art of the Possible – Interpreting Statutes under the Human Rights Act' [1999] EHRLR 665; Bennion, F, 'What Interpretation is 'Possible' under Section 3(1) of the Human Rights Act' [2000] PL 77; Edwards, R, 'Reading down Legislation under the Human Rights Act' (2000) 20 LS 353; Gearty, C, 'Reconciling Parliamentary Democracy and Human Rights' (2002) 118 LQR 248; Phillipson, G, '(Mis)Reading Section 3(1) of the Human Rights Act' (2003) LQR 183.
107 *R v A (Complainant's Sexual History)*; [2002] 1 AC 45 (HL); [2001] 2 WLR 1546; [2001] 2 Cr App R 21.

into the legislative provision in question – in order to render it compatible with Art 6. The case concerned a form of 'rape shield' law, under s 41(3)(c) of the Youth Justice and Criminal Evidence Act 1999, that prevented a woman being questioned as to an alleged previous sexual relationship with the defendant, although evidence as to the existence of such a relationship could be adduced by the defence in relation to his belief in her consent. Thus, arguably, s 41(3)(c) protected the woman's Art 8 Rights. Lord Steyn said:

> Under ordinary methods of interpretation a court may depart from the language of the statute in order to avoid absurd consequences: section 3 goes much further. Undoubtedly, a court must always look for a contextual and purposive interpretation: section 3 is more radical in its effect. It is a general principle of the interpretation of legal instruments that the text is the primary source of interpretation: other sources are subordinate to it . . . Section 3 qualifies this general principle because it requires a court to find an interpretation compatible with the Convention rights if it is possible to do so . . . . In accordance with the will of Parliament . . . it will sometimes be necessary to adopt an interpretation which linguistically will appear strained. The techniques to be used will not only involve the reading down of express language in a statute but also the implication of provisions. A declaration of incompatibility is a measure of last resort . . .
>
> It is therefore possible under s 3 to read . . . s 41(3)(c) [of the Youth Justice and Criminal Evidence Act 1999] . . . as subject to the implied provisions that *evidence or questioning which is required to ensure a fair trial under Article 6(1) . . . should not be treated as inadmissible* [emphasis added].[108]

In taking this stance Lord Steyn arguably went beyond using interpretative techniques and – in effect – rewrote a sub-section of the legislation. In *R v A*, Lord Steyn very clearly accepted that a declaration under s 4 was indeed a last resort and that s 3 could be used in an extremely creative fashion in order to avoid having to make one. A somewhat more cautionary note was sounded regarding the application of s 3 in *Poplar Housing and Regeneration Community Association Limited v Secretary of State for the Environment, Transport and the Regions*.[109] Lord Woolf said that s 3 'does not entitle the court to legislate; its task is still one of interpretation but interpretation in accordance with the direction contained in s 3'.[110] He went on to say that the most difficult task of the courts is that of distinguishing between interpretation and legislation.

Similarly, in *Wilson v the First County Trust Ltd*[111] the Court of Appeal found that s 127(3) of the Consumer Credit Act 1974 was incompatible with Art 6 and with Art 1 of the First Protocol to the Convention since it imposed an inflexible prohibition against the making of an enforcement order in an instance where a loan agreement did not contain the terms prescribed for the purposes of s 61(1) of the Act. The effect of s 127(3) was therefore to prevent the creditor from obtaining a judicial remedy where the loan agreement did not contain all the prescribed terms. The Court considered the possibility

---

108 Ibid, paras 44 and 45.
109 [2001] 3 WLR 183; [2001] 4 All ER 604; [2002] QB 48.
110 At paras 75 and 76.
111 [2001] 3 All ER 229.

of finding 'some other legitimate interpretation' of the words of the section which would avoid the finding of incompatibility.[112] It said that a court is 'required [by s 3] to go as far as but not beyond what is legally possible . . . the court is not required or entitled to give to words a meaning which they cannot bear'.[113] In the instance in question, the court did not think that the words would bear a Convention-compliant interpretation and so a declaration of the incompatibility was issued. Clearly, the Court of Appeal considered that there are limits to what can be achieved even under s 3, although their finding is hardly consonant with that of the House of Lords in *R v A*. That declaration was reversed in the House of Lords on the basis that applying the 'retrospectivity provisions' discussed below, the HRA was inapplicable to the factual situation. Clearly, it would not have appeared possible for the Lords to accept the interpretation of Art 6 and Art 1 of Protocol 1 adopted by the Court of Appeal, but then go on to find that the words of s 127(3) could be forced to take a Convention-compliant meaning.

The approach in *R v A* can also be contrasted with the decision of the Privy Council in *Brown v Stott*,[114] the first decision of the Law Lords under the HRA. The decision illustrated, it is suggested, the problems that may arise due to the adoption of a form of 'purposive' approach and of 'reading down' Convention rights by reference to the purpose in question. The decision is discussed fully below, but a number of central findings in it illustrate the approach adopted. Lord Steyn found: 'national courts may accord to the decisions of national legislatures some deference where the context justifies it . . . the subject [road safety] invites special regulation . . . some infringements [of Art 6] may be justified.' Lord Hope said:

> the jurisprudence of the Court of Human Rights tells us . . . that [in the case of a non-absolute right] the . . . restriction contended for has to have a legitimate aim in the public interest. If so is there a reasonable relationship of proportionality between the means employed and the aim sought to be realised?

He found that, in relation to s 172 of the Road Traffic Act, which requires that drivers identify themselves, on pain of a fine, as driving a car at the material time, the answer to both questions, in terms of limiting the right not to incriminate oneself under Art 6(1), was in the affirmative. This decision exemplifies, it is suggested, the possibilities of undermining the Convention rights by taking a particular view as to the general purposes of the Convention and then by 'reading down' a particular right in order to do so. This approach is considered further below in relation to the notions of judicial activism and minimalism.

In *re W and B*[115] the Lords accepted that, following *R v A*, words could be read into a statute, but took a more cautious stance in relation to s 3(1). The Lords refused to use s 3 to bring about the radical changes to the Children Act 1989 put in place by the Court of Appeal, and a restrained reading of section 3 was advocated. As Kavanagh observes, 'The Court of Appeal had read into the Children Act 1989 a range of new

---

112 Ibid, para 41.
113 Ibid, para 42.
114 [2001] 2 WLR 817; [2001] 2 All ER 97, the Judicial Committee of the Privy Council. See, for the Scottish decision, *Stott v Brown* 2000 SLT 379.
115 *Re W and B (Children) (Care Plan)* [2002] 2 WLR 720.

powers and procedures by which courts could supervise and monitor the implementation of care orders by local authorities, so as to protect children against violations of their rights under Art.8 ECHR'.[116] Lord Nicholls found that s 3(1) is 'a powerful tool whose use is obligatory. It is not an optional canon of construction. Nor is its use dependent on the existence of ambiguity. Further, the section applies retrospectively'.[117] But he found as to a reading of legislation under section 3(1):

> [I]t is sufficient to say that a meaning which departs substantially from a fundamental feature of an Act of Parliament is likely to have crossed the boundary between interpretation and amendment. This is especially so where the departure has important practical repercussions which the court is not equipped to evaluate.[118]

This decision is broadly consistent with *R v A* on the assumption that the change made in *R v A* did not depart substantially from a fundamental feature of the Youth Justice and Criminal Evidence Act. But Lord Nicholls showed a concern to identify the point at which reading in words would be inappropriate.

The factor of departure from a fundamental feature of the statute was of relevance in *Anderson*.[119] The incompatibility lay in the involvement of the Secretary of State in sentencing adult life prisoners. The Secretary of State's role in the legislation was a pervasive feature of it. The Secretary of State's role in sentencing was found to be incompatible with Art 6 since he could not be viewed as an independent and impartial tribunal. A declaration of incompatibility was made rather than seeking to use s 3(1) since the Secretary of State's role was such a fundamental feature of the statute as a whole – any other approach would have been against the grain of the statute. Since the use of s 3 was therefore rejected, the House of Lords instead issued a declaration of incompatibility on the ground that a power conferred on the Home Secretary by s 29 of the Crime (Sentencing) Act 1997 to control the release of mandatory life sentence prisoners was inconsistent with the right to have a sentence imposed by 'an independent and impartial tribunal', under Art 6 ECHR.

Lord Hope took a similar stance in *R v Lambert*.[120] He said as to section 3 that:

> Resort to it will not be possible if the legislation contains provisions, either in the words or phrases which are under scrutiny or elsewhere, which expressly contradict the meaning which the enactment would have to be given to make it compatible. The same consequence will follow if legislation contains provisions which have this effect by necessary implication . . . It does not give power to the judges to overrule decisions which the language of the statute shows have been taken on the very point at issue by the 'legislator'.[121]

---

116 Kavanagh, A, 'Statutory interpretation and human rights after Anderson: a more contextual approach' [2004] PL 537 at p 538.
117 At para 37.
118 At para 40.
119 *R (on the application of Anderson) v Secretary of State for the Home Department* [2003] 1 AC 837.
120 *R v Lambert* [2001] 3 All ER 577.
121 At para 79.

The legislation at issue in *Lambert* was the Misuse of Drugs Act 1971; the Lords found that a reverse onus clause in the statute appeared to violate Art 6(2), ECHR. It placed a legal burden on the accused: he had to prove that he was ignorant of the fact that the substance that he had in his possession was a controlled drug; if he did not prove his ignorance of the fact he would be convicted. Their Lordships re-interpreted this provision, relying on s 3(1), so that it imposed an *evidential* burden only on the accused. The Lords read the words, 'proves that he neither believed or suspected that the substance in question was a controlled drug' as meaning, 'leads evidence such as to raise an issue as to whether he knew that the substance in question was a controlled drug'.[122] Thus although Lord Hope stated that the courts should not change a Parliamentary decision which it is clear has been taken on the very point at issue by the legislator, it appears that that is in fact what the Lords managed to do.

Lambert was one of a group of decisions taken in the context of a governmental demand for the use of reverse onus provisions in response to global concerns about terrorism and organised crime, especially drug trafficking, people trafficking and serious fraud.[123] In this context the lawbreaking in question tends to be systematically planned by professional criminals, providing encouragement to a policy of imposing a greater burden on the defendant despite the accompanying impact on the presumption of innocence. The 'reading down' under s 3 HRA of reverse burdens to evidential ones, has provided something of a check to this governmental tendency[124] and a reassertion of the fundamental right encapsulated in Art 6(2),[125] and long recognised under common law principle.[126] This tendency was also evident in *Sheldrake v DPP*.[127] *Sheldrake* concerned the offence of belonging to a proscribed terrorist organisation contrary to s 11, Terrorism Act 2000.[128] The defendant argued that at the time when he became a member or professed to become a member of the organisation it had not yet been proscribed (the defence provided by s 11(2)). The Court of Appeal found that s 11(2) did not relate to an element of the offence, but that in any event if it did it was compatible with Art 6(2). The House of Lords, by a three to two majority, reversed this decision,

122 See, e.g., Lord Hope at para 94. See further Fenwick, H and Phillipson, G, *Media Freedom under the Human Rights Act* 2006, pp 160–61.

123 In *R v DPP ex p Kebilene* [2000] 2 AC 326 (HL) (see pp 1347–52); *R v Lambert (Steven)* [2001] UKLH 37, discussed above; *R v Johnstone (Robert Alexander)* [2003] UKHL 28; Attorney-General's Reference (No 1 of 2004) [2004] 1 WLR 211; *Sheldrake v DPP* [2004] UKHL 43 (two conjoined appeals, one of which is discussed below).

124 Williams in 'The Logic of Exceptions' [1988] Cambridge Law Journal 261 argues that the word 'prove' in an English statute can legitimately be interpreted as imposing only an 'evidential burden' on the defendant. See further, Tadros, V and Tierney, S, 'The Presumption of Innocence and the Human Rights Act', (2004) 67 MLR 402, at 403; Simester, AP and Sullivan, GR, *Criminal Law: Theory and Doctrine*, 2nd edn, 2004, esp p 69; Dennis, I, 'Reverse Onuses and the Presumption of Innocence: In Search of Principle' [2005] CLR 901; Dingwall, G, 'Statutory Exceptions, Burdens of Proof and the Human Rights Act 1998' (2002) 65 MLR 40; Ashworth, A, 'Four Threats to the Presumption of Innocence' (2006) 10 *International Journal of Evidence and Proof* 241; Ashworth, A, 'Criminal Justice Reform: Principles, Human Rights and Public Protection' [2004] Crim LR 516.

125 See Chapter 2, pp 64–65.

126 See *Woolmington* [1935] AC 462, 481–82. See further Ashworth, A and Blake, M, 'The Presumption of Innocence in English Criminal Law' [1996] CLR 306.

127 *Sheldrake v DPP* [2004] UKHL 43; [2005] 1 AC 264; [2005] 1 All ER 237.

128 See further Chapter 14, pp 1391–92.

Lord Bingham finding that a person who had not engaged in any blameworthy conduct could come within s 11(1) and that the presumption of innocence was infringed by requiring him or her to disprove involvement in the organisation at the time in question. Thus the Lords found that s 11(2) imposes an evidential burden only. A majority of the House of Lords relied on s 3 to read the word 'prove' as though it meant 'adduce sufficient evidence to raise an issue in the case'.

In a further decision in the terrorism context, *R(MB) v Secretary of State for the Home Department*,[129] the Court of Appeal reversed the judgment of Sullivan J who had made a declaration of incompatibility, in holding that the procedure available under the Prevention of Terrorism Act 2005 to challenge a non-derogating control order breached Art 6. The Court of Appeal reversed his decision on the basis that s 3 of the HRA could be applied to read down s 11(2) of the 2005 Act; the Court found: 'we consider that section 3(10) can and should be 'read down' [under s 3 HRA] so as to require the court to consider whether the decisions of the Secretary of State in relation to the control order are flawed as at the time of the court's determination'.[130]

As fully discussed in Chapter 6, radically differing views of the effect of s 3 were expressed in the Court of Appeal[131] and in the House of Lords[132] in *R (on the application of Pro-Life Alliance) v BBC*.[133] The Court of Appeal's approach resembled that taken in *R v A*; Laws LJ, having concluded that both common law and Art 10 protection for freedom of expression forbade censorship of the Pro-Life Alliance video, did not seek to explain what *should* be done in relation to the statutory provision at issue – s 6(1)(a) of the Broadcasting Act 1990 – in order to render it compatible with Art 10. Laws LJ did not rely expressly on s 3 HRA; he merely found, 'the Broadcasting Act 1990 . . . must be read conformably with this principle'.[134] As Chapter 6 points out, the House of Lords also virtually ignored s 3 but on the basis of a very different stance taken towards Art 10; as discussed in that chapter, the House was determined to defer to the views of the broadcasters; in so doing it appeared to overlook the duty placed on it by s 3 to interpret the legislation in issue – the Broadcasting Act – compatibly with the Convention rights if possible. The provision at issue could in fact readily have been re-interpreted in order to achieve Art 10 compliance.[135]

In *Bellinger v Bellinger*,[136] W, a post-operative transsexual, appealed against a decision under the Matrimonial Causes Act 1973 that she was not lawfully married to her husband, H, because she, W, was not female. Section 11 of the 1973 Act states: 'A marriage . . . shall be void on the following grounds only, that is to say . . . that the parties are not respectively male and female . . .'. W argued that the word 'female' should be interpreted as including her and other post-operative transsexuals, relying on her right to private and family life under Art 8 ECHR. As Phillipson has argued, 'All that was required was the re-interpretation of the single word "female",

---

129 [2006] EWCA Civ 1140.
130 At para 46.
131 [2002] 2 All ER 756.
132 [2004] 1 AC 185.
133 See Chapter 6, pp 534–43.
134 Ibid at para 44.
135 See Chapter 6, p 543.
136 [2003] 2 AC 467 (HL).

to reflect modern understandings of the protean nature of gender, so that it included post-operative male to female transsexuals.'[137] However, the House of Lords refused to reinterpret the word 'female' to include transsexuals as had been argued for. They were influenced by the fact that the government had already accepted that the area of law in question had become incompatible with Art 8 and had stated that it intended to bring legislation before Parliament to remedy the matter. In those circumstances, it appeared that the Lords preferred to leave reform of the law to Parliament which would be able to take a far more comprehensive and systematic view of the issue. A range of policy matters were involved; as Kavanagh observes: 'the resulting change in the law would have [had] far-reaching practical ramifications, raising issues whose solution calls for extensive inquiry and the widest public consultation and discussion which was more appropriate for Parliament than the courts'.[138]

In *Ghaidan v Godin-Mendoza*,[139] discussed fully in Chapter 15,[140] the Court of Appeal found that Sched 1, para 2 of the Rent Act 1977 was incompatible with Art 14 read with Art 8. But it found that the potential incompatibility could be remedied under s 3 HRA by construing the words 'as his or her wife or husband' in Sched 1, para 2 as if they meant 'as if they were his or her wife or husband'. The House of Lords in *Ghaidan v Godin-Mendoza* agreed with the Court of Appeal, and used s 3 HRA to interpret the statute to avoid the discrimination against homosexuals so that they had the same rights to succeed to tenancies upon the death of their partner as were enjoyed by heterosexual couples. This meant not merely changing the meaning given to certain words, but the addition of (a few) words that were not included in the provision.

Lord Nicholls made a number of very significant points on s 3 which are worth quoting in full since *Ghaidan* is now the leading decision on s 3:[141]

> [T]he first point to be considered is how far, when enacting section 3, Parliament intended that the actual language of a statute, as distinct from the concept expressed in that language, should be determinative. Since section 3 relates to the "interpretation" of legislation, it is natural to focus attention initially on the language used in the legislative provision being considered. But once it is accepted that section 3 may require legislation to bear a meaning which departs from the unambiguous meaning the legislation would otherwise bear, it becomes impossible to suppose Parliament intended that the operation of section 3 should depend critically upon the particular form of words adopted by the parliamentary draftsman in the statutory provision under consideration. That would make the application of section 3 something of a semantic lottery. If the draftsman chose to express the *concept being enacted* in one form of words, section 3 would be available to achieve Convention-compliance. If he chose a different form of words, section 3 would be impotent (emphasis added).

---

137 Phillipson, G, 'Deference, Discretion and Democracy in the Human Rights Act Era' (2007) CLP 40 at p 65.

138 'Statutory interpretation and human rights after Anderson: a more contextual approach' [2004] PL 537 at 541.

139 [2003] 2 WLR 478; [2002] 4 All ER 1162; [2004] 2 AC 557 (HL).

140 See pp 1525–26.

141 At paras 31–34.

From this the conclusion which seems inescapable is that the mere fact the language under consideration is inconsistent with a Convention-compliant meaning does not of itself make a Convention-compliant interpretation under section 3 impossible. Section 3 enables language to be interpreted restrictively or expansively. But section 3 goes further than this. It is also apt to require a court to read in words which change the meaning of the enacted legislation, so as to make it Convention-compliant. In other words, the intention of Parliament in enacting section 3 was that, to an extent bounded only by what is "possible", a court can modify the meaning, and hence the effect, of primary and secondary legislation.

Parliament, however, cannot have intended that in the discharge of this extended interpretative function the courts should adopt a meaning inconsistent with a fundamental feature of legislation. That would be to cross the constitutional boundary section 3 seeks to demarcate and preserve. Parliament has retained the right to enact legislation in terms which are not Convention-compliant. The meaning imported by application of section 3 must be compatible with the underlying thrust of the legislation being construed. Words implied must, in the phrase of my noble and learned friend Lord Rodger of Earlsferry, "go with the grain of the legislation". Nor can Parliament have intended that section 3 should require courts to make decisions for which they are not equipped. There may be several ways of making a provision Convention-compliant, and the choice may involve issues calling for *legislative deliberation* (emphasis added).

Both these features were present in *In re S (Minors)(Care Order: Implementation of Care Plan)* [2002] 2 AC 291. There the proposed "starring system" was inconsistent in an important respect with the scheme of the Children Act 1989, and the proposed system had far-reaching practical ramifications for local authorities. Again, in *R (Anderson) v Secretary of State for the Home Department* [2003] 1 AC 837 section 29 of the Crime (Sentences) Act 1997 could not be read in a Convention-compliant way without giving the section a meaning inconsistent with an important feature expressed clearly in the legislation. In *Bellinger v Bellinger* [2003] 2 AC 467 recognition of Mrs Bellinger as female for the purposes of section 11(c) of the Matrimonial Causes Act 1973 would have had exceedingly wide ramifications, raising issues ill-suited for determination by the courts or court procedures.

The majority in the Lords took a broadly similar view.[142] Thus, it is now accepted, as Lord Nicholls stated, that section 3 may require legislation to bear a meaning which departs from the unambiguous meaning the legislation would otherwise bear, since the particular form of words used by the draftsman to express the concept of the statute – its underlying policy – should not be allowed to prevent the courts from achieving Convention-compliance. But in using s 3 to modify the meaning of the statute a meaning cannot be adopted, he said, that goes against a fundamental feature of the legislation or requires legislative deliberation.

---

142   For discussion of the other judgments, including the dissenting judgment of Lord Millett, see Kavanagh, A, in *Judicial Reasoning under the HRA* (2007) fn 1 above, Chapter 5.

The House of Lords thus went on to adopt the course taken in the Court of Appeal, and found that the words 'living with the tenant as his or her wife or husband' could be read as: 'living with the tenant, as *if they were* his or her wife or husband'. This change was much more radical than the change argued for in *Bellinger*. The Lords appeared to be prepared to take this stance since, unlike the position in *Bellinger v Bellinger*, the change in meaning to the law was a straightforward one and affected only one provision of the statute; also it did not appear to have the wide-ranging policy ramifications that the change argued for in *Bellinger* might have had. It provided, as Lord Steyn pointed out, a remedy that would not otherwise have been available for the claimant:

> It is necessary to state what section 3(1), and in particular the word 'possible', does not mean. First, section 3(1) applies even if there is no ambiguity in the language in the sense of it being capable of bearing two *possible* meanings. The word 'possible' in section 3(1) is used in a different and much stronger sense. Secondly, section 3(1) imposes a stronger and more radical obligation than to adopt a purposive interpretation in the light of the ECHR. Thirdly, the draftsman of the Act had before him the model of the New Zealand Bill of Rights Act which imposes a requirement that the interpretation to be adopted must be reasonable. Parliament specifically rejected the legislative model of requiring a reasonable interpretation.
>
> Instead the draftsman had resort to the analogy of the obligation under the EEC Treaty on national courts, as far as possible, to interpret national legislation in the light of the wording and purpose of Directives.[143] . . . Given the undoubted strength of this interpretative obligation under EEC law, this is a significant signpost to the meaning of section 3(1) in the 1998 Act.
>
> Parliament had before it the mischief and objective sought to be addressed, viz the need 'to bring rights home'. The linch-pin of the legislative scheme to achieve this purpose was section 3(1). Rights could only be effectively brought home if section 3(1) was the prime remedial measure, and section 4 a measure of last resort. How the system modelled on the EEC interpretative obligation would work was graphically illustrated for Parliament during the progress of the Bill through both Houses . . . It was envisaged that the duty of the court would be to strive to find (if possible) a meaning which would best accord with Convention rights. This is the remedial scheme which Parliament adopted.[144]

Furthermore, the change did not go against the grain of the statute; as Klug and Starmer put it,[145] the re-interpretation was 'fairly viewed as compatible with the thrust of the

---

143 He noted that in *Marleasing SA v La Comercial Internacional de Alimentación SA* (Case C-106/89) [1990] ECR I-4135, 4159 the European Court of Justice defined this obligation as follows: 'It follows that, in applying national law, whether the provisions in questions were adopted before or after the directive, the national court called upon to interpret it is required to do so, as far as possible, in light of the wording and the purpose of the directive in order to achieve the result pursued by the latter and thereby comply with the third paragraph of Article 189 of the Treaty'

144 At paras 44–46.

145 'Standing Back from the Human Rights Act: How Effective is it Five Years On?' (2005) PL 716, p 720.

statute, which was intended to include cohabiting as well as married couples, but on its face discriminated against homosexuals'. Nevertheless, *Ghaidan* obviously takes a radical approach which appears at first glance to take a stance towards s 3 very similar to that taken in *R v A*. Kavanagh argues that the Lords went too far in *Ghaidan* in appearing to take the stance that there are no textual limits to the operation of s 3(1).[146] This point is returned to below.

A further possibility arises. This point has not yet been relied upon, but it could be put forward in relation to post-HRA statutes, or statutes enacted in order to achieve Convention-compliance after an adverse ruling in the ECHR, such as the Contempt of Court Act 1981. If in such an instance the judges were prepared to accept that Parliament had partially failed to achieve its aim in enacting the provisions in question, then reading words into the statute to achieve Convention-compliance *even* where it was arguable that they came close to going against the grain of the statute, could be seen, not as *defeating* Parliament's intention, but as perfecting it. This could be argued in relation to post-HRA statutes on the basis that a declaration of the compatibility of the statute with the Convention had been made under s 19 and that therefore Parliament must have intended to enact provisions that did achieve compatibility. However, that would only be the case where it was clear that the Convention under the HRA demanded the change, which had been overlooked by Parliament.

Summing-up the current approach to s 3[147]

Clearly, 'the precise limits of the s 3 rule of construction remain controversial'.[148] But, as indicated, those limits are becoming apparent. Following the lead of the House of Lords in the key decisions mentioned, in particular *R v A, Donoghue, Alconbury*,[149] *Bellinger, Ghaidan*, it is apparent that a number of steps are being taken when the argument is put that a legislative provision is incompatible with a Convention right. First, whether or not a declaration of incompatibility has already been made in a lower court (or, if in a court unable to make a formal declaration, an informal finding of incompatibility), the Strasbourg jurisprudence and the provision itself are considered

---

146 See *Judicial Reasoning under the HRA* (2007) fn 1 above, Chapter 5.
147 See further: Clayton and Tomlinson, op. cit., fn 1, (2006) Part II; Phillipson, G, '(Mis)Reading Section 3(1) of the Human Rights Act' [2003] LQR 183; Young, A, 'Judicial Sovereignty and the Human Rights Act 1998' [2002] CLJ 53; Kavanagh, A, 'Statutory interpretation and human rights after Anderson: a more contextual approach' [2004] PL 537; Kavanagh, A, 'Unlocking the Human Rights Act: the 'radical approach' to section 3(1) revisited' (2005) 3 EHRLR 259; Kavanagh, A, in *Judicial Reasoning under the HRA* (2007) fn 1 above, Chapter 5. For two recent decisions on the effect of s 3 which relied on the *Ghaidan* approach, see *R v Holding* [2006] 1 WLR 1040 in which the Court of Appeal read down s 75 of the Representation of the People Act 1983 and *Culnane v Morris* [2006] 2 All ER 149 in which s 10 of the Defamation Act 1952 was re-construed under s 3 HRA.
148 Gearty, C, 'Reconciling Parliamentary Democracy and Human Rights' (2002) 118 LQR 248; Phillipson, G, '(Mis)Reading Section 3(1) of the Human Rights Act' (2003) LQR 183 (a response to C Gearty); Young, A, 'Judicial Sovereignty and the Human Rights Act 1998' [2002] CLJ 53; Kavanagh, 'Statutory interpretation and human rights after Anderson: a more contextual approach' [2004] PL 537, which responds to Nicol, D 'Statutory interpretation and human rights after Anderson' [2004] PL 273.
149 *R (on the application of Alconbury Ltd) v Secretary of State for the Environment, Transport and the Regions* [2001] 2 All ER 929; (2001) NLJ 135.

afresh in order to determine whether there is, on close scrutiny, a problem regarding compatibility. That may be the end of the matter, as in *Alconbury*.

Second, if there does appear to be potential incompatibility, it may be resolvable using accepted interpretative techniques as in *Brown v Stott*,[150] without relying on s 3.[151] Third, if the use of such techniques alone would almost certainly mean that a declaration of incompatibility has to be made, the court will consider the use of s 3. Section 3 may be used in a very creative fashion, as indicated by Lord Steyn in the majority in *R v A*, and by Lord Nicholls in *Ghaidan*, in order to avoid a finding of incompatibility unless, according to *Donoghue*, so doing would mean crossing the boundary between interpreting and legislating. *Bellinger* and *Ghaidan* indicate that the word 'possible' in s 3(1) relates to matters ranging well beyond linguistic possibility. Clearly, they appear to view it as denoting something that is possible linguistically but that may be undesirable, for a range of reasons. So when will the courts be prepared to read words into a statute, or to reinterpret an existing word, in order to avoid incompatibility? In other words, which factors will persuade them to the more radical approach adopted in *R v A* and in *Ghaidan*? Their approach appears to be that they will adopt that more radical approach where it appears to them to be proper and desirable to do so. What factors will strike them as bringing a particular instance into that category of desirableness? The word 'desirable' is used deliberately in preference to the more neutral 'appropriate' used by Kavanagh. She points out that the courts will take a more radical approach to compatibility under s 3, not where it is 'possible' to do so, but where they think it is *appropriate*, taking various matters into account, to do so.[152]

The following discussion is based on Dr Kavanagh's analysis of the s 3(1) cases[153] which the author finds compelling in the sense that it is the most accurate analysis of the wide range of factors that the courts are relying on in determining how radical their approach should be in particular instances under s 3. Clearly, the courts are concerned that they should not cross the line between interpretation and legislation. Kavanagh argues that the decision in *re S and re W*,[154] shows that, while the courts are prepared to read words into statutes, as in *R v A*, or *Ghaidan*, they will not do so, 'as a way of radically reforming a whole statute or writing a quasi-legislative code granting new

---

150   This approach receives support from *Donoghue v Poplar Housing and Regeneration Community Association Ltd and the Secretary of State for the Environment* [2001] 3 WLR 183; [2001] 4 All ER 604. The Lord Chief Justice said that, 'unless legislation would otherwise be in breach of the Convention s 3 can be ignored; so courts should always ascertain whether, absent s 3, there would be any breach of the Convention (at para 75).'

151   See *Ghaidan* at para 24; see also *International Transport Roth GmbH v Secretary of State for the Home Dept* [2002] 3 WLR 344.

152   'Statutory interpretation and human rights after *Anderson*: a more contextual approach' [2004] PL 537 at pp 544–45.

153   See Kavanagh, A, 'Unlocking the Human Rights Act: the 'radical approach' to section 3(1) revisited' (2005) 3 EHRLR 259; see in particular 'The elusive divide between interpretation and legislation under the HRA' (2004) 24(2) OJLS 259; and 'Statutory interpretation and human rights after Anderson: a more contextual approach' [2004] P.L. 537, which is a response, in part, to Nicol, D, 'Statutory interpretation and human rights after Anderson' [2004] PL 273. The analysis below (pp 184–85) partially follows my co-author's in *Media Freedom under the Human Rights Act*, pp 161–62.

154   [2002] 2 AC 291. This decision was reversed unanimously by the House of Lords.

powers and setting out new procedures to replace that statute'.[155] As discussed, the Court of Appeal had written a number of provisions into the statute in *re S* under s 3 – an approach that was rejected by the House of Lords.

Another aspect of this stance is to find that the change proposed, to ensure compatibility, will probably be rejected where it would run counter to a pervasive feature of the statute – where the objectionable provisions permeate the statute. This factor was decisive in *Anderson*.[156] In *R v A*, or *Lambert* or *Ghaidan* the objected-to provision was not viewed as fundamental to the statute as a whole or a substantial part of it. Where the change is viewed as fundamental it would probably require extensive statutory modification to achieve compatibility. Clearly, different views could be taken as to the fundamental nature or otherwise of a provision.

The subject-matter of the provision at issue is relevant. If it relates to matters peculiarly within the judicial domain, including the ordering of the criminal or civil justice system, in matters of sentencing, or admissibility of evidence, the judges are more likely to be prepared to take a radical approach, as they did in *R v A* and in *R v Offen*.[157] In taking such a stance in that context they would not view themselves as stepping outside their own area of constitutional responsibility.

If, however, a case involves issues of social policy or resource allocation, the courts are much less likely to be bold. This factor was of relevance in *re S:* the proposed 'interpretation' of the statute that had been accepted in the Court of Appeal would also have had, 'far-reaching practical ramifications for local authorities and their care of children, including the authority's allocation of scarce financial and other resources'.[158] Those policy and resource factors were also of relevance, as indicated above, in *Bellinger v Bellinger* and persuaded the court to take a cautious approach to s 3.[159] As discussed, the change brought about in *Ghaidan v Godin-Mendoza*[160] did not engage significant countervailing policy or resource-based factors. In both *Lambert* and *Sheldrake* the judges were arguably therefore pulled in opposing directions; in confronting reverse onus clauses aimed at combating organised crime or terrorism, both decisions concerned matters that could be viewed as within the judicial area of particular competence, but they also related to resource allocation in terms of the costs and difficulties of combating organised crime and bringing those allegedly involved to trial, as the culmination of a resource-intensive process.

Kavanagh further argues, referring to Lord Steyn's judgment in *Ghaidan*, that the key to understanding the various uses of s 3 is to see it as a remedial provision.[161] In other words, where the use of s 3 rather than s 4 is the only means of providing a remedy in the particular situation, the judges will tend to employ s 3. As she notes, in

---

155 'Statutory interpretation and human rights after *Anderson*: a more contextual approach' [2004] PL 537 at p 540.
156 *R (on the application of Anderson) v Secretary of State for the Home Department* [2003] 1 AC 837.
157 [2001] 1 WLR 253. The case concerned the 'reading down' of provisions governing mandatory sentences for repeat offenders.
158 Kavanagh, 'Statutory interpretation and human rights after *Anderson*: a more contextual approach' [2004] PL 537 at p 540.
159 [2003] 2 AC 467 (HL).
160 [2004] 2 AC 557 (HL).
161 See *Judicial Reasoning under the HRA* (2007) fn 1 above, Chapter 5.

Bellinger, a remedy was about to be provided for the applicant by planned legislation, whereas in *Ghaidan* Mr Mendoza would have had no means of succeeding to a statutory tenancy had s 3 not been employed as it was.

So it appears that the courts are prepared to depart from the literal meaning of the section and to read words into it where the new interpretation does not go against a pervasive feature of the statute.[162] At the same time the court will feel most comfortable with this stance where the reform proposed is largely a matter of interpretation rather than one of implying into the statute an entirely new provision that was absent from it.[163] If the area in question is one that is clearly within the judicial domain in terms of constitutional competence and role they are also more inclined to boldness.[164] The argument will be aided if Parliament is not otherwise addressing this issue – there are no plans to reform the objected-to provision – and no issues of resource allocation arise. In such circumstances there will be positive reasons for activism and none for deference.

As a final step, if one or more of the other countervailing factors discussed are present, so that the use of s 3 is viewed as inappropriate in order to find compatibility, a declaration of the incompatibility will have to be made, when and if the matter reaches a court able to make such a declaration, under s 4.[165] It now appears that the courts tend to view s 3, not s 4, as the main remedial mechanism of the HRA, only turning to s 4 exceptionally as a last resort, so normally this fourth step will not be needed.[166] If no remedy is available or in prospect, except by way of s 3, it appears that the courts may be strongly inclined towards the more radical use of s 3.

Conclusions

It is argued that the approach being taken to s 3, especially the stance taken in *R v A*, is not one that it is entirely easy to feel comfortable with in terms of the doctrine of Parliamentary sovereignty. Space precludes extended analysis of *R v A* here,[167] but some differences between it and *Ghaidan* – the other most radical s 3 case – can be identified which could be viewed as building in further indicators as to when the radical s 3 approach is appropriate and when it is not. *R v A* is singled out since it is argued that Art 6 did *not* clearly demand the change that Lord Steyn imposed on the statute,[168]

---

162 Cf *R (on the application of Anderson) v Secretary of State for the Home Dept* [2003] 1 AC 837.

163 As in the Court of Appeal in *re S and re W (Care Orders)*; HL: [2002] 2 AC 291.

164 The context is relevant in terms of both expertise and constitutional role: *R v A* [2002] 1 AC 45; *R v Offen* [2001] 1 WLR 253.

165 As in *Wilson v First County Trust Ltd* [2001] 3 All ER 229; [2001] EWCA Civ 633, although arguably, it is unclear that the Convention absolutely demanded this result.

166 See Lord Steyn's remarks on this point in *Ghaidan* [2004] 2 AC 557 (HL) at para 50.

167 See for debate on *R v A*, Kavanagh, A, 'Unlocking the Human Rights Act: the radical approach to section 3(1) revisited' (2005) 3 EHRLR 259 (she defends the decision in terms of the use of s 3). See also Young, A, 'Judicial Sovereignty and the Human Rights Act 1998' [2002] CLJ 53.

168 See Chapter 13, p 1292. It is pointed out that the Convention leaves a wide margin of appreciation to member states as to evidential matters. Lord Steyn's analysis was less rooted in the Art 6 jurisprudence than was that of the House of Lords in *Ghaidan*; no decision at Strasbourg under Art 6 directly supports Lord Steyn's stance.

whereas it is argued that Art 8 *did* demand the change imposed in *Ghaidan*.[169] Therefore *R v A* sits uneasily with the leading s 2 cases, discussed below,[170] in which it has been found that courts should 'interpret the Convention rights in a way which keeps pace with rather than leaps ahead of the Convention jurisprudence as it evolves over time.'[171] Even if, as argued below, the view is taken that the courts are free to broaden the ambit of a Convention right, unless that jurisprudence imposes a clear limit on its ambit, it may be argued that where there are countervailing constitutional and Convention-based considerations, that course should not be taken. In *Ghaidan* an individual right was at stake and opposed only by a societal concern – an interest in entering into an agreement on a certain contractual basis even if in a discriminatory fashion. In such instances, as documented throughout this book, the starting-point is always the primacy of the right and the exception to it is to be narrowly construed.[172]

In *R v A*, on the other hand, it is arguable that a clash of two Convention rights occurred – between Arts 6 and 8,[173] and possibly between Arts 6 and 3 – although the Lords did not recognise this. The Lords were bound by all the rights under s 6 HRA and, it is contended, should have respected the balance that Parliament had very recently struck between them in the statute at issue. In terms of separation of powers, arguably, a very difficult moral clash occurred which Parliament, not the courts, had already resolved, taking full account of the issues involved, and Parliament's solution should have remained undisturbed. The change did have policy and resource-based implications since it affected the use of police and CPS resources in rape cases as the decision may have had some impact in hindering a rise in the rape conviction rate.[174] In terms of the remedial role of s 3, it should be noted that the change imposed by Lord Steyn could be said to have *removed* a remedy for a harm suffered by victims – that of the humiliation endured if sexual behaviour evidence is admitted. The psychological harm suffered by the victim whose rapist is acquitted, either because she withdraws in the face of the threat that such evidence will be admitted,[175] or because the evidence undermines her credibility, arguably could be viewed as Art 3 treatment.[176]

---

169 See Chapter 15, pp 1525–26.

170 See pp 191–97.

171 *R (on the application of Marper) v Chief Constable of South Yorkshire* [2004] 1 WLR 2196 at para 78, *per* Baroness Hale.

172 See, e.g., Chapter 9, p 951, fn 669 and associated text.

173 In part, on the basis that Art 8 gives protection to information pertaining to sexual behaviour: see Chapter 9, pp 927–28. There is also the question of humiliation; see Chapter 12, p 1207. Clearly, the clash might be resolved in favour of Art 6 since Art 8 is materially qualified, but the fact that the victim's Art 8 right was arguably at stake should have been recognised.

174 See Temkin, J, *Section 41: An Evaluation Of New Legislation Limiting Sexual History Evidence In Rape Trials*, Home Office Online Report 20/2006, with Kelly, L and Griffiths, S. She found that judges tend to interpret *R v A* broadly and to admit sexual behaviour evidence on the ground that otherwise a fair trial could be jeopardised. She found that this did have an impact on conviction rates (Conclusions section).

175 See Temkin, J, *Section 41: An Evaluation Of New Legislation Limiting Sexual History Evidence In Rape Trials*, Home Office Online Report 20/2006, with Kelly and Griffiths on this point: she notes that victims did withdraw once an application to admit sexual behaviour evidence was made, and this appeared to be because they did not want to face a humiliating cross examination.

176 It may be noted that a complaint under Art 3 in respect of degrading treatment of a woman in a UK rape trial was declared admissible at Strasbourg: *JM v UK* (2001) 2 EHRLR 215. The woman was

Moreover, the change imposed by Lord Steyn on the statute did go against the grain of the provision in question, whereas in *Ghaidan* the provision appeared to be intended to protect co-habiting couples, which in 2003 were much more likely to be homosexual couples than would have been contemplated in 1977, when the Rent Act was passed. The Rent Act may have been intended to create discrimination against homosexual couples, but it was passed at a time when homosexual acts had only been legal for a short period of time, and therefore the social and human rights implications of importing discrimination were not thoroughly investigated and debated in the way that they would have been had the statute been passed post-HRA. Parliament may have intended that discrimination should occur, but it did not and could not contemplate all the consequences of its decision at the time.

On the other hand, s 41 of the 1999 Act was deliberately intended by Parliament, after weighing the evidence, to improve the position of the victim of rape and to increase the number of rape convictions. The argument against the change in *Ghaidan* was unmeritorious: it was that private landlords should be able to discriminate on grounds of sexual orientation in housing provision although they are forbidden by law to do so on grounds of race or gender. That argument opposed fundamental values enshrined in the European Convention and strongly recognized in EU law, as Chapter 15 demonstrates.[177] Perhaps most crucially, it should be noted that had *R v A* been decided the other way, and the defendant had taken the case to Strasbourg arguing for a breach of Art 6, the success of the application could not have been assured, whereas it is argued that Ghaidan would have succeeded under Art 8 at Strasbourg.[178] That test – the chances of success of the 'losing' party at Strasbourg if the case were to go the other way – should, it is contended, be pivotal in determining whether a radical interpretation should be imposed on statutory provisions, since the intention of Parliament expressed in the HRA, and accepted in post-HRA judgments, was that citizens should be able to claim their rights in the domestic courts against public authorities where they would be able to claim them at Strasbourg. As the House of Lords has found, the HRA should not offer less than Strasbourg would offer.[179] Where the Strasbourg standard is in accord with that maintained in other comparable jurisdictions and under international human rights standards, this argument would be even stronger. It is argued then that *Ghaidan* can be seen as entirely in accordance with the spirit of the Convention, which Parliament wished to see fully received into UK law, while *R v A* was an exercise in illegitimate judicial legislation in the sense that it was very doubtfully in accordance with that spirit.

These two decisions, both on the borderline between legislating and interpreting, arguably illustrate the factors that, it is contended, should legitimately be taken into

---

subjected to prolonged cross-examination – over a period of days – by the rapist himself, who was deliberately wearing the clothes in which he had raped her. The experience, which was extremely humiliating and distressing, could no longer recur thanks to the provision of the Youth Justice and Criminal Evidence Act 1999, s 34, introduced as a result of that case.

177 See pp 1525–26.

178 See Chapter 15, pp 1519–21.

179 See *R (on the application of Ullah) v Special Adjudicator* [2004] UKHL 26; in the context of s 2 Lord Bingham said: 'The duty of domestic courts is to keep pace with the Strasbourg jurisprudence as it evolves over time: no more but certainly no less' at para 20.

account in determining whether to adopt a radical approach. It is argued that a hierarchy of factors should be identified, founded strongly on the differing constitutional roles and competences of the courts and Parliament, and that the two most significant are the demands of the Convention, taking the jurisprudence into account, and the difficulty of bringing about the change in question in the sense that it opposes a fundamental feature of the statute. In terms of weighing up what is to count as a 'fundamental feature', it is argued that a number of factors might be relevant. Where a provision in a Bill is the product of wide-ranging consultation with interested parties, and Parliament, after weighing up the issues fully, clearly intended the provision in question to have the effect that it has – as in *R v A*, as opposed to an instance in which the effect is merely incidental – as arguably was the case in *Ghaidan*, the courts should be more inclined to accept that interference goes against the grain of the statute. Where the converse is the case, interference is more readily justifiable.

The use of the range of factors identified clearly allows the senior judiciary a great deal of leeway to allow their own values to have an influence on legislation, under the cloak of deploying neutral factors and using interpretative techniques. Reliance mainly on s 3 tends to marginalise the democratic process: if s 3 is used, even if it emasculates a legislative provision, as in *R v A*, Parliament will not have been asked – under the s 4 procedure – to amend the provision. The whole process remains in the hands of the judiciary. In this sense, *R v A* has, it is contended, placed the whole carefully crafted scheme of the HRA in jeopardy. The tensions inherent in the scheme have been explored and heightened, since it appears that s 3 will almost always be used to outflank s 4 and s 10. The idea, which seemed to be inherent in s 4, that declarations of incompatibility would be made, even in criminal cases, seems to have been shown to be misconceived. Clearly, it is hard to see that they could be where Art 6 is concerned: if a conviction is obtained in breach of Art 6, it is unsafe;[180] therefore, if a conviction is obtained after a declaration of the incompatibility of a relevant legislative provision with Art 6, it is likely to be viewed as unsafe, unless it could be argued that the provision had had in its effects, ultimately, no or virtually no impact on the conviction.[181] The possibility of convictions obtained in breach of the Convention was inherent in the compromise effected under s 3. But in general it is argued that the judges should show a greater preparedness to use the s 4 route, bearing in mind that the government has been receptive to declarations of incompatibility, as discussed below.

In response to *R v A*, in which arguably the Art 8 rights of the victim were disregarded, it would have seemed on the face of it possible for Parliament merely to reinstate the offending provision, using words that left no leeway at all for the bold interpretation placed upon s 41(3)(c) of the Youth Justice and Criminal Evidence Act 1999,[182] although the findings in *Ghaidan* did not give much encouragement to that possibility. It should

---

180   *Condron v UK* (2001) 31 EHRR 1. See also *Forbes* [2001] 2 WLR 1, p 13, para 24.

181   Bearing in mind the fact that jurors do not give reasons for conviction and cannot be asked about them, it would be difficult in some instances to be sure that this was the case. But if, as in *R v A* itself, the allegedly incompatible provision concerned the admission of evidence, and ultimately the evidence was not admitted, it would be possible to say that the conviction was not unsafe.

182   In similar circumstances in Canada, noted below at p 260, the reinstated rape shield law (Criminal Code as amended, s 276) survived a human rights challenge in 2000: *R v Darrach* (2000) 191 DLR (4th) 539.

be noted that the House of Lords considered that the provision had provided a 'gateway' for the very creative interpretation adopted.[183] But it would not have been realistic to reinstate the provision using a notwithstanding clause to protect it, such as 'this provision is to be applied notwithstanding the provisions of Art 6(1)', since its use in practice would have appeared to render convictions obtained unsafe, while the government would have suffered the international embarrassment attendant on appearing to legislate deliberately in breach of the Convention.

Again, under the HRA there is nothing theoretically to prevent the over-turning of *Ghaidan* by a statute with one single, overriding purpose – to discriminate against homosexual couples in provision of housing.[184] Not only could a government commanding a majority in Parliament probably ensure that such legislation was passed (it certainly could as far as the HRA itself is concerned), but the judges would have to apply it so long as the provisions incompatible with Arts 8 and 14 were pervasive enough to be viewed as a fundamental feature of the statute. It is perhaps somewhat ironic that the more pervasive and clear the incompatibility, the less that can be done in response to it in remedial terms under s 3. But as a matter of constitutional practice a government would be very unlikely to be seek to reinstate provisions found authoritatively by the House of Lords to be in breach of the Convention. Seeking to do so would not only breach the UK's obligations at the international level (although possibly not in the *R v A* instance), it would also undermine the judges' constitutional role as the guardian of human rights. Further, although this is a less significant point, the HRA as currently conceived is quite a blunt instrument to be used for the purpose of passing legislative provisions already found at the domestic level to have breached the Convention (although of course on a face value reading it appeared to be intended that it could be used for that purpose). It itself contains no safeguards against passing such legislation – such as a demand that if such legislation is passed it must be in response to a particular pressing social need (a requirement that would not be as demanding as the requirements of Art 15,[185] but which would at least place an express burden on government to justify the introduction of apparently incompatible legislation into Parliament). These points illustrate not only the constitutional realities of the HRA, but also the obvious difference between the position in Canada and that in the UK – Canada is dealing with its own Charter, while the UK is adhering domestically to an international human rights instrument which also binds it at the international level.

The conclusion must be, then, that s 3 provides the judges with more power – in terms of adopting what is in essence a legislative role – than the notwithstanding clause used in Canada does. Clearly, the other side of the coin is that they can read down the Convention right in question – as in *Brown* – in order to avoid using s 3 or s 4. It is arguable that a factor determining their choice of approach may be their view of the desirableness of the outcome, in social policy rather than legal terms.[186] The strength of the obligation under s 3 is not, it is suggested, without its dangers. The strong

---

183 *R v A, per* Lord Steyn, para 42.

184 Clearly, this is in practice highly improbable at present, given that the government intends to introduce Regulations in response to EU law making such discrimination unlawful; see Chapter 15, p 1526.

185 See Chapter 2, pp 110–11.

186 They may favour a legislative regime that aids in the maintenance of road safety, whereas their 'common sense' may inform them that a woman who has allegedly had sex with a man on one occasion may

interpretative obligation on the judiciary can be viewed as a double-edged sword. They are enjoined to strive to find a Convention-friendly interpretation, but in certain instances the Convention standards are diluted as courts adopt the least liberal interpretation of the Convention right in order to make it harmonise with UK legislation (as in *Brown*). An interpretative approach which leads to the dilution of Convention standards can be avoided only if a vigorous, activist approach is taken, not only to foisting Convention-based interpretations onto statutory language, but also to ensuring that Convention standards are fully upheld by means of that interpretation. But as discussed in relation to *R v A*, there is a strong argument for using the declaration of incompatibility procedure where a clash of rights concerning an arguably incommensurable moral issue is in question, one that has been consciously and systematically addressed by Parliament after full and wide-ranging consultation with the groups representing those directly affected by the provision in question.[187]

The effect of s 2

Introduction

In seeking to interpret statutory provisions compatibly with the Convention rights under the HRA, the domestic judiciary 'must take into account' any relevant Strasbourg jurisprudence,[188] under s 2. Thus, they are not bound by it. Section 2 creates on its face quite a weak obligation, since it is open to the judiciary to consider but disapply a particular decision. It may be noted that only the Convention rights themselves are binding on public authorities, under s 6. As Chapter 2 indicated, the rights appear, in certain respects, quite out of date today. But since 1950, they have been subject to a rich and extensive jurisprudence which has extended and clarified their ambit. On the other hand, adoption of the Strasbourg jurisprudence may sometimes have the effect of 'reading down' the right due to the effect of the margin of appreciation doctrine.[189] In such instances it may be that departure from such decisions would give a 'successful lead to Strasbourg'.[190] The Lord Chancellor explained the role of s 2 at the Committee stage in Parliament: '[s 2] would permit UK courts to depart from Strasbourg decisions where there has been no precise ruling on the matter and a Commission opinion which does so has not taken into account subsequent Strasbourg case law . . .'.[191] At the Report stage, the Lord Chancellor further explained: 'Courts will often be faced with

---

be likely to consent to have sex with him on another. This implications of this latter issue are pursued below, pp 260–61.

187 This very difficult issue is discussed further below in relation to judicial activism; see pp 266–67.

188 The term exhaustively covers any 'judgment, decision, declaration or advisory opinion of the Court', any 'opinion of the Commission given in a report adopted under Article 31', any 'decision of the Commission in connection with Article 26 or 27(2)' or any 'decision of the Committee of Ministers taken under Article 46'. The words 'in connection with' appear to mean that all findings which may be said to be linked to the admissibility procedure, including reports prepared during the preliminary examination of a case, could be taken into account.

189 See *Salabiaku v France* (A 141-A) (1988) and see further pp 270–73, below. See also the discussion of the margin of appreciation doctrine in Chapter 2, pp 36–39.

190 583 HL 514, 515, 8 November 1997.

191 583 HL 514, 515, 8 November 1997.

cases that involve factors perhaps specific to the UK which distinguish them from cases considered by the European Court . . . it is important that our courts have scope to apply that discretion so as to aid in the development of human rights law . . .'.[192]

In the course of such development, it was always clear that the courts could also consider jurisprudence from other jurisdictions; s 2 clearly leaves open the possibility of so doing. It is important for the judiciary to consider other international human rights treaties to which the UK is a signatory, as well as human rights jurisprudence from other jurisdictions, since it is often found that the same issues have arisen elsewhere. The Canadian and New Zealand jurisprudence is of relevance, since their Bills of Rights are of relatively recent origin and show strong similarities with the HRA. Post-HRA the House of Lords has shown itself willing to consider jurisprudence from other jurisdictions.[193] While such jurisprudence cannot merely be transplanted wholesale into the UK situation,[194] it can aid both in using the under-theorised Strasbourg jurisprudence, with its dependence on the margin of appreciation doctrine, and in encouraging the domestic judiciary to adopt a more theorised approach to human rights.[195]

Legal status of the jurisprudence and the role of the judges under the HRA?

Although the Strasbourg jurisprudence is not technically binding, it has been treated in a fashion that comes close to giving it binding force.[196] Clearly, it is a well-established international law principle that when treaty obligations are incorporated into domestic law, the obligation will be construed by reference to the principles of international law governing its interpretation.[197] On the other hand, it is a recognised constitutional principle that constitutional instruments, unlike statutes, should be applied in a flexible manner.[198] The Lords' acceptance that they should rely heavily on Strasbourg decisions was made apparent in the early post-HRA decision of *R (on the application of Alconbury) v Secretary of State for the Environment*.[199] The Divisional Court made a declaration of incompatibility in relation to planning law provisions, finding them incompatible with Art 6 since the Secretary of State for the Environment, in determining a planning appeal, is acting in a dual capacity in both hearing the appeal and applying his or her own policy guidelines. Under Art 6, as Chapter 2 explained,[200] a person's civil rights and obligations must be determined by an independent and impartial tribunal. The Minister, the Divisional Court found, could not be viewed as independent and impartial owing to his dual role.

---

192 484 HL 1270, 1271, 9 January 1998.
193 See *R v A* [2001] 2 WLR 1546. See, e.g., below, pp 288–91.
194 See for discussion Watson, A, *Legal Transplants in Comparative Law*, 1993.
195 See the criticisms of their traditional approach advanced in Fenwick, H and Phillipson, G, 'Public protest, the HRA and judicial responses to political expression' [2000] PL 627–50.
196 See further Masterman, R, 'Aspiration or Foundation? The Status of the Strasbourg Jurisprudence and 'the Convention Rights' in Domestic Law' in Fenwick, H, Masterman, R and Phillipson, G (eds), *Judicial Reasoning under the UK Human Rights Act*, 2007
197 See, for example, *In re H* [1998] AC 72 at para 87, *per* Lord Browne-Wilkinson.
198 See, e.g., *Minister of Home Affairs v Fisher* [1980] AC 319.
199 [2001] 2 All ER 929; (2001) *The Times*, 24 January.
200 See pp 59–61.

On appeal to the House of Lords the declaration was overturned;[201] reliance on the Strasbourg jurisprudence was crucial to this decision. The House of Lords found that the requirements of Art 6 can be satisfied by the possibility of judicial review. If the Minister does not act impartially, his or her decision can be judicially reviewed. Therefore, it was found, a remedy was available. The House considered the question whether judicial review could be viewed as providing a sufficient remedy, bearing in mind the findings that it could not in *Lustig-Prean v UK*[202] and *Kingsley v UK*.[203] It came to the view, after extensively reviewing the Strasbourg jurisprudence in planning cases, that judicial review could now be viewed as providing a sufficient remedy, owing to the need to consider proportionality under the HRA. But it also considered that even without considering proportionality, judicial review could provide a sufficient remedy in the context in question, bearing in mind findings of that jurisprudence which suggested that a light touch review would be appropriate, taking into account the complex and wide ranging policy issues involved in what was essentially a socio-economic matter. Lord Slynn found that the domestic courts should follow any 'clear and constant' Strasbourg jurisprudence, except in special circumstances.[204] As indicated throughout this book this is, in general, the course that the courts are following.[205] Thus, the obligation under s 2 as interpreted by the House of Lords comes close to affording binding force to the jurisprudence.

This stance appears to indicate that the domestic courts cannot provide greater Convention protection for citizens than is available at Strasbourg – that they are inhibited in developing a more expansive domestic Convention jurisprudence. On this point in *R (on the application of Ullah) v Special Adjudicator*,[206] in the context of s 2, Lord Bingham said: 'In determining the present question, the House is required by section 2(1) of the Human Rights Act 1998 to take into account any relevant Strasbourg case law. While such case law is not strictly binding, it has been held that courts should, in the absence of some special circumstances, follow any clear and constant jurisprudence of the Strasbourg court.[207] This reflects the fact that the Convention is an international instrument, the correct interpretation of which can be authoritatively expounded only by the Strasbourg court. From this it follows that a national court subject to a duty such as that imposed by section 2 should not without strong reason dilute or weaken the effect of the Strasbourg case law. It is indeed unlawful under section 6 of the 1998 Act for a public authority, including a court, to act in a way which is incompatible with a Convention right. It is of course open to member states to provide for rights more generous than those guaranteed by the Convention, but such provision should not be

---

201 *R (on the application of Alconbury Ltd) v Secretary of State for the Environment, Transport and the Regions and* other cases [2001] 2 All ER 929; (2001) NLJ 135.
202 (1999) 29 EHRR 548.
203 (2001) *The Times*, 9 January.
204 At para 26.
205 See, e.g., Chapter 9, p 914. See further: Masterman, R, 'Taking the Strasbourg Jurisprudence into Account: developing a 'municipal law of human rights' under the Human Rights Act 1998' (2005) 54 *International and Comparative Law Quarterly* 907–32; Masterman, R, 'Section 2(1) of the Human Rights Act 1998: Binding Domestic Courts to Strasbourg?' [2004] *Public Law* 725–37
206 [2004] UKHL 26.
207 He relied on *R (Alconbury Developments Ltd) v Secretary of State for the Environment, Transport and the Regions* [2001] UKHL 23, [2003] 2 AC 295, at para 26.

the product of interpretation of the Convention by national courts, since the meaning of the Convention should be uniform throughout the states party to it. The duty of national courts is to keep pace with the Strasbourg jurisprudence as it evolves over time: no more, but certainly no less. The duty of domestic courts is to keep pace with the Strasbourg jurisprudence as it evolves over time: no more but certainly no less.'[208]

Similar findings were made in a decision on the retention of fingerprints and samples under the Police and Criminal Evidence Act 1984 by the House of Lords in *Marper*.[209] Lord Steyn followed *Ullah* in rejecting the idea, which had been put forward by Lord Woolf in the Court of Appeal, that domestic cultural traditions should determine the ambit of the Convention rights.[210] However, he considered that such traditions would be relevant in determining whether the infringement of the right was justified:

> While I would not wish to subscribe to all the generalisations in the Court of Appeal about cultural traditions in the United Kingdom, in comparison with other European states, I do accept that when one moves on to consider the question of objective justification under article 8(2) the cultural traditions in the United Kingdom are material. With great respect to Lord Woolf CJ the same is not true under article 8(1) . . . The question whether the retention of fingerprints and samples engages article 8(1) should receive a uniform interpretation throughout member states, unaffected by different cultural traditions. And the current Strasbourg view, as reflected in decisions of the Commission, ought to be taken into account.

Similarly, in *N v Secretary of State for the Home Department*,[211] which concerned the deportation of an AIDS sufferer to a country that would not have the medical facilities of the UK, the House of Lords, having criticised the reasoning of the Strasbourg court,[212] accepted that the case law had to be applied. The Strasbourg Court had found that such deportation could create a breach of Art 3 in *D v United Kingdom*.[213] The Lords considered that it would be inequitable to single out the appellant for treatment on humanitarian grounds since many immigrants suffering from AIDS would have

---

208 At para 20.
209 *R (on the application of Marper) v Chief Constable of South Yorkshire* [2004] 1 WLR 2196 e.g. at para 78, *per* Baroness Hale.
210 At para 27. Lord Woolf CJ in the Court of Appeal expressed this view at [2002] 1 WLR 3223, para 34.
211 [2005] 2 WLR 1124.
212 Lord Steyn said [at paras 11–13]: 'the Strasbourg jurisprudence, it has to be said, is not in an altogether satisfactory state. The difficulty derives from the decision in *D v United Kingdom* (1997) 24 EHRR 425, concerning the expulsion of an AIDS sufferer to St Kitts, and the basis on which the Strasbourg court has subsequently sought to distinguish that case. In the case of *D* the court extended the reach of article 3. The court noted, at paragraph 46, that contracting states have the right, as a matter of well-established international law and subject to their treaty obligations including the European Convention, to control the entry, residence and expulsion of aliens. Having noted the *Chahal* type of case, the court said it must reserve to itself sufficient flexibility to consider the application of article 3 in other contexts: paragraph 49. The court then applied Art 3 in what it described as the "very exceptional circumstances"'of that case. The difficulty posed by this decision is that, with variations in degree, the humanitarian considerations existing in the case of *D* are not 'very exceptional' in the case of AIDS sufferers.
213 (1997) 24 EHRR 425.

their lives shortened if returned to their home countries due to the higher level of medical expertise and resource available in the UK. However, the Lords found that a careful and fact-sensitive consideration of the Strasbourg cases meant that an over-broad interpretation of Art 3 could be avoided, allowing for the deportation of the appellant, even though deporting her was viewed as the equivalent of switching off her life support machine. Lord Steyn said 'on this subject the Strasbourg jurisprudence lacks its customary clarity'.[214] Lord Hope in *N* considered that:[215]

> It is not for us to search for a solution to [the appellant's] problem which is not to be found in the Strasbourg case law. It is for the Strasbourg court, not for us, to decide whether its case law is out of touch with modern conditions and to determine what extensions, if any, are needed to the rights guaranteed by the Convention. We must take its case law as we find it, not as we would like it to be.

The view that the purpose of the HRA is not to enlarge the rights or remedies offered at Strasbourg, but only to ensure that those rights and remedies can be enforced by the domestic courts, also finds a basis in *Aston Cantlow and Wilmcote with Billesley Parochial Church Council v Wallbank*;[216] *R (Greenfield) v Secretary of State for the Home Department*;[217] and *R (Quark Fishing Ltd) v Secretary of State for Foreign and Commonwealth Affairs*.[218] That view was also reiterated and afforded further explanation in *R(SB) v Denbigh High School*.[219] In *Kay v Lambeth London Borough Council; Leeds City Council v Price*,[220] discussed below, Lord Bingham, with whom the other Law Lords agreed on this issue, said that domestic courts are not strictly required to follow rulings of the Strasbourg court, but that they must give practical recognition to the principles it expounds. On the other hand, Lord Nicholls said in *Campbell*, a case that did not involve re-writing statutory provisions:

> The values embodied in articles 8 and 10 are as much applicable in disputes between individuals or between an individual and a non-governmental body such as a newspaper as they are in disputes between individuals and a public authority. In reaching this conclusion *it is not necessary to pursue the controversial question whether the European Convention itself has this wider effect* (emphasis added).[221]

(Obviously in relation to a statute this approach has limits as indicated above, dictated by the doctrine of parliamentary sovereignty.) Lord Nicholls' finding could be interpreted as meaning that if the jurisprudence is not on its face 'clear and constant'

---

214 At para 14.
215 [2005] 2 WLR 1124, para 25.
216 [2004] 1 AC 546, paras 6–7, 44.
217 [2005] 1 WLR 673, paras 18–19.
218 [2005] 3 WLR 837, paras 25, 33, 34, 88 and 92.
219 [2006] 2 WLR 719, para 29.
220 [2006] UKHL 10.
221 [2004] 2 WLR 1232 at paras 17 and 18. (But see now the post-*Campbell* decision in *Von Hannover v Germany* (2006) 43 EHRR 7 (App no. 59320/00), discussed in Chapter 9, pp 819–23).

it can be disregarded completely and the case decided on the basis of what could arguably be called a constitutional human rights jurisdiction.[222] This approach is, it is contended, appropriate, bearing in mind the stance of Strasbourg that states have the primary responsibility for affording protection for the Convention rights,[223] and the whole constitutional enterprise of the HRA which demands a generous interpretation of the rights.

As Masterman argues, the minimalist approach taken in *Ullah* towards the jurisprudence, which does not allow domestic courts to expand the ambit of a Convention right where clear and constant Strasbourg jurisprudence stands in the way, creates a tension with the status of the HRA as a constitutional instrument.[224] Clayton similarly finds that there is a tension between 'established perceptions of the judicial role' and the constitutional status of the HRA.[225] The over-generous and over-expansive approach of Lord Steyn to Art 6 in *R v A* was criticised above, but that was on the basis that there were strong countervailing Convention-based and constitutional objections to the course taken on the particular facts at issue. That approach, absent those objections, is in keeping with the redefined role of the judges now mapped out for them under the HRA, but it is clearly in tension with the approach in *Ullah* since it did much more than keep pace with the Strasbourg jurisprudence.

If the judges are to realise the role that the HRA appears to give them, and which was contemplated in Parliament during the passage of the Human Rights Bill, there are a number of avenues that can be explored in the interests of maximizing judicial discretion under s 2. If the jurisprudence in question is *not* clear and constant it can be disregarded, as Lord Nicholls indicated in *Campbell*. In fact, as Chapter 9 argues, the relevant Art 8 jurisprudence came very close to determining the question at issue before the House of Lords.[226] Therefore, impliedly, Lord Nicholls could be viewed as demanding quite a high degree of constancy and clarity in the jurisprudence before he was prepared to apply it. His disregard for the relevant jurisprudence could be viewed as indicating that even if it is *approaching* the requisite level of clarity it need not be applied. Further, if the jurisprudence itself *conflicts* with Strasbourg principles it need not be applied; Lord Bingham made it clear in *Price* that the principles, not necessarily the jurisprudence, are to be given effect domestically. As Chapter 8 argues, this is particularly the case in relation to certain Strasbourg decisions in the context of public protest which conflict with underlying Convention principles.[227] If the jurisprudence is heavily affected by the influence of the margin of appreciation doctrine it can be marginalized on the basis that that doctrine is not applicable in domestic law, and to rely on Strasbourg cases influenced by it is to import the doctrine impermissibly into domestic law by the back door.[228]

---

222   See the comments of Lord Justice Laws in *Pro-Life Alliance* [2002] 3 WLR 1080 at 6 para 36.
223   See Chapter 2, pp 17–20.
224   See further Masterman, R, 'Aspiration or Foundation? The Status of the Strasbourg Jurisprudence and 'the Convention Rights' in Domestic Law' in Fenwick, H, Masterman, R and Phillipson, G, (eds), *Judicial Reasoning under the UK Human Rights Act*, (2007).
225   See Clayton, R, 'Judicial Deference and Democratic Dialogue' : the legitimacy of judicial intervention under the HRA' [2004] PL 33,34.
226   See pp 911–13.
227   See pp 686–88.
228   See below pp 270–72.

Conflict with domestic precedents

If clear and constant jurisprudence is apparent it must be followed, although not strictly binding, except where a domestic precedent stands in the way. This was made clear by the House of Lords in *Kay v London Borough of Lambeth; Leeds City Council v Price.*[229] The case concerned rights to possession of property in domestic law which appeared to violate Art 8. The Court of Appeal in the *Leeds* case had concluded that the decision in *Connors v United Kingdom,*[230] which was relied upon by the applicants in resisting possession proceedings, was inconsistent with the earlier House of Lords decision in *Harrow London Borough Council v Qazi,*[231] and that they were bound to apply the House of Lords decision.[232] The later Strasbourg case suggested that the earlier House of Lords' decision had not correctly reflected the Convention position. As indicated above, Lord Bingham, with whom the other Law Lords agreed on this issue, said that domestic courts must give effect to the principles expounded by the Strasbourg court. He pointed out that that court is the highest judicial authority to interpret Convention rights as they are to be understood uniformly by all member states, and domestic courts have to determine initially how the principles it lays down are to be applied in the domestic context. Adherence to precedent, he said, is a cornerstone of the domestic legal system whereby some degree of certainty in legal matters is most effectively achieved. He found that therefore where judges consider that a binding domestic precedent is inconsistent with a Strasbourg decision, they should follow the ordinary rules of precedent, except in an extreme case where the pre-HRA decision of a superior court could not survive the introduction of the HRA 1998.

Lord Hope agreed on the precedent issue. He found that *Connors* was not incompatible with *Qazi,* but that *Qazi* should not in any event be departed from; however, in the light of subsequent Strasbourg cases he found that greater emphasis should be placed on the need for the court to provide a remedy in those special cases not considered in *Qazi* where it was seriously arguable that the right to possession afforded by domestic law violated the Convention right.

The rule from *Price* means that citizens might have to seek the vindication of their Art 8 rights at Strasbourg. This position is in tension, not only with the UK's obligations at Strasbourg under Arts 1, 8 and 13 of the Convention, but with the constitutional status of the Convention in domestic law and with Lord Bingham's finding in *Ullah* that the duty of domestic courts is to keep pace with the Strasbourg jurisprudence as it evolves over time. Therefore, it is argued, the courts should explore methods of marginalising the rule from *Price* in any affected areas of law while technically adhering to domestic precedent. For example, where a statute has been interpreted domestically in a superior court in a post-HRA decision in a manner that conflicts with Strasbourg jurisprudence, the court should strive to find an interpretation of the domestic precedent that avoids the conflict, but if this is impossible it should issue a declaration of the incompatibility, leaving Parliament to over-turn the precedent. That course would be preferable to minimising the interpretation of the right in order to avoid the conflict.

---

229 [2006] UKHL 10.
230 [2006] 40 EHRR 189.
231 [2004] 1 AC 983.
232 See *Price v Leeds CC* [2005] 1 WLR 1825.

Section 2 and the common law

The HRA does not expressly mention the interpretation of the common law. But it is clear that s 2 makes the rights relevant to its interpretation since its application is not confined to statutory interpretation, but to the determination of any question, in a court or tribunal, that has arisen in connection with a Convention right. Further, since the courts themselves are public authorities under s 6, they are expected to ensure, through their interpretation of the common law, that the Convention rights are not breached. As discussed below, the precise duty placed on the courts in this respect is a matter of debate. But it is clear that, where a legislative provision is not in question, but one party in the case before a court is a public authority, or in any event in reliance on the court's own s 6 duty, the court should apply s 2. Section 2 contains no words which limit its application to an instance in which one party before the court is a public authority. The limitation would arise if it was argued in such an instance that a private body does not possess Convention rights as against another private person and therefore that no question has arisen in connection with a Convention right, but that argument was rejected, impliedly, by the courts in early decisions under the HRA.[233]

It is now clear, as Chapter 9 in particular points out,[234] that the Convention rights are as much at issue in private common law disputes as in public law ones, assuming that a cause of action is applicable. In such an instance ss 2 and 6 in combination might be viewed at first glance as placing an interpretative obligation on courts which is, in one sense, stronger than that created by s 3, since no provision allowing incompatible common law doctrines to override Convention rights appears in the Act. However, this is not the case, for two reasons. As discussed further below, the precise duty placed on the court by s 6 in relation to the development of the common law in private common law adjudication has not yet been fully resolved, and it certainly cannot yet be said that s 6 places a s 3-like interpretative obligation on courts in common law adjudication.[235] Moreover, the decision in *Price* is of particular relevance in common law adjudication since, obviously, such adjudication is reliant on the doctrine of precedent unaffected by statutory intervention. Following *Price*, the odd position has been reached whereby a decision of a superior court inconsistent with Convention principle must be followed, whereas a statutory provision apparently inconsistent with a Convention right can be rendered compatible with it, if possible, even if that means reading words into the statute, under s 3. Therefore, while s 2 is of relevance in common law adjudication as discussed in this section, the Strasbourg jurisprudence may perhaps have a more limited effect in this context in practice. In the key context of privacy, however, in which ss 6 and 2 have had a very significant impact in transforming the common law doctrine of confidence, the problem of incompatibility between common law precedent and Convention principle has not arisen since the key precedents were pre-HRA ones.[236]

---

233   It is clear under s 3 that legislation should be construed compatibly with the Convention rights regardless of the fact that both parties are private bodies. In *Wilson v First County Trust* [2001] 3 All ER 229, the Court of Appeal accepted that s 3 does indeed apply in such instances.

234   See pp 825–28, 911–15.

235   See pp 252–55.

236   It may be noted that the key decision of *Campbell* was taken before *Price*. See further Chapter 9, pp 911–15.

Conclusions

The pursuit of the s 2 endeavour is witnessing the attempt to interweave into a mass of existing statutory and common law provisions, the uneven and often flawed jurisprudence of the European Court of Human Rights. In so doing the judges are adopting a more theorised approach to fundamental rights.[237] It is often pointed out that the inception of Bills of Rights tends to have the effect, as in Canada, of requiring courts to grapple with justification for limitation of fundamental rights, taking a more philosophical approach to legal reasoning as they attempt to resolve conflicts between rights and competing societal and individual interests. However, the limitations placed on the judicial role under the HRA by both *Price* and *Ullah*, create a clear tension, as discussed, with the HRA's constitutional status and with the development of a domestic doctrine of constitutional rights.

Meaning of primary and secondary legislation

Which measures then can override the Convention even if incompatible with it under s3(2)? Section 21(1) defines 'primary legislation' as used in s 3(2) to include Measures of the General Synod of the Church of England and, most significantly, Orders in Council made under the royal prerogative. Thus, executive power as well as parliamentary sovereignty are preserved under the HRA.[238] This is clearly an anomalous provision, since it renders individual rights subordinate to powers which may be used to infringe them and which cannot claim legitimacy derived from the democratic process.

Subordinate legislation covers Orders in Council not made under the royal prerogative, orders, rules, regulations, bylaws or other instruments made under primary legislation unless 'it operates to bring one or more provisions of that legislation into force or amends any primary legislation'. The last provision is significant, since it means that where provision is made under primary legislation for amendment by executive order, subject to the negative, or even the affirmative resolution procedure, the amendment, which will almost certainly have received virtually no Parliamentary attention, will still be able to override Convention provisions. This is of particular importance in relation to, for example, the Terrorism Act 2000 and the Regulation of Investigatory Powers Act 2000, since a number of gaps were left in the provisions, to be filled in this manner.[239]

The 'declaration of incompatibility' under s 4

Section 4(2) applies under s 4(1) when a court is determining in any proceedings whether a provision of primary legislation is incompatible with a Convention right. If a court is satisfied that the provision is incompatible with the right, 'it may make a declaration of that incompatibility' – a declaration that it is not possible to construe the legislation in question to harmonise with the Convention. Section 4(4) applies to

---

237 See, e.g., Chapter 9, pp 911–15 and below, pp 289–91.
238 For discussion of the effect of treating this exercise of prerogative powers as primary legislation, see Squires, N, 'Judicial review of the prerogative after the HRA' [2000] 116 LQR 572–75.
239 See, e.g., Chapter 10, p 1064 and Chapter 14, p 1398.

incompatible secondary legislation where incompatible primary legislation prevents the removal of the incompatibility. Again, the incompatibility can be declared. Thus, s 4 may seem to come close to allowing an infringement of parliamentary sovereignty since, as Feldman observes, 'For the first time Parliament has invited the judges to tell it that it has acted wrongly by legislating incompatibly with a Convention right'.[240] But, as Feldman also notes, the court is not informing Parliament that it has acted unlawfully, since, as explained below, Parliament is not bound by the Convention (s 6(3)). Nevertheless, the House of Lords has made it clear, in *R v A*, as indicated above, that it views the making of a declaration as a last resort to be avoided if at all possible, and this was reaffirmed in *Ghaidan*.[241]

But only certain courts can make the declaration. Section 4(5) provides that this applies to the House of Lords, the Judicial Committee of the Privy Council, the Courts-Martial Appeal Court; in Scotland, the High Court of Justiciary sitting otherwise than a trial court, or the Court of Session; in England and Wales, the High Court or the Court of Appeal. Under s 5(1), when a court is considering making a declaration, the Crown must be given notice so that it can, under s 5(2), intervene by being joined as a party to the proceedings.

A court falling within s 4(5) has a *discretion* to make a declaration of incompatibility. Section 4(2) clearly leaves open the possibility that such a court, having found an incompatibility, might nevertheless decide not to make a declaration of it. As indicated above, in *Wilson v First County Trust Ltd*,[242] the Court of Appeal found that s 127(3) of the Consumer Credit Act 1974 was incompatible with Art 6 and with Art 1 of the First Protocol to the Convention. The Court considered that, having found an incompatibility, it should make a declaration of it for three reasons.[243] First, the question of the incompatibility had been fully argued at a hearing appointed for that purpose. Second, the order required by s 127(3) could not lawfully be made on the appeal unless the court was satisfied that the section could not be read in such a way as to give effect to the Convention rights, and that fact should be formally recorded by a declaration that 'gives legitimacy to that order'. Third, a declaration provides a basis for a Minister to consider whether the section should be amended under s 10(1) (see below). The Court duly went on to make the declaration. The second reason given is of particular interest, since it suggests that a court would not feel that it could make an order required by an incompatible legislative provision without making a declaration, since the order would lack legitimacy. It may be noted that lower courts, which cannot make a declaration, are being asked under the HRA to do precisely that. This finding indicates the reluctance such courts are likely to feel in this situation. It further suggests, as do the other reasons, that courts within s 4(5) are unlikely to find incompatibility without declaring it. In other words, the discretion under s 4(2) appears to be narrow. It is hard to imagine circumstances in which a higher court would find an incompatibility without declaring it.

240 Feldman, D, 'The Human Rights Act 1998 and constitutional principles' (1999) 19(2) LS 165, p 187.
241 See *Ghaidan* [2004] 2 AC 557 (HL) at para 50.
242 [2001] 3 All ER 229.
243 Ibid, para 47.

A further early declaration was made by the Court of Appeal in relation to the system of appeals for prisoners detained on mental health grounds in *R (H) v Mental Health Tribunal, North and East London Region and Another*.[244] The Court found that s 73 of the Mental Health Act was incompatible with Art 5 since it in effect reversed the burden of proof against the detained person. The declaration was surprising in the sense that s 3 could have been used more strenuously to find that the system of appeals in such mental health cases could be viewed as compliant with the Convention.[245]

In the early months of the HRA, the lower courts took an approach to s 3 which differed considerably from that taken in *R v A*, in the sense that there was a preparedness to make declarations of incompatibility, rather than using s 3 in order to impose compatibility on the legislation. A declaration of incompatibility was made by the Divisional Court in respect of four planning cases, in *Alconbury*, but the declaration was then reversed by the House of Lords,[246] on the basis that a close reading of the Convention jurisprudence revealed that no incompatibility arose.[247]

When a declaration of incompatibility has been made, the legislative provision in question remains valid (s 4(6)). Section 3 provides that the interpretative obligation does not affect the validity, continuing operation or enforcement of any incompatible primary legislation, and this is equally the case under s 4(6) if a declaration of incompatibility is made. The Convention guarantee in question is disapplied by the court in relation to that incompatible provision. Once a declaration has been made, there will be a period of time during which the Convention right can still be utilised in respect of other relevant non-incompatible provisions until and if compatibility is achieved by amendment via the s 10 procedure considered below. The Convention provision does not appear to suffer a diminution of status except, to an extent, in relation to the incompatible legislative provision itself. In other words, it is not impliedly repealed in domestic law.

During the period after the declaration, while amendment of the legislative provision is awaited as a possibility, other courts might have to consider the same issue. Owing to the doctrine of precedent, the lower courts are bound by the declaration. The HRA leaves open the possibility – in a higher court than the one which made the declaration – of eventually finding compatibility in respect of the incompatible legislative provision itself once it is revisited in a subsequent suitable case (assuming that the original declaration has not already been overturned on appeal). In other words, a different court can take a different view on incompatibility. Possibly, in so doing, it might be aided by jurisprudential developments occurring at Strasbourg, after the initial finding of incompatibility. But following the decision of the House of Lords in *Price*,[248] a court in a similar case, raising a similar issue of compatibility, would be bound by a declaration already made in a superior court, despite such development.

---

244 (2001) *The Times*, 2 April.
245 This is not a comment on the merits of the judgment; it is unfortunate that the system of appeals in such mental health cases was not rendered compliant with the Convention prior to the coming into force of the HRA.
246 *R (on the application of Alconbury Ltd) v Secretary of State for the Environment, Transport and the Regions and other cases* [2001] 2 All ER 929; (2001) NLJ 135.
247 This point is considered further below; see p 276.
248 See above p 197.

If legislation is found to be incompatible with a Convention guarantee in a court that cannot make a declaration of incompatibility or in one that can, but exercises its discretion not to do so, the position is broadly the same: the legislative provision remains valid and the Convention guarantee in question is disapplied in relation to the incompatible provision. There is less likelihood that it will be amended until and if a declaration of incompatibility is made, although obviously it could, theoretically, be amended without waiting for a declaration.[249] Clearly, the case might not be appealed up to a court which could make the declaration. Thus, there will probably be a longer period of time during which a Convention guarantee cannot be utilised in relation to that legislative provision, than there would be once a declaration had been made. In order to avoid this period of uncertainty, the courts are using fast track procedures to resolve the issue, as in *R v A*[250] and *Alconbury*.

Since, under s 4(5), only higher courts can make a declaration of incompatibility, the pressure on courts to find compatibility is increased since otherwise a citizen has to suffer a breach of their Convention rights without a remedy.[251] The pressure is particularly strong in criminal proceedings. However, where essential, as discussed earlier, it is preferable that a declaration of incompatibility should be made rather than 'reading down' the Convention right in question in order to find compatibility.

The declaration is likely to trigger off amending legislation by means of the s 10 so-called 'fast track' procedure. However, it need not do so – very significantly, the declaration is non-binding. Declarations of incompatibility are playing a part in ensuring that domestic law is being brought into a state of conformity with the human rights norms embodied in the jurisprudence of the European Court of Human Rights.[252] However s 4 is having less impact in this respect, as discussed above, than s 3. The government's stance appears to be that it will seek to bring forward amending legislation once a declaration has been made; it has not sought to argue that a declaration should be ignored. Since October 2000 there have been 15 declarations of incompatibility which have not been reversed on appeal. All the declarations so far made under the HRA have either been remedied or are currently under consideration with a view to being remedied.[253] The most well-known and far-reaching declaration was made by the House of Lords in *A v Secretary of State for the Home Department*;[254] it is discussed in full in Chapter 14.[255] The declaration was accepted by the government and the

---

249 Since such amendment would occur outside the s 10 procedure, the normal time constraints would apply.

250 [2001] 2 WLR 1546.

251 This was very clearly a pressing concern in *R v A* [2001] 2 WLR 1546; the ruling was awaited, not only in that case, but in a number of pending rape cases.

252 Apart from the declarations mentioned a number of other examples may be given: in *R (H) v London North and East Region Mental Health Review Tribunal (Secretary of State for Health intervening)* [2002] QB 1 the Mental Health Act 1983 s 73 was found to be incompatible with Arts 5(1) and 5(4); in *R (D) v Secretary of State for the Home Department* [2003] 1 WLR 1315 the Mental Health Act 1983 s 74 was found to be incompatible with Art 5(4); *R (Uttley) v Secretary of State for the Home Department* [2003] 1 WLR 2590 the Criminal Justice Act 1991 ss 33(2), 37(4)(a) and s 39 were found to be incompatible with Art 7.

253 See for examples fn 267 below.

254 [2004] QB 335.

255 See pp 1430 *et seq*.

offending provisions in the Anti-Terrorism, Crime and Security Act 2001 were repealed. A recent significant declaration was made by the Court of Appeal in *Westminster City Council v Morris*.[256] The Court of Appeal held that the Housing Act 1996 s 185(4) was incompatible with Art 14. Section 185(4) permitted a difference in treatment based on national origin or on a combination of nationality, immigration control, settled residence and social welfare which, the Court found, could not be justified.

Use of s 4 may eventually mean that a certain amount of non-Convention-compliant legislation is amended. A future, less liberal, government, wishing to restore the provisions thus removed, although not formally constrained in any way (assuming that it could command a majority in Parliament), would do so in the face of public knowledge that it was resurrecting provisions which the courts had authoritatively determined to be in breach of Britain's obligations under the ECHR.[257] In this sense, both the 'adverse publicity' and the 'manifest breach' types of protection for the Convention discussed below[258] bestowed by a 'notwithstanding clause' have been given – albeit to a lesser degree[259] – to the rights protected by the Convention.

A declaration is clearly an empty remedy as far as the majority of litigants are concerned. Clearly, it cannot be viewed as an effective remedy in Convention terms;[260] this was reaffirmed in the Chamber judgment in *Burden v United Kingdom*.[261] It was found that the applicants had not needed to exhaust that remedy. The Court stated that it did not consider that the applicants could have been expected to have brought a claim for a declaration of incompatibility under s 4 of the 1998 Human Rights Act before bringing their application to the European Court of Human Rights, since it was a remedy that was dependent on the discretion of the executive and so ineffective on that ground. The Court expressed the view, however, that it was possible that at some future date, evidence of a long-standing and established practice of Ministers giving effect to the courts' declarations of incompatibility might be sufficient to persuade it of the effectiveness of the procedure. Since the government has so far accepted that declarations should be responded to and has not resisted a declaration it is possible that the Court may find eventually that a declaration amounts to an effective remedy.

Since the ability to make the declaration is confined to certain higher courts, a litigant in a lower court or tribunal, who is affected by incompatible legislation, appears to be

---

256 [2006] 1 WLR 505.
257 And, quite possibly, also of common law principle; see, e.g., the statements in the House of Lords in *Derbyshire CC v Times Newspapers* [1993] 1 All ER 1011 to the effect that Art 10 of the ECHR and the English common law are substantively similar.
258 See p 206.
259 Lesser, because even where no statement of compatibility had been made, the courts would not be empowered to strike down the legislation in question.
260 The applicant only needs to exhaust those possibilities which offer an effective remedy, so if part of the complaint is the lack of a remedy under Art 13, then the application is not likely to be ruled inadmissible on this ground: *X v UK* (1981) (Appl 7990/77); 24 D & R 57. A remedy will be ineffective if according to established case law there appears to be no chance of success: Appl 5874 172, Yearbook XVII (1974). Until recently (see below) Strasbourg had not had the opportunity to rule on the question whether a Declaration of Incompatibility could amount to an effective remedy, since no analogous procedure exists in the contracting states. Since it offers nothing which has previously been recognised as a remedy to the individual in question, it was clear that there were strong grounds for considering that the system would not be viewed as offering an effective remedy.
261 (2006) App no 93378/05.

completely remediless, since even the empty remedy of a declaration is unavailable. The forum at the next level might be equally powerless. In the circumstances covered by this book, the picture is mixed as regards the ability of litigants to get into a court which can issue a declaration.[262] The litigant has little incentive to appeal in the hope of eventually reaching a court able to make a declaration, especially as there is no provision requiring the Crown to bear its own costs where it intervenes in accordance with s 5(2) of the HRA. In criminal proceedings, however, the courts appear to be taking the view that to convict a defendant in breach of Art 6 of the Convention would be an abuse of process.[263]

It is impossible not to conclude that this aspect of the system of remedial action is inadequate to the task of providing a domestic remedy for violation of Convention rights.[264] If, at the least, legislation is not forthcoming within the next few years to amend s 4 of the HRA with a view to allowing lower courts to make declarations, the pressure on the judiciary to find compatibility, already very high, will become increasingly severe.

The remedial process under s 10

Section 10 provides the remedial process to be followed if a declaration of incompatibility is made. Under s 10(2) if a Minister of the Crown considers 'that there are compelling reasons for proceeding under this section, he may by order make such amendments to the legislation as he considers necessary to remove the incompatibility'.[265] In a departure

---

262   E.g., an appeal from a magistrates' court to the Crown Court would require a further appeal in order to obtain a declaration. A declaration could be obtained using only one level of appeal if an appeal was by way of case stated to the Divisional Court. Appeals from the Proscribed Organisations Appeal Commission are, by leave, to the Court of Appeal in England and Wales, and to the equivalent courts in Scotland and Northern Ireland (see further Chapter 14, pp 1399–1400).

263   See the views of Lord Steyn in *R v DPP ex p Kebilene* [1999] 4 All ER 801.

264   See Leigh, I and Lustgarten, L, 'Making rights real: the courts, remedies and the Human Rights Act' (1999) 58(3) CLJ 509, p 543. They conclude that rights may be less well protected than previously as a result of the HRA.

265   Section 10(1): This section applies if:

   (a)   a provision of legislation has been declared under section 4 to be incompatible with a Convention right and, if an appeal lies-
   (i)   all persons who may appeal have stated in writing that they do not intend to do so;
   (ii)   the time for bringing an appeal has expired and no appeal has been brought within that time; or
   (iii) an appeal brought within that time has been determined or abandoned; or
   (b)   it appears to a Minister of the Crown or Her Majesty in Council that, having regard to a finding of the European Court of Human Rights made after the coming into force of this section in proceedings against the United Kingdom, a provision of legislation is incompatible with an obligation of the United Kingdom arising from the Convention.

(2) If a Minister of the Crown considers that there are compelling reasons for proceeding under this section, he may by order make such amendments to the legislation as he considers necessary to remove the incompatibility.

(3) If, in the case of subordinate legislation, a Minister of the Crown considers:

   (a)   that it is necessary to amend the primary legislation under which the subordinate legislation in question was made, in order to enable the incompatibility to be removed, and
   (b)   that there are compelling reasons for proceeding under this section, he may by order make such amendments to the primary legislation as he considers necessary.

from the New Zealand scheme, s 10 allows a Minister to make amendments to the offending legislation by means of a 'fast track' procedure. Section 10 may also be used where a decision of the European Court of Human Rights suggests that a provision of legislation has become incompatible with the Convention. Therefore, campaigning groups could lobby the government to make amendments under s 10 following any such decision. However, as indicated above, the Minister is under no obligation to make the amendment(s), either after any such decision or after a declaration of incompatibility under s 4, and may only do so if he or she considers that there are 'compelling reasons for proceeding under this section'. In other words, the fact that a declaration of incompatibility has been made will not necessarily *in itself* provide a compelling reason, although the circumstances in which it is made may do so.

Schedule 2 provides two procedures for making a 'remedial order' which must, under s 20, be in the form of a statutory instrument. Sched 2, para 2(a) and para 3 provide for a standard procedure whereby the Minister must lay a draft of the Order before Parliament, together with the required information – an explanation of the incompatibility and a statement of the reasons for proceeding under s 10 – for at least 60 days, during which time representations can be made to the Minister. It must then be laid before Parliament again and does not come into effect until it is approved by a resolution of each House within 60 days after it has been laid for the second time. The emergency procedure under Sched 2, para 2(b) and para 4 follows the same route, apart from the very significant provision for allowing the Minister to make the order before laying it before Parliament. Thus, the amendment can be made outside the full Parliamentary process, which would be required for primary legislation, but otherwise the responsibility for amending primary legislation remains firmly in Parliamentary hands, retaining 'Parliament's authority in the legislative process'.[266] In fact, so far the government has shown a clear preference for using the standard procedure.

Clearly, it is preferable in human rights terms to follow the Convention exception system rather than the HRA one. The response of the Labour Government to the declarations of incompatibility made so far indicates that it accepts this argument. It has moved to address all of them and in no instance has it stated that it merely intends to maintain the incompatibility – although the HRA clearly allows it to do so.[267] So although the HRA theoretically leaves the last word to Parliament in terms of creating

(4) This section also applies where the provision in question is in subordinate legislation and has been quashed, or declared invalid, by reason of incompatibility with a Convention right and the Minister proposes to proceed under paragraph 2(b) of Sched 2.

(5) If the legislation is an Order in Council, the power conferred by subsection (2) or (3) is exercisable by Her Majesty in Council.

(6) In this section 'legislation' does not include a Measure of the Church Assembly or of the General Synod of the Church of England.

(7) Schedule 2 makes further provision about remedial orders.

266 Ewing, K, 'The Human Rights Act and parliamentary democracy' (1999) 62(1) MLR 79, p 93.

267 E.g. in *R (H) v London North and East Region Mental Health Review Tribunal (Secretary of State for Health intervening)* [2002] QB 1 the Mental Health Act 1983 s 73 was found to be incompatible with Arts 5(1) and 5(4); the Mental Health Act 1983 (Remedial Order) 2001 was introduced to address the incompatibility by way of the fast track procedure. In *A and Others* [2004] QB 335 the House of Lords declared Part 4 ACTSA 2001 incompatible with Art 5 and 14 ECHR; Part 4 was repealed by the Prevention of Terrorism Act 2005, as discussed further in Chapter 14 pp 1438 *et seq.*

compatibility, thereby preserving Parliamentary sovereignty, in practice the government accepts the ECHR constraints, rather than the more lax HRA ones.

Declarations as to the compatibility of new Bills with the Convention rights

Under s 19(1)(a) HRA, in introducing legislation into Parliament, a Minister, before Second Reading of the Bill, must state that the Bill is compatible with the Convention or that while unable to make such a declaration, the government nevertheless wishes to proceed with the Bill (s 19(b)). When the relevant Minister has made a declaration of compatibility under s 19(a), its effects may be viewed as additional to the duty the courts are already under, arising from s 3(1), to ensure that the legislation is rendered compatible with the guarantees if at all possible. The Lord Chancellor has said: 'Ministerial statements of compatibility will inevitably be a strong spur to the courts to find the means of construing statutes compatibly with the Convention.'[268] The guidance given to Ministers is to the effect that for a s 19(1)(a) statement to be made it must be 'more likely than not that the provisions . . . will stand up to challenge on Convention grounds'.[269] But if a s 19(1)(b) statement is made this does not have to be taken to mean that 'the provisions of the Bill are incompatible . . . but that the Minister is unable to make a statement of compatibility'. There is no procedure within the HRA allowing the government or Parliament to declare that the judiciary should not strive to achieve compatibility even when dealing with almost certainly incompatible provisions.

The idea behind s 19 is that governments will not be willing, in general, to introduce incompatible Bills, although it does open the door to that possibility. In relation to Bills of Rights in general, Dawn Oliver has offered two reasons why a government would be unwilling to state openly that it was legislating in breach of a Bill of Rights.[270] First, there would be the general political embarrassment which would be caused to the government (this may be termed the 'adverse publicity' type of protection). Second, a declaration of intent to infringe constitutional rights would be tantamount to a declaration of the government's intention to breach its obligations under international law; this would undoubtedly provoke widespread international condemnation which would be highly embarrassing (this may be termed the 'manifest breach' type of protection). The stance taken towards the Communications Act 2003, which was not accompanied by a statement of compatibility, as discussed below, bears out this prediction.

It may be said that in one respect, s 19 bears comparison with a 'notwithstanding clause', but there is the very significant difference that, as discussed above, the judiciary are not empowered to strike down legislation which contains no such clause, but which is inconsistent with the Convention. Further, s 19 does not expressly provide for the possibility that the government deliberately wishes to achieve incompatibility with the Convention. It merely leaves open the possibility or – in practice – the strong

---

268   Lord Irvine [1998] PL 221.
269   Department of Constitutional Affairs, *Human Rights Act 1998 Guidance for Ministers* (2nd edn), para.36, www.dca.gov/hract/guidance.htm#how, para.36. See further Feldman, D, 'The Impact of Human Rights on the UK Legislative Process' (2004) 25(2) Stat.LR 91.
270   'A Bill of Rights for the UK', in *Government and the UK*, 1991.

probability that the legislation, or at least certain of its provisions, are incompatible. But s 19 resembles a 'notwithstanding clause' in the sense that a government that intends to introduce measures which are probably or certainly rights-abridging must be open about the fact – at least in the sense that the relevant Minister has to state that a declaration is not being made. The government can nevertheless take the position that while a statement is not being made, it considers the legislation in question to be compatible with the Convention.

The statement of compatibility does not necessarily indicate that compatibility has been achieved once the legislation comes into force. A declaration under s 19(1)(a) might be made and challenged in Parliament. The opposition parties might argue that the legislation had not achieved compatibility, but their amendments intended to achieve compatibility might be defeated due to the large majority of the government. It could hardly be said of such legislation that Parliament was genuinely satisfied that compatibility had been achieved. Further, Parliament might be misled into believing that the legislation was compatible. The legal advice behind the declaration might be flawed. It is arguable that legislation has been passed which gives an appearance of achieving compatibility only because a minimalist interpretation of the Convention was adopted in drafting it. It is suggested in Chapters 10 and 14 that certain provisions of the Terrorism Act 2000 and the Regulation of Investigatory Powers Act 2000 arguably provide examples of such a tendency.[271] Further, legislation, which was arguably compatible with the Convention when passed, might become incompatible due to the effect of subsequent decisions of the European Court of Human Rights taken before the legislation comes into force. Section 2 HRA requires a court to take such decisions into account 'whenever made or given'.

At the time of the inception of the HRA, it was not necessarily apparent that Bills would almost always be accompanied in future by a declaration of their compatibility with the Convention rights, or that a derogation would be sought where otherwise a declaration could not be made. The response of the Conservative Government in the 1990s to certain decisions of the European Court of Human Rights, in particular to its decision in *McCann, Farrell and Savage v UK*,[272] the first judgment of the Court to find a breach of Art 2, did not suggest that future governments would necessarily be deterred on 'manifest breach' or 'adverse publicity' grounds from passing legislation clearly in breach of the Convention without seeking a derogation. The same can be said of the reaction to the findings of the Strasbourg Court in *Jordan, Kelly, Arthurs, Donelly and Others v UK*[273] in 2001. A breach of Art 2 was found in respect of the killing of eight IRA members by the SAS in 1987. The Conservative and Unionist Parties were outraged by the verdict.

After the decision in *McCann*, Michael Heseltine, the then Deputy Prime Minister, declared that the then Conservative Government would not change the administrative policies or rules which had led to the deaths in question in that case; members of the government also voiced strong disapproval of the decision, and their stance was welcomed in the right wing sections of the UK press. A future government might

---

271 See pp 1391–92 and p 1042.
272 (1995) 21 EHRR 97, A 324, Council of Europe Report.
273 (2001) *The Times*, 18 May; see further Chapter 2, p 40.

take the view that passing a certain measure in overt breach of the Convention was necessary on crime control and/or anti-terrorist grounds, but this stance has *not* been taken by the current Labour Government, as Chapter 14 indicates.[274]

As discussed below, the Communications Act 2003 is the only Act so far since the Human Rights Act came into force in 2000 not to be accompanied by a statement of compatibility. Apart from the Communications Act, all legislation passed since the obligation to make a statement of compatibility came into force[275] has been accompanied by a declaration of its compatibility with the Convention rights, under s 19. But this need not mean that all such legislation is in fact compatible: the mere fact that a declaration is made does not mean that it can be assumed that compatibility was in fact achieved.[276] As indicated, a statement of compatibility is far from conclusive of the matter.

Thus, the s 19 procedure should be viewed as the expression of an executive opinion based on legal advice, nothing more. As far as s 3 is concerned, the courts are expected to satisfy their obligation under s 3 in respect of legislation passed prior to the inception of the HRA in 1998, but are under an even stronger obligation, as indicated above, in respect of legislation accompanied by a statement of compatibility since it can be assumed that Parliament intended that the legislation should be compatible with the Convention. Where no declaration is made, it can be said that the courts are placed in a dilemma. Section 3 still applies, but Parliament's intention can be viewed as being that the legislation in question should not be compatible with the Convention. However, if no derogation from the Convention right is sought, the dilemma could be resolved by adopting the view that Parliament could be presumed not to wish to legislate compatibly with the Convention except where it had expressly stated that such was its intention. A court could then apply s 3 as it would to legislation passed after 1950, but before 1998. This point is returned to below, in relation to the Communications Act 2003.

As Chapter 11 indicates, in order to ensure that a declaration could be made, and more significantly, to ensure full compliance with the Convention in a more general sense, the Terrorism Act 2000 contained provisions that allowed the government to abandon the embarrassing derogation from Art 5.[277] Thereafter, the Labour Government, which introduced the HRA, has not sought to introduce Bills, with the one exception mentioned, that could not be accompanied by a declaration under s 19.

The view taken by the government in introducing the Communications Bill containing a statutory prohibition on political advertising in broadcasting was that the 2003 Act could not be declared to be compatible with the ECHR. The government had taken the decision, in introducing the 2003 reforms, not to relax or modify the ban, despite the fact that this meant that it considered that it could not issue a statement of the compatibility of the Act with the European Convention on Human Rights, under s 19(a) HRA. The government was not prepared to modify the section by creating exceptions in order to seek to ensure compatibility. The government was supported in

---

274 See, e.g., p 1438.
275 The obligation to make a statement of compatibility came into force on 24 November 1998, not on 2 October 2000, under the HRA 1998 (Commencement) Order 1998 (SI 1998/2882).
276 See Feldman, D, 'Institutional Roles and meanings of 'compatibility' under the HRA' in Fenwick, Masterman and Phillipson (eds) (2007), fn 1 above.
277 See pp 1168–69.

this decision by the Parliamentary Committees that considered the matter prior to the introduction of the new Act.[278] Sections 319 and 321, it was considered, could not be declared to be compatible with Art 10 and so, in accordance with s 19(1)(b) HRA, no statement of compatibility was issued accompanying the Bill, but the point was made in Parliament that the provisions need not be viewed as incompatible and that they would be defended if necessary.[279]

Thus the use of the broadcast media for paid political advertising is prohibited by ss 319 and 321 of the Communications Act 2003. Section 319(2)(g) imposes a duty on Ofcom, the broadcast regulator, to ensure that political advertising is not included in television or radio services. Section 321(2) provides that for the purposes of section 319(2)(g) an advertisement will contravene the prohibition on political advertising if it is:

(a) an advertisement which is inserted by or on behalf of a body whose objects are wholly or mainly of a political nature; (b) an advertisement which is directed towards a political end; or (c) an advertisement which has a connection with an industrial dispute.

The ban appears to be even wider then these rules would warrant.[280] Section 321(3) provides a non-exhaustive definition of 'objects wholly or mainly of a political nature', which covers: influencing the outcome of elections, bringing about changes in the law, influencing political policy and influencing persons with public functions, including functions conferred via international agreements. These provisions make it clear that this is an extremely broad and comprehensive prohibition. It may be noted that the objectives mentioned are not confined to the UK, but include influencing foreign governments and policy. This statutory definition of 'political advertising', for the purposes of the ban, is more detailed and explicit than in any previous legislation.

Since this is an absolute ban it probably contravenes Art 10 of the European Convention on Human Rights.[281] An interest group, such as *Make Poverty History*, might decide to mount a challenge to the ban under the HRA, relying on Art 10. The action would be likely to be brought in the form of judicial review of a decision of

---

278 See Joint Committee on the Draft Communications Bill, *the Draft Communications Bill* HL 169-I/HC876-I (2001–2) para 301; Committee on Standards in Public Life *Fifth Report: the Funding of Political Parties in the UK* Cm 4057 (1998) recommendation 94.

279 See *Hansard*, HC Vol.395, col 789 (Dec 3, 2002); *Hansard*, HL Vol. 646, cols 658–59 (March 25, 2003).

280 Rule 4 of the Television Advertising Standards Code of the Broadcast Committee of Advertising Practice (BCAP) reflects the ban; it prohibits commercials that: (a) may be inserted by or on behalf of any body whose objects are wholly or mainly of a political nature; (b) may be directed towards any political end; (c) may have any relation to any industrial dispute (with limited exceptions); or (d) may show partiality as respects matters of political or industrial controversy or relating to current public policy. It may be noted that the statute does not contain an equivalent to Rule 4(d) of the Television Advertising Standards Code; the Code is therefore wider than the statute and so creates a broader restriction.

281 In *VGT v Switzerland* (2002) 34 EHRR 159 the Strasbourg Court had found that a similar refusal to broadcast an advertisement had amounted to an interference by a public authority in the exercise of the rights guaranteed by Art 10 (at para 48).

Ofcom's upholding a ban on *Make Poverty History* broadcast advertising.[282] It could first be asked whether the ban based on ss 319(2)(g) and 321 Communications Act 2003 combined is in fact incompatible with Art 10. The fact that the 2003 Act was not declared compatible with the Convention due to the prohibition in s 321 indicates that the finding of such a breach, while not inevitable, would be probable. Parliament did make a deliberate decision in relation to a post-HRA statute to pass provisions that were arguably in breach of Art 10, having been given notice under s 19(1)(b) HRA that this was possibly the case. Clearly, the courts do not have to accept that the provisions did in fact create such a breach,[283] but it may be argued at first glance that they should show some deference to Parliament's decision to pass them, a different issue.

But the question is what does showing deference entail in this highly exceptional context? The courts have not so far tackled the question of deference in relation to provisions that Parliament itself has accepted are probably incompatible with a Convention Article. In this context deference appears to mean taking account of the probability that the provisions are indeed incompatible with Art 10 as the s 19(1)(b) HRA statement signalled. This is objectively evidenced on the face of the Bill in the statement – there is no difficulty in determining Parliament's intention. A finding by a court that the provisions are in fact incompatible would not therefore be out of line with the intention of Parliament – which on one rational reading of the debates, intended to pass incompatible provisions. The government's own position in the debates was, it is suggested, contradictory. It used the s 19(1)(b) HRA statement procedure but stated that it did not accept that the provisions were incompatible. Had it thought that the provisions could be viewed as compatible on a 'more likely than not' test then presumably it would have issued a statement under s 19(1)(a) HRA to that effect. Therefore Parliament must have considered that it was passing provisions that were probably incompatible with Art 10. Paying deference to that decision of Parliament does not appear to be incompatible with bringing an intense form of scrutiny to bear on the question of proportionality since Parliament has in a sense invited the courts to do just that.

Lewis argues that s 321 could be seen as 'merely an opening gambit' in a conversation between the organs of governance about the essence of rights whose content is 'essentially contestable'.[284] He cites in support Jack Straw's speech made during the passage of the Human Rights Bill to the effect that 'Parliament and the judiciary must engage in a serious dialogue about the operation and development of the rights in the Bill . . . this dialogue is the only way in which we can ensure the legislation is a living development that assists our citizens'.[285] This comment of Jack Straw's supports the argument that the government were opening a dialogue with the courts in making the s 19(1)(b) statement in the passage of the Communications Bill regarding the standard of scrutiny to be used. In general, courts may be prepared to defer to Parliament's view

---

282   See further Fenwick and Phillipson (2006) fn 1 above, Chapter 20.

283   In *R v A* [2002] 1 AC 45 Lord Hope said, obiter, that s 19 statements are merely expressions of opinion by the Minister. He found that they are not binding on courts and do not have even persuasive authority (at para 69).

284   Lewis, T, 'Political Advertising and the Communications Act 2003' [2005] 3 EHRLR 290–300 at p 299.

285   *Hansard*, HC Vol. 314, col 1141 (June 24, 1998).

that provisions are compatible with the Convention rights. Thus, in this instance, the use of deference might conceivably be more likely to lead to a finding that the ban is compatible with Art 10.

As discussed in Chapter 14, when the Anti-Terrorism Crime and Security Act 2001 was passed the government sought a derogation from Art 5 in respect of the detention without trial provisions of Part 4, rather than seeking to pass them through Parliament unaccompanied by a statement of compatibility.[286] In general it is argued, for obvious reasons, that seeking a derogation from the relevant Article in question in order to achieve compatibility is preferable to merely pushing incompatible legislation through Parliament, even though the HRA allows for that latter possibility. A derogation under Art 15, as discussed in Chapters 2 and 14, can only be sought under very limited circumstances that can then be subject to judicial scrutiny.[287] In contrast, the HRA allows for exceptions to the Convention to be made in any circumstances – no limitations at all are contained in the HRA itself, except the limitation that can be implied from the wording of s 3. No requirement of proportionality is imported into the HRA itself in relation to the introduction of incompatible Bills. A requirement could have been imposed in the HRA that a detailed explanation for the reasons behind seeking to legislate in breach of the Convention must be given to Parliament and that only in certain circumstances, including emergency ones, should Parliament accept them. But, clearly, such a requirement would have been overtly incompatible with the doctrine of Parliamentary sovereignty.

Clearly, legislating in deliberate and overt breach of the Convention would eventually invite a successful challenge to the measure in the European Court of Human Rights, but the government in its legislative programme has not sought to take advantage even of the time lapse that would have occurred.

Special protection for the media and religious freedom?

Protecting religious organisations

The Church of England lobbied fiercely during the passage of the Human Rights Bill to be given special protection for religious freedom. The amendments to the Bill adopted in the House of Lords, which would have provided a defence where religious organisations breached human rights in the pursuance of religious belief, suggested that the Church wished to be allowed to disregard human rights values in the name of respect for religious belief, and that while protecting its own Art 9 rights, it was prepared to use them to invade the Convention rights of others.[288] The Church appeared to hope that it would be able to discriminate against persons on the ground, for example, of gender or sexual orientation in respect, *inter alia*, of employment in Church schools. Those amendments were removed in the Commons and s 13 was substituted, on the basis that Church concerns could be met without compromising the integrity of the Bill.[289] Section 13 does not allow the Church, and other religious organisations, to

---

286 See Chapter 14, pp 1422 *et seq*.
287 See p 110 and pp 1431–38.
288 See 585 HL Official Report Cols 747–60, 770–90, 805, 812–13, 5 February 1998.
289 The Home Secretary, 312 HC Official Report, Col 1019 (1998).

disregard human rights, but on its face it appears to give special protection to their Art 9 rights. It provides: 'If a court's determination of any question arising under this Act might affect the exercise by a religious organisation . . . of [its Art 9 rights] the right to freedom of . . . religion, it must have particular regard to the importance of that right.' Arguably, s 13 impliedly accepts, therefore, what some commentators regard as a regrettable dislocation between human rights values and religious ones which could present judges with problems of interpretation.[290] Ian Loveland has dubbed the amendment 'a substantive obscenity'.[291] However, since, as Chapter 9 indicates, s 12 has not been found to enhance the weight to be given to Art 10 on the basis that Arts 8–11 must be viewed as standing on an equal footing,[292] it is probable that this would also be found to be the case in respect of s 13 in relation to Art 9.

Protecting the media

The press also lobbied for special protection. Press lobbying focused overwhelmingly upon the fear that the Act would introduce a right to privacy against the media 'through the back door', due either to judicial development of the common law in the post-HRA era, or to the probable status of the Press Complaints Commission as a public authority, itself bound to act compatibly with the Convention under s 6 HRA.[293] Sometimes the basic point was missed that the Convention rights would not directly bind newspapers, since they are not public authorities.[294] The amendment became s 12, which applies 'if a court is considering whether to grant any relief [which could] affect the exercise of the Convention right to freedom of expression'.

Section 12(2)–(3) provides special provision against the grant of ex parte injunctions, which is discussed further in Chapters 8[295] and 9.[296] Under s 12(3), no relief which, if granted, might affect the exercise of the Convention right to freedom of expression is to be granted so as to restrain publication before trial 'unless the court is satisfied that the applicant is likely to establish that publication should not be allowed.' Section 12(3) therefore affects the grant of interim injunctions generally. The use of injunctions is discussed in Chapter 9 in the context of restraining misuse of private information. The discussion considers in particular the use of s 12 HRA where interim injunctions are sought in civil proceedings against newspapers.[297]

Under s 12(5), the term 'relief' includes 'any remedy or order other than in criminal proceedings'. Section 12(4) provides that the court must have special regard to the Convention right to freedom of expression and, in particular, to the extent to which it is about to become or has become available to the public, the public interest in its

---

290 See further Cumper, P, 'The protection of religious rights under s 13 of the HRA' [2000] PL 254.
291 Loveland, I, *Constitutional Law*, 2000, p 603.
292 See pp 950 *et seq*.
293 See Chapter 9, pp 848–49 on this point.
294 The definition of 'public authority' appears in ss 6(1), 6(3)(b) and 6(5)) of the Act, discussed in HL Deb Vol 582 Cols 1277, 1293–94 and 1309–10, 3 November 1997, and ibid, Vol 583, Cols 771–811, 24 November 1997.
295 See p 795.
296 See pp 985–90.
297 See pp 988–89.

publication and 'any relevant privacy code'.[298] Section 12(4) is therefore highly relevant in actions originating under the breach of confidence doctrine. Section 12 has not protected the media from the impact of a privacy law. Media fears that a 'privacy law' would develop under the HRA were not misplaced and are currently in the process of being realised. But there was an enjoyable irony in the fact that it was s 12(4) that was used, at least initially, to provide such a law with impetus, ensnaring the group that lobbied for its inclusion. Clearly, from a human rights perspective, this can be viewed as a welcome development, since it means that a group – media proprietors – with the ability and the evident desire to infringe the rights of others, while protecting its own, can be curbed in its ability to do so.

The position of the Scottish Parliament, the Northern Ireland Assembly and the Welsh Assembly

The devolution legislation places the Scottish Parliament, the Northern Ireland Assembly and the Welsh Assembly in a different position from that of the Westminster Parliament as regards the legal status of the Convention rights. The Welsh Assembly is not able to pass primary legislation and it is bound by the Convention under s 107(1) of the Government of Wales Act 1988. The Scottish Parliament cannot act incompatibly with the Convention under s 29(2)(d) of the Scotland Act 1998. The Executive and law officers in Scotland are also bound.[299] Under s 21 HRA, legislation passed by the Scottish Parliament and by the Northern Ireland Assembly is regarded as secondary legislation. Under s 3 HRA, any primary legislation[300] passed by the Westminster Parliament and applicable to Scotland, Northern Ireland and Wales will be binding, even if it is not compatible with the Convention. These arrangements mean that Scotland has, in effect, a Bill of Rights in the traditional sense since the Parliament is bound by the Convention and therefore cannot pass primary legislation which conflicts with it.[301] The references to 'legislation' so far, and below, are to legislation emanating from the Westminster Parliament.

Conclusions

It can now be said that the rules of interpretation relating to legislation affecting Convention rights differ, depending on when it was passed. Prior legislation passed before 1950 is subject to a compatible construction rule only, arising under s 3. Prior legislation passed after 1950 is subject to a 'legislative intention plus compatible construction rule'[302] since, as indicated above, Parliament can be presumed not to

---

298 See further on s 12(4): Griffiths, J and Lewis, T, 'The HRA s 12 – press freedom over privacy' (1999) 10(2) Ent LR 36–41. They argue that s 12(4) did not in fact provide the protection the media had hoped for, although their spokespersons believed that it had.

299 See Scotland Act 1998, s 57. Thus, in Scotland and Wales, the Convention became binding from 1 July 1999, when the devolution legislation came into force, over a year before the HRA came fully into force.

300 Scotland Act 1998, s 29(2)(b) and Sched 5, and Government of Wales Act 1988, Sched 2.

301 See further Tierney, S, 'Devolution issues and s 2(1) of the HRA' (2000) 4 EHRLR 380–92.

302 See Bennion, F, 'What interpretation is possible under s 3(1) of the HRA?' [2000] PL 77.

have intended to legislate incompatibly with the Convention. Subsequent legislation – passed after the inception of the HRA – is subject to the general legislative intention rule, the presumption which may be said to be embodied in the s 19 procedure and to the compatible construction rule under s 3. If no declaration of compatibility is made, subsequent legislation is subject to the compatible construction rule and probably to the legislative intention rule too.

In so far as the possibility of incompatibility arises in either prior or subsequent legislation, the stance taken by the House of Lords in *Ghaidan* is that it should be dealt with under s 3, without resorting to a declaration of incompatibility under s 4, except as a last resort. After *R v A* and *Ghaidan* Parliament's theoretical ability under the HRA to pass incompatible legislation has been undermined. It may be concluded, therefore, that s 3 places the Convention in a strong position when compared with ordinary legislation, although, in a very technical sense, as a matter of constitutional theory, parliamentary sovereignty is preserved.

But at the same time the HRA is in a weak position compared to, for example, the US Bill of Rights, since it is subject to express repeal or amendment by subsequent enactments. This is a significant weakness, bearing in mind the continuing hostility of the Conservative Party to the HRA,[303] and indeed the lack of support for its values exhibited by members of the Labour Government. As already indicated, the intention of the Conservative Party is to repeal the HRA if it is elected at the next General Election, expected to be in 2009 or 2010. Although in terms of express repeal, the doctrine of Parliamentary sovereignty is preserved, the other HRA mechanisms apparently intended to show adherence to that doctrine now look tokenistic. The possibilities of passing incompatible legislation, or of disregarding declarations of incompatibility, have not been exploited over the last seven years of the HRA's existence. Aside from certain provisions of the Communications Act 2003, Parliament has shown little evidence of an intent to employ the leeway allowed for under the HRA to pass incompatible legislation in the years 2000–7.

Instead, the Convention exceptions system has been deployed domestically so that at the least parity with Strasbourg is maintained. When Part 4 Anti-Terrorism Crime and Security Act 2001 was passed, a derogation from Art 5 accompanied it.[304] Otherwise, Parliament and the courts have relied on the doctrine of proportionality in finding that exceptions to the Convention rights can be justified. The stance taken under s 3 appears to be, as discussed, a remedial one. In other words, the courts have shown a determination to take measures to avoid a breach of a Convention right at the domestic level, largely disregarding the possibility of dealing with Convention restraints offered by s 3(2) and s 4 HRA. The government and Parliament have largely followed suit, as the discussion of the use of ss 4, 10 and s 19(1)(a) and (b) over the last seven years indicates. The stance of the senior judges in the leading s 3 cases is in accordance with the redefinition of their role that the HRA has brought about, and with the status of the HRA as a constitutional instrument. However, as the discussion of the leading s 2 decisions reveals, the traditional constraints of the doctrine of precedent are creating a

303 Such hostility became ever more evident once the Conservatives had lost the 2001 General Election, owing to the change of leadership. At the 2005 General Election it was stated that the HRA would be modified if the Conservatives were elected.
304 See Chapter 14, pp 1422 *et seq.*

countervailing pressure that is holding back the development of a British constitutional rights jurisprudence.[305]

4 The Position of Public Authorities under the HRA

The binding effect of Convention rights

Section 6 is the central provision of the HRA. Section 6(1) provides: 'It is unlawful for a public authority to act in a way which is incompatible with a Convention right.' This is the main provision giving effect to the Convention rights: rather than incorporation of the Convention, it is made binding against public authorities. Under s 6(6), an 'act' includes an omission, but does not include a failure to introduce in or lay before Parliament a proposal for legislation or a failure to make any primary legislation or remedial order. Section 6(6) was included in order to preserve Parliamentary sovereignty and prerogative power: in this case, the power of the executive to introduce legislation.

Thus, apart from its impact on legislation, the HRA also creates obligations under s 6 which bear upon 'public authorities'. Such obligations have a number of implications. Independently of litigation, public authorities have had to put procedures in place in order to ensure that they do not breach their duty under s 6. Guidance was issued prior to the coming in to force of the HRA[306] to a number of central government departments by the Human Rights Unit (HRU), now the Human Rights Division of the Department for Constitutional Affairs, and a number of the departments undertook a human rights audit, reporting back to the HRU.[307] However, beyond central government departments, practice was very variable,[308] although certain bodies, including the police, undertook quite extensive preparation before the HRA came fully into force.[309] The Human Rights Task Force was set up by the Home Office to aid in the preparations, and it has received reports from certain public authorities regarding completion of internal human rights reviews. It is clear that internal human rights reviewing and auditing in public authorities is an ongoing process, one that intensified once the HRA was fully in force. The level of awareness of the implications of the HRA in the various public authorities has been and will remain extremely variable for some considerable period.

Clearly, an exception had to be made under s 6 in order to bring it into harmony with s 3 and to realise the objective of preserving Parliamentary sovereignty. Section

---

305 See further Masterman, Chapter 3, in Fenwick, Masterman, Phillipson (eds)) (2007) fn 1 above.

306 A number of documents have been issued by the HRU, including *Putting Rights into Public Services*, July 1999; *Core Guidance for Public Authorities: A New Era of Rights and Responsibilities; The Human Rights Act 1998: Guidance for Departments*, now *A Guide to the Human Rights Act 1998*, 3rd edn, 2006.

307 See further the Department for Constitutional Affairs website: www.dca.gov.uk; the DCA Human Rights Division website: www.dca.gov.uk/peoples-rights/human-rights/index.htm.

308 See for comment at that time Pleming, 'Assessing the act: a firm foundation or a false start' (2000) 6 EHRLR 560–79. See further Clements and Thomas (eds) *The HRA: A Success Story?* (2005).

309 The Association of Chief Police Officers set up a Human Rights Working Group in November 1998; it appointed a Human Rights Programme Team in 1999. Twelve areas of police work were selected as especially significant in HRA terms, including covert policing, discipline, hate crimes, domestic violence and public order. An audit of those areas was undertaken in order to determine whether procedures and policies required modification.

6(2) provides: 'sub-section (1) does not apply to an act if, (a) as the result of one or more provisions of primary legislation, the authority could not have acted differently; or (b) in the case of one or more provisions of, or made under, primary legislation which cannot be read or given effect in a way which is compatible with the Convention rights, the authority was acting so as to give effect to or enforce those provisions'. Thus, s 6(2)(a) creates a strong obligation requiring public authorities to do their utmost to act compatibly.

It may be noted that s 6(2)(a) applies to primary legislation only, whereas s 6(2)(b) applies also to subordinate legislation made under incompatible primary legislation. This is implicit in the use of the words 'or made under' used in the latter sub-section, but not the former. The exception under s 6 applies to legislation only (which, as indicated above, includes Orders in Council made under the royal prerogative, under s 21(1)). If a common law provision conflicts with a Convention right binding on a public body under s 6, it appears that the right will prevail. No provision was included in the Act allowing the common law to override the Convention or creating restrictions as to those courts that can find incompatibility between the two.

Relationship between ss 3 and 6

Where legislation is applicable to a public authority, a court, as itself a public authority must, in addition to its duty under s 3, seek to ensure that the Convention is adhered to. It must bear in mind that it is considering the obligations of another public authority which is bound by the rights. But its duty under s 3 relates to its interpretation of the legislation itself, its duty under s 6 to the application of the legislation by the public authority and by itself in relation to the Convention rights. The courts in the post-HRA cases do not always advert expressly to their use of either ss 3 or 6 in applying legislation.[310] A court can first apply s 6 and ask whether the public authority has, by its action or omission, breached the Convention guarantee(s) in question. If it appears that it has, the court should look to the relevant legislation to determine whether, even when the attempt is made to construe it compatibly with the Convention, it remains incompatible and therefore provides the public authority with a loophole under s 6(2). An alternative method is to consider the legislation first in relation to the public authority, affording it a Convention-friendly interpretation, and then asking whether, under such an interpretation, it appeared that the body had the power to do what it had done. If it appeared that it had not, it could be found to have acted ultra vires.

Distinguishing between public authorities and private bodies

'Standard' and 'functional' public authorities

Under s 6, Convention guarantees are binding only against 'public authorities'. The terms 'public authority' and 'public function' were left deliberately undefined in the HRA. Nor was an exhaustive list of public authorities attempted, on the model provided

---

310 See, e.g., Chapter 8, p 797. In the cases discussed it was not clear whether ss 6 or 3 were being relied upon in applying the Convention.

by the Freedom of Information Act 2000.[311] Under s 6(3)(b) the term covers 'any person certain of whose functions are functions of a public nature'. So the crucial question in relation to many bodies concerns the meaning of the term 'functions of a public nature' – if the body is not self-evidently a public authority, as explained below. Only two bodies are categorised under the HRA itself – the courts and Parliament. Under s 6(3)(a), the term 'public authority' includes a court or under sub-section (b) a tribunal. Parliament 'or a person exercising functions in connection with proceedings in Parliament' is expressly excluded from the definition. This refers to the Westminster Parliament; the Scottish Parliament, the Northern Ireland Assembly and the Welsh Assembly.

Not only is the definition under s 6(3) non-exhaustive, it also leaves open room for much debate on the meaning of 'functions of a public nature'. The definition was explained in the Notes on Clauses accompanying the Bill as indicating that where a body is clearly recognisable as a public authority, there is no need to look at the detailed provisions of s 6(3)(a)–(b). Thus, the term 'public authority' includes firstly bodies which are self-evidently of a public nature, such as the police, government departments, the Probation Service, local authorities, the Security and Intelligence Services, and the BBC. They are usually referred to as 'standard public authorities'.

Second, certain bodies, which have both public and private functions, are quasi-public or hybrid bodies. They are generally referred to as 'functional public authorities', the terminology used in the Notes on Clauses accompanying the Bill. Under s 6(5), 'in relation to a particular act, a person is not a public authority by virtue only of s 6(3)(b) if the nature of the act is private'. Since, in relation to standard public authorities, there is no need to consider s 6(3)(b), this provision refers to functional public authorities and has the effect of excluding the private acts of functional public authorities from the scope of the HRA (but see the discussion of 'horizontal effect', below). This is a very significant matter, since the private acts of standard public authorities are *not* excluded. So under s 6(5), functional public authorities are bound by the Convention rights in respect of their public functions only. Therefore, for example, assuming that acts relating to employment are private acts, an employee of a standard public authority could use the HRA directly against the authority, as explained below, while the employee of a functional public authority could not. A hospital, for example, might be viewed as exercising a public function in relation to NHS patients, a private one in relation to private patients. But some room was clearly created for debate as to those bodies that should be classified as standard rather than functional.[312] Classic functional bodies include privatised fuel or water companies and other contracted-out services.

Thus, under the generally accepted view of s 6(3) and (5), the provisions create three categories of body in relation to the Convention rights. First, there are standard ('pure') public authorities which can *never* act privately, even in respect of matters governed by private law, such as employment relations. Such bodies are obliged under s 6 to act in accordance with Convention rights in relation to all of their activities, whether they can be accounted public or private functions. Secondly, there are functional (quasi-public) authorities which have a dual function and which can act privately; these are

---

311 See Chapter 7, pp 632–34.
312 See Grosz, Beatson and Duffy, op. cit., fn 1, on this point: para 4–10 et seq.

bodies having several functions, some public and some private; they are caught by the Convention in respect of the former functions but not the latter. In other words, they are not bound by the Act to adhere to the Convention rights when engaged in *private* acts. It is possible, it is suggested, that they could operate privately in respect of *aspects* of carrying out their public functions, while they would always act privately respect of their private functions. Thirdly, there are purely private bodies which have no public function at all. It was accepted in Parliament in debate on the Human Rights Bill that this was the correct reading of s 6.[313]

It follows from the three categorisations that, for example, the prison service has a mainly public function in respect of managing prisons and providing services in relation to prisoners, but a private function in relation to the employment of prison officers. Nevertheless, as a core public authority it is bound by the Convention in respect of both functions. An example of a body in the second category arose in respect of Railtrack (now abolished and re-nationalised), which had a public function in respect of rail safety (see *Cameron v Network Rail*),[314] but might also have dealt with ancillary matters linked to safety, including employment, which could have been viewed as private. The other, private, function of such bodies (British Telecom and British Gas may provide examples) would relate, *inter alia*, to their dealings with shareholders and property development, and in respect of those functions it is probable that such bodies could never act publicly.[315] A further example was given by the Lord Chancellor; he stated in debate on the Human Rights Bill that 'doctors in general practice would be [functional] public authorities in relation to their National Health Service functions, but not in relation to their private patients'.[316] Similarly, a private security company that has a contract with the government to transport prisoners to and from court, and especially if it has a statutory duty in so doing, is probably a functional public authority for the purposes of the HRA when it is transporting prisoners, but not when it is guarding private property under a contract with a private organisation since that is a private function. Therefore, when performing that latter function, it is not under a direct duty to respect Convention rights. It would only be affected by the rights – assuming that no statute was applicable – if an incident occurred in which another cause of action was applicable. If a cause of action, such as trespass to the person, applied and an action was brought, the court in adjudicating on that action, would have to take the Convention rights into account since the court is itself a public authority under s 6. This difficult point is pursued below, in relation to the duties of private bodies under the HRA.

The discussion below, and in this book in general, proceeds on the basis, therefore, that s 6 creates three categories of bodies – standard, functional and private – and that the private acts of functional bodies are excluded from the scope of the s 6 obligation, while standard public authorities are bound in respect of all their functions. They are not excluded from the effects of the HRA entirely, owing to its creation of indirect horizontal effects (discussed below).

---

313 See Straw, HC Official Report, Cols 409–10 (1998).
314 [2006] EWHC 1133 QB.
315 See HL Deb Col 811, 24 November 1997.
316 *Hansard*, HL Deb, Vol 583, Col 811 (24 November 2001). See further Clayton and Tomlinson, *The Law of Human Rights*, 1st edn, 2000, para 5–3.

Tests determining core and functional public authority status

The relevant test determining that a public authority is a 'core' authority was considered in detail in the leading decision of the House of Lords in *Aston Cantlow PCC v Wallbank*.[317] The question facing the Lords was whether the action of a parochial church council (PCC) seeking to enforce liability to repair a church was taken as an aspect of a public function. Lord Nicholls first considered whether the PCC should be viewed as a core public authority, finding that there no single test was available to determine whether a public body carried out a public function. He said:[318]

> The expression 'public authority' is not defined in the Act, nor is it a recognised term of art in English law, that is, an expression with a specific recognised meaning. The word 'public' is a term of uncertain import, used with many different shades of meaning: public policy, public rights of way, public property, public authority (in the Public Authorities Protection Act 1893), public nuisance, public house, public school, public company. So in the present case the statutory context is all important. As to that, the broad purpose sought to be achieved by section 6(1) is not in doubt. The purpose is that those bodies for whose acts the state is answerable before the European Court of Human Rights shall in future be subject to a domestic law obligation not to act incompatibly with Convention rights. If they act in breach of this legal obligation victims may henceforth obtain redress from the courts of this country. In future victims should not need to travel to Strasbourg.
>
> Conformably with this purpose, the phrase 'a public authority' in section 6(1) is essentially a reference to a body whose nature is governmental in a broad sense of that expression . . . under the Human Rights Act a body of this nature is required to act compatibly with Convention rights in everything it does. The most obvious examples are government departments, local authorities, the police and the armed forces. Behind the instinctive classification of these organisations as bodies whose nature is governmental lie factors such as the possession of special powers, democratic accountability, public funding in whole or in part, an obligation to act only in the public interest, and a statutory constitution . . . . One consequence of being a 'core' public authority, namely, an authority falling within section 6 without reference to section 6(3), is that the body in question does not itself enjoy Convention rights . . . . A core public authority seems inherently incapable of satisfying the Convention description of a victim: "any person, *non-governmental organisation* or group of individuals" (Article 34, with emphasis added). Only victims of an unlawful act may bring proceedings under section 7 of the Human Rights Act, and the Convention description of a victim has been incorporated into the Act, by section 7(7) . . . It must always be relevant to consider whether Parliament can have been intended that the body in question should have no Convention rights.

---

317   [2004] 1 AC 546. For discussion, see Meisel, F, 'The *Aston Cantlow* case: blots on English jurisprudence and the public/private law divide' [2004] PL 2–10.

318   At paras 6–8.

Applying these tests, the House of Lords found that parochial church councils (PCCs) are not 'core' public authorities. Lord Nicholls noted that as the established church the Church of England has special links with central government, but he considered that it remains essentially a religious organisation. He found that the constitution and functions of PCCs do not support the view that they should be characterised as core public authorities. Lord Nicholls said that the essential role of a PCC is to provide a formal means, prescribed by the Church of England, whereby ex officio and elected members of the local church promote the mission of the Church and discharge financial responsibilities in respect of their own parish church; he viewed these as acts of self-governance and PCCs as far removed from the type of body whose acts engage the responsibility of the state under the European Convention. As indicated, he further noted that if PCCs could be characterised as core public authorities that would mean that they would not be capable of being victims within the meaning of the HRA and, *inter alia*, would not be able take advantage of s 13, which gives express mention to the exercise by religious organisations of the Art 9 right of freedom of thought, conscience and religion.[319] Lord Hope noted that the Strasbourg jurisprudence supports this approach.[320] He also considered that the case law on judicial review might not provide much assistance as to functions of a public nature because the cases were not decided for the purposes of identifying the liability of the state in international law.[321]

The question of categorising core public bodies has not proved unduly problematic[322] since, as Lord Nicholls stated, such bodies are normally self-evidently governmental. But the tests for determining 'hybrid' public authority status are still less than clear. A clear definition of a 'public' function has proved elusive.[323] The precise distinction to draw between standard and functional bodies, and between functional and private bodies, has already given rise to quite a lot of litigation. This latter issue has proven to be a complex and difficult area for the courts, and the cases have not yet succeeded in establishing a clear, coherent and workable test as to the nature of the function that will cross the threshold between private and public. The tests that are currently emerging, as discussed below, do not, it will be argued, accord with the spirit of the Convention or with the government's intention in deciding on the wording of s 6.

One of the leading decisions, which was also discussed above, is *Poplar Housing & Regeneration Community Association Ltd v Donoghue*.[324] A local authority, Tower Hamlets, was under a statutory duty under s 188 of the Housing Act 1996 to provide or secure the provision of housing to certain homeless people. Donoghue was provided with interim accommodation in Council property – a flat – by Tower Hamlets pending the Council's decision in relation to her application as a homeless person under the Housing Act. The local council set up a housing association, Poplar Housing and

---

319 See paras 13–15.
320 At para 62. *Holy Monasteries v Greece* (1995) 20 EHRR 1 and *Hautanemi v Sweden* (1996) 22 EHRR CD 156.
321 Ibid, para 52.
322 See further for early comment Oliver, D, 'The Frontiers of the State: Public Authorities and Public Functions under the Human Rights Act', [2000] PL 476; Clayton and Tomlinson, *The Law of Human Rights*, 1st edn 2000 para 5.08.
323 See Oliver, D, 'Functions of a public nature under the Human Rights Act' [2004] PL 329.
324 [2002] QB 48; [2001] EWCA Civ 595.

Regeneration Community Association Ltd, as a registered social landlord, with the specific purpose of receiving its housing stock; it then transferred a lot of its property, including the applicant's flat, to the Association. By the transfer, the applicant's tenancy became an assured short-hold tenancy. Poplar Housing began possession proceedings; Donoghue claimed that this would violate her right to a home under Art 8 ECHR and that Poplar Housing was bound under s 6 HRA to respect this right because it was a public authority under the Act. Poplar claimed, *inter alia*, that it was not a standard public authority, and the Court of Appeal accepted this. It further claimed that it was not a body performing a function of a public nature. On this point, Lord Woolf said:

> What can make an act, which would otherwise be private, public, is a feature or a combination of features which impose a public character or stamp on the act. Statutory authority for what is done can at least help to mark the act as being public; so can the extent of control over the function exercised by another body which is a public authority. The more closely the acts that could be of a private nature are enmeshed in the activities of a public body, the more likely they are to be public. However, the fact that the acts are supervised by a public regulatory body does not necessarily indicate that they are of a public nature. This is analogous to the position in judicial review, where a regulatory body may be deemed public but the activities of the body which is regulated may be categorised private.[325]

The Court concluded that the role of the housing association was so closely intertwined with that of the Council that it was to be considered as discharging a public function in relation to the management of the social housing it had taken over from Tower Hamlets: '. . . in providing accommodation for the defendant and then seeking possession, the association's role was *so closely assimilated* to that of the authority that it was acting as a public authority.'[326] On the other hand, the Court considered that the raising of finance by Poplar was probably a private function. Also, the fact of providing accommodation for rent was not viewed 'without more, a public function',[327] even where the accommodation being provided had been previously the responsibility of a local authority.

So the finding of a public function in the particular case was not based on whether the function should be viewed as inherently 'public' in nature – using the wording of the statutory test. Instead, the Court of Appeal stressed a number of factors other than that of taking over the role of a public authority providing a public service, the provision of accommodation, although that factor was obviously of great significance. It stressed that the definition of what is a public authority should be given a generous interpretation, but the approach, it said, 'is clearly inspired by the approach developed by the courts in identifying the bodies and activities subject to judicial review'. It took into account the fact that the tenant had been a tenant of the council at the time of the transfer and should not be disadvantaged.

---

325 Ibid at p 69.
326 Ibid at p 70.
327 Ibid at p 69.

The Court thus identified a number of factors which would suggest that a function was public. If the function was carried out under statutory authority and there was control over the function by another body which was a public authority that would be of significance. If there were acts which could be of a private nature – providing accommodation for rent – which were enmeshed in the activities of a public body that would also aid in finding that the function was public, as would the closeness of the relationship with the public body, and that a transfer of responsibilities between the public and private sectors had occurred. The relationship between the two bodies in this instance was close: five members of Tower Hamlets were on the board of Poplar and it was subject to the guidance of the Council as to the manner in which it acted towards its tenants. So the fact that Poplar was carrying out a function of public interest value that the Council would otherwise have had to carry out was not in itself enough to determine that the function should be accounted public. The Court also identified considerations that it viewed as either neutral or irrelevant in making the determination as to the 'public' nature of a function. They included supervision by a regulatory body and the carrying out of functions which would be public if they were carried out by a public bodies.

The problem with this decision is that it demands that a number of criteria should be satisfied other than the inherently 'public' nature of the role in question. The provision of social housing is a public service that serves the public interest since it addresses the problem of homelessness. On the face of it the function appears to be 'public'. The demand that other criteria should be satisfied obviously limits the potential generosity of the statutory term which, it is argued, invites, and was intended to invite, an expansive interpretation. The government's intervention in *R (on the application of Johnson) v Havering London Borough Council/YL v Birmingham City Council*,[328] discussed below, confirms that this was the intention.

The purpose behind s 6 was obviously to impose Convention obligations on those carrying out public functions and to disallow the avoidance of those obligations simply because functions had been transferred from the public to the private sector. But in making 'public function' the central criterion under the HRA, the intention was to single out only those functions that should be accounted public – and which therefore should be discharged in a Convention-compliant fashion. So the function in question, *not* the nature of institution discharging it, should be the crucial factor. This decision however concentrates on institutional factors – in particular the closeness of the relationship between the private and the public body. Dawn Oliver argues:

> The problem here is that not all of the considerations and criteria identified by Lord Woolf relate to the nature of the functions or acts in question, which is what s 6 is about, but are institutional (the institutional arrangements of the housing association) and relational (the relationship of the local authority with the housing association and the prior relationship between the local authority and the tenant).[329]

---

328 [2007] All ER 271.
329 Oliver, D, 'Functions of a Public Nature under the Human Rights Act [2004] PL, pp 329–51.

It is suggested that the first factor that Oliver terms 'relational' can in fact be assimilated to the other institutional factors since the relationship between the two bodies relates to the institutional nature of Poplar. The factor of the prior relationship between Tower Hamlets and the tenant is, it is argued, relevant to the inherently public function in question; in other words it is suggested that it is a factor that the court could properly take into account as a functional factor. The Court of Appeal did identify a number of functional factors, of which that was one, but failed to confine its findings to them.

The same tendency was evident in *R (on the application of Heather) v Leonard Cheshire Foundation*[330] in which it was found that the body in question was not carrying out a public function. The Foundation (hereafter LCF; it should be noted that LCF is the UK's leading voluntary sector provider of care and support services for the disabled) was a large charitable trust providing residential care homes for those with disabilities. The claimants, who had been placed in the home run by LCF by social services under s 26 National Assistance Act 1948, were long-stay residents in it. Their fees were partly paid from their benefits and partly by the local authority. The claimants had been promised that it would be their home for life. The LCF decided to close the home, and the claimants sought to challenge this decision by way of judicial review as a breach of their rights under Art 8.

Lord Woolf said:[331]

> (i) It is not in issue that it is possible for LCF to perform some public functions and some private functions. In this case it is contended that this was what has been happening in regard to those residents who are privately funded and those residents who are publicly funded. But in this case except for the resources needed to fund the residents of the different occupants of [the home], there is no material distinction between the nature of the services LCF has provided for residents funded by a local authority and those provided to residents funded privately. While the degree of public funding of the activities of an otherwise private body is certainly relevant as to the nature of the functions performed, by itself it is not determinative of whether the functions are public or private.[332] . . . (ii) There is no other evidence of there being a public flavour to the functions of LCF or LCF itself. LCF is not standing in the shoes of the local authorities. Section 26 of the [National Assistance Act 1948] provides statutory authority for the actions of the local authorities but it provides LCF with no powers. LCF is not exercising statutory powers in performing functions for the appellants. (iii) In truth, all that [counsel on behalf of the applicants] can rely upon is the fact that if LCF is not performing a public function the appellants would not be able to rely upon art 8 as against LCF. However, this is a circular argument. If LCF was performing

---

330 [2002] 2 All ER 936; [2002] EWCA Civ 366. For discussion see Sachdeva, V [2002] JR Law 249. See for the first instance decision: [2001] EWHC Admin 429 [2001] ACD 75. For discussion see Johnston [2001] JR 250. See also Carss-Frisk QC, M, 'Public Authorities: The Developing Definition' [2002] EHRLR 319.

331 At para 35.

332 He relied on the case of *R v HM Treasury ex parte Cambridge University* [2000] 1 WLR 2514 (ECJ) at pp 2523 2534/5, argued as relevant on behalf of LCF, as an interesting illustration in relation to European Union legislation in different terms to s 6.

a public function, that would mean that the appellants could rely in relation to that function on art 8, but, if the situation is otherwise, art 8 cannot change the appropriate classification of the function. On the approach adopted in *Donoghue*, it can be said that LCF is clearly not performing any public function.

The court thus held that this was not a case where the local authority was trying to divest itself of its obligations under Art 8 by contracting out its obligations under the National Assistance Act 1948. The local authority still retained its obligations under Art 8. The court noted that if the placements in the home had begun after the HRA came into force it would have been possible for the residents to require the local authority to ensure that their rights under Art 8 were protected by contract. The Court identified three decisive factors which led it to the conclusion that LCF's functions were not public. The home was publicly funded, but there was no other evidence of a 'public flavour' to the activities of LCF. It was not, it was found, standing in the shoes of the local authority. It was noted that the nature of the service provided by LCF did not differ between those residents of the Home who were publicly funded and those who were privately funded. The fact that the claimants would lose the protection of Art 8 against LCF if it was not viewed as performing a public function was viewed as a circular argument. It was observed that the need to secure the protection of Art 8 could not in itself change the classification of a function.

It is argued that this decision is also out of accord with the purpose behind s 6. In a number of respects this appeared to be a case tailor-made for the use of s 6 to impose Convention obligations on a particular body. The function in question – the provision of accommodation to a particularly vulnerable group in society – had been placed on a statutory basis in order to address a social need. The local authority's function in addressing that need was taken over by LCF in the sense that persons in the home in the position of the claimants were there due to the discharge by the local authority of its statutory obligations. In that sense LCF *was* standing in the shoes of the local authority. The fact that in such circumstances, depending on timing in relation to the HRA, residents could protect their rights through a contract with the public body misses the point of s 6 – it should not be necessary to impose contractual obligations on a body due to its institutional status to adhere to the Convention since under s 6 those obligations should be imposed due to the nature of the function in question. As McDermont observes, this decision 'reject[ed] by implication any 'public interest' arguments'.[333]

In *R (A) v Partnerships in Care Ltd*,[334] however, the High Court took a stance that did accept public interest arguments and which, it is argued, was more in accord with the spirit of s 6. This decision was handed down before the decision of the Court of Appeal in *Cheshire*. The managers of a private psychiatric hospital decided to alter the nature of care provided in one of its wards. A detained patient brought a challenge to the hospital's decision to change the nature of a ward's activities with the result that

---

333 McDermont, M, 'The Elusive Nature of the 'Public Function': *Poplar Housing and Regeneration Community Association Ltd v Donoghue*' (2003) 66(1) MLR 113, at 121.
334 [2002] EWHC 529.

there would be less treatment available for those who were mentally ill. The issue was as to the legality of that decision. A preliminary issue arose as to whether in taking that decision the hospital was acting as a functional public authority under s 6. In other words, was the provision of the treatment for the mentally ill a public function? It was found that the reason for the hospital's decision, which was that staff had left, should not be viewed as having an effect on the nature of the function at issue. There was also a public interest in the provision of adequate facilities, since the detention of the patients might otherwise be prolonged. It was found to be decisive that the hospital was under a statutory duty to provide adequate professional staff and adequate treatment facilities. The Court also thought it significant that the patients' Health Authority had probably discharged its statutory obligations, but those placed on the hospital were freestanding. The functions at issue, the provision of staff and facilities, had a 'statutory underpinning'. Further, detained patients had no choice about receiving the service; their position was therefore analogous to that of those detained in private prisons. Keith J held that the decision was an act of a public nature, and was also amenable to judicial review. The two issues, it was found, would stand together. So the Court found that such a hospital would be a public authority as far as the functions of making the arrangements for the level of care to be provided were concerned.

Public interest factors were also found to be relevant in the decision of the House of Lords in *Aston Cantlow v Wallbank*.[335] Having decided that a PCC was not a core public authority, as discussed above, the question still remained whether the action of the parochial church council in seeking to enforce liability to repair the church should be characterised as an aspect of a public function. In other words, was the parish council to be viewed as a functional public authority acting in a public function? Lord Nicholls said on the general test for 'public authority' under the HRA:

> What, then, is the touchstone to be used in deciding whether a function is public [for the purpose of s 6(3)]? Clearly there is no single test of universal application. There cannot be, given the diverse nature of governmental functions and the variety of means by which these functions are discharged today. Factors to be taken into account include the extent to which in carrying out the relevant function the body is publicly funded, or is exercising statutory powers, or is taking the place of central government or local authorities, or is providing a public service.[336]

In considering the 'public' nature of functions he took account, as noted above, of factors such as 'the possession of special powers, democratic accountability, public funding in whole or in part, an obligation to act only in the public interest, and a statutory constitution'.[337]

The majority of the House of Lords found that the PCC was a functional authority; but went on to decide that the PCC was not carrying out a public function in this particular instance. Lord Hope found that:

---

335 [2004] 1 AC 546 [2003] 3 WLR 283.
336 Ibid at para 12.
337 Ibid at para 8.

[I]t may be said that, as the church is a historic building which is open to the public, it is in the public interest that these repairs should be carried out. [But] the nature of the act is to be found in the nature of the obligation which the PCC is seeking to enforce. It is seeking to enforce a civil debt. The function which it is performing has nothing to do with the responsibilities which are owed to the public by the state. The nature of the act is to be found in the nature of the obligation which the PCC is seeking to enforce . . . [namely] a civil debt. The function it is performing has nothing to do with the responsibilities which are owed to the public by the state.[338]

The Court of Appeal had seen the liability as a tax and therefore as pertaining to a public function because it was enforced on people who were not necessarily church members and, using circular reasoning, because it was imposed by a public authority. The House of Lords saw it as a civil liability that arose from occupation of a particular type of land. It was stressed in particular that the liability was taken on with notice – and therefore voluntarily – when purchasing the land. This, it was found, distinguished it from a tax,[339] which would apply generally.

The Lords appeared to focus more on a generous functional approach than the Court of Appeal had been doing. But in *R v Hampshire Farmers Market ex parte Beer*,[340] the Court of Appeal returned to its largely institutional approach. It noted that neither *Poplar* nor *Leonard Cheshire* had been overruled or expressly disapproved by the House of Lords.[341] Having done so, it went on to apply an approach in which institutional factors played an important part. It held that the question under the HRA would remain the same as that under judicial review unless the Strasbourg case law required otherwise. The Court of Appeal concluded that the farmers' market was a public authority. This was first because the power of access to a public market had a public element or flavour.[342] Second, it was because the market owed its existence to the local authority and had stepped into its shoes, in the sense that it performed functions which had previously been performed by the local authority.[343] Further, the company exercised public functions so as to be amenable to judicial review, and therefore it was also a public authority under the HRA.

In the recent case of *R (on the application of Johnson) v Havering London Borough Council*;[344] *YL v Birmingham City Council*[345] the Court of Appeal again returned to the question of defining a public function under s 6. The claimants in both sets of appeals in *Johnson v Havering* and in *YL v Birmingham City Council* were residents in a care home maintained by the defendant local authority under the provisions of s 21 of the National Assistance Act 1948. The local authorities decided to transfer their accommodation into private sector control. The claimants sought to prevent the

---

338 Ibid at para 64.
339 Ibid at para 66, *per* Lord Hobhouse.
340 [2003] EWCA Civ 1056.
341 *Hampshire*, op. cit., at para 15.
342 *Leonard Cheshire*, op. cit., at para 30.
343 *Hampshire*, op. cit., at paras 35–36.
344 [2007] EWCA Civ 26.
345 [2007] EWCA Civ 27. The approach of the Court of Appeal was confirmed when the case reached the House of Lords: [2007] UKHL 27, although, arguably, the Lords relied on *functional* rather than institutional factors in finding that the care home was *not* a functional public authority.

transfer, arguing that it would amount to a breach of the residents' rights under the European Convention on Human Rights, principally under Art 8. The two appeals were heard together since they raised similar issues of public importance.

In *Johnson* the key point of the appellants' complaint was that as a result of the transfer they would lose a remedy that they would have been able to deploy to assert Art 8 protection against the local authority directly. The Council, it was argued, would be removing or diminishing the human rights that they formerly guaranteed to the claimants. Therefore in discharging its statutory obligations to the claimants under ss 21 and 26, the Council would be failing to ensure real and effective protection of their rights and so it would be acting incompatibly with the Convention and unlawfully under s 6 HRA. The Court of Appeal dismissed this argument on various grounds. It followed the previous decision of the Court of Appeal in *R (on the application of Heather) v Leonard Cheshire Foundation*[346] to the effect that in the event of a transfer of obligations by a public authority to a private care home, the home would not be viewed as 'exercising functions of a public nature' under s 6. (As will be seen below, the argument that that decision was inconsistent with that of the House of Lords in *Aston Cantlow* was not accepted.) The Court of Appeal considered in any event that it was doubtful whether Art 8 placed on a member state an obligation to make welfare provision of the type and extent required by s 21 of the 1948 Act. It also noted that the public authority would continue to have Art 8 obligations towards a resident, as well as its s 21 obligations, notwithstanding the transfer.

In *YL* it also had to be determined whether a private care home was a 'public authority.' In *YL*'s case the court was concerned only with the preliminary issue whether the private care home, when accommodating the claimant under arrangements made with the Council under the 1948 Act, was exercising a public function for the purposes of s 6(3)(b). The Court of Appeal again noted its earlier decision in *Cheshire*, where the status of the care home in that case was not materially different from that of the home at issue on the facts in *YL*. The Secretary of State however intervened, submitting that *Cheshire* was wrongly decided, on the basis that it was inconsistent with Strasbourg authority, and that it could not stand with the subsequent decision of the House of Lords in *Aston Cantlow*.

As indicated above, the judgment in *Aston Cantlow* dealt primarily with the issue of what is a 'core' public authority. But the House did deal briefly with the issue of what qualified as a 'hybrid' public authority. It found that the courts should have regard to the Strasbourg jurisprudence. It also said that domestic cases addressing amenability to judicial review do not provide the 'touchstone', although they can provide useful guidance. The Lords also said, as considered above, that if the body in question is 'taking the place of Central Government or the local authority' and is providing 'a public service' those factors are relevant to determining whether that body is exercising functions of a public nature under s 6(3)(b) HRA. The Court of Appeal rejected the Secretary of State's submission that *Aston Cantlow* had overruled the decision in *Cheshire*. The Court said that it was bound to follow both the reasoning and the decision in the factually similar *Leonard Cheshire Foundation*. The Court of Appeal further noted that in its previous decision in *R (on the application of Beer) v Hampshire Farmers Market Ltd,*[347] the Court of Appeal on that occasion did not accept that *Aston Cantlow* had necessarily disturbed the judgment in *Cheshire*, which it considered to remain good law.

The stance of the Court indicated that it took the same view as had been taken in the previous Court of Appeal decisions. It found that a state may be found to have breached a Convention right if it arranges its legislative system in such a way as to fail to enable or facilitate conduct consistent with the Convention by a private party. Further it found that the state, in its administrative rather than its legislative capacity, cannot avoid one of its own Convention responsibilities by delegating that responsibility to a private body. It also noted in relation to the facts of the instant case that the state could be impleaded for the European Court of Human Rights in a care home case because of the inadequacy of its judicial provision. This, it said, arose from a positive obligation of the state, under Art 8, to respect, and therefore to promote, the interests of private and family life. The effect of all the European Court of Human Rights authorities, it found, is that there are various ways in which complaints about the conduct or policy of a private care home might be brought before that Court, but none of them would involve or require any finding or assumption that the care home was itself a 'public authority'.

The Court had the opportunity of providing some detailed guidance as to what it considered the test of general application to be, taking into account the observations of the House of Lords in *Aston Cantlow*, and the role of Strasbourg case law. However, the Court declined to provide such guidance, and indicated some general principles only. It will be argued below that these comments failed to clarify the test for determining that bodies are hybrid public authorities, and indeed that they muddy the waters still further. Buxton, LJ said:[348]

> I therefore venture to suggest that the approach to the issue of whether a particular body is a (hybrid) 'public authority' should respect the instrumental nature of section 6 of the 1998 Act, and its purpose in promoting access to the Convention jurisprudence. That does not exclude the conclusion that a hybrid body may be directly impleaded in the protection of some Convention rights but not of others. Nor does it exclude consideration of the necessity of imposing liability on a body even where that significantly distorts the balance required by some articles of the Convention. What is not likely to be helpful is to ask whether in performing a particular function a hybrid body falls under the Convention for all purposes and at all times, in the same way as the status of a core public authority is fixed without reference to the instant context.

Thus the Court concluded that the private care home in accommodating the appellants was not performing the functions of a public authority under s 6(3)(b) of the 1998 Act. In so finding it reaffirmed its own approach to the public function issue rather than that of the House of Lords, despite the attempt by the Secretary of State of Constitutional Affairs, intervening in the case, to persuade it that its approach was out of kilter with

---

347   [2003] All ER 356.
348   [2007] EWCA Civ 26 at para 78.

that of the Lords in *Aston Cantlow*. It had been hoped in the *Johnson* case, given the intervention of several key parties, including the Secretary of State of Constitutional Affairs, that the confusion surrounding the 'public function' test might be resolved and a clear test might emerge. The case however failed to produce such a test, which must wait until and if the House of Lords considers the matter on appeal.

The Court of Appeal's conclusion that it was bound by its previous decision in *Cheshire*, was unsurprising. Its general observations as to the scope of s 6(3)(b) re-emphasise the uncertainty in this area, and make it more imperative that a clear test is laid down. The observation that 'a hybrid body may be directly impleaded in the protection of some Convention rights but not of others' runs counter to s 6(3)(b) HRA. If a body is exercising a public function it must be bound in respect of that function by all the Convention rights in Sched 1 HRA.

It is argued that the observation that the Strasbourg authorities do not require that care homes should be deemed public authorities in order for states to satisfy their Art 8 obligations completely misses the point of the HRA. The European Court of Human Rights and the domestic courts are placed in very different situations in relation to applicants. At Strasbourg, the state would be the respondent where it was argued that the legislative arrangements in the state meant that residents in private care homes were not receiving their Art 8 rights. Domestically, either remedies can be claimed against the care home itself, or no remedy can be made available, via court action. The purpose of ss 6–9 HRA was to provide for the delivery of effective remedies in the domestic courts. If the term 'public function' is defined too narrowly, that creates a situation where claimants could obtain a remedy at Strasbourg, by claiming against the state, but could not obtain it directly, under the HRA. It is suggested that the Court did not take fully into account the purpose behind ss 6–9 HRA, as stressed by Lord Hope in *Aston Cantlow:*[349]

> There is one vital step that is missing from the Court of Appeal's analysis. It is not mentioned expressly in the Human Rights Act 1998, but it is crucial to a proper understanding of the balance which sections 6 to 9 of the Act seek to strike between the position of public authorities on the one hand and private persons on the other. The purpose of these sections is to provide a remedial structure in domestic law for the rights guaranteed by the Convention. It is the obligation of states which have ratified the Convention to secure to everyone within their jurisdiction the rights and freedoms which it protects . . . The source of this obligation is article 13. It was omitted from the articles mentioned in section 1(1) which defines the meaning of the expression 'the Convention rights', as the purpose of sections 6 to 9 was to fulfil the obligation which it sets out. But it provides the background against which one must examine the scheme which these sections provide.'

Critiquing the tests for 'public function'

Dawn Oliver has pointed out that a corollary of drawing as many bodies as possible into the category of standard public authorities is that they cannot also be 'victims' and therefore cannot assert rights against other public authorities, possibly resulting,

---

349 At para 44.

if the 'state pigeon-hole becomes too full' in 'the imposition by the body politic of regulations and checks which could inhibit the development of institutions of civil society'.[350] But this point does not apply to functional public authorities, and there are a number of arguments in favour of drawing bodies within that category.

It is clear that the House of Lords' approach in *Aston-Cantlow* to the public function test in s 6 (3)(b) focuses more upon whether the *function* in question should be seen as public, and less upon the institutional factors relied upon in the Court of Appeal, most notably by Lord Woolf in *Poplar* and in *Leonard Cheshire*. The Joint Committee on Human Rights noted in its Fourth Report[351] that Lord Nicholls said that the definition of 'public function' in the HRA should be given a 'generously wide' interpretation,[352] while Lord Hope found that: 'It is the function that the person is performing that is determinative of the question whether it is, for the purposes of the case, a 'hybrid' public authority.'[353]

From the case law discussed it is apparent that a variety of factors are currently being taken into account in order to determine whether a body has a public function, but the most significant one is, in the Court of Appeal decisions, consideration of the principles deriving from judicial review case law on the question whether the decision-maker is a public body.[354] Commentators agree that this is the case,[355] and it was contemplated that it would be from the debates on the Human Rights Bill.[356] Most commentators considered at the inception of the HRA that this would be the primary, or at least a very significant method, of answering the question[357] whether a body was discharging a public function.

However, the House of Lords indicated in *Aston Cantlow* that the judicial review cases should not be definitive, partly because the Strasbourg jurisprudence takes an autonomous approach to the nature of public bodies that differs from the judicial review approach. This was also pointed out by a number of commentators pre-HRA.[358] The question of amenability to judicial review is a matter that is irrelevant in most contexts

---

350 'The frontiers of the State: public authorities and public functions under the HRA' [2000] Autumn PL 476, p 477.

351 'The Meaning of Public Authority under the Human Rights Act' HC 382, HL 39 (2003–4) 12.

352 *Aston Cantlow* at para 11. See Sunkin, M, 'Pushing Forward the Frontiers of Human Rights Protection: the meaning of public authority under the HRA' [2004] PL 643.

353 Ibid at para 41.

354 See generally on this point Oliver, D, 'The frontiers of the State: public authorities and public functions under the HRA' [2000] PL 476.

355 See McDermont, M, 'The Elusive Nature of the 'Public Function': *Poplar Housing and Regeneration Community Association Ltd v Donoghue*' (2003) 66(1) MLR 113; Morgan, J, 'The Alchemist's Search for the Philosopher's Stone: the Status of Registered Social Landlords under the Human Rights Act (2003) 66(5) MLR 700; Cane, P, 'Church, state and human rights: are parish councils public authorities?' (2004) 120 (Jan) LQR, 41–48.

356 See Straw, J, HC Deb Cols 408, 409, 17 June 1998.

357 See Clayton and Tomlinson, op. cit., fn 1, p 194, Lester and Pannick, op. cit., fn 1, para 2.6.3.

358 See Grosz, Beatson and Duffy, op. cit., fn 1, para 4–4; they rely on the decision in *Chassagnou v France* (1999) 7 BHRC 151, Judgment of 29 April 1999, para 100, in which it was found that the classification of a body as public or private in national law is only a starting point. See further Bamforth, N, 'The application of the HRA to public authorities and private bodies' [1999] 58 CLJ 159. Bamforth argues that the definition under s 6(1) is out of kilter with the criteria used in judicial review for determining whether a body is a public one.

covered by this book since most relevant bodies are obviously subject to judicial review, and it will, therefore, be considered briefly.[359] The starting-point used in judicial review cases is the finding that the body is statutory or is acting under prerogative powers. But the source of a body's power is now viewed as far less significant than the public element in its functions.[360] However, in the cases considered so far the question whether there is statutory authority for or underpinning the function in question has been viewed as near-decisive or as significant (*Poplar, R (A) v Partnerships in Care, Aston Cantlow*). Clearly, the *Aston Cantlow* approach, in which amenability to review is taken into account but is not conclusive, is the more authoritative and also the more appropriate one.

Where a body is non-statutory, a further determining factor in terms of amenability to judicial review concerns the question whether there is evidence of government support or control for the body,[361] while a relevant, although not a conclusive factor, is whether it has monopoly power.[362] A further factor concerns the question whether, had the body not existed, the government would have set up an equivalent body.[363] Similarly, the cases considered on s 6 HRA have taken account of whether the body is publicly funded and whether it is controlled by a public authority (*Aston Cantlow, Poplar*). The strength of the link between the two bodies is relevant; in *Poplar* it was relevant that board members were also members of the public authority. It can also be asked whether the function is being exercised over public land and whether there is a difference between the way a service is provided when it is publicly funded and when it is privately funded, as in *Johnson*. The Joint Committee has concluded that, absent a situation in which the body in question is exercising coercive powers or powers of a public nature directly assigned to it by statute, its institutional connection with government is likely to remain a significant factor in determining whether any of its functions are public.[364]

But in *Aston Cantlow* the House of Lords focused on the inherently public nature of the function, taking account of functional as opposed to institutional factors, such as whether there is a public interest in the function. It is argued that this approach should prevail – a point that is pursued below.

The House of Lords now has the task, after *Johnson*, of determining how far the tests developed so far should be influential, and how far the test of public function under s 6(1) should be allowed to denote a different, more generous ambit. A proper understanding of the demands of the Strasbourg jurisprudence and of the institutional

---

359 An administrative law textbook obviously provides far fuller consideration. See, e.g., Bradley, A and Ewing, K, *Constitutional and Administrative Law*, 14th edn, 2006, Part IV); Halliday, S, *Judicial Review* (2004), CUP; DeSmith, Woolf (Lord) and Jowell, J, *Judicial Review of Administrative Action*, 6th edn, 1999, Sweet and Maxwell; Pannick, 'Who is subject to judicial review and in respect of what?' [1992] PL 1.

360 This can now be said due to the influence of the finding to this effect in *R v Panel of Take-Overs and Mergers ex p Datafin* [1987] QB 815, p 838. See further Bamforth, N, 'The scope of judicial review: still uncertain' [1993] PL 239.

361 *R v Disciplinary Committee of the Jockey Club ex p Aga Khan* [1993] 1 WLR 909.

362 *R v Football Assoc ex p Football League* [1993] 2 All ER 833.

363 *R v Disciplinary Committee of the Jockey Club ex p Aga Khan* [1993] 1 WLR 909. Even if this is case, if the source of the body's power is contractual, this will be a strong indication that it is a private body: *Aga Khan*.

364 Seventh Report 2003–4, at para 16.

difference between the position of the domestic courts and the Strasbourg one is necessary, one that does not fall into the error found in *Johnson*.

It is argued that, in principle, the more generous House of Lords interpretation should prevail; the courts should be prepared to take a generous stance towards the public function test in order avoid excluding bodies from the direct scope of the HRA. So doing seems to reflect the intention underlying the Act[365] and would be consonant with the general approach taken to human rights instruments. It would also mean that the contracting out of public services to the private sector would not result in a failure of that sector to observe Convention standards in respect of such services. This is a very significant matter due to the diminution of the public sector that has occurred over the last 20 years and is still occurring.

Many commentators have criticised the failure of the Court of Appeal in the cases described above to take the more generous approach to the interpretation of 'public function'.[366] The Joint Committee on Human Rights concluded in 2003 that: 'A serious gap has opened in the protection which the Human Rights Act was intended to offer, and a more vigorous approach to re-establishing the proper ambit of the Act needs to be pursued.'[367] The group *Liberty* argued in 2006:

> [G]aps in human rights protection have arisen because some courts have sought to identify Functional Public Authorities by looking at the character of the institutional arrangements of the body, i.e. the extent to which the body is controlled or funded by a core public body, rather than the character of the function that it is performing. . . . The appropriate question for the courts to ask is, however, whether the function in question is one for which the state has taken responsibility in the public interest . . . the best response to ill-informed and misleading claims that the HRA is no more than a charter for terrorists and criminals . . . [is that] the Act [while offering traditional protection in those contexts against state abuse of power] must be shown also to provide visible and accessible protection for children, disabled people and older people at the most vulnerable times in their lives.[368]

The *Johnson* case, which was expected to provide a more workable test and to accept the more generous approach of the House of Lords, failed, as discussed above, to do so. This matter remains problematic and may demand an amendment to the HRA, defining 'public function' in a manner that overturns the *Leonard Cheshire* decision.

---

365   The Lord Chancellor said at Second Reading of the Bill in the House of Lords: 'We . . . decided that we should apply the Bill to a wide rather than a narrow range of public authorities so as to provide as much protection as possible for those who claim that their rights have been infringed'. HL Official Report Cols 1231–32, 3 November 1997.

366   See the Seventh Report of the Joint Committee on Human Rights, 2003–4, HL Paper 39/HC 382, in particular at paras 41–44 and paras 45–74; JCHR, Thirty-Second Report, *The Human Rights Act: the DCA and Home Office Reviews*, esp para 92. See also Kate Markus in 'What is Public Power?: the Courts' Approach to the Public Authority definition under the Human Rights Act', in *Delivering Rights*, Jowell and Cooper, eds (Hart, 2003), at pp 106–14.

367   Seventh Report of JCHR for 2003–4 at para 43.

368   Evidence from Liberty to the JCHR, December 2006.

Categorising specific bodies

At present, the point at which it is possible to draw a line between functional and private bodies is unclear.[369] If a body is subject to judicial review, it is clear that it is almost certainly a functional public authority. Standard public authorities are clearly subject to judicial review,[370] although not necessarily in relation to all their functions.[371] This book is centrally concerned with the relationship between the citizen and the state, and so most of the bodies covered by it are standard public authorities, such as the police. But some bodies are in a slightly more uncertain position.[372] A number of regulators or watch-dog bodies are considered in this book, including the Equal Opportunities Commission (EOC), the Commission for Racial Equality (CRE), the new Commission for Equality and Human Rights (CEHR),[373] and Ofcom, the broadcast media regulator. As Chapter 6 finds, Ofcom is clearly a public authority for the purposes of the HRA. All these regulators are set up under statute and have been given coercive powers and duties that are clearly governmental in nature. They are probably standard public authorities since they are statutory government regulators/administrative bodies. In any event they are functional public bodies since in their regulatory functions they are clearly bound by the Convention due to s 6(3)(b). As Chapters 9 and 6 argue, the regulators of the press and the film industry, the Press Complaints Commission,[374] the British Board of Film Classification (BBFC) and the Video Appeals Commission are probably functional public bodies.[375] These bodies are not set up under statute but they have a footing in statutory provisions, as the relevant chapters point out. The BBFC's functions are recognised, for example, in the Video Recordings Act 1984, as amended.

As Chapters 6 and 9 note, the private media bodies, including newspaper companies and broadcasters, such as ITV, Channel 5 and Sky are clearly not public authorities since they have no public functions. As Chapters 9 and 6 point out, the BBC, and possibly Channel 4, may be considered to be functional public authorities.[376] If so, they are bound to adhere to the Convention rights in their public functions, but not their private ones. The BBC is a 'state broadcaster'; it was created under a Royal Charter – in other words, by a direct act of government. It is also fully funded through state funds – the licence fee. As Chapter 6 notes, as a 'public service' broadcaster it has various duties relating to the contents of its programmes that are designed to ensure that it serves the public interest.[377]

---

369 See further Oliver, D, 'The frontiers of the State: public authorities and public functions under the HRA' [2000] PL 476. See also for extensive discussion of the definition of public authorities, Clayton and Tomlinson, op. cit., fn 1, pp 186–204.

370 See Clayton and Tomlinson, op. cit., fn 1, pp 197–98, for an extensive list.

371 *R v Jockey Club ex p RAM Racecourses Ltd* [1993] 2 All ER 225, p 246.

372 It is possible that many – although not all – of those bodies that are listed in Sched 1 to the Freedom of Information Act 2000, as public authorities (see Chapter 7, pp 632–33) can probably be assumed to be public authorities for HRA purposes. But at present that list can only be viewed as a starting-point.

373 See Chapter 15, p 1595.

374 As Chapter 9 notes, this point appears to have been impliedly accepted in *R (on the application of Ford) v Press Complaints Commission* [2002] EMLR 5; see at pp 846–47.

375 See Chapter 6, p 567.

376 See Chapter 6, pp 530–31 and Chapter 9, pp 848–49.

377 See Chapter 6, at pp 519, 521.

As Chapter 9 will discuss, the BBC is probably not a standard public authority; if it was so deemed it could not also be a victim, a definition that includes: 'any person, non-governmental organisation or group of individuals' a 'non-governmental organisation' within the terms of Art 34 ECHR.[378] As discussed below, those terms are also used to determine who can be a 'victim' for the purposes of s 7(1)(a) HRA.[379] Clearly, it would be strange if the BBC was unable to resist governmental attempts to curb its freedom of expression on the ground that it is a standard public authority. So, although the point has not finally been settled, that is probably the better view. Channel 4 is set up under statute,[380] but it is funded in the same way as the private broadcasters, through the normal commercial means. However, it receives free spectrum in return for fulfilling its statutory public service obligations. As Chapter 6 notes, it has a particular remit in relation to broadcasting innovative, diverse, creative or educational programmes.[381]

In this book the question whether either body has public functions arises in two areas, discussed in Chapters 6 and 9. First, it is relevant in the kind of context that arose in the *Pro-Life Alliance*[382] case, which is discussed in full in Chapter 6.[383] As that discussion will make clear, the BBC in that instance acted in its regulatory role; it refused to broadcast a video in the form that Pro-Life had submitted it (Pro-Life's party election broadcast) since it considered that the video offended against good taste and decency. In that instance Art 10 was pleaded directly against the BBC on judicial review of the decision; the House of Lords did not state explicitly that the BBC was acting in its public function when it acted as a regulator, but clearly that was implicit in the decision.

The other situation in which functional public authority status could be of some pertinence would arise where it was alleged that either of these broadcasters had breached the right of privacy of a person in a broadcast, for example by showing him or her engaged in some private activity.[384] This issue is no longer of great significance since, as Chapter 9 points out, there is now quite a comprehensive privacy law in this country, albeit arising from a range of sources. So there would not be many situations in which one of the laws in question – especially the new tort of misuse of private information – would not apply where Art 8 would. Assuming that the new tort would apply, there would probably be no advantage to a litigant to argue as an alternative possibility that, for example, Channel 4 was acting in its public function when it breached the claimant's privacy, since the parameters of Arts 8 and 10 would determine the outcome in any event. The litigant would obviously prefer to pursue the tort measure of damages rather than the Strasbourg measure.[385] It is conceivable, however, that the broadcaster might have harassed a person in a manner not covered by either the new tort or by the Protection from Harassment Act 1997. In that instance it

---

378   In *BBC Scotland v UK*, no 34324/96 (1997) (discussed Chapter 5, pp 325–26); *BBC v UK*, no 25798/94 (1996). In both instances, the cases were found to be inadmissible on other grounds; therefore it was not found necessary to decide the point.

379   See *Leonard Cheshire Foundation* [2002] 2 All ER 936 on this point.

380   By the Broadcasting Act 1990.

381   See s 265(3) of the 2003 Act. See further p 519.

382   [2002] 2 All ER 756 CA; [2004] 1 AC 185, HL.

383   See p 534 *et seq.*

384   See Chapter 9, at pp 848–50, 883–86.

385   See pp 241–47.

would be worth trying to demonstrate that Channel 4 was a functional public authority and acting in a public function at the time in question.

Phillipson argues that the BBC is probably a functional public authority:

> . . . insofar as institutional factors are still taken into account . . . the fact that the BBC is a creature of the state, rather than having a private status, will increase the chances of its being found to have some public functions, as will its public funding. Channel 4, a private and commercial broadcaster, is much less likely, under these criteria, to be found to have such functions. Although it was created by statute, it is entirely privately funded.

Having noted that it is implicit in *Pro-Life* that the BBC was carrying out a public function in deciding not to broadcast the video, Phillipson goes on to find:

> . . . the least unsatisfactory resolution is to accept the apparent anomaly [of differentiating in this respect between broadcasters] and hold that whenever the BBC decides to broadcast a programme, it is performing a public function, whilst the commercial broadcasters are not . . . Further, it could be argued that since the BBC is a state broadcaster, and benefits from full public funding, it is fair for it to accept obligations that lie upon other organs of the state.[386]

This author agrees, but considers for the reasons given that there are very few situations in which anything would turn on this issue. At the points in this book at which this question does arise, it will be considered further.

Invoking the Convention rights against public authorities

This is a detailed and complex area; extended discussion of the procedural issues involved would not be appropriate in a book of this nature; full discussion is available in Clayton and Tomlinson, *The Law of Human Rights*.[387]

'Victims'

Section 7(1)(a) HRA allows a person who claims that a public authority has acted or proposes to act in breach of a Convention right to bring proceedings against the public authority. Section 7(1)(b) allows a person to rely on the Convention in any legal proceedings against a public authority. Section 7(1)(b) means that Convention points can be raised in judicial review proceedings. But in either case, the person relying on the Convention must be (or would be) a 'victim' of the unlawful act. Section 7(7) provides: 'a person is a victim of an unlawful act only if he would be a victim for the purposes of Art 34 of the Convention if proceedings were brought in the European Court of Human Rights in respect of that act'. It was accepted in Parliament that the Strasbourg interpretation of 'victim' would be used, rather than the wider test for

---

386 See Fenwick and Phillipson, *Media Freedom under the HRA*, 2006, pp 121–22.
387 2nd edn, 2006.

standing which, under the UK judicial review doctrine, allows pressure groups to bring actions so long as they satisfy the 'sufficient interest' test.[388] The UK group Liberty had argued for adoption of the latter as the test, since it is broader. But the idea behind s 7(5) is that the HRA should create symmetry with the protection for human rights provided by Strasbourg.[389] In order to obviate the possibility of circumvention of the victim test by use of judicial review outside the HRA but raising Convention points, s 7(3) provides: 'if the proceedings are brought on an application for judicial review, the applicant is taken to have sufficient interest in relation to the unlawful act only if he or she is a victim.'

The Strasbourg test was discussed further in Chapter 2.[390] It is now contained in Art 34 (formerly 25): a person (or group or non-governmental organisation) may not bring an application unless he or she has been personally affected by the alleged violation.[391] However, as Miles points out, it cannot be said that the concept of 'victim' has been interpreted consistently at Strasbourg, although it is clear that those indirectly affected may be covered.[392] There will, therefore, be substantial room for domestic litigation on this issue. But s 7(3) means that pressure groups cannot in general bring actions claiming breach of Convention rights in reliance on s 7(1)(a), although such groups are able to challenge public bodies by way of judicial review, on the test of 'sufficient interest'.[393] They can use the s 7(1)(a) route if they can demonstrate that although part of a pressure group, they have been directly affected by the violation or intended violation of the right in question.[394]

Thus, although the definition of the bodies covered under s 6 is potentially wide and brings quite a large number of them within its scope, the application of the Convention by using the s 7(1)(a) route is narrowed by adopting quite a limited definition of a 'victim'. But for s 7(3), a non-victim body – normally a pressure group – could challenge executive action relying on judicial review and raising Convention points.[395] Had s 7(3) not been included, a pressure group might have been able to bring an action relying on the wider judicial review standing provisions, but then obtained the stricter scrutiny available when it is argued that a public authority has breached s 6.

Due to s 7(3) non-victim groups with sufficient interest must rely on judicial review only. Thus in a very few instances a dual system of judicial review arises, with more generous standing rules but weaker scrutiny, outside the HRA, while the reverse applies

---

388 See the ruling of Rose LJ in *Secretary of State for Foreign Affairs ex p World Development Movement* [1995] 1 All ER 611, pp 618–20.

389 See HC Official Report Col 1083, 24 June 1998.

390 For extensive discussion, see Clayton and Tomlinson, op. cit., fn 1, pp 1484–98.

391 *X v Austria* No 7045/75, 7 DR 87 (1976); *Knudsen v Norway* No 11045/84, 42 DR 247 (1985).

392 Miles, 'Standing under the Human Rights Act: theories of rights enforcement and the nature of public law adjudication' (2000) 59(1) CLJ 133–67, p 137. She further points out that while pressure groups cannot bring actions in their own name, there are other public interest enforcement mechanisms at Strasbourg including the possibility, exceptionally, of third party intervention which can be used to seek to ensure that the rights are secured.

393 It may be noted that s 11 HRA would bar the way to any narrowing of those rules.

394 See Cane [1995] PL 276.

395 Section 11 provides: 'A person's reliance on a Convention right does not restrict . . . (b) his right to make any claim or bring any proceedings which he could make or bring apart from ss 7–9.'

under s 7(1).[396] A court, although bound by s 6, confronted by a Convention issue in such an application, would have to apply traditional review principles only;[397] the Strasbourg proportionality doctrine would not appear to be applicable. There would be very few instances, however, in which this limitation would be of significance since members of a pressure group might also be able to show that they were victims, and moreover public interest groups can support victims, acting as third party intervenors in cases brought under s 7.[398] But this limitation does apply to the new Commission for Equality and Human Rights, as discussed below.[399]

When administrative action is purportedly taken under statutory powers, non-victim groups with sufficient interest who wish to challenge it by way of judicial review can rely on s 3 and argue that the action is *ultra vires* on the basis that the statute does not give powers to the executive to act incompatibly with the Convention rights, unless the statute is irretrievably incompatible with them. This is possible because s 3, as indicated above, applies to all statutes and is not limited by the s 7(7) test regarding victims. This is a significant matter since it broadens the reach of the Convention rights, possibly in an unintended fashion.[400] If freedom of expression was in issue, in an instance similar to those of *Brind*[401] or *Simms*,[402] s 12, providing special protection for freedom of expression would apply, as well as s 3. In respect of non-statutory actions or decisions s 12 alone would apply if freedom of expression was in issue. If so, the fact that the applicant was a non-victim would be irrelevant.

Relying on s 7(1)

Section 7(1) provides: 'A person who claims that a public authority has acted or proposes to act in a way which is made unlawful by s 6(1) may (a) bring proceedings against the authority under this Act in the appropriate court or tribunal . . .' or (b) rely on the Convention right or rights concerned in any legal proceedings . . .'. Section 7(1)(b) allows for Convention points to be raised once an action has begun under an existing cause of action, where the other party is a public authority. Under s 7(1)(b), there are a number of possible instances in which a victim can raise Convention arguments in proceedings in which a public authority is involved. In the contexts covered by this book, the Convention is frequently invoked in criminal proceedings. Questions of exclusion of evidence or abuse of process could be raised in relation to breaches of Convention rights, and these possibilities are pursued in Chapter 13.

The Convention guarantees can also afford a defence in criminal proceedings. They can also be used to afford a defence in common law civil proceedings where the

---

396 See Steyn, K and Wolfe, D, 'Judicial review and the Human Rights Act: some practical considerations' (1999) EHRLR 614.

397 As stated *obiter* in *Alconbury* [2001] 2 All ER 929; (2001) NLJ 135, para 53.

398 See Hannett [2003] PL 128. There is no express right on intervention under the HRA, but it has been allowed by the House of Lords and Court of Appeal. See, e.g., *Sepet v Secretary of State for the Home Dept* [2003] UKHL 15.

399 See pp 293–94.

400 See further on this point Elliott, M, 'The HRA and the standard of substantive review' (2001) 60 CLJ 301.

401 *R v Secretary of State for the Home Dept ex p Brind* [1991] 1 AC 696.

402 *R v Secretary of State for the Home Department ex p Simms* [1999] 3 WLR 328.

plaintiff is a public authority. Other existing tort actions, such as false imprisonment, which are coterminous with Convention rights (in that instance, Art 5) can be brought against public authorities under s 7(1)(b) with a view to expanding the scope of the action by reference to the right.[403] The possibilities presented by the use of tort actions are discussed at various points in this book, but most extensively in Chapter 13.[404] A litigant would be best advised to rely on an existing action, but seek to persuade the court as a public authority, if necessary, that regard should be had to the Convention principles in determining its scope.

Section 7(1)(a) does not demand reliance on an existing cause of action or claim. It allows a victim of a breach or threatened breach of a Convention right to bring an action against a standard public authority or a functional body acting in its public capacity.[405] It was said in the Parliamentary debates on the Bill: '[Persons who believe that their Convention rights have been infringed] will also be able to bring proceedings against public authorities on Convention grounds even if no other cause of action is open to them.'[406] The action must be brought in 'the appropriate court or tribunal' which will be determined 'by rules' (s 7(2)). As was said in debate on the Bill: 'They may [rely on the Convention rights by . . . bringing proceedings under the [Act] in an appropriate court or tribunal; seeking judicial review; as part of a defence . . . or in the course of an appeal.'[407] Proceedings can be brought in the High Court for breach of statutory duty – the duty under s 6. Under s 7(9), the term 'rules' in s 7(2) means: 'in relation to proceedings in a court or tribunal outside Scotland rules made by the Lord Chancellor or the Secretary of State for the purpose of this section or rules of court . . .'. Claims go to the appropriate court or the tribunal dealing with claims closest in nature to the particular situation in which it is alleged that Convention rights were breached. Claims, relying on Convention rights, not existing causes of action or defences, might take the form of private law claims or counter-claims, or defences in civil or criminal law proceedings. A number of post-HRA statutes have designated certain fora as 'appropriate tribunals'. The most significant of these is the Tribunal set up by s 65(2) of the Regulation of Investigatory Powers Act 2000.[408]

The possibility of creating what has been termed a 'constitutional tort' of breach of Convention rights was left open by the HRA and by the Lord Chancellor in parliamentary debate.[409] Section 7(1)(a) is able to encourage the growth of new tort actions. Litigation concerning the private functions of standard public authorities, in relation to matters not tortious under existing tort law, could occur under s 7(1)(a), and could be relevant in, for example, the context of discrimination.[410] In an important article, Dawn Oliver argues that the creation of such new areas of tortious liability operating against public authorities can also tend to lend an impetus to the

---

403 Such actions are, of course, also available against purely private bodies; see discussion below of horizontal effects and Chapter 9, pp 825–28. For early comment on this matter see Phillipson, G, 'The Human Rights Act and the common law' [1999] 62 MLR 824, esp pp 834–40. See also Bamforth, N, 'The true 'horizontal effect' of the HRA' (2001) 117 LQR 34.

404 See pp 1306–9.

405 The term 'public authority' will be used to encompass both types of body for the purposes of the rest of the discussion.

406 Lord Chancellor, 582 HL 1232, 3 November 1997.

407 The Home Secretary, 306 HC Official Report Col 780, 16 February 1998.

408 See Chapter 10, pp 1080 *et seq*.

409 HL Deb Vol 585 Cols 853–56, 24 November 1997.

410 See Chapter 15, pp 1483–85.

creation of tortious liability against private bodies, arising out of existing tort actions.[411] As indicated below and considered fully in Chapter 9, a right to privacy has already arisen from the doctrine of confidence. However, the House of Lords is not receptive to the argument that new causes of action against public authorities should be created outwith the s 7(1)(a) action. In *Watkins (Respondent) v Home Office (Appellants)*[412] Lord Rodger held: 'In general, at least, where the matter is not already covered by the common law but falls within the scope of a Convention right, a claimant can be expected to invoke his remedy under the Human Rights Act rather than to seek to fashion a new common law right'. In finding this, he relied on *Wainwright v Home Office*.[413]

Where actions are brought as judicial review applications, they are brought in the High Court and are subject to the Civil Procedure Rules. Actions can also be brought in the county court where a claim for damages is made.[414] The majority of actions brought under s 6 via s 7(1)(a) against public authorities contemplated in this book raise purely public law issues.

Leigh and Lustgarten have pointed out, however, that the judicial review procedure may not be adequate as a means of determining the crucial issue of proportionality.[415] It is far less likely in judicial review proceedings, as opposed to private law actions, that discovery would be ordered or cross-examination allowed. Therefore, there are inadequacies in its fact-finding role. These limitations of judicial review in human rights matters are significant. But it could also be pointed out that, in practice, some persons are virtually precluded from taking this course owing to its inaccessibility, the fact that judicial review may only be initiated in the High Court in London and the extent to which most solicitors/law centres or advisers on legal helplines have awareness of the availability or appropriateness of such review in any particular instance.[416]

Retrospectivity

Under s 22(4)(b): 'para (b) [of s 7(1)] applies to proceedings brought by or at the instigation of a public authority whenever the act in question took place; but otherwise that sub-section does not apply to an act taking place before the coming into force of that section'. Where the Convention is used as a 'shield' against public authorities, therefore, pre-commencement action is covered if, following *R v Lambert*[417] the proceedings are brought 'by or at the instigation of a public authority'. Thus, before the Act came fully into force, public authorities were seeking to abide by it in bringing proceedings, including prosecutions, against citizens. But it was found in *Lambert* that a decision of a trial judge taken before the HRA came into force was not found to amount to such proceedings. [418]

411 'The HRA and public law/private law divides' (2000) 4 EHRLR 343.
412 [2006] UKHL 17.
413 [2004] 2 AC 406, 423, para 33, *per* Lord Hoffmann.
414 HRA 1998: Rules CP5/00, March 2000, para 12.
415 Leigh, I and Lustgarten, L, 'Making rights real: the courts, remedies and the Human Rights Act' (1999) 58(3) CLJ 509.
416 See Le Sueur, AP and Sunkin, M, *Public Law*, 1997, Chapters 21–28, esp Chapter 21, 'Access to judicial review'.
417 [2001] 3 All ER 577.
418 Following the decision of the House of Lords in *R v Lambert* [2001] 3 All ER 577, appeals against pre-commencement convictions are not within s 22(4)(b).

Lord Woolf CJ observed in *Wainwright v Home Office*[419] that there has been considerable uncertainty as to whether the HRA can apply retrospectively in situations where the conduct complained of occurred before the Act came into force. Lord Hope in *Aston Cantlow*[420] considered that the position could be summarised as follows:

> The only provision in the Act which gives retrospective effect to any of its provisions is section 22(4). It directs attention exclusively to that part of the Act which deals with the acts of public authorities – sections 6 to 9. It has been said that its effect is to enable the Act to be used defensively against public authorities with retrospective effect but not offensively . . .[421] Section 22(4) states that section 7(1)(b) applies to proceedings brought by or at the instigation of a public authority whenever the act in question took place, but that otherwise subsection (1)(b) does not apply to an act taking place before the coming into force of section 7. Section 7(1)(b) enables a person who claims that a public authority has acted in a way which is made unlawful by section 6(1) to rely on his Convention rights in proceedings brought by or at the instigation of the public authority. Section 6(2)(a) provides that section 6(1) does not apply if as a result of one or more provisions of primary legislation the authority could not have acted differently.

He went on to find that, therefore, acts of courts or tribunals which took place before 2 October 2000 which they were required to make by primary legislation and were made according to the meaning which was to be given to the legislation at that time are not affected by s 22(4) (*R v Kansal*).[422] He said that the interpretative obligation in s 3(1) cannot be applied to invalidate a decision which was good at the time when it was made by changing retrospectively the meaning which the court or tribunal previously gave to that legislation. He noted that the same view has been taken where the claim relates to acts of public authorities other than courts or tribunals. It has been held that the Act cannot be relied upon retrospectively by introducing a right of privacy to make unlawful conduct which was lawful at the time when it took place: *Wainwright v Home Office*.[423]

Time limits

If proceedings are brought against a public authority alleging breach of a Convention right, they must be brought, under s 7(5), within one year 'beginning with the date on which the act complained of took place' or 'such longer period as the court or tribunal considers equitable having regard to all the circumstances', but that is subject to any rule imposing a stricter time limit in relation to the procedure in question'.

419   [2001] EWCA Civ 208, [2002] QB 1334, p 1344G para 22.
420   [2004] 1 AC 546, at paras 27 and 28.
421   He noted the annotations to the Act by the late Peter Duffy QC in *Current Law Statutes*, vol 3 (1999).
422   [2002] 2 AC 69, 112, para 84; *Wainwright v Home Office* [2002] QB 1334, 1346A-1347C, paras 29–36.
423   [2002] QB 1334, 1347G–H, para 40.

Judicial review proceedings are subject to a stricter rule, since the limitation period of three months for judicial review is applicable.[424] But in certain circumstances, the longer period might apply; a *Pepper v Hart* statement suggests that the one year period could, exceptionally, apply: 'someone with a genuine grievance will be able to pursue it under s 7(1)(a) whether or not within the judicial review time limit.'[425] In *R (Burkett) v Hammersmith and Fulham LBC*[426] the House of Lords said that the time limit for judicial review proceedings could be extended only for good reason.

Remedies

Under s 8(1) a court which has found that an act or proposed act of a public authority is unlawful, is authorised to grant 'such relief or remedy or . . . order within its powers as [the court] considers just and appropriate'. Assuming that a breach of the Convention is found, all the familiar remedies, including damages, certiorari (now a quashing order), a declaration or mandamus (a mandatory order), a prohibiting order (now a prohibition) are available so long as they are within the jurisdiction of the relevant court or tribunal. The remedies include all those available in criminal or civil proceedings. The various remedies are considered at the relevant points in the following chapters. Under s 8(2), damages cannot be awarded in criminal proceedings. Traditionally, the courts have been reluctant to award damages in public law cases and s 8(3) of the HRA encourages the continuance of this tradition in requiring consideration to be given first to any 'other relief or remedy granted or order made', the consequences of the court's decisions and the necessity of making the award. If damages are awarded it is on the basis of 'just satisfaction' (s 8(3)).

A line of authorities seeks to emphasise that a declaration of a breach of human rights should be considered 'just satisfaction' and no more should be required by way of redress. In *Anufrijeva and Another v Southwark London Borough Council; R (Mambakasa) v Secretary of State for the Home Office; R (N) v Secretary of State for the Home Office*[427] it was held that: 'Where an infringement of an individual's human rights has occurred, the concern will usually be to bring the infringement to an end and any question of compensation will be of secondary, if any, importance.' *Anufrijeva* involved three Art 8 claims for damages for maladministration in the handling of housing and asylum applications. The Court of Appeal found that there was a wide discretion as to whether damages should be awarded, and that an award should be made only when it was 'necessary' (s 8(3) HRA) so to do in order to afford just satisfaction. The finding of a violation would often itself be just satisfaction, it found, and damages are to be viewed as a 'remedy of last resort'.[428] The Court further found that the exercise of the discretion as to damages should include consideration of the balance between the interests of the victim and of the public as a whole.[429]

---

424 CPR Sched 1 r 53.4(1). See further on a number of these matters, Supperstone and Coppel, 'Judicial review after the Human Rights Act' (1999) 3 EHRLR 301–29; Nicol, D, 'Limitation periods under the HRA and judicial review' [1999] LQR 216.
425 HC Deb Vol 314 Col 1099, 20 May 1998.
426 [2002] UKHL 23.
427 [2004] QB 1124; [2004] 2 WLR 603.
428 At para 56.
429 At para 56.

It was reaffirmed in *R (Greenfield) v Home Office*[430] that damages need not be awarded. A prisoner who failed a mandatory drugs test was charged and convicted under the Prison Rules 1999 and ordered to serve an additional 21 days' imprisonment. The prisoner alleged that in being denied legal representation at the hearing before the deputy controller of the prison his right to a fair trial had been infringed. The Divisional Court and Court of Appeal dismissed the prisoner's appeal on the grounds that the offence was a prison disciplinary offence and not a criminal offence for the purposes of Art 6. Following a decision of the ECHR it was conceded that the proceedings did involve a criminal charge; the deputy controller was not an independent tribunal and the prisoner was wrongly denied legal representation. On the prisoner's claim for damages, the Lords held that the approach of the ECHR, that a finding that Art 6 had been violated was, in itself, just satisfaction, should be followed and that there should be no award of damages to the prisoner.

A somewhat similar approach was taken in *re P.*[431] The Court of Appeal considered whether the judge at first instance had been correct in considering that a declaration of a breach of Art 8 amounted to 'just satisfaction' where a breach of Art 8 had been found on the basis that a mother had been insufficiently involved in the decision by the local authority to abandon a care plan for her rehabilitation with her child. The mother had appealed on the basis of a number of Strasbourg authorities which she claimed entitled her to damages in addition to the declaration. The appeal was ultimately unsuccessful, but their Lordships did indicate that such loss of opportunity cases could attract a damages award.

Under s 8(4), the court in deciding to award damages must take into account the principles applied by the European Court of Human Rights. The Court can award compensation under what is now Art 41.[432] The purpose of the reparation is to place the applicant in the position he would have been in had the violation not taken place. Compensation will include costs unless the applicant has received legal aid, although where only part of a claim is upheld, the costs may be diminished accordingly.[433] It can also include loss of earnings, travel costs, fines and costs unjustly awarded against the applicant.[434] Compensation is also available for intangible or non-pecuniary losses such as loss of future earnings[435] or opportunities,[436] unjust imprisonment,[437] stress or loss of personal integrity.[438]

---

430 [2005] 2 WLR 240.
431 [2007] EWCA Civ 2.
432 Previously Art 50 under the old numbering of the Articles.
433 *Steel v UK* (1999) 28 EHRR 603, para 125.
434 See as to heads of loss Burns, N (2001) NLJ 164.
435 E.g., in *Young, James and Webster v UK*, Judgment of 13 August 1981, A 44 (1981), pecuniary and non-pecuniary costs, taking such loss into account, were awarded: the Court ordered £65,000 to be paid.
436 *Weekes v UK*, A 114-A (1988).
437 In *Steel v UK* (1999) 28 EHRR 603, para 122, the three successful applicants were each imprisoned for seven hours. The Court, without giving reasons, awarded them £500 each in compensation for non-pecuniary damage.
438 See further Mowbray, A, 'The European Court of Human Rights' approach to just satisfaction' [1997] PL 647; Feldman, D, 'Remedies for violation of Convention Rights under the HRA' [1998] EHRLR 691; Amos, M, 'Damages for breach of the Human Rights Act' [1999] EHRLR 178; Fairgrieve, D, 'The Human Rights Act 1998, damages and tort law', PL 2001, pp 695–716; Sir Robert Carnwath,

But there are difficulties in following the principles of the European Court. One is, as Mowbray has pointed out, that the method of determining the award in any particular judgment is frequently unclear.[439] Also, the Court, prior to the changes introduced under Protocol 11, had no independent fact finding role[440] and therefore, where it was unclear that the breach had occasioned the effect in question, it has at times refused to award compensation. The October 2000 Law Commission report '*Damages Under The Human Rights Act 1998*'[441] noted that the Strasbourg Court normally applies a strict causation test which bars the majority of claims for pecuniary loss; it argued that the tort measure should be employed under the HRA. Awards at Strasbourg have tended to be modest and its practice is not to award exemplary damages.[442] This is a clear instance in which domestic courts could create higher standards than those maintained at Strasbourg, both in terms of dealing with this issue of causality and in creating a clearer rationale for awards, although they will be able to derive guidance from post-1998 decisions taken under the Protocol 11 reforms.

The decision of the Court in *R (on the application of KB and Others) v Mental Health Review Tribunal and Another*[443] set out a number of guidelines in relation to awards of damages by the courts under the HRA. The claimants were patients detained under powers conferred by the Mental Health Act 1983. They made applications to the Mental Health Review Tribunal for the review of their respective detentions. There were delays in the hearings of the applications. In two earlier judgments, *R (on the application of KB and others) v Mental Health Review Tribunal*[444] and *R (on the application of B) v Mental Health Review Tribunal*,[445] the Court had held that the claimants' rights under Art 5(4) (to the speedy determination by a court on the lawfulness of their detention) of the Convention had been infringed. In this judgment, Burnton J considered whether the claimants were entitled to awards of damages, and if so in what sum. All of the damages claims raised issues of principle concerning awards of damages under the HRA. None of the claimants' claims were for pecuniary loss: their claims were for the frustration and distress they allegedly suffered by reason of the delay in the hearings of their applications. In addition, four of the claimants claimed that the breaches of Art 5(4) had resulted in deprivation of their liberty and/or damage to their mental health.

Burnton J first considered the extent to which the High Court must follow the rules applied by the European Court of Human Rights in awarding damages. He noted that the Strasbourg Court tended to award damages on an 'equitable' basis, and its judgments did not analyse the basis of calculation nor give a breakdown between different items of damages. These characteristics rendered it difficult to identify more than very general principles. Burnton J considered it to be understandable that a Court composed of many members from different legal backgrounds should express its conclusions on damages in

---

'ECHR Remedies from a Common Law Perspective' (2000) 49 ICLQ 517. The question of the level of damages is addressed further in Chapter 2, p 34.

439 Mowbray, ibid, p 650.

440 As Leigh and Lustgarten point out in 'Making rights real: the courts, remedies and the Human Rights Act' (1999) 58(3) CLJ 509, p 529.

441 Report No 266, 2000.

442 *BB v United Kingdom* (2004) 39 EHRR 635, para 36.

443 [2003] 2 All ER 209.

444 [2002] EWHC 639.

445 [2002] EWHC 1553.

such general terms, but concluded that the domestic courts' own jurisprudence and legal culture required a more analytical approach. Burnton J next considered whether an award of damages was compulsory in cases where a breach of the HRA had been established. He took account of the wording of section 8(3) HRA, and concluded that there could be findings of infringement of ECHR rights without a consequential award of damages.

The judge went on to consider whether a European measure of damages or a UK measure should be applied to breaches of the HRA by domestic courts. He concluded that the measure of damages should be the national measure. This was on the basis that it was understandable that the Strasbourg Court should apply a constant scale of damages to all cases that came before it, but the UK courts should take account of the scale of damages awarded by the Strasbourg Court and should be free to depart from it in order to award adequate, but not excessive, compensation in UK terms. He considered whether damages awards should be modest and lower than in comparable English tort cases. He concluded that there was no justification for awarding a lower level of damages under the HRA than would be awarded in a comparable tort claim. Applying those principles, the damages awarded to the claimants by the court ranged from a determination that a finding of a breach of Art 5(4) ECHR amounted to 'just satisfaction' in respect of sums of up to £4,000.

Thus the court followed the approach of the Strasbourg Court in holding that an award of damages may in certain circumstances not be necessary, on the basis that a finding of violation may itself constitute 'just satisfaction'. But in holding that damages awards for breaches of the HRA should be comparable with and in line with damages for tort claims, the judgment indicated that a successful claim under the HRA could potentially be of considerably more value to a claimant than the traditionally modest awards of damages usually offered by the Strasbourg Court.

But in a departure from this stance, in the House of Lords in *R (Greenfield) v Home Office*,[446] these findings were overruled; it was held that at least in cases involving a breach of Art 6, damages should not be assessed on the same basis as in tort cases. There was no need, it was found, to go beyond the level of damages that would be awarded at Strasbourg.

Lord Bingham found[447] that 'the routine treatment of a finding of violation as, in itself, just satisfaction for the violation found reflects the point already made that the focus of the Convention is on the protection of human rights and not the award of compensation'.[448] He noted that where Art 6 is found to have been breached, the outcome will often be that a decision is quashed and a retrial ordered, which will vindicate the

---

446 [2005] 1 WLR 673.
447 At paras 9–12.
448 He said: 'Thus the Court of Appeal (Lord Woolf CJ, Lord Phillips of Worth Matravers MR and Auld LJ) were in my opinion right to say in *Anufrijeva v Southwark London Borough Council* [2003] EWCA Civ 1406, [2004] QB 1124, paras 52–53:

52. . . . The remedy of damages generally plays a less prominent role in actions based on breaches of the articles of the Convention, than in actions based on breaches of private law obligations where, more often than not, the only remedy claimed is damages.

53. Where an infringement of an individual's human rights has occurred, the concern will usually be to bring the infringement to an end and any question of compensation will be of secondary, if any, importance.

victim's Convention right. He noted that the Court has 'acknowledged the principle of *restitutio in integrum*'.[449] As he found, the Court has:

> ... ordinarily been willing to depart from its practice of finding a violation of Art 6 to be, in itself, just satisfaction under Art 41 only where the Court finds a causal connection between the violation found and the loss for which an applicant claims to be compensated. Such claim may be for specific heads of loss, such as loss of earnings or profits, said to be attributable to the violation. The Court has described this as pecuniary loss, which appears to represent what English lawyers call special damage. This head does not call for consideration here. It is enough to say that the Court has looked for a causal connection, and has on the whole been slow to award such compensation.

He considered the question of general damages, that the Strasbourg Court tends to call non-pecuniary damage. He found that:

> A claim under this head may be put on the straightforward basis that but for the Convention violation found the outcome of the proceedings would probably have been different and more favourable to the applicant, or on the more problematical basis that the violation deprived the applicant of an opportunity to achieve a different result which was not in all the circumstances of the case a valueless opportunity. While in the ordinary way the Court has not been easily persuaded on this last basis, it has in some cases accepted it.[450]

---

449 He referred to: *Piersack v Belgium* (1984) 7 EHRR 251, para 11; *De Cubber v Belgium* (1987) 13 EHRR 422, para 21). He also referred to *Bönisch v Austria* (1985) 13 EHRR 409, para 11, where the Court noted

> ... that in the present case an award of just satisfaction can only be based on the fact that the applicant did not have, before the Austrian courts, the benefit of the guarantees of Article 6(1).'

He said that similar statements could be found in *Delta v France* (1990) 16 EHRR 574, para 43; *Vidal v Belgium* (Appn No. 14/1991/266/337, 28 October 1992, unreported), para 8; *Pelissier and Sassi v France* (1999) 30 EHRR 715, para 80; *Zielinski and Others v France* (1999) 31 EHRR 532, para 79; *Davies v United Kingdom* (2002) 35 EHRR 720, para 34; *Polskiego v Poland* (Appn No. 42049/98, 21 September 2004, unreported), para 47; *Edwards and Lewis v United Kingdom* (Appn Nos. 39647/98 and 40461/98, 27 October 2004, unreported), para 49, in which the Grand Chamber endorsed the earlier finding of a Chamber. He also noted that a recent statement of particular authority, was recently given by a Grand Chamber on a reference specifically directed to the issue of just satisfaction under article 41: *Kingsley v United Kingdom* (2002) 35 EHRR 177, para 40:

> 'The Court recalls that it is well established that the principle underlying the provision of just satisfaction for a breach of Article 6 is that the applicant should as far as possible be put in the position he would have enjoyed had the proceedings complied with the Convention's requirements. The Court will award monetary compensation under Article 41 only where it is satisfied that the loss or damage complained of was actually caused by the violation it has found, since the state cannot be required to pay damages in respect of losses for which it is not responsible.'

450 He referred to: *Goddi v Italy* (1984) 6 EHRR 457, para 35 ('a loss of real opportunities'); *Colozza v Italy* (1985) 7 EHRR 516, para 38 ('a loss of real opportunities'); *Lechner and Hess v Austria* (1987) 9 EHRR 490, para 64 ('some loss of real opportunities'); *Weeks v United Kingdom* (1988) 13 EHRR 435, para 13 ('a loss of opportunities'); *O v United Kingdom* (1988) 13 EHRR 578, para 12 ('some loss of real opportunities'); *Delta v France* (1990) 16 EHRR 574, para 43 ('a loss of real opportunities').

In other words it has made an award if it considers that the applicant had been deprived of a real chance of a better outcome. He further found[451] that where, 'having found a violation of article 6, the Court has made an award of monetary compensation under article 41, under either of the heads of general damages considered in this opinion, whether for loss of procedural opportunity or anxiety and frustration, the sums awarded have been noteworthy for their modesty'.[452]

On the question whether reliance should be placed on the tort measure of damages or the Strasbourg standard, he said:

> First, the 1998 Act is not a tort statute. Its objects are different and broader. Even in a case where a finding of violation is not judged to afford the applicant just satisfaction, such a finding will be an important part of his remedy and an important vindication of the right he has asserted. Damages need not ordinarily be awarded to encourage high standards of compliance by member states, since they are already bound in international law to perform their duties under the Convention in good faith, although it may be different if there is felt to be a need to encourage compliance by individual officials or classes of official. Secondly, the purpose of incorporating the Convention in domestic law through the 1998 Act was not to give victims better remedies at home than they could recover in Strasbourg but to give them the same remedies without the delay and expense of resort to Strasbourg. Thirdly, section 8(4) requires a domestic court to take into account the principles applied by the European Court under article 41 not only in determining whether to award damages but also in determining the amount of an award. There could be no clearer indication that courts in this country should look to Strasbourg and not to domestic precedents . . . The Court routinely describes its awards as equitable, which I take to mean that they are not precisely calculated but are judged by the Court to be fair in the individual case. Judges in England and Wales must also make a similar judgment in the case before them. They are not inflexibly bound by Strasbourg awards in what may be different cases. But they should not aim to be significantly more or less generous than the Court might be expected to be, in a case where it was willing to make an award at all'.[453]

According to the Department of Constitutional Affairs, 2006 *Review of the Implementation of the Human Rights Act*,[454] there are only three reported cases where HRA damages

---

451 At para 17.

452 He relied on *Nikolova v Bulgaria* (2001) 31 EHRR 64, para 76, an Art 5 case, where the Court referred to to the award of 'relatively small amounts', and in *Migon v Poland* (Appn No 24244/94, 25 September 2002, unreported, para 91), another Art 5 case, where it referred to 'modest awards'. He said that it made this plain in *Osman v United Kingdom* (1998) 29 EHRR 245, para 164: 'The Court notes that it conducts its assessment of what an applicant is entitled to by way of just satisfaction in accordance with the principles laid down in its case law under Art 50 [now Art 41] and not by reference to the principles or scales of assessment used by domestic courts'. He noted that it made the same point in an Art 5 case, *Curley v United Kingdom* (2000) 31 EHRR 401, para 46: 'It does not, however, consider that the domestic scales of compensation applicable to unlawful detention apply in the present case where there has been no equivalent finding of unlawfulness.'

453 At para 19.

454 At p 17.

have been awarded: *R (Bernard) v Enfield LBC*[455] where £10,000 was awarded to two claimants to reflect the impact on the profoundly disabled wife of living in unsuitable accommodation; *R (KB) v Mental Health Review Tribunal*[456] where damages of £750 to £4,000 were awarded for delays in tribunal hearings and *Van Colle v Chief Constable of Hertfordshire*[457] in which substantial HRA damages were awarded for breaches of Arts 2 and 8. The award was to parents of a witness murdered due to inadequate police protection and despite pleas to the police for greater protection. In assessing HRA damages Cox J took account of the character and conduct of the parties and the extent and seriousness of the breach; this included: the failure of the police to appreciate the escalating pattern of intimidation or to consider the need to protect the witness; the failure to implement the witness protection protocol. Also relevant was the minor disciplinary sanction imposed on the police officer concerned (a fine of five days' pay); the enormous distress and grief of the parents, and the failure of the police to make a suitable apology. Cox J therefore awarded HRA damages of £15,000 for the son's distress in the weeks leading up to his death and £35,000 for the claimants' own grief and suffering.

The cautious approach of the House of Lords in *R (Greenfield) v Home Office* is clearly of concern, in terms of upholding the Convention rights, given the Strasbourg approach to damages. Further, if applied in relation to other Convention rights, it potentially creates anomalies. In particular, if a public authority breached a claimant's Art 8 right within the context now covered by the new tort of misuse of private information, the claimant could obtain the tort measure of damages. But if the claim fell outside that context, but was still within the ambit of Art 8, and no existing cause of action appeared to be applicable, the claimant would only be entitled to the more meagre Strasbourg measure.

Conclusions – possible reform?

It now appears that the failure to define the terms 'public authority' and 'public function' created a significant flaw in the HRA. As indicated above, commentators and the Joint Committee on Human Rights (JCHR) have criticised the ungenerous approach taken in the Court of Appeal to determining which bodies are to be accounted public authorities for the purposes of the HRA. As discussed, in a number of cases relating to the delivery of public services by private suppliers, in particular the *Leonard Cheshire* case, the UK courts have adopted a restrictive interpretation of the meaning of 'public function'. The effect has been to exclude large numbers of very vulnerable people, including disabled or elderly people in long term private care, from the protection offered by the Convention rights under the HRA. Since the trend towards the contracting out of public functions is continuing, the problem is becoming more acute.

In an attempt to address this problem, in 2007 the Chairman, of the JCHR, Mr Andrew Dismore MP, introduced a Private Member's Bill in the House of Commons on the meaning of 'public authority' for HRA purposes.[458] In 2007 the Joint Committee on

---

455   (2003) HRLR 111.
456   [2004] QB 836.
457   [2006] EWHC 360 QB.
458   HC Deb, 9 January 2007, col 152. The Bill is listed for Second Reading on Friday 15 June 2007.

Human Rights also published its Ninth Report of Session 2006–7 on *The Meaning of Public Authority under the Human Rights Act*.[459] The Committee noted that interventions by the government in cases in order to seek to persuade the courts to adopt 'a more functional interpretation of the meaning of public authority' had proved an unsuccessful strategy and found that the approach taken by the Court of Appeal in the *Leonard Cheshire* case was still dominant.[460] It found that a solution had become a matter of some urgency. The Committee put forward a range of possible legislative solutions. It recommended that urgent consideration should be given to the amendment of existing statutes to ensure that the sectors most seriously affected by the narrow interpretation of public authority were made subject to the HRA.[461] As an alternative, the Committee proposed that Bills providing for the contracting-out or delegation of public functions to private bodies should provide that the body performing the functions will be a public authority for the purposes of the HRA.[462] The Committee did not recommend direct amendment of the HRA itself 'because of its status as a significant and important constitutional measure', but made the case for 'a separate, supplementary and interpretative statute, specifically directed to clarifying the interpretation of "functions of a public nature" in s 6(3)(b) HRA.'[463] The new provision could state, it suggested: 'For the purposes of s 6(3)(b) of the Human Rights Act 1998, a function of a public nature includes a function performed pursuant to a contract or other arrangement with a public authority which is under a duty to perform the function.'

This reform if implemented would make it clear that s 6 relates to the function that has been contracted out and not to the institution that is performing the function, However, there are a number of signs, which are documented in the JCHR's Report, that the government is not very receptive to this reform or is ambivalent. In particular, it appears to take the view that service providers in the private sector might be less prepared to take over the services or facilities in question if they had to accept human rights obligations.[464] From the government's perspective, in contemplating the Dismore Private Member's Bill or the JCHR's proposals, a straightforward moral choice has to be made between denying certain vulnerable members of society the protection, not only of the public sector generally but also of the Convention, or of ensuring that in divesting the state of expensive obligations at the least a basic level of Convention protection is retained for those affected. The protection would clearly be materially qualified. In the context of tenancies in *Kay v Lambeth London Borough Council; Leeds City Council v Price*[465] the House of Lords found that a public authority landlord's unqualified right to possession under domestic law would automatically supply the justification under Art 8(2) of the Convention for interference with an occupier's right to respect for his home under Art 8(1) except in an exceptional case where it was seriously arguable that domestic law was not compatible with the Convention. A claim based on the defendant's personal circumstances was not found to be permissible.

---

459   HL Paper 77, HC 410, published on 28 March 2007.
460   Paragraph 22.
461   Paragraph 142.
462   Paragraph 143.
463   Paragraph 150.
464   Section 3 of the Report, esp para 62.
465   [2006] UKHL 10.

Possibly the acceptance of Art 8 obligations would create some disincentive to private sector providers since their ability to maximise profits could be affected if they could not obtain vacant possession of property or oust persons from private homes. But the fact that private sector providers might want to infringe the Art 8 rights of certain persons – persons who are not viewed as desirable tenants or care home residents – provides an argument either for retaining the resource in the public sector or imposing Art 8 obligations on the provider. Otherwise, the base level protection of the Convention, and in particular Art 8, is denied to some of those persons who most need it. As far as private sector providers are concerned financial incentives to take over public sector resource are high and would have to be balanced, if the definition of 'public function' was broadened, against the effect of the acceptance of Art 8 obligations.

5 Private bodies and indirect horizontal effect

Private bodies

Private bodies are defined as such by virtue of the fact that they have no public function at all. This category covers, for example, individual citizens, newspapers, and other private companies, so long as they have no public function, such as discharging contracted-out governmental services. Therefore, they are not directly bound by the Convention guarantees under the HRA. This does not mean, however, that they are entirely unaffected by them; apart from the creation of indirect effects under the HRA, discussed below, any legislation that affects them has to be interpreted compatibly with the Convention under s 3. Functional public bodies acting in their private function are in the same position as purely private bodies, and therefore where the discussion below refers to 'private bodies' it should also be taken to be referring to such bodies but only in relation to their private functions.

The division between public and private bodies under the HRA is immensely significant and s 6 can be said to create an arbitrary division between the two. Bodies such as nursery schools, which have little power or desire to infringe human rights, are covered, while corporate bodies, such as Shell or media oligopolies, which may well have the ability, the will and the means to do so, are not. From this perspective, it may be said that the definition of 'public' authorities does not allow the HRA to have an impact that correlates fully with the location of power in the UK. Where power exists, it may be used in a manner which infringes human rights. But the HRA may be unable to address a number of instances of abuse of rights, while allowing certain powerful bodies to use it to enhance their power. For example, corporate media bodies can use the Act and can continue to rely on rights-based arguments for the enhancement of their power. The Act does not directly limit what has been termed 'the ability of corporate media giants to further their own commercial ends while acting in ways that run counter to maximising the provision of information upon which the claim is premised'.[466] In other words, certain powerful bodies are able to use the Act for rights-abridging ends, or in order to curb the expression of the values that underlie

466 See Feintuck, M, *Media Regulation, Public Interest and the Law*, 1999, Edinburgh University Press, Part 1, Chapter 3.

the Convention guarantees. For example, powerful media bodies can rely on their right to freedom of expression under Art 10 as a means of defending their invasion of the privacy of private citizens, protected under Art 8.[467]

Under a purposive approach, a court confronted with a large supranational company as a 'victim' of a breach of a Convention right (for example, a corporate press body invoking Art 10 against a media regulator which is itself a public authority), should take into account the values underlying Art 10 in adjudicating on the claim. This was what, it is suggested, the Supreme Court of Canada failed to do when finding that a ban on tobacco advertising infringed the free expression guarantee,[468] since the arguments underlying freedom of expression were hardly engaged by such advertising.

These criticisms could be and are levelled at Bills of Rights in general on the basis that they identify the elected government as the enemy, not recognising that the elected government can be the protector of the people, who need protection not from it, but from powerful multinational corporations. While, clearly, the elected government does sometimes act as the enemy, through the agency of the police or intelligence services, there is also a need for the HRA to play a very significant role in protecting rights threatened not by the state, but by powerful rights-holders. This point raises the vexed issue of 'horizontal effect'. The horizontal effect of the HRA means that private bodies also to have to respect the Convention rights in certain circumstances, as discussed below.

'Horizontal effect'

As indicated above, s 6 HRA seeks to prevent the creation of full direct 'horizontal' effect. 'Direct horizontal' effect arises if private bodies are directly bound by the Convention in their legal relations with each other. If direct horizontal effect was available under the HRA, it would mean that a private body or person claiming that her Convention rights had been breached by another private body could bring proceedings on that basis directly against that other body. The term 'indirect horizontal' effect is used to refer to effects on the legal relations between private parties arising indirectly – by relying on another cause of action as the vehicle by which the rights can have an impact on the legal relations between the two parties. The term 'vertical effect' is used to refer to the binding effect of the Convention on public authorities.

Thus, legal effects between private parties (for example, citizens, newspapers) are limited to the creation of indirect horizontal effect, that is, the use of the Convention in relation to existing causes of action. In other words, it is argued that the Act affects the legal relations between private persons and bodies although, since they are outside the scope of s 6, they are not bound by it directly. A key concern of this book is with vertical liability – the relations between citizen and state – but the question of horizontal effect arises in certain contexts, most notably that of the assertion of privacy rights against the media; this is considered fully in Chapter 9 on the privacy of personal information.

---

467 See Chapter 9, pp 950 *et seq.*
468 *RJR MacDonald Inc v Canada* (1995) 127 DLR (4th) 1.

Statutes which affect the legal relations between private parties are affected by s 3 of the HRA and therefore, in this sense, the Act clearly creates indirect horizontal effects.[469] The position was initially much less clear in relation to the common law. Even before the HRA was fully in force there was a strong consensus that the courts' inclusion under s 6 within the definition of those bodies bound not to infringe Convention rights was the key to the horizontal effect of the Act upon the common law.[470] As regards the precise effect of the courts' status as a public authority under s 6, this created the area of greatest uncertainty under the Act and it therefore proved to be a focus for academic debate.[471] The academic debate was initially polarised, Professor Wade perceiving no distinction between the obligations of private and public bodies (direct horizontal effect)[472] and Buxton LJ taking the stance that no horizontal effects are created.[473] Wade argued that a citizen claiming that a private body had breached her Convention rights could claim that the court as a public authority under s 6 must afford a remedy itself for the breach once she had found a cause of action in order to get into court.[474] But the problem was that even if this were possible (for example, a very weak claim in reliance on an uncertain area of the common law), it was always unlikely that the courts would accept that Parliament could have intended to allow the distinction between private and public bodies under s 6 to be destroyed by this means.[475]

The third edition of this book took the middle ground in perceiving the creation of indirect horizontal effect under s 6. This position was endorsed in certain early decisions

---

469   It could have been argued that as private individuals do not have Convention rights against each other, there is no need to construe the statute in question compatibly with the rights. However, since s 3 applies to itself, it is suggested that it would not have been appropriate to construe it in a fashion which would have led to the denial of such rights where they would have been afforded to the individual at Strasbourg, bearing in mind the purpose of the HRA, to 'bring rights home'. On this point see Bamforth, N, 'The true 'horizontal effect' of the HRA' (2001) 117 LQR 34. See further Chapter 9, esp p 824. It is clear in any event that the courts have not adopted this stance (see pp 179–80 above) so that statutes affecting private parties create horizontal effect for the rights.

470   See Hunt, M, 'The "horizontal" effect of the Human Rights Act' [1998] PL 423; Phillipson, G, 'The Human Rights Act, "horizontal effect" and the common law: a bang or a whimper' (1999) 62 MLR 824.

471   For earlier comment, see Hunt, M, 'The 'horizontal' effect of the Human Rights Act' [1998] PL 423; Graber, CB and Teubner, G, 'Art and money: constitutional rights in the private sphere?' (1998) 18(1) OJLS 61; Leigh, I, 'Horizontal rights, the Human Rights Act and privacy: lessons from the Commonwealth' (1999) 48 ICLQ 57; Wade, 'The United Kingdom's Bill of Rights', 1998, pp 62–64. See on the horizontal effect of the Convention generally: Clapham, A, *Human Rights in the Private Sphere*, 1993, Clarendon; Clapham, A, *The Privatisation of Human Rights* [1995] EHRLR 20; Phillipson, G, 'The Human Rights Act, "horizontal effect" and the common law: a bang or a whimper?' (1999) 62 MLR 824; Buxton LJ, 'The Human Rights Act and private law' [2000] LQR 48. Clayton and Tomlinson (2006) (op. cit., fn 1) provide a very full discussion of the various aspects of 'horizontal effect' that also considers the position in a variety of jurisdictions – Part II. See also Hare, I (2001) 5 EHRLR 526.

472   *The United Kingdom's Bill of Rights*, 1998, pp 62–63.

473   'The Human Rights Act and private law' (2000) 116 LQR 48. Wade, having set out his position in favour of full direct horizontal effect, 'The United Kingdom's Bill of Rights', 1998, pp 62–64 as indicated above, then returned to the attack, replying to Buxton in 'Horizons of horizontality' (2000) 116 LQR 217.

474   Phillipson, ibid, pp 828–29.

475   See Hunt, 'The 'horizontal' effect of the Human Rights Act' [1998] PL 423. Further, s 9(3) HRA precludes an award of damages in respect of a judicial act done in good faith.

under the HRA[476] and by the majority of commentators at that time.[477] Pre-HRA, courts were already under a duty to take account of the Convention where the common law was unclear.[478] The majority of commentators considered, pre-HRA and in the first post-HRA years, that the inclusion of courts as public authorities under s 6 would at the least heighten the impact of the Convention on the common law,[479] but the nature of that impact remained uncertain for some time.

So under the HRA the courts had to answer two questions in relation to private common law disputes. First, did the Convention have indirect horizontal effect under the HRA? In other words, did the courts, as an aspect of their s6 duty, have to give effect to the Convention in relation to adjudications between two private parties? Second, if so, did they have an absolute duty to render the common law Convention-compliant or were they merely under a duty to have regard to it? Their duty was viewed as a qualified one by Phillipson[480] and an absolute one by Hunt.[481] Phillipson suggested that the obligation would only be to have regard to the Convention rights as guiding principles, having a variable weight depending on the context. Leigh considered that the HRA 'does not formally change the approach to Convention questions in the common law, although there may be a change of atmosphere post-incorporation'.[482]

Sedley LJ made it clear in the important early post-HRA decision in *Douglas and Others v Hello! Ltd*,[483] that once a plaintiff is in court presenting an arguable case, based on the existing doctrine of breach of confidence, for an injunction, which would affect freedom of expression, the court clearly has a duty to take account of s 12(4) since s 12 is applicable in all instances in which freedom of expression is in issue, not merely those in which the other party is a public authority. Section 12(4) requires the Court to have particular regard to Art 10 – the right to freedom of expression. So Art 10 must be applicable as between one private party to litigation and another; in other words, it has indirect horizontal effect. However, Art 10(2) is qualified in respect of the reputation and rights of others and the protection of information received in confidence. Therefore, in having particular regard to Art 10, it is also necessary to have such regard to the other Convention rights, including Art 8. Section 12(4) does

---

476 *Michael Douglas, Catherine Zeta-Jones, Northern and Shell plc v Hello! Ltd* [2001] 2 WLR 992, CA; *Thompson and Venables v Associated Newspapers and Others* [2001] 1 All ER 908.

477 Hunt 'The 'horizontal' effect of the Human Rights Act' [1998] PL 423; Phillipson, G, 'The Human Rights Act, 'horizontal effect' and the common law: a bang or a whimper?' (1999) 62 MLR 824. Hunt's and Phillipson's positions differ as to the scope of the duty under s 6, but the concept of indirect horizontal effect as argued for by both has been accepted by Lord Lester and Pannick in op. cit., fn 1, p 32 and by Clayton and Tomlinson, 1st edn, op. cit., fn 1, pp 236–38.

478 See above, Chapter 3, p 137.

479 See Hunt 'The "horizontal" effect of the Human Rights Act' [1998] PL 423; Phillipson, G, 'The Human Rights Act, "horizontal effect" and the common law: a bang or a whimper?' (1999) 62 MLR 824; Lord Lester and Pannick in op. cit., fn 1, p 32 and by Clayton and Tomlinson, op. cit., fn 1, pp 236–38. This was precisely the basis of the findings in the early post-HRA decision in *Thompson and Venables v Associated Newspapers* [2001] 1 All ER 908 (discussed Chapter 9, pp 906, 909).

480 Phillipson, G, 'The Human Rights Act, "horizontal effect" and the common law: a bang or a whimper' (1999) 62 MLR 824.

481 'The "horizontal" effect of the Human Rights Act [1998] PL 423.

482 See Leigh, I, 'Horizontal rights, the Human Rights Act and privacy: lessons from the Commonwealth' (1999) 48 ICLQ 57 pp 82–83.

483 *Douglas, Zeta-Jones, Northern and Shell plc v Hello! Ltd* [2001] 2 WLR 992, CA.

not, therefore, merely give freedom of expression priority over the other rights; equal weight must also be given to Art 8 as a right recognised under Art 10(2). In other words, Sedley LJ found that in so far as there is doubt as to the scope of the duty of the court under s 6 of the HRA, s 12(4) makes the matter crystal clear where interference with the right to freedom of expression is in issue.

This technique was also adopted in *Jon Venables, Robert Thompson v News Group Newspapers Ltd, Associated Newspapers Ltd, MGN Ltd*,[484] but as well as Art 8, the Arts 2 and 3 rights of the applicants were taken into account and were determinative of the issue. In taking Arts 10 and 8 (and other Convention rights) into account under s 12, as Chapter 9 explains further,[485] the domestic courts clearly accepted in early post-HRA decisions that, as interpreted at Strasbourg, the guarantees affect the relations between private parties.

So from early post-HRA decisions it appeared that once adjudication on an existing cause of action was occurring, and freedom of expression was in question, s 12(4) would apply, thus creating indirect horizontal effect. Section 12 made it clear that the Convention rights indirectly affected the legal relations between private parties. However, it was apparent that anomalies would be created if other Convention rights, such as Art 8, protecting privacy, could be considered in private common law adjudication when freedom of expression was in question, but could not be considered when it was not. So, as discussed in Chapter 9, the courts began more overtly to rely on s 6 in taking all the rights into account in relation to the common law.

The seminal decision in *Campbell*[486] in the House of Lords, discussed fully in Chapter 9,[487] rejected the Buxton and Wade positions, and gave some endorsement to Hunt's argument. Naomi Campbell complained of the publication of details of her treatment at Narcotics Anonymous for drug addiction, including a photograph of her taken outside the clinic. She relied upon an existing cause of action – breach of confidence; however, to provide her with a remedy since the body infringing her privacy was clearly not a public authority; it was a purely private body – a newspaper company. The question to be determined was the duty of the court under s 6 in private common law adjudication. Lady Hale took an unambiguous and clearly stated position on this matter:[488]

> Neither party to this appeal has challenged the basic principles which have emerged from the Court of Appeal in the wake of the Human Rights Act 1998. The 1998 Act does not create any new cause of action between private persons. But if there is a relevant cause of action applicable, the court as a public authority must act compatibly with both parties' Convention rights. In a case such as this, the relevant vehicle will usually be the action for breach of confidence, as Lord Woolf CJ held in *A v B plc*, para 4.[489]

---

484 [2001] 1 All ER 908, HC, 8 January 2001.

485 See pp 902–5, 950 *et seq.*

486 [2004] 2 WLR 1232. See for discussion Phillipson, G, 'Clarity postponed? Horizontal Effect after *Campbell* and *re S'* in Fenwick, Masterman and Phillipson (eds) (2007), see fn 1 above.

487 At pp 911–13.

488 Op. cit., at para 132

489 That paragraph reads: 'Under section 6 of the 1998 Act, the court, as a public authority, is required not to "act in a way which is incompatible with a Convention right". The court is able to achieve this

Lord Hope found:

> In the present case it is convenient to begin by looking at the matter from the standpoint of the respondents' assertion of the article 10 right and the court's duty as a public authority under section 6(1) of the Human Rights Act 1998, which section 12(4) reinforces, not to act in a way which is incompatible with that Convention right.[490]

Having considered also Ms Campbell's Art 8 right, and balanced the two against each other as discussed in Chapter 9, Lord Hope concluded:

> Despite the weight that must be given to the right to freedom of expression that the press needs if it is to play its role effectively, I would hold that there was here an infringement of Miss Campbell's right to privacy that cannot be justified.[491]

Lord Carswell agreed with Lords Hope and Hale. Phillipson observes on this:

> ... both Lord Hope and Lady Hale appear to engage in what can be termed strong indirect horizontal effect reasoning. The difference between the two is that while Lady Hale expressly accepted the application of strong horizontal effect as a duty that must be carried out in each case involving common law actions that are in the sphere of Convention rights, Lord Hope did not.[492]

Thus, it now appears that the courts accept a duty to abide by the Convention rights in private common law adjudication, in the context of misuse of personal information.[493] It cannot yet be said that they have accepted such a duty in other contexts.

In the Court of Appeal in *McKennitt v Ash*[494] Buxton LJ appeared to accept something akin to an absolute duty under s 6 HRA to develop the common law consistently with the Convention rights, at least in the context of Arts 8 and 10. He found:

> ... difficulty has been experienced in explaining how that state obligation is articulated and enforced in actions between private individuals. However, judges of the highest authority have concluded that that follows from section 6(1) and (3) of the Human Rights Act, placing on the courts the obligations appropriate to a public authority: see Baroness Hale of Richmond in *Campbell* at 132; Lord Phillips of Worth Maltravers in *Douglas v Hello!* at 53; and in particular Lord Woolf in *A v B plc*:[495] Under section 6 of the 1998 Act the court, as a public authority, is required not to act in a way which is incompatible with a Convention right. The court is able

by absorbing the rights which articles 8 and 10 protect into the long-established action for breach of confidence.'

490 Ibid at para 114.
491 At para 125.
492 See Fenwick and Phillipson (2006) fn 1 above, Chapter 3 at 136–37.
493 See Chapter 9, pp 826–28, 911–15.
494 [2006] EWCA Civ 1714 at paras 10 and 11.
495 [2003] QB 195[4].

to achieve this by absorbing the rights which articles 8 and 10 protect into the long-established action for breach of confidence. This involves giving a new strength and breadth to the action so that it accommodates the requirements of those articles. The effect of this guidance is, therefore, that in order to find the rules of the English law of breach of confidence we now have to look in the jurisprudence of articles 8 and 10 . . . '.

As Chapter 9 argues, although the courts are very reluctant to take an explicit position on this matter, it is implicit in *Campbell* that a form of indirect horizontal effect has been accepted, which appears from *McKennitt* to impose something close to an absolute duty to develop the common law compatibly with the rights rather than a requirement merely to have regard to them.[496] The courts do not appear to have reached this position purely by reference to the extent to which the Convention itself accepts horizontal effect. The House of Lords in *Campbell*[497] considered that it could go beyond the demands of the Convention at Strasbourg in determining that indirect horizontal effect arises under the HRA.[498] But that stance is in harmony with the approach of the Convention since it demands that remedies should be available which can be used against private bodies,[499] not merely against the state. The dramatic alteration, documented in Chapter 9, that has been effected to the domestic doctrine of confidence in order to transform it into a remedy for misuse of private information, suggests that the courts accept implicitly that the s 6 duty is an absolute one – at least in the context of privacy. The demands that the duty imposes appear to be determined by the scope of the Convention rights, at least in the context of Arts 8 and 10, following *McKennitt*.

This clearly does not mean that direct horizontal effect is created – that citizens can simply take another private person or body to court in reliance solely on a claim of breach of a Convention right. But under the HRA litigants can rely on an obligation of the court in respect of the common law under s 6 that is beginning to resemble that under s 3 in respect of legislation. There is still not a complete consensus on this matter, either among academics[500] or the judiciary. But this appears to be the stance that the courts are taking as the HRA beds in. As Chapter 9 argues, the extent to which a duty to develop the common law under the doctrine of indirect horizontal effect has been accepted places pressure on the courts to go further towards accepting *direct* horizontal effect in that context since the gaps and anomalies appear more obvious.[501]

So while the eventual impact of s 6 is not a matter that can be regarded as settled, it is possible that eventually, through the development of the common law, we will arrive

---

496 See pp 827–28, 913–15.
497 [2004] 2 WLR 1232.
498 See Chapter 9, p 826.
499 See the discussion of *Spencer v UK* (1998) 25 EHRR CD 105; [1998] EHRLR 348 in Chapter 9, pp 816–17. See further *Von Hannover*, discussed Chapter 9 pp 818–23.
500 See: Beatson, J and Grosz, S, 'Horizontality: A Footnote' (2000) 116 LQR 385; Morgan, J, 'Questioning the True Effect of the HRA' (2002) *Legal Studies* 259; see also Morgan, J, 'Privacy, Confidence and Horizontal Effect: "Hello" Trouble' (2003) CLJ 443. Professor Beyleveld and Shaun Pattinson have put forward a sophisticated argument in favour of direct horizontal effect: 'Horizontality applicability and horizontal effect' (2002) 118 LQR, 623. See Fenwick and Phillipson (2006) op. cit. fn 1, Chapter 14 which broadly takes the stance that indirect horizontal effect is being created.
501 See pp 828, 991.

at a position that in its effects is equivalent to the creation of direct horizontal effects for the rights. In other words, it is possible that, in the long term, citizens will not be deprived of a remedy in respect of a breach of their Convention rights, although the body infringing them is a private one. This point is explored further in Chapter 9.[502] But at present reliance must be placed on an existing cause of action in order to be able to invoke the court's s 6 duty in private common law adjudication. Although it would seem hard for a court to resist the argument that indirect horizontal effect cannot be confined to the context of privacy, the question of the courts' duty in relation to the other Convention rights has not yet been settled.[503] Clearly, either statutory provisions or common law doctrines provide citizens with protection in most of the areas now covered by the Convention rights. The context in which it appeared that indirect horizontal effect might be relevant, apart from privacy, was that of discrimination: in particular, since the Convention offered protection against discrimination on grounds of sexual orientation at Strasbourg,[504] there was a strong case for arguing that such protection should be available under the HRA. The problem was that no existing cause of action was available to rely on since the common law was markedly inadequate in protecting persons from discrimination.[505] The problem is currently being addressed by means of EU-driven legislation; had it not been, that area would have highlighted very clearly one of the deficiencies of the HRA, as Chapter 15 explains.[506]

6 The stance of the judiciary in adjudicating on the Human Rights Act

Introduction

Clearly, the response of the judiciary to the interpretation and application of the Convention rights and HRA provisions is crucial to the success of the human rights project. Lord Hope of Craighead, for example, found: 'everything will depend on the ability of the judges to give effect to its provisions in a clear and consistent manner in a way which matches the intentions of the legislature.'[507] Lord Lester and David Pannick have written: 'The challenge and the opportunities for the judiciary are probably going to be the most dramatic.'[508] Clearly, judicial training is a significant factor in relation to the performance of the judiciary.[509] As indicated above, in the whole discussion of the HRA, a number of areas of uncertainty were created and left for the judges to deal with when the HRA was passed through Parliament. This is clearly true in particular

---

502 See pp 826–28, 991.
503 See Chapter 9, pp 824 *et seq.* on this point.
504 See Chapter 15, pp 1519–21.
505 See p 1485.
506 See pp 1479–81, 1519–21.
507 'The HRA 1998: the task of the judges' (1999) 20(3) Statute L Rev pp 185–97, p 185.
508 Preface to Human Rights Law and Practice, 1999. See also Martens, S, 'Incorporating the Convention: the role of the judiciary' [1998] EHRLR 5.
509 The Judicial Studies Board (JSB) held a series of 60 one-day training seminars for all full- and part-time members of the judiciary. Magistrates' training was undertaken by Magistrates' Courts Committees. The JSB also provided training for Chairs of Tribunals and provided a training pack for Chairs and members of Tribunals.

of the interpretation of s 3, the definition of 'public' function' and the issue of indirect horizontal effect.

The interpretation of the Convention rights demands that the judges consider both the competing claims of individual rights and societal interests and conflicts between individual rights. Under s 2 HRA they have some leeway in using imported principles and relevant doctrines in interpreting and developing the HRA provisions and the rights themselves. The often untheorised Strasbourg jurisprudence and the impact of the margin of appreciation doctrine leaves them quite a lot of room for the interpretation of the rights in applying them to new contexts. Thus both the Convention and the HRA create wide scope for the exercise of judicial discretion and for the development of the law. The extent to which they have discretion in human rights claims raises, it is suggested, a number of issues which are indicated below and considered further at relevant points in the following chapters.

The composition and independence of the judiciary – reform

At the time of the inception of the HRA, a number of commentators criticised the judicial appointments system,[510] and in particular the role of the Lord Chancellor in relation to it,[511] thereby making the case for its reform in order to create a more objective and impartial system, with a view to changing the composition of the judiciary. In response to such criticisms, the Labour Government accepted that some reform was necessary.[512] The Judicial Appointments and Training Commission was set up in 2000; it oversaw all stages of the appointments process, but had an advisory role only. In February 2001 the Lord Chancellor was criticised for soliciting funds for the Labour Party at an event held for barristers who would thereafter be candidates for judicial appointment. Subsequently, in his statement to Parliament regarding the matter, he said that the possibility of an independent Appointments Commission – which would have an active role in the appointments process – was under consideration. In 2003 the government announced its intention to change the system for making appointments to judicial offices in England and Wales. The reform was a central part of a reform of the judiciary intended to enshrine judicial independence in law and to enhance accountability, public confidence in the judges and effectiveness.

Following extensive consultation, the Constitutional Reform Act (CRA) received Royal Assent in March 2005. The Judicial Appointments Commission (JAC) was set up by the Constitutional Reform Act 2005 and launched in 2006.[513] It is an independent Non Departmental Public Body (NDPB) established to select judicial office holders. Its remit is to do so on merit, through fair and open competition, from the widest range of eligible candidates. The intention in setting it up was to maintain and strengthen

---

510 See, e.g., Fredman, S, 'Bringing rights home' (1998) 114 LQR 538.
511 See Bradley, AW and Ewing, K, *Constitutional Law*, 12th edn, 1997, p 419.
512 See the Peach Report, December 1999, www.open.gov.uk/lcd/judicial/Peach/reportfr.htm. The Judicial Appointments and Training Commission was proposed: see Access to Justice Labour Party, 1995. See further Brazier, 'The judiciary', in Blackburn and Plant (eds), *Constitutional Reform: The Labour Government's Constitutional Reform Agenda*, 1999, Longman, p 329. See also The Rt Hon B Hale [2001] PL 489.
513 The JAC was officially launched on 3 April 2006.

judicial independence by taking responsibility for selecting candidates for judicial office out of the hands of the Lord Chancellor and making the appointments process clearer and more accountable. Therefore for the first time in 900 years, the Lord Chancellor no longer has the sole power to select the judges to appoint. Instead, the JAC selects the candidates, and makes a recommendation to the Lord Chancellor. He can reject that recommendation but he is required to provide his reasons for doing so to the JAC. The 2005 Act also set up a new Judicial Appointments and Conduct Ombudsman (JACO) responsible for investigating and making recommendations concerning complaints about the judicial appointments process and the handling of judicial conduct complaints

The Act brought about other relevant and fundamental changes. It reformed the post of Lord Chancellor, transferring his judicial functions to the President of the Courts of England and Wales (the new title given to the Lord Chief Justice). It will launch a new independent Supreme Court in 2008, distinct from the House of Lords. It establishes the Directorate of Judicial Offices for England and Wales (DJO) comprising the Judicial Office, the Judicial Studies Board and the Judicial Communications Office. The Act also imposes a duty on government Ministers to uphold the independence of the judiciary.

The argument for the more radical reform of the appointments system that has occurred has a number of aspects, but centrally it concerns the unrepresentative nature of the judiciary. Apart from the likelihood that the judges' backgrounds and experiences may differ radically from those whose rights they are considering, a matter that can have relevance in a number of circumstances, a system that – in effect – tends to exclude women from the highest office also excludes some of the most meritorious candidates, while arguably overestimating the merits of others. It may be noted that in the first 20 months of the Labour Government from 1997, the Lord Chancellor made 17 exclusively male appointments to higher judicial office.[514] At the present time, the House of Lords, which is often the ultimate arbiter in the most controversial human rights cases, is, with one exception – Baroness Hale – all-male, with no ethnic minority representation. So far, only one woman has ever been appointed to the House of Lords. The over-representation of men offends against the merit principle since under normal competitive conditions the representation would be unlikely to be so heavily weighted towards one gender.

The primary rationale, as Malleson argues, for promoting gender equality on the bench should be based on principles of equity and legitimacy.[515] She rejects as strategically dangerous and empirically doubtful the argument that women will bring a unique contribution to the bench as a result of their different life experiences, values and attitudes.

Judges are still largely drawn from a tiny minority group: upper-middle-class, rich, white, elderly males who were public school and Oxbridge educated. As positions

---

514   See (1999) 5 Legal Action, February.

515   Malleson, K, 'Justifying Gender Equality on the Bench: Why Difference Won't Do' (2003) 11(1) Feminist Legal Studies 1–24. She finds that arguments, derived from difference theory, have had a strong appeal since they appear to give legitimacy to the undervalued attributes traditionally associated with the feminine while also promoting the merit principle by claiming to improve the quality of justice. However, the article argues that difference theory arguments are theoretically weak and empirically questionable.

of power in Britain are often filled by persons drawn from this group, it appears incongruous to afford them – in effect – the responsibility under the HRA of protecting the rights of minority groups, who by definition tend to be weak or unpopular. John Griffiths, in *The Politics of the Judiciary*,[516] argues that the senior judges:

> ... define the public interest, inevitably, from the viewpoint of their own class. And the public interest, so defined, is ... the interest of others in authority. It includes the maintenance of order, the protection of private property, the containment of the trade union movement.

The Griffiths' argument, which is echoed by other leftist commentators, has led the left to view the domestic reception of the Convention as likely to lead to a diminution in the protection of civil liberties in the UK.[517] In particular, it is thought that the judiciary, in the UK and abroad, cannot be trusted to protect the interests of minorities and/or unpopular groups, but tends to protect commercial interests[518] and the interests of those in authority.[519] Therefore, Convention rights may be enforced by powerful bodies, including rich individuals and large corporations. Such enforcement can be to the detriment of civil liberties or to the detriment of general public interests of a social welfare nature. This is a powerful argument even to those who do not accept the conclusion which the left draws from it – that the HRA should never have been introduced.

However, the causal link between the judges' backgrounds and their decisions may not be as clear as Griffiths suggests. Other variables may be present influencing particular decisions, and judges, despite similar backgrounds, sometimes display markedly differing degrees of liberalism. As Lee points out,[520] a number of House of Lords' decisions on human rights issues have been reached on a three–two majority,[521] while in others, a unanimous Court of Appeal has been overturned by a unanimous House of Lords.[522] Clearly, judges aspire to objectivity and impartiality, but it is obvious that sometimes they will be influenced, unconsciously or otherwise, by the interests of their class and by their experiences in general, including their sexual experiences.

It is apparent, however, that despite the fact that they largely belong to a particular societal group, they do not always display attitudes which tend to be associated with that group. At the least, it is fair to say that during the Conservative years 1979–97, the judges demonstrated on the whole a greater eagerness to protect the rights of 'weak' or minority groups than did their counterparts in government. A number of highly significant decisions taken in the 1980s and 1990s relating to the rights of, for example, poorly paid women, asylum seekers or of suspects in police custody are documented

---

516 4th edn, 1991, p 327.
517 See Ewing and Gearty, (1997) 2 EHRLR 149, on Labour's plans to incorporate the Convention.
518 The Supreme Court of Canada struck down as an unjustifiable restriction on freedom of expression a Canadian statute prohibiting advertising: *RJR MacDonald Inc v Canada (AG), SCC, 21* September 1995, a decision that could support the leftist thesis.
519 See Ewing, K, 'The Futility of the Human Rights Act', Public Law (2004), 829–52.
520 *Judging Judges*, 1989, p 36.
521 E.g. *Gillick v West Norfolk and Wisbech AHA* [1986] AC 112; [1985] 3 WLR 830, HL.
522 *Mandla v Dowell Lee* [1983] 2 AC 548; [1983] 1 All ER 1062, HL.

in this book in which judges may be said to have acted against the interests of their class.[523] The 'judicial supremacism' controversy discussed by Loveland illustrates this tendency.[524] As he points out, a number of decisions on immigration policies taken during the second Major Government in the early-mid 1990s inflamed Conservative MPs as well as right wing commentators.[525] Certain decisions under the HRA, in particular *A and Others*,[526] have had a similar impact. The argument that the judges will almost inevitably be influenced by the interests of those in authority is not, it is suggested, fully supported by the evidence.

How far can it be said that male judges are able to overcome a lack of experience or understanding, or straightforward prejudice, based on gender and particular sexual experiences? Given the current dominance of male judges at the higher levels of the judiciary, this is a very pertinent question. Rights of especial relevance to women may often come before all-male courts under the HRA, raising fears of a lack of impartiality and understanding. In particular, Art 6 has been used to diminish the value of special protections for rape victims within the criminal justice system.[527] In Canada, the so called 'rape shield', which prevented the defence asking questions about a complainant's sexual history or reputation, was struck down by the Supreme Court under the Canadian Charter on the ground of fairness to the accused (*R v Seaboyer*),[528] although the rape shield law was reinstated.[529]

In 2001, as discussed above, a challenge to a law similar in certain respects to the one in Canada was considered by the House of Lords in *R v A*.[530] It may be noted that the change in the law had been campaigned for by women's groups over a long period of time, and that one of the most persuasive arguments for its introduction concerned the strong tendency of Crown Court judges to allow humiliating questions regarding the complainant's sexual history even where irrelevant to the issue of consent. Women's groups were allowed to intervene in the appeal by making written representations that the law should be retained. Further, an application was made on behalf of the Fawcett Society, a group campaigning for women's rights, to intervene on the basis that the House of Lords is insufficiently impartial to decide the case. The argument was that an all-male court might be influenced, unconsciously, by their attitudes towards sexuality and therefore would not be able to decide impartially where the balance should lie between the rights of the female complainant and the Art 6 fair trial rights of the male defendant.

523 E.g. *Hayward v Cammell Laird* [1988] 2 All ER 257; *Pickstone v Freemans* [1988] 3 WLR 265. See Chapter 15, p 1496. Chapter 13, pp 1281–82.
524 *Constitutional Law*, 2000, pp 587–95.
525 See, e.g., *Secretary of State for Home Affairs ex p Leech (No 2)* [1993] 4 All ER 539.
526 See Chapter 14, pp 1430 *et seq*.
527 *R v A*, discussed above at pp 176–91. It is also possible that the current anonymity of rape complainants in the UK might be challenged on similar grounds under Art 6 or possibly under Art 8 in conjunction with Art 14 (on grounds of equal rights to privacy).
528 [1991] 2 SCR 577; 83 DLR (4th) 193.
529 The reinstated rape shield law (Criminal Code as amended, s 276), however, survived a human rights challenge in 2000: *R v Darrach* (2000) 191 DLR (4th) 539.
530 [2001] 2 WLR 1546. The Court of Appeal considered the possibility of incompatibility between the rape shield provision and Art 6: *R v Y (Sexual Offence: Complainant's Sexual History)* (2001) *The Times*, 13 February 2001; the House of Lords may issue a declaration of incompatibility: *R v A (Joinder of Appropriate Minister)* (2001) *The Times*, 7 March. For comment, see the *Guardian*, 19 March 2001. The provision in question is the Youth Justice and Criminal Evidence Act 1999, s 41.

The House of Lords refused to accept the case made by the group and went on to find that the provision in question could be rendered compatible with Art 6, since s 3 of the HRA could be used in order to allow for the reading of words into the section, allowing the possibility of the admission of relevant evidence relating to a previous (alleged) sexual relationship between defendant and complainant. This was, as indicated above, an extremely activist interpretation of what s 3 requires. In reaching its decision as to the requirements of s 3, the Lords did not rehearse the relevant Strasbourg jurisprudence in any detail. Therefore, it is arguable that the legislative role being adopted was almost overt. The Art 8 rights of the complainant were not mentioned, although Art 8 concerns were considered. It is suggested that this was an instance in which the House of Lords read up the Convention right in question – and read down the domestic legislative provision – the reverse of the position the Law Lords adopted in *Brown v Stott*.[531] This approach may be termed a selectively activist one.

This example indicates the nature of the problem: it is hard to acquit the male judiciary of lacking understanding of women's experiences and of making decisions that at times appear to be tinged by sexism. Possibly, the practice of accepting interventions from women's campaigning groups in human rights cases is an interesting development that has the potential, to address this problem, to a limited extent.[532] Part of a broader solution to the problem is to appoint more women to higher judicial office, especially to the House of Lords. In the case of the 'rape shield' law, the solution, put forward on behalf of the Fawcett Society, was to appoint two female Law Lords in order to ensure that the decision was not taken by an all-male court. It was not expected that this would occur in this instance, but intervention aided in making the general case for reform. Reform of the appointments system may eventually change the gender make-up of the higher courts.

Learning lessons from the Canadian experience

In adjudication on the HRA, domestic judges at times refer to decisions of courts from other jurisdictions, and Canadian cases have been considered with some frequency,[533] although it cannot be assumed that the judiciary will invariably welcome the use of Canadian precedents.[534] Canadian judges share a similar constitutional background with UK judges and Canada has adopted the Charter of Rights and Freedoms relatively recently.

As indicated below, opinions differ as to the success of the Supreme Court of Canada, as compared to that of other equivalent courts throughout the world, in upholding human rights. As well as taking the Court's jurisprudence into account in human rights cases, lessons can be drawn from the Canadian experience that are relevant to UK judges. It should be pointed out, however, that there had been judicial review of legislation in Canada since before Confederation in 1867. It has been argued that they

---

531 See above, p 176.
532 See Samuels, H, 'Feminist Activism, Third Party Interventions and the Courts' (2005) 13(1) Feminist Legal Studies 15–42.
533 See *R v A* [2001] 2 WLR 1546; [2001] UKHL 25, esp paras 76, 77, 100, 101. See also *Montgomery v Lord Advocate* [2001] 2 WLR 779, p 810.
534 See *Brown v Stott* [2001] 2 WLR 817, pp 853–55, *per* Lord Hope of Craighead.

have adjusted successfully to applying the Canadian Charter of Rights and Freedoms 1982. Professor Russell of the University of Toronto wrote in 1988 (six years after the Charter was adopted): 'In *Skapinker*[535] [the first Charter decision of the Canadian Supreme Court] the Court made it clear that it was prepared to take the Charter seriously, to give its terms a liberal interpretation and to strike down laws and practices of government found to be in conflict with it.'[536] Writing on two decisions in which freedom of expression was upheld under the Charter, Judge Strayer of the Federal Court of Canada has said:

> Such vague paternalistic laws had long been recognised as posing a threat to freedom of expression and they could not survive long in a country which had so recently dedicated itself to guaranteeing that freedom. One can only speculate that such laws would long since have been amended and particularised had inertia not been the line of least political resistance.[537]

In passing, it is worth noting that one of the laws in question was a provincial law dealing with film censorship which did not prescribe standards for such censorship; its counterpart can be found at present in the UK in the power of local authorities to license films, which derives from legislation passed in 1909.[538]

Decisions under the Charter have not, however, gone uncriticised from the political left: it has been said that 'the Charter is being used to benefit vested interests in society and to weaken the relative power of the disadvantaged and under-privileged',[539] referring to a decision condoning restriction of the collective bargaining power of unions in *Retail, Wholesale and Department Store Union*.[540] On the other hand, Russell has contended that the Supreme Court 'is sensitive to the left's concerns and is struggling to avoid an approach to the Charter which will give credence to them'.[541] These relatively early favourable evaluations of the impact of the Charter have received mixed support in later analysis. It has been suggested that the Charter 'has transformed the rights' agenda in Canada positively and creatively – sometimes even inspirationally'.[542] There have been, however, a number of suggestions that the record of the Supreme Court of Canada must be viewed as timorous and unflattering since it has failed to take a bold and innovative approach, one which could be viewed as showing the way forward for other such courts throughout the world.[543]

Clearly, any assessment of the record of the Supreme Court must be subject to later revision. A number of decisions of the Supreme Court are considered at various points in this book, since it will be suggested that despite the reservations expressed, they will provide a very valuable source of jurisprudence. Techniques developed by

535 [1984] 1 SCR 357.
536 Russell, P [1988] PL 385, p 388.
537 [1988] PL 347, p 359.
538 The Cinematograph Act 1909, which was concerned with the fire risk posed by films at that time.
539 (1988) 38 UTLJ 278, p 279.
540 (1986) 33 DLR (4th) 174; [1986] 1 SCR 460; for comment, see also (1987) 37 UTLJ 183.
541 Op. cit., p 388.
542 Penner, R, 'The Canadian experience with the Charter of Rights' [1996] PL 125. See further Hogg, PW, *Constitutional Law of Canada*, 1996, Carswell.
543 See Beatty, D, 'The Canadian Charter of Rights: lessons and laments' [1997] 60(4) MLR 487.

the Supreme Court in relation to the Charter will also be of relevance. The Court adopts a purposive approach: 'the purpose of the right or freedom is to be sought by reference to the . . . larger objects of the Charter itself, to the historical origins of the concept enshrined and, where applicable, to the meaning and purpose of [other associated rights and freedoms] . . .'.[544]

The Court has also shown a strong tendency to draw upon international human rights law and to consider decisions from other jurisdictions.[545] It is, it is suggested, valuable to adopt a similar approach to the Convention rights under the HRA, bearing in mind the meagre, under-theorised nature of much of the Strasbourg jurisprudence and the fact that it is not binding. By considering Canadian human rights jurisprudence and jurisprudence from other jurisdictions, it is arguable that the judiciary will be able to settle human rights issues in a manner that will not depend on their own personal moral outlook. As Raz puts it, the judges have available 'distancing devices . . . devices the judges can rely on to settle [such issues] in a way that is independent of the personal tastes of the judges'.[546]

Many commentators have remarked on the growing tendency of courts to refer to the human rights jurisprudence of other jurisdictions.[547] However, the legitimacy of relying on such jurisprudence has been doubted. For example, if a Canadian decision is relied upon which has itself been especially heavily influenced by jurisprudence from other jurisdictions (as has that other jurisprudence itself), could that decision be viewed as having a particular legitimacy because it reflects an accepted multinational standard of human rights? Or should it be viewed with suspicion on the basis that without looking more closely at the possible decisions that could have influenced it, it might merely reflect a selective use of jurisprudence in order to reach a desired end? It has been suggested that the invocation of foreign jurisprudence may merely obscure rather than guard against moral arbitrariness.[548] However, it is unlikely that such criticisms will lead to a reversal of such an established trend. What is needed is a deeper understanding of the use of foreign jurisprudence in domestic courts with a view to answering a number of questions, especially regarding its effect on the legitimacy of decisions. As McCrudden argues in an important article, a systematic examination of this complex phenomenon is required so that we could 'at least understand it better'.[549]

Domestic approaches to the margin of appreciation doctrine

The part to be played by the margin of appreciation doctrine, discussed in Chapter 2,[550] in some form in the domestic courts is not fully resolved. A central issue under the HRA

---

544 *R v Big M Drug Mart Ltd* (1985) 18 DLR (4th) 321, pp 395–96.

545 See Schabas, W, *International Human Rights Law and the Canadian Charter*, 1991, Carswell; Hogg, PW, *Constitutional Law of Canada*, 1996.

546 Raz, J, 'On the authority and interpretation of constitutions: some preliminaries', in *Constitutionalism: Philosophical Foundations*, 1998, p 190.

547 See Nelken, D, 'Disclosing/invoking legal culture: an introduction' (1995) 4 SLS 435.

548 See Ghai, Y, 'Sentinels of liberty or sheep in Woolf's clothing? Judicial politics and the Hong Kong Bill of Rights' [1997] 60 MLR 459.

549 'A common law of human rights? Transnational judicial conversations on constitutional rights' (2000) 20(4) OJLS 499–532.

550 See pp 36–39.

from its inception concerned the domestic reception of the doctrine. Since it has probably been the key dilutant of Convention standards, as Chapter 2 indicated,[551] it was clearly essential that UK judges should reject it as a relevant factor in their own decision-making under the Convention, although it became clear that there would be instances, as indicated below, when it would be appropriate to recognise a 'discretionary area of judgment'. This is a domestic doctrine with some similarities to the margin of appreciation doctrine, but the two doctrines are distinct, although their effects may not always be. As indicated in Chapter 2, the margin of appreciation doctrine is a distinctively international law doctrine, based on the need to respect the decision making of Nation states within defined limits. Therefore, it would not appear to have any application in national law.[552] However, under s 2 of the HRA, the domestic judiciary 'must take into account' any relevant Strasbourg jurisprudence, although they are not bound by it.[553] A central concern is, therefore, the reconciliation of the requirement under s 2 of the HRA with the domestic rejection of the margin of appreciation doctrine, taking into account its international character.

As indicated above, s 2 in its face creates quite a weak obligation, since it is open to the judiciary to consider, but disapply a particular decision. Only the Convention rights themselves are binding under s 6. As pointed out above, the rights appear, in many respects, quite out of date today. But since 1950 they have been subject to a rich and extensive jurisprudence. The domestic judiciary would view a number of the Articles as far too bald and imprecise unless their interpretation at Strasbourg was taken into account.[554] But in so doing it was also open to them to consider whether it was possible and desirable to avoid applying the margin of appreciation aspects of the jurisprudence.[555] While it was clear at the time of the inception of the HRA that the doctrine itself had no application in national law,[556] the obligation to disapply it can be viewed as going much further than merely refusing to import it into domestic decision-making. The judiciary have accepted that they should not import the doctrine wholesale into domestic law, but they have shown that they are prepared to rely on decisions at Strasbourg which have been influenced by it. To an extent, this was the approach adopted in the leading pre-HRA case of *R v DPP*

---

551 See p 36–39.

552 As Sir John Laws put it in 1998: 'The margin of appreciation doctrine as it has been developed at Strasbourg will necessarily be inapt to the administration of the Convention in the domestic courts for the very reason that they are domestic; they will not be subject to an objective inhibition generated by any cultural distance between themselves and the state organs whose decisions are impleaded before them.' 'The limitations of human rights' [1998] PL 254, p 258.

553 The term exhaustively covers any 'judgment, decision, declaration or advisory opinion of the Court', any 'opinion of the Commission given in a report adopted under Article 31', any 'decision of the Commission in connection with Article 26 or 27(2)' or any 'decision of the Committee of Ministers taken under Article 46'. The words 'in connection with' appear to mean that all findings which may be said to be linked to the admissibility procedure, including reports prepared during the preliminary examination of a case, could be taken into account.

554 It may be noted that this is not necessarily the case; the Strasbourg jurisprudence may have the effect of 'reading down' the right; see the discussion of *Khan v UK* (2000) 8 BHRC 310 in Chapter 13, pp 1291–92; see also *Salabiaku v France*, A 141-A (1988).

555 See Hunt, M, Singh, R and Demetriou, M, 'Is there a role for the margin of appreciation in national law after the Human Rights Act?' [1999] EHRLR 15.

556 In *R v Stratford JJ ex p Imbert* (1999) *The Times*, 21 February, Buxton LJ confirmed obiter that the doctrine had no such application. This was also the advice given by the Judicial Studies Board.

ex p Kebilene:[557] although the doctrine itself was rejected, the outcomes of applications at Strasbourg were taken into account without adverting to the influence the doctrine had had on them.[558] As discussed below, it was also open to the judiciary at the inception of the HRA to develop their own version of the doctrine of the margin of appreciation (under a different name) based upon common law acceptance of judicial deference to Parliament and to aspects of executive power.

Discretionary areas of judgment, deference and proportionality[559]

Lord Woolf recently said this on the post-HRA approach to deference:

> Where a court is applying . . . human rights, such as those contained in the European Convention, the court is given an additional responsibility in the case of most of the rights. The right to life and the right not to be subjected to cruel and unusual punishment are absolute rights, but the majority are qualified so as to preserve the needs of a democratic society . . . A balance has therefore to be drawn between the state and the individual and a judge is responsible for determining where the balance lies. This is a task new to the English judiciary . . . How the balancing act is done is extremely important. To be too favourable to the citizen can frustrate the ability of the government to govern and to be too favourable to the government can devalue the rights. To assist the English judges to strike the balance correctly, we have developed a doctrine of deference which they extend both to the legislature and the Executive when appropriate. On matters of national security, for example, a high degree of deference is shown. Similarly, in relation to matters of economic policy. There will be situations, however, in which that the public body whose actions are being challenged is no better qualified to determine the issue than a judge. The position of the individual making the challenge also has to be taken into account. Such is the scale of the change involved in moving from a jurisdiction where the courts enforce public duties to one where the courts are required to enforce public rights, that a degree of conservatism is a virtue. Insofar as this is possible, the objective should be to convince the legislative and the Executive that the supervision of the courts is wholly constructive. It results in better administration, better government and better legislation.[560]

557 [1999] 3 WLR 372.
558 Such applications included *H v UK*, Appl No 15023/89 and *Bates v UK*, Appl No 26280/95.
559 For the notion of respect for a 'discretionary area of judgment' see Pannick, D, 'Principles of interpretation of Convention rights under the Human Rights Act and the discretionary area of judgement' (1998) PL 545. See further also: Craig, P, 'The Courts, the Human Rights Act and Judicial Review' (2001) 117 L.Q.R. 589; Edwards, R, 'Judicial Review under the Human Rights Act' (2002) 65 CLJ. See further Edwards, R, 'Judicial Deference under the Human Rights Act' 65(6) MLR 859; Klug, F, 'Judicial Deference under the Human Rights Act' (2003) 2 EHRLR 125; Jowell, J and Lord Steyn, Deference: A Tangled Story' [2005] PL 346; Hickman, T, 'Constitutional Dialogue, Constitutional Theories and the Human Rights Act 1998' [2005] PL 306; O'Cinneide, C, 'Democracy and Rights: New Directions in the Human Rights Era' [2004] 57 *Current Legal Problems*.
560 'Current Challenges in Judging' Speech to the 5th Worldwide Common Law Judiciary Conference 2003, Sydney, Australia.

It should now be clear – and it is readily evident from Lord Woolf's speech – that the Human Rights Act and the Convention itself leave open a great deal of leeway for diverse judicial approaches. This chapter has sought to indicate that the judges are hesitating between accepting a role in developing an autonomous constitutional rights jurisprudence and merely applying Strasbourg standards, often in a traditional deferential fashion – adding in what Phillipson has termed a 'double dose of deference'.[561] The complexity of the position described below is the result of the reliance on an international instrument and thus on a body of jurisprudence affected by the influence of the margin of appreciation doctrine. In public law cases a number of stages can be discerned in judicial decision-making, and what occurs at each one can be characterised as minimalist or activist, using those terms as shorthand for a 'constitutional rights' or a 'minimal compliance with Convention standards' approach. Although the discussion is largely concerned with public law cases, some of the points, in particular the use of the Strasbourg jurisprudence, are also applicable in private law and criminal cases, and reference is made to case law outside the public law sphere.

Before moving on and accepting that activism is necessary in order to realise the full benefits of the Convention, it is essential to pause briefly to consider both what activism means and what its effects may be. The main concern of this book is with vertical effects in the classic arenas of state power and therefore it avoids the most problematic issues since activism is usually welcomed by most commentators in such arenas.[562] Indeed, as indicated above, some, although by no means all, commentators looked to the HRA in 1998 as a means of undoing the effects in such contexts of years of untrammelled parliamentary sovereignty.[563] As this book indicates, especially in relation to state surveillance in Chapter 10, counter-terrorist and public order measures in Chapters 14 and 8, the Security and Intelligence Services in Chapter 10, such effects are readily evident.

But unbridled judicial activism can also have the effect, in certain contexts, of imposing particular moral views on individuals and thereby infringing their Convention rights. The proper role of activism is to uphold individual rights in the face of state interference or state neglect of the right, not to substitute judicial for state interference, in intruding on rights, even in the name of upholding competing rights. Judicial activism is justified where it results in an enhancement of the fairness and justice of public policy making, rendering public authorities accountable by reference to constitutional principle.[564] The most obvious example of such a stance is that taken by the House of Lords in *A v Secretary of State for the Home Department*,[565] discussed in full in Chapter 14.[566] Activism is unjustified as a means of imposing particular judicial views of morality on individuals. As Sir John Laws puts it, that is a matter 'upon which the

561 See Fenwick and Phillipson (2006) fn 1 above, Chapter 3 p149 .

562 See, e.g., Ewing, KD and Gearty, CA, *Freedom under Thatcher*, 1989.

563 See Chapter 3, pp 116–19. Some commentators, however, have continued to view the allocation of any further power to the judiciary as a dangerous step and therefore consider that the protection of civil liberties should be left to Parliament; see Griffiths, 'The brave new world of Sir John Laws' [2000] March MLR 159; Ewing, K, 'The Futility of the Human Rights Act', Public Law (2004), 829–52.

564 See Feldman, D, 'The Human Rights Act 1998 and constitutional principles' (1999) 19(2) LS 165; Laws LJ, 'The limitations of human rights' [1998] PL 254.

565 [2004] QB 335.

566 See pp 1430 *et seq*.

judges have no special voice'.[567] This point was canvassed above,[568] and is returned to below.

Three stages in judicial reasoning in public law cases can be identified for the sake of clarity, while readily acknowledging that judicial reasoning in these contexts cannot frequently be so easily pigeon-holed, and that aspects of activist or minimalist reasoning are often unconsciously adopted. In some instances of judicial reasoning, two or all of the three stages may collapse into each other. Below, examples are given of minimalist or activist reasoning, using this somewhat artificial staged approach as a deliberate means of seeking to pin down elusive ideas of deference, proportionality and the domestic reception of the margin of appreciation doctrine; these points are then developed in the various human rights contexts covered in this book.

The first stage is to find that the case falls within the ambit of a right and to determine the Strasbourg case law to be applied. In fact, under the post-HRA case law this is not necessarily the first step in the reasoning, but there is normally a point in the judgment at which the relevant Strasbourg jurisprudence is assessed. As discussed above, in *R (on the application of Marper) v Chief Constable of South Yorkshire*[569] Lord Steyn, following *R (on the application of Ullah) v Special Adjudicator*,[570] found that where Strasbourg had determined the ambit of a Convention right, the domestic court would not be free to determine it by reference to domestic cultural traditions. In *N v Secretary of State for the Home Department*[571] Lord Nicholls similarly stated: 'We are dealing here with a decision of the Strasbourg court which created what the Court of Appeal rightly accepted was an "extension of an extension" to the article 3 obligation[572] . . . Our task is determine the limits of that extension, not to enlarge it beyond the limits which the Strasbourg Court has set for it'. However, those findings still leave some leeway for the courts to interpret the Strasbourg jurisprudence as to the ambit of the rights, especially where it is meagre or heavily affected by the influence of the margin of appreciation doctrine. Also, instances may arise which are not covered, or not unambiguously covered by the relevant jurisprudence, creating leeway for the domestic court to adopt a more or a less generous view of the ambit. There may be compelling and exceptional reasons to depart from the Convention jurisprudence; this was recognised in the House of Lords in *Kay v Lambeth LBC*[573] by Lord Bingham. In *R v Spear*,[574] for example, the domestic court challenged the application by the Strasbourg court of Convention principles to the detailed facts of a particular class of case which it viewed as peculiarly within the knowledge of national authorities. The determination as to ambit can itself be viewed as activist or minimalist – and arguably

---

567 Laws, ibid For the view that the judiciary, and Sir John Laws in particular, are, in effect, claiming the power to determine moral and political matters, see Griffiths, 'The brave new world of Sir John Laws' [2000] 63(2) MLR 159.
568 See pp 190–91.
569 [2004] 1 WLR 2196. See p 194 above.
570 [2004] UKHL 26.
571 [2005] 2 WLR 1124
572 [2003] EWCA Civ 1369, *per* Laws LJ, para 37; Dyson LJ, para 46.
573 [2006] 2 WLR 570 para 28
574 [2003] 1 AC 734, paras 12 and 92

autonomous, activist domestic concepts of the ambit are already being developed.[575] But so are minimal ones, as will be seen below. In many instances, clearly, there will be no assessment of the ambit since it will be self-evident that the right is engaged. The key, but not the only, difference between an activist and a minimalist approach at this stage lies in the stance taken towards the margin of appreciation aspects of the Convention jurisprudence that is to be applied domestically.

The second stage is to determine whether and how far deference should be paid to the decision-maker in the context in question. Under a minimalist approach it may readily be found that the decision-maker should be afforded a 'discretionary area of judgment', meaning that the court is minded to adopt a deferential, non-rigorous standard of review. Under an activist approach a court will not readily adopt a deferential stance; it will tease out the factors more properly making for deference – this point is returned to below. The key point is that once the court has made a determination as to deference or no, and degree of deference, the standard of review it wishes to adopt is then apparent.

At the third stage, the court, having settled on the standard of review it views as appropriate, chooses the proportionality test that will most effectively deliver that standard. In other words, it settles on the test that best reflects the standard of review it deems appropriate. Thus, adopting a soft-edged standard of review, a court might take the stance that the decision-maker had not acted unreasonably in interfering with the guarantee in question. At the other extreme – under a very hard-edged standard – it could be asked whether the interference was entirely necessary in the sense that a less intrusive means was available – one that would have invaded the right more minimally. As Chapter 2 indicated, and as discussed at various points in this book,[576] Strasbourg has employed a range of proportionality tests, some of them allowing for a far from hard-edged scrutiny.

In describing judicial reasoning in this way it is accepted that, clearly, a judge does not necessarily consciously decide that deference is appropriate, and then go on to select a proportionality test that will deliver the desired result; moreover, every stage of the reasoning process may be redolent of deference. In *Brown v Stott*,[577] for example, considered below, the reason for adopting a restrained approach to the Strasbourg jurisprudence was that the judges were minded to accord deference to the decision-maker. In some instances the second and third stages collapse into each other in the sense that having decided that a decision is outwith the area of judicial competence, a court may proceed to refuse to conduct a proportionality exercise at all; it is suggested that this occurred in *Pro-Life Alliance*, discussed below.[578] But unpacking the stages of the reasoning in this fashion has its uses in seeking to tease out the processes that are in reality occurring.

575　See *Ghaidan v Godin-Mendoza* [2003] 2 WLR 478; [2002] 4 All ER 1162; [2004] 2 A.C. 557 (HL) in relation to the need for a connection between Arts 8 and 14; the determination that a tenuous connection was sufficient could be viewed as extending the ambit of Art 14. See further Baker, A, *The Enjoyment of Rights and Freedoms: a New Conception of the Ambit under Article 14 ECHR*, (2006) 69 MLR 714, and see further Chapter 15, pp 1525–26.

576　See Chapter 5, p 414 and Chapter 6, pp 539–41.

577　[2001] 2 WLR 817, the Judicial Committee of the Privy Council. See, for the Scottish decision, *Stott v Brown* 2000 SLT 379; see also, for discussion, Kerrigan [2000] J Civ Lib 193.

578　See pp 274–75.

A minimalist approach

At the first stage, a restrained approach to the ambit of a right may be adopted. For example, in *Pro-Life Alliance*,[579] in relation to the banning of the party's election video from broadcasting, Lord Hoffmann said:

> First, the primary right protected by article 10 is the right of every citizen not to be *prevented* from expressing his opinions. He has the right to "receive and impart information and ideas without *interference* by public authority". In the present case, that primary right was not engaged. There was nothing that the Alliance was prevented from doing (emphasis in original).

This narrow view of Art 10(1) is critiqued in Chapter 6.[580]

Similarly, in *R (on the application of Gillan) v Commissioner of Metropolitan Police*,[581] a case concerning a blanket stop and search power introduced as a counter-terrorist measure, Lord Bingham found on the application of Art 5(1) to a stop and search conducted without reasonable suspicion: 'there is no deprivation of liberty. That was regarded by the Court of Appeal as "the better view",[582] and I agree'. In other words, a restrained view of the ambit of Art 5 was adopted which meant, it appeared, that stops and searches would be unlikely to fall within it. Article 8(1) was similarly viewed in a restrictive manner:

> I am, however, doubtful whether an ordinary superficial search of the person can be said to show a lack of respect for private life. It is true that "private life" has been generously construed to embrace wide rights to personal autonomy. But it is clear Convention jurisprudence that intrusions must reach a certain level of seriousness to engage the operation of the Convention, which is, after all, concerned with human rights and fundamental freedoms, and I incline to the view that an ordinary superficial search of the person . . . can scarcely be said to reach that level.[583]

Under this approach, it is not stated bluntly that the primary right is inapplicable; rather, its applicability is doubted, leading to an extremely superficial proportionality review when justification for the interference is considered – for which, in *Gillan*, see below.

If the ambit of the right is not defined in such a way as to exclude, or virtually exclude, the case in question from falling within it, and the justification for interfering with the right is considered, the jurisprudence tends to be applied in an unselective fashion. As Phillipson observes:[584]

---

579 [2004] 1 AC 185 at paras 55 and 56.
580 pp 533–44.
581 See [2006] UKHL 12. For full discussion see Chapter 11, pp 1119–21.
582 At para 46 of the Court of Appeal judgment.
583 At para 28.
584 Fenwick and Phillipson (2006) op. cit., fn 1, Chapter 2, p 147.

when judges are minded to carry out a minimalist audit of UK law against Convention law, they merely examine the outcomes of particular cases – even when those decisions were heavily influenced by the doctrine and, comparing the two, declare that because UK law cannot be seen clearly to breach findings of law made in the Strasbourg jurisprudence, there is no breach of the Convention'.

A minimalist judicial approach to the HRA tends to include a full reliance on the margin of appreciation aspects of the Strasbourg jurisprudence, resulting at the third stage, below, in the operation of a restrained review jurisdiction only, in determining issues covered by any 'relevant' jurisprudence. This does not mean openly importing the margin of appreciation doctrine into domestic decision-making; rather, it means applying such aspects regardless of the influence it had had on them. In a sense, it means importing the doctrine by the back door.

An example of adoption of this model in the pre-HRA era was arguably provided by *R v Khan*.[585] The House of Lords relied on an exclusion of evidence decision at Strasbourg, *Schenk v Switzerland*,[586] where a very wide margin of appreciation had been allowed, without acknowledging that this was the case. For example, it was said in the Lords in Khan: 'the discretionary powers of the trial judge to exclude evidence march hand in hand with Article 6(1) of the Convention . . . the decision of the Court in *Schenk* . . . confirms that the use at a criminal trial of material obtained in breach of privacy enshrined in Article 8 does not of itself mean that the trial is unfair.'[587] The House of Lords, therefore, appeared impliedly to reassure itself that sufficiently high standards would be maintained by following *Schenk*. But the decision in *Schenk* in fact confirms that admitting evidence obtained due to such a breach is within the margin of appreciation conceded to the national courts; it does not therefore confirm that a domestic practice of so doing meets nationally recognised standards of procedural justice.[588]

In various contexts covered by this book the balance struck in the common law between civil liberties and societal concerns, such as public order, has already been found to accord with the Convention at Strasbourg.[589] Thus the judges are able to find, without adverting to the influence at Strasbourg of the margin of appreciation doctrine, that the national legal system has already achieved the requisite balance within the margin it is allowed at Strasbourg. Under this approach it can be argued that having reviewed aspects of the balance struck in the national law of one or more of the signatory states, Strasbourg is satisfied with it and therefore it is necessary only to ensure that that standard is maintained in any particular instance. A number of examples of this approach in the early post-HRA period are documented in this book.[590] An obvious example in which this stance was taken arose in respect of the exclusion of improperly or illegally obtained non-confession evidence, where the *Khan* approach was continued;

---

585 [1997] AC 558.
586 (1988) 13 EHRR 242.
587 [1997] AC 558, p 583, *per* Lord Nicholls.
588 See, e.g., the decision of the Canadian Supreme Court in *R v Burlingham* [1995] 2 SCR 206.
589 E.g., in the public order and freedom of assembly context: see Chapter 8, p 691.
590 See, e.g., Chapter 6, pp 534–44.

the common law tradition could be viewed as 'amoral',[591] but it was not out of accord with the Strasbourg one – since Strasbourg had declined to take an interventionist stance to matters of evidence in the member states.[592] Under this approach, a court might ostensibly refuse to apply the margin of appreciation doctrine and yet adopt a restrained stance in some circumstances.

The minimalist approach is most problematic when it is confronted by a much more robust and clearly analogous decision at Strasbourg, adopting a stance opposed to the previous general trend of UK law.[593] This may not arise very frequently, as this book indicates, but it arose in the significant Privy Council decision in *Brown v Stott*,[594] a decision which, it is suggested, exemplified the minimalist approach in the sense that it required a 'reading down' of the Convention right in question. *Brown* is discussed more fully in Chapter 12,[595] but it is used as an example of this approach here. In *Saunders v UK*[596] it was found that, if a penalty formally attaches to silence in questioning by state agents, and the coerced statements are then used in evidence, a breach of Art 6 is almost bound to occur. Section 172 of the Road Traffic Act (RTA) 1988 makes it an offence for motorists not to tell police who was driving their vehicle at the time of an alleged offence. The coerced statement can then be used in evidence at trial for the RTA offence in question.

In *Brown*, the Law Lords found a way of distinguishing the instant case in the particular circumstances, from *Saunders*. It was pointed out that s 172 could be distinguished from s 437 of the Companies Act 1985, the provision at issue in *Saunders*, on a number of grounds, including the degree of coercion and the length of questioning. The Lords did not find that s 172 was incompatible with Art 6 and therefore it was not necessary to rely on s 6(2)(b). The Lords also used an equivalent doctrine, that of according a discretionary area of discretion to the legislature, in coming to its decision. Bearing that doctrine in mind, it was further argued that Art 6 itself does not expressly require that coerced statements should be excluded from evidence and that although a right to freedom from self-incrimination could be implied into it, the right had not been treated at Strasbourg as an absolute right. Following *Ex p Kebilene*, the Lords relied on decisions to that effect at Strasbourg that had been influenced by the margin of appreciation doctrine. Lord Bingham found: 'Limited qualification of [Art 6] rights is acceptable if reasonably directed by national authorities towards a clear and proper public objective and if representing no greater qualification than the situation calls for'. The objective in question was the laudable one of curbing traffic accidents. On that basis, by importing a form of balancing test into Art 6, it was found that answers given under s 172 could be adduced in evidence at trial.

While it is understandable that the Lords wished to find a method of preserving the effect of s 172, with the aim of serving an important societal interest, it is suggested

---

591 Zander, M, The Police and Criminal Evidence Act 1984, 1995, p 236. See further Chapter 13, pp 1289–91.

592 See Chapter 13, pp 1291–92.

593 This occurred in *Osman v UK* (2000) 29 EHRR 245. In criticising the Strasbourg decision, at the time, Lord Hoffman made it clear that he viewed the House of Lords as having a limited role in adjudicating on human rights' issues: 'Human rights and the House of Lords' (1999) 62(2) MLR 159, p 161.

594 [2001] 2 WLR 817, the Judicial Committee of the Privy Council.

595 See pp 1252–53.

596 (1997) 23 EHRR 313; No 19187/91.

that their decision has the effect of undermining the right not to incriminate oneself in Art 6(1), in a range of circumstances. The combination of the uses of the doctrine of deference to the legislature, combined with the use of Strasbourg decisions affected by the margin of appreciation doctrine, led, it is argued, to a decision that affords the right a lesser significance than Strasbourg has accorded it. If the intention had been to balance the rights in Art 6 against a range of societal interests, a paragraph could have been included, as in Arts 8–11, setting out the exceptions and the tests to be applied in using them. Alternatively, a general exception could have been included, as in section 1 of the Canadian Charter. The decision not to adopt either of these courses implies that there is little or no room for the use of implied exceptions. In so far as Strasbourg has suggested that the Art 6 rights are qualified, the Lords should have considered whether adoption of that stance was due to the use of the doctrine of the margin of appreciation.

Thus, in approaching decisions at Strasbourg not heavily influenced by the doctrine, a court, following notions of common law restraint expressed in a manner similar to the *Kebilene* 'area of discretionary judgment' doctrine, might find that it could adopt a cautious interpretation to Strasbourg decisions if to do so appeared to be in accordance with common law tradition. As Chapter 5 argues, an example is provided by *Camelot Group Ltd v Centaur Communications*[597] in the Court of Appeal in which a restrained approach to the Strasbourg decision in *Goodwin v United Kingdom*[598] – a decision in which the margin of appreciation conceded was very narrow – was taken.

At the second stage, the court tends to identify reasons for restraint in the particular context. Signs of judicial adherence to a minimalist approach to the Convention by way of a domestic doctrine of deference were found in *Ex p Kebilene*.[599] Lord Hope said:

> This technique [the margin of appreciation] is not available to the national courts when they are considering Convention issues arising within their own countries [but] . . . In some circumstances it will be appropriate for the courts to recognise that there is an area of judgment within which the judiciary will defer, on democratic grounds, to the considered opinion of [the democratic body or person] whose act or decision is said to be incompatible with the Convention.

In the context of the case, which concerned the compatibility of primary terrorist legislation with the Convention, these findings were used to justify a deferential approach. Indeed, they sought to introduce qualifications into a guarantee which on its face was unqualified. The term used by Lord Hope to describe the area in which choices between individual rights and societal interests might arise was 'the discretionary area of judgment';[600] he found that it would be easier for such an area of judgment to be recognised:

---

597   [1998] EMLR 1; [1999] QB 124.

598   (1966) 22 EHRR 123.

599   [1999] 3 WLR 172; [2000] AC 326. The Lord Chief Justice, Lord Bingham, had found that the provisions in question undermined the presumption of innocence under Art 6(2) 'in a blatant and obvious way' due to the use of presumptions and the possibility of conviction on reasonable suspicion falling short of proof under the PTA, s 16A, as amended. See further Chapter 14, pp 1347–51.

600   First coined by Pannick, D, 'Principles of interpretation of Convention rights under the Human Rights Act and the discretionary area of judgement' [1998] PL 545, pp 549–51.

where the Convention itself requires a balance to be struck, much less so where the right [as in Art 6(2)] is stated in terms which are unqualified . . . But even where the right is stated in [such] terms . . . the courts will need to bear in mind the jurisprudence of the European Court which recognises that due account should be taken of the special nature of terrorist crime and the threat which it poses to a democratic society.[601]

In support of his balancing approach, Lord Hope referred to Lord Woolf's findings in *AG of Hong Kong v Lee Kwong-kut*.[602] Lord Woolf considered the Canadian approach when applying the Canadian Charter of Rights and Freedoms, s 1 of which states that the rights and freedoms which it guarantees are: 'subject only to such reasonable limits prescribed by law as can be demonstrably justified in a free and democratic society.' He said: 'In a case where there is real difficulty, where the case is close to the borderline, regard can be had to the approach now developed by the Canadian courts in respect of section 1 of their Charter.'

The approach of Lord Hope towards the development of a broad domestic doctrine of deference was therefore based on a watering down of the Convention rights since a provision equivalent to s 1 of the Charter was omitted from the basic Convention rights under Arts 2–7. A somewhat similar approach was taken in *R v Chief Constable of Sussex ex p International Ferry Traders Ltd*.[603] The decision was taken in the context of EC, not Convention, law but the principles referred to were the familiar ones. Lord Slynn, in a speech with which the other Law Lords agreed, found: 'the courts have long made it clear that . . . they will respect the margin of appreciation or discretion which a Chief Constable has', and, in this instance, that margin had not been exceeded. Lord Hoffmann found:

> on the particular facts of this case the European concepts of proportionality and margin of appreciation produce the same result as what are commonly called *Wednesbury* principles . . . in this case I think that the Chief Constable must enjoy a margin of discretion that cannot differ according to whether its source be found in purely domestic principles or superimposed European principles.

In other words, it is possible to discover, as in *Khan* and *Kebilene*,[604] a judicial approach under which traditional notions of deference on expertise grounds to executive bodies or to Parliament may be coterminous with the expression of the margin of appreciation doctrine, or that Strasbourg principles happen to yield the same result as *Wednesbury* ones. Thus, a court may find that, having relied on Strasbourg case law, affected by the margin of appreciation doctrine, in order to determine what the law is that is to be applied, still further deference can then be built into the decision at the second stage of reasoning, since it is found to be possible, following Strasbourg principle, to afford the decision-maker a 'margin of appreciation'. In the early post-HRA period, it

601 He gave the example of the ruling of the Court in *Murray v UK* (1994) 19 EHRR 193, p 222, para 47.
602 [1993] AC 951, p 966.
603 [1999] 1 All ER 129; [1999] 2 AC 418.
604 [1999] 3 WLR 172; discussed in Chapter 14.

became apparent that the judiciary were continuing to find that certain matters, most obviously those relating to national security, were peculiarly matters for Parliament and the institutional body in question to determine. *Gillan* provides an obvious example of that tendency, in relation to the decision of the police officers on the ground[605] as, it is argued, does *Pro-Life Alliance*[606] in relation to both Parliament and the BBC acting as regulator. In *Pro-Life* the House of Lords had to consider rules on taste and decency contained in the Broadcasting Act 1990 and the BBC's decision, taking account of those rules and acting in its self-regulatory capacity, not to broadcast the video showing graphic pictures of abortion.

In *Pro-Life* Lord Hoffmann began by expounding the legal principles on which, he said, decision-making powers are allocated to different branches of government:

> The courts are the independent branch of government and the legislature and executive are, directly and indirectly respectively, the elected branches of government. Independence makes the courts more suited to deciding some kinds of questions and being elected makes the legislature or executive more suited to deciding others. The allocation of these decision-making responsibilities is based upon recognised principles. The principle that the independence of the courts is necessary for a proper decision of disputed legal rights or claims of violation of human rights is a legal principle. It is reflected in Article 6 of the Convention. On the other hand, the principle that majority approval is necessary for a proper decision on policy or allocation of resources is also a legal principle. Likewise, when a court decides that a decision is within the proper competence of the legislature or executive, it is not showing deference. It is deciding the law.[607]

He went on to find that the decision made by Parliament in imposing standards of taste and decency was an entirely proper decision for it as representative of the people to make. He further found that the decision of the broadcasters was one that they were entitled to make; he said: 'Once one accepts that [they] were entitled to apply generally accepted standards, I do not see how it is possible for a court to say that they were wrong.'[608] Thus Lord Hoffmann insisted that as a matter of law the decision was not within the competence of a court but within that of Parliament. He further appeared to view it as outwith the courts' competence, as a legal principle, to interfere with the decision of the BBC as a regulator. This stance did not, it is argued, take account of the courts' own role under s 6 HRA to ensure that the Convention rights – in this case Art 10 – are not infringed. It also avoided the question whether, assuming that the BBC is a functional public function authority and acting in its public function when it took the decision not to broadcast the video,[609] the BBC had fully adhered to Art 10. It was not enough to note that the BBC had taken account of the value of political expression in deciding to ban the video; the question whether they had adhered to Art 10 was for the court to decide. The decision was so determinedly deferential that the basic

---

605 See pp 1119–21.
606 [2004] 1 AC 185 at paras 55 and 56.
607 At para 76.
608 At para 79.
609 See above pp 216–18, 233–35.

point as to the legal effect of s 6 HRA was missed and the courts' role as guardian of the Convention rights was, it is argued, not discharged. Lord Hoffmann's point that a court, in allocating competencies to different spheres of government, 'is deciding the law' ignores the fact that that determination has already been made by s 6.

A somewhat similar approach was taken in *R (SB) v Denbigh High School*.[610] While, under the activist stance discussed below, the courts are adopting a nuanced approach to the notion of deference to Parliament or the executive, they are prepared to show deference where the decision-maker appears to have weighed up the competing considerations in an effective fashion due to its special expertise. In that instance the House of Lords had to consider whether a school had breached Art 9 in refusing to allow the 16-year-old Muslim schoolgirl-claimant to wear the stricter jilbab form of dress which contravened its uniform policy. The Lords concluded that the school was fully justified in maintaining its policy. Lord Bingham found:[611]

> [T]he school . . . had taken immense pains to devise a uniform policy which respected Muslim beliefs but did so in an inclusive, unthreatening and uncompetitive way. The rules laid down were as far from being mindless as uniform rules could ever be. The school had enjoyed a period of harmony and success to which the uniform policy was thought to contribute. On further enquiry it still appeared that the rules were acceptable to mainstream Muslim opinion. It was feared that acceding to the respondent's request would or might have significant adverse repercussions. It would in my opinion be irresponsible of any court, lacking the experience, background and detailed knowledge of the head teacher, staff and governors, to overrule their judgment on a matter as sensitive as this. The power of decision has been given to them for the compelling reason that they are best placed to exercise it, and I see no reason to disturb their decision.

Although it is argued that the House of Lords was right to reject the over-formalistic approach of the Court of Appeal which had demanded that the school follow a Convention-based procedure in reaching its decision, it is argued that the House of Lords itself still had to decide, under s 6, whether the decision of the school was correct in terms of proportionality under Art 9(2). Lord Bingham's approach, it is suggested, comes too close to abdicating responsibility for making that decision.

At the third stage of the reasoning process, where the Strasbourg jurisprudence applies a weak proportionality review, close to ensuring only that the view taken of the need for a particular restriction was not unreasonable, a domestic court fully applying it, including its margin of appreciation aspects, will find itself able to defer to the judgment of the executive. Clearly, this approach is distinguishable from that

---

610 [2006] 2 WLR 719 para 30. For discussion of the Court of Appeal decision see: Poole, 'Of headscarves and heresies: The *Denbigh High School* case and public authority decision making under the Human Rights Act' [2005] PL 685; Linden and Hetherington, 'Schools and Human Rights' [2005] Educational Law Journal 229; Davies, 'Banning the Jilbab: Reflections on Restricting Religious Clothing in the Light of the Court of Appeal in *SB v Denbigh High School* (2005) 1.3 European Constitutional Law Review 511.

611 At para 34.

of heightened *Wednesbury* unreasonableness,[612] but it may tend to lead to the same outcome.[613] This, it is suggested, was the approach taken, for example, in *Alconbury*[614] in which it was found that the *Wednesbury* unreasonableness test satisfies the Strasbourg demand for an effective remedy. As discussed above, the House of Lords came to the view that judicial review could now be viewed as providing a sufficient remedy, owing to the need to consider proportionality under the HRA. But it also considered that even without considering proportionality, judicial review could provide a sufficient remedy in the socio-economic context in question.

The 'third' stage of reasoning in *Pro-Life* followed logically from the second one. Having decided that 'deference' was appropriate, although he did not use that term, Lord Hoffmann went on to find that the weaker version of 'proportionality' that is sometimes used by Strasbourg, and is closer to *Wednesbury* or 'heightened' *Wednesbury* review,[615] may be viewed as appropriate in some contexts. He made this clear in *Pro-Life Alliance* in stating:

> The test applied in the letter from the Registrar, namely, whether the restriction on the content of the PEB was 'arbitrary or *unreasonable*', seems to me precisely the test which ought to be applied. It is more in accordance with the jurisprudence of the ECHR and a proper analysis of the nature of the right in question than the fundamentalist approach of the Court of Appeal (emphasis added).[616]

Similarly, Moses J in *Ismet Ala v Secretary of State for the Home Department*[617] said:

> It is the Convention itself and, in particular, the concept of proportionality which confers upon the decision maker a margin of discretion in deciding where the balance should be struck between the interests of an individual and the interests of the community. A decision-maker may fairly reach one of two opposite conclusions, one in favour of a claimant, the other [against him]. Of neither could it be said that the balance had been struck unfairly. In such circumstances, the mere fact that an alternative but favourable decision could reasonably have been reached will not lead to the conclusion that the decision-maker has acted in breach of the claimant's human rights. Such a breach will only occur where the decision is outwith the range of reasonable responses to the question as to where a fair balance lies between the conflicting interests.

---

612 See *Ministry of Defence ex p Smith and Others* [1996] 1 All ER 257, p 263.

613 It could collapse into it if in some instances a test of 'reasonableness' rather than of necessity and proportionality was adopted under the cloak of using the terminology of proportionality. *Gillan* arguably provides an example of this tendency. Beatty suggests that this has occurred in Canada under the Charter: see Beatty, D, 'The Canadian Charter of Rights: lessons and laments' [1997] 60(4) MLR 487, p 493.

614 *R v Secretary of State for the Environment, Transport and the Regions ex p Holding & Barnes Plc (Alconbury)* [2001] 2 WLR 1389, HL.

615 See Chapter 3, pp 128–30.

616 At para 72.

617 [2003] EWHC 521 at para 44.

As Chapters 8, 11 and 14 point out, courts have traditionally shown deference to decisions of the police regarding public order and national security.[618] At this third stage the proportionality test chosen by Lord Bingham in *Gillan* in considering the interference with the Art 8 guarantee was strongly reflective of that traditional stance:

> If, again, the lawfulness of the search is assumed at this stage, there can be little question that it is directed to objects recognised by article 8(2). The search must still be necessary in a democratic society, and so proportionate. But if the exercise of the power is duly authorised and confirmed, and if the power is exercised for the only purpose for which it may permissibly be exercised (i.e. to search for articles of a kind which could be used in connection with terrorism: section 45(1)(a)), it would in my opinion be impossible to regard a proper exercise of the power, in accordance with Code A, as other than proportionate when seeking to counter the great danger of terrorism.[619]

Clearly, there is no real proportionality review here.

In *Gillan* Arts 10(2) and 11(2) received an even more cursory treatment, bearing in mind that the stop and search affected persons reporting on or going to a protest at an arms fair. In this instance, even in terms of lip-service, proportionality vanished from the analysis completely:

> The power to stop and search under sections 44–45 may, if misused, infringe the Convention rights to free expression and free assembly protected by articles 10 and 11 . . . I find it hard to conceive of circumstances in which the power, properly exercised in accordance with the statute . . . could be held to restrict those rights in a way which infringed either of those articles. But if it did . . . I would expect the restriction to fall within the heads of justification provided in articles 10(2) and 11(2).[620]

As Chapter 11 argues, Lord Bingham was unwilling to constrain the exercise of the police discretion to stop persons, even where there was nothing to suggest a connection with terrorism, in any way.[621] Jeffrey Jowell has described certain *dicta* of Lord Hoffman as 'heavy with deference'.[622] The findings of Lord Bingham in *Gillan*, at every stage in the reasoning, could equally be described as redolent of deference.

It might appear that a minimalist approach would provide a little more protection for human rights than was provided under pre-HRA judicial review principles, since the domestic courts in theory have to consider proportionality, not merely *Wednesbury* reasonableness. The court might be expected to ask whether an interference goes beyond the aim in question, or whether evidence of the need for it has been advanced by the state. But Lord Bingham's approach in *Gillan* demonstrates that proportionality review

---

618 See, e.g., pp 1337, 1347–51, 1425–26.
619 At para 29.
620 At para 30.
621 See pp 1119–21; see also p 726.
622 'Judicial Deference: servility, civility or institutional capacity?' [2004] PL 592, 600.

can readily be rendered an empty exercise. Minimalist approaches under the HRA are discussed further in Chapters 5 and 14.[623]

Activism

An approach that takes a more expansive stance towards the Convention rights may be termed activist. Such an approach might be viewed as continuing the activism shown in developing a common law of human rights in the pre-HRA era, as discussed in Chapter 3.[624] Such an approach assumes that the common law recognises and upholds fundamental human rights[625] and that therefore, an approach which takes an activist stance towards such rights under the HRA is in accordance with UK legal tradition. But it recognises that a constitutional shift has occurred since the HRA has placed the courts under a legal duty, in s 6, to uphold the Convention rights, even in circumstances in which deference has been accorded.

At the first stage of reasoning, under an activist approach, a court is wary of applying decisions at Strasbourg that are heavily influenced by the margin of appreciation doctrine, looking instead to fundamental Convention principles. Strasbourg has found that the purpose of the Convention is to 'maintain and promote the ideals and values of a democratic society',[626] which include tolerance of views offensive to the majority,[627] and to provide 'rights that are practical and effective' rather than 'rights that are theoretical or illusory'.[628] These concepts have not always found expression in practice, partly due to the diluting effect of the margin of appreciation doctrine. But in support of the 'activist' approach, it can be pointed out that much of the more deferential Strasbourg jurisprudence is very heavily influenced by decisions of the Commission, which, as indicated in Chapter 2, is not a fully judicial body[629] and therefore has less authority than the Court. It is in accordance with the Strasbourg principles to have regard to the balance struck between individual rights and societal interests in other European courts, and perhaps also to that struck by the International Covenant on Civil and Political Rights and in other jurisdictions, including the US or Canada. By so doing, it may be possible to determine what the outcome of a decision at Strasbourg would have been had a lesser or no margin been conceded to the state. Human rights jurisprudence from other jurisdictions can clearly prove valuable where the Strasbourg

623 See, e.g., Chapter 5, pp 373–79.
624 See pp 127–33.
625 It may be noted that s 11 HRA affords recognition to the protection for fundamental rights already achieved under the common law, in providing that reliance on a Convention right does not restrict existing rights or freedoms, or a person's right to make any claim 'which he could make or bring apart from ss 7–9'.
626 *Kjeldsen v Denmark* (1976) 1 EHRR 711, p 731; see also the comments of the Court in *Socialist Party v Turkey* (1998) 27 EHRR 51 as to the need for pluralism in a democracy.
627 In *Handyside v UK* (1976) 1 EHRR 737, para 49 the Court said: '[Article 10] . . . is applicable not only to "information" or "ideas" that are favourably received or regarded as inoffensive . . . but also to those which offend, shock or disturb the state or any sector of the population. Such are the demands of that pluralism, tolerance and broadmindedness without which there is no "democratic society".'
628 *Airey v Ireland* (1979) 2 EHRR 305, p 314.
629 Chapter 2, pp 22–23.

jurisprudence is exiguous, which is frequently the case. Indeed, the domestic courts showed a willingness pre-HRA to take such jurisprudence into account.[630]

A national court which afforded greater protection to the substantive rights than accorded at Strasbourg could not exceed the margin conceded to the state, unless two fundamental Convention rights came into conflict. The rejection in the Lords during debate on the Human Rights Bill of a Conservative amendment which would have required that the Strasbourg jurisprudence should be binding on the UK courts also lends support to this argument. In rejecting the amendment the government spokesperson, the Lord Chancellor, implied, as discussed above in relation to s 2 HRA,[631] that the possibility would thereby be left open of applying higher standards than those applied at Strasbourg.[632] A further Conservative amendment to the Bill, which was also rejected, sought to ensure that the domestic judiciary would be obliged to adhere to the margin of appreciation doctrine in interpreting and applying the Convention. Any domestic judge uncertain whether to disregard a Commission decision on admissibility or a deferential decision of the Court can therefore find some justification under the *Pepper v Hart*[633] doctrine for so doing. The rejection of these two amendments suggests that the judiciary have a discretion under the HRA to afford greater weight to the Convention rights than Strasbourg affords, although they are not placed under an obligation to do so. It follows, it may be argued, that this approach allows the HRA to recognise the difference between the roles of a national and an international court, and in particular the need for the latter, but not the former, to take a sensitive approach to varying cultural standards and practices in the member states.

Clearly, the leading decisions on s 2, *Ullah*[634] and *Price*,[635] place, as discussed above, a very significant constraint on this possibility. But where no clear and constant Strasbourg jurisprudence stands in the way, the courts have some leeway to give a lead to Strasbourg. Under this approach, judges could regard themselves, where such leeway applies, as able to go somewhat *beyond* the minimal standards applied in the Strasbourg jurisprudence,[636] given that Strasbourg's view of itself as a system of protection firmly subsidiary to that afforded by national courts has led it in certain contexts to intervene only where clear and unequivocal transgressions have occurred. Such a stance recognises that the national authorities have not always been required to demonstrate convincingly that the test of 'pressing social need' has been met, or conducted any meaningful analysis of the proportionality of the particular measures taken to restrict the expression in question.[637]

---

630 In *Albert Reynolds v Times Newspapers* [1999] 4 All ER 609, the House of Lords took into account authorities from Canada, Australia and New Zealand, although they found that the Strasbourg jurisprudence was more influential.

631 See pp 193–96.

632 'The Bill would of course permit UK courts to depart from existing Strasbourg decisions and upon occasion it might well be appropriate to do so and it is possible they might give a successful lead to Strasbourg.' HL Deb Col 514, 18 November 1997.

633 [1993] AC 593; [1993] 1 All ER 42.

634 See p 193 above.

635 See p 197 above.

636 In the words of Judge Martens, '[the task of domestic courts] goes further than seeing that the minimum standards laid down in the ECHR are maintained' ('Opinion: Incorporating the Convention: The Role of the Judiciary' [1998] 1 EHRLR 3).

637 See Chapter 2, e.g. at pp 84–85.

It tends to require consideration to be given primarily to the core principles developed at Strasbourg as underlying the Convention rights, rather than following specific decisions, whether as to admissibility or otherwise. But, in contrast to Lord Hope's approach in *Ex p Kebilene*, it would use such principles to enhance rather than constrain the utilisation of the rights. As Laws LJ observed in *Runa Begum v Tower Hamlets London Borough Council*:[638]

> the court's task under the HRA . . . is not simply to add on the Strasbourg learning to the corpus of English law, as if it were a compulsory adjunct taken from an alien source, but to develop a municipal law of human rights by the incremental method of the common law, case by case, taking account of the Strasbourg jurisprudence as HRA s 2 enjoins us to do.

As far as the second stage of reasoning under this approach is concerned, it is argued that the courts are developing a nuanced stance towards the notion of deference that, in contrast to the minimalist approach at this stage, allows them to satisfy their role under s 6 HRA, even in relation to matters traditionally viewed as particularly within the purview of the government or Parliament, including matters of national security or social policy. The stance taken in *Pro-Life* by Lord Hoffmann – that certain matters are allocated to different branches of government on the basis of legal principle – has been rejected, although *Pro-Life* has not been expressly overruled. The courts have taken the stance that the democratic quality of the rights-infringing rule can be considered: legislation should be treated with greater deference than executive decisions,[639] but in very recent decisions, as discussed below, they have refined that stance. Precisely what deference might require under this nuanced approach is considered below.

At this point the argument that the HRA itself represents a choice as to the division of responsibility between Parliament and the judiciary for resolving moral and political issues should be considered. Under it, it can be argued, judicial activism is inherently limited as a result of the attempt to reconcile conflicting constitutional aims that lies at the heart of the HRA. Lord Steyn has said, 'It is crystal clear that the carefully and subtly drafted [HRA] preserves the principle of parliamentary sovereignty.'[640] Klug concludes:[641] 'The issue of judicial deference to the legislature was settled through the intersection of [ss 3 and 4]. If they are applied as intended, no further doctrine of judicial deference to the legislature . . . is required.'[642] However, the arguments put forward in this chapter have sought to problematise Lord Steyn's stance, to an extent. If, as argued here, the constitutional reality of the HRA is that in practice the carefully and subtly drafted HRA mechanisms are on the whole *not* being used in a manner that fully preserves the principle of parliamentary sovereignty, then a degree of deference to the legislature does retain a role under it. As already noted, s 3, not s 4, is now accepted as the prime remedial mechanism of the HRA.[643] This point must

---

638 [2002] 2 All ER 668 at para 17.
639 *See International Transport Roth Gmbh v Secretary of State for the Home Dept* [2002] 3 WLR 344.
640 *R v DPP ex p Kebilene* [2000] 2 AC 326, 327.
641 'Judicial Deference under the Human Rights Act' (2003) 2 EHRLR 125.
642 Ibid, p 128.
643 See pp 184–86 above.

not be over-stated since the power under s 3 does have limits, as described above, but this argument would support the stance that the judges appear to be taking in certain very recent decisions under the activist approach.

Lord Steyn's argument would support a refusal to accord any deference at all to the legislature. The senior judges are not currently taking that stance. Instead, a more subtle and differentiated version of deference is being developed, which builds in safeguards against the excessive servility seen in pre-HRA decisions. Section 6 HRA itself guards against the stance taken in *Pro-Life*, and, as discussed below, Lord Bingham has recently expressly given a reminder of the straightforward effect of s 6 – to examine whether the executive in its decision-making has adhered to the Convention rights. Sections 3 and 4 go some way towards delineating constitutional roles, but the HRA failed to create in s 6(1) itself any nuanced method of addressing the issue of deference. The current version of deference seen in the decisions below avoids the extremes of excessive activism, based on the argument that the HRA itself has already allocated institutional competencies, or excessive deference, flowing from a disregard for the straightforward, face-value meaning of s 6 (perhaps on the basis that taken literally it was initially too radical a change for the judges to accept).[644]

Simon Brown LJ in *International Transport Roth GmbH v Secretary of State for the Home Department*[645] made a clear statement as to the effect of s 6 in finding that: '. . . the court's role under the 1998 Act is as the guardian of human rights. It cannot abdicate this responsibility.' He further observed:

> But judges nowadays have no alternative but to apply the Human Rights Act 1998. Constitutional dangers exist no less in too little judicial activism as in too much. There are limits to the legitimacy of executive or legislative decision-making, just as there are to decision-making by the courts.[646]

Lord Nicholls' findings in *Ghaidan* are to similar effect in relation to a claim based firmly on core Convention values but within the social policy area in which pre-HRA a deferential stance would probably have been adopted:

> arguments based on the extent of the discretionary area of judgment accorded to the legislature lead nowhere in this case . . . Parliament is charged with the primary responsibility for deciding the best way of dealing with social problems. The court's role is one of review. The court will reach a different conclusion from the legislature only when it is apparent that the legislature has attached insufficient importance to a person's Convention rights. The readiness of the court to depart from the view of the legislature depends upon the subject matter of the legislation and of the complaint. National housing policy is a field where the court will be less ready to intervene. Parliament has to hold a fair balance between the competing interests of tenants and landlords, taking into account broad issues of social and economic policy. But, even in such a field, where the alleged violation comprises

---

644 See the analysis of Leigh, I,, 'Taking Rights Proportionality: Judicial Review, the Human Rights Act and Strasbourg' [1997] PL 265.
645 [2003] QB 728, para 27.
646 At para 54.

differential treatment based on grounds such as race or sex or sexual orientation the court will scrutinise with intensity any reasons said to constitute justification. The reasons must be cogent if such differential treatment is to be justified.

In the present case the only suggested ground for according different treatment to the survivor of same sex couples and opposite sex couples cannot withstand scrutiny. Rather, the present state of the law as set out in paragraph 2 of Schedule 1 of the Rent Act 1977 may properly be described as continuing adherence to the traditional regard for the position of surviving spouses, adapted in 1988 to take account of the widespread contemporary trend for men and women to cohabit outside marriage but not adapted to recognise the comparable position of cohabiting same sex couples. I appreciate that the primary object of introducing the regime of assured tenancies and assured shorthold tenancies in 1988 was to increase the number of properties available for renting in the private sector. But this policy objective of the Housing Act 1988 can afford no justification for amending paragraph 2 so as to include cohabiting heterosexual partners but not cohabiting homosexual partners. This policy objective of the Act provides no reason for, on the one hand, extending to unmarried cohabiting heterosexual partners the right to succeed to a statutory tenancy but, on the other hand, withholding that right from cohabiting homosexual partners. Paragraph 2 fails to attach sufficient importance to the Convention rights of cohabiting homosexual couples.[647]

This was not a case in which there was a doubt as to the Convention protection available since Strasbourg has clearly found that discrimination on grounds of sexual orientation falls within Art 14 read with Art 8.[648] Although the decision was taken in an area of social and economic policy, the underlying thrust of the legislation did not provide a reason, under strict scrutiny, for up-holding the discriminatory rule in question. Close scrutiny was required since the fundamental right to freedom from discrimination was at stake. Lord Nicholls referred to the context and stated that the readiness of the court to depart from the view of the legislature is affected by the particular context in question. But in fact it is difficult to see that the context had any impact on the level of scrutiny to which the provisions and the policy underlying them were subjected. It is argued below that Lord Nicholls' approach, in refusing to accord deference, was appropriate in this context.

A somewhat similar stance was taken by Lord Bingham in *A and Others v Secretary of State for the Home Department*.[649] But in that instance, in the very sensitive context of national security – one in certain respects more within the area of competence of the executive rather than that of the judiciary – he gave indications as to the circumstances in which a degree of deference would be appropriate. Rather than accept that deference should be paid to the legislature or executive in a general sense, he considered that different institutional competences might make *degrees* of deference appropriate. He considered that the Home Secretary was entitled to take the view that an emergency situation was in being, on the basis that a degree of deference should be paid on the

---

647 At paras 20 and 21.
648 See Chapter 15, pp 1519–21.
649 [2005] 2 WLR 87; [2005] 3 All ER 169.

grounds of 'institutional competence,' in the sense that the Home Secretary had to make an essentially political judgment. Nevertheless, he went on to find that the measures taken to meet it were disproportionate to the aims pursued. As indicated below, he refused to accept the *full* claim made for deference:

> . . . I would accept that great weight should be given to the judgment of the Home Secretary, his colleagues and Parliament on this question, because they were called on to exercise a pre-eminently political judgment. It involved making a factual prediction of what various people around the world might or might not do . . . It would have been irresponsible not to err, if at all, on the side of safety. As will become apparent, I do not accept the full breadth of the Attorney General's argument on what is generally called the deference owed by the courts to the political authorities. It is perhaps preferable to approach this question as one of demarcation of functions or what Liberty in its written case called "relative institutional competence". The more purely political (in a broad or narrow sense) a question is, the more appropriate it will be for political resolution and the less likely it is to be an appropriate matter for judicial decision. The smaller, therefore, will be the potential role of the court . . . The present question seems to me to be very much at the political end of the spectrum:[650] . . . the appellants have shown no ground strong enough to warrant displacing the Secretary of State's decision on this important threshold question.[651]

The findings in these three decisions suggest that the courts are taking their role as guardians of the Convention rights under s 6 HRA seriously. Taking account also of his findings below, Lord Bingham, while accepting that deference may be accorded, is, to an extent, seeking to unpack the reasons for it, the areas to which it extends, and its extent within those areas. His findings indicate that where deference is demanded due to the very political nature of a security-based decision, that does not mean that deference should be extended equally to all aspects of that decision. He therefore created differentiation in terms of the deference to be accorded to the threshold decision as to the existence of an emergency and to the decision as to the measures required to be adopted to meet it.

These decisions indicate that the discretionary area of judgment accorded to the executive or legislature is narrowing considerably, in some contexts almost to vanishing point, which is in accordance with s 6 HRA. Clearly, if a court accepts that a decision-maker is acting within a discretionary area of judgment, and then proceeds as a result to choose a weak proportionality test, then it is deliberately disabling itself from being able to discover whether the rights-infringing decision was genuinely necessary. Since the Convention itself allows for exceptions to the rights, the building in of further deference is unnecessary, except where there are compelling reasons to do so, such as that, in the national security context, the decision-maker is in possession of sensitive information not available to the judiciary. Even then, as Lord Bingham indicated, aspects of the

---

650 In this finding he relied on *Secretary of State for the Home Department v Rehman* [2001] UKHL 47, [2003] 1 AC 153, para 62, *per* Lord Hoffmann.
651 At para 29.

decision can still be subjected to a more rigorous proportionality test. It should be noted, however, that Lord Bingham was referring, in somewhat more delphic fashion, to the intensely political nature of certain decisions rather than to the possession of sensitive information. Clearly, considerations relating to the political nature of decisions relating to national security or the possession of sensitive information were not applicable in *Ghaidan*, and therefore the stance taken was in accordance with the role accorded to the judges under the HRA.

At this point the problem of unbridled judicial activism should be addressed. If the judges are putting their s 6 duty fully into practice, and in reality they are relatively unconstrained by the HRA scheme under ss 3 and 4, over-activism could become apparent. It has already been argued that *R v A*[652] may provide an example. It could have the effect, in certain contexts, of imposing particular moral views on individuals and thereby infringing their Convention rights. The example of abortion was used by the Lord Chancellor in Parliamentary debate on the Human Rights Bill in order to illustrate the possibilities which might arise. In that scenario, if activism was simply taken to mean a requirement to 'read up' the Convention rights, and if necessary to 'read down' the domestic statute, the ideological views of particular judges could be given expression by means of the HRA. Under the Lord Chancellor's example, that could mean affording the Abortion Act 1967, as amended, a very restrictive interpretation (which would not be difficult, given its potentially limited application) and reading up the right to life under Art 2. The government would probably subsequently bring forward legislation to restore the broader application of the Act,[653] but there might be a period of time during which the social effects of the judgment were strongly apparent.

However, at Strasbourg, Art 2, the right to life guarantee, does not prevent abortion, since the Commission has declined to find that the foetus is protected,[654] and the Court has avoided confronting the issue so far.[655] Strasbourg is clearly taking account of the varying abortion laws in the member states which would be severely affected if the foetus was brought within Art 2. Further, the stance so far adopted avoids the conflict of rights, between Arts 8 and 2, that could potentially arise. So at present the abortion issue does not involve a clash of Convention rights. Clearly where the underlying principles at stake can be viewed as entirely opposed, and largely incommensurable, as in this instance, so that a moral choice would have to be taken in an area of irreconcilable

---

652 [2001] 2 WLR 1546.

653 It may be noted that if the government brought forward such legislation, it would not need to state that it could not issue a declaration of compatibility under s 19 HRA since it would be overruling a precedent of the House of Lords, not the Convention guarantees themselves. As already argued, it is *not* clear that Art 6 demanded the result in *R v A* – see above pp 174–77, 187–90.

654 *Paton v UK* (1981) 3 EHRR 408; *H v Norway*, No 17004/90 (1992) 73 DR 155.

655 See *Vo v France* [GC], judgment of 8 July 2004, No 53924/00 in which on unusual facts, the Grand Chamber avoided the question of a foetal right to life within Art 2. *D v Ireland* No 26499/02, oral hearing on admissibility and merits, 6 September 2005, concerned access to abortion for foetal anomaly, an application made under Arts 3, 8, 10 and 14 of the European Convention. If the case of *D* had been declared admissible, the Court would then have had to consider whether a denial of access to abortion for foetal anomaly constitutes inhuman and degrading treatment contrary to Art 3, or an interference with a pregnant woman's right to respect for private life under Art 8. *D* was declared inadmissible on procedural grounds on 13 June 2006. For discussion see Barbara Hewson 'Dancing on the head of a pin? Foetal life and the European Convention' (2005) 13(3) Feminist Legal Studies 363–75.

conflict, Strasbourg prefers to defer to the member states.[656] Where such a difficult choice has to be taken, with such wide-ranging social implications, Strasbourg clearly prefers to leave it to the member states to take it, taking account of particular cultural or religious sensitivities in their own jurisdictions.[657]

At present then, interference with abortion law domestically is unlikely since the duty under s 6 HRA relates to the Convention rights, not to free-standing moral principles. It would be a very radical move to find that Art 2 covered the foetus domestically where Strasbourg had not taken that step. There are reasons for deference to the legislature in the sense that the judiciary is not well placed to assess the wide-ranging social and economic implications of according Art 2 rights to the foetus.[658] But such reasons are currently being rejected in somewhat similar areas of social policy. Adoption of an interventionist stance under s 3 in relation to the Abortion Act is unlikely since the judges would be entering a policy arena, something that they are reluctant to do, as discussed above. Moreover, they would be out of accord with international human rights standards if they did so.[659] However, if in future Strasbourg does find that the foetus is within the ambit of Art 2, it has to be accepted that under an activist stance interference with abortion law would be a possibility.

At the third stage of reasoning under the activist approach the stricter versions of the Strasbourg proportionality tests are adopted. In *Smith and Grady v United Kingdom*[660] the traditional *Wednesbury* approach to judicial review was held to afford inadequate protection for the Convention rights. In *R (Daly) v Secretary of State for the Home Department*[661] it was accepted that the 'domestic courts must themselves

---

656 An example is provided by *Evans v United Kingdom* in which the Grand Chamber gave judgment on 11 April 2007. In *Evans* the claimant and her then partner J commenced fertility treatment when she was told that she had pre-cancerous tumors in both ovaries. She and J signed consent forms to IVF treatment on the understanding that under the Human Fertilisation and Embryology Act 1990, either could withdraw consent at any time before the embryos were implanted in her uterus. The couple then attended a clinic, eggs were harvested and fertilised; six embryos were created and put in storage. She then had an operation to remove her ovaries. The relationship subsequently broke up and when J notified the clinic that he was withdrawing his consent, the clinic informed the claimant that it was under an obligation to destroy the embryos. Evans argued that under Art 8 there exists a positive obligation on the state to ensure that a woman who has embarked on treatment for the specific purpose of giving birth to a genetically related child should be permitted to proceed to the implantation of an embryo even though her former partner had withdrawn his consent. She failed to win her case in the domestic courts (*Evans v Amicus Healthcare* [2005] Fam 1) and also failed at Strasbourg. The Grand Chamber found that an irreconcilable conflict between her interests and those of her partner had arisen and declined to find a breach of Art 8 if the eggs were destroyed on the basis that there is no consensus in the member states on the question when the sperm donor's consent would become irrevocable.

657 See Chapter 2, pp 36–38 and Chapter 6, pp 463–67.

658 See *Wilson v First County Trust Ltd (No 2)* [2003] 3 WLR 568, 589, para 70.

659 E.g. in *R v Morgentaler* [1988] 1 SCR 30, the decision of the Supreme Court of Canada which found the abortion provision in the Criminal Code to be unconstitutional, since in placing restrictions on access to abortion it violated a woman's right under section 7 of the Canadian Charter of Rights and Freedoms to 'security of person'. Ever since that ruling, there have been no laws regulating abortion in Canada. See 'Abortion: Ensuring Access' (2006) 175(1) CMAJ.

660 (1999) 29 EHRR 493.

661 [2001] UKHL 26; [2001] 2 WLR 1622; [2001] 2 AC 532; [2001] 3 All ER 433; HL, paras 23, 27. The decision concerned rights of privacy of prisoners in respect of correspondence. See further Steyn, Lord, 'Deference: A Tangled Story' (2005) Public Law 346.

form a judgment whether a Convention right has been breached' and that 'the intensity of review is somewhat greater under the proportionality approach'.

In *R(SB) v Denbigh High School*[662] Lord Bingham reiterated this principle: '. . . the court's approach to an issue of proportionality under the Convention must go beyond that traditionally adopted to judicial review in a domestic setting. The inadequacy of that approach was exposed in *Smith and Grady v United Kingdom*[663] and the new approach required under the 1998 Act was described by Lord Steyn in *R (Daly) v Secretary of State for the Home Department*,[664] in terms which have never to my knowledge been questioned'. There is no shift to a merits review, but the intensity of review is greater than was previously appropriate, and greater even than the heightened scrutiny test adopted by the Court of Appeal in *R v Ministry of Defence ex p Smith*.[665] The domestic court must now make a value judgment, an evaluation, by reference to the circumstances prevailing at the relevant time: *Wilson v First County Trust Ltd (No 2)*.[666] Proportionality must be judged objectively, by the court: *R (Williamson) v Secretary of State for Education and Employment*.[667]

The House of Lords in *Ex p Daly* adopted the relatively rigorous proportionality tests from *de Freitas*.[668] Following *de Freitas*, it is first necessary to ask whether a significant and pressing interest, falling within one or more of the exceptions in para 2 of Arts 8–11 has been identified since so doing is part of the threshold test for 'necessity' under para 2. The second and third *de Freitas* tests cover the issue of proportionality. Under the second it is necessary to consider the suitability of the interference in question – the extent to which it is rationally connected to the aim pursued. (This was the test that Lord Nicholls appeared to have in mind in *Ghaidan* in finding that the policy objective of the Act did not have a rational connection with creating discrimination against homosexual couples.) The third *de Freitas* test concerns the need to choose the least intrusive measure – the measure that creates a minimal degree of harm to the primary right consistent with affording protection to the aim pursued. The seriousness of the interference has to be balanced against the importance of the aim sought to be pursued. This is means/end balancing – if there is another way of achieving the aim pursued that is less restrictive, it should be used. This can also be termed 'the least intrusive means' test.

A further test was utilised in *Goodwin v UK*.[669] In that instance Strasbourg made it clear that in the context in question – source disclosure – the strictest form of scrutiny should be afforded to the application of the tests for proportionality, and the more rigorous version of the test should be deployed due to the strong link between protection of sources and freedom of expression. *Goodwin* relied largely on speech/harm balancing as the proportionality test.[670] The Court found: 'Having regard to the importance of the

---

662 [2006] 2 WLR 719 para 30.
663 (1999) 29 EHRR 493, para 138.
664 [2001] 2 AC 532, paras 25–28.
665 [1996] QB 556.
666 [2004] 1 AC 816, paras 62–67.
667 [2005] 2 AC 246, para 51
668 *de Freitas v Permanent Secretary of Ministry of Agriculture, Fisheries, Lands and Housing* [1999] 1 AC 69, 80. This test was also utilized by the Supreme Court of Canada in *R v Oakes* [1986] 1 SCR 103, paras 69–70.
669 (1996) 22 EHRR 123.
670 See Chapter 5, pp 413–14.

protection of journalistic sources for press freedom in a democratic society . . . such a measure cannot be compatible with article 10 of the Convention unless it is justified by an overriding requirement in the public interest.'[671] As discussed in Chapter 5, the seriousness of the harm caused by the disclosure of the confidential information by the source was weighed up against the weightiness of the expression interest. The Court carefully scrutinised the state's case regarding the degree of harm that the company in question had suffered, and took a view of it that differed significantly from that of the state. It found that the interference was very severe, bearing in mind the significance for free expression of protection for journalistic sources. In coming to this conclusion the Court scrutinised the balance between the two interests very strictly – had it conceded a wider margin of appreciation to the national authorities, it might have adopted a less rigorous standard of review and been satisfied that the balance struck between the two was not manifestly unreasonable. Thus the Court found that the proportionality test had not been met. This test can be termed speech/harm balancing or, more generally, rights/harm balancing. Clearly, the extent to which any balancing could occur would depend on whether the right in question was materially qualified.

In two of the more activist decisions of the House of Lords under the HRA, *Laporte*[672] and *A and Others*, the key proportionality test adopted was the relatively hard-edged *De Freitas* 'least intrusive means' one. In *A and Others* the second *De Freitas* test – demanding that the state demonstrate a rational connection between the means employed and the aim pursued – was also relevant, and the rights/harm balancing test used in *Goodwin* was also relevant, although *Goodwin* itself was not referred to. *Laporte* concerned the detention of protesters on a coach which had been turned back by the police from an anti-war demonstration. The House of Lords found, in a seminal decision for freedom of protest and assembly, that the actions of the police in preventing the protesters travelling to the site of the protest and detaining them on a coach travelling back to London, were disproportionate to the aims pursued, in terms of para 2 of Arts 10 and 11. On the question of proportionality, Lord Bingham declined to take a deferential approach to the decision of the police on the ground:

> I would acknowledge the danger of hindsight, and I would accept that the judgment of the officer on the spot, in the exigency of the moment, deserves respect. But making all allowances, I cannot accept the Chief Constable's argument.[673]

Having rejected a fully deferential approach, he went on to find that less intrusive measures could have been taken in that the detention of the protesters had been premature; arrests if necessary could have been made at a later point:

> . . . Nor was it reasonable to anticipate an outburst of disorder on arrival of these passengers in the assembly area or during the procession to the base, during which time the police would be in close attendance and well able to identify and arrest those who showed a violent propensity or breached the conditions to which the

---

671 At para 39.
672 [2006] UKHL 55, para 34. CA: *R (on the application of Laporte) v CC of Gloucester Constabulary* [2004] EWCA Civ 1639. See Chapter 8 for discussion at pp 757–71.
673 At para 55.

assembly and procession were subject. The focus of any disorder was expected to be in the bell-mouth area outside the base, and the police could arrest trouble-makers then and there . . . There was no reason (other than her refusal to give her name, which however irritating to the police was entirely lawful) to view the claimant as other than a committed, peaceful demonstrator. It was wholly disproportionate to restrict her exercise of her rights under articles 10 and 11 because she was in the company of others some of whom might, at some time in the future, breach the peace . . . the claimant was not suspected of having personally committed or of being about to commit any crime, or any breach of the peace.[674]

This was a significantly more intrusive stance than has traditionally been taken in public protest decisions; the common law approach pre-HRA did not fully reflect the Convention since the focus of concern was, broadly, on proprietorial rather than protest rights,[675] and there was a distinct reluctance to interfere with the decisions of police officers unless they were manifestly unreasonable. In *Kent v Metropolitan Police Commissioner*[676] that most attenuated form of *Wednesbury* review was adopted. This decision was taken on the basis of affording the Commissioner a very wide margin of discretion to impose a ban leading to the prohibition of a march expected to be entirely peaceful. Similarly, Slynn J (as he was) said 'if the Commissioner took a view of the circumstances which was wholly untenable I consider that the court could intervene'.[677] Under that standard of review the decision of the police to detain the protesters in *Laporte* could readily have been viewed as not unreasonable.

A and Others, discussed in full in Chapter 14,[678] concerned indefinite detention of non-nationals without trial under ss 21 and 23 of Part 4, Anti-Terrorism, Crime and Security Act 2001, a measure adopted to avert the threat of terrorism, taking account of the fact that the suspects could not be deported due to the risk of Art 3 treatment in the receiving country. Lord Bingham, having found – at the second stage of the reasoning process – that a fully deferential approach would not be appropriate, even in relation to executive decisions taken on grounds of national security in relation to anti-terrorist measures, then went on to adopt a relatively hard-edged proportionality test. Relying on a number of Strasbourg decisions,[679] he noted:[680] 'Even in a terrorist situation the

---

674 At para 55.
675 See Gray and Gray, 'Civil rights, civil wrongs and quasi-public places' (1999) 1 EHRLR 46, and see further Chapter 8, esp p 719.
676 (1981) *The Times*, 15 May. The court found that it could not say that the Commissioner was at fault in making the order, although the reasons for it seemed meagre
677 Quoted in Brownlie's *Law of Public Order and National Security*, 2nd edn, 1981, Butterworths p 52.
678 See pp. 1430 *et seq*.
679 He relied on *Brogan v United Kingdom* (1989) 11EHRR 117, para 80; *Fox, Campbell & Hartley v United Kingdom*, (1990) 13 EHRR 157 paras 32–34. In *Aksoy v Turkey* (1996) 23 EHRR 553, para 76, he noted that the Court, clearly referring to national courts as well as the Convention organs, held:

> 'The Court would stress the importance of Article 5 in the Convention system: it enshrines a fundamental human right, namely the protection of the individual against arbitrary interference by the state with his or her right to liberty. Judicial control of interferences by the executive with the individual's right to liberty is an essential feature of the guarantee embodied in Article 5(3), which is intended to minimise the risk of arbitrariness and to ensure the rule of law.'

680 At para 41.

Convention organs have not been willing to relax their residual supervisory role'. He further quoted from *Korematsu v United States*:[681] '. . . in times of distress the shield of military necessity and national security must not be used to protect governmental actions from close scrutiny and accountability.' He therefore went on to find, at the third reasoning stage, that proportionality review was appropriate, and accepted that a relatively strict proportionality test should be used:

> It follows from this analysis that the appellants are in my opinion entitled to invite the courts to review, on proportionality grounds, the Derogation Order and the compatibility with the Convention of section 23 and the courts are not effectively precluded by any doctrine of deference from scrutinising the issues raised.[682]

The appellants founded on the proportionality principles discussed above, adopted by the Privy Council in *de Freitas v Permanent Secretary of Ministry of Agriculture, Fisheries, Lands and Housing*.[683] As to the second test from *de Freitas*, the appellants argued that ss 21 and 23 of Part 4, Anti-Terrorism, Crime and Security Act 2001 did not rationally address the threat to the security of the UK presented by Al-Qaeda terrorists and their supporters because (a) it did not address the threat presented by UK nationals, (b) it permitted foreign nationals suspected of being Al-Qaeda terrorists or their supporters to pursue their activities abroad if there was any country to which they were able to go, and (c) the sections permitted the certification and detention of persons who were not suspected of presenting any threat to the security of the UK as Al-Qaeda terrorists or supporters.

As to the third test from *de Freitas* – the 'less intrusive means' proportionality test – they argued that if the threat presented to the security of the United Kingdom by UK nationals suspected of being Al-Qaeda terrorists or their supporters could be addressed without infringing their right to personal liberty, it had not been shown why similar measures could not adequately address the threat presented by foreign nationals.[684] In other words, less intrusive means were available, and were being used, which could therefore also have been used against foreign nationals suspected of terrorist activity. Lord Bingham viewed these arguments as to the disproportionality of the Part 4 scheme with the aims pursued as sound.

Lord Bingham's stance in relation to indefinite detention of the appellants further recalled that of the Strasbourg Court in *Goodwin* in that he was not prepared to accept that the grave intrusion into liberty represented by indefinite detention could be justified by the harm sought to be averted – the terrorist threat:[685]

> In urging the fundamental importance of the right to personal freedom, as the sixth step in their proportionality argument, the appellants were able to draw on the long libertarian tradition of English law, dating back to chapter 39 of Magna

---

681   584 F Supp 1406 (1984) para 21, *per* Judge Patel in relation to the Supreme Court's earlier decision (323 US 214 (1944).
682   At para 42.
683   [1999] 1 AC 69, p 80.
684   At para 31.
685   At para 36.

Carta 1215, given effect in the ancient remedy of habeas corpus, declared in the Petition of Right 1628, upheld in a series of landmark decisions down the centuries and embodied in the substance and procedure of the law to our own day . . . The authors of the Siracusa Principles . . . were of the opinion . . . that . . . 'no person shall be detained for an indefinite period of time, whether detained pending judicial investigation or trial or detained without charge . . .'.

He further referred to the recognition of the 'prime importance of personal freedom' in the Strasbourg jurisprudence, noting: 'the fundamental importance of the guarantees contained in Art 5 for securing the right of individuals in a democracy to be free from arbitrary detention at the hands of the authorities' and the need to interpret narrowly any exception to 'a most basic guarantee of individual freedom'.[686]

Jeffrey Jowell has found that 'the courts are charged by Parliament with delineating the boundaries of a rights-based democracy'.[687] In *A and Others* and in *Laporte* a recognition of the courts' role in relation to the core values of the Convention is evident. A purely tokenistic approach to the review of executive decisions is rejected on the basis that this would be an abrogation of the constitutional role accorded to the judges under the HRA. Lord Bingham referred in *A and Others* to the fact that s 6 of the 1998 Act renders unlawful any act of a public authority, including a court, that is incompatible with a Convention right.[688] Thus, as he found, courts must carry out scrutiny of executive decisions that curtail fundamental rights, even in the sensitive context of national security.

Lord Nicholls captured the role of the courts as the guardians of constitutional rights under the HRA effectively in *A and Others* in finding:

I see no escape from the conclusion that Parliament must be regarded as having attached insufficient weight to the human rights of non-nationals. The subject matter of the legislation is the needs of national security. This subject matter dictates that, in the ordinary course, substantial latitude should be accorded to the legislature. But the human right in question, the right to individual liberty, is one of the most fundamental of human rights. Indefinite detention without trial wholly negates that right for an indefinite period.[689]

These two decisions make it plain that where common law tradition had diverged from Strasbourg in developing in a less rights-oriented manner, the HRA has provided the impetus for change, under an activist approach. This approach clearly leads to greater interference with executive decision-making, and departs, to an extent, from common law tradition in so doing. This approach starts from the premise that the reception of the

---

686 In *Kurt v Turkey* (1998) 27 EHRR 373, para 122. He also mentioned *Garcia Alva v Germany* (2001) 37 EHRR 335, para 39, where the Court referred to 'the dramatic impact of deprivation of liberty on the fundamental rights of the person concerned'.

687 See 'Judicial Deference: servility, civility or institutional capacity?' [2003] PL 592, 597'. See also Clayton, 'Judicial deference and 'democratic dialogue': the legitimacy of judicial intervention under the Human Rights Act 1998' [2004] PL 33.

688 At para 42.

689 At para 81.

Convention into UK law represents a decisive break with the past. Activism can occur in accordance with a synthesis of Strasbourg and national constitutional principles. As Beatty puts it:

> the same set of principles and analytical framework . . . are used by [the judiciary] in Washington, Tokyo, New Delhi, Strasbourg, Rome, Karlsruhe . . . [principles] which lie at the core of the concept of constitutional rights that allow judges to act out their role as guardians of the constitution in an objective, determinate and ultimately very democratic way.[690]

7 Scrutiny of the workings of the HRA

Under the Green Paper, *Bringing Rights Home*, a very significant aspect of the reception of the Convention into domestic law was to be the eventual setting up of a Human Rights Commission. The consultative paper suggested that such a Commission would probably have a number of roles which would include: providing guidance and support to those wishing to assert their rights, along the lines of the role of the Equal Opportunities Commission; instituting proceedings in its own name; scrutinising new legislation to ensure that it conforms with the Convention and monitoring the operation of the new Act.[691] Setting up such a Commission would therefore have been a significant step towards ensuring the efficacy of the Convention, in a number of respects. However, it was not provided for under the HRA. The Belfast Agreement 1998 promised that Northern Ireland would have such a Commission and the Northern Ireland Human Rights Commission came into existence in 1999.[692] The experiment in Northern Ireland provides a model, although the Northern Ireland Commissioner has particular concerns

---

690 See Beatty, D, 'The Canadian Charter of Rights: lessons and laments' [1997] 60(4) MLR 487, p 481.

691 See *Bringing Rights Home: Labour's Plans to Incorporate the ECHR into UK Law: A Consultation Paper*, December 1996 (1997), p 11. For discussion of the possible roles of the Commission, see Spence, S and Bynoe, I (1997) 2 EHRR 152; Spencer, S, 'A Human Rights Commission', in Blackburn, R and Plant, R (eds), *Constitutional Reform: The Labour Government's Constitutional Reform Agenda*, 1999, p 395.

692 It was created by s 68 of the Northern Ireland Act 1998, in compliance with the commitment made by the UK Government in the Belfast (Good Friday) Agreement. The current full-time Chief Commissioner Prof. Monica McWilliams, succeeded the first holder of the office, Prof. Brice Dickson, in 2005. It has a variable number of part-time Commissioners (currently nine). The NIHRC's role is to promote awareness of the importance of human rights in Northern Ireland, to review existing law and practice and to advise the Secretary of State and the Executive Committee of the Northern Ireland Assembly (when it is functioning) on what legislative or other measures ought to be taken to protect human rights in Northern Ireland. The Commission is also able to conduct investigations, and (subject to anticipated legislaton) will soon have new powers to enter places of detention, and to compel individuals and agencies to give oral testimony or to produce documents. The Commission also has the power to assist individuals when they are bringing court proceedings, to intervene in proceedings and to bring court proceedings itself. It receives inquiries from people who believe that their human rights have been violated, and provides training and information on human rights. It is specifically charged with advising on the scope for a Bill of Rights to supplement the European Convention on Human Rights (which is part of the law in Northern Ireland as a result of the passing of the Human Rights Act 1998). It is recognised as a member of the worldwide network of National institutions for human rights. For discussion, see Harvey, C and Livingstone, S, 'Human rights and the Northern Ireland peace process' [1999] EHRLR 162, pp 168–74.

regarding religious discrimination which are not applicable in England and Wales. The decision in the early post-HRA years not to set up a Human Rights Commission, as proposed in the Green Paper, created a clear weakness in the extra-judicial enforcement of the Act.[693]

A Joint Parliamentary Committee on Human Rights (JCHR) was set up under the chairmanship of Professor David Feldman, and now of Murray Hunt, in order, *inter alia*, to advise on legislation.[694] It has fulfilled a very valuable role. But the responsibility for the extra-judicial promotion and enforcement of the HRA was clearly fragmented between 2000–6. As indicated above, the Human Rights Unit (now the Human Rights Division of the Department for Constitutional Affairs) and the Human Rights Task Force, set up by the Home Office, have a role in providing guidance to public authorities as to their responsibilities under the HRA, and in monitoring their progress. Further responsibility for monitoring the compliance of the key public authorities with the Convention has tended to devolve to existing bodies, all of which are bound by s 6, such as the Police Complaints Authority (now Independent Police Complaints Commission), the Parliamentary Intelligence and Security Committee, the Interception of Communications and Surveillance Commissioners,[695] the EOC, the Commission for Racial Equality and the Disability Rights Commission. It may be argued that the proliferation of such bodies tends to lead to the maintenance of inconsistent standards of human rights.[696]

In March 2003 the JCHR published its report on *The Case for a Human Rights Commission*.[697] In the Report the JCHR considered that there had not been a rapid development of awareness of a culture of respect for human rights; instead ill-informed and distorted views of the HRA were apparent. The Committeee thought that awareness of human rights was ebbing, rather than developing. It found that:

> the development of a culture of respect for human rights in this country was in danger of stalling, and that there was an urgent need for the momentum to be revived and the project driven forward . . . [the Report] concluded that this task could not be undertaken by the courts alone, and that . . . an independent commission would be the most effective way of achieving the shared aim of bringing about a culture of respect for human rights.[698]

It argued that the original vision that the Human Rights Act should aid in developing a culture of human rights would not be realised through litigation alone. In October 2003 the government announced that it had decided to proceed with the single equality body, and to give it a human rights dimension as well as an equality remit. The government's

---

693 See Wadham 'The HRA: one year on' [2001] EHRLR 620.
694 See Blackburn, R, 'A Parliamentary Committee on Human Rights', in Blackburn and Plant, ibid
695 See Chapter 10, pp 1039, 1047 for discussion of the current position.
696 See further Beckett, S and Clyde, I, 'A Human Rights Commission for the UK: the Australian Experience' (2000) 2 EHRLR 116.
697 Sixth Report, Session 2002–3, *The Case for a Human Rights Commission*, HL Paper 67-I and II, HC 489-I and II; see also Twenty-second Report, Session 2001–2, *The Case for a Human Rights Commission: Interim Report*, HL Paper 160, HC 1142.
698 Sixth Report, Session 2002–3, op. cit., para 99.

written statement announced that the new Commission would '. . . promote a culture of respect for human rights, especially in the delivery of public services'.[699]

As the JCHR pointed out in its Eleventh Report of 2004, the most fundamental issue in relation to the powers and functions of the CEHR is the nature of its human rights remit. The Commission will have a broad human rights mandate and will have a free-standing power to promote human rights. However, it will not have enforcement powers as part of its human rights remit. In the Lords' debate on the JCHR's Sixth Report, Lord Falconer said:

> . . . human rights include but go beyond equality issues. That is to be reflected in the new body: therefore, human rights will not be a seventh strand but will inform and support the six equality strands. It will be a free-standing subject for the body to promote whether or not there is a linked equality issue.[700]

Similarly, in the House of Commons, the Deputy Minister for Women and Equality, just prior to publication of The White Paper: *Fairness For All: A New Commission for Equality and Human Rights*,[701] Jacqui Smith MP, said:

> . . . we are putting human rights at the heart of the new politics of equality . . . The new body will be able to work to embed a culture of respect for human rights in public services and help public bodies to understand their obligations under the Human Rights Act . . . human rights values will help the new body to balance one person's rights against another's.[702]

The Commission for Equality and Human Rights (CEHR) was set up as a Non-Departmental Public Body (NDPB) under Part 3 Equality Act 2006 and will come into operation in October 2007.[703] As Chapter 15 explains, the CEHR will bring together the work of the three existing equality Commissions discussed in that chapter,[704] as well as taking on new responsibilities in relation to the Human Rights Act. The government's intention is that the CEHR will have a promotional rather than coercive role in relation to human rights. It will have investigatory powers, but in contrast to its powers in relation to equality matters, it will not have special enforcement powers. The new Commission can launch inquiries but not investigations, in respect of human rights matters. As discussed in Chapter 15, investigations are more serious matters since they

---

699 HC Deb, 30 October 2003, cols 18–20WS.
700 On 16 January 2004, HL Deb, 16 January 2004, Cols 765–66.
701 May 2004, Cm 6185.
702 On 4 March 2004, HC Deb, 4 March 2004, col 1141.
703 See the Equality Act 2006 (Commencement No.1) Order 2006, SI 2006/1082. It may be noted that Scotland will also soon have a Human Rights Commission. The Justice Minister, Jim Wallace, stated in 1999 that he is in favour of a Scottish Human Rights Commission: *The Scottish Executive: An Open Scotland*, SE/1999/51, November 1999. There are Scottish proposals to set up a Scottish Human Rights Commission (SHRC), and a Bill to that effect was announced by First Minister Jack McConnell in his Statement on the Scottish legislative programme to 2007. As a result, a Scottish 'Commissioner for Human Rights Bill' was introduced in the Scottish Parliament on 7th October 2005.
704 See pp 1595 *et seq*.

can lead to legal consequences.[705] It will have to publish terms of reference before launching an inquiry, and must publish reports at the end of the process, which could include recommendations for changes to policies, practices or legislation.

The CEHR power to carry out general inquiries means that it can promote improved human rights practice in public authorities. If during an inquiry the Commission suspects that an unlawful act has been committed – a breach of a Convention right by a public authority – it must stop the inquiry, but it cannot launch an investigation. The CEHR has not been given additional enforcement powers relating to the HRA on the somewhat doubtful basis that legal aid is available.[706] If an inquiry reveals that a body appears to be engaging in non-Convention-compliant practices, but no victim is willing to bring an action, the CEHR can merely make a recommendation. It does not appear that it could challenge the practices by way of judicial review in its own name, as discussed below. Assuming that it commenced an investigation on grounds of suspected unlawful discrimination in a public authority, it might find that a suspected breach of Art 14, probably read with Art 8, was also occurring.[707] That would be of some significance if Art 14 in the particular circumstances had a wider ambit than the relevant domestic anti-discrimination instrument. The CEHR is likely to be placed in a difficult position since it appears that it would be expected to close its eyes to Convention breaches while investigating breaches of such instruments.

The CEHR will have an advisory role in relation to individuals and pressure or community groups. Under s 13 of the 2006 Act, which covers its advisory role, it will publish information; undertake research; provide education or training; give advice or guidance. Its guidance could be about the Convention implications of a proposed Bill. The CEHR will also act in an advisory capacity in relation to proposed legislation[708] under s 12. It is intended that it should give Ministers advice or make proposals on any aspect of current or proposed law that relates to any part of its remit.

While the CEHR can advise and assist, it cannot take representative actions on behalf of individuals in either equality or human rights matters. However, the EOC and CRE were able to bring about general changes in discriminatory practices by seeking a direct change in domestic law in reliance on European Union law (*Secretary of State for Employment ex p EOC*),[709] and the CEHR will be able to do this in much wider range of circumstances in the field of discrimination.[710] Clearly, in respect of its human rights remit the CEHR would not have the same role in relation to EU law. However, it could have sought judicial review of executive actions and decisions that arguably breach the Convention rights[711] were it not for the narrow 'victim' provisions of the HRA which seem to preclude this possibility.

---

705 See pp 1594–98.
706 White Paper (2004), para 4.2.
707 See Chapter 15, pp 1482–84.
708 See the White Paper *Fairness for All* (2004) Cm 6185, paras 3.35, 3.36.
709 [1994] All ER 910; [1994] ICR 317.
710 See Chapter 15, pp 1596, 1600.
711 See, e.g., *R (Amin) v Secretary of State for the Home Dept* [2003] 4 All ER 1284 in which a declaration was made that a public inquiry investigation into a death in a Young Offenders' Institution should have been held; the failure of the Home Secretary to do so had created a breach of Art 2.

The JCHR proposed that the Commission, in addition to the power to assist as a friend of the court or to intervene as a third party in significant cases raising questions of public interest relating to human rights, should have an exceptional power to seek judicial review on compliance by public authorities with their duties under the Human Rights Act.[712] The government, however, took the view that the narrow victim provisions of s 7 HRA should remain undisturbed. As argued above, however, when administrative action is purportedly taken under statutory powers, a non-victim group such as the CEHR (assuming that it was viewed as having sufficient interest), who wished to challenge it by way of judicial review could rely on s 3 and argue that the action was *ultra vires* since the statute did not give powers to the executive to act incompatibly with the Convention rights, unless the statute was irretrievably incompatible with them. The obligation under s 3 is not limited by the s 7(7) test regarding victims.

But as a general comment on its human rights remit, the lack of an investigative power and the inability of the CEHR to rely on the use of judicial review creates, it is argued, a weakness in its ability to ensure adherence to the HRA among public authorities. Nevertheless, it may have some impact in making the case for the HRA to the general public that was not made seven years ago.

8 Conclusions

This book examines the emerging effects of the HRA in various contexts. It argues that its impact is immensely variable, depending on the context, but that it provides a means of reversing the erosion of fundamental freedoms which occurred under the Thatcher, Major, and now Labour Governments in the contexts of public protest, state surveillance and suspects' rights, especially those of terrorist suspects. The Labour Government has in some respects carried on the illiberal traditions of the previous Conservative Governments in showing, in its 'state power' legislation, especially counter-terrorist legislation, a 'corrupting insensitivity to liberty'.[713] The HRA has taken a role in providing a basic protection for human rights in the face of ill-thought out and arguably counter-productive anti-terrorism legislation. In the completely different context of privacy rights asserted against the media, it has provided a very significant impetus to the developments that were already occurring in the pre-HRA era.

The HRA incorporates a set of moral values under the Convention into UK law; the Convention represents a series of moral choices in that some of the rights are absolute, while some have presumptive priority over competing social interests.[714] The Convention jurisprudence employs concepts recognised and developed across the world by judges who may be viewed as defending a particular set of liberal values. These may be employed in a counter-majoritarian fashion in the sense that they aid in the protection of the rights of weak and unpopular groups. But in the case of the HRA, their judicial use

---

712 Research Paper 05/28: The Equality Bill para 39.
713 Dworkin, R, *Index on Censorship* (1988) pp 7–8. See also Dworkin, R, *A Bill of Rights for Britain?* (1988) pp 9–10.
714 The rights fall into three groups: those which are absolute: Arts 3, 4, 6(2), 6(3), 14 and First Protocol Art 3; those which are very narrowly qualified: Arts 2, 5, 6(1), 7, Sixth Protocol Art 1 (read with Art 2) and those which are materially qualified: Arts 8–12, First Protocol Art 1. See further Chapter 2, pp 18, 68.

is subject, theoretically, to the possibility of using the parliamentary override. Under the ECHR exceptions to the rights can only be utilised if both necessary and proportionate, and a number of the rights are not qualified at all or not materially qualified. The ECHR only allows for derogation from the rights in an emergency situation, and even then not from all of the rights.[715] Under the HRA ss 3(2) and 6(2) in theory derogation is completely unconstrained, in accordance with the theory of Parliamentary sovereignty. Further, it is not required in those sections that the demands of proportionality should be satisfied before rights can be abrogated. On a face-value reading of those sections, Parliament is entirely free to pass rights-abridging legislation and the judges must give effect to it if s 3 cannot be utilized to impose compatibility since the infringement of the right is such a fundamental feature of the statute. So on the face of it the HRA represented a compromise between Parliamentary sovereignty and rights-protection that left the rights entirely at the mercy of a government that could command a majority in Parliament. As far as the courts were concerned, the s 4 declaration of incompatibility procedure left the rights to the mercy of an unfettered executive discretion. So, as argued above, a contradiction was created between Parliamentary sovereignty and rights protection: rights were not, apparently, brought home since Parliament could simply override them and the government could disregard declared incompatibility. The HRA itself on its face appeared to be incompatible with the stated aim of reversing erosions of liberty effected via legislative changes in the Thatcher years.

But although the HRA provided mechanisms supposed to allow for an overt resolution of the contradiction between enhanced rights protection and Parliamentary sovereignty – ss 3(2), 6(2), 4, 10, 19 – they have hardly been utilized by the Labour Government.[716] The battle between parliamentary sovereignty and rights protection is playing out much more subtly, in the interpretation given by the judges to s 3 and in the interpretation of 'public function' under s 6. The question whether Parliament has passed rights-abridging legislation is in essence a determination as to which measures satisfy the demands of proportionality. That decision, as a matter of constitutional practice, is now for the judges, not Parliament, to make. The question whether the government can transfer large amounts of public sector resource to the private sector, without imposing Convention obligations on private sector providers, has arguably resolved itself into an issue as to whether judges take an institutional or a functional view of s 6. The government has not passed legislation overtly denying Convention rights to persons whose lives are affected when the accommodation they are living in passes into the private sector. The government has not relied on the HRA to force legislation that is overtly rights-abridging through Parliament, preferring instead to utilise the Convention derogation system.[717] It has not refused to respond to a declaration of incompatibility even though it set up the HRA as a mechanism for so doing. In relying on the ECHR system for creating exceptions to the rights, rather than the HRA one, it has indicated its acceptance of its ECHR obligations.

Thus the moral values captured in the Convention are filtering in to domestic law, essentially without being subject to certain of the overt constraints that the HRA appeared

---

715 See Chapter 2, pp 110–11.
716 Except in respect of the Communications Act 2003.
717 See, e.g., Chapter 14, pp 1438–42.

to create. The constraints that are apparent are more subtle. They are arguably largely rooted in common law values that are being imposed on the HRA and Convention by the judiciary. This is apparent, as discussed above, in the post-HRA use of deference. The public function question has to an extent been addressed in a manner that reflects a reluctance to constrain market values in the private sector, relying on judicial review principles. Thus s 6 has been quite narrowly interpreted, whereas s 3 has received on the whole a wide interpretation where common law principles, such as the presumption of innocence or the admissibility of probative evidence, are at stake. A key area in which the judges have given an appearance of departing from common law values in favour of Convention ones, where the two appeared to be in conflict, is in respect of the creation of indirect horizontal effect. But even in that instance the common law was poised pre-HRA to take the leap in the direction of protecting privacy that was then taken. Perhaps a clearer departure from common law values can be seen in *Laporte* in which the Lords used Convention principle to curb, not the effect of rights-abridging legislation, but the effect of their own creation – the common law doctrine of breach of the peace,[718] which has had a far more significant impact in the last 20 years in limiting public protest than have the statutory public order provisions.

In the chapters that follow, then, a doctrinal analysis of the use of the HRA mechanisms in various contexts is accompanied by perspectives that take account of government reluctance to breach the Convention in an overt manner, and of the stances taken by the judiciary as they apply those mechanisms in Convention-based adjudication. These perspectives may aid in explaining, not only why certain Convention values are finding a more ready reception in domestic law than others, but also in revealing why the HRA mechanisms themselves are being deployed in Parliament and in the courts in a manner that does not entirely comport with the expectations of 2000.

The still unresolved choice before the courts is whether to treat the HRA as a domestic Bill of Rights in the sense that autonomous constitutional rights are being developed, or whether to treat it merely as a means of affording a readier access to Strasbourg principles in the domestic courts. This chapter has identified developments tugging in opposing directions; the book as a whole reveals similarly opposing stances. But certain recent decisions of the House of Lords suggest that a movement in the Bill of Rights direction is occurring, most clearly *Campbell, Ghaidan, A and Others*[719] and *Laporte*.[720]

As this chapter has argued, the HRA itself, in terms of its basis in constitutional theory, potentially stood in the way of the development of an autonomous human rights jurisprudence. Taking account of the s 3 jurisprudence, it allowed, in accordance with the doctrine of parliamentary sovereignty, for completely unconstrained derogations from the Convention rights, unrelated to emergency situations and not dependent on satisfying the demands of proportionality, so long as the incompatibility in primary legislation was strong and far-reaching enough – so long as it permeated the statute or could be said to be a fundamental feature of it. Thus, *Ghaidan* could have been overturned by a statute with one single, overriding purpose – to distinguish between homosexual

---

718 See Chapter 8, p 759.
719 See Chapter 14, pp 1430–38.
720 See Chapter 8, pp 695, 757–71.

and heterosexual couples in provision of housing to the detriment of the former. That stance was hardly consonant with the idea of developing a domestic Bill of Rights. But, as discussed in this chapter, that leeway has hardly been utilised: the theoretical constraints built in to the HRA have been marginalised in favour of an assertion of judicial power in defence of the Convention rights. That position seems to open the door to the development of a domestic Bill of Rights. If as a matter of constitutional reality the true constraints on parliamentary and judicial power are Convention ones, not HRA ones, then the way is open to develop a synthesis of common law and Convention principle unconstrained by the key dilutant of the Convention standards – the margin of appreciation doctrine. On this basis it is unnecessary – leaving aside the conceptual incoherence of the Conservative position on this matter[721] – to repeal the HRA in order to introduce a 'modern' British Bill of Rights, since Britain already has one.[722]

---

721 See fn 50 above.
722 See on this point 'A Bill of Rights: Do we need one or do we already have one?' Francesca Klug, 2 March 2007, Irvine Human Rights Lecture 2007, University of Durham, Human Rights Centre (to be published in *Public Law*, Winter 2007). It may be noted that Labour is also drawn to the idea of replacing the HRA with a 'British Bill of Rights'. As Chapter 3 (p 156) pointed out, Gordon Brown in his inaugural speech as Prime Minister on 24 June 2007 indicated his interest in this possibility. The driving force appears to be a perception that a new instrument could enable a 'better' balance to be struck between human rights concerns and counter-terrorist measures. Also, as indicated above (p 163), Labour is concerned about the image that the media have created of the HRA. A 'British Bill of Rights' could possibly be 'sold' to the British people more readily as an instrument rooted in British tradition than can an instrument that incorporates a European Human Rights Treaty.

Part II

Expression

Introduction

Part II covers a number of aspects of expression including political expression, in the form of public protest, and pornographic expression. It also covers access to official information as an essential precursor to expression since, without such access, some expression will be curbed or cannot occur at all. This introduction considers the justifications underlying the legal protection offered to freedom of expression, their recognition in the Strasbourg and domestic jurisprudence and the implications of the justifications for the legal restrictions on expression. The chapters contained in Part II consider the restrictions domestic law places on expression – the traditional starting point for discussion of expression in the UK – but then they go on to consider the impact of the HRA on those restrictions. In so doing, it will take account of the discussion, in Chapter 2, of the freedom of expression guarantee under Art 10 of the European Convention on Human Rights, and of a number of the other aspects of the Strasbourg jurisprudence. The main focus of these chapters will be on the changes that are occurring in the protection for expression under the HRA as the Strasbourg jurisprudence permeates this area of law. This part is concerned with *expression*, since that is the term used in Art 10 – a wider term than speech: Art 10 protects expression, which could only very doubtfully be termed 'speech'. However, where the expression in question consists of speech, that term will be used.

In this Part, it will be found that the right to freedom of expression comes into conflict with the freedom to manifest racial hatred and with the right to a fair trial. It has also been viewed as conflicting with the right to freedom of religion. It is apparent from the Convention jurisprudence that, where two Convention rights come into conflict, some kind of balancing act between the two needs to be undertaken.[1] Although jurisprudence in this area is limited, it appears that the margin of appreciation tends to become particularly significant here, so that states have a fairly wide discretion in resolving the conflict.[2] Domestic courts therefore, have an appreciable degree of

---

1 *Otto-Preminger Institut v Austria*, Series A 295-A; (1994) 19 EHRR 34, para 55. The two Convention rights in conflict there were free speech itself and – so the Court found – the right to religious freedom, protected by Art 9.
2 See Chapter 9, pp 943–950. See in particular, *Otto-Preminger Institut v Austria*, Series A 295-A; (1994) 19 EHRR 34. The restriction on Art 10 entailed by the seizure of an allegedly blasphemous film was justified by reference to the Art 9 right to freedom of religious belief. The Court applied a wide margin of appreciation, and simply said that 'the content of the film cannot be viewed as

latitude in determining where to strike the balance between the two interests involved. Section 12 HRA, which, as Chapter 4 indicated, enjoins the courts to have 'particular regard' to Art 10 when making any order which might infringe it, appears on its face to suggest a higher weighting for speech interests. Such imbalance is also prima facie suggested by the strength of the 'speech' jurisprudence at both the Strasbourg and domestic levels discussed above. In *Ex p Simms*,[3] Lord Steyn referred to free speech as 'the primary right . . . in a democracy' and some commentators take the view that Art 10 attracts an especially high level of protection at Strasbourg.[4]

However, save for admitting the distinction between those rights stated in absolute terms, such as Arts 3, 4 and 7 and those subject to generalised exceptions (8–11), Strasbourg has never sought to establish a hierarchy of Convention rights. Rather, where rights collide, it has advocated a careful examination of the competing claims of each in the light of all the circumstances of the case.[5] There is no indication that Parliament, in passing the HRA, intended to alter this position and create a serious imbalance between the two rights;[6] rather, it is evident that the sponsors of the amendment saw it merely as a domestic reflection of the Strasbourg approach.[7] Moreover, the un-balanced American approach is out of line with other jurisdictions and flows from factors peculiar to that jurisdiction, in particular the absolute nature of the First Amendment.[8] It is now clear that, despite the wording of s 12, the courts have rejected an approach under the HRA that gives Art 10 a higher status than the other qualified Convention rights.[9]

Free expression justifications

All countries which have a Bill of Rights protect freedom of expression because it is perceived as one of the most fundamental rights. But why should this particular freedom be viewed as so worthy of protection? Why, as Barendt puts it, should speech which offends the majority have any special immunity from government regulation 'while there would be no comparable inhibition in restraining conduct [such as public] love-making which has similar offensive characteristics?'.[10] Four main justifications for offering protection to free speech have been offered and will be considered here in turn. In each case, an indication will be given as to the kinds of expression the various justifications will support because all the theories will not be relevant to all forms of

incapable of grounding' the conclusion of the national authorities that seizure was justified (para 56). Thus the test applied was reminiscent of the narrow *Wednesbury* standard of unreasonableness. See further Chapter 6, pp 487–491. See also *Wingrove v UK* (1997) 24 EHRR 1.

3 [1999] 3 All ER 400, CA; [1999] 3 WLR 328, HL

4 Leigh, I and Lustgarten, L, 'Making rights real: the courts, remedies, and the Human Rights Act' (1999) 58 CLJ 509, p 524 and n 79.

5 See the views of Lord Steyn and Lord Cooke in *Reynolds v Times Newspapers* [1999] 4 All ER 609, pp 631 and 643.

6 An amendment providing that a court should 'normally' give precedence to Art 10 over Art 8 was rejected (HC Deb Vol 315 Cols 542–43, 2 July 1998).

7 See, e.g., the speech of Jack Straw on cl 12: HC Deb Vol 315 Cols 535–39, 2 July 1998.

8 See below, pp 311–12.

9 See Chapter 9, pp 956–58.

10 Barendt, E, *Freedom of Speech*, 1987, p 1. References will normally be to the 2nd edn, (2006) unless otherwise stated.

expression. Initially, it should be noted that three of the justifications are inherently more contingent and therefore precarious than the first. These three justifications – the arguments for the opportunity to arrive at the truth through free discussion, for the necessity of free speech to enable meaningful participation in democracy and for individual self-fulfilment – all ultimately argue that speech is to be valued not for its own sake, but because it will lead to some other outcome we think desirable; thus, they may be characterised as teleological justifications. If, therefore, when considering a particular form of speech, a persuasive argument can be made out that allowing the speech is likely to achieve a result antithetical to the desired outcome, protection will no longer be justifiable. By contrast, as will be seen below, it is inherent in the first main justification for free speech – the argument for moral autonomy – that arguments about the likely effects of allowing the particular speech are not relevant to the question whether the justification applies – although clearly, such arguments may still be relevant in deciding whether the speech should nonetheless be abrogated.

The argument from moral autonomy

This argument was outlined in Chapter 1 as one of the most powerful justifications for human rights in general and so will only briefly be rehearsed here. Ultimately, whether the particular argument used is Rawls's hypothetical social contract[11] or Dworkin's basic postulate of the state's duty to treat its citizens with equal concern and respect,[12] this justification for free expression is centred around the liberal conviction that matters of moral choice must be left to the individual. In either case, the conclusion reached is that the state offends against human dignity,[13] or treats certain citizens with contempt if the coercive power of the law is used to enforce the moral convictions of some upon others. The argument perhaps has a more common and conspicuous application with regard to sexual autonomy and so is often disregarded in arguments about free speech.[14]

The justification is less contingent than the others, as mentioned above, because any restriction on what an individual is allowed to read, see or hear, clearly amounts to an interference with her right to judge such matters for herself. Thus, the argument consistently defends virtually all kinds of speech and other forms of expression,[15] whereas the arguments from truth and democracy[16] will tend to have a somewhat less comprehensive range of application. Since the argument also sets up freedom of speech as a strong 'trump' right,[17] or as part of the individual's claim to inviolability,[18]

---

11 See Chapter 1, p 6.
12 See Chapter 1, pp 7–8.
13 Barendt makes the point, however, that unlimited speech may also assault human dignity (Barendt, E, *Freedom of Speech*, 1987, pp 16–17). This argument is considered in relation to pornography below: Chapter 6, pp 455–61.
14 Barendt, e.g., comments (ibid, p 16) that the 'general freedom to moral autonomy [is] perhaps without much relevance to free speech arguments'.
15 It also covers material which could only doubtfully be classified as speech, e.g., photographic pornography.
16 See below, pp 302–5.
17 Ronald Dworkin's phrase; see Chapter 1, p 12.
18 The idea is Rawls's; see Chapter 1, p 11.

the right in both cases overrides normal utilitarian arguments about the benefit or detriment to society of the particular form of speech under consideration.[19] By contrast, the justifications from democracy and truth both set out goals for society as a whole and, therefore, would seem reasonably to allow abrogation of speech in the interests of other public concerns which may be immediately and directly damaged by the exercise of speech. As Barendt puts it, in discussing the argument from truth: 'a government worried that inflammatory speech may provoke disorder is surely entitled to elevate immediate public order considerations over the long-term intellectual development of the man on the Clapham omnibus.'[20]

The argument from truth

The most famous exposition of this argument is to be found in JS Mill's *On Liberty*.[21] The basic thesis is that truth is most likely to emerge from free and uninhibited discussion and debate. It is worth noting that this is a proposition about a causal relationship between two phenomena – discussion and truth – which of course has never been conclusively verified. However, its general truth is taken as virtually axiomatic in the Western democracies and forms the basic assumption underpinning the whole approach of reasoned, sceptical debate which is the peculiar hallmark of Western civilisation. Nonetheless, the crude assumption that more free speech will always lead to more truth has been attacked by certain feminist writers, who consider that the free availability of pornography leads not to the revelation of truth, but to the creation of false and damaging images of women or, more controversially, that pornography actually 'constructs the [sexist] social reality of gender'[22] – a claim which will be examined in detail in Chapter 6.

It appears that Mill envisaged his argument as applicable mainly to the expression of opinion and debate, but it can equally well be used to support claims for freedom of information, since the possession of pertinent information about a subject will nearly always be a prerequisite to the formation of a well-worked-out opinion on the matter. However, prima facie, it may be thought that the theory does not immediately make it clear when we need to know the truth about a given subject. Thus, it could be argued that a delay in receiving certain information (owing, for example, to government restrictions) would not greatly matter, as long as the truth eventually emerged. In response to this, it may be argued that if truth is valued substantively – a position most would assent to[23] – then any period of time during which citizens are kept in ignorance of the truth or form erroneous opinions because of such ignorance, amounts to an evil, thus giving rise to a presumption against secrecy. If, alternatively or in addition, knowledge of the truth is valued because of its importance for political participation, then clearly it will be most important to know the information at the time that the issue it concerns is most likely to affect the political climate. This rationale would thus provide a strong

---

19   For a discussion of justifications allowing strong rights to be overridden, see Chapter 1, pp 12–14.
20   Barendt, E, *Freedom of Speech*, 1987, p 10.
21   Mill, JS, *On Liberty*, in Cowling, M (ed), *Selected Writings of John Stuart Mill*, Everyman, 1972.
22   MacKinnon, C, *Feminism Unmodified*, 1987, Harvard University Press, p 166.
23   Mill, as a utilitarian, would probably not see truth as inherently valuable, but rather as a very important means of ensuring the overall welfare of society.

argument against the propensity of UK Governments to attempt to conceal political secrets until revelation would no longer have a damaging effect on their interests.[24]

Clearly, whether truth is valued instrumentally – for example, as essential to self-development – or as a good in itself, some kinds of truths must be regarded as more important than others.[25] Thus, in the context of a collision between free speech and privacy rights, the small intrinsic value of knowing the facts about (say) a film star's sexual life juxtaposed with the implausibility of the notion that such information would enable more effective political participation or individual growth, provides reasonable grounds for favouring the privacy interest in such a case. By contrast, revelations about corruption amongst prominent politicians will arguably not only have a more important part to play in the formation and development of individuals' general opinions, they will also play a vital role in enabling informed contribution to be made to the political process. Thus, a compelling argument for favouring free speech in this situation is readily made out. We will return to this argument in Chapter 9.

The argument from participation in a democracy

Barendt describes this theory as 'probably the most attractive of the free speech theories in modern Western democracies' and concludes that 'it has been the most influential theory in the development of 20th-century free speech law'.[26] The argument, which is associated primarily with the American writer Meiklejohn,[27] is simply that citizens cannot participate fully in a democracy unless they have a reasonable understanding of political issues; therefore, open debate on such matters is essential. In so far as democracy rests upon ideas both of participation *and* accountability, the argument from democracy may be seen to encompass also the function which a free press performs in exposing abuses of power,[28] thereby allowing for their remedy and also providing a deterrent effect for those contemplating such wrong-doing.[29] The influence of this argument can be seen in the fact that directly political speech has a special protected status in most Western democracies.

Such speech now has a legal guarantee in the UK under Art 10, taking into account the Strasbourg political speech jurisprudence. Pre-HRA, when the British judiciary considered the claims of free speech, they seemed in general to be particularly concerned to protect the free criticism of the political authorities. Thus, in the seminal House of Lords decision in *Derbyshire v Times Newspapers*,[30] Lord Keith, in holding that neither local nor central government could sustain an action in defamation, said: 'It is of the highest importance that a democratically elected governmental body should be open to

---

24 As seen, e.g., in the so called 'Thirty-Year Rule' now contained in the Public Records Act 1958, as amended. See below, Chapter 7, p 629.

25 It is outside the scope of this work to attempt a full-scale normative inquiry into the relative value of different truths. A commonsensical consensus approach is all that is employed in the text, where it is suggested only that the mere satisfaction of curiosity without more is of a relatively low value compared to the ending of a deception.

26 Barendt, E, *Freedom of Speech*, 1987, pp 20 and 23 respectively.

27 See, e.g., his 'The First Amendment is an absolute' (1961) Sup Ct Rev 245.

28 See Blasi, V, 'The checking value in First Amendment theory' (1977) Am B Found Res J 521.

29 See Greenwalt, K, 'Free speech justifications' (1989) 89 Columbia L Rev 119, p 143.

30 [1993] AC 534; [1993] 1 All ER 1011; [1992] 3 WLR 28, HL.

uninhibited public criticism'. The fact that he based his decision on *this* justification for free speech and not on, for example, the individual right of journalists to express themselves freely, is evidence of judicial endorsement of the argument from democracy – and also, possibly, of their failure to give much consideration to other, rights-based justifications. The fact that the judiciary have mainly, or even only, this interest in mind when considering threats to free speech, helps to explain why they are so often prepared to allow speech to be overridden by other considerations. This is because this argument sees speech as a public interest and as justified instrumentally by reference to its beneficial effects on democracy, rather than seeing it as an individual right of inherent value. Therefore, clearly, it can render speech vulnerable to arguments that it should be overridden by competing public interests which are also claimed to be essential to the maintenance of democracy. Hence Margaret Thatcher's well-known justification for the media ban challenged unsuccessfully in the *Brind* case:[31] 'We do sometimes have to sacrifice a little of the freedom we cherish in order to defend ourselves from those whose aim is to destroy that freedom altogether.' Clearly, to a judge who sees the value of free speech only in terms of its contribution to the political process, an argument that allowing the speech in question will do more harm than good to the maintenance of democracy will always seem compelling. This is not to argue that this justification is fundamentally flawed – clearly its basic premise is correct and offers an important reason to protect speech – but rather that one should be wary of using it as the sole justification even for directly political speech.

There is, however, an argument which does see the justification as fundamentally flawed because it would appear to allow suppression of free speech by the democracy acting through its elected representatives. However, this objection may be answered by the argument that certain values, such as protection for minorities and fundamental freedoms generally, are implicit in any mature conception of a democracy.[32] Therefore, the term 'democracy' or the furtherance of democracy should not be narrowly defined to include only the decisions of the particular government in power, but should also encompass the general principles mentioned; by affording respect to such principles, democracy will ultimately be preserved. This argument would suggest that the justification would appear to have little direct relevance to sexually explicit forms of expression or blasphemous speech but, on the other hand, since freedom of expression is arguably one of the freedoms the suppression of which would undermine democracy, protection for these forms of speech can also be argued for by the justification. It should be borne in mind, however, that as this argument depends on a separate and somewhat controversial contention about the nature of democracy, it offers only an indirect defence of non-political speech.[33] Nevertheless, if the above contention is accepted, one may

31 *Secretary of State for the Home Dept ex p Brind* [1991] 1 AC 696; [1991] 1 All ER 720; [1991] 2 WLR 588, HL.
32 Such a view is in fact endorsed by a number of legal philosophers and civil libertarians, and amounts to the most satisfactory reply to the charge that an entrenched Bill of Rights is undemocratic. See Dworkin, *A Bill of Rights for Britain*, 1990; the view also clearly underpins his general political philosophy, see, e.g., 'Liberalism', in *A Matter of Principle*, 1985. See also Hart, HLA, *Law, Liberty and Morality*, 1963 and Lester, A, *Democracy and Individual Rights*, 1968.
33 Most commentators seem to assume that the argument from democracy has little, if any, application to pornographic material. See, e.g., Dworkin, A, 'Do we have a right to pornography?' op. cit., fn 38, p 335. Similarly, the Williams Committee did not regard the argument as pertinent to their

then conclude that the argument from democracy is actually concerned to further two values: maintenance of the democracy and effective participation in it. The two values are distinct in that although effective as opposed to passive or inert participation may help to secure maintenance of the democracy, nevertheless some of its members, while wishing to see its continuance, might not wish to participate actively in it. Thus, political speech would contribute to the maintenance of both values, while other forms of speech would contribute only to the first, confirming what was suggested at the outset, namely that this justification argues for special protection of political speech.

The argument from individual self-fulfilment

Finally, we may turn to the thesis that freedom of speech is necessary in order to enable individual self-fulfilment. It is argued that individuals will not be able to develop morally and intellectually unless they are free to air views and ideas in free debate with each other. However, as Barendt notes,[34] it may be objected that free speech should not be singled out as especially necessary for individual fulfilment; the individual might also claim that, for example, foreign travel or a certain kind of education was equally necessary. On the other hand, freedom of speech represents a means of furthering individual growth which it is possible to uphold as a 'negative freedom'; other methods of furthering individual freedom would require positive action on the part of the government.

This justification is clearly rights-based and, as such, in theory at least, is less vulnerable to competing societal claims; however, it does not value speech in itself, but rather, instrumentally, as a means to individual growth. Therefore, in situations where it seems that allowing free expression of the particular material will be likely to retard or hinder the growth of others or of the 'speaker', the justification does not offer a strong defence of speech.[35] Precisely this argument has been used by feminist commentators to justify the censorship of pornography. Thus, MacKinnon asserts that far from aiding in the growth of anyone, 'Pornography strips and devastates women of credibility'[36] through the images of women it constructs in its readers' minds. The thesis which forms the basis of the UK law on obscenity – that certain kinds of pornography actually damage the moral development of those who read it by depraving and corrupting them, similarly fastens onto the argument that this kind of material achieves the opposite of the outcome which allowing freedom of expression is designed to ensure.[37] The apparent vulnerability of the argument from self-development when

---

deliberations (*Report of the Committee on Obscenity and Film Censorship*, Cmnd 7772, 1979; see below, p 455).

34   Barendt, E, *Freedom of Speech*, 1987, p 15.

35   Barendt argues (ibid, pp 16–17) that justifications for suppressing some forms of speech could be advanced on the basis that human dignity (the value promoted by allowing self-development) would thereby receive protection. He cites the finding of the German Constitutional Court that there was no right to publish a novel defaming a dead person as such publication might violate the 'dignity of man' guaranteed by Art 1 of the German Basic Law (*Mephisto* (1971) BVerfGE 173).

36   MacKinnon, C, *Feminism Unmodified*, 1987, p 193.

37   It should be noted first that pro-censorship feminists deny that their arguments have anything in common with conservative objections to pornography, e.g., MacKinnon, ibid, p 175, and secondly that the feminist thesis on pornography is far more complex than this. It will be explored in more detail in Chapter 6.

used to justify the protection of material which is arguably degrading[38] leads Barendt to suggest[39] that a sounder formulation of the theory is one which frames it in terms of the individual's right to moral autonomy. It is submitted that moral autonomy does provide the most persuasive defence of sexually explicit 'speech' and this argument will be developed when obscenity law is discussed. However, it will also be argued that autonomy is conceptually distinct from the notion of self-fulfilment and that nothing is to be gained by conflating the two concepts.

Implications for restrictions on expression

It is argued that the justifications considered would support the following propositions, which will be used as analytical tools to examine the soundness of the legal responses to expression considered in this Part, including those from Strasbourg. But the complex issues raised by these propositions cannot possibly be considered in sufficient depth here; full treatment can be found in books dealing specifically with theories underlying freedom of expression,[40] and it may be noted that the literature dealing with the domestic potential for importing free expression jurisprudence from other jurisdictions,[41] which has addressed many of the hard issues, is likely to become more extensive as one of the results of the inception of the HRA.

Content and form-based interferences

As a starting point, content-based restrictions should clearly be regarded with more suspicion than those based on *form*, since all of the free speech justifications potentially argue against such restrictions. Content-based restrictions, other than those constraining deliberate lies, prevent certain messages from ever entering the arena of debate and therefore run counter to the arguments from truth and self-fulfilment. Such restrictions prevent persons from knowing of, let alone evaluating, a particular message, thereby infringing their autonomy and, where the message is a political one, running counter to the argument from democracy. Thus, a regime committed to free speech would strongly condemn such restrictions. On this argument, a scholarly thesis arguing that the Holocaust caused far fewer deaths than is generally accepted would fall within the area of protected expression, while the handing out of leaflets and the putting up of posters by a Nazi group in a Jewish community designed to demonstrate precisely this point, might not.[42]

---

38 Dworkin also concludes that the argument from self-fulfilment fails to defend pornographic speech: 'Do we have a right to pornography?' in *A Matter of Principle* 1985; he founds his defence on moral autonomy and, like the present writer, clearly regards this concept as offering a separate head of justification.

39 Barendt 1987, p 17.

40 See Schauer, F, *Free Speech: A Philosophical Enquiry*, 1982, CUP; Barendt, E, *Freedom of Speech*, 2nd edn, 2006, esp Chapter 1; Waluchow, WJ (ed), *Free Expression: Essays in Law and Philosophy*, 1994, Clarendon; Campbell, T and Sadurski, W (eds), *Rationales for Freedom of Communication*, 1994, Dartmouth.

41 A provocative and interesting forerunner of such books is Loveland, I (ed), *Importing the First Amendment, Freedom of Expression in Britain, Europe and the USA*, 1998, Hart. See also Fenwick, H and Phillipson, G, *Media Freedom under the Human Rights Act* (2006).

42 This example is, of course, reminiscent of the famous 'Nazis at Skokie' affair. A group of Nazis wished to demonstrate, wearing Nazi uniforms and displaying swastikas, in a predominantly Jewish community.

But the idea of seeking to ensure content neutrality (an inquiry into the validity of restrictions that completely ignores the *content* of expression) in an absolutist fashion immediately runs into some difficulties.[43] Two key problems are identified here. First, while the idea can be sustained in the example given above, it is clear that in others, the manner in which a message is conveyed may be as significant, or more significant, than the message itself.[44] The examples of symbolic protest, mime, music and art are only some of those that come to mind. The use of various techniques, such as imagery and symbolism, is not only significant, but indissociable from the message. Indeed, such techniques convey a message. In a crude sense, they are the vehicle by means of which the 'message' is conveyed, but they not only interact with it, but also convey a host of emotive and cognitive 'messages' themselves. Secondly, form-based restrictions cannot be fully divorced from content-based ones, since it is only in relation to certain contents that the issue of form is raised. Time, place and access (based on age) restrictions are less problematic, since the infringement of freedom of expression they represent may tend to be insignificant in relation to achieving the ultimate goals indicated by the free speech justifications.

Thus, while it is suggested that all four free speech justifications (depending on the message) would argue against content-based restrictions, they might all also be engaged by form-based restrictions. Moreover, when one examines the justifications themselves, it can be found that they will support restrictions on expression in the furtherance of non-expression values. The feminist argument in this respect is considered below. In relation to forms of hate speech, it can be argued that it is an invasion of moral autonomy and militates against self-fulfilment for someone to be *forced to witness* expression deeply offensive to her (either because it is so pervasive as to be unavoidable or because it is likely that she will encounter it unwittingly). *A fortiori* this is the case when the speech goes beyond offensiveness and becomes threatening.[45] Speech that is impliedly or expressly threatening or intimidatory (so-called 'fighting words') may well impair an individual's autonomy since it has such a direct impact on her in the free ordering of her life.

It is concluded, first, that while content-based restrictions should be viewed with great caution, an engagement in the nature of the content when considering restriction is necessary, especially in terms of the impact on identifiable individuals, defined by their

They relied, successfully, on their First Amendment right to do so, in a case that divided civil libertarians: *Collin v Smith* (1978) 578 F 2d 1197, 7th Cir; (1978) 436 US 953; (1978) 439 US 916.

43   See Feldman, D, 'Content neutrality', in Loveland, I (ed), *Importing the First Amendment, Freedom of Expression in Britain, Europe and the USA*, 1998, Chapter 8.

44   See *Cohen v California*, (1971) 403 US 15, below, p 491.

45   As in the case of attacks on religious faith or homophobic, racist or sexist expression targeted directly at specific individuals. Examples of offensive behaviour that might readily become threatening would include putting up pornographic posters of women in the work place, sexist, homophobic or racist remarks directed at an employee, displaying an offensive symbol such as a swastika at work (see Chapter 15, pp 1556–63) or targeting persons in their homes as part of a racist campaign and, e.g., putting leaflets through the door, painting racist graffiti on the house. Cf *RAV v City of St Paul, Minnesota* (1992) 112 S Ct 2538; 120 L Ed 2d 305 in which a group of racist youths burnt a home-made cross in the front yard of a black family. It was found in the Supreme Court that the Ordinance under which one of the youths was charged was overbroad and content-based: expressive conduct of this nature causing offence was protected speech under the First Amendment.

group status. Secondly, the argument in favour of creating simplistic distinctions between content and form is unsustainable. The extent to which the form of the expression can be said to engage the free speech justifications has to be considered. Third, while time, place and access restrictions should be rigorously scrutinised on the basis of proportionality, they are prima facie less disturbing than content or form-based ones.

Market freedom and creative freedom

The second proposition is, contrary to the US 'marketplace' model,[46] that market freedom is far from consonant with creative freedom. As Barendt puts it, in relation to US thinking: 'A market-place which few can enter does nothing for the principle that debate on public issues should be uninhibited, robust and open.'[47] Promoting market freedom will tend to mean the dominance of the media by certain conglomerates.[48] It may, therefore, lead to homogenous expression which reflects unchallenged majority viewpoints. Thus, some intervention in the market, with the free speech justifications in mind, is warranted, with a view to furthering creative freedom. Such intervention would limit cross-media ownership – the concentration of ownership in different media sectors – and would seek to protect a public service element – as opposed to the reflection of purely commercial values – in, for example, the granting of licences to broadcast and in the monitoring of output. Such an element might include requirements to observe due impartiality, and to broadcast at peak times programmes reflecting minority interests, experimental and original drama, investigative documentaries ('must carry' requirements).[49] Toleration of such intervention is founded on the understanding that commercial television has a dual concern which will influence its output. It must satisfy the companies who use it to advertise their products that it can deliver a mass audience, which means that it must be able to provide programming which attracts and satisfies such an audience. Therefore, unlike books, music, art, or, to an extent, newspapers, a central concern is to satisfy the advertisers. Regulation is therefore warranted in order to prevent creative freedom from being outweighed by commercial concerns.

This is a matter that is, of course, especially pertinent in relation to media regulation, but the general proposition has implications going beyond current regulatory schemes[50] and, indeed, is relevant in relation to the HRA itself.[51] The proposition covers the use of libel laws by big business,[52] rights of access to the broadcast media,[53] interpretations

---

46 See Schauer, F, 'The political incidence of the free speech principle' (1993) 64 US Colorado LR 935.
47 See 'The First Amendment and the media', in Loveland, I (ed), *Importing the First Amendment, Freedom of Expression in Britain, Europe and the USA*, 1998, Chapter 8, pp 43–44. The quotation is from *New York Times v Sullivan* (1964) 376 US 254, 270. Barendt goes on to attack the market place model on a number of further grounds; he argues that the pressures of advertisers will influence mass communication and, further, that when corporate interests determine the media agenda, and do not provide access to the means of communication for dissenters, certain ideas cannot enter the 'free' market.
48 See Feintuck, M, *Media Regulation, Public Interest and the Law*, 1999.
49 See Chapter 6, pp 511–13.
50 See Chapter 6, pp 512–15.
51 See Chapter 4, pp 249–50.
52 See Wilmo, P and Rodgers, W (eds), *Gatley on Libel and Slander*, 1998, para 2.19.
53 See Chapter 6, p 539.

of contempt law,[54] access to publicity at election times, the suppression of protest (by, for example, environmental activists) in the corporate interest.[55]

Both these propositions suggest that the US freedom of expression model should be treated with caution, although this is not to say that it should not be referred to domestically, under the HRA, as providing an extensive and rich source of jurisprudence. Under the US model, all content-based restrictions on protected speech – speech protected under the First Amendment – are self-evidently unconstitutional, as indicated below.

The US model has been strongly influenced by the 'American's characteristically profound suspicion of government and the whole-hearted belief in the socially beneficial effects of unfettered economic freedom and individual endeavor . . . these traits have generated a model of the state which precludes government and courts from offering protection against significant forms of social and personal harm'.[56] The Strasbourg model, as this part will indicate, contrasts strongly with the American one in tolerating content-based restrictions that relate to the exceptions under Art 10(2).

Recognition of these justifications in Strasbourg and UK expression jurisprudence

The high regard in which freedom of expression, and particularly press freedom, is held by the Strasbourg institutions was indicated in Chapter 2. The Court has repeatedly asserted that freedom of expression 'constitutes one of the essential foundations of a democratic society',[57] and that it 'is applicable not only to "information" or "ideas" that are favourably received or regarded as inoffensive or as a matter of indifference, but also to those that "offend, shock or disturb" '.[58] Particular stress has been laid upon 'the pre-eminent role of the press in a state governed by the rule of law' which, 'in its vital role of "public watchdog" ' has a duty 'to impart information and ideas on matters of public interest' which the public 'has a right to receive'.[59]

However, while the rhetorical attachment to free speech is always strong, it is a marked feature of the Strasbourg jurisprudence that clearly political speech, which may be seen as directly engaging the self-government rationale, receives a much more robust degree of protection than other types of expression. Barendt's contention that this is 'the most influential theory in the development of 20th century free speech law'[60] is supported by examination of the approach of UK and Strasbourg judges. As indicated above, the basic thesis is that citizens cannot participate fully in a democracy unless they have a reasonable understanding of political issues; therefore, open debate on such

---

54 See Chapter 5, pp 330–34.
55 See Chapter 8, pp 793–94.
56 See Feldman, 'Content neutrality', in Loveland, I (ed), *Importing the First Amendment, Freedom of Expression in Britain, Europe and the USA*, 1998, Chapter 8, p 140.
57 *Observer and Guardian v UK* A 216 (1991), para 59.
58 See, e.g., *Thorgeirson v Iceland* (1992) 14 EHRR 843, para 63.
59 *Castells v Spain* A 236 (1992), para 43.
60 Barendt *Freedom of Speech* (1987), pp 20 and 23 respectively.

matters is necessary to ensure the proper working of a democracy; as Lord Steyn has put it: 'freedom of speech is the lifeblood of democracy.'[61]

Thus, the 'political' speech cases of *Sunday Times*,[62] *Jersild*,[63] *Lingens*[64] and *Thorgeirson*[65] all resulted in findings that Art 10 had been violated and all were marked by an intensive review of the restriction in question in which the margin of appreciation was narrowed almost to vanishing point.[66] By contrast, in cases involving artistic speech, supported by the values of autonomy and self-development rather than self-government, an exactly converse pattern emerges: applicants have tended to be unsuccessful and a deferential approach to the judgments of the national authorities as to its obscene or blasphemous nature has been adopted.[67]

A similar pattern may be discerned in the domestic jurisprudence: when speech supported by the arguments from self-development or autonomy rather than self-government is in question, decisions have tended to be cautious,[68] or downright draconian,[69] and accompanied by little or no recognition of these underlying values. The most lofty rhetorical assertions of the importance of free speech and the strongest determination to protect it have been evident in cases where journalistic material raises political issues, broadly defined.[70] In such cases, the courts have either overtly adopted the Strasbourg principles described above[71] or have strongly emphasised the high status freedom of

61 *R v Secretary of State for the Home Dept ex p Simms* [1999] 3 All ER 400, p 408.

62 *Sunday Times v UK* A 30 (1979). The case concerned a contempt of court action brought against the newspaper in respect of revelations it published concerning the dangers of the drug Thalidomide (for discussion, see Chapter 5, pp 336–37).

63 *Jersild v Denmark* (1994) 19 EHRR 1 concerned an application by a Danish journalist who had been convicted of an offence of racially offensive behaviour after preparing and broadcasting a programme about racism which included overtly racist speech by the subjects of the documentary.

64 *Lingens v Austria* (1986) 8 EHRR 103 concerned the defamation of a political figure.

65 *Thorgeirson v Iceland* (1992) 14 EHRR 843 concerned newspaper articles reporting allegations of brutality against the Reykjavik police.

66 See the discussion of the doctrine in Chapter 2, pp 36–39.

67 *Müller v Switzerland* (1991) 13 EHRR 212; *Gibson v UK*, Appl No 17634 (declared inadmissible by the Commission); *Handyside v UK*, A 24 (1976) (not a case involving artistic speech but where the issue was that of obscenity); *Otto-Preminger Institut v Austria* (1994) 19 EHRR 34; *Gay News v UK* (1982) 5 EHRR 123. In *Wingrove v UK* (1997) 24 EHRR 1, the Court remarked: 'Whereas there is little scope under Article 10(2) of the Convention for restrictions on political speech or on debate of questions of public . . . a wider margin of appreciation is generally available to the Contracting states when regulating freedom of expression in relation to matters liable to offend intimate personal convictions within the sphere of morals or, especially, religion' (para 58). These cases are discussed in Chapter 6, pp 463–66 and pp 487–91. See Harris, J, O'Boyle, M and Warbrick, C, *Law of the European Convention on Human Rights*, 1995, pp 397 and 414.

68 *Gibson* [1990] 2 QB 619. See Chapter 6, pp 482–83.

69 *Knuller v DPP* [1973] AC 435. In *Lemon* [1979] AC 617, the House of Lords held that the common law offence of blasphemy required no mental element, and that there was no defence of public interest. See further Chapter 6, p 485.

70 *Reynolds v Times Newspapers* [1999] 4 All ER 609; *Derbyshire CC v Times Newspapers* [1993] AC 534; *R v Secretary of State for the Home Dept ex p Simms* [1999] 3 WLR 328. However, deference to widely drafted primary legislation (*Secretary of State for Home Affairs ex p Brind* [1991] 1 AC 696) or governmental arguments from national security (*Attorney General v Guardian Newspapers (No 2)* [1990] 1 AC 109) has resulted in the ready upholding of restrictions on directly political speech.

71 See the approach of the Court of Appeal in *Derbyshire* [1993] AC 534 and in *Ex p Leech* [1994] QB 198, of the House of Lords in *Reynolds* [1999] 4 All ER 609, pp 621–22, *per* Lord Nicholls, pp 628

speech holds in the common law, as 'a constitutional right', or 'higher legal order foundation'.[72] Earlier pronouncements to the effect that: 'The media . . . are an essential foundation of any democracy'[73] were emphatically reinforced by pronouncements in the House of Lords' decision in *Reynolds v Times Newspapers*[74] which afforded an explicit recognition to their duty to inform the people on matters of legitimate public interest. Press freedom in relation to political expression has clearly been recognised as having a particularly high value in UK law and Convention jurisprudence.

The theory that freedom of speech is necessary for the discovery of truth[75] has been a strong influence in US jurisprudence,[76] but not historically at Strasbourg[77] or in the UK courts.[78] The argument from self development – that the freedom to engage in the free expression and reception of ideas and opinions in various media is essential to human development[79] – has received some recognition at Strasbourg[80] and recently in the House of Lords.[81]

Free speech protection in practice[82]

In the US, the country with perhaps the greatest commitment to freedom of speech, the First Amendment to the Constitution provides: 'Congress shall make no law abridging

---

and esp 635, *per* Lord Steyn, p 643, *per* Lord Cooke and *Ex p Simms* [1999] 3 WLR 328, p 407, *per* Lord Steyn and pp 419–20, *per* Lord Hobhouse.

72 *Reynolds v Times Newspapers* [1999] 4 All ER 609, pp 628–29 (Lord Steyn). In *Ex p Simms* [1999] 3 WLR 328, p 411, Lord Steyn described the right as 'fundamental', as did Lord Hoffmann, p 412.

73 *Francome v MGN* [1984] 2 All ER 408, p 898, *per* Sir John Donaldson.

74 *Per* Lord Steyn [1999] 4 All ER 609, pp 633–34; Lord Nicholls: 'freedom to disseminate and receive information on political matters is essential to the proper functioning of the system of parliamentary democracy cherished in this country' (p 621).

75 See above, pp 302–3; see further Greenwalt, K, 'Free speech justifications' (1989) 89 Columbia L Rev 119, pp 130–41 generally.

76 See the famous *dicta* of Judge Learned Hand in *United States v Associated Press* 52 F Supp 362, p 372 (1943); and of Holmes J, dissenting but with the concurrence of Brandeis J, in *Abrams v United States* 250 US 616, p 630 (1919).

77 The repeated reference by the ECtHr to freedom of expression being one of the 'basic conditions for [society's] progress' (see, e.g., *Otto-Preminger Institut v Austria* (1994) 19 EHRR 34, para 49) could be seen as a reference to the justification.

78 But see *Secretary of State for the Home Department ex p Simms* [1999] 3 All ER 400, p 408, *per* Lord Steyn.

79 E.g., Emerson argues that the right to free expression is justified as the right of the individual to realise his character and potentialities through forming his own beliefs and opinions ('Towards a general theory of the First Amendment' (1963) 72 Yale LJ 877, pp 879–80); see also Redish, M, *Freedom of Expression*, 1984, pp 20–30 and K, 'Free speech justifications' (1989) 89 Columbia L Rev 119, pp 143–45.

80 One of the stock phrases of the European Court of Human Rights in relation the value of freedom of expression asserts that it is one of the 'essential foundations for the 'development of everyone' (e.g., *Otto-Preminger* (1995) 19 EHRR 34, para 49).

81 *Per* Lord Steyn in *Ex p Simms* [1999] 3 All ER 400, p 498.

82 For comment, see Marshall, G, 'Freedom of speech and assembly', in *Constitutional Theory*, 1971, OUP, p 154; Barendt, *Freedom of Speech*, 2nd edn, 2006; Gibbons, *Regulating the Media*, 1998, Sweet and Maxwell; Robertson, G and Nichol, L, *Media Law*, 1999, Penguin; Boyle, A, 'Freedom of expression as a public interest in English law' [1982] PL 574; Singh, 'The indirect regulation of speech' [1988] PL 212; Clayton, R and Tomlinson, H, *The Law of Human Rights*, 2006, Chapter 15; Lester (Lord) and Pannick, D (eds), *Human Rights Law and Practice*, 1st edn, 2000, Chapter 4, p 197.

the freedom of speech or of the press.' This stricture is not interpreted absolutely literally, but it does mean that US citizens can challenge a law on the sole ground that it interferes with freedom of expression. However, freedom of expression is not absolute in any jurisdiction; other interests can overcome it, including the protection of morals, of the reputation of others, the preservation of public order, national security and protecting the interest in a fair trial. In fact, freedom of expression comes into conflict with a greater variety of interests than any other liberty and is therefore in more danger of being curtailed. Most Bills of Rights list these interests as exceptions to the primary right of freedom of expression, as does Art 10 of the European Convention on Human Rights. This does not mean that the mere invocation of the other interest will lead to displacement of freedom of expression; it is necessary to show that there is a pressing social need to allow the other interest to prevail.[83]

Although, until the inception of the Human Rights Act, the UK had no Bill of Rights protecting freedom of expression, Art 10 of the European Convention on Human Rights was taken into account by the courts in construing ambiguous legislation on the basis, as Chapter 3 indicated, that as Parliament must have intended to comply with its Treaty obligations, an interpretation should be adopted which would allow it to do so.[84] It has also, on occasion, been taken into account where there is ambiguity in the common law. Combined with the effects of certain very significant decisions against the UK at Strasbourg, Art 10 had a greater impact on UK law pre-HRA than its fellow Article, Art 11. However, its impact has been variable. It has not had as much influence as might perhaps have been expected as far as the laws of obscenity and decency are concerned. As Chapter 8 explains, it has also had little effect on expression in the form of public protest. This part covers access to information which, as Chapter 7 indicates, is not covered by Art 10, although such access may be viewed as associated with expression.

Under s 3 of the HRA, the obligation to interpret legislation compatibly with Art 10, and the related Arts 9[85] and 11, is much stronger than it was in the pre-HRA era, while the courts and other public authorities, including the police, are bound by the Convention under s 6 to uphold freedom of expression. As Chapter 2 indicated, Art 10 provides a strong safeguard for freedom of expression in relation to competing interests, since it takes the primary right as its starting point. The content of speech will rarely exclude it from the protection of Art 10, although not all speech is included.[86] Article 10(2) demands that interferences with the primary right should be both necessary and proportionate to the legitimate aim pursued. But the interferences with expression, considered in the following chapters, have not all been subject to the same intensity of scrutiny at Strasbourg. The reasons why this is so will be considered in those chapters.

---

83 See Chapter 2, pp 94–95 for discussion of this point and p 336, below.
84 See further Chapter 3, pp 134–37.
85 See Chapter 2, p 91.
86 In *Jersild v Denmark* (1994) 19 EHRR 1 it was assumed that the actual racist utterances of racists in a broadcast were not protected. In *Janowskki v Poland* (1999) 5 BHRC 672 it was found that insults to civil servants acting in their public capacity were protected, although the interference was found to be justified.

As the following chapters indicate, there are two methods of protecting the other competing interests mentioned: prior and subsequent restraints on freedom of expression. Prior restraints are generally seen as more pernicious and therefore countries with a Bill of Rights either outlaw them or keep them to a minimum. In the case of censorship, such restraints are viewed as particularly inimical to free speech, since they may operate outside the public domain and may therefore generate little or no publicity. Decisions will be taken by an administrative body, often with no possibility of challenge in the courts. On the other hand, subsequent restraints operate after publication of the article in question: the persons responsible may face civil or criminal liability. The trial may then generate publicity and the defendants may have an opportunity of demonstrating why they published the article in question. In other words, the case for allowing the speech in question is given a hearing.[87] However, the distinction between the two kinds of restraint may not be as stark as this implies. Subsequent restraints may have a chilling effect on publications; editors and others may well not wish to risk the possibility of incurring liability and may therefore themselves take the decision not to publish without reference to any outside body. In the case of prior restraints granted by the courts, usually injunctions, the case in favour of publication will normally be heard.

When one turns to consider UK law in this area, one confronts a mass of common law and statutory restrictions on freedom of expression and on expressive activities associated with it, such as marches or demonstrations. Traditionally, in order to determine how far freedom of expression was protected, it was necessary to consider the width of these restrictions in order to determine how much of an area of freedom was left within which expression could be exercised. Historically, in English law, there was no such thing as 'media freedom' as a constitutional or legal concept: as Dicey said, 'Freedom of discussion is in England little else than the right to write or say anything which a jury, consisting of twelve shopkeepers, think it expedient should be said or written.'[88] It was indeed crucial to the Diceyan paradigm that, insofar as press freedom was protected, it was a result of ordinary court judgments determining the rights of private citizens. In some areas of law affecting the media, where the media sought to make claims that could not be made by individual speakers, they were denied completely: perhaps the most notorious example is Lord Templeman's trenchant assertion at the beginning of his speech in a major case on protection of journalists' sources: 'This case is not about freedom of the press . . .'.[89] More typically, under the traditional English view, freedom of the press was simply the absence of a prior system of censorship, but other than that, simply a negative liberty. As Lord Wilberforce observed in 1981: 'Freedom of the press imports, generally, freedom to publish without pre-censorship, subject always to the laws relating to libel, official secrets, sedition and other recognised inhibitions.'[90]

As the above passage suggests, 'the law of media freedom' consisted merely of a mechanical application of the law deriving from statute and common law precedents; and media freedom, like any other negative liberty, was simply what was left over after

---

87 See Barendt, E, 'Prior restraints on speech' [1985] PL 253.
88 Dicey, AV, *Introduction to the Study of the Law of the Constitution*, 10th edn, 1959, Chapter VI .
89 *British Steel Corp v Granada Television Ltd* [1981] AC 1096; see further Chapter 5 at p 424.
90 [1981] 1 All ER 417, 455.

the scope of the restrictions had been determined. The HRA has altered that position in the sense that the media and citizens generally are able to rely on the Art 10 guarantee, against public authorities. Therefore, domestic freedom of expression should be determined by the scope of the Art 10 protection, bearing in mind the duty of national courts, discussed in Chapter 4, to disapply the margin of appreciation doctrine. The extent to which the judiciary are taking an activist or a minimalist approach to that doctrine in relation to expression is of particular significance, since Strasbourg has applied a review of very varying intensity in this context. The development of the domestic law, whether by way of legislation or the common law, is still highly significant, since all of it is being tested more directly against Art 10, in Parliament or in the courts.

It will be found that the law in this area has developed in an incoherent fashion. A willingness to accept the values of freedom of expression,[91] rather than relying strongly on those that traditionally attracted protection, especially proprietorial rights, became apparent in the 1990s, as Chapter 3 indicated. But where expression came into conflict with those values that had traditionally gained acceptance, such as maintaining public order, such values remained in the ascendant. The lack of a consistent pattern was arguably due to the lack of a free expression clause against which the other interests had to be measured. The emphasis of these chapters has to be on the judges' concern to strike a balance between free expression and a variety of other interests in the pre-HRA era, and the impact of Art 10 on the stance adopted. A pervasive critical theme will be the exposure of the judges' readiness to allow freedom of expression to be restricted on uncertain or flimsy grounds. It will be found in certain contexts that some of the interests identified by judges as justifying such restrictions would not qualify as sufficient grounds for outweighing the right of free expression under the liberal conception of rights outlined in Chapter 1. In such contexts, the impact of Art 10 will, therefore, be of especial significance. In others, it will become apparent that domestic law already satisfies Art 10 requirements.

In considering UK law it will be argued that outside the public order or anti-terrorist context statutes in this area give, in general, greater protection to freedom of expression than does the common law and that during the 1980s and 1990s it came particularly under threat, partly, but not exclusively, through common law developments, although, as indicated above, there were also a number of recent important judgments favouring freedom of speech. A theme which runs through this part concerns the extent to which the common law has undermined statutory safeguards for freedom of speech. This is a matter of especial significance under the HRA, since inconsistent common law provisions are not protected under s 6(2) HRA when applying the guarantee under Art 10 to a public authority. As Chapter 4 explained, incompatible common law provisions do not enjoy the protection afforded to statutory ones, although their precise legal position in relation to the Convention is complex.[92]

Clearly, this is not to argue that no English statute governing freedom of expression has to be modified by interpretation under Art 10 relying on the Human Rights Act. In examining the statutory provisions considered in this Part, it will become apparent that

---

91 See the House of Lords' decisions in the *Derbyshire* case [1993] AC 534; [1993] 1 All ER 1011; [1992] 3 WLR 28 and in *Ex p Simms* [1999] QB 349, considered above in Chapter 3, pp 125–26.
92 See pp 254–55.

some of them, especially in the field of public protest, provide extremely wide powers intended to protect other interests. It must, however, be remembered that they were framed by a parliament which had no domestic legal brake upon its powers, although post-1951 the UK was bound by the Convention at the international level. At times, it has been prepared to frame laws which, if fully enforced, would severely damage freedom of expression. Post-2000, as Chapter 4 argues, new legislation affecting freedom of expression has almost invariably been accompanied by a statement of its compatibility with the Convention (the exception is the Communications Act 2003), but this does not mean that incompatibility will not be found. Further, the statement may be issued on the basis of an interpretation grounded in a minimal version of the Convention. It is suggested that this is true of parts of the Terrorism Acts 2000 and 2006, discussed further in Chapter 14, in relation to its effects on freedom of expression.

But pre- and post-Human Rights Act legislation affecting freedom of expression shares the same characteristic: the laws are not – in normal circumstances - fully enforced; if they were, the consequent clash between the media and the government would bring the law into further disrepute. Thus, although by examining the provisions of these statutes, an indication of the 'balance' Parliament had in mind may be gained, other more nebulous factors, including the influence of powerful media bodies, must also be taken into account. Such factors may not apply in relation to public protest, and one of the concerns of this Part is to reveal the different emphasis placed on expression arising as protest rather than as an aspect of media freedom.

But a key concern of this Part is to evaluate whether any change in this 'balance' is occurring under the Human Rights Act and to consider the extent to which any such a change reflects the theoretical justifications underpinning various aspects of freedom of expression. The extent to which such justifications are likely to play a part in determining the resolution of the conflict between expression and a number of societal and individual interests, under the Human Rights Act, will form a central theme.

Chapter 5

Restraining Freedom of Expression under the law of contempt

1 Introduction[1]

This chapter is essentially concerned with two interests which are frequently perceived as being in conflict - the administration of justice and media freedom. The protection of the administration of justice is a general aim which is not concerned solely with protecting the right of the individual to a fair trial, although it may have that effect. Domestically, the interest in the administration of justice has been protected by the law of contempt, although obviously the main responsibility for ensuring fairness in criminal trials or civil actions remains with the judge. A number of aspects of contempt law are discussed below, including its use in curbing pre-trial discussions and publicity in the media which might influence those involved in forthcoming proceedings; threats to justice in the long-term sense, and requirements to disclose journalistic sources. It is apparent that, prima facie, contempt law creates interferences with the guarantee of freedom of expression under Art 10. The interference may be justified where it has the legitimate aim of 'maintaining the authority and impartiality of the judiciary' under para 2. This phrase may be taken to cover the preservation of the integrity of the administration of justice, including the rights of litigants. Since contempt law has a role to play in preventing prejudice to proceedings or in deterring the media from causing such prejudice, it may be viewed as a means of protecting Art 6 rights,[2] although the main responsibility for providing such protection falls on the trial judge.[3] Viewed as exceptions to Art 10, such rights fall within the rubric 'the rights of others' in para 2, as well as that of 'maintaining the authority of the judiciary'. (Since court proceedings may bring an individual to the attention of the media, with the result that details of their

---

1 Texts referred to in this chapter: Miller, CJ, *Contempt of Court*, 1999, OUP; Barendt, E, *Freedom of Speech*, 1st edn, 1987, 2nd edn, 2007, Chapter 8; Sufrin, B and Lowe, N, *The Law of Contempt*, 1996, Butterworths; Fenwick, H and Phillipson, G, *Media Freedom under the Human Rights Act*, 2006; Robertson, G, *Media Law*, 1999, Chapter 6; Arlidge, A and Smith, ATH, *Arlidge, Eady and Smith on Contempt*, 2nd edn, 1999, Sweet and Maxwell; Barendt, E and Hitchens, L, *Media Law: Cases and Materials*, 2000, Chapters 12, 13 and 14; Clayton, R and Tomlinson, H, *The Law of Human Rights*, 2nd edn, 2006, Chapter 15; Marshall, G, 'Press freedom and free speech theory' [1992] PL 40; Laws LJ, 'Problems in the law of contempt' (1990) CLP 99; Naylor, B [1994] CLJ 492; Laws LJ (2000) 116 LQR 157. For a historical overview, see: Fox, *The History of Contempt of Court*, 1927, Butterworths; Goodhart, AL, 'Newspapers and contempt of court in England' (1935) 48 Harv LR 885.
2 See Chapter 2, pp 59–66.
3 See the comments of Simon Brown LJ regarding the differing roles of the judge in contempt proceedings and at trial: *Attorney General v Birmingham Post and Mail Ltd* [1998] 4 All ER 49.

personal lives are revealed, the guarantee of respect for private life under Art 8 may also be relevant; the implications of this possibility are discussed in Part III, Chapter 9). Contempt law therefore comes into conflict with free expression, either on the basis of protecting general societal interests or other individual rights. Article 6 is not engaged where the threat is to the administration of justice in a general or long-term sense. Similarly, the use of contempt law to require the disclosure of sources would not normally engage Art 6, although it clearly does create an interference with the Art 10 guarantee, and moreover one which is viewed at Strasbourg as particularly serious, as indicated below.

But the notion that free speech and the administration of justice are likely to come into conflict should be examined further. This Part began by arguing that one of the most influential justifications for free speech arises from the part it plays in furthering democratic values. Speech which, under strict scrutiny, undermines the fairness of a trial can be viewed as attacking such values rather than upholding them. Chapter 9 argues that the conflict between speech and privacy is more apparent than real since, as Emerson puts it, the rights are 'mutually supportive in that both are vital features of the basic system of individual rights'.[4] It is suggested that, to an extent, this may also be said of free speech and fair trials. In a democracy, free speech serves the ends of justice since the free debate of conceptions of justice may allow for the inclusion of a variety of views within the process of justice which will therefore enhance its moral authority.[5] Thus, if one of the justifications for speech is that it supports the fairness of trials by scrutinising justice, as an aspect of the 'open' justice principle, speech which, on careful scrutiny, creates unfairness may legitimately be restricted since it undermines that central justification. In other words, freedom of speech has a key role as an essential aspect of a fair system of justice, but speech which affects the impartiality of a hearing may undermine public confidence in the role of the courts and the administration of justice, and can therefore undermine its key role.

Further, it is a central tenet of a democracy that justice should not be arbitrary, and therefore the state has a duty to ensure that all have equal access to justice. As Chapter 1 indicated, rights are premised on the notion that the state has a duty to treat all its citizens with equal concern and respect. That notion underlies, it is argued, both free speech and fair trials. If the fair trial of an individual is arbitrarily affected by media coverage, since that individual is accused of a crime which has caught public attention, the state has failed to secure equal access to justice. Therefore, restrictions on such coverage may be justified on the basis that free speech which creates such an interference undermines an aspect of its own underlying rationale.

In many such instances, no sufficient competing aspect is available in order to found the argument that the restrictions are unjustified, since the speech in question may be trivial and sensationalist, motivated solely by profit-making concerns. The fact that newspaper coverage constitutes 'speech' should not be allowed to obscure the failure of some sensationalist coverage of certain cases to participate in almost all the justifications for affording speech primacy over competing interests. Moreover, the

---

4 Emerson, C, 'The right to privacy and the freedom of the press' (1979) 14(2) Harvard Civil Rights-Civil Liberties L Rev 329, p 331.
5 See further Allan, TRS, 'Procedural fairness and the duty of respect' [1988] 18 OJLS 497, esp pp 507–10.

guarantee under Art 10 is most strongly engaged, not only when those justifications, especially the argument from democracy, are at stake, but when the promulgator of the speech is also observing the duties and responsibilities which accompany the exercise of the freedom.[6] Such responsibilities include that of avoiding the invasion of the interests protected under para 2 in a manner which is unnecessary in a democratic society and which is motivated and determined merely by market considerations. Thus, it may be concluded that careful differentiation must be maintained between speech which conflicts with the underlying aims of both free speech and justice, and speech which furthers those aims.

But the argument regarding the harmony between the furtherance of the ends of both justice and speech may break down, it is suggested, where the dominant conception of justice is itself arguably flawed and an instance arises, related to a specific trial, which is especially illustrative of that flaw. In other words, it provides a strikingly paradigmatic example, which may not soon be repeated. For example, the percentage of convictions for rape is extremely low. In a rape trial, the fact that a defendant had a number of rape convictions, or had been acquitted of rape on numerous occasions, would not normally go before the jury. If a newspaper, which was campaigning for improvement in the conviction rate for rape, disclosed such facts pre-trial, as part of its campaign, and, in particular, as part of an argument that rape convictions should be disclosed to the jury, it might seek to justify its publication on the basis that it would influence debate as to conceptions of justice in such trials and might therefore serve the ends of both free speech and justice. The interest in the *efficacy* of speech as well as in its justifications in a formal sense could be relied on in an effort to outweigh the argument that the use of this particular trial in order to give bite to the campaign had undermined the principle of equal access to justice.

This example illustrates the difficulty of formulating a general principle of harmony between the interests involved. But, as a general proposition, subject to exceptions, it is argued that the idea of antinomy between free speech and fair trials is misconceived. If these underlying ideas are taken into account, they provide a means of analysing domestic and Convention rules for their legitimacy in terms of the harmony between the principles underlying free speech and the administration of justice. Where they fail to promote such harmony, reforms will be suggested. It will be argued that the Convention jurisprudence has gone somewhat further than domestic jurisprudence in recognising such harmony, bearing in mind the central aim of the Convention, which is to protect and promote democratic values. However, in certain instances, it will be suggested that the influence of the margin of appreciation doctrine has led to failures in this respect.

The central concern of this chapter is the impact, actual and potential, that the European Convention on Human Rights under the Human Rights Act is having and could have on aspects of domestic contempt law. It will indicate that the domestic development of the law of contempt was quite strongly influenced by the Strasbourg jurisprudence, pre-HRA. While the common law afforded supremacy to the administration of justice, Strasbourg aided in the creation of a shift in favour in freedom of expression. Nevertheless, despite the influence of the Convention, this Chapter will contend that

---

6 Article 10, para 1.

domestic contempt law still fails to satisfy the demands of Art 10 in certain respects. It will also be argued that, as currently administered, it fails to protect the administration of justice and, in some respects, to meet the demands of Art 6. The response of UK contempt law to findings at Strasbourg and the judicial domestic interpretations of the Convention have not shown a sufficient appreciation, it will be argued, of its key underpinning values. In particular, the extent to which the apparent conflict between Arts 10 and 6 may be resolvable at the level of principle has largely gone unrecognised. These failings are revealed, it will be contended, by testing contempt law and practice more directly against Convention standards under the Human Rights Act.

2 Publications prejudicing proceedings: the strict liability rule

A central area of contempt law is that which is concerned with publications potentially interfering with the course of justice in civil or criminal proceedings. Media bodies may incur liability for contempt due to potentially prejudicial reporting of and discussion of, or relating to, pending proceedings. This form of contempt is therefore intended to limit the freedom of the media to report on or comment on issues arising from, or related to, the administration of justice. Such restriction answers to a genuine public interest in ensuring that justice is properly administered and is unaffected by bodies who are unlikely to judge the merits of a case fairly. If, for example, a large number of tabloids, in pursuit of a newsworthy story, take the view that a defendant is guilty, they may slant stories and pictures so that they seem to give that impression and such coverage may affect the jury. If so, the conviction will have been influenced by the partial views of a certain group of people who do not have all the evidence available to them and are influenced by concerns other than the concern to ensure fairness in decision making. If a trial seems to have been prejudiced by unfair reporting, a successful appeal may be brought on that basis,[7] but this method only creates a remedy for the defendant; it does not deter the media from such behaviour in future. No one would argue that this is a desirable method of preventing prejudice to the administration of justice, since it may allow the factually guilty to be acquitted or the innocent to be convicted.

In seeking to avoid such interferences with the course of justice while also affording protection to the freedom of the press, states have chosen to adopt either a *protective* or a *neutralising* model,[8] or a mixture of both. Under the protective model, the state seeks to protect court proceedings by deterring the media from the publication of potentially prejudicial material, while allowing non-prejudicial reporting of proceedings and of discussion relating to them. This model has traditionally been used in the UK. Under the neutralising model, the emphasis is placed on dealing with the potential effects of prejudicial material, by means of procedural devices aimed at ensuring the impartiality of the jury. The aim is to ensure that the potential effect of prejudicial publicity is neutralised. Such devices include the use of strong directions to the jury, jury challenges, changing the trial venue, stays, and sequestration of the jury. If neutralising measures

---

7 See the successful appeal on this basis in *Taylor* (1993) 98 Cr App R 361, CA (for discussion, see below, p 345).
8 See Cram, I [1998] EHRLR 742.

fail, the remedial measure of acquittal may be the last resort. Both models seek to ensure fair hearings, but the former seeks to do so by curbing media freedom to an extent, the latter by insulating the hearing from potentially prejudicial publications, while leaving media freedom largely intact.

Since the First Amendment provides an unqualified guarantee, the emphasis in the US has been on neutralising measures rather than on sanctions intended to deter the media from publishing potentially prejudicial material.[9] In *Nebraska Press Association v Stuart*[10] the Supreme Court held that adverse publicity before a trial would not necessarily have a prejudicial effect on it and that therefore, a prior restraint would not be granted. Barendt, commenting on this decision, argues that subsequent restraints might therefore also be unconstitutional; thus, a conviction might not be obtained in respect of an already published article which created a risk of prejudicial effect.[11] Therefore witnesses' statements may be obtained pre-trial, while assertions of guilt or confessions and hearings to determine the admissibility of evidence[12] may all be made public. The use of procedural devices such as delaying the trial, or changing its venue, as an alternative to restraining the media, are not always very effective, leaving open the possibility that defendants may appeal against conviction and obtain an acquittal owing to the publicity. Certain US commentators therefore favour adoption of the protective approach used in Britain.[13] A further possible model is directly *preventive* of prejudicial effects in the sense that certain material is barred from publication by means of prior restraint, pre-trial.

When Canada adopted the Charter of Rights and Freedoms in 1982, the Supreme Court considered that the common law stance of affording the fairness of trials priority over free speech had been changed by the Charter and that therefore, adherence to a neutralising rather than a protective or preventive model had become appropriate. The Court found that a ban on pre-trial publication should only be ordered when 'alternative measures', such as jury sequestration, could not prevent the risk of prejudice.[14] In contrast, Australia has adopted a stance more akin to that of domestic common law, although somewhat less restrictive of freedom of expression.[15]

---

9 See *Knapp* (1990) 114 L Ed 2d 763 on the detailed questioning of jury members; see Chesterman (1997) 'OJ and the dingo: how media publicity for criminal jury trials is dealt with in Australia and America' 45 Am Jo Comp Law 109 and *Cram* [1998] EHRLR 742 on the US neutralising approach generally. As the most extreme neutralising measure, a conviction may be quashed and a retrial ordered. In *Shepherd v Maxwell* (1966) 384 US 333, a re-trial was ordered because of the extensive media coverage. For comment on *Shepherd v Maxwell*, see Grant, A, 'Pre-trial publicity and fair trial' (1976) 14 Osgoode Hall LJ 275. The neutralising measure of sequestration of the jury was used in the trial of OJ Simpson in 1995 and attracted widespread criticism in the UK.

10 (1976) 427 US 539.

11 Barendt, E, *Freedom of Speech*, 1987, 1987, p 228.

12 *United States v Brooklier* (1982) 685 F 2d 1162; *Re Application of Herald Co* (1984) 734 F 2d.

13 See Krause (1996) 76 Boston UL Rev 357.

14 See *Dagenais v Canadian Broadcasting Corpn* (1995) 120 DLR (4th) 12, p 37. For comment, see Horwitz, 'Jury selection after *Dagenais*: prejudicial pre-trial publicity' (1996) 42 CR 220.

15 For discussion of the Australian approach, which contrasts it with that adopted in the US, see Chesterman (1997) 45 Am Jo of Comp Law 109. In Australia, contempt cannot be committed until proceedings are pending: *James v Robinson* (1963) 109 CLR 593.

It is argued below that, contrary to the view which some commentators have taken,[16] Strasbourg has on the whole adopted a protective or preventive rather than a neutralising approach and that therefore, the Convention under the Human Rights Act, unlike the Canadian Charter, does not demand a radical change in the stance of UK law, in this context. Moreover, bearing in mind the arguments outlined above, regarding the underlying harmony of values between free speech and the fair administration of justice, it is argued that the preventive is, in general, to be preferred to the neutralising model since much speech which, under close scrutiny, creates prejudice to trials runs counter to its own underlying justifications, while at the same time the quality of justice may be affected by using neutralising measures.[17] It must be pointed out, however, that the preventive model may become unworkable owing to current technological changes, particularly the use of the internet and the proliferation of websites, a point which will be developed further below. Bearing these points in mind, the central argument will be that while radical change is unnecessary in this area of contempt law, certain reforms are necessary in order to meet, in full, the demands both of media freedom and the administration of justice, as recognised under the Convention, but interpreted domestically under the Human Rights Act.

The Strasbourg stance

Under Art 10, an interference with the guarantee of freedom of expression can be justified if it is prescribed by law, has a legitimate aim and is necessary in a democratic society. Proceedings against a media body for contempt in respect of its coverage of a forthcoming or ongoing action, or of issues impliedly or expressly linked to it, may be justified if they have the legitimate aims of protecting the 'rights of others' and/or of 'maintaining the authority and impartiality of the judiciary'. The 'rights of others' exception covers Art 6 rights. The 'authority' of the judiciary refers to the acceptance of the courts as the proper forums for the settlement of disputes.[18] The term 'impartiality' refers to the preservation of confidence in the courts by persons engaged in dispute settlement and the public in general.[19] This exception was apparently included in the Convention at the instigation of Britain precisely to cover contempt of court.[20] The other European signatories have no clearly comparable law, although laws regulating pre-trial publicity are common.

As indicated, this form of contempt law can be viewed as protecting the right to a fair trial, together with the societal interest in preserving the integrity of the administration of justice. It can be argued, therefore, that where this other 'strong' right is at stake,

---

16 Mann, FA has written: 'In a potentially wide variety of cases the European Court may assume a revising function and impose continental standards or, perhaps one should say abuses, upon this country which, in the name of freedom of the press and discussion are likely to lower English usages by the substitution of trial by media for trial by courts' (1979) 95 LQR 348, p 352.

17 This point has been made by Chesterman (1997) 45 J Comp Law 109 and by Krause (1996) 76 Boston UL Rev 357. Clearly, devices such as delaying the trial may mean that defendants will spend longer in custody; the stress of victim-witnesses may be increased; memories of the relevant events may fade.

18 *Chorherr v Austria* (1994) 17 EHRR 358.

19 *Fey v Austria* (1994) 16 EHRR 387; *Worm v Austria* (1998) 25 EHRR 454, p 473.

20 See the Joint Dissenting Opinion in *Sunday Times v UK* (1979) 2 EHRR 245, p 285, para 2.

Strasbourg would accept that free speech must be more readily compromised, unless in the particular instance the speech would in fact further the ends of justice.[21] But resolving these matters under the Convention is not entirely straightforward owing to the particular approach it adopts, which is influenced by its own structural constraints. This approach is revealed by a consideration of the stance taken at Strasbourg to claims that Art 10 has been violated by prosecutions of journalists in respect of publications bearing upon legal proceedings in the line of authority stemming from *Sunday Times v UK*,[22] *Worm v Austria*[23] and *News Verlags v Austria*.[24]

Clashes between the administration of justice and media freedom

The *Sunday Times* case is discussed in full below. The state argued that the interference with freedom of expression could be justified since it served the legitimate aim of preserving the authority and impartiality of the judiciary. The stance adopted by the Court in finding a breach of Art 10 was explicable on the basis that the interest in protecting such authority or, at a more general level, the administration of justice, was very weak: little threat could be discerned since the litigation in question was dormant. Although, as an aspect of its application of the requirements of proportionality, the Court took the view that the strong free speech interest outweighed the slight impact on the administration of justice, a more satisfactory way of viewing the case is, it is argued, to say that the speech in question engaged strongly in the debate as to the proper ends of justice, but no countervailing considerations regarding equal access to justice or the creation of unfairness genuinely arose.

In contrast, in *Worm*, the interference with the freedom of speech guarantee had a link with the Art 6 guarantee. *Worm v Austria*[25] is now the leading authority on balancing expression and fair trial values. Unlike the *Sunday Times* case, it addressed a real clash between the two since in the circumstances the Art 6 guarantees were clearly engaged. The article in question created a high risk of prejudice: it was published during a criminal trial, clearly imputed guilt and made specific allegations against the defendant. In all these respects, therefore, it created a strong contrast with the article at issue in *Sunday Times*. Thus *Worm*, unlike *Sunday Times*, is properly characterised as a clashing rights case. A political periodical had published an article by Worm, a journalist, about the criminal trial for tax evasion of Hannes Androsch, a former Minister of Finance. The article, published while the trial was ongoing, stated that it had been known for a substantial period of time that Androsch was evading taxes and that it had been proved for some time, by the investigating judge, that Androsch was lying on this key point. In general, the article was highly critical of Androsch and clearly evinced a belief in his guilt. Worm was convicted and fined under s 23 of the Austrian Media Act which provides for the punishment of those who discuss 'subsequent to the indictment and before the judgment at first instance . . . the probable outcome of those proceedings or the value of evidence in a way capable of influencing the outcome.'

---

21 See the discussion as to when 'strong' individual rights may be infringed in Chapter 1, pp 11–14.
22 (1979) 2 EHRR 245.
23 (1997) 25 EHRR 557; (1998) 25 EHRR 454.
24 (2001) 31 EHRR 8.
25 (1998) 25 EHRR 454.

There is no need to establish that the proceedings have in fact been influenced. The Vienna Court of Appeal considered that the article had a potential influence on the criminal proceedings since it had the capacity to affect at the least the two lay judges involved. It also found that Worm had intended to influence the proceedings.

The European Court of Human Rights accepted that Worm's conviction constituted an interference with the freedom of expression guarantee. The state argued that the prosecution had the legitimate aims of preserving the authority and impartiality of the judiciary and the 'rights of others.' The Court accepted that the conviction had a link with the Art 6(1) guarantee, although it did not pursue the question whether the article had created an interference with the rights of others by undermining the presumption of innocence which is guaranteed under Art 6(2). It found:

> In this regard, the Court has consistently held that the expression 'authority and impartiality of the judiciary' has to be understood 'within the meaning of the Convention'. For this purpose, account must be taken of the central position occupied in this context by Art 6 which reflects the fundamental principle of the rule of law. The phrase 'authority of the judiciary' includes, in particular, the notion that the courts are, and are accepted by the public at large as being, the proper forum for the settlement of legal disputes and for the determination of a person's guilt or innocence on a criminal charge; further, that the public at large have respect for and confidence in the courts' capacity to fulfil that function. 'Impartiality' normally denotes lack of prejudice or bias. However, the Court has repeatedly held that what is at stake in maintaining the impartiality of the judiciary is the confidence which the courts in a democratic society must inspire in the accused, as far as criminal proceedings are concerned, and also in the public at large ... It follows that, in seeking to maintain the 'authority and impartiality of the judiciary', the Contracting states are entitled to take account of considerations going – beyond the concrete case – to the protection of the fundamental role of courts in a democratic society.[26]

As to the question whether the interference was necessary in a democratic society, the Court found that although the limits of acceptable comment are wider as regards politicians than as regards a private individual, public figures are still entitled to the enjoyment of the guarantee of a fair trial set out in Art 6(1), which in criminal proceedings includes the right to an impartial tribunal. It went on:

> [T]his must be borne in mind by journalists when commenting on pending criminal proceedings since the limits of permissible comment may not extend to statements which are likely to prejudice, whether intentionally or not, the chances of a person receiving a fair trial or to undermine the confidence of the public in the role of the courts in the administration of criminal justice. [27]

The Court conceded a certain margin of appreciation to the state in relation to the particular choice made by the domestic authorities in relation to what was needed to

26 Ibid, at para 40.
27 Ibid, at para 50.

protect the administration of justice, since – as it does not adopt the role of a domestic appellate court – it did not second guess the evidence. It accepted that there was no necessity to demonstrate that prejudice to the proceedings had actually arisen. It found that it was,

> ... in principle for the appellate court to evaluate the likelihood that at least the lay judges would read the article to ascertain the applicant's criminal intent in publishing it. It cannot be excluded that the public's becoming accustomed to the regular spectacle of pseudo-trials in the news media might in the long run have nefarious consequences for the acceptance of the courts as the proper forum for the determination of a person's guilt or innocence on a criminal charge.[28]

The sanction was found to be proportionate to the aim pursued since a fairly minor penalty only – a fine – was imposed and the publishing firm was ordered to be jointly and severally liable for its payment. Thus the proportionality analysis was based on means/end balancing[29] – the measures taken, it was found, did not go further than necessary to protect the right to a fair trial in the circumstances. No breach of Art 10 was therefore found.

This was an instance in which it could more readily be argued than in the *Sunday Times* case that the speech ran counter to the underlying speech-supporting rationales discussed above, in the sense that it was more likely to cause prejudice to the trial. The Court's approach rested on the possibility that the article had made it very difficult to ensure that the tribunal was impartial. It took the stance that the Art 10 guarantee could be justifiably infringed in order to protect Androsch's right to a fair trial under Art 6(1). But it also spoke of the general principles encapsulated under Art 6. The Court explicitly refused to look at the question whether the proceedings in question had actually been affected by the publication; it refused to consider whether the Austrian media law should have concerned itself with that issue. Therefore it explicitly denied that there was a need to show an actual interference with Art 6 rights (or at least a very strong probability that such an interference had occurred) before an interference with the Art 10 guarantee – in the context of political expression – could be justified. Thus, it seemed to adopt both a protective and a preventive approach, though laying more stress on the former. An obvious unfairness was potentially created by the article, but the Court also concentrated on the longer term harm that it might have created to the administration of justice in a broader sense. The state's case was obviously problematic in *Sunday Times* since the litigation in question was dormant. In contrast, in *Worm*, the state had acted to avert a genuine risk to the trial; the Court made it clear that Art 6 will take precedence over Art 10 where it can be said that there is a real likelihood of prejudice.

The stance adopted in *Worm* had been foreshadowed to an extent in the Commission's decisions in *C v UK*[30] and *BBC Scotland v UK*.[31] *C v UK* concerned a broadcast reproducing parts of the appeal in the *Birmingham Six* case. The intention of the

---

28 Ibid, para 54.
29 See Chapter 4, p 286.
30 (1989) 61 DR 285.
31 (1997) 25 EHRR CD 179.

broadcasters was that it should be shown before the final judgment in the appeal, but the Court of Appeal hearing the case granted an injunction preventing the broadcast of the programme until after the appeal had been heard. The Commission found no breach of Art 10 on the basis that there was a pressing social need to delay the programme; the portrayal of the hearing by actors would condition the response of the audience since the actors would be bound to communicate suggestions about the reliability of the witnesses they were portraying. Also the Commission accepted the view of the Court of Appeal that while the Courts' judgment would normally be unaffected, the appellants had the right to be assured that the Court had been unaffected by external matters.[32]

The application in *BBC Scotland v UK*[33] arose from the prohibition of a broadcast which featured allegations that prisoners moved to Barlinnie Prison after prison riots had been assaulted there by prison officers. The broadcast 'Beaten by the System' was an update on one previously broadcast on the same subject. An indictment had been served on three prison officers alleging that they had assaulted prisoners, about three weeks before the programme was to be broadcast. The Scottish High Court relied on its inherent equitable jurisdiction to issue an order prohibiting the broadcast until the completion of the trial of the officers, on the ground that the programme would create a risk of prejudice to the trial. The risk of prejudice arose, so the High Court found, since at least one of the jurors might have obtained from the programme the impression that the prison doctor interviewed, who was a witness for the prosecution, was a witness of considerable credit. The Court noted that the broadcast was not particularly urgent and that there was a more than minimal risk of prejudice. The applicants complained that the order of the High Court constituted a breach of Art 10.

The Commission accepted that the order constituted an interference with the freedom of expression guarantee. It went on to find that the order had the legitimate aim of protecting the right of the officers to a fair trial; therefore it was for the preservation of the authority and impartiality of the judiciary and for the protection of the 'rights of others'. In considering the question whether the order was necessary in a democratic society it might have been expected that the Commission would have subjected it to that 'most careful scrutiny' which prior restraints demand.[34] Instead the Commission largely adopted the High Court's assessment of the necessity and proportionality of the order. The Commission appeared to be assessing the reasonableness of the High Court's findings in balancing the free speech and fair trial interests, rather than considering the issues itself. In speaking of the 'balancing act' carried out by the High Court, the Commission clearly did not view itself as applying a principle of freedom of expression subject to exceptions to be narrowly construed. Thus the need for the interference was not subjected to a strict scrutiny. Had it been, it is possible that a breach of Art 10 might have been found, bearing in mind the uncertainty of the risk of prejudice and the probability that the programme would never be broadcast once it had been postponed.

32 Ibid, p 294.
33 (1997) 25 EHRR CD 179.
34 *Observer and Guardian v UK* (1991) 14 EHRR 153, at para 60.

The stance taken in this line of authority was confirmed in *News Verlags v Austria*.[35] At first sight *News Verlags* presents something of a contrast to *Worm v Austria*, *C v UK* and *BBC Scotland v UK* in terms of the intensity of the review, but ultimately the findings are consistent with the previous ones. The case concerned a somewhat weaker Art 10 claim; the 'rights of others' exception was invoked to justify the restriction on the speech in question, but the application succeeded. The case concerned the prosecution of the News Company for the publication of a photograph of a right wing extremist, B, who was accused of sending letter bombs as part of a political campaign. The text accompanying the photograph accused him of being the perpetrator of the attacks. The applicant company complained that court decisions prohibiting it from publishing the photograph in the context of reports on the criminal proceedings against it, violated its right to freedom of expression. The aims pursued were to protect the rights of others and the authority of the judiciary. The Court noted that the 'rights of others' exception was relevant since, *inter alia*, the injunctions were intended to protect B against violations of the presumption of innocence, protected by Art 6(2).

The case turned on the proportionality of the interference with the legitimate aims pursued. The Court subjected this question to a detailed review, conceding only a narrow margin of appreciation to the state. It took into account the possible effect on the Art 6(2) rights of B. But it also took account of the facts that he had sought publicity as a Nazi activist and that the offences in question had a political background and were 'directed against the foundations of a democratic society'.[36] Reiterating the significance of the essential function of the press in a democratic society, the Court pointed out that the duty of the press to inform the public extends to reporting and commenting on court proceedings and noted the consonance of its discharge of such a duty with the requirement under Art 6(1) that hearings should be public. The injunctions restricted the choice of the newspaper as to its presentation of reports. The Court in particular took account of the fact that, although objection was taken only to the picture in conjunction with the adverse comments, the injunction created an absolute prohibition on publishing a picture of B with or without such comments. It may be argued that the intensity of the review undertaken in this instance was due partly to the special circumstances of the case, especially the fact that, as a right wing extremist, B had himself sought publicity for his views in the past. But the key point was that the photograph alone was unlikely to cause prejudice to the proceedings and yet the effect of the injunction was to prohibit any publication of it, even if accompanying a fair and accurate factual report of the proceedings. The injunction, therefore, was manifestly overbroad since it caught harmless publications. Thus the proportionality analysis was again based on means/end balancing[37] – the measures taken, it was found, went further than needed to serve the end in question. The Court concluded on that basis that there was no reasonable relationship of proportionality between the interference and the aims pursued.

The injunction also affected the openness of the proceedings, since publication of such reports was found to be consonant with that aspect of Art 6(1). Although it might be argued that the publication of this particular photograph had little impact on

---

35 (2001) 31 EHRR 8; (2000) 9 BHRC 625.
36 Ibid, at paras 54 and 55.
37 See Chapter 4, p 286.

open justice, the judgment may be said to protect both the substance and the form of reporting on court proceedings. Thus, the Court made explicit, in a partial sense, the consonance between Arts 10 and 6. That line of argument could have been taken further and the broader harmony between the aims of free speech and the protection for the administration of justice could have been more clearly articulated. *News Verlags* differs somewhat from the previous line of authority in terms of the intensity of the review that was undertaken, but does not represent a significant departure from it since the potential impact on the trial was thought to be very slight, whereas the effect on media freedom was viewed as quite significant. Moreover, the case concerned an obviously overbroad injunction.

Given the tendency of the Court to view its approach to the interests of freedom of expression and the administration of justice as 'the balancing of competing interests'[38] where a claim raising these issues arises under Art 10, it is arguable that the stance taken would have differed had the Austrian Court refused to grant the injunction and *B* had brought a claim to Strasbourg, arguing for a violation of Art 6(2). In *Ribemont v France*[39] an application brought on the basis of a violation of the Art 6(2) guarantee owing to the effect of publicity succeeded once the violation was found since, apart from provisions allowing for the exclusion of persons from a hearing in certain circumstances (see below), Art 6 is not qualified. The Court went on to find that the comments made about Ribemont went beyond merely providing information and had created a breach of Art 6(2):

[S]ome of the highest-ranking officers in the French police referred to Mr Allenet de Ribemont, without any qualification or reservation, as one of the instigators of a murder and thus an accomplice in that murder. This was clearly a declaration of the applicant's guilt which, firstly, encouraged the public to believe him guilty and, secondly, prejudged the assessment of the facts by the competent judicial authority.'[40]

Once the violation of Art 6(2) was found, the application succeeded since, apart from provisions allowing for the exclusion of persons from a hearing in certain circumstances, Art 6 is not qualified.

In contrast, in *Wloch v Poland*[41] an allegation that numerous newspaper comments shortly after the applicant's arrest had led to a violation of Art 6(2) was rejected on the basis that on the facts it was extremely unlikely that the comments could have affected the judges who were to preside over the trial. Long after the time of publication – a matter of about six years – the judges who would preside over the trial had still not been empanelled. It was clearly highly unlikely that the newspaper comments would be remembered with any clarity by the judges when they were eventually empanelled

---

38 Paragraph 56, relying on the judgment in *Bladet Tromsø and Stensaas v Norway* (2000) 29 EHRR 125; (1999) 6 BHRC 599.
39 (1995) 20 EHRR 557. The Court found that Art 6(2) had been breached by a statement made by the French Minister of the Interior and senior police officers at a press conference in which they named the applicant as involved in a murder.
40 Ibid, at para 41.
41 March 2000, Information note No 16; for the other aspects of the application see (2002) 34 EHRR 9.

and even more unlikely that they would have any influence. Thus it was found that there was no evidence that the presumption of innocence had been violated and so this aspect of Wloch's application was dismissed as manifestly ill-founded. This decision is of little value in terms of supporting the argument that the British media have some leeway to comment on the guilt or innocence of a potential defendant, since it could only be utilised where there had been a very significant time lapse between publication and trial. A lapse of around six years would not normally occur in the UK.

Balance created between Article 6 and Article 10

As a preliminary comment on the above jurisprudence, it may be found that where a matter comes before the Court in the form of an Art 10 claim, the Court's reasoning follows the contours of that Article, which require it to afford presumptive primacy to freedom of expression and to regard the administration of justice as an exception to that right. It is perhaps inevitable, then, that the two interests will be viewed, broadly, as competing. Where the same or similar issues arise, exceptionally, in the form of an Art 6 claim, it appears that there can be no balancing of competing interests,[42] except as regards the requirements of a public hearing in Art 6(1), since Art 6 is otherwise unqualified. The question is merely whether, on the facts, a breach of Art 6 could have arisen due to media comment – no question of justification arises. The choices thereby apparent, informing the moral framework of the Convention, indicate that in this context Art 6 takes precedence over Art 10. Therefore where an infringement of the guarantee under Art 6 might genuinely arise as a result of a publication, the Court is almost bound to find no breach of Art 10, despite the fact that when it is dealing with an Art 10 claim it has to treat an arguable violation of Art 6 as arising, technically, in the form of an exception under Art 10(2).

The Court's statement in *Worm* to the effect that 'the limits of permissible comment may not extend to statements which are likely to prejudice, whether intentionally or not, the chances of a person receiving a fair trial' bears out this finding. This comment suggests that speech (including political speech) which infringes the presumption of innocence, or is likely to infringe it, will readily be overridden by the fair trial guarantee. This is not because the speech is seen as of low value, but because the competing interest is so weighty.[43] In other words, the treatment of speech that invades another right protected by the Convention may tend to cut across the established categories of expression as 'political,' 'artistic' and 'commercial'. This is especially the case where the expression affects one of the unqualified, or not materially qualified, rights. Even where the speech is within the category occupying the highest place in the hierarchy of speech, as in *Worm*, that factor does not appear to play a significant role in the

---

42 See the discussion of the 'parallel analysis' in *re S* [2003] 2 FCR 577, CA; [2004] UKHL 47; the decision is discussed in Chapter 9, pp 958–79.

43 To a lesser extent this is also the case in relation to privacy-invading speech and speech offensive to religious sensibilities – breaching Art 9. See *Otto-Preminger* (1994) 19 EHRR 34 in relation to speech that the Court has viewed as clashing with the Art 9 guarantee of freedom of religion. *Tammer v Estonia* (2003) 37 EHRR 43 and *N v Portugal* (Appl No 20683/92, 20.2.1995) both indicated that quite draconian penalties for invasion of privacy are compatible with Art 10. See further Chapter 9, pp 945–46.

stance taken – the value of the speech does not appear to be weighed up against the effect on the other Convention right.

One difficulty with the Court's approach is that it can allow interferences with freedom of expression even where the Art 6 rights of a particular defendant are only doubtfully threatened – as *BBC Scotland* indicates. A further difficulty is that the Court is also prepared to draw the line at allowing comments that 'are likely to . . . undermine the confidence of the public in the role of the courts in the administration of criminal justice.'[44] On the other hand, it avoided such a stance in the *Sunday Times* case. The exception – the 'authority of the judiciary' – is not linked to criminal proceedings alone and many of the comments made by the Court in *Worm* regarding the fear of undermining public confidence in such authority could have equal validity in relation to civil actions. It considered that one aspect of the mischief to be avoided was that of a threat to the administration of justice in a general sense. It justified such a stance by reference to the rule of law principle encapsulated in Art 6 regarding the need to maintain confidence in the courts. In other words, it sought to reconcile the stance taken under Art 10(2) with that taken in relation to Art 6, partly on the basis of infringing Art 10 in order to avoid a concrete harm in Art 6 terms, but *also* at a broader level of principle. The difference of approach may partly be explicable on the basis that the Court is particularly concerned with the protection of the administration of justice in criminal rather than *civil* proceedings. Clearly, where laypersons are concerned in the justice process – which is more likely to be the case in criminal proceedings[45] – the risk of unfairness due to the influence of publications may be higher. The fear of 'trial by newspaper' that exercised the House of Lords in *Attorney General v Times* appeared to strike the Court as of especial significance in relation to criminal proceedings.

The Court's differences of approach to Art 10 claims in this context are therefore explicable by reference to the question whether the term 'the authority of the judiciary' can or cannot be viewed as covering interests that are quite closely linked to the concrete demands of Art 6 in that instance. The effect of the margin of appreciation doctrine is variable. Where the rhetoric of 'protection for the administration of justice' in a non-concrete sense is used in relation to a publication that in actuality relates closely to particular proceedings, especially criminal ones, and creates some risk to those proceedings, a margin of appreciation may be conceded in assessing the *degree* of risk. The *Sunday Times* case established that the interference with freedom of expression represented by curbing media freedom to comment on a forthcoming action or on issues linked to it must answer to a pressing social need.[46] Where, as in that instance, the interference is aimed – broadly – at the protection of the administration of justice, but has only a very indirect and uncertain justification in terms of protecting particular litigation, the review of the existence of such a need is likely to be intense. But where the interference appears to be fairly strongly linked to the preservation of Art 6 rights, since a particular trial is quite clearly affected, the margin of appreciation doctrine may not have a significant role, and the interference may be found to be justified, as in *Worm* and *BBC Scotland v UK*, since, where two rights are viewed as in conflict, the

---

44 (1998) 25 EHRR 454, at para 50.
45 In the UK juries are used in certain civil proceedings, notably libel actions and in certain civil actions against the police: see Supreme Court Act 1981 s 69.
46 (1979) 2 EHRR 245, at para 62.

Court will prefer the (almost) unqualified right under Art 6. Free expression has a role in supporting confidence in the administration of justice; this is made explicit under the Art 6 guarantee of a public hearing and by the Court; but as the Court made plain in the cases considered, speech that undermines that confidence may be fairly readily displaced by the competing administration of justice interest. Within the Strasbourg rhetoric, therefore, regarding competing interests, a recognition of the consonance between the values underlying them is evident.

Approaches to the domestic impact of the Convention under the Human Rights Act

A court, adjudicating on an action for contempt against a media organ is bound by all the Convention rights under s 6 HRA and in this context must ensure that Arts 10 and 6 – as particularly relevant – are satisfied. It must also interpret the provisions of the Contempt of Court Act 1981 compatibly with the Convention under s 3 if a potential incompatibility arises; the common law could potentially be modified in reliance on the courts' duty under s 6, although, as discussed below, significant change in the key common law contempt area is now unlikely. Section 2 HRA requires the courts to take the Convention jurisprudence into account in satisfying their duties under ss 6 or 3. But the discussion above has indicated that the impact of the Convention on this area of domestic contempt law is complex. It is not enough to argue merely that the Convention demands a shift towards freedom of expression, since such an argument fails to take account of the demands of Art 6 and the need to protect the administration of justice in a general sense.

In so far as, traditionally, domestic contempt law favoured the protection of the administration of justice over the protection of freedom of expression, it failed to strike a balance which is consistent with the Convention. The domestic inquiry pre-HRA always began by considering the law governing the interference with the negative liberty of expression. The domestic courts have traditionally been preoccupied with the administration of justice rather than with individual rights to free speech. This approach was modified in the pre-HRA era under the Contempt of Court Act 1981, which was a response to the finding at Strasbourg[47] that common law contempt had failed to afford sufficient weight to freedom of expression, as explained below. The approach adopted may now require further modification under the HRA, but the structure of domestic decision-making need not fully follow the Strasbourg model since Art 10 and, in some instances, Art 6 issues normally arise during a contempt action[48] rather than as aspects of an Art 10 claim. Article 6 issues may also be raised during a criminal trial or on appeal as part of an argument that the jury or others would be or had been affected by the publication of prejudicial journalistic material.

As argued above, although the overturning of a conviction or a stay of proceedings can be used as a remedy where there has been a violation of Art 6 rights due to media publicity, it would be more satisfactory to use preventive measures where the possibility

---

47   In the *Sunday Times* case (1979) 2 EHRR 245 (see below, pp 334–37).
48   They might also arise in judicial review proceedings; this is discussed below in relation to *Taylor*, p 345.

of prejudice to proceedings genuinely arises. Strasbourg tends to favour such measures, as indicated, although where the connection between protecting the right to a fair trial and suppressing the speech in question is doubtful, it will subject them to an intense scrutiny. It will be argued that, at the present time, contempt law is not fulfilling this preventive role, but that neutralising measures have not fully taken its place. Common law contempt afforded primacy to the interest in the administration of justice, but it is suggested that statutory contempt is not engaging fully with the core values underlying either free speech or the administration of justice. In particular, it will be argued that contempt law is failing to meet Art 6 demands that the relevant legislation, and executive decisions taken in relation to it, should be efficacious in protecting the right to a fair trial.[49] This failure is partly due to the height of the bar that must be surmounted if a contempt action is to be successful – this point is considered below. The failure also relates, it is argued, to the role of the Attorney General, who has the responsibility under s 7 of the Contempt of Court Act 1981 for initiating prosecutions against media bodies.[50] Theoretically, superior courts[51] can punish contempts on their own motion. This inherent power is preserved under s 7. In practice, the courts do not exercise this power in respect of publications subject to the strict liability rule (see below). A party to proceedings in a superior court could put, through counsel, the argument that a publication is prejudicial. The judge could then refer the matter to the Attorney General. This would not necessarily mean, however, that proceedings would be brought.[52]

The Attorney General can also seek an injunction to restrain a planned publication and, in this respect, can be viewed as having a limited vetting role.[53] He may also issue warnings to the media regarding coverage of cases which have attracted public attention.[54] The Attorney General is a member of the Cabinet. Theoretically, he or she acts in two distinct capacities – as a member of the government and as an independent law officer. His role as law officer places him, theoretically, at a distance from the government. In practice, his impartiality may be questioned, owing to the conflict of interests inherent in his dual role. He may come under pressure to initiate prosecutions in cases in which the government itself has an interest. As Borrie and Lowe observe: 'in cases such as these the Attorney's role . . . does smack of partisanship'.[55] Conversely, it is possible that he may be reluctant to initiate proceedings when to do so would mean bringing the government – in effect – into conflict with powerful media proprietors.

---

49   Such demands are those indicated in *BBC Scotland v UK* (1998) 25 EHRR CD 179. See also *Worm v Austria* (1998) 25 EHRR 454 or *News Verlags* (2001) 31 EHRR 8, although the laws at issue in those instances were not contempt laws.

50   Section 7 provides: 'Proceedings for a contempt of court under the strict liability rule shall not be instituted except by or with the consent of the Attorney General or on the motion of a court having jurisdiction to deal with it.'

51   In England and Wales, the House of Lords, the Court of Appeal, the High Court of Justice, the Crown Court, the Restrictive Practices Court, the Employment Appeals Tribunal, the Courts-Martial Appeal Court.

52   See *R v Taylor and Taylor* (1993) 98 Cr App R 361 (discussed below, p 345).

53   This occurred in *Attorney General v Times Newspapers Ltd* [1974] AC 273 (see below, pp 335–36).

54   He issued such warnings in respect of the 'Yorkshire Ripper' case and in the case of Frederick and Rosemary West.

55   *The Law of Contempt*, 1996, p 485.

Clearly, there will be variable practice between the office-holders in these respects, but this inconsistency itself has a questionable effect on the quality of justice and the protection for media freedom. As certain of the decisions discussed below indicate, it cannot be said that when the massed tabloids act, effectively, in concert in their coverage of a trial-related story, they are immune from prosecutions. But it will be argued that a reluctance to prosecute a large number of media organs simultaneously, especially those with large circulations, is evident. The result is arguably that the tendency to prosecute those parts of the press which have the most central role in furthering the values underpinning political speech is not in proportion to their tendency to affect the fairness of trials.

The Attorney General is bound by s 6 HRA and, therefore, must ensure that both Arts 10 and 6 are satisfied. While it may be argued that contempt law does not directly provide a remedy where a publication has prejudiced a trial or may be about to do so, it has a link with Art 6, as indicated in the Strasbourg jurisprudence. Injunctions are infrequently granted,[56] but would be of value as a preventive measure. An injunction against one newspaper would prevent it from pursuing a story, while it would tend to deter others from running variations on the same story, since they might incur criminal liability for contempt.[57] The use of injunctions could prevent the risk of prejudice arising from a wide-ranging and relentless coverage of issues relevant in a forthcoming trial. More generally, prosecutions for contempt, where Art 6 rights were violated, might have a future deterrent effect. In other words, the link between the use of contempt law and Art 6 should be given some weight in the current situation in which the judiciary understandably do not at present use neutralising measures, such as stays, extensively to combat possibly prejudicial publicity.[58]

As indicated above, once a contempt action is in being, the national court is not in the same position as Strasbourg since the part played by the margin of appreciation at Strasbourg should not be reflected in domestic decision making. Thus, where Arts 6 and 10 rights appear to be at stake, detailed and rigorous review could determine how far this is the case. The central concern should be the need to isolate the fundamental values at stake in terms of both free speech and fair trials and to tailor domestic law in order to protect them.

In a contempt action, the court is bound by the Convention rights under s 6 of the HRA and, where the statutory provisions were in question, could seek to ensure that it discharged that obligation by interpreting them compatibly with the relevant guarantees. It is suggested that the domestic court could examine the effect of finding liability in terms of both Arts 10 and 6. In so doing, it is argued, it would not only escape the structural constraints of the Strasbourg approach, but might more readily recognise the underlying harmony between the two Articles.

---

56 In *Attorney General v News Group Newspapers* [1987] 1 QB 1, an injunction would have been granted.

57 This would normally be under the *Spycatcher* doctrine discussed below at pp 369–70. But, depending on timing of the third party publication, liability could arise under the 1981 Act – see p 380.

58 See the comments of Simon Brown LJ regarding the failure to use stays in certain instances in which prejudice to proceedings was found: *Attorney General v Birmingham Post and Mail Ltd* [1998] 4 All ER 49.

In order to illustrate this approach, two instances will be considered taken from the cases discussed below. In the first example, based on the *Taylor* case,[59] it is assumed that all the tabloid newspapers have reported, in sensationalist and misleading terms, on a forthcoming trial which has happened to catch the public eye. They are prosecuted for contempt. (In fact, in *Taylor*, no prosecution was forthcoming, a factor which may have played a part in recent tabloid excesses.) Assuming that prima facie liability could be established under the 1981 Act, it must also be asked whether the creation of such liability would be unjustified under Art 10. The first question would be whether it would constitute an interference with the freedom of expression of the tabloids. Despite the lack of value of the speech, such an interference would be found, since Strasbourg rarely denies Art 10 protection to speech on the basis of its content. The interference would clearly be found to be prescribed by law – the 1981 Act. The legitimate aims in view would be the preservation of the authority and impartiality of the judiciary and of the rights of others. Those aims would probably be established, on the facts; they have been established in all the relevant claims considered at Strasbourg.

The key question would be whether the interference represented by the creation of liability would be necessary in a democratic society. In determining necessity, the proportionality of the potential interference would require careful scrutiny. This would be the point at which the domestic court would be expected to take a somewhat different stance from that taken by Strasbourg, in relation to the 'rights of others' exception, in that its scrutiny of this question should be much more intensive. Factors to be taken into account would include the extent to which the various newspapers had in fact misled readers and the ability of jurors to disregard the coverage, on strong directions from the judge. But the central importance of fair trials in a democratic society should also be considered, as should the lack of value of the speech. The question of proportionality can encompass such matters, as the decisions in *News Verlags* and *Sunday Times* demonstrated. On the facts, it is argued that a finding of liability against the newspapers under the 1981 Act would be justified under Art 10. The same result would be likely to arise if the liability was then considered from the Art 6 perspective since, on the facts, it could readily be found that the fairness of the trial had been affected and possibly that the presumption of innocence had also been undermined. The court would have discharged its duty under s 6 of the HRA. (Had it appeared that it would fail to do so if it found against the newspapers, it would then have had to examine the statutory provisions in detail for their compatibility with the Convention under s 3 of the HRA.) If, on the above facts, the Attorney General failed to bring a prosecution, it is argued that he would have failed to discharge that duty.

The opposing result would be reached, it is argued, in a case in which certain newspapers comment on a matter of grave public importance, relating to the possibility of abuse of power in part of the executive, where no criminal trial is affected. The comment may, however, affect the ability of the Attorney General to continue a breach of confidence action with a view to suppressing debate on the matter. Publications in other jurisdictions in fact render it extremely unlikely that the rights can be preserved

---

59 See below, p 236. For comment on the case and its implications within the Convention, see Borrie and Lowe, *The Law of Contempt*, 1996, Butterworths, pp 481–82.

in any event. This example is based on *Attorney General v Times Newspapers*,[60] which is discussed below. In this instance, the speech in question concerns a matter of great public significance while hardly affecting Art 6 rights. The interest in question, which might conceivably be viewed as falling within Art 6, concerns the preservation of the rights of one party to a civil action. (Strasbourg, however, did not view that right as engaging the 'rights of others' exception as a distinct exception when it considered the interference with freedom of expression created by the grant of an injunction on grounds of breach of confidence.)[61] The sanction of contempt of court would be, in this instance, disproportionate to the aim of preserving the authority of the judiciary since it could not in fact be preserved by that means.[62] Thus, the action would fail, since the imposition of liability on the newspapers would be unjustified.

These two examples illustrate the harmony that exists between the values underlying Arts 6 and 10. They also, it is argued, indicate the proper approach to the infusion of Convention values into this area of contempt law. Essentially, it is an approach that seeks out and protects the core values at stake in relation to both media freedom and the administration of justice. In identifying the consonance which exists between such values it differentiates sharply between speech supported by the justifications from truth, democracy or self-fulfilment, and speech which is promulgated mainly to further the ends of media conglomerates. It seeks to preserve impartiality and fairness, especially in criminal proceedings, but demands a rigorous and careful scrutiny of the possibility that unfairness may arise.

Domestic provisions: the development of the common law pre-1981

This section discusses the background to the inception of the Contempt of Court Act 1981. The reasons for introducing the Act are key to understanding its provisions. Prior to the inception of the Act, this particular area of criminal contempt at common law curtailed the freedom of the media to discuss and report on issues arising from criminal or civil proceedings on the basis that those proceedings might suffer prejudice. However, it went further than was necessary to deal with very clear risks of interference with the administration of justice. The media was restricted in its reporting of issues relevant to civil or criminal proceedings which were, or were soon to be, in being. It is important to note that civil proceedings can also be prejudiced, even though usually no jury is involved, but obviously this danger may be less likely to arise. It is apparent that more weight was given to protecting the administration of justice rather than free speech, from the ease with which it was possible to satisfy the common law tests.

The elements of common law contempt pre-1981 consisted of the creation of a real risk of prejudice (the *actus reus*) and an intention to publish; it was therefore a crime of strict liability. The *actus reus* could be fulfilled if it were shown that the publication in question had created a risk that the proceedings in question might be prejudiced; it was irrelevant whether they actually had been. This distinction was clearly illustrated by *Thompson Newspapers Ltd ex p Attorney General*.[63] While the defendant was awaiting

---

60 [1992] 1 AC 191; discussed below, p 369.
61 *Observer and Guardian v UK* (1991) 14 EHRR 153; discussed below, pp 620–22.
62 See pp 620–22.
63 [1968] 1 All ER 268; [1968] 1 WLR 1.

trial, The *Sunday Times* published his photograph and commented on his unsavoury background as a brothel keeper. This was held to amount to contempt. He was convicted and then appealed on the ground that the trial had been prejudiced by the article, but his appeal failed on the basis that jurors had not in actuality been so prejudiced. This case further illustrates the nature of the *actus reus*: it was not necessary to publish very damaging comments in order to create the risk in question.

At common law, there was a certain time before and a certain time after the action, known as the *sub judice* period, when there was a risk that any article published relevant to the action might be in contempt. The starting point of this period occurred when the proceedings were 'imminent' (*Savundranayagan and Walker*).[64] This test attracted much criticism because of its vagueness and width; it was obviously capable of applying a long time before the trial and it therefore had an inhibiting effect on the media out of proportion to its value. In particular, it gave rise to the restriction caused by so-called 'gagging writs'. A newspaper might be discussing corruption in a company. If a writ for libel was then issued – although there was no intention of proceeding with the case – the newspaper might find itself in contempt if it continued to discuss the issues. Thus, this method could be used to prevent further comment.

The need for reform which would, in particular, address the width of the imminence test was apparent and led to the setting up of the Phillimore Committee in 1974,[65] but it might not have come about without the influence of the European Court of Human Rights. The ruling that UK contempt law had breached Art 10 arose through the decision of the House of Lords in *Attorney General v Times Newspapers Ltd.*[66] The case concerned litigation arising out of the Thalidomide tragedy. The parents of the Thalidomide children wished to sue Distillers, the company which had manufactured the drug, because they believed that it was responsible for the terrible damage done to their unborn children. Distillers resisted the claims and entered into negotiation with the parents' solicitors. Thus, the litigation was dormant while the negotiations were taking place. Meanwhile, the *Sunday Times* wished to publish an article accusing Distillers of acting ungenerously towards the Thalidomide children. The article came close to saying that Distillers had been negligent, although it was balanced in that it did consider both sides.

The Attorney General obtained an injunction in the Divisional Court preventing publication of the article on the ground that it amounted to a contempt of court. The Court of Appeal then discharged the injunction in a ruling which weighed up the public interest in freedom of speech against the need to protect the administration of justice and found that the former value outweighed the latter: the article concerned a matter of great public interest and, since the litigation in question was dormant, it would probably be unaffected by it. The House of Lords then restored the injunction on the ground that the article dealt with the question of negligence and therefore prejudged the case pending before the court. It held that such prejudgment was particularly objectionable as coming

---

64 [1968] 3 All ER 439; [1968] 1 WLR 1761, CA.
65 See *Report of the Committee on Contempt of Court*, Cmnd 5794, 1974. For comment, see Dhavan, R, 'Contempt of court and the Phillimore Committee Report' (1976) 5 Anglo-Am L Rev 186–253.
66 [1974] AC 273; [1973] 3 All ER 54; [1973] 3 WLR 298, HL. For case notes, see Miller, CJ (1974) 37 MLR 96; O'Boyle, M (1974) 25 NILQ 57; Williams, DGT (1973) 32 CLJ 177 and Miller, CJ [1975] Crim LR 132.

close to 'trial by media' and thereby leading to an undermining of the administration of justice: a person might be adjudged negligent by parts of the media with none of the safeguards available in court. The confidence of the public in the courts might be undermined, thus creating a long-term detriment to the course of justice generally.

This ruling created a possible new test for the *actus reus* of contempt. Termed the 'prejudgment' test, it was wider than the test of real risk of prejudice, in that little risk to proceedings might be shown, but it might still be possible to assert that they had been prejudged. This test was heavily criticised by the Phillimore Committee; it had a potentially grave effect on freedom of speech because it was very difficult to draw the line between legitimate discussion in the media and prejudgment. Since it was easier to satisfy the prejudgment test than the old test for the *actus reus* of common law contempt, the Phillimore Committee considered that the *Sunday Times* ruling strengthened the case for reform. Meanwhile, the case was on its way to the European Court of Human Rights. The editor of the *Sunday Times* applied to the European Commission of Human Rights seeking a ruling that the imposition of the injunction breached Art 10 of the European Convention, and five years after the judgment of the House of Lords, the case came before the European Court of Human Rights (*Sunday Times* case).[67]

As indicated in the introduction to this Part, the Art 10 guarantee of freedom of expression is subject to exceptions to be narrowly construed. The Court found that the injunction clearly infringed Art 10(1) and that this was not a trivial infringement; the free speech interest involved was very strong, because the matter was one of great public concern. However, the injunction fell within Art 10(2) because it had an aim permitted by one of the exceptions – maintenance of the authority of the judiciary.

The next question was whether the injunction was 'necessary in a democratic society' in order to achieve the aim in question: it was not enough merely to show that the injunction was covered by an exception. In order to make a determination on this point, the Court considered the meaning of the term 'necessary'. It ruled that this did not mean indispensable, but connoted something stronger than 'useful', 'reasonable' or 'desirable'. It implied the existence of a 'pressing social need'. Was there such a need? The Court employed the doctrine of proportionality in determining the existence of such a 'need' in the circumstances: it weighed up the strength of the free speech interest in considering whether the injunction was disproportionate to the aim of preserving the authority of the judiciary. It found that although courts are clearly the forums for settling disputes, this does not mean that there can be no newspaper discussion before a case. The article was couched in moderate terms and explored the issues in a balanced way. Moreover, the litigation in question was dormant and therefore unlikely to be affected by the article. Nevertheless, the injunction created an absolute prohibition on discussion of the issues forming the background to the case. Thus, on the one hand, there was a strong free speech interest; on the other, there was a weak threat to the authority of the judiciary. If the free speech interest had been weaker, it might have been more easily overcome. The Court, therefore, concluded that the interference did not correspond to a social need sufficiently pressing to outweigh the public interest in freedom of expression. In reaching its conclusion that a breach of Art 10 had therefore

---

67 Judgment of 26 April 1979, A 30; (1979) 2 EHRR 245. For case notes, see Duffy, PJ, 5 H Rts Rev 17; Mann, FA (1979) 95 LQR 348; Wong, W-WM (1984) 17 NY Univ JIL and Pol 35.

taken place,[68] the Court also adverted briefly to the value of the Article in furthering the aim of preserving the authority of the judiciary since 'in bringing to light certain facts it might have served as a brake on speculative and unenlightened discussion'. In other words, the speech in question served the ends of justice in a general sense.

The UK Government responded to this decision in the enactment of the Contempt of Court Act 1981 which was supposed to take account of the ruling of the European Court and was also influenced to an extent by the findings of the Phillimore Committee.[69]

The Contempt of Court Act 1981

The 1981 Act was designed to introduce provisions based on a modification of the common law tests without bringing about radical change. It introduced various liberalising factors, but it was intended to maintain the stance of the ultimate supremacy of the administration of justice over freedom of speech, while moving the balance further towards freedom of speech.[70] In particular, it introduced stricter time limits, a more precise test for the *actus reus* and – in a departure from the common law rules – allowed some articles on matters of public interest to escape liability even though prejudice to proceedings was created.

These reforms brought about under the Act will be considered below, bearing the obligation of s 3 HRA in mind, in terms of their ability to satisfy the Convention, in particular Art 10, interpreted domestically. In any particular instance, the *current* Strasbourg standards should be taken into account in strictly scrutinising interferences with the Art 10 guarantee. It would not be sufficient to assume that such standards will be met on the basis that the 1981 Act was introduced in order to take account of the Strasbourg ruling in the *Sunday Times* case. In order to determine whether liability is created, the following steps must be taken under the Act. Possible modifications of the statutory tests under the HRA will be considered taking account of the Strasbourg standards discussed.

The publication falls within s 1 of the Act

Under s 1, conduct will be contempt if it interferes with the administration of justice in particular proceedings regardless of intent to do so. Thus, not all publications which deal with issues touching on the administration of justice will fall within the 1981 Act. The starting point under s 1 is to ask whether the publication touches upon particular legal proceedings. In other words, if the article appears to have a long-term effect on the course of justice generally, without affecting any particular proceedings, it would fall outside the Act and might be considered at common law. This point will be considered below.

It is important to note that it is not necessary to show that the defendant intended to prejudice proceedings: the 'strict liability rule' under s 1 continues the position as

---

68 It may be noted that the Court was divided 11–9 in reaching this determination.

69 See *Report of the Committee on Contempt of Court*, Cmnd 5794, 1974; Green Paper, Cmnd 7145, 1978.

70 For comment on the 1981 Act, see Miller, CJ [1982] Crim LR 71; Lowe, NV [1982] PL 20; Smith, JC [1982] Crim LR 744; Zellich, GF [1982] PL 343; Redmond, M [1983] CLJ 9.

it was at common law. After establishing that the publication might affect particular proceedings, a number of other tests must be satisfied if the strict liability rule is to be established. If the publication does affect particular proceedings, but one of these tests is unsatisfied, it might still be possible to consider it at common law. It should be noted that the proceedings must be 'court' proceedings. This test includes certain tribunals in the contempt jurisdiction.[71]

The proceedings are 'active'

This test, which arises under s 2(3), is more clearly defined than the test at common law and therefore proceedings are 'active' (or *sub judice*) for shorter periods. Thus, the test is intended to have a liberalising effect. The starting and ending points for civil and criminal proceedings are defined in Sched 1. For criminal proceedings, the starting point (Sched 1, s 4(a)–(e)) is: the issue of a warrant for arrest, an arrest without warrant or the service of an indictment (or summons or an oral charge); the ending point is acquittal, sentence, any other verdict or discontinuance of the trial. The starting point for civil proceedings occurs when the case is set down for a hearing in the High Court or a date for the hearing is fixed (Sched 1, ss 12 and 13). This provision was clarified in *Attorney General v Hislop and Pressdram*:[72] it was found that s 2(3) was fulfilled because the proceedings in question (an action for defamation) had come into the 'warned' list at the time the articles in question were published. This starting point addresses the problem of gagging writs: the mere issuance of a writ would not mean that any further comment could give rise to an action for contempt because the issue of a writ is not the starting point. The end point of the active period for civil proceedings comes when the proceedings are disposed of, discontinued or withdrawn. The precision of these provisions, which allows the media to determine with reasonable certainty the point at which a risk of liability arises, means that they can be viewed as meeting the demands of Art 10.

Surprisingly, appellate proceedings are also covered by Sched 1. The starting point occurs when leave to appeal is applied for, by notice of appeal or application for review or other originating process; the end point occurs when the proceedings are disposed of or abandoned. Section 9 of the Criminal Appeal Act 1995 provides that a reference by the Criminal Cases Review Commission to the Court of Appeal is to be treated as an appeal under the Criminal Appeal Act 1968 for all purposes, and therefore, appellate proceedings become active when such a reference is made.

These provisions are less restrictive than the previous ones under the common law, which also covered the period during which notice to appeal could be given, but the key question is why appellate proceedings are covered at all. The Phillimore Committee recommended that most appellate proceedings should not be covered.[73] Given the principles at stake, discussed above, it is suggested that the ends of justice are unlikely to be served by seeking to stifle media comment that refers specifically to appeals, since the openness of the discussion supports confidence in the quality of

---

71 Section 19 provides that 'court' includes 'any tribunal or body exercising the judicial power of the state'. See further Borrie and Lowe, op. cit., fn 1, pp 485–91.

72 [1991] 1 QB 514; [1991] 1 All ER 911; [1991] 2 WLR 219, CA.

73 Phillimore Committee Report, para 132.

justice which is unafraid of comment. The misinformed or biased nature of aspects of such discussion would not be expected to affect the judiciary, especially the senior judiciary. Therefore, no fear of arbitrariness due to prejudice should arise. As Lord Reid said in the *Sunday Times* case: 'It is scarcely possible to imagine a case when comment could influence judges in the Court of Appeal or noble and leaned Lords in this House.'[74] Nevertheless, Channel 4 was enjoined from broadcasting a re-enactment, in the form of a dramatic 'reconstruction', of the appeal of the Birmingham Six, until after the decision on the appeal had been taken.[75] This was a doubtful decision, since it was highly unlikely that the judges would have been influenced by the programme. The injunction was therefore obtained on the basis that the public's view of the judgment of the court might have been affected by it. This justification is flawed, since it does not appear to be covered by s 2(2) of the Act,[76] and also because the public's view of that judgment and of the Appeal Court generally would be more greatly influenced, it is suggested, by the impression given that a ban was necessary in order to prevent the programme from influencing the judges.

It is probable that prosecutions in respect of contempt of appellate courts will not be brought in future. In *re Lonhro plc and Observer Ltd*,[77] the House of Lords relied on Art 10 in finding that since the possibility that a professional judge would be influenced by media coverage of a case is extremely remote, it would be extremely hard to establish a 'pressing social need', as required by Art 10, to suppress the speech in question. This stance has now been reinforced by the inception of the Human Rights Act.

The publication creates 'a substantial risk of serious prejudice or impediment to the course of justice in the proceedings in question' (s 2(2))

Introduction

The s 2(2) test can be viewed as taking a protective stance since it is intended to deter media bodies from publishing prejudicial material. Arguably, it goes further in terms of protecting the fairness of trials than neutralising or remedial measures (acquittals, abandonment of the proceedings) do. Section 2(2) can be said to punish media bodies who have created prejudice even where – from the point of view of the *trial* judge, as opposed to the judge in the contempt proceedings – a stay of proceedings or other measures are not viewed as necessary. Section 2(2) is an objective test; it is unconcerned with the question whether prejudice has actually been caused. The inclusion of a substantial risk of 'impediment' could be viewed as making it clear that UK law adheres more to a protective rather than a neutralising model in terms of seeking to ensure the fairness of trials. The more far-reaching neutralising measures, such as changing the

---

74 *Attorney General v Times Newspapers*, [1974] AC 273; [1973] 3 All ER 54; [1973] 3 WLR 298, HL.

75 *In re Channel 4 Television Co Ltd* (1988) *The Times*, 2 February; [1988] Crim LR 237.

76 Since it could not have been shown that a substantial risk of prejudice to the proceedings – the appeal – would arise. Section 2(2) does not refer to a substantial risk of prejudice to the course of justice in a general sense.

77 [1989] 2 All ER 1100, HL.

venue of the trial or delaying it, would clearly tend to have an impeding effect on it. On the other hand, the use of lesser neutralising measures, such as warnings to the jury to disregard media coverage, are matters which may properly be taken into account when considering the risk in question. In *Attorney General v Times Newspapers*[78] it was found that jurors were able to ignore possibly prejudicial comment in newspapers. That case concerned a relatively trivial incident which happened to attract publicity because of the fame of one of the persons involved, a factor which jurors might be expected to appreciate, leading them to discount the press coverage. Recently, it has become more common for consideration to be afforded to the likelihood that the jury will be strongly directed to ignore prejudicial coverage of the trial.[79] Thus, responsibility is shifting to an extent from the media and is being placed upon judges and jurors. Perhaps, as indicated above, that shift of responsibility is not fully in accordance with the notion that the 'duties and responsibilities' of Art 10 are placed upon those exercising the right to freedom of expression it protects, that is, the media.

Moreover, as Simon Brown LJ pointed out in *Attorney General v Birmingham Post and Mail*,[80] 's 2(2) postulates a lesser degree of prejudice than is required to make good an appeal against conviction. Similarly, it seems to me to postulate a lesser degree of prejudice than would justify an order for a stay'. He went on to conclude that where s 2(2) was satisfied, it would not follow that a conviction was imperilled or that a stay was required, but that the converse was not the case: 'I find it difficult to envisage a publication which has concerned the judge sufficiently to discharge the jury and yet is not properly to be regarded as a contempt.' Clearly, although this may be an accurate statement of the effect of s 2(2) where a particular publication creates a likelihood of prejudice to a criminal trial, the preventive or punitive effect can only occur if (a) the prejudicial effect is not the result of cumulative media coverage of issues relevant to or arising from a particular case, and (b) if contempt proceedings are actually brought. As the discussion below indicates, both these matters are problematic.

According to the Court of Appeal in *Attorney General v News Group Newspapers*,[81] both limbs of the test under s 2(2) must be satisfied: showing a slight risk of serious prejudice or a substantial risk of slight prejudice would not be sufficient. The question to be asked under the first limb could be broken down as follows: can it be argued that there is a substantial risk that a person involved in the case in question such as a juror would: (a) encounter the article; (b) remember it; and (c) be affected by it so that he or she could not put it out of his or her mind during the trial? Clearly, a person cannot be affected at all by something he or she has never encountered or has forgotten about. Thus, a number of factors may be identified which will be relevant to one or more of these questions. Having considered factors that are taken into account in determining whether a 'substantial risk' has arisen, the discussion will then consider the less problematic question of 'serious prejudice'.

78 (1983) *The Times*, 12 February, DC. See also *Attorney General v MGN* [1997] 1 All ER 456.
79 See, e.g., *Attorney General v MGN* [1997] EMLR 284.
80 [1998] 4 All ER 49, pp 57, 59. See further *Mcleod* (2000) *The Times*, 20 December.
81 [1987] 1 QB 1; [1986] 2 All ER 833; [1986] 3 WLR 365, CA.

Key factors

The circulation of a publication/viewing figures for a broadcast is a relevant factor in relation to the 'substantial risk' limb of the s 2(2) test.[82] This factor potentially has a greater impact on broadcasters than on newspapers, since the viewing figures for popular programmes tend to far exceed the circulation figures of individual newspapers: one broadcast will in general reach far more people than will one article. However, not many prosecutions have been brought against broadcasters, probably because they tend to take a more responsible stance than the press due to the strict regulatory regime to which they are subject, discussed in Chapter 6.[83] An exception arose in *Attorney General v BBC, Attorney General v Hat Trick Productions Ltd.*[84] During a programme on BBC2 in the irreverent, satirical series *Have I Got News for You*, remarks were made by celebrities which assumed that the Maxwell brothers were guilty of defrauding the *Daily Mirror* pensioners. The broadcast occurred six months before the trial of the Maxwells, but was viewed by an audience of several millions. An action for contempt was brought and it was found that despite the humorous context, the remarks assuming the guilt of the defendants might have been taken seriously by viewers and that therefore s 2(2) was satisfied.

Clearly, circulation figures cannot be calculated only on the basis of viewing or selling figures. The impact of newspapers depends on their readership, not just their circulation figures. Further, front-page, banner headlines may reach many more people in a range of contexts. The existence of the internet clearly increases the circulation figures of both newspapers and broadcasts. All newspapers and some broadcasts have their own website on which material is archived. Internet-users could access trial-related material on such websites, either by putting a key word into Google (or another search engine), or by choosing to search the website of a particular media organ in the expectation that some reporting would cover such material.[85]

The temporal proximity between the publication and the trial or civil action is the single most significant factor under s 2(2). However, the rapidly increasing popularity of the internet may be calling the current stance into question. The reliance on temporal proximity between publication and proceedings in relation to the 'substantial risk' limb of s 2(2) arguably favours the particular operational methods of the tabloid press. As Chapter 9 points out, the press are not restrained, as are broadcasters, by quite a strict statutory regime governing privacy and accuracy. The result is that tabloid newspapers

---

82 If a publication has a small circulation, this risk might be seen as too remote. This point was considered in *Attorney General v Hislop and Pressdram* [1991] 1 QB 514; [1991] 1 All ER 911; [1991] 2 WLR 219, CA which concerned the effect of an article in *Private Eye* written about Sonia Sutcliffe, wife of the Yorkshire Ripper. She began an action for defamation in respect of the article. Shortly before the hearing of the action, *Private Eye* published two further articles defamatory of Mrs Sutcliffe. The Attorney-General brought proceedings for contempt of court in respect of the second articles, and on appeal it was determined that as *Private Eye* had a large readership, many of whom might live in London, where the libel action was held, it could not be said that the risk of prejudice was insubstantial.

83 At pp 518–22.

84 [1997] EMLR 76; *The Times*, 26 July 1996. See also *Attorney General v LWT* 3 All ER 116; *Attorney General v Jones and BBC* (1995) (unreported).

85 See further, C Walker, 'Fundamental Rights, Fair Trials and the New Audio-Visual Sector' [1996] 59 MLR 517.

are able to rely on sensationalist and frequently misleading reporting as a marketing tool. Such reporting is very unlikely to attract liability under the strict liability rule so long as it occurs some months or even weeks before the proceedings in question. It is very clear from decisions over the last ten years that the time at which coverage is most at risk is getting closer and closer to the time at which the proceedings occur. Prosecutions would probably no longer be brought where a time lag of the order of ten months between publication and proceedings had occurred. By 2007 it became possible to say that imputations of guilt in the active period probably would not incur liability unless they occurred contemporaneously with the trial.

In 1987 the ruling in *Attorney General v News Group Newspapers*[86] made it clear that the proximity of the article to the trial is highly relevant to the question of risk. The Court of Appeal held that a gap of ten months between the two could not create the substantial risk in question because the jury would be likely to have forgotten the article by the time the trial came on and even if it were faintly recollected at the time of the trial, it would be likely to have little impact. Similarly, in *Attorney General v Independent TV News and Others*[87] one of the factors founding the ruling that s 2(2) was not satisfied was the lapse of time before the trial; the risk that any juror who had seen the offending item would remember it was not seen as substantial. ITV News and certain newspapers had published the fact that a defendant in a forthcoming murder trial was a convicted IRA terrorist who had escaped from jail where he was serving a life sentence for murder. However, the trial was not expected to take place for nine months, there had only been one offending news item, and there had been limited circulation of only one edition of the offending newspaper items. In contrast, in *Attorney General v Hislop and Pressdram*,[88] a gap of three months between publication of the article and the trial of the libel action was not viewed as long enough to negate the risk. A publication during the trial is clearly most likely to create a risk.

In the late 1990s judges began to show a readiness to assume that somewhat smaller time lapses in months would still diminish the risk in question to the point where it could be viewed as negligible or minimal. In *Attorney General v Unger*[89] the article in question, discussed further below, was published about three-and-a-half months before the trial in a tabloid with a large circulation. It was found that its impact should be looked at at the time of publication and at the time of the trial – its residual impact on jurors should be taken into account. Over that period of time its impact would have faded; taking that 'fade factor' into account, it was determined that a substantial risk of prejudice did not arise. A similar stance was taken in *Attorney General v Unger*.[90] The respondent newspapers, the *Daily Mail* and *Manchester Evening News*, published newspaper articles, relating how the defendant, who was a home help, had been caught red-handed on video stealing money from a pensioner in her care. In other words, they imputed guilt. Simon Brown LJ found that articles of this nature which plainly prejudged guilt could influence jurors. But when he considered the 'crucial' matter of the residual impact of the publication on a notional juror at the time of trial, he attached great significance to

---

86 [1987] QB 1.
87 [1995] 2 All ER 370.
88 [1991] 1 QB 514; [1991] 1 All ER 911; [1991] 2 WLR 219, CA.
89 [1997] 1 All ER 456.
90 *Attorney General v Unger* (1998) EMLR 280 at 319.

the 'fade' factor, the effect of the lapse of time between publication and trial. Here the time lapse was of the order of nine months. He considered that this would greatly affect the recollections of the article by any juror who had happened to read it. He noted that this factor had been stressed in a number of the cases.[91] He considered that publications are most dangerously prejudicial when they are published contemporaneously with the trial, because then jurors read them with 'particular interest rather than merely as part of an everyday media diet', or when they disclose prejudicial material which is itself inadmissible in evidence, most obviously an accused's previous convictions. Neither of those two factors were present. But in *Attorney General v Newsgroup Newspapers*,[92] the *Sun* published a serious allegation regarding a defendant in a murder trial at the point at which the jury had retired to consider its verdict. The murder charge was dropped, and the *Sun* was prosecuted, convicted and fined for contempt.

The existence of the internet is highly relevant to temporal proximity. Trial-related material is often placed on a newspaper's website prior to or early in the active period – at the time when the reporting occurs of a high profile investigation or of an arrest. However, that material is likely to remain on the website, whereas the newspaper itself will be discarded by its readers very rapidly, often on the day that it is obtained. Thus the material may still be on the website and accessible as the trial date approaches. Jurors might decide deliberately to search newspapers' websites with a view to discovering more about the trial and, perhaps, the background of defendants. Where publicity is potentially prejudicial, but is subject to a significant face-factor, newspapers could ensure that such material is removed from the website's archives. However, if they fail to do so they clearly place themselves at risk of a prosecution for contempt even though there has been a significant time lapse between initial publication and trial. This factor, and the accessibility of the web-based material, should be taken into account when assessing the risk created by press material that has been published some time before the trial. It may be noted that where the internet Service Provider maintaining a website on which trial-related material is stored is not a domestic newspaper or broadcaster, but is a body outside the jurisdiction, it would not be possible to bring a prosecution even if highly prejudicial material was uploaded to an easily accessible website and maintained on it before and during the trial. It might be argued that the chance of a juror accessing the website could be viewed as remote, but the rapidly increasing use of the internet is undermining that argument.[93]

On the face of it, the factor of proximity in time cannot be considered in isolation from other relevant ones: the celebrity status of defendants/plaintiffs; the subject matter of the publication; the language used. These three factors may make it more likely that a publication will be remembered even over a fairly substantial period of time. However, temporal proximity, combined with the effect of neutralising directions, is by far the most important factor. We now seem to have arrived at the point when it is almost possible to say that the active period runs *de facto* only from the start of the trial – from the point at which the jurors are empanelled, since from that point they are likely to take especial interest in articles relating to that particular trial. From that

---

91 *Attorney General v NGN* [1987] QB 1; *ex p Telegraph plc* [1993] 1 WLR 980; *Attorney General v Independent TV News* [1995] 1 Cr App R 204.
92 16 April 1999 (unreported).
93 See Chapter 6, p 572, fn 477.

point judges view publications or broadcasts as no longer part of an ephemeral media diet (they have not yet, it seems, taken account of the fact that the use of the internet means that it is much less ephemeral than it used to be), but as of especial significance. In other words, even where other factors founding a 'substantial risk' are quite clearly present, unless material is disclosed that would be inadmissible in evidence, prejudicial publication/broadcasts, even very close to the trial, but not during it, may not reach the s 2(2) threshold.

This reliance on proximity means that where a high profile crime, such as the Soham murders in 2002 or the attempted terrorist bombings in London in July 2005,[94] occurs, the tabloids can report on the arrestees in lurid terms, as they did in both instances, in the knowledge that although the proceedings are 'active,' there is likely to be quite a significant time lapse before the trial, and that therefore the risk of prejudice will probably be viewed as diminished to the point where it cannot be regarded as 'substantial'. Therefore newspapers that are – in contrast to broadcasters – already unrestrained in such reporting by a statutory regulatory scheme enjoining accuracy and impartiality on them, are likely to be equally unrestrained by the strict liability rule. In the instance of Soham the Attorney General did issue warnings to the tabloids reminding them of the rule, but no action was taken. Clearly, if the aim of s 2(2) is to protect the fairness of particular trials, it is inevitable that the proximity in time of a publication will be taken into account. But there may be instances, such as that of Soham, or of the terrorist incidents in 2003 and 2005, where the coverage is so extreme and so unremitting at the time of an arrest, that a fair trial, even months later, is likely to be prejudiced. The more recent rulings on temporal proximity suggest that the judges would not accept that s 2(2) was satisfied in such circumstances, especially when the findings from *Attorney General v MGN* regarding totality of coverage were also taken into account, since it would be difficult to ascribe responsibility for the creation of prejudice to any one newspaper. Once a substantial period of time had elapsed, it would be likely that a potential juror would merely remember an impression, rather than the specifics of the coverage of any one newspaper. But that impression – that the arrestees were guilty – might be deep-rooted and insidious.[95]

The totality of the news coverage is a relevant factor in the sense that where a large amount of arguably prejudicial publicity has occurred, it is difficult to isolate the contribution that one publication has made. Obtaining a conviction under the s 2(2) test, as currently interpreted, is especially difficult or impossible where a substantial risk of serious prejudice or impediment is created by the totality of the news coverage, rather than by the coverage of a particular article or broadcast. *Attorney General v MGN*[96] concerned the coverage of a case involving the notorious boyfriend of a soap opera actress, Gillian Taylforth, by five tabloid newspapers, which mentioned his previous criminal record and presented a misleading picture of the incident in question. It was found that none of the

94 See p 362, fn 168.

95 There would be the possibility of bringing an action for common law contempt in respect of such coverage, but editors would be able to show that due to the lapse of time they did not foresee the creation of a real risk of prejudice as a virtual certainty (oblique intent). So far, apart from cases relating to material covered by an injunction against another media body, it is only in cases in which a newspaper has a personal interest that a desire to prejudice proceedings (simple intent) has been shown: see discussion below pp 364–65, 368.

96 [1997] 1 All ER 456.

articles, considered separately, reached the required threshold under s 2(2). The judge, Schiemann LJ, said that where, in such an instance, the totality of the coverage had prejudiced the trial, it might be proper to stay the proceedings. This decision reveals a weakness in the use of the strict liability rule, since it means that the creation of serious prejudice to a trial by a large number of newspaper articles in combination cannot be addressed by means of contempt law where individual articles just fail to satisfy the strict test of s 2(2) as interpreted in *Attorney General v Guardian Newspapers*.[97] As discussed below, that decision significantly raised the s 2(2) bar. The use of a stay means that the coverage has had the effect of impeding the course of justice in the proceedings in question, but that the detriment thereby created cannot be laid at the doors of those responsible.

It is argued that the courts need to distinguish more clearly between 'threshold,' 'generic' and prejudicial publicity.[98] 'Generic' publicity can be taken to indicate coverage that is not in itself prejudicial since it does not relate specifically enough to the trial. But it may have a general and all-pervasive effect in terms of painting 'the defendant with an incriminating brush.'[99] 'Threshold' publicity is merely coverage relating to someone involved in proceedings, making his or her name memorable. The existence of threshold or generic publicity tends to mean that prejudicial publicity has more impact.[100] Therefore such publicity is more, not less, likely to satisfy the s 2(2) test. On the other hand, where a number of newspapers publish material that does relate specifically to a case and which, combined, satisfies s 2(2), it may be difficult to show that any particular publication, alone, satisfies the test.

Some of the prosecutions discussed above, and in particular that in *Attorney General v BBC, Attorney General v Hat Trick Productions Ltd*,[101] may be contrasted with the lack of action taken in respect of the facts of *R v Taylor*.[102] A large number of tabloid newspapers published a photograph which was taken of one of the defendants in a murder trial giving the husband of the victim a polite kiss on the cheek; it was distorted in such a way as to give the impression that it was a passionate mouth-to-mouth kiss and was captioned 'Cheats Kiss.' It was found that this was part of an 'unremitting, extensive, sensational, inaccurate and misleading press coverage' and had led to a real risk of prejudice to the trial. This determination was made on appeal in overturning the convictions of the two defendants. The Attorney General refused to bring an action against the newspapers for contempt, possibly because he considered that no individual publication would attract liability, and it was found that his decision not to act was non-reviewable.[103] The failure to act did not therefore have to be justified, but the uncertain nature of the s 2(2) test as applied to individual newspapers could be viewed

97 [1999] EMLR 904. See pp 347, 353 below.

98 See e.g., Doppelt, JC, 'Generic Prejudice: How Drug War Fervor Threatens the Right to a Fair Trial' (1991) 40 *American University Law Review* 821.

99 See Chesterman, M, Chan, J and Hampton, S, *Managing Prejudicial Publicity*, 2001, Justice Research Centre, Law and Justice Foundation of New South Wales, p 9.

100 Ibid, pp 111, 121, 122, 235.

101 [1997] EMLR 76.

102 (1993) 98 Cr App R 361, CA.

103 *R v S-G, ex p Taylor*, *The Times*, 14 August 1995. For comment on the case see Stephens, M and Hill, P, 'The Role and Impact of Journalism' in Walker, C and Starmer, K (eds) *Miscarriages of Justice: A Review of Justice in Error*, 1997, Blackstone, 263, pp 264–67. For comment and the implications of the case within the European Convention on Human Rights, see Borrie and Lowe, *The Law of Contempt* (1996), pp 481–82.

as providing a degree of justification for it. On the other hand, the possibility cannot entirely be ruled out, as argued above, that government reluctance to take on a large number of press proprietors played a part in the decision.

In a number of the cases discussed below judges have taken account of the potential use of neutralising measures in assessing the risk of prejudice. They have stressed the ability of jurors to disregard media comment, especially when properly directed to do so. In taking the use of such 'neutralising' directions into account, they have also stressed the need for contempt law to use the same standards as those that would determine the need for a stay or the success of an appeal. The courts have, increasingly, emphasised the unlikelihood that jurors will be unaffected by prejudicial media comment. The probability that the lesser neutralising measure of warning the jury to disregard media coverage will be employed is increasingly taken into account when a court is considering the risk of prejudice, although two schools of thought can be discerned among the judiciary on this matter – broadly speaking, those of juror susceptibility and juror invulnerability.[104]

It was pointed out in *Attorney General v Times Newspapers*[105] that jurors are able to ignore possibly prejudicial comment in newspapers. That case concerned a relatively trivial incident which happened to attract publicity because of the fame of one of the persons involved, a factor which jurors might be expected to appreciate, leading them to discount the press coverage. Recently, it has become more common for consideration to be afforded to the likelihood that the jury will be strongly directed to ignore prejudicial coverage of the trial.[106] In *Attorney General v BBC*,[107] however, Staughton LJ said that he did not have the confidence expressed by certain judges in 'the ability of jurors to disregard matters which they do remember but which they are not entitled to take into account.'

In contrast, in *Attorney General v Unger*[108] Simon Brown LJ found that the 'fade factor' should be coupled with the presumption that juries would decide cases solely according to the evidence put before them and the directions they were given. He considered that in the case before him, if the accused woman had elected jury trial and had been convicted, she could not have won an appeal on the basis of the published articles. A similar stance was taken in *Attorney General v Guardian Newspapers*.[109] The case concerned the trial of one Kelly for stealing body parts, apparently for artistic purposes; during the trial the *Observer* published an article suggesting in strong terms that Kelly had had no artistic purpose in stealing the parts, but was motivated merely by a morbid fascination with dead people. The writer linked Kelly's fascination to that experienced by a number of named serial killers. Since Kelly's honesty was a key issue in the trial, the article was very damaging to his case since in the jury's eyes it could have undermined his credibility. Both Collins LJ and Sedley LJ concluded that the article therefore created a risk of serious prejudice.

104 See the National Heritage Committee Second Report (1997) *Press Activity Affecting Court Cases*, pp 33–34.
105 *The Times*, 12 February 1983.
106 See e.g., *Attorney General v MGN* [1997] EMLR 284.
107 1 December 1995 (unreported).
108 (1998) EMLR 280 at 319.
109 [1999] EMLR 904.

Sedley LJ wrestled with the question whether the risk should be described as substantial:

> In the end, and not without anxiety, I have concluded that it is simply not possible to be sure that the risk created by the publication was a substantial risk that a jury, properly directed to disregard its own sentiments and any media comment, would nevertheless have its own thoughts or value judgments reinforced by the article to a point where they influenced the verdict. As a first cross-check, I doubt whether an appeal would have been allowed had the jury which convicted Mr Kelly read the article. As a second cross-check, it seems to me that the threat from this article, published when it was, to the course of justice in Mr Kelly's trial was not sufficient to make either prior restraint or subsequent punishment a proportionate response in a society which, as a democracy, values and protects the freedom of the press.

In other words, some degree of serious prejudice had been caused, but it was accepted that the degree of risk was likely to be diminished by the use of such directions. Collins LJ also took into account the effect of judicial directions on the jury in terms of neutralising any prejudice created by the publication, although he differed from Sedley LJ in finding that once it could be assumed that 'serious prejudice' had arisen it would be difficult to be sure that it had been dispelled by the use of neutralising directions. However, Collins LJ felt that the issue was so finely balanced that he would not dissent from Sedley LJ's conclusion on this point. It was therefore found that the test of 'serious prejudice,' but not that of 'substantial risk,' was satisfied.

Sedley LJ's approach, which appears to be the dominant one, shifts the emphasis impliedly from the protective to the neutralising stance since it makes the assumption that directions to the jury will be effective and can therefore properly undermine the need for protective measures. That approach also, to an extent, shifts the responsibility for the effect of prejudicial material from the media to judges and jurors. Arguably, that shift of responsibility is not fully in accordance with the Art 10 notion that the 'duties and responsibilities' it mentions in paragraph 1 are placed upon those exercising the right to freedom of expression it protects – that is, the media. As pointed out in Chapter 6, Strasbourg has interpreted para 1, in general, to enhance media freedom rather than to limit it.[110] So any reliance on it in the sense suggested here would probably therefore have to be a development in the *domestic* Art 10 jurisprudence.[111]

There has been uncertainty as to the relationship between s 2(2) and the tests used to make good an appeal against conviction or to found a stay. Simon Brown LJ found in *Attorney General v Birmingham Post and Mail*:[112] 's 2(2) postulates a lesser degree of prejudice than is required to make good an appeal against conviction. Similarly, it seems to me to postulate a lesser degree of prejudice than would justify an order for a stay'. He went on to conclude that where s 2(2) was satisfied, it would not follow

---

110   Cf its use in *Otto-Preminger Institute v Austria* (1995) 19 EHRR 34.

111   See p 463. A notion of protection only for responsible journalism already appears to be impliedly occurring, as discussed in Chapter 9, pp 970, 977–78, but not at present in reliance on the wording of Art 10(1).

112   [1999] 1 WLR 361, at 369H; [1998] 4 All ER 49, at 57, 59. See further *McLeod, The Times*, 20 December 2000.

that a conviction was imperilled or that a stay was required, but that the converse was not the case:

> I find it difficult to envisage a publication which has concerned the judge sufficiently to discharge the jury and yet is not properly to be regarded as a contempt . . . In short, s 2(2) is designed to avoid (and where necessary punish) publications even if they merely risk prejudicing proceedings, whereas a stay will generally only be granted where it is recognised that any subsequent conviction would otherwise be imperilled, and a conviction will only be set aside . . . if it is actually unsafe.

However, Sedley LJ and Collins LJ in *Attorney General v Guardian Newspapers*[113] considered that the tests for contempt and for the risk of actual prejudice to a trial should be harmonised. Collins LJ said:

> It seems to me that the prejudice required by s 2(2), which must be serious, is not of a lesser degree than that required to make good an appeal against conviction. To establish contempt it needs only be shown that there was a substantial risk that serious prejudice, which must in my view mean such prejudice as would justify a stay or appeal against conviction, would result from the publication. That such prejudice does not in the event result is nothing to the point. Thus uniformity of approach is achieved by requiring that the prejudice within the meaning of s 2(2) must be such as would be likely to justify at least a stay.

These words were echoed by in *Attorney General v Unger*[114] by Simon Brown LJ in something of a departure from his previous stance:

> It seems to me important in these cases that the Courts do not speak with two voices, one used to dismiss criminal appeals with the Court roundly rejecting any suggestion that prejudice resulted from media publications, the other holding comparable publications to be in contempt, the Courts on these occasions expressing grave doubts as to the jury's ability to forget or put aside what they have heard or read . . . generally speaking it seems to me that unless a publication materially affects the course of trial in that kind of way, or requires directions from the court well beyond those ordinarily required and routinely given to juries to focus their attention on evidence called before them rather than whatever they may have heard or read outside court, or creates at the very least a seriously arguable ground for an appeal on the basis of prejudice, it is unlikely to be vulnerable to contempt proceedings under the strict liability rule.

Thus a growing perception among the judiciary can be discerned of a need to bring contempt law into line with criminal appeals, so that in Simon Brown LJ's words, the courts do not 'speak with two voices'. This stance, it is argued, encourages newspapers to publish prejudicial material in the hope that the risk it poses to proceedings is not

---

113 [1999] EMLR 904.
114 (1998) EMLR 280 at 319.

substantial enough. The problem with this approach is that it detracts from the role of contempt law in protecting particular proceedings. It seems to assume that unless the resulting effect might approach one that had to be dealt with by a stay or an appeal, s 2(2) would not be satisfied. This stance undermines the role s 2(2) seemed to be intended to have – that of setting the threshold before that stage would be likely to be reached, thus protecting the criminal justice system. The fact that the judges are taking this stance is not surprising, given that the division of responsibility between contempt law and trial judge has always been problematic. But arguably it poses an unacceptable level of risk to the system.

Having established a substantial risk that jurors and others will be influenced by the article, it is then necessary to ask if the influence can be characterised as of a prejudicial nature or would be likely to impede the proceedings in question. A publication which was in some way relevant to a trial might be likely to create a substantial risk that it would influence persons involved in the trial, bearing the factors identified in mind, but without leading to prejudice to it. An article published in every national newspaper in the land on the day of the trial and discussing certain issues relevant to it in a striking and interesting, but fair and impartial manner would have an influence, but not a prejudicial one. In considering whether it would be prejudicial, the two limbs of the test must be considered together: it must be shown that the language used, the facts disclosed or sentiments expressed would lead an objective observer to conclude that a substantial risk had been established that persons involved in the proceedings would be prejudiced, before going on to consider whether that effect could properly be described as serious.

Prejudice and its seriousness can be established in a number of ways: the article (or other publication) might be likely to have the effect of influencing relevant persons against or in favour of the defendant; it might be likely to affect either the outcome of the proceedings in question or their very existence – as where pressure is placed on one party to drop[115] proceedings. In re Lonhro plc,[116] Lord Bridge said:

> [Pre-trial] it is easy to see how critical public discussion of the issues and criticism of the conduct of the parties, particularly if a party is held up to public obloquy, may impede or prejudice the course of the proceedings by influencing the conduct of witnesses or parties in relation to the proceedings. If [a jury is involved] the possibility of prejudice by advance publicity directed at an issue which the jury will have to decide is obvious.

It is assumed that laypersons are more likely to be affected by media coverage than professionals; as indicated above, it would be readily assumed that a judge would be unaffected.[117] Therefore, civil proceedings are less at risk of being prejudiced than

---

115 See *Hislop and Pressdram* [1991] 1 QB 514; [1991] 1 All ER 911; [1991] 2 WLR 219, CA: this aspect of the case is discussed in relation to common law contempt, below, p 368.

116 [1990] AC 154, p 209B.

117 This is the general view expressed in the relevant jurisprudence in Britain and in other common law jurisdictions. e.g., Lord Salmon said in *Attorney General v BBC* [1981] AC 303, p 342: 'I am and always would be satisfied that no judge would be influenced by what may be said by the media.' Of course, it should be borne in mind that this stance is taken by the judges themselves.

criminal ones, except in those instances in which a jury is used.[118] But, as indicated, civil actions can be affected in other ways. Also, witnesses, especially lay witnesses, in both civil and criminal actions might be affected by media coverage. They might be deterred from coming forward[119] or they might be intimidated or influenced[120] by it.

As noted above, the proximity in time between the article and the proceedings can affect this limb of s 2(2), as can the extent to which it may be said that the trial concerns a person in the public eye. If the article is published some time before the trial, as in *Attorney General v News Group Newspapers*, its probable effect on the minds of jurors will be lessened because it may only exist there as a faint memory: any effect it has is unlikely to be of a seriously prejudicial nature. This might be the case even though the article would have been likely to have such an effect had it been fresh in their minds. In the *Hislop* case, however, the vitriolic nature of the article did suggest that it would be likely to have a seriously prejudicial effect. The serious allegations in question were held to blacken the plaintiff's character and might well have influenced the jurors against her. The fact that Peter Sutcliffe was well known also made it more likely that the article would have an impact. However, courts will not be quick to assume that jurors are incapable of ignoring prejudicial publications. In *Attorney General v Guardian Newspapers*[121] the publication of the fact that one unidentified defendant out of six in a Manchester trial was also awaiting trial elsewhere was not found to satisfy s 2(2), since it was thought that it would not cause a juror of ordinary good sense to be biased against the defendant.

The test of 'impeding' proceedings is treated in a more specific fashion. It may be satisfied where the publication can be said to have led to the delay of the proceedings owing to the risk of prejudice.[122]

Use of s 2(2) in the post-HRA era

The post-HRA prosecutions have tended to occur in the more clear-cut cases. In two of them liability was not contested. In *Attorney General v BBC*[123] the BBC mistakenly released details about a complainant witness during a trial relating to charges of sexual abuse in an approved school, breaching his anonymity. The police had undertaken not to allow such details to be released and his anonymity was protected by s 1(1) of the Sexual Offences (Amendment) Act 1992. The witness was very distressed since his family had not known that he had – as he alleged – suffered sexual abuse. The BBC accepted that the publication of the details had satisfied the tests under s 2(2) and therefore the only question was as to the penalty to be imposed. It was accepted that the publication of the details had resulted from negligence and that the journalist responsible had had an exemplary record in relation to such matters. The penalty – a fine – was not excessive; it was imposed both on the BBC and on the journalist

---

118 In respect of defamation and in certain actions against the police.
119 See *Vine Products Ltd v Green* [1966] Ch 484, p 495.
120 See *Re Doncaster and Retford Co-operative Societies Agreement* [1960] LR 2 PC; *Hutchinson v Amalgamated Engineering Union, Re Daily Worker* (1932) *The Times*, 25 August.
121 [1992] 3 All ER 38, CA.
122 See *Attorney General v BBC* (1992) *The Independent*, 3 January 1992.
123 [2001] EWHC Admin 1202.

involved. The HRA was not mentioned during the case, although Art 10 would have been relevant to the heaviness of the fine[124] and to the decision to impose a separate penalty on the journalist.

Attorney General v MGN[125] concerned a somewhat similar instance in that liability was not disputed and the articles in question were apparently published in error. The articles, in the *Sunday Mirror*, concerned the trial of certain Premiership footballers for affray and causing grievous bodily harm with intent. The article revived allegations that the attack was racially motivated. The article was published at the time when the jury were considering their verdicts and, as the publishers recognised, its thrust was at variance with the evidence as presented in the criminal trial. The publishers recognised that the judge had given a clear direction that there was no evidence of a racial motive. The second article concerned a co-accused, Duberry. He had been acquitted, but his credibility and his evidence were still relevant in relation to the guilt or innocence of the four remaining defendants, in respect of whom verdicts had not been returned. Liability was not disputed but the court gave some consideration to the s 2(2) tests, finding that they were satisfied due to the timing of the article and the probability that the jurors might have been influenced for or against the four defendants. The trial had been abandoned as a result of the article and a retrial ordered. It was found that: '"substantial" in that context connotes a risk which is more than remote and not merely minimal . . . and it has to be accepted that within the range of strict liability contempts, this case is towards the top end.' This indicates that a test akin to that of Lord Diplock in *Attorney General v English* is still influencing judges, particularly at first instance. Again the HRA was not mentioned and the fine imposed was high but not excessive.

A somewhat similar instance arose in *Attorney General v Express*.[126] The *Daily Star* published an article relating to the alleged gang rape of a 17-year-old girl at a London hotel by up to eight footballers on 27 September 2003. Between 30 September 2003 and 22 October 2003 the Attorney General and the Metropolitan Police had repeatedly issued advice and guidelines stating that identification was in issue and that suspects should not be identified by name or photograph or other likeness. There was a great deal of media interest, but the article in the *Daily Star* was unique in that it identified two potential defendants. The Attorney General contended that it was sufficient to establish a substantial risk that the course of justice would be prejudiced to show that there was a risk that the complainant did not know the identity of the footballers revealed in the *Daily Star*. It was found that at the point when the *Daily Star* published the article the complainant had not identified to the police either of the two footballers by name or by effective description. The Court found that the inference could be drawn therefore that the complainant did not know the identities of the accused at the time of the publication. Accordingly, the publication to millions in the *Daily Star* of items identifying the two individuals created a substantial risk that the course of justice would be seriously impeded or prejudiced. The HRA played no part in the judgment.

---

124   See *Tolstoy Miloslavsky v UK* (1995) 20 EHRR 442.
125   [2002] EWHC 907.
126   [2005] EMLR 13.

Given the nature of these cases, no careful scrutiny of the s 2(2) tests in the light of the HRA was necessary, although it might have been expected that Art 10 would not have been entirely disregarded. The cases were clear-cut: either specific details relating to identity were released, or the prejudicial material was published during the trial.

The threshold created by the s 2(2) test

The decisions on s 2(2) have not fully clarified its meaning, but it may be concluded quite firmly that the threshold to be reached under the test can now be viewed, nearly 30 years after the inception of the 1981 Act, as quite a high one *in practice*. Therefore newspapers may risk publishing material concerning high-profile trials that they would not have published 25 years ago when the 1981 Act was introduced. A steady, if unacknowledged, raising of the bar denoted by the term 'substantial risk' can be discerned from the case law, which can largely be attributed to the influence of Art 10 of the European Convention, even before the HRA had come into force. It will be questioned below whether this raising of the bar is really in accord with Art 10 values, as some of the judges appear to assume.

Two years after the 1981 Act was introduced the bar was placed at a low level. In *Attorney General v English*[127] Lord Diplock interpreted 'substantial risk' as excluding a 'risk which is only remote,'[128] a finding which still strongly influences the *formal* approach to s 2(2).[129] The finding that only remote risks would be excluded allowed the House of Lords to find that the reference in the article to the mercy-killing of handicapped babies might prejudice the jury in the trial of a consultant charged with the murder of a Down's syndrome baby. The article, published in the *Daily Mail* after the trial had begun, made no direct reference to him, but was written in support of a pro-life candidate, Mrs Carr, who was standing in a by-election. Mrs Carr had no arms; the article referred to this fact and continued: 'today the chances of such a baby surviving are very small – someone would surely recommend letting her die of starvation. Are babies who are not up to scratch to be destroyed before or after birth'? The Lords considered that jurors would be likely to take the comments to refer to the trial; therefore, the assertion that babies were often allowed to die if handicapped might influence them against the consultant. The timing of the article predisposed the court to find that s 2(2) was satisfied. Nevertheless, on any view the risk was quite low but could be viewed as more than remote. (Incidentally, the consultant was acquitted; therefore, the article presumably did not in fact influence the jurors against him.) The

---

127 [1983] 1 AC 116; [1982] 2 All ER 903.

128 *Attorney General v English* [1983] 1 AC 116; [1982] 2 All ER 903; for comment, see Zellick G, 'Fair trial and free press' [1982] PL 343 (especially on the question of the degree of risk); Ward, A, 'A Substantial Change in the Law of Contempt?' (1983) 46 MLR 85; Redmond M, 'Of Black Sheep and too much Wool' [1983] 42 CLJ 9. It may be noted that aspects of *Attorney General v English* were the subject of an unsuccessful application to Strasbourg: *Times Newspapers Ltd and others v UK* (1983) 8 EHRR 45, p 54. Bearing in mind the comments in Chapter 2 pp 22–23 as to the effect of the Commission on the Convention jurisprudence, especially in its older decisions, it is suggested that this finding of inadmissibility would be unlikely to be repeated today and that the decision is somewhat out of line with the generality of the jurisprudence relating to pre-trial publicity and the reporting of issues relating to litigation.

129 See Zellick G, ibid, on this point, p 344.

finding that only remote risks are excluded appears to lessen the impact of the term 'substantial', and it is hard to see that there is a difference between this test and the old common law 'real risk' one.

In *MGN Pension Trustees Ltd*[130] it was found that the term meant 'not insubstantial' or 'not minimal' rather than weighty. In *Attorney General v Independent TV News and Others*,[131] the same view was taken – the risk of prejudice was found to be too small to be termed substantial, although arguably it could have been viewed as more than minimal. The term 'substantial' has been afforded *de facto* greater weight in the instances discussed below,[132] effectively excluding fairly low but non-remote risks. *Attorney General v Guardian Newspapers*,[133] *Attorney General v Unger*[134] and *Attorney General v MGN*[135] marked the turning point in the approach. These cases were all decided around the time of the inception of the HRA but before it had come into force. The imminent reception of Art 10 into domestic law affected the judicial approach.

In *Attorney General v MGN*[136] an article creating the inference that a defendant in forthcoming proceedings was guilty was not found in itself to create a sufficiently substantial risk of serious prejudice, despite the fact that that article in combination with others had led the trial judge to stay the proceedings. A straightforward imputation of guilt was made in *Attorney General v Unger*, but the time lapse led to the conclusion that the risk was not substantial enough. In *Attorney General v Guardian Newspapers* Sedley LJ in the Court of Appeal considered that he was placing a strong reliance on the Art 10(2) tests as interpreted in *Worm v Austria*[137] in finding that although a risk of serious prejudice arose, it was not certain that it could be viewed as a substantial one.

The previous rulings clearly do not give as much weight to the term 'substantial' as Sedley LJ did. The facts of *Guardian Newspapers*, discussed above, were in some respects far more compelling than those of *English* as far as s 2(2) was concerned. The *Observer* article at issue in *Guardian Newspapers* was centrally about the trial, whereas the comments in the *Daily Mail* article in *English* were only obliquely or inferentially linked to it; they were ambiguous and did not necessarily impute guilt. Both the articles at issue were published contemporaneously with the trial. Yet s 2(2) was found to be satisfied in *English*, whereas in *Guardian Newspapers* the opposing result was reached, indicating the incremental, stealthy raising of the bar which has occurred. The imminent inception of the Human Rights Act, encouraging the judiciary to afford a strong weight to the relevant Art 10 jurisprudence, appears to explain the difference. In *Worm*, which was relied on in *Guardian Newspapers*, the test used was that of 'likelihood' of risk; as discussed below, this appears to mean that the risk is more likely than not to materialise. This test denotes a higher threshold than does Lord Diplock's test in *English* of excluding only remote risks.

---

130 [1995] EMLR 99.
131 [1995] 2 All ER 370.
132 See in particular Lord Lane's comments in *Attorney General v Times Newspapers Ltd*, *The Times*, 12 February 1983.
133 [1999] EMLR 904.
134 *Attorney General v Unger* (1998) EMLR 280 at 319. The decision is discussed above at pp 342–43.
135 [1997] 1 All ER 456. The decision is discussed above at pp 344–45.
136 [1997] 1 All ER 456.
137 (1998) 25 EHRR 454.

The only case to succeed under the strict liability rule in the late 1990s was *Attorney General v BBC and Hat Trick Productions Ltd*[138] where the words in question were spoken by celebrities during a popular television programme. Auld LJ said of them:

> The offending words are strikingly prejudicial and go to the heart of the case which the jury are to try, and . . . the offending publicity is great both because of its medium and repetition, and because both the speakers and the victims are already much in the public eye.

Taking account of the case law as a whole, it seems fair to conclude that although the courts continue in most instances to pay lip-service to Lord Diplock's dictum in *Attorney General v English*, they are not prepared to find that s 2(2) is satisfied on the basis of risks just above the 'minimal' threshold. And, clearly, a strict approach to s 2(2) seemed to be likely to prevail after the Human Rights Act came into force, on the basis that the judiciary in general were likely to accept that the *Guardian Newspapers* approach to the Strasbourg jurisprudence, and especially to *Worm v Austria*, was the correct one.

Following Simon Brown LJ's approach in *Unger* and Sedley LJ's in *Guardian Newspapers*, it seems to be clear that the s 2(2) bar is being raised. Clearly, this is a media-friendly approach. Whether it is protective of free speech values is more open to doubt. Collins LJ said, 'in applying s 2(2) due weight must be given to the protection of freedom of speech.' This assumes a complete convergence between the claims of the media and those of free speech, although it is questionable whether speech that undermines the presumption of innocence has a strong claim to protection, bearing in mind underlying free speech rationales.[139] This approach may also be under-protective of trials since it confuses the role of protective measures with that of neutralising ones. If the administration of justice is not protected from prejudicial comment on the ground that the courts should not 'speak with two voices' then the criminal justice system is potentially placed under strain. It may be exposed to prejudicial comment and have to take measures, such as stays, which may themselves cause impairment to trials,[140] in order to protect itself. If the less responsible sections of the media[141] perceive that they can cause prejudice just short of that sufficient to create a demand for a stay, then they will do so, and in pushing at that boundary they may overstep it. In particular they may do so where, amidst a mass of sensationalist, partial reporting, it is very difficult to ascribe responsibility to individual newspapers.

Reform of s 2(2) under the HRA in reliance on *Worm v Austria*?

The s 2(2) test appears at first glance to be in harmony with the Convention standards as indicated in *Worm v Austria*,[142] *News Verlags*[143] and *BBC Scotland v UK*.[144] But

---

138 [1997] EMLR 76; *The Times*, 26 July 1996.
139 See Part II, pp 300–6.
140 See Chapter 2, pp 63–64.
141 Generally, the tabloids in the lower and middle sectors of the market.
142 (1998) 25 EHRR 454.
143 (2001) 31 EHRR 8.
144 (1997) 25 EHRR CD 179.

in requiring a substantial risk of serious prejudice, it could be said to set too high a threshold: publications merely creating a risk of serious prejudice will not be covered, although it is arguable that Art 6 demands that they should be. The discussion has sought to demonstrate that the strict liability rule, based on the protective approach, sets a high threshold, is unworkably imprecise and therefore ineffective in operation. As a result, in relation to high profile cases, it allows too much strain to be placed on the criminal justice system (and on individual defendants, witnesses and victims) which has to seek to combat the effects of prejudicial publicity by taking neutralising measures. It has been suggested that the adoption of such measures can create, in itself, unfairness in the system.[145] But at the same time, since the s 1 rule is capable of going beyond what is necessary to protect fair trials, freedom of expression can be unnecessarily curtailed. (And the very uncertainty of the rule can of course have a chilling effect.) This is especially apparent in relation to those decisions on proceedings, including civil actions, which are heard by a judge or judges, not by a jury or other layperson.

The inefficacy of s 2(2) considered here – in terms of protecting fair trials – could be addressed to an extent by adopting a change of interpretation under s 3(1) HRA. The s 2(2) test, on its face, differs from that accepted at Strasbourg as in harmony with the Convention standards indicated in *Worm v Austria*,[146] *News Verlags*[147] and *BBC Scotland v UK*.[148] In *Worm* Strasbourg set the limits of permissible comment at the point at which the material creates a likelihood of prejudice to the chances of a person receiving a fair trial.[149] This is, on its face, a test that is in one respect close to the old common law one in that it requires only that prejudice, as opposed to serious prejudice, should be caused. In this respect it is less strict than the terms used in s 2(2). However, the requirement of 'likelihood' appears to denote a stricter requirement in terms of risk than the term 'substantial' in s 2(2). 'Likely' appears to mean 'more likely than not',[150] whereas substantial may be taken to mean 'not insubstantial' or not negligible. According to Lord Diplock, the term is cognate to the terms 'more than minimal' or not remote. The domestic courts, following the interpretation adopted by Lord Diplock in *Attorney General v English*, have, as discussed above, paid lip-service to this interpretation of the term 'substantial'.

Post-HRA, the test for the degree of risk could have relied on the test of likelihood from *Worm* under s 2 HRA. That test would have sounded the death knell for Lord Diplock's interpretation. An (unacknowledged) departure from Lord Diplock's interpretation has indeed occurred, but the interpretation of s 2(2) adopted in *Attorney General v Guardian*,[151] although influenced by *Worm*, created a higher threshold for the test than is denoted by the likelihood test. It appears then that the minimising interpretation adopted in *Attorney General v English* does not represent the current

145   See Corker D and Levi M, 'Pre-trial publicity and its Treatment in the English Courts' [1996] Crim LR 622. See also pp 328–29, above.

146   (1998) 25 EHRR 454.

147   (2001) 31 EHRR 8.

148   (1998) 25 EHRR CD179.

149   *Worm v Austria* (1998) 25 EHRR 454, at para 5.

150   See *Cream Holdings v Bannerjee* [2005] 1 AC 253; [2004] 3 WLR 918 which in a different context found that the term 'likely to succeed' meant 'more likely than not'. See Chapter 9 pp 988–89.

151   [1999] EMLR 904.

test, although the courts have not acknowledged that this is the case. The term 'serious prejudice' has not been afforded a minimising interpretation. Thus it is clear that there is a difference of emphasis between the domestic and the Strasbourg tests – at least in relation to the need for serious prejudice, and probably in relation to the need for a substantial risk, on the basis that that term as currently interpreted domestically still denotes, on the face of it, a lower risk than the term 'likelihood' does. Confusion is created since the courts, as discussed, are not relying in practice on establishing only a low level of risk.

This problem could be addressed if the domestic courts decided to rely on the *Worm* test to minimise the term 'serious' and to clarify the meaning of the term 'substantial' with a view to creating greater certainty as to the threshold to be reached under s 2(2). The need to show serious prejudice may go too far in protecting speech at the expense of fair trials under Art 6, even taking account of the use of neutralising measures. At the same time the high threshold that apparently needs to be reached under the term 'substantial' following *Attorney General v Guardian* and *Attorney General v MGN* may also be overprotective of speech, although Lord Diplock's non-remote risks test was under-protective. It is suggested that the test of 'likelihood' from *Worm* should be used under ss 2 and 3 HRA and should be used to re-interpret the term 'substantial' in s 2(2) of the Act. So doing would only involve a minimal departure from Lord Diplock's test, since remote risks would still be excluded; it would merely mean that some non-remote risks were also excluded – which has been occurring in practice in any event since the late 1990s.

The result of this change would ultimately be that the strict liability rule could have more impact in curbing prejudicial comment and therefore on the fairness of trials since a greater deterrent effect could be created. It must be acknowledged that it could exacerbate the likelihood of interfering with freedom of expression unnecessarily since this is inevitable under the protective approach based on a test with a fairly low threshold. If the threshold was clarified in this way by interpretation under s 3 HRA, relying on s 2, the courts and Attorney General would then have leeway within the broader test to target only those publications which are genuinely likely to cause prejudice. For example, it would be possible and easier to target individual newspapers even where a number of papers had engaged in prejudicial reporting. Where, amid such reporting, one newspaper had given prominence to a single, highly telling, item of prejudicial information, it would clearly fall within s 2(2), even if it could be assumed that jurors would be told to disregard it. Instead of trying to disentangle the responsibility of individual newspapers from the collective impact of the reporting, the test should be: if one article by itself would have satisfied s 2(2), had there been no other prejudicial publications, liability should be established, taking all the circumstances into account, including the effect of generic and threshold reporting in raising the profile of the defendant and in focusing the public mind on the trial. It would be as legitimate to take account of the reporting as a whole in the manner suggested – considering generic reporting but not the cumulative effect of reporting – as it is to take account of the probability that neutralising measures such as directions from the judges, would minimise the impact of the reporting. All such factors are part of the context within which the potentially prejudicial reporting should be judged.

The article amounts to 'a discussion in good faith of public affairs or other matters of general public interest' and 'the risk of impediment or prejudice to particular legal proceedings is merely incidental to the discussion' (s 5)

Introduction

Section 5 reflects the guarantee under Art 10. It affords a high value to political speech, broadly defined, and therefore reflects the value placed upon such speech at Strasbourg. If it appears that s 2(2) is fulfilled, it must next be established that s 5 does not apply. Section 5 does not, therefore, operate as a defence. If it did, it would not follow the contours of the inquiry to be conducted under Art 10. Section 5 conveys the message to the media that they can create a substantial risk of serious prejudice to a trial without incurring liability so long as they can also satisfy s 5, and they do not have the burden of proof in so doing. The existence of s 5 therefore offers further confirmation that the 1981 Act is partly based on the protective model since it accepts that a substantial risk of serious prejudice to a trial can be created but that no liability may arise. Section 5 is founded on the assumption that the prejudice would have to be dealt with by the adoption of neutralising measures in relation to trials, and it is only by taking that possibility into account that s 5 can be viewed as compatible with Art 6, as *Ribemont* and *Worm* make clear.

Interpretation of s5

Attorney General v English[152] is the leading case on s 5 and is generally considered to provide a good example of the kind of case for which s 5 was framed. After the trial had begun of a consultant who was charged with the murder of a Down's syndrome baby, an article was published in the *Daily Mail* which made no direct reference to him, but was written in support of a pro-life candidate, Mrs Carr, who was standing in a by-election. Mrs Carr had no arms; the article referred to this fact and continued: 'today the chances of such a baby surviving are very small – someone would surely recommend letting her die of starvation. Are babies who are not up to scratch to be destroyed before or after birth?' The trial judge referred the article to the Attorney General, who brought contempt proceedings against the *Daily Mail*. First, it was determined that the article did fulfil the test under s 2(2) on the basis that jurors would be likely to take the comments to refer to the trial; therefore, the assertion that babies were often allowed to die if handicapped might influence them against the consultant, Dr Arthur.

The burden then fell on the prosecution to show that s 5 did not apply. Lord Diplock adopted a two-stage approach in determining this issue. First, could the article be called a 'discussion'? The Divisional Court had held that a discussion must mean the general airing of views and debating of principles. However, Lord Diplock considered that the term 'discussion' could not be confined merely to abstract debate, but could include consideration of examples drawn from real life. Applying this test, he found that a discussion could include accusations without which the article would have been

152 [1983] 1 AC 116; [1982] 2 All ER 903.

emasculated and would have lost its main point. Without the implied accusations, it would have become a contribution to a purely hypothetical issue. It was about Mrs Carr's election and also the general topic of mercy killing. The main point of her candidature was that killing of sub-standard babies did happen and should be stopped; if it had not asserted that babies were allowed to die, she would have been depicted as tilting at imaginary windmills. Thus, the term 'discussion' could include implied accusations.

Second, was the risk of prejudice to Dr Arthur's trial merely an incidental consequence of expounding the main theme of the article? Lord Diplock held that in answering this, the Divisional Court had applied the wrong test in considering whether the article could have been written without including the offending words. Instead, the Court should have looked at the actual words written. The main theme of the article was Mrs Carr's election policy; Dr Arthur was not mentioned. Therefore, this article was the antithesis of the one considered in *Attorney General v Times Newspapers*,[153] which was concerned entirely with the actions of Distillers. Clearly, Dr Arthur's trial could be prejudiced by the article, but that prejudice could properly be described as incidental to its main theme.

Thus, s 5 applied; the article did not, therefore, fall within the strict liability rule. This ruling was generally seen as giving a liberal interpretation to s 5.[154] Had the narrow interpretation of the Divisional Court prevailed, it would have meant that all debate in the media on the topic of mercy killing would have been prevented for almost a year – the time during which the proceedings in *Arthur's* case were active from charge to acquittal. (It may be noted that Dr Arthur was acquitted; therefore, the article presumably did not influence the jurors against him. That fact, however, as pointed out above, would not have precluded a finding that there was a substantial risk of serious prejudice to his trial.) Lord Diplock's test under s 5 may be summed up as follows: looking at the actual words written (as opposed to considering what could have been omitted), was the article written in good faith and concerned with a question of general legitimate public interest which created an incidental risk of prejudice to a particular case? It seems that the discussion can be triggered off by the case itself; it need not have arisen prior to it.

This ruling gave an emphasis to freedom of speech which tended to bring the strict liability rule into harmony with Art 10 as interpreted by the European Court of Human Rights' ruling in the *Sunday Times* case. However, despite this broad interpretation of s 5, the media obviously does not have *carte blanche* to discuss issues arising from or relating to any particular case during the 'active' period.

The *Attorney General v English* ruling did not concern a direct reference to a particular case and therefore it was uncertain until the ruling in *Attorney General v Times Newspapers*[155] whether s 5 would cover such references. The *Sunday Times* and four other newspapers commented on the background of an intruder into the Queen's bedroom, Michael Fagin, at a time when he was about to stand trial. The comments of *The Mail on Sunday* about Fagin, which included the allegation that he had had

---

153 [1974] AC 273; [1973] 3 All ER 54; [1973] 3 WLR 298, HL.
154 See, e.g., Robertson, G, *Media Law*, 1999, Chapter 6, p 216.
155 (1983) *The Times*, 12 February.

a homosexual liaison with the royal bodyguard and that he was a 'rootless penniless neurotic', satisfied the s 2(2) test as it was thought that they would affect the jury's assessment of his honesty. However, they fell within s 5 as they were part of a discussion of the Queen's safety, which was a matter of general public concern. In contrast, the *Sunday Times'* allegation that Fagin had stabbed his stepson could not fall within s 5, as it was irrelevant to the question of the Queen's safety, but had nevertheless been considered in detail.

It must also be shown that the article was written in good faith. In *Attorney General v Hislop* the articles in question did not fall within s 5 because it could not be said that they were published in good faith: the finding – relevant to the question of contempt at common law – that the editor had intended to prejudice the relevant proceedings – was held to be incompatible with a finding of good faith under s 5.

It can be concluded that the term 'a discussion in good faith of public affairs or other matters of general public interest' has received quite a broad interpretation in the courts. However, this is less clearly the case in relation to the question whether the risk is 'merely incidental' to the discussion. In this respect s 5 clearly requires some fine lines to be drawn. Where a piece merely discusses a particular case and makes no attempt to address wider issues, s 5 will not apply (*Daily Express* case).[156] *Attorney General v TVS Television, Attorney General v HW Southey and Sons*[157] concerned a TVS programme entitled 'The New Rachman' which made allegations about certain landlords in the South of England, alleging that they were obtaining money by deceiving the DHSS. The programme focused on landlords in Reading and coincided with the charging of a Reading landlord with conspiring to defraud the DHSS. It was found that the focus on Reading landlords meant that the article could not be viewed as creating a merely incidental risk of prejudice. In *Attorney General v Guardian Newspapers*[158] the article in question dealt with the tendency of judges in fraud trials to impose reporting restrictions, and stated that the judge in a criminal trial in Manchester had banned all reporting of the trial under s 4(2) of the 1981 Act on the ground that it could influence a separate trial involving one of the defendants. When the judge's attention was drawn to the article, he discharged the jury. It was readily found that the effect on the trial, if any, should be viewed as 'merely incidental' to the wider discussion[159] since the inclusion of examples was no more than 'an incidental consequence of expounding the main theme of the article.'[160]

Reform of s 5?

These findings indicate that there can be a difficulty in more borderline cases in drawing lines between the creation of risks in an incidental and a non-incidental fashion. Since s 5 was adopted as a response to *The Sunday Times* case, as a measure intended to protect media freedom, it might be expected to be capable of creating a clear demarcation between two types of prejudicial publications – those consisting of

156 (1981) *The Times*, 19 December.
157 *The Times*, 7 July 1989.
158 [1992] 3 All ER 38, CA.
159 It had already been found that s 2(2) was not satisfied.
160 [1992] 3 All ER 38, p 49.

inaccurate, misleading coverage of forthcoming proceedings and those that concern a general issue of public interest where the proceedings are used as an example – in a way that satisfies s 2(2). Section 5 does not fully succeed in creating such differentiation since, although reporting in the latter category would fall within s 5 as 'a discussion of public affairs,' following the ruling in *English*, it might fail the 'incidental' test, as occurred in *Attorney General v TVS Television, Attorney General v HW Southey and Sons*. A clearer test is needed.

One possibility would be to re-interpret s 5 in reliance on ss 3 and 2 HRA and Art 10. Section 5 was intended to afford scope to the speech/harm balancing proportionality test under Art 10(2), as a response to *Sunday Times v UK*. But it fails to do so, since it does not provide an effective means of weighing up the seriousness of the prejudice against the significance of the speech in question. In contrast to the previous common law position, it clearly does provide a means of affording value to political speech, broadly defined, and to that extent it reflects the value placed upon such speech at Strasbourg. However, it is not the equivalent of a proportionality test since it depends on problematic determinations as to the central focus of a publication, as opposed to its peripheral aspects. The courts are being asked to engage in literary as opposed to legal analysis. The 'incidental' test is not apt to encapsulate the notion of proportionality and it is hard to import that notion through interpretation of the term. It would, however, be possible to go some way in doing so, which could mean stretching the notion of 'incidental' under s 3(1) HRA where a publication would be viewed as of especial value at Strasbourg in terms of the justifications for free expression.[161] If, as discussed above, the threshold under s 2(2) was lowered in reliance on s 3(1), such a development would allow a counter-balancing value to be afforded to media freedom.

The problematic term 'incidental' can only be stretched so far, and if the courts were to seek to adopt a proportionality test within the terms of s 5, they would have to be prepared to depart from the literal meaning of the section and to read words into it.[162] A strong argument for so doing is that the Parliamentary intention behind the introduction of the 1981 Act was to bring English law into compliance with the Convention. If the judges were prepared to accept that Parliament had partially failed to achieve its aim, then even reading words into the statute to achieve such compliance could be seen, not as *defeating* Parliament's intention, but as perfecting it. The new interpretation, moreover, does not go against a pervasive feature of the statute.[163] At the same time the reform proposed is largely a matter of interpretation rather than of implying into

---

161 See above, pp 309–11.

162 This might be possible: see *R v A* [2001] 2 Cr App R 21; [2002] 1 AC 45; for discussion see Chapter 4, pp 175–83. Kavanagh's writings on s 3(1) have influenced this analysis. See in particular 'The elusive divide between interpretation and legislation under the HRA' (2004) 24(2) OJLS 259. A court could read in the words 'if the proportionality test under Article 10(2) is not satisfied, or' after the word 'if'.

163 Cf *R (on the application of Anderson) v Secretary of State for the Home Dept* [2003] 1 AC 837 in which the Secretary of State's role in sentencing was found to be incompatible with Art 6 since he could not be viewed as an independent and impartial tribunal. However, a declaration of incompatibility was made rather than seeking to use s 3(1) since the Secretary of State's role was such a fundamental feature of the statute as a whole – any other approach would have been against the grain of the statute.

the statute an entirely new provision that was absent from it.[164] Moreover, the area in question – protecting the judicial process – is one that is clearly within the judicial domain in terms of constitutional competence and role.[165] Parliament is not otherwise addressing this issue – there are no plans at present to reform the 1981 Act.[166] No issues of resource allocation arise; thus there are positive reasons for activism in this context and none for deference.

The Defence of 'ignorance' under s 3

A defendant charged with the s 1 offence can seek to use s 3 as a defence. Section 3 is a true defence, since the burden of proof lies on the defendant. The publisher or distributor will not be strictly liable if, having taken all reasonable care, he or she does not know and has no reason to suspect that the proceedings are active or that the publication contains the type of material likely to give rise to strict liability under s 2. It may be noted that since the common law (see below) does not depend on the use of the active test, liability could still arise outside the statute even where, within the statute, s 3 would have been applicable.

Conclusions: re-balancing the 1981 Act

It has been argued in this chapter that contempt law is failing as a means of protecting fair trials, but also that it is not sufficiently effective in protecting freedom of expression. A rarely enforced rule of a high but uncertain threshold such as that under s 2(2) inevitably tends to leave the ultimate responsibility for avoiding unfairness with trial judges. The current division of responsibility, almost inevitable under a largely protective model, between contempt law and trial judges, is deeply problematic. The current position may mean that freedom of expression is not fully protected since the media are uncertain at times whether or not a publication might infringe the imprecisely expressed rule under s.2(2). But at the same time the existence of the rule fails to provide protection for trials. Certain newspapers, especially the less responsible sections of the press, at times engage in reporting at the outer limits of what can be tolerated under s.2(2). They may do so in the knowledge that if a number of newspapers are involved, it may be hard to identify the responsibility of any particular one. Or they may merely take a risk, motivated by determination to maintain commercial advantage, on the basis that the uncertainty of the s.2(2) test (and of the common law test of real risk of prejudice), and the high threshold it appears to represent, make it difficult for a prosecution to succeed and quite probable, therefore, that it will not be undertaken.

---

164 As in the Court of Appeal in *re S and Re W (Care Orders)* – as discussed in Chapter 4, pp 176–77 – the decision was overturned: it was made clear by the House of Lords [2002] 2 AC 291 that the Court of Appeal had gone too far under s 3.

165 In terms of both expertise and constitutional role the context is similar to those in *R v A* [2002] 1 AC 45 and in *R v Offen* [2001] 1 WLR 253; but not that in *Bellinger* [2003] 2 All ER 513– where the court declined to read words into the statute in question under s 3 HRA. For discussion, see Chapter 4, pp 183–86.

166 Cf *Bellinger* ibid, where Parliament was about to address the situation at issue regarding the law relating to transsexuals.

The imprecision of the s 2(2) test is exacerbated precisely because the roles of contempt law and of the trial judge overlap. Judges in contempt cases must take account of the likelihood that neutralising measures will be or have been used. The use of such measures, including directions to the jury, make it hard to determine whether the risk in question at the time of publication still subsisted at the time of trial. Different judges take varying views as to the efficacy of such measures and the ability of the jury to disregard media comment. Thus contempt law is failing to delineate the boundary between the use of protective and of neutralising measures and therefore allowing too much pressure to be placed on the criminal justice system in high-profile cases. Possibly that boundary cannot be delineated effectively unless, as discussed below, a far more precise 'protective' test is adopted and preventive measures are used more extensively, accompanied by robust safeguards for media freedom. Most worryingly, parts of the media may rely, not merely on the uncertainty of s 2(2), but on some kind of complicity with the government in relation to their coverage, especially in terrorist cases. The uncertainty of s 2(2), and the high bar it appears to create in practice, clearly aid the Attorney General in justifying refusals to prosecute. As indicated above, such refusals probably do not in any event have to be justified in court.[167]

The reforms proposed could re-balance the statute by focussing it more closely on fair trial and free speech rights. Where prejudice has probably been caused and the speech in question consists of reportage with a misleading gloss,[168] s 5 could not be used, under the current interpretation of the section. But the speech might in any event escape liability since it would be probable that no prosecution would be brought for the reasons given above, founded partly on the unsatisfactory nature of s 2(2). The reform proposed under s 5 would not afford greater protection to such speech since its misleading quality would undermine its public interest value. Section 2(2), if interpreted more clearly, as discussed above, could provide an increased protection for fair trials; s 5 could only be viewed as providing a satisfactory countervailing protection for free speech if the courts were prepared to take this course. But the result might be – in something close to a reversal of the current situation – that near worthless and probably prejudicial speech would be caught by an enhanced s 2(2), while speech of the most value in Art 10 terms would be more likely to escape under the reformed s 5. Thus a re-balancing of the statute, based more firmly on both fair trial and free speech principles, could occur. This would accord more strongly with the speech/harm balancing test from *Sunday Times v UK*. Speech of value would be less likely to be caught but where there was a real possibility of harm to a trial, liability would be more likely to be established. This approach would echo the Strasbourg one as encapsulated in both *Sunday Times* and *Worm* more closely than is the case under the current position, but it would not replicate it. The problem would still remain that Art 10 values can overcome Art 6 ones under s 5 since the section allows speech to cause serious prejudice to a trial but escape liability due to its value. It is only possible to meet this argument by relying on the use of neutralising measures at trial, but for the reasons already discussed, this is not an entirely satisfactory position.

---

167 See above fn 103 and p 345.
168 E.g. the *Sun* headline 'Got the Bastards!' in relation to the arrests of terrorist suspects in July 2005 referred to earlier, fn 94, above.

3 Intentionally prejudicing proceedings: common law contempt

Introduction

As explained above, the common law of contempt pre-1981 created an offence of strict liability. A residual and narrow area of common law contempt was preserved under the 1981 Act, based on a *mens rea* requirement. Section 6(c) of the 1981 Act preserves liability for contempt at common law if intention to prejudice the administration of justice can be shown. 'Prejudice [to] the administration of justice' clearly includes (and may solely denote – see below) prejudice to particular proceedings. Once the requirement of intent is satisfied, it is easier to establish contempt at common law rather than under the Act since it is only necessary to show 'a real risk of prejudice' and proceedings need only be imminent, not 'active'. Clearly, liability can be established at common law in instances when it might also be established under the 1981 Act, as occurred in the *Hislop* case, and also in instances when the Act will not apply because proceedings are inactive. Possibly, it might also be established where one of the statutory tests other than the 'active' requirement was not satisfied. These preliminary observations are developed below, taking Convention standards into account under the HRA. Section 3 HRA does not apply (except to s 6(c) itself) since intentional contempt arises at common law, but the court has a duty to ensure that that the common law is compatible with the Convention under s 6. It will be suggested, in particular, that the common law requirements should be subjected to a strict scrutiny in so far as they represent the possibility of circumventing a measure adopted specifically to meet Art 10 standards. A publication will fall within the area of liability preserved by s 6(c) if three elements are present – a specific intention to prejudice the administration of justice in *imminent* proceedings, and the creation of a real risk of prejudice to those proceedings.

Intention to prejudice the administration of justice

The test for intention to prejudice the administration of justice was established in *Attorney General v Times Newspaper*[169] and *Attorney General v News Group Newspapers plc*.[170] It was made clear that 'intention' connotes specific intent and therefore cannot include recklessness. The test may be summed up as follows: did the defendant either wish to prejudice proceedings or ('oblique' intent) foresee that such prejudice was a virtually inevitable consequence of publishing the material in question? Thus, it is not necessary to show a desire to prejudice proceedings or that where there was such a desire, that it was the sole desire. This test is based on the meaning of intent arising from rulings on the *mens rea* for murder: *Hancock and Shankland*,[171] *Nedrick*[172] and *Woollin*.[173]

169 [1992] 7 AC 191; [1991] 2 All ER 398; for a report of the Divisional Court proceedings, see *Re Attorney General v Observer and Guardian Newspapers Ltd* (1989) *The Times*, 9 May; for comment, see [1989] PL 477. For comment on the *mens rea* issue, see Laws (1990) 43 CLP 99, pp 105–10.
170 [1989] QB 110; [1988] 3 WLR 163; [1988] 2 All ER 906.
171 [1986] AC 455; [1986] 1 All ER 641; [1986] 3 WLR 1014.
172 [1986] 3 All ER 1; [1986] 1 WLR 1025.
173 [1999] 1 AC 82.

This is a subjective test, but the Court of Appeal in *Attorney General v Newspaper Publishing plc* (the *Spycatcher* case)[174] appeared to be asking whether or not the consequences in question were 'foreseeable', suggesting not that the defendant should actually have foreseen them, but that an objective observer would have done so. This would, of course, be an easier test to satisfy, although since, in practice, it will be necessary to infer that the defendant foresaw the consequences, the difference between the two tests may be of only theoretical importance. This argument is put forward on the basis that in general, if an objective observer would have foreseen a risk of prejudice, it will be hard for an editor to show that he or she did not, because, unlike some defendants to whom this test is applied (in other areas of criminal law), an editor must make a decision as to publication unaffected by mental incompetence (it is assumed), emotion or the need to act in the heat of the moment. Nevertheless, a concept of 'objective intent' is insufficiently distinguishable from recklessness; as it is established that recklessness will not suffice for common law contempt, intention clearly refers to subjective intent.

A number of circumstances may allow the inference of intention to prejudice the proceedings to be drawn, although it is suggested that the relevance of the circumstances will depend on the form of intent – desire or oblique intent – which seems to be in question. In *Attorney General v News Group Newspapers plc*,[175] the newspaper's support for the prosecution in its columns and in funding a private prosecution allowed the inference to be made. A Dr B was questioned about an allegation of rape made against him by an eight-year-old girl, but eventually the county prosecuting solicitor decided that there was insufficient evidence to prosecute him. *The Sun* obtained the story and decided that it should offer the mother financial help in order to fund a private prosecution. It published various articles attacking Dr B: 'Rape Case Doc: Sun acts'; 'Beast must be named, says MP', etc. The Attorney General brought a prosecution against *The Sun* for contempt. The articles could not come within the strict liability rule because the proceedings in question – the private prosecution – were not active. The contempt alleged, therefore, arose at common law. It was found that intention could be established, either on the basis of a desire to prejudice the proceedings (presumably in order to vindicate the paper's stance) or because the editor must have foreseen that Dr B would almost certainly not receive a fair trial. The judgment would support either view, but probably favours the former: in his ruling, Watkins LJ said: '. . . they could only have printed articles of such a kind if they were campaigning for a conviction as they clearly were.' However, if he had the latter form of intent in mind, it may be said that although the newspaper had acted reprehensibly in using its power to attempt to influence a trial it had itself become involved in, it is arguable that intent should not have been so readily established. The fact that *The Sun* was personally involved was not, it is argued, relevant to oblique intent. The proceedings were clearly not going to occur for some time; therefore, although the defendants probably foresaw some risk of prejudice to them, it was not clear that such prejudice could be said to be a virtually inevitable consequence of publication. In fact, Dr B was acquitted; the jury were clearly able to put out of their minds any influence articles may have had.

174   [1988] Ch 333; [1987] 3 All ER 276; [1988] 3 WLR 942, CA.
175   [1989] QB 110; [1988] 3 WLR 163; [1988] 2 All ER 906.

The Sun case may be contrasted with *Attorney General v Sport Newspapers Ltd*[176] in which the test for intention was somewhat more strictly interpreted. One David Evans, who had previous convictions for rape, was suspected of abducting Anna Humphries. He was on the run when *The Sport* published his convictions; the proceedings were not therefore active, and so the case arose at common law. It did not appear that *The Sport* wished to prejudice proceedings. Was it foreseen as a virtual certainty that prejudice to Evans's trial would occur as a result of the publication? It was held that there was a risk of such prejudice of which the editor of *The Sport* was aware, but that such awareness of risk was not sufficient. Clearly, had the *mens rea* of common law contempt included recklessness, it would have been established. The requirement to prove intent was re-affirmed post-HRA in *Attorney General v Punch*, which is discussed below.

Imminence

At common law, the *sub judice* period began when proceedings could be said to be 'imminent' (*Savundranayagan*).[177] This test would of course be readily satisfied where proceedings were active. However, it may not always be necessary to establish imminence. In *Attorney General v News Group Newspapers plc*[178] it was held *obiter* that where it is established that the defendant intended to prejudice proceedings, it is not necessary to show that proceedings are imminent. In his judgment, Watkins LJ approved *obiter* of David Pannick's contention that 'no authority states that common law contempt cannot be committed where proceedings cannot be said to be imminent but where there is a specific intent to impede a fair trial, the occurrence of which is in contemplation'. It was found that even if the trial of Dr B was too far off to be said to be pending or imminent, the conduct of *The Sun* in publishing stories at the same time as assisting the mother in the private prosecution could still amount to contempt.

Bingham LJ concurred with this dilution of the imminence test in *Attorney General v Sport*,[179] although in the same case Hodgson J considered that proceedings must be 'pending'. He interpreted 'pending' as synonymous with 'active', an interpretation which would at one and the same time have curtailed the scope of common law contempt, but focused it more closely on the harm caused by deliberately creating prejudice to proceedings. This point, therefore, remains unresolved, leaving the media without a clear guide as to the period during which publication of matter relevant to proceedings will be risky. If proceedings need not even be imminent, it appears that reporting of matters which may give rise to proceedings at some point in the future could be curbed, assuming that the other tests were satisfied. The test of 'imminence' is itself too wide and uncertain, but would be preferable to the uncertainty on this point which was exacerbated by *Attorney General v Sport*. It is uncertain what the alternative test contemplated by Bingham LJ could be. There cannot be an intention to prejudice something which cannot even be identified as a possibility. Thus the test at its least stringent must be that proceedings can be identified as a possibility before this head of common law contempt can be in question. At the same time it would only

---

176 [1991] 1 WLR 1194.
177 [1968] 3 All ER 439; [1968] 1 WLR 1761, CA.
178 [1989] QB 110; [1988] 3 WLR 163; [1988] 2 All ER 906.
179 [1991] 1 WLR 1194.

be possible to rely on this diluted imminence test in relation to instances of simple rather than oblique intent. Desired consequences can never be viewed as too remote, assuming that they in fact arise, but it would be almost impossible to show that a virtually certain consequence of prejudice had been foreseen in instances of a very lengthy time lag between publication and proceedings. Obviously, even in relation to simple intent the *actus reus* of a real risk of prejudice still has to be established, which would also be very difficult in relation to a lengthy time lag, except possibly in exceptional instances, such as that in *Attorney General v News Group Newspapers* itself, where the newspaper is personally involved. This development in common law contempt is therefore of little practical significance. It may have some slight curtailing impact on media freedom, but at the same time it is unlikely to protect the fairness of proceedings. The more uncertain the test becomes, the more, it is argued, common law contempt is divorced from a focus on such fairness.

This test – that proceedings need merely be in contemplation or highly likely to occur – is also used in New Zealand.[180] If a suitable post-HRA case ever arises, it is possible that reinterpretation of this common law doctrine as an aspect of the courts' duty under s 6 HRA[181] might reintroduce certainty into the timing test. It is questionable whether the interference with freedom of expression represented by a prosecution for common law contempt could be said to be 'prescribed by law' due to the lack of precision and therefore of forseeability inherent in the current interpretations of the *sub judice* period. As Chapter 2 indicated, an interference must not only have a basis in law, that basis must be of sufficient quality.[182] Probably the most satisfactory method of ensuring that the requirements of quality are met would be to adopt the course suggested by Hodgson J in *Attorney General v Sport*. The 'active' test is laid down with reasonable precision and would, therefore, probably meet those requirements. It may be noted that, as Hodgson J pointed out, Scottish and Australian cases have held that imminent proceedings are not covered by contempt law.[183] At the least, reinterpretation might demand a return to the original requirement of imminence. Obviously, if the active test was adopted, this would confine common law contempt to instances in which the statute could also be used. It would still have a role since, where intention to prejudice was shown, a much higher fine could be imposed on the media body in question. Such a development would be, it is suggested, appropriate in the post-HRA era since it would prevent the common law, as interpreted in accordance with Art 10 under s 6, from circumventing a statute that had been adopted in order to meet a Strasbourg ruling.[184] If common law contempt could be viewed as prescribed by law, the timing test could nevertheless be narrowed down by reference to the Art 10(2) tests of necessity and proportionality. It could readily be argued that holding open the possibility of liability for such an indeterminate length of time was disproportionate to the legitimate aim pursued.

This development in common law contempt could theoretically be curtailing press freedom, since it clearly does nothing to help editors who wish to determine whether

---

180 *Television New Zealand Ltd v Solicitor-General* [1989] 1 NZLR 1, at 3.
181 See *Douglas v Hello!* [2001] QB 967.
182 See pp 68–69.
183 See *Hall v Assoc Newspapers Ltd* 1978 SLT 241; *Attorney General for NSW v TCN Channel Nine Pty Ltd* (1990) 20 NSWLR 368.
184 In the *Sunday Times* case (1979–80) 2 EHRR 245.

or not a publication might attract a criminal prosecution. In practice, unless a media body can be shown to have *desired* to prejudice proceedings through a publication, by creating bias in the minds of those involved such as jurors, it is almost impossible to show that such prejudice is a virtually certain consequence of publication if the proceedings are merely imminent but not active. *Virtual certainty* of such prejudice could normally only arise where publication occurred close to the action or during it. Therefore the 'imminence' test is only nominally of significance in most instances – it can be assumed that it may have become virtually otiose and that currently the strict liability rule will almost always be used rather than the common law in relation to the *Sun* type of case. The only reason for using the common law during the active period would be to seek a higher penalty where *mens rea* could be shown. But this could be done in any event if reforms to the 1981 Act abolished this form of common law contempt but allowed for higher penalties to be applied where the media body was shown to have *mens rea*. There would be an argument for including recklessness. Intentionally or recklessly creating a substantial risk of serious prejudice during the active period could become a new offence, creating an alternative to the strict liability rule, and attracting a higher sentence. The current common law rule has however a residual relevance in relation to other forms of creating prejudice to proceedings, as discussed below.

In practice, unless a media body can be shown to have *desired* to prejudice proceedings through a publication, by creating bias in the minds of those involved such as jurors, it is almost impossible to show that such prejudice is a virtually certain consequence of publication if the proceedings are merely imminent but not active. *Virtual certainty* of such prejudice could normally only arise where publication occurred close to the action or during it. Therefore the 'imminence' test is only nominally of significance in most instances – it can be assumed that it may have become virtually otiose and that currently the strict liability rule will almost always be used rather than the common law in relation to the *Sun* type of case. The only reason for using the common law during the active period would be to seek a higher penalty where *mens rea* could be shown. But this could be done in any event if reforms to the 1981 Act abolished this form of common law contempt but allowed for higher penalties to be applied where the media body was shown to have *mens rea*. There would be an argument for including recklessness. Intentionally or recklessly creating a substantial risk of serious prejudice during the active period could become a new offence, creating an alternative to the strict liability rule, and attracting a higher sentence. The current common law rule has however a residual relevance in relation to other forms of creating prejudice to proceedings, as discussed below.

A real risk of prejudice

Methods of fulfilling this test

It must be shown that the publication amounts to conduct which creates a real risk of prejudice to the administration of justice (*Thompson Newspapers*).[185] There are a number

185 [1968] 1 All ER 268; [1968] 1 WLR 1.

of different methods of fulfilling this test. In *Hislop and Pressdram*[186] it was found that the defendants, who were one party in an action for defamation, had interfered with the administration of justice because they had brought improper pressure to bear on the other party, Sonia Sutcliffe, by publishing material in *Private Eye* intended to deter her from pursuing the action. There was a substantial risk that the articles might have succeeded in their aim; had they done so, the course of justice in Mrs Sutcliffe's action would have been seriously prejudiced, since she would have been deterred from having her claim decided in a court. Counsel for *Private Eye* had argued that defamatory material which the defendant seeks to justify should not be restrained, because until it is clear that the alleged libel is untrue, it is not clear that any right has been infringed (*Bonnard v Perryman*).[187] This argument was rejected because the question of deterrence did not depend on the truth or falsity of the allegations. The possibility of justification was thus irrelevant. In this instance, it might also be noted that the relevant tests under the 1981 Act had been satisfied; therefore, it would seem that, *a fortiori*, common law contempt could be established, it having already been accepted that the articles had been published with the intention of putting pressure on Mrs Sutcliffe to discontinue the defamation action, thereby satisfying the *mens rea* requirement at common law. In *Attorney General v News Group Newspapers plc*[188] it was found that there was a risk of prejudice since jurors might have been influenced by the newspaper coverage which came close to imputing guilt to the defendant. This was however a doubtful finding due to the lapse of time between publication and trial. The almost dismissive treatment of the *actus reus* in that case came close to implying that the *Sun* was being punished for acting reprehensibly in seeking to prejudice the proceedings, rather than in relation to the risk it actually created.

The particular use of common law contempt in *Hislop* represents a clear and quite precisely defined area of liability targeted at a particular mischief. There is no division of responsibility between trial judge and contempt law: if contempt law did not fulfil this role, it could not be fulfilled at all, under the existing law. But the form of common law contempt based on creating bias in the minds of those involved in proceedings seems to be serving no useful purpose, since it overlaps with the use of the strict liability rule, and should be abolished. The imprecision and over-breadth of the tests for the *actus reus* sit uneasily with the demands of proportionality under Art 10. Since it is now hard to satisfy s 2(2) of the 1981 Act unless a publication occurs close to or during the trial, it is hard to imagine an instance in which it would be useful to invoke the test of imminence: if a publication was merely imminent as opposed to active it would not satisfy the 'real risk of prejudice' test under the more recent s 2(2) rulings on the creation of risk.[189]

A further very significant special form of common law contempt can arise if part of the media frustrates a court order (including orders made under s 4(2) of the 1981 Act)[190] against another part. Usually the order is made to restrain the publication of

---

186 1991] 1 QB 514; [1991] 1 All ER 911; [1991] 2 WLR 219, CA.
187 [1891] 2 Ch 269, p 289.
188 [1989] QB 110.
189 See pp 343–44, 350 above.
190 Section 4(1) provides that a fair and accurate report of proceedings held in public published contemporaneously in good faith will not be a contempt. Section 4(2) of the 1981 Act provides

confidential material.[191] The three tests applicable are the same as those discussed above: proceedings must (probably) be imminent; specific intent to prejudice proceedings must be shown, and a real risk of prejudice must arise. But the last test has had to be interpreted in a very particular fashion in order to allow this particular form of contempt to arise.

Frustrating an injunction against another media body

The *Spycatcher* doctrine

This highly significant extension of common law contempt arose from one strand of the *Spycatcher* litigation. In 1985, the Attorney General commenced proceedings in Australia in an attempt to restrain the publication of *Spycatcher* by Peter Wright. The book included allegations of illegal activity engaged in by MI5. In 1986, after the *Guardian* and the *Observer* had published reports of the forthcoming hearing which included some *Spycatcher* material, the Attorney General obtained temporary *ex parte* injunctions preventing them from further disclosure of such material on the ground of breach of confidence.[192] While the temporary injunctions were in force, the *Independent* and two other papers published material covered by them. It was determined in the Court of Appeal,[193] and confirmed in the House of Lords,[194] that such publication constituted the *actus reus* of common law contempt on the basis that publication of confidential material, the subject-matter of a pending action, damaging its confidentiality and thereby probably rendering the action pointless, created an interference with the administration of justice. Once the material had been published it was no longer confidential; therefore the subject-matter of the action for breach of confidence in which a permanent injunction was being sort had been destroyed. The case therefore affirmed the principle that once an interlocutory injunction has been obtained restraining one organ of the media from publication of allegedly confidential material, the rest of the media may be in contempt if they publish that material, even if their intention in so doing is to bring alleged iniquity to public attention. This case thus allowed the laws of confidence and contempt to operate together as a significant prior restraint on media freedom, and in so doing created an inroad into the general principle that a court order should only affect the party to which it is directed as only that party will have a chance to argue that the making of the order would be wrong.

The decision in *Attorney General v Newspaper Publishing plc and Others*[195] seemed to represent an attempt to narrow down the area of liability created by the decision in *Attorney General v Times Newspapers Ltd*. The case arose from the reporting of

---

that during any legal proceeding held in public, a judge may make an order postponing reporting of the proceedings if such action 'appears necessary for avoiding a substantial risk of prejudice to the administration of justice in those proceedings'. For discussion of s 4, see below 384–89.

191   See, for discussion of breach of confidence in the context of state secrecy, Chapter 7, pp 616–24.

192   For discussion of this branch of the litigation, see Chapter 7, pp 618–19.

193   *Attorney General v Newspaper Publishing plc*, *The Times*, 28 February 1990.

194   *Attorney General v Times Newspapers Ltd* [1992] 1 AC 191; [1991] 2 All ER 398; [1991] 2 WLR 994, HL: for comment see NLJ (1991) 141 (6516), 1115.

195   [1997] 3 All ER 159; *The Times*, 2 May 1997, CA.

the appeals in the *Ordtech* case,[196] a case which bore strong similarities to the *Matrix Churchill* case.[197] The appellants appealed against their convictions for exporting arms; public interest immunity certificates were issued,[198] but the Court of Appeal ordered that the material covered by them, which was crucial to the appeal, should be disclosed in summarised and edited form to the appellants and their legal advisers. The order restricted the use of the material to the appeal and requested its return on conclusion of the appeal. In Court, in directing return of the documents, the Lord Chief Justice indicated that breach of the order would result in the matter being referred to the Attorney General.

In its report of the proceedings, the *Independent* published a small amount of material from the documents which did not also appear in the written copy of the judgment. The Attorney General brought proceedings for contempt against the *Independent*, relying on the ruling in *Attorney General v Times Newspapers* to the effect that if a third party with the requisite intent acts in a way that frustrates the basis on which a court has determined that justice should be administered, then it will be guilty of contempt. On behalf of the *Independent* it was argued that the *Times* case represented an extension of the law as it had previously been understood and that the Court should be slow to extend the law any further since any such extension represented a further encroachment on freedom of expression and inhibited the media in its function of informing the public. The Court did not accept that any conduct by a third party inconsistent with a court order was sufficient to amount to the *actus reus* of contempt: it was found necessary to show that a significant and adverse effect on the administration of justice in the relevant proceedings had occurred. The Court of Appeal used the wording of Art 10 of the Convention in finding that restraints on freedom of expression should be no wider than necessary in a democratic society, and considered that conduct which is inconsistent with a court order in a trivial way should not create the risk of a conviction for contempt. The application of the Attorney General was therefore dismissed.

The principle laid down in the *Times* case was again reconsidered in the HRA era by the House of Lords in *Attorney General v Punch*.[199] The case arose from the publication by *Punch* magazine of an article by David Shayler. Shayler had served as an officer with MI5 and when he left MI5 he took with him copies of confidential documents containing sensitive information relating to intelligence activities of MI5. According to the Attorney General, Mr Shayler then disclosed some of this material to a newspaper publisher, Associated Newspapers Ltd. Articles written by Mr Shayler, or based on information provided by him, were published in *The Mail on Sunday* and the *Evening Standard* in August 1997. The Attorney General then intervened and brought civil proceedings against Mr Shayler and Associated Newspapers. Hooper J granted an interlocutory injunction against Mr Shayler based on breach of confidence.[200] A similar order was made against Associated Newspapers. By this order, expressed to

---

196　See *Blackledge and Others* (1996) 1 Cr App R 326, CA.

197　See *The Report of the Inquiry into the Export of Defence Equipment and Dual Use Goods to Iraq and Related Prosecutions*, 1995–96, HC 115. See further [1996] PL 357–527; PL [1997] pp 211–14.

198　Certificates rendering the material covered immune from scrutiny.

199　[2003] 1 AC 1046; [2003] 2 WLR 49; [2003] 1 All ER 289. For discussion of the case, see Smith, ATH 'Third Parties and the Reach of Injunctions' [2003] 62(2) CLJ 241.

200　On 4 September 1997.

continue until the trial of the action, Mr Shayler was restrained from disclosing to any newspaper or anyone else,

> . . . any information obtained by him in the course of or by virtue of his employment in and position as a member of the Security Service (whether presented as fact or fiction) which relates to or which may be construed as relating to the Security Service or its membership or activities or to security or intelligence activities generally.

Two provisos were attached to the order. First, the order did not apply to any information in respect of which the Attorney General stated in writing that the information was not information the publication of which the Crown was seeking to restrain. Second, the order did not preclude repetition of the information disclosed in *The Mail on Sunday* on 24 August 1997. Neither Mr Shayler nor Associated Newspapers objected to the making of these orders.

Mr Shayler then began writing for *Punch* magazine; the editor, Mr Steen, was aware of the terms of the interlocutory non-disclosure orders made against Mr Shayler. The article which became the subject of the contempt proceedings dealt with the Bishopsgate bomb in 1993 and the death of WPC Yvonne Fletcher outside the Libyan Embassy in 1984. At first instance, in the contempt proceedings, Silber J concluded[201] that the *actus reus* of common law contempt had been established on the basis that the defendants had published the article in breach of the terms of the injunctions, with the result that the purpose of the Court in making those injunctions was subverted and, in consequence, there had been some significant and adverse effect on the administration of justice. The judge held that the purpose of the Court in granting the injunctions was not to protect national security, but to ensure that until trial there should be no disclosure of information obtained by Mr Shayler in his employment, so that the confidentiality of the information could be kept intact until the trial of the permanent injunctions.[202] The judge also found that the necessary *mens rea* had been established since Mr Steen knew that publication of the article was a breach of the injunctions, and he intended to act in breach of them. Therefore it was found that he intended by the publication to impede or prejudice the administration of justice by thwarting or undermining the intended effect of the injunctions.[203]

The Court of Appeal, by a three to two majority, overturned this decision.[204] Lord Phillips MR characterised the Court's purpose in granting the injunctions differently. He found that the correct approach was to proceed on the basis that Hooper J's purpose in granting the injunctions was 'to prevent the disclosure of any matter that arguably risked harming the national interest'.[205] He noted the Attorney General's case that the effect of the injunctions was that 'no newspaper could knowingly publish any matter that fell within the wide terms of the Associated Newspapers' injunction without first obtaining clearance from himself or from the court'. Lord Phillips objected to this

---

201 *Attorney General v Punch*, 6 October 2000 (unreported), QB, at para 62.
202 Ibid, at para 52.
203 Ibid, at para 78.
204 [2001] QB 1028; [2001] 2 All ER 655.
205 Ibid, at para 100.

contention on the basis that it would subject the press to the censorship of the Attorney General. He found that it would result in an imposition of a restriction on freedom of the press that would be disproportionate to any public interest and thus in breach of Art 10 of the European Convention. He further considered that such a proposition could not be reconciled with the duty imposed on the Court by s 12(3) HRA.[206] Section 12(3) has established a higher threshold for granting injunctions against the media but it is not applicable in criminal proceedings. Lord Phillips's point appeared to be that if an injunction could be granted which then affected another media body through the threat of criminal proceedings, that would not appear to accord with the spirit of the section. However, he found that the article in question included three items of previously unpublished material which *did* risk harming the national interest and therefore defeated the purpose of the injunction. The *actus reus* of common law contempt was therefore established. Lord Phillips went on, however, to hold that in order to satisfy the test for *mens rea* it had to be shown that Mr Steen knew that publication would interfere with the course of justice by defeating the purpose underlying the injunctions. It was found that the Attorney General had failed to establish this; Mr Steen had contended that he thought that the purpose of the court order was to restrain publication of material dangerous to national security and that he had no intention of publishing any such information.

This decision of the Court of Appeal sought to focus closely on the values and interests at stake, and refused to allow an uncertain threat to the administration of justice to overcome freedom of expression. Although the Convention was not relied on extensively, and there was virtually no recitation of the relevant jurisprudence, the Court showed itself determined to adopt a stance which relied on close examination of the necessity of the interference in question, eventually concluding that a pressing social need to allow such an interference with freedom of political expression was not present. The Court was not impressed by the claim that it was necessary to preserve this area of liability in order to prevent impediments to the administration of justice. Thus, the Court sought to identify another interest – in this instance national security – which could genuinely support the grave interference with freedom of expression represented by the *Spycatcher* doctrine, and found that the alleged harm was not serious enough to justify such a grave interference with media freedom. In some rare instances it might be possible to show that the journalist or other person in question, due to his or her background and/or specialist knowledge, did recognise that publication of the material in question would be likely to damage national security. It may be noted that the Official Secrets Act 1989, s 5 presupposes that it will sometimes be possible to show that a person in the position of a journalist recognised that possibility.[207]

Nevertheless, this decision would have narrowed down and virtually destroyed the *Spycatcher* area of liability, since if the purpose of interim orders was accepted to be to prevent disclosure of any matter that arguably risked harming the national interest, then proof of *mens rea* for contempt would involve proving to the criminal standard that third parties, including editors and journalists, knew that materials published arguably risked harming that interest. This would probably have proved to be a difficult, if not

---

206 For the provision of s 12(3) and discussion, see Chapter 9, pp 985–90.
207 See Chapter 7, pp 602–4 for discussion of s 5.

impossible, task for the Crown in most instances. Editors would have been able to insist that they had no reason to believe that even arguable damage to national security might result from such publication. Since the *mens rea* required is specific intent, it would not be possible merely to show that a reasonable person in the defendant's position would have known that such a risk arose – a possible means of satisfying the test required under the Official Secrets Act 1989 s 5. Thus, the result would have been that the grant of such injunctions in most circumstances could not have lead to the imposition of criminal liability against third parties such as Mr Steen.

However, the House of Lords overturned the decision of the Court of Appeal. Lord Nicholls, in a speech with which the other Law Lords agreed, found that the underlying purpose of the Attorney General, as the plaintiff in the proceedings against Mr Shayler, in seeking the order against Mr Steen, was irrelevant. He said:

> The reason why the court grants interim protection is to protect the plaintiff's asserted right. But the manner in which this protection is afforded depends upon the terms of the interlocutory injunction. The purpose the court seeks to achieve by granting the interlocutory injunction is that, pending a decision by the court on the claims in the proceedings, the restrained acts shall not be done. Third parties are in contempt of court if they wilfully interfere with the administration of justice by thwarting the achievement of this purpose in those proceedings. This is so, even if in the particular case, the injunction is drawn in seemingly over-wide terms.[208]

In that instance, he found, the remedy of the third party whose conduct is affected by the order is to apply to the court for the order to be varied. He also pointed out that the act in question would only be contemptuous if the act done has some 'significant and adverse effect on the administration of justice in the proceedings'. Lord Hope characterised the purpose of the interim injunction in similar terms: '[i]ts purpose is to ensure that the other party to the dispute does not assume the responsibility of deciding for himself whether the material is of such a nature that the Attorney General is entitled in law to protection against its publication.'[209]

In the instant case the Lords found that the purpose of the judge in making the order was to preserve the confidentiality of the information specified in the order pending the trial so as to enable the court at trial to adjudicate effectively on the disputed issues of confidentiality arising in the action. It was to ensure that the court's decision on the claims in the proceedings should not be pre-empted by disclosure of any of the information specified in the order before the trial. The *actus reus* of contempt was satisfied by the thwarting of this purpose by destruction of the confidentiality of the material, through its publication in *Punch*, which it was the purpose of the injunction to preserve. Mr Steen had accepted that the publication of the offending magazine article had constituted the *actus reus* of contempt. Bearing in mind the purpose of the injunctions as already established, Lord Nicholls went on to find that the *mens rea* of common law contempt was also satisfied and so concluded that contempt of court was established. He said:

---

208 [2003] 1 AC 1046; [2003] 2 WLR 49; [2003] 1 All ER 289, at paras 43 and 44.
209 Ibid, at 114.

> The facts speak for themselves. Mr Steen . . . knew that the action against Mr Shayler raised confidentiality issues relating wholly or primarily to national security. He must, inevitably, have appreciated that by publishing the article he was doing precisely what the order was intended to prevent, namely, pre-empting the court's decision on these confidentiality. That is knowing interference with the administration of justice.[210]

Clearly, the finding of contempt represented an interference with freedom of expression as guaranteed by Art 10. However, Lord Nicholl's consideration of the impact of the HRA was brief and superficial. He noted, before coming to the argument as to the purpose of the injunction, that national security, one of the list of exceptions in Art 10(2), can justify a restraint on freedom of expression. He then went on to find, '[t]he rule of law requires that the decision on where this balance lies in any case should be made by the court as an independent and impartial tribunal established by law' and in the meantime the court must be able to prevent the information being disclosed. He went on to find that therefore:

> . . . the law must be able to prescribe appropriate penalties where a person deliberately sets the injunction at nought. Without sanctions an injunction would be a paper tiger. Sanctions are necessary to maintain the rule of law; in the language of the Convention, to maintain the authority of the judiciary.

This analysis did not address the questions of necessity and proportionality; it implied that once a court had decided that material should be kept confidential before the trial of a permanent injunction and had imposed an interim injunction with that object in mind, it would *always* be justifiable to restrict freedom of expression by way of common law contempt in order to provide a sanction against publication of the material by third parties where publication would have a significant and adverse effect on the administration of justice in that trial. But the need to show such an effect does not necessarily satisfy the requirements of proportionality since the adverse effect would always be caused by publication of material covered by the injunction which was not already, or not to a significant extent, in the public domain. Further, in such circumstances the *mens rea* requirement would virtually always be satisfied since journalists would normally be aware that the material was covered by an injunction against another body or person.

Lord Hope gave brief consideration to the question of proportionality, but without citing any Strasbourg jurisprudence, although he came to the same conclusion as Lord Nicholl. He found that there can be no objection to an interim injunction against the publication of information on the ground of proportionality if three requirements are satisfied. He considered that the general principles from which the requirements are to be derived are well established and are indicated in three leading cases: *R (Daly) v Secretary of State for the Home Department*,[211] *R (Pretty) v Director of Public*

---

210 Ibid, at paras 51 and 52.
211 [2001] 2 AC 532, at p 547A–B, *per* Lord Steyn.

Prosecutions,[212] *R v Shayler*.[213] He found that in the context in question the requirements are: first, that there is a genuine dispute as to whether the information is confidential because its publication might be a threat to national security; second that there are reasonable grounds for thinking that publication of the information before trial would impede or interfere with the administration of justice and third, that the interference with the right of free speech is no greater than is necessary. Lord Hope concentrated on the third requirement and found that the requirements of proportionality were satisfied since the opening words of the interim injunction were qualified by the proviso allowing newspapers to apply to the Attorney General to publish innocuous material; the extent of the injunction remained subject to the further order of the court and that court itself would have to observe the principle of proportionality when it dealt with any application before the trial for the relaxation of the scope of the injunction.[214] He insisted that in each instance the analysis of proportionality should be fact-sensitive.

However, objection can be made to his findings on the basis that all interim injunctions would satisfy the second and third of these requirements and the first is open to the objection that it places a power of censorship in the hands, not only of a member of the executive but also in those of one party to the original and forthcoming actions, creating an appearance of bias. The Attorney General is the very person (or office) whose rights are being upheld by the threat of the invocation of the contempt of court jurisdiction. To determine whether liability under that jurisdiction can be justified as an interference with freedom of expression, partly by reference to his powers to allow publication, does not appear to provide an adequate safeguard for the media. This was far from the hard look at the proportionality that one would expect of a court which took its duty under s 6(1) HRA seriously.

Critique of *Punch*

The requirements of both the *actus reus* and *mens rea* of common law contempt, as interpreted by the House of Lords in *Punch*, do little to temper the rigour of this doctrine. In particular, the demands of proportionality do not appear to be satisfied when it is borne in mind that if the party to whom the interim injunction was originally addressed published material covered by it, it would only be subject to civil sanctions, whereas third parties such as *Punch* who published such material would be criminally liable. It is clearly anomalous that this should be the case. In the instant case the Attorney General had fair warning that *Punch* was likely to publish Shayler material and could have sought a separate injunction, backed up by civil sanctions, against it.[215]

The requirements of proportionality could have been satisfied by accepting the test put forward by the Court of Appeal. That test clearly did depart from the test for common law contempt established in the *Spycatcher* case since it focused on the underlying as

---

212 [2001] 3 WLR 1598, at 1637A–B.
213 [2002] 2 WLR 754, at 783F–H, 786A–B.
214 *Attorney General v Punch* [2003] 1 AC 1046, at paras 114–120.
215 It is in fact arguable that if the first party violated an injunction as indicated, it could be punished under the law of criminal contempt in the sense that it had interfered with the administration of justice in the proceedings against itself, but since the civil sanction is available, this sanction is not used in such circumstances. *Attorney General v Punch* [2003] 1 AC 1046, at paras 114–20.

opposed to the expressed purpose of the injunctions. But it is the duty of the courts under s 6 HRA to develop the common law by reference to the Convention rights,[216] taking account of the jurisprudence (s 2 HRA). In this instance the scrutiny afforded to the proportionality review would be expected to be particularly intense since the expression to be suppressed was political expression.

The alternative is to expect the media to apply to the Attorney General to have injunctions varied, something that – it appears – they will only be able to do if the original order makes provision for such applications,[217] and an avenue that the Court of Appeal saw in any event as amounting almost to executive vetting and censorship. Where the original order made no such provision there would appear to be a strong case for asking the court in contempt proceedings to take account of the over-breadth of the original order.

In so far as the *Spycatcher* doctrine is of value in preserving national security, whether that is viewed as an indirect or direct effect of its application, such liability would also provide protection against disclosures that might harm national security, and of course liability could also arise under s 5 of the Official Secrets Act 1989.[218] The Attorney General could merely seek injunctions against each media body separately on grounds of breach of confidence if it seemed likely that it would publish the material in question. Thus the continuance of this form of liability overlaps in most instances with other possible remedies or sanctions.

The net result of the House of Lords' ruling in *Punch* is that the *Spycatcher* contempt principle has been re-affirmed, unchanged, in the HRA era. The cursory treatment of the HRA is perhaps the most interesting aspect of the ruling. It had little impact on the reasoning and none on the outcome. The immense implications of the *Spycatcher* contempt principle for media freedom went largely unrecognised in the Lords' findings. Those findings mean that the whole of the media can continue to be threatened with a criminal sanction for an indefinite period of time – a period that could well exceed one year – as a result of civil proceedings for an interim injunction within which media third parties are not represented. The contrast with other leading cases on journalistic speech, such as *Reynolds*,[219] is particularly striking in this regard: in that case the central point was to mark out discussion of important public affairs in the media as deserving of special protection under the common law and the European Convention because of its vital role in maintaining a democratic society.

The value of the speech in question was hardly touched upon in the rulings. The rich Strasbourg jurisprudence on political speech was not referred to: the Lords managed to decide the case without mentioning one Strasbourg precedent. A clear preference for referring to UK precedents decided post-HRA, such as *R v Shayler*,[220] was evinced.

---

216 The position is more complex where both parties are private; for discussion, see Chapter 4, pp 249–56.

217 Arguably, a third party could invoke s 7(1)(a) HRA as a route to seek variation of the original order. A third party could also seek permission to publish some of the material covered by the injunction (see *Attorney General v Observer Ltd, Re An Application by Derbyshire CC* [1988] 1 All ER 385), but of course this would be likely to be denied since such publication would amount to the *actus reus* of common law contempt unless a minimal amount of confidential material was included.

218 For discussion of s 5, see Chapter 7, pp 602–4.

219 [1999] 4 All ER 609.

220 [2003] 1 AC 247; see further Chapter 7, pp 606–12.

Free speech jurisprudence on the matter from other jurisdictions played no part in the decision. The approach of their Lordships in general was so narrow and blind to the free speech values at stake, that the judgment as a whole cannot but leave an advocate of such values with a sense of strong unease. Despite the inception of the HRA, their reasoning proceeded largely on the basis of an orthodox approach to an analysis of the common law with a brief nod in the direction of Art 10.

This is essentially not only a minimalist but a defensive approach to the HRA. Under this approach a case is decided by reference to established common law principle. The outcome is then checked briefly against HRA standards in order to ensure that incompatibility with the relevant Convention right is not clearly manifest. If a reasonable person could come to the conclusion that compatibility has been achieved, that appears to be sufficient. This approach compares strikingly with that taken in *Simms*[221] and *Reynolds*,[222] decided prior to the inception of the HRA. In those decisions, freedom of expression, both as a common law 'constitutional right' and as embodied in Art 10 of the Convention, was 'the starting point' of legal reasoning.[223] *Reynolds* included extensive citation and consideration of relevant Convention jurisprudence.[224] The values underpinning freedom of expression in general, and those particularly engaged by the instant case were identified; in *Simms* the demands of freedom of expression were treated as the touchstone by which the legality of subordinate legislation was to be assessed, and were found to demand a reading of it which ran clearly counter to its literal meaning. The explicit treatment of the free speech dimension in *Punch* was one which sought its marginalisation. Lord Hope made token references to it, although there was no consideration of Strasbourg jurisprudence, despite the fact that a number of relevant cases were cited to their Lordships in argument – again, a sharp contrast with the approach of the House of Lords in the leading pre-HRA free speech cases.

Lord Nicholls appeared to be uninterested in the Convention and the HRA: the latter was mentioned only once in a lengthy speech of 63 paragraphs. He claimed that his view of the law was not inconsistent with Art 10 since paragraph 2 provides exceptions to the right, but he made little attempt to apply the Art 10(2) tests; he stated that third parties 'must' respect the rule of law – i.e. the effect of an interim injunction against another party – but, as pointed out above, he did not subject this contention to a Convention-based analysis, by establishing a pressing social need to enforce such respect and by considering the demands of proportionality. Lord Hoffmann similarly showed a marked unwillingness to engage with the HRA and the Art 10(2) tests, merely remarking that 'national security is a well-established exception to the freedom conferred by Article 10.' However, the pertinent exception in question was that relating to 'maintaining the authority of the judiciary' if, as their Lordships were contending, the purpose of the injunction was to preserve the right of the Attorney General to have an effective hearing of the final injunction rather than to safeguard national security. So the wrong exception

---

221   [1999] 3 All ER 400.
222   [1999] 4 All ER 609.
223   See *Ex p Simms* [1999] 3 All ER 400, at 407, *per* Lord Steyn and at 412, *per* Lord Hoffmann (referring to 'fundamental rights' generally); *Reynolds* [1999] 4 All ER 609, at 629, *per* Lord Steyn.
224   (1999) 4 All ER 609, at 621–22, *per* Lord Nicholls, at 628 and esp. 635, *per* Lord Steyn, at 643, *per* Lord Cooke.

was identified and in any event, the well-established status of the exception is beside the point: since it is expressly mentioned in Art 10(2) it is clearly 'well-established'; the question was whether in the circumstances it was necessary to achieve the end of maintaining the authority of the judiciary by continuing the *Spycatcher* doctrine and, in the instant case, by imposing liability for contempt on Mr Steen.

This superficial approach to Art 10 was applied also to the HRA itself. Lord Hoffmann's approach echoed that of all the other Law Lords, in ignoring the question of the *content* of the courts' duty under s 6 HRA when developing the common law. Section 12 was also ignored by Lords Nicholls and Hoffmann and this was all the more remarkable since Lord Hoffmann did embark on some consideration of the effect of *American Cyanamid*, a decision which has been superseded by s 12(3) HRA.[225] Although this was a case with the gravest of implications for media freedom, consideration of the meaning and effect of s 12(4)[226] played no part in the majority of the speeches. Lord Hope merely repeated the words of the statute in noting that s 12(4) demands that particular regard should be had to freedom of expression. He did not consider whether this adds anything to the duty the court is already under due to s 6 to apply Art 10. He was content to find that s 12(4) and Art 10 had been satisfied since 'the restriction on the publication of the information before trial can be justified as being in the public interest in a democratic society'. He gave some consideration to proportionality, as discussed above, but none to necessity or to the particular 'public interest' involved. It is now reasonably clear that s 12(4) is being treated judicially either as a means of drawing other Convention rights into consideration in private law cases or – as far as the demand to have particular regard to Art 10 in its opening words are concerned – as an unnecessary and superfluous reminder of the effect of Art 10.[227] Since s 6 covers both effects in any event, the latter stance is probably the correct one. In other words, in essence s 12(4) is being found – in effect –to add nothing to the demands of Art 10 and s 6 combined. However, at the time of deciding *Punch* one would have expected their Lordships to consider the question whether s 12(4) could have had any significant impact in the instant case. Having marginalised s 12(4), they proceeded in effect to do the same with Art 10. Whatever s 12(4) means, this stance appears to represent the converse of the intention behind it.

Their Lordships were content with the idea that while the right of freedom of expression and the public's right to know are of great importance, their exercise can be subject – in effect – to the dictat of the Attorney General. Freedom of expression under Art 10 is subject to exceptions to be narrowly construed. It must be questioned whether the scope of the exception re-affirmed in this case can be viewed as narrow. In terms of the acceptance or non-recognition of the anomalies created and the likelihood that in may instances, once an interim injunction is obtained, the material in question will lose its newsworthiness, their Lordships showed no awareness of the practical

---

225 See *Douglas v Hello!* [2001] QB 967. It is now clear after the House of Lords decision in *Cream Holdings v Bannerjee* [2005] 1 AC 253; [2004] 3 WLR 918 that s 12(3) raised the bar for awarding an injunction – the test is that the injunction is more likely than not to be awarded at final trial; for further discussion, see Chapter 9, pp 988–90.

226 Section 12(4) provides that the court must have 'particular regard' to the importance of Art 10. For full citation of the sub-section and further discussion, see Chapter 9, pp 953–58.

227 See Chapter 9, pp 957–58.

realities of media freedom. Not only does this approach display a characteristically exaggerated attachment to the value of the right to bring litigation, it also exemplifies the tendency of English judicial reasoning to assume a narrow and technical basis, abstracted from any meaningful context.

Abolition of the *Spycatcher* doctrine?

The effect on third parties of the *Spycatcher* doctrine flows from findings in hearings for interim relief in which the burden on the Attorney General is not weighty, as discussed in Chapter 7.[228] Bearing in mind the relative ease with which such relief may be granted – despite the effect of s 12(3) HRA[229] – it must be questioned whether this is a satisfactory basis for the consequential far-reaching impact on the media. One unsatisfactory consequence of the continuance of this doctrine has already been pointed out – that third parties who publish information covered by an interim injunction can be subject to a harsher penalty than would be available if the first party published the same information. A further anomaly arises: the litigant who has obtained the interim injunction is thereby placed, in effect, in a more advantageous position than he or she will be in if the final injunction is obtained, since the *Spycatcher* doctrine has been found to cease to have effect once that injunction is granted.[230] In a sense, the litigant who has obtained the interim injunction obtains a very significant benefit, not enjoyed by the litigant who wins the final action, since the whole of the media will be deterred from publication of the confidential material during the period between the interim and the final injunction. In other words, the litigant is worse off after establishing his substantive right to confidentiality at trial. Clearly, in instances in which no final injunction is obtained since the other party – usually a newspaper – does not continue to contest the interim injunction because the information in question loses its newsworthy quality, a greater anomaly is created because the period of time during which the *Spycatcher* doctrine is applicable is likely to be longer. The applicability of that doctrine in relation to interim but not final injunctions follows logically from the emphasis on preserving the litigant's right to the final hearing of the action. However, if the emphasis was instead on the underlying purpose of the injunction, as the Court of Appeal in *Punch* advocated, it would still be possible in a narrow range of circumstances that a third party could attract liability for criminal contempt by undermining the final order in the sense of negating its purpose in protecting national security by publishing material covered by it. This would be less anomalous than the current position.

This form of common law contempt remains of very doubtful compatibility with Art 10, bearing in mind the emphasis placed upon the role of the media in *Goodwin v UK*[231] by the European Court of Human Rights. Although trivial or technical breaches of court orders made against other parties will not attract liability, the area of liability which remains creates a curb on media freedom which is out of accord with the crucial

---

228 See pp 618–23.
229 As mentioned above, fn 225, s 12(3), as interpreted in *Cream Holdings and Bannerjee* [2005] 1 AC 253, has raised the bar for the grant of injunctions.
230 *Jockey Club v Buffham* [2003] 2 WLR 178; [2003] EMLR 5.
231 *Goodwin v UK* (1996) 22 EHRR 123.

role of the press in a free society.[232] It is unlikely after *Attorney General v Punch* that reform can be expected in the domestic courts and therefore it can now only come from Strasbourg or Parliament. If a Strasbourg ruling eventually leads to abolition of this form of common law contempt, certain instances of the *Spycatcher* type could still fall within the statutory strict liability rule, if – which would rarely occur – the hearing of the permanent injunction had been set down at the time of publication. In such instances, however, s 5 would apply; therefore liability might be avoided, depending on a difficult application of the 'incidental' test where the information had public interest value.

For obvious reasons the political will to introduce reform to abolish this head of common law contempt is likely to be absent. From the government perspective the doctrine remains valuable as a means of creating secrecy that is in executive hands in terms of instigation – since in the *Punch* and *Spycatcher* category of case the initial temporary injunction will be sought by the Attorney General. Having obtained it on the basis of a test satisfied with relative ease, he need do nothing more to ensure that all the rest of the media are silenced on the matter at hand since criminal contempt at common law, after *Punch*, will do the job for him. If reform of this area of contempt eventually occurs as a result of a Strasbourg ruling, it will represent an indictment of the stance of a number of the senior judiciary in relation to a fundamental freedom in a democratic society. *Attorney General v Punch* is one of the most disappointing rulings there has been so far under the HRA: it represents a judicial acquiescence to the executive's predilection for secrecy, coupled with a determination to cling to anti-speech values reflected in common law doctrine even where they fly in the face of Convention principles.

The relationship between the 1981 Act and the common law

Common law contempt represents not only an alternative, but also, where proceedings are active, an additional possibility of establishing liability. It presents such an alternative in all instances in which proceedings are not active, assuming, of course, that the *mens rea* requirement can be satisfied, and it has proved to be of great significance in this context owing to the readiness with which it has sometimes been accepted that the common law tests have been fulfilled. The doctrine has therefore attracted criticism as circumventing the 1981 Act[233] but it may also, even more controversially, present an alternative in instances where proceedings are active, but liability under the Act cannot be established. If, as suggested above, the 'active' test replaces that of imminence in respect of common law contempt under the HRA, this would be the only significant role of common law contempt. It would open up the possibility that the Act and, in particular, the provisions of s 5, could be undermined. This is of particular significance given that s 5 was adopted to take account of the ruling in the European Court of Human Rights that UK contempt law had breached the Art 10 guarantee of freedom of speech.

232 These issues are discussed further in Chapter 7, pp 618–23, in relation to the breach of confidence issue, the other strand of the *Spycatcher* litigation.
233 Miller has written: 'I think it is at best messy and may also be dangerous to allow the common law to outflank the Act' ([1992] Crim LR 112).

Common law contempt was established in the *Hislop* case in an instance in which proceedings were active and, therefore, the relationship between the concept of good faith under s 5 and the question of intention under s 6(c) came under consideration. It appeared that a finding of intention to prejudice the administration of justice necessary to found liability for contempt at common law would probably preclude a finding of good faith under s 5. This finding seemed to obviate the possibility of proceeding at common law in appropriate instances in order to avoid the operation of s 5 – a course which would have undermined the policy of the Act as providing some safeguards for media freedom. However, the point is open to argument. It could be said that in the majority of cases, a finding of good faith under s 5 would indeed preclude a finding of intention to prejudice proceedings, but in one instance it might not. It might be shown that where a newspaper recognised a strong risk that proceedings would be prejudiced, but did not desire such prejudice (as may have been the case in *Attorney General v Newspaper Publishing plc*), a finding of good faith might not be precluded. A publisher might argue that his or her recognition of the risk to proceedings was outweighed (in his or her own mind) by the need to bring iniquity or other matters of public interest to public attention. The good faith requirement under s 5 might cover such a situation, thereby preventing liability under statute, although it might still arise at common law. Thus, for example, the principle arising from *Attorney General v Newspaper Publishing plc* might apply where proceedings were active and where publication of material covered by an injunction fell within s 5. In this sense, therefore, common law contempt may have the ability to undermine the statutory protection for freedom of speech,[234] unless requirements similar to those under s 5 can be implied into the common law in reliance on Art 10, a matter which is discussed further below.

The possibility envisaged is unlikely to arise. However, there are other circumstances in which a prosecution at common law could succeed in an instance in which proceedings are active but prosecution under the Act fails. For example, s 5 might be irrelevant because it might be clear that the article does not concern a discussion in good faith of public affairs. However, s 2(2) might not be satisfied on the basis that, although some risk of prejudice arose, it could not be termed serious enough. In such an instance, there appears to be no reason why the common law could not be used instead on the basis that the test of showing 'a real risk of prejudice' is less difficult to satisfy. If so, it would be possible to circumvent the more stringent s 2(2) requirement. Of course, it would be necessary to prove an intention to prejudice the administration of justice. Bearing in mind the fact that the 1981 Act was introduced in order to satisfy Art 10, it is suggested that its circumvention under the common law should be resisted.

Conclusions

This overview of this form of contempt, taking account also of the strict liability rule from the 1981 Act, gives rise, it is argued, to the conclusion that at present it is out of accord with Convention values and requirements in terms of both law and practice. Although, as discussed above, its jurisprudence in this context is open to criticism,

---

234 For comment on these developments in common law contempt, see Stone, 'Common law contempt' (1988) 138 NLJ 136; Halpin, A, 'Child's play in the Lords' (1991) 141 NLJ 173; McHale, J, 'Common law contempt' (1991) 141 NLJ 1115.

certain thematic strands can be discerned. As *Worm*, *Ribemont*,[235] *News Verlags*[236] and *Sunday Times* indicate, Strasbourg seeks to protect fair trials where they appear to be genuinely threatened by media coverage. Where the threat is nebulous and the value of the speech in question is high, restraints on the media are not found to be justified. A comparison between the *Taylor*[237] and the *Spycatcher* or *Punch* cases[238] suggests that both statute and common law are insufficiently focused on the core Convention values at stake. In *Taylor*, the individual's right to a fair trial under Art 6 was genuinely threatened; at the same time, the speech in question was of virtually no value in Art 10 terms, since it was misleading. Yet no prosecution was forthcoming. In contrast, *Spycatcher* and *Punch* concerned political speech to which Strasbourg accords the highest value, while in both instances the Art 6 guarantee was only doubtfully engaged. A successful prosecution for contempt in *Taylor* on the basis that the trial in question had been severely affected by relentless and misleading publicity could almost certainly have justified under Art 10(2) as proportionate in terms of speech/harm balancing to the aim pursued – that of protecting the Art 6 rights of the defendants. The reverse is true, it is contended, of both *Spycatcher* and *Punch*.

A possible explanation for current practice in these and other similar instances is that where speech is directly critical of a part of the executive and therefore, impliedly, of government itself, the interests of the government in stifling it are most obviously engaged. Such an instance arose in both *Spycatcher* and *Punch*, arguably providing an example of the failure of Attorney Generals to ensure that an appearance of distance from the government was maintained. In contrast, as in *Taylor*, when the trial of an obscure personage, accused of a highly-publicised crime, is in question, there is little or no political advantage to be gained in seeking to prevent or punish interferences with it. But there may be quite severe political disadvantage in appearing to attack the massed ranks of the tabloids. As indicated above, it is not entirely possible to dismiss misgivings as to the ability of Attorney Generals to distance themselves fully from their political colleagues, who are likely to have such considerations in mind.

The problems created by the willingness of newspaper proprietors to damage the fairness of trials in pursuit of competitive advantage are likely to continue so long as they view contempt actions as improbable. Certain trials such as those of the Taylor sisters, of Harold Shipman in 2000, the trial in 2001 of the suspect charged with the murder of the television presenter Jill Dando, the arrest of the terrorist suspects in connection with the Ricin incident in 2003, the trial of Ian Huntley for the Soham murders in 2003 and the arrest of terrorist suspects in July 2005 tend to attract a misleading and sensationalist media coverage, which has, in the case of a number of newspapers, little connection with free speech values but is motivated merely by profit-making concerns. Obviously, horrifying incidents, especially terrorist ones, will be reported in extensive detail using untempered language, but the aim of some of the coverage appears to be to come closest to expressing the baser instincts of readers, however prejudicial to a fair trial such expression might be. Assuming that in the very competitive media market, one newspaper is unlikely to forego the chance of attracting

235 (1995) 20 EHRR 557.
236 (2001) 31 EHRR 8.
237 [1993] 98 Cr App R 361. See pp 345–46 above.
238 See above p 369 and pp 373–76.

readers by its coverage of such cases, further intervention by Parliament appears to be essential if the criminal justice system and certain deeply unpopular defendants are not to bear the burden created by the demands of the media market.

The protective approach, as recognised under the 1981 Act and the common law, is not achieving its objective. At the same time, a shift towards the neutralising model has occurred in a piecemeal and incoherent fashion. The most extreme method of remedying the effects of prejudicial press coverage – acquittal – is used with some readiness despite its effect upon the administration of justice, while certain lesser measures, such as the use of a *voir dire* in order to determine jury knowledge of the case from the media,[239] or the delay of the trial, are shunned or rarely used. As argued above, such measures place burdens on the criminal justice system, while having, in many instances, no genuinely beneficial consequences in terms of freedom of speech. The question whether the use of such measures as a safeguard is warranted where contempt law is ineffective should be addressed as part of a general review of this area of law. In the meantime, it is suggested that judicial reliance on the Convention and especially on its underlying principles under the HRA could address certain of the deficiencies indicated above.

4 Prior restraints restricting reports of court proceedings

The general principle that justice should be openly administered is well established.[240] This principle is recognised in the Art 6 requirement that everyone is entitled to a 'fair and *public* hearing'. This Art 6 requirement is subject to a number of exceptions contained in para 1: 'the press and public may be excluded from all or part of the trial in the interests of morals, public order or national security in a democratic society, where the interests of juveniles or the protection of the private life of the parties so require or to the extent strictly necessary in the opinion of the court in special circumstances where publicity would prejudice the interests of justice'. In this respect, Arts 10 and 6 are not in conflict, since Art 10 may be said to require impliedly that restrictions on allowing journalists to attend hearings should be strictly scrutinised. Conflict is more likely to arise between the interest in open justice and the Art 8 guarantee of a right to respect for privacy. This issue is considered in Chapter 9.[241]

In general, in accordance with the open justice principle, courts are open to the public and therefore a fair and accurate factual report of the proceedings, in good faith, will not amount to a contempt. This is provided for under s 4(1) of the 1981 Act. The reverse is true of private sittings, a report of which will usually prima facie amount to a contempt. Section 4(1), therefore, creates an exception from strict liability in respect of proceedings held in public, so long as the other elements mentioned are present. Another way of putting this is to say that fair and accurate reports of proceedings would be unlikely to fall within s 2(2) in any event: s 4(1) merely makes this explicit, in statutory

---

239 In *Andrews (Tracey)* [1999] Crim LR 156, the Court of Appeal re-stated its view that juries should not be questioned regarding their knowledge of the case they are to judge upon.

240 See the comments to this effect and on the need to limit use of private hearings in *Preston* [1993] 4 All ER 638; 143 NLJ 1601.

241 See pp 851–66.

form. However, a number of exceptions to the principle of openness have been created to allow the withholding of information, either temporarily or indefinitely. For example, at common law, a judge can order prohibition of a publication in order to prevent, for example, the disclosure of the identity of a witness. The leading authority is *Attorney General v Leveller Magazine Ltd*[242] in which it was accepted that departure from the principle of openness would be warranted if necessary for the due administration of justice, and that therefore if a court made an order designed to protect the administration of justice, then it would be incumbent on those who knew of it not to do anything which might frustrate its object. All these exceptions must be considered for their compatibility with Art 10, since all clearly represent interferences with freedom of expression. In relation to reporting restrictions, as opposed to restrictions on those who may attend the hearing, a conflict between Arts 10 and 6 may arise where the restrictions are aimed at avoiding prejudice to the trial.

Postponing reporting of information to avoid a risk of prejudice

Section 4 provides:

(1) Subject to this section a person is not guilty of contempt of court under the strict liability rule in respect of a fair and accurate report of legal proceedings held in public, published contemporaneously and in good faith.

(2) In any such proceedings the court may, where it appears to be necessary for avoiding a substantial risk of prejudice to the administration of justice in those proceedings, or in any other proceedings pending or imminent, order that the publication of any report of the proceedings, or any part of the proceedings be postponed for such period as the court thinks necessary for that purpose.

(3) For the purposes of subsection (1) of this section . . . a report of proceedings shall be treated as published contemporaneously (a) in the case of a report of which publication is postponed pursuant to an order subsection (2) of this section, if published as soon as practicable after that order expires.

Thus s 4(1) contains an exception to the strict liability rule under s 1 of the Act. It may be noted that s 2(2) speaks of the creation of '*serious* prejudice', whereas s 4(2) speaks only of 'prejudice'. So in this respect s 4(2) creates a lower threshold than s 2(2). The effect of s 4(1) is that, even where the contemporaneous publication of a fair and accurate report of court proceedings creates a substantial risk that the course of justice will be seriously impeded or prejudiced (under s 2(2)), the publisher is not to be guilty of contempt of court under the strict liability rule. Clearly, it is highly unlikely in most circumstances that such fair and accurate reporting could cause prejudice. However, this exception is intended to reassure newspaper editors in relation to trial-related reporting.

The freedom of the media to report proceedings is itself then limited, however, by the provision of s 4(2). Section 4(2) provides a discretion to be exercised during any legal proceeding held in public, allowing a judge to make an order postponing reporting of those proceedings, if such action 'appears necessary for avoiding a substantial risk

---

242 [1979] AC 440; [1979] 2 WLR 247, HL.

of prejudice' to the proceedings or any other imminent proceedings, thus creating an exception to s 4(1).[243] In other words, despite the fairness and accuracy of such reporting – and its importance in relation to the open justice principle – there are special circumstances that mean that it should nevertheless be curbed. Section 4(2) is limited in one respect – it only covers reports *of* the proceedings, not reports of extraneous matters *relating to* the proceedings that could create the risk in question. They can be dealt with by way of subsequent sanctions, as discussed above. It is also important to note that reports of the proceedings can be postponed, not because they might affect the proceedings in question, but because *other* proceedings could be affected. Those other proceedings need only be 'imminent', not 'active',[244] and it is clear that the term 'imminent' denotes a longer and more imprecise period of time. Thus the period during which reporting is postponed can be very lengthy.

Lord Taylor CJ found in *R v Central Criminal Court ex parte Telegraph plc*[245] that s 4(2) contains two requirements for the making of an order. The first is that publication would create 'a substantial risk of prejudice to the administration of justice' and the second is that postponement of publication 'appears to be necessary for avoiding' that risk. He continued:

> It has been said that there is a third requirement, derived from the word "may" at the beginning of the sub-section, namely, that a court, in the exercise of its discretion, having regard to the competing public interests of ensuring a fair trial and of open justice, considers it appropriate to make an order.

In fact whether the element of discretion is to be regarded as part of the 'necessity' test or as a third requirement, the courts as a matter of practice have tended to merge the requirement of necessity and the exercise of discretion.[246] As regards the second element, it is important to note that the risk in question can concern 'any other proceedings pending or imminent'. This appears to mean that reports that would not satisfy the strict liability rule – since the other proceedings are merely imminent, not *active* – could nevertheless be the subject of a s 4(2) order. The term 'imminent' has been found to cover the possibility that those other proceedings might never in fact arise.[247] Orders under s 4(2) might typically involve the reporting of matters which the defence wished to argue should be ruled inadmissible.

Section 4(3) is not free from ambiguity, but appears to allow an order to be made relating to reports which would have been published – but for the s 4(2) order – some time after the proceedings in question had concluded.[248] A right of appeal against such orders in relation to trials on indictment was created by s 159 of the Criminal Justice

---

243 For comment on s 4 of the 1981 Act, see Walker, C, Cram, I and Brogarth, D, 'The Reporting of Crown Court Proceedings and the Contempt of Court Act 1981' (1992) 55 MLR 647.

244 See above, at pp 365–67.

245 [1993] 1 WLR 980, p 984 D–G.

246 See *BBC, Petitioners* [2002] SLT 2.

247 See *R v Horsham Justices ex parte Farquharson and West Sussex County Times* [1982] QB 762, p 797 E. In *Galbraith v HM Advocate* [2001] SLT 465, p 468 J–K opinion was reserved on this matter.

248 See *Attorney General v Guardian Newspapers* [2001] EWCA Crim 1351 (see below pp 388–89).

Act 1988 (CJA) in order to take account of a challenge under Art 10 at Strasbourg.[249] The position of the media when a s 4(2) order is made in respect of reporting a summary trial is less clear. However, it was established in *R v Clerkenwell Metropolitan Stipendiary Magistrate, ex parte The Telegraph*[250] that in such circumstances, the media have a right to be heard and must be allowed to put forward the case for discharging the order. When the applicants, publishers of national newspapers, became aware of the existence of the order, they were granted a hearing before the magistrate at which they submitted that the court had power to hear representations from them as to why the order should be discharged. The magistrate held that the court had no power to hear from anyone but the parties to the proceedings. The applicants sought a declaration that the court did have the power to hear their representations, and it was determined, relying on *R v Horsham Justices ex parte Farquharson*,[251] that they had sufficient standing to apply for judicial review. It was found to be implicit in s 4(2) that a court contemplating use of the section should be able to hear representations from those who would be affected if an order was made. In determining whether the order should be maintained, it was found to be necessary to balance the interest in the need for a fair trial before an unprejudiced jury on the one hand and the requirements of open justice on the other. In performing this balancing exercise, the magistrate would need to hear representations from the press as being best qualified to represent the public interest in publicity.

A Practice Direction relating to the use of s 4(2) orders was issued by Lord Lane CJ on 6 December 1982:[252]

> . . . a court may, where it appears necessary for avoiding a substantial risk of prejudice to the administration of justice in the proceedings before it or in any others pending or imminent, order that publication of any report of the proceedings or part thereof be postponed for such period as the court thinks necessary for that purpose. It is necessary to keep a permanent record of such orders for later reference. For this purpose all orders made under section 4(2) must be formulated in precise terms having regard to the decision of *Horsham Justices, ex parte Farquharson* . . . and orders under both sections must be committed to writing either by the judge personally or the clerk of the court under the judge's directions. An order must state (a) its precise scope, (b) the time at which it shall cease to have effect, if appropriate, and (c) the specific purpose of making the order. Courts will normally give notice to the press in some form that an order has been made . . . and court staff should be prepared to answer an inquiry about a specific case, but it is, and will remain, the responsibility of those reporting cases, and their editors, to ensure that no breach of any order occurs and the onus rests with them to make inquiry in any case of doubt.

The ruling of the Court of Appeal in *Horsham Magistrates ex parte Farquharson* was to the effect that such orders should be made sparingly; judges should be careful not to

249 *Hodgson, Woolf Productions and NUJ and Channel Four Television* (1987) 10 EHRR 503.
250 [1993] 2 All ER 183; *The Times*, 22 October 1992.
251 [1982] 2 All ER 269, [1982] QB 762, (1982) 76 Cr App R 87, CA.
252 [1982] 76 Cr App R 78.

impose a ban on flimsy grounds where the connection between the matters in question and prejudice to the administration of justice was purely speculative. If other means of protecting the jury from possibly prejudicial reports of the trial were available, they should be used. Moreover, it must be ensured that the ban covers only the matters in question. This ruling was reinforced by the decision in *Central Independent Television plc.*[253] During a criminal trial, the jury had to stay overnight in a hotel and in order that they could watch television or listen to the radio, the judge made an order under s 4(2) postponing reporting of the proceedings for that night. The applicants, broadcasters, appealed against the order under s 159 CJA on the basis that there was no ground on which the judge could have concluded that there was a substantial risk of prejudice to the administration of justice. Further, they argued that the judge had incorrectly exercised his discretion under the sub-section and failed to take proper account of the public interest in freedom of expression and in the open administration of justice. The Court of Appeal found that it had not been necessary to make the order as there was little, if any, evidence of a risk to the administration of justice: the previous reporting of the case had not suggested that reporting on the day in question would be anything other than fair and accurate. Even had there been a substantial risk, it might have been possible to adopt alternative methods of insulating the jury from the media. Where such alternative methods were available, they should be used. Accordingly, the appeal was allowed.

The emphasis in this judgment on the need to restrict reporting only where clearly necessary is in accordance with Art 10 requirements: the convenience of the jury is not a sufficient reason for invoking the sub-section, since it would not fall within one of the legitimate aims of Art 10(2). Similarly, in *Ex parte The Telegraph plc*,[254] the Court of Appeal found that even where a substantial risk to proceedings might arise, this need not mean that an order must automatically be made. The court based this finding on the need to consider the two elements of s 4(2) separately; first, a substantial risk of prejudice to the administration of justice should be identified flowing from publication of matters relating to the trial, and, secondly, it should be asked whether it was necessary to make an order in order to avoid the risk. In making a determination as to the second limb, a judge should consider whether, in the light of the competing interest in open justice, the order should be made at all, and if so, with all or any of the restrictions sought. In the case in question, the order should not have been made, since the risk of prejudice was outweighed by the interest in open justice. In *MGN Pension Trustees Ltd v Bank of America National Trust and Saving Association*,[255] the Serious Fraud Office applied for an order postponing reporting of civil actions brought by trustees of the pension fund until after the criminal proceedings were concluded. Six newspapers opposed the application. The judge followed the steps indicated in *Ex parte The Telegraph* in determining that no order would be made.

These decisions suggests a concern on the part of the judiciary to prevent a ready use of s 4(2) orders, which would be prejudicial to the principle of open justice.[256]

---

253 [1991] 1 All ER 347.
254 [1993] 2 All ER 971.
255 [1995] EMLR 99.
256 See also *Saunders* (the Guinness trials) [1990] Crim LR 597; *Barlow Clowes Gilt Managers v Clowes*, *The Times*, 2 February 1990; *R v Sherwood ex p The Telegraph Group plc*, *The Times*, 12 June 2001.

Incidentally, it is of some interest to note that this decision followed closely on that in *Attorney General v Guardian Newspapers (No 3)*[257] which concerned an article written while a ban on reporting of a major fraud trial was in force, criticising the alleged propensity of judges in such trials to impose bans. It was held that the article created too remote a risk to constitute a contempt under the strict liability rule (see below), and Brooke J took the opportunity of re-emphasising the importance of the news media as the 'eyes and ears' of the general public. This approach was developed in *R v Beck ex parte Daily Telegraph*.[258] Beck, who had been a social worker in charge of children's homes, was charged with offences involving sexual abuse, and owing to the number of charges, the trial was split into three. At the first trial, a s 4(2) order was made, owing to the risk of prejudice to the subsequent two trials. On appeal, the Court of Appeal accepted that there was a substantial risk of prejudice, but went on to find that the public interest in the reporting of the trial outweighed the risk. In so finding, the Court emphasised the concern which the public must feel because of the particular facts of the case and the right of the public to be informed and to be able to ask questions about the opportunities created for those in public service to commit such offences.

The decisions discussed indicate that pre-HRA the domestic courts were already taking into account the demands of Arts 10 and 6 by reference to the principles underlying those two Articles. The stance taken towards the role of journalists closely parallels that taken at Strasbourg, as indicated in Chapter 3.[259] A further Practice Direction, which also appears to be intended to ensure that the use of s 4(2) is Convention-compliant, was issued in 2002:

From 'Practice Direction (Criminal: consolidated)':[260]

3 *Restrictions on reporting proceedings*
. . .
3.2. When considering whether to make such an order [under s 4(2) or s 11] there is nothing which precludes the court from hearing a representative of the press. Indeed it is likely that the court will wish to do so . . . . [The Order continues in the same terms as the previous order.]'

The important point is that this Direction indicates that media representatives should be heard before the order is made, thus allowing them to challenge it in general and also to raise Art 10 points. However, even where the Practice Directions are followed, courts in making s 4(2) orders are under a duty due to s 6 HRA to ensure that the tests of necessity and proportionality under Art 10 are satisfied. This duty was not explicitly adverted to in the post-HRA decision in *Attorney General v Guardian Newspapers*[261] in which the reach of s 4(2) was widened and the tension between s 4(2) and s 2(2)

---

257   [1992] 3 All ER 38.
258   [1993] 2 All ER 177.
259   See pp 125–26.
260   [2002] 3 All ER 904, at pp 906–7.
261   [2001] EWCA Crim 1351.

was exacerbated. The order in question in the case had been made in the criminal trial[262] of four Premiership footballers. During the trial the judge had given a direction that there was no evidence of a racial motive in the case. The jury retired to consider their verdicts and were eventually sent home for the weekend, still undecided.[263] That Sunday the *Sunday Mirror* published an interview with the father of the victim which in a double-page spread, with photographs, revived the allegations of racism.[264] The judge decided in consequence to discharge the jury. The *Sunday Mirror* article and the halting of the trial attracted a great deal of media publicity in a number of newspapers. The judge ordered that a retrial should take place and provisionally fixed the date for the retrial.

The judge had agreed to make an order under s 4(2) of the 1981 Act imposing stringent reporting restrictions. They covered any reference to material from the offending article and to racist motives in the case.[265] This order under s 4(2) was designed to obviate the possibility of prejudice to the future retrial. This order was the subject of the appeal by a number of newspapers under s 159 CJA. The main ground for the appeal was that the terms of the order were not limited to the publication of a report of the proceedings, or part of the proceedings, and therefore the order was made without jurisdiction. Without referring to the HRA, the Court of Appeal found that since the order concerned an article that had led to the halting of the trial: '[a]ny similar reporting or republication of [the *Sunday Mirror*] article or its contents, or discussion of the judge's reasons, after 10th April . . . would albeit indirectly, be a "report of part of the proceedings."' The order was able to cover reports intended to be published some time after the trial had been halted since it was found that such reporting could be treated as 'contemporaneous' due to the provision of s 4(3). It might have been expected, taking Art 10 into account, that a more media-friendly reading of s 4(3) – affording a more limited meaning to the term 'contemporaneous' – would have been adopted under s 3(1)HRA. However, this judgment exhibits the tendency, noted in other chapters of this book, to disregard the HRA even where a Convention article is clearly relevant.

262   The order in question in the case had been made in the trial of four Premiership footballers, Woodgate, Bowyer, Clifford and Caverney, for offences of affray and causing grievous bodily harm with intent to Sarfraz Najeib. The case had of course attracted a considerable amount of publicity. See, for further discussion of the trial and the effect of the *Sunday Mirror* reporting, p 351, above.
263   On 4 April 2001.
264   It also included comments commending the evidence of a co-accused (who had by that time been acquitted) in suggesting that some of the remaining defendants, in relation to whom the jury were still considering their verdicts, were guilty.
265   The order was in the following terms:

> 1 There should be no further publication or broadcast of any matter contained within the headlines or the body of the article which appeared on pages 8 and 9 of the *Sunday Mirror* on 8 April 2001. 2 There should be no further reference in any publication or broadcast to the said article or headline, save for reference to the fact that this jury was discharged as a result of an article in the *Sunday Mirror*. 3 No publication or broadcast should make reference to racism or racist motivation in relation to the above proceedings. 4 For the avoidance of doubt, the above Order does not preclude publication or broadcast of any material relating to, or comment upon, the Macpherson Report, or issues of racism generally, provided that no reference in such publications or broadcasts is made to these proceedings.

Prohibiting reporting of information

Section 11 of the 1981 Act allows a court which has power to do so to make an order prohibiting publication of names or other matters if this appears necessary 'for the purpose for which it was so withheld'. Thus, s 11 does not itself confer such a power and therefore refers to other statutes[266] and to the imprecise common law powers. The leading authority is the House of Lords' decision in *Attorney General v Leveller Magazine Ltd*.[267] The majority found that if, in the course of regulating its own proceedings, a court makes an order designed to protect the due administration of justice, it is then incumbent on those who know of the ruling to do nothing which would frustrate the object of the ruling. At present, there are signs that a robust interpretation will be given to s 11 similar to that being taken to s 4(2): the fundamental importance of open justice will be outweighed only by a very clear detriment which answers to a general public interest flowing from publication of the matters in question – economic damage to the interests of the defendant will not suffice.[268] Nor will a concern to protect the 'comfort and feelings of the defendant'.[269] The courts may be prepared to make anonymity orders to protect the privacy of those involved in proceedings,[270] but only where the failure to afford anonymity would, under strict scrutiny, render the attainment of justice very doubtful.[271] Witnesses are placed in a somewhat different position. There is a clear public interest in encouraging witnesses to come forward and to co-operate in proceedings. Therefore, courts have shown a greater willingness to ensure the anonymity of witnesses.[272] If a court takes measures to protect the anonymity of witnesses such as sitting *in camera* or allowing the use of screens, there may be no need to make an express s 11 order.

Section 12(1) Administration of Justice Act 1960 adheres to the open justice principle in indicating that in general the reporting of private proceedings will not amount to a contempt in itself, before going on to specify the exceptional circumstances in which it will do so. It could therefore be said that in a sense the legal scheme relating to the first aspect of the open justice principle – that court hearings should be public – is more restrictive than that relating to the third – open reporting. Clearly, in practical terms, reporting of private hearings is often likely to be problematic, although those involved or witnesses may disclose matters to journalists, and so doing will not amount to a contempt so long as none of the exceptions under the 1960 Act apply.[273] Thus the mere fact that a hearing occurs in private does not automatically mean that reporting of the proceedings is restricted. Under s 12(1) of the 1960 Act it will only be a contempt

---

266 A number of statutory provisions impose restrictions such as allowing certain persons concerned in a case to remain anonymous.

267 [1979] AC 440; [1979] 2 WLR 247, HL. For comment on s 11 of the 1981 Act, see Walker, C, Cram, I and Brogarth, D, 'The Reporting of Crown Court Proceedings and the Contempt of Court Act 1981' (1992) 55 MLR 647.

268 *R v Dover JJ ex p Dover DC and Wells* (1991) 156 JP 433; [1992] Crim LR 371.

269 *R v Evesham JJ ex p McDonagh* [1988] 1 QB 553, p 562.

270 See *H v Ministry of Defence* [1991] 2 QB 103 and *Criminal Injuries Compensation Board ex p A* [1992] COD 379.

271 *R v Westminster CC ex p Castelli and Tristan-Garcia* (1995) *The Times*, 14 August.

272 See *R v Watford Magistrates' Court ex p Lenman* [1993] Crim LR 388; *Taylor* [1994] TLR 484.

273 *Clibbery v Allan* [2001] FLR 819.

to report on proceedings held in private where they relate to: wardship, adoption, guardianship, custody upbringing of or access to an infant; where they are brought under Part VII Mental Health Act 1983 or under any provision of the 1983 Act authorising an application or reference to be made to a mental health review tribunal or county court; where the court sits in private for reasons of national security; where the information relates to a secret process or invention at issue in the proceedings; where the court, acting within its powers, expressly prohibits the publication of all information relating to the proceedings or of information of the description which is published.

A report of information relating to all such proceedings is prima facie a contempt; it is not *automatically* a contempt since the section preserves all defences a person accused of contempt would normally have. Thus a conviction was not obtained where a newspaper editor published material relating to wardship proceedings without being aware of the connection.[274] It has been found that the press cannot report any aspect of wardship proceedings,[275] but this is not an absolute restriction: it has been found to cover 'statements of evidence, reports, accounts of interviews' and similar information.[276] The restrictions on reporting relating to children are largely intended to protect privacy, although the open justice principle may also be relevant.

The restrictions on the use of s 11 appear to render it compatible with Art 10. In *Atkinson Crook and the Independent v UK*[277] a journalist, Crook, had attempted to challenge a s 11 anonymity order: *Central Criminal Court ex parte Crook.*[278] When the challenge failed, Crook took the case to Strasbourg, arguing a breach of Art 10. In the circumstances of the trial it had been feared that matters disclosed in open proceedings might put the defendant's family at risk. The Commission found that the interest of the media in reporting arguments about the sentencing of a convicted defendant could be outweighed if, on reasonable grounds, the prosecution, the judge, and the defendant himself, wished to hear them in private.[279]

Witnesses are placed in a somewhat different position. There is a clear public interest in encouraging witnesses to come forward and to co-operate in proceedings. Therefore, courts have shown a greater willingness to ensure the anonymity of witnesses.[280] And, clearly, if a court takes measures to protect the anonymity of witnesses, such as sitting in camera or allowing the use of screens, there may be no need to make an express s 11 order. Exceptionally, an injunction granted to protect the anonymity of a child may be extended, on grounds of the doctrine of confidence, once the child reaches 18. This was found in *Venables, Thompson v News Group Newspapers Ltd, Associated Newspapers Ltd, MGM Ltd.*[281] Although such a restraint relates to the administration of justice since it concerns an interference with the reporting of criminal justice matters, the object of the injunction is to protect privacy, not to protect a fair hearing, and therefore it is discussed in Chapter 9.[282]

---

274 *Re F (A Minor) (Publication of Information)* [1977] Fam 58.
275 See *Re X (A Minor) (Wardship: Injunction)* [1984] 1 WLR 1422 (the Mary Bell case).
276 *Re F (A Minor) (Publication of Information)* [1977] Fam 58, at 105.
277 (1990) 67 DR 244.
278 (1984) *The Times*, 8 November.
279 See further Chapter 9, p 971.
280 See *R v Watford Magistrates' Court, ex parte Lenman* [1993] Crim LR 388; *Taylor* [1994] TLR 484.
281 [2001] 1 All ER 908, Fam Div.
282 See pp 851–65.

A number of reporting restrictions are aimed at the protection of children. These reporting restrictions are discussed in Chapter 9[283] since they are mainly aimed at protecting privacy. However, it can also be argued that an aspect of the fair trial provision under Art 6(1) is to provide special protections for juveniles in the criminal justice system,[284] whether involved as witnesses or defendants. Under s 39 of the Children and Young Persons Act 1933 (CYPA), a court (apart from a Youth Court) could direct that details relating to a child, 'who was a witness or defendant, including his or her name', should not be reported and that 'no picture of the child should be broadcast or published'. The media could make representations to the judge, arguing that the demands of media freedom outweigh the possibility of harm to the child. Section 49 of the Act, as amended,[285] which relates to Youth Courts, now provides for an automatic ban on publishing certain identifying details relating to a juvenile offender, including his or her name and address, although the court can waive the ban. Under s 45 Crime (Sentences) Act 1997 (C(S)A), the court can lift reporting restrictions where it considers that a ban would be against the public interest.[286]

The s 39 restrictions were extended under s 44 of the Youth Justice and Criminal Evidence Act 1999, which now covers children involved in adult proceedings. The CYPA did not cover the period before proceedings begin. In contrast, the 1999 Act prohibits the publication once a criminal *investigation* has begun, of any matter relating

283 See pp 853–65.
284 See *Thompson and Venables v UK* (2000) 7 BHRC 659. It may be noted that Rule 5 of the Beijing Rules recommends that every juvenile justice system emphasise the well being of the juvenile and ensure that all reactions to such offenders are proportionate to the offence. The UN Convention on the Rights of the Child links fairness and privacy in relation to juveniles, Art 40(2)(b): every child has the right to the presumption of innocence, to informed promptly at the charges against him/her, to have the matter determined without delay by a competent and independent body, the right to silence, a right to an appeal, to understand the language used in proceedings and to have their privacy respected at each stage of the trial.
285 As amended by Sched 2 to the Youth Justice and Criminal Evidence Act 1999.
286 Section 45 provides:

'(1) After subsection (4) of section 49 of the 1933 Act (restrictions on reports of proceedings in which children or young persons are concerned) there shall be inserted the following subsections-

(4A) If a court is satisfied that it is in the public interest to do so, it may, in relation to a child or young person who has been convicted of an offence, by order dispense to any specified extent with the requirements of this section in relation to any proceedings before it to which this section applies by virtue of subsection (2)(a) or (b) above, being proceedings relating to-
   (a) the prosecution or conviction of the offender for the offence;
   (b) the manner in which he, or his parent or guardian, should be dealt with in respect of the offence;
   (c) the enforcement, amendment, variation, revocation or discharge of any order made in respect of the offence;
   (d) where an attendance centre order is made in respect of the offence, the enforcement of any rules made under section 16(3) of the Criminal Justice Act 1982; or
   (e) where a secure training order is so made, the enforcement of any requirements imposed under section 3(7) of the Criminal Justice and Public Order Act 1994.
(4B) A court shall not exercise its power under subsection (4A) above without-
   (a) affording the parties to the proceedings an opportunity to make representations; and
   (b) taking into account any representations which are duly made.'

to a person involved in an offence while he is under 18 which is likely to identify him. Thus, juveniles who are witnesses are also covered. Under s 44(4), the court can dispense with the restrictions if it is satisfied that it is in the public interest to do so. Thus, s 44 brings the restrictions relating to juveniles in adult proceedings into line with those under s 49 relating to youth proceedings, placing the onus on the court to find a good reason for lifting the restriction rather than having to find a good reason for imposing it. The discretion of the court is therefore more narrowly confined.[287] This is clearly an instance in which, as between the demands of press freedom and the interest in the protection of the privacy and reputation of juveniles, the latter interest has prevailed.[288]

A number of special restrictions also apply to the victims of certain sexual offences. Under s 4(1)(a) of the Sexual Offences (Amendment) Act 1976, once an allegation of rape was made it was an offence to publish or broadcast the name, address or photograph of the woman who was the alleged victim. Once a person was accused of rape, nothing could be published by the media which could identify the woman. These restrictions were extended under s 1(1) of the Sexual Offences (Amendment) Act 1992.[289] Section 1(1) covers a number of sexual offences as well as rape, and makes wider provision for anonymity: 'where an allegation has been made that an offence to which the Act applies has been committed against a person,[290] no matter relating to that person shall during that person's lifetime be included in any publication.' This restriction, unlike those considered above, is not subject to any exception. Therefore, in that respect, it affords less recognition to freedom of speech, although it does not prevent the reporting of the case or discussion of it once it is over, so long as details likely to identify the victim are not revealed.

Restrictions on the reporting of proceedings intended to preserve anonymity are likely to create conflict between Art 10, especially in relation to the interest in open justice, and the Art 8 guarantee of a right to respect for privacy. The main safeguard for media freedom is the possibility that the restrictions, apart from that of anonymity in relation to certain sexual offences, may be dispensed with in the public interest. In the HRA era, it would be expected that Art 10 jurisprudence would become an increasingly important influence upon the development of the public interest test. The granting of anonymity raises a number of Convention issues. From the perspective of Art 10, the imposition of anonymity clearly limits what can be reported about a case and may inhibit later reporting or discussion of any issues arising out of the case. However, such restrictions may be justifiable within the paragraph 2 exceptions which include 'for the rights of others'. The right to respect for privacy would therefore be covered, as would Art 6 rights. Therefore, the current emphasis on granting anonymity only on the basis that otherwise, the administration of justice would suffer, is questionable. Courts are bound by Art 8; therefore witnesses, plaintiffs and defendants are able to argue in certain circumstances that anonymity should be granted even where such administration does not clearly demand it. If an order preserving anonymity is lifted it would appear

287 See the discussion in *Lee* [1993] 1 WLR 103, pp 109–10.
288 See further Cram, I, *A Virtue Less Cloistered: Courts, Speech and Constitutions*, 2002, Hart, Chapter 4. See also Chapter 9, pp 854–55.
289 As amended by s 48 of the Youth Justice and Criminal Evidence Act 1999 and Sched 2.
290 Male victims are also covered, under the Criminal Justice and Public Order Act 1994, s 142.

that a breach of Art 6 would arise if the subject of the order had no means of challenging the lifting of the order, whether on the basis of the potential infringement of Art 8 that might arise or on the basis of his or her welfare within the criminal justice system. This argument was put in *R v Manchester Crown Court ex parte H and D*[291] in relation to the lifting of a s 39 CYPA order; the lifting of the order was challenged in the Divisional Court which found that it had jurisdiction to restore it under s 29(3) S(C)A. The Court however considered that clarifying legislation as to the scope of s 29(3) and s 159 CJA was required.

While Arts 6 and 10 may come into conflict in respect of anonymity granted to the defendant, they may have similar demands in respect of anonymity granted to witnesses. Allowing witnesses to give evidence behind screens or by means of a video link clearly raises Art 6 issues, as Strasbourg has accepted,[292] but it also raises Art 10 considerations. Again, argument could be raised under both Articles to the effect that any measures affording anonymity to witnesses should be strictly scrutinised. But while arguments for anonymity might prevail under Art 10 since it is materially qualified, they would be less likely to do so under Art 6.

5 Protecting justice as a continuing process

Publications which interfere with the course of justice as a continuing process, as opposed to publications which affect particular proceedings, may occasionally attract liability. The forms which a risk to justice as a continuing process might take are considered below. A key issue to be considered concerns the mental element under this form of contempt. Such publications must fall outside the Contempt of Court Act 1981, which according to s 1 is concerned only with publications which may affect *particular* proceedings. They must, therefore, arise at common law; the question is whether *mens rea* must be shown, as s 6(c) seems to provide. It could be argued that the words 'administration of justice' used in s 6(c) could be interpreted to mean 'in particular proceedings only', in which case forms of strict liability contempt may still exist at common law. Support could be found for such an interpretation on the basis that s 6(c) is concerned to demonstrate that where intention can be shown, nothing prevents liability arising at common law. Given the context in which this statement is made (appearing to present a contrast to the strict liability rule) it might seem that the area of liability preserved by s 6(c) would cover the same ground as s 1, but only in instances in which *mens rea* could be shown. This point is not settled: there is no post-Act authority on it.

If, on the other hand, s 6(c) covers all interferences with the administration of justice at common law, whether in relation to particular proceedings or not, it would appear to cover the form of contempt known as 'scandalising the court' (considered below) which would run counter to the ruling of the Divisional Court in *Editor of New Statesman*[293] and to some persuasive authority from other jurisdictions.[294] Nevertheless,

---

291 [2000] 2 All ER 166.
292 See *Doorson v Netherlands* (1996) 22 EHRR 330.
293 (1928) 44 TLR 301.
294 *Solicitor General v Radio Avon* [1978] 1 NZLR 225; cf *S v Van Niekirk* (1970) 3 SA 655. See Miller, op. cit., fn 1, pp 378–79 and Borrie and Lowe, *The Law of Contempt*, 1996, pp 359–60.

this may be the more satisfactory approach, since it would be more likely to allow the UK to fulfil its Art 10 obligations under the HRA. Otherwise, common law contempt might have too wide a potential and the intention of the European Court of Human Rights in the *Sunday Times* case would not be given full effect. This would mean that liability for 'scandalising the court' would arise only where intention to interfere with the course of justice generally was shown. However, this point cannot yet be regarded as settled.[295]

It is possible to interfere with the course of justice in the long term in various ways. In *Attorney General v News Group Newspapers* it was found that 'the purpose of the contempt jurisdiction is to prevent interference with the course of justice'. It may be argued that these comments apply where no trial or other proceeding is in contemplation. An interference might arise where a part of the media made a prejudgment on a particular issue with legal implications, although no court had made a determination on the issue or where a court had made a contrary determination. In most instances of prejudicial comment in the media, particular proceedings are soon to occur, or at least exist as a possibility in the future. Therefore, s 6(c) would apply, as would s 1, if the proceedings were active. Thus, attention focuses on the effect of the comment upon those proceedings. However, instances may arise in which no proceedings ever occur. For example, in 1997, the *Daily Mirror* published pictures of five men with the caption 'Murderers!' Proceedings against three of them for the racially motivated murder of Steven Lawrence[296] had led to their acquittal. At the time of the *Mirror*'s comment, no proceedings which could be influenced by it were in being, although there were future possibilities. It was possible that the family of the victim might bring a civil action against the men for battery; thus, the *Mirror* might possibly have been found to have caused prejudice to that action. (However, since the action would have been heard by a judge only, it would have been improbable that a finding of such prejudice would have been made.) Prosecutions against two of the suspects were still possible. The suspects could, of course, have sued the *Mirror* for defamation. That might have provided them with a remedy, but it does not address the possibility that the action of the *Mirror* could be viewed as undermining the authority of the judiciary since it usurped the function of the courts. The ruling of the House of Lords in *Attorney General v Times Newspapers*,[297] which has not been overruled, lends some support to the possibility that a sanction, other by way of a defamation action, is available in respect of 'trial by newspaper', although it may also be said that the spirit of the judgment of the European Court of Human Rights in the *Sunday Times* case[298] might be flouted if it was found that one existed.[299] At present, domestic law does not appear to recognise

---

295 In the pre-HRA era, the weight of academic opinion was to the effect that *mens rea* was not required: Borrie and Lowe (ibid) consider, p 360, that the common law is left untouched by the 1981 Act in relation to publications interfering with the course of justice as a continuing process. This view is also taken by Walker, C (1985) 101 LQR 359, pp 369–70.

296 See Chapter 11, pp 1112–13.

297 [1974] AC 273; [1973] 3 All ER 54; [1973] 3 WLR 298, HL.

298 Judgment of 26 April 1979, A 30; (1979) 2 EHRR 245.

299 In *re Lonhro plc* [1990] 2 AC 154, p 208; [1989] 2 All ER 1100 and 1116, Lord Bridge said that it was 'extremely doubtful' that the *Sunday Times* case could still be relied upon owing to the decision at Strasbourg, although that decision was not direct authority. However, he did not entirely rule out the possibility that the prejudgment test could still be used.

liability for any form of interfering with the course of justice in the long term, apart from the form discussed below. If such a form does exist in respect of prejudgments it may, as argued above, be covered by s 6(c).

The form of contempt termed 'scandalising the court'[300] arose in order to protect the judicial system from media attacks. The idea behind it is that it would be against the public interest if the media could attack judges and cast doubt on their decisions – suggest, for example, that a judge had shown bias – because the public confidence in the administration of justice would be undermined. It has not been affected by the 1981 Act because there are normally no proceedings which could be influenced; any relevant proceedings will usually be concluded. If an attack on a judge occurred during the 'active' period, it would probably fall outside the Act, since any risk it created would tend to be to the course of justice as a continuing process rather than to the particular proceeding. Prosecutions are rare (and, in recent times, almost unheard of in the UK), but Lord Hailsham said in *Baldry v DPP of Mauritius*,[301] a Privy Council decision, that although it was likely that only the most serious or intolerable instances would be taken notice of by courts or Attorney Generals, nothing had happened in the intervening 80 years to invalidate the analysis of this branch of contempt put forward in *Gray*.[302] Thus, this branch of contempt law is probably still alive, and cannot merely be disregarded by the media.

As noted above, the weight of authority is probably to the effect that this is a form of strict liability contempt arising at common law, but this point cannot be regarded as settled. If the view taken in *Editor of New Statesman*[303] is correct, there would be no need to show an intention to lower the repute of the judge or court in question, merely an intention to publish. The *actus reus* of this form of contempt consists of the publication of material calculated to lower the reputation of a court or judge, thereby creating a real risk of undermining public confidence in the due administration of justice.

There are two main methods of fulfilling this *actus reus*. First, a publication which is held to be scurrilously abusive of a court or judge may provide the classic example of scandalising the court. The leading case is *Gray*,[304] which arose from the trial of one Wells on a charge of obscene libel in which Darling J warned the press not to publish a full account of court proceedings (because details of obscene matter might have been included). After they were over, the *Birmingham Daily Argus* published an article attacking him and referring to him as an 'impudent little man in horsehair' and 'a microcosm of conceit and empty-headedness [who] would do well to master the duties of his own profession before undertaking the regulation of another'. This article was held by the Divisional Court to be a grave contempt as it was 'not moderate criticism; it amounted to personal, scurrilous abuse of the judge in his capacity of judge'. On the other hand, in *Ambard v Attorney General for Trinidad and Tobago*,[305] reasoned criticism of certain sentences was held by the Privy Council not to constitute contempt on the

---

300 For general comment on this head of contempt, see Walker, C (1985) 101 LQR 359.
301 [1983] 2 AC 297; [1983] 3 All ER 973.
302 [1900] 2 QB 36; (1900) 69 LJ QB 502.
303 (1928) 44 TLR 301.
304 Above, fn 302.
305 [1936] AC 322; [1936] 1 All ER 704.

basis that 'Justice is not a cloistered virtue: she must be allowed to suffer the scrutiny and respectful, even though outspoken, comments of ordinary men'. In a more recent case, *Metropolitan Police Comr ex p Blackburn*,[306] the Court of Appeal reaffirmed this position.

Secondly, a publication may scandalise a court if it imputes bias to a judge – even if it does so in a moderate way – on the basis that allegations of partiality will undermine confidence in the basic function of a judge. The leading case in this area is *Editor of New Statesman*.[307] The pioneer of birth control, Dr Marie Stopes, lost a libel action and an article commenting on the case stated: '. . . the verdict represents a substantial miscarriage of justice (we are not in sympathy with Dr Stopes but prejudice against her aims should not be allowed to influence a Court of Justice as it appeared to influence Mr Justice Avory in his summing up. Such views as those of Dr Stopes cannot get a fair hearing in a court presided over by Mr Justice Avory.' The editor was found to be in contempt, because although the article was serious and seemingly respectful, it imputed unfairness and lack of impartiality to the judge in the discharge of his judicial duties. The most notorious instance of this variety of scandalising the court occurred in *Colsey*.[308] A moderate article had imputed unconscious bias to a judge because in making a determination as to the meaning of a statute, he might have been influenced by the fact that he had himself earlier, as Solicitor General, steered it through Parliament.

Until 1999, there were no further successful prosecutions for this form of contempt in the UK. Prosecutions may have been discouraged owing to the attacks on the *Colsey* ruling, which clearly laid itself open to the charge of amounting to an unjustified encroachment on the free speech principle.[309] In 1999, the Attorney General sought to jail a defendant, Scriven, from whom an undertaking not to scandalise the court had been obtained, but subsequently breached. The defendant had agreed not to make further accusations, including accusations of bias, against the judiciary, but in November 1999 he placed material on a website which criticised a number of judges.[310] Lawyers in the Lord Chancellor's department complained to the service provider, who closed the website down. Scriven signed an undertaking not to breach the terms of an injunction requiring him to refrain from further criticism. The material was subsequently published on a US website. Proceedings for contempt were brought against him in respect of breach of the undertaking.[311]

It will not be surprising to learn that this is an area of contempt law which has attracted particular criticism,[312] and such criticism has especial pertinence in the post-HRA era. Some critics argue that the offence of scandalising the court should be abolished altogether on the grounds that the rationale of the offence – undermining public confidence in the administration of justice – is too imprecise to justify imposing restrictions on freedom of speech. They argue that a system of justice should not be

306   [1968] 2 All ER 319, CA.
307   (1928) 44 TLR 301.
308   (1931) *The Times*, 9 May.
309   See, e.g., Goodhart, AL (1935) 48 Harv L Rev 885, pp 903–4; (1931) 47 LQR 315.
310   *R v Hulbert* (1999) unreported; see News Report, the *Guardian*, 8 November 1999.
311   See News Report, the *Guardian*, 31 January 2001.
312   See Borrie and Lowe, *The Law of Contempt*, 1996, p 360 *et seq*; Law Commission Report No 96, *Offences relating to Interference with the Course of Justice*, pp 67–68.

so lacking in self-confidence that it must suppress attacks on itself. Harold Laski has written: 'To argue that the expression of doubts as to judicial impartiality is an interference in the course of justice because the result is to undermine public confidence in the judiciary is to forget that public confidence is undermined not so much by the comment as by the habit which leads to the comment.'[313] It may be argued that the public will have more confidence in the judiciary if it can be freely discussed. Moreover, because no jury sits in such cases, the judicial system is in a sense prosecution and judge in the same case, thereby giving rise to a suggestion of bias. It may be asked why only judges and not, for example, politicians or members of the clergy, should receive this special protection from criticism? Why single out judges for such insulation? The position may be compared to that in America where this form of contempt is almost extinct owing to the ruling in *Bridges v California*;[314] it was held that the evil of displaying disrespect for the judiciary should not be averted by restricting freedom of expression, as enforced silence on a subject is more likely to engender resent, suspicion and contempt. This is, therefore, a further instance in which the ends of both justice and free speech would be served by curtailing or abolishing this area of liability.

On the other hand, it might be argued that an action for defamation is not a sufficient remedy where bias has been imputed to a judge because it would place him or her in an invidious position while the action was being held. More doubtfully, it might also be said that the singling out of judges can be justified on the basis that, unlike many other public figures, judges may be more reluctant to use available fora from which to reply to criticism. A compromise between these two positions could be effected by adopting the course advocated by the Law Commission – replacement of this form of liability with a narrowly drawn offence covering the distribution of false matter with intent that it should be taken as true, and knowing or being reckless as to its falsity when it imputes corrupt conduct to any judge.[315] Narrowing down the current offence and affording it much greater precision would be, it is suggested, much more in accordance with the demands of Art 10, including the 'prescribed by law' requirement. As currently conceived, it may allow for an interference with truthful and highly significant speech which may readily be viewed, not only as unjustifiable in a democratic society, but also as too imprecise to form a basis for criminality.

6 Disclosure of jury deliberations

This chapter now moves on to consider a specific preventive measure – the ban on media reporting of jury deliberations. Apart from the various specific restraints on reporting already discussed, there is a complete ban in the Contempt of Court Act 1981 on the reporting of jury deliberations; it is aimed not at preventing prejudice to particular proceedings, but at preserving the administration of justice by protecting the confidentiality of such deliberations. Section 8(1) of the 1981 Act bars the revelation of statements, opinions, arguments or votes of the members of the jury in the course of their

---

313 (1928) 41 Harv L Rev 1031, p 1036.
314 (1941) 314 US 252.
315 This was the view of the Law Commission in their report (No 96), *Offences Relating to Interference with the Course of Justice*.

deliberations,[316] except in very narrow circumstances, to a court, as discussed below. It is accepted that there is a *mens rea* element of intention: the section refers only to deliberate revelations. A similar but less absolute rule has prevailed in Commonwealth countries;[317] it does allow for research.[318]

Therefore jurors are prevented from exercising their freedom of expression, except in one narrow circumstance, and the media are barred from discussing such deliberations in two ways. First, the source of information that they would need is withheld from them since it would be an offence for a juror to disclose information about the deliberations, while it would also be an offence under s 8 for a reporter to solicit it. Second, any reporting of the deliberations would itself infringe s 8.[319] Therefore, apart from general and abstract discussions, the media cannot act in their watchdog role[320] in relation to the very significant function of the jury in society. Further, due to s 8 research into the deliberations of jurors in real trials, even if anonymised, is so highly constrained in the UK as to be impossible.

The pre-HRA stance, from the ruling in *Attorney General v Associated Newspapers Ltd and Others*,[321] was that s 8 should be interpreted literally. In that instance, jury deliberations were not disclosed directly to the defendant newspaper, but to researchers who made a transcript of them. The paper then used the transcript in order to gather information for the article in question. It was argued on behalf of the defendants that

316 Section 8 provides in full:

'Confidentiality of jury's deliberations.

(1) Subject to subsection (2) below, it is a contempt of court to obtain, disclose or solicit any particulars of statements made, opinions expressed, arguments advanced or votes cast by members of a jury in the course of their deliberations in any legal proceedings.

(2) This section does not apply to any disclosure of any particulars--
  (a) in the proceedings in question for the purpose of enabling the jury to arrive at their verdict, or in connection with the delivery of that verdict, or
  (b) in evidence in any subsequent proceedings for an offence alleged to have been committed in relation to the jury in the first mentioned proceedings, or to the publication of any particulars so disclosed.

(3) Proceedings for a contempt of court under this section (other than Scottish proceedings) shall not be instituted except by or with the consent of the Attorney General or on the motion of a court having jurisdiction to deal with it.'

317 For Australia, see: *R v Andrew Brown* [1907] 7 NSWSR 290; *R v Medici* (Court of Criminal Appeal, Victoria, 5 June 1995); for Canada, see: *R v Pan; R v Sawyer* [2001] 2 SCR 344; for New Zealand, see: *R v Papadopoulos* [1979] 1 NZLR 621.

318 A particularly important piece of research was completed five years ago in New Zealand (Young, W, Cameron, N and Tinsley, Y, *Law Juries in Criminal Trials, Part Two: A Summary of the Research Findings*, Law Commission of New Zealand Prelim Paper 37, Vol 2, 1999). It relied on the experience of jurors in 48 completed criminal trials, many of them high-profile cases. 19% of the jurors recalled seeing some pre-trial publicity. The main conclusion of the report was that in only one case was there some evidence that pre-trial publicity might have influenced the deliberations of the jury. 34% per cent of jurors recalled encountering publicity *during* the trial but considered that it had had no influence on them. Jurors consciously made an effort to put aside the effects of any publicity, and the researchers said that it was impossible to know whether this was due to directions from the judge or because they thought that to take such publicity into account would be unfair.

319 See *Attorney General v. Associated Newspapers* [1994] 2 AC 538, HL.

320 See the discussion below of *Goodwin v UK* (1996) 22 EHRR 123 at pp 413–15.

321 [1994] 2 WLR 277; [1994] 1 All ER 556; (1994) 142 NLJ 1647, HL; [1993] 2 All ER 535; (1993) 144 NLJ 195, CA.

the word 'disclose' used in s 8 is capable of bearing two meanings; it could mean disclosure by anyone, or it could mean disclosure by a member of the jury to the defendant. As Chapter 3 indicated, it was well established in the pre-HRA era that where a statute contains an ambiguous provision, it should be construed so as to conform with the relevant Convention guarantee.[322] On that basis, the narrower meaning should have been adopted, allowing the defendants to escape liability. However, it was found that the word 'disclose' was not ambiguous: in its natural and ordinary meaning, which Parliament clearly intended it to bear, it denoted disclosure to anyone; the defendants therefore clearly fell within its provisions.

The closing up of a potential loophole in s 8 achieved by this ruling means that the important institution of the jury is largely immune from media scrutiny, at least as regards the manner in which they discharges their role.[323] The section does not prevent interviewing of jurors that does not touch upon their deliberations in the jury room, but such inquiries should only be undertaken with the leave of the trial court or after verdict and sentence, by the Court of Appeal.[324] Jury deliberations are clearly a matter of very significant public interest, and it is therefore argued that s 8 should have been framed much less widely. The only current constraint is the requirement of the Attorney General's consent to a prosecution, but even this is not necessary where proceedings are instituted on the motion of a court.

The absolute nature of s 8 means that it may be incompatible with Art 10 since jurors are denied freedom of expression, and media discussion and reporting on a matter of great public interest is so greatly curbed. Section 8 probably answers to the exceptions under Art 10(2), of preserving confidentiality and perhaps 'for maintaining the authority of the judiciary'. But assuming that one of these exceptions applies, the absolute nature of the section means that it creates an interference arguably disproportionate to the end in view. On the face of it, it might have been expected, therefore, that s 8 would be found at some point after 2000 to be prima facie incompatible with Art 10 under the Human Rights Act, and s 3 would have had to be invoked to impose a different interpretation on it. Alternatively, it might have been expected that a declaration of the incompatibility would have to be made under s 4 HRA.

The two leading post-HRA cases concerned the compatibility of s 8 with Arts 6 and 10; they indicate that the senior judges are not minded to create exceptions to the section, relying on s 3 HRA, apart from one very narrow one. It seems clear therefore that they would not be prepared to create an exception which would allow for some limited, anonymised disclosure of jury deliberations to the media. In *R v Mirza; R v Connor*[325] the House of Lords largely reaffirmed the accepted understandings as to the interpretation of s 8.[326] However, it was found that s 8(1) does not apply to the trial court or to the Court of Appeal. In other words, there is an exception to s 8 allowing a judge to inquire into a juror's disclosure of impropriety in the jury's deliberations during proceedings. Thus matters can be disclosed without either the juror or court

---

322 See pp 136–37.

323 For consideration of the effect of the restriction, see the Royal Commission on Criminal Justice Report (1993) Cm 2263, p 2.

324 *McCluskey* (1993) 94 Cr App R 216, CA. See also *Mickleborough* [1995] 1 Cr App R 297, CA.

325 [2004] 1 All ER 925; [2004] 2 WLR 201.

326 See *R v Qureshi* [2002] 1 WLR 518; *Roylance v GMC (No 2)* [2000] 1 AC 311.

facing liability under s 8. Prior to this decision the general assumption in the English courts was that the terms of s 8(1) were so broad as to apply to any court, whether the trial court or the Court of Appeal (Criminal Division), which might otherwise have wished to inquire into a matter relating to the jurors' deliberations. Section 8(1), it had been thought, in effect ruled out such inquiries by the courts.[327]

Subsequently, in *R v Smith*[328] the House looked further at what form the trial judge's inquiries might take when a matter was drawn to his/her attention during the trial. It was found that it would not be appropriate for a judge to question jurors about the contents of a letter received during proceedings from one of the jurors making allegations about impropriety in the jury deliberations, and a judge was not obliged to do so. In relation to the case it was said: 'If he had gone into the allegations, he would inevitably have had to question them about the subject of their deliberations and whether S were guilty of any of the offences charged.' The common law prohibition against inquiring into events in the jury room extended, it was found, to matters connected with the subject matter of the jury's deliberations. Thus, following *Mirza* and *Smith*, s 8 does not disallow inquiry into the jury's deliberations, but once an inquiry has been made the judge cannot under the common law question the jury as to allegations made. He or she would only have a choice between discharging the jury or redirecting them in terms that took account of the allegations. In *Smith* it was found on appeal that the redirection had not taken sufficient account of the allegations and therefore the appeal was allowed.

Mirza also concerned the admissibility into evidence of jurors' expressed concerns about the jury's deliberations – concerns that suggested that the jury had not acted fairly. The majority determined, by virtue of a long-standing common law rule,[329] that after the jury have returned their verdict, evidence directed to matters intrinsic to the jurors' deliberations is inadmissible.[330] Exceptionally, however, evidence of extraneous influences on the verdict is admissible. So jury concerns could not be admitted into evidence after the conclusion of proceedings unless the jury had been subjected to, for example, bribery. The bar thereby created was found not to be incompatible with the Art 6 guarantee of a fair trial. The residual possibility of a miscarriage of justice was, it was found, the necessary price to be paid for the preservation and protection of the jury system, although Lord Steyn, in the minority, delivered a powerful dissenting judgment. He said:

> In my view it would be an astonishing thing for the ECHR to hold, when the point directly arises before it, that a miscarriage of justice may be ignored in the

---

327 See *R v Young* [1995] QB 324, 330.

328 [2005] 1WLR 704.

329 There is a long line of decisions holding that it is never permissible to admit evidence of what happened during jury deliberations. See: *Ellis v Deheer* [1922] 2 KB 113, 117–18, *per* Bankes LJ at 121; *R v Thompson* [1962] 1 All ER 65, 66, *per* Lord Parker CJ; *Attorney General v New Statesman and National Publishing Company Ltd* [1981] QB 1,10, *per* Lord Widgery CJ; *R v Miah* [1997] 2 Cr App R 12, 18–19, *per* Kennedy LJ; *Roylance v General Medical Council* (No 2) [2000] 1 AC 311, 324B, *per* Lord Clyde; *R v Qureshi* [2002] 1 WLR 518, *per* Kennedy LJ. The position is similar in Scotland: *Stewart v Fraser* (1830) 5 Murray 166; *Swankie v H M Advocate* (1999) SCCR 1.

330 *R v Hood* [1968] 1 WLR 773; R *v Brandon* (1969) 53 Cr App R 466; *R v Young (Stephen)* [1995] QB 324.

interests of the general efficiency of the jury system. The terms of Article 6(1) of the European Convention, the rights revolution, and fifty years of development of human rights law and practice, would suggest that such a view would be utterly indefensible.[331]

Clearly, the Lords were not concerned with the compatibility of s 8 with Art 10. However, the findings demonstrate that the Lords are not minded to create implied exceptions to s 8 except in relation to the courts themselves: they were prepared to find that a court itself cannot be in contempt of court on the narrow basis that to hold otherwise would be self-evidently absurd and that therefore s 8 must be read as including that exception. Otherwise, the Lords were content to continue the previously established approach.

In the key post-HRA authority, *Attorney General v Scotcher*,[332] the House of Lords reaffirmed the approach in *Mirza* and also found that s 8 is compatible with Art 10. It should be pointed out that *Scotcher* did not concern media free expression – at least, not directly - but the exercise of free speech rights by a juror. The facts of *Scotcher* were as follows. In January 2000 the appellant, Scotcher, was summoned for jury service in the Crown Court. Like all the other potential jurors, Scotcher was informed that disclosing the deliberations of the jury to anyone would be contempt of court under s 8 Contempt of Court Act 1981. The jury convicted the two defendants (brothers) by a majority verdict of ten votes to one.

The appellant then wrote to the defendants' mother, telling her that he had been the one juror who had wanted an acquittal and criticising the basis on which the other jurors had reached their decision. He said, *inter alia*, that they had not weighed up the evidence properly and that some of them had convicted merely because they wanted to get home. He also indicated that in his view the police had framed the defendants but that the other jurors had failed to appreciate this. He suggested that she should appeal and also asked her not to disclose the fact that he had sent the letter to the court or to the police. The defendants' mother's solicitor brought the matter to the attention of the Court of Appeal; eventually Scotcher admitted that he had written the letter, and he was convicted of the offence under s 8. He appealed, arguing that he had a defence based on the Human Rights Act, and specifically Art 10, on the basis that he had written the letter since he was seeking to prevent a miscarriage of justice. This was of relevance also in relation to Art 6, although that Article was not directly engaged. It was argued that in the particular circumstances of this case, by virtue of s 3 HRA, s 8(1) had to be interpreted as including the defence argued for so as to make it compatible with Art 10 of the European Convention. It was further argued that if this could not be done, then the House should make a declaration of incompatibility under s 4 HRA.

Both sides accepted that, in the terms of s 8, the appellant had revealed 'statements, opinions, arguments or votes' of the members of the jury in the course of their deliberations. It was also accepted that the *mens rea* for the offence is an intention to disclose those matters and that the appellant had deliberately disclosed these aspects of the jury's deliberations to the defendants' mother. So unless a defence was available

---

331 *R v Mizra; R v Connor* [2004] 1 All ER 925; [2004] 2 WLR 201, at para 19.
332 [2005] 1 WLR 1867.

to the appellant he was guilty of contempt of court in the terms of s 8(1). Just before the appeal in this case, the House of Lords had given judgment in *R v Mirza*.[333] That decision corrected the previous interpretation of s 8(1), which the Divisional Court had applied in Scotcher's case. As a result, the arguments before the House were different from those in the Divisional Court. The House had held in *Mirza*, however, as indicated above, that if a trial judge was informed about any misconduct during the jury's deliberations, but before they had returned their verdict, then s 8(1) did not prevent him/her from looking into the matter. Since jurors might well not appreciate that they could tell the judge about any misconduct of their fellow jurors, the House suggested that in future they should be given further guidance. This suggestion led Lord Woolf CJ to issue Practice Direction (Crown Court: Guidance to Jurors) in 2004[334] which amended Practice Direction (Criminal Proceedings: Consolidation)[335] so as to provide, *inter alia*: 'Trial judges should ensure that the jury is alerted to the need to bring any concerns about fellow jurors to the attention of the judge at the time, and not wait until the case is concluded.'

However, this amended advice was not available at the time when Scotcher served as a juror: the advice he received was the previous, blanket advice. It was accepted that if he had written his letter to the Crown Court or to the Court of Appeal, he would not have been in contempt of court in the terms of s 8(1). Taking Art 10 and s 3 HRA into account, the defence argued that s 8 should be interpreted as being subject to a defence that it did not apply to a juror who disclosed the jury's deliberations to a third party rather than to the court, if the juror was motivated by a desire to expose a miscarriage of justice and he did not contact the court authorities because he had been told that he could not disclose the deliberations to anyone. Any other argument would, it was suggested, lead to a breach of Art 10 on the ground of the disproportionality of the penalty to the aim pursued. This argument was rejected by the House on the basis that s 3 HRA comes into play only where it is needed in order to make a legislative provision compatible with a Convention right. But when properly interpreted, according to ordinary principles of construction (as it was in *Mirza*), it was considered that s 8(1) is compatible with Art 10 of the Convention and that, therefore, s 3 did not apply. So the warnings to the jurors at the time were incorrect, but the statutory provision was not. In any event, the House found, any such potential defence would have been inapplicable to Scotcher since he disregarded warnings not to contact anyone and therefore the warnings could not be viewed as having affected him. Therefore he would not have contacted the court had the warnings been correct. Scotcher's conviction was therefore upheld since the defence argued for in his favour was not found to exist.

A number of comments may be made on this decision in relation to the balance it strikes between free expression and the administration of justice. Although this was not a decision about media reporting of jury deliberations, it is clear that the House had the possibility of disclosures to the media in mind. The Lords appeared to be concerned that the creation of exceptions to s 8, allowing disclosure to anybody apart from a court, might open the floodgates to such disclosures. The discussion will

---

333   [2004] 1 AC 118.
334   [2004] 1 WLR 665.
335   [2002] 1 WLR 2870.

concentrate on the current position in relation to Art 10 and ask whether an absolute bar on disclosure to the media, taking account of the possibility of anonymising the reporting, is acceptable under Art 10. The defence Counsel conceded that, once the 2004 Practice Direction came into force, s 8(1) did not infringe a juror's Art 10 rights, since he would know that he could draw his concerns to the attention of the trial judge before the jury returned their verdict. However, this is questionable. As matters stand at present certain bodies have been exempted from the application of s 8 via interpretation. The exception arose since it appeared strange to hold that a court could itself be in contempt of court.

But, following *Mirza*, a *juror* may avoid liability for contempt if she or he discloses to the court what is said or done during the jury's deliberations with the intention of prompting an investigation. She or he is also exempt from being in contempt of court in terms of s 8(1) – a further exception and one not dependent on the anomaly of finding a court to be in contempt. Jurors can make representations to the court regarding jury deliberations both during and after the trial. Doing so after the trial is, however, of no efficacy since such evidence is inadmissible, unless the representations concern external influences. Section 8 itself does not appear to import such an exemption for jurors. Once this inroad had been made, it could be argued that in an exceptional instance a further exemption should be created, using the powerful interpretative tool of s 3 HRA. For example, after acquittal, a female juror in a rape trial might come to the conclusion on reasonable grounds that both the court and fellow-jurors were affected by highly sexist views of rape victims. For example, a juror might have expressed the view that 99 per cent of victims in rape trials are liars. Or a group of jurors might have expressed the view that since the woman was wearing a short skirt and had flirted with the alleged rapist, she must have given consent. If despite her concern about the court's stance, she exposed the sexist views of jurors to the court she would not be acting unlawfully, but her action would have no effect in averting a miscarriage of justice (the wrongful acquittal of a rapist) or in alerting the public to failings in the jury system in rape cases. Her action would be ineffective in relation to miscarriages since the verdict could not be appealed. Therefore after an acquittal tainted by sexism the female juror might consider that the only way of exposing this matter, and thus helping to address the very low conviction rate in rape cases, was to contact the media. If a newspaper published her allegations, but anonymised the case itself, it would nevertheless face liability for contempt under s 8, as would the juror.

In a similar instance, if a juror considered that fellow jurors and the court were influenced by racism in reaching a conviction, disclosure to the court would not be unlawful but would not avert a miscarriage of justice since on appeal the evidence would be inadmissible. Lord Steyn gave this example in *Mirza*: 'A juror reveals after verdict that during the jury deliberations it emerged that some members of the jury were associated with a Neo-Nazi group and that they urged the conviction of the accused because he was a black immigrant;' he considered that there could be no serious dispute as to the perversion of justice that would have occurred in that instance.[336] Nevertheless, the disclosure could not be admitted in evidence on appeal. The juror who realised that his/her revelation had had no effect might be tempted to write to a newspaper,

---

336 *R v Mirza* [2004] 1 AC 118 [1].

revealing what had happened as a matter that the public should be informed about. If he did, he would incur liability under s 8 even if he anonymised his letter.

Under the present state of the law, disclosure by a juror *during* the case of the fact that a juror was evincing sexist or racist views, could be received by the court. But it is clear, following the Lords' decision in *R v Smith*,[337] that it could not lead to an inquiry by the judge into the matter; the judge appears only to have the options of discharging the jury or re-directing them. If a mere redirection was given, which in fact appeared to have little impact, disclosure to the court might be viewed as having been ineffective by the juror. Recourse to the media might appear to be the only way of alerting the public to the miscarriage of justice and also possibly prompting a change in the law.[338] Consideration of such instances indicates that s 8 may be incompatible with Art 10 since the free expression of jurors and of the media is severely curbed in relation to jury deliberations.

The position in England prior to the enactment of s 8 is of some interest in this context. *Attorney General v New Statesman*[339] was the decision that led to the introduction of s 8. Following the acquittal of a prominent politician on a charge of conspiracy to murder, the *New Statesman* magazine published an article, based on an interview with one of the jurors, which gave an account of significant parts of the jury's deliberations. The Attorney General applied for an order for contempt of court against the *New Statesman*. The Divisional Court held that a juror's disclosure of the jury's deliberations was not a contempt of court unless it 'tended, or would tend, to imperil the finality of jury verdicts, or to affect adversely the attitude of future jurors and the quality of their deliberations'. The Court held that the article in question would not have that effect and the Attorney General's application was refused. Lord Widgery CJ found:[340]

> The evidence before us shows that for a number of years the publication of jury room secrets has occurred on numerous occasions. To many of those disclosures no exception could be taken because from a study of them it would not be possible to identify the persons concerned in the trials. In these cases, jury secrets were revealed in the main for the laudable purpose of informing would-be jurors what to expect when summoned for jury service. Thus, it is not possible to contend that every case of post-trial activity of the kind with which we are concerned must necessarily amount to a contempt. Looking at this case as a whole, we have come to the conclusion that the article in the *New Statesman* does not justify the title of contempt of court. That does not mean that we would not wish to see restrictions on the publication of such an article because we would.

---

337 [2005] 1WLR 704.
338 A possible change that might be prompted by media outcries would be to allow for inquiries into jury debate to be made by a judge during trial if an allegation of jury prejudice is made by a juror (contrary to the finding in *R v Smith* [2005] 1WLR 704). This would have been valuable in domestic courts in relation to the domestic case (*R v Gregory*, Manchester Crown Court, between 26 and 28 November 1991; leave to appeal refused) resulting in *Gregory v UK* [1997] 25 EHRR 577, discussed below.
339 [1981] QB 1.
340 At p11.

These findings suggest that an absolute bar on publication of jury deliberations was not needed and was not being asked for by the court. They also suggest that the courts did not view anonymised publications as problematic, while even nominate ones – as in the *New Statesman* case – were not viewed as imperilling the jury system in a significant manner. These remarks provide a starting-point from which to examine the compatibility of s 8 in its current manifestation – post-*Mirza* – with Art 10. It may be noted that in *Scotcher* the House relied on *Gregory v UK*,[341] discussed below, in noting that the European Court of Human Rights had acknowledged that the rule governing the secrecy of jury deliberations is a crucial and legitimate feature of English trial law. The House took the view that this finding was relevant to the compatibility of s 8 with Art 10, Lord Rodger of Earlsferry stating:

> Therefore, in so far as section 8(1) serves to reinforce that rule by making it an offence for a juror to disclose the information which he receives in confidence from his fellow jurors, the objective is sufficiently important to justify limiting the juror's freedom of expression in this way. The provision is rationally connected to its aim and the means adopted are no more than is reasonably necessary, since the restriction does not apply to bona fide disclosures to the court authorities. The measure is accordingly reasonably justifiable in a democratic society.[342]

However, that is not necessarily the end of the matter as far as Art 10 is concerned. *Gregory* concerned the right to a fair trial under Art 6(1) and specifically whether, in the circumstances of the trial in question, impartiality had been achieved so as to satisfy Art 6(1). Article 10 was not in question. On the facts the Court was satisfied that no breach had occurred. The applicant in that case had been tried for robbery and on the final day of the trial the jury had retired to consider their verdict. After some time a note was passed by the jury to the judge. It read: 'Jury showing racial overtones. One member to be excused.' The trial judge consulted counsel for the prosecution and defence and decided to redirect the jury as to the need to decide the case on the evidence, although he did not mention racial prejudice specifically. He could not inquire directly into any racial bias on the part of jury members due to s 8. Eventually the jury convicted. The European Court decided that the note was ambiguous and that the judge had taken reasonable measures to ensure that impartiality had been safeguarded. Thus the decision turned on the particular circumstances of the case and did not determine that in all circumstances the application of s 8 on its current interpretation could cause no breach of Art 6 or of Art 10.

If s 8 serves a legitimate aim under Art 10(2) and satisfies the tests for necessity and proportionality in relation to that aim then there is no incompatibility. However, it is suggested that Lord Rodger in *Scotcher* did not take full account of all the tests for proportionality or subject s 8 in relation to them to a sufficiently high level of scrutiny, despite citing *de Freitas v Permanent Secretary of Ministry Agriculture*.[343] Clearly, the preservation of jury confidentiality serves a significant societal interest – it can be said

341 (1997) 25 EHRR 577, 594, at para 44.
342 At para 29.
343 [1999] 1 AC 69, p 80.

that it answers to a pressing social need. It is important that there should be free debate in the jury room; jurors should be able to deliberate without fear of possible future repercussions. Does s 8 go further than is necessary to serve that need? A number of tests for proportionality should be applied (those from *Goodwin v UK*[344] and from *de Freitas v Permanent Secretary of Ministry Agriculture*).[345] It is also suggested that the level of scrutiny to be adopted should be strict, bearing in mind the significance of the speech in question and the importance of the media's role – a juror disclosing material to a newspaper about a miscarriage of justice would be in position analogous to that of a source disclosing malpractice in, for example, the police service. Thus the strict level of scrutiny determined upon in *Goodwin v UK* in relation to source disclosure should apply.[346]

The *de Freitas* tests for proportionality cover first the suitability of the interference in question. In this instance, the penalty under s 8 constitutes the interference. This test is arguably met on the basis that criminal liability for disclosing information is effective while the penalties imposed are not excessive: a custodial sentence is unlikely to be imposed, although a suspended sentence might be. The second test concerns the need to choose the least intrusive measure. It is arguable that this test is not met since a less intrusive measure – an injunction obtained on grounds of breach of confidence – is available and subject to a public interest test that meets Art 10's demands. More significantly, near-absolute bars to the exercise of expression rights invade the right almost as far as it is possible to do so. A parallel could be drawn with *Open-Door Counselling and Dublin Well-Woman v Ireland*[347] in which the interference with speech rights was also very serious. Pamphlets on the availability of abortions outside Ireland were – in effect – banned by an injunction granted by the Irish courts. The European Court of Human Rights was struck by the absolute nature of the interference – there were no grounds, including that of health, on which it could be waived. On that basis it was found to be a disproportionate interference with expression rights. In the instance of s 8 there is an *absolute* bar to the exercise of *media* expression rights since jurors cannot disclose matters relating to the trial to the media, however significant the public interest involved. Media reports of such matters could adopt anonymity and therefore protect the confidentiality of jury deliberations. Therefore absolute bars to media reporting may be viewed as unnecessarily restrictive. The strictness of the test for scrutiny means that it is not sufficient to find a reasonable relationship between the restrictiveness of s 8 and the aim pursued.

Third, the seriousness of the interference has to be balanced against the importance of the aim sought to be pursued. Clearly, the interference is especially severe, since it amounts to an absolute bar despite the significance of the expression in question. The aim pursued is important – the efficient working of the jury system. But is that efficiency best served by hiding the failings of the system from public scrutiny? Could it be served more effectively by allowing reports of jury deliberations, but anonymised? In coming to a conclusion on this point it would not be enough to be satisfied that

344 (1996) 22 EHRR 123.
345 [1999] 1 AC 69, 80. The tests are discussed fully in Chapter 4, pp 286–90.
346 (1992) 15 EHRR 244. See further below, pp 413–15 for discussion of the proportionality test used in this instance and for discussion of the standard of scrutiny from *Goodwin* (1996) 22 EHRR 123.
347 (1993) 15 EHRR 244.

the balance struck between the two interests was not manifestly unreasonable. On a stricter level of scrutiny it would appear that the balance struck between the two is not satisfactory since it is does not appear that the serious invasion of expression rights is warranted by the aim pursued. The efficacy of the jury system might ultimately be enhanced by media scrutiny accompanied by the safeguards mentioned: an absolute bar is not therefore needed. Thus it appears that two of the key tests for proportionality are unsatisfied by s 8. If its effects are disproportionate to the aim pursued, they cannot be viewed as necessary in a democratic society under Art 10(2).

Arguably it would be possible to imply an exception into s 8 via s 3 HRA on similar lines to the exception created by the House of Lords in *R v A*[348] to s 41 Youth Justice and Criminal Evidence Act 1999: s 8 could be read subject to the need to ensure compatibility with Art 10 by allowing for a defence where a juror was genuinely motivated by a desire to expose a miscarriage of justice in the public interest and where the material was anonymised. Such a reinterpretation would not be contrary to the underlying intention behind s 8 since, as the House accepted in *Scotcher*, the main intention behind introduction of the section was to prevent the harassment of jurors by the media. The new exception could be made applicable only where the jury member had spontaneously contacted the media in the exceptional circumstances envisaged; thus the exception could be found not to apply where a journalist had contacted the juror or offered money. There is also a strong Art 10-based argument for creating a further exception covering anonymised research into jury trials on the basis that the confidentiality of jury deliberations is unlikely to be threatened but the material discovered is of very high public interest value. The creation of implied exceptions to s 8, which allow for serious debate as to the fairness of the jury system would be a desirable result in terms of the values enshrined not only in Art 10 but also in Art 6 and possibly Arts 8 and 3. If the creation of such exceptions using s 3 HRA was viewed as too radical, a declaration of incompatibility between Art 10 and s 8 could be made. Clearly, in order to import these exceptions into s 8 under s 3 HRA, the House of Lords would probably have to decide in a suitable case to overturn *Scotcher*. The only alternative in terms of creating compatibility at the domestic level, in the absence of legislative change, would be for the courts to find that *Scotcher* is confined to its own special facts.

7 Protection of sources[349]

Introduction

The protection of sources is clearly vital to the role of journalists. As the Strasbourg Court put it in the seminal case of *Goodwin v UK*: 'Protection of journalistic sources is one of the basic conditions for press freedom.'[350] If sources do not believe that their identity will be protected, they will not normally contact journalists and therefore, the most potent source of information, that of a person who is, in some sense, an 'insider', will be denied to them. If sources are afraid to come forward, the result will be that the

---

348 [2001] 2 WLR 1546.
349 For comment on s 10, see Allan [1991] CLJ 131; Miller, CJ [1982] Crim LR 71, p 82; Palmer, S [1992] PL 61.
350 (1996) 22 EHRR 123, at para 39.

public will not be informed on matters which are frequently of grave public interest. These may relate to crime, when the source may be a person involved in, or in some way linked to, forms of criminal activity. Or, they may relate to national security; the source may be a civil servant who is activated by conscience in seeking to disclose an abuse of power by the executive. They may relate to improper practices in large commercial organisations, in which case the source is likely to be an employee, who is prepared to 'blow the whistle'. Such an employee would now have protection from dismissal under the Public Interest Disclosure Act 1998, but nevertheless is likely to want to protect her identity.

Thus, the use of and protection of sources serves a vital function in relation to the role of the media. In recognition of this, journalists view themselves as morally obliged to protect the identity of their sources, a principle which is recognised in cl 15 of the Press Commission Code.[351] Where the media exposes executive malpractice, it performs a vital constitutional role. In general, the speech generated, which relates to the matters mentioned, is of great value in a democracy and would be viewed as of the first importance within Art 10. Nevertheless, the protection it is afforded under UK law, is, it will be argued, inadequate.

Having suggested that source protection is largely in harmony with free speech values, it is necessary to look somewhat more closely at that argument. Information deriving from sources is not *intrinsically* of any greater value than information obtained by other means. Sources, especially those linked to government, may have their own agenda; this may also be true of corporate sources. Source-based information may consist of a slanted mixture of substance and disinformation. The government may well wish to leak information into the public domain for a range of purposes, such as that of 'smearing' political opponents, or those whose published opinions run counter to an important aspect of government policy. The well-known US *Judith Miller* case in 2005,[352] linked to the 'evidence' of WMD justifying the war in Iraq, may provide an example of the latter tendency of governments. In that instance it appeared that Miller's source had leaked information to her deliberately designed to discredit an insider who had challenged evidence of Saddam Hussein's possession of WMD. Clearly, the Bush administration wanted to rely on that evidence in order to justify the war in Iraq. Therefore the administration had a strong motivation to leak information to journalists that in some way aided in its attempts to justify its stance on the war. Miller was eventually found to be in contempt of court when she refused to reveal her sources. This was not an instance – it appeared – in which a journalist was acting to protect her source in order to serve the public interest, but one in which such protection led to the promulgation of misinformation and so was opposed to that interest. On the other hand, Miller went to prison rather than reveal her source, sending a general message to sources about journalists' commitment to their ethical code. As discussed below, the application of the doctrine of proportionality under a strict level of scrutiny can potentially provide a means of determining how far speech values are truly at stake in any given instance.

---

351 For further comment on the Code, see Chapter 9, pp 833–37.
352 *Judith Miller, Petitioner v US and M Cooper and Time inc, Petitioners v US*, Supreme Court (2005) No 04–1508; opinion of the court of appeals (Miller Pet. App. 1a–77a; Cooper Pet. App. 1a–85a) is reported at 397 F 3d 964.

The Norwich Pharmacal *jurisdiction*

Under the common law there are – imprecisely defined – circumstances in which a journalist can be ordered to disclose the identity of a source. Questions may be asked in existing legal proceedings that might lead to disclosure,[353] and orders for disclosure outside such proceedings are based on the jurisdiction established by the House of Lords in *Norwich Pharmacal Co v Customs and Excise Commissioners*.[354] Under the pre-HRA cases, on one view the jurisdiction was exercisable where the defendant (normally this will be the journalist) had become 'mixed up' in the tortious acts of the source so as to facilitate his/her wrongdoing, and as a result had to co-operate in righting the wrongs he had unwittingly facilitated (*Norwich Pharmacal Co*;[355] *British Steel Corp v Granada Television*).[356] The wrongdoing would normally consist of breaching confidence although, as the cases discussed below indicate, there are other possibilities. Typically, a source would divulge confidential information to a journalist, thus potentially incurring liability under the equitable doctrine of breach of confidence.[357] The journalist would become 'mixed' up in the wrong-doing if he or she published the information.

It is generally accepted that the *Norwich Pharmacal* jurisdiction is discretionary, and in its exercise the Court, pre-1981, was both entitled and bound to perform a balancing exercise weighing the public interest in advancing the course of justice against any countervailing feature of the public interest.[358] That balancing exercise is now conducted in accordance with s 10 Contempt of Court.

Section 10 of the Contempt of Court Act

Until the inception of the Human Rights Act, receiving Art 10 into domestic law, very little formal recognition was given in UK law to the constitutional role of the press. However, an exception to this rule was afforded by s 10 of the 1981 Act which provides:

> No court may require a person to disclose, nor is any person guilty of contempt of court for refusing to disclose, the source of information contained in a publication for which he is responsible, unless it be established to the satisfaction of the court

---

353 However, under the common law a court order to disclose sources would not be made in the context of the preliminary proceedings in a defamation action: see *Adam v Fisher* (1914) 110 LT 537; *Hennessy v Wright* (1888) 21 QBD 509. See further, Wilmo, P and Rogers, W (eds) *Gatley on Libel and Slander*, 9th edn, 1998, Sweet and Maxwell, para 30, 112.

354 [1974] AC 133. See Mathews and Malek, *Discovery* (1992) on the law and practice relating to this jurisdiction.

355 [1974] AC 133 at 175, *per* Lord Reid.

356 [1981] AC 1096.

357 See Chapter 9, pp 895–915 for discussion of the doctrine. As the chapter argues, it appears to have undergone a transformation in order to become the tort of misuse of private information. But in terms of commercial and state secrets, it appears to have retained its original form and ingredients (see pp 616–20, 877, 895, below).

358 See [1974] AC 133, 175, *per* Lord Reid; pp 181 and 182, *per* Lord Morris of Borth-y-Guest; pp 188 and 190, *per* Lord Dilhorne; pp 198–99, *per* Lord Cross of Chelsea; and p 205, *per* Lord Kilbrandon.

that disclosure is necessary in the interests of justice or national security or for the prevention of disorder or crime.

The exceptions under s 10 regarding national security and the prevention of crime answer to the exceptions to Art 10. The term 'the interests of justice' is not repeated in para 2 of Art 10, although it may be covered to an extent by the term 'the preservation of the authority and impartiality of the judiciary' and, possibly, by the 'rights of others' exception. The key issue, therefore, is whether the interpretation of the term 'necessary' is compatible with the Strasbourg view of what is necessary in a democratic society in order to further those aims.

Section 10 does not provide any new power to require a journalist to disclose the identity of a source. As Lord Diplock put it in *Secretary of State for Defence v Guardian Newspapers*,[359] the leading case: 'Section 10 confers no powers upon a court additional to those powers, whether discretionary or not, which already existed at common law or under rules of court, to order disclosure of sources of information, its effect is restrictive only.' It was also determined in that case that s 10 will apply to the disclosure of information which might reveal the identity of the source. Thus, s 10 creates a presumption in favour of journalists who wish to protect their sources, which is, however, subject to four wide exceptions, the widest of which arises where the interests of justice require that disclosure should be made. It was found in *Secretary of State for Defence v Guardian Newspapers*[360] that disclosure of the identity of the source would only be ordered where this was necessary in order to identify him or her; if other means of identification were reasonably readily available, they should be used. On the other hand, this did not mean that all other means of inquiry which might reveal the identity of the source must be exhausted before disclosure would be ordered. The term 'necessary' was found in *re an Inquiry under the Companies Security (Insider Dealing) Act 1985*[361] to mean something less than indispensable, but something more than useful. In *Guardian Newspapers* a civil servant, who considered that Parliament was being misled as regards the arrival of cruise missiles in Britain, sent a photocopy of a memorandum regarding the timing to the *Guardian*, who published. The Secretary of state wished to discover the identity of the civil servant and sought the return of the photocopy, since it would reveal the identity. The Secretary of State, the plaintiff, claimed that the national security exception under s 10 applied on the basis that the fact of a secret document with restricted circulation relating to defence having come into the hands of a national newspaper was of great significance in relation to the maintenance of national security. The minority in the House of Lords were not convinced by this evidence, but the majority accepted it, Lord Bridge stating that any threat to national security ought to be eliminated by the speediest and most effective means possible. The identity of the source was duly discovered when the photocopy was returned and she was prosecuted.[362] The majority, therefore, took the traditional stance of failing to afford a full scrutiny to imprecise claims of a threat to national security made by the executive. However, the House of Lords did suggest that more convincing evidence would be needed in future.

359 [1984] 3 All ER 601; [1985] AC 339, 347, HL.
360 [1985] AC 339.
361 [1988] 1 All ER 203.
362 See Chapter 7, p 593.

The House of Lords clarified the nature of the balancing exercise to be carried out under s 10 in *X v Morgan Grampian Publishers*.[363] A confidential plan was stolen from the plaintiffs, a company named Tetra; information apparently from the plan was given by an unidentified source by phone to William Goodwin, a journalist. The plaintiffs applied for an order requiring Goodwin to disclose the source and sought discovery of his notes of the phone conversation in order to discover his or her identity. The House of Lords had to consider the application of s 10 to these facts. It found that when a journalist relies on s 10 in order to protect a source, it must be determined whether the applicant's right to take legal action against the source is outweighed by the journalist's interest in maintaining the promise of confidentiality made to him or her. The House of Lords took into account various factors in balancing these two considerations, including the threat to the plaintiffs' business and the complicity of the source in 'a gross breach of confidentiality'. Lord Bridge, with whom the other Law Lords unanimously agreed, found that the interest of the plaintiffs in identifying the source outweighed the interests of the journalist in protecting it. Goodwin refused to reveal the identity of the source and was fined £5,000 for refusing to obey the court's order.

The findings in the Lords were significant since they made it clear that a newspaper publishing information deriving from an employee of the plaintiff body in question would very frequently be ordered to disclose his or her identity, since the factors identified by Lord Bridge would almost always apply. In such instances there would almost always have been a breach of confidence (the judiciary are remarkably unwilling, in this context, to find that the public interest defence could have been made out)[364] and there would almost always be a threat, based on speculation, to the company. It would almost always be virtually impossible to rule that threat out, and the judiciary, as noted earlier, have not required any evidence to accept that the threat actually exists in any given instance: the mere fact that one disclosure has occurred is apparently sufficient. Clearly, an employee who has leaked information on one occasion might leak it again, but the likelihood of that occurring requires scrutiny, depending on the facts.

Thus, following the *Morgan Grampian* findings, the 'balancing' exercise appeared to be virtually a misnomer since once the factors identified were in the equation, it was unclear that they would ever be likely to be outweighed by the value of the information.[365] The term 'necessary' was being afforded very little weight: the key question was in reality whether the 'interests of justice' could be viewed as being at stake at all, and, as contended above, they inevitably would be. The Lords did find that very clear cases of exposing iniquity might mean that disclosure would not be ordered on the basis that the factors identified could be outweighed, but they made it clear that in most instances – outside such clear-cut cases – disclosure would be ordered. Lord Bridge mentioned the interest in protecting sources. However, when it

---

363   [1991] AC 1; [1991] 2 All ER 1, HL.
364   See pp 437–38 below.
365   However, in *Chief Constable of Leicestershire v Gravelli* [1997] EMLR 543, DC, a case concerning revelations of malpractice in the police, it was found that in the circumstances of the case in question – disciplinary proceedings – it appeared that the interests of justice would not in fact be served by requiring the journalist to name her source. In other words, there could be no necessity to make such a demand when it was of viewed as of no, or virtually no, utility in the particular context that arose.

came to conducting the balancing exercise, he considered that the public interest value of material would be a relevant factor, but he did *not* avert to the *general* and constant public interest in protecting sources in order to serve the interests of investigative journalism. That was the key error in the analysis. He did not set *that* factor against the need of the company to identify the untrustworthy employee. Since both interests would almost always be present in a source disclosure case they would always tend to need to be balanced against each other.

When Goodwin took his case to Strasbourg, it was made clear, it is argued, that the House of Lords had indeed failed to give proper weight to the term 'necessary' in s 10. Goodwin applied to the European Commission on Human Rights[366] which gave its opinion that the order against Goodwin violated his right to freedom of expression under Art 10 of the Convention on Human Rights. When the case came before the Court it found that there was a vital public interest in protecting journalistic sources, since so doing was essential to the maintenance of a free press.[367] Thus, the margin of appreciation was circumscribed by that interest. It considered that limitations placed on the confidentiality of such sources would require the most careful scrutiny. Was the vital public interest in protecting sources outweighed by Tetra's interest in eliminating the threat of damage due to the dissemination of confidential material? The injunction was already effective in preventing the dissemination of such material and therefore the additional restriction on freedom of expression entailed by the disclosure order was not supported by sufficient reasons to satisfy the requirements of Art 10(2). Tetra's interest in disclosure, including its interest in unmasking a disloyal employee, was not outweighed by the public interest in the protection of journalistic sources. Taking these matters into account, it was found that the order was disproportionate to the purpose in question and therefore could not be said to be necessary. A breach of Art 10 was therefore established. The Court found:

> The court recalls that freedom of expression constitutes one of the essential foundations of a democratic society and that the safeguards to be afforded to the press are of particular importance. Protection of journalistic sources is one of the basic conditions for press freedom, as is reflected in the laws and the professional codes of conduct in a number of contracting states and is affirmed in several international instruments on journalistic freedoms. Without such protection, sources may be deterred from assisting the press in informing the public on matters of public interest. As a result the vital public watchdog role of the press may be undermined and the ability of the press to provide accurate and reliable information may be adversely affected. Having regard to the importance of the protection of journalistic sources for press freedom in a democratic society and the potentially chilling effect an order of source disclosure has on the exercise of that freedom, such a measure cannot be compatible with article 10 of the Convention unless it is justified by an overriding requirement in the public interest.[368]

366 *Goodwin v UK* (1994) No 17488/90 Com Rep.
367 *Goodwin v UK* (1996) 22 EHRR 123. See also *Fressoz and Roire v France* (1999) 5 BHRC 654.
368 At para 39.

Thus *Goodwin* made it clear that in *this* context the strictest form of scrutiny should be afforded to the application of the tests for proportionality. As Chapter 4 indicates, less strict forms can be seen as applicable.[369] *Goodwin* relied largely on speech/harm balancing as the proportionality test.[370] In other words, the seriousness of the harm caused by the disclosure of Tetra's confidential information was weighed up against the weightiness of the expression interest. The Court insisted on looking closely at the State's case regarding the degree of harm that Tetra had suffered, and took a view of it that differed significantly from that of the state. The interference was very severe, bearing in mind the significance for free expression of protection for journalistic sources. In coming to this conclusion the Court applied a strict test for scrutinising the balance between the two interests – had it conceded a wider margin of appreciation to the national authorities, it might have been satisfied that the balance struck between the two was not manifestly unreasonable. Thus the Court found that the proportionality test had not been met.

The Court did not fully refer to the tests for necessity and proportionality that answer to the *de Freitas*[371] three-stage test discussed in Chapter 4,[372] but it is worth placing the facts of *Goodwin* within that reasoning framework in order to demonstrate that the application of the key *Goodwin* proportionality test, as opposed to the key *de Freitas* tests, may well lead to a different outcome. Following *de Freitas*, it is first necessary to ask whether a significant and pressing interest, falling within one or more of the Art 10(2) exceptions, has been identified since so doing is part of the test for 'necessary' under para 2. That is the first test, and impliedly it was not met in *Goodwin* since the Court did not find that the harm caused to Tetra outweighed the value of protecting the source. The second and third *de Freitas* tests cover the issue of proportionality. Under the second it is necessary to consider the suitability of the interference in question – the extent to which it is rationally connected to the aim pursued. In this instance, the source disclosure order constituted the interference; the Court did not address this question directly, but in many source disclosure cases this is a relevant issue. It is relevant, for example, where an injunction would probably be effective in preventing further disclosures, or where, due to the circumstances, little likelihood of a further disclosure by the same source arose. In *Goodwin* an injunction had already been obtained and the Court could have adverted specifically to the question of its efficacy in the circumstances.

The third *de Freitas* test concerns the need to choose the least intrusive measure – the measure that creates a minimal degree of harm to the primary right consistent with affording protection to the aim pursued. The seriousness of the interference has to be balanced against the importance of the aim sought to be pursued. This is means/end balancing – if there is another way of achieving the aim pursued that is less restrictive, it should be used. This can also be termed 'the least intrusive' means test. The Court's judgment might be viewed as implying that this test had not been met since a less intrusive measure – the injunction – was available and had been used. The problem is

---

369 See Chapter 4, pp 276–77.
370 See Chapter 4, pp 286–89.
371 From the decision of the Privy Council in *de Freitas v Permanent Secretary of Ministry of Agriculture, Fisheries, Lands and Housing* [1999] 1 AC 69, 80.
372 See Chapter 4, p 286.

that this test does not lend itself readily to the principled analysis of the harm caused in relation to the value of the speech that can occur under the *Goodwin* speech/harm balancing test.[373] It remained to be seen whether the domestic courts would apply this test under a strict level of scrutiny.

In order to comply with this ruling, it might have been thought to be necessary to amend the 'interests of justice' head of s 10. The then Conservative Government stated, however, in response to the ruling, that it had no plans to amend the 1981 Act.[374] Thus, before the HRA came fully into force it appeared that under s 3(1) HRA, when a suitable case arose, s 10 would be found to require re-interpretation: clearly, the established interpretation of the term 'necessary' did not accord with the test for necessity under Art 10(2). But in any event it was probable that the judges would react to the ruling in *Goodwin,* regardless of the HRA, although there was subsequently disagreement among them as to the effect of *Goodwin*. The argument that the UK stance on source disclosure differed from that taken at Strasbourg was far from fully accepted.[375]

Therefore it appeared to be quite possible that before the HRA was in force, the judges would already have brought about harmony between the established domestic interpretation of s 10 and the demands of Art 10 as indicated by *Goodwin*. However, in *Camelot Group Ltd v Centaur Communications*[376] the Court of Appeal allowed the 'necessary in the interests of justice' exception under s 10 a scope which was arguably as wide as that afforded to it in *X v Morgan Grampian*. The company, Camelot, runs the UK national lottery. An anonymous source sent Camelot's draft accounts to the newspaper, which published them. It appeared that Camelot was misleading the public regarding the dedication of the funds generated to charitable concerns. Camelot sought return of the documents in order to identify the source, and the newspaper relied on s 10.

Camelot had already obtained an injunction preventing any further dissemination of its accounts. Once the injunction had been obtained against Centaur, any other newspaper that published information covered by it would have risked liability for contempt of court as a result of the contempt ruling in the *Spycatcher* case, discussed in Chapter 7.[377] Therefore the disclosure order might have been viewed as disproportionate to the end in view. This was found to be the case in *Goodwin* in similar circumstances. The significance of the information itself might also have been taken into account in reaching this finding, since it concerned the accountability of a large and very profitable company, engaged, at least to an extent, in funding public and community services. On the *Goodwin* model the Court of Appeal could have balanced the weightiness of the expression interest against the degree of harm caused. In relation to the expression interest it could have taken account, not only of the significance of protecting sources, but also of the issues of public interest that are raised by the question of the proportion of lottery money that is diverted to community projects, and the like, and the proportion

373 See further Chapter 4, pp 287–90. This depends on the interpretation of the means/end balancing test. If the *nature* and extent of the interference is examined, it overlaps with the speech/harm balancing test.

374 *Hansard* (Lords) 13 April 1996 Vol 571, Col 6147, Written Answer.

375 See fn 388 above.

376 [1998] EMLR 1; [1999] QB 124.

377 See above, pp 369–79.

which is straightforward profit. There is clearly an important political dimension to Camelot's activities that might not arise to the same extent in respect of the activities of many private companies. In relation to the question of harm, it could have taken account of the effect of the injunction that was already in place.

Schiemann LJ, with whom the other judges concurred, concentrated, not on the public interest value of the information, but on the speculative harm to Camelot that might arise in future if the employee who had leaked the information, perpetrated further leaks:

> There is no threat now posed to the plaintiffs by further disclosure of the draft accounts. Such threat as there was has been dealt with by injunction or undertaking in relation to that material and the passage of time. There is however a continuing threat of damage of a type which did not feature significantly in the *Goodwin* case or in the *X v Morgan Grampian* case ... Clearly there is unease and suspicion amongst the employees of the company which inhibits good working relationships. Clearly there is a risk that an employee who has proved untrustworthy in one regard may be untrustworthy in a different respect and reveal the name of, say, a public figure who has won a huge lottery prize.[378]

This speculative threat of damage was found to be sufficient to outweigh the interest in protecting sources. On the question of necessity the court found that the interests of Camelot in ensuring the loyalty of its employees and ex-employees should outweigh the public importance attached to the protection of sources. In the present instance, the Court considered that in any event, there was no public interest in protecting the source.[379] The Court of Appeal took the view that in reaching this finding it was applying the same test of necessity as was applied by the European Court of Human Rights in *Goodwin*.

Clearly, the term 'necessary in the interests of justice' used in s 10 leaves room for varying interpretations. Nevertheless, the determinations as to necessity in *Camelot* and in *Goodwin* do not, it is contended, afford equal weight to the role of the media in informing the public. In asking whether the interference in question was proportionate to the legitimate aim pursued, the Strasbourg Court in *Goodwin* unpacked the 'harm' apparently caused, and applied a very high weight to the speech interest. In *Camelot* the court did not consider the question of proportionality as a distinct aspect of necessity and did not accord a high weight to source protection or look closely at the harm caused by the leak. Further, since the European Court of Human Rights allowed the domestic authorities a margin of appreciation (albeit highly circumscribed) in determining the issue of proportionality in *Goodwin*, one might have expected an even stricter view of the issue to be taken at the domestic level. It is argued that this threat did not provide a weighty enough basis for finding that the key *Goodwin* test for proportionality was satisfied, taking account of the strict scrutiny required. Bearing the use of the injunction in mind, it could also have been argued that the *de Freitas* means/end balancing test was not satisfied. In fact in *Goodwin* there was the same speculative harm.

---

378 At p 138.
379 See e.g. p 139 of the judgment.

Greater weight was, however, accorded to the term 'necessary' in two further pre-HRA decisions and the balance struck was more in accord with that endorsed in *Goodwin*. Both concerned apparent leaks from lawyers' offices. In *Saunders v Punch Ltd*,[380] in which an injunction had been granted to restrain use of the information in question, it was found that the interests of justice were not so pressing as to require the statutory privilege against disclosure to be overridden. Saunders had been the subject of interviews by the DTI in relation to a criminal prosecution that had eventually been challenged under Art 6 at Strasbourg.[381] No report made by the inspectors to the DTI had been published, but the inspectors' deliberations had got to that stage at which extracts of their provisional findings had been sent to those persons potentially affected by them, including Mr Saunders. He took legal advice and had a number of meetings with solicitors and leading counsel. An article appeared in *Punch* magazine that led Mr Saunders to think that confidential material as to communications between him and his solicitors had been leaked and he began proceedings against *Punch*. An injunction restraining further publication was immediately granted and its continuation until judgment was not resisted by *Punch*. However, Mr Saunders wanted *Punch* to be compelled to disclose its source for the information in the article. The article stated that Mr Saunders was expected 'to fight tooth and nail to prevent publication of the report by DTI inspectors' and it then raised the question why that should be the case, concluding that Saunders was trying to protect his earning power at the last stages of his career.[382]

The judge, Lindsay J, found that an issue of legal professional confidence arose, but that there was some public interest in knowing why, so many years after the relevant events, no report had been published regarding the DTI prosecutions, a matter that presumptively should be reported upon by a free press. He also took into account the more general public interest against disclosure, as summed up in *Goodwin v UK*. He found that there was a relatively insubstantial risk of foreseeable future damage and a relative unlikelihood of repetition. The 'residual threat of damage through dissemination'[383] was much less weighty, he found, than it had been in *X Ltd*.[384] He found that the great importance of the protection of sources constituted 'a very substantial counterweight' and, conducting the balancing act under s 10, he found that relief going beyond that provided by the injunction already granted, in the interests of justice, was not of such preponderating importance as to override the statutory privilege against disclosure. This was a pre-HRA case, but Lindsay J conducted, without using that terminology, the speech/harm balancing act required by the proportionality test from *Goodwin*.

In *John v Express Newspapers*,[385] a similar approach was taken by the Court of Appeal. The first four claimants, who included the well-known singer, Elton John, were involved in litigation in which their solicitors, the fifth claimants, had instructed

---

380 [1998] 1 WLR 986.
381 *Saunders v UK* (1996) 23 EHRR 313.
382 The article went on: 'The answer lies in previous unpublished records of meetings between Saunders and his then lawyers in 1996. The documents show that Saunders was worried that the DTI would choose to publish immediately after the verdict from the European Court last October and that his real fear was that this would affect his earning power in the last few years of his business career.'
383 He took the phrase from *Goodwin v UK* (1996) 22 EHRR 123, 145.
384 [1991] AC 1, discussed above.
385 [2000] 1 WLR 1931; [2000] 3 All ER 257.

counsel to advise them. A copy of counsel's draft advice was leaked to a journalist; the chambers did not institute an internal inquiry into the leak. A source disclosure order was made, but on appeal Lord Woolf, in giving the leading judgment, found that disclosure of a journalist's source might be necessary to protect the interests of justice pursuant to s 10 of the 1981 Act, but that, before the courts would require journalists to break what they regarded as a most important professional obligation to protect a source, the minimum requirement was that other means of identifying that source should be explored; it could not merely be assumed that it would not be possible to identify the culprit. He indicated that the failure of the plaintiffs to take other steps to find out the identity of the source (such as instituting an internal inquiry) was very significant since it affected the assessment of what was 'necessary' in the circumstances. He found that the first instance judge had attached insufficient importance to the failure of counsel's chambers to conduct an inquiry into the leak and too much significance to the threat that that single incident posed to legal confidentiality.

Therefore the claimants had not established that disclosure of the journalist's source was necessary in the interests of justice and, in any event, the judge should have exercised his discretion to refuse disclosure. Lord Woolf laid emphasis on the role of the press in exposing corruption and stressed the importance of protecting sources in order that that role should be fulfilled. These findings clearly refer to aspects of the *Goodwin* tests for proportionality discussed above.

Thus it may be concluded that these two decisions took some account of such tests, rather than focusing on identifying and stressing the countervailing need to order source disclosure to further the aim in question. However, the different context in these two cases, as compared to that in *Camelot* appeared to be of relevance. *John* and *Saunders* did not concern an employee of a company – someone who might potentially leak confidential information in future. In both instances it appeared probable that the leak would not recur. Thus in both instances the judges seemed to view themselves as free to impose a strict standard of scrutiny: they were not trammelled by the concern to protect a business from an untrustworthy employee – the 'ticking bomb' notion – that exercised the courts so much in *X v Morgan-Grampian* and in *Camelot*.

The discussion indicates that although there were signs that a different balance was being struck between the value of protecting of sources and the interests of justice in the immediate pre-HRA period, the domestic approach was still flawed. In deciding whether or not to order disclosure of sources the test of necessity demanded that the Court then had to balance the public interest in confidentiality of sources against that of advancing the cause in question. But the interpretation of the test of 'necessary in the interests of . . .' did not appear to depend sufficiently on differentiation between the concepts of necessity and proportionality, especially in *Camelot*. The pre-HRA test was not therefore fully in harmony with that under Art 10(2) since the factor of proportionality was not being given full weight. It was also apparent that the test for necessity appeared to differ depending on the exception being invoked, a weaker test operating under the 'national security' exception than under that concerning the 'interests of justice'. This stance has some basis in the Strasbourg jurisprudence under Art 10(2),[386] but it is nevertheless unclear that the readiness with which this weaker test has been satisfied in this context would be acceptable at Strasbourg.

---

386 See above, p 336, and compare with Chapter 6, p 464.

Post-Human Rights Act jurisprudence

It has been argued that a number of the leading pre-HRA cases – *Secretary of State for Defence v Guardian Newspapers, British Steel* and *Camelot* – reveal that a media-friendly stance was not adopted by the judiciary in respect of the step-by-step analytical exercise to be taken in a source disclosure case. Those steps are: first, that jurisdiction must be established; second, that the applicability of one or more of the s 10 exceptions must be determined; and third, that the necessity of ordering disclosure to serve the aim of the exception must be considered. As cases arose under the HRA, bearing in mind the importance accorded at Strasbourg to the protection of sources under Art 10 as a vital part of the media's role, it was reasonable to expect at the least that the reasoning on the question of necessity – the third step – would be affected by a determination to afford a stronger weight to the various media interests at stake[387] by applying the *Goodwin* test for proportionality under a strict form of scrutiny. It appeared possible that an order to disclose the identity of a source would only be obtained in the most exceptional of circumstances and that Art 10 under the Human Rights Act would satisfy the role that had been assigned by some to s 10 of the 1981 Act, but which it had not fulfilled.

Under the HRA attention was always likely to turn exclusively to the s 10 term 'necessary', which now clearly covered the Art 10 tests of necessity and proportionality. It was in this respect, after *Goodwin*, that Art 10 of the Convention most clearly demanded a greater protection for sources than had been provided under domestic law. This was partly due to the Strasbourg Court's insistence on the constant, unvarying interest in protecting sources, and partly to the strictness of the standard of scrutiny applicable to the use of the tests for proportionality. The argument that *Goodwin* established a stricter standard than *Morgan Grampian* was put forward in *Camelot Group plc v Centaur Communications Ltd*[388] and rejected by Schiemann LJ; he held that the different result merely reflected the fact that different courts can reach different conclusions while applying the same legal principles to the same facts. However, Sedley LJ commented on this point in the post-HRA decision in *Interbrew SA v Financial Times Ltd*:[389] 'the decisions of the European Court of Human Rights demonstrate that the freedom of the press has in the past carried greater weight in Strasbourg that it has in the courts of this country'.

But it was already apparent that the strong established domestic traditions governing the approach of the courts ran counter to the Strasbourg jurisprudence. Therefore the possibility of departure from the jurisprudence, while appearing to adhere to it in a superficial or tokenistic fashion, became apparent. The key issue, therefore, in the post-HRA era was whether the interpretation of the term 'necessary' in s 10 would become fully consonant with the Strasbourg view of what is 'necessary in a democratic society' in order to further the aims in question.

In *Interbrew SA v Financial Times Ltd*[390] the claimant, the company Interbrew, maker of Stella Artois lager, was contemplating a possible takeover bid for another company, S. Interbrew's advisers prepared a presentation which they submitted to the company.

---

387 See, for example, Feldman, D, in *Civil Liberties and Human Rights*, 2nd edn, 2002, p 856.
388 [1999] QB 124 (pp 415–16 above) at p 135.
389 [2002] EMLR 24 at para 97.
390 [2002] EMLR 24; [2002] EWCA Civ 274, CA.

Subsequently, an unidentified person obtained a copy of the presentation. The document referred to the intention of Interbrew to launch the bid. Most of the document was genuine, but whoever leaked it also doctored it to include a fabricated offer price and timetable. He or she then sent copies of the doctored version to various news media, including the defendants. The defendants then published articles about the takeover bid. The claimants applied for a *Norwich Pharmacal* order requiring the defendants to deliver up the copies of the presentation they had received so that there could be an attempt to identify the source. The defendants invoked s 10 of the Contempt of Court Act 1981, but the judge made the order sought. He took the view that the doctored leak had been perpetrated in order to affect S's share price. Since this would, on the face of it, be a criminal act, he considered that it would be in the public interest for Interbrew to be given the documents to try to trace the source. The defendants appealed.

The appeal therefore concerned the scope of the right of a newspaper to refuse to reveal its sources within the bounds of Art 10, applied under ss 3 and 6 HRA. The source had passed on information which he must have known was confidential, and therefore a breach of confidence was made out. Each defendant, by disseminating the leaked information, had innocently lent itself to the source's wrongful purpose. It was found that the jurisdiction recognised in *Norwich Pharmacal Co v Customs and Excise Commissioners*[391] allowed the Court to make an order requiring the yielding up of the documents. The appellants argued that even if there was jurisdiction to grant the order it should not have been granted, taking into account s 10 of the Contempt of Court Act 1981 and Art 10 ECHR, under the HRA.

The Court began by considering the effect of reading and applying s 10, so far as possible, compatibly with the Convention rights under s 3(1) HRA. Sedley LJ said, on the question of the meaning of the term 'interests of justice' in s 10 of the 1981 Act, that the Court of Appeal in *Ashworth*[392] (discussed below) had followed the line of authority now accepted as dominant which attributes a broader meaning to the phrase 'the interests of justice' in s 10 of the Contempt of Court Act 1981 than was initially given to it in *Secretary of State for Defence v Guardian Newspapers*,[393] where Lord Diplock had limited it to the technical interests of the administration of justice in court proceedings. He said: 'By common consent our approach is that of Lord Bridge in *X v Morgan-Grampian*:[394] the phrase is large enough to include the exercise of legal rights and self-protection from legal wrongs, whether or not by court action.' He further found that the term 'interests of justice' in s 10 means 'interests that are justiciable' and said that he could not envisage any such interest that would not fall within one or more of the catalogue of legitimate aims in Art 10(2). This approach to the first and second steps to be taken in a source disclosure case was the expected and readily predictable one.

The Court went on to consider whether the use of the disclosure order was necessary and proportionate to the aim in view – to protect the interests of justice, and one or more of the Art 10(2) aims. Lord Justice Sedley went on to find that the term 'necessary' within s 10 must mean what is 'necessary in a democratic society' within Art 10(2).

391 [1974] AC 133.
392 [2001] 1 WLR 515 1 All ER 991, CA.
393 [1985] AC 339 at p 350.
394 [1999] 1 AC 1 at p 43.

He found that this meant, 'to be necessary within what is now the meaning of section 10, disclosure must meet a pressing social need, must be the only practical way of doing so, must be accompanied by safeguards against abuse and must not be such as to destroy the essence of the primary right. He also asked whether the importance of disclosure outweighed the public interest in protecting journalist's sources. He went on to find that it was clear that a democratic society accepts the need to protect press sources. Therefore it must be possible to identify a strong countervailing 'pressing social need' to set on the other side of the scale. The need was, he found, in terms of s 10, to enable Interbrew to restrain by court action any further breach of confidence by the source and possibly to recover damages for losses already sustained. In terms of Art 10(2) it was to protect the rights of Interbrew. No less invasive alternative had to be available – which appeared to be the case. So there were two significant interests on both sides of the scale. On the one hand, then, it was found that there was 'the legitimacy of Interbrew's intended resort to law'. On the other there was a constant public interest in the confidentiality of media sources.

The critical factor identified by the court in determining where the balance lay between the two interests was the source's evident purpose. Sedley LJ found that it was clearly a malevolent one. The public interest in protecting the source of such a leak was not, he considered, sufficient to withstand the countervailing public interest in letting Interbrew seek justice in the courts against the source. Therefore the order of disclosure was upheld, and the House of Lords refused leave to appeal[395] on the ground that the issues had been dealt with in the *Ashworth* case, below.

As will be contended in more detail below, this judgment did not fully apply the *Goodwin* speech/harm balancing test. It did not examine the two interests at stake in a sufficiently rigorous fashion. In particular it appeared to give less weight to the unvarying and strong interest in protecting sources than *Goodwin* did – in a fairly similar situation – although in *Goodwin* the source did not seem to be activated by malice. As part of the subsequent saga, lawyers for Interbrew immediately wrote to the organisations demanding that the document be handed over. Interbrew went on to ask the High Court to seize the *Guardian*'s assets for refusing to hand over a copy of the leaked document. However, after an outcry against the company in the media and in government, which might have affected its brand image, Interbrew withdrew its threat to seize the assets. It announced that it had abandoned its legal action against the *Guardian* and three other media organisations, the *Financial Times*, *The Times*, the *Independent* and Reuters, in the attempt to recover the leaked documents.[396] The newspapers stated that they intended to take the case to the European Court of Human Rights.[397]

The decision attracted adverse comment from a range of sources in the press, from civil libertarians, the House of Commons and abroad.[398] An interesting analogy might

---

395 On 11 July 2002.
396 On July 26 2002.
397 See the *Guardian* 12 July 2002.
398 Aidan White, general secretary of the Brussels-based International Federation of Journalists, said that the decision created further intolerable pressure on journalistic ethics from corporate interests. John Wadham, the (then) Director of *Liberty*, said that the principle of press freedom, 'a fundamental protection for democracy', would be substantially eroded if journalists had to disclose their sources.

be drawn between Interbrew's actions in seeking to seize the *Guardian*'s assets and those of the Turkish Government in the Strasbourg case of *Ozgur Gundem v Turkey*.[399] The Court found in that instance that a search operation at the newspaper's premises, which resulted in newspaper production being disrupted for two days, constituted a serious interference with the applicants' freedom of expression under Art 10. No justification had been provided for the seizure of the newspaper's archives, documentation and library. The Turkish case was concerned with state actions, Interbrew with those of a large corporate body. But arguably media freedom was severely threatened in both instances. Judges in a mature democracy such as that in the UK already recognise the threat posed by the *State* to that freedom; they appear to be less ready at present to recognise the threat posed by multi-nationals.

In the ruling in *Ashworth Hospital Authority v MGN Ltd*[400] a somewhat stricter approach was taken, under the HRA, to the interests of the media in protecting sources, although the process of reasoning and the outcome were similar to those in *Interbrew*. The appeal concerned the right of a newspaper to refuse to reveal its sources. It arose from the publication of an article in the *Daily Mirror* which included extracts from the medical records of Ian Brady (one of the Moors murderers), a patient at Ashworth Security Hospital ('Ashworth'). He was, at the time of the publication, engaged on a hunger strike which had received a great deal of publicity.[401] In April 2000, Rougier J ordered the defendant, MGN Ltd, the publisher of the *Daily Mirror*, to make and serve upon the authority a witness statement aimed at identifying the source who had passed on the medical records.[402]

In the course of their appeal against that order, MGN contended that Rougier J had no jurisdiction to grant the order, but that if he did have such jurisdiction, he was not entitled to do so in the circumstances of this case. The *Daily Mirror* reporter stated that he did not know the identity of the initial source of the information, but that he assumed it to be an employee of Ashworth. However, he accepted that he did know the identity of the intermediary who supplied the material to him. It was also accepted

Chris Mullin, chairman of the all-party Commons Home Affairs committee, commented: 'The right to protect sources is a fundamental part of a free press. I am very disappointed that the courts have not recognised this.' Tom Watson, a member of the all-party Commons Home Affairs Select Committee, said: 'This legal action is corporate bullying.' Jeremy Dear, General Secretary of the National Union of Journalists, attacked the decision: 'The idea that a brewer is prepared to send a team of accountants to sequestrate and run a newspaper is one of the biggest threats to press freedom for decades.' See the *Guardian* website: guardian.co.uk.

399 (2001) 31 EHRR 49. See further pp 446–47, below.

400 [2002] 1 WLR 2033; [2002] 4 All ER 193 HL; [2001] 1 WLR 515 1 All ER 991, CA.

401 On 2 February 2000, Ian Brady obtained permission to apply for judicial review, in order to challenge the continuing decision to force-feed him (see *R (Brady) v Ashworth Hospital Authority* [2000] Lloyd's Med R 355; (2001) 58 BMLR 173). Maurice Kay J ruled that force-feeding was lawful since it was reasonably administered as part of the medical treatment given for the mental disorder from which Ian Brady was suffering.

402 The statement, to be served within two working days, demanded of the publisher that it: (i) explain how it came to be in the possession or control of any medical records kept by the claimant in respect of Ian Brady whether that possession or control be of originals, copies or extracts; (ii) identify any employee of the claimant and the name of the person or persons (and any address, telephone and fax numbers known for such a person or persons) who were involved in the defendant acquiring possession or control of the said records.

that knowledge of the intermediary would in all probability lead to the identity of the original source. The reporter had previously dealt with the intermediary on the understanding that he would be paid for stories supplied.

It was found by the Court of Appeal (and was not later disputed in the House of Lords), that it was overwhelmingly likely that the source provided the intermediary with a print-out from Ashworth's computer database which was used to record data about patients ('PACIS'). This meant that the source was probably an employee of the authority. The importance of the confidentiality of medical records was emphasised when a new member of staff was engaged at Ashworth and the contract of employment included a confidentiality clause. It was accepted that leaks to the press have a detrimental effect on security, treatment of patients and staff morale for a number of reasons: they may inhibit proper recording of information about patients; may deter patients from providing sensitive information about themselves; may damage the patient-doctor relationship, which rests on trust; may lead to assaults by patients on a patient about whom information is disclosed; may create an atmosphere of distrust amongst staff, which is detrimental to efficient and co-operative work; and they may give rise to fear of future leaks.

The Court of Appeal found that the jurisdiction to order the disclosure of the identity of a wrongdoer did not have to be confined to cases involving tort but should be of general application. The Court considered the approach that should be taken to s 10, taking into account the requirements of the HRA. It considered that there is no difference in principle between English law and Art 10,[403] and that in interpreting s 10 the Court should, where possible, (a) equate the specific purposes for which disclosure of the source was permitted under s 10 with 'legitimate aims' under Art 10 of the Convention, and (b) apply the same test of necessity as that applied by the European Court. Applying that test to the instant case, it was found that in general the disclosure of confidential medical records to the press was misconduct which was contrary to the public interest. The exceptional circumstances making this argument more compelling were stressed: it was said that there is a very clear need to protect patient confidentiality, especially the confidentiality of medical records, which should be safeguarded in any democratic society and, further, in this case it was considered that there was a risk of further leaks. So the Court of Appeal dismissed the appeal and disclosure was ordered.

When MGN appealed, it argued in the House of Lords that the order should not have been granted, taking account of s 10 of the 1981 Act and Art 10. The House of Lords found that both s 10 and Art 10 have a common purpose in seeking to enhance the freedom of the press by protecting journalistic sources. They relied on the approach of the European Court of Human Rights as to the role of Art 10 as set out by the

---

403 It found that two views had been expressed in the House of Lords as to the meaning of the expression 'interests of justice'. As discussed above, in *Defence Secretary v Guardian Newspapers* [1985] AC 339 at 350 Lord Diplock had sought to confine the exception to the administration of justice in the course of existing court proceedings. But in *X Ltd v Morgan Grampian* [1991] 1 AC 1 at 43 Lord Bridge had found that this interpretation was too narrow and that the exception included facilitating the exercise of legal rights even where resort to legal proceedings was not occurring, and whether or not it would need to do so. The Court of Appeal favoured Lord Bridge's much broader approach.

Court in *Goodwin v United Kingdom*,[404] and in particular on these phrases from the judgment:

> Protection of journalistic sources is one of the basic conditions for press freedom. . ... source disclosure cannot be compatible with article 10 of the Convention unless it is justified by an overriding requirement in the public interest.[405]

It was accepted that the same approach should be applied equally to s 10 since Art 10 is part of domestic law under the Human Rights Act. It had to be determined whether it was a necessary precondition of the exercise of the jurisdiction to make an order of disclosure that the applicant (Ashworth) should have begun, or had an intention to begin, legal proceedings in respect of the allegedly wrongful act against the source. The Lords relied on the speeches in *British Steel Corp v Granada Television Ltd*[406] and in particular on the judgments of Lord Denning MR,[407] and of Templeman LJ,[408] in the Court of Appeal in finding that this was unnecessary. Lord Woolf confirmed that the approach of Lord Bridge in *Morgan Grampian* was the correct one.[409] In other words, it was confirmed that s 10 allows for the making of orders in the interests of justice, and such interests are widely defined – they are not confined to the administration of justice within legal proceedings and it is not necessary that such proceedings should be brought. This was, clearly, a crucial finding, demonstrating that, despite the effect of the HRA and Art 10, the Lords were determined to keep open the possibility of seeking source disclosure orders in a very wide range of circumstances.

The Lords considered whether the use of the disclosure order was necessary and proportionate to the aim in view – to protect the interests of justice, under s10 and Art 10. On the interpretation of the term 'necessary in the interests of justice', Lord Woolf said:

> Construing the phrase 'in the interests of justice' in [the sense determined upon] immediately emphasises the importance of the balancing exercise. It will not be sufficient, per se, for a party seeking disclosure of a source protected by section 10 to show merely that he will be unable without disclosure to exercise the legal right or avert the threatened legal wrong on which he bases his claim in order to establish the necessity of disclosure. The judge's task will always be to weigh in the scales the importance of enabling the ends of justice to be attained in the circumstances of the particular case on the one hand against the importance of protecting the source on the other hand. In this balancing exercise it is only if the judge is satisfied that disclosure in the interests of justice is of such preponderating importance as to override the statutory privilege against disclosure that the threshold of necessity will be reached.[410]

---

404 (1996) 22 EHRR 123.
405 At para 39.
406 [1981] AC 1096.
407 At p 1127.
408 At p 1132.
409 At para 39.
410 At para 39.

The hospital had to establish 'an overriding public interest, amounting to a pressing social need, to which the need to keep press sources confidential should give way' since, as Laws LJ had pointed out in the Court of Appeal,

> . . . the public interest in the non-disclosure of press sources is constant, whatever the merits of the particular publication and the particular source. It is in no way lessened and certainly not abrogated, simply because the case is one in which the information actually disclosed is of no legitimate, objective public interest.[411]

Lord Woolf found that any restriction on the otherwise unqualified right to freedom of expression must meet the requirements under Art 10(2) of answering to a 'pressing social need' and also the restriction should be proportionate to a legitimate aim which is being pursued.[412] In this instance, it was found, an overriding public interest could be identified, as Lord Woolf determined:

> The situation here is exceptional, as it was in *Financial Times Ltd v Interbrew SA* and as it has to be, if disclosure of sources is to be justified. The care of patients at Ashworth is fraught with difficulty and danger. The disclosure of the patients' records increases that difficulty and danger and to deter the same or similar wrongdoing in the future it was essential that the source should be identified and punished. This was what made the orders to disclose necessary and proportionate and justified. The fact that Ian Brady had himself disclosed his medical history did not detract from the need to prevent staff from revealing medical records of patients.

Lord Woolf also referred to the approach of the European Court to medical records in relation to Art 8 in *Z v Finland*.[413] The Court had found that:

> . . . the protection of personal data, not least medical data, is of fundamental importance to a person's enjoyment of his or her right to respect for private and family life as guaranteed by Article 8 of the Convention. Respecting the confidentiality of health data is a vital principle in the legal systems of all the contracting parties to the Convention. The domestic law must therefore afford appropriate safeguards to prevent any such communication or disclosure of personal health data as may be inconsistent with the guarantees in Article 8 of the Convention.

Taking account of the significance of preserving the confidentiality of health data, Lord Woolf went on to dismiss the appeal. He did not examine the question of proportionality in detail, but appeared to assume impliedly that since there was such a pressing need to protect medical records in the instant case, the measure in question was proportionate to the aim pursued. Thus he did not engage in a full application of the *Goodwin* proportionality tests under a strict level of scrutiny.

411 At para 101.
412 At para 62.
413 (1998) 25 EHRR 371 at paras 94 and 95.

The other Law Lords agreed with his findings. Therefore the order of disclosure was upheld. The test of necessity from *Ashworth* may be taken to have superseded the test from *Interbrew* in so far as the two decisions differ on this point. The Lords, however, appeared to take the view that they do not differ significantly since they refused leave to appeal in the *Interbrew* case. The nature of the current domestic tests for proportionality and its consonance with the Strasbourg tests is considered further below.

Ackroyd v Mersey Care NHS Trust[414] arose as a result of the findings in the *Ashworth* case. MGN proceeded to disclose the identity of the intermediary through whom it had obtained the notes – Ackroyd. He was an investigative journalist who had been involved in previous investigations into mismanagement at the hospital; he therefore had an established and lengthy interest in it. Some of Mr Ackroyd's revelations about failings at the hospital had previously led to the Fallon Inquiry which produced the Fallon Report.[415] The conclusion of the Report had been that Ashworth should close due to poor management. In evidence Ackroyd said that over the years he had developed contacts with a number of sources at the hospital and that in the instance in question in *Ashworth* he had not paid the source for the notes. The claimant, Ashworth, brought proceedings against the defendant, Ackroyd, seeking an order for disclosure of his source. He resisted, relying first on an argument that the *Norwich Pharmacal* jurisdiction was not applicable. He argued that the source would have had a public interest defence to a claim by the hospital for breach of confidence or contract and that therefore he was not mixed up' in wrong-doing by the source since there was no wrong-doer.

He also relied on s 10. Ashworth argued that Mr Ackroyd's position was indistinguishable from that of *The Mirror* in the *MGN* case and that the decision of the House of Lords had concluded the issue. Ackroyd argued that the facts relevant to an application for an order for disclosure against him were materially different from those advanced by *The Mirror* in the *MGN* case. The judge took the view that the issues had been settled by the *MGN* case, and made the order of disclosure sought. The view was taken that the expressed purpose of the order made in the *MGN* case would be subverted if Mr Ackroyd were to succeed in keeping his source anonymous on the basis that the judgments in that case, to which Mr Ackroyd was not a party, were determinative of his defence also.

Ackroyd appealed, contending as his ground of appeal that the judge had been wrong to find that he had no real prospect of successfully resisting the claim that he should be ordered to disclose the source of the clinical notes. He put forward an argument based on the public interest in the disclosures, which went both to establishing that there was no jurisdiction to make the disclosure order and to the s 10 contentions. In support of this argument he said in evidence that he had been approached by sources at Ashworth and provided with information, including the PACIS notes covering Brady's first month on hunger strike. He had promised not to reveal the identity of the sources.

The sources were not, Ackroyd said, motivated by monetary gain; he had made no payment to them; their purpose in providing him with information was: 'to enable the public disclosure of the way in which Mr Brady had been treated, which, consistent with the findings of the Fallon Report in other matters, had not been disclosed by

414 [2003] EMLR 820.
415 *The Report of Committee of Inquiry in to the Personality Disorder Unit at Ashworth Special Hospital* (1999).

Ashworth'.[416] Thus, according to Ackroyd, the sources were acting in the public interest since they were exposing various serious flaws in the running of the hospital. In particular, they had revealed that the treatment of Brady was improper. Ackroyd had relied on a number of confidential journalistic sources in order to help him expose incompetence at the hospital and to subject the institution to public scrutiny. The Fallon Report had revealed that there was a history of secrecy and non-disclosure of reports at the hospital. Therefore exposure of improper practices at the hospital might not have occurred had sources not made revelations to Mr Ackroyd. He further argued that in any event the hospital had failed to establish an overriding public interest in disclosure of the identity of the source, making it necessary for that identity to be revealed in the interests of justice under s 10, and Art 10, HRA.

The Court of Appeal found that that it was not necessary to reach any conclusion as to whether Ackroyd might be able to establish, on the facts presented, that the source who provided the clinical notes to him might have had a public interest defence to a claim by the hospital for breach of confidence or contract. The Court accepted that, if this were established, a *Norwich Pharmacal* claim would not have been available for want of a 'wrongdoer', but also accepted that if the defence was not established the source had clearly acted in breach of confidence and in breach of contract.[417] The Court went on to find that if its inquiry was confined to disclosure of the clinical notes alone, a public interest defence might be difficult to sustain. However, it did not decide that question since it found that the 'separate public interest defence', depending on s 10 and Art 10 encompassed the same facts and considerations and provided 'a more promising defence'. It was clearly found that a failure to establish that the source had a public interest defence would *not* have meant, automatically, that the hospital would be able to establish that their public interest in disclosure was sufficient to override Mr Ackroyd's public interest in maintaining the confidentiality of his source. The difference between the two arguments was indicated in the findings of the Court in relation to the effect of Art 10 on the protection of sources.

The Court relied on the statement of principle in the judgment of the European Court of Human Rights in *Goodwin*[418] – re-stated in the *Ashworth v MGN* case – that protection of journalistic sources is one of the basic conditions of press freedom, and since an order of source disclosure undermines the exercise of that freedom, such a measure cannot be compatible with Art 10 unless it is justified by an overriding requirement in the public interest.[419] The Court found that it might be hard to identify a particular public interest in the disclosure of Brady's clinical notes in the context in which they were disclosed and looked at alone since Brady had himself already published the details that they contained. Further, it was found that the notes did not contain matter giving rise to legitimate criticism of the hospital. The argument had been advanced, relying on the decision of the European Court of Human Rights in *Fressoz and Roire v France,*[420] that the notes provided 'much needed corroboration of

---

416 At para 36.
417 The Court noted that Lord Woolf had said, in paras 32–34 of his Opinion in the *MGN* case, that Lord Phillips was almost certainly correct in coming to this conclusion.
418 At p 143, para 39.
419 At para 66 of the *Ackroyd* judgment.
420 *Fressoz and Roire v France* (2001) 31 EHRR 2, para 55.

what would otherwise be Brady's own bald and unconvincing narrative'. This argument was rejected, partly on the basis that the *Mirror* article did not use the notes for that purpose. However, this argument was found in any event to be redundant since, relying on *Goodwin*, it was clear that Ackroyd did not have to establish an overriding public interest in his source's disclosure of the clinical notes. On the contrary, the hospital had to establish 'an overriding public interest, amounting to a pressing social need, to which the need to keep press sources confidential should give way', since it was clear, relying on Laws LJ's comments in the *MGN* case, that the public interest in the non-disclosure of press sources was established and unvarying.[421]

This was found to be the basis for accepting that Ackroyd could argue plausibly that his case differed from the MGN one. The Court went on to consider the differences between the two cases and the factors that might be capable of swinging the balance from the preservation of confidentiality in patient records, to preserving the anonymity of sources in order to further the ends of journalism. In so doing the Court did in fact identify a public interest *other than* that of protecting sources, despite its earlier remarks on the point. The factors identified included: the unhappy history at the hospital which did not feature prominently in the *MGN* case, but was very significant in Ackroyd's; Ackroyd's arguable entitlement to enlarge the ambit of his defence to encompass other sources on the basis of the chilling effect of a requirement to disclose one source that might extend to other sources whom the hospital was not seeking to have identified; the fact that Mr Ackroyd's sources received no payment. The Court also noted that Ackroyd might be entitled to argue that, in the different circumstances of his case, the finding of the need for disclosure of his source in order to deter other breaches of confidence ought to be re-considered.

The Court concluded that Mr Ackroyd had established a sufficient case to entitle him to a trial since the focus of his defence was significantly different factually from that of MGN. Therefore the decision in that case should not have been regarded as summarily determinative of his case under the Civil Procedure Rules.[422] An order for source disclosure would only be compatible with Art 10 of the Convention if justified by an overriding requirement in the public interest. There was a clear public interest in preserving the confidentiality of medical records but that alone could not be regarded as an *automatically* overriding requirement without examining the facts of a particular case. It would only be in exceptional circumstances that a journalist could be ordered to disclose the identity of his source without the facts of *his* case being fully examined. The nature of the subject-matter was therefore found to indicate that there should be a trial in most cases.

421　At para 67 of the judgment.
422　For the purposes of Pt 24 of the Civil Procedure Rules (CPR). It was also found that he was entitled to point to Pt 24.2(b) CPR to the effect that there was another compelling reason why the case should be disposed of at a trial. Part 24 CPR provides: 'The court may give summary judgment against a claimant or defendant on the whole of a claim or on a particular issue if – (a) it considers that (i) the claimant has no real prospect of succeeding on the claim or issue; or (ii) that the defendant has no real prospect of successfully defending the claim or issue; and (b) there is no other compelling reason why the case or issue should be disposed of at a trial.' This conclusion of the Court was reached without according the CPR itself a Convention-friendly interpretation under s 3(1) HRA, but that would have been a possibility.

Flaws in the post-HRA judicial reasoning

The discussion above reveals that post-HRA a stance unsympathetic to the media's watchdog role was still found in relation to the first two steps in a source disclosure case – those of finding jurisdiction and applying one or more of the s 10 exceptions. The discussion of the findings in the leading post-HRA decision in *Ashworth* makes this clear. The key post-HRA change occurred in the third step – the determination as to the test of necessity – due to the influence of Art 10 under the HRA, a change that was prefigured in *John v Express Newspapers* and in *Saunders v Punch*. In relation to the first two steps the judges have always taken and continue to take an approach that enhances the chances of ordering disclosure.

The decisions discussed concerned two very different interests which were opposed to the public interest in media freedom and the protection of sources. In *Ashworth* (and in *Ackroyd*) there was a risk of further leaks and the source had revealed confidential medical records. A number of reasons for preserving the confidentiality of such records, especially in a hospital treating dangerous patients, were taken into account. In *Interbrew*, on the other hand, the decision protected a company's interest in bringing a legal action against a person who had leaked confidential information (although the institution of the action was not essential to the obtaining of the order – a very important point, discussed further below). The decisions in *Interbrew* and in *Ashworth* took account of the effect of the HRA and the courts considered that the outcomes were consistent with the demands of Art 10 of the Convention, as interpreted in *Goodwin*.[423]

Nevertheless, the decisions clearly do not offer reassurance to sources who are uncertain whether to come forward. It could be argued that the source in the *Interbrew* case came forward for his or her own (arguably improper) motives and was hardly in the position of the source who is activated by conscience in seeking to reveal wrong-doing but is afraid of the repercussions. But potential sources are unlikely to understand the nuances of the decisions, but may merely receive the message that the protection for their anonymity is in jeopardy. It might appear in general that the courts are over-zealously protecting the right of institutions or companies to bring actions against employees and others. Their tendency to envisage the potential harm that could be done to companies in clear and concrete terms remains very apparent, although they now also afford at least some degree of recognition to the interest in source protection. Although it is understandable that the courts would want to protect the right to bring an action where there is a legitimate grievance, the net result may be that companies are aided in seeking to maintain effective cover-ups.

In *Ashworth*, wrongdoing was not perceived as being revealed. It appears that unless it is revealed, freedom of expression may be at risk of being outweighed by varying

---

423   The demands of Art 10 in relation to source protection are a matter of interpretation and do not arise from the wording of para 2 itself, so they could have been departed from since under s 2 HRA the jurisprudence itself is not binding; it is the rights themselves which must be adhered to if at all possible under s 3(1), not the jurisprudence. Thus the leeway that existed to allow departure from the Strasbourg standard in the pre-HRA era, still existed post-HRA. Nevertheless, the judges, post-HRA, stated, possibly disingenuously, that they were following *Goodwin* rather than refusing to treat the case as binding, despite the established tendency within the pre-HRA domestic jurisprudence to afford less weight to source protection than that afforded at Strasbourg.

public interests in disclosure of the identity of the source, *despite* the unvarying nature of the interest in protecting sources. The findings in *Ashworth* and in *Interbrew* stand in contrast to each other, to an extent. In *Ashworth*, now the leading decision, the importance of protecting sources was recognised in the test laid down for determining the 'necessity' of ordering disclosure. If the protection of sources is regarded as an inherent and constant public interest, the other party is forced into the position of seeking to establish very weighty reasons for displacing that interest. Thus the judgment of the court has to focus on the particulars of that other party's claim. This was a significant departure from *Interbrew*, since in that instance the focus of the decision was on the source's culpability rather than on identifying a clear public interest in disclosure of his or her identity. In *Ackroyd* the test from *Ashworth* was applied, resulting in the finding that the need to preserve patient confidentiality could not represent an automatic justification for ordering disclosure: it would be necessary to consider the facts in any particular instance.

The House of Lords in *Ashworth* purported to do what the European Court did in *Goodwin*, but, it is argued, mis-weighed both the harm done to the privacy interest and the value of the speech. The Lords took the view that the protection of sources is in *itself* a highly significant public interest, regardless of the specifics of the case in question and the objective value of the information disclosed. That finding, relying on *Goodwin*, was clearly correct. But the point was not made clearly enough that the *converse* finding does not apply. In other words, where the information *is* of value in public interest terms it should weigh in the calculus as *another* weighty factor in favour of non-disclosure of the source, meaning that the other party would have to provide reasons of an exceptionally weighty nature pointing in the direction of disclosure. This point is of relevance to the key *Goodwin* proportionality test – weighing up the seriousness of the interference with speech against the importance of the aim that the plaintiff is seeking to pursue and the harm done to that interest. The seriousness can be judged in terms of its *extent* or its nature, or both. In this instance both aspects were at stake. In terms of *nature* the interference was serious for the reasons indicated: two weighty speech-based arguments went in favour of non-disclosure of the source's identity – the general interest in protecting sources, affirmed in *Goodwin*, and the public interest value of the information. In terms of extent, the interference was also serious (the third *de Freitas* test) since, unlike an injunction, which can be tailored to a particular situation, a source disclosure order is an all-or-nothing measure. The consequences for the source would have been very serious, and other sources at the hospital would have been deterred from coming forward. Thus it is arguable that, on strict scrutiny, this test would not have been found to be satisfied in *Ashworth*, meaning that the infringement of Art 10 would not have been viewed as justified.

This analysis is now, however, complicated where another Convention Article – usually Art 8 – can be invoked as part of the justification for source disclosure. This was the case in *Ashworth*, as the House of Lords impliedly indicated in its references to *Z v Finland*. The term 'parallel analysis' was not used, but after the House of Lords' decisions in *Campbell*[424] and in *re S*,[425] it is now clear that this is the proper means of

---

424 [2004] 2 WLR 1232; see Chapter 9, pp 975–76 for further discussion of the decision.
425 [2005] 1 AC 593; [2004] UKHL 47. See Chapter 9, pp 958–59 for further discussion of the decision.

weighing up two Convention Articles against each other,[426] except in certain narowly defined (and anomalous) exceptional circumstances.[427] In fact, prior to *Ashworth*, it had already been found in *Douglas v Hello!*[428] that this was the proper method of proceeding where an apparent clash of rights arose. It might be thought at first sight that where another Convention right is engaged the standard of scrutiny from *Goodwin* is not applicable since *Goodwin* was not a clashing rights case, but a case in which an exception based on a societal concern had to be narrowly construed. At Strasbourg a wide margin of appreciation tends to be afforded in the case of clashing rights and therefore the standard of scrutiny is less strict.[429] However, as argued in Chapter 9, this is not and should not be the approach taken at the domestic level.[430] There are a number of reasons why the approaches at the domestic and the international levels inevitably differ. The most valuable precedent for future source disclosure cases involving a clash of rights is that of the House of Lords in *Campbell* in which in a different context, but where Arts 8 and 10 were both engaged, a strict standard of scrutiny was adopted.[431] The precedent of *Von Hannover*[432] could also be taken into account, in which, unusually, Strasbourg did not concede a wide margin of appreciation in a case of a collision between Arts 8 and 10.

Had the parallel analysis been fully conducted in *Ashworth*, as arguably it should have been, it would have reached the stage of balancing the underlying values of both Arts 8 and 10 against each other. It would have been necessary to examine the restriction each Article proposed to lay on the other and to ask which right would suffer the greater harm if the other prevailed. The question whether the invasion of Art 10 (via the source disclosure order) went further than necessary to protect the Art 8 right at stake should have been asked.

On the other side, the interference with the Art 8 rights of Brady as a patient was serious: the preservation of the confidentiality of medical records is itself recognised at Strasbourg as an unvarying and consistent public interest.[433] But in terms of *this particular context* the interference was of a less serious nature. The history of mal-management at the hospital was not viewed as relevant in *Ashworth* for various reasons. In fact it was highly relevant in relation to the weightiness of the patient confidentiality claim *and* the claim for non-disclosure of the source. It was relevant to the former claim due to the particular context in question in which the key argument for preserving patient confidentiality was put forward. It could readily be argued that where patients themselves have deliberately breached their own confidentiality in order to serve a more pressing cause – to reveal the abuses suffered by patients at the hospital – that creates a particular focus from which to view the interest in preserving confidentiality. In the

---

426 See Chapter 9, pp 950–81 for a full discussion of the use of the 'parallel analysis'.
427 See Chapter 9, pp 864–65, 972–74 for further discussion. It is possible that eventually the courts may decide that there are no exceptional circumstances – there are merely instances in which the speech in question is especially valuable since it relates to the open justice principle (but see pp 972–74).
428 [2001] QB 967. See Chapter 9, pp 904–5 for further discussion of the decision.
429 See Chapter 9, pp 943–48 for discussion.
430 See Chapter 9, pp 956–57 for discussion.
431 See Chapter 9, pp 975–77 for discussion.
432 (2004) Appl No 59320/00, judgment of 24 June 2004; see in particular paras 63, 64, 65, 66.
433 See *Plon Société v France* No. 58148/00.

instance in question two patients, including Brady himself, had breached confidentiality with that end in view. In general, in terms of the experience of being in a secure hospital and in terms of treatment, patients are likely to view the interest in confidentiality as outweighed by the interest in preventing the suffering and humiliation of patients due to maltreatment. In the hierarchy of interests relating to the hospital experience, the prevention of maltreatment – by exposing it – looms higher than the preservation of confidentiality.

It must be re-emphasised that this argument is being applied to the value of preserving patient confidentiality in a highly context-sensitive fashion, and on the basis, endorsed by *Goodwin*, of an intense scrutiny. It is undoubted that there is *general* value in enabling persons to be reassured that their medical records will remain confidential, and the Lords were clearly right to refer to that value. It has since been endorsed by the European Court of Human Rights in *Plon* (*Société*) *v France*[434] as an interest that can win out even when opposed by the countervailing interest in political speech. But while the Lords were right to place weight on the *general* value of preserving patient confidentiality, they failed to examine the very particular context in question which, it is argued, undermined that value as an individual right, or countered it. Thus, the general societal interest in preserving medical confidentiality remained of significance, but the interference with Brady's Art 8 right was of less significance than it would have been in a different context. The value of the parallel analysis and of concentration on the speech/harm balancing test from *Goodwin* is precisely that this method teases out the values genuinely at stake.

In the context of maltreatment, then, the preservation of patient confidentiality, generally of very high importance, may be viewed as a near-meaningless abstraction divorced from the idea of serving any worthwhile purpose. Indeed, it came close to being used in *Ashworth* in a perversion of its original purpose. Preservation of patient confidentiality is rooted in ideas about the intimacy of details of medical treatment – in itself linked to notions of humiliation and embarrassment. If that treatment itself directly causes humiliation – as was alleged in abundance in relation to Ashworth Hospital – then the underlying basis for maintaining confidentiality is undermined. Although it was true that the *Mirror* article in question did not directly concern mal-management at Ashworth, disclosure of the identity of the source was clearly likely to aid in the continuing attempt of the Ashworth management to cover up the failings there, documented in the Fallon Report. Thus the ruling preserved patient confidentiality in a technical or formal sense without succeeding in examining the *real* value of that confidentiality in the circumstances. Lord Woolf relied on *Z v Finland* in relation to the value of confidentiality of medical records encapsulated in Art 8. But he failed to take account of other competing values underlying Art 8, including the preservation of dignity and privacy of patients in hospitals such as Ashworth, or the general interest in the prevention of harm to patients, which would have pointed in the direction of protecting the source in order to aid in uncovering abuses of power in the hospital. However, there are precedents in a different context for weighing up such competing values.

434 No. 58148/00, 18 May 2004.

In a series of cases the courts have recognised that the public interest in protecting patients, or potential patients, from harm outweighs the interest in maintaining the confidentiality of medical records.[435] In *re A (Disclosure of Medical Records to the GMC)*,[436] it was found that production of medical records could be justified on the ground of protecting persons from possible medical misconduct, even where the risk of such conduct is not established. Similarly, in *A Health Authority v X*,[437] at first instance, it was found that there was a public interest in the disclosure of health care records in order to aid in an investigation into a certain GP. Serious allegations had been made of misconduct and unsatisfactory standards of care, although these had not been substantiated. Further, in *Woolgar v Chief Constable of Sussex*[438] a patient in a nurse's care had died in suspicious circumstances. Disclosure of the medical records was authorised for disciplinary purposes to the United Kingdom Central Council for Nursing, Midwifery and Health Visiting on the basis of the general public interest of the proper regulation of the nursing profession in the interests of those receiving nursing care.

It was essential in *Ashworth* to identify the relevant Art 8 values at stake, under a strict level of scrutiny, in order to determine the seriousness of the interference, weighing it against the importance of the speech, without affording either value presumptive priority. In this instance, although interference with patient confidentiality had occurred, the more significant value at stake was that of the humiliation and indignity suffered by patients at the hospital, especially Brady. Publicity *aided* in addressing that matter and thus affected both aspects of the speech/privacy balancing analysis. The more significant privacy interest – the humiliation suffered by patients, which sought publicity – overcame, it is argued, the interest in confidentiality. Therefore the interference with the right to respect for private life – the disclosure of the notes to the newspaper – was proportionate to the legitimate aim pursued, that of preserving the Art 10 rights of the newspaper (under the Art 8(2) 'rights of others' exception). No breach of Art 8 occurred on this analysis.

In terms of the second half of the parallel analysis, conducted under Art 10(2), it is clear that under a strict scrutiny a very serious interference with speech rights occurred which was not justified by the aim pursued – the Art 8 rights of others. The discussion reveals that the unhappy history of the hospital was relevant to the claim for non-disclosure of the identity of the source in *Ashworth* on a basis other than that of the general interest in protecting sources: thus there was a *heightened* interest in non-disclosure. That interest arose in the context of a matter of grave public interest – a context that the House of Lords was aware of but chose not to place weight on. The fact that in the instance in question the revelations arguably did not add much of significance to discussions of the situation at Ashworth was not the end of the matter. Any order of disclosure was bound to have some broad stifling effect in a number of respects in relation to a matter of grave public interest. In other words, their Lordships

---

435 This has also been recognised legislatively: the Data Protection (Processing of Sensitive Personal Data) Order 2000 (SI 2000/417), Sched para 2, allows disclosure for regulatory purposes if in the public interest.

436 [1998] 2 FLR 641, p 644.

437 *X* [2001] 2 FLR 673, p 677.

438 [1999] 3 All ER 604 at p 615.

should have looked beyond the specifics of the revelations in question, to that general effect in such a significant context. Had these factors been taken into account, and then weighed up in the calculus of proportionality, under the speech/harm balancing test, it is argued that the decision would have gone the other way since the doubly strong public interest on the side of non-disclosure would have outweighed the relatively weak public interest – in the particular context – of preserving patient confidentiality. The values enshrined in Art 3 could also have been taken into account in the balancing act since the disclosures were relevant to the use of degrading treatment.[439] Revelations leading to the uncovering of Art 3 treatment should surely be afforded a high value in speech terms.

Despite purporting to take account of Art 10, and in particular of the test of necessity, the House of Lords' decision fell into the trap, typical of British judicial reasoning, of assuming a narrow and technical basis, divorced from the realities of the context in question. Further, in terms of the third limb of the *de Freitas* test, it may be argued that the source disclosure order went further than was needed to serve the end of preserving the value of confidentiality since an action for breach of confidence was available against the newspaper (although it might have failed on public interest grounds), and consequently the interference was disproportionate to the end pursued. Therefore it should have been found that a breach of Art 10, but not of Art 8, would occur if the source disclosure order was upheld.

In following *Ashworth*, *Ackroyd* dealt more fully with the proportionality aspects of the instance before it, although the parallel analysis was not conducted. The decision focused on the lack of payment to the source and the chilling effect on other sources at the hospital if disclosure was ordered. If the interest in protecting sources is viewed as constant, those are significant factors in terms of *heightening* that interest. The unhappy history of mismanagement and abuse of power at the hospital was considered in relation to the nature of the interference, but it should have been taken into account both in relation to the preservation of confidentiality *and* in respect of the claim for non-disclosure of the source, as argued above. In other words, it potentially affected both sides of the speech/harm equation, diminishing the importance of the aim pursued (medical confidentiality) and enhancing the significance of the interference with freedom of expression. Following this argument, *Ackroyd* reached the right result.

If the more complete version of the doctrine of proportionality argued for here – speech/harm balancing - had been applied to the facts of *Interbrew*, there is a strong argument that a breach of Art 10 would have been found. In *Interbrew* any weighing up of Arts 10 and 8 against each other would have had to concern the 'privacy' of a company. Although companies may have certain rights to private life and to protection for correspondence,[440] that argument has been accepted at Strasbourg only in

---

439 For example, Brady was quite seriously injured in the course of subjecting him to force-feeding, and a child was allowed unsupervised visits in the hospital and was subjected to sexual abuse on a number of occasions. Article 3 provides 'No-one shall be subjected to torture or inhuman or degrading treatment.'

440 See *R v Broadcasting Standards Commission ex p BBC* [2000] 3 WLR 1327 (concerning the privacy of the company Dixons). The decision is discussed further in Chapter 9, pp 849–50.

relation to search and seizure of material from a company's premises.[441] It is unlikely that disclosure of information relating to a company could be viewed as 'private" information'. Revelations as to share prices and the like are prima facie of a public character: Article 8 would be found to be unengaged or only peripherally engaged in such an instance. In *Interbrew* then it may be argued that the Art 10 claim did not have to be balanced by a strong – or any – Art 8 claim. So the case was arguably correctly viewed as one in which Art 10 had presumptive priority, subject to exceptions to be narrowly construed.

Since another Convention right was not at stake, or barely at stake, the parallel analysis was not applicable and the interests of Interbrew were rightly viewed by Sedley LJ as protected only by Art 10(2) exceptions to be narrowly construed. The exception in question appeared to be that of 'the rights of others'. In this context, the case of *Chassagnou v France*[442] is of relevance. The Court said in that case that when dealing with 'rights of others' that are not themselves competing Convention rights, 'only indisputable imperatives can justify interference with enjoyment of a Convention right.' *Chassagnou* was not referred to in *Interbrew*, but it might be asked whether Interbrew's interest in bringing a legal action was an indisputable imperative. In any event, the public interest involved in requiring source disclosure was clearly less significant than that in *Ashworth* since an individual Convention right was not involved, and therefore the case for allowing it to outweigh the interest in protecting the confidentiality of media sources was less strong. Following *Goodwin*, that is a strong and unvarying interest; it would have had to be outweighed by a very compelling countervailing interest if it was to be overcome; on the facts that did not appear to be the case.

Clearly, *aside* from the interest in source protection, the speech in *Interbrew* was *not* of high value since it appeared to be intended to be misleading; therefore it ran counter to the truth-based rationale. (In making this point it must be borne in mind that although it is possible or even probable that the source had behaved reprehensibly and from reprehensible motives, his or her motives could not be known since (obviously) he or she could not come to court to answer accusations.) In this respect the speech differed from that at issue in *Ashworth* which was of a higher value in terms of all the speech-based rationales. But that factor did not detract from the general significance of protecting sources.

Lord Justice Sedley relied partly on a test akin to means/end balancing in conducting the proportionality analysis. But such a test does not provide a sufficiently effective or nuanced mechanism for weighing up the value of the speech in relation to the harm caused. Moreover, in applying this test he did not take account of the possibility that an injunction on grounds of breach of confidence could have been obtained against the newspapers banning publication of similar material from the same source. If other

441 In *Société Colas Est v France* (2002) Application no. 37971/97 at para 41 the Court found: 'the time has come to hold that in certain circumstances the rights guaranteed by Article 8 of the Convention may be construed as including the right to respect for a company's registered office, branches or other business premises . . .'. However, the protection at present extends only to physical searches of the company's premises; it would not appear to cover information relating to it or held by it (although obviously the company personnel would have individual Art 8 rights to their own private information held in the company's files).

442 (2000) 29 EHRR 615.

newspapers had then published such material they would have faced liability under the doctrine of common law contempt.[443] Clearly, an injunction would not have covered the doctored part of the document published by the newspapers, but it is argued that no source disclosure order should have been made in relation to that part in any event since the *Norwich Pharmacal* jurisdiction was not available in relation to it (this point is discussed further below).

Sedley LJ purported to use the *Goodwin* speech/harm balancing test, but when it came to weighing up the two interests against each other he allowed the apparently malevolent attitude of the source to undermine the interest in protecting sources, despite accepting at an earlier point in the judgment that that interest should be viewed as constant. If that interest had been viewed as constant it is argued that it would have outweighed the interest of Interbrew in resorting to law since source disclosure cases inevitably involve a desire to seek legal redress: thus there was no especially pressing need in this instance to aid Interbrew in seeking such redress. He said on this point: 'the relatively modest leak of which they are entitled to complain does not diminish the prospective seriousness for them of its repetition'.[444] This point could also have been made in *Goodwin*; it was highly speculative, and relied only on a possibility of future harm. It is suggested that this nebulous possibility of harm should not have been allowed to outweigh the constant interest in protecting sources. Had the *Goodwin* test been properly applied at this crucial point in the analysis, it is argued that a different outcome would have been reached.

The *Interbrew* decision is likely to deter those who have, prima facie, purer motives for leaking information – to expose malpractice in a powerful corporate player. Arguably, if the *Goodwin* speech/harm balancing test is applied, it is clear that the impact of such deterrence was not given sufficient weight when balanced against the interest of the company in the right to pursue an action for breach of confidence. Moreover, the other possible sanctions which could be brought to bear in relation to this (arguably successful) attempt to 'rig' the market by the Financial Services Authority (FSA) could have been taken into account and afforded greater weight in the reasoning on proportionality in relation to the 'least intrusive means' inquiry. In other words, in so far as wrong-doing had occurred, another means of redress was potentially available which was likely to deter many persons from seeking to promulgate financial misinformation. The interests of Interbrew were not therefore without protection due to the existence and powers of the FSA. Therefore, not only was the speech interest more weighty than the countervailing interest of Interbrew, but the interference represented by the source disclosure order went further than necessary to pursue the aim of protecting those interests.

The argument here is not only that an intense focus on the true values at stake in any particular instance is necessary in the proportionality analysis. It is also that judges should be wary of making unfounded assumptions about sources. Although, following *Ashworth*, the protection of sources has been accepted as a strong and unvarying interest, it appears that particular factors in a situation can strengthen the free speech

443 See above, pp 369–82. If it had been published during the 'active' period under the Contempt of Court Act 1981 they could arguably also have faced liability under the strict liability rule for impeding the proceedings.
444 At para 54.

claim under the *Goodwin* proportionality test. In *Ackroyd*, for example, they did so. But in *Interbrew* they were viewed as weakening it, and this appears now to be an illegitimate stance to take since it takes no account of the general deterrent effect on potential sources of source disclosure in a particular instance. This point may be made about a number of the cases discussed in this chapter; it is further enhanced since the matters that have sometimes tipped the balance in relation to the test of necessity often turned out to rest on judicial 'commonsense' and assumptions. Many of the pre- and post-HRA cases discussed rested on uncertain assumptions, which then turned out to be erroneous.[445] In *Ashworth* the assumption was made that the source was a dishonest employee motivated by greed. *Ackroyd v Mersey Care NHS Trust* showed that the sources were in fact motivated by the desire to expose malpractice at the hospital. The assumption is also often made that the source, if undetected, will continue to leak confidential information. But, as argued above, *Guardian Newspapers* indicated that this is not necessarily the case.

The judicial reasoning in the post-HRA cases is, it is argued, also flawed in a further respect. The cases considered rested on the *Norwich Pharmacal* jurisdiction: in order to consider whether a journalist was mixed up in wrong-doing it was necessary to examine the claim for breach of confidence (or of contract) in relation to the source. If no justiciable claim had been found to exist there could be no wrong-doing for the journalist to be mixed up in and therefore no jurisdiction to make the disclosure order. But the courts failed to recognise that they have a duty under s 6 HRA to develop common law and equitable doctrines in order to render them compatible with Art 10.[446] Indeed, arguably, s 6 may possibly make *greater* demands on the common law in terms of modification, than s 3 does on statutes since there is no provision in s 6 equivalent to s 3(2) HRA[447] in relation to the common law. This duty should have affected their approach to that jurisdiction: rather than merely following the pre-HRA authorities as to its nature, they should have considered whether it itself should be modified post-HRA. In this instance this means firstly taking account of post-HRA developments in the doctrine of confidence, and secondly applying s 6 to the jurisdiction itself.

The Court of Appeal in *Ackroyd* considered whether the source would have a defence to an action for breach of confidence based on public interest, but did not need to come to a conclusion on the subject. The Lords in *Ashworth* did not consider this point. It is argued that they should have done so, taking account of the post-HRA breach of confidence jurisprudence. So doing means, where Art 8 is engaged in relation to the confidentiality claim (which would not inevitably be the case in this context), conducting a parallel analysis based on Art 8(2) and Art 10(2).[448] Since *Ashworth* concerned an important privacy interest the Court should have considered whether the balancing

---

445 For example, as mentioned earlier, the assumption was made in *Guardian Newspapers* that the source was a senior Civil Servant, which turned out to be not to be the case.

446 See Chapter 4, pp 253–56.

447 See Chapter 4, pp 171–72, 254–55 on this point. It may be noted that as Chapter 9, p 905 points out, s12 HRA in any event puts paid to any doubts as to the duty of the court in relation to Art 10 and the common law.

448 See Chapter 9, pp 957–59.

of Arts 10 and 8 – as in *A v B*[449] (and now, *Campbell*)[450] would have resulted in a finding that no wrong-doing had occurred. If a case such as that of *Ashworth* arises in future post-*Campbell* this is the course that should be taken. The public interest defence has been subsumed within the consideration of the Art 10 claim. The argument at this stage is not the same as at the latter, s 10, stage since the unvarying interest in protection of sources is not yet at stake – the speech case at *this* point depends only on the public interest dimension of the information disclosed by him or her. Therefore, as the Court correctly pointed out in *Ackroyd*, the failure to put forward a convincing public interest argument at this point would affect but not preclude the success of the s 10 argument later on.

The argument then is that a court in an action for source disclosure appears to be in the unfortunate position of having to take the steps that would be taken in the hypothetical breach of confidence action – where that cause of action would constitute the wrong-doing in question. Where any other claim, such as a claim for breach of contract, has a link to the preservation of privacy, those steps would also be applicable, by analogy with the confidence jurisprudence, since contract doctrine is clearly also subject to modification via s 6 HRA where a Convention right is engaged. Although *Campbell* concerned a breach of confidence claim, the balancing act would surely bring about the same outcome in relation to breach of contract. On the face of it, had this step been taken in *Ashworth* the chance of identifying a 'wrong-doer' would have been *enhanced*, since the parallel analysis enhances the privacy claim; as Chapter 9 argues, the analysis is based on the view that Arts 8 and 10 are presumptively equal. On the face of it this would obviously be an unwelcome argument for the defendant to pursue.

However, subjecting the privacy claim to the intense scrutiny of the parallel analysis allows its true value to be revealed. As argued above in relation to Art 10, there were compelling Arts 8 and 10-based reasons in favour of disclosure of the conditions at Ashworth, had the arguments relating to disclosures of malpractice at the hospital figured more fully in the case. On the face of it a strong Art 8 claim could have been identified, based on the significant privacy interest in preserving the confidentiality of medical records – as in fact it was, based on *Z v Finland*, but *Z* was not considered at the jurisdictional stage of the argument. However, bearing in mind the arguments above as to the *true* value in the circumstances of such preservation of confidentiality, it is argued that the balancing act – using the parallel analysis – would have come down on the side of Art 10 since other Art 8 values – in preventing humiliation and preserving dignity – would have spoken in favour of publicity, even without assistance from the strong argument in favour of protecting sources. Thus, having conducted the parallel analysis, it could be found in a case such as *Ashworth*, that no jurisdiction for making the source disclosure order could be found as the source could not be viewed as a wrong-doer.

As indicated above, not all confidentiality cases in this context engage Art 8. In *Interbrew* it was unnecessary to weigh up Arts 10 and 8 against each other at the

---

449 [2002] 3 WLR 542.

450 [2004] 2 WLR 1232; (2004) UKHL 22. For comment see Morgan, J, 'Privacy in the House of Lords – Again' (2004) 120 LQR 563–66. See further Chapter 9 pp 975–77.

jurisdictional stage on the basis that the 'private life' of a company was not engaged[451] – for the reasons already discussed. Article 10 had presumptive priority, subject to exceptions to be narrowly construed; therefore the speech argument could have prevailed at the jurisdictional stage, in relation to the potential confidentiality claim. However, that argument was not considered at that stage. It is possible that the case could have been decided merely on the basis that there was a lack of jurisdiction to make the order. The fact that there was no competing Art 8 right in question would clearly have *enhanced* the possibility that any potential breach of confidence action would have failed.[452]

Thus the hypothetical breach of confidence action offering the restraint of an injunction represented an interference with the Art 10 rights of the newspaper that had to be necessary and proportionate to the aim pursued – that of the preservation of confidentiality, narrowly construed. It is argued that the true grievance of Interbrew was that the disinformation was promulgated and the share price went down. But, as Sedley LJ noted, the disinformation presumably emanated largely from the *source itself* and therefore would not qualify in itself as confidential information. Possibly Interbrew might have argued on this point that some of the information was confidential and that in order to deter persons from producing doctored information it was necessary to pursue the breach of confidence action, even though the confidential information leaked was in itself innocuous. But could it not be argued that the pursuit of such an action would have been disproportionate to the aim pursued, under a strict level of scrutiny,[453] on the basis that the remedy was not suitable for the purpose (the second limb of the *De Freitas* test) since the appropriate remedy answering to the true grievance of Interbrew lay with the FSA? It could also be argued that the speech/harm balancing test from *Goodwin* was not satisfied: since part of the information – the more significant part – was not confidential, the importance of the aim pursued was thereby undermined. If the general value in protecting sources (the speech interest) had been balanced against the harm done to the confidentiality of the information, it might have been found that the latter outweighed the former.

On this basis it could be argued that in *Interbrew* the source would have had an answer based on the application of Art 10 to the potential breach of confidence action and therefore should not have been viewed as a wrong-doer. With no wrong-doer the journalist could not have been viewed as mixed up in wrong-doing and so no jurisdiction to make the order would have arisen. Clearly, the reason for this arguable flaw in the reasoning is that although Art 10 was taken properly into account at the later stage in the reasoning, it was not taken fully into account at the earlier stage – when the *Norwich Pharmaceutical* rule was being considered. Had Art 10 been allowed to affect both the statutory and the common law rule, the outcome might have been different.

---

451 See fn 441 above regarding the extent to which companies can claim Art 8 rights.

452 As Chapter 4 discusses (pp 253–55), whenever a common law doctrine coincides with the area covered by a Convention right(s), it may need to be modified by reference to the demands of that right(s) (established so far in relation to Art 8). But the modification that must occur differs depending on whether the doctrine protects (a) a legitimate interest that has to be viewed as an exception to a competing interest arising in the form of a right (in *Interbrew* the interest was that of a company in preserving confidentiality under that exception in Art 10(2)) or (b) where a common law doctrine covers a right, not a societal interest.

453 On the strict level of scrutiny deriving, not from *Goodwin* since no source disclosure action is at this point in contemplation, but from the Strasbourg cases defending the media's watchdog role. See above, pp 309–10 for discussion of such cases.

Seizure of journalistic material

This section moves on to look at the seizure of journalistic material in order to aid in criminal or terrorist investigations. Clearly, journalists will quite frequently possess material in the form of documents or film obtained as a result of pursuing a particular investigative story. The next section considers a selection of the key powers allowing for the seizure of journalistic material. In each case the information obtained might include material identifying sources. Even where that is not the case, seizure of such material affects press freedom, not only because it hampers the collection of information, but also because if journalists are viewed as likely to be forced to aid police investigative efforts, contacts and others may refuse to cooperate with them. Journalists might also be put at risk when, for example, trying to film or report on demonstrations, since those involved would be likely to be concerned about the use to which the material gathered could be put.

A partial 'shield' against seizure of journalistic material is provided in the key seizure power under the Police and Criminal Evidence Act (PACE) 1984. But despite the significance of the other powers, they contain no express protection for media freedom. No common law privilege against seizure of press material exists[454] and it appears, as discussed below, that where sources might be revealed by such seizure s 10 of the 1981 Act nevertheless does not apply to any of the powers. However, some protection for press material could be imposed upon them since all these powers should of course be rendered compatible with Art 10, taking account of *Goodwin*, under s 3(1) HRA if at all possible. Following *Goodwin* some mechanism should be available within these powers to allow for the weighing up of the interest in protecting sources against the countervailing public interest in preventing crime or protecting national security that the power in question seeks to serve. Article 8 may also be applicable. As indicated above, Strasbourg has found that companies may have certain rights to private life and to protection for correspondence in the context of search and seizure of material from their premises.[455] A search and seizure of journalistic material could therefore engage both Articles. Further, since all those involved in using the powers are public authorities (the police, the courts, civil servants), they should, under s 6 HRA, comply with Art 10 and 8 in exercising them. The real possibilities of protecting the identity of sources where the varying powers are exercised are discussed below.

Search and seizure of journalistic material under the Police and Criminal Evidence Act 1984

The main search and seizure powers are provided in PACE, Part II.[456] The orders allowed for are intended to force journalists to disclose material where so doing is

---

454 See *Senior Holdsworth ex p Independent TV News* [1976] 1 QB 23.

455 In *Société Colas Est v France* (2002) Application no. 37971/97 at para 41 the Court found: 'the time has come to hold that in certain circumstances the rights guaranteed by Article 8 of the Convention may be construed as including the right to respect for a company's registered office, branches or other business premises . . .'.

456 For comment on these provisions see: Stone, R, *The Law of Entry, Search and Seizure*, 4th edn, 2005, OUP; Zander, M, *The Police and Criminal Evidence Act 1984*, 4th edn, 2003, Sweet and Maxwell; Feldman, D, *The Law Relating to Entry, Search and Seizure*, 1986, Butterworths; Stone, R, [1988] Crim LR 498.

likely to assist in a criminal investigation, but certain restrictive conditions have to be met. Under s 9 PACE a search warrant cannot be issued in respect of journalistic material; a production order has to be sought under Sched 1, which can be challenged in an *inter partes* hearing before a circuit judge on the basis that the access conditions have not been met. This position is similar to that applying in the US, where such a hearing can be held, if necessary, and investigators cannot obtain the specified material by applying only for a search warrant.[457]

The protection is afforded to journalists against seizure of journalistic material by designating it as either excluded or special procedure material and then placing special conditions on obtaining access to it. Section 11 governs excluded material. Such material consists, *inter alia*, of documentary journalistic material[458] held in confidence[459] and can only be seized if the special restrictions under Sched 1 to PACE are satisfied. The provisions allow for production orders to be made by a judge only if there is reasonable suspicion that the material is on the premises specified and that but for s 9(2) PACE it would have been possible and appropriate for a search warrant to have been issued.[460] Under s 14 non-confidential journalistic material is termed special procedure material and can only be seized if a serious arrestable offence has been committed and the material is on the premises and is likely to be of substantial value to the investigation. It must also be in the public interest to make the order, taking account of the benefit to the investigation and the circumstances under which it is held.[461] It is clearly of significance that the public interest requirement only applies to non-confidential journalistic material. It was intended as a safeguard but it has been subverted by judicial interpretation; pre-HRA it appeared that it would always be assumed to be served where the material would be of substantial benefit to the investigation or relevant in evidence.[462] However, this interpretation renders the inclusion of the public interest requirement otiose. This point is discussed further below.

Section 8(1) PACE covers general powers of search and seizure for material other than excluded material (s 8(1)(d)). The ruling in *Guildhall Magistrates' Court ex p Primlacks Holdings Co (Panama) Ltd*[463] made it clear that a magistrate must satisfy him or herself that there are reasonable grounds for believing that the items covered by the warrant do not include material subject to the special protection. The Criminal Justice and Police Act 2001 (CJP) s 50 extends the power of seizure very significantly. The further new power of seizure under s 50(2) allows the person in question to seize

---

457 94 Stat 1879 (1980).

458 Defined in s 13 as material created or acquired for the purposes of journalism – a circular definition that obviously is unhelpful in determining the limits of the privilege. It clearly covers material gathered for such purposes even if the material itself is not eventually published. See further Feldman, D, (2002) ibid on this point at 104–6.

459 S11(1)(c). Journalistic material is not afforded as much protection as legally privileged material, covered by s 10; no access to such material is allowed at all.

460 Sched 1, para 3.

461 Sched 1, para 2.

462 See: *R v Bristol Crown Court ex p Bristol Press and Picture Agency Ltd* (1986) 85 Cr App R 190; *Chief Constable of Avon and Somerset Police v Bristol United Press, Independent*, 4 November 1986.

463 [1989] 2 WLR 841. The magistrates had issued search warrants authorising the search of two solicitors' firms. Judicial review of the magistrates' decision to issue a warrant was successfully sought; it was found that the magistrate had merely accepted the police officer's view that s 8(1)(d) was satisfied rather than independently considering the matter.

material which he has no power to seize but which is attached to an object he does have the power to seize, if it is not reasonably practicable to separate the two, and this includes the specially protected material.[464] Section 50 may serve to undermine the protection for journalistic certain material since where such material is part of other material and cannot practicably be separated, it can be seized.

Sections 50, 54 and 55 CJP taken together provide avenues to the seizure and use of journalistic material.[465] The provisions thus circumvent the limitations placed on the seizure of excluded material and, most importantly, mean that information contained in the material, identifying sources, will have been passed to the police even though the material is subsequently returned. It can be said that for the first time journalistic material has lost part of the protection it was accorded under PACE. These wide CJP powers are 'balanced' by the provisions of ss 52–61 which provide a number of safeguards.[466] Under s 60 a duty to secure the property arises which includes the obligation under s 61 to prevent, *inter alia*, copying of it. But despite these safeguards, it is unclear that the new powers, especially to seize and use journalistic material, are compatible with the requirements of the Convention under the HRA, as discussed below.

Production Orders under the Terrorism Act 2000; requirements to provide information under the terrorism legislation

Schedule 7, para 3(5) of the Prevention of Terrorism (Temporary Provisions) Act 1989 provided for the production of material relating to terrorism if such production would be in the public interest. When inquiries relating to terrorist offences were made, Sched 7, para 3(5) allowed access to special procedure and excluded material. This provision was replaced by an equivalent provision under the Terrorism Act 2000, Sched 5. The judge only needs to be satisfied that there is a terrorist investigation in being, that the material would substantially assist it and that it is in the public interest that it should be produced. This procedure creates an exception to the PACE, Sched 1 special-access conditions[467] and so can be viewed as undermining the PACE shield provisions. A

---

464 The further powers of seizure it provides in s 50 apply to police powers of search under PACE and also to powers of seizure arising under a range of other statutes and applicable to bodies other than police officers, as set out in Sched 1 of the CJP. This provision is significant since, *inter alia*, it allows police officers to remove items from premises even where they are not certain that – apart from s 50 – they have the power to do so. Thus a number of items can now be seized from media premises although no power of seizure – apart from that now arising under s 50 – in fact arises. It can also be seized where a police officer takes the view on reasonable grounds that it is something that he has the power to seize, although it turns out later that it falls within one of the special categories.

465 Special provisions are made under the 2001 Act for, *inter alia*, the return of excluded material. Under s 54 such material must be returned unless it falls within s 54(2). Section 57(3) provides that ss 53–56 do not authorise the retention of property where its retention would not be authorised apart from the provisions of Part 2 of the CJP. Under s 62 inextricably linked property cannot be examined or copied, but under sub-section (4) can be used to the extent that its use facilitates the use of property in which the inextricably linked property is comprised.

466 Notice must be given to persons whose property has been seized under s 52, and under s 59 he or she can apply to the 'appropriate judicial authority' for the return of the whole or part of the seized property, on the ground that there was no power to seize, or that excluded material is not comprised in other property as provided for in ss 54 and 55.

467 This is also the case in respect of drug trafficking: see Drug Trafficking Act 1994, SS 55, 56.

police officer of the rank of superintendent or above can authorise a search if satisfied that immediate action is necessary since the case is one of great urgency.[468] It appears that once the first two requirements are satisfied, it will be rare to find that the third is not.[469]

It was assumed in *Director of Public Prosecutions v Channel Four Television Co Ltd*[470] that the existence of the Sched 7 provision meant that the making of an order precluded a defence under s 10 Contempt of Court Act. The potential danger of Sched 7 – now Sched 5 – in terms of media freedom was shown in that case. Channel 4 screened a programme in its Dispatches series called 'The Committee', which was based on the allegations of an anonymous source (Source A) that the RUC and Loyalist paramilitaries had colluded in the assassination of Republicans. The police successfully applied under Sched 7, para 3(5) for orders disclosing information which would probably uncover the identity of Source A. Channel 4 refused to comply with the orders on the ground that to do so would expose Source A to almost certain death and it was then committed for contempt of court. It attempted to rely on the public interest provision of Sched 7 in arguing that it was in the public interest for the identity of Source A to be protected, but this was rejected on the following grounds. Channel 4 should not have given an unqualified assurance of protection to the source even though had it not done so, the programme could probably not have been made, because so doing was likely to lead to flouting of the provisions of the Prevention of Terrorism (Temporary Provisions) Act 1989. Thus, giving such assurances could inevitably undermine the rule of law and therefore, it was held, help to achieve the very result that the terrorists in Northern Ireland were seeking to bring about. Channel 4 was therefore fined for non-compliance with the orders. In determining the amount of the fine, it was borne in mind that the defendants might not have appreciated the dangers of giving an unqualified assurance, but a warning was given that this consideration would be unlikely to influence courts in future cases of this nature. This ruling fails to accord sufficient weight to the public interest in the protection of journalistic sources in order to allow the media to fulfill its role of informing the public. The comment that the assurances given to Source A as a necessary precondition to publication of this material would undermine the rule of law, ignores the possibility that undermining of the rule of law might be most likely to flow from the behaviour alleged in the programme: it might appear that nothing would be more likely to undermine the rule of law than collusion between state security forces and terrorists. The decision not to impose a rolling fine on Channel 4 or make a sequestration order may be welcomed in the interests of press freedom, but it is clear that such indulgence may be refused in future, thereby creating a significant curb on investigative journalism. Schedule 7, para 3(5), as interpreted in that instance, arguably breached Art 10. The power under the Terrorism Act 2000 affords primacy to national security without explicitly providing a defence for journalists. It now must be interpreted compatibly with Art 10, in a manner which may impliedly provide such a defence. Some means of conducting the balancing act demanded by Art 10(2) should be imported if possible, as discussed below.

468 Para 31.
469 See above fn 462.
470 [1993] 2 All ER 517.

The current terrorism legislation, discussed fully in Chapter 14, provides a number of provisions criminalising failures to disclose information. They contain no journalistic shields at all, although they could clearly have an application to journalists. On their face, the obtaining of journalistic material is treated in precisely the same way as seizure of other material. Under s 19 Terrorism Act 2000 it is an offence to fail to report information to the police that comes to one's attention in the course of a trade, profession, business or employment and which might be of material assistance in preventing an act of terrorism or in arresting someone carrying out such an act.[471] Section 38B Anti-Terrorism Crime and Security Act 2001 broadens this provision immensely: it makes it an offence, subject to an un-explicated defence of reasonable excuse, for a person to fail to disclose to a police officer any information which he knows or believes *might* be of material assistance in preventing an act of terrorism or securing the apprehension or conviction of a person involved in such an act. A further wide range of people are potentially subject to criminal penalties under s 58(1) Terrorism Act 2000, the provision relating to the collection of information, which is based on section 16B Prevention of Terrorism (Temporary Provisions) Act 1989. Section 58(1) provides: 'A person commits an offence if (a) he collects or makes a record of information of a kind likely to be useful to a person committing or preparing an act of terrorism, or (b) he possesses a document or record containing information of that kind.' The offence lacks any requirement of *knowledge* regarding the nature of the information or any requirement that the person *intended* to use it in order to further the aims of terrorism, although a defence of 'reasonable excuse' is provided.

Powers under the Official Secrets Act 1989 s 8(4)

The Official Secrets Act 1989 s 8(4) makes it an offence for a person (this would normally be a journalist) to fail to comply with an official direction for the return or disposal of information which is the subject of s 5, and which is in their possession or control. Section 5, discussed in Chapter 7,[472] is headed 'information resulting from unauthorised disclosures or entrusted in confidence'. This is not a new category of information. Information will fall within s 5 if it falls within one or more of the previous categories (under ss 1, 2, 3, 4, discussed in Chapter 7) and it has been disclosed to the defendant by a Crown servant or falls within s 1 of the Official Secrets Act 1911. Section 5 is primarily aimed at journalists who receive information leaked to them by Crown servants, although it could of course cover anybody in that position.[473]

As s 5 is aimed at journalists and potentially represents an interference with their role in informing the public, it requires a very strict interpretation under s 3(1) HRA, in accordance with Art 10, bearing in mind the emphasis placed by Strasbourg on

---

471 Subsection (5) preserves an exemption in respect of legal advisers' privileged material.
472 See pp 603–4.
473 It is also aimed at the person to whom a document is entrusted by a Crown servant 'on terms requiring it to be held in confidence or in circumstances in which the Crown servant or government contractor could reasonably expect that it would be so held' (s 5(1)(ii)). The difference between entrusting and disclosing is significant in that, in the former instance, the document – but not the information it contains – will have been entrusted to the care of the person in question.

the importance of that role.[474] The fact that journalists were included at all in the net of criminal liability under s 5 has been greatly criticised on the basis that some recognition should be given to the important role of the press in informing the public about government policy and actions.[475] In arguing for a restrictive interpretation of ss 8(4) and 5 under s 3 of the HRA, a comparison could be drawn with the constitutional role of the press recognised in America by the *Pentagon Papers* case.[476]

Human Rights Act implications

Where journalistic material is seized, potentially revealing the identity of sources, Art 10 is engaged, as *Goodwin* made clear. The powers discussed, apart from the PACE power, make no express provision themselves for balancing the needs of criminal investigations against the requirements of Art 10. The powers must, however, be read and applied under the HRA compatibly with Art 10. If a source might be revealed by the exercise of the power, it would appear prima facie that s 10 of the Contempt of Court Act would apply. In *Secretary of State for Defence v Guardian Newspapers*,[477] it was found that on its true construction, s 10 applied to all judicial proceedings irrespective of their nature, or the claim or cause of action in respect of which they had been brought.[478] However, the later decision in *Director of Public Prosecutions v Channel Four Television Co Ltd and Another* found otherwise, in relation to the Terrorism Act production power. Thus by analogy it might be argued, if the question of source disclosure arose, that s10 does not apply to the other provisions, in PACE and the Official Secrets Act. One way out of this problem would be to argue that since there is ambiguity as to the question of the applicability of s 10 to all the powers discussed, it should be taken to apply, overruling the *Channel Four* case on that point. It is a pre-HRA case and therefore subject to over-ruling via s 3 HRA. The argument would be that s 10 should be read, in reliance on s 3(1), as applying to all provisions requiring the production of material, where that would lead to the disclosure of the identity of a source.

If this argument is not accepted in a suitable case, it could in any event be argued that Art 10 could be applied to the provisions via ss 6 and 3 HRA, and since s 10 has been rendered virtually synonymous with Art 10, as discussed in the main part of this chapter, source protection could be made available by that route. Clearly, the problem would be that these provisions do not make specific provision for source protection, so the courts would have to seek to read into them defences that do not exist. It could be argued at the least that it would be anomalous, given the protection offered to sources by both Art 10 and s 10, to consider ordering the seizure of journalistic material, revealing sources, without taking account of the free expression implications

474 See, e.g., *Goodwin v UK* (1996) 22 EHRR 123.
475 See, e.g., Ewing, K and Gearty, C, *Freedom under Thatcher*, 1990, Chapter 6, pp 196–201.
476 *New York Times Co v US* (1971) 403 US 713. the Supreme Court determined that no restraining order on the press could be made in order to protect the role of journalism in relation to government scrutiny.
477 [1984] 3 All ER 601; [1985] AC 339, 347, HL.
478 At pp 349B–D, 356E–F, 362D–G, 368G–369A, 372A–C.

as a specific and distinct exercise. So where the provisions offer any discretion to the court as to application or sentence, the factor of source protection should be influential via ss 3 and 6 HRA. That factor affected the sentence, as discussed, in the *Channel Four* case.

The special procedure under s 9 of and Sched 1 to PACE allow for production orders to be made only if the material is likely to be of *substantial* value to the investigation. That term could be used to limit the authorising of such orders where the identity of sources might be likely to be disclosed. A similar argument could be used in relation to the production power under the Terrorism Act 2000, Sched 5 since it can be invoked only if the material would substantially assist the investigation. Further, and more significantly, it must be in the public interest under PACE Sched 1, para 2 and under the Terrorism Act 2000 for the order to be made. That term would allow leeway to a court to impose an Art 10-based interpretation on the provisions, relying on s 3 HRA, Art 10 and *Goodwin*. The public interest could be read as requiring that the court should balance the needs of the investigation against the public interest in source protection. Indeed, Sched 1 para 2 lends itself to this interpretation since it requires the court to consider the benefit to the investigation *and* the circumstances under which the material was held.[479] In other words, a strong countervailing public interest would have to be shown in order to overcome the strong and constant interest in protecting sources.

Where journalistic material was seized *without* revealing the identity of a source, Art 10 would still be applicable via ss 3 and 6 HRA, but the strong interest in protecting sources would not be engaged. It must be noted that it is not a prerequisite of the engagement of Art 10 that the seizure of the material would inevitably reveal the source; it is sufficient that it would be likely to do so.[480] The provisions under the terrorism legislation requiring provision of information are subject to defences of a reasonable excuse for failing to comply. That term would allow leeway to a court to impose an Art 10-based interpretation on the provisions, relying on s 3 HRA and Art 10. Once a journalist had put forward the excuse that the material had been collected for the purposes of journalism, this would enable a court to balance the value of the information in revealing terrorist activity against the public interest in protecting journalistic material in determining its reasonableness.

As mentioned above, companies can claim Art 8 rights to private life and to protection for correspondence where search and seizure of material from their premises has occurred.[481] Where a search and seizure of journalistic material takes place on the premises of a media organisation Art 10 as well as Art 8 is relevant. Even where a production order had been properly obtained, argument could be raised regarding the *effects* of the search, as *Ozgur Gundem v Turkey*[482] demonstrates. The Court found that

---

479   Sched 1, para 2.
480   In *Guardian Newspapers* ibid. Lord Bridge said (at p 372): 'Secondly, is it sufficient to attract the protection of the section that the order of the court in dispute *may*, although it will not necessarily, have the effect of disclosing a "source of information" to which the section applies? In agreement with Griffiths LJ and with all your Lordships I would answer both these questions in the affirmative for the reasons given in the judgment of Griffiths LJ [1984] Ch 156, and in the speeches of my noble and learned friends, Lord Diplock and Lord Roskill, with which I fully agree.'
481   See *Société Colas Est v France* (2002) Application no. 37971/97 at para 41, fn 441 above.
482   (2001) 31 EHRR 49.

the search operation at the newspaper's premises, which resulted in newspaper production being disrupted for two days, constituted a serious interference with the applicants' freedom of expression. It accepted that the operation was conducted according to a procedure 'prescribed by law' for the purpose of preventing crime and disorder within the meaning of the second paragraph of Art 10. It did not, however, find that a measure of such dimension was proportionate to this aim. No justification had been provided for the seizure of the newspaper's archives, documentation and library.

It has been argued that the judiciary have not provided sufficient protection for journalistic material.[483] Both Arts 8 and 10 could be relied upon in arguing that a production order under s 9 and Sched 1 PACE should not be issued on grounds of disproportionality. This occurred in *R v Central Criminal Court ex p Bright*.[484] Judicial review was sought of production orders under s 9 PACE. The orders concerned material relating to David Shayler, a former employee of MI5 who had made allegations about the involvement of MI6 in a plot to assassinate Colonel Gadafy. The *Guardian* had published an emailed letter from Shayler; the *Observer* had published an article about his allegations; production orders were sought to obtain material from both newspapers regarding Shayler.

The court had to consider the principles to be applied. Lord Justice Judge found that the judge personally must be satisfied that the statutory requirements have been established. The question to be asked was not whether the decision of the constable making the application was reasonable, nor whether it would be susceptible to judicial review on *Wednesbury* grounds. He found that this followed from the express wording of the statute: 'if . . . a circuit judge is satisfied that one . . . of the sets of access conditions is fulfilled' and considered that, '[t]he purpose of this provision is to interpose between the opinion of the police officer seeking the order and the consequences to the individual or organisation to whom the order is addressed, the safeguard of a judgment and decision of a circuit judge.'[485] Further, the material to be produced or disclosed could not be merely general information which might be helpful to police inquiries, but relevant and admissible evidence. Once it was found that the relevant set of access conditions was fulfilled, it was made clear that the judge is empowered, but not bound, to make the order. The basis for refusing the order was found in the conditions stated to be relevant to the 'public interest' in paragraph 2(c). It was found that this provision allows the judge to take account of matters not expressly referred to in the set of relevant access conditions including fundamental principles.

In adopting this approach the judge relied on *R v Bristol Crown Court ex p Bristol Press and Picture Agency Ltd*[486] in which Glidewell LJ noted with approval that the judge at the Crown court had rightly taken into account both 'the importance of the impartiality and independence of the press', and 'the importance of ensuring that members of the press can photograph and report what is going on without fear of their personal safety'. In the case of journalistic material the judge considered that the potential stifling of public debate could be taken into account. He did not consider that it was necessary to take account of Art 10 of the European Convention on the basis

---

483 Costigan, R [1996] Crim LR 231.
484 [2001] 2 All ER 244.
485 At para 73 of the judgment.
486 (1987) 85 CAR 190.

that the principles it encapsulates are: 'bred in the bone of the common law'.[487] Taking the public interest in freedom of expression into account, the judge decided that the orders must be quashed. The findings in that case were made just before the HRA came fully into force. The comments of Mr Justice Judge as to the relationship between the ECHR jurisprudence and common law principle provide encouragement to argument that under the HRA such orders should not be made where the journalistic material is sought and there is a strong public interest in the material in question. The judge making the order would be bound by s 6 HRA and therefore he or she would have to take account of Strasbourg jurisprudence, unless it was clear that a result consistent with that required by Art 10 would be arrived at by following common law principles. Where the material revealed the identity of sources that jurisprudence should be relied on since it provides the strongest statement of principle, as discussed above, regarding the significance of protecting sources.

Conclusions

Where s 10 of the 1981 Act applies, source protection has been enhanced in the UK post-HRA. But it is clear that where it does *not*, journalistic material that may reveal the identity of a source may be obtained under coercion in a range of circumstances, and that little leeway for Art 10 arguments has so far been made available. The duties of the courts under ss 6 and 3 HRA make this position no longer sustainable; where scope is available under the relevant provisions for speech/harm balancing, it must be explored, and in particular the 'public interest' provision under Sched 1, para 2 PACE requires reinterpretation.

In relation to s 10, the inception of the Human Rights Act has made a difference to source protection in the sense that efforts are being made to ensure that the tests for necessity and proportionality under Art 10 are being fully applied when examining the need for ordering disclosure of the identity of a source. But no narrowing of the *Norwich Pharmacal* jurisdiction or re-interpretation of the s 10 exceptions has occurred, and this is due, it is argued, to the strong and well-established attachment of the judiciary to values opposed in this instance to journalistic ones. The tests devised for the determination of jurisdiction and for the applicability of the s 10 exception 'in the interests of justice' show a hollow judicial attachment to the values at stake since they are almost invariably fulfilled due to the very nature of the case. The new framework for judicial reasoning under the HRA outlined here would allow for a very different approach – one that would demand a lot more of the plaintiff.

The pre-HRA domestic decisions discussed above reveal that despite the introduction of s 10 the domestic courts were not affording the same weight to media freedom in examining the need for source disclosure as that afforded at Strasbourg, as revealed in the strong judgment in the *Goodwin* case. In particular, the 'interests of justice' exception was being applied in a manner that afforded greater weight to the right of institutions to take legal action than to the principle of freedom of expression. This approach has now been modified by the decision in *Ashworth*, which did evince a determination to apply Art 10 under the HRA correctly, since it fully recognised

---

487 At para 82 of the judgment.

the constant and unvarying interest in protecting sources. The findings in *Ashworth* demonstrate, however, that there is still a failure to engage fully with the Strasbourg reasoning process in respect of the doctrine of proportionality. The courts' approach to this journalistic privilege still appears to depend very much on the *nature* of the other interest at stake. The real *extent* to which it might be damaged still appears to be a largely subordinate consideration. If an employee of a company appears to be the source, that fact continues to have a very significant influence on the judicial response, while the stance taken under the national security exception presumably would not differ significantly from that taken in *Guardian Newspapers*.

The judges consider that the stance they are now taking is in accordance with the Strasbourg one. This chapter has argued that this is not the case – the judges have misapplied *Goodwin*. *Interbrew* suggests that they appear to prefer the means/end balancing proportionality test from *de Freitas* rather than the speech/harm balancing act. Where speech/harm balancing has occurred, as in *Ashworth,* the level of scrutiny adopted has not been strict enough. If that level of scrutiny was used, and use was made of the parallel analysis from *Campbell* where Art 8 is engaged, the analytical tools made available to the judiciary would allow for a more effective teasing out of the values at stake in any particular instance. The true value of confidentiality in the circumstances could be gauged. But on the other side of the coin, where sources appeared to be motivated by a desire to 'spin' or doctor the information in question, the general interest in source protection would remain unvarying, but other speech arguments, based on the public interest value of the information, would be undermined since the speech rationale from truth would be lightly engaged at best.

The judicial reasoning in source disclosure cases is typical of that found in other common law areas covered by this book, such as common law contempt and breach of confidence. There is a strong tendency to erect apparent legal barriers that in reality can inevitably be crossed, thus giving the appearance of protection to an interest that the judges are not in sympathy with. The first barrier is normally created by the *Norwich Pharmacal* jurisdiction, but its demands will inevitably be satisfied since it is hard to imagine a source disclosure case in which a breach of confidence will not have occurred. The court then considers the next apparent barrier, the need to show that one of the s 10 exceptions applies. But the 'interests of justice' exception will always apply since a possible action for breach of confidence will always be available. The need to show that a *serious* legal wrong has occurred appears to have no inhibiting effect at this stage: it appears to be assumed that a breach of confidence is always a serious matter. Pre-*Goodwin* the courts would always then find that disclosure was necessary. Even in *Interbrew* Sedley LJ was preoccupied by the 'legitimacy' of Interbrew's intended resort to law, which of course would always be a factor for the reasons given. In the vast majority of cases considered in this chapter, including the post-HRA ones, disclosure has been ordered. So has any further protection for sources really been created due to *Goodwin* and the inception of the HRA?

In relation to the question of necessity a change has occurred. The difference, post-*Goodwin*, is that the Strasbourg Court has found that there is an unvarying interest in source protection. So there has to be a clear and strong interest to set on the other side *other than* the plaintiff's apparent desire to bring an action. The unvarying interest in protecting sources cannot be outweighed by the legitimacy of a resort to law alone since that would always be a factor. In *Interbrew* the other special feature was the malevolent purpose of the source; in *Ashworth* it was the interest in medical confidentiality. In both instances it is arguable that the courts did not examine the nature of that other factor closely since they were inclined towards the outcome achieved. There has been no post-HRA case yet where it would be difficult to identify a special factor *but* the source might perpetrate further leaks (unlike the situation in *Saunders* and in *John*). *Camelot* arguably provided an example pre-HRA. How would the courts react in such an instance? In reality two interests would be opposed. First, there would be the interest of the company or institution in protecting its confidential information – something that the judges take very seriously. On the other side, there would be an imported notion, from *Goodwin,* of the need to protect sources – a matter that has not traditionally struck the judiciary as appealing. If a *Camelot* type of case arose post-*Ashworth* it would pose an interesting dilemma for the judges.

It may be asked *why* the British judiciary are traditionally disinclined to protect sources. First, it seems to be for the reason given earlier, that they can readily envisage the concrete harm done to a company by a leak, the 'ticking bomb argument, but the opposing interest strikes them as much more nebulous. Second, there appears to be a suspicion of s 10. It was introduced by a Labour Government as a deliberate means of overturning a House of Lords' decision in the wake of a case with a controversial political dimension. The judges appear to view s 10 with some suspicion, partly because they may have expected the *government* to have been the main beneficiary of the protection s 10 offers – since leaking information is often associated with government activity.[488] No exception contained in s 10 would have covered leaked governmental information, unless there was a national security dimension, without the broad interpretation given to the interests of justice exception which would now cover it. Thus the courts have removed some of the protection government may have arrogated to itself for its own purposes.

It may be concluded that in the UK investigative journalism relying on sources has received some encouragement from legal developments and that post-HRA the judiciary have shown an enhanced determination to apply *Goodwin* to domestic decisions. But the protection for sources is still fairly precarious and is not embedded fully in the judicial consciousness as a common law principle to which they are strongly wedded.

---

488 In *Interbrew* fn 389 above, at para 7, Sedley LJ said: 'It should not be forgotten that in this country, then as now, the principal source of unattributable leaks to the media – in the form of off-the-record briefings – and therefore the principal beneficiary of a rule protecting the secrecy of sources, was government itself.'

Chapter 6

Offensive speech

1 Introduction[1]

*Freedom of expression constitutes one of the essential foundations of a [democratic]
society, one of the basic conditions for its progress and for the development of every
man. Subject to paragraph 2 of Article 10, it is applicable not only to 'information'
or 'ideas' that are favourably received or regarded as inoffensive, but also to those
that offend, shock or disturb the state or any sector of the population. Such are the
demands of that pluralism, tolerance and broadmindedness without which there is
no democratic society. – Handyside v UK (1976).*

This chapter in essence asks three questions. Where is the borderline in the twenty-first
century between the images or words that can and cannot be published in the UK on
the ground of causing offence? How satisfactory is that borderline in free speech terms?
Since the criminal law regulates expression on grounds of offence, how satisfactory
is it that the important mediums of film and broadcasting are regulated beyond what
the law allows?

---

1 Texts referred to below: Fenwick, H and Phillipson, G, *Media Freedom under the Human Rights Act*,
2006, Chapters 8, 9, 10, 11, 12; Barendt, E, *Freedom of Speech*, 2nd edn, 2005, Chapters 10, 12
and 13, (1st edn will also be referred to); Feldman, D, *Civil Liberties in England and Wales*, 2002;
Robertson, G and Nichol, D, *Media Law*, 1999, Chapter 14; Bailey, Harris and Jones, *Civil Liberties
and Human Rights Cases and Materials*, 5th edn, 2002, Chapter 6; Carey, P and Sanders, J, *Media
Law*, 3rd edn, 2004, Sweet and Maxwell, Chapters 5 and 9 (basic guide); Gibbons, T, *Regulating the
Media*, 1998; Dworkin, R, 'Do we have a right to pornography?', in *A Matter of Principle*, 1985; Itzen,
C (ed), *Pornography: Women, Violence and Civil Liberties*, 1993, OUP; Feinberg, J, *The Moral Limits
of the Criminal Law: Offense to Others*, 1985, OUP; MacKinnon, C, *Feminism Unmodified*, 1987;
'Feminism, Marxism, method and the state', in Bartlett and Kennedy (eds), *Feminist Legal Theory*,
1991, HarperCollins. See also Hare, I, 'Legislating Against Hate: the Legal Response to Bias Crimes'
(1997) 17 OJLS 415; Weinstein, J, 'First Amendment challenges to hate crime legislation: where's the
speech?' (1992) 11 Criminal Justice Ethics 6; Sumner, LW, *The Hateful And The Obscene: Studies in
the Limits of Free Expression*, 2004, University of Toronto Press. Background: Marsh, J, *Word Crimes:
Blasphemy, Culture, and Literature in Nineteenth-century England*, 1998, University of Chicago
Press; O'Higgins, P, *Censorship in Britain*, 1972, Nelson; Robertson, G, *Obscenity*, 1979, Weidenfeld
and Nicolson, and (with Nichol, D), *Media Law*, 1999, Chapter 3; MacMillan, PR, *Censorship and
Public Morality*, 1983, Ashgate; Simpson, AWB, *Pornography and Politics: the Williams Committee in
Retrospect*, 1983, Pergamon Press; Travis, A, *Bound and Gagged – A Secret History of Obscenity in
Britain*, 2000, Profile Books.

This chapter covers a variety of forms of expression. Much of it is primarily visual and also falls outside the category of political expression. This may be said of some films, of music, opera, mime, plays, paintings, all of which are covered by aspects of the law and regulation considered below. But aspects of political expression are also covered, since some regulation of political expression is a feature of broadcasting regulation, while hate speech almost inevitably has a political message. Under the HRA 1998, the judiciary are finding that the stance they traditionally tend to take towards the different types of expression is being reinforced by the hierarchy of expression recognised within the Strasbourg jurisprudence, as the Introduction to this Part indicated.[2] The Strasbourg stance tends to accord with their own leanings as expressed in the free expression decisions taken in the pre-HRA era that are discussed in Chapter 3,[3] although the value placed upon political speech at Strasbourg is arguably higher. However, if the justifications for freedom of expression considered in the Introduction are taken into account, particularly those from truth and self-fulfilment, it is suggested that there is no convincing basis for relegating 'artistic' expression to a lowly place in such a hierarchy, at the domestic level.

The inception of the HRA meant that the UK courts were faced with the difficult theoretical problems associated with a positive right to freedom of expression as opposed to a negative liberty. This is a matter that is especially pertinent in relation to the forms of expression considered in this chapter. Instead of merely determining whether a particular statute or a doctrine of the common law applies to a factual situation, the courts must consider the weight to be given to a particular manifestation of expression, when considering the claim that an interference with it is justified. As Chapter 3 indicated, they were already going down this path in creating a common law right to freedom of expression. But they now have to consider the ambit of such a right in a much wider range of situations, and have to grapple with the doctrinal constraints of the Art 10(2) exceptions. Restraints on explicit expression are found in a range of rules deriving from a number of common law doctrines, statutes, and the Codes or Guidelines of regulatory bodies. Some of the rules, based on concepts of obscenity, indecency or insult are far too subjective, imprecise and broad to be fully in harmony with the free speech justifications. If the propositions advanced in the Introduction to Part II are accepted, media regulation designed to intervene in the market can be defended even when it affects the content of broadcasts in terms of 'must carry' requirements designed to reflect the values of plurality and creativity. On the other hand, such regulation based on the content of broadcasts as indicated by such uncertain terms as 'taste and decency' will be in a far more doubtful position. Further, the distinctions founded on such uncertain terms that will be discussed below, based partly on the medium in question, must also be called into question.

This is a context in which it is suggested that the HRA will not have and has not had a radical impact as far as the general statutory regime governing explicit expression is concerned. It will be argued that it has some potential to have an impact as regards specific decisions taken under that statutory regime; in relation to the common law,

2 See pp 309–11.
3 See pp 124–27.

especially the law of blasphemy, and in relation to aspects of media regulation. But the relevant Strasbourg jurisprudence is not of assistance to arguments in favour of close scrutiny of decisions taken in this context. The Introduction to Part II is intended to provide a theoretical framework, based on the free speech justifications, within which to view the laws that are discussed below. As the domestic Art 10 explicit expression jurisprudence takes form, the stance taken in relation to those propositions is determining its distinctive quality.

This chapter begins by examining the free speech justifications in their application to explicit speech. It moves on to examine the stance taken towards such speech at Strasbourg, and then proceeds to examine and evaluate the key substantive criminal offences relevant in this area, including offences relating to religious and racial sensibilities. Such offences form the backdrop to the following discussion of the regulatory regimes applicable to broadcasting and film. That discussion also covers the special position of the internet.

2 Law and pornography: theoretical considerations

The question as to how far sexually explicit speech deserves the same protection as other forms of expression and if it does not, how far and for what reasons it should be suppressed, has, as Barendt notes, '. . . almost certainly elicited more academic commentary than any other [free speech] topic'.[4] As striking as the amount of writing on the subject is the failure by academics of different persuasions to reach a consensus view. Thus, for example, AWB Simpson, a former member of the Williams Committee appointed in 1977 to review obscenity law, recalls that the law certainly did not represent such a consensus: 'Before, during and after the Committee sat, the chorus of abuse against the law continued; virtually everyone claimed that it was unworkable.'[5] In a similar vein, conservatives,[6] liberals[7] and feminists[8] have all attacked the Committee's findings and all for different reasons. In addition, even to speak of 'feminist' and 'liberal' positions necessitates a conscious simplification, because these two opposing positions, at first sight monolithic, are in fact riven by internal debate; in particular,

---

4 Barendt, E, *Freedom of Speech*, 1987, 1st edn, p 245.

5 Simpson, AWB, *Pornography and Politics: the Williams Committee in Retrospect*, 1983, p 80.

6 See, e.g., the comments of Mary Whitehouse in *The Sunday Times* that, as a result of the Committee's report, '. . . we are going from a quicksand into . . . a very, very mucky quagmire . . .', quoted in Simpson, ibid, p 44; he also quotes (p 45) a *Daily Telegraph* leader which criticised the 'some would say excessively liberal principle' it endorsed.

7 See, e.g., the detailed analysis in Dworkin, R, 'Do we have a right to pornography?', in *A Matter of Principle*, 1985, in which he broadly endorses the Committee's conclusions, but argues that these cannot be supported by the arguments they deployed.

8 The whole approach of the feminists is hostile to the broadly liberal stance adopted by the Committee; see, e.g., Brownmiller, S, *Against Our Will*, 1975, where it is asserted that all previous value systems, including the liberal tradition, have worked against the interests of women. For explicit criticism of the Committee by a more moderate feminist, see Eckersley, R, 'Whither the feminist campaign? An evaluation of feminist critiques of pornography', 15 Int J Soc of Law 149. Eckersley dismisses Williams as having 'simply fail[ed] to register the feminist objection' (p 174).

the feminist camp displays a conspicuous lack of unanimity.[9] Nevertheless, an attempt will be made, in what follows, to outline briefly the 'core' of each stance and evaluate the strength of their arguments, both against each other and directly on the subject of the permissibility of censorship in this area.

The conservative position

The conservative position, which in the popular consciousness is probably most associated with Mary Whitehouse, finds its academic and somewhat more abstract exposition in Lord Devlin's work, *The Enforcement of Morals*, 1965. In essence, Devlin's view is that since a shared set of basic moral values is essential to society, it is as justified in protecting itself against attacks on these values (such as that mounted by pornography) as it is in protecting itself against any other phenomena which threaten its basic existence, such as violent public disorder. On this thesis, moral corruption of the individual is to be prevented in order to ensure the ultimate survival of society. By contrast, Whitehouse's concerns are presumably more with damage to individuals *per se*, a position which, as argued below, appears to reflect that taken by the case law in this area. Devlin's position, by contrast, is clearly not compatible with most existing UK law:[10] it could neither support nor even account for the existence of the public good defence in s 4 of the Obscene Publications Act 1959,[11] or indeed any similar defence: it would appear somewhat absurd to argue that material which threatened the very survival of society should be allowed to circulate freely on the grounds that it was somehow also in the public good.[12]

Devlin's position also appears to have been placed in doubt on the theoretical level by Hart's incisive critique.[13] Briefly, Hart's objections are as follows: on the more favourable reading of Devlin's position, he is not assuming, but trying to establish the truth of the proposition that a shared set of moral standards (going on Devlin's account far beyond simple prohibitions on violence, theft, etc) is an essential attribute of society. If this is the case, argues Hart, Devlin fails to establish the proposition for the simple reason that he offers no empirical evidence to support it. This leads one, Hart continues, to the suspicion that Devlin actually *assumes* the truth of the proposition and thus builds his theory on a tautology: having defined society as a system of shared beliefs he then concludes, with perfect logic but some futility, that if those shared beliefs change radically or unanimity is lost, the society has disintegrated. Devlin's position, therefore does not strike one as particularly strong.

---

9   For comments on the divisions in the feminist critique of pornography see Eckersley, ibid. See also Lacey, N, 93 JLS 93.

10 It may however find reflection in some of the more obscure common law offences such as conspiracy to corrupt public morals and outraging public decency. The Lords, in *Knuller v DPP* [1973] AC 435; [1972] 3 WLR 143; (1972) 56 Cr App R 633, HL, a much criticised decision, arguably gave some support to the Devlin thesis. For discussion of the decision, see below, p 482.

11 For discussion of the defence, see below p 472 *et seq*.

12 Under the 1959 Act, the defence of public good only comes into play once it has been decided that the material is likely to deprave and corrupt: *Penguin Books* [1961] Crim LR 176 (the *Lady Chatterley's Lover* trial). See below, p 473.

13 For a summary of Hart's critique, see 'Social solidarity and the enforcement of morality', in *Essays in Jurisprudence and Philosophy*, 1983.

The liberal position

The liberal position on pornography is broadly united around general opposition to censorship in the absence of clear evidence of a concrete harm caused by its free availability.[14] However, unanimity does not exist as to the rationales for free speech most applicable to defending a liberty to read or view pornographic material. There is general agreement that Meiklejohn's argument from participation in democracy[15] is of little relevance; as Dworkin caustically remarks, 'No one is denied an equal voice in the political process . . . when he is forbidden to circulate photographs of genitals to the public at large'.[16]

A variant of Mill's argument from truth[17] was avowedly the free speech justification adopted by the Williams Committee convened in 1979 to report on obscenity; although they expressed some scepticism at Mill's perhaps rather naive conviction that in a *laissez faire* market of ideas, truth would always win out,[18] they endorsed the main thrust of his theory. Interference with the free flow of ideas and artistic endeavour was unacceptable since it amounted to ruling out in advance possible modes of human development, before it was known whether or not they would be desirable or necessary. Since they also reached the conclusion that '. . . no one has invented or in our opinion *could* invent, an instrument that would suppress only [worthless pornography] and could not be turned against something . . . of [possibly] a more creative kind',[19] they concluded that this risk of suppressing worthwhile creative art ruled out censorship of the written word. (They regarded standard photographic pornography as not expressing anything that could be regarded as an 'idea' and so as unprotected by the argument from truth.)

Ronald Dworkin has mounted a sustained attack on this rationale;[20] it rests, he contends, on the instrumental justification that allowing the free circulation of ideas is necessary to enable individuals to make intelligent and informed choices about how they want to lead their lives and then flourish in them. He finds that such an argument is unable to support its own conclusion against censorship; for, he urges, it must be accepted that allowing the free availability of pornography will 'sharply limit' the ability of some (perhaps the majority) to shape their cultural understanding of sexuality in a way they think best – a way in which sexuality has dignity and beauty. His argument appears to conclude that the justification from self-development does not argue conclusively against censorship, because of the plausible case that forbidding some pornography will for many people greatly assist in their self-development. Dworkin is surely correct when he concludes that not self-development, but the straightforward argument from *moral autonomy* amounts to the strongest case against censorship in this area. This argument simply points out that judging for an individual what will and will not be beneficial for

---

14 See Feinberg, J, *The Moral Limits of the Criminal Law: Offense to Others*, 1985. For a brief discussion of the possible link between pornography and the commission of sexual offences, see below, p 565.
15 See above, pp 303–4 and fn 27, p 303.
16 Dworkin, R, op. cit., fn 1, p 336.
17 See above, pp 302–3.
18 Report of the Committee on Obscenity and Film Censorship (Williams Committee), Cmnd 7772, 1979, para 5.20.
19 Ibid, para 5.24.
20 Dworkin, R, op. cit., fn 1.

him or her to read represents a clear invasion of the strong individual right to decide moral issues concerned with one's own life for oneself.[21] Such an invasion could therefore only be justified if a serious risk of substantial damage to the concrete well being of society was shown.[22] Since the law does not posit such a risk, censorship is unacceptable. Whether this argument also provides a convincing answer to the radical feminist objections to free access to pornography will be considered below; this position must first be sketched out.

It should finally be noted that liberals are willing to support restrictions on the outlets and public display of pornography[23] on the grounds that such restrictions do not necessarily spring from contempt for those who read pornography, but may simply reflect the genuine and personal aesthetic preferences of those who would rather not have to suffer the continual and ugly spectacle of publicly displayed pornography.[24]

The pro-censorship feminist position

The views of feminist writers on the harms pornography does, on the justifications offered for allowing its free availability and on what, if anything, the law should do about it are many and varied.[25] However, the pro-censorship feminist position on the possibility of legal control of pornography is generally equated with the views of Catherine MacKinnon and Andrea Dworkin, who framed an Indianapolis Ordinance giving rise to civil liability for trafficking in pornography or forcing it upon unwilling recipients; its constitutionality was successfully challenged on the grounds of incompatibility with the First Amendment.[26] The essence of this variant of feminist thought is that while pornography is regarded as causing harm to some individual women, by causing some individual men to perpetrate rape, battery and sexual abuse,[27] pornography causes a

---

21 See above, Chapter 1, pp 7–8.
22 It is submitted that other possible justifications for abrogating speech (described in Chapter 1, pp 13–14) are not in most instances applicable here. But see below, p 565 for consideration of a possible link between pornography and sexual offences.
23 Such as, e.g., the recommendations of the Williams Committee; see their 'Summary of our proposals', above, fn 1.
24 See Dworkin, R, op. cit., fn 1, pp 355–58, where he broadly endorses the Williams Committee's proposals.
25 For feminist writers who take a different stance on pornography from that broadly examined here, see any of the following: the chapters on pornography in Smart, *Feminism and the Power of Law*, 1989, Routledge, in which the author expresses distrust of using the law to control pornography; Rhode, *Justice and Gender*, 1989, Harvard University Press, in which the extent to which feminism has framed a puritanical ideology of sexuality and pornography is deplored: it is argued that women who find explicit depictions of, e.g., bondage or anonymous sex don't 'need more sexual shame, guilt and hypocrisy, this time served up as feminism'. See also Jackson, 'Catherine MacKinnon and feminist jurisprudence: a critical appraisal' (1992) JLS, pp 195–13 for a moderate critique, particularly of MacKinnon's views on the impossibility of non-coercive heterosexual activity in contemporary society.
26 For the first instance decision, see *American Booksellers Assoc, etc v Hudnitt III, Mayor, City of Indianapolis et al.* 598 F Supp 1316. For the (unsuccessful) appeal, see 771 F 2d 323.
27 See, e.g., MacKinnon, C, *Feminism Unmodified*, 1987, pp 184–91; 'Pornography as Sex Discrimination.' *Law and Inequality: A Journal of Theory and Practice* 38 (1986): 4; *In Harm's Way: The Pornography Civil Rights Hearings.* edited and introduced (with Andrea Dworkin), 'The Roar on the Other Side of Silence' (introduction), 1997; *Only Words*, 1993, Harvard University Press.

far more subtle and all-pervasive harm to all women. It is on the latter argument that the remainder of the discussion will concentrate.

In some of their more terse, dramatic statements, such as 'Pornography is violence against women',[28] and 'We define pornography as a practice of sex discrimination',[29] it sounds as if MacKinnon and A Dworkin regard the very existence of pornography as a concrete harm to women which goes far beyond mere offence and yet is not a physical harm. However, in the more precise explanations they offer, it seems clear that the harm is caused through the effect it has on men's view of women: 'Men treat women as who they see women as being. Pornography constructs who that is.' In other words, the argument does remain, as R Dworkin claims, 'a causal one'.[30] At this point, having posited a link between pornography and the way men treat women, the explanation draws in the more general radical feminist thesis that men have near total power over women and that consequently, 'the way men see women defines who women can be'.[31] Elsewhere, MacKinnon explains that this power is generated by the fact that men have managed to establish the total 'privileging' of their interests and perceptions and the concomitant complete subordination of women and then passed this off as reality or 'just the way things are'. MacKinnon calls the resulting illusion 'metaphysically nearly perfect'.[32] Several more moderate feminists have pointed out[33] that this view places feminism in the bizarre position of having to deny the possibility of its own existence because it entails assuming that all available modes of thought and perception are male, although masquerading as neutral. If this were true, it is hard to see how women could even come to realise that they were oppressed, let alone frame proposals for affirmative action to free themselves from male dominance. MacKinnon has indeed asserted that 'Feminism affirms women's point of view by ... explaining its impossibility',[34] but since MacKinnon herself has in fact somehow managed to construct a substantive and highly influential feminist point of view – including the analysis of pornography under consideration – this reply is not fully convincing. It might be thought at this point that since acceptance of the radical feminist thesis on pornography is apparently only possible if one also accepts a metaphysical theory which seems both to deny its own existence and to involve acceptance of the most comprehensive conspiracy theory ever devised, the thesis can be summarily dismissed.

This, however, would be premature. The most significant feminist point with respect to pornography is the effect it is said to have on men's view of women and therefore on the way they treat them. One does not have to accept the general radical feminist thesis in order to give *some* consideration to the proposition that pornography, through

---

28 The basic thesis of Dworkin, A, *Pornography: Men Possessing Women*, 1979, The Women's Press, quoted in Simpson, op. cit., fn 1, p 71.
29 MacKinnon, op. cit., fn 1, p 175. The quotation given refers specifically to the Indianapolis ordinance, but equally summarises MacKinnon's analysis of pornography.
30 Dworkin, R, 'Liberty and pornography', *The New York Review of Books*, 15 August 1991, p 12.
31 MacKinnon, op. cit., fn 1, p 172.
32 See 'Feminism, Marxism, method and the state', in Bartlett and Kennedy (eds), *Feminist Legal Theory*, 1991, HarperCollins, p 182, and 'Feminism, Marxism, Method and the State: An Agenda for Theory' *Signs: Journal of Women in Culture and Society*, 1983, University of Chicago Press, 515: 7.
33 See, e.g., Sandra Harding's introduction to MacKinnon's 'Feminism, Marxism, method and the state', in Harding, S, *Feminism and Methodology*, 1987, Indiana University Press.
34 Bartlett and Kennedy (eds), *Feminist Legal Theory*, 1991, p 181.

the effect it has on men, oppresses women. Consequently, the discussion will now turn to considering whether the feminist thesis can still provide a justification for restrictions on the freedom to consume pornography even if the notion of total female subordination is rejected.

The oppression of women caused by pornography is claimed to manifest itself in the following three distinct ways. First, women are discriminated against, sexually harassed and physically assaulted in all walks of life; this constitutes a denial of their civil right to equality. Secondly, women are denied their positive liberty, their right to equal participation in the political process because of the image in men's minds constructed by pornography which 'strips and devastates women of credibility',[35] and consequently prevents women's contributions from being taken seriously. Finally, pornography 'silences' women – even their negative ability to speak is denied because they are not seen as fully human agents, but rather as dehumanised creatures who 'desperately want to be bound, battered, tortured, humiliated and killed'.[36] The argument that the state should, therefore, seek to ban pornography on the basis of furtherance of equality, just as it seeks to outlaw discrimination in employment, is developed in *Only Words*.[37]

Two points may be made in response to the above. First, this thesis attributes to men a uniformly passive and receptive attitude to all pornographic images.[38] Nowhere in a long essay on pornography[39] does MacKinnon appear to advert to the possibility that many men may completely reject the 'message' of violent misogynistic pornography, even though some may be aroused by it. Her theory thus, in effect, amounts to a profound refusal to recognise the immense difference which men's backgrounds, education and life experiences will have on their responses,[40] and more generally, the enormous variety of human responses to any given phenomena which will be found even amongst those of similar backgrounds; ultimately, her theory denies (male) free will and with it men's individual voices.[41]

The second point is that if one leaves aside the extreme idea of the total control of men over women described above, it then becomes impossible to accept the immense influence that is attributed to the consumption of pornography. The idea, for example, that pornography silences women in all walks of life remains quite simply, 'strikingly

---

35 MacKinnon (1987), op. cit., fn 1, p 193.

36 MacKinnon, (1987) op. cit., fn 1, p 172. Cf Andrea Dworkin's description of the view that rape law evinces of women as one in which rape is not really against a woman's will, 'because what she wants underneath is to have anything done to her that violates or humiliates or hurts her': *Pornography: Men Possessing Women*, 1979.

37 MacKinnon, C, *Only Words*, 1993. For criticism of the notion that banning pornography should be viewed as an aspect of the furtherance of equality, see Sadurski, 'On 'Seeing speech through an equality lens': a critique of egalitarian arguments for suppression of hate speech and pornography' (1996) 16(4) OJLS 713.

38 Andrea Dworkin attributes a similarly monolithic character to men; consider, e.g., the following description of the male sex: 'Terror issues forth from the male; illuminates his essential nature and his basic purpose' (*Pornography: Men Possessing Women*, 1979, p 74).

39 MacKinnon, 1987, Chapter 14.

40 For criticism of this characteristic failing in MacKinnon's work generally, see Jackson, 'Catherine MacKinnon and feminist jurisprudence: a critical appraisal' (1992) JLS, pp 195–13.

41 An ironic point, since MacKinnon often talks of men 'silencing' women.

implausible'[42] perhaps precisely *because* it is so eloquently expressed and it is hard to take seriously the notion that pornography denies women the right to participate in political life. One could only accept such arguments if one regarded women as defined completely by the images of pornography; as has been seen, that argument in turn could only have force if one first accepted that men's view of women is almost wholly constructed by pornography and then could agree to the assertion that men's view of women is all that women are. The impossibility of accepting such counter-intuitive propositions means, it is submitted, that the radical feminist argument does not convincingly establish that the availability of pornography represents or causes actual infringements of the rights of women. In strict liberal theory, therefore, the argument from moral autonomy would, in the absence of competing individual rights, require that the choice as to which kinds of explicit literature to read and which to shun, remains properly with the individual. However, a number of comments may be made as to this finding. First, in contrast to many other types of speech, we have found that the only convincing argument for free speech in this area rests upon the interest in moral autonomy, unbolstered by other free speech justifications. Secondly, it seems self-evident that some invasions of autonomy – those which interfere with choices which go to the core of the individual's identity – must be more grave than invasions with respect to more peripheral areas. Interference with the individual's choice to view violent misogynistic pornographic films with no pretension to artistic expression is surely less of an infringement of his autonomy than, say, interfering with the right of the individual to have homosexual relations. If this argument is accepted, it follows that the autonomy interest here is comparatively weak.

These two points, taken together, would suggest that the total case for protecting inartistic violent pornography is not a particularly strong one. This case, such as it is, must then be balanced against the risk that there may possibly be a link between pornography and the commission of sexual offences. The argument as to this link is still ongoing and it is submitted that a proper evaluation of the evidence in this area falls within the ambit of the social sciences rather than a study of civil liberties. *Some* evidence has been produced of a link, although this evidence is disputed by other studies;[43] what is clear is that there may be said to be a chance of a risk that pornography contributes towards the motivation of sex offenders. It is submitted that until a consensus on the evidential question emerges, the law is entitled, given the relative weakness of the argument for protecting violent hardcore pornography, to take a pragmatic stance and allow narrow and selective censorship of at least sexual violence in films, subject to an artistic merits defence, rather than insist that pornography should be unrestricted

---

42 Dworkin, R, op. cit., fn 1, p 14; Rhode also asks how, if women are silenced by pornography, a small group of feminists managed to mount a challenge to some of the most cherished principles of American constitutionalism and one of its most successful entertainment industries: Rhode, D, *Justice and Gender*, 1989, Harvard University Press.

43 Evidence for a causal link is quoted in MacKinnon (1987), op. cit., fn 1, pp 184–91, while R Dworkin, cites a recent UK study which finds against such a link: Cumberbatch, G and Howitt, D, *A Measure of Uncertainty – the Effects of the Mass Media*, 1989, University of Luton Press. The findings of this latter study were published in the *Daily Telegraph*, 23 December 1990. Eckersley discusses the issue (Eckersley, R, 'Whither the feminist campaign? An evaluation of feminist critiques of pornography', 15 Int J Soc of Law 149, pp 161–63). See also Itzen, C (ed), *Pornography: Women, Violence and Civil Liberties*, 1993, which puts forward a body of evidence supporting a causal link.

until the hypothesised link with sex offences has been established beyond reasonable doubt. Further, the case for withdrawal of restrictions must also be balanced against the possibility that while a particular group of men may be influenced by pornography towards the commission of sexual offences, a further group may also be influenced by it towards psychologically damaging treatment of women falling short of any criminal offence. If the link discussed above were established, this further argument would come into play, since it would seem strange if pornography could have a highly significant influence on one group of men but none at all on any other. Thus, this point supports the pragmatic stance advocated above, although it falls well short of accepting the general pro-censorship feminist position.

A further, distinct argument concerns the harm that may be done to the *participants* in the making of hardcore pornographic films. This will depend on the nature of the pornographic industry in the particular jurisdiction. If such films portray a variety of actual sexual acts, including sado-masochistic ones, the participants may suffer psychological or even physical harm. This point is of especial pertinence to women since, typically, the female participants are subjected to sexual acts in which they are more victim than perpetrator. For example, a typical scenario might include one woman having sex with a large number of men and being 'roughed up' by them. In such circumstances, it is arguable that the woman's consent may be undermined owing to uncertainty as to what will occur, intimidation into accepting certain acts, such as anal sex, and, more generally, owing to the power disparity between the woman and the almost exclusively male directors of such films. The women participants are, typically, young and from economically deprived groups. If, for example, a woman is alone with a group of men in a house at which filming is taking place and has already been bullied and intimidated, the question whether she is continuing to give informed consent to a variety of sexual acts, which have been occurring for a period of time, begins to lose any reality.[44] If it *was* fairly clear that she was no longer giving such consent, it is hard to imagine that it would be possible, in practice, for her to seek the protection of the law, a fact of which she, and the film-makers, will be aware. The film-makers are under commercial pressures to push participants into accepting more extreme acts. If it appears from the nature of a film that participants may have been intimidated and subjected to actions verging on sexual abuse (owing to the circumstances, including the duration of one session), both feminists and liberals, on the arguments indicated, would unite in accepting regulation. On this argument, films depicting simulated sado-masochism or actual sexual acts would not necessarily be banned completely, but the conditions under which such filming could take place would be subject to rigorous controls, with the welfare of the participants in mind, and designed to be certain that

---

44 During the making of a documentary into the making of hard core pornographic films in Los Angeles, *Hard Core* (broadcast on Channel 4 on 7 April 2001), the director of the Channel 4 documentary intervened when it appeared that due to bullying and intimidation by the director of the pornographic film, the woman participant was no longer capable of giving informed consent. She had already been subjected to painful and humiliating acts to which it appeared probable that she had not given consent. In other words, consented-to acts had verged into actions going beyond the apparent boundaries of what she had consented to beforehand. Despite her distress occasioned by painful, forceful oral sex, the director wished to continue filming and she was told that she must next participate in a group orgy scene in which she would be the only woman. She appeared to acquiesce but, after the intervention, she, and the film crew, had to leave immediately. See further *The Times*, 9 April 2001, p 27.

full, informed consent had always been given. But where it was clear that such controls had not been in place, and that harm, such as psychological trauma, had occurred, censorship would clearly be warranted, except in exceptional cases owing to the strong artistic merits of the film. Where it could only be said that a risk of such harm was possible, it could be viewed as a further factor to be weighed in the balance, along with those identified above.

As a matter of interest, it is worth considering what the position would be if radical feminist scholars could somehow establish that pornography really did construct the social reality of women's identity. How would the feminist argument fare in competition with the liberal arguments for free speech? In the case of the three instrumental justifications, the arguments from democracy, truth and self-development,[45] the feminist thesis would be able to demonstrate how, in the case of pornography, each argues for restraint on speech. They would argue that free circulation of pornography hinders, even prevents women's participation in the democratic process; it assists not in finding the truth, but in constructing false and all-pervading images of women; it does *not* assist in the healthy development of those who take advantage of its free availability: rather they become rapists, abusers, misogynists.

The one liberal defence of free speech not *explicitly* addressed by the feminist argument is the argument from moral autonomy, which it was suggested above[46] provides the only arguable defence of the right to choose to read pornography. How would this argument fare if it was shown that the basic rights to equality, political participation and speech were in reality denied to all women by the consumption of pornography? Ronald Dworkin has considered this hypothetical position, in which he does not accept that pornography causes individual men to rape and assault women, but accepts the remainder of the feminist claims. One might consider that he would conclude that the massive infringements of women's strong individual rights and the concomitant loss of their moral autonomy would clearly override the comparatively minor invasions of men's free speech and autonomy represented by restrictions on pornography. Somewhat surprisingly, however, Dworkin argues that even if it were the case that the posited harms were actually visited upon all women by pornography, still this would provide no justification for restraining its free availability.[47] Such a view places the right to consume hardcore pornography over the rights of half the population to be treated with dignity and respect, to equal participation in democratic government and to free speech itself. Such a conclusion represents, it is submitted, a complete betrayal of the premise on which Dworkin's whole theory of rights is based, namely the overriding duty of the state to treat all its citizens with equal concern and respect.

3 Legal responses to explicit expression

That the above conclusions on pornography are not in general accepted by states, is revealed by the fact that almost all Bills or Charters of Rights, apart from the US Bill of Rights, contain an exception to the free speech clause which, *inter alia*, allows restraint

---

45 See the Introduction to Part II, above, pp 305–6.
46 See pp 455–6.
47 Dworkin, R, op. cit., fn 1, p 15.

on freedom of speech on the broad ground of protection of morality. The 'absolute' nature of the First Amendment, in contrast, has led the US courts to interpret the First Amendment so as to exclude obscene speech from the category of protected speech.[48] Section 14 of the New Zealand Bill of Rights protects freedom of expression, but the protection is subject to such 'reasonable limits prescribed by law as may be justified in a free and democratic society'. Such limits include the regulation of obscenity and pornography.[49] The justification borne in mind in interpreting such exceptions is the harm to be guarded against which seems to include three possibilities: the corruption of persons, particularly children as the more vulnerable; the shock or outrage caused by public displays of certain material and the commission of sex crimes.[50] The development of UK law has been based on the avoidance of the first two possibilities mentioned, although in relation to the visual media, the third has had some influence. On the ground of causing shock, the public display of certain publications can be regulated, while others viewed as having the potential to corrupt can be prohibited entirely, either by punishment of those responsible after publication or by being suppressed or censored before publication.

The type of restraint used tends to depend on the type of publication in question because it seems to be accepted that the harm which may be caused will vary from medium to medium. The print media are subject to a far more lax regime than the visual media. Printed matter, including magazines, newspapers and books, is not subject to censorship before publication, but punishment is available afterwards if indecent or corrupting material is published. Books are less likely to be punished than magazines because it is thought that something which has a visual impact is more likely to cause harm. Thus, films and broadcasts are censored because of their visual nature and are also subject to punishment. The theatre, however, is in an odd position; it has not been censored since 1968 despite its visual impact. Possibly, this may be due to the idea that theatre audiences are more sophisticated and less likely to be affected by what they have seen than cinema audiences. As indicated below, the internet is also in an anomalous position: although it may be viewed as broadly analogous to the visual media, it is not, and, under current proposals, will not be subject to the same regime.

The likelihood that sweeping change will not occur is partly due to the Strasbourg stance in relation to explicit expression in general, indicated below. It is also due to the fact that, in practice, much of the material subject to seizure consists merely of photographs of various sexual acts and of genitals, with no conceivable artistic merit. Therefore, since the statutory regime is in most respects almost certainly within the margin of appreciation conceded to the member state, it is unlikely that the judiciary would be inclined to bring about significant change in it, through challenging interpretation, since the result would merely be to increase the trafficking in hardcore pornography. There are grounds for arguing that this change would be desirable, but decisions under the HRA hardly provide the appropriate forum for bringing it about.

---

48 See *Roth v US* (1957) 354 US 476; *Memoirs v Massachusetts* (1966) 383 US 413.

49 *Society for Promotion of Community Standards Inc v Waverley International (1988) Ltd* [1993] 2 NZLR 709.

50 These were the key notions of harm considered by the Williams Committee appointed in 1977 to review obscenity and indecency law (Williams Report, Cmnd 7772, 1979). Broadly, the Committee endorsed regulation of pornography with a view to preventing the second of the harms mentioned.

If radical change is to come about, due in part to the impact of the internet, it would have to be brought about by Parliament.

The Strasbourg stance

Article 10(1) specifically provides that the Article 'shall not prevent states from requiring the licensing of broadcasting, television or cinema enterprises'. It is significant that this provision arises in the *first* paragraph of Art 10, thereby providing a limitation of the primary right that on its face is not subject to the test of para 2. However, a very restrictive approach to this sentence has been adopted. It has been found to mean that a licensing system is allowed for on grounds not restricted to those enumerated in para 2; the state may determine who is to have a licence to broadcast. But in general, other decisions of the regulatory bodies who normally grant licences and oversee broadcasting, etc, are not covered by the last sentence of para 1 and must be considered within para 2.[51] Thus, content requirements must be considered under para 2. The preservation of a state monopoly on broadcasting must also be considered within para 2.[52]

As discussed in Chapter 2, under Art 10(2), an interference with the guarantee of freedom of expression under Art 10 can be justified if it is prescribed by law, has a legitimate aim and is necessary in a democratic society. As the Introduction to this Part indicated, Strasbourg affords a very high value to freedom of expression and, in particular, views the scope for interference with political expression as very limited.[53] Even in respect of artistic expression, which appears to have a lower place in the hierarchy of expression,[54] the discussion below indicates that no decisions defending restrictions on the freedom of expression of adults can be found, except in respect of hardcore pornography, or where a risk to children is also present, or in the context of offending religious sensibilities.

As the Introduction to Part II indicated, certain forms of expression which may be said to be of no value may fall outside the scope of Art 10(1) and it is arguable that, for example, material gratuitously offensive to religious sensibilities[55] or depictions of genitals in pornographic magazines intended merely for entertainment[56] may fall outside its scope. On the other hand, 'hardcore' pornography has been found by the Commission to fall within Art 10(1).[57] Given the breadth of para 2, it is unnecessary to seek to draw lines between artistic erotica and forms of pornography aimed at entertainment alone, even assuming that such line-drawing has any validity.[58] The jurisprudence under Art 10 in this context, as in others, concentrates on the para 2 tests.

Interferences with explicit expression may be justified if they have the legitimate aim of providing for the protection of morals or – in certain circumstances – the 'rights of

---

51 *Groppera Radio AG v Switzerland* (1990) 12 EHRR 321.
52 *Informationsverein Lentia v Austria* (1993) 17 EHRR 93.
53 See Chapter 2, pp 94–96.
54 See above, pp 309–11
55 *Otto-Preminger Institut v Austria* (1994) 19 EHRR 34.
56 In *Groppera Radio AG v Switzerland* (1990) 12 EHRR 321, it was thought that mere entertainment might not fall within Art 10(1).
57 *Hoare v UK* [1997] EHRLR 678.
58 See Kearns, P, 'Obscene and blasphemous libel: misunderstanding art' [2000] Crim LR 652.

others'. The use of laws on obscenity, indecency or blasphemy against explicit expression or regulation of the media with a view to upholding 'standards of taste and decency' are matters that, potentially, could be addressed under the HRA, relying on Art 10. Specific possibilities are considered below, at relevant points. Here, the Strasbourg stance on the application of Art 10 to explicit expression is considered.

The line of authority stemming from the *Handyside* case[59] suggests that although explicit expression, including some pornographic expression, is protected within Art 10(1), interference with it can be justified quite readily in certain circumstances. It is clear that the scope of the domestic margin of appreciation is not the same in respect of all the aims listed in Art 10(2). The protection of morals would appear to be viewed as requiring a wide margin owing to its subjective nature, in contrast with the protection of the authority of the judiciary, which is seen as a more objective notion.[60] The uncertainty of the notion of the protection of morals appears in the lack of a clearly discernible common European standard.

In the *Handyside* case, the European Court of Human Rights had to consider the test of 'deprave and corrupt'. A book called The *Little Red Schoolbook*, which contained chapters on masturbation, sexual intercourse and abortion was prosecuted under the Obscene Publications Act 1959 (which is discussed below) on the basis that it appeared to encourage early sexual intercourse. The publishers applied for a ruling under Art 10 to the European Commission and the case was referred to the Court, which determined that the book fell within Art 10(1). In a famous passage, which strongly favours freedom of artistic or creative expression (the expression of information or ideas), it found: 'Freedom of expression constitutes one of the essential foundations of a democratic society, one of the basic conditions for its progress and for the development of every man. Subject to paragraph 2 of Art 10, it is applicable not only to information or ideas that are favourably received, or regarded as inoffensive but also to those that offend, shock or disturb the state or any sector of the population. Such are the demands of that pluralism, tolerance and broadmindedness without which there is no democratic society.'[61]

However, as this passage indicates, the interference could be justified under para 2. The Court then considered the protection of morals provision under Art 10(2), in order to determine whether the interference with the expression was necessary in a democratic society. It suggested that the 'protection of morals' exception refers to the corruption of individuals rather than to an effect on the moral fabric of society.[62] The Court found that the requirements of morals vary from time to time and from place to place and that the domestic authorities were therefore best placed to judge what was needed. They must 'make the initial assessment of the reality of the pressing social need implied by the notion of necessity in this context'.[63] The judgment thus accepted that domestic authorities would be allowed a wide margin of appreciation in attempting to secure the freedoms guaranteed under the Convention in this area, although this

---

59 Eur Ct HR, A 24; (1976) 1 EHRR 737.
60 See the judgment of the Eur Ct HR in the *Sunday Times* case (1979) 2 EHRR 245, discussed in Chapter 2, p 94.
61 Ibid, para 49. The 1959 Act is discussed below, pp 468–75
62 Ibid, para 52.
63 Ibid, para 48.

was not to be taken as implying that an unlimited discretion was granted: the power of appreciation 'goes hand in hand with a European supervision' which concerns the legislation in question – the Obscene Publications Act – and the decision applying it. The Court placed particular weight on the fact that the book was aimed at children between the ages of 12 and 18 and that it might encourage them 'to indulge in precocious activities harmful for them or even to commit certain criminal offences'.[64] Thus, the English judges were entitled to find that the book would have a 'pernicious effect on the morals' of the children who would read it. In finding that the tests under para 2 were satisfied, it was said that the fact that the book was circulating freely in the rest of Europe was not determinative of the issues, owing to the application of the margin of appreciation doctrine.

A similar stance was taken in *Müller v Switzerland*[65] in respect of a conviction arising from the exhibition of explicit paintings: the fact that the paintings had been exhibited in other parts of Switzerland and abroad did not mean that their suppression could not amount to a pressing social need. The Court took into account the fact that the paintings were exhibited to the public at large, without a warning as to their content, and that a young girl had seen them.

It is notable that the Court in *Handyside* based its justification for the protection of freedom of expression on the arguments from democracy and self-fulfilment rather than on those from truth or moral autonomy.[66] As indicated above, in the Introduction to Part II, these justifications, as instrumental arguments, are open to attack in the way that the argument from moral autonomy is not. This stance of the Court is especially relevant in the context of explicit expression since the argument may provide, as indicated above, the sole justification. (It is not suggested that this was the case in *Handyside* itself; on the contrary, on the basis of the content of the book, three of the four justifications could have applied.) In the other contexts covered by Part II, all four justifications may be present. The Court's stance may have some bearing on the cautious nature of its jurisprudence in this area, although unlike the Supreme Court of Canada, it has not explicitly addressed this issue.[67]

These two decisions give a strong indication as to the stance taken by the Court in respect of Art 10, para 2, but may be viewed as turning on their special facts, particularly the fact that children might have been affected. The thinking behind the *Handyside* decision can find some parallels from the US[68] and Canada.[69] In the US, however, there has been a greater concentration on the question whether restrictions aimed at children might impinge also on the freedom of expression of adults and on the extent to which this should be tolerated,[70] a matter which was in issue in *Handyside*, although not afforded weight by the Court.

---

64 Ibid, para 52.
65 (1991) 13 EHRR 212. See Chapter 2, p 95.
66 See the Introduction to Part II.
67 See *R v Butler* [1992] 1 SCR 452.
68 *Ginsberg v New York* 390 US 629 (1968).
69 *Irwin Toy Ltd v AG (Quebec)* [1989] 1 SCR 927 (broad limitation on broadcast advertising aimed at children).
70 *Reno v American Civil Liberties Union* (1997) 521 US 844.

These decisions at Strasbourg do not determine the question of the consumption of explicit material solely or mainly by a willing adult audience. These decisions at Strasbourg do not determine the question of the consumption of explicit material solely or mainly by a willing adult audience – a matter that is especially pertinent in relation to films and videos, bearing their age classifications in mind. That question was considered in *Hoare v UK*,[71] which concerned the possession of 'hardcore' pornographic videos. The applicant had been convicted of possessing obscene material under s 2 of the Obscene Publications Act. The Commission found quite easily that the restriction on his freedom of expression had the legitimate aim of protecting morals and was not disproportionate to that aim. But the decision was largely based on the risk that children might view the videos since once they had left the applicant's possession he would not have been able to control their eventual audience. The Commission may have been influenced by the nature of the material: it had no artistic or political value and therefore the justifications underlying freedom of expression, referred to above, were not present, apart from the justification based on moral autonomy.

That decision is broadly in harmony with that of the Commission in *Scherer v Switzerland*;[72] it was found that the conviction of the proprietor of a sex shop for showing obscene and explicit videos had breached Art 10, since access was restricted to adults and no one was likely to confront them unwittingly. *Scherer* demonstrates that Strasbourg (or at least, the Commission) is prepared to defend adult autonomy in relation to the consumption of explicit material, so long as control is retained over the ultimate consumer of the material. The difference between *Hoare* and *Scherer* related to the question of the restrictions on access to the material; in *Hoare* the penalty imposed was proportionate to the aim pursued since it was viewed as capable of protecting the 'rights of others' – the rights appeared to be those of minors to be protected from harmful material; in *Scherer* such rights could not be protected by the imposition of the penalty since they were not threatened by the showing of the videos.[73] Thus, in contrast to the stance taken in the US,[74] Strasbourg is clearly content to restrict the expression rights of adults in order to protect children.

---

71 [1997] EHRLR 678.

72 A 287 (1993) Com Rep (the case was discontinued in the Court owing to the death of the applicant).

73 In *Hoare* the Commission, having found that the material fell within Art 10(1), went on to find under Art 10(2): 'In the present case, the sole question which arises in the context of the relationship of proportionality between the interference with the applicant's right to freedom of expression and the aim pursued is the question of whether, given that the applicant only distributed his video cassettes to people who expressed a clear interest, it can be said that the penalty imposed was capable of protecting the "rights of others" (see, in this context, *Scherer v. Switzerland*, Comm Report 14.1.93, Eur Court HR, Series A no 287, p 20, para 65). Where no adult is confronted unintentionally or against his will with filmed matter, there must be particularly compelling reasons to justify an interference (above-mentioned Scherer Report, p 20, para 65). The Commission considers that it cannot therefore be said with any degree of certainty that only the intended purchasers of the film would have access to it and not minors. To that extent the present case is different from the case of *Scherer*, where the only adults who saw the applicant's videos were those who had access to his shop (above-mentioned *Scherer* Report, p 19, para 62).'

74 See below, p 581.

In *Otto-Preminger Institut v Austria*,[75] the Court considered the question of restrictions on freedom of expression in respect of a film where the expression was aimed at a willing adult audience. A warning had been given and therefore viewers knew what to expect. Nevertheless, owing to the shock caused to particular religious sensibilities in the local region, it was found, in a much criticised decision,[76] that the interference could be justified despite the fact that the measure had the effect of preventing the showing of the film across the whole country. That decision can be contrasted with the findings of the Commission in the same case that Art 10 had been violated.[77]

Applying the Strasbourg jurisprudence under the Human Rights Act

The decisions in this line of authority confirm that where there is a chance that children might be affected or religious sensibilities offended, Strasbourg is particularly cautious. Even accepting the effect of the margin of appreciation doctrine, its stance is very significantly out of line with that taken under a number of national Bills of Rights at the end of the Twentieth century and the beginning of the Twenty-First. It is one of the weakest and most out-dated areas of its jurisprudence, which entirely fails to follow up the principles established in *Handyside* in relation to Art 10(1). However, *Scherer* provides a basis of sorts from which to attack the current censorship of films for cinematic release in the UK since age restrictions are in place and are enforced. That decision and the jurisprudence in general provide, on its face, no basis for attacking the regulation and censorship of videos and broadcasting since there is a risk that children will encounter the material. In general the Strasbourg jurisprudence in this area does not set precise standards that could be followed effectively by regulators or by the courts; the standards may readily be referred to as 'soft-edged'. But clearly it can be argued that the Convention was never intended to set such standards since it provides a 'floor', not a 'ceiling', of rights.

The expectation deriving from the margin of appreciation doctrine is that the state, via legislation, decisions of the courts and the practice of regulators, will devise its own standards which will be higher than those maintained at Strasbourg. Only where the margin of appreciation is over-stepped – as in especially restrictive decisions – is Strasbourg expected to intervene. Thus, used at the *domestic* level under the HRA, the Strasbourg jurisprudence can be misleading and could be used to underpin a very restrictive stance since it could be applied without regard to the influence of the margin of appreciation doctrine on it: the *outcome* of decisions such as *Handyside*, rather than the free speech pronouncements, could be influential. (However, so far, in judicial reasoning under the HRA there has been no recognition of the need to 'strip away' the margin of appreciation aspects of Strasbourg decisions before applying them domestically.) Therefore, below, although the jurisprudence is referred to, it is not fully relied upon as though it provided or was intended to provide a definitive set of standards.

---

75 (1994) 19 EHRR 34.
76 For an incisive critique, see Pannick, D, 'Religious feelings and the European Court' [1995] PL 7.
77 See also *Wingrove v UK* (1996) 24 EHRR 1; *Gay News v UK* (1982) 5 EHRR 123.

Restrictions based on the idea of avoiding offence or maintaining certain standards of taste and decency tend to have a greater impact on 'artistic' rather than political expression – using the term 'artistic' very broadly. As indicated, the margin of appreciation doctrine has an especially significant impact on such expression due to the lack of consensus in Europe as to the proper extent of restrictions on it intended to prevent offence. So if the established Strasbourg hierarchy of expression is rigidly applied in relation to such restrictions they can be justified quite readily. However, if the justifications for freedom of expression considered are taken into account, particularly those from truth and self-fulfilment, it is suggested that there is no convincing basis for relegating 'artistic' expression to a lowly place in such a hierarchy. Possibly its place should be below that of political speech, but too sharp a distinction should not be drawn. Moreover, it is readily apparent that some forms of political speech are clearly less valuable than some forms of artistic speech. For example, a number of classic films that fall outside the category of political speech engage a number of the justificatory free speech arguments more strongly than do the more minor manifestations of political speech. An autonomous free speech jurisprudence in the UK under the HRA could begin to grapple with this matter more effectively than Strasbourg is able to do due to the effects of the margin of appreciation doctrine. There is little sign as yet, however, that such a development is likely to occur in relation to post-HRA regulatory decisions. But at the Strasbourg level there may be developments in the explicit expression jurisprudence. The effects of EU driven harmonisation may begin to influence the margin of appreciation doctrine: if greater consistency of standards in this context can be discerned in the EU member states, the case for conceding such a broad margin of appreciation to state authorities may come to be viewed by the Strasbourg Court as less compelling.

Statutory obscenity[78]

Obscenity law operates as a subsequent restraint and is largely used in relation to books, magazines and other printed material, material posted on web-pages or videos;[79] theoretically it could also be used against broadcasts and films. The harm sought to be

---

78 Texts referred to in this section: Barendt, E, *Freedom of Speech*, 2nd edn, 2005, Chapters 10, 12 and 13, (1st edn will also be referred to); Feldman, D, *Civil Liberties in England and Wales*, 2002; MacMillan, PR, *Censorship and Public Morality*, 1983; Robertson, G and Nichol, D, *Media Law*, 1999, Chapter 14; Bailey, Harris and Jones, *Civil Liberties and Human Rights Cases and Materials*, 5th edn, 2002, Chapter 6; Carey, P and Sanders, J, *Media Law* 3rd edn, 2004, Chapters 5 and 9 (basic guide); Gibbons, T, *Regulating the Media*, 1998; Dworkin, R, 'Do we have a right to pornography?', in *A Matter of Principle*, 1985; Itzen, C (ed), *Pornography: Women, Violence and Civil Liberties*, 1993; Feinberg, J, *The Moral Limits of the Criminal Law: Offense to Others*, 1985; MacKinnon, C, *Feminism Unmodified*, 1987; 'Feminism, Marxism, method and the state', in Bartlett and Kennedy (eds), *Feminist Legal Theory*, 1991; Baker, R, *Media Law*, 1995; background: O'Higgins, P, *Censorship in Britain*, 1972, Nelson; Robertson, G, *Obscenity*, 1979, and (with Nichol, D) *Media Law*, 1999, Chapter 3; MacMillan, PR, *Censorship and Public Morality*, 1983; Baker, R, *Media Law*, 1995, Chapter 15; Simpson, AWB, *Pornography and Politics: the Williams Committee in Retrospect*, 1983, Pergamon; Travis, A, *Bound and Gagged – A Secret History of Obscenity in Britain*, 2000.

79 In *AG's Reference (No 5 of 1980)* [1980] 3 All ER 816, CA, it was found that a video constituted an "article" for the purposes of the 1959 Act.

prevented is that of a corrupting effect on an individual. In other words, it is thought that an individual will undergo a change for the worse after encountering the material in question. The rationale of the law is thus overtly paternalistic. Of course, if all material which might appear capable of causing corruption were suppressed, a severe infringement of freedom of speech would occur. Thus, the statute which largely governs this area – the Obscene Publications Act 1959[80] – takes the stance that in preventing material which may deprave and corrupt, a line must be drawn between erotic literature and the truly obscene on the basis that hardcore pornography does not deserve special protection.[81] This echoes the approach in America, where this form of pornography is not defined as 'speech' because it is thought that the justification for the constitutional protection for freedom of speech does not apply.[82] In fact, oddly enough, this may mean that pornography is more likely to be prohibited in the US than in the UK. Now that the HRA is in force, it is fair to say that pornography is, in a sense, in a better position in the UK than in the US since, as indicated above, it will probably fall within the range of expression protected by Art 10(1).

The idea of preventing corruption had informed the common law long before the 1959 Act; it sprang from the ruling in *Hicklin*.[83] Determining whether material would 'deprave and corrupt' was problematic, especially as it was unclear to whom the test should be applied. Two cases in 1954 showed the uncertainty of the law. In *Martin Secker and Warburg*[84] it was determined that the test applied to persons who might encounter the material in question. But at the same time, in *Hutchinson*,[85] the Court held that the test should be applied to the most vulnerable person who might conceivably encounter the material and that the jury could therefore look at the effect it might have on a teenage girl. Moreover, the jury could find that something which could merely be termed 'shocking' could deprave and corrupt.

The 1959 Act was passed in an attempt to clear up some of this uncertainty, although it failed to lay down a test for the meaning of the term 'deprave and corrupt'. The *actus reus* of the offence involves the publication for gain (s 2(1)) or having for such publication (s 1(2) of the Obscene Publications Act 1964) an article which tends, taken as a whole, (or where it comprises two or more distinct items, the effect of one of the items) to deprave and corrupt a significant proportion of those likely to see or hear it (s 1(1)). This is a crime of strict liability: there is no need to show an intention to

---

80 The Obscene Publications Act 1959 does not apply in Scotland; the Civic Government (Scotland) Act 1982 makes it an offence to publish obscene material and prosecution is the responsibility of the Procurator Fiscal Service. Under the Scotland Act 1998, Scottish criminal law generally has been devolved and this includes the law on obscenity; however, the Video Recordings Act has been reserved to the UK Parliament. The Obscene Publications Act does not extend to Northern Ireland; nor do the relevant provisions of the Local Government (Miscellaneous Provisions) Act 1982. Obscene material, including videoworks, is generally dealt with under the common law offence of publishing an obscene libel.

81 See, for argument on this point, Dworkin, R, 'Is there a right to pornography?' (1981) 1 Ox JLS 177.

82 *Miller v California* (1973) 413 US 15. It should be noted that under the argument from moral autonomy, it is irrelevant whether the material concerned is classified as 'speech' or not.

83 (1868) 3 QB 360.

84 [1954] 2 All ER 683; [1954] 1 WLR 1138.

85 (1954), unreported. For an account of the proceedings, see St John Stevas, N, *Obscenity and the Law*, 1956, p 116.

deprave and corrupt, merely an intention to publish. Once it is shown that an article is obscene within the meaning of the Act, it will be irrelevant, following the ruling of the Court of Appeal in *Calder and Boyars*,[86] that the defendant's motivation could be characterised as pure or noble. The Act does not cover live performances on stage which fall within the similarly worded Theatres Act 1968.

'Deprave and corrupt'

This test could be applied to any material which might corrupt; it is clear from the ruling in *Calder (John) Publishing v Powell*[87] that it is not confined to descriptions or representations of sexual matters and it could therefore be applied to a disturbing book on the drug-taking life of a junkie. This ruling was followed in *Skirving*,[88] which concerned a pamphlet on the means of taking cocaine in order to obtain maximum effect. In all instances, the test for obscenity should not be applied to the type of behaviour advocated or described in the article in question, but to the article itself. Thus, in *Skirving*, the question to be asked was not whether taking cocaine would deprave and corrupt, but whether the pamphlet itself would.

This test is hard to explain to a jury and uncertain of meaning, with the result that directions such as the following have been given: '. . . obscenity, members of the jury, is like an elephant; you can't define it, but you know it when you see it.'[89] However, it is clear from the ruling of the Court of Appeal in *Anderson*[90] that the effect in question must be more than mere shock. The trial judge had directed the jury that the test connoted that which was repulsive, loathsome or filthy. This explanation was clearly defective, since it would have merged the concepts of indecency and obscenity and it was rejected by the Court of Appeal on the basis that it would dilute the test for obscenity which, it was said, must connote the prospect of moral harm, not just shock. The conviction under the Act was therefore overturned because of the misdirection. The House of Lords in *Knuller v DPP*[91] considered the word 'corrupt' and found that it denoted a publication which produced 'real social evil' – going beyond immoral suggestions or persuasion.

This was quite a strict test, but it was qualified by the House of Lords in *DPP v Whyte*.[92] The owners of a bookshop which sold pornographic material were prosecuted. Most of the customers were old men who had encountered the material on previous occasions and this gave rise to two difficulties. First, the old men were unlikely to engage in anti-social sexual behaviour and therefore the meaning of 'corrupt' had to be modified if it was to extend to cover the effect on them of the material: it was found that it meant creating a depraved effect on the mind which need not actually issue forth in any particular sexual behaviour. Secondly, it was suggested that the old men were already corrupt and therefore would not be affected by the material. However,

---

86 [1969] 1 QB 151; [1968] 3 WLR 974; [1968] 3 All ER 644; (1968) 52 Cr App R 706.
87 [1965] 1 QB 159.
88 [1985] QB 819.
89 Robertson, *Obscenity* op. cit., fn 1, p 45.
90 [1972] 1 QB 304.
91 [1973] AC 435; [1972] 3 WLR 143; (1972) 56 Cr App R 633, HL.
92 [1972] AC 849; [1972] 3 All ER 12, HL.

it was held that corruption did not connote a once-only process: persons could be 'recorrupted' and, on this basis, a conviction was obtained. (Interestingly, this finding suggests that there is a presumption that the 'deprave and corrupt' test is of universal application: no person or group of persons can be excluded in principle from its ambit. In this sense it differs from the test as put forward in *Hicklin*; that test applied only to those whose minds were open to immoral influences.) The test will not be satisfied if the material in question causes feelings of revulsion from the immorality portrayed. This theory, known as the 'aversion theory', derives from *Calder and Boyars*, which concerned *Last Exit from Brooklyn*; it was found that the horrific pictures it painted of homosexuality and drug taking in New York would be more likely to discourage than encourage such behaviour.[93]

The 'deprave and corrupt' test must be applied to those likely to see or hear the material in question and, therefore, the concept of relative obscenity is imported into the Act. In other words, the obscenity or otherwise of material cannot be determined merely by its consideration or analysis but, rather, will depend on the character of the consumer and, in this sense, the test presents a contrast with German obscenity law which absolutely prohibits hard core pornography, although soft core material is quite freely available.[94] It was held in *DPP v Whyte*[95] that in order to make a determination as to the type of consumer in question, the Court could receive information as to the nature of the relevant area, the type of shop and the class of people frequenting it. The jury must consider the likely reader in order to determine whether the material would deprave and corrupt him or her rather than considering the most vulnerable conceivable reader. In *Penguin Books*,[96] which concerned the prosecution of *Lady Chatterley's Lover*, the selling price of the book was taken into account and the fact that being in paperback, it would reach a mass audience.

The jury has to consider whether the article would be likely to deprave and corrupt a *significant proportion* of those likely to encounter it. It was determined in *Calder and Boyars*[97] that the jury must determine what is meant by a 'significant proportion' and this was approved in *DPP v Whyte*, Lord Cross explaining that 'a significant proportion of a class means a part which is not numerically negligible, but which may be much less than half'. This formulation was adopted in order to prevent sellers of pornographic material claiming that most of their customers would be unlikely to be corrupted by it. The effect of the article as a whole on persons likely to encounter it should be considered, not merely the effect of specific passages of a particularly explicit nature. However, in *Anderson*[98] it was made clear that where the article consists of a number of items, each item must be considered in isolation from the others. Thus, a magazine which is, on the whole, innocuous, but contains one obscene item, can be suppressed, although a novel could not be.

---

93 [1969] 1 QB 151; [1968] 3 WLR 974; [1968] 3 All ER 644; (1968) 52 Cr App R 706. For comment, see Robertson, *Obscenity*, 1979, pp 50–53.
94 German Criminal Code, s 184(3).
95 [1972] AC 849; [1972] 3 All ER 12, HL.
96 [1961] Crim LR 176; see Rolph, CH, *The Trial of Lady Chatterley*, 1961, Andre Deutsch.
97 [1969] 1 QB 151.
98 [1972] 1 QB 304.

It may be reasonably straightforward to identify a group, of whom a significant proportion might encounter the material, but it is unclear how it can then be determined that they would be likely to experience depravity and corruption as a result. The ruling in *Anderson* was to the effect that in sexual obscenity cases and normally in other obscenity cases, the defence cannot call expert evidence as to the effect that an article may have on its likely audience. Thus, the view taken in *DPP v A and BC Chewing Gum Ltd*[99] that such evidence would be admissible may be regarded as arising only due to the very specific circumstances of that case. However, it was decided in *Skirving*[100] that in cases concerned with alleged depravity and corruption arising from factors other than the sexual nature of the material, expert evidence will, exceptionally, be admissible, although the evidence can only be as to the effects of the behaviour described in the material, not as to the likely effects of the material itself. Thus, generally, where the material deals with matters within their own experience, the jury will receive little help in applying the test. However, it seems clear that a jury will be able to take into account changing standards of morality (the 'contemporary standards' test from *Calder and Boyars*) in considering what will deprave and corrupt. Therefore, the concept of obscenity is, at least theoretically, able to keep up to date. The application of these tests at the present time was seen in the trial for obscenity of the book *Inside Linda Lovelace*[101] which suggested that a prosecution brought against a book of any conceivable literary merit would be unlikely to succeed. Thus, in December 1991, the DPP refused to prosecute the Marquis de Sade's *Juliette*, even though it was concerned (fictionally) with the torture, rape and murder of women and children. But – aside from forfeiture proceedings, discussed below, the use of obscenity law is currently of great significance in relation to the internet; as discussed below the decision in *R v Perrin*[102] sought to adapt obscenity law to explicit web-based expression. Current proposals to introduce a new offence aimed at extreme pornography are also discussed below since they are aimed mainly at the internet, although they would also apply to other media, if implemented.[103]

The defence of public good

This defence, which arises under s 4 of the 1959 Act (as amended by s 53 of the Criminal Law Act 1977) and s 3 of the Theatres Act 1968, was intended to afford recognition to artistic merit. Thus it may be seen as a highly significant step in the direction of

---

99   [1968] 1 QB 159.
100 [1985] QB 819.
101 For comment see (1976) NLJ 126. The prosecution failed.
102 [2002] EWCA Crim 747, CA. This case involved a French national based in the UK who was publishing from abroad (in the USA). The appellant was convicted of publishing an obscene article and appealed. The obscene article in question was a web page on the internet. It depicted people covered in faeces, coprophilia or coprophagia, and men involved in fellatio. That web page was in the form of a trailer, a preview, available free of charge to any one with access to the internet. Any one wanting more of the type of material which it displayed could click on to a link marked 'subscription to our best filthy sites' and could gain access to a further web-page by providing credit card details. The preview web-page was accessed by an officer with the Obscene Publications Unit. To reach it a viewer would have to type in the name of the site, or conduct a search for material of the kind displayed.
103 See pp 585–86 below.

freedom of speech, acknowledging the force of a variant of the free speech argument from truth which was also used by the Williams Committee.[104] Under the 1959 Act, it is a defence to a finding that a publication is obscene if it can be shown that 'the publication of the article in question is justified as for the public good in that it is in the interests of science, literature, art, learning or of other objects of general concern'. Under the 1968 Act, the similarly worded defence which covers 'the interests of drama, opera, ballet or any other art or of literature or learning' is somewhat narrower as omitting the concluding general words. Under s 53(6) of the 1977 Act, this narrower defence applies to films. Expert evidence will be admissible to prove that one of these possibilities can be established and it may include considering other works.

It was determined in *Penguin Books* in respect of *Lady Chatterley's Lover* that the jury should adopt a two-stage approach, asking first whether the article in question is obscene and if so, going on to consider whether the defendant has established the probability that its merits are so high as to outbalance its obscenity so that its publication is for the public good. The failure of the prosecution was seen as a turning point for literary freedom and the jury allowed it to be known that the second stage of the test afforded the basis on which the novel escaped suppression. In *DPP v Jordan*,[105] the House of Lords approved this two-stage approach and the balancing of obscenity against literary or other merit.

In *DPP v Jordan*, the attempt was made to widen the test. The main question was whether the articles in question – hardcore pornography – could be justified under s 4 as being of psychotherapeutic value for persons of deviant sexuality in that the material might help to relieve their sexual tensions by way of sexual fantasies. It was argued that such material might provide a safety valve for such persons, which would divert them from anti-social activities and that such benefit could fall within the words 'other objects of general concern' deriving from s 4. The House of Lords, however, held that these words must be construed *ejusdem generis* with the preceding words 'art, literature learning, science'. As these words were unrelated to sexual benefit, the general words which followed them could not be construed in the manner suggested. It was ruled that the jury must be satisfied that the matter in question made a contribution to a recognised field of culture or learning which could be assessed irrespective of the persons to whom it was distributed.

Although the test of public good has clearly afforded protection to freedom of expression in relation to publications of artistic merit, it has been criticised. It does not allow for consideration of the benefits of pornography and may be inapt as a means of considering 'new art at the cutting edge of art development'.[106] It requires a jury to embark on the very difficult task of weighing a predicted change for the worse in the minds of the group of persons likely to encounter the article, against literary or other merit. Thus, an effect or process must be imagined which, once established, must be measured against an intrinsic quality. Geoffrey Robertson has written: 'the balancing act is a logical nonsense [because it is not] logically possible to weigh such disparate

---

104 See above, p 270.
105 [1977] AC 699.
106 Kearns, P, 'Obscene and blasphemous libel: misunderstanding art' [2000] Crim LR 652, p 654.

concepts as 'corruption' and 'literary merit'.[107] The test seems to create an almost complete paradox: it assumes that an individual can be corrupted, which suggests a stultifying effect on the mind and yet can also experience an elevating effect due to the merit of an article. However, such an interpretation of the test is open to two objections. First, a person could experience corruption in the sense that her moral standards might be lowered, but she might retain a sense of literary or artistic appreciation. Secondly – and this might seem the more satisfactory interpretation – the *message* of the article and its general artistic impact (through, for example, its influence on other works which followed it) might be for the public good although some individuals who encountered it were corrupted. Thus the term 'publication' in s 4 must mean publication to the public at large, not only to those who encounter the article if the test is to be workable.[108]

It should be noted that, as discussed below, the defence can be avoided by bringing a charge of indecency at common law; as *Gibson*[109] demonstrated, the merits of an obscene object may, paradoxically, prevent its suppression while the merits of less offensive objects may not.

Forfeiture proceedings

The vast majority of actions against allegedly obscene material take the form of forfeiture proceedings. Under s 3 of the 1959 Act, magazines and other material, such as videos, can be seized by the police if it is suspected on reasonable grounds that they are obscene and have been kept for gain. No conviction is obtained; if found to be obscene, the material is merely destroyed; no other punishment is imposed and therefore s 3 may operate at a low level of visibility. Seizure may mean that the safeguards provided by the Act can be bypassed: consideration is not given to the possible literary merits of such material because the public good defence is not taken into account in issuing the seizure warrant. The merits of an article can be taken into account in the forfeiture hearing in determining whether it out-balances its obscenity, but there is not much evidence that magistrates take a very rigorous approach to making such a determination. They do not need to read every item, but need only look at samples selected by the police[110] and seem, in any event, more ready than a jury to find that an item is obscene.[111] It seems, therefore, that the protection afforded by the 1959 Act to freedom of speech may depend more on the exercise of discretion by the police as to the enforcement of s 3 or on the tolerance of magistrates, rather than on the law itself. However, s 3 can be used only in respect of material which may be obscene rather than in relation to

---

107 Robertson, *Obscenity* op. cit., fn 1, p 164.
108 The House of Lords in *Jordan* [1977] AC 699 appeared to take this view. See also Robertson, ibid, on the point (pp 168–69).
109 [1990] 2 QB 619; [1991] 1 All ER 439; [1990] 3 WLR 595, CA.
110 *Crown Court at Snaresbrook ex p Metropolitan Police Comr* (1984) 148 JP 449.
111 Bailey, Harris and Jones note (1st edn op. cit., fn 1, p 328) that comment arose when forfeiture proceedings of an edition of the magazine *Men Only* coincided with the jury acquittal of the editors of *Nasty Tales* of the offence under s 2 ((1973) 127 JPN 82). Robertson argues (*Obscenity*, 1979, p 96) that as the hearing is before a tribunal which has already decided that the material is – at least prima facie – obscene, it is likely to have an appearance of unfairness. The Bench may be unlikely to be convinced that in effect, it was wrong in the first place in issuing the summons.

any form of pornography; it was held in *Darbo v DPP*[112] that a warrant issued under s 3 allowing officers to search for 'sexually explicit material' was bad on its face, as such articles would fall within a much wider category of articles than those which could be called obscene.

Statutory obscenity, the HRA and the protection of morals exception under Art 10(2)

Clearly, any prosecutions under the Act or forfeiture actions constitute interferences with the Art 10 guarantee of freedom of expression under the HRA, although subject to justification. In relation to any particular decision, the public authorities involved are bound by s 6 of the HRA to ensure that the tests under Art 10 are satisfied, while the provisions of the 1959 Act must be interpreted consistently with Art 10, if necessary, under s 3 HRA. As Chapter 4 indicated, s 12 HRA does not apply to criminal proceedings. Forfeiture proceedings have the hallmarks of criminal proceedings in certain respects, although a conviction is not obtained, and therefore they are probably outside the ambit of s 12.

Given the wide margin of appreciation afforded to the domestic authorities in the relevant decisions, little guidance as to the requirements of Art 10 in this context is available, especially where the material is directed at a willing adult audience. The domestic judiciary are, therefore, theoretically free to take a different stance. The decisions considered above at Strasbourg on the 1959 Act indicate that the statutory regime relating to publication of an obscene article under s 2 is broadly in harmony with Art 10 of the European Convention. Nevertheless, a specific decision might not meet the proportionality requirements, scrutinised more intensively than at Strasbourg.

The UK forfeiture regime has not itself been tested at Strasbourg. The HRA requirements may be especially pertinent in relation to forfeiture: the magistrates conducting the proceedings are, of course, bound by Art 10 and therefore would be expected to approach the task with greater rigour. In particular, it is arguably necessary to examine each item, even where a large scale seizure has occurred, rather than considering a sample of items only.[113] But since, in practice, a vast amount of material is condemned as obscene in legal actions for forfeiture, the practical difficulties facing magistrates make it possible, especially initially, that the impact of the HRA will be more theoretical than real. It seems probable that, in practice, magistrates will not examine each item and will give only cursory attention, if any, to considering the application of the somewhat elusive Strasbourg case law. However, if on occasion publishers seek to contest s 3 orders before a jury, the proportionality of the measures adopted may receive more attention. Moreover, it is arguable that Art 6 might be breached by the procedure since it could be said to lack impartiality, given that the same magistrate may sign the seizure order, and determine forfeiture.[114]

---

112 (1992) *The Times*, 4 July; [1992] Crim LR 56.
113 It was found that such sampling was acceptable in *Snaresbrook Crown Court ex p Comr of the Metropolis* (1984) 79 Cr App R 184. For discussion, see Stone, R [1986] Crim LR 139.
114 See above, Bailey, Harris and Jones (1st edn op. cit., fn 1, p 328).

Statutory indecency[115]

The concept of indecency, as opposed to obscenity, is contained in certain statutes and also exists at common law. The idea of prohibiting indecency is, essentially, to prevent *public displays* of offensive material or the possibility that such material will impinge in some way on the general public, or a part of it. Such prohibition is aimed at protecting persons from the shock or offence occasioned by encountering certain material, rather than at preventing moral deterioration. Therefore, except perhaps in a very broad sense, it may be said not to be aimed at the protection of morals and so might not fall within that exception to Art 10. The general lowering of moral standards or attacks on the moral fabric of society must occur – if it is assumed that it is likely to occur at all – through the medium of individual persons who are affected by encountering obscene material;[116] it would seem, therefore, that the 'moral fabric of society' would be unaffected by material which only serves to shock. However, it might be very broadly argued on a conservative view that indecent material might have a corrupting effect if it was repeatedly encountered because it might lead at each encounter to less outrage as sensibilities became blunted. In any event, the European Court of Human Rights has found that material which was, arguably, merely shocking, fell within the protection of morals exception.[117]

If the material is not obscene and is either stored with a view to sale, or offered for sale, it will not attract liability, unless the provision of s 160 of the Criminal Justice Act 1988 apply (below). Indecency is easier to prove than obscenity because there is no defence of public good, there is no need to consider the whole article and there is no need to satisfy the difficult test of deprave and corrupt. Prosecuting authorities have taken note of these distinctions and have therefore tended at times to rely on the law against indecency where, arguably, the article in question could be said to be obscene.[118] It will be seen that the existence of these two strands of law has led to some anomalies.

Meaning of indecency

The test for indecency was discussed in *Knuller v DPP*;[119] it was determined by Lord Reid to be satisfied by material which creates outrage or utter disgust in 'ordinary decent-minded people'. This statement, coupled with the general tenor of Lord Reid's comments, suggested that the level of shock would have to be fairly high. In *GLC ex*

---

115 Texts referred to: Robertson, op. cit., fn 1, Chapter 7; Robertson, G and Nichol, AGL, *Media Law*, 1992, pp 115–24; Chaps 8, 9, 10, 11, 12; Barendt, E, *Freedom of Speech*, 2nd edn 2005, Chaps 10, 12 and 13 [or 8–12] (1st edn will also be referred to); Feldman, D, *Civil Liberties in England and Wales*, 2002; Robertson, G and Nichol, D, Media Law (Penguin, 1999) Chapter 14; Bailey, Harris and Jones, *Civil Liberties and Human Rights Cases and Materials*, 5th edn (2002).

116 For criticism of the view that preventing the lowering of the moral tone of society justifies censorship, see the introduction to this Chapter, p 454.

117 *Müller v Switzerland* (1988) 13 EHRR 212.

118 This trend is reflected in Lord Denning's comments in *GLC ex p Blackburn* [1976] 1 WLR 550, p 556.

119 [1973] AC 435, p 457; [1972] 3 WLR 143; (1972) 56 Cr App R 633.

p Blackburn,[120] Lord Denning approved the simple test of 'is this indecent?' since he considered that if jurors were asked the more complex question 'will it deprave and corrupt?' they would allow very offensive articles into circulation. However, Lord Bridge wondered whether asking whether something is shocking or disgusting could be a suitable test of criminality. Sir Robert Megarry has said that 'indecency' is too subjective and emotional a concept[121] to be workable as a legal test. It seems that the test is not confined to sexual material; Lord Reid in *Knuller* considered that 'indecency is not confined to sexual indecency'.[122] This is supported by the finding in *Gibson*[123] that the use of freeze-dried foetuses as earrings on a model of a head was indecent.

Uncertainty arises as to whether the term 'indecency' denotes a relative concept: a concept which, like that of relative obscenity, depends on its context or on the nature of the audience or recipient. According to the ruling of the Court of Appeal in *Straker*,[124] such considerations are irrelevant: indecency is an objective quality discoverable by examination in the same way that, for example, a substance might be discovered to be a certain chemical. However, *Wiggins v Field*[125] suggests otherwise; the ruling specifically demanded that the circumstances in which the alleged indecency occurred should be taken into account. A prosecution was brought in respect of a reading of Allen Ginsberg's poem 'America' on the basis of a charge of using indecent language in contravention of a local bylaw. The Divisional Court held that if the context was considered – this was the work of a recognised poet, read without any intention of causing offence – the charge of indecency could not be supported. This stance was taken by the Court of Appeal in *AG ex rel McWhirter v IBA*;[126] it was agreed that the film in question 'taken as a whole' was not offensive, although a small percentage of it depicted indecent incidents. Thus it may be that the Straker ruling, to the effect that indecency may be treated as an objective concept, is confined to cases arising under the Post Office Act 1953, but the point cannot yet be regarded as settled. However, it is clear that the notion of indecency will vary from generation to generation and that the jury will be expected to apply current standards.[127]

The variety of specific statutory offences

The word 'indecent' is contained in a number of statutes and bylaws. Therefore, only specific areas are covered, but if no statute affects a particular area, the gap may be filled by the common law. Taking an indecent photograph or film of a person under the age of 18 is prohibited under s 1 of the Protection of Children Act 1978 (as amended by the Sexual Offences Act 2003), as is possessing it with a view to sale, showing it or distributing it. The only intention needed is the intention to take a photograph;

120 [1976] 3 All ER 184.
121 *A Second Miscellany at Law*, 1973, p 316.
122 [1973] AC 435, p 458.
123 [1990] 2 QB 619; [1991] 1 All ER 439, CA.
124 [1965] Crim LR 239; this approach was affirmed by the Court of Appeal in *Stamford* [1972] 2 WLR 1055; [1972] 2 All ER 427.
125 [1968] Crim LR 50.
126 [1973] QB 629.
127 *Shaw v DPP* [1962] AC 220, p 292. This approach was accepted in *Stamford* [1972] 2 WLR 1055; [1972] 2 All ER 427.

whether the photograph is indecent depends on the view of the jury regarding recognised standards of propriety.[128] No artistic merits defence is available, although the distributor of the photographs, not the taker of them, can seek to show that he had a 'legitimate reason' for distributing or showing the photographs or for having them in his possession. Section 84 of the Criminal Justice and Public Order Act 1994 amended the 1978 Act to add 'pseudo-photographs' of children in order to cover digitally created photographs.[129] It also amended the Act so that the storage of data on computer disk or by other electronic means capable of conversion to a photograph is covered. Section 160 of the Criminal Justice Act 1988 created an additional offence of merely possessing the indecent picture of a child without a view to sale, display or distribution. The offence under either the 1978 or the 1988 Act can be committed merely by downloading an image onto a computer;[130] automatic storage of an image on a hard disk would not amount to making a photograph or pseudo-photograph.[131] Further, it has been found that possession requires knowledge.[132] In *Oliver, Hartrey and Baldwin*[133] the Court of Appeal found that pornographic images were to be categorised by the a number of levels of seriousness, beginning with images depicting erotic posing with no sexual activity.

The breadth of these offences was illustrated when the Saatchi Gallery in London was threatened with prosecution in March 2001 for showing pictures of children playing naked on the beach, taken by their mother, a professional photographer, as what one commentator called 'a celebration of the wonderment and joie de vivre of her children'.[134] The prosecution did not materialise, apparently on the basis that no element of lewdness was present. Similarly, when the Mapplethorpe Exhibition was shown at the Hayward Gallery in London in Autumn 1996, the Gallery took legal advice owing to the sexually explicit nature of some of the exhibits. Prosecution under the 1959 and/or under the 1978 Act appeared to be a possibility. It decided not to show three photographs, one of which was of a child.[135]

Offensive displays fall under the Indecent Displays (Control) Act 1981.[136] The Act provides, under s 1(1): 'If any indecent matter is publicly displayed the person making the display and any person causing or permitting the display to be made shall be guilty of an offence.' The Act provides in s 1(2) that 'Any matter which is displayed in or so as to be visible from any public place shall, for the purposes of this section, be deemed to be publicly displayed.' 'Public place' is then defined as 'any place to which the public have or are permitted to have access (whether on payment or otherwise)

---

128   *See R v Graham-Kerr* (1988) 88 Cr App R 302: this offence is discussed further at pp 556–58 below in relation to films.
129   See further Manchester, C, 'Criminal Justice and Public Order Act 1994: obscenity, pornography and videos' [1995] Crim LR 123, pp 123–28.
130   *R v Bowden* [2000] 2 All ER 418.
131   *Atkins v DPP* [2000] 2 All ER 425.
132   Ibid.
133   [2003] Cr App R 28. See further below at p 557.
134   See the *Guardian*, Report, 10 March 2001, p 9.
135   See further Warbrick, 'Federalism and free speech', in Loveland (ed), *Importing the First Amendment*, 1997, pp 177–79 and 190–92.
136   For discussion of the effect of the Act, see: (1982) Stat LR 31; (1981) 45 MLR 62; (1981) 132 NLJ 629.

while that matter is displayed'.[137] There are various exceptions to the definition of 'public places': the Act does not apply to the theatre, cinema, broadcasting, museums, art galleries, local authority or Crown buildings (s 1(4)). Shops which display an adequate warning notice are exempted[138] as far as adults are concerned; thus, as will be seen below, art galleries are, anomalously, more constrained in their displays than sex shops, in that they will fall within the common law on indecency and will not be able to take advantage of this exception.

Mailing of obscene or indecent items is covered by s 85 of the Postal Services Act 2000;[139] sexual literature in luggage is covered by s 49 of the Customs and Excise Management Act 1979. In the 1970s, customs officials interpreted the term 'indecency' widely; in 1976, for example, they seized and destroyed 114,000 books and magazines and 4,000 films. It also appeared that the test was being used in an arbitrary and indiscriminate manner. For example, in 1985 books ordered by the bookshop 'Gay's the Word' were impounded, including books by Oscar Wilde and Gore Vidal. The trial was about to commence, but the proceedings were withdrawn because of the ruling of the European Court of Justice in *Conegate Ltd v Customs and Excise Comrs*.[140] It was held that under Art 36 of the Treaty of European Union[141] that Britain could not apply a more stringent test – indecency – to imported goods when the equivalent in terms of domestically produced ones could circulate freely because they were not obscene. Thus, where obscenity or indecency existed as alternatives, the easier test should not be used to favour domestic goods since that would amount to arbitrary discrimination on trade between member states contrary to Art 36. Customs officers now apply this ruling but not just to EU imports, because it would be too impracticable to apply different tests to imports from different countries. This ruling has therefore resulted in a major relaxation of censorship. 'Hard core' pornography is, however, still seized; this is justifiable under Art 36 because it would also be prohibited if disseminated internally under the Obscene Publications Act.

Anomalies have arisen from the dichotomy between the tests for indecency on the one hand and obscenity on the other in other contexts. In *Straker*,[142] obscenity charges which resulted in an acquittal were brought in respect of the sale of artistic nude studies. The defendant then sent the pictures by post to persons interested in photographic art and was prosecuted successfully under s 11 of the Post Office Act 1953. In other words, the mere fact that the articles happened to be transferred through the post meant that criminal liability could arise, although otherwise it could not have done so. The DPP has recognised the anomalies created by cases of this nature and therefore he indicated – in 1981 – that prosecutions under the Post Office Act would be confined to cases where the indecent material sent through the post was unsolicited.

Apart from statutes prohibiting the promulgation of indecent material in specific situations, the possibility also arises of using the Sexual Offences Act 1956 to prevent

---

137 Section 1(3).
138 Section 1(3)(b).
139 Formerly, the Post Office Act 1953, s 11.
140 [1987] QB 254; [1986] 2 All ER 688. Figures quoted by Robertson, *Obscenity*, 1979, p 193.
141 Formerly Art 30 of the Treaty of Rome.
142 [1965] Crim LR 239; this approach was affirmed by the Court of Appeal in *Stamford* [1972] 2 WLR 1055; [1972] 2 All ER 427.

displays of indecency in stage plays and perhaps in the context of other live performances. A play, *The Romans in Britain*, which was staged in 1982 by the Royal National Theatre, included a depiction of the homosexual rape of a young druid priest by three Roman soldiers. Mary Whitehouse wanted to bring an action in respect of this scene, but the Attorney General refused permission as required under s 8 of the Theatres Act. Under s 2 of the Act, liability at common law could not arise in respect of a stage performance. Therefore, Mary Whitehouse invoked s 13 of the Sexual Offences Act 1956, which proscribes the procurement by one male of an act of gross indecency on another. This was arguably fulfilled by the procurement by the male director of the commission of an act of gross indecency by one actor on another. Had a female director been in charge, no prosecution would have been possible. It was determined on a preliminary ruling that prima facie liability might be established using this method.[143] At that point the prosecution was withdrawn; Mary Whitehouse had established the point in question and did not wish to take the risk that the prosecution would fail, as it might have done on various grounds. In particular, it was uncertain whether it could be shown that any indecency took place: it was unclear whether the actor's penis or thumb was shown in the scene. The significance of this possibility should not be over-emphasised; nevertheless, it clearly subverts the purpose of the Theatres Act, which should therefore be amended to prohibit liability arising under other statutes.

Statutory indecency, the HRA and the protection of morals exception under Art 10(2)

Prosecutions under these provisions will normally constitute interferences with freedom of expression under the HRA. The public authorities involved are bound by s 6 of the HRA to ensure that the tests under Art 10 are satisfied, while the provisions of the various statutes must be interpreted consistently with Art 10 under s 3. As Chapter 2 indicated, state interference with the Art 10 guarantee must be in accordance with the law, under para 2, if it is to be justified. This requirement covers not only the existence of national law, but its quality. In *Kopp v Switzerland*[144] the Court clearly stated that the essential requirements of a national legal basis are those of accessibility and foreseeability. These requirements require precision so that, in this context, the citizen is sufficiently aware of the meaning of the term 'indecency'. It is suggested that, as currently interpreted, the term is so uncertain that there is at least room for argument that these statutory provisions do not meet the 'prescribed by law' requirement. In *Hashman and Harrup v UK*,[145] the Court found that the *contra bono mores* doctrine was too uncertain to meet this requirement, since it depended on a vague concept of anti-social behaviour. Arguably, the concept of indecency considered in *Knuller v DPP*,[146] which depends on considering whether material would disgust 'ordinary decent-minded people', is almost equally imprecise; as pointed out above, doubts have been expressed as to the suitability of such a concept as a basis for criminality.

143 *The Romans in Britain*: see [1982] PL 165–67.
144 (1999) 27 EHRR 91, paras 70–71.
145 (2000) 8 BHRC 104. See Chapter 9, pp 751–52.
146 [1973] AC 435, p 457; [1972] 3 WLR 143.

It would, of course, be a bold domestic court that was prepared to find such a significant flaw in a large number of statutory provisions (and in respect of common law indecency, discussed below). The Commission has had the opportunity of making such a finding but has not done so,[147] and neither did the Court in *Muller*,[148] although this is not conclusive of the issue. It is much more likely that certain aspects of this statutory regime will be found to be disproportionate to the legitimate aim pursued, either in terms of the provisions themselves or in respect of decisions made under them. The Indecent Displays Act comports readily with the findings on adult autonomy from Scherer and Hoare since it impliedly does allow adults to choose to acquire explicit material, but does not allow it to be foisted upon an unwilling public, and makes special provision to protect children. However, it is suggested that the provisions of s 160 of the Criminal Justice Act 1988, affecting the downloading of pseudo-photographs of persons under 16 onto a computer, presumably from a website, might be viewed as disproportionate to the aim in view. The provisions criminalise a person merely for possessing a photograph, or its equivalent, which has been created without the involvement of a child. It is hard to view the use of the criminal law in this way as proportionate, since it is unclear that morals could be protected by this means. The breadth of the offences under the Protection of Children Act was indicated by the possibility of prosecution in respect of the Saatchi Exhibition. Arguments regarding proportionality could be raised in a similar instance, especially regarding the lack of an artistic merits defence or a defence of legitimate reason applicable to the creator of the photographs, so that the taking and distributing of photographs of children by paedophiles is not distinguished from the taking of them for artistic or scientific purposes.

Common law offences of indecency and obscenity

Prosecutions for conspiracy to corrupt morals can be brought at common law, as can prosecutions for outraging public decency. Thus, common law indecency creates a much wider area of liability than is created under statute because the law is not confined to specific situations such as using the mail. In *Shaw v DPP*,[149] the House of Lords determined that the offence of conspiring to corrupt public morals existed on the basis that the law conferred a general discretion to punish immoral (not merely criminal) conduct which could injure the public. Thus, any subject-matter which could lead others astray – although not necessarily amounting to a criminal offence – could be the subject of a prosecution if two or more persons were involved. Lord Reid, in his dissenting judgment, argued that the decision offended against the principle that the criminal law should be certain; it would be very difficult to determine beforehand what a jury would consider to fall within the area of liability created. The DPP then used this form of liability in instances where the material in question appeared to fall outside the Obscene Publications Act or added a charge of conspiracy to corrupt public morals to a charge of obscenity as an alternative in case the obscenity charge failed.

---

147 *Gibson v UK*, Application No 17634.
148 See p 465 above.
149 [1962] AC 220; [1961] 2 WLR 897, HL; for comment, see (1961) 24 MLR 626; (1964) 42 Canadian Bar Review 561.

The decision in *Shaw* has been especially criticised on the basis that it left it unclear whether an agreement to commit adultery could amount to a criminal conspiracy.[150]

Despite such criticism, the House of Lords confirmed the existence of the offence of conspiring to corrupt public morals and also the existence of the substantive offence of outraging public decency and conspiring to commit it in *Knuller v DPP*,[151] which concerned publication of homosexual contact advertisements. The conviction on the latter count was, however, overturned because the trial judge had misdirected the jury as to the ingredients of the offence. The House of Lords ruled that the necessary 'public' element would be present even if the indecency was not immediately visible, since it appeared on an inside page, so long as there was an express or implied invitation to penetrate the cover and partake of the lewd contents; therefore there must be a reference on the cover to the contents. Furthermore, the contents must be so offensive that the sense of decency of the public would be outraged by seeing them. Whether or not a member of the public *would* be so outraged, would be determined by reference to that section of the public likely to frequent the place where the publication in question was sold. In this respect, conspiracy to outrage public decency differs from conspiracy to corrupt public morals, which requires that the public at large must be considered. The motive in offering the article will be irrelevant, although it will be necessary to show that the defendant was aware both of the lewd nature of the material in question and that it was being placed on public sale.

Both these offences were preserved in s 5(3) of the Criminal Law Act 1977, and in *Gibson*[152] the Court of Appeal reaffirmed the ruling of the House of Lords in *Knuller* as to the ingredients of the offence of outraging public decency. The defendants were convicted of the offence after displaying in an art gallery a model of a human head with earrings made out of freeze-dried human foetuses of three to four months gestation. It may be noted that, at first instance, the jury was directed that they were entirely free to use their own standards in deciding whether the model was indecent. Argument on appeal centred on s 2(4) of the 1959 Act which provides that where a prosecution is brought in respect of an obscene article, it must be considered within the Act, not at common law, 'where it is of the essence of the offence that the matter is obscene'. 'Obscene' could denote something which disgusted the public or something which had a tendency to corrupt; if it carried the first meaning, the prosecution failed, as there was no suggestion that the exhibition of the earrings had a tendency to corrupt. Moreover, if the second, more restricted meaning were accepted, that would undermine the defence contained in s 4 of the Act which could be invoked if the material in question was, *inter alia*, of artistic worth. However, Lord Lane held that the words of s 1(1) were plain and clearly indicated that the restricted meaning of 'obscene' applied throughout the Act; he refused to depart from the normal canons of statutory construction.

If the defence argument on the meaning of obscene had been accepted, a greater number of publications would have fallen within the Obscene Publications Act and could have benefited from the s 4 defence, although this would also have meant extending the ambit of the Act, including the powers of seizure under s 3. As it is, the anomaly

---

150   See Robertson, op. cit., fn 1, p 215.
151   [1973] AC 435; [1972] 3 WLR 143; (1972) 56 Cr App R 633, HL.
152   [1990] 2 QB 619; [1991] 1 All ER 439; [1990] 3 WLR 595; for comment, see Childs [1991] PL 20–29.

has been continued that the artistic merit of objects which more seriously breach normal moral standards – objects which may corrupt – can prevent their suppression while the merits of less offensive objects cannot. This anomaly could have been addressed not by extending the meaning of obscenity, but by introducing a defence of public good which would have applied to common law indecency. A further anomaly arises due to the exclusion from the Indecent Displays (Control) Act 1981 of art galleries which, as noted above, are actually more restricted under common law. It was found in *Gibson* that the prosecution did not have to prove an intent to outrage public decency or recklessness as to the risk of such outrage; it was only necessary to prove that a defendant had intentionally done an act which in fact outraged public decency; he could not escape liability merely because his own standards were so base that he could not appreciate that outrage might be caused. This requirement may be contrasted with the full *mens rea* required for conspiracy to corrupt public morals. In *Knuller*, the House of Lords found that the defendant must intend to corrupt morals.

In the HRA era, the opportunity may arise to consider whether the continued existence, unmodified, of these common law doctrines is justifiable, in the light of the statutory regimes with which they overlap. A court in the discharge of its duty under s 6 HRA could curtail these offences, by reference to Art 10. These two common law offences are each aimed at a distinct mischief. Conspiracy to corrupt public morals clearly stems from the same roots as the offence under the Obscene Publications Act, rather than forming a part of the laws against indecency. Its existence is therefore perhaps even less defensible than that of conspiracy to outrage public decency, since it covers an area of liability which cannot be distinguished from that covered by the 1959 Act and is therefore most likely to allow escape from the statutory safeguards. It can exist only on the basis that its *actus reus* is the agreement between the parties rather than the risk of corruption of morals, whereas common law indecency can be distinguished from the offence under the 1959 Act on the more substantial basis that it is concerned in essence with indecency rather than obscenity.

On the other hand, it may be argued that the protection of morals answers to a more weighty public interest than the prevention of shock or outrage, and this contention is reflected in Art 10, which contains an exception expressed in terms of the former interest, but not the latter. However, when the defendants in *Gibson* applied to the European Commission alleging a breach of Art 10,[153] the application was found inadmissible, suggesting either that in the particular circumstances, the conviction might have appeared to have the effect of protecting morals, as opposed to merely preventing outrage, or that the protection of morals exception may sometimes cover material which merely shocks. It must be said that at present, the European Court has not always drawn a clear distinction between the two mischiefs: in *Müller v Switzerland*,[154] paintings found to offend morals under Swiss law fell within Art 10(2) as likely to 'grossly offend the sense of sexual propriety of persons of ordinary sensitivity'. This sounds like indecency rather than corruption, but the Court blurred the distinction between them in implying that the former would merge with the latter once a certain level of offensiveness was reached. That level may be reached, it is suggested, by speech

---

153 *Gibson v UK*, Appl No 17634.
154 (1991) 13 EHRR 212.

which may best be termed 'very shocking'. The Court made it clear that speech which would merely be termed 'shocking' or 'disturbing' would not reach it. Thus, it seems that these common law offences may be viewed as having a legitimate aim under Art 10(2), although their curtailment is nevertheless warranted because of their uncertain ambit and the anomalies they create.

It may be noted that the development of the wide ranging and flexible doctrine of common law indecency and conspiracy to corrupt public morals bears some resemblance to that of common law contempt: both doctrines work in tandem with statutes which create a more precise area of liability and which provide a defence which may ensure compatibility with Art 10 of the European Convention on Human Rights. In both instances, therefore, the common law tends to undermine the safeguards for free speech provided by the statute. However, testing the use of common law indecency and obscenity against the para 2 requirements under the HRA would import into them an ingredient akin to a defence of public good, since giving consideration to the question whether their use in a particular instance was necessary in a democratic society would require giving some consideration to the content of the expression in question. Where it could be said to have clear artistic merit, a court would be expected to give that factor some weight in assessing the question of proportionality.

4 Blasphemy, seditious libel, religious and racial hatred

Blasphemous and seditious libel

The existence of the offence of blasphemous libel[155] stems from the seventeenth century when it was tried in the Ecclesiastical courts. It was then thought to be a form of sedition due to the close relationship between the Church and the state. Therefore, it only protected the Anglican Church; other sects of the Christian Church such as Catholicism, or other religions, received no protection. Its basis, which derives from *Taylor's* case,[156] was that the defendant had aspersed the Christian religion. By the middle of the nineteenth century, and in particular after the case of *Ramsay and Foote*,[157]

---

155 Texts referred to, or for further reading: see Robertson, (1979) op. cit., fn 1, Chapter 8, pp 236–43; Robertson and Nichol, op. cit., fn 1, Chapter 3, pp 124–27; Bailey, Harris and Jones, op. cit., fn 1, Chapter 9; Robilliard, JA, *Religion and the Law*, 1984, Manchester University Press, Chapter 2; Barendt, op. cit., fn 1; for historical discussion of the development of blasphemy law see Kenny, CS, 'The evolution of the law of blasphemy' [1992] CLJ 127–42 and Walter, *Blasphemy Ancient and Modern*, 1990, Rationalist Press; Marsh, J *Word Crimes: Blasphemy, Culture, and Literature in Nineteenth-century England*, 1998; Lawton, D, *Blasphemy*, 1993, University of Pennsylvania Press. For a discussion of the theoretical issues lying behind blasphemy law, see Feinberg, J, *Offense to Others*, 1985; Sumner, LW, *The Hateful And The Obscene: Studies in the Limits of Free Expression*, 2004; Weinstein, J, 'First Amendment challenges to hate crime legislation: where's the speech?' (1992) 11 Criminal Justice Ethics 6 and, in the context of possible reform, see Law Commission Report No 145, *Offences against Religion and Public Worship*, 1985. For recent comment, see: Hare, I, 'Crosses, Crescents and Sacred Cows: Criminalising Incitement to Religious Hatred' (2006) Autumn PL 2006, 521–38; Goodall, K, 'Incitement to Religious Hatred: All talk and no substance' [2007] 70(1) MLR 89–113; Hare, I, 'Legislating Against Hate: the Legal Response to Bias Crimes' (1997) 17 OJLS 415; Kearns, P, 'Obscene and blasphemous libel: misunderstanding art' [2000] Crim LR 652.
156 (1676) 1 Vent 293.
157 (1883) 15 Cox CC 231.

it became clear that the basis of blasphemy had changed: it required a scurrilous attack on Christianity rather than merely reasoned and sober arguments against it. It was thought by 1950 that the offence was a dead letter.[158] However, it was resurrected in *Lemon*.[159] *Gay News* published a poem – 'The Love that dares to speak its name' – by a Professor of English literature, James Kirkup. It expressed religious sentiment in describing a homosexual's conversion to Christianity and in developing its theme it ascribed homosexual practices with the Apostles to Jesus and made explicit references to sodomy. Mary Whitehouse obtained leave to bring a private prosecution against *Gay News* and the editor and publishing company were convicted of the offence of blasphemous libel.

The Court of Appeal held that the intention or motive of the defendants was irrelevant since blasphemy was a crime of strict liability. It could therefore be committed by a Christian as there was no need to show that the material had mounted a fundamental attack on Christianity (as had been thought). There was no defence of publication in the public interest; serious literature could therefore be caught. The work in question need not be considered as a whole. All that needed to be shown was that the material in question, which was published with the defendant's knowledge, had crossed the borderline between moderate criticism on the one hand and immoderate or offensive treatment of matter sacred to Christians on the other. It was only necessary to show that resentment would be likely to be aroused, not that it actually was aroused. The past requirement to show that a breach of the peace might be occasioned by publication of the material was no longer necessary. The case was considered by the House of Lords on the question of the mental element required. The judgment confirmed the Court of Appeal ruling that it was only necessary to show an intent to publish the material. This decision has been much criticised[160] as it inhibits many, if not most, juxtapositions of sexuality with aspects of the Anglican religion by writers and broadcasters. In common with other parts of the common law, it allows the Obscene Publications Act to be circumvented because it admits of no public good defence. Moreover, there are already various areas of liability, discussed above, arising at common law and under statute which could be used to prevent offence being caused to Christians.

Gay News applied to the European Commission on Human Rights on a number of grounds including that of a breach of Art 10.[161] This application was ruled inadmissible in a cautious judgment. It was found that the Art 10 guarantee of freedom of expression had been interfered with, but that the interference fell within the 'rights of others' exception of Art 10(2). Was the interference necessary in a democratic society? It was found that once it was accepted that the religious feelings of citizens may deserve protection if attacks reach a certain level of savagery, it seemed to follow that the domestic authorities were best placed to determine when that level was reached. In other words, the argument used in the *Handyside* case, that a very wide margin of appreciation was required, was again invoked.

---

158 This was Lord Denning's description of it in *Freedom under the Law*, 1949, p 46.
159 [1979] AC 617; [1979] 2 WLR 281; [1979] 1 All ER 898, HL.
160 See Robertson, op. cit., fn 1, p 242; Law Commission Report, 1985.
161 (1979) 5 EHRR 123.

It seemed fairly clear in the pre-HRA era that this offence was unlikely to be extended beyond Anglicanism. The Law Commission in their 1985 Report[162] concluded, rather, that it should be abolished, in finding that an offence of wounding the feelings of adherents of any religious group would be impossible to construct because the term 'religion' could not be defined with sufficient precision. The argument in favour of extension of the offence was put and rejected in *Chief Metropolitan Magistrate ex p Choudhury*,[163] a case which arose out of the publication of Salman Rushdie's *The Satanic Verses*.[164] The applicants applied for judicial review of the refusal of a magistrates' court to grant summonses against Salman Rushdie and his publishers for, *inter alia*, the common law offence of blasphemous libel. The Court of Appeal found that the expression of views in an artistic context would not prevent them from amounting to a blasphemous libel, a finding that has been criticised as revealing a 'lack of judicial awareness of the right to artistic expression and its theoretical basis . . . [and an ignorance of] the autonomy of art as a specific cultural category with its own symbolic methods'.[165] But it was determined after reviewing the relevant decisions that the offence of blasphemy was clearly confined only to publications offensive to Christians. Extending the offence would, it was found, create great difficulties since it would be virtually impossible to define the term 'religion' sufficiently clearly. Freedom of expression would be curtailed as authors would have to try to avoid offending members of many different sects.

The applicants did not, however, rely only on domestic law; during argument that the offence should be extended, it was said that UK law must contain a provision to give effect to the Convention guarantee of freedom of religion under Art 9.[166] In response, it was argued and accepted by the Court of Appeal that the Convention need not be considered because the common law on the point was not uncertain. However, the respondents nevertheless accepted that in this particular instance, the Convention should be considered. It was found that the UK was not in breach of the Convention because extending the offence of blasphemy would breach Arts 7 and 10; the exceptions of Art 10(2) could not be invoked, as nothing in the book would support a pressing social need for its suppression. Furthermore, Art 9(1) could not be treated as absolute; implied exceptions to it must include the lack of a right to bring criminal proceedings for blasphemy where no domestic law had been infringed. Article 9 might be infringed, it was found, where Muslims were prevented from exercising their religion, but such restrictions were not in question. It should be noted that that last finding, and probably the finding regarding Art 10(2), can now be said to be wrong, as a matter of Convention law, in the light of the findings in *Otto-Preminger* in the Strasbourg Court (below).

---

162 Report No 145, Offences Against Religion and Public Worship. This was preceded by the Law Commission Working Paper No 79 of the same title (1981). See Robertson [1981] PL 295; Spencer, JR [1981] Crim LR 810; Robilliard (1981) 44 MLR 556 for comment on the 1981 Working Paper. The direction reform might take is considered further below, pp 491–97.

163 [1991] 1 QB 429; [1991] 1 All ER 306, DC; for comment, see Tregilgas-Davey, M (1991) 54 MLR 294–99.

164 For discussion of Muslim and Western reactions to publication of *The Satanic Verses*, see Abel, R, *Speech and Respect*, 1994, Chapter 1 (iii).

165 See Kearns, P, 'Obscene and blasphemous libel: misunderstanding art' [2000] Crim LR 652, p 656.

166 For discussion of the particular question whether blasphemy law can be defended by reference to the rights of others to freedom of religion, see below, pp 494–97.

On behalf of the applicants, it was further argued that if Art 9 provided no protection for Muslims, they had suffered discrimination in the exercise of their freedom of religion and therefore a violation of Art 14 had occurred. This interpretation of Art 9, read alongside Art 14, had been rejected by the European Commission in the *Gay News* case.[167] In this case, it also failed on the ground that the envisaged extension of UK law to protect Islam would involve a violation of Art 10, which guarantees freedom of expression. Such an extension was not, therefore, warranted. It seems clear from this ruling and from statements made by Lord Scarman in the House of Lords in *Lemon*,[168] which were relied upon in the *Choudhury* case, that the judiciary are not minded to extend this offence, considering that only Parliament should do so.

The applicants also argued that the crime of seditious libel would extend to the image of Islam presented by *The Satanic Verses*. This offence at one time seemed to cover any attack on the institutions of the state, but in modern times, it has been interpreted to require an intention to incite to violence and the words used must have a tendency to incite to violence.[169] It was not, therefore, apt to cover the offence caused to Muslims by the book, which could be said to be intended to arouse general hostility and ill will between sections of the community, but not against the public authorities. This finding, which was contrary to the ruling in *Caunt*,[170] means that incitement to religious hatred is not covered by any part of the law, although attacks on Anglicanism would in most instances fall within blasphemy, while attacks on religious groups which are also racial groups would fall within incitement to racial hatred (discussed below).

An application was made to the European Commission on Human Rights by the applicants in *Choudhury*,[171] but it was declared inadmissible on the ground that Art 9 does not include a positive obligation on the part of the state to protect religious sensibilities. The discriminatory application of blasphemy law therefore remains a source of discontent among Muslims. Parliament had the opportunity of abolishing the offence of blasphemy in 1994 when a Bill was put forward by Lord Lester which would have achieved this. However, it was withdrawn after the government opposed it,[172] partly on the ground that no clear consensus as to the value of abolishing this offence could be discerned. When the government brought forward the Racial and Religious Hatred Bill 2006 it did not include provision to abolish blasphemy law.

Blasphemy law in the HRA era

The Strasbourg jurisprudence

Consideration of the Strasbourg jurisprudence suggests that the inception of the HRA is unlikely to bring about reform of UK blasphemy law since such reform is not required in order to ensure harmony with Art 10 of the European Convention on Human Rights

---

167 (1982) 5 EHRR 123.
168 [1979] AC 617, p 620. Lord Scarman considered that there was a case for extension, however.
169 *Burns* [1886] 16 Cox CC 333; *Aldred* (1909) 22 Cox CC 1; *Caunt* (1947) unreported, but see case note 64 LQR 203; for comment see Barendt, op. cit., fn 1 (1st edn), pp 152–60.
170 (1947) 64 LQR 203.
171 *Choudhury v UK* (1991) No 17349/1990; (1991) 12 HRLJ 172.
172 555 HL Deb Cols 1891–1909, 16 June 1994.

as interpreted at Strasbourg. This suggestion is borne out by the findings of the European Commission in the *Gay News* case.

But the most significant ruling is that of the European Court of Human Rights in *Otto-Preminger Institut v Austria*.[173] An order was made for the seizure and forfeiture of a film, *Das Lieberkinzil (Council in Heaven)*, which caricatured aspects of Christianity, on the basis that it disparaged religious doctrines and was 'likely to arouse justified indignation'. The film was based on a satirical play by Oskar Panizza, published in 1894. The play bases itself on the assumption that syphilis was God's punishment for man's fornication and sinfulness at the time of the Renaissance. The film begins and ends with a depiction of Panizza's trial for blasphemy in 1895 in respect of the play. It shows the performance of the play, by the *Teatro Belli* in Rome, which portrays God as a senile old man, prostrating himself before the devil. Jesus is portrayed as a mental defective and is shown attempting to kiss and fondle his mother's breasts. God, Jesus and the Virgin Mary agree with the Devil to punish the world; the Devil suggests infecting the world with a sexually transmitted disease; as his reward, he demands freedom of thought. Apart from satirising aspects of religious belief, the film explores the idea of the limitations of artistic freedom, explicitly in relation to the trial and impliedly (in the context of the trial) in the case of the play.

In an Opinion that strongly emphasised the need to protect artistic freedom, the Commission found a breach of Art 10. In considering whether the interference was necessary in a democratic society for protecting the right to freedom of religion under Art 9, the Commission took into account the role of works of art in a democratic society and relied on the observation in *Müller*[174] to the effect that 'those who create, perform, distribute or exhibit works of art contribute to the exchange of ideas and opinions which is essential for a democratic society. Hence, the obligation of the state not to encroach unduly on their freedom of expression'. A warning was given to the public as to the nature of the film, and although access was not specifically restricted, the film was to be shown in a 'cinema of art' at a late hour. Therefore, it was unlikely that young children would be present. These factors affected the Commission's view. The Commission considered that recourse to certain artistic methods (satirisation and caricature) would not 'justify the imposition of a restriction on a work of art even if it deals with religion'.[175] Further, 'a complete prohibition which excludes the chance to discuss the message of the film *must* be seen as a disproportionate measure' (emphasis added).[176]

The Court took a strikingly different stance. The Austrian Government maintained, and the Court accepted, that the seizure and forfeiture were aimed at protecting the 'rights of others' within Art 10(2). The Court found that 'the manner in which religious doctrines are opposed or denied is a matter which may engage the responsibility of the state, notably its responsibility to ensure *the peaceful enjoyment of the right under Article 9*' (emphasis added).[177] The Court found that the responsibilities of those exercising the right under Art 10 include 'an obligation to avoid as far as possible expressions

---

173 (1994) 19 EHRR 34.
174 (1991) 13 EHRR 212.
175 (1994) 19 EHRR 34, para 72.
176 Ibid, para 77.
177 Ibid, para 47.

that are gratuitously offensive to others and thus an infringement of their rights and which therefore *do not contribute to any form of debate capable of furthering progress in human affairs*' (emphasis added).[178] Therefore, it might be considered necessary to prevent such expressions.

The Court took into account the lack of a uniform conception in Europe of the significance of religion in society in finding that it was not possible to arrive at a comprehensive definition of what constitutes a permissible interference. It therefore left a wide margin of appreciation to the Austrian Government in respect of assessing the extent of the interference necessary. It considered, however, that the necessity for the restriction 'must be convincingly established'. In finding that the seizure and forfeiture were necessary, the Court accepted the view of the Austrian authorities that the offensive nature of the film was not outweighed by its artistic merits and left them a wide margin of appreciation in determining the measures needed in the light of the local situation, bearing in mind the fact that the Roman Catholic religion was the dominant religion in the local region, the Tyrol. The Court did not give a specific reason for finding that the case for adopting the measures had been convincingly established, merely asserting that the Austrian authorities had not overstepped their margin of appreciation. No breach of Art 10 was therefore found.

Harris, O'Boyle and Warbrick criticised the breadth of the decision in these terms: 'It is hard to know which aspect of the majority's judgment more threatens freedom of expression interests: that outrage of people based only on knowing of, not being confronted with, certain expression provides justification for interfering with the expression, or, this being the case, that the indignation of people in a discrete geographic area is sufficient to justify the interference across the entire state.'[179] Bearing in mind the completeness of the interference, and its theoretical basis, this judgment is, it is argued, entirely unsatisfactory in the light of the free speech justifications discussed in the Introduction to Part II. The Court appeared to afford little weight to the value of the speech in question in terms of providing worthwhile dissent from established thought. In finding that the film did not contribute to 'debate capable of furthering progress in human affairs' it revealed a failure to understand the principle of moral autonomy which demands that citizens should be free not only to choose to view works of art, but to decide for themselves whether they have value.[180] It also showed a misunderstanding of the nature of the argument from truth, which it appeared to be referring to, in that it excluded the possibility that the film's message might in future be viewed as winning out in the market place of ideas. In other words, it allowed an interference in that free market of ideas which sought to preclude that possibility. In attacking the *manner* of the dissent from established religious ideas, the Court, in contrast to the Commission, failed to understand the nature of artistic endeavour, which often uses techniques such as satire in order to make an impact on an audience. In this respect, it disregarded its own earlier statement to the effect that 'Article 10 protects not only the substance of the ideas and information but also the form in which they are conveyed'.[181] It further

---

178 Ibid, para 49.
179 *Law of the European Convention on Human Rights*, 1995, p 402.
180 See the statement to this effect in the well known free expression decision in the US: (1966) *Ginzburg v US* 463, p 498.
181 *Oberschlick v Austria* (1991) 19 EHRR 389.

failed to differentiate between taking account of the possibility that the expression in question had value, based on an understanding of the free speech justifications, and assessing that value itself.[182] Clearly, the Court possessed no special expertise allowing it to arbitrate as to the artistic worth of the film. The judgment was also unsatisfactory even in its own terms, since it failed to conduct a strict evaluation as to whether the need for such a wide ranging restriction had been convincingly established. In short, this was an unconvincing, under-theorised judgment of the Court which is unworthy of its freedom of expression jurisprudence in general. The Opinion of the Commission was, it is suggested, far more in tune with that jurisprudence.

The judgment of the Court in *Wingrove v UK*[183] applied the reasoning from *Otto-Preminger* and therefore showed very similar tendencies. Again, the decision can be contrasted with the finding of the Commission that there had been a violation of Art 10.[184] The Court had to consider whether a refusal of the BBFC to issue a certificate licensing a video, *Visions of Ecstasy*, constituted a breach of Art 10. The film depicts erotic visions experienced by St Theresa of Avila, a 16th-century Carmelite nun. In the short, silent film she is depicted in a white habit suspended from a cord being erotically embraced by her own psyche, represented by a half-naked woman. That scene is intercut by scenes showing St Theresa, as part of her fantasies, kissing and embracing Christ who is fastened to the cross. She kisses his wounds and sits astride him in a manner reflecting intense arousal. The BBFC took the view that if the video had been granted a classification certificate and shown in the UK, a private prosecution for blasphemy might have been brought successfully.

The Court found that the restriction was prescribed by law, taking into account the fact that the BBFC was acting within its powers under s 4(1) of the Video Recordings Act 1984 and that no general uncertainty was apparent as to the definition of blasphemy formulated in the *Lemon* case. The refusal of the certificate had the aim of protecting the rights of others within Art 10(2) and was consonant with the aim of the protection afforded by Art 9 to religious freedom. In considering the necessity and proportionality of the restriction, the Court went on to find that while the margin of appreciation allowed to states would be narrow in relation to political speech, it would be wide in relation to offending 'intimate personal convictions within the field of morals or, especially, religion'.[185] It also placed strong emphasis on the fact that views hostile to Christianity could be expressed under the English law of blasphemy: 'it is the manner in which the views are advocated rather than the views themselves which the law seeks to control . . . The high degree of profanation that must be attained [is] . . . itself a safeguard against arbitrariness.'[186] The Court found, having viewed the video, that the decision of the BBFC that it would outrage and insult the feelings of believing Christians could not be said to be arbitrary or excessive. The national authorities had not overstepped their margin of appreciation: the exception applied and therefore no breach of Art 10 had occurred.

---

182 See further Pannick, D, 'Religious Feelings and the European Court' [1995] PL 7.
183 Opinion of the Commission: (1994) 19 EHRR CD 54. Judgment of 25 November 1996, Case 19/1995/525/611; (1996) 24 EHRR 1. For further discussion, see Ghandi, S and James, J, 'The English law of blasphemy and the European Convention on Human Rights' [1998] EHRLR 430.
184 *Wingrove v UK* (1994) 76-A DR 26.
185 Judgment in draft form, p 22.
186 Ibid, para 60.

It is suggested that this judgment strongly resembles that in *Otto-Preminger* in revealing a strange failure in a court of human rights to understand or afford weight to the familiar free speech justifications. The judgment reveals an inability to appreciate that a *complete* ban on a film is especially difficult to defend if the principle of moral autonomy is to be given any weight. It failed to understand the value of allowing dissent, not only from established views of religious figures, but also from such views as to their proper portrayal. In placing so much emphasis on the question of the *manner* of the portrayal, it shows a readiness to stifle artistic initiative, thereby preventing the free debate of the ideas the film portrays and also preventing, or at least strongly curbing, the outgrowths in terms of further artistic exploration of similar ideas, that it might have fostered.

Domestic approaches to blasphemy law under the HRA

Where the European Court of Human Rights leaves a wide margin of appreciation to member states in determining the extent of the exceptions to a Convention right, this could be taken to imply that, at least until a common European conception of the width of the exception emerges, states have the main responsibility for ensuring that rigorous human rights standards are maintained. It is suggested that the ease with which publications can infringe blasphemy law in the UK does not represent a maintenance of such standards and that therefore, reform of blasphemy law should be attempted, now that the HRA is in force, by domestic judges who are not trammelled by the margin of appreciation doctrine. Moreover, given the widespread criticism of the decisions in *Otto-Preminger* and *Wingrove*, and the failure to understand basic principles of freedom of expression that they reveal, there are strong grounds for arguing that the domestic courts should not follow them, but should look for guidance to the Commission in both instances, and to courts in other jurisdictions in order to achieve a more developed understanding of those principles.

For example, in the well known judgment in *Cohen v California*,[187] the US Supreme Court found that a political view expressed in profane terms was protected by the First Amendment; it said: 'much linguistic expression serves a dual communicative function: it conveys not only ideas capable of relatively precise, detached explication, but otherwise inexpressible emotions as well . . . words are often chosen as much for their emotive as their cognitive force. We cannot sanction the view that the Constitution, while solicitous of the cognitive content of individual speech, has little regard for that emotive function which, practically speaking, may often be the most important element of the overall message sought to be communicated.' These words would clearly be equally applicable to a film such as Council in Heaven, which had both an emotive and a cognitive function, or to *Visions of Ecstasy*, which had a largely emotive function.

There are at least two clear reasons why some change is needed in the current law. First, from a pragmatic point of view, the present situation, since it is perceived

---

187 (1971) 403 US 15, 25–6. The decision, regarding the words 'Fuck the draft', could be viewed as affected by being taken in the context of political speech. Nevertheless, lower courts have applied the words regarding emotive communication to visual expression that cannot be regarded as political expression: *Cinevision Corp v City of Burbank* 7456 F 2d 560, p 569 (concerning music) and *Birkenshaw v Haley* (1974) 409 F Supp 13 ED Mich (concerning mime).

by Muslims as unfair, is a considerable source of racial tension: it both engenders feelings of anger and alienation in the Muslim community and, when these feelings are expressed through such activities as book burning and attacks on booksellers stocking *The Satanic Verses*, increased feelings of hostility towards Muslims in certain sections of the non-Muslim population. Secondly, from the liberal point of view broadly endorsed in this book, it is indefensible that the state should single out one group of citizens and protect their religious feelings while others are without such protection. In what follows, therefore, the question whether blasphemy law should be extended, abolished or replaced by an offence of incitement to religious hatred, will be considered from the point of view of the philosophical justifications which would support each alternative. The probable effect of each course of action on racial tension will also be briefly considered. This discussion is premised upon the argument outlined in Chapter 1 that free speech, as a strong individual right, should be infringed only if a similar individual right is threatened by speech, or if the values which lead us to support free speech are not at issue in the instant case, or if the speech carries a real risk of substantial damage to the well being of society.

When blasphemy law is considered in suitable instances under the HRA, the arguments for its abolition or extension are likely to be canvassed. Since blasphemy is a common law doctrine, the judges are, it is suggested, at liberty to abolish, extend or curtail it, under s 6 of the HRA. The argument to extend the blasphemy law to cover other faiths would clearly find support in principle if the present law is viewed as having a firm basis in Convention values.[188] It receives strong support, it is suggested, from the decision in *Otto-Preminger* which would have to be taken into account by the domestic judiciary, under s 2 of the HRA, in a suitable case. It could be argued that since the Strasbourg Court has found that Art 9 covers a right to be free from the knowledge that expression offensive to one's religious beliefs is occurring in one's locality, and that that right further covers the a ban on such speech that covers the whole country, the reach of Art 9 has been greatly extended. Muslims could readily argue that the sale of a book or showing of a film with a theme similar to that of *The Satanic Verses*, amounts on this argument to a violation of their Art 9 rights and that a complete ban, as opposed to a very restricted sale, confined to certain localities, would therefore be warranted. Article 14 could also be invoked in conjunction with Art 9. The argument of the European Commission on Human Rights in *Choudhury*,[189] to the effect that Art 9 does not include a positive obligation on the part of the state to protect religious sensibilities, may be doubted on the basis that positive obligations have been accepted

188 For general discussion of this issue, see 'Speech, religious discrimination and blasphemy' (1989: Proceedings of the American Society of International Law, p 427 *et seq*. and, in particular, Reisman's article, pp 435–39: he makes out an elegant thesis that attempts such as Ayatollah Khomeni's, to punish and deter unorthodox references to the Koran, amount to a 'claim of the right to exclusive control of major symbols of global culture and the prerogative of deciding how they are to be used artistically' (p 437). He expresses concern over 'the support lent by religious leaders in the West' to this claim and the criticism of Rushdie expressed by some of them. He warns that imposing censorship on artists or forcing them to internalise such censorship through insisting that free expression amounts to a form of religious intolerance will lead to the deterioration of the arts: creative endeavour will become a kind of 'communal Rubik cube in which a limited number of approved elements are moved feverishly round in an ever decreasing number of "new" combinations' (p 439).

189 *Choudhury v UK* (1991) No 17349/1990; (1991) 12 HRLJ 172.

under Art 8.[190] The Art 7 problem would still have to be overcome and it is suggested that, since the decision as to the reach of rights to freedom of religion in *Otto-Preminger* is out of line with the stance in most 'civilised nations',[191] the exception under Art 7(2) could not be invoked successfully.[192]

There are practical difficulties, based on the nature of the HRA, in seeking to rely on Art 9 in relation to a bookseller or a film producer or a broadcaster. Probably a Muslim group would not have standing (s 7(3)) under s 7(1)(a) to bring an action based on a free standing application of Art 9 and, in any event, the other party would not normally be a public authority. The 'victim' provision under s 7(3) would obviously still create a difficulty, but there would be the possibility of bringing an action based solely on Art 9 where a public authority, such as a media regulator, or the BBC, was involved. If a remedy was available, it would presumably take the form of an injunction, since the Convention cannot be used to create criminal liability. But the most obvious, and, as indicated, probably the only, vehicle existing in domestic law on which to base an Art 9 argument is blasphemy law. The result of an attempt to use the blasphemy law might end in an application for judicial review, as in *Choudhury*. A Muslim group would base their application on the ordinary standing rules, as in *Choudhury*, and then rely on s 7(1)(b) in order to argue that their Art 9 and 14 rights should be afforded recognition.

But, practical issues aside, the key issue of principle concerns the validity of the arguments that freedom of expression should give way to a right to freedom of religion that includes the right not to be offended by the promulgation of expression that offends against religious sensibilities. To evaluate the force of this argument, it is necessary first to identify which, if any, of the rationales for blasphemy law would provide support for both its continued existence and extension, and which would not. Three rationales will be considered in turn: the argument from the protection of society, the argument from preventing individual distress and the argument from the right to religious freedom. The point of view which sees blasphemy law as protecting those shared beliefs of a society which are essential to its survival[193] would not, it is submitted, support the extension of the law to cover other faiths; the law would then be protecting a whole set of conflicting beliefs and thus supporting religious pluralism, not the survival of religious conformity. It may be argued that the law should uphold religious pluralism

---

190 See Chapter 9, pp 816–20.

191 The fact that, as the Court noted in *Wingrove*, para 57, 'the application of [blasphemy laws in Europe] is becoming increasingly rare and several states . . . have recently repealed them altogether . . .' would also support this contention. In the US, the First Amendment provides expressly that 'Congress shall make no law respecting an establishment of religion, nor prohibiting the free exercise thereof' and in *Joseph Burstyn Inc v Wilson* (1952) 343 US 495, an attempt to stop the screening of a film on the ground that it was blasphemous failed. The decision made it clear that the offence of blasphemy could not be sustained since it was entirely opposed to First Amendment principles. See also the famous 'Nazis at Skokie' decisions: *Collin v Smith* (1978) 578 F 2d 1197, 7th Cir, (1978) 436 US 953, (1978) 439 US 916; *Skokie v Nat Socialist Party* (1978) 373 NE 2d 21; it raised issues which have parallels with those in *Otto-Preminger*.

192 See Chapter 2, pp 66–68.

193 Lord Devlin is usually associated with the thesis that society may justifiably protect its shared moral beliefs through the criminal law: see his *The Enforcement of Morals*, 1965, OUP. It is arguable that the protection of society was, historically at least, one of the purposes of blasphemy law: see, e.g., *Taylor's case* [1676] 1 Vent 293 in which it was said: 'For to say, Religion is a cheat is to dissolve all those obligations whereby civil societies are preserved.'

as a shared belief, but abolition of the offence of blasphemy would do this far more simply than extension.

The argument that blasphemy laws are justified because they protect individual believers from mental anguish immediately runs into a host of problems over extension of the law. For if one is concerned to protect individuals from the mental distress which can flow from attacks on deeply held beliefs,[194] it is not readily apparent that society should not also outlaw attacks upon deeply held non-religious beliefs, such as a deep belief in the equality of the sexes.[195] But one would then arrive at a position in which the criminal law would be being used to prevent people from attacking or insulting the deep beliefs of others. Arguably, such a law would be unworkable, since it would require judgments to be made about indeterminable matters such as the depth at which a belief was held. More importantly, not only would such a law represent a major infringement of the individual's freedom of speech, offering only the prevention of distress as a justification, it would be philosophically indefensible besides. If we are really committed to the notion that free discussion is the best way to arrive at the truth,[196] it seems nonsensical to abandon that position when our most important beliefs are at stake; if anything, we should be most concerned precisely to *encourage* free discussion of our deep beliefs since, almost axiomatically, it is our deepest beliefs which we most wish to be true.

It is submitted that the only justification for continuance of the blasphemy law which could offer it even prima facie support is the argument from the right to religious freedom, which is protected under Art 9 of the Convention. The need to provide such protection is also viewed as falling within the 'rights of others' exception to Art 10 and, therefore, as arguably justifying the banning of publications that might offend religious sensibilities, as the Court of Human Rights found in *Otto-Preminger* and *Wingrove*. It is contended that the argument accepted by the Court that such publications infringe Art 9 is deeply flawed. In order to demonstrate this, it is necessary to consider the substantive contention that, as Poulter puts it:

> Freedom of religion is . . . a valuable human right and it may be doubted whether it can be fully enjoyed in practice if the state allows religious beliefs to be vilified and insulted in a gratuitous manner.[197]

The first assertion made here, about the value of religious freedom, is of course readily conceded. However, the argument, as expressed by the Court of Human Rights, then goes on to assume that the state is under a positive duty to facilitate the full enjoyment

---

194 Note, e.g., the *dicta* of Lord Scarman in *Lemon* [1979] AC 617, p 620 to the effect that 'there is a case for legislation extending [blasphemy law] to protect the religious beliefs and feelings of non-Christians'. Arguably, however, he saw protection of feelings as ultimately aimed at 'the internal tranquillity of the Kingdom'.

195 Recognising this, a number of commentators have attempted to frame definitions of 'religious belief' in which the term includes both actual religious convictions and those beliefs which hold a place in people's minds analogous to that held by religious belief. See, e.g., Clements, 'Defining 'religion' in the First Amendment: a functional approach' (1989) 74 Cornell LR 532.

196 For an exposition of this theory, see above, pp 302–3.

197 Poulter, S, 'Towards legislative reform of the blasphemy and racial hatred laws' [1991] PL 371, p 376.

in practice of its citizens' right to freedom of religion, taking that term to encompass a duty to prevent attacks on religion which take a certain objected-to form. This is surely a mistaken view; rather, it is submitted, the right to religious freedom is violated if one is not free to choose, express and manifest one's religious beliefs:[198] the right is not so violated simply because one is not protected from mental suffering caused by verbal attacks upon one's religion or offensive portrayals of it. As Van Dijk and Van Hoof put it in one of the leading texts: 'this decision [in *Otto-Preminger*] is mistaken. The screening of the film in no way would have limited or inhibited Roman Catholics in manifesting their religion . . . a right [not to be insulted in one's religious views] is not included in Article 9 but is on the contrary inconsistent with the "pluralism indissociable from a democratic society"[199] embedded in Article 9.'[200]

Even if it were to be accepted for the purposes of argument that the religious freedom of those from Christian faiths should be protected by the blasphemy law, it is denied that this finding would be a conclusive argument for continuing or, *a fortiori*, extending the protection. If Poulter's contention, and that of the Court of Human Rights, are correct, then we are confronted by a situation in which two important individual rights – freedom of religion and freedom of speech – come into conflict with each other. In such a situation, it is surely reasonable not simply to assume that freedom of religion should override freedom of speech, but rather to attempt to weigh up which right would suffer most if the other was given precedence. If this is done, the argument runs as follows: if there was no offence of blasphemy, this might mean that on occasion some distress, perhaps acute, would be associated with the practice of one's religion, although those aware that they might suffer distress can normally take steps to ensure that they do not encounter the offending publication. If there is such an offence, it might mean that use of the coercive sanctions of the law would severely damage the liberty to write creatively or speak one's mind freely on religious matters.[201] Clearly, the damage done to freedom of religion if there is no blasphemy law is far less than the damage done to freedom of speech if there is one.

In any event, the argument that regards a blasphemy law as essential because the right to religious freedom demands it, immediately runs into difficulties since it is clearly necessary to define religion. One could not follow the path described above and define religion to include secular but deeply held beliefs, as one would then be placed in the absurd position of defending secular ideas from attack by reference to a right to *religious* freedom. Nor could one overcome this difficulty by adopting a pragmatic stance and framing a statute protecting only the five major world religions. If the individual's right to religious freedom demands protection against vilificatory

---

198 Thus, Art 18 of the Universal Declaration of Human Rights provides that: 'Everyone has the right to freedom of thought, conscience and religion; this right includes freedom to change his religion or belief and freedom . . . in public or private to manifest his religion or belief in teaching, practice, worship and observance.' Both the International Covenant on Civil and Political Rights (Art 18) and the European Convention (Art 9) contain very similar provisions.

199 *Kokkinakis v Greece* A 260-A, p 18.

200 Van Dijk, P and Van Hoof, F, *Theory and Practice of the European Convention on Human Rights*, 1998, p 551.

201 See Poulter S, 'Towards legislative reform of the blasphemy and racial hatred laws' [1991] PL 371, p 376. Poulter concedes that his proposed extension of the blasphemy law (pp 378 *et seq.*) might well have caught *The Satanic Verses* (pp 384–85).

attacks upon her religion,[202] and since presumably members of less well known religions are as entitled to religious freedom as members of the major religions, it follows that they must also be entitled to protection against such attacks. Clearly, therefore, a satisfactory definition of religion would have to be arrived at. The difficulties of framing such a definition have already been noted. In this connection, it is also worth recalling that the UN General Assembly *Declaration on the Elimination of All Forms of Intolerance and Discrimination Based on Religion and Belief*, as one commentator notes, 'does not seek to define religion or belief'. He explains: 'This is because no definition could be agreed upon, as none could be agreed when the texts of Article 18 of the Universal Declaration and Article 18 of the ICCPR were drafted.'[203] Since, therefore, the impossibility of framing such a definition seems to be well attested to, it may reasonably be concluded that the project to extend blasphemy law to cover other faiths is fraught with difficulty.

On all these grounds, it is concluded that the argument that freedom of religion demands a blasphemy law, fails. It follows, if this view is accepted, that the abolition of the current law can readily be defended on Art 10 grounds without fear of offending against Art 9. Christian beliefs and doctrines could, therefore, be placed in the same position as Islamic or deeply held secular beliefs in that its adherents can choose to avert their eyes from distasteful portrayals of their beliefs, and to combat what they regard as untrue or unfair representations with – in their view – more truthful or more inspirational speech. In both *Wingrove* and *Otto-Preminger*, it was very unlikely that a religious adherent who might be offended would unwittingly view the film.

Abolition of the blasphemy law would tend to ease racial tension since at least it would be clear that Muslims and Christians were being accorded an equal lack of protection. This would be the better solution, since it is by no means clear that extending blasphemy law would ease the problem. Indeed, it is possible that if, for example, Muslims had been able to use an extended blasphemy law to suppress *The Satanic Verses*,[204] considerable resentment might well have been engendered in the non-Muslim community. The justified grievance felt by Muslims about the unfairness of the present law would, to a certain extent, be remedied if blasphemy was abolished altogether as an offence.

At present, however, this is not in prospect, although it is also probably fair to point out that blasphemy prosecutions have not been undertaken in recent years. The 25th anniversary of the conviction in *Lemon* of the publishers of *Gay News* and Professor Kirkup for blasphemy in relation to the poem, 'The Love that Dares to Speak its Name' was re-visited by a public reading of the poem in Trafalgar Square in 2002.[205] 11 speakers,[206] including writers, academics and MPs, each took a turn to read a verse of the poem. The event was intended as an act of civil disobedience, both to protest

---

202 This proposition is not conceded, as indicated. It is put forward by Poulter, 'Towards legislative reform of the blasphemy and racial hatred laws' [1991] PL 371–85.

203 Boyle, K, 'Religious intolerance and the incitement of hatred', in Coliver (ed), *Striking a Balance: Hate Speech, Freedom of Expression and Non-discrimination*, 1992, Article 19.

204 See Poulter S, 'Towards legislative reform of the blasphemy and racial hatred laws' [1991] PL 371.

205 See the account given at http://www.petertatchell.net/religion/blasphemy.htm.

206 Namely, Barry Duke, Shirley Dent, Jim Herrick, Jonathan Meades, George Melly, Professor Richard Norman, Sam Rimmer, Brian Sedgemore MP, Hanne Stinson, Peter Tatchell and Keith Wood.

against the infringement of free speech represented by the original prosecution, and in effect to defy the prosecuting authorities either to bring a prosecution, or declare the offence 'dead'. The police took no action against those reading the poem, but filmed the event and sent the film to the DPP, who decided not to bring a prosecution. The offence however cannot yet be dismissed as a dead letter. In 2005, in a written answer, a government spokesperson said: 'If material or conduct is gratuitously offensive to Christians, and is prosecuted as such, a finding of blasphemy may be the appropriate response by a court to ensure that the rights of others under Article 9 [of the Convention] are protected.'[207] In debate on the Religious Hatred Bill, however, the government did recognise that there was a serious issue to be considered in relation to the abolition of the law of blasphemy, but took the view that that Bill was not the right vehicle to achieve it, further consultation and consideration being necessary.[208] The offence may be viewed in Art 10 terms as deeply problematic, not least because its *actus reus* is so imprecise as to render it almost unusable in practice. Thus, until the introduction of the offence of incitement to religious hatred in 2006, Islamic belief and Muslims generally had no protection from speech-based attacks, while Christianity, subject to the caveats already noted, was over-protected. It is to the new religious hatred offence that this chapter now turns.

Incitement to racial and religious hatred

Hate speech: stirring up racial hatred[209]

Domestic provisions

The offence of stirring up racial hatred was introduced under s 6 of the Race Relations Act 1965, in order to meet public order concerns and protect persons from the effects on others of provocative and inflammatory racist expression. The Public Order Act 1936 was amended in order to include this offence, but Part III (ss 17–23) of the Public Order Act 1986 extends its ambit. Section 18 provides that liability will arise if threatening, abusive or insulting words or behaviour are used or written material of that nature is displayed, intended by the defendant to stir up racial hatred or which make it likely that racial hatred will be stirred up against a racial group (not a religious

---

207 *Official Report*, 3 March 2005; co WA 40.
208 See HL Deb, col 540 (8 Nov 2005).
209 For recent discussion and literature referred to below, see: Hare, I, 'Crosses, Crescents and Sacred Cows: Criminalising Incitement to Religious Hatred' (2006) Autumn PL 2006, 521–38; Goodall, K, 'Incitement to Religious Hatred: All talk and no substance' [2007] 70(1) MLR 89–113; Hare, I, 'Legislating Against Hate: the Legal Response to Bias Crimes' (1997) 17 OJLS 415. For general discussion of this offence and its background, see: Cotterell, R [1982] PL 378; Dickey [1968] Crim LR 489; Gordon, *Incitement to Racial Hatred*, 1982; Leopold, P [1977] PL 389; Wolffe [1987] PL 85; Bindman, G (1982) 132 NLJ 299; Williams, DGT [1966] Crim LR 320; Weinstein, J, 'First Amendment challenges to hate crime legislation: where's the speech?' (1992) 11 Criminal Justice Ethics 6; Law Commission Report No 145, *Offences against Religion and Public Worship*, 1985. See Chapter 14, pp 1416–21 for discussion of the new offence of 'glorifying' terrorism.

group) in Great Britain.[210] Where intent is not shown, it is necessary to show that the accused realised that the words used might be threatening, abusive or insulting.[211] Section 18(2) catches private or public meetings (unless held in a 'dwelling'). Section 19 makes it an offence to publish threatening, abusive or insulting material, either intended by the defendant to stir up racial hatred or which make it likely that racial hatred will be stirred up against a racial group. Section 21 extends the offence to the distributing, showing or playing of visual images or sounds. Section 20 makes it an offence to stir up racial hatred in the public performance of a play, but the likelihood that hatred will be stirred up must be judged by reference to 'all the circumstances' and 'in particular taking the performance as a whole'. Therefore, the context in which, for example, a character is racially abused must be considered: where the message of the play as a whole could not be viewed as one aimed at stirring up racial hatred, the offence will not be committed. Thus, plays that explore the theme of racism in society should escape liability.

Section 22 makes it an offence to use threatening, abusive or insulting visual images or sounds in a programme, intended by the defendant to stir up racial hatred, or which make it likely that racial hatred will be stirred up against a racial group. Section 164(2) of the Broadcasting Act 1990 amended s 22 so that it covers 'programme services', including cable programme services. The offence under s 22 can be committed by the programme producer, director, the television company and any person 'by whom the offending words or behaviour are used'. This is a broadly worded offence which encourages caution in producing programmes about the problem of racism, since it can be committed without any intent on the part of the producer or the company. Programmes can only be shown if it is made clear, editorially, that the message of racists is disapproved of. Section 23 of the 1986 Act places further obstacles in the way of those producing programmes about racism, particularly historical programmes. Section 23, as amended by s 164(4) of the Broadcasting Act 1990, creates an offence of possessing racially inflammatory (threatening, abusive or insulting) material with a view, in the case of written material, to publication or distribution and, in the case of a recording, to its being distributed, shown, played or included in a programme service, intended by the person possessing it to stir up racial hatred or which makes it likely, having regard to all the circumstances, that racial hatred will be stirred up. Television researchers must be sure that historical material will be placed in a context which makes it clear that its message is disapproved of.

These offences have a number of elements in common. None of them requires a need to show that disorder was caused, or that there was an intent to cause disorder, and there is no need to show that racial hatred is actually stirred up. It is not an essential ingredient to show that there was an intent to stir up racial hatred. It is sufficient to show that hatred *might* actually be stirred up. In that circumstance, s 18 imports an element of *mens*

---

210 'Racial group' is defined using the same terms as under the Race Relations Act; see Chapter 15, pp 1507–8. The result is that, e.g., hatred may be stirred up against Muslims – so long as the offence under the 1986 Act, s 5 (see Chapter 8, pp 780–85) is not committed – but not against Sikhs.

211 Section 18(5) governs the *mens rea* if it is not shown that the defendant intended to stir up racial hatred. He must intend the words, etc, to be or be aware that they might be, threatening, abusive or insulting. 'Awareness' as used in the 1986 Act seems to mean subjective recklessness.

rea, but the other sections do not, a very significant difference.[212] The offence might be committed by broadcasting or using or promulgating words or material by the methods indicated above, threatening, abusive or insulting matter which, objectively speaking, is incapable of stirring up racial hatred so long as the accused intended that it should do so. It may be noted that the s 18 offence is the only public order offence which may be committed by words alone unaccompanied by the need – as an essential ingredient – to show any likelihood that they would cause distress, since the offence could be committed by uttering words which were greeted with delight by those who heard them. But of most significance is the possibility that criminal liability can arise owing to the promulgation of material likely to stir up racial hatred unintentionally. These offences represent a restriction based on manner rather than content due to their specific requirements. Reasoned argument of a racist nature would not incur liability, since the racist words or material must be threatening, abusive or insulting. Further, the term 'hatred' is a strong one: merely causing offence or bringing into ridicule is not enough and nor is racial harassment. The difficulty of showing that race hatred would be likely to be stirred up or that the defendant intended to stir up race hatred was demonstrated when jurors cleared Nick Griffin of using words or behaviour intended to stir up racial hatred in 2006. He was accused of using words or behaviour intended to stir up racial hatred, and faced two alternative counts of using words or behaviour likely to stir up racial hatred. He was charged after making a speech to British National Party (BNP) supporters at a pub in Keighley, West Yorkshire, in January 2004. In it, he described Islam as a 'wicked, vicious faith' and said that Muslims were turning Britain into a 'multiracial hellhole'. The BNP's head of publicity, Mark Collett, was cleared of similar charges. He had referred to asylum seekers as 'cockroaches' and had told the Keighley gathering: 'Let's show these ethnics the door in 2004'. Nick Griffin told the jury that his speech was not an attack on Asians in general, but on Muslims. Mark Collett said that the speeches had only been intended to motivate BNP members to take part in 'legal and democratic' campaigning.[213] The speeches had been filmed by an undercover BBC reporter and were later broadcast as part of the documentary *The Secret Policeman*. The verdict caused a furore amongst anti-racist campaigners since, as a number of organisations stated, had the two been convicted that would not only have indicated the point at which racist speech would not be tolerated by the law, but also it would have indicated the law's intolerance of Islamophobia in British society.[214] The acquittals led to comments from Cabinet members to the media about the possible need for a review of the race hatred law in Parliament.[215] The new religious hatred offences, discussed below, would cover attacks on Muslims, as opposed to attacks on Asians generally, but it is unclear that they would have led to convictions had they been deployed in the *Griffin* case since they are so narrowly drawn.

212 See above, fn 211. The other sections provide a defence – in effect, a reversed *mens rea*: the defendant could prove that he was not aware of the content of the recording/material/broadcast and had no reason to suspect that it was threatening, etc.

213 See the *Guardian*, 10 November 2006.

214 A spokesman for the Islamic Human Rights Commission said: 'I am very disappointed. I think this judgment is going to have very grave consequences indeed. It gives a very wrong message to the whole of society, both to the victims of his words and to those who are supporters of his racist and Islamophobic views and the promotion of them.' Sabby Dhalu, of Unite Against Fascism, commented in similar terms. (See the *Guardian* 10 November 2006.)

215 See the *Guardian*, 11 November 2006.

Thus, the current race hatred offences are relatively narrowly conceived; although they cover political expression, they concentrate on the *manner* of the expression. Further, it is hard to conceive that the manner – the form of threats – could itself be defended by reference to the free speech justifications discussed in the Introduction to Part II. The terms 'abuse, insults' are significantly broader. Where the threat, etc, is thematically appropriate since it is placed within a context, such as a play or film touching on the theme or subject of racism, it would probably fall outside the area of liability, since all the circumstances must be taken into account. The breadth of the offences relating to broadcasting are particularly problematic, since, as suggested above, they are likely to deter the production of documentaries dealing with the subject of racism. This position has been exacerbated by the addition of offences of incitement to religious hatred as discussed below.

Impact of the HRA?

Is the expression 'likely to stir up racial hatred' covered by Art 10(1)? In other words, would it be viewed as protected expression at all? In *Lehideux and Isornia v France*[216] it was found that if material is directed towards attacking the Convention's underlying values, it will be outside the protection of Art 10.[217] In that instance, the material supported a pro-Nazi policy. However, in *Kuhnen v FRG*,[218] Art 10 was found to cover the conviction of the applicant for advocating the reinstitution of the Nazi Party, although the interference was justified under Art 10(2). Similarly, Art 10 applied in *Glimmerveen and Hagenbeeck v Netherlands*. The applicants had been convicted of possessing leaflets which incited racial discrimination. The interference was found to be justified under Art 10(2). In that instance, Art 17 was relied upon.[219] Where racist expression is concerned, reliance on Art 17, either in addition to Art 10(2) or alone, tends to produce the same result: the interference is found to be justified and the review is not intensive.[220]

Jersild[221] concerned an application by a Danish journalist who had been convicted of an offence of racially offensive speech after preparing and broadcasting a programme about racism which included overtly racist speech by the subjects of the documentary. A breach of Art 10 was found. The interference with expression was found to be disproportionate to the aim pursued – protecting the rights of others. The Court stressed that its finding was directed to the value of enabling the media to act as a public watchdog. The news value of the programme was a matter that could be best assessed by professional journalists. The Court also considered that the mode of presenting the broadcast should be determined by journalists. Had the racists who spoke on the programme applied to Strasbourg, their own convictions would have been found to be justified under Art 10(2), if indeed Art 10(1) would have been applicable, which is doubtful.

216 (1998) 5 BHRC 540.
217 Ibid, p 558, para 53.
218 (1988) 56 DR 205.
219 (1979) 18 DR 187. See Chapter 2, p 112.
220 See *X v Germany* (1982) 29 DR 194; *T v Belgium* (1983) 34 DR 158; *H, W, P and K v Austria* (1989) 62 DR 216.
221 *Jersild v Denmark* (1994) 19 EHRR 1.

It seems to be clear that persons directly using threatening or abusive or insulting speech likely to stir up racial hatred would not obtain any benefit by invoking Art 10. But the position of those who aid in the dissemination of such speech, who do not have the purpose of stirring up racial hatred, is different. It is arguable that UK law does not draw a sufficiently clear distinction between the two groups. *Jersild* suggests that the restrictions on broadcasting in relation to racial hatred are open to challenge under the HRA since it would seem possible that if an equivalent situation arose in the UK, the presenter and producer of the programme could be convicted of the offence under s 22 of the 1986 Act. Possibly television researchers involved could also be convicted of the broader offence under s 23.

It is argued as a matter of principle that the prohibition of incitement to racial hatred under the Public Order Act creates an unacceptable infringement of freedom of speech since the offences as currently conceived go beyond the mischief that they are intended to prevent. There is an argument that some provision should be available to prevent some forms of racist speech owing to its special propensity to lead to disorder and that such protection should be extended to religious groups, but it is argued that the Public Order Act offences require reform to encompass a much more narrowly targeted area of liability. Such reform could be effected by narrowing them on the model now represented by the new offence of religious hatred. Possibly s 3 HRA could be relied upon, if necessary, to interpret the term 'circumstances' used in Part 3 of the 1986 Act narrowly. The term is used, as indicated above, in respect of material likely to stir up racial hatred rather than in respect of instances where the defendant intended to do so. No 'public good' defence is included in the 1986 Act. But consideration of the 'circumstances' could include consideration of the extent to which the broadcast or other material was for the public good in terms of its artistic or other merit. Since this is a strained interpretation, s 3 of the HRA might need to be relied upon, in order to achieve compatibility with the demands of Art 10 in respect of a particular provision, in particular ss 22 and 23 of the 1986 Act. Section 6 of the HRA could be relied upon, to find an application of the provision in question which would ensure compatibility with Art 10. For example, in 2007 competitors in the Channel 4 show *Big Brother* made allegedly racist remarks during the live show. If the presenter and producer of the programme were prosecuted under the s 22 offence of the 1986 Act *Jersild* would be relevant under s 2 HRA. It could be argued that s 22 should be narrowly construed in order to avoid bringing anyone other than the competitors themselves within the net of liability, on the grounds of proportionality. [222]

Incitement to religious hatred

The International Covenant on Civil and Political Rights, to which the UK is a signatory, requires contracting states to prohibit the advocacy of 'national, racial or *religious* hatred that constitutes incitement to discrimination, hostility or violence' (Art 20, emphasis added). In practical terms, it is fairly straightforward to amend ss 17–23

---

222   A somewhat similar argument was used in *Percy v DPP*; [2001] EWHC 1125 (Admin).

of Part III of the Public Order Act 1986 prohibiting incitement to racial hatred,[223] to include religious groups.[224] The first attempt to introduce an offence of inciting religious hatred was made by Lord Avebury's Bill in 2000, which was remitted to a committee for consideration; Cl 38 the Anti-Terrorism, Crime and Security Bill 2001 provided for such amendation but was defeated by the Lords; the third attempt appeared in the Serious and Organised Crime Bill 2004; the provision was dropped in order to allow the Bill to go through Parliament in time for the 2005 General Election. The Racial and Religious Hatred Act 2005 now represents the successful conclusion of the fourth attempt to introduce the new offence.

The Racial and Religious Hatred Act 2005 outlaws incitement to religious hatred. Under s 9B, amending Part 3 of the 1986 Act, a person who uses threatening words or behaviour, or displays threatening written material is guilty of an offence if he intends thereby to stir up religious hatred, and the subsequent sections apply this offence to the media.[225] The Act leaves unchanged the five main ways in which the offence can be committed. These are:

---

223 For discussion of racial hatred in the context of freedom of speech, see Robertson and Nichol, op. cit., fn 1, Chapter 3, pp 129–32; Barendt, op. cit., fn 1 (1st edn), pp 161–67 and generally Cotterell, R [1982] PL 378; Dickey [1968] Crim LR 489; Gordon, *Incitement to Racial Hatred*, 1982; Leopold, P [1977] PL 389; Wolffe [1987] PL 85. For the argument that the state should seek to ban racially motivated hate speech on the basis of furtherance of equality just as it seeks to outlaw discrimination in employment, see MacKinnon, op. cit., fn 1. For criticism of the argument, see Sadurski, W, 'On 'Seeing speech through an equality lens': a critique of egalitarian arguments for suppression of hate speech and pornography' (1996) 16(4) OJLS 713.

224 The definition under the Race Relations Act of 'racial group' which will be used under the Public Order Act 1986 does not include religious groups; see *Mandla v Dowell Lee* [1983] 2 AC 548; [1983] 1 All ER 1062, HL. But discrimination on grounds of religion can be viewed as indirect racial discrimination.

225 In the Public Order Act 1986 (c. 64), after Part 3 insert –
'Part 3A
Hatred against persons on religious grounds
Meaning of 'religious hatred'

    29A Meaning of 'religious hatred'

        In this Part 'religious hatred' means hatred against a group of persons defined by reference to religious belief or lack of religious belief.

Acts intended to stir up religious hatred

    29B Use of words or behaviour or display of written material
        (1) A person who uses threatening words or behaviour, or displays any written material which is threatening, is guilty of an offence if he intends thereby to stir up religious hatred.
        (2) An offence under this section may be committed in a public or a private place, except that no offence is committed where the words or behaviour are used, or the written material is displayed, by a person inside a dwelling and are not heard or seen except by other persons in that or another dwelling.
        (3) A constable may arrest without warrant anyone he reasonably suspects is committing an offence under this section.
        (4) In proceedings for an offence under this section it is a defence for the accused to prove that he was inside a dwelling and had no reason to believe that the words or behaviour used, or the written material displayed, would be heard or seen by a person outside that or any other dwelling.

- the use of words or behaviour or display of written material (s 18, Public Order Act 1986);
- publishing or distributing written material (s 19);
- the public performance of a play (s 20);
- distributing, showing or playing a recording (s 21); and
- broadcasting or including a programme in a programme service (s 22).
- publishing or distributing written material (s 19).

The version of the Bill that received Royal Assent included a number of Lords' amendments aimed at protecting freedom of expression. Ministers had urged MPs to reject the Lords' amendments and back instead a government compromise. On 1 February the government suffered two defeats over its attempts to overturn changes

> (5) This section does not apply to words or behaviour used, or written material displayed, solely for the purpose of being included in a programme service.
>
> 29C Publishing or distributing written material
> (1) A person who publishes or distributes written material which is threatening is guilty of an offence if he intends thereby to stir up religious hatred.
> (2) References in this Part to the publication or distribution of written material are to its publication or distribution to the public or a section of the public.
>
> 29D Public performance of play
> (1) If a public performance of a play is given which involves the use of threatening words or behaviour, any person who presents or directs the performance is guilty of an offence if he intends thereby to stir up religious hatred.
> (2) This section does not apply to a performance given solely or primarily for one or more of the following purposes –
>   (a) rehearsal,
>   (b) making a recording of the performance, or
>   (c) enabling the performance to be included in a programme service;
> but if it is proved that the performance was attended by persons other than those directly connected with the giving of the performance or the doing in relation to it of the things mentioned in paragraph (b) or (c), the performance shall, unless the contrary is shown, be taken not to have been given solely or primarily for the purpose mentioned above.
> (3) For the purposes of this section –
>   (a) a person shall not be treated as presenting a performance of a play by reason only of his taking part in it as a performer,
>   (b) a person taking part as a performer in a performance directed by another shall be treated as a person who directed the performance if without reasonable excuse he performs otherwise than in accordance with that person's direction,
>   and
>   (c) a person shall be taken to have directed a performance of a play given under his direction notwithstanding that he was not present during the performance;
> and a person shall not be treated as aiding or abetting the commission of an offence under this section by reason only of his taking part in a performance as a performer.
> (4) In this section 'play' and 'public performance' have the same meaning as in the Theatres Act 1968. (5) The following provisions of the Theatres Act 1968 apply in relation to an offence under this section as they apply to an offence under section 2 of that Act –
>   section 9 (script as evidence of what was performed),
>   section 10 (power to make copies of script),
>   section 15 (powers of entry and inspection).

that the Lords had imposed on Racial and Religious Hatred Bill.[226] The votes came after large numbers of persons protested against the Bill outside Parliament. The Lords did some excellent work in free speech terms: they imposed an amendment ensuring that only 'threatening' words should be banned, not those which are only abusive or insulting. This was a very significant amendment since 'insulting' is clearly the most problematic term used in the 1986 Act, in free speech terms. They also ensured that the offence could only be committed intentionally. Under the 1986 Act, the offence can be committed either by means of specific intent – if the 'speaker' . . . 'intends thereby to stir up racial hatred' – *or* if, 'having regard to all the circumstances, racial hatred is likely to be stirred up thereby.'[227] This part of the Act, allowing for a conviction without intention to incite racial hatred, and indeed, in situations in which no racial hatred was in fact stirred up,[228] has been subject to criticism. The amendments introduced in the House of Lords[229] mean that it is harder to establish that the offence of incitement to religious hatred has been committed than it is to establish incitement to racial hatred since there is no alternative to proving that specific intent is present.

The Lords further imposed a saving clause for freedom of expression (now s 29J), specifying that:

Nothing in this Part shall be read or given effect in a way which prohibits or restricts discussion, criticism or expressions of antipathy, dislike, ridicule, insult

> 29E　Distributing, showing or playing a recording
> (1) A person who distributes, or shows or plays, a recording of visual images or sounds which are threatening is guilty of an offence if he intends thereby to stir up religious hatred.
>
> 29F　Broadcasting or including programme in cable programme service
> (1) If a programme involving threatening visual images or sounds is included in a programme service, each of the persons mentioned in subsection (2) is guilty of an offence if he intends thereby to stir up religious hatred. (2) The persons are –
> (a) the person providing the programme service,
> (b) any person by whom the programme is produced or directed, and
> (c) any person by whom offending words or behaviour are used.
>
> Inflammatory material
>
> 29G　Possession of inflammatory material
> (1) A person who has in his possession written material which is threatening, or a recording of visual images or sounds which are threatening, with a view to –
> (a) in the case of written material, its being displayed, published, distributed, or included in a programme service whether by himself or another, or
> (b) in the case of a recording, its being distributed, shown, played, or included in a programme service, whether by himself or another, is guilty of an offence if he intends religious hatred to be stirred up thereby.
> (2) For this purpose regard shall be had to such display, publication, distribution, showing, playing, or inclusion in a programme service.

226 In the first vote MPs voted by 288 votes to 278 to back the Lords amendments to the Bill. In the second vote, MPs voted by 283 votes to 282 to back the Lords.
227 Section 18 POA 1096; similar wording is used in all the other offences in ss 19–22.
228 Possible because the Act only requires that it be likely that hatred be stirred up, not that it actually was.
229 The measures referred to are those in the Bill as they were amended by the Lords on 15 October 2005.

or abuse of particular religions or the beliefs or practices of their adherents, or of any other belief system or the beliefs or practices of its adherents, or proselytising or urging adherents of a different religion or belief system to cease practising their religion or belief system.

So satirising religion in films or plays or broadcasts by comedians cannot be an offence. The saving for free expression which is now s 29J makes it hard to imagine situations in which this offence could be used – since the saving is so broad. It could only be used where 'threatening' words were used intended to incite religious hatred, as opposed to being intended to express antipathy to religion. That leaves a very narrow area of liability. It is possible to imagine a situation in which a person was seeking, via such words, to arouse persons to hatred against eg Muslims, as opposed merely to expressing antipathy to Islamic beliefs, but the lines drawn are fine indeed.

However, the offences under the new Act could have been narrowed further. The new offences do not require a need to show that disorder was caused, or that there was an intent to cause disorder, and there is no need to show that religious hatred is actually stirred up, or even that in the circumstances it was likely to be stirred up. The offences might be committed by using or promulgating threatening words or material by the methods indicated above, which, objectively speaking, were incapable of stirring up religious hatred so long as the accused intended that they should do so. The various offences could be committed by uttering words or promulgating material which were greeted with delight by the audience. It may be pointed out that the cl 29B offence is noteworthy as a public order offence which may be committed by words alone unaccompanied by the need – as an essential ingredient – to show any likelihood that they would cause distress.

The fact that in all the media contexts mentioned offences of stirring up religious hatred can now also be committed, creates a serious inroad into freedom of expression. However, the impact of the provisions can be curbed. Prosecutions for the offences of stirring up racial or religious hatred can only be brought with the consent of the Attorney General, which has so far been sparingly given in respect of race hatred. Since the Attorney General is a public authority under the HRA, he or she should give careful consideration to Art 10 before giving consent. If prosecutions are brought, the courts are in the same position. They need not, as argued above, give weight to Art 9, on the ground that protection for religious freedom does not include protection against attacks on religion. The term 'hatred' should be given full weight, while the term 'insulting' should, it is argued, be interpreted as meaning – insulting to the reasonable, tolerant religious adherent rather than in relation to adherents of a particular sect (or group within a religion) which may be of an extreme nature.

Possibly s 3 HRA could be relied upon, if necessary, to narrow down relevant terms used in Part 3 of the 1986 Act, as amended by the 2005 Act. The 2005 Bill was accompanied by a statement of compatibility under s 19 of the HRA. But, as Chapter 2 argues, such a statement leaves the judges free to consider compatibility afresh. It may be argued that rather than strive to ensure compatibility, a declaration of incompatibility should be made in order to mark the dangerous potential of the new provisions and to invite Parliament to think again. The view of the Joint Committee on Human Rights on the compatibility of the Bill as originally drafted with Art 10 was as follows:

We accept the existence of a serious, albeit limited, problem of incitement to hatred on religious grounds. We consider that the measures proposed in the Bill are unlikely to give rise to any violation of the right to freedom of expression under Article 10 of the ECHR.[230]

The recent decision in *Norwood v UK*,[231] indicates that this view is correct. The applicant belonged to the BNP. The facts were as follows:

Between November 2001 and 9 January 2002 he displayed in the window of his first-floor flat a large poster . . . supplied by the BNP, with a photograph of the Twin Towers in flame, the words 'Islam out of Britain – Protect the British People' and a symbol of a crescent and star in a prohibition sign.[232]

He was convicted in a magistrates court of the offence under section 5 of the Public Order Act of displaying 'any writing, sign or other visible representation which is threatening, abusive or insulting, within the hearing or sight of a person likely to be caused harassment, alarm or distress thereby'. He was moreover convicted of having committed the offence in religiously aggravated way. He unsuccessfully appealed his conviction to the High Court,[233] which found that the restriction upon his freedom of expression right represented by the offence was proportionate to the legitimate aim of protecting the rights of others, given also the fact that the speech arguably fell within Art 17 ECHR.[234] One of the applicant's arguments was that there was no evidence that any Muslim had in fact seen the poster. The Strasbourg Court, in a brief judgment, found the application inadmissible; in doing so it referred to Art 17:

Such a general, vehement attack against a religious group, linking the group as a whole with a grave act of terrorism, is incompatible with the values proclaimed and guaranteed by the Convention, notably tolerance, social peace and non-discrimination. The applicant's display of the poster in his window constituted an act within the meaning of Article 17, which did not, therefore, enjoy the protection of Articles 10 or 14.[235]

Given this judgment, it seems likely that prosecutions under the new law, provided they were used only in clear-cut cases, would be found to be compatible with Art 10. But ss 3 and 6 could possibly be relied upon in more doubtful cases, in which less grossly offensive statements were made than in *Norwood*. *Dehal v Crown Prosecution Service* provides an example of the application of the doctrine of proportionality under

---

230 Eighth Report of the Joint Committee on Human Rights at [2.59].
231 (2005) 40 EHRR SE11.
232 Ibid at [A].
233 *Norwood v DPP* (2003) WL21491815.
234 This provides: 'Nothing in [the] Convention may be interpreted as implying for any state, group or person any right to engage in any activity or perform any act aimed at the destruction of any of the rights and freedoms set forth herein or at their limitation to a greater extent than is provided for in the Convention.'; see Chapter 2 at p 112. For comment on Art 17 by the House of Lords see *DPP v Collins* [2006] UKHL 40.
235 Op. cit.

s 6 HRA in this type of context.[236] The appellant, a Sikh man, put up a notice at a Sikh Temple that he had attended for many years. It was written in Punjabi and attacked the President of the Temple and other members of the Committee. Mr Dehal intended the notice to be read by those it was aimed at and other worshippers. He was convicted of the offence under the Public Order Act 1986, s 4A (1) (it is discussed in Chapter 8 and contains elements similar to those of s 5).[237] His appeal concerned in essence the relationship between Art 10 of the European Convention on Human Rights and the s 4A offence. The Court had to examine the following questions: was the prosecution of the appellant a proportionate response to his conduct and did Art 10 provide him with a defence, therefore making the interference with the appellant's freedom of expression unnecessary? In allowing the appeal, the Court determined that although all the elements of the offence were present, the prosecution had not presented enough evidence to establish that bringing a criminal prosecution was a proportionate response to the appellant's conduct.

The problem of defining religion, of course, still remains. The Explanatory Notes to the Bill state:

> It includes, though this list is not definitive, those religions widely recognised in this country such as Christianity, Islam, Hinduism, Judaism, Buddhism, Sikhism, Rastafarianism, Baha'ism, Zoroastrianism and Jainism. Equally, branches or sects within a religion can be considered as religions or religious beliefs in their own right. The offences also cover hatred directed against a group of persons defined by reference to a lack of religious belief, such as Atheism and Humanism.[238]

Religion is also undefined in relation to discrimination on the grounds of religion and belief in the Employment Equality (Religion or Belief) Regulations 2003.[239] Further, since such incitement represents a far narrower area of liability than blasphemy, the danger that a wide interpretation of 'religion' would lead to controversy when prosecutions in relation to claims from obscure groups were refused is accordingly less great. Furthermore, prosecutions in this area can only be brought with the consent of the DPP, so the possibility of frivolous prosecutions being brought is slight. The justification sometimes put forward for abrogating free speech in this area is that prohibiting the advocacy of racial hatred does not strike at the core value of free speech because neither individual self-fulfilment, nor the opportunity to arrive at the truth through free discussion, nor the chance to participate meaningfully in democracy[240] seem to be strongly threatened by such a prohibition.

However, the gap in the law which is filled by the new offences is either tiny or non-existent since a range of existing offences, most notably s 5 Public Order Act

---

236 [2005] EWHC 2154.

237 See pp 785, 797.

238 Explanatory Notes to the Bill, at para 13, available: http://www.publications.parliament.uk/pa/ld200506/ldbills/015/en/06015x--.htm

239 Reg 2 (the interpretation section) offers no definition of "religion" or "belief". See Chapter 15, p 1482.

240 See above, pp 303–4.

1986, or incitement to criminal offences, would cover it in most circumstances.[241] The gap is prima facie only of significance when incitement to hatred, not to a criminal offence, occurs on grounds of religion, and such incitement would not be covered by the existing race hatred laws. But ss 5 and 4A of the 1986 Act would still be available. The obvious beneficiaries of the new law are therefore Muslims. The rationale for introducing the law was that the BNP and other groups were exploiting that gap by making pronouncements intended to stir up racial hatred, but hiding behind attacks on Isalm. As Goodall argues, 'it is not difficult to decode . . . statements, from a BNP article called "The Islamic Menace" . . . as not simply anti-Muslim but racist, and [they] will be read so by BNP supporters'. The argument used by Nick Griffin in 2006 at his trial for incitement to racial hatred was that he was only inciting hatred against Islam – so the law may have some benefit in curbing Islamophobia stirred by BNP supporters, since the BNP is seeking to stay within the law, in order to seek to make itself electable.[242] But s 5 of the 1986 Act could have been used against Griffin.

The existence of the new offences represents an interference with the individual's moral autonomy, since it amounts to judging both for him and his possible audience what is and is not fit for them to hear.[243] The state is supposed to leave such judgments to the individual because to do otherwise would be to violate the individual's basic right to equal concern and respect.[244] But there is an arguable case for the introduction of the new offence: the interference with moral autonomy involved is necessary to avoid discrimination and there is an argument that the free speech interest involved is relatively weak; in addition, there are strong utilitarian arguments that such a measure would considerably ease racial tension since Muslims now have at least some protection. Nevertheless, it may be argued that the present situation, in which the advocacy of hatred against Muslims or Christians is allowed in a range of circumstances wider than those covered by the race hatred provisions, so that Sikhs and Jews enjoy a stronger (and dual) protection from hate speech,[245] still amounts to a denial of equal respect for Muslims.[246] Christians can fall back on the doubtful, but very broad protection offered by blasphemy law. The argument that laws against religious hatred are justified because they protect individual believers from experiencing hatred directed at them because of their beliefs, and from mental anguish due to the nature of the attack, runs into further difficulty if justified on equality grounds. If one is concerned to protect individuals from the mental distress which can flow from the incitement of hatred against them

---

241 See on this point: Goodall, K, 'Incitement to Religious Hatred: All talk and no substance' [2007] 70(1) MLR 89–113; Hare, I, 'Legislating Against Hate: the Legal Response to Bias Crimes' (1997) 17 OJLS 415.

242 Goodall, K, 'Incitement to Religious Hatred: All talk and no substance' [2007] 70(1) MLR 89–113.

243 On this point see: Hare, I, 'Crosses, Crescents and Sacred Cows: Criminalising Incitement to Religious Hatred' (2006) Autumn PL 521–38.

244 See, e.g., Dworkin, R, 'Do we have a right to pornography?', in *A Matter of Principle*, 1985.

245 Muslims, unlike Sikhs and Jews, are not defined as a racial, as well as religious, group. See the definition from *Mandla v Dowell Lee* [1983] 2 AC 548; [1983] 1 All ER 1062, HL, discussed below, p 1508. But prejudice against Muslims can possibly be viewed as indirect racial discrimination; see Chapter 15, pp 1544–47, but that is not relevant in this context.

246 It might be argued from this that all measures prohibiting incitement to racial hatred should be repealed, but this is not a practicable possibility and would involve the UK in an even clearer breach of Art 20 of the ICCPR than is currently being committed by the lack of protection for Muslims.

due to their deeply held beliefs, it is not readily apparent that society should not also outlaw such incitement based upon deeply held non-religious beliefs, such as a deep belief in the equality of the sexes,[247] or in the evil of homophobia. Moreover, the case for introducing laws prohibiting incitement of hatred on grounds of sex or on grounds of sexual orientation could readily be made out on grounds similar to those used to justify the new offences. Certain extremist Muslim groups have made deeply homophobic pronouncements. There is a case for criminalising such pronouncements if made in threatening terms and intended to incite hatred on the grounds of sexual orientation. But ss 5, 4 and 4A Public Order Act are available to punish such conduct,[248] and it may be concluded that the damage to free speech if further incitement offences were included in the law would be too great, while the benefit it too uncertain. This argument clearly also applies to the new offence and, as argued above, to the racial hatred offences.

5 Regulating broadcasting

Introduction[249]

This section considers the regulation of broadcasting[250] and concentrates on the regulatory regime that was put in place for broadcasting in 2003. The statutory regime currently in place includes elements of licensing and content regulation by an administrative body. Broadcasting is treated differently from the print media which is subject only to the criminal law. The stricter system of controls seems to have been adopted in answer to the view that owing to their particular impact on audiences, broadcasting requires regulatory restraint, whereas it is now accepted that books and other printed material do not. Owing to such restraint, it is very unlikely that a broadcast could attract liability under the Obscene Publications Act;[251] nevertheless, it provides a further possibility of restraint and can also be used as a guide as to the standards censorship will observe. Thus, the regulatory regime in place means that broadcasting

---

247 On this point see, e.g., Clements, 'Defining 'religion' in the First Amendment: a functional approach' (1989) 74 Cornell LR 532.

248 In *Hammond* [2004] EWHC 69 the appellant took a placard with the words 'Stop Immorality', 'Stop Homosexuality', 'Stop Lesbianism', and 'Jesus is Lord' to the centre of Bournemouth and began preaching. This attracted a large group of people who were provoked by the preaching and physically attacked the appellant. He was requested by two police officers to stop preaching. Upon refusing to comply with this request the appellant was arrested and subsequently charged and convicted of a s 5 offence. Although Art 10 was taken into account on appeal, it was found that the conviction was proportionate to the harm sought to be averted. The decision is discussed further in Chapter 8, p 797.

249 Texts referred to below: Barendt, E, *Freedom of Speech*, 2nd edn, 2005, Chapters 10, 12 and 13; Robertson, G and Nichol, D, *Media Law*, 1999, Chapter 14; Bailey, Harris and Jones, *Civil Liberties and Human Rights Cases and Materials*, 5th edn, 2002, Chapter 6 at pp 650–67; Carey, P and Sanders, J *Media Law*, 3rd edn, 2004, Chapters 5 and 9 (basic guide); Gibbons, T, *Regulating the Media*, 2nd edn, 1998.

250 For a comprehensive treatment, see Gibbons, *Regulating the Media*, 1998.

251 The Obscene Publications Act, s 1 covers these media under s 1(2) since the Broadcasting Act 1990, s 162, has brought radio and television within its ambit.

is censored beyond what the law demands. The impact of the HRA is complicated by the fact that a number of the media bodies involved are private bodies, while the administrative body is a public authority.

Historically, in the UK the scarcity of frequencies was thought to provide part of the rationale for broadcast regulation.[252] But it is not apparent that this rationale can support content-based curbs, although it might support rights of access to a scarce resource[253] of such significance in terms of the efficacy of expression. In any event, cable and satellite television have enormously increased the number of actual and potential channels. Digital technology is continuing to increase the number of channels available. There are far more channels available at present in the UK than there are individual newspaper titles. The high level of regulation to which broadcasting continues to be subject must now therefore be attributed mainly to its status as the most influential means of communication.[254] Since it comes into the home and since so much time is spent watching television, it has been viewed as having a unique impact on people and particularly on children who form a large part of the broadcast audience, especially at certain times of the day. Further, the potential for flouting viewer expectations by inadvertently causing offence when people tune in and out of programmes is thought to provide a cogent rationale for content regulation.[255] In other words, a viewer might be unexpectedly confronted by offensive broadcast material. That is the main reason usually advanced for providing a different and stricter regime for broadcasting as opposed to videos. But as this chapter will reveal, the UK regulatory regime has incrementally moved away from the *general* imposition of certain standards of 'taste and decency' on broadcasting, in favour of curbs premised mainly, although not solely, on protection for children. Thus it has focused more on the use of protective devices – such as the use of the watershed or of encryption[256] – as opposed to outright bans on the showing of explicit and offensive material. Nevertheless, broadcasting is still restrained to a greater extent than other media.

Adherence to a regulatory regime aimed at the avoidance of offence has been viewed as a part of a 'contract' for the privilege of coming directly into the home which should be adhered to by responsible broadcasters. The Broadcasting Standards Commission made this point by referring in its Code on Standards to an implied contract between viewer and broadcaster about the terms of admission to the home.[257] Lord Hoffmann pointed out in *Pro-Life Alliance v BBC*[258] that a similar point was made by Stevens J giving the opinion of the United States Supreme Court in *Federal Communications Commission v Pacifica Foundation*[259] in a case about the use of obscene language on sound radio:

---

252 See Briggs, A, *The History of Broadcasting*, Vols 1 and 2, 1961 and 1965, OUP; Barendt and Hitchens, *Media Law* 2000, Longman.

253 See the discussion of the US Supreme Court on this point in *Red Lion Broadcasting Co v FCC* (1969) 395 US 367.

254 See Barendt and Hitchens, 2000, pp 5–9.

255 See pp 516–17 below.

256 The broadcasting of adult material and '18'-rated films later in the evening. The provision of warnings and of consumer advice has also become much more prevalent. See pp 525–28 below.

257 Para 2 of the Code. The Code is discussed at pp 525–29 below.

258 [2004] 1 AC 185; [2003] 2 All ER 977.

259 (1978) 438 US 726, 748–49.

[T]he broadcast media have established a uniquely pervasive presence in the lives of all Americans. Patently offensive, indecent material presented over the airwaves confronts the citizen, not only in public, but also in the privacy of the home, where the individual's right to be left alone plainly outweighs the First Amendment rights of an intruder . . . Because the broadcast audience is constantly tuning in and out, prior warnings cannot completely protect the listener or viewer from unexpected program content. To say that one may avoid further offence by turning off the radio when he hears indecent language is like saying that the remedy for an assault is to run away after the first blow.

However, although these points may have been valid in 1978, they are clearly losing their cogency today, at least in relation to television, as it becomes more and more interactive. Viewers usually tune in and out of programmes using a menu, which also provides them with consumer advice on programmes. 'Adult material' can be Pin-protected or made available on pay-per-view channels only, decreasing the chance that children could access it and obviating the risk of coming across it inadvertently. Thus the chances of involuntary encounters with offensive material have diminished; the argument that children should be protected from material that they deliberately choose to view, continues retain some cogency.[260] As the interactivity of television broadcasting and the provision of consumer information increases, while improvements occur in the use of security devices such as encoding, its position comes closer to that of the internet which also comes into the home. Therefore there is a degree of tension in free speech terms between the lack of regulation for the internet and the high level of content-based regulation to which broadcasting is currently subject.

A very different rationale can be advanced to argue that regulation is necessary in order to preserve pluralism – in order to seek to ensure that a range of views, including a variety of political ones, are heard.[261] This can be achieved by imposing requirements to broadcast minority interest programmes, 'must carry' requirements,[262] or by imposing more general responsibilities that tend to support diversity, including impartiality requirements.[263] The unregulated press are openly partisan in the UK, and

---

260 See the 2005 research conducted by Ofcom on the efficacy of PIN protection systems, p 527, fn 328, below.

261 See Feintuck, M, *Media Regulation, Public Interest and the Law*, 1999.

262 See Communications Act 2003 ss 296 and 309. Under s 296 C4C has obligations in relation to school programming. Under s 309 10% of the air time must be allocated to a range and diversity of independent productions in digital services.

263 The due impartiality requirements are now contained in the Communications Act 2003, ss 319(c) and 320; they are reflected in s 5 of Ofcom's Broadcasting Code which came into force in 2005. There are three key statutory requirements. First, under s 319(2)(c), news included in television and radio services must be presented with due impartiality. Second, under s 320(1)(a), the opinions of persons providing a programme service on matters of industrial or political controversy or current public policy must be excluded, and third, under s 320(1)(b), all programming should preserve due impartiality on those matters, although this last requirement can be satisfied in relation to 'a series of programmes taken as a whole'. The BBC's Charter (Cm 6925) was renewed with effect from 2007 until 2016; if a complaint relates to the accuracy and impartiality of a programme, the BBC remains finally responsible and this continued to be the case when the BBC Charter was renewed at the end of 2006, although under a new body – the BBC Trust.

right wing and anti-liberal views predominate.[264] Therefore a significant threat to free expression – in terms of diversity – comes not from government, but from private corporate bodies. As Barendt puts it, referring to the free speech rationale from truth:[265] 'it is . . . reasonable to doubt whether any truth will emerge from an unregulated market-place in which a handful of media corporations draw up the agenda of political and social discourse and carefully limit the access of individuals and groups which dissent from their programme'.[266] Therefore this argument provides a rationale for broadcast regulation, even in the context of a rapidly changing technological landscape, in so far as plurality and impartiality can be ensured by this means. It does not, however, provide a necessary justification for restraints based on offence-avoidance. Indeed, such restraints tend to run *counter* to the enhancement of plurality and diversity since they may curb the more controversial forms of broadcast speech, including that reflective of the practice of sexual minorities. The regulatory regimes for broadcast regulation in the UK have tended at one and the same time to impose curbs based on generally accepted standards of taste and decency, while making some efforts in the direction of diversity. The contradiction between the two goals appears to have gone unrecognised both by the legislation and by the regulators.

Market-based 'deregulation' in the UK

The Broadcasting Act 1990 brought about the so-called 'deregulation' of independent television, a trend culminating at present in the Communications Act 2003. The trend represents a movement towards enhancing the influence of media regulators but exerted post-transmission in terms of content, as explained below. An underlying policy objective of deregulation was that of enhancing the ability of corporate bodies to maximise commercial success by furthering and developing concentrations of media power, especially in the sectors of the press and satellite broadcasting. The 1990 Act raised questions about the influence of the owners of broadcasting stations who might wish to use broadcasting as a means of exerting political influence. The Broadcasting Act 1996 further eased some of the restrictions on media ownership created by the 1990 Act, with a view to balancing 'proper commercial demands and the wider public interest which includes plurality, diversity of opinion'.[267] The dominant theme governing the regulatory regime is the continuance of light-touch regulation, in terms of commercial freedom, which was introduced under the Conservative Government's 1990 Act. The changes introduced by the Labour Government's Communications Act 2003 continue to represent a business-oriented scheme that recognises the convergence of the separate technological sectors. It favours corporate interests, not necessarily those of plurality and diversity. It does not address substantive media freedom issues. For example,

---

264 Feintuck 1999, ibid at 54–56; Gibbons, T, 'Freedom of the Press: ownership and editorial values' (1992) Summer PL 279. The *Telegraph*, the *Mail* and the *Sun* are the highest selling newspapers in their different sections of the market. Editorially, they tend towards the right and to anti-liberal views.

265 See Part II introduction, pp 302–3.

266 See *Importing the First Amendment* (1998) Loveland, I, (ed), Barendt, E, Chapter 3 at p 46.

267 Bottomley, V, Dept of National Heritage Press Release DNH 219/96. For discussion of regulation of cross-media ownership and concentrated media ownership see Feintuck *Media Regulation, Public Interest and the Law* 1999; Fleming, H (1997) 60(3) MLR 378; Hitchens (1994) 57 MLR 585.

while corporate advertising remains central to the commercial viability of independent television, political advertising is still disallowed. Thus, in so far as groups such as Greenpeace or Amnesty may wish, *inter alia*, to criticise and challenge corporate interests by means of such advertising, they are unable to do so.

The Communications Act 2003 is influenced by the 'Television Without Frontiers' ('TVWF') Directive,[268] as discussed below, and is based to a significant extent on the model of deregulation put in place by the 1990 Act.[269] This continued movement away from market regulation may have the effect of *detracting* from the exercise of creative freedom since small independent broadcasters may be unable to gain a foothold in the market, while investigative journalism (especially investigations into corporate matters) and alternative film-making may be marginalised and discouraged in the pursuit of commercially safe, but bland, homogenous broadcasting, in the form of game shows, soap operas, gardening and home-decorating programmes. On this view, further movement towards privatisation of the means of communication, deregulation and the freer expression of commercial values is unwelcome. Moreover, it provides a strong argument for retaining the licence fee for the BBC, and its independence, on the basis that certain programmes would not be made if BBC programming was subject to a largely or wholly market-driven regime. Further, programmes made under such a regime – and the choices underlying the selection of programmes – are likely in themselves to have an impact in influencing the public's choices. Therefore leaving BBC programming largely to market forces by removing the licence fee would tend to have a pro-corporate, anti-plural impact. The contemporary political agenda would be more likely to go unchallenged, while the anti-liberal agenda apparent in much of the press would have a greater chance of gaining ascendancy since programmes challenging it might not be made.

The thesis can be put forward that in general regulation is an essential precondition for securing the objectives inherent in the familiar free speech justifications,[270] although this argument is not applicable to the current offence-avoidance rules. As Feintuck argues, media regulators are concerned to limit 'the ability of corporate media giants to further their own commercial ends while acting in ways that run counter to maximising the provision of information upon which the claim is premised'.[271] However, the ethos underlying the regulatory regime considered below is unclear, although it could be broadly expressed as intended to be in the public interest.

The EU's role in UK broadcasting regulation reflects the various values that are being balanced. It may be argued that since economic integration is a central constitutional value for the EU, its regulatory agenda might be expected to bear more resemblance to that of the US, in terms of economic values, than to the public interest values evident in the regimes of its member states.[272] At the same time EU audio-visual policy reflects the values embodied in Arts 8 and 10 ECHR; in particular it focuses on the protection

---

268 Council Directive 89/552/EEC, as amended by Directive 97/36/EC of the European Parliament and of the Council, adopted in 1989. See pp 514, 526.
269 See also the proposals in the White Paper *A New Future for Communications* Cm 5010, published 12 December 2000.
270 See Part II, pp 300–8.
271 See Feintuck, (fn 261, above) 1999.
272 Ibid, p 170.

of minors and of human dignity. These varying – and arguably conflicting – values are reflected in the TVWF Directive,[273] which deals with the protection of minors from harmful content disseminated via broadcasting. Technological and market developments necessitated the revision of the TVWF in 1997, as discussed below. The need to ensure the effective protection of minors was also reflected in the Recommendation adopted in 1998[274] and in the Commission's proposal for an additional Recommendation in 2004.[275]

The TVWF Directive, the original and the proposed Recommendation, seek to reconcile the protection for minors and human dignity with both freedom of expression and market freedom. One aspect of such reconciliation is reflected in the focus on the protection of minors, as opposed to the imposition of 'standards of taste and decency' on programmes aimed at adults. It will be made clear below that this emphasis is reflected in the Communications Act 2003, s 319, and in the current policy of Ofcom, the broadcast regulator. This is quite a significant departure from the stance adopted under the previous UK regulatory regime. However, the Act provides no clear mechanisms for co-operation with the sectors not covered by the Act, in particular that of film. The Act leaves Ofcom to determine how far content regulation in broadcasting should be harmonised with that relating to film. No express guidance on that matter is provided, save for that which can be viewed as flowing implicitly from the provisions of s 319.[276] This is acceptable under the TVWF, but it does not appear to accord with the aims of the proposed 2004 Recommendation.

Thus the reforms that have occurred under the Communications Act 2003 may already have been shown to be inadequate since the question of harmonisation of content regulation across the various media sectors has not been addressed. The new regulatory regime created under the Act leaves the internet, films and videoworks unaffected since the decision was taken to leave such sectors outside Ofcom's remit. While this decision is readily defensible, as it means that regulation in those sectors can remain flexible and sensitive to the particular needs of consumers and the industry involved, it means that both freedom of expression and the protection of minors may not receive effective protection. On the one hand Ofcom may continue the previous practice of indicating to broadcasters (via its Code) that the broadcast of a film may not be appropriate without cuts, or at all, even though it has been released on video with an '18' classification. On the other, the availability of (arguably) harmful material on the internet may pose a danger to children[277] and may also call into question disharmony between restraints on internet and broadcast content.

The EU creates pressure for harmonisation, not only across the member states of the EU, but also between the various audio-visual sectors. The promotion of national

273 Council Directive 89/552/EEC, as amended by Directive 97/36/EC of the European Parliament and of the Council, adopted in 1989.
274 *The Council Recommendation concerning the protection of minors and human dignity* 24 September 1998 98/560/EC, OJL 270, 7.10.1998, p 48.
275 *Proposal for a recommendation of the European Parliament and Council on the protection of minors and human dignity and the right to reply in relation to the competitiveness of the European audiovisual and information services industry*, COM(2004) 341 final 2004/0117 (COD) 30.4.04, press release 04/598. The legal basis proposed for the Recommendation is Art 157 of the EC Treaty.
276 See fn 313, p 522 below.
277 See pp 575–82.

frameworks aimed at achieving an effective level of protection for minors can, clearly, come into conflict with the promotion of competitiveness within and between those sectors. Further, the extent to which public interest values can be furthered in broadcasting while promoting competition is debatable. 'Must carry' requirements[278] can be viewed as anti-competitive, as can regulation via a legislative scheme, as opposed to self- or co-regulation.[279] The Human Rights Act may have a role to play in relation to broadcast regulation in terms of providing a counter to the expression of commercial values, although that role should not be over-stated. If the public interest has so far been defined within the regulatory regime considered below in too nebulous a manner, the Strasbourg jurisprudence might provide a means of creating greater certainty, in terms of the part to be played by media regulation in a democratic society. The jurisprudence of the European Convention on Human Rights, especially that relating to Art 10, is centrally premised on the notion that the purpose of the Convention is to 'maintain and promote the ideals and values of a democratic society'.[280] Article 10 arguments, taking such jurisprudence into account, could be raised in relation to the adjudication of Ofcom, the super-regulator set up under the Communications Act 2003, since it is bound by s 6 HRA.[281] It is at least arguable that the infusion of clear substantive values into media regulation, organised around the concept of the public interest, could occur under the HRA. At the least, the HRA could play a part in allowing such an infusion to occur since it provides media regulators with a benchmarking document with its jurisprudential accretions – domestic and international[282] – which is highly relevant to the argument that a version of media freedom informed by Strasbourg principles is not necessarily coterminous with market freedom.

Content regulation on grounds of offence-avoidance

Arguments based on pluralism and autonomy do not underpin the ethos of the current broadcasting *content* regulatory regime, particularly the continued offensive material restrictions, now contained in the Communications Act 2003. Further, since the restrictions apply to all forms of broadcasting, including political broadcasting, a matter discussed further below, they militate against plurality since they may mean that minority forms of expression are curbed. In terms of restrictions on grounds of offence avoidance, the UK has traditionally operated one of the strictest regulatory regimes for broadcasting within Western Europe. The constraints created by the imposition of content-based responsibilities on broadcasters have inevitably meant that their creative freedom is curtailed. The government had the opportunity to overhaul the regime in 2000 when it was considering the changes to the regulatory regime that eventually came about under

---

278 Requirements to carry certain forms of material in broadcasting, usually imposed in the interests of ensuring impartiality (see fn 263, above) or in order to serve minority interests.
279 See further, Part II, pp 308–9.
280 *Kjeldsen v Denmark* (1976) 1 EHRR 711, p 731; see also the comments of the Court in *Socialist Party v Turkey* (1999) 27 EHRR 51 as to the need for pluralism in a democracy.
281 As a regulator of private sector broadcasting set up under statute, it can be classified as a core public authority (or at the least, a functional one) on the basis that it is acting in a governmental capacity: see below pp 530–31 and Chapter 4, pp 233–35.
282 See *Sunday Times v UK* A 30 (1979); *Jersild v Denmark* (1994) 19 EHRR 1; *Lingens v Austria* (1986) 8 EHRR 103; *Thorgeirson v Iceland* (1992) 14 EHRR 843.

the Communications Act 2003,[283] but it drew back from seeking to bring about radical change. The traditional particularly strict regime in relation to matters of taste and decency was continued with some modification and presented in more detail under Part 3 of the 2003 Act. It is a regime that would clearly appear intolerable if applied to the print media. Broadcasting has also been subject to greater restraints than have videos, and such greater restraint continued under the post-2003 regime, although the regime itself is less restrictive and the current broadcast regulator, Ofcom, is taking a relatively liberal stance under its Broadcast Code. This special regime for broadcasting can only be justified by reference to the notion of intrusion into the home, discussed above. Previously, s 6(1)(a) of the Broadcasting Act 1990 imposed on independent broadcasters an obligation to ensure that programmes contained nothing that would offend against good taste and decency or was likely to be offensive to public feeling, and the BBC Charter and Agreement 1996 (now 2007) contained equivalent provisions. The Broadcasting Act 1996 gave statutory recognition to the Broadcasting Standards Commission which was set up to monitor standards of taste and decency in public sector and independent broadcasting, and its role was then taken over by Ofcom, which under the 2003 Act now has to set standards whereby the public is protected from offensive material.

The emphasis placed on protection from offence rather than on adult autonomy was not seriously questioned in the White Paper preceding the 2003 Act, *A New Future for Communications*,[284] and the current statutory regime does not differ from the previous one in essentials. There are, however, certain significant differences which may, depending on their interpretation by Ofcom, tend in the direction of liberalisation. Proportionality issues must now be considered when creating standards under the 2003 Act (s 3(3)(a)); the notion of maintaining standards of 'taste and decency' has been replaced by a duty to avoid offence and harm,[285] judged by context and by generally accepted standards; Ofcom has an express duty to abide by free expression principles in relation to that duty.[286] However, this of course adds nothing to the duty it is already under, as a public authority, under s 6 HRA.

In making decisions as to offence-avoidance Ofcom is faced with choices on a spectrum of extreme liberality or extreme restraint. It can either deny all viewers the chance of watching explicit or disturbing material or it can operate a highly liberal regime, allowing broadcast audiences the freedom to view such material but expecting them to protect themselves from offence. It is clearly arguable that people have a responsibility to protect themselves from offensive material merely by accessing information via a remote control before tuning into a programme where such material might be present. As warnings, encoding, Pin-protection and consumer advice become more effective, this argument becomes more compelling. The small burden placed on viewers in expecting them to take responsibility for their own viewing could readily be viewed as proportionate to the aim of allowing others autonomy in terms of choosing for themselves what they wish to see or hear. In other words, the small chance that someone might inadvertently view something they find offensive provides a doubtful

---

283 See the White Paper, *A New Future for Communications*, published 12 December 2000; www. communicationswhitepaper.gov.uk.
284 Ibid.
285 Sections 3(2)(e) and 319.
286 Section 3(3)(g).

justification for the infringement of autonomy involved in denying all viewers the chance to watch unexpurgated disturbing or sexually explicit material, within the limits created by the criminal law. This argument would apply in particular to the showing of films on television since they would already have been subject to the possibility of cuts to achieve a particular rating.

The warning contained in the classification of videos which also come into the home is viewed as going a long way towards providing a basis for ensuring that young children will not watch explicit material: the regime for videos is founded largely on the idea of parental responsibility, although there is of course some infringement of adult autonomy since videos must not contain material that prevents them from achieving a classification.[287] Broadcasting is based on the same foundation, since 'adult' material is shown after the watershed, but the offence-avoidance regime discussed below is potentially more restrictive than that in place for videos, and therefore goes further in the direction of paternalism. This regime affecting broadcasting in the interests of preventing offence to viewers clearly curbs the freedom of broadcasters.

The pervasive notion that broadcasts, as opposed to video-based material, are aspects of an 'intrusive' medium is largely based, it is suggested, on an out-of-date model for television. The large number of channels currently available and the increased possibilities of interactivity (in particular, checking on information about a programme via a remote control) undermine the idea of intrusiveness. In the past the small number of channels made it more probable that in tuning in and out of programmes a viewer might inadvertently encounter offensive material. The possibility of encoding also offers protection to those who do not wish to view such material. At present two issues in particular arise. Under the previous regulatory regime for broadcasting '18' rated films were shown but normally long after the cinematic or video release, when the '18' rating had in general become less significant, as standards changed.[288] Since such films are viewed in the home on videos, is there any basis for refusing to show them on general television channels without cuts and not long after the video release, so long as adequate consumer advice is provided? Secondly, if videos classified 'R18' (which now do contain 'hard core' material, as discussed below)[289] can be bought from restricted outlets, are there cogent reasons for barring the showing of such material on domestic or EU-based television subscription channels, using encoding as a protection for children? There are indications that a different stance is being taken towards such issues under the current Ofcom regime. An approach based not on general restrictions intended to avoid offence, but on the protection of minors only will become more firmly established if the recommendation under the TVWF Directive is adopted.

This part of this chapter will focus on the question of how far the current model of broadcast regulation, as compared with the previous one, comports with free speech principles. It will consider what part, if any, is played by the European Convention on Human Rights under the Human Rights Act in guaranteeing media freedom and media responsibility in the context of the maintenance of broadcasting standards relating to offence-avoidance. This is a context, however, in which it will be suggested that the HRA as mediated by the judiciary has not had and will not have a radical impact as

---

287 See pp 563–65.
288 See pp 555–60 for discussion of the standards applied to films by the BBFC and the ratings system.
289 At pp 562–66.

far as modifying the general statutory regime governing explicit or violent expression in broadcasting is concerned. It may, however, have an impact as regards specific decisions taken under that statutory regime by courts and regulators. Although the regime is governed by a post-HRA statute, the Communications Act 2003, the Act itself was not, it is argued, heavily influenced by the European Convention on Human Rights. The 2003 Act was *not* declared compatible with the Convention under s 19 HRA. However, the incompatibility is due to the continuance of the ban on political advertising under ss 321 and 319(g),[290] and it can be assumed that the rest of the provisions are intended to be compatible. Case law on the Act's provisions governing broadcast content is, however, likely to be sparse, providing few opportunities for examining its compatibility with the Convention rights.

The basic regulatory regime

In the 1950s, with the advent of commercial television, it was considered necessary to impose direct statutory regulation on broadcasting. Special duties were imposed on independent broadcasting to maintain standards of taste and decency and of impartiality; the responsibility for maintaining standards was given to the Independent Broadcasting Authority (IBA), established in 1954. Prior to the introduction of the Broadcasting Act 1990, the IBA was charged with the regulation of independent television. As part of the policy of deregulation of television, the 1990 Act set up the Independent Television Commission (ITC) to replace the IBA as a public body charged with licensing and regulating non-BBC television services.[291] The function of the ITC in this respect was similar to that of the Radio Authority (RA), which had the statutory function, under Part III of the 1990 Act, of licensing and monitoring the independent radio stations.

The regime established under the 1990 Act, and then taken further under the 1996 Act, represented an attempt to deregulate broadcasting, in the sense of enhancing market freedom, especially by affording further leeway to cross-media ownership, that is, ownership in more than one media sector. In contrast, in terms of creative freedom it would be misleading to speak of 'deregulation' when the system not only led to the establishment of an overlapping and strict set of controls over broadcasting, but also had a tendency to suppress diversity. As Gibbons puts it: '[the 1990 Act created the danger that cross-media ownership would] create pressure for more homogenised editorial positions or, as has occurred, cross-media promotion.'[292] Section 106 of the Broadcasting Act 1996 established the Broadcasting Standards Commission (BSC); until 2003 the Commission monitored BBC and independent programming.[293] Its role

---

290 The s 3(1)HRA obligation applies to s 321 of the 2003 Act as it would to any statutory provision Therefore, in a challenge to the ban, a judge would be free to re-examine the presumptive incompatibility. This would be of particular significance if relevant developments had occurred since 2003 in the Strasbourg jurisprudence. But in any event it would be open to a judge to seek to reinterpret the relevant provisions in order to determine whether exceptions to the ban could be created.

291 For discussion of the change in regime introduced under the 1990 Act, see Jones, T, 'The deregulation of broadcasting' (1989) 52 MLR 380–88.

292 'Aspiring to pluralism: the constraints of public broadcasting values on the deregulation of British media ownership' (1998) 16 Cardozo Arts and Entertainment Journal 475, p 485.

293 BSC Annual Report 1988–89 and Code of Practice 1989, p 41. For comment on the work of the BSC, see Coleman, F, 'All in the best possible taste – the Broadcasting Standards Council 1989–1992' [1992] PL 488.

was taken over in 2003 by the new regulator, Ofcom, which created legally enforceable controls over public broadcasting for the first time. Thus, until the Communications Act 2003 came into force, *independent* broadcasting was governed by the Broadcasting Acts 1990 and 1996.

Public broadcasting was and – to an extent – still is governed by the Royal Charter of the BBC which partly comprises a Licence Agreement. The 1996 Act drew the BBC partly into the regulatory regime, as discussed below, and the 2003 Act takes that process somewhat further, but still leaves many regulatory matters to the BBC Charter and Agreement, which were renewed at the end of 2006.[294] Thus the BBC still operates under this Agreement and also under the terms of its new Charter. Under the old Charter this included the undertaking to comply generally with the statutory duties placed on the IBA and then the ITC.[295] The current position of the BBC under the 2003 Act in relation to Ofcom is discussed below. Under the Charter and Agreement, the Board of Governors of the BBC has the responsibility for maintaining standards of taste and decency and of impartiality. The (1996) Charter and Agreement, amended in 2003, set out in more detail the obligations of the BBC as a public broadcaster operating by means of the licence fee, in particular its obligation to maintain independence. Although it is commercially funded, Channel 4 also has a public service remit governed by statute – previously s 25 of the 1990 Act – and now contained in s 265 of the 2003 Act.

Thus, under the pre-2003 regime commercial broadcasting was subject to dual, overlapping regulation from the ITC and BSC. The key difference under the pre-2003 regime, between the regulators, was in terms of sanctions: the BSC could only require a broadcaster found to be in breach of its code to broadcast its findings and an apology if appropriate; the ITC could, in addition to these sanctions, fine a broadcaster, and, in extreme cases, withdraw its licence. The BBC was still largely self-regulatory although it was regulated by the BSC in relation to taste and decency and privacy.[296] Thus the BBC was under a much 'lighter touch' scheme of regulation than the commercial broadcasters. As indicated below, the Ofcom regime has harmonised these regimes to an extent, but the BBC remains self-regulatory in terms of its public service remit.[297]

Regulation on grounds of avoiding offence under the Communications Act 2003

The BSC's and ITC's roles in relation to the maintenance of standards of taste and decency were taken over in 2003 by Ofcom, the inclusive regulator set up under powers provided for in the Office of Communications Act 2002 and with the powers and

---

294 The Charter (Cmnd 6925) for the continuance of the BBC came into force in 2007 (previously Cmnd 8313); 2006 Agreement: Cmnd 6872.

295 This undertaking was annexed to the Corporation's licence agreement. This includes the requirement to observe due impartiality. See Gibbons, T, 'Impartiality in the media' (1985) *Archiv für Rechts- und Sozialphilosophie*, Beiheft, Nr 28 pp 71–81. The requirements are similar under the current Charter – see below.

296 See Chapter 9, pp 839–51 for discussion of broadcast regulation and privacy.

297 See First Report of Select Committee on Culture, Media and Sport (2004) *A Public BBC* HC 82-I.

duties designated under the 2003 Act.[298] They include the licensing[299] and regulation of broadcasting and of telecommunications. Thus the regime was rationalised under the 2003 Act and the dual system of control – by the ITC and BSC – was modified: during 2004-early 2005 independent television only had to refer to one Code, the ITC Programme Code monitored by Ofcom. In 2005 the ITC Code was superceded by Ofcom's own Code once it came into force.

Section 325 Communications Act 2003 covers observance of the Code in licensed TV services. Under s 325 the conditions included in Broadcasting Act licences must ensure that the s 319 standards for offence avoidance (see below) are observed in the service provision and a duty is imposed on Ofcom to establish procedures for handling and resolving complaints regarding adherence to the standards. Section 237 allows for the imposition of penalties, including financial penalties, for the contravention of licence conditions or of directions given by Ofcom. If Ofcom is satisfied that a licensee has contravened a provision of a licence or failed to comply with a direction from Ofcom, a penalty can be imposed.[300] Under its own penalty Guidelines[301] Ofcom states that the amount of any penalty must be appropriate and proportionate to the contravention in respect of which it is imposed. It states that it must have regard to any representations made by the regulated body in breach, and accepts therefore that in setting the level of penalty, it will consider all relevant circumstances. In particular it states that it will take account of the seriousness of the contravention, precedents set by previous cases, and the need to ensure that the threat of penalties will act as a sufficient incentive to comply. The penalty will be higher where there are repeated contraventions by the same regulated body, where the contravention continues after the body becomes aware of it, or after it has been notified of it by Ofcom.

The Ofcom regime and the position of the BBC

Ofcom also affects public sector broadcasting.[302] Such broadcasting was also regulated under the BSC regime, but the BSC did not have the power to impose financial penalties on the BBC. This power, introduced under the current regime, represents a highly

---

298　Section 2(1), (2) 2003 Act.

299　Television Licensable Content Services and the licensing regime which applies to them are described in ss 232–40 of the Communications Act 2003. They replace the separate categories of satellite television services and licensable programme services which were established under the Broadcasting Act 1990 (as amended by the Broadcasting Act 1996). A television licensable content service is a service provided in digital or analogue form broadcast from a satellite or distributed using an electronic communications network that is to be made available for reception by members of the public and consists of television programmes (which for this purpose also comprises text services) or electronic programme guides, or both. It does not constitute a service which is a television multiplex service, a restricted television service, a digital television programme service, a service provided under a Channel 3 licence, a service provided under the Channel 4 licence, a service provided under the Channel 5 licence, a service provided under the public teletext licence or an additional television service.

300　This cannot exceed a fine of £250,000. See further fn 304.

301　From its website: www.Ofcom.org.uk/codes_guidelines/penalty.

302　Section 198(1): 'It shall be a function of OFCOM, to the extent that provision for them to do so is contained in–
　(a) the BBC Charter and Agreement, and (b) the provisions of this Act and of Part 5 of the 1996 Act, to regulate the provision of the BBC's services and the carrying on by the BBC of other activities for purposes connected with the provision of those services.'

significant change from the previous regime. It undermines the BBC's independence and brings the BBC far more into conformity with independent television. But at the same time the current statutory regime represents a compromise between BBC editorial freedom and greater regulation by a government regulator[303] since the regime for the BBC has to operate within the parameters of its Charter and Agreement. Section 198 provides that Ofcom may impose financial penalties on the BBC within the powers conferred by the Charter and Agreement if it contravenes the provisions of Part 3 2003 Act or of its Charter and Agreement.[304] The Agreement was amended in 2003 in anticipation of the changes to be introduced under the 2006 Agreement, the amendment coming into force in 2004. Clause 13 of the amended BBC Agreement allowed Ofcom to impose penalties, including financial ones, on the BBC[305] if it contravenes a 'relevant enforceable requirement'. A 'relevant enforceable requirement' includes the current Ofcom Broadcasting Code. Thus complaints about harm and offence may be addressed by the BBC, by Ofcom, or by both.

When the BBC's Charter was renewed at the end of 2006 this system changed, but not radically. Under the current Royal Charter[306] the government has created a new body called the BBC Trust to take on the oversight role previously discharged by the Governors.[307] Thus the responsibility previously shared between Ofcom and the Governors for ensuring offence-avoidance was from January 2007 shared between the BBC Trust and Ofcom. This is also true of complaints about fairness and privacy, as discussed in Chapter 9. But if a complaint relates to the accuracy and impartiality of a programme, the BBC will remain finally responsible.[308] The BBC Trust will now deal with such complaints from 2007 onwards – for the 10 years of the new Charter's life. The Hutton Report formed a significant background to the renewal of the Charter.[309]

So the BBC is now subject to a dual and overlapping system for complaints regarding offence, and this will continue to be the case from 2007. Under s 46 of the BBC's 2006 Agreement the Programme Content standards that must be observed are set by s 319 of the 2003 Act, which is discussed below. This system hardly makes for clarity

303 See further First Report of Select Committee on Culture, Media and Sport (2004) *A Public BBC* HC 82-I.

304 Section 198 (2): 'For the purposes of the carrying out of that function OFCOM- (a) are to have such powers and duties as may be conferred on them by or under the BBC Charter and Agreement; and (b) are entitled, to the extent that they are authorised to do so by the Secretary of State or under the terms of that Charter and Agreement, to act on his behalf in relation to that Charter and Agreement.'
The maximum penalty that can be imposed is £250,000 (s 198(5)), although the 2003 Act also confers power on the Secretary of State to substitute a different sum (s 198(6)).

305 See Chapter 9, pp 842–43 for further discussion of the position of the BBC in relation to Ofcom.

306 The Green Paper that reviewed the BBC's Royal Charter stated that the government intended to create a new body called the BBC Trust (Review of BBC's Royal Charter *A strong BBC, independent of government*, published May 2005). The White Paper was published in 2006, and the Charter came into force in January 2007. It may be noted that parts of the Green Paper are to be treated as 'White', including the part on governance and accountability. See HL Paper 50-I, 15.3.05 at para 47.

307 Ibid at p 10, para 3.1.

308 For discussion see Fenwick and Phillipson, fn 1 above, Chapter 20.

309 Lord Hutton, Report of the Inquiry into the Circumstances Surrounding the Death of Dr David Kelly CMG (hereafter 'the Hutton Report'). For comment on the Report, see Smith, G and Sandelson, D, 'The Future Shape of the BBC – the Hutton Inquiry, Charter Review and the Challenges Facing the BBC and the Government' [2004] Ent LR 15(5) 137–46.

in terms of content-based control and could lead to a confused and even conflicting application of standards. In its response to the Green Paper Ofcom proposed that the government should move towards greater clarity and consistency in content; it argued that the current arrangement, dividing regulation between Ofcom and the BBC, 'risks implying to the public that there are no common standards of acceptability and quality . . .'.[310] The effect of this change on the BBC's traditional independence depends to quite a significant extent on the stance that Ofcom takes under its Code. The possibilities open to Ofcom are discussed below.

Protection from offensive material under s 319 Communications Act

The key provision under the 2003 Act in terms of curbing the broadcasting of offensive material is s 319.[311] Section 319(1) of the 2003 Act requires Ofcom to set standards whereby the public is protected from offensive material.[312] The standards objectives for the Code are set out in s 319(2)[313] and include protection for children and a warning that responsibility must be exercised in relation to the content of religious programmes.[314] The specific obligation set out in s 319(2)(a), to protect persons under the age of eighteen, is new; the 1990 Act contained no such obligation.

The most general restriction is contained in s 319(2)(f) which provides that 'generally accepted standards are applied to the contents of television and radio services so as to provide adequate protection for members of the public from the inclusion in such services of offensive and harmful material'. The term 'generally accepted standards' can be assumed to refer to changing contemporary ideas of what is offensive material.

Section 319(4) gives further guidance as to the matters to be taken into account by Ofcom in securing the standards objectives;[315] they are particularly pertinent in relation

---

310 House of Lords Select Committee on BBC Charter Renewal, HL Paper 50-I, 15.3.05 at para 104.
311 See also s 3(2)(e), concerning the general duty of Ofcom to secure the application of standards to television and radio services, 'that provide adequate protection for members of the public from the inclusion of offensive and harmful material in such services'. That duty is then encapsulated in more detail in s 319.
312 (1) It shall be the duty of OFCOM to set, and from time to time to review and revise, such standards for the content of programmes to be included in television and radio services as appear to them best calculated to secure the standards objectives.
313 (2) The standards objectives are-

   (a) that persons under the age of eighteen are protected;

   (b) that material likely to encourage or to incite the commission of crime or to lead to disorder is not included in television and radio services . . .

   (e) that the proper degree of responsibility is exercised with respect to the content of programmes which are religious programmes

   (f) that generally accepted standards are applied to the contents of television and radio services so as to provide adequate protection for members of the public from the inclusion in such services of offensive and harmful material;
314 In relation to the statutory obligation regarding religious sensibilities, see Ofcom's ruling on the BBC's broadcast of *Jerry Springer – the Opera* in 2005, fn 332 below.
315 Section 319(4) provides: 'In setting or revising any standards under this section, OFCOM must have regard, in particular and to such extent as appears to them to be relevant to the securing of the standards objectives, to each of the following matters – the degree of harm or offence likely to be caused by the inclusion of any particular sort of material in programmes generally, or in programmes of a particular

to the objective of s 319(2)(f). Section 319(4) does not contain an exhaustive list of the matters that Ofcom must take into account in setting or revising the standards referred to, and, while minimum standards must be apparent under s 319(5)(a) which impliedly reflect the matters listed, Ofcom can take the listed matters into account to the extent that it deems them to be relevant to the securing of the standards objectives. Ofcom is warned not to be too interventionist since it must bear in mind the desirability of maintaining the independence of editorial control over programme content. At the same time it has to consider the extent to which harm or offence may be caused by the inclusion of certain forms of material in programmes.

A distinction is drawn in s 319(4) between material which could give offence in programmes generally, or where it is included in programmes of a particular description. Clearly, this is a crucial distinction: some forms of material may be viewed by Ofcom as too offensive or harmful to be broadcast at all, whereas in most instances the context is the determining factor. The issues most often encountered are likely to concern the suitability of showing particular forms of material before the watershed, or at what point after it, or in the context of a particular type of programme. Context clearly strongly influences audience expectations, and Ofcom is enjoined to take those expectations into account. In coming to such decisions as to contextual suitability, Ofcom must take into account the probable size and composition of the potential audience for particular radio and television programmes. But Ofcom also has to consider the nature of the audience for television and radio services generally. This appears to mean that Ofcom must look beyond the audience that might be attracted to, for example, a sexually explicit film shown late at night and take account of the expectations and wishes of the more general audience who might happen to tune in to it. Clearly, this provision might encourage Ofcom to take a more restrictive approach. The possibility that persons might be unintentionally exposed to the content of a programme, and the extent to which the nature of a programme's content can be brought to the attention of potential members of the audience, are specifically identified as relevant factors, but it is clearly implicit in this approach that even where a person could take steps to ascertain the content of a programme beforehand (ie outside the context of trailers or adverts which come upon the audience without warning), the programme makers must take their susceptibility to offence into account.

Section 319 has nothing to say about the responsibility of audience members to seek to avoid shock or offence by looking up the guidance given as to the nature of the programme beforehand or using interactive features to do so. The nod in the direction of editorial freedom in s 319(4)(f) does not amount to the far more comprehensive guidance which could have been given as to the showing of material at the boundaries of acceptability, such as material from films with an '18' rating which are towards the further end

description; the likely size and composition of the potential audience for programmes included in television and radio services generally, or in television and radio services of a particular description; the likely expectation of the audience as to the nature of a programme's content and the extent to which the nature of a programme's content can be brought to the attention of potential members of the audience; the likelihood of persons who are unaware of the nature of a programme's content being unintentionally exposed, by their own actions, to that content; the desirability of securing that the content of services identifies when there is a change affecting the nature of a service that is being watched or listened to and, in particular, a change that is relevant to the application of the standards set under this section; and the desirability of maintaining the independence of editorial control over programme content.'

of the '18' classification band.[316] For example, specific guidance could have been given as to the conditions under which such material could be broadcast. The use of the term 'offensive' clearly implies that the material covered falls well outside the boundaries of criminal liability created by the common law, statutory indecency provisions, or the Obscene Publications Act 1959,[317] taking account of the 'public good' defence under s 4, which was discussed above. As discussed in Chapter 8, those provisions set variable but higher bars in terms of establishing the impact of the material in order to attract liability than is inherent in the term 'offensive'. Section 319 therefore indicates that there is a body of material that cannot be broadcast, although it lies well outside the boundaries created by the criminal law relating to explicit expression. At present, the statutory emphasis on the possibility that persons might view such material unawares appears to outweigh the emphasis on seeking to ensure that willing adult audiences can view such material. It is arguable that a full plurality of standards is not being maintained.

As indicated, it is extremely unlikely that a broadcast could fall foul of the Obscene Publications Act 1959. However, given the 'likely audience' test used in obscenity law, as discussed above, an argument could conceivably be made that the transmission of a film on television changes the analysis of that audience since individuals, including children or teenagers, switching between channels at random, could be confronted by explicit images without warning. Since obscenity is a relative concept, judged to its effect on a significant proportion of the likely audience, a televised film could be adjudged obscene where that would not be the case if it was made available only by hiring a DVD, since the publicity material on the DVD case, together with the age rating for the film, would give the individual some warning of its likely content. It would be even less likely that the same film could be viewed as obscene when shown in the cinema, since entrance to the cinema would be age-restricted; further, the advertisements for the film would provide a warning. Given therefore, that when a film is broadcast on television, there is the likelihood of a number of younger people stumbling upon it unawares, it is possible to conceive of a particular broadcast being deemed obscene, though the film itself obviously had not been – by the film regulator, the British Board of Film Classification (BBFC).[318] Since 'hard core' pornography – film material rated R18 – is not broadcast on television under the current regulatory regime,[319] this is highly improbable but the possibility cannot be completely ruled out.

Ofcom's Broadcast Code[320]

Until 2005 Ofcom relied on the ITC Code and on the BSC Standards Code, although it was in the process of developing its own Code. The 2005 Code now applies[321] to

---

316 The nature of the '18' rating is discussed below in relation to the current stance of the British Board of Film Classification (BBFC). See pp 553–61.

317 Under Broadcasting Act 1990 s 162 the 1959 Act is applied to broadcasting; s 162 was not repealed by the Communications Act 2003.

318 For the standards the BBFC currently uses in classifying films, see pp 555–61 below. Clearly, it would not classify a film that might be obscene within the meaning of the OPA 1959.

319 See p 528 below.

320 See s 324(1).

321 It came into force on July 25 2005.

programmes, advertisements[322] and text broadcast on all forms of television services and radio, including satellite and cable channels. Ofcom made a deliberate decision to discard the ITC and BSC Codes on offence-avoidance and to make a fresh start with its own Code. Clearly, one option would have been merely to adopt the ITC Programme Code as it stood, with some modifications due to Ofcom's broader remit. The ITC Code would have had the advantage of familiarity as far as the independent broadcasters were concerned, and also it had evolved over a number of years, taking into account the ITC's experience in monitoring it. It had also undergone an incremental process of liberalisation. However, Ofcom decided instead to make a clean break and to introduce a new Code which, while it retains certain basic features of the ITC Code, differs from it significantly in a number of respects.

Ofcom's current Code places the emphasis more strongly than the ITC Code did on the avoidance of harm, rather than on the imprecise and subjective idea of avoidance of offence and the maintenance of standards of 'good taste'. It also places greater emphasis on the use of warnings rather than on restricting the broadcast of certain forms of material. Thus it assumes up to a point that the audience can exercise choice and protect itself from shock. It further assumes that people are entitled to view a wide and diverse range of programmes. It is less prescriptive, comprehensive and detailed than the last (2003) version of the ITC Code. Ofcom's Code places quite a strong emphasis on free expression principles and on editorial responsibility since it is less extensive and prescriptive than the ITC and BSC Codes. Nevertheless, in a number of specific instances it is very precise and provides clear and unequivocal rules.[323] The prescriptive terms used indicate that a number of the rules are mandatory rather than advisory or discretionary. In those instances, then, broadcasters clearly lay themselves open to the possibility of an adverse adjudication for breach of the Code if they do not follow the rules. However, the use of clear and precise rules, so long as their restraining effect is kept to a minimum, does obviate the potentially chilling effect of imprecision.

The Code is more firmly based on the principle of allowing for creative freedom than the two previous Codes were. To this end, Ofcom's Code creates a clear dividing line between provisions applicable to children and to adults, whereas the ITC Code provisions applied, on their face, to both. The ITC Programme Code, s 1.2 was headed 'Family Viewing Policy, Offence to Good Taste and Decency, Portrayal of Violence and Respect for Human Dignity'. However, it did not seek to ensure that unsuitable material would never be viewed by a few children. The rules assumed a 'progressive decline throughout the evening in the proportion of children present in the audience'. Section 1 of Ofcom's Code is headed 'Protecting the under-18s', while s 2 relates to protection from harmful or offensive material generally. It can be assumed therefore that s 2 relates mainly, although not exclusively, to adults. Ofcom's stance is welcome since it allows for a greater focus on the need for restrictions applicable largely to adult programming. Under the ITC Code there appeared to be a greater possibility that adult viewing would be restricted in order to protect children. Ofcom's Code also lays greater emphasis – depending on Ofom's interpretation of it in practice – on protecting persons

---

322 Broadcast advertisements are under the remit of the Advertising Standards Authority, working in partnership with Ofcom.
323 See eg ss 1.1, 1.2 and 1.5 of the Code.

from the inadvertent viewing of offensive material, not by barring it from broadcasts, but by requiring that it is accompanied by extensive warnings.

Ofcom's Code places a strong emphasis on protecting children, not by restricting or banning the showing of explicit material completely, but by showing it at certain times, either after the watershed or by avoiding times when 'children are particularly likely to be listening'. Ofcom's Code is also more specific than the ITC one in relation to what should not be shown when children are likely to be viewers. Only 'material that might *seriously* impair the moral, mental or physical development of children (emphasis added)' must not be broadcast.[324] (The wording is taken from the Television Without Frontiers Directive, 1997, Art 22.1.)[325] Ofcom's Code begins with the Directive's wording, indicating that it is focusing on the avoidance of serious harms, whereas the ITC Code began with the wording from s 6(1)(a) of the 1990 Act concerning the avoidance of material that is offensive to good taste and decency. In other words, the Code is focused on the avoidance of serious and specific harms to children (defined as those under 15). But under s 1.2 material that might merely *impair* their development in the ways specified *can* be shown so long as 'appropriate scheduling or technical devices' are used. The reference to scheduling means, following ss 1.3 and 1.4, that the material must be shown after the watershed and the probable number and age of the children present in the audience must be taken into account. If encoding is not used, 'a clear verbal warning' must be given prior to the programme. Encoding may provide an effective means of protecting children while allowing adults to view a range of material, including explicit or potentially disturbing material.

The use of the term 'seriously impair' creates, on its face, a standard that appears similar to that employed in the Obscene Publications Act 1959 with its use of the terms 'deprave and corrupt'. In fact the test under the OPA is not currently interpreted in this fashion,[326] but the apparent closeness of the boundaries between the two tests is of interest since, taking the previous regime into account, one would expect a broadcast regulatory body to impose standards lying well within the borders of the basic OPA test. In general, the emphasis of Ofcom's Code as regards children is on the use of various devices to protect them (the use of the watershed, detailed warnings, PIN-protection and encoding of material), rather than on bans or on making cuts in the material. '18' rated films can be shown at any time while 'adult-sex' material can be shown between 2200 and 0530 so long as protections are in place to ensure that children cannot view the material.[327] A very clear distinction is drawn between pay-per-view and ordinary

---

324   Section 1.1.

325   Dir 89/552, as amended by Directive 97/36.

326   See pp 00; see also Edwards, S, 'On the Contemporary Application of the Obscene Publications Act' (1998) Crim LR 843.

327   1.23 Pay per view services may broadcast up to BBFC 18-rated films or their equivalent, at any time of day provided: there is a protection system pre 2100 and post 0530 (a mandatory PIN or other equivalent protection), that seeks satisfactorily to restrict access solely to those authorised to view when material other than BBFC U-rated or PG-rated or their equivalents is shown; information is provided about programme content that will assist adults to assess its suitability for children; there is a detailed billing system for subscribers which clearly itemises all viewing including viewing times and dates; and those security systems which are in place to protect children are clearly explained to all subscribers.

broadcasting, although 'R18' material still cannot be broadcast.[328] The convergence that appears to be occurring between video and pay per view broadcasting suggests that the current distinction between what can be shown on the two media may eventually disappear. In fact, ironically, it may now be less likely that children would view R18 material in Pin-protected broadcasts than on video, once videos are brought into the home by adults.

Section 2 of the Code, focusing more on adult viewing, is aimed at ensuring that broadcasters provide 'adequate protection for viewers and listeners from the inclusion of harmful or offensive material', judged against 'generally accepted standards'. It is noticeable that the 'protection' to be provided in s 2 centres more on the provision of information, than on making cuts in the material. This is made clear in s 2.3. At the same time s 2.3 makes it clear that if the use of potentially offensive language and material, in particular, the inclusion of scenes of violence or sex, sexual violence, or scenes of humiliation, distress or the use of discriminatory treatment or language must be justified by the context, implying that otherwise they should not be broadcast or should be cut. The term 'context' refers, *inter alia*, to a number of the factors outlined in s 319(4)(a), (b), (c) and (d) of the Communications Act.[329] But s 2.3 also accepts that if information is included, presumably in the form of consumer advice and detailed warnings as to content, it can assist in preventing offence.

Section 2, in contrast to the provisions of the ITC Code, is far more specific. After the general provisions regarding the broadcasting of explicit material in ss 2.1 and 2.3, it focuses, in the following sections on a range of specific harms to be avoided.[330]

1.24 Premium subscription services and pay per view/night services may broadcast 'adult-sex' material between 2200 and 0530 provided that in addition to other protections mentioned above: there is a mandatory PIN protected encryption system, or other equivalent protection, that seeks satisfactorily to restrict access solely to those authorised to view; and there are measures in place that ensure that the subscriber is an adult.

1.25 BBFC R18-rated films or their equivalent must not be broadcast.

328 In May 2005 Ofcom conducted a research study, *Research into the Effectiveness of PIN Protection Systems in the UK*. It found that a high percentage of children (about 50% of those in the relevant houses surveyed) knew that a PIN number was needed to access blocked channels and of those children about 50% knew of their parents' PIN number; of those just under half had used the number to access pay-per-view programmes without their parents' permission. Ofcom concluded that security methods in the current PIN environment are not likely to prevent children from accessing 'R18' material.

329 See above fn 315.

330 2.4 Programmes must avoid anything that individually, and/or taken as a whole and in context, is likely to encourage violent, dangerous or seriously antisocial behaviour.

2.5 The means or methods of suicide and self harm must not be included in programmes except where the context, scheduling and likely audience can justify them.

2.6 Demonstrations of exorcism, the occult, the paranormal, divination and related practices must be treated with due objectivity. Entertainment programmes that contain such demonstrations must be clearly labelled as such for the audience. No potentially life changing advice may be given. (Religious programmes are exempted from the rule about life-changing advice but must, in any event, comply with the provisions in the section regarding religious programmes in this Code.) (Please also note the scheduling restrictions contained in section 1 of this Code.) Films, dramas and fiction generally are not bound by this rule. Meaning of 'life-changing': Life-changing advice includes advice about health, finances, employment, relationships etc.

2.7 Broadcasters must prevent hypnosis being induced in susceptible viewers and listeners . . .

Beginning with the opening words about taste and decency in s 1.1, the ITC Code was more general and much more extensive.[331] In relation to films, Ofcom's Code provides, in s 1.20: 'No version of a film or programme refused certification by the British Board of Film Classification (BBFC) may be broadcast.' Material rated 'R18' cannot be shown; '18' rated films can be shown after 9.00 pm, but even after that point they may be viewed as 'unsuitable' (s 1.21). As to suitability, Ofcom presumably takes the view that the provisions relating to the portrayal of sex and violence and the showing of disturbing material in general in s 1 regarding children and in s 2 cover the scheduling of films. But it is clear that Ofcom's Code is somewhat less prescriptive in this respect and leaves greater discretion to the broadcasters. But the BBFC standards are regarded as minimum ones; the mere fact that a film has an '18' certificate is not to be taken as implying that it is clearly proper to broadcast it.

It can be said that Ofcom's Code accords with the liberal free speech account of restrictions on broadcasting discussed above in so far as it concentrates on the avoidance of specific harms, and largely avoids the use of broad statements about ensuring the promotion of 'good taste and decency'. It strikes a balance between offence avoidance and the right of adult television audiences to receive a diverse range of broadcast expression, which differs somewhat from the balance struck under the superceded Codes. The ability of people to take responsibility for protecting themselves from offence is more strongly emphasised. The restrictions placed on films shown

2.9 Programmes must not use techniques which exploit the possibility of conveying a message to viewers or listeners, or of otherwise influencing their minds, without their being aware, or fully aware, of what has occurred.

2.10 Television broadcasters must minimise the risk to viewers who have photosensitive epilepsy . . .

3.1 Material likely to encourage or incite crime, or likely to lead to disorder must not be included in television or radio services.

3.2 Material that enables viewers or listeners to commit crime must not be included in television or radio services . . .

3.6 Material must not be broadcast that could endanger lives or prejudice the success of attempts to deal with a hijack or kidnapping.

331 1.6 Sex and Nudity. Similar considerations apply. Much great fiction and drama have been concerned with love and passion which can shock and disturb. Popular entertainment and comedy have always relied to some extent on sexual innuendo and suggestive behaviour but gratuitous offence should be avoided. Careful consideration should be given to nudity before the watershed but some nudity may be justifiable in a non-sexual and relevant context. Representations of sexual intercourse should not occur before the watershed unless there is a serious educational purpose. Any portrayal of sexual behaviour must be defensible in context. If included before the watershed it must be appropriately limited and inexplicit. Sex scenes of a more adult nature, which are more graphic and prolonged, should be limited to much later in the schedule. (See also Section 1.3(i))

1.7 Violence. The real world contains violence in many forms. It is reasonable for television to reflect this but it is clear that the portrayal of violence, whether physical, verbal or psychological, can upset, disturb and offend and can be accused of desensitising viewers, of making them unduly fearful or of encouraging imitation. These are legitimate public concerns requiring careful consideration whenever violence, real or simulated, is to be shown. The treatment of violence must always be appropriate to the context, scheduling, channel and audience expectations.

a) Offensive violence. At the simplest level, some portrayed acts of violence may go beyond the bounds of what is tolerable in that they could be classified as material which, in the words of the Broadcasting Act, is 'likely to be offensive to public feeling'.

on television appear to be more in line with those placed on videos, as discussed in Chapter 00, although it remains the case that 'hardcore' pornography cannot be broadcast. Since videos and the internet also come into the home this relaxation of the rules is readily defensible.

An indication of the stance Ofcom is currently taking was given when, in 2005, Ofcom cleared the BBC of flouting the BSC Code in relation to *Jerry Springer – the Opera*. The programme, which satirised features of Christianity, received 16,801 complaints.[332] Ofcom considered in particular the question of offence against religious sensibilities and balanced the possibility of offence against the need to protect freedom of expression. In coming to this finding, Ofcom took into account the significance of the work. This was a very important and telling decision, bearing in mind the subject-matter

332 The BBC's Governors Programme Complaints Committee had also considered the complaints; it found: ' in all the circumstances, the outstanding artistic significance of the programme outweighed the offence which it caused to some viewers and so the broadcasting of the programme was justified'.
      Extracts from Ofcom's adjudication: Sections 26 and 27 – Respect and Dignity. The Code states that 'challenging and deliberately flouting the boundaries of taste in drama and comedy is a time-honoured tradition. Although these programmes have a special freedom, this does not give them unlimited licence to be cruel or to humiliate individuals or groups gratuitously'. Ofcom recognises that a great number of complainants felt that the *Opera* denigrated the Christian religion. The show was created as a caricature of modern television. Importantly, in Ofcom's view the *Opera* did not gratuitously humiliate individuals or any groups and in particular the Christian community. Its target was television and fame. Conclusion: The programme did not contravene these sections of the Code. Sections 43–45 – Offences against Religious Sensibilities. The Code states that: 'Although religions should not be exempt from (the) critical scrutiny . . . particular care should be taken when referring to religion in entertainment.' Many complainants accused the BBC of committing the crime of blasphemy. However, criminal law is not a matter for Ofcom but for the courts. Ofcom is not required to determine whether the BBC committed blasphemy, but whether, in this case, the provisions of the Code had been contravened . . . Ofcom has sought to achieve the appropriate balance between, on the one hand the standards set in the Code (ex-BSC Code on Standards) and the need to apply those standards to give adequate protection from harmful and offensive material, and on the other hand the need, as appropriate, to guarantee freedom of expression. Freedom of expression is particularly important in the context of artistic works, beliefs, philosophy and argument . . . Their main concern arose from the depictions of figures at the heart of the complainants' religious beliefs. In considering offence against religious sensibilities, Ofcom took into account the clear context of the Opera. The fictional Jerry Springer lay dying in a delusional state. As he hallucinated, this character was asked to pitch Jesus against the Devil in his own confessional talk show. This 'dream' sequence was emphasised by the fact that the same actors, who played guests on his show in the first act, played the characters in the second act. What resulted was a cartoon, full of grotesque images, which challenged the audience's views about morality and the human condition. The production made clear that all the characters in the second act were the product of the fictional Springer's imagination: his concepts of Satan, God, Jesus and the others and modelled on the guests in his show . . . In light of this, Ofcom did not believe that the characters represented were, in the context of this piece, conveyed as faithful or accurate representations of religious figures, but were characterisations of the show's participants . . . It is not within Ofcom's remit to record a contravention of the Code on the basis that Christianity, as opposed to another faith, was the subject of *Jerry Springer: The Opera*. In considering freedom of expression, Ofcom recognises the UK's long-standing tradition of satirising political and religious figures and celebrities. Ofcom must consider each programme on its merits. No contravention was found. Ofcom broadcast bulletin 34, 9 May 2005. See Ofcom's web-site 10 May 2005. An application to seek judicial review of the BBC's decision to screen the film, by the Christian Institute and other groups was refused by the Honourable Mr Justice Crane, judgment dated 27 May 2005.

of the programme and the extremely large number of complaints; it may be taken to indicate that Ofcom is taking a robust stance in relation to creative freedom.[333]

It may be concluded that in so far as the ITC Code in its various manifestations was gradually becoming more liberal, Ofcom's Code takes this process further. But although the Code is, on its face, a liberalising measure when compared with the ITC and BSC's Codes, a number of open-ended terms are used and the level of detail of those Codes is missing. Thus Ofcom has a great deal of leeway to take a range of approaches in terms of liberality and the preservation of creative freedom when it adjudicates on alleged breaches of the Code. It also has a lot of room for manouevre in drafting future manifestations of the Code. Since it is unlikely that there will be much or any court intervention in Ofcom's regulatory scheme, after the *Pro-Life* decision, the provisions of the Code and Ofcom's stance towards them provide the key mechanisms for protecting free speech in broadcasting. Nevertheless, it is to the possibilities of court intervention under the HRA that this chapter now turns.

The potential effects of the Human Rights Act and the implications of the Pro-Life Alliance decision for the current regime

The public authority/private body distinction

Ofcom and the public sector broadcasters are susceptible to challenge under the Human Rights Act. Ofcom is probably a core public authority under s 6(1) HRA; it has clear governmental functions since it is a regulator set up by government. In any event, it is clearly a functional public authority as is reasonably clear from the discussion of the meaning of 'public function' under s 6(3)(b) HRA in Chapter 4.[334] It can be viewed as a governmental body in being set up under a Royal Charter. Acceptance of its status as a functional public authority appeared to be implicit in the decision in the case of *Pro-Life Alliance*,[335] although, as discussed, the judges were reluctant to engage in argument as to the mechanisms of the HRA.

Assuming that the BBC is a functional public authority, there is then immense room for argument as to those functions it has that are 'public'. There is nothing inherently public about broadcasting, and if the BBC were to be viewed as acting publicly in relation to all aspects of programme-making, this would set up a clear anomaly in relation

---

333 The stance it took in relation to *Jerry Springer* may be contrasted with its stance in relation to the timing of the broadcast of *Pulp Fiction* by the BBC Report: *Pulp Fiction BBC 2, 7 August 2004, 21:10* Nine viewers complained about the transmission of this film. The majority were concerned that its transmission shortly after the 21:00 watershed, when young people watch television, could encourage anti-social behaviour. Overall, viewers felt that the strong content, including graphic violence, seriously offensive swearing and scenes of drug abuse, made the film unsuitable at a time in the evening when young people and children were still part of the audience. It was found that such intense material is not normally expected so soon after the watershed and that the scheduling of this film at 21:10 was too early, given the strong, adult content from the start. The scheduling of this film was found to be in contravention of the Code. It may be noted that the case was appealed three times by the BBC. This decision was made by the Content Board following the BBC's third and final appeal.

334 See pp 216–35.

335 [2003] 2 WLR 1403, see pp 534–43.

to the private broadcasters since they would be performing the same function but would not bound by the HRA. A distinction could be drawn between the BBC's function as a broadcaster and as a regulator, finding that it is providing a public function in the latter role but not the former. This would be a sensible line to draw, although it is not without its difficulties. This stance could be viewed as implicit in *Pro-Life*. This would mean that when the BBC regulates its *own* programmes it is performing a public function. Thus, decisions as to filming techniques and the making of programmes might not be viewed as 'public' while decisions to allow a programme to be broadcast taken at senior level would be. Decisions taken in relation to offence-avoidance could be viewed as public as so closely associated with the BBC's core role in providing programming for public consumption. Clearly, s 6 HRA inevitably creates difficult decisions and anomalies in relation to the public/private divide. The BBC provides an especially difficult example. But it must be noted for the purposes of this chapter that assuming it is a public authority in relation to decisions to broadcast, it is hard to imagine a situation in which a Convention right could be invoked against it in response to a positive decision to broadcast a programme that then caused offence. There is no Convention right not to be offended – the only possible candidate would be Art 9 in relation to offending against religious sensibilities.[336] The public/private function divide is far more significant in relation to invasion of privacy, discussed in Chapter 9.

Channel 4 may possibly have the status of a functional public authority since it has public service functions, but the independent broadcasting companies are almost certainly private bodies for HRA purposes. Thus the independent broadcasters cannot be challenged directly under the HRA. However, in any court action against Ofcom or the BBC concerning relevant sections of the 2003 Act, an interpretation of the provisions should of course be adopted, under s 3(1) HRA, which accords with the demands of Art 10. Any resultant modification of the Act by interpretation, or as a result of a declaration of incompatibility under s 4 HRA, would then affect the independent broadcasters. If s 319 itself were affected in this way the effect would be indirect, as a result of a change in Ofcom's stance. Also, as public authorities, Ofcom and the BBC must take the demands of Art 10 into account in coming to any decisions relating to content restrictions.

The *Pro-Life Alliance* decision, discussed below, with its strong emphasis on deference to the regulatory scheme and the regulator, gave little encouragement to the use of the HRA as a means of challenging restrictive decisions relating to broadcast material or the restrictions themselves. However, using a different approach, or on other, more compelling, facts a successful challenge remains a possibility. Overly restrictive decisions of public sector broadcasters and of Ofcom under the 'offensive material' provisions of s 319 of the 2003 Act and the current Code could theoretically be challenged by a programme-maker under s 7(1)(a) HRA, relying on Art 10. A challenge to Ofcom's use of its powers would normally have to occur after the event since Ofcom does not have censorship powers.

There are some grounds for thinking that the inception of the Human Rights Act might have called the previous regime into question and that it might still do so as regards the current one. In this context the restraints on broadcast expression relate to offence-avoidance. Such restraints can be justified only where they meet the Art 10(2)

---

336 See *Otto-Preminger* (1994) 19 EHRR 34, discussed at pp 488–90, above.

tests.[337] In particular they have to be proportionate to the aims of protecting morality or the rights of others. On the face of it, one might not expect the restrictions on the basis of avoiding offence – essentially of a similar nature under the previous and the current regimes – to meet those tests since the term 'offence' is so broad and imprecise. However, as discussed above, the Convention jurisprudence interpreting Art 10(2) notoriously does not uphold freedom of expression very strongly where restrictions protecting children from offence in respect of non-political speech are concerned. Thus the possibility of mounting challenges to the decisions of regulators or broadcasters in court was always likely to be problematic since the regulatory regime tends to have its greatest impact on artistic rather than political speech. The message of political expression can frequently, although not invariably, be conveyed without the use of potentially offensive words or images. As discussed, a strong pronouncement was made in *Handyside*[338] to the effect that Art 10(1) covers speech which some might find offensive, but the Court went on to find that in the instance before it such speech (albeit of ideological significance) could justifiably be suppressed, and it reached this decision on the basis of conceding a wide margin of appreciation to the state since there is no uniform European conception of moral standards.[339] It can therefore readily be said in this context that the Art 10 standard is 'soft-edged': applied domestically, it very clearly leaves room for the adoption of either an activist or a minimalist approach, and *Pro-Life* adopted the latter approach. It might well support quite far-reaching restrictions on broadcasting owing to the possibility that children might be affected.

But, as discussed above, in the line of authority stemming from *Handyside*[340] a broad margin of appreciation was conceded to the state in finding against the applicant, especially where offensive 'artistic' speech was concerned – using that term loosely.[341] The pronouncement in *Handyside* to the effect that Art 10(1) covers offensive speech runs presumptively directly counter to the previous provision against such speech in broadcasting in s 6(1)(a) 1990 Act, aspects of the BBC's Agreement, s 108 1996 Act and now s 319 of the 2003 Act. As the domestic courts are not required to concede a margin of appreciation to the state, there is a case for expecting them to take a stricter stance in relation to restraints on broadcast speech. The use of the Convention jurisprudence on both political and, if afforded a creative interpretation, artistic expression,[342] has in principle the potential, applied domestically, to challenge accepted conceptions of offence-avoidance in broadcasting. This argument is reasonably strong in relation to restrictions on all forms of broadcasting on the ground of offence-avoidance, including soap operas, 'reality' TV programmes, and films. It is even stronger in relation to forms of political broadcasting, such as Party Political Broadcasts, Election Broadcasts, news programmes and documentaries since the Strasbourg jurisprudence defends political expression in the media very strongly – as decisions such as that in *Jersild*,[343] discussed in Chapter 2, demonstrate. *Handyside*, as discussed above, concerned expression that

---

337 Discussed in Chapter 2, pp 92–96.
338 See pp 464–65.
339 See p 464.
340 See pp 465–67.
341 As discussed, the effect of the doctrine should be irrelevant in the domestic courts since the margin of appreciation doctrine is an international one with no application domestically. See Chapter 2, pp 36–39.
342 See above, pp 467–68.
343 (1994) 19 EHRR 1. See further Chapter 2, p 93.

could be viewed only as a very marginal form of political speech. Mainstream, 'core', political expression, even accompanied by explicit images, could in principle be treated as far more analogous with the expression in *Jersild*, which concerned the broadcast of a programme containing grossly racist language. If this argument were to be accepted, restraints based on offence-avoidance, particularly if applied to such speech, would be found to breach Art 10 as impermissibly over-broad.

Pro-Life Alliance v BBC

This chapter goes on to discuss *R. (on the application of) Pro-Life Alliance v BBC*,[344] in which the taste and decency provisions of the pre-2003 regime were considered against Art 10 standards. The decision is considered at length since it is one of the most significant (and disappointing) post-HRA free speech decisions and has very important implications for the current Ofcom regime. The divergent approaches towards political expression, the effect of the HRA and the stance as to the impact of the taste and decency rules in the House of Lords as compared to that taken by the Court of Appeal make this decision remarkable.

Restraints created by regulation based on maintaining standards of 'taste and decency' are especially problematic in relation to political broadcasting. Many types of political expression in the form of documentaries, discussions, interviews with politicians are broadcast, but the opportunities for political groups to speak directly to television audiences by producing their *own* programmes for broadcasting are very constrained. Political advertising is prohibited in independent broadcasting[345] and the BBC is prohibited from accepting payment in return for broadcasting. Party Political Broadcasts (PPBs) and Party Election Broadcasts (PEBs), transmitted free, are an exception to this rule. These PPBs and PEBs provide the only opportunity for political parties to have access to television to obtain broadcast time for programmes they produce in order to promote their party and their political agenda. But this narrow opportunity for this particular form of political communication is on its face restricted by the taste and decency requirements, which in this instance operate as a *prior* restraint since the broadcasters have the opportunity to reject material or insist on cuts to the proposed broadcast beforehand.

The taste and decency provisions of the BSC Standards Code, the ITC Code and the BBC Agreement applied to all forms of broadcasting expression, including political expression. Therefore PPBs and PEBs were covered (and are still covered under the current regime, as discussed below). This position was endorsed by a document produced jointly by the BBC and the independent broadcasters entitled 'Guidelines for the Production of Party Election Broadcasts' which indicated that PEBs had to comply with the ITC Programme Code and the BBC Producers' Guidelines, 'having regard to the political context of the broadcast'. Paragraph 4 of the BBC *Producers' Guidelines* 'Impartiality and Accuracy', states:

> The content of party political broadcasts, party election broadcasts, and Ministerial broadcasts (together with Opposition replies) is primarily a matter for the originating party or the Government and therefore it is not required to achieve impartiality. The

---

344 [2003] 2 WLR 1403; [2003] 2 All ER 977.
345 Communications Act 2003, ss 319 and 321.

BBC remains responsible for the broadcasts as publisher, however, and requires the parties to observe proper standards of legality, taste and decency.

Paragraph 4.2 of the ITC Programme Code stated:

> Editorial control of the contents of [PPBs and PEBs] normally rests with the originating political party. However, licensees are responsible to the ITC for ensuring that nothing transmitted breaches the Programme Code, notably the requirements on matters of offence to good taste and decency set out in section 1 ... Licensees should issue parties with general guidelines on the acceptability of content ... These guidelines, which are agreed between all relevant broadcasters, are designed to reconcile the editorial standards of the broadcaster, and audience expectations, with the freedom of political parties to convey their political messages.

The Guidelines for the Production of Party Election Broadcasts issued by the broadcasters for the 2001 election stated that PEBs had to comply with the ITC Programme Code and the BBC *Producers' Guidelines* relating to taste and decency and the codes concerning fairness and privacy, 'having regard to the political context of the broadcast'.

The application of these constraints to political broadcasting was challenged in *R (on the application of Pro-Life Alliance) v BBC*.[346] The case arose from a refusal of a PEB by the BBC and independent broadcasters; eventually the House of Lords had to consider the application of the taste and decency provisions to a PEB – the first time that such restraints had been looked at by the senior judiciary. The Pro-Life Alliance is a registered political party which opposes abortion. At the 1997 General Election the applicant put up enough parliamentary candidates to qualify for a party election broadcast. The applicant submitted a video showing, *inter alia*, an abortion being carried out. The broadcasters refused to broadcast the video on the grounds that it offended against good taste and decency and would cause widespread offence. The applicant's application for permission to seek judicial review was refused by Dyson J and by the Court of Appeal, and its application to the European Court of Human Rights was declared inadmissible by the Commission.[347] At the 2001 General Election the applicant put up enough parliamentary candidates to qualify for a PEB[348] in

---

346 [2003] 2 WLR 1403; [2003] 2 All ER 977.

347 See: *R v British Broadcasting Corpn, ex p Pro-Life Alliance Party* (unreported) 24 March 1997; *R v BBC ex p Quintavalle* (1997) 10 Admin LR 425; *Pro-Life Alliance v United Kingdom* (Application No 41869/98) 24 October 2000.

348 Section 36 of the 1990 Act provides that licences for certain descriptions of broadcasters must include 'conditions requiring the licence holder to include party political broadcasts in the licensed service' (subsection (1)(a)) and to observe 'such rules with respect to party political broadcasts as the [ITC] may determine' (subsection (1)(b)). The BBC is not under a formal obligation to offer PPBs or PEBs but has agreed to the same rules of allocation. Section 4 of the ITC Programme Code contains the rules for PPBs and PEBs. PPBs are offered to the major parties in Great Britain (the Labour, Conservative and Liberal Democrat parties and, in Scotland and Wales respectively, the Scottish National Party and Plaid Cymru) at the time of significant events in the political calendar. PEBs are offered at election times. In the 2001 General Election, the major parties were each offered a separate series of PEBs in each of the four nations of the United Kingdom. A smaller party could qualify for a PEB for transmission in the territory of any nation if it fielded candidates in at least one-sixth of its seats. Thus a party could qualify if it put up 88 candidates in England, 12 in Scotland, 6 in Wales,

Wales.[349] The applicant submitted a modified form of the video it had submitted in 1997; it had been edited to remove the most graphic images but still showed aborted foetuses in a mutilated state. The video described the processes involved in different forms of abortion, and included, as Simon Brown LJ put it: 'prolonged and graphic images of the product of suction abortion'. Again, representatives of the broadcasters refused to screen the images as part of the proposed broadcast. They did not raise any objection, however, to the soundtrack proposed. Therefore the Pro-Life Alliance was able to make various anti-abortion points verbally. Eventually a version of the video was submitted by the Alliance and unanimously approved by the broadcasters. It replaced the offending images with a blank screen on which the word 'censored' appeared, and which was accompanied by a sound track describing the images shown in the banned pictures. This version was then broadcast in Wales before the General Election.[350]

The Pro-Life Alliance then applied for permission to seek judicial review of the broadcasters' refusal to broadcast the original version of the video, showing the offending images. The application was dismissed by Scott-Baker J. Like Dyson J, Scott-Baker J held that the broadcasters' decision was not irrational, and the applicant appealed. The challenge was not to s 6(1)(a) of the Broadcasting Act 1990, imposing the requirement to adhere to the taste and decency standards, itself, or the equivalent standards of the BBC's Licencing Agreement, as inconsistent with Art 10 under the HRA; so a declaration of the incompatibility of s 6(1)(a) with Art 10 was not sought under s 4 HRA. (Given that the case was brought against the BBC which was not subject to s 6(1)(a) it is hard to see that a declaration could have been made, in any event. This point was avoided by the judges in the proceedings.) The applicant argued rather that the broadcasters had not properly *applied* those standards, on the basis that they had failed to attach sufficient significance to the electoral context – a context in which freedom of expression was especially crucial.

The Court of Appeal found that under the HRA it itself had to decide whether the censorship (as it put it) in question was justifiable under Art 10(2) of the European Convention. The prohibition of the claimant's PEB was found to be 'prescribed by law' since the broadcasters' obligations arose under the Agreement between the BBC and the Secretary of State and under s 6(1) Broadcasting Act 1990. It was further found that they did not offend against the required standard of legal certainty. The factors of taste, decency and offence were found to be capable of justifying a prohibition upon free expression under Art 10(2) since they could be viewed as aspects of the 'rights of others' – a term that required, it was found, a broad interpretation: the

3 in Northern Ireland. These rules and the fact that abortion is not at present available in Northern Ireland obviously dictated the tactical choice of Wales for the Pro-Life Alliance.

349 The rules governing PEBs, and the fact that abortion is not at present available in Northern Ireland, obviously dictated the tactical choice of Wales for the Pro-Life Alliance since the cost would be far less when the candidates lost their deposits than it would have been had candidates been put up in England. The loss of deposits was almost certainly inevitable in the case of an extremist single-issue party, and in the event all the deposits were duly lost. The six Alliance candidates in Wales received a total of 1,609 votes, or 0.117% of the total votes cast.

350 It may be noted that had the Alliance succeeded in the application discussed below, and put the offending version of the same video forward for broadcasting in the 2005 election campaign, the broadcasters would have had to broadcast it if the Alliance had put up enough candidates to qualify for a PEB.

'rights' were not limited to the Convention rights.[351] In considering the necessity and proportionality of the interference with the freedom of expression of the Alliance and the potential audience, Laws LJ, for the majority, examined the question of deference, considering that 'the degree of deference which the Court would pay to the view of the legislature in imposing requirements of taste and decency, and to the expertise of the broadcasters, depended on the context'. In the context of broadcast *entertainment*, he found, a very high degree of respect to the broadcasters' judgment would be accorded, while the broadcasters' margin of discretion would be only slightly diminished in the context of day-to-day news reporting. However, in the context of a general election the broadcasters' margin, it was found, would be *very* constrained since the court's duty to protect political speech would be viewed as 'over- arching'.[352]

Citing the *Bowman* case,[353] Laws LJ went on to find that under the Strasbourg jurisprudence the state in principle possesses very little discretion to interfere with free political speech, especially at election time. But he acknowledged that a wide margin of appreciation is conceded to states in the context of speech liable to offend against personal moral or religious convictions, on the basis that the signatory states are in such instances at greater liberty to choose between more restrictive or more liberal regimes. Therefore, he went on to find, the national authorities in question can make choices as to the approach to be taken to restrictions on political speech, where such convictions may also be at stake.

He considered that in extreme cases concerns regarding taste and decency might prevail even over political speech, but found that this was not the case in the instance before him. Such an instance might, he found, involve factors of gratuitous sensationalism and dishonesty, rather than the mere promulgation of graphic and disturbing images. Having decided that gratuitous sensationalism was not present, Laws LJ found that considerations of taste and decency could not prevail over freedom of speech by a political party at election time, except wholly exceptionally – and this instance did not, he found, require an exception to be made. Very little deference to the broadcasters' expertise and experience was accorded by the court.[354] A declaration was made that the BBC's refusal to broadcast the Pro-Life Alliance's party election broadcast was unlawful.

But this was a seminal free speech ruling. It was entirely consistent with the argument expressed at the beginning of this chapter, that content-based regulatory schemes tend to run counter to free speech rationales. It was a principled ruling that looked closely at the importance of the type of speech in question and found that flexibility had to be imposed on the regulatory scheme in order to accommodate it. Taking account of the high value of the speech, it found that it could not be treated in a monolithic fashion, despite the fact that the regulatory scheme implied that it could. It rejected the idea of deference to a regulator where speech of this nature was in question.

---

351 *Muller v Switzerland* (1988) 13 EHRR 212; *VGT v Switzerland* (2002) 34 EHRR 159 and *Chapman v UK* (2001) 33 EHRR 399 applied.
352 Para H7 4.
353 *Bowman v UK* (1998) 26 EHRR 1.
354 For discussion and criticism of this decision, see: Geddis, A, 'What Future For Political Advertising on The United Kingdom's Television Screens?' [2002] PL 615. See also Rowbottom, J, 'Freedom of Expression in Election Campaigns' (2002) 152 New Law Journal 679.

When the BBC appealed to the House of Lords[355] the majority in the Lords considered that the Court of Appeal decision amounted to a finding that the taste and decency standards should not be applied to Party Election Broadcasts. However, they found that Parliament had decided that such broadcasts should not be exempt from those standards – despite the importance of free speech at such times – and that decision of Parliament as encapsulated in the Broadcasting Acts 1990 and 1996 (in respect of both the ITC and BSC)[356] had not itself been challenged – although it could have been, under ss 3(1) and 4 HRA. Thus, according to the majority in the Lords, once it was accepted that those standards should be applied to PEBs, the question was whether the broadcasters had applied them wrongly. That did not appear to be the case on the facts, bearing in mind the clear findings of expert broadcasters; and in giving weight to their views the Lords made it clear that a degree of deference should be accorded to the broadcasters on the basis that, due to their audience research, they were likely to be thoroughly in touch with audience expectations.

Lord Nicholls of Birkenhead and Lord Hoffmann, who gave the leading speeches, considered the scope of the application of Art 10 in the context in question. Whereas the Court of Appeal had treated the BBC's findings as censorship, both agreed that Art 10 does not provide an entitlement to make television broadcasts: it provides, they found, a right to expression, but not a right to have access to a particular medium – broadcasting – in order to exercise that right.[357] However, a right to broadcast a PEB had already been provided by the relevant legislation to those who qualified. Therefore, Lord Nicholls found:

> the principle underlying article 10 requires that access to an important public medium of communication should not be refused on discriminatory, arbitrary or unreasonable grounds . . . or . . . granted subject to discriminatory, arbitrary or unreasonable conditions.[358]

Both accepted that a restriction on the content of a PEB had to be justified under Art 10(2). They also accepted that this was a particularly pressing matter in relation to political communication at election time, especially where, as in the instant case, the restriction operated as a prior restraint.[359]

In relation to the question of justification Lord Nicholls considered that two questions appeared, at first glance, to arise. First, he asked whether the content of party broadcasts should be subject to the same restriction on offensive material as other programmes. He said that, clearly, this was the case since the statutory and non-statutory regimes in question demanded that they should be. (In fact, it is suggested that questions could

---

355 [2004] 1 AC 185; [2003] 2 All ER 977.
356 Section 108 of the 1996 Act relating to the standards Code of the Broadcasting Standards Commission was relevant, but the discussion as to the effect of s 3(1) HRA focused on s 6(1)(a) of the 1990 Act.
357 See para 8 of the judgment. See also the decisions of the European Commission of Human Rights in *X and the Association of Z v United Kingdom* (1971) 38 CD 86; *Haider v Austria* 83-A DR 66; *Huggett v United Kingdom* 82-A DR 98.
358 Para 8 of the judgment.
359 The BSC and ITC operated, as explained above, by way of *subsequent* restraint only in relation to matters of taste and decency, arising in contexts outside the PEB one, and this continues to be the case under the 2003 Ofcom regime.

be raised about the legal status of the non-statutory BBC regime in relation to the HRA – a matter that all the judges decided not to consider, making the assumption that nothing turned on the distinction between the two regimes. This matter is returned to below.) He found that in considering this question at all, the Court of Appeal had fallen into error:

> The flaw in this broad approach is that it amounts to rewriting, in the context of party broadcasts, the content of the offensive material restriction imposed by Parliament on broadcasters. It means that an avowed challenge to the broadcasters' decisions became a challenge to the appropriateness of imposing the offensive material restriction on party broadcasts . . . this was not an issue in these proceedings.[360]

He said that the Court of Appeal had 'carried out its own balancing exercise between the requirements of freedom of political speech and the protection of the public from being unduly distressed in their own homes', but that the Court had done so illegitimately since Parliament had already decided where the balance should be struck. The second question was whether, on the basis that the restrictions applied, the broadcasters had applied the right standards in the instant case.

So the only pertinent question to consider, in Lord Nicholls' view, was the second one. In viewing the matter in this way, however, he ignored the effect of s 3(1) HRA. The judges themselves are under an obligation to render legislative provisions compatible with the Convention; whether the applicant had challenged the provision itself or not should therefore have been viewed as irrelevant. It is argued that there were in fact *three* questions to be answered; the second one should have concerned the proper interpretation, in the light of Art 10, of the taste and decency provisions when applied to political communication. It could have been argued that they should have been given a narrow interpretation in that context, under s 3(1) HRA in relation to the demands of Art 10, and then the third question would have been whether the broadcasters had correctly applied those standards once they had been subjected to that more narrow interpretation.

Lord Nicholls assumed impliedly that there was no need to consider the effect of s 3(1) since the Pro-Life Alliance had accepted that the taste and decency regimes were not incompatible with its Art 10 right. Therefore he considered that the Court of Appeal had been wrong to find that the regimes could only rarely and exceptionally be relied upon in censoring a PEB. Lord Hoffmann, however, did examine the question of the interpretation of the statutory (and, by implication, the non-statutory) rules. He considered that the thrust of the applicant's submissions, which the Court of Appeal had been receptive to, was that the statute should be 'disregarded' or taken lightly. However, it must be pointed out that the application of s 3(1) HRA to a statute, narrowing, if necessary, the meaning of a provision in order to achieve compliance with the Convention, does not amount to *disregarding* it. Lord Hoffmann was the only judge who considered the compatibility of Art 10 with the taste and decency rules; he considered that despite its apparent stance on compatibility in relation to s 4 HRA, this was really the gravemen of the Pro-Life Alliance argument. He agreed with Lord

---

360 Para 15.

Nicholls in finding that Art 10 does not provide a right of access to the broadcast media, relying on *Haider v Austria*.[361] In that instance the Commission had found:

> The Commission recalls that article 10 of the Convention cannot be taken to include a general and unfettered right for any private citizen or organisation to have access to broadcasting time on radio or television in order to forward his opinion, save under exceptional circumstances, for instance if one political party is excluded from broadcasting facilities at election time while other parties are given broadcasting time.

Lord Hoffmann found that under Art 10, 'The emphasis, therefore, is on the right not to be denied access on discriminatory grounds,'[362] not on a right to broadcast. He considered whether the Strasbourg jurisprudence would require the taste and decency requirement to be regarded as unreasonable or discriminatory. Pro-Life Alliance was claiming that the requirements did not operate as 'neutral' or non-discriminatory restrictions. They applied, on their face, to all PEBs of any party, but the Pro-Life Alliance wished to express a particular message which, it claimed, had to be presented visually in order to depict the reality of abortion and therefore to arouse people against it. It inevitably breached the rules which therefore, it claimed, bore unfairly upon it alone since it was unable to present its political message in its chosen manner. On this basis it may be noted that the taste and decency rules could be viewed as discriminatory in relation not only to the Alliance PEB, but potentially in relation to any PEB dependent on visual material likely to cause offence.

Lord Hoffmann accepted that the rules had a prima facie discriminatory effect. So the next question was whether they could be objectively justified. In considering this matter, Lord Hoffmann analysed the proportionality of the restrictions in relation to the political value of the Alliance PEB. He noted that the broadcast time allocation for PEBs had been introduced in order to further informed choice in general elections. However, he found that the Pro-Life Alliance message was not related to making such a choice since abortion is not a party political issue in the UK. In his view the message was significant only in relation to the six Welsh constituencies in which the party's candidates were standing since, having seen the broadcast, the electorate in those constituencies could have chosen to vote for those candidates. Therefore the value and significance of the PEB was limited if considered in the context of the purpose behind providing for PEBs in general. That limited value then had to be weighed up, he said, against the right of viewers of broadcasts not to be shocked and offended in the privacy of their homes. It was, he considered, legitimate for Parliament to lay down certain conditions governing PEBs to protect those viewers' rights.

He noted that in *VGT Verein gegen Tierfabriken v Switzerland*,[363] in which a ban on political advertising was found to be discriminatory, the European Court had made it clear that it was not considering a case in which the objection to an advertisement was that its content was offensive. He also considered the response of the Court to the

---

361 (1995) 83-A DR 66.
362 At para 61.
363 34 EHRR 159, at para 76, p 177.

complaint of the Alliance about the previous rejection of its PEB in the 1997 election. The Registrar of the Court had written to the Alliance, stating: 'in accordance with the general instructions received from the court' he drew their attention to 'certain shortcomings' in the application. The indication given by the Registrar was that the Court might consider that the taste and decency requirements were not an 'arbitrary or unreasonable' interference with the access of the Alliance to television. The Court then rejected the application as inadmissible as not disclosing 'any appearance of a violation of the rights and freedoms set out in the Convention . . .'. Lord Hoffmann concluded therefore that there 'is no public interest in exempting PEBs from the taste and decency requirements on the ground that their message requires them to broadcast offensive material.'[364]

Thus Lords Nicholl and Hoffmann came to the same conclusion – that the only significant question was whether the broadcasters had applied the 'taste and decency' rules correctly. Having arrived at that finding, with which Lords Millett and Walker agreed, the outcome of the case became virtually inevitable. Once Lord Nicholls had configured the issue as indicated he found that it resolved itself into one question only: 'should the court, in the exercise of its supervisory role, interfere with the broadcasters' decisions that the offensive material restriction precluded them from transmitting the programme proposed by Pro-Life Alliance?' He answered this question by considering the broadcasters' decision and went on to find that the broadcasters' application of the statutory criteria was not at fault. He noted that the broadcasters would have accepted that some images of abortion could be included to convey the message, but that the images put forward were too graphic and prolonged. The BBC representative had stated: 'What is unacceptable in your client's broadcast is the cumulative effect of several minutes primarily devoted to such images.' The broadcasters had, Lord Nicholls found, applied an appropriate standard in assessing the question whether transmission of the images in question would be likely to cause offence to viewers. In other words, if the only matter at issue was the application by the broadcasters of the statutory criteria, not the *interpretation* of those criteria, then it appeared that the broadcasters had taken the correct stance.

Lord Hoffmann arrived at the same conclusion. Having found that Parliament was entitled to impose standards of taste and decency which were 'meant to be taken seriously', he went on to consider the application of those standards by the broadcasters. In considering the standards applied he rejected the idea that they could be 'a matter of intuition on the part of elderly male judges' and took into account the expertise of the broadcasters and the audience research they had conducted.[365] He also took account of the feelings of women who had had abortions who might have viewed the PEB inadvertently. He found that the broadcasters were well placed to determine whether members of the public would be likely to find the images offensive, and that they had found that the images did not fall at the margin of acceptability, but well below it. He therefore accepted that the broadcasters' decision should not be interfered with. So the appeal of the BBC was allowed.

364 At para 73.
365 Paras 78–80.

It is argued that the majority judges in the House of Lords failed to apply the Art 10 correctly because the effect of s 3(1) HRA was misunderstood. The striking thing about their ruling was the extraordinarily contorted reasoning; the Lords assumed that Pro-Life was challenging the statute itself – seeking to set it aside. Section 3(1)'s very function is to create compatibility with the Convention rights and, as discussed, this would not have involved damaging the statute, let alone setting it aside.

The outcome would also have been the same had the House of Lords accepted that s 3(1) *could* be used to narrow down the rules, but come to the conclusion that the Strasbourg jurisprudence did not require that the broadcasters' decision should be declared unlawful. It could have been argued that the effect of s 3(1) HRA would depend on the application of the tests of proportionality and necessity under Art 10(2) in relation to the conditions applied to the Alliance's PEB. (The argument that there is no right to broadcast air-time under Art 10(1) is irrelevant since the Alliance had already qualified for a PEB.) Lord Hoffmann appeared to be of the view that the jurisprudence gave little support to the Alliance's claim, although he did not make it clear that his argument was linked to the potential effect of s 3(1). He made two points in relation to his proportionality argument. The first was that the value of political expression in this instance was limited.[366] This argument has been roundly condemned by two of the academics who have commented on the House of Lords' decision[367] and, although it was argued that the Court of Appeal decision makes more 'appeal to rhetoric than to reason',[368] its findings on the matter were preferred. The applicant's video was a form of political communication and therefore still of particular significance in Art 10 terms. Where Lord Hoffmann fell into error, it is argued, was in his dismissal of the speech in question as of limited value. It remained a form of highly significant political expression, partly due to its very nature, and partly due to the less central election-related values underlying it. Therefore there was a strong case for narrowing down the taste and decency rules where they led to a restriction on such expression. This was the case that the majority in the House of Lords failed to acknowledge,[369] while at the same time Laws LJ in the Court of Appeal arguably over-stated it.

---

366 Note that this concern was raised in a report published in 2003: *Party Political Broadcasting: Report and Recommendations*, by the Electoral Commission. It considered that there was a case for deterring organisations from fielding candidates so as to qualify for a PEB for their own publicity purposes rather than for genuine electoral purposes. Lord Hoffmann also noted this concern in *Pro-Life Alliance v BBC* [2004] 1 AC 185, at para 35.

367 See: Barendt, E, 'Free Speech and Abortion' 2003] PL 580–91 and Hare, I, 'Debating Abortion – the Right to offend Gratuitously' [2003] 62(3) CLJ 525–28. Rowbottom, J, 'Article 10 and Election Broadcasts' [2003] 119 LQR 553–57 favours the House of Lords' approach. MacDonald, A's analysis appears to favour the stance of the House of Lords, but concentrates on the general issue of 'the role, if any, of judicial "deference" in a democratic constitution': *R (on the application of Pro-Life Alliance v BBC* 6 EHRLR 651–57. Geddis, A, 'If Thy Right Eye Offend Thee, Pluck it Out' [2003] 66 MLR 885–93 strongly favours the House of Lords' approach and attacked that of the Court of Appeal in 'What future for political advertising on the UK's television screens?' [2002] PL 615.

368 Hare, I, ibid at p 527.

369 Lord Hoffmann touched on this point, but did not, it is argued, give enough weight to political speech. He appeared to take the stance that even political speech of the highest value could be restricted or banned in response to the application of taste and decency rules: 'Even assuming that the Alliance broadcast had been an ordinary PEB, relevant to the general election, I do not think it would have been unreasonable to require it to comply with standards of taste and decency' (para 70).

Lord Hoffmann's second point was linked to his first. He found that Strasbourg endorsed his view that the form of political expression in question was of low value, meaning that interferences with it could readily be justified. In coming to this conclusion he relied most strongly on the adverse Strasbourg admissibility decision against the Alliance in respect of their 1997 video.[370] (In strong contrast, the Court of Appeal made little attempt to engage with the relevant jurisprudence, deciding the case largely on the basis of common law free speech principles.) Lord Hoffmann did not take account of the less offensive nature of the 2001 video and, more importantly, ignored the impact of the margin of appreciation doctrine on the jurisprudence, and the fact that under s 2 HRA it is non-binding. The failure to deal with the impact of the margin of appreciation doctrine was most significant. As argued elsewhere in this book, the stance of the UK judiciary in relation to the implications of the effects of this doctrine amounts to one of their most significant failures in confronting the application of the HRA.[371] The line of cases stemming from *Handyside*[372] is deeply affected by this doctrine, which is not applicable at the national level. Therefore the admissibility decision relied upon by Lord Hoffmann should have been applied – as far as that is possible – after stripping away the effects of the doctrine upon it. Since it was a decision upon admissibility alone, the decision would have been rendered almost an empty one once that process had been undertaken. It may be noted that the Court of Appeal accepted – correctly – that this admissibility decision was non-determinative of the issue before it. Had the Lords taken that stance that would have left the judges with little guidance as to the Strasbourg stance on the matter, except from the *Handyside* line of authority and from general Strasbourg free speech principles.

Lord Hoffmann noted that *VGT Verein gegen Tierfabriken v Switzerland*,[373] in which a breach of Art 10 was found in relation to discrimination in allocation of broadcast time, did not deal with an instance in which the objection to an advertisement was that its content was offensive. However, that left the point at issue open. Therefore the general principle from *Handyside* should have been applied, bearing in mind that *Handyside* was itself to an extent in point in relation to the instant case. It dealt with speech that could be termed political, if that term is broadly interpreted, including information about abortion, taking impliedly a pro-abortion stance. The book in question in *Handyside* informed children and teenagers about matters related to sexuality, and its implicit message could be viewed as a liberal one. As discussed above, the Court took a strong stance in favour of offensive speech under Art 10(1) but then applied the tests of necessity and proportionality under Art 10(2) in a manner that was heavily influenced by the margin of appreciation doctrine. If the influence of that doctrine on the decision was to be disapplied at the domestic level, the decision could be taken to endorse a very restricted role for rules aimed at avoidance of offence in relation to semi-political speech. *A fortiori* the decision would endorse such a role in relation to political speech of *higher* value – as in the *Pro-Life Alliance* case.[374]

370 *Pro-Life Alliance v United Kingdom* (Application No 41869/98) 24 October 2000.
371 See Chapter 4 pp 263–65, 270–72.
372 Eur Ct HR, A 24; (1976) 1 EHRR 737. See pp 465–67.
373 34 EHRR 159, at para 76, p 177.
374 See further on these points Part II, pp 309–10.

Therefore, if the effects on the findings of the margin of appreciation doctrine could have been disapplied, *Handyside* would arguably favour a stance closer to that of the Court of Appeal than that of the House of Lords, although whether, bearing in mind the view taken by the BBC of the gravity of the offence that would be caused by the video, it could have supported the findings of the Court of Appeal as to the *outcome*, is debatable. It is concluded that the treatment of the Strasbourg jurisprudence in both the House of Lords and Court of Appeal was flawed: Lord Hoffmann did not take account of the effects of the margin of appreciation doctrine and severely under-stated the value placed by Strasbourg on speech in general and political speech in particular, while the Court of Appeal failed to analyse the implications of the jurisprudence relating to such speech, choosing instead to rely on more familiar common law principles.

The House of Lords' judgment does nothing to mitigate the dangers of content-based regulatory schemes in free speech terms, discussed at the beginning of this chapter. In this instance all the free rationales were engaged in relation to Pro-Life itself as a speaker and in relation to the audience. Lord Hoffmann's key point was that deference should be paid to the expertise of the regulator, as well as to Parliament. Presumably, therefore, even if he had explicitly rejected the effects of the margin of appreciation doctrine on Strasbourg jurisprudence, he would still have been wedded to a domestic doctrine of deference. But it is argued that the notion of deferring to a regulator needs to be unpacked. Regulators have expertise as to matters of fact and can also give expert opinions. In this instance the regulator – the BBC – had expertise as to accepted standards of taste and decency in broadcasting and therefore as to audience expectations. Therefore it was entitled to take the stance that the Pro-Life video infringed those standards and it was reasonable for the Court to defer to those findings. But the regulator did not have expertise in *balancing* the concerns relating to taste and decency against free speech. That was a normative exercise for the court, basing itself on Strasbourg principles. It is precisely the role of the courts to conduct that balancing exercise under Art 10(2) between the right to freedom of expression and societal concerns. Lord Hoffmann fudged the issue – he elided the issue of deference on the basis of expert findings with the question of balancing those findings against free speech demands. Lord Hoffmann made much also of deference to Parliament, but Parliament had enacted not only s 6(1)(a) of the 1990 Act, but also the HRA and had placed a responsibility on the judges to abide by the Convention rights, under s 6. Lord Hoffmann appeared almost to abrogate his responsibility as a judge to conduct the necessary balancing exercise. His motivation appeared to be a determination to avoid subjecting a regulator's decision to a real, systematic Strasbourg scrutiny.[375]

Leaving aside the *Pro-Life Alliance* decision, it would have appeared to follow from the Strasbourg free speech principles, and ss 3 and 6 HRA, that the Ofcom regulatory regime upholding offence-avoidance standards might have been found to conflict with the standards maintained by Art 10 in the realm of political speech. However, the decision now appears to render improbable a successful challenge to the current regime governing offence-avoidance.

---

375 For further criticism of Lord Hoffmann's findings on deference in this instance, see Lord Steyn, 'Deference is a tangled web' (2005) PL 346–59.

The appeal of the BBC in the *Pro-Life Alliance* case was allowed on the basis that there was no ground for interfering with the decision reached by the BBC as regulator and the broadcasters, taking account of their special expertise. The outcome means that the broadcasters' freedom within that particular statutory framework - which in essence is now encapsulated in s 319 of the 2003 Act – was re-affirmed. The HRA did not operate as a mechanism enabling the courts to wield (or claim) significantly greater powers of interference in broadcasters' decisions as to their responsibilities in respect of maintaining standards of taste and decency – even in respect of political speech. The same stance is now likely to be taken in respect of the current statutory framework if a similar case arises.

If, for example, an independent broadcaster wished to broadcast a documentary which relied on very disturbing, explicit images from a war or disaster zone, but it was clear from Ofcom's Code that so doing would be likely to attract a financial penalty, the broadcaster could, as a last resort, mount a challenge under Art 10 against Ofcom, relying on s 7(1)(a) HRA. The *Pro-Life Alliance* decision, however, suggests that such a challenge would be unlikely to succeed due to the high level of deference conceded to the expert regulator, and therefore indirectly to Parliament.

Successful challenges to the current regulatory regime?

Nevertheless, successful HRA challenges to the current regime under the 2003 Act are conceivable, despite the *Pro-Life* decision. A claim could occur in relation to any form of broadcasting affected by the offence-avoidance Ofcom Code rules, but clearly it would be most likely to succeed in the context of political broadcasting. It is nevertheless important to point out that the following remarks could also apply to, for example, films of strong artistic merit if the relevant Art 10 jurisprudence was applied, but the effects of the margin of appreciation doctrine were disapplied,[376] when applied at the domestic level. Thus while the strongest impetus for change could come in the realm of political expression, it is not ruled out in relation to other forms.

A departure from the *Pro-Life Alliance* decision could come about if a case on a similar factual basis arose but the challenge was to the new statutory framework itself – specifically on s 319 – as requiring re-interpretation under s 3(1) HRA in order to achieve compatibility with the demands of Art 10. The decision in *Pro-Life Alliance* does not stand in the way of such a reinterpretation since the House of Lords deliberately considered only the application of the statutory provisions and not the provisions themselves.[377] The 2003 Act does not exempt PEBs from the s 319 requirements or the Ofcom Code, which applies to all forms of broadcasting. Thus, post-HRA Parliament did make the deliberate decision to continue to subject PEBs to the offence-avoidance requirements. Courts will inevitably consider that they should pay some deference to that decision, following *Pro-Life*. Nevertheless, the majority in the House of Lords left open the possibility that a challenge to the equivalent provisions under the previous regime might have succeeded. It may be noted that, as discussed above, the 2003 Act was *not*

---

376   As discussed above, a case can be made for arguing that comments of the Strasbourg Court support forms of artistic expression quite strongly. See pp 465–68.

377   If a challenge was mounted to the application of the rules themselves the outcome would probably be the same as in *Pro-Life* unless the decision to ban an election video was a far more marginal one.

declared compatible with the Convention rights under s 19 HRA.[378] However, it can be assumed that the rest of the Act was viewed by Parliament as compatible with Art 10 and therefore it should be treated in the same way as any other Act of Parliament.[379]

Section 3(1) HRA could be used to impose a different interpretation on s 319, reducing its impact quite dramatically in relation to PEBs or other forms of political broadcasting. As a result, where such forms were concerned, quite a radical modification of ss 1 and 2 of Ofcom's Code could be brought about by interpretation. The demands of offence-avoidance as a standards objective could be minimised in the context of political broadcasting. Such a modification may be possible since, although s 319 does cover PEBs, it is more nuanced and goes into more detail regarding context and audience expectations than s 6(1)(a) of the 1990 Act or s 108 of the 1996 Act did. Such matters were only taken into account previously by the ITC Programme Code and the BSC Standards Code. Section 319(4)(a) – (d) could be viewed as a gateway to allowing the radical re-interpretation suggested. For example, the term 'generally accepted standards' used in s 319(f) in relation to the protection of the public from 'offensive material' could be interpreted to mean that greater leeway should be accorded to PEBs since such standards can be assumed to accord particular weight to the nontramelling of political expression. The comments of the Court of Appeal in *Pro-Life* as to the greater public tolerance of controversial and explicit images in the context of serious political speech should be borne in mind. There is a case for limited deference to Parliament here since the re-interpretation argued for would not go against the grain of the statute or necessitate reading words into it, and the question of balancing the societal interest in maintaining standards of decency in broadcasting against the demands of free speech is very much one within the Courts' constitutional sphere under the HRA.[380]

Such a re-intepretation of s 319(f), and the resultant effect on ss 1 and 2 of the Code, could also affect other forms of political broadcasting. Such a result would in one sense enhance the freedom of broadcasters since it would widen choice as to what could be shown in documentaries, discussion programmes, etc. In relation to PEBs it would tend to remove some control from their hands in relation to their interpretation of their responsibilities and place it in the hands of the courts. Challenging and explicit images could be shown, if justified by context. A more effective representation of a plurality of views, including the views of minority groups, in broadcasting might occur.[381]

EU-based satellite broadcasting

In the 1990s, the regulatory regime controlling broadcasting was confronted with the dissemination of material by methods which seemed to fall outside its compass since

---

378 As noted earlier, the lack of a declaration was due to the view taken that s 321(2) (the ban on political advertising) was incompatible with Art 10. This decision was based on the decision of the ECHR in *VGT v Switzerland* [2001] ECHR 408.

379 Indeed, it is argued that the lack of a statement of compatibility under s 19(1)(b) HRA has no effect on the ability of judges to seek to achieve compatibility under s 3(1) in relation to s 321(2)).

380 See for discussion of the use of s 3, Chapter 4, pp 174–91.

381 As a further resort, there would also be the possibility of issuing a declaration of the incompatibility under s 4 HRA between Art 10 and s 319. Amendment in relation to PEBs might then come about in reliance on the s 10 procedure.

the material originated from outside the UK, but could be accessed from within it. The concern was that obscene or indecent material would be disseminated by non-terrestrial broadcasters outside the jurisdiction of the UK. The difficulties of attempting to regulate material when it is transmitted by these means, since it is outside the regulatory regime for broadcasting, are discussed below. EU-based satellite broadcasting created particular difficulties, in the view of the government, difficulties that, it will be argued, are currently being evaded rather than resolved.

The ITC Code did not apply to broadcasters who were not licence holders of the ITC. Under s 43 of the 1990 Act, a satellite service was required to hold an ITC licence if it was a 'domestic satellite service' or a 'non-domestic satellite service'. A domestic service was defined as one that used direct broadcasting by satellite on one of the five frequencies allocated to the UK at the World Administrative Radio Conference in 1977. A non-domestic satellite service was one which either used a lower powered satellite to transmit programmes from the UK or transmitted from outside the territory of prescribed countries, but a UK supplier dictated the service. 'Non-domestic' satellite services were not subject to the same regime as domestic services in the sense that they had to transmit on allocated frequencies and had public service responsibilities.

If a service is licensed from within an EU member state, it must receive freedom of reception within other member states under the EU Directive on Transfrontier Television, *Television without Frontiers* (89/552/EEC). In *Commission of EC v UK*[382] it was found that s 43 of the Broadcasting Act 1990 applied different regimes to domestic and non-domestic satellite services and that in exercising control over certain broadcasters falling under the jurisdiction of other member states, the UK had failed to fulfil its obligations under Arts 2(1), (2) and 3(2) of the Directive. Thus, in 1997, the distinction between domestic and non-domestic services was abolished: only one category was created – satellite television services.[383] Section 89 of the Broadcasting Act 1996 amended s 45 of the 1990 Act to allow for the immediate revocation of the licence of a satellite television service which breached s 6(1)(a) of the 1990 Act. These sections in both statutes were repealed by the Communications Act 2003. Under ss 232–40 of the 2003 Act satellite services are 'television licensable content services'. That term replaces the separate categories of satellite television services and licensable programme services which were established under the Broadcasting Act 1990, as amended.

But satellite services licensed from within another EU member state are not licensable services and are not therefore covered by Ofcom's broadcast Code. Therefore material that might infringe the Code, particularly 'hardcore' pornography, could be received in the UK via EU satellite broadcasting. The solution adopted in the Broadcasting Act 1990 was to allow for the proscription of such material. The government took the view in the 1990s that although such material was available in other EU countries, it should not be available in the UK. It appeared at the time that the use of proscription would not infringe EU law. Directive 89/552 was amended by Directive 97/36 to provide that member states must not restrict retransmissions on their territory of broadcasts from other member states for reasons within the fields co-ordinated by the Directive, but it

382 Case 222/94 [1996] ECR-I 4025.
383 Satellite Television Service Regulations 1997 SI 1997/1682. Further amendment was made under the Television Broadcasting Regulations 1998 SI 1998/3196.

allowed them to derogate provisionally from the obligation to allow the free movement of broadcasts where a broadcast 'manifestly, seriously and gravely' infringes Art 22 and/or Art 22a. Article 22 allows for restrictions where programmes might 'seriously impair the physical, mental or moral development of minors'. This is not confined to their violent or sexual content, and individual nations have a wide margin of discretion in relation to such matters.

Proscription orders are made under ss 177 and 178 of the 1990 Act.[384] Proscribing a channel is not, formally speaking, a means of banning it. When a channel is proscribed it becomes an offence for it to advertise in the UK or to supply (or offer to supply) any decoding equipment primarily for the purpose of enabling the reception of the proscribed service within the UK. Proscription therefore does not prevent the channel from broadcasting, but in practical terms it means that UK citizens are unable to access it. Once the television service in question has been drawn to the attention of the Secretary of State he or she can only make an order if satisfied that it is in the public interest and compatible with any international obligations of the UK (s 177(3)). Section 177 was not repealed by the 2003 Act and the ITC's role in this respect has now been taken over by Ofcom. Under s 177 of the 1990 Act; the ITC could draw 'unacceptable' foreign satellite services to the attention of the Secretary of State if satisfied that 'there is repeatedly contained on programmes included in the service matter which offends against good taste and decency or is likely to . . . be offensive to public feeling'. This procedure was thought to be allowed for by Art 2a of the *Television without Frontiers* Directive. Under s 177 the National Heritage Secretary has issued a number of proscription orders against satellite channels from EU member states which beam 'hard core' pornography into Britain. Channels proscribed have included *Eurotic Rendez-vous* in 1999 and *Eros TV* in 1998.[385] But proscription orders have not been issued since 2000, and this is probably due to their doubtful compatibility with EU law.

So far, the question whether proscription orders breach EU law has not been addressed by the European Court of Justice. Article 22 presupposes that there is a reasonable likelihood that minors would be affected, and it is arguable that the likelihood is minimal. Thus it seems possible that a breach would be found, taking account of the wording of Art 2a, since children would be highly unlikely to be exposed to the broadcast of hard core pornography due to recent advances in technology. Channels can be digitally encrypted and scrambled so that non-subscribers are unable to view any signal. It is possible to PIN-protect channels to prevent unauthorised access.[386] Adult supervision of the equipment provides a further level of protection. Where the service is transmitted very late at night and accessible only by using a smart card

---

384 Note that ss 329–32 of the 2003 Act allow for the use of proscription orders by the Secretary of State at the instigation of Ofcom, but not against satellite broadcasts.
385 See *R v Secretary of State for Culture Media and Sport ex p Danish Satellite TV* 9.7.99 (CD) in which the Court of Appeal held that the Secretary of State was entitled to proscribe the service *Eurotic Rendez-vous*; it was found that the order was based on the protection of minors and not on wider grounds. Some of the images shown on the service were so explicit that if shown in the cinematic or video release of a film, an R18 certificate would not have been granted (see below pp 553–54). *Eros TV* was proscribed under SI 1998 No 1865.
386 The most recent Sky systems have PIN-protection by default on adult channels, as does Telewest; the PIN can be automatically disabled after three failed attempts at access.

– as was the case in respect of *Eurotic Rendez-vous* – it seems to be improbable that children would be affected. The provisions relating to the protection for children under the Directive are likely in themselves to be amended in 2005 in the light of such technological developments.[387]

At present the evidence that children would be harmed to any significant extent if they were exposed to hardcore material is inconclusive.[388] This was high-lighted by the High Court ruling in 2000 in *R v Video Appeals Committee of the BBFC ex p BBFC*,[389] discussed below; the BBFC lost their judicial review in relation to the promulgation of hard core material on videos largely because they had not provided cogent evidence of any harm to children caused by such material. That decision led to the relaxation of BBFC Guidelines in relation to videos. Since hard core material is now legally on sale under the 'R18' classification, DVDs and videos from more than 120 licensed sex shops in the UK, the claim by the government that such material would seriously impair the development of children would probably fail in the European Court of Justice. Its availability from UK shops means that the risk that children might view hard core videos cannot be entirely ruled out. It is also hard to sustain the argument that greater protection should be available for children in the UK than in other parts of the EU. The Italian hard core channel *Satisfaction TV* was recommended for proscription by the ITC in December 2000. However, no proscription order has yet been raised. In itself this is telling since if harm to children was genuinely likely it would not appear to be acceptable to delay the order. It is also notable that the old notion of maintaining 'taste and decency' is applied as the basis for raising proscription orders, while domestic services are subject to the current apparently less stringent offence-avoidance standard, under the 2003 Act, as discussed above. Since the legalisation of hard core material on the BBFC 'R18' video classification in 2000 the government appears to have abandoned proscription of foreign satellite channels. The government presumably has concerns that using an order would breach EU law, in the light of the factors identified.

The possibility that some proscription orders may be incompatible with Art 10 under the HRA should be considered. The protection of children is a significant theme running through the Convention explicit expression cases discussed in this chapter,[390] and restrictions on such expression tend to be readily justified under Art 10(2) at the Strasbourg level. It is theoretically possible for the domestic courts to apply a strict proportionality analysis in this context, which Strasbourg has never done due to the effects of the margin of appreciation doctrine. This is possible since the domestic courts are not bound by that doctrine. However, as discussed above, this need not be the case at the domestic level if the requirements of proportionality are applied absent the effects on them of the margin of appreciation doctrine. It could be argued that the restriction created by a proscription order was disproportionate to the harm to be avoided since the risk to children appeared to be minimal. It would arguably be

---

387   Commission: Second Evaluation Report on the application of Council Recommendation of 24 Sept 1998 concerning the protection of minors and human dignity. COM (2003) 776 final (12.12.2003).

388   See BBFC News Release 26 Oct 2000, *Abused children most at risk from pornography*, below, p 565 fn 439.

389   (2000) EMLR 850. See pp 564–65 below.

390   See eg *Müller v Switzerland* (1991) 13 EHRR 212; *Scherer* A 287 (1993) Com Rep; for discussion, see above pp 465–66.

acceptable under Art 10 to distinguish between modern satellite subscription services under which viewing is very restricted, and open to air broadcasts where any viewer can access any programme. The rights of others to be protected from offence under Art 10(2) would be only minimally at stake due to the impact of such restrictions.

Conclusions

The discussion above suggests that a number of matters should have been addressed with greater clarity under the 2003 reforms. Over the last 15 years' broadcasting content regulation has moved from a system based on censorship under the IBA, to one based on post-transmission sanctions reflecting standards of taste and decency under the ITC and BSC, to the use of such sanctions to ensure offence avoidance and to protect minors, under Ofcom. The vexed question as to the basic standard to be used in relation to material aimed at adults was left open by the 2003 Act and, as discussed, it is still largely unanswered, despite the promulgation of the new Code. The current controls over broadcasting appear to be aimed more at preserving market rather than creative freedom. Their tendency is to make for cautious rather than explorative and challenging broadcasting.

When the power of the owners of the television companies to influence the nature of broadcasting is compared with that of the media regulators or of the public service broadcasters, a human rights scheme in which the exercise of the powers of the latter, but not the former, can be challenged on free expression grounds looks fundamentally flawed. There is clearly a mismatch between the areas in which the HRA can intervene and the location of the main influences over the medium of most significance in terms of its cultural and opinion-forming impact. But the impact of the HRA on broadcasting is unlikely to be radical. This is in part because the regulatory regime already adheres to free expression principles in a reasonably comprehensive and advanced fashion. Nevertheless, this chapter has described quite significant restraints to avoid causing offence contained in Ofcom's Code and the 2003 Act. Currently broadcast material is subject both to special regulation in terms of a regime based on warnings, and use of the 'watershed', and *also* to restraint which in effect amounts to a form of censorship since the broadcasters must exercise self-censorship in order to adhere to the offence-avoidance aspects of Ofcom's Code. Despite quite significant liberalisation relative to the old ITC and BSC Codes, the new Code is potentially quite restrictive in certain respects, depending on Ofcom's interpretation of it. Ofcom retains significant leeway in adopting a range of free expression standards.

This regime is not applied to any other medium and since, as discussed below, the BBFC appears to be operating a regime in respect of films and videos that has recently become much more liberal, the differences between the regimes for films and for broadcasting are becoming more marked. As technology advances, the range of channels widens and a wider range of information about programmes becomes more readily available to viewing audiences, these differences are arguably becoming less defensible. Although it might appear that Art 10 under the HRA could play a part in bringing about a greater liberalisation of the current offence-avoidance decency regime, it is probable, for the reasons discussed above, that its effect will continue to be marginal, especially after the *Pro-Life* decision. Regulation of UK broadcasting is in effect insulated from free speech principles applied by means of the HRA due to the excessive deference to the regulators enjoined upon the courts by *Pro-Life*.

6 The internet, films and videos

Introduction[391]

This section considers the regulation of the internet, films and videos.[392] The regimes in place at present for each of these media differ from each other quite considerably. But they also contrast strongly with the regime in respect of books, newspapers, magazines and other printed matter. Broadcasting, films and videos are subject to regulatory schemes, which (as discussed) are wholly statute-based in the case of broadcasting and videos, and partly statute-based in respect of films. At present, there is no state regulation of the internet, apart from the application of the ordinary law. The new regulatory regime put in place for broadcasting in 2003 does not cover use of the internet.

The statutory regimes currently in place include elements of licensing, regulation by administrative bodies and censorship. The reasons behind treating broadcasting and films differently from the print media differ in a number of respects, but have a common historical basis. The stricter system of controls seems to have been adopted in answer to the view that owing to their particular impact on audiences, films, videos and broadcasting require a system of prior restraints, whereas it is now accepted that books and other printed material do not. These media are viewed as beneficial to the public in a number of respects, but are also seen as possible sources of harm. Owing to the availability of censorship, it is very unlikely that a film or broadcast could attract liability under the Obscene Publications Act;[393] nevertheless, it provides a further possibility of restraint and can also be used as a guide as to the standards censorship will observe. Thus, the regulatory regimes in place mean that the visual media are censored beyond what the law demands. The impact of the HRA in these areas is variable and its effects are complicated by the fact that a number of the media bodies involved are private bodies, while the administrative 'watchdog' bodies are public authorities.

Regulation of films, videos and the internet differs sharply from the 'command and control' model of regulation provided by the Ofcom system. Regulation of films for cinematic release has some features in common with the self-regulation of the internet since it was originally entered into voluntarily by the film-makers themselves. However, the regulation of films is far less fragmentary and has achieved far greater recognition

---

391 Texts referred to below: Barendt, E, *Freedom of Speech*, 2nd edn, 2005, Chapters 10, 12 and 13; Robertson, G and Nichol, D, *Media Law*, 1999, Chapter 14; Bailey, Harris and Jones *Civil Liberties and Human Rights Cases and Materials*, 5th edn, 2002, Chapter 6 at pp 650–67; Carey, P and Sanders, J, *Media Law*. 3rd edn, 2004, Chapters 5 and 9 (basic guide); Gibbons, T, *Regulating the Media*, 2nd edn, 1998; Akdeniz, Y, Walker, C and Wall, D, (eds), *The Internet, Law and Society*, 2000, Longman; for background, see Hunnings, N, *Film Censors and the Law*, 1967, Allen and Unwin.
392 For a comprehensive treatment, see Gibbons, *Regulating the Media*, 1998.
393 The Obscene Publications Act, s 1 covers these media under s 1(2) since the Broadcasting Act 1990, s 162, has brought radio and television within its ambit.

than the system for the internet. In relation to videoworks, the film regulatory scheme does bear quite a strong resemblance to the Ofcom one. Generally, film regulation does not have a *full* statutory under-pinning, but is strongly associated with a number of statutes. As discussed below, a range of bodies set up by Internet Service Providers, such as the Internet Watch Foundation, provide a self-censoring service for the internet. None of these bodies has a statutory underpinning or have so far received any statutory recognition. Nor can they be viewed as affecting the internet in a comprehensive fashion since, unlike the system for films, they do not apply controls at source but are consumer-driven. In other words, they rely on a voluntary engagement with their services by the public or by institutions, whereas films and videos are affected by regulation prior to release. The remit of the Advertising Standards Authority now not only covers broadcasting, but runs across all these different media; it is most significant in relation to the internet, so it will be discussed in the different contexts, below.

The British Board of Film Classification

Classification and censorship of films and videoworks is undertaken by the British Board of Film Classification (BBFC), a self-censoring body set up by the film industry itself in 1912. It is an independent, non-governmental body which is funded by the fees it charges to those who submit films, videos, DVDs for classification. The video release of films has a firmer statutory under-pinning deriving from the Video Recordings Act 1984, and so the regulation of videos has a greater resemblance in that respect to the system for broadcasting.

The BBFC provides an interesting example of a body that does not possess statutory powers, in relation to the cinematic release of films, and yet whose decisions as to film classification are adhered to as though they had statutory force. It was originally set up in response to the Cinematograph Act 1909 (now Cinemas Act 1985), which allowed local authorities to grant licences in respect of the films to be shown in their particular area; the idea was that the film industry would achieve a uniformity of decision-making by local councils by providing authoritative guidance to them. So when the BBFC classifies films it does so, formally speaking, on behalf of the local authorities who license cinemas under the Cinemas Act 1985. The idea behind this system, from the point of view of the film-makers and distributors, was that they would have a guide as to whether a film would be shown and as to where to make cuts in order to achieve a wider audience.

Statutory powers to control what is shown at cinemas still remain with local councils who may over-rule any of the Board's decisions. Thus, films – not videos – can be classified on two levels: first, the BBFC may insist on cuts before issuing a certificate allowing the film to be screened or may refuse to issue a certificate at all. Second, the local authority may on occasion decide to depart from the BBFC classification or may refuse to allow a film to be shown despite the fact that it has received an '18' classification. Clearly, this is an anomalous system since it means that films are the only medium subject to censorship on a local level. But although the BBFC originates from an arbitrary and now out-dated system, it performs a function that would otherwise be performed by a regulator such as Ofcom with statutory powers. The BBFC is not a creation of statute although, as discussed below, it does have statutory powers in relation to videos. Arguably, a regulator that has worked closely with the industry for a substantial period of time and which is not a governmental creation, or subject to government appointments, may be able to take a more effective, sensitive and nuanced stance in relation to classification and censorship than a government body, a point that is returned to below. The matter of self-censorship by film companies prior to submission to the BBFC must not be disregarded, but over the last 10 years the BBFC has adopted an increasingly liberal attitude to censorship: in 1995 27 films were censored; in 2005 the figure was four.[394] However, at present, as the BBFC itself accepts, films and videos are still more likely to be subject to censorship in the UK. The reasons for this and the current pressure for change form a central focus of the discussion below. Below, the general classification and censorship system operated by the BBFC is considered, before turning to the differences between the way films are treated for cinematic release and for release on video-works.

The classification and censorship system

In relation to the theatrical release of films the BBFC operates within a broad statutory framework, but unlike Ofcom its decisions on classification are not driven by that statutory basis. This is also broadly true in relation to videoworks, although the statutory basis in question is more prescriptive. The BBFC classifies and censors films and videos against the background of the relevant criminal law,[395] including the Obscene Publications Act 1959. Section 4(1)(a) Video Recordings Act 1984, as amended,[396] requires the BBFC to apply an additional test with regard to the classification of videos, that of suitability for viewing in the home. This requirement reflects the fact that, in the BBFC's words,

> unlike cinema films where age restrictions may be 'policed' by box office staff, videos in the home are more likely to be viewed by younger age groups and could be replayed many times with individual scenes taken out of context and repeated in slow motion or even frame by frame.[397]

In relation to videos there is a right of appeal from the decisions of the BBFC to the Video Appeals Committee (VAC). No such right exists in relation to films.

The BBFC makes its decisions on the basis of published Guidelines.[398] As it acknowledges, the application of the Guidelines goes further in terms of creating restraints than the relevant law itself does. It states in the Guidelines that it is complying with the requirements of the European Convention on Human Rights to make the classification criteria clear. It considers that it has fulfilled this duty by the publication of the Guidelines and their availability on the BBFC website or directly from the Board. However, the mere fact that the Guidelines can be readily accessed clearly does not mean

394 Source – the *Guardian* 13.9.05. The figure of four in 2005 is based on decisions from Jan–Sept 05. However, the figure is unlikely to rise significantly: only five films were censored in 2004.
395 The relevant criminal law is discussed above. Note also that the Cinematograph Films (Animals) Act 1937 makes it illegal to show any scene if animals were treated cruelly in the making of that scene.
396 Discussed below at p 562.
397 See the 2000 BBFC Response to the Home Office Consultation Paper on *the Regulation of R18 Videos* at para 2.1.
398 Available from the BBFC website: http://www.bbfc.co.uk.

that the criteria are sufficiently clear, and it is arguable that in a number of respects sufficient clarity has not been achieved. This is an especially significant matter since the BBFC is the only UK media regulator which operates by means of prior restraint: it can order cuts in films before they can be seen by the public. Adherence to the Guidelines is intended to mean – and so far has meant – that the producers or distributors of a film are very unlikely to be prosecuted under the Obscene Publications Act 1959 (OPA) or other provisions imposing criminal liability in respect of explicit expression. Thus, as is the case in relation to broadcasting, it is probable that films do not fully explore the boundaries of the criminal law, but stop instead somewhere short of them.

Age restrictions

Films and videos are classified by age, creating a number of categories that restrict viewing. The age restrictions are more significant, for obvious reasons, in relation to films as opposed to videos. Clearly, children and teenagers under 15 or 18 may well be able to view videos privately that have the higher age rating; they are able to do so much more readily than in the cinema. This is a matter that the BBFC takes into account in its classification. There are seven classification categories. 'U' and 'Uc' films are open to anybody as, in effect, are 'PG' (parental guidance) classified films; these categories are advisory only. After that are '12'/'12A', '15' and '18' certificate films; '12A' is a new, recently introduced, category, which allows children under 12 to see '12'-rated films at their parents' discretion; it requires such children to be accompanied into the cinema by an adult. Children over 12 will be able to see the film unaccompanied, as previously. Thus the '12A' rating recognises that parents have a better understanding of the particular sensitivities of their individual children than a regulator can have. The introduction of the '12A' rating is a step in the direction of recognising the applicability of the free speech autonomy rationale to children as well as to adults.

The advice at the '18' rating is obviously crucial since it represents the outer limits of acceptability for mainstream films and sets the boundaries for most adult viewing. The '18' rating does not fully perform that function in relation to videos since the BBFC takes into account the possibility that people under 18 may see the film, although that is far from meaning that only material suitable for, say, 15-year-olds is promulgated. The majority of classifications issued by the BBFC are not 18; at the '18' classification cuts are usually minor. 'R [restricted viewing] 18' films are intended for viewing only on segregated premises. The 'R18' classification certificate was introduced by the BBFC following the introduction of the 1982 Local Government (Miscellaneous Provisions) Act which required the licensing of all cinema exhibitions operated for private gain, including those clubs which showed films containing more explicit sexual depictions than would be acceptable in the public adult – '18' – category. This classification is also used in the context of classifying sexually explicit videoworks following the implementation of the Video Recordings Act 1984. There are strict controls on the sale of videoworks which are given an 'R18' classification. Under s 12 of the 1984 Act, such videos can only be sold in a licensed sex shop to adults aged 18 and over. They cannot be legally sold by mail order, supplied through ordinary video outlets or shown on television. Their supply other than in a licensed sex shop is a criminal offence.[399]

---

399 The offence is subject to a fine of up to £5,000, 6 months' imprisonment, or both.

The issue of an 'R18' certificate means that the BBFC considers that the film or video would survive an OPA prosecution; it will refuse a certificate if a film is thought to be obscene within the meaning of the Act. Thus BBFC decisions as to the borderline between what can be shown in an 'R18' film and what would fall foul of the OPA are probably the best guide to the meaning and application of the problematic term 'obscenity' available in the UK. The BBFC may of course err on the side of caution: it may not wish to patrol very closely to that borderline, and the very uncertainty of the term 'obscenity' is likely to engender caution.

R v Video Appeals Committee of the BBFC ex p BBFC,[400] discussed further below, marked a very significant change in the use of the 'R18' certificate for videos. The decision resulted in the promulgation of new, more relaxed Guidelines for 'R18' videos by the BBFC. The BBFC nevertheless takes the view that despite this relaxation the UK 'still probably has the strictest Guidelines of any European or Western nation'.[401] As film-makers outside the pornography industry obviously do not want to receive an 'R18' rating for their work, the vast majority of films aimed at adults must respect the BBFC Guidelines in order to secure the UK adult market, as far as the UK cinema release of films is concerned. The BBFC states that it 'respects the right of adults to chose their own entertainment, within the law. It will therefore expect to intervene *only rarely* in relation to '18'-rated cinema films' (emphasis added).[402]

In coming to its decision, the BBFC will take the 'public good' defence under s 4(1A) of the 1959 Act, as amended, into account.[403] This defence is the more restricted defence under s 3 of the Theatres Act 1968; s 4(1A) provides that a film or soundtrack can be justified as being for the public good 'on the ground that it is in the interests of drama, opera, ballet or any other art or of literature or learning'. Therefore, the BBFC may grant a certificate on the grounds of artistic merit to a film which contains some obscene matter.

The '12A' to 'R18' classifications are mandatory, not recommendatory. In most of Europe and in the US the age classifications are intended to provide guidance to parents and to children, but children under the age in question can enter the cinema and view films in the 'older' category. For example, in the US the 'PG13' rating is roughly the equivalent of the '12A' rating in the UK; younger children in the US can view 'PG13'-rated films, but in the UK they can only view an equivalent rated film if accompanied by an adult. Thus in this respect the autonomy of children and teenagers is more fully acknowledged than it is in the UK. This restriction is not – in effect – applicable to videos and, as discussed further below, influences the BBFC in relation to determining the classification of videos and in deciding on cuts.

Most film distributors have no interest in achieving only a restricted publication for a film and are therefore prepared to make cuts to achieve a wider circulation. This

---

400 (2000) EMLR 850. The appeal to the VAC was brought by Sheptonhurst Ltd and Prime Time Promotions (Shifnal) Ltd and involved seven titles: *Horny Catbabe, Nympho Nurse Nancy, TV Sex, Office Tart, Carnival International Version (Trailer), Wet Nurses 2 Continental Version* and *Miss Nude International Continental Version*.

401 See the 2000 BBFC Response to the Home Office Consultation Paper on *the Regulation of R18 Videos* 28.7.00.

402 BBFC Guidelines, '18' ratings.

403 See above pp 472–74.

is especially the case in relation to the '18' and 'R18' certificates. But profitability is also highly significant and determinative of pre-censorship: the system of control may be driven largely by commercial motives: studios may make relatively stringent cuts in order to ensure that, for example, a film receives a 'PG' or '15' certificate and so reaches a wider audience. The BBFC normally avoids having to impose cuts because film directors effectively pre-censor films in order to fall within a particular classification.

Explicit depictions of sex and violence in films and videoworks

The BBFC states in its Guidelines that the acceptability of a particular theme at levels of classification is determined by 'the context and sensitivity of its presentation'. The Guidelines state that the very problematic themes such as drug abuse or paedophilia are almost bound to be unacceptable below the '15' level of classification. Therefore it is accepted that in principle *any* theme could be viewed as acceptable if properly handled at '18' or even at '15'. But this must now be read subject to new restrictions, discussed below, on the depiction of teenage sexuality created by the inception of the Sexual Offences Act 2003. The Guidelines state that the portrayal of human sexual activity is not permitted at 'U', 'Uc' or 'PG'; it may be implied in '12'-rated video works and in '12A' cinema works. Thereafter, 'progressively more graphic portrayal' may be included at the '15' and '18' classifications,[404] but the extent of the portrayal is context-dependent, and the emphasis given to 'responsible, loving and developing' relationships will be relevant. In taking this stance the BBFC lays itself open to the charge that it is engaging in ideological censorship – in other words, only an authorised view of sexuality is acceptable. Again, the effect of the 2003 Act is to create a further age-based constraint even within the depiction of such relationships. Certain forms of simulated consenting heterosexual or homosexual sexual behaviour can no longer be shown involving 16- or 17-year-old actors, or older actors portraying younger people. The 'R18' category is primarily reserved for explicit videos of consenting sex between adults. In contrast, nudity, providing there is 'no sexual context or sub-text', is stated to be acceptable at all classification levels. Films rarely depict actual as opposed to simulated, sexual acts, including intercourse. The film *9 Songs*, however, achieved an '18'-rating in 2004 for the cinematic release despite frequent and graphic portrayals

---

404 At '12A'/'12': 'sexual activity may be implied. Sexual references may reflect the familiarity of most adolescents today with sex education through school'. At '15': 'sexual activity and nudity may be portrayed but without strong detail. The depiction of casual sex should be handled responsibly.' At '18': the Board may cut or reject the 'more explicit images' of sexual conduct unless, exceptionally, they are justified by context. The following are not acceptable, even at 'R18': 'any material which is in breach of the criminal law; material (including dialogue) likely to encourage an interest in abusive sexual activity (e.g., paedophilia, incest) which may include depictions involving adults role-playing as non-adults; the portrayal of any sexual activity, whether real or simulated, which involves lack of consent; the infliction of pain or physical harm, real or (in a sexual context) simulated. Some allowance may be made for mild consensual activity. Any sexual threats or humiliation which do not form part of a clearly consenting role-playing game are disallowed, as are the use of any form of physical restraint which prevents participants from withdrawing consent, for example, ball gags, penetration by any object likely to cause actual harm or associated with violence, activity which is degrading or dehumanising (examples include the portrayal of bestiality, necrophilia, defecation, urolagnia)'.

of non-simulated sexual intercourse. Previously, *Ai No Corrida* was classified '18' in 1991, as were *Romance* (1999) and *Intimacy* (2001) – all three films contain images of non-simulated intercourse. No '18'-rated film has yet depicted actual homosexual intercourse (the term is used here to include oral sex as well as anal intercourse).

Significantly, the Guidelines state that the standards set for *legal* heterosexual and homosexual behaviour are equal (emphasis added). The use of the term 'legal' is important: in the past there has been legal differentiation between homosexual and heterosexual behaviour. For example, the age of consent for heterosexual intercourse is 16, whereas until 1994 it was 21 for homosexual intercourse; until quite recently it was 18.[405] However, under recent legislative changes the two forms of behaviour are now equal under the law. Under the Sexual Offences (Amendment) Act 2000, s 1, the age of consent was equalised at 16. When the Sexual Offences Act 2003 came into force,[406] a range of forms of heterosexual and homosexual sexual behaviour were placed on an equal footing. These changes could potentially have some impact on depictions of homosexual behaviour on film, and some liberalisation in terms of what can be shown may occur, due indirectly to changes in the criminal law.

The 2003 Act also made a very important change in this context, which has further implications for the distribution of films and videos made prior to 2003. The change concerns the definition of a 'child' under the terms of the Protection of Children Act 1978 (PCA), discussed above in relation to offences of indecency.[407] Previously the PCA s 7(6) defined a 'child' as a person under 16 years of age and made illegal the manufacture, possession and distribution of indecent photographs of children under 16. Section 45(2) of the new Sexual Offences Act amended the PCA by raising the age of a 'child' for the purposes of this Act to 18. The effect of this is retrospective, applying to all such images, regardless of when they first came into circulation. The Act in effect bans from the screen all depictions of sexual activity involving someone under 18 that could fall within the term 'indecent'. It is uncertain whether older actors whose features have been digitally manipulated to make them appear to be under 18 could be used since this might amount to the use of a 'psuedo-image' of a child.[408] Section 51 of the 2003 Act introduced a new offence of 'facilitating' child pornography. The new restraints are mainly aimed at internet pornography, but place film-makers exploring depictions of teenage sexuality in a very difficult position, and mean that 16- and 17-year-olds are constrained in relation to viewing people of the same age involved in sexual activity.

Sexual intercourse between over-16s is legal, and other forms of sexual activity short of intercourse were legal even before the age of consent was raised to 16, but although the acts themselves are legal, depictions of them may not be. It is anomalous,

---

405 Under the Sexual Offences Act 1967, s 1, the age of consent was 21; this was amended by the Criminal Justice and Public Order Act 1994 s143 to 18. Until recently, when the Sexual Offences Act 2003 came into force, there were a number of legal differentiations between illegal heterosexual and homosexual acts/behaviour, apart from that stemming from the age of consent; the more restrictive laws applied to homosexual behaviour.

406 On 1 May 2004.

407 See pp 477–79.

408 Section 84 of the Criminal Justice and Public Order Act 1994 amended the 1978 Act to add 'pseudo-photographs' of children in order to cover digitally created photographs. This would of course depend on whether in the context the image would be seen as 'indecent'.

to say the least, that heterosexual or homosexual intercourse between 16-year-olds or with adults, is lawful, whereas depictions of forms of sexual activity involving 16- or 17-year-old actors, falling far short of intercourse, might not be. Clearly, depictions of some forms of sexual activity involving 16- and 17-year-old actors would not attract criminal liability, but the 2003 Act has created a number of grey areas in relation to such depictions which did not previously exist. The BBFC may find itself seeking to classify films that could fall foul of the PCA 1978.

Clearly, the key question is whether the depiction of the 'child' could be viewed as 'indecent'. Whether a photograph is indecent depends on the view of the jury regarding recognised standards of propriety.[409] In *Oliver, Hartrey and Baldwin*[410] the Court of Appeal found that pornographic images were to be categorised by the following levels of seriousness: (1) images depicting erotic posing with no sexual activity; (2) sexual activity between children, or solo masturbation by a child; (3) non-penetrative sexual activity between adults and children; (4) penetrative sexual activity between children and adults, and (5) sadism or bestiality. Thus level (1), covering a very wide range of images,[411] represents the 'lowest' level at which an image of a child could be termed 'indecent'. A number of films have depicted teenage actors, most frequently those aged between 16 and 18, in the situations described in (1)–(3).[412] The definition of indecency is obviously context-dependent. Where *Gillick*-competent child or teenage actors above the age of 13 engage in depictions of fairly restrained, non-nude, consensual heterosexual activity with each other it may perhaps be assumed that this would not violate recognised standards of propriety. Clearly, the older the teenager, the more this would be the case. The fact that a teenage actor of 17 had been made up or (perhaps) digitally altered to look, say, 13 would also be taken into account in relation to a determination as to indecency. But the uncertainty of the definition of indecency hardly favours erotic creativity, and places film-makers and the BBFC in a difficult position. The Court of Appeal may have to revisit and clarify its definition of indecency under the PCA due to the effect of the 2003 Act. The retrospective effect of the current definition of a 'child' is also highly problematic since certain cinematic depictions of sexuality, using 16- or 17-year-old actors, would not have fallen foul of the constraints

---

409 *R v Graham-Kerr* (1988) 88 Cr App R 302. See further: Manchester, C, 'Criminal Justice and Public Order Act 1994: obscenity, pornography and videos' [1995] Crim LR 123, pp 123–28; Cram, I, 'Criminalising Child Pornography – a Canadian Study' [2002] 66 J Crim L 359.

410 [2003] Cr App R 28.

411 As discussed above (p 478), recent developments involving art galleries showing pictures of naked children have illustrated the breadth of the definition of indecency in this context. See further Warbrick, 'Federalism and free speech', in Loveland, I (ed), *Importing the First Amendment*, 1997, pp 177–79 and 190–92.

412 A number of examples could be given; in *The Ice Storm* a sequence depicted actors Elijah Wood and Christina Ricci 'dry-humping'; another scene depicted Christina Ricci and Adam Hann-Byrd half-naked and kissing in bed together. All three actors were very young teenagers at the time. Both scenes appear to fall within level (2) from *Oliver, Hartrey and Baldwin*. In *The Name of the Rose* Christian Slater, who was 17 at the time and depicting a teenager, had simulated sex with an adult woman. The film *Kids* depicted a number of teenagers engaging in sexual activity. In *Trainspotting* Kelly McDonald, 17 at the time, engaged in simulated intercourse with an adult male actor, Ewan McGregor. The key question, of course, would be whether such scenes in the context of acting, and taking account of the fact that the actors were teenagers and *Gillick*-competent, would violate accepted standards of propriety and so be viewed as 'indecent'.

of the 1978 Act at the time.[413] In 2007 the film *Hounddog* was released in America and caused some controversy since it concerned the rape of a 12-year-old girl, played by an actress of that age, Dakota Fanning. The actress did not have to participate in the scene in a physical fashion since the rape sequence was created by a mélange of shots of her face or hand when alone in a studio – so it was suggested, not simulated. On its face, the scene would appear to fall well within the *Oliver* boundaries of indecency – at level 4. But presumably the context would mean that the images would not violate accepted standards of propriety.

Theoretically, homosexual acts (including simulated or actual intercourse) between 16- or 17-year-old actors or between such actors and an adult could be shown on screen. But if viewed as indecent such acts cannot be seen on screen regardless of the equalisation of the age of consent. This is now also true of heterosexual acts, and in this sense the effect of the 2003 Act was to 'level down' in terms of equalising cinematic depictions of sexuality involving teenagers or apparent (digitally manipulated images of adults or CGI) teenagers. But it is probable that homosexual acts might be more likely to be seen as indecent, and in this sense BBFC decisions might – in effect – indirectly discriminate against depictions of homosexuality. This point is pursued below in relation to the HRA.

This might also be true even outside the purview of the 1978 Act, where other criminal law provisions are or might be applicable, including the anomalous common law doctrine of outraging public decency.[414] Such other provisions create differentiation in the legal position, thereby creating difficulties affecting depictions of homosexual behaviour short of intercourse, and simulated sexual acts, even between actors on screen, since such acts might be more likely to be viewed as indecent. Therefore depictions of homosexual behaviour on films have been, and still are, subject to greater restriction.

The classification system also addresses the degree and nature of violence depicted in films,[415] while accepting that violence is an inevitable aspect of entertainment at all

---

413   The change might not be compatible with the demands of Art 7(1) in HRA, Sched 1. Article 7 provides: '(1) No one shall be held guilty of any criminal offence on account of any act or omission which did not constitute a criminal offence under national or international law at the time when it was committed. Nor shall a heavier penalty be imposed than the one that was applicable at the time the criminal offence was committed. (2) This Article shall not prejudice the trial and punishment of any person for any act or omission which, at the time when it was committed, was criminal according to the general principles of law recognised by civilised nations. Article 7 was found to have been breached in *Welch v UK* (1995) 20 EHRR 247. Before the trial of the applicant for drug offences, a new provision came into force under the Drug Trafficking Offences Act 1986, making provision for confiscation orders. This was imposed on the applicant, although the legislation was not in force at the time when he committed the offences in question. It clearly had retrospective effect and was found to constitute a 'penalty' within Art 7(1). The 2003 Act was not declared compatible with the Convention under HRA, s 19(1)(a), but only in respect of ss 319 and 321 (the ban on political advertising), so the government legal advice must have been to the effect that Art 7 had been complied with, probably on the basis that the exception under Art 7(2) applied. In any event compatibility remains a matter for the judiciary to determine.

414   See pp 481–84 above.

415   At '12A'/'12': 'Violence must not dwell on detail. There should be no emphasis on injuries or blood. Sexual violence may only be implied or briefly indicated and without physical detail.' At '15': 'Violence may be strong but may not dwell on the infliction of pain, and of injuries. Scenes of sexual violence

ages, 'an element in many serious representations of the human condition'. But the Guidelines advise against the portrayal of violence as 'a normal solution to problems' and against callousness to victims or the encouragement of aggression. The Guidelines state that works which 'glorify or glamorise violence' will receive a more restrictive classification and may be cut. Sexual violence is of particular concern. The BBFC states that it has a strict policy on rape and sexual violence. Cuts may be made in material that associates sex with non-consensual restraint, pain or humiliation. If a portrayal eroticises or endorses sexual assault, the Board is likely to require cuts at any classification level. Cuts are more likely in video rather than film portrayals due to the possibility of repeat viewing of video scenes. The Guidelines indicate that portrayals of the use of weapons easily accessible to young people will be restricted, and imitable combat techniques may be cut, as may imitable detail of criminal techniques. Works that promote or encourage or glamorise the use of illegal drugs will not in general receive even an '18' classification. Clear instructive detail as to drug use is only acceptable at the '18' classification 'if there are exceptional considerations of context'.

The Guidelines highlight the use of expletives in films, a matter that is more problematic in relation to UK film audiences than it is in the rest of Europe. The BBFC finds that the degree of offence caused by the use of expletives varies according to age, background and beliefs; ethnicity may also be relevant. The context will also be significant. In the light of these variables it offers only general guidance rather than providing a comprehensive listing of unacceptable words. Specific terms are advised against at different classification levels only where there is a reasonable consensus of opinion.[416]

The 1984 Act does not make reference specifically to avoiding offence to religious sensibilities. In general videos are more restricted than films in respect of the depiction of sex and violence, but this does not appear to be the case in relation to filmic portrayals of religion. Under the BBFC Guidelines for both films and videos:

> The acceptability of a theme depends significantly on its treatment, i.e. the context and sensitivity of its presentation. However, the most problematic themes (for example . . . incitement to racial hatred) are unlikely to be appropriate at the most junior levels of classification. Correspondingly, there is no reason in principle why most themes, however difficult, could not be satisfactorily handled at "18" or even "15".

The BBFC will have to up-date its Guidelines in 2007 to add the words 'or religious' to them after the word 'incitement' in the light of the introduction of the new offence of inciting to religious hatred, discussed above. The Guidelines also state: 'Many people are offended, some of them deeply, by bad language, including the use of expletives with a religious or racial association.' Thus, the BBFC makes very little specific provision

---

must be discreet and brief.' There should be no 'detailed portrayal of violent or dangerous acts which is likely to promote the activity'.

416 The Guidelines state, at '12'/'12A': 'The use of strong language (eg 'fuck') should be rare'. At '15': 'there may be frequent use of strong language; the strongest terms (eg 'cunt') are only rarely acceptable. Continued *aggressive* use of strong language and sexual abuse is unacceptable.' At '18' there are no constraints on language.

in relation to the portrayal of religion. However, it does state that it takes account of the criminal law, which includes the laws relating to blasphemy and religious hatred.

The theatrical release of films

This section looks at the different considerations that apply to the theatrical, as opposed to the video, release of films. The BBFC Guidelines discussed are applied somewhat differently to films in relation to the cinematic and the video release. Since cinema films are viewed by an adult, willing audience who has access to information about the nature of the film, it might have been expected that '18'-rated films would fall just outside the boundaries of criminal liability as determined by the Obscene Publications Act, as amended, and common law offences. There is a greater risk in relation to videos that children might view adult films. The difficulty with the availability of the 'R18' classification in relation to the cinematic release is that it may mean that the BBFC are not exploring the boundaries of the legal definition of obscenity in adult films in general, those that receive the '18' classification. The 'R18'-classification may, in effect, drive a wedge between such films and the outer limits of acceptability under the criminal law.

Consideration of recent decisions by the BBFC suggests that there is some basis for these concerns. However, at the 'PG' to '15' levels the BBFC has shown a willingness in some instances to place films within a non-restrictive category, even where they fall at the outer limits of that category. For example, the BBFC took a creative approach in 2001 to the classification of *The Lord of the Rings – the Fellowship of the Ring*. The Board found that the battle violence and fantasy horror in the film were a matter for concern since children under the age of eight might be frightened or disturbed. However, it decided to give the film a 'PG' rating, on the basis that the film's distributor had agreed that all advertising and publicity for the film would carry the consumer advice that the film contained scenes which might not be suitable for children under eight years of age. Most films do not carry such advice, over and beyond the classification rating; the only other films to carry consumer advice on all publicity and advertising were *Jurassic Park* and *The Lost World – Jurassic Park*, both of which were rated 'PG'.[417] The BBFC was presented with greater difficulties in relation to the film *Spiderman*. It was aimed at a young audience by the film-makers, and Hollywood had marketed it with that audience in mind. But the BBFC considered it 'possibly the most violent film . . . aimed at a young audience that the BBFC has classified.' Therefore the Board considered that it was clearly unsuitable for a 'PG' rating since very young children would then be able to view the film. Classifying it as '12', the BBFC found that the film '[carries] . . . a clear message that the use of violence is the normal and appropriate response when challenged'.[418] The '12A' rating was not available at the time.

At the '18' level the BBFC has to deal with the even more problematic issue of censorship of material aimed at adults, as opposed to the issues raised by restrictive age classifications. In 2002 the BBFC decided to classify the French film *Irreversible* as '18' uncut for the cinema release. The film centres around a graphically depicted rape

417 See BBFC press release, 22 November 2001.
418 See BBFC press release, 13 June 2002.

and its consequences. The Board found, in line with its current classification guidelines and having taken advice from a clinical forensic psychiatrist, that the depiction of the rape did not eroticise or appear to endorse sexual violence. The Board considered that the rape scene was a harrowing and vivid portrayal of the brutality of rape which was not designed to titillate.[419] In contrast, in the same year the BBFC passed the French language cinema film, *The Pornographer*, as '18' but required a cut to a graphic unsimulated sex scene in which a woman was seen with semen on her face following oral sex.[420] This cut was in line with the BBFC's Guidelines at '18' which state that the Board may cut or reject 'the more explicit images of sexual activity – unless they can be exceptionally justified by context'. The Board did not find that the context justified the scene. As mentioned above, the film *9 Songs* obtained an '18' rating in 2004 for the cinematic release, although it depicted actual as opposed to simulated sexual intercourse. The Board decided that the film's sensitive exploration of the relationship between the two people provided sufficient contextual justification. The consumer advice provided a warning of the content.

The emphasis on context as providing a justification for portrayals of sexual activity or violence is questionable since it depends on value judgments made by the Board members as to 'acceptable' contexts. Films are a very significant medium for the exploration of controversial themes and such themes may depend on the use of images from outside the boundaries of those contexts. There is a case for arguing that the 'R18' classification should be abolished for the theatrical release of films and that mainstream films should therefore be able to explore the boundaries created by the criminal law more vigorously and closely. If a film viewed only by adults is to be cut, the starting-point should be the demands of the criminal law. Clear justification based on the avoidance of specific harms, as opposed merely to offence-avoidance, should be available for cuts made reaching beyond those demands. The possibility of more extensive use of detailed consumer guidance should be pursued in order to avoid the causing of offence.

The second level of classification is operated, as discussed above, by local authorities under the Cinemas Act 1985 which continues the old power arising under the Cinematograph Act 1909. The local authority will usually follow the Board's advice; authorities are reluctant to devote resources to viewing films and will tend to rely on the BBFC's judgment.[421] But authorities may, on occasion, choose not to grant a licence to a film regardless of its decision. Films which have been licensed but which nevertheless have been banned in some areas include *A Clockwork Orange, The Life of Brian, The Last Temptation of Christ* and *Crash*. Conversely, local authorities may come under pressure to change the classification of a film in order to make it less restrictive. Two local authorities downgraded *Spiderman* to a 'PG' rating for that reason, since some parents had been disappointed by the '12' rating.[422] There is no requirement of consistency between authorities and thus discrepancies have arisen between different local authority areas. It is notable that the cinema is the only art form subject to moral judgment on a local level and clearly it may be asked why it should be so singled

---

419 See BBFC press release, 21 October 2002.
420 See BBFC press release, 2 April 2002.
421 See Holbrook (1973) 123 NLJ 701.
422 See BBFC press release, 13 June 2002.

out. This dual system of censorship was criticised unavailingly over 25 years ago by the Williams Committee in 1979,[423] partly on the ground of the anomalies caused by having two overlapping levels of restraint and partly due to the inconsistency between local authorities. It considered that a unified system should be adopted. In particular, it criticised a system which allowed adult films to be censored beyond the requirements of the OPA.

Statutory regulation of video works

The Video Recordings Act 1984 was introduced after a campaign about the dangers posed by 'video nasties' to children. The campaign, by the *Daily Mail* and a group called the Festival of Light, managed to convince Parliament that legislation was necessary in order to address the problem.[424] Under the Video Recordings Act 1984, the BBFC was established as the authority charged with classifying videos for viewing in the home.[425] It currently classifies videos, DVDs and some digital works under the 1984 Act. Videoworks[426] are classified and therefore censored in almost the same way as films, and under s 9 of the 1984 Act, it is an offence to supply a video without a classification certificate, unless it is exempt on grounds of its concern with education, sport, music or religion. Under s 2(2) the exemption will not apply if the video portrays human sexual activity or gross violence or is designed to stimulate or encourage this. Section 4 of the 1984 Act requires that the BBFC should have 'special regard to the likelihood of videoworks being viewed in the home'. Thus, makers of videos may find that videos are censored well beyond the requirements of the OPA.

The regime in respect of videos was made potentially more restrictive in 1994. Fears that children might be more likely to commit violence after watching violent videos[427] led the government to include a number of provisions in the Criminal Justice and Public Order Bill 1994, which was then before the Commons. Under s 90 of the Criminal Justice and Public Order Act 1994, inserting s 4A into the 1984 Act, the BBFC must have 'special regard' to harm which may be caused to 'potential viewers or through their behaviour to society' by the manner in which the film deals with criminal behaviour, illegal drugs, violent behaviour or incidents, horrific incidents or behaviour or human sexual activity. These criteria are non-exhaustive. The BBFC can consider any other relevant factor. 'Potential viewers' include children, but it is not necessary to show that children had in fact viewed the video. The kind of harm envisaged, to a child or to society, is not specified and nor is the degree of seriousness envisaged although the use of the word 'may' implies that there must be some likelihood of harm. Section 4A does not prescribe the Board's response once it has taken the above factors 'into

---

423 See Williams Committee on Obscenity and Film Censorship, which conducted a review of the area, Cmnd 7772, 1979.

424 See Petley, J, *Screen*, Vol 25 No 2, p 68.

425 After the introduction of the Video Recordings Act 1984, the President and Vice-Presidents of the Board were designated by the Home Secretary under s 4(1) as the authority responsible for applying the statutory classification system for videoworks set out in the Act.

426 When the term 'videowork' or 'video' is used it will be used to cover video material presented on DVDs and digital games.

427 See further, Home Affairs Committee, *Video Violence and Young Offenders*, Fourth Report (1994) HC 514.

account'.[428] Section 89 of the 1994 Act also amended s 2(2) in respect of the scope of the exemptions mentioned above. These exemptions will not apply if a video 'depicts techniques likely to be useful in the commission of offences' or 'criminal activity likely to any significant extent to stimulate or encourage the commission of offences'. It is not necessary to show that the video is designed to stimulate or encourage the activity mentioned above, but only that it is likely to do so. If the BBFC considers that a particular work is unacceptable for viewing, it can, and does, refuse to issue a classification certificate altogether. This has the effect of banning the videowork concerned since under the 1984 Act, ss 9–11 it is a criminal offence to supply, offer or possess for supply an unclassified video. It is also an offence to supply a video in breach of the classification certificate issued by the BBFC.[429]

A right of appeal from the decisions of the BBFC to the Video Appeals Committee (VAC), which operates as a Tribunal, was created under the provisions of s 4(3) of the 1984 Act.[430] No other party has the right of appeal under the Act. The Home Secretary has sought to intervene in this classification and appeals scheme, with the result that in the 1990's the BBFC and the VAC came into conflict in respect of a number of explicit videos which depicted actual, rather than simulated, sexual scenes. The Board relaxed their Guidelines in 1997 and classified a number of videos containing more explicit material than had been classified before, including scenes of actual penetration and oral sex. The Home Secretary was apparently concerned that this action would create a potential conflict with the enforcement policies of both Customs and Excise and the police who may seize material of similar explicitness for forfeiture proceedings via Magistrates' Courts under the Customs Consolidation Act 1876 and the Obscene Publications Act 1959 respectively. He instructed the Board to rescind their policy change. The Board set up an Enforcement sub-group which was established to consider the issue of consistency of standards between the Board and the prosecuting authorities.[431]

In 1998 the Board refused to classify an explicit sex video, *Makin' Whoopee*, to which they had given, but subsequently withdrawn, an interim classification certificate under their revised Guidelines. The publishers appealed to the VAC who found in their favour, rejecting arguments that the video might be obscene within the meaning of the 1959 Obscene Publications Act. The Board classified the video in the 'R18' category

---

428 See on this issue, Manchester, C, 'Criminal Justice and Public Order Act 1994: obscenity, pornography and videos' (1995) Crim LR 123, pp 129–30.

429 It may be noted that it is a defence under the Video Recordings Act 1993 to a charge of any offence under the 1984 Act to prove that the offence was due to the act or default of another person or that the accused took all reasonable precautions to avoid the commission of the offence 'by any person under his control'.

430 Under s 4(3) of the 1984 Act the Home Secretary must be satisfied that the designated authority (in practice this meant the principal officers at the BBFC) have adequate arrangements for appeals against classification determinations which producers or distributors feel are too restrictive. This may be because the video works in question have been given too high a classification or because they have been refused a classification altogether. The 1984 Act itself is silent as to the nature of the appeals body but the BBFC itself set up the VAC. The BBFC was responsible for the mechanics of recruitment and appointment of its members.

431 See BBFC Response to the Home Office Consultation Paper on *The Regulation of R18 Videos*, paras 2.3 and 1.4.

but did not accept that the judgment, which was limited to the issue of obscenity, set a precedent for consideration of similar videos.[432] A further seven videos were subsequently refused classification certificates and the Board then faced appeals against their decisions in respect of the videos. The VAC found in favour of the appellants and the Board subsequently sought leave to apply for judicial review of the VAC's judgement: *R v Video Appeals Committee of the BBFC ex p BBFC*.[433] The Board was unsuccessful on the basis that the VAC had taken all the relevant factors into account, including any risk to children. It was thought that since the videos were to be sold in adult sex shops, the risk that they would come into the hands of children and the risk that they would cause harm to them was very slight. In the proceedings, Mr Justice Hooper concluded 'I have no doubt that the conclusion "that the risk of [the videos in question] being viewed by and causing harm to children or young persons is, on present evidence, insignificant" is one that a reasonable decision maker could reach . . .'. He found that the VAC had acted reasonably in reaching the decision they did on the basis of the arguments put before them, and dismissed the Board's application. In other words, it could not be said that this was a decision that no reasonable regulator could have come to – the familiar low threshold. Thus the judgment was based on the *Wednesbury* unreasonableness standard only, not on Art 10 demands, and indicated quite a high degree of deference, common in this context, to the expert decision-maker – the VAC.[434] It was *consistent* with the view that the access of adults to explicit material should not be prevented on the basis that there was an unquantifiable risk of harm to children if it happened to come into their hands. However, it would be overstating the matter to find that the judgment laid down a statement of principle of this nature.

The then Labour Home Secretary, Jack Straw, attacked the decision of the VAC, and the Home Office published a Consultation Paper indicating that new legislation on the VAC and the use of the 'R18' classification might be necessary.[435] The possibility that the VAC could be newly set up under statute, with government-appointed officers, was raised.[436] In response the BBFC did not accept the government's criticisms of the VAC, but recommended that its jurisdiction should be confined to deciding whether the Board, as the Designated Authority under the Video Recordings Act, had been 'fair, consistent and legally correct in the application of its published policy and Guidelines'.[437] It may be noted that the VAC has not always been so bold: it did not reverse the decision of the BBFC in relation to the video *Visions of Ecstasy*, on the basis that it was possibly blasphemous. This decision turned, however, on the problematic nature of the law of blasphemy.[438]

The decision in *R v Video Appeals Committee of the BBFC ex p BBFC* highlighted one of the problems inherent in the 1984 Act, a flaw that became especially apparent in relation to 'R18'-rated videos, under the more relaxed Guidelines. Section 4A of

---

432 Ibid.
433 (2000) EMLR 850.
434 See further Chapter 4, pp 273–78 on deference in this context.
435 Home Office Consultation Paper on *The Regulation of R18 Videos* 28.7.00; see also the *Guardian*, 17 May 2000.
436 Home Office Consultation Paper on *The Regulation of R18 Videos*, paras 3.16–3.21.
437 BBFC Response to the Home Office Consultation Paper on *The Regulation of R18 Videos*.
438 See pp 490–91.

the Act operates on the assumption that children may be harmed if they view sexually explicit or very violent videos. However, there is no firm evidence that this is the case in relation to explicit depictions of sexuality,[439] as the government itself accepts,[440] and therefore it is very difficult to establish that harm is likely. Also, the connection between violence on film and violent behaviour in children has not been firmly established. It appears to be possible that there is a greater likelihood, not that children may perpetrate violence as an immediate reaction to exposure to violent films, but that they may be de-sensitised to violence in a long-term sense if they watch a great deal of it.[441] However, psychologists disagree as to the creation of this effect and there is no clear consensus among them as to the general proposition that watching violent films harms children.[442]

Likelihood of harm should arguably be established on the balance of probabilities,[443] and on the basis of the current research it is unclear that it can be. If a greater risk of harm could be established it would at the least support the continuance of the restrictions on the sale of 'R18' videos. There are clearly two separate issues – that of the likelihood of harm and that of the likelihood that children might view the video. The small chance that they might do so in respect of videos with the 'R18' classification due to the restrictions on sale makes it difficult to give effect to s 4A in relation to such videos, as the High Court accepted in *R v Video Appeals Committee of the BBFC ex p BBFC*. It could also be argued that it is difficult to give legal effect to s 4A, even in relation to videos classified '15' or '18', since although there is a higher probability that children may view them, it is even harder to establish that they might be harmed

---

439 BBFC News Release, 26 October 2000, *Abused children most at risk from pornography*: 'The BBFC commissioned the research in response to the Video Appeals Committee's ruling that the Board had failed to provide sufficient evidence of harm to children from viewing pornography in an appeal to the VAC by two porn distributors in 1999. The research was focused on finding out whether pornography by itself harmed children . . . The majority of those interviewed [child psychologists] believed that viewing pornography would be harmful to any child, and that they should be protected from it. They were, however, able to quote very little in the way of evidence to support this belief, either from their own case loads or those of their colleagues. Some felt that viewing pornography depicting consensual sex would *not* be harmful to children who were well cared for and not being harmed in other ways. Determining the harm pornography does is not easy because it is difficult to disentangle it from other features of a child's situation, especially as the majority of children who are exposed to pornography are usually being harmed in other ways. Several of the experts argued that pornography was less regulated and more readily available in Europe and the USA. Yet they were not aware of any evidence that a higher proportion of children in those countries needed professional help because seeing pornography had upset them. Nor were related outcomes like teenage pregnancies or marital breakdowns higher in countries where pornography circulated more freely . . . Robin Duval, Director of the BBFC, said: ". . . this research shows that there is in fact little clear evidence to support the natural view that 'accidental' viewing will have seriously harmful effects. It is reasonable to assume that a sample of 38 leading professionals would have been able to cite more anecdotal evidence from their case loads if harm to children, outside abusive or negligent situations, were significant or common".'

440 Home Office Consultation Paper on *The Regulation of R18 Videos*, para 1: 'There is little conclusive evidence of harmful effects'.

441 See further, Home Affairs Committee, *Video Violence and Young Offenders*, Fourth Report (1994) HC 514.

442 See M Barker and J Petley *Ill Effects: The Media Violence Debate* (London: Routledge, 1997).

443 See further above, pp 459–60 on this point.

if they do. Possibly s 4A has become legally ineffectual. Therefore it is unclear that there is a sound legal basis for creating distinctions between videos and films in terms of cuts at those classification levels .

The 1984 Act places the BBFC in the position of official censors and in that role their work has in the past been criticised as over-strict and arbitrary.[444] Taking account of s 4 of the 1984 Act, the BBFC uses cuts and restrictive classification more stringently with videos than with films partly because of the greater possibility that younger children will view them, despite the age classification, and also because – as it states – certain techniques, such as the use of weapons or of drugs, can be watched repeatedly 'until the lesson is learned'. The possibility of repeat viewings may also, in the Board's view, be a matter of concern in relation to sexually explicit and violent scenes. So the age classifications may be used more restrictively in relation to videos and cuts are more likely to be made to videos before being rated '18'. For example, after taking specialist advice, the BBFC required a cut of one minute 28 seconds to the video version of *A Ma Soeur!*, a film about the rape of a young girl, to achieve an '18' rating. The Board had previously passed the film version '18' uncut, but took the advice of a leading consultant clinical psychologist who considered that the rape scene was similar to material which paedophiles use to groom their victims.[445] This was perceived as more of a problem in relation to the video, as opposed to the cinematic, release due to the possibility that the scene in question could be played repeatedly and in a private context.

The impact and influence of the Human Rights Act

The stance of the BBFC is obviously influenced by the composition of the Board. Its effect on film-makers has been criticised as militating against creativity. It has been suggested that a cosy relationship has developed with film-makers that is insufficiently challenging – the acceptable boundaries are not fully explored in the name of artistic integrity and creative freedom.[446] Although there has been liberalisation, it is still arguable that commercial judgments rather than artistic considerations tend to dominate. The most pressing consideration for distributors is to find the widest possible audience, which may mean instituting cuts in order to obtain a '15' or '12A' certificate. The fact that the classifications are mandatory is also relevant, since distribution in the UK is therefore more restricted by age restraints than in countries in which it is recommendatory. Children under the age in question are still part of the targeted market in such countries. The relationship between 'artistic' and 'commercial' considerations is, clearly, a complex one. There is clear commercial mileage in obtaining the widest possible release of a film by way of the 'PG' certificate. But there may also be commercial advantage in producing sexually explicit and controversial films. In both instances, in a very competitive market where backers and distributors are unwilling to take commercial risks, directors and producers may be forced to institute cuts for the UK release of a film where clearly they would prefer to release it uncut. The BBFC accepts that its application of its Guidelines leads to a more restrictive censorship and classification of films in the UK than in almost all of Europe or the US.

---

444 See Hunnings, N, 'Video censorship' [1985] PL 214; Robertson, G, *Freedom, the Individual and the Law*, 7th edn, 1993, Penguin, pp 263–72.
445 See BBFC press release, 25 June 2002.
446 See Robertson and Nichol, op. cit., fn 1, p 593.

It seems possible that the inception of the HRA could have some impact on this situation, although ultimately by far the most significant matter is the stance of the BBFC. For example, a film-maker whose film was refused a classification without certain cuts, could refuse to institute the cuts and seek to challenge the decision of the BBFC or, in the case of a video, that of the VAC, if it upheld the BBFC's decision. The VAC is a body set up under statute with a public function in the sense of hearing appeals regarding the classification of material to be promulgated to the public; it is also subject to judicial review. It is therefore almost certainly a functional public authority under s 6 HRA. The BBFC has a public function which is also statutory in respect of providing classification certificates for videos. Its function in relation to films is not statutory, but can clearly be termed public. Had it not undertaken the classification of films, the government would have been likely to set up a statutory body.[447] It is suggested therefore that it too is also almost certainly a functional public authority under s 6.[448] If this is correct, private bodies or persons could bring an action against either body under s 7(1)(a) of the HRA, or by way of judicial review, relying on Art 10. In such an action, a court would have to give effect to s 12(4) HRA.[449]

Assuming that the VAC and BBFC are public authorities and so bound by the Convention rights under s 6, they should also ensure that their decisions do not breach Art 10, or any other relevant Article. For example, a film-maker whose film portraying actual homosexual intercourse or other explicit homosexual activity did not receive a certificate, could put forward the argument that Art 10 read with Art 14 (the freedom from discrimination Article)[450] should affect the interpretation, under s 3 HRA of the term 'indecency' in the PCA (if one of the actors was 17) or 'obscene' in the OPA. The argument would be that the same standards should be applied as would be applied to films showing explicit heterosexual activity. Importantly, as a public authority, the VAC cannot be confined to considering only whether the BBFC's decisions are 'fair, consistent and legally correct'; it also has to consider whether its own decisions on appeals might breach Art 10. It can of course be argued that 'legally correct' includes consideration of the BBFC's own duty under s 6(1) HRA not to breach Art 10 in its decisions,

---

447 See Chapter 4, pp 220–24, 233–35, on functional public authorities.

448 The BBFC takes the view that because of its public functions in respect of the statutory classification of videoworks, it is a 'public authority' under the HRA. In taking this view it has not distinguished between its function in relation to videos and that in relation to films. Clearly, it would be anomalous if such a distinction was drawn given the similarity of the two functions. (See the 2000 BBFC Response to the Home Office Consultation Paper on *The Regulation of R18 Videos* at para 1.16.) See also Chapter 4, pp 233–35.

449 See further Chapter 4, pp 215–37, on the provisions of s 12(4), and see Chapter 9 pp 938, 953–58 on the stance that the courts have taken towards it.

450 Article 14 provides: 'The enjoyment of the rights and freedoms set forth in this Convention shall be secured without discrimination on any ground such as sex, race, colour, language, religion, political or other opinion, national or social origin, association with a national minority, property, birth or other status.' Thus, Art 14 does not provide a general right to freedom from discrimination, only that the rights and freedoms of the Convention must be secured without discrimination. In the context under discussion Art 14 could be employed in order to argue that the right under Art 10 should be secured without discrimination on grounds of sexual orientation. This ground of discrimination is clearly covered by Art 14 (*Salgueiro da Silva Mouta v Portugal*, judgment of 21 December 1999); the question that would arise in this context would be whether differentiation between film-makers' output on the grounds of the *nature* of the output would be covered.

and therefore the VAC must decide whether the BBFC has acted compatibly with the demands of Art 10. Nevertheless, the VAC has a duty in relation to Art 10 under the HRA distinct from that of the BBFC itself. The 1984 Act, as amended, must be interpreted compatibly with the Convention rights under s 3(1) HRA. Given that a number of its terms are very open-ended, there is room for a range of interpretations.

However, in the case of a sexually explicit or violent film, the problem would be, as indicated above, that the Strasbourg jurisprudence appears to support quite far-reaching restrictions. It might be argued that where the risk of children viewing the cinema release of a film is very slight due to the use of age restrictions, *and* the question of offending religious sensibilities does not arise, the jurisprudence could be viewed as supporting the availability of even very explicit films.[451] This contention would be based on the unavailability of the margin of appreciation doctrine at the domestic level, and also derives from the principles underlying the jurisprudence, which, as indicated above, relate to the familiar free speech justifications, including that of self-fulfilment.[452]

But it must be acknowledged that this argument is not situated firmly in the Strasbourg jurisprudence at present. It rests mainly on one decision of the Commission – that of *Scherer*.[453] The decisions of the Court, in particular those of *Handyside*[454] and *Otto-Preminger*,[455] lend it only speculative support. The Court may have found it easier, in those decisions, to rest its argument on risks to children or to religious sensibilities, rather than enter the extremely difficult debate as to the proper limits of adult autonomy in relation to controversial, offensive and explicit speech. The argument that decisions at Strasbourg heavily influenced by the margin of appreciation doctrine should be applied domestically 'stripped' of its effects, is an appealing and compelling one that has been canvassed elsewhere in this book.[456] But the judges have shown little receptivity to it under the HRA so far.[457]

If a suitable case in this context arose domestically – which in itself is unlikely – a judge who wanted to impose a liberalising interpretation on the domestic law would have to have a *pre-existing* determination to take a liberal stance in relation to the PCA 1978 or the OPA 1959. If so, he or she would be able to find some, admittedly meagre, support in the jurisprudence for that stance. But equally the opposing, conservative stance could be taken and could find support in the jurisprudence, particularly from *Gibson v UK*.[458] The OPA itself clearly takes an overtly paternalistic stance since it assumes that judgments can be made and imposed on others as to what might deprave

451 See p 466, above.
452 See above, pp 305–6.
453 A 287 (1993). See, for discussion, pp 466–68.
454 (1976) 1 EHRR 737. See, for discussion, p 464.
455 (1994) 19 EHRR 34. See further pp 488–89.
456 See Chapter 4, pp 262–63, 270–73.
457 For example, in *R v Perrin* [2002] EWCA Crim 747, a recent case on the OPA 1959 (discussed at pp 584–85 below) in relation to the internet, *Handyside* and other relevant Strasbourg decisions were fully considered. The Court noted that the margin of appreciation doctrine was relevant in them, especially *Handyside*. But it did not appear to appreciate that by applying *Handyside* without seeking to disregard as far as possible the parts of the decision affected by the doctrine, it was in effect allowing the doctrine to have an impact on domestic law.
458 See p 483. For discussion of the domestic case, see Childs, M, 'Outraging Public Decency' (1991) PL 20.

and corrupt them. The HRA could be viewed as legitimising this existing position since the Strasbourg jurisprudence, especially the decisions of the Court on explicit expression, is itself paternalistic. Recent case law on the OPA and PCA in the context of internet pornography indicates that the courts are taking the latter stance. On the other hand, in this context, courts are likely to defer to the expertise of the regulators,[459] rather than rely on the Strasbourg jurisprudence, however it could be interpreted. So if the BBFC adopts a liberal stance – and it appears, increasingly, to be doing so[460] – the courts are unlikely to interfere with its decisions.

On the assumption that the relevant Strasbourg freedom of expression jurisprudence lends a degree of support to adult autonomy in this context, it can be argued that there is fairly limited scope under Art 10(2) for interferences with the freedom of expression of film-makers in respect of the theatrical release of films targeted at adults. It would be expected that they would be afforded an '18' certificate and appropriate warnings should be posted at cinemas and on the internet so that an unwitting viewer would not be offended. Article 10 might be viewed as underpinning the policy of awarding 'R18' certificates to films not viewed as obscene since there is virtually no chance of children viewing them due to the restrictions.

Taking account of *Scherer*[461] and *Hoare*,[462] different considerations might appear to apply to *videos*, owing to the possibility that, despite the restrictions on sale they might be viewed by children in the home, but this argument should be considered carefully, in terms of its impact on adults. The effect of the margin of appreciation doctrine on those decisions should be taken into account, following the argument discussed above.[463] The question of the harm that might be caused should also be considered, bearing in mind the lack of evidence mentioned above regarding a connection between behaviour seen on film and actual behaviour. The mere invocation of the possibility that children might view a video might not appear to be enough to satisfy the demands of proportionality, although it was found to be enough in *Hoare*. Theoretically, a domestic court could take a harder look at those demands than the Commission did in *Hoare*, since the margin of appreciation doctrine would be inapplicable. In practice, as discussed, the court would probably defer to the BBFC or VAC decision as in *R v Video Appeals Committee of the BBFC ex p BBFC*; possibly the HRA would add little in this context to the reasonableness standard applied in that instance although a nod in the direction of proportionality would be expected. In respect of videos, the small chance that children might view a video with an 'R18' certificate (bearing in mind the controls on buying such videos), and the unquantifiability of the risk that a child might be harmed by it, could be taken to mean that refusing to classify a video at 'R18', even where it is not obscene, would be disproportionate, under Art 10(2), to the aim pursued. Guidance on this matter might also usefully be sought from other jurisdictions,[464] since it is not a matter that Strasbourg has inquired into in any depth.

---

459 This is strongly indicated by the House of Lords' decision in *Pro-Life Alliance v BBC* [2004] 1 AC 185; [2003] 2 All ER 977 (for discussion, see pp 533–44) and by the *R v Video Appeals Committee of the BBFC ex p BBFC* decision [2000] EMLR 850.
460 See pp 555–62 above.
461 A 287 (1993) Com Rep.
462 [1997] EHRLR 678.
463 At pp 466–68.
464 See above, p 465.

The stance taken by Strasbourg in relation to films likely to offend religious sensibilities was indicated in the leading decision, *Otto-Preminger*,[465] discussed above.[466] The film in question was not likely to be viewed by children, but was found to be offensive to religious sensibilities. The seizure and forfeiture of the film was not found to breach Art 10. Further guidance derives from the decision of the Court of Human Rights in *Wingrove v UK*.[467] It concerned a decision of the BBFC, upheld by the VAC, to refuse a certificate to the short, explicit film, *Visions of Ecstasy*. The Court found that the decision to refuse a certificate was within the national authorities' margin of appreciation. But the film, which was to be promulgated as a short video, was viewed as offensive to religious sensibilities and as quite likely to come to the attention of children, since it could be viewed in the home.[468] No breach of Art 10 was found.

Conclusions

The view of the Williams Committee on Obscenity and Film Censorship, which conducted a review of the area in 1979,[469] was that the censorship of films should continue. The Committee considered that in the light of some psychiatric evidence to the effect that violent films might induce violent behaviour, a policy based on caution was justified.[470] The point has often been made, however, that the evidence that films have a very different impact from books or magazines is not strong: the difference in treatment may be due to historical reasons: new forms of expression take time to gain the acceptance accorded to traditional mediums and are viewed with some suspicion.[471] Many of the BBFC Guidelines are aimed at preventing specific forms of harm which might come about as a result of the viewing of films. Clearly, the causal relationship between the viewing and the harm in many instances may be debatable, but the BBFC does have the prevention of particular harms – over and above the causing of offence – in mind. For example, rejecting or cutting the depiction of imitable combat techniques in films aimed at children is defensible on that basis. Glamorisation of images of sexual violence, including rape, may have some effect on the incidence of male aggression towards women, or other men. However, the avoidance of specific harms cannot be said to be the sole aim of cutting explicit sexual images in films aimed at adults, where they are not linked to non-consensual acts or violence. If such images are not obscene, although, admittedly, as pointed out above, that concept creates its own grave difficulties of interpretation, the basis for cutting them is unclear.

Although the BBFC clearly has in mind the invasion of adult autonomy created by imposing constraints on films beyond those demanded by the criminal law, it continues to accept that such constraints are necessary, even though they create a stricter censorship regime in the UK than in the rest of Europe. Such constraints are partly based on

---

465   (1994) 19 EHRR 34.
466   See pp 488–89.
467   (1996) 24 EHRR 1. The question of the validity of taking the stance adopted in *Wingrove* and *Otto-Preminger* is considered above, at pp 491–97.
468   See paras 61 and 63 of the judgment.
469   Cmnd 7772, 1979. See Simpson, AWB, *Pornography and Politics: The Williams Committee in Retrospect*, 1983, pp 35–37.
470   See Simpson, AWB, ibid p 37.
471   See eg Barendt, *Freedom of Speech*, op. cit., fn 1, 1st edn, p 125.

necessarily subjective interpretations of the contextual validation of explicit images. In taking its particular stance towards the censorship and classification of films the BBFC appears to an extent to be bowing to government pressure, as the story behind *R v Video Appeals Committee of the BBFC ex p BBFC* reveals. The possibility of mounting successful challenges to restrictive BBFC decisions in reliance on Art 10, as discussed above, remains open and would provide a counter to the paternalistic stance sometimes taken by the government.

But it is not suggested that the only consideration that should inform BBFC decisions is that of moral autonomy. In dealing with the portrayal of sexuality the BBFC is in a position to shift the focus from traditional concerns as to offence and the undermining of traditional moral values, to the protection of what may be termed 'constitutional morality'.[472] Indeed there are some signs in the stance it takes to the classification of films portraying sexual violence that it is already beginning to do so. In other words, on the model provided by the Supreme Court of Canada which reconceptualised the concern of obscenity law as focused on the protection of foundational values such as equality and dignity,[473] the BBFC could increasingly bring such factors into its deliberations into the portrayal of sexual activity in film.

The internet[474]

Introduction

The question of the regulation of the internet is immensely complex.[475] The issues raised can only be touched on here, but one of the most significant concerns its regulation in the converged environment, which is considered below. The obvious problem which arises if one considers the regulatory regime applied to broadcasting under the 1990 Act, is that the internet provides a complex global communications network which cannot be fully subject to regulation applied within the boundaries of one state. The application of criminal and civil law to the internet is also challenging.

The internet is already a highly significant medium in terms of the provision of both information and entertainment. Its current and future significance as a medium cannot be over-stated – it is probably overtaking broadcasting as the culturally supreme medium. Its role in providing information has been recognised for some time; its role in relation to entertainment has perhaps been less emphasised. Many websites seek to provide both information and entertainment by the provision of video clips, photographs, narrative. The association between the use of the internet and the other media considered here is very strong; for example, a number of websites, official and unofficial, are dedicated to a range of films and broadcasts and show trailers, advertisements and clips.

---

472 See Fenwick, H and Phillipson, G, (2006), op. cit., fn 1 at Chapter 9, pp 450–62.

473 See *R v Butler* [1992] 1 SCR 452. See also Harel, A, 'Bigotry, Pornography and the First Amendment' 65 (1992) S Cal L Rev 1887, 1897.

474 See generally: Barendt, E, *Freedom of Speech*, 2nd edn, 2005, Chapter 13; Akdeniz, Y, Walker, C and Wall, D (eds), *The Internet, Law and Society*, 2000; Graham, G, *The Internet: A Philosophical Inquiry*, 1999, Routledge.

475 For detailed treatment, see Akdeniz, Y, Walker, C and Wall, D (eds), *The Internet, Law and Society*, 2000.

But the internet is also a strongly *participatory* medium;[476] it not only enables ideas to be expressed by individuals in their live journals or on websites and discussion forums, it also affords – more significantly – efficacy to such expression in terms of audience access.[477] The internet is taking on a new and important role as a platform for the mass expression and exchange of ideas, globally. Individuals in general are largely excluded from mainstream discourse in the media. Journalists may claim to speak for them, and also their views find a very limited opportunity for expression in 'Letters' pages or audience-participation broadcasts, but such expression hardly overcomes the dominance of the media by professionals, meaning that it is unrepresentative, especially of the views of women and minority groups, since journalism in general, and the higher positions in the media hierarchy, still tend to be a white male domain. In this sense the internet can be compared to public protest since protest also provides a means of affording efficacy to the speech of individuals, and particularly of minority or excluded groups.[478] The German Supreme Court, in the *Brokdorf* case, viewed participation in protest as a form of 'active engagement in the life of the community'.[479] But the internet provides opportunities for the mass exchange of ideas that far transcend the role of protest since it allows for such engagement with the global community, providing a means of exchanging views across national boundaries that has never existed before with such efficacy. Further, such ideas include, but are not confined to, the political arena. As Barendt notes:

> The Net certainly affords much more equal opportunities for communication than the traditional press and broadcasting media, where the entry costs are high and which are in practice for the most part available only to professional journalists and to the political and social elite.[480]

It may be said therefore that it engages with the broadly based speech justifications, engaging values of autonomy[481] and self-development. [482]

There might appear then to be a strong case for viewing regulation of the internet with suspicion in free speech terms. The US Supreme Court has found that it should not be equated with broadcasting in relation to regulation, but, impliedly, with the

476 See Barendt (2005), op. cit., fn 1, at p 451.
477 According to a major research study published in April 2005 (*UK Children Go Online*, Sonia Livingstone and Magdalena Bober, April 2005: www.children-go-online.net), 75% of 9–19-year-olds surveyed had accessed the internet from a computer at home. The *Guardian* reported in October 2005 that one third of UK teenagers had their own website or live journal.
478 See: Chapter 8, pp 663–65; Barnum, DG, 'The Constitutional Status of Public Protest Activity in Britain and the US' [1977] PL 310; Barendt, op. cit., at pp 9, 14–15; Williams, D, *Keeping the Peace: the Police and Public Order* 1967, Hutchinson, pp 10 and 130–31; see also Sherr, *Freedom of Protest, Public Order and the Law* 1989, Blackwell, at pp 10–12.
479 69 Bverfge 315, 343–47 (1985).
480 See Barendt, E, *Freedom of Speech*, 2nd edn, 2005, Chapter 13, p 452.
481 See generally, Dworkin, R, 'Do We Have a Right to Pornography?' Chapter 17, in *A Matter of Principle*, 1985; Scanlon, T, 'A Theory of Freedom of Expression' (1972) 1 Phil & Pub Aff. 216.
482 See generally, Emerson, C, 'Towards a General Theory of the First Amendment' (1963) 72 Yale LJ 877, at pp 879–80; Redish, M, *Freedom of Expression*, 1984, Lexis, pp 20–30 and Greenwalt, K, (1989) 89 Columbia Law Review 119, at pp 143–45.

print media.[483] The argument that the choice that can be exercised over encountering online expression differentiates it from broadcasting is reasonably persuasive, although as argued above, it is becoming increasingly possible to exercise greater choice over broadcast expression as it becomes more interactive. In other words, it is becoming less of an intruder into the home and more of a deliberately invited visitor. Thus there is an argument for relaxing the regulation of broadcasting – which Ofcom appears to accept – but not for extending that model of regulation to the internet.

But the strength of the internet – its ready accessibility and susceptibility to choice – can also be viewed as its weakness. Its use by groups excluded from the mainstream media is not necessarily benign. For example, a range of racial hatred offences can be committed by broadcasters, film-makers or playwrights under the Public Order Act 1986 ss 20, 21, 22 and 23. As discussed above, Part 3 of the 1986 Act was amended to include religious hatred under the Racial and Religious Hatred Act 2005. The Public Order Act offences have not been specifically amended to apply to the internet, although s 21 probably covers it, but in any event the general difficulty of prosecuting ISPs, discussed below, would apply. Hate speech can be available from websites which would not appear in UK newspapers and could not appear in broadcasting due to Ofcom's regulation, and it can also be much more rapidly disseminated throughout the world. The ready dissemination of hate speech (and possibly of extreme depictions of sexual violence) arguably cannot be supported by the free speech argument from self-fulfilment.[484] Thus, as Barendt puts it:

> it is surely wise at least to retain those controls on Internet speech which are justifiable in the case of speech disseminated by other means. The mere facts that the Internet is easy and cheap for most people to use, and that they enjoy equal access as speakers and receivers on it, does not constitute an argument for a bonfire of controls.[485]

The discussion below of law and regulation of the internet is not therefore premised on the desirability of a complete relaxation of control over the internet.

This concern as to the 'weakness' of the internet particularly exercises the authorities in relation to the availability of pornography and the protection of children. This is the case at EU level and in relation to the UK Government, as discussed below. As a UK Government Consultation Paper put it in 2005:

> [The Internet is a] spectacular communications development . . . transforming our lives, offering unparalleled opportunities to communicate, to discover and to learn. Alongside these benefits, the Internet also brings challenges for, amongst other things, the regulation of potentially illegal pornographic material which is readily accessible . . . In pre-Internet days, individuals who wished to view this kind of material would need to seek it out, bring it into their home or have it delivered in physical form as magazines, videos, photographs etc, risking discovery and

---

483 *Reno v ACLU* 521 US 844. For further discussion of this point, see Barendt (2005), Chapter 13, p 455.

484 For discussion, see above, pp 305–6.

485 See Barendt, *Freedom of Speech*, 2nd edn, 2005, Chapter 13, p 454.

embarrassment at every stage. Now they are able to access it from their computers at home . . .[486]

Concern about the use of the internet is not confined to the availability of extreme or child pornography. It expresses itself in the UK partly through prompting developments in the criminal law, but also in supporting other initiatives aimed at regulation. Below, issues relating to UK law and regulation of the internet are considered, followed by consideration of the current efforts at regulation and the application of the current and proposed criminal law, taking account of free speech arguments.

Regulation of the internet

Internet advertising is regulated in the UK by the Advertising Standards Authority (ASA), but otherwise the internet is not at present regulated in accordance with any of the models considered above. In the White Paper, *A New Future for Communications*,[487] the government did not propose a means of drawing the internet within the Ofcom regime in relation to the regulation of programme services on the internet, or otherwise. Visual images available on a service provided by the internet prima facie fall within the definition, in the 2003 Act, of a 'licensable programme service', but such services also appear to fall within the exception provided for 'two-way' services, depending on the interpretation given to that exception. It is clearly intended to cover internet services. However, even on the very doubtful assumption that it could do, Ofcom, like the ITC,[488] has not sought so far to apply its powers to the internet. There would be severe practical difficulties in doing so, although it could in relation to broadcast material placed on websites by licensed broadcast services already under its purview. The result is that material is shown on various websites that clearly could not be shown in a broadcast.[489]

The internet provides a complex global communications network which cannot be fully subject to regulation applied within the boundaries of one state. The government has recognized the problems of seeking to applying regulation on the Ofcom model to the internet.[490] It has been contended that: 'By creating a seamless global-economic zone, borderless and unregulatable, the internet calls into question the very idea of a nation-state.'[491] But in considering controls over the internet, as over the other media considered here, it is necessary to distinguish between the application of the ordinary law and the use of a general regulatory regime monitored and policed by a regulatory body. In relation to the use of the law, a range of views have been expressed. It has been argued that the internet is not inherently unregulatable, even at the national level, on the ground that 'the Internet creates new contexts for old problems rather than new

---

486 *Consultation Paper on The Possession of Extreme Pornographic Material*: Home Office 30.8.05 – URL: news.bbc.co.uk/1 shared/bsp/hi/pdfs/30 08 05 porn doc.pdf.

487 Published 12 December 2000: www.communicationswhitepaper.gov.uk.

488 See the ITC website: http://www.itc.co.uk.

489 For example, Channel 4 has shown material on its website that has been excluded from films broadcast on television. See e.g. *Guardian* Unlimited Special Report 27.4.04.

490 See *Regulating Communications: The Way Ahead* June 1999, www.dti.gov.uk/convergence-statement.htm at para 3.20.

491 Barlow, JP, 'Thinking locally, acting globally' (1996) Cyber-Rights Electronic List 15 January.

problems *per se*'.[492] Robin Duval, President of the BBFC from 1999-2004, has also argued that the internet can be regulated, pointing out that corporations have successfully brought actions against ISPs on commercial grounds.[493] This is also the stance of the EU Commission, which is discussed further below. But as the UK Government pointed out in a recent Consultation Paper,[494] the general application of the criminal law in one jurisdiction to ISPs based abroad faces almost insuperable problems, as discussed below. The solutions being canvassed at present include reaching international agreements, particularly on the availability of pornography, and adapting or developing offences aimed at consumers and only indirectly at ISPs.

The availability of explicit and pornographic material on the internet has prompted significant changes in EU audio-visual policy. *The Council Recommendation concerning the protection of minors and human dignity*[495] was the first legal instrument at EU-level that was concerned with the content of material on the internet. The European Parliament and the Council had already taken measures in 1999 with a view to protecting minors from harmful material on the internet.[496] But in 2002 the Commission found that the development of the internet was continuing to create difficulties in relation to the policy of protecting children.[497] It noted that the volume of material on the internet is immense in comparison to broadcasting and also that in traditional broadcasting (analogue or digital) it is not difficult to identify the individual broadcaster, while it may be impossible to identify the source of content on the internet. At the same time access to harmful and illegal content is very easy and may even be unintentional. As a result the Commission proceeded in 2004 to propose an additional *Recommendation*[498] which calls on the member states, the industry and other interested parties to:

---

492 Akdeniz, Y, Walker, C and Wall, D (eds), *The Internet, Law and Society*, 2000, Chapter 1, p 17.

493 See RSA lecture 21.2.01, available from the BBFC website, www.bbfc.co.uk.

494 *Consultation Paper on The Possession of Extreme Pornographic Material*, Home Office 30.8.05 – URL: news.bbc.co.uk/1 shared/bsp/hi/pdfs/30 08 05 porn doc.pdf.

495 24 September 1998 98/560/EC, OJ L 270, 7.10.1998, p 48.

496 In order to promote a safer internet, the European Parliament and the Council adopted on 25 January 1999 a multi-annual Community Action plan on promoting safer use of the internet by combating illegal and harmful content on global networks Decision No 276/1999/EC, OJ L33, 6/2/1999 p 1 (the 'Safer Internet Action Plan'). On 16 June 2003, the European Parliament and the Council adopted a two-year extension to the Safer Internet Action Plan Decision No. 1151/2003/EC amending Decision No 276/1999/EC, OJ L 162, 1.7.2003, p 1.

497 In accordance with section III of the Recommendation, para 4. The implementation of the Recommendation was evaluated for the first time in 2000, and the first report was published in 2001: Evaluation Report to the Council and the European Parliament on the application of Council Recommendation of 24 September 1998 on protection of minors and human dignity COM(2001) 106 final, 27.2.2001. Parliament adopted a resolution on the report on 11 April 2002: C5-0191/2001 – 2001/2087(COS), in which it called on the Commission to draw up a further report preferably before 31 December 2002. This was produced in 2003: SECOND EVALUATION REPORT FROM THE COMMISSION TO THE COUNCIL AND THE EUROPEAN PARLIAMENT on the application of Council Recommendation of 24 September 1998 concerning the protection of minors and human dignity, Brussels, 12.12.2003, COM(2003) 776 final.

498 *Proposal for a recommendation of the European Parliament and Council on the protection of minors and human dignity and the right to reply in relation to the competitiveness of the European audiovisual and information services industry*, COM(2004) 341 final 2004/0117 (COD) 30.4.04, press release 04/598.

take steps to enhance the protection of minors and human dignity in the . . . Internet sector . . . Illegal, harmful and undesirable content and conduct on the Internet continues to be a concern for law-makers, industry and parents. There will be new challenges both in quantitative (more 'illegal' content) and qualitative terms (new platforms, new products) . . . . [states should take] into account the ever-increasing processing power and storage capacity of computers . . .[499]

The original and the proposed *Recommendations* favour the development of co-regulatory and self-regulatory mechanisms for the internet rather than regulation based on the imposition of an external regulatory regime via legislation. Such approaches, especially the co-regulatory one, are viewed by the Commission as more likely to be 'flexible, adaptable and effective . . . with regard to the protection of minors'.[500] At present the approach in the UK is largely self- rather than co-regulatory. At the same time it may be said that self-regulation is giving way to an extent to co-regulation at present since a loose co-operative framework covering public authorities, the industry and the other interested parties, including consumers, is becoming apparent, as indicated below.

So in accordance with the EU stance, which is reflected in current government policy as indicated below, Ofcom is likely to continue to take the approach that the ITC took – that it will support and contribute to the voluntary regulation of the internet in relation to television programme material and advertisements on web-sites.[501] It will be argued below, however, that current policy may not result in the creation of the level of protection for minors envisaged in the proposed 2004 Recommendation. A more overt and formal movement towards co-regulation may be necessary.

The remit of the Advertising Standards Authority covers standards of taste and decency in internet advertising. But the ASA does not seek to apply the British Code of Advertising, Sales Promotion and Direct Marketing (the CAP Code) to all internet advertising. It only applies it to online advertisements in 'paid for' space, such as banner and pop-up advertisements;[502] advertisements in commercial e-mails and sales promotions wherever they appear online (including in organisation's websites or in e-mails). It does not apply the CAP Code, which includes requirements of offence-avoidance and 'decency' in advertising,[503] to organisations' claims on their own websites.

---

499 Para 2 of the proposal for a recommendation.
500 Fn 495 above, Introduction.
501 See further: Ballard, T, 'Main Developments in Broadcasting Law' Yearbook of Copyright and Media Law, 2001–2, 329 at pp 334–35; Ballard, T, 'Survey of the Main Developments in the Field of Broadcasting Law in 1999' Yearbook of Copyright and Media Law, 2000, p 367 at pp 373–74.
502 In relation to these forms of internet advertising, the ASA states: 'There are a number of different online advertising formats (or Interactive Marketing Units (IMUs) as they are sometimes called) that are available to marketers. Banner advertisements are probably the best known, but other forms of IMUs include interstitials, superstitials, buttons, pop-ups, skyscapers, floating ads, advertorials and text links. A banner is an advertisement found on a website page. Banners appear on a rotating basis in windows, usually at the top, bottom or side of web pages, and are used by marketers to make consumers aware of their products and services and to drive consumers directly to a particular website.'
503 The Code states: 'Decency (ie avoiding serious or widespread offence) 5.1 Marketing communications should contain nothing that is likely to cause serious or widespread offence. Particular care should be taken to avoid causing offence on the grounds of race, religion, sex, sexual orientation or disability.

This is mainly because it would be almost impossible to apply sanctions effectively for breach of the Code in such advertising. When the ASA and CAP apply sanctions against companies that do not co-operate with their requests, they usually rely on third parties, such as the owners of newspapers, magazines and poster sites, to enforce decisions by refusing to accept advertising by the company in question. As the ASA acknowledges on its website: 'the direct relationship between the internet user and the organisation bypasses any middleman and makes the medium almost impossible to regulate effectively'.[504] The ASA also views the relationships between consumers who visit an organisation's own website as direct rather than involuntary: 'the information is therefore "pulled to" rather than "pushed at" them unlike traditional forms of advertising'. In relation to the forms of online advertising that it does seek to regulate, it appears to have a very high compliance rate.[505] It reacts to consumer complaints, if upheld, by contacting the organisations in question and requesting changes to internet adverts.[506] The advertisers appear to perceive commercial advantage in complying with the CAP Code – on the 'tit-for-tat' principle. If one advertiser defaults by refusing to comply, others are also likely to do so, thus damaging the level-playing field for marketers within each sector. Also the ASA could seek to apply sanctions against that company's advertising in other media sectors where middle-men can be utilised.

Thus the ASA has informal, commercial sanctions that can be brought to bear in relation to online advertising. They are aimed more at misleading adverts rather than at offensive ones. A general UK internet regulator would not have such sanctions at its command. Nor could it have the licensing power that Ofcom possesses or the classification power of the BBFC since ISPs may well be based outside the jurisdiction. The internet is clearly not as susceptible to control on the basis of offence-avoidance as the other visual media are. In relation to explicit and pornographic speech in films and photographs on websites, the internet has the potential in a sense to undermine the regulatory regimes applied to the other media, precisely because no regulatory body stands between it and the criminal law, creating a regulated 'no-go' area beyond the requirements of the law. In other words, there is no one regulator monitoring explicit internet material via a code with sanctions attached – a code that would, on the Ofcom model, impose standards for offence-avoidance going beyond those demanded by the relevant criminal law. This is not an argument for seeking to impose regulation on that model on the internet, even assuming that that could be done. The argument is that

Compliance with the Code will be judged on the context, medium, audience, product and prevailing standards of decency. 5.2 Marketing communications may be distasteful without necessarily conflicting with 5.1 above. Marketers are urged to consider public sensitivities before using potentially offensive material. 5.3 The fact that a particular product is offensive to some people is not sufficient grounds for objecting to a marketing communication for it.'

504 See asa.org.uk.

505 See *Compliance Report: Internet banner and pop-up adverts Survey* (2002), available from the ASA website: asa.org.uk.

506 The ASA upheld its first complaint against a banner advertisement in May 2000. The advertisement, by an internet service provider, appeared on a financial web page and a complaint was upheld on the ground that the advertiser did not make it sufficiently clear that the banner was an advertisement, not editorial content. Since that time, complaints against a further six banner advertisements have been upheld by the ASA.

the availability of legal, explicit material on the internet that at present could not be broadcast, places Ofcom's regulation under pressure.

Since there is no regulatory regime on the broadcasting model, material posted on the internet is more likely to come directly into conflict with the criminal law in relation to explicit expression. The internet is subject to the criminal law just as the other media considered here are, although the law has required adaptation in order to bring websites within its ambit. Procedurally and substantively speaking, there are problems in securing convictions in respect of web-based material which do not arise in relation to broadcasts or films. The use of the criminal law to strike directly at the consumer of pornography rather than at the supplier immediately engages speech-based autonomy arguments balanced against weaker countervailing justifications, as discussed below.

Voluntary Regulation

The UK, in accordance with EU policy, has followed the path of self-regulation of the internet, against the backdrop of the relevant criminal law. Thus, in the UK there has been so far no general attempt to draw the internet within the system of restraints used for broadcasting, or the system used for films. Instead the internet is restrained, as discussed above, by the general criminal law relating to expression, and also by self-regulation. The White Paper, *A New Future for Communications*,[507] and the Communications Act itself endorse this self-regulatory approach.

Section I(1) of the EU Council *Recommendation*[508] provides that the member states should encourage the establishment of national frameworks for self-regulation by operators of online services. A number of UK Internet Service Provider Associations (ISPAs) are established in the UK, and in a number of member and accession states.[509] The ISPAs from eight member states, including those from the UK are members of the European Internet Service Providers Association organisation (EuroISPA). Section II(2) of the Recommendation proposes that the industries and the parties concerned should draw up codes of conduct for, *inter alia*, the protection of minors and human dignity, in order to create an environment favourable to the development of new services.[510]

---

507 White Paper, para 6.10: 'OFCOM should ensure continuing and effective mechanisms for tackling illegal material on the internet, such as those being pursued under the auspices of the internet Watch Foundation. It will also promote rating and filtering systems that help internet users control the content they and their children will see. 6.10.1: The Government sees enormous benefits in promoting new media, especially the internet. But it is important that there are effective ways of tackling illegal material on the internet and that users are aware of the tools available, such as rating and filtering systems, that help them control what they and their children will see on the internet. Research suggests that this is what people want in relation to the internet, rather than third party regulation.'

508 Fn 495 above.

509 The member states are: Belgium, Germany, Spain, France, Ireland, Luxembourg, Netherlands, Austria, Sweden. Hungary, Estonia, Slovenia, Turkey, Iceland and Norway have also established ISPAs. In Denmark, Greece, Portugal and Finland, the ISPs are represented through other trade organisations (Commission Report, see fn 495 above).

510 The Commission has given guidance as to the content of such Codes. In particular, the Codes should cover the complaints mechanisms, with a view to facilitating the making and handling of complaints. They should also facilitate a co-regulatory approach by covering the procedures for ensuring cooperation between the operators and the public authorities. These should address the issues of basic rules (i)

The UK has stated that codes of conduct have been established and has also proposed to the Commission that such codes should be drawn up by the industry representatives, rather than within a cooperative venture, involving public authorities. In a number of the member states, in contrast, including Germany and France, public authorities have been involved in drawing up the codes.

A number of the member states also have in place additional specific legal requirements dealing with the operators' obligations in relation to any illegal content on the internet. This includes, for example, the imposition of positive obligations to prevent the further distribution of information clearly covered by the provisions of the country's penal code or obligations to preserve data in order to assist in investigations and prosecutions. This is not the case at present in the UK. The Commission has also encouraged the development of 'notice and take down' procedures in relation to illegal content on the internet.[511]

The development of rating systems is encouraged by the Commission. They allow the carers of children to decide for themselves whether particular websites are suitable for children to access. The systems can be voluntary or mandatory. The UK relies on a voluntary system established by the Internet Content Rating Association (ICRA); under it website managers can apply for a rating on a voluntary basis. Once this rating is available, parents and others, such as teachers, can use it to restrict access to websites with the most suitable rating. ICRA receives funding under the Safer Internet Action Plan and has produced a content rating system that is viewed as suitable for the EU. Rating systems can also be accompanied by filtering systems – systems that block access to certain websites, in the interests of protecting minors.[512] Once a quality charter of websites has been drawn up filter programmes can ensure that users in a particular forum, such as a library or school, are restricted to the websites on the list and such programmes are used in a number of the member states.

The above discussion indicates that the UK favours a regime that is towards the 'lighter touch' end of the spectrum, in comparison with the regimes established in a number of the other member states. The regime relies on a number of voluntary bodies and the involvement of public authorities in the UK has so far been very low-key. While this regime creates flexibility and avoids an overly restrictive approach to website access where controlled by public authorities, it also opens the way to misuse

on the nature of the information to be made available to users, its timing and the form in which it is communicated, (ii) for the businesses providing the online services concerned and for users and suppliers of content, (iii) on the conditions under which, wherever possible, additional tools or services are supplied to users to facilitate parental control, (iv) on the handling of complaints, encouraging operators to provide the management tools and structures needed so that complaints can be sent and received without difficulty and introducing procedures for dealing with complaints and (v) on cooperation procedures between operators and the competent public authorities (op. cit., fn 495 above, para 3.1.1).

511 See fn 495 above. These are methods of receiving complaints from members of the public via hotlines, which can then be screened and passed on to the police or to an internet service-provider. One of the key aims of the Safer Internet Action Plan 1999–2004 (ibid, para 3.1.2, 9) was the creation of a European network of hotlines to span the EU. The Commission found that although hotlines had been established in a number of states, no respondents appeared to have made provision for assessing the efficiency of the hotlines in practice.

512 A particular filtering system utilises 'walled gardens', consisting of special portals allowing access only to sites of guaranteed quality.

of power by the voluntary bodies in question. In the UK a self-regulatory system for the internet is being established by a number of voluntary bodies, including in particular the Internet Watch Foundation with a remit to reduce the availability of illegal material on the internet.[513] The Internet Watch Foundation (IWF) was founded by the UK Internet Industry in 1996. It is funded by the EU and the UK internet industry;[514] it also has the support of the DTI and the Home Office.[515] In its own words the IWF:

> is the only authorised organisation in the UK which provides an Internet 'hotline' for the public to report their exposure to illegal content online. We aim to minimise the availability of Internet content that contains: child abuse images originating anywhere in the world; criminally obscene content hosted in the UK; criminally racist content hosted in the UK.[516]

The IWF has produced a Consultation Paper on developing the use of rating systems in the UK to block undesirable internet content.[517] Thus its activities appear to be extending beyond the enforcement of the criminal law; they may have a hidden ideological basis and may in particular invade the expression of sexual minorities. It is argued that government backing should be withdrawn from the IWF unless its activities, and any apparent ideological predilections, are subject to some form of accountability.

Rating, or vetting,[518] and filtering systems[519] can be used as an aspect of the self regulation of the internet. Filtering systems are commonly used in the US by state bodies such as schools or universities and also by parents. Such systems are supported by the government in the UK[520] and also by the EU.[521] Rating or filtering systems are problematic in free speech terms since they limit consumer choice and are frequently over-inclusive. They may also be under-inclusive in the sense that they do not affect a

---

513 For further information, see: www.iwf.org.uk.
514 This includes Internet Service Providers (ISPs), Mobile Operators and manufacturers, Content Service Providers (CSPs) and telecommunications and software companies.
515 See the DTI statement Secure Electronic Commerce Statement (London 1998 at www.dti.gov.uk/CII/ana27p.html) para iv; Memorandum by John Battle MP, Minister for Science, Energy and Industry, House of Commons Adjournment Debate 'HMG Strategy for the Internet' 18.3.98, www.dti.gov.uk/Minspeech/btkspch3.htm.
516 It claims on its website that the use of its hotline reporting system has reduced the amount of illegal content hosted in the UK from 18% in 1997 to less than 1% in 2003. Under this system ISPs can combat abuse of their services by operating a 'notice and take down' service which alerts them to any illegal content found on their system; they can report material to the IWF which then passes on any relevant details to the law enforcement agencies.
517 'Rating and Filtering Internet Content – A UK Perspective' March 1998, at www.Internetwatch.org.uk/rating.html.
518 The Platform for internet Content Selections is a vetting system that prevents the display on the computer of certain material. It can cover a range of specified material and is added by an independent vetting body, the publisher of the material, or an ISP.
519 Filtering software, such as Cyberpatrol, can also be used to block or limit access to certain websites.
520 See notes 515 and 495 above.
521 See European Commission Communication, *Illegal and Harmful Content on the Internet* (COM(96) 487, Brussels,1996); but cf the Opinion of the Economic and Social Committee of the European Commission – OJEC, 98/C 214/08, 1998 at 29–32. See also Akdeniz, Y, 'The EU and illegal and harmful content on the Internet' (1998) 3(1) Journal of Civil Liberties 31.

number of aspects of internet-related communication, such as the use of chat-rooms. Thus, the objective of protecting children by the use of rating or filtering systems may not in fact be met, while at the same time adults may be prevented from accessing material posted on the internet. The free speech implications of the use of filtering software by state bodies was considered in the US in *Mainstream Loudoun v Board of Trustees*.[522] The Loudoun County public libraries provided internet access to their patrons subject to a number of restrictions; in particular, library computers were equipped with site-blocking software to block all sites displaying child pornography and obscene material and material deemed harmful to juveniles. The plaintiffs and the intervenors alleged that this policy violated their First Amendment rights since it 'impermissibly discriminates against protected speech on the basis of content and constitutes an unconstitutional prior restraint'. It was found that the policy should be subject to strict scrutiny; having examined it it was found that the policy was not necessary to prevent sexual harassment or access to obscenity or child pornography since other, less intrusive measures could have been adopted. Further, it was found that it was not narrowly tailored to meet the objectives asserted since less restrictive means were available to further the defendant's interests.[523]

The decision in *Loudoun* indicates that the pursuit of self-regulation by the use of rating or filtering systems by public authorities, such as schools, libraries or universities could be viewed as incompatible with rights of expression under Art 10. Clearly, as discussed above, the standards demanded under Art 10 at Strasbourg where children might be affected by explicit speech, are not as high as those maintained under the First Amendment. However, if, rather than use a filtering system, less restrictive measures were available in order to protect children, while leaving adults unaffected, state bodies might be expected to adopt them, although it must be noted that the European Court of Human Rights has not yet used the 'less restrictive measures' test in the context of explicit material.[524] This is in an instance in which, if a successful challenge to the policy of a particular public authority, such as a library, was mounted under Art 10, using s 7(1)(a) HRA, the body would merely have to change its policy; it would not be able to rely on s 6(2) HRA since no legislation mandates the use of filtering systems or provides public authorities with a discretion as to their use. However, as discussed in relation to films, it is unlikely that a challenge would be successful since the relevant Art 10 jurisprudence is so weak in its defence of explicit speech.

A less restrictive approach might involve relying on the Internet Content Rating Association (ICRA). The ICRA is an international, non-profit organisation of internet leaders. It states that its objective is to make the internet safer for children, by warning parents and others of the content of websites. It believes in an approach it terms: 'user empowerment - giving families the tools to control their online experience. When used voluntarily, tools like ICRA's empower families to match their online experience with their values, without compromising free expression or undermining other users' access to information and while respecting the rights of content providers'. The ICRA claims to make no ideological judgment about various sites. This labelling system would be

---

522 2 FSupp 2d 783 (EDVa 1998) 24 FSupp 2d 552 (1998).
523 *Sable Communications of California, Inc v FCC*, 492 US 115 (1989) was relied upon.
524 See further Chapter 4, pp 276, 287–90.

less restrictive than a general filtering system such as the one used in *Loudoun* since the questionnaire used is specific.[525] However, it would still create the problem of blocking adult access to sites in pursuit of the objective of protecting children.[526]

It is perhaps understandable that the UK Government has not sought so far to follow the example of the US Government in terms of seeking to impose cyber-censorship. But concerns may be raised as to the regulation by the IWF. It is a private, not a public, body although it could be viewed as having a public role of sorts, since it has government backing. But its role as an essentially private self-regulatory body means that it is not formally accountable to the public. In particular, any infringement of free speech principles by its activities would probably be outside the HRA since it may not be a functional public authority[527] and no statute governs its activities.

Applying criminal law to web-based material

The US has sought to suppress and restrict sexually explicit expression on the internet; initially by means of the Communications Decency Act 1996; but its main provisions were struck down as unconstitutional on the basis of over-breadth.[528] In so doing, the Supreme Court found, following a number of precedents relating to other media, that if restraints aimed at protecting children also affect adults disproportionately, they may not be used as the means of denying children access to sexually explicit material. In other words, traditional free speech principles were applied to the internet. So a more narrowly targeted provision in terms of cyber-censorship was needed, if it was to survive challenges. The 1996 Act was followed by the more narrowly drafted Child Online Protection Act 1998.

In contrast, no statute with special application has so far been introduced in the UK. Instead, amendments have been made to existing statutes creating criminal liability in

---

525 It employs 'the ICRA questionnaire'. This asks content providers to check which of the 45 elements in the questionnaire are present or absent from their websites. This then generates a short piece of computer code known as an ICRA label that the webmaster then adds to his/her site. Users can then use filtering software to allow or disallow access to websites, based on the information declared in the label. The ICRA does not itself rate internet content; the content providers do that, using the ICRA labelling system.

526 See further Lessig, L and Resnick, P, 'Zoning Speech on the Internet: A Legal and Technical Model' (1999) 98 Michigan Law Rev 395, discussing methods of seeking to ensure that ISPs can recognise that the recipient of a communication is a child.

527 In particular, it is not strongly linked to a core public authority, although as indicated it does have the support of government Departments. It is the weakest regulator discussed in this book, but it is similar in some respects to the Press Complaints Commission which probably is a public authority. For example they both have no statutory underpinning or association with statutes, apart from the recognition of the PCC in the HRA, s 12. See further Chapter 4, pp 216–35 on the emerging legal explanations of the functional public authority concept.

528 *Reno v ACLU* 521 US 844. For further information on the struggle between the American Civil liberties Union (ACLU) and official attempts to curb expression on the internet, see the ACLU site: www.aclu. org/issues/cyber/hmcl.html, 2000. The CDA made it a crime, punishable by up to two years in jail and/or a $250,000 fine, for anyone to engage in speech that is 'indecent' or 'patently offensive' on computer networks, if the speech can be viewed by a minor. The ACLU argued that the censorship provisions are unconstitutional because they would criminalize expression that is protected by the First Amendment and because the terms 'indecency' and 'patently offensive' are unconstitutionally overbroad and imprecise. See Vick, D [1998] 61 MLR 414 on the Supreme Court decision.

relation to explicit expression in order to apply them to web-based material. The situation is similar in Australia where the Broadcasting Services Amendment (Online Services) Act 1999 (Cth) drew the internet within the generally applicable prior restrictions on sexually explicit expression.[529] As discussed above, explicit web-based material can be considered within the Obscene Publications Act 1959, as amended (OPA). Section 168 of the Criminal Justice and Public Order Act 1994 added the transmission of electronically stored data to the Obscene Publication Act's definition of 'publication'. Creating a link from a UK-based web-page to another in another jurisdiction on which obscene material is posted arguably amounts to 'publication'.[530] In *Graham Waddon*,[531] the defendant was convicted of the offence under s 2(1) of the 1959 Act on the basis that he had maintained a website in the USA onto which he had uploaded obscene material from the UK. Thus the fact that the material was placed on a US-based website did not prevent the defendant from being charged and convicted of the s 2(1) offence in England.

But in general there are, in practice, particular problems in applying the Obscene Publications Act (and its equivalent in Scotland – the Civil Government (Scotland) Act 1982) to web-based material. For example, the definition of obscenity is a relative one, dependent on the susceptibilities of those who are likely to encounter the material.[532] Web-based erotic and pornographic material, including material from '18'- or 'R18'- rated films, is available on a range of websites to any user who possesses a computer of the correct specification, although a credit card would often have to be used to gain access to it. Children can therefore gain access to such material and images, and the question of the obscenity of the material might therefore have to be determined by reference to that likely audience, depending on the circumstances, including the nature of the website and the likelihood that children would be able to access it. It would be harder to establish the extent of the likelihood that children might access the information than it is to make the same calculation in relation to print material, although probably it would be as hard as it is in relation to videos. But videos are of course regulated by the BBFC and it is an offence in itself to publish an unclassified video, without reference to its obscenity or indecency. Further, the BBFC has already taken the decision to continue to censor video films beyond the demands of the criminal law, thereby obviating the possibility of a prosecution under the 1959 Act, a decision which is, in effect, as discussed above, a compromise between defending adult autonomy and risking the promulgation of pornography to children. Since the internet is not subject to the policing of an equivalent regulator, this problem is more significant in that context.

Although the thrust of UK policy in relation to web-based pornography is against individual consumers under the OPA, where the manager of the ISP happens to be in this jurisdiction successful prosecution can occur. At least one successful prosecution

---

529 For discussion and criticism of the Act, see Chen, P 6(1) UNSWLJ.

530 See Akdeniz, Y, 'To link or not to link?' (1997) 11(2) International Review of Law, Computers and Technology 281.

531 (1999) Southwark Crown Court, 30 June; appeal dismissed 6 April 2000.

532 See pp 470–72 above.

has been brought against a web page provider – *R v Perrin*.[533] In that judgment a number of findings were made that were intended to adapt obscenity law so as to catch web-based pornography, addressing some of the issues discussed above. The defence argued that the only relevant publication of the web page was to the police officer who had downloaded it, and therefore it was wrong to test obscenity by reference to others who might have gained access to the preview page, and it was very unlikely that it would be visited by accident. However, the Court of Appeal accepted that there was publication whenever anyone accessed the preview page. No evidence that children would be likely to access it or had accessed it was put forward, but the Court appeared to assume that this was a possibility and that therefore the obscenity of the material could be judged against that likely audience. The lack of interest in the evidence in relation to children could be viewed as creating an appearance of departure from the basic principle of relative obscenity. The Court also rejected the suggestion that a prosecution should only be brought against a publisher where the prosecutor could show that the major steps in relation to publication were taken within the jurisdiction of the court. The possibility that the main steps towards publication might have occurred in another jurisdiction with less restrictive laws (the US) was not accepted as relevant. In relation to Art 10 the Court found: 'In the result we are satisfied that the statutory provision relied upon does fall within the scope of Article 10:2. For a legitimate purpose the offence was prescribed by law. Parliament was entitled to conclude that the prescription was necessary in a democratic society.' In other words, the Court refused to look beyond the balance that Parliament had struck in amending the OPA in 1994 order to include the internet. This was a highly restrictive interpretation of Art 10 since the Court refused to accept that it itself had a responsibility, under s 6 HRA, to examine the application of the law, taking the requirements of proportionality into account, in the instant case.

In general the gravest problem facing the UK authorities is the practical one of seeking to bring prosecutions against ISPs operating abroad. Clearly, jurisdictions differ greatly as to the speech that they criminalise. This potentially places both the national authorities and the Internet Service Providers in a difficult, almost impossible, position. If national laws *could* be enforced against ISPs regardless of jurisdiction, they would be forced to limit the provision of material on websites very severely since they would have to obey the most draconian and restrictive of the speech laws available.[534]

---

533   [2002] EWCA Crim 747, CA. This case involved a French national based in the UK who was publishing from abroad (in the USA). The appellant was convicted of publishing an obscene article and appealed. The obscene article in question was a webpage on the internet. It depicted people covered in faeces, coprophilia or coprophagia, and men involved in fellatio. That webpage was in the form of a trailer, a preview, available free of charge to any one with access to the internet. Any one wanting more of the type of material which it displayed could click on to a link marked 'subscription to our best filthy sites' and could gain access to a further webpage by providing credit card details. The preview webpage was accessed by an officer with the Obscene Publications Unit. To reach it a viewer would have to type in the name of the site, or conduct a search for material of the kind displayed.

534   This was pointed out on behalf of the defence in *R v Perrin* [2002] EWCA Crim 747, CA, referring to 'the world wide accessibility of the Internet' and the opinion of the United States Court of Appeal was relied on to the effect that (Third Circuit) in *ACLU v Reno (No 3)* [2000] 217 F.3d 162 at 168–69 any court or jury asked to consider whether there has been publication by a defendant of a webpage which is obscene should be instructed to consider first where the major steps in relation to publication took place, and only to convict if satisfied that those steps took place within the jurisdiction of the court. As discussed, this argument was not accepted by the Court of Appeal.

As Barendt points out:

> Website operators and other senders may have no idea who picks up their messages and which jurisdiction they live in, so the law imposes a great burden of them if they can be prosecuted whenever, say, a sexually explicit communication is accessed by a child, or extremist speech is accessed by anyone living in a country with strict hate speech laws.[535]

On the other hand, the national authorities are placed in an impossible position since they may well be unable to enforce sanctions against ISPs who are in another jurisdiction that is unlikely to aid in the enforcement of stricter national laws than it itself recognises. Such countries would be likely to have little interest in prosecuting. Publishers might take the main steps towards internet publication in countries with the most relaxed laws. According to the UK Government, very little potentially illegal pornographic material found on the internet originates from within the UK.[536] It appears probable that the lack of UK-hosted material is the result of the deterrent effect of the OPA and the Civil Government (Scotland) Act 1982.

Thus the UK is a more restrictive jurisdiction which the government views as in an especially difficult position in terms of holding the line against internet material hosted on websites outside the jurisdiction. The UK is addressing these problems, as discussed below, partly by enforcing laws against explicit expression against the ultimate consumer rather than against the ISP, and partly through voluntary regulation of the internet. In relation to extreme adult pornography the government stated recently in its *Consultation Paper on The Possession of Extreme Pornographic Material*:[537] 'the global nature of the internet means that it is very difficult to prosecute those responsible for publication who are mostly operating from abroad'. The paper is consulting on the introduction of a new offence of mere possession of 'extreme pornographic' material – an offence that has not existed previously in UK law. In its *Consultation Paper* the government noted that it is already illegal to publish such material under the Obscene Publications Act 1959 and, in Scotland, under the Civic Government (Scotland) Act 1982. However, it pointed out that the global nature of the internet means that it is very difficult to prosecute those responsible for publication who tend to operate from abroad.

So the proposal is to make illegal the possession of a limited range of extreme pornographic material featuring adults. The intention is that the new legislation would introduce provisions to operate alongside the OPA that would mirror the provisions already in place in respect of indecent photographs of children.[538] A new offence would be created of 'simple possession of extreme pornographic material which is graphic and sexually explicit and which contains actual scenes or realistic depictions of serious violence, bestiality or necrophilia.' The intention is not to add an offence of possession to the OPA but to create a new freestanding offence to operate alongside the OPA

---

535 See Barendt *Freedom of Speech* 2nd edn (2005) Chapter 13 p 452.
536 It notes in its 2005 Consultation paper (fn 537 below) that the Internet Watch Foundation (IWF) received no reports of UK-hosted material in 2003 or 2004.
537 Home Office 30.8.05 – URL: news.bbc.co.uk/1 shared/bsp/hi/pdfs/30 08 05 porn doc.pdf.
538 The offence of possession of child pornography under the Protection of Children Act 1978 s1, discussed below.

1959 and the Civic Government Act and to increase the sentence for publishing under those other two statutes in order to emphasise the difference between possession and publication. The Consultation paper states: 'We believe the material which is under consideration would be abhorrent to most people and has no place in our society. Our intention in proposing a possession offence is to try to break the demand/supply cycle.' The offence would be limited to explicit actual scenes or realistic depictions of the specified types of material. The term 'explicit' indicates that the offence would cover activity which can be clearly seen and is not hidden, disguised or implied. The intention is also only to cover actual images or realistic depictions of the activities listed. It is not intended therefore to cover text or cartoons. This follows the precedent of the Protection of Children Act (PCA) 1978, s 1 of which covers pseudo-photographs.

The similar child pornography offence under the PCA s 1 requires possession for gain. However, as far as the internet is concerned, possession has been criminalised since downloading child pornography from the internet is covered by the PCA; it has been found to constitute the 'making' of a photograph or pseudo-photograph.[539] It is not intended that the new offence will depend on bringing the material within the definition of 'obscenity'. The aim is to close a gap in the OPA: at present it only covers possession for gain. Thus, downloading adult pornography is not covered by the OPA since making a photograph not for gain is not covered. The new offence would close that gap and bring the OPA into line with the PCA. It would also possibly criminalise the possession of some material that might not be deemed obscene. The obscenity of material is judged by reference to its likely audience; the current proposal appears to proceed on the basis that some material should not be possessed, regardless of the likelihood that it would be encountered by anyone other than members of a willing audience. The new offence is aimed at the internet, but would not be confined to it. It would represent an extremely significant extension of the law relating to explicit speech. The justifications for its introduction are weak: it is unlikely that it would break the demand/supply link since the ISPs involved would still have an audience in a range of countries with less restrictive laws. The evidence that the availability of such material causes harm is inconclusive, as the government admits in the Paper.

The experience in the US indicates that forms of self-regulation of the internet provide a more sensitive, nuanced and, arguably, more effective form of restraint than creating broad criminal sanctions relating to explicit material on websites. However, the restraints on the internet described above indicate that the situation in the UK is a confused and anomalous one. The criminal law has been applied in an arguably over-inclusive fashion. An imprecise and archaic law – the Obscene Publications Act – has been afforded a very broad interpretation in *R v Perrin*[540] that applies it to a relatively new medium. The same could be said of the interpretation of the PCA in *R v Bowden*.[541] The OPA creates restrictions in the UK that are not duplicated in a number of other jurisdictions; if the new possession offence is introduced, that position will be exacerbated. At the same time public authorities, such as libraries and schools, are drifting into a situation similar to that appertaining in the US, whereby rating and

539 [2000] 2 All ER 418. See further p 478 above.
540 [2002] EWCA Crim 747, CA.
541 [2000] 2 All ER 418.

filtering systems are used to block access to a number of websites, without full inquiry into the over-inclusiveness of such systems or the value judgments underlying them. The decision so far of the UK Government not to follow the dubious US example in seeking to introduce general legislation to protect children in this context is a readily defensible one, but the lack of government intervention or – it appears – of recognition of the potential problems could lead to an overly restrictive stance. The analogy of book-burning has been used quite frequently[542] to describe the scenario that might arise in the UK, whereby cyber-censorship creates the same effect, but in a hidden fashion, in relation to controversial and explicit expression in cyberspace.

7 Conclusions

The Williams Committee recommended in 1979 that the printed word should not be subject to any restraint and that other material should be restrained on the basis of two specific tests: first, material which might shock should be available only through restricted outlets; second, material should not be *prohibited* unless it could be shown to cause specific harm.[543] Clearly, these proposals would give greater weight to freedom of expression than is currently given, in that they would allow greater differentiation between the kinds of harm which might be caused by different forms of material, an emphasis on inquiring into whether harm is or could be caused by the promulgation of pornography to a willing adult audience, and in particular they could have led to the abolition of the uncertain and almost unworkable 'deprave and corrupt' test. The Committee emphasised a fundamental difference between the *prohibition* and the *restriction* of the sale of pornography and other explicit material.

These proposals found partial expression in the Indecent Displays (Control) Act 1981, the provisions under the Local Government (Miscellaneous Provisions) Act 1982 for regulating 'sex establishments' and the Cinematograph (Amendment) Act 1982, which changed the classification of films and in particular introduced the 'R18' rating. The proposal as to removing the prohibition as opposed to restriction from the written word and from much other pornographic material has not been implemented[544] and various far-reaching restraints remain, including the use of forfeiture proceedings and the uncertain offence of outraging public decency, both tending to undermine the safeguards for artistic freedom contained in the 1959 Act.

It seems that, if there is to be radical reform of the law relating to obscenity, indecency, regulation and censorship, the government will have to take the initiative. As indicated, the inception of the HRA has not brought about sweeping change, and is very unlikely to do so. The UK position in respect of restraints on freedom of speech in the name of the protection of morality does not appear to breach Art 10. In any event, the preoccupation of the domestic judiciary with the value of *political* expression and decisions such as those in *Knuller* and *Gibson* do not suggest that there is a determination on the part of the judiciary to import greater certainty and liberality into the restriction and regulation

---

542 See the ACLU Report www.aclu.org/issues/cyber/burning.html, 1997.

543 See the recommendations of the Williams Committee (*Report of the Committee on Obscenity and Film Censorship* Cmnd 7772, 1979); Simpson, op. cit., fn 1; for commentary, see McKean, WA [1980] CLJ 10; Coldham, S (1980) 43 MLR 306; Dworkin, op. cit., fn 1.

544 For further discussion of the Committee's position, see above, p 455.

of explicit expression. Similarly, after the decisions in the *Handyside* case and in *Müller v Switzerland*,[545] it seems unlikely that there will be any UK move towards greater protection of freedom of speech in this area by recourse to the European Convention on Human Rights at Strasbourg. It may be assumed that the exception contained in Art 10(2) in respect of the protection of morals will continue to be widely interpreted because the European Court of Human Rights will continue to allow a wide margin of appreciation to member states in this very sensitive area. However, as indicated above, there are strong grounds for expecting the domestic judiciary to take a stance under the HRA towards expression offensive to religious sensibilities which differs from that taken at Strasbourg. In so far as political expression is affected, especially by aspects of media regulation, the domestic judiciary now have the opportunity to take a more intrusive stance towards furthering the protection of such expression, under the HRA. This may be a very important development in the domestic *political* expression jurisprudence.

The most significant decisions about what it is acceptable for people to see or hear are taken by media regulators, not by courts. The discussion demonstrated that regulation is subject to rapid change which to an extent reflects the rapidly changing technological environment in the visual as opposed to the print sector. But it is suggested that regulation has not kept pace with such technological change, and in particular with the impact of the internet and with developments in Western broadcasting. Developments in broadcasting and in internet access have lead to a globalisation of outlook in the current younger generation – an expectation that standards relating to explicit expression in the more progressive Western countries will be broadly in harmony with each other, while strongly differing standards will not be apparent across the different audio-visual sectors. The discussion reveals that such expectations are not being met, while justifications for maintaining anomalous differences between the sectors or for taking a specifically UK-based stance on offence-avoidance have not been forthcoming. At present, it will be suggested, the government is tending to avoid the difficult questions that harmonisation in both respects would create, in particular the question of the anomaly of non-regulation of the internet alongside regulation of broadcasting by Ofcom. The judiciary continues to prefer to defer to the decisions of regulators rather than accepting that it has a duty under the HRA to call them to account in terms of maintaining free expression standards.

The position of the visual media is particularly difficult in relation to such forms of expression. From a liberal standpoint, cuts in film or broadcast material on the basis of avoiding offence may be condemned as an infringement of autonomy, especially where they go beyond what is demanded by the criminal law.[546] There is general opposition to such censorship in other mediums in the absence of clear evidence of the concrete harm caused by the material.[547] However, explicit images conveyed in the print as

545 See further Feingold, C, 'The Little Red Schoolbook and the European Court of Human Rights' (1978) Revue des Droits de l'Homme 21.

546 See Schauer, F, *Free Speech: A Philosophical Enquiry*, 1982, Chapters 5 and 6; Feldman, D, *Civil Liberties and Human Rights*, 2nd edn, 2002, 13.2; Tucker, DFB, *Law, Liberalism and Free Speech*, 1985, 11–56; Barendt, E, *Freedom of Speech*, 2nd edn, 2005, Chapter 1; see also above, pp 301–2.

547 See Feinberg, J, *The Moral Limits of the Criminal Law: Offense to Others*, 1985. For a brief discussion of the possible link between pornography and the commission of sexual offences, see above, pp 456–60.

opposed to the visual media may not only have less impact on people, but the encounter with them may represent more of a genuine choice. Liberals are willing to support restrictions on the outlets and public display of explicit material[548] on the ground that such restrictions do not necessarily spring from contempt for those who wish to view such material, but may simply reflect the genuine and personal aesthetic preferences of those who would rather not be confronted unexpectedly with offensive images.[549] The position of the broadcast media, film, the internet is more problematic since adults can normally protect themselves from offence. Following the liberal argument from autonomy, the provision of information and advice in order to warn persons of the content of particular films or broadcasts is clearly acceptable. Provision of such information, far from infringing personal autonomy, upholds it. But cuts or outright bans of visual material aimed at adult audiences, beyond the requirements of the criminal law, represent a failure to respect the right of adults to choose their own diverse forms of entertainment, within the law.

548 Such as, e.g., the recommendations of the Williams Committee (*Report of the Committee on Obscenity and Film Censorship* Cmnd 7772, 1979); see their 'Summary of our proposals'.
549 See Dworkin, R, 'Do we have a right to Pornography?' in *A Matter of Principle* (1985) pp 355–58, where he broadly endorses the Williams Committee's proposals.

Chapter 7

Official secrecy; access to state information

1 Introduction[1]

This chapter is concerned with restraints upon access to information created directly or indirectly by the law governing the release of sensitive government information, of 'official secrets'. It also considers the corollary – the positive rights to access to information held by public authorities now granted by the Freedom of Information Act 2000 (FoI), which came into force on 1 January 2005. This Act is not, strictly speaking, an aspect of the law of freedom of expression; since it gives positive rights to information, it does not, strictly, affect media free expression: it does not place restraints upon what the media may publish; rather it assists media bodies in their attempts to extract information from public authorities.[2] This is the stance taken at Strasbourg: Article 10 does not, as discussed below, offer rights of access to information. The Act is of concern in free expression terms in that it is very likely that journalists, along with opposition politicians and campaigners, as well as concerned individuals, will make particular use of it, in order to obtain information. This Chapter offers a brief treatment, taking account of developments since the Act came into force, because the Act is relevant to the overall position of the media as it seeks to hold government to account. For example, the law on disclosure of journalistic sources is difficult to assess without some knowledge of the means by which information about bodies such as hospitals, the police, and local authorities may be freely obtainable.

In contrast, the law on official secrecy has some direct application in free expression terms: there are indeed particular provisions of the Official Secrets Act that are aimed specifically at journalists,[3] while the restrictions the Act lays upon, for example, members

---

1 General reading, see: Birkinshaw, P, *Freedom of Information: The Law, the Practice and the Ideal*, 4th edn, 2005; Vincent, D, *The Culture of Secrecy, Britain 1832–1998*, 1998, OUP; Feldman, D, *Civil Liberties and Human Rights in England and Wales*, 2nd edn, 2002, Chapter 14; Bailey, SH, Harris, DJ and Jones, BL, *Civil Liberties: Cases and Materials*, 5th edn, 2001, Chapter 7; Baxter, JD, *State Security, Privacy and Information*, 1990, Macmillan; Shetreet, S (ed), *Free Speech and National Security*, 1991, Dordrecht; Gill, P, *Policing Politics: Security, Intelligence and the Liberal Democratic State*, 1994, Frank Cass; Lustgarten, L and Leigh, I, *In From the Cold: National Security and Parliamentary Democracy*, 1994, Clarendon; Whitty, N, Murphy, T and Livingstone, S, *Civil Liberties Law*, 2001, Chapter 7.
2 See for example Austin, R, 'Freedom of information: – a Sheep in Wolf's Clothing?', in Jowell, J and Oliver, D, *The Changing Constitution*, 5th edn, 2004, OUP.
3 See below at pp 602–5.

of the security services, directly affects their ability to tell their stories through the media, as in the notorious David Shayler affair,[4] considered in detail below.

The overall concern of this chapter is with the degree to which a proper balance has been and is currently being struck between the interest of the individual in acquiring information and the interest of the state and public authorities in withholding it. Clearly, there are genuine public interests, including that of protecting national security, in keeping some information out of the public domain; the question is whether other interests that do not correspond with and may even be opposed to the interests of the public are also at work. Initially, it may be said that in the UK, the area of control over government information is one in which the state's supposed interest in keeping information secret has in general prevailed very readily over the individual interest in question. It has often been said that the UK is more obsessed with keeping government information secret than any other Western democracy.[5] It is clearly advantageous for the party in power to be able to control the flow of information in order to prevent public scrutiny of certain official decisions and in order to be able to release information selectively at convenient moments. The British Government has available a number of methods of keeping official information secret, including the deterrent effect of criminal sanctions under the Official Secrets Act 1989, the Civil Service Conduct Code,[6] around 80 statutory provisions engendering secrecy in various areas and the civil action for breach of confidence. The situation of the civil servant in the UK who believes that disclosure as to a certain state of affairs is necessary in order to serve the public interest may therefore be contrasted with the situation of his or her counterpart in the US, where he or she would receive protection from detrimental action flowing from whistle-blowing[7] under the Civil Service Reform Act 1978. A weak form of a public interest defence might have been adopted under proposals in the then government's White Paper on freedom of information, published in July 1993.[8] It was proposed that the disclosure of information would not be penalised if the information was not 'genuinely confidential'. But when the Labour Government introduced the Public Interest Disclosure Act 1998, crown servants involved in security and intelligence activities, or those whose 'whistle-blowing' breaches the 1989 Act, were expressly excluded from its ambit, leaving them unprotected from employment detriment.

The UK has traditionally resisted freedom of information legislation and, until 1989, criminalised the unauthorised disclosure of any official information at all, however trivial, under s 2 of the Official Secrets Act 1911, thereby creating a climate of secrecy in the Civil Service which greatly hampered the efforts of those who wished to obtain and publish information about the workings of government. The Freedom of Information Act 2000 (FoI) signalled a break with the traditional culture of secrecy: 'the principle

---

4 For an overall look at the implications of that episode, see Best, K 'The Control of Official Information: Implications of the Shayler Affair' (2000) 5(6) *Journal of Civil Liberties* 18.

5 E.g., Robertson, G, *Freedom, the Individual and the Law*, 1989, pp 129–31.

6 See Drewry, G and Butcher, T, *The Civil Service Today*, 1991, Blackwell. It should be pointed out that the Civil Service Code, which came into force on 1 January 1996, contains a partial 'whistle-blowing' provision in paras 11–12.

7 For discussion of the situation of UK and US civil servants and developments in the area, see Cripps, Y, 'Disclosure in the public interest: the predicament of the public sector employee' [1983] PL 600; Zellick, 'Whistle-blowing in US law' [1987] PL 311–13; Starke (1989) 63 ALJ 592–94.

8 *Open Government*, 1993, HMSO.

that communication was the privilege of the state rather than of the citizen was at last ... reversed.'[9]

2 Official secrets

Section 2 of the Official Secrets Act 1911[10]

During the nineteenth century, as government departments grew larger and handled more official information, the problem of confidentiality grew more acute. Internal circulars such as the 1873 Treasury minute entitled *The Premature Disclosure of Official Information* urged secrecy on all members of government departments and threatened the dismissal of civil servants who disclosed any information; a Treasury minute issued in 1875 warned civil servants of the dangers of close links with the press.[11] The need for a further safeguard was emphasised in 1878 when one Marvin, who worked in the Foreign Office, gave details of a secret treaty negotiated between England and Russia to a particular newspaper. His motive appeared to be dissatisfaction with his job. He was prosecuted, but it was then discovered that no part of the criminal law covered the situation. He had memorised the information and thus had not stolen any document. He was not a spy and could not, therefore, be brought within the provisions of the Treason Act 1814. No conviction could be obtained and the Official Secrets Act 1889 was passed largely as a means of plugging the gap which had been discovered.

The 1889 Act made it an offence for a person wrongfully to communicate information obtained owing to his employment as a civil servant. However, the government grew dissatisfied with this measure; under its terms, the state had the burden of proving both *mens rea* and that the disclosure was not in the interests of the state. It was thought that a stronger measure was needed, and this led eventually to the passing of the Official Secrets Act 1911. It has often been suggested that the manner of its introduction into Parliament was disingenuous and misleading.[12] It was introduced apparently in response to fears of espionage and by the Secretary of State for War, not by the Home Secretary, giving the impression that it was largely an anti-espionage measure. Section 1 did deal largely with espionage, but s 2 was aimed not at enemy agents, but at English civil servants and other Crown employees. It was called, innocuously, 'an Act to re-enact the 1889 Act with amendments'. These disarming measures seem to have succeeded; it was passed in one afternoon and s 2 received no debate at all.

Section 2, which appeared to create a crime of strict liability, imposed a complete prohibition on the unauthorised dissemination of official information, however trivial. It is thought that the government clearly intended s 2 to have such a wide scope and had wanted such a provision for some time in order to prevent leaks of *any* kind of official information, whether or not connected with defence or national security.[13] It lacked any provision regarding the substance of the information disclosed so that technically it criminalised, for example, disclosure of the colour of the carpet in a minister's office.

---

9 Vincent, *The Culture of Secrecy, Britain 1832–1998*, 1998, p 321.
10 See Hooper, D, *Official Secrets*, 1987, Coronet, for history of the use of s 2.
11 See Robertson, op. cit., fn 5, at 53.
12 See *The Franks Report*, Cmnd 5104, 1972, para 50; Birkinshaw, op. cit., fn 1 at 76.
13 See ibid, at para 50.

It criminalised the receiver of information as well as the communicator, although there did appear to be a requirement of *mens rea* as far as the receiver was concerned; he or she had to know that the disclosure had occurred in contravention of the Act. Thus, it afforded no recognition to the role of the press in informing the public.

There were surprisingly few prosecutions under s 2; it seems likely that it created an acceptance of secrecy in the civil service which tended to preclude disclosure. In one of the few cases which did come to court, *Fell*,[14] the Court of Appeal confirmed that liability was not dependent on the contents of the document in question or on whether the disclosure would have an effect prejudicial to the interests of the state. The eventual demise of s 2 came about owing to a number of factors, of which one appears to have been the realisation that its draconian nature was perceived as unacceptable in a modern democracy and that therefore, convictions under it could not be assured. Such a realisation probably developed in response to the following three decisions.

Aitken and Others[15] arose from the disclosure by a reporter, Aitken, that the UK Government had misled the British people as to the amount of aid the UK was giving Nigeria in its war against Biafra. The government had suggested that it was supplying about 15% of Nigeria's arms, whereas the figure should have been about 70%. This figure derived from a government document called the Scott Report, which Aitken disclosed to the press. Aitken was then prosecuted under s 2 for receiving and passing on information, but the judge at trial, Caulfield J, clearly had little sympathy with a case seemingly brought merely to assuage government embarrassment and which disclosed no national security interest. Furthermore, the facts obtained from the Scott Report were obtainable from other sources. The judge found that a requirement of *mens rea* was needed and, moreover, effectively directed the jury to acquit in a speech which placed weight on the freedom of the press and suggested that it should prevail given the lack of a significant competing interest. He considered that s 2 should be 'pensioned off'.

Tisdall[16] also created some adverse publicity for the government owing to what was perceived as a very heavy handed use of s 2. Sarah Tisdall worked in the Foreign Secretary's private office, and in the course of her duties she came across documents relating to the delivery of cruise missiles to the RAF base at Greenham Common. She discovered proposals to delay the announcement of their delivery until after it had occurred and to make the announcement in Parliament at the end of question time in order to avoid answering questions. She took the view that this political subterfuge was morally wrong and therefore leaked the documents to the *Guardian*. However, they were eventually traced back to her. She pleaded guilty to an offence under s 2 and received a prison sentence of six months – an outcome which was generally seen as harsh.[17]

A similar situation arose in *Ponting*,[18] the case which is usually credited with sounding the death knell of s 2. Clive Ponting, a senior civil servant in the Ministry of Defence, was responsible for policy on the operational activities of the Royal Navy at a time when

14 [1963] Crim LR 207.
15 Unreported. See Aitken, J, *Officially Secret*, 1971, Weidenfeld and Nicolson.
16 (1984) *The Times*, 26 March.
17 See Cripps, op. cit., fn 7.
18 [1985] Crim LR 318; for comment, see Brewry, G, 'The *Ponting* case' [1985] PL 203, 212 and [1986] Crim LR 491.

opposition MPs, particularly Tam Dalyell, were pressing the government for information relating to the sinking of the *Belgrano* in the Falklands conflict. Michael Heseltine,
then Secretary of State for Defence, decided to withhold such information from
Parliament and therefore did not use a reply to Parliamentary questions drafted by
Ponting. He used instead a much briefer version of it and circulated a confidential minute
indicating that answers on the rules of engagement in the Falklands conflict should not
be given to questions put by the Parliamentary Select Committee on Foreign Affairs.
Feeling that opposition MPs were being prevented from undertaking effective scrutiny of
the workings of government, Ponting sent the unused reply and the minute anonymously
to the Labour MP, Tam Dalyell, who disclosed the documents to the press.

Ponting was charged with the offence of communicating information under s 2. The
relevant sub-section reads:

> ... it is an offence for a person holding Crown office to communicate official
> information to any person other than a person he is authorised to communicate it
> to or a person to whom it is *in the interests of the state* his duty to communicate
> it. [Emphasis added.]

The defence relied on the phrase the 'interests of the state', arguing that the term 'the
state' should be interpreted as 'the organised community' rather than the government.
This interpretation seemed to be warranted by part of Lord Reid's judgment in *Chandler
v DPP*.[19] Thus, it could be argued that it was in the interests of the nation as a whole
that Parliament should not be misled and that there was a moral duty to prevent this.
The word 'duty' in s 2, it was claimed, therefore connoted a moral or public duty.
However, the Crown relied upon other comments of Lord Reid in *Chandler* to the
effect that where national security was a factor, the government would be the final
arbiter of the state's interests. The judge, McCowan J, accepted this argument, finding
that the 'interests of the state' were synonymous with those of the government of the
day, and he therefore effectively directed the jury to convict. Despite this direction,
they acquitted, presumably feeling that Ponting should have a defence if he was acting
in the public interest in trying to prevent government suppression of matters of public
interest. The prosecution and its outcome provoked a large amount of adverse publicity,
the public perceiving it as an attempt at a cover up which had failed, not because the
judge showed integrity, but because the jury did.[20]

The decision in *Ponting* suggested that the very width of s 2 was undermining its
credibility; its usefulness in instilling a culture of secrecy owing to its catch-all quality
was seen as working against it. The outcome of the case may have influenced the decision
not to prosecute Cathy Massiter, a former officer in the Security Service, in respect of her
claims in a Channel 4 programme screened in March 1985 (*MI5's Official Secrets*) that
MI5 had tapped the phones of trade union members and placed leading CND members
under surveillance.[21] Section 2's lack of credibility may also have been a factor in the

---

19 [1964] AC 763; [1962] 3 All ER 142, HL.
20 For comment on the decision, see Ponting, C, *The Right to Know*, 1985, Sphere; Brewry, G, op. cit.,
    fn 18.
21 The Independent Broadcasting Association banned the programme pending the decision as to whether
    Massiter and the producers would be prosecuted. The decision not to prosecute was announced by

decision to bring civil as opposed to criminal proceedings against the *Guardian* and *The Observer* in respect of their disclosure of Peter Wright's allegations in Spycatcher: civil proceedings for breach of confidence were, in many ways, more convenient and certainly less risky than a s 2 prosecution. No jury would be involved and a temporary injunction could be obtained quickly in *ex parte* proceedings. However, the government did consider that the criminal rather than the civil law was, in general, a more appropriate weapon to use against people such as Ponting, and therefore thought it desirable that an effective criminal sanction should be available. When the government was eventually defeated in the *Spycatcher* litigation, the need for such a sanction became clearer.[22]

There had already been a long history of proposals for the reform of s 2. The Franks Committee, which was set up in response to Caulfield J's comments in *Aitken*, recommended[23] that s 2 should be replaced by narrower provisions which took into account the nature of the information disclosed. The Franks proposals formed the basis of the government's White Paper on which the Official Secrets Act 1989 was based. There had been various other attempts at reform; those put forward as Private Members' Bills were the more liberal. For example, Clement Freud MP put forward an Official Information Bill[24] which would have created a public right of access to official information, while the Protection of Official Information Bill,[25] put forward by Richard Shepherd MP in 1987, would have provided a public interest defence and a defence of prior disclosure.

The Official Secrets Act 1989[26]

Once the decision to reform the area of official secrecy had been taken, an opportunity was created for radical change, which could have included freedom of information legislation along the lines of the instruments in America and Canada. However, it was made clear from the outset that the legislation was unconcerned with freedom of information.[27] It decriminalises disclosure of some official information, although an official who makes such disclosure may, of course, face an action for breach of confidence as well as disciplinary proceedings, but it makes no provision for allowing the release of any official documents into the public domain. Thus, claims made, for example, by Douglas Hurd (the then Home Secretary) that it is 'a great liberalising

---

Sir Michael Havers on 5 March 1985. An inquiry into telephone tapping by Lord Bridge reported on 6 March that all authorised taps had been properly authorised. This, of course, did not address the allegation that some tapping had been carried out although unauthorised.

22 *AG v Guardian (No 2)* [1990] 1 AC 109 (see below, at 618–22).

23 *Report of the Committee on s 2 of the Official Secrets Act 1911*, Cmnd 5104, 1972; see Birtles, W, 'Big brother knows best: the Franks Report on section 2 of the Official Secrets Act' [1973] PL 100.

24 1978–79, Bill 96.

25 1987–88, Bill 20.

26 For comment on the 1989 Act see Palmer, S, 'The Government proposals for reforming s 2 of the Official Secrets Act 1911' [1988] PL 523; Hanbury, W, 'Illiberal reform of s 2' (1989) 133 Sol Jo 587; Palmer, S, 'Tightening secrecy law' [1990] PL 243; Griffith, J, 'The Official Secrets Act 1989' (1989) 16 JLS 273; Feldman, D, *Civil Liberties and Human Rights*, 1st edn, 1993, Chapter 14.3.

27 See the White Paper on s 2, Cmnd 7285, 1978; the Green Paper on *Freedom of Information*, Cmnd 7520, 1979; White Paper: *Reform of the Official Secrets Act 1911*, Cmnd 408, 1988.

measure' clearly rest on other aspects of the Act. Aspects which are usually viewed as liberalising features include the categorisation of information covered which makes relevant the *substance* of the information, the introduction of tests for harm, the *mens rea* requirement of ss 5 and 6, the defences available and decriminalisation of the receiver of information. In all these respects, the Act differs from its predecessor, but the nature of the changes led commentators to question whether they would bring about any real liberalisation.[28] Other aspects of the Act have also attracted criticism: it applies to persons other than Crown servants, including journalists; it contains no defences of public interest or of prior disclosure and no general requirement to prove *mens rea*. Thus, what is omitted from its provisions, including the failure to provide any right of access to information falling outside the protected categories, is arguably as significant as what is included. The Human Rights Act may provide a means of tempering the effects of the 1989 Act. There is obviously a tension between the two statutes, since the one binds public authorities – which includes government departments – under s 6 to observe the Convention rights, including the right to freedom of expression, while the other creates criminal liability for disclosure of information whether or not the disclosure is in the public interest. Further, the 1989 Act must be interpreted under s 3 of the HRA so as to render it compatible with the Convention rights. The tension between the two was explored in the preliminary hearing in the *Shayler*[29] case (discussed below) in which it was argued unsuccessfully that s 1 of the 1989 Act is incompatible with Art 10. Below, the possible effects of Art 10 on the Official Secrets Act are indicated.

Criminal liability for disclosing information

The general prohibition on disclosing information under the Official Secrets Act 1911 was replaced by the more specific prohibitions under the Official Secrets Act 1989. Sections 1–4 of the 1989 Act (excepting the provisions of s 1(1)), which also determine the categorisation of the information, all concern unauthorised disclosures by any present or former Crown servant or government contractor of information which has been acquired in the course of his or her employment. If a civil servant happens to acquire by other means information falling within one of the categories which he or she then disclosed, the provisions of s 5 apply. Section 7 (below) governs the meaning of 'authorisation', while ss 5 and 6 apply when *any* person – not only a Crown servant – discloses information falling within the protected categories.

Security and intelligence information is covered by s 1. The category covers 'the work of or in support of, the security and intelligence services' and includes 'references to information held or transmitted by those services or by persons in support of . . . those services'.[30] It is, therefore, a wide category and is not confined only to work done by members of the security and intelligence services. Section 1(1) is intended to prevent members or former members of the security services (and any person notified that he is subject to the provisions of the sub-section) disclosing anything at all relating or appearing to relate

---

28 E.g., Ewing and Gearty, *Freedom under Thatcher* (1989), at 200.
29 Preparatory hearing: (2001) *The Times*, 10 October, 98(40) LSG 40; CA.
30 Section 1(9).

to[31] the operation of those services. All such members thus come under a lifelong duty to keep silent even though their information might reveal a serious abuse of power in the security services or some operational weakness. There is no need to show that any harm will or may flow from the disclosure, and so all information, however trivial, is covered. On its face, this blanket ban raises one of the most serious prima facie incompatibilities with Art 10. It is therefore worth examining briefly the government arguments for such a ban. Essentially, four main reasons are put forward.[32]

First, it is argued that disclosures by agents or former agents carry particular credibility; however this is presumably only relevant if the disclosure is in fact harmful. If the disclosure itself is anodyne, then its extra authority makes no difference. This therefore does not provide an argument for a blanket ban.

Second, it is said that such disclosures reduce confidence of the public in the security services' ability and loyalty. This is (a) speculative and (b) not very convincing. If non-harmful revelations were made, it is unlikely that they would affect the publics' view. Moreover, it begs the question why the public should have an exaggeratedly positive view of the ability of the security services. Why is it especially important that the public at large have a positive view of the abilities of the security services, any more than, say, the armed forces or the Cabinet?

Third, it is said that disclosures by agents or former agents ought to be criminal because of the special duty of secrecy that the members of the security service accept. This is a circular argument: that special duty of secrecy is imposed by the law – of the OSA, and the law of confidence. This cannot be an argument for determining what the law should in fact be.

Fourth, it is said that because governments do not traditionally comment on assertions about the security services, a false report made by a former agent could be as damaging as a true one, because it would go un-denied. Against this, it may be said that governments could simply make an exception to this general rule when a former agent is involved. Moreover, this argument again posits only a possible harm, that might come about in particular cases, not an invariable one. In fact, the government did deny aspects of the claims made by former agent David Shayler: in particular his assertion that the SIS had planned for the assassination of Colonel Gadaffi was vigorously rebutted.[33]

A further point to be noted about s 1(1) is that there is no defence that the material released was already in the public domain. This runs clearly counter to the finding both in *Attorney General v Guardian Newspapers Ltd (No 2)*[34] and in *Observer and Guardian v UK*[35] that the maintenance of a ban on the publication of information when it has entered the public domain is contrary to both common law and Art 10.[36]

Similar in nature to the blanket prohibition in section 1(1), and therefore considered here, is s 4(3), which covers information obtained by the use of intercept and security

---

31 Under s 1(2), misinformation falls within the information covered by s 1(1) as it includes 'making any statement which purports to be a disclosure of such information or which is intended to be taken as being such a disclosure'.

32 They are summarised in the White Paper, op. cit., fn 27 at para 40.

33 See Best, op. cit. fn 4, at 20.

34 [1990] 1 AC 109.

35 (1991) 14 EHRR 153; for comment see Leigh, I, '*Spycatcher* in Strasbourg' [1992] PL 200–8.

36 As was argued in the *Shayler* case: see fn 52 below.

service warrants.[37] There is no harm test under this category. Thus, in so far as it covers the work of the security services, it creates a wide exception to the general need to show harm under s 1(3) when a Crown servant who is not a member of the security services makes a disclosure about the work of those services.

The government's defence of this blanket ban is as follows: '*no* information obtained by means of interception can be disclosed without assisting terrorism or crime, damaging national security or seriously breaching the privacy of private citizens.'[38] This is simply implausible. As for the privacy point, the *nature* of the information gained through phone tapping (e.g., details of a large drug transaction) may barely engage private life, although the mode of interception does, and there may be very strong public interest arguments on the other side sufficient to make the interference with private life proportionate. The fact that privacy is in question does not begin to justify a blanket ban on disclosure: to have such a ban does not allow for a balancing between Arts 10 and 8 but simply creates an abrogation of one at the expense of the other. It is not clear that the first part of the statement can be taken seriously: whether any damage would be caused by such revelations would plainly depend upon what was disclosed, and what information revealed thereby about the techniques of the security services.

The White Paper also addressed the argument that there should be a general public interest to which all the offences in the Act would be subject. It first of all deliberately mis-characterises this argument – that there should be a defence of making revelations that were in the public interest, judged objectively – as being an argument that a defendant's good *motivation* should be a defence. The White Paper correctly states that the general rule is that motive is not relevant and that there are good grounds for sticking to this general rule.[39] This is true, but simply irrelevant: the argument about the public interest test does not revolve around motivation. The White Paper adds to this:

> the proposals in this White Paper are designed to concentrate the protection of the criminal law on information which demonstrably requires its protection in the public interest. It cannot be acceptable that a person can lawfully disclose information which he knows may, for example, lead to loss of life simply because he conceives that he has a general reason of a public character for doing so.[40]

This is extraordinarily poor reasoning. The first sentence is simply question-begging: by including a blanket ban on all disclosures by members and former members of the security services, it clearly covers information that is *not* required to be protected in the

---

37 This applies to (a) any information obtained by reason of the interception of any communication in obedience to a warrant issued under s 2 of the Regulation of Investigatory Powers Act 2000, any information relating to the obtaining of information by reason of any such interception and any document or other article which is or has been used or held for use in or has been obtained by reason of any such interception; and (b) any information obtained by reason of action authorised by a warrant issued under s 3 of the Security Service Act 1989, any information relating to the obtaining of information by reason of any such action and any document or other article which is or has been used or held for use in or has been obtained by reason of any such action.

38 The White Paper, op. cit., fn 27 at para 53.

39 Ibid at paras 59–60.

40 Ibid at para 60.

public interest. The example given is simply a gross exaggeration. No one is arguing for a defence for those who release information risking life; second, the wording 'because *he* conceives' implies that what is being argued for is a subjective test, rather than, of course, the actual objective public interest that is being proposed.

A more general, final concern about the White Paper is that it nowhere mentions Art 10 ECHR. As Lord Hope commented in *Shayler*, this 'leaves one with the uneasy feeling that . . . the problems which it raises were overlooked'.[41] The point is returned to below.

Section 1(3), which criminalises disclosure of information relating to the security services by a former or present *Crown servant* as opposed to a member of the security services, does include a test for harm under s 1(4) which provides that:

a disclosure is damaging if:

(a) it causes damage to the work of or any part of, the security and intelligence services; or

(b) it is of information or a document or other article which is such that its un-authorised disclosure would be likely to cause such damage or which falls within a class or description of information, documents or articles the unauthorised disclosure of which would be likely to have that effect.

Taken at its lowest level, it is clear that this test may be very readily satisfied: it is not necessary to show that disclosure of the actual document in question has caused harm or would be likely to cause harm, merely that it belongs to a class of documents, disclosure of which would be likely to have that effect. Disclosure of a document containing insignificant information and incapable itself of causing the harm described under s 1(4)(a) can, therefore, be criminalised, suggesting that the importation of a harm test for Crown servants as opposed to members of the security services may not inevitably in practice create a very significant distinction between them. However, at the next level, harm must be likely to flow from disclosure of a specific document where, owing to its unique nature, it cannot be said to be one of a class of documents.

In such an instance, the ruling of the House of Lords in *Lord Advocate v Scotsman Publications Ltd*[42] suggests that the test for harm may be quite restrictively interpreted: it will be necessary to show quite a strong likelihood that harm will arise and the nature of the harm must be specified. The ruling was given in the context of civil proceedings for breach of confidence, but the House of Lords decided the case on the basis of the principles under the 1989 Act even though it was not then in force. The ruling concerned publication by a journalist of material relating to the work of the intelligence services. Thus, the test for harm had to be interpreted, according to s 5, in accordance with the test under s 1(3) as though the disclosure had been by a Crown servant. The Crown conceded that the information in question was innocuous, but argued that harm would be done because the publication would undermine confidence in the security services. The House of Lords, noting that there had already been a degree of prior publication, rejected this argument as unable alone to satisfy the test for harm. The case therefore

41 [2003] 1AC 247, at para 41.
42 [1990] 1 AC 812; [1989] 2 All ER 852, HL; for criticism of the ruling, see Walker [1990] PL 354.

gives some indication as to the interpretation the harm tests may receive. This ruling affords some protection for journalistic expression concerning the intelligence services which, under the HRA, would be in accordance with the high value Strasbourg has placed on expression critical of the workings of the state and state agents.[43]

Even taken at its highest level, the harm test is potentially very wide because of its open-textured wording. It states, in effect, that a disclosure of information in this category is damaging if it causes damage to the area of government operation covered by the category. No clue is given as to what is meant by 'damage'; in many cases it would, therefore, be impossible for a Crown servant to determine beforehand whether or not a particular disclosure would be criminal. The only safe approach would be non-disclosure of almost all relevant information; the position of Crown servants under the 1989 Act in relation to information in this category is therefore only with some difficulty to be distinguished from that under the 1911 Act. However, the fact that there is a test for harm at all under s 1(3), however weak, affirms a distinction of perhaps symbolic importance between two groups of Crown servants because the first step in determining whether a disclosure may be criminalised is taken by reference to the *status* of the person making the disclosure rather than by the nature of the information, suggesting that s 1(1) is aimed at underpinning a culture of secrecy in the security services rather than at ensuring that no damaging disclosure is likely to be made.

Section 2 covers information relating to defence. What is meant by 'defence' is set out in s 2(4):

(a) the size, shape, organisation, logistics, order of battle, deployment, operations, state of readiness and training of the armed forces of the Crown;
(b) the weapons, stores or other equipment of those forces and the invention, development, production and operation of such equipment and research relating to it;
(c) defence policy and strategy and military planning and intelligence;
(d) plans and measures for the maintenance of essential supplies and services that are or would be needed in time of war.

It must be shown that the disclosure in question is or would be likely to be damaging as defined under s 2(2):

(a) it damages the capability of, or of any part of, the armed forces of the Crown to carry out their tasks or leads to loss of life or injury to members of those forces or serious damage to the equipment or installations of those forces; or
(b) otherwise than as mentioned in para (a) above, it endangers the interests of the United Kingdom abroad, seriously obstructs the promotion or protection by the United Kingdom of those interests or endangers the safety of British citizens abroad; or
(c) it is of information or of a document or article which is such that its unauthorised disclosure would be likely to have any of those effects.

43 See *Thorgeirson v Iceland* (1992) 14 EHRR 843; *The Observer* and the *Guardian v UK* (1991) 14 EHRR 153.

The first part of this test under (a), which is fairly specific and deals with quite serious harm, may be contrasted with (b), which is much wider. The opening words of (b) may mean that although the *subject* of the harm may fall within (a), the level of harm can be considered within (b) since it does not fall within terms denoting harm used in (a). This could occur where, for example, there had been *damage* as opposed to 'serious damage' to installations abroad. Clearly, this interpretation would allow the harm test to be satisfied in a wider range of situations. On this interpretation, as far as disclosures concerning UK armed forces operating *abroad* are concerned, it would seem that (b) renders (a) largely redundant, so that (a) would tend to play a role only where the disclosure concerned operations within the UK. It may be noted that parts of this test are mere verbiage; it would be hard to draw a significant distinction between 'endangering' and 'seriously obstructing' the interests of the UK abroad. In fact, the overlapping of the harm tests within the categories and across the categories is a feature of this statute; the reasons why this may be so are considered below.

Information relating to international relations falls within s 3(1)(a). This category covers disclosure of 'any information, document or other article relating to international relations'. Clarification of this provision is undertaken by s 3(5), which creates a test to be used in order to determine whether information falls within it. First, it must concern the relations between states, between international organisations or between an international organisation and a state; second, it is said that this includes matter which is capable of affecting the relation between the UK and another state or between the UK and an international organisation. The harm test arises under s 3(2) and is identical to that arising under s 2(2)(b) and (c).

Section 3(1)(b) refers to confidential information emanating from other states or international organisations. This category covers 'any confidential information, document or other article which was obtained from a state other than the United Kingdom or an international organisation'. Clearly, the substance of this information might differ from that covered under s 3(1)(a), although some documents might fall within both categories. Under s 3(6), the information will be confidential if it is expressed to be so treated due to the terms under which it was obtained or if the circumstances in which it was obtained impute an obligation of confidence. The harm test under this category contained in s 3(3) is somewhat curious: the mere fact that the information is confidential or its nature or contents 'may' be sufficient to establish the likelihood that its disclosure would cause harm within the terms of s 3(2)(b) (which uses the terms of s 2(2)(b)). In other words, once the information is identified as falling within this category, a fiction is created that harm may automatically flow from its disclosure. This implies that there are circumstances (such as a particularly strong quality of confidentiality?) in which the only ingredient which the prosecution *must* prove is that the information falls within the category.

Given that s 3(3) uses the word 'may', thereby introducing uncertainty into the section, there is greater leeway for imposing a Convention-friendly interpretation on it. If the word 'may' is interpreted strictly, the circumstances in which it would be unnecessary to show harm would be greatly curtailed. It could then be argued that since harm or its likelihood must be shown, the harm test itself must be interpreted compatibly with Art 10. It would have to be shown that the interference in question answered to a pressing social need.[44] Depending on the circumstances, it could be argued that if, ultimately, the 'interests of the UK abroad' would be benefited by the disclosure, or on balance little affected, no pressing social need to interfere with the expression in question could be shown.

Section 4 is headed 'crime and special investigation powers'. Section 4(2) covers any information the disclosure of which:

(a) . . . results in the commission of an offence; or facilitates an escape from legal custody or the doing of any other act prejudicial to the safekeeping of persons in legal custody; or impedes the prevention or detection of offences or the apprehension or prosecution of suspected offenders; or

(b) which is such that its unauthorised disclosure would be likely to have any of those effects.

'Legal custody' includes detention in pursuance of any enactment or any instrument made under an enactment (s 4(6)). In contrast to s 3(3), in which the test for harm may be satisfied once the information is identified as falling within the category, in s 4(2), once the test for harm has been satisfied, the information will necessarily be so identified. As with s 2, parts of this test could have been omitted, such as 'facilitates an escape', which would have been covered by the succeeding general words.

Section 5 is headed, 'information resulting from unauthorised disclosures or entrusted in confidence'. This is not a new category. Information will fall within s 5 if it falls within one or more of the previous categories and it has been disclosed to the defendant by a Crown servant or falls within s 1 of the Official Secrets Act 1911. Section 5 is primarily aimed at journalists who receive information leaked to them by Crown servants, although it could of course cover anybody in that position. It is also aimed at the person to whom a document is entrusted by a Crown servant 'on terms requiring it to be held in confidence or in circumstances in which the Crown servant or government contractor could reasonably expect that it would be so held'.[45] The difference between entrusting and disclosing is significant in that, in the former instance, the document – but not the information it contains – will have been entrusted to the care of the person in question.[46]

These provisions are presumably aimed mainly at the journalist or other non-Crown servant who receives the information from another journalist who received it from the civil servant in question. However, this does not apply where the information has been entrusted to the defendant, but has never been disclosed to him or her; in that case, it must come directly from the civil servant, not from another person who had it entrusted to him or her.[47] The disclosure of the information or document by the person into whose possession it has come must not already be an offence under any of the six categories.

44 *Sunday Times v UK* (1979) 2 EHRR 737.
45 Section 5(1)(ii)).
46 If the Crown servant has disclosed or entrusted it to another who discloses it to the defendant, this will suffice (s 5(1)(a)(i) and (iii)).
47 Section 5(1)(b)(ii)).

Since s 5 is aimed at journalists and potentially represents an interference with their role of informing the public, it requires a very strict interpretation under s 3 of the HRA, in accordance with Art 10, bearing in mind the emphasis placed by Strasbourg on the importance of that role.[48] In contrast to disclosure of information by a Crown servant under ss 1–4, s 5 does import a requirement of *mens rea* under s 5(2) which, as far as information falling within ss 1, 2 and 3 is concerned, consists of three elements. The defendant must disclose the information knowing or having reasonable cause to believe that it falls within one or more of the categories, that it has come into his possession as mentioned in sub-section (1) above and that it will be damaging (s 5(3)(b)). As far as information falling within s 4 and probably s 3(1)(b) is concerned, only the first two of these elements will be relevant. Under s 5(6), only the first of these elements need be proved if the information came into the defendant's possession as a result of a contravention of s 1 of the Official Secrets Act 1911. Thus, as far as disclosure of such information is concerned, the *mens rea* requirement will be fulfilled even though the defendant believed that the disclosure would not be damaging and intended that it should not be. Indeed, since the *mens rea* includes an objective element, it may be satisfied under all the categories where the defendant did not in fact possess the belief in question, but had reasonable cause to possess it.

The requirement of *mens rea*, although not as strict as may at first appear, represents the only means of differentiating between journalists and Crown servants. The test for damage will be determined as it would be if the information was disclosed by a Crown servant in contravention of ss 1(3), 2(1) or 3(1) above. A court could afford recognition to the significance of the journalistic role, as required by Art 10, by placing a strong emphasis on the *mens rea* requirement. Where a journalist appeared to be acting in the public interest in making the disclosure, it would be possible for a court to interpret the *mens rea* requirement as disproved on the basis that it would be impossible to show that the defendant knew or should have known that the disclosure was damaging to the interest in question if on one view (even if mistaken) it could be seen as beneficial to it, and that was the view that the journalist took.

Section 4 is not mentioned, because the information will not be capable of falling within s 4(1) unless the harm test is satisfied. As already mentioned, there is no harm test under s 4(3). Thus, an interesting anomaly arises: if, for example, information relating to the work of MI5 is disclosed to a journalist by a security service agent, a distinction is drawn between disclosure by the agent and by the journalist: in general, it will not be assumed in the case of the latter that the disclosure will cause harm, but if the information relates to (say) telephone tapping, no such distinction is drawn. If the journalist is then charged with an offence falling within s 5 due to the disclosure of information under s (3), both he or she and the agent will be in an equally disadvantageous position as far as the harm test is concerned. The apparent recognition of journalistic duty effected by importing the harm test under s 1(3) into the situation where a security service member discloses information to a journalist, may therefore be circumvented where such information also falls within s 4(3).

Another apparent improvement which might tend to affect journalists more than others is the decriminalisation of the receiver of information. If he or she refrains from publishing it, no liability will be incurred. Of course, this improvement might be said

---

48 See, e.g., *Goodwin v UK* (1996) 22 EHRR 123.

to be more theoretical than real in that it was perhaps unlikely that the mere receiver would be prosecuted under the 1911 Act even though that possibility did exist. The fact that journalists were included at all in the net of criminal liability under s 5 has been greatly criticised on the basis that some recognition should be given to the important role of the press in informing the public about government policy and actions.[49] In arguing for a restrictive interpretation of s 5 under s 3 of the HRA, a comparison could be drawn with the constitutional role of the press recognised in America by the *Pentagon Papers* case:[50] the Supreme Court determined that no restraining order on the press could be made so that the press would remain free to censure the government.

Section 6 covers the unauthorised publication abroad of information which falls into one of the other substantive categories apart from crime and special investigation powers. It covers the disclosure to a UK citizen of information which has been received in confidence from the UK by another state or international organisation. Typically, the section might cover a leak of such information to a foreign journalist who then passed it on to a UK journalist. However, liability will not be incurred if the state or organisation (or a member of the organisation) authorises the disclosure of the information to the public (s 6(3)). Again, since this section is aimed at journalists, a requirement of *mens rea* is imported: it must be shown under s 6(2) that the defendant made 'a damaging disclosure of [the information] knowing or having reasonable cause to believe that it is such as is mentioned in subsection (1) above and that its disclosure would be damaging'. However, it is important to note that under s 6(4), the test for harm under this section is to be determined 'as it would be in relation to a disclosure of the information, document or article in question by a Crown servant in contravention of s 1(3), 2(1) and 3(1) above'. Thus, although it appears that two tests must be satisfied in order to fulfil the *mens rea* requirement, the tests may in fact be conflated as far as s 3(1)(b) is concerned because proof that the defendant knew that the information fell within the relevant category may satisfy the requirement that he or she knew that the disclosure would be damaging. The requirement that *mens rea* be established is not, therefore, as favourable to the defendant as it appears to be because – as noted in respect of s 5 – it may be satisfied even where the defendant believes that no damage will result. Once again, aside from this particular instance, this applies in all the categories due to the objective element in the *mens rea* arising from the words 'reasonable cause to believe'.

The requirement that the information, document or article is communicated in confidence will be satisfied as under s 3 if it is communicated in 'circumstances in which the person communicating it could reasonably expect that it would be so held' (s 6(5)). In other words, it need not be expressly designated 'confidential'.

A disclosure will not lead to liability under the Act if it is authorised and so it is necessary to determine whether or not authorisation has taken place. The meaning of 'authorised disclosures' is determined by s 7. A disclosure will be authorised if it is made in accordance with the official duty of the Crown servant or a person in whose case a notification for the purposes of s 1(1) is in force. As far as a government contractor is concerned, a disclosure will be authorised if made 'in accordance with an official authorisation' or 'for the purposes of the functions by virtue of which he is a government

49 See, e.g., Ewing and Gearty, op. cit., fn 28, at 196–201.
50 *New York Times Co v US* (1971) 403 US 713.

contractor and without contravening an official restriction'. A disclosure made by any other person will be authorised if it is made to a Crown servant for the purposes of his functions as such; or in accordance with an official authorisation.

Defences; disproving mens rea – a reversed burden

The defence available to Crown servants arises in each of the different categories and reads:

> . . . it is a defence to prove that at the time of the alleged offence he did not know and had no reasonable cause to believe that the information, document or article in question was such as is mentioned (in the relevant subsection) or that its disclosure would be damaging within the meaning of that subsection.

Belief in authorisation will also provide a defence under s 7. Thus, the Act appears to provide three defences for Crown servants: first, that the defendant did not know and had no reasonable cause to believe that the information fell into the category in question; secondly, that he or she did not know and had no reasonable cause to believe that the information would cause harm, and thirdly, that he or she believed that he had lawful authorisation to make the disclosure *and* had no reasonable cause to believe otherwise. However, very significantly, in *R v Keogh*[51] it was found that the imposition of reverse legal burdens is incompatible with the demands of Art 6(2), so they should be read down under s 3 HRA to an evidential burden only. So it is a defence for a defendant to prove lack of knowledge in the different categories if he adduces evidence sufficient to raise an issue with respect to it; the court or jury should then assume that the defence is satisfied, unless the prosecution proved beyond reasonable doubt that it is not.

The first two defences may be conflated in certain categories, largely because the second defence is intimately tied up with the harm tests and therefore, like them, operates on a number of levels. Where the harm test operates at its lowest level, only the first defence is available. Thus, a person falling under ss 1(1) or 4(3) has no opportunity at all of arguing that, for example, the triviality of the information or the fact that it was already in the public domain had given rise to an expectation that its disclosure would cause no harm at all. At the next level, under s 3(1)(b), because the test for harm may be satisfied merely by showing that the information falls within the sub-section, the second defence could be viewed as more apparent than real and could therefore be categorised along with the defence under s 1 as non-existent. However, following the argument regarding the interpretation of the harm test under this section above, this defence could be afforded some substance, under s 3 of the HRA. Under s 1(3), the second defence is extremely circumscribed. It would not necessarily avail the defendant to prove that for various reasons, it was believed on reasonable grounds before the disclosure took place that it would not cause harm. So long as the prosecution could prove a likelihood that harm would be caused from disclosure of documents falling into the same class, the harm test under the section would be satisfied and the defendant would be forced to prove that he or she had no reasonable cause to believe

---

51 [2007] All ER (D) 105 (Mar). For further discussion see Chapter 14 pp 1347–54.

that disclosure of documents of that class would cause harm – a more difficult task than showing this in relation to the particular disclosure in question.

Generally, under all the other categories the harm test allows for argument under both the first and second defences, assuming that they are expressed disjunctively. However, under s 4(4), the second defence alone applies to information falling within the category under s 4(2)(a), while the first alone applies to information likely to have those effects under s 4(2)(b). This is anomalous, as it means that the disclosure of information which had had the effect of preventing an arrest could be met by the defence that it was not expected to have that effect, while information which had not yet had such an effect, but might have in future, would not necessarily be susceptible to such a defence. So long as the disclosure of the document was in fact likely to have the effect mentioned, it would be irrelevant that the defendant, while appreciating that it might in general have such effects, considered that they would not arise in the particular instance. Thus, a broader defence would be available in respect of the more significant disclosure, but not in respect of the less significant. This effect arises because, under s 4(2), the first defence is contained in the second owing to the use of the harm test as the means of identifying the information falling within the section.

Thus, it is clear that the Act is even less generous towards the defendant in terms of the defences it makes available than it appears to be at first glance. Moreover, it is important to note that, although it is a general principle of criminal law that a defendant need have only an honest belief in the existence of facts which give rise to a defence, under the Act a defendant must have an honest and reasonable belief in such facts. However, as indicated, s 3 of the HRA could be used to broaden the defences in certain respects.

The Act contains no explicit public interest defence and it follows from the nature of the harm tests that one cannot be implied into it; on the face of it, any good flowing from disclosure of the information in question cannot be considered, merely any harm that might be caused. Thus, while it may be accepted that the Act at least allows argument as to a defendant's state of knowledge (albeit of very limited scope in certain instances) in making a disclosure to be led before a jury, it does not allow for argument as to the good intentions of the persons concerned, who may believe with reason that no other effective means of exposing iniquity exists. In particular, the information may concern corruption at such a high level that internal methods of addressing the problem would be ineffective. Clearly, good intentions are normally irrelevant in criminal trials: not many would argue that a robber should be able to adduce evidence that he intended to use the proceeds of his robbery to help the poor. However, it is arguable that an exception to this rule should be made in respect of the Official Secrets Act. A statute aimed specifically at those best placed to know of corruption or malpractice in government should, in a democracy, allow such a defence. The fact that it does not argues strongly against the likelihood that it will have a liberalising impact. However, s 3 of the HRA could be used creatively, as indicated, to seek to introduce such a defence – in effect – through the back door.

The Shayler litigation

Whether or not such a use of the HRA is possible in respect of categories of information covered by a harm test, it appears that it is not possible in respect of s 1(1) and s 4(1).

David Shayler, a former member of MI6, was charged with an offence under s 1(1) and s 4(1) in respect of his allegations that MI6 had been involved in a plot to assassinate Colonel Gadaffi; further allegations exposed, Shayler claimed, serious illegality on the part of MI6, and were necessary to avert threats to life and limb and to personal property.[52] A preliminary hearing was held regarding the effect of the Human Rights Act on s 1(1). It was argued that since s 1(1) and s 4(1) are of an absolute nature, they are incompatible with Art 10 of the Convention, under the Human Rights Act, owing to the requirement that interference with expression should be proportionate to the legitimate aim pursued. In other words it was not possible, using s 3 of the HRA to harmonise these provisions of the 1989 Act with the requirements of the Convention would not be possible, since the two were plainly incompatible. Therefore a declaration of incompatibility should be granted, under section 4 of the Act. This argument was rejected in *Shayler*;[53] Judge Moses at first instance found that there was no need to rely on s 3 HRA since no incompatibility between Art 10 and s 1(1) arose.[54] He reached the conclusion that s 3 could be ignored in reliance on the finding of the Lord Chief Justice in *Donoghue v Poplar Housing and Regeneration Community Assoc Ltd and the Secretary of State for the Environment*;[55] he said that 'unless legislation would otherwise be in breach of the Convention s 3 can be ignored; so courts should always first ascertain whether, absent s 3, there would be any breach of the Convention'.[56] The conclusion that ss 1(1) and 4(1) were not in breach of Art 10 was reached on the basis that Mr Shayler did have an avenue by which he could seek to make the disclosures in question. There were various persons to whom the disclosure could be made, including those identified in s 12. Further, significantly, under s 7(3) of the 1989 Act a disclosure can be made to others if authorised; those empowered to afford authorisation are identified in s 12. Shayler could have sought authorisation to make his disclosures from those identified under s 21 or from those prescribed as persons who can give authorisations. Such persons or bodies now include the Tribunal established under the Regulation of Investigatory Powers Act 2000 s 65[57] and a Minister of the Crown. Such persons could have authorised disclosure to other persons *not* identified in s 12 or prescribed.

Also, Mr Justice Moses found, a refusal of authorisation would be subject, the Crown accepted in the instant case, to judicial review. The refusal to grant authority would have to comply with Art 10 due to s 6 HRA; if it did not, the court in the judicial review proceedings would be expected to say so.[58] Mr Justice Moses went on to say:

> It is not correct . . . to say that a restriction [under s 1(12) and 4(1)] is imposed irrespective of the public interest in disclosure. If there is a public interest it is . . . not unreasonable to expect at least one of the very large number of persons

---

52 *R v Shayler* [2003] 1 A.C. 247.
53 (2001) 28 September, CA.
54 Paragraph 78 of the transcript.
55 [2001] 3 WLR 183.
56 Ibid para 75.
57 The old tribunals set up under s 7 of the Interception of Communications Act, s 5 of the Security Services Act 1989 and s 9 of the Intelligence Services Act 1994 were prescribed for this purpose under the Official Secrets Act 1989 (Prescription) Order 1990 SI 1990/200, as amended by SI 1993/847. That prescription now applies to the single Tribunal.
58 Paragraphs 25 and 26 of the Transcript.

identified [by reference to s 12 and to the bodies prescribed] to recognise the public interest and to act upon it.[59]

He went on to call the suggestion that all those so identified would not authorise the disclosure in such circumstances far fetched. But he thought that even if that possibility might arise,

> . . . it is a step too far to say that the proportionality of this legislation must be judged in the light of the possibility that the courts themselves [in judicial review proceedings in respect of a refusal of authorisation] would countenance suppression of a disclosure which they considered necessary to avert injury to life, limb or serious damage to property even before October 2000.

Therefore he found that no absolute ban on disclosure was imposed.

The Court of Appeal agreed that the interference with freedom of expression was in proportion to the legitimate aim pursued – that of protecting national security on the basis that the members of the security services, and those who pass information to them, must be able to be sure that the information will remain secret. The Court of Appeal also agreed that for the reasons given the absence of a 'public interest' defence in the 1989 Act does not breach the Convention. Mr Justice Moses had stated that had he found otherwise he would have considered the use of s 3 of the HRA, but would have rejected the possibility put forward on behalf of Shayler, of inserting the word 'lawful' into s 1(9) so that s 1(1) would only cover the *lawful* work of the secret services. He also rejected the similar argument in respect of s 4. In so finding he again relied on *Donoghue v Poplar Housing and Regeneration Community Association Ltd and the Secretary of State for the Environment*[60] in which Lord Woolf said that s 3 does not entitle the court to legislate.[61] This decision means that s 3 need not be used in relation to s 1(1) and s 4(1) and it is probable that the same arguments would apply if, in respect of disclosure of information falling within other categories, the defence sought to introduce a public interest defence.

The House of Lords' judgment in the case contains some encouraging signs, in terms of the influence of Art 10 ECHR upon the judgment, but is ultimately open to the same criticisms as the earlier judgments. Essentially, the House found that the OSA 1989 did need to be read compatibly with the requirements of proportionality under Art 10, but that the method of seeking permission to reveal information provided in the Act rendered the relevant provisions proportionate. The encouraging point that was stressed by their Lordships, especially Lord Hope, was that, upon any judicial review of a refusal to authorise release of information, a full Art 10 analysis would apply and be used. However, as argued below, this is likely to be a moot point. Looking at the decision more closely, the problem with it appears to lie, not in the assessment of what Strasbourg case law on Art 10 demands, but upon the conclusions drawn from that case law as applied to the OSA. Thus Lord Bingham states:

---

59 Ibid para 54.
60 Ibid See fn 55.
61 Ibid paras 75 and 76.

The acid test is whether, in all the circumstances, the interference with the individual's Convention right prescribed by national law is greater than is required to meet the legitimate object which the state seeks to achieve.[62]

It was accepted generally that a truly blanket ban could not, by its nature, be proportionate. Lord Bingham conceded that such a ban 'permitting of no exception' would be inconsistent with 'the rigorous and particular scrutiny required to give effect to article 10(2).'[63] Differences of approach were apparent between Lords Bingham and Hutton on the one hand, who were quite readily convinced of the compatibility of the challenged provisions with Art 10, and the analysis of Lord Hope, which was both more sceptical on this point and gave more detailed consideration to the Strasbourg requirements. Thus, Lord Bingham did not consider the proportionality test in any detail, or give much consideration to the type of expression in issue. Indeed, his Lordship appeared to assume that once it was shown that the ban was not technically a blanket one, proportionality was automatically satisfied.

There was no detailed examination as to whether such routes were likely to prove effective – indeed, his Lordship's view on this matter appeared positively naïve – a point returned to below. Lord Hutton found that in the absence of any attempt by the applicant to lay his case before the authorities under the relevant provisions of the Act,[64] there was no evidence to show that these procedures would have been ineffective. This essentially turns the proportionality exercise on its head. Under Art 10(2) the state has the burden of showing that the restrictions placed upon the right in question are justifiable; Lord Hutton's approach essentially asks the applicant to prove that the state's alternative means of protecting expression are *in*effective, rather than requiring the state, by adducing 'relevant and sufficient reasons',[65] to show their effectiveness.

In contrast, Lord Hope did look at proportionality closely: identifying the second and third parts of the proportionality test from the *Daly* case he said;

> The problem is that, if they are to be compatible with the Convention right, the nature of the restrictions [placed upon the right] must be sensitive to the facts of each case if they are to satisfy the second and third requirements of proportionality. The restrictions must be rational, fair and not arbitrary, and they must impair the fundamental right no more than is necessary. As I see it, the scheme of the Act is vulnerable to criticism on the ground that it lacks the necessary degree of sensitivity.[66]

But he then examined the fact that the authorisation system would be subject to judicial review, which would provide the necessary safeguard. Lord Hope did address the point that technically it would be impossible for an agent or former agent to bring judicial review, since the disclosure by him to his lawyer for the purposes of preparing the case of the information he wished to disclose would itself breach s 1 OSA. Therefore an

---

62   Ibid at para 26.
63   Ibid at p 275.
64   Under sections 7(3)(a) or (b),
65   The standard often referred to under Art 10: see *Sunday Times v UK* (1979) 2 EHRR 245.
66   Ibid at paras 69–70. The case referred to is *R (on the application of Daly) v SSHD* [2001] 2 AC 532.

implied right to legal advice was read into the scheme – a right, that is, to disclose the substance of the information covered by s 1(1) to a legal adviser, in order to prepare for a judicial review to challenge the refusal of the authoriser to give permission to disclose. As Lord Hope said:

> I think that it follows that he has an implied right to legal assistance of his own choosing, especially if his dispute is with the state. Access to legal advice is one of the fundamental rights enjoyed by every citizen under the common law.[67]

Having granted this point, Lord Hope went on to hold that where permission to reveal information was sought and refused, the appropriate test on judicial review challenging that refusal would be as follows:

> (1) What, with respect to that information, was the justification for the interference with the Convention right? (2) If the justification was that this was in the interests of national security, was there a pressing social need for that information not to be disclosed? And (3) if there was such a need, was the interference with the Convention right which was involved in withholding authorisation for the disclosure of that information no more than was necessary. This structured approach to judicial control of the question whether official authorisation should or should not be given will enable the court to give proper weight to the public interest considerations in favour of disclosure, while taking into account at the same time the informed view of the primary decision maker. By adopting this approach the court will be giving effect to its duty under [s 6(1) HRA] to act in a way that is compatible with the Convention rights . . .[68]

Essentially therefore the broad choice is between a legislative scheme in which the applicant makes disclosure and the court judges directly whether the disclosure should be permitted (whether under the OSA or under the breach of confidence doctrine) and the actual scheme of the Act, which rests on 'judicial review of decisions taken beforehand by administrators'[69] as to whether disclosure should be permitted. The first choice of course would require an Act which, *unlike* the OSA, subjects all the offences to a 'harm' test. Lord Hope came down in favour of the second system (judicial review) on the basis of a number of factors. First, the would-be discloser may not be in a position to appreciate all the harm that his disclosures might do; second, gathering evidence of harm to bring a criminal prosecution could do more damage than the original disclosure.[70] This argument was constantly floated but no examples given; moreover, this argument ignores the point that on judicial review, the government would have to put forward evidence of harm to justify its prior refusal to authorise disclosure. Therefore this argument, although possibly true, does not help us to choose between the two choices of system, since it applies equally to each. Finally, Lord Hope makes the point that a successful prosecution would not in fact remedy the harm done by the original disclosure.[71]

---

67 Ibid at para 73.
68 Ibid at para 79.
69 Ibid at para 83.
70 Ibid at para 84.
71 Ibid at para 85.

The basic problem with the reliance placed by all the judges who heard this case upon the internal complaint route and judicial review is that the means they viewed as available to members or former members of the security services to expose iniquity are so unlikely to be used. It seems, to say the least, highly improbable that such a member would risk the employment detriment that might be likely to arise, especially if he then proceeded to seek judicial review of the decision. It would appear that it would place him in an impossible position in relation to colleagues and superiors. Of course, simply making the disclosure directly and then being prosecuted for it would also risk such detriment, even if the person was acquitted. However, the obvious route in such circumstances would be to make the disclosure anonymously. Former members of the services would not be subject to the same constraints in terms of employment detriment, but might be deterred from using this route for the simple reason that they would probably view it as inefficacious. Lord Bingham cannot but sound naïve when he says:

> If . . . the document or information revealed matters which, however, scandalous or embarrassing, would not damage any security or intelligence interest or impede the effective discharge by the service of its very important public functions, [a] decision [in favour of disclosure] might be appropriate.[72]

The Act has been in force for 18 years at the time of writing and no such member has ever availed themselves of this route, although persons other than Shayler have made or sought to make disclosures to the public at large, as this chapter reveals. Moreover, one point that Lord Hope and the others wholly fail to recognise is that requiring a person wishing to speak to the media to take legal action *before* he can do so (judicial review of the refusal to allow disclosure) is to place a very weighty fetter upon his freedom of expression. Effectively, such a system reverses the principle under Art 10(2) that the state must justify interference with freedom of expression. It places upon the would-be speaker the burden of forcing the state, through legal action, to allow him to speak. One would not normally think of human rights as being those which cannot be exercised without prior legal action. Moreover, one of the most important principles recognised at Strasbourg is that rights must be real, not tokenistic or illusory. It is argued that the right to freedom of expression – one of the central rights of the Convention – is rendered illusory by ss 1(1) and 4(1) of the OSA in relation to allegedly unlawful activities of the security services – a matter of great significance in a democracy.

One of the specific arguments heavily relied upon by their Lordships was one previously cited by the courts. Lord Hutton cited dicta of Lord Nicholls in *Attorney General v Blake*:[73]

> It is of paramount importance that members of the service should have complete confidence in all their dealings with each other, and that those recruited as informers should have the like confidence. Undermining the willingness of prospective informers to co-operate with the services, or undermining the morale and trust

---

72 Ibid at para 30.
73 [2001] 1 AC 268, 287.

between members of the services when engaged on secret and dangerous operations, would jeopardise the effectiveness of the service. An absolute rule against disclosure, visible to all, makes good sense.

The obvious rejoinder to this argument that members of the service and others must be able to trust each other to keep information secret is that such trust would surely be expected to extend only to information which did not reveal illegality. Otherwise the policy of ss 1(1) and 4(1) of the OSA seems to be to promote criminal conspiracies among members of the services or between members and informants to conceal information revealing unlawful activities. Moreover, whilst it is common sense to believe that the willingness of informants to give information to the security services would be undermined if they feared that their identities might be later unmasked, this argument *cannot* support a blanket ban on *any* disclosures by members or former members of the services. It is highly doubtful that those considering giving information to the services are aware of the precise legal position under the OSA: a simple guarantee by the agent cultivating the source that their identity would always be kept secret would suffice.

As noted above, the impact of the OSA in terms of freedom of expression is further exacerbated since no general defence of prior publication is provided; the only means of putting forward such argument would arise in one of the categories in which it was necessary to prove the likelihood that harm would flow from the disclosure; the prosecution might find it hard to establish such a likelihood where there had been a great deal of prior publication because no further harm could be caused. Obviously, once again, this will depend on the level at which the harm test operates. Where it operates at its lowest level, prior publication would be irrelevant. Thus, where a member of the security services repeated information falling within s 1 which had been published all over the world and in the UK, a conviction could still be obtained. This position is out of accord with Art 10: in such an instance, the imposition of criminal liability would be unable to preserve national security and therefore, it would be disproportionate to the aim of so doing.

If such publication had occurred, but the information fell within s 1(3), the test for harm might be satisfied on the basis that although no further harm could be caused by disclosure of the particular document, it nevertheless belonged to a class of documents the disclosure of which was likely to cause harm. However, where harm flowing from publication of a specific document is relied on, *Lord Advocate v Scotsman Publications Ltd* suggests that a degree of prior publication may tend to defeat the argument that further publication can still cause harm. However, this suggestion must be treated with care, since the ruling was not given under the 1989 Act and the link between the Act and the civil law of confidence may not form part of its *ratio*.[74] It should also be noted that s 6 provides that information which has already been leaked abroad can still cause harm if disclosed in the UK. The only exception to this arises under s 6(3), which provides that no liability will arise if the disclosure was authorised by the state or international organisation in question.

---

74 [1990] 1 AC 812; [1989] 2 All ER 852, HL. Only Lord Templeman clearly adverted to such a link.

Conclusions

The claim that the Act is an improvement on its predecessor rests partly on the substance or significance of the information it covers. Such substance is made relevant first by the use of categorisation; impliedly, trivial information relating to cups of tea or colours of carpets in government buildings is not covered (except in security services buildings) and second, because even where information *does* fall within the category in question, its disclosure will not incur liability unless harm will or may flow from it. Thus, on the face of it, liability will not be incurred merely because the information disclosed covers a topic of significance such as defence. In other words, it does not seem to be assumed that because there is a public interest in keeping information of the particular type secret, it inevitably relates to any particular piece of information. However, in relation to many disclosures it is, in fact, misleading to speak of using a second method to narrow down further the amount of information covered because, as noted above, establishing that the information falls within the category in question is in fact (or may be; no guidance is given as to when this will be the case) synonymous with establishing that harm will occur in a number of instances.

Clearly, if only to avoid bringing the criminal law into disrepute, 'harm tests' which allow the substance of the information to be taken into account are to be preferred to the width of s 2 of the 1911 Act. However, although the 1989 Act embodies and emphasises the notion of a test for harm in its reiteration of the term 'damaging', it is not necessary to show that harm has *actually occurred*. Bearing this important point in mind, it can be seen that the test for harm actually operates on four different levels:

(a) The lowest level arises in two categories, s 1(1) and s 4(3), where there is no explicit test for harm at all – impliedly, a disclosure is of its very nature harmful.
(b) In one category, s 3(1)(b), the test for harm is more apparent than real in that it may be identical to the test determining whether the information falls within the category at all.
(c) In s 1(3), there is a harm test, but the harm need not flow from or be likely to flow from disclosure of the specific document in question.
(d) In three categories, ss 2, 3 and 4, there is a harm test, but it is only necessary to prove that harm would be *likely* to occur due to the disclosure in question, whether it has occurred or not.

Even at the highest level, where it is necessary to show that the actual document in question would be likely to cause harm, the task of doing so is made easy due to the width of the tests themselves. Under s 2(2), for example, a disclosure of information relating to defence will be damaging if it is likely to seriously obstruct the interests of the UK abroad. Thus, the harm tests may be said to be concerned less with preventing damaging disclosures than with creating the *impression* that liability is confined to such disclosures.

These tests for harm are not made any more stringent in instances where a non-Crown servant – usually a journalist – discloses information since, under s 5, if anyone discloses information which falls into one of the categories covered, the test for harm will be determined by reference to that category. The journalist who publishes information and the Crown servant who discloses it to him or her are treated differently in terms of the test for harm only where the latter is a member of the security services disclosing information relating to those services.

One of the objections to the old s 2 of the 1911 Act was the failure to include a requirement to prove *mens rea*. The 1989 Act includes such a requirement only as regards the leaking of information by non-Crown servants; in all other instances, it creates a 'reversed *mens rea*': the defence can attempt to prove that the defendant did not know (or have reasonable cause to know) of the nature of the information or that its disclosure would be damaging. However, under ss 5 and 6 the prosecution must prove *mens rea*, which includes a requirement to show that the disclosure was made in the knowledge that it would be damaging. This is a step in the right direction and a clear improvement on the 1911 Act; nevertheless, the burden of proof on the prosecution is very easy to discharge where the low level harm tests of ss 1(3) and 3(1)(b) apply once it was shown that the defendant knew that the information fell within the category in question.

Under s 3 of the HRA it is strongly arguable that the Act needs to afford greater recognition to the important constitutional role of the journalist in order to bring it into line with the recognition afforded to that role at Strasbourg under Art 10. But unless s 3 is used creatively in order to create such recognition, a journalist who repeated allegations made by a future Peter Wright as to corruption or treachery in MI5 could be convicted if it could be shown first, that he or she knew that the information related to the security services and, secondly, that disclosure of that *type* of information would be *likely* to cause damage to the work of the security services, regardless of whether the particular allegations would cause such damage. In the case of a journalist who repeated allegations made by a future Cathy Massiter, it would only be necessary to show that the allegations related to telephone tapping and that the journalist knew that they did. Clearly, this would be a burden which would be readily discharged.

It may be argued – bearing in mind the scarcity of prosecutions under the 1911 Act – that the Official Secrets Acts were put in place mainly in order to create a deterrent effect and as a centrepiece in the general legal scheme engendering government secrecy, rather than with a view to their invocation. The 1989 Act may be effective as a means of creating greater government credibility in relation to official secrecy than its predecessor. It allows the claim of liberalisation to be made and gives the impression that the anomalies in existence under the 1911 Act have been dealt with. It appears complex and wide ranging partly due to overlapping between and within the categories and, therefore, is likely to have a chilling effect because civil servants and others will not be certain as to the information covered except in very clear cut cases. It may, therefore, be proving more effective than the 1911 Act in deterring the press from publishing the revelations of a future Peter Wright in respect of the workings of the security services. Thus, it may rarely need to be invoked and, in fact, may have much greater symbolic than practical value.

In considering the impact of the Act, it must be borne in mind that many other criminal sanctions for the unauthorised disclosure of information exist and some of these clearly overlap with its provisions. Sections 1 and 4(3) work in conjunction with the provisions of the Security Services Act 1989 to prevent almost all scrutiny of the operation of the security services. Even where a member of the public has a grievance concerning the operation of the services it will probably not be possible to use a court action as a means of bringing such operations to the notice of the public: under s 5 of the Security Services Act, complaint can only be made to a tribunal and under s 5(4), the decisions of the tribunal are not questionable in any court of law. In a similar manner s 4(3) of the Official Secrets Act, which prevents disclosure of information about telephone tapping, works in tandem with the Regulation of Investigatory Powers Act 2000. Under the 2000 Act, complaints can be made only to a tribunal whose decisions are not published, with no possibility of scrutiny by a court. Moreover, around 80 other statutory provisions provide sanctions to enforce secrecy on civil servants in the particular areas they cover. For example, s 11 of the Atomic Energy Act 1946 makes it an offence to communicate to an unauthorised person information relating to atomic energy plant. Further, s 1 of the Official Secrets Act 1911 is still available to punish spies. Thus, it is arguable that s 2 of the 1911 Act could merely have been repealed without being replaced.

A number of the provisions of the 1989 Act look increasingly anomalous in the Human Rights Act era. Although repeal of the Act is unlikely, the pressure to amend s 1(1), as the most pernicious section – in terms of its impact on state accountability – may eventually become irresistible, although the decision in *Shayler* now makes it clear that it will not come from the judiciary.

Prosecutions under the Act are rare, and, where they attempt to punish a member of the security services for revealing illegality or abuse of power by the security services, are likely to expose the government to a huge amount of negative publicity, particularly if the matter to which the revelation relates is a sensitive one. The Katharine Gunn affair in 2003 illustrated these points powerfully. Ms Gunn was an employee at GCHQ, the government's listening installation. She discovered, through correspondence that crossed her desk, that the UK Government had been requested by the US Government to give assistance in spying on the diplomats of states who were temporary members of the UN Security Council, at UN Headquarters in New York, in order to gain information making it easier to convince such states to vote for the US–UK resolution in favour of military action. Such action would plainly have violated the Vienna Convention on diplomatic relations[75] and Gunn disclosed the request to the *Observer* newspaper, which, not surprisingly, splashed the story on its front cover on 2 March 2003. Gunn was arrested and a prosecution commenced for breach of s 1(1) of the OSA. However, the prosecution was abandoned in February 2004, when it emerged that the CPS would offer no evidence.[76] Gunn had stated her intention to plead a defence of necessity – the revelation of illegal conduct by the security services, and the avoidance of an illegal war, and thus the saving of lives; specifically, she had intimated that her lawyers would seek disclosure, as part of her defence, of the Attorney General's advice on the legality or otherwise of the Iraq war, before its inception, a matter of enormous political sensitivity to the government. The case not only illustrated the undesirability from a government's point of view of using the Act against a seemingly honest and concerned whistleblower, but raised questions as to the real independence of the decision to drop the prosecution, given the intense embarrassment the case looked likely to cause the

---

75 As well, seemingly, as the 1946 General Convention, Article 2(3), which provides the premises of the UN shall be immune from any form of search or interference.

76 See the statement by Harriet Harman QC to the House of Commons: HC Deb, col 427 (26 Feb 2004).

government. The indefensible nature of s 1(1), leaving Gunn no ability to raise a public interest defence, even in an instance of such enormous public importance, was once more vividly illustrated.

3 Breach of confidence

Introduction[77]

Breach of confidence is a civil remedy affording protection against the disclosure or use of information which is not generally known and which has been entrusted in circumstances imposing an obligation not to disclose it without authorisation from the person who originally imparted it. This area of law developed as a means of protecting secret information belonging to individuals and organisations.[78] However, it can also be used by the government to prevent disclosure of sensitive information and is, in that sense, a back-up to the other measures available, including the Official Secrets Act 1989.[79] It is clear that governments are prepared to use actions for breach of confidence against civil servants and others in instances falling outside the protected categories – or within them. In some respects, breach of confidence actions may be more valuable than the criminal sanction provided by the 1989 Act. Their use may attract less publicity than a criminal trial, no jury will be involved and they offer the possibility of quickly obtaining an interim injunction. The latter possibility is very valuable because, in many instances, the other party (usually a newspaper) will not pursue the case to a trial of the permanent injunction since the secret will probably be stale news by that time. However, where the government, as opposed to a private individual, is concerned, the courts will not merely accept that it is in the public interest that the information should be kept confidential. It will also have to be shown that the public interest in keeping the information confidential due to the harm its disclosure would cause is not outweighed by the public interest in disclosure.

Thus, in *AG v Jonathan Cape*,[80] when the Attorney General invoked the law of confidence to try to stop publication of Richard Crossman's memoirs on the ground that they concerned Cabinet discussions, the Lord Chief Justice accepted that such public secrets could be restrained, but only on the basis that the balance of the public interest came down in favour of suppression. As the discussions had taken place ten years previously, it was not possible to show that harm would flow from their disclosure; the public interest in publication therefore prevailed.

The nature of the public interest defence – the interest in disclosure – was clarified in *Lion Laboratories v Evans and Express Newspapers*.[81] The Court of Appeal held that

---

77 General reading: Gurry, F, *Breach of Confidence*, 1985, Clarendon; Bailey, Harris and Jones, op. cit., fn 1 at 435–52; Robertson, G and Nichol, AGL, *Media Law*, Chapter 4; Wacks, R, *Personal Information*, 1989, Clarendon, Chapter 3; Feldman, op. cit., fn 1 at 648–68; the general development of the doctrine is discussed in Chapter 9 at p 876 *et seq*.

78 See Chapter 9, at p 877.

79 For comment on its role in this respect see Bryan, MW, 'The Crossman Diaries: developments in the law of breach of confidence' (1976) 92 LQR 180; Williams, DGT, 'The Crossman Diaries' (1976) CLJ 1; Lowe and Willmore, 'Secrets, media and the law' (1985) 48 MLR 592.

80 [1976] QB 752.

81 [1985] QB 526; [1984] 2 All ER 417, CA.

the defence extended beyond situations in which there had been serious wrongdoing by the plaintiff. Even where the plaintiff was blameless, publication would be excusable where it was possible to show a serious and legitimate interest in the revelation. Thus, the *Daily Express* was allowed to publish information extracted from the manufacturer of the intoximeter (a method of conducting breathalyser tests) even though it did not reveal iniquity on the part of the manufacturer. It did, however, reveal a matter of genuine public interest: that wrongful convictions might have been obtained in drink driving cases owing to possible deficiencies of the intoximeter.

Just as the Official Secrets Act creates a direct interference with political speech, the doctrine of confidence as employed by the government can do so too. Therefore, the use of the doctrine in such instances requires careful scrutiny, with Art 10 in mind. Since this is a common law doctrine, s 3 will not apply. But the courts have a duty under s 6 of the HRA to develop the doctrine compatibly with Art 10. Thus a court, as itself a public authority under s 6, is obliged to give effect to Art 10, among other provisions of the Convention, when considering the application of this doctrine. In so doing, the courts arguably have nearly as much leeway as they do under s 3 of the HRA, and it must be remembered that no provision was included in the HRA allowing the common law to override the Convention rights. Since, in an action between the individual and the state, the vexed issue of horizontal effect does not arise,[82] this matter can be regarded as settled, since the state as employer is also presumably a public authority under s 6. Section 12(4) is also applicable where interference with the right to freedom of expression is in issue, as it inevitably will be in this context. Section 12(4) requires the Court to have particular regard to the right to freedom of expression under Art 10. Thus, s 12(4) provides added weight to the argument that in the instance in which the state seeks to suppress the expression of an individual using this doctrine, the court must consider the pressing social need to do so and the requirements of proportionality very carefully, interpreting those requirements strictly. In considering Art 10, the court should, under s 12(4)(a), take into account the extent to which the material is or is about to become available to the public and the public interest in publication. These two matters are central in breach of confidence actions. They imply that the state's task in obtaining an injunction where a small amount of prior publication has taken place – or is about to – has been made harder.

In breach of confidence actions the state, as indicated below, typically seeks an interim injunction and then, if it has obtained it, may proceed to the trial of the permanent injunction. However, s 12(3) of the HRA provides that prior restraint on expression should not be granted except where the court considers that the claimant is 'likely' to establish at trial that publication should not be allowed, which the House of Lords has found will generally mean 'more likely than not'.[83] Moreover, *ex parte* injunctions cannot be granted under s 12(2) unless there are compelling reasons why the respondent should not be notified or the applicant has taken all reasonable steps to notify the respondent. All these requirements under the HRA must now be taken into account in applying the doctrine of confidence. The result is likely to be that the doctrine will undergo quite a radical change from the interpretation afforded to it in the *Spycatcher* litigation, which is considered below.

---

82 See Chapter 4, pp 249–57.
83 See Chapter 9 at pp 988–90.

The Spycatcher *litigation*

The leading case in this area is the House of Lords' decision in *AG v Guardian Newspapers Ltd (No 2)*,[84] which confirmed that the *Lion Laboratories Ltd v Evans* approach to the public interest defence is the correct one and also clarified certain other aspects of this area of the law. In 1985, the Attorney General commenced proceedings in New South Wales[85] in an attempt (which was ultimately unsuccessful)[86] to restrain publication of *Spycatcher* by Peter Wright. The book included allegations of illegal activity engaged in by MI5. In the UK on 22 and 23 June 1986, the *Guardian* and *The Observer* published reports of the forthcoming hearing which included some *Spycatcher* material and on 27 June the Attorney General obtained temporary *ex parte* injunctions preventing them from further disclosure of such material. *Inter partes* injunctions were granted against the newspapers on 11 July 1986. On 12 July 1987, *The Sunday Times* began publishing extracts from *Spycatcher* and the Attorney General obtained an injunction restraining publication on 16 July.

On 14 July 1987, the book was published in the US, and many copies were brought into the UK. On 30 July 1987, the House of Lords decided[87] (relying on *American Cyanamid Co v Ethicon Ltd)*[88] to continue the injunctions against the newspapers on the basis that the Attorney General still had an arguable case for permanent injunctions. In making this decision, the House of Lords were obviously influenced by the fact that publication of the information was an irreversible step. This is the usual approach at the interim stage: the court considers the balance of convenience between the two parties and will tend to come down on the side of the plaintiff because of the irrevocable nature of publication. However, since an interim injunction represents a prior restraint and is often the most crucial and, indeed, sometimes the *only* stage in the whole action, it may be argued that a presumption in favour of freedom of expression should be more readily allowed to tip the balance in favour of the defendant. This may especially be argued where publication from other sources has already occurred which will be likely to increase, and where the public interest in the information is very strong.

It is arguable that the House of Lords should have been able in July 1986 to break through the argument that once the confidentiality claim was set up, the only possible course was to transfix matters as at that point. The argument could have been broken through in the following way: the public interest in limiting the use of prior restraints could have been weighed against the interest in ensuring that everyone who sets up a legal claim has a right to have it heard free from interference. A prior restraint might be allowed even in respect of a matter of great public concern if the interest it protected was clearly made out, it did not go beyond what was needed to provide such protection and it was foreseeable that the restraint would achieve its objective. If it seemed probable that the restraint would not achieve its objective, it would cause an erosion of freedom of speech to no purpose. In the instant case, although the first

84   [1990] 1 AC 109; [1990] 3 WLR 776; [1988] 3 All ER 545, HL.
85   [1987] 8 NSWLR 341.
86   HC of Australia (1988) 165 CLR 30; for comment see Mann, FA (1988) 104 LQR 497; Turnbull, M (1989) 105 LQR 382.
87   *AG v Guardian Newspapers Ltd* [1987] 3 All ER 316; for comment, see Lee, S (1987) 103 LQR 506.
88   [1975] AC 396; [1975] 1 All ER 504, HL.

of these conditions may have been satisfied, the other two, it is submitted, were not; the restraint should not, therefore, have been granted. Such reasoning would bring the law of confidence closer to adopting the principles used in defamation cases as regards the grant of interim injunctions.[89] When cases of this nature recur under the HRA, such reasoning would be taken into account under s 12(4) and s 6; since relying on either section the demands of Art 10 must be met, so an injunction should not be granted where it is probable that it will not be able to serve the legitimate aim in question, owing to the probability that further publication abroad, or on the internet, will occur.

The judgment of the House of Lords did nothing to curb the use of 'gagging injunctions' in actions for breach of confidence where there had not been prior publication of the material. In any such action, even where the claim was of little merit, and the public interest in publication strong, it was possible to argue that its subject matter should be preserved intact until the merits of the claim could be considered. Even in an instance where the plaintiff (the state) then decided to drop the action before that point, publication of the material in question could be prevented for some substantial period of time. The House of Lords' decision was found to be in breach of Art 10 of the European Convention on Human Rights, as discussed below, but on the ground of prior publication, rather than public interest in the material.

In the trial of the permanent injunctions, *AG v Guardian (No 2)*,[90] the Crown argued that confidential information disclosed to third parties does not thereby lose its confidential character if the third parties know that the disclosure has been made in breach of a duty of confidence. A further reason for maintaining confidentiality in the particular instance was that the unauthorised disclosure of the information was thought likely to damage the trust which members of MI5 have in each other and might encourage others to follow suit. These factors, it was argued, established the public interest in keeping the information confidential.

On the other hand, it was argued on behalf of the newspapers that some of the information in *Spycatcher*, if true, disclosed that members of MI5 in their operations in England had committed serious breaches of domestic law in, for example, bugging foreign embassies or effecting unlawful entry into private premises. Most seriously, the book included the allegations that members of MI5 attempted to destabilise the administration of Mr Harold Wilson and that the Director General or Deputy Director General of MI5 was a spy. The defendants contended that the duty of non-disclosure to which newspapers coming into the unauthorised possession of confidential state secrets may be subject, does not extend to allegations of serious iniquity of this character.

It was determined at first instance and in the Court of Appeal that whether or not the newspapers would have had a duty to refrain from publishing *Spycatcher* material in June 1986 before its publication elsewhere, any such duty had now lapsed. The mere making of allegations of iniquity was insufficient, of itself, to justify overriding the duty of confidentiality, but the articles in question published in June 1986 had not contained information going beyond what the public was reasonably entitled to know

---

89 See *Bonnard v Perryman* [1891] 2 Ch 269; *Herbage v The Times Newspapers and Others* (1981) *The Times*, 1 May.

90 [1990] 1 AC 109; [1990] 3 WLR 776; [1988] 3 All ER 545, HL; in the Court of Appeal [1990] 1 AC 109; [1988] 3 All ER 545, p 594.

and in so far as they went beyond what had been previously published, no detriment to national security had been shown which could outweigh the public interest in free speech, given the publication of *Spycatcher* that had already taken place. Thus, balancing the public interest in freedom of speech and the right to receive information against the countervailing interest of the Crown in national security, continuation of the injunctions was not necessary. The injunctions, however, continued until the House of Lords rejected the Attorney General's claim (*AG v Guardian Newspapers Ltd (No 2))*[91] on the basis that the interest in maintaining confidentiality was outweighed by the public interest in knowing of the allegations in *Spycatcher*. It was further determined that an injunction to restrain future publication of matters connected with the operations of the security services would amount to a comprehensive ban on publication and would undermine the operation of determining the balance of public interest in deciding whether such publication was to be prevented; accordingly, an injunction to prevent future publication which had not yet been threatened was not granted.

It appears likely that the permanent injunctions would have been granted but for the massive publication of *Spycatcher* abroad. That factor seems to have tipped the balance in favour of the newspapers. It is arguable that the operation of the public interest defence in this instance came too close to allowing for judicial value judgments rather than application of a clear legal rule. Without a Bill of Rights to protect freedom of speech, the Law Lords, it is suggested, showed a tendency to be swayed by establishment arguments. The judgment also made it clear that once the information has become available from other sources, even though the plaintiff played no part in its dissemination and indeed tried to prevent it, an injunction would be unlikely to be granted. This principle was affirmed in *Lord Advocate v Scotsman Publications Ltd*,[92] which concerned the publication of extracts from *Inside Intelligence* by Antony Cavendish. The interlocutory injunction sought by the Crown was refused by the House of Lords on the ground that there had been a small amount of prior publication and the possible damage to national security was very nebulous. The decision suggests that the degree of prior publication may be weighed against the significance of the disclosures in question: if less innocuous material had been in issue, an injunction might have been granted.

The Observer and the *Guardian* applied to the European Commission on Human Rights claiming, *inter alia*, that the grant of the temporary injunctions had breached Art 10 of the Convention, which guarantees freedom of expression. Having given its opinion that the temporary injunctions constituted such a breach, the Commission referred the case to the court. In *Observer and Guardian v UK*,[93] the Court found that the injunctions clearly constituted an interference with the newspapers' freedom of expression; the

---

91 [1990] 1 AC 109; [1990] 3 WLR 776; [1988] 3 All ER 545, p 638; for comment, see Williams (1989) 48 CLJ 1; Cripps, Y, 'Breach of copyright and confidence: the *Spycatcher* effect' [1989] PL 13; Barendt, E, '*Spycatcher* and freedom of speech' [1989] PL 204; Michael, J, 'Spycatcher's end?' (1989) 52 MLR 389; Narain, BJ (1988) 39 NILQ 73 and (1987) 137 NLJ 723 and 724; Burnett, D and Thomas, R (1989) 16 JLS 210; Jones, G, 'Breach of confidence – after *Spycatcher*' (1989) 42 CLP 49; Kingsford-Smith, D and Oliver, D (eds), *Economical With the Truth*, 1990, ESC, chapters by Pannick and Austin; Ewing and Gearty, op. cit., fn 28 at 152–69; Turnbull, M, *The Spycatcher Trial*, 1988; Bailey, Harris and Jones, op. cit., fn 1 at 435–50.
92 [1990] 1 AC 812; [1989] 2 All ER 852, CA.
93 (1991) 14 EHRR 153; for comment see Leigh, I, '*Spycatcher* in Strasbourg' [1992] PL 200–8.

question was whether the interference fell within one of the exceptions provided for by para 2 of Art 10. The injunctions fell within two of the para 2 exceptions: maintaining the authority of the judiciary and protecting national security. However, those exceptions could be invoked only if the injunctions were necessary in a democratic society in the sense that they corresponded to a pressing social need and were proportionate to the aims pursued.

The Court considered these questions with regard first to the period from 11 July 1986 to 30 July 1987. The injunctions had the aim of preventing publication of material which, according to evidence presented by the Attorney General, might have created a risk of detriment to MI5. The nature of the risk was uncertain as the exact contents of the book were not known at that time because it was still only available in manuscript form. Further, they ensured the preservation of the Attorney General's right to be granted a permanent injunction; if *Spycatcher* material had been published before that claim could be heard, the subject matter of the action would have been damaged or destroyed. In the court's view, these factors established the existence of a pressing social need. Were the actual restraints imposed proportionate to these aims? The injunctions did not prevent the papers pursuing a campaign for an inquiry into the operation of the security services and, though preventing publication for a long time – over a year – the material in question could not be classified as urgent news. Thus, it was found that the interference complained of was proportionate to the ends in view.

The court then considered the period from 30 July 1987 to 30 October 1988, after publication of *Spycatcher* had taken place in the US. That event changed the situation: in the court's view, the aim of the injunctions was no longer to keep secret information secret; it was to attempt to preserve the reputation of MI5 and to deter others who might be tempted to follow Peter Wright's example. It was uncertain whether the injunctions could achieve those aims and it was not clear that the newspapers who had not been concerned with the publication of *Spycatcher* should be enjoined as an example to others. Further, after 30 July it was not possible to maintain the Attorney General's rights as a litigant because the substance of his claim had already been destroyed; had permanent injunctions been obtained against the newspapers, that would not have preserved the confidentiality of the material in question. Thus, the injunctions could no longer be said to be necessary either to protect national security or to maintain the authority of the judiciary. Maintenance of the injunctions after publication of the book in the US therefore constituted a violation of Art 10.

This was a cautious judgment. It suggests that had the book been published in the US after the House of Lords' decision to uphold the temporary injunctions, no breach of Art 10 would have occurred, despite the fact that publication of extracts from the book had already occurred in the US[94] and the UK. The Court seems to have been readily persuaded by the Attorney General's argument that a widely framed injunction was needed in July 1986, but it is arguable that it was wider than it needed to be to prevent a risk to national security. It could have required the newspapers to refrain from publishing Wright material which had not been previously published by others until (if) the action to prevent publication of the book was lost. Such wording would have taken care of any national security interest; therefore, wording going beyond that was disproportionate to that aim.

---

94 The *Washington Post* published certain extracts in the US on 3 May 1987.

Thus, although the newspapers 'won', the judgment is unlikely to have a significant liberalising influence on the principles governing the grant of temporary injunctions on the grounds of breach of confidence. The minority judges in the court set themselves against the narrow view that the authority of the judiciary is best preserved by allowing a claim of confidentiality set up in the face of a strong competing public interest to found an infringement of freedom of speech for over a year. Judge Morenilla argued that prior restraint should be imposed in such circumstances only where disclosure would result in immediate, serious and irreparable damage to the public interest.[95] It might be said that such a test would impair the authority of the judiciary in the sense that the rights of litigants would not be sufficiently protected. However, following the judgment of the Lords, the test at the interlocutory stage allowed a case based on a weak argument to prevail on the basis that the court could not weigh the evidence at that stage and therefore had to grant an injunction in order to preserve confidentiality until the case could be fully looked into. As noted above, this stance can mean that the other party does not pursue the case to the permanent stage and, therefore, freedom of speech is suppressed on very flimsy grounds. Thus, a greater burden to show the well founded nature of the claim of danger to the public interest – even if not as heavy as that under the test proposed by Judge Morenilla – should be placed on the plaintiff, and such a burden would be, it is argued, more in accord with the duties of the court under ss 6 and 12 of the HRA.

The result of the ruling in the European Court of Human Rights appears to be that where there has been an enormous amount of prior publication, an interim injunction should not be granted, but that it can be when there is at least some evidence of a threat to national security posed by publication coupled with a lesser degree of prior publication. It meant that the action for breach of confidence was still of great value as part of the legal scheme bolstering government secrecy.

The position, however, has now been affected by the decision of the House of Lords in *Cream Holdings Ltd v Banerjee*.[96] This decision gives the definitive interpretation of the meaning of s 12(3) HRA, which provides, *inter alia*, that no relief affecting the Convention right to freedom of expression '. . . is to be granted so as to restrain publication before trial unless the court is satisfied that the applicant is likely to establish that publication should not be allowed'. It is discussed in detail in Chapter 9 and it is not proposed to repeat that discussion here. The key point is that the effect of the decision of the House of Lords, in nearly all cases – absent the claim of immediate and serious danger to life, limb, or presumably national security – is that the party seeking the injunction, that is the government in these kinds of cases, must show not only an arguable case, as previously, but that it is 'more likely than not' that they will succeed at final trial.[97] This approach, assuming it is applied consistently to *Spycatcher*-type cases, should make it significantly harder for future governments to obtain gagging injunctions against the media. The post-HRA decision discussed below, although made before *Cream Holdings*, was taken under s 12(3) and appears to confirm this.

---

95 He relied on the ruling to this effect of the US Supreme Court in *Nebraska Press Association v Stuart* (1976) 427 US 539.
96 [2004] 3 WLR 918. For comment see Smith ATH, [2005] 64(1) CLJ 4.
97 See further Chapter 9 at pp 988–90.

Case law subsequent to Spycatcher and conclusions

The decision in *AG v Times*[98] suggest that Art 10 is having a greater impact in breach of confidence actions than it had at Strasbourg. Tomlinson, a former MI6 officer, wrote a book, *The Big Breach*, about his experiences in MI6[99] which *The Sunday Times* intended to serialise. There had been a small amount of publication of the material in Russia. The Attorney General sought an injunction to restrain publication. The key issue concerned the degree of prior publication required before it could be said that the material had lost its quality of confidentiality. The Attorney General proposed the formula: 'publication has come to the widespread attention of the public at large.'[100] This formula would have meant that injunctions could be obtained even after a high degree of prior publication and therefore it was unacceptable to *The Sunday Times*. However, the two parties agreed on a formula: that the material had already been published in any other newspaper, magazine or other publication whether within or outside the jurisdiction of the court, to such an extent that the information is in the public domain (other than in a case where the only such publication was made by or caused by the defendants). The Attorney General, however, contended that the defendants had to demonstrate that this was the case, which meant that they had to obtain clearance from the Attorney General before publishing.

In arguing against this contention at first instance, the newspaper invoked Art 10 and also relied on sub-sections 12(3) and (4) of the HRA.[101] It was argued that the restriction proposed by the Attorney General would be disproportionate to the aim pursued and therefore could not be justified in a democratic society. The decision in *Bladet-Tromsø v Norway*[102] was referred to, in which the Court said that it is incumbent on the media 'to impart information and ideas concerning matters of public interest. Not only does the press have the task of imparting such information and ideas, the public has the right to receive them'.[103] Taking these arguments into account, it was found at first instance that the Attorney General had to demonstrate why there was a public interest in restricting publication. No injunction was granted since it was found that he had not done so. On appeal, the same stance was taken. It was found that the requirement to seek clearance should not be imposed: the editor had to form his own judgment as to whether the material could be said to be already in the public domain. That position was, the Court found, most consonant with the requirements of Art 10 and s 12.

This decision suggests that, bearing in mind the requirements of the HRA, an injunction is unlikely to be granted where a small amount of prior publication has already taken place. It does not, however, decide the question of publication where no prior publication has taken place, but the material is of public interest (which could clearly have been said of the Wright material). Following *Bladet-Tromsø v Norway* it is suggested that an injunction should not be granted where such material is likely, imminently, to come into the public domain, a position consistent with the demands

---

98 [2001] EMLR 19.
99 Tomlinson was charged with an offence under the Official Secrets Act, s 1, pleaded guilty and was imprisoned for six months.
100 Ibid para 2.
101 For discussion of s 12(4) HRA, see Chapter 9, pp 950–54.
102 (1999) 6 BHRC 599.
103 Ibid at para 62.

of s 12(4), which refers to such a likelihood. Even where this cannot be said to be the case, it would be consonant with the requirements of Art 10 and s 12 to refuse to grant an injunction on the basis of the duty of newspapers to report on such material. The burden would be placed on the state to seek to establish that a countervailing pressing social need was present and that the injunction did not go further than necessary in order to serve the end in view.[104]

4 Defence Advisory notices[105]

The government and the media may avoid the head-on confrontation which occurred in the *Spycatcher* litigation by means of a curious institution known until 1992 as the 'D' (Defence) notice system. This system, which effectively means that the media censor themselves in respect of publication of official information, can obviate the need to seek injunctions to prevent publication. The 'D' Notice Committee was set up with the object of letting the Press know which information could be printed and at what point: it was intended that if sensitive political information was covered by a 'D' notice, an editor would decide against printing it. The system is entirely voluntary and in theory the fact that a 'D' notice has not been issued does not mean that a prosecution under the Official Secrets Act 1989 is precluded, although in practice it is very unlikely. Further, guidance obtained from the Secretary to the Committee does not amount to a straightforward 'clearance'. Press representatives sit on the committee as well as civil servants and officers of the armed forces.

The value and purpose of the system was called into question due to the injunction obtained against the BBC in respect of *My Country Right or Wrong*, a programme that concerned issues raised by the *Spycatcher* litigation; the BBC consulted the 'D' Notice Committee before broadcasting and were told that the programme did not affect national security. However, the Attorney General then obtained an injunction preventing transmission on the ground of breach of confidence, thereby disregarding the 'D' Notice Committee.

Some criticism has been levelled at the system: in the Third Report from the Defence Committee,[106] the 'D' notice system was examined and it was concluded that it was failing to fulfil its role. It was found that major newspapers did not consult their 'D' notices to see what was covered by them and that the wording of 'D' notices was so wide as to render them meaningless. The system conveyed an appearance of censorship which had provoked strong criticism. It was determined that the machinery for the administration of 'D' notices and the 'D' notices themselves needed revision. The review which followed this reduced the number of notices and confined them to specific areas. The system was reviewed again in 1992 (*The Defence Advisory Notices: A Review of the D Notice System*, MOD Open Government Document No 93/06) leading to a reduction in the number of notices to six. They were renamed Defence Advisory notices to reflect their voluntary nature.

---

104 The manner in which the law of common law contempt may allow for the imposition of widespread restrictions upon the media on the back of an initial breach of confidence injunction is considered in detail in Chapter 5 at pp 363 *et seq*.

105 On the system generally, see Jaconelli, J, 'The 'D' Notice system' [1982] PL 39; Fairley, D (1990) 10 OJLS 430.

106 (1979–80) HC 773, 640 i–v, *The 'D' Notice System*.

5 Freedom of information: general principles and the position prior to the 2000 Act

Principles of freedom of information and Article 10 ECHR

The citizen's 'right to know' is recognised in most democracies including the USA, Canada, Australia, New Zealand, Denmark, Sweden, Holland, Norway, Greece and France. In such countries, the general principle of freedom of information is subject to exceptions where information falls into specific categories. In terms of principle, and in particular, as seen through the lens of Art 10 ECHR, an assertion of a right to access to information can be distinguished from an assertion of a free speech right, [107] although the two are clearly linked. This distinction receives support from the wording of Art 10 itself, which speaks in terms of the freedom to 'receive and impart information', thus appearing to exclude from its provisions the right to demand information from the unwilling speaker. Moreover, the phrase 'without interference from public authorities' does not suggest that governments should come under any duty to act in order to ensure that information is received.

There are at least three reasons why access to information is often treated as a distinct interest by commentators and constitutional courts. First, freedom of information can be justified by reference to values that go beyond those underlying freedom of speech. It is generally accepted that the quality of decision-making will improve if access to official information allows citizens to scrutinise the workings of the government and public authorities generally. Moreover, the accountability of the government to the public is increased, since pressure can more readily be brought to bear on the government regarding the effects of its policies and citizens are able to make a more informed choice at election times, in accordance with the argument from democracy.

Second, information may be sought even though it is not intended that it should be communicated to others. It is not clear that the free speech justifications considered in the Introduction to Part II would apply to such a situation, and therefore it would tend to be considered purely as an access to information or privacy issue. Indeed, in such instances, the seeker of information might well be asserting a right not merely to gain access to the information, but also to have its confidential quality maintained. Access rights under the Data Protection Act 1998[108] often take account of both interests, and therefore may be said to be opposed to free speech interests. Thus, it is clear that many demands for access to information are not based on an assertion of free speech interests. Rights of access to information overlap with certain privacy interests since they may cover many situations in which a person might wish to receive information, apart from that of the individual who wishes to obtain and publicise government information. However, freedom of information is most readily associated with the demand for the receipt of information with a view to placing it in the public domain.

Third, information intended to be placed in the public domain may be sought when there is no speaker willing to disclose it, or where the body which 'owns' the information is unwilling that it should be disclosed. Whether such communication of

---

107 *Leander v Sweden* (1987) A 116; *Guerra v Italy* (1998) 26 EHRR 357, esp. at para 53.
108 For discussion, see Chapter 9 at pp 926 *et seq*.

confidential information should be regarded as 'speech' or not,[109] it is clearly a necessary precondition for the production of speech and therefore can be treated as deserving of the same protection as 'speech' in that the result will be that the public will be informed and debate on issues of public interest will not be stifled. The argument that such dissemination of information will render the government more readily accountable is strongly related to the justification for free speech discussed in the Introduction to Part II,[110] which argues that it is indispensable to democracy, since it enables informed participation by the citizenry.

However, freedom of speech guarantees, including Art 10, do not tend to encompass the imposition of positive obligations and therefore, in general, are violated when a willing speaker is prevented from speaking rather than in the situation where information deriving ultimately from an unwilling speaker – usually the government – is sought, entailing the assertion of a positive right. Thus, a distinction should be drawn between gaining access to the information and then placing it in the public domain – the second situation giving rise to a free speech interest. However, these issues have tended to arise together within the legal scheme in the UK, which has traditionally protected a 'closed' system of government; it is therefore convenient to consider both within the same chapter.

As these remarks indicate, Art 10 of the ECHR cannot be expected to have much impact on access to information, in the sense of using Art 10 to create an access right. The Freedom of Information (FoI) Act, introduced in 2000, provides for the first time a statutory right of access to official information. However, it is suggested that the basic values underlying Art 10, in particular the argument from democracy,[111] may be able to be relied upon in as a means of interpreting the provisions of the new FoI Act.

Probably the most important value associated with freedom of information is the need for the citizen to understand as fully as possible the working of government, in order to render it accountable. The following discussion therefore places a strong emphasis on the choices that were made as to the release of information relating to public authorities – not only to central government – in the FoI Act 2000.

Rights of access to information prior to the Freedom of Information Act[112]

The UK has traditionally resisted freedom of information legislation and, until 1989, criminalised the unauthorised disclosure of any official information at all, however trivial, under s 2 of the Official Secrets Act 1911, thereby creating a climate of secrecy in the Civil Service which greatly hampered the efforts of those who wished

---

109 The European Court of Human Rights takes the view that it should not. In the *Gaskin* case (1990) 12 EHRR 36 it viewed a demand for access to information which the body holding it did not wish to disclose as giving rise only to an Art 8 issue, not an Art 10 issue. The US Supreme Court has held that the First Amendment does not impose an affirmative duty on government to make information not in the public domain available to journalists (417 US 817). For discussion of this issue generally, see Barendt, *Freedom of Speech* (2005), at 108 *et seq.*

110 See pp 303–5.

111 For discussion of the Court's 'privileging' of political speech, see Part II introduction, pp 309–10.

112 See, generally, Birkinshaw, op. cit., fn 1; *Reforming the Secret State*, 1990; 'The White Paper on open government' [1993] PL 557.

to obtain and publish information about the workings of government. The attitude to secrecy exemplified by US freedom of information legislation, which is founded on the presumption that information must be disclosed unless specifically exempted, may be contrasted with this traditional position in the UK. American freedom of information provision can, in particular, be contrasted with provision under the UK Public Records Act 1958, which is considered below. It provides a measure of access to official information, but only after 30 years or more have passed. Considering all the various and overlapping methods of preventing disclosure of official information in the UK, and bearing in mind the contrasting attitude to this issue evinced in other democracies, it is fair to say that that until 2000, the UK was being increasingly isolated in its stance as a resister of freedom of information legislation. Since virtually all other democracies had introduced such legislation, that stance was indefensible in a mature democracy. It was finally abandoned when the Freedom of Information Act 2000 was introduced.

However, even before that point, and before the Labour Government came to power in 1997, there had been certain developments under the Conservative Governments of 1989–97, especially under the Major Government, which suggested that a gradual movement towards more open government was taking place in the UK. The Data Protection Act 1984 allowed access to personal information held on computerised files. A very limited right to disclosure of information in the field of local government was created.[113] The Campaign for Freedom of Information had, from 1985 onwards, brought about acceptance of the principle of access rights in some areas of official action. It supported Private Members' Bills, which allowed for rights of access to information in certain limited areas. Disclosure of a range of information was decriminalised under the Official Secrets Act 1989, as indicated above.

After the 1992 general election, the Prime Minister promised a review of secrecy in Whitehall to be conducted by William Waldegrave, the minister with responsibility for the Citizen's Charter, which would concentrate on the large number of statutory instruments which prevent public disclosure of government information in various areas, with a view to removing those which did not appear to fulfil a pressing need. It was also promised that a list of secret Cabinet committees with their terms of reference and their ministerial membership would be published. It was proposed that reform of the Official Secrets Act 1989 would be undertaken, so that disclosure of a specific document would be criminalised as opposed to disclosure of a document belonging to a class of documents which might cause harm. In fact, this reform did not take place. A White Paper on *Open Government* (Cm 2290) was published in July 1993 and a Code of Practice on Access to Government Information was introduced in 1994. The Code has now been replaced by the Freedom of Information Act when the latter came into force on 1 January 2005. However, it is important to have a basic understanding of how the Code worked, and the scope of its exemptions, in order to decide how much of an advance the 2000 Act really was.

---

113 Part VA of the Local Government Act 1972 (introduced by the Local Government (Access to Information) Act 1985. The right allowed members of the public to inspect local authority minutes, reports and background papers and to take copies of them. However, a number of significant areas were exempt from the access right; also, council 'working parties' are exempt.

The Code provided that non-exempted government departments should publish 'facts and analysis of the facts which the government considers relevant and important in framing major policy proposals and decisions',[114] 'explanatory material on departments' dealings with the public', and 'reasons for administrative decisions to those affected', and information in accordance with the Citizen's Charter on the operation of public services.[115] Such departments would also provide information on receipt of specific requests. A key limitation of the Code was that it afforded access only to information, as opposed to documents. As the Campaign for Freedom of Information has pointed out, this was: 'a potentially overwhelming defect: the opportunities for selective editing are obvious.'[116]

The Code was of course subject to exemptions. Particular exemptions are compared with those under the 2000 Act below, but it is useful to give a general indication of the scope and number of exemptions which existed under the Code. The exemptions could be divided into two groups: those subject to a harm test and those which were not. The key exemptions within the former group covered information relating to: defence, security and international relations, internal discussion and advice, law enforcement and legal proceedings, effective management of the economy and collection of tax, effective management and operations of the public service, third parties' commercial confidence, immigration and nationality information, medical information given in confidence, information which is soon to be published or where disclosure would be premature, and research, statistics and analysis where disclosure could be misleading. The latter group included information within the following categories: communications with the royal household, public employment, public appointments and honours, privacy of an individual, information given in confidence, information covered by statutory and other restrictions. Unreasonable, voluminous and vexatious requests, or requests requiring an 'unreasonable diversion of resources', were also exempt.

The Act was 'enforced' by means of complaint to the Ombudsman. There were two main issues in relation to this method. First, members of the public could not complain directly to the Ombudsman, but had to complain initially to an MP, who was then supposed to pass on the complaint to the Ombudsman. This was a widely criticised system.[117] Second, the Ombudsman, in keeping with the nature of his role, had no power to enforce his findings. His office worked by persuasion and there had been instances of refusals by government departments to comply with recommendations for disclosure,[118] although these were rare instances. The Ombudsman's lack of powers to compel release of information merely highlighted the fact that the Code was ultimately a 'grace and favour' system, which gave no *right* to government information. The Freedom of Information Act 2000 thus signalled a break with the traditional culture of secrecy: 'the principle that communication was the privilege of the state rather than of the citizen was at last . . . reversed.'[119]

---

114 Paragraph 3(i).
115 Paragraph 3(ii) and (iii).
116 Appendices to the Minutes of Evidence taken before the Select Committee on the PCA, session 1993–94, HC 33 (1993–94), Vol II, p 258.
117 See, e.g., the *Public Service Committee First Special Report*, HC 67 (1996–97), para 9.
118 See below, fn 179.
119 Vincent, *The Culture of Secrecy, Britain 1832–1998*, 1998, p 321.

The Public Records Acts

The UK Public Records Act 1958, as amended by the Public Records Act 1967, provides that public records will not be transferred to the Public Records Office in order to be made available for inspection until the expiration of 30 years, and longer periods can be prescribed for 'sensitive information'. Such information will include personal details about persons who are still living and papers affecting the security of the state. Some such information can be withheld for 100 years or for ever, and there is no means of challenging such decisions. For example, at the end of 1987, a great deal of information about the Windscale fire in 1957 was disclosed, although some items are still held back. Robertson argues that information is withheld to prevent embarrassment to bodies such as the police or civil servants rather than to descendants of persons mentioned in it; and in support of this he cites examples such as police reports on the NCCL (1935–41), flogging of vagrants (1919), and decisions against prosecuting James Joyce's *Ulysses* (1924) as instances of material which in January 1989 was listed as closed for a century.[120]

However, a somewhat less restrictive approach to the release of archives became apparent in 1994. In 1992–93, a review was conducted of methods of ensuring further openness in government and its results were published in a White Paper entitled *Open Government* (Cm 2290).[121] The White Paper, as well as proposing the Code of Practice on Access to Government Information already discussed, promised that there would be a reduction in the number of public records withheld from release beyond 30 years. A review group established by Lord Mackay in 1992 suggested that records should only be closed for more than 30 years where their disclosure would cause harm to defence, national security, international relations and economic interests of the UK; information supplied in confidence; personal information which would cause substantial distress if disclosed. Under s 3(4) of the 1958 Act, records may still be retained within departments for 'administrative' reasons or for any other special reason.

The FoI, Part VI and Sched 8 amends the 1958 Act. Part VI amends the exemptions of Part II of the 1958 Act in respect of historical records, with a view to enhancing the ease of access to them. Section 63(1) of the FoI Act reduces the number of exemptions that apply to such records. This is done in three tranches. First, exemptions are removed after 30 years in respect of a number of categories of information, including information prejudicial to the economic interests of the UK, information obtained with a view to prosecution, court records, information prejudicial to public affairs and commercial interests. Second, one exemption is removed after 60 years – in respect of information concerning the conferring of honours. Third, a large number of exemptions under s 31 relating to various investigations and the maintenance of law and order are removed after 100 years. These modest provisions are to be welcomed, as easing the task of historians, but their limited nature should be questioned; especially, it must be asked why any absolute exemptions, in particular those relating to intelligence information, remain.[122]

---

120 See Robertson, G, *Media Law*, 1999, Chapter 10 'Public Records'.
121 The White Paper proposals in relation to public records are considered by Birkinshaw, P, 'I only ask for information – the White Paper on open government' [1993] PL 557.
122 Cf the provision in respect of intelligence information held in the Public Record Office of Northern Ireland, which will no longer be subject to an absolute exemption, under FoI Act, s 64(2).

6 The Freedom of Information Act 2000

Introduction

The position of the UK prior to the 2000 Act may be contrasted with the position in other democracies which have introduced freedom of information legislation[123] within the last 30 years. Canada introduced its Access to Information Act in 1982, while America has had such legislation since 1967. Its Freedom of Information Act 1967 applies to all parts of the Federal Government unless an exemption applies. Exempted categories include information concerning defence, law enforcement and foreign policy. The exemptions can be challenged in court and the onus of proof will be on the agency withholding the information to prove that disclosure could bring about the harm the exemption was intended to prevent. However, although the principle of freedom of information in America has attracted praise, its application in practice has often been criticised.[124] In particular, the American business community considers that the system is being abused by persons who have a particular financial interest in uncovering commercial information. A number of reforms have been suggested since 1980 and, in 1986, a major FoI Act reform was passed which extended the exemption available to law enforcement practices.

With the example set by other democracies in mind, commentators have been arguing for a number of years that the voluntary Code should be replaced by a broad statutory right of access to information, enforceable by another independent body or through the courts.[125] In particular, many commentators considered that one of the messages of the Scott Report published in February 1996 was that the UK needed an FoI Act, although it is impossible to know whether FoI could have prevented the Matrix Churchill affair.[126] The report tellingly revealed the lack of 'openness' in government: the system appeared to accept unquestioningly the need to tell Parliament and the public as little as possible about subjects which were seen as politically sensitive. It was apparent that the voluntary Code could not provide a sufficient response to the concerns which the report aroused. The Matrix Churchill affair, which led to the Scott Inquiry, would not, it seems, have come to the attention of the public but for the refusal of the judge in the *Matrix Churchill* trial to accept that the information covered by the PII certificates, relating to the change in the policy of selling arms to Iraq, could not be revealed. As the Select Committee on the PCA pointed out in its Second Report, an FoI Act would tend to change the culture of secrecy in government departments.

Nevertheless, the Conservative Governments of 1979–97 had no plans to enact FoI legislation. The Select Committee on the PCA recommended the introduction of an FoI Act,[127] but this proposal was rejected by the then Conservative Government.[128] The Labour Government which came into office in 1997 had made a manifesto commitment

123 See McBride, T, 'The Official Information Act 1982' (1984) 11 NZULR 82; Curtis, LJ, 'Freedom of information in Australia' (1983) 14 Fed LR 5; Janisch, HN, 'The Canadian Access to Information Act' [1982] PL 534; for America, see Supperstone, M, *Brownlie's Law of Public Order and National Security*, 1982, pp 270–87; Birkinshaw, op. cit., fn 1, Chapter 2.
124 For discussion of criticism in the US see Birkinshaw, op. cit., fn 1 at 39–40.
125 See Birkinshaw, op. cit., fn 1; Tomkins, A, *The Constitution after Scott: Government Unwrapped*, 1998, Clarendon, Chapter 3, at 124–26.
126 See Birkinshaw, P, 'Freedom of information' (1997) 50 *Parliamentary Affairs*, at 166; Tomkins, op. cit., at 93, Chapter 3, at 123–26.
127 Paragraph 126.
128 HC 75, HC 67 (1996–97).

to introduce an FoI Act. The White Paper, *Your Right to Know*,[129] was published on 11 December 1997. The White Paper stated: 'Unnecessary secrecy in government leads to arrogance in governance and defective decision-making ... the climate of public opinion has changed: people expect much greater openness and accountability from government than they used to.'[130] A comprehensive statutory right of access to information was finally introduced with the inception of the Freedom of Information Act 2000.

The Act is the latest of the Labour Government's major measures of constitutional reform, receiving Royal Assent on 30 November 2000.[131] As will be indicated below, the White Paper proposed an FoI regime that would have had a radical impact.[132] Had it been implemented, not only would it have brought the UK into line with other democracies as regards its freedom of information provision, but also in a number of respects the legislation would have been more bold and radical than that in place in other countries. When the Bill appeared, it was a grave disappointment,[133] but a number of improvements were made to it during the Parliamentary process. The Act that has emerged cannot be termed radical – far from it – but it shows an adherence to the principle of openness which was absent in the Bill.

In what follows, the aim is to provide an overview of the key provisions of the Act and an indication of some of the main criticisms made of it during its passage through Parliament. It should be noted that initially the Act does not extend to Scotland, which has introduced its own, somewhat tougher legislation, via the Scottish Parliament.[134]

Fundamentals of FoI and the 2000 Act[135]

Rodney Austin identifies a number of common features of FoI regimes, which, together, indicate in essence how FoI legislation differs from the approach taken by the UK up until the 2000 Act.[136] As indicated above, the historical approach of the UK has been to make no comprehensive statutory provision for disclosure of official information,

129 Cm 3818.
130 White Paper, *Your Right to Know*, Cm 3818, 1997.
131 The best source of detailed critical analysis of the Bill may be found on the website of the Campaign for Freedom of Information (http://www.cfoi.org.uk), which contains numerous briefing notes and press releases. None of these is on the final text of the Act, but those prepared for the House of Lords' Committee, Report and Third Reading stages are extremely useful, provided they are read alongside the Act itself, and the following analysis has relied on those notes.
132 See Birkinshaw, P, 'An "All singin' and all dancin'" affair: New Labour's proposals for FoI' (1998) PL 176.
133 See Birkinshaw, P and Parry, N, 'Every trick in the book: the Freedom of Information Bill 1999' (1999) 4 EHRLR 373.
134 The Freedom of Information (Scotland) Act 2002, ASP 13.
135 It should be noted that environmental information is covered separately by the Environment Information Regulations, which also came into force on 1 January 2005 and which cover '... information about pollution, energy, noise and radiation ... GMOs, air and water borne disease agents, food contamination, planning, road building and transport schemes'. The basic scheme of the Regulations is that of the 2000 Act, but 'The exemptions are fewer, all are subject to a public interest test and there is no upper cost limit for requests.' See 'Freedom of Information for Journalists' – CFOI website.
136 'Freedom of information: a Sheep in Wolf's Clothing?', in Jowell, J and Oliver, D (eds), *The Changing Constitution*, 5th edn, 2004, p 362.

except under the very limited provisions of the Public Records Act 1958; the starting point instead was the criminalisation of disclosure in certain categories under the Official Secrets Acts and by virtue of numerous other statutory provisions. By contrast, the essence of FoI regimes, identified by Austin, are: the creation of public rights of access to official information; placing the determination and enforcement of those rights in the hands of 'an authority independent of government', whether the courts or an information commissioner; the extension of the basic right to information to cover 'all official information other than that specified to be exempt'.[137] The assumption lying behind FoI legislation is that the release of information is something which is desirable in general terms, the burden lying upon government to justify refusal to release in particular cases.

The 2000 Act may be said partially to share the bases of FoI legislation identified above; as will be explained below, it will give UK citizens, for the first time, a statutory right to official information, which will extend to all such information except that which the Act defines as exempt. In terms of enforcement, there is a mixed picture: as will also appear below, the right to information given by the Act is enforceable by an independent Information Commissioner, who, in the final resort, can enforce her orders through invoking the courts' power to punish for contempt of court. However, the Commissioner's power to force government to disclose information will not apply to some of the information that may be released under the Act: her disclosure orders can in some cases be quashed by Ministerial veto. This is perhaps the first major concern about the Act. The second is the great number and width of the exemptions it contains and the fact that many of these amount to 'class exemptions' where, in order to refuse release of the information, it is not necessary to satisfy a 'harm test', that is, show that release of the particular information requested would prejudice a particular interest, but merely that the information falls into a specified class and is, for that reason alone, exempt.

The scope of the Act

The Act covers 'public authorities'. Section 3 sets out the various ways in which a body can be a public authority. Instead of using the method adopted in the HRA, which, similarly, covers only 'public authorities' and which defines them by means of a very broad and general, non-exhaustive definition, the FoI Act takes the different route of listing a number of public authorities in Sched 1. The list is divided into two halves. First, Parts I–V list those bodies that are clearly public authorities; under s 6 of the HRA they would be standard public authorities.[138] Second, Parts VI–VII list those bodies that are only public authorities so long as they continue to meet the conditions set out in s 4(2) and (3) – that they have been set up by government and their members appointed by central government. Such bodies would probably also be viewed as standard public authorities under the HRA. But the list is not exhaustive, since s 4(1) gives the Secretary of State the power to add bodies to the list in Parts VI–VII if they meet the conditions set out in s 4(2) and (3), by Order. Further, s 5

137 Ibid.
138 See Chapter 4 at pp 216–20.

provides the Secretary of State with a power to designate a body as a public authority even though it is not listed in Sched 1, and does not meet the conditions set out in s 4(2) and (3), but which appears to him to be exercising public functions. These bodies would probably be viewed as functional public authorities under s 6 of the HRA.[139] Under s 3(1)(b), a publicly owned company as defined in s 6 is automatically a public body; no formal designation is needed. Section 6 defines such bodies as those wholly owned by the Crown or any public authority listed in Sched 1, other than government departments.

Some public authorities are covered only in respect of certain information they hold, in which case the Act only applies to that class of information (s 7(1)). Rather disturbingly, under s 7(3), the Secretary of State can amend Sched 1 so that a particular public authority becomes one which is subject only to such limited coverage by the Act – in effect potentially drastically limiting the range of information which can be sought from that authority.

It is suggested that although the FoI follows the model of the HRA in differentiating between public authorities as indicated, and between private and public bodies, Sched 1 read with ss 3–6 does *not* provide an exhaustive list of those bodies that are public authorities for the purposes of s 6 of the HRA, although these provisions provide a useful guide. The security and intelligence services, which are presumably standard public authorities under s 6 of the HRA, are omitted from Sched 1 and therefore they are completely excluded from the Act. They meet the conditions set out in s 4(2) and (3), but are – it is readily apparent – unlikely to be added to Sched 1, Parts VI–VII. The difference of approach between the two statutes is defensible; there may be cogent reasons why a body, such as the security service, should not provide information (although a *complete* exclusion is hard to defend), although it would be expected to observe the Convention rights in its operations.

Thus, the Act covers, in Sched 1, all government departments, the House of Commons, the House of Lords, quangos, the NHS, administrative functions of courts and tribunals, police authorities and chief officers of police, the armed forces, local authorities, local public bodies, schools and other public educational institutions, public service broadcasters. Under s 5, private organisations may be designated as public authorities in so far as they carry out statutory functions, as may the privatised utilities and private bodies working on contracted-out functions. The coverage of the Act is therefore far greater than under the Code and it is notable that some private sector bodies may be covered, although the government made it clear in debate on the Bill that a distinction between private and public bodies in terms of their obligations under the FoI Act should be strictly maintained and that s 5 should be used only to designate bodies discharging public functions.[140] The FoI is clearly *not* to be extended into the realm of business. The Act has been praised for the very wide range of bodies which it covers; in comparison with FoI regimes abroad, the coverage is very generous. But it should be noted that in fact, its coverage of private bodies discharging public functions is subject to the exercise of a discretion by the Secretary of State.

---

139 See Chapter 4 at pp 219–35.
140 HC Standing Committee B, 11 January 2000, Col 67.

The basic rights granted by the Act

The Act begins with an apparently broad and generous statement of the rights it confers. The Act grants two basic rights. Section 1(1) states:

> Any person making a request for information to a public authority is entitled –
>
> (a) to be informed in writing by the public authority whether it holds information of the description specified in the request [this is referred to in the Act as 'the duty to confirm or deny']; and
> (b) if that is the case, to have that information communicated to him.

It may be noted that the right conferred under s 1(1)(b) can cover original documents as well as 'information',[141] and in this respect the Act is clearly an improvement on the Code.

Both these fundamental rights are subject to the numerous exemptions that the Act contains. In other words, broadly, where an authority is exempt from providing information under the Act, it is also entitled to refuse even to state whether it holds the information or not, although in some cases, it may only do this where stating whether it holds the information would have the effect of causing the prejudice that the exemption in question is designed to prevent. Such cases will be considered below.

Exemptions under the Act

Under the White Paper, certain public bodies were to be completely excluded from the Act. One was Parliament, on the ground that, as stated in the White Paper, its deliberations are already open and on the public record. The security services, including GCHQ, were also excluded on the ground that they would not be able to carry out their duties effectively if subject to the legislation. Thus, the security services were to be subject to a blanket agency exemption. Apart from these exemptions, there were no exempt categories of information at all held by bodies which are subject to the Act. But seven specified interests were indicated in the White Paper, which took the place of the exemptions under the Code. The test for disclosure was based on an assessment of the harm that disclosure might cause and the need to safeguard the public interest. The test was: will this disclosure cause *substantial* harm to one of these interests? The first of these interests covered national security, defence and international relations. Obviously, this interest covered a very wide range of information. A further five interests were: law enforcement, personal privacy, commercial confidentiality, the safety of the individual, the public and the environment, and information supplied in confidence. Finally, there was an interest termed 'the integrity of decision-making and policy advice processes in government'. In this category, a different test was used: it was not necessary to show that disclosure of the information would cause substantial harm; a test of simple harm only was used. The reason for placing this information in a special category was, in the words of the White Paper: 'now more than ever, government needs space and time in

---

141 Section 84 defines information broadly to cover information 'recorded in any form', and in relation to matters covered by s 51(8) this includes unrecorded information.

which to assess arguments and conduct its own debates with a degree of privacy . . . [decision making in government] can be damaged by random and premature disclosure of its deliberations under Freedom of Information legislation.' This exemption was possibly the most controversial, since it meant that the full background to a decision could remain undisclosed, tending to restrict debate and challenge to it.

Thus, the exemptions under the White Paper were relatively narrow and were subject to quite a strict harm test. They may be sharply contrasted with those that emerged under the Act which include a number of 'class'-based exemptions. Nevertheless, the exceptions under the Act will be, on the whole, less wide ranging than those under the Code, taking into account the limitations of the PCA's remit. In certain respects, however, the Code was, on its face, more generous, as indicated at various points below. In particular, the total exemption under s 21 did not appear in the Code in as broad a form,[142] and the exemption under s 35 is broader than the equivalent exemption was under the Code – in para 2.

The exemptions under the Act rely on the key distinction between 'class-' and 'harm-based' exemptions mentioned above. The harm-based exemptions under the Act are similar to those indicated in the White Paper: they require the public authority to show that the release of the information requested would, or would be likely to, cause prejudice to the interest specified in the exemption. However, it should be noted that even in relation to the 'harm-based' exemptions, the test used has been substantially watered down from that proposed in the White Paper. That document, as noted above, had used a 'substantial harm' test; the Act itself refers simply to 'prejudice' – a test that is evidently easier to satisfy. It may be noted that the equivalent Scottish Act uses the tougher test of 'substantial prejudice'. The Commissioner has issued a series of guidance notes on the interpretation and operation of the Act,[143] one of which deals with the 'prejudice' test.[144] Firstly, as to the meaning of prejudice, the Commissioner indicates how the term is to be interpreted, in general terms:

> In legal terminology, prejudice is commonly understood to mean harm and the Information Commissioner regards them as being equivalent. So, when considering how disclosure of information would prejudice the subject of the exemption being claimed, the public authority may find it more helpful to consider issues of harm or damage. Although prejudice need not be substantial, the Commissioner expects that it be more than trivial. Strictly, the degree of prejudice is not specified, so any level of prejudice might be argued. However, public authorities should bear in mind that the less significant the prejudice is shown to be, the higher the chance of the public interest falling in favour of disclosure.

This indicates that, at the least, the Commissioner is not minded to countenance trivial claims of prejudice.

As noted above, the prejudice-based exemptions can be pleaded on the basis that prejudice would be 'likely' to be caused by the release of information; it is not necessary to show that it would definitely occur. As to this, the Commissioner has said:

---

142 Paragraph 8 of the Code refers to information obtainable under existing statutory rights.
143 Available on the Commissioner's website: see www.foi.gov.uk.
144 *Freedom of Information Act Awareness Guidance No 20.*

The phrase 'likely to prejudice' has been considered by the courts in the case of *R (on the application of Alan Lord) and The Secretary of State for the Home Department*. Although this case concerns the Data Protection Act, the Commissioner regards this interpretation as persuasive. The judgment reads:

> " 'Likely' connotes a degree of probability where there is a very significant and weighty chance of prejudice to the identified public interests. The degree of risk must be such that there 'may very well' be prejudice to those interests, even if the risk falls short of being more probable than not."

In other words, the probability of prejudice occurring need not be 'more likely than not', but there should certainly be substantially more than a remote possibility.

Once again, this approach will help to rule out flimsy or implausible claims of prejudice.

A number of exemptions are in any event class-based, meaning that in order to refuse the request, the authority only has to show that the information falls into the class of information covered by the exemption, not that its release would cause or be likely to cause harm or prejudice. It may be noted that the class exemptions can be further divided into two groups: those that are content-based, in the sense that no access to the information under the FoI or any other interest is available; and others, which relate not to the content of the information, but to the process of acquiring it. These distinctions are made clear below, in the first group of exemptions considered.

The Act complicates matters further by providing that, in relation to some, but not all, of the class exemptions, and almost all the 'harm exemptions', the authority, having decided that the information is prima facie exempt (either because the information falls into the requisite class exemption, or because the relevant harm test is satisfied, as the case may be), must still then go on to consider whether it should be released under the public interest test set out in s 2. This requires the authority to release the information unless 'in all the circumstances of the case, the public interest in maintaining the exemption outweighs the public interest in disclosing the information'. It should be noted that this provision was amended in the Lords so as to require release unless the interest in maintaining secrecy *'outweighs'* the interest in disclosure. This was thought to provide greater protection for freedom of information, since it must be demonstrated that the need for secrecy is the more compelling interest in the particular case.

The strengthening of the public interest test which took place in the Lords led some Liberal Democrat peers to claim that its application to class exemptions in effect transformed them into 'harm-'based exemptions. However, it should be noted that the Campaign for Freedom of Information (CFOI) emphatically rejected this view, on cogent grounds. While the application of a public interest test to the class exemptions does provide for the opportunity to balance the interest in disclosure against that in secrecy, the test is not the same as it would be if considering a harm test. As the CFOI notes, where information falls into a class exemption, and an authority objects to disclosure even under the public interest test, it will be able not only to argue that the specific disclosure would have harmful effects, *but also that the public interest would be harmed by any disclosure from within the relevant class of documents, regardless of the consequences of releasing the actual information in question.*[145] By contrast, under a prejudice test, the authority must be able first to identify that harm would be caused by releasing the *specific information* requested, and then go on to show that that specific harm outweighs the public interest in disclosure.

In the result, the exemptions under the Act can actually be broken down into four different categories, starting with the most absolute exemptions and moving to the least. It is helpful to consider them in the order suggested by this categorisation, because the Act does not set out the exemptions in any systematic way, but rather randomly, so that class exemptions are mixed in with 'harm-based' exemptions, and 'absolute exemptions' with both. It should be noted that the following categorisation relates to categories of exemptions not necessarily to categories of information, although the two may be synonymous. The four suggested categories are as follows, and are described in order of their illiberality.

(a) 'Total' exemptions: that is, class exemptions to which the public interest test in s 2 *does not apply*. Thus, the public authority concerned only has to show that information sought falls into the exempt class, not that its disclosure would cause any harm or prejudice; and, there is no duty to consider whether the public interest in maintaining the exemption outweighs the public interest in disclosing the information.

(b) Class exemptions to which the s 2 public interest test does apply. This is self-explanatory.

(c) Harm-based exemptions to which the s 2 public interest test does not apply. In these exemptions, the authority has to show that the release of the particular information concerned would cause or be likely to cause the relevant prejudice, but then need not go on to consider whether this prejudice outweighs the public interest in disclosure: once prejudice is established, that is the end of the matter.

(d) Harm-based exemptions to which the s 2 public interest test *does* apply. These are the exemptions under which it is hardest for the public authority concerned to resist the release of information. To do so, it must first demonstrate prejudice or likely prejudice from the release of the particular information request and then, even if prejudice is shown, go on to consider whether the public interest in forestalling that prejudice outweighs the public interest in disclosing the information under s 2.

These categories are important, not only in terms of the substantive legal tests which must be satisfied before information may be withheld: they also have crucial practical consequences in terms of time limits and enforcement. As explained below, the 20-day deadline for releasing information does not apply to information released only on public interest grounds. More importantly, the Commissioner's decision to order release on such grounds can, in relation to information held by certain governmental bodies, be vetoed by Ministers (a matter discussed further below).

145 Freedom of Information Bill, House of Lords Third Reading, 21 November 2000 briefing notes, p 10.

As to what 'the public interest' in the Act means, the Commissioner has again given guidance.[146] Defining 'the public interest' as 'simply something which serves the interests of the public', the Commissioner guidance asserts that therefore when applying the public interest test to a request for disclosure 'the public authority is simply deciding whether in any particular case it serves the interests of the public better to withhold or to disclose information'. This, it has to be said, is not particularly helpful. However, the guidance goes on to make a number of rather more detailed points.

> It is also important to bear in mind that the competing interests to be considered are the public interest favouring disclosure against the public (rather than private) interest favouring the withholding of information. There will often be a *private* interest in withholding information which would reveal incompetence on the part of or corruption within the public authority or which would simply cause embarrassment to the authority. However, the public interest will favour accountability and good administration and it is this interest that must be weighed against the public interest in not disclosing the information.[147]

This should be self-evident, but it is worth stating. More usefully perhaps, the Commissioner takes the view that 'There is a presumption running through the Act that openness is, in itself, to beregarded as something which is in the public interest.' The Guidance goes on to enumerate, non-exhaustively some of the specific public-interest arguments in favour of disclosure generally:

* furthering the understanding of and participation in the public debate of issues of the day. This factor would come into play if disclosure would allow a more informed debate of issues under consideration by the government or a local authority;
* promoting accountability and transparency by public authorities for decisions taken by them. Placing an obligation on authorities and officials to provide reasoned explanations for decisions made will improve the quality of decisions and administration;
* promoting accountability and transparency in the spending of public money. The public interest is likely to be served, for instance in the context of private sector delivery of public services, if the disclosure of information ensures greater competition and better value for money that is public. Disclosure of information as to gifts and expenses may also assure the public of the personal probity of elected leaders and officials;
* allowing individuals and companies to understand decisions made by public authorities affecting their lives and, in some cases, assisting individuals in challenging those decisions;
* bringing to light information affecting public health and public safety. The prompt disclosure of information by scientific and other experts may contribute not only to the prevention of accidents or outbreaks of disease but may also increase public confidence in official scientific advice.[148]

---

146 *Freedom of Information Act Awareness Guidance No 3.*
147 Ibid at para C.
148 Ibid at para D.

This is an encouraging statement of general principles. In particular, bearing in mind the sweeping exemptions relating to health and safety matters which might lead to an investigation, the last point made above is of great interest, as is the general weight placed upon the desirability of transparent decision-making and accountability.

We now turn to enumerating and commenting upon the numerous exemptions the Act contains, classifying them in accordance with the scheme outlined above.

Class exemptions not subject to the public interest test

First, there are the total exemptions – class exemptions that are not subject to the public interest test. Most of these exemptions are fairly self-explanatory; therefore, explanation is given where necessary. Section 21 covers information that is reasonably accessible to the applicant from other sources. It should be noted that this exemption applies even if the applicant would have to pay a higher fee than that provided by the Act to obtain the information (s 21(2)(a)) so long as the information can still be viewed as reasonably accessible. If the fee is excessive, this may no longer be the case. But, in order to be reasonably accessible, the information must be provided *as of right*. The duty to confirm or deny *does* apply, so an applicant would at least have to be told whether the authority to which he applied was holding the information. This is not an exemption in the usual sense of the word – as applied to freedom of information schemes – since it is not content-based and does not deprive the applicant of access to the information in general; it merely prevents her from obtaining it under the Act itself.

Section 23(1) covers information supplied by or which relates to the intelligence and security services, GCHQ, the special forces and the various tribunals to which complaints may be made about their activities and about phone tapping. It should be noted that, as indicated above, the bodies mentioned in this exemption are not themselves covered by the Act at all. This exemption therefore applies to information which is held by *another public authority*, but which has been supplied by one of these bodies. Since it is a class exemption, it could apply to information which had no conceivable security implications, such as evidence of a massive overspend on MI5 or MI6's headquarters. The duty to confirm or deny does not apply to information in this category where complying with it would itself involve disclosure of information covered by this exemption. Bearing in mind the complete exclusion of the security and intelligence services from the Act, the use of this exemption unaccompanied by a harm test, and not subject to the public interest test, is likely to mean that sensitive matters of great political significance remain undisclosed, even if their disclosure would ultimately benefit those services or national security.

Section 32 covers information *which is only held* by virtue of being contained in a document or record served on a public authority in proceedings or made by a court or tribunal or party in any proceedings or contained in a document lodged with or created by a person conducting an inquiry or arbitration, for the purposes of the inquiry or arbitration. The duty to confirm or deny does not apply. Section 34 covers information where exemption from s 1(1)(b) is required for the purpose of avoiding an infringement of the privileges of either House of Parliament. The duty to confirm or deny does not apply to information in this category where compliance with it would entail a breach of Parliamentary privilege.

The exemption under s 40(1) is a complex one, but essentially it covers two classes of data. The first is information which the inquirer would be able to obtain under the Data Protection Act (DPA) 1998 because it is personal information which relates to himself; the second covers personal information which relates to *others*, the disclosure of which would contravene one or more of the data protection principles or the right under the Act to prevent processing likely to cause damage or distress. The first part of this exemption is designed to ensure that the FoI Act does not give rights which overlap with those granted by the DPA; the second, to ensure that the FoI Act does not give rights which contravene the DPA.

There are a number of further total exemptions. Vexatious requests (s 14) and unduly costly requests (those where compliance would cost more than a reasonable amount, to be specified (s 12)), are exempt, but the duty to confirm or deny applies. Information the disclosure of which would contravene any other Act of Parliament (for example, the Official Secrets Act 1989), or would be incompatible with any EU obligation, or constitute a contempt of court, is exempt[149] and the duty to confirm or deny does not apply to the extent that compliance with it would itself amount to a contravention of any of these provisions. This exemption ensures that the FoI Act cannot be seen impliedly to repeal the numerous provisions that criminalise the release of information, but rather preserves them all.

Information the disclosure of which would be an actionable breach of confidence (s 41) is exempt and the duty to confirm or deny does not apply if compliance with it would itself amount to a breach of confidence. This exemption requires some comment. While it is expressed as an absolute exemption, with no need to show that prejudice would be caused by release of the information, and no requirement to consider the public interest in disclosure, in fact the doctrine of confidence may contain the first of these requirements (that is, a need to show detriment – there are conflicting *dicta* on the matter)[150] and certainly contains the second – a need to consider any countervailing public interest in disclosure. This is clearly recognised by the relevant guidance.[151] The CFOI expressed concern at the time of the passage of the Act that while there is clearly some need to protect genuine confidences, governments could seek to protect all information supplied by third parties simply by agreeing with the third party at the time of the communication of the information that it would be treated in confidence. The information would then become confidential, provided that it was not already in the public domain, and subject to the public interest test and, possibly, to the need to show detriment. This potential problem – of 'contracting out' of the obligations under the Act – has however been recognised. The Access Code issued by the Lord Chancellor[152] takes a clear stance on this issue:

> When entering into contracts public authorities should refuse to include contractual terms which purport to restrict the disclosure of information held by the authority and relating to the contract beyond the restrictions permitted by the Act. Public authorities cannot 'contract out' of their obligations under the Act. Unless an

---

149 Section 44.
150 See Chapter 9, p 877.
151 *Freedom of Information Act Awareness Guidance No 2.*
152 Under s 45 of the Act.

exemption provided for under the Act is applicable in relation to any particular information, a public authority will be obliged to disclose that information in response to a request, regardless of the terms of any contract.'[153]

What however remains of concern is that when adjudicating upon this exemption under the Act, the Commissioner reproduces as faithfully as possible the common law doctrine of confidence, which is now, of course, heavily influenced by Art 10 ECHR, meaning that the duty of confidence must also be tested against the requirements of that Article. In that respect, it is unfortunate that the Guidance published on this exemption does not mention this.

Class exemptions subject to the public interest test

The second category covers class exemptions subject to the public interest test. It will be recalled in relation to these exemptions that in practice, while the Commissioner will always have the last word on whether the information falls into the class in question, she will not always be able to enforce a finding that it should nevertheless be released on public interest grounds if the information is held by certain governmental bodies, since the Ministerial veto may be used.

It is most convenient to quote the Act itself for the first of these exemptions. Under s 30(1):

> Information held by a public authority is exempt information if it has at any time been held by the authority for the purposes of –
>
> (a) any investigation which the public authority has a duty to conduct with a view to it being ascertained –
> (i) whether a person should be charged with an offence, or
> (ii) whether a person charged with an offence is guilty of it,
> (b) any investigation which is conducted by the authority and in the circumstances may lead to a decision by the authority to institute criminal proceedings which the authority has power to conduct, or
> (c) any criminal proceedings which the authority has power to conduct.

This exemption, together with that contained in s 35, is one of the most widely criticised provisions in the Act. It is a sweeping exemption, covering all information, whenever obtained, which relates to investigations that may lead to criminal proceedings. It represents a specific rejection of the recommendation of the MacPherson Report[154] that there should be no class exemption for information relating to police investigations. It overlaps with the law enforcement of s 31, which does include a harm test. The exclusion of police operational matters and decisions echoes the approach under s 4 of the Official Secrets Act, but unlike s 4, no harm test is included. There are certain aspects of information relating to investigations which would appear to require disclosure in

---

153 Quoted in *Freedom of Information Act Awareness Guidance No 2*.
154 The *MacPherson Report on the Stephen Lawrence Inquiry*, Cm 4262, 1999, proposed that all such matters should be covered by the FoI Act, subject only to a substantial harm test.

order to be in accord with the principle of openness enshrined in the Act. For example, a citizen might suspect that his or her telephone had been tapped without authorisation or that he or she had been unlawfully placed under surveillance by other means. Under the Act, no satisfactory method of discovering information relating to such a possibility will exist. It is therefore unfortunate that telephone tapping and electronic surveillance were not subjected to a 'substantial harm' or even a 'simple harm test'.

This exemption extends beyond protecting the police and the CPS. Other bodies will also be protected: it will cover all information obtained by safety agencies investigating accidents. Thus, it will cover bodies such as the Health and Safety Executive, the Railway Inspectorate, Nuclear Installations Inspectorate, Civil Aviation Authority, Marine and Coastguard Agency, environmental health officers, trading standards officers and the Drinking Water Inspectorate. It will cover routine inspections as well as specific investigations, since both can lead to criminal prosecution. Thus, anything from an inspection of a section of railway track by the Railway Inspectorate, to a check upon hygiene in a restaurant by the Health and Safety Executive could be covered. The duty to confirm or deny does not apply (s 30(3)). As the CFOI commented:

> Reports into accidents involving dangerous cars, train crashes, unsafe domestic appliances, air disasters, chemical fires or nuclear incidents will go into a permanently secret filing cabinet. The same goes for reports into risks faced by workers or the public from industrial hazards. The results of safety inspections of the railways, nuclear plants and dangerous factories would be permanently exempt. This is the information that most people assume FoI legislation exists to provide.[155]

It is particularly hard to understand the need for such a sweeping class exemption when s 31 specifically exempts information which could prejudice the prevention or detection of crime, or legal proceedings brought by a public authority arising from various forms of investigation. That exemption will ensure that no information is released which could damage law enforcement and crime detection, while we have noted above that information which could amount to a contempt of court is also exempted. The CFOI noted that the recently retired director general of the Health and Safety Executive has said publicly that the work of the HSE does not require such sweeping protection.[156] It should be noted that, where it has been decided that the information falls into the protected class, the authority must then go on to consider whether it should be released under the public interest test. Since most of the information above will not be held by a government department (see below), the Commissioner will be able to order disclosure if she thinks the information should be released under this provision, with no possibility of a Ministerial veto. The Commissioner's own views on this exemption are therefore of particular importance.[157] One point the Commissioner makes in the relevant published guidance relates to timing and is of considerable importance:

---

155 Freedom of Information Bill, House of Lords Committee Stage, 19 October 2000, briefing, notes. Under the Act as passed, information under this exemption would not go into a *permanently* sealed filing cabinet': after 30 years it would become a historical record; the s 30 exemption would no longer apply.

156 Ibid.

157 See generally Freedom of Information Act Awareness Guidance No. 16.

As a general rule, the Commissioner recognises that the public interest in the disclosure of information is likely to be weaker whilst an investigation is being carried out. However once an investigation is completed, the public interest in understanding why an investigation reached a particular conclusion or in seeing that the investigation had been properly carried out is more likely to outweigh the public interest in maintaining the exemption. By the same token, there is likely to be a weaker public interest in disclosure of information about investigations which have been suspended but which may be reopened, than about those which have been concluded or abandoned.

If applied in a thorough-going way, this approach would lay to rest some of the more negative views as to the effect of this exemption, such as those of the CFOI, quoted above. The reports and safety records *will* be made public, under the public interest test, once completed or abandoned; the exemption will be seen as one designed to provide time-limited protection for sensitive on-going investigations, rather than the very sweeping one that it first appears to be. Moreover, the Commissioner adds:

> It should be noted that the presumption that information relating to ongoing investigations will not be released is not invariable. Much will depend upon the effect of disclosure with a stronger case for maintaining the exemption where the confidentiality of the information is critical to the success of the investigation.

This very strongly suggests that the exemption, although a class one, will be tested strongly against the public interest test: once into the balancing act, the public authority, to maintain the exemption, will have to produce real evidence of harm *in the particular case* to outweigh the public interest in disclosure.

One of the few decisions made by the Commissioner under the Act so far is of relevance here. It was made under s 31, not s 30, but, since the two categories cover such similar ground, it is a useful indicator in relation to both. The facts are scarcely dramatic:[158] an individual requested from Bridgend County Borough Council 'A copy of the last hygiene inspection report of the Heronston Hotel'; the Council refused the request,[159] arguing that to reveal it would prejudice the exercise of its function of 'ascertaining whether circumstances which would justify regulatory action in pursuance of any enactment exist or may arise.'[160] The enactment in question was the Food Safety Act 1990. The Council's argument was that:

> ... the release of inspection reports would undermine the way it carries out food hygiene inspections. It promotes an informal approach to the inspection of premises, where advice and practical assistance is given to businesses ... If information was publicly available, businesses would no longer be willing to have open discussions with inspectors. The Council would then be forced to adopt a formal inspection regime without the ability to protect the public by what it believes to be more

---

158 Decision Notice dated 9 December 2005; ref: FS50073296.
159 Citing section 31(1)(g).
160 A function listed in s 31(2)(c).

effective means. This, it argues, would be prejudicial to the purpose at section 31(2)(c) of the Act.

The Commissioner rejected the Council's view. It is important that she did so without having to rely on the public interest test: she decided that the exemption itself was not fulfilled. This was because she took the view that 'that the release of this information would bring greater clarity to, and reinforce public confidence in, the inspection system.'[161] She also found that whilst release of the information might, as the Council argued, prejudice its informal inspections system, it would not affect the specific duties the Council had under the Food Safety Act, because it would still be obliged to carry out inspections and, if necessary, 'pursue formal regulatory action'. These points indicate a robust upholding of transparency as a good in itself and a sceptical attitude to the arguments of public authorities against it. More strikingly still, whilst the Commissioner did not formally have to consider the argument based on the public interest, since she did not find the exemption to apply at all, she did 'note that there is an overwhelming public interest in the disclosure of this category of information'. This is a significant statement, and indicates that robust policing by the Commissioner, who will not in this area be subject to the Ministerial veto, may lay to rest some of the fears generated by s 30, as to the transmission of information to the public about issues affecting health and safety.

The other major class exemption in this category, under s 35, has been just as criticised. It amounts to a sweeping exemption for virtually all information relating to the formation of government policy. Under s 35(1):

Information held by a government department or by the National Assembly for Wales is exempt information if it relates to –

(a) the formulation or development of government policy,
(b) Ministerial communications,
(c) the provision of advice by any of the Law Officers or any request for the provision of such advice, or
(d) the operation of any Ministerial private office.

The duty to confirm or deny does not apply.

This exemption is presumably intended to prevent government from having to decide policy in a goldfish bowl – to protect the freeness and frankness of Civil Service advice and of internal debate within government – but, once again, it appears to go far beyond what would sensibly be required to achieve this aim. Section 36 contains a harm-based exemption which covers almost exactly the same ground: it exempts government information which would, or would be likely to, inhibit (a) the free and frank provision of advice, or (b) the free and frank exchange of views for the purposes of deliberation, or (c) would otherwise prejudice, or would be likely otherwise to prejudice, the effective conduct of public affairs. Since this covers all information whose release might cause damage to the working of government – and is framed in

161 Statement of Reasons, op. cit.

very broad terms – it appears to be unnecessary to have a sweeping class exemption covering the same ground. Moreover, this exemption is not restricted to Civil Service advice; it covers also the background information used in preparing policy, including the underlying facts and their analysis. As the CFOI commented:

> There would be no right to know about purely descriptive reports of existing practice, research reports, evidence on health hazards, assumptions about wage or inflation levels used in calculating costs, studies of overseas practice, consultants' findings or supporting data showing whether official assertions are realistic or not.[162]

The sole, and very limited exception to this exemption appears in s 35(2); it applies only 'once a decision as to government policy has been taken', and covers 'any statistical information used to provide an informed background to the taking of the decision'. This was a concession made by the government fairly late in the Bill's passage through Parliament and it is very limited. First, unlike most other FoI regimes, by excluding only statistical information from the exemption, it allows the *analysis* of facts to be withheld. Second, it only applies once a decision has been taken. Thus, where the government gave consideration to introducing a new policy but then shelved the matter without a decision, statistics used during the consideration process would, bizarrely, remain exempt. However, the Commissioner's interpretation of the Act is again somewhat encouraging. As to the statistical exception, the published guidance firmly states:

> Statistical information incorporates analyses, projections and meta-data, as well as the statistics themselves; numerical data which may take the form of a table or graph or simply be a sum total. Statistics must be derived from a recorded or repeatable methodology, and commentary on this is also statistical information.[163]

This suggests a somewhat broader reading of the phrase 'statistical information' than that given in the Act itself.

The Act is much more restrictive in this respect than the previous voluntary Code of Practice on Access to Government Information. The latter required both facts and the analysis of facts underlying policy decisions, including scientific analysis and expert appraisal, to be made available, once decisions were announced. Material relating to policy formation could only be withheld under a harm test – if disclosure would 'harm the frankness and candour of internal discussion'. The White Paper preceding the Bill proposed that there should be no class exemption for material in this area, but rather that, as under the Code, a harm test would have to be satisfied to prevent disclosure. However, the Commissioner has issued important guidance on this provision which all but changes it into a 'harm-based' test. In one of the strongest pronouncements made on the interpretation of the Act, the guidance states:

---

162 Freedom of Information Bill, House of Lords Committee Stage, 19 October 2000 briefing notes, p 1.
163 *Freedom of Information Act Awareness Guidance No 24.*

> The Information Commissioner's view is that there must be some clear, specific and credible evidence that the formulation or development of policy would be materially altered for the worse by the threat of disclosure under the Act.[164]

It will be immediately seen that this approach, by requiring 'specific . . . evidence' of a change 'for the worse', means that the Commissioner is in effect requiring prejudice to be shown: the whole point about a class exemption, in theory at least, is that it is unnecessary to show any such evidence; it is required only to show that the information in question falls within the exemption as defined. If carried through – and subject of course to use of the Ministerial veto, this requirement would greatly ameliorate the negative effects of the s 35 exemption. The Commissioner adds specific factors to be taken into account in deciding whether the exemption is made out:

- In this particular case, would release of this information make civil servants less likely to provide full and frank advice or opinions on policy proposals? Would it, for example, prejudice working relationships by exposing dissenting views?
- Would the prospect of future release inhibit the debate and exploration of the full range of policy options that ought to be considered, even if on reflection some of them are seen as extreme?
- Would the prospect of release place civil servants in the position of having to defend everything that has been raised (and possibly later discounted) during deliberation?
- On the other hand, would the possibility of future release act as a deterrent against advice which is ill-considered, vague, poorly prepared or written in unnecessarily brusque or defamatory language? Would the prospect of release in fact enhance the quality of future advice?
- Is the main reason for exempting the information to spare a civil servant or a Minister embarrassment? If so, then it is not appropriate to use this exemption.[165]

 Two things are noteworthy about the above guidance: first of all, the whole thrust of it is that the effect of the release of the particular information under consideration is what is crucial: as just discussed, this comes very close to re-working this exemption into one based on harm or prejudice. Second, the guidance adverts to reasons why disclosure may actually *improve* the quality of advice and of policy deliberation. This runs directly against the notion of a class-based exemption, which of course is a legislative *presumption* that release will be harmful: by instructing public authorities, and being prepared itself to consider reasons why release may in fact be beneficial, this presumptive quality of the exemption is radically undermined.

The guidance on the application of the public interest test to this exemption is also positive. It emphasises two distinct interests in disclosure in this area – participation and accountability. In terms of the former, the Guidance notes that 'A key driver for FOI legislation is allowing people access to information that will allow informed participation in the development of government proposals or decisions which are of

---

164 Ibid at para e.
165 Ibid.

concern to them',[166] and that participation 'cannot be meaningful' without access to information about how decisions are reached, including rejected policy options. These are powerful statements of principle in favour of disclosure. In terms of accountability, the Guidance specifically recognises the role of FOI legislation in counterbalancing government control over the release of information by 'spin doctors', seeking to put the most favourable gloss upon it: release of information under the Act would, it asserts: 'better enable the public to make objective judgments on the facts.'[167] It also sets out two situations in which there will generally be a 'strong public interest in disclosure'. One is where the policy decision 'is going to lead to large amounts of public expenditure on a particular project'; the other is where there is a departure from 'routine procedures' or 'standard practices'. In other words, in cases where Ministers appear to be bending or breaking the rules, the public interest in finding out why will be heightened. Overall, the guidance given in relation to this section, if followed by government departments, or enforced upon them by the Commissioner, will have a notably liberalising effect upon one of the most critical exemptions in the Act. It should however be recalled that, because, by definition, it will generally be information held by a government department, if the Commissioner orders disclosure on public interest grounds, the Ministerial veto will be available to override her. It is too soon to tell what the governmental view on use of the veto will be.

Information intended for future publication where it is reasonable that it should be withheld until that future date is exempt (s 22), and the duty to confirm or deny does not apply to the extent that complying with it would itself entail disclosing such information. The problem with the class exemption under s 22 is its imprecision: it does not specify a period within which the information has to be intended for publication for this exemption to apply. The government repeatedly rejected amendments that would have provided that this exemption could only be relied upon if a date for publication within a short, specified period had already been fixed.

There are a number of further class exemptions. Information subject to legal privilege (s 42) is exempt. The duty to confirm or deny does not apply if compliance with it would itself breach legal privilege. Trade secrets (s 43(1)) are exempt, but the duty does apply. 'Communications with Her Majesty, with other members of the Royal Family or with the Royal Household' are exempt, as is information relating to 'the conferring by the Crown of any honour or dignity' (s 37), and the duty to confirm or deny does not apply. It is unclear why it is necessary to bestow a class exemption relating to the royal household and honours and dignities, although this follows the practice under the previous voluntary Code. A separate class exemption covers information obtained for the purposes of conducting criminal proceedings and a very wide variety of investigations (specified in s 31(2)) carried out under statute or the prerogative, and which relate to the obtaining of information from confidential sources.

Harm-based exemptions not subject to the public interest test

This third category of exemptions has only one member. There is a general, harm-based exemption under s 36 for information the disclosure of which would be likely to

---

166 Ibid.
167 Ibid at para f.

prejudice the effective conduct of public affairs or inhibit free and frank discussion and advice. This exemption is subject to the general public interest test with one exception: for a reason that is not readily apparent; where the information in question is held by the Commons or Lords, the public interest test cannot be considered.

Harm-based exemptions which are subject to the public interest test

As harm-based exemptions, these are in one respect the least controversial aspect of the Act. But it should be noted that the Act departed from one of the most liberal and widely praised aspects of the White Paper, namely, the requirement that in order to make out such exemptions, the authority concerned would have to demonstrate 'substantial' harm. This has been changed to a test of simple prejudice, although government spokespersons attempted to deny that the change would make any difference in practice. In each case, the duty to confirm or deny does not apply if, or to the extent that, compliance with it would itself cause the prejudice which the exemption seeks to prevent.

These exemptions cover information the disclosure of which would prejudice or would be likely to prejudice: defence and the armed forces (s 26); international relations (s 27); the economy (s 29); the mental or physical health or safety of any individual (s 38); auditing functions of other public authorities (s 33); the prevention, detection of crime, legal proceedings brought by a public authority arising from an investigation conducted for any of the purposes specified in s 31(2) (above) and carried out under statute or prerogative; collection of tax; immigration controls; good order in prisons; the exercise by any public authority of its functions for any of the purposes specified in s 31(2) (above); relations between administrations in the UK (for example, between the government and the Scottish Executive) (s 28). These exemptions are relatively straightforward, although they go beyond the information covered by the Official Secrets Act.

A number of these exemptions are more contentious. Section 24 covers information the disclosure of which would prejudice or would be likely to prejudice national security. The use of the national security exemption, albeit accompanied by the harm test, may mean that sensitive matters of great political significance remain undisclosed. In particular, the breadth and uncertainty of the term 'national security' may allow matters which fall only doubtfully within it to remain secret. Had the Act been in place at the time of the change in policy regarding arms sales to Iraq, the subject of the Scott Report, it is likely that information relating to it would not have been disclosed since it could have fallen within the exception clauses. The whole subject of arms sales will probably fall within the national security exception and possibly within other exceptions as well.[168]

Under s 43, information the disclosure of which would prejudice or would be likely to prejudice the commercial interests of any person (including the public authority holding it) is exempt. The CFOI commented that under this exemption, the prejudice referred to could be caused by consumers refusing to buy a dangerous product. Thus they noted that the fact that a company had sold dangerous products, or behaved in

---

168 See further the Minutes of Evidence before the Public Service Committee HC 313-1 of 1995–96 QQ 66 *et seq.*

some other improper manner, could be suppressed if disclosure would lead customers to buy alternative products or shareholders to sell their shares.[169] This is clearly correct; however, in the case of unsafe products, the public interest test would surely require disclosure. The Commissioner has indeed said specifically that:

> There would be strong public interest arguments in allowing access to information which would help protect the public from unsafe products or unscrupulous practices even though this might involve revealing a trade secret or other information whose disclosure might harm the commercial interests of a company.[170]

Section 36 covers information which, in the reasonable opinion of a qualified person, would prejudice or be likely to prejudice collective Ministerial responsibility, or the work of the Executives of Northern Ireland and Wales, or which would be likely to inhibit the free and frank provision of advice, or the free and frank exchange of views for the purposes of deliberation, or would otherwise prejudice, or would be likely otherwise to prejudice, the effective conduct of public affairs. Two main criticisms of this exemption can be made. First, the test is not a wholly objective one, but is dependent upon 'the reasonable opinion of a qualified person'. The intention behind this provision is apparently to allow a person representing the department or body in question to make the primary determination of prejudice, with the Commissioner only being able to take issue with such a finding if it is irrational in the *Wednesbury* sense. The second main objection to this section is the 'catch-all' provision covering information the release of which could 'prejudice the effective conduct of public affairs', a phrase which is so vague and broad that it could mean almost anything.

Expiry of certain exemptions

As indicated above, the Act, through amendments to the Public Records Act, provides that some of the exemptions will cease to apply after a certain number of years, although these limitations are hardly generous. The following exemptions will cease to apply at all after 30 years (s 63(1)): s 28 (inter-UK relations); s 30(1) (information obtained during an investigation); s 32 (documents generated in litigation); s 33 (audit functions); s 35 (information relating to internal government discussion and advice); s 36 (information which could prejudice effective conduct of public affairs); s 37(1)(a) (communications with royal household); s 42 (legal professional privilege) and s 43 (trade secrets and information which could damage commercial interests). The exemptions under s 21 (information accessible by other means) and s 22 (information intended for future publication) will cease to apply after 30 years where the relevant document is held in a public record office (s 64(1)). Still less generously, information relating to the bestowing of honours and dignities (s 37(1)(b)) only ceases to be exempt after 60 years, while we will have to wait 100 years before the expiry of the exemption for information falling within s 31, that is, information which might prejudice law enforcement, the administration of justice, etc.

---

169 Freedom of Information Bill, House of Lords Committee Stage, 19 October 2000 briefing notes, p 1.
170 Freedom of Information Act Awareness Guidance No 5, at para 2.

Additionally, one of the absolute exemptions – information provided by the security, intelligence, etc services (s 23(1)) – *will cease to be absolute* after 30 years, that is, the public interest in disclosure must be considered once 30 years has expired.

Applying for information and time limits

Requests for information must be in writing (s 8) and, under s 9, a small fee may be charged. Information requested must generally be supplied within 20 days of the request (s 10(1)). However, there is an important exception to this: where an authority finds that information is prima facie exempt, either because it falls within a class exemption, or the requisite prejudice is thought to be present, but then goes on to consider whether the information should nevertheless be released under the public interest test, it does not have to make a decision within the normal 20-day deadline. Instead, it must release the information only within an unspecified 'reasonable period'.

Clearly, there are practical problems in using the Act. The citizen may have difficulty in obtaining the document he or she requires. He or she may not be able to frame the request for information specifically enough in order to obtain the particular documents needed. The request may be met with the response that several hundred documents are available touching on the matter in question; the citizen may lack the expert knowledge needed to identify the particular document required. If so, under s 1(3), the authority arguably need not comply with the request and can continue to postpone its compliance until and if the requester succeeds in formulating the request more specifically. Section 1(3) does not allow the authority to postpone the request until it has had a chance to obtain further information, enabling it to deal with the request. However, the duty to provide advice and assistance so far as reasonable, provided for in section 16 of the Act,[171] would apply to an instance in which the authority was itself able to identify the requisite documents and did not genuinely require further information to do so. It would then come under a duty to assist the applicant in choosing the relevant documents. The Code of Practice published by the Department for Constitutional Affairs[172] deals with the section 16 duty. In relation to the instant point, it states:

> 8. Authorities should, as far as reasonably practicable, provide assistance to the applicant to enable him or her to describe more clearly the information requested.
>
> 10. Appropriate assistance in this instance might include:
>
> - providing an outline of the different kinds of information which might meet the terms of the request;
> - providing access to detailed catalogues and indexes, where these are available, to help the applicant ascertain the nature and extent of the information held by the authority;

---

171 (1) It shall be the duty of a public authority to provide advice and assistance, so far as it would be reasonable to expect the authority to do so, to persons who propose to make, or have made, requests for information to it.

172 Under s 45 of the Act. The Code is available at: http://www.dca.gov.uk/foi/reference/statCodesOfPractice.htm.

- providing a general response to the request setting out options for further information which could be provided on request.[173]

This is a helpful clarification that authorities cannot rely upon the applicant's ignorance as to the documents available, without seeking to provide a reasonable level of assistance in identifying the relevant documents. Early indications are that central government has a very mixed record on compliance with the Act's requirements within the time limits set down.[174] In a press release, the Campaign for Freedom of Information said 'the government's figures showed that a "disturbing" level of requests were not being dealt with within the Act's time limits'.[175] Overall, more than a third (36 per cent) of government departments failed to meet the deadline of 20 working days. 25 per cent failed even to tell the applicant that they needed extra time, as required by the Act. The Home Office had by far the worst record amongst government departments. In 60 per cent of all requests it failed either to respond to the request within 20 days, or even to inform the applicant that it needed more time within that period. The Campaign said this represented 'routine disregard for the Act's requirements'.[176] Other important Ministries did much better:

> the Department for Transport and the Department for Constitutional Affairs both answered 83% of their requests within the basic 20 working day period. The Department for Work and Pensions met this time limit in 81% of cases and the Ministry of Defence, which received far more requests than any other department, met the 20 day limit for 71% of its requests.[177]

There was also a disturbing variation in the extent to which the department concerned answered the requests put to it in full. The Department of Transport provided full answers in 76 per cent of cases, followed by the MOD which managed 67 per cent. However, 'at the other end of the scale the Department of Trade and Industry provided full answers in only 21 per cent of cases, the Home Office in 28 per cent and the Cabinet Office in 29 per cent of cases.' The Campaign said 'it's ... clear that some parts of Whitehall are more committed to freedom of information than others'.

The enforcement mechanism

The basic mechanism

The enforcement review mechanism under the Act is far stronger than the mechanism established under the Code. The internal review of a decision to withhold information, established under the Code, was formalised under the Act and the role of the Ombudsman was taken over by that of the Information Commissioner. The Commissioner's powers

---

173 Op. cit. at paras 8–10.
174 See 'Freedom of Information Act 2000. Statistics on Implementation in Central Government. Q1. January-March 2005; published on the website of the Department for Constitutional Affairs.
175 Press Release, dated 23 June 2005, available on the Campaign's website: http://www.cfoi.org.uk.
176 Ibid.
177 Ibid.

are also much more extensive than those of the Ombudsman. As indicated below, she has the power to order disclosure of the information and can report a failure to disclose information to the courts who can treat it in the same way as contempt of court. Under the White Paper, it was to be a criminal offence to destroy, alter or withhold records relevant to an investigation of the Information Commissioner. It was also to become a criminal offence to shred documents requested by outsiders, including the media and the public. However, the two offences are omitted from the Act. No civil liability is incurred if a public authority does not comply with any duty imposed by the Act (s 56).

The rights granted under the Act are enforceable by the Data Protection Commissioner, now known as 'The Information Commissioner'. Importantly, the Commissioner has security of tenure, being dismissible only by the Crown following an address by both Houses of Parliament. An appeal lies from decisions of the Commissioner to the Information Tribunal, which is made up of experienced lawyers and 'persons to represent the interests' of those seeking information and of public authorities (Sched 2, Part II).

Under s 50: 'Any person (in this section referred to as "the complainant") may apply to the Commissioner for a decision whether, in any specified respect, a request for information made by the complainant to a public authority has been dealt with in accordance with [the Act].' The Commissioner must then make a decision unless the application has been made with 'undue delay', is frivolous or vexatious or the complainant has not exhausted any complaints procedure provided by the public authority (s 50(1)). If the Commissioner decides that the authority concerned has failed to communicate information or confirm or deny when required to do so by the Act, she must serve a 'decision notice' on the authority stating what it must do to satisfy the Act. She may also serve 'Information Notices' upon authorities, requiring the authority concerned to provide her with information about a particular application or its compliance with the Act generally.

The Commissioner may ultimately force a recalcitrant authority to act by serving upon it an enforcement notice, which (*per* s 52(1)) 'requir[es] the authority to take, within such time as may be specified in the notice, such steps as may be so specified for complying with those requirements'. If a public authority fails to comply with a Decision, Enforcement or Information Notice, the Commissioner can certify the failure in writing to the High Court, which, the Act provides (s 52(2)):

> may inquire into the matter and, after hearing any witness who may be produced against or on behalf of the public authority, and after hearing any statement that may be offered in defence, deal with the authority as if it had committed a contempt of court.

In other words, the Commissioner's decisions can, in the final analysis, be enforced just as can orders of the court. These powers are buttressed by powers of entry, search and seizure to gain evidence of a failure by the authority to carry out its obligations under the Act, or comply with a Notice issued by the Commissioner (detailed in Sched 3).

There does, however, appear to be a developing problem of overload. The Campaign for Freedom of Information reports that, as at November 2005, only 11 months after the Act came into force, there was a backlog of over 1,300 cases, and that some complaints had been with the Commissioner's office for more than six months without even being allocated to an investigating officer. This is of particular concern to the media, given that news stories may have a temporary shelf life. Where a response is made to a public authority for documents that would reveal some embarrassing failure or scandal, and media interest in the matter is temporarily intense, the authority may well be tempted just to refuse the request, in the knowledge that even though the Information Commissioner will almost certainly overturn its decision, by the time that is done, media interest in the story will have died down, and the interest generated by the eventual release of the documents will be minimal.

Appeals

The Commissioner's decisions are themselves subject to appeal to the Tribunal, and this power of appeal is exercisable upon the broadest possible grounds. The Act provides that either party may appeal to the Tribunal against a decision notice, and a public authority may appeal against an enforcement or information notice (s 57(2) and (3)), either on the basis that the notice is 'not in accordance with the law', or 'to the extent that the notice involved an exercise of discretion by the Commissioner, that he ought to have exercised his discretion differently' (s 58(1)). The Tribunal is also empowered to review 'any finding of fact on which the notice in question was based' and, as well as being empowered to quash decisions of the Commissioner, may 'substitute such other notice as could have been served by the Commissioner'. There is a further appeal from the Tribunal to the High Court, but on a 'point of law' only (s 59). In practice, this will probably be interpreted so as to allow review of the Tribunal's decisions, not just for error of law, but also on the other accepted heads of judicial review. Early indications are however that the Tribunal is in fact taking a more robust, pro-FOI stance than the Commissioner, which is a welcome development.[178]

The ministerial veto of the Commissioner's decisions

The ministerial veto is another highly controversial aspect of the Act. The White Paper made no provision for such a power of veto, on the basis that to do so would undermine confidence in the regime. Such a veto clearly dilutes the basic FoI principle that a body independent from government should enforce the rights to information and since, in cases where the release of information could embarrass ministers, it constitutes them judge in their own cause, it is objectionable in principle.

For the veto to be exercisable, two conditions must be satisfied under s 53(1). First, the Notice which the veto will operate to quash must have been served on a government department, the Welsh Assembly or 'any public authority designated for the purposes of this section by an order made by the Secretary of State.' Second, the Notice must order the release of information which is prima facie exempt but which the Commissioner has decided should nevertheless be released under the public interest test in s 2. (By prima facie exempt, it will be recalled, is meant information that either falls into a

---

178 For details see 'Information Tribuanl's Early Decisions Lead to Greater Open-ness' – 20 Dec 2005; available http://www.cfoi.org.uk/pdf/tribunalnote.pdf.

class exemption or, where prejudice is required to render it exempt, the Commissioner has adjudged the prejudice to be present).

The veto is exercised by means of a certificate signed by the Minister concerned, stating that he has 'on reasonable grounds formed the opinion that, in respect of the request or requests concerned, there was no failure' to comply with the Act. The decision must be made at a relatively senior level. If the information is sought from a department of the Northern Irish Executive or any NI public authority, it must be exercised by the First and Deputy Minister acting together; if sought from a Welsh department or any Welsh public authority, the Assembly First Secretary makes the decision; if it is sought from a UK government department or any other public authority, the person responsible is a Cabinet Minister. The reasons for the veto must be given to the complainant (s 56), unless doing so would reveal exempt information (s 57), and the certificate must be laid before Parliament or the Welsh/NI assembly as applicable. How much resort will be made to the veto, only time will tell. However, as the Campaign for FOI pointed out, a worrying precedent exists in that the government has on several occasions refused to comply with rulings by the Ombudsman (PCA) under the previous Code of Practice on Access to Information. Examples include:[179] refusals to comply fully with a recommendation by the PCA as to the release information on Ministerial gifts; preventing the PCA from seeing papers of Cabinet committees which were dealing with the Human Rights Act; and the issuance of a certificate blocking disclosure of information about Ministerial conflicts of interest on the grounds that it would be contrary to the public interest. These precedents are far from encouraging: it may be doubted that the additional safeguards built into the use of the veto in the Act will be enough to dissuade or deter Ministers from making use of it, although one may confidently predict an outcry in the media if and when the veto is first used. The Phillis Committee on Government Communications, amongst other matters, called on the government to publicly renounce the use of the veto.[180]

Publication schemes

Under ss 19 and 20, public authorities must adopt 'publication schemes' relating to the publication of information by that authority, that is, schemes by which information is made generally available to the public, without a specific request having to be made. This is a significant aspect of the Act, since more citizens will thereby gain access to a wider range of information. The difficulty and expense of making a request will be avoided. The scheme can be devised by the authority or, under s 20, a model scheme devised by the Information Commissioner can be used. If a tailor-made scheme is used, it must be approved by the Commissioner (s 19(1)(a)). Therefore, authorities are likely to use the model schemes, thereby avoiding the need to submit the scheme for approval. Consistency between authorities is probably desirable as promoting transparency and thereby enhancing access to information. For early indications as to the schemes prepared by central government departments, see a report by the CFOI.[181]

---

179 For the full report ((HC 951 (2002–3), see http://www.ombudsman.org.uk/pca/document/aoi03nj/index.htm.
180 See http://foi.missouri.edu/internatfoinews/FinalReport.pdf.
181 'Central Government Publication Schemes: Good Practice' http://www.cfoi.org.uk/pdf/ps_report.pdf.

Proposals to restrict the use of the Act

One year after the Act came fully into force, the Department of Constitutional Affairs published a Report on the Act, *Freedom of Information – one year on*, to which the government responded in[182] The Report found that implementation of the FOI Act had already brought about significant and new releases of information and that this information was being used in a constructive and positive way by a range of different individuals and organisations. The report stated: '. . . This is a significant success.' A number of examples of releases of information were noted in the Report; they included the disclosure of information relating to: the heart surgery survival rates for different hospitals in England and Wales; the safety of Britain's nuclear plants; the best and worst performing schools in each county; information on restaurant hygiene. The government in its response also noted that public authorities had continued to make substantial efforts to comply with the FOI Act. Public authorities were proactively publishing information; an example of this was the Rural Payments Agency's release of figures relating to Common Agricultural Policy payments. However, it also became apparent in 2006 that the government had reservations about the impact of the Act.

In 2006 the Department for Constitutional Affairs ordered an independent review of the economic cost of the Act.[183] Implementation of FoI is estimated to cost roughly £35m a year. Under the current financial regime, public bodies do not make a charge for considering requests if the work involved does not exceed £600's worth of a civil servant's time. The independent Report looking at the economic impact of the legislation found that journalists make up 10 per cent of the volume of central government requests and 21 per cent of the cost. In response the government took the view that implementing the Act has become too expensive, and in December 2006 the Department for Constitutional Affairs published draft Regulations intended to restrict use of the Act.[184]

The existing Regulations are the Freedom of Information and Data Protection (Appropriate Limit and Fees) Regulations 2004, which came into force in January 2005. Their key provisions are: the 'appropriate limit', above which public authorities may decline to comply with a request for information, is set at £600 for central government and Parliament, and £450 for the wider public sector; when estimating whether the costs of complying with a request for information would exceed the appropriate limit, public authorities may only include the costs of determining whether the information is held, and then locating, retrieving and extracting it; where those costs relate to the time spent by officials or other people carrying out the relevant activities on behalf of the authority, they must be calculated at a standard rate of £25 per hour; and when estimating whether the costs of complying with a request for information would exceed the appropriate limit, public authorities may aggregate the costs of two or more requests received from the same person, or persons who appear to be acting in concert or in pursuance of a campaign, provided the requests relate to the same or similar information and are received within a period of 60 working days.

---

182 Select Committee's Report – Freedom of Information – one year on, October 2006, Cm 6937.
183 *An Independent Review of the Impact of FoI*, A Report for the Dept of Constitutional Affairs, October 2006.
184 Draft FoI and Data Protection (Appropriate Limit and Fees) Regulations 2007, Consultation Paper 28/06, 14.12.06.

Under the new draft Regulations restrictions can be placed on the type of information requested: it must not be too frivolous; and restrictions can be placed on the cost of collecting it; officials' reading time, consideration time and consultation time must be included in the estimate of the charge to be made. Public authorities can refuse an application if the cost of dealing with the request exceeds £450 or, in the case of government departments, £600. Only the cost of searching for the information can be included in this calculation at the moment. Under draft regulation 7 a public authority, when calculating the appropriate cost limit, could aggregate the costs of requests for information received from the same person (or persons who appear to be acting in concert or in pursuance of a campaign) where they were made within a period of 60 working days and where:

> ... (as under the 2004 Regulations) the requests related to the same or similar information (draft regulation 7(2)(b)(i); or b) the requests did not relate to the same or similar information, but it was reasonable in all the circumstances to aggregate the requests (draft regulation 7(2)(b)(ii)).

Thus, restrictions could be placed on the frequency of requests from any one individual or body (the aggregation proposal). Under that proposal any one organisation would be limited in the number of requests that could be made when the aggregated costs of dealing with requests from that organisation exceeded the cost limits. Thus, if a very large media organisation made a request, that would mean that further requests from a member of that organisation, even working in a completely separate sector of the organisation and pursuing a very different story, could be refused once the cost limit had been reached. Clearly, under the proposed regulations, not only can aggregation of requests occur much more readily, but the costs that can be included in the calculation have increased. The regulations could put the ability of such an organisation to submit FOI requests on a par with those of an individual wanting to obtain access to his or her personal records. The government considers that the number of requests made by individual pressure groups and media outlets add disproportionately to the costs of the legislation.

The restrictions also create leeway for delay and for the creation of bureaucratic obstacles to obtaining access to the information while, for example, costs of obtaining it were worked out. The proposed restrictions indicate that the government, in the very early life of the Act, is already becoming concerned about its use. Arguably, the Act is being used more successfully than the government predicted that it would be.

If the proposals were implemented they would create approximately a 10 per cent saving, meaning that about £5m-£12m would be saved.[185] The proposals would lead to a significant dilution of the freedom of information regime. For example, the BBC would be caught by the aggregation proposal. It could mean that if one BBC journalist were to submit a request that took the organisation to the limit of the number of requests it could make, the BBC could not make further further requests for three months.

---

185 Estimation from an article in the *New Statesman* 5.3.2007. The figure of £12 million was mentioned in Parliament in debate on the regulations. It was also argued that the Act was working reasonably well, despite the flaws (7 Feb 2007: Column 315 WH).

In Parliamentary debate on the proposals Mark Fisher MP made some pertinent criticisms:

> Money is not the explanation of what is proposed . . . in a really participatory democracy the legislation would be used much more, which is perhaps what the Government fear . . . In the present generation, Parliament is getting weaker and weaker in relation to Governments who are growing more and more mighty . . . The imbalance between the Executive and the legislature has reached a critical point. If we pass the regulations it will be only a small drop of water into the balance, but it will tip it in the wrong direction for Parliament and the public realm, and the investigative press . . .[186]

Maurice Frankel, director of the Campaign for Freedom of Information, has argued: 'These proposals would make it harder for requesters to ask penetrating questions and easier for authorities to avoid scrutiny.' One of the biggest costs in considering requests is when it triggers a referral to a Minister. Mr Frankel considers that the new rules, if implemented, would mean more interventions by Ministers and therefore more requests declined for reasons of costs. 'It means Ministers will be deciding requests on whether the release makes headlines or not – and that's not what the legislation is about. Ministers should leave these decisions to the experienced FOI officers.'[187]

Conclusions

Despite its weaknesses, this is a constitutional development whose significance can hardly be over-stated. The FoI Act, enforceable by the Information Commissioner, will be a clear improvement on the Code introduced by the Major Government. Rodney Austin described the draft Bill as 'a denial of democracy'.[188] It is suggested that the improvements made to the Bill during its passage through Parliament, while still leaving it a far weaker and more illiberal measure than the scheme proposed by the widely praised White Paper which preceded it, render this view no longer accurate. In particular, the public interest test has been strengthened, and applies to most of the exemptions in the Act, including, crucially, the key class exemptions relating to investigations and to the formation of government policy; however, as the CFOI points out, it is misleading to view this as converting class exemptions into 'harm-based' ones, since the very existence of a class exemption is based upon a presumption, built into the Act, that such information is, as a class, of a type which generally should not be released. Nevertheless, although it is still too early to tell, the attitude of the Information Commissioner as expressed in the published guidance indicates that, in reality, evidence of individual damage that would be done by publication will be required where a public authority seeks to resist the argument that publication should take place on public interest grounds.[189]

---

186 Hansard 7 Feb 2007 : Column 310WH.
187 See CFOI web-site.
188 Austin, R, 'Freedom of information: a Sheep in Wolf's Clothing?', in Jowell, J and Oliver, D (eds), *The Changing Constitution*, 5th edn, 2004, at 237.
189 See above at 645–46.

The Act does represent a turning point in British democracy in, for the first time in its history, removing the decision to release many classes of information from government and placing it in the hands of an independent agency, the Information Commissioner, and in giving a statutory 'right' to information, enforceable if necessary through the courts, to citizens. However, as seen, the Act fences this basic right around with so many restrictions that, depending upon its interpretation, much information of any conceivable interest could still be withheld. Whether this turns out to be the case in practice will depend primarily upon the robustness of the stance taken by the Commissioner, particularly in applying the public interest test to the class exemptions under the Act, where it will provide the only means of obtaining disclosure. Early signs in this respect are hopeful, but only the experience of several years will make clear what the Act has achieved. The current 2007 proposals to limit access to information on grounds of costs would, if implemented, have a significantly restrictive effect on the operation of the Act. There have been a number of suggestions, from the media, from MPs and from the CFOI that the proposals are less about curbing the cost of the use of the Act, since the savings would be relatively minor, and more about retreating from the principle of openness enshrined in the Act.

Chapter 8

Freedom of protest and assembly

1 Introduction[1]

In the UK in the twenty-first century the legal response to protest is changing. The terrorist acts of 9/11, the rise of terrorism thereafter and of awareness of terrorism, the Iraq war, have all had an impact. The deployment of criminal sanctions in 2006 to seek to rid Parliament Square of a lone, peaceful anti-war protester is only the most obvious manifestation of this change. Since the main statutory framework governing protest was put in place in 1986 and extended in 1994 under the Conservative government, there has been, this chapter will argue, a continued creeping criminalisation, and even terrorisation, of many forms of dissent over the ten years of Labour rule since 1997. The over-broad provisions introduced in 1986 and 1994 have been extended incrementally

---

1 For texts referred to below and further reading, see: Bailey, SH, Harris, DJ and Jones, BL, *Civil Liberties: Cases and Materials*, 5th edn, 2002, Chapter 3; Whitty, N, Murphy, T and Livingstone, S, *Civil Liberties Law*, 2001, Part V; Feldman, D, *Civil Liberties and Human Rights in England and Wales*, 2002, Chapter 17; Fenwick, H, *Civil Rights: New Labour, Freedom and the Human Rights Act*, 2000, Chapter 4; Waddington, PAJ, *Liberty and Order*, 1994; Clayton, R and Tomlinson, H, *The Law of Human Rights*, 2nd edn, 2006, Chapter 16; Mead, D, *The New Law of Peaceful Protest – Rights and Regulation in the Human Rights Act Era*, forthcoming 2007. For discussion and criticism of the Public Order Act 1986, see Bonner, D and Stone, R, 'The Public Order Act 1986: steps in the wrong direction?' [1987] PL 202; Card, R, *Public Order: the New Law*, 1987, Butterworths; Smith, ATH, 'The Public Order Act 1986 Part I' [1987] Crim LR 156; Gearty, CA, 'Freedom of assembly and public order', in *Individual Rights and the Law in Britain*, 1994, p 55; Harris, J, O'Boyle, M and Warbrick, C, *Law of the European Convention on Human Rights*, 1995. For discussion and criticism of the Criminal Justice and Public Order Act 1986, see Allen, MJ and Cooper, S, 'Howard's way: a farewell to freedom?' 58(3) MLR 364, p 378; Fenwick, H and Phillipson, G, 'Public protest, the Human Rights Act and judicial responses to political expression' (2000) PL 627–50. For post-HRA criticism of the provisions of the two statutes, see: Geddis, A, 'Free Speech Martyrs or Unreasonable Threats to Social Peace? – "Insulting" Expression and Section 5 of the Public Order Act 1986' (2004) *Public Law* 853; Newman, C, (2006) 'Divisional Court: Public Order Act 1986, s 4A: Proportionality and Freedom of Expression' 70 *Journal of Criminal Law* 191; Ormerod, D, *Smith and Hogan Criminal Law*, 11th edn, 2005, OUP; Ward, R and Wragg, A, *Walker and Walker's English Legal System*, 9th edn, 2005, OUP. For background, see: Williams, DGT, *Keeping the Peace*, 1967 (excellent historical account); Brownlie, I and Supperstone, M, *Law Relating to Public Order and National Security*, 1981; Marshall, G, 'Freedom of speech and assembly', in *Constitutional Theory*, 1971, p 154; Bevan, VT, 'Protest and public disorder' [1979] PL 163; Uglow, S, *Policing Liberal Society*, 1988, OUP; Smith, ATH, *Offences Against Public Order*, 1997, Sweet and Maxwell; Sherr, A, *Freedom of Protest, Public Order and the Law*, 1989; Ewing, KD and Gearty, CA, *The Struggle for Civil Liberties*, 1999; Ewing, KD and Gearty, CA, *Freedom under Thatcher*, 1990, Chapter 4.

in a range of statutes that, on their face, are not concerned mainly with public order, such as the Anti-Social Behaviour Act 2003. Accompanying incrementally increasing criminalisation of forms of dissent, there has recently been a more worrying trend – to use sanctions based on the civil standard of proof against protesters. For most of those ten years the Human Rights Act has also been in force – an intriguing contradiction that forms one of the main themes of this chapter. But in exploring the contradictions in recent UK civil rights statutory policy, it must be remembered that the common law doctrine of breach of the peace overshadows all the statutory changes over the last ten years. Breathtakingly broad, bewilderingly imprecise in scope, it provides the police with such wide powers to use against protesters as to render the statutory frameworks almost redundant.

It is often said that toleration of public protest is a hallmark of a democratic, free society. The logic of such a society is that it is prepared to take at least some account of the wishes of its citizens and will not wish to stray too far from the path of majority acceptance in decision making. Further, it does not impose one vision of the good life on its citizens; therefore, it tolerates and even encourages the public expression of various political visions. Public protest as a form of expression is therefore tolerated in free societies.[2] However, the public interests which may be threatened by public protest – the maintenance of order, the preservation of property, freedom of movement, respect for personal autonomy – may also be viewed as essential to democracy.[3] Thus, a tension clearly exists between the legitimate interest of the state in maintaining order on the one hand and, on the other, the protection of the freedoms of protest and assembly.

Therefore, in seeking to discover the limits of the legal acceptance of freedom of protest and assembly, and the value that the law places upon it, this chapter focuses on those provisions of the criminal and civil law most applicable in the context of demonstrations, marches, meetings, direct action. The legal regime relies on the use of both prior and subsequent restraints. Prior restraint on assemblies may mean that an assembly cannot take place at all or that it can take place only under various limitations. Subsequent restraints, usually arrests and prosecutions for public order offences, may be used after the assembly is in being. Although the availability of subsequent restraints may have a 'chilling' effect, they are used publicly and may receive publicity. If an assembly takes place and, subsequently, some of its members are prosecuted for public order offences, it will have achieved its end in gaining publicity and may in fact have gained greater publicity due to the prosecutions. If the assembly never takes place, its object will probably be completely defeated.

Prior and subsequent restraints arise from a large number of wide ranging and sometimes archaic powers which spring partly from a mix of statutory provisions, partly from the common law and partly from the royal prerogative.[4] To an extent, the number of restraints available is unsurprising because the range of state interests

---

2 See, e.g., Nimmer, MB, 'The meaning of symbolic speech under the First Amendment' (1973) 21 UCLA L Rev 29, 61–62; Kalven, H, 'The concept of the public forum' (1965) Sup Ct Rev 1, p 23.

3 See Bailey, Harris, and Jones, op. cit., fn 1, 4th edn, p 167.

4 For discussion of the various offences, see Ormerod, D, *Smith and Hogan Criminal Law* 11th edn, 2005 (standard criminal law text), Chapter 21; Thornton, P, *Public Order Law*, 1987; Smith, ATH, *Offences Against Public Order*, 1987, Blackstone.

involved is wider than any other expressive activity would warrant: they include the possibilities of disorder, of violence to citizens and damage to property. Clearly, the state has a duty to protect citizens from the attentions of the mob. The need to give weight to these interests explains the general acceptance of freedom of assembly as a non-absolute right,[5] even though it may be that violent protest is most likely to bring about change.

Most of these restraints are not aimed specifically at assemblies and protesters, but generally at keeping the peace. Nevertheless, they severely affect the freedoms of protest and of assembly. Therefore, those seeking to exercise the freedoms of protest and assembly have historically been in a vulnerable position[6] and currently they are in an especially precarious legal position since such a web of overlapping and imprecise public order provisions now exists and is constantly increasing. But they can now rely on an express recognition in domestic law of rights to protest and assemble within Arts 10 and 11 of the European Convention on Human Rights as received into UK law under the Human Rights Act (HRA) 1998. This constitutes a potentially climactic break with the traditional UK constitutional position. That position was that citizens might do anything which the law did not forbid, whereas, under the HRA, they are able to exercise rights to protest and assembly, circumscribed, as Chapters 2 and 4 explain, only in a manner compatible with specified Convention exceptions or, exceptionally, by incompatible domestic legislation.[7]

As Sedley LJ put it in *Redmond-Bate v DPP*:[8]

> A liberty, as AP Herbert repeatedly pointed out, is only as real as the laws and bylaws which negate or limit it. A right, by contrast, may be asserted in the face of such restrictions and must be respected, subject to lawful and proper reservations, by the courts.[9]

Since, as indicated, the extent of such reservations, which may undermine the right, will largely be determined by police officers and magistrates, it is important to bear in mind their obligations to abide by the Convention rights under s 6 of the HRA. Most significantly, this means that, for the first time, the constitutional duty placed personally on individual police officers[10] and magistrates to keep the Queen's Peace is coupled with a corresponding duty to uphold public freedom of expression under s 6 HRA.

The focus of this chapter is on the mass of common law and statutory public order provisions, in the light of the rights to freedom of assembly and protest given further effect in domestic law under the Human Rights Act. Having considered the justifications underpinning such rights, it will evaluate the potential and actual responses of the judiciary to the acceptance of the substantive values underlying public expression under Arts 10 and 11 in UK public order law. It will be argued that the common

---

5 See the leading US case, *Hague v Committee for Industrial Organisation* (1938) 307 US 496. For further discussion, see Williams, DGT [1987] Crim LR 167.

6 See Ewing and Gearty (1990), op. cit., fn 1.

7 HRA 1998, s 3(2). The government has not sought to rely on this exception post-HRA.

8 [1999] All ER (D) 864; (1999) *The Times*, 28 July; see below, pp 778–79 for discussion.

9 Transcript, para 15.

10 See *Humphries v Connor* (1864) 17 ICLR 1.

law had signally failed to provide the recognition for the value of public protest as a form of political expression which is evident in respect of media expression. Such failings are due, it will be contended, to the desire to protect countervailing interests, particularly proprietorial rights, but the judiciary in general did not make this explicit: the express balancing act which may be carried out at Strasbourg between political expression and other societal interests has not occurred until very recently – post-HRA – in the judgments of domestic courts, often because the former value is merely afforded no recognition at all. Parliament also failed, it will be argued, to provide that recognition while incrementally adding to the public order legislation. Moreover, prior to the inception of the HRA, the guarantees of freedom of expression and peaceful assembly under Arts 10 and 11 of the Convention were hardly adverted to in the domestic courts as aids to statutory interpretation, or to resolve common law policy issues in public protest cases, as the decisions discussed below reveal. The close nexus between assembly and expression failed to receive recognition when low level public order offences, committed in the course of, or directly through, the exercise of political protest, were adjudicated upon. But that nexus has been recognised at Strasbourg for some time.[11] But this chapter will demonstrate that the HRA is encouraging a change in the judicial response, and the central theme of this chapter will concern the impact the Act has had and is likely to have within the established context of the existing and increasing web of prohibitory rules.

Lord Bingham tellingly described the impact that the HRA is having in this context in the House of Lords decision in *R (on the application of Laporte) (FC) v Chief Constable of Gloucestershire:*[12]

> The approach of the English common law to freedom of expression and assembly was hesitant and negative, permitting that which was not prohibited. Thus although Dicey in *An Introduction to the Study of the Law of the Constitution*[13] in Part II on the 'Rule of Law', included chapters VI and VII entitled 'The Right to Freedom of Discussion' and 'The Right of Public Meeting', he wrote of the first[14] that 'At no time has there in England been any proclamation of the right to liberty of thought

---

11 See, for example, *Ezelin v France* (1991) 14 EHRR 362, paras 37, 51; *Plattform "Ärzte für das Leben" v Austria* (1988) 13 EHRR 204; *Djavit An v Turkey* (2003) Reports of Judgments and Decisions, 2003-III, p 233, para 39; *Christian Democratic People's Party v Moldova* (Appl No 28793/02, 14 May 2006, unreported) para 62; *Öllinger v Austria* (Appl No 76900/01, 29 June 2006, unreported), para 38. In the protest case of *Steel and Others v United Kingdom* (1998) 28 EHRR 603, para 101, freedom of expression was said to constitute 'an essential foundation of democratic society and one of the basic conditions for its progress and for each individual's self-fulfilment'. In *Ezelin v France* at para 53, the Court found that the 'freedom to take part in a peaceful assembly – in this instance a demonstration that had not been prohibited – is of such importance that it cannot be restricted in any way, even for an *avocat*, so long as the person concerned does not himself commit any reprehensible act on such an occasion'. In *Ziliberberg v Moldova* (Appl No 61821/00, 4 May 2004, unreported), para 2, the Court made the association between assembly and expression explicit: 'the right to freedom of assembly is a fundamental right in a democratic society and, like the right to freedom of expression, is one of the foundations of such a society'.

12 [2006] UKHL 55, para 34. CA: *R (on the application of Laporte) v CC of Gloucester Constab* [2004] EWCA Civ 1639. See below for discussion pp 757–62.

13 10th edn, 1959.

14 At pp 239–40.

or to freedom of speech' and of the second[15] that 'it can hardly be said that our constitution knows of such a thing as any specific right of public meeting'. Lord Hewart CJ reflected the then current orthodoxy when he observed in *Duncan v Jones*[16] that 'English law does not recognize any special right of public meeting for political or other purposes'. The Human Rights Act 1998, giving domestic effect to articles 10 and 11 of the European Convention, represented what Sedley LJ in *Redmond-Bate v Director of Public Prosecutions*,[17] aptly called a 'constitutional shift'.

Underlying justifications

In considering the justifications underlying rights of protest and assembly it should be pointed out that the two rights are distinguishable, although they will often be exercised together. Some protest of the symbolically or actually obstructive type, such as standing in front of grouse shooters or lying down in front of earth moving machinery, is primarily expression-based: the assembly element may not be significant. A lone anti-war protester reading out names of those killed in the Iraq war in a symbolically significant location is not relying on group impact to make the point. Equally, while persons may assemble in a group in order to make a more effective protest, not all groups come together in order to protest: the assembly may be of a ceremonial, albeit political nature; the Orange parades in Northern Ireland fall into this category. In such instances, the fact of assembling is significant in itself and, although the assembly is expressing a message, it could not readily be characterised as a protest. In other words, in some instances the 'assembly' element is dominant; in others, it is almost absent.

The individual rights to assemble and make public protest are bolstered by the interests justifying freedom of speech – furthering the search for truth, the participation of the citizen in the democracy and the exercise of autonomy. The justification based on the argument from truth[18] is present in the sense that citizens must be able to communicate with each other if debate which may reach the truth is to occur: public protest provides one means of ensuring that speech reaches a wider audience. Political speech is justified instrumentally on the basis that it allows participation in the democracy;[19] public protest is one particular and direct means of allowing such participation to occur outside election periods. Public protest is probably one of the most effective means by which ordinary citizens can bring matters to the attention of others, including Members of Parliament. Ordinary citizens are unlikely to be able to gain access to the media to publicise their views; they may, for example, distribute leaflets or posters without assembling in order to do so, but such methods are probably less effective if they are not part of a public protest. A clear example was provided by the anti-poll tax marches in the 1990s. As the Introduction to Part II indicates, this justification for expression is the one most favoured by the European Court of Human Rights,[20] which has also given

15 At p 271.
16 [1936] 1 KB 218, 222.
17 (1999) 163 JP 789, 795; for discussion of the decision, see below at pp 778–79.
18 Mill, JS, *On Liberty*, 1972.
19 See Meiklejohn, 'The First Amendment is an absolute' (1961) Sup Ct Rev 245.
20 See *Castells v Spain* A 236 (1992), paras 42, 46; *Goodwin v UK* (1996) 22 EHRR 123.

a very wide meaning to the concept of political expression. Therefore, allowing forms of protest suggests that a society wishes to encourage participation in the democratic process since citizens will thereby be able to signal their response to government policies, encourage changes in policy and deter the government from repressive measures. Public protest provides a direct means of allowing democratic participation to occur outside election periods. On this argument, the acceptance of the freedom to protest poses no threat to the established authorities, but rather underpins the democratic process which placed them where they are and from which they derive their legitimacy. In particular, protesters could be viewed as exercising, through the protest, a choice as to their mode of participation in political activity, a choice, which in the case of some minority groups, may not be a real one, in the sense that they may be, in effect, excluded from mainstream politics. Its exercise may also be bolstered, therefore, by arguments in favour of equality of democratic participation.

Thus, one of the most significant justifications underpinning public protest is that it provides a means whereby the free speech rights of certain groups can be substantively rather than formally exercised. Disadvantaged and marginalised groups, including racial or sexual minorities and groups following 'alternative' lifestyles, may be unable to exercise such rights in any meaningful sense since they cannot obtain sufficient access to the media. At the same time the media, particularly the tabloid press, may tend to misrepresent them. However impoverished members of such groups may be, they are able to band together to chant slogans, display placards and banners and demonstrate by means of direct action. By these means they may be able both to gain access to methods of communication through publicity and to persuade members of their immediate audience to sympathise with their stance. As Barnum puts it: 'the *public* forum may be the *only* forum available to many groups or points of view.'[21] Thus, public protest can act both as a means of access to the media and as a substitute for fair media exposure.[22] The truism that speech in general generates speech is especially applicable to speech or expression as protest.

These methods may provide the only avenue available to such groups if they wish to participate in the democracy and it is of crucial importance that they should be able to take it since, by its very nature, the democratic process tends to exclude minorities with whom the majority may be out of sympathy. Minority interests may be safeguarded only indirectly within that process, by persuading sufficient numbers of people to sympathise with causes which do not directly affect them. There is a reasonable degree of academic consensus regarding the need to protect public protest in order to safeguard minority interests:[23] while it has frequently been suggested that state regulation of the media, far from inhibiting free expression, tends to safeguard it,[24] that argument has been applied to public protest only in respect of the regulation of counter-protest. Unsurprisingly,

---

21 Barnum, DG, 'The constitutional status of public protest activity in Britain and the US' (1977) PL 310, p 327. See also Williams, op. cit., fn 1, p 10.

22 As indicated below (see fn 60), public protest websites may act as one such substitute.

23 See, e.g., Allen and Cooper, op. cit., fn 1, p 378; Barnum, 'The constitutional status of public protest activity in Britain and the US' (1977) PL 310.

24 See, e.g., Abel, R, *Speech and Respect*, 1994, Sweet and Maxwell, pp 48–58. Abel argues, using examples of media regulation by the market, that 'state withdrawal exposes speech to powerful market forces'. See also Feintuck, M, *Media Regulation, Public Interest and the Law*, 1999.

the intense debate on these issues derives from the First Amendment jurisprudence; within the American academic community there appears to be agreement, not only that the state cannot deny a forum to those whose ideas it finds acceptable while denying it to those expressing unpopular views,[25] but also that 'equality of status in the field of ideas' or equality in the exercise of speech rights[26] requires substantive protection. Denial of a public forum for the exercise of expressive rights bears unequally on different groups: it may amount in effect to a denial of the free speech rights of certain minority groups since equal access to other means of exercising those rights will tend to be unavailable. This has also been recognised in the UK context; as Bevan has put it: '[public protest] assists the "unknowns", those who do not have the capability or resources to exercise expression through the conventional media'.[27]

A further justification for speech based on moral autonomy[28] counters public protest in one respect, since the right of a citizen to choose what she will see or hear would seem to include a right not to be forced to encounter protest which she finds offensive.[29] Article 10 of the European Convention on Human Rights protects the 'freedom of expression and the freedom . . . to receive . . . information and ideas . . .'. This includes a right not to speak, according to the Commission in *K v Austria*,[30] and may therefore include a right not to be forced to encounter speech. In the context of public protest, this would probably depend on the duration of the protest and its probable impact on passers-by and others. It might also depend on the extent to which the protesters could be viewed as exercising, through the protest, a choice as to their mode of participation in political activity, a choice which, in the case of some minority groups, may not be a real one, in the sense that they may be, in effect, excluded from mainstream politics. Its exercise may also be bolstered, therefore, by arguments in favour of equality of democratic participation, in addition to those reliant on the values most readily viewed as underlying expressive rights. As Barendt points out, in relation to the German *Brokdorf* case,[31] freedom of assembly (protected, in Germany, by Art 8 of the Basic Law) 'enables people, especially minorities, to participate in the political process. Participation rights are not exhausted by membership of political parties . . . the exercise of the right enables protesters to express their personalities by their physical presence . . .'.[32]

Thus justifications deriving from free speech values and from the choice as to the mode of participation in the democracy underpin freedom of assembly and public protest. Even an assembly which publicised anti-democratic views would fall within the justification from the argument from truth. But it is clear that these justifications are not equally present in relation to all assemblies or all forms of what may loosely be termed protest.

25 See *Police Dept of the City of Chicago v Mosley* (1972) 408 US 92, pp 95–96. The case concerned an anti-racist protest by a single black protester.

26 See Karst, K, 'Equality as a central principle in the First Amendment', 43 University of Chicago L Rev 20.

27 Bevan, VT, 'Protest and public disorder' [1979] PL 163, p 187.

28 See Scanlon, T, 'A theory of freedom of expression' (1972) 1 Phil and Public Affairs 204; see p 201, above.

29 Cf Dworkin's distinction between display and distribution: 'Do we have a right to pornography?' in *A Matter of Principle*, 1985, pp 355–58.

30 A 255-B (1993), Com Rep, paras 45, 49.

31 (1985) 69 BVerfGE 315.

32 Paper given February 2000 at the Cambridge public law conference.

Public assembly and protest occurs in various forms, admittedly overlapping, ranging from the peaceful expression of a message or views to rioting and extreme violence; it can be categorised as: peaceful persuasion,[33] offensive or insulting persuasion,[34] intimidation,[35] symbolic or persuasive physical obstruction or interference,[36] actual physical obstruction or interference,[37] forceful physical obstruction[38] and violence.[39] The argument from democracy most clearly supports peaceful assemblies or marches that use speech in some form to persuade others, including the authorities, to a particular point of view. The second and third forms, which may occur by means of both speech and conduct, may be supported by the arguments from truth and democracy so long as they are not outweighed by the threat posed by the action. Since these justifications are goal- as opposed to rights-based, they would support only public protest which did not run counter to the goals in question (such as a racist protest).[40] Further, since they set out goals for society as a whole, they would seem to allow interference with speech in the interests of other public concerns which may be immediately and directly damaged by the exercise of speech. As Barendt puts it, in discussing the argument from truth: '. . . a government worried that inflammatory speech may provoke disorder is surely entitled to elevate immediate public order considerations over the long term intellectual development of the man on the Clapham omnibus.'[41]

The last four forms, often loosely referred to as 'direct action', cannot be termed 'speech', but may be viewed as forms of expression and as having, to varying extents, the same role as political speech. If, as in the last three, a group seeks not to persuade others, but by its actions to bring about the object in question, the democratic process may be said to have been circumvented rather than underpinned. Some forms of non-violent action may well be combined with attempts at verbal persuasion, but may also be intended in themselves to bring about the object in question or at least to obstruct others in their attempts to bring about various objects. Such action would include industrial and other forms of picketing and protests such as those of hunt or fishing saboteurs who physically obstruct the activity in question, albeit usually by non-violent means. Does such action fall within the justifications for freedom of protest at all? If it is non-violent, it may be lawful in itself on the principle that everything which is not legally forbidden is allowed. Sleeping in a tree in order to prevent it being cut down or throwing twigs into water to disrupt angling is not intrinsically unlawful, but if no rights-based justification protects such activity and if it impinges on the lawful activity of others, it may appear reasonable to proscribe it. Such activity could, however, be viewed as symbolic speech – message-bearing expression – and therefore as deserving of a degree of protection on that basis. It could be viewed both as obstructing the activity in question but also as calling attention to it, fuelling debate and thereby

33 E.g., offering innocuous leaflets or chanting inoffensive slogans.
34 E.g., carrying racist banners, displaying pictures of dead foetuses.
35 E.g., shouting and gesturing at individuals crossing picket lines.
36 E.g., lying passively in front of earth moving machinery, conducting a vigil.
37 E.g., blowing horns during a hunt or chaining oneself to a tree.
38 E.g., resisting official attempts to remove members of a sit-in.
39 E.g., attacking counter demonstrators or police officers.
40 See *Kuhnen v FRG* No 12194/86 (1988) 56 DR 205.
41 *Freedom of Speech*, 1987, 1st edn, p 10.

potentially activating the democratic process. However, such action is also likely to create an invasion of personal autonomy. This argument may be countered where strong justification for the direct action is put forward. An obvious example is its use by the Suffragettes in order to persuade and to draw attention to a cause of immense importance in a democracy. It is clearly questionable whether, short of violence, such protest should be placed, in the eyes of the law, in the same category as late night high street rowdiness. The same cannot be said so readily of direct action which seeks to prevent an outcome of lesser significance – such as the building of a bypass – which has been determined upon by an application of the democratic process.[42]

The fourth form of protest, persuasive physical obstruction or interference, is in a rather different position, although the line between the fourth and fifth tiers will often be hard to draw. Such action is not intended to bring about the object in question directly, but to draw attention to a cause. Of course, some direct action may exemplify both purposes. This may be said of the actions of hunt or fishing saboteurs and motorway protesters.[43]

Direct action may include, in its most extreme form, group violence intended to force others into compliance with a certain view. This would include political riots intended to overthrow the government. This would be unjustifiable in relation to a democratically elected government following the arguments above. However, some forceful action may not be intended in itself to bring about the object in question directly, but may be used as a desperate expedient to draw attention to a cause where peaceful means have failed. It may be distinguished from violent direct action, since it is still intended to bring about its object by democratic means; it may be used to draw attention to a cause and to persuade the electors and Parliament that action is necessary. Such action may be preferred to direct action due to the nature of the object in question. The history of the Suffragette movement shows that after peaceful protest had failed, forceful or violent protest was adopted.

Political riots do not present states with the dilemmas normally associated with public protest. The difficulty usually lies in determining whether a protest, which is justified by reference to the arguments above, has the potential to threaten public order. This possibility clearly raises issues as to the scope of state duties to keep the peace and to safeguard the interests of citizens upon whom protests may impinge. Forms of direct action may infringe privacy rights and the freedom from physical attack or threats. The substance of the protest may be offensive and hurtful to others. The manner of the protest may involve intimidation, thereby potentially infringing the rights of persons to security of the person, freedom of movement and possibly to freedom of assembly. Non-violent or more vulnerable groups may require a calm public order situation in

---

42 In the case of road building, the extent to which the outcome may be said to represent an application of the democratic process is debatable, especially where the road is within the remit of the Department of Transport rather than a local council. In both instances, under the Highways Act 1980, s 258, objections may be made by those directly and indirectly affected and usually a public inquiry will be arranged and conducted by an 'independent' inspector – a civil servant in the Department of Transport – who then makes a recommendation to the Secretary of State.

43 A good example is the protest at Newbury against the A34 bypass. Between 1994 and 1998 every form of protest was used, from non-violent direct action to criminal damage; see the Newbury Bypass website: geocities.com/newburybypass/index.html.

order to be enabled to make an effective protest. Protecting the freedom to protest can mean protecting powerful and well-organised groups at the expense of the weak.

In a mature democracy, it would be expected that the extent to which a protest was persuasive rather than simply obstructive would tend to determine the extent of its constitutional protection, although even obstructive protest may be viewed as falling within the range of expressive rights,[44] as raising issues of association and, arguably, of participation in the democracy. The direct action forms of protest might be justified, particularly when exercised by minority groups, on the grounds that they provide a substantive means of engaging in the more *effective* means of communicating with others (since such forms are most likely to attract media attention) and of participating freely in political activity.[45] The same arguments could be applied to persuasive protest requiring a particular forum and time for its exercise. In other words, the equality principle in terms of free expression and rights to engage in political activity might be taken to demand that minorities should be allowed access to forms and places of protest going beyond the relatively innocuous or convenient. Such an argument might allow interference with forms of direct action exercised by minority groups to be considered as interferences with the freedoms of expression, assembly and association though subject to justification, although this raises the difficult issue of the relationship between equality and freedom.[46] Constitutional protection for such freedoms might be expected to override societal interests in preventing mere inconvenience or preserving decorum but, depending on considerations of proportionality, might give way to justifications based on moral autonomy, the risk of personal harm and, perhaps, economic loss. If the value of minority political participation is at stake, a protest expressing a minority viewpoint tending to marginalise a further minority might undermine any special claim it might otherwise have had to access to a particular place.[47] These are the issues with which, on the whole, the domestic courts have not had to grapple in determining public order questions,[48] but with which they are now confronted under the HRA 1998.

The legal response

The development of public order law

Taking the justifications underpinning public protest considered above into account and weighing them against the interest of the state and its citizens in the maintenance of

---

44 Such protest will be viewed as an expression of opinion according to the findings of the European Court of Human Rights in *Steel v UK* (1999) 28 EHRR 603 and *Hashman and Harrup v UK* (1999) 30 EHRR 241, both discussed below. The protests at issue in those decisions might be viewed as having both persuasive and destructive elements, but it might be argued that a protest intended by the protesters to be purely obstructive could also be viewed as the expression of an opinion; it could also lead incidentally to publicity for the cause and on that basis also could be viewed as a form of expression.

45 See Barendt's argument (Barendt, *Freedom of Speech*, 1st edn, 1987) above, Part II, p 303.

46 See Karst, 'Equality as a central principle in the First Amendment', 43 University of Chicago L Rev 20, p 43.

47 E.g., racist groups were diverted from marching through Asian communities in Leicester in 1974 and 1979, by the imposition of conditions under the Public Order Act 1936, s 3(1). Such conditions could now be imposed under the 1986 Act, s 12.

48 As Feldman puts it: 'the central value [in UK public protest cases] is public order . . .' (*Civil Liberties and Human Rights in England and Wales*, 1993, 1st edn, p 785).

public order, it is clear that some restraint on public protest is needed and is justifiable. The difficulty is that, in furtherance of the interest in public order (which in itself protects freedom of protest and assembly), the constitutional need to allow freedom of assembly in a democracy may be obscured. Historically, the UK has had no formal constitutional or statutory provision providing rights to protest and assemble. Instead, it has seen a series of often ill-considered and needlessly broad statutory responses to disorder. Thus, the activities of the followers of Mosley underpinned the Public Order Act 1936,[49] while in the period leading up to the inception of the Public Order Act 1986 there were a series of disturbances beginning with the Brixton riots in 1981[50] and continuing with the disorder associated with the miners' strike in 1984–85, probably the most significant event in British public order history. The strike largely provided the justification for the introduction of the Public Order Act 1986, although it does not appear that further police powers to control disorder were needed. The police did not seem to have lacked powers to deal with the disturbances; on the contrary, a number of different common law and statutory powers were invoked, including powers to prevent a breach of the peace, s 3 of the Public Order Act 1936, offences of unlawful assembly, of obstruction of a constable and of watching and besetting under s 7 of the Conspiracy and Protection of Property Act 1875.[51] However, the government took the view that the available powers were confused and fragmented and that there was scope for affording the police additional powers to prevent disorder before it occurred.[52] It therefore introduced a number of low level public order offences and created a cumbersome, unwieldy framework for the policing of processions and assemblies under the 1986 Act.

The late 1980s and the early 1990s witnessed some similar protests, notably the anti-poll tax demonstrations, protests against *The Satanic Verses* and against the Criminal Justice and Public Order Act (CJPOA) 1994 itself ('Kill the Bill' protests). Mass protest was not a hallmark of the 1990s, but the period did see an enormous growth in the use of direct action by a variety of groups, usually protesting about environmental and animal rights issues. These included hunt saboteurs, fishing saboteurs, motorway and bypass protesters, and veal calf protesters. The protests at Newbury, Twyford Down and Oxleas Wood against bypasses[53] and at Brightlingsea and Shoreham Ferry Port against the export of veal calves were particularly notable. The growth in the use of direct action was arguably traceable to the perception of animal rights and environmental groups that the government's pursuit of free-market policies meant that it had little concern with environmental as opposed to commercial values.[54] Therefore, during its lengthy period in office, it was assumed that it would be unresponsive to a minority view, and peaceful protest as part of the democratic process would be ineffective. The

---

49 For an excellent account of this period, see Ewing and Gearty, op. cit., fn 1, 1999.

50 See the inquiry by Lord Scarman, *The Brixton Disorders*, Cmnd 8427, 1981.

51 See McCabe, S and Wallington, P, *The Police, Public Order and Civil Liberties: Legacies of the Miners' Strike*, 1988, Routledge, esp Appendix 1; Wallington, P, 'Policing the miners' strike' (1985) 14 ILJ 145. During the miners' strike, over 10,000 offences were charged; see Wallington, ibid.

52 See: House of Commons, Fifth Report from the Home Affairs Committee, Session 1979–80, *The Law Relating to Public Order*, HC 756–1; Lord Scarman, *The Brixton Disorders*, Part VI, Cmnd 8427, 1981; Smith, ATH, 'Public order law 1974–1983: Developments and proposals' [1984] Crim LR 643; White Paper, *Review of Public Order Law*, Cmnd 9510, 1985.

53 See Bryant, B, *Twyford Down: Roads, Campaigning and Environmental Law*, 1996, E and FN Spon; 'Roads to nowhere', Green Party Election Manifesto 1997, Transport section.

54 See Monbiot, G, 'The end of polite resistance', TLS, 8 March 1997; Bryant, ibid.

rise in direct action suggested that the traditional aim of protest – to persuade – was being abandoned. The response of the Major Government was to introduce more draconian measures under the CJPOA 1994 aimed largely at direct action in order to suppress it.[55]

The coming into power of the Labour Government in 1997 did not herald any diminution of the direct action form of protest, on the government's own analysis of its predicted prevalence.[56] The concerns of protesters against motorway development, abuse of human rights and on environmental matters, including the introduction of genetically modified crops, continued to be expressed in this form.[57] Diverse groups continued to view protest as a valuable means of drawing attention to viewpoints which tended to be excluded from what may be termed the mainstream communications market place, particularly the tabloid press. Direct action protest may indirectly generate debate and scrutiny of the issues it raises – in the media, and sometimes in the form of official inquiries. The use of direct action at Huntingdon Life Sciences against the use of animals in medical research currently provides an example of the effect of such action in terms of re-igniting serious debate on aspects of the issue.[58] Demonstrations against the impact of trading globalisation took place in London in 1999, 2000 and 2001, and human rights groups, including Amnesty, attempted to protest against the abuse of human rights in China on the occasion of the visit of the Chinese President in October 1999,[59] but were met by heavy-handed policing. Flags and banners were forced from the hands of protesters and removed from the windows of private houses. The availability of a range of other means of communication, particularly via the internet, did not appear to lead to the marginalisation of protest as a means of communicating and of participating in the democratic process. Indeed, the internet, far from providing an alternative means of communication, facilitates protest and publicises it.[60] The movement away from socialist policies under Labour, and the similarities between the criminal justice policies of the two main parties, appeared to give rise to a continued perception that radical views could find no place within mainstream politics.

---

55 For the background to the 1994 Act, which received the Royal Assent on 3 November 1994, see the introduction in Wasik and Taylor's *Guide to the Act*, 1995, p 1. For discussion of the public order offences, see Smith, ATH [1995] Crim LR 19.

56 *Legislation Against Terrorism: A Consultation Paper*, Cm 4178, 1998.

57 See the Newbury Bypass website: geocities.com/newburybypass/index.html; reports of protests at Newbury, *Daily Telegraph*, 11 January 1999 and 30 April 1999; the Greenpeace website: greenpeace. org.uk/.

58 See, e.g., the *Guardian*, 16 January 2001, p 7 and 22 January 2001, p 5, Radio 4's *World At One*, 15 January 2001 and two lengthy Channel 4 documentaries in the same week. See further www. huntingdon.com; www.vivisectioninfo.org/HLS.html;www.freezone.co.uk/liberationmag/huntingex. htm.

59 The Home Office stated that it had not placed pressure on the Metropolitan Police to prevent demonstrators disrupting the visit of the Chinese President (national news reports, 25 October 1999). A routine internal review was carried out which exonerated the police; report published on 17 March 2000. Eventually, in judicial review proceedings brought by lawyers for the Free Tibet campaign, the Metropolitan Police admitted that that the treatment of the demonstrators had been unlawful: news reports, 4 May 2000.

60 The Newbury Bypass website – geocities.com/newburybypass/index.html – for example, runs to 23 pages and has links to a mass of connected pages.

Anti-terrorism law and policy are considered in Chapter 14. But the blurring of the distinction between terrorist groups and protest groups in s 1 Terrorism Act 2000 (TA) should be mentioned at this point since the potential use of anti-terrorist law against protest groups has arisen. Terrorism and protest are the antithesis of each other and the legislation should make the distinction clear. Terrorism is about intimidating people and undermining the democratic process; protest is *part* of that process; it is about seeking to persuade, to change minds in a manner that may be reflected at the ballot box. Causing deaths by setting off bombs on the London Underground – as in June 2005 – is a classically terrorist activity. It could be dealt with by the ordinary criminal law since many criminal offences were committed, but if groups are to be labelled 'terrorist' then groups such as Al-Qaeda, that send suicide bombers onto crowded tube trains, clearly fall within that category. It is understandable, if misjudged, that governments might wish to use special terrorist sanctions outside the criminal justice process or the use of the substantive criminal law, against suicide bombers. But it is not understandable to apply the label 'terrorist' to groups that are in essence protest groups.

The response of the Labour Government to the likelihood that the direct action form of protest would continue in evidence during its period of office resembled that of the Major Government. It passed the Terrorism Act (TA) 2000, partly aimed, like the 1994 Act, at this form of protest, but – in a departure from previous policies – it used the technique, as Chapter 14 explains, not of introducing new, draconian offences, but of applying the established terrorism offences to the new targets. The TA allows for the application of a number of provisions developed to combat Irish terrorism to be applied to a much wider range of targets. By using the rubric 'terrorist' to denote the groups to be targeted, it sought to deflect the opposition which would have arisen had the terrorism offences merely been used overtly as a means of curbing the activities of animal rights groups, anti-war protesters, environmental activists and the like, under a new public order Act. However, the constantly reiterated plea of government ministers to the effect that the TA is aimed only at those who are likely to undermine democracy, has not prevented the perception from arising among some protest groups that they are the target of its provisions, for the straightforward reason that the definition of terrorism in s 1 is not remotely confined to combating a threat to democracy. Rather, as Chapter 14 argues, it connotes, quite clearly, the notion of stifling dissent.[61] Since it is aimed at certain groups which put forward a political or ideological message,[62] a potential conflict with Art 10 under the HRA arises. In particular, it could be asked, if a suitable case arises, whether a proportionate response to the activities of a number of groups which fall within the s 1(1) definition would not have been merely to use the ordinary criminal law against them, where necessary.

The introduction of the TA, as the government's consultation paper preceding the Act explains,[63] could only be justified in relation to non-Irish domestic groups, including groups motivated by ideological as well as political concerns; two of the key target groups expressly mentioned are animal rights or environmental activists. The offences discussed in Chapter 14 could probably only have been introduced in the context of the

---

61 See pp 1377–81.
62 They must fulfil the other criteria of s 1(1); see Chapter 14, pp 1377–78.
63 *Legislation Against Terrorism: A Consultation Paper*, Cm 4178, 1998, Chapter 2.

threat from Irish terrorism, in some instances at a time when the number of deaths from bomb attacks had been very high in the preceding years. At the time, MPs obviously could not know that in 2000 they would be asked to apply all these offences to groups which, in terms of their ability to create a serious threat to life and their willingness to do so, cannot be compared with the IRA. Moreover, certain of these offences appeared only in the Emergency Powers Act (applicable only in Northern Ireland), partly on the basis that the threat was greatest in Northern Ireland and that without some apparently strong justification, they should not be included in the Prevention of Terrorism Act (PTA). Unless and until the Home Secretary proscribes a range of domestic animal rights and environmental groups, the proscription-related offences will not apply to them. But all the special terrorist offences and the special arrest and detention powers apply,[64] meaning that although 'terrorist' groups can lawfully exist, they are potentially trammeled in exercising public freedom of expression or engaging in direct action since the terrorism offences discussed in Chapter 14, including the offence of being involved in the organisation of a terrorist group, could be invoked against them. Where 'terrorist' groups are also proscribed their rights of expression, assembly and association are almost entirely abrogated by the provisions considered in that Chapter. A member or supporter of a non-proscribed 'terrorist' group, such as a group advocating direct action against a dictatorship abroad, can still speak in public. But they run the risk of falling foul of the 'leader/organiser' TA offence or of the new offence introduced by the Terrorism Act 2006, discussed in Chapter 14, of 'glorifying' terrorism.

Aside from the broader application of terrorist offences, the attacks on the World Trade Centre in 2001, the entry of Britain into the Iraq war, which sparked large-scale protests, and the London bombings in 2005, also had an impact in leading to the introduction of a range of new offences aimed at stifling anti-war dissent, a number of which are relevant in this area. The Serious and Organised Crime and Police Act 2005 ushered in severe restrictions on demonstrations in Parliament Square, which were clearly aimed mainly at anti-war demonstrators. The Anti-Social Behaviour Act 2003 was employed to broaden a number of the already broad provisions in order to deploy them in a wider range of circumstances against protesters. The Act deleted reference to activity taking place in the 'open air' in s 68 of the Criminal Justice and Public Order Act 1994, a broad provision aimed originally at animal rights and environmental activists. It also reduced the number of persons who can constitute a 'public assembly' for the purpose of banning it or imposing conditions on it under the 1986 Act, from twenty to two. A number of the wide range of statutory provisions already in place, as well as the ancient common law doctrine of breach of the peace, were deployed against anti-war protesters. The broadening of the definition of 'public assembly' means that two people reading out names of those killed in the Iraq war are now subject to the 'assembly' provisions of the Public Order Act 1986.

The nature of public order law

Although the method adopted by the TA 2000 differs, as indicated, from that of its predecessors, the effect is the same: it follows the tradition they established, whereby

---

64 See Chapters 11, 12 and 14.

provisions likely to affect public protest and assembly are simply added to the existing and extensive ones. A number of trends inimical to public protest are discernible, carried through from the Public Order Act 1986, to the CJPOA 1994, the Protection from Harassment Act 1997, ss 1 and 25 of the Crime and Disorder Act 1998, the TA 2000, the Criminal Justice and Police Act 2001 and, at present, they culminate in ss 132–38 of the Serious and Organised Crime and Police Act 2005 which apply to demonstrations in the vicinity of Parliament.

Certain features of these statutes exhibit the traditional hallmarks of UK public order law, but in the more recent legislation their illiberal tendency is more greatly marked. These statutes are littered with imprecise terms such as 'disorderly' or 'insulting' or 'disruptive', all objectionable under rule of law notions since protesters cannot predict when a protest may lead to criminal liability. Reliance on the likelihood that police, magistrates or the CPS will under-enforce the law is unsatisfactory due to the likelihood that their decisions, in any particular instance, will not be subjected to independent scrutiny. Such reliance hardly provides the firm basis for the exercise of rights to assemble and to protest which one would expect to find in a mature democracy.

The more recent statutory offences tend to have the ingredients of a minimal *actus reus* and an absent, minimal or reversed *mens rea*.[65] This tendency contributes to the conflation of substantive offences with police powers, evident in the 1986 Act, which has recently become more marked. The CJPOA 1994 continued the trend begun by the 1986 Act of introducing a number of offences which depended on taking orders from the police and which were based on the reasonable suspicion of a police officer.[66] For example, s 60 of the 1994 Act was amended by s 25 of the Crime and Disorder Act 1998 to provide a power under s 60(4A)(a) to demand the removal of a face covering 'if the constable reasonably believes that person is wearing [it] wholly or mainly for the purpose of concealing his identity' and to create an offence punishable by one month's imprisonment of failing to remove the covering. A reasonable, if erroneous, belief is sufficient and no *mens rea* need be established, so that the wearing of a covering for religious reasons could be irrelevant. No defence of reasonable excuse is provided, so that, for example, it would be unavailing for a farm worker protesting against hunting to claim to wish to conceal her identity not from the police, but from her employer. This trend was strongly continued under the TA 2000.[67]

The more recent provisions affecting public protest also exhibit a tendency not only to create restrictions at the outer limits of what might be tolerated in a democratic society, but to impose criminal penalties while marginalising the criminal process in dealing with disorder. Thus, s 69 of the 1994 Act allows for the conviction of the defendant due to disobedience to a ban on entering land imposed by a police officer, even if the original order was based on an error.[68] Section 3 of the Protection from Harassment

---

65 See discussion of the Public Order Act 1986, ss 14A, 14C; the Criminal Justice and Public Order Act 1994, s 69 and the Crime and Disorder Act 1998, s 1, below.

66 See the 1986 Act, ss 12 and 14. Sections 14A and C, introduced under the 1994 Act, s 70, are discussed below, as are the 1994 Act, ss 68 and 69.

67 See Chapter 14, pp 1381–1421 and see also below, p 698 for brief discussion of the relevant counter-terrorist provisions.

68 See *Capon v DPP*, Case CO/3496/97 judgment 4 March 1998, LEXIS transcript, discussed Mead, D, 'Will peaceful protesters be foxed by the Divisional Court decision in *Capon v DPP*?' [1998] Crim LR 870; considered below, pp 742–43.

Act 1997 and s 1 of the Crime and Disorder Act 1998 provide criminal penalties for disobedience to civil orders. Section 1 of the 1998 Act provides a penalty of a maximum of five years' imprisonment for failing to obey an order obtained on the civil standard of proof,[69] forbidding any form of 'anti-social' behaviour.[70] As Chapter 14 explains, s 3(4) of the TA 2000 empowers the Home Secretary to add a group to the list of those proscribed 'if he believes that it is concerned in terrorism'. There is no express requirement of reasonable belief; nor is it necessary for the group to fall within the definition of terrorism under s 1.[71] No criminal or other proceedings are necessary and there is initially no right of appeal to a court.[72] Not only do the proscription provisions have immense implications for the rights of the groups proscribed to association, expression and assembly, they also provide the basis for criminalising a wide range of persons who are in some way associated with such groups, including those who merely organise informal meetings at which a member of a proscribed group is speaking, regardless of the purpose of the meeting as a whole.[73]

These recently introduced statutes tend to provide a minimal recognition of a need to protect freedom of expression and assembly by including certain defences of 'reasonableness' without attempting to define the meaning of the term[74] and without making any reference to expression. Such defences stand in contrast to those provided in statutes affecting *media* freedom of expression, such as s 5 of the Contempt of Court Act 1981, s 4 of the Obscene Publications Act 1959, and s 12 of the HRA, all of which provide explicit and detailed defences, allowing, in effect, for a balancing act between protecting expression and the societal interest at stake.

Clearly, the nature of the statutory provisions is only one factor contributing to the real extent of rights to protest and assemble. The common law power to prevent a breach of the peace or to be of good behaviour arguably outdoes such provisions in terms of exhibiting many of the features just criticised, and, as indicated, judicial influence in developing and interpreting public order law has been significant. The key factor, however, continues to be the working practice of the police.[75] The police may already have developed a practice which renders a statutory power irrelevant, or they may consider that the use of the power would exacerbate a public order situation, rather than defusing it. The police may therefore tend to pick and choose among the available powers, tending to prefer familiar or very broad ones, particularly the power to prevent a breach of the peace. These factors appear to explain why certain of the far reaching provisions of the Public Order Act 1986, including the obligation to notify the police of a march,[76] the powers to impose conditions on marches[77] and assemblies,[78] and to ban

---

69 According to the 1998 Magistrates' Courts Rules applicable to these orders.
70 Section 1(10)(b).
71 See the TA 2000, s 3(5) and Chapter 14, pp 1383–84.
72 See Chapter 14, pp 1385, 1397–1401.
73 See further Chapter 14, pp 1392–96.
74 E.g. the Public Order Act 1986, ss 5(3)(c) and 4A(3)(c); the Protection from Harassment Act 1997, s 1; the Crime and Disorder Act 1998, s 3(1)(c) and s 1(10).
75 See Waddington, *Liberty and Order*, 1994.
76 Section 11.
77 Section 12.
78 Section 14.

assemblies on the basis of a reasonable belief in the risk of serious public disorder[79] have hardly been used.[80] In contrast, there is emerging evidence that the broader, less cumbersome provisions discussed below, including the recently introduced statutory powers, are being utilised against protesters. The accountability of the police has lain in this context largely in the hands of magistrates due to the dominance of summary offences and the use of binding over powers; therefore, the reality of freedom of protest has frequently been determined at that level. As Palmer puts it, 'prosecutions before magistrates' courts [which] may give rise to [frequently unreported] decisions of the Divisional Court of the Queen's Bench . . . are the gauge by which the health of civil liberties in this country can be measured'.[81]

Methods of policing disorder are also significant. Developments in the law during the 1980s and 90s, which provided the police with new and extensive powers to control public protest, have been matched to an extent by developments in such methods. Equipment has become more effective; in 1981, the Home Secretary announced that stocks of CS gas, water cannon and plastic bullets would be held in a central store available to chief officers of police for use in situations of serious disorder, although only as a last resort.[82] However, CS gas has not been used to control disorder since 1981 and water cannon were withdrawn from availability in 1987.[83] The possibility that the use of forceful tactics may exacerbate public order situations has been recognised since Lord Scarman's report into the Brixton disorders in 1981.[84]

The conditions under which various weapons and tactics may be used are not defined in any statute and before the inception of the HRA it appeared that their use was subject to a very low standard of scrutiny by the courts. When a local police authority tried to prevent the Chief Constable applying for plastic bullets from the central store, the Court of Appeal declared that the Crown had a prerogative power to keep the peace which allowed the Home Secretary to 'do all that was reasonably necessary to preserve the peace of the realm'.[85] As the power is undefined, it appeared to render lawful any measures taken by the Home Secretary which can be termed 'reasonably necessary' in order to keep the peace. However, this position cannot be sustained under the HRA, since a court is expected to examine the proportionality of the measures taken to the aim of preventing disorder.[86]

Meetings on private premises

Although the emphasis of the discussion so far has largely been on meetings and demonstrations in public places, meetings held on private land or premises with the permission

79 Section 13.
80 See Waddington, op. cit., fn 1, 1994.
81 Palmer, S, 'Wilfully obstructing the freedom to protest?' [1987] PL 495.
82 Report of HM Chief Inspector for Constabulary for 1981, 1981–82, HC 463. For discussion of police riot control techniques and equipment, see Waddington, *The Strong Arm of the Law*, Chapter 6.
83 See Jason-Lloyd, L (1991) 141 NLJ 1043.
84 *The Brixton Disorders*, Cmnd 8427, 1981.
85 *Secretary of State for the Home Dept ex p Northumbria Police Authority* [1989] QB 26; [1988] 2 WLR 590; [1988] 1 All ER 556, CA; for criticism, see Beynon [1987] PL 146 (on the Divisional Court decision); Bradley, AW, 'Police powers and the prerogative' [1988] PL 298.
86 See further Chapter 2, pp 92–97, Chapter 4, pp 287–88.

of the owner are, nevertheless, affected by a number of public order provisions. Under the Public Order Act 1986, still the central statute governing this area, any meeting held in wholly enclosed premises will be a private meeting (s 16), including a meeting held in a town hall, although the town hall is owned by a public body. The provisions of ss 11–14A of Part II of the Public Order Act 1986, creating a statutory framework for marches and assemblies, do not cover private meetings. But the public order provisions of ss 5, 4A and 4 do apply to 'private places'. However, if the place in question is a 'dwelling', the words or behaviour must affect a person outside the dwelling. Thus, in theory, these provisions are applicable to private meetings not held in a person's home. Provisions aimed at violent disorder – ss 1, 2, 3 – apply equally to private and public places, without any qualification regarding dwellings. The counter-terrorism measures discussed below could also be used in respect of private meetings.

Aside from the powers of arrest under the provisions of Part I of the 1986 Act which, with the qualifications mentioned regarding dwellings, are available, the power of the police to enter indoor meetings is uncertain. It was generally thought that the police had no power to enter unless they were invited in. However, such a power may derive from the decision in *Thomas v Sawkins*.[87] A meeting was held in a hall to protest regarding the provisions of the Incitement to Disaffection Bill which was then before Parliament. The police entered the meeting and its leader, who considered that they were trespassing, removed one of the officers, who resisted the ejectment. In response, the leader brought a private prosecution in which he sought to show that the officers were trespassers and that therefore he had a right to eject them, in which case their resistance would amount to assault and battery. The court found that the officers had not been trespassing. Although the meeting had not constituted or given rise to a breach of the peace, the officers had reasonably apprehended a breach because seditious speeches and incitement to violence might have occurred. The police had therefore been entitled to enter the premises. This decision has been much criticised.[88] Nevertheless, it does not hand the police *carte blanche* to enter private meetings; it should mean that the police can enter the meeting only if there is a clear possibility that a breach of the peace may occur. The nature of this doctrine and the probable effect on it of the HRA is considered below. Under the Strasbourg jurisprudence, an element of immediacy is necessary.[89] Therefore the power to enter meetings indicated in *Thomas v Sawkins* is likely to undergo limitation.

A more narrow right to enter premises, which might be applicable in respect of some meetings, arises under s 17(1)(c) of the Police and Criminal Evidence Act 1984. A police officer has the right to enter and search premises with a view to arresting a person for the offence arising under s 1 of the Public Order Act 1936 of wearing a uniform in connection with a political object. Furthermore, the police can enter premises in order to arrest a person for an offence under s 4 of the Public Order Act 1986. It should be noted that the offence under s 4 (discussed below) can be committed in a private or public place, although not in a dwelling. Presumably it could therefore be committed in a town hall. Thus, a meeting during which violence might be threatened

---

87 [1935] 2 KB 249.
88 See Goodhart, AL [1936–38] CLJ 22.
89 *McLeod v UK* (1998) 27 EHRR 493 RJD 1998-VII 2774. See below, p 776.

to persons present[90] would give police officers the right to enter if they had reasonable suspicion that such could be the case. If it was thought that one of the serious public order offences under ss 1, 2 or 3 of the 1986 Act was occurring or about to occur, the police could arrest under the general arrest power of s 24 of the Police and Criminal Evidence Act 1984. We will return to this arrest power and police powers of entry to premises in Chapters 10 and 11 below.

Conclusions

Thus, the domestic focus of attention has been, and still is, on the many areas of law which delimit the residual freedom to make public protest. Clearly, it is understandable that public protest suffers greater circumscription than political expression generally, since it conflicts with a large number of societal interests and may create invasions of individual autonomy,[91] damage to property and even personal injury. But the traditional marked judicial reluctance to consider the free expression claims of public protest in a democracy provides, it will be argued, too great a contrast not only with the stance taken in Strasbourg, but with that taken by the domestic judiciary, and the House of Lords in particular, in relation to the political expression of the media.[92]

In considering public protest, Strasbourg has viewed it as a form of political expression and has therefore relied on case law in other areas of expression.[93] In contrast, in the domestic courts, 'rights' to the freedoms of protest and assembly are occasionally mentioned,[94] but their content is hardly considered; far more typically, the interest of the judgment centres on the legal content of proprietorial rights. Perhaps even more significantly, the status of Arts 10 and 11 as providing claim rights subject to exceptions which are 'necessary in a democratic society', has provided Strasbourg, as *Handyside v UK*[95] makes clear, with the opportunity of considering the hallmarks of such a society. Strasbourg is therefore able to consider what is required in terms of the necessity of an interference with public protest, both in terms of the maintenance of the democracy and of effective participation in it. In contrast, the domestic judiciary have been confined to applying the law, whether or not its restrictions go beyond those nationally and internationally deemed necessary in democracies. The UK courts have hardly participated in the ongoing debate in democracies regarding the permissible extent of such restrictions, and to an extent this is due to their inevitable preoccupation, under a constitution based on negative liberties, with the legal content of the restriction in question. As indicated above, this position has, formally, changed under the HRA. Its possible effects in this context form the central theme of this chapter.

---

90 In general, the control of indoor meetings is the responsibility of the persons holding the meeting and to that end, a reasonable number of stewards should be appointed (Public Order Act 1936, s 2(6)) who may use reasonable force to control disorder and to eject members of the public whose behaviour does not constitute reasonable participation in the meeting.

91 In the sense that the protest must be experienced by those who may not wish to experience it. It may also interfere with individual choices as to activities and movement.

92 See *Derbyshire CC v Times Newspapers* [1993] AC 534 and *Reynolds v Times Newspapers* [1999] 4 All ER 609.

93 See, e.g., *Steel and Others v UK* (1999) 28 EHRR 603, para 101.

94 See, e.g., Lord Denning's comments in *Hubbard v Pitt* [1975] 3 All ER 1.

95 (1976) 1 EHRR 737.

Judicial uncertainty in applying the Convention is arising in a number of contexts, but public protest cases present them with an especially stark choice, since the HRA provides that public authorities must not infringe Arts 10 and 11; on its face, this requirement demands a break, not only with the traditional acceptance that there is no legal right to assemble or engage in public protest in the UK, but with the failure to prevent encroachment on the negative liberty. As indicated above, references to 'rights' were occasionally made, but they appeared to be, loosely, to negative liberties.[96] The HRA requires more of public authorities than a mere voluntary tolerance of public protest or a recognition of freedom of assembly that can be readily abrogated.[97] There were signs in the early post-HRA years that the judiciary, while paying lip-service to rights to freedom of protest, were maintaining something close to the previous balance between public order and freedom of assembly, thereby failing to give full effect to Arts 10 and 11. However, *Laporte* in the House of Lords signalled not only a change of stance and a willingness to break with previous tradition, but also an acknowledgement that the previous common law protection for protest and assembly was deeply flawed and inadequate.

2 Rights to assemble and to protest

Traditional legal recognition of freedom of assembly[98]

It is generally thought that there is a right to assemble in certain places, such as Trafalgar Square or Hyde Park, but it is a fallacy that UK law has recognised any legal right to do so.[99] Until the Convention was received into domestic law, it continued to afford virtually no recognition to rights to meet or to march. However, there are two instances in which such recognition is given. There is a very limited right to hold meetings, applying only to parliamentary candidates before a general election, which arises under ss 95 and 96 of the Representation of the People Act 1983. This right will normally be upheld even when it appears that it is being abused by a minority group: in *Webster v Southwark LBC*[100] the Labour council had wished to deny it to a National Front candidate, but the court upheld the statutory right of the group to meet. Once an election meeting is in being, the law will afford a limited protection: it is an offence under s 97 of the 1983 Act to use disorderly conduct in order to break up a lawful public election meeting and this will include meetings held on the highway.[101] This limited provision may be

---

96 It may be noted that when approval has been expressed of Lord Denning's defence of 'rights to protest', the 'right' has become a freedom: *per* Otton J in *Hirst and Agu v Chief Constable of West Yorkshire* (1987) 85 Cr App Rep 143: having quoted Lord Denning's findings with approval, he went on to say: 'the freedom of protest on matters of public concern would be given the recognition it deserves.'

97 See *DPP v Jones* [1999] 2 WLR 625. The decision is discussed in detail below, pp 711–20.

98 See Barnum, DG, 'The constitutional status of public protest activity in Britain and the US' (1977) PL 310, and (1981) 29 Am Jo of Comparative Law 59; see also Stein, LA [1971] PL 115 for discussion of the constitutional status of public protest.

99 In respect of Trafalgar Square, see *Ex p Lewis* (1888) 21 QBD 191. By statutory instrument, an application must be made to the Department of the Environment to hold a meeting in Trafalgar Square (SI 1952/776). There is no right to hold meetings in the royal parks: see *Bailey v Williamson* (1873) LR 8 QB 118.

100 [1983] QB 698; [1983] 2 WLR 217.

101 *Burden v Rigler* [1911] 1 KB 337.

compared with more general provisions from other jurisdictions making it an offence to disrupt any meeting that has not been prohibited.[102]

Further, s 43 of the Education (No 2) Act 1986 provides that university and college authorities are under a positive duty to 'ensure that freedom of speech within the law is secured for members, students and employees of the establishment and for visiting speakers'.[103] Although there may be an argument that this provision is to be welcomed as promoting free speech interests, it is somewhat anomalous, to say the least, that a right to meet arises in certain specified buildings but not in others, such as town halls, while it does not arise at all in public places such as town squares or parks. In *Caesar-Gordon ex p University of Liverpool*,[104] the University gave permission, under a number of limitations, allowing a South African speaker to speak at a meeting. Concerns were expressed about the possibility of disorder in the nearby area of Toxteth, an area with large ethnic population. The Divisional Court upheld the limiting conditions imposed which included the right to charge the organisers, the Conservative Association, for the cost of security, and a ban on publicity. Thus, quite severe limits can be placed on this right in practice.

But apart from these narrow rights, arising from specific provisions, a group which is prevented from holding an effective meeting due to the activities of other groups had no special protection.[105] A group which wished to assemble in a particular place had no right to do so, although a very limited freedom to assemble on the highway was recognised prior to the inception of the HRA, as discussed below.[106] On the other hand, the law affords great prominence to the freedom to pass and re-pass along the highway. Section 137 of the Highways Act 1980 provides that a person will be guilty of an offence if he 'without lawful authority or excuse wilfully obstructs the free passage of the highway'. It might appear, therefore, that the negative freedom to assemble is entirely abrogated so far as the highway is concerned since most assemblies will create some obstruction. However, according to *Hirst and Agu v Chief Constable of West Yorkshire*,[107] the term 'lawful excuse' refers to activities which are lawful in themselves and which are reasonable, and this was found to cover peaceful demonstrations. This decision supports the view that freedom of assembly has found some recognition as a common law principle.

Further, s 14 of the Public Order Act 1986 impliedly recognises the freedom to meet so long as the statutory requirements are complied with, and this argument may be supported by the existence of certain specific statutory prohibitions on meetings in certain places or at certain times, such as s 3 of the Seditious Meetings Act 1817 which prohibits meetings of 50 or more in the vicinity of Westminster during a Parliamentary

102 See, e.g., Arts 284 and 285 of the Austrian Criminal Code.
103 For discussion of this provision see Barendt, E, *Freedom of Speech*, 1st edn, 1987, pp 321–22; Barendt, E, 'Freedom of speech in the universities' [1987] PL 344.
104 (1990) 3 All ER 821.
105 See discussion of this point in the European Court of Human Rights in *Plattform 'Ärzte für das Leben' v Austria* (1988) 13 EHRR 204; it was found that freedom of assembly could not be reduced to a mere duty on the part of the state not to interfere; it did require the state to take some positive steps to be taken although the state was not expected to guarantee that a demonstration was able to proceed.
106 See pp 680, 711–20.
107 (1986) 85 Cr App R 143. See also *Nagy v Weston* [1966] 2 QB 561; [1965] 1 WLR 280; cf *Arrowsmith v Jenkins* [1963] 2 QB 561; [1963] 2 All ER 210; for comment, see [1987] PL 495.

session. Such restrictions impliedly support the existence of a general freedom to meet or march that will exist if not specifically prohibited. The decision in *Burden v Rigler*[108] that, for the purposes of s 97 of the Representation of the People Act 1983, the fact that the meeting is held on the highway will not of itself render it unlawful, also supports this view. However, it will be indicated throughout this chapter that common law recognition of freedom of assembly was patchy, limited and precarious. Therefore, the rights of freedom of expression and assembly recognised in domestic law under the effects of the HRA are of especial significance.

Rights to make public protest within Arts 10 and 11

Under s 6 HRA, those seeking to exercise rights of protest and assembly can rely on Arts 10 and 11 of the Convention, and any other relevant right,[109] against public authorities, in particular the police. All the legislation already mentioned and discussed below must where necessary be interpreted compatibly with those rights, under s 3, taking the Strasbourg jurisprudence into account under s 2. But, in order to evaluate the actual and potential impact of the Convention, under the HRA, it is necessary to consider the scope and content of the Art 10 and 11 rights of protest and assembly.

Existing Strasbourg jurisprudence on the right to protest is scanty,[110] and very few cases deal with direct action protest, which has been analysed under Art 11[111] and also Art 10.[112] Owing to the existence of Art 11, it is fair to say that until recently, Strasbourg had not developed a distinct Art 10 jurisprudence on expression as public protest. However, recent decisions, discussed below, suggest that such a jurisprudence is developing and that Strasbourg currently views freedom of assembly simply as an aspect of freedom of expression.[113] In *Ziliberberg v Moldova*[114] the Court made the association between assembly and expression explicit: 'the right to freedom of

108 [1911] 1 KB 337.
109 Article 5 may have particular applicability. See Chapter 2, pp 51 *et seq.*
110 There have been comparatively few decisions by the Court (*Plattform 'Ärzte für das Leben' v Austria* A 139 (1988); *Ezelin v France* A 202 (1991); *Steel v UK* (1998) 28 EHRR 603; *Chorherr v Austria* A 266-B (1993); *Hashman and Harrup v UK* (1999) 30 EHRR 241; (2000) 8 BHRC 104). Most of the jurisprudence consists of admissibility decisions in the Commission, finding that the application was manifestly ill founded.
111 *G v FRG* No 13079/87 (1980) 21 DR 138.
112 See *Steel v UK* (1999) 28 EHRR 603 and *Hashman and Harrup v UK* No 25594/94, 25 November 1999, [1999] EHRLR 342, (2000) 8 BHRC 104. Previously, the general tendency was to treat Art 11 as *lex specialis* in such cases, with Art 10 requiring no separate consideration *per se*, but nevertheless providing relevant principles to assist in the consideration of the Art 11 claim (see, e.g., *Ezelin v France* A 202 (1991), para 35).
113 *Ezelin v France* A 202-A (1991). However, it may be noted that in his partly dissenting opinion, Judge de Meyer took the view that the two Articles were inextricably linked in their bearing on the instant situation and that there had been a violation of both (p 31). *Plattform 'Ärzte für das Leben' v Austria* (1988) 13 EHRR 204; *Djavit An v Turkey* (2003) Reports of Judgments and Decisions, 2003-III, p 233, para 39; *Christian Democratic People's Party v Moldova* (Appl No 28793/02, 14 May 2006, unreported) para 62; *Öllinger v Austria* (Appl No 76900/01, 29 June 2006, unreported), para 38. In the protest case of *Steel and Others v United Kingdom* (1998) 28 EHRR 603, para 101, freedom of expression was said to constitute 'an essential foundation of democratic society and one of the basic conditions for its progress and for each individual's self-fulfilment'.
114 (Appl No 61821/00, 4 May 2004, unreported), para 2.

assembly is a fundamental right in a democratic society and, like the right to freedom of expression, is one of the foundations of such a society'. This stance is appropriate given the deliberate adoption of the wider term 'expression' rather than 'speech' in Art 10; it also avoids the problems experienced in the US, in distinguishing between message-bearing conduct and conduct *simpliciter*. The conduct element of assemblies and protests may exclude it from Art 11 protection due to the requirement that they should be 'peaceful' but it is argued that this restriction should not also be read into Art 10(1) even though that fails to ensure the consistency and coherence of the two Articles. This does not imply that the 'assembly' element within the exercise of Art 11 rights is necessarily subordinate to the 'expression' element or that it is unnecessary to distinguish between the two elements. In *Chorherr v Austria*[115] the expression of protesters appeared likely to offend some spectators, leading to an interference with their peaceful enjoyment of a parade. The interference of the state with the Art 10 rights of the protesters was justified since it had the aim of upholding freedom of assembly.

Freedom of assembly under Art 11

Article 11 is specifically aimed at freedom of assembly. Forms of public protest as examples of both assembly and expression will fall within Art 10 also. Some forms of protest, such as handing out leaflets or expressing an opinion through direct action – where the 'assembly' element of the protest may be insignificant – may be considered only within Art 10. The value of freedom of choice as to the *manner* of participation in political activity may, however, fall most readily within Art 11 which, in this instance, should not therefore be viewed simply as providing assembly rights interchangeable with expression rights under Art 10. Article 11 protects both association and assembly, and in its judgement in *Socialist Party and Others v Turkey*[116] the Court linked the three guarantees together in finding that the dissolution of the Socialist Party of Turkey had breached Art 11. The individuals affected by the interference in question could be viewed as exercising rights to participate in political activity, of a central nature in a democracy. As indicated above, such participation can occur by various means, including direct action, and is clearly not confined to activity associated only with general elections. The persons participating may be viewed as exercising a choice as to the particular manner of their participation. The close connection which the Court perceived between the freedoms of association and expression echoes the findings of Judge Harlan in the US Supreme Court in 1958: 'Effective advocacy of both public and private points of view, particularly controversial ones, is undeniably enhanced by group association, as this Court has more than once recognised in remarking upon the close nexus between the freedoms of speech and assembly.'[117]

If the argument in favour of rights of association and participation in political activity is applied to public protest, it may in certain circumstances provide a foundation for the claims of protesters that might not readily arise if Art 10 alone was relied on. As Barendt has pointed out,[118] the US Supreme Court has shown itself willing to protect

---

115 A 266-B (1993).
116 Judgment of 25 May 1998 (Appl No 20/1997/804/1007); (1999) 27 EHRR 51, paras 41, 47, 50.
117 *NAACP v Alabama* (1958) 357 US 449, p 460.
118 In 'Freedom of assembly', in Beatson and Cripps (eds), *Freedom of Expression and Freedom of Information*, 2000.

rights of access to particular public places in order to hold meetings or demonstrations, in contrast to its stance in respect of the exercise of speech rights. Although this stance flows from the wording of the First Amendment which, in contrast to Art 10, refers to speech rather than expression, the argument may be of relevance in relation to 'manner' issues and have value in carving out a distinctive, or any, role for Art 11 which is not at present apparent in the recent Strasbourg public protest jurisprudence. Thus, once domestic courts begin to develop a distinctive Convention jurisprudence on public protest, it is suggested that they should question the treatment of protest as simply a form of political expression. Although protest is thereby bolstered by the arguments outlined supporting the special position of such expression, there may be instances in which other arguments based on the exercise of autonomy in relation to political activity, deriving solely or mainly from Art 11, should be utilised. If protesters rely on both Arts 10 and 11, the argument that other means of communication, such as the internet, are available or that free expression justifications may not fully support rights to determine the place, manner and time of the protest, will carry less weight since each protester may be viewed as exercising rights to self-determination in choosing both to associate with a particular group and to participate in the political process in a particular manner, time and place.

Article 11 leaves a great deal of discretion to the judiciary. It is not a far-reaching provision since, as explained in Chapter 2, it protects only freedom of *peaceful* assembly and since, in common with Arts 8–10, it contains a long list of exceptions in para 2.[119] In interpreting it, the UK judiciary are obliged, under s 2 of the HRA, to take the relevant Strasbourg jurisprudence into account. That jurisprudence is not, on the whole, of a radical nature, although the Court has found that the right to organise public meetings is 'fundamental'[120] and includes the right to organise marches, demonstrations and other forms of public protest. Article 11 may impose limited positive duties on the state to ensure that an assembly or a protest can occur even though it is likely to provoke others to violence; the responsibility for any harm caused appears to remain with the counter-demonstrators.[121] The acceptance of further positive duties, including a duty to require owners of private land to allow some peaceful assemblies on their property, has not yet been accepted under the Convention but remains a possibility,[122] especially, as Harris, O'Boyle and Warbrick point out,[123] in view of the growth of quasi-public places such as large, enclosed shopping centres and the privatisation of previously public places.

---

119 See Chapter 2, p 96.

120 *Rassemblement Jurassien Unite Jurassienne v Switzerland* No 819/78, (1979) 17 DR 93, 119.

121 *Plattform 'Ärtze fur das Leben' v Austria* A 139 (1988), para 32; Judgment of 21 June 1988; 13 EHRR 204.

122 See *De Geillustreede Pers v Netherlands* No 5178/71, 8 DR 5 (1976) Com Rep; the Commission accepted that states may have positive obligations to uphold freedom of expression in the context of media ownership. In the US, the 'access' issue was initially resolved in favour of the property right, but now seems to be moving towards acceptance of exceptions favouring expressive rights; see Nardell, 'The Quantock Hounds and the Trojan Horse' [1995] PL 27 on *R v Somerset CCV ex p Fewings*, [1995] 1 All ER 513 for discussion of the shopping mall/'constitutional fora' cases. See further below, pp 453–54. In *Appleby v UK* 6 May 2003 no violation of Arts 10 or 11 was found where protesters were unable to exercise rights of protest in a privately owned shopping mall. The state had not failed in its obligation to secure such rights.

123 *Law of the European Convention on Human Rights*, 1995, p 419.

'Direct action' used in a symbolical sense has been found to fall within Art 11.[124] The key factor in determining whether a protest counts as a peaceful assembly appears to be whether it is violent in itself or whether any violence arises incidentally.[125] *G v FRG*[126] concerned a sit-in that had blocked the road to a US Army barracks in a protest against nuclear weapons.[127] Under the distinction suggested above,[128] the protest would be viewed as primarily symbolic, rather than obstructive, since the demonstrators blocked the road for only 12 minutes in every hour. The applicant ignored an order to leave the road, was arrested and convicted of the offence of coercion by force or threats.[129] It was found that 'the applicant's conviction . . . interfered with his [Art 11] rights'.[130] However, the interference was again quite readily found to be justified. The Commission considered that the applicant's conviction for having participated in the sit-in could be viewed as necessary in a democratic society for the prevention of disorder and crime, since the blocking of a public road had caused more obstruction than would normally arise from the exercise of the right of peaceful assembly. The applicant and the other demonstrators had thereby intended to attract broader public attention to their political opinions concerning nuclear armament. However, 'balancing the public interest in the prevention of disorder and the interest of the applicant and the other demonstrators in choosing the particular form of a sit-in, the applicant's conviction for the criminal offence of unlawful coercion does not appear disproportionate to the aims pursued'. The application was dismissed as manifestly ill founded.

The Court found an infringement of freedom of assembly under Art 11 in the very significant judgment, *Ezelin v France*,[131] discussed below. In *Steel v UK*[132] and *Hashman v UK*,[133] a violation of Art 10 was found in respect of public protest and the Court therefore did not find it necessary to consider Art 11. It has been a feature of the practice that applications did not reach the Court since the Commission has readily found them to be manifestly ill founded.[134] The Commission has since been abolished but the admissibility criteria used by the Court continue to mean that many applications will not obtain a full hearing.[135] This cautious stance largely arises from the wide margin of appreciation that has been afforded to national authorities in determining what is needed to preserve public order at local level.

---

124 *G v Federal Republic of Germany* No 13079/87, (1989) 60 DR 256, 263. Currently, the Court views such protest as falling most readily within Art 10; see below, 776–78.

125 *Christians against Racism and Fascism v UK* No 8440/78, (1980) 21 DR 138, 148.

126 No 13079/87, (1980) 21 DR 138.

127 The protest was intended to mark the third anniversary of the NATO Twin-Track Agreement (NATO-Doppelbeschluß).

128 See pp 666–67.

129 Under the German Criminal Code, s 240.

130 It accepted that 'the applicant and the other demonstrators had not been actively violent in the course of the sit-in concerned'.

131 A 202-A (1991).

132 In *Steel and Others v UK* (1999) 28 EHRR 603, a violation of Art 10 was found in respect of interferences with public protest.

133 (2000) 8 BHRC 104; (1999) 30 EHRR 241. Both judgments are discussed below, pp 684–85, 776–79.

134 *Friedl v Austria* Appl No 15225/89 (1992) unreported; *Christians Against Racism and Fascism v UK* Appl No 8440/78; 21 DR 138 (1980).

135 See Chapter 2, pp 28–31.

Protest as expression under Art 10

The Art 10 jurisprudence relating specifically to public protest is meagre, as this chapter will indicate. However, the extensive jurisprudence on expression generally, especially political expression, is clearly applicable to public protest.[136] The *content* of speech will rarely exclude it from Art 10 protection: thus, speech as part of a protest likely to cause such low level harm as alarm or distress may be protected according to the *dicta* of the Court in *Müller v Switzerland*[137] to the effect that the protection of free speech extends equally to ideas which 'offend, shock or disturb'. The Court has repeatedly asserted that freedom of expression 'constitutes one of the essential foundations of a democratic society', that exceptions to it 'must be narrowly interpreted and the necessity for any restrictions . . . convincingly established'.[138] As the Introduction to this part indicates, it is a marked feature of the Strasbourg jurisprudence that political expression receives a high degree of protection. One of the leading works on the Convention concludes: 'It is clear that the Court ascribes a hierarchy of value' to different classes of speech, attaching 'the highest importance to the protection of political expression . . . widely understood.'[139]

Prima facie all forms of protest that can be viewed as the expression of an opinion fall within Art 10 according to the findings of the Court in *Steel v UK*.[140] Thus the direct action form of protest, such as symbolic or actual physical obstruction, does fall within the scope of Art 10,[141] a finding that was reiterated in *Hashman v UK*.[142] In *Steel*, protesters who were physically impeding grouse shooters and road builders were found to be engaging in 'expression' within the meaning of Art 10. These findings are clearly of the highest significance, but, unfortunately, since they were made without the slightest attempt at explanation or justification,[143] it is impossible to ascertain with any certainty either the limits of the protection thereby extended to such protests, or whether Strasbourg views such expression as having a lower status than 'purely' expressive protest activities – carrying banners, handing out leaflets, shouting slogans, and the like. *Steel* also concerned third, fourth and fifth applicants, who had engaged

---

136 *Steel and Others v UK* (1999) 28 EHRR 603.

137 (1991) 13 EHRR 212.

138 *Observer and Guardian v UK* judgment of 26 November 1991, A 216, pp 29–30, para 59; 14 EHRR 153.

139 Harris, J, O'Boyle, M and Warbrick, C, *Law of the European Convention on Human Rights*, 1995, pp 397 and 414. The second rank is artistic speech, the third commercial speech, e.g., advertising. They acknowledge that these terms may be too narrow (p 397, fn 14 and associated text). In particular, the term 'artistic' is too restrictive since it does not cover all speech, including some forms of protest, which may be said to be supported by the free speech arguments.

140 (1999) 28 EHRR 603.

141 See *Steel v UK* (1999) 28 EHRR 603, para 92: 'It is true that the protests took the form of physically impeding the activities of which the applicants disapproved, but the Court considers nonetheless that they constituted expressions of opinion with the meaning of Article 10.'

142 *Hashman* (2000) 8 BHRC 104; (1999) 30 EHRR 241 does not offer much guidance as to the scope of protection for direct action since, having found that a sanction applied to the applicants for blowing a horn with the intention of disrupting a hunt was a form of expression within Art 10, the Court went on to find that the interference was not 'prescribed by law': the domestic law – the *contra bono mores* doctrine – was found to be insufficiently precise.

143 The like finding made by the Commission in *G v FRG*, No 13079/87, (1980) 21 DR 138, similarly took the form of a bare assertion.

in purely peaceful protests with no element of obstruction or other 'action'. Since no justification for the arrest of such purely peaceful protesters was apparent, a breach of Art 10 was found. As explained below, no breach was found in respect of the first two applicants and the Court did not scrutinise the question of proportionality very closely. This stance suggests that while actual obstruction falls within Art 10, it may have a lower status than protest in the form of pure speech.

In *Steel*, the Court drew no distinction between actual and symbolic obstruction, and has not therefore considered the means by which any such distinction might manifest itself in the assessment of the lawfulness of state interferences with these forms of obstruction. It is clear only that violent or threatening protest – which, according to the Commission, includes 'demonstration[s] where the organisers and participants have violent intentions that result in public disorder' – falls outside Art 11 and, possibly, Art 10.[144] In any event, interference with such protest would be likely to be found to be justified under Art 10(2).

Justifications for interferences with the primary rights

Owing to the likelihood that, as indicated, most forms of protest will fall within Art 10, and probably also Art 11, the emphasis of Strasbourg findings is on the para 2 exceptions which include 'in the interests of national security . . . public safety . . . for the prevention of disorder or crime . . . for the protection of the . . . rights of others'. Under the familiar formula discussed in Chapter 2, in order to be justified, state interference with Art 10 and 11 guarantees must be prescribed by law, have a legitimate aim, be necessary in a democratic society and be applied in a non-discriminatory fashion (Art 14). In carrying out this assessment, the domestic courts are obliged to take the Strasbourg public protest jurisprudence into account although they are not bound by it.[145]

In freedom of expression cases, Strasbourg's main concern has been with the 'necessary in a democratic society' requirement; the notion of 'prescribed by law' has been focused upon to some extent but almost always with the result that it has been found to be satisfied. The 'legitimate aim' requirement will normally be readily satisfied; as Harris, O'Boyle and Warbrick point out, the grounds for interference are so wide that 'the state can usually make a plausible case that it did have a good reason for interfering with the right'.[146] The provision against non-discrimination arising under Art 14 is potentially very significant, especially in relation to minority public protests, but so far it has not been a significant issue in the relevant freedom of expression jurisprudence.

The requirements of precision and foreseeability connoted by the term 'prescribed by law'[147] have been flexibly applied in this context; for example, in *Rai, Allmond and 'Negotiate Now' v UK*,[148] the Commission had to consider the ban on public demonstrations or meetings concerning Northern Ireland in Trafalgar Square. The ban was the subject of a statement in the House of Commons and many refusals of demonstrations had been made subsequent to it. The Commission found that the ban was sufficiently

---

144 But see above, p 681.
145 HRA 1998, s 2(1).
146 *Law of the European Convention on Human Rights*, 1995, p 290.
147 *Sunday Times v UK* A30, para 49 (1979).
148 81-A D & R 46 (1995).

prescribed by law: 'It is compatible with the requirements of foreseeability that terms which are on their face general and unlimited are explained by executive or administrative statements, since it is the provision of sufficiently precise guidance to individuals . . . rather than the source of that guidance which is of relevance'.[149] In *Steel and Others v UK*[150] the Commission introduced a very significant qualification to the requirement: 'The level of precision required depends to a considerable degree on the content of the instrument, the field it is designed to cover, and the number and status of those to whom it is addressed.'[151] Although the term 'margin of appreciation' was not used, this finding appears to allow the member state a certain leeway in public protest cases in relation to the 'prescribed by law' requirement. As indicated below, that leeway was overstepped by the *contra bono mores* (contrary to a good way of life) power arising under the Justices of the Peace Act 1361, due to its imprecision.[152]

The Court tends to afford a wide margin of appreciation when reviewing the necessity of interferences with expression in the form of protest, viewing measures taken to prevent disorder or protect the rights of others as peculiarly within the purview of the domestic authorities, in contrast to its stance in respect of 'pure' speech. Therefore, expression as protest tends to be in a precarious position. The notion of a margin of appreciation conceded to states permeates the Art 10(2) and 11(2) public protest jurisprudence, although it has not influenced the interpretation of the substantive rights.

In finding that applications are manifestly ill founded, the Commission has been readily satisfied that decisions of the national authorities to adopt quite far-reaching measures, including complete bans, in order to prevent disorder are within their margin of appreciation.[153] The Court has also found 'the margin of appreciation extends in particular to the choice of the reasonable and appropriate mean to be used by the authority to ensure that lawful manifestations can take place peacefully'.[154] Thus, states are typically *not* required to demonstrate that lesser measures than those actually taken would have been inadequate to deal with the threats posed by demonstrations – disorder, interferences with the rights of others and so on.

The effect of this 'light touch' review may also be seen in the tendency to deal with crucial issues – typically proportionality, but also in some cases the scope of the primary right[155] – in such a brusque and abbreviated manner that explication for the findings is

149 Ibid, p 152. The power in question arose from the Trafalgar Square Regulations 1952 SI 1952/776, para 3, made under the Parks Regulation (Amendment) Act 1926. The Act allowed the Secretary of State to 'make any regulations considered necessary . . . for the preservation of order . . .' in the parks.

150 (1998) 28 EHRR 603; [1998] Crim LR 893.

151 Paragraph 145. The Commission based these findings on the judgments of the Court in *Chorherr v Austria* Series A 266-B (1993), para 23 and in *Cantoni v France* para 35 (1996) RJD 1996-V 1614.

152 See *Hashman and Harrup v UK* (1999) 30 EHRR 241; Appl No 25594/94 (European Court of Human Rights); (2000) 8 BHRC 104.

153 See *Christians against Racism and Fascism v UK* No 8440/78, 21 DR 138; and *Friedl v Austria* No 15225/89 (1992) unreported.

154 *Chorherr v Austria* A 266-B (1993), para 31.

155 See the crucial findings in *Steel v UK* (1999) 28 EHRR 603, *Hashman and Harrup v UK* (2000) 8 BHRC 104; (1999) 30 EHRR 241 and *G v FRG* 21 DR 138 (1980) that direct action fell within the scope of Arts 10 and 11.

either non-existent or takes the form of mere assertion.[156] Moreover, the jurisprudence is, in general, markedly under-theorised, in notable contrast to that concerning media expression. 'It is fair to say that little recognition of the distinctive value of public protest as compared to other forms of political discussion is apparent from the case law; moreover . . . general principles have not played [a] great . . . part in cases involving public protest.'[157] In *Steel*,[158] for example, which, as indicated, concerned interferences with the freedom of expression of five applicants, the proportionality of the arrest and 17 hour detention of the second applicant and her subsequent imprisonment for seven days on refusing to be bound over is airily determined, in a mere two sentences. The applicant was physically impeding digging equipment by sitting on the ground. The Court's finding was that her arrest and detention was justified as necessary to prevent disorder and protect the rights of others.[159] But these grounds had scant substantiation: it was accepted that no violent incidents or damage to property had been caused by the road protesters (para 15) and the conduct of the applicant had been entirely peaceful: she had never resisted being removed from the area by security guards – so it is hard to see wherein lay the 'risk of disorder',[160] still less why it was sufficient to justify such comparatively drastic action. As for 'the rights of others', the court, rather extraordinarily, nowhere said what these 'rights' were, although presumably the judges had in mind the fact that the road builders were engaged in a lawful activity – building a road – which the protesters were disrupting. The issue of the gravity of the interference with these 'rights' was not touched upon: the road builders did have security guards, and were apparently able to carry on with their work, at the cost of some inconvenience. In neither case was the question of alternative means of protecting the road builders even adverted to, much less subjected to any analysis. In other words, one of the justificatory grounds for the interference with Art 10 rights was unsubstantiated by any real evidence; the other was subject to no analysis at all.

In *Pendragon*[161] and *Chappell*,[162] Commission cases on challenges to blanket bans[163] on assemblies at and around Stonehenge, these tendencies are even more marked. In both cases, the bans under challenge prevented Druids from holding bona fide religious ceremonies, which had been held for over 80 years during the summer solstice period. Since such bans constitute prior restraint, and in both cases resulted in the criminalisation

---

156 While such terse reasoning is a typical feature of the Strasbourg case law (see, e.g., Dickson, B, 'The common law and the European Convention', in *Human Rights and the European Convention*, 1997, pp 216–17), the tendency is particularly marked in protest cases: cf, e.g., the reasoning devoted to the proportionality issue in *News Verlags v Austria* (2001) 31 EHRR 8 (a case concerning media freedom discussed in Chapter 5) – six lengthy paragraphs – with that in *Steel v UK* ibid (one paragraph).

157 See Fenwick and Phillipson (2000) op. cit., fn 1, pp 629–30.

158 (1998) 28 EHRR 603.

159 (1998) 28 EHRR 603, para 109.

160 The first applicant, it found, 'had created a danger of serious physical injury to herself and others and had formed part of a protest which risked culminating in disorder and violence': (1998) 28 EHRR 603, para 105). Neither of these factors was present in relation to the second applicant, so the reference was not only worthless, but positively misleading (though the Court did note that the risk of disorder was 'arguably less serious than that caused by the first applicant' (para 109)).

161 No 31416/96 (1998).

162 No 12587/86 (1987).

163 In *Chappell*, these were made under the National Heritage Act 1983, and the Ancient Monuments and Archaeological Areas Act 1979, in *Pendragon*, under s 14A itself.

of those engaged in purely peaceful gatherings, it might have been expected that they would have been subjected to that 'most careful scrutiny' which prior restraints in other contexts demand.[164] In *Pendragon*, the ban caught a group of Druids conducting a ceremony *near* Stonehenge; the justification for it put forward by the Chief Constable was that in the previous year, about 40 people had tried to gain access to the monument itself, during the solstice period. The Commission cited no evidence whatever to justify the assertion that the use of a blanket order – the most serious interference possible – was the *only way* of protecting Stonehenge,[165] an assertion which must be seriously open to question, given the plethora of other powers available.[166] In fact, the Commission made no inquiry at all as to whether less intrusive means could have been used: it merely asserted blandly: 'it cannot be considered to be an unreasonable response to prohibit assemblies at Stonehenge for a given period.'

In *Chappell*, the Commission found that the decision to enforce a total ban 'was a necessary public safety measure, and that any implied interference with the applicants' rights under Article 9[167] ... was ... necessary ... in the interests of public safety, for the protection of public order or for the protection of the rights and freedoms of others'. It may be noted that this purported determination consists of a mere assertion that the Convention tests were fulfilled. A similar finding was made in relation to Art 11. As in *Steel*, part of the justification for the restrictions was asserted to be 'for the protection of the rights and freedoms of others' although there was no mention of what these rights might be, still less any analysis of why they should outweigh the primary Convention rights of freedom of religion and assembly, exercised in a wholly peaceful manner. The dismissal of both cases as 'manifestly ill founded' indicated the Commission's view that the applications raised no serious issues of law. The specific problems these characteristics raise when attempting to 'apply' the case law to particular domestic facts are considered at various points in this chapter.

But in *Ezelin v France*[168] the Court took a 'hard look' at the issue of proportionality. The applicant, an advocate, took part in a demonstration against the judicial system generally and against particular judges, involving the daubing of slogans attacking the judiciary on court walls, and eventual violence. Ezelin did not himself take part in any illegal acts, but did not disassociate himself from the march, even when it became violent. He was disciplined by the Bar Association and eventually given a formal reprimand, which did not impair his ability to practice. No fine was imposed. The French Government's argument was that, 'By not disavowing the unruly incidents that had occurred during the demonstration, the applicant had ipso facto approved them [and that] it was essential for judicial institutions to react to behaviour which, on the part of an 'officer of the court' ... seriously impaired the authority of the judiciary

---

164 *Observer and Guardian v UK* (1991) 14 EHRR 153, para 60.
165 The government simply asserted that 'the other powers in the Act did not provide adequate protection'.
166 In respect of breach of the peace, attempted or actual criminal damage, breach of conditions applied to specific assemblies (i.e., to keep clear of Stonehenge), POA 1986, s 5, and possibly CJPOA, s 69, breach of an order imposed under the powers used in *Chappell*.
167 See Chapter 2, p 91; Art 9 guarantees the right to 'freedom of thought, conscience and religion', including the right 'either alone or in community in others and in public or private, to manifest [one's] religion ... in worship ... practice and observance'.
168 A 202 (1991).

and respect or court decisions'.[169] The argument was rejected; Art 11 was found to have been violated. In an emphatic judgment, the Court found: '. . . the freedom to take part in a peaceful assembly – in this instance a demonstration that had not been prohibited – is of such importance that it cannot be restricted in any way, even for an advocate, so long as the person concerned does not himself commit any reprehensible act on such an occasion.'[170]

Conclusions

The broad phrasing of Arts 10 and 11[171] inevitably leave a great deal of interpretative discretion to the UK judiciary in considering their application to existing law. But certain conclusions can be drawn: the Court will not tolerate the arrest and detention of purely peaceful protesters, even if the protest degenerates into violence, so long as the protesters in question have not themselves committed 'reprehensible acts'. The finding of the Court in *Steel v UK*,[172] reiterated in *Hashman v UK*,[173] that direct action protest, such as physical obstruction, does fall within the scope of Art 10[174] is of great significance, as is the finding of the Commission that protesters engaged in a 'sit-in' blocking a road are covered by Art 11.[175] It appears to be the case that Strasbourg views such expression as having a lower status than 'purely' expressive and speech-based protest activities, but a distinction has not been drawn between actual and symbolic obstruction,[176] although it may be inferred that actual obstruction might be viewed as reprehensible.

Thus, apart from violent or threatening protest, most forms of protest and assembly are within the scope of both Arts 10 and 11, although ceremonious processions and assemblies will probably be considered only within Art 11,[177] while the recent tendency is to consider forms of direct action within Art 10. All the forms of protest mentioned above, apart from the last two,[178] appear to be covered. Thus, forms of protest including those far removed from the classic peaceful assembly holding up banners or handing out leaflets engage these Articles, but interference with direct action protest can be readily justified, even where it is primarily of a symbolic nature.

Nevertheless, it is evident that the application of the above case law without more, would do little to structure the domestic judicial discretion, leaving the courts free to apply Arts 10 and 11 so that they constitute little or no check upon police discretion over assemblies and demonstrations on the ground. Whether this turns out to be the case depends crucially upon two factors: first, the attitude of the domestic courts towards

---

169   Ibid, para 49.
170   Ibid, para 53.
171   Articles 5 and 6 may also be relevant in some circumstances.
172   (1998) 28 EHRR 603.
173   (1999) 30 EHRR 241; No 25594/94 25 November 1999; (2000) 8 BHRC 104.
174   In *Steel v UK* (1999) 28 EHRR 603, para 92: 'It is true that the protests took the form of physically impeding the activities of which the applicants disapproved, but the Court considers nonetheless that they constituted expressions of opinion with the meaning of Article 10.'
175   *G v FRG* Appl No 13079/87 (1980) 21 DR 138.
176   Above, p 666.
177   See *Chorherr v Austria* A 266-B (1993); see above, p 681.
178   See pp 684–85.

the margin of appreciation doctrine and any domestic equivalent; secondly, whether they are prepared to make any use of the more fundamental principles underlying Convention jurisprudence on political expression generally.

The domestic application of Arts 10 and 11

In Chapter 4, two opposing judicial approaches were indicated to the application of the Convention, although it was pointed out that judicial reasoning cannot always be neatly pigeonholed. It is suggested below that the two approaches are of especial significance in this context, since the common law has failed to afford the protection to freedom of protest and assembly which has been evident at Strasbourg. This is clearly not a context in which the tendency of the common law has been to achieve high standards of human rights protection, as Lord Bingham acknowledged in *Laporte*. If the judges fail to abandon their traditional approach in favour of a more activist stance, under the impetus of the HRA, it will continue to be the case that the freedoms of protest and assembly receive less recognition in the UK than in other comparable democracies.

As commentators have agreed[179] and as the House of Lords has stressed,[180] the margin of appreciation doctrine, as such, should not be applied by domestic courts, since it is a distinctively international law doctrine. Applying the Convention without such reliance has two aspects. It means, first, refusing to import the doctrine into domestic decision making on the Convention where no Strasbourg decision is in point, and, secondly, where such a decision is in point, seeking to apply it but to disentangle the margin of appreciation aspects from it. This might mean giving consideration to the likely outcome of the case at Strasbourg had the doctrine been disregarded. However, as discussed above, the reasoning in much of the case law is quite sparse and tokenistic, the doctrine having had the effect, not of influencing a particular part of the judgment in a clear way, but simply of rendering the whole assessment quite rudimentary. Therefore, stripping away the effects of the doctrine might merely mean treating certain judgments as non-determinative of the points raised at the domestic level. Certainly, domestic courts minded to make an intensive inquiry into questions of proportionality will receive little aid from the cases described above in so doing. So far in the post-HRA domestic case law, there is little evidence that the judges appreciate the fact that they are in a sense importing the margin of appreciation aspects of Strasbourg decisions into domestic law by the back door.

Minimalism

This is a context in which the possible stances that the domestic judiciary might adopt when confronted with public order cases raising Art 10 and 11 issues are, it

---

179   See Laws, J (Sir), 'The limitations of human rights' [1999] PL 254, p 258; Feldman, D, 'The Human Rights Act and constitutional principles' (1999) 19(2) LS 165, p 192; Pannick, D, 'Principles of interpretation of Convention rights under the Human Rights Act and the discretionary area of judgment' (1998) PL 545; Hunt, M, Singh, R and Demetriou, M, 'Is there a role for the 'margin of appreciation' in national law after the Human Rights Act?' (1999) 1 EHRLR 15, esp p 17.

180   *R v DPP ex p Kebilene and Others* [1999] 3 WLR 972, p 1043, *per* Lord Hope: '[the doctrine] is not available to the national courts . . .'; see *dicta* to like effect in *R v Stratford JJ ex p Imbert* (1999) *The Times*, 21 February, *per* Buxton LJ.

is argued, quite clearly opposed. A minimalist approach might be, in this context, almost indistinguishable from what might be termed a 'traditionalist' one and might yield similar results, since this is a field in which the judiciary have, since *Beatty v Gillbanks*,[181] almost invariably eschewed an activist approach. A minimalist approach could be justified on the basis that a balance has always been struck in UK law between freedom of assembly and public order by reference either to common law principle or parliamentary restraint; with only two exceptions,[182] that balance has been found to accord with Arts 10 and 11 at Strasbourg[183] and therefore there is no reason to disturb it now. Under this approach, the courts, while pronouncing the margin of appreciation doctrine inapplicable, would not take the further step of recognising and making due allowance for its influence on the cases applied. Thus, judges could rely simplistically and solely on the *outcomes* of decisions at Strasbourg – most of which are adverse to the applicants – without adverting to its influence on those outcomes. Thus, they could import its effects – 'light touch' review and therefore a 'soft-edged' proportionality standard likely to catch only grossly unreasonable decisions – into domestic decision making. Anticipation of such an approach pre-HRA was not unduly pessimistic: arguably it was already evident in the pre-HRA era in Convention-based reasoning.[184]

The traditionalist judge would tend to take the view that common law principle has long recognised values which are coterminous with the factors taken into account at Strasbourg in evaluating the balance in question, and that, in most instances, the outcome of cases would not differ whether freedom of expression was viewed as a common law principle or as protected under the Convention. Occasional judicial pronouncements suggest that the common law recognises legal rights to assemble and protest. In *Hubbard v Pitt*,[185] in a well-known minority judgment, Lord Denning referred to 'the right to demonstrate and the right to protest on matters of public concern'.[186] In the immediate pre-HRA period, Eady J found, in a decision concerning animal rights' activists, that the Protection from Harassment Act 1997 'was . . . not intended by Parliament to be used to clamp down on . . . the rights of political protest and public demonstration which are so much a part of our democratic tradition'.[187] The traditionalist judge might note, however, that the two decisions at Strasbourg which have found that the UK had breached Art 10 in interfering with public protest, both concerned common law doctrines. Such a judge might perhaps also acknowledge that there has been more

---

181 [1882] 9 QBD 308, discussed below, p 772.
182 See the findings of the Court under Art 10 regarding the third, fourth and fifth applicants in *Steel, Lush, Needham, Polden and Cole v UK* Appl No 24838/94 (1999) 28 EHRR 603 above, pp 684–87, and below, pp 776–77, and *Hashman and Harrup v UK* (1999) 30 EHRR 241; (2000) 8 BHRC 104.
183 See, e.g., *Chappell v UK* (1988) 10 EHRR 510; *Christians Against Racism and Fascism v UK* Appl No 8440/78 (1980) 21 DR 138; the findings as regards Steel and Lush in *Steel, Lush, Needham, Polden and Cole v UK* Appl No 24838/94 (1999) 28 EHRR 603.
184 See the House of Lords' decision in *Ex p Kebilene* [1999] 3 WLR 972 and the earlier case of *Khan* [1997] AC 558, HL. Sedley J, in *Redmond-Bates* (1999) Crim LR 998; (1999) *The Times*, 28 July, also appeared to follow this tendency in remarking merely that the decision in *Steel* 'demonstrates that the common law [of breach of the peace] is in conformity with the Convention'.
185 [1975] 3 All ER 1.
186 Ibid, pp 10D and 11B.
187 *Huntingdon Life Sciences Ltd and Another v Curtin and Others* (1997) *The Times*, 11 December; (1998) 3(1) J Civ Lib 37.

reluctance to accept that the freedoms of protest and assembly, as opposed to media freedom of speech, are recognised as reflecting common law values[188] coterminous with Convention ones.[189] As mentioned above, Lord Bingham in 2006 in *Laporte* gave precisely this acknowledgment.

Since, under the HRA, the courts have to take account of rights to protest as opposed to negative liberties,[190] these approaches had to be modified in order to provide a little more protection for such rights than was provided previously. Under pre-HRA judicial review principles, the domestic courts had to consider proportionality: a restriction would be deemed disproportionate where there was insufficient need for it or where no evidence of such need was advanced by the state. Under the HRA the courts can no longer apply the reasonableness standard or an attenuated proportionality doctrine. But where different views might be taken of the need for a particular interference, such as a ban imposed on a march under s 13 of the Public Order Act 1986, a domestic court fully applying the Strasbourg jurisprudence, including its margin of appreciation aspects, under s 2 HRA, would tend to defer to the judgment of the executive. Clearly, this approach is distinguishable from that of heightened *Wednesbury* unreasonableness,[191] but it can often lead to the same outcome.

Pre-HRA, the likelihood that a domestic doctrine of judicial restraint would be developed in relation to aspects of executive decision making, including the policing of public protest, found support from the decision of the House of Lords in *Chief Constable of Sussex ex p International Ferry Traders Ltd*.[192] International Ferry Traders Ltd, who were engaged in exporting live cattle, had sought judicial review of the decision of the Chief Constable of Sussex to limit the policing of animal rights protesters at Shoreham ferry port. The Lords had to consider the discretion of a Chief Constable

---

188 Compare the following pronouncement of Lord Hewart CJ in finding that where a public meeting might lead others to breach the peace, the speaker could be arrested: 'There have been moments during the argument in this case where it appeared to be suggested that the court had to do with a grave case involving what is called the right of public meeting. I say "called" because English law does not recognise any right of public meeting for political . . . purposes . . .' (*Duncan v Jones* [1936] 1 KB 218, p 221), with these pronouncements from *Derbyshire CC v Times Newspapers* in which it was found that local (or central) government cannot sue for libel. Lord Keith said: 'I find it satisfactory to be able to conclude that the common law of England is consistent with the [freedom of expression] obligations assumed under [the Convention]' [1993] AC 534, p 551, HL. Butler-Sloss LJ said: 'I can see no inconsistency between English law upon this subject and Article 10 . . . This is scarcely surprising, since we may pride ourselves on the fact that freedom of speech has existed in this country perhaps as long, if not longer than . . . in any other country in the world' ([1992] 3 WLR 28, p 60, CA). Admittedly, in view of the dates of these findings, this comparison might be viewed as mischievous and unfair, since the later decisions might be said to have been reached in the 'shadow' of the Convention. But the decision of the House of Lords in *DPP v Jones and Lloyd* [1999] 2 All ER 257, discussed below, pp 711 *et seq.*, could hardly be viewed as upholding the right to protest and assemble as strongly as *Derbyshire* upheld media freedom of speech.
189 The Divisional Court decision in *Jones and Lloyd v DPP* [1997] 2 All ER 119, discussed below, pp 711–20, found that there is no right to assemble on the highway, merely a voluntary toleration of such assemblies. No reference was made to an acceptance of Convention values within the common law except to say that Art 11 did not need to be referred to since the law was not ambiguous.
190 The Convention rights will be claim rights in the sense that they are binding on public authorities under the HRA, s 6. See Chapter 1, p 15.
191 See *Ministry of Defence ex p Smith and Others* [1996] 1 All ER 257, p 263.
192 [1999] 1 All ER 129.

to deploy powers to prevent a breach of the peace against protesters and the relevance of the margin of appreciation allowed to member states in respect of satisfying their Community obligations under the free movement of goods provisions of Art 34 of the Treaty of Rome. Lord Slynn, in a speech with which the other Law Lords agreed, found: 'the courts have long made it clear that . . . they will respect the margin of appreciation or discretion which a Chief Constable has,' and in this instance that margin had not been exceeded. As to the European aspects of the case, Lord Hoffmann found 'on the particular facts of this case the European concepts of proportionality and margin of appreciation produce the same result as what are commonly called Wednesbury principles . . . in this case I think that the Chief Constable must enjoy a margin of discretion that cannot differ according to whether its source be found in purely domestic principles or superimposed European principles'.

The decision illustrated the attachment of the judiciary to the doctrine of deference to policing decisions, even where the application of European law might have led to a different result. Lord Hoffmann's judgment above suggested that in the post-HRA era, the application of the Strasbourg public protest jurisprudence in order to determine questions of proportionality might lead to the same results as the application of the *Wednesbury* doctrine, since decisions of Chief Constables as to the needs of public order might tend to be as readily deferred to within the 'review' model as those in respect of the allocation of resources. This decision was in keeping with the only judicial review case involving a challenge to the decision of a Chief Constable to seek a ban on processions – *Kent v Metropolitan Police Comr*[193] – the most attenuated form of *Wednesbury* review was adopted, the courts affording the Commissioner a very wide margin of discretion. Courts adopting this approach could continue to apply traditional notions of deference to assessments of police officers and trial courts in respect of the possibility of disorder and the action thought necessary to avert it, interfering only if grossly disproportionate action had been taken. This would, as Lord Hoffmann's *dicta* make clear, entail the type of low-intensity inquiry into the existence of a 'pressing social need' to restrict rights to protest typified by the Strasbourg case law, albeit adopted for somewhat different reasons. The issue of whether less intrusive means could have been adopted would either be ignored or treated as an issue of police expertise, to which the courts should likewise defer.

Under the HRA, this approach has now become established as a domestic version of the margin of appreciation doctrine, recognising and respecting an 'area of discretionary judgment'.[194] The application of this discretionary area in this context is likely to

---

193 (1981) *The Times*, 15 May.
194 In *R v DPP ex p Kebilene* [1999] 3 WLR 972, Lord Hope rejected any domestic application of the margin of appreciation doctrine, but went on: 'In some circumstances it will be appropriate for the courts to recognise that there is an area of judgment within which the judiciary will defer, on democratic grounds, to the considered opinion of [the democratic body or person] whose act or decision is said to be incompatible with the Convention.' See also Lord Hoffmann, 'The Human Rights Act and the House of Lords' (1999) 62(2) MLR 159, esp p 161; Laws, *'Wednesbury'*, in Forsyth and Hare (eds), *The Golden Metwand and the Crooked Cord: Essays in Honour of Sir William Wade QC*, 1998, Clarendon, p 201; Pannick, D, 'Principles of interpretation of Convention rights under the Human Rights Act and the discretionary area of judgment' (1998) PL 545, pp 549–51; Hunt, M, Singh, R and Demetriou, M, 'Is there a role for the 'margin of appreciation' in national law after the Human Rights Act?' (1999) 1 EHRLR 15. In *Brown v Stott* [2001] 2 WLR 817, p 835, Lord Bingham found that a

encourage the continuance of a deferential approach to the decisions of police officers and other bodies,[195] either on democratic grounds, or on the well established and familiar basis that the issue is one of expertise and on-the-spot discretionary decision making that should be interfered with only in cases of manifest injustice.[196]

It is contended that under both the 'minimalist' and 'traditionalist' approaches, the clear danger exists that the change brought about by the HRA in relation to protest is not much more than cosmetic only: while the rhetoric of legal reasoning is changing, the actual standards applied and the results obtained are not, or are only marginally enhanced. Indeed, the inception of the HRA has the ability to exacerbate the failures of the pre-HRA era as evinced in a number of the decisions discussed below;[197] executive interferences with public protest could be given an appearance of human rights auditing, but successful challenges would be as rare as ever. Thus, the executive could stifle political accountability in the form of criticisms of such interferences by asserting that the courts have found that such actions do not infringe the basic Convention rights to expression and assembly. Legal protection, therefore, would not be enhanced, while political accountability would actually be hampered. Moreover, the opportunity offered, under an activist approach, of differentiating between forms of protest, such as the physical obstruction of the fuel protest in November 2000[198] and the symbolically obstructive protests in *Steel*, would be lost. A domestic jurisprudence that in its development would call upon the underlying Convention values in order to create such a differentiation, would thus fail to come into existence.

It appeared pre-HRA that the domestic judiciary might find an 'activist' approach problematic, especially in determining whether a restriction is necessary in a democratic society in an instance covered by an adverse Commission decision on admissibility. It appeared inevitable, at least in the early decisions under the HRA, that in such circumstances some practitioners, magistrates or judges, lacking familiarity with the Strasbourg system, would view the finding of manifest ill-foundedness in a number of Strasbourg public protest cases as virtually conclusive of the issue since, on its face, it appears to mean that the case was almost unarguable.[199] It appeared that this problem would be exacerbated since public protest issues are usually adjudicated on in low-level

discretionary area of judgment would be accorded to the legislature and the government; in the post-HRA cases of *Profile Alliance* [2004] 1 AC 185 and *Wilson v First County Trust* [2001] 3 All ER 229 the House of Lords and the Court of Appeal respectively accepted that this was the case. See further Chapter 4, pp 272–75.

195 I.e., Parliament's decision to enact the relevant legislation in the first place.

196 See Fenwick, H, *Civil Rights: New Labour, Freedom and the Human Rights Act*, 2000, pp 138–39, and Ewing and Gearty, op. cit., fn 1, pp 91–93.

197 In particular, *Winder* and *Capon*; see below, pp 739–43.

198 See Fenwick, H and Phillipson, G, 'Direct action, convention values and the Human Rights Act' [2001] 21 (4) LS 535–568.

199 Under Art 27(2) of the Convention, the Commission shall consider inadmissible any petition submitted under Art 25 which it considers . . . manifestly ill-founded . . . The Court has said: 'rejection of a complaint as "manifestly ill-founded" amounts to a decision that there is not even a prima facie case against the respondent state . . .': *Boyle and Rice v UK* A 131 (1988), paras 53–54. However, Harris, O'Boyle and Warbrick, in *Law of the European Convention on Human Rights*, 1995, p 627 observe: '[the manifestly ill-founded provision] is possibly the only provision in the Convention where the Commission, in its practice, has departed from the literal and ordinary meaning of the words employed.'

courts. The early post-HRA decisions discussed in this chapter suggest that a minimalist approach was, to an extent adhered to, especially in the lower courts.

Activism

The approach under the HRA, which was adopted in 2006 by the House of Lords in *Laporte*, may be referred to as 'activist';[200] it starts from the premise that the reception of the Convention into UK law represents a decisive break with the past. Under this approach, judges regard themselves as required to go *beyond* the minimal standards applied in the Strasbourg jurisprudence,[201] given that Strasbourg's view of itself as a system of protection firmly subsidiary to that afforded by national courts has led it, particularly in public protest cases, to intervene only where clear and unequivocal transgressions have occurred. Such a stance recognises that, as a consequence, most of the cases on peaceful protest have not in fact required national authorities to demonstrate convincingly that the test of 'pressing social need' has been met. Furthermore, significantly, the courts can look for assistance to the general principles developed by Strasbourg.[202]

A foundational Strasbourg principle, repeated in a number of cases, is that 'the right to freedom of peaceful assembly . . . is a fundamental right in a democratic society, and, like the right to freedom of expression, is one of the foundations of such a society . . .'.[203] As indicated in Chapter 3 and the Introduction to Part II above, the House of Lords demonstrated that it can take such principles seriously and give them real efficacy in the field of media freedom, even prior to the coming into force of the HRA.[204] The HRA opened the way for the domestic courts to take to heart the principle – declared by Strasbourg. but not given practical effect by it – that peaceful protest has equal weight to freedom of expression generally, a freedom which is accorded 'special importance' within the Strasbourg jurisprudence,[205] and now, with the House of Lords judgment in *Laporte*, within the common law. That judgment clearly marked a turning point, not only in the UK public protest jurisprudence generally, but also in the post-HRA jurisprudence. It stands in marked contrast to the other relatively recent House of Lords' decision in this context – in *DPP v Jones*, taken immediately prior to the coming into force of the HRA, which is discussed below. Now that the freedom of expression dimension of public protest has been given domestic recognition in *Laporte*, following *Steel*, the principles developed in the Strasbourg and domestic

---

200 Fenwick, H, *Civil Rights: New Labour, Freedom and the Human Rights Act*, 2000, pp 502–5.

201 In the words of Judge Martens, '[the task of domestic courts] goes further than seeing that the minimum standards laid down in the ECHR are maintained . . . because the ECHR's injunction to further realise human rights and fundamental freedoms contained in the preamble is also addressed to domestic courts'. ('Opinion: incorporating the Convention: the role of the judiciary' (1998) 1 EHRLR 3.)

202 See Fenwick, H, *Civil Rights: New Labour, Freedom and the Human Rights Act*, 2000, pp 502–3. As the House of Lords recently stressed: 'in the national courts also the Convention should be seen as an expression of fundamental principles rather than as a set of mere rules' (*R v DPP ex p Kebilene* [1999] 3 WLR 972).

203 *Rassemblement Jurassien v Switzerland* (1980) 17 DR 93, p 119.

204 See Chapter 3, pp 125–26, 137, and the Introduction to Part II, pp 310–11.

205 The court referred to 'the special importance of freedom of peaceful assembly and freedom of expression, which are closely linked in this instance' (*Ezelin v France* A 202 (1991), para 51).

media freedom jurisprudence can be utilised in protest cases, thus underpinning and guiding judicial activism.

If a more Convention-friendly approach continues to develop post-HRA courts may begin to make a real attempt to 'strip away' or 'disapply' the effects of the margin of appreciation doctrine in applying Strasbourg jurisprudence. Thus, they may eventually apply a more rigorous approach to proportionality than has Strasbourg, making use as indicated of underlying Convention values in the attempt to flesh out the meagre Strasbourg jurisprudence, and to construct out of it a coherent set of openly stated principles. Under the 'activist' model, then, it appears to be unlikely that justifications for judicial restraint in public protest decisions, if any, will remain fully coterminous with Strasbourg restraint.

In this context, such an approach leads to much greater interference with executive decision making. It would be in accordance with this approach to have regard to the balance struck in public protest matters in other European courts within the margin of appreciation, and perhaps also to that struck by the International Covenant on Civil and Political Rights and in the US or Canada.[206] In support of this approach, it might also be pointed out that the Strasbourg public protest jurisprudence is very heavily influenced by decisions of the Commission, which was not a fully judicial body[207] and therefore has less authority than the Court. As Chapter 2 indicates, within the Court there is disagreement as to the interferences which fall within a state's margin of appreciation,[208] and this is particularly so in the key decision of the Court finding a violation of the freedom of assembly guarantee of Art 11, *Ezelin v France*.[209] Two of the partly dissenting judges considered that the interference in question fell within that margin,[210] although the majority found that the state had exceeded it.

Direct action

Direct action has been a tactic adopted by animal rights groups, environmentalists and anti-war protesters. It has been employed by anti-hunting groups, by groups opposed to the use of GM crops and protesters against the war in Iraq. A number of recent cases discussed in this chapter concern, not traditional assemblies or marches, but direct action. Under the HRA courts are required to consider the extent to which Convention rights should be abrogated *in a democratic society*, taking the values and hallmarks of such a society – 'pluralism, tolerance and diversity'[211] into account. Such an approach

---

206 See, e.g., *Brandenburg v Ohio* (1969) 395 US 444 in which it was found that an interference with public protest was acceptable only where incitement to unlawful action occurred. This may be compared with the decision on breach of the peace in *Nicol v DPP* (1996) 1 J Civ Lib 75 (discussed below, pp 773–74) in which such interference was permitted on the ground that it would not be unreasonable for others to react violently; no element of incitement was necessary.

207 See Chapter 2, pp 22–23.

208 E.g., in *Cossey v UK* A 184 (1990), para 3.6.5, Judge Martens, in his dissenting opinion, differed sharply from the majority in the Court in finding: '. . . I think that the Court should not have built its reasoning on the assumption that "this is an area in which the Contracting Parties enjoy a wide margin of appreciation" . . . In this context there simply is no room for a margin of appreciation.'

209 A 202-A (1991).

210 Judges Ryssdal and Pettiti, pp 26 and 28–30.

211 *Handyside v UK* (1976) 1 EHRR 737, para 49.

does *not* provide a charter for those bent on disrupting the lawful activities of others. It means that the expressive dimension of 'direct action' protest can be recognised and given due weight in legal assessment as a basic value enshrined in law. But it also requires proper analysis of the extent to which direct action, which aims to disrupt the lawful pursuits of others, can be permitted in a democracy governed by the rule of law. This is not the place to consider this debate at length, but it is certainly arguable that those who attempt directly to prevent such activities are in fact undermining both the democratic process (by attempting to marginalise its role in determining which pursuits are to remain lawful) and the rule of law (by attacking the basic liberty of the citizen to do that which the law does not forbid). Both of these are core values of the Convention. The clash of such values and the method of their resolution must now be made explicit in the legal discourse surrounding the limits of public protest: they must not be simply ignored or marginalised as at present in most domestic courts, or recognised in a purely tokenistic sense as in too many decisions at Strasbourg.

Where, as is frequently the case, various provisions discussed below[212] are used in respect of a conflict between two groups, such as hunters and hunt saboteurs, the argument might be raised in court that those provisions should be interpreted in such a way as to protect freedom of assembly in the sense of allowing persons to engage in group activities, such as hunting, shooting or fishing, free from interference by others.[213] The provisions might appear to allow the state to discharge a positive obligation to ensure that such groups are able to assemble. This argument finds some support from the ruling in *Chorherr v Austria*.[214] The expression of protesters appeared likely to offend some spectators, leading to an interference with their peaceful enjoyment of a parade. The interference of the state with the Art 10 rights of the protesters was justified since it had the aim of upholding freedom of assembly. This argument would place the law in the position of choosing between the Art 11 rights of opposing groups or between the Art 10 rights of one group and the Art 11 rights of another. This would be the case, of course, only if the activities of hunters, fishers and the like were able to take advantage of the Art 11 guarantee. As noted above, the Commission has found that Art 11 does not cover peaceful assembly for purely social purposes[215] and it is therefore probable that it does not cover the activities in question. However, this decision is not directly in point and, in any event, the domestic courts would not be bound by it.

The group activities in question might also, or alternatively, find protection under Art 8 since, depending on the circumstances, the activities of the protesters in coming onto private land in order to protest against activities taking place there could be viewed as interfering with the right to respect for private life, the home and the family.[216] The

---

212 In particular, the Criminal Justice and Public Order Act 1994, ss 68 and 69 and the Public Order Act 1986, ss 14A and 14C.
213 See *Plattform 'Ärtze fur das Leben' v Austria* A 139 (1988), para 32; 13 EHRR 204.
214 A 266-B (1993).
215 *Anderson v UK* Case No 33689/96, (1998) 25 EHRR CD 172. This application arose from *CIN Properties Ltd v Rawlins* [1995] 2 EGLR 130.
216 See, e.g., *Spencer (Earl) v UK* (1998) 25 EHRR CD 105. The applicants complained that English law provided no remedy for the invasion of their privacy through the publication in the press of various (truthful) stories relating to the bulimia and mental health problems of Countess Spencer, including photographs taken of her walking in the grounds of the clinic. The Commission dismissed the claim as manifestly ill-founded, not on the basis that the Convention did not require a remedy in such

interference with the Art 10 and 11 rights of protesters under the domestic provisions could then be justified on the basis that it allowed discharge of the state obligation under Art 8 to ensure that the exercise of the rights it guarantees is not threatened by the interference of private persons.[217] The court itself would have to ensure that it did not fail to protect the Art 11 or 8 rights of the hunters or shooters,[218] if it was prepared to countenance the argument that those rights were at stake. It would then have to perform a balancing act between the exercise of two conflicting rights with very little guidance from Strasbourg, because where such a conflict arises, Strasbourg allows a very wide margin of appreciation.[219]

Some groups advocating or perpetrating direct action fall within the current definition of 'terrorism', in s1 TA, discussed in Chapter 14. The definition potentially allows many protest-based activities, to be re-designated as terrorist. The definition now expressly covers threats of serious disruption or damage to, for example, computer installations or public utilities. The definition is therefore able to catch a number of forms of public protest. Danger to property, violence or a serious risk to safety that can be described as 'ideologically, politically, or religiously motivated' may arise in the context of many demonstrations and other forms of public protest, including some industrial disputes. The government stated in the Consultation paper preceding the TA, paper that it had 'no intention of suggesting that matters that can properly be dealt with under normal public order powers should in future be dealt with under counter-terrorist legislation'.[220] But once special arrest and detention powers are handed to the police, they can be used, at their discretion, if a particular person or group falls, or appears to fall, within the current TA definition. Some direct action against property by animal rights or environmental activists may well fall within it. As pointed out, some 'direct action' by such groups may be viewed as forms of expression and as having, to varying extents, the same role as political speech.[221] Some direct action, such as the destruction of genetically modified crops, may be intended both to disrupt and to draw attention to a cause. Direct action forms of protest going beyond persuasion may provide a substantive means of engaging in the more effective means of communicating with others (since such forms are most likely to attract media attention). To label forms of such action 'terrorist', as the current legislation does, is not only to devalue that term, but to take a stance towards forms of protest more characteristic of a totalitarian state than of a democracy. Chapter 14 returns to these points.

---

circumstances, but on the basis that such a remedy – breach of confidence – did exist in UK law, but had not been exhausted.

217 In *X and Y v Netherlands* (1985) 8 EHRR 235 the Court stated: 'these [Article 8] obligations may require the adoption of measures even in the sphere of relations between individuals.' In other words, the term 'interference by a public authority' used in Art 8 can mean 'unjustified failure to prevent interference by others'.

218 Since, as Chapter 4 points out, the court is itself a public authority under the HRA, s 6, and is itself bound to respect the Convention rights.

219 See *Otto-Preminger Institut v Austria* (1994) 19 EHRR 34. The conflict in the case between Arts 10 and 9 played a part in the concession of a very wide margin of appreciation to the state.

220 Ibid, para 3.18.

221 Such action is likely to be already tortious or criminal but, as Chapter 4 notes, defendants can raise Art 10 and 11 arguments in defence.

Positive obligations

The particularly thorny question of affording positive rights of access to land is likely to arise in the post-HRA case law. It is now established that the right of access to the highway may include holding an assembly on it.[222] But prima facie assemblies on other quasi-public or private land will virtually always be trespassory, unless in the circumstances it is found that permission to hold some peaceful protests was given. Strasbourg has not yet accepted that there is a positive obligation on the public authorities to require private individuals to allow the exercise of protest and assembly rights on their land. But an activist domestic court might be prepared to uphold such a claim, thereby anticipating the stance on this matter which some commentators view Strasbourg as not unlikely to adopt.[223]

When the issue of exclusion of persons from a quasi-public place, a shopping mall, was raised before the Commission, it declared the application inadmissible, on the basis that Art 11 was not applicable, since the applicants were gathering there for a purely social purpose.[224] Clearly, had Art 11 been engaged, a different outcome might have been achieved. However, *Appleby v UK*[225] does not afford encouragement to this proposition. The applicants were stopped from setting up a stand and distributing leaflets in a privately owned shopping centre. The Court found that in determining whether or not a positive obligation exists, regard must be had to the fair balance that has to be struck between the general interest of the community and the interests of the individual, the search for which is inherent throughout the Convention. The scope of this obligation will inevitably vary and it must not, the Court found, be interpreted in such a way as to impose an impossible or disproportionate burden on the authorities.[226] The Court said that while freedom of expression is an important right, it is not unlimited. Regard, it was found, must also be had to the property rights of the owner of the shopping centre under Art 1 of Protocol No 1. The Court found that Art 10 does not bestow any 'freedom of forum' for the exercise of that right. Where the bar on access to property has the effect of preventing any effective exercise of freedom of expression or it can be said that the essence of the right has been destroyed, the Court stated that it might be prepared to find that a positive obligation could arise for the state to protect the enjoyment of the Convention rights by regulating property rights.[227] But in this instance the restriction on the applicants' ability to communicate their views was limited only to certain areas. They were able to campaign in the old town centre and to employ other alternative means of making their protest. The Court therefore found no breach of Art 10 and stated that as the same issues arose under Art 11 it did not require separate consideration.

In the US, the courts are moving away to an extent from a position of upholding proprietorial rights and towards providing protection for expressive activity in quasi-

---

222 *DPP v Jones* [1999] 2 WLR 625.
223 Harris, J, O'Boyle, M and Warbrick, C, *Law of the European Convention on Human Rights*, 1995, p 419.
224 *Anderson v UK* [1998] EHRLR 218. As the Commission implied, the outcome would probably have been different had the UK ratified Protocol 4, Art 2, which guarantees freedom of movement.
225 6 May 2003; see for discussion J Morgan [2003] J Civ Lib 98–112.
226 Ibid para 40.
227 Ibid para 48.

public forums.[228] This can also be said of the Canadian and Australian courts.[229] In contrast, the traditional stance of the UK judiciary is to favour the property right when it conflicts with rights of protest. In general, they tend to uphold proprietorial rights in an abstract fashion, regardless of any real harm that may occur due to their infringement.[230] But Art 10 and 11 arguments might persuade them in future to consider the possibility of recognising broader access rights to quasi-public land. *DPP v Jones*[231] has already found that this can be the case as far as the highway is concerned, in respect of non-obstructive assemblies, but a large number of quasi-public places exist to which the public has limited rights of access, such as unenclosed shopping malls, parks, the grounds and forecourts of town halls or civic centres, monuments and their surrounding land or rights of way across private land.[232] At present, such rights of access would not include assemblies for the purpose of protests and demonstrations. In other words, it is clear from *DPP v Jones* that an assembly on the highway will not necessarily be unlawful. However, there is no right to trespass: orders affecting private land, or assemblies on the highway which are unlawful – because they are obstructive, or disorderly – based on the concept of trespass are valid and enforceable.

The issue of access to private land might arise in two ways. A group seeking access to a forum for the holding of an assembly or demonstration might seek to bring an action against the relevant land-owning body if it was a public authority under ss 6 and 7(1)(a) of the HRA, claiming that a refusal to allow an assembly in a particular place had constituted an interference with its Art 10 and 11 rights. For example, it might seek judicial review of the decision of a local authority refusing it access to a park in order to hold a meeting. Where a group was charged with infringing a ban on assemblies under ss 13 or 14A of the Public Order Act 1986 (discussed below), it could raise the issue under s 7(1)(b) of the HRA.

Procedural problems

A key factor affecting the reception of Arts 10 and 11 into UK law is, as indicated, the model favoured by the senior UK judiciary. But there are also procedural difficulties in bringing about statutory change. Relying on Arts 10 and 11, protesters are able to challenge public order provisions in criminal proceedings under s 6(1)(b) and s 7(1)(b) of the HRA, or they can seek judicial review of public order decisions made by police or local authorities under s 6(1)(a) and s 7(1)(a). However, as Chapter 4 explains, s 6 of the HRA provides that it is lawful for a public authority to act in a way which is incompatible with Convention rights if it is authorised to do so by primary legislation. If the legislation is thought to be incompatible, the court must nevertheless apply it; the higher courts can make a declaration of incompatibility which will have no impact on the instant decision but which will probably trigger off a legislative change by ministerial

---

228 See *Shad Alliance v Smith Haven Mall* 484 NYS 2d 849, esp p 857.
229 See *Harrison v Carswell* (1975) 62 DLR (3d) 68 Supreme Court of Canada; *Gerhardy v Brown* (1985) 159 CLR 70.
230 See on this point Gray and Gray, 'Civil rights, civil wrongs and quasi-public places' [1999] EHRLR 46.
231 [1999] 2 WLR 625; [1999] 2 All ER 257 HL
232 See further below, pp 719–20, 749–50.

amendment.[233] Public order questions are rarely adjudicated on in those courts which are able to make a declaration,[234] and some defendants would have little interest in appealing to a higher court in order to obtain the declaration since it would be of no personal benefit. However, members of some protest groups are likely to wish to appeal test cases to the higher courts in order to obtain changes in the law. But unless they do so as defendants in criminal proceedings, this will be possible under s 7(1)(a) HRA only if they themselves have been 'victims' or are likely to become victims in future, within the meaning of s 7(7) of the HRA.[235] Owing to the effect of s11 of the HRA they could, however, have raised Convention points in judicial review proceedings based on the old standing rules but for s 7(3) HRA.[236] This course would have been an attractive one since executive action under statutory powers which breaches Convention rights is unlawful unless the statute cannot be rendered compatible with the rights.[237]

Reform of common law powers under s 6, or the curbing of such powers is already occurring and can occur quite readily. As Sedley LJ said in *Redmond-Bate v DPP*,[238] before the HRA was fully in force, 'it is now accepted that the common law should seek compatibility with the values of the Convention'. This finding was reinforced, in a different context, in the post-HRA decisions in *Douglas and Others v Hello!*[239] and in the House of Lords in *Campbell*.[240] If incompatibility is found, it is arguable that the Convention guarantee should prevail, since no provision was included in the Act allowing the common law to override the Convention or creating restrictions as to those courts which can find incompatibility between the two. However, the stance taken by the judiciary on this issue is complex: they have avoided fully clarifying the matter at the level of principle.[241]

3 Legal regulation of meetings and marches: the statutory framework

The Public Order Act 1986, as amended by the CJPOA 1994, put in place a cumbersome statutory framework for the policing of marches and assemblies which was much more extensive than that put in place by the predecessor of the 1986 Act, the Public Order Act 1936. The scope of the 1986 Act was widened when the Anti-Social Behaviour Act 2003 was employed to reduce the number of persons who can constitute a 'public assembly', for the purpose of banning it or imposing conditions on it under the 1986 Act, from twenty to two. The scheme was also added to when ss 132–38 of the Serious

---

233 See Chapter 4, pp 204–6; the HRA, s 10(2), provides: 'If a Minister of the Crown considers that there are compelling reasons for proceeding under this section, he may by order make such amendments to the legislation as he considers necessary to remove the incompatibility.'
234 See s 4(4) and (5) of the Act which provide that no court lower than the High Court or Court of Appeal may make a declaration of incompatibility.
235 See Chapter 4, pp 235–36.
236 See Chapter 4, p 236.
237 See Chapter 4, pp 171–72.
238 (1999) *The Times*, 28 July; [1999] All ER (D) 864.
239 [2001] 2 WLR 992, CA.
240 See Chapter 4, pp 252–55.
241 See for further discussion Chapter 9, pp 911–15.

and Organised Crime Act 2005 were introduced, specifically applying to demonstrations in the vicinity of Parliament. The interaction between this statutory framework and the HRA forms the central focus of the following discussion.

Advance notice of public processions

Sections 12 and 13 of the Public Order Act 1986, which allow banning or limitation of a march, are underpinned by s 11, which provides that the organisers of a march (not a meeting) must give advance notice of it to the police in the relevant police area[242] six clear days before the date when it is intended to be held.[243] This national requirement was at the time an entirely new measure, although in some districts a notice requirement was already imposed under local regulations. It represents the first step to involving the police so that they have an opportunity to impose conditions. It should be remembered, of course, that organisers of a sizeable march would probably have to involve the police in any event, as they might need traffic to be held up while crossing busy roads. As the main purpose of s 11 is to allow conditions to be imposed on marches that might disrupt the community, but as those are the very marches that the police would tend to know of in any event, the need for a national provision of this nature is questionable.

However, the notice requirement does not apply under s 11(1) if it was not reasonably practicable to give any advance notice. This provision was intended to exempt spontaneous demonstrations from the notice requirement, but is defective because of the use of the word 'any'. Strictly interpreted, this word would suggest that a telephone call made five minutes before the march set off would fulfil the requirements, thereby exempting very few marches. In most circumstances, even though a march sets off suddenly, it might well be reasonably practicable to make such a telephone call. However, it can be argued that the word 'any' should not be interpreted so strictly as to exclude spontaneous processions where a few minutes was available to give notice, because to do so would defeat the intention behind including the provision. If read in combination with the requirements as to giving notice by hand or in writing, it should be interpreted to mean 'any written notice' under s 3 of the HRA. If it were not so interpreted, it might be argued that s 11 breaches the guarantees of freedom of assembly under Art 11 and of expression under Art 10, since it could criminalise the organiser of a peaceful spontaneous march. Punishing the organisers of such a march by way of criminal sanctions could be viewed as disproportionate to the legitimate aim pursued – to obviate the risk of disorder – since other measures, such as limiting the numbers of persons taking part in the march or a careful choice of route could achieve the same result. In any event, giving very short notice of a spontaneous march would not give the police enough time to impose conditions and therefore the aim in question could not, in fact, be attained by that means.

Advance notice must be given if the procession is held 'to demonstrate support or opposition to the views or actions of any person or body of persons, to publicise a cause or campaign or to mark or commemorate an event'. This provision was included

---

242 Section 11(4).
243 Section 11(5) and (6).

in order to exempt innocuous crocodiles of children from the requirement. Processions customarily held are expressly exempted.[244] The notice must specify the date, time and proposed route of the procession and give the name and address of the person proposing to organise it. Under s 11(7), the organisers may be guilty of an offence if the notice requirement has not been satisfied or if the march deviates from the date, time or route specified. If it does, an organiser may have a defence under s 11(8) or (9) that he or she either had no reason to suspect that it had occurred or that it arose due to circumstances outside his or her control.

Section 11 criminalises what may be trivial administrative errors and, although police officers will use a discretion in bringing prosecutions under it, this leaves the power open to abuse and means that potentially, at least, it could be more rigidly enforced against marchers espousing unpopular causes. At present, prosecutions under s 11 are very rarely being brought and therefore its deterrence value to organisers may be diminishing.[245] For example, the organisers of a large peace march, held on the date the UN Security Council ultimatum against Iraq[246] expired, failed to comply with the notice requirements under s 11 but no prosecution was brought. However, organisers of the 'veal calves' protest at Brightlingsea in April 1995 were threatened with prosecution under s 11. On the other hand, the fact that the notice requirement has not been fully adhered to may provide the police with a basis for taking very harsh measures against a protest when it is in being, or beforehand, and may predispose a judge, if a case comes to court, to take a stance that is very sympathetic to the police action, even though no prosecution for the breach of s 11 itself is brought.

In *Austin and Saxby v Commissioner of Police of the Metropolis*[247] it was found that the organisers of a large Mayday protest in London in 2001 had complied with the notice requirement under s 11, but had stated that the march would start at 4.00 whereas in fact it began at 2.00. The police stated in court that this was a deliberate move designed to impede the difficult policing operation. The march was ordered to cease and the protesters were trapped inside a police cordon in Oxford Square for seven hours. In effect, all the protesters – about 3,000 – were detained for seven hours. It was found that this detention was lawful in order to prevent a breach of the peace, and the judgment made some references to the deliberate decision of protesters to take part in an 'unlawful' assembly. The assumption appeared to be that it was unlawful partly because the notice requirement had not been fully complied with. However, the failure to comply with it could only give rise to liability on the part of the organisers, under s 11(7), not the participants. Also it is a notice requirement; it is not an application for *authorisation* of the march. So *Austin and Saxby* indicates that s 11 is of significance in terms of the control of the protest, although it is unlikely that a breach of s 11 itself would lead to a prosecution. So s 11 probably does have a significant impact on organisers and on policing, but indirectly. *Austin and Saxby* is discussed fully below.[248]

244 Section 11(2). Funeral processions are also covered by this exemption.
245 Waddington, *Liberty and Order*, 1994, pp 37–40.
246 Contained in SC resolution 678, 15 January.
247 [2005] HRLR. 20; 2005 WL 699571 (QBD), (2005) 155 NLJ 515, 2005) *The Times* 14 April, 699,571, [2005] EWHC 480; 23 March 2005, Queen's Bench Division of the High Court.
248 At pp 763–71.

The notice requirement in itself may have some inhibiting effect on organisers of marches, but except in that sense, it cannot readily be characterised 'an interference' with freedom of expression or assembly under the HRA since it is not a request for *permission* to hold the march. Once notice is correctly given, the march can take place, although conditions may be imposed on it, the matter considered in the next section. As indicated above, prior restraints on marches, including complete bans, have been upheld at Strasbourg, although the margin of appreciation doctrine was influential.[249] Owing to its relatively minimal impact on marches, which means that it is probably – depending on the circumstances of a particular case – proportionate to the aims pursued, the notice requirement, assuming that it exempts spontaneous marches, appears to be compatible with Arts 10 and 11. But if tendencies are evinced by the police to treat a march more restrictively when the notice given is defective, and judges then accept that those tendencies are lawful, the case for adopting a restrictive approach to s 11 and for emphasising that non-compliance does not render a march 'unlawful', becomes stronger. From a public order perspective it can clearly be said that a march which does not comply with the notice requirement may be more difficult to police since the organisers are non-cooperative or less cooperative. But the extent to which lack of cooperation regarding the notice legitimises very restrictive policing tactics still requires very strict scrutiny under s 6 HRA from the freedom of protest perspective.

Imposing conditions on meetings or marches

The s 12 power

Section 12 of the 1986 Act reproduces in part the power under s 3 of the Public Order Act 1936 allowing the Chief Officer of Police to impose conditions on a procession if he apprehended serious public disorder. However, the power to impose conditions under s 12 may be exercised in a much wider range of situations than the old power. It arises in one of four situations that may be known as 'triggers'. In making a determination as to the existence of one of these 'triggers', the senior police officer in question should 'have regard to the time or place at which and the circumstances in which, any public procession is being held or is intended to be held and to its route or proposed route'. Bearing these factors in mind, he or she must reasonably believe that 'serious public disorder, serious damage to property or serious disruption to the life of the community' may be caused by the procession (s 12(1)(a)).

The third phrase used is a very wide one which clearly offers police officers some scope for interpretation and may be said to render the other two 'triggers' redundant. This 'trigger' has attracted particular criticism from commentators. It has been said that 'some inconvenience is the inevitable consequence of a successful procession. 'The Act threatens to permit only those demonstrations that are so convenient that they become invisible.'[250] Bonner and Stone have warned of 'the dangers that lie in the vague line between serious disruption and a measure of inconvenience'.[251] Further, it has been

---

249 E.g., *Christians Against Racism and Fascism v UK* (1980) 21 DR 138.
250 Ewing and Gearty, *Freedom under Thatcher*, 1990, p 121.
251 'The Public Order Act 1986: steps in the wrong direction?' [1987] PL 202, p 226.

noted that the term 'the community' is ambiguous. In the case of London, it is unclear whether the term could be applied to Oxford Street or central London or the whole Metropolitan area.[252] The more narrowly the term is defined, the more readily a given march could be said to cause serious disruption. Serious obstruction of traffic might arguably amount to some disruption of the life of a small area which might be said to constitute a 'community'.

Imposition of conditions allows police officers to cut down the cost of the policing requirement for an assembly and therefore may encourage them to interpret 'the community' or 'disruption' in the manner most likely to bring the 'trigger' into being, since the conditions then imposed, such as requiring a limit on the numbers participating, might lead to a reduction in the number of officers who had to be present. However, in answer to some of these fears, it can be noted that in *Reid*[253] it was determined that the 'triggers' should be strictly interpreted: the words used should not be diluted. This third 'trigger' causes particular concern under Arts 10 and 11 since it does not readily equate to any of the legitimate aims under the second paragraph of those Articles. Probably, it could cover the prevention of disorder, as opposed to 'serious disorder' (the first 'trigger'); it would probably also also cover protecting 'the rights of others', an aim which has received a broad and imprecise interpretation at Strasbourg.[254] But in a suitable case the police and courts would have to consider whether either of those aims applied, bearing in mind the need for a stricter approach at the domestic level.

The fourth 'trigger', arising under s 12(1)(b), consists of an evaluation of the purpose of the assembly rather than an apprehension that a particular state of affairs may arise. The senior police officer must reasonably believe that the purpose of the assembly is 'the intimidation of others with a view to compelling them not to do an act they have a right to do or to do an act they have a right not to do'. This requires a police officer to make a political judgment as to the purpose of the group in question because it must be determined whether the purpose is coercive or merely persuasive. Asking police officers to make such a judgment clearly lays them open to claims of partiality in instances where they are perceived as out of sympathy with the aims of the group in question. It should be noted that the fourth 'trigger' requires a reasonable belief in the presence of two elements – intimidation and coercion. Therefore, a racist march through an Asian area would probably fall outside its terms since the element of coercion would probably be absent. It might, however, fall within the terms of the third 'trigger'. On the other hand, a march might be coercive without being intimidatory. In *Reid*, the defendants shouted and raised their arms; it was determined that such behaviour might cause discomfort, but not intimidation, and that the two concepts could not be equated. In *News Group Newspapers Ltd v SOGAT*[255] it was held that mere abuse and shouting did not amount to a threat of violence for the purposes of intimidation under s 7 of the Conspiracy and Protection of Property Act 1875. Thus, behaviour of a fairly threatening nature would have to be present in order to cross the boundary between discomfort and intimidation.

252 Ewing and Gearty, *Freedom under Thatcher*, 1990, p 121.
253 [1987] Crim LR 702.
254 See the discussion in *Steel v UK* (1999) 28 EHRR 603 relating to the first and second applicants.
255 [1986] ICR 716.

The conditions that can be imposed under s 12 if one of the above 'triggers' is thought to be present are very wide, in contrast to those that can be imposed on static assemblies: any condition may be imposed which appears necessary to the senior police officer in order to prevent the envisaged mischief occurring. The conditions imposed may include changes to the route of the procession or a prohibition on it entering a particular public place. If the march is already assembling, the conditions may be imposed by the senior police officer present at the scene who may be a constable; if the conditions are being considered some time before this point, the Chief Officer of Police must determine them.

The very wide discretion allowing a range of conditions to be imposed is now subject to the proportionality requirement of Arts 10 and 11, para 2. Such a requirement should now be read into the term 'necessary' under s 12 under s 3 of the HRA. The duty of the police under s 6 of the HRA means that they must seek to ensure that conditions are not imposed which go beyond the legitimate aim pursued. The interpretation of s 12 which is compatible with Arts 10 and 11 under the HRA is considered below. The post-HRA case law so far is meagre and the key case, *R (Brehony) v Chief Constable of Greater Manchester*,[256] does not suggest that the courts are eager to take a restrictive approach to the use of this power in reliance on Arts 10 and 11.

The s 14 power

Section 14 of the 1986 Act allows the police to impose conditions on assemblies.[257] It was introduced in the 1986 Act as an entirely new power. Conditions may be imposed only if one of four 'triggers' under s 14(1) – identical to those arising under s 12 – is present. However, once it is clear that one of the 'triggers' is present, the conditions that may be imposed are much more limited than those that may be imposed on marches. They are confined to such 'directions . . . as to the place at which the assembly may be (or continue to be) held, its maximum duration or the maximum number of persons who may constitute it' as appear to the senior police officer 'necessary to prevent the disorder, damage, disruption or intimidation'. It must be clear that the condition was communicated to the members of the march. In *Brickley and Kitson v Police*,[258] anti-apartheid demonstrators outside the South African embassy were asked to move away from the front of the embassy to a nearby street, Duncannon Street. The pickets in Duncannon Street increased and four of the demonstrators moved back in front of the embassy. The Chief Officer of Police feared that further disorder might be caused and imposed a condition under s 14 requiring the pickets to stay in Duncannon Street. This was conveyed to them over a megaphone. However, it was uncertain whether this information was actually communicated to the pickets and therefore their convictions in respect of failure to abide by the condition were quashed. The defences available if

---

256 [2005] EWHC 640.
257 Under s 16, as amended by the Anti-Social Behaviour Act 2003, an assembly consists of 2 or more people in a public place; a public place is defined as one which is wholly or partly open to the air. Section 16 defines a public procession as one in a place to which the public have access. No further guidance is given. Presumably the procession must be moving and will become an assembly if it stops and if it consists of 2 or more people, in which case different rules will apply.
258 *Legal Action*, July 1988, p 21 (Knightsbridge Crown Court).

there is a failure to comply with the conditions are identical to those under s 12, as is the power of arrest arising under s 14(7).

Liability under ss 12 and 14

A member of the march or assembly will incur liability under s 12(5) or 14(5) if he or she knowingly fails to comply with a condition. An organiser[259] will incur liability under ss 12(4) or 14(4) if he or she knowingly fails to comply with the conditions imposed, although he or she will have a defence if it can be shown that the failure arose from circumstances beyond his or her control. Thus, the *organiser* must actually breach the condition in question; he or she would not incur liability merely because some members of the march or assembly did so and therefore, where a march contains an unruly element which deliberately breaches conditions imposed, the persons involved will incur liability, but the organiser may escape it. An organiser may also incur liability if he or she incites another knowingly to breach a condition that has been imposed (ss 12(6) and 14(6)). According to the Court of Appeal in *Hendrickson and Tichner*,[260] incitement requires an element of persuasion or encouragement; moreover, following *Krause*,[261] the solicitation must actually come to the notice of the person intended to act on it. Therefore, merely assuming the position of leader of a march or assembly which is in breach of a condition would not seem to be sufficient of itself to amount to incitement. However, express or implied encouragement to bring about or continue a breach, such as leading the group in a certain forbidden direction, would amount to incitement if the leader was aware of the breach of the condition.

Imposing banning orders on marches

As indicated above, the 1986 Act for the first time gave the police the power to impose very wide ranging conditions[262] if they were thought necessary for the prevention of serious public disorder, serious damage to property or (the least grave trigger condition) 'serious disruption to the life of the community'.[263] This latter trigger attracted widespread criticism for its imprecision[264] and for decisively lowering the level and nature of risk that must be shown before conditions can be imposed. However, the 1986 Act did make some attempt to strike a balance between speech and public order

---

259 The 1986 Act does not define the term 'organiser' and there is no post-Act case law on the issue. It is submitted that on the dictionary definition of the term, stewards and others who have some role as marshals will be organisers. This contention is supported by the ruling from *Flockhart v Robinson* [1950] 2 KB 498 that a person who indicated the route to be followed should be designated an organiser as well as the person who planned the route. Thus, it appears probable that the term includes stewards as well as leaders of the assembly or march.

260 [1977] Crim LR 356.

261 (1902) 18 TLR 238.

262 Directions may be given as to the number of persons who may attend an assembly, its duration and location.

263 These conditions were considerably broader than the single one of anticipated 'serious public disorder' which alone could trigger the power to impose conditions upon processions under the Public Order Act 1936, s 3.

264 See, e.g., Bonner and Stone, op. cit., fn 1, p 226; Ewing and Gearty, op. cit., fn 1, p 121.

interests. It provided, as did its predecessor, for the possibility of an outright ban on public processions,[265] but only if the Chief Constable reasonably believed that his powers to impose conditions on processions under s 12 (based on the same 'trigger' conditions as for assemblies)[266] would be inadequate to prevent 'serious public disorder'.

Under s 13(1) of the 1986 Act, a ban must be imposed on a march if it is thought that it may result in serious public disorder. This power is exercised as follows. If, at any time, the Chief Officer of Police reasonably believes that, because of particular circumstances existing in any district or part of a district, the powers under s 12 will not be sufficient to prevent the holding of public processions in that district or part from resulting in serious public disorder, he shall apply to the council of the district for an order prohibiting for such period not exceeding three months as may be specified in the application the holding of all public processions (or of any class of public procession so specified) in the district or part concerned.

In response, the council may make the order as requested or modify it with the approval of the Secretary of State. It should be noted that once the Chief Officer of Police has come to the conclusion in question he or she must, not may, apply for a banning order. This power is exercised in respect of London by the Commissioner of Police for the City of London or the Commissioner of Police of the Metropolis. A member of the march or a person who organises it knowing of the ban will commit an offence under s 13(7) and (8) and can be arrested under s 13(10).

This reproduces the old power under s 3 of the Public Order Act 1936. Assuming that a power was needed to ban marches expected to be violent, this power was nevertheless open to criticism in that once a banning order had been imposed, it prevented all marches in the area it covered for its duration. Thus, a projected march likely to be of an entirely peaceful character could be caught by a ban aimed at a violent march. The Campaign for Nuclear Disarmament attempted to challenge such a ban after it had had to cancel a number of its marches (*Kent v Metropolitan Police Comr*),[267] but failed because of the finding that an order quashing the ban could be made only if there were no reasons for imposing it at all. The court found that the Commissioner had considered the relevant matters and, further, that CND had a remedy under s 9(3) (now s 13(5) of the 1986 Act) as they could apply to have the order relaxed.

It is arguable that the 1986 Act should have limited the banning power to the particular marches giving rise to fear of serious public disorder, but this possibility was rejected by the government on the ground that it could be subverted by organisers of marches who might attempt to march under another name. It would therefore, it was thought, have placed too great a burden on the police, who would have had to determine whether or not this had occurred. However, in making this decision, it is arguable that too great a weight was given to the possible administrative burden placed on the police and too little to the need to uphold freedom of assembly. A compromise solution – banning all marches putting forward a political message similar to that of the offending march – could have been adopted and this possibility is considered further below in relation to the effects of the HRA.

265 Section 13.
266 I.e., serious public disorder, serious damage to property or serious disruption to the life of the community.
267 (1981) *The Times*, 15 May.

This power was being used with increased frequency up to the mid-1980s: there were 11 banning orders in the period 1970–80 and 75 in the period 1981–84[268] (39 in 1981, 13 in 1982, nine in 1983 and 11 in 1984). Interestingly, however, as Waddington has noted, there have been few bans of marches in London since the passing of the 1986 Act.[269] The power may have been used sparingly because police officers preferred to police a march known about for some time as opposed to an assembly formed hastily in response to a ban or a hostile, unpredictable and disorganised march. As Waddington has argued, such considerations may account for the police refusal to ban the third anti-poll tax march to Trafalgar Square, although such a march had previously led to a riot, and in the face of fierce pressure to ban from Westminster City Council, local MPs and the Home Secretary.[270] However, the power to ban and to impose conditions gives the police bargaining power to use in negotiating with marchers and enables them to adopt a policy of strategic under-enforcement as part of the price of avoiding trouble when a march occurs. Moreover in some circumstances there may appear to be no alternative but to ban a march.[271]

It might seem that the s 13 banning power would be in breach of Arts 10 and 11, in that the banning of a march expected to be peaceful would not appear to be justified under para 2 of those Articles in respect of the need to prevent disorder. In *Christians Against Racism and Fascism v UK*,[272] however, the applicants' argument that a ban imposed under s 3(3) of the Public Order Act 1936 infringed *inter alia* Art 11 was rejected by the Commission as manifestly ill founded, on the ground that the ban was justified under the exceptions to Art 11 contained in para 2, since there was a real danger of disorder which it was thought could not be 'prevented by other less stringent measures'. However, this is a relatively elderly decision of the Commission alone that was strongly affected by the margin of appreciation doctrine. Therefore, the domestic judiciary would be free to scrutinise the extent of the risk and the proportionality of a particular ban, bearing in mind the possibility that a particular march affected by the ban was unlikely in itself to give rise to disorder. While a ban is allowable under the Convention, it is a prior restraint and therefore should be scrutinised with especial rigour.[273] The approach that might be taken is considered further below, in conjunction with the impact of the HRA on s 14A of the 1986 Act.

Imposing banning orders on assemblies

Prior to the Public Order Act 1986, there was no statutory power at all to place prior restraints, still less a ban, upon assemblies as opposed to marches. The police had therefore dealt with outbreaks of disorder at such assemblies using their powers to

---

268 White Paper, (1985) Cmnd 9510, para 4.7.
269 Waddington, op. cit., fn 1, pp 58–61.
270 Waddington, op. cit., fn 1.
271 E.g., in August 2001 a march of a far-right group against asylum-seekers, intended to go through Sunderland town centre to coincide with the gathering of football match supporters for an important match, was banned.
272 (1984) 24 YB ECHR 178.
273 Since the ban would affect freedom of expression, the jurisprudence under Art 10 on prior restraints could be considered. This point was stressed in *Wingrove v UK* (1997) 24 EHRR 1 by the Commission, in pointing out that scrutiny of such restraints should be especially strict.

arrest for breach of the peace and for specific common law[274] and statutory public order offences.[275] When s 13 of the 1986 Act was passed, no parallel power to ban assemblies was included, on the grounds, apparently, that the then Thatcher Government considered that it would represent too serious an inroad upon freedom of speech.[276]

Only eight years later, the power to ban assemblies was introduced in the CJPOA 1994 by inserting s 14A into the 1986 Act.[277] Although the power is only to ban assemblies taking place on private land, the widespread 'privatisation' of previously common land means that there is in fact little land on which demonstrations may take place without the landowner's consent which are non-trespassory.[278] The introduction of a banning power, deemed unnecessary and too draconian less than 10 years previously and not even requested by the police,[279] itself represented a decisive movement towards authoritarianism. However, the Act compounded this trend by basing the power to ban not, as in the case of processions, upon the most grave risk – a belief in otherwise uncontrollable serious public disorder – but the least and most ill defined: anticipation of 'serious disruption to the life of the community'. In this respect, it is a much wider power than that arising under s 13.

Section 14A provides that a Chief Officer of Police may apply for a banning order if he reasonably believes that an assembly is likely to be trespassory and may result in serious disruption to the life of the community or damage to certain types of buildings and structures. Section 14A(1) provides that a Chief Officer of Police may apply for a banning order[280] if he reasonably believes (a) that an assembly is likely to be trespassory and (b) may result in serious disruption to the life of the community or damage to certain types of buildings and structures, in particular, historical monuments. The requirement of trespass is made out where the Chief Constable believes that an assembly is intended to be held on land (a) to which the public has no right of access and is likely to be held without the permission of the occupier of the land or (b) on land to which the public has only a limited right of access and the assembly is likely to exceed the limits of any permission of the landowner or the public's right of access. If an order is made, it will subsist for four days, operate within a radius of five miles around the area in question, and prohibit any trespassory assembly held within its temporal and geographical scope.[281]

Just as s 13 catches peaceful processions, the provisions of s 14A mean that assemblies that are not likely *in themselves* to cause the prohibited harm under s 14A(1) or 14A(4) may nevertheless be banned once the ban is in place, triggered by trepassory assemblies expected to cause that harm. Section 14A is backed up by s 14C (inserted into the 1986 Act by s 71 of the 1994 Act). Section 14C provides a very broad power to stop persons within a radius of five miles from the assembly if a police officer reasonably

---

274 Namely the offences of riot, rout, unlawful assembly and affray.

275 E.g., Public Order Act 1936, s 5: using threatening, abusive or insulting words or behaviour likely to cause, or with intent to provoke a breach of the peace.

276 'Meetings and assemblies are a more important means of exercising freedom of speech than are marches.' *Review of Public Order Law*, Cmnd 9510, 1985, pp 31–32).

277 Under s 70.

278 See further below, pp 749–50.

279 See Marston, J and Tain, P, *Public Order Offences*, 1996, p 124.

280 Orders are granted by the local authority, with the approval of the Secretary of State.

281 Section 14A(5).

believes that they were on their way to it and that it is subject to a s 14A order. If the direction is not complied with and if the person to whom it has been given is aware of it, he or she may be arrested and may be subject to a fine if convicted. Thus, this power operates before any offence has been committed and hands the police a very wide discretion.[282]

Jones and Lloyd v DPP

This decision is considered in detail since it is the currently the leading decision on public protest and because it indicates, tellingly, that the assimilation of Art 10 and 11 values into domestic law will be especially problematic in the field of protest.

Section 14A was considered in *Jones and Lloyd v DPP*.[283] The case concerned an assembly on the route leading to Stonehenge, at a time when a s 14A order was in force. The order prohibited the holding of trespassory assemblies within a four-mile radius of Stonehenge and covered the period from 29 May to 1 June 1995. While the ban was still in force, a protest was held against it, in the form of an assembly on a road near Stonehenge, within the five-mile radius covered by the ban. It was found as a fact at trial that the assembly was non-obstructive, orderly and wholly peaceful.[284] Nevertheless, the protesters were asked by the police to move on; some did, but others refused and were arrested and charged with the offence under s 14A. The main question that arose was whether the assembly in question was subject to the s 14A order. This depended on s 14A(5) of the 1994 Act which provides that once an order is in being, it operates to prohibit any assembly which is held on land to which the public has no or only a limited right of access and which takes place without the permission of the owner of the land or exceeds the limits of the permission or of the public's right of access. In this instance, the assembly was simply present on the highway, but within the relevant four-mile radius. Section 14A(9) provides that 'limited' in relation to a right of access by the public to land means that their use of it is restricted to a particular purpose.

The key question was, therefore, whether the category of legitimate purposes for which the highway might be used included use of it by peaceful assemblies. Thus, the main issue that arose was whether the assembly was 'trespassory', so as to fall within the s 14A order. The question, therefore, was whether the category of legitimate purposes for which the public might lawfully use the highway included peaceful, non-obstructive assembly. The Divisional Court,[285] disagreeing with the Crown Court on the point, found that it did not.[286] The Divisional Court found that the highway was to be used for passing and repassing only and that assembling on it was outside the purpose for which the implied licence to use it was granted. In so finding, the court relied on *Hickman v Maisey*.[287] The decision concerned the defendant's use of the highway in

---

282 See further below, pp 719–20.
283 [1997] 2 All ER 119.
284 See p 15 of the Crown Court's judgment, cited at [1999] 2 WLR 625, p 627, *per* Lord Irvine.
285 For the Crown Court's reasoning on the point, see the speech of Lord Hutton ([1999] 2 WLR 625, p 657); the DPP appealed the point by way of case stated to the Divisional Court.
286 [1997] 2 All ER 119.
287 [1900] 1 QB 752, CA.

order to gain information by looking over the plaintiff's land. The defendant was on the highway watching the plaintiff's land. It was found that the plaintiff owned the sub-soil under the highway and that the defendant was entitled to make ordinary and reasonable use of it. Such watching was held not to be reasonable; the defendant had gone outside the accepted use and therefore had trespassed.

On behalf of the respondents it was argued that any assembly on the highway is lawful so long as it is peaceful and non-obstructive, since such an assembly is making a reasonable use of the highway. The Divisional Court, however, took the view that s 14A(5) operates to prohibit any assembly which exceeds the public's limited right of access. The right of access was found to be limited to the right to pass along the highway, not to hold a meeting or demonstration on it. Such activities might be tolerated, but there could be no legal right to engage in them. Section 14A(5) was found to operate to prevent assemblies which would otherwise be permitted. Thus, since the assembly had exceeded the limited rights of access to the highway, it fell within s 14A(5) and the fact that, but for the s 14A order, it would probably have been permitted, could not affect this argument. It was also argued on behalf of the respondents that unless there was a right to hold an assembly as opposed merely to a toleration, Art 11 of the European Convention on Human Rights would be breached. However, the court found that recourse to the Convention was unnecessary since the law in question was not ambiguous and, further, that since peaceful assemblies are normally permitted, the law was in any event in conformity with the Convention. The case was remitted to the Crown Court for a rehearing.

John Wadham of Liberty said of this decision: 'A peaceful non-obstructive gathering is a reasonable use of a public highway. To say that it is a form of trespass seems extraordinary.'[288] Nevertheless, this decision represented a reasonable interpretation of the very restrictive provisions of s 14A. No authority clearly suggests that there is a legal right to assemble on the highway since it is difficult to support an argument that assembling on the highway and remaining there for a substantial period of time is incidental to passage along it. Therefore, if the term 'right' within s 14A(1) means 'legal right', then any activity on the highway, other than passing along it, involving 20 or more people, is illegal if a s 14A order is in force. The limits of the rights to use the highway was the main question before the House of Lords when it considered the case.[289]

Despite the advent of the HRA (although it was not fully in force at the time), the Lords declined the opportunity to move beyond the traditional limited judicial perspective adopted in protest cases and to consider instead the political expression dimension of public protest. By a three to two majority, the Lords upheld the defendants' appeal. Since all those in the majority delivered substantial and quite different speeches, it is a matter of some difficulty to identify the ratio, but the key finding in common was that since *the particular assembly in question* had been found by the tribunal of fact to be a reasonable user of the highway, it was therefore not trespassory and so not caught by the s 14A order. The conduct of the protesters, according to the majority, thus had

---

288 (1997) *The Times*, 24 January.
289 *Jones and Lloyd v DPP* [1999] 2 WLR 625. The following discussion is drawn in part from Fenwick and Phillipson, 'Public protest, the Human Rights Act and judicial responses to political expression' (2000) PL 627–50.

the classic character of an English negative liberty: since it was not unlawful, it was permitted, and the police had 'no right' to remove the protesters. This was the basis of the judgment, not any finding that the protesters had a positive right to peaceful protest which the police were under a corresponding duty to respect.[290] The majority, therefore, apparently found a liberty to peaceful assembly on the highway. A liberty generally is precarious for two reasons: there is no duty upon the state (or anyone else) to respect it or facilitate its exercise, and the legislature (or the judiciary through the common law) may encroach upon it at any time. The liberty identified by their Lordships shares both these enervating characteristics; what is remarkable, however, is the exceptionally precarious footing upon which its status even as a currently lawful activity rests. Not one of their Lordships was prepared to find that assemblies on the highway which were both peaceful and non-obstructive were invariably lawful. Lord Irvine stipulated that in addition, they would also have to be 'reasonable' in the eyes of the tribunal of fact,[291] without defining what was meant by 'reasonable' in this context.[292] Lord Clyde agreed, explicitly limiting his finding to the statement that a peaceful, non-obstructive assembly on the highway 'does not necessarily constitute a trespassory assembly'.[293] Similarly, Lord Hutton said: '. . . I desire to emphasise that my opinion that this appeal should be allowed is based on the finding of the Crown Court that the assembly on this particular highway . . . at this particular time, constituted a reasonable use of the highway. I would not hold that a peaceful and non-obstructive public assembly on a highway is always a reasonable user and is therefore not a trespass.'[294]

Since, therefore, their Lordships explicitly contemplated that a peaceful (and non-obstructive) assembly could nevertheless be found to be unreasonable and therefore unlawful, it is in fact correct to say that they declared no liberty to hold such assemblies on the highway.[295] Rather, what the judgment upholds is a liberty to use the highway in a way which a trial court as the tribunal of fact finds to be reasonable, nothing more.[296] The lawfulness of such assemblies is thus placed in the hands of magistrates' courts.[297] The legal reasoning by which the majority reached their conclusion is no more reassuring. Clayton notes that Lord Clyde, with the minority, 'considered that

---

290 Lord Hutton did appear to assert this ([1999] 2 WLR 625, p 660), but his conclusion (p 666), upholds only the narrow and precarious liberty formulated by Lords Irvine and Clyde.

291 '[A] public highway [may be used] for any reasonable purpose provided the activity in question does not amount to a public or private nuisance and does not obstruct the highway by unreasonably impeding the primary right of the public to pass and re-pass: within these qualifications there is a public right of peaceful assembly on the highway': [1999] 2 WLR 625, pp 632–33.

292 [1999] 2 WLR 625, p 633. He added the words 'in the sense defined' after the word 'reasonable' (p 633B), but it is not clear what this refers to. It cannot mean 'reasonable' in the sense of 'not unreasonably impeding the right to pass and re-pass' since this would render otiose the separate stipulation that an assembly must be 'non-obstructive'; in any event, at an earlier point, his Lordship explicitly stated that the test of 'reasonable user' was additional to that of not impeding the public's right to pass and re-pass (ibid, pp 632H–633A).

293 Ibid, p 655.

294 Ibid, p 666 (emphasis added).

295 Still less did they uphold any right to assembly on the highway, as one commentator has erroneously declared: Foster (1999) 33(3) L Teach 329–36, p 330.

296 [1999] 2 WLR 625, p 667, *per* Lord Hutton.

297 The offence under s 14A is triable summarily, subject to the normal right of appeal to the Crown Court.

the law of trespass defined the issue',[298] but it is apparent that this was also the case for Lord Irvine. Neither of their Lordships thought that they were liberalising the law in order to facilitate public protests. Their reasoning proceeded on the basis of an orthodox approach to analysis of the common law; from this, Lord Irvine deduced and stated explicitly that he was merely declaring what the law was already and had been probably since *Harrison v Duke of Rutland*[299] and certainly since *Hickman v Maisey*[300] in 1900: namely, that reasonable users of the highway include not only activities strictly related to passing and re-passing, but also those which are customary and reasonable, such as taking a sketch, stopping to talk to a friend, carol singing, and so on. He strictly based his judgment on prior authority[301] and stated explicitly that he found it unnecessary to have regard to the Convention.[302] He made no mention of any common law right to peaceful assembly and, indeed, the only principle which went to his decision[303] was that the Divisional Court's judgment would have rendered many activities commonly carried on in the street unlawful, and 'the law should not make unlawful what is commonplace and well accepted'.[304] Lord Clyde's approach was to like effect.[305] While one commentator describes this approach as 'refreshing and positive',[306] it gives a higher place to the uncertain value of preserving accepted custom than to the supposedly fundamental human right declared in Art 11. Lord Clyde's approach differed only in that he expressly disclaimed any human rights dimension to the case at all, remarking: 'I am not persuaded that the . . . case has to be decided by reference to public rights of assembly.'[307] To both of their Lordships it appeared to make no difference whether a given group of people were meeting to engage in political protest or to look at an interesting shop window; neither indicated that a magistrates' court should take into account any expressive dimension of a given assembly of people in arriving at the determination of reasonableness.

It was, therefore, only Lord Hutton who based his findings at least partly upon the broad right at stake: 'the common law recognises that there is a right for members of the public to assemble together to express views on matters of public concern and I consider that the common law should now recognise that this right, which is one of the fundamental rights of citizens in a democracy, is unduly restricted unless it can be exercised in some circumstances on the public highway.'[308] However, it is apparent from

---

298 Clayton, G, 'Reclaiming public ground: the right to peaceful assembly' (2000) 63(2) MLR 252, p 257.
299 [1893] 1 QB 142.
300 [1900] 1 QB 752, CA.
301 'I conclude that the judgments of Lord Esher MR and Collins LJ are authority for the proposition that the public have the right to use the public highway for such reasonable and usual activities as are consistent with the general public's primary right to use the highway for purposes of passage and repassage': [1999] 2 WLR 625, p 631D.
302 Ibid, p 635.
303 His references to the Convention are expressly *obiter* only: ibid, p 635B.
304 Ibid, p 631.
305 Ibid, pp 654–55.
306 Clayton, G, 'Reclaiming public ground: the right to peaceful assembly' (2000) 63(2) MLR 252, p 254.
307 [1999] 2 WLR 625, p 654.
308 [1999] 2 WLR 625, p 660.

this conclusion that in his view, as in Lord Irvine's,[309] the demands of this 'right' are satisfied provided merely that an assembly on the highway is not invariably tortious. Moreover, this consideration was only one of his three reasons for his conclusion.[310]

Thus, Lord Irvine considered compatibility with Art 11[311] (strictly, *obiter*),[312] but recognised no equivalent common law right. Lord Hutton ignored the Convention, thought that there was a common law right to peaceful assembly, but gave it minimal recognition. Aside from a brief citation by Lord Hutton,[313] human rights jurisprudence on the matter from other jurisdictions played no part in the decision. By no stretch of the imagination, therefore, could human rights considerations be said to have played a leading role in the decision. Furthermore, there was no awareness of the background to the case – the unprecedented legislative attack upon the right to peaceful assembly of which s 14A was the culmination.[314] For two out of three of their Lordships, the issues raised were to be resolved by reference to the interpretation of nineteenth-century case law on real property.

This approach compares strikingly with that taken in the media freedom cases of *Simms*[315] and *Reynolds*,[316] decided within a few months of *Jones*. In those decisions, freedom of expression, both as a common law 'constitutional right' and as embodied in Art 10 of the Convention, was 'the starting point' of legal reasoning.[317] *Reynolds* included extensive citation and consideration of relevant Convention jurisprudence.[318] The values underpinning freedom of expression in general, and those particularly engaged by the instant case were identified; in *Simms* the demands of freedom of expression were treated as the touchstone by which the legality of subordinate legislation was to be assessed, and were found to demand a reading of it which ran clearly counter to its literal meaning.

It was common ground between all their Lordships that any users of the highway other than passage must not be incompatible with that primary use; they must therefore be peaceful and non-obstructive. The very narrow distinction which divided their Lordships was whether such other users had to be 'reasonable and usual'[319] (as the majority thought) or 'reasonable and associated with passage' (the view of the minority – Lords

---

309 '. . . in my judgment our law will not comply with the Convention unless its starting point is that assembly on the highway will not necessarily be unlawful': [1999] 2 WLR 625, pp 634H–635A.

310 The second was the need to harmonise the civil law of trespass with the criminal law on obstruction of the highway ([1999] 2 WLR 625, p 664); his third was that the authorities themselves indicated that extensions to the lawful uses of the highway might be necessary and desirable in response to changing circumstances ([1999] 2 WLR 625, pp 660 and 664–66).

311 Lord Clyde made a glancing reference to it, but only to the fact that Art 11 laid down 'express limitations' to the right it declared! ([1999] 2 WLR 625, p 654).

312 Above, fn 303.

313 He cited *The Queen in Right of Canada v Committee for the Commonwealth of Canada* (1991) 77 DLR (4th) 385, p 394) ([1999] 2 WLR 625, pp 661–62).

314 See above, pp 709–10.

315 [1999] 3 All ER 400.

316 [1999] 4 All ER 609. See Chapter 3, p 126.

317 See *Simms* [1999] 3 All ER 400, p 407, *per* Lord Steyn and p 412, *per* Lord Hoffmann (referring to 'fundamental rights' generally); *Reynolds* [1999] 4 All ER 609, p 629, *per* Lord Steyn.

318 (1999) 4 All ER 609, pp 621–22 (*per* Lord Nicholls), p 628 and esp p 635 (*per* Lord Steyn), p 643 (*per* Lord Cooke).

319 See, e.g., Lord Irvine: [1999] 2 WLR 625, p 631C.

Slynn and Hope). The case law was clearly capable of supporting both interpretations,[320] as the ability of the majority to base their judgment on prior authority indicates.[321] In any event, regardless of the interpretation adopted of the cases, no recognition was shown of the fact that those upon which the minority principally relied – *Hickman v Maisey*[322] and *Harrison v Duke of Rutland*[323] – were nineteenth-century authorities, not decided in the House of Lords. Nevertheless, these hundred year old findings from inferior courts were treated almost as if they were binding. Remarkably, in fact, their Lordships clearly preferred to rely on these dated authorities, even though, as the appellants pointed out, this involved rendering the civil law inconsistent with the criminal law of obstruction of the highway,[324] as interpreted in a more recent Court of Appeal decision.[325] The fact that their approach would logically have entailed the implied repeal of that authority[326] and a consequent considerable broadening in scope of the related criminal offence did not appear to be a matter of concern. So reluctant, indeed, were the minority to depart from the nineteenth-century view of the law that they formulated a series of extremely questionable arguments against adopting the majority's view of the case law. Lord Slynn clearly misstated the possible adverse impacts which would flow from it.[327] Lord Hope made the novel proposition that where Parliament

320 For the wider view see, e.g., *Hickman v Maisey* [1900] 1 QB 752, pp 757–58, *per* Collins LJ: 'in modern times a reasonable extension has been given to the use of the highway as such . . . the right of the public to pass and repass . . . is subject to all those reasonable extensions which may from time to time be recognised as necessary to its exercise in accordance with the enlarged notions of people in a country becoming more populous and highly civilised but they must be such as are not inconsistent with the maintenance of the paramount idea that the right of the public is that of passage'. For the narrower view see, e.g., *Harrison v Duke of Rutland* [1893] 1 QB 142, p 154, *per* Lopes LJ: 'If a person uses the soil of the highway for any purpose other than that [of passage and repassage] he is a trespasser'; and Kay LJ, p 158: 'the right of the public upon a highway is that of passing and repassing over land the soil of which may be owned by a private person . . . any other purpose is a trespass.'
321 See [1999] 2 WLR 625, p 665, *per* Lord Hutton. The leading text (Clerk and Lindsell, *The Law of Torts*, 17th edn, 1995, p 861) cited by Lord Slynn ([1999] 2 WLR 625, p 638) appeared to favour the majority view, although his Lordship did not take it so.
322 [1900] 1 QB 752.
323 [1893] 1 QB 142.
324 The Highways Act 1980, s 137(1), provides: 'If a person, without lawful authority or excuse, in any way wilfully obstructs the free passage along a highway he is guilty of an offence . . .'
325 *Hirst and Agu v Chief Constable of West Yorkshire* (1987) 85 Cr App R 143. See below, pp 734–35.
326 In *Hirst*, the crucial issue was whether peaceful protest on the highway constituted a reasonable user, thus amounting to a 'lawful excuse' for obstruction. Glidewell LJ pointed out that, logically, 'for there to be a lawful excuse . . . the activity in which the person causing the obstruction is engaged must itself be inherently lawful. If it is not, the question whether it is reasonable does not arise': (1987) 85 Cr App R 143, p 151. The court then went on to find that peaceful assembly was a reasonable user and thus constituted a lawful excuse. The minority in *Jones* simply dismissed the comparison ([1999] 2 WLR 625, pp 640 and 651). However, on the interpretation of the case law which they upheld, the activities in question in *Hirst* – protesters holding a banner and giving out leaflets – would clearly have been unlawful, as a trespass; therefore, on the logic of Glidewell LJ's argument, the decision in *Hirst* that such activities were reasonable and thus a lawful excuse would have been wrong.
327 Lord Slynn contended: 'the defendants' argument in effect involves giving to members of the public the right to wander over or to stay on land for such a period and in such numbers as they choose so long as they are peaceable, not obstructive, and not committing a nuisance': [1999] 2 WLR 625, p 639. This is clearly inaccurate: the judgment concerned the highway, not 'land' generally, and it is only reasonable and customary users that are to be allowed.

has legislated by reference to common law principles,[328] the effect of that reference is to forbid any subsequent judicial development of the common law in that area;[329] at another point, his Lordship resorted to virtual tautology, arguing that the proposed development of the law would be incompatible with the previous law.[330]

It is when the concrete, practical distinction between users which are 'reasonable and associated with passage' and 'reasonable and usual' is grasped that this dogged refusal to contemplate a modest development of the law from one formulation to another appears all the more remarkable. The narrower view apparently permits activities such as stopping to consult a map or tie a shoelace, since these are directly connected to the activity of travelling along a highway, but not activities such as carol singing, leafleting, assembly, all of which become acts of trespass. However, since *all* agreed that no use could be lawful which impeded the primary right of passage, even the majority view would not have allowed activities which caused any obstruction to passage or were otherwise unreasonable. It therefore entailed no actual *detriment* to the highway owner or anyone else. The minority were not then protecting a property owner from detrimental interference with his property. They invoked as the sole justification for the criminalisation of entirely peaceful protesters an entirely technical, abstract right: the entitlement of a highway owner to have the highway used only for activities which, as well as being peaceful, non-obstructive, customary and reasonable, were also 'associated with passage'.[331]

This tendency to rely upon artificial legal reasoning may also be seen in the lack of any appreciation of the fact that the normative context of the decisions relied upon differed markedly from that in *Jones*, a tendency present equally in the majority judgments. In both *Hickman*[332] and *Harrison*,[333] the plaintiffs owned the highway in question and had brought legal action to stop activities taking place on them which were actually detrimental to them. Moreover, neither defendant was engaging in peaceful protest. By contrast, the peaceful protest which took place in *Jones* was presumably a matter of complete indifference to the highway authority and amounted to a political expression. At no point were these significant differences adverted to.[334] Lord Hope

---

328 By relying on the notion of civil trespass, as s 14A does.

329 '... the intention of Parliament as disclosed by the language of that section was to rely upon the existing state of the law relating to trespass ... this ... makes the ... [a]symmetry [between civil and criminal law] inevitable.' ([1999] 2 WLR 625, p 651).

330 'I do not think that this broad argument can be reconciled with Lord Esher MR's statement of the law.' ([1999] 2 WLR 625, p 648).

331 The idea of a highway owner actually taking legal action to protect this right, by, for example, suing a group of carol singers for 'trespass' to the highway is evidently absurd; the authors are aware of no recorded case of a highway authority suing persons who have committed such a technical trespass: see Bailey, Harris and Jones, op. cit., fn 1, 4th edn, p 182.

332 [1900] 1 QB 752. The defendant, a racing tout, was using the highway to observe the plaintiff's race horses being trained.

333 [1893] 1 QB 142. The defendant was using the highway to disrupt grouse shooting on the plaintiff's land.

334 This tendency is a marked feature of English law on public order: Glidewell LJ in *Hirst and Agu* (1987) 85 Cr App R 143, a case concerning peaceful protest, applied *Nagy v Weston* [1965] 1 WLR 280, where the facts concerned a hot-dog stall and expressly compared the case with 'persons distributing advertising material ... outside stations'. See Bailey, Harris and Jones, op. cit., fn 1, p 167.

indeed made a point of 'stress[ing] that the purpose for which the appellants were seeking to remain where they had gathered is not material in this context'.[335] As noted above, the majority, particularly Lords Irvine and Clyde, found in favour of the defendants on the basis that their activity was *no more harmful* than other inoffensive activities customarily carried out on the highway, such as carol singing and queuing, which they were reluctant to stigmatise as unlawful. The contrast with leading cases on journalistic speech, such as *Reynolds*, discussed above, is particularly striking in this regard: in that case, the central point was to mark out discussion of important public affairs in the media, as deserving of special protection under common law and the European Convention because of its vital role in maintaining democratic society.[336]

Not only does this approach display a characteristically exaggerated attachment to the value of property rights,[337] it also exemplifies the tendency of English judicial reasoning to assume a narrow and technical basis, abstracted from any meaningful context. The property right at stake in *Jones* was treated, in Sunstein's phrase, as a 'purposeless abstraction',[338] unrelated to any human interests or values. As Professor Gray puts it, 'property' exists in the law as 'an abstract "bundle of rights" – an artificial construct – interposed between the possessor of land and the land itself . . .'[339] There was no recognition of the fact that, as the Supreme Court of New Jersey has put it: 'property rights serve human values. They are recognised to that end, and are limited by it,'[340] a proposition explicitly recognised also by the German Constitution.[341]

The explicit treatment of the human rights dimension by the minority was – like Lord Clyde's – one which sought its marginalisation. Both of their Lordships claimed that there was no need to advert to the Convention because there was no ambiguity in the common law[342] – this despite the fact that the House had split 3:2 on its interpretation. Both, nonetheless, made token references to it, although, as with the majority, there was no consideration of Strasbourg jurisprudence, despite the fact that a number of relevant cases were cited to their Lordships in argument – again, a sharp contrast with the approach of the House of Lords in the recent cases relating to media freedom, discussed in Chapter 3, above. Lord Slynn was plainly uninterested in the Convention: he claimed that his view of the law was not inconsistent with Arts 10 and 11 because both 'provide for exceptions to the rights created', but made no attempt even to specify those exceptions which might be relevant.[343] Lord Hope was clearly also disposed to ignore the Convention altogether,[344] preferring to take the relevant principles on

---

335 [1999] 2 WLR 625, p 650.

336 Albeit that the Lords did not find that 'political speech' should automatically attract privilege as a generic class.

337 See below, fn 338 and fn 349 and associated text.

338 The phrase is taken from Sunstein, who uses it to describe the approach of the US Supreme Court to the First Amendment: Sunstein, C, *Democracy and the Problem of Free Speech*, 1993, The Free Press.

339 Author of the leading text, *Elements of Land Law*, 1993.

340 *State v Shack* (1971) 277 A 2d 369, p 372.

341 Article 14(2) of the German *Grundgesetz* provides: 'Property imposes duties. Its use should also serve the welfare of the community.'

342 [1999] 2 WLR 625, p 640, *per* Lord Slynn and, p 651, *per* Lord Hope.

343 [1999] 2 WLR 625, p 640.

344 See the opening words of his speech: [1999] 2 WLR 625, p 641.

free speech from a case some 90 years old.[345] Their Lordships were content with the idea that while the right to demonstrate was 'of great importance' it could simply be exercised somewhere else. Klug, Starmer and Wier,[346] noting Forbes J's similar attitude in *Hubbard v Pitt*,[347] describe this as the 'working assumption of most judges when restricting the activity of protesters' and as 'simply wrong'. As Clayton puts it: 'There is not some other place where the public have a better right. If freedom of assembly cannot be exercised in the streets, it is in effect denied.'[348] Once again, their Lordships showed no awareness of the practical realities of human rights.

The one substantive Convention argument which Lord Hope did consider was, characteristically, related to the defence of property rights. His view was that any possible restrictions on Art 11 entailed by s 14A could be justified as necessary to protect the rights of property holders to peaceful enjoyment of their possessions under Protocol 1 of the Convention.[349] Indeed, he said that a construction of Art 11 which gave a right to peaceful assembly on the highway could 'deprive' owners of 'their right to the quiet enjoyment of their possessions contrary to Art 1 of the First Protocol'.[350] Since his Lordship expressly drew no distinction as to the position between publicly owned highways and private ones,[351] his view entailed the novel proposition of attributing to emanations of the state (highway authorities) 'rights' under the Convention.

The decision of the police in this case to arrest and seek the prosecution of an entirely peaceful protest group lends credence to the civil libertarian and leftist thesis that enormous discretion has been placed in the hands of the police which may be used to harass marginal groups.[352] The response of the House of Lords suggests very little preparedness to restrict that discretion and indicates how far judicial attitudes currently are from a real appreciation of the importance and practical realities of the right to peaceful protest. The decision of the House of Lords has attracted favourable reviews: Barendt considers that Lords Irvine and Hutton 'formulated a broad common law right of public assembly'.[353] Another commentator describes the decision as 'the endorsement of the right to peaceful assembly . . . an important vindication of a fundamental civil

---

345 *McAra v Magistrates of Edinburgh* 1913 SC 1059, p 1073: '. . . there is no such thing as a right in the public to hold meetings as such in the streets . . . the right of free speech is a perfectly separate thing from the question of the place where that right is to be exercised.'

346 *The Three Pillars of Liberty*, 1996, p 193.

347 [1976] QB 142: 'They are free at some other place and by legitimate means, to bring their dislike . . . before the public.'

348 'Reclaiming public ground: the right to peaceful assembly' [2000] MLR 252, p 257. Similarly, Sherr notes: 'Highways are the most probable places for outdoor protests to be held . . .', *Freedom of Protest, Public Order and the Law*, 1989, p 61.

349 'Every natural and legal person is entitled to the peaceful enjoyment of his possessions . . .' See Chapter 2, pp 104–5.

350 [1999] 2 WLR 625, p 652.

351 Ibid, pp 643 and 650–51, rejecting counsel's suggestion that statutory highway authorities should be treated differently from private owners.

352 For a general survey of repressive police tactics against leftist working class demonstrations, see Bowes, *The Police and Civil Liberties*, 1966, Lawrence and Wishart; Sherr, A, *Freedom of Protest, Public Order and the Law*, 1989, pp 30 *et seq.*; Ewing and Gearty, *Freedom under Thatcher*, 1990, Chapter 4.

353 Freedom of assembly', in Beatson and Cripps (eds), *Freedom of Expression and Freedom of Information*, 2000, OUP, p 3.

liberty'.[354] It is suggested, reluctantly, that such assessments are overly generous. It is contended that the concession granted by the majority was so limited and precarious, and the approach of their Lordships in general[355] so narrow and blind to the human rights values at stake, that the judgment as a whole cannot but leave a civil libertarian with a sense of strong unease, despite the fact that the outcome could have been so much worse. Gray and Gray have spoken of the manner in which, in other jurisdictions, 'the operation of the private law of trespass is inevitably and increasingly qualified by the paramountcy of human rights considerations'.[356] Such qualification was, it is suggested, barely present in the decision of the majority and stoutly resisted by the minority.

Impact of the HRA on ss 12–14A of the 1986 Act

Section 13 catches all marches once a ban is in place, not merely trespassory ones. Sections 12 and 14 can affect peaceful marches and assemblies which, in the judgment of a police officer, could disrupt the life of the community. The disruption could be caused by the size of the group or the particular circumstances applicable: it is not necessary for the group to be disorderly. The decision in *Jones* makes it clear that peaceful non-obstructive assemblies are not inevitably non-trespassory and therefore they can fall foul of s 14A, if a ban is already in place. Thus, those assemblies recognised at Strasbourg as most worthy of protection can attract liability under the statutory framework created by the 1986 Act. It would appear that this position is incompatible with Arts 10 and 11. There is not much post-HRA case law on this statutory framework but, as will be argued below, the stance taken by the courts so far has been far from activist. It does not suggest that the HRA will have much impact on it. This section will consider whether there are any grounds for nevertheless expecting a radical change in approach under the HRA.

Human Rights Act mechanisms

In criminal proceedings brought in reliance on these provisions, defendants can rely on s 7(1)(b) of the HRA, using the argument that in the circumstances, the interference with the freedoms of expression and assembly was disproportionate to the aims pursued. Since ss 12 and 14 confer a *discretion* on the police, it could be argued that the imposition of the particular conditions in question was disproportionate to the aims pursued – aims which would have to fall within Arts 10 or 11 para 2. In other words, it could be argued that although the statutory language was compatible with those Articles, the police had not applied the power in question compatibly, thereby failing in their duty under s 6 HRA. Alternatively, argument could be raised that the current interpretation of the relevant section creates incompatibility; it could then be argued that ss 12 and 14, due to their broad wording, should be read or given effect in a way which rendered them compatible with the Convention rights (for example, by adopting a strict interpretation of the meaning of the third 'trigger' or by reading s 14 as allowing only the imposition of conditions of a narrow ambit).

---

354 Clayton, G, 'Reclaiming public ground: the right to peaceful assembly' (2000) 63(2) MLR 252.
355 The approach of the Divisional Court was in line with that taken by the minority; thus, of the seven judges who adjudicated upon this case in the two courts, a majority found against the applicants.
356 'Civil rights, civil wrongs and quasi-public places' [1999] EHRLR 46, p 100.

Decisions under these provisions can also be challenged in judicial review proceedings. Prior to the inception of the HRA, the scope for challenging the conditions was very limited: there was no method of appealing from them and it was only possible to have them reviewed for procedural errors or unreasonableness in the High Court. The power to impose any condition thought necessary under s 12 is so subjective that until Arts 10 and 11 were given further effect in domestic law under the HRA, the courts had little scope for assessing the human rights-compatibility of the decision made.[357] The condition had to relate to the mischief it was designed to avert but that still left the police with a very broad discretion. In dealing with police action to maintain public order, the courts have been very unwilling to find police decisions to have been unlawful.[358] Applying the rule from *Kent v Metropolitan Police Comr*[359] one could infer pre-HRA that a challenge to a condition would almost certainly fail. It would only have been where a challenge mounted where an officer had evinced a belief in the existence of a 'trigger' which no reasonable officer could entertain, that it could succeed due to the need to show a reasonable belief in relation to the 'triggers'. No presumption in favour of freedom of assembly was imported.

A very 'light touch' review is now no longer appropriate under the HRA, since the courts have to consider proportionality. The extent to which this can have any real impact in practice will depend on the approach adopted, as indicated above, and on the willingness of judges to examine the evidence available to the police at the time as to the likelihood that, for example, a particular group would be likely to cause disruption or disorder. The findings of the House of Lords in *Jones* strongly suggest that the traditionally blinkered and deferential judicial approach to public protest prevails, although *Laporte* may signal a change of stance. Therefore challenges to ss 12–14A present the judiciary with an opportunity to step away from that approach in construing existing law so that it complies with the Convention, 'in so far as it is possible' under s 3 of the HRA, or in relation to the application of the law in any particular instance under s6. The demands of proportionality are the key issue. There are at least two entry points in ss 12 and 14 enabling Art 10 or 11 considerations to be taken into account. 'Serious disruption to the life of the community' is a very wide phrase and clearly offers wide scope for interpretation. It could be argued that since the determination as to the meaning of the phrase allows for conditions to be imposed on protesters, a strict interpretation of it is required since otherwise interference with protests could occur too readily, thereby failing to satisfy the demands of proportionality under para 2 of the two Articles. Such demands could also be taken into account in relation to the degree of interference represented by the conditions imposed. If lesser measures were available which would still achieve the end in view, it can be argued that they should have been imposed.

In an instance such as *Jones*, or in respect of ss 12–14, the courts' approach has changed, at least in methodology. Rather than focusing primarily upon the limitations upon otherwise lawful conduct that these sections create, the Convention rights in issue must be taken into account. The court is bound to find that a protest which

---

357 See, e.g., *Secretary of State for Education and Science v Tameside* [1977] AC 1014.
358 See, e.g., *Secretary of State for the Home Department ex p Northumbria Police Authority* [1989] QB 26; [1988] 2 WLR 590; [1988] 1 All ER 556, CA.
359 (1981) *The Times*, 15 May.

is wholly peaceful falls within Art 11 and, following *Steel*, it may also find Art 10 applicable.[360] Prima facie interference with the right(s) would clearly have occurred, including the arrests of the defendants and any convictions sustained.[361] Having made this determination, the court then has to consider the exceptions within para 2 of those Articles. It is bound under s 3 of the HRA to find an interpretation of ss 12–14A which is compatible with the Convention if at all possible, but the question of what is required in order to achieve compatibility is open to interpretation, depending on the view of the Strasbourg jurisprudence adopted. Under s 6 a court must ensure that the application of the provisions complies with Arts 10 and 11.

However, although the methodology has changed, under the HRA, the courts have as yet made little attempt to curb ss 12 and 14 as they impact upon protesters. In *R (Brehony) v Chief Constable of Greater Manchester*[362] a very light touch approach was taken to the demands of proportionality in the circumstances. A regular demonstration had occurred outside a Marks and Spencers, protesting about the firm's support for the government of Israel; a counter-demonstration had also occurred, supporting the government. The Chief Constable had issued a notice under s 14 requiring the demonstration to move to a different location due to the disruption it would be likely to cause to shoppers over the Christmas period when the number of shoppers was likely to treble in number. The demonstrators sought judicial review of this decision; the judge refused the application on the basis that, in Art 10 and 11 terms, the restraint was proportionate to the aim, of maintaining public order, pursued. This decision confirms that 'serious disruption to the life of the community' can mean mere anticipated inconvenience to shoppers. The decision indicates that ss 12 and 14 provide the police with extremely wide scope for interfering in demonstrations and marches, depite the inception of the HRA.

The conditions that can be imposed if one of the above 'triggers' is thought to be present are very wide in the case of processions: prima facie, any condition may be imposed which appears necessary to the senior police officer in order to prevent the mischief envisaged occurring. Obviously, they are not completely unlimited; if the condition imposed bears no relationship to the mischief it was intended to avert, it may be open to challenge. Feldman argues 'Conditions which are so demanding that they amount in effect to a ban are an improper use of the power and so are unlawful on ordinary public law principles.'[363] In *Austin and Saxby v Commissioner of Police of the Metropolis*[364] it was found that both ss 12 and 14 allow for the imposition of extremely broad and restrictive conditions. It was found that s 12 gives a power to bring a procession that is in progress to an end. The section refers to 'the circumstances in which any public procession is being held . . .' and specifically states that directions may be 'as to the route of the procession or prohibiting it from entering any public

---

360 See above, text to fn 112.
361 Where an arrest and police detention took place but no charges were laid, or no conviction sustained, there would still be a prima facie violation of Arts 10 and 11, following *Steel* (1999) 28 EHRR 603: violations were found in relation to the third, fourth and fifth applicants who were arrested and detained but not tried (the prosecution adduced no evidence).
362 [2005] EWHC 640.
363 Feldman, D, *Civil Liberties and Human Rights in England and Wales*, 2nd edn, 2002, at p 1063.
364 [2005] HRLR 20; 2005 WL 699571 (QBD); (2005) 155 NLJ 515;(2005) *The Times* 14 April 2005, 699, 571; [2005] EWHC 480.

place specified in the directions'. So, it was found, if a procession is intended to go to a certain destination, a direction prohibiting that falls within s 12(1). The judge did find in that instance that a condition imposed could not amount to a ban, but could be imposed – even if amounting to a ban on the continuance of the march – where the march had already taken place to an extent. It was found that if the conditions do no more than is necessary and proportionate in the circumstances of the case to achieve the statutory public order objectives, then bringing the procession to an end will not be unlawful. That point clearly raises the question of strict scrutiny of the police action in order to be certain that bringing the march to an end was proportionate, or whether a *post facto* justification is being put forward.[365] Section 12 also, it was found, includes a power to detain persons who are part of a protest if that is necessary in order to achieve the objectives of preventing disorder or disruption of the life of the community. This is discussed below under s 14; *a fortiori* it must be possible under s 12 if it was found to be possible under s 14 since a much broader range of conditions can be imposed under s 12 than under s 14.

It was further found in *Austin and Saxby* that the police do not need to have either ss 12 or 14 in mind when imposing conditions. So if police give directions to protesters to limit or disperse the protest, thinking that they are doing so under other powers, the conditions can be retrospectively justified by reference to ss 12 or 14 even if the police did not advert specifically to the trigger conditions under ss 12 and 14 at the time. It was also confirmed in that decision that a protest could have conditions applied to it, including far-reaching ones even where the protest itself was not the source of the disruption. In other words, if counter-protesters were causing a disruption the police would be justified in imposing conditions on the original protest, not the counter-protest. This is technically correct; the wording of ss 12(1)(a) and 14(1)(a) does not refer to any need for the protest in question to be the *source* of the disruption, disorder etc. However, it is contrary to the principle enunciated in *Beatty v Gillbanks*[366] to the effect that the responsibility for causing disruption should be placed on those who are disruptive, not on those who are peaceful but whose protest has provoked a disorderly counter-protest a principle that was also enunciated in *Redmond-Bate*[367] by Sedley LJ. It is also, it is argued, contrary to the pronouncements in *Ezelin*[368] on Art 11 of the Convention.

The conditions which may be imposed under s 14 are, on their face, much more limited in scope. In *DPP v Jones*[369] conditions as to the movement of the assembly had been imposed; and were found to be *ultra vires* on the basis that they could only have been imposed under s 12; they could not be imposed under s 14 since the demonstration in question was clearly a static assembly, not a march. The decision in *Austin and Saxby v Commissioner of Police of the Metropolis*[370] concerned a protest

---

365 See the discussion of this case below in which it is suggested that since the police did not have s 12 in mind at the time of the march it is arguable that they were seeking to find justifications for their very controversial actions after the event.

366 (1882) 15 Cox CC 138.

367 See pp 778–79 below.

368 See pp 688–89 above.

369 [2002] EWHC 110.

370 [2005] HRLR 20; 2005 WL 699571 (QBD); (2005) 155 NLJ 515; *The Times* 14 April 2005, 699, 571; [2005] EWHC 480.

against globalisation in 2001, discussed in full below, which the police controlled by trapping all the protesters behind a police cordon in Oxford Square, London for seven hours. The decision gave an interpretation to the conditions that can be imposed under s 14 that gave them a much broader scope than their face value wording warrants.

It was found that s 14 gives a power to detain people for a very substantial period of time to prevent them leaving an assembly, even when they specifically ask to do so. The judge noted that, on its face, the section is aimed at limiting the numbers who may attend, or continue to attend, but that the purpose of the power is to prevent public disorder, damage, disruption and intimidation. He considered that if the only direction apt to achieve those ends in the particular circumstances is a controlled dispersal, which in turn involves a period of preliminary detention, then s 14 would allow for that condition also. In coming to this conclusion he relied on *DPP v Meaden*.[371] In that instance, in finding that the search warrant in that case carried with it a power to detain the occupants of the premises, the judge found: 'The authority [to search premises and person], to be meaningful, had . . . to enable the search to be effective. It could not be effective . . . if the occupiers were permitted to move about freely within the premises while the search was going on.' Relying on this observation, the judge found that there may be a greater implied power to detain when the police act pursuant to ss 12 and 14 of the 1986 Act than there would be if they acted pursuant to their common law powers. The judge concluded that a direction under s 14 that some or all members of an assembly disperse, can include a direction that they disperse by a specified route, and that they stay in a specified place for as long as is necessary for the dispersal to be effected, consistently with the objective of preventing disorder, damage, disruption or intimidation, and of taking reasonable care for the safety of themselves and others. This was, it is argued, a very doubtful extension of the law. Had Parliament wished to allow for the imposition of a broad range of conditions in s 14, as in s 12, the two sections could have been framed in the same terms. It was also found, somewhat less controversially, that a direction under s 14 may bring an existing assembly to an end. The judge said that this would be allowable since the section refers to 'the circumstances in which any public assembly is being held . . .' and authorises a direction imposing the 'maximum duration'.

European Convention on Human Rights jurisprudence

A much more radical approach could be taken to ss 12 and 14. It is suggested that there are, in fact, two contrasting lines of authority in ECHR jurisprudence relevant to these issues. In *Steel v UK*,[372] the Court found that the interference with an entirely peaceful protest which had occurred was disproportionate to the aim of preventing disorder, and in *Ezelin v France*[373] the Court made a significant statement of basic principle:[374]

---

371   [2003] EWHC 3005 (Admin); [2004] 1 WLR 945.
372   (1999) 28 EHRR 603. The applicants had been holding a banner and giving out leaflets outside an arms exhibition.
373   A 202 (1991).
374   Note that within the Convention system, there is no difference in weight between '*obiter* comments' and those which, in common law terms, form part of the 'ratio' of the case: see Harris, O'Boyle and Warbrick, op. cit., fn 1, pp 18–19.

'The Court considers ... that the freedom to take part in a peaceful assembly ... is of such importance that it cannot be restricted in any way ... so long as the person concerned *does not himself* commit any reprehensible act on such an occasion.'[375] On its face,[376] this finding would prohibit the application of criminal sanctions to peaceful protesters[377] as a result of the use of blanket bans, a possibility which, as noted above, is left open by *Jones*. This possibility is also supported to an extent by the jurisprudence of the Court on prior restraint outside the context of public protest.[378] It would also prohibit the imposition of conditions which can, depending on the circumstances, have an effect on an assembly almost as severe as that created by a ban. As indicated above, conditions can be imposed on peaceful assemblies where it is thought that a risk of disruption to the life of the community may arise.

On the other hand, there is a consistent line of case law from the Commission which indicates that bans – therefore, *a fortiori* the imposition of conditions – on assemblies and marches are in principle compatible with Art 11 even where they criminalise wholly peaceful protests[379] or prevent what would have been peaceful demonstrations from taking place at all.[380] The cases, particularly *Pendragon* and *Chappell*, also exhibit an unwillingness to examine the proportionality of bans to the threatened risks with any rigour.

It is therefore open to a court inclined to a minimalist response to the HRA to follow the Commission case law on the basis that it is more directly applicable to ss 12–14A, since it deals directly with prior restraints, unlike *Steel* and *Ezelin*. On such an approach the imposition of conditions under ss 12 or 14, or of bans under s 13, can be substantively unaffected by the HRA since the police assessment of the need to impose the condition or seek the ban can be deferred to. This approach also leave *Jones* substantially untouched, although it probably requires the court to engage in an inquiry not relevant to *Jones*,[381] namely to satisfy itself that there was some risk of disorder or property damage to justify the making of the original s 14A order. However, provided some evidence to this effect was produced, such a court could take the view that its sufficiency to justify the ban was a matter within the 'area of discretion' of police decision making. Such courts could thus continue to find such assemblies lawful or unlawful, depending on the view of the trial court as to their 'reasonableness' in the circumstances.

---

375 A 202 (1991), para 53.
376 The Crown might argue that it is inapplicable beyond its particular facts: it concerned professional disciplinary sanctions applied to a lawyer who took part in a march that became violent and disorderly, but who conducted himself peacefully.
377 It might be argued that a distinction should be drawn between protesters who take part in a peaceful demonstration which they know to be banned, arguably thereby committing a 'reprehensible act', and those who obey the ban by abandoning their proposed demonstrations, but bring proceedings to test its legality.
378 See Chapter 7, pp 620–21.
379 *Pendragon v UK* Appl No 31416/96 (1998); *Chappell v UK* Appl No 12587/86 (1987) (both discussed above, p 444).
380 *Christians Against Racism and Fascism v UK* (1980) 21 DR 138 is a particularly clear example. See also *Rassemblement Jurassien v Switzerland* Appl No 8191/78 (1980) 17 DR 93; *Rai, Allmond and 'Negotiate Now v UK'* 81-A D & R 146 (1995).
381 The point of law certified for consideration by the Lords in *Jones* related to whether the particular assembly fell within the s 14A order; they were not asked to consider the adequacy of the grounds for granting of the original order.

Under this approach these provisions probably do not require reinterpretation under s 3 HRA; they can be viewed as compatible with Arts 10 and 11 of the Convention since they allow only for limited intervention. Sections 12 and 14 only allow for intervention necessary to avert the risk in question; they do not provide for the ban of the assembly. Section 13 bans are only available to avert the risk of serious disorder. The prohibitory powers provided under s 14A apply only in a limited area, for a limited period. Orders under s 14A can only be made if the police, the local authority (outside London) and the Secretary of State are all satisfied that the order is necessary. Only those organising or knowingly taking part in a prohibited assembly commit an offence. The powers under s 14C can only be exercised within the area covered by the order. The orders are aimed at preventing crime or disorder or the protection of the rights of landowners and others (the right, for example, to free passage) in accordance with Arts 10(2) and 11(2). The limited interference with Convention rights can therefore be seen as prescribed by law in order to serve legitimate aims. The prohibitory orders available can be viewed as both necessary in a democratic society and proportionate to the aims pursued following *Pendragon v UK*[382] in which the Commission found an order under s 14A POA 1986 compatible with Convention, even though the assembly in question was peaceful. The interference with Art 11 rights was viewed as justified and the application was declared inadmissible. At present *DPP v Jones* and *Brehony* indicate that this is the approach that the courts are continuing take to these orders. *R (on the application of Gillan) v Commissioner of Metropolitan Police*[383] also encourages a pessimistic view: the House of Lords found that, assuming that Art 10 was applicable in an instance in which a protester had been stopped and searched – arguably an interference that had occurred in order to impede him in joining the protest,[384] the exception for the prevention of crime under para 2 was satisfied, without engaging in any proportionality analysis.

A more radical approach?

A court inclined to take a more rigorous approach to its duties under the HRA than was taken in *Brehony* could go into the matter a little more deeply. In relation to ss 13 or 14A, it could start by noting that the *effect* of a blanket ban under either of those provisions is that those organising or taking part in demonstrations caught by it can be subject to criminal penalties and hence to an interference with their Art 10 and 11 rights even though they themselves were behaving wholly peacefully. This is apparently contrary to the statement of principle set out in *Ezelin*, above, since the arrest and conviction of such demonstrators cannot be seen to be directly serving one of the legitimate aims of preventing public disorder or ensuring public safety. Prima facie it is therefore arguable that such bans always constitute breaches of Arts 10 and 11, when they catch entirely peaceful protesters, since the 'legitimate aim' test is

---

382 (1999) EHRLR 223.
383 [2006] UKHL 12. See also Chapter 11, pp 1119–21, 1131–36.
384 It is arguable that Arts 10 and 11 were not engaged: in *McBride v UK* (Case 27786/95) the applicant was arrested, detained but released without charge to prevent a breach of the peace. She was bound for an arms fair about 15 minutes away from an anti-arms demonstration that she had attended when she was arrested. The application was deemed inadmissible.

unsatisfied. At the least it may be argued that since such bans are so repugnant to the Convention in principle, the burden should be on the authorities to show that a ban was, genuinely, the only way of dealing with the threatened disorder. The court could attribute the Commission's failure to take this approach in the Strasbourg cases to the effects of the margin of appreciation.[385] It could also note the fact that the cases on blanket bans are merely admissibility decisions of the Commission, which clearly have a lower status in the Convention case law than decisions of the Court[386] especially where, prima facie, they run counter to its decisions. Thus, s 3 HRA could be used to limit and structure the tests allowing for the use of these curbs on protests.

There are therefore, strong grounds of principle to justify a departure from *DPP v Jones*,[387] on the basis that it affords too precarious a level of protection to a fundamental right in allowing peaceful, non-obstructive protests to be interfered with, not after satisfying the rigorous standard suggested above, but merely because a magistrates' court has found the assembly to be 'unreasonable'. The question is then, how far a court might wish to go in establishing a new approach to s 14A. The civil trespass finding could be modified: a court could find that if an assembly is peaceful and non-obstructive, it must *always* be termed reasonable, therefore non-trespassory, and so outside the terms of any s 14A order in force. A court could go further, and find that even obstructive assemblies are not necessarily trespassory: as noted above, the criminal law on obstruction of the highway provides for peaceful protest to constitute a lawful excuse to such conduct.

A further, more contentious possibility, might arise where a group was charged with infringing a ban imposed under s 14A POA in respect of land owned by a public authority. A possible recourse (apart from a challenge to the ban itself, discussed above), since prima facie the assembly would appear to be trespassory, would be to argue that in the circumstances it had a constructive licence to enter the land on the basis of the demands of the guarantees under Arts 10 and 11. A failure to accept such an argument could lead, potentially, to a serious interference with those guarantees.[388] A successful claim of such access rights would mean reinterpreting s 14A(5) in order to find that rights of access to certain areas, going beyond the highway, exist for the purpose of holding peaceful assemblies. If such a claim was upheld, it would also preclude the imposition of tortious liability.

However, such an approach would still leave untouched the more fundamental objection to s 14A, that it allows for the criminalisation of purely peaceful protests

---

385 In one case, the Commission argued that such bans were justified since they were 'based on considerations designed to ensure an even application of the law in that it aims at the exclusion of any possibility for the taking of arbitrary measures against a particular demonstration' (*Christians against Racism and Fascism v UK* (1980) 21 DR 138, p 150).

386 See Harris, O'Boyle and Warbrick, op. cit., fn 1, p 18: 'If the Court interprets the Convention differently from the Commission, the Court's view prevails,' as, they note, the Commission has accepted.

387 The break with precedent could be justified on the basis that the new interpretative approach under s 3 rendered the decision non-binding; the opinion of Lord Irvine on the decision's compatibility with the Convention was *obiter* only and made without the benefit of full argument on the point.

388 The members of the assembly would be convicted of various offences arising under s 14B, however peaceful or non-obstructive the assembly was. Its organiser could be imprisoned (s 14B(5)), as could anyone who could be proved to have incited a member of the assembly to come onto the land (s 14B(7)).

through prior restraint, on the basis only of a risk of 'serious disruption to the life of the community' and civil trespass. There are two aspects to this objection: the first is to blanket bans *per se*; the second is to the use of 'serious disruption to the life of the community'[389] as the test for their imposition. A court which formed the view that blanket bans *per se* were essentially incompatible with Arts 10 and 11 could enforce this view through a radical reinterpretation of s 14A under s 3(1) of the HRA. It would entail reading into s 14A(5)[390] the requirement that a given assembly, as well as being trespassory and within the geographical and temporal scope of a subsisting s 14A order, also must itself pose a threat of disorder, or otherwise satisfy one of the exceptions to Art 11. Since such an interpretation would mean that s 14A effectively ceased to bestow a power to impose blanket bans, and as only doubtfully necessary under the Convention, it is very unlikely to be adopted.

Under s 14A, if a suitable post-HRA arises, which has not yet occurred, attention may therefore focus upon scrutiny of the risk of 'serious disruption to the life of the community'. This method could also be used to bring ss 12 and 14 into line with the Convention. Courts might be required to determine that the nature of the risk anticipated is one which would constitute one of the legitimate aims for limiting the primary rights under Arts 11 and 10. It has been pointed out that this vague and ambiguous phrase,[391] 'would appear to subsume, and indeed go beyond, the criteria for restricting public protest laid down in Art 11(2)'[392] of the Convention. Given the terms of these criteria, the grounds for the ban would have to be justified, either on the basis of protecting 'the rights of others' (discussed above),[393] or because the 'serious disruption' feared amounted to 'disorder' for the purposes of Art 11(2). But if it was feared merely that serious traffic congestion might occur, which could be seen as disrupting the 'life of the community', by making it more difficult for activities such as shopping and commuting from work to carry on, this would not appear to amount to 'disorder' under para 2.

Under a more subtle approach, consideration could be given to the question of the compatibility with general Convention principles of the concept of 'community' used in s 14A. As Fitzpatrick and Taylor comment, the use of the term:

> begs the question of how the 'community' in question is actually constituted . . . [under] the Act . . . the community . . . is defined implicitly by a notionally uniform way of life of those who inhabit the . . . area in question . . . one result of the Act is that certain groups become socially and politically authorised to undertake practices of exclusion on the basis that it is they who represent 'the community'.[394]

---

389   Such a claim could be raised collaterally as a defence to criminal proceedings (*Boddington v British Transport Police* [1998] 2 WLR 639, and see HRA 1998, s 7(1)(b)). Those aggrieved by the making of a s 14A order could also challenge it directly by relying on HRA 1998, s 7(1)(a).

390   Above, p 711.

391   The alternative ground is reasonable anticipation of 'significant' damage to historical, etc, buildings (s 14A(1)(b)(ii)).

392   Fitzpatrick, P and Taylor, N, 'Trespassers might be prosecuted: the European Convention and restrictions on the right to assemble' [1998] EHRLR 292, p 297.

393   See pp 687–88.

394   Fitzpatrick and Taylor, ibid, p 298.

Under ss 12, 14, 14A those engaging in protest – which could be seen as an 'intrinsically communal' activity – 'are constructed by [it] as being inherently in opposition to the exercise of the day-to-day rights of members of the community within which the assembly takes place'.[395]

There is a compelling argument to the effect that this aspect of the 1986 Act is in opposition to one of the most basic values underlying the Convention, insisted upon by the Court in a number of freedom of expression judgments, although not in the context of public protest: that the key characteristics of that 'democratic society', the values of which are the touchstone by which the legality of restrictions on individual rights must be determined, are 'pluralism, tolerance and broadmindedness'.[396] An activist approach to the HRA would lead a court to recognise the concrete relevance and applicability of such constitutive values underlying the Convention, rather than the 1986 Act's 'monolithic'[397] conception of the community: the Court would thus view its duty under s 6 of the HRA as including a duty to respect and uphold pluralism and diversity within communities, and in determining whether the life of a given community will be 'seriously disrupted' by a given protest, to ascribe to that community the qualities of tolerance and broadmindedness towards the values and activities of others. Such an attitude would raise decisively the value of peaceful protest and place quite a heavy burden upon those arguing that serious disruption to the community justified prior restraint of such assemblies.

Section 13 is not open to amelioration in order to achieve compatibility with Arts 10 and 11, by way of reinterpretation of the meaning of trespass, since it provides a power to ban all marches for a period, not merely trespassory ones. However, a court confronted with the kind of situation that arose in *Christians Against Racism and Fascism*[398] under the HRA could take a hard look at the question of proportionality. The court could take the view that the geographical or temporal scope of the ban had been greater than was needed to obviate the risk of serious disorder. Or it could find that the ban need not have been imposed at all since the imposition of conditions under s 12 would have been sufficient. More controversially, it could find that the banning order applied for could have excluded the peaceful march caught by the ban. It could do this in one of two ways. Either it could be found that the duty of the Chief Officer of Police under s 6 of the HRA required him to exclude the march from the ban, where it was reasonable to expect him to know that it was imminent. It could be argued that a power to seek an order to ban all marches could be interpreted as a power to ban all marches espousing a particular message, using s 3 of the HRA creatively as the House of Lords did in *R v A*[399] and *Ghaidan v Mendoza*.[400] Alternatively, the words 'or any class of public procession' used in s 13(1) could be utilised to afford leeway to include

---

395   Fitzpatrick and Taylor, ibid They further point out that protests, such as that at Newbury, attracted both support and opposition from the local communities: 'thus . . . the intra-community factions could be simultaneously causing each other "serious disruption".' See also Gray and Gray, 'Civil rights, civil wrongs and quasi-public places' [1999] EHRLR 46, p 51.
396   *Handyside v UK* (1976) 1 EHRR 737, para 49.
397   Fitzpatrick and Taylor, ibid.
398   See above, p 709.
399   See Chapter 4, pp 174–75.
400   See Chapter 4, pp 180–83 respectively.

potentially disruptive marches (using 'disruptiveness' as the method of defining their membership of the class) and therefore to exclude marches expected to be entirely peaceful. As indicated above, this interpretation does not reflect Parliament's intention in passing s 13. However, s 3 HRA allows Parliament's intention to be disregarded, since it imposes a later requirement of achieving compatibility with the Convention rights.

Conclusions

It is predicted that the courts will continue to take a non-activist line in relation to this statutory framework; the HRA will continue to have little impact on it, except in terms of judicial methodology. Remarks from Lord Bingham in *Laporte*, which is discussed below, suggest that when the judges confront statutory provisions that have a relatively limited impact on Convention rights, either because they regulate the enjoyment of the right rather than removing it, or because they may only be invoked in relatively narrow circumstances, they are happy to assume that the task of satisfying the demands of proportionality has already been undertaken satisfactorily by Parliament. However, it has been argued above that in fact these provisions provide powers that are over-broad and that it should not be assumed that those demands have already been met. These suggestions indicate the impact that the HRA could have on the legal framework within which marches and assemblies operate. They indicate opposing lines of thought within the Convention jurisprudence, but also demonstrate that the *Ezelin* and *Steel* line is more in tune with the Convention stance on prior restraint generally. Clearly, the stance of the House of Lords in *Jones* gives little cause for expecting a rigorous approach to the Convention jurisprudence or an understanding of Convention values. However, as Chapter 4 indicated, and as *Laporte* confirmed, there are signs that recent decisions taken under the HRA, rather than in the period immediately before it came fully into force, show a much greater understanding and appreciation of those values.[401]

The far-reaching nature of the prohibitory orders under discussion argues strongly for establishing further protection for freedom of assembly under the HRA, by re-interpretation of a number of the provisions under s 3. Or, and this is the more probable course, a more rigorous examination of the application of the provisions could be undertaken, under s 6. To say this is not to argue that the scheme is completely out of harmony with Arts 10 and 11. The scheme is to an extent pursuing legitimate aims—the protection of the rights of others and prevention of disorder and crime—under those Articles, but in so far as certain of its provisions allow for interference with peaceful assemblies, it appears, as indicated, that in certain respects it goes further than is necessary in a democratic society. Ironically, the very fact that the scheme employs imprecise phrases such as 'serious disruption of the life of the community', possibly in an attempt to afford maximum discretion to the police, works against it in favour of freedom of protest, since it provides entry points for Arts 10 and 11 that render the task of re-interpretation under s 3 HRA, or rigorous scrutiny under s 6, relatively straightforward.

Demonstrations in the vicinity of Parliament

The Serious and Organised Crime Act 2005 ss 132–38 provides controversial new powers which were introduced partly as a response to the presence near Parliament

---

401 See, in particular, pp 278–90.

of a peace protester, Brian Haw, against the war in Iraq; he set up a peace protest site outside Parliament in 2001 which he maintained until it was largely dismantled under the new powers in 2005. The new provisions restrict the right to demonstrate within an exclusion zone of up to one kilometre from any point in Parliament Square. Demonstrators have to apply to the Commissioner of the Metropolitan Police for an authorisation for the protest six days in advance, or if this is not reasonably practicable, then no less than 24 hours in advance (s 133). No equivalent provision is made for any other Parliament in the UK. Under s 132(1) any person who

(a) organises a demonstration in a public place in the designated area, or
(b) takes part in a demonstration in a public place in the designated area, or
(c) carries on a demonstration by himself in a public place in the designated area,
   is guilty of an offence if, when the demonstration starts, authorisation for the demonstration has not been given under section 134(2).

It is a defence under s 132(2) for a person accused to show that he reasonably believed that authorisation had been given. Under s 133 the person seeking the authorisation must give written notice to that effect to the Commissioner of Police of the Metropolis. Under s 132(4) the notice must state: the date, time and duration of the demonstration; the place where it is to be carried on; whether it is to be carried on by a person by himself or not. Section 132(1) does not apply if the demonstration is a public procession for which notice must given under s 11(1) of the POA, or for which (under s 11(2)) notice is not required to be given. Section 134 allows for the imposition of an extensive range of conditions on the demonstration. Under s 134 the Commissioner may impose conditions that are:

in the Commissioner's reasonable opinion . . . necessary for the purpose of preventing any of the following:

(a) hindrance to any person wishing to enter or leave the Palace of Westminster,
(b) hindrance to the proper operation of Parliament,
(c) serious public disorder,
(d) serious damage to property,
(e) disruption to the life of the community,
(f) a security risk in any part of the designated area,
(g) risk to the safety of members of the public (including any taking part in the demonstration).

The conditions that can be imposed are not exhaustively enumerated. Under s 132(4):

The conditions may, in particular, impose requirements as to:

(a) the place where the demonstration may, or may not, be carried on,
(b) the times at which it may be carried on,
(c) the period during which it may be carried on,
(d) the number of persons who may take part in it,
(e) the number and size of banners or placards used, (f) maximum permissible noise levels.

The area itself that is covered is defined by Statutory Instrument[402] rather than by the Act. It specifically excludes Trafalgar Square, traditionally a site of protest, on the northern boundary of the area. Apart from Parliament, it also includes Whitehall, Downing Street, Westminster Abbey, the Middlesex Guildhall, New Scotland Yard, and the Home Office. It also covers a sliver of land on the other bank of the River Thames, including County Hall, the Jubilee Gardens, St Thomas' Hospital and the London Eye.

These provisions were invoked against Brian Haw and he challenged the decision to use them by way of judicial review (*R (Haw) v Secretary of State for the Home Dept*).[403] It was argued on his behalf that the provisions could not be applied retrospectively; and that as his demonstration had begun before the provisions came into force, he was not caught by them. The Court of Appeal found, however, in construing the Act that it was clearly Parliament's intention that such demonstrations should be deemed to have started on the date that they came in to force. The Court found that the statutory purpose of ss 132–38 was to regulate all demonstrations in the vicinity of Parliament and no rational basis had been suggested as to why Parliament should have intended entirely to exclude demonstrations which had begun before the commencement date of the relevant provisions. The Court concluded that the Parliamentary intention was clear. It was to regulate all demonstrations within the designated area, whenever they began. The Court considered that s 132(1) had clearly been intended to include demonstrations actually starting before the commencement of the Act. Those starting before commencement, like the claimant's, were therefore, it was found, deemed to start at commencement. In such instances, the Court held, the words 'when the demonstration starts' referred to the time of commencement.[404]

---

402 The Serious Organised Crime and Police Act 2005 (Designated Area) Order 2005 (SI 2005 No 1537), which came into force on 1 July 2005.

403 [2006] EWCA Civ 352.

404 Brian Haw was arrested and his site dismantled under these powers but he was eventually granted permission to maintain a greatly reduced site. His whole site is now part of an exhibition entitled 'State Britain' at Tate Britain, on the very edge of the zone delineated by the SOCA powers. On 30 June 2006 Westminster City Council granted Brian Haw the right to use his megaphone at certain times. All use of megaphones (with particular exemptions) is banned but the Council can grant permission. Brian initially sought permission in September 2005; the Council refused. A High Court judge quashed the refusal after Westminster lawyers conceded that the decision could not stand and that a legal challenge should be allowed, and agreed to pay Brian Haw's legal costs. It was also agreed that a differently-constituted licensing sub-committee should consider his application again in 21 days. The Committee agreed to Brian's limited use of the megaphone subject to noise level tests and various other criteria. He can use it for half an hour in the morning, half an hour in the early evening, and for a short while as Tony Blair drives past to face prime minister's question time. This Early Day Motion 2146 in support of Brian Haw may be noted: 25 May 2006: *That this House notes the verdict of Monday 9th May in the case of Brian Haw, peace protestor in Parliament Square for over four and a half years, which overturned the original High Court ruling allowing him to continue his peace vigil; notes with concern that Mr Haw may now be forced to end his protest should the Police Commissioner fail to grant him permission to remain; further notes that Mr Haw's silent protest causes no hindrance to the proper operation of Parliament, nor does it create a public disorder; further notes that this House owes Mr Haw a debt of gratitude for his long-term active engagement in democracy; believes that Mr Haw should be allowed to remain in Parliament Square; and calls upon the Government to nurture engagement by the public with politicians and to support the democratic right of all to protest where they can be seen by hon. Members.*

It is debatable whether this decision is in accord with Art 7 ECHR.[405] It is also possible that if a suitable case arises the provisions could be narrowed down or applied narrowly in reliance on ss 3 and 6 HRA and Arts 10 and 11. No defence of 'reasonableness' is provided – or any other equivalent defence – and therefore Art 10 and 11 considerations must employ the statutory language and the application of the statute in particular instances as their entry points. If a suitable case arises in which an authorisation is sought, a court will be able to consider first, whether the statutory language should be narrowed down by reference to s 3 HRA and second, whether, under s 6 HRA, the choice of conditions in question was proportionate to the aims pursued. These questions were discussed above in relation to the conditions that can be imposed on demonstrations under ss 12 and 14 of the 1986 Act. Proportionality considerations could also be applied to the evaluation of the triggers undergone by the Commissioner before imposing conditions. The 'trigger situations' are wider than those available under ss 12 and 14 of the 1986 Act, but one of them must be established, and can be subject to a strict scrutiny, before conditions can be imposed. The 'triggers' appear to go well beyond the 'legitimate aims' enumerated in Arts 10 and 11 para 2. However, Strasbourg generally finds very readily that one or more of the aims has been satisfied;[406] so argument is much more likely to centre on the question of proportionality. The trigger relating to 'hindrance' to persons entering Parliament is particularly broad since any large demonstration would be likely to cause some hindrance. On its face, it is hard to see that the use of this trigger complies with proportionality requirements under Arts 10 and 11 para 2, and is therefore a clear candidate for narrowing down under s 3 HRA. The restrictions as to noise and size of demonstrations clearly have the potential to destroy their impact almost completely. The robust approach taken to the right to freedom of assembly in *Laporte*[407] by the House of Lords, discussed below, indicates that if a suitable case arises, the courts may be prepared to use ss 3 or 6 HRA to limit the application of these broad provisions.

4 Criminalisation of trespass and obstruction of the highway

In order to assemble or demonstrate, protesters require access to land. But in order to create an impact, persons normally assemble in large groups. If they are on the highway, they are very likely to cause some obstruction to free passage and therefore may fall foul of the offence of obstructing the highway. Further, the tendency for public spaces to be privatised has been reinforced by the direction of UK law. Not only are there virtually no positive rights of access to forums for the holding of meetings,[408] but under the provisions discussed below, a 'creeping criminalisation of trespass'[409]

---

405 See Chapter 2, pp 66–67.

406 See Chapter 2, p 68.

407 [2006] UKHL 55. See also pp 757–62, below.

408 See the Representation of the People Act 1983, ss 95 and 96 (providing a right for Parliamentary candidates to hold meetings at election times) and the Education (No 2) Act 1986, s 43 (providing that university and college authorities must secure freedom of speech for persons, including visiting speakers, within their establishments).

409 See Wasik and Taylor, *The Criminal Justice and Public Order Act 1994*, 1995, Blackstone, p 81.

has occurred, denying protesters access to private or quasi-public land on pain of the risk of arrest and conviction, not merely of incurring tortious liability. There are now a number of circumstances in which a person who merely walks onto land may incur criminal liability. A central issue, therefore, is the impact of the HRA on the creation of such liability, and on the offence of obstructing the highway when used against assemblies.

Obstructing the highway

The pre-HRA interpretation

Section 137 of the Highways Act 1980 provides that a person will be guilty of an offence if he 'without lawful authority or excuse in any way wilfully obstructs the free passage of the highway'. The only right in using the highway is to pass and re-pass along it – to make an ordinary reasonable use of it as a highway. Since obstruction of the highway is a criminal offence, it might therefore appear that all assemblies on the highway are prima facie unlawful since they are bound to cause some impediment to those passing by and therefore they can only take place if the police refrain from prosecuting. However, the courts seem to take the stance that not every such assembly will be unlawful; the main issue will be what was reasonable in the circumstances.

In *Arrowsmith v Jenkins*[410] it was determined that minor obstruction of traffic can lead to liability under the 1980 Act. A pacifist meeting was held in a certain street which linked up two main roads. The meeting blocked the street and the organiser co-operated with the police in unblocking it. It was completely blocked for five minutes and partly blocked for 15 minutes. The police had advance notice of the meeting and the organiser was under the impression that the proceedings were lawful, especially since other meetings had been held there on a number of occasions without attracting prosecutions. Nevertheless, the organiser was convicted. This use of the Highways Act is open to criticism; it places such meetings in a very precarious position since it seems to hand a power to the police to license them, thereby seriously undermining freedom of assembly. However, in *Nagy v Weston*[411] it was held that a reasonable user of the highway will constitute a lawful excuse and that in order to determine its reasonableness or otherwise, the length of the obstruction must be considered, its purpose, the place where it occurred and whether an actual or potential obstruction took place.

The purpose of the obstruction, mentioned in *Nagy*, was given greater prominence in the significant decision in *Hirst and Agu v Chief Constable of West Yorkshire*:[412] it was said that courts should have regard to the freedom to demonstrate. This was found in relation to the behaviour of a group of animal rights supporters who had conducted a demonstration in a busy street. The crucial issue was whether peaceful protest on the highway constituted a reasonable user, thus amounting to a 'lawful excuse' for obstruction. Glidewell LJ pointed out that, logically: 'for there to be a lawful excuse . . . the activity in which the person causing the obstruction is engaged must itself be

---

410 [1963] 2 QB 561; [1963] 2 All ER 210; for comment, see [1987] PL 495.
411 [1966] 2 QB 561; [1965] 1 WLR 280.
412 (1987) 85 Cr App R 143.

inherently lawful. If it is not, the question whether it is reasonable does not arise.'[413] The Court then went on to find that peaceful assembly was a reasonable user and thus constituted a lawful excuse.

However, doubt was cast on the notion that there is a right to demonstrate on the highway by the decision in *Birch v DPP*.[414] The defendant was arrested under s 137 for lying down in the road in front of a vehicle destined for the premises of a chemical wastage plant, SARP UK. The defendant alleged that the company was engaging in unsafe and illegal practices, putting residents in the area at risk.[415] Both this vehicle and other (public) vehicles were obstructed. On appeal against his conviction he argued that the activity of lying down in the road was a reasonable one, that gave rise to a defence of 'lawful authority or excuse' under the Highways Act 1980. He relied on this defence as used in the cases of *Hirst and Agu v Chief Constable of West Yorkshire* and *Nagy v Weston*. His second argument was that the activity was undertaken in order to prevent crime, in accordance with s 3 of the Criminal Law Act 1967. Therefore, he argued, the magistrate should have allowed him to lead evidence about the alleged unlawful activities of SARP before he could dismiss this defence. The first ground of defence was dismissed by distinguishing *Hirst and Agu* on the basis that the question which arose in that instance was whether the lawful activity of handing out leaflets was a reasonable activity providing lawful excuse. In the present case, deliberately lying down in the road so as to obstruct the highway and traffic flowing along it was not, it was found, a lawful activity; the appellant's actions gave rise to trespass, public nuisance and private nuisance, so they were not within any category of lawful excuse, aside from the question of prevention of crime. The prevention of crime argument failed on a number of grounds. It was found that the test of whether something is a 'crime' is an objective not a subjective test: it is not a matter of 'belief' but of proving that an action actually is criminal. The crime being prevented must be an imminent breach of the peace or other serious offence. There has to be an actual (or imminent) crime on or near the highway itself: you cannot obstruct a vehicle that could merely be contributing to crime elsewhere. The activity would have to actually prevent (or be capable of preventing) the crime, not merely draw attention to it. The decision in *Birch* clearly makes it very hard to defend any action as part of a protest or demonstration that is clearly deliberately obstructive in terms of the 'lawful authority or excuse' part of the defence.

The impact of the HRA

Following the interpretation accorded to s 137 in *Hirst and Agu*, the purpose of an assembly as a means of legitimate protest may suggest that it can amount to a reasonable user of the highway. If an assembly is a reasonable user then it is a lawful use of the highway. It may be noted that this finding is consonant with the finding of two of the Law Lords in *DPP v Jones* in the context of s 14A of the 1986 Act to the effect that there is a right of peaceful assembly on the highway providing right of passage is not

---

413   Ibid, p 151.
414   [2000] Crim LR 301.
415   On May 30 1988 SARP leaked a cloud of nitric-dioxide gas over the village of Killamarsh in north Derbyshire and surrounding areas.

obstructed. This finding was not conclusive of the issue, however, as the third Law Lord in the majority did not endorse it. *Hirst* meant that the use of s 137 against protesters was less likely or less likely to succeed unless the obstruction becomes unreasonable. Therefore, the stance taken in *Hirst* under s 137 may be in accord with the values of Arts 10 and 11. But the decision in *Birch* is not fully in accordance with those values since it means that any peaceful protest or demonstration that is obstructive cannot rely on the 'lawful authority or excuse' part of the s 137 defence. It means that most, perhaps all, direct action forms of protest on the highway are unlawful, however peaceful they are, and regardless of the significance of the protest.

However, it could be argued that the argument in the *Birch* judgment is somewhat circular since blocking the highway is only 'patently unlawful' under the Highways Act 1980 itself. Aside from the Act (and the actions for nuisance and trespass), lying in the road is no more unlawful than handing out leaflets; it is arguably circular to find that it is the Act itself that prevents you from raising a defence under it. Following *Birch*, the defence appears to apply only to non-obstructive activities on the highway. However, if the activity is non-obstructive no charge could be brought in any event. The better argument is that the defence applies to (otherwise) lawful obstructive activities that are also reasonable. *Birch* could be reconciled with *Hirst* on the basis that the one instance concerned a reasonable activity on the highway – handing out leaflets – and the other concerned an unreasonable activity. Therefore the protesters in *Hirst* had a lawful excuse on the basis that the defence renders reasonable obstructions lawful. Since two possible arguments are available under s 137, s 3 HRA could be utilised to employ the Convention-friendly one.

If this argument is accepted in the post-HRA era, the question of the reasonableness of an obstruction would provide a key entry point for Art 10 and 11 arguments. It could also be argued that the use of a criminal charge against peaceful protesters who had caused some obstruction cannot be defended on proportionality grounds, utilizing the argument from the post-HRA case of *Dehal* in a different context, which is discussed below. The courts' approach to this issue should undergo a change, when protesters are charged with the offence under s 137, at least in terms of methodology in suitable post-HRA cases: the impact of the Convention rights in issue now have to be considered. An assembly that is obstructive (due to numbers or circumstances), but wholly peaceful, falls within Art 11 and, following *Steel*, Art 10 is also applicable.[416] Prima facie interference with the right(s) would clearly have occurred; the court would therefore have to consider the exceptions within para 2 of those Articles. It could use s 3 HRA to find an interpretation of s 137 which was compatible with those rights, if it viewed compatibility as in issue, or it could apply s 137 compatibly with those rights under s 6.

It is suggested that compatibility is in issue. *Pendragon* in which the convictions of peaceful protesters were not found to create a breach of Art 11 could be disregarded as a decision of the Commission only and one heavily influenced by the use of the margin of appreciation doctrine. Most significantly, in *Pendragon* a ban on the use of the highway under s 14A of the 1986 Act was in force at the time in question. In this instance, *Steel* and *Ezelin* are most clearly applicable since s 137 does not amount to

---

416 See above, pp 684–85.

a prior restraint. The finding in *Ezelin v France*[417] that freedom of peaceful assembly cannot be restricted in any way so long as the person in question has not committed any reprehensible act[418] would be applicable, since the obstructiveness of an assembly may frequently have nothing reprehensible about it – as appeared to be the case in *Arrowsmith and Jenkins*. Further, the conviction of persons taking part in a peaceful assembly does not appear to serve one of the legitimate aims of preventing public disorder or ensuring public safety. Obstruction is not necessarily equivalent to disorder. It is therefore arguable that the use of s 137 in such an instance would constitute a breach of Arts 10 and 11 since, in relation to disorder or public safety, the 'legitimate aim' test would be unsatisfied. The rights of others would, however, be in question, depending on the circumstances, in which case the issue would be one of proportionality. (It should be noted that since the right of free passage on the highway is not a Convention right, it should amount to an 'indisputable imperative'[419] in order to qualify as a legitimate aim; however, the Strasbourg Court has not consistently adopted such a strict stance.) Since s 137 uses the imprecise term 'excuse', which, as indicated, has been found to mean a reasonable user, a Convention-friendly interpretation could be adopted quite readily, possibly without needing to rely on s 3 HRA. It could be found that a peaceful, albeit obstructive, assembly would normally amount to a reasonable user of the highway, but that where the obstruction created a risk to safety or impinged disproportionately on the right of others to free movement,[420] due to its length, it could no longer be viewed as reasonable. Such an interpretation would impose a proportionality on s 137 that it currently lacks, after *Birch*.

Criminalising trespass

Wasik and Taylor note that 'The criminalisation of various forms of trespass in the 1994 Act . . . has been vigorously opposed by those who fear that it will provide an inappropriate disincentive to group protest'.[421] As argued in the Introduction to this chapter, forms of direct action are less justifiable under rights-based arguments than other forms of protest. But the concern generated by the provisions discussed below is that over-reaction to the activities of hunt saboteurs has led to an unnecessary distortion of this area of the criminal law, to the detriment of freedom of protest.

The statutory scheme: mass trespass

Simple trespass – walking onto someone's land without permission or refusing to leave when asked to do so – has never been a crime under UK law. However, the 1986 Act created a special form of criminal trespass under s 39[422] which involved the application

---

417   A 202 (1991).
418   Ibid, para 53.
419   See *Chassagnou v France* (2000) 29 EHRR 615.
420   It may be noted that, as indicated above, Strasbourg has not indicated with any precision which 'rights' are in question. See above, p 688.
421   *The Criminal Justice and Public Order Act 1994*, 1995, p 81.
422   For comment on this offence, see Vincent-Jones (1986) 13 JLS 343; *Stonehenge* (1986) NCCL; Ewing and Gearty, op. cit., fn 1, 1990, pp 125–28.

of a two-limb test. Under the first limb (s 39(1)), it had to be shown that two or more persons had come onto the land as trespassers with the common purpose of residing there for some period of time and that reasonable steps had been taken to ask them to leave on behalf of the occupier. Further, they must have brought 12 or more vehicles onto the land or threatened or abused the occupier or his agents or family or damaged property on the land. If the senior police officer believed that these conditions were satisfied, he could direct the persons to leave.

Under the second limb (s 39(2)), if they then failed to comply with the direction or came back onto the land within three months, they committed a criminal offence punishable with three months imprisonment. Section 39 was aimed at certain forms of assemblies, including animal rights activists and the 'peace convoys' which gather for the summer solstice festival at Stonehenge. As a number of commentators pointed out, it was probably unnecessary to enact this offence given the availability of civil remedies and the possibility of using powers to prevent a breach of the peace against mass trespassers or of charging them with low level public order offences.[423] It has also been suggested that the provision failed to confine itself to preventing the mischief it was created to prevent.[424] It could also be criticised as adding to the number of offences which can occur due to disobedience of police orders; it has been argued that a person should be obliged to take orders from the police only in the narrowest of circumstances.[425]

Section 39 was repealed by the CJPOA 1994 and its provisions replaced by s 61. Section 61, however, closely resembles s 39 and the changes it makes tend to have the effect of widening the offence. Under s 61, the persons in question need not have entered the land originally as trespassers; the question is whether they are trespassing, whether or not they originally entered the land as trespassers. If they did not enter as trespassers, the power to eject them only arises if there is a reasonable belief that the other conditions under s 61(1) are satisfied. The conditions under s 61(1) are similar to those under s 39(1), but the number of vehicles has been reduced from 12 to six and damage to the land itself has been included as well as damage to property on the land.

Aggravated trespass

The CJPOA 1994 also created the offence of aggravated trespass under s 68, which is aimed at certain groups, such as hunt saboteurs or motorway protesters.[426] In its original manifestation s 68 created a two-stage test; first, it had to be shown that the defendant trespassed on land in the open air and second, in relation to lawful activity which persons are engaging in or are about to engage in, that he did there anything intended by him to have the effect of either intimidating those persons so as to deter them from the activity or of obstructing or disrupting that activity.[427] No defence is provided and, crucially, it is not necessary to show that the activity was actually affected.

---

423   Smith, ATH, *Offences Against Public Order*, 1987, paras 14–18.
424   Card, R, *Public Order: The New Law*, 1987, takes this view: see pp 146–48.
425   See [1987] PL 211.
426   See HC Deb Col 29, 11 January 1994.
427   Section 69(1)(a).

The corollary of this requirement, which potentially narrows the application of the section, is that if persons engaging in a lawful activity are in fact impeded in carrying it out by the protest, but the protesters did not intend to impede or intimidate those persons since the intention was to engage in a protest of a purely symbolic nature it would appear that s 68 would not apply. Reckless, negligent or accidental intimidation or obstruction would not be enough.

This is a broadly worded provision; its impact in practice depends in part on the meaning attached to the imprecise terms 'disrupt' and 'obstruct'. A great many peaceful but vociferous demonstrations may have some impact of an obstructive nature on lawful activities. It is, however, limited in its application in that it does not apply to demonstrations on a metalled highway, although it does include public paths such as bridleways, and it excludes most, but not all buildings.[428] The original object of the section was to penalise the activities of trespassing hunt saboteurs and animal rights activists hence the inclusion of the limiting requirement that the activity must occur in the open air, but the section was later widened by deleting the reference to the open air under s 57 Anti-Social Behaviour Act 2003. By virtue of s 172(10) the section applies throughout the UK.

Section 68 has been used against hunt saboteurs and other protesters on a number of occasions and some of the decisions on the section have had the effect of widening the area of liability created still further. In *Winder v DPP*[429] the appellants had been running after the hunt. It was accepted that they did not intend to disrupt it by running but it was found that running after it was a more than a preparatory act and that it was close enough to the contemplated action to incur liability. The defendants could not have been charged with attempting to commit the offence[430] but, rather remarkably, the courts used the statutory test for attempts – whether the actions were 'something more than merely preparatory to the commission of the offence' – in support of their finding that the defendants had committed the actual offence,[431] thus appearing to conflate attempts to commit offences with the offences themselves. The willingness of the court to extend the boundaries of s 68 to catch such activities was all the more disturbing given that s 69 allows a direction to be given where it is suspected that the s 68 offence will be committed, a provision surely intended to cover precisely this set of circumstances. Thus, it was found that the offence under s 68 could be established if the appellants were trespassing on land in open air with the general intention of disrupting the hunt and were intending when in range to commit the acts in question with the required intention. This decision comes very close to punishing persons for their thoughts rather than for their actions.

---

428 'Land' is defined in s 61(9); it does not include metalled highway or buildings apart from certain agricultural buildings and scheduled monuments; common land and non-metalled roads are included.

429 (1996) *The Times*, 14 August.

430 There is no offence of attempting to commit summary offences unless specifically provided for in the statute creating the offence: Criminal Attempts Act 1981, s 1(4).

431 'The running after the hunt was, in the undisputed circumstances of the present case, sufficiently closely connected to the intended disruption as to be, in the words of the Criminal Attempts Act 1981, 'more than merely preparatory'.

Laws LJ's findings in *DPP v Barnard and Others*,[432] a decision that also concerned the breadth of s 68 when applied to direct action protest, showed similar tendencies, which are also found in Lord Bingham's willingness in *DPP v Capon*[433] (discussed below) to entertain the notion that mere presence on land *per se* might constitute 'doing there anything' intended to be intimidatory, obstructive or disruptive under s 68(1), a construction of the offence which could effectively remove the need to prove one if its constituent elements.[434] The decision concerned protesters against open cast mining who came onto land at an open cast site. The information against them alleged that having trespassed on land in the open air, they then, in relation to a lawful activity of open cast mining which persons were about to be engaged in on that land, did an act of unlawfully entering on that land, intended by them to have the effect of intimidating those persons so as to deter them from engaging in that activity, or obstructing or disrupting that activity, contrary to s 68(1). The magistrate, relying on *Winder*, found that three elements were required to establish the offence of aggravated trespass: namely, trespass, an intention to disrupt a lawful activity and an act done towards that end. The magistrate found that the allegation in the informations that the respondents 'unlawfully entered on land' alleged no more than that they had trespassed, and therefore was not capable of amounting to the second aggravating act required by the words in s 68(1): '. . . does there anything which is intended by him to have the effect . . .'. The magistrate refused an application by the prosecution to amend the informations to allege the act of 'unlawfully occupying the site in company with numerous other people' on the ground that it still would not have disclosed an offence, as occupation of the site was the act of trespass, and not an additional act aggravating that trespass. Reference to the number of people was no more than an indication that some were trespassing.

Laws LJ found that the magistrate was clearly correct in finding the original information to be defective. Proof was required of trespassing on land in the open air and of doing a distinct and overt act other than the act of trespassing which was intended to have the effects specified under sub-sections (a)–(c) of s 68(1). Unlawful occupation could equate to no more than the original trespass, but there might, he found, be circumstances where it could constitute the second act, other than trespass, required under the offence. However, a bare allegation of occupation was insufficient. It had to be supported by particulars of what the defendant was actually doing, and the occupation had to be distinct and overt from the original trespass. The proposed amendment would, he found, have disclosed an offence under s 68(1) of the 1994 Act, but it would not have been appropriate to allow the amendments; accordingly, the appeal was dismissed.

This decision suggests at first sight that when a group of protesters merely come onto land to protest about something taking place there, they do not thereby commit a criminal offence. It reiterates that the offence under s 68 consists of distinct elements, all of which must be shown to be present. But the potential blurring of the distinction

---

432 Before Laws LJ and Potts J (judgment of 15 October 1999); (1999) *The Times*, 9 November.
433 Below, fn 440.
434 'If the Police Sergeant had been found to have based his reasonable belief [that the s 68 offence was being committed] simply on the fact that [they] were present at the scene then . . . it would be necessary . . . to consider whether presence alone might be intimidatory . . . obstructive . . . or disruptive.' (Lord Bingham LCJ, *obiter*.)

between the first two to the effect that for the purposes of the offence of aggravated trespass, the occupation of land could constitute an act intended to intimidate, obstruct or disrupt, if it was distinct from a mere act of trespass, might lead to confusion as to the difference between simple and aggravated trespass. The circumstances in which an occupation of land will be viewed as distinct from a trespass on it are left unclear. The mere fact that the defendants unlawfully (that is, committing the tort of trespass) occupied the site in company with numerous other people does not necessarily mean that the offence under s 68 is made out unless the group do there anything which, in relation to others engaging in a lawful activity, is intended to have the effects mentioned in sub-sections (a)–(c) of s 68(1). If, for example, a large group walked onto land and engaged in a peaceful sit-in without making any effort to approach the persons the protest was aimed at, it is unclear that any of the effects mentioned above could be said to have occurred. The terms are ambiguous, but bearing Arts 10 and 11 in mind, they should now be interpreted more strictly under s 3 HRA, or applied more restrictively under s6. On the facts, the protesters' behaviour was quite closely analogous to that of the successful applicants in *Steel* in that the protest clearly constituted an expression of opinion, albeit occurring by means of action rather than speech, which was peaceful and unlikely to lead to disorder. As discussed below, the post-HRA case of *Tilly*[435] has in fact adopted the argument suggested above.

Directions under s 69

Far-reaching provisions under s 69 underpin s 68. Section 69(1)(a) provides that if the senior officer present at the scene reasonably believes that a person is committing, has committed or intends to commit the offence under s 68, or (b) that two or more persons are trespassing and have the common purpose of intimidating persons so as to deter them from engaging in a lawful activity or of obstructing or disrupting that activity, he can direct any or all of those persons to leave the land. Under s 69(3), if the person in question, knowing that the s 69 direction has been given that applies to him, fails to leave the land[436] or re-enters it as a trespasser within three months,[437] he commits an imprisonable offence. It is a defence for the person to show that he or she was not trespassing on the land[438] or that he or she had a reasonable excuse[439] for failing to leave the land or for returning as a trespasser.

It may be noted that s 69 is the equivalent of s 14C of the Public Order Act 1986, which was discussed above. Section 14C allows a constable to stop a person whom he reasonably believes is on her way to an assembly in an area to which a s 14A order applies, and to direct her not to proceed in that direction. The power can only be used within the area to which the order applies. Failure to comply is an offence and renders the person liable to arrest. The similarities between s 14C and s 69 mean that much of the discussion below would apply also to s 14C.

---

435 (2001) *The Times* November 27.
436 Section 69(3)(a).
437 Section 69(3)(b).
438 Section 69(4)(a).
439 Section 69(4)(b).

Although s 68 may not lead to the criminalisation of persons who simply walk on to land as trespassers, s 69 has the potential to do so, depending on the interpretation given by the courts to the 'reasonable excuse' defence. For example, where a person is in receipt of the direction under s 69, even though it was erroneously given (since in fact, although she was trespassing, she did not have the purpose of committing the s 68 offence), she may still commit an offence if thereafter she re-enters the land in question during the specified time. The fact that on the second occasion she was merely walking peacefully on to land in order to engage in a non-obstructive public protest would be irrelevant unless she could also produce an excuse which could be termed reasonable. Whether the erroneousness of the senior police officer's original 'reasonable belief' would amount to a reasonable excuse is left unclear.

Capon v DPP[440] made it clear that the offence under s 69 could be committed even though the offence under s 68 was not established. The defendants were videoing the digging out of a fox when they were threatened with arrest under s 68 by a police officer if they did not leave and were asked whether they were leaving the land. This exchange and question was found to be sufficient, in the circumstances, to constitute the direction necessary under s 69. Their intention in undertaking the videoing was not found to be to disrupt, intimidate or interfere with the activity in question. Despite the fact that the protesters had been peaceful and non-obstructive throughout,[441] and it was very doubtful whether the officer had directed his mind towards all the elements of the offence, including the *mens rea*,[442] it was found that there was sufficient evidence. It was further found that there was no defence of 'reasonable excuse' in the circumstances,[443] even though the protesters were still in the process of trying to find out what offence they were being arrested for[444] when they were, in fact, arrested, and genuinely believed that no direction under s 69(1) had been made against them.

The judgment consisted of a fairly orthodox exercise in statutory interpretation, coupled with a generous approach to the reasonableness of the officer's belief.[445] Since criminalisation of what will often, in Convention terms, be an act of political expression,[446] rests primarily upon the state of belief of a single officer, perhaps formed in a few moments, a court with any appreciation of the enormous discretion that this statute affords the police to interfere with political protest would have been expected to conclude both that it should construe the statute as strictly as possibly against

---

440   Case CO/3496/97 Judgment of 4 March 1998 LEXIS; considered: Mead [1998] Crim LR 870.
441   In the exchange with the officer, one said, 'I have no intention of disrupting [the hunt] . . .'; another, 'We're here quite peacefully . . . simply videoing what is going on' (Mead [1998] Crim LR 870, p 871).
442   As Mead notes, ibid, p 875.
443   'The fact that the appellants were not . . . committing an offence under s 68 plainly . . . does not provide a reasonable excuse for not leaving the land. So to hold would emasculate the obvious intention of the section' (*per* Lord Bingham, Case CO/3496/97 (1998), transcript).
444   The first protester said, immediately before he was arrested, 'I'm not prepared to leave the land because I don't believe I'm committing any offence'; the second, 'I don't understand' (Mead [1998] Crim LR 870, p 871).
445   In particular, as Mead points out, no inquiry was made as to whether he had directed his mind towards all the elements of the offence, including the *mens rea* (ibid, pp 874–75).
446   The ECHR had not delivered judgment in *Steel* at this point (judgment was delivered on 23 September 1998) and *Capon* was decided on 4 March 1998; however, the decision of the Commission, which made a like finding as to the applicability of Art 10, was delivered on 9 April 1997.

the executive, and, further, that it should scrutinise the actions of the police officer, especially the clarity of his instructions,[447] and the findings of the trial court with particularly anxious care. Further or alternatively, the court could have found that where the defendants were in fact engaged in peaceful protest, they could plead 'reasonable excuse'; the very broad phrasing of that defence provides the most obvious means by which to import human rights values into s 69. The court, unfortunately, showed no awareness of any of these factors, engaging instead in a purely mechanistic interpretation of the law; indeed, there was no (explicit) *normativity* in its approach at all.

Under this approach, the outcome in instances similar to *Winder* or *Capon* might not differ in the post-HRA era, although the reasoning process by which it was reached would, since the value of political expression – taking that term to encompass an animal rights' protest – receive some consideration. It is suggested that the decisions reveal a judicial approach that, far from engaging with the thorny issues raised by the direct action form of protest, shows a continuance of traditional, formalist reasoning, coupled with marked executive-friendly tendencies: a willingness to widen the scope of already widely drafted offences and a reluctance to interfere with the exercise of broad police discretion. Such tendencies proceeded directly, it appeared, from the evident lack of judicial recognition of the issues of principle at stake.

The impact of the HRA on ss 61, 68 and 69

In *Tilly v DPP*[448] the defendant was charged on two occasions with aggravated trespass. The case in question involved the damaging of genetically modified crops, where the farmer was not present at the time. It was argued on behalf of the defendant that aggravated trespass could not be established since no one was engaging in a lawful activity at the time in question. The question that was asked on appeal was whether the element of 'engaging in a lawful activity' in s 68(1) required the physical presence of a person engaged in such activity. It was found, significantly, that a person cannot be convicted of aggravated trespass if no one is physically engaged in lawful activity on the land at the time of the disruption. It was found that aggravated trespass was designed to deal with situations where people were intimidated or prevented from carrying out activity as they wished. It therefore followed that it could not be applied to situations where there was no one actually present. *Tilly* is of significance in relation to a number of forms of direct action protest, occurring before the lawful activity – the subject of the protest – gets underway, such as disabling traps or 'prebeating' a hunt, in order to rid an area of foxes before the hunt arrives. *Tilly* appears to establish, not only that persons engaging in a lawful activity must be present, but that the defendants must intend to intimidate them or impede them in engaging in it. If persons engaging in such an activity were present, but a protest was aimed at a different activity, s 68 would not apply. If such persons were present and engaging in the protested-about activity, but the protest was not intended to impede the activity, being only of a symbolic nature, it would also appear that s 68 would not apply.

447 As Mead remarks: '. . . it must be very difficult to "know" within section 69(3) that a direction has been given if the police are permitted such wide and uncertain language as this' (Mead, op. cit., fn 440, p 872).
448 (2001) *The Times* 27 November.

The situation in *DPP v Bayer*[449] differed from that in *Tilly* since disruption to a lawful activity had clearly occurred. The defendants went on to private land which was being drilled with genetically modified (GM) maize. The crop had been granted a marketing consent and could be grown legally anywhere in the UK. The defendants attached themselves to tractors engaged in the drilling process, thereby disrupting that activity. They were charged with aggravated trespass contrary to s 68(1) and (3) of the Criminal Justice and Public Order Act 1994. At trial the defendants submitted that their actions were justified to protect damage to the environment since GM crops could cause damage to surrounding property. The district judge dismissed the charges, finding that the defendants' actions were reasonable in the circumstances and came within the common law private defence of property. The question for the opinion of the High Court on appeal was whether the finding that the actions of all four defendants was reasonable in the defence of property was a finding properly open to the district judge, judging the issue of reasonableness objectively. The appeal was allowed. It was found that where the common law private defence of property was raised the court had first to ask itself whether the defendants were contending that they had used reasonable force in order to defend property from actual or imminent damage, which constituted or would constitute an unlawful or criminal act. If the answer to that was 'no' then the defence was not available. If the answer was 'yes' then the court had to go on to consider the facts as the defendants honestly believed them to be and then had to determine objectively whether the force that had been used was reasonable in all the circumstances. In the instant case, it was found that it was clear that the defendants were well aware that there was nothing unlawful about the drilling of GM maize on the land, whether or not the seed might be transferred by one means or another to the neighbouring land. They had acted as they had because they considered that the seed represented a danger to neighbouring property, not to prevent an activity that was unlawful or criminal. It followed that the district judge should have directed himself as a matter of law that the private defence of property was not available to the defendants on the facts. These findings were unsurprising.

In *R v Jones*; *R v Milling*; *R v Olditch*; *R v Pritchard*; *R v Richards*; *Ayliffe v Director of Public Prosecutions*; *Swain v Director of Public Prosecutions*[450] a further argument was put forward in an attempt to escape from the rigours of s 68. Again the argument centred on the 'lawful activity' that was being disrupted, the argument being that it was not lawful. The appellants had all been charged with or convicted of aggravated trespass or criminal damage arising out of their separate, independent actions taken at military bases by way of protest against the war in Iraq. It was claimed on their behalf that they were entitled to rely upon s 3 of the Criminal Law Act 1967, on the basis that they were using reasonable force to prevent the commission of a crime, or that their acts of disruption were not aggravated trespass because the activities of the Crown at the military bases were not lawful within the meaning of s 68(2) of the Criminal Justice and Public Order Act 1994, since they were being carried out in pursuance of a crime of aggression under customary international law. The questions certified were

---

449 [2003] EWHC 2567 (Admin), 167 JP 666, [2003] All ER (D) 28 (Nov), High Court.
450 [2006] UKHL 16. For the previous decisions in the cases, see: [2004] EWCA Crim 1981; [2005] QB 529 and [2005] EWHC 684; [2005] 3 WLR 628.

whether the crime of aggression was capable of being a 'crime' within the meaning of s 3 of the 1967 Act and, if so, whether the issue was justiciable in a criminal trial, and whether the crime of aggression was capable of being an 'offence' within s 68(2) of the 1994 Act and, if so, whether the issue was justiciable in a criminal trial. It was contended that: (1) customary international law was, without the need for any domestic statute or judicial decision, part of the domestic law of England and Wales; (2) at all times relevant to the instant appeals customary international law recognised a crime of aggression; (3) crimes recognised in international customary law were, without the need for any domestic statute or judicial decision, recognised and enforced by the domestic law of England and Wales; (4) 'crime' in s 3 covered a crime established in customary international law, such as the crime of aggression; (5) alternatively, 'crime' in s 3 meant a crime in the domestic law of England and Wales, and the crime of aggression was such; (6) 'offence' in s 68(2) covered an offence established in customary international law, such as the crime of aggression; (7) alternatively, 'offence' in s 68(2) meant a crime in the domestic law of England and Wales, and the crime of aggression was such.

The House of Lords found that it was very unlikely that Parliament had understood 'crime' in s 3 as covering crimes recognised in customary international law but not assimilated into domestic law by any statute or judicial decision. Therefore, 'crime' in s 3 did not cover a crime established in customary international law, such as the crime of aggression.[451] The House concluded that the crime of aggression was neither capable of being a 'crime' within the meaning of s 3 of the Criminal Law Act 1967, nor an 'offence' within s 68(2) of the Criminal Justice and Public Order Act 1994. Therefore, individuals facing charges for criminal damage and aggravated trespass arising out of their actions in protesting against the war in Iraq could not argue that they were using reasonable force to prevent the commission of a crime, or that the activities of the Crown at the military bases were unlawful. The appeals were therefore dismissed.

In *Jones* and in *Bayer* it was not very surprising that these arguments failed. The lack of a defence in s 68 clearly prompts defendants in protest cases to seek to persuade the courts to establish one that would enable account to be taken of the significance of the protest. But the defendants could have sought instead to rely on the *Steel* case which established that Art 10 was engaged by their activity. *R v Jones* was argued before the House of Lords in 2006 but Art 10 arguments were not relied on. Following the findings in *Dehal*, discussed below,[452] it could then have been argued that the bringing of the prosecution was disproportionate to the aim pursued, and/or that s 68 should be applied restrictively, narrowing down its application. The effect of the Convention on prosecutions brought under ss 61, 68 and 69 could be, at least superficially, quite dramatic, whether a minimalist or an activist approach is followed. As indicated above, judicial consideration of these provisions pre-HRA gave no recognition to the Convention rights at stake. By contrast, as discussed above,[453] the European Court

---

451 *R (Rottman) v Commissioner of Police for the Metropolis* (2002) UKHL 20 , (2002) 2 WLR 1315 was applied.
452 See p 797.
453 See pp 683–85 above. The findings in *Steel* were to the effect that protesters who were arrested and detained after, respectively, obstructing a grouse shoot and sitting in the path of road making equipment had suffered a prima facie violation of Art 10.

made a clear finding in *Steel*,[454] confirmed in *Hashman*,[455] that protest which takes the form of physical obstruction nevertheless falls within the protection of Art 10 – and probably Art 11.[456] Unless the courts simply refuse to follow this aspect of the *Steel* and *Hashman* judgments – as they arguably could do under s 2 HRA[457]– they are bound to find that the actions of similar protesters engage Arts 10 and 11.[458] Acceptance of such engagement, at least in formal terms, could entirely change the approach to the determination of such cases. Instead of merely undertaking a standard exercise in statutory interpretation, the courts could decide whether the interference with the protesters' Convention rights is justifiable under the second paragraphs of those Articles.

In the absence of further direct guidance from Strasbourg apart from *Steel*, it is necessary both to resort to inference from the *outcomes* of direct action and other cases, and to attempt to draw conclusions from the more general Convention principles enunciated at Strasbourg. As indicated above, it appears that while there is no express statement to the effect that 'expression' in the form of direct action has a lower status than 'pure' expression, such a finding can be inferred from the case law. In *Steel* itself, the Court appeared to be readily convinced of the necessity and proportionality of the interferences with the two direct action protests complained of by the first two applicants.[459] In contrast, as discussed above, the Court in *Ezelin*[460] found that it was impossible to justify interferences with the freedom of peaceful assembly unless the person exercising the freedom himself committed a 'reprehensible act'. The first two applicants in *Steel* were both acting 'peacefully' in the sense that they were not themselves offering violence. In order to reconcile the two decisions, therefore, it must be assumed either that *obstructive* protest, while it does fall within at least Art 10, does not constitute that class of purely 'peaceful' protest which, according to *Ezelin*, 'cannot be restricted in any way' or that any restriction is more readily justifiable.

---

454 (1999) 28 EHRR 603.
455 (2000) 8 BHRC 104; (1999) 30 EHRR 241.
456 The Court in *Steel* found that there was no need to consider the applications under Art 11, implying that since the matter had been resolved under Art 10, consideration of Art 11 would be otiose, as raising the same issues. It may be noted that Art 11 protects only freedom of 'peaceful' assembly. On the face of it, there is no need to read this restriction should also be read into Art 10; the words were not expressly included and reading them in potentially reduces the scope of the primary right.
457 The domestic courts generally follow ECHR judgments where they are viewed as reflecting settled jurisprudence (see Chapter 4, pp 193–94); however, a court might take the view that the jurisprudence is not sufficiently 'settled'.
458 Even where an arrest and detention had occurred, but no further action had been taken, an interference might be viewed as subsisting on the basis that protesters would not be able to exercise their Convention rights free from the fear of arrest and charges: see *Dudgeon v UK* (1982) 4 EHRR 149.
459 The case also concerned third, fourth and fifth applicants, who had engaged in purely peaceful protests with no element of obstruction or other 'action'. The first applicant, who had been impeding grouse shooters, was detained for 44 hours and sentenced to 28 days' imprisonment upon refusing to be bound over; the second, who had been lying down in front of digging equipment, suffered a 17-hour detention and seven-days' imprisonment. The Court found that these were 'serious interference[s]' with the applicants' Art 10 rights. However, it had little difficulty in going on to find them to be both necessary and proportionate.
460 (1991) 14 EHRR 362.

It seems clear from the findings in *Steel* as to the first and second applicants, and from the Commission decision in *G v FRG*,[461] that where a protester is engaged in obstructive, albeit non-violent activity, arrest and imprisonment are in principle justifiable under the Convention. Such an acceptance does not, however, entail a finding that s 68 is Convention-compliant. Section 68 is aimed only at disruptive protesters, not at those engaged purely in verbal persuasion, and therefore the powers it provides may, depending on their interpretation, be compatible with Art 10 as interpreted in *Steel*. However, it must be recalled that in *Steel, actual disruption* had been caused by the protesters: by contrast, s 68 makes clear on its face that it is necessary only that 'acts' additional to trespass, committed with the *intention* of causing disruption, obstruction or intimidation are required to make out the offence. Thus, in cases where the protesters have engaged in action intended to be disruptive, etc, but no such disruption has actually been caused, it is doubtful whether the imposition of criminal liability could be seen as 'necessary' under the Convention. Its imposition would arguably be incompatible with *Steel* and would amount to a clear departure from the principle set out in *Ezelin*, that peaceful protest cannot be interfered with, unless the particular protesters arrested commit 'reprehensible acts'.[462]

If this argument is accepted, a significant narrowing of the area of liability generated by s 68 will be required: the offence would have to be re-interpreted under s 3(1) of the HRA so that it catches only 'acts' that actually have some disruptive, etc, effect. This would entail a clear departure from the literal meaning of the section, but it is presumably a 'possible' interpretation under s 3. On this basis, *Winder*, which allows the criminalisation of protest at a stage even further away from actual obstruction, would also have to be reconsidered and, it is suggested, overruled.

Section 69, as interpreted by *Capon*, is similarly problematic. As *Capon* made clear, s 69 allows peaceful protesters to be arrested even though in fact there was no obstruction, intimidation or disruption of others and no risk of disorder, as long as a police officer reasonably believed that such factors were present. This belief is supposed to be 'reasonable',[463] but as *Capon* vividly demonstrates, the inhibiting effect of this requirement in practice can all but disappear due to the courts' marked disinclination to take issue with the judgments of police officers on the spot.[464] Therefore, it may be argued, depending on the particular circumstances, that certain s 69 'bans' may be unjustifiable under para 2 of Arts 10 and 11, bearing in mind the extent of the discretion to interfere with peaceful protest which this section vests in the police without any independent check, and the extent of the interference – in effect, a complete ban on entering the land in question, potentially lasting for three months. Since s 69 can operate as a prior restraint, Art 10 would demand that any direction given should be strictly scrutinised.[465]

---

461 (1980) 21 DR 138.

462 Reading *Steel* and *Ezelin* together, it must be assumed that the 'reprehensible acts' mentioned in *Ezelin* included obstructive behaviour.

463 Section 69(1).

464 (1999) 28 EHRR 603, pp 609–10, 638–39 and 647: the arrest of purely peaceful protesters (the third, fourth and fifth applicants) was found to create breaches of Arts 5(1) and 10.

465 See pp 687–89.

Peaceful protesters – like the two defendants in *Capon* – have clearly committed no 'reprehensible' acts, as *Ezelin* requires. One possible response, therefore, would be to reinterpret s 69 under s 3(1) of the HRA so as to allow for a lawful direction to be given only where in fact one of the above elements is actually present. Reasonable belief would have to be taken to mean reasonable and true belief.[466] While such a reading renders s 69 largely otiose (since s 68 would cover such a situation) it is again, a 'possible' reading under s 3(1). A further, more likely, possibility would be to find by reference to Arts 10 and 11 that the erroneousness of the senior police officer's original 'reasonable belief' should amount to a reasonable excuse. It would also be possible to find that purely peaceful protesters have a 'reasonable excuse' for not obeying a s 69 direction under s 69(4)(b). Moreover, under this view, courts could surely find that the Convention requires officers to use the clearest possible words when ordering persons to leave the land, precisely what the court failed to do in *Capon*.

That decision also raises the possibility that a direction under s 69, if it can be given in such an imprecise form, might be found in a future post-HRA case to fail to satisfy the test denoted by the term 'prescribed by law' under Arts 10 and 11, assuming that the activity in question could be viewed as constituting the expression of an opinion so as to engage those Articles. It might well be argued that if a direction can be given in the form of a question, as in *Capon*, the term is too imprecise to satisfy that test. But, equally, the domestic court would be free to apply a doctrine of deference to the executive, whereby the nature of the direction should not be scrutinised too closely since the circumstances could be best assessed by the police officer on the ground. In the words of Lord Slynn, in the *International Ferry Traders* case,[467] the courts might show respect to 'the margin of appreciation or discretion' of the police officers in question in refusing to undertake a rigorous review of the wording of a direction. But since the courts should recognise that they are dealing with the exercise of a fundamental right under the Convention, it would be problematic to allow for its abrogation on the exceptionally flimsy grounds upheld in that case.

The discussion so far has not centred on the question of rights of access to land, except in relation to the highway, under s 14A of the 1986 Act.[468] It is now established that the 'right' of access to the highway may include holding an assembly on it. But prima facie assemblies on other quasi-public or private land will virtually always be trespassory, and therefore could attract liability under ss 68, 69 or 61 of the CJPOA unless, in the circumstances, it is found that express or implied permission to hold some peaceful protests was given. A large number of quasi-public places exist to which the public has limited rights of access, such as unenclosed shopping malls, parks, the grounds and forecourts of town halls or civic centres, monuments and their surrounding land or rights of way across private land. At present, such rights of access would not include assemblies for the purpose of protests and demonstrations. Strasbourg has not yet accepted that there is a positive obligation on the state to require public

---

466   It should be noted that s 69 raises an issue distinct from that of arresting under s 68(4) on the basis of reasonable suspicion of committing the offence under s 68. Since s 68(4) requires reasonable suspicion as to the commission of an offence, it is in principle compatible with Art 5 under the exception of para (1)(c).

467   [1999] 1 All ER 129; see above, pp 692–93.

468   See above, pp 711–19.

authorities or private individuals to allow the exercise of protest and assembly rights on their land. But an activist domestic court might be prepared to uphold such a claim in respect of a public authority, thereby anticipating the stance on this matter which some commentators view Strasbourg as not unlikely to adopt.[469] When the issue of exclusion of persons from a quasi-public place, a shopping mall, was raised before the Commission, it declared the application inadmissible, on the basis that Art 11 was not applicable, since the applicants were gathering there for a purely social purpose.[470] Clearly, had Art 11 been engaged, a different outcome might have been achieved.

In the US, the courts are moving away from a position of upholding proprietorial rights and towards providing protection for expressive activity in quasi-public forums.[471] This can also be said of the Canadian and Australian courts.[472] In contrast, the traditional stance of the UK judiciary, as indicated above, is to favour the property right when it conflicts with rights of protest. In general, they tend to uphold proprietorial rights in an abstract fashion, regardless of any real harm which may occur due to their infringement.[473] But Art 10 and 11 arguments might persuade them in future to consider the possibility of recognising broader access rights to quasi-public land.

The issue might arise in two ways. A group seeking access to a forum for the holding of an assembly or demonstration might seek to bring an action against the relevant landowning body, if it was a public authority, under ss 6 and 7(1)(a) of the HRA, claiming that a refusal to allow an assembly in a particular place had constituted an interference with its Art 10 and 11 rights. Where a group was charged with infringing s 61 of the CJPOA in respect of private or quasi-public land, its main recourse, since prima facie it would appear to be trespassory, would be to argue under s 7(1)(b) of the HRA that in the circumstances it had an implied licence to enter the land on the basis of the demands of the guarantees under Arts 10 and 11. A failure to accept such an argument could lead, potentially, to a serious interference with those guarantees.[474] A successful claim of such access rights would mean reinterpreting s 61 in order to find that rights of access to certain areas, going beyond the highway, exist for the purpose of holding peaceful assemblies. If such a claim was upheld, it would also preclude the imposition of tortious liability.

Similar arguments could be raised under ss 68 or 69 of the CJPOA; a group charged with aggravated trespass could argue, as a preliminary issue, that they had not trespassed since they were within the limited rights of access to the land. Upholding such a claim would mean, in effect, deeming under s 68 that an implied or constructive licence to enter the land existed, imposed by the HRA. Any such implied licence would no doubt be highly circumscribed. For example, it would have to avoid allowing any infringement

---

469 Harris, O'Boyle and Warbrick, op. cit., fn 1, p 419.

470 *Anderson v UK* [1998] EHRLR 218.

471 See *Shad Alliance v Smith Haven Mall* 484 NYS 2d 849, esp p 857.

472 See *Harrison v Carswell* (1975) 62 DLR (3d) 68 Supreme Court of Canada; *Gerhardy v Brown* (1985) 159 CLR 70.

473 See, on this point, Gray and Gray, 'Civil rights, civil wrongs and quasi-public places' [1999] EHRLR 46.

474 The members of the assembly would be convicted of various offences arising under s 14B, however peaceful or non-obstructive the assembly was. Its organiser could be imprisoned (s 14B(5)), as could anyone who could be proved to have incited a member of the assembly to come onto the land (s 14B(7)).

of Art 8 rights, including respect for the home. It would probably apply for a limited period and possibly only to peaceful protests, such as sit-ins.

The status of the landowning body under s 6 of the HRA would be relevant. Further, since the offences in question are statutory, the court would have to satisfy its obligation under s 3. If the landowning body was itself a standard public authority, it would clearly be bound by the Convention rights. If it was a functional body,[475] it would depend whether its public function could be said to be engaged by the claims of the protesters. As Chapter 4 indicated, s 6 of the HRA has brought a number of bodies which manage or own land within its ambit, including bodies such as Network Rail, which are classic hybrid bodies. If, for example, Network Rail bought land, perhaps by means of a Compulsory Purchase Order, in order to place railway lines across it, it would then own the land for the purpose of satisfying its public function as the manager of rail infrastructure, but such ownership is nevertheless probably part of its private function.[476] But if it acted in order to secure the lines by, for example, placing fences round them, it would be doing so in pursuance of its statutory duty in respect of rail safety and therefore might be viewed as acting in that respect as a public authority.[477] A body exercising a private function, or a fully private body, would not be bound by s 6, but would still be affected by s 3 of the HRA. If, for example, an assembly took place, in the period to which a s 14A ban applied, on land owned by a privatised body which could not be viewed as related to the public function of that body, a court would still have to interpret s 14A(5) in order to ensure compatibility with Arts 10 and 11. If, alternatively, a person was charged with an offence under ss 61, 68 or 69 in respect of such an assembly, the court would have to ensure compatibility with those Articles in respect of the term 'trespass' in ss 61, 68(1) or 69(1).

5 Breach of the peace, binding over and bail conditions[478]

Justices and any court of record having criminal jurisdiction have a power at common law[479] to bind over persons to keep the peace. Under the Justices of the Peace Act 1361, there is also a power – the *contra bono mores* (contrary to a good way of life) power – to bind over persons to be of good behaviour. If a person refuses a binding over order, he or she can be imprisoned for up to six months. These ancient powers are of great significance in relation to direct action, demonstrations and public protest generally due to the wide discretion they hand to police and magistrates. Academic writers agree that the notion of maintaining the Queen's peace continues to be the central one in public

---

475 See Chapter 4, pp 216–35.

476 There was a *Pepper v Hart* statement in Parliament to this effect: 583 HL 796, 811 (24 November 1997).

477 Clearly, it does not necessarily follow in any particular circumstance that Arts 10 and 11 would require that access to the land should be allowed for protesters. Both Articles contain exceptions in the interests of public safety.

478 For discussion of this power, see Grunis, A [1976] PL 16; Law Commission Paper, *Binding Over: The Issues*, 1987, Paper 103: for comment, see [1988] Crim LR 355; 'The roots and early development of binding over powers' [1988] CLJ 101–28; Kerrigan, K, 'Breach of the peace and binding over – continuing confusion' (1997) 2(1) J Civ Lib 30.

479 See the Justices of the Peace Act 1968, s 1(7) and the Administration of Justice Act 1973, Sched 5.

order law.[480] It has been said to express the idea that 'people should be free to act as they choose so long as they do not cause violence'.[481] This simple concept appears to be unobjectionable in civil libertarian terms, since it would not sanction interference with the freedom to protest peacefully. However, it will be argued below that this concept no longer expresses the central value underlying the doctrine of breach of the peace. In many respects, it has been replaced by a notion of freedom of action so long as serious inconvenience is not caused. The concept itself has also changed and grown in a way that has taken it some distance from the values it may originally have expressed. Since the breach of the peace doctrine has the potential to curb all forms of protest – not excluding peaceful persuasion – it has come into domestic conflict with Arts 10 and 11 of the Convention. Where a balance has been struck between the rights of protesters and the control of disorder by the statutory schemes discussed in this chapter, the use of the common law by police in preference leads to a failure to accord proper weight to such rights. The extraordinary width of this common law doctrine has been somewhat narrowed by the seminal House of Lords' decision in *Laporte* in 2006. Nevertheless, it still retains the capacity to undermine the statutory schemes discussed. This doctrine provides the most significant power for use against protesters discussed in this chapter; it provides the police with almost limitless powers unless the protest remains anodyne. Protests containing protesters with a history of causing disorder, protests including a few who are disorderly or who may become so, all become subject to an array of restraints, including the ending of the march or detention for several hours with or without arrest, under this doctrine.

The contra bono mores power

The *contra bono mores* power under the 1361 Act allows the binding over of persons whose behaviour is deemed by a bench of magistrates to be anti-social although not necessarily unlawful. This vague and broad power hands an unacceptably wide discretion to magistrates to determine the standards of good behaviour; it has been severely criticised as a grave breach of rule of law standards.[482] The power has been used in this century against those engaging in political public protest and against groups such as animal rights activists. In *Hughes v Holley*,[483] the Court of Appeal confirmed the existence of the power and its availability regardless of the lawfulness of the behaviour in question.

However, following the decision in *Hashman v UK*[484] it is probable that the doctrine will become a dead letter. The case concerned the behaviour of hunt saboteurs. One of the applicants had blown a horn with the intention of disrupting a hunt. There was no threat of violence and no breach of the peace. Blowing a horn is not unlawful. However, it was probable that he would have repeated the behaviour in question, which

---

480 See, e.g., Feldman, *Civil Liberties and Human Rights in England and Wales*, 1993 1st edn, p 786; 'Breaching the peace and disturbing the quiet' (1982) PL 212; Williams, op. cit., fn 1.
481 Feldman, ibid, p 787.
482 Williams, G, 'Preventive justice and the rule of law' (1953) 16 MLR 417. See also Hewitt, P, *The Abuse of Power*, 1984, p 125.
483 (1988) 86 Cr App R 130.
484 (2000) 8 BHRC 104; (1999) 30 EHRR 241.

was found to be anti-social by the magistrates. He was therefore bound over to be of good behaviour and the binding over order was upheld on appeal. The case led to an application to the European Commission on Human Rights under Arts 10, 11 and 5; it was declared admissible under Arts 10 and 11.[485] The Court went on to find that the power was too vague and unpredictable in its operation to satisfy the 'prescribed by law' requirement under Arts 10 and 11.[486] The finding of the court in *Sunday Times v UK*,[487] that 'a norm cannot be regarded as a "law" unless it is formulated with sufficient precision to enable the citizen to regulate his conduct', was not satisfied. Thus, it may be assumed that, although this decision is not binding, the *contra bono mores* power is unlikely to be used now that the HRA is in force.

Breach of the peace

Introduction

The notion of breaching the peace is less vague and uncertain than the *contra bono mores* doctrine, but it has quite frequently been interpreted very broadly. If a police officer suspects that a breach of the peace is likely to be committed – for example, a march is expected to be disorderly – a person or persons can be arrested without a warrant under common law powers to prevent a breach of the peace and can be bound over to keep the peace, in other words not to continue the behaviour thought likely to lead to the breach of the peace. Thus, the march could be prevented from occurring. If the person refuses the binding over order, he or she can be imprisoned. Under s 6 HRA, this power is being re-evaluated when applied to protesters, as discussed below. The tendency of the judiciary – as shown, for example, in *Piddington v Bates*[488] – to accept the finding of the police officer on the ground, is undergoing a change.

This flexible common law power[489] overlaps with a number of the powers arising under the 1986 and 1994 Acts and is in general more useful to the police than they are, since its definition is so imprecise and the powers that can be exercised to prevent a breach are so broad. This imprecision means that it can readily be used in such a way as to undermine attempts in the statutory provisions to carve out more clearly defined areas of liability. The leading case is *Howell*,[490] in which it was determined that a breach of the peace will arise if an act is done or threatened to be done which either: harms a person or *in his presence* his property or is likely to cause such harm or which puts a person in fear of such harm. Under this definition, threatening words might not in themselves amount to a breach of the peace, but they might lead a police officer to apprehend a breach. Another and rather different definition of the offence was offered

---

485 *Hashman and Harrup v UK* (1996) 22 EHRR CD 184.
486 Article 8 uses the formulation 'in accordance with the law', but it was established in *Silver v UK*, judgment of 25 March 1983, A 61; (1983) 5 EHRR 347 that both formulations are to be read in the same way.
487 Judgment of 26 April 1979, A 30, para 49.
488 [1961] 1 WLR 162.
489 For comment, see 'Breaching the peace and disturbing the quiet' [1982] PL 212; Williams, op. cit., fn 1.
490 [1981] 3 All ER 383.

in *Chief Constable for Devon and Cornwall ex p CEGB*[491] by Lord Denning. His view was that violence, or the threat of it, was unnecessary; he considered that 'if anyone unlawfully and physically obstructs a worker – by lying down or chaining himself to a rig or the like – he is guilty of a breach of the peace'. On this view, peaceful protest could be severely curtailed. It is generally considered that the view taken in *Howell* is the correct one,[492] but the fact that as eminent an authority as Lord Denning could offer such a radically different definition of the offence[493] from that put forward in *Howell* only a year earlier, epitomises the disturbingly vague parameters of breach of the peace. The *Howell* definition in itself is extremely wide, largely because it does not confine itself to violence or threats of violence. Nor does it require that the behaviour amounting to a breach of the peace, or giving rise to fear of a breach of the peace, should be unlawful under civil or criminal law. Further, it has been recognised for some time by the courts that a person may be bound over for conduct which is not itself a breach of the peace and which does not suggest that the individual concerned is about to breach the peace, but which may cause another to breach the peace.[494] This third possibility is arguably implicit in the *Howell* definition itself and indeed is not sufficiently distinguished, within that definition, from conduct which in itself amounts to a breach of the peace. This additional possibility is of great significance in the context of public protest since it means that in certain circumstances peaceful, lawful protest can lead to the arrest and binding over of the protesters.

The width of powers to prevent a breach of the peace means that they can be used to curtail freedom of assembly in situations in which statutory powers might be inapplicable. For example, *Piddington v Bates*[495] suggested that the courts could be, at times, very unwilling to disagree with the finding of the police officer on the ground. In that case, the defendant wished to join other pickets at a printer's works but was told by police officers that only two men were to be allowed to picket each of the main entrances. The defendant then tried to push 'gently' past the police officer and was arrested for obstructing a police officer in the course of his duty. On appeal, it was held that the officer had reasonably apprehended that a breach of the peace might occur and the limiting of the number of the pickets was designed to prevent it; however, the main reason for fearing trouble was apparently merely that there were 18 pickets at the works. In effect, therefore, a condition was imposed on a static assembly, reducing its numbers to four. It is interesting to note that if that situation were to occur today, with the 1986 Act in force, the powers under s 14 allowing control of assemblies could not be used, since less than 20 people were present and even had more than 20 pickets been there, it seems probable that none of the 'trigger' conditions would have been satisfied. The case illustrates the readiness of the common law to sanction police interference with free assembly on production of what can only be described as minimal evidence of a risk of disorder.

---

491 [1982] QB 458.
492 See, e.g., Thornton, P, *Public Order Law* 1987, p 74. In *Percy v DPP* [1995] 3 All ER 124, DC, the *Howell* definition as opposed to that of Lord Denning, was preferred. Lord Denning's definition was rejected as erroneous.
493 It should be noted that breach of the peace, though arrestable, is not a criminal offence.
494 *Wise v Dunning* [1902] 1 KB 167; *Lansbury v Riley* [1914] 3 KB 229.
495 [1961] 1 WLR 162.

Immediacy

A constable or citizen has the power and duty to seek to prevent, by arrest or other action short of arrest, any breach of the peace occurring in his presence, or any breach of the peace which (having occurred) is likely to be renewed, or any breach of the peace which is about to occur. Three key issues arise in relation to the question of immediacy. First, it is necessary to determine the degree of imminence. In other words, does it indicate that the officer predicts that the breach will occur in the very near future? At what point could it be said that the point at which it was expected to arise was too distant to justify intervening action, including arrest? Second, assuming that a breach can be said to be imminent, who can be arrested or otherwise affected by police intervention? If, as may frequently occur in relation to protests, an innocent party is in the company of those who are, in the view of the police officers, about to commit the breach, can the police arrest or take other interventionary action against the innocent party? In the interests of maintaining public order this might be argued for on the basis that it was difficult for the police to distinguish between those about to breach the peace and others.[496] Or it might be argued for on the basis that those remaining present while others, part of the same protest, become more confrontational, condoned or even encouraged the breach by their very presence or by their verbal support for the protest. This issue is a difficult one since police consider that some activist groups use protests as a cover for acts of violence and aggression.[497] Third, if a breach can *not* be said to be imminent, can the police take action short of arrest, such as directing protesters away from the protest, or detaining them without arresting them, on the basis that otherwise the breach will become imminent? In other words, is the degree of intervention linked to the degree of immediacy?

The last two issues tend to arise in the context of protests rather than in the context of other activities that could lead to a breach of the peace. Their resolution is of great significance in that context since it determines whether and how far the police have extremely broad and ill-defined powers to prevent or curb freedom of protest or deter persons from taking part in it. The statutory framework contained in the Public Order Act 1986, discussed above, provides a range of far-reaching powers intended to allow the police to control protests. The 1986 Act also provides (s 40(2)) that nothing in it 'affects the common law powers . . . to deal with or prevent a breach of the peace'. At present the statutory framework is marginalised since the police prefer to rely on the much less precisely defined common law powers. In fact, at first glimpse the statutory powers might appear to offer the police more than the common law powers do. The statutory powers rely on a lower threshold of harm as protests can be controlled on the basis only of an apprehended serious disruption to the life of the community rather than on an apprehension of violence to persons or property. Also the powers make it clear, on their face, that a range of actions short of arrest can be taken against individual members of protests, whether or not they themselves are creating or are expected to create the disruption. Arrest powers are available on the same basis, providing that reasonable suspicion as regards the *mens rea* elements of the offences in question under ss 11, 12, 14 is present. But the statutory framework is more precise, more detailed

---

496 This was the case in both *Laporte* and *Austin and Saxby*, which are considered below.
497 Ibid.

and more complex; it appears to present the police with a greater challenge in terms of defending their actions at a later point. For example, if an assembly is static it cannot be subject to the same range of conditions as a march can, so if the police purport to apply the wrong set of conditions their actions may be found later on to have been unlawful.[498] Until the House of Lords' decision in *Laporte*, discussed below, the police had good grounds for thinking that the invocation of powers to prevent a breach of the peace offered them far more scope for intervention in a protest than the statutory powers did. This was especially the case in relation to an assembly rather than a march. But even in relation to a march the statutory powers were far more precise and complex to operate than the common law ones. The three issues identified are taken in turn in the following discussion in relation to pre and post-HRA case law in order to determine how far the common law powers have been kept in check by the courts in relation to protests, especially in the HRA era.

The leading authority on the question of what is an imminent breach of the peace (which was accepted in the House of Lords in *Laporte*, discussed below) is *Albert v Lavin*.[499] That case reflected the trend of existing authority. In *Humphries v Connor*[500] Fitzgerald J summarised a constable's duty:

> With respect to a constable, I agree that his primary duty is to preserve the peace; and he may for that purpose interfere, and, in the case of an affray, arrest the wrongdoer; or, if a breach of the peace is imminent, may, if necessary, arrest those who are about to commit it, if it cannot otherwise be prevented.

Once it is accepted that an arrest may be made in respect of an apprehended breach of the peace, the question of the necessary degree of immediacy (the first issue identified) arises. A number of authorities establish that the duty to arrest for breach of the peace arises only when the police officer apprehends that a breach of the peace is 'imminent' (*O'Kelly v Harvey*;[501] *Foulkes v Chief Constable of the Merseyside Police*)[502] or is 'about to take place' or is 'about to be committed' (*Albert v Lavin*) or will take place 'in the immediate future' (*R v Howell*).[503] His apprehension 'must relate to the near future' (*McLeod v Commissioner of Police of the Metropolis*).[504] If the officer reasonably apprehends that a breach of the peace is likely to occur in the near future, the officer's duty is to take reasonable steps to prevent it.

When this power, in conjunction with the offence of obstruction of an officer in the execution of his duty, was used extensively during the miners' strike,[505] it was made clear that an arrest can occur well before the point is reached at which a breach of the peace is apprehended. The most notorious[506] instance of its use occurred in *Moss*

---

498 *DPP v Jones* [2002] EWHC 110. See above p 723.
499 [1982] AC 546.
500 (1864) 17 ICLR 1, 8–9.
501 (1883) 14 LR Ir 105, 109.
502 [1998] 3 All ER 705, 711b–c.
503 [1982] QB 416, 426.
504 [1994] 4 All ER 553, 560F.
505 March 1984 to March 1985.
506 The case has attracted widespread criticism; see Ewing and Gearty, op. cit., fn 1, pp 111–12; Newbold [1985] PL 30.

v McLachlan.[507] A group of striking miners in a convoy of cars were stopped by the police a few miles away from a number of collieries and prevented from travelling on to pits a few miles away where non-striking miners were working. The police officers had reason to believe that violent clashes would break out, not at the motorway exit where their cordon was positioned, but at the pits. The police told them that they feared a breach of the peace if the miners reached the pits and that they would arrest the miners for obstruction if they tried to continue. After some time, a group of miners tried to push past the police, were arrested and convicted of obstruction of a police officer in the course of his duty. Their appeal on the ground that the officers had not been acting in the course of their duty was dismissed. It was said that there was no need to show that individual miners would cause a breach of the peace, nor even to specify at which pit disorder was expected. A reasonable belief that there was a real risk that a breach would occur in close proximity to the point of arrest (the pits were between two and four miles away) was all that was necessary. (A case in Kent in which striking miners were held up over 200 miles away from their destination suggested that this requirement of close proximity might become otiose.)[508] In assessing whether a real risk existed, news about disorder at previous pickets could be taken into account; in other words, there did not appear to be a requirement that there was anything about these particular miners to suggest they might cause a breach of the peace.[509] Thus, a number of individuals were lawfully denied their freedom of both movement and assembly apparently on no more substantial grounds than that other striking miners had caused trouble in the past, without having themselves provided grounds on which violence could be foreseen. Skinner J, giving the judgment of the Divisional Court, also introduced a significant modification to the doctrine. Dealing with the requirement of imminence, Skinner J said,[510] 'The imminence or immediacy of the threat to the peace determines what action is reasonable.' In *Minto v Police*[511] Cooke P said that 'the degree of immediacy is plainly highly relevant to the reasonableness or otherwise of the action taken by the police officer'. On this approach, a police officer has the power – and duty – to take action short of arrest (such as stopping cars or directing protesters away from a protest) at an earlier stage than that at which he would have the power and duty to arrest persons on the grounds of breach of the peace.

The decision in *Peterkin v Chief Constable of Cheshire*,[512] taken one year before the HRA came fully into force, took a strongly differing stance. Peterkin, a hunt protester, had access to intelligence that told him when and where the Cheshire Hunt was to meet. He was making his way to the hunt in a convoy of vehicles carrying other protesters

---

507 [1985] IRLR 76.

508 *Foy v Chief Constable of Kent* (1984) unreported, 20 March. It has also been noted by Thornton, P *Public Order Law*, 1987, pp 97–98 that the Attorney General, in a written answer to a parliamentary question tabled during the miners' strike, omitted the requirement of an imminent threat to public order.

509 The miners apparently gave a hostile reception to passing NCB coaches but this, it appears, occurred after the police had stopped them and informed them that they could not proceed. It does not appear, therefore, that it could have formed part of the basis for the police decision that a breach of the peace was to be expected.

510 At p 79, para 24.

511 [1987] 1 NZLR 374, 377.

512 (1999) *The Times*, 16 November.

when he was arrested for conduct likely to cause a breach of the peace. The arresting officer said that he anticipated that Peterkin and the other protesters would enter private land, causing a serious breach of the peace. Peterkin argued that he was arrested merely for walking on a country lane, half a mile from where the hunt was taking place, and was not in sight of it at the time. He claimed unlawful arrest, false imprisonment and assault and battery against the Cheshire police on the basis that they had no legal grounds for the arrest and therefore any actions used to effect it were unlawful. In awarding damages, Manchester County Court found that there were no such grounds, since there was no apprehension or imminent threat of any breach of the peace.

The highly significant decision of the House of Lords in *Laporte* did not add much to the established understanding of the meaning of immediacy. However, it did address the question of action that can be taken when a breach is *not* imminent (the second issue identified above). The stance taken in *Moss* to the effect that action short of arrest can be taken if a breach of the peace is not imminent was decisively rejected by the House of Lords in *Laporte*.[513] The case arose in relation to the detention of protesters on a coach which had been turned back by the police from an anti-war demonstration. The House of Lords found, in a seminal decision for freedom of protest and assembly, that the actions of the police in preventing the protesters travelling to the site of the protest and detaining them on a coach travelling back to London, were disproportionate to the aims pursued, in terms of para 2 of Arts 10 and 11. The case arose because the claimant, a peace protester, wanted to protest against the policy and conduct of the UK and US Governments in relation to the Iraq war, and wished to join a protest at RAF Fairford in order to do so. RAF Fairford was used for hostile operations against Iraq, and the base became a focus for protest against the war. A protest group calling themselves Gloucestershire Weapons Inspectors, in conjunction with other anti-war groups, organised a protest demonstration to take place at RAF Fairford in March 2003. As required by s 11 of the 1986 Act, the Gloucestershire Weapons Inspectors gave the Chief Constable the proper written notification of their proposed demonstration. There was to be a rally at the main gate of the base which would last from 1.30–4.0 pm. There were to be several speakers and the numbers attending were estimated at 1,000–5,000.

It was not suggested that Laporte was anything other than entirely peaceful in her conduct. The Chief Constable, as head of the Gloucestershire Constabulary, had overall responsibility for policing the demonstration at Fairford. Various demonstrations had already occurred and on one occasion an otherwise peaceful protest was attended by a hardcore activist anarchist group known as the Wombles (White Overalls Movement Building Libertarian Effective Struggles). This led to serious disorder. Three coaches set off from London to Fairford on the relevant day; the claimant was on one of them. It appeared from the contents of websites advertising the protest that members of the Wombles might be on one of them.

The Chief Constable's plan for the demonstration was to allow it take place peacefully and to minimise the risk of serious public disorder. The Chief Constable decided not to invoke the power and duty under s 13 of the Public Order Act 1986 to seek an

---

513 [2006] UKHL 55, para 34. CA: *R (on the application of Laporte) v CC of Gloucester Constab* [2004] EWCA Civ 1639. See below for further discussion p 770.

order prohibiting all processions in the Fairford area for a period of time.[514] The Chief Constable took a number of other measures as part of a policing operation which was the largest ever undertaken by the Gloucestershire Constabulary. The Chief Constable issued a direction under s 12 of the Act, prescribing (in accordance with the notification) the time, place of assembly and procession route, prescribing where the procession route should end and drawing attention to the criminal offence of failing to comply with the conditions laid down. The Chief Constable promulgated several thousand leaflets, provided to websites advertising the event and (in due course) to protesters, describing the arrangements and warning that those who deviated from the conditions (as by leaving the prescribed route) were liable to arrest. Attention was drawn to the danger of entering military premises. There were to be designated drop-off points, policed by officers, where protesters would get out of their vehicles. The Chief Constable formulated a detailed plan:

> . . . to control the march and protest from the initial assembly area directing march along the prescribed route as per the attached plan (highlighted) and allowing the protest to take place in the bell-mouth area of the gate, thereby giving them a point of focus. The protest will be allowed until a predetermined time when they will be encouraged to disperse. In order to ensure the protesters keep to the prescribed route, certain minor roads will be closed as per attached plan.

Protesters were to be escorted along the procession route by officers. The Chief Constable considered in his assessment of the protest that the protesters would include hard-line activists intent on violence and entry to the base. Police officers were mustered in large numbers, supported by anti-climbing teams, patrols on both sides of the perimeter fence, dog teams, a member of the Metropolitan Police Public Order Intelligence Unit (to recognise those known to be extreme protestors), a facial recognition team, Forward Intelligence Teams, three Police Support Units ('PSUs') and helicopters. A statutory stop and search authorisation under s 60 of the Criminal Justice and Public Order Act 1994 was issued.[515] It applied to an area around Fairford, and was extended on the following day. An authority under s 60AA of the 1994 Act, giving power to require the removal of disguises, was also issued.

On the day in question the claimant joined a group of about 120 passengers who boarded three coaches at Euston bound for Fairford. Eight members of the Wombles were also on the coaches. The three coaches were stopped by the police at Lechlade near Fairford. The police searched the coaches and found a few items that could possibly have been used in a non-peaceful protest, such as face masks, spray paint, two pairs of scissors and a safety flare, home-made shields. All these articles were seized. It appeared that all or some of the passengers were not questioned about their intentions or affiliations. After the search the coaches and passengers were directed by the officer in charge to be escorted by the police back to London. The officer took the view that had the coaches been permitted to continue to RAF Fairford the protesters on the coaches would have been arrested upon arrival at RAF Fairford, as a breach of the peace would then have been 'imminent'. He stated that he had concluded that

---

514 See above, pp 708–9.
515 See Chapter 11, p 1122.

he had a choice of either allowing the coaches to proceed and managing a breach of the peace at RAF Fairford, arresting the occupants of the coaches in order to prevent a breach of the peace, or turning the coaches around and escorting them back away from the area in order to avert a breach of the peace. Officers stood by the doors as the coaches moved off, holding them shut to prevent passengers from disembarking, as some had tried to do on learning that they were to be returned to London. The coaches were driven to the motorway, where police motorcycle outriders prevented them from stopping on the hard shoulder or turning off to motorway services, even to allow passengers to relieve themselves.

The claimant issued an application for judicial review, seeking to challenge the actions of the Chief Constable in (1) preventing her travelling to the demonstration in Fairford, and forcing her to leave the area, and (2) forcibly returning her to London, keeping her on the coach and preventing her from leaving it until she had reached London. At first instance her first complaint was rejected but her second was upheld.[516] In upholding the claimant's second claim, May LJ concluded that the claimant had been detained on the coach back to London and that such detention could not be held to be covered by Art 5(1)(b) or 5(1)(c) of the Convention. The Court of Appeal (Lords Woolf CJ, Clarke and Rix LJJ) upheld the Divisional Court's decision, dismissing an appeal by the Chief Constable and a cross-appeal by the claimant.[517]

Relying on *Sunday Times v United Kingdom (No 2)*[518] and *Hashman and Harrup v United Kingdom*,[519] Lord Bingham found that:

> . . . any prior restraint on freedom of expression calls for the most careful scrutiny . . . . The Strasbourg Court will wish to be satisfied not merely that a state exercised its discretion reasonably, carefully and in good faith, but also that it applied standards in conformity with Convention standards and based its decisions on an acceptable assessment of the relevant facts.[520]

He noted that the protection of the Articles may be denied 'if the demonstration is unauthorised and unlawful' (as in the case of *Ziliberberg*),[521] or if conduct is such as actually to disturb public order (as in *Chorherr v Austria*).[522] But he noted this finding in *Ziliberberg*:

> . . . an individual does not cease to enjoy the right to peaceful assembly as a result of sporadic violence or other punishable acts committed by others in the course of the demonstration, if the individual in question remains peaceful in his or her own intentions or behaviour.[523]

---

516 The case came before the Queen's Bench Divisional Court (May LJ and Harrison J) [2004] EWHC 253 (Admin), [2004] 2 All ER 874.
517 [2004] EWCA Civ 1639; [2005] QB 678.
518 (1991) 14 EHRR 229, at para 51.
519 (1999) 30 EHRR 241, at para 32.
520 Lord Bingham took this phrase from *Christian Democratic People's Party v Moldova*, unreported Appl No 28793/02, 14 May 2006, at para 70.
521 Appl No 61821/00, 4 May 2004, unreported.
522 (1993) 17 EHRR 358.
523 At para 2.

The key argument on behalf of Laporte was that subject to Arts 10(2) and 11(2) of the Convention, the claimant had a right to attend the lawful assembly at RAF Fairford in order to express her strong opposition to the war against Iraq. The conduct of the police, in stopping the coach on which the claimant was travelling at Lechdale, and not allowing it to continue its intended journey to Fairford, was an interference by a public authority (s 6 HRA) with the claimant's exercise of her rights under Arts 10 and 11. The burden of justifying an interference with the exercise of a Convention right such as those protected by Arts 10 and 11 was on the public authority which has interfered with such exercise, in this case the Chief Constable. The interference by the Chief Constable in this case was for a legitimate purpose – the interests of national security, for the prevention of disorder or crime or for the protection of the rights of others – but (a) was not prescribed by law, because it was not warranted under domestic law, and (b) was not necessary in a democratic society, because it was (i) premature and (ii) indiscriminate and was accordingly disproportionate. As regards the argument, which is discussed further in Chapter 11,[524] that the Chief Constable's interference was not prescribed by law because it was not warranted by domestic legal authority, it was argued that there is a power and duty resting on constables to prevent a breach of the peace which reasonably appears to be about to be committed. The test is the same whether the intervention is by arrest or (as in *Humphries v Connor*, *King v Hodges* and *Albert v Lavin* itself) by action short of arrest. But it was argued that there is nothing in domestic authority to support the proposition that action short of arrest may be taken when a breach of the peace is not so imminent as would be necessary to justify an arrest. Here, the officer in charge did not think that a breach of the peace was so imminent as to justify an arrest. Counsel for the police relied on *Moss v McLachlan*,[525] discussed above, in support of an argument that it is not necessary to show that the breach of the peace was so imminent as to justify an arrest. But the House of Lords rejected this argument and accepted that there is nothing in domestic authority to support the proposition that action short of arrest may be taken when a breach of the peace is not so imminent as would be necessary to justify an arrest. Lord Bingham took this view partly on the basis that otherwise the common law doctrine would undermine the 1986 Act:

> Parliament conferred carefully defined powers and imposed carefully defined duties on chief officers of police and the senior police officer. Offences were created and defences provided. Parliament plainly appreciated the need for appropriate police powers to control disorderly demonstrations but was also sensitive to the democratic values inherent in recognition of a right to demonstrate. It would, I think, be surprising if, alongside these closely defined powers and duties, there existed a common law power and duty, exercisable and imposed not only by and on any constable but by and on every member of the public, bounded only by an uncertain and undefined condition of reasonableness.[526]

---

524 See pp 1142–43.
525 [1985] IRLR 76.
526 Ibid at para 46.

He found that *Albert v Lavin* had laid down a simple and workable test readily applicable to constable and private citizen alike which recognised the power and duty to act in an emergency to prevent a breach of the peace, and that there would in almost all circumstances be little doubt as to whom to take action against. He further found little support in the authorities for the proposition that action short of arrest may be taken to prevent a breach of the peace which is not sufficiently imminent to justify arrest. Since the police officer in charge did not consider that the claimant could properly be arrested when the coaches were stopped before reaching Fairford, it followed that action short of arrest could not be taken as an alternative. He also did not accept the finding of the Court of Appeal that the present case is 'very much on all fours with the decision in *Moss v McLachlan*'.[527] He found that *Moss* carried the notion of imminence to extreme limits, but that it was not unreasonable to view the apprehended breach as imminent. But he considered that the situation in *Moss* differed greatly from that in the instant case in which 120 passengers, by no means all of whom were or were thought to be Wombles' members, had been prevented from proceeding to an assembly point which was some distance away from the scene of a lawful demonstration. So he concluded that the actions of the police in turning away the passengers on the coach and then detaining them on the coach were not prescribed by law.

Counsel for the claimant also contended that the police action at Lechlade failed the Convention test of proportionality because it was premature and indiscriminate. It was argued that the action was premature because there was no hint of disorder at Lechlade and no reason to apprehend an immediate outburst of disorder by the claimant and her fellow passengers when they left their coaches at the designated drop-off points in Fairford. Since the action was premature it was necessarily indiscriminate because the police could not at that stage identify those (if any) of the passengers who appeared to be about to commit a breach of the peace. Lord Bingham found that it was not reasonable to suppose that the passengers, apart from the Womble members, wanted a violent confrontation with the police. It was also unreasonable, he found, to anticipate that disorder would immediately occur on arrival of the passengers at the protest site. He noted that during that time the police would be in close attendance and able to identify and arrest those who showed a violent propensity or breached the conditions to which the assembly and procession were subject. He found therefore that it was wholly disproportionate to restrict the claimant's exercise of her rights under Arts 10 and 11 because she was in the company of others, some of whom might, at some time in the future, breach the peace.

This decision is broadly in accordance with the stance taken in *McLeod v UK*,[528] in which it was found that it is insufficient to find that a breach may occur at some future point, but is not immediately probable. In the third edition of this book it was predicted that *McLeod* would be taken into account in findings as to the application of the breach of the peace doctrine under s 2 HRA and that therefore the stance taken in *Peterkin* would be likely to prevail. As discussed above, much of the case law is in accordance with *McLeod* in establishing that (a) an arrest for breach of the peace can only occur when the breach is imminent, meaning – to occur in the near future

---

527 At para 45 of the judgment.
528 (1998) 27 EHRR 493, RJD 19998-VII 2774, Judgment of the Court, 23 September 1998.

– and (b) that if it is not imminent action short of arrest cannot be taken. However, in *Laporte*[529] the Divisional Court and the Court of Appeal both adopted the approach in *Moss*, which allowed for preventive action short of arrest in relation to apprehended breaches of the peace that were not imminent. The House of Lords has now rejected that possibility as representing an illegitimate broadening of the breach of the peace doctrine. In requiring a clear element of immediacy, this decision has created a strong inhibitory rule, not as to the powers that can be invoked under this doctrine, but as to the point at which it can be invoked. However, the Lords could have made a clearer pronouncement on the requirements of immediacy. They accepted that *Moss* took a somewhat lax view of what could be termed imminent, but did not reject that view. The Lords also accepted that preventive action short of arrest can be used under this doctrine where an arrest could be made for an imminent breach of the peace. Thus the police still retain wide powers under this doctrine to interfere with the actions of protesters so long as the element of immediacy is present. That element has to be judged by the officer on the ground who may well take a very broad view of what constitutes an imminent breach of the peace. When such a view is taken it is unlikely in practice that decisions to, for example, disperse protesters or impede them in travelling to the site of the protest will ever be challenged in court, and the impact of the protest will merely be diminished. Nevertheless, this decision is likely to have some impact in protest situations in which it would be very difficult to argue that a breach of the peace was imminent.

This judgment took ss 2 and 6 HRA seriously. The Strasbourg jurisprudence was quite closely analysed and the facts in question were subjected to close scrutiny under the doctrine of proportionality. The very real possibility that the common law could undermine a carefully crafted statutory scheme was recognised and, at least to an extent, avoided. Interestingly, the actions of the police were found not only to be disproportionate to the aim pursued, they were also found not to be prescribed by law. The starting-point was the significance of upholding rights to protest. *Laporte* has offered a check to further development of the doctrine of breach of the peace and has recognised the 'constitutional shift' that the HRA has brought about in this context. Had the judgment gone the other way, it would have left intact a position whereby the police had *carte blanche* to order peaceful protesters away from the scene of a protest, stop cars proceeding to it, and detain persons, without arresting them, whenever a few of the protesters appeared likely to cause disorder or were causing it. That would have continued to render much of the Public Order Act 1986, as amended, effectively redundant, since it would continue to be unnecessary in most circumstances, to rely on ss 12 and 14. It would also have undermined the arrest power under s 24 PACE,[530] and the safeguards for arrest contained in PACE and in Code of Practice G, since in public order situations police could have continued to decide merely to use common law powers to detain short of arrest.

But the impact of *Laporte* must not be over-stated. It curbed the use of common law powers only where a breach of the peace could not be said to be imminent. A range of interventions, including arrest or action short of arrest, is still available to the police so long as it can be said that a breach of the peace is imminent. Thus the statutory

529 [2004] EWCA Civ 1639; [2005] QB 678.
530 See Chapter 11, pp 1144–45.

scheme is still highly likely to be marginalised. If a large group of protesters appears to the police to contain some unruly, or aggressive, or potentially aggressive, elements, the police appear, post-*Laporte*, to retain very broad powers to intervene. This point brings this discussion to the third issue identified above, which arose in the highly controversial case of *Austin and Saxby v Commissioner of Police of the Metropolis.*[531] The decision concerned a political demonstration against capitalism and globalisation that was organised in the heart of the West End of London on May Day 2001. Publicity material had given the police reason to believe that it would begin at 4 pm, but in fact it started two hours earlier. About 3,000 people had gathered in Oxford Circus and thousands more in the surrounding streets. The protest was made up of disparate groups, some of whom, according to police intelligence, had been involved in violent acts during protests in the past. The first claimant, Austin, took part in the demonstration and made political speeches using a megaphone. The second claimant, Saxby, had come to London on business and had inadvertently become caught up in the crowd. The police faced a difficult public order situation, and stated that they had been taken by surprise by the timing of the demonstration; in order to prevent a breakdown of law and order, they detained thousands of demonstrators for about seven hours by forming a cordon around them. The cordon was absolute, in that persons were completely trapped in the area for the whole seven-hour period in cold and uncomfortable conditions and without recourse to any facilities. The police planned to release the crowd slowly, but this was hindered, according to the police evidence, by some outbreaks of disorder or violence either from the trapped group or from persons outside the cordon. It was considered unsafe to release groups but a few individuals were released because, for example, they were suffering panic attacks. The claimants asked to be released but were refused on the ground that some protesters were threatening a breach of the peace. The claimants had not created a threat; nor had they provoked others. They remained peaceable throughout the period.

The claimants brought a claim for damages, alleging false imprisonment and also deprivation of liberty, contrary to Art 5, ECHR, raising the claim under s 7 HRA. Some 150 other persons trapped that day had given notice of, or commenced, legal proceedings for damages against the Commissioner. The two cases of the claimants, Austin and Saxby, were not strictly test cases, but the decisions on the issues arising in the two cases were considered by the judge to enable most, if not all, of the other claims to be settled by agreement. The issues under the tort action and under Art 5 were dealt with separately since the judge found that different factors were relevant in both claims. He found that in a claim for false imprisonment the burden of proof rested on the claimant to prove the imprisonment and on the defendant to prove the justification for it. If the detention fell within Art 5, the burden of proof, he found, lay on the defendant to bring the case within one of the exhaustive list of exceptions to Art 5(1), but if the question was whether the detention fell within Art 5(1) the burden was on the claimant.

The judge noted that in *HL v United Kingdom*,[532] the Strasbourg Court had explained that the meaning of imprisonment in the tort is not the same as the meaning of deprivation

---

531 [2005] HRLR 20; 2005 WL 699571 (QBD), (2005) 155 NLJ 515; (2005) *The Times* 14 April, 699, 571, [2005] EWHC 480; 23 March 2005, Queen's Bench Division of the High Court.
532 Appl No 45508/99.

of liberty in Art 5. It had held that, as Chapter 2 pointed out, the distinction for the purposes of Art 5 between a deprivation of, and restriction upon, liberty is merely one of degree or intensity and not one of nature or substance.[533] The House of Lords (in *R v Bournewood Community and Mental Health NHS Trust ex p L*, the domestic case that was then considered at Strasbourg)[534] had considered the question from the point of view of the tort of false imprisonment, and considerable emphasis had been placed by the domestic courts on the fact that the applicant was compliant and had never attempted, or expressed the wish, to leave. The Court found, however, that the right to liberty is too important in a democratic society for a person to lose the benefit of Convention protection for the single reason that he may have given himself up to be taken into detention,[535] especially when it was not disputed that that person was legally incapable of consenting to, or disagreeing with, the proposed action. The Court went on to find that the applicant was of unsound mind within Art 5(1)(e), but that there had been a violation of Art 5(1)[536] due to the absence of procedural safeguards designed to protect against arbitrary deprivations of liberty on grounds of necessity. So, as the judge in the instant case noted, the position was that the tort, and the claim under s 6 HRA and Art 5, although both concerned with liberty, are using that term in different senses. He considered that a claim could fail under the tort, but succeed under Art 5, and *vice versa*. It may be noted that it would arguably have been open to the judge to import the Convention concept of deprivation of liberty into the tort of false imprisonment under s 6 HRA, thus – in relation to the concept of imprisonment – aligning the tort with Art 5, but that having briefly considered this, he did not do so.[537] He accepted that the tort must not be interpreted inconsistently with Art 5, under s 6. Clearly that would mean, under s 6, that a claim could not succeed under Art 5 but fail under the tort, although the converse would be possible.

There were other relevant factors, including that of the application of ss 11, 12 and 14 POA 1986; the consideration of those sections in the case is discussed further above.[538] It may be noted that the police did not state at the time in question that they were relying on ss 12 or 14; nor did they mention the sections in their written submissions on the case. The possible application of the sections was raised by the judge in the case, and it was found that the police could be viewed as imposing conditions under the sections even though they did not have them in mind at the time and appeared to consider that they were exercising common law powers only to control the protest. It was found that conditions were properly imposed under ss 12 or 14 on the march and were breached. It was also found that s 11 was breached since the organisers had not given the correct time of the march in the notice. The breach of s 11 appeared to influence the judge in relation to the breach of the peace and Art 5 issues. Neither

---

533 *Guzzardi v Italy* judgement of November 6, 1980, Series A no.39, at para 92 and *Ashingdane v UK* (1985) 7 EHRR 528, at para 41. See also Chapter 2 pp 52–53 for brief discussion of the concept of deprivation of liberty.
534 [1999] 1 AC 458.
535 *De Wilde, Ooms and Versyp v Belgium* (judgement of June 18, 1971, Series A no 12, paras 64–65.
536 At para 124.
537 See the discussion of the impact of the Convention under the HRA on the common law, Chapter 4, pp 252–56.
538 See pp 703 and 722–23.

claimant, however, was an organiser and there appeared to be no evidence that Austin, who was part of the demonstration, was aware of the breach. Saxton obviously could not have been aware of it. The judge appeared to view the march as unlawful since the notice requirement had been breached and therefore viewed Austin as deliberately taking part in an unlawful march. However, as discussed above, s 11 provides a notice requirement; it does not require that marches should be *authorised* by the authorities. The *organisers* can incur liability under s 11(7) if the requirement is breached, but the participants can not, even if they are aware of the breach, and the march in general is not rendered unlawful.

The case raised the question, if the detention of the claimants fell within Art 5(1), whether Art 5(1)(c) in particular was capable of authorising the detention of individuals whom the police neither suspected of criminality nor – it appeared – intended to bring before a court on reasonable suspicion of having committed an offence or to prevent them doing so. Once the cordon was lifted and dispersal occurred, it did not appear from the evidence of both sides that any consideration at all was given to arresting Austin or Saxby. When they asked to be allowed to leave earlier they were not told by police that at some point they personally might be arrested.

The claimants argued that Art 5(1) was engaged by a deprivation of liberty short of arrest, especially one that was more than brief.[539] It was found that Art 5(1) applied to the detentions: no one in the crowd was free to leave without permission; the detention was sufficient physically to amount to a deprivation of liberty. The measure was a close confinement, with minimal liberty, in Oxford Circus; so the detention was a deprivation of liberty, rather than a restriction. If the only reason why police had detained the crowd had been to take temporary measures for the protection of members of the crowd themselves, this would not, it was found, amount to a deprivation of liberty. However, this was not found to be the case, and so there was a deprivation of liberty within Art 5(1).

The detention was imposed, the judge then found, with the conditional purpose of arresting those whom it would be lawful and practicable to arrest and bring before a judge, and to prevent such persons as might be so identified from committing offences of violence. This was found to be capable of falling within Art 5(1)(c). In order to fall within Art 5(1)(c) the police had to be exercising a lawful power. It was found that powers to prevent a breach of the peace do not depend upon the threat of violence and that there was a power of temporary detention for so long as was necessary to protect the rights of others and consistent with public safety.

The judgment is not entirely clear, but essentially it proceeded on the basis that the police actions could be justifiable under Art 5(1)(c) on the ground that the detention was effected partly in order to arrest some persons at some future point on grounds of breach of the peace. The claimants relied on the finding in *Lawless v Ireland (No.3)*[540] that persons detained must be brought before the court in all cases to which Art 5(1)(c) refers. Their counsel also relied on *Guzzardi v Italy*,[541] *Fox, Campbell and Hartley v*

---

539 *Guenat v Swizerland*, Appl No 24722/94 (1995) 810A DR 130; *Hojemeister v Germany* 9179/80 on July 6, 1981 were relied on. The domestic case of *DPP v Meaden* [2003] EWHC 3005 (Admin); [2004] 1 WLR 945 was also relied upon.

540 (1961) 1 EHRR 15 at paras 13–14.

541 (1980) 3 EHRR 333 at para 102.

UK,[542] and *Berktay v Turkey*[543] for the proposition that the suspicion has to relate to the person detained and to a concrete and specific offence. It was argued on behalf of the police that if the detainee is not taken before a court, but is released instead, then Art 5(1)(c) may be satisfied on the basis that the police had a 'conditional' purpose to arrest.[544] The test for deciding whether a measure short of arrest could lawfully be taken against a given individual was, it was found, reasonable suspicion that that individual was presenting the relevant threat. It may be noted that the two claimants were trapped within the cordon for a total of seven hours and during that time, on the evidence, committed no act that could be interpreted as meaning that they themselves were about to breach the peace. Saxby was – in effect – not in the company of the protesters voluntarily.

In assessing the preventive action that can be taken against persons who do not threaten to breach the peace, the judge relied on the Court of Appeal decision in *Laporte*; it was held:

> The important feature to note about the ability to take preventive action is that its justification is not derived from the person against whom the action is taken having actually committed an offence, but based upon a need to prevent the apprehended breach of the peace. In some situations, preventing a breach of the peace will only be possible if action is taken which risks affecting a wholly innocent individual.[545]

The judge found that in *R v Jones and Mirrless*,[546] mere voluntary presence which in fact encouraged the principal was not enough; nor was mere voluntary presence coupled with a secret intention to assist, if required. He said that none of the cases make it clear whether mere voluntary presence, which in fact encourages the principal, and which is intended to do so, is sufficient, but he found that this should be the case and that that conclusion was consistent with the leading case of *R v Coney* on the point.[547] He found that the voluntary presence of a defendant as part of a crowd engaged in threatening behaviour over a period of time and/or distance was sufficient to raise a prima facie case against him on a charge of threatening behaviour, notwithstanding the absence of evidence of any act done by himself.[548] The court commented that a high degree of respect should be shown towards a police officer's assessment of the risk of what a crowd might do were it not contained, whilst also bearing in mind individuals' human rights.

---

542 (1990) 13 EHRR 157 at para 34.
543 Appl No 22493/93 March 1, 2001 at para 199.
544 The defence relied on *Brogan v UK* (1988) 11 EHRR 11 in which it was found at paras 52–53 that a 'conditional' purpose can suffice to bring a case within Art 5(1)(c).
545 *(Laporte) v Chief Constable of Gloucestershire Constabulary* [2004] EWCA Civ 1639; [2005] All ER 473; [2005] HRLR 6 at para 48.
546 65 Cr App R 250, CA (following *R v Allan* [1965] 1 QB 130, 47 Cr App R 243, CCA.
547 (1882) 8 QBD 534, CCR (non-accidental presence at an unlawful prize-fight capable of being encouragement); he also found it consistent with *Wilcox v Jeffrey* [1951] 1 All ER 464, DC (intentional encouragement in fact by voluntary attendance at a concert performance known to be unlawful).
548 *Allan v Ireland*, 79 Cr App R 206, DC.

The judge further found that there was a public procession or assembly being held at Oxford Circus at 2 pm and the senior police officer reasonably believed that it might result in serious public disorder, serious damage to property, or serious disruption to the life of the community. The claimants argued that those powers could not provide a power to detain people, and could not be relied on after the event if not relied on at the time. But the judge found that directions pursuant to ss 12 and 14 POA were given, and the fact that none of the officers had the sections in mind was, the judge found, immaterial. The directions imposed conditions prohibiting the procession from entering any public place specified. Those directions, the judge found, were necessary to prevent disorder, damage, disruption or intimidation, and the police had reasonable grounds to take this view.

The judge noted that it appeared to the officers detaining each claimant that a breach of the peace was about to be committed. The judge found that whilst this inference could be properly drawn in the instant case, it was unlikely to be capable of being drawn in all crowd cases. It was found that the police also have a right, and perhaps a duty, to take measures short of arrest, sometimes called self-help, when there is unlawful conduct which does not amount to a breach of the peace. (In so far as this finding formed a part of the part of the judgment, it has now been overruled by the House of Lords' judgment in *Laporte*.) The limits on these common law powers, he noted in passing, are by no means clear.

The measures that the officers took – in containing the claimants in Oxford Street – were found to be reasonable steps to prevent each claimant from breaking or threatening to break the peace. In determining reasonableness the judge took account of the fact that members of the assembly were in breach of the conditions imposed under ss 12 or 14 of the 1986 Act, although there had been no advertence to the imposition of conditions under the Act by the police. The judge did not make this entirely clear, but appeared to indicate that the police detention of the assembly related to the breach of ss 12 or 14. That would have to presuppose that one of the conditions that could be imposed under ss 12 or 14 was to detain the assembly for a substantial period of time. Leaving aside the question whether the police can invoke conditions under either ss 12 or 14 without adverting to those powers, or communicating their use to the protesters, that finding is doubtful since once the march becomes a static assembly it is subject to s 14 which does not, on its face, allow for detention of the assembly, and case law has established that the condition must be imposed under the right section.[549] However, as discussed above, the judge found that s 14 could be interpreted to include a power to impose detention.[550]

In assessing whether an arrest of the applicants, if undertaken, would have been reasonable, the judge noted that it is now recognised that 'domestic courts must themselves form a judgment whether a Convention right has been breached' and that 'the intensity of review is somewhat greater under the proportionality approach' [than under the *Wednesbury* approach].[551] In relation to the intensity of scrutiny, the judge

549 See *DPP v Jones* (2002), above p 723.
550 See pp 722–23.
551 *R (Daly) v Secretary of State for the Home Department* [2001] UKHL 26, [2001] 2 AC 532; [2001] HRLR 49, paras 23, 27.

found that the Court should accord a high degree of respect for the police officers' appreciation of the risks of what the members of the crowd might have done if not contained. At the same time he found that the Court should subject to a very close scrutiny the practical effect which derogating measures have on individual human rights, the importance of the rights affected, and the robustness of any safeguards intended to minimise the impact of the derogating measures on individual human rights. The judge found that when each claimant came forward and asked to be released, the police did suspect that all those present within the cordon, including each claimant, were demonstrators, and that in the particular circumstances of the case, that meant that they also appeared to the police to be about to commit a breach of the peace.[552] The judge accepted the police evidence that it was not possible to differentiate between violent and non-violent demonstrators in order to determine who could in principle be subject to arrest. The judge held that the burden of proof was on the claimants to show that the exercise of the discretion to detain was unreasonable, either to the *Wednesbury* threshold, or to a more intense level of scrutiny.

So, in summary, the detention of the claimants amounted to a breach of Art 5 but, it was found, it was justified because they appeared to the police to be protesters and, as such, might commit a breach of the peace. The detention was imposed with the conditional purpose of arresting those whom it would be lawful and practicable to arrest and bring before a judge, and to prevent such persons as might be so identified from committing offences of violence. It appeared to the officers detaining each claimant that each one, as members of the demonstration, was about to commit a breach of the peace and, the judge found, it so appeared on reasonable grounds. So the detention was found to be justified under Art 5(1)(c). On the basis of the use of the breach of the peace doctrine, taking account of the breach of s 12 or s 14, the claims of breach of Art 5 were found to fail in respect of both claimants.

It was further found, in relation to the claim of false imprisonment, that the claimants had been imprisoned within the cordon, but that the police had a defence of necessity in so trapping them, which defeated the false imprisonment claim. In putting forward that defence, it was found that the police had to show that they reasonably suspected that the claimants presented a relevant threat and that it had been reasonable to use their discretion to detain them. The existence of the defence of necessity in tort had been affirmed by the House of Lords in *Esso Petroleum Co Ltd v Southport Corp.*[553] The police, it was found, can take measures for the protection of everyone, and a reasonable measure taken in this instance, involving minimum use of force, was, it was found, to detain the crowd until dispersal could be arranged safely. The claimants argued that there were alternative and less restrictive measures open to the police and that therefore the police had acted negligently, defeating the defence of necessity. This was rejected by the judge on the basis that in the difficult circumstances the police had acted reasonably. The need to take the action of creating the cordon did not arise out of any negligence on the part of the police, it was found. The claimants, he found, as members of the crowd, would, if not subject to police control, have presented as

---

552 At para 129.
553 [1955] 3 All ER 864, [1956] AC 218.

much of an innocent threat to other members of the crowd as every other innocent member presented to them. He found that one of the reasons for which the police took the contested actions was to prevent serious injury, and possible death, to persons for whom they were responsible, including police officers, members of the crowd and third parties, as well as to protect property.

The judge concluded by saying that no case was advanced at the trial to the effect that the police were adopting tactics designed to interfere with rights of assembly and freedom of speech. He ended by stating that the case was about the right to liberty, and public order, and not about freedom of speech or freedom of assembly.[554]

This is a very significant and very worrying judgment for public protest. It means that the police can use this doctrine against protesters in order to: arrest them; detain them for several hours, without arresting them; or to stop an assembly or march or divert it or to disperse most or all of it. The power to do all this arises if some members of the group have been involved in disorder in the past, or intelligence suggests that this is the case, or if some members are disorderly, or appear likely to become disorderly. The 'conditional purpose' to arrest some persons is sufficient to allow the power of prolonged detention to be exercised, even if in the event no attempt to arrest those detained is made or – it appears – even considered. These powers are so broad that the use of the statutory scheme under the 1986 or 1994 Acts becomes almost irrelevant. In most circumstances all the ss 12 or 14 powers can be exercised by way of the breach of the peace doctrine. The degree of deference accorded to the police in this judgment makes it very difficult to assess after the event the risk in fact posed at the time by protesters. The situation was particularly volatile, but the judgment came very close to suggesting that taking part in any protest during which a few protesters were disorderly, or showed a propensity to disorder, could render all members of the protest liable to all the powers listed, and a range of other ones as well. For example, as the protesters (and any bystanders, such as Saxby, trapped with them) were allowed to filter through the cordon, names and addresses were taken and they were filmed.

The key point, it is argued, at which this judgment fell into error was in finding that if protesters are in the company of other protesters who are disorderly or may become disorderly, even though they themselves have shown no propensity at all to disorder over a long period of time, they become liable to detention or arrest. It is argued that that finding is completely opposed to the spirit of Art 5 (and Arts 10 and 11), and that a notional, tokenistic 'conditional purpose to arrest' on that basis is not sufficient to justify the detention under Art 5(1)(c), given the strong findings in *Guzzardi v Italy*,[555] *Fox, Campbell and Hartley v UK*,[556] and *Berktay v Turkey*[557] as to the need for suspicion of a specific offence relating to the person in question. The specific 'offence' would have to be breaching the peace, but it is greatly stretching the definition from *Howell* to find that protesters such as Austin who have behaved entirely peacefully throughout the whole period of time can be said to be liable to arrest for that 'offence'. *A fortiori* those remarks can be applied to bystanders such as

---

554 At paras 607 and 608.
555 (1980) 3 EHRR 333 at para 102.
556 (1990) 13 EHRR 157 at para 34.
557 Appl No 22493/93 March 1, 2001 at para 199.

Saxby who are only in the company of the protesters because they have been forced into it by the police! Saxby could not have been said to have encouraged those breaching the peace by his presence or as intending to do so since he was not part of the protest. Clearly, he, in common with the others, was annoyed at being trapped by the police – although he remained peaceful – but that was a consequence of the actions of the police, not part of encouragement to others to engage in disorderly or violent protest. Austin's only 'offence' was to take part in a protest during which some people, not the majority, were disorderly or aggressive. It is argued that the police had ample opportunity – seven hours in total, or more – to observe the behaviour of the protesters and could have made greater efforts to allow some persons to leave, differentiating between peaceful and non-peaceful protesters in so doing. Article 5 was breached, it is argued, at some point during those seven hours in relation to both Austin and Saxby. It was, it is contended, breached at the point when an argument that they personally could be liable to arrest at some future point would have become implausible had even superficial inquiries been made. Both Austin and Saxby communicated with police about their circumstances; that could have been the point at which both should have been allowed to leave, in a carefully controlled dispersal from the Square. After that point had come and passed, the continued detention, it is argued, breached Art 5 and damages should have been awarded that reflected the length of that period.

The House of Lords' decision in *Laporte* differs greatly from this one in its treatment of the Convention dimension. It takes the Convention rights in question more seriously and adopts a stricter level of scrutiny in relation to the judgments of the officers at the time. The situations in the two instances were roughly comparable in certain respects, in that in each officers chose to detain protesters on grounds of apprehension of breach of the peace rather than arresting them or allowing them to proceed with the protest. In each instance completely peaceful protesters were engaged in a protest in the company of a small number of disorderly or potentially violent protesters, and in each instance this led to their detention. The House of Lords indicated that the police should have made more effort to distinguish between peaceful and non-peaceful protesters in exercising powers to prevent a breach of the peace. However, in *Laporte* the police, crucially, did not think that a breach of the peace was imminent, although they thought one might arise if the protesters continued, whereas in *Austin and Saxby* it appeared that the police did think that a breach was imminent at the point when the detention occurred. The House of Lords' decision merely limited the use of the immense panoply of powers available under the breach of the peace doctrine to situations where the imminence of the breach of the peace would warrant arrest. Since in *Austin* the police appeared to take the view that they could have made arrests at the entrance to Oxford Square, the outcome of the decision is not out of harmony – except on the point noted above – with that of the House of Lords. Therefore most of the findings in *Austin* still stand, despite the later House of Lords' decision in *Laporte*.

The judge considered that Arts 10 and 11 were not engaged in this instance since Saxby was not seeking to exercise rights under those Articles on that occasion and Austin had already had an opportunity to exercise them. She had used her loudspeaker to broadcast political messages before the march arrived at Oxford Square and thereafter for a period. When she was told that she could not leave and was imprisoned in the cordon she used her loudspeaker to comfort those who were trapped in the Square. It is, however, argued that the judge's conception of the exercise of Art 10 and 11 rights was a very narrow one. Austin was tramelled as to the place and time that she could exercise those rights and the situation in which she could exercise them. The messages she could broadcast were circumscribed by the situation. Austin's intentions in joining the protest would have been to exercise the rights as part of the march, when they could have been publicised more effectively to passers-by, not as part of a group of prisoners trapped by the police on one spot in very uncomfortable conditions. Further, the judgment – which confirms and extends already very broad powers – is not in harmony with the spirit of Arts 10 or 11. If protesters risk arrest or detention when joining protests they may be deterred from doing so.

Was the tort of false imprisonment interpreted consistently with Art 5 in this case? It is suggested that the application of the defence of necessity as interpreted in this case is inconsistent with Art 5 since none of the exceptions in Art 5 cover the defence. In order to align the two, the tort should be reinterpreted to exclude that defence; the position should be that a detention cannot be tortious if a lawful arrest, or a detention short of arrest, based on a clear power, and covered by Art 5(1)(c) (or (b)) has occurred. If the judge considered that apprehension of breach of the peace provided a lawful power to detain for a substantial period without arrest, it is unclear why it was thought that the defence of necessity was relevant in any event.

Austin and Saxby has confirmed that the police have a very wide range of powers to use even against entirely peaceful protesters if a few protesters are or may be disorderly. Clearly, the police are faced with serious difficulties in controlling a protest such as that which occurred on Mayday in 2001. However, trapping 3,000 people for seven hours is a highly unusual event; it has not occurred before or since. That suggests that the police do not normally need to resort to such tactics which of course could be counter-productive. It is suggested that if further powers to control protests are needed Parliament should enact them, in preference to any further distortions of an already very broad common law doctrine, in order to provide a legal underpinning for police action. This judgment gave the impression of trying to find, after the event, legal justification for the police action; in so doing it created a number of extensions to the doctrine. The decision in *Laporte* may signal to judges that they need to rein in this doctrine rather than extend it, so it is possible that a repeat of decisions such as this one will not occur. The police in *Austin* could have employed ss 12 and 14 of the 1986 Act against the protest beforehand, but chose not to. Curtailment of this common law doctrine might encourage the police to employ the statutory framework that is already in place in order to manage protests – and Lord Bingham clearly signalled in *Laporte*, not only that the Convention rights under the HRA had brought about a clear change in the constitutional position of rights to expression and assembly, but that the common law should not be allowed to marginalise or undermine that framework.

Provoking a breach of the peace

Cases such as *Moss v McLachlan* concerned the use of preventive powers against those who could be viewed as likely to breach the peace at some future point. The courts have taken an equally broad view of conduct which might provoke others to breach the peace. *Beatty v Gillbanks*[558] established the important principle that persons acting lawfully could not be held responsible for the actions of those who were thereby induced to act unlawfully. However, in *Duncan v Jones*,[559] a speaker wishing to address a public meeting opposite a training centre for the unemployed, was told to move away to a different street because the police apprehended that her speech might cause a breach of the peace. A year previously there had been some restlessness among the unemployed following a speech by the same speaker. She refused to move away from the centre and was arrested for obstructing a police officer in the course of his duty. On appeal, it was found that the police had been acting in the course of their duty because they had reasonably apprehended a breach of the peace.

The case therefore clearly undermined the *Beatty v Gillbanks* principle in that the freedom of the speaker was infringed, not because of her conduct, but because of police fears about the possible response of the audience. In the later case of *Jordan v Burgoyne*,[560] it was found that a public speaker could be guilty of breach of the peace if he spoke words which were likely to cause disorder amongst the particular audience present, even where the audience had come with the express intention of causing trouble. In *Wise v Dunning*[561] it was found that a breach of the peace would arise if there is an act of the defendant 'the natural consequence of which, if the act be not unlawful in itself would be to produce an unlawful act by other persons'. An extremely wide interpretation of this possibility was accepted in *Holmes v Bournemouth Crown Court*;[562] an anti-smoking campaigner who held up a placard and shouted anti-smoking slogans, but in no way threatened violence, was arrested on the ground that if he stayed in his position – outside the designated lobbying area at a Conservative Party Conference – a breach of the peace might arise. The finding that in arresting him, the officer had acted in the execution of his duty, was upheld on appeal.

A similar stance was taken in *Kelly v Chief Constable of Hampshire*[563] which concerned an altercation between a hunt saboteur and a huntsman, resulting in the arrest of the saboteur. According to the Court of Appeal, if a constable reasonably believes that a breach of the peace is about to occur due to a dispute, he may arrest one of the participants: he has complete discretion as to which participant to arrest, and this may even be the case where the evidence suggests that the one not arrested has committed an assault on the other.[564] In other words, the victim of the assault may be arrested to prevent a fight between the two from breaking out.

In *Percy v DPP*,[565] Collins J ruled: 'The conduct in question does not in itself have to be disorderly or a breach of the criminal law. It is sufficient if its natural consequence would, if persisted in, be to provoke others to violence.'[566] Similarly, in *Morpeth Ward*

---

558   (1882) 9 QBD 308.
559   [1936] 1 KB 218; for comment, see Daintith, T [1966] PL 248.
560   [1963] 2 QB 744; [1963] 2 All ER 225, DC. It should be noted that the case was concerned with breach of the peace under the Public Order Act 1936, s 5.
561   [1902] 1 KB 167. See also *Duncan v Jones* [1936] 1 KB 218.
562   (1993) unreported, 6 October 1993, DC; cited in Bailey, Harris and Jones, op. cit., fn 1, p 256.
563   (1993) *The Independent*, 25 March.
564   *Obiter* comment from Lloyd LJ. The huntsman had assaulted Kelly with his whip.
565   [1995] 3 All ER 124, DC.
566   Ibid, p 131.

JJ ex p Ward,[567] which concerned the behaviour of protesters against pheasant shooting, Brooke J stated: '. . . provocative disorderly behaviour which is likely to have the natural consequence of causing violence, even if only to the persons of the provokers, is capable of being conduct likely to cause a breach of the peace.'[568] Thus, the reasonableness of the shooters' behaviour or potential behaviour was not called into question. The court did not lay down a test to determine the point at which a violent reaction to provoking behaviour might be termed an unnatural consequence of such behaviour. It focused simply on the question whether the natural consequence of the behaviour in question was to provoke violence, thus leaving open the possibility that an extreme reaction from those provoked, although probably unreasonable, might be termed natural. The reasonableness of the shooters' behaviour or potential behaviour (one of the shooting party had threatened to kill a protester) was not called into question. The response of the shooters was viewed as the natural and probable consequence of the protest; the attribution of responsibility for the apprehended breach of the peace on the basis of proportionality between the provocation and the reaction was avoided.

This very wide finding received a more restrictive interpretation in *Nicol v DPP*,[569] which concerned the behaviour of fishing protesters. During an angling competition the protesters blew horns, threw twigs into the water and attempted verbally to dissuade the anglers from fishing. This provoked the anglers so that they were on the verge of using force to remove the protesters. The protesters were arrested for breach of the peace. It was found that they were guilty of conduct whereby a breach of the peace was likely to be caused since their conduct, although lawful, was unreasonable and was likely to provoke the anglers to violence. Thus, the reasonableness of the behaviour of those provoked was considered. Simon Brown LJ found that a natural consequence of lawful conduct could be violence in another only where the defendant rather than the other person could be said to be acting unreasonably, and, further, that unless the anglers' rights had been infringed, it would not be reasonable for them to react violently. It was assumed that their rights had been infringed,[570] and that as between the two groups the behaviour of the fishing protesters was clearly unreasonable. The need to show an infringement of 'rights' and the findings as to reasonableness place a limitation on the 'natural consequence' test which was not present in *Wise v Dunning*. This finding offers some clarification of the 'natural consequence' test although, since there is no right to fish, the rights referred to are unclear. The term 'liberties' rather than 'rights' would have been more appropriate. Possibly in referring to an infringement of rights Simon-Brown J was seeking to distinguish so called direct action from other forms of protest.

It is unclear at present whether the test from *Nicol* or from *Ex p Ward* will prevail. Clear adoption of the *Nicol* test would go some way towards restoration of the *Beatty v Gillbanks* principle since following it, behaviour which has as its natural consequence the provoking of others to violence will not amount to a breach of the peace unless it

---

567 (1992) 95 Cr App R 215.
568 Ibid, p 221.
569 (1996) 1 J Civ Lib 75. See further *Steel v UK* (1999) 28 EHRR 603.
570 The rights referred to were left unclear. There is, of course, in general no right to fish, merely a freedom to do so; fishing rights may be obtained under a contract with the landowner, but this does not appear to have been the case in this instance since the anglers were fishing in a public park.

is also unreasonable. But, of course, the test depends upon a wide and uncertain test of reasonableness; the judiciary may well be disinclined to find that the behaviour of groups espousing minority, 'alternative' viewpoints, such as hunt saboteurs or tree protesters, while lawful, was also reasonable. The decision may well be interpreted to mean that any activities as part of peaceful protest, which may provoke those whose behaviour is the subject of the protest to use force, should be accounted behaviour likely to give rise to a breach of the peace, so long as the protesters can be said to have infringed 'rights'. The judiciary may be disinclined to find that the behaviour of groups such as hunt saboteurs or tree protesters, while lawful, was reasonable.

Adoption of the *Nicol* test in relation to protest by speech rather than by means of direct action might allow a distinction to be drawn between forceful speech calling the attention of others to arguments, issues or events, and speech which consists of an attack upon the hearers with the intent of causing extreme provocation. The crucial difference should be the verbal attack which renders the speaker directly responsible for awakening hatred and violence. Arguably, the first type of speech should never be restrained, but it may be acceptable to restrain the second when it offers extreme provocation to its hearers.[571] Sections 4, 4A and 5 of the Public Order Act 1986 (below) appear to be aimed only at the latter, deliberately provocative form of speech, although they are not confined to instances of extreme provocation. However, as seen above, the power to prevent a breach of the peace fails to distinguish at present clearly between the two situations.

Bail conditions

Binding over to keep the peace may form part of a bail condition, but bail conditions may be more specific than this. A person charged with any offence may be bailed as long as they promise to fulfil certain conditions.[572] This aspect of criminal procedure can readily be used by the police against protesters or demonstrators; they can be charged with a low level public order offence or bound over to keep the peace, thus allowing the imposition of conditions which may prevent participation in future protest. If the conditions are broken, the bailee can be imprisoned. The Bail Act 1976 requires that applications for bail should be individually assessed in order to determine whether conditions should be imposed, thereby reflecting concern that the bailing procedure should not result in any further deprivation of liberty than is necessary. Despite this, during the miners' strike there was evidence that conditions were being routinely imposed without regard to the threat posed by the individual applicant. The Divisional Court, however, found that such practices were lawful (Mansfield JJ *ex p Sharkey*).[573]

Impact of the HRA

On the basis of the decisions discussed, the breach of the peace doctrine not only fails to distinguish fully between the forms of protest referred to above, but also makes

571 For comment on this issue, see Birtles, W (1973) 36 MLR 587. For discussion in the context of race hatred, see Chapter 6, pp 497–509.
572 See Feldman, op. cit., fn 1, 1st edn, pp 835–42.
573 [1985] QB 613.

no attempt to inquire into their significance in terms of free expression. The doctrine in itself provides no means of distinguishing between rowdy football supporters and protesters. There is no recognition of the particular need to protect the communicative rights of minority groups, on the basis that their views may find little expression within mainstream speech, or of the likelihood that the provision of such broad police powers, while neutral on their face as between collective and minority standpoints, will tend to bear disproportionately on the latter. The domestic decisions discussed here tend to exhibit an arbitrariness which fuels the general argument that these powers provide the police with an unacceptably wide discretion which is not fully held in check by the courts. Even where cases do not come to court, or where decisions to bind over are overturned on appeal, as in *Percy v DPP*,[574] the detention of the defendant will have occurred on what is often a flimsy and imprecise legal basis. Post-HRA *Laporte* established that preventive action short of arrest cannot be used under this doctrine where an arrest could not be made for an imminent breach of the peace. But that is the only sense in which *Laporte* curbed this very broad doctrine. Within the models indicated above, what further effect could Arts 10 and 11 have on the development of the doctrine of breach of the peace?

As noted above, any interference with freedom of peaceful assembly must be 'prescribed by law' according to Arts 10(2) and 11(2). These words import requirements of certainty and fair warning and therefore under the HRA, the arrest and bind over powers may be reviewed by the judiciary in order to determine whether they meet these standards. The view of the Law Commission is that '. . . binding over falls short of what ought to be two elementary principles of criminal or quasi-criminal law. These require the law to be both certain and readily ascertainable'.[575] However, as indicated above, the actual standards connoted by the words 'prescribed by law' may not be very high, particularly where public order matters are in issue. In *Steel and Others v UK*,[576] which concerned the arrest and detention of applicants engaged in various forms of public protest, the European Commission on Human Rights took note of the findings of the Law Commission regarding certainty, but, taking account of the notion of varying levels of precision referred to above, it found that 'the concept of "breach of the peace" is sufficiently certain to comply with the notion of "prescribed by law" under Article 10 para 2'.[577] The Court found that the breach of the peace doctrine provided sufficient guidance and was formulated with sufficient precision to satisfy the requirement of Art 5(1)(c) that arrest and detention should be in accordance with a procedure prescribed by law, and that the prescribed by law requirement of Art 10

---

574 [1995] 3 All ER 124. The case concerned a solitary protester who trespassed at a US military base; it was found that her conduct was likely to give rise to a breach of the peace and, when she refused to be bound over, she was imprisoned. However, on appeal, the Divisional Court found that trained military personnel were unlikely to be provoked into responding to her trespass with violence.

575 Law Commission Report No 222, para 4.16. The Law Commission relied in part on the failure of these powers to meet the standards laid down by the European Convention on Human Rights.

576 (1999) 28 EHRR 603.

577 Para 148. Usually, Strasbourg will find a violation of the 'prescribed by law' requirement only where the interference has no legal basis: *Malone v UK* A 82 (1984) 7 EHRR 14; *Halford v UK* [1997] IRLR 471. But, exceptionally, in *Hashman and Harrup v UK* (2000) 8 BHRC 104, a basis in law was present but did not satisfy the requirements of this test; discussed above, pp 751–52.

was also satisfied.[578] In *McLeod v UK*,[579] the Court found that the breach of the peace doctrine was 'in accordance with the law' under Art 8. Thus, in respect of the key elements of 'prescribed by law' – legal basis, certainty and accessibility – the breach of the peace doctrine meets Strasbourg standards. The House of Lords was not directly confronted with this question in *Laporte*; it merely found that the use of powers short of arrest to deal with non-imminent breaches of the peace were not prescribed by law. The Lords impliedly took the stance that the power to arrest for an imminent breach is prescribed by law. Within the 'minimalist' model it is almost inconceivable that domestic courts will seek to import higher standards under the 'prescribed by law' rubric. Within the 'activist' model, however, this might occur on the argument that the findings in question in *McLeod* depended on the application of relatively low standards of precision and accessibility.

Clearly, reappraisal and reform of the doctrine of breach of the peace is far more likely to occur by reference to the notion of what is 'necessary in a democratic society' within Arts 10 and 11 para 2, which includes the need to show that the action taken was proportionate to the aim pursued. This issue was extensively considered by the Court in *Steel v UK*, but the findings were quite strongly influenced by the doctrine of the margin of appreciation.[580] The first applicant had taken part in a protest against a grouse shoot and had stood in the way of participants to prevent them taking shots. Since this behaviour was likely to be provocative, the Court found that her arrest and detention, although constituting serious interferences with her freedom of expression, could be viewed as proportionate to the aim of preventing disorder and of maintaining the authority of the judiciary,[581] and this could also be said of her subsequent detention in the police station for 44 hours,[582] bearing in mind the findings of the police or magistrates that disorder might have occurred. The Court made little attempt to evaluate the real risk of disorder, taking into account the margin of appreciation afforded to domestic authorities in determining what is necessary to avoid disorder in the particular domestic situation.[583] It may be noted that this conclusion was reached only by a five to four majority; the partly dissenting opinions of Judges Valticos and Makarczyk termed the measures taken against the first applicant, Helen Steel, 'so manifestly extreme' in proportion to her actions during the protest that a violation of Art 10 had occurred. The second applicant had taken part in a protest against the building of a motorway, placing herself in front of the earth-moving machinery in order to impede it. The Court found unanimously that her arrest also could be viewed as proportionate to the aim of preventing disorder, even though it accepted that the risk of immediate disorder was not so high as in the case of the first applicant.[584] The Court accepted the finding of the magistrates' court that there had been such a risk.

578 *Steel and Others v UK* (1999) 28 EHRR 603.
579 Above, fn 528.
580 This was acknowledged by the Court, para 101.
581 Paras 104 and 107.
582 Para 105. The Commission acknowledged (para 156) 'some disquiet as to the proportionality of a detention of this length' which continued long after the grouse shoot was over.
583 Para 101.
584 Para 109.

The third, fourth and fifth applicants were peacefully holding banners and handing out leaflets outside a fighter helicopter conference when they were arrested for breach of the peace. The Court found that there was no justification for their arrests at all since there was no suggestion of any threat of disorder.[585] A violation of Art 10 was therefore found in respect of those applicants. These findings draw a distinction between the first category of protest and the fourth and fifth forms – symbolic physical action and obstructive action – suggesting that interferences with protest as direct action may frequently fall within the national authorities' margin of appreciation. But, significantly, the findings also make it clear that the fourth and fifth forms constitute expressions of opinion and therefore fall within Arts 10 and 11. This was re-affirmed in *Hashman and Harrup v UK*.[586]

The stance of the Court in *Steel* in fact implies less tolerance of peaceful direct action than the stance taken in *Nicol*, since the Court required only an interference with the rights of others and the possibility of disorder in order to be satisfied regarding proportionality; no added requirement to show that the defendant rather than the other party was acting unreasonably was imposed. The dissenting minority judgments in *Steel* made an oblique reference to such a comparison in noting that the behaviour of the first applicant, albeit 'extreme', was aimed at preserving the life of an animal.[587] The findings of the Court provide little basis for curbing interference under the breach of the peace doctrine with certain forms of public protest of the direct action type, although they do require a re-structuring of the domestic scrutiny of such interference, which takes the primary right as the starting point. *Steel* clearly affords the domestic judiciary a wide discretion in interpreting the requirements of the Convention in an analogous case. In evaluating the risks posed by a protest, the courts might tend to adopt notions of deference to decisions of the executive in respect of the possibility of disorder in accordance with the tradition in such cases, and take the view that the courts should be reluctant to interfere with the decision of the police officer or magistrate (as the tribunal of fact) in question. A minimalist approach to Arts 10 and 11 would lead to a similar result. If *Steel* was simply applied regardless of the influence of the margin of appreciation, little protection would be available for most direct action forms of protest. But following an activist approach, the domestic judiciary, faced with similar facts, but disapplying the margin of appreciation aspects of *Steel,* would find that the interference was unjustified since their review of the decisions of the police or of magistrates would be less restrained. Within this model, some interferences with freedom of expression would be allowed, where direct action was likely to provoke immediate disorder due to the degree of provocation offered, but the measures taken in response, such as the length of detention, would be much more strictly scrutinised for their proportionality with the aims pursued.

The decision in *Steel* is of most value in placing the form of protest most deserving of protection, peaceful persuasion, in a specially protected position. Therefore, it is problematic, even within the 'review' or minimalist model, to uphold arrest or bind over decisions in such instances or in cases of the *Holmes v Bournemouth*[588] type. This

---

585 Para 110.
586 (2000) 8 BHRC 104; (1999) 30 EHRR 241.
587 Partly dissenting opinions of Judges Valticos and Makarczyk.
588 6 October 1993, unreported, DC.

would be a welcome restriction and clarification of the breach of the peace doctrine but, in terms of protecting public protest, it would achieve no more than *Nicol* has already done. Both *Steel* and *Nicol* leave open leeway for deciding when it should be found that protest, which has some provocative effect, should nevertheless be termed peaceful. In other words, in terms of the categories of protest indicated, their application to the second form of protest – insulting or offensive persuasion – is dependent on the degree of provocation. The findings in *Steel* impliedly drew a distinction in terms of reasonableness between action which is directly and physically provocative and speech which might have some provocative effect, but which could nevertheless be viewed as part of a peaceful protest. It is not clear that they simply drew a distinction between physical and verbal protest. Such a distinction would fail to take account of forms of hate speech which may be far more provocative to hearers than forms of physical obstruction such as the ones at issue in *Steel*. Thus, a minimalist approach to *Steel* would be to confine it to speech which had little provocative effect. In *Steel* itself, in respect of the successful applicants, there was no evidence that the audience in question – those participating in the fighter helicopter conference – were provoked. A traditionalist approach would be to defer to the opinion of the officer on the ground as to the likelihood that disorder would follow the provocation.

But a more activist approach would be to afford protection to insulting or offensive persuasion or symbolic direct action, following *Steel*, and this approach would also receive some endorsement from *Plattform 'Ärtze fur das Leben' v Austria*[589] which adopted a version of the *Beatty v Gillbanks*[590] approach. Such an approach to the decision in *Steel* was, in some respects, taken by Sedley LJ in *Redmond-Bate v DPP*[591] in the period just before the HRA was fully in force. Ms Redmond-Bate and other women, a group of fundamentalist Christians, were preaching forcefully on the steps of Westminster Cathedral. A large crowd gathered, who were angered by their preaching. Fearing a breach of the peace, a police officer asked the women to desist; when they refused, he arrested them. The Divisional Court found that in the circumstances, two questions should be asked of the action of the police officer. First, was it reasonable to believe that a breach of the peace was about to be caused? Secondly, where was the threat coming from? These questions could have been answered by distinguishing the facts from those relating to the successful applications in *Steel* and bringing them, at the same time, within the rule from *Nicol*, on the basis that the women did in fact provoke their audience and could have been viewed as acting unreasonably since they continued to preach despite the growing restlessness of the crowd. It could have been said that the natural consequence of the lawful but arguably unreasonable conduct of the women was the provocation of others. Applying *Steel*, however, the Divisional Court found, in answer to both the questions posed, that there were no sufficient grounds on which to determine that a breach of the peace was about to be caused or, moreover, on which to determine that the threat was coming from Ms Redmond-Bate, bearing in mind the tolerance one would expect to be extended to offensive speech. Sedley LJ said: 'Free speech includes not only the inoffensive, but the irritating, the contentious, the eccentric, the heretical, the unwelcome and the provocative providing it does not

---

589 A 139 (1988), para 32; judgment of 21 June 1988; 13 EHRR 204.
590 (1882) 9 QBD 308, discussed above, p 772.
591 (1999) *The Times*, 28 July; [1999] All ER (D) 864.

tend to provoke violence. Freedom only to speak inoffensively is not worth having.'[592] He went on to find that the Crown Court had correctly directed itself that 'violence is not a natural consequence of what a person does unless it clearly interferes with the rights or liberties of others so as to make a violent reaction not wholly unreasonable'[593] and he emphasised that the court should make its own independent judgment of the reasonableness of the police officer's belief.

This decision simplified the tests from *Nicol* of determining which party was acting reasonably where one was provoked to violence and as to which was exercising rights. The key test put forward was one of reasonableness: a breach of the peace will occur where violence was threatened or provoked, in the sense of infringing rights or liberties, unless the provoked party acts wholly – not partly – unreasonably. Sedley LJ then categorised certain of the decisions mentioned above into those where the provoked party was reasonable or unreasonable, in order to offer some guidance on this matter. He placed *Beatty v Gillbanks* and *Percy v DPP* in the first category, but, strangely, put *Wise v Dunning* and *Duncan v Jones* in the second. In *Duncan*, there was little evidence on which to base an apprehension of a breach of the peace and it was unclear that persons provoked by the speech in question could be said to have acted reasonably. Thus, although *Redmond-Bate* applies *Steel* quite broadly, it still leaves some uncertainty as to the status of provocative speech; the test of reasonableness will be, it is suggested, no more certain in its application than the tests from *Nicol* and will therefore have some chilling effect on protest.

Indications of a more restrictive domestic approach also come from *Bibby v Chief Constable of Essex*,[594] which is not a public protest case; it concerned the arrest of a bailiff who was seeking to seize goods. But various requirements were laid down in the findings of the Court of Appeal, which would be of significant applicability in a protest case. The threat to the peace must be real and present in order to justify depriving a person of his liberty when he is not himself at that point acting unlawfully. Following *Redmond-Bate*, the threat must come from the person under arrest, overturning *Kelly*. The other conditions confirmed those laid down in *Nicol* to the effect that the violence provoked must not be wholly unreasonable.

In the post-HRA era, a more activist approach to *Steel* could afford the substantive rights under Arts 10 and 11 greater weight in cases of persuasive or provocative speech by disallowing interferences with these forms of protest unless incitement to violence or to hatred of racial, religious or sexual groups had occurred. (It may be noted that in *Laporte* the question of provoking others was not relevant.) A presumption that it is normally unreasonable to be provoked to violence or the threat of it by speech could be imported into the doctrine, a stronger test than the one put forward by Sedley LJ. In response to the finding in *Steel* that breaching the peace is a criminal offence, it would appear that the courts could create a clearer distinction if a suitable case arises, between conduct likely to cause a breach, allowing for a preventive arrest, and conduct actually amounting to a breach. The former could not, it seems, if *Steel* is followed on this point, lead to binding over, since no offence has been committed which would allow for this punishment. Since such preventive powers are frequently, although not

---

592 Transcript, para 12.
593 Transcript, para 16.
594 (2000) *The Times*, 24 April.

exclusively, used where the arrestee may cause another to breach the peace, *Steel* might therefore herald a return to the more minimal interpretation in *Howell*, leaving the possibility of causing another to breach the peace to the statutory provisions discussed below, in particular ss 5 and 4A of the Public Order Act 1986, which cover much of the same area. Admittedly, ss 5 and 4A, unlike the breach of the peace doctrine, criminalise offensive speech *per se* without requiring a public order rationale. The 'victim' need only be distressed rather than likely to react violently. However, the nature of the language required for both provisions curtails their ambit, in contrast to the breach of the peace doctrine. Almost all the cases concerning peaceful persuasion discussed above, in which the doctrine was successfully invoked, would fall outside ss 5 and 4A, apart, probably, from *Wise v Dunning* in which abusive or insulting words or behaviour were used. The peaceful direct action cases of *Nicol* and *Percy* probably would not be covered, although they would fall within s 68 of the CJPOA, as discussed above. In other words, if the use of provocative speech requires a legal response at all, such a response should be left to those provisions which lay down a more precise test for liability than the breach of the peace doctrine.

But such determinations, which would have the effect of greatly narrowing down the doctrine, would not be fully rooted in the application of *Steel* or other analogous decisions at Strasbourg: they would have to be based largely on an appeal to a notional 'higher' standard of human rights, articulated by the general principles informing the Strasbourg jurisprudence, which might have been adhered to but for the margin of appreciation doctrine.[595] If one of the key principles at stake is the need to protect the communicative rights of minority groups, such as pacifists, animal rights or environmental activists, reliance might be placed, by analogy, on strong pronouncements of the need to protect minority rights and plurality within democracies which, as indicated above, are scattered across the Convention jurisprudence.[596]

6 Criminalising public disorder and anti-social behaviour

Introduction

The criminalisation of low level forms of anti-social behaviour, allowing for curbs to be placed on protests has been a feature of recent public order law. The process was begun under s 5 of the Public Order Act 1986, continued under s 154 of the CJPOA 1994,[597] and was taken further under the Protection from Harassment Act 1997, s 1 of the Crime and Disorder Act 1998 and s 42 of the Criminal Justice and Police Act 2001. These provisions target similar forms of anti-social behaviour which had previously been viewed as too trivial or too imprecise to attract criminal or, in most instances, civil liability. All are aimed at behaviour causing harassment, alarm or distress or, under the

---

595　E.g., the Court in *Handyside v UK* (1976) 1 EHRR 737, para 49 found, in a famous passage, that Art 10 is applicable 'not only to ideas that are . . . regarded as inoffensive, but also to those which offend, shock or disturb', although in the particular instance, due to the operation of the margin of appreciation doctrine, the application failed.

596　Above, pp 681–82.

597　Which inserted s 4A into the 1986 Act.

1997 Act, amounting to harassment, and all are targeted at particular social problems, largely unrelated to public protest. Section 5 of the 1986 Act was aimed at the perceived problem of disturbance from football hooligans or late night rowdies; the 1997 Act at the problem of so called 'stalkers'; s 1 of the 1998 Act at anti-social neighbours. Section 41 of the 2001 Act was, however, aimed at the direct action form of protest and, in particular, at the actions of protesters against the use of animals in experiments at Huntingdon Life Sciences. The offences under ss 5, 4A and 4 of the 1986 Act can be charged as racially or religiously aggravated as provided by ss 28 and 31 of the Crime and Disorder Act 1998 (as amended by s 39 of the Anti-terrorism, Crime and Security Act 2001). The 1998 Act, as amended, introduced a statutory aggravation to a number of offences, including s 5 of the 1986 Act, carrying with it higher maximum penalties. According to ss 28(1)(b) and 31(1)(c) of the 1998 Act, an offence under s 5 of the 1986 Act is 'racially or religiously aggravated' if it is 'motivated (wholly or partly) by hostility towards members of a racial or religious group based on their membership of that group'. Section 18 POA also covers incitement to racial hatred if expressed in threatening or abusive or insulting terms, and the Racial and Religious Hatred Act 2006 has added a new Part 3A to the Public Order Act, to cover incitement to religious hatred expressed in threatening terms. These offences are also applied in the context of a range of media and therefore they are considered in Chapter 6.[598]

Section 5 of the 1986 Act is the most problematic provision in that it catches a very wide range of relatively trivial behaviour. All these provisions, due to their breadth, have a potential application to protest within all the categories indicated above,[599] probably not in all circumstances excluding the first – peaceful persuasion. These offences can be used against various forms of anti-social behaviour, but they can also catch forms of public protest. The HRA is having a significant effect, especially on the application of ss 5 and 4A of the 1986 Act: a key distinction is being created between the application of the offences to hooliganism/rowdiness and to protesters.[600]

Criminalising use of threats, abuse, insults

The offences under ss 5 and 4A of the 1986 Act, as amended, require establishment of a minimal and imprecise *actus reus*. Section 5 is the lowest level public order offence contained in the 1986 Act and the most contentious, since it brings behaviour within the scope of the criminal law which was previously thought of as too trivial to justify the imposition of criminal liability.[601] It criminalises the person who 'uses threatening, abusive or insulting words or behaviour or disorderly behaviour' or 'displays any writing, sign or other visible representation which is threatening or abusive or insulting' which takes place within the 'hearing or sight of a person likely to be caused harassment,

598 See pp 497–509.
599 See pp 666–67.
600 See: Geddis, A, 'Free Speech Martyrs or Unreasonable Threats to Social Peace? – "Insulting" Expression and Section 5 of the Public Order Act 1986' (2004) *Public Law* 853; Newman, C, 'Divisional Court: Public Order Act 1986, s 4A: Proportionality and Freedom of Expression' (2006) 70 *Journal of Criminal Law* 191.
601 For background to s 5, see Law Commission Report No 123, *Offences Relating to Public Order*, 1983.

alarm or distress thereby'. The word 'likely' imports an objective test into the section: it is necessary to show that a person was present at the scene, but not that he or she actually experienced the feelings in question, although it must be shown that in all the circumstances, he or she would be likely to experience such feelings. In so showing, it is not necessary to call the person in question as a witness. In *Swanston v DPP*[602] it was found that if a bystander gives evidence to the effect that the 'victim' perceived the threatening, abusive or insulting words, then the court can draw the inference that they were so perceived. There is no need to aim the words or behaviour at a specific individual, so long as an individual can be identified and the inference can be drawn that he or she would have perceived the words or behaviour in question. It was determined in *DPP v Orum*[603] that a police officer may be the person caused harassment, alarm or distress, but in such instances Glidewell LJ thought it might be held that a police officer would be less likely to experience such feelings than an ordinary person. These two decisions enhance the ease with which this offence may be deployed, as does *DPP v Fidler*,[604] in which it was found that a person whose own behaviour would not satisfy the requirements of s 5 may be guilty of aiding and abetting this offence if he or she is part of a crowd who are committing it. In the Divisional Court ruling in *R v DPP*[605] on s 4, which is discussed below, it was found that an insult to a police officer, from a 12-year- old boy (he called the officer, who was arresting his sister at the time, a 'wanker') had not caused distress. The evidence did not establish that the police officer had suffered 'any real emotional disturbance'. Thus the harm caused, or likely to be caused, must be real emotional disturbance. The term 'distress' is used in both ss 5 and 4 and so will be interpreted in the same way, although under s 4 it is necessary to establish that the person concerned actually suffered distress.

Whether the words used were insulting, etc, is a question of fact for the magistrates. The terms used must be given their ordinary meaning: *Brutus v Cozens*.[606] Following *Ambrose*,[607] rude or offensive words or behaviour may not necessarily be insulting, while mere swearing may not fall within the meaning of 'abusive'. However, threatening gestures such as waving a fist might suffice. Whether or not the words are insulting is not a purely subjective test and therefore the mere fact that the recipient finds them so will not be sufficient. The House of Lords so held in *Brutus v Cozens*[608] in respect of disruption of a tennis match involving a South African player by an anti-apartheid demonstrator. Some of the crowd were provoked to violence, but the conduct of the demonstrator could not be described as insulting. The conviction of the defendant under the predecessor of s 4 was therefore overturned. The test appears to be whether a reasonable person sharing the characteristics of the persons at whom the words in question are directed would find them insulting. However, whether or not the speaker knows that such persons will hear the words is immaterial as far as this ingredient of

---

602 (1997) *The Times*, 23 January.
603 [1988] 3 All ER 449.
604 [1992] 1 WLR 91.
605 [2006] All ER (D) 250.
606 [1973] AC 854; [1972] 2 All ER 1297; [1972] 3 WLR 521, HL.
607 (1973) 57 Cr App R 538.
608 [1973] AC 854; [1972] All ER 1297; [1972] 3 WLR 521; (1973) 57 Cr App R 538, HL.

s 4 is concerned (*Jordan v Burgoyne*).[609] It was found in *DPP v Fidler*[610] that a person whose own behaviour would not satisfy the requirements of s 5 may be guilty as aiding and abetting this offence if he or she is part of a crowd who are committing it.

Post-HRA a key question to be asked, it is contended, is whether to label the words 'insulting', etc in order to criminalise them is a proportionate response to the aim pursued, to prevent crime or disorder or protect the rights of others, under Art 10(2). In *Hammond*[611] it was found that Art 10 considerations apply when determining whether something is insulting.[612] However, in determining this question it was merely asked whether it was reasonable for the lower court to take the view that the words were insulting. As Geddis argues, the Court only applied the *Wednesbury* test rather than one of proportionality when considering the magistrate court's conclusion on the question whether the words were 'insulting'.[613] This was the wrong approach. Article 10 should be considered in relation to the *actus reus* and in relation to the defences of reasonableness in these provisions, which are discussed below. In *Dehal*[614] the question of proportionality under Art 10 was examined as a free-standing inquiry, but it would have been more appropriate to have considered it in relation to the *actus reus* (in that instance of s 4A), as indicated, and in relation to the question of reasonableness. This question is returned to below.

Taken at its lowest level, s 5 criminalises a person who displays disorderly behaviour calculated to create harassment. Section 5 was included as a measure aimed at anti-social behaviour generally, but its breadth and vagueness have given rise to the criticism that the police have been handed a very broad power.[615] The criminalisation of speech which causes such low level harm as alarm or distress may be contrary to dicta of the European Court of Human Rights in *Müller v Switzerland*[616] to the effect that the protection of free speech extends equally to ideas which 'offend, shock or disturb'.[617] Section 5, far from being confined to restraining rowdy hooligans, has been used against political speech. In the so called *Madame M* case, four students were prosecuted for putting up a satirical poster depicting Margaret Thatcher as a 'sadistic dominatrix';[618] the students were acquitted, but the fact that such a case could even be brought in a democracy is highly disturbing. This was not an isolated use of s 5 against political speech: protesters outside abortion clinics have been prosecuted[619] and, in Northern

---

609 [1963] 2 QB 744; [1963] 2 All ER 225.
610 [1992] 1 WLR 91; for comment, see Smith, JC [1992] Crim LR 63.
611 [2004] EWHC 69.
612 At para 21.
613 Geddis, A, 'Free Speech Martyrs or Unreasonable Threats to Social Peace? – "Insulting" Expression and Section 5 of the Public Order Act 1986' (2004) *Public Law* 853 at 865.
614 [2005] EWHC 2154.
615 See comment on s 5 in [1987] PL 202.
616 (1991) 13 EHRR 212.
617 It should be noted that in *Brutus v Cozens* [1973] AC 854; [1972] 2 All ER 1297; [1972] 3 WLR 521; (1973) Cr App R 538, HL, Lord Reid said that the previous Public Order Act 1936, s 5 was 'not designed to penalise the expressions of opinion that happen to be disagreeable, distasteful or even offensive, annoying or distressing'. The current s 5 offence precisely does cover 'distressing' speech, but use could be made of Lord Reid's *dicta* to argue that expression of opinions *per se* should not be criminalised.
618 Thornton, P, *Decade of Decline: Civil Liberties in the Thatcher Years*, 1990, p 37.
619 *DPP v Fidler* [1992] 1 WLR 91; *DPP v Clarke* [1992] Crim LR 60.

Ireland, s 5 has been used against a poster depicting youths stoning a British Saracen with a caption proclaiming 'Ireland: 20 years of resistance'.[620] Similarly, as one commentator noted when the Act was passed: 'In the context of pickets shouting or gesturing at those crossing their picket lines, the elements of this offence will usually be established without difficulty.'[621]

However, the Strasbourg Court indicated recently that Art 10 may not be engaged where the speech in question is offensive on racial or religious grounds since Art 17 of the Convention may apply, depending on the gravity of the attack on the group in question in terms of the Convention rights. Article 17 provides:

> Nothing in [the] Convention may be interpreted as implying for any state, group or person any right to engage in any activity or perform any act aimed at the destruction of any of the rights and freedoms set forth herein or at their limitation to a greater extent than is provided for in the Convention.

The recent decision in *Norwood v UK*,[622] took this stance. The applicant, who belonged to the BNP, displayed in the window of his first-floor flat a large poster. . .supplied by the BNP, with a photograph of the Twin Towers in flame, and the words 'Islam out of Britain – Protect the British People' and a symbol of a crescent and star in a prohibition sign.[623] He was convicted in a magistrates' court of the offence under s 5 of displaying 'any writing, sign or other visible representation which is threatening, abusive or insulting, within the hearing or sight of a person likely to be caused harassment, alarm or distress thereby'. He was convicted of having committed the offence in religiously aggravated way. He unsuccessfully appealed his conviction to the High Court;[624] one of the applicant's arguments was that there was no evidence that any Muslim had in fact seen the poster. The High Court rejected this argument on the basis that s 5 does not require that a person should actually experience distress, and found that the restriction upon his freedom of expression right represented by the offence was proportionate to the legitimate aim of protecting the rights of others, given also the fact that the speech arguably fell within Art 17 ECHR.[625] The Strasbourg Court found his application inadmissible; referring to Art 17, the Court found that an attack of this nature against a religious group, linking them to a grave act of terrorism, was not compatible with the values proclaimed and guaranteed by the Convention, notably 'tolerance, social peace and non-discrimination'. The applicant's display of the poster in his window constituted an act within the meaning of Art 17 and therefore it did not enjoy the protection of Arts 10 or 14.

The *mens rea* requirements of the s 5 offence offers a degree of protection to free expression. Under s 6(4), it must be established that the defendant intended his words, etc, to be threatening, abusive or insulting or was aware that they might be. In *DPP v*

---

620   Reported in *The Independent*, 12 September 1988; mentioned in Ewing and Gearty, op. cit., fn 1, 1990, p 123.
621   Williams, op. cit., fn 1.
622   (2005) 40 EHRR SE11.
623   Ibid at [A].
624   *Norwood v DPP* (2003) WL 21491815.
625   See Chapter 2 at p 112. For comment on Art 17 in a different context by the House of Lords, see *DPP v Collins* [2006] UKHL 40.

Clarke[626] it was further found that to establish liability, it is insufficient to show only that the defendant intended or was aware that he might cause harassment, alarm or distress; it must also be shown that he intended his conduct to be threatening, abusive or insulting, or was aware that it might be. Both mental states have to be established independently. Thus, showing that the defendant was aware that he might cause distress was not found to be equivalent to showing that he was aware that his speech or behaviour might be insulting. Applying this subjective test, the magistrates acquitted the defendants and this decision was upheld on appeal. Using this test, it was found that anti-abortion protesters had not realised that their behaviour in shouting anti-abortion slogans, displaying plastic models of foetuses and pictures of dead foetuses would be threatening, abusive or insulting. This decision allows those who believe fervently in their cause, and therefore fail to appreciate that their protest may insult or offend others, to escape liability. It therefore places a significant curb on the ability of ss 5 and 4A to interfere with Art 10 and Art 11 rights. Persons participating in forceful demonstrations may sometimes be able to show that behaviour which could be termed disorderly and which might be capable of causing harassment to others, was intended only to make a point and that it had not been realised that others might find it threatening, abusive or insulting. Once a particular group of protesters has been prosecuted, however, and it has been found, as in *Clarke*, that others found their protest threatening, abusive or insulting, the subjective element of the *mens rea* will be in future readily made out, even if the instant prosecution fails. The burden imposed by the subjective test for intention or awareness is to be welcomed, since it means that an offence which strikes directly at freedom of expression and can only doubtfully be justified is harder to make out.

Section 154 of the CJPOA 1994 inserted s 4A into the 1986 Act, thereby providing a new and wide area of liability which to some extent overlapped with s 5. Section 4A of the 1986 Act criminalises threatening, abusive, insulting words or behaviour or disorderly behaviour which cause a person harassment, alarm or distress thereby. Thus, the *actus reus* under s 4A is the same as that under s 5, with the proviso that the harm in question must actually be caused as opposed to being likely to be caused. As noted above, the Divisional Court ruling in *R v DPP*[627] will apply – the harm caused will have to amount to real emotional distress. The *mens rea* differs somewhat from that under s 5, since the defendant must intend the person in question to suffer harassment, alarm or distress. Section 4A provides another possible level of liability with the result that using offensive words is now imprisonable, without any requirement (as under s 4, below) to show that violence was intended or likely to be caused. Like s5 its use against protesters or demonstrators can come into conflict with Art 10 due to its protection for forms of forceful or offensive speech.[628] As discussed in relation to s 5, the *actus reus* should be considered in terms of proportionality; the court failed to do this in *Dehal*, which is discussed below, instead examining proportionality as a free-standing enquiry. Section 4 is also subject to a defence of reasonableness, providing a further entry point for Art 10 considerations; this is discussed below.

---

626 [1992] Crim LR 60.
627 [2006] All ER (D) 250.
628 See Newman, C, (2006) 'Divisional Court: Public Order Act 1986, s 4A: Proportionality and Freedom of Expression' 70 *Journal of Criminal Law* 191.

Section 4 of the Act covers somewhat more serious behaviour than s 5. It is couched in the same terms except for the omission of 'disorderly behaviour', but instead of showing that a person present was likely to be caused harassment, etc, it is necessary to show 'intent to cause that person to believe that immediate unlawful violence will be used against him or another by any person or to provoke the immediate use of unlawful violence by that person or another or whereby that person is likely to believe that such violence will be used or it is likely that such violence will be provoked'. One or more of these four possibilities must be present. The behaviour in question must be specifically directed towards another person. If the defendant does not directly approach the person being threatened, he or she might be unlikely to apprehend immediate violence. However, there might remain the possibility that the defendant intended his or her words to provoke others to violence against the victim. Under s 6(3), it must also be established that the defendant intended his words, etc, to be threatening, abusive or insulting or was aware that they might be.

It was found in *Horseferry Road Metropolitan Stipendiary Magistrate ex p Siadatan*[629] that 'violence' in this context must mean immediate and unlawful violence. The case arose from publication and distribution of *The Satanic Verses* by Salman Rushdie. The applicants alleged that the book contained abusive and insulting writing whereby it was likely that unlawful violence would be provoked contrary to s 4. On appeal from the decision of the magistrates not to issue a summons against the distributors of the books, Penguin Books, Watkins LJ found:

> We find it most unlikely that Parliament could have intended to include among sections which undoubtedly deal with conduct having an immediate impact on bystanders, a section creating an offence for conduct which is likely to lead to violence at some unspecified time in the future.

The finding that the violence provoked must be immediate, although not necessarily instantaneous, led to dismissal of the appeal. This strict interpretation was confirmed in *Winn v DPP*[630] and it was made plain that the prosecution must ensure that all the ingredients of the particular form of the offence charged under s 4 are present. The appellant threatened and abused a Mr Duncan who was attempting to serve a summons on him. On appeal, the ingredients of the s 4 offence were considered. It was clear from the provision of s 7(2) of the Act that s 4 creates only one offence; however, it is clear that the offence can be committed in one of four ways. Common to all four are the requirements, first, that the accused must intend or be aware that his words or behaviour are or may be threatening, abusive or insulting (s 6(3), which governs the *mens rea* requirement) and secondly, that they must be directed to another person. The offence charged included a statement of the required intention and was based on the fourth way it could be committed: that he used threatening and abusive words and behaviour whereby it was likely that violence would be provoked. The charge, therefore, required proof of a likelihood that Mr Duncan would be provoked to immediate unlawful violence and as there was no evidence to that effect, the direction to the justices was

629 [1991] 1 QB 260; [1991] 1 All ER 324; [1990] 3 WLR 1006.
630 (1992) 142 NLJ 527.

that the charge under s 4 should have been dismissed. Had the charge related to the first form of the offence – 'intent to cause that person to believe that immediate unlawful violence will be used against him' – it might have succeeded. It should be noted that such intent must be shown in addition to the *mens rea* under s 6(3).

The decision in *Siadatan* places a curb on the use of s 4A which might otherwise have occurred under the HRA. As it currently stands, it is clear that the ingredients of this offence relate to a much higher harm threshold than those of ss 4A and 5; therefore, although its use may on occasion be viewed as creating an interference with the Art 10 rights of protesters, the interference is likely to be found to be proportionate to the aim pursued.

Section 5 clearly covers quite trivial forms of harm and therefore can readily be resorted to in a wide range of situations. The sheer number of prosecutions being brought under s 5 conclusively demonstrates that the police are not showing restraint in using this area of the Act. The old s 5 offence under the Public Order Act 1936, an offence with a higher harm threshold,[631] accounted for the majority of the 8,194 charges brought in connection with the miners' strike of 1984. In a survey of 470 public order cases in 1988, conducted that year, in two police force areas, it was found that 56 per cent of the sample led to charges under s 5. Research has also shown that during the period 1986–88, the number of charges brought for public order offences doubled and this was thought to be due not to increased unrest, but to the existence of the new offences, particularly s 5 with its low level of harm.[632]

Harassment

Section 42 of the Criminal Justice and Police Act 2001, as amended, allows a constable to give any direction to persons, including a direction to leave the scene where they are outside or in the vicinity of a dwelling, if the constable reasonably believes (a) that they are seeking to persuade a person living at the dwelling not to do something that he/she has a right to do or to do something she/he is not under any obligation to do, and (b) that the presence of the persons (normally protesters) is likely to cause harassment, alarm or distress to the person living at the residence. Disobedience of a direction is an arrestable offence. Section 42 was broadened by amendments introduced under the Criminal Justice Act 2003 Sched 26, para 56. It now includes a provision (s 42(4)) that if a direction is given it will be an offence to return to the vicinity for a specified period, which can be for up to three months. The penalty was increased to a maximum of 51 weeks imprisonment. Section 42 clearly draws on the ingredients of ss 5 and 4, although there are also significant differences. There are also similarities with the offences under s 14C of the 1986 Act and s 69 of the 1994 Act. Section 42 of the 2001 Act is problematic in the sense that it hits directly at peaceful protest – protest that need not be abusive, etc, but is aimed only at persuading. The protesters need have no intention of causing harassment, alarm or distress so long as a constable reasonably believes that the target of the protest might experience those feelings. In

---

631 It was similar to the offence which replaced it (the 1986 Act, s 4).
632 Newburn, T *et al.*, 'Policing the streets' (1990) 29 HORB 10 and 'Increasing public order' (1991) 7 Policing 22; quoted in Bailey, Harris and Jones, *op. cit.*, fn 1, pp 229–30.

catching peaceful protest, this offence comes directly into conflict with Arts 10 and 11. Section 42 can also be viewed as protecting Art 8 rights. However, a court would be expected to consider the extent to which those rights could be said to be at stake and the proportionality of the police response, in using s 42 as opposed to a lesser measure.

Section 41 of the 2001 Act is an offence with a minimal *actus reus*, as is apparent when it is compared with the requirements of s 5 of the 1986 Act or ss 69 and 68 of the 1994 Act. The requirement that the words or conduct should be abusive, etc, in s 5 is missing; the requirements of ss 69 or 68 that the persons in question should be trespassing and must do something intended to be obstructive or intimidatory or disruptive are also absent. But s 41 is similar to s 69, and a number of the other recent offences discussed in this chapter, in that it conflates the exercise of police powers with the substantive offence. The key limiting requirement is that the persons must be outside or in the vicinity of a dwelling, although the term 'the vicinity' is open to quite a wide interpretation. The need for the introduction of this offence must be questioned, bearing in mind that ss 5 or 4A could be used against intimidation by protesters gathered outside the home of the person targeted. The offence of harassment under the 1997 Act would also be available.

Section 1 of the Protection from Harrassment Act 1997 is available to cover harassment in a broader sense. It defines harassment as a course of conduct which a reasonable person would consider amounted to harassment of another where the harasser knows or ought to know that this will be its effect; s 2 makes harassment an offence. An interim injunction, breach of which is an offence (s 3(6)) punishable by up to five years' imprisonment (s 3(9)), can be obtained under s 3 in civil proceedings. No definition of a course of conduct which might amount to harassment is offered.

Section 1 of the Crime and Disorder Act 1998 provides a penalty of a maximum of five years' imprisonment for failing to obey an order obtained on the civil standard of proof,[633] an ASBO, forbidding any form of 'anti-social' behaviour,[634] defined under s 1(1)(a) as behaving: 'in an anti-social manner, that is to say in a manner that caused or was likely to cause harassment, alarm and distress to one or more persons' other than those of the same household as the defendant. Any person over the age of nine who behaves n this manner can be the subject of an ASBO. The Police Reform Act 2002 extended the power to seek an order to persons registered under the Housing Act 1996 as 'social landlords' and to the Chief Constable of the British Transport Police. The Anti-Social Behaviour Act 2003 added housing action trusts and county council councils.

Both statutes provide a defence of reasonableness, discussed below, which assumes especial significance in relation to the 1997 and 1998 provisions, since in contrast to the earlier ones, under the 1986 Act, there is either no need to establish *mens rea* or its establishment is likely to have little inhibitory effect. Thus, the decision in *Clarke* will not have a ready application under those Acts. Sections 1 and 2 of the 1997 Act makes it a requirement of establishing the offence that the harasser knows or ought to know that the course of conduct amounts to harassment. However, since an interim injunction

---

633 According to the 1998 Magistrates' Courts Rules applicable to these orders.
634 Section 1(10)(b).

can be obtained under s 3 of the Act, in *ex parte* proceedings, the establishment of that state of mind would be aided in proceedings for its breach once it had been served on the defendant. Breach of such an injunction is punishable by five years' imprisonment. Therefore, although prima facie the 1997 Act imports a *mens rea* requirement, the existence of punishment on the civil standard of proof allows for its circumvention. Criminal proceedings relating to the same course of conduct, but under s 2, may also be affected, as explained below, once an injunction has been obtained.

Section 1 of the 1998 Act requires no circumvention of *mens rea* requirements, since it merely abandons them. They could be re-introduced only in the form of a 'reversed' *mens rea*, under the defence of reasonableness, unless, in a public protest case, with a view to narrowing down the potential of this section to interfere with Art 6, 10 or 11 rights, a judge was prepared to import the additional *mens rea* element identified in *Clarke*.

These matters are linked to the key difference between these two recent provisions and the previous ones – their hybrid nature in allowing for criminal sanctions, including imprisonment, on the civil standard of proof for breach of an injunction or order. The 1997 Act allows for an injunction to be obtained at the instigation of the 'victim' in *ex parte* proceedings, merely on his or her affidavit. This probably explains why the 1997 Act is proving to offer a primary means of curbing various forms of protest. It provides a contrast to ss 5 and 4A of the 1986 Act, which are widely used, but not, research suggests, frequently in the context of political protest.[635] Unlike the 1997 Act, they appear, on the whole, to have been used to target those at whom they were originally aimed. The features of the 1997 Act which have made it attractive as a measure to be used against protesters, are, it should be noted, also present in the 1998 Act in the sense that the subject of the protest can (indirectly) instigate proceedings[636] and criminal sanctions, including imprisonment, may be imposed on the civil standard.

The relevance of the civil standard of proof in the 1997 and 1998 Acts was always likely to raise questions about the compatibility of these provisions with Art 6, under the HRA. At Strasbourg, the fact that national law classifies an act as non-criminal is relevant but not conclusive. In *Benham v UK*,[637] the leading case on 'criminal charge', the Court found that although the legislation in question[638] clearly did not create a criminal offence in UK law, it should be accounted criminal for Art 6(1) purposes. The proceedings against the applicant[639] had been brought by the public authorities; the proceedings

---

635   Waddington explains the reluctance to arrest in this context on the basis that it risks sparking off hostility among other protesters and can create trouble later, since the arrest may be scrutinised in court: see op. cit., fn 1, pp 54–55. Independent records of arrests may be available since supporters of the protest may photograph them and reporters may well also be present. Records and reports of arrests may help to lead to acquittals and may fuel public criticism of the police. This would be unlikely to be the case in relation to the arrest of, e.g., drunken football supporters.

636   The application for the order is made by the 'relevant authority' under s 1(1), but it may be triggered off by allegations made to the police or housing authority.

637   (1996) 22 EHRR 293. See also *Lauko v Slovakia* (1999) 1 EHRLR 105 in which it was found that a penalty for anti-social behaviour was inherently criminal in nature. *Han v Customs and Excise Comrs* [2001] 1 WLR 2253, 2269–2273, paras 55–64 reviewed the European case law.

638   The Local Government Changes for England (Community Charge and Council Tax, Administration and Enforcement) Regulations 1995, SI 1995/247, s 41.

639   In respect of default on payment of the community charge or poll tax.

had some punitive elements and the bringing of them implied fault on the part of the applicant. Further, the penalty was severe (committal to prison for up to three months).[640] In *Engel v The Netherlands (No 1)*[641] the European Court established three criteria for determining whether proceedings are 'criminal' within the meaning of the Convention: (a) the domestic classification, (b) the nature of the offence, and (c) the severity of the potential penalty which the defendant risks incurring.

Prior to the inception of the HRA it appeared that if, for example, a defendant in a magistrates' court raised the issue of the compatibility of the proceedings for an order under s 1 of the 1998 Act with Art 6, it might be necessary to stay the proceedings while the issue is dealt with on an appeal by way of case stated. Owing to the provision of s 3 of the HRA, it would appear that a national court could not merely redefine ss 1 and 2 as creating criminal offences if that involved finding that Art 6 and ss 1 and 2 were incompatible.

Once the HRA was in force the national courts had to face the difficulty directly that s 3 of the 1997 or s 1 of the 1998 Act classifies an act as non-criminal, but Art 6 could be viewed as suggesting that it is criminal. The fair trial guarantee under Art 6(1) applies to both 'the determination of a (person's) civil rights' and 'the determination of any criminal charge'. But only the determination of a criminal charge attract the additional protections under Art 6(2) and 6(3). Anti-social behaviour orders, according to the applicable 1998 Magistrates' Courts Rules, are made on the civil standard of proof, no legal aid is available and, under s 1(10)(b) of the 1998 Act, there is the possibility of five years' imprisonment if the order is breached. The consequence for the subject of an order of the making of it are serious in the sense that their reputation is damaged and if they breach it they are subject to criminal penalties. Clearly, once the order is made, in proceedings accompanied only by safeguards applicable in civil actions, a person is at greater risk of attracting criminal penalties than they would be if a criminal offence had been charged against them in the first place, since the offence would have to be proved on the criminal standard of proof and the proceedings would be accompanied by a higher level of safeguards.

In *B v Chief Constable of Avon and Somerset Constabulary*[642] the question arose whether proceedings for a sex offender order under s 2 of the Act are civil. Section 2 is different in conception from s 1 in as much as an order can only be made in respect of a person who has already been convicted as a sex offender. But there are similarities since its purpose is preventative 'to protect the public from serious harm from him'. Lord Bingham of Cornhill CJ held:[643]

> The rationale of section 2 was, by means of an injunctive order, to seek to avoid the contingency of any further suffering by any further victim. It would also of course be to the advantage of a defendant if he were to be saved from further offending. As in the case of a civil injunction, a breach of the court's order may attract a sanction. But, also as in the case of a civil injunction, the order, although

---

640 The magistrates could only exercise their power of committal on a finding of wilful refusal to pay or culpable neglect (para 56 of the judgment).
641 (1976) 1 EHRR 647, 678–79, para 82.
642 [2001] 1 WLR 340.
643 At p 352, para 25.

restraining the defendant from doing that which is prohibited, imposes no penalty or disability upon him. I am accordingly satisfied that, as a matter of English domestic law, the application is a civil proceeding, as Parliament undoubtedly intended it to be.

Gough v Chief Constable of the Derbyshire Constabulary[644] took the same view. It was held that football banning orders under ss 14A and 14B of the Football Spectators Act 1989 do not involve criminal penalties and are therefore civil in character. The House of Lords in *McCann v Manchester Crown Court*[645] had to consider this issue. It was argued on behalf of the defendants that the purpose of Parliament was to cast proceedings under the first part of s 1, as opposed to proceedings for breach, in a civil mould but that in reality and in substance such proceedings are criminal in character. The House of Lords noted that in proceedings under the first part of s 1 the Crown Prosecution Service is not involved at all; there is no formal accusation of a breach of criminal law; the proceedings are initiated by the civil process of a complaint; *mens rea* as an ingredient of particular offences need not be proved; the making of the order results in no penalty; it cannot be entered on a defendant's record as a conviction. It was considered that the true purpose of the proceedings is preventative and therefore it was found to follow that the making of an anti-social behaviour order is not a conviction or condemnation that the person is guilty of an offence.

Counsel for the defendants argued that the procedure leading to the making of an order under s 1(4) must be considered together with the proceedings for breach under s 1(10), the latter being undoubtedly criminal in character. The House of Lords did not accept this argument since the making of the order would sometimes serve its purpose and there would be no proceedings for breach. It was considered that in principle it is necessary to consider the two stages separately. Counsel for the defendants also argued that the making of an anti-social behaviour order may have very serious consequences for a defendant since they are made in cases which satisfy the threshold of persistent and serious anti-social behaviour. So the making of such an order against a person inevitably reflects seriously on his character. However, the House of Lords noted that, for example, Mareva injunctions, may have serious consequences as may Anton Piller orders. It was concluded that proceedings to obtain an anti-social behaviour order are civil proceedings under domestic law.

The House went on to consider whether, despite its domestic classification, an anti-social behaviour order nevertheless has a criminal character in accordance with the autonomous concepts of Art 6. The minimum right under Art 6(3)(d) of everyone charged with a criminal offence to examine or have examined witnesses against him, or to obtain the attendance and examination of witnesses on his behalf under the same conditions as witnesses against him was significant in the instant case. If the proceedings under s 1 of the Act were criminal within the meaning of Art 6, this provision was clearly applicable. If they were deemed civil, then Art 6(3)(d) would be inapplicable. The Law Lords accepted that this was not an instance where the proceedings fell outside Art 6 altogether; it was found to be clear that a defendant has the benefit of the

---

644 [2002] QB 459; and on appeal at [2002] 3 WLR 289.
645 [2002] 4 All ER 593.

guarantee applicable to civil proceedings under Art 6.1. The House of Lords applied the criteria from *Engel v The Netherlands (No 1)*. Clearly the proceedings are domestically classified as civil. The order under the first part of s 1 does not constitute a finding that an offence has been committed. This was contrasted with the community charge decision in *Benham v United Kingdom*.[646] But the third factor was the most important. Here the position was that the order itself involved no penalty. The established criteria suggested that the proceedings were not in respect of a criminal charge.

It was noted that there is, as Lord Bingham of Cornhill CJ pointed out in *B v Chief Constable of Avon and Somerset Constabulary*,[647] no case in which the European Court has held proceedings to be criminal even though an adverse outcome for the defendant cannot result in any penalty. The Lords considered that there was scope for the law to be developed in that direction. However, the Lords relied on the interpretation of Art 6 by the Lord President (Rodger) in *S v Miller*[648] in finding that the proceedings are not criminal. Section 52(2) of the Children (Scotland) Act 1995 provides that a child may have to be subjected to compulsory measures of supervision when he 'has committed an offence'. The question arose whether in such proceedings Art 6 is applicable. The Lord President said on this point:[649]

> S was arrested and charged by the police . . . He remained 'charged with a criminal offence' in terms of article 6 until the procurator fiscal decided the following day – in the language of section 43(5) of the Criminal Procedure Act – 'not to proceed with the charge'. At that point the criminal proceedings came to an end and the reporter initiated the procedures under the 1995 Act by arranging a hearing in terms of section 63(1) . . . The subsequent proceedings under the 1995 Act are not criminal for the purposes of article 6. Although the reporter does indeed intend to show that the child concerned committed an offence, this is not for the purpose of punishing him but in order to establish a basis for taking appropriate measures for his welfare . . . So the specific guarantees in article 6(2) and (3) do not apply.

The Lords accepted this reasoning as correctly reflecting the purpose of Art 6 and found that it applied *a fortiori* to proceedings under s 1. Therefore it was found that an application for an anti-social behaviour order does not involve the determination of a criminal charge in Art 6 terms. However, despite this finding the House adopted a curious compromise in considering that an order should be made on the criminal standard of proof. This creates the odd situation whereby the standard of proof is criminal but the evidence that can be put forward to achieve that standard is not bound by the rules applicable in criminal trials, including the rule against hearsay evidence. Also the safeguards of Art 6(2) and (3) do not apply.

These findings would seem also to apply to injunctions issued under the 1997 Act. The extent to which the hybrid nature of s 3 of the 1997 Act has the potential to allow interferences with the Art 6, 10 and 11 guarantees in protest cases was illustrated in

646 (1996) 22 EHRR 293.
647 [2001] 1 WLR 340.
648 2001 SC 977.
649 At pp 989–90.

two significant decisions. In *Huntingdon Life Sciences Ltd and Another v Curtin and Others*[650] the company (HLS) obtained an *ex parte* injunction against six groups under s 3 of the Act, which prohibited conduct amounting to harassment within the terms of the Act, or entering HLS research sites. HLS was engaged in animal experimentation and was the subject of a campaign by a number of animal rights' organisations. One of the defendants, the British Union of Anti-Vivisectionists (BUAV), a peaceful campaigning group, applied to have the injunction varied so that it was not covered. Eady J found, in the *inter partes* proceedings, that the plaintiff had not provided sufficient evidence to support the claim that the defendants should be covered by the injunction. He also considered it unfortunate that the provisions of the Act were couched in such wide terms that they could appear to cover 'the rights of political protest and public demonstration which are so much a part of our democratic tradition'. This judgment clearly recognised, as the legislators did not, the general need to seek to delineate forms of anti-social behaviour sufficiently clearly so as to avoid infringing the rights in question.

The BUAV was exempted from the injunction, but the case illustrates the ease of obtaining interim injunctions against a wide range of persons and groups in these circumstances. In practice, once such an injunction is obtained, the police are likely to enforce it against a number of persons who are not covered or are only doubtfully covered by it, on the basis that they appear to be acting under the authority of, or in concert with, one of groups which are enjoined. This will commonly occur in such situations.

A rather similar situation arose in *DPP v Moseley, Woodling and Selvanayagam*.[651] One of the defendants, Ms Selvanayagam, had been served with an *ex parte* interim injunction under s 3 of the 1997 Act, which she was seeking to challenge. After she had been served with the injunction, she and the other two defendants continued to demonstrate peacefully against the fur trade, at a fur farm. They were arrested and charged with the offence under s 2 of the 1997 Act. All of them relied on the defence that the conduct was reasonable in the circumstances under s 1(3)(c), and this defence was accepted by the magistrate. He further found that the injunction was obtained only on the basis of affidavit evidence and could not as a matter of law preclude the finding of reasonableness. Therefore, he acquitted all three. On appeal, the High Court found that pursuit of a course of harassment in breach of an injunction would preclude establishing the defence of reasonableness and that the magistrate had not been entitled to go behind the terms of the injunction. The other two respondents were not named in the injunction and there was no basis for considering that they were acting in concert with Ms Selvanayagam. Therefore, they were not precluded from putting forward the defence of reasonableness. Accordingly, Ms Selvanayagam was convicted under s 2.

The most striking feature of this case is the acceptance that a central issue in a criminal trial can be predetermined in civil proceedings, particularly uncontested *ex parte* proceedings, in which the only evidence is 'on the papers'. The Act, as indicated, provides a remedy of imprisonment for breach of an injunction; there is therefore no reason why its breach should also be determinative of separate criminal proceedings. This matter clearly raises Art 6 issues; it comes close to obtaining a conviction 'on

---

650 (1998) 3(1) J Civ Lib 37.
651 Judgment of 9 June 1999; reported [1999] J Civ Lib 390.

the papers' since, if an injunction has been previously obtained, the burden on the prosecution will be considerably eased. Although Strasbourg has not dealt with the precise point regarding the usurpation of the function of the criminal court by previous civil proceedings, it has made it clear in a series of cases that the use of written statements from witnesses who are not present at the trial will contravene Art 6(3)(d) except in limited, exceptional circumstances.[652] It may be said that an injunction obtained at an uncontested hearing is analogous to such statements. The use of such an injunction to predetermine a key issue in the criminal trial might also be viewed as infringing the presumption of innocence under Art 6(2) since the defendant may be confronted with an irrebuttable presumption against her. In *Salabiaku v France*[653] it was found that while Art 6(2) 'does not . . . regard presumptions of fact or of law provided for in the criminal law with indifference', it permits the operation of such presumptions against the accused so long as the law in question confines such presumptions 'within reasonable limits which take into account the importance of what is at stake and maintain the rights of the defence'.[654] It is debatable whether the rights of the defence can be said to be preserved where no means at all of going behind an injunction is available. These issues will probably, after *McCann*, have to be raised at Strasbourg.

Clearly, the use of injunctions as in *Huntingdon Life Sciences* and *Moseley* represents an interference with the Art 10 and 11 rights of the protesters, which must be justified under the para 2 exceptions. The fact that the injunction operates as a prior restraint is not conclusive of the issue since, as indicated above, Strasbourg has accepted that the use of such restraint may be justified in certain circumstances in public protest cases.[655] The leading case on prior restraints is *Observer and Guardian v UK*,[656] in which the Court considered the compatibility with Art 10 of interim injunctions preventing those newspapers from publishing *Spycatcher* material. The Court laid down the basic principle that: 'while Art 10 does not in terms prohibit the imposition of prior restraints on publication . . . the dangers inherent in [them] are such that they call for the most careful scrutiny on the part of the Court . . .'.[657] These findings were based on the perishable nature of news, a relevant consideration on the facts. But there is no reason to view the stance of the Court as precluding consideration of other values which are threatened by the use of injunctions as a prior restraint on expression, bearing in mind the arguments set out at the beginning of this chapter as to the value of public protest. Injunctions may not prevent the protest completely, but they may prevent it from being effective by excluding it from the place where it will have most impact. Moreover, arguments opposed to prior restraint need not rest only on values associated with expression, but may take into account the value of rights of participation in the political process, and such arguments may be raised under Art 11. In other words, while

652 *Unterpinger v Austria* (1991) 13 EHRR 175; *Van Mechelen v Netherlands* (1998) 25 EHRR 647; *Kostovski v Netherlands* (1989) 12 EHRR 434; *Delta v France* (1993) 16 EHRR 574; *Doorson v Netherlands* (1996) 22 EHRR 330.
653 (1988) 13 EHRR 379.
654 See p 388, para 28.
655 See, e.g., the decision of the Commission in *Christians Against Racism and Fascism v UK*, Appl No 8440/78 (1980) 21 DR 138.
656 (1991) 14 EHRR 153; for comment, see Leigh, I, '*Spycatcher* in Strasbourg' [1992] PL 200.
657 Ibid, para 60.

it might be argued that the terms of an injunction under s 3 of the 1997 Act preventing protesters from demonstrating, say, outside the detention centre for asylum seekers at Oakington, Cambridge on the anniversary of its opening, would not prevent them from distributing leaflets or holding a peaceful protest elsewhere, it would undermine the exercise of rights of effective expression and of participation in the political process.

Such arguments, where linked to Art 10, could be given added impact by invoking s 12 of the HRA in relation to the use of *ex parte* injunctions in cases analogous to *Moseley*.[658] Section 12(1) provides: 'this section applies if a court is considering whether to grant any relief which, if granted, might affect the exercise of the Convention right to freedom of expression . . . (2) if the person against whom the application for relief is made (the respondent) is neither present nor represented no such relief is to be granted unless the court is satisfied . . . that the applicant has taken all practical steps to notify the respondent or that there are compelling reasons why the respondent should not be notified.' Under s 12(4) 'the court must have particular regard to the importance of the convention right to freedom of expression . . .'. Section 12(2) provides a strong adjuration against the use of *ex parte* injunctions which, it is suggested, is as applicable in public protest cases as it is in those for which it was intended – injunctions against publications by the media. It may be noted that Art 10 only is referred to and therefore, as far as s 12 is concerned, the Art 11 argument would be irrelevant, an unfortunate effect of seeking to afford added weight to the Art 10 rights of one group – the media – while disregarding those of another – protesters. Section 12 may have been limited in its application to civil proceedings[659] with the intention, *inter alia*, of excluding public protest from its ambit. If so, the failure to take account of the use of injunctions and orders obtained in civil proceedings in protest cases may have led to this unintended result.

Section 12 may apply to orders made under s 1 of the 1998 Act, which potentially could also operate as prior restraints. The procedure to be followed appears to allow the grant of *ex parte* orders, but the defendant should be informed before the hearing that an application for an order has been made.[660] In a public protest case, the defendant would be likely to attend the hearing in order to raise the question of the interference with Art 10 and 11 rights which would occur if the order was made. Section 12(2) would not therefore normally be of relevance, but s 12(4) would be, and might tip the scales against the grant of an order in a protest case.

The arguments which can be raised under the HRA in relation to injunctions or anti-social behaviour orders when used in protest cases, are creating a clear distinction, which the architects of the 1997 Act and s 1 of the 1998 Act failed to create, between their operation in relation to those at whom they were targeted, and protesters. Under the activist model, such orders or injunctions would be subject to strict scrutiny under Arts 6, 10 and 11. The Art 8 rights, if in question, of those subject to the protest would also be relevant. Where an order or injunction was issued, the result might be that it would be carefully limited in order to answer to the strict requirements of proportionality.

---

658 See also the discussion of injunctions more generally in Leigh, I and Lustgarten, L, 'Making rights real: the courts, remedies and the Human Rights Act' (1999) 58 CLJ 509.
659 Under s 12(5).
660 Magistrates' Courts (Sex Offender and Anti-Social Behaviour Orders) Rules 1998.

Defences of reasonableness

These statutory provisions all provide defences of reasonableness, none of which is defined or specifically aimed at protecting expression.[661] Demonstrators shouting at passers-by to support their cause, whose behaviour could readily be termed threatening or disorderly, etc, and likely to cause one of the passers-by harassment, distress or alarm,[662] will have a defence under s 5(3)(c) if they can show that their behaviour was reasonable. The Act gives no guidance as to the meaning of the term, but it was determined in *DPP v Clarke*[663] that the defence is to be judged objectively, and it will therefore depend on what a bench of magistrates considers reasonable. In that case, the behaviour of the protesters outside an abortion clinic was not found to be reasonable. The use of pictures and models of aborted foetuses appeared to contribute to this conclusion.

This decision, which would clearly also apply to charges under s 4A, and, where appropriate, to s 12(3) of the 1997 Act and s 1(5) of the 1998 Act as well, obviously does not give much guidance to protesters seeking to determine beforehand the limits or meaning of 'reasonable' protest. As a deliberately ambiguous term, it obviously leaves enormous discretion to the judiciary to adopt approaches to its interpretation in accordance with Arts 10 and 11 as interpreted in *Steel*, ranging from the minimalist to the activist. Under the former approach, it might be found that only innocuous, peaceful persuasion could be termed reasonable. Such a finding might be of value where, for example, a large number of groups were served with injunctions under s 3 of the 1997 Act since it might serve to allow differentiation between those whose peaceful persuasion had nevertheless been viewed by its target as 'harassment' and those groups which had adopted more forceful means. But a more 'activist' interpretation of this defence would have to find a basis in the general principles articulated above,[664] especially applicable in relation to protest expressing minority viewpoints. This would be a matter of significance, since such viewpoints may be unlikely to be favourably received by others. Thus, offensive words used by protesters could be found to fall within this defence on the basis that in the context of a particular demonstration which had a legitimate political aim, such behaviour was acceptable and therefore reasonable. An argument for giving such a wide interpretation to the term 'reasonable' can be supported on the basis that, as argued above, to criminalise such behaviour would arguably amount to a very far reaching curb on the freedom to protest which might be found to be in breach of Art 10 or Art 11, bearing in mind the need to interpret statutory provisions in conformity with the Convention.

---

661 Under s 5(3)(c) and s 4A(3)(b) of the 1986 Act, s 1(3) of the 1997 Act and s 1(5) of the 1998 Act. It may be noted that under the 1997 and 1998 provisions, the 'defence' operates as partially reversed *actus reus*, in the sense that if the defence is proved (the burden of so doing is on the defendant), then harassment or anti-social behaviour is not established.

662 It is not necessary to prove that anyone actually experienced harassment, merely that this was likely.

663 Above, fn 626.

664 See above, pp 681–89.

The decisions in *Norwood*[665] and *Hammond*[666] indicate that this view is correct. The facts of *Norwood* are discussed above. The defence of reasonableness under s 5 of the 1986 Act was employed as the entry-point for the consideration of proportionality under Art 10 and it was found that the restriction upon his freedom of expression right represented by the offence was proportionate to the legitimate aim of protecting the rights of others. In *Hammond* the appellant took a placard with the words 'Stop Immorality', 'Stop Homosexuality', 'Stop Lesbianism', and 'Jesus is Lord' to the centre of Bournemouth and began preaching. This attracted a large group of people who were provoked by the preaching and who physically attacked the appellant. He was requested by two police officers to stop preaching. Upon refusing to comply with this request the appellant was arrested and subsequently charged and convicted of a s 5 offence. It was found that the interference with the appellant's right to freedom of expression under s 5 was a proportionate response in view of the fact that the appellant's behaviour went beyond legitimate protest, was provoking violence and disorder and interfered with the rights of others. In those circumstances it was found that the appellant's conduct was not reasonable. The conclusion on appeal was that the lower court had embarked upon the necessary exercise and had reached a decision that was open for them to take, namely, that the defendant's conduct was not reasonable in the particular circumstances.[667] It was accepted that Art 10 considerations apply to the evaluation of a reasonableness defence.[668] Thus, although Art 10 was taken into account on appeal, it was again found that the conviction was proportionate to the harm sought to be averted.

Aside from the defence of reasonableness, the prosecution may also have to demonstrate – where Art 10 or 11 is engaged – that bringing a prosecution under ss 4 or 5 is a proportionate response to the conduct in question. This was established in *Dehal v Crown Prosecution Service*[669] in which an application of the doctrine of proportionality under Art 10, relying on s 6 HRA, occurred, as a free-standing exercise. The appellant, a Sikh man, had put up a notice at a Sikh Temple that he had attended for many years. It was written in Punjabi and attacked the President of the Temple and other members of the Committee. Mr Dehal intended the notice to be read by those it was aimed at and other worshippers. He was convicted of the offence under the Public Order Act 1986, s 4A (1).[670] His appeal concerned in essence the relationship between Art 10 of the European Convention on Human Rights and the s 4A offence. The Court had to examine the following questions: was the prosecution of the appellant a proportionate response to his conduct and did Art 10 provide him with a defence, therefore making the interference with the appellant's freedom of expression unnecessary? In allowing the appeal, the Court determined that although all the elements of the offence were present, the prosecution had not presented enough evidence to establish that bringing a criminal prosecution was a proportionate response to the appellant's conduct.

---

665 [2004] EWHC 69.
666 [2004] EWHC 69.
667 At para 33.
668 At para 22.
669 [2005] EWHC 2154.
670 The case is also discussed in Chapter 6; see pp 506–7.

Public nuisance

The statutory offences discussed bear similarities with the common law doctrine of public nuisance, which has occasionally been used against public protest. This common law offence will arise if something occurs which inflicts damage, injury or inconvenience on all members of a class who come within the sphere or neighbourhood of its operation.[671] Liability for committing a public nuisance may arise by blocking the highway; however, according to *Clarke (No 2)*,[672] the disruption caused must amount to an unreasonable user of the highway in order to found such liability. Thus, once obstruction has been shown, the question of reasonableness arises. It would appear from *News Group Newspapers Ltd v SOGAT*[673] that to cause a minor disruption for a legitimate purpose such as a march does not constitute an unreasonable user of the highway and will not therefore amount to a nuisance. It might seem that an assembly could not constitute a reasonable user of the highway under the Highways Act and yet nevertheless amount to a public nuisance. However, *dicta* in *Gillingham BC v Medway Dock Co*[674] suggest that this might, exceptionally, be possible.

Public nuisance, as a common law doctrine of a broad and imprecise nature, might not meet the requirement of 'prescribed by law' under Arts 10 and 11. Moreover, given its lack of precision and the lack of any defence of reasonableness it is suggested that, in satisfying their duty to observe proportionality under Arts 10 and 11, in pursuance of their duty under s 6 of the HRA, the police and CPS should not employ a common law offence of this width when a more precisely defined statutory offence – arising under s 137 of the Highways Act – is available. There is a case therefore, for suggesting that this offence should not be used in future against assemblies on the highway.

Private common law remedies

Apart from control by the police, meetings and demonstrations can be prevented or curbed by private persons who seek injunctions to that end.[675] An interim injunction may be obtained very quickly in a hearing in which the other party is not represented. Even if a permanent injunction is not eventually granted, the aim of the demonstration may well have been destroyed by that time. In *Hubbard v Pitt*,[676] the defendants mounted a demonstration outside an estate agent in order to protest at what was seen as the ousting of working class tenants in order to make way for higher income buyers, thereby effecting a change in the character of the area. They therefore picketed the estate agents. The plaintiffs sought an injunction to prevent this on various grounds, including that of nuisance. At first instance, it was held that a stationary meeting would not constitute a reasonable user of the Highway and the grant of the interim injunction

---

671 See *Halsbury's Laws of England*, 4th edn, Vol 34, para 305. For discussion of the offence, see Spencer, JR [1989] CLJ 55.
672 [1964] 2 QB 315; [1963] 3 All ER 884, CA.
673 [1986] ICR 716; [1986] IRLR 337.
674 [1992] 3 All ER 931.
675 For discussion of such use of injunctions, see Wallington, P, 'Injunctions and the right to demonstrate' [1976] CLJ 82. For discussion of their use in the context of labour disputes see (1973) 2 ILJ 213; Miller, *Contempt of Court*, 1989, pp 412–22.
676 [1976] QB 142.

was upheld by the Court of Appeal, Lord Denning dissenting on the ground that the right to demonstrate is so closely analogous to freedom of speech that it should be protected.

Under the HRA, the use of such injunctions raise a number of issues. They resemble injunctions available under s 3 of the 1997 Act. However, since they are based on the common law, s 3 of the HRA does not apply. Section 6 of the HRA does not apply directly unless the party seeking the injunction is a public authority or a private body discharging a public function. In *Hubbard*, those seeking the injunctions would not have fallen within either of those categories. But, as Chapter 4 indicated, s 6 has implications even for private parties.[677] Thus, the Strasbourg protest jurisprudence should be taken into account when considering the grant of an injunction in similar circumstances, arguably even where the common law is not ambiguous.

7 Riot, violent disorder and affray

Serious offences under the 1986 Act

Section 9 of the Public Order Act 1986 abolishes the common law offences of riot, unlawful assembly and affray and replaces them with similar statutory offences of riot (s 1), violent disorder (s 2) and affray (s 3).[678] Each of these offences may be committed in a public or a private place and it is not necessary that any person should actually have feared unlawful violence. Violent disorder would be most commonly used against unruly demonstrations, since it can be committed by words alone.

In order to establish an affray, it must first be shown that the defendant used or threatened unlawful violence towards another, secondly that his conduct was such as would cause a person of reasonable firmness present at the scene to fear for his personal safety and thirdly, under s 6(2), that he intended to use or threaten violence or was aware that his conduct might be violent or threaten violence. Under s 3(3), a threat cannot be made by the use of words alone. A demonstration in which threatening gestures were used might fulfil the first limb of s 3(1), but a strong argument can be advanced that it does not fulfil the second. If the gestures are part of a demonstration, it is probable that a person of reasonable firmness would not fear unlawful violence even though such a person might feel somewhat distressed. In *Taylor v DPP*,[679] Lord Hailsham, speaking of the common law offence, said 'the degree of violence must be such as to be calculated to terrify a person of reasonably firm character'. The Act, of course, refers to 'fear' as opposed to terror, but this ruling suggests that 'fear' should be interpreted restrictively.

Violent disorder was introduced in the 1986 Act as a completely new offence which was aimed in part at curtailing the activities of violent pickets. It is couched in the same terms as affray, but requires that three or more persons are involved. In order to establish violent disorder, it must first be shown that the defendant was one of three or more persons who used or threatened unlawful violence; secondly, that his conduct was

---

677 See pp 250–56.
678 For comment on the offences, see 'Public Order Act offences' (1989) December LAG.
679 [1973] AC 964.

such as would cause a person of reasonable firmness present at the scene to fear for his personal safety and thirdly, that the defendant himself actually used or threatened violence. The mental element under s 6(2) is the same as for affray. It may be argued that in the context of a demonstration, threatening gestures would not be termed a threat of violence. 'Violence' is a strong term which should not be watered down. In one respect, however, violent disorder is wider than affray since it may be committed by the use of words alone. If no threats are used by a defendant, he could not incur liability under s 2 even if it was found that he encouraged violence by others.[680]

Riot is the highest level public order offence created by the Act and is similar to the offence of violent disorder. However, it is narrower in that it requires that 12 or more persons who are present together use or threaten unlawful violence for a common purpose and that the defendant must actually use violence intending to do so or being aware that his conduct may be violent. The requirement that the conduct of them (taken together) is such as would cause a person reasonable firmness present at the scene to fear for his personal safety is common to all three offences.

Impact of the HRA

The behaviour covered by these provisions will in general fall outside Art 11, which covers only peaceful assemblies, and possibly outside Art 10 as well. Even assuming that a disorderly assembly could be viewed as expressing an opinion and therefore as within the principle from *Steel*, the measures used against it would readily be viewed as proportionate to the aims of preserving order and public safety. However, the HRA may allow differentiation to be created between the application of these offences to protesters and to hooligans. In respect of protesters, the proportionality of the measures adopted would be considered, although, depending on the circumstances, the court might view the choice of measures as falling within the area of discretionary judgment likely to be accorded to the police.

8 Conclusions

Before the HRA came into force, the true boundaries of public protest were drawn, not by reference to the constitutional significance in a democracy of rights of political participation or of affording expression, through the medium of forms of protest, to a variety of viewpoints, but often arbitrarily due to the imprecision of the law and the approach frequently taken to it in low level courts or by the police. In 2000 it was tempting to look forward to the use of Arts 10 and 11 in the post-HRA era in the expectation, not only that the boundaries would eventually be re-drawn more precisely, but also that legal discourse in this area would no longer focus simply on disorder, but rather would seek to engage in the ongoing debate, at Strasbourg and in other jurisdictions, as to the values underlying the constitutional significance of protest and the weight they should be afforded. The question whether that expectation would be fulfilled depended partly on the readiness of the domestic judiciary to disregard the

---

680 *McGuigan and Cameron* [1991] Crim LR 719; *Fleming and Robinson* [1989] Crim LR 658; cf *Caird* (1970) 54 Cr App R 499.

outcomes of many of the public protest cases that Strasbourg has considered. But it was also suggested that the impact of the HRA on public protest would be principally determined, not by the Strasbourg jurisprudence it introduced, but by the prevailing and established judicial attitude to public protest, and the extent to which the judiciary might be prepared to move away from it, by giving practical effect to the core values underlying the Convention. Vital, also, was the way that the judiciary were likely to deal with the problematic issue of the margin of appreciation and its role in the Strasbourg jurisprudence. As we have seen, reliance on the outcomes of cases at Strasbourg provide no secure grounding for such protection – rather the reverse.

How far have those expectations been answered, nearly seven years on? This chapter has on the whole painted a dismal picture. Over-broad statutory provisions have been broadened still further by incremental extension. In post-HRA cases lip service only has tended to be paid to questions of proportionality. The breach of the peace doctrine has been used extensively by police against protesters over most of the HRA period with little attempt by the judiciary, except in *Redmond-Bate*, to hold it in check, the low point being *Austin and Saxby*. The finding that 3,000 mainly peaceful protesters could be trapped for seven hours in a London Square, and that an entirely peaceful protester and a bystander caught up in the protest had no redress for the detention must be one of the low points of the domestic public protest jurisprudence. However the House of Lords' decision in *Laporte* may signal a change of stance. But it is not enough to view the breach of the peace doctrine as far too broad and as needing a check. Many of the statutory provisions are also excessively broad. Far more recognition of the value of expression and assembly is still needed in this context. The judiciary are still too prone to accept police assessments of public order risks.

In future post-HRA decisions judges inclined to take a more activist or pro-free assembly stance may be prepared to find where necessary that their decision making can be rooted in the general principles upheld at Strasbourg as underpinning the Convention, rather than in its particular application. The judiciary can draw upon the general principles and values underlying the Convention – free expression, pluralism, tolerance and the maintenance of diversity as essential characteristics of a democratic society – if the HRA is to provide more than a cosmetic change in approach to the protection of the right of peaceful protest.[681] The justification for affording greater weight to communicative rights than that afforded at Strasbourg in findings under Arts 10 and 11 can be found in the need to ensure the genuine efficacy of the rights, with a view to realising the free expression and assembly objectives referred to above, especially in the case of minority groups or viewpoints. As argued, the Convention jurisprudence clearly recognises the need to protect a plurality of views in a democracy, even in the face of offence caused to the majority.[682] It would be in accordance with the Convention concept of a democratic society to refuse to place those seeking to exercise communicative rights in the same position as football hooligans and to reject a legal tradition of valuing the general societal interest in public order over the exercise of such rights. In accordance with the values of the Convention, safeguarding the interests of

---

681 They will also, of course, be free to draw upon the rich US and Canadian jurisprudence on public protest as a basic civil right.
682 Above, pp 681–84.

minorities in a democracy is not to circumvent the democratic process, but to uphold it by obviating the danger that those interests will be marginalised.

If the judiciary are prepared to take this stance more strongly in the coming years, the nature and structure of judicial argument in public protest cases, as well as the likely outcomes, will change significantly. Although some judges have tended post-HRA towards approaches which have been termed 'minimalist' or 'traditionalist', the rather tokenistic changes in legal reasoning which are resulting may still eventually come to influence judicial attitudes. In public order cases such judges are hearing, even if they are unreceptive to, arguments from counsel as to the value of this form of political expression. Now that the judiciary are placed in the position of considering such value and the need nevertheless to circumscribe protest within a democracy, they may eventually come to view this matter from a broader perspective[683] and to participate in the debate which has been occurring in other jurisdictions for many years. Ultimately, in this particular area of political expression, the HRA may be beginning to have a more profoundly educative effect than in others, not only on the public, but on the judiciary.

---

683 Comparison may be made here with the manner in which the jurisprudence of the Canadian Supreme Court changed radically following the enactment of the Charter of Fundamental Rights, from orthodox 'black letter' analysis to a far more theorised and philosophical approach: see Leigh, I and Lustgarten, L, 'Making rights real: the courts, remedies and the Human Rights Act' (1999) 58 CLJ 509.

Part III

The protection of privacy

Introduction[1]

The right to respect for privacy is now accepted as part of the domestic law of a number of countries[2] and of international human rights instruments.[3] However, the limits of the right are still unclear and a generally accepted definition of privacy has not emerged. As Raymond Wacks has observed, 'the voluminous [theoretical] literature on the subject has failed to produce a lucid or consistent meaning of [the] concept'.[4] It may be said, therefore, that privacy has become a complex and very broad concept due to the variety of claims or interests which have been thought to fall within it.[5] The European Court of Human Rights has accommodated many disparate issues within the concept of privacy arising under Art 8 of the European Convention on Human Rights: they range from the rights of homosexuals[6] to the right to receive information about oneself.[7] As Feldman has argued, the scope of Art 8 is continuing to widen.[8]

---

1 Texts referred to in this Part: Wacks, R, *The Protection of Privacy*, 1980, Sweet and Maxwell; Westin, AF, *Privacy and Freedom*, 1970, The Bodley Head; Wacks, R (ed), *Privacy*, 1993, New York University Press; Fenwick, H and Phillipson, G, *Media Freedom under the Human Rights Act*, 2006, Chapters 13–17; Tugendhat and Christie, *The Law of Privacy and the Media*, 2002, OUP; Feldman, *Civil Liberties and Human Rights in England and Wales*, 2nd edn, 2002, Part 3; Markesinis, B (ed), *Protecting Privacy*, 1999, OUP; Birks, R (ed), *Privacy and Loyalty*, 1997, Clarendon; Clayton and Tomlinson, *The Law of Human Rights* (2006), Chapter 12; Eady, D, 'A statutory right to privacy' (1996) 3 EHRLR 243; Winfield, P 'Privacy' (1931) 47 LQR 23; Yang, TL 'Privacy: A Comparative Study of English and American Law' (1966) 15 ICLQ 175; Wacks, R, 'The poverty of privacy' (1980) 96 LQR 73; Seipp, D, 'English judicial recognition of the right to privacy' (1983) 3 OJLS 325; Leigh, I, 'Horizontal rights, the Human Rights Act and privacy: lessons from the Commonwealth?' (1999) 48 ICLQ 57; Grosz, S and Braithwaite, N, 'Privacy and the Human Rights Act', in Hunt and Singh (eds), *A Practitioners Guide to the Impact of the Human Rights Act*, 1999; Wright, J, 'How private is my private life?' in Betten, L (ed), *the Human Rights Act 1998: What it Means*, 1999, Brill. Whitty, N, Murphy, T and Livingstone, S, *Civil Liberties Law: the Human Rights Era* (2001) Chapter 6; Fenwick, H and Phillipson, G, 'Breach of confidence as a privacy remedy in the Human Rights era (2000) 63 (5) MLR 660–93.

2 For example, the US Privacy Act 1974 and the tort or torts of invasion of privacy, the Canadian Protection of Privacy Act 1974, Art 1382 of the French Civil Code; German courts can protect privacy under s 823(1) of the Civil Code and a right to privacy arises under the German Basic Law Art 10 (albeit limited to posts and telecommunications).

3 It appears in the European Convention on Human Rights, Art 8 and the International Covenant on Civil and Political Rights, Art 17.

4 'Introduction', in Wacks, op. cit., fn 1, p xi.

5 See Wacks, op. cit., fn 1, Chapter 1, pp 10–21.

6 *Dudgeon* (1982) 4EHRR 149.

7 *Gaskin* (1990) 12 EHRR 36.

8 (1997) 3 EHRLR 264.

The Convention does not attempt to define privacy,[9] but various definitions have been put forward which tend to be very broad: it has been termed 'a circle around every individual human being which no government . . . ought to be permitted to overstep' and 'some space in human existence thus entrenched around and sacred from authoritative[10] intrusion'. Feldman has found that the desire for a private area in life derives its justification from personal autonomy, which is linked to the idea of 'defensible space', and from the 'idea of utility' – the idea that 'people operate more effectively and happily when they are allowed to make their own arrangements about domestic and business matters without interference from the state'.[11] Such phrases suggest that some aspects of an individual's life, which can be identified as private aspects, are of particular value and therefore warrant special protection from state intrusion. At an intuitive level, the notion that boundaries can and should be placed around such aspects of an individual's life, preventing such intrusion and thereby protecting personal autonomy, seems to be accepted as the fundamental basis of the idea of privacy[12] and underlies decisions under Art 8.[13] However, as recognised at Strasbourg, the guarantee under Art 8 goes further than simply requiring that the individual should be let alone – in two respects. As indicated below, the right also encompasses positive obligations on the part of the state authorities. It also places obligations on private bodies, which can include positive obligations. In *X and Y v Netherlands*[14] the Court stated: 'these [Art 8] obligations may require the adoption of measures even in the sphere of relations between individuals.'

The disparate obligations created by this right are reflected in the different concerns of the two chapters in Part III. Chapter 9 deals with the protection of personal information from non-consensual use by public and private bodies. It particularly concentrates on invasion of privacy by the media and considers protection for both family and private life. Chapter 10 considers state surveillance and searches of property; it covers a variety of intrusions of state agents into private live and considers the safeguards available to the individual. It will be argued that in each of these contexts the Human Rights Act (HRA), which has imported the Strasbourg conceptions of privacy into domestic law, will be of great significance. The statues which now have a central impact in this context, the Data Protection Act 1998 and the Regulation of Investigatory Powers Act 2000, have to be interpreted compatibly with the Convention rights under s 3 HRA. The HRA has provided the impetus for the development of further protection for private information by effecting a transformation of the doctrine of confidence.

Theoretical considerations

Privacy can be associated with a range of underlying values. The key values are, it is argued, informational autonomy (control over private information), self-fulfilment,

---

9   See further Chapter 2, pp 69–91.
10   Mill, JS, *Principles of Political Economy*, 1970, Penguin, p 306.
11   See *Civil Liberties and Human Rights in England and Wales*, 1st edn, 1993, pp 353–54.
12   See Seipp, op. cit., fn 1, at p 333.
13   See, e.g., *Leander v Sweden* (1987) 9 EHRR 433; *McVeigh, O'Neill and Evans v United Kingdom* (1981) 45 EHRR 71.
14   (1985) 8 EHRR 235.

dignity, substantive autonomy.[15] As will be discussed below, these values are often strongly associated with each other. It has often been argued that privacy is associated with self-fulfilment in the sense that protection for the private life of the individual tends to provide the best conditions under which he or she may flourish.[16] In other words, self-fulfilment may be fostered if the individual is able to enjoy the benefits most obviously associated with the private: the dropping of the public mask, the communion of intimates, and the expression of the deepest emotions.

If it is accepted that a key value underlying differing conceptions of privacy is that of personal autonomy,[17] it is necessary to draw a distinction between what may be termed 'substantive' and 'informational' autonomy. The former denotes the individual's interest in being able to make certain substantive choices about personal life for him or herself, such as the choice to engage in certain sexual practices, or follow certain life styles without state interference or coercion.[18] Privacy derives its value partly from its close association with personal autonomy, in the sense that freedom from interference by the authorities will foster the conditions under which autonomy can be exercised. Thus, some authoritative invasions of privacy may be said to lead to interference with individual autonomy.

The term 'informational autonomy', on the other hand, refers to the individual's interest in controlling the flow of personal information about herself, the interest referred to by the German Supreme Court as 'informational self-determination',[19] or as Beardsely has put it, the right to 'selective disclosure'.[20] In accordance with the views of a number of writers, it is suggested that this interest is one of the primary concerns of the law in this area.[21] The ability to exercise control in this manner also affords some protection to other values, as Feldman[22] has pointed out: 'If people are able to release [private] information with impunity, it might have the effect of illegitimately constraining a person's choices as to his or her private behaviour, interfering in a major way with his or her autonomy'.[23] In other words, control over information thus indirectly protects

---

15   See further Feldman, D, 'Secrecy, dignity or autonomy? Views of privacy as a civil liberty' (1994) 47(2) CLP 42.

16   See Feldman, fn 1 above (2002) at 512.

17   See Wacks, op. cit., fn 1, pp 10–21; Westin, op. cit., fn 1, p 7; Miller, A, *Assault on Privacy*, 1971, University of Michigan Press, p 40.

18   See further Chapter 2, pp 74–87, Chapter 9, p 961, Chapter 15, pp 1520–21.

19   BGH, 19 December 1995, BGHZ 131, pp 322–46.

20   'Privacy: autonomy and selective disclosure', in Nomos XIII 54.

21   Ruth Gavison's definition of privacy – 'a limitation of others' access to an individual' – has three aspects: information; attention; physical access (Privacy and the limits of law' (1980) 89(3) Yale LF 421); see also Gross's similar definition: 'The concept of privacy' (1967) 42 NYULR 34, p 36. The issue of physical access is adequately dealt with by the law of trespass; it will be argued below that the issue of 'attention' can be addressed within an 'informational' paradigm, provided that term is conceived of with sufficient sensitivity and flexibility. Cf Wacks, op. cit., fn 1, p 76 (acknowledging the point as from unpublished work by Ruth Gavison). Parent agrees ('A new definition of privacy for the law' (1932) 2 Law and Philosophy 305, p 326).

22   Feldman, D, 'Secrecy, dignity or autonomy? Views of privacy as a civil liberty' (1994) 47(2) CLP 42, p 54.

23   Ibid, p 51. Feldman's view is that privacy protects persons operating in a given sphere from interference within that sphere by those who are outside it. He argues that within each different sphere of existence, privacy operates in four dimensions: 'space (including access to and control over material goods), time: action; and information' (ibid, p 52). Chapters 9 and 10 deal mainly with 'information'; control

substantive autonomy. Personal dignity, which must be diminished when information relating to intimate aspects of a person's life is widely published, giving rise to feelings of violation, shame and embarrassment, is also afforded a measure of protection. Informational control also protects what Feldman identifies as the value in forming and maintaining spheres of social interaction and intimacy – for example, work colleagues, friends, family, lovers – which may be seen as essential to human flourishing.[24] It is clear that the intimacy that such relationships entail is predicated upon an ability of the individual to ensure that information which may be circulated within one sphere is not, without her knowledge or consent, transferred to another sphere or the outside world. A privacy law gives legal force to that ability.

Since considerations of this nature involve an implied contrast between the public and the private, it may be helpful at this point to consider the division between the two spheres in order to come closer to examining what may be encompassed by the notion of privacy. A variety of referents may be used. The public includes state activity, aspects of the world of work, the pursuit of public interests, while the private includes the home, the family the expression of sexuality and of the deepest feelings and emotions. Postulating such a division need not obscure the fact that these spheres are not entirely distinct, but may interact; the distinction is not, it is argued, dependent on physical space.[25]

The strength of claims that respect for individual autonomy has not been accorded may be affected, as the following chapters explain, by the nature of the obligation sought to be imposed on public authorities on private bodies, and by their potential effect on competing interests. 'Control over personal life' is treated under Art 8 as covering areas as disparate as allowing a homosexual to choose to express his or her sexuality free from state interference,[26] and enabling an individual to enjoy his or her property free from the attentions of reporters. On the one hand, the individual's privacy is invaded through the criminalisation of certain activities, while on the other the citizen is seeking a legal remedy to prevent an invasion of privacy. Thus both negative and positive obligations are placed on the state.

In the former case, if the homosexual were to be prevented from expressing his sexual orientation, the government would be using its coercive powers to give effect to the moral conviction that the homosexual's way of life is contemptible. Thus, it would clearly be failing in its duty to treat its citizens with equal respect; to prevent this, under the liberal analysis of rights; the homosexual should be given a 'strong' right to sexual autonomy which would overcome any competing claims of society. In contrast, the state, in failing to control the activities of the reporter, is not thereby giving expression to feelings of contempt for the individual's way of life; it is erring on

over 'space' is dealt with by the law of trespass and property and is considered in Chapter 9; the 'action' and 'time' categories clearly raise issues of substantive autonomy, considered in Chapter 9, pp 961, 973. As regards the attempt to bring both informational and substantive autonomy under one definition: see Parent, W ('A new definition of privacy for the law' (1932) 2 Law and Philosophy 305), at pp 309 and 316 and Wacks, op. cit., fn 1, esp p 79.

24   Ibid, pp 51–69. As Fried notes, privacy is essential for 'respect, love, friendship and trust' – 'without it they are simply inconceivable' (Privacy' (1968) 77 Yale LJ 477, p 483).

25   See E Paton-Simpson, 'Privacy and the Reasonable Paranoid: the Protection of Privacy in Public Places' (2000) 50 *University of Toronto Law Journal* 305.

26   See Chapter 2, pp 74–87.

the side of free expression as it collides with the interest of the individual in securing her privacy. In this case, the individual's claim has to compete with the claim to free expression which the interest in moral autonomy does not face. In the case of public figures claiming privacy rights against the press, the argument that views free speech as essential in order to ensure meaningful participation in a democracy may have particular strength, depending on the nature of the free speech claim. This would be the case in relation to public figures where the information gained was clearly related to their fitness to carry out their public functions.[27] In the case of a purely private figure, or of private facts unrelated to the public function of public figures, freedom of expression would also compete with the claim of privacy. However, two of the important justifications for free speech – the arguments from truth and from political participation – would be largely irrelevant so that the strength of the free expression claim would be appreciably diminished.

It may be concluded that privacy is in a difficult position in so far as its ability to overcome other individual rights is concerned – *if* the values underpinning that other right are genuinely at stake. However, as Chapter 9 argues, the strength of both claims have to be weighed up when an apparent conflict arises.[28] Where preservation of privacy may lead to upholding an individual's moral autonomy, it is more clearly evident that it should be treated as a strong individual right able to overcome various public interests.

Domestic protection for privacy

Traditionally, UK law recognised no general right to respect for privacy, although there was some evidence, as will be seen, that the judges considered this to be an evil which required a remedy.[29] It has been argued that various areas of tort or equity, such as trespass, breach of confidence, copyright and defamation are instances of a general right to privacy,[30] but it is reasonably clear from judicial pronouncements that these areas and others were treated as covering specific and distinct interests which only incidentally offered protection to privacy[31] – despite the fact that the term 'privacy' was used in a number of rulings.[32] In such instances, it can usually be found that a recognised interest such as property actually formed the basis of the ruling. Thus, prior to the inception of the HRA, UK law offered only a piecemeal protection to privacy and therefore a number of privacy interests were largely unprotected. In so far as the protection for privacy broadened in the years immediately prior to the inception of the HRA, the initiative came not from the courts or the government, but from Europe – either from

---

27   See Markesenis, B and Nolte, N, 'Some Comparative Reflections on the Right of Privacy of Public Figures in Public Places', in Birks, R, (ed), *Privacy and Loyalty*, 1997, Oxford, pp 118 *et seq.*

28   See pp 937–62.

29   Seipp, D, 'English judicial recognition of the right to privacy' (1983) 3 OJLS 325.

30   See Warren and Brandeis, 'The right to privacy' (1890) 4 Harv L Rev 193.

31   See the comments of Glidewell LF in *Kaye v Robertson* [1991] FSR 62, CA: 'It is well known that in English law there is no right to privacy . . . in the absence of such a right the plaintiff's advisers have sought to base their claim on other well-established rights of action'.

32   E.g., *Prince Albert v Strange* (1848) 2 De Gex & Sm 652; *Clowser v Chaplin* (1981) 72 Cr App R 342.

European Union Directives[33] or from decisions under the European Convention on Human Rights.[34]

When Art 8 of the Convention was received into domestic law under the HRA 1998, UK citizens acquired, for the first time, a guarantee of respect for their privacy. Under ss 6 and 7(1)(a) of the HRA the right is directly enforceable against public authorities, such as the police or security services, as discussed in Chapter 10, but not against private bodies, including the press, as discussed in Chapter 9. But citizens can sue private bodies relying on an existing cause of action, breach of confidence, looking to the court itself as a public authority under s 6 of the HRA, and to its obligations under s 12, to develop the action by reference to Art 8. In other words, as Chapter 4 argued, Art 8 can have indirect horizontal effect.[35] The precise nature of this effect is a complex matter which is not yet fully settled, as explored in Chapter 9.

33   See the section on Data Protection, Chapter 9, pp 926–37.
34   For decisions against the UK, see Chapter 9, pp 813–18.
35   See pp 249–56.

Chapter 9

Protection for personal information

I Introduction[1]

The recent creation of a tort of invasion of privacy aimed at the protection of personal information has filled one of the most serious lacunae in English law. Described by the Law Commission as 'a glaring inadequacy',[2] and condemned by the Court of

---

1 This chapter draws in places upon Fenwick, H and Phillipson, G, 'The Doctrine of Confidence as a Privacy Remedy in the Human Rights Act Era' [2000] 63 (5) MLR 660–93. Texts and articles that will be referred to in this chapter: Fenwick, H and Phillipson, G, *Media Freedom under the Human Rights Act*, 2006; Tugendhat and Christie, *The Law of Privacy and the Media*, 2002; Tambini, D and Heyward, C (eds), *Ruled by Recluses? Privacy, Journalism and the Media after the Human Rights Act*, 2002, Institute for Public Policy Research; Wacks, R, *Personal Information, Privacy and the Law*, 1993; Wacks, R, *Privacy and Press Freedom*, 1996, Blackstone; Markesinis, B (ed), *Protecting Privacy* (a collection of essays reviewing the concept of privacy and the law relating to it, especially in the context of personal information, in a number of jurisdictions), 1999; Paul, E, Miller, F and Paul, J (eds) *The Right to Privacy*, 2000, CUP; Harris, D, O'Boyle, K and Warbrick, C, *Law of the European Convention on Human Rights*, 1995; Younger Committee, *Report of the Committee on Privacy*, Cmnd 5012, 1972 (criticised: MacCormick, DM, 'A note on privacy' (1973) 84 LQR 23); *Report of the Committee on Privacy and Related Matters*, Chairman David Calcutt QC (Calcutt Report), Cmnd 1102, 1990; Calcutt, *Review of Press Self-regulation*, Cm 2135, 1993; National Heritage Select Committee, 'Privacy and media intrusion', Fourth Report, HC 291, 1993; Lord Chancellor's Green Paper, *Infringement of Privacy*, 30 July 1993, CHAN J060915NJ.7/93; *Privacy and Media Intrusion*, White Paper (1995) Cm 2918; Phillipson, G, 'Transforming breach of confidence? Towards a common law right of privacy under the Human Rights Act', (2003) 66(5) MLR 726 and 'Judicial Reasoning in Breach of Confidence Cases under the Human Rights Act: not taking privacy seriously? [2003] EHRLR (*Privacy Special*) 53; Morgan, J, 'Privacy in the House of Lords – Again' (2004) 120 *Law Quarterly Review* 563; Fenwick, H and Phillipson, G, 'The Doctrine of Confidence as a Privacy Remedy in the Human Rights Act Era' [2000] 63 (5) MLR 660–93; Feldman, D, 'Secrecy, dignity or autonomy: views of privacy as a civil liberty' (1994) 47(2) CLP 42; Phillipson, G, 'The Human Rights Act, 'horizontal effect' and the common law' (1999) 62 MLR 824; Eady, D, 'A statutory right to privacy' (1996) 3 EHRLR 243; Markesinis, B, 'The right to be let alone versus freedom of speech' [1986] PL 67; Wilson, W, 'Privacy, confidence and press freedom' (1990) 53 MLR 43; Markesinis, B, 'Privacy, freedom of expression, and the horizontal effect of the Human Rights Bill: lessons from Germany' (1999) 115 LQR 47; Leigh, I, 'Horizontal rights, the Human Rights Act and privacy: lessons from the Commonwealth?' (1999) 48 ICLQ 57; Singh, 'Privacy and the media after the Human Rights Act' (1998) EHLR 712; Grosz, S and Braithwaite, N, 'Privacy and the Human Rights Act', in Hunt, M and Singh, R (eds), *A Practitioner's Guide to the Impact of the Human Rights Act*, 1999; Wright, J, 'How private is my private life?', in Betten, L (ed), *The Human Rights Act 1998: What it Means*, 1999; Elliott, M, 'Privacy, confidentiality, horizontality: the case of the celebrity wedding photographs' [2001] CLJ 231.
2 Law Commission Report No 110, *Breach of Confidence*, para 5.5. The Commission was referring specifically to the fact that 'the confidentiality of information improperly obtained . . . may be unprotected'.

Appeal,[3] *dicta* in a pre-HRA decision of the House of Lords[4] remarked upon '. . . the continuing, widespread concern at the apparent failure of the law' in this area.[5] That failure has now been remedied under a largely HRA-driven legal development. As this chapter will describe, this development, together with the Data Protection Act 1998, has led to the provision of quite a high degree of protection for personal information in UK law, although, as the House of Lords stated in *Wainwright v Home Office*,[6] there is still no general, comprehensive tort of invasion of privacy.

The developments discussed below are driving forward a respect for the privacy of personal information still not fully evident in the publishing of a number of media bodies, especially the tabloid press. The acquisition and use of personal information by state agents, with the purpose of preventing or detecting crime or protecting national security, is considered in Chapter 10. While Chapter 10 considers the laws relating to interception of communications and surveillance aimed at the regulation of investigative techniques by state agents, it must be remembered that they can also be used against intrusive methods employed by the media to gather information.[7] The laws and Codes regulating the use of personal information by a range of private and public bodies considered here should be examined in tandem with those 'privacy statutes' considered in Chapter 10, since all are part of a complex web of 'privacy' law. The press is one of the worst offenders, in terms of acquiring and publishing personal information non-consensually, and therefore the use of various legal provisions against the press forms a central theme in this chapter.

This chapter gives approval to the development of a tort of misuse of personal information that is occurring. However, in doing so the danger to media freedom must not be over-looked. That danger does not arise only from the operation of the new tort. The mass of laws that this chapter and Chapter 10 cover reveal a dangerous potential for their misuse by powerful private or public figures seeking to cover up matters of genuine public interest value. Injunctions represent one of the main remedies employed to protect private information. As Chapter 5 pointed out, once an injunction has been granted, any party that has notice of it, can under the *Spycatcher* doctrine,[8] be found to be in contempt if they publish the information covered by it.

But the new privacy tort is genuinely needed so long as it is balanced by protection for speech, so as to allow the publication of matters of genuine public interest. Warren and Brandeis' verdict in the nineteenth century, 'The Press is overstepping in every direction the obvious bounds of propriety and decency . . . [inflicting] through invasions

---

3   *Kaye v Robertson* [1991] FSR 62, CA.
4   *Khan* [1997] AC 558.
5   Ibid, *per* Lord Nicholls.
6   [2004] 2 AC 406 paras 28–35. See for discussion of *Wainwright* Chapter 11, pp 1176–79.
7   Clive Goodman, the royal editor of the *News of the World*, pleaded guilty in November 2006 to plotting to intercept private phone messages involving the royal family. Glenn Mulcaire also admitted the same charge. Mulcaire further admitted five charges of unlawfully intercepting voicemail messages left by a number of people, including publicist Max Clifford and Elle Macpherson. The charges, under the Regulation of Investigatory Powers Act 2000, related to interceptions between February 16 2006 and June 16. The conspiracy charge, under the Criminal Law Act, related to conspiring to intercept voicemail messages between November 1 2005 and August 9 2006 (the *Guardian* 29 November 2006).
8   See Chapter 5, pp 369–70.

of privacy ... mental pain and distress far greater than could be inflicted by mere bodily injury',[9] is still alarmingly true today, over 100 years later. Anyone familiar with the output of our print media will be wearily aware of its penchant for publishing what one journalist has described as 'toe-curlingly intimate details' about the sex lives not only of celebrities, but of 'quite obscure people'.[10] Intrusive prurience is not the only complaint: Victim Support has detailed a large number of case histories in which ordinary victims of crime and their families had had their suffering markedly exacerbated by intrusive and insensitive publications in local and national newspapers describing their plight in quite needless detail, causing in some cases diagnosable psychiatric harm, making others feel forced to move from the area where the crime had been committed; causing all intense emotional distress.[11] In contrast to the position in the US and virtually every other Western democracy, such injuries had until recently no remedy in a privacy law in this country: a toothless Press Complaints Commission could only request the offending newspaper to print its adjudication on the matter.[12] It is frequently remarked of countries which have a privacy law, such as France and Germany, that their media does not exhibit the 'gutter' quality associated with the UK tabloid press.[13] In our cut-throat media market, the tendency of debased and lurid 'news' coverage in one newspaper to drive down the standards in another is very marked. Within this pervasive 'gutter' culture, which will influence the choices of readers, a newspaper which is unwilling to debase its standards may not survive, detracting from the diversity of opinion one would expect of a free press.

While the notion of respect for individual privacy could be said to be a clear underlying common law value,[14] it failed pre-HRA to find full expression, perhaps because intermittent governmental interest in the latter half of the twentieth century in statutory protection for privacy distracted the courts with the chimera of possible

---

9   'The right to privacy' (1890) IV(5) Harvard L Rev 193, p 196.

10 Marr, A, *The Independent*, 25 April 1996. In a conference speech, the editor of the *Guardian*, Alan Russbridger, listed a string of recent examples in which newspapers had published intimate details about the personal lives of celebrities, in some cases surreptitiously obtained, with either no or the flimsiest of 'public interest' justifications (Human Rights, Privacy and the Media, organised by the Constitution Unit, and the Centre for Communication and Information Law, UCL, 8 January 1999).

11 See Fourth Report of the National Heritage Select Committee on Privacy and Media Intrusion Minutes of Evidence, Appendix 24 HC 294-II (1993).

12 See below, pp 833–39 for discussion of the role of the Commission.

13 As Markesinis remarks, '. . . the possible extra-marital affairs of German politicians and businessmen hold little or no appeal for most readers of German newspapers.' (Markesinis, op. cit., fn 1.) See also: J Seaton, 'Public, Private and the Media' (2003) *Political Quarterly* 174.

14 See *dicta* of Laws J in *Hellewell v Chief Constable of Derbyshire* [1995] 1 WLR 804, p 807; *Francome v Mirror Group Newspapers* [1984] 1 WLR 892, in which the Court of Appeal recognised (in effect) a right to privacy in telephone conversations; *Stephens v Avery* [1988] Ch 449; *dicta* of Lord Keith in *AG v Guardian Newspapers (No 2)* [1990] 1 AC 109, p 255, 'The right to personal privacy is clearly one which the law [of confidence] should seek to protect'. In the decision in *Dept of Health ex p Source Informatics Ltd* [2001] 2 WLR 953; (2000) *The Times*, 21 January, Simon Brown LJ stated clearly that in cases involving personal information, 'The concern of the law [of confidence] is to protect the confider's personal privacy'. In *R v Khan* [1997] AC 558, Lords Browne-Wilkinson, Slynn and Nicholls left open the question whether English law already recognised a right to privacy.

legislative action.[15] Quite clearly, however, no government in the past grasped this nettle, out of a fear of press hostility.[16]

The Human Rights Act 1998 (HRA), however, introduced Art 8 of the European Convention on Human Rights into UK law, providing for a right to respect for private life.[17] While the general view is that Art 8 is not directly justiciable against the press or other private bodies,[18] it will be argued that its reception into UK law nevertheless provided an impetus for the notion of respect for privacy finally to find expression through the common law. The Data Protection Act 1998 (DPA) represents a further legislative development of immense significance for the protection of personal information. The Act has a very significant impact on all bodies that process personal data, including the press, and the interaction between the DPA and the HRA is complex and intriguing. Inevitably, tension has been generated by the incursion of the HRA and DPA into an area which previously was largely unregulated, being governed partly by media codes of practice and partly by relatively narrow (albeit expanding) common law doctrines.

This chapter will examine the impact that the HRA is having on the currently available measures protecting personal information and aspects of privacy more generally. Above all, it will concentrate on the development of the doctrine of confidence into a privacy remedy. The implications of this development of protection for privacy for freedom of expression will be considered, as will jurisprudence from other jurisdictions, including the jurisprudence generated by the American 'private facts' tort.[19] The developments discussed below, under the Communications Act 2003 and the DPA, were influenced by

15   The Younger Committee, *Report of the Committee on Privacy* (Cmnd 5012, 1972), Calcutt Committee on Privacy and Related Matters, hereafter *The Calcutt Report* (Cmnd 1102, 1990), Review of Press Self Regulation (Cm 2135), Fourth Report of the National Heritage Select Committee in 1993, HC 294-II (1993), all proposed the introduction of statutory measures to protect privacy, as did the Lord Chancellor's Green Paper of the same year (CHAN J060915NJ.7/93).

16   Such fear was clearly evident during the passage of the HRA itself. In response to the press outcry over the possibility that the Act would create a right to privacy, the government introduced a specific amendment in favour of press freedom (HRA, s 12, discussed below), and repeatedly and explicitly sought to reassure the press during the Bill's debate. As Lord Ackner put it, the Lord Chancellor devoted 'a very large part of his [second reading] speech . . . to trying to pour oil on ruffled waters.' (HL Deb Col 473, 18 November 1997). In fact, bearing in mind the effect of s 12(4)(b), discussed below, the government may have deceived the press as to the impact that s 12 was actually likely to have. For an example of blanket hostility from the press' representative body – the Newspaper Society – to the possible development of any privacy law in the UK, see Rasaiah, 'Current legislation, privacy and the media in the UK' (1998) 3(5) Communications Law 183.

17   As Chapter 2 explained, pp 69–91, Art 8 of the Convention provides a person with a right to respect for four different rights: 'his private and family life, his home and his correspondence'. Paragraph 2 then specifies a number of grounds permitting interference by 'a public authority' with this right.

18   See below, pp 824–29.

19   See below, esp p 855–87 for a discussion of the tort. Some emphasis is placed on the American tort since, in comparison with other common law jurisdictions, the case law is particularly rich, having been generated over a considerable period of time; further, the American tort had its genesis in the Warren and Brandeis reading of a number of English decisions, including some breach of confidence cases (in particular, *Prince Albert v Strange* (1848) 2 De Gex & Sm 652; *Duke of Argyll v Duchess of Argyll* [1967] 1 Ch 302; *Pollard v Photographic Company* (1888) Ch 345), and therefore is of relevance to the development of a cause of action growing from the same roots. However, as will become apparent, this chapter takes the stance that the protection offered in the UK is more effective and is much more soundly based in principle than that offered in the US; therefore the lessons to be learnt post-HRA from the US tort are becoming less relevant.

Art 8, but the work in developing the privacy rights was done initially by Parliament and then by the Regulator in both cases – the Data Protection Registrar and Ofcom (the broadcast regulator). The difficult area, and the one which has seen dynamic and dramatic development, was the transformation of the doctrine of confidence into a privacy law, under the impetus of the HRA.

The chapter begins by examining the protection offered under the HRA and Art 8. It then considers protection for privacy under media regulation; it moves on to look at specific reporting restrictions under statute and, in relation to children, under the jurisdiction of the court. It proceeds (in section 5) to consider the protection for privacy offered by trespass and defamation and against harassment by the Protection from Harassment Act 1997. That section acts partly as an introduction to the main part of this chapter, which (in section 6) examines the transformation of the doctrine of confidence into a privacy tort. The chapter then moves on to consider the over-lapping and further protection for personal information offered by the DPA. It ends with an examination of the method of balancing the protection for privacy offered by all these measures with protection for free speech under Art 10 ECHR, followed by a look at the remedies available for privacy-invasion.

2 Protection for personal information under the Human Rights Act

Strasbourg jurisprudence on protection for personal information

As Chapter 2 explained, Art 8(1) provides a 'right to respect for private and family life, the home and correspondence'; para (2) states:

> There shall be no interference by a public authority with the exercise of this right except such as is in accordance with the law and is necessary in a democratic society in the interests of national security, public safety or the economic well-being of the country, for the prevention of disorder or crime, for the protection of health or morals, or for the protection of the rights and freedoms of others.[20]

There is a substantial Strasbourg jurisprudence on the data protection obligations of public authorities. It is clear that the actions of such bodies in the gathering, storing and use of information relating to private or family life, including photographs,[21] engages Art 8.[22] Certain categories of material, such as those relating to health[23] or sexual orientation or activity[24] are regarded as 'particularly sensitive or intimate',[25] requiring especially

---

20 See further Chapter 2, p 72.
21 *Murray and Others v United Kingdom* (1994) 19 EHRR 193 (photographing of a person at a police station without her consent was found to be a prima facie violation of Art 8).
22 See, e.g., *Leander v Sweden* (1987) 9 EHRR 433; *McVeigh, O'Neill and Evans v United Kingdom* (1981) 45 EHRR 71.
23 *Z v Finland* (1998) 25 EHRR 371.
24 *Lustig-Prean v United Kingdom* (1999) 29 EHRR 548; 7 BHRC 65.
25 Feldman, D, 'Information and privacy'; conference paper, Cambridge Centre for Public Law, Freedom of Expression and Freedom of Information, 19–20 February 2000.

compelling grounds to justify interference. As Chapter 10 will indicate, surreptitious methods of obtaining information, such as telephone tapping, are seen potentially as particularly serious breaches of Art 8 at Strasbourg.[26] This identifiable general trend suggests that this is another instance in which the emphasis should be on the evolutive nature of the Convention[27] rather than on the outcome of particular applications to the Commission, such as that in *X v United Kingdom*.[28] The Commission found that the actions of the police in taking and filing photographs without consent of a woman arrested for taking part in a political demonstration disclosed no prima facie breach of Art 8. The reasoning was unclear, but a central factor appeared to be the public and voluntary nature of her activities. The decision has been viewed as out of line with the trend of Art 8 jurisprudence: 'In the opinion of some scholars, the . . . decision may well be an outdated aberration in the case law of the Strasbourg organs'.[29]

The collection of personal information by *private* bodies, including, in particular, the press, sometimes using surreptitious means, and its publication, is in reality only one, often highly objectionable manifestation of data collection and processing. The strength of the jurisprudence on interferences with personal information by public bodies indicates that the interest in being free from such intrusion is one which, in general terms, falls within the ambit of Art 8. As a leading text in the area put it over ten years ago: 'the obligation of the state to respect private life by controlling the activities of its agents [in collecting personal information] ought to extend also to similar operations by private persons such as . . . newspaper reporters'.[30]

The simple transposition of Convention obligations upon public authorities onto private agents cannot be assumed in all instances covered by Art 8. But the Court found over 20 years ago[31] that Art 8 obligations may require the adoption of measures even in the sphere of relations between individuals. In other words, 'interference by a public authority' can mean 'unjustified failure by that authority to prevent interference by others'. Thus, the state is likely to be under a positive obligation to provide legal protection for the individual, even when public authorities are not themselves responsible for an interference with the Art 8 right.

However, Strasbourg originally approached the notion of an obligation to intervene between private parties with caution. It found that, in deciding whether there is even

---

26 *Kopp v Switzerland* [1998] HRCD 6 (356), para 72.
27 The Convention must be given an 'evolutive' interpretation (*Johnstone v Ireland* A 112, para 53 (1986)), which takes account of current standards in European society (*Tyrer v UK* A 26, para 31 (1978)). These would be expected to include the presence of privacy laws across Europe.
28 Appl 5877/72; (1973) 16 YBCHE, 328.
29 Bygrave, LA, 'Data protection pursuant to the right to privacy in human rights treaties' [1999] 6(3) IJLIT 247, p 265. Bygrave notes: '. . . there are good grounds for holding that it ought to be accorded little weight in present and future interpretation of Article 8'. In spite of these comments, however, Bygrave concedes that in the later decision of *Friedl v Austria* (1995) A 305B (not treated by the Court on the merits due to friendly settlement), 'the Commission laid weight upon the same . . . kind of factors as those mentioned in *X v United Kingdom*' (ibid, p 266). See also *Stewart-Brady v UK* (1999) 27 EHRR 284, in which a claim of an interference with Art 8 rights due to the taking of a photograph was declared inadmissible (although these findings were made in the context of positive state obligations and there was a conflict with Art 10).
30 Harris, D, O'Boyle, K and Warbrick, C, *Law of the European Convention on Human Rights*, 1995, p 310.
31 *X and Y v Netherlands* (1985) 8 EHRR 235.

a prima facie engagement of Art 8 in such a context, 'regard must be had to the fair balance that has to be struck between the general interest of the community and the interests of the individual'.[32] Thus, it appeared over 15 years ago that the gathering and subsequent publication of personal information by private bodies, including the press, would not automatically engage Art 8, as such actions would if carried out by a public body. When one turns to the case law directly on the question of the obligations of private parties to protect private information, a brief survey reveals both that it is quite meagre, and that until recently there were no directly relevant successful applications.

In order to understand quite why the Court took until recently such a cautious stance, it is necessary to appreciate the significance which the margin of appreciation doctrine has had in this context. The essence of the doctrine,[33] as Chapter 2 explained, is that in assessing compliance with the Convention, the Court will afford states a certain latitude, principally in deciding what kinds of interferences with Convention rights are necessary. The margin can widen or narrow depending on the circumstances of the case, resulting in a variation of the intensity of the Court's review of the state's actions. Three principal factors influence Strasbourg in conceding a particularly wide margin of appreciation: first, where a complainant seeks to lay a positive obligation on the state; second, where the harm complained of flows from the action of a private party, rather than the state itself, so that the so-called 'horizontal effect' of the Convention is in issue; third, where there is a potential conflict with another Convention right. Clearly, these factors may arise independently of each other. Or they may, as in the context under discussion, arise contiguously, thereby demanding that an especially wide margin should be allowed. In a number of the earlier private life decisions to be discussed, all three were present,[34] which may explain the somewhat unsatisfactory and misleading nature of some of those judgments.

Winer v UK,[35] decided over 20 years ago, is often seen as an unsatisfactory decision in privacy terms. The applicant complained that various aspects of his private life had been publicised in a book; he had settled a defamation case in respect of some of the statements made, but argued that he had no remedy under national law in respect of those which were truthful. His application was declared inadmissible, the Commission stating briefly that it viewed the available remedies, in particular that of defamation,[36] as satisfactory, and that no positive obligation to provide further remedies in respect of the truthful statements should be imposed, bearing in mind the wide margin of appreciation to be afforded in this area, the limitation of the Convention right to freedom of expression which such remedies would entail and the availability of a remedy in defamation. The applicant's privacy 'was not wholly unprotected'. However,

---

32 *Cossey v UK* A 184, para 37 (1990).

33 For discussion, see Chapter 2, pp 36–39; see also Fenwick, H, 'The right to protest, the Human Rights Act and the margin of appreciation' (1999) 62(4) MLR 491, pp 497–500.

34 All three were present in: *Winer v UK* (1986) 48 DR 154; *Spencer (Earl) v UK* (1998) 25 EHRR CD 105 and *N v Portugal* Appl No 20683/92, 20 February 1995; however, the third was influential only in *Winer*.

35 (1986) 48 DR 154.

36 The remedy represented by the doctrine of confidence was not explicitly adverted to, presumably because at the time of the application it was still viewed as having only marginal application to privacy.

the possibility was clearly left open of imposing a positive obligation on the state in an instance in which no national remedy was available.

The obvious example at that time, impliedly envisaged, would be an instance in which truthful, personal facts about an individual were published without consent and it was apparent that a defamation action had no or virtually no hope of success. In such circumstances, then, it was clear that an individual might be viewed as holding a privacy right, which the state would come under a positive obligation to respect, a finding which received some indirect support from the decision in *N v Portugal*.[37]

In *Barclay v United Kingdom*,[38] the Court accepted that a lack of a remedy in respect of the filming of a private home by reporters could in principle constitute a breach of Art 8, although on the facts no invasion of private life had occurred.[39] The decision made it clear that there was therefore no bar in principle to the application of the Court's general approach to interferences with personal information to the actions of private bodies. A decision that can be seen as something of a turning point in this context was *Spencer (Earl) v United Kingdom*.[40] The Commission dismissed as inadmissible Earl Spencer's claim that the UK Government had failed to protect him from invasions of privacy by the press[41] on the basis that he had failed to exhaust domestic remedies, namely breach of confidence. This judgment accepted that an interference with the right to respect for privacy had arguably occurred, and required a remedy, but that the doctrine of confidence would have provided one and should have been used. Had the Commission considered that the pleaded facts disclosed no arguable breach of Art 8, it would simply have so held – as the Court did in *Barclay* – and would not have instead decided the case on non-exhaustion of domestic remedies.

It was therefore clear that *Spencer*, far from suggesting that Art 8 did not require the UK to develop a privacy law, was decided on the assumption that it already had one, albeit at a relatively early stage of development. As Harris *et al.* put it in relation to the efficacy of domestic remedies for exhaustion purposes, the key issue in *Spencer*: 'in a common law system it [is] incumbent on an aggrieved individual to allow the domestic courts the opportunity to develop existing rights by way of interpretation'.[42] Thus, since the Commission in both *Winer* and *Spencer* could identify a remedy which, applying a wide margin of appreciation, it could view as sufficient, it found against the applicant. Had no remedy been identifiable, there are therefore grounds for assuming that the applications would have been declared admissible.

---

37 *N v Portugal*, Appl No 20683/92, 20 February 1995. A magazine publisher's application complaining of a breach of Art 10 after being convicted of defamation and invasion of privacy in respect of the publication of photographs of a well known businessman engaged in sexual activities was rejected as manifestly ill-founded. The Commission considered that the sanction was proportionate and necessary for the protection of the rights of others, one of which was clearly the right to protection from invasion of privacy through publication of true facts by other private individuals.

38 (1999) Appl No 35712/97 (admissibility only).

39 The property filmed was the island of Brecqhou, owned by the Barclay brothers. They had no home there, and were not present when the filming occurred.

40 (1998) 25 EHRR CD 105.

41 The applicants complained of publication in the press of various (truthful) stories relating to the bulimia and mental health problems of Countess Spencer, including photographs taken of her walking in the grounds of a health clinic.

42 Harris, O'Boyle and Warbrick, op. cit., fn 1, p 611.

Individual decisions are not the only matters of relevance here, however. As the House of Lords stressed in *ex p Kebilene*: 'in the national courts also the Convention should be seen as an expression of fundamental principles rather than as a set of mere rules . . .'.[43] Strasbourg has found that the purpose of the Convention is to 'promote the ideals and values of a democratic society',[44] and to provide 'rights that are practical and effective' rather than 'rights that are theoretical or illusory'.[45] The Convention must be given an 'evolutive' interpretation[46] which takes account of current standards in European countries,[47] in which legal protection for privacy is the norm.[48] In the context of Art 8 it has been said: 'The Court has not perceived the rights in Article 8 in wholly negative terms – the right to be left alone. Instead it has acknowledged that states must ensure . . . the effective enjoyment of liberty'.[49] As suggested earlier, effective enjoyment of liberty cannot occur when persons who are constantly afraid of betraying information to the media are forced to order their choices in life as a consequence,[50] and it would appear to be a hallmark of a democratic society that it seeks to protect a person from any such curtailment of liberty.

Such general principles did not until recently receive enough attention in this context; the significance of the *Spencer* decision took some time to achieve widespread recognition,[51] perhaps due to a failure on the part of some commentators to appreciate the considerations outlined above, coupled with a tendency to concentrate on the apparently disappointing outcomes of the individual applications. Thus, a number of commentators, writing before the HRA had come fully into force, concluded that the Art 8 jurisprudence could not be said to require the courts to develop the common law so as to provide a remedy for non-consensual use of true but personal information. One commentator bluntly concluded: '. . . Strasbourg case law . . . does not require a specific remedy between private individuals'.[52] Another commented: 'The still unanswered question is whether Article 8 also requires a member state to provide a right of action against

43 *R v DPP ex p Kebilene* [1999] 3 WLR 972.
44 *Kjeldsen v Denmark* (1976) 1 EHRR 711, p 731; *Socialist Party v Turkey* (1999) 27 EHRR 51.
45 *Airey v Ireland* (1979) 2 EHRR 305, p 314.
46 *Johnstone v Ireland* A 112, para 53 (1986).
47 See Chapter 2, p 38; *Tyrer v UK* A 26 (1978), para 31. There are also numerous resolutions of the Council of Europe on effective protection for personal information (Nos 73(22) and 74(29)).
48 For discussion of the law in Germany, see Markesenis, B and Nolte, N, 'Some comparative reflections on the right of privacy of public figures in public places', in Birks, P (ed), *Privacy and Loyalty*, 1997; in relation to Germany, France and Italy see Chapters 2–5 of Markesenis, B (ed), *Protecting Privacy*, 1999; *The Calcutt Report*, op. cit., fn 1, paras 5.22–5.28 also discusses privacy protection in Denmark and the Netherlands.
49 Harris, O'Boyle and Warbrick, op. cit., fn 1, p 303.
50 See above, pp 805–7.
51 One of the leading works on the Convention has no discussion at all of the issue of intrusion by the press into private life: Van Dijk, P and Van Hoof, F, *Theory and Practice of the European Convention on Human Rights*, 1998, pp 489–504; similarly the discussion of Art 8 in a pre-HRA textbook on media law makes no mention of the decision (Carey, P, *Media Law*, 1999, pp 79–81); Leigh in a 1999 article dealing with horizontality, the HRA and privacy, cites *Winer*, but not *Spencer* (1998) 25 EHRR CD 105, p 86 (op. cit., fn 1). The decision receives some attention from Grosz and Braithwaite (op. cit., fn 1), Singh (op. cit., fn 1) and Wright (op. cit., fn 1).
52 Leigh, op. cit., fn 1.

intrusions into private life by private persons . . .'.[53] Even pre-HRA it is contended that this question was *not* unanswered: the cases discussed above strongly implied that it should be answered in the affirmative.

Prior to the decision in *Von Hannover*, discussed below, Strasbourg had been prepared to extend the notion of private space beyond obvious places such as the home; as Harris, O'Boyle and Warbrick put it: 'it is not enough just for the individual to be himself: he must be able to a substantial degree to keep to himself what he is and what he does . . . the idea of private space need not be confined to those areas where the person has some exclusive rights of occupancy'.[54] In this respect, the Strasbourg approach had been developing for some time in a direction which went beyond the pre-HRA UK common law approach. It was said over 10 years ago: 'the expanding understanding of private life set out in the *Niemetz* case indicates that a formal public/private distinction about the nature of the location will not always be decisive'.[55] *Niemetz v FRG*[56] concerned office premises, making it clear that rights to respect for privacy are not dependent on an interest in property or on a domestic environment. This approach was already taking root in the UK to an extent, and in other jurisdictions. In *Broadcasting Standards Commission ex p BBC*[57] it was found that privacy can be retained even in a place to which the public have access, such as a shop. The Canadian Criminal Code also reflects such a stance.[58]

So when the case of *Von Hannover v Germany*[59] was decided, making it clear that Art 8 *does* require that there should be a remedy for invasions of privacy by private parties, it was already apparent that this was the course that Strasbourg was preparing to take.[60] A significant decision pre-dating *Von Hannover*, and arguably highly indicative of the Court's eventual stance in that case, was *Peck v United Kingdom*.[61] *Peck* was a case about the obligations of public authorities, but it made it clear that media intrusion into privacy can lead to a breach of Art 8. The applicant had been captured on Council CCTV cameras, wandering through the street carrying a knife, immediately after he had attempted to commit suicide by cutting his wrists. This footage was passed by the local authority on to a news broadcast and a popular television programme, *Crime Beat*, both of which showed extracts from the CCTV footage, from which the applicant was recognisable, to an audience of hundreds of thousands.

The Court said that the relevant moment was viewed to an extent which far exceeded any exposure to a passer-by or to security observation and to a degree surpassing that

---

53 Nicol, D, 'Media freedom after the Human Rights Act 1998', conference paper (Human Rights, Privacy and the Media, organised by the Constitution Unit, and the Centre for Communication and Information Law, UCL, 8 January 1999); see also Naismith, 'Photographs, privacy and freedom of expression' (1996) 2 EHLR 150, p 156.
54 Harris, O'Boyle and Warbrick, op. cit., fn 1, p 309.
55 Ibid, p 309.
56 A 251-B (1992).
57 [2000] 3 WLR 1327.
58 Section 487.01(4).
59 (2005) 40 EHRR 1; [2004] EMLR 21– for a summary and comment, see (2004) 5, EHLR pp 593–96.
60 See further: *Stjerna v Finland*, judgment of 25 November 1994, Series A no 299-B, p 61, § 38; and *Verliere v Switzerland* (dec), no 41953/98, ECHR 2001-VII).
61 (2003) 36 EHRR 41. For comment, see Welch, J [2003] EHRLR (Privacy Special) 141.

which the applicant could possibly have foreseen. Therefore the Court found that the disclosure by the Council of the relevant footage constituted a serious interference with the applicant's right to respect for his private life.[62] In terms of the proportionality of the interference, the Court accepted that the state has a strong interest in detecting and preventing crime and that the CCTV system plays an important role in furthering that interest. But the Court noted that the Council had other options available to it to allow it to achieve the same objectives. It could have identified the applicant through inquiries with the police and thereby obtained his consent prior to disclosure. Alternatively, the Council could have masked the relevant images itself, thereby concealing his identity. A further alternative would have been to take the utmost care in ensuring that the media, to which the disclosure was made, masked those images. The Court noted that the Council did not explore the first and second options, and considered that the steps taken by the Council in respect of the third were inadequate. It was concluded that the disclosure constituted a disproportionate and therefore unjustified interference with his private life and a violation of Art 8 of the Convention. The Court also found that the applicant had no effective remedy in relation to the violation of his right to respect for his private life. Therefore the Court also found a breach of Art 13.

Thus *Peck* established that for a public authority to release footage portraying private acts without consent to the broadcast media is prima facie a breach of Art 8, albeit subject to a freedom of expression defence, as discussed below. It appeared apparent that this principle could also be transposed into a situation in which the public authority dropped out of the picture and its place was taken by a broadcaster which was itself a public authority, such as (arguably) the BBC.[63] If BBC reporters had happened to be filming at the time in question for other purposes and had caught Peck's actions on camera, it would appear that the same principles would have applied, so there would have been a breach of Art 8 in that instance too. *Peck* did not make it clear that Art 8 would have been breached had a private, commercial broadcaster, such as ITV or Channel 5, made and broadcast such a film, and the Court expressly declined to consider whether such bodies could be considered organs of the state. But it can be said to be clear from the judgment that in principle a breach of Art 8 should be found to arise in that instance too on the basis that the state is under an obligation to afford victims a proper remedy even against private bodies.

Von Hannover[64] finally made it clear that had the filming of Peck been undertaken by a private media body which had then published the information, a breach of Art 8 would probably have arisen if Peck had been unable to obtain a domestic remedy. The word 'probably' is used since the facts of *Peck* and of *Von Hannover* differ significantly. However, *Von Hannover* made it clear that Art 8 rights are applicable in the private sphere and there is a positive obligation on the state to provide a remedy in national law. The case represented the culmination of a long legal fight by Princess Caroline of Monaco in the German courts to stop pictures of herself and her children, obtained by paparazzi without consent, appearing in various newspapers and magazines across Europe. The pictures were of the Princess engaged in various everyday acts: shopping,

---

62 At paras 62 and 63.
63 See discussion in Chapter 6, pp 530–31 as to whether the BBC is a functional public authority and as to its functions that may be considered public functions. See also Chapter 4, pp 233–35.
64 (2005) 40 EHRR 1; no 59320/00 [2004] EMLR 21.

horse-riding, at a beach club, or a restaurant. The German courts had afforded her a privacy remedy in relation to the more intrusive photographs she had complained of. The German Supreme Court[65] had refused to follow the approach of the Appeal Court that privacy 'stopped at the doorstep' and that therefore no action lay for invasion of privacy in respect of events which had taken place outside the home or other clearly private spaces. The approach indicated was that one may still be entitled to respect for privacy in semi-public places if, as the court put it, it is clear by reference to 'objective criteria' that one wishes to 'left alone' so that one can, 'relying on the fact of seclusion, act in a way that [one] would not have done ... in public'. In other words, the interest in privacy was clearly distinguished from property interests. But the German court's approach still left the Princess's privacy unprotected to an extent. The Court found, unanimously, that the failure of the German courts to provide her with a remedy in relation to a number of the unconsented-to paparazzi pictures amounted to a breach of Art 8:

> The Court reiterates that although the object of Art 8 is essentially that of protecting the individual against arbitrary interference by the public authorities, it does not merely compel the State to abstain from such interference: in addition to this primarily negative undertaking, there may be positive obligations inherent in an effective respect for private or family life. These obligations may involve the adoption of measures designed to secure respect for private life even in the sphere of the relations of individuals between themselves.[66]

The Court found in relation to the specific facts of the case:

> In the present case there is no doubt that the publication by various German magazines of photos of the applicant in her daily life either on her own or with other people falls within the scope of her private life.[67]

The Court did not articulate the underlying reasoning behind this finding in any detail. However, this finding suggests that the Court equated the idea of 'daily life' with that of 'private life'. This was made clear in the following passage: 'the photos of the applicant in the various German magazines show her in scenes from her daily life, thus engaged in activities of a purely private nature such as practising sport, out walking, leaving a restaurant or on holiday.[68] These findings are discussed further below.[69]

In other words, although the photographs were taken in places that could be viewed as 'public' in the sense of open or semi-open to the public, the activities captured on film acquired a private quality since they self-evidently related to every-day life activities with no 'public life' dimension. The Princess was obviously not acting in her public capacity at the times in question – as when taking part in a ceremonious occasion. She was not engaging in activity of a more borderline private/public nature such as, for example, visiting war graves or paying homage to local monuments or dignitaries

---

65 BGH, 19 December 1995 BGHZ 131, pp 322–46.
66 Ibid at para 57.
67 Op. cit. at para 53.
68 Ibid para 61.
69 See pp 892–94.

while visiting a city informally. The Court stated that it had previously 'had regard to whether the photographs related to private or public matters'. It had also found that there is 'a zone of interaction of a person with others, even in a public context, which may fall within the scope of 'private life'.[70] These findings could be taken to suggest that the *place* in which activities occur is of secondary importance to the *nature* of the activities. In other words, while activities occurring in obviously private places such as the home are normally – not always – to be viewed as private activities by virtue of that fact, the converse is not the case.

The question is whether the activity need be of particular significance in privacy terms,[71] despite occurring in public, in order to overcome the 'public' character it might thereby appear to acquire, or whether the fact that the activity has all the hallmarks of a private activity while occurring in public should be the determining factor. Many of the 'every-day' activities engaged in by the Princess could have occurred in either public or private places. Swimming or dining or playing with her children provide obvious examples. It would not appear to comport readily with the values Art 8 is seeking to protect to impose an obligation on celebrities to confine such activities to private places in order to avoid paparazzi attention. This may be inferred from the finding at Strasbourg that Art 8 is 'primarily intended to ensure the development, without outside interference, of the personality of each individual in his relations with other human beings.'[72]

It is instructive to compare the stance of the Strasbourg Court in *Von Hannover* with that of the Californian Supreme Court in *Gill v Hearst Publishing Co*.[73] A husband and wife were photographed without consent while affectionately cuddling each other at a confectionery stand in a public marketplace. The Supreme Court of California ruled that the publication of the photograph did not in itself constitute an actionable invasion of privacy, stating:

> Here plaintiffs . . . had voluntarily exposed themselves to public gaze in a pose open to the view of any persons who might then be at or near their place of business. By their own voluntary action plaintiffs waived their right of privacy . . . In short, the photograph did not disclose anything which until then had been private, but rather only extended knowledge of the particular incident to a somewhat larger public . . .'

The objection to the Californian decision is that, echoing the argument of Paton-Simpson,[74] it demands that people adopt a paranoid, defensive stance towards interactions

---

70 Ibid at para 50. The findings referred to are from the previous decisions in *PG and JH v United Kingdom*, Appl No 44787/98, (2001), at para 56, and *Peck v United Kingdom* (2003) 36 EHRR 41, at para 57.

71 For example, sexual activity, relating to intimate relationships, health, medical treatment.

72 *Botta v Italy* (1998) 26 EHRR 241, at para 33.

73 253 P2d 441 (Cal. 1953); see also *De Gregorio v. CBS, Inc*, 473 NYS2d 922 (Sup 1984). Obviously the comparison is somewhat unfair to the Californian Court since its decision is over 50 years old.

74 See Paton-Simpson, E, 'Privacy and the Reasonable Paranoid: the Protection of Privacy in Public Places' (2000) 50 *University of Toronto Law Journal* 305. See also Paton-Simpson, E, 'Private circles and public squares: invasion of privacy by the publication of "private facts"' (1998) 61 MLR 318; McClurg, AJ, 'Bringing Privacy Law Out of the Closet: A Tort Theory of Liability for Intrusions in Public Places' (1995) 73 NCL Rev 989, esp at 990.

with each other in public. Confining interactions with others to an obviously private place would clearly have a stifling impact on them; it could further be argued that being forced in effect to confine solitary activities, such as swimming or walking, to private spaces would have a general deleterious effect on personal development. Homes and other private places are now subject to surveillance due to recent developments in surveillance technology in a way that 50 years ago was not possible. Thus, merely retiring behind a front door or a garden wall is no longer any safeguard against intrusion – intrusion can still be expected. If everyday activities are occurring in a home or semi-secluded place and could be viewed by paparazzi, the only argument against allowing such intrusion is that the person in question had sought seclusion – had had a legitimate expectation of privacy. But if that expectation could be transferred into non-private spaces – and *Von Hannover* indicates that it can – then the argument that a distinction between the two can be created is undermined. In other words, the question of affording a remedy should now turn on a changing cultural understanding of privacy and not on a simplistic distinction between places, based on physicality.

One commentator on *Von Hannover* found:

> In V*on Hannover* the Court accepted almost without question that Art 8 was engaged by the publication of the photographs. This might be thought to sit rather ill with its own judgment in *Peck*, where it seemed to be the fact that CCTV footage of the applicant was disseminated to a much wider audience than he could 'possibly have foreseen' together with the nature of the act he was engaged in (an unsuccessful suicide attempt) that led the Court to find that Art 8 was engaged.[75]

However, another reading of *Peck* might be to the effect that it was of most significance that the *place* in which an extremely private and intimate act occurred was not taken to be the deciding factor. Further, *Peck* did not close the door to a finding that less dramatically intimate activities occurring in public places could also engage Art 8.

The finding as to unexpectedly wide dissemination is, it is argued, irrelevant in *Von Hannover:* the Princess might have guessed – where Peck did not – that her activities would attract attention and that widespread dissemination would occur, but that factor could not stand in the way of Art 8 engagement since it would amount to accepting an implied consent to the publication of personal information whenever a celebrity, due to their celebrity status, was aware that dissemination would occur. Peck, as a non-celebrity, would not have attracted any attention, nor would there have been any dissemination of his activities had it not been for their dramatic nature. (Presumably, like thousands of others, he would have been captured on the CCTV cameras walking innocuously on the street and no dissemination of the pictures would have occurred.) Thus, unless celebrities are to lose much of their Art 8 protection purely by virtue of their celebrity status, account must be taken of the reality of paparazzi concerns: persons in Peck's position must perforce engage in activities of a striking, newsworthy nature – and therefore often inherently intimate and private – in order to attract journalistic attention. Persons in the Princess's position will constantly attract attention purely by virtue of their position, so there are strong reasons for differentiating between the positions of

---

75 (2004) 5 EHRLR, 593–96 (case comment).

celebrities and non-celebrities under Art 8 in order to recognise the risk to which the
one is exposed while the other is not. In common parlance, being photographed and
followed while engaging in daily life activities is an invasion of privacy. So is being
photographed when engaging in an activity of great personal significance in public.
It is not evident, it is argued, that the unwelcome feelings generated in each instance
– of outrage, humiliation, resentment of intrusion and so on – are conceptually distinct
from each other.

Some scholars have tended to define the notion of 'private facts' restrictively. WA
Parent's proposed definition of personal information, for example, is 'information about
a person which most individuals in a given time do not want widely known [or which]
though not generally considered personal, a particular person feels acutely sensitive
about.'[76] This is, it is suggested, an out-dated and impoverished view of privacy. The
trend in the Strasbourg jurisprudence has been incrementally to discard the simplistic
public/private space dichotomy in favour of focusing on the public/private nature of
activities.[77] The mere fact that an activity occurs in public should not be strongly
determinative of Art 8 engagement. If a private life activity occurs in a public space,
it is likely to fall within Art 8. To argue that because a 'private life' activity happens
to occur in a public space it is required that the plaintiff demonstrate that an extra
dimension of privacy was present, where this would not be necessary in a private place,
is to place too much emphasis on the private/public place analysis – it is to allow it to
re-enter by the back-door, having discarded it as initially determinative. If the activity
is one that could readily occur in a public or a private place, and it is one which is
self-evidently within the daily life sphere as opposed to the formal one, the case for
Art 8 engagement that the Court clearly accepted in *Von Hannover* is a strong one. To
fail to recognise this is to fail to understand the harm caused to personal every day
life choices if they must be made under threat of surveillance. The Court took account
of the reality of celebrity life in which constant surveillance by paparazzi amounts to
harassment and even persecution:

> [The Princess] alleged that as soon as she left her house she was constantly hounded
> by paparazzi who followed her every daily movement, be it crossing the road,
> fetching her children from school, doing her shopping, out walking, practising sport
> or going on holiday[78] . . . The context in which these photos were taken – without
> the applicant's knowledge or consent – and the harassment endured by many public
> figures in their daily lives *cannot be fully disregarded*.[79]

But the concluding words of this statement make it clear that the Court is *not* basing
its judgment on the element of harassment that was present, although that element

---

76 Parent, WA, 'A New Definition of Privacy for the Law' (1983) 2 *Law and Philosophy* 305,
pp 306–7.
77 See on this point in relation to the privacy protection available in the US, Canada and New Zealand:
Paton-Simpson, E, 'Privacy and the Reasonable Paranoid: the Protection of Privacy in Public Places'
(2000) 50 University of Toronto Law Journal 305. Paton-Simpson notes: 'There are signs that Canadian
and New Zealand courts may be more open to developing a degree of protection for privacy in public
places than their American counterparts.'
78 *Von Hannover v Germany* (2005) 40 EHRR 1 at para 44.
79 Ibid, para 68 (emphasis added).

was taken into account. The judgment makes it clear that every-day activities of a personal nature can find Art 8 protection from press intrusion regardless of the place in which they occur and without the need to demonstrate that an especially intimate act was occurring. It was indicated in *Sciacca v Italy*[80] that there is no need for press harassment in order to bring reporting of daily life details within the scope of Art 8; the Strasbourg Court applied *Von Hannover* to a case that was not one of press harassment, and cited the jurisprudence of *Von Hannover* in general terms.[81]

The German approach in its reliance on seeking seclusion was less expansive – obviously – than the one adopted in *Von Hannover*. The *Von Hannover* approach is closest to that taken in France; one commentator summarised the French position in these terms: 'As a principle, acts pertaining to private life but performed in a public place deserve the protection of the law.' [82] Clearly, this stance could appear at first sight to threaten freedom of expression. However, the activities captured by photographers and complained of by the Princess were, it is argued, devoid of public interest value. As discussed in Section 8, below, the courts are developing a means of balancing Arts 8 and 10 against each other which should offer reassurance to those parts of the media which do not rely on relaying celebrity gossip as their staple fare.

The 'horizontal effect' of Art 8 under the Human Rights Act

Most public authorities and a number of private bodies engage in the processing of personal information. They are therefore subject to the provisions of the Data Protection Act (DPA) 1998[83] and any other relevant statute, such as the Protection from Harassment Act 1997, and such statutes must be interpreted compatibly with the Convention rights under s 3 of the HRA, whether or not both parties concerned are private bodies.[84] In ensuring that such statutes are interpreted compatibly with the Convention, it is clear that Art 8 is of particular relevance. In determining whether information is to count as private, Art 8 must now be viewed as the source of interpretation under ss 3 and 2 HRA. This is made explicit in the PCC Code, cl 3, and is clearly the case in respect of all statutory provisions which mention or could relate to personal information, including the DPA 1998. By virtue of ss 2 and 6 of the HRA, it is also the case in relation to the common law.

---

80 (Application 50774/99), at paras 27 and 29 of the judgment.
81 It should be noted however that the facts of *Sciacca* differed from those of *Von Hannover* in a number of respects and the breach of Art 8 was found on the basis that the interference was not in accordance with the law. The applicant had submitted that the dissemination of her photograph at the press conference had infringed her right to respect for her private life, contrary to Art 8 (right to respect for private life) of the Convention. The Court noted that the photograph, taken for the purposes of drawing up an official file, had been released to the press by the tax inspectors. According to the information in its possession, there was no law governing the taking of photographs of people under suspicion or arrested and assigned to residence and the release of photos to the press. It was rather an area in which a practice had developed. As the interference with the applicant's right to respect for her private life had not been 'in accordance with the law' within the meaning of Art 8, the Court concluded that there had been a breach of that provision.
82 Picard, E, 'The Right to Privacy in French Law', in Markesenis (ed), *Protecting Privacy*, op. cit., fn 1 at 91.
83 Unless they are excluded from its ambit: see p 929.
84 Due to the effect of HRA, s 3(1) which, in covering all statutes, also covers those which create a number of rights binding private bodies.

Where a body processing personal information (which includes its publication) is also a public authority it can be sued directly under s 7(1)(a) of the HRA in respect of breaches of Art 8 – thus creating a statutory tort of invasion of privacy applicable only against public authorities. But it now seems fairly clear that there is no possibility under the HRA of suing *private* bodies for breach of Art 8 of the Convention directly under s 7(1)(a), principally because, as Chapter 4 explained, s 6 of the Act makes the Convention rights binding only upon 'public authorities'. However, since the courts, as 'public authorities'[85] themselves have a duty not to act incompatibly with the Convention rights, this creates a role for the rights even in litigation between private parties, thus giving rise to indirect 'horizontal effect'. As discussed below, it now seems clear that this does not require the courts to create new causes of action in such litigation;[86] rather, the s 6(1) duty to act compatibly with the Convention rights can bite upon their adjudication of existing common law actions. This was confirmed by the House of Lords in *Wainwright*.

What precisely s 6(1) requires of the courts in private common law adjudication is a vexed and much discussed issue.[87] Space precludes full rehearsal of the numerous and complex arguments here; while one commentator has argued that the courts have an absolute duty to render all private common law compatible with the Convention rights,[88] others in the early post-HRA years perceived a much more limited duty.[89] This chapter will argue, as indicated in Chapter 4,[90] that it is now apparent in the context of privacy that the courts are coming much closer to accepting the absolute duty just mentioned, but that their position has not yet been fully resolved. Their initial reluctance in this context appeared to be due to a number of factors: the decision not to make

---

85 Section 6(3)(a).

86 See Chapter 4, pp 249–56. It was expected that this would be the case: there are clear *Pepper v Hart* statements in Parliament to this effect: see HL Deb Vol 583 Col 784, 24 November 1997 and op. cit., Vol 585 Col 841, 5 February 1998; HC Deb Vol 314 Col 406, 17 June 1998. There is also virtually unanimous agreement amongst the commentators on the point: Phillipson, G, 'The Human Rights Act, 'horizontal effect' and the common law' (1999) 62 MLR 824, pp 826–28; Hunt, M, 'The horizontal effect of the Human Rights Act' [1998] PL 423, p 442; Buxton LJ, 'The Human Rights Act and private law' [2000] 116 LQR 48; Markesenis, op. cit., fn 1, pp 72–73; Leigh, op. cit., fn 1, pp 84–85; Singh, op. cit., fn 1; cf Wade, W (Sir), 'The United Kingdom's Bill of Rights', in Forsyth, C and Hare, I (eds), *The Golden Metwand and the Crooked Cord: Essays in Honour of Sir William Wade QC*, 1998, pp 62–63; Beyleveld, D and Pattinson, S, 'Horizontality applicability and horizontal effect' (2002) 118 LQR, 623.

87 See further Markesenis, B, 'Privacy, Freedom of Expression, and the Horizontal Effect of the Human Rights Bill: Lessons from Germany' (1999) 115 LQR 47; Leigh, I, 'Horizontal Rights, the Human Rights Act and Privacy: Lessons from the Commonwealth?' (1999) 48 ICLQ 57; Singh, R, 'Privacy and the Media after the Human Rights Act' (1998) EHRLR 712; Grosz, S and Braithwaite, N, 'Privacy and the Human Rights Act' in Hunt, M and Singh, R, (eds) *A Practitioner's Guide to the Impact of the Human Rights Act*, 1999, Hart (only partially concerned with media intrusion); Sir Brian Neill, 'Privacy: A Challenge for the Next Century' in Markesenis (ed) *Protecting Privacy*, 1999, Clarendon; Wright, J, 'How Private is my Private Life?' in Betten, L, (ed), *The Human Rights Act 1998: What it Means*, 1999. See further Chapter 4, pp 252–56.

88 Hunt, M, 'The horizontal effect of the Human Rights Act' [1998] PL 423, pp 439–43.

89 See, e.g., Leigh, I: the HRA 'does not formally change the approach to Convention questions in the [private] common law' (op. cit., fn 1, pp 82–83). See also Feldman, D, 'The Human Rights Act 1998 and constitutional principles' (1999) 19 LS 165, p 201.

90 See pp 255–56.

the Convention rights themselves binding upon private bodies meant that in the private sphere they could be viewed not as rights to enforce but only as legal values;[91] such a duty would have required courts to overturn settled common law rules and principles;[92] it would 'indirectly impose a very significant degree of liability on private bodies . . . contrary to the general scheme of the Act and the clear intention of its sponsors'.[93] It appeared at one point that the courts were only obliged, when engaged in common law adjudication, to develop and apply the law by reference to relevant Convention rights, treating them as legal principles having a variable weight, depending on the context.[94] But, as Chapter 4 indicates, the courts are close to accepting – in the context of privacy, but not, so far, in other contexts – that the common law must be developed compatibly with the rights. Lord Nicholls said in *Campbell*:

> The values embodied in articles 8 and 10 are as much applicable in disputes between individuals or between an individual and a non-governmental body such as a newspaper as they are in disputes between individuals and a public authority. In reaching this conclusion it is not necessary to pursue the controversial question whether the European Convention itself has this wider effect.[95]

In *Douglas III*,[96] Lord Phillips considered that the House of Lords had accepted the doctrine of indirect horizontal effect in *Campbell v MGN*[97] and in *Re S (a child)*.[98] Lord Phillips summarised Lady Hale's comments on the matter:

> Baroness Hale said that the Human Rights Act did not create any new cause of action between private persons. Nor could the courts invent a new cause of action

---

91 Phillipson, op. cit., fn 1 (1999) pp 834–37. It now appears that this is not, however, the case so far as HRA, s 3 is concerned: see *Wilson v First County Trust* [2001] 3 All ER 229, discussed in Chapter 4, p 149.

92 Phillipson, ibid, pp 838–40.

93 Phillipson, ibid, p 848; see also p 840.

94 Phillipson, ibid, pp 843–44. Buxton LJ (Buxton LJ, 'The Human Rights Act and private law' [2000] 116 LQR 48) argued that the HRA would have no impact at all on private common law: the rights could not even figure as principles or values in such a context, he argued, since they 'remain, stubbornly, values whose content lives in public law' (ibid, p 59). This argument, it is suggested, could not be reconciled, even pre-HRA, with the findings of the Commission in *Spencer*, and the Court in *Barclay* (discussed above) that the actions of private agents can engage Art 8, requiring domestic courts, through the common law, to offer redress. Nor could it be reconciled with the approach of the House of Lords pre-HRA in the decision in *Reynolds v Times Newspapers* [1999] 4 All ER 609 where, in the context of a private defamation action, their Lordships regarded the Convention as of great importance; (see esp ibid, pp 621–22, *per* Lord Nicholls; ibid, pp 628, 635, *per* Lord Steyn). Lord Nicholls specifically stated that, following the coming into force of the HRA 1998, 'the common law is to be developed in a manner consistent with Art 10' (ibid, p 622); Lord Steyn observed that, with the coming into force of the HRA 1998, 'The constitutional dimension of freedom of expression is reinforced' (ibid, p 628). Neither of their Lordships appeared to consider the private nature of the proceedings of significance in this respect.

95 [2004] 2 WLR 1232 at paras 17 and 18. (But now, as discussed, the post-*Campbell* decision in *Von Hannover v Germany* (2004) Appl No 59320/00, affirmed that the Convention does have this effect.)

96 [2005] EWCA 595.

97 [2004] 2 WLR 1232.

98 [2005] 1 AC 593.

to cover types of activity not previously covered. But where there is a cause of action the court, as a public authority, must act compatibly with both parties' Convention rights.[99]

It is perhaps too soon to say that the Courts have fully accepted a position in which they are bound to act compatibly with the Convention rights in developing private common law actions, but it is suggested that they are on the cusp of doing so, and this chapter will proceed on the basis that that is the position they are in the process of adopting. In *HRH Prince of Wales v Associated Newspapers Ltd*[100] Lord Phillips in the Court of Appeal said:

> The English court has recognised that it should also, in so far as possible, develop the common law in such a way as to give effect to Convention rights. In this way horizontal effect is given to the Convention. This would seem to accord with the view of the Strasbourg court as to the duty of the court as a pubic authority; see: *Von Hannover v Germany*.[101]

The caveat contained in the words 'so far as possible' may indicate that the courts are holding back from accepting the absolute duty to give effect to the rights within the common law in the sense that it might be impossible to give effect to the rights where they conflicted with clear common law rules. But Buxton LJ in the Court of Appeal in *McKennit v Ash*[102] summed up the post-*Campbell* position without any such caveat:

> . . . judges of the highest authority have concluded that that follows from section 6(1) and (3) of the Human Rights Act, placing on the courts the obligations appropriate to a public authority: see Baroness Hale of Richmond in *Campbell* at 132; Lord Phillips of Worth Matravers in *Douglas v Hello!* at 53; and in particular Lord Woolf in *A v B plc* [2003] QB 195[4]: under section 6 of the 1998 Act the court, as a public authority, is required not to act in a way which is incompatible with a Convention right. The court is able to achieve this by absorbing the rights which articles 8 and 10 protect into the long-established action for breach of confidence. This involves giving a new strength and breadth to the action so that it accommodates the requirements of those articles.

The word 'accommodate' suggests that the action in question should reflect the Convention rights, even if the Convention requirements *do* conflict with established common law rules.

In the area of privacy with which this chapter is concerned, the distinction between having regard to the Convention rights and having an absolute duty to act compatibly with them when applying existing common law, appeared in relation to the early post-HRA 'privacy' cases to be of little practical significance. That is because the difference between the two models would be of most practical importance when a clear imperative

---

99 Op. cit. at para 52.
100 [2006] EWCA Civ 1776, [2006] All ER (D) 335.
101 (2005) 40 EHRR 1 at paras 74 and 78.
102 [2006] EWCA Civ 1714.

from the Convention clashed with a well-defined pre-existing common law rule or principle. A judge accepting an absolute duty would be bound to override the common law, whereas under the weaker model, the Convention would provide only a reason for changing it. However, until the ruling in *Von Hannover* such a direct clash appeared to be unlikely to occur in this area. The indeterminacy and paucity of pre-*Von Hannover* Strasbourg jurisprudence on this aspect of Art 8 meant, as explored above, that English courts were likely to glean from it general principles and guidance, rather than clear-cut rules, which might have conflicted with the common law. *Von Hannover* provided the clear-cut rule which was previously lacking, and so brought the courts closer to confronting the decision to adopt either the 'absolute duty' rule or the 'giving regard to' test. But although this argument suggests that the judges may now have to extend the boundaries of the doctrine of confidence further than they have done in order to accommodate the *Von Hannover* rule, it is also suggested that confidence does not present them with a clear-cut common law rule that would have to give way. While the common law doctrine of trespass continues to lack flexibility, the currently very fluid and flexible boundaries of the doctrine of confidence, discussed below, made it unnecessary to override clear pre-existing rules of the action in order to achieve Convention-compliance, and this still appears to be the case in the face of the current more well defined and more radical Strasbourg privacy jurisprudence. On the other hand, the doctrine of confidence *has* changed out of all recognition under the impetus of the HRA, so although they may not have fully acknowledged it, the judges appear to be accepting the absolute duty to give effect to the rights.

There were, moreover, always strong arguments of principle which in the post-HRA years may have persuaded judges inclined to treat the Convention rights only as relevant principles to afford them an especially high weight when dealing with invasions of privacy by the media,[103] or other powerful conglomerates, thus minimising the difference between the stronger and weaker models of indirect horizontal effect. The power of such bodies to invade privacy is arguably equal to that of the state, rendering the drawing of a sharp, formalistic distinction between the state and the private agent, whereby rights are upheld against the one but not the other, unjustified at the level of principle. Moreover, in contrast with certain instances in the private sphere in which a plaintiff might have freely agreed to a diminution of his rights by another,[104] the invasion of individual rights by certain private bodies, particularly the press, may be as involuntary as if perpetrated by the state. Thus, for a number of reasons the course that has been taken in this context, by the incremental steps described below, was not one that required difficult decisions to be made at each stage. The favoured common law mode of reasoning, resembling the creeping in of the tide rather than the breaching of a dam, lent itself very readily to this new context.

---

103 For further argument on this point, see Phillipson, 1999, op. cit., fn 1, pp 846–47.
104 E.g., where a schoolteacher accepted a job at a Catholic school and signed a contract which provided that s/he would not publicly deny any of the fundamental doctrines of the Catholic Church. Strasbourg has quite readily accepted restrictions on Convention rights where these are said to have been voluntarily accepted by the applicant as a result of their employment: see, e.g., *Ahmed v UK* (1982) 4 EHRR 125; *Stedman v UK* (1997) 23 EHRR CD 168; *Rommelganger v Germany* (1980) 62 D&R 151 (no violation of Art 10 when employee of Catholic hospital dismissed for expressing pro-abortion views).

Judicial responses to the Strasbourg jurisprudence

Under the HRA, then, courts began by allowing Art 8 to figure as a relevant, weighty principle in considering privacy complaints raised within the common law. They have now reached a point at which they appear to accept that they must develop the common law so as to be compatible with Art 8, even where that quite fundamentally changes the nature of the law. A key factor has been the response of the courts to the Strasbourg jurisprudence on that Article examined above, since it is that case law, rather than Art 8 itself, which articulates the need for protection for personal information intrusion. When considering any issue under the Convention, s 2(1) HRA requires the domestic judiciary to take any relevant Strasbourg jurisprudence into account.[105] Since they are not bound by the case law, the courts could depart from it when so minded. However, as Chapter 4 pointed out, the courts tend to follow Strasbourg jurisprudence where it is of a settled nature.

If the courts had merely attempted to reach the same decisions as Strasbourg would have done, they would in effect have been applying the international law doctrine of the margin of appreciation in a domestic setting. As Chapter 4 pointed out, commentators have agreed,[106] and the House of Lords[107] has stressed, this would be wholly inappropriate. But a further and more difficult step is required: in applying Strasbourg jurisprudence under s 2 HRA, judges should attempt to disregard those aspects of the judgment which were attributable to the doctrine, difficult though this task clearly is.[108] Judges of a conservative bent, who wish to adopt a minimalist approach to the domestic application of the Convention,[109] might not take this further step or it might be merely overlooked: thus, while pronouncing the margin of appreciation doctrine inapplicable, judges could in fact rely fully on the outcomes of decisions at Strasbourg, without adverting to the influence of the doctrine on those outcomes.

This indeed was the approach arguably adopted in the House of Lords decision in *Ex p Kebilene*,[110] and the earlier case of *Khan*.[111] This approach would have been wholly mistaken in considering the application of *Winer* and *Spencer* to domestic law, and in fact it was not adopted: it could have lead to the mistaken assumption that the failure of both applications reflected the lack of a requirement under Art 8 to provide a remedy for non-consensual disclosures of true but personal information. As indicated below,

---

105 See Chapter 4, pp 191–99.

106 See Laws LJ, speaking extra-judicially ('The limitations of human rights' (1999) PL 254, p 258): 'The margin of appreciation . . . will necessarily be inapt to the administration of the Convention in the domestic courts'; Feldman, D, 'The Human Rights Act 1998 and constitutional principles' (1999) 19 LS 165, p 192: 'The doctrine will have no application in national law'; see further Chapter 4, p 263–65.

107 In *DPP ex p Kebilene and Others* [1999] 3 WLR 972, p 1043, Lord Hope of Craighead said: 'This technique [the doctrine] is not available to the national courts when they are considering Convention issues arising in their own countries.'

108 See Chapter 4, pp 278–79.

109 E.g., Buxton LJ, who believes that it has no place in private common law proceedings (Buxton LJ, 'The Human Rights Act and private law' [2000] 116 LQR 48).

110 [1999] 3 WLR 972. The decisions concerned included *H v UK* Appl No 15023/89 and *Bates v UK* Appl No 26280/95; see further Chapter 4, pp 270–73.

111 [1997] AC 558, HL; the Strasbourg decision in question was *Schenk v Switzerland* A 140 (1988).

the courts have not adopted a minimalist approach in this context.[112] Their acceptance that they should provide such a remedy in fact pre-dated *Von-Hannover*. But *Von Hannover* now confirms that the UK courts took an approach which was consistent with the developments occurring at Strasbourg in adopting an increasingly strong line in relation to privacy complaints. At Strasbourg and domestically it is possible to say that from 2004 to 2007 a clear shift occurred in fully recognising a right to privacy to be exercised against the media.

Moreover, in this area, there is no justification for the replacement of the margin of appreciation doctrine with a domestic version, whereby the courts take a restrictive approach to the protection of Convention rights, in deference to the 'area of judgment' or 'discretion' of another body,[113] in this case, to Parliament's presumed intent in not enacting a law of privacy. It is quite clear that the sponsors of the HRA explicitly contemplated the creative development of the common law to protect privacy. During the debate on the Bill, Lord Irvine said: 'it must be emphasised that the judiciary are free to develop the common law in their own independent judicial sphere', remarked that the judges were 'pen-poised' to develop a right to privacy through the common law, and contended that 'it will be a better law if [they] developed it after incorporation because they will have regard to Articles 8 and 10 [of the Convention]'.[114] The introduction of s 12 of the Act, strengthening press freedom, was clearly premised on the understanding that the Act might well drive forward the development of common law causes of action protecting privacy against the press.

Since there were, therefore, no grounds for deference to the judgment of another body in this context, and given the clear need to strip away its margin of appreciation aspects from the Strasbourg jurisprudence, the 'activist' approach to the application of such jurisprudence,[115] which led to positive development of the law in this area, was justified.

3 Broadcasting regulation and press self-regulation

Introduction

Successive governments have considered that the press should regulate itself as regards protection of privacy rather than using civil or criminal sanctions. Self-discipline has been preferred to court regulation in order to preserve press freedom. In contrast,

---

112 See pp 882–83, 889–90, 893–94.
113 See further Chapter 4, pp 265, 274–78, 280–84 for post-HRA discussion of decisions on the subject; it was pointed out that Lord Hope in *Ex p Kebilene* [1999] 3 WLR 972 said: 'In some circumstances it will be appropriate for the courts to recognise that there is an area of judgment within which the judiciary will defer, on democratic grounds, to the considered opinion of [the democratic body or person] whose act or decision is said to be incompatible with the Convention.' See also Lord Hoffmann, 'The Human Rights Act and the House of Lords' (1999) 62(2) MLR 159, esp p 161; Laws LJ, 'Wednesbury', in Forsyth and Hare (eds), *The Golden Metwand and the Crooked Cord: Essays in Honour of Sir William Wade QC*, 1998, p 201; Pannick, D, 'Principles of interpretation of Convention rights under the Human Rights Act and the discretionary area of judgment' [1998] PL 545, pp 549–51.
114 HL Deb Col 784, 24 November 1997.
115 For further discussion of this term, see Chapter 4, pp 278–81.

as Chapter 6 indicated, broadcasting privacy regulation has a statutory basis and the broadcast regulators are government-appointed. The model used for broadcasting has diverged in a number of respects from the press self-regulatory scheme.

Certain especially sensitive information is covered by these regulatory models, but is also the subject of specific reporting restrictions, discussed in Section 4 below. In some instances, these were adopted once it was clear that self-regulation could not be trusted to ensure that some newspapers would behave responsibly.[116] The media are also subject to the DPA 1998 in respect of their processing of personal information, although, as explained below, the Act does not provide a full protection against intrusion on privacy by the media.

There is an obvious tension between press self-regulation, broadcasting regulation and the demands of Art 8 of the Convention, introduced into UK law by the HRA. As discussed below, the Press Complaints Commission (PCC) and Ofcom (previously the Broadcasting Standards Commission (BSC)) have powers to adjudicate upon violation of their respective privacy codes. Their adjudications will be published by offending newspapers or broadcasters and Ofcom can also fine offenders; this arguably constitutes some 'respect' for private life.[117] The requirement to broadcast Ofcom adjudications is statutory in the case of the independent broadcasters; it arises under its Agreement in the case of the BBC. Thus Ofcom, which has powerful sanctions at its command, as detailed further in Chapter 6,[118] might be viewed as more likely to provide an effective remedy for breaches of Art 8. But the press is subject to no similar constraints.

When the European Commission on Human Rights considered the PCC in *Spencer (Earl) v UK*,[119] it made no suggestion that its activities could satisfy the requirement of respect for private life. Rather, it pointedly remarked: 'the PCC has no legal power to prevent publication of material, to enforce its rulings or to grant any legal remedy against the newspaper in favour of the victim'. Thus, it is reasonably clear that reliance on the PCC alone is inconsistent with the Convention principle that rights should be 'practical and effective', not 'theoretical or illusory'.[120] *Peck v UK*[121] made it clear that self-regulation cannot be considered an adequate way of protecting Art 8. In relation to the relevant regulation of the broadcast media, which are subject to a much tougher regulatory regime on privacy matters than the press, the Court found, in relation to the provision of a remedy for breach of Art 8:

> The Court finds that the lack of legal power of the Commissions to award damages to the applicant means that those bodies could not provide an effective remedy to him. It notes that the ITC's power to impose a fine on the relevant television company does not amount to an award of damages to the applicant.[122]

---

116 The law regarding the anonymity of rape complaints was prompted by public outrage in 1986 after the *Sun* published without her consent a picture of a rape victim in the 'Ealing vicarage' rape case taken as she was leaving church. The Press Council adjudication one year later censured the *Sun* for its unwarranted invasion of privacy: *Press Council, the Press and the People* 1987, p 241.

117 See further Wright, op. cit., fn 1, pp 137–38.

118 See pp 519–22.

119 (1998) 25 EHRR CD 105.

120 *Airey v Ireland* (1979) 2 EHRR 305, p 314.

121 (2003) 36 EHRR 41.

122 Op. cit. at para 109.

Thus, *a fortiori*, the PCC system cannot be viewed as providing an effective remedy. The Ofcom regime, although it is more effective, does not appear to satisfy the demands of Art 8 either: no damages for the complainant are available and the sanctions only operate post-broadcast. This question is considered further below. So it is apparent that self-regulation of the press is no longer sufficient to protect privacy. Judicial recognition of the need to provide further protection for privacy, reflecting the demands of the HRA, is now fully apparent.[123] The self-regulatory regime described below, therefore, may become increasingly marginalised by actions relying on common law privacy liability under the impetus of the HRA, which is considered in Section 6 below. The broadcasting regime is also influenced by the HRA, but less radically.

Press self-regulation

The Press Council

The Press Council was created in 1953 with a view to allowing the press to regulate itself. It issued guidelines on privacy and adjudicated on complaints. It could censure a newspaper and require its adjudication to be published. In practice, however, a number of deficiencies became apparent: the Council did not issue clear enough guidelines, its decisions were seen as inconsistent and in any event ineffective: it had no power to fine or to award an injunction.[124] Moreover, it was seen as too lenient; it would not interfere if the disclosure in question could be said to be in the public interest, and what was meant by the public interest was uncertain. Its inefficacy led the Younger Committee, convened in 1972, to recommend a number of proposals offering greater protection from intrusion by the press.[125] These proposals were not implemented but, by 1989, a perception had again begun to arise, partly influenced by *Kaye v Robertson*,[126] (discussed below) that further measures might be needed to control the press, although at the same time there was concern that they should not prevent legitimate investigative journalism. This perceived need led eventually to the formation of the Committee on Privacy and Related Matters chaired by Sir David Calcutt (hereafter 'Calcutt 1') in 1990[127] which considered a number of measures, some relevant to actual publication and some to the means of gathering information. The Committee decided that improved self-regulation should be given one final chance and recommended the creation of the Press Complaints Commission, which was set up in 1991 to police a Code of Practice for the press.

---

123 See pp 876–915 below.
124 See further Levy, HP, *The Press Council*, 1967.
125 The Committee considered the need for legal curbs on the press; it recommended the introduction of a tort of disclosure of information unlawfully acquired and a tort and crime of unlawful surveillance by means of a technical device. See Younger Committee, Cmnd 5012, 1972; criticised: MacCormick, op. cit., fn 1.
126 [1991] FSR 62.
127 *Report of the Committee on Privacy and Related Matters*, Cm 1102, 1990 (Calcutt Report); for comment see Munro, C, 'Press freedom – how the beast was tamed' (1991) 54 MLR 104.

The Press Complaints Commission

After self-regulation by the Press Complaints Commission in accordance with the revised Code of Practice had been in place for a year, Sir David Calcutt (hereafter 'Calcutt 2') reviewed its success[128] and determined that the Press Complaints Commission 'does not hold the balance fairly between the press and the individual (it is in essence a body set up by the industry (dominated by the industry'. He therefore proposed the introduction of a statutory tribunal which would draw up a revised code of practice for the press and would rule on alleged breaches of the code; its sanctions would include those already possessed by the Press Complaints Commission and in addition the imposition of fines and the award of compensation. When the matter was considered by the National Heritage Select Committee[129] in 1993, it rejected the proposal of a statutory tribunal in favour of the creation of another self-regulatory body to be known as the Press Commission, which would monitor a Press Code and which would have powers to fine and to award compensation. It also decided that a regulatory level beyond the commission was needed and recommended the setting up of a statutory Press Ombudsman.

However, the then Conservative Government did not respond to these proposals, making no move to appoint a new self-regulatory body or to give the Press Complaints Commission new powers. It responded to the National Heritage Select Committee in 1995,[130] stating that the system of voluntary self-regulation was to be preferred to statutory measures. It also noted various improvements in that system. The Commission itself had decided in January 1994 to appoint a Privacy Commissioner with the power to recommend that newspaper editors should be disciplined for breaching the Press Code. In January 1995, Lord Wakeham was appointed Chairman of the Commission and served until 2001; he was strongly in favour of continued self-regulation and pointed to a number of improvements made in the system, including the fact that the Commission by that point had a strengthened lay majority. The government did, however, make some suggestions for improvement in the system, including the establishment of a press hotline whereby the PCC could warn editors, thought likely to publish a story in breach of the Code, of the consequences of so doing. It also proposed that a fund should be set up in order to compensate members of the public whose privacy has been invaded. Neither proposal was implemented.

Policing the Code of Practice

The Press Complaints Commission agreed a Code of Practice in 1990, which the newspapers accepted. In 1997, the Code was made more restrictive; it was revised again in 2004 and 2005. The PCC Code was given added status in 2000 since it, and the Ofcom Broadcasting Code discussed below, are recognised in s 12(4)(b) of the HRA

---

128 Review of Press Self-regulation, Cm 2135.

129 Fourth Report of the Committee 294–91, *Privacy and Media Intrusion*, Fourth Report, HC 291–1 (1993).

130 *Privacy and Media Intrusion*, Cm 2918, 1995.

and in s 32(3)of the DPA.[131] Section 12(4)(b) requires that when a court is considering a grant of relief that could affect the exercise of Art 10 rights it should, *inter alia*, have regard to 'any relevant privacy code'. In this sense the HRA affords the PCC statutory recognition and s 12 provides the balancing act between free expression and privacy that should be carried out by the PCC code with a statutory basis.

The Commission can receive and pronounce on complaints of violation of the Code and can demand an apology for inaccuracy, or that there should be an opportunity for reply. It receives around 200 privacy complaints annually.[132] The current Chair is Sir Christopher Meyer; there are 17 Commission members; a majority of them have no connection with the press. There are three classes of members: the Chairman, Public Members and Press Members. The independent Chairman is appointed by the newspaper and magazine publishing industry. He must not be engaged in or, otherwise than by his office as Chairman, connected with or interested in the business of publishing newspapers, periodicals or magazines. The same constraint applies to the Public Members. Each of the Press Members must be a person experienced at senior editorial level in the press.

Code provisions

Clause 3(i) of the PCC Code incorporates part of the wording of Art 8(1) into the Code; it provides: 'Everyone is entitled to respect for his or her private or family life, home, health and correspondence,' and that publications intruding into private life without consent must be justified. When Clause 3 was amended in 2004 it added 'everyone is entitled to respect for his or her private . . . correspondence, including digital communications'. The Code makes special mention of hospitals and similar institutions in cl 8 and requires that the press must identify themselves and obtain permission before entering non-public areas of such institutions. Intrusion into grief and shock must be done with sympathy and discretion under cl 5.

Children receive special protection under cl 6: they must not be interviewed or photographed on subjects involving the welfare of the child or any other child in the absence of or without the consent of a parent or other adult who is responsible for the children. Children must not be approached or photographed at school without the permission of the school authorities. In 1999, Tony Blair complained to the PCC regarding a news story about Kathryn, his daughter.[133] The complaint was upheld. It was in fact the first complaint to be made under cl 6 regarding the privacy of the children of public figures at school. The PCC said: 'if every story about the PM's children which

---

131 The Secretary of State has power to designate the Code by order for the purposes of the sub-section, under s 32(3)(b).

132 In 2005, the Commission received 228 complaints about privacy from those directly affected by an alleged breach of the Code, a small increase on the 2004 figure. Of these, the Commission found 119 possible breaches of the Code, of which it successfully resolved 97 to the express satisfaction of the complainant. It obtained proportionate offers to resolve the matter in 17 more, which were not immediately accepted by the complainant, and adjudicated 18 (figures from PCC Annual Report for 2005).

133 Press Complaints Report (1999). Complaint upheld: 17 July 1999.

relates to their education is to be justified on the basis that he has made statements about education, then the Code provides no protection for his children or others in a similar position.' But the PCC also said that the press should be free to report on matters relating to children of public figures if such stories revealed hypocrisy or had an impact on policy. It said further that the child should only be identified if that child alone had to be the centre of the story.

Under cl 9, the press must avoid identifying relatives and friends of persons convicted or accused of crime without their consent. Clause 3(ii) provides that it is 'unacceptable to take photographs of individuals in private places without their consent'. Thus in comparison with the previous version cl 3 was tightened to prevent *all* photography of people in private places, irrespective of whether a long-range lens had been used. Private places are stated to be public or private property 'where there is a reasonable expectation of privacy'. The taking of photographs in private places, persistent phoning, questioning, photographing or pursuit of individuals after being asked to desist, or failing to leave private property after being asked to do so (cl 4(ii)), harassment (cl 4(i)), and the use of listening devices or phone interception (cl 10), are also all proscribed. Clause 8 (Listening Devices) of the previous Code has now been subsumed into the previous cl 11 (misrepresentation) and its provisions expanded to prevent the interception of 'private or mobile telephone calls, messages or emails'. The clause, which became cl 10 (clandestine devices and subterfuge), reads:

i) The press must not seek to obtain or publish material acquired by using hidden cameras or clandestine listening devices; or by intercepting private or mobile telephone calls, messages or emails; or by the unauthorised removal of documents or photographs.

ii) Engaging in misrepresentation or subterfuge can generally be justified only in the public interest and then only when the material cannot be obtained by other means.

It is notable that editors are enjoined in cl 4, the harassment clause, not only to ensure that those working for them comply with the cl 4 requirements, but also not to publish material from other sources which do not meet those requirements. The requirement as regards other sources – usually freelance journalists – is not expressly included in the other privacy clauses, most notably cl 3.

Further provisions of the Code reflect certain of the statutory reporting restrictions mentioned below, but go further than they do. Under cl 7, the press must not, even where the law does not prohibit it, identify children under 16 who are involved in cases concerning sexual offences, whether as victims or witnesses. Equally, cl 11 provides that the press must not identify victims of sexual assault unless they are free to do so by law and there is 'adequate justification'.

All the clauses of the Code that relate to intrusion into private life, except cl 5, are subject to exceptions in the public interest; this is defined non-exhaustively as including 'detecting or exposing crime or serious impropriety (previously 'serious anti-social conduct'), protecting public health or safety or preventing the public being misled by some statement or action of an individual or organisation'. The Code also states that 'There is a public interest in freedom of expression itself.' The Code requires that

'Whenever the public interest is invoked, the PCC will require editors to demonstrate fully how the public interest was served.'

The most notable amendments to the Code made in 2004 reflected the need for it to respond to changes in technology. Other clauses were tightened in order to allow them better to respond to particular ethical issues. For example, cl 12 (Discrimination) now emphasises that pejorative, prejudicial or irrelevant reference to 'an individual's race, colour, religion, sex, sexual orientation, physical or mental illness or disability' is unacceptable. In May 2005 cl 12 of the Code was expanded to cover discriminatory press reporting of transgendered people. The Commission took the view that the discrimination clause, in its previous form, gave protection to transexuals, but it decided, following the Gender Recognition Act 2004, that more specific cover should be given. It was decided that the word 'gender' would replace 'sex' in sub-clause 12(i), thus widening its scope to include transgendered individuals. Clause 9 (Reporting of Crime) now makes the specific central point that relatives or friends of persons convicted or accused of crime should not generally be identified, 'unless they are genuinely relevant to the story'.

Interpretation of the privacy provisions of the Code

The PCC's interpretation of the very significant privacy clause, cl 3, suggests that the non-consensual publication of specific identifying personal information, including addresses, is not necessarily a breach of the Code unless the person in question may be thereby put at risk from stalkers,[134] or the person involved may be 'potentially vulnerable'.[135] If this is the case, it is suggested that it is not in accord with the principle of informational autonomy under Art 8.

Clause 3 states that it is unacceptable to photograph individuals in private places without consent, making it clear that a private place is either public or private property in which there is a reasonable expectation of privacy. The interpretation of the term 'a reasonable expectation of privacy' is clearly a significant matter. Since the PCC, which monitors the Code and its interpretation, is probably a public authority under s 6 HRA,[136] it is suggested that it should adopt the post-*Von Hannover* Strasbourg interpretation of a 'reasonable expectation of privacy', thus extending it well beyond obviously private places or places accessible to the public, but semi-private, such as restaurants. *Von Hannover* obviously takes an approach that renders privacy no longer dependent on location. As argued above, public/private distinctions based on location are too simplistic, and a test of a reasonable expectation of privacy or, more broadly still, of control of private information is more satisfactory.[137] On the basis of such a test, if, for example, one person engages in a whispered exchange with another in the street, and this exchange is recorded by a reporter using a listening device, it is contended that an invasion of privacy has occurred which falls within Art 8.

---

134 Complaint by a well-known entertainer, complaint dated 16 July 2000.
135 Complaint of Mrs Renate John, adjudication, 2000.
136 See Chapter 4, pp 233–35 and fn 170, below.
137 The PCC's Code of Practice defines 'private places [as] public or private property where there is a reasonable expectation of privacy'. Such a test was recommended by the Irish Law Reform Commission: *Privacy, Surveillance and Interception* (1996), Consultation Paper.

The PCC does appear to accept a fairly expansive interpretation of a 'reasonable expectation of privacy', but not one that is clearly in full harmony with *Von Hannover* as it has not been made fully clear that people have such an expectation in the street. It said in a 2006 adjudication, for example:

> The Commission has previously ruled that publicly accessible places such as restaurants, hotels and offices can be those in which a person would have a reasonable expectation of privacy. In this instance, it was clear to the Commission that the publication of a photograph of the complainant in his workplace – a high street bank – without permission was a breach of Clause 3.[138]

It has also found that publication of pictures of children in crowds on public occasions, such as sporting events, do not amount to breaches of the Code.[139]

The interpretation of the public interest test in the Code is also of crucial significance. In making a determination, the PCC takes into account the extent to which the material is already in the public domain, and the specific issues of public interest that are raised.[140] At present, despite the requirements of s 6 HRA, it is not apparent that it takes Art 8 or 10 jurisprudence into account in making its determinations.[141]

Sanctions

The Commission does not require the complainant to waive any legal right of action as the Press Council was criticised for doing. However, it has the same limited sanctions

138   Adjudication on 28 April 2006, as regards Mark Kisby. The article was a feature on millionaire 'lottery lout' Michael Carroll and included a picture of him withdrawing £15,000 from his local bank. The complainant was the cashier at the branch and was included in the picture. He had not consented to his photograph being taken or published. The complainant considered that the publication of his image intruded into his private life and could have led to security problems for him and his family. The magazine said that the complainant represented the public face of a high street bank and could not therefore have any expectation of having his identity concealed. The PCC disagreed. Nonetheless, in the circumstances – given the innocuous nature of the photograph (published in *Loaded* magazine in Feb 2006) – the Commission decided that the magazine's offer of an apology which acknowledged its error represented sufficient and proportionate remedial action on its part.

139   In an Adjudication issued 23 June 2006 as regards such a picture the Commission stated that it would not normally consider that a photograph of a child in a crowd at an FA Cup tie – a public event at which there would be many photographers and television cameras, as well as tens of thousands of people – was intrusive or involved the child's welfare. It said that it is not the case that any picture of a child taken and published without the consent of the parent will always breach the Code. It went on: 'The Code says that children under 16 must not be photographed on issues involving their welfare without the consent of a custodial parent. While the complainant – her custodial parent – may not have actively consented for the photograph to be used, the Commission could not ignore the context in which it was taken. The complainant was at a significant sporting occasion, where he and his daughter would have been seen by a large number of people, and where the complainant must have been aware of the possibility of being photographed by press photographers or even appearing on television'. No breach was found.

140   See PCC, Report No 43 (1998), paras 3.0–3.2.

141   See e.g., Adjudication on 28 April 2006, as regards Mark Kisby complaining in respect of a photograph taken of him in his work place. The adjudication occurred post-*Von Hannover* but the decision was not mentioned; nor was Art 8 referred to.

as the Press Council: it has no coercive powers at all; it can do only what newspaper proprietors have agreed to allow it to do. At present, this is limited to adjudicating upon complaints received, making a public finding as to whether the Code was violated, and requesting newspapers to publish its adjudication – a request invariably complied with, to date. The Code preamble states that any publication criticised by the PCC must publish the adjudication 'in full and with due prominence'. Editors and publishers are required by the preamble to ensure that the Code is observed. The terms of the Code are incorporated into the conditions of employment of many members of the staff of newspapers, although not all. It still has no power to award fines, damages or prevent publication of offending items. It has not established a hotline, which – if editors were prepared to accept the PCC's implicit recommendation or advice not to publish – might have an effect similar to that of obtaining an *ex parte* injunction to prevent publication. No fund has been set up in order to compensate members of the public whose privacy has been invaded.

Conclusions

It is suggested that various fundamental problems are still apparent. Arguably, the PCC's own policing of the Code still errs on the side of generosity towards the newspapers.[142] Most importantly, the lack of punitive remedies means that the PCC has to rely on consent to the Code and so on the self-discipline of reporters and editors. Employees of newspapers may on occasion simply ignore the Code. Or newspapers may publish material obtained by freelance journalists or others in breach of the Code. In particular, despite the Code, they have been prepared to publish pictures of individuals in obviously private places (such as holiday villas), often taken with a long-range lens, without consent, even when it is virtually impossible to argue that a public interest in publication exists. A pre-*Von Hannover* example of such flouting of the Code occurred in the case of *Holden (Amanda) v The Star*.[143] Holden, the star of a sitcom, was holidaying in a private villa in Italy when, without her consent, agency reporters took photographs of her sunbathing topless. One of the photographs was published in *the Star*. She obtained an *ex parte* injunction on grounds of breach of confidence, as interpreted in *Douglas and Others v Hello!*[144] preventing further publication of the photographs. Although the case was clearly covered by cl 3(ii) of the PCC's Code of Practice, she did not make a complaint, preferring – for obvious reasons – to go straight to the courts to obtain the injunction. She claimed damages in respect of the publication which did occur.[145] A number of more recent examples are given below in which celebrities disregarded the PCC route.[146] The *Holden* case indicates that the Code alone was not proving a sufficient deterrent to newspapers which, for obvious commercial reasons, were prepared to invade privacy.

---

142 See further Tambini, D and Heyward, C, 'Regulating the trade in secrets: policy options', in Tambini and Heyward (2002) op. cit., fn 1. See also Rozenberg, J, *Privacy and the Press*, 2004, OUP.
143 Unreported; see the *Guardian*, 2 July 2001; (2001) *The Observer*, 15 July.
144 [2001] 2 WLR 992.
145 See *The Observer*, 15 July 2001.
146 See pp 882–83, 889–90 below.

The PCC cannot prevent publication of material obtained even in gross breach of the Code and, ultimately, the PCC cannot enforce its adjudications. Absent radical changes to its powers, which would have to be agreed by the industry, it is clear that it cannot be regarded as providing an effective remedy for violations of privacy under Art 8. This does not mean that it has no role now that effective remedies have been developed under the impetus of the HRA. It continues to provide an alternative to using the law for those who cannot or do not wish to incur legal costs. It continues, in conjunction with the National Union of Journalist's Code, to set benchmarking ethical standards for the profession. It also provides a means of appeasing and satisfying complainants, which may be less stressful and more speedy than court action. But taking the right to private life seriously obviously requires that a court remedy is available – the PCC route alone would clearly be inadequate. As discussed above, Strasbourg has made it clear that the PCC does not satisfy the Convention requirement under Art 13 of providing an effective remedy for breach of a Convention right.

Regulation of broadcasting

Introduction

The regime governing broadcasting in relation to privacy is (anomalously) much tougher than the one just described. It is set up under statute and the broadcast regulator has a number of relatively strong sanctions at its command.

Under s 142 of the Broadcasting Act 1990, the Broadcasting Complaints Commission (BCC) had a role similar to that of the PCC in adjudicating on complaints of infringement of privacy 'in or in connection with the obtaining of materials included in BBC or independent licensed television or sound broadcasts'. The term 'privacy' could receive quite a wide interpretation according to the ruling in *Broadcasting Complaints Commission ex p Granada Television Limited*.[147] Granada Television challenged a finding of the BCC that matters already in the public domain could, if republished, constitute an invasion of privacy. In judicial review proceedings, it was found that privacy differed from confidentiality and went well beyond it because it was not confined to secrets; the significant issue was not whether material was or was not in the public domain but whether, by being broadcast, it caused hurt and anguish. There were grounds on which it could be considered that publication of the matters in question had caused distress, and therefore the BCC had not acted unreasonably in the *Wednesbury* sense in taking the view that an infringement of privacy had occurred. However, the alleged infringement of privacy could be found to have occurred only when the broadcast was over, and not earlier.[148] A broad view of privacy was also taken in *Broadcasting Standards Commission ex p BBC*;[149] it was found that a company – in this instance, Dixons – can complain of an invasion of privacy in respect of secret filming in one of its shops. The 'public' nature of the shop and the fact that the goods which were being filmed, with a view to showing that they were second-hand, were

---

147 (1993) *The Times*, 31 May; affirmed [1995] EMLR 163; (1994) *The Times*, 16 December, CA.
148 *Broadcasting Complaints Commission ex p Barclay and Another* (1997) 9 Admin LR 265; (1996) *The Times*, 11 October.
149 [2000] 3 WLR 1327.

clearly on public display, did not affect this finding. Pre-2003 control was exercised by the Independent Television Commission, the Broadcasting Standards Commission and the Radio Authority; it is now exercised by one broadcast regulator – Ofcom.[150]

The role of the Independent Television Commission (ITC) was considered in Chapter 6, and it was made clear that it had a number of significant sanctions to use against broadcasters who failed to adhere to the ITC Programme Code.[151] Although, as that chapter discussed, its role was taken over by the super-regulator, Ofcom, in 2003, the model used for broadcasting regulation did not undergo radical change, either in relation to privacy or 'taste and decency'. The ITC's Programme Code had a section on privacy, also covering the gathering of information, which overlapped with the BSC Code on privacy. Clause 2.1 provided that the public interest had to be balanced against individual privacy and stated that the public interest includes detecting or exposing crime or a serious misdemeanour; protecting public health or safety; preventing the public from being misled by some statement or action of the individual or organisation concerned; exposing significant incompetence in public office. The Code echoed Art 8 in also providing that any act relying on the defence of public interest must be in proportion to the interest served.

The Broadcasting Complaints Commission was replaced by the Broadcasting Standards Commission (BSC) which was set up under s 106 of the Broadcasting Act 1996. The BSC was in a somewhat different position from that of the PCC in that it was set up under statute and had certain statutory powers. The BSC was charged with the duty of drawing up a Code in respect of programme standards under s 107, which was based on s 152 of the 1990 Act, but for the first time the Code also had to cover matters of fairness and privacy. The BSC adjudicated upon complaints received, made findings as to whether the Code had been violated, and requested broadcasters to publish its adjudications. In this respect, s 119 of the 1996 Act afforded the BSC a significant power, since it placed the requirement to publish the BSC findings and a summary of the complaint on a statutory basis.

The Ofcom privacy regime

Ofcom has now taken over the role of the BSC under the Communications Act 2003. However, it is still necessary to consider the previous Broadcasting Act 1996, and the Fairness and Privacy code published under s 107 of that Act, and now revised and policed by Ofcom. The 2003 Act may readily be seen as clarifying and stream-lining the position in relation to protection for privacy in broadcasting. As Chapter 6 describes, it set up a single regulator for the broadcast media – Ofcom. Previously, the Broadcasting Standards Commission (BSC) regulated all the broadcast media, while the Independent Television Commission (ITC) regulated the independent television channels. Both the BSC and the ITC had drafted, and enforced, two codes each; one on taste and decency (covering, broadly, the portrayal of sex and violence) known as 'the standards code', which is discussed in Chapter 6, and one on fairness and privacy, covering intrusion into privacy, misrepresentation, inaccuracy.

---

150 See Chapter 6, pp 519–20.
151 See p 518.

Under the position before the 2003 Act, the BSC code covered all the broadcasters, including the BBC, whereas the ITC code only covered the independent broadcasters. Thus the independent broadcasters were actually subject to two codes on privacy, and two Regulators – clearly an unsatisfactory and confusing position; the Codes overlapped and yet were not identical. Certain clauses of the ITC Code were more specific and appeared to be somewhat less generous to broadcasters than similar clauses in the BSC Code. For example, cl 2.7 of the ITC Code, dealing with children, went into greater detail regarding what could be shown than did cl 32, the equivalent clause under the BSC Code.

The key difference between the two regimes for the BBC and for independent broadcasting prior to the inception of the 2003 Act arose in terms of sanctions: the BSC could only require a broadcaster found to be in breach of its code to broadcast its findings and an apology if appropriate;[152] the ITC could, in addition to these sanctions, fine a broadcaster, and, in extreme cases, withdraw its licence.[153] Thus the BBC was under a much 'lighter touch' scheme of regulation. The position under the 2003 legislation is in essentials the same as that under the old regime, except that the position of the BBC was brought into line with that of independent television. The model adopted is the one described in Chapter 6 regarding the control of potentially offensive material in broadcasting. Court sanctions are not provided under the regulatory regime; persons aggrieved by privacy-invading broadcasting can complain to the regulator, Ofcom, which can provide redress, if it finds that the Code on privacy that it polices has been breached. Ofcom's remedies do not, however, extend to the provision of injunctions or damages.

Ofcom took over the previous duties of the BSC[154] to draw up, revise, and hear complaints under the fairness and privacy code issued under s 107 of the Broadcasting Act 1996.[155] It also took over the BSC's powers under s 119 of that Act[156] to force

152 Under s 119, Broadcasting Act 1996.
153 Under the Broadcasting Act 1990; see Chapter 6, p 519.
154 Schedule 1, para 14 of the 2003 Act provides:

'The following functions of the Broadcasting Standards Commission under Part 5 of the 1996 Act are transferred to OFCOM –

    (a) the Commission's function of drawing up and from time to time revising a code of practice under section 107 of that Act (codes of practice relation to fairness and privacy); and
    (b) their functions in relation to fairness complaints under that Part.

155 Section 107 provides:

(1) It shall be the duty of the BSC to draw up, and from time to time review; a code giving guidance as to principles to be observed, and practices to be followed, in connection with the avoidance of –

    (a) unjust or unfair treatment in programmes to which this section applies, or
    (b) unwarranted infringement of privacy in, or in connection with the obtaining of material included in, such programmes.

(2) It shall be the duty of each broadcasting or regulatory body, when drawing up or revising any code relating to principles and practice in connection with programmes, or in connection with the obtaining of material to be included in programmes, to reflect the general effect of so much of the code referred to in subsection (1) (as for the time being in force) as is relevant to the programmes in question.

(3) The BSC shall from time to time publish the code (as for the time being in force). Ss 4 relates to consultation and is omitted.

156 Section 119 provides:

(1) Where the BSC have –

broadcasters to carry apologies and statements of findings following complaints. The substantive provisions of that Code, and the meagre case law relating to the interpretation of its predecessors, probably still a reliable guide to the interpretation of the current Code, are considered below.

The 2003 Act opened the way for the BBC to be able, for the first time, to be fined by an independent regulator – Ofcom. Section 198 of the 2003 Act gives power to Ofcom to regulate the BBC in so far as that is provided for in the BBC's Agreement with the government.[157] In other words, it created the possibility of regulation by Ofcom on privacy matters. The amendments subsequently made in December 2003 to the BBC Agreement inserted, for the first time, the requirement to observe the fairness and privacy Code drawn up under the Broadcasting Act 1996. Previously, the BBC Agreement had no provisions relating to invasion of privacy.

The BBC's current Charter and Agreement came into force in 2007 and will expire in 2016.[158] Paragraph 45 of the Agreement provides:

   (a) considered and adjudicated upon a fairness complaint, or
   (b) considered and made their findings on a standards complaint, they may give directions of the kind specified in subsection (2).

(2) Those directions are –

   (a) where the relevant programme was broadcast by a broadcasting body, directions requiring that body to publish the matters mentioned in subsection (3) in such manner, and within such period, as may be specified in the directions, and;
   (b) where the relevant programme was included in a licensed service, directions requiring the appropriate regulatory body to direct the licence holder to publish those matters in such manner, and within such period, as may be so specified.

(3) Those matters are –

   (a) a summary of the complaint;
   (b) the BSC's findings on the complaint or a summary of them;
   (c) in the case of a standards complaint, any observations by the BSC on the complaint or a summary of any such observations.

(5) The form and content of any such summary as is mentioned in subsection (3)(a), (b) or (c) shall be such as may be approved by the BSC.

(6) A broadcasting or regulatory body shall comply with any directions given to them under this section.

157 Section 198 provides:

   (1) It shall be a function of OFCOM, to the extent that provision for them to do so is contained in-

     (a) the BBC Charter and Agreement, and
     (b) the provisions of this Act and of Part 5 of the 1996 Act, to regulate the provision of the BBC's services and the carrying on by the BBC of other activities for purposes connected with the provision of those services.

   (2) For the purposes of the carrying out of that function OFCOM –

     (a) are to have such powers and duties as may be conferred on them by or under the BBC Charter and Agreement; and
     (b) are entitled, to the extent that they are authorised to do so by the Secretary of State or under the terms of that Charter and Agreement, to act on his behalf in relation to that Charter and Agreement.

158 July 2006; Cm 6872. It came into force on 1 January 2007.

(1) The BBC must comply with the Fairness Code—

    (a) in connection with the provision of the UK Public Broadcasting Services, and

    (b) in relation to the programmes included in those services.

(2) 'The Fairness Code' means the code for the time being in force under section 107 of the Broadcasting Act 1996.[159]

The second change was discussed in Chapter 6; it was foreshadowed by s 198(3) of the 2003 Act, which allows for the imposition of penalties upon the BBC for breach of provisions in its Agreement and Charter.[160] The 2007 Agreement provides for the imposition by Ofcom upon the BBC of financial penalties for breach of various enforceable requirements,[161] which includes the fairness Code in para 45.[162] Moreover, cl 93 provides that if Ofcom is satisfied that the BBC has breached an enforceable requirement, it may require the BBC to carry a correction or statement of Ofcom's findings upon its adjudication on any complaint.[163]

The independent broadcasters are regulated by the 2003 Act directly. Section 326 provides that they too are bound by the fairness and privacy code;[164] they may be

---

159 Previously contained in Clause 5A of the amended Agreement.
160 Section 198(3) provides: The BBC must pay OFCOM such penalties in respect of contraventions by the BBC of provision made by or under –

(a) this Part, or
(b) the BBC Charter and Agreement,as are imposed by OFCOM in exercise of powers conferred on
    them by that Charter and Agreement.

161 Clause 94 provides:

1 If OFCOM are satisfied that the Corporation has contravened a relevant enforceable requirement, they may serve on the Corporation a notice requiring it to pay them, within a specified period, a specified penalty.

2 The amount of the penalty that may be imposed on any occasion under this clause shall not exceed the maximum specified for the time being in subsection 198(5) of the Communications At 2003 [that is, £250,000].

162 By virtue of clause 95(1)(a).
163 Clause 93 provides:

1 This clause applies if OFCOM are satisfied- (a) that the Corporation has, in relation to any of its services, contravened a relevant enforceable requirement; and (b) that the contravention can be appropriately remedied by the inclusion in that service of a correction or a statement of findings (or both), OFCOM may direct the Corporation to include a correction or statement of findings (or both) in the service.

2 A direction may require the correction or statement of findings to be in such form, and to be included in programmes at such times, as OFCOM may determine. Clause 93 applies to contravention of the fairness code by virtue of clause 93(7) and clause 95.

164 Section 326 provides:

'The regulatory regime for every programme service licensed by a Broadcasting Act licence includes the conditions that OFCOM consider appropriate for securing observance-

    (a) in connection with the provision of that service, and;

    (b) in relation to the programmes included in that service,of the code for the time being in force under section 107 of the 1996 Act (the fairness code).'

directed by Ofcom to carry statements of findings and corrections;[165] they can be fined for breach of the Code,[166] and, in extreme cases, licences may theoretically be revoked.[167]

These provisions are bolstered by s 3(2) of the 2003 Act under which Ofcom has the duty of ensuring the application of standards that provide adequate protection to members of the public and all other persons from what the Act calls 'unwarranted infringements of privacy', balanced of course against freedom of expression. Thus the BBC is now in the same position as the other broadcasters in relation to standards of privacy protection, correcting the anomalous position that existed previously.

Ofcom's Privacy Code

Ofcom's rules on privacy, taken over from the BSC Code, are part of its 2005 Broadcasting Code, discussed in Chapter 6. Ofcom's Code, like the PCC Code, goes beyond what the law demands in a number of respects; it is binding in the sense that Ofcom can apply sanctions if it is breached. This Code is similar to that of the PCC, but in certain respects, it is more extensive and offers greater guidance on the operation of the overriding public interest test. However, since its revision in 2004 and 2005 it is arguable that, on its face, the PCC Code offers as much protection for privacy as Ofcom's current Code does, and even in certain respects takes a stricter stance. It states for example in cl 4 that journalists should leave property when asked to do so, although this is subject to the public interest defence. Ofcom's code contains no equivalent provision.

Section 8 of the Broadcasting Code contains the privacy rules. The privacy of persons suffering grief or distress must in particular be respected, under cl 8.16, but footage of accidents etc can be broadcast without consent if 'warranted'. Such persons should be approached with sensitivity, and they should not be put under pressure to provide interviews unless this is warranted. Clauses 8.13–8.15 provide that surreptitious filming, the use of hidden microphones etc must be justified by an overriding public interest. Clause 25 of the BSC Code provided that people who are currently in the news cannot object to interviewing in public places, but that persistent questioning of

---

165 Under section 236.
166 Section 237 provides:

   If OFCOM are satisfied that the holder of a licence to provide a television licensable content service –
      (a) has contravened a condition of the licence, or
      (b) has failed to comply with a direction given by OFCOM under or by virtue of a provision of this Part, Part 1 of the 1990 Act or Part 5 of the 1996 Act, they may serve on him a notice requiring him to pay them, within a specified period, a specified penalty.

   (2) The amount of the penalty under this section must not exceed the maximum penalty given by ss (3).

   (3) The maximum penalty is whichever is the greater of—
      (a) £250,000 and
      (b) 5 per cent. of the qualifying revenue for the licence holder's last complete accounting period falling within the period for which his licence has been in force ('the relevant period').

167 Under s 238.

individuals after being asked to desist could constitute an unwarranted infringement of privacy. Clause 8.1 of Ofcom's Code is more nuanced and in this instance accords more readily with current Art 8 jurisprudence:

> Legitimate expectations of privacy will vary according to the place and nature of the information, activity or condition in question, the extent to which it is in the public domain (if at all) and whether the individual concerned is already in the public eye. There may be circumstances where people can reasonably expect privacy even in a public place. Some activities and conditions may be of such a private nature that filming or recording, even in a public place, could involve an infringement of privacy. People under investigation or in the public eye, and their immediate family and friends, retain the right to a private life, although private behaviour can raise issues of legitimate public interest.

But under cl 8.11 filming of people in the news can occur in public places without prior warning. Clause 8.11 does not state that this can occur only if 'warranted'. In other words, it does not, on its face, demand that broadcasters perform a balancing act between Arts 8 and 10. In light of *Von-Hannover*, and the developing UK privacy jurisprudence discussed below, it is argued that cl 8.11 requires amendment.

Children receive special protection under cll 8.20–8.22. If under 16 they must not be interviewed without the consent of a parent or other adult who is responsible for them. If consent is refused a decision to go ahead must be justified by an overriding public interest. Under cl 2.6 of the ITC Code children could not be interviewed regarding private, family matters. This requirement was not subject to the public interest test. But under cl 8.22 such interviewing can be warranted The Code makes special mention of agency operations in cl 8.8 (such as police investigations) and requires that the broadcasters should obtain consent to film unless it is warranted to proceed without consent. Clause 8.8 also covers filming in institutions, such as hospitals, and requires that the broadcasters must obtain consent to transmit material when persons are shown in sensitive situations, such as in psychiatric hospitals, unless exceptions can be made in the public interest. The previous ITC Code covered the filming of police operations or the investigations of similar bodies and required that the broadcasters must identify themselves and should normally leave private property if asked to do. Since a trespass could occur in such an instance, the licensee's most senior programme executive had to be consulted before transmission and had to be convinced that showing the material serves the public interest. This provision does not appear in the current Code. Broadcasters can record phone calls if they identify themselves (cl 8.12); door-stepping can occur on private property if there is an overriding public interest (cl 8.11).

Under the public interest test, an infringement of privacy can be justified (warranted) on a number of grounds. They include: revealing or detecting crime or disreputable behaviour, protecting public health or safety, exposing misleading claims made by individuals or organisations or disclosing significant incompetence in public office (cl 8.1). The Code also impliedly adopts a nuanced approach to public domain issues. The BSC Code spoke of determining whether when filming events in public places it was clear that information was sufficiently in the public domain to make it justifiable to broadcast it without consent (clause16). Ofcom's Code states in its preamble: 'Legitimate expectations of privacy will vary according to the place and nature of the information, activity or condition in question, the extent to which it is in the public domain . . .'. Clause 8.10 provides: 'Broadcasters should ensure that the re-use of material, i.e. use of material originally filmed or recorded for one purpose and then used in a programme for another purpose or used in a later or different programme, does not create an unwarranted infringement of privacy'.

The relationship between the HRA and media regulation

Marginalisation of the PCC?

The indirect effect of the HRA on the media regulatory schemes is becoming apparent and is most significant as far as the PCC is concerned since, as indicated above, the problem of invasion of privacy by the press, not the broadcast media, is more pressing and the PCC has no statutory basis or powers. The most significant effect is that the PCC has been to an extent marginalised in respect of its role in relation to privacy, because persons, particularly celebrities, whose privacy has been or is about to be invaded by the press are seeking *ex parte* injunctions and/or damages on grounds of breach of confidence/privacy, as discussed below, rather than complaining to the PCC, which has no such remedy at its command (and might be viewed, if it had, as reluctant to use it). As such a trend became apparent, the PCC reviewed its Code with a view to tightening it up, in 2004 and 2005. Clearly, it faces the possibility that the self-regulation system might become a dead letter – at least as far as celebrities are concerned. It may eventually have to adopt some of the proposals it has at present rejected, such as the hotline system and the award of compensation to complainants.

Clearly, *ex parte* injunctions can also be obtained restraining the showing of a broadcast, on grounds of breach of confidence/privacy or, in the case of any media bodies that are also public authorities, on grounds of invasion of privacy under Art 8, using s 7(1)(a) of the HRA. But it is clear that marginalisation of Ofcom as a body charged, *inter alia*, with protecting privacy, is less likely to occur, since the problem posed by invasion of privacy by the broadcast media is not of the proportions of that posed by the press, and the sanctions available to Ofcom create greater confidence in its ability to address it.

In debate on the Human Rights Bill, a great deal of concern was voiced in Parliament about the possibility, as regards the PCC, that it would be deemed a public authority for the purposes of the HRA. It was thought that it would be subject to judicial review for violation of the Convention in its rulings and therefore in some way in a position to threaten press freedom.[168] Although it appears that it is subject to the Convention,[169] it is unlikely in practice that this route will frequently be explored: it would be likely to provide, even if proceedings succeeded, a merely paper remedy. Those expressing that concern appeared to overlook the fact that the PCC has no coercive powers. As far as the PCC is concerned, it is also hard to see what impact a finding of breach of the Convention could have on the bodies it is regulating. If a finding was made that the PCC had violated the Convention rights, for example by finding that someone's privacy had not been invaded when, in the court's view, Art 8 required a contrary

---

168   See Hansard, HL Col 784, 24 November 1997.
169   See *R (on the application of Ford) v PCC* [2002] EMLR 5.

conclusion,[170] the very most that the court could do would be to quash the finding of the PCC by a quashing order (formerly *certiorari*) and require it to reconsider the case by a mandatory order (formerly *mandamus*). Damages could conceivably be awarded against it also under s 8 HRA.

But this would not affect the newspapers themselves, in the sense that none of this would change the fact that the only 'remedies' they would be subject to would be those available at present: the publication of the PCC's adjudications although they could not be forced to do this. However, an action brought directly against Ofcom under s 7(1)(a) on grounds of failing to use sanctions in respect of an invasion of privacy in breach of its Privacy Code could lead to a mandatory order requiring it to use the sanctions it has available, including, ultimately, withdrawal of its licence, against the broadcaster concerned. This possibility could have some impact, although it would apply post-broadcast; it would not prevent the broadcast of the material. Nevertheless, it would still not provide an effective remedy for breach of Art 8, following the *Peck* ruling discussed above, since Ofcom cannot award damages to complainants. The effective remedy for breach of Art 8 rights is provided in most circumstances by the action for breach of confidence/privacy discussed below. The Data Protection Act 1998 could also be invoked, as will be discussed, in order to provide such a remedy in certain circumstances against data-processing by newspapers or broadcasters.

The only way in which the PCC could acquire greater powers than it has at present (for example, to levy fines against newspapers adjudged to have breached the Code) would be if the newspaper industry collectively agreed that it should have the power to demand fines, and even then, it is hard to see what the sanction for non-payment would be, other than adverse publicity. It is possible that if actions are successfully brought against it, the PCC may seek agreement from the industry that breach of the PCC Code should lead to disciplinary action, including dismissal. But again, it could not enforce such action. Or it could ask newspapers to indemnify it against possible actions under the HRA. It goes without saying that the PCC, not having any statutory basis or powers (other than the recognition of its Code in s 12 HRA), could not be given by the industry more than the power to request a newspaper not to publish a given article; it could never require non-publication. In short, therefore, the effect of the HRA on the PCC may be in the short term that a layer of judicial supervision was added onto what remains a mere self-regulatory body, with powers to do only that which the industry agrees voluntarily to submit to. In the longer term, the HRA may play a crucial part in the dismantling of the whole self-regulatory system – at least as far as privacy complaints are concerned – if it becomes marginalised due to actions based on breach of confidence/privacy. In fact it is most probable that the system will remain as it is at present – a poor man's substitute for court action.

Impact of the Convention rights

Clearly, the statutory powers affecting Ofcom must all be interpreted compatibly with the Convention under s 3 HRA. Thus, in so far as the concept of privacy at Strasbourg

---

170 Anna Ford, a BBC journalist, applied to the High Court for judicial review of the PCC's decision to reject her claim that the *Daily Mail* breached her right to privacy by publishing pictures of her on holiday with her partner (*The Observer*, 15 July 2001). The PCC's decision was vindicated.

in this context has undergone a change post-*Von Hannover*, the duties placed upon Ofcom under the statute should be interpreted relying on ss 3 and 2 HRA to reflect that change.

The Convention rights of course also have a direct impact on the regulators via s 6 HRA. The BSC and ITC were subject to judicial review,[171] as is Ofcom;[172] and this is also probably the case in respect of the PCC.[173] As Chapter 6 indicated, it is clear that Ofcom is a functional public authority under s 6 HRA and it is probably a core authority.[174] The PCC is probably also a functional public authority.[175] The duties of Ofcom under s 6 HRA can be viewed as additional and complementary to those it has under the 2003 Act and the Broadcasting Act 1996. If these bodies fail to uphold complaints relating to invasion of privacy, proceedings can be brought against them under s 7(1)(a) HRA. In any such proceedings, a court now has to satisfy s 12(4)(b) HRA, which means that the privacy Codes of these bodies are admissible in evidence and can be considered. By this means, the PCC Code has acquired, it is suggested, a quasi-legal status. Ofcom's Code already has such a status since it was set up under statute, but its status can be viewed as enhanced under s 12 HRA. It may be noted that the BSC Code was taken into account in any event in the pre-HRA ruling in *Broadcasting Standards Commission ex p BBC*.[176]

But the private media bodies – the newspapers and non-public service broadcasters – are not bound by the Convention rights under s 6. So if they invade privacy the aggrieved individual has three options. He or she could use the complaints mechanisms represented by Ofcom or the PCC. If an adjudication occurs the individual would not receive damages, but would have the satisfaction of an acknowledgement that a breach had occurred. He or she might be appeased and would not have had to incur the cost, risk and publicity of a court action. Clearly, a court action seeking to uphold privacy runs the risk of drawing attention to the subject-matter of the original complaint. Most members of the public are not in a position to take newspapers/broadcasters to court. So the benefits of these non-court-based methods of obtaining redress should not be over-looked.

If the complaint was not upheld he or she could seek review of the Ofcom or PCC decision, relying on Art 8 and s 7(1)(a) HRA. This possibility was discussed above, and as indicated, would not provide an effective remedy for the individual whose privacy had been invaded, even assuming that the action was successful. Finally, he or she could bring an action relying on breach of confidence/privacy, possibly coupled with action under the DPA 1998. But the position would be different if the media body itself was a public authority for HRA purposes. The BBC and possibly Channel 4, as bodies

---

171   The bodies they replaced were so subject and this was found to be the case in respect of the BSC: see *R v BCC ex p Owen* [1985] QB 1153; *R v BSC ex p BBC* [2000] 3 WLR 1327; *R v IBA ex p Whitehouse* (1985) *The Times*, 4 April.

172   See the *Pro-Life Alliance* case, discussed Chapter 6, pp 533–44.

173   See *PCC ex p Stewart-Brady* (1997) 9 Admin LR 274; *R (on the application of Ford) v PCC* [2002] EMLR 5.

174   See Chapter 6, p 530; Chapter 4, p 233.

175   It is subject to judicial review and receives some recognition under statute – the HRA, s 12. See further on regulators as functional public authorities, Chapter 6, pp 530–31 and Chapter 4, pp 233–35.

176   [2000] 3 WLR 1327.

with a public service remit, are probably functional public authorities.[177] If this is the case, under s 6 HRA, these bodies are bound to comply with the Convention rights in exercising their public functions. The question then would be whether decisions as to filming are part of that function. Assuming that they are, an effective remedy would potentially be available under s 8 HRA.

Deference

If an aggrieved individual brought an action directly against the BBC or against Ofcom (assuming that Ofcom had refused to uphold a privacy complaint) in respect of an invasion of privacy, relying on s 7(1)(a) HRA and Art 8, the chances of success would be low. The courts take a markedly deferential approach to reviewing decisions of the regulator, being reluctant to interfere in the exercise of its expert judgment unless Ofcom has made a plain error of law, or abused its discretion. This stance has also been taken in respect of the BBC. In *R v Broadcasting Complaints Commission ex p Granada Television Ltd*,[178] in an application for judicial review of the then Commission's finding under a privacy code, Balcombe LJ found:

> It is a reasonable inference that another reason why Parliament did not provide a definition of privacy in the [Broadcasting Act 1990] is because it considered it more appropriate that the difficult questions of fact and degree and value judgment, which are raised by the concept of an infringement of privacy, are best left to a specialist body, such as the BCC, whose members have experience of broadcasting[179] . . . Unless on no interpretation of the word "privacy" could the findings of the BCC be justified . . . there is no basis for the grant of judicial review . . . Whether in such a case there is an unwarranted infringement of privacy is a matter of fact and degree and as such for the decision of the BCC with which the court cannot interfere . . .[180]

The leading decision in this area is *R v BSC ex p BBC*;[181] this case concerned an application by the BBC for judicial review of the BSC's findings that the privacy of a company, in this case Dixon's, had been invaded by secret recording in one of its stores by the BBC. Lord Woolf observed:

> So long as the approach which [the Regulators] adopt is one to which, in their statutory context, the words 'infringement of privacy' are capable of applying

---

177 This seemed to be assumed in the *Pro-Life Alliance* case, as discussed in Chapter 6, pp 533–44. There is a possible difficulty with this proposition which may need to be addressed by the courts. Arguably, the BBC (and Channel 4) may also, exceptionally, be viewed as both public authorities and victims for HRA purposes. They appear to satisfy the test for victims at Strasbourg, which is encapsulated under HRA 1998, s 7(7), since, although in a sense they are emanations of the state, they are editorially independent from it. It would of course be bizarre if they could not be viewed as victims since that would run contrary to the scrutinising role over the state that one would expect these bodies, especially the BBC, to exercise.

178 [1995] EMLR 163.

179 Ibid at p 167.

180 Ibid at p 168.

181 [2000] 3 WLR 1327, p 1332.

then the courts should not interfere. It is only if an approach to 'infringement of privacy' by [them] goes beyond the area of tolerance that the courts can intervene. There will be situations which fall within the grey area where it will be very much a matter of judgment whether they fall within [their] ambit or not. In the latter situations, having regard to the role the legislation gives to [them], the answer to the scope of their remit is that it is something for [them] to determine not the courts. The nature of their work and their membership are important when considering the role of the courts in relation to adjudications by [them]. What constitutes an infringement of privacy or bad taste or a failure to conform to proper standards of decency is very much a matter of personal judgment. This is not an area on which the courts are well equipped to adjudicate.[182]

In the post-HRA *Anna Ford* case,[183] which concerned an application for judicial review of the decision of the PCC on a complaint under its own privacy code, the judge found:

> English courts will continue to defer to the views of bodies like the [Press Complaints] Commission even after the HRA came into force. In summary, the type of balancing operation conducted by a specialist body such as the Commission is still regarded as a field of activity to which the courts *should and will* defer. The Commission is a body whose membership and expertise makes it much better equipped than the courts to resolve the difficult exercise of balancing the conflicting rights of Ms Ford and Mr Scott to privacy and of the newspapers to publish[184] ... My task is not to determine if Ms Ford's rights to privacy were infringed by the surreptitious taking of the photographs or their subsequent publication but to decide whether Ms Ford has an arguable case for exercising the limited supervisory powers of the Administrative Court.[185]

The decision of the House of Lords in *R (on the application of Pro-Life Alliance) v BBC*,[186] discussed in detail in Chapter 6, gives very strong endorsement to the notion that a high degree of deference should be paid to media regulators and to media bodies due to their special expertise.[187] In that instance the BBC was acting in effect in its regulatory role in deciding whether the film in question offended too greatly against taste and decency to be broadcast in its original form. *Pro-Life* indicates that the courts do not regard it as their task to decide what the outcome of a privacy complaint should have been. They view their role as merely demanding that they review the decisions of the regulators, or media bodies, affording them a very broad area of discretion, even where the Convention rights are in issue. They take this stance, as Chapter 6 pointed out, partly on the basis that the primary determination as to the requirements of privacy

---

182 Ibid at p 1332.
183 *R (on the application of Ford) v Press Complaints Commission* [2002] EMLR 5.
184 Ibid, at para 28 – emphasis added.
185 Ibid, at para 29.
186 [2003] 2 WLR 1403.
187 In this case to the BBC Governors, in deciding not to broadcast a PEB submitted to the BBC by the Pro-Life Alliance party. See Chapter 6, pp 537–40.

has been entrusted to the regulators by Parliament, not the courts, but perhaps mainly on the ground of institutional competence – on the basis that the courts are not well equipped to adjudicate in this context due to lack of the special expertise possessed by the media bodies in question. It might appear that the HRA should have affected this stance radically since under s 6, the courts must ensure that Convention standards are adhered to. But this was not the stance that was adopted in *Pro-Life*.

It can however be argued that *Pro-Life* concerned a matter that the courts are arguably not well equipped to inquire into – the acceptability to television audiences of disturbing material in election broadcasts. But the courts are, clearly, well equipped to consider the proper means of balancing conflicting legal rights. As discussed below, they have shown themselves readily capable of performing the balancing act between Arts 8 and 10 of the Convention in the context of breach of confidence/privacy claims and of the inherent jurisdiction of the court to protect children. Thus, it is arguable that if a privacy claim, as opposed to a claim relating to offensive broadcast material, is considered at the highest level under the HRA, the court might be prepared to take a stance that differed from that taken in *Pro-Life*. The degree of deference shown to the media body in that instance might, and should, be repudiated.

In the *Campbell* case discussed below, the House of Lords showed no inclination to defer to the newspaper's expertise in determining how far it had balanced public interest and privacy factors in taking the decision to publish the photos of Naomi Campbell. Instead, the Lords engaged in a rigorous scrutiny of that decision. It is hard to see why the mechanism by which the claimants get into court (breach of confidence or s 7(1)(a) HRA) should affect this stance. It is also difficult to see why greater deference should be paid to a broadcaster as opposed to a newspaper editor. Possibly there is an argument that Ofcom has greater expertise than a media body in this matter, but it would be hard to argue that it would have the experience or authority of a court in dealing with the quintessentially legal problem of the balancing act between Arts 8 and 10 based on proportionality.

4 Specific reporting restrictions

Victims of sexual offences

A number of special restrictions also apply to the victims of certain sexual offences. Under s 4(1)(a) of the Sexual Offences (Amendment) Act 1976, once an allegation of rape was made it was an offence to publish or broadcast the name, address or photograph of the woman who was the alleged victim. Once a person was accused of rape, nothing could be published by the media which could identify the woman. These restrictions were extended under s 1(1) of the Sexual Offences (Amendment) Act 1992 as amended by s 48 of the Youth Justice and Criminal Evidence Act 1999 and Sched 2. Section 1(1) covers a number of sexual offences as well as rape, and provides: 'where an allegation has been made that an offence to which the Act applies has been committed against a person,[188] no matter relating to that person shall during

---

188   Male rape victims are also covered under the CJPOA 1994, s 142, as are offences of incitement, attempt, conspiracy.

that person's lifetime be included in any publication.' So it is a specific offence to publish a picture of the alleged victim, or her name and address, once an allegation of a rape offence has been made. Once a person has been charged with a rape offence, no matter or article likely to lead members of the public to identify an individual as the complainant in relation to the offence may be published.[189] However, the courts do have powers to direct the restrictions to be removed; this may be done on the narrow ground of encouraging witnesses to come forward,[190] or on the broader ground that a refusal to lift the restrictions 'would impose a substantial and unreasonable restriction upon the reporting of proceedings at the trial and it is in the public interest to remove the restriction'. This clearly allows a judge to undertake a broad balancing act between the privacy rights of the woman – and the policy of encouraging women to bring cases to trial, given that rapes are notoriously under-prosecuted – and the media interest in reporting on trials, including, specifically the open justice principle.

Trial-related reporting restrictions – adults

There are a number of other statutory reporting restrictions,[191] including stringent limitations upon the reporting of pre-trial hearings,[192] details of vulnerable witnesses,[193] and the reporting of assertions made about others during a plea in mitigation. An order may be made prohibiting the reporting of such assertions where:

> an assertion forming part of the speech or submission is derogatory to a person's character (for instance, because it suggests that his conduct is or has been criminal, immoral or improper), and . . . that the assertion is false or that the facts asserted are irrelevant to the sentence.[194]

This provision, in catching derogatory and false allegations, is clearly intended primarily to safeguard the *reputations* of those caught up in the commission of criminal offences; it could cover, for example, an assertion that an individual had been unfaithful to her partner, put forward in a plea of mitigation about violent conduct towards that individual. But, where the allegation is true but irrelevant, the interest protected may be privacy, if, of course, the allegation relates to the person's private life, as in the example given. Again, the court has a discretion (it 'may make an order') rather than a binding duty to order the restriction: presumably under these provisions also, the open justice principle may be balanced against any relevant privacy or reputational interests.

This restriction, unlike those considered above, is not subject to any exception. Therefore, in that respect, it affords less recognition to freedom of speech, although it does not prevent the reporting of the case or discussion of it once it is over, so long as details likely to identify the victim are not revealed.

---

189 Section 4(1)(b).
190 Upon the application of the person accused of rape; the defendant must additionally show that his defence is likely to be substantially prejudiced without such a direction.
191 See for further discussion Barendt, E and Hitchens, L, *Media Law: Cases and Materials*, 2000, Chapter 7.
192 Sections 37 and 38, Criminal Procedure and Investigations Act, 1996.
193 Under s 25 of the Youth Justice and Criminal Evidence Act 1999.
194 Section 58(4), Criminal Procedure and Investigations Act, 1996.

Reporting restrictions relating to children

Introduction

The discussion concerns a range of restrictions on reporting, usually, although not invariably, linked to court proceedings, mainly intended to protect the identity of children. Reporting restrictions engage the 'privacy' of the child in the sense that the injunctions or orders are intended to protect the child's identity or other personal information. Thus in many instances her family life, her mental stability and her ability to form and develop relationships are also indirectly protected.[195]

Private hearings; statutory restrictions on identification

The restrictions in question could be variously categorised. A certain group of them affect the reporting of proceedings held in private and a substantial proportion of such proceedings involve cases concerning children. The common law rule is that all courts, in the exercise of their inherent power to regulate their own proceedings in order to ensure that justice is done, have a discretion to sit in private, but, due to the importance of the open justice principle, the discretion is to be exercised only in exceptional circumstances.[196] Certain statutes expressly provide for hearings to be held in private in relation to matters involving children.[197] However, the mere fact that a hearing occurs in private does not automatically mean that *reporting* of the proceedings is restricted. Under s 12(1)(a) of the Administration of Justice Act 1960 it will be a prima facie contempt to report on proceedings held in private[198] where they relate to: wardship, adoption, guardianship, custody, upbringing of or access to an infant.[199] It has been found that the press cannot report any aspect of wardship proceedings,[200] but this is not an absolute restriction:[201] it has been found to cover 'statements of evidence, reports, accounts of interviews' and similar information.[202] In relation to other information linked to the proceedings the test is whether the information is 'within the mischief which the cloak of privacy in relation to the substance of the proceedings is designed to guard against'.[203]

---

195 See *Bensaid v UK* [2001] 33 EHRR 10, para 47; *A and Byrne and Twenty-Twenty Television v UK* [1998] 25 EHRR CD 159.

196 *Scott v Scott* [1913] AC 417.

197 Adoption Act 1976 s 64; Magistrates' Courts Act 1980 s 69(2), as amended by the Children Act 1989 s 97. The Civil Procedure Rules 1998, Part 39 provide that a number of categories of hearing may take place in private; the decision whether to hold the hearing in private or in public is for the judge conducting it.

198 Under the 1960 Act s 12(2) it is permissible to publish the text of all or part of an order made by a court sitting in private unless the court, having power to do so, expressly prohibits its publication.

199 *Re F* [1977] Fam 58.

200 See *Re X (A Minor) (Wardship: Injunction)* [1984] 1 WLR 1422 (the Mary Bell case).

201 In *Pickering v Liverpool Daily Post and Echo Newspapers plc* [1991] 2 AC 370; [1991] 1 All ER 622, HL at 423 and 635 Lord Bridge observed: 'The essential privacy which is protected by each of the exemptions in paras (a)–(d) of s 12(1) attaches to the substance of the matters which the court has closed its doors to consider . . .'

202 *Re F (A Minor) (Publication of Information)* [1977] Fam 105.

203 *Pickering v Liverpool Daily Post and Echo Newspapers plc* [1991] 2 AC 370; [1991] 1 All ER 622 at 422–3 and 634.

Juveniles involved in criminal proceedings

Under s 39 of the Children and Young Persons Act (CYPA) 1933, a court (apart from a youth court) could direct that details relating to a child, who was a witness or defendant, including his or her name, should not be reported and that no picture of the child should be broadcast or published. The media could make representations to the judge, arguing that the demands of media freedom outweigh the possibility of harm to the child. In relation to any proceedings in any court the court may make an order under s 39 of the 1933 Act prohibiting publication of particulars calculated to lead to the identification of any child concerned in the proceedings.[204] Section 39 orders are especially problematic for journalists since they frequently provide insufficient guidance as to what can safely be published.[205]

Section 49 of the CYPA, as amended,[206] which relates to youth courts, places restrictions on the identification of children or young persons convicted in the youth court.[207] Section 49 provides for an automatic ban on publishing certain identifying details relating to a juvenile offender, including his or her name and address, although the court can waive the ban. Under the Crime (Sentences) Act 1997, the court can lift reporting restrictions where it considers that a ban would be against the public interest.

The s 39 restrictions were extended under s 44 of the Youth Justice and Criminal Evidence Act 1999, which now covers children involved in adult proceedings. The 1933 Act did not cover the period before proceedings begin. The 1999 Act prohibits the publication once a criminal investigation has begun, of any matter relating to a person involved in an offence while he is under 18 which is likely to identify him. Thus, juveniles who are witnesses are also covered. Under s 44(4), the court can dispense with the restrictions if it is satisfied that it is in the public interest to do so. Thus, s 44 brings the restrictions relating to juveniles in adult proceedings into line with those

---

204 Section 39 provides:

> 'In relation to any proceedings in any court the court may direct that–
>
> (a) no newspaper report of the proceedings shall reveal the name, address, or school, or include any particulars calculated to lead to the identification, of any child concerned in the proceedings, either as being the person by or against or in respect of whom the proceedings are taken, or as being a witness therein;
>
> (b) no picture shall be published in any newspaper as being or including a picture of any child or young person so concerned in the proceedings as aforesaid; except in so far (if at all) as may be permitted by the direction of the court.'

This section applies to sound and television broadcasts, and to cable programme services, as it applies to newspapers (Children and Young Persons Act 1963, s 57(4); Broadcasting Act 1990, Sched 20, para 3(2)).

205 See *Briffett v DPP; Bradshaw v DPP* [2001] EWHC 841 (Admin) and commentary: Dodd, M 'Children, the press – and a missed opportunity' [2002] 14(1) CFLQ 103–8.

206 As amended by Sched 2 to the Youth Justice and Criminal Evidence Act 1999.

207 Under the Crime Sentences 1997 s 45, which inserted s 49(4)(A) into the 1933 Act. The Youth Justice and Criminal Evidence Act 1999 s 44 creates an earlier starting point for the imposition of anonymity: protection against disclosure of identity for suspects, victims, witnesses now begins at the point of commencement of the criminal investigation. The Anti-Social Behaviour Act 2003 amended the Crime and Disorder Act 1998 s 1 to provide that s 49 does not apply to proceedings for orders under the 2003 Act, but that s 39 does apply.

under s 49 relating to youth proceedings, placing the onus on the court to find a good reason for lifting the restriction rather than having to find a good reason for imposing it. The discretion of the court is therefore more narrowly confined.[208] This is clearly an instance in which, as between the demands of press freedom and the interest in the protection of the privacy and reputation of juveniles, the latter interest has prevailed.

The ECHR (previously inherent) jurisdiction of the court

Where s 12(1)(a) or s 39 do not apply, the High Court may nevertheless grant an injunction restraining reporting that might reveal a child's identity or other matters relating to a child as an aspect of its inherent jurisdiction to protect minors.[209] After the decision in *In re X (A Minor) (Wardship: Jurisdiction)*[210] (the Mary Bell case), it can be seen that there was an increasing recourse to the court's asserted power to grant injunctions to restrain the publication of information about its wards or other children. The invention of this jurisdiction was described by Hoffmann LJ in *R v Central Independent Television*[211] in the following terms: 'the courts have, without any statutory or . . . other previous authority, assumed a power to create by injunction what is in effect a right of privacy for children'.

Instances in which the High Court is exercising its inherent jurisdiction tend to create the most wide-ranging impact on media freedom to publish since the reporting is not necessarily linked to court proceedings. The decisions discussed below suggest that the conflict between free expression and privacy is most likely to occur where the inherent jurisdiction is being exercised. It must be noted that after the House of Lords decision in *In re S*,[212] as discussed below, this term was replaced by the term 'the Convention jurisdiction'.

The inherent jurisdiction pre-HRA

In the pre-HRA era the courts sought to establish the boundaries between media freedom (recognised as an aspect of a common law right to freedom of expression)[213] and the privacy of the child in a series of decisions, culminating in the decision in *In re Z (A Minor) (Identification: Restrictions on Publication)*.[214] It was accepted that there was no need to strive to create a balance between media freedom and privacy once it was

---

208 See the discussion in *Lee* [1993] 1 WLR 103, pp 109–10.

209 In *In re M and N (Minors) (Wardship: Publication of Information)* [1990] Fam 211 Butler-Sloss LJ found: 'The power of the courts to impose restrictions upon publication for the protection of children is derived from the inherent jurisdiction of the High Court exercising the powers of the Crown as *parens patriae*. It is not restricted to wardship . . .' She relied on Lord Donaldson of Lymington MR who said in *In re C (A Minor) (Wardship: Medical Treatment) (No 2)* [1990] Fam 39, 46 that wardship 'is the machinery for its exercise'. Ibid, 223.

210 [1975] Fam 47.

211 [1994] Fam 192, 204.

212 *In re S (a child)* [2004] UKHL 47; [2005] 1 AC 593.

213 See: *R v Secretary of State for the Home Department ex p Simms* [1999] 3 WLR 328; *Reynolds v Times Newspapers* [1999] 4 All ER 609; *Derbyshire CC v Times Newspapers* [1993] AC 534.

214 [1995] 4 All ER 961 (CA).

found that the matter at issue related to 'upbringing', and so the paramountcy principle[215] applied: where it did so it determined the issue without any doubt in favour of the child's 'welfare'.[216] However, where the reporting at issue could be viewed as unrelated directly to 'upbringing', some sort of balancing act had to be undertaken. The tendency was to allow freedom of publication to prevail due to the perceived strength of the value of freedom of expression under the common law. Where a court viewed a case as raising a genuine public interest, it was unlikely to restrain publication, or place only minimal restraints on it. In *re W (A Minor) (Wardship: Freedom of Publication)*,[217] for instance, it was found that the placing of a ward who had previously suffered homosexual abuse, with a male homosexual couple as foster parents, raised public interest questions about the fostering policy of the local authority in question and therefore the newspaper in question had a right to raise such questions, despite the fact that it was accepted as quite possible that the identity of the ward would be disclosed.[218]

An outcome even more favourable to media freedom was reached in *R v Central Independent Television*.[219] A programme was made depicting a police investigation into a man subsequently convicted of offences of indecency. His wife, the plaintiff, did not wish her daughter, aged five, who knew nothing of his convictions, to know what had occurred and therefore sought to have the programme altered so that it would not be possible to recognise her husband. The Court of Appeal refused the injunction, finding that the protection for the privacy of children under the inherent jurisdiction would not extend to covering publication of facts relating to those who were not carers of the child in question and which had occurred before the child was born. In other words, the limits of the protection for children's privacy were indicated: no overt balancing exercise between privacy and freedom of expression was found necessary.

These decisions were clearly beginning to establish a spectrum of categories of case covering the balance to be struck between the privacy of the child and freedom of reporting. In the leading pre-HRA case, *In re Z (A Minor) (Identification: Restrictions on Publication)*,[220] these categories were made explicit. A first category of cases was recognised in which freedom of publication would *always* prevail over the welfare of the child. These were cases, it was found, which would fall beyond the proper limit for the invocation of the wardship or inherent jurisdiction since upbringing was not in issue and the risk of harm to the child by invading her privacy could be viewed as

---

215 Following s 1(1) of the Children Act 1989 (CA), the child's welfare is the court's paramount consideration when it determines any question with respect to the upbringing of the child. In *J v C* this was explained to mean: 'when all the relevant facts, relationships, claims and wishes of parents, risks, choices and other circumstances are taken into account and weighed, the course to be followed will be that which is most in the interests of the child's welfare.' [1970] AC 668, 710–11, *per* Lord McDermott.

216 Freedom of publication can be viewed as a 'circumstance' which a responsible parent would take into account; see discussion of this point in *In re Z (A Minor) (Freedom of Publication)* [1995] 4 All ER 961.

217 [1992] 1 All ER 794 (CA).

218 See also *In re C (A Minor) (Wardship: Medical Treatment) (No 2)* [1990] Fam 39, 46; *In re W (A Minor) (Wardship: Restrictions on Publication)* [1995] 2 FLR 466 (CA).

219 [1994] Fam 192.

220 [1995] 4 All ER 961 (CA).

incidental;[221] as Ward LJ put it: 'the freedom of the press is so fundamental that in this category it must triumph over welfare'. A further, second, category of cases was recognised – those in which the court does not have to determine an issue relating to upbringing but where the child's privacy is directly affected. In this category the child's interests would not be paramount and a balancing exercise had to be performed between the child's privacy and media freedom.[222] The third category covered instances where a question of the child's upbringing or of the exercise of parental responsibility *was* being determined, where the welfare of the child would be the paramount consideration, and her privacy interests would therefore trump competing free expression claims.[223]

In *In re Z* itself the issue before the court was found to relate to the upbringing of the child; a television company wished to make a film about Z (the daughter of Cecil Parkinson and Sarah Keays) and the treatment she was receiving for her particular educational needs at a specialised institution. It was envisaged that in demonstrating the methods and results of the institution Z would be identified and play an active part in the film. The court found that Z would be directly involved and that the proposed publicity would be harmful to her welfare. Therefore the instance was found to fall within the third category of case since the paramountcy principle applied. The court did not therefore need to perform a balancing act and refused to vary the injunction that was already in place preventing commentary on her situation.

In relation to the inherent jurisdiction, as the cases discussed from the pre-HRA era reveal, the courts had established a method of dealing with conflicts between the child's welfare and media freedom that largely excluded cases involving 'upbringing' from the battleground. It was only in respect of the second category of cases – where the child's privacy was at stake and at risk from media invasion – that the conflict had to be resolved, and in such instances, as indicated, it tended to be resolved in favour of the media, albeit with minimal restrictions on reporting. Doubtful distinctions were relied upon, as *In re Z* reveals, in pursuit of avoidance of the conflict. Once cases could be assigned to the 'upbringing' category on the one hand (the third grouping from *In re Z*) or the 'incidental' category on the other (the first grouping), conflict could be avoided. The general academic view was that adoption of these approaches had led to a failure to deal satisfactorily with the issues of both privacy and free speech at the level of principle.[224] That failure appeared to spring from the resistance of the

---

221 The court compared *In re X (A Minor) (Wardship: Jurisdiction)* [1975] Fam 47 with *In re X (A Minor) (Wardship: Injunction)* [1984] 1 WLR 1422. In the first case, concerning a book about X's father, the material was not a story about her or about the way she had been brought up, except indirectly since it revealed that her father was a philanderer. By contrast, the story in 1984 about X, Mary Bell's daughter, was directly about the fact that the authorities were permitting her to be brought up by a mother who was viewed by some as too evil to be entrusted with the care of a young child. See also *In re M and N (Minors) (Wardship: Publication of Information)* [1990] Fam 211, 231; *M v British Broadcasting Corpn* [1997] 1 FLR 51.

222 In *re W (Freedom of Publication)* [1992] 1 All ER 794 the child's upbringing was a central focus of the publicity, although at the same time the court did not consider that it was determining a question relating to upbringing.

223 This occurred in *Re C (A Minor) (Wardship: Medical Treatment) (No 2)* [1990] Fam 39 and in *In re M and N (Minors) (Wardship: Termination of Access)* [1990] Fam 211. In this category the court was seen as exercising its 'custodial' jurisdiction.

224 See: Cram, I, 'Minors' Privacy, Free Speech and the Courts' [1997] PL 410; Woods, L, 'Freedom of Expression and the protection of minors' (2001) 13(2) CFLQ 209.

courts, especially the Family Division, to the notion of individual rights as opposed to welfare.[225]

Effect of the HRA

However, the somewhat simplistic or mechanistic analysis from *In re Z* was thrown into jeopardy by the inception of the Human Rights Act, since where the third category was applicable the Art 10 guarantee was almost automatically abrogated, while where the first or second applied, the Art 8 rights of the child were likely to be afforded no or insufficient weight. The pre-HRA treatment of both rights appeared therefore to become inconsistent with the courts' duty under s 6(1) HRA and also with the interpretative obligation under s 3(1): it might have been expected that s 3(1) would be used to reinterpret the paramountcy principle under s 1(1) CA so that Art 10 no longer suffered automatic abrogation where restrictions on publication related to upbringing.

In what follows certain significant decisions are examined in which the *In re Z* categories were considered in the light of the HRA. However, by subtly manipulating the concept of 'upbringing', either under s 3(1) HRA or by using ordinary principles of interpretation, the courts have managed so far to avoid confronting the most difficult question of all – the compatibility of the paramountcy principle as currently conceived with Art 10. Instead the courts have succeeded in confining themselves to considering instances falling within the middle category from *In re Z* – wherein a balancing act between the two interests could be performed. But even in conducting that less difficult exercise, unsatisfactory reasoning processes were followed since there was, at least initially, a reluctance to accord Art 8 its status as a fully-fledged Convention right, once it came into conflict with Art 10.

The European Convention on Human Rights did not play a significant part in the decisions considered so far since, despite increasing reliance on the Convention in other areas of law pre-HRA,[226] the Family Division was content to balance media freedom against the child's welfare on the basis of common law understandings of those values. In *Kelly v BBC*,[227] however, the imminent inception of the Human Rights Act influenced the court to take Art 10 of the Convention fully into account. The case concerned a boy of 16, Kelly, who was made a ward of court after he disappeared from home to join a religious cult group. The BBC obtained an interview with him, but an order restraining publication of the detail of any report or interview with him or with members of the religious group was made, which the BBC challenged. It was accepted by both sides that the case was one in which the court did have jurisdiction to grant injunctive relief. The dispute between the parties was as to whether the case fell within the second or third of the three categories identified in *In re Z*. Clearly, if it was found to fall within the third, the paramountcy principle would apply and the interest in freedom of expression would be almost automatically overcome. Therefore it was crucial for counsel for the BBC to convince the Court that the case fell within the second category and then to argue that the injunction could not be justified as necessary in a democratic society, under Art 10(2).

225 See Butler Sloss LJ in *Re L (A Child) (Contact: Domestic Violence)* [2001] Fam 260 CA, para.294.
226 See, e.g., the Court of Appeal decision in *Derbyshire CC v Times Newspapers* [1993] AC 534.
227 [2001] 1 All ER 323; [2001] 2 WLR 253; [2001] Fam 59.

The Court did not find it entirely easy to decide what distinguishes cases in the second category from those in the third. Clearly, this turned on the meaning assigned to the term 'upbringing'.[228] Munby J concluded:

> Upbringing . . . involves a process in which the parent, or other person in *loco parentis*, is the subject and of which the child is the object . . . Section 1(1)(a) CA therefore applies only to those processes or actions of which the child is the object, and not to those in which the child is the subject.

Munby J went on to find that *In re Z* had created a distinction between cases such as *In re W*, in which four boys without their father's involvement had given interviews to journalists, and cases in which the parent actively encourages or brings about the involvement of the child with the media. *In re Z*, he found, fell within the latter category in which the child is the object since, as he put it, referring to the words of Ward LJ, Z's mother wished to 'bring up her child as one who will play an active part in a television film'. The *In re W* case was viewed as similar to the instant one since Kelly had given the interview without the involvement of his grandmother or mother. The case was therefore viewed as one not involving upbringing and as a result as within the second category; the paramountcy principle was inapplicable and therefore a 'so-called balancing exercise has to be performed.'[229]

In considering the claim of freedom of expression as compared with the need to safeguard the welfare of the child, Munby J pointed out that this exercise had in general been carried out in an unsatisfactory fashion in the Family Division due to its 'child-centred' approach.[230] He found that there was no question of 'balancing' freedom of expression against one or more of the interests identified in para 2 of Art 10: those who sought to bring themselves within the protection of para 2 had to demonstrate convincingly that the protection applied. He went on to find that the arguments in favour of suppressing the interview were not sufficiently convincing.[231] Since the arguments were fairly evenly balanced, and he had already found that Art 10(2) places the burden on those seeking to make the case for interference with freedom of expression, he determined that injunctive relief could not be justified. He further found that the grant of an injunction framed as widely as the one he was being invited to make would have been wholly disproportionate to any aim that could legitimately be pursued on Kelly's behalf.

---

228 See *In re Z* at p 29.
229 [2001] 1 All ER 323, 341.
230 'As Thorpe LJ [noted] in *In re G (Celebrities: Publicity)* [1999] 1 FLR 409, 418 . . . Hoffmann LJ rightly said in his judgment in *R v Central Independent Television plc* there is an inevitable tendency for the Family Division judge at first instance to give too much weight to welfare and too little weight to freedom of speech.'
231 It had been argued, *inter alia*, that Kelly would find it harder to reconcile himself with his family if the interview were broadcast. Munby J found that the argument that further publicity might be in his best interests was as plausible as the contrary argument put forward – that it would be opposed to them.

A similar instance arose in *In the matter of X (a child)*,[232] but the significant difference was that in the few months since *Kelly* the HRA had come into force. It prompted the Court to go even further than *Kelly* had done in accepting the primacy of media freedom once it was free to do so, having once again succeeded in excluding the instance from the third 'upbringing' category.[233] The Court proceeded to make the important finding, foreshadowed in *Kelly*, that while the exercise of its discretion had been referred to many times before October 2000 as a balancing exercise, such an exercise was no longer appropriate after the coming into force of the HRA. The Court determined that it must rely on s 12(4) HRA and Art 10 in reaching its decision, and went on to find: '[this] is not a balancing exercise in which the scales are evenly positioned at the commencement of the exercise. On the contrary, the scales are weighted at the beginning so that Article 10 prevails unless one of the defined derogations applies when given a narrow interpretation.' The application was, however, granted on the basis that the injunction was too wide and it was varied accordingly. The same stance was taken in *Medway Council v BBC*[234] in an instance, which once again was not found to involve a question of upbringing, the scales were weighted so that Art 10 prevailed, subject to an application of one of the derogations, narrowly defined.[235] Interestingly, a narrow construction under s 3(1) HRA of s 1(1) CA, allowing the case to be excluded from the 'upbringing' category, was found to accord with the demands of Art 10 and s 12(4) HRA.[236]

Although the recognition of the importance of media freedom in *Kelly*, *In the matter of X* and *Medway Council* was arguably welcome, when compared to the possibility of an *over*-protective child-centred approach, the analysis in relation to Arts 8 and 10 in this line of authority was quite clearly flawed. This meant that Art 8 lost its Convention status as a fully-fledged right, and became instead merely a narrowly interpreted exception to the Art 10 right of 'freedom of expression.' But conversely it is also hard to reconcile dicta in this line of authority with the Convention under the HRA since it assumes that where the paramountcy principle *is* found to apply, Art 10 can be almost automatically abrogated. However, judicial recognition of a need for a proper resolution of the conflict between Arts 8 and 10 in this context under the HRA where the principle does *not* apply was apparent in the most authoritative decision to touch on the issues raised in *Kelly* and in *Re X*.

---

232   [2001] 1 FCR 541.
233   A newspaper publisher had applied for an order to vary an injunction granted to the local authority restraining foster parents from disclosing to the newspaper information concerning the local authority's policies in respect of trans-racial fostering. Relying on the analysis of Munby J in *Kelly*, Mrs Justice Bracewell found that in this instance the child should be viewed as the subject of the process of upbringing, not the object, since the issue before the court concerned restrictions on media reporting of issues alleged to be raised by the child's history.
234   [2002] 1 FLR 104.
235   The case concerned the inherent jurisdiction of the court to restrain a broadcast of a consented-to interview with a boy of 13 who had been made one of the first subjects of an anti-social behaviour order.
236   At para 29.

Impact of Re S

In *re S (A Child)*[237] the Court of Appeal had to adjudicate on an appeal against an order made by Hedley J in the Family Division of the High Court.[238] The appeal raised a short but difficult point: 'can or should the court [under the inherent jurisdiction] restrain the publication of the identity of a defendant and her victim in a murder trial to protect the privacy of her son who is the subject of care proceedings'? The victim was S's brother and there was psychiatric evidence to the effect that S, as an already vulnerable child, would suffer greater trauma and be at greater risk of later mental illness if he was subjected to bullying and harrassment at school once the identity of his mother became known. Hedley J made an interim order restraining reporting that would identify S but modified it to include in para 8 the proviso that 'Nothing in this order shall of itself prevent any person (a) publishing any particulars of or information relating to any part of the proceedings before any court other than a court sitting in private . . .' At the *inter partes* hearing the newspapers argued that they should be able to publish the names and photographs of both parents and of S's dead brother. In particular, they wanted to publish photographs of S's brother with his mother. Since S was the same age as his brother was when he died and they resembled each other, the photographs would indirectly identify S. The judge decided that the exception in para 8(a) should remain in the order.

On appeal by the child, the Court of Appeal found, unanimously, that the question before them did not concern a matter of upbringing since, as Lady Justice Hale found:

> In deciding whether or not to make this order, the court is not exercising its jurisdiction over how CS is to be brought up. That is being done in the care proceedings. Nor is it deciding how any aspect of parental responsibility should be met.'[239]

Therefore this was not an instance in which the paramountcy principle applied. Interestingly, the first instance judge had considered that even if the child's welfare had been the paramount consideration, he would have decided in the same way. The Court of Appeal disagreed, Lady Justice Hale finding that when the child's welfare is the paramount consideration, 'it rules on or determines the issue before the court. It is the trump card' (emphasis in the original).[240]

Despite this finding, it must be asked whether *Re S* was not in fact concerned with upbringing, albeit indirectly. According to the evidence of an expert psychologist S

---

237 [2003] 2 FCR 577; (2003) 147 SJLB 873. See also *Harris v Harris* [2001] 2 FLR 895 in which, while there was no detailed consideration of the balancing exercise between Art 10 (and 11) on the one hand and Art 8 on the other, Munby J accepted (at para 384) that the approach adopted by Sedley LJ in *Douglas v Hello!* [2001] QB 967 should be followed in which Art 10 was *not* given presumptive priority.

238 19 February 2003.

239 As she put it: 'Parents cannot prohibit press reporting of criminal proceedings in order to protect their children from harm, however much they might like to be able to do so' (para 22).

240 *Per* Lady Justice Hale, para 62. In *Clayton v Clayton* [2007] 1 All ER 1146 the Court of Appeal agreed that the father's Art 10 rights must be balanced against the child's Art 8 rights but still took the view that the issue was governed by s 1 CA 1989. They avoided tackling the problem posed by the paramountcy principle. See also *Re Webster* [2007] 1 FLR 1146.

was more likely to suffer mental illness due to the results of the publicity and the father, who was his main carer, would have to deal with those effects. If the child had to move school or home due to bullying after the publicity that would again affect his upbringing. Perhaps most pertinently of all, the placement of the child with the father was also likely to be affected by the publicity since the father was barely coping with the situation and might have failed to cope with further stress and trauma suffered by an already vulnerable child as a result of the publicity. S might have encountered it himself since he might have seen articles and pictures in the media about his dead brother and his mother. He was also likely to suffer harassment and teasing at school once the identity of his mother and further details of the crime became more widely known, during the period of the trial. That was also the period during which his own trauma and stress due to loss of his brother were likely to be at their height.

In comparison, the upbringing of the child in *In re Z* was unlikely to be directly affected to her detriment or as an indirect effect of the broadcasting of the documentary, although possibly she might have become aware of secondary publicity as a result of it. Thus the only way in which the documentary could have been detrimentally linked to Z's upbringing would have been via the ultimate effects of the publicity. This was also the case in *In re S*. The only difference between the two instances was that in the one instance the child was directly involved in the documentary, while in the other the child was not directly the subject of the press coverage. Taking account of the view of the mother in Z that the child would *benefit* from participation in the documentary, while all those involved in S's upbringing, and expert opinion, considered that the media coverage would be extremely detrimental to him, it is suggested that the distinction between direct and indirect effects on 'upbringing' is a spurious one.

The *Re S* findings also indicate that it is very unlikely that the welfare principle will ever be found to apply in these instances of indirect effects on upbringing via media reporting. This is clearly the preferred course for the *courts* since it avoids a problematic conflict between s 1(1) CA and Art 10. But it might also mean that the courts are likely to be reluctant to focus too strongly on the effect of reporting on the family and private life of a child, since so doing appears to draw the effects on upbringing back into the equation. It creates tension in the decision since at one stage in the reasoning upbringing is excluded, but at a later stage it potentially re-enters the reasoning process when the private and family life claim is being balanced against the speech claim. This is precisely what occurred, as discussed below, in the House of Lords decision in *In re S*. The better solution, considered further below, is to reinterpret the welfare principle under s 3(1) HRA in order to avoid a conflict with Art 10 and to accept a broad definition of the term 'upbringing'. So doing might encourage the courts to focus strongly on the effects of reporting on upbringing, meaning that the significant issues truly at stake under the private and family life claim manage to obtain a hearing.

Having found that the welfare principle did not apply, the Court of Appeal went on to find that the case fell within the scope of the inherent jurisdiction of the High Court.[241] But following the House of Lords decision in *Re S*[242] it is no longer necessary

---

241 At para 40.
242 *In re S (a child)* [2004] UKHL 47; [2005] 1 AC 593.

in these cases to show that the inherent jurisdiction applies. The House of Lords in *Re S* found unanimously that since the 1998 Act came into force, the earlier case law about the *existence* and scope of inherent jurisdiction did not have to be considered in the instant case or in 'similar cases'. Lord Steyn said: '*The foundation of the jurisdiction to restrain publicity in a case such as the present is now derived from convention rights under the ECHR* (emphasis added).'[243] In other words, the jurisdiction is not the 'vehicle' allowing for the balancing exercise to occur – the Convention rights themselves provide the vehicle.

At first glimpse this looks like the creation of a form of direct horizontal effect, discussed in Chapter 4, since it would appear that in relation to assertions of a need for restraint to protect the privacy of the child there would be no need for the inherent jurisdiction even to *exist*. Further, the rights under the HRA would not be expected to deliver less than the existing cause of action which could have acted as the vehicle for their delivery. Possibly they could deliver *more* and that would then represent a form of direct horizontal effect since it would mean that there would not be an infusion of the right into the existing cause of action, but a replacement of that existing cause with an extended protection based only on the rights. In other words, Lord Steyn appeared to be stating that the technicalities of the inherent jurisdiction could be discarded and its place taken by the Convention rights. That would be direct horizontal effect as normally understood – the creation of a new cause of action allowing private parties to rely on the rights against each other. There would be no need to rely on an existing cause of action, as was thought to be the case in *Campbell*,[244] in the context of privacy generally.

But this part of Lord Steyn's judgment was highly problematic since it was ambiguously expressed; it might appear that *adults* could seek to rely on it in instances in which the action for breach of confidence would not be available, but where a Convention right – normally Art 8 – arguably applied. The obvious example would be in harassment cases where there were difficulties in relying on the Protection from Harassment Act 1997.[245] However, leaving aside the question of Art 8's applicability to harassment, it is suggested that Lord Steyn did not intend that the new 'ECHR jurisdiction' could be extended to adults. The true explanation for the creation of the new jurisdiction is, it is contended, that the court is taking the place of the state in terms of protecting the child and that in this instance alone a form of direct horizontal effect has been created since there is little to be gained from seeking to distinguish the courts' duty under s 6 HRA from its former duty under the inherent jurisdiction. It is arguable that at the international level the Convention allows for vindication of the right to private life in instances (such as adopting intrusive means in order to obtain information)[246] where the Human Rights Act provides for no such vindication, due to its inherent limitations – the need to find a public authority to sue, or an existing cause of action, or an

---

243 At para 23.
244 [2004] 2 WLR 1232; see above pp 826–27.
245 See pp 871, 873 below.
246 See *Von Hannover v Germany* (2005) 40 EHRR 1; (2004) Appl No 59320/00; on one view the use of intrusive methods by reporters appeared to play a part in the decision to find that a breach of Art 8 had occurred. However, it now appears that that is not the reading of the decision that is being adopted domestically; see p 914 below.

applicable statutory provision. But Lord Steyn's remarks, ambiguous as they were, do not appear to provide a basis for affording Art 8 an ability to operate beyond those limitations, at the domestic level. The only instance in which, conceivably, a cause of action could arise outside those limitations after *Re S*, would be one where, had it arisen in the past, the child's welfare would have been viewed as so doubtfully at stake that the inherent jurisdiction could not have been found to apply but where, now, Art 8 could be viewed as applicable. It should also be noted that the jurisdiction of the High Court to protect juveniles caught up in the criminal justice system has been extended to cover vulnerable adults with mental health problems.[247]

The House of Lords' decision in *Re S* demanded abandonment of the reliance on the inherent jurisdiction in favour of reliance on the Convention rights. Therefore if a child had an Art 8(1) claim to respect for his/her private life, even if previously the inherent jurisdiction would have been inapplicable, a cause of action appears to arise and the claim has to be tested against the competing Art 10 claim of the media. The problem, however, with speaking of the application of the ECHR jurisdiction, or indeed the extension of the inherent jurisdiction in reliance on s 6 HRA, is that, as touched on earlier, tension between accepting indirect horizontal effect and creating direct effect arises. If it is assumed, in any event, that a cause of action arises, it is clear that as the Article 8 claim is weak, the Art 10 claim will probably prevail, but this should not be an *automatic* presumption.

Thus, Lady Justice Hale's judgment in *Re S* – endorsed by the House of Lords in *Campbell*[248] – represents the closest approach yet, not only to a proper understanding of the method of resolving conflicts between Convention rights, but also to a partial acceptance of the need for the Family Division to confront fully the changes in judicial reasoning that the Human Rights Act necessitates. It demonstrates a complete break with the mistaken approach adopted in *Kelly*, *X* and *Medway Council* in which freedom of speech was given automatic priority once it was found that the paramountcy principle did not apply. However, highly significantly, by excluding the case on somewhat doubtful grounds from the 'upbringing' category, the Court of Appeal in *Re S* backed away from a confrontation between that principle and Art 10 under the HRA. That principle, if it is to act as a 'trump card', is clearly incompatible with the Convention values. Below, the general question of the proper reconciliation of the conflict between Arts 8 and 10, even where upbringing *is* in issue, or where the child's privacy is only indirectly or inferentially affected, is considered in more detail in relation to all reporting restrictions designed to protect children.

The path forward does not involve, it is argued, continuing to refine the definition of upbringing almost out of existence in this context by the use of exclusionary interpretations under s 3(1)HRA so as to avoid invoking the paramountcy principle (as in *Re S* or *Medway Council*) in order to avoid the difficult questions raised in a conflict with Art 10. Instead, it involves re-defining the paramountcy principle under s 3(1) so that even where it *is* in play, the conflict between Arts 8 and 10 can be properly resolved. At present resolution of the conflict is merely precluded since due

247 *In re A Local Authority (Inquiry: Restraint on Publication)* [2003] EWHC 2746 (Fam); [2004] 2 WLR 926 at paras 66 and 86–97.
248 [2004] 2 WLR 1232.

to the effect of the absolutist presumption of the principle, the Art 8 right to respect for family life of the child[249] will – in effect – always win out where it clashes with Art 10, thereby denying Art 10's status as an individual right. The Strasbourg approach to clashes between Arts 8 and 10 not only indicates that the paramountcy principle as currently conceived is incompatible with the demands of the HRA, but also underpins and confirms the *Re S* and *Campbell* approach[250] – that Art 10 should not be afforded presumptive priority where the principle does not apply. At present the courts have not accepted that approach, preferring instead to interpret cases of media publicity in this context as not engaging the paramountcy principle, and it is predicted that they will continue to take this course unless a case too similar to *In re Z* arises. Thus in these cases the key question in this context is now simply – is the child's Art 8 right engaged? If so it must be balanced against the media's Art 10 right, on the *Campbell* model, as discussed below, in Section 8. The *In re Z* categories appear to have lost their significance after *Re S*.

Impact of the HRA

The most important concern arising from the use of these reporting restrictions is the fear that they may create unacceptable curbs on the freedom of the press and broadcasters. The main safeguard for media freedom is the possibility that the restrictions, apart from that of anonymity in relation to certain sexual offences, may be dispensed with in the public interest. In the HRA era, Art 10 jurisprudence is becoming an increasingly important influence upon development of the public interest test, so that it is now the principal mechanism for a balanced resolution of rights to privacy (and, on occasion, to life) and to freedom of expression. It is apparent from the Convention jurisprudence that, where two Convention rights come into conflict, some kind of balancing act between the two needs to be undertaken.[251] Although jurisprudence in this area is still quite limited, it appears that the margin of appreciation becomes particularly significant here, so that states tend to have a fairly wide discretion in resolving the conflict.[252] Domestic courts therefore have an appreciable degree of latitude in determining where to strike the balance between the two interests. Section 12 of the HRA, which enjoins the court to have 'particular regard' to Art 10 when making any order which might infringe it, is relevant when civil matters, including wardship proceedings, or the doctrine of confidence, are in question. Since throughout this chapter the effect of s 12 and

---

249 It has been accepted in a number of the domestic cases that the welfare of the child can be viewed as an aspect of his or her Art 8 rights. See, e.g., *Medway Council v BBC* [2002] 1 FLR 104, para 29.

250 [2004] 2 WLR 1232.

251 *Otto-Preminger Institut v Austria* (1994) 19 EHRR 34, para 55. The two Convention rights in conflict there were free speech itself and – so the court found – the right to religious freedom, protected by Art 9.

252 Ibid The restriction on Art 10 entailed by the seizure of an allegedly blasphemous film was justified by reference to the Art 9 right to freedom of religious belief. The Court applied a wide margin of appreciation, and simply said that 'the content of the film cannot be viewed as incapable of grounding' the conclusion of the national authorities that seizure was justified (para 56). Thus, the test applied was reminiscent of the narrow *Wednesbury* standard of unreasonableness. See also *Wingrove v UK* (1997) 24 EHRR 1. Both decisions are discussed in Chapter 6, pp 488–91.

of public interest tests in relation to Art 8 rights is a central theme, the question of seeking to resolve the conflict between Arts 8 and 10 is considered fully in one section, below.[253] The courts have more leeway in the context of the ECHR jurisdiction to consider solutions to this conflict, the arguments below as to the engagement of Arts 8 and 10, and the discussion of methods of resolving the conflict between them, would apply equally to the automatic reporting restrictions and to orders made under the other current powers.

5 Trespass, defamation, harassment; proposals for a new privacy tort

This section begins by considering a range of proposals put forward pre-HRA by government-appointed bodies for providing protection for privacy, which provide the backdrop to the recent development of the doctrine of confidence into a privacy law. Although a privacy law has now emerged, it is not an all-encompassing one that could cover, for example, persistent pursuit of a person by reporters or the use of bugging devices. The Protection from Harassment Act 1997 might cover such intrusions as considered below. This section then moves on to demonstrate why other tortious remedies proved inadequate to protect personal information, leading the courts to develop the doctrine of breach of confidence, under the impetus of the HRA.

Proposals for civil and criminal liability for invasion of privacy

No general, comprehensive tort of invasion of privacy exists in the UK, as in the US,[254] to control the activity of the media or others in intruding on the privacy of individuals, using harassment or surreptitious techniques to obtain information regarding an individual's private life, and then publishing the details, perhaps in exaggerated, lurid terms. It was recently confirmed in *Wainwright v Home Office*[255] that there is no English common law tort of invasion of privacy. But there is, as indicated above, a statutory tort of invasion of privacy, under the HRA, applicable only against public authorities, relying on Art 8 and s 6 HRA. Also, protection for personal information is now available under the new privacy liability discussed below, and under a number of statutory provisions.

In the early 1990s, prior to these developments, comprehensive legal controls were proposed, intended to be used against the media and others when private information was published. These controls were to affect both the publication of the information and the methods used to obtain it. When information such as a photograph is obtained, there may often be some kind of intrusion on property, albeit of a nebulous kind, such as long-range surveillance. Proposals regarding legal controls relevant to the publication of information will be considered first, followed by proposals regarding the legal control of intrusions.

---

253 See pp 937–81.
254 US Restatement 2d Torts (1977) No 652A.
255 Lord Hoffmann's speech to this effect was agreed with in full by Lord Hope of Craighead and Lord Hutton: [2004] 2 AC 406, paras 28–35. See for discussion of *Wainwright*: Chapter 11, pp 1176–81.

Proposals for the enactment of a tort of invasion of privacy in the UK centred around the protection of personal information. Article 8 ECHR under the HRA, as interpreted in *Douglas and Others v Hello!*,[256] but more importantly now in *Campbell*,[257] has brought about a dramatic development of the existing doctrine of breach of confidence, with the result that greatly increased protection for control of personal information has been created. However, there is still an argument for providing further protection for privacy by means of a statutory tort balanced by wide ranging and carefully drawn specific public interest defences. Such a tort could provide a more comprehensive protection for privacy, including protection from intrusions where no publication occurs. Although such comprehensive protection may now be available, as the discussion below and in ss 6 and 7 indicates, it is provided on a piecemeal basis and is not available in dedicated statutory privacy provisions.

Support for a statutory tort was, however, far from unanimous in the relevant committees which have considered the issue. Thus, while the Younger Committee in 1972[258] recommended the introduction of a tort of disclosure of information unlawfully acquired, Calcutt 1[259] decided against recommending a new statutory tort of invasion of privacy relating to publication of personal information, although the Committee considered that it would be possible to define such a tort with sufficient precision. Calcutt 2[260] recommended only that the government should give further consideration to the introduction of such a tort, but the National Heritage Select Committee[261] recommended its introduction, as did the later Lord Chancellor's Consultation Paper, the Green Paper.[262] As indicated above, these proposals were abandoned in July 1995,[263] although they found some expression in the DPA 1998.[264] It may be noted that the Lord Chancellor's Paper did not propose an extension of legal aid to those seeking redress under the proposed new civil privacy liability.

The possible definition of the proposed tort put forward by Calcutt 1 was designed to relate only to personal information which was published without authorisation. Such information was defined as those aspects of an individual's personal life which a reasonable person would assume should remain private. The main concern of the Committee was that true information which would not cause lasting harm, was already known to some, and was obtained reputably might be caught by its provisions. The Lord Chancellor's proposals were wider: there should be a new cause of action for 'infringement of privacy causing substantial distress' (para 5.22). No definition of

---

256 [2001] 2 WLR 992.
257 [2004] 2 WLR 1232. See pp 911–13 below. For comment, see: Lindsay, D, 'Naomi Campbell in the House of Lords: Implications for Australia' (2004) 11 *Privacy Law & Policy Reporter* 4–11; Morgan, J, 'Privacy in the House of Lords – Again' (2004) 120 LQR 563–66.
258 Op. cit., fn 1.
259 Op. cit., fn 1.
260 Op. cit., fn 1.
261 Op. cit., fn 1.
262 The paper was released on 30 July 1993 – CHAN J060915NJ.7/93. See 143 NLJ 1182 for discussion of these proposals.
263 The White Paper, *Privacy and Media Intrusion: The Government's Response*, Cmnd 2918, July 1995, found against creation of a statutory tort.
264 See below, pp 920–37.

privacy was offered, although it was stated to include matters relating to health, personal relationships and communications, and freedom from harassment.

Legatt LJ asserted confidently in *Kaye* that a right to privacy exists in the US which will be enforced and suggested that such a right should be imported into UK law, but this proposition has come under attack,[265] on the basis that the scope of US privacy rights is severely limited by a general defence of 'newsworthiness'[266] which allows many stories disclosing embarrassing and painful personal facts to be published. Clearly, there is little value in looking to the US for a model if a UK statutory right to privacy is ever enacted. The Calcutt Committee did not consider that liability should be subject to a general defence of public interest on US lines, although it did favour a tightly drawn defence of justified disclosure. Under Calcutt 2 (para 12.23) it was proposed that it would be a defence to show that the defendant had reasonable grounds for believing that publication of the personal information would contribute to preventing, detecting or exposing the commission of a crime or other seriously anti-social conduct; or to preventing the public from being misled by some public statement or action of the individual concerned; or that the defendant had reasonable grounds for believing that publication would be necessary for the protection of public health or safety. The Green Paper invited comments on these defences and in particular on the question whether the public interest defence should be defined in general terms or whether it should be more specific (paras 5.62–5.67). The Green Paper proposed (para 5.45) that there should be a defence that the defendant had acted under any lawful authority. Prima facie, these defences seemed to range widely enough to prevent public figures from being able to use the tort to stifle legitimate investigative journalism. The defence of seeking to prevent the public from being misled by some public statement or action of the individual concerned would be, it is submitted, essential to draw a clear distinction between the private citizen and the public figure, and to ensure the accountability of the latter.

Further proposals for reform aimed at methods of obtaining information were also put forward. The Younger Committee proposed the introduction of a tort and crime of unlawful surveillance by means of a technical device, and both Calcutt Committees[267] recommended the creation of a specific criminal offence providing more extensive protection – a recommendation which was backed by the National Heritage Select Committee[268] when it considered the matter.

The clause creating the offence under Calcutt 2 also offered the individual whose privacy has been invaded the possibility of obtaining injunctions in the High Court to prevent publication of material gained in contravention of the clause provisions; it was also proposed that damages should be available to hold newspapers to account for any profits gained through publication of such material. Under the proposal criminal liability would have been made out if the defendant did any of the following with

---

265 Bedingfield, D, 'Privacy or publicity: the enduring confusion surrounding the American tort of invasion of privacy' (1992) 55 MLR 111.

266 Bedingfield ibid cites the example of *Kelley v Post Publishing Co Mass* [1951] 98 NE 2d 286. A father was unable to restrain publication of a picture of the severely injured body of his daughter due to the finding that the accident was newsworthy.

267 Op. cit., fn 1.

268 Op. cit., fn 1.

intent to obtain personal information or photographs, in either case with a view to their publication: entering or remaining on private property without the consent of the lawful occupant; placing a surveillance device on private property without such consent; using a surveillance device whether on private property or elsewhere in relation to an individual who is on private property without his or her consent; taking a photograph or recording the voice of an individual who is on private property without his or her consent and with intent that the individual should be identifiable. This clause seemed to specify the forbidden acts fairly clearly and to be aimed at preventing what would generally be accepted to be, on the face of it, undesirable invasions of privacy; it is worth noting that France, Germany, Denmark and the Netherlands all have similar offences on the statute books. (It should be noted that the offence would not have covered persistent telephoning,[269] or photographing, interviewing or recording the voice of a vulnerable individual such as a disaster victim or a bereaved relative in a public place.)

Calcutt 1 and the Green Paper[270] proposed defences to the proposed criminal offences which were wider than the defences suggested in relation to a tort of invasion of privacy. Calcutt 1 proposed (para 6.35) that it would be a defence to any of the actions above to show that the act was done:

(a) for the purpose of preventing, detecting or exposing the commission of a crime or other seriously anti-social conduct; or
(b) for the purpose of preventing the public from being misled by some public statement or action of the individual concerned; or
(c) for the purpose of informing the public about matters directly affecting the discharge of any public function of the individual concerned; or
(d) for the protection of public health or safety; or
(e) under any lawful authority.

Calcutt 1, 2 and the Green Paper were silent as to the mental element required with respect to the defences. There appear to be three possibilities here which, for the purposes of exposition, will be examined using the example of a claim of defence (a). First, the defence would succeed only if it was shown that the forbidden act actually could have led to the exposure of crime, so that if it turned out that in fact no criminal activity had been present – though perhaps a reasonable person would have thought that it was – the defence would fail. Secondly, the defence would succeed if the defendant could show that she honestly and reasonably believed that she was acting with the purpose of exposing crime. Thirdly, it would succeed if the defendant could show that she honestly believed that she was acting with this purpose. It is submitted that the first possibility would be undesirable for three reasons: first, it could lead to serious injustice where a reporter had a reasonable suspicion which turned out later to be untrue; secondly, it would offend against the principle of criminal law formulated in *DPP v Morgan*[271] that the defendant should be judged on the facts as she believed them to be, and thirdly, it could act as a serious deterrent to investigative journalism.

---

269 This might be covered by the Protection from Harassment Act 1997, as discussed above.
270 Op. cit., fn 1.
271 [1976] AC 182.

The second possibility is an improvement, but it again falls foul of the *Morgan* principle; moreover, there would be a risk that judges might demand quite a high standard of reasonable belief so that journalists would have to produce substantial evidence justifying their suspicions in order to make out the defence – a burden which would again exercise a deterrent effect.

It is suggested that the third possibility was preferable; a journalist who honestly believes that she is acting in the public interest (within the terms of one of the defences) should not be criminalised. It may be feared that such a fully subjective test would always provide an escape from liability and thus render the offence useless. However, a journalist who merely asserted that she thought she was acting within the terms of one of the specific public interests, but was unable to adduce any grounds at all for her belief, would probably not be believed by the court. The other advantage of adopting this third possibility would be that it could come into play while the journalistic investigation was still at an inchoate stage so long as some evidence could be adduced supporting the necessary belief. On this basis, the proposed offence would provide a remedy against some unjustifiable invasions of privacy, but would be unlikely to deter serious journalism. However, the Lord Chancellor's Consultation paper favoured narrowing the defences by omitting the words 'seriously anti-social conduct' from defence (a) and curtailing defences (b) and (c). If this proposal was ever implemented, the public lives of public figures such as Ministers would be protected from scrutiny, an instance of curtailment of freedom of speech which would clearly prevent the full participation of the citizen in the democratic process.

Causing harassment, alarm or distress, and anti-social behaviour

The Protection from Harassment Act 1997 (PHA), which was also discussed in Chapter 8,[272] offers a remedy in respect of some forms of repeated intrusions on privacy. It was not aimed at persons such as reporters or photographers, but at 'stalkers'; however, it could be utilised in relation to repeated intrusions by journalists or on privacy. The use of the new tort of misuse of personal information discussed above does not provide a remedy in respect of intrusions aimed at obtaining information; it can only provide a remedy if information is obtained and sought to be published. It is *not* a new comprehensive privacy tort, covering all forms of privacy-invasion and no such tort is recognised in UK common law.[273] The use of the PHA against reporters would have to be balanced by Art 10 arguments; this point is returned to below.

PHA offences and civil liability

Sections 1 and 2 PHA make it an offence to pursue a course of conduct that amounts to harassment of another where the harasser knows or ought to know that this will be its effect. Apart from creating criminal liability for stalking, the Act also provides a

---

272 See pp 788–97.

273 There is no English domestic law tort of invasion of privacy. Previous suggestions to the contrary were dismissed by Lord Hoffmann, whose speech was agreed with in full by Lord Hope of Craighead and Lord Hutton, in *Wainwright v Home Office* [2004] 2 AC 406, paras 28–35.

civil remedy in s 3 in the form of damages or a restraining order. 'Conduct' includes speech (s 7(4)). The harassment must occur on more than one occasion (s 7(3)) and a defence of reasonableness is available (s 1(1)(c)).[274]

Use of the PHA against press intrusion

Since the remedies provided by the Act are statutory, s 3 of the HRA applies. The PHA is not dependent on acquiring or attempting to acquire information, but it might be applicable where individual reporters had pursued a particular individual on a number of occasions. The possibility that the Act could be used in respect of the invasion of privacy that occurs when a person – often a journalist – is seeking to obtain information about an individual by, for example, watching the home, interviewing neighbours, or planting bugging devices arises since such activities fall within Art 8. Thus, if there was any doubt in the matter, the term 'harassment' could be interpreted to cover such activities. Section 6 HRA applies to the *application* of the Act in particular instances.

Use of the PHA in respect of publication of information causing distress

It may be argued that s 3 of the PHA could also be used in respect of the publication of information. Bearing in mind the obligation of a court to interpret the PHA compatibly with Art 8 under the HRA, it could be argued that if on more than one occasion an article was published in a newspaper which caused profound distress to its subject due to its publication of private facts creating the indirect possibility of harassment or injury from members of the public who had read it, an injunction or damages could be obtained under s 3. An argument similar to this one was used successfully against the *Sun* newspaper in 2001.[275] The *Sun* had published an article and, on a further occasion, readers' letters, attacking a black woman who was a civilian employee in a London police station. She had reported a racist incident relating to an asylum seeker, with the result that two police officers were disciplined. The *Sun*, in an article attacking 'political correctness gone mad' and omitting a number of key facts (including the fact that a white police officer had also reported the racist incident), identified her and the police station where she worked and invited readers to express their views as to her conduct. A number did so, in very hostile terms. She received hate mail and was also very distressed by the items; since she worked on the front desk she felt very vulnerable to attack from members of the public. She left her job as a consequence. Damages were awarded against the *Sun* under s 3 of the 1997 Act and the decision was affirmed on appeal.

This was an interesting and entirely novel use of s 3 of the 1997 Act; it suggests that the judiciary are determined to find a remedy for the plaintiff who has suffered a gross breach of the right to respect for privacy under Art 8 even where no obvious remedy for the particular breach in question is available, and despite the effect of s 12 of the HRA. However, had there been one item of publication only – in which identifying as well as distressing details were given – it is doubtful whether the 1997 Act could

274 See further Chapter 8, pp 796–97.
275 *Thomas (Esther) v News Group Newspapers* (2001) WL 753464; judgment of 18 July 2001.

have been used, unless a particular article could be viewed as, say, being in two parts. This decision emphasises the need for specific remedies for invasion of privacy by the publication of identifying and distressing details. It is not clear that the new tort of misuse of private information discussed above, would cover all the circumstances in which publication of information might lead to harassment or threats. In this instance, for example, it was not self-evident that the information as to the location of the police station could be viewed as private.

A similar example would arise where a tabloid newspaper published a story in sensationalist terms about a person who had been acquitted of a serious offence, or about a person bringing an action for race discrimination, identifying the individual involved and/or their place of work. He or she might suffer distress due to the articles themselves and also severe harassment from neighbours and others, which might make it impossible to avoid abandoning their home. It is arguable that a remedy should be available in such a situation, although it would have to be balanced against the right to freedom of expression of the newspaper, since s 12 of the HRA would be applicable and Art 10 would in any event be relevant, due to the effect of s 3 HRA. The defence of reasonableness could be used as the mechanism for recognising the value of freedom of expression. Alternatively, it could merely be argued that in applying the statutory provisions, the duty of the court under s 6 HRA demanded that it should examine the effect of affording the remedy in Art 10 terms.

Similar offences

Similar arguments could also be used in respect of the offences created under the 1997 Act and of the similar offences created under the Public Order Act 1986,[276] s 1 of the Crime and Disorder Act 1998 and s 41 of the Criminal Justice and Police Act 2001, all of which were discussed in Chapter 8,[277] although, of course, the police would have to take the initiative. All, except s 41 of the 2001 Act, contain similar defences which would allow for recognition to be given to freedom of expression under s 3 of the HRA, although s 12 of the HRA would not be applicable since the proceedings would be criminal. The court in applying the PHA is bound to adhere to both Arts 8 and 10. Methods of balancing expression and privacy rights are considered below.

Conclusions

The discussion below of the balancing act between Arts 8 and 10 could be used under the PHA when its provisions are deployed against journalists, assuming that Art 8 covers

276 See the use of the 1986 Act, s 5, in *Vigon v DPP* [1998] Crim LR 298; (1998) 162 JP 115. (The defendant had positioned a video camera in the changing room attached to his market stall, in which women were changing into swimming costumes. He was charged with the offence under s 5 since it was found that the switching on and use of the camera had caused the women harassment, alarm and distress, and his behaviour was insulting to them.) However, the requirement of immediacy which has been found to apply to s 4 of the 1986 Act and which therefore probably also applies to ss 5 and 4A may preclude the use of these provisions in the circumstances envisaged (see *R v Horseferry Road Metropolitan Stipendiary Magistrate ex p Siadatan* [1991] 1 All ER 324). See further Chapter 8, pp 781–87, esp 786.
277 See pp 780–97.

journalistic harassment. The PHA may not be an appropriate means of curbing press intrusion, partly because it depends on a course of conduct and so would arguably not capture a very intrusive activity occurring on one occasion only. Also it contains no obvious mechanism protecting freedom of expression. It would therefore be more desirable to enact certain very specific and narrowly defined areas of liability, relating to particularly intrusive invasions of privacy, including harassment. However, there seems to be no prospect of this at present. So the PHA remains the key mechanism that can fill the gaps left by the new privacy liability.

Defamation and malicious falsehood

The law of defamation offers some protection to an individual who has suffered from the unauthorised disclosure of private matters, but the interest protected by defamation – the interest of the individual in preserving his or her reputation – is far from coterminous with the interest in preserving privacy. A reputation may not suffer, but the fact that personal information is spread abroad may nevertheless be hurtful in itself for the individual affected. Thus, no remedy was available in *Corelli v Wall*[278] which arose from publication by the defendants, without the plaintiff's permission, of postcards depicting imaginary events in her life. Such publication was not found to be libellous, and no remedy lay in copyright as the copyright was in the creator of the cards.

The ruling in *Kaye v Robertson and Another*[279] made clear the inadequacy of defamation as a remedy for invasions of privacy. Mr Kaye, a well-known actor, was involved in a car accident and suffered severe head injuries. While he was lying in hospital two journalists from the *Sunday Sport*, acting on Mr Robertson's orders, got into his room, photographed him and interviewed him. Owing to his injuries, he did not object to their presence and shortly after the incident had no recollection of it. The resultant article gave the impression that Mr Kaye had consented to the interview. His advisers sought and obtained an injunction restraining the defendants from publishing the photographs and the interview. On appeal by the defendants the Court of Appeal ruled that the plaintiff's claim could not be based on a right to privacy as such a right is unknown to English law. His true grievance lay in the 'monstrous invasion of privacy' which he had suffered but he would have to look to other rights of action in order to obtain a remedy, namely libel and malicious falsehood. The basis of the defamation claim was that the article's implication that Mr Kaye had consented to a first 'exclusive' interview for a 'lurid and sensational' newspaper such as the *Sunday Sport* would lower him in the esteem of right thinking people. The Court of Appeal held that this claim might well succeed, but that as such a conclusion was not inevitable it could not warrant grant of an interim injunction, basing this ruling on *Herbage v Times Newspapers and Others*.[280]

278 (1906) 22 TLR 532 (Ch).
279 [1991] FSR 62; (1991) *The Times*, 21 March; for comment, see Prescott, P, '*Kaye v Robertson*: a reply' (1991) 54 MLR 451; Bedingfield, D, 'Privacy or publicity: the enduring confusion surrounding the American tort of invasion of privacy' (1992) 55 MLR 111; Markesinis, BS, 'The Calcutt Report must not be forgotten' (1992) 55 MLR 118.
280 (1981) *The Times*, 1 May.

The court then considered malicious falsehood. First, it had to be shown that the defendant had published about the plaintiff words which were false. Their Lordships considered that any reasonable jury would find that the implication contained in the words of the article was false. As the case was, on that basis, clear cut, an interim injunction could in principle be granted. Secondly, it had to be shown that the words were published maliciously. Malice would be inferred if it was proved that the words were calculated to produce damage and that the defendant knew them to be false. The reporters clearly realised that Mr Kaye was unable to give them any informed consent. Any subsequent publication of the falsehood would therefore be malicious. Thirdly, damage must have followed as a direct result of the publication of the falsehood. The words had produced damage in that they had diminished the value of Mr Kaye's right to sell the story of his accident at some later date. That ground of action was therefore made out.

Therefore, an injunction restraining the defendants until trial from publishing anything which suggested that the plaintiff had given an informed consent to the interview or the taking of the photographs was substituted for the original order. However, this was a limited injunction which allowed publication of the story with certain of the photographs, provided that it was not claimed that the plaintiff had given consent. Thus, it seemed that no effective remedy was available for the plaintiff. Legatt LJ concluded his ruling by saying: 'We do not need a First Amendment to preserve the freedom of the Press, but the abuse of that freedom can be ensured only by the enforcement of a right to privacy.'[281] *Kaye* was a very telling decision: it is possible that had breach of confidence been argued in that instance it could have succeeded; but the case highlighted the need for the judges to develop a privacy remedy, if Parliament continued to refuse to do so. Confidence was not argued in Kaye because at the time it was not readily apparent that it covered situations in which there was no prior confidential relationship.

Trespass

It was suggested over 15 years ago[282] that there are sufficient remedies in the common law of trespass to cover at least the kind of situation which arose in *Kaye v Robertson*.[283] The physical intrusion into the hospital involved trespass on to property (because the reporters, given their purpose, could have no implied licence to be there). Kaye obviously could not have brought an action on his own account as his property had not been trespassed upon, but the solution would have been to join the hospital as co-plaintiff in the action. Once trespass had been established, the court could exercise its equitable jurisdiction to grant an injunction to prevent the defendants from profiting from their own wrong by publishing the material obtained by the trespass for gain. The case of *Chappell and Co Ltd v Columbia Gramophone Co*[284] was cited as support for this course of action. In that case, the defendants had wrongfully used the plaintiff's sheet music to make gramophone records. Although the making of the records themselves was not a violation of the plaintiff's legal rights, the court ordered their destruction on the grounds that the defendants should not be allowed to 'reap all the proceeds of their

281 [1991] FSR 621, p 104.
282 Prescott, P, '*Kaye v Robertson*: a reply' (1991) 54 MLR 451.
283 [1991] FSR 62.
284 [1914] 2 Ch 745, pp 752, 754, 756, CA.

wrongdoing'. However, it is clear that there is no guarantee that possible co-plaintiffs (such as hotel owners) would agree to join in such actions.

Thus, the remedy available even in a case of physical intrusion onto private land would not be certain. Further, an action in trespass would be of limited application in relation to the interviewing of disaster or accident victims and their relatives generally: a person might be interviewed at or near the scene of a disaster in a public place or in a semi-private place, such as a shopping mall, which reporters could be viewed as having an implied licence to enter. Where, in such instances, victims of a disaster did not consent to be interviewed, it would not appear that interviewing them could found a cause of action in trespass. Further, it should be noted that if detailed information regarding Mr Kaye's condition had been obtained without physically entering the hospital – by photographing him with a long range lens or perhaps by interviewing him over the telephone – an action in trespass, as the cause of action is currently conceived, would not be possible. Specific remedies for invasion of privacy are clearly more appropriate, subject to a broad public interest defence.

However, although it is clear that in the HRA era the doctrine of confidence has developed into a privacy remedy, and that therefore there is no longer a need to look to trespass to provide such a remedy, it is possible that eventually trespass will also show some development, under the impetus of the HRA. The findings in *Campbell*[285] and in *Douglas and Others v Hello!*,[286] considered below, as to the effect of the Act on the common law, would be equally applicable to trespass. As discussed above, a judge has a duty, under s 6 HRA and – where freedom of expression is in issue – s 12, to ensure that the common law reflects the Convention rights. In a case similar to that of *Kaye*, freedom of expression would be in issue and therefore, if a judge was faced with a plaintiff who was seeking to bring an action in trespass rather than in confidence, it is arguable that she should adapt the doctrine of trespass in order to provide a remedy for the invasion of privacy. This could arise where breach of confidence was inapplicable since the complaint concerned the *method* used to obtain the information, not the threatened disclosure of the information. It is now clear that trespass will not be developed under the HRA to provide a remedy in relation to the processing and publication of information, but possibly it could develop in respect of the invasion of privacy which occurs due to an intrusion which is not a physical intrusion on property – for example, watching the home, using a long range lens to take photographs of persons on private property, etc.

Conclusions

As indicated above, the proposals for new forms of liability for invasion of privacy were eventually abandoned. Obviously, there is now less need to create a new tort, since the doctrine of confidence has taken over the role such a tort would have had, in relation to the misuse of person information. Nevertheless, the development of the doctrine to cover the requirements of Art 8 of the Convention under the HRA 1998 may eventually prompt Parliament to introduce a new tort since they highlight areas covered by Art 8 but not by the new formulation of the doctrine.

285 [2004] 2 WLR 1232.
286 [2001] 2 WLR 992.

6 Liability for disclosing personal information under the new privacy doctrine

Introduction

The following discussion traces the creation for the first time in UK law of common law liability for invasion of privacy by the unauthorised disclosure of personal information. Of all the areas of law covered by this book, this one has undergone the most dramatic transformation under the impetus of the HRA. The discussion documents the incremental transformation of the doctrine of confidence into a privacy remedy.[287]

It covers liability for publishing personal information outside reliance on s 7(1)(a) of the HRA. In other words, it covers a remedy for invasion of privacy that can be utilised against private and public bodies. The previous section demonstrated why other tortious remedies proved inadequate to protect personal information, leading the courts to develop the doctrine of breach of confidence, under the impetus of the HRA, into a new 'law of privacy'. The doctrine of confidence has now established itself as a cause of action able to protect personal information from disclosure in most circumstances. It is coming to be termed a 'privacy law' – more specifically, a tort of misuse of private information – with increasing frequency.[288]

The general thesis of this discussion is that the doctrine of confidence has now shown that it can afford far more protection in this area than was previously thought,[289] but that an enormous amount of judicial labour has been and still is required to flesh out and give definition to the current action in order to give it a clear legal profile. It will be argued that any law protecting a person from unwanted publication of personal information must inevitably become 'a legal porcupine, which bristles with difficulties',[290] but that workable and principled solutions to the problems associated with the legal right to respect for privacy under Art 8 are being developed. In particular, it will be strongly contended that the perception of conflict between speech and privacy is often exaggerated and simplistic, and indeed that an examination of the values underlying each reveals them to be in many respects mutually supportive, rather than invariably antagonistic. In conclusion, it will be contended that the goals in view in developing a privacy law – the protection of human dignity and autonomy, the movement away from the demeaning and debasing pursuit of certain figures and the destruction of their privacy in order to sell newspapers, the consequent enhancement of the speech of the press and enrichment of our cultural life – are proving sufficient to encourage the judiciary to grasp at the possibilities which the HRA offers to develop a privacy law.

---

287 This section draws on parts of Fenwick, H and Phillipson, G, 'The Doctrine of Confidence as a Privacy Remedy in the Human Rights Act Era' [2000] 63(5) MLR 660–93.

288 See the comments in *McKennitt v Ash* [2006] EWCA Civ 1714, below, p 913.

289 The possibilities available under the doctrine were apparent pre-HRA: see the comments of Laws J in *Hellewell v Chief Constable of Derbyshire* [1995] 1 WLR 804, p 805 and the findings of the European Commission on Human Rights in *Spencer (Earl) v United Kingdom* (1998) 25 EHRR CD 105, discussed below. See also the post-HRA comments in *Douglas and Others v Hello!* [2001] 2 WLR 992, discussed below.

290 The phrase is borrowed from *dicta* in an administrative law case: *Inner London Education Authority ex p Westminster CC* [1986] 1 WLR 28.

Traditionally, the common law doctrine of breach of confidence protected some confidential communications,[291] and the breadth of the doctrine had for some time supported the view that it could provide a general means of protecting personal information, although this area of law had developed largely as a means of protecting commercial secrets. The Younger Committee, which was convened to report on privacy,[292] considered that confidence was the area of the law which offered the most effective protection for the privacy of personal information. For a time, however, less emphasis was placed on the ability of the doctrine to protect privacy in the discussions of both privacy and confidence which occurred following the *Kaye* case.[293]

The House of Lords in *AG v Guardian Newspapers (No 2)*[294] found that the ruling in *Coco v AN Clark (Engineers) Ltd*[295] conveniently summarised the three traditionally accepted key elements of the law of confidence: 'First the information itself . . . must have the necessary quality of confidence about it. Secondly, that information must have been imparted in circumstances importing an obligation of confidence. Thirdly, there must be an unauthorised use of that information to the detriment of the party communicating it.' Even if these elements were made out, publication of the information was still possible if the defence of public interest applied.

To satisfy the requirements of the first element, information must, it seemed, not be in the public domain and must not be trivial. The third element, unauthorised use of information, was fairly self-explanatory; as to detriment, it appeared from the cases either that unwanted revelation of private facts *per se* might constitute detriment for the purposes of the law of confidence,[296] or, alternatively, that detriment might not always be necessary.[297] However, it is in the second element – the circumstances in which the courts will find an obligation of confidence to have been imposed – that the most radical development has occurred. Under the traditional model of confidence, one of two ingredients had to be satisfied for such an obligation to arise. The first was that, at least in cases involving personal, as opposed to commercial information, there had to be some identifiable pre-existing intimate or necessarily confidential relationship between confider and confidant, such as a professional relationship of trust,[298] or marriage,[299] from which the obligation of confidence could be inferred, in the absence of an express agreement on the matter.

---

291 See generally Dworkin, G, *Confidence in the Law*, 1971, University of Southampton; Gurry, F, *Breach of Confidence*, 1991; Jones, G (1970) 86 LQR 463.

292 See *Report of the Committee on Privacy*, Cmnd 5012, 1972.

293 See the Calcutt Committee on Privacy and Related Matters (Cmnd 1102, 1990, para 32) and Wacks, op. cit., fn 1, p 56); compare the earlier view of the Younger Committee (*Report of the Committee on Privacy*, Cmnd 5012, 1972, p 26).

294 [1990] 1 AC 109.

295 [1969] RPC 41, p 47.

296 *AG v Guardian Newspapers (No 2)* [1990] 1 AC 109, p 265, *per* Lord Keith.

297 Ibid Lord Goff explicitly left the point open (ibid, pp 281–82), while Lord Griffiths (ibid, p 270) thought that it was required. The remainder of the House did not address the point. In *X v Y* ([1988] 2 All ER 650, pp 651 and 657) it was held *per curiam* that actual or possible detriment to the plaintiff was 'not a necessary precondition to injunctive relief' ([1988] 2 All ER 650, pp 651 and 657). In the recent *Source Informatics* case [2000] 2 WLR 953, the Court of Appeal did not attempt to resolve the matter, but appeared to favour Lord Keith's view.

298 See, e.g., *W v Egdell* [1990] Ch 359 (doctor-patient); *X v Y* (ibid); *AG v Guardian Newspapers (No 2)* [1990] 1 AC 109 (both employer-employee).

299 As in *Duchess of Argyll v Duke of Argyll* [1967] 1 Ch 302.

As discussed above, the courts have now accepted in this context that their duty under s 6 HRA means that they should develop the common law to reflect the Convention rights, including the right to respect for private life under Art 8. The discussion shows that each element of the traditional doctrine of confidence has undergone a remarkable change, allowing it to become a workable remedy for the unauthorised disclosure of personal information. The landmark decision was that of the House of Lords in *Campbell v MGN*.[300] While the new privacy law can now provide protection from the invasion of privacy that occurs when personal information is published, causing distress, it cannot directly protect persons from invasions of privacy – such as persistent telephoning or the planting of bugs – created by information-seekers. Section 8 below considers the means of balancing the new privacy remedy against speech.

The discussion below proceeds on the basis that there are now three main steps in a privacy claim: (1) the first question is whether the threshold test of a reasonable expectation of privacy has been passed on the basis that private information is involved; this includes considering whether the information should escape protection as being banal, trivial or anodyne; (2) it should be asked whether the 'limiting factor' that the information is in the public domain should be applied; (3) it should be asked whether publication of the information is in the public interest as part of the speech/privacy balancing act. These tests are drawn from *Campbell v MGN*, *McKennit v Ash*[301] and *HRH Prince of Wales v MGN Newspapers Limited and Others*.[302] The latter test is now best considered as part of the balancing act between Arts 10 and 8. However, it is still relevant in traditional confidence cases, so it will be considered below.

These three steps will be considered in turn. However, it must be remembered, not only that the privacy action has grown out of the confidence doctrine, but that the confidence doctrine is still relevant in non-privacy cases – and may also be pleaded within them as an alternative possibility. The fact that a traditional confidence claim would have succeeded is no longer an essential element of the new doctrine but, as discussed below, it will weigh heavily in the balance in favour of the privacy claim when it is balanced against the competing speech interest.

Confidence is also relevant in commercial cases, which are not the concern of this book, and in state cases, in which the government asserts a breach of confidence claim in respect of a leak or other use of government information, as in the well-known *Spycatcher* case, discussed in Chapter 7. So in order to trace the steps by which the privacy action has arisen from the confidence doctrine, while examining both the scope of the new privacy action and the nature of confidence claims, the discussion will begin by considering the transformation of the test for 'confidential' information into a test for 'private' information. If there is a reasonable expectation of privacy, the information can be viewed as private. This is not necessarily self-evident – the use of the term 'reasonable' precludes claims in which the claimant happened to be unusually sensitive about trivial or anodyne information relating to him. The discussion will move on to consider the question of the 'public domain' which is relevant in both confidence and

---

300 [2004] 2 WLR 1232. For further comment see: Lindsay, D, 'Naomi Campbell in the House of Lords: Implications for Australia' (2004) 11 *Privacy Law & Policy Reporter* 4–11; Morgan, J, 'Privacy in the House of Lords – Again' (2004) 120 LQR 563–66.
301 [2006] EWCA Civ 1714.
302 [2006] EWCA Civ 1776, [2006] All ER (D) 335.

privacy actions. It will then examine a test that is no longer needed in privacy actions – that of imposing an obligation of confidentiality. Indeed, the discarding of this test was the crucial step in the transformation of confidence into a privacy action. But it is still relevant in old-style confidence actions, and in any event an explanation of the steps by which it was discarded is crucial to an understanding of the method by which the present position has been reached. After a brief consideration of the 'public interest' test, the discussion concludes by returning to the key theme of discarding limiting factors that were aspects of the doctrine of confidence. The discarding of the so-called defence of waiver and the need to demonstrate detriment arising from the breach of confidence, have also aided in the transformation of the doctrine into a privacy remedy.

What is 'private' information?

What 'information' is protected under the new privacy law? The key factor is that the information is accounted private. In order to engage Art 8 at all, information must be viewed as private and, if already in the public domain, must be capable of causing further harm in terms of privacy-invasion by being re-publicised.[303] Therefore, the discussion below will begin by considering what constitutes personal information, and then go on to ask when it can be said to be in the public domain, two separate but linked issues. Since until recently most of the case law concerned commercial information,[304] the courts pre-HRA had not evolved any workable tests to decide what kinds of personal information should be protected, save for the requirement that the information must not be 'in the public domain' – a negative requirement considered below – and that it must not be mere trivial tittle-tattle. The traditional view was that equity would not intervene to protect trivial information.

Initially it appeared that the possibly inadequate scope of the confidence action in this area created a further potential problem. Confidence requires unauthorised use of personal 'information',[305] like many privacy torts which take as the root of the complaint the publication of 'private facts'.[306] On its face, therefore, it did not appear to encompass situations where there had clearly been some invasion of privacy, assessed intuitively, but where it was difficult to conceptualise what had occurred as concerning 'information'. An example would be a broadcast showing mourners at a funeral in acute emotional anguish.[307] The root of the complaint in such situations, it is suggested, is not that the 'fact' that a person is weeping, or that details of their appearance in mourning have been disclosed, but rather of mass intrusion through unwanted attention into a highly

---

303 See *Mills v News Group Newspapers* (2001) WL 720, below, p 889, on this point.
304 In such cases, the issue of whether the information is 'confidential' may be readily resolved by reference to its potential or actual commercial value.
305 See the definition in *Coco* [1969] RPC 41.
306 Privacy torts in the United states and New Zealand require the disclosure of identifiable private facts. A number of Canadian cases have also stressed this requirement, although it is not required by the strict words of the relevant section of the Canadian Charter: see Paton-Simpson, E, 'Private circles and public squares: invasion of privacy by the publication of "private facts"' (1998) 61 MLR 318.
307 Ibid, p 337.

personal situation.[308] Moreover, a requirement of identifiable 'information' could find it difficult to accommodate the importance of anonymity and context. For example, some people may be happy to appear on a public beach nude or topless when surrounded by others doing likewise, because in this situation their nudity becomes unremarkable and therefore un-remarked upon. If, however, a photograph is taken and given mass publicity through the pages of a newspaper or magazine, feelings of intrusion and violation justifiably arise.[309] The difficulty is that it might seem problematic to define such situations as involving protected information: the mere 'fact' that a person is weeping at a funeral seems too innocuous to count as 'personal information', while the normally private nature of the appearance of someone's unclothed body might appear to be lost by the voluntary public exposure of it on a beach.

Such an approach would have been, however, simplistic. Wacks has made the important point that 'any definition of "personal information" must . . . refer both to the quality of the information and to the reasonable expectation of the individual concerning its use'.[310] In other words, one cannot assess whether information is 'personal' or not, without looking at the use which the defendant has made or proposes to make of it. It now appears that the doctrine of confidence can accommodate such delicate assessments, as discussed below. It should be recalled that the doctrine protects against unauthorised use of information and so is capable of singling out particular actions of defendants as giving rise to liability. Moreover, there was never any reason why the 'reasonable man' test employed at one point to decide whether an obligation of confidentiality should be imposed, could not be pressed into service to determine what was to count as protected information in the first place. A reasonable man might be expected to understand that the activities of mourners at a funeral, or nude sunbathers on a beach, could be seen as personal in so far as such people reasonably expected that their behaviour would not be subject to unwanted mass attention. Thus, contrary to the doubts expressed on this point,[311] it is suggested that a duty of confidentiality was always able to attach in respect of particular uses of information, such as mass publicity.

It should be pointed out that the question whether information is personal can either pre-date the 'public domain' inquiry, considered below, or can be indistinguishable from it. Thus, it may be necessary to consider whether information remains viewed personal when it relates to an event occurring in a public environment. *Von Hannover* suggests that it can still retain that quality. If it is determined that it can be viewed as personal, a court can go on to consider whether nevertheless it has been disseminated to such an extent that it has lost the personal quality that it otherwise would have had.

---

308 For the argument that such matters should be included within the definition of privacy, see Gavison, R, 'Privacy and the limits of law' (1980) 89(3) Yale LJ 421; Paton-Simpson, ibid, pp 337–38; Reinman, J, 'Driving to the Panopticon: a philosophical exploration of the risks to privacy posed by the highway technology of the future' (1995) 11 Computer & High Tech LJ 27, p 30. For a contrary view, see Parent, op. cit., p 805, fn 21, above, at pp 306–7.

309 This example is used because of the propensity of press photographers to take photographs of celebrities in such situations.

310 Wacks, *Personal Information: Privacy and the Law*, 1980, p 24.

311 Wacks, op. cit., fn 1, p 56.

It appeared from *Stephens v Avery*[312] and *Michael Barrymore*[313] that information relating to an individual's sexual life would merit protection,[314] a decision clearly in harmony with the approach of Strasbourg[315] and the DPA 1998.[316] The US 'private facts' tort requires that 'the matter made public must be one which would be offensive and objectionable to a reasonable man of ordinary sensibilities'.[317] However, if, as has been argued, protection for informational autonomy provides the theoretical underpinning of the action to protect privacy, objective notions of offensiveness should not be the essential issue, since it is a person's ability to apply their own standards of openness which should – within limits – be protected.[318]

Well before the HRA era there were signs that the categories of information capable of being accounted sufficiently substantial were widening: information concerning an individual's sexual orientation (*Stephens v Avery*)[319] and physical appearance (*HRH Princess of Wales*) has been found to merit protection. Post-HRA in the 2005 decision in *Douglas v Hello!*[320] the Court of Appeal found:

> It seems to us that information will be confidential if it is available to one person (or a group of persons) and not generally available to others, provided that the person (or group) who possess the information does not intend that it shall become available to others.

Dealing at paragraph 83 of the same case with the issue of privacy, the Court said:

> What is the nature of 'private information'? It seems to us that it must include information that is personal to the person who possesses it and that he does not intend shall be imparted to the general public. The nature of the information, or the form in which it is kept, may suffice to make it plain that the information satisfies these criteria.

---

312 [1988] Ch 449.
313 [1997] FSR 600.
314 The decision in *HRH Princess of Wales* Transcript, Association of Official Shorthandwriters Limited, 8 November 1993 (which concerned photographs taken of the Princess exercising while wearing a leotard) gave some weak prima facie evidence that information regarding physical appearance may attract protection in some circumstances.
315 See *Lustig-Prean v UK* (1999) 29 EHRR 548; discussed in Chapter 15, pp 1520–21.
316 As indicated below, p 928, such information is classified as 'sensitive personal data' along with matters such as a person's religious and political opinions, and his physical and mental health (s 2). The processing of 'sensitive personal data' attracts a higher level of safeguards than normal data under Data Protection Principle 1(b) (Sched 1) as elucidated by Sched 3.
317 Prosser, D, 'Privacy' (1960) 48 Calif L Rev 383, p 396. The tort grew out of the Warren and Brandeis article ('The right to privacy' (1890) IV(5) Harvard L Rev 193, p 196). The Restatement (Second) of the Law of Torts, 625D defines the tort as follows: 'One who gives publicity to a matter concerning the private life of another is subject to liability to the other for invasion of his privacy, if the matter publicised is of a kind that (a) would be highly offensive to a reasonable person and (b) is not of legitimate concern to the public.'
318 See above, pp 805–6.
319 [1988] Ch 449.
320 (No 3) [2005] EWCA Civ; [2006] QB 125, at para 55.

Lord Nicholls of Birkenhead in *Campbell v MGN Ltd* found:[321] 'Essentially the touchstone of private life is whether in respect of the disclosed facts the person in question had a reasonable expectation of privacy'. Lord Hope of Craighead advanced a similar test:[322] '. . . a duty of confidence will arise whenever the party subject to the duty is in a situation where he knows or ought to know that the other person can reasonably expect his privacy to be protected'. He further said:[323] 'The underlying question in all cases where it is alleged that there has been a breach of the duty of confidence is whether the information that was disclosed was private and not public.'[324] His Lordship also referred to 'the right to privacy, which lies at the heart of the breach of confidence action'.[325] Lady Hale advanced the same test[326] and Lord Carswell endorsed this.[327] These tests were approved of by Lord Phillips in the Court of Appeal in *HRH Prince of Wales v Associated Newspapers Ltd*.[328]

In *Douglas v Hello!*,[329] the court accepted that the basis of the action is now the notion of a 'reasonable expectation of privacy',[330] and its purpose is the protection of 'the individual's informational autonomy'.[331] The Court summed up its view of the development of this area of law:

> Megarry J in *Coco v A N Clark* identified two requirements for the creation of a duty of confidence. The first was that the information should be confidential in nature and the second was that it should have been imparted in circumstances importing a duty of confidence. As we have seen, it is now recognised that the second requirement is not necessary if it is plain that the information is confidential, and for the adjective 'confidential' one can substitute the word 'private'.[332]

The Court went on to find that:

> . . . the House of Lords in *Campbell* . . . agreed . . . that the knowledge, actual or imputed, that information is private will normally impose on anyone publishing that information the duty to justify what, in the absence of justification, will be a wrongful invasion of privacy.[333]

So all that is needed is that the information is obviously private. That appears to cover all sorts of obviously private activities such as medical treatment (*Campbell*); it also

---

321 At para 21.
322 At para 85.
323 Ibid para 88.
324 Ibid para 92.
325 Ibid para 105.
326 At para 34.
327 At para 165.
328 [2006] EWCA Civ 1776, [2006] All ER (D) 335.
329 [2005] EWCA Civ 595 (Court of Appeal judgment on appeal from final trial); hereafter *Douglas III*.
330 *Douglas III* [2005] EWCA Civ 595 at para 80.
331 Ibid para 81.
332 Ibid para 83.
333 Ibid para 82.

covers private functions such as weddings (*Douglas*), and, according to *Von Hannover*, daily life activities that happen to be carried out in public. *Von Hannover* has received recent endorsement in the Court of Appeal in *McKennit v Ash*;[334] it was found that in considering an action to prevent the publication of confidential material and looking to Arts 8 and 10 of the European Convention on Human Rights, the Court was not prevented by Court of Appeal authority to contrary effect from applying the later case of *Von Hannover* in the European Court of Human Rights.

The first question, it was said in a complaint of wrongful publication of private information, was to ask whether the information was private in the sense that it was in principle protected by Art 8. In considering this issue, it was found that the first instance judge[335] had been entitled to consider *Von Hannover v Germany*[336] when considering whether Art 8 was engaged. The defendants had submitted that the court was bound to follow *A v B plc*[337] by the rule of precedent in *Kay v Lambeth London Borough Council*.[338] Having found that the width of the rights given to the media by *A v B* could not be reconciled with *Von Hannover*, Buxton LJ rejected the submission: the court in *A v B* had not ruled definitively on the content and application of Art 10; and thus, where *A v B* was not binding on the content of Arts 8 and 10, the court, it was found, had to look for that content to *Von Hannover*. The terms of *Von Hannover* were very far away from the automatic limits placed on the privacy rights of public figures by *A v B*; and, applying the correct considerations, including regard to *Von Hannover*, no error of law was disclosed. Buxton LJ concluded by stating that in an action for misuse of private information the first question to be asked is: 'is the information private in the sense that it is in principle protected by Article 8?'[339] That is now the test for determining whether information can receive protection or not.

The *form* of the information can be relevant in two respects. The form in which the plaintiff recorded the information may enhance the privacy claim – making it clearer that the information should be viewed as private.[340] It is more invidious in privacy terms to breach the privacy of, for example, a private diary or an obviously confidential document, expressly marked confidential. Both factors were relevant in the *Prince of Wales* case.

The form in which the defendant recorded the information may be relevant – text, still photographs, video footage. A number of decisions suggest that the courts pre-HRA had for some time been adopting a flexible approach to the *form* of the information.[341] In *HRH Princess of Wales*, Drake J had no hesitation in granting interim injunctions to prevent the *Daily Mirror* and others from publishing photographs of the Princess exercising in a gymnasium, taken by the gymnasium owner without her knowledge or

334 [2006] EWCA Civ 1714. First instance: [2005] EWHC 3003; [2006] EMLR 10.
335 Eady J sitting in private in the Queen's Bench Division ([2005] EWHC 3003 (QB)).
336 (2005) 40 EHRR 1.
337 [2003] QB 195.
338 [2006] 2 AC 465.
339 At para 11.
340 In the *Prince of Wales* case the Court of Appeal said at para 36: 'we consider that its form and content would clearly have constituted it private information entitled to the protection of Article 8(1) as qualified by Article 8(2)'.
341 See Fenwick, H and Phillipson, G, 'Confidence and privacy: a re-examination' (1996) 55 CLJ 447, pp 449–50.

consent. The plaintiff's case was based both on breach of contract and on confidence, but Drake J appeared to take the view that although the contractual claim was more clearly made out, either limb of the claim would have justified the injunction.[342] Similarly, in *Shelley Films Ltd v Rex Features Ltd*[343] the defendant was restrained by injunction from publishing photographs, which had been taken without permission on the set of the film *Frankenstein*.

The possibility that the taking of photographs can amount to the acquiring of confidential information was also expressly accepted by Laws J in *Hellewell v Chief Constable of Derbyshire*.[344] These three decisions go further, it is suggested, than simply affirming that photographs can carry information for the purposes of the law of confidence.[345] A photograph is merely a record and as such may be treated as any other means of recording information. However, in these instances, the 'information' had not been captured and contained in any particular form until the defendant brought that about. It would seem to follow that had the gymnasium owner in the *HRH Princess of Wales* case merely observed Princess Diana's appearance in the gymnasium without recording it, he would have been in possession of 'information', and an interim injunction to restrain publication of the observations would have been available. At that time it appeared, it is submitted, that a record in any form of any matter of substance not already in the public domain could amount to confidential information for the purposes of the doctrine of confidence. In general it is suggested that the form in which the information was captured or received for its later dissemination was becoming no longer a relevant factor.

As privacy values became dominant, the form in which the information was captured became no longer a focus of attention, except in the sense that it could enhance the privacy claim. In *Campbell*, *Von Hannover* and *Peck* photographs were in issue. If an eye-witness had seen Peck walking down the street and had later sent a detailed account to the press that would not, it is suggested, have affected the privacy analysis in that instance, due to the nature of the information at issue. But in terms of privacy-invasion photographs do represent a very effective way of conveying minute details, including facial expressions, in a way that cannot be replicated by reporting. So photographs appear to represent a particularly pernicious form of privacy-invasion. The fact that photographs have been taken may give weight to the argument that the invasion of privacy at stake should be accounted serious enough to allow prima facie for the grant of relief. Arguably, this factor could also be taken into account at the stage of conducting the balancing act between Arts 8 and 10, below. However, the distinction between the private information inquiry and the balancing act should not be blurred: this is currently becoming a doctrinal problem which is returned to in the discussion below.[346]

The new action thus covers information that is clearly private in character, and the Art 8 jurisprudence should be taken into account in order to determine whether information should be viewed as private or not. While the basis of the action is a reasonable expectation of privacy, that may not create a clear test to be used to determine

---

342 Ibid, pp 4–5.
343 [1994] EMLR 134.
344 [1995] 1 WLR 804, p 807.
345 As earlier indicated by *Pollard v Photographic Company* (1888) Ch 345.
346 See pp 967–81.

whether specific items of information should be viewed as private or not, since in particular circumstances the claimant – such as Princess Caroline – may have little *expectation* of privacy, although the information is private in the sense that it relates to her personal life. This test encapsulates the crucial distinction between breach of privacy and defamation, since the latter action is concerned with untruthful matter. The word 'private' is used in order to seek to make a distinction between information which a person wishes to keep secret because it is personal or intimate to her, and information (such as the fact that she had lied to Parliament) which raises no privacy issues, but which she wishes to conceal because it would hurt her reputation.

But the invasion of privacy must be viewed as *serious*. The facts that photos were taken surreptitiously and deliberately, and that it was clear that the person in question would not have consented to their being taken, are relevant factors informing the inquiry as to whether the information should be adjudged private; they might arguably also re-enter the equation at the stage of considering the balancing act. In relation to the question whether it was obvious that the person in question would not have consented to the taking of the pictures, prior contacts with the newspaper or with the PCC, asking for privacy to be respected by reporters and editors, could be taken into account, as could prior PCC adjudications.

Admittedly, there will be borderline cases in which it will not be possible to determine whether information can be said to relate to a person's private or public life. In that case, the information could be viewed as private and the question of its public nature would be relevant in determining the public interest in disclosure – in other words, at the stage of balancing speech and privacy rights. This test provides much more satisfactory protection than is provided by the US private facts tort in covering those cases where the matter disclosed, although not ordinarily considered 'offensive', is of great import to the individual concerned. In the well known case of *Sidis v F-R Publishing Corporation*[347] the *New York Times* revealed the identify and history of a former mathematical genius, who had given up his research and retired into obscurity. The article had a devastating effect on Sidis, but despite the court's finding that the article was 'merciless in its dissection of intimate details of the subject's personal life',[348] his action for breach of privacy failed on the basis that nothing was revealed which would have been offensive to the reasonable man.

The *Von Hannover* and *Peck* approach goes some way to resolving a possible objection to the use of confidence in privacy cases, namely the fear that precisely because the action – unlike the American privacy torts[349] – does not require wide publicity, but only 'unauthorised use' of information, it could in principle catch mere gossip between friends and neighbours. It has been argued that the intervention of the blunt tool of the law into the delicate area of social life and friendship which this would entail would both create intolerable legal uncertainty and also wrongly introduce the possibility of legal sanctions into an area which depends upon the unenforceable trust of one who confides for its moral integrity.[350] One solution to this problem would be to adapt the

---

347 113 F 2d 806 (2d Cir 1940).
348 Ibid, p 807.
349 This applies to the US 'false light' and 'private facts' torts. See Wacks, op. cit., fn 1, pp 56–59, for an extended comparison of confidence with the American torts.
350 Wilson, op. cit., fn 1, p 56.

rule from defamation for cases of personal, as opposed to commercial information and, as suggested by Warren and Brandeis,[351] to develop a rule that no cause of action would lie in respect of oral publication by private individuals in the absence of actual financial loss to the plaintiff.[352] Such a limitation is justifiable in principle, on the approach just indicated: our reasonable expectations or concerns as to the uses made of personal information probably encompass the possibility of a certain amount of social gossip, as opposed to mass circulation, as part of the price of living within a relatively free society. On a more pragmatic level, such a limitation would be necessary in the interests of legal certainty. As Zimmerman points out: '. . . most courts limit the private facts tort's scope by requiring mass or widespread communication as an element of the cause of action. American judges either tacitly or expressly recognise that they would create an impossible legal tangle if they subjected back-fence and front-parlour gossip to liability.'[353]

Public domain?

Introduction

Information could be protected by the doctrine of confidence if it retained a quality of confidentiality. But, clearly, information is not confidential if it is already in the public domain. As discussed, it is now only necessary to ask whether the information qualifies as private information. However, information will be neither confidential nor private if it is already in the public domain. A better way of putting this is to say that public information – such as photographs of the Prince of Wales at a ceremonial occasion – by its nature cannot be private. So the discussion begins by considering the point at which information can be said to have lost its quality of confidentiality or, now, of privacy. It will be found that privacy values, such as seeking to prevent humiliation, distress, indignity, and to preserve informational autonomy, have come to dominate the public domain inquiry to a very significant extent.

Information could be viewed as public, as opposed to private, either because it is already known to many people, so it has lost its private quality, or because it was made available in a public place. Obviously if the information became available in a public place it would then be known to anyone who happened to be present, but that was not the only factor viewed at one time as of relevance in relation to location. Section 12(4) HRA confirms that, when considering when to grant an injunction, the court must 'have regard to the extent to which the information has become, or is about to become, available to the public.'

---

351 'The right to privacy' (1890) IV(5) Harvard L Rev 193, p 196, p 217.

352 E.g., where a friend or acquaintance disclosed the secret of a person's homosexuality to an employer where it was foreseen that this would probably damage the plaintiff's career. Publication by radio or television would not be counted as 'oral', for obvious reasons.

353 Zimmerman, D, 'Requiem for a heavyweight: a farewell to Warren and Brandeis's privacy tort' (1983) 68 Cornell L Rev 291, p 337; at fn 246 she cites the decision in *La Fontaine v Family Drug Stores, Inc*, 33 Conn Supp 66, p 73; 360 A 2d 899, p 902 (Conn CP 1976) where the court commented that the abandonment of the mass publicity requirement 'would expand the concept of invasion of privacy beyond manageable limits'.

Information already known to a number of people

Making a determination on this first public domain matter has often been problematic. In the US prior publicity generally negatives liability.[354] For example, it might be argued that a celebrity had deliberately revealed sensitive personal information about his sexuality in the past and that therefore details regarding his current sexual partners or practices can now be published. It has been argued in the American context that celebrities may be seen to have waived their right to privacy so that a defence of implied consent may be used against any privacy actions they may bring.[355] The US courts have at times failed to draw a distinction between voluntary and involuntary publicity.[356] As Wacks has remarked: 'It is in principle unacceptable that merely because an individual seeks favourable publicity . . . his entire private life might be laid bare with impunity'.[357]

In contrast, the English doctrine of confidence and s 12(4)(a)(i) of the HRA have adopted a more nuanced approach, whereby the existence of prior publicity is a relevant but not conclusive factor. Thus, in the leading decision, *AG v Guardian Newspapers Ltd (No 2)*,[358] Lord Keith argued that whether information is in the public domain will often be a matter of degree and therefore prior disclosure to a limited group of people might not rob the information of its confidentiality, an approach which received general support in the case.[359] His Lordship was referring to the possibility of publication abroad, but the principle behind his comments – that the true test is whether further and more serious damage will flow from the fresh disclosure contemplated[360] – clearly applied in a case in which the relevant information had been previously disclosed in this country but in such a manner or at such a distance in the past that the information could not fairly be characterised as being currently in the public domain. Further, even 10 years ago, it was clear that where information conveys a particular message which is itself already in the public domain, the level of detail which accompanies it, which is not in the public domain, may allow the information to be termed confidential.[361]

---

354 See, e.g., *Sidis* 113 F 2d 806 (2d Cir 1940) and *Forsher v Bugliosi* 26 Cal 3d 792, 608 P 2d 716, 163 Cal Rptr 628 (1980); cf the earlier decision in *Melvin v Reid* 112 Cal App 283 (1931). See also, the decision in *Ann-Margret v High Society Magazine Inc* (1980) 498 F Supp 401 in which a well-known actress was denied relief in respect of the publication of a nude photograph of her

355 Elwood 'Outing, privacy and the First Amendment' [1992] Yale LJ 747.

356 Thus in *Metter v Los Angeles Examiner* (1939) 35 Cal App 2d 304, a person committed suicide by jumping from a high building and the court found that the victim had made herself a public figure 'for a brief period' through her own actions. However, the same result – denial of any right to privacy – was reached in *Kelly v Post Publishing Co* (1951) 327 Mass 275, where there was no element of voluntariness at all, the victim having died in a car accident.

357 Wacks, op. cit., fn 1, p 24.

358 [1990] 1 AC 109; [1990] 3 WLR 776; [1988] 3 All ER 545, HL.

359 Ibid, p 260. His Lordship was referring specifically to the possibility of publication abroad – *Spycatcher* had been published in the United States – but the principle is of general application. Sir John Donaldson in the Court of Appeal took the same approach, remarking that 'it is a matter of degree' (ibid, p 177), as did Scott J (ibid, p 149). See also *AG v Guardian Newspapers* [1987] 1 WLR 1248 (the first *Spycatcher* case).

360 Note the similar findings in the privacy context on this point in *Broadcasting Complaints Commission ex p Granada TV Ltd* (1993) *The Times*, 31 May; affirmed [1995] EMLR 163; (1994) *The Times*, 16 December, CA.

361 See *Barrymore v NGN Ltd* [1997] FSR 600.

The claim that prior, voluntary revelations mean that implied consent to future invasions of privacy has been given is clearly incompatible with the core privacy value: the individual's right to control over the release of personal information – the right to selective disclosure. When such selectivity is exercised in the context of disclosures to the media, and resulted in a public deception on a matter of importance, there would be an arguable public interest in correcting it by revealing the truth – the situation that arose in *Campbell*. But the information would not be robbed of its private quality merely because revelations had been made in the past relating to a similar area of the plaintiff's private life.

The public domain issue could be problematic where the information now disclosed had previously been recorded in a public record or given some earlier publicity. Once again, the US courts have opted for an absolutist stance in such situations: the Second Restatement of Torts states: 'there can be no [privacy] liability for giving publicity to facts about the plaintiff's life which are matters of public record.'[362] The Law Commission, in its final report on the doctrine of confidence,[363] decided not to follow its own earlier suggestion[364] that information should automatically be classified as in the public domain if it is on a register or other record required by law to be open to the public. This, it is suggested, reflected a realistic recognition of the fact that there is a world of difference between, as Ingber puts it, 'the disclosure of a personal fact in a dusty public record hidden somewhere in the bowels of a county courthouse and a similar disclosure disseminated through the mass technology of the modern press'.[365] This approach was followed in cases involving disclosure of past criminal convictions, despite the fact that such convictions are arrived at and announced in open court.[366] While such approaches have been attacked,[367] it is notable that under the DPA 1998, information relating to a person's criminal record forms one of the seven categories of 'sensitive personal data',[368] the processing of which attracts a higher level of safeguards than normal data.[369] It should also be borne in mind that the public interest would often require disclosure in such cases, as it did in the two cases just cited.

Similarly, the Law Commission has found that prior publicity some time ago in local newspapers should not preclude later legal protection for such information. Instead, their recommendation was simply that information could be said to be in the public domain only if 'having regard to its nature and the circumstances of its

---

362 Restatement, 625D.

363 Commission Report No 110, *Breach of Confidence*, para 6.74; see also para 6.68.

364 Set out in their Working Paper No 58, para 103.

365 Ingber, S, 'Rethinking intangible injuries: a focus on remedy' (1985) Cal L Rev 772, pp 848–49, cited in Paton-Simpson, E, 'Private circles and public squares: invasion of privacy by the publication of "private facts"' (1998) 61 MLR 318 p 327; see also p 890, below.

366 *R v Chief Constable of North Wales Police ex p AB* [1997] 3 WLR 724, CA; in *Hellewell*, the applicant complained that his 'mug shot', lawfully taken by the police, had been passed on to local retailers as part of their own anti-crime efforts, thus revealing the fact of his arrest. Laws J treated the fact that the complainant had been involved with the police as 'not . . . a public fact' but 'prima facie at least . . . a piece of confidential information' ([1995] 1 WLR 804, p 810).

367 See Thompson [1995] Conv 404, pp 406–7.

368 Along with matters such as a person's sexual life, religious and political opinions, and his physical and mental health (s 2).

369 Markesenis points out that the German courts have also afforded privacy protection to ex-criminals whose records are revealed, hampering their rehabilitation (op. cit., fn 1, p 123).

disclosure, it is generally available to the public'.[370] They considered that information was not in the public domain if 'it is only accessible to the public after a significant contribution of labour, skill or money'.[371] Such a flexible definition would allow courts to draw distinctions both between readily accessible public records and those buried in obscurity,[372] and between matters reported some years previously in a local newspaper and the contemporary mass reporting of the same matter.[373]

In any event, it is now clear from the recent privacy cases that information can remain 'private' or confidential even though it is known to a number of persons. In *Mills v News Groups Newspapers*,[374] which concerned the threatened publication of the applicant's address in the *Sun*, the judge said: 'The fact that information may be known to a limited number of members of the public does not of itself prevent it having and retaining the character of confidentiality, or even that it has previously been very widely available.'[375] The fact that information might be known to a limited number of members of the public did not of itself prevent it having and retaining the character of confidentiality.[376] It is also said that even if it had previously been very widely available, the restraint of further dissemination of the confidential material might be justified to prevent harm.[377]

In *Campbell*, there was no suggestion that the limited number of people who knew the details of the model's attendance at Narcotics Anonymous had robbed the information of its confidential quality. Similarly, in *Blair v Associated Newspapers*,[378] in which Cherie Blair was granted a series of injunctions against various parties to prevent the publication of details of her domestic arrangements, provided by a former nanny, the fact that one print-run of the *Mail on Sunday* carrying the offending article had already been distributed was held not to have robbed the information of its confidential quality. That was a significant decision since thousands of people would have read the article. In principle, it is argued, it was correct since the mere fact that a newspaper manages to put out one print run before the plaintiff can obtain an interim injunction should not preclude the grant of relief on the basis that the defendant should not be able to

370 Commission Report No 110, *Breach of Confidence*, para 6.74(i).
371 Ibid, para 6.74(ii). They gave the example of a reporter who combs through the back copies of a local newspaper in order to find out information about a now famous person; she would be gathering information not in the public domain, as she is expending considerable labour in the task (para 6.67).
372 It is clear that if the controller of the record is under a statutory duty not to disclose it to others, for example under the Rehabilitation of Offenders Act 1974 or the Data Protection Act 1998, then the information should be regarded as prima facie confidential at common law also.
373 A similar approach was followed in the New Zealand case, *TW3 Network Services Ltd v Broadcasting Standards Authority* [1995] 2 NZLR (HC) 720, p 731: 'Although information has been made known to others, a degree of privacy, entitled to protection, may remain. In determining whether information has lost its private character it would be appropriate to look realistically at the nature, scale and timing of previous publications.'
374 [2001] EMLR 41.
375 Ibid at para 25.
376 It referred to *Stephens v Avery*, p 454; *R v Broadcasting Complaints Commission ex p Granada Television Ltd* [1995] EMLR 163, p 168; *Creation Records Ltd v News Group Newspapers Ltd* [1997] EMLR 444, p 456.
377 *AG v Guardian Newspapers (No 2)*, p 260, *per* Lord Keith of Kinkel.
378 Case no HQ0001236.

profit from his own wrong-doing. In *McKennit v Ash* Mr Justice Eady said at first instance: 'in matters of privacy the Courts should be slow to allow public domain as a defence, and it is permissible to allow a controlled release of private information'. In other words, the judges are strongly adhering to a key principle of informational autonomy – that persons constantly choose the forums and the persons to whom they disclose some personal information: the fact that it is disclosed in a particular setting to a particular group – as in *McKennitt* in respect of some of the information – does not mean that the individual condones its mass dissemination.

This approach is clearly to be preferred to the more absolutist stance. While the latter has the advantage of making it relatively easy to predict in advance what can be disclosed with impunity, it relies, as Paton-Simpson has persuasively argued, on a simplistic and misleading attitude whereby privacy is treated as an all or nothing concept, rather than as a matter of degree.[379] Nevertheless, in rejecting this approach, it is stressed that s 12 HRA and Art 10 of the Convention require the judiciary to have regard to the possible impact on press freedom in developing remedies against privacy: this must be considered in terms of the certainty or otherwise of the new privacy law. Editors and journalists must be able to foresee to a reasonable extent whether given actions will result in liability. Zimmerman notes, 'The [US Supreme] Court has stated repeatedly that vague proscriptions against speech may chill the willingness of individuals and the media to take part in those communicative activities that are clearly protected by the First Amendment.'[380] However, if it is clear – which is the position that the law is approaching – that the publication of personal information without consent, including information known to a large number of persons, may attract liability under the new privacy doctrine, that is a rule giving the press reasonably precise warning as to what can safely be published. Attention should then focus on the value of the speech, not on a mechanistic application of a public domain test – a test that fails to focus on the key issue: the distress caused by the disclosure of the information.

Bearing in mind that confidence became the key mechanism to be used to prevent non-consensual disclosures of personal information, a tension between privacy values and confidence ones may be apparent, suggesting that Sedley LJ's approach in *Douglas*[381] may be more satisfactory than that of Dame Butler-Sloss in *Venables*.[382] Where the claimant has deliberately placed her sexual life in the public domain and has profited from it (for, example, where it is part of a certain image that she wishes to project) it is suggested that in terms of privacy it has lost its personal quality and in terms of confidence it is no longer secret. This approach is, as noted above, consonant with that under the DPA since it is one of the conditions for processing sensitive personal data. But where others have previously placed her sexual life in the public domain it is suggested that in terms of privacy the information retains its personal quality in the sense that each re-revelation causes her distress, whereas in terms of confidence it is

---

379 See Paton-Simpson, E, 'Private circles and public squares: invasion of privacy by the publication of "private facts"' (1998) 61 MLR 318.
380 Zimmerman, D, 'Requiem for a heavyweight: a farewell to Warren and Brandeis's privacy tort' (1983) 68 Cornell L Rev 291.
381 [2001] 2 WLR 992.
382 [2001] 1 All ER 908, Fam Div (High Court of Justice, Queen's Bench Division).

no longer secret despite her lack of acquiescence in the disclosures.[383] But the courts have not so far made anything of this distinction in the recent privacy cases.

Information obtained in public places

As to the second public domain matter, it used to be the case that confidence would not cover instances where the information was initially obtained through observation in a public place. However, nearly 15 years ago the decision in *HRH Princess of Wales v MGN Newspapers Ltd and Others*[384] cast some doubt on this contention, since the information in question was obtained in a gymnasium attended by other club members and therefore, clearly, it had been disseminated to an extent, albeit in a manner limited enough to prevent it from being viewed as in the public domain. An interim injunction to protect the information was nevertheless granted. Thus, at the time it appeared to be clear that information obtained by means of observation in similar semi-public places, such as restaurants, might be found to retain the necessary quality of confidence.

A particular problem arises where information, alleged to be personal, relates to a matter occurring within a public or semi-public environment and it is consequently argued that it cannot be seen as 'personal information'. Two basic approaches to this problem and other variants of it may be discerned concerning the borderline of the public/private divide.[385] The first is the straightforward, but anti-privacy, approach adopted by the US courts, which hold, with apparent logic, that what takes place in 'public' cannot by definition be 'private'. As Prosser puts it:

> the decisions indicate that anything visible in a public place may be recorded and given circulation by means of a photograph [or] . . . written description, since this amounts to no more than giving publicity to what is already public and what any one present would be free to see.[386]

The advantages of this approach in terms of legal certainty and predictability are apparent. However, it entirely misses the point that privacy need not be an absolute state of affairs[387] to be valuable and that everyday lives are in fact a constant trade-off between human interaction and the formation of relationships on the one hand, and the maintenance of a reasonable degree – not an absolute state – of privacy on the other. The alternative legal approach is therefore far more nuanced and subtle; it focuses, as the US one does not, on core privacy values. UK law recognised some years ago that a degree of privacy might be retained in a semi-public environment, such as a

---

383 The difference between the two was encapsulated in *Broadcasting Complaints Commission ex p Granada Television* [1995] EMLR 163.
384 Transcript, Association of Official Shorthandwriters Limited, 8 November 1993. Discussed below.
385 See further below, pp 912–15.
386 Prosser, D, 'Privacy' (1960) 48 Calif L Rev 383, p 396, pp 394–95.
387 Gavison suggests that an individual 'enjoys perfect privacy when he is completely inaccessible to others' (Gavison, R, 'Privacy and the limits of law' (1980) 89(3) Yale LJ 421, p 428) without suggesting that this is anything other than an unrealistic and undesirable scenario.

restaurant,[388] or gymnasium.[389] The step towards accepting that privacy might be retained in *entirely* public locations was not taken until recently.

English courts initially found that the Strasbourg jurisprudence provided little specific guidance on this particular matter, although it appeared that it probably did not require the narrow approach characterised by the US jurisprudence.[390] The approach of the German Supreme Court[391] over 10 years ago provided a useful contrast to the US stance. Princess Caroline of Monaco complained of photographs taken by the press of her having an intimate dinner with her boyfriend in a garden restaurant in France. The Supreme Court refused to follow the approach of the Appeal Court that privacy 'stopped at the doorstep': they found that the Princess had clearly 'retreated to a place of seclusion where [she wished] to be left alone' and that she was entitled to respect for that wish. The approach indicated was that one may still be entitled to respect for privacy in semi-public places, recognising, as the court put it, that people may 'transfer their private sphere of life to a place outside their home'. While the presumption of the Court was that events taking place in such places do not attract privacy protection, this could be rebutted if, as the Court put it, it is clear by reference to 'objective criteria' that one wishes to be 'left alone' so that one can, 'relying on the seclusion of the place, behave in a manner which [one] would not have done if . . . in full view of the public'.[392] Thus, identifying such places of seclusion was not to be done simplistically by reference solely to locality,[393] an approach implicitly approved in a decision of the Canadian Supreme Court involving the publication, without consent, of a photograph of the plaintiff taken in public.[394]

This flexible attitude to privacy is confirmed implicitly by the Press Complaints Commission's Code of Practice drawn up by the press itself, to which, as noted above, the courts have to have regard under s 12(4) of the HRA. As indicated above, the Code defines 'private places [as] public or private property where there is a reasonable expectation of privacy'. It does *not* draw a simplistic locational distinction between private places such as homes and public ones such as the street. The fact that an event

388   See the decision of the German Federal Court: BGH 19 December 1995 BGHZ 131, 322–46, discussed below.

389   The location where surreptitious photographs were taken of the former Princess of Wales in *HRH Princess of Wales*.

390   The Commission found in *X v United Kingdom* ((1973) Appl 5877/72 16 YBCHE, p 328) that the actions of the police in taking and then filing photographs taken without consent of a woman arrested for taking part in a political demonstration disclosed no prima facie breach of Art 8, partly it seems because of what was described as the 'public and voluntary' nature of her activities (emphasis added). This decision has however, been described as 'an outdated aberration' in the case law of the Commission: Bygrave, 'Data protection pursuant to the right to privacy in human rights treaties' (1999) 6(3) IJLIT 247, 265; see also *Niemetz v Germany* (1992) 16 EHRR 97.

391   BGH 19 December 1995 BGHZ 131. See the discussion of this decision in Markesenis, B and Nolte, N, 'Some comparative reflections on the right of privacy of public figures in public places', in Birks, P (ed), *Privacy and Loyalty*, 1997, pp 118 *et seq*.

392   Ibid.

393   Feldman (1994) expresses strong support for this view: op. cit., fn 1, pp 59–62.

394   *Les Editions Vice Versa Inc v Aubry* [1999] 5 BHRC 437 (appeal from decision of Quebec courts under the Charter of Rights and Freedoms which protects the right to privacy (s 5)). The photograph did not show the plaintiff engaged in any private act, or partially unclothed, but it was held that the right to privacy included the right to control over one's image.

takes place in a semi-public environment could, however, possibly be a factor which could be used in assessing the 'weight' of the privacy claim, when it is placed in the balance against any public interest in disclosure, including the interest in media freedom, a matter discussed below. This flexible attitude to personal information was also reflected in the pre-HRA case law on the doctrine of confidence; as indicated above, the courts had been prepared for some time to protect information already – in essence – in the public domain in the sense of being known to some people, such as the physical appearance of Princess Diana.[395] In those instances, protection for the details of an individual's personal appearance on a specific occasion was available. Even pre-HRA 'public domain' was clearly becoming a much more flexible concept.

But it became much clearer post-HRA that the courts were prepared to view information already partly in the public domain as worthy of protection on the grounds that it could still be viewed as private.[396] *Campbell*, in which both types of public domain issue arose – made it clear that the gathering of information in a public location did not mean that it was robbed of its confidentiality. *Von Hannover* confirmed that that is clearly the position adopted at Strasbourg. Baroness Hale in *Campbell* qualified her finding on the public domain point by demanding that where a private/daily life activity takes place in public, it must have an *added* privacy element in order to overcome the argument that the material was in the public domain since the activity occurred in a public location. She said: 'The activity photographed must be private.'[397] *Von Hannover* as discussed above, did *not* demand this added privacy element. But Lord Hope did not demand that the activity captured by photographers should be of an especially significant nature in terms of privacy; he said: 'But these were not just pictures of a street scene where she happened to be when the photographs were taken. They were taken deliberately, in secret and with a view to their publication in conjunction with the article'.[398] Those dicta comport quite readily with the findings of the Strasbourg Court.

In any event, depending on its interpretation, the term 'private' used by Baroness Hale could cover daily life activities, although that was not the sense she appeared to be using it in. In order to impose liability the invasion of privacy must be accounted serious. It could be said that *Von Hannover* turned on the state's failure to create a remedy in respect of the campaign of invasion of privacy by the press and that the decision need not be fully applied in a domestic case concerning the taking of photographs of daily life activities by one magazine photographer. But, as discussed above, in *McKennitt*[399] Buxton LJ rejected that explanation of *Von Hannover*. In fact, no liability in a *Von Hannover* situation (where the information was prima facie anodyne) has yet been imposed in the UK courts. Further, in the *Prince of Wales* case it was found that the question whether the revelation of the information was serious was to be regarded from the point of view of a person standing in the shoes of the claimant, not merely from the point of view of the reasonable person.[400] The latter test, it is argued,

395 See p 891.
396 See *Mills v News Group Newspapers* (2001) WL 720322, above p 889 on this point.
397 Campbell ibid at para 154.
398 Ibid, at para 123
399 [2006] EWCA Civ 1714.
400 At para 33.

would have been too limiting since it would have excluded too much information from the 'private' category.

What is the guiding principle to be derived from these findings, including those in *Peck* and *Von Hannover*? It is suggested that it is simply that of recognising the value of allowing persons control over the mass dissemination of private information, taking private information to mean information relating to a person's personal, as opposed to public, life. This principle does *not* depend on the specific *expectation* of the person 'holding' the information at issue. In other words, although that factor was taken into account in *Peck*, it should not be determinative of the matter since it places the moral responsibility for privacy invasion on the wrong party. If Peck had been a very high profile celebrity whose every movement in public was the subject of interest to the press, and had known, when he walked down the street after cutting his wrists, that he was probably being followed and photographed, he would therefore have expected that widespread publicity would follow. But the fact of his celebrity status should not change the privacy analysis since otherwise the moral responsibility for privacy invasion shifts to the victims of it.

Clearly, in some circumstances a person may control the dissemination of information and may expect to do so, as where a person invites guests to a wedding and takes measures to exclude unwanted persons, including the press (the *Douglas* situation). In other circumstances, such as that arising in *Von Hannover*, a person may wish to or seek to control the dissemination of information but have little expectation of doing so. In *Douglas v Hello (No 3)*[401] the Court of Appeal said: 'What is the nature of "private information"? It seems to us that it must include information that is personal to the person who possesses it and that he does not *intend* shall be imparted to the general public' (emphasis added). The Court of Appeal in the *Prince of Wales* case expressly endorsed those findings as sound. Obviously there will be circumstances where mass dissemination of the information has already occurred to the point where the information cannot be viewed as private. But the courts appear to be reluctant, as the *Blair* case indicated, to accept that a person has *lost control* of their private information, unless prior mass publicity forces them to that conclusion. In taking this stance it is clear that the judges have shown recognition of the underlying values of dignity and autonomy at stake.

Conclusions

So it is reasonable to conclude that the law is now seeking to protect the ability of the individual to control the mass dissemination of private information. The fact that the information is already known to some or that it was obtained in an inherently uncontrolled environment, such as the street, are not the key factors. Private life activities ranging from the everyday (walking with a friend), to the intensely intimate (attempting suicide), can occur in public. Private *facts* – such as a revelation that a person, thought to be straight, is in a gay relationship, or that a person is having an affair – can be revealed in public locations. The *location* of the activities has already been discarded as non-determinative and, as indicated, is ceasing to play even a residual role in UK

401   [2005] EWCA Civ; [2006] QB 125 at para 83.

privacy cases. It does not appear to be necessary that the information should be of an especially private nature: daily life activities can also be viewed as personal.

In general, then, the role of 'public domain' as a limiting factor in terms of location is clearly diminishing in privacy claims, although arguably it can still play an important part in confidentiality ones. The first public domain issue is still of significance where the plaintiff, not the defendant, deliberately placed the information in the public domain by revealing it to reporters or others.[402] The second – location – is becoming increasingly insignificant.

It may be noted that *state* confidentiality claims appear to be moving in a direction entirely opposed to that indicated in *Campbell* and in *Von Hannover*. In other words, a *contrary* development is apparent, it is suggested, in relation to *government* assertions of a breach of confidence. As Chapter 7 indicated, *AG v Times*, the Tomlinson case,[403] suggested that a tendency to find that information is already in the public domain, even where it has been disseminated only to a small group of persons, is apparent.[404] If it can eventually be said that the interpretation of 'public domain' differs depending on whether the plaintiff is the government or a private individual, this would accord with the requirements of Strasbourg jurisprudence as recognised under s 2 HRA since in the former instance, the strong individual right under Art 8 is not also at stake.

Section 12(4)(a)(i) HRA requires a court to 'have particular regard' to 'the extent to which the material has, or is about to become available to the public' when considering the grant of relief which, if granted, might affect the exercise of the Art 10 right (s 12(1)). If the development indicated becomes a settled one, this would mean that the courts had accepted that differing approaches should be taken to the interpretation of s 12(4)(a)(i) of the HRA, depending on whether Art 8 was or was not at stake. The requirement to take into account the extent to which the material is *about to* become available (emphasis added) could have the effect of widening the public domain test in a manner reconcilable with the spirit of *AG v Times* (Tomlinson case), but not with *Von Hannover* or *Campbell*. So since s 12(4) should be interpreted compatibly with Art 8 under s 3 HRA, a differentiated use of the public domain argument in privacy cases and in state ones under the doctrine of confidence, would be justified.

The obligation of confidentiality – a discarded test; the new action for breach of privacy

The discarding of this test was the single most important step in the transformation of the doctrine of confidence into a privacy remedy. It therefore warrants lengthy discussion. Three stages of development can be discerned. First, the traditional categories of

---

402 It can also be argued that in a number of circumstances a person has impliedly consented to the placement of the information in the public domain; this is true of reporting of public occasions such as sporting events or ceremonies where the person in question is taking part in a public sense in the event. The position of spectators is not so clear-cut. See the comments of the Major Government in *Privacy and Media Intrusion: The Government's Response*, Cm 2918, para 3.14 and the rejoinder by Bingham LJ (writing extra-judicially), (1996) 5 EHRLR 450. Under the US tort, the test for consent is whether the complained of publicity differed 'materially . . . in kind or extent' from the informational material in relation to which consent was actually given (Prosser, D, 'Privacy' (1960) 48 Calif L Rev 383, p 420

403 See Chapter 7, p 623.

404 See pp 623–24.

relationship imposing obligations of confidence were broadened and it was recognised that the relationship between the parties was not the determining factor. The key factor appeared to be that the receiver of the information was bound by conscience not to disclose it. The focus on conscience transmuted into a different test: it began to be recognised that the obligation could be imposed whenever a reasonable man would recognise that the information was confidential.[405] Thus the need for some kind of prior bond of trust between the parties began to disappear. Second, these developments were consolidated under the impetus of the HRA, but in general the courts considered that they were dealing with an extension of the doctrine of confidence. Finally, the notion of imposing an obligation of confidence was discarded entirely: the only requirement was that the information was private in Art 8 terms; if that was the case the other party came under a duty not to disclose it. In other words, the action in question became that of breach of privacy (that term is used as short-hand for liability for misuse of private information). In identifying these stages of development, it must be borne in mind that the traditional relationships imposing an obligation of confidence, such as master/servant or patient/doctor are still relevant: they can figure as weighty factors tipping the balance in favour of privacy at the stage of balancing the speech and privacy interests.[406]

Discarding the need for a confidential relationship

Since *Stephens v Avery*,[407] the basic principle on which the doctrine of confidence was founded was that confidentiality would be enforced if the information was received 'on the basis that it is confidential'.[408] This depended on all the circumstances of the case, and the imposition of confidence was not limited (as had previously been thought) to instances in which there was a pre-existing relationship between the parties: 'The basis of equitable intervention to protect confidentiality is that it is unconscionable for a person who has received information on the basis that it is confidential, subsequently to reveal that information . . . The relationship between the parties is not the determining factor.'[409] It is suggested that this explanation of the basis of the doctrine weakened the requirement to identify the specific public interest, such as the interest in preserving the stability of the family,[410] which would be served by protecting the information in question.

The fact that the information was given in confidence could be expressly communicated to the defendant (as in *Stephens v Avery*), but it could also be implied from the circumstances surrounding the communication. In *Fairnie (Dec'd) and Others v Reed and Another*[411] the confidential information (the format of a board game which the plaintiff wished to market) was mentioned by him incidentally during conversation

---

405 For further discussion see: Phillipson, G, 'Transforming breach of confidence? Towards a common law right of privacy under the Human Rights Act' (2003) 66(5) MLR 726 and 'Judicial Reasoning in Breach of Confidence Cases under the Human Rights Act: not taking privacy seriously? [2003] EHRLR (*Privacy Special*) 53.

406 See below p 977.

407 [1988] Ch 449.

408 Ibid, p 482.

409 Ibid.

410 As in *Duchess of Argyll v Duke of Argyll* [1967] 1 Ch 302.

411 20 May 1994, CA, transcript from LEXIS.

with a virtual stranger about another matter; it was therefore transmitted only in passing, and the recipient was not told that it was given in confidence. The Court of Appeal found that there was an arguable case that the information had been transmitted in confidence, relying primarily on the fact that the information was of clear commercial value.[412]

It used to be thought that confidence was of limited value in protecting privacy, since it only covered those specific instances in which information was communicated in confidence. Thus, for example, it was not thought to cover situations where reporters took unauthorised photographs by means of telephoto lenses or surreptitiously recorded conversations with a view to publication. Where there was no formal relationship, the alternative ingredient traditionally required for a duty of confidence to arise was an express or implied agreement between the parties, or promise by the defendant, that the information received would be treated as confidential.[413] The notion of 'implied agreement' denoted an agreement which, although unspoken, was in fact mutually assumed between the parties. Owing to this requirement, it was thought that the action caught only those specific instances in which information was (voluntarily) communicated in confidence. Thus, it was not thought to cover the paradigm example of an invasion of privacy where reporters surreptitiously took photographs by means of telephoto lenses or recorded private conversation, with a view to publication, because in such cases there is no possibility of agreement between the parties or a promise (express or implied) of confidentiality: it would be absurd to say that the defendant journalist had 'agree[d] to treat the information as confidential'[414] when his whole purpose was to publish it, while the plaintiff 'confider' was blissfully unaware that any communication of information was taking place at all.

It appeared that an obligation of confidence could be imposed even where the information was not intentionally communicated to the defendant by the plaintiff. In *AG v Guardian Newspapers (No 2)*[415] Lord Goff suggested *obiter* that the nature of the information and the fact that it was not intended that the defendant should acquire it[416] could in itself impose the duty, using the example of '. . . an obviously confidential document . . . dropped in a public place and then picked up by a passer-by . . .'. He said:[417]

---

412 '[Plaintiff's counsel] submits that in the context [the plaintiff] disclosed to [the defendant] a confidential idea which he believed could be commercially successful, particularly with his endorsement. In my judgment, that is an arguable inference . . . It all depends precisely on the language used, and the circumstances in which the conversation took place . . . [defendant's counsel] points out that . . . if the plaintiff simply blurted out or casually referred to the number one game . . . then the defendant could not be taken as understanding that he was being given that information in confidence. That may be so, but in my judgment it is not possible to say . . . precisely what inference should be drawn by the reasonable man who was the bystander and observer of the conversation', *per* Stuart Smith LJ, pp 7–8. The hearing was an appeal upon an application to strike out, so the Court did not have to decide whether an obligation of confidence was in fact imposed.

413 See the Law Commission Report No 110, *Breach of Confidence*, para 6.11: for an obligation to be imposed, 'any confidant must agree to treat the information as confidential'.

414 The requirement which the Law Commission thought necessary (ibid).

415 [1990] 1 AC 109.

416 *Fairnie*, 20 May 1994, CA, transcript from LEXIS, suggests that it will not always be essential to show that this element is present.

417 At p 281.

I start with the broad principle (which I do not in any way intend to be definitive) that a duty of confidence arises when confidential information comes to the knowledge of a person (the confidant) in circumstances where he has notice, or is held to have agreed, that the information is confidential, with the effect that it would be just in all the circumstances that he should be precluded from disclosing the information to others . . . in the vast majority of cases . . . the duty of confidence will arise from a transaction or relationship between the parties . . . but it is well settled that a duty of confidence may arise in equity independently of such cases . . .'

Francome v Mirror Group Newspapers,[418] in which the information was obtained by means of a telephone tap, suggested that a duty of confidence could arise on the basis of such factors,[419] as did *Shelley Films Ltd v Rex Features Ltd*.[420]

These findings further confirmed that the duty could still be imposed (or perhaps imposed *a fortiori*) where the defendant set out deliberately to acquire the information without the plaintiff's knowledge, as opposed to stumbling across it inadvertently.[421] Presumably, this was also the case where the defendant acquired the information with the awareness, but without the consent of the plaintiff and where, as in *Hellewell v Chief Constable of Derbyshire*,[422] the defendant was acting under a legal power in acquiring the information for one specific purpose but wished to use it for another.[423] The decisions in *Rex Features*, *HRH Princess of Wales* and *Hellewell* also indicated that there was no need for anything recognisable as a 'communication' from the plaintiff to any other person for the duty to arise,[424] although presumably the information concerned had in some sense to emanate from the plaintiff. Thus, the obligation of confidence was able to be imposed unilaterally; it was not founded on the express or implied agreement of

---

418 [1984] 1 WLR 892.

419 *Cf* the *obiter* remarks in *Malone v Comr of Police of the Metropolis (No 2)* [1979] Ch 344, p 376, to the effect that those who spoke of confidential matters in situations in which it was foreseeable that they could be overheard (e.g., on the telephone) could not claim that any eavesdroppers were bound by a duty of confidentiality. However, in *Malone v UK* (1984) 7 EHRR 14, the European Court of Human Rights reaffirmed (p 38) the place of telephone conversations within Art 8 and therefore must be taken to have rejected the notion that citizens assume a lack of confidentiality in communication by telephone.

420 [1994] EMLR 134, *per* Mr Mann QC (sitting as a deputy judge): '. . . [the photographer] was not an invitee and assuming that he saw the signs [forbidding photography] . . . (I am not convinced that it would be fatal to Shelley's case if he did not) . . . it is impossible . . . not to conclude that what he saw and understood from his location might not have fully and sufficiently fixed him with knowledge [that the plaintiff wished to keep the appearance of "the Creature" and its costume secret] according to any of the relevant standards . . .'. The Australian case of *Franklin v Giddins* [1978] 1 Qd R 72 was relied upon as persuasive authority.

421 For the contrary view that a duty will only be imposed where there is unlawful action by the taker of information, see Wei, G, 'Surreptitious takings of confidential information' (1992) LS 302. For critical discussion of Wei's view, see the articles cited by him, p 309.

422 The case concerned the taking of photographs under Code of Practice D made under the Police and Criminal Evidence Act 1984 of a suspect in police custody. The police wished to allow a 'shop watch' scheme to use the photographs. An injunction was refused on the basis that the public interest was clearly served by the disclosure in question.

423 See also *Marcell and Others v Comr of Police of the Metropolis* [1992] Ch 224, esp pp 236–37.

424 See Thompson, *Confidentiality and the Law*, 1990, LLP, p 73.

the parties that the communication would be confidential.[425] In *Maudsley v Palumbo and Others*[426] Knox J said (*obiter*) that while the absence of actual belief on the part of the defendants that they were being given confidential information was 'quite capable of being significant', he '[did] not accept that . . . a person who forms no belief on the question is thereby absolved from being found to have received information in confidence'.

The developments described above significantly widened the circumstances in which the duty of confidence would be imposed, with the result that many of the activities of reporters engaged in uncovering private facts could be caught by the law of confidence. As Laws J remarked *obiter* in *Hellewell*:

> If someone with a telephoto lens were to take . . . a photograph of another engaged in some private act, his subsequent disclosure of the photograph would in my judgment . . . amount to a breach of confidence . . . In such a case the law would protect what might reasonably be called a right of privacy, although the name accorded to the cause of action would be breach of confidence.[427]

Care had to be taken in extrapolating general principles applicable at the time from some of the decisions discussed here, since a number of them concerned interim injunctions only[428] and therefore it was only necessary for the plaintiff to make out an arguable case. Others concerned appeals from applications to strike out[429] in which, as Stuart Smith LJ emphasised in *Fairnie*, the plaintiff must succeed unless his case is 'unarguable'.[430] Nevertheless, it is suggested that in the pre-HRA era, the courts were inclining towards a position regarding imposition of the duty to maintain confidence which may be indicated as follows. It was not necessary to establish a pre-existing relationship, an express imposition of the duty, an agreement between the parties or anything resembling a communication of the information by the plaintiff to the defendant or anyone else.[431] That ingredient could be established in a number of ways. Since *Stephens v Avery*,[432] it appeared that the existence of a formal relationship was 'not the determining factor'.[433] Instead, confidentiality would be enforced simply on the basis that the information was received 'on the basis that it is confidential',[434] since to allow such a recipient to reveal the information would be 'unconscionable'.

---

425 An approach indicated earlier in *Coco v AN Clark (Engineers) Ltd* [1969] RPC 41, p 48.

426 (1995) *The Times*, 19 December, transcript from LEXIS; the case concerned an application for an injunction to restrain the defendants from making use of an idea for a dance club disclosed to them by the plaintiff.

427 [1995] 1 WLR 804, p 807.

428 *Rex Features*; *HRH Princess of Wales*, fn 166; *Francome v Mirror Group Newspapers Ltd*.

429 *Fairnie*, 20 May 1994, CA, transcript from LEXIS, above; *Stephens v Avery* [1988] Ch 449.

430 Ibid, p 1.

431 Following *AG v Guardian Newspapers (No 2)* [1990] 1 AC 109; [1990] 3 WLR 776; [1988] 3 All ER 545, HL, the defendant did not need to be the person to whom the information was originally 'communicated'.

432 [1988] Ch 449: the plaintiff brought an action against a friend to whom she had confided that she had had a lesbian affair; the friend sold the story to a newspaper.

433 [1988] Ch 449, p 482, *per* Browne-Wilkinson VC.

434 Ibid.

To sum up – in a number of pre-HRA cases, including *Francome v Mirror Group Newspapers*,[435] *Shelley Films*,[436] *Creation Records*,[437] and *Hellewell*,[438] no prior relationship was present. As a result of the successful actions in *Shelley Films*,[439] *Creation Records*[440] and *HRH Princess of Wales*[441] (all involving surreptitiously taken photographs), *Francome*,[442] (where information was obtained by a newspaper using a telephone tap) and *Lam v Koo and Chiu*[443] (involving the surreptitious obtaining of a document), any requirement for a communication between plaintiff and defendant disappeared, a development also supported by *dicta* of Lord Goff in *AG v Guardian Newspapers (No 2)*.[444] This was possible because the requirement of an 'implied agreement' of confidentiality was radically re-interpreted: the approach of the courts was to imply the agreement of confidentiality into the dealings between the parties, not on the basis of any mutual agreement on the matter, but instead on the basis that the reasonable man in the position of the defendant would have assumed such an obligation.[445]

The test appeared to be wholly objective.[446] What factors were assumed to lead a reasonable person to realise that the information was confidential? The authorities suggested that they would include the following: where it had clear commercial value, as in *Fairnie* and *Rex Features*, and where it was obvious that the plaintiff did not

---

435 [1984] 1 WLR 892. The information concerned (that the plaintiff, a well-known jockey, had breached various rules of racing) was obtained by means of tapping the plaintiff's telephone; the tapes so made were sold to the press.

436 *Shelley Films v Rex Features Limited* [1994] EMLR 134. An injunction was granted to prevent the use of a photograph taken surreptitiously on the film set of Frankenstein.

437 *Creation Records Ltd v News Group Newspapers Ltd* [1997] EMLR 444; an injunction was granted against a newspaper to prevent it from publishing a photograph of a new album cover designed for the group Oasis which had been taken surreptitiously on the set where the album cover was being shot.

438 *Hellewell v Chief Constable of Derbyshire* ([1995] 1 WLR 804). The 'information' here was a 'mug'-shot of the plaintiff taken by the police which was later passed by them to local shopkeepers to aid the prevention of shoplifting.

439 [1994] EMLR 134. The case was discussed extensively in the *Spencer* decision (1998) 25 EHRR CD 105.

440 *Creation Records Ltd v News Group Newspapers Ltd* [1997] EMLR 444.

441 *HRH Princess of Wales v MGN Newspapers Limited and Others* (1993) Transcript, Association of Official Shorthandwriters Ltd, 8 November 1993. Photographs of the plaintiff exercising in a private gymnasium taken by a hidden camera were sold to and published by a tabloid newspaper.

442 [1984] 1 WLR 892.

443 [1992] Civil Transcript No 116, CA (a Hong Kong case): a medical researcher accidentally or surreptitiously obtained a confidential research document produced by the plaintiff.

444 *AG v Guardian Newspapers (No 2)* [1990] 1 AC 109; [1990] 3 WLR 776; [1988] 3 All ER 545, HL. Lord Goff considered *obiter* that confidentiality would be imposed in instances where, e.g., '. . . an obviously confidential document is wafted by an electric fan out of the window into a crowded street, or when an obviously confidential document . . . is dropped in a public place and is then picked up by a passer-by . . .' (ibid, p 281).

445 Thus, in *Creation Records* ([1997] EMLR 444), Lloyd J reasoned: '. . . the circumstances were such that any reasonable man in the shoes of [the photographer] would have realised on reasonable grounds that he was obtaining the information, that is to say the view of the scene, in confidence . . .'.

446 In *Li Yau-wai v Genesis Films Ltd* [1987] HKLR 711, a Hong Kong decision, an 'officious bystander' test was used to impose the duty of confidence (*per* Rhind J, p 719). An objective test was also employed in *Lam v Koo and Chiu* (1992) Civil Transcript No 116, see esp p 30 (Hong Kong Court of Appeal). See Wacks, *Privacy and Press Freedom*, op. cit., fn 1, pp 62–63; Loh, E, 'Intellectual property: breach of confidence?' (1995) 17 EIPR 405–7.

wish the information to be obtained (as in *HRH Princess of Wales* and *Rex Features*). Conversely, where the plaintiff deliberately refrained from mentioning confidentiality to the defendant, this could prevent the imposition of the duty, as in *Palumbo*.

This bold development, a clear departure from the view of the Law Commission on the matter,[447] radically increased the potential scope of the confidence action: it was able to cover cases where personal information was surreptitiously obtained by the media and then published without consent,[448] since in many such instances, it would be open to the court to say that the reasonable man would have assumed an obligation of confidence. This possibility – as indicated above – received further clear recognition from the European Commission in *Spencer*;[449] in the well-known *Hellewell* case,[450] Laws J said: 'If someone with a telephoto lens were to take . . . a photograph of another engaged in some private act, his subsequent disclosure of the photograph would in my judgment . . . amount to a breach of confidence.'

When used in this way, the central interest served by protecting confidences ceased to be enforcing promise-keeping, or preserving certain kinds of relationships; rather, it became simply that of preventing private or personal information entering the public domain without the plaintiff's consent. The action, therefore, while still termed 'breach of confidence',[451] became almost indistinguishable from a 'pure' privacy tort.[452] The Law Commission on breach of confidence explained the difference between confidentiality and privacy by saying that the former 'arises from the nature of the information itself: it would be based on the principle that certain kinds of information are categorised as private and *for that reason alone* ought not to be disclosed'.[453] The 'new' model of confidence outlined allowed a duty of confidentiality to be imposed solely on the basis of matters relating to the information: as noted above, it had to be of substance and not already in the public domain; it had to be such that the reasonable person standing in the defendant's shoes would have realised that it should be kept confidential.

---

447 'It would in our view, extend the idea of breach of confidence too far to cover situations where the potential defendant has not expressly or by inference accepted an obligation of confidence in respect of information which has come into his possession' (Law Commission Report No 110, *Breach of Confidence*, para 6.11).

448 Provided that the information 'has the necessary quality of confidence about it' (*Coco* [1969] RPC 41). See discussion below.

449 (1998) 25 EHRR CD 105. There is some recognition amongst the commentators as well; see, e.g., Singh, Grosz and Braithwaite, Wright (all op. cit., fn 1).

450 [1995] 1 WLR 804, p 807.

451 As Laws J remarked in *Hellewell*: 'In such a case the law would protect what might reasonably be called a right of privacy, although the name accorded to the cause of action would be breach of confidence' (ibid).

452 Confidence does, however have one limitation in such a guise: it cannot directly cover cases where there is intrusion but no information is gained or where information is gathered but never used (the Protection from Harassment Act 1997 might apply in cases of persistent intrusion). However, a reporter could be prevented by the terms of an injunction from passing any information gained on to anyone else in a newspaper, and presumably from processing and storing the information in the newspaper's archives (activities which might also engage the Data Protection Act 1998 (see below, pp 927–30). Moreover, the availability of a remedy in confidence against the publication of private information obtained by, e.g., a bugging device, might give rise to a perception that such use was pointless if lawful publication of the material gained was not possible; it might thus come to have a 'chilling effect' upon this form of intrusion.

453 Law Commission Report No 110, *Breach of Confidence*, para 2.3 (emphasis added).

When the doctrine was dealing with personal information, this realisation could come purely from the nature of the information itself, coupled sometimes with the manner in which it was acquired: the fact that the defendant had to intrude on the plaintiff in some way in order to gather the information was evidence to the defendant that the plaintiff would regard what he was doing as private.[454]

One final aspect of the utility of confidence in this area should be mentioned: in many cases, newspapers obtain private information about the plaintiff from his or her friends and acquaintances, as in *Stephens v Avery*[455] and *Michael Barrymore v News Group Newspapers Ltd.*[456] In such a case, an obligation of confidence can be imposed upon the newspaper on the orthodox basis that they knew or ought to have known that they had received the fruits of a broken confidence;[457] alternatively, under the developed model of the doctrine, applicable around ten years ago, the obligation could have been imposed upon the newspapers directly, on the basis that the reasonable man would have realised that the information received should be kept confidential, due its clearly private character.[458]

The initial effect of Art 8 and the HRA

What, then, was the role of Art 8 in the development of confidence, given that the judges already apparently had to hand a serviceable tool with which to tackle invasions of privacy? It is suggested that it performed two, linked, functions. First, it provided the normative impetus for the consolidation of the radical developments outlined above. Secondly, given the somewhat inchoate nature of the new model of confidence, Art 8, together with s 12 of the HRA, provided an organising principle around which the uncertainties inherent in the action, particularly the conflict between the demands of privacy and press freedom, could be resolved, a matter addressed below. It is suggested that Art 8, together with s 12 of the HRA, performed the first of these functions and also gave indications as to the means of resolving that conflict in the significant post-HRA decision of the Court of Appeal in *Douglas and Others v Hello! Ltd.*[459]

---

454 In *AG v Guardian Newspapers (No 2)* [1990] 1 AC 109, Lord Goff stated that the courts should take account of 'all the circumstances, including the manner in which the information was acquired' (at p 283).

455 [1988] Ch 449.

456 [1997] FSR 600. A man with whom Mr Barrymore had allegedly had a homosexual affair passed the details to the *Sun* newspaper.

457 See *AG v Guardian Newspapers* [1987] 1 WLR 1248, esp p 1265, *per* Lord Browne-Wilkinson, and the Law Commission report: 'The third party is liable to be restrained from disclosing or using information which he knows or it would seem, he ought to know, was subject to an obligation of confidence' (Law Commission Report No 110, *Breach of Confidence*, para 4.11).

458 The view of the Law Commission (ibid, para 5.9) was that cases such as *Fraser v Evans* [1969] 1 QB 349 meant that the doctrine could give no remedy to the 'owner' of personal information where the promise of confidentiality is given to another, as where a newspaper promises a journalist that information he obtains on a celebrity will not be published in her lifetime, and then breaches that promise, leaving, so the Commission thought, the celebrity with no remedy. See also the doubts of Wacks on this point (*Privacy and Press Freedom*, 1996, p 56).

459 [2001] 2 WLR 992. See, for discussion Moreham, N [2001] 64(5) MLR 767–74; Elliott, M [2001] CLJ 231–33.

The magazine *OK!* secured an agreement with two celebrities, Michael Douglas and Catherine Zeta-Jones, eight days before their wedding under which it agreed to pay a very large sum of money to them in respect of rights to publish exclusive photographs of the wedding and an article about it. The couple trusted *OK!* to project only the images they wanted projected to the public. They also retained rights of approval in relation to anything that was to be published. Mr Douglas and Ms Zeta-Jones undertook to use their best efforts to ensure that: 'no other media (including but not limited to photographers, television crews or journalists) shall be permitted access to the wedding, and that no guests or anyone else present at it (including staff at the venues) shall be allowed to take photographs'. The rival magazine *Hello!* had tendered for the rights but had failed. *Hello!* clearly knew that exclusive rights were to be granted for coverage of the wedding, and that it had not secured them. However, the security operation at the wedding failed to prevent some unauthorised photos from being taken and *Hello!* obtained them. The couple were informed after the wedding that copies of *Hello!* were already in the UK with a photo of the wedding on the front cover and that they would be distributed very shortly. They rapidly obtained an *ex parte* injunction restraining publication.

The Court of Appeal had to decide whether an injunction restraining the publication should be continued in force until trial, thereby effectively 'killing' that issue of *Hello!*. The key issues were (a) the applicability of the law of confidence; (b) the relevance of the HRA 1998; (c) whether the injunction should be continued until the trial of the action or whether the claimants should be left to seek to obtain damages at the trial. The Court noted that the doctrine of confidence originally arose from the exercise of the equitable jurisdiction to restrain freedom of speech in circumstances in which it would be unconscionable to publish private material. It said that it was clearly established that where information was accepted on the basis that it would be kept secret, the recipient's conscience would be bound by that confidence, and it would be unconscionable for him to break his duty of confidence by publishing the information to others.[460]

Sedley LJ found that the law of confidence had developed to the point at which it could provide a right to privacy, in so far as a privacy right could be viewed as covering matters which are distinct from those which confidence has come to be viewed as capable of covering. He accepted that it might have reached that point even independently of the HRA. In particular, he found that it is arguable that confidence does not cover surreptitious takings of personal information by someone whose conscience cannot be said to be bound to maintain confidence – a 'stranger' – and that such takings are more readily covered by a right to privacy, albeit originating from confidence. His point appeared to be that although such takings could be covered by confidence, as indicated

---

460 *Stephens v Avery* [1988] Ch 449, p 456. The court noted that in *Argyll v Argyll* [1967] Ch 302, 329f–330b it was said: 'It . . . seems to me that the policy of the law, so far from indicating that communication between husband and wife should be excluded from protection against breaches of confidence given by the court in accordance with *Prince Albert v Strange* ((1848) 2 De Gex & Sm 652; on appeal 1 Mac & G 25), strongly favours its inclusion . . .'. The court also relied on *Michael Barrymore v News Group Newspapers Ltd* [1997] FSR 600; Jacob J had followed those principles in a case in which a newspaper sought to publish information concerning an intimate homosexual relationship.

above,[461] the notion of an implied obligation to maintain confidence might be viewed as artificial, depending on the circumstances. In this instance the photographs might have been taken by a guest (who would come under an obligation of confidence since his or her conscience would be bound, in which case it would be immaterial whether the cause of action was called confidence or privacy). But even in the case of a taking by a stranger a cause of action, he found, would be available.

However, if the photos in the instant case had been taken by a 'stranger', the cause of action in his view could arguably be termed a right to privacy, and the HRA aided that conclusion since it provided a clear impetus to develop the law on the lines indicated obiter by Laws LJ in *Hellewell*.[462] Thus, the HRA gave a force to the above argument – that confidence had developed in such a way as to provide a right to privacy – which it might not otherwise have had. Sedley LJ made this clear: 'we have reached a point at which it can be said with confidence that the law recognises and will appropriately protect a right of personal privacy'. He based this finding in part on the coming into force of the HRA since it required the courts – as public authorities under s 6 HRA – to give effect to the right to respect for private and family life set out in Art 8 of the European Convention on Human Rights. He said that the jurisprudence of the Court and the common law:

> now run in a single channel because, by virtue of s 2 and s 6 of the Act, the courts of this country must not only take into account jurisprudence of both the Commission and the European Court of Human Rights which points to a positive institutional obligation to respect privacy; they must themselves act compatibly with that and the other Convention rights. This, for reasons I now turn to, arguably gives the final impetus to the recognition of a right of privacy in English law.[463]

His key point in relation to a possible difference between confidence and privacy was:

> a concept of privacy does . . . accord recognition to the fact that the law has to protect not only those people whose trust has been abused, but those who simply find themselves subjected to an unwanted intrusion into their personal lives. The law no longer needs to construct an artificial relationship of confidentiality between intruder and victim: it can recognise privacy itself as a legal principle drawn from the fundamental value of personal autonomy.[464]

461 See *Francome v MGM* [1984] 1 WLR 892 and *dicta* in *AG v Guardian Newspaper (No 2)* [1990] 1 AC 109, p 281, discussed above.

462 In *Hellewell v Chief Constable of Derbyshire* [1995] 1 WLR 804 Laws LJ said: 'I entertain no doubt that disclosure of a photograph may, in some circumstances, be actionable as a breach of confidence. If someone with a telephoto lens were to take from a distance and with no authority a picture of another engaged in some private act, his subsequent disclosure of the photograph would, in my judgment, as surely amount to a breach of confidence as if he had found or stolen a letter or diary in which the act was recounted and proceeded to publish it. In such a case the law would protect what might reasonably be called a right of privacy, although the name accorded to the cause of action would be breach of confidence.'

463 [2001] 2 WLR 992 at para 111.

464 Ibid, para 126.

He pointed out that Art 8(1) of the Convention creates a right to respect for private and family life, although Art 8(2), and ss 6, 7 and 8 of the HRA, make it clear that these rights are enforceable only against public authorities. However, he noted that, as indicated above, the European Court of Human Rights has relied on the positive duty imposed on the member states by Art 1 of the Convention,[465] and therefore found that Art 8 does recognise the applicability of its guarantee as between private parties.

Clearly, in an action between private parties – as in the instant case – it could not be said that the defendant was bound by the Convention since it was not a public authority under s 6 of the HRA. Sedley LJ found that the Court, as itself a public authority under s 6, was obliged to give some effect to Art 8, among other provisions of the Convention. Its duty, he said, appears to allow it to 'take the step from confidentiality to privacy'.[466] Significantly, he found that in so far as there was doubt as to the scope of the duty of the Court under s 6, s 12(4) made the matter crystal clear where interference with the right to freedom of expression was in issue. He noted that s 12(4) requires the Court to have particular regard to the right to freedom of expression under Art 10. Therefore, it was clear that Art 10 was applicable as between one private party to litigation and another; in other words, it has indirect horizontal effect.

However, Art 10(2) is qualified in respect of the reputation and rights of others and the protection of information received in confidence. Therefore, in having particular regard to Art 10, it was also necessary to have such regard to the other Convention rights, including Art 8. Section 12(4), it was found, does not, therefore, merely give freedom of expression priority over the other rights. In weighing up the competing claims, the Court also had to take the Code policed by the Press Complaints Commission into account under s 12(4)(b); it did not appear that the photographer had complied with the provision of cl 3 (which, as indicated above, provided at that time, in part, that, 'A publication will be expected to justify intrusions into any individual's private life without consent . . . The use of long lens photography to take pictures of people in private places without their consent is unacceptable.'). This clause is qualified by the exceptions where a public interest can be demonstrated to apply. That was not the case in this instance, since knowing of the details of the wedding could not serve a legitimate public interest. The court concluded that the claimants had an arguable case that they had suffered a breach of their privacy; this claim was based on the law of confidence, interpreted compatibly with Art 8, due to the requirements of s 12(4). Although the court was unanimous in reaching this conclusion, Sedley LJ differed from the other two judges in differentiating between confidence and privacy in respect of surreptitious takings of information.

The ultimate outcome of what was essentially a commercial case was of little interest in terms of future privacy claims; the case was of interest since it afforded confirmation to the development of confidence into a privacy remedy, a development which was accepted and relied upon in *Venables, Thompson v News Group Newspapers Ltd, Associated Newspapers Ltd, MGM*.[467] The case concerned the identity of the killers of Jamie Bulger; exceptionally, an injunction granted to protect the anonymity of a child

---

465 See the judgment of the court in *A v United Kingdom* (1999) 27 EHRR 611.
466 He noted that this argument is supported by Hunt, op. cit., fn 1.
467 [2001] 1 All ER 908 Fam Div (High Court of Justice, Queen's Bench Division).

may be extended, on grounds of the doctrine of confidence, once the child reaches 18. Jon Venables and Robert Johnson were claimants in proceedings for injunctions. In 1993 they had murdered a boy of two, James Bulger, when they were 10 years old. The murder was particularly shocking and distressing and the facts were widely publicised in the media. They were sentenced to be detained under s 53(1) of the Children and Young Persons Act 1933 (CYPA 1933), and they were placed in separate secure units. At the conclusion of their trial, the judge granted comprehensive injunctions restricting publication of further information about the two boys, with no limit of time, based both under s 39 of the CYPA 1933 (which is discussed above) and the inherent jurisdiction of the High Court to deal with children. The claimants reached 18 and wanted the injunctions to continue. The injunctions were principally designed to protect their new identities when they were released into the community. The court had to decide whether there was jurisdiction to grant an injunction under the law of confidence against the whole of the media in respect of an adult to protect his identity and other relevant information. That issue raised the question of the effect of the implementation of the HRA 1998 and, in particular, the applicability of the Convention, since the proceedings were private ones.

A number of newspapers made representations to the court, arguing that on grounds of press freedom, an injunction should not be granted to protect the claimants' identities. The key issue in the case for the injunctions concerned the grave danger to the claimants if their new identities and whereabouts became known, since threats against them had frequently been made, including threats to their lives. They were also likely to suffer serious and relentless invasions of privacy. The court found that in the light of the judgments in the *Douglas* case[468] regarding the effect of s 12(4) of the HRA it was clear that Art 10 had to be applied directly. Dame Butler-Sloss P in the High Court found that,[469] taking into account the effect of the Convention on domestic law, that the law of confidence could extend to cover the injunctions sought in the instant case. She said that 'the common law continues to evolve, as it has done for centuries, and it is being given considerable impetus to do so by the implementation of the Convention into our domestic law'.

Her view was that the duty of confidence could arise in equity independently of a transaction or relationship between the parties. She said that the duty of confidence placed upon the media arises when confidential information comes to their knowledge in circumstances in which the media have notice of its confidentiality. This was a very significant finding since it relied on the nature of the information and not on other factors giving rise to an obligation of confidence. She further said that it was also recognised that it would be just in all the circumstances that information known to be confidential should not be disclosed to others, in this case by publication in the press.[470] The issue in question was whether the information leading to disclosure of the claimants' identity and location came within the confidentiality brackets. In answering that crucial question, she found that she could rely upon the European case law and the duty on the court, where necessary, to take appropriate steps to safeguard the physical safety

---

468   [2001] 2 WLR 992.
469   [2001] 1 All ER 908 at pp 1064–65, paras 80–81.
470   She relied on Lord Goff in *AG v Guardian Newspapers Ltd (No 2)* [1990] 1 AC 109.

of the claimants, including the adoption of measures even in the sphere of relations of individuals and/or private organisations between themselves. She said that under the umbrella of confidentiality there would be information which might require a special quality of protection. In the present case the reason for advancing that special quality was that, if the information was published, the publication would be likely to lead to grave and possibly fatal consequences.

Bearing that finding in mind, Dame Butler-Sloss found that the appropriate measures to be taken were to grant the injunctions since they would substantially reduce the risk to each of the claimants. The court therefore proceeded to grant the injunctions 'against the world'. It was not thought that this extension of the law of confidence would lead to the granting of general restrictions on the media in cases where anonymity would be desirable since, under the strict application of Art 10(2), it would only be appropriate to grant injunctions to restrain the media where it could be convincingly demonstrated, within those exceptions, that it was strictly necessary. The court left open the question whether it would be appropriate to grant injunctions to restrict the press in this case if only Art 8, as opposed to Arts 2 and 3, had been likely to be breached. Although the breach of the claimants' right to respect for family life and privacy would have been likely to be serious, it might not have been sufficient to meet the importance of the preservation of the freedom of expression in Art 10(1). This was a very significant ruling since it provided for the anonymity of adults. However, the question whether the injunction would have been issued on grounds of the threat of a very serious invasion of privacy alone was left open. It may be noted that the injunction was varied in July 2001 to absolve internet service providers (ISPs) from liability if matter identifying Venables or Thompson were to be posted on a website accessed through ISPs without their knowledge, if they had no knowledge that the material was on the site and had taken all reasonable steps to prevent publication of the banned material.[471] However, the varied injunction did not specify the steps that ISPs would be expected to take. This episode highlighted the potential inefficacy of the use of injunctions in the internet era.

The decisions in *Douglas* and *Venables* were followed in *Mills (Heather) v News Group Newspapers Ltd*.[472] Mills was a well-known and successful model who had, since 1999, been publicly associated with Sir Paul McCartney. She contracted to buy a property, and in view of a number of very disturbing e-mails she received, and in the light of the circumstances surrounding the death of John Lennon, and the attack on George Harrison, she was anxious to ensure that details of her address were not given public circulation, since she feared that she might be subject to physical threats or even injury. She bought the property under an alias. However, the *Sun* was informed by a person, who had obtained the information from a friend who lived nearby, that she had information that Mills was buying a house. The editor of the *Sun* decided, owing to the good relationship of the newspaper with Sir Paul McCartney, not to run the story. He was asked for confirmation that the paper would not publish the address and/or a photograph and/or a description of the property in breach of the Code of

---

471 See the *Guardian*, 11 July 2001, p 2. See further guardian.co.uk/bulger.
472 [2001] EMLR 41, 4 June, High Court No HC 0102236, WL 720322. See also *A v B and C* (2001) WL 1251798.

Practice of the Press Complaints Commission (PCC). He would not confirm this in writing because he thought that other newspapers would run the story, and that were others to publish, he could not guarantee that the *Sun* would not publish it by way of 'secondary publication'. He said, however, that he could run it within the PCC Code but had decided not to. In view of this response there seemed to be a risk of publication; Mills then sought and obtained an *ex parte* injunction against the publishers of the *Sun* newspaper to restrain publication of material which might identify her new address.

The Court noted that the case for an injunction was on the ground of breach of confidence since, in general, the rights in the Convention, as incorporated by the 1998 Act, and in particular Art 8, did not justify the creation of new causes of action to give effect to them where the common law or statute law is deficient.[473] It said that the English courts had not, unlike the American courts which applied and developed the views expressed by Warren and Brandeis in their famous article in the *Harvard Law Review* in 1890,[474] developed a separate right of privacy prohibiting unreasonable and offensive intrusion on the interest of a person in solitude or seclusion, or objectionable publicity of private information about a person. However, it thought that this deficiency was being remedied, as was made clear by Sedley LJ in *Douglas v Hello! Ltd*.[475]

Assuming that the information in question – Ms Mills' address, or information that would reveal it – was therefore confidential information, the question was whether it should be protected by an injunction. The court found that there was no evidence that the newspaper had learned of it from or through some person who learned of it through some confidential relationship or transaction. But it said that it is no longer a necessary element of the cause of action that the information arises from a confidential relationship. In so finding it relied on the findings of Dame Elizabeth Butler-Sloss P in *Venables v News Group Newspapers Ltd*[476] to the effect that the court had jurisdiction to restrain the publication of material about Venables and Thompson, to protect information about their identities and whereabouts, because the disclosure of the information would have disastrous consequences for them.

Thus, the court found that there is jurisdiction to restrain a newspaper from publishing the address of a person in certain circumstances. However, it said that the mere publication of an address may not be a breach of confidence, or an unwarranted invasion of privacy. It said that, as the *Venables* case shows, one of the necessary additional elements may be the risk of injury or death to the person involved. In so finding, the court noted the practice of the PCC in applying the privacy provision of its Code of Practice (cl 3) which it said indicated that the rationale for prohibiting newspapers from publishing the address of the home of a celebrity (or material which might enable people to find its whereabouts) is not simply that the address is protected information, but that a risk to the safety of the person might thereby be created.

---

473 In so finding it relied on *Venables v News Group Newspapers Ltd* [2001] 2 WLR 1038, pp 1048–49, 1075, paras 24–25, 111, and disagreed with *Douglas v Hello! Ltd*, p 1026, para 129, *per* Sedley LJ.

474 Vol 4, p 193.

475 [2001] 2 WLR 992, p 1025, paras 125–26. Sedley LJ said: the 'two first-named clients have a right of privacy which English law will today recognise and, where appropriate, protect. To say this is in my belief to say little, save by way of a label, that our courts have not said already over the years . . .'. Cf Brooke LJ, para 95; Keene LJ, paras 165–67. See further Jack J in *A v B and C* (2001) unreported, 30 April. (The Court of Appeal decision in *A v B* is discussed below, p. 911.)

476 [2001] 2 WLR 1038.

Similarly the judge in *Theakston v MGN*,[477] a case concerning surreptitiously taken photographs of a minor celebrity's encounter with prostitutes, was prepared to injunct any photographs of Theakston's encounter, despite the absence of any circumstances imposing the obligation save the intimate nature of the events recorded. Theakston clearly had had no pre-existing relationship with the surreptitious photographer and on the evidence he had not (obviously) made any express stipulation that the occasion was a confidential one. The decision therefore gave support to the findings in *Douglas* and in *Venables*, that there was no need to identify further circumstances imposing the obligation of confidence. The judge did not however consider what the basis of the action would be.

After these decisions it was possible to say, with a certainty that was not previously appropriate, that the law recognised and protected a right of personal privacy. That right found its roots in an existing cause of action, the doctrine of confidence. The HRA had, as commentators had predicted, given the courts the impetus to develop confidence to this point. But it is important to be clear about the method of reaching this stage. The *Douglas* decision did not rely on the creation of so-called direct horizontal effect in the sense of the creation of a new free-standing cause of action: the HRA precludes an action directly against newspapers based on Art 8, since newspapers are not public authorities within the meaning of s 6 of the HRA.

But once the plaintiffs were in Court presenting an arguable case for an injunction on grounds of confidence, the Court had a duty, under s 12(4) HRA (if not under s 6 as a public authority) to develop that action by reference to Art 10, which meant also giving full weight to Art 8 as a right recognised under Art 10(2). In taking Art 8 into account, the domestic courts also accepted that, as interpreted at Strasbourg, its guarantees clearly affect the relations between private parties. The most important aspect of the findings in *Douglas* related to the possibility of a surreptitious taking of the photographs since that was the instance in which the doctrine of confidence as traditionally conceived gives way to privacy. In other words, where surreptitious takings of information were in question, privacy values were able to determine the issue, although both *Mills* and *Venables* found that these values were reflected in an extension of the doctrine of confidence, not in a common law doctrine of privacy. As indicated above, this development was already occurring, but the reliance on privacy values gave it a grounding in case law and in principle which it had previously lacked.

These early post-HRA decisions provided a consolidation of the developments in the law of confidence described above, which was clearly needed. While, prior to the inception of the HRA, confidence had the potential to be applied in the archetypal privacy case, the developments outlined above had a relatively slight grounding in authority: there were comparatively few cases involving personal, as opposed to commercial information; moreover, in those which dealt with such information, there was only one decision, at the interlocutory stage,[478] where the obligation of confidence was imposed without there being an express or implied promise that the information would be kept secret[479] or where there had not at least been a pre-existing relationship

---

477 [2002] EMLR 22.
478 *Francome* [1984] 1 WLR 892.
479 As there was in *Stephens v Avery* [1988] Ch 449 and *HRH Princess of Wales* (1993) Transcript, Association of Official Shorthandwriters Ltd, 8 November 1993.

between confider and confidant.[480] All but one of the cases[481] involving surreptitious takings of information (where there was no pre-existing relationship or agreement of confidentiality) occurred in the commercial or professional context. It had been argued that in such cases, the courts were only protecting the plaintiffs' rights to the fruits of their labour;[482] conversely, it was said that the basis of intervention in personal information cases had historically been to protect the integrity of certain kinds of relationship. Thus, where personal information was revealed in circumstances where there was no such prior relationship, it was argued that there was no clear social need to protect confidentiality[483] and in the absence of such a need, the judges should not use the law to enforce 'free-standing' moral convictions,[484] such as a belief that private information should not be disclosed without consent. Lord Bingham had said of the claim that confidence could have been used to remedy the violation of privacy which occurred in *Kaye v Robertson*,[485] that such use would have done 'impermissible violence to the principles upon which that cause of action is founded'.[486]

Thus, had it not been for the advent of the HRA, a conservative appellate court, determined to restore the action to the founding principles which Lord Bingham invoked, could well have found that the use of confidence to protect privacy was weakly supported by authority, an illegitimate distortion of the law and lacking any underpinning in clear legal principle.[487] But, as *Douglas* demonstrates, under the HRA, the right to respect for privacy declared by Art 8 has become, as discussed above, an important legal value or principle, which may properly inform the direction of the common law. The Strasbourg jurisprudence examined above indicates that unremedied invasions of privacy by the media are in principle a violation of Art 8. Thus, the consolidation of the developments described above, far from being regarded as an illegitimate exercise in judicial activism, has now been underpinned by legal principle, and justified by the need identified at Strasbourg to answer to the requirements of Art 8 in this area through the common law.

Somewhat ironically, s 12 HRA, introduced after intense media lobbying to provide greater protection for the press to counterbalance the possible effect of Art 8, in fact encouraged the courts to provide remedies against the worst excesses of intrusive journalism. In particular, it afforded further status, as the decisions emphasised, to the PCC Code, which is, as indicated above, quite extensively concerned with privacy.

480 In *Duchess of Argyll v Duke of Argyll* [1967] 1 Ch 302, there was a prior relationship of husband and wife, in *HRH Princess of Wales* (1993) Transcript, Association of Official Shorthandwriters Ltd, 8 November 1993, a commercial relationship, and in *Michael Barrymore* ([1997] FSR 600), a close friendship and a sexual relationship (there was also a written agreement of confidentiality).

481 *Francome* [1984] 1 WLR 892 is the exception.

482 Wilson, op. cit., fn 1, p 49.

483 This view ignored the argument, notably advanced by Feldman, that the right to privacy does serve a strong social function in protecting the integrity of the different spheres of business, social and personal life within which we operate as individuals ('Secrecy, dignity or autonomy: views of privacy as a civil liberty' (1994) 47(2) CLP 42, pp 51–53).

484 Wilson, op. cit., fn 1, pp 54–55.

485 [1991] FSR 62. The argument is put in Fenwick and Phillipson, 'Confidence and Privacy: a Re-examination' [1996] 55(3) CLJ 447, pp 449–50.

486 Bingham LJ, 'Should there be a law to protect rights of personal privacy?' (1996) 5 EHRLR 450, p 457.

487 See, however, the Court of Appeal judgment in *Dept of Health ex p Source Informatics Ltd* [2000] 2 WLR 953.

Breach of privacy

The following decisions make more explicit the shift from confidence to privacy. Most importantly, the House of Lords in *Campbell* afforded relief in a situation in which, very clearly, the only basis for doing so was the nature of the information itself. In the decisions considered so far this was contemplated but relief was denied (*Theakston, Mills*), or the engagement of Art 8 was not the determining factor (*Venables*), or the decision dealt with a situation in which, either the more traditional confidence analysis applied, or in any event the message that the information was not to be disclosed was made explicit (*Douglas*).

In *A v B plc* the Court of Appeal dealt with the vexed issue of the requirement of an obligation of confidentiality very straightforwardly as follows:

> The need for the existence of a confidential relationship should not give rise to problems as to the law ... A duty of confidence will arise whenever the party subject to the duty is in a situation where he either knows or ought to know that the other person can reasonably expect his privacy to be protected.[488]

This passage created the possibility that the obviously private nature of the information itself could create the reasonable expectation of privacy. It made it clear that a duty of confidentiality could be imposed purely on the basis of such a reasonable expectation. That meant that the test of imposing an obligation of confidence had disappeared. These comments were, however, obiter since on the facts of the case a duty of confidence in the more traditional sense could arguably have arisen. The case concerned a 'kiss and tell' story: the applicant, a premiership footballer, had had a pre-existing relationship with the women who then sold the story of their relationship to the newspaper. On the other hand, there was not much reason to suppose that there was a public interest in preserving the confidentiality of a relationship based on casual sex.[489] It is argued that the finding is not to be viewed as *obiter* on that basis. It is *obiter* because it could have depended on the 'reasonable man' test already in existence.

The seminal case of *Campbell*[490] in the House of Lords was the turning point in the final transformation of confidence into privacy. Naomi Campbell complained in an action both in breach of confidence and under the Data Protection Act 1998 after the *Mirror* newspaper had published details of her treatment for drug addiction with Narcotics Anonymous, including surreptitiously-taken photographs of her leaving the clinic and hugging other clients. Importantly, this photo made the location of the NA centre that Campbell had been attending clearly identical to anyone familiar with the area.[491] In the trial the information in question was divided into five classes as follows:

(1) the fact of Miss Campbell's drug addiction;
(2) the fact that she was receiving treatment;

---

488 [2002] 3WLR 542, at 551B.
489 Lord Woolf said, in *A v B* at para 45: 'Relationships of the sort which A had with C and D (the women in question) are not the categories of relationships which the court should be astute to protect when the other parties to the relationships do not want them to remain confidential.'
490 [2004] 2 WLR 1232.
491 As Lord Nicholls found: ibid, at para 5.

(3) the fact that she was receiving treatment at Narcotics Anonymous;

(4) the details of the treatment – how long she had been attending meetings, how often she went, how she was treated within the sessions themselves, the extent of her commitment, and the nature of her entrance on the specific occasion; and

(5) the visual portrayal [through photographs] of her leaving a specific meeting with other addicts and being hugged before such a meeting by other members of the group receiving treatment [492]

The applicant had conceded that the *Mirror* was entitled to publish the information in categories (1) and (2) – the vital fact that Campbell was a drug addict and was receiving treatment for her addiction;[493] the dispute therefore centred around the question whether publishing the further details and the photographs (categories (3)–(5)) could attract liability. The Court of Appeal found that the extra details in these categories were too insignificant to warrant the intervention of the courts.

It was clear that most of the 'information' in the case – the fact of, and details of the treatment – were provided to the *Mirror* by another patient at Narcotics Anonymous or one of Campbell's staff, sources who would have been caught by the obligation of confidence even under the traditional doctrine of confidence.[494] But the photographs had clearly been covertly taken. Morland J at first instance found that the taking of such photographs imposed an obligation of confidentiality.[495] The Court of Appeal reversed this finding only on the basis that the photographs disclosed no fresh confidential information, *not* on the basis that under the circumstances no obligation of confidentiality could be imposed.

The finding that no relief should be granted in respect of the photographs was over-turned in the Lords. A majority of the House of Lords found liability in confidence in respect of the publication of surreptitiously-taken photographs of the model outside Narcotics Anonymous, in the street. There were clearly no circumstances that could impose an obligation of confidentiality in the traditional sense. There was obviously no pre-existing relationship between Campbell and the photographer. Clearly, there had been no express or implied promise by the photographer of confidentiality. Those factors appeared to be no longer necessary in any event, according to the findings in *Douglas* and in *Venables* discussed above. The duty to refrain from disclosing the information arose purely from the private nature of the information itself. In *Douglas* there were warning signs forbidding photography which could be viewed as indicating to the reasonable person that the information was to remain confidential. In *Venables*, although obviously there was no pre-existing relationship or agreement between the claimants and the newspapers, it was not clear that relief would have been granted purely on the basis that the information in question was private. The engagement of Arts 2 and 3 was crucial. So this was the first time that the nature of the information

---

492 Ibid, at para 23.

493 This was because it was accepted that the press was entitled to expose the falsity of Campbell's previous public statements that she did not take drugs and was not a drug addict.

494 On the basis of an express or implied promise of confidentiality (with a fellow patient) or relationship of trust and confidence (with clinic staff).

495 Ibid, at para 40(2).

alone was allowed to impose a duty not to publish it. As Lord Nicholls put it: 'This cause of action has now firmly shaken off the limiting constraint of the need for an initial confidential relationship.'[496]

So if the private nature of the information in itself imposes that obligation, then the test of an obligation to maintain confidentiality becomes redundant. The photographs were found to attract liability only by the majority, but the minority rejected this finding, not on the basis that there was no obligation of confidence, but because of their finding that the photographs contained no information worthy of protection. Lord Nicholls – one of the minority – made it clear the test of an obligation to maintain confidentiality was no longer a necessary part of the action in stating: 'the law imposes a "duty of confidence" whenever a person receives information he knows or ought to know is fairly and reasonably to be regarded as confidential'.[497]

Lord Hope said: 'If the information is obviously private, the situation will be one where the person to whom it relates can reasonably expect his privacy to be respected.'[498] He further said that the only element required to give rise to the reasonable expectation of privacy is the fact that the information is obviously private. So all that is needed is that there is private information which the defendant publishes without consent, or seeks to publish. With the decision in *Campbell* the action therefore become one for breach of privacy. The 2005 Court of Appeal judgment in *Douglas v Hello! Ltd*,[499] strongly re-affirmed this development, and was prepared to discard the terminology of confidence in favour of that of privacy. Buxton LJ in *McKennitt v Ash*[500] also referred to 'the rechristening of the tort as misuse of private information' which had occurred in *Campbell*.[501]

A similar stance regarding the need to show only that the information was private was taken in *McKennitt v Ash* in the Court of Appeal. The case concerned the publication in 2005 of a book *Travels with Loreena McKennitt: My Life as a Friend*. The book was written by the defendant, Niema Ash, who was formerly a friend of Ms McKennitt, a well-known folk star with a global reputation. She had often travelled and socialised with Ms McKennitt and she entertained her while she was in England.

Ms McKennitt claimed that a substantial part of the book revealed personal and private detail about her which she was entitled to keep private. Ms McKennitt had always very carefully guarded her personal privacy. But she accepted that she had occasionally released some personal information which she felt comfortable with, and in respect

---

496 *Campbell v MGN Ltd* [2004] 2 AC 457 at paras 13–14. Part of the argument on *Campbell* draws on that of my co-author, Gavin Phillipson, in *Media Freedom under the Human Rights Act* (2006) at pp 738–39

497 [2004] 2 AC 457 at para 14. Lady Hale also summarised the essential requirement of the new-style action very clearly: 'The position we have reached is that [prima facie liability is made out] when the person publishing the information knows or ought to know that there is a reasonable expectation that the information in question will be kept confidential': ibid, para 134.

498 Ibid, para 96.

499 [2005] EWCA Civ 595. This is the decision of the Court of Appeal on the appeal from the decision to award damages at final trial made by Lindsay J: [2003] 3 All ER 996 (*Douglas II*), the Court of Appeal having in 2001 declined to grant an injunction in the case: [2001] QB 967.

500 [2006] EWCA Civ 1714.

501 In *McKennitt* at para 8. Lord Nicholls of Birkenhead had used this term in *Campbell* [2004] 2 AC 457 at para 14.

of which she was able to control the boundaries herself.[502] This occurred mainly in connection with a charity which she had founded and the personal information she divulged was highly relevant to the charity's key purposes. The information sought to be restrained contained in the book included: Ms McKennitt's personal and sexual relationships; her personal feelings and, in particular, in relation to her deceased fiancé and the circumstances of his death; matters relating to her health and diet; matters relating to her emotional vulnerability, and as to the specifics of the interior of her home. Buxton LJ found that all of it was obtained within a pre-existing relationship of confidence, in the traditional sense. He found that not only would a reasonable man standing in Ms Ash's shoes have realised that the information was confidential, but that Ms Ash herself clearly realised that it was, from comments that she had made in the book.

Against that background he found that the information in relation to which relief was sought could be accounted private information – the key question – because, he noted, relying on *Von Hannover*:

> . . . private life, in the Courts view, includes a person's physical and psychological integrity; the guarantee afforded by Article 8 of the Convention is primarily intended to ensure the development, without outside interference, of the personality of each individual in his relations with other human beings. There is therefore a zone of interaction of a person with others, even in a public context, which may fall within the scope of private life. Based on that general principle, the ECtHR held that there [was] no doubt that the publication by various German magazines of photos of the applicant in her daily life either on her own or with other people falls within the scope of her private life.[503]

The defendant had sought to suggest that the ECtHR went no further in *Von Hannover* than to hold that the Princess's privacy had been invaded by a campaign of media intrusion into her life, and otherwise the taking and publication of the photographs would not have been in itself an invasion of privacy. Buxton LJ rejected that contention, on the basis that the findings in *Von Hannover* were not confined to an instance of a campaign of media intrusion. It was concluded on that basis that the information in question was covered by Art 8. Although *Von Hannover* was taken into account, it was clear that the information was of a more personal nature than the information about the Princess. But the references to *Von Hannover* indicated that the Court of Appeal would probably have been prepared to find that less intimate information was also covered. As discussed above, the key question was whether Article 8 was engaged, as determined by reference to *Von Hannover*.[504]

It is clear that the findings in the appeal ranged widely, well beyond the narrow limits of the facts of the case. The Court of Appeal made it clear that it was not necessary to identify factors giving rise to an obligation of confidence – even though such factors were in fact present. It was also made clear that the determination as

502 At para 6.
503 At para 38.
504 See p 883.

to whether information is private must be made by reference to Art 8, and that *Von Hannover*, as the leading case, should be applied without limiting its scope to an instance of media harassment. Thus, personal facts could be covered even if partly in the public domain. Some of the information at issue was partly in the public domain due to its controlled release by Ms McKennitt as part of her charity work. Clearly, the information complained of was not acquired in public in the way that the information at issue in *Von Hannover* was acquired, but Buxton LJ's judgment indicated that if it had been, it would have been viewed as private information.

In *McKennitt* and in *Campbell* it can be seen that the need to demonstrate that an obligation of confidentiality had been imposed was entirely discarded. Both judgments clearly accepted – as *Venables* and *Mills* did not – that the step from confidence to privacy had been taken, and that the determination as to whether the information should be accounted private, relying on Art 8, had become the only necessary step in deciding that relief could be afforded, subject to the speech/privacy balancing act. The acceptance that a key element of confidence could and should be discarded in favour of relying on Art 8 is indicative of an acceptance in this context of an absolute duty to develop the common law by reference to the Convention rights, under the s 6 HRA doctrine of indirect horizontal effect.

The public interest defence

Perhaps the most important concern relating to the development of confidence as a remedy for invasion of privacy is the fear that the action will pose an unacceptable risk to media freedom. The main insurance against this possibility pre-HRA rested with the public interest defence, whereby disclosure of admittedly private or confidential information was permitted if this would serve the public interest.[505] A recent example of the working of this defence was provided by the 2007 'Cash for Honours' inquiry. The Attorney General sought to obtain injunctions to prevent disclosure of the identity of one of the persons involved on the ground of breach of confidence.[506] The injunction was refused on the basis of the public interest value of the information.

---

505 While originally only allowing disclosure if it would reveal wrongdoing on the part of the plaintiff (*Gartside v Outram* (1856) 26 LJ Ch 113, p 114 and in relation to copyright, *Glyn v Weston Feature Film* Co [1916] 1 Ch 261) the strength of the public interest in question rather than the individual wrongdoing of the plaintiff is now the determining factor: see *Fraser v Evans*, ([1969] 1 QB 349), *Schering Chemicals v Falkman* [1981] 2 WLR 848, esp p 869, *X v Y* ([1988] 2 All ER 648) and *AG v Jonathan Cape* [1976] 1 QB 752; *Lion Laboratories v Evans and Express Newspapers* [1984] 1 QB 530, *W v Egdell* ([1990] Ch 359) and *Hellewell* [1995] 1 WLR 804; *AG v Guardian Newspapers (No 2)* [1990] 1 AC 109, p 282, *per* Lord Goff, and p 268, *per* Lord Griffiths. Note that where disclosure has been said to be in the public interest because it exposes particular criminal or anti-social behaviour or reveals some specific risk to public health, it has been held this will not always justify disclosing the matter in the press: see *Francome* ([1984] 1 WLR 892); *Initial Services Ltd v Putterill* [1968] 1 QB 396, pp 405–6, *per* Lord Denning; *AG v Guardian Newspapers (No 2)* [1990] 1 AC 109, p 269, *per* Lord Griffiths; ibid, p 282, *per* Lord Goff; ibid, p 177, *per* Sir John Donaldson in the Court of Appeal.

506 The *Guardian* revealed that a meeting between Lord Levy, the Labour Party's chief fund-raiser and Ms Turner, a Downing St aide, was central to the police inquiry into the Cash for Honours affair. Lord Levy was arrested in connection with the affair. A High Court judge refused the injunction against the *Guardian* sought by the Attorney General (see the *Guardian* 7 March 2007). An injunction against the BBC covering the same story was also lifted.

None of the cases in which the public interest defence was discussed at length pre-HRA concerned the paradigmatic privacy claim, and Art 10 of the Convention had little influence upon it prior to the inception of the HRA.[507] The traditional public interest defence is discussed at this point; its role now is to weigh in the balance when Arts 8 and 10 are weighed up against each other, as discussed below. If weighty public interest factors are present, that may tip the balance in favour of Art 10. It is discussed here in order to indicate the development that has occurred and to identify the factors that are viewed as relevant.

Traditionally, confidential information would not be protected if the public interest served by disclosing the information in question outweighed the interest in preserving confidentiality. This aspect of the doctrine was often termed the 'public interest' defence. It was traditionally said that there is no confidence in iniquity: the plaintiff could not use the law of confidence to cover up his or her own wrong-doing and therefore the public interest in disclosure would prevail. However, it appears that the 'public interest defence' was not limited to cases of iniquity. The House of Lords found *obiter* in *British Steel Corporation v Granada Television*[508] that publication of confidential information could legitimately be undertaken only where there was misconduct,[509] but in *Lion Laboratories v Evans*[510] Stephenson LJ said that he would reject the 'no iniquity, no public interest rule' agreeing with Lord Denning's statement in *Fraser v Evans*[511] to the effect that 'some things are required to be disclosed in the public interest in which case no confidence can be prayed in aid to keep them secret and [iniquity] is merely an instance of just cause and excuse for breaking confidence'. These rulings concerned confidential information held by private companies and seemed to leave open the possibility of the existence of a broad public interest defence which, it seemed from *Woodward*, might also sometimes apply in the case of public figures.

Where personal information relating to a private individual was in issue, the ruling in *X v Y*[512] suggested that the public interest defence was confined to cases of iniquity. On the other hand, *Lion Laboratories v Evans and Express Newspapers*,[513] *W v Egdell*[514] and *Hellewell* suggested that the defence had broadened its focus of concern with the result that the strength of the public interest in question rather than the individual wrongdoing of the plaintiff might tend to be the determining factor. In *W v Egdell*, no such wrongdoing was relied upon in finding that the medical report relating to the plaintiff's condition should be placed before the appropriate authorities where it was in the public interest to do so. It should be noted that this decision placed some limitations on the ability of the public interest defence to afford protection to press freedom: it was found that it might sometimes be appropriate to pass information to

---

507   Remarkably, Jacob J's pre-HRA judgment in *Michael Barrymore* [1997] FSR 600 – a case relating to the unauthorised disclosure of personal information and thus clearly raising both privacy and speech issues – did not once advert to the Convention.
508   [1981] AC 1096; [1981] 1 All ER 417, HL.
509   See Cripps (1984) 4 OJLS 184 on the public interest defence.
510   [1985] QB 526, p 537.
511   [1969] 1 QB 349, p 362.
512   [1988] 2 All ER 648.
513   [1985] QB 526; [1984] 2 All ER 417, CA.
514   [1990] Ch 359; see also *X v Y* [1988] 2 All ER 658 and *dicta* of Lord Goff in *AG v Guardian Newspapers (No 2)*, p 659.

a particular body rather than disclosing it to the public at large. On the other hand, where the public itself had previously been misled by the plaintiff, it appeared that wide disclosure might be warranted.

These points should not be taken as assuming that the public interest always required disclosure of information and would therefore invariably be in competition with the interest of the plaintiff in suppressing it. Clearly, there was a general public interest in allowing the transmission of information from one person to another without interference, and in certain circumstances such as those which arose in *X v Y*[515] there might be a further specific public interest in maintaining confidentiality. A newspaper wished to publish information deriving from confidential hospital records which showed that certain practising doctors were suffering from the AIDS virus. In granting an injunction preventing publication, Rose J took into account the public interest in disclosure, but weighed it against the private interest in confidentiality and the public interest in encouraging AIDS patients to seek help from hospitals, which would not be served if it was thought that confidentiality might not be maintained.

Where public bodies are in possession of personal information, their obligations in relation to disclosure may differ from those applicable in private law. In *Chief Constable of the North Wales Police ex p Thorpe*,[516] the police had confidential information to the effect that the occupants of a caravan on a particular site were paedophiles, with a number of convictions for sexual offences. They sought judicial review of the decision of the police to disclose their convictions to the owner of the caravan site. It was found by the Court of Appeal that the duty of the police in such a circumstance differs from that under private law. The police as a public authority were not free to publish the information despite the fact that it could be viewed as being in the public domain, but that the information could be used if that was what was required to protect the public, as in the instant case. Both Art 8 and English administrative law would accept that the police were entitled to use the information in such an instance.

The approach of the domestic courts in the pre-HRA era was becoming very similar to that of the House of Lords in the important decision on defamation in *Reynolds v Times Newspapers*,[517] which concerned the proper balance to be struck between the individual right to reputation on the one hand and the freedom of the press on the other. The issue for determination was whether qualified privilege[518] should attach to good-faith political speech in the media. Their Lordships, while recognising for the first time that it could, showed a marked preference for the retention of a very broad and flexible test which asked simply whether, in all the circumstances, the public interest required publication of the material in question.[519] While Lord Nicholls showed some recognition of the possible 'chilling effect' which could arise if the imprecision of the test left the media uncertain as to the boundaries of permissible speech, he thought some uncertainty

---

515 [1988] 2 All ER 648.
516 [1999] QB 396.
517 [1999] 3 WLR 1010; [1999] 4 All ER 609.
518 If the defendant can establish the privilege, then even though he cannot prove the truth of the defamatory allegations, the plaintiff can succeed only if he can show that the defendant had known the allegations to be false or was indifferent to their veracity.
519 This approach was thought to be in harmony with Strasbourg jurisprudence on Art 10: see p 610 (the head note) and p 625 (*per* Lord Nicholls), an issue discussed below.

unavoidable and regarded its likely extent as relatively small in any case.[520] It thus seemed plausible to assume that a similar approach was likely to prevail in relation to the breach of confidence action,[521] as recommended by the Law Commission.[522]

It may be concluded that there were two key developments in the defence in the pre-HRA era. First, while originally only allowing disclosure if it would reveal wrongdoing on the part of the plaintiff,[523] the strength of the public interest in question rather than the individual wrongdoing of the plaintiff became the determining factor.[524] Secondly, where disclosure was said to be in the public interest because it exposed particular criminal or anti-social behaviour, or revealed some specific risk to public health, it was clear that this would not always justify disclosing the matter in the press.[525]

The public interest defence provided a means of reconciling the demands of speech and privacy. Under the impetus of the HRA, this balancing exercise is becoming, as indicated below, more sophisticated since it is largely undertaken as a balancing act between Arts 8 and 10 with their associated jurisprudence. Section 12 HRA is relevant as discussed below and draws in the PCC Privacy Code. The Strasbourg principles of necessity and proportionality determines the balance between the conflicting demands of speech and privacy, as indicated below, but it is likely that these domestic decisions will nevertheless be drawn upon since they provide some useful guidance aiding determinations as to the resolution of that conflict. Section 8 below examines the speech/privacy conflict that the new law has had to grapple with, since the issues raised are pertinent in all speech/privacy clashes considered in this chapter.

Further redundant elements

A defence of waiver?

In *Woodward v Hutchins*,[526] intimate facts about Tom Jones and another pop star were revealed to the *Daily Mirror* by a former agent who had been their confidante. The plaintiffs sought an injunction on the ground of breach of confidence. There had been a confidential relationship and they claimed that the agent should not be able to take unfair advantage of that confidentiality. The Court of Appeal failed to uphold the claim on the basis that the plaintiffs had sought to publicise themselves in order to present a certain

---

520 Ibid, pp 623–24.
521 The defence will always involve somewhat different considerations: in privacy cases, matters concerning the defendant's attempts to verify the allegations and give a balanced account will be inapplicable.
522 The Commission considered that the courts should retain a 'broad power' to decide whether 'in the particular case' the public interest required disclosure (op. cit., fn 2, at para 6.77).
523 *Gartside v Outram* (1856) 26 LJ Ch 113, p 114 and in relation to copyright, *Glyn v Weston Feature Film Co* [1916] 1 Ch 261.
524 See *Fraser v Evans* [1969] 1 QB 349; *Schering Chemicals v Falkman* [1981] 2 WLR 848, esp p 869; *X v Y* [1988] 2 All ER 648 and *AG v Jonathan Cape* [1976] 1 QB 752; *Lion Laboratories v Evans and Express Newspapers* [1984] 1 QB 530, *W v Egdell* [1990] Ch 359; and *Hellewell* [1995] 1 WLR 804; *AG v Guardian Newspapers (No 2)* [1990] 1 AC 109, p 282, *per* Lord Goff, and p 268, *per* Lord Griffiths.
525 See *Francome* [1984] 1 WLR 892; *Initial Services Ltd v Putterill* [1968] 1 QB 396, pp 405–6, *per* Lord Denning; *AG v Guardian Newspapers (No 2)* [1990] 1 AC 109, p 269, *per* Lord Griffiths; ibid, p 282, *per* Lord Goff; ibid, p 177, *per* Sir John Donaldson in the Court of Appeal.
526 [1977] 1 WLR 760, CA.

'image' and therefore could not complain if the truth were later revealed. This decision has been criticised on the basis that a need to reveal the truth about the plaintiffs was irrelevant to the breach of confidence on the part of the agent,[527] but it has not been overruled. The public interest in knowing the truth about the plaintiffs seemed to rest on a refusal to use the law to protect their attempt to mislead the public.

In *Campbell* it was made clear that there is no general defence of waiver. The applicant herself had conceded that *the Mirror* was entitled to publish the fact that she was a drug addict and was receiving treatment for her addiction; it was accepted that the press was entitled to expose the falsity of her previous public statements that she did not take drugs and was not a drug addict. As Phillipson puts it, 'This, however, was on the basis that there was a public interest in preventing the public from being misled,[528] *not* on any notion that that publicity-seeking *in itself* destroys an individual's reasonable expectation of privacy'.[529] Campbell's general statements that she was not a drug addict did not defeat, it was found, her expectation of privacy in relation to the *details* of her treatment for drug addiction. Lord Hoffmann found, '[Campbell] is a public figure who has had a long and symbiotic relationship with the media. A person may attract or even seek publicity about some aspects of his or her life without creating any public interest in the publication of personal information about other matters.'[530] None of their Lordships accepted that Campbell's publicity-seeking in the past would destroy protection for her private life.

It is concluded that the 'defence of waiver' is being marginalised, although *Woodward* has not been expressly over-ruled.[531] A person who has placed details of her private life in the public domain by giving interviews to magazines etc may find that that defeats her expectation of privacy, because the matters are not accounted private. Or if a person has misled the public that may provide a public interest argument that the record should be set straight. In *Campbell* her denial of her drug addiction meant that the fact that she was receiving drug treatment lost protection on the basis that there was a public interest in knowing the truth which defeated her expectation of privacy. Thus the defence of waiver appears to have been swallowed up, mainly in the balancing act between speech and privacy which is discussed below. The attempt by the defendant to put such a defence forward in *McKennitt* on the basis of the plaintiff's alleged hypocrisy was rejected on the ground that the charge of hypocrisy had not been substantiated, but the tone adopted was not propitious: Buxton LJ implied that the courts would not be receptive to attempts to rely on the defence. He said of *Woodward*:

---

527 Wacks, R, *The Protection of Privacy*, 1980, p 85.

528 See, e.g., Lord Nicholls (ibid) at para 24: 'where a public figure chooses to present a false image and make untrue pronouncements about his or her life, the press will normally be entitled to put the record straight.' This approach was endorsed by Lord Hoffmann at para 58 and Lord Hope at para 82.

529 *Media Freedom under the Human Rights Act* (2006) at 776. For a now out-dated view, see the remarks of Lord Wakeham, former Chair of the Press Complaints Commission, to the effect that the former Princess of Wales had made herself 'fair game' for public analysis of her private life by discussing it herself on television (*The Times*, 2 May 1996). A similar argument was also put forward in *Mills v News Group Newspapers* [2001] EMLR 41, 4 June, High Court No HC 0102236, WL 720322 by the *Sun*.

530 [2004] 2 WLR 1232, at para 57.

531 Brooke LJ in *Douglas* dismissed the argument that the couple's admitted previous courting of publicity precluded protection for their privacy; he said that he 'did not obtain any assistance' by citation of *Woodward v Hutchins*': [2001] QB 967, 995.

This case dates back to an era when the Convention had not invaded the consciousness of English lawyers. I bear well in mind the warning of Lord Woolf in [9] of *A v B* that authorities which relate to the action for breach of confidence prior to the coming into force of the 1998 Act are largely of historic interest only.[532]

Detriment arising from unauthorised use of the information

The discussion ends by briefly considering the third element identified as essential in *Coco v AN Clark (Engineers) Ltd*; it appeared to require two ingredients – unauthorised use of the information and detriment arising from such use. This point was addressed by the House of Lords in *AG v Guardian Newspapers (No 2)*, but the Law Lords were divided as to the need to show detriment where a private individual was claiming a breach of confidence. Lord Griffiths considered that detriment had to be shown even in such a case;[533] Lords Brightman and Jauncey were silent as to the issue, while Lord Goff considered that the question should be left open.[534] Lord Keith, however, was of the view that in this respect a private individual should not be treated in the same way as a state body:

> The right to personal privacy is clearly one which the law should in this field seek to protect . . . I would think it is sufficient detriment to the confider that information given in confidence is to be disclosed to persons who he would prefer not to know of it even though the disclosure would not be harmful to him in any positive way.[535]

Obiter dicta in *Shelley Films Ltd v Rex Features Ltd* appeared to favour the position taken by Lord Goff,[536] while Lord Keith's view received some support from the finding in *HRH Princess of Wales v MGN Ltd and Others*[537] which suggested that in relation to private individuals, the courts may be prepared to assume the presence of detriment. The recent privacy cases, including *Campbell* have implicitly taken the latter view. So while showing detriment is a necessary element in state or commercial cases based on the doctrine of confidence, it is now apparent that this is not the case in relation to misuse of private information.

7 The Data Protection Act 1998

Introduction

Until 1998, there was no statute in the UK equivalent to the US Privacy Act 1974 which enables persons to obtain access to information held on them in paper-based and electronic state files. In the UK, certain categories of information covered by the

---

532 At para 33.
533 [1990] 1 AC 109, pp 269–70.
534 Ibid, pp 281–82.
535 Ibid, pp 255–63.
536 10 December 1993, transcript from LEXIS, p 16.
537 Transcript, Association of Official Shorthandwriters Limited, 8 November 1993.

Official Secrets Act 1989 could not be disclosed, but if personal information fell outside those categories there was still no general right of access to it. Central government and public authorities in general hold a vast amount of personal information in manual and computerised files. The police, for example, use a national system which stores an immense amount of personal information, as does the Inland Revenue. But private bodies, including the media, also process personal information; until relatively recently, the citizen had no means of knowing what information was held on him or her by private or public bodies, and no control over the nature or use of such information. However, an inroad into the principle of secrecy was made in 1984 by the Data Protection Act 1984,[538] which was adopted in response to the Council of Europe Convention of 1980.[539] Once access to certain computerised files became possible, access rights to some manual files began to follow, although no general statutory rights of access to personal information or control over the processing of such information were created until the Data Protection Act 1998 (DPA) was passed, and therefore much personal information still remained inaccessible and its processing was uncontrolled. A right of such access was proposed in the 1993 White Paper on freedom of information and open government,[540] but was not implemented in the 2000 Act which came into force in 2005.[541] Prior to the passing of the 1998 Act, the access to information measures discussed below merely provided exceptions to the general denial of access. Therefore the 1998 Act is of immense significance in terms of protecting the privacy of personal information by seeking to ensure that processing is conducted in accordance with the Data Principles.

Background to and context of the Data Protection Act

Control over personal information held electronically[542]

In response to the steady computerisation of information, the government decided in 1975 that those who use computers to handle personal information cannot remain the sole judges of the extent to which their own systems adequately safeguard privacy. The Committee on Data Protection was therefore set up, and the Council of Europe promulgated the Convention on Data Protection in 1980.[543] In response, the DPA 1984,

---

538 The provisions of the 1984 Act were extended by the Data Protection (Subject Access Modifications) Health Order 1987, SI 1987/1903.

539 Convention for the Protection of Individuals with regard to the Automatic Processing of Personal Data, 17 September 1980.

540 Cm 2290. For further discussion of the Code of Practice on Access to Government Information, which was introduced in 1994 as promised in the White Paper, see Chapter 7, pp 627–28, above. The previous Code, and the Freedom of Information Act 2000, which took over its role, were not designed to protect personal information, except in the sense that it is exempted from the access.

541 Section 40(1) FoI: Any information to which a request for information relates is exempt information if it constitutes personal data of which the applicant is the data subject.

542 Texts referred to and further reading: see Lloyd, I, *Information Technology and the Law*, 3rd edn, 2000, LexisNexis UK; Reed, C (ed), *Computer Law*, 1990, Blackstone, Chapter 9; Sieghart, P, *Privacy and Computers*, 1977, Latimer; Tapper, C, *Computer Law*, 1989, Longman; Hewitt, P (ed), *Computers, Records and the Right to Privacy*, 1979, Input Two-Nine; Wacks, op. cit., fn 1, Chapter 6.

543 Convention for the Protection of Individuals with regard to the Automatic Processing of Personal Data, 17 September 1980.

applying to personal information in both the public and private sectors, was passed.[544] It was seen as a measure to protect privacy and a first step towards freedom of information. However, clearly it was difficult to defend allowing access only to electronically held information, as opposed to access to all personal information. As indicated below, the DPA 1998 recognised that most of the arguments regarding the electronic storage of information could also be applied to manual files.

It may be argued that the electronic storage of information presents a partcular threat to privacy because computers exacerbate the problems which also exist with respect to manual files. For example, an error may creep into information held on manual files, but where information is collated from a large number of sources, as may be more likely in respect of computerised files, an error may be more likely to occur. Moreover, once it does occur, the speed with which information can be retrieved and disseminated means that an error can reach far more persons and may do more damage than a record on a manual file. It is possible to transmit data from one data bank to another much more easily than can be done using manual files. Personal information gathered for a purpose acceptable to its subject may be transferred to another data bank without the subject's knowledge or consent. It may also be linked up with other information, thus creating what may be a distorted picture.

There is a danger that the confidentiality of information may be placed at risk. Information may be given to an employer by an employee on the understanding that because there is a confidential relationship between the parties it will go no further. If it is then stored in a data bank, there is a danger that the confidentiality will be lost. An action for breach of confidence could lie, but the individual affected would have to be aware of the breach. The retention of data may also create disadvantages. Although a person's circumstances or behaviour may change, old data may not be updated, but may follow him or her around with the result that (for example) he or she is refused credit. Manually held information is less likely to follow an individual so effectively. It may therefore be said that no difference in principle between problems associated with the storage of manually held and computerised information can be discerned, but that there is a difference of degree.

The regime created by the DPA 1984

The 1984 Act attempted to address the problems of protecting personal information by placing certain obligations on persons storing personal data. Below, the key features of the regime created by the DPA 1984 are indicated; they will be compared with those of the regime created under the 1998 Act.

Any person using a computerised system in order to store data relating to people was designated the 'data user', while the person who was the subject of the data was the 'data subject'. Any data relating to a living person was termed 'personal data'.[545] The data user had to register with the Data Protection Registrar. Section 5 provided that the data user must not use the data for any purpose other than the one it was collected for and under Sched 1, it had to be kept up to date. Also, it had to be adequately

---

544   For commentary, see 'Confidential: computers, records and the right to privacy' (NCCL); Savage, N and Edwards, C, *A Guide to the Data Protection Act*, 1985, Blackstone.
545   These definitions were found in ss 4 and 5 of the Act.

protected; appropriate security measures were to be taken. Under ss 10 and 11, if the Data Registrar was satisfied that the data user was not complying with the Act, she could serve an enforcement notice, and if this measure was not adequate, she could serve a deregistration notice. It was a criminal offence for an unregistered person or body to store personal data.

Section 21 provided that if the data user was asked by the data subject whether personal data was held on her or him, that information had to be given and the data subject had to be allowed access to such data. Schedule 1 also provided that if the data was found to be inaccurate, the data subject could have it corrected or erased. If the data user did not comply, the subject could apply to court under s 24 for an order erasing or rectifying the data. Under s 22, compensation could be awarded if loss or damage had resulted from inaccurate data. However, compensation was available only if the data user compiled the inaccurate information, not if the data user compiled inaccurate material supplied by a malicious or careless third party. No compensation was available for circulating the inaccurate data; nor could the data subject know the third party's name.

A number of aspects of the 1984 Act attracted criticism, especially the wide subject access exemptions which included information relating to crime, national security, and a person's physical or mental health. A broad interpretation tended to be given to these exemptions; thus, the results of the lack of protection for privacy were unchecked in those categories. Moreover, there was still the possibility of transferring data to manual files and as provisions relating to manual files were narrow in scope, especially those under the Access to Personal Files Act 1987, it appeared to be the case that the manual file did not fall within any of the provisions affording access. The transfer of data from a registered data user such as the Department of Employment to an unregistered user, such as the security services, remained secret, and national security was exempt from the principle that data users could not allow data to be used for a purpose other than the original one.

Further, the budgetary restraint on the Data Protection Registry made it impossible to keep a check on all data users. In any event, it was considered relatively straightforward to devise an information retrieval system which only provided an incomplete copy of an individual's record. In such an instance, it appeared probable that no action for breach of the Act was likely to follow due to the inability of the Data Registrar Officer to check up on what had occurred. It would have taken a specialist a long time to work out what had happened, and, given the constraints on the Data Registrar, that time was unlikely to be available. Thus, it may be said that the Act was certainly a step in the direction of control over personal information, but it contained many loop-holes.

The Computer Misuse Act 1990

Unauthorised access to information electronically held falls within the Computer Misuse Act 1990[546] which criminalises such conduct whether or not the 'hacker' has a sinister purpose. It may be wondered why it should be an offence to access files held on an office computer, but not files held in the filing cabinet. One answer is that hacking presents a more widespread and pernicious danger: it is possible to access the files from

---

546 For comment, see 'The Computer Misuse Act 1990' (1990) 140 NLJ 1117.

a different part of the country – there is no need for the would-be hacker to break into the office, as in the case of the unauthorised seeker of information in manual files. Thus, the possibility that persons may gain unauthorised access to personal information may now be diminished, although use of the 1990 Act in practice has proved problematic.[547] Together, the 1984 and 1990 Acts formed a code which, until the inception of the 1998 Act, provided a relatively comprehensive protection for privacy in relation to computerised files containing personal information, when compared with that available in respect of manually held files.

Protection for manually held personal information prior to the inception of the DPA 1998

In the wake of the DPA 1984, access rights to manual files were gradually extended under the influence of the Campaign for Freedom of Information, although without government support. The measures that were introduced were of limited effect, as indicated below, and provided inadequate and piecemeal protection.

The Access to Personal Files Bill was put forward as a Private Members' Bill and would have allowed access to a wide range of personal information. However, the government forced its proponents to accept an eviscerated Bill covering only housing and social security files. Thus, the Bill was restricted to local government because central government was resistant to any measure allowing individuals access to personal files. The Bill became the Access to Personal Files Act 1987. It allowed access to 'accessible information' and therefore provided for the rectification of errors. However, it was acknowledged in the passage of the Bill that there was nothing to prevent the keeping of a secret file behind the accessible file. Moreover, the Act did not have retrospective effect; thus, it did not apply to information collected before it came into effect. It was eventually repealed under the DPA 1998.

The findings of the European Court of Human Rights in the *Gaskin* case[548] illustrated the inadequacy of the available measures. Graham Gaskin wanted to gain access to the personal files on his childhood in care kept by Liverpool City Council because he wanted to sue the council in negligence. He sought to invoke Art 8 and also Art 10. However, the files did not fall under the DPA 1984 since they were manually held; nor did they fall within the Access to Personal Files Act 1987 because they were collected before it came into force. The first question to be determined under Art 8 was whether it could apply to such a situation since it was considered that the essential object of Art 8 is to protect the individual from arbitrary interference by the authorities. However, the court found that there could also be a positive obligation on the authorities to act in certain situations. Here, the information consisted of the only coherent record of the whole of Gaskin's early childhood. It was therefore found that prima facie an obligation to protect privacy arose, because individuals should not be obstructed by the authorities from obtaining information so closely bound up with their identity as human beings. Thus, a positive obligation could arise although it was thought that Art 8 would not normally import such an obligation.

---

547 See Charlesworth, A, 'Between flesh and sand: rethinking the Computer Misuse Act 1990' (1995) 9 International Yearbook of Law, Computers and Technology 33.
548 *Gaskin v UK* (1990) 12 EHRR 36.

The Court then considered whether the exception under Art 8(2) in respect of the rights of others could apply. On the one hand, there was the need to demonstrate respect for Gaskin's privacy; on the other, the contributors of the information wanted it kept confidential. It was found that the two interests should be weighed against each other by invoking the principle of proportionality. However, the local authority had not put in place any means of independently weighing the two values; thus the preference would automatically be given to the interest in maintaining confidence. Therefore, the principle of proportionality was offended and a breach of Art 8 was found. Gaskin was awarded damages on the basis of the distress he had suffered. No breach of Art 10 was found. It was determined that the right to receive information protected by Art 10 meant that the government should not interfere if a willing speaker wished to impart information, but that there was no positive obligation on the government to impart it.

The government complied with this ruling by introducing the Access to Personal Files (Social Services) Regulations 1989, as amended,[549] which provided that social services departments must give personal information to individuals unless the contributor of the information could be identified and he or she did not consent to the access. Certain personal health information was also exempted. Thus, local authorities had to weigh against each other the two values considered by the Court of Human Rights. The Regulations were also eventually repealed by the DPA 1998. One further possible result of the *Gaskin* case was likely to be that test cases would be encouraged in relation to central government files if they were not covered by the DPA 1998 (see below).

A method of obtaining access to medical information relating to oneself arises under the Medical Reports Act 1988[550] which also started life as a Private Members' Bill. It provides for limited circumstances in which a person can obtain access to personal medical information: if an insurance company or prospective insurer asks for a medical report for employment purposes, the individual in question can see it beforehand to read it and check it for errors. An example was given in Parliamentary debate on the Bill of a woman who had had mistakenly included in her medical record a sheet from another record indicating that she was dying of cancer. She was refused insurance and would never have been able to obtain insurance since she had no chance of putting the mistake right. Similarly, a misdiagnosis might remain on a medical record and never be corrected. These possibilities are of particular significance because a medical record contains information on a person's sexual habits and family circumstances; it does not merely contain purely medical information.

The Act, however, creates only a limited right of access; it does not mean that a person has a general right of access to all his or her medical files. There is a view in the medical profession that patients who do not have medical knowledge will not be able to place medical notes in their context, and moreover that knowing of certain conditions may exacerbate their illness since they may worry and therefore come under greater stress. Concerns may also be raised that a general right of access might increase the likelihood of a negligence action; clearly such an action might fail, but they do not welcome the waste of time and energy which fighting an action, even successfully, would entail. The darker side to this argument is, of course, that lack of access rights might preclude a legitimate negligence action: in some instances a patient might never realise that a mistake had been made.

The Access to Health Records Act 1990,[551] took the principle of access in this area much further.[552] Since the introduction of the DPA 1984, patients had been entitled to have access to their computerised health records, but the 1990 Act was intended to provide an equivalent right of access to information recorded in manually held health records. The access to health records allows people to examine exactly what has been recorded about them – thus satisfying personal curiosity – but, more importantly, it will allow for mistakes to be noted and rectified. The emphasis of the Act is on an individual's control of personal and private information. However, several exceptions curb the actual scope of the access. First, as in the Access to Personal Files Act, no pre-commencement material must be shown, unless it is necessary for a full understanding of something which has been shown. It is clear that no right of access to pre-commencement material arises at common law.[553] Second, if the holder of the information – the doctor – considers that disclosure of information would result in serious physical or mental harm to the patient, access can be denied. Third, patients need not be told when information is being withheld. Although the 1990 Act is a move in the direction of enabling individuals to enjoy a degree of control over personal medical information and should ensure higher standards of accuracy and objectivity on the part of doctors and other record holders, it remains the case that patients whose documents are held as computerised records enjoy greater legal protection.

In general, the anomalous situation whereby an individual had greater access to and control over his or her personal information held in computerised as opposed to manual files changed once the DPA 1998 was fully in force.

The Data Protection Act 1998[554]

The DPA 1998 was passed in response to the European Data Protection Directive on the protection of individuals with regard to the processing of personal data and the free movement of such data.[555] The aim of the Directive was to ensure that the same level of data protection was established in all member states in order to facilitate the transfer of personal data across national boundaries within the European Union. The DPA 1998[556] creates a far more comprehensive protection for personal information

---

551 It came into force on 1 November 1991.
552 See 'Access to health records' (1990) 140 NLJ 1382.
553 *Mid-Glamorgan Family Health Services and Another ex p Martin* (1993) *The Times*, 2 June.
554 For a basic guide, see Carey, P, *The Data Protection Act 1998*, 1998, Blackstone; for early discussion of the impact of the Act on the media, see Tugendhat, M, 'The Data Protection Act 1998 and the Media' [2000] YBMCL 115; Rasaiah, S and Newell, D, 'Data protection and press freedom' [1997–98] YBMEL 209.
555 Directive 95/46/EC of the European Parliament and of the Council of 24 October 1995 (1995) OJ L281/31, mainly Art 6. Recital 10 reads: 'Whereas the object of the national laws on the processing of personal data is to protect fundamental rights and freedoms, notably the right to privacy, which is recognised both in Article 8 of the European Convention for the Protection of Human Rights and Fundamental Freedoms and in the general principles of Community law . . .'
556 Certain sections came into force on the date of the passing of the statute – 16 June 1998. Most of the provisions came into force in 1999. As indicated below, certain provisions came into force after the first transitional period, ending on 24 October 2001; further provisions are about to come into force

than has ever previously been available. The 1998 Act is based on the 1984 Act but it is far more extensive; in particular, unlike its predecessor, it covers both manual and computerised files. This follows from s 1(1), which defines data as information processed by equipment operating automatically or recorded with the intention that it should be processed by means of such equipment or recorded as part of a relevant filing system or which forms part of an accessible record. The most significant part of this definition refers to data recorded as part of 'a relevant filing system'. Such a system is defined in s 1(1) as any set of information relating to individuals that is structured by reference to individuals or by reference to criteria relating to individuals 'in such a way that specific information relating to individuals is readily accessible'. This definition is clearly imprecise, but it seems that most, if not all, structured filing systems relating to paper-based materials containing personal information will be covered. Thus 'data' is caught by the Act either if it is held on any electronic storage system, typically a computer, or if it forms part of a filing system.[557]

The Act protects against the wrongful processing of 'personal data'. 'Personal data' means 'data which relate to a living individual who can be identified (a) either from those data', or (b) 'from those data and other information which is in the possession of, or is likely to come into the possession of, the data controller.' Any data relating to a living person is termed 'personal data'.[558] Personal data covers expressions of opinions about an individual, but now also covers indications of intentions in relation to that individual. This would include, for example, the intentions of a personnel manager regarding the promotion or demotion of an employee. Photographs of an individual clearly fall within the Act. The Court of Appeal's decision in *Durant v Financial Services Authority*[559] narrowed the prima facie meaning of these terms to an extent. It was held that the interpretation of personal data should be guided by the principle of respect for privacy. It means: 'information that affects his privacy, whether in his personal or family life, business or professional capacity'. Thus it was held that, to be personal, data about an individual must go beyond:

> the recording of the putative data subject's involvement in a matter or an event that has no personal connotations . . . The information should have the putative data subject as its focus rather than some other person with whom he may have been involved or some transaction or event in which he may have figured or have had an interest.[560]

after the end of the second transitional period, ending on 24 October 2007. Transitional provisions under Sched 14 provide for the transition from the regime of the 1984 Act to that of the 1998 Act while transitional relief from the full rigour of the Act is provided in Sched 8. Schedule 16 repeals the whole of the 1984 Act.

557 Under s 1(1) DPA: 'data' means information which –

(a) is being processed by means of equipment operating automatically in response to instructions given for that purpose,

(b) is recorded with the intention that it should be processed by means of such equipment,

(c) is recorded as part of a relevant filing system or with the intention that it should form part of a relevant filing system . . . .

558 The definition of 'personal data' is found in s 1(1) of the Act.

559 [2003] EWCA Civ 1746; [2004] FSR 28.

560 Ibid, at para 28.

Especially intimate private information is classified as 'sensitive personal data'; this covers a person's sexual life, along with matters such as a person's religious and political opinions, and his or her physical and mental health (s 2). It also includes some other, more wide-ranging categories of information, including information relating the racial or ethnic origin of the data subject, his or her political opinions, membership of a trade union and information relating to the commission by the individual of any offence and any proceedings relating to that offence.[561]

Under the law of confidence, as discussed above, and under the American private facts tort, once it can be determined that information is in the public domain, through, for example, previous media attention or other participation in a public process, such as a trial, an individual is no longer able to protect it through legal action. This is confirmed by s 12(4)(a)(i) of the HRA under which courts must have regard to the extent to which the material has, or is about to, become available to the public. As indicated, the courts are reluctant, under the new privacy liability, to find that information is unprotected as already in the public domain. The public domain issue is addressed only in a very limited fashion by the DPA, in Sched 3, para 5, which provides that one of the conditions for the processing of sensitive personal data is that the data subject has deliberately placed the information in the public domain. This stance is not far from the one the courts are reaching under the new privacy doctrine.

The following discussion is not intended as a comprehensive guide to the 1998 Act, something that would be out of place in a book of this nature. Instead, it will focus on certain specific privacy issues, and especially on their relationship with freedom of expression.

The Data Principles

The Data Principles, contained in Sched 1 of the Act, form its central core. The rest of the Act elaborates on the system for ensuring that these principles are adhered to. Subject to the exemptions, *all* personal data must be processed in accordance with the Data Protection Principles. The principles set out a number of fundamental privacy rights which encapsulate the value of informational autonomy. They accept that personal information must be stored and used by others, but surround such use by safeguards intended to preserve informational autonomy so far as possible, consistent with such acceptance.

Part II of Sched 1 deals with interpretation of the principles and makes the following provision in relation to the first principle:

1   (1) In determining for the purposes of the first principle whether personal data are processed fairly, regard is to be had to the method by which they are obtained, including in particular whether any person from whom they are obtained is deceived or misled as to the purpose or purposes for which they are to be processed.'

---

561   Under s 2, the definition includes: '(g) the commission or alleged commission by him of any offence, or (h) any proceedings for any offence committed or alleged to have been committed by him, the disposal of such proceedings or the sentence of any court in such proceedings.'

The most important of the Principles is Data Principle 1 which states that personal data must be processed fairly and lawfully and shall only be processed if at least one of the conditions in Sched 2 is met. The conditions include the requirement that the data subject has given consent to the processing, or it is necessary for the administration of justice or for the exercise of statutory functions, of functions of a Minister or government department or for the exercise of other functions of a public nature exercised in the public interest, or for the purposes of legitimate interests pursued by the controller or a third party, except where the processing is unwarranted by reason of prejudice to the legitimate rights or freedoms of the subject. Thus, in the case of all data, one of the conditions in Sched 2 must be met while in the case of sensitive personal data, one of the conditions in Sched 3 must also be met.

Thus the processing of 'sensitive personal data' attracts a higher level of safeguards than normal data under Data Principle 1(b) (Sched 1), as elucidated by Sched 3. The conditions include the requirement that the data subject has given her explicit consent to the processing, or the information has deliberately been made public by the subject, or it is necessary for medical purposes, or for the administration of justice, or for the exercise of statutory functions, of functions of a Minister or government department, or for the purposes of legitimate interests pursued by certain non-profit-making bodies.

Data Principle 2 provides that the data may be obtained only for one or more specified purposes and shall not be processed in any manner incompatible with that purpose. Under Data Principles 4 and 5, data must be accurate and, where necessary, kept up to date; when it is kept for a specific purpose, it must not be kept for longer than is necessary for that purpose. Also, data must be processed in accordance with the rights of data subjects under Data Principle 6, and under Data Principle 7 it must be adequately protected; appropriate security measures must be taken.

A number of subject exemptions, however, allow certain activities to be exempted from a number of the new provisions. The Data Principles and most of the key provisions of the Act do not apply where the exemption is required for the purpose of safeguarding national security. Thus, the security and intelligence services are exempt. Data related to the prevention and detection of crime are exempt from the first Data Principle and the subject access provisions in s 7. As indicated below, there is a special exemption for journalistic purposes; where the media exemption operates, the media will be exempt from a number of the provisions, including all the Data Principles, except the seventh.

Obligations of data controllers

Any person using a computerised system in order to store data relating to people is now designated the 'data controller' (s 1(1)), while the person who is the subject of the data remains the 'data subject'. However, the processing of personal data no longer requires the performance of operations by reference to a data subject (s 1(1)). Under s 17, the data controller must register with the Data Protection Registrar, now renamed the Data Protection Commissioner. The data controller must notify the holding of data to the Commissioner under s 17(1), who will then make an entry in the register maintained under s 19 unless, under s 17(3), processing is unlikely to prejudice the rights or freedoms of data subjects or unless, under s 23(1), the data controller has an approved in-house supervision scheme. However, the Act requires compliance with the

Data Principles and therefore such compliance is not dependent on the registration of the data holder .

Section 7 provides that if the data controller is asked by the data subject in writing whether personal data is being processed by or on behalf of the data controller, that information must be given within 40 days. If such data is being processed, the data subject is entitled to a description of the data, of the purposes for which it is being processed and of the recipients to whom it may be disclosed. Also, the data subject is entitled to have the data communicated to her and any information available to the controller as to the source of the data, in a form which is capable of being understood. Under Sched 1, Part II in relation to the fourth principle it is provided that if the data is found to be inaccurate, the data subject can notify the controller of the fact, which should then be indicated in the data. If it is so indicated, the fourth principle is not contravened. If a court is satisfied on the application of a data subject that personal data of which the applicant is the subject is inaccurate the court under s 14 can make an order erasing, blocking, destroying or rectifying the data.

Under s 10, the data subject has a new right, enforceable by court order, to prevent the processing of data likely to cause substantial damage or distress, if that damage or distress is or would be unwarranted.

Impact of the DPA on the media

The media are regarded as data controllers under the DPA 1998 and this is a very significant matter, since personal information stored manually is covered. The Act covers the 'processing' of data, which is defined extremely widely; of particular significance for the media is the fact that the definition covers both the obtaining and the publishing of data.[562] The 'data' controller – the person who has responsibilities under the Act, is the person[563] who controls the manner in which and the purposes for which the data is processed. In relation to newspapers, this will generally be the editor or editorial board.

In so far as the DPA offers remedies that can affect media freedom, s 12 HRA is relevant, whether the body against which relief is sought is a private body or a public authority under the HRA.[564] The 1998 Act has very significant implications for the media[565] and, on its face, it appears that in certain respects it has, in effect, favoured the protection of Art 8 over Art 10 rights. However, any tension therefore created between the DPA 1998 and the HRA is resolvable, as discussed below.

---

562 'Processing', in relation to information or data, means obtaining, recording or holding the information or data or carrying out any operation or set of operations on the information or data, including-

    (a) organisation, adaptation or alteration of the information or data,
    (b) retrieval, consultation or use of the information or data,
    (c) disclosure of the information or data by transmission, dissemination or otherwise making available, or
    (d) alignment, combination, blocking, erasure or destruction of the information or data; 'using' or 'disclosing', in relation to personal data, includes using or disclosing the information contained in the data.

563 Either alone or in company with others.

564 Since s 12 is not limited in its application to public authorities; see above p 905.

565 See further Tugendhat, M, 'The Data Protection Act 1998 and the Media' [2000] YBMCL 115; Rasiah and Newell, 'Data protection and press freedom' [1997–98] YBMEL 209.

Conditions

A key question in relation to the First Data Protection Principle is, as indicated above, that of consent, since data cannot be processed unless one of the conditions in Sched 2, in relation to all personal data, or Sched 3, in relation to sensitive personal data, is met. The obvious condition which would apply in relation to journalism would be that consent had been obtained, since in most circumstances it is unlikely that one of the other conditions could be met. But consent by the data subject would rarely be present in a privacy case. Schedule 3 refers to explicit consent. Thus, in relation to non-sensitive personal data, implied consent is sufficient. In relation to sensitive data, it is sufficient if the information has deliberately been made public by the subject. The Act does not explain what is meant by consent.

It could be claimed, as it has been successfully under the American private facts tort, that the plaintiff has sought publicity in the past and therefore has impliedly consented to a current publication of data to which he or she now objects. English judges in breach of confidence cases have in the past shown some receptivity to this claim, as discussed above, although there has often been a tendency to conflate it with the different claim that the plaintiff's private information has lost its quality of confidentiality. For example, in *Woodward v Hutchins*,[566] the Court of Appeal denied the plaintiffs (pop singers) an injunction against a former employee in respect of a series of newspaper articles giving detailed accounts of the singers' private lives. Bridge LJ reasoned that:

> those who seek and welcome publicity of every kind bearing upon their private lives so long as it shows them in a favourable light are in no position to complain of an invasion of their privacy by publicity which shows them in an unfavourable light.[567]

A similar approach was taken in *Lennon v News Group Newspapers*[568] in which one party to a marriage was denied relief in respect of personal information concerning the relationship on the grounds that both had sought publicity about it on previous occasions.

The proper approach to the question of consent under the DPA is to align it with that discussed above under the new privacy doctrine. It should be asked therefore whether the plaintiff has in fact robbed the information disclosed of its private quality through prior, voluntary publicity of the information in question or related information. It is essential that this test is applied in a nuanced fashion, basing it on the core privacy value of informational autonomy.[569] The notion of 'consent', then, should be used only

---

566 [1977] WLR 760.

567 Ibid, p 765. The decision is not clearly reasoned; Lord Denning also found (p 763): 'There is no doubt whatever that this pop group sought publicity . . . [relating to] their private lives also.' But this finding may also have been directed towards the idea that, having sought publicity themselves, they had effectively placed their private lives in the public domain; the decision also seems to have motivated by the idea that it was in the public interest to correct the false favourable impression that early publicity had given (ibid, p 764).

568 [1978] FSR 573.

569 Prosser suggests that consent is only impliedly given 'if the plaintiff has industriously sought publicity of the same kind' (Prosser, D, 'Privacy' (1960) 48 Calif L Rev 383, p 396, pp 420–21).

where there is an arguable claim of actual consent to the publication in question, express in respect of sensitive personal data or implied in respect of personal data. In relation to non-sensitive personal data, it is clear that implied consent is sufficient.

The only other condition that could be fulfilled by a media body is that the processing is necessary for the purposes of legitimate interests pursued by the data controller, or by the third party or parties to whom the data are disclosed, except where the processing is unwarranted in any particular case by reason of prejudice to the rights and freedoms or legitimate interests of the data subject. While this provision is imprecise, it would appear, in the context of press publication, to require the Court to examine, in the light of Arts 8 and 10, whether it was 'necessary' to publish the complained of data for the purposes of exercising the Art 10 right to freedom of expression. Thus, it might be relied upon by the press generally to argue that the data had been gathered and published in order to carry out the press's legitimate role as watchdog.[570] However it will not assist a newspaper which had obtained information surreptitiously, as will often be the case in privacy cases, and which therefore cannot claim to have obtained it 'fairly'. The Act, however, gives the media quite generous conditional exemptions from many of its provisions, and protection from the possibility of interim injunctions to restrain publication. Where data is processed for the 'special purpose' of journalism[571] under s 32(1) and (2), the key protective provisions (including Data Principles 1 and 2 and s 10) do not apply at all if the processing is undertaken with a view to publication, the data controller reasonably believes that, having regard to the special importance of the public interest in freedom of expression, publication is in the public interest, and compliance with the protective principles is incompatible with journalistic activity.[572] In considering the belief of the data controller that publication is in the public interest, regard may be had under s 32(3) to his compliance with any relevant code of practice that has been designated by the Secretary of State for the purposes of the sub-section. Journalists are not exempt from Data Principle 7, which in essence requires that care must be taken of the personal data, but this provision alone does not provide a significant protection for privacy.

Media exemptions

Although the Act gives an individual the right to apply to the Court for an order that a journalist, as a data controller, cease processing information about him which is causing or is likely to cause substantial, unwarranted distress (s 10), the mere claim that the processing is for the purposes of journalism with a view to publication stays the proceedings and the case is referred to the Data Commissioner for a determination on the point (s 32(4)). Thus, interim injunctions to prevent unfair processing by the press – a critical remedy in privacy cases – are not available. Even if a journalist was found to have breached the Act due to a failure to take such care, no interim injunction could be granted – under s 32. Where the exemption applies, it may be said then that the DPA 1998 probably has only a marginal impact on non-consensual media use of

---

570 This was not, however, accepted in *Campbell*.
571 Section 3.
572 For further discussion, see Carey, P, *The Data Protection Act 1998*, 1998, pp 196–98.

personal information. The remedies under the Act, discussed below, for breach of the Data Protection principles include a right to compensation[573] and a right to prevent processing likely to cause damage or distress.[574] However, there is a specific exemption designed to benefit the media in s 32 of the Act. In essence, it both prevents the media from being subject to interim injunctions preventing the publication of personal data[575] and allows them to be exempted from the Data Protection Principles[576] if the media body in question was acting for journalistic purposes and the data controller reasonably believed publication to be in the public interest and that he could not comply with the provisions of the Act, given the journalistic purposes he was carrying out. This provision has been held, controversially, to apply both before and after publication,[577] so that it provides a comprehensive media defence.

The right under s 10 to demand that the data controller ceases processing and the right if they do not to seek a remedy in court is unlikely, in any event, to bite against the media since the data subject must first notify the data controller to require that she cease processing, and the controller has 21 days to reply stating the action she intends to take. In the case of the media it seems probable that if publication of the personal data is intended, the media body in question would publish it, if possible, within the 21-day period.

However, these protections for the media do have limits. If data is being processed for the special purposes without a view to publication – which could be the case if it has already been published – the exemption does not apply. Equally, it does not apply to unpublished personal information if no reasonable belief could be demonstrated that publication of the information would be in the public interest. Clearly, there would also be cases where it was uncertain whether that belief could be demonstrated. Thus, journalists would be subject to the requirements of the Act in certain circumstances.

Use of the DPA against the media

Thus the DPA gives the public broad rights against the publication of sensitive personal data without consent by the media, and against the publication of any unfairly obtained personal data, subject however to a broad defence of public interest. Phillipson has observed that the DPA may provide one of the few ways that English law can provide a remedy for the publication of photographs of daily life activities that might not attract the protection of the law of confidence,[578] although, taking account of the expansive interpretation of *Von Hannover* in *McKennitt*, it now appears that they might be covered.

---

573 Section 13: it applies either where the individual suffers damage as a result of unlawful processing under the Act or suffers distress and the processing is done for the purposes of (*inter alia*) journalism.
574 Under s 10.
575 See s 32(4)–(5), under which the Court must stay any proceedings under the DPA relating to the publication of hitherto unpublished material, including proceedings under section 10(4) (obtaining an order preventing processing – i.e. an injunction) *if* the data is being processed for journalistic purposes with a view to publishing it.
576 Except for Principle 7, which, however, merely provides that the data controller shall take appropriate measures against accidental loss of or damage to data or unauthorised processing of it.
577 See the finding of the Court of Appeal in *Campbell*: op. cit. at paras 129–31.
578 *Media Freedom under the Human Rights Act*, at 767–68. See also above at p 893, for Baroness Hale's comments on the point in *Campbell*.

The DPA has not, however, proved popular with litigants, probably largely because interim injunctions cannot be obtained under it against the media. It was pleaded in *Campbell*, but it was virtually ignored in the House of Lords findings. The DPA was relied upon by Naomi Campbell alongside breach of confidence in her case against *Mirror Group Newspapers*,[579] discussed above, after the *Mirror* had published details of her treatment for drug addiction with Narcotics Anonymous, including surreptitiously taken photographs.[580] The case confirmed the application of the Act to the media. At first instance it was found:

> Under s 1(1), the claimant was termed a 'data subject', the information, including the details and photographs, that the claimant was receiving therapy at Narcotics Anonymous was 'personal data', the defendant was the 'data controller', the obtaining, preparation and publication of the claimant's personal data was 'processing'.[581]

These findings were not questioned on appeal; the Court of Appeal in fact specifically confirmed that the publication of hard copies of newspaper does fall within the definition of processing of data.[582] In relation to the media, it was found in *Campbell* at first instance, that the obtaining of information by surreptitious photography was unfair, and that if information is obtained in breach of confidence, it will not be obtained 'lawfully'.[583] *Campbell* demonstrated that the position of the media in relation to sensitive personal data, is particularly difficult. Under Sched 3, the media body has to show that the data subject has given 'explicit consent' to the processing or the data was deliberately 'made public' by the subject. Otherwise the media body must bring itself within the conditions set out in the Data Protection (Processing of Sensitive Personal Data) Order 2000, which essentially requires a very weighty 'public interest defence' involving the revelation of criminality, dishonesty, malpractice or mismanagement.[584] It would clearly be very difficult to make out such a defence in a normal case concerning the revelation of private facts; it was not made out in *Campbell*.[585] It is clear from *Campbell* that the DPA claim will normally stand or fall with the privacy claim.

---

579 The first instance decision: *Campbell v MGN* [2002] EMLR 30 (QB).
580 [2004] 2 AC 457.
581 [2002] EMLR 30, at para 85.
582 [2003] QB 633, at para 107.
583 [2002] EMLR 30, at paras 108–110.
584 The only circumstances which could normally apply to journalism under Sched 3 are:
3(1) the disclosure of personal data –

    (a)   is in the substantial public interest;
    (b)   is in connection with –

        (i)   the commission by any person of any unlawful act (whether alleged or established),
        (ii)   dishonesty, malpractice, or other seriously improper conduct by, or the unfitness or incompetence of, any person (whether alleged or established), or
        (iii) mismanagement in the administration of, or failures in services provided by, any body or association (whether alleged or established);

    (c)   is for the special purposes [of, *inter alia*, journalism] as defined in section 3 of the Act; and
    (d)   is made with a view to the publication of those data by any person and the data controller reasonably believes that such publication would be in the public interest.'
585 As the Court of Appeal confirmed: op. cit., fn 582, above at paras 88–89.

It is concluded, therefore, that the 1998 Act does have an impact on the media[586] since, except in a narrow range of instances, they are not exempt from the requirement to obtain consent where one or more of the conditions set out in s 32 do not apply. Although, from the point of view of protecting privacy, it may be argued that this is a welcome development, it may be suggested that the Act does not properly hold the balance between Arts 10 and 8. If so, since s 3 HRA applies, the courts have to consider the scope within the Act for creating a fairer balance in accordance with the demands of both those Articles. For example, s 10 speaks of unwarranted disclosures, a terminology which creates leeway for arguments based on Art 10. Although publication or processing in the public interest is not a general defence under the Act there is, as indicated, scope for interpreting what is meant by the public interest in s 32 in order to create such a balance, a matter that is considered further below.[587] Once the stage of considering the balancing act between Arts 8 and 10 is reached, it should be conducted as for the privacy claim.

Enforcement

The enforcement mechanisms allow for the enforcement of privacy rights against a range of bodies, including private ones, thus affording greater respect for Art 8 rights than is afforded under the HRA, since under it only public authorities are directly bound. The Act creates a number of offences in relation to data processing and the Act's requirements. In particular, it is a criminal offence for an unregistered person or body to store personal data under s 21(1).

Under s 13, compensation can be awarded if damage has resulted from the contravention by a data controller of any of the requirements of the Act, including the requirement to rectify, destroy, block or erase inaccurate data. However, it is a defence for the controller to prove that he had taken such care as is reasonable in the circumstances to comply with the requirement.

The rights granted under the Act are largely enforceable by the Data Protection Commissioner. Importantly, the Commissioner has security of tenure, being dismissible only by the Crown following an address by both Houses of Parliament. Under s 47, a failure to comply with a ruling of the Commissioner is a criminal offence. But the Commissioner can only make such a ruling after serving an enforcement notice under s 40 and such a notice may only be served if one or more of the Data Principles has been breached. The enforcement mechanism under the 1998 Act is based on the serving of notices on data controllers. If a person thinks that data of which she is the subject is being processed in contravention of the Act she can apply to the Commissioner for an assessment as to whether this is the case (s 42). The Commissioner can serve an information notice under s 43 on a data controller requiring the controller to furnish information to her within certain time limits.

Where the Commissioner is satisfied that a controller is contravening the Act, she may ultimately force the controller to act by serving upon it an enforcement notice, which (under s 40(1)) requires the controller to take, within such time as may be specified

586 See, for further discussion of the impact of the Act on the media, Tugendhat, 'The Data Protection Act 1998 and the media' [2000] YBMCL 115.
587 See pp 937 et seq.

in the notice, such steps as may be specified for complying with the requirements of the Act. The notice may either ask the controller to rectify, block, erase or destroy any inaccurate data or data containing an expression of opinion or take steps to check the accuracy of the data. If a controller fails to comply with an enforcement or information notice, it will commit a criminal offence.

Under s 48, an appeal lies from decisions of the Commissioner to the Tribunal which is made up of experienced lawyers and 'persons to represent the interests' of data subjects under (s 6(6)). This power of appeal is exercisable upon the broadest possible grounds. The Act provides that any person may appeal to the tribunal against an enforcement or information notice (s 48) either on the basis that the notice is not in accordance with the law, or that the Commissioner ought to have exercised her discretion (if any) differently' (s 49). The Tribunal is also empowered to substitute such other notice as could have been served by the Commissioner. There is a further appeal from the Tribunal to the High Court, but on a 'point of law' only (s 49(6)). In practice, this will probably be interpreted so as to allow review of the Tribunal's decisions, not just for error of law, but also on the other accepted heads of judicial review.

Thus, the Commissioner's decisions can, in the final analysis, be enforced, just as can orders of the Court. These powers are buttressed by powers of entry, search and seizure to gain evidence of a failure by the authority to carry out its obligations under the Act or of the commission of a criminal offence under the Act (detailed in Sched 9).

Relationship between the HRA and DPA

The DPA 1998 is precisely aimed, *inter alia*, at the preservation of informational autonomy in a very broad sense, going far beyond the obligations created by the HRA, under Art 8, which is directly applicable only to public authorities. The provisions of the 1998 Act must of course be interpreted compatibly with the Convention rights, including those under Arts 8 and 10, under s 3 of the HRA. But as Chapter 4 explained, s 3 is only an interpretative obligation, not a means of binding persons to abide by the rights. Thus, the 1998 Act is of immense significance as a privacy measure which reaches fully into the private sphere. In so far as they are reflected in the 1998 Act, the rights under Art 8 also bind private bodies.

A number of the bodies processing data are public authorities and therefore will be bound to observe the Convention rights in relation to such processing, under s 6 of the HRA. The bodies charged with the enforcement of the 1998 Act are also public authorities, and therefore must abide by the Convention rights in relation to any adjudications. Since the 1998 Act implements an EU Directive, the obligation to take the Convention into account in relation to processing of data, and adjudications relating to such processing, stems not only from s 3 but from the reliance on the Convention as a source of principles informing EU legislation.[588] This could be a matter of significance, as articles of the Convention, in particular Art 13, that have not been received into domestic law under the HRA, Sched 1, should be considered. Further, EU law can override domestic law and it has a greater impact than the HRA due to the possibility

588 See Chapter 3, pp 138–40.

of bringing a *Francovich* action.[589] The Directive could override incompatible primary legislation; if it has been inadequately implemented, an action could be brought directly against the state, thereby extending the impact of the privacy rights it encompasses, which should reflect Art 8 principles. The 1998 Act therefore reflects an acceptance of the value and significance of privacy interests which was not previously present in domestic law. It also arguably affords those interests priority – in certain respects – over free expression interests – a priority which is further reinforced by the complex relationship between the HRA and other domestic provisions and between the HRA and EU law.

The Data Protection Commissioner and Tribunal operating under s 6 of the DPA 1998 are public authorities and therefore they are directly bound, under s 6 of the HRA, by the Convention rights. Both bodies are consequently subject to judicial review for violation of the Convention in their rulings. Because under s 47 a failure to comply with a ruling of the Commissioner is a criminal offence, a significant possibility of enforcing Art 8 rights might appear to arise.

The exemptions under the Act are broad; where they apply to bodies that are public authorities under s 6 of the HRA, Art 8 could be relied upon to seek to prevent the unfair processing of data where an infringement of its guarantee had occurred or appeared likely to occur. This is a matter that is considered further in Chapter 10, but it may be noted here that Art 8 clearly views the processing of personal data as prima facie falling within para 1.[590]

8 Balancing speech and privacy claims under the HRA

Introduction

This chapter has set out to demonstrate that far more protection for privacy is available in UK law now than ever before. It is no longer possible for the press to treat privacy merely as a commodity that can be used to sell newspapers. But along with enhanced protection for privacy, it is necessary to seek to ensure that media freedom is preserved, in the sense that speech of genuine public interest is not suppressed. Since two Convention rights are involved – Arts 8 and 10 – it is necessary to find a way of striking a fair balance between them.

All the privacy measures discussed above provide some mechanism allowing for a balancing of expression and privacy rights. This may be by means of some form of public interest or 'reasonableness' test. This is true, albeit to quite a limited extent, of the DPA 1998 and of the PHA 1997. The PHA leaves some leeway for taking account of Art 10, under ss 3 and 6 HRA, as discussed above, where the provisions are used against journalists. Under s 3 DPA, leeway in the data protection provisions as applied

---

589   *Francovich v Italy* [1993] 2 CMLR 66 (circumstances in which national governments have a duty to compensate individuals for loss caused by failure to implement Directives and for other breaches of EC law).

590   In *MS v Sweden* (1997) 3 BHRC 348, the applicant complained that disclosure of her medical records in respect of a compensation claim infringed Art 8. The Court found that disclosure was an interference with private life but justified – economic wellbeing of state information relating to an individual's sexual life may merit protection, a decision clearly in harmony with the approach of Strasbourg.

to the media can be explored, allowing consideration to be paid to Art 10, in particular the question of the public interest in s 32 and the notion of an 'unwarranted' invasion of privacy in s 10. But s 12(3) HRA, discussed below,[591] will not be applicable since, as indicated above, the DPA does not appear in most circumstances to allow for the use of injunctions against the media; it contains no general defence, although the public interest is an important factor in the media exemption under s 32. If the data controller is also a public authority it will be directly bound by the Convention rights under s 6. The Privacy Codes affecting broadcasting and the press overtly strike a balance between privacy and the public interest, and if the policing of the Codes is challenged under the HRA, a balance is again overtly struck under s 12 HRA, which, as Chapter 4 discussed,[592] provides, in s 12(4), that if restraint on freedom of expression is contemplated the Court must have regard not only to Art 10 but also to any relevant privacy code. In making determinations as to the application of Strasbourg concepts in a particular instance, a form of public interest test is arguably drawn into the equation under s 12(4)(b) since the relevant privacy codes, in particular that of the PCC, are heavily influenced by the test.

Where a statute is in question the balance between Arts 8 and 10 must be struck by means of ss 3 and 6 HRA. Section 12 may also be relevant. In relation to s 6 a court must ensure in applying the statute that it strikes a proper balance between the two rights. If no statutory provision applies the court is in any event bound to strike that balance due to its own duty under s 6.

The most significant protection for privacy is provided by the new tort of misuse of private information. As indicated throughout this chapter, the notion of the public interest was pre-HRA, the key domestic mechanism allowing for the balancing of speech and privacy rights. Under the HRA, it was thought originally, as *Venables*[593] and *Mills*[594] indicated, that the balancing act would occur by reference to s 12 HRA which refers to any relevant privacy codes. *Campbell* now gives far more extensive guidance on the balancing act and makes it clear that it is not affected by the apparent priority given to Art 10 by s 12. Where an action for breach of Art 8 is brought directly against a media body, which is a public authority, the same balancing act occurs but is arrived at by a slightly different route. The public authority will be bound by Arts 8 and 10 under s 6 of the HRA.

In relation to all the privacy measures, then, the statutory scheme of the HRA, the Convention rights and the relevant privacy codes – usually the PCC code – provide the ground rules for determining when material should be published despite the invasion of privacy which will occur. This scheme is affected by the importation of the Strasbourg concepts of necessity and proportionality as applied under the HRA, Arts 10 and 8. The second paragraphs of Arts 8 and 10 under the HRA provide the principal mechanism by which to seek to create a balanced resolution of the two rights of privacy and speech. The privacy codes may be relevant in terms of the weight to be placed on the Art 8 side of the equation. Equally, public interest factors may go to the value to be placed on the speech. If the balancing act is to produce consistent, principled and reasonably

---

591 See pp 987–90.
592 See pp 212–13.
593 [2001] 1 All ER 908, Fam Div (High Court of Justice, Queen's Bench Division).
594 (2001) WL 720322.

foreseeable resolutions of the conflicting interests at stake, rather than amounting merely to an *ad hoc* exercise of judicial 'common sense', it is, it is suggested, essential that it be approached with an awareness of the values underlying both freedom of the press and privacy itself. In this section, therefore, principles are discussed which may be derived from an examination of the main free speech theories in the context of possible conflicts with privacy rights. The discussion then moves on to consider the Strasbourg jurisprudence on clashing rights, and particularly on clashes between Arts 8 and 10, before examining the way that the courts are resolving the conflict domestically. The courts have very recently developed quite a sophisticated method of resolving the conflict, relying on the Convention jurisprudence.

Free speech theories and privacy

The theory that freedom of speech is necessary for the discovery of truth, discussed in the Introduction to Part II,[595] has been a strong influence in US jurisprudence[596] but not historically at Strasbourg[597] or in the UK courts.[598] It has been persuasively argued that this rationale has little application to the paradigm privacy case, in which intimate facts about an individual are revealed. Barendt has contended that 'Mill's argument . . . applies more strongly to assertions of opinion . . . than to . . . propositions of fact'.[599] The argument is that since privacy actions attempt to prevent the publication of private facts only, and not general expressions of opinion, they will pose little threat to that free and unhindered public debate about matters of importance which Mill's argument seeks to protect. Moreover, as Schauer has argued,[600] on finding out a new fact, it may not replace a previously false belief, but merely add to what was previously 'epistemologically empty space'. Much intrusive journalism merely communicates a set of probably trivial facts about a given figure and it is very hard to maintain plausibly that the simple acquisition of such factual information has any inherent truth value. However, this is not the case in relation to some investigative journalism. For example, the revelation of the paedophile tendencies of a right wing evangelist leading a campaign against homosexual rights would contribute to various strands of public debate. Anonymity orders covering relatives of children involved in criminal proceedings may also indirectly stifle debate.

---

595 See pp 302–3. The most famous exposition of the 'truth' argument is to be found in Mill's *On Liberty*, in Cowling (ed), *Selected Writings of John Stuart Mill*, 1968, p 121.

596 See the famous *dicta* of Judge Learned Hand in *United States v Associated Press* (1943) 52 F Supp 362, p 372; and of Holmes J, dissenting but with the concurrence of Brandeis J, in *Abrams v United States* (1919) 250 US 616, p 630.

597 The repeated reference by the ECtHR to freedom of expression being one of the 'basic conditions for [society's] progress' (see, e.g., *Otto-Preminger Institut v Austria* (1994) 19 EHRR 34, para 49) could be seen as a reference to the justification.

598 But see *R v Secretary of State for the Home Department ex p Simms* [1999] 3 All ER 400, p 408, *per* Lord Steyn.

599 *Freedom of Speech*, 1st edn, 1985, p 191.

600 Schauer, F, 'Reflections on the value of truth' (1991) 41 Case Western Reserve L Rev 699, p 708. His other categories are: 'one's belief may be unjustified [though possibly true]; [and] one's belief can be false.'

Similarly, the justification for speech which may be referred to as the argument from autonomy[601] arguably has minimal application in this area, and indeed the values it espouses actually point to a reasonable degree of privacy protection. The basic thesis is that matters of substantive moral choice must be left to the individual as an autonomous, rational agent (subject, of course, to his duty to respect the basic rights of others); therefore, the state offends against human dignity, or treats certain citizens with contempt, if the coercive powers of the law are used to enforce the moral convictions of some upon others by, say, banning certain kinds of pornography or extreme political discourse.[602] It is immediately apparent that much privacy-invading speech, by both directly assaulting informational autonomy and indirectly threatening the individual's freedom of choice over substantive issues,[603] far from being bolstered by the autonomy rationale, is in direct conflict with it. The state, in restricting what one citizen may be told about the private life of another, is not acting out of a paternalistic desire to impose a set of moral values thereby, but rather to assure an equal freedom to all to live by their own values.

The argument from self development – that the freedom to engage in the free expression and reception of ideas and opinions in various media is essential to human development[604] – has received some recognition at Strasbourg[605] and in the House of Lords.[606] As with the argument from autonomy, it is immediately apparent that this justification, since it seeks to facilitate human flourishing, far from inevitably opposing the right to privacy, must support it to some extent since, as argued above,[607] a reasonable degree of privacy is a requirement, not a threat, to individual self-development, particularly the human capacity to form intimate relationships, without which the capacity for individual growth would be severely curtailed.

Moreover, as Barendt has argued,[608] it is implausible to view most newspaper reporters as freely serving their own human need for self-development. The focus must therefore be on the readers of such material. Joseph Raz has proposed a theory of freedom of expression which he argues provides a reader-based justification for expression and is concerned not with 'serious' public debate, but with the type of speech which is 'often overlooked' or seen as 'trivial'.[609] He points out that much public expression in the

---

601 The argument has been most influentially put by writers in the revived tradition of deontological liberalism. See Chapter 1, pp 6–7.

602 The particular concern of Thomas Scanlon's influential approach set out in 'A theory of freedom of expression' (1972) 1 Phil & Pub Aff 216.

603 See pp 805–6, above.

604 See the Introduction to Part II, pp 204–5. Emerson, C, for example, argues that the right to free expression is justified as the right of the individual to realise his character and potentialities through forming his own beliefs and opinions: 'Towards a general theory of the First Amendment' (1963) 72 Yale LJ 877, pp 879–80; see also Redish, M, *Freedom of Expression*, 1984, pp 20–30.

605 One of the stock phrases of the European Court of Human Rights in relation the value of freedom of expression asserts that it is one of the 'essential foundations for the development of everyone' (e.g., *Otto-Preminger Institut v Austria* (1994) 19 EHRR 34, para 49).

606 *Per* Lord Steyn in *R v Secretary of State for the Home Department ex p Simms* [2000] 2 AC 115, p 498.

607 See p 806.

608 Barendt and Hitchens, *Media Law, Cases and Materials*, 2000, p 68; he concedes that such arguments may have some applicability to the writers of 'fringe or underground journals'.

609 Raz, J, 'Free expression and personal identification' (1991) 11(3) OJLS 303, p 310.

media portrays and expresses aspects of forms of different lifestyles[610] which, he argues, 'validate the styles of life portrayed'. Conversely, censorship is not only an 'insult' to the persons leading the lifestyle censored – a point which sounds very like Dworkin's argument for freedom of expression based on equal respect for citizens[611] – but it also, in a more instrumental vein, denies those living the lifestyle the opportunity for reassurance, the sense that they are not alone in their lifestyles and its problems, and also the chance for the public to learn about the widest possible range of lifestyles, thus maximising their freedom of choice.[612]

Raz considers that his argument does not in general justify revelations about particular individuals, but may do so in relation to 'individuals who have become symbols of certain cultures, or ideologies, or . . . styles of life'.[613] It is clear, however, that if speech which invades the privacy of such individuals is restricted, the 'message' sent by the state thereby, far from suggesting condemnation or contempt for the lifestyle revealed, in fact displays respect for the ability of the individual to decide for himself whether he wishes to share his life-decisions with the public at large. Moreover, the reassuring knowledge that control of such information rests with the individual will surely further the core aim of the self-fulfilment justification – the ability of persons to make free choices to experience and experiment with the widest possible range of lifestyles and activities. Conversely, the inability of the individual to exercise such control would, as argued above, amount to a significant 'chilling effect' upon the willingness of individuals to make controversial choices about their personal lives. On both deontological and consequentialist arguments, then, this justification tends to support a reasonable degree of protection for informational autonomy.

As the Introduction to Part II explained, the 'self-governance' or argument from democracy is viewed as 'the most influential theory in the development of 20th century free speech law',[614] an assertion supported by examination of the approach of UK and Strasbourg judges, discussed in the Introduction to Part II. Its basic thesis is that citizens cannot participate fully in a democracy unless they have a reasonable understanding of political issues; therefore, open debate on such matters is necessary to ensure the proper working of a democracy;[615] as Lord Steyn has put it, 'freedom of speech is the lifeblood of democracy'.[616] In so far as democracy rests upon ideas both of participation and accountability, the argument from democracy may be seen to encompass also the function which a free press performs in exposing abuses of power,[617] thereby allowing for their remedy and also providing a deterrent effect for those contemplating such wrong-doing.[618]

---

610   Ibid: 'Views and opinions, activities, emotions etc, expressed or portrayed are an aspect of a wider net of opinions, sensibilities, habits of action or dressing, attitudes etc which taken together form a distinctive style of form of life.'

611   Dworkin, *A Matter of Principle* 1985, esp pp 272–74.

612   Raz, J, 'Free expression and personal identification' (1991) 11(3) OJLS 303, p 312.

613   Ibid, p 316.

614   See pp 303–5.

615   See Meiklejohn, A, 'The First Amendment is an absolute' (1961) Sup Ct Rev 245 and *Political Freedom*, 1960, esp pp 115–24.

616   *R v Secretary of State for the Home Department ex p Simms* [2000] 2 AC 115, p 408.

617   See Blasi, V: 'The checking value in First Amendment theory' (1977) Am B Found Res J 521.

618   See Greenwalt, K, 'Free speech justifications' (1989) 89 Columb L Rev 119, p 143.

As has been indicated previously, it is a marked feature of the Strasbourg jurisprudence that clearly political speech receives a much more robust degree of protection than other types of expression.[619] Thus, the 'political' speech cases discussed in this book[620] all resulted in findings that Art 10 had been violated and all were marked by an intensive review of the restriction in question. In contrast, in cases involving artistic speech, supported by the values of autonomy and self-development rather than self-government, an exactly converse pattern emerges: applicants have tended to be unsuccessful and a deferential approach to the judgments of the national authorities as to its obscene or blasphemous nature has been adopted.[621] As indicated in Part II a similar pattern may be discerned in the domestic jurisprudence: the most lofty rhetorical assertions of the importance of free speech and the strongest determination to protect it have been evident in cases where journalistic material raises political issues, broadly defined.[622] In such cases, the courts have either overtly adopted the Strasbourg principles described above[623] or have strongly emphasised the high status freedom of speech holds in the common law, as 'a constitutional right'.[624] Media freedom in relation to political expression has clearly been recognised as having a particularly high value in UK law and Convention jurisprudence. In contrast, when speech supported by the arguments from self-development or autonomy rather than self-government is in question, decisions have tended to be far more cautious.[625]

Two points emerge from this discussion. Where speech is supported mainly by arguments from autonomy, truth and self-development, there will in general be little or no justification at the level of principle for allowing it to override privacy; indeed, the discussion above reveals the truth of Emerson's remark that, far from being invariably in conflict, the twin rights to freedom of speech and to privacy 'are mutually supportive, in that both are vital features of the basic system of individual rights'.[626] In more

---

619   See Part II, pp 309–10 above.
620   See, e.g., *Jersild v Denmark* (1994) 19 EHRR 1; *Lingens v Austria* (1986) 8 EHRR 103, discussed above, p 209.
621   See Chapter 6, pp 277–81, at which the following cases are discussed: *Müller v Switzerland* (1991) 13 EHRR 212; *Gibson v UK*, Appl No 17634 (declared inadmissible by Commission); *Handyside v UK*, A 24 (1976) (not a case involving artistic speech but where the issue was obscenity); *Otto-Preminger Institut v Austria* (1994) 19 EHRR 34; *Gay News v UK* (1982) 5 EHRR 123. In *Wingrove v UK* (1997) 24 EHRR 1, the Court remarked: 'Whereas there is little scope under Article 10(2) of the Convention for restrictions on political speech or on debate of questions of public . . . a wider margin of appreciation is generally available to the Contracting states when regulating freedom of expression in relation to matters liable to offend intimate personal convictions within the sphere of morals or, especially, religion' (para 58). See Harris, O'Boyle and Warbrick, op. cit., fn 1, pp 397 and 414.
622   *Reynolds v Times Newspapers*; *Derbyshire CC v Times Newspapers* [1993] AC 534; *R v Secretary of State for the Home Department ex p Simms* [2000] 2 AC 115. However, deference to widely drafted primary legislation (*Secretary of State for Home Affairs ex p Brind* [1991] 1 AC 696) or governmental arguments from national security (*AG v Guardian Newspapers* [1987] 1 WLR 1248) has resulted in the ready upholding of restrictions on directly political speech.
623   See the approach of the Court of Appeal in *Derbyshire* (ibid) and in *Ex p Leech* [1994] QB 198, of the House of Lords in *Reynolds* (ibid, pp 621–22), *per* Lord Nicholls, pp 628 and esp 635, *per* Lord Steyn, p 643, *per* Lord Cooke and *Ex p Simms*, p 407 *per* Lord Steyn and pp 419–20 *per* Lord Hobhouse.
624   *Reynolds v Times Newspapers*, pp 628–29 (Lord Steyn). In *Ex p Simms* (ibid, p 11), Lord Steyn described the right as 'fundamental', as did Lord Hoffmann (ibid, p 412).
625   *Gibson* [1990] 2 QB 619; *Knuller v DPP* [1973] AC 435; *Lemon* [1979] AC 617.
626   Emerson, T, 'The right of privacy and the freedom of the press' (1979) 14(2) Harvard Civil Rights – Civil Liberties L Rev 329, p 331.

practical terms, the type of speech which, as we have seen, receives the highest level of protection, namely political speech, is by its nature most unlikely to conflict with the right to privacy. In many cases it will not raise privacy issues, as where it consists of the discussion of political ideas, institutions, and policies. Where political speech does concern individuals, as where it reveals abuse of state power, the conflict is more likely to be with reputation than privacy.[627] Conversely, the paradigm cases of journalistic invasions of privacy which, by definition, involve the personal, not the public-political affairs of its subject, usually involve celebrities rather than public servants, and are driven by purely commercial considerations. Such publications simply do not engage core Art 10 values such as the furtherance of a democratic society. Thus, it will only be in a fairly narrow category of cases that any real conflict will arise – those where the publication in question relates to the personal life of a particular figure,[628] but there is a serious argument that it serves a valuable purpose in revealing a matter relevant to that person's fitness for office, or in furthering public knowledge or debate about matters of serious public concern. The remainder of this section will consider approaches to the resolution of such hard cases.

The developing Strasbourg jurisprudence on clashing rights

Save for admitting the distinction between those rights stated in absolute or near-absolute terms, such as Arts 2, 3, 4, 6 and 7 and those subject to generalised qualifications (in particular Arts 8–11), Strasbourg has never sought to establish a hierarchy of Convention rights. In this respect it is in accord with the stance in other jurisdictions, such as Germany, France and Canada which have rejected any notion of establishing an *a priori* ranking of rights.[629]

It is fair to say that in some extreme instances clashes can be resolved by refinements of the definition of the ambit of the right. For example, as has recently been argued, speech which 'amounts to a *gross* invasion of privacy . . . [is] considered [by the Commission] to have little or no informational value worth protecting (emphasis added)'.[630] But in general, as indicated below, where rights collide Strasbourg speaks of taking account of both and striking a fair balance under para 2 of the Article pleaded before the Court. While the reasoning process inevitably follows the structure demanded by the Article(s) invoked by the applicant at Strasbourg, the other Convention right is given greater weight at the stage of determining the necessity of the interference (to support that right) in a democratic society, since it is axiomatic that all the Convention rights must be afforded a high value in such a society. This contrasts with the general

---

627 As in the case of *Reynolds v Times Newspapers* [1993] AC 534, in which the former Irish Taoiseach sued newspapers which published reports accusing him of lying to the Irish Dail; see also, e.g., *Lingens* (1986) 8 EHRR 103 and *Thorgeirson* (1992) 14 EHRR 843.

628 See the conclusions of the Calcutt Report on this point (op. cit., fn 1, at paras 12.24–12.29).

629 The German Supreme Court has remarked of the right to protection of personality (including privacy) and of free expression that 'neither can claim precedence in principle over the other' (BVerfGE 35, 200). For the Canadian approach, see *Hill v Church of Scientology* [1995] 2 SCR 1130, 1179 and the recent decision in *Les Editions Vice Versa Inc v Aubry* [1999] 5 BHRC 437; for the French approach, see Picard, E, 'The Right to Privacy in French Law' in Markesinis (ed) *Protecting Privacy*, 1999, at 93–96.

630 Tugendhat, M, QC and Christie, I, *The Law of Privacy and the Media* 2002, pp 420–21.

Strasbourg approach to Arts 8-11 which is that where *societal* interests potentially threaten the primary guarantee, the issue is not 'a choice between two conflicting principles but . . . a principle . . . that is subject to a number of exceptions which must be narrowly interpreted'.[631] Although Strasbourg has not made this difference of approach explicit, it is clearly consistent with the Convention's foundational values to assume that a Convention right, albeit considered under the para 2 exceptions, must be viewed as a conflicting principle rather than as a narrow exception to the primary guarantee.

Otto-Preminger Institut v Austria[632] provides a striking example of this approach. The Court found that the seizure and forfeiture of a film mocking Christianity was aimed at protecting the 'rights of others' within Art 10(2). The Court found that 'the manner in which religious doctrines are opposed or denied is a matter which may engage the responsibility of the state, notably its responsibility to ensure *the peaceful enjoyment of the right under Article 9*' (emphasis added).[633] The Court found that the responsibilities of those exercising the right under Art 10 include

> an obligation to avoid as far as possible expressions that are gratuitously offensive to others and thus an infringement of their rights and which therefore *do not contribute to any form of debate capable of furthering progress in human affairs* (emphasis added).[634]

The Court considered that the necessity for the restriction 'must be convincingly established' but did not give a specific reason for finding that this was the case, merely asserting that the Austrian authorities had not overstepped their margin of appreciation.[635] Although the reasoning as to the *applicability* of Art 9 in this judgment is viewed by a number of commentators as deeply flawed,[636] the decision demonstrates, it is argued, that the Court follows a different approach within para 2 of Arts 8–11 where the 'rights of others' exception that is engaged concerns another Convention right.

The Art 8 'family' cases on clashes of rights – where the right of the parent to family life appears to clash with that of the child – have not in general been resolved by reference to a principle of paramountcy – as that is understood domestically. Nor has it been assumed that the child's Art 8 rights can be viewed as exceptions to be narrowly construed. In *Elsholz v Germany*,[637] the applicant father claimed that his Art 8 rights had been breached by the refusal of the national court to allow him access to his child. The European Court of Human Rights, in finding that a violation of the

---

631 *Sunday Times v UK* (1979) 2 EHRR 245, para 65.
632 (1994) 19 EHRR 34.
633 Ibid, para 47.
634 Ibid, para 49.
635 Ibid As Chapter 6 explained, the restriction on Art 10 entailed by the seizure of an allegedly blasphemous film was justified by reference to the Art 9 right to freedom of religious belief. The Court applied a wide margin of appreciation, and simply said that 'the content of the film cannot be viewed as incapable of grounding' the conclusion of the national authorities that seizure was justified (para 56). Thus the test applied was reminiscent of the narrow *Wednesbury* standard of unreasonableness.
636 See, e.g., Harris, O'Boyle and Warbrick *Law of the European Convention on Human Rights*, 1995, p 402.
637 [2000] 2 FLR 486.

father's Art 8 rights had occurred, reiterated the principle from *Johansen v Norway*[638] that a fair balance must be struck between the interests of the child and those of the parent. Similarly, in *Hansen v Turkey*,[639] a case in which the mother argued that failure to enforce contact had breached her Art 8 right to respect for family life, the Court found, citing *Hokkanen*[640] and *Ignaccolo-Zenide*:[641] 'the rights and freedoms of all concerned must be taken into account, and more particularly the best interests of the child and his or her rights under Art 8 of the Convention. Where contacts with the parent might appear to threaten those interests or interfere with those rights, it is for the national authorities to strike a fair balance between them'. In other words, within the margin of appreciation of the member state, a fair balance must be struck between the Art 8 rights of the child and those of the parent, thereby ruling out the use of a presumption that precludes that balancing exercise, although the welfare of the child will be of especial significance.

Similar reasoning has informed the protection of Art 8 rights where there is a conflict with Art 10. Initially it seemed possible in *Winer v UK*[642] that the presence of such a clash might lead to a narrowing down of the ambit of 'private life' under Art 8(1) in order to avoid interfering with the guarantee of freedom of expression.[643] However, a different stance was taken in *Spencer (Earl) v United Kingdom*:[644] it was indicated impliedly not only that the conflict of rights should not be resolved by re-defining the ambit of the primary right to respect for private life, but also that a clash with Art 10 still leaves the privacy right with significant protection. The later decisions in *Tammer v Estonia*,[645] *N v Portugal*[646] and *Barclay v United Kingdom*[647] also support this stance.

638 (1996) 23 EHRR 33.
639 (2004) 1 FLR 142, Appl No 36141/97, para 98. Cf the previous decision in *Yousef v Netherlands* (2003) 1 FLR 210. It is argued that, bearing *Hansen* and the decision in *Hoppe v Germany* (2004) 38 EHRR 15 at para 44 in mind, *Yousef* is out of line with the Court's established and continuing line of reasoning on the interests of the child.
640 (1994) A 299-A, 22
641 (2000) Reports of judgments and decisions 2000-I, 265.
642 (1986) 48 DR 154.
643 The applicant complained that various aspects of his private life had been publicised in a book. His application was declared inadmissible, the Commission stating briefly that it viewed the available remedies, in particular that of defamation, as satisfactory and that no positive obligation to provide further remedies in respect of the truthful statements made should be imposed, bearing in mind the wide margin of appreciation to be afforded in this area, the limitation of the Convention right to freedom of expression which such remedies would entail and the availability of a partial remedy.
644 (1998) 25 EHRR CD 105. The applicants complained of publication in the press of various (truthful) stories relating to the bulimia and mental health problems of Countess Spencer, including photographs taken of her walking in the grounds of a health clinic.
645 (2003) 37 EHRR 43; (2001) 10 BHRC 543.
646 *N v Portugal*, Appl No 20683/92, 20 February 1995. A magazine publisher's application complaining of a breach of Art 10 after being convicted of defamation and invasion of privacy in respect of the publication of photographs of a well-known businessman engaged in sexual activities was rejected as manifestly ill-founded. The Commission considered that the sanction was proportionate and necessary for the protection of the rights of others, one of which was clearly the right to protection from invasion of privacy through publication of true facts by other private individuals.
647 (1999) Appl No 35712/97 (admissibility only). The Court accepted that a lack of a remedy in respect of the filming of a private home, the island of Brecqhou, owned by the Barclay brothers, by reporters could in principle constitute a breach of Art 8, although on the facts no invasion of private life had occurred.

Tammer v Estonia is an especially significant decision in this context since the process of reasoning and the outcome is highly reminiscent of those in *Otto-Preminger*. The journalist applicant had been subject to a criminal penalty in respect of the publication of a hard-hitting interview relating to a former political aide, alleging that she had broken up the Prime Minister's marriage by having an affair with him and had deserted her own children. His application under Art 10 failed before the Court, which found that the remarks in question related to the former aide's private life; the restriction upon the journalist's Art 10 rights, taking into account the lightness of the penalty imposed, was therefore a necessary and proportionate response to the need to uphold the privacy of the aide. In coming to this conclusion the Court afforded a very wide margin of appreciation to the national authorities since the case concerned a clash of rights: 'In considering the way the domestic authorities dealt with the case, the Court observes that the Estonian courts fully recognised that the present case involved a conflict between the right to impart ideas and the reputation and rights of others. It cannot find that they failed properly to balance the various interests involved in the case'.[648]

As discussed above, *Peck v United Kingdom*[649] provides further confirmation that the Court is prepared to find a breach of Art 8 rights even where significant restrictions on Art 10 rights are thereby created. The case concerned CCTV footage of an attempted suicide in the street, which was then shown on national television. The applicant was identifiable from the footage and the broadcasting of it was found to create a breach of Art 8. The decision is of significance, not only because it allowed for the suppression of freedom of expression on a matter of some significant public interest, but also because it demonstrates that freedom of expression can be curbed even where the speech suppressed is already partly in the public domain. It might have been found, taking account of *Observer and Guardian Newspapers v UK*,[650] that the suppression of speech in such circumstances was disproportionate to the legitimate aim pursued. But *Guardian Newspapers* was not a case that concerned a clash between two opposing individual rights. Rather, it concerned a clash between societal interests – in national security and the authority of the judiciary – and freedom of expression. The comparison between *Peck* and *Guardian Newspapers* provides a further indication that the Court is prepared to adopt a different approach – one that more readily accepts interferences with freedom of expression – where another individual Convention right is at stake.

A and Byrne and Twenty-Twenty Television v. United Kingdom[651] is of particular significance in this line of authority. Decided prior to *Tammer* and *Peck*, it is nevertheless in line with the findings in those decisions, and also reveals the stance taken at Strasbourg to the paramountcy principle where a clash with Art 10 arises. The clash of rights which occurred was resolved in favour of the Art 8 rights of the child (although the case was not argued in those terms), but it was also, most significantly, made clear that even in respect of a child's welfare, Art 8 does not take *automatic* priority over Art 10. The case concerned the restriction of freedom of expression represented by the refusal to vary the injunction in *In re Z*, discussed above.

---

648 At para 69. It may be noted that a civil penalty could have been imposed rather than a criminal conviction for insulting the aide.

649 *Peck v United Kingdom* (2003) 36 EHRR 41; (2003) Appl No 44647/98. See above pp 818–19.

650 (1991) 14 EHRR 153.

651 (1998) 25 EHRR CD 159.

The first applicant, the child (C)'s mother, argued that the Court's refusal to accept her decision that C should take part in the television programme had constituted a breach of her Art 8 right to respect for family life. The mother and the media applicants both complained of a breach of Art 10. The Commission took into account, in the context of Art 10, that the right to freedom of expression is one of the essential foundations of a democratic society and that prior restraints call for the 'most careful scrutiny'.[652] In addition, it found that, in considering the 'duties and responsibilities' of the applicants as persons exercising their freedom of expression through the making and production of a television programme, the potential impact of the programme on the public and consequently on C, had to be viewed as an important factor.[653] The Commission noted that by continuing the injunctions, the domestic courts prevented all the applicants from making a television programme featuring the education and development of C in an educational and behavioural institute; it found that the continuance of the injunction by the domestic courts constituted an interference with all three applicants' right to freedom of expression within the meaning of Art 10(1).

In relation to the question whether the interference could be considered 'necessary' under para 2 of both Arts 8 and 10, the Commission afforded a certain margin of appreciation in assessing whether the need existed. It conducted the examination of necessity under Art 8(2) but stated that the same principles and considerations would apply under Art 10(2). It took into account the purpose of the documentary programme and the acceptance of the applicants' *bona fides* in this respect. The applicants submitted that the programme was of significant public interest in that it would inform the educational authorities in the United Kingdom, the families of those who suffer from similar problems as C and those sufferers themselves about other educational and behavioural methods which could significantly improve the latter's potential. The first applicant (C's mother) submitted that since her decision to allow C to participate in the television programme was taken in good faith, for C's benefit and with the proper advice, the courts should have followed her decision unless they found it irrational or in bad faith.[654]

The Commission found that it was for the national authorities to strike a fair balance between the relevant competing interests: what would be decisive would be whether the national authorities had made such efforts 'as can be reasonably demanded under the special circumstances of the case' to accommodate the parents' rights.[655] The Commission took into account the fact that the applicant had jointly applied for the first of the injunctions under consideration with the express intention of protecting the privacy of C, and also the High Court's conclusion that the 'overwhelming probability' was that the transmission of the programme would attract extended secondary tabloid publicity largely because of C's parents' high profile. The High Court had taken the

---

652 *Observer and Guardian v United Kingdom*, (1991) 14 EHRR 153, paras 59–60.

653 *Jersild v Denmark* (1995) 19 EHRR 1, para 31.

654 She further submitted that the courts were not well placed to make the assessment they did; the judges were elderly males of an elite class unlikely to have had experience of raising children with handicaps like C and they could not possibly know how the transmission of the programme would affect C. She argued that the judges were wrong in considering that the transmission of the programme would adversely affect C.

655 *Olsson v Sweden (No 2)*, (1994) 17 EHRR 134, para 90 and *Hokkanen v Finland* (1995) 19 EHRR 139, para 57.

view that any short-term benefit for C deriving from the publicity was outweighed by the 'serious consequences' which transmission of the programme would entail for her. The Commission concluded that, in the circumstances of the present case and in view of the margin of appreciation accorded to states in this area, the imposition by the courts of their view as to the best interests of C was supported by 'relevant' as well as 'sufficient' reasons. The domestic courts had made such efforts as could be reasonably demanded to accommodate the first applicant's rights and the interference was accordingly proportionate to the legitimate aim pursued. The restriction was not therefore found to create a breach of Art 10 or, on the particular facts, of the Art 8 right to family life of the mother. The Commission added that the High Court considered that if it had had to carry out a balancing exercise (for the purposes of Art 10 of the Convention or otherwise) between the welfare of C and the public interest in the programme, it would have 'firmly seen the scales as coming down in favour of there being an order against the programme being made'. Importantly, the Commission did *not* find that where the UK courts had applied the paramountcy principle, the media's right should be narrowly interpreted to avoid an invasion of the child's interests (viewed as aspects of her Art 8 rights).

In the very significant recent case of *Von Hannover v Germany*,[656] concerning an Art 8 claim in respect of journalism that invaded the applicant's privacy, the Court, in an approach reminiscent of that in *Otto-Preminger*, balanced Arts 8 and 10 against each other without a strict application of the Art 8(2) tests. As indicated above, journalists had followed Princess Caroline, photographing and recording trivial details of her personal life, such as dining with her children or shopping. The German Constitutional court had granted her relief in respect of journalistic intrusions in instances in which she had deliberately sought solitude. But it had refused relief where it considered that there was a public interest value in certain of the photographs. The German Court had found:

> The public had a legitimate interest in knowing where the applicant was staying and how she behaved in public.'[657] Nor can mere entertainment be denied any role in the formation of opinions . . . Entertainment can also convey images of reality and propose subjects for debate that spark a process of discussion and assimilation relating to philosophies of life, values and behaviour models. In that respect it fulfils important social functions . . . The same is true of information about people. Personalization is an important journalistic means of attracting attention. Very often it is this which first arouses interest in a problem and stimulates a desire for factual information. Similarly, interest in a particular event or situation is usually stimulated by personalised accounts. Additionally, celebrities embody certain moral values and lifestyles. Many people base their choice of lifestyle on their example. They become points of crystallisation for adoption or rejection and act as examples or counter-examples. This is what explains the public interest in the various ups and downs occurring in their lives. As regards politicians this public interest has always been deemed to be legitimate from the point of view of transparency and

---

656 *Von Hannover v Germany* (2005) 40 EHRR 1; (2004) Appl No 59320/00, judgment of 24 June 2004; see in particular paras 63, 64, 65, 66, 76.
657 Quoted ibid at para 25.

democratic control. Nor can it in principle be disputed that it exists in respect of other public figures. To that extent it is the function of the press to show people in situations that are not limited to specific functions or events and this also falls within the sphere of protection of press freedom'.[658]

The European Court did not accept this analysis of the public interest dimension:

> ... the publication of the photos and articles in question, of which the sole purpose was to satisfy the curiosity of a particular readership regarding the details of the applicant's private life, cannot be deemed to contribute to any debate of general interest to society despite the applicant being known to the public.[659]

The Court further found:

> a fundamental distinction needs to be made between reporting facts – even controversial ones – capable of contributing to a debate in a democratic society, relating to politicians in the exercise of their functions, for example, and reporting details of the private life of an individual who, moreover, as in this case, does not exercise official functions. While in the former case the press exercises its vital role of 'watchdog' in a democracy by contributing to 'impart[ing] information and ideas on matters of public interest ... it does not do so in the latter case[660] ... The situation here does not come within the sphere of any political or public debate because the published photos and accompanying commentaries relate exclusively to details of the applicant's private life.[661]

Since the photographs and publications 'made no contribution' – due to their banal and anodyne nature – to a debate of general interest, the interest in press freedom under Art 10 had to give way it was found to the Princess's privacy interests. Thus, the Court found that the reporting of the private life of a public figure is not an aspect of the media's watchdog role, except in special circumstances where aspects of his or her private life relate to political or public debate. In the instant case the details related exclusively to the applicant's private life and in those circumstances, it was determined, freedom of expression had to be narrowly interpreted. That narrow interpretation appeared to mean impliedly that while the reporting was viewed as constituting expression, interferences with it would almost inevitably be justified due to its nature. The Court did appear to accept that Art 10 was engaged, but it made it clear that the type of speech in question would always, as a general rule, tend to be afforded a very low weight.[662] The Court appeared to be making the assumption that of their nature the photographs could *not* relate to a debate of public interest, since the Princess was not exercising official functions. This seems to miss the point that private life details might relate to social trends in a much more significant fashion,

---

658 Ibid, para 25.
659 Ibid, para 65.
660 *Von Hannover v Germany* (2005) 40 EHRR 1 at para 63.
661 Ibid, para 64.
662 See further *Media Freedom under the Human Rights Act* (2006) at p 695.

in different circumstances, and therefore could have some public interest value. On the other hand, material consisting merely of photographs showing daily life activities of celebrities accompanied by no reporting attempting to create links to wider issues is the staple fare of many magazines and newspapers. So the possible public interest value of such photographs should not be exaggerated. Further, it must be borne in mind that consented-to photographs of celebrities are readily available. Any desires of the audience to see their life-styles ratified, or to observe social trends embodied in the lives of celebrities, already have a ready outlet.

These decisions reveal the stance at Strasbourg in relation to clashes of rights and particularly to conflicts between Arts 10 and 8. It can now be said to be clear that neither Article can be viewed as having presumptive priority where such conflicts occur. In such instances, the matter may be resolved by something close to definitional balancing of the rights on the model offered by *Von Hannover* where the speech interest is very weak – consisting of mere celebrity gossip. Where a full application of the tests of necessity and proportionality occurs, Strasbourg engages within those tests in something more akin to a balancing exercise in which a broad margin of appreciation tends to be conceded to the national authorities. Since the protection of both rights is axiomatically necessary in a democratic society, the Court is prepared to leave the national authorities with a wide discretion as to the precise balance to be struck in the member state between them.

Domestic approaches to the speech–privacy balance

Thus, where two Convention rights come into conflict, some kind of balancing act between the two needs to be undertaken and the margin of appreciation tends to be particularly significant here, so that states have a fairly wide discretion in resolving the conflict. Domestic courts therefore have an appreciable degree of latitude in determining where to strike the balance between the two interests. Section 12 HRA, which enjoins the court to have 'particular regard' to Art 10 when making any order which might infringe it, appears, on its face, to suggest a higher weighting for speech interests. Such imbalance is also prima facie suggested by the strength of the 'speech' jurisprudence discussed in the Introduction to Part II.[663] Free speech is by far the more accepted and established right.[664] The contrast with the relatively meagre case law on privacy at the European level, with, until recently, its cautious approach to intervention between private individuals, and the historic failure of English judges to recognise such a right in the common law, might suggest that the twin rights to speech and privacy do not currently occupy an equal footing. At one time it was therefore feared – or hoped – that English law would come to replicate the position in the US where, as Wacks puts it, 'It is widely acknowledged that the . . . 'newsworthiness' defence has effectively demolished the private-facts tort'.[665]

663 See pp 309–11.
664 See Fenwick and Phillipson (2006), fn 1 above, Chapters 1 and 2.
665 Wacks, op. cit., fn 1, p 113.

In *Reynolds*, a libel case, where expression interests also function as a defence, the House of Lords took this approach. 'The starting point,' Lord Steyn stated,[666]

> is now the right of freedom of expression, a right based on a constitutional or higher legal order foundation. Exceptions . . . must be justified as being necessary in a democracy. In other words, freedom of expression is the rule, and regulation of speech is the exception requiring justification.[667]

These findings were echoed in the *Mills* case.[668]

These findings appear at a superficial glance to be in line with the general Strasbourg approach which finds that in cases in which other interests potentially threaten free speech, the concern is not with 'a choice between two conflicting principles but with a principle of freedom of expression that is subject to a number of exceptions which must be narrowly interpreted'.[669] If this approach had been applied in domestic privacy cases, as seemed possible until recently,[670] the result would have been that privacy lost its Convention status as a fully fledged right, becoming instead merely a narrowly interpreted exception to the right of freedom of expression. A higher weighting for speech interests was suggested by the strength of the 'speech' jurisprudence at both the Strasbourg and domestic levels. In *Ex p Simms*[671] Lord Steyn referred to free speech as 'the primary right . . . in a democracy' and some commentators have taken the view that Art 10 attracts an especially high level of protection at Strasbourg.[672] In *Central Independent Television plc*[673] Hoffmann LJ in an oft-quoted statement said: freedom of speech is 'a trump card which always wins'.[674] The statement, however, should be placed in context, as discussed below.

A number of other judicial pronouncements have accepted the presumptive primacy of Art 10, in particular that of Butler-Sloss LJ in *Venables*. The decision has been superceded on the question of the presumptive priority for Art 10, but it is still of interest in relation to taking account of interests to be weighed against Art 10, other than Art 8 interests. A number of newspapers made representations to the Court. They pointed out that the speech of Lord Steyn in *Secretary of State for the Home Department ex p Simms*[675] supported the presumption in favour of freedom of expression. The speech of Lord Templeman in *AG v Guardian Newspapers*,[676] the judgment of Hoffmann LJ in

---

666 An approach echoed by Lord Nicholls: 'My starting point is freedom of expression' (*Reynolds* [1999] 4 All ER 609, p 621).

667 Ibid, p 629.

668 [2001] EMLR 41; see pp 907–8 above.

669 *Sunday Times v UK* A 30 (1979), para 65.

670 There were signs of this approach in *Mills v NGN* [2001] EMLR 41, 4 June, High Court No HC 0102236, WL 720322.

671 [1999] 3 All ER 400, CA; [1999] 3 WLR 328, HL at p 407.

672 Leigh, I and Lustgarten, L, 'Making rights real: the courts, remedies, and the Human Rights Act' (1999) 58 CLJ 509, 524 and n 79.

673 [1994] Fam 192.

674 Ibid, at pp 203 and 204.

675 [1999] 3 WLR 328, p 337.

676 [1987] 1 WLR 1248, p 1297.

Central Independent Television[677] and the judgment of Munby J in *Kelly v BBC*[678] also provided support. It was not, it was argued, a question of a balancing exercise by the Court, since freedom of expression had presumptive priority. The newspapers further argued that, if either of the claimants was discovered by a journalist, it should be left to the judgment of the editor whether or not to publish the information. Instances could be found, it was pointed out, where the press was asked by the Court not to publish and did not do so.[679]

It was found that the Court had to carry out a balancing operation, weighing the public interest in maintaining confidence against the interest in disclosure. However, s 12 HRA and Art 10(1) of the Convention gave, it was found, an enhanced importance to freedom of expression and so to the right of the press to publish. The Court went on to find that the freedom of the media to publish could only be restricted if the need for those restrictions could be shown to fall within the exceptions set out in Art 10(2). In considering the limits to the law of confidence, and whether a remedy is available to the claimants within those limits, it was found that the exceptions must be narrowly interpreted. The claimants' right under Art 2 (right to life), Art 3 (right to freedom from torture and inhuman and degrading treatment) and Art 8 (right to respect for private life) were in issue. The rights under Arts 2 and 3 are not capable of derogation. In *Osman v United Kingdom*,[680] the European Court held that the provisions of Art 2 enjoined a positive obligation upon contracting states to take measures to secure the right to life. The case, discussed in Chapter 2,[681] concerned the failure of the police to act to protect a family from criminal acts, including murder. The European Court said:[682]

> The Court notes that the first sentence of Art 2(1) enjoins the state not only to refrain from the intentional and unlawful taking of life, but also to take appropriate steps to safeguard the lives of those within its jurisdiction . . . it must be established that the authorities knew or ought to have known at the time of the existence of a real and immediate risk to life of an identified individual or individuals from the criminal acts of a third party and that they failed to take measures within the scope of their powers which, judged reasonably, might have been expected to avoid that risk.

Since in the instant case the Court found that there was a real possibility that the claimants might be the objects of vigilante or revenge attacks, the potential breaches of Arts 2, 3 and 8 had to be scrupulously evaluated. Further, since a restriction on freedom of expression was in issue, all the criteria in Art 10(2), narrowly interpreted, the judge considered, had to be met. The Court was satisfied that confidence could extend to cover the injunctions sought and that therefore, the restrictions proposed were in accordance with the law. It was found that the common law continues to evolve and was given 'considerable impetus' to do so by the implementation of the Convention

677 [1994] Fam 192, p 203E, p 204C.
678 [2000] 3 FCR 509, p 525.
679 See *Broadmoor Hospital Authority and Another v R* [2000] 2 All ER 727.
680 [1999] 1 FLR 193.
681 See p 41.
682 At paras 115–16.

into domestic law by the HRA. Also, it was a strong probability that on the release of the claimants there would be great efforts to find them and some of those seeking to do so would be determined upon revenge. The requirement in the Convention that there can be no derogation from the rights under Arts 2 and 3 provided strong support for the very pressing social need that their confidentiality should be protected. The provision of injunctions to achieve the object sought also had to be proportionate to the legitimate aims they pursued. The aim was to protect the claimants from serious and possibly irreparable harm. Dame Butler-Sloss noted that Lord Woolf said in *Lord Saville of Newdigate ex p A*:[683]

> ... when a fundamental right such as the right to life is involved, the options open to the reasonable decision-maker are curtailed. They are curtailed because it is unreasonable to reach a decision which contravenes or could contravene human rights unless there are sufficiently significant countervailing considerations. In other words it is not open to the decision-maker to risk interfering with fundamental rights in the absence of compelling justification ...

Dame Butler-Sloss went on:

> The onus of proving the case that freedom of expression must be restricted is firmly upon the applicant seeking relief ... I can only restrict the freedom of the media to publish if the need for those restrictions can be shown to fall within the exceptions set out in Art 10(2) ... I must interpret narrowly those exceptions.'[684]

The significant point is that these remarks were made in the context of countervailing Convention rights – Arts 2 and 3 – not in relation to societal interests.[685] Similarly, in *Mills* the High Court had to consider whether to grant an interim injunction. The judge said that the starting point was s 12 of the HRA since it applies 'if a court is considering whether to grant any relief which, if granted, might affect the exercise of the Convention right to freedom of expression' (s 12(1)) and, in particular, provides that 'no such relief is to be granted so as to restrain publication before a trial unless the court is satisfied that the applicant is likely to establish that publication should not be allowed' (s 12(3)). The court also noted the provision of s 12(4):

> The court must have particular regard to the importance of the Convention right to freedom of expression and, where the proceedings relate to material which the respondent claims, or which appears to the court, to be journalistic, literary or artistic material (or to conduct connected with such material), to
>
> (a) the extent to which –
>   (i) the material has, or is about to, become available to the public; or
>   (ii) it is, or would be, in the public interest for the material to be published;
>
> (b) any relevant privacy code.

---

683 [2000] 1 WLR 1885, p 1857.
684 [2001] 1 All ER 908, 921 and 931.
685 See further Phillipson, G, n 1 above, (2003) 749–52.

The Court went on to refer briefly to 'frequent and authoritative expressions of the importance of a free press and freedom of speech'. It was noted that in *Reynolds v Times Newspapers Ltd*[686] the House of Lords stressed that there is a basic and fundamental right to freedom of expression, that freedom of expression would be buttressed by s 12 of the HRA, and that when the Act was fully in force the common law would have to be developed and applied in a manner consistent with Art 10. It was found that, to be justified,

> . . . any curtailment of freedom of expression must be convincingly established by a compelling countervailing consideration, and the means employed must be proportionate to the end sought to be achieved; and the interest of a democratic society in ensuring a free press weighs heavily in the balance in deciding whether any curtailment of this freedom bears a reasonable relationship to the purpose of the curtailment.[687]

Thus, it was found that freedom of expression 'is the rule and regulation of speech is the exception requiring justification. The existence and width of any exception can only be justified if it is underpinned by a pressing social need.'[688] Reliance was also placed in *Venables* on the findings of Hoffmann LJ in *Central Independent Television plc*:[689]

> Newspapers are sometimes irresponsible and their motives in a market economy cannot be expected to be unalloyed by considerations of commercial advantage. Publication may cause needless pain, distress and damage to individuals or harm to other aspects of the public interest. But a freedom which is restricted to what judges think to be responsible or in the public interest is no freedom. Freedom means the right to publish things which government and judges, however well motivated, think should not be published. It means the right to say things which "right-thinking people" regard as dangerous or irresponsible. This freedom is subject only to clearly defined exceptions laid down by common law or statute. . . .

The Court noted that cl 3 is plainly based on Art 8 of the Convention and that although Art 8 is not directly applicable in England in the sense of creating new causes of action, the English Court (a) must, in determining a question which has arisen in connection with a Convention right, take into account, *inter alia*, the decisions of the European Court of Human Rights (under s 2(1) of the HRA) and (b) because the court is a public authority (s 6(3)(a) of the HRA), must not act in a way which is incompatible with a Convention right. The Court went on to consider the exception under Art 10(2) in respect of 'the protection of the reputation or rights of others', which it said must include Convention rights such as Art 8 when being given effect by such means as

---

686 [1999] 3 WLR 1010.
687 Referring to Lord Nicholls, p 1023.
688 Referring to Lord Steyn, pp 1029–39. The court also noted the findings in *McCartan Turkington and Breen v Times Newspapers Ltd* [2000] 3 WLR 1670, p 1686 (HL), where Lord Steyn said that the European Convention fulfilled the function of a Bill of Rights, and considered *Secretary of State for the Home Department ex p Simms* [2000] 2 AC 115, p 126.
689 [1994] Fam 192, pp 202–4.

the law of confidentiality; and also the exception 'for preventing the disclosure of information received in confidence'.

In applying the Convention jurisprudence under s 12(3) of the HRA, and bearing in mind that the qualifications in Art 10(2) are as relevant as the basic right of freedom of expression in Art 10(1), the Court noted that the European Court of Human Rights has emphasised that the national court has to strike a fair and proportionate balance between the respective Convention rights, depending on such factors as the nature and seriousness of the interests at stake and the gravity of the interference. Further, one of the matters which the Court has to take into account in deciding whether prior restraint is justified is 'any relevant privacy code', and the PCC Code of Practice is clearly such a code.[690] It noted that the rules on privacy under cl 3 are 'disarmingly simple' and found that the existence of the statutory provisions, coupled with the current wording of the relevant privacy code, meant that in any case where the Court was concerned with issues of freedom of expression in a journalistic, literary or artistic context, it was bound to pay particular regard to any breach of the rules set out in cl 3 of the Code, especially where none of the public interest claims set out in the preamble to the Code was asserted.

It found that a newspaper which flouts cl 3 of the Code is likely in those circumstances to have its claim to an entitlement to freedom of expression trumped by Art 10(2) considerations of privacy, and said that unlike the court in *Kaye v Robertson*,[691] Parliament had recognised that it had to acknowledge the importance of the Art 8(1) respect for private life, and it was able to do so untrammelled by any concerns that the law of confidence might not stretch to protect every aspect of private life. Therefore, in making a determination in the instant case, the Court found that it was not necessary to go beyond s 12(3) of the 1998 Act and cl 3 of the Press Complaints Commission's Code to find the ground rules by which to weigh the competing considerations of freedom of expression on the one hand and privacy on the other.

However, the Court had to be satisfied, if it was to restrain publication before trial, that the claimant was likely to establish that publication should not be allowed. In deciding not to grant the injunction, the Court took into account the fact that the risk to personal safety which arose was only slight, and the fact that the *Sun* had repeatedly said that it would not publish the address and that it would abide by the PCC Code. It also found that whether or not the information appeared in the press, it would, at least to a limited extent, become available to the public, simply as a result of Ms Mills living in a busy and populous town. The Court said that that was not in itself a reason for denying her a remedy, but that it was relevant both in assessing the degree to which publication should be restrained, and the impact of publication on her privacy and security. The Court did not take account of the fact that Ms Mills had for several years courted publicity, and had herself stimulated public interest in her lifestyle, sex life, and her homes.

---

690 The judge noted that in *Douglas v Hello! Ltd* [2001] 2 WLR 992, Brooke LJ said (p 1018, paras 92–94): '. . . the Code of Practice ratified by the Press Complaints Commission in November 1997 states that all members of the press have a duty to maintain the highest professional and ethical standards, and that the code sets the benchmarks for those standards: it both protects the rights of the individual and upholds the public's right to know.'

691 [1991] FSR 62.

This approach – affording Art 10 priority – clearly does not accord with that of Strasbourg in the clashing rights cases discussed above: a careful examination of the competing claims of each right was undertaken on a basis of the equal value of the two rights,[692] except in exceptional instances where expression is narrowly defined. The decision in *Von Hannover* clearly established the presumptive equality of the two rights. There is no indication that Parliament, in passing the HRA, intended to alter this position and create a serious imbalance between the two rights;[693] rather, it is evident that the sponsors of the amendment which became s 12 saw it merely as a domestic reflection of the Strasbourg approach.[694] Moreover, the unbalanced American approach is out of line with other jurisdictions and flows from factors peculiar to that jurisdiction, namely the absolute nature of the First Amendment, and the fact that it is not balanced by any constitutional right to informational privacy.[695] Where privacy has such a status, as in Germany and Canada, courts have rejected any notion of establishing an *a priori* ranking of rights.[696] The *Venables* and *Mills* approach would have introduced a striking asymmetry: the protection of the right to privacy would have to be justified as necessary in a democratic society, while the claims of free speech would be simply assumed. The cases make it clear that where a restriction on a Convention right is justified not as serving one of the societal interests the Convention enumerates,[697] such as economic well being or protection of morals, but as ensuring the protection of another Convention guarantee, a different approach must be followed.

In cases where Convention rights have clashed, Strasbourg has still formally followed the standard approach, treating one right as primary, so that restrictions upon it by a competing right have to be justified as necessary in a democratic society. However, this is because when Strasbourg hears cases brought by individuals alleging a violation of a Convention right, other, competing rights, figure only as possible means of justification for the respondent state. By contrast, the position of a domestic court is fundamentally different: both sides before are claiming that their rights are equally in issue. Only one party before the Strasbourg Court is claiming to be a right-holder: competing rights figure only as possible means of justification for the respondent state and thus as an exception to the primary right whose infringement is alleged. At the same time Strasbourg does not view the other right as an exception to be interpreted narrowly but in practice conducts something more akin to a balancing act between the two, if both

---

692 See the views of Lord Steyn and Lord Cooke in *Reynolds v Times Newspapers* [1999] 4 All ER 609, at 631 and 643.

693 An amendment providing that a court should 'normally' give precedence to Art 10 over Art 8 was rejected (HC Deb Vol 315 Cols 542–43, 2 July 1998).

694 See, e.g., the speech of Jack Straw on cl 12: HC Deb Vol 315 Cols 535–39, 2 July 1998.

695 The US Supreme Court has fashioned a constitutional right to what it has termed 'privacy', but by this it signifies choice over substantive matters, such as sexual activity and abortion: see, e.g., *Griswold v Connecticut* (1965) 381 US 479 and *Roe v Wade* (1979) 410 US 113.

696 The German Supreme Court has remarked that the protection of personality [including privacy] and of free expression are both 'essential aspects of the liberal democratic order . . . with the result that neither can claim precedence in principle over the other' (BVerfGE 35, 200) – this point relies on Markesenis's translation (op. cit., fn 1, p 123). For an example of the Canadian approach, see *Hill v Church of Scientology* [1995] 2 SCR 1130, p 1179 and the recent decision in *Les Editions Vice Versa Inc v Aubry* [1999] 5 BHRC 437, which involved a careful balancing of the rights to privacy and speech.

697 See the second paragraph of Arts 8–11.

are found to be engaged. The national court is in a different position, not only because the margin of appreciation doctrine is inapplicable,[698] but also because the process by which the cases arise at Strasbourg differs from the way they arise domestically. Therefore the domestic court has to find a way of affording weight to both rights and of balancing them against each other, as opposed to reviewing the balance already struck. Thus, while the process of domestic reasoning needs to take account of the Strasbourg stance in terms of principle, it is able to differ from it in terms of structure and of depth of scrutiny.

Section 12(4) HRA, which enjoins the courts to have 'particular regard' to Art 10 when making any order which might infringe it, appears, on its face, to suggest a higher weighting for speech interests than for privacy. However, it is now evident that this is not the correct reading.[699] In the context of the law of confidence the equal weighting of the two rights has now gained clear general acceptance. Lightman J found in *Campbell v Frisbee*: 'The right to privacy and to freedom of expression are of equal value.'[700] The notion that Art 10 has presumptive priority in relation to other Convention rights under s 12(4) was also disapproved of by the Court of Appeal in *Cream Holdings v Bannerjee*.[701] This trend was reaffirmed in the Court of Appeal decision in *Re S*, setting out the proper approach to speech/privacy claims (in a different context and also only within cases in the second category from *In re Z*). That approach to such claims was then ratified by the House of Lords in their seminal decision in *Campbell v MGN*: Lord Hoffmann said of balancing speech/privacy claims: 'There is in my view no question of automatic priority. Nor is there a presumption in favour of one rather than the other.'[702] When the House of Lords in *Re S* reached the stage of considering the conflict between Arts 8 and 10 in its reasoning, it strongly endorsed the parallel analysis from *Campbell in general*, confirming that presumptive priority for speech where it competes with another Convention right, not a societal concern, has been decisively rejected.

It can now therefore be said with confidence that where the two rights collide, the notion of affording presumptive priority to Art 10 has been abandoned in favour of affording presumptive equality to the two rights.[703] Any other approach would probably

---

698 See *R v DPP ex p Kebilene and Others* [1999] 3 WLR 972, 1043, *per* Lord Hope.

699 Further, this was probably not the intention behind the government's reluctant inclusion (in the face of pressure from the press lobby) of the clause that became s 12; see, e.g., the speech of Jack Straw on cl 12: HC Deb. Vol 315 Cols 535–39, 2 July 1998.

700 [2002] EMLR 31, para 24. Lindsay J also accepted that s 12 was not intended to afford special weight to freedom of expression when *Hello!* was found liable to pay damages for breach of confidence: *Douglas v Hello! (No 5)* [2003] EMLR 31, [2003] EWHC 786, para 185(v).

701 See Simon Brown LJ, speaking for the majority: [2003] 2 All ER 318, at para 41. Rogers and Tomlinson, commenting on this finding, concluded that where free expression collides with Art 8 there will be 'presumptive equality' between the two: [2003] EHRLR (Privacy Special Issue) 38 at 41.

702 [2004] 2 WLR 1232; (2004) 154 NLJ 733; [2004] UKHL 22, at para 55. Baroness Hale of Richmond (at paras 138–41) made it clear that her own approach in *Re S* should be adopted in order to conduct the balancing exercise, and an exercise based on the presumptive equality of the two Articles was also adopted unanimously by the other Law Lords (see Lord Nicholls at paras 19 and 18, Lord Hope at paras 103–11 and Lord Carswell at para 167).

703 As pointed out in *Campbell*, ibid at para 138 this is consistent with Resolution 1165 (1998) of the Parliamentary Assembly of the Council of Europe, para 10, which affirms the equal value of the two rights.

have necessitated a declaration of the incompatibility of s 12(4) with Art 8. The sub-section can now be viewed therefore either merely as a (superfluous) reminder of the demands of Art 10, or as a means of drawing in the conflicting right under Art 8 since s 12(4) clearly covers Art 10(2) as well as Art 10(1).[704] The former view accords more comfortably with the notion of presumptive equality. As far as the latter view is concerned, s 6 obviously renders this role for s 12 redundant.

The parallel analysis or 'ultimate balancing act'

Once the equal value of the rights has been accepted, it follows that the courts should consider the grant of a prior restraint, or other remedy, in instances similar to those mentioned, from the perspectives of both Art 10 and Art 8.[705] The notion of undertaking a parallel exercise and informing it by reference to the justificatory arguments underlying both guarantees was first put forward some years ago pre-HRA.[706] The Court of Appeal decision in *Re S* made it clear that this balancing act must occur, and its findings on that matter were accepted by the House of Lords in *Campbell*. Those findings were not disputed in the Lords in *Re S*.[707] Indeed, they were strongly reaffirmed. Lady Hale in the Court of Appeal in *Re S* found that it was not merely necessary to consider Art 8 as an exception to Art 10 under Art 10(2); it was also necessary to consider Art 10 as an exception to Art 8, under Art 8(2). Thus, the Court must ask whether Art 10 is engaged. The standard Convention tests should then be followed, under Art 10(2) asking whether the interference with the Art 10 guarantee proposed by the plaintiff would be necessary in a democratic society and proportionate to the legitimate aim of protecting private life, as a 'right of others'. The Court should then consider the issue from the opposing perspective under Art 8, with the rights reversed in position, so that the speech interest is treated as an exception to the primary right to respect for privacy under Art 8. The same inquiries as to necessity and proportionality should then be made from this opposing perspective, again under the rights of others exception which also appears in Art 8(2). Lord Steyn, in a speech with which the other members of the House concurred, deduced a number of principles from the decision of the House in *Campbell v MGN*:

> First, neither article has as such precedence over the other. Secondly, where the values under the two articles are in conflict, an intense focus on the comparative importance of the specific rights being claimed in the individual case is necessary.

---

704   See Sedley LJ in *Douglas v Hello!* [2001] QB 967, 1003 at para 137. Section 12(4) is not needed to perform the task of drawing Art 8 into the frame since it is performed by s 6; however, Sedley LJ's interpretation accords with the impact of s 3 (which applies to s 12(4)) and refutes the notion that s 12(4) affords presumptive priority to Art 10. Lord Hope in *Campbell* approved of this approach to s 12(4): ibid at para 111.

705   Other Convention rights may also be relevant. If, for example, the *Re W* case ([1992] 1 All ER 794) had arisen after the HRA was in force it might have been possible to argue, under Art 14 read with Art 8, that there was also a discriminatory dimension to the findings: had the child been placed with a heterosexual couple after suffering heterosexual abuse the Court of Appeal might not have concluded so readily that public interest questions arose. The principle of open justice under Art 6(1) may add weight to the Art 10 argument.

706   Fenwick, H and Phillipson, G, 'The Doctrine of Confidence as a Privacy Remedy in the Human Rights Act Era' [2000] 63 (5) MLR 660–93. The following analysis draws to an extent on the ideas put forward at pp 682–87.

707   *In re S (a child)* [2004] UKHL 47; [2005] 1 AC 593.

Thirdly, the justifications for interfering with or restricting each right must be taken into account. Finally, the proportionality test must be applied to each.'

This process may be termed the 'parallel analysis':[708] the steps to be taken under it are considered in more detail below.

In this way, useful insights can be gleaned as to the strength of both the speech and the privacy claim, by asking, for example, both whether the publication in question was more intrusive than was necessary to its legitimate aim of provoking discussion on matters of public interest or revealing a lack of fitness for public office, and, conversely, whether the remedy sought by the plaintiff would go further than necessary in order to protect the legitimate privacy interest. In a manner reminiscent of the approach of the German[709] and Canadian courts,[710] the claims of both parties are thus subject to a searching, but balanced examination.

In all instances in which a power to restrict or penalise publicity arises based on all the causes of action discussed above, including powers to protect children (whether based on the ECHR jurisdiction of the court or on the other restrictions discussed) the court should seek if possible to balance the two rights on the *Re S* and *Campbell* model in accordance with the demands of the HRA. In cases involving children, however, the welfare of the child would appear to determine the issue if s 1(1) CA applies. But it is highly probable that the courts will continue if possible to find ways of defining the concept of 'upbringing' so that it does not apply in most cases of media publicity relating to children. In that way, they preserve the possibility of conducting the balancing act between Arts 8 and 10 and avoid the difficult issue of the incompatibility of the paramountcy principle with Art 10. So, for example, in a case such as *In re Z*, arising under the HRA, the court can fulfil its duty under s 6(1) HRA, s 12(4) and s 2 by adopting an approach which weighs up the strength of both the Art 10 and Art 8 claim. Where a restriction on publicity is statutory s 3(1) could bite and could also demand that if possible a reinterpretation of it that took account of both Articles should be adopted. Where the restriction itself allowed no leeway for the parallel analysis in order to achieve compatibility with Art 10, a declaration of incompatibility should be issued under s 4.[711] Section 12(1) of the 1960 Act might be likely in future to attract such a declaration since it offers little leeway for media freedom.

The discussion below of conducting the parallel analysis begins by noting that the values underlying Arts 8 and 10 may in fact mean that both Articles come down against publicity, or at times against restraint of speech. It proceeds to identify the steps to be taken in conducting the balancing exercise. It then proceeds to consider the rationales underlying both Articles, making it possible to identify factors that have been found to weigh strongly in the balance on one side or the other – where a clash between the two Articles does appear to arise. It finally looks at the steps taken and the outcomes in certain recent seminal cases in which the parallel analysis has been conducted.

---

708 Tomlinson, H, QC and Rogers, H, coined the term 'parallel analysis': 'Privacy and Expression: Convention Rights and Interim Injunctions' [2003] EHRLR (Special Issue: Privacy) 37, 50.

709 See Markesenis, B and Nolte, N, 'Some comparative reflections on the right of privacy of public figures in public places', in Birks, P (ed), *Privacy and Loyalty*, 1997, pp 122–24.

710 See, e.g., *Les Editions Vice Versa Inc v Aubry* [1999] 5 BHRC 437.

711 See further, Cram, I, 'Young Persons, Criminal Proceedings and Open Justice – A Comparative Perspective' Yearbook of Copyright and Media Law, Vol V (2000) 141–65.

Articles 8 and 10 as mutually supportive guarantees

In balancing Arts 8 and 10 against each other in cases when the media wishes to reveal private facts, it becomes clear as discussed that the justificatory arguments underlying media freedom are quite frequently partially or largely inapplicable. In some instances speech that invades privacy is likely to gain little, if any, support from the arguments from autonomy and self-development, so there will often be little or no justification at the level of principle for allowing it to override privacy. It may also be found that the rationales underlying *both* Arts 8 and 10 come down on the side of secrecy or, conversely, publicity. The rights to freedom of speech and to privacy are in many respects, 'mutually supportive'[712] since the principles of autonomy and self-development underlie both Articles.

Millian justificatory arguments based on truth tend to have little application to the paradigmatic celebrity privacy case, in which facts relating to private and family life are revealed. Reporting restraints attempting to prevent the publication of private facts only, and not general expressions of opinion, will pose little threat to that free and unhindered public debate about matters of importance which Mill's argument seeks to protect.[713] However, in certain of the cases concerning children considered, such as *In re Z*, this argument would support disclosure since the matters sought to be revealed would have formed part of a wider debate about the value of certain forms of education or upbringing.

The justification for speech based on the argument from autonomy may have an application in the child privacy cases, depending on whether the child *herself* is seeking publicity as in *In re W (Wardship: Restrictions on Publication)* and *Kelly v BBC*. The value of autonomy underlying Art 8 could *also* speak in favour of publicity: where the child is *Gillick*-competent and seeks publicity, her informational autonomy is at stake in the sense that she is exercising a choice as to disclosure of aspects of her private life. Her informational autonomy would be invaded if disclosure was disallowed. Where a responsible and devoted parent or carer seeks publicity on behalf of the child, as in *Oxfordshire CC*[714] or *In re Z*, invocation of both Arts 8 and 10 could also point in the direction of disclosure. Indeed, in *Twenty-Twenty Television v UK* the mother as applicant at Strasbourg sought to invoke both Articles in support of her claim for publicity on the ground that her freedom of expression and right to respect for her family life were both at stake. The child herself could have invoked her own Art 8 and 10 rights in support of publicity.

In such instances no real conflict between Arts 8 and 10 arises, except in so far as it is arguable under Art 8 that disclosure ran counter to the child's own welfare. Where publicity would clearly not further her best interests, a court, affording weight to her welfare in accordance with the stance of the Court of Human Rights discussed in relation to the family cases at Strasbourg and, if applicable, s 1(1) CA (possibly

---

712 See: Emerson, C, 'The Right of Privacy and the Freedom of the Press' (1979) 14(2) *Harvard Civil Rights – Civil Liberties Law Review* 329, p 331. See also Fenwick, H and Phillipson, G, *Media Freedom under the Human Rights Act*, 2006, Chapter 13.

713 See Barendt, E, *Freedom of Speech*, 1st edn, 1985, p 191.

714 [1997] 1 FLR 235.

encapsulating a new primacy principle), would uphold non-disclosure. Clearly, even a *Gillick*-competent child might fail to appreciate the harm that publicity could do and could be over-persuaded by reporters or by a parent/carer. In such instances the court would be expected to consider, not only the autonomy argument and the short-term benefits to the child in terms of, for example, enhanced self-esteem, but also the long-term detriment, including any impact on his development or ability to form or sustain relationships with his peers or others. However, where, as in the *Mary Bell* case,[715] or *Re S*, such arguments are not applicable, the child and her carers are opposed to publicity and there are also weighty welfare grounds for such opposition, it can be argued that disclosures could directly assault the informational autonomy of the child and those caring for her, and indirectly threaten their freedom of choice over substantive issues.[716] In such instances the speech in question, far from being bolstered by the autonomy rationale, is in direct conflict with it. But arguments based on the idea of uncertain and nebulous detriment to the child's welfare would hardly engage Art 8 and would be readily overcome where core values under both Arts 8 and 10 weighed on the other side of the balance. Where the speech was essential to inform a wider debate the justificatory arguments under Art 10 would be strengthened.

It is clearly apparent that the argument for speech from self development, since it seeks to facilitate human flourishing, far from inevitably opposing the right to privacy, must support it to some extent since a reasonable degree of privacy is a requirement for individual self development, particularly the ability to form relationships, without which the capacity for individual growth would be severely curtailed. This argument applies in many of the privacy cases discussed in this chapter; referred to in *Bensaid v UK*, it clearly has an especially significant application in relation to the upbringing and welfare of the child. As indicated above, a version of the paramountcy principle – in which the child's welfare has primacy – is inevitably going to continue to obtain recognition on the basis of arguments based on the requirements for individual self development under Art 8. Where publicity threatens the welfare of the person in question, the argument that it should be suppressed would be readily to hand, not only under Art 8, but also under Art 10, on the basis that it would not further the fulfilment of the values underlying its free speech guarantee. This may be particularly the case in relation to children. This argument could readily have been used successfully in *Re S* to justify the restriction on reporting: the majority judges in the Court of Appeal and the Law Lords assumed too readily in that case, it is contended, that Arts 8 and 10 were entirely opposed in relation to the circumstances.

Conversely, where speech might *further* the welfare of the child, the values underlying both Articles speak in favour of publicity. Such instances arise where she might gain in self esteem through publicity (as the mother argued in *In re Z*) or where she desires publicity in order to reveal and express feelings of frustration or persecution (as in *In re W (Wardship: Restrictions on Publication)*) or, more controversially, where publication of true facts about the relationship with a parent, as a corrective to the parent's

---

715 *Re X (A Minor) (Wardship Proceedings Injunction)* [1984] 1 WLR 1422.
716 Such matters could include choice of abode or of schools. See the discussion on this issue at p 973 below.

version already successfully placed in the public domain, could vindicate and ratify the child's own stance in respect of that relationship (*Harris v Harris*).[717]

Finally, the argument that prior restraints intended to safeguard the privacy might inhibit journalistic debate on matters of significant public interest must be fully confronted. Clearly, political speech by its nature is unlikely in many instances to conflict with the Art 8 rights to private and family life. Such a conflict will not arise where political speech consists of the discussion of political ideas, institutions, and policies. The paradigmatic cases of journalistic invasions of privacy in this context tend to the private and family life, or children of celebrities, or sometimes relate to criminal activity involving children, and may amount to mere 'infotainment' or be driven simply by a desire for sensationalism for purely commercial purposes. Such publications hardly engage the press's right under Art [10] to impart 'information on matters of serious public concern'[718] or more general Convention values such as the furtherance of a democratic society.

The findings of principle discussed should, it is argued, inform the balancing act between Arts 8 and 10. When examining instances in which the media wish to reveal private facts it becomes clear that the justificatory arguments underlying media freedom are quite frequently partially or largely inapplicable. In some instances speech invasive of privacy is likely to gain little, if any, support from the arguments from autonomy and self-development, so there will often be little or no justification at the level of principle for allowing it to override privacy. As indicated, it may sometimes be found in child privacy cases that the rationales underlying *both* Arts 8 and 10 come down on the side of publicity. But in all cases they are more likely to come down in favour of secrecy. As the discussion indicates, the rights to freedom of speech and to privacy are in many respects, 'mutually supportive'[719] since the principles of autonomy and self-development underlie both Articles.

The structure of the reasoning process

In terms of the *structure* of the reasoning process, the court should begin as a first step by considering the issue from the perspectives of both Arts 8(1) and 10(1) in turn, on the *Re S* model. In exceptional instances at the extremes the matter might be resolvable largely by reference to the scope of media rights under Art 10(1). Speech that invades the privacy of a person and which relates exclusively to her private life could be viewed as a form of expression that will inevitably be overcome by the strong Art 8 claim, requiring no justification under para 2 for its suppression.[720] Alternatively, it could be

---

717 Munby J contended in that instance: 'Mr Harris has manipulated the press by feeding it tendentious accounts of these proceedings, enabled to do so because he has been able to . . . shelter behind the very privacy which hitherto has prevented anyone correcting his misrepresentations . . . the remedy for Mr Harris's antics . . . is publicity for the truth . . . the children's own best interests will be furthered by the public being told the truth . . . ' [2001] 2 FLR 895, paras 386–89.

718 *Bladet Tromso and Stensaas v Norway* (2000) 29 EHRR 125, para 59.

719 Emerson, C, 'The Right of Privacy and the Freedom of the Press' (1979) 14(2) Harvard Civil Rights–Civil Liberties Law Review 329, 331.

720 See *Von Hannover v Germany* (2005) 40 EHRR 1, at para 66. The findings in *Von Hannover* would clearly cover not only celebrities but the children of celebrities or children who had attracted publicity due to their own or their parents' actions or situation, where the speech related purely to their private

viewed as a form of expression that only marginally deserves to fall within that term and therefore as very vulnerable to interference.[721] There is possibly more scope for resolution of the conflict within Art 8(1). Where speech relating to an adult which has only the most incidental and tenuous connection with the private or family life of a child is concerned, on factual bases even less compelling than that in *Central Television*, it might be argued that Art 8(1) is not engaged at all, in which case no conflict arises requiring resolution. Under s 6(1) HRA, as argued above, the inherent jurisdiction must be exercised in accordance with the Convention rights, thereby arguably extending its ambit via the doctrine of indirect horizontal effect. Following this argument a power to restrict publication would prima facie be available where the child's claim had the *potential* to fall within Art 8(1); if on close examination it was found that the connection was too tenuous on the particular facts, the case could be resolved in favour of the Art 10 claim without recourse to Art 8(2).

But it is clear that 'definitional balancing' on the American model – that is, in this context, redefining the nature and content of the primary rights under either Article to create demarcations between those two rights – will only very rarely be possible, as will identifying and utilising the underlying values at stake in order to avoid the conflict within para 1. In most instances, then, the extent to which the rationales discussed are at stake will be relevant, but in relation to the exercise of proportionality under para 2 of both Articles – the second step. The structure of the reasoning process would follow the contours laid down by Baroness Hale in *Re S* and in *Campbell*, but the parallel analysis accepted as appropriate should also arguably be used in cases relating to children and involving upbringing.

The court should consider the issue of any conflict between Arts 8 and 10 from at least two parallel perspectives.[722] The court should follow the standard Convention tests under Art 10(2), asking whether the interference with the primary guarantee proposed would be prescribed by law, necessary in a democratic society and proportionate to the legitimate aim of protecting private and family life – 'the rights of others' protected under Art 8(1). The court should then consider freedom of expression as creating an exception to the right to respect for private and family life, under Art 8(2), again applying the tests of legality, necessity and proportionality.

But in each instance the application of the test of necessity would not require strict scrutiny in accordance with the findings deriving from the Strasbourg clashing rights cases such as *Tammer v Estonia*, since, as argued above, it is axiomatic that there is a pressing need to protect both rights in a democratic society. The test of proportionality would clearly be much more significant, as Sedley LJ indicated in a different context in *London Regional Transport v Mayor of London*,[723] since while it is clear that both privacy and speech must be protected, the particular restriction under consideration must be tailored towards satisfying this test under both Articles.

---

life. As discussed above, the term 'private life' was *not* found to cover especially intimate matters or secluded situations or activities, but the normal incidents of private life such as shopping expeditions (paras 49 and 61).

721 See Tugendhat, M, QC and Christie, I, *The Law of Privacy and the Media*, 2002, pp 420–21.

722 As pointed out above, other Convention Articles might also be relevant.

723 [2003] EMLR 4, para 49.

The Strasbourg proportionality test can be broken down into a number of stages in this context, partly relying on the analysis put forward by Paul Craig.[724]

(i)   Some view must be taken as to whether certain interests can be traded off to achieve other goals at all. This is the point at which it might be argued, following *Von Hannover*, that the fundamental right of respect for privacy can rarely be traded off in order to allow the publication of speech of no public interest value.

(ii) The importance of the privacy aim served by restricting expression should be balanced against the importance of the expression itself, a method that may be referred to as 'speech/privacy balancing.' Equally, this question could be asked from the opposing perspective: the importance of the speech aim served by restricting privacy should be balanced against the importance of the privacy interest itself. This balancing act would become almost tokenistic if a fact-sensitive examination of the values underlying both Articles demonstrated that both point in the direction of secrecy, or conversely, publicity. Thus, a very serious invasion of privacy, in the sense of mass dissemination of a particularly private moment, as in *Peck*, could not be justified by reference to speech even of some public interest value.

(iii) It should finally be asked (and this test is of especial pertinence in relation to an injunction) – is the disputed measure the least restrictive which could be adopted in the circumstances to serve the aim in question; is the challenged act suitable and necessary for the achievement of its objective, and one which does not impose excessive burdens on the individual; what are the relative costs and benefits of the disputed measure? For example, in many privacy cases, the aims of privacy might be sufficiently served by concealing the identity of the person in question, while still allowing aspects of the story in question to be published.

The first test will not normally be of any significance in this context since Arts 8 and 10 clearly protect important values which, as the Strasbourg jurisprudence discussed establishes, are of equal value. But there might be instances in which either the speech or the privacy interest at stake is so weak that, although Arts 8 and 10 can both be viewed as engaged, it is clear that no trade off can occur. In fact, as pointed out above, Strasbourg tends to rely mainly on the second test when conducting the proportionality analysis.[725] The Strasbourg proportionality test tends essentially to focus on the balancing of the seriousness of the interference with the right against the importance of the aim pursued. Thus the hierarchy of values that can be discerned in relation to each Article aids the balancing act since it should be apparent whether a very weighty speech or privacy interest is at stake. The specific factors identified below, relating to those hierarchies, will strengthen either the privacy or the speech claim in relation to the exercise of proportionality at that second stage. Any harmony that can be discerned between the underlying rationales of both Articles in respect of the factors relevant in the particular instance should be identified. A greater and

724   P Craig, *Administrative Law*, 4th edn, 1999, Sweet and Maxwell, p 590. See further Chapter 3, pp 127–33 and Chapter 4, pp 268, 275–78. 285–90. See also Fenwick and Phillipson (2006) op. cit., fn 1, Chapter 2.
725   See pp 946–50.

more nuanced insight into privacy claims in general and, in cases related to children, into the best interests of the child might be attained; the notion that publicity might in some circumstances serve those interests might begin to take hold. At the same time the claims of the media in this context would be subjected to greater scrutiny than they have been in the past: dissonance between the values of free speech and the commercial interests of the media would tend to be revealed.[726]

Underlying rationales of both Articles; the hierarchy of values

Lord Hoffmann in *Campbell* made it clear that the values underlying both Articles should be utilised as a means of balancing the two interests:

> Take the example . . . of the ordinary citizen whose attendance at NA is publicised in his local newspaper. The violation of the citizen's autonomy, dignity and self-esteem is plain and obvious. Do the civil and political values which underlie press freedom make it necessary to deny the citizen the right to protect such personal information? Not at all . . . there is no public interest whatever in publishing to the world the fact that the citizen has a drug dependency. The freedom to make such a statement weighs little in the balance against the privacy of personal information.[727]

The rationales underlying both Articles make it possible to identify a number of factors that can be taken into account in conducting the parallel analysis in order to resolve clashes between the two guarantees. The identification of weighty speech or privacy factors allows the balance to be pushed one way or the other. A starting-point is to examine the extent to which the values accepted as underlying either Article are at stake in any particular instance. Where they are not fully at stake, an interference with the primary right is likely to be more readily justifiable. The significance of such arguments is already well accepted under Art 10: while the rhetorical attachment of Strasbourg to free speech has always been strong, commentators have accepted for some time that a hierarchy of speech categories has been developed, and that the place of speech within the hierarchy in a particular instance is likely to determine the outcome of a case. Thus it is clear that claims of media freedom in this context do not necessarily partake fully in the classic justificatory rationales of free speech[728] – a point that is developed below. Although the hierarchy of speech is well established this did not lead until recently to strict scrutiny of the *speech* claim in domestic cases concerning clashes between speech and privacy.

As Part 2 of this book made clear, it is a marked feature of the Strasbourg jurisprudence that clearly political speech, which may be seen as directly relating to the bases of

---

726 See further on this point Cram, I, 'Minors' Privacy, Free Speech and the Courts' [1997] PL 410. As Cram puts it in relation to minors' privacy claims: 'the courts [have failed] at times to probe free speech claims advanced by the media by reference to accepted free speech rationales' (at p 419; see also pp 411–12). See further Barendt, E, 'Press and Broadcasting freedom: Does anyone have any rights to free speech?' (1991) 44 CLP 63, 65.

727 [2004] 2 WLR 1232 para 56.

728 See further Barendt, E, 'Press and Broadcasting freedom: Does anyone have any rights to free speech?' (1991) 44 CLP 63, 65.

democracy[729] in terms of both participation and accountability,[730] receives a much more robust degree of protection than other types of expression. Thus the 'political' speech cases of *Sunday Times v UK*,[731] *Jersild v Denmark*,[732] *Lingens v Austria*,[733] and *Thorgeir Thorgeirson v Iceland*[734] all resulted in findings that Art 10 had been violated.[735] By contrast, in cases involving non-political speech supported by the values of autonomy[736] and self-development,[737] applicants have almost invariably been unsuccessful since a deferential approach to the judgment of the national authorities has been adopted.[738]

A similar pattern can be found at the domestic level. When non-political speech supported by the arguments from truth,[739] self-development or autonomy is in issue, domestic decisions have tended to be cautious.[740] In contrast, political expression has clearly been recognised as having a particularly high value in UK law,[741] partly as a response to the Strasbourg stance,[742] although the high status of political expression in the common law is also emphasised.[743]

---

729 See Meiklejohn, A, 'The First Amendment is an Absolute' (1961) Sup Ct Rev 245 and *Political Freedom* (1960) esp pp 115–24.

730 See Barendt, E, *Freedom of Speech*, 1st edn, 1985, Oxford: Clarendon at pp 20 and 23; Blasi, V, 'The Checking Value in First Amendment Theory' (1977) Am B Found Res J 521.

731 A 30 (1979).

732 (1994) 19 EHRR 1.

733 (1986) 8 EHRR 103.

734 (1992) 14 EHRR 843.

735 In *Wingrove v UK* (1997) 24 EHRR 1 the Court remarked: 'there is little scope under Article 10(2) of the Convention for restrictions on political speech or on debate of questions of public interest' (para 58).

736 The argument from moral autonomy – that matters of substantive moral choice must be left to the individual as an autonomous, rational agent. See Scanlon, T, 'A Theory of Freedom of Expression' (1972) 1 Phil & Pub Aff 216.

737 The argument from self development is that the freedom to engage in the free expression and reception of ideas and opinions in various media is essential to human development. See Emerson, C, 'Towards a General Theory of the First Amendment' (1963) 72 Yale LJ 877, 879–80; Redish, M, *Freedom of Expression*, 1984, pp 20–30 and Greenwalt, K, 'Free Speech Justifications' (1989) 89 Columbia Law Review 119, pp 143–45. The ECtHR has repeatedly asserted that freedom of expression is one of the 'essential foundations for the development of everyone' (e.g. *Otto-Preminger Institute v Austria* (1994) 19 EHRR 34, para 49).

738 See *Handyside v UK*, A 24 (1976); *Müller v Switzerland* (1991) 13 EHRR 212; *Gibson v UK*, Appl No 17634 (declared inadmissible by the Commission); *Gay News v UK* (1982) 5 EHRR 123. See further Harris, D, O'Boyle, M and Warbrick, C, *Law of the European Convention on Human Rights*, 1995, pp 397 and 414.

739 Mill's *On Liberty* in Cowling, M, (ed) *Selected Writings of John Stuart Mill*, 1968, Cambridge: CUP, p 121; for discussion see Greenwalt, K, 'Free Speech Justifications' (1989) 89 *Columbia Law Review* 119, pp 130–41. The ECtHr has repeatedly referred to freedom of expression as being one of the 'basic conditions for [society's] progress' (see e.g. *Otto-Preminger Institute v Austria* (1994) 19 EHRR 34, para 49).

740 *Gibson* [1990] 2 QB 619; *Knuller v DPP* [1973] AC 435; *Lemon* [1979] AC 617.

741 *Reynolds v Times Newspapers* [1999] 4 All ER 609; *Derbyshire CC v Times Newspapers* [1993] AC 534; *R v Secretary of State for the Home Dept ex p Simms* [1999] 3 WLR 328.

742 See the approach of the Court of Appeal in *Derbyshire* [1993] AC 534 and in *Ex p Leech* [1994] QB 198, of the House of Lords in *Reynolds* [1999] 4 All ER 609, 621–22, *per* Lord Nicholls, 628 and esp 635, *per* Lord Steyn, 643, *per* Lord Cooke and *Ex p Simms* [1999] 3 WLR 328, 407, *per* Lord Steyn and 419–20, *per* Lord Hobhouse.

743 Lord Steyn has referred to free expression as the 'lifeblood' of democracy (*R v Secretary of State for the Home Dept ex p Simms* [1999] 3 All ER 400, p 408). In *Reynolds v Times Newspapers*

These indications as to the established hierarchy of forms of speech at Strasbourg and domestically and of the values underlying them are of utility in seeking to identify factors that will weigh in favour or against the media claim. It is also necessary to examine the values underlying Art 8 claims in general, although it is fair to say that a hierarchy of such values is not so readily apparent. Such claims may, especially in the case of children, be viewed as relating to both their private and their family life. As argued in the Introduction to this Part, the justification of autonomy generally accepted as one of the key values underlying Art 8, can be broken down into 'substantive' and 'informational' autonomy.[744] The term 'informational autonomy', refers to the individual's interest in controlling the flow of personal information about herself. Substantive autonomy, on the other hand, denotes the individual's interest in being able to make substantive choices about personal life without interference from the state or from other bodies, including the media itself. It is not only fear of media publicity that might drive personal choices, but fear of media opprobrium that might, for example, drive Hollywood actors and other celebrities to conceal their sexual orientation. The media is far from a neutral informing mechanism; media proprietors and editors may well have their own value-laden agendas which may include disapproval of certain life-styles.

Self-fulfilment may also be associated with privacy as a free-standing value in the sense that protection for the private life of the individual – which may take many forms – may provide the best conditions under which he or she may flourish. In *Bensaid v UK* the Court of Human Rights recognised the value of self-development, especially mental development, as an aspect of private life.[745] It is possible to identify further categories of material, in particular those relating to health[746] or sexual orientation or activity[747] that are regarded under Art 8 and under the DPA 1998 as 'particularly sensitive or intimate',[748] requiring especially compelling grounds to justify interference. These values may be particularly pertinent in relation to the privacy of children, as the primacy of the child's welfare, considered above in relation to certain of the 'family' cases under Art 8,

---

[1999] 4 All ER 609, the House of Lords afforded an explicit recognition to the duty of the media to inform the people on matters of legitimate public interest *per* Lord Steyn, 633–34 and 629–29; Lord Nicholls: 'freedom to disseminate and receive information on political matters is essential to the proper functioning of the system of parliamentary democracy cherished in this country' (621). Nevertheless, it should be noted that even political expression can be curbed when courts view other societal interests as especially pressing. This is clear from a number of significant post-HRA decisions: *Pro-Life Alliance*, [2003] 2 WLR 1403 (this decision is in the tradition of deference to widely drafted primary legislation (*Secretary of State for Home Affairs ex p Brind* [1991] 1 AC 696)); *AG v Punch* [2003] 1 AC 1946; *R v Shayler* (governmental arguments from national security (*AG v Guardian Newspapers (No 2)* [1990] 1 AC 109)) have also in the past resulted in the ready upholding of restrictions on directly political speech).

744 See above, pp 804–6.

745 'Private life is a broad term not susceptible to exhaustive definition ... Mental health must also be regarded as a crucial part of private life ... Article 8 protects a right to identity ... personal development, and ... to develop relationships ... The preservation of mental stability is in that context an indispensable precondition to effective enjoyment of the right to respect for private life.' [2001] 33 EHRR 10, para 47.

746 See *Z v Finland* (1998) 25 EHRR 371. See now the findings as to information relating to health matters in the House of Lords in *Campbell* [2004] 2 WLR 1232.

747 See *Lustig-Prean v United Kingdom* (1999) 29 EHRR 548; 7 BHRC 65.

748 Feldman, D, 'Information and privacy' in Beatson, J and Cripps, Y, *Freedom of Expression and Freedom of Information: Essays in Honour of Sir David Williams* 2000, Chapter 19.

indicates. The unauthorised disclosure of personal information relating to children is highly likely to have a greater impact on their personal development, including their ability to recover from traumatic events or sustain or develop beneficial relationships, than it would have on adults. Strasbourg recognised this possibility in the 'family cases' and in *Twenty-Twenty Television*; it has also been recognised domestically, as indicated above.[749]

Far more so than in the typical 'celebrity privacy' cases,[750] political speech, broadly defined, does sometimes come into conflict with the Art 8 rights of children, as where it reveals failings or good practice of state representatives or within state institutions (*Re S, In re Z, Re C (A Minor), Re W(A Minor)(Restriction on Publication)), Re W (A Minor) (Freedom of Publication)), Oxfordshire Council v L and F)*,[751] or opposes gendered concepts of parenting (*Re W (A Minor) (Restriction on Publication))*, or the techniques of cult groups (*Kelly*), or concerns criminal activity where there is an arguable public interest dimension (*Central Independent Television*).

Nevertheless, it is only in a fairly narrow category of cases that any genuine and serious conflict arises – those where a publication would reveal material furthering public knowledge or debate about matters of legitimate public concern *and* the privacy or autonomy or family life of the child would be adversely affected. Where a real conflict appeared to arise – as in *Re S* – the privacy interest could frequently be protected while invading the speech interest only minimally by means of a temporary order intended to conceal identity, so long as the order provided sufficient guidance to the media as to the material that could be published.

The difference between the 'child privacy' cases and those of adult celebrities should be recognised. In the case of children, the facts revealed, as in *Re S*, can be of an order of intimacy, and the publicity can lead to a level of suffering, that is not normally applicable in the celebrity cases. Equally, due to the nature of the facts, the public interest in the cases of children may be much higher. This may also be the case in respect of ordinary adults who happen to be caught up in or engage in activities of a very newsworthy nature – as in *Peck*. In the celebrity cases, the true issue at stake is often not so much the depth of intimacy of the facts revealed – although it may be – it is more likely to concern the relentless intrusion into daily life perpetrated by the paparazzi – as in *Von Hannover*. But at the same time the arguments that the daily life details revealed have public interest value tend to be readily overcome. So the most difficult clashes between Arts 8 and 10 tend not to arise in the typical celebrity privacy cases. This is readily apparent if the facts of *Campbell* and of *Re S* – the two recent and most significant House of Lords' decisions – are compared.

Factors weighing on either side of the balance

Taking account of the underlying values of both Articles as discussed, it is now possible then to identify a range of factors that will weigh strongly in the balance on one

---

749 See e.g.: *In re Z* [1995] 4 All ER 961; *October Films* [1999] 2 FLR 347; Lady Justice Hale's judgment in *Re S*, pp 971–72 below.

750 Such as: *Douglas v Hello!* [2001] QB 967; *Theakston* [2002] EMLR 22; *Campbell* [2002] EMLR 30, CA; [2004] [2004] 2 WLR 1232; [2004] 2 WLR 1232; UKHL 22, HL; *A v B Plc* [2002] 3 WLR 542.

751 [1997] 1 FLR 235.

side or the other at the second stage of the proportionality enquiry.[752] Clearly, that inquiry will be highly fact-sensitive. As *Campbell* made clear, the speech claim will be weakened if the speech fails to partake in the justificatory speech rationales discussed. The decision in *Von Hannover* identified a category of speech – 'infotainment' – that will in most circumstances be overridden by privacy interests since it is devoid of the speech value indicated by those rationales.[753] It has been pointed out that, '[The] media uses people's names, statements, experiences, and emotions to personalise otherwise impersonal accounts of trends or developments.'[754] Clearly, this is the case, although how far it can justify invasions of privacy depends on the facts in each instance. In many instances consented-to publicity could be equally illustrative. But in any event it is suggested that the speech at issue in *Von Hannover* was not illustrative of social trends; it had no wider purpose than to entertain; it was aimed at an audience motivated purely by curiosity. The photograph at issue in *Campbell* was also of very little value in speech terms, as Lord Hoffmann pointed out. Conversely, the speech claim will be strengthened if one of the speech-based rationales is present, even if it cannot be viewed as political expression. If the interest in open justice is at stake that will tend to strengthen it very strongly (as the House of Lords found in *Re S*), but it will not inevitably overcome the privacy claim. Where speech of public interest value is in issue, taking account *inter alia* of the public interest factors discussed above,[755] it would have a higher value than the speech at issue in *Von Hannover*.

The privacy claim will be strengthened if sensitive personal data as designated by the DPA 1998 is at stake. In a case concerning a child, if matters relating to upbringing are involved, that will also strengthen the claim (as in *Re S, In re Z* and in the recent *Re W* case discussed below), even if it is found, as it probably would now be in a media case, that the paramountcy principle is inapplicable. If intrusive methods such as telephone tapping are used to obtain the information, particularly those that could potentially attract criminal sanctions,[756] that will weigh in the balance in favour of privacy. In assessing the gravity of the invasion of privacy involved, further considerations might be of relevance. It could be asked whether the events reported happened in a very intimate setting (for example, the plaintiff's home) or in a more 'public' environment, such as a restaurant, a beach, or the street. On the other hand, if selective disclosure of personal information appears to be part of a deliberate, systematic attempt to manipulate the media by giving a false impression of the claimant's life to the public on a matter of some importance that might arguably weaken the privacy claim,[757] although great caution must be used in deploying this argument since selective disclosure of certain personal matters is entirely in accord with informational autonomy; the

---

752 For further discussion of such factors see Fenwick and Phillipson (2006) op. cit., fn 1 at Chapters 15 and 16.

753 It may be noted that the Supreme Court has found this category of speech is covered by the First Amendment in the US: 'There is no doubt that entertainment, as well as news, enjoys First Amendment protection': *Zaccchini v Sciprrs-Howard Broad Co*, 433 US 562, 578 (1978).

754 Anderson, D, 'The Failure of American Privacy Law' in Markesenis, B, (ed), *Protecting Privacy*, 1999, p 142.

755 See pp 915–18.

756 See p 810, fn 7 above, which refers to the conviction of Goodman, editor of the *News of the World*, in relation to phone-tapping.

757 See Tugendhat and Christie on this point (2002), op. cit., fn 1 at 344.

mere fact that a person is a celebrity does not mean that they under a duty to reveal intimate details of their sex life. The fact that the public is in ignorance as to certain aspects of it should be irrelevant.

If breaches of the PCC Code occurred, including breaches relating to the use of clandestine devices and subterfuge, it is suggested that that is a matter a court can properly take into account in terms of strengthening the privacy claim, under s 12(4) HRA. The *Mills* case in particular made it clear that the PCC Code provides a valuable guide to the weight to be accorded to privacy factors. If traditional duties of confidence are involved, including in particular contractual duties, that will also add strongly to the privacy claim (as in *HRH Prince of Wales v Associated Newspapers Ltd*).[758] The *form* in which the information is recorded, or the form in which it is captured by the defendant may also be relevant in enhancing the privacy claim, as discussed above. The fact that other Convention rights are also implicated may strengthen the privacy claim. Indeed, the engagement of other rights as in *Venables* would be the determining factor if they were absolute or near absolute (for example Arts 2 and 3). If the values underlying other rights could be viewed as engaged, as in *Re S*, in respect of Art 6(1), that might strengthen either claim.

In terms of the third proportionality test the appropriateness of affording relief by way of an injunction, and the ambit of the proposed injunction in terms of the information and time period covered, is relevant. The potential use of injunctions in other similar cases could also be taken into account where a novel use of an injunction is argued for. In *Venables* it was pointed out on behalf of the press that if injunctions were granted, they would not only bind all of the media for an indefinite period, they would also become a precedent for the future. One example put forward at the time was that similar arguments for an injunction could have been used in relation to the release of Myra Hindley. It was pointed out that the Court of Appeal in *Chief Constable of the North Wales Police*[759] had refused to grant injunctions to prevent the Chief Constable from revealing to the owner of a caravan site the past convictions of two paedophiles living on the site. In *Douglas*, in the Court of Appeal, an injunction was not granted on the basis that the plaintiffs had in effect 'sold' the privacy they were seeking to protect; damages alone were awarded.

The balancing act between Articles 8 and 10 – examples of outcomes

This section considers four significant cases in which the parallel analysis was conducted in order to resolve the clash between speech and privacy in each instance – *Re S*, *Re W*, *Campbell* and the *Prince of Wales* case. In these instances *Re S* was, it is argued, a case in which a real and especially problematic conflict between speech and privacy arose – so the balancing act was especially delicate. *Prince of Wales* also raised some fairly difficult issues.

In *re S* the Court of Appeal found that the 'information in the case lay somewhere in between that in *Re X* and *R v Central Television* and that in *Re M and N* or

---

758 [2006] EWCA Civ 1776, [2006] All ER (D) 335 (Dec); the first instance judgment: Blackburne J's judgment [2006] EWHC 522 (Ch).
759 [1999] QB 396.

Re W.[760] The proposed publication indirectly identifying S did not, it was considered relate directly to S's current upbringing. But equally it did not constitute 'the sort of remote and unconnected information about a deceased or long-absent parent' at issue in *Re X* and *R v Central Independent Television plc*. The reports related to recent events in his family life and therefore could be expected to have a real bearing on his future upbringing. So there a very significant privacy interest was involved.

But there was also an important speech interest – the information related to the identity of the defendant and her alleged victim in a murder trial. It was concluded, relying on *ex parte Crook*,[761] that the important public interest in the identification of defendants, in particular those found guilty of serious crimes, can be outweighed in certain circumstances by the need to protect those affected by the crime from further harm. It was accepted that Art 6(1) would not be breached by the concealment of the defendant's identity: it was found that its importance lay in the relationship between the values it protects – the furtherance of the transparency of the administration of justice[762] – and the right to freedom of expression under Art 10(1). Unhampered media reports would play a part in safeguarding the public character of justice. Thus Art 6(1) provided an added dimension in the case, strengthening the speech argument, but not conclusive of the matter.

Clearly it was then necessary to conduct a *dual* exercise in proportionality – the parallel analysis. Lady Hale began by considering the proportionality of the proposed interference with freedom of expression, and in so doing took into account not only the importance of press freedom in principle, but also the features of the case which made its exercise of especial importance. Such enhancing features were found to include: the particular importance attached to the reporting of criminal trials; the right of the public to receive the information in question; the important issues raised regarding an unusual and controversial form of child abuse and about the conduct of the world famous children's hospital in which it was allegedly allowed to take place. Thus the public interest in allowing unrestricted reporting was found to be strong. However, that was not found to mean that it was impossible to justify any restriction, however limited, under Art 10(2). The Court had to consider what restriction, if any, was needed to meet the legitimate aim of protecting the rights of S. If prohibiting publication of the family name and photographs was needed, the Court had to consider how great an impact that would in fact have upon the freedom protected by Art 10, taking into account the greater public interest in knowing the names of persons convicted of serious crime rather than of those who are merely suspected or charged.

The important step in the judicial reasoning process, in accordance with the principle of presumptive equality of the two rights, was the next one. Lady Justice Hale then went on to consider the matter from the perspective of S's Art 8 rights, media freedom under Art 10 figuring this time as an exception to them under Art 8(2). In considering the proportionality of the proposed interference with the right of S to respect for his private and family life, she found that account had to be taken of the magnitude of the

---

760 Para 37.
761 [1995] 1 WLR 139. In that instance it was found that the likely harm to the surviving children of the defendants outweighed the effect on freedom of expression created by the restrictions on publication.
762 *Diennet v France* [1995] 21 EHRR 554, para 33, was referred to.

interference proposed. Factors to be taken into account included the extent to which the additional intrusion would add to the interference which had already taken place; the extent of any further harm that identifying publicity about the trial would do to the child's private and family life, in which his mental health was a 'crucial part'; the impact upon his father, other carers and his school, and the extent to which their task would be made harder by this kind of publicity, and the impact on his relationship with his mother in the short and the longer term. The nature of the publicity would be relevant in minimising the interference: prolonged identifying publicity, with photographs, during the trial, would have a far greater impact than would publicity during the rather shorter period when the family might be identified if there was a conviction. In other words, Lady Justice Hale drew a distinction between the different periods of time during which publicity would occur, if unrestrained: the strength of the free expression claim (bolstered also by the values underlying the guarantee of open justice under Art 6(1)) would be at its greatest at the point at which the argument against publicity would be at its weakest.

Lady Justice Hale came to the conclusion that since the judge had not considered each Article independently, and so had not conducted the difficult balancing exercise required by the Convention, the appeal should be allowed, in order that the exercise could be properly carried out by the first instance Family Division court. The two judges in the majority disagreed, finding that although the balancing exercise outlined by Lady Justice Hale should have been carried out, the result reached – that the restraining order should be discharged – would have been reached even if it had been properly carried out. They considered that the first instance judge had not carried out the exercise correctly, but had had factors relevant to the question of proportionality under Art 8 sufficiently in mind.

In the House of Lords, Lord Steyn, giving the leading judgment, found that the interest in open reporting or criminal trials outweighed the privacy interest of the child. He made an ambiguous finding as to the strong general rule allowing for the reporting of criminal trials. On one possible reading of his findings, he appeared to suggest that that rule created something almost amounting to an exception to the presumptive equality of Arts 8 and 10. The rule, he found, could only be displaced by unusual or exceptional circumstances.[763] Lord Steyn's judgment is confused on this matter since at one point[764] he accepted that both Art 8(1) and 10(1) are engaged and yet then

---

763 Lord Steyn, at para 18: 'the ordinary rule is that the press, as the watchdog of the public, may report everything that takes place in a criminal court. I would add that in European jurisprudence and in domestic practice this is a strong rule. It can only be displaced by unusual or exceptional circumstances. It is, however, not a mechanical rule. The duty of the court is to examine with care each application for a departure from the rule by reason of rights under article 8 . . .' At para 37: 'In my view [Hedley J] analysed the case correctly under the ECHR. Given the weight traditionally given to the importance of open reporting of criminal proceedings it was in my view appropriate for him, in carrying out the balance required by the ECHR, to begin by acknowledging the force of the argument under Article 10 before considering whether the right of the child under Article 8 *was sufficient to outweigh it* (emphasis added). He went too far in saying that he would have come to the same conclusion even if he had been persuaded that this was a case where the child's welfare was indeed the paramount consideration under s 1(1) of the Children Act 1989. But that was not the shape of the case before him.'

764 At paras 26 and 28.

that Hedley J's analysis should be endorsed.[765] Hedley J had considered that since the speech related to the open justice principle Art 8 would figure only as an exception to Art 10 – an implicit rejection of the parallel analysis model of reasoning. Lord Steyn found that Hedley J's approach at first instance – of affording presumptive priority to Art 10 and then allowing Art 8 to figure only as an exception to it, was appropriate in this context. Clearly, as discussed above, this approach denies Art 8's status as a fully-fledged Convention right, where there is a clash between private life and the reporting of criminal proceedings. In other words the House of Lords appeared to go back in this instance to the flawed reasoning adopted in the *Kelly* line of authority. For the reasons given above, and rooted in the Convention clashing rights jurisprudence, it is clear that this is the wrong approach, and that even in relation to such reporting Arts 10 and 8 should have presumptive equality. The creation of this exception is not rooted in the ECHR jurisprudence as Lord Steyn appeared to think. A number of cases were cited that supported the notion of the significance accorded to the open reporting of criminal proceedings[766] but those cases were not decided in the context of a clash with Art 8 rights. *Tammer v Estonia* demonstrates that even where a very significant form of expression is in issue, it may have to give way where a significant privacy interest arises. This could also be applied in relation to the form of expression in question in *Re S*.

In *re S* the private and family life claim was very strong in terms of both informational and substantive autonomy. The revelation of the mother's identity was likely to affect S's ability to recover from the impact on him of his brother's death and mother's trial for the murder, and therefore it was especially crucial that her identity should not be revealed in the immediate aftermath of his brother's death. S was a victim in a very real sense of the alleged offence: he lost his mother (who was later imprisoned for the murder of his brother) and his brother and his high risk of psychiatric harm was likely to be enhanced, according to expert evidence, depending on the level of publicity.[767] The suffering he was likely to undergo as a result of the publicity in terms of bullying and teasing was thought likely to have such an impact on him, in terms of exacerbating the inevitable psychiatric harm he would suffer, that the precarious placement with his father was thought to be likely to break down. So very intimate relationships were at stake in extremely compelling circumstances. A range of Art 8 values were very strongly engaged. Nevertheless, Lord Steyn gave the privacy claim a very cursory treatment, dismissing it in two paragraphs of his speech.

In contrast to the privacy claim in *Re S*, the speech claim was weak; Lord Steyn was obviously right to identify the interest in open justice as a very significant matter in terms of speech values, but wrong, it is argued, to proceed to the assumption that knowledge of S's identity was necessary in order to serve that interest. The speech interest engaged in publishing photographs of the mother with the dead boy and revealing the mother's name was minimal: discussion of the circumstances surrounding the murder could have occurred in the press on a basis of anonymity, at least during the mother's trial. The mother's name would clearly mean nothing to the vast majority of the readers of the newspapers in question. Thus the public interest could have been served, since the

765 At para 37.
766 At para 15.
767 Hale LJ made these points at para 39 of the CA judgment.

case raised certain wider issues, while still protecting S. This judgment suggests that the courts are more comfortable with free speech than with privacy claims: as discussed above, free speech values have traditionally had far more hold on the common law than privacy values have. There are real dangers as a result that the privacy claim of the child will be minimised as – it is argued – it was in the House of Lords in *Re S*. Although the parallel analysis was formally conducted in *Re S*, it is suggested that it was undertaken in a tokenistic fashion – no real effort was made to subject the true value of the speech claim to scrutiny; conversely, the privacy claim was accorded insufficient weight.

Thus, although the Lords in *Re S* endorsed *Campbell*, there seemed to be no recognition of the fact that the decision gave the impression of departing in spirit from the fundamental approach of *Campbell*, that of presumptive equality. However, the interpretation given to the Lords' ruling in the later case of *Re W* made it clear that the interest in open justice should figure in the parallel analysis as a weighty factor rather than as determinative of the matter in favour of Art 10. That is clearly the better interpretation. It is further contended that even on that analysis the wrong outcome was reached since the factual situation in *Re S* was more strongly supportive of Lady Justice Hale's minority judgment: the revelation of the mother's identity was likely to affect S's ability to recover from the impact on him of his brother's death and mother's trial for the murder, and therefore it was especially crucial that her identity should not be revealed in the immediate aftermath of his brother's death. The interest in open justice and the public interest in the issues surrounding the trial could have been served with relative efficacy at a later date, bearing in mind those compelling arguments for postponement. In this instance the balancing exercise, it is argued, reached the wrong outcome since too much weight was afforded to the open justice factor.

The more satisfactory explanation of Lord Steyn's judgment in *Re S* was adopted in a significant subsequent case in the High Court, *Re W (Children)*.[768] In that instance the mother of two children (T, aged three, and R, aged six months), who was HIV positive, had pleaded guilty to knowingly infecting the father of R with HIV; she was awaiting sentence under s 20 of the Offences Against the Person Act. It was apparent that the children were likely to suffer the hostility of the community if it was thought that they might be infected by the disease and their connection with the criminal trial of their mother was fully revealed. It seemed quite possible that their long-term care placement would be jeopardised. The local council therefore sought an injunction to restrict publicity relating to the trial which might connect the children to it. As in *Re S*, the injunction was intended to conceal the identity of the defendant and victim in the trial in order to protect the children, indirectly. Thus the facts of the two cases were very similar.

The President of the Family Division in *Re W* had to determine how to reconcile Lord Steyn's findings as to the presumptive equality of Arts 8 and 10 with his finding as to the strong general rule relating to the open justice principle. As indicated above, it appeared on one reading of Lord Steyn's findings that Art 10 was to be viewed as having presumptive priority where reporting relating to criminal trials was concerned. However, the President managed to find an explanation of Lord Steyn's findings that allowed Arts 8 and 10 to be balanced against each other on a basis of equality:

---

768 *A Local Authority v (1) W (2) L (3) W (4) T & R (By The Children's Guardian)* [2005] EWHC 1564 (Fam).

. . . the starting point is presumptive parity, in that neither article has precedence over or 'trumps' the other. The exercise of parallel analysis requires the court to examine the justification for interfering with each right and the issue of proportionality is to be considered in respect of each. It is not a mechanical exercise to be decided upon the basis of rival generalities. An intense focus on the comparative importance of the specific rights being claimed in the individual case is necessary before the ultimate balancing test in terms of proportionality is carried out. Having so stated, Lord Steyn strongly emphasised the interest in open justice as a factor to be accorded great weight in both the parallel analysis and the ultimate balancing test . . . However, nowhere did he indicate that the weight to be accorded to the right freely to report criminal proceedings would invariably be determinative of the outcome.[769]

On this basis it is argued that the factual situations in both *Re S* and *Re W* supported restraint on the media: as indicated above, in *Re S* the revelation of the mother's identity was likely to have a strong psychological impact on S. His risk of psychiatric harm was dependent on the level of publicity.[770] It was also quite possible that his placement with his father might break down so that he would have to go into care; thus the potential impact on his family life of he disclosure of his identity could also have been severe. In other words, the private and family life claims were very strong. The same was clearly true of the claim in *Re W*. But in contrast to Lord Steyn, the President of the Family Division examined the privacy claims of the children concerned in detail, finding that their Art 8 rights were very strongly engaged.

As discussed, the public interest could have been served in *Re S* since the case raised certain wider issues, while still protecting S by an injunction concealing his identity. This was the stance taken towards the speech claim in *Re W*. In granting the injunction in order to protect the children, the President found:

> . . . granting the injunction is [not] in fact likely to inhibit the press from reporting the case, nor should well-informed debate be significantly impaired simply because of the non-identification of the defendant or victim. It is said that the editor's principal wish is to be free to identify and publish a picture of the defendant *so as to report and convey an adequate understanding to the public*. I do not think the former is essential to the latter'.[771]

It can be concluded that Baroness Hale's balancing test is to be used in cases where the child's Art 8 right is engaged and clashes with the media's Art 10 right, including instances where the reporting relates to a criminal trial and the child would be indirectly identified.

The balancing act set out in the Court of Appeal in *Re S* between Arts 8 and 10 – the dual exercise in proportionality, or 'parallel analysis' – was endorsed by the House of

---

769 Ibid at para 53.
770 Ad indicated above, Hale LJ made these points at para 39 of the CA judgment.
771 *A Local Authority v (1) W (2) L (3) W (4) T & R (By The Children's Guardian)* [2005] EWHC 1564 (Fam) at para 63 (emphasis in original).

Lords in the seminal decision in *Campbell*.[772] *Campbell* was remarkable since as part of the 'parallel analysis' of proportionality, the poverty of the speech claim was made clear. Lord Nicholls found: 'The need to be free to disseminate information regarding Miss Campbell's drug addiction is of a lower order than the need for freedom to disseminate information on some other subjects such as political information.'[773] Lady Hale similarly held: 'there are undoubtedly different types of speech' and that some of those 'are more deserving of protection in a democratic society than others'; speech would be valuable where it included:

> . . . revealing information about public figures, especially those in elective office, which would otherwise be private but is relevant to their participation in public life. Intellectual and educational speech and expression are also important in a democracy, not least because they enable the development of individuals' potential to play a full part in society and in our democratic life. Artistic speech and expression is important for similar reasons, in fostering both individual originality and creativity and the free-thinking and dynamic society we so much value.[774]

Lord Hope found:

> But it should also be recognised that the right of the public to receive information about the details of her treatment was of a much lower order than the undoubted right to know that she was misleading the public when she said that she did not take drugs. In *Dudgeon v United Kingdom* (1981) 4 EHRR 149, para 52 the European Court said that the more intimate the aspects of private life which are being interfered with, the more serious must be the reasons for doing so before the interference can be legitimate. Clayton and Tomlinson, *The Law of Human Rights* (2000), para 15.162, point out that the court has distinguished three kinds of expression: political expression, artistic expression and commercial expression, and that it consistently attaches great importance to political expression and applies rather less rigorous principles to expression which is artistic and commercial. According to the court's well-established case law, freedom of expression constitutes one of the essential foundations of a democratic society and one of the basic conditions for its progress and the self-fulfilment of each individual: *Tammer v Estonia* (2001) 37 EHRR 857, para 59. But there were no political or democratic values at stake here, nor has any pressing social need been identified.[775]

He concluded that a person's right to privacy can be limited by 'the public's interest in knowing about certain traits of her personality and certain aspects of her private life . . .'.[776] But he found that in order to deprive Miss Campbell of her right to privacy it would not be enough to argue 'that she is a celebrity and that her private life is newsworthy'.

772 [2004] 2 WLR 1232; for further discussion of *Campbell*, see above pp 911–13.
773 Ibid para 29.
774 Ibid para 148.
775 *Campbell v MGN Ltd* [2004] 2 AC 457 at para 117.
776 He relied on L'Heureux-Dubé and Bastarache JJ in the Supreme Court of Canada recognised in *Aubry v Les Editions Vice-Versa Inc* [1998] 1 SCR 591, paras 57–58.

Treating the complained-of details merely as background was to undervalue the importance that was to be attached to the need, if Miss Campbell was to be protected, to keep these details private. And it is hard to see that there was any compelling need for the public to know the name of the organisation that she was attending for the therapy, or for the other details of it to be set out.[777]

Therefore he found that in relation to the details complained of, including the picture taken of Ms Campbell outside the NA clinic, other than the fact of receiving drug treatment, a remedy should be granted, a conclusion with which the Lords in the majority agreed.

In *HRH Prince of Wales v Associated Newspapers Ltd*[778] the Court of Appeal had to consider a claim for breach of privacy and confidence brought by the Prince against the *Mail on Sunday* which had published details from his private diary. The diary in question was one of eight given to the paper by Sarah Goodall, a secretary in his private office from 1988 to 2000. The journals were handwritten accounts that Charles made following foreign visits over the past 30 years and which he circulated 'in confidence' to between 50 and 75 people, including politicians, actors, journalists and other people in the media. The employment contracts of each of those in Prince Charles' service provided that any information in relation to him that was acquired during the course of his or her employment was subject to an undertaking of confidence and was not to be disclosed to any unauthorised person.

Prince Charles alleged that the publication of the extracts from the journal interfered with his right to respect for his private life and his correspondence under Art 8 of the Convention, so that it constituted in a breach of privacy. The *Mail on Sunday* denied this but alleged, in the alternative, that any interference with this right was justified under Art 8(2) as necessary to protect the rights of the newspaper and the public under Art 10. Prince Charles had accepted that the relief that he claimed amounted to a restriction on the newspaper's right of freedom of expression under Art 10, but he alleged that this restriction was justified under Art 10(2) as necessary to protect his right to privacy, his copyright and to prevent the disclosure of information received in confidence.

The Court of Appeal found that the action was not concerned with a claim for breach of privacy that involved an extension of the old law of breach of confidence. It found that all the elements of a claim for breach of confidence under the old law were evident since the information was disclosed in breach of a 'well-recognised relationship of confidence, that which exists between master and servant'.[779] So a weighty element that weighed in the balance was the importance in a democratic society of upholding duties of confidence between individuals. It was argued on behalf of the newspaper that Prince Charles, as heir to the throne, was a public figure who had controversially courted public attention and used the media to publicise views, particularly in relation to the Chinese, of a similar kind to those expressed in the journal, so he could have no

777 Ibid at para 120.
778 [2006] EWCA Civ 1776, [2006] All ER (D) 335 (Dec); the first-instance judgment: Blackburne J's judgment [2006] EWHC 522 (Ch).
779 Ibid at para 28.

reasonable expectation that the journal would remain confidential.[780] The first instance judge had found, and the Court of Appeal agreed, that this factor did not go to the question of whether the content of the journal was confidential, but rather to the question whether that confidentiality would have to give way when weighed against the rights of freedom of expression enjoyed by the newspaper and its readers. It was concluded that the publication by the newspaper of extracts from the journal interfered with Prince Charles' right to respect for his private life, and it was noted that this was even more clearly made out since the right extended to protect Prince Charles' 'correspondence' under Art 8. The Court noted that the cause of action was now focused upon the protection of human autonomy and dignity, the right to control the dissemination of information about one's private life and the right to the esteem and respect of other people.[781]

In relation to balancing Arts 8 and 10 the Court found that in general the Strasbourg Court views with disfavour attempts to suppress publication of information which is of genuine public interest and noted that where it relates to a matter of major public concern, even medical confidentiality may not prevail.[782] The Court noted that where no breach of a confidential relationship is involved, the balance will be between Art 8 and Art 10 rights and will usually involve weighing the nature and consequences of the breach of privacy against the public interest, if any, in the disclosure of private information. But the Court found that position would be different where the disclosure related, as it did in the instant case, to 'information received in confidence'. It found:

> . . . the test to be applied when considering whether it is necessary to restrict freedom of expression in order to prevent disclosure of information received in confidence is not simply whether the information is a matter of public interest but whether, in all the circumstances, it is in the public interest that the duty of confidence should be breached. The claimant is as much entitled to enjoy confidentiality for his private thoughts as an aspect of his own 'human autonomy and dignity' as is any other.[783]

The newspaper identified a number of matters of public interest revealed by the diary: (1) the nature of lobbying to which Prince Charles subjected this country's elected leaders; (2) the political conduct of the Heir to the Throne; (3) the conduct of Prince Charles in failing to attend the 1999 Chinese banquet; (4) Prince Charles' public statements about his non attendance at that banquet. He had termed Chinese officials 'waxworks'. However, the first instance judge concluded that the contribution that the journal or the articles in the newspaper made to providing information on any of those matters was minimal, and the Court of Appeal took the same view. The Court concluded that the first instance judge had been correct to hold that Prince Charles had an unanswerable claim for breach of privacy. When the breach of a confidential relationship was added into the balance, the Court found that his case was overwhelming. This case was of interest in that matters of some public interest were revealed – matters of much greater

---

780 Para 45.
781 Para 51.
782 The Court relied on *Editions Plon v France* (2006) 42 EHRR 36.
783 Para 68.

interest than those revealed by the reporting in *Von Hannover*, but the Court had little difficulty in finding that the privacy and confidentiality interest outweighed them.

Arguably, this case followed a pattern rather similar to that taken in the Lords in *Re S*, in the sense that one of the claims was dealt with in a somewhat cursory fashion, while still paying lip service to the balancing act. The speech claim was dismissed with rapidity, after a fairly cursory examination of its weight. If the future monarch exhibits tendencies that could be viewed as non-diplomatic in relation to Chinese officials, that is a matter of public interest which the public have a right to know about. The speech claim required far more thorough consideration. The strength of the privacy claim, the morally reprehensible methods used to obtain the information, and the public interest in protecting the Prince's ability to protect his record of his confidential thoughts seemed to obscure the competing strengths of the speech claim.

Conclusions

There are doctrinal difficulties, as this chapter has revealed, in determining whether to assign 'privacy factors' to the private information stage of the claim or to the balancing act. The trend is clearly away from accepting *limiting* factors at that stage, such as the defence of waiver or of public domain, although they may re-enter the equation to an extent at the balancing act stage. But factors *enhancing* the privacy claim are more problematic. Judicial work is still required in this respect.[784] The media might complain that the new liability therefore creates too much uncertainty, having a chilling effect on press freedom. But if the press are put on notice that publishing unconsented-to photographs of celebrities or other private information, might attract liability if the information is of little or no speech value, and where it is obvious that the celebrity would not have consented to the photograph if asked, that is not, it is argued, an invasion of freedom of speech that is worthy of concern. The recent cases discussed have revealed the 'Emperor's new clothes' aspect of press free speech claims in the context of celebrity gossip, revealing them to be in reality purely commercial ones.

Full use of the parallel analysis in all instances creates strong scrutiny of the real basis of media free speech claims, with the result, in the wake of *Campbell* and *Von Hannover*, that privacy may tend to prevail where speech in the infotainment category is at stake. In other instances, both claims should be probed with a view to considering how crucial it is to the speech value of reporting that a person's identity is revealed. Obviously, if the story concerns malpractice by a public figure, identity is crucially relevant. But, despite very recent developments, it is argued that the courts continue to be more comfortable with free speech than with privacy claims. This is probably one of the most significant points emerging from this chapter. As discussed above, the common law accorded a very high value to free speech, elevating it, pre-HRA, to the status of a common law right. In *ex parte Simms*[785] Lord Steyn referred to free speech as 'the *primary* right . . . in a democracy' (emphasis added). In contrast, the judges pre-HRA failed to create a common law tort of invasion of private life or of the non-consensual use of personal

---

784 See further: Markesinis, BS, O'Cinneide, C, Fedtke, J and Hunter-Henin, M, 'Concerns and Ideas about the Developing English Law of Privacy (and how Knowledge of Foreign Law Might Be of Help)' (2004) LII(1) *American Journal of Comparative Law* 133 at pp 158–60.

785 [1999] 3 All ER 400, CA; [1999] 3 WLR 328, HL.

information.[786] Thus, in substantive terms, the strong common law tradition of free speech influenced the decision in *Re S* to the detriment of the more nebulous demands of privacy – demands that appear to have less of a hold on the judicial imagination. Where the judiciary perceive a clash between common law and Convention values, their tendency, despite the inception of the HRA, is to give preference to the former.

Clearly, the HRA's primary role is to protect the citizen against the arbitrary and oppressive use of state power – the main concern of the other chapter in this Part. But the ability of large media corporations to invade privacy is equal to, or even arguably surpasses, that of the state, as the state does not possess the power *in itself* to create widespread dissemination of private information. Therefore provision of protection for the citizen against the mass media is equally necessary. It is, it is argued, a standing embarrassment to the members of the House of Lords, and in particular Lord Steyn, that that outcome was not achieved in *Re S*.

The more sensitive and sophisticated reasoning of the President of the Family Division in *Re W*, which succeeded in examining the real weight of both the speech and the privacy claims put forward, may be indicative of the path that judicial reasoning is now likely to take in this context. Clearly, it could be viewed at first glimpse as rooted in the child-centred approach of the Family Division – as merely reflecting the values underpinning the paramountcy principle and therefore as flawed in its desire to afford primacy to privacy as Lord Steyn's approach was, it is contended, in relation to speech. Its claim to be viewed as a model of HRA judicial reasoning – as exhibiting a nuanced and sensitive approach to the clash of rights in question which outdoes the reasoning in a number of Strasbourg cases, including *Twenty-Twenty TV* – is based, however, precisely on its avoidance of the creation or acceptance of a presumption on the lines of those accepted in either *Re S* or *In re Z*.

The discussion above has sought to reveal the flaws in judicial reasoning in early post-HRA clashing rights cases. It has suggested that in relation to this speech/privacy clash the new privacy liability or 'ECHR jurisdiction' could develop in a distorted manner: it could fall into the trap of failing to provide privacy protection even where very strong claims for such protection arise, despite the harmony that can be found between free speech and private life values. The Lords' decision in *Re S* not only fails to demonstrate a strong grasp of the values at stake in difficult clashing rights cases, it also exhibits the tendency of common law judicial reasoning to prefer form over substance. In other words, the judiciary tend to be more comfortable with a fairly mechanistic approach to reasoning, as opposed to the more value-laden type of reasoning demanded by the Convention. *Re S* exemplifies the uneasy fusion in post-HRA judicial reasoning between Convention values and common law ones. We can find in the judgment firstly a partial abandonment of the needlessly rigid *Re Z* categories, but then a re-entrance of the more mechanistic approach, by way of a device allowing avoidance of an examination of the true values at stake. Clearly, this analysis is complicated by

---

786   See *Kaye v Robertson* [1991] FCR 62. The caveat to the above remarks was entered by the author in 1996 in *Confidence and Privacy: A Re-examination* [1996] 55(3) CLJ 447 (with Phillipson, G). The article traces the somewhat uncertain steps that the judges were taking towards the creation of such a tort by utilising the action for breach of confidence, which this chapter has focused upon. However, it is highly unlikely that members of the judiciary would claim that private life had attained the same common law recognition as free speech had by the time of inception of the HRA.

the value-laden nature of that device – a near-automatic presumption in favour of speech based on the value of the open justice principle. But in Convention terms any such presumption is flawed since it creates a barrier to the full examination of both the speech and the private life claim, taking account of both speech and privacy values in a democratic society. The presumption is flawed since, as *Re S* illustrated, it precludes a genuine attempt to weigh up the strength of the competing privacy claim. A converse presumption, that unauthorised publication of a private diary would tend to outweigh competing speech claims, as arguably occurred in the *Prince of Wales* case, is equally flawed. On the other hand, a presumption that privacy-invading speech amounting only to infotainment is unlikely to be capable of displacing the privacy claim, is easier to justify since its focus is precisely on the weakness of the speech claim. In other words, placing a presumptively strong speech or privacy factor in the balance should not be, in effect, the end of the matter. As further clashing speech/privacy cases arise before the domestic courts, this danger, that the parallel analysis might be conducted in a tokenistic fashion as unspoken presumptions begin to pervade it, is likely to continue to arise, due in part to the preference of the judges for follow established common law modes of reasoning that avoid dealing with moral conflict.

9 Remedies

Introduction

The privacy measures considered in this chapter – apart from the 'powers' of the PCC in relation to the PCC Code – offer a variety of remedies. Ofcom has a number of internal remedies at its command and since it is a public authority under s 6 HRA, it must act in accordance with Arts 10 and 8 in applying them. Various criminal offences arise under the DPA 1998, while reporting restrictions can be enforced in contempt proceedings. Compensation is available under s 13 of the DPA in respect of unfair processing by data controllers. However, as indicated above, it appears that interim injunctions are not obtainable under s 32 DPA unless the claimant is seeking to prevent re-publication of the material. The PHA creates criminal offences and also provides a power to obtain an injunction to prevent harassment. If the doctrine of confidence/privacy is relied on, a number of civil remedies are available, and those remedies are also available under s 8 HRA where an action is brought directly for invasion of privacy under Art 8 under s 7(1)(a) of the HRA against a media body which is a public authority.[787]

Where an action is brought directly against a media body, either under the doctrine of confidence/privacy or, in the case of the BBC or Channel 4 under the HRA, the claimant would normally be seeking an injunction. In the case of Ofcom, the order sought by the claimant under s 8 HRA could be a declaration or a mandatory order, since he or she would be asking Ofcom to use its powers either to punish a broadcaster or to prevent a future broadcast. Orders against Ofcom would presumably take the form of mandatory orders or declarations. These remedies are considered below, together with the impact on them of s 12 HRA. The discussion below revolves round the privacy cases brought under the privacy/confidence action. But it is probable that the same

787 See further Chapter 4, pp 241–47.

principles would apply if an action was brought directly against a media body who was also a public authority under s 7 HRA.

Damages and accounts of profit

An account of profits[788] is available in confidence cases. On this matter, the Court in *Douglas III* said:

> If, however, *Hello!* had made a profit on the publication, we would have had no hesitation in accepting that the Douglases would have been entitled to seek an account of that profit. Such an approach may also serve to discourage any wrongful publication, at least where it is motivated by money. [789]

Damages are also available, in addition to, or in substitution for, injunctive relief, [790] and regardless of whether or not the court could also have ordered injunctive relief in the particular circumstances.[791] Until *Campbell* there was no authority for the award of damages for emotional distress, but precedents exist in other areas of law.[792] It is now established that damages for emotional distress may be awarded in 'private fact' cases. In *Campbell* damages were assessed at a little over £14,000, including £1,000 for aggravated damages, in respect of the 'trashing' of Campbell's character in articles published after she commenced her action against the *Mirror*.

In *Archer v Williams*[793] it was accepted that damages could be awarded for emotional distress, in this case caused by publication of details of plastic surgery: they were assessed at £2,500. As discussed, damages are also available under the Data Protection Act. An account of profits may alternatively be ordered.[794] The Court of Appeal in *Douglas III* said as to damages in confidence/privacy cases:

---

788 The court will not award both, on the basis that this would compensate the plaintiff twice over. See the comments of the Law Commission in its Working Paper No 58, Cmnd 5012, 1972, para 123.

789 Ibid at para 249.

790 Under Lord Cairns' Act; see Wacks, op. cit., fn 1, pp 149, 151, and fns 28 and 44. Damages were awarded in the decisions in *Douglas II* (2003) EWCA Civ 139 (affirmed in *Douglas III* [2005] EWCA 595) and in *Campbell v MGN* [2004] 2 WLR 1232.

791 Provided the court has jurisdiction to grant an injunction: see *Hooper v Rogers* [1975] 1 Ch 43, p 48, *per* Russell LJ. See also *Race Relations Board v Applin* [1973] 1 QB 815 and the views of Capper, D ('Damages for breach of the equitable duty of confidence' (1994) 14 LS 313) and Gurry, F, *Breach of Confidence* 1984, Chapter 23. See Wacks, op. cit., fn 1, p 151, fn 46; cf the views of Megarry VC in *Malone v Comr of Police for the Metropolis (No 2)* [1979] 1 Ch 344.

792 Examples include contract (*Jarvis v Swans Tours Ltd* [1973] 1 QB 233), copyright and under the Sex Discrimination Act 1975, which gives the courts power to award damages on the same basis as in tort actions (see Chapter 15, pp 1586–90) and which under s 66 allows courts to award damages for injury to feelings alone. Space precludes full discussion of the point, but it was until *Campbell* an area free of authority; but to decide that as a blanket rule, such damages could never be available, by leaving the plaintiff potentially remediless, would be clearly have been out of line with the Convention notion of effective protection for rights; Strasbourg has recognised the need to compensate for 'moral damage', including emotional distress (see Van Dijk and Van Hoof, *Theory and Practice of the European Convention on Human Rights*, 1998, pp 179–82).

793 [2003] EMLR 38.

794 Op. cit., at para 123.

The sum [of damages awarded] is also small in the sense that it could not represent any real deterrent to a newspaper or magazine, with a large circulation, contemplating the publication of photographs which infringed an individual's privacy.
Accordingly, particularly in the light of the state of competition in the newspaper
and magazine industry, the refusal of an interlocutory injunction in a case such
as this represents a strong potential disincentive to respect for aspects of private
life, which the Convention intends should be respected.[795]

In *Douglas* the High Court and the Court of Appeal accepted that there had been
a breach of the couple's privacy by virtue of the publication of the unauthorised
photographs, and awarded around £14,000 damages. The Court of Appeal in *Douglas
III*[796] found that this interference with an exclusive contract gave no cause of action to
OK! – the original beneficiaries of it. It therefore overturned the award of £1 million
damages to *OK!*, but the award was restored by the House of Lords.

The Court of Appeal referred to the damages awarded to the Douglases as 'a very
modest sum in the context of this litigation'.[797] Clearly, these meagre awards of damages
provide little financial disincentive to journalists inclined to invade privacy in pursuit
of profit-making photographs and stories.

Interim injunctions

Clearly, the most important issue both for privacy and for media freedom is the question
of the basis on which the courts will grant an interlocutory injunction to restrain
publication. The main flaw of the Data Protection Act, as indicated, as a statutory
privacy remedy, is its bar on interim injunctions against the press. From the plaintiff's
perspective, obtaining an injunction is vital in privacy cases, far more so than in
defamation. This is because the damage done to reputation by initial publication can
be subsequently restored by a public finding that the allegation was false. By contrast,
if private information is made public, the law can compensate for this harm at final
trial by awarding damages, but it cannot in any way cure the invasion of privacy: it
cannot erase the information revealed from people's memories. From the defendant's
perspective, on the other hand, if the story is topical, even an interim injunction might
kill it off completely. Thus, as Robertson and Nichol put it: 'In breach of confidence
. . . the critical stage is usually the application for an interim injunction . . . If the
publisher is able to publish . . . the action will often evaporate . . . If the story is
injuncted the publisher will often lose interest . . .'[798] Similarly, Leigh and Lustgarten
comment: 'the interim stage is the critical one . . . [it is] effectively the disposition of
the matter'.[799] However, while all privacy is lost if the story is published, the speech
claim could be served by a limited injunction designed to protect identity – it might,

---

795 Op. cit. at paras 225–57.
796 *Douglas II* (2003) EWCA Civ 139 was affirmed in *Douglas III* [2005] EWCA 595. HL decision:
      [2007] UKHL 21.
797 Op. cit. at para 110.
798 *Media Law*, 1992, p 190.
799 Leigh, I and Lustgarten, L, 'Making rights real: the courts, remedies, and the Human Rights Act'
      (1999) 58 CLJ 509 p 533 (referring to the granting of interim injunctions generally); and see also
      p 551.

depending on the circumstances, still be possible to publish the story itself. This point is returned to below.

Prior to the inception of the HRA it was only necessary for the plaintiff to make out an arguable case for confidentiality[800] in order to obtain an injunction; the courts then sought to maintain the *status quo*, on the basis that if the story was published, the material would lose its confidential character, and there would be nothing to have a final trial about.[801] However, this consideration could be outweighed by the defence of public interest at the interlocutory stage. The view of Lord Denning in *Woodward v Hutchins*,[802] that the mere fact that defendants intend to plead public interest at final trial should preclude interim relief, did not find wide support; instead, it appeared that, whilst a plea of public interest could defeat a claim for such relief, the defence had to be supported by evidence and have a credible chance of success at final trial.[803] Since the judges have the confidential information in question before them at that stage, they may be able to find quite readily that the defence is made out (as Laws J did in *Hellewell*) or will probably succeed (as in *Lion Laboratories*) or that it does not justify publication at large (as in *Francome*). Since, as suggested above, the paradigmatic privacy claim often involves speech of little or no value in public interest terms,[804] it is fairly easy, at least in some instances, to determine that the publication in question raises no serious speech or public interest issue.

However, that test was thought to be potentially unfavourable to the media because, in balancing the rights of the two parties, courts took the view that while the plaintiff's right to confidentiality would be wholly defeated by publication, the press could always still publish the story if they won at trial; they were thus inclined toward protecting the more fragile right of the plaintiff.[805]

---

800 E.g., *HRH Princess of Wales*; *Shelley Films Ltd*; *Francome*.
801 See *AG v Guardian Newspapers (No 2)* [1990] 1 AC 109. Thus in *Francome* [1984] 1 WLR 892, p 900, Fox LJ said: 'Unless Mr Francome is given protection until the trial, I think that a trial might be largely worthless from his point of view even though he succeeded.' Similarly, in *Lion Laboratories* [1984] 1 QB 530, p 551, Griffiths LJ said: 'there will usually be a powerful case for maintaining the status quo by the grant of an interlocutory injunction to restrain publication until trial of the action.'
802 [1977] 1 WLR 760, CA.
803 See *Lion Laboratories* [1984] 1 QB 530, pp 538 and 553, *per* Stephenson LJ (explicitly rejecting Lord Denning's approach in *Woodward*); ibid, p 548 *per* O'Connor LJ and p 553 *per* Griffiths LJ; similarly in *Hellewell*, where the public interest argument prevented the award of an injunction.
804 E.g., Alan Russbridger, the editor of the *Guardian*, in a conference speech, listed a string of examples in which newspapers had published intimate details about the personal lives of celebrities, in some cases surreptitiously obtained, with either no or the flimsiest of 'public interest' justifications; he instanced a story in the *News of the World* in January 1999, in which a lap dancer gave full details of a recent sexual encounter with the singer Tom Jones (Human Rights, Privacy and the Media, organised by the Constitution Unit, and the Centre for Communication and Information Law, UCL, 8 January 1999).
805 This generally followed under the 'balance of convenience' test (*American Cyanamid Co v Ethicon* [1975] AC 396). See *AG v Guardian Newspapers* [1987] 3 All ER 316, which concerned an application for an interim injunction to restrain publication of confidential information (extracts from *Spycatcher*). Lord Brandon remarked (ibid, p 1292): 'the choice lies between one course [allowing publication] which may result in permanent and irrevocable damage to the cause of [the plaintiff] and another course which can only result in temporary and in no wary irrevocable damage to the cause of the newspapers ... it seems to me clear that the second ... course should ... be preferred ...'; see also the similar reasoning of Lord Ackner, ibid, p 1305.

The HRA addresses this issue directly. In this context, s 12 is of interest in respect of injunctions or other orders granted under its own powers, contained in s 8,[806] and at common law, where freedom of expression is affected. It will be recalled from Chapter 4 that s 12 applies (*per* sub-section (1)): '. . . if a court is considering whether to grant any relief which, if granted, might affect the exercise of the Convention right to freedom of expression';[807] it provides (*per* sub-section (3)) that: 'no such relief is to be granted so as to restrain publication before trial unless the court is satisfied that the applicant is likely to establish that publication should not be allowed'. Section 12(4) specifically instructs the courts that when they are dealing with, *inter alia*, journalistic material, they should consider the extent to which 'it is, or would be, in the public interest for the material to be published' and thus remove any lingering doubts as to whether the court should consider the strength of the public interest defence at the interim stage. Sub-section (3), in allowing the court to grant injunctions only where it believes that the plaintiff will succeed at trial, requires the court to undertake a substantial balancing test at the interim stage; it also makes it clear that the burden is on the plaintiff to show that the privacy interest would probably succeed at trial.[808]

Undertaking this evaluation at the interlocutory stage is not proving to be an especially difficult task, as the findings in *Douglas*,[809] *Venables*[810] and *Mills*[811] suggested. The position in defamation, in which the courts refuse an interim injunction if the defendants intend to plead justification, may be distinguished: justification is a factual claim, the investigation of which will often require sifting through a mountain of evidence and so cannot be resolved at the interlocutory stage; by contrast, the defence in confidence cases generally requires not an empirical, but an evaluative judgment. When undertaking this inquiry, the courts obviously have to take account of Art 10 jurisprudence on interim injunctions since s 12 instructs them to have 'particular regard' to Art 10. The leading Strasbourg case on prior restraints is *Observer and Guardian v UK*,[812] in which the Court considered the compatibility with Art 10 of interim injunctions preventing those newspapers from publishing *Spycatcher* material. The Court laid down the basic principle that:

. . . while Art 10 does not in terms prohibit the imposition of prior restraints on publication . . . the dangers inherent in [them] are such that they call for the most careful scrutiny on the part of the Court . . . news is a perishable commodity and delay of its publication, even for a short period, may well deprive it of all its value and interest.[813]

806 See Chapter 4, p 241.
807 See pp 212–13.
808 Sub-section (2) provides some procedural protection against interim injunctions. It provides: 'If the person against whom the application for relief is made ('the respondent') is neither present nor represented, no such relief is to be granted unless the court is satisfied –

 (a) that the applicant has taken all practicable steps to notify the respondent; or

 (b) that there are compelling reasons why the respondent should not be notified.' This clearly limits the circumstances in which *ex parte* injunctions against publication can be granted.
809 [2001] 2 WLR 992.
810 [2001] 1 All ER 908, Fam Div.
811 [2001] EMLR 41, 4 June, High Court No HC 0102236, WL 720322.
812 (1991) 14 EHRR 153; for comment see Leigh, I, '*Spycatcher* in Strasbourg' [1992] PL 200.
813 Ibid, para 60.

While the court's actual decision in the case seemed to suggest that the need to preserve the plaintiff's rights would in itself point strongly towards the imposition of an interim injunction,[814] the relatively cautious approach adopted may have been influenced by the fact that the very sensitive issue of national security was at stake. It is suggested that the domestic judiciary should look rather to the general principle laid down in the case that the granting of interim injunctions is a particularly significant prima facie infringement of Art 10, given the perishable qualities of news. This factor would then have to be weighed against the strength of the privacy claim, in the manner suggested earlier and, in accordance with s 12, a court should award the interim injunction only if it considers that the privacy argument is the stronger one.

In *Douglas* the Court of Appeal had to consider whether the injunction against *Hello!* should be continued. Section 12(3) HRA provides that prior restraint on expression should not be granted except where the court considers that the claimant is 'likely' to establish at trial that publication should not be allowed. Under s 3 HRA the court has a duty to construe all legislation, which must include the HRA itself, compatibly with the Convention rights 'so far as it is possible to do so'. Therefore, clearly, both sub-sections must be read in such a way as to ensure that all the rights are given full weight; s 12(3) must not accord more weight to Art 10 than to the other rights. The outcome, in any particular instance, would be determined, the Court found, principally by considerations of proportionality. Sedley LJ said that the Court has to:

> . . . look ahead to the ultimate stage and to be satisfied that the scales are likely to come down in the applicant's favour. That does not conflict with the Convention, since it is merely requiring the Court to apply its mind to how one right is to be balanced, on the merits against another right, without building in additional weight on one side.

Taking into account the fact that the claimants had in a sense already 'sold' their privacy, Sedley LJ found that their rights to privacy were outweighed by the right of publication and considered that they should be left to a claim for damages at the trial of the action.

But the Court also had to consider the effects of leaving the claimants to a damages claim. In *American Cyanamid Company v Ethicon Ltd*[815] it was found that a judge must weigh the respective risks that injustice may result from his deciding one way or the other at the interim stage. If an injunction is refused, but the claimant does succeed in establishing his legal right at the trial which he sought to protect by means of the injunction, he might in the meantime suffer harm which could not adequately be compensated for by an award of money. On the other hand, there was the risk that

---

814 It was found that the initial injunctions, which prevented publication for over a year, had the aim of maintaining the Attorney General's ability to bring a case claiming permanent injunction, a case which would have been destroyed if *Spycatcher* material had been published before that claim could be heard. This factor was found to establish the existence of a pressing social need justifying the restriction of Art 10. The finding that the continuation of the injunctions after the book had been published in the US could not be justified was based simply on the fact that such publication had destroyed the confidentiality of the material, making it impossible to maintain the Attorney General's rights as a litigant. See Chapter 7, pp 620–21.

815 [1975] AC 396.

if the injunction was granted, but the claimant failed at the trial, the defendant in the meantime might have suffered harm which was also irrecompensable. This weighing up is sometimes termed 'the balance of convenience'. Brooke LJ found that the balance of convenience appeared to favour leaving *OK!* to assert its legal rights at the trial of what he said was 'essentially a commercial dispute between two magazine enterprises'. Therefore, although the Court found that the claim might succeed at trial and result in an award of compensation, it also found that the injunction should be discharged. Thus, *Hello!* could publish the issue which contained the wedding photographs.

In *Venables* the Court was satisfied that there was a real and serious risk to the rights of the claimants under Arts 2 and 3, and it was found that, in principle, jurisdiction to grant the injunctions to protect the claimants was present. The Court went on to assess the strength of the evidence relating to those risks; finding that a real risk existed and that the protection represented by the injunctions was proportionate to the need for confidentiality, the injunctions were granted. The injunctions were intended to last for their whole lives, although, as noted above, the existence of the internet makes their efficacy in practice somewhat doubtful.[816]

The Court found in *Mills* in considering the grant of the injunction that the combination of Art 10 and s 12 had a number of consequences. It was clear, relying on *Douglas v Hello! Ltd*[817] *per* Sedley LJ, that Art 10 is directly applicable as between the parties to private litigation. Further, it found that an injunction should not be granted to restrain publication before trial unless the Court was satisfied that the applicant was likely to establish that publication should not be allowed. It said that s 12(3) makes it clear that the applicant must show more than the *American Cyanamid* threshold of a serious issue to be tried. It noted that in *Douglas v Hello! Ltd* Sedley LJ said, in applying the test set out in s 12(3), and taking s 3 HRA into account, that by virtue of s 12(1), (4) the qualifications set out in Art 10(2) are as relevant as the right set out in Art 10(1).[818] Therefore, the rights of others, including their Convention rights, are, it found, as material as the defendant's right of free expression and so is the prohibition on the use of one party's Convention rights to injure the Convention rights of others. He also found that the term 'likely' in s 12(3) should not be read as requiring simply an evaluation of the relative strengths of the parties' evidence. He said that a wholly unjustifiable invasion of privacy is entitled to no less regard, by virtue of Art 10(2), than is accorded to the right to publish by Art 10(1): 'neither element is a trump card. They will be articulated by the principles of legality and proportionality which, as always, constitute the mechanism by which the court reaches its conclusion on countervailing or qualified rights.' The Court also noted the findings of Keene LJ in the same case. He said that s 12(3) deals with the interlocutory stage of proceedings and requires the Court to look at the merits of the case and not merely to apply the *American Cyanamid* test.[819] This meant that the Court had to look ahead to the ultimate stage and be satisfied that the scales were likely to come down in the applicant's favour.

---

816 See above, p 907.
817 [2001] 2 WLR 992, p 1027, para 133.
818 Ibid, p 1028, para 136.
819 [1975] AC 396, p 1032, para 150.

The Court further noted in *Mills* that in *Venables v News Group Newspapers Ltd*[820] the President had held that the court has jurisdiction to grant an injunction against the world in order to protect individuals from the criminal acts of others. That jurisdiction, it said, has a wider and more direct effect than the decision in *AG v Times Newspapers Ltd*[821] that newspapers which know of an injunction against another newspaper would, if they were to publish the information, be guilty of contempt. The rationale of that decision was that publication of the material by other newspapers would nullify the purpose of the proceedings against the defendant by putting into the public domain material which the applicant claimed should remain confidential, and they would be in contempt by impeding or interfering with the administration of justice. In the instant case, the Court found that it would not be right to grant an injunction against the world on the *Venables* basis because the balancing exercise would not support so doing, especially in view of the absence of evidence of the apprehended harm and the other relevant matters.

The leading case on the interpretation of section 12(3) is now *Cream Holdings Ltd and Others v Banerjee and Others*.[822] Banerjee was a senior accountant for Cream Holdings. She was dismissed and took with her copies of documents that appeared to show illegal and improper financial activities by the company, which she then passed to the *Echo* newspaper. The *Echo* published articles allegedly showing corruption involving a director of Cream and a council official. Cream sought injunctions to prevent further publication. The Court had to consider the proper test to be applied in deciding whether to grant such an injunction taking account of the terms of s 12(3) HRA. The old test, as indicated above, was that the applicant as a threshold test, had to show that he or she had a 'real prospect of success' at final trial. If so, the court would consider where the 'balance of convenience' lay[823] between the case for granting an injunction and that of leaving the applicant to his or her remedy in damages. So the Court had to consider the modification of that test under the HRA. Lord Nicholls noted that press concerns under the old 'balance of convenience' test which were discussed above lay behind the enactment of s 12(3). The leading speech was delivered by Lord Nicholls, with whom all their Lordships agreed. His Lordship said:

> 'Likely' in section 12(3) cannot have been intended to mean 'more likely than not' in all situations [emphasis added] . . . [Section 12(3)] makes the likelihood of success at the trial an essential element in the court's consideration of whether to make an interim order. But . . . there can be no single, rigid standard governing all applications for interim restraint orders. Rather, on its proper construction, the effect of section 12(3) is that the court is not to make an interim restraint order unless satisfied that the applicant's prospects of success at the trial are sufficiently favourable to justify such an order being made in the particular circumstances of the case. As to what degree of likelihood makes the prospects of success 'sufficiently favourable', the general approach should be that courts will be exceedingly slow to make interim restraint orders where the applicant has not satisfied the court he

---

820 [2001] 2 WLR 1038, p 1071, para 100.
821 [1992] 1 AC 191; see Chapter 5, p 369.
822 [2004] 3 WLR 918. For comment, see Smith, ATH [2005] 64(1) CLJ 4.
823 *American Cyanamid Co v Ethicon Ltd* [1975] AC 396.

will probably ('more likely than not') succeed at the trial. In general, that should be the threshold an applicant must cross before the court embarks on exercising its discretion, duly taking into account the relevant jurisprudence on article 10 and any countervailing Convention rights. But there will be cases where it is necessary for a court to depart from this general approach and a lesser degree of likelihood will suffice . . .[824]

Lord Nicholls said that he had in mind, as instances in which a lesser degree of likelihood would suffice, two categories of case. As to the first, he clearly had the *Venables* situation in mind, where the claimant would be placed in immediate danger if the injunction was not granted. It is contended that he was right to take this stance since arguably the courts' duty under s 6 HRA would not be satisfied if an injunction was not granted in such circumstances, since the court is bound to observe Arts 2 and 3. He said:

> Cases may arise where the adverse consequences of disclosure of information would be extremely serious, such as a grave risk of personal injury to a particular person. Threats may have been made against a person accused or convicted of a crime or a person who gave evidence at a trial. Disclosure of his current whereabouts might have extremely serious consequences. Despite the potential seriousness of the adverse consequences of disclosure, the applicant's claim to confidentiality may be weak. The applicant's case may depend, for instance, on a disputed question of fact on which the applicant has an arguable but distinctly poor case. It would be extraordinary if in such a case the court were compelled to apply a 'probability of success' test and therefore, regardless of the seriousness of the possible adverse consequences, refuse to restrain publication until the disputed issue of fact can be resolved at the trial.[825]

Lord Nicholls further had in mind the less contentious instance in which an injunction of short duration (days or hours) is required in order to give a judge time to consider the case properly:

> . . . an application [may be] made to the court for an interlocutory injunction to restrain publication of allegedly confidential or private information until trial. The judge needs an opportunity to read and consider the evidence and submissions of both parties. Until then the judge will often not be in a position to decide whether on balance of probability the applicant will succeed in obtaining a permanent injunction at the trial. In the nature of things this will take time, however speedily the proceedings are arranged and conducted . . . Confidentiality, once breached, is lost for ever. Parliament cannot have intended that, whatever the circumstances, section 12(3) would preclude a judge from making a restraining order for the period needed for him to form a view on whether on balance of probability the claim would succeed at trial. That would be absurd . . . Similarly, if a judge refuses to grant an interlocutory injunction preserving confidentiality until trial the court ought

824 Ibid, at para 22
825 Ibid, at para 19.

not to be powerless to grant interim relief pending the hearing of an interlocutory appeal against the judge's order.[826]

Thus, it is now clear that an injunction will be awarded only if the judge considers it more likely than not that the applicant will succeed at final trial. If the scales appear to be evenly balanced between the parties, injunctive relief will be refused, as set out in *A v B*.[827] It is argued that this stance does not necessarily comport readily with the establishment of the presumptive equality of Arts 8 and 10. Once privacy has been breached, it cannot be reinstated while the speech claim could be served at a later date, or could be served by a limited injunction concealing identity. In other words, there are nuanced methods of answering to the speech claim but not the privacy claim. The findings in *Bannerjee*, it is argued, elevate the speech claim over the privacy one in a manner which is not fully in accordance with the Strasbourg clashing rights jurisprudence. Since s 12(3) must be interpreted compatibly with the Convention rights under s 3 HRA, and the Convention jurisprudence must be taken into account under s 2, it is arguable that the test from *Bannerjee* should be re-visited in future by the House of Lords.

   Ironically, the pre-HRA test gave a more equal weight to the two competing claims. The idea that newspapers would lose interest if the reporting was enjoined arose in a climate in which free speech had primacy and newspaper editors considered that their working practices should remain unfettered, confusing this idea quite frequently with free speech claims. Such confusion is also evident in early post-HRA decisions, such as *Venables*. But in the changed privacy-valuing culture that is now becoming established, the idea of maintaining relatively unfettered media working practices might need to be revisited: if the press did have to face the grant of interim injunctions quite frequently, they would have to modify their working practices accordingly. The need to show that it is more likely than not that the privacy claim would succeed at final trial can distort, it is argued, the parallel analysis, encouraging a judge inclined towards the privacy claim to over-state it in order to find it possible to award an interim injunction. Equally, and perhaps most worryingly, it might lead a judge to overstate the speech claim, in the face of a strong competing privacy interest, in order to avoid the grant of an injunction.

10 Conclusions

So what can finally be said as to the current state of legal protection for privacy in the UK, taking account also of the protections against state invasion of privacy detailed mainly in Chapter 10? As far as private actors are concerned, the main focus of this chapter, the position has changed dramatically in the post-HRA years. A comprehensive but complex and piecemeal protection against invasion of privacy can now be identified. It has a number of strands. First, misuse of private information can now give rise to liability. The new privacy liability has shaken itself free of the constraints previously

---

826   Ibid at paras 17–18.
827   Ibid at pp 240 ff.

imposed by the doctrine of confidence. Second, if a public authority breaches Art 8, ss 7 and 8 HRA can be relied on to obtain a remedy against it. That liability is much broader than the privacy liability that has grown out of the doctrine of confidence since it potentially reaches beyond providing protection for personal information and into a range of substantive privacy areas. Obviously the new privacy liability could also be relied upon as an alternative against a public authority. Thirdly, children and vulnerable adults can rely on the ECHR jurisdiction of the Court in seeking reporting restrictions. Since that jurisdiction is based on Art 8 it could cover invasions of privacy within the ambit of that Article *other than* misuse of private information. In cases of harassment, for example, a child or vulnerable adult could seek to rely on the ECHR jurisdiction; anyone could seek to rely on it against a public authority via ss 6 and 7 HRA. In all cases of harassment persons could seek to rely on the PHA. So it is apparent that although a quite comprehensive protection from invasion of privacy is now available, gaps and anomalies are still evident.

Nevertheless, the existence of the new privacy liability, together with the provisions of the DPA and PHA, indicate that the available comprehensive domestic protection against invasion of privacy is almost as extensive as the protection provided by Art 8 at Strasbourg. In terms of rapidity of development, it out-stripped the Strasbourg protection at certain stages. The pronouncement in *Wainwright* as to the lack of a tort of invasion of privacy in UK law remains correct, but is becoming irrelevant since the protection provided by the developments under the HRA, together with that available under the various privacy statutes (including those discussed in Chapter 10), is so comprehensive.

However a note of caution must be sounded. Apart from the doubts expressed above as to the *Bannerjee* decision, it must also be pointed out that no appellate court has yet to deal with the *Von Hannover* situation in which snatched paparazzi photographs of daily life activities taken in the street or in public places, such as beaches, are published. The *Campbell*, *Prince of Wales* and *McKennitt* cases all dealt either with especially sensitive information, or with situations in which the old style doctrine of confidence would have applied in any event, or with both. However, the tone of the relevant decisions, especially in *McKennit*, suggests that the courts are now prepared to grant relief in the *Von Hannover* situation, so long as the invasion of privacy can be viewed as *serious*, since the parameters of Art 8 created by the jurisprudence are being allowed to determine whether information should or should not be viewed as private. But the seriousness of the invasion of privacy can be evaluated on the basis of a range of factors, as this chapter has indicated and *not* merely on the basis either of the nature of the location or of the especially intimate nature of the information. Those factors appear more likely to be relevant to the Art 8 and 10 balancing act, as opposed to being allowed to deny relief to the plaintiff at the stage of considering the private information claim.

The new ECHR jurisdiction, the new privacy liability and the liability of public authorities not to breach Art 8 are essentially the same cause of action since all are based on Art 8 and s 6 HRA. Something close to an absolute duty to bring the common law into line with the Convention rights has clearly been accepted in the transformation of confidence into privacy – the change that has been brought about to the doctrine of breach of confidence is dramatic. The pressure to accept direct horizontal effect in respect of privacy is becoming greater as an Art 8-based jurisdiction sweeps into domestic law like an incoming tide through the mechanisms of a range of separate causes of action.

The lacunae that are still apparent[828] appear less defensible and more anomalous. This is not, however, to suggest that the judges would accept this argument; indeed, for obvious reasons, they are likely to resist it, just as they have largely avoided acknowledging that an absolute duty to align domestic private common law with the Convention has now been accepted under s 6 HRA. If it can be accepted in this context, what arguments of principle are available to avoid accepting it in a number of others?

Legitimisation of the judicial enterprise in creating the new privacy liability was found in the HRA: its introduction of the Convention into UK law allowed the courts to draw upon the general principles expressed in the Strasbourg privacy jurisprudence.[829] As this chapter has sought to demonstrate, that enterprise is also grounded in universal human rights values as expressed in other jurisdictions. The achievement of the judges documented in this chapter is impressive; they have shown, it is argued, moral courage in imposing privacy values on a popular culture that pre-HRA resembled the impoverished US one in many respects.[830] The principal objection to the development of privacy rights has always been the perceived threat to media freedom. This chapter has argued that that fear is largely misplaced, and indeed that the right to free speech and to protection for privacy are 'mutually supportive',[831] because, as the German Supreme Court has put it, both are 'essential aspects of the liberal democratic order'.[832] The introduction of legal protection for privacy may be encouraging a movement away from the prurient trivia currently infesting so much of the print media, and therefore, far from threatening free speech in the press, could enhance it. As factors limiting the circumstances in which privacy claims can be raised at all, such as 'public domain' and the defence of waiver, are diminishing in importance, so the focus of attention becomes – even more clearly – the true strength of the speech claim.

---

828 It may be noted that in July 2007 the House of Commons Media Select Committee decided in favour of the continued self-regulation of the press, despite various lapses in journalistic standards, including breaches of the PCC Code earlier in 2007, which led to the examination of the current system operated by the PCC. The conviction of Clive Goodman, the *News of the World*'s former Royal editor (see fn 7 above, and see for discussion of the offences in question, Chapter 10, for unlawfully intercepting voicemail left on the mobile phones of members of the Royal family and other public figures was taken into account by the Committee. Goodman's actions breached the Code as well as the criminal law.

829 A comparison may be drawn with Canada; see: Craig, JDR, 'Invasion of Privacy and Charter Values: The Common-Law Tort Awakens' (1997) 42 McGill LJ 355.

830 See further Anderson, D, 'The Failure of American Privacy Law' in Markesenis, B, (ed) *Protecting Privacy* op. cit., fn 1.

831 Emerson, C, 'The right of privacy and the freedom of the press' (1979) 14(2) Harvard Civil Rights–Civil Liberties Law Review 329. See also Kenyon, A and Richardson, M (eds), *New Dimensions in Privacy Law* (2007), CUP, Chapters 7 and 8.

832 BGH 19 December 1995 BGHZ 131, 322–46.

Chapter 10

Powers of the security and intelligence services; state surveillance; search and seizure of property

1 Introduction

The state possesses a myriad of methods of invading privacy in the course of seeking to prevent and detect crime or terrorist activity. It can place persons under surveillance, watch citizens on CCTV cameras, tap telephones, enter and search homes, or seek to build up a picture of a person's mind by examining websites visited or mobile numbers called. Agents of the state invade privacy with increasing frequency as technology allowing them to do so becomes more advanced. The method of obtaining information creates an invasion of privacy; its use creates a further invasion. These actions are undertaken by the police, other law enforcement agencies and the security and intelligence services with the aim of promoting internal security or preventing and detecting crime. Such aims are clearly legitimate; the question is whether the safeguards against unreasonable or arbitrary intrusion are adequate. Under the requirements of the Human Rights Act (HRA), such safeguards have to include a clear remedy for the citizen who has been the subject of unauthorised surveillance or other intrusion, and should create strict Convention-compliant controls over the power to effect such intrusion or issue authorisation for it. The latter safeguard is particularly crucial since the citizen may not even be aware that intrusion is taking place. This is particularly true of telephone tapping and the use of surveillance devices.

However, not only have legal developments failed to keep pace with technological ones, the principles which in a liberal democracy should inform the law governing such invasions of privacy have largely failed to find expression in it. It will be argued that the value of privacy still finds little place in it despite the fact that the central statute now governing this area, the Regulation of Investigatory Powers Act 2000, was introduced specifically in order to meet the demands of the European Convention on Human Rights.

The common law has always given a high priority to preventing interference with personal property[1] and therefore, prior to the inception of the HRA, privacy received some incidental protection. Remedies for intrusion on property are found in the torts of trespass and nuisance, while seizure of goods is also prima facie tortious.[2] Trespass is defined as entering on to land in the possession of another without lawful justification. It is confined to instances in which there is some physical entry; prying with binoculars

---

1 See *McLorie v Oxford* [1982] 1 QB 1290.
2 Under the torts of trespass to goods and conversion.

is not covered and, obviously, nor is electronic eavesdropping. The limitations of the law have been determined in certain decisions. In *Hickman v Maisey*[3] the defendant, who was on the highway, was watching the plaintiff's land. It was found that the plaintiff owned the land under the highway and that the defendant was entitled to make ordinary and reasonable use of it. Such watching was held not to be reasonable; the defendant had gone outside the accepted use and therefore had trespassed. Thus, it was made clear that intention in such instances is all important, but that unless behaviour could be linked to some kind of physical presence on land, trespass would not provide a remedy.

This decision can be contrasted with that in *Bernstein v Skyviews and General Ltd*[4] in order to determine the limits of trespass. The defendants flew over the plaintiff's land in an aircraft in order to take photographs of it and the question arose whether the plaintiff had a right in trespass to prevent such intrusion. It was held that either he had no rights of ownership over the air space to that height or, alternatively, if he did have such rights, s 40 of the Civil Aviation Act 1942 exempted reasonable flights from liability. The Court was not prepared to find that the taking of one photograph was unreasonable and a remedy could not be based solely on invasion of privacy as, of course, there is no such tort. The distinction between this decision and that in *Hickman* arises partly because the plaintiff could not show that he had an interest in what was violated – the air space – and so he fell outside the ambit of trespass.

The tort of nuisance has not provided a means of protecting privacy except in extreme instances. Liability for nuisance will arise if a person is disturbed in the enjoyment of his or her land to an extent that the law regards as unreasonable. There is a dearth of authority on the issue of straightforward surveillance but, in an Australian case, *Victoria Park Racing Company v Taylor*,[5] where a platform was erected in order to gain a view of a racecourse which diminished the value of the plaintiff's business, no remedy in nuisance was available. The activity was held not to affect the use and enjoyment of the land, but dicta in the case suggested that there would, in general, be no remedy in nuisance for looking over another's premises. However, *dicta* in *Bernstein* favoured the possibility that grossly invasive embarrassing surveillance would amount to a nuisance and that possibility was followed up (though not explicitly) in somewhat different circumstances in *Khorasandjian v Bush*.[6] An injunction was granted against the defendant restraining him from using violence to or harassing, pestering or communicating with the plaintiff, the child of the owner of the property in question. This decision, which sought to extend the tort to cover interference with rights to privacy, was criticised by the House of Lords in *Hunter v Canary Wharf*[7] in which it was confirmed that the tort is essentially concerned with injury to land. Thus, it is fair to conclude that trespass and nuisance offer only limited protection in this area from the crudest and most obvious forms of invasions of privacy.

---

3 [1900] 1 QB 752, CA.
4 [1978] QB 479; [1977] 2 All ER 902.
5 (1937) 58 CLR 479.
6 [1993] 3 All ER 669. For discussion of this decision, see (1993) 143 NLJ 926 and (1993) 143 NLJ 1685.
7 [1997] AC 655, pp 691G–692B.

Therefore, under the common law, when an invasion of privacy did not fall within these narrow areas of tortious liability, it did not require lawful authority. Thus police search and seizure of property required such authority, but the interception of communications and much state surveillance had no comprehensive legal basis. This chapter demonstrates that the European Convention on Human Rights, both before and after the inception of the HRA, has been the driving force for change. The state has been forced, incrementally, to accept that a legal basis for the invasion of privacy by state agents must be put in place. Such a basis is now in place, contained in a range of statutes of which the most comprehensive is the Regulation of Investigatory Powers Act 2000. However, the creation of a legal basis for state invasion of privacy does not necessarily mean that the requirements of Art 8 have been met. Moreover, there is now pressure to extend that legal basis to cover the imposed retention of communications data by mobile phone operators and other communications providers in order to aid in state surveillance. The main concern of this chapter is to consider how far Art 8 principles are in actuality reflected in these statutes, a concern that was given a sharper focus after the HRA came into force.

This chapter begins by considering police powers of entry and search. That section must be placed in the context of Chapters 11, 12 and 13 which consider a range of other aspects of police powers. The chapter moves on to consider the powers of the security and intelligence services and the procedures for creating accountability. The chapter concludes with consideration of a vast range of state surveillance powers, including powers to intercept communications. The provisions considered in this chapter are immensely extensive, complex and detailed, so in a book of this breadth and comprehensiveness, only an overview can be undertaken.

2 Police powers of entry and search[8]

In America, the Fourth Amendment to the Constitution guarantees freedom from unreasonable search and seizure by the police, thus recognising the invasion of privacy which a search of premises represents. A search without a warrant will normally[9] be unreasonable; therefore, an independent check is usually available on the search power.[10] In contrast, the common law in Britain, despite some rulings asserting the importance of protecting the citizen from the invasion of private property,[11] allowed

---

8 Texts referred to below: Feldman, D, *The Law Relating to Entry, Search and Seizure*, 1986; Stone, RTH, *Entry, Search and Seizure*, 4th edn, 2005 Chapter, 4; Lidstone, K and Bevan, V, *Search and Seizure under the Police and Criminal Evidence Act 1984*, 1992, University of Sheffield; Clayton, R and Tomlinson, H, *Civil Actions Against the Police*, 2nd edn, 2005, Sweet and Maxwell, Chapter 7; Ashworth, A, *The Criminal Process*, 3rd edn, 2005, OUP; Feldman, D, *Civil Liberties and Human Rights in England and Wales*, 2nd edn, 2002, Chapters 5 and 9; Sanders, A and Young, R, *Criminal Justice*, 3rd edn, 2007, LexisNexis UK; Zander, M, *The Police and Criminal Evidence Act 1984*, 2003; Clark, D, *Bevan and Lidstone's The Investigation of Crime*, 2004, LexisNexis UK.
9 *Coolidge v New Hampshire* (1973) 403 US 443: exception accepted where evidence might otherwise be destroyed.
10 For comment on the efficacy of this check, see Lafave, W, *Search and Seizure*, 1978, West.
11 See, e.g., rulings in *Entinck v Carrington* (1765) 19 St Tr 1029; *Morris v Beardmore* [1981] AC 446; [1980] 2 All ER 753.

search and seizure on wide grounds, going beyond those authorised by statute.[12] Thus, the common law did not provide full protection for the citizen and the Police and Criminal Evidence Act 1984 (PACE) went some way to remedy this by placing powers of entry, search and seizure on a clearer basis and ensuring that the person whose premises are searched understands the basis of the search and can complain as to its conduct if necessary. Whether the procedures actually do provide sufficient protection for the privacy interests of the subject of the search is the question to be examined by this section. PACE provides for procedures to be followed where statutory applications for search warrants are made, under PACE itself or other statutes,[13] including post-PACE provisions; it also provides non-warrant-based powers of entry, search and seizure. In this respect it strongly resembles the provisions regarding stop and search in PACE, discussed in Chapter 13. On the stop and search model, the procedures to be followed in exercising entry and search powers and the safeguards for suspects and others are partly in a Code of Practice – Code B (2006 version). The Serious and Organised Crime and Police Act 2005 (SOCA) provided for significant extensions to entry and search powers, as indicated below.

Entry without warrant

Powers under the Police and Criminal Evidence Act (PACE)

The power to enter premises without warrant conferred by PACE, as amended, is balanced in a manner similar to the method employed in respect of stop and search, which is discussed in Chapter 13. A power of entry arises under s 18 if a person has been arrested for an indictable offence and the intention is to search the person's premises immediately after arrest:

> . . . a constable may enter and search any premises occupied or controlled by a person who is under arrest for an indictable offence, if he has reasonable grounds for suspecting that there is on the premises evidence, other than items subject to legal privilege, that relates:
>
> (a)   to that offence; or
> (b)   to some other arrestable offence which is connected with or similar to that offence.

The power can be exercised under s 17 to: execute a warrant of arrest arising out of criminal proceedings; where an officer wants to arrest a person suspected of an indictable offence; to recapture someone unlawfully at large (such as, for example, an escapee from a prison, court or mental hospital); to save life or limb or prevent serious damage to property. This provision regarding criminal proceedings allows an entry to be made to search for someone wanted under a warrant for non-payment of a fine. Apart from

---

12   The ruling in *Ghani v Jones* [1970] 1 QB 693 authorised seizure of a wide range of material once officers were lawfully on premises. *Thomas v Sawkins* [1935] 2 KB 249 allowed a wide power to enter premises to prevent crime (see below, p 1000).

13   For example, powers under s 23 Misuse of Drugs Act 1971 or Terrorism Act 2000, Sched 5, para 1.

the life or limb or serious damage provisions, a constable can only exercise the powers if he or she has reasonable grounds for believing that the person in question is on the premises.

Thus, the power is subject to some significant limitations; in particular it does not arise in respect of an arrest for a non-indictable offence. If a search is considered necessary in situations in which ss 17 or 18 are inapplicable after an arrest, a search warrant would have to be obtained unless the provisions of s 32 applied. Section 32(2)(b) allows a search of premises after arrest, if there are reasonable grounds for thinking that the arrestee, who has been arrested for an indictable offence, may present a danger to himself or others if the arrestee was arrested on those premises or was on them immediately before the arrest.

Search powers under the Terrorism Act 2000

The provisions for warrantless search of premises under PACE after arrest are wide enough to cover many circumstances in which police officers might wish to search for items relating to a terrorist investigation. But they are supplemented by special powers under warrant which are discussed below and also, in an emergency, by a power in the Terrorism Act 2000, Sched 5, para 3. Sections 33–36 of the Terrorism Act 2000 allow police officers of at least the rank of superintendent, engaged in a terrorism investigation, to establish in certain circumstances a police cordon around an area. Under s 33(1) 'An area is a cordoned area for the purposes of this Act if it is designated under this section. (2) A designation may be made only if the person making it considers it expedient for the purposes of a terrorist investigation.' Once the cordon is in place Sched 5, para 3 gives a power of search. It must be authorised in writing by an officer of at least the rank of superintendent who must have reasonable grounds for believing that material which would be of substantial value to the investigation, and which is not excluded or special material or material covered by legal privilege (see below), is on specified premises within the cordon. The power is exercised by a constable who may enter and search premises and may seize items not protected by legal privilege if he has reasonable grounds for believing that they will be of substantial value to the investigation. Under para 3(1): 'Subject to sub-paragraph (2), a police officer of at least the rank of superintendent may by a written authority signed by him authorise a search of specified premises which are wholly or partly within a cordoned area.' Under para 3(2) 'A constable who is not of the rank required by sub-paragraph (1) may give an authorisation under this paragraph if he considers it necessary by reason of urgency.' This power of search previously arose under s 16C and para 7 of Sched 6A which were added to the PTA by the Criminal Justice and Public Order Act 1994. Para 7 of Sched 6A gave a power of search. There is evidence that the use of special search powers without the need to rely on reasonable suspicion or on a warrant have some value in terrorist investigations.[14] Nevertheless, the use of such powers represents an invasion of liberty which requires a strong and clear justification rather than a reliance on an uncertain phrase such as 'expedient'.

14 See Walker, C, *The Prevention of Terrorism*, 2nd edn, 1992 p 195.

Search powers under the Police Act 1997

As discussed below, this Act places police powers of surveillance on a statutory basis. It also provides powers of entry, search and seizure. An authorisation may be issued if the search is believed to be necessary because it will be of substantial value in the prevention and detection of serious crime and the objective cannot reasonably be achieved by other means (s 93(2)). Under s 93(4)

> 'For the purposes of subsection (2), conduct which constitutes one or more offences shall be regarded as serious crime if, and only if –
>
> (a) it involves the use of violence, results in substantial financial gain or is conduct by a large number of persons in pursuit of a common purpose, or
> (b) the offence or one of the offences is an offence for which a person who has attained the age of twenty-one and has no previous convictions could reasonably be expected to be sentenced to imprisonment for a term of three years or more . . .'

As explained below,[15] the main check on these extensive powers is provided by the special commissioners appointed from the senior judiciary (s 91(1)). Where the entry and search contemplated is of a dwelling house, prior approval by the commissioner is necessary, but this requirement is waived where the authorising officer believes that the search is urgent (s 94(2)). Since the belief does not need to be based on reasonable grounds, such a safeguard may have little impact in practice. These controversial extensions of the police powers of entry under the 1997 Act are therefore subject to very limited independent oversight and, unlike the s 18 power, they may be divorced from the needs of an immediate criminal investigation.

Search warrants

Searching of premises other than under ss 17 and 18 can also occur if a search warrant is issued under s 8 of PACE, as amended, by a magistrate or if a warrant is applied for under other statutory powers, including post-PACE powers. Applications for all warrants by police officers, and the execution of the warrant must comply with the procedures set out in ss 15 and 16 of PACE. The application for the warrant must be supported, under s 15(3), by an 'Information' in writing. It must specify the enactment under which it is issued, the premises to be searched[16] and the articles or persons to be sought (s 15(6)). Section 8(1C), inserted by s 113(4) of the Serious and Organised Crime and Police Act 2005 (SOCA), provides that multiple entry can be authorised. Section 15(5A), also introduced in 2005 by SOCA, provides that if the warrant authorises multiple entry it must specify whether the multiple entries are limited to a specified maximum or unlimited. Previously, the warrant authorised entry to premises on one occasion only.

Section 16 governs the procedure to be followed in executing the warrant. The warrant must be produced to the occupier (although it seems that this need not be at the time of entry if impracticable in the circumstances)[17] under s 16(5) (b) and (c) and

---

15 See p 1065.
16 *Southwestern Magistrates' Court ex p Cofie* [1997] 1 WLR 885.
17 *Longman* [1988] 1 WLR 619, CA; for comment, see Stevens, R, *Justice of the Peace*, 1988, p 551.

must identify the articles to be sought, although once the officer is on the premises, other articles may be seized under s 19 if they appear to relate to any other offence. The warrant does not necessarily allow for a general search of the premises[18] since the search can only be for the purpose for which the warrant was issued (s 16(8)). The extensiveness of the search depends upon that purpose.

Under s 16, the copy of the warrant issued to the subject of the search must identify the articles or persons sought and the offence suspected, but need not specify the grounds on which it was issued or give the name of the constable conducting the search. A warrant, like the Notice of Powers and Rights (discussed below) therefore provides the occupier with limited information. Moreover, as noted above, it need not be produced to the occupier before the search begins if the purpose of the search might be frustrated by such production.[19] However, within these limitations, the courts seem prepared to take a strict view of the importance of complying with this safeguard. In *Chief Constable of Lancashire ex p Parker and McGrath*[20] police officers conducted a search of the applicant's premises in the execution of a search warrant issued under s 8 of PACE. However, after the warrant had been signed by the judge, the police detached part of it and reattached it to the other original documents. In purported compliance with s 16 of PACE, the police produced all these documents to the applicants. Thus, the police did not produce the whole of the original warrant and moreover, did not supply one of the documents constituting the warrant. The applicants applied for judicial review of both the issue and the execution of the warrants. It was determined that s 16(5)(b) of PACE had been breached in that the warrant produced to the applicants was not the original warrant as seen and approved by the judge and a declaration was granted to that effect. The police had admitted that there was a breach of the requirement under s 16(5)(c) that a copy of the warrant should be supplied to the occupier of the premises.

A warrant under s 8 will only be issued if there are reasonable grounds for believing that an indictable offence has been committed and where the material is likely to be of substantial value to the investigation of the offence and which will be admissible evidence at trial. A large number of other statutes also provide for the issuing of warrants to the police and to other public officials. Special provisions arise, *inter alia*, under s 27 of the Drug Trafficking Act 1994, s 2(4) of the Criminal Justice Act 1987 (in relation to serious fraud) and, as discussed below, in relation to the security and intelligence services under the Intelligence Services Act 1994. Section 8 covers 'all premises' searches and under certain circumstances, and as indicated, under changes introduced by s 113 SOCA, multiple entries to the same premises are possible.

A warrant authorising the police to search premises does not of itself authorise officers to search persons on the premises. The Home Office circular on PACE stated that such persons could be searched only if a specific power to do so arose under the warrant (for example, warrants issued under s 23 of the Misuse of Drugs Act 1971).

A wide power to search premises also arose under Sched 7, para 2 of the Prevention of Terrorism (Temporary Provisions) Act 1989[21] which, in contrast to the warrant

---

18 See *Chief Constable of Warwick Constabulary ex p Fitzpatrick* [1999] 1 WLR 564.
19 *Longman* [1988] 1 WLR 619, CA.
20 (1992) 142 NLJ 635.
21 See Walker, C, *The Prevention of Terrorism*, 2nd edn, 1992, pp 185–97.

power under PACE, was not dependent on the need to allege a specific offence and could therefore take place at a very early stage in the investigation. This power was reproduced in the Terrorism Act 2000, Sched 5 which, as Chapter 14 indicates, applies to a wider range of groups. A justice of the peace must be satisfied that a terrorist investigation is being carried out and that there are reasonable grounds for believing that there is material which is likely to be of substantial value to the investigation. Also, it must appear that it is impracticable to gain entry to the premises with consent and that immediate entry to the premises is necessary. A warrant could also be issued under s 15(1) of the PTA in order to allow entry to premises to effect an arrest under s 14(1)(b). This power was thought necessary since the general PACE powers would not be applicable due to the broad nature of s 14(1)(b).[22] It was continued in the Terrorism Act 2000, Sched 5.

Power to enter premises at common law

Section 17(5) PACE abolished all common law powers to enter premises, subject to s 17(6), which preserves powers to enter without consent to deal with or prevent a breach of the peace. At common law, a power to enter premises in order to prevent crime arises from the much criticised case of *Thomas v Sawkins*.[23] Lord Hewart CJ contemplated that a police officer would have the right to enter private premises when 'he has reasonable grounds for believing that an offence is imminent or is likely to be committed'. This judgment received some endorsement from the provision of s 17(5) and (6), common law powers to enter were only preserved to deal with or prevent a breach of the peace; this narrowed down the power of entry, since it did not arise in respect of any offence. *Thomas v Sawkins* arose in the context of a public meeting held on private premises, but common law powers are not confined to such circumstances; in *McGowan v Chief Constable of Kingston on Hull*[24] it was found that police officers were entitled to enter and remain on private premises when they feared a breach of the peace arising from a private quarrel. The powers are even broader than s 17(6) would appear, on its face, to indicate: in *R (on the application of Rottnam) v Commissioner of Police for the Metropolis*[25] the House of Lords found that s 17 was concerned with powers to enter to arrest and that it did not limit the common law power to enter premises without consent *after* arrest.

Voluntary searches

Code of Practice B (2006 version) made under PACE,[26] which governs powers of entry, search and seizure, makes special provision for voluntary searches. Paragraph 4 of Code B as originally drafted provided that a search of premises could take place with the consent of the occupier and provided under para 4(2) that he must be informed that he need not consent to the search; in requiring that the consent should be in

---

22 See below, Chapter 11, pp 1147–48.
23 [1935] 2 KB 249; for criticism, see Goodhart, ALG (1947) 6 CLJ 222; see further Chapter 9, p 433.
24 [1968] Crim LR 34. But see the ruling in *McLeod v UK* (1998) 27 EHRR 493.
25 [2002] 2 All ER 865.
26 See Chapter 11, pp 1106–8 for discussion of the PACE Codes of Practice.

writing, it recognised that there might sometimes be a doubt as to the reality of such consent and went some way towards resolving that doubt. After revision in 1991, para 4 went further in that direction and under the 2006 version para 5 reiterated its provisions. Under sub-para 5.1 the officer concerned must ensure that the consent is being sought from the correct person, whereas previously this problem was only addressed in a Note for Guidance (4A), and then only in respect of lodgings. Sub-para 5.3 provides that the search must cease if the consent is withdrawn during it and also contains an express provision against using duress to obtain consent.[27] However, it has been doubted whether these provisions have had much effect on ensuring that use of consensual search is not abused because it is not always made clear to occupiers that they can withhold consent.[28]

Power of seizure

At common law prior to PACE, a wide power of seizure had developed where a search was not under warrant. Articles could be seized so long as they either implicated the owner or occupier in any offence or implicated third parties in the offence for which the search was conducted.[29] However, the power of seizure under PACE is even wider than this. Under s 8(2), a constable may seize and retain anything for which a search has been authorised. Section 8(2) provides that: 'A constable may seize and retain anything for which a search has been authorised under sub-section (1) above.' The power of seizure without warrant under the power of entry and search after arrest is governed by s 18(2), which provides that: 'A constable may seize and retain anything for which he may search under sub-section (1) above.' This power is greatly widened, however, by the further power of seizure arising under s 19:

The constable may seize anything which is on the premises if he has reasonable grounds for believing:

(a) that it has been obtained in consequence of the commission of an offence; and
(b) that it is necessary to seize it in order to prevent it being concealed, lost, damaged, altered or destroyed.

The constable may seize anything which is on the premises if he has reasonable grounds for believing:

(a) that it is evidence in relation to an offence which he is investigating or any other offence; and
(b) that it is necessary to seize it in order to prevent the evidence being concealed, lost, altered or destroyed.

Under s 22(1), anything which has been so seized may be retained 'so long as is necessary in all the circumstances'. It was made clear in *Chief Constable of Lancashire ex p*

---

27 For criticism of these provisions, see Bevan, K and Palmer, C, *Bevan and Lidstone's The Investigation of Crime*, 1996, pp 117–21.
28 See further Dixon, D, 'Consent and the legal regulation of policing' (1990) 17 JLS 345–62.
29 *Ghani v Jones* [1970] 1 QB 693; *Garfinkel v MPC* [1972] Crim LR 44.

Parker and McGrath[30] that the above provisions assume that the search itself is lawful; in other words, material seized during an unlawful search cannot be retained and if it is, an action for trespass to goods may arise. It was accepted in this instance that the search was unlawful (see below), but the Chief Constable contended that the material seized could nevertheless be retained. This argument was put forward under the provision of s 22(2)(a), which allows the retention of 'anything seized for the purposes of a criminal investigation'. The Chief Constable maintained that these words would be superfluous unless denoting a general power to retain unlawfully seized material. However, it was held that the sub-section could not bear the weight sought to be placed upon it: it was merely intended to give examples of matters falling within the general provision of s 22(1). Therefore. the police were not entitled to retain the material seized.

Excluded or special procedure material or material covered by legal privilege

Under s 9, excluded or special procedure material or material covered by legal privilege cannot be seized during a search not under warrant and it is exempt from the s 8 search warrant procedure under s 8(1). However, the police may gain access to excluded or special procedure material by making an application to a circuit judge in accordance with Sched 1 or, in the case of special procedure material only, to a magistrate for a search warrant. Access to excluded material may only be granted where it could have been obtained under the previous law relating to such material. Excluded material is defined under s 11 to consist of material held on a confidential basis, personal records,[31] samples of human tissue or tissue fluid held in confidence and journalistic material held in confidence. Personal records include records held by schools, universities, probation officers and social workers. 'Special procedure material' defined under s 14 operates as a catch-all category which is, it seems, frequently used[32] to cover confidential material which does not qualify as personal records or journalistic material.[33] A production order will not be made unless there is reasonable suspicion that a serious arrestable offence has been committed, the material is likely to be of substantial value to the investigation and admissible at trial. It should be noted that when inquiries relating to terrorist offences are made, Sched 7, para 3 of the Prevention of Terrorism (Temporary Provisions) Act 1989 (PTA) allowed access to both special procedure and excluded material. This power is reproduced in Sched 5 to the Terrorism Act 2000 which allows for orders to be made in relation to obtaining access to such material.[34] The judge only

---

30   [1993] 2 WLR 428; [1993] 1 All ER 56; (1992) 142 NLJ 635.
31   Defined in s 12.
32   See Lidstone, K (1989) NILQ 333, p 342.
33   For comment on these provisions, see Stone, R, 'PACE: Special Procedures and Legal Privilege' [1988] Crim LR 498.
34   Sched 5, para 5:

   (1) A constable may apply to a Circuit judge for an order under this paragraph for the purposes of a terrorist investigation.

   (2) An application for an order shall relate to particular material, or material of a particular description, which consists of or includes excluded material or special procedure material.(3) An order under this paragraph may require a specified person –

needs to be satisfied that there is a terrorist investigation in being, that the material would substantially assist it and that it is in the public interest that it should be produced. It may well be that once the first two requirements are satisfied, it will be rare to find that the third is not.

The ruling in *Guildhall Magistrates' Court ex p Primlacks Holdings Co (Panama) Ltd*[35] made it clear that a magistrate must satisfy him or herself that there were reasonable grounds for believing that the items covered by the warrant did not include material subject to the special protection. The magistrates had issued search warrants authorising the search of two solicitors' firms. Judicial review of the magistrates' decision to issue a warrant was successfully sought; it was found that the magistrate had merely accepted the police officer's view that s 8(1) was satisfied rather than independently considering the matter.

The strongest protection extends to items subject to legal privilege, since they cannot be searched for or seized by police officers and therefore, the meaning of 'legal privilege' is crucial. Under s 10, it will cover communications between client and solicitor connected with giving advice or with legal proceedings. However, if items are held with the intention of furthering a criminal purpose they will not, under s 10(2), attract legal privilege. It seems that this will include the situation where the solicitor unknowingly furthers the criminal purpose of the client or a third party. In *Crown Court at Snaresbrook ex p DPP*[36] it was found that only the solicitor's intentions regarding the criminal purpose were relevant, but the House of Lords in *Central Criminal Court ex p Francis and Francis*[37] rejected this interpretation in finding that material which figures in the criminal intentions of persons other than solicitor or client will not be privileged. A judge must give full consideration to the question whether particular documents have lost legal privilege.[38]

This interpretation of s 10(2) was adopted on the basis that otherwise, the efforts of the police in detecting crime might be hampered, but it may be argued that it gives insufficient weight to the need to protect the special relationship between solicitor and client and, as argued below, is arguably vulnerable to challenge under the HRA.

Powers of seizure under the Criminal Justice and Police Act 2001

The Criminal Justice and Police Act 2001 (CJP) extended the power of seizure very significantly. The further powers of seizure it provides in s 50 apply to police powers of search under PACE and also to powers of seizure arising under a range of other statutes and applicable to bodies other than police officers, as set out in Sched 1 to the

> (a) to produce to a constable within a specified period for seizure and retention any material which he has in his possession, custody or power and to which the application relates;
>
> (b) to give a constable access to any material of the kind mentioned in paragraph (a) within a specified period;
>
> (c) to state to the best of his knowledge and belief the location of material to which the application relates if it is not in, and it will not come into, his possession, custody or power within the period specified under paragraph (a) or (b).

35 [1989] 2 WLR 841.
36 [1988] QB 532; [1988] 1 All ER 315.
37 [1989] AC 346; [1988] 3 All ER 375. For comment, see Stevenson (1989) Law Soc Gazette 1 February, p 26.
38 *R v Southampton Crown Court ex p J and P* [1993] Crim LR 962.

CJP. The power of seizure under s 50(1) depends on three conditions. The person in question must lawfully be on the premises. Once there, if he finds something which he has reasonable grounds for thinking is something he is authorised to seize, and it is not reasonably practicable at the time to determine whether what he has found *is* something he is authorised to seize, he can seize as much of it as is necessary to make that determination. A further power of seizure under s 50(2) allows the person in question to seize material which he has no power to seize but which is attached to an object he does have the power to seize, if it is not reasonably practicable to separate the two.

This provision is significant since, *inter alia*, it allows police officers to remove items from premises even where they are not certain that – apart from s 50 – they have the power to do so. Thus a number of items can now be seized from premises although no power of seizure – apart from that arising under s 50 – in fact arises.

As indicated above, the seizure of excluded or special procedure material is restricted, while material covered by legal privilege cannot be seized. Most significantly, s 50 may serve to undermine these protections for certain material since where such material is part of other material and cannot practicably be separated, it can be seized. It can also be seized where a police officer takes the view on reasonable grounds that it is something that he has the power to seize, although it turns out later that it falls within one of the special categories.

Special provisions are made for the return of excluded or special procedure material or material covered by legal privilege. For obvious reasons, these provisions are most significant in relation to material covered by legal privilege since they could aid in undermining the privilege. Under s 54 such material must be returned unless it falls within s 54(2). Section 54(2) covers a legally privileged item comprised in other material. Such an item will fall within that sub-section if the retention of the rest of the property would be lawful and it is not reasonably practicable to separate the legally privileged item from the rest of the property without prejudicing the use of the rest of that property. Section 57(3) provides that ss 53–56 do not authorise the retention of property where its retention would not be authorised apart from the provisions of Part 2 of the CJP. Under s 62 inextricably linked property cannot be examined or copied but under sub-section 4 can be used to the extent that its use facilitates the use of property in which the inextricably linked property is comprised.

The provisions of ss 57 and 62, taken together with the provisions of ss 54 and 55 appear to create two categories of property. Property within the first can be retained as it would have been but for the CJP. Property within the second is not subject to an obligation to return but cannot be treated as it would have been had it fallen within the first category. It can be used to a limited extent in accordance with s 62(4). Section 62 makes it clear that s 62(4) applies to excluded or special procedure material or material covered by legal privilege which has not been returned since it is comprised in other lawfully held property.

Thus, ss 50, 54 and 55 taken together do provide avenues to the seizure and non-return of the specially protected material. The provisions thus circumvent the limitations placed on the seizure of excluded or special procedure material and, most importantly of all, provide an avenue to the seizure and use of legally privileged material. It can be said that for the first time legally privileged material has lost part of the protection it was accorded under the common law and under PACE.

These wide powers are 'balanced' by the provisions of ss 52–61 which provide a number of safeguards. Notice must be given to persons whose property has been seized under s 52, and under s 59 he or she can apply to the 'appropriate judicial authority' for the return of the whole or part of the seized property, on the ground that there was no power to seize, or that excluded or special procedure material, or legally privileged material, is not comprised in other property as provided for in ss 54 and 55. Under s 60 a duty to secure the property arises which includes the obligation under s 61 to prevent *inter alia*, copying of it. But despite these safeguards, it is unclear that these powers, especially to seize and use legally privileged material, are compatible with the requirements of the Convention under the HRA.

Procedural safeguards for searches under Code of Practice B

As revised in 1991, 1995, 2005, Code of Practice B made under PACE provides for an increase in the amount of information to be conveyed to owners of property to be searched by use of a standard form, the Notice of Powers and Rights (para 6.7). It covers certain information including specification of the type of search in question, a summary of the powers of search and seizure arising under PACE and the rights of the subjects of searches. This notice must normally be given to the subject of the search before it begins, but under para 6.8 need not be if to do so would lead to frustration of the object of the search or danger to the police officers concerned or to others. These exceptions also apply under para 6.8 to leaving a copy of the warrant where the search is made under warrant. As explained above, s 18(4) provides that premises occupied or controlled by a person arrested for an arrestable offence may be searched after the arrest if an officer of the rank of inspector or above gives authority in writing. Under para 4.3, the authority should normally be given on the Notice of Powers and Rights. This clears up previous confusion[39] as to the form the authority should take.

Under original paras 4 and 5, the amount of information to be conveyed to the subject of a search depended on its status. Before any non-consensual search, an officer had to convey certain information orally to its subject: his identity, the purpose of the search and the grounds for undertaking it. In the case of a consensual search, it was only necessary to inform its subject of its purpose. Thus, the subject of an apparently consensual search dissatisfied with its conduct or intimidated by the officers concerned would have found it more difficult to make a complaint than would the subject of a non-consensual search. Under current para 6 as revised, the subjects of all searches, regardless of the status of the search, must receive a copy of the Notice of Powers and Rights and, under para 6.8 where a consensual search has taken place but the occupier is absent, the Notice should be endorsed with the name, number and station of the officer concerned. Oddly enough, it is not stated expressly that this information must be added to the Notice where the subject of a consensual search is *present*. Sub-paragraph 6.5 provides that officers must identify themselves except in the case of inquiries linked to terrorism or where this might endanger them (para 2.9), but this provision appears to apply only to non-consensual searches due to the heading of that section. It might

---

39 In *Badham* [1987] Crim LR 202 it was held that merely writing down confirmation of an oral authorisation was insufficient.

be thought that a person who voluntarily allows police officers to come onto his or her premises does not need the information mentioned, but this is to ignore the possibility that such a person might wish to withdraw consent during the search but might feel too intimidated to do so.

The power to search and seize is balanced by the need to convey certain information to the subject of the search in question, thereby rendering officers (at least theoretically) accountable for searches carried out. However, it is arguable that the provisions are largely of a presentational nature: they ensure that a large amount of information is conveyed to the occupier and make an attempt to ensure that community relations are not adversely affected by the operation of the search power,[40] but have little to say about the way the search should be conducted. In other words, the regulation of the search power under Code B emphasises the provision of information to the owner of premises so that officers can be rendered accountable for searches made, rather than regulating circumstances relating to the nature of the search itself in order to minimise the invasion of privacy represented by such searches.

In contrast, searches made in order to gain evidence relating to civil proceedings, under orders known as *Anton Piller* orders,[41] must observe a number of safeguards: they must be organised on weekdays in office hours so that legal advice can be obtained before the search begins; the defendant must be allowed to check the list of items to be seized before items can be removed and in some circumstances, an independent solicitor experienced in the execution of such orders must be present, instructed and paid for by the plaintiff.[42] It may be argued that there is a greater public interest in the prevention of crime than in ensuring that evidence is obtained by a party to civil proceedings, and therefore the police need at times to make an immediate search of premises, but the power to do so without judicial intervention should, it is submitted, be narrowed down to instances where the urgency of the search was demonstrable, while Code B should, it is argued, contain clearer safeguards applicable to all searches, allowing, for instance, for a legal advisor to be present during a non-urgent search and including a clear prohibition on non-urgent searches at night. At present, searches should be conducted at 'a reasonable hour'[43] and under Note for Guidance 5A this was explained to mean at a time when the occupier or others are unlikely to be asleep. This Note has been dropped from the 2006 version of Code B, although a rather vague provision appears in para 6.10 to the effect that search must be conducted with 'due consideration' for the privacy of the occupier. A prohibition on the non-urgent entry and search of property at night by state agents – perhaps one of the most unpleasant invasions of privacy possible – requires a clearer and more certain basis. The question of the meaning of a 'reasonable hour' was raised in *Pharmaceuticals Ltd v Director*

---

40 There is provision under para 3.5 for informing the local police community relations officer before a search of premises takes place if it is thought that it might adversely affect the relationship between the police and the community, subject to the proviso that in cases of urgency it can be performed after the search has taken place.

41 From *Anton Piller KG v Manufacturing Processes Ltd* [1976] Ch 55; [1976] 1 All ER 779, CA.

42 These conditions, and others, were laid down in *Universal Thermosensors Ltd v Hibben* (1992) 142 NLJ 195. For discussion of the concern created by such orders prior to this decision, see (1990) 106 LQR 601.

43 Code B, para 6.2.

of the SFO,[44] and the Divisional Court took the view that a search of premises at 6.00 am was at a reasonable hour, partly because the members of the household would be more likely to be present, bearing in mind the time at which people normally leave for work. This view is clearly open to doubt and the application of the search powers in that instance is, it is suggested, in doubtful compliance with Art 8. Provision appears in Note 6C to the effect that the number of persons involved in the search shall be determined by what is reasonable and necessary in the circumstances. But, as discussed elsewhere,[45] the Notes for Guidance are not part of the Codes and are of very uncertain legal status. The provision that an occupier may ask a friend or neighbour to witness the search unless there are reasonable grounds for believing 'that this would seriously hinder the investigation' would usually be completely inadequate to allow the occupier to obtain legal advice or the presence of a solicitor.[46]

Impact of the HRA and police accountability

The PACE search and seizure provisions are clearly intended to make lawful actions which would otherwise amount to trespass to property and to goods only in very specific circumstances and only where a certain procedure has been followed. Invasion of a person's home has traditionally been viewed as an infringement of liberty which should be allowed only under tightly controlled conditions and in the exercise of a specific legal power. Article 8 ECHR under the HRA affords specific expression to these values.[47] But it also goes further, and under ss 6 and 8 HRA a public authority is acting unlawfully and is liable to pay compensation for a breach of Art 8 in conducting a search of premises[48] even where pre-HRA, no liability would have arisen in tort. The PACE provisions suggest some determination to strike a reasonable balance between the perceived need to confer on the police a general power to search property and the need to protect the privacy of the citizen. It is less clear that this is true of the TA and CJP provisions.

Breaches of Code of Practice B

Although Code B plays a part in creating safeguards for individual privacy, breaches of Code B will not attract tortious liability[49] and unlike Codes C, D and E (discussed in Chapters 11, 12 and 13), exclusion of evidence will rarely operate as a form of redress because the courts are very reluctant to exclude physical evidence[50] and therefore it can have little impact on Code B provisions. Such reluctance may be justifiable since the significance of Code B can be attributed to its regulation of invasive procedures

---

44 [2002] EWHC 3023.
45 See Chapter 11, p 1108.
46 Paragraph 5.11.
47 See Chapter 2, pp 69–70, 72–74, 75, 89–91 for discussion of relevant aspects of Art 8.
48 See, e.g., *Keegan v United Kingdom* (2003) App 28867/03. The decision concerned the obtaining of compensation in the European Court of Human Rights for breach of Art 8 and Art 13 following a police search.
49 PACE 1984, s 67(10).
50 See below Chapter 14, pp 1287–99.

rather than to its concern to ensure the integrity of the evidence thereby obtained. As Chapter 12 demonstrates, Codes C, D and E, on the other hand, are arguably concerned more with outcome than with rights (with the exception of access to legal advice) which are fundamental in themselves. This difference is due partly to the nature of the rights involved: privacy of the home or of the person represents an important value in itself, unlike a person's right to the contemporaneous recording of an interview. However, this does leave something of a gap as far as a means of redress for breaches of Code B is concerned in comparison with the other three Codes, since the only means available will normally be by way of a complaint. The possibility of raising arguments in criminal proceedings under s 7(1)(b) of the HRA which might lead – in effect – to an enhancement of the status of the Codes of Practice is discussed in Chapters 11 and 12.[51]

Reliance on Art 8

Article 8 values are reflected in this scheme to an extent and may be coming to influence it more strongly due to the use of arguments under s 7(1)(b) of the HRA, either raised in criminal proceedings, in civil actions against the police for trespass, trespass to goods or for conversion, or as freestanding actions under s 7(1)(a) of the HRA. The use of Art 8 arguments in the different context of police custody is considered in Chapter 11 and those arguments would arguably also have applicability here in relation to the level of intrusiveness represented by a search; the proportionality of the search to the aim of preventing crime could be raised.[52] It could be argued that whether or not a basis in law for an entry to property is established, rendering the action non-trespassory, various features of the police actions might amount to infringements of Art 8. Where it was clear that a legal basis for the entry itself was likely to be established, a freestanding action could be brought against the police as a public authority under s 7(1)(a), arguing that although the entry had such a basis, such features amounted to a breach of Art 8, as Chapter 13 considers.[53] The use of Art 8 arguments in criminal proceedings under s 7(1)(b) is discussed in Chapters 12 and 13.[54]

The European Court of Human Rights has found that entry, search and seizure can create interferences with all the Art 8 guarantees apart from that of the right to respect for family life.[55] Search for and seizure of documents is covered by the term 'correspondence' and the documents do not have to be personal in nature.[56] Such interferences can be justified only if they are in accordance with the law (Art 8(2)). This requirement covers not only the existence of national law, but its quality.[57] The statutory and common law powers probably meet this requirement[58] and have the legitimate aim of preventing crime or protecting national security.

---

51 See Chapters 11 and 12, pp 1174–81 and 1207–8.
52 See pp 1178–81.
53 See pp 1308–9.
54 See pp 1289–95, and also Chapter 12, pp 1207–8.
55 See *Funke v France* (1993) 16 EHRR 297; *Mialhe v France* (1993) 16 EHRR 332.
56 See *Niemetz v Germany* A 251-B (1992).
57 *Kopp v Switzerland* (1999) 27 EHRR 91, paras 70–71.
58 In *McLeod v UK* (1998) 27 EHRR 493 powers to enter to prevent a breach of the peace were found to meet this requirement (paras 38–45).

It must further be shown that the interference 'corresponds to a pressing social need and, in particular, that it is proportionate to the legitimate aim pursued'.[59] It was found in the context of intercept warrants in *Klass v FRG*[60] that judicial or administrative authority for warrants would provide a degree of independent oversight: sufficient safeguards against abuse were available. This requirement was also stressed in *Kopp v Switzerland*.[61] It could be argued that the arrangements whereby magistrates issue search warrants might fail to meet this requirement since, although in appearance an independent judicial check is available before the event, the 'check' may be almost a formality in reality.[62] These provisions provide a scheme which is reasonably sound in theory, but which is dependent on magistrates observing its requirements. Research suggests that in practice, some magistrates make little or no attempt to ascertain whether the information a warrant contains may be relied upon, while it seems possible that magistrates who do take a rigorous approach to the procedure and refuse to grant warrants are not approached again.[63] It might be considered, therefore, that a breach of Art 8 might be established in respect of the practice of certain magistrates. It may be noted, however, that this argument failed in the Scottish case of *Birse v HM Advocate*.[64]

It is also arguable that the decision of the House of Lords in *Central Criminal Court ex p Francis and Francis*[65] regarding material subject to legal professional privilege may require re-consideration in relation to Art 8. As indicated above, the House of Lords found that privilege is lost when the material is innocently held, but is for a third party's criminal purpose. The approach in *Niemetz v Germany*[66] was to the effect that a search of a lawyer's office had led to a breach of Art 8 since it was disproportionate to the aims of preventing crime and of protecting the rights of others. That decision also raises questions about the provisions of Part 2 of the CJP. Since the CJP was accompanied by a declaration of its compatibility with the Convention rights, legal advice to the government must have been to the effect that Part 2 was compatible with Art 8. Clearly, this advice could subsequently be found to be flawed; the judiciary remain entirely free (in the higher courts, as Chapter 4 explained) to make a declaration of incompatibility between one or more of the Part 2 provisions and Art 8.

Clearly it could be argued that the limitations placed on the seizure and the use of legally privileged material by Part 2 may represent a proportionate response to the aim of preventing crime under Art 8(2). In other words, an interference with the Art 8 rights represented by the existence of legislation or in any particular instance could be viewed as relatively minimal, consistent with the need to serve that aim. On the other hand, the use of Part 2 provisions in practice may undermine the relationship between client and solicitor. The attitude of the courts in this context as indicated in decisions

59 *Olsson v Sweden* A 130 (1988), para 67.
60 (1978) 2 EHRR 214.
61 (1999) 27 EHRR 91.
62 See the comments of Feldman, D, *Civil Liberties and Human Rights in England and Wales*, 1st edn, 1993, p 414 and of Clayton, R and Tomlinson, H, *The Law of Human Rights*, 2000, p 863.
63 This point is made by Dixon, D (1991) 141 NLJ 1586.
64 Unreported, 13 April 2000.
65 [1989] AC 346; [1988] 3 All ER 375. For comment, see Stevenson (1989) *Law Soc Gazette* 1 February, p 26.
66 A 251-B (1992).

such as *Pharmaceuticals Ltd v Director of the SFO* does not at present demonstrate a clear determination to afford the Convention rights real efficacy.

3 Powers of the security and intelligence services

Introduction

Traditionally, the security and intelligence services were governed by informal non-statutory mechanisms. The Security Service (MI5) was governed by the unpublished Findlater-Stewart Memorandum and then by the Maxwell-Fyfe Directive published in 1952. The Intelligence Service (MI6) was governed by a Directive to 'C' – the title given to the Chief of the Service. Until 1994, MI6 'maintained [its] existence in legal darkness'.[67] After an existence which spanned almost all of the twentieth century, it was only in 1989 that the government admitted to the existence of the Security Service[68] and only in 1994 to the existence of the Secret Intelligence Service.[69] GCHQ, the signals intercept body, was also placed on a statutory basis in 1994.

The central impetus for change arose from the need to comply with the demands of the European Convention on Human Rights,[70] well before the introduction of the HRA. Once a model for the statutory framework of MI5 had been devised in the form of the Security Service Act 1989, based on the model used for the Interception of Communications Act 1985, also introduced to comply with the Convention, the model was extended to the Secret Intelligence Service and GCHQ in the Intelligence Services Act 1994. A complaints mechanism relying on deliberation in secret by a Commissioner and tribunals was created. At the same time, a level of parliamentary oversight of the agencies was added. Thus, in 1997, the Labour Government inherited a particular statutory framework. It largely adopted, it will be argued, the model that framework provided when it made changes to the agencies' accountability in the Regulation of Investigatory Powers Act 2000.

In the era of the Northern Irish peace process, fragile as it is, and of the HRA, with its guarantee of protection for individual privacy in Art 8, the powers of the three agencies raise a number of concerns. The government considers that current levels of terrorist activity provide a justification for increasing the funding for the services. This view of the government is reflected in the recent budgets for the three agencies and, as the government puts it, it has 'set spending plans which will enable the agencies to face up to the formidable tasks, old, new and changing, which confront them'.[71] The Security Service has had a role in countering terrorist threats since the 1960s. But

---

67 Leigh, I and Lustgarten, L, 'The Security Service Act 1989' (1989) 52 MLR 801, p 802.
68 The Secret Service bureau was established in 1909 and became known as MI5 in January 1916.
69 See also Leigh, I and Lustgarten, L, *In From the Cold: National Security and Parliamentary Democracy*, 1994, *Coda* for discussion of the statutory framework for MI6, and Wadham (1994) 57(6) MLR 916. For discussion of aspects of the changed position of MI6, see Davies, P, 'Integrating intelligence into the machinery of British central government' (2000) 78(1) Public Administration 29.
70 See *Harman and Hewitt v UK*, Appl No 1211 75/86; (1992) 14 EHRR 657.
71 *The Government Response to the Intelligence and Security Committee's Annual Report*, Cm 4089, 1998, p 3, para 1. The figure for 1999/2000 was £743.2m for all three services; in 2000/2001 it was £745.0m: *The Intelligence and Security Committee Report 1997–98*, Cm 4073, p 9. Individual figures for the three services were not published.

that role is undergoing some redirection in response to the redefinition of terrorism, discussed in Chapter 14,[72] which is currently contained in s 1(1) of the Terrorism Act 2000. The government and the Parliamentary committee charged with oversight of the agencies, the Intelligence and Security Committee, agree in considering that such redirection aids in justifying the maintenance of the services: 'The [Intelligence and Security] Committee acknowledges the continued need for the intelligence and security agencies in a changed but still dangerous world and believes they must be maintained and funded in a sustainable way. The government reached the same conclusions in the Comprehensive Spending Review.'[73]

In its Third Report in 1998, the Committee raises concerns regarding the continued existence of the services in the current era:

> So far from being invented to justify the agencies' continued existence [new challenges to the services] are real enough, and the country rightly expects to be protected against them . . . However, the agencies face these tasks in a new environment of greater openness and accountability. They also face them with new technologies available to bring new capacities for the collection of information in many forms, which may pose new challenges to ensuring that the privacy of law-abiding individuals is respected . . . [in times of no grave national threat] public confidence can be very fragile. That is the inevitable consequence of operating within a 'ring of secrecy' which prevents a more balanced public view of their activities. The public must therefore be confident that there is adequate independent scrutiny and democratic accountability on their behalf by people within that ring of secrecy. That is the task of this Committee.[74]

The Fourth Report, for 1998/99, also adopted a robust tone.[75] It took particular exception to the continuing refusal of the government to publish a national audit office report on the excessive spending of the agencies on refurbishment. The Chairman, Tom King, said: 'The cloak of secrecy has been used to cover up inadequacies and serious lapses in expenditure control.' The Chairman of the Commons Public Accounts Committee endorsed this view on the day the Intelligence Committee's Fourth Report was published.

The Intelligence and Security Committee, in both its Third and Fourth Reports, was clearly signalling its concern at the probable tension between the continued existence of doubtfully accountable agencies, with an increasing remit, in an age when the expectations of accountability have never been higher. The implication is that the confidence in the balance supposedly struck by the statutory mechanisms between individual rights, especially to privacy, and the demands of secrecy, has never been more fragile.

---

72 See pp 1377–81; see also Home Office and Northern Ireland Office, *Legislation against Terrorism: A Consultation Paper*, Cm 4178, 1998.
73 *The Government Response to the Intelligence and Security Committee's Annual Report*, Cm 4089, 1998.
74 Third Report of the Intelligence and Security Committee for 1997–1998, Cm 4073, p vii.
75 Cm 4532, published on 25 November 1999.

While making gestures in the direction of openness and accountability, the statutory mechanisms, including the most recent one, the Regulation of Investigatory Powers Act 2000 (RIPA), are still, it will be argued, imbued with the culture of secrecy.[76] Therefore, it is questionable whether the more extensive statutory basis for the agencies' activities which is now available can create confidence in them. It has been shaken by a number of allegations from ex-MI5 or MI6 agents. *Spycatcher*, written by Peter Wright, a former member of MI5, alleged that MI5 had 'bugged and burgled its way around London', that the Service had tried to destabilise the Labour Government of Harold Wilson, and that the Director General from 1956 to 1965, Roger Hollis, was a Soviet agent.[77] Richard Tomlinson, a former MI6 officer, was prosecuted in 1998, as was David Shayler, a former MI5 officer, in 2001[78] under the Official Secrets Act, in both instances for seeking to make public a number of grievances and concerns about the services. Concerns were also raised over MI5's and MI6's handling of the Vasili Mitrokhin affair in 1999[79] and regarding allegations of involvement in the attempt to assassinate Colonel Gadafy.

It will be contended below that Ministerial responsibility, Parliamentary oversight and the complaints and checking mechanisms of the relevant Commissioners and tribunals create only a limited and flawed control of the agencies. Although the changes to the tribunal system that occurred under the Regulation of Investigatory Powers Act 2000 represented a step in the direction of greater accountability, they are, it will be argued, unlikely to have much impact in terms of creating stricter control, since in various respects, including the role of parliamentary oversight, the current tribunal system is based on the old model.[80] Without radical structural change to these methods, which could allow for some breaching of the ring of secrecy, no real control will be achieved. The HRA may be aiding in providing some of the impetus for such change, but its direct impact on the agencies, in terms of ensuring protection for privacy, is likely to continue to be minimal, for the reasons discussed below.

---

76 Admittedly, the specifically operational aspects of the work of the security and intelligence services it covers would be secret anywhere in the world. But the tendency to curb the scrutinising role of the ordinary courts discussed in this chapter, especially in relation to the interception of communications, suggests that secrecy remains the dominant value.

77 See *AG v Times Newspapers Ltd* [1991] 2 All ER 398; [1992] 1 AC 191, discussed in Chapter 7. The last two allegations appear to be unreliable, see *MI5: The Security Service*, 3rd edn, 1998, pp 39–40; Mitrokhin, V and Andrew, C, *The Mitrokhin Archive*, 1999, confirmed that the allegation regarding Roger Hollis was untrue.

78 He was imprisoned in France pending determination of the extradition request which was so that he could face charges under the Official Secrets Act, s 1. France refused to extradite him. Once he returned to the UK, in August 2000, he was charged with an offence under s 1(1) of the Act: see *Shayler*, Transcript of the Preparatory hearing on 14 May 2001 and the judgment of the Court of Appeal on 28 September 2001. It was found that no defence to a charge under s 1(1) could arise by reliance on s 3 HRA, but that a defence of necessity could arise. For the House of Lords' decision see further Chapter 7, pp 606–11. For discussion of the background to the prosecution and the civil actions brought against Shayler, see Best, K, 'Implications of the Shayler affair' (2001) 6 J Civ Lib 18.

79 Mitrokhin was a KGB defector who identified Melita Norwood and others as Soviet agents in *The Mitrokhin Archive*, 1999 .

80 See below, pp 1080 *et seq.*

The framework for the agencies

The functions of MI5 are set out in s 1 of the Security Services Act 1989. Section 1(1) provides: 'the function of the Service shall be the protection of national security and, in particular, its protection against threats from espionage, terrorism and sabotage, from the activities of agents of foreign powers and from actions intended to overthrow or undermine parliamentary democracy by political, industrial or violent means.' Section 1(3) adds the function of safeguarding 'the economic well-being of the UK' but only from external threats. The Act was amended to add sub-section 1(4) by s 1 of the Security Services Act 1996 in order to add to the two existing functions of the Security Service a third function: 'to act in support of the activities of police forces, [the National Criminal Intelligence Service (NCIS), the National Crime Squad and other law enforcement agencies in the prevention and detection of serious crime].' The words in square brackets were added by s 134(1), Sched 9, para 60 of the Police Act 1997. In 2006 these bodies were amalgamated.

The Serious Organised Crime Agency (SOCA) was set up under SOCA 2005 and became officially operationally active from April 2006. The Agency is an Executive Non-Departmental Public Body sponsored by, but operationally independent from, the Home Office. The Agency has been formed from the amalgamation of the National Crime Squad (NCS), National Criminal Intelligence Service (NCIS), that part of HM Revenue and Customs (HMRC) dealing with drug trafficking and associated criminal finance and a part of UK Immigration dealing with organised immigration crime (UKIS). SOCA is an intelligence-led agency with law enforcement powers and harm reduction responsibilities. Harm in this context is stated to be the damage caused to people and communities by serious organised crime. The Home Secretary may set SOCA strategic priorities and will judge the success of its efforts. Within that framework, SOCA plans its priorities, including how it will exercise the functions given to it by statute, and what performance measures it will adopt.

As indicated above, the definition of terrorism was greatly widened under the Terrorism Act 2000. This means that the functions of the Service have been widened quite significantly since the 1989 Act was passed. Sections 1(2) and 3(2) of the Intelligence Services Act 1994 (ISA) provide that the function of MI6 and of GCHQ is exercisable only in the interests of national security with particular reference to the defence and foreign policies of HM Government and in the 'interests of the economic well-being of the UK' and 'in support of the prevention and detection of serious crime'. MI6 is empowered under s 1(1) to obtain and provide information relating to the actions or intentions of persons outside the British Isles and perform tasks relating to such actions and intentions. Thus, MI6 is geared to external rather than internal security, in accordance with its traditional role, but this does not mean that it does not carry out operations on British soil. Targeted individuals may temporarily come to Britain and information relating to them may be found here. The police have pointed out that NCIS is a more open and accountable body than MI5 and, further, that there is little point in putting resources into a police intelligence body if MI5 then removes some of its main functions.

In order to perform their functions, the agencies operate their broad powers under a secrecy and a lack of accountability which would not be acceptable in respect of the police or other law enforcement agencies. But under a model which gave a high priority to oversight and democratic accountability, it would be found that the agencies should carry out no function which could be carried out by a service, such as the police, which was more open to scrutiny. A confusion of functions between such services and MI5 is occurring due to the fact that this principle has not been followed, although given the secrecy surrounding the operations of the agencies, it is not possible to come to any conclusion as to the genuine necessity of affording them a serious crime function or of allowing them to investigate the activities of a wider range of groups by designating them 'terrorist'. MI5 is specifically empowered to function against terrorist groups. MI6 and GCHQ can operate against them, since part of their function is to further the interests of national security which terrorism is assumed to threaten. Thus, widening the definition of terrorism widens the function of all three agencies.

The Intelligence and Security Committee

The 1989 Act provided for no real form of Parliamentary oversight of the Security Service.[81] But the 1994 Act set up, under s 10, the Parliamentary Committee, the Intelligence and Security Committee, to oversee the 'expenditure, administration and policy' of MI5, MI6 and GCHQ.[82] Operational matters were omitted from their remit. The Committee has wide access to the range of Agency activities and to highly classified information. Its cross–party membership of nine from both Houses is appointed by the Prime Minister after consultation with the Leader of the opposition. The Committee is supported by a Clerk and secretariat in the Cabinet Office and can employ an investigator to pursue specific matters in greater detail.

Thus, for the first time, all three services were made, to an extent, accountable to Parliament. The Committee's annual Report is not, however, presented directly to Parliament but to the Prime Minister, who may censor it before presentation on broad grounds – it need not be damaging to national security, merely to the continued discharge of the functions of the Services. After deletions of sensitive material, the Reports are placed before Parliament by the Prime Minister. The Committee also provides ad hoc reports to the Prime Minister from time to time. Appointment to the Committee is by the Prime Minister.

As the Committee is not a Select Committee, it has no powers to compel witnesses to appear before it. But in practice it has exercised greater powers than a select committee: in its inquiry into the Vasili Mitrokhin affair it was able to obtain papers from former administrations and official advice to Ministers, both of which are forbidden to select committees. After each general election the Prime Minister appoints the nine Parliamentarians to the Committee in consultation with the Leader of the opposition. Members are mainly from the House of Commons, but at least one must be from the House of Lords. Serving Ministers are not allowed to be members, but several members have previously held Ministerial positions. Details of the membership of the most recent committee, including its final report and the government's response, are on its web page.[83] The committee ceases to exist when Parliament is dissolved; after the election the Prime Minister reforms the committee.

---

81 See further Leigh and Lustgarten, *In from the Cold* 1994.
82 For discussion of the introduction of the Committee in 1994 see Leigh and Lustgarten, ibid.
83 Cabinetoffice.gov.uk/intelligence.

The members of the Committee are notified that s 1 of the Official Secrets Act will apply to them as though they were members of the services themselves and therefore, they will commit a criminal offence if they disclose any information or document they have obtained as a result of their work. They would have no defence that the disclosure revealed a serious abuse of power which could not be otherwise addressed, or that the information was already in the public domain. 'Sensitive' information can be withheld from the Committee by agency heads[84] and non-sensitive information can be withheld by the Secretary of State.[85]

It was clear at its inception that the extent to which the work of the Committee was likely to have a real impact on the agencies depended on its appointees and on the way they interpreted their role. The 1996–97 Report of the Intelligence and Security Committee made no recommendations as to independence at all, in quite strong contrast to the 1997–98 Report, which adopted a more adversarial approach. Tom King chaired the Committee over this period of time and appears to have adopted an increasingly robust stance. The 1998 Report signalled a change of direction towards a more rigorous scrutiny, and this continued in the 1999 Report, also under his chairmanship.

The 1998 Report was completed after the system had been in place for four years. In its section on oversight, it looked especially at the oversight available in other countries, the Committee having talked in the past year to counterpart bodies. They found that other countries have 'more extensive forms of "independent" oversight'.[86] One feature of such 'more extensive' models of oversight is the Inspector General (IG), a full time appointment who has wide powers of access to operational and other information. The Commissioner for the Security Service has similar powers of access, but it is not his function to review operations and the tribunals only do so in response to a direct complaint. Clearly, many members of the public who might have grounds for complaint would not be able to bring one, since they would be unaware of the operation. An IG would be able to consider operational abuse of power without depending on a complaint. The Committee pointed out that it cannot 'investigate directly different aspects of the Agencies' activities' and it found that the Committee's reach should be extended by an additional 'investigative capacity'.[87] It considered that without this capacity, it cannot make authoritative statements and needed some reinforcement of authority. In its 'Future Programme of Work' it set forth a number of issues to be pursued in 1998 and 1999, including the question whether individuals should have rights in connection with the destruction or otherwise of any file held on them; protections against storage and use, against individuals' interests, of inaccurate information, and the implications of the European Convention. Following this Report, additional support was given to the Committee on a non-statutory basis, reflecting their interest in an 'Inspector General' model of accountability. This is a step forward in those terms, but since no powers are granted, the co-operation of the services will be on a consensual basis only.

84 Schedule 3, para 3(2).
85 Schedule 3, para 3(4).
86 See p 24, para 62.
87 See p 25, para 69.

Warrant procedure

The legal constraints on targets in the UK may be compared with those in Canada and the US. In the US, warrants are only issued if there is 'probable cause' that the target is a foreign power or agent of a foreign power and collection is for the purpose of obtaining foreign intelligence.[88] In Canada, warrants may be issued only if there are 'reasonable grounds' for believing that the warrant is required to investigate a threat to national security.[89] It is apparent that the constraints in these jurisdictions are narrower and, in particular, that serious crime work is not included. The functions of the agencies in assisting in preventing or detecting serious crime is likely to form a much smaller percentage of their work than will widening the definition of terrorism. The MI5 booklet published in 1998[90] mentions 'arrangements' governing the role of the Service in assisting in serious crime work and the need for a close working relationship with the other agencies in question.[91] The arrangements are not published. Therefore, two executive bodies are left to determine, in a barely accountable and 'invisible' manner, the key issue of principle at stake here.

The warrant procedure for all three agencies is governed partly by ss 5 and 6 of the Intelligence Services Act 1994 and partly by Part II of RIPA. Under s 5(2) of the 1994 Act, the Home Secretary can issue a warrant authorising the 'taking of any such action as is specified in the warrant in respect of any property so specified or in respect of wireless telegraphy so specified'. In other words, members of the agencies can interfere in any way with property so long as it appears that the action would be of 'substantial value' to the agency in carrying out any of its functions.

The Security Services Act 1996 added sub-ss 3, 3A and 3B to s 5 of the 1994 Act. Section 5(3) provides that warrants issued to GCHQ and MI6 in respect of their 'serious crime' function 'may not relate to property in the British Islands'. Section 5(3A) provides that in respect of the Security Service's serious crime work a warrant may not relate to property within Britain unless s 3B applies. Section 3B applies if the conduct in question appears to constitute one or more offences and either involves the use of violence, results in substantial gain or is conduct by a large number of persons in pursuit of a common purpose or is an offence for which a person of 21 or over with no previous convictions could be expected to receive a sentence of imprisonment of three years or more.

The purpose of the 1996 Act was to allow the Security Service to aid the police in preventing and detecting serious crime, by which the government stated that it meant organised crime. However, the terms of the Act do not limit its application to serious or organised crime. It could be used, for example, against persons engaging in public protest who might well (given the breadth and vagueness of some public order law), commit an offence, such as obstruction of the highway, and who can be said to be acting in pursuit of a common purpose. Thus, a distinction is created between the agencies in terms of what they may do in relation to property, and this was continued in Part II RIPA. But, clearly, all three were able to engage in other activities in relation

---

88   Under the Foreign Intelligence Surveillance Act.
89   Under the Canadian Security Intelligence Service Act 1984, s 2.
90   *MI5: The Security Service*, 3rd edn, 1998.
91   Ibid, p 18.

to persons in the British Islands, whether under warrant or not, so long as, formally speaking, the activities were in accordance with their functions. This position became untenable under the HRA and therefore, in anticipation of its coming into force, such activities were provided with a statutory basis under the RIPA. 'Directed surveillance' and covert 'human intelligence sources' can be used by MI6 and GCHQ, but 'intrusive surveillance', which entails an intrusion onto 'residential premises', can normally be used only by MI5 in respect of its serious crime work.[92]

It was suggested in debate in Parliament that the 1994 Act should contain a clear set of principles which would govern and structure the operations of the services in carrying out these statutory functions. It was suggested that they should include the requirements that the more intrusive the technique, the higher the authority should be to authorise its use, and that except in emergencies, less intrusive techniques should be preferred to more intrusive ones.[93] The government rejected these amendments to the 1994 Act on the ground that they were implicit in s 5 of the Act. Section 5 provides that the Secretary of State should be satisfied that 'what the action seeks to achieve cannot reasonably be achieved by other means'. This imprecise requirement is clearly no substitute for the more detailed set of principles suggested. If a member of the Service wishes to intercept communications on the public telephone system, another level of control is imposed, since the procedure under the Interception of Communications Act 1985 applies (discussed below). The RIPA addressed the anomaly that members of the services could engage in various forms of surveillance in reliance merely on the procedure under the 1994 Act, but that in respect of this particular form, an extra layer of control was added.

The result of s 5 is that a private individual can have surveillance devices placed on his or her premises or can be subject to a search of the premises even though engaged in lawful political activity which is not intended to serve any foreign interest. An amendment to the Security Services Bill was put forward that would have exempted such a person from the operation of the legislation, but it was rejected by the government.

The authorisation must be by the Home Secretary, personally, under s 6(1) of the 1994 Act, except in the case of emergency warrants which may be authorised by a senior official, with express authorisation from the Home Secretary. The arrangements for intrusive surveillance under the RIPA are similar, as explained below,[94] but no independent authorisation procedure is necessary in respect of the other two forms of surveillance. The s 6 warrant procedure begins with a letter from the agency to the Home Office. It is considered in the warrants division which may require further information in order to strengthen the application. As Leigh and Lustgarten point out, this process could be viewed as a gulling of their political master by collusion between 'the Security Service and its Whitehall counterpart', or it could be seen as 'conscientious control' over the requests, endowing stronger ones with greater credibility and rejecting weaker ones.[95] Under s 5 of the 1994 Act, the Home Secretary should then consider whether it is necessary for the action to be undertaken on the ground that 'it is likely to be of substantial value in assisting the agency in question in carrying out its function, as indicated above'. He must be satisfied that what is sought to be achieved could not be achieved by other means and as to the arrangements for disclosure of information obtained. It is not possible to ascertain how far each of these matters is subjected to serious scrutiny or how far, assuming that they were taken seriously, a Home Secretary would be able to detect weaknesses in the application. Obviously, these matters would depend partly on the particular Home Secretary in question. But applications are very rarely rejected and, as Lustgarten and Leigh point out, political considerations as well as legal ones enter into the approval.[96] The warrants are issued for six months initially by the Home Secretary and may be renewed by him for that period so long as it is thought necessary for them to continue. There is no overall maximum period and some warrants may therefore be, in effect, permanent. If issued by a senior official, the warrant ceases to have effect after two working days.

The warrant procedure has been compared unfavourably with that in other mature democracies. The Canadian Security Intelligence Service may only be granted warrants on the authorisation of a Federal Court judge, thus ensuring a measure of independent oversight. Moreover, the warrant will not be issued unless the facts relied on to justify the belief that a warrant is necessary to investigate a threat to national security are set out in a sworn statement.[97] In the US, the warrants are authorised by special Foreign Intelligence Surveillance Act courts comprising selected federal judges, although in certain circumstances, the Attorney General can authorise searches or warrants by executive order only. These arrangements present a strong contrast with those in the UK, since there is no judicial involvement at all in the UK in the issuing of warrants under either the 1994 or 2000 Acts. Any judicial involvement can occur only after the warrant has been issued. Thus, the crucial stage of the procedure is entirely in executive hands – one part of the executive is authorising another to interfere with individual rights. The impact of judicial authorisation must not be overestimated; clearly, some judges may develop a tendency to rubber-stamp requests. But the fact of placing papers before a judge may foster internal scrupulousness in their preparation. Since many persons will have no means of knowing that they have been targeted and therefore will have no ability to make a complaint, judicial involvement at the complaints stage only is of marginal importance. The failure to allow such involvement in the warrant procedure may be viewed as one of the key weaknesses in the scheme.

Under s 7 ISA the Secretary of State (in practice the Foreign Secretary) can authorise SIS (MI6) to carry out acts outside the United Kingdom which are necessary for the proper discharge of one of its functions. As with s 5 warrants, before the Secretary of State gives any such authority, he must first be satisfied of a number of matters: (a) that the acts being authorised (or acts in the course of an authorised operation) will be necessary for the proper discharge of an SIS function (s 7(3)(a)); (b) that satisfactory arrangements are in force to secure that nothing will be done in reliance on the authorisation beyond what is necessary for the proper discharge of an SIS function (s 7(3)(b)(i)); (c) that satisfactory arrangements are in force to secure that the nature and likely consequences of any acts which may be done in reliance on the

---

96   Ibid, p 58.
97   For discussion of the impact of this system in practice, see Leigh, I, 'Secret proceedings in Canada' (1996) 34 Osgoode Hall LJ 113.

authorisation will be reasonable having regard to the purposes for which they are carried out (s 7(3)(b)(ii)); and (d) that satisfactory arrangements are in force to secure that SIS shall not obtain or disclose information except in so far as is necessary for the proper discharge of one of its functions (s 7(3)(c)). By virtue of s 7(4)(a) of ISA, authorisations may be given for acts of a specified description. These are known as class authorisations. They could cover, for example, the obtaining of documents which might involve theft, or payment to an agent which might involve bribery. Section 7 was amended in 2001 so as to apply also to GCHQ. The amendment was effected by s 116 of the Anti-Terrorism, Crime and Security Act 2001 and arose from a further consideration of the powers available to the intelligence services in the light of the events of 9/11. As amended, s 7 allowed GCHQ to be authorised to carry out acts outside the United Kingdom for the proper exercise of its functions in the same manner as SIS and (by a new sub-section (9)) made it clear that any question as to whether activities taking place in the UK but intended only to relate to apparatus situated outside the UK are covered by s 7 authorisations.

The system for accountability therefore relies mainly on a level of Ministerial control, but only as regards activities of the agencies which are under warrant or require Ministerial authorisation under the RIPA. As indicated, a further, judicial level of control is then added which relates only to the warrant procedure. The Commissioner is supposed to provide oversight of the procedure, but only after the event. At present, the same Commissioner operates as Commissioner in respect of all three agencies, and can be re-appointed to continue his role as 'the Intelligence Services Commissioner' under s 59 RIPA. Section 59 of the Act provides for the Prime Minister to appoint the Commissioner, who must hold or have held high judicial office within the meaning of the Appellate Jurisdiction Act 1876. He or she is appointed for a period of three years with the possibility of re-appointment. His job is to keep under review the issue of warrants by the Secretary of State authorising intrusive surveillance (e.g. eavesdropping) and interference with property in order to make sure that the Secretary of State was right to issue them. Like the Interception of Communications Commissioner, the Intelligence Services Commissioner reviews warrant applications and visits the Security Service and other agencies to discuss any case he wishes to examine in more detail. He must be given access to whatever documents and information he needs and at the end of each reporting year he submits a report to the Prime Minister; it is subsequently laid before Parliament and published. The Intelligence Services Commissioner is also responsible for reviewing the internally authorised use of directed surveillance (the covert monitoring of targets' movements, conversations and other activities) and of covert human intelligence sources (i.e. agents) to check that the agencies are acting in accordance with the requirements of the law.

The oversight is, however, limited. The Commissioner can only oversee the issuance of warrants under ss 5 and 6 of the 1994 Act; he cannot order that they should be quashed; nor can he order an operation against a particular group to cease. The Commissioner cannot address instances in which no warrant was necessary, since the procedure in question is not unlawful. The remit of the Commissioner precludes consideration of unauthorised actions since he can only consider whether a warrant was properly authorised. If an action does not require a warrant, such a question becomes irrelevant. This is also true of actions which are unlawful and unauthorised by warrant, such as burgling a property.

Personal files

The Intelligence and Security Committee has taken a particular interest in the creation and use of personal files stored by the agencies, particularly those on British citizens. A particular concern was to consider 'the protection for an individual against having information inappropriately or inaccurately gathered, stored and used against their interests.'[98] These files play a significant role in security vetting, which affects a wide range of jobs in the UK. It applies to senior staff in a range of government departments, to independent bodies such as the BBC and in the private sector.[99] Security checks will include consideration of information, if any, held on an applicant by MI5.

For example, in 1998 the Security Service was holding 250,000 hard copy files on individuals and a further 4,000 were archived on microfiche. Of these, 17,500 were coded 'green'[100] or active, and 13,000 related to British citizens. The Service is currently reviewing files for destruction by category. The Committee expressed concern that reviewing was restricted to individuals over 55. Thus, files may be retained on individuals under that age because they had 20 years ago joined an organisation then classed as subversive, whereas a file would not be opened on a person joining the same organisation today.[101] The Committee found: 'We believe . . . that some form of independent check should be built into the process . . .'[102] The government response to this recommendation suggested that secrecy remained the overriding priority. 'The government does not believe that the process of reviewing files for destruction would be assisted by independent scrutiny.'[103]

The Committee took a somewhat less robust view of the SIS and GCHQ records and data. In 1998 SIS had 86,000 records, half of which related to UK citizens. Many of them related to the staff of the Agency and its contacts. Of these, 75% were closed and some related back to 1909. Thus, it appears to have no destruction policy and of course no independent check that it was not holding files on British citizens needlessly. The argument for an independent check may not be as pressing as in respect of the Security Service, but it is clearly applicable, especially as internal procedures reveal an unawareness of the abuses which can arise if files are stored for many years without review.

Like SIS, GCHQ does not hold and create personal records in the same way that MI5 does. But its rationale is to hold personal data collected by intercepting communications. GCHQ informed the Committee that such data 'which may arise from collection under warrant *or otherwise* (emphasis added) is a necessary and sometimes key analytical

---

98 *Report of the Intelligence and Security Committee for 1997/98*, Cm 4073, p 16, paras 39 and 40.
99 See First Report from the Select Committee on Defence, Session 1982–83, Positive Vetting Procedures in Her Majesty's Services and the Ministry of Defence HC (182/83) 242 and the Radcliffe Report, Cmnd 1681, 1962, Chapter 7; Linn, I, *Application Refused: Employment Vetting by the State*, 1990, Civil Liberties Trust; Hollingsworth, M and Norton-Taylor, R, *Blacklist: The Inside Story of Political Vetting*, 1988, Hogarth. The vetting guidelines were set out in a statement made at HC Deb Vol 251–766w, 15 December 1994.
100 This is part of the 'traffic lighting' process for files: 'green' files are active; 'amber' ones are closed but may have papers added; 'red' ones are closed and retained for research only.
101 Ibid, p 19, para 47.
102 Ibid, p 20, para 50.
103 *The Government Response to the Intelligence and Security Committee's Annual Report*, Cm 4089, 1998, p 5, para 16.

tool'. GCHQ has a lawful basis for interception under s 5 of the 1994 Act and under s 3(2)(a)(i) of the 1985 Act. But these words imply that GCHQ is currently holding some personal data without a basis of legal authorisation. Since such holding of data was not a criminal offence or civil wrong, this practice of GCHQ could not be said to be unlawful until the HRA came fully into force. Assuming that it amounts to an infringement of Art 8, it is now unlawful, since it cannot be said to be in accordance with the law. As discussed below, it may well be the case that no avenue, other than the complaints mechanism, is available to an individual to challenge the holding of his or her personal information which has been obtained unlawfully. Such a matter could be brought before the tribunal set up under the RIPA; this is discussed below. The government has said that all GCHQ interception, use and retention of material is carried out only in accordance with the 1994 and, where appropriate, 1985 Acts and 'these arrangements are subject to continuing scrutiny by the Commissioners' under the two Acts.[104]

One means of allowing a check on the retention and use of personal information would be to allow some access, with use of editing, under the Freedom of Information Act 2000 to the personal data held by all three agencies. However, the three agencies are all excluded from the Act as Chapter 7 explains.[105] They are also now fully exempt from the obligation to apply the data protection principles under the Data Protection Act 1998, on the basis that the files are held for national security purposes. Under the 1984 Act, personal data held on national security grounds was not exempt from the principles, although the agencies did not register under the Act on national security grounds. The protection is therefore weaker under the 1998 Act, although a person directly affected by the exemption can appeal against the issue of a national security certificate, under s 28 of the 1998 Act. Since the agencies, and MI5 in particular, have a role in relation to serious crime, this position is anomalous. As the Data Protection Registrar (now Commissioner) has argued, MI5 should be placed in the same position as the police in relation to this role.[106] The Commissioner has no general statutory remit to obtain access to files for monitoring purposes. But individual cases referred to him or her may raise general issues of file keeping. The position may be compared to that in Canada, where the agencies are subject to privacy and access to information legislation, although individuals have no right of access to their files and are not informed that the file exists. An edited version of the file may be made available which will be limited to information already in the public domain. The key point is that the *Commissioners* in Canada have access to the files. In the US, records may only be established and held if they are relevant to the conduct of authorised intelligence operations and they are subject to the Freedom of Information Act. Individuals can ask to see files; they may be given an edited version and the agency can choose neither to confirm nor deny that material has been withheld. These arrangements, qualified as they are, represent an improvement on the complete exclusion of the agencies from the relevant privacy and FoI legislation, as in the UK.

---

104 Government Response, p 6, para 19.
105 See pp 633.
106 Our Answers: Data Protection and the EU Directive (95/46/EC), the Data Protection Registrar, July 1996. This position was also strongly criticised by Justice in its report *Under Surveillance: Covert Policing and Human Rights Standards*, 1998, p 90. For the position of the police under the 1998 Act, see Chapter 9, p 929.

Complaints

Taking the Interception of Communications Act as a model, the 1989 Act set up a Commissioner under s 4 and a tribunal under s 5 as a means of oversight for MI5. The procedure for complaints and composition of the tribunal are dealt with in Scheds 1 and 2. The 1994 Act adopted the same model for MI6 and GCHQ under ss 8 and 9 and Scheds 1 and 2.

No duty is imposed on the agencies to disclose the fact to an individual that an operation has occurred, after it is over. Most individuals will have no means of knowing that it has occurred and therefore will be unlikely to bring a complaint. If an individual brings a speculative complaint to the tribunal, uncertain whether surveillance or intrusion has occurred, the result may leave him or her none the wiser. The tribunals only reported that the result was unfavourable to the complainant, not whether an operation was indeed taking place, but was viewed as justified. The tribunals were not permitted to give reasons for their decisions.[107] Service personnel who felt that they had been required to act improperly in bugging or searching a person's property may not disclose the matter.

As discussed in Chapter 7, s 1 of the Official Secrets Act 1989 prevents members or former members of the security and intelligence services disclosing anything at all about the operation of those services. These provisions also apply to anyone who is notified that he or she is subject to the provisions of the section. Similarly, s 4(3) of the Act prohibits disclosure of information obtained by, or relating to, the issue of a warrant under the Interception of Communications Act 1985 or the Security Services Act 1989.

The 1989 and 1994 Acts provide no avenue for members of the agencies to complain to the Commissioner or Tribunals. Therefore, any disclosure of information to them or to the individual citizen concerned by such members would be a criminal offence under the Official Secrets Act. Thus, the persons who would be most aware of an abuse of power are denied this means of either supporting a complaint or enabling the individual concerned to instigate one. They can complain to the Security and Intelligence Services Staff Counsellor, appointed by the Prime Minister in 1987, but the office is, as Leigh and Lustgarten put it, 'a safety valve for conscience-troubled officials, rather than a form of oversight'.[108] The Reports of the Counsellor for the Prime Minister, Home Secretary and Foreign Secretary are unpublished and therefore there is no means of knowing whether his work has any benefit in terms of terminating unlawful or improper agency activities.

Under Sched 1, para 2 to the 1989 Act, the Security Service Tribunal could investigate two types of complaint: that the agency had instituted inquiries about the complainant and, if so, whether it had reasonable grounds for so doing. If the inquiries were due to a person's membership of a category of persons, the only question to be asked was whether there were reasonable grounds for believing him or her to be a member of that category, not whether the Service had reasonable grounds for investigating the group in question. Where information had been disclosed to an employer, the tribunal would investigate whether there were reasonable grounds for believing the information

---

107 Schedule 1, para 5(3) to the 1989 Act and Sched 1, para 6 to the 1994 Act.
108 Ibid, p 430.

to be true. No inquiry is to be made into the misleadingness of the information or its factual truth. Nor can the tribunal consider the reasonableness of the categorisation of a particular group, or part of a group. The final ground for complaint was apparently wide: a person 'may complain to the tribunal if he is aggrieved by anything which he believes the Service has done in relation to him or any property of his'.[109] But the tribunal cannot investigate a complaint which relates to property and must pass it to the Commissioner who would utilise the principles applied by a court on an application for judicial review.[110]

The standard of scrutiny in the tribunals was always unlikely to be rigorous: in *Secretary of State for Home Affairs ex p Ruddock*[111] (determined prior to the coming into force of the 1985 Act) the question was whether the decision of the Home Secretary in granting the warrant was 'so outrageous in its defiance of logic or accepted moral standards that no sensible person who applied his mind to the question to be decided could have arrived at it'. Since the tribunals can merely ask whether the agency had 'reasonable grounds' for its action, they cannot consider the questions whether the action was proportionate to the invasion of privacy and whether the action could have been carried out by the police. The tribunals both sit in secret and the complainant has no right to be informed of the findings of the investigation, only whether it is favourable or unfavourable. The Commissioner is operating under severe constraints, which arguably render his office a merely tokenistic one. He sits as a full time judge, has no staff and takes roughly two weeks' leave plus his own free time to carry out his role. He has been appointed to carry out his task in respect of all three agencies, and therefore he is expected to oversee bodies with, in 1998, a combined budget of £747m and a staff of around 5,000.[112] In the US, Canada and Australia, the equivalent bodies have a full time staff. The Commissioner's Report for 2002[113] was typical. It was mainly descriptive and contained a secret annex. In relation to specific cases it stated:

> Five breaches of a particular agency's internal authorisation procedures and one separate breach of ISA have been reported to me in 2002. As it is not possible for me to explain any details of these breaches without revealing information of a sensitive nature, I have referred to them in more detail in the confidential annex. However, I can report that four of the five breaches that occurred in an agency's internal authorisation procedures were due to administrative failures to renew existing RIPA internal authorisations before they expired with the fifth reflecting their failure to obtain internal authorisation ahead of an operation commencing.[114]

The Report of the Intelligence Services Commissioner for 2004 was similarly bland; it resembled the annual report by Sir Swinton Thomas, the Interception Commissioner, in that it said little about specific cases and had a secret annex to the report.

---

109 1989 Act, Sched 1, para 1; 1994 Act, Sched 1, para 1.
110 1989 Act, Sched 1, para 4; 1994 Act, Sched 1, para 3(b).
111 [1987] 1 WLR 1482.
112 This is an estimate; the numbers have been censored from the Parliamentary Committee's Report 1998, pp 42 and 47.
113 9.9.03, HC 1048.
114 Para 36.

Given these limitations, it is unsurprising to find that no complaint has ever been upheld by the tribunals or Commissioner. Between the introduction of the 1989 Act and the end of 1997, the tribunal set up under s 4 of the 1989 Act investigated 275 complaints; none was upheld.[115] The Report of the Security Services Commissioner presented to Parliament in June 1999[116] reported that the tribunal received 28 complaints in 1998, of which 18 were investigated and none was upheld. The Commissioner received 16 complaints and upheld none.[117] The Prime Minister has the power to censor the report before it is presented to Parliament, a power which is clearly exercised routinely. It appeared to be almost impossible, in practice, for a member of the public who was dissatisfied with the outcome of the complaints procedure to seek a remedy in the courts. The tribunals were set up as the only avenue of complaint and, under s 5(4) of the 1989 Act and s 9(4) of the 1994 Act, the decisions of the tribunals, including decisions as to their jurisdiction, were not questionable in any court of law.

Commentators have not viewed this system for complaints as a success and the Commissioner has implied that it was flawed from the outset. He has said that the limitations of the complaints mechanism are the fault of the 'architects' of the statutory provisions.[118] It has been said: 'A major cause for concern . . . is the failure to confront adequately the need for accountability and review of the Services.'[119] John Wadham of *Liberty* described the Security Service Tribunal as 'useless'.[120] Gill found: 'this structure . . . has been constructed neither for elegance nor impact'.[121] Lustgarten and Leigh sum up the problem: 'in so far as the government believed that by creating these new structures it would reassure the public that all is well it seriously miscalculated.'[122] As indicated below, a different complaints system was established under the RIPA. A new tribunal replaced the previous ones and it took over the Commissioner's complaints' role. An Interception of Communications Commissioner as well as a Chief Surveillance Commissioner was appointed under the RIPA. The remit of those Commissioners overlaps with that of the Intelligence Services Commisisoner, since it includes some oversight of surveillance undertaken by the agencies.[123]

Impact of the HRA

Under the HRA, it can be said that the Convention represents a set of principles which the 1989, 1994 and 2000 Acts can be tested against. The statutes were introduced with the Convention in mind, so it may be the case that no irremediable incompatibility between the statutory provisions and the rights exists.[124] The three agencies in question, the

---

115 *MI5: The Security Service*, 3rd edn 1998, p 33.
116 Report of the Commissioner for 1998, Cm 4365.
117 Ibid, p 5.
118 Leigh and Lustgarten, *In from the Cold* 1994 p 438.
119 Ewing, KD and Gearty, CA, *Freedom under Thatcher*, 1989, p 178.
120 Leigh and Lustgarten, *In from the Cold*, 1994 p 439.
121 Gill, P, *Policing Politics: Security Intelligence and the Liberal Democratic State*, 1994, p 295.
122 Leigh and Lustgarten, *In from the Cold*, 1994, p 439.
123 See p 1065. For the role of the Chief Surveillance Commissioner, see the same page.
124 HRA, s 3.

relevant Ministers and the oversight bodies (apart from the Parliamentary Committee)[125] as public authorities are bound by the rights under s 6 of the HRA. Although, formally, this is the legal position, the means whereby the Convention rights can be enabled to have a real rather than a theoretical impact on the agencies are highly circumscribed. They are discussed below, but although possible methods of bringing the HRA to bear on the agencies in court are considered, it is contended that the main impact of the HRA in this context is an educative and cultural one: it provides the openness the Parliamentary Committee has favoured with a clearer basis, and it may have an eventual, incremental impact on the work of the oversight bodies, in terms of the attitude they bring to their work. Most significantly, it may help to provide the impetus for the further evolution of the oversight.

Convention requirements

The Art 8(1) guarantees of respect for private life, the home and correspondence are clearly of most relevance to the activities of the agencies. The Introduction to Part III argued for a broad view of what constitutes invasion of privacy, based on the notion of control of personal information.[126] An interference with property normally creates an interference with one or more of the guarantees, as indicated above.[127] This would include planting a 'bug' on the premises in question, or entering them in order to remove property.[128] Less obvious invasions can also engage Art 8. The provisions of the Acts themselves may constitute a continuing invasion of privacy.[129] In *Harman and Hewitt v UK*,[130] the European Commission of Human Rights found that secret surveillance by MI5 of two former NCCL officers, Patricia Hewitt and Harriet Harman, had infringed Art 8(1), although they had not been subjected to direct intrusion. The intrusion was termed 'indirect' since information about them obtained from the telephone or mail intercepts of others had been recorded.

The use made of personal information, including disclosure to others, can also engage Art 8(1). In *MS v Sweden*,[131] the applicant complained that the use of medical records in respect of a compensation claim had infringed Art 8. The Court found that the disclosure did constitute an interference with the respect for private life, although it was found to be justified under Art 8(2).[132] The findings in *G, H and I v UK*[133] implied that the compiling and use of personal files by the Security Service can fall within Art 8, although they also raised questions regarding the onus placed on applicants to establish that they were likely to have been the victims of surveillance – in that instance

---

125 Parliament itself is not a public body under s 6 and nor is a person exercising function in connection with proceedings in Parliament (s 6(3)(b)). It is probable that the Committee is not a public authority under this definition.
126 See pp 803–6.
127 See p 1008–9.
128 See below, pp 1068–72.
129 See *Klass v FRG* (1978) 2 EHRR 214.
130 Appl No 121175/86; (1992) 14 EHRR 657.
131 (1999) 28 EHRR 313.
132 On the grounds of being necessary in a democratic society to further the economic wellbeing of the state.
133 15 EHRR CD 41.

of positive vetting for civil service posts. *Esbester v UK*[134] confirmed that a security check based on personal information could fall within Art 8. It may be concluded that many, if not almost all, activities of the agencies in obtaining, collecting, using and disclosing personal information tend to engage Art 8.

Once Art 8(1) is engaged, the question is whether the interference can be justified under para 2. To be justified, state interference with the Art 8 guarantee must first be in accordance with the law. As indicated in Chapter 2, interpreting 'prescribed by law' (treated as an equivalent provision at Strasbourg), Strasbourg has asked first whether the interference has some basis in domestic law, and secondly whether it is of the right 'quality'.[135] In *Huvig v France*[136] and in *Kruslin v France*[137] the Court said that the requirement of quality means that the law 'should be accessible to the person concerned, who must moreover be able to foresee its consequences for him, and compatible with the rule of law'. The application in *Harman and Hewitt v UK*[138] was declared admissible since the activities of MI5 in placing the applicants under surveillance were not in accordance with the law. No sufficient basis in law existed at the time, and the successful application led to the passing of the 1989 Act. Although there is room for argument that certain of the terms used in the 1989 and 1994 Acts are too imprecise and broad to satisfy the 'in accordance with the law' requirement, it is unlikely that this would be found to be the case in respect of primary legislation in this context, unless the domestic courts are prepared to take a much stricter view of that requirement than that taken at Strasbourg. In *Christie v UK*,[139] the Security Service and Interception of Communications Acts were both found to meet this requirement and the Commission noted: 'the [Strasbourg] case law establishes that the requirements of forseeability in the special context of sectors affecting national security cannot be the same as in many other fields'. Nevertheless, in criticising the provisions of the 1996 Act, Peter Duffy and Murray Hunt have argued that it breaches Art 8[140] since it probably does not pass the Convention requirement that an interference with private life should comply with rule of law principles. Executive discretion is so unfettered under the Act that any interference may not be 'in accordance with the law' as interpreted in *Huvig v France*[141] and *Kruslin v France*.[142] The 'in accordance with the law' question cannot be regarded as finally settled.

In *Esbester v UK*,[143] which concerned the alleged supply of information by MI5 regarding the applicant's membership of the Communist Party of Britain and of CND, leading to the revocation of a job offer, the Commission found that the 1989 Act complies with the 'in accordance with the law' requirement since the grounds under s 3 were expressed sufficiently precisely. This was a cautious, narrow application of

---

134 18 EHRR CD 72. See also *Harman v UK* Appl No 20317/92 (1993) unreported.
135 See also *Sunday Times v UK* A 30, para 49 (1979) and *Hashman v UK*, discussed in Chapter 8, pp 751–52.
136 (1990) 12 EHRR 528, para 26.
137 (1990) 12 EHRR 547, para 27.
138 Appl No 121175/86; (1992) 14 EHRR 657.
139 78-A DR E Com HR 119.
140 See (1997) 1 EHRR 11.
141 (1990) 12 EHRR 547.
142 (1990) 12 EHRR 528.
143 18 EHRR CD 72. See also *Harman v UK* Appl No 20317/92 (1993) unreported.

the Convention requirements by the Commission. In *Leander v Sweden*,[144] which concerned the holding of information in a secret police register, the Court found that unpublished statements explaining the law could not meet the accessibility requirement. Since, as indicated above, vetting procedures are either unpublished or have not been placed on a statutory basis, it might have been expected that they would fail to meet this requirement. The Commission in *Esbester* seemed to fail to distinguish between the different invasions of privacy created by vetting, and to have failed to look for a satisfactory basis in law in relation to the interference created when the information is supplied. Possibly this is a context in which the Court will eventually allow a narrower margin of appreciation in scrutinising the quality of the domestic basis for vetting more rigorously, bearing in mind its deterrent effects which may undermine freedom of association. The Court's freedom of association jurisprudence in the context of membership of political groups has recently become somewhat more interventionist.[145] Since security vetting tends to raise issues under both Art 8 and Art 11, it is possible that such a stance may also become more evident under Art 8.

Any residual activities undertaken by the Security and Intelligence Services which at present are not covered by the procedures under the 1994 and 2000 Acts may not be in accordance with the law, assuming that the primary right under Art 8(1) is engaged. For example, at present, agents must acquire a warrant if they intend to enter property or interfere with it. They are also bound by the terms of Part I of the RIPA; under s 1, as discussed below, it is a criminal offence to tap into a public or private telecommunications system without authorisation. But certain surveillance techniques may not be covered by Parts I or II of the RIPA. Until the inception of the HRA, use of such techniques was lawful under civil or criminal law in the sense that since no law forbade them, they were assumed to be permitted. The Intelligence and Security Committee in its 1998 Report[146] spoke of 'executive and judicial checks that intelligence and security services are obeying the law, in particular on acts which would be unlawful but for express authorisation'.[147] The implied distinction is between acts which do not require such authorisation and acts which do. But under the HRA it is unlawful for a public authority to fail to abide by the Convention rights and therefore, as explained below, this distinction between acts which require express authorisation and those which do not may tend to break down. All these activities require a basis in law under the HRA since all, or almost all of them, represent an infringement of privacy. Following the principle laid down in *Harman and Hewitt v UK*,[148] it is clear that placing the use of certain surveillance activities on a legal basis, which includes requiring warrant applications, is insufficient if others remain unregulated.

Christie v UK[149] concerned an interference, telephone tapping, which requires a warrant if it is not to amount to a criminal offence, as the Commission pointed out. No breach of Art 8 was found. It is unclear, but possible, that had the complaint

---

144 (1987) 9 EHRR 443.
145 See *Socialist Party and Others v Turkey* Judgment of 25 May 1998 (Appl No 20/1997/804/1007); (1999) 27 EHRR 51, paras 41, 47, 50. See also p 681, above.
146 Cm 4073.
147 Ibid, p 23.
148 Appl No 121175/86; (1992) 14 EHRR 657.
149 78-A DR E Com HR 119.

concerned a procedure which did not require a warrant but which infringed Art 8, its basis in law might have been viewed as insufficient, given that no involvement of the Secretary of State in checking warrants or, under s 6 of the 1985 Act, in reviewing the use of resultant material, would have been necessary.

This contention must be put forward tentatively. It may be that activities which did not require authorisation until the inception of the HRA might be said to have a form of legal basis under the statutory provisions if they are carried out in accordance with the stated functions of the agencies in the 1989 and 1994 Acts. But it is suggested that this basis is so exiguous and leaves discretion so unfettered that it may in future be found to fail to satisfy the 'accordance with the law' requirement. The case of *G, H and I v UK*[150] raised questions concerning the efficacy of the 1989 Act, although the applications failed. As indicated above, the RIPA is intended to provide the necessary legal basis. Clearly, there may still be activities of the agencies which fall outside it. Further, it is questionable whether the RIPA itself provides a basis of sufficient quality, a matter that is discussed further below.

Assuming that an interference is 'in accordance with the law', under the 1989, 1994 or 2000 statutes, it must also, under Art 8(2), have a legitimate aim, be necessary in a democratic society and be applied in a non-discriminatory fashion (Art 14). In cases of invasion of privacy by the state, Strasbourg's main concerns have been with the requirements of 'in accordance with the law' and 'necessary in a democratic society'. In this context, the 'legitimate aim' requirement has always been found to be satisfied. This is unsurprising since the grounds available for interference are so broad. They are: the interests of national security, public safety or the economic well being of the country, the prevention of disorder or crime, the protection of health or morals, the protection of the rights or freedom of others. The provision against non-discrimination under Art 14 has not been so far a significant issue in the state-invasion of privacy jurisprudence. But possibly Art 14 argument could be raised domestically in conjunction with Art 8 ones on the basis that certain racial or religious groups were being were being singled out as the target for surveillance in relation to suspected terrorist activity. The question would then be one of proportionality.[151] The Court has interpreted 'necessary in a democratic society' as meaning: 'an interference corresponds to a pressing social need and, in particular, that it is proportionate to the legitimate aim pursued.'[152] As explained in Chapter 4, the doctrine of proportionality is strongly linked to the principle of the margin of appreciation. The width of that margin appears to depend partly on the aim of the interference in question and partly on its necessity. In relation to the aim of national security, the Court has allowed a very wide margin to the state.

In *Klass v Federal Republic of Germany*[153] the European Court of Human Rights found, bearing the margin of appreciation doctrine in mind, that German telephone tapping procedures were in conformity with Art 8 since, *inter alia*, they provided for compensation in proceedings in the ordinary courts for persons whose phones had been unlawfully tapped. The legality of such interceptions could be challenged in the ordinary courts. No such provision is available under the Security Services Act 1989

---

150   15 EHRR CD 41.
151   See Chapter 2, p 109.
152   *Olsson v Sweden* A 130 (1988), para 67.
153   (1978) 2 EHRR 214.

or the Intelligence Services Act 1994 in respect of analogous intrusions, although, theoretically, the old tribunals could award compensation, either of their own motion or on a reference from the Commissioner.[154] This system would appear to represent a significantly lower standard of accountability than the West German one in respect of phone tapping and it is at least possible that a breach of Art 8 would have been found in *Klass* had the margin allowed to Germany been narrower.

Leander v Sweden[155] concerned rather similar complaints mechanisms. Information on the applicant was stored on a secret police register for national security purposes and used for employment vetting. This created an interference with Art 8(1), but a wide margin was allowed to the state in choosing the means of protecting national security. The aggregate of remedies available, recourse to an independent Ombudsman and Chancellor of Justice, were found to be sufficient to satisfy Art 13. In *Harman v UK*[156] and *Esbester v UK*,[157] the Commission found that the 1989 Act complied with the procedural requirements of Art 8(2), at least in the national security context. In *Christie v UK*,[158] in respect of the almost identical mechanisms under the 1985 Act, the Commission found, 'having regard to the wide margin of appreciation in this area', the safeguards provided by the tribunal and the Commissioner were sufficient in the instant case.

These findings need not be taken to mean that the oversight mechanisms provided under the 1989 and 1994 Acts, and now under the 2000 Act, clearly meet Convention requirements. They were made in relation to the particular case, not as abstract comment on such mechanisms in general, and they were heavily influenced by the margin of appreciation, especially wide where national security is in issue. As argued in Chapter 4, that doctrine is not available at national level and this, it is contended, means that it should not influence national decision makers. An activist domestic judge considering, judicially or extra-judicially (assisting the new tribunal, or as a member of it, or on appeal) whether the domestic complaints or reference provisions meet Strasbourg standards, and untrammelled by the margin of appreciation doctrine, might conclude that the controls built into the UK system under the 1989, 1994 and 2000 Acts are insufficient to prevent abuse. The framework is largely based on scrutiny of the procedure after the event and in a manner which keeps most of its key aspects in the hands of the executive. In this respect it fails to accord with the rule of law, since a part of the executive is authorising another part to invade rights; the checking procedure which is then marginally available appears to provide a largely illusory protection and in respect of key aspects of it, the only recourse is to the executive again. Arguably, the safeguards would not appear to satisfy Art 8(2).

But it is more probable that the judiciary would find that traditional notions of deference in the national security context would yield the same result as the application of the margin of appreciation doctrine.[159] There are signs, however, that at Strasbourg,

---

154 Schedule 1, para 6(1) and para 7(2) to the 1989 Act; Sched 1, para 8(1)(b) and para 8(2)(b) to the 1994 Act.
155 (1987) 9 EHRR 443.
156 Appl No 121175/86; (1992) 14 EHRR 657.
157 18 EHRR CD 72.
158 78-A DR E Com HR 119.
159 See further Chapter 4, pp 264–67, 272–73, and Chapter 14, pp 1349–52. See also the *Rehman* case, discussed briefly in Chapter 14, pp 1426, 1431.

in quite recent decisions, the Court is becoming less deferential towards claims of national security, although admittedly they have been in the context of Art 6 rather than Art 8, a significant difference due to the qualifications under Art 8.[160] The question whether the current, single tribunal provides an effective remedy for the citizen is discussed below.[161]

Using the HRA in practice

Clearly, there have always been, theoretically, methods of seeking to curb the agencies' powers when they impinge on individual citizens. Agents could be prosecuted for burglary, for example, if the action was unauthorised or improperly authorised. Prosecution of agents is, however, highly unlikely, since no means of referring an investigation to the police is provided in the statutes; further, any risk of revealing secrets would probably be avoided simply by taking a decision not to prosecute. It would also be difficult to acquire evidence due to the provisions against providing evidence to complainants. Actions for trespass to property or other tortious liability could be brought against agents, although the secrecy of operations makes this very unlikely. Any such action brought in the post-HRA era would have to accord with the Convention. The HRA extends the theoretical protection available for the citizen since, under ss 6, 7 and 8, it creates civil liability where activities are carried out that were not previously unlawful, but which breach the Convention guarantees. However, allegations that such breaches have occurred would have to be brought in the tribunal created under s 65 of the RIPA, not in the ordinary courts, as indicated below.[162]

The single tribunal has a duty under s 6 HRA to comply with the Convention in adjudicating on complaints, and the Commissioner has such a duty in overseeing not only warrants, but also the discharge of the duties of the Home Secretary and the agencies under the RIPA. The tribunal, Commissioner and Home Secretary are bound by the Convention under s 6; they are also providing oversight of bodies which are themselves so bound.

However, reliance on court action in efforts to secure the agencies' compliance with the Convention guarantees is very unlikely, largely due to the secrecy of the operations. Action in the ordinary courts at the citizen's instigation may in any event be almost entirely ruled out. As indicated above, ouster clauses contained in s 5(4) of the 1989 Act and s 9(4) of the 1994 Act barred the way to obtaining judicial review of the decisions of the Commissioner and tribunals. Both were post-*Anisminic*[163] ouster clauses in that they covered decisions of the tribunals and Commissioner as to their jurisdictions. The current tribunal is also protected by such a clause, although there is also a very narrow right of appeal, as discussed below. Judicial review of Ministerial decisions in the ordinary courts appears to be ruled out since complaints should be brought to the relevant tribunal or Commissioner and now to the single tribunal. However, judicial review could be sought, it was made clear in the preparatory hearing in *Shayler*,[164] of

---

160   *Tinnelly v UK* (1998) 27 EHRR 249 (discussed below, p 1088); *McElduff v UK* Appl No 21322/92.
161   See pp 1089–90.
162   See pp 1080 *et seq.*
163   *Anisminic Ltd v Foreign Compensation Commission* [1969] 2 AC 147. See further p 1085, fn 411.
164   Transcript of the Hearing of 14 May 2001, para 25.

the refusal of a Minister or other person within s 12 of the Official Secrets Act 1989 to authorise a member of the agencies to disclose matters relating to the work of the services.[165] Any such refusal would have to comply with the Convention rights, and a court considering the matter would not merely consider whether the decision was reasonable, but whether it had so complied.

Security vetting in the UK, taking into account information held on an applicant by MI5, raises a number of Convention issues. The position of applicants who are dismissed or refused employment as regards obtaining recourse to industrial tribunals has improved due to the government response to the findings of the European Court of Human Rights in *Tinnelly v UK*.[166] The Court found that a Ministerial certificate, stating that the reasons for the failure to employ the applicants were national security ones, effectively blocked the applicants' claim, since the judge could not go behind its terms and consider the claim, and therefore a breach of Art 6 had occurred. As a result of the ruling, the law as regards employment hearings in which national security is a factor was changed. Section 90 of the Northern Ireland Act 1998 provides for the creation of a tribunal, modelled on the Special Immigration Appeals Tribunal, to review the issue of Ministerial certificates in Northern Ireland.[167] Thus, the issue of national security will be justiciable. However, the extent to which the evidence can be tested will be questionable. As White puts it: 'the central difficulty with the type of Tribunal set up by the 1998 Act is that it attempts to create an adversarial forum where one of the parties is severely hampered in presenting his or her case.'[168] This tribunal provided a model for the tribunal set up under the RIPA; the discussion of its procedure and its compatibility with the Convention below are therefore of relevance. Section 193 of the Employment Rights Act 1996 and s 10 of the Employment Appeals Tribunals Act 1996 were amended[169] so that complaints of unfair dismissal cannot be dismissed on national security grounds unless it is demonstrated that the reason for dismissal was on those grounds. All these tribunals, including the one in Northern Ireland, are bound by s 6 of the HRA, and therefore their procedure must comply with the Convention, and the Convention points considered above could be raised before them. In industrial tribunals, under the previous position, the assertion of national security grounds would have precluded their consideration.

The possibility of further actions at Strasbourg in future cannot be ruled out, probably under Arts 8, 6 or 13, despite the fact that at the present time, as indicated below, the domestic arrangements probably satisfy the Convention requirements in a number of respects. As Chapter 2 points out, decisions of the Commission, taken some years ago and heavily influenced by the margin of appreciation, may not reflect the current stance of the Court. Given the arguments canvassed here, it might be argued that no domestic remedy which must be exhausted, other than that represented by the single tribunal

---

165 Under the Official Secrets Act 1989, ss 7(3)(b) and s 7(5); see further Chapter 7, p 605.

166 (1998) 27 EHRR 249. For discussion, see McEvoy, K and White, C, 'Security vetting in Northern Ireland' (1998) 61 MLR 341, pp 349–54.

167 For discussion, see White, C, 'Security vetting, discrimination and the right to a fair trial' [1999] PL 406–18.

168 Ibid, p 413.

169 By the Employment Rights Act 1999, Sched 8, Security and Intelligence service members may also have access to industrial tribunals, under Sched 8.

procedure exists; such absence would speed up the process of taking a case. In other fields, the HRA itself might offer such a remedy which would require exhaustion in the ordinary courts, but in this one that argument is much weaker owing to the provisions of ss 65 and 67(8) of the RIPA.

Conclusions

Consideration of the oversight and accountability system above indicates that no fundamental change has taken place and is unlikely to do so as a result of the inception of the HRA. There are signs of a strengthening accountability, taking into account the RIPA changes, particularly the introduction of the single tribunal, but the mechanisms are still, it is contended, too weak to live up to the expectations currently created in the new era of openness and accountability under the HRA. At the time when they were put in place, the mechanisms were viewed as a radical departure from the old order and all that could be expected of the governments in question. Now, although their inadequacies are apparent, they have provided the model for the mechanisms provided under the RIPA. In the current era, the assumptions underlying them look more questionable.

But the introduction of such mechanisms and the extension of a statutory basis for the agencies, under the RIPA, are first steps in a process. It is perhaps no longer likely, now that these first steps have been taken, that the impetus for greater accountability will come from Strasbourg, and the barriers in the way of using the HRA in the domestic courts to create more accountability look almost insurmountable, except, to an extent, in criminal proceedings. It has been suggested that the impetus is most likely to come from pressure from the current oversight mechanisms themselves, especially the Parliamentary Committee, from MPs and from commentators. It is possible that greater accountability will be achieved through the operation of the single tribunal but, as argued below, its efficacy is clearly open to question.

4 The interception of communications

Introduction

The interception of communications clearly presents a profound threat to the core value of privacy identified in the Introduction to Part III, informational autonomy. However, a state has a duty to preserve national security and to prevent and detect crime. But, as Leigh and Lustgarten put it: 'in attempting to protect democracy from threats such as terrorism there is the ever-present risk that . . . that which was to be preserved has been lost.'[170] The approach which succeeds in preserving respect for democracy and for the value of individual privacy, as a hallmark of democracy, while affording respect to state interests, is one which is increasingly reflected in the jurisprudence of the European Court of Human Rights, even taking into account the wide margin of appreciation conceded in this particular area.[171]

---

170 Leigh and Lustgarten, *In from the Cold* 1994, p 41.
171 See, e.g., the pronouncements of the Court in *Klass v FRG* (1978) 2 EHRR 214.

Methods of communication and, in response, methods of interception have become increasingly sophisticated. Telephonic interception was possible for much of the twentieth century, but its incidence and the interception facilities have recently increased.[172] In other words, its value in terms of combating crime and terrorism has long been recognised. But legal recognition of the harm interception causes, in terms of creating invasions of privacy, has lagged behind. Prior to 1985, there was no requirement to follow a particular legal procedure when authorising the tapping of telephones or the interception of mail. The tapping of telephones was neither a civil wrong[173] nor a criminal offence. Interference with mail was a criminal offence under s 58 of the Post Office Act 1953, but under s 58(1) such interference would not be criminal if authorised by a warrant issued by the Secretary of State. The conditions for issuing warrants for interception of postal or telephonic communications were laid down in administrative rules which had no legal force.[174] Under these rules, the interception could be authorised in order to assist in a criminal investigation only if the crime was really serious, normal methods had been tried and had failed, and there was good reason for believing that the evidence gained by the interception would lead to a conviction. If the interception related to security matters, it could be authorised only in respect of major subversion, terrorism or espionage, and the matters obtained had to be directly useful to the Security Service in compiling information allowing it to carry out its function of protecting state security.

The Interception of Communications Act 1985 was introduced as a direct result of the ruling in the European Court of Human Rights in *Malone v UK*[175] that the existing British warrant procedure violated the Art 8 guarantee of privacy. The Court held that UK domestic law did not regulate the circumstances in which telephone tapping could be carried out sufficiently clearly or provide any remedy against abuse of the power. This meant that it did not meet the requirement of being 'in accordance with the law' under Art 8(2). The decision therefore required the UK Government to introduce legislation to regulate the circumstances in which the power to tap could be used.

Thus, the driving force behind the response of the UK Government in the Interception of Communications Act 1985 was the need to provide a statutory basis for interception. Nevertheless, it was an incomplete reform. Despite its misleading name, the 1985 Act only covered certain limited means of intercepting communications. It did not cover interception by means of listening devices or all forms of telephone tapping. It covered the interception of only one means of telephonic communication – communication via the public telecommunications system. This covered telephone, fax, telex and any other data transmission on the system, such as e-mail.[176] Given the immense increase in the use of mobile phones,[177] pagers, cordless phones, the potential for e-mail transmission

---

172 Report of the Commissioner under the Interception of Communications Act 1998, published June 1999, Cm 4364, p 2, para 13 and p 11.
173 *Malone v MPC (No 2)* [1979] Ch 344.
174 See Report of the Committee of Privy Councillors, Cmnd 283, 1957.
175 (1984) 7 EHRR 14; for comment, see (1986) 49 MLR 86.
176 Prior to the inception of the RIPA 2000, the government maintained that some use of email was covered by the 1985 Act where public telephone lines were used.
177 Mobile-to-mobile communication would appear to fall outside the 1985 Act. Mobile communication which partially uses the telecommunications system (when a system such as BT Cellnet or Vodafone sends a signal to the telecommunications system) may be within it.

outside the telecommunications system, and the growth of internal telephone systems over recent years, the Act became increasingly marginalised. Marginalisation was likely to increase since e-mails are likely to be sent more frequently via mobile phones, using satellites.[178] It was therefore apparent that the statutory basis for interception provided by the 1985 Act was inadequate and would probably be shown to be so in reliance on the HRA.[179] The Labour Government responded by introducing a far more comprehensive basis under the Regulation of Investigatory Powers Act 2000, Part I.

The Regulation of Investigatory Powers Act 2000, Part I (RIPA)

The intention of the Labour Government was to bring all forms of interception within the RIPA, Part I so that the 1985 Act would be superseded and could be repealed.[180] Under s 2(1) of the RIPA, the term 'public telecommunications system' used in s 2(1) of the 1985 Act, covers any system 'which exists (whether wholly or partly in the UK or elsewhere) for the purpose of facilitating the transmission of communications by any means involving the use of electrical or electro-magnetic energy'. This includes all such systems which provide or offer a telecommunications service to the public or part of it. This definition would cover all the forms of communication, including e-mail, mentioned above, provided by any private company.[181] Section 2(1) of the RIPA also covers private telecommunications systems – most obviously those confined to a particular company or body – although its coverage of private systems is limited to those which are attached to the public system directly or indirectly.[182] Its wording appears to be wide enough to cover most forms of telecommunication currently available, apart from entirely self-standing private systems,[183] although not necessarily those which may arise in the near future. Ironically, the point was made in Parliamentary debate that 'the Bill does not recognise the changing technologies'.[184]

Issuance of warrants

The 1985 Act provided very wide grounds under s 2(2) on which warrants for the purposes of interception could be authorised by the Secretary of state, and the same grounds appear in the RIPA, with one addition. Under s 5(3) RIPA, a warrant may be issued if necessary '(a) in the interests of national security'; '(b) for the purpose of preventing or detecting serious crime';[185] or '(c) for the purpose of safeguarding the economic

---

178   Possibly without use of a 'server' computer.
179   See the Consultation Paper 'Interception of Communications in the UK' (1999) Cm 4368.
180   Part I has repealed the key sections of the 1985 Act: ss 1–10, s 11(2)–(5), Sched 1.
181   These would include, e.g., BT, Orange, Vodafone. It would also cover other providers of e-mail systems such as Freeserve or Yahoo. However, it is in fact unclear that the technology to intercept emails sent via the internet is available. Such emails are sent by so called 'split package' technology; the message is split into a number of different packages, sent by different global routes. If a hundred million messages are sent a day, split into tiny particles, interception of particular messages may be difficult.
182   Its coverage of private systems is a direct response to *Halford v UK* [1997] IRLR 471.
183   Such as intranet systems not connected to any public system.
184   HC Deb Col 806, 6 March 2000.
185   Defined in s 81(3).

well-being of the UK'. In relation to the third ground, the information must relate, under s 5(5), to 'the acts or intentions of persons outside the British Isles'. This wording almost exactly reproduces that used under s 2(4) of the 1985 Act. These grounds are significantly wider than those under the old Home Office guidelines previously relied upon in order to authorise warrants. The last ground falls under sub-para (d): 'in circumstances appearing to the Secretary of state to be equivalent to those in which he would issue a warrant by virtue of paragraph (b), for the purpose of giving effect to the provisions of any international mutual assistance agreement.' This ground relates to Art 16 of the EU draft Convention on Mutual Assistance in Criminal Matters.[186] Its purpose is to require satellite operators based in the UK to provide technical assistance to another member state. The discussion below reveals that the safeguards relating to warrants issued on this ground are significantly weaker than those relating to the other three. This is an instance in which the EU's 'Third Pillar' policies relating to law and order and national security have allowed decisions to be taken on matters which may infringe human rights, possibly to the extent of breaching the Convention. Such decisions are taken within 'a framework where the EU's democratic deficit is most prominent'.[187]

Section 5(2) of the RIPA, however, contains a stronger proportionality requirement than that which was contained in s 2(3) of the 1985 Act. The Secretary of State 'shall not' issue an interception warrant unless he believes that the conduct it authorises 'is proportionate to what is sought to be achieved'. This includes asking, under s 5(4), whether the information which it is thought necessary to obtain under the warrant could reasonably be obtained by other means. This question also had to be asked under s 2(3). But s 5(2) implies that further matters should be considered. For example, where the information *cannot* reasonably be obtained by other means, the proportionality of the particular interception warrant with its objective could still be considered. This might involve considering its contents and duration. Clearly, s 5(2) was introduced in an effort to meet the proportionality requirement under Art 8(2), discussed below. Under s 7(1) of the RIPA, the warrants must be personally signed by the Secretary of State or, under s 7(2) in urgent cases, or cases under the fourth ground, by 'a senior official' with express authorisation from the Secretary of State. A 'senior official' is defined in s 81(1) as 'a member of the Senior Civil Service' and under s 81(7) the Secretary of State 'may by order make . . . amendments [to] the definition of "senior official"'. Under the 1985 Act the official had to be 'an official of his Department of or above the rank of Assistant Under Secretary of State'. In this respect, the requirements have been relaxed under the RIPA.

This procedure is based on the model previously provided by the 1985 Act in that it allows for administrative oversight, but maintains executive authorisation of interception; it may therefore be contrasted with that in the US, where prior judicial

---

186 The EU draft Convention on Mutual Assistance in Criminal Matters (5202/98-C4–0062/98) was set out in the EU-FBI telecommunications plan adopted by the EU in January 1995. Under ENFOPOL, the information required includes e-mail addresses, credit card details, passwords, IP addresses, customer account numbers.

187 Norton-Taylor, R, in Blackburn, R, and Plant, R, (eds), *Constitutional Reform: The Labour Government's Constitutional Reform Agenda*, 1999, p 208. See also *Enhancing Parliamentary Scrutiny of the Third Pillar,* Select Committee of the European Communities, HL Session 1997–98, 31.7.97.

authorisation is required,[188] and with that in Denmark where authorisation is by an investigating magistrate.[189] A Commissioner was appointed under s 8 of the 1985 Act; the appointment is now of the Interception of Communications Commissioner under s 57(8) of the RIPA. The Commissioner has a role in overseeing the issuance of warrants, but this is a general review role, which occurs after the event. The possibility of replacing an executive with a judicial mechanism was entirely rejected by the Labour Government. In debate on the Bill, it received support only from the Liberal Democrats.[190] Judicial involvement only at the complaint stage (discussed below) is of little significance as a safeguard since many persons will have no means of knowing that tapping is occurring. Nevertheless, prior judicial involvement in authorising warrants cannot be said at present to be a requirement of Art 8.[191]

Under s 4(5) and (6) of the 1985 Act, the warrants were issued for an initial period of two months and could be renewed for one month in the case of the police and for six months in the case of the security and intelligence services. Under s 9(6) of the 2000 Act, warrants are issued for an initial period of three months if by the Secretary of State and can be renewed for six months if he states his belief that the grounds under s 5(3)(a) or (c) apply. If the other grounds apply, the renewal period is three months. If signed by a senior official, they can be issued initially for five working days but renewed for three months. In the case of all warrants, particularly those issued in respect of the prevention or detection of serious crime, to the police, these are significant increases. The period in respect of the serious crime ground may be compared with that in Denmark, which is four weeks, renewable.[192]

As was the case under the 1985 Act, there is no overall limit on renewals and so some warrants are very long standing. The number of interception warrants issued is increasing. The Commissioners' Reports only cover the warrants authorised by the Home Office and Scottish Office. These figures show that at the end of 1989, 315 warrants were in force and 522 were issued during the year.[193] By 1993, a clear upward trend in the numbers of warrants issued was evident: in 1993, 1,005 warrants for telephone tapping and 115 for mail interceptions were issued; 409 warrants were in force at the end of the year.[194] The trend continued: in 1996 1,795 telecommunications warrants were in force or were issued during the year; by 1998, the figure had risen to 2,251.[195] In 2003 2525 warrants were issued by the Home Office.[196] As the Commissioner accepts,

---

188 *Berger v NY* (1967) 388 US 41.
189 Code of Criminal Procedure, Art 126m.
190 HC Deb Col 8076, March 2000.
191 *Klass v FRG* (1978) 2 EHRR 214; *Mersch v Luxembourg* 43 D & R 34 (1985).
192 Code of Criminal Procedure, Art 126m.
193 Report of the Commissioner for 1989, Cm 1063, p 2. Similar figures are available for other years; see reports for 1986, Cm 108 and for 1987, Cm 351.
194 See Report of the Commissioner for 1993, Cm 2522.
195 For example, the figure for postal interceptions rose from 115 in 1996 to 167 in 1998. Figures from the Report of the Commissioner under the Interception of Communications Act for 1998 published June 1999, Cm 4364, p 11.
196 The full figures of Warrants (a) in force, under the Regulation of Investigatory Powers Act, as at 31 December 2003 and (b) issued during the period 1 January 2003 and 31 December 2003 are: Home Secretary 705 1878, the total number of RIPA modifications from 01/01/2003 to 31/12/03 = 2525; Scottish Executive 41 105, the total number of RIPA modifications from 01/01/2003 to 31/12/03 = 319. Under the Regulation of Investigatory Powers Act 2000 there is no longer a breakdown of the

these figures do not provide a satisfactory guide as to the number of persons subject to interception, since a single warrant can cover a large organisation. The figures do not cover all the warrants authorised, since those authorised by other departments, including the Foreign Office, are viewed as too sensitive.

Section 8(1) of RIPA suggests that the warrants should be precise; they must specify a person or an address. However, a 'person' can equal 'any organisation and any association or combination of persons'.[197] Once a warrant is obtained, all communications to or from the property or 'person' specified must be intercepted, if that is what is required in order to give effect to the warrant.[198] Failure to comply with the warrant is an offence under s 11(7) carrying a maximum sentence of two years. Under s 11(4), telephone tapping and mail interceptions are conducted by Post Office or 'public telecommunications employees' or by persons controlling or partly controlling private systems wholly or partly in the UK.[199]

Under s 6(2), the request for the warrant may be made by a number of persons from a non-exhaustive list. They include: the Director General of the Security Service, the Chief of MI6, the Director of GCHQ, the Director General of the National Criminal Intelligence Service, the Commissioner of Police of the Metropolis; the Chief Constable of the RUC, Chief Constables in Scotland,[200] the Commissioners of Customs and Excise; the Chief of Defence; the relevant person for the purposes of any international mutual assistance agreement. The Bill originally provided: 'or any such other person as the Secretary of State may by order designate.' The government was eventually persuaded to omit the last provision. A number of other such powers are, however, scattered throughout the Act, meaning that this statute, comprehensive as it is, leaves open a great deal of leeway for significant and more covert extension. On Second Reading of the Bill in the Commons this list was criticised on two grounds. The Conservative opposition considered that the list was not extensive enough and that, in particular, the Benefits Agency of the DSS[201] and the Inland Revenue[202] should be added to it. The Liberal Democrats, supported by Tom King, Chair of the Intelligence and Security Committee, argued that primary legislation, not a statutory instrument, should be used in order to add bodies to the list.[203]

Lawful interception without a warrant

Sections 3 and 4 of the RIPA allow for lawful interception without a warrant. Section 3(2) covers instances where it is reasonably believed that both parties to the communication

---

figures between Telecommunications and Letters. Figures from the Report of the Commissioner under the Interception of Communications Act for 2003.

197 RIPA 2000, s 78(1) which, with the addition of an 'association', reproduces s 10(1) of the 1985 Act.

198 Section 11(4).

199 Bearing in mind the range of companies which are affected and the difficulty of complying, especially in relation to the internet, a provision regarding practicality was necessary. Section 11(5) recognises that there may be circumstances under which it is not reasonably practicable to comply with the duty to implement the warrant. The prosecution must prove that it was practicable.

200 'Of any police force maintained under or by virtue of section 1 of the Police (Scotland) Act 1967.'

201 HC Deb Cols 778 and 831, 6 March 2000.

202 HC Deb Col 821, 6 March 2000.

203 HC Deb Cols 768 and 831, 6 March 2000.

have consented to the interception.[204] In such circumstances, the interception must also be authorised within Part II, s 26. This provision effects a compromise in relation to so called 'participant monitoring' (where one party is aware of the interception). It was pointed out in the leading Canadian authority[205] that the consent of one party does not affect the infringement of privacy suffered by the other. But s 3(2) does not demand that 'participant monitoring' should be subject to the controls necessary for other interceptions; it is subject only to the lesser controls for 'directed' surveillance, discussed below. Section 4 covers persons whose communications are intercepted who are believed to be outside the UK, instances where the Secretary of State has made regulations covering the interception for business[206] purposes (s 4(2)), and instances in psychiatric hospitals or prisons (within the relevant applicable statutes). These provisions may raise questions as to their compatibility with the Convention, which are considered below.

Use of the intercepted material

Section 15 provides safeguards regarding the use of the intercepted material. They are intended to limit the persons who can see the material and to ensure that it is destroyed once it is no longer necessary to retain it for the authorised purposes. However, the Act does not state how these objectives are to be achieved; it is left to the Secretary of State to put arrangements into place to secure them. Further, s 15 does not apply to material obtained without warrant, under ss 3 or 4. Since, as indicated below, personal criminal intelligence information obtained from interceptions and then stored and processed electronically is not subject to the stronger controls under the data protection regime of the 1998 Data Protection Act, it is clear that the controls created under s 15 are potentially crucial in protecting this aspect of privacy.

Unauthorised interceptions

Section 1 of the 1985 Act dealt with unauthorised interceptions and made it a criminal offence to intercept a postal communication or telecommunication intentionally without authorisation. It did not cover taps outside the public telecommunications system. So, for example, no criminal or even civil wrong was committed by the Chief Constable of Merseyside when a tap on the internal police phone system was used against Alison Halford in order to seek to discredit her and undermine her sex discrimination claim against the police service.[207] The RIPA, which under s 1 reproduces the old s 1 offence with extensions, also covers interception of private systems, unless they are entirely freestanding. However, it is subject to an exception under s 1(6) which might have been applicable in the *Halford* case.[208] Section 1(6) provides that conduct is excluded from criminal liability if the interceptor 'is a person with a right to control the operation

---

204 This provision is clearly more protective of privacy than its counterpart under the 1985 Act, s 1(2), which relied on the consent of one party only.
205 *Duarte* [1990] 53 CCC (3d) 1.
206 'Business' includes government departments.
207 See *Halford v UK* (1997) 24 EHRR 523.
208 Ibid.

or the use of the system; or he has the express or implied consent of the [person intercepted]'. Section 1(3) creates civil liability in relation to unauthorised interception of a private, not a public system. Possibly in future, therefore, a person in a situation similar to that of Alison Halford might be able to bring a civil action only.

The role of the Commissioner

The Commissioner is a senior judge appointed by the Prime Minister on a part time basis to monitor the warrant procedure and to consider complaints. He had a duty under s 8(1)(a) of the 1985 Act, which is now continued under s 57(2)(a) of the RIPA, to keep the warrant procedure under review. Apart from the statutory limitations of his powers, the practical constraints on them have been overwhelming. He had no staff and carried out the checking procedure personally on a part time basis. Clearly, as he accepts, these constraints precluded consideration of every warrant which is brought to his attention. His powers were very limited. He could not order that warrants should be quashed or that the material obtained should be destroyed; under s 8(9) he could merely report a contravention of ss 2–5 to the Prime Minister, which had not already been the subject of a tribunal report, or a contravention of s 6 which covered destruction of material, and he had to prepare an annual report for the Prime Minister under s 8(6). These arrangements regarding checking of warrants were largely continued under RIPA, under ss 57[209] and 58 when the office became that of the Interception of Communications Commissioner, although staff can be appointed. His complaints role was taken over by the single tribunal.

The remit of the Commissioner gave him the opportunity to note that unauthorised tapping had occurred, but only when he was informed of it by the agencies concerned. Where he was so informed, he was told at the same time that the unauthorised action had been recognised, usually 'immediately', and all resultant material destroyed. His view was that these unauthorised actions, that is, criminal offences under s 1, termed 'errors' were 'comparatively few in number when considered in the context of the volume and complexity of the operations carried out'.[210] In his 2003 Report the Commissioner stated: 'A significant number of errors and breaches have been reported to me during the course of the year – 39 in all. Although the level of errors is the same as that in 2002, the number is still unacceptably high.'[211] In 2004 45 errors were reported to him and again he commented that his was unacceptable. In his annual reports, the Commissioner found no instance in which a warrant was issued unjustifiably. Although Crown servants, telecommunications and postal workers were under a duty to provide the Commissioner with the information he required to carry out his task, under s 8(3) of the 1985 Act (continued and extended to a wider range of people under the 2000 Act),[212] he had no effective means of checking that information had not been withheld.

209 Under s 57(2), 'Subject to subsection (5), the Interception of Communications Commissioner shall keep under review the exercise and performance by the Secretary of State of the powers and duties conferred or imposed on him by or under sections 1 to 11'.
210 Report of the Commissioner under the Interception of Communications Act 1998, published June 1999, Cm 4364, p 10.
211 Report of the Interception of Communications Commissioner for 2003, para 32.
212 See s 58(1), s 21(4) and s 49.

He received a list of warrants issued, renewed, modified or cancelled since the last visit, and checked a sample of them. He had no means of knowing whether the list was in fact complete, and unauthorised interception was not, unsurprisingly, recorded on it. These basic limitations affecting his role remained unchanged under the RIPA arrangements. The key reform under the RIPA was to the tribunal system.

It may be noted that the Interception of Communications Commissioner claims not to be a public body under the FoI. Technically, the Interception of Communications Commissioner may not be designated as a public body yet, but the office certainly meets both of the conditions in the Freedom of Information Act 2000, s 4 (Amendment of Schedule 1 to be included in the list of Public Bodies by Order). The first condition is that the body or office – (a) is established by virtue of Her Majesty's prerogative or by an enactment or by subordinate legislation, or (b) is established in any other way by a Minister of the Crown in his capacity as Minister, by a government department or by the National Assembly for Wales. The second condition is (a) in the case of a body, that the body is wholly or partly constituted by appointment made by the Crown, by a Minister of the Crown, by a government department or by the National Assembly for Wales, or (b) in the case of an office, that appointments to the office are made by the Crown, by a Minister of the Crown, by a government department or by the National Assembly for Wales. It appears that both of these criteria are clearly fulfilled by Regulation of Investigatory Powers Act 2000, s 57 and by the appointment process for the Interception of Communications Commissioner.

Reform of the tribunal system

Section 7 of the 1985 Act established a Tribunal to consider complaints from people who believed that their telephone had been tapped or their mail intercepted. It should be noted that the statutory provisions had no retrospective effect. Thus, complaints could relate only to post-commencement activities. The RIPA set up a new tribunal, under s 65, which as indicated above, replaced the old one and also those set up under the Security Services Act and the Intelligence Services Act. It also took over the role of Commissioners in hearing complaints under s 102, and Sched 7 to the Police Act 1997, (discussed below) and it also acquired a role in considering surveillance undertaken by other public authorities. It is able to consider pre-commencement activity, within certain limitations. Thus, its role extends well beyond that of the old Interceptions of Communications Tribunal. It therefore has immense significance as the central mechanism protecting citizens against abuse of state surveillance powers. Apart from the President of the Tribunal and Vice-President, both of whom are senior judges, seven senior members of the legal profession serve on the Tribunal. A Registrar has also been appointed to help in the process of hearing claims alleging infringements of the Human Rights Act. The Tribunal is discussed fully below.[213]

The old tribunal set up under the 1985 Act (which consisted of five senior lawyers) had a duty under s 7(3) of that Act, on receiving a complaint, to investigate whether a warrant had been issued and if so, whether it was properly issued – whether there were adequate grounds for issuing it and whether statutory procedures were complied with. Under s 7(4), the tribunal applied 'the principles applicable by a court on an

213 Pages 1080 *et seq.*

application for judicial review' to this exercise. The tribunal could only consider the matters referred to in ss 2–5 of the 1985 Act concerning the issuance of warrants; it could not consider the questions whether the action was proportionate to the invasion of privacy and whether the action could have been carried out by other means.

The Report of the Commissioner for 1998 stated that the tribunal received 75 complaints in 1998, of which 72 were investigated and none was upheld.[214] The 1997 Report[215] stated that since it was established in 1986, the tribunal had received 568 complaints and that none had ever been upheld. According to the Report, in only eight of these cases was interception being carried out by a government agency and in each case it was properly authorised. The possibility that in some of the other 560 cases, or in others, unauthorised interception was occurring was seen in the Report as 'very remote' since it would involve a criminal conspiracy between the agency and the Public Telecommunications Operators. It may be noted that the 1985 Act did not provide any possibility of recognising that an invasion of privacy could occur due to the possibility that a phone had been tapped. The European Court of Human Rights accepted in *Klass v Federal Republic of Germany*[216] that this possibility represented a continuing invasion of privacy, since conversations would be inhibited.

Parliamentary oversight

Under the 1985 Act, parliamentary oversight, such as it was, was limited to interceptions which fell within the statute. Under RIPA, the oversight is equally limited, but it covers a far wider range of interceptions. Modelled on the old arrangements, the annual report of the current Commissioner must be presented to Parliament and published as a Command Paper, under s 58(6). The Prime Minister may censor the report under s 58(7) if it appears to him that it contains matter 'prejudicial to national security, to the prevention and detection of serious crime or to the economic well-being of the UK'. These grounds are the same as the previous ones under the 1985 Act. A new, broad one was added: the matter may be excluded if it appears to be prejudicial to 'the continued discharge of the functions of any public authority whose activities include activities that are subject to review by that Commissioner'. It appears to be unnecessary, in any event, for the Prime Minister to censor the report; the practice has been for the Commissioner to designate the part to be withheld.

Thus, parliamentary oversight continues to be highly circumscribed under the current oversight system since no Committee is directly charged with monitoring state surveillance. Bearing in mind the brevity of the Commissioner's reports, the opportunity for Parliament to oversee these arrangements is very limited. The parliamentary oversight is clearly much weaker than that applicable in Germany, as considered in the *Klass* case[217] (below). The opportunity of enabling the comprehensive interceptions statute to reflect notions of openness and accountability to Parliament in the era of the Human Rights and Freedom of Information Acts was lost.

---

214 Report of the Commissioner under the Interception of Communications Act 1998, published June 1999, Cm 4364, p 10.
215 Cm 4001.
216 (1978) 2 EHRR 214.
217 Ibid.

The impact of the HRA

As indicated, Part I of the RIPA was intended to be compatible with the requirements of the Convention. Since it allows for state invasion of privacy, the Convention Article of most relevance is Art 8. The discussion below identifies some of the aspects of Part I which are arguably of doubtful compatibility with Art 8. It then goes on to consider the effect of the HRA in this context and the means available under it of seeking to ensure that the Convention rights are adhered to when interception is used.

Interference with the primary rights

As indicated above, the interception of communications is likely to represent an interference with the Art 8(1) rights to respect for private life, the home and correspondence. The Strasbourg Court found in *Klass*[218] that the possibility that an interception was occurring could infringe Art 8, and this was also accepted in *Malone v UK*.[219] In *Klass*, the Court said: 'in the mere existence of the legislation itself there is involved, for all those to whom the legislation could be applied, a menace of surveillance; this menace necessarily strikes at freedom of communication between users of the postal and telecommunications services . . .'[220] Thus, the provisions of the 1985 Act could be viewed as representing a continuing invasion of privacy, whether or not in any individual case an intercept had actually been used, and the same can now be said of Part I of the RIPA.

As the Strasbourg Court explained in *Halford v UK*,[221] under the Convention the issue would be whether, on the particular facts, the essence of the complaint concerned the actual application to her of the measures of surveillance or that her Art 8 rights were menaced by the very existence of the law and practice permitting such measures. *Halford v UK* concerned the tapping of the applicant's office telephone by the police at a time when she was bringing a claim of sex discrimination against the police authority in question. The government argued that in using the private internal office system, the applicant could not expect to retain her privacy and that an employer should in principle be able to monitor calls made by an employee on the internal system without prior warning or consent.[222] The Court disagreed, finding that calls made from business premises as well as the home may be covered by the notions of 'private life' and 'correspondence' within the meaning of Art 8(1). This stance was also taken in *Kopp v Switzerland*.[223] The Court emphasised in that case that the interception of the telephone calls constituted the interference with the right under para 1; the fact that the recordings were not subsequently used was irrelevant. Thus, the Court has taken quite a broad approach, strongly protective of informational autonomy, to the meaning of the terms used in Art 8(1), thereby widening their application beyond obviously private spheres, including the home. The use made of material obtained from intercepts, including disclosure to others, may also fall within Art 8(1).[224]

218 (1978) 2 EHRR 214.
219 (1984) 7 EHRR 14.
220 See p 21, para 41.
221 [1997] IRLR 471; (1997) 24 EHRR 523.
222 Para 43.
223 (1999) 27 EHRR 91, paras 70–71.
224 *MS v Sweden* (1999) 28 EHRR 313.

In accordance with the law

As indicated above, state interference with the Art 8 guarantees must be in accordance with the law, under para 2, if it is to be justified and this requirement covers not only the existence of national law, but its quality. In *Halford v UK*,[225] the interception of the internal office telephone was clearly not in accordance with the law since domestic law provided no regulation at all of such interception, and therefore the Court found a breach of Art 8.

Part I of the RIPA was introduced in response to the findings in *Halford v UK*[226] and, generally, to provide a statutory basis for interception outside the public telecommunications system. Thus, a basis in national law currently exists. Once such a basis is found, its quality must be considered; it must be asked whether it is 'compatible with the rule of law . . . there must be a measure of legal protection in domestic law against arbitrary interferences by public authorities with [the right to respect for private life under Art 8(1)]. Especially where a power of the executive is exercised in secret, the risks of arbitrariness are evident.'[227] In *Kopp v Switzerland*[228] the Court clearly stated that the essential requirements of a national legal basis are those of accessibility and foreseeability so that, in this context, the citizen is sufficiently aware of the circumstances allowing interception. It must be clear as to the 'circumstances in and conditions on which public authorities are empowered to resort to any such secret measures'.[229]

In *Christie v UK*,[230] the 1985 Act was found to meet this requirement in relation to the terms 'national security' and 'economic well being'. The Commission viewed those terms as sufficiently precise since they had been explained by 'administrative or executive statements'. The Interception of Communications Tribunal had investigated and had found no breach in relation to the warrant procedure; this could be taken to mean that no warrant had been issued, a matter outside the jurisdiction of the tribunal, or that one had been properly issued. The other issue concerned the retention of information collected through the tap by the Security Service. It is notable, however, that this was a decision of the Commission only, that it was influenced by the margin of appreciation doctrine and that it was not made in the context of the 'serious crime' provision under the Act.

In *Kruslin v France*,[231] a basis in law was found for interception but it was not found to be of sufficient quality owing to its imprecision, which was found to fail to satisfy the requirement of foreseeability.[232] Similarly, in *Kopp v Switzerland*, which was also concerned with crime, not national security, the Court said: 'interception . . . constitutes a particularly serious interference with private life and correspondence and

---

225 (1997) 24 EHRR 523.
226 Ibid.
227 *Malone v UK* A 82, para 67; 4 EHRR 330. The Court reaffirmed this in *Halford v UK* (1997) 24 EHRR 523 above: 'this expression . . . relates to the quality [of domestic law], requiring it to be compatible with the rule of law' (para 49).
228 (1999) 27 EHRR 91, paras 70–71.
229 *Halford v UK* (1997) 24 EHRR 523, para 49.
230 78-A DR E Com HR 119.
231 (1990) 12 EHRR 528.
232 Ibid, para 30. See also *Huvig v France* (1990) 12 EHRR 528, para 29.

must accordingly be based on a "law" that is particularly precise.'[233] In another case outside the realm of national security or economic well being, *Valenzuela v Spain*,[234] the Court also found that the legal basis available for interception did not satisfy the requirements of foreseeability. In particular, the conditions necessary under the Convention to satisfy that requirement, including the nature of the offences which might give rise to an intercept order, were not included in the relevant provisions.[235] A development towards greater stringency appears to be evident in the jurisprudence, at least within the 'prevention of crime' context.

It is arguable that the 1985 Act did not fully meet the 'in accordance with the law' requirement since, *inter alia*, the serious crime ground was not defined as *Valenzuela v Spain* requires. It is defined in the RIPA, albeit in broad terms.[236] The question whether Part I of the RIPA meets this requirement in all respects remains open, bearing in mind the possible future development of the Strasbourg jurisprudence on this matter. The grounds under s 5(3), including the 'mutual assistance' ground, are clearly ill defined.

The fact that the Act provides for authorisation by executive, rather than judicial warrant, is also relevant to the requirement of foreseeability. In *Kopp v Switzerland*, in finding a breach of Art 8 for failure to satisfy that requirement, the Court said: 'it is . . . astonishing that this task should be assigned to an official of the Post Office's legal department, who is a member of the executive, without supervision by an independent judge.'[237]

The provision under s 3 of the RIPA allowing for interception with consent on the basis of reasonable belief may be questionable under Art 8, depending on the steps which must be taken in practice to establish the consent, especially in relation to the *recipient* of the communication.[238] Moreover, the authorisation procedure is less demanding than that in relation to interception by warrant and might appear, therefore, to be out of accord with the requirement of quality. However, at the present time the procedure is in principle in accordance with Art 8. The Court has found that where one party to the conversation had given consent under the equivalent provision of the 1985 Act, s 1(2), Art 8 was not breached since citizens would be sufficiently aware of the risk.[239]

Legitimate aims and necessit·· in a democratic society

If an interference is 'in accordance with the law', it must have a legitimate aim and be necessary in a democratic society. The legitimate aims under Art 8(2), set out above,[240] are very broad and echo those used under s 5(3), apart from the fourth one. But since

233 Ibid, para 44.
234 (1998) 28 EHRR 483.
235 Ibid, para 75.
236 In s 81(3).
237 Ibid, para 46.
238 See *Lambert v France* (1999) 1 EHRLR 123. In *Kruslin v France* (1990) 12 EHRR 547, para 26, it was accepted that although the line of a third party had been tapped, an interference with the applicant's Art 8 rights had occurred, since his conversations on that line had been intercepted and recorded.
239 *Nadir Choudhary v UK* (1999) 1 EHRLR 522. See also *Smith v UK* [1997] EHRLR 277.
240 See pp 1027–28.

the aim of that ground is to prevent crime, this aim would almost certainly be viewed as legitimate. Thus, this requirement appears to be satisfied.

The Court has interpreted 'necessary in a democratic society' as meaning: 'an interference corresponds to a pressing social need and, in particular, that it is proportionate to the legitimate aim pursued.'[241] The scrutiny of proportionality in a particular instance, as Chapters 2 and 4 indicated, is strongly linked to the extent of the margin of appreciation conceded to the state. The width of that margin appears to depend partly on the aim of the interference in question. In relation to the aim of national security, the Court has allowed a very wide margin to the state.

In *Klass v Federal Republic of Germany*[242] the European Court of Human Rights found, bearing the margin of appreciation doctrine in mind, that German telephone tapping procedures were in conformity with Art 8 since they contained a number of safeguards. An oversight body, a Parliamentary board,[243] could consider, on an application from an aggrieved individual or *ex officio*, whether the interception had been authorised and its necessity. There was also quite a substantial degree of Parliamentary scrutiny: the Minister in question had to report to a parliamentary board and also to give an account of the interceptions ordered to a Commission. The possibility was available of compensation for persons whose phones had been unlawfully tapped and of challenges to interception in proceedings in the ordinary courts, and the individual warrants had to be reviewed by a Commission headed by a person qualified for judicial office.

The Court did not, however, state that these were the minimal safeguards necessary; it said:

> The Court considers that in a field where abuse is so easy in individual cases and could have such harmful consequences for democratic society as a whole, it is in principle desirable to entrust supervisory control to a judge. Nevertheless, having regard to the supervisory and other safeguards provided . . . the Court concludes that the exclusion of judicial control does not exceed the limits of what may be deemed necessary in a democratic society. The Parliamentary Board and the . . . Commission are independent of the authorities carrying out the surveillance, and are vested with sufficient powers and competence to exercise an effective and continuous control. Furthermore, the democratic character is reflected in the balanced membership of the Parliamentary Board. The Opposition is reflected on this body and is therefore able to participate in the control of the measures ordered by the . . . Minister . . .[244]

In *Christie v UK*,[245] the Commission found: 'having regard to the wide margin of appreciation in this area' the safeguards provided by the Interception of Communications Tribunal and the Commissioner were sufficient in the instant case where the applicant was a trade unionist with links with communist Eastern Europe and his phone was

---

241 *Olsson v Sweden* A 130 (1988), para 67.
242 (1978) 2 EHRR 214.
243 Under Law G10.
244 Ibid, p 235.
245 78-A DR E Com HR 119.

being tapped on the grounds of 'national security' and 'economic well-being'. The interception was proportionate to those legitimate aims, on the facts of the case. Similar findings were made, rather readily, by the Commission in *Remmers and Hamer v The Netherlands*[246]in the context of serious crime.

Bearing in mind the findings in *Klass*, the findings in *Christie* need not be taken as absolutely conclusive evidence that the oversight mechanisms provided by the 1985 Act, and maintained, with modifications, under Part I of RIPA, meet Convention requirements. They were made in relation to the particular case, not as abstract comment on the mechanisms or on the warrant procedure in general, and they were heavily influenced by the margin of appreciation. As indicated in Chapter 4, that doctrine is not available at national level and this, it is contended, means that it should not influence national decision makers, including judges acting judicially or extra-judicially, and other national bodies. The government and the Commissioner have assumed that the decision in *Christie* closes the question as far as the 1985 Act is concerned and as the statement of compatibility accompanying it demonstrates, the government takes this stance in respect of Part I, Chapter I of the RIPA as well. But in respect of interception under warrant, under the RIPA, the issue could be re-opened at Strasbourg in future, under developments in the Court's jurisprudence, bearing in mind the possibility of changing standards in other member states.

Domestically, a national judge (probably sitting in the single tribunal,[247] not in an ordinary court) is theoretically free under the HRA to take a more rigorous look at the safeguards provided by the RIPA and at the necessity and proportionality of an interference. The approach taken in practice would depend on the tendency of the judge to follow the traditionalist model: it might well be found that traditional notions of deference to the executive in this sensitive area would yield the same result as adherence to the margin of appreciation doctrine. But a judge might be prepared to depart from a deferential stance outside the national security context. As indicated above, it is a statutory requirement for the Secretary of State or Senior Official to consider proportionality[248] in issuing a warrant. Therefore, the single tribunal is expected to consider whether the statutory requirements have been met, taking Strasbourg guidance into account under s 2 HRA, but adopting a more rigorous scrutiny. The continued lack of judicial authorisation under the RIPA should be considered, when looking at the necessity of an interference, bearing in mind the fact that the other safeguards available, including parliamentary oversight, are weaker than those considered in *Klass*. Complaints to the Tribunal cannot easily be 'categorised' under the three tribunal system that existed prior to RIPA, so it is not possible to detail those complaints that relate solely to the interception of communications. The Tribunal received 109 new applications during 2003 and completed its investigation of 43 of these during the year as well as concluding its investigation of 57 of the 67 cases carried over from 2001/2002. Seventy six cases have been carried forward to 2004[249] and 90 new applications were made in 2004. On no occasion has the Tribunal concluded that there has been a contravention of RIPA or the Human Rights Act 1998.

---

246 (1999) 27 EHRR CD 168.
247 Note that tribunal members, apart from the President, need not be judges (see Sched 3).
248 Section 5(2).
249 Report of the Interception of Communications Commissioner for 2003, para 30.

*Obligations of oversight bodies, of those applying for warrants
and of those carrying them out*

As a public authority under s 6 of the HRA, the Interception of Communications Commissioner has a duty to abide by the Convention rights in discharging his oversight role. The Commissioner should ensure that the agencies he oversees are themselves ensuring Convention compliance. The members of the agencies and telecommunications and postal workers are bound by s 6 not to infringe the Convention in carrying out their work. In other words, all the public authorities involved should comply with the requirements of the Convention.

Parliament is not bound by s 6, but in considering reports of the Commissioner or in debating any issues arising from the operation of the RIPA, it would be expected that the Convention requirements would be strictly borne in mind, especially as a statement of compatibility accompanied the Act.

Raising Convention issues in court proceedings

Under s 7(1)(b) of the HRA, Convention issues could be raised in prosecutions against agency members, police officers, telecommunications or postal workers or other public authorities in respect of the various offences arising from non-co-operation with state interception created under the 2000 Act. But this would not normally involve consideration of the key issue – the invasions of privacy allowed for under the RIPA. Consideration of the compatibility of intercepts with Art 8 in court proceedings appears to be almost entirely precluded by s 17 of the RIPA. Section 17 is based on s 9 of the 1985 Act which provided: 'In any proceedings before any court or tribunal, no evidence shall be adduced and no question asked in cross-examination which . . . tends to suggest that 'the offence under s 1 has been or is to be committed by postal or telecommunications workers or Crown Servants or 'that a warrant has been or is to be issued to any of those persons'.

Section 17 provides:

> subject to s 18, no evidence shall be adduced, question asked, assertion or disclosure made or other thing done in, for the purposes of or in connection with any legal proceedings which (in any manner) –
>
> (a) discloses, in circumstances from which its origin in anything falling within subsection (2) may be inferred, any of the contents of an intercepted communication or any related communications data; or
> (b) tends (apart from any such disclosure) to suggest that anything falling within subsection (2) has or may have occurred or be going to occur.

Section 17(2) covers:

> (a) conduct . . . that was or would be an offence under s 1(1) or (2) of this Act or under s 1 of the . . . 1985 Act;
> (b) a breach by the Secretary of State of his duty under section 1(4) of this Act;
> (c) the issue of an interception warrant or of a warrant under the . . . 1985 Act;

(d) the making of an application by any person for an interception warrant, or for a warrant under that Act;

(e) the imposition of any requirement on any person to provide assistance with giving effect to an interception warrant.

This is clearly a far more comprehensive clause than s 9, although it is subject to certain exceptions under s 18, which may allow Convention points to be raised, in accordance with the courts' duty under s 6 of the HRA. This rule is clearly arbitrary, since material deriving from the use of bugging and other surveillance devices can be adduced, as discussed below.

Section 18(1) provides that s 17(1) does not apply in proceedings before the tribunal, for an offence under the RIPA, s 1 of the 1985 Act, s 4(3)(a) of the Official Secrets Act, and a number of other provisions relating to the secrecy of interceptions. Section 18(4), (6), (7) and (9) provide a number of very significant exceptions not previously included. Section 18(4) applies, *inter alia*,[250] where the interception was by consent under s 3; s 18(6) provides that s 17(1)(b) does not prevent doing anything which discloses conduct for which a person has been convicted under ss1(1), 11(7), 19 or s 1 of the 1985 Act. Under s 18(7), s 17(1) does not prohibit disclosure of '(a) any information that continues to be available for disclosure' to the prosecution 'for the purpose only of enabling that person to determine what is required of him by his duty to secure [its] fairness' or (b) disclosure to a relevant judge[251] by order of the judge 'to be made to him alone'. Under s 18(8), a judge shall not order such a disclosure unless satisfied that 'the exceptional circumstances of the case make the disclosure essential in the interests of justice'. If disclosure is ordered, s 18(9) allows the judge, in 'exceptional circumstances', to 'direct the prosecution to make any admission of fact . . . that the judge thinks is essential in the interests of justice'. But any such direction must not, under s 18(10), contravene s 17(1). Thus, where intercept material is still available, its disclosure to the judge or to the prosecution may be ordered. It may be noted that the material may still be in existence at the time of the trial, since it is preserved, for the benefit of the prosecution, under s 15(4)(d). Communications data (details of calls made) may be adduced in evidence, since it is not an intercepted communication as defined in s 17(4), so long as it does not suggest that the offences in question have been committed.[252]

Section 9 of the 1985 Act meant that if an intercept had been used to obtain material, whether unauthorised or not, the information gained would be inadmissible in evidence. But s 9 only applied to the forms of interception which the Act covered. Section 9 was considered in two House of Lords' decisions, which led to a bizarre

---

250 Section 18(4) also provides that s 16(1)(a) does not apply if the interception was lawful by virtue of s 1(5)(c) (relating to stored material obtained under another statutory power), or s 4(1) (persons believed to be outside UK). For discussion of ss 17 and 18, see Mirfield, P, 'Regulation of Investigatory Powers Act 2000: Part 2: Evidential Aspects' [2001] Crim LR 91.

251 *Inter alia*, a judge of the High Court or Crown Court. This provision amends the Criminal Procedure and Investigations Act 1996, s 3(4).

252 This position continues that established under the 1985 Act in *Morgans v DPP* [2000] 2 WLR 386, HL; [1999] 1 WLR 968, CA in which it was found that s 9 of that Act does not preclude a court from receiving evidence of printouts obtained by a logging device.

and anomalous situation. In *Effick*,[253] the defendants were prosecuted for conspiracy to supply controlled drugs and police officers obtained part of the evidence against them by means of intercepting and taping their telephone calls. The offence under s 1 had not been committed since the calls taped were made on a cordless telephone which was not found to be part of 'a public telecommunications system' as required under s 1. The appellants were convicted, and appealed on the ground that the evidence deriving from the intercepted telephone calls should have been ruled inadmissible under s 9 of the Interception of Communications Act 1985, or under s 78 of the Police and Criminal Evidence Act 1984 (PACE), since they were made without a warrant for interception.

The House of Lords determined that argument under s 9 failed because its provisions were aimed at preventing disclosure of information which tended to suggest that the offence of unauthorised interception (under s 1(1) of the 1985 Act) had been committed by specified persons, or that a warrant had been or was to be issued to such persons. These matters were not in issue since the interception was not within the Act. Section 9 was not intended to render inadmissible evidence obtained which would not reveal such matters. Clear statutory language would have been needed to oust the principle that all logically probative evidence should be admitted. As this was not the case, and as the instance in question did not appear to fall within s 9, the evidence was admissible. The submission in respect of s 78 of PACE failed because it was not suggested that the police officers had deliberately contravened the 1985 Act. It was found that no unfairness to the defendants had occurred due to the admission of the evidence, but this begs the question whether the manner in which the evidence was obtained – on no legal basis and by means of a surreptitious act – could affect the fairness of the trial.

In *Preston*,[254] in contrast, a lawful intercept had occurred and the defence wanted admission of the material derived from it which, it was alleged, might have led to the acquittal of the defendants. In a decision which accepted somewhat reluctantly that the 1985 Act created a scheme designed to elevate the interests of secrecy above individual rights to privacy or to a fair trial, the House of Lords found that s 9 was designed to prevent information as to the manner of authorising and carrying out the intercepts from being uncovered at the trial. It was intended, *inter alia*, to prevent the defendant from seeking to uncover the source of information behind the decision to use an intercept. Thus, the defence had no right to obtain disclosure of the material deriving from the intercepts. Further, since on the proper interpretation of s 2(2) read in conjunction with s 6(3), destruction of material gained by the intercepts had to be undertaken once the criminal investigation (not the prosecution) was complete, such material would not be available.

The result of this decision was that although telephone tapping could be used as an investigative tool in the criminal process, material deriving directly from an intercept would not be admissible and the defence would not be allowed to ask any questions

---

253 [1994] 3 WLR 583; (1994) 99 Cr App R 312, HL; (1992) 95 Cr App R 427, CA. For criticism of the Court of Appeal decision, see Leigh, I (1992) 142 NLJ 944–45, 976–77; Smith, JC [1992] Crim LR 580. See generally Spencer (1999) 58 CLJ 43.

254 [1993] 4 All ER 638; (1994) 98 Cr App R 405, HL. For discussion, see Tomkins, A (1994) 57 MLR 941.

designed to discover whether an intercept was used. Thus, the prosecution might at times be disadvantaged, since some probative material would not be admissible,[255] but the other side of the coin was that material deriving from the intercept could not be disclosed to the defence even if (as the defence alleged in *Preston*) it might show the innocence of the defendants. One exception, favourable to the prosecution, to the rule deriving from s 9, as interpreted in *Preston*, was allowed in *Rasool* and *Choudhary*.[256] It was determined that where intercepts are consensual, material deriving from them will be admissible. The rule in s 9(1)(a) was not found to be sufficient to make consensual material inadmissible; it was found to be irrelevant to the question of admissibility that an offence had been committed in obtaining the evidence. *Choudhary's* appeal was dismissed while *Rasool's* was allowed on that ground. Similarly, in *Owen*,[257] the evidence deriving from an intercept was found to be admissible, on the basis that it did not suggest that the offence under s 1 had been committed. The defendant, in prison on remand, had admitted the offence with which he was charged in a phone call to his wife. He was deemed to have consented to the interception since notices warning of the likelihood of interception had been posted near telephones in the prison. The defendant claimed that he had not seen any such notice. But it was found that, on the basis that one of the parties had impliedly consented, the admission of the evidence would not suggest that the offence under s 1 of the Act had been committed.[258]

The anomalous result of *Effick* and *Preston* was that in one, unlawfully obtained evidence, favourable to the prosecution, could be used as part of the prosecution evidence, while in another, lawfully obtained evidence could not be used at the behest of the defence. However, the decision in *Morgans*[259] addressed this anomaly. The House of Lords found that s 9 covers intercepts both with and without warrant. These decisions appear to have influenced Part I of the RIPA. Most obviously, that statute covers most forms of communication so that the argument used in *Effick* regarding cordless phones cannot be raised. Section 18(4), which refers *inter alia* to interceptions without a warrant where one party has consented to the interception (s 3), covers the findings from *Rasool* and *Owen*. Significantly, in certain imprecisely defined circumstances, disclosure relating to intercept material can be made to the prosecution and, if ordered, to the judge. But the defence may remain unaware of the source of the material. The fact that the use of the intercept led to the uncovering of other evidence, which is adduced, might be relevant to any challenge the defence could mount to the evidence. This position may not accord with the equality of arms principle under Art 6 of the Convention, since prosecution and defence may not be equally affected by the unavailability of the evidence.[260] The compatibility of ss 17 and 18 with the Art 6(1) guarantee of a

---

255 This factor influenced the Commission in declaring the application from Preston inadmissible: *Preston v UK*, 2 July 1997, Appl No 24193/94; available from the Commission's website.

256 [1997] 4 All ER 439. Choudhary applied, unsuccessfully, to Strasbourg: *Choudhary v UK* (1999) 1 EHRLR 522. For a further exception, see *Aujla* [1998] 2 Cr App R 16.

257 [1999] 1 WLR 949.

258 Since under s 1(2) of the Act, interceptions without warrant but with consent is not an offence.

259 [2000] 2 WLR 386. For an interesting application of the *Morgans* argument, see *Sargent* [2001] UKHL 54.

260 This could be argued by analogy with the decisions in *Windisch v Austria* (1990) 13 EHRR 281 and *Kostovski v Netherlands* (1989) 12 EHRR 434.

fair trial may be raised. If the use of interception is lawful, and probative evidence is obtained, it is hard to identify the legitimate purpose of refusing to adduce it directly in court. Section 18 addresses the question of proportionality to a very limited extent, but the question arises whether the requirements of equality of arms can be satisfied by a provision which allows the intercept material to be disclosed to the prosecution but not to the defence. More generally, the question of the fairness of the trial arises in relation to the exclusion of probative evidence.

In circumstances similar to those in *Preston* in which the defence seeks disclosure of the intercept material which has evidential value, whether or not it has been disclosed to the prosecution, the defence could make representations to the judge under s 18(9)(b), arguing that the term 'exceptional circumstances' must be rendered compatible with Art 6 under s 3 of the HRA, taking into account the requirements of fairness in the particular instance.[261] If the material is crucial to the defence, but the judge refuses to make an order, an appeal could be mounted on the basis that the judge had not complied with Art 6. Perhaps the most difficult situation would arise where, as in *Malone*, the defence suspected that an unauthorised intercept had been used. The defence might wish to mount an argument that evidence causally related to such use, rather than directly deriving from it, should be excluded since it would not have been obtained but for the illegality. Such exclusion could be argued for under s 78 of PACE, interpreted compatibility with Art 6.[262] But ss 18(10) and 17(1) stand in the way of obtaining an admission that an unauthorised intercept had been used. Possibly where an activist view of the exclusion of evidence requirement under Art 6 was taken, the only recourse would be to obtain a declaration of incompatibility between those provisions and Art 6(1) under s 4 of the HRA on the basis of unfairness under Art 6(1). However, if it was assumed that no appeal could succeed since those provisions would have to be applied, the defendants might view seeking such a declaration as worthless since it could not provide them individually with any redress. It appears therefore that although ss 17 and 18 show signs of seeking to escape from certain of the effects of s 9 of the 1985 Act, they nevertheless provide a scheme whose central aim is to preserve the secrecy surrounding interceptions, whether or not the interests of justice are thereby compromised.

Sections 17 and 18 are most likely to be relevant in criminal proceedings, but other proceedings are also affected. As discussed below, the route to judicial review of the decisions of the single tribunal may be barred by the ouster clause contained in s 67(8) of the RIPA[263] and based on s 7(8) of the 1985 Act. Section 65(2), which provides that the jurisdiction of the tribunal is to be 'the only appropriate tribunal' for the purposes of s 7(1)(a) of the HRA, also stands in the way of review. Section 65 is discussed further below,[264] and it is suggested that judicial review of executive decisions in the ordinary

---

261 See pp 1075–77. The findings in *Rowe and Davis v UK* (2000) 30 EHRR 1, although in a different context, which concerned unfairness arising from the non-disclosure of evidence, would be applicable.

262 See further Chapter 13, pp 1290–95.

263 Replacing s 7(8) of the 1985 Act and replacing s 91(10) of the 1997 Act in so far as complaints are concerned, and creating a new ouster clause in relation to complaints regarding surveillance by a range of other public authorities.

264 See pp 1081–82.

courts is possible in respect of some surveillance. But in respect of the interception of communications, s 17 would also have to be circumvented. Since s 18(9) applies to criminal proceedings only, the way to judicial review in the ordinary courts appears to remain barred. The only, faint, possibility seems to be that eventually, a declaration of incompatibility under s 4 of the HRA between s 17 and Art 6 might eventually be made on appeal from proceedings for permission to seek review.

The possibility of a tort action, including that of a cause of action based on breach of Art 8, is also probably ruled out on the same grounds. Where the existing law fails to cover interceptions which infringe Art 8, new tortious liability could have been created. Under the 1985 Act, the possibility would have been open of bringing an action once the HRA was fully in force in respect of forms of phone tapping outside the 1985 Act. This position was unsatisfactory and anomalous. But it did leave open the possibility, now probably closed down under Part I of RIPA, of raising such matters in the ordinary courts. At present, apart from prosecutions for the offences created by the RIPA, or enforcement of interception in the civil courts, the tribunal appears to provide the only judicial forum in which the Convention points discussed above can be raised.

Conclusions

The discussion suggests that court action as a method of seeking to ensure that the HRA is fully complied with in this context is highly circumscribed and uncertain. No clear and effective method is currently available, unless the tribunal proves to be more effective than its predecessor. Parliamentary oversight is also limited. If the Convention rights are to have any real impact domestically in this context, this may be most likely to occur through incremental internal change in procedures, rather than through the courts or the complaints mechanisms.

It is notable that the inception of proceedings in the ordinary courts in relation to interception under Part I of the RIPA is at present a privilege intended to be accorded only to the state. The role of the judiciary in the ordinary courts in protecting individual citizens, at their instigation, from abuse of state power in conducting interceptions has been almost entirely removed. Instead, the intention is that the courts should be used only to seek to further state ends – as a means of enforcing the use of intercepts. Thus, civil or criminal proceedings can be used under ss 11(7) and (8) in order to compel private companies to intercept the communications of their customers. At the same time, a citizen whose communications appear to have been unlawfully intercepted has no means of challenging the interception in the ordinary courts, even assuming that she becomes aware of it. It is a criminal offence under s 19, a classic 'reverse onus' clause, for a telecommunications worker, for example, to inform a member of the public that her phone has been tapped under an unlawfully issued warrant. The unsatisfactoriness of this regime leads to the conclusion that further safeguards against arbitrary invasion of privacy by interception, and consequent modifications of Part I of the RIPA, may eventually be introduced as a result of Strasbourg findings, or possibly as a result of relying on Art 8 under the HRA in applications to the new tribunal.

5 State surveillance[265]

Introduction

The last 25 years have seen an immense and still increasing expansion in the availability and use of a range of highly sophisticated surveillance devices, and state surveillance has become more intensive since the Labour Government came to power in 1997.[266] The recent growth in state use of such devices as part of intelligence-led policing has received encouragement from official studies.[267] The growth in such policing, which involves using covert investigative techniques proactively to target suspects, is due, as the group *Justice* has pointed out, to the need to respond to terrorist activity,[268] to organised crime, to the availability and efficacy of the new technology, and to the wider use of criminal intelligence following the growth of national and transnational agencies, including Europol and the National Criminal Intelligence Service[269] (amalgamated since 2006 into the Serious and Organised Crime Agency) and transnational agreements.[270] 'Bugging' equipment has become much more sophisticated in the last 25 years, with the result that it is now very powerful, readily concealable and relatively cheap.[271]

265 For texts referred to below and further discussion see: Mckay, S, *Covert Policing: Law and Practice*, 2007, OUP; Starmer, K, Strange, M and Whitaker, W, *Criminal Justice, Police Powers and Human Rights*, 2001, Blackstone; Uglow, S, Covert Surveillance and the European Convention on Human Rights [1999] *Criminal Law Review*, April, pp 287–99; Akdeniz, Y, Taylor, N and Walker, C, 'Regulation of Investigatory Powers Act 2000: Bigbrother.gov.uk: State Surveillance in the Age of Information and Rights' (2001) *Criminal Law Review*, February: 73–90; Taylor, N, 'State Surveillance and the Right to Privacy' *Surveillance & Society* 1(1) 84; Davies, S, (1996) *Big Brother: Britain's Web of Surveillance and the New Technological Order*. London: Pan; Etzioni, A, *The Limits of Privacy* 1999, Basic Books Inc.; Fenwick, H, *Civil Rights: New Labour, Freedom and the Human Rights Act*, 2000; Fitzpatrick, B and Taylor, N, 'Human Rights and the Discretionary Exclusion of Evidence', 2001, *Journal of Criminal Law*, 65(4): 349–59; Feldman, D, 'Secrecy, Dignity or Autonomy? Views of Privacy as a Civil Liberty' (1994) *Current Legal Problems*, 47(2): 41–71; Home Office, *Interception of Communications in the United Kingdom* Cm.4368 (1999); JUSTICE, *Under Surveillance*, 1998; Leigh, I, 'A Tapper's Charter?' [1986] *Public Law*, Spring: 8–18' Lustgarten, L and Leigh, I, *In From The Cold: National Security and Parliamentary Democracy*, 1994; Lyon, D, *Surveillance Society: Monitoring Everyday Life*, 2001, Open University Press; Norris, C and Armstrong, G, 'Introduction: Power and Vision', in Norris, C, Moran, J and Armstrong, G, (eds) *Surveillance, Closed Circuit Television and Social Control*, 1998, Ashgate, pp 3–20; Norris, C and Armstrong, G, *The Maximum Surveillance Society: The Rise of CCTV*, 1999, Berg; Taylor, N and Walker, C, 'Bugs in the System' (1996) *Journal of Civil Liberties*, 1: 105–24; Leigh, I, 'The security service, the press and the courts' [1987] PL 12–21.
266 See Mckay, S, *Covert Policing: Law and Practice*, 2007. See also below, pp 1058–59.
267 Audit Commission, *Helping with Enquiries*, 1993; *Home Office Review of Police Core and Ancillary Tasks*, 1995. See Manwaring-White, S, *The Policing Revolution*, 1983; *Report of the Commissioner for 1993*, Cm 2522; *Security Services Work Against Organised Crime*, Cm 3065, 1996.
268 See also Chapter 14, p 1332.
269 *Justice: Under Surveillance*, 1998, p 7. Walker and Taylor have pointed out that the use of surveillance techniques by police avoids adherence to the PACE interviewing rules and makes it less likely that evidence will be excluded: 'Bugs in the system' (1996) J Civ Lib 105, pp 107–8.
270 See the *Memorandum of Understandings on the Lawful Interception of Communications*, EU JHA-Council, 25 October 1995.
271 See Taylor and Walker, 'Bugs in the system' (1996) J Civ Lib 105; Mckay, S, *Covert Policing: Law and Practice*, 2007.

The criminal intelligence information obtained can be matched and disseminated with increasing rapidity using the new technology.

Thus, surveillance devices and techniques offer an important weapon to the police and security services in the maintenance of law and order and the protection of national security. However, as the Supreme Court of Canada has said of them: '. . . one can scarcely imagine a state activity more dangerous to individual privacy than electronic surveillance.'[272] This was also the view of the Younger Committee, which considered the range of devices then in use.[273] The use by state bodies of surveillance techniques and their legal basis resembles the pattern considered above in relation to the interception of communications. Despite the development of such techniques and the increased use of them by the police and the security services, they had until quite recently no or a quasi-legal basis – a position which was possible under a constitution based on negative liberties since the state, like the ordinary citizen, was, according to a key decision, entitled to do anything which the law did not forbid.[274] They operated until quite recently outside the realms of Parliamentary, judicial or administrative control. Bearing in mind the power of the state to conduct surveillance and its intrusiveness, this was an especially anomalous position.

Prior to the inception of the Police Act 1997, under administrative guidelines,[275] the use of listening devices could be authorised by Chief Constables in order to assist in a criminal investigation, if the crime was really serious, normal methods had been tried and had failed, and there was good reason for believing that the use of such equipment would lead to a conviction. Also, the authorising officer had to weigh the seriousness of the offence against the degree of intrusion necessary. When it became apparent in 1996 that this regime was inadequate, as explained below, since it did not meet the demands of the European Convention on Human Rights, the use of certain surveillance techniques by the police was placed on a statutory basis in the Police Act 1997. Following the lead of the Interception of Communications Act 1985, it gives an impression of covering the use of surveillance devices by the police, while in fact leaving many areas of their use outside its statutory framework.

The imminence of the HRA, and the effect of Art 8 in particular, was the driving force for further change. The unsatisfactory nature of the arrangements was pointed out in 1998 by *Justice* in a report[276] which argued for integration of surveillance techniques with interception, in one comprehensive statute. The Regulation of Investigatory Powers Act provides that comprehensive basis. Overlapping with the 1997 Act, most of which it does not repeal, Part II of the RIPA covers a far wider range of both techniques and public authorities, including the police. It places the use of surveillance by the security and intelligence services on a clearer statutory basis, overlapping with the Intelligence Services Act 1994. By providing a comprehensive statutory basis that

---

272   *Duarte* (1990) 65 DLR (4th) 240.
273   *Report of the Committee on Privacy*, Cmnd 5012, 1972.
274   See Megarry VC in *Malone v MPC* [1979] Ch 344.
275   *Guidelines on the Use of Equipment in Police Surveillance Operations*, House of Commons Library, 19 December 1984.
276   *Under Surveillance*, 1988.

coincided (roughly) with the coming fully into force of the HRA, Part II sought to avoid the embarrassment of the findings in *Malone v UK*,[277] *Halford v UK*[278] and *Khan v UK*.[279] As indicated above, *Malone* led to the inception of the Interception of Communications Act 1985 since it was found at Strasbourg that the interference with privacy represented by telephone tapping was not in accordance with the law, as it had no satisfactory legal basis. In *Halford* it was found that the tapping of the applicant's internal office phone had no such basis, while the same finding was made as regards the use of 'bugging' devices in *Khan*. The finding in *Halford* was addressed in Part I of the RIPA, that in *Khan* in Part III of the 1997 Act.[280] Assuming that the forms of surveillance covered by Part II of the RIPA engage Art 8 in the sense that they represent an interference with the respect for private life guaranteed under that Article,[281] the Convention arguments raised in those cases would have been raised in the domestic courts under the HRA (under s 7(1)(a) or (b)), particularly in respect of forms of so called 'directed' surveillance (see below) if Part II of the RIPA had not been introduced. Part II also provides a fuller complaints mechanism, with a view to keeping most scrutiny of surveillance out of the ordinary courts, but nevertheless satisfying the demands of the Convention. In contrast with the position under Part I, it does not create a criminal offence of conducting unauthorised surveillance. Part II also seeks to deal with the problem of encryption by requiring disclosure of the key to information under s 49,[282] rendering refusal punishable under s 53, a classic 'reverse onus' clause.

Thus, for the first time a statutory basis for a number of investigative techniques was created, clearly a welcome development. But it is questionable whether Part II is any more adequate at the level of principle than the previous scheme. It is clearly not as vulnerable to challenges under the Convention at Strasbourg or under the HRA. Nevertheless, its compatibility with the Convention remains in doubt, as discussed below. The *Justice* Report (1998) influenced its introduction, but while the first of their key recommendations – that there should be an integrated, comprehensive statutory basis for surveillance – has largely been met, it is questionable whether this is true of the second – using a 'coherent set of principles as required by Art 8' to underpin the scheme.[283]

---

277 A 82 (1984); 7 EHRR 14.
278 [1997] IRLR 471.
279 (2000) 8 BHRC 310.
280 By the time that the European Court of Human Rights made this finding, Part III of the 1997 Act had already been passed. Nevertheless, at the time when the police used the bugging device to obtain evidence against Khan, no sufficient basis in law was available to meet the demands of Art 8.
281 The Strasbourg decisions, discussed pp 1068–71, strongly suggest that this would be the case.
282 A s 49 notice requires service providers to disclose encryption keys and to keep secret the fact that a key has been disclosed. This provision may lead to adoption of a 'voluntary' key escrow system – a system whereby private encryption keys are deposited with a third party. Such a system would provide protection from prosecution for those who had genuinely lost or deleted their keys. But it clearly has significant privacy implications. See further Akedeniz, Y, 'UK Government policy on encryption' [1997] WSCL 1.
283 *Under Surveillance: Covert Policing and Human Rights Standards*, 1998; see Recommendation 1, p 107.

The Police Act 1997, Part III

The House of Lords in *Khan*,[284] confronted with evidence obtained by police bugging involving trespass, recommended legislation, taking into account the fact that the regime governing the use of bugging devices was not on a statutory basis and therefore might not comply with the 'in accordance with the law' requirement under Art 8.[285] Their recommendation was one of the factors behind the passing of the Police Act 1997, which therefore represents another instance in which powers posing a grave threat to privacy and other individual rights were governed only by administrative guidelines until it became apparent that such a course could not be justified under the Convention.

The authorisation procedure

The Police Act, Part III placed the practice under the relevant Home Office guidelines[286] on a statutory basis, with certain changes. It only covers the installation of devices which could have attracted liability under trespass, criminal damage or unlawful interference with wireless telegraphy, under the Wireless Telegraphy Acts 1949 and 1967. Therefore, it does not cover 'stand off' devices. Also, it does not cover devices installed with the consent of the person able to give permission in respect of the premises in question.[287] The use of surveillance devices in a range of circumstances therefore falls outside it, as do a range of techniques, in particular the use of informants.[288] Such matters continued to be governed by the Guidelines until Part II of the RIPA (see below) came into force.

Part III of the Police Act is largely modelled on the Interception of Communications Act and therefore contains certain similar objectionable features. The basis for allowing the use of bugging is very broad. An authorisation may be issued if the action is expected to be of substantial value in the prevention and detection of serious crime and the objective cannot reasonably be achieved by other means (s 93(2)). Serious crime is defined under s 93(4) to include crimes of violence, those involving substantial financial gain, and those involving a large number of people in pursuit of a common purpose.[289] These definitions appear to be significantly wider than those under the old guidelines. The last possibility could allow bugging to be used against, for example, members of CND or anti-road protesters, if it was expected, *inter alia*, that their activities might

---

284 [1996] 3 All ER 289; [1996] 3 WLR 162; (1996) 146 NLJ 1024, HL; [1995] QB 27, CA.

285 See the comments of Lord Nolan [1996] 3 WLR 162, p 175 and Lord Slynn, p 166. See also the Home Affairs Select Committee 3rd Report for 1994–5, Organised Crime HC 18–1, which recommended a statutory basis. It may be noted that *Khan v UK* Appl No 35394/97 was declared admissible at Strasbourg: (1999) 27 EHRR CD 58, and the application was successful (Judgment of the Court of 12 May 2000, 8 BHRC 310) since at the time there was no sufficient basis in law for the interference with Art 8. See further Chapter 15, pp 1291–92.

286 HO Circular to Chief Constables, *Guidelines on the Use of Technical Equipment in Police Surveillance Operations*.

287 Under the Guidelines and the previous Code of Practice, *Intrusive Surveillance*. One example would be the placing of listening devices in a police station: see *Bailey and Smith* [1993] Crim LR 861; *Musqud Ali* [1966] QB 668.

288 See *H* [1987] Crim LR 47 and *Jelen and Katz* [1990] 90 Cr App R 456. The use of a wired informant may require permission under the HO Circular; Part II of the RIPA – provisions covering covert human sources – now applies.

289 Or the crime is one for which a person of 21 or over with no previous convictions could reasonably be expected to receive a prison sentence of three or more years.

infringe s 68 of the Criminal Justice and Public Order Act 1994.[290] The 1999 Code of Practice, however, adopted under s 101 of the Act, emphasised that the bugging powers must only be used in cases of serious crime such as drug trafficking.

Under s 93(5), an authorisation to interfere with property may be issued by the Chief Officer of Police or, if that is not practicable, by an officer of the rank of Assistant Chief Constable of the force in question (s 94), if s 93(2) applies. The authorisation will be given in writing, except in cases of emergency, when it may be given orally by the Chief Officer in person (s 95(1)). A written authorisation will last for three months, an oral one for 72 hours. Both forms may be renewed in writing for a further three months. The commissioners appointed under s 91(1) must be notified of authorisations as soon as they are made (s 96), but this does not prevent the police acting on the authorisation. There is no administrative check under the 1997 Act, as there is under the 1985 one: no Minister is involved in the bugging authorisations. Apart from authorisations falling within s 97 (below), no other independent prior check is available, although special Information Commissioners (who became Surveillance Commissioners under the RIPA, Part II) have an oversight role. As has been pointed out in relation to the checking procedure under the 1985 Act, subsequent independent checks are clearly not as effective as prior ones. Again, these arrangements may be compared with those in Denmark, where authorisation of the use of listening devices, wherever placed, and including 'participant monitoring', must be by an investigating magistrate.[291]

As initially drafted, the Bill made no provision for any prior independent scrutiny of the bugging warrants at all, thereby adopting the model used for the 1985 Act, but without even the intervention of Home Office officials. The warrants were to be issued by the Chief Constable of the force in question, continuing the old practice. Michael Howard, the then Home Secretary, considered that exclusion of an independent authorising body was necessary since the police must be able to react instantly to prevent crime. This proposal was severely criticised from various quarters[292] and amendments requiring prior independent approval were put forward by Labour and the Liberal Democrats.[293] The Labour amendment is reflected in s 97; however, prior approval of authorisation is not required in all instances. Under s 97(2), such approval by a Commissioner is required where the specified property is believed to be a dwelling, hotel bedroom or office premises. It is also needed where the authorising officer believes that information of a more sensitive nature may be acquired – matters subject to legal privilege; confidential personal information; confidential journalistic material.

---

290 See Chapter 9, pp 738–41.
291 Art 126 1 and Code of Criminal Procedure.
292 The criticism came from the pressure group, *Liberty*, and from some sections of the press, including sections of the tabloid press. It was argued that other countries accept prior judicial authorisation for bugging warrants and the UK accepts judicial involvement in other aspects of the policing process such as the authorisation of search warrants.
293 Labour proposed that an information commissioner appointed from the judiciary should be involved in checking the warrants, while the Liberal Democrats proposed that a judge acting in his or her capacity as a judge should undertake this role. See Standing Committee F Fifth Sitting Cols 131 *et seq.*, 11 March 1997. The House of Lords accepted both amendments and Michael Howard then reached an agreement with Jack Straw, then the Shadow Home Secretary, that an information commissioner appointed from the judiciary should be involved in checking warrants if certain authorisations were in question.

The special Commissioners are appointed by the Prime Minister from among the senior judiciary (s 91(1)). The involvement of special Commissioners, even such a limited involvement, provides a degree of independent oversight and scrutiny, although the Commissioners tend to accept and agree with police representations. Nevertheless, apart from other considerations, the involvement of Commissioners may mean that internal procedures are tightened up before representations are made. No provision is made under the Act for independent review of the authorisations in the ordinary courts. Nevertheless, under the Labour amendment, scrutiny of police practices is, arguably, somewhat more effective than scrutiny of those of the Security Service, not weaker, as Michael Howard originally proposed. Clearly, this is a more satisfactory situation, since the arguments for excluding the judiciary from the process are weaker when matters pertaining to national security are not in question. This is quite a thin veneer of judicial supervision, but at present the Court of Appeal takes the view that the Police Act arrangements satisfy Article 8 under the HRA.[294]

Various groups and bodies had put forward pleas for exemption from the provisions of the Bill. These included Catholic priests – who were afraid that the confessional would be bugged – doctors and solicitors. Section 97(2)(b) and the Code of Practice, *Intrusive Surveillance*, adopted under s 101 of the Act[295] reflected the concerns of these groups to an extent. Where the action authorised is likely to result in 'any person acquiring knowledge of matters subject to legal privilege, confidential personal information or confidential journalistic material', prior authorisation is required. Under s 98, 'matters subject to legal privilege' include communications between a professional legal advisor and his or her client connected with the giving of legal advice or relating to legal proceedings. Once approval for an authorisation has been given, allowing, for example, for a solicitor's office to be bugged, all conversations between solicitors and clients would be recorded. Under s 99, 'confidential personal information' includes information relating to a person's physical or mental health or to spiritual counselling.

A key weakness in the authorisation procedure is that under s 97(3), even where s 97 applies, no approval is needed if the authorising officer 'believes that the case is one of urgency'. No requirement that the belief should be based on reasonable grounds is included. However, the Code of Practice provided that in all but exceptional cases the police must obtain prior approval of the authorisation where s 97 applies: the 'urgency' provision was not to be used routinely. Section 101 was repealed by RIPA and this Code was replaced by a Code issued under s 71 of that Act, *Covert Surveillance* (2005). Para 5.23 of the current RIPA Code repeats the provision that the urgency provision should not be used routinely and provides that the reason for the urgency must be explained to the Commissioner. The RIPA Code is discussed further below.

The Regulation of Investigatory Powers Act, Part II [296]

Part II of the RIPA 2000 covers surveillance activities of immense potential to infringe privacy that previously had no – or only a narrow – basis in law. For the first time,

---

294 *R v Lawrence* [2002] Crim LR 584.
295 It was issued on 27 October 1998.
296 It may be noted that under s 46, there are restrictions on Part II authorisations extending to Scotland.

a comprehensive statutory basis has been created for the expanding use of covert surveillance. The growth in proactive intelligence-led policing (targeting suspects using covert surveillance rather than investigating a crime after it has happened) and the proliferation of various forms of surveillance devices provided part of the impetus for reform.[297] Unlike Part III of the Police Act 1997 or s 5 of the Intelligence Services Act 1994 with which it overlaps,[298] Part II of the RIPA covers a very wide range of public authorities. It also covers a much wider range of circumstances. Prior to the introduction of Part II, invasions of privacy by means of covert surveillance falling outside the narrow scope of the 1997 or 1994 provisions were occurring, not on the basis of a legal power, but on the basis that the state is in the same position as the individual citizen in being free to do that which the law does not forbid. Since there was no legal right to privacy – in a broad, general sense – no legal power to invade it was needed.[299]

The pre-existing statutory provisions were mainly (although not exclusively) aimed at the form of surveillance termed 'intrusive' by Part II. Most significantly, a warrant or authorisation was required where there was a physical invasion of property by the police or security and intelligence services. So a wide area of surveillance fell outside those statutes, and the need to cover this particular form of surveillance – in anticipation of the effects of the HRA – provided the immediate impetus for the introduction of Part II. Under the HRA it is clearly necessary for surveillance to be placed on a statutory basis even where previously it would not have attracted any form of liability, if it would amount to an invasion of privacy under Art 8 of the European Convention on Human Rights, since para 2 provides that an interference with individual privacy must be 'in accordance with the law'. The key aim of Part II is therefore to meet a central requirement under the Convention – that of legality. The RIPA Code on *Covert surveillance* (2005) makes this clear:

> Para 2.2: Part II of the 2000 Act does not impose a requirement on public authorities to seek or obtain an authorisation where, under the 2000 Act, one is available (see s 80 of the 2000 Act). Nevertheless, where there is an interference by a public authority with the right to respect for private and family life guaranteed under Art 8 of the European Convention on Human Rights, and where there is no other source of lawful authority, the consequence of not obtaining an authorisation under the 2000 Act may be that the action is unlawful by virtue of section 6 of the Human Rights Act 1998.

---

297 The use of covert surveillance together with other targeting methods, including the use of informers, has expanded rapidly and is seen as immensely useful by the police: see, e.g., *Policing with Intelligence* HMIC Thematic Inspection Report, 1997/99; Mckay, S, *Covert Policing: Law and Practice*, 2007.

298 Under the Police Act 1997, Part III, s 92: 'No entry on or interference with property or with wireless telegraphy shall be unlawful if it is authorised by an authorisation having effect under this Part'. Thus, forms of directed surveillance involving an actual interference with property (see below) – on non-residential premises – were covered by the Police Act 1997, Part III. Under the 1994 Act, s 5, the Home Secretary, on an application from a member of the Intelligence Service, can issue a warrant authorising the 'taking of any such action as is specified in the warrant in respect of any property so specified or in respect of wireless telegraphy so specified'.

299 See above, pp 807, 873–75; clearly, certain aspects of privacy received protection in the pre-HRA era, especially under the doctrine of trespass.

2.3 Public authorities are therefore strongly recommended to seek an authorisation where the surveillance is likely to interfere with a person's Art 8 rights to privacy by obtaining private information about that person, whether or not that person is the subject of the investigation or operation.

It is clear that Part II has gone some way towards achieving this aim in the sense that it has provided a much more comprehensive statutory underpinning for covert surveillance than the pre-existing one. A basis in national law has been created which purports to meet the requirements of legality under the Convention. Below, it will be considered whether it has succeeded in meeting those requirements and whether the further Convention requirements of necessity and proportionality have also been met. In order to do so, the provisions governing so called 'intrusive' and 'directed' surveillance will be examined with a view to contending that when the two regimes are contrasted, the inadequacies of the latter, in Convention terms, are starkly revealed. The Code provides:

2.5 . . . if the activities are necessary, the person granting the authorisation must believe that they are proportionate to what is sought to be achieved by carrying them out. This involves balancing the intrusiveness of the activity on the target and others who might be affected by it against the need for the activity in operational terms. The activity will not be proportionate if it is excessive in the circumstances of the case or if the information which is sought could reasonably be obtained by other less intrusive means. All such activity should be carefully managed to meet the objective in question and must not be arbitrary or unfair.

Intrusive surveillance

Under s 26(3) of the RIPA, 'intrusive' surveillance occurs when a surveillance device is used or an individual undertaking surveillance is actually present on residential premises, or in a private vehicle, or it is carried out by such a device in relation to such premises or vehicle without being present on the premises or vehicle. 'Residential' is defined in s 48(1) of the RIPA as premises used as living accommodation, while 'premises' includes movable structures and land. The definition expressly excludes common areas of residential premises and clearly does not cover office premises (s 48(7)(b)). Thus, covert surveillance of office premises falls within the term 'directed', rather than intrusive, surveillance. Section 26(3), read with s 48(7), creates confusion, since it covers all forms of covert surveillance taking place in relation to residential premises. Some forms of such surveillance can be treated as directed surveillance, as indicated below, and it is in relation to residential premises that an area of uncertainty is created as to the category into which surveillance falls.

Under s 32(3) of the RIPA authorisation of intrusive surveillance is on the grounds of 'the interests of national security, for the purpose of preventing or detecting serious crime or of preventing disorder, in the interests of the economic well-being of the UK'. 'Serious crime' is defined in s 81(3)[300] in substantially the same terms as in s 93(4)

---

300   Section 81(2) provides that such crime satisfies the tests of sub-section 3(a) or (b). Under s 81(3), those tests are (a) that the offence is one for which a person of 21 with no previous convictions could

of the Police Act 1997. Proportionality requirements are introduced under s 32(2): the authorising person must be satisfied that the action to be taken is proportionate to what is hoped to be achieved by carrying it out. Authorisations for such surveillance are granted by the Home Secretary under s 41 or, for police or customs officers, by senior authorising officers, who are the highest-ranking police officers in Britain (see s 32(6)). There is also provision for the grant of authorisations in a case of urgency by persons of almost equally high rank, other than the senior authorising officer.[301]

The provisions for urgent and non-urgent authorisations under ss 33, 34, 35 and 36 mirror those under the Police Act, Part III in that, under s 35, notice must be given to a 'Surveillance Commissioner' and, under s 36, the authorisation will not take effect until it has been approved, except where it is urgent and the grounds for urgency are set out in the notice, in which case the authorisation will take effect from the time of its grant. Under s 38, senior authorising officers can appeal to the Chief Surveillance Commissioner against decisions of ordinary Surveillance Commissioners. The Commissioners have responsibility for the destruction of material obtained by surveillance, under s 37, but there is no requirement that material no longer needed for proceedings and no longer subject to an authorisation *must* be destroyed.

Under s 43, authorisations can be granted or renewed urgently orally by senior authorising officers or in writing by persons authorised to act on their behalf in urgent cases. If, under s 43(3)(a), an authorisation is granted or renewed by a person entitled to act only in urgent cases, or was renewed by such a person or orally, it ceases to take effect after 72 hours. Section 42 provides special rules for the intelligence services which overlap with those of s 5 of the Intelligence Services Act 1994. Under s 42, the security and intelligence services can undertake intrusive surveillance on grant of a warrant. The grounds are those under s 32(3). As far as intrusive surveillance is concerned, the function of the services in support of the prevention or detection of serious crime is excluded where the application is by a member of GCHQ or the SIS (under s 42(3)). Under s 44(3), a warrant authorising intrusive surveillance issued by a senior official, and not renewed under the hand of the Secretary of State, 'shall cease to have effect at the end of the second working day' after its issue. In the case of other such warrants, that point will be at the end of the period of six months from the day of issue or renewal.

This authorisation regime follows the model adopted for telephone tapping under the Interception of Communications Act 1985 and continued with minor modifications under Part I of the RIPA. That regime has been subjected to criticism on the basis that the mechanisms for creating executive accountability are so weak,[302] but it may meet Strasbourg requirements.[303] The regime for intrusive surveillance provides for independent checks and for the possibility that an authorisation will not be able to take

---

reasonably expect a sentence of three years' imprisonment or more, or (b) that the conduct involves the use of violence, results in substantial financial gain, or is conduct by a large number of persons in pursuit of a common purpose.

301 Under s 34(4), such persons are of a rank almost as high as such officers. In the case of police forces, this means a person holding the rank of Assistant Chief Constable or, in the case of the Metropolitan or City of London forces, of Commander.

302 See: Lloyd (1986) 49 MLR 86; Leigh [1986] PL 8.

303 As discussed above, pp 1027–28, the regime created under the 1985 Act was considered in *Christie v UK* 78-A DR E Com HR 119; on the facts of the case no breach of Art 8 was found.

effect if it does not satisfy the requirements, including those of proportionality. Clearly, the standard of scrutiny may be variable, but the very fact that an authorisation will be checked independently may tend to foster rigour in preparing the papers.

Directed surveillance

Under s 26(2) of the RIPA, all covert surveillance is directed surveillance if it is not intrusive and it is undertaken 'otherwise than by way of an immediate response to events or circumstances, the nature of which is such that it would not be practicable for an authorisation to be sought', and for the purposes of 'a specific investigation or . . . operation', and 'in such a manner as is likely to result in the obtaining of private information about a person', even if he is not identified in relation to the investigation. If the device or person is not on the premises or in the vehicle, the surveillance is 'directed', not 'intrusive' unless 'the device is such that it consistently provides information of the same quality and detail as might be expected to be obtained from a device actually present on the premises or in the vehicle' (s 26(5)). The Code of Practice on Covert Surveillance made under s 71(3)(a) of the RIPA seeks to draw a distinction between general law enforcement functions carried out covertly as an immediate response, and the systematic targeting of an individual (para 4); only the latter may amount to directed surveillance. Anomalously enough, the term 'directed surveillance' also covers an interception of communications in the course of its transmission that is consented to by the sender or recipient and in respect of which there is no interception warrant (s 26(4)(b) and s 48(4)).

From the above, it appears that directed surveillance would occur where a 'bugging' device is placed in the hallway of a block of flats that provides information of a lesser quality than would be obtained if the device was inside one of the flats. Intrusive surveillance would occur, for example, when a 'bugging' device is placed in a car parked near a private house that normally provides information of the same quality as would be obtained if the device was inside the house. These examples make it clear that very fine lines may be drawn between the two forms of surveillance, although, as indicated below, the two regimes differ so sharply. Moreover, the distinction between directed surveillance and 'general law enforcement' functions, such as observing persons entering or leaving a house, turns on the question whether or not the observation can be viewed as an immediate response – another instance in which fine lines may be drawn. If observation of a house occurs over a period of time, it can be argued that an invasion of privacy is occurring that can no longer be viewed as an immediate response. In such an instance an authorization should be sought. It could also be argued that such surveillance requires a more specific statutory underpinning.[304]

Section 47(1) provides powers for the Secretary of state to extend or modify the authorisation provisions. He can provide for any directed surveillance 'to be treated for the purposes of this Part as intrusive surveillance'. Under s 47(2), this power is subject to the negative resolution procedure, but clearly that does not provide the same safeguards as the full Parliamentary process.

---

304 Such an underpinning can be created, by order of the Secretary of State, under s 47.

'Directed' surveillance may be authorised on the grounds under s 28. The grounds include 'the interests of national security, for the purpose of preventing or detecting crime or of preventing disorder, in the interests of the economic well-being of the UK, in the interests of public safety; for the purpose of protecting public health; for the purpose of assessing or collecting any tax, duty . . . or other . . . charge payable to a government department'; or for any other 'purpose specified for the purposes of this sub-section by an order made by the Secretary of State'. This order must be approved by Parliament. Proportionality requirements are introduced under s 28(2) to the effect that the authorising person must believe that the authorisation or authorised conduct is 'proportionate to what is sought to be achieved by carrying it out'.

The authorisation for directed surveillance is granted by a 'designated person' under s 28. Under s 30, such persons are 'the individuals holding such offices, ranks or positions with relevant public authorities as are prescribed for the purposes of this sub-section by an order' made by the Secretary of State. The Secretary of State can himself be a designated person under s 30(2). The 'relevant public authorities' (set out in Sched 1) include the police, the security and intelligence services, Customs and Excise, Inland Revenue, the armed forces, the Departments of Health; Social Security; Trade and Industry; Environment, Transport and the Regions. Further authorities can be designated by order of the Secretary of State. The prescribed persons in the relevant public authorities are now set out in the Regulation of Investigatory Powers Act 2000 (Prescription of Offices, Ranks and Positions) Order 2000.[305] In police forces, the prescribed office is that of Superintendent; in urgent cases, that of Inspector. The Code of Practice, para 4.14 recommends that authorising officers should not 'be responsible for authorising their own activities . . . however, it is recognised that this may sometimes be unavoidable . . .'

Under s 43, written authorisations cease to have effect after three months, although they may be renewed for additional three month periods (security or intelligence service authorisations may be renewed for six months). Urgent authorisations cease to have effect after 72 hours unless they are renewed either orally (if the urgency subsists) by a person whose entitlement to act is not confined to urgent cases, or in writing. Authorisations cannot be granted orally except in urgent cases and by a person whose entitlement to act is not confined to such cases. Under s 43(3)(b) 'in a case not falling within paragraph (a) in which the authorisation is for the conduct or the use of a covert human intelligence source', the period is 12 months from its grant or last renewal. In a case falling outside s 43(3)(a) or (b), it is three months under s 43(3)(c). Under s 44(5)(a), when an authorisation for the carrying out of directed surveillance is granted by a member of any of the intelligence services and renewed by an instrument 'endorsed under the hand of the person renewing [it] with a statement that the renewal is believed to be necessary on grounds falling within section 32(3)(a) or (c), the authorisation (unless renewed again) shall cease to have effect at the end of the period of six months'.

A Chief Surveillance Commissioner, who may be assisted by Assistant Commissioners, has a general oversight role in relation to this regime, under s 62. But, this independent check occurs only after the event. Therefore, its impact on accountability may be minimal.

---

305 SI 2000/2417.

Other surveillance

Under s 47, the Secretary of State may also by order 'apply this Part, with such modifications as he thinks fit, to any . . . surveillance that is neither directed nor intrusive'. The power is intended to afford, if necessary, a statutory basis for the use of other powers which may be found to have fallen outside this Act. The compatibility of this the legal basis for the powers with the Convention is questionable, partly because, it is suggested, it is so uncertain and so dependent on the exercise of executive power. The term 'such modifications' implies that lesser safeguards than those available for directed surveillance might be adopted, a possibility which would be likely to have Art 8 implications. These matters are considered below.

Confidential information

Certain safeguards relating to the type of information that can be gathered using directed or intrusive surveillance are created, but the relevant rules appear only in the draft Code of Practice, not in the Act itself. Paragraph 2.3 relates to certain types of confidential information: confidential personal information (relating to physical or mental health or to spiritual counselling), matters subject to legal privilege and confidential journalistic material. Under para 2.10, if it is 'possible that a *substantial* proportion of the material acquired could be confidential material' (emphasis added), applications should be granted 'only in exceptional and compelling circumstances, with full regard to the proportionality issues'. Paragraph 2.8 reminds those granting the authorisation that an undertaking has been given that material subject to the seal of the confessional will not be the subject of operations. General principles apply to confidential material, under para 2.11; they include the requirement to destroy the material 'as soon as it is no longer necessary to retain it for a specified purpose' and to refrain from dissemination of it unless 'an appropriate officer [having sought legal advice] is satisfied that is necessary for a specific purpose'. These rules fail to introduce any independent check into the process even where material is most clearly of a private nature. As far as directed surveillance is concerned, the question of acquiring and using confidential material is subject, in essentials, to the same regime as is available for non-confidential material.

The use and storage of information obtained by surveillance techniques is governed as far as the police are concerned by the Data Protection Act. The Surveillance Commissioners also have power, when quashing authorisations of intrusive surveillance under s 37, to order the destruction of records. Storage and retention of police information are also governed by a detailed ACPO Code[306] which instructs on the applicability of data protection principles to such information. As indicated above, concerns have been raised regarding record keeping by the Security Service, bearing in mind the fact that it does not have to comply with the Data Protection Act 1998, even in its criminal function.[307] Under the 1998 Act, in relation to personal information, the police do not have to comply with the fair and lawful processing provisions of the first data

---

306 Code of Practice for Data Protection, 2002.
307 See pp 928–29.

protection principle,[308] subject access requests, or restrictions on disclosure of personal information, if to do so would be likely to prejudice the prevention and detection of crime or the apprehension and prosecution of offenders. These are not blanket exemptions; they should be considered in their application to individual cases. But it is unclear that careful scrutiny on this basis occurs.[309] The ACPO Code of Practice is therefore of significance since it provides greater clarity and safeguards a significant aspect of privacy. But it is argued that such a significant task should not be undertaken by quasi-legislation.[310]

The oversight role of the Commissioners

The Police Act 1997 set up a complaints system which, apart from the lack of a special tribunal, strongly resembled that under the 1985 Act, considered above. The similarity was the more striking since the system related to ordinary crime, not necessarily to terrorism or other activities, having a potential impact on national security. This model was continued under s 62 of the RIPA which added additional functions to those of the 'Chief Surveillance Commissioner', so that his role mirrors that of the Interceptions of Communications Commissioner. The office of Commissioner under s 91 of the 1997 Act is continued, but the Commissioners are re-designated 'Surveillance Commissioners' and their complaints role was removed. Assistant Surveillance Commissioners can be appointed under s 63 of the RIPA to aid the Chief Surveillance Commissioner. Such aid is clearly needed since the Commissioner provides oversight, not only of police surveillance, but also of surveillance carried out by all the persons covered by Part II of the RIPA. Thus, the oversight role of the Surveillance Commissioners is broader than their role in relation to authorisations, since the latter relates only to the police and customs, while the former covers other public authorities and the Home Secretary's authorising role under s 41. Thus, the role of the Surveillance Commissioners overlaps with that of the Intelligence Services Commissioner who has an oversight role which, as indicated above, covers, *inter alia*, surveillance carried out by those services.

Under s 107 of the Police Act 1997, the Chief Commissioner has reporting duties similar to those of the Intelligence Services Commissioner. (His duty under s 106, to report to the Prime Minister if an appeal is allowed and where a finding in favour of a complainant is made by a Commissioner, was repealed under Sched 4 to the 2000 Act.) He must make an annual report on the discharge of his functions. The report must be presented to Parliament and published as a Command Paper. The Prime Minister may exclude matters from the report under s 107(4) of the Act if it appears to him that it contains matter 'prejudicial to the prevention and detection of serious crime' or to the discharge of the functions of a police authority, the service authorities for the National Criminal Intelligence Service or the duties of the Commissioner for Customs and Excise.

---

308 Except in relation to 'sensitive' data.
309 See the 1998 *Justice* report (*Under Surveillance*) Chapter 4, esp pp 92–95.
310 See Chapter 11, pp 1105–8 for analogous discussion in relation to the PACE Codes.

The RIPA Code of Practice on Covert Surveillance

The current Code of Practice on *Covert Surveillance* (2005), made under s 71 RIPA and one of four RIPA Codes,[311] applies to every authorisation of covert surveillance or of entry on or interference with property or with wireless telegraphy carried out under s 5 of the Intelligence Services Act 1994, Part III of the Police Act 1997 or Part II of the Regulation of Investigatory Powers Act 2000 by public authorities.

The previous Code of Practice *Intrusive Surveillance* was revised in November 1999.[312] The revision appeared to be intended to limit further the power of intrusive surveillance in relation to the especially sensitive categories of information. Surveillance operations were banned in churches or temples where a minister of religion is giving spiritual counselling such as absolution. In order to use bugging equipment in such circumstances, it was not only necessary for the provisions of the Act have to be complied with, but the police also had to seek permission from the head of the appropriate church or faith. This provision brought the Church of England and other churches and faiths into line with the Roman Catholic Church: the sacramental confessional was given added protection under the original Code. The position differs under the current RIPA Code, *Covert Surveillance*.

> Under para 3.1: The 2000 Act does not provide any special protection for 'confidential information'. Nevertheless, particular care should be taken in cases where the subject of the investigation or operation might reasonably expect a high degree of privacy, or where confidential information is involved. Confidential information consists of matters subject to legal privilege, confidential personal information or confidential journalistic material. So, for example, extra care should be given where, through the use of surveillance, it would be possible to acquire knowledge of discussions between a minister of religion and an individual relating to the latter's spiritual welfare, or where matters of medical or journalistic confidentiality or legal privilege may be involved.
>
> 3.2: In cases where through the use of surveillance it is likely that knowledge of confidential information will be acquired, the use of surveillance is subject to a higher level of authorisation. Annex A lists the authorising officer for each public authority permitted to authorise such surveillance.

The relationship between the current Code of Practice and the statutes is significant. The statutes grants broad discretionary powers to conduct intrusive surveillance and inter-fere with property to senior law enforcement officials, but seeks to constrain and structure these powers in two main ways. First, there are general precedent conditions for the exercise of such powers, the most significant being the requirement that the action is likely to be of substantial value in preventing or detecting serious crime. Secondly, there are specific countervailing provisions intended to protect privacy and

---

311   The others are: the Covert Human Intelligence Sources (CHIS) Code of Practice (2005); Interception of Communications Code of Practice (2005); The Acquisition and Disclosure of Communications data draft Code (2005).

312   The revised Code was published by the Home Office on 18 November 1999. As noted, it was replaced under s 71 RIPA.

confidentiality. Part II RIPA and the other provisions mentioned above provide the key powers, but the Code of Practice, a set of quasi-legal rules, provides a due process underpinning. The statutory provisions, together with the Code provisions, could be viewed as providing a detailed domestic scheme satisfying the demands of Art 8. But this view fails to take account of the rule of law implications of placing a number of key protective provisions on a quasi-legislative basis within what Baldwin has termed 'tertiary rules', or government by circular.[313]

In common with many of the Codes accompanying 'state power' legislation discussed in this book,[314] the Code provisions are not on their face discretionary; they are in general phrased in the precise terms of mandatory instructions. Nevertheless, no formal sanction, apart from an internal disciplinary one, is provided for their breach (s 72(2) RIPA).[315] This is also true of the statutory provisions. However, they cloak otherwise tortious actions with authority, while the mere fact that they are statutory may appear to give them greater weight than the Code provisions in the eyes of those to whom they are directed, and of the judiciary. If the provisions were not followed, it would be, theoretically, an internal disciplinary matter and in practice, police officers might pay more attention to this than to the theoretical possibility of being sued. But, as Chapter 13 points out, the same sanction is used for breach of the PACE Codes and does not appear to be effective, taking into account the very few disciplinary charges laid for their breach.[316] Thus, senior law enforcement officials are in effect given at least a partial discretion as to whether to follow the Code rules and thus whether to respect the Art 8 rights which they reflect.[317] As pointed out in Chapter 1, the concept of a right precludes the idea of an open-ended discretion to infringe it in the pursuit of competing interests.[318] It is however possible that the principle from *Wainwright v UK*,[319] discussed in Chapter 11, might come to influence this position, under the HRA.

Unless rigorous, independent review of rule-compliance and a clear remedy for breach are available, the Code rules will remain, in effect, largely discretionary, and the rights protected by them illusory. This is a concern in respect of the statutory

313 See Baldwin, R, *Rules and Government*, 1995, Clarendon.

314 The Codes of Practice made under the Police and Criminal Evidence Act 1984 considered in Chapters 11, 12 and 13 were the forerunners of the similar Codes considered in this book – the Codes adopted under the Terrorism Act 2000 and the Regulation of Investigatory Powers Act 2000.

315 On the model provided by the PACE Codes (adopted for all the Codes mentioned in this book) it is admissible in evidence under s 72(3). It should be taken into account by courts, the single tribunal and relevant Commissioners under s 72(4).

316 See pp 1310–18.

317 Ronald Dworkin has argued that if an official's decision whether to comply with a given rule is final and unreviewable, he is endowed with a form of discretion (*Taking Rights Seriously*, 1977, p 69). In practice, decisions taken by police officers in relation to the provisions of the Codes of Practice discussed in this book (see, in particular, Chapter 11, pp 1116–17 and Chapter 13, pp 1311, 1317) are in general unlikely to be considered in courts or in police disciplinary proceedings. In a minority of instances, however, such provisions may be considered in relation to exclusion of evidence. Even then, the 'sanction' of such exclusion is unlikely to be used in respect of most forms of non-confession evidence, the form of evidence to which the provisions of the RIPA Code are most likely to relate. See, generally, Davis, KC, *Discretionary Justice*, 1980, Greenwood, pp 84–88.

318 See pp 12–14. Dworkin argues that it only makes sense to denote an interest as a right if it will generally win any battle with competing societal considerations: see ibid, p 191.

319 See pp 1179–81.

provisions, but it arises *a fortiori* in respect of the Code made under s 71 RIPA. It is suggested below that the single tribunal system is not proving ineffective, and that since no clear Parliamentary or administrative means of seeking to enhance rule compliance is available, recourse to court-based remedies under the influence of the HRA would be of especial significance in this context if, which is very doubtful, they could find expression.

Closed circuit television

The increasing use by local authorities of closed circuit television as a form of visual surveillance is not regulated by RIPA 2000, Part II. It is not either directed or intrusive surveillance since it is not undertaken for a specific purpose. Section 163 of the Criminal Justice and Public Order Act 1994 clarifies the power of local authorities to install closed circuit cameras for surveillance purposes.[320] The fact of capturing the image of a person on CCTV may not, in all circumstances, in itself constitute an invasion of privacy, although the mere fact that a person is in a public place should not preclude that possibility.[321] Even where it is arguable that an invasion of privacy has not occurred, the use of the information later on may create one.[322]

The HRA and state surveillance

Interference with the guarantees of Art 8

A preliminary question in terms of the Convention requirements might, in this context, concern the status of the individual in question as a victim, where he or she was uncertain whether surveillance had occurred. The Court put forward the following reason in *Klass v Federal Republic of Germany*[323] for regarding the applicants as 'victims' under Art 25 despite the fact that they were uncertain whether or not their phones had been tapped: '[normally an applicant cannot challenge a law *in abstracto* ... the position is different [when] owing to the secrecy of the measures objected to, he cannot point to any concrete measure specifically affecting him'. Thus the existence of legislation permitting secret measures, including the RIPA and the Police Act 1997, may allow a person to claim to be the victim of a breach of Art 8 although she would also have to show a 'reasonable likelihood that surveillance had occurred'.[324] Given that the provisions in the HRA regarding the status of 'victims' rely on the Convention jurisprudence,[325] this finding would aid the claim of such a person in the ordinary courts. The remit of the single tribunal under s 65 RIPA, discussed below, might not allow it to consider such a claim, unless it interprets its jurisdiction more widely.

---

320 See *Brentwood Council ex p Peck* [1998] CMLR 697, now in the Strasbourg system. For further discussion see Norris, Moran and Armstrong (eds), *Surveillance, CCTV and Social Control*, 1999. See also Data Protection Commissioner (2000) CCTV Code of Practice. Available at: http://www.dataprotection.gov.uk/dpr/dpdoc.nsf.
321 See above, pp 819–20, and below, pp 1069–70.
322 See further the *Justice* report, *Under Surveillance* 1998, p 31.
323 (1978) 2 EHRR 214.
324 *G, H and I v UK* 15 EHRR CD 41.
325 See Chapter 4, pp 235–37.

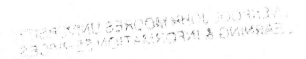

Assuming that there is a reasonable likelihood that surveillance had occurred, a key question for the tribunal or a court is whether in the particular circumstances it fell within Art 8(1). The extent to which Art 8 provides protection from surveillance outside the home or other living accommodation such as hotel rooms might be considered. The principles at stake are similar to those discussed above in relation to interception: all these forms of surveillance interfere with informational autonomy. But while it is now clearly settled in the Strasbourg jurisprudence that in most circumstances interception (at least in the form of telephone tapping) creates an interference with Art 8 guarantees, this cannot be said with equal certainty of all the diverse forms of surveillance covered by Part II of the RIPA or Part III of the 1997 Act.

However, 'the state [has an obligation] to respect private life by controlling the activities of its agents [in collecting personal information]'.[326] It has been indicated that interference with property for surveillance purposes by the security and intelligence services has been found to fall within Art 8.[327] Collection and use of information derived from covert investigative techniques may do so unless the applicant is already involved in criminal activity.[328] The acquiring of information represents one form of invasion of informational autonomy; further invasions may occur due to the storage and dissemination of the information. In a number of cases, Strasbourg has found that the collection of information about an individual by the state without his or her consent will, in principle, interfere with the right to respect for private life[329] and it has contemplated the possibility that compiling and retaining the information will also do so.[330] The use of listening devices has been found to create an interference with the Art 8(1) guarantee.[331] Systematic or even indirect targeting of an individual is also very likely to involve such an interference.[332]

The Strasbourg case law suggests that where an interference occurs in an obviously 'private' place, an infringement of the primary right will be found. The extent to which, outside such places, an invasion of privacy might be found in respect of surveillance is a matter which is subject to a developing jurisprudence at Strasbourg and nationally. An individual may expect to retain a degree of privacy in a semi-public environment, such as a restaurant,[333] gymnasium,[334] solicitor's office,[335] pub or shop.[336] Strasbourg has been prepared to extend the notion of private space beyond obvious places such

---

326 Harris, D, O'Boyle, K and Warbrick, C, *Law of the European Convention on Human Rights*, 1995, p 310.
327 See pp 1025–28.
328 *Ludi v Switzerland* A 238 (1992).
329 See: *Murray v UK* A 300 (1994), paras 84, 85; *McVeigh v UK* (1981) 25 DR 15, p 49.
330 See *G, H and I v UK* 15 EHRR CD 41 (application of first and third applicants failed on the basis that they had not shown sufficient likelihood that such compiling or retention had occurred).
331 See *Govell v UK* (1997) 4 EHRLR 438; *Khan v UK* Appl No 35394/97 (declared admissible on 20 April 1999) (1999) 27 EHRR CD 58; judgment of the Court: 8 BHRC 310.
332 *Harman and Hewitt v UK* (1992) 14 EHRR 657.
333 A situation considered in a decision of the German Supreme Court: BGH 19 December 1995 BGHZ 131, pp 322–46.
334 The location where surreptitious photographs were taken of the former Princess of Wales, in *HRH Princess of Wales v MGN Newspapers Ltd and Others* (1993) Transcript, Association of Official Shorthand Writers, 8 November 1993.
335 See *Niemetz v FRG* A 251-B (1992).
336 See *R v Broadcasting Standards Council ex p BBC* [2000] 3 WLR 1327.

as the home; as Harris, O'Boyle and Warbrick put it: 'it is not enough just for the individual to be himself: he must be able to a substantial degree to keep to himself what he is and what he does . . . the idea of private space need not be confined to those areas where the person has some exclusive rights of occupancy'.[337] In this respect, the Strasbourg approach may be developing in a direction which will take it away from the current UK statutory approach: 'the expanding understanding of private life set out in the *Niemetz* case[338] indicates that a formal public/private distinction about the nature of the location will not always be decisive.'[339]

This identifiable general trend suggests that this is another instance in which the emphasis should be on the evolutive nature of the Convention[340] rather than on the outcome of particular applications to the Commission, such as that in *X v United Kingdom*.[341] The Commission found that the actions of the police in taking and filing photographs without consent of a woman arrested for taking part in a political demonstration disclosed no prima facie breach of Art 8. The reasoning was unclear, but a central factor appeared to be the public and voluntary nature of her activities. The decision has been viewed as out of line with the trend of Art 8 jurisprudence: 'In the opinion of some scholars, the . . . decision may well be an outdated aberration in the case law of the Strasbourg organs.'[342] The decision in *Von Hannover*,[343] although taken in a different context, suggests that the 'public' nature of activities will not necessarily take them outside the ambit of Art 8. This issue is discussed in Chapter 9.[344]

The approach in other jurisdictions may also indicate the direction in which the Strasbourg jurisprudence is likely to develop. The German Supreme Court[345] has refused to follow the approach of the Appeal Court that privacy 'stopped at the doorstep' and that therefore, no action lay for invasion of privacy in respect of events which had taken place outside the home or other clearly private spaces. The approach indicated was that one may still be entitled to respect for privacy in semi-public places if, as the Court put it, it is clear by reference to 'objective criteria' that one wishes to be

---

337   Harris, O'Boyle and Warbrick, op. cit., fn 326, p 309.

338   *Niemetz v FRG* A 251-B (1992).

339   Harris, O'Boyle and Warbrick, op. cit., fn 326, p 309. *Niemetz v FRG* A 251-B (1992) concerned office premises, making it clear that rights to respect for privacy are not dependent on an interest in property.

340   The Convention must be given an 'evolutive' interpretation (*Johnstone v Ireland* A 112 (1986), para 53), which takes account of current standards in European society (*Tyrer v UK* A 26 (1978), para 31). These would be expected to include the presence of privacy laws across Europe.

341   (1973) Appl No 5877/72 16 YBCHE, 328.

342   Bygrave, LA, 'Data protection pursuant to the right to privacy in human rights treaties' (1999) 6(3) IJLIT 247, p 265. Bygrave notes: '. . . there are good grounds for holding that it ought to be accorded little weight in present and future interpretation of Article 8'. In spite of these comments, however, Bygrave concedes that in the later decision of *Friedl v Austria* (1995) A 305B (not treated by the Court on the merits due to friendly settlement) 'the Commission laid weight upon the same . . . kind of factors as those mentioned in *X v United Kingdom*' (ibid, p 266). See also *Stewart-Brady v UK* (1999) 27 EHRR 284, in which a claim of an interference with Art 8 rights due to the taking of a photograph was declared inadmissible (although these findings were made in the context of positive state obligations and there was a conflict with Art 10).

343   See p 819.

344   See pp 822–24.

345   BGH 19 December 1995 BGHZ 131, pp 322–46.

'left alone' so that one can, 'relying on the fact of seclusion, act in a way that [one] would not have done . . . in public'. In other words, the interest in privacy was clearly distinguished from property interests. The Canadian Criminal Code also reflects such a stance.[346] Thus, it may be argued that public/private distinctions based on location are too simplistic and that a test of a reasonable expectation of privacy or, more broadly still, of control of private information is more satisfactory.[347] On the basis of such a test, if, for example, one person engages in a whispered exchange with another in an almost empty street, and this exchange is recorded by means of a listening device, it is contended that an invasion of privacy has occurred which may fall within Art 8(1). It may be noted that this test would bring some use of CCTV – where it captures private actions in semi-public or even public places – within Art 8(1).

As Leigh and Lustgarten observe: 'An atmosphere in which people practise self-censorship . . . is stultifying and fearful . . . Citizens should be able to assume that unless there are overwhelming reasons to the contrary, their thoughts and feelings will be communicated only to those to whom they choose to utter them.[348]' These comments clearly apply equally to conversations in the street, in a vehicle, in pubs, in hotel rooms. Obviously, there may be circumstances in which it is impossible to speak without expecting to be overheard, as in a crowded train. But in other circumstances, this expectation would depend entirely on the circumstances. In a reasonably quiet street it would be viewed as socially and probably morally unacceptable to approach two persons speaking quietly together with the obvious intention of eavesdropping on their conversation, since the two would have a reasonable expectation of enjoying a degree of privacy. It follows, therefore, that the issue as to whether the respect for private life has been infringed by the secret recording of a communication should be resolved not by reliance on fine distinctions regarding the degrees of 'privacy' to be associated with different locations, but according to the intentions and reasonable expectations of at least one of the parties to it.[349] In other words, a shift in the meaning of 'privacy' would have to occur, one which appears to be in accordance with the notion of informational autonomy as the core privacy value and with changing perception of privacy at Strasbourg. Therefore, there is a sound argument that the use of surveillance devices or techniques in most circumstances will lead to findings that an interference with the rights to respect for private life and, where appropriate, to the home and correspondence, under Art 8 has occurred.

In accordance with the law

Once it is established that such an interference has occurred, it cannot be justified if it is not in accordance with the law. Until the 1997 Act and then the RIPA 2000, Part II

---

346 Section 487.01(4).
347 The Press Complaints Commission's Code of Practice defines 'private places [as] public or private property where there is a reasonable expectation of privacy'. Such a test was recommended by the Irish Law Reform Commission Consultation Paper: *Privacy, Surveillance and Interception*, 1996.
348 *In from the Cold* 1994, p 40.
349 This proposition finds support from the position in the US. The US Supreme Court has found: 'the Fourth Amendment protects people not places'; the significant issue was not the location of the covert device, but the existence of a reasonable expectation that privacy would be protected (*Katz v US* (1967) 389 US 347, pp 351–53).

were introduced, the use of various techniques had no sufficient basis in law.[350] Such a basis is now established, but it is questionable whether it is of sufficient quality.[351] The regimes governing the forms of surveillance show dissimilarities, especially between 'intrusive' and 'directed' surveillance. The position regarding the use of intrusive surveillance is broadly the same as that discussed above, in relation to interception, under Part I of the RIPA, since the provisions are equally foreseeable and accessible.[352] The same may be said of the regime under s 97 of the 1997 Act.

Bearing in mind the strictness of these requirements in this context, discussed above,[353] it is not entirely clear that the requirement as to quality would be found to be satisfied in respect of certain of these provisions. This may be said in relation to the use of directed surveillance, and of listening devices within the 1997 Act, but outside s 97. The definition of directed surveillance is confusing and imprecise and creates an uncertain divide between directed and intrusive surveillance. Despite such uncertainty, the regime for intrusive surveillance is much stricter. This uncertainty creates, it is suggested, a fundamental flaw in RIPA 2000, Part II, which may mean that it cannot meet the requirement of quality, in that respect. As indicated above, ss 28, 29 and 30 allow the Secretary of State, by order, to make provision regarding 'designated persons', further grounds, and for allowing further bodies to engage in directed surveillance on the very broad grounds under ss 28 and 29. The extent to which, in all these instances, power is placed in executive hands so that it might be exercised in an unpredictable fashion calls into question the quality of the law, even accepting that in some, but not all, of these instances there is a lesser invasion of privacy, calling for less precision.[354] The accessibility of the law would also be questionable, bearing in mind the opportunities for its extension by executive order, albeit with the approval of Parliament. In respect of all these provisions, the means of keeping a check on their arbitrary use is in doubt due to the failure to include any independent check at all on authorisations of directed surveillance, outside the public authority in question.[355] No judicial or administrative check is necessary, in contrast to the provisions for intrusive surveillance and interception.

The 'in accordance with the law' requirement was considered for example, in *Amann v Switzerland*.[356] In the early 1980s the applicant, a businessman, imported depilatory appliances into Switzerland which he advertised in magazines. In 1981 a woman telephoned the applicant from the former Soviet embassy in Berne to order a depilatory appliance. That telephone call was intercepted by the Federal Public Prosecutor's Office which then requested the Intelligence Service of the police of the Canton of Zürich to

---

350 See above, pp 1054–56 and pp 1058–60.
351 As indicated above, it is clear that Art 8 is not necessarily satisfied merely on the ground that interferences with privacy have a basis in primary legislation. See pp 1008–9.
352 See p 1043.
353 See pp 1043–44.
354 This may be argued by analogy with the findings in *Malone v UK* (1984) 7 EHRR 14 regarding telephone metering as opposed to interception.
355 In *Leander v Sweden* (1987) 9 EHRR 433, the Court said: 'in view of the risk that a system of secret surveillance poses . . . the court must be satisfied that there exist adequate and effective guarantees against abuse' (para 60).
356 (2000) ECHR 87.

carry out an investigation into the applicant. In December 1981 the Public Prosecutor's Office filled in a card on the applicant for its national security card index on the basis of the report drawn up by the Zürich police. In particular, the card indicated that the applicant had been 'identified as a contact with the Russian embassy' and was a businessman. It was numbered (1153:0) 614, that code meaning 'communist country' (1), 'Soviet Union' (153), 'espionage established' (0) and 'various contacts with the Eastern block (614). He could not obtain an effective remedy domestically and applied to Strasbourg, alleging a breach of Art 8. The Court found that the legal provisions relied on by the government, in particular the Federal Council's Decree of 29 April 1958 on the Police Service of the Federal Public Prosecutor's Office, the Federal Criminal Procedure Act and the Federal Council's Directives of 16 March 1981 applicable to the Processing of Personal Data in the Federal Administration, did not contain specific and detailed provisions on the gathering, recording and storing of information. It also pointed out that domestic law, particularly s 66(1ter) FCPA, expressly provided that documents which were no longer 'necessary' or had become 'purposeless' had to be destroyed; the authorities had failed to destroy the data they had gathered on the applicant after it had become apparent, as the Federal Court had pointed out in its judgment in 1994, that no criminal offence was being prepared. The Court concluded that there had been no legal basis for the creation of the card on the applicant and its storage in the Confederation's card index. Therefore it was found that there had been a violation of Art 8 of the Convention. The case concerned interception of telephone communications but the issues of storage and destruction of data apply equally in relation to data acquired by covert surveillance.

Legitimate aims

Assuming that an interference with the Art 8(1) guarantee occurs, which is found, in the particular circumstances which confront a court or the new tribunal, to be in accordance with the law, it must be shown that it had a legitimate aim. The 'legitimate aim' requirement would probably be readily satisfied in respect of intrusive surveillance and the use of surveillance devices under the 1997 Act since the grounds justifying interference under Art 8(2) correspond with the three grounds under s 32(3) of the RIPA and with the 'serious crime' ground under the 1997 Act. This is also probably true of the power to use CCTV under s 163 of the Criminal Justice and Public Order Act 1994.

There may be room for argument that certain of the grounds for the use of directed surveillance under s 28(3) are less clearly within para 2 since they cover, *inter alia*, the purpose of collecting any contribution due to a government department. However, they would probably fall within the 'economic well-being' exception.[357] The possibility is left open of including other grounds, by order of the Secretary of State. Any such further grounds would also have to fall within the para 2 aims. So far, under Art 8(2), the state has always satisfied the legitimate aim requirement.

---

357 *MS v Sweden* (1999) 28 EHRR 313, para 38.

Necessary in a democratic society

It must further be shown that the interference 'corresponds to a pressing social need and, in particular, that it is proportionate to the legitimate aim pursued'.[358] In assessing proportionality in relation to the aim of national security, the Court has allowed a very wide margin of appreciation to the State,[359] but it is less wide in relation to the prevention of crime and arguably also in respect of the other grounds. In any event, the margin of appreciation doctrine should be irrelevant in domestic decisions. In terms of the outcomes of applications, Strasbourg has not provided clear guidance on the question of when a pressing social need would be discerned in this context. In a number of key cases, including *Khan v UK*,[360] which concerned the use of a listening device, it was found that the interference had no basis in law.[361] In a further group of cases, it was found that the interference had such a basis and the safeguards available, particularly in the context of national security, were found to be sufficient, taking the margin of appreciation into account.[362] But some analogous jurisprudence is available.

As indicated above, it was found in *Klass v FRG*[363] that judicial or administrative authority for warrants would provide a degree of independent oversight. While the arrangements for intrusive surveillance under the RIPA 2000, Part II or under s 97 of the 1997 Act may meet this requirement, those under s 93 or for directed surveillance might fail to do so since no independent administrative or judicial check is available before the event. In this respect, the contrast with the arrangements for intrusive surveillance is very clear, bearing in mind the fact that directed surveillance is a means of acquiring large amounts of personal information; the only distinction between it and intrusive surveillance may be the quality of the sound or vision – the content of the information may be almost identical. Therefore, the strong distinction created between the two types of surveillance may be unwarranted. In particular, where a person has authorised himself to conduct surveillance, the requirement of independence could be said to be completely abrogated; it is hard to see that in such an instance, it can be said that a check on the requirements of proportionality is in place.

The key criticism of Part II is that a twin-track scheme is created under it whereby a much more rigorous regime is in place for intrusive as opposed to directed surveillance: intrusive surveillance requires authorisation at a higher level within the public authority and at an external level. Directed surveillance requires lower level internal authorisation and no external authorisation – merely review after the event by the Surveillance Commissioner. This markedly different regime leads to the suggestion that the regime for directed surveillance fails to meet Convention requirements. The general principles espoused at Strasbourg may also be indicative. If it is accepted that informational autonomy lies in the 'core' of Art 8, as a value which a democratic society should respect,[364] interferences with it by a public authority should receive the strictest scrutiny. Such scrutiny would be of the arrangements for authorisation and their application

---

358   *Olsson v Sweden* A 130 (1988), para 67.
359   *Leander v Sweden* (1987) 9 EHRR 433.
360   (2000) 8 BHRC 310.
361   E.g., *Malone v UK* (1984) 7 EHRR 14, *Halford v UK* [1997] IRLR 471; (1997) 24 EHRR 523.
362   E.g., *Christie v UK* 78-A DR E Com HR 119.
363   (1978) 2 EHRR 214.
364   See *Kjeldsen v Denmark* (1976) 1 EHRR 711, p 731.

in the particular instance. Even where the authorisation process itself was found to satisfy Art 8(2), a particular authorisation might be found to allow an interference disproportionate to the legitimate aim pursued. In particular, issues of proportionality might also arise where a listening device placed outside a house provided information of only a marginally lower quality than would be provided were it on the premises. The use of CCTV may be proportionate to the legitimate aim – of preventing crime – pursued, but the lack of regulation of the use of the information obtained may mean that there are insufficient safeguards available.

Using the HRA

Duties of Commissioners

All the Commissioners should comply with the Convention in relation to their review-ing functions under the 1997 Act and Part II of the RIPA. The position is very similar to that in respect of the Interception of Communications Commissioner, since all the Commissioners are bound by the Convention under s 6 of the HRA and are also pro-viding oversight of bodies which are so bound. The Surveillance Commissioners are providing oversight of police officers and other 'public authorities' using surveillance while the Intelligence Services Commissioner is providing oversight of the Services' activities under the RIPA and the Intelligence Services Act.

Criminal proceedings

Significantly, there is no equivalent in the Police Act or Part II of the RIPA to s 17 in Part I of the RIPA, which, as indicated above, largely disallows reference to interceptions in any court or tribunal proceedings. Clearly, any such provision would be counter-productive in prosecution terms. But this does mean, depending on the extent of disclosure to the defence, that a defendant may become aware at some point during criminal proceedings that a surveillance operation has occurred, and therefore will be able to take any avenues of redress that may be open, including raising Convention arguments in the trial itself.

The issues of exclusion of evidence and of disclosure will be most significant. The duty of disclosure to the defence is restricted under the Criminal Procedure and Investigations Act 1996 and the residual common law rules on the public interest.[365] The fact that a particular surveillance technique has been used may not be disclosed on the basis that it is 'sensitive' material. Under that Act, the duty of the CPS is to disclose to the defence all material which it considers might undermine the prosecution case, except sensitive material which should not be disclosed in the public interest. The sensitivity of the material may be based on the need to use the technique in question in a future operation. If the prosecutor considers that the material is sensitive, an application to a court for a ruling to protect it on grounds of public interest immunity must be made.[366] It can be made *ex parte* with notice to the defence or, in an exceptional case,

---

365 The 1996 Act, s 21(2).
366 See ss 3(6) and 7(5).

without notice. In any such application, a judge, bound by s 6 of the HRA, would have to consider Art 6 requirements in respect of such disclosure.[367]

Where it is clear in criminal proceedings that surveillance has been used in order to obtain evidence against the defendant, the defence could seek to establish in a suitable case that it was unauthorised or improperly authorised or was not covered by Part III of the 1997 Act or Part II of the RIPA. The defence could also raise the argument, under s 7(1)(b) of the HRA, that therefore a breach of Art 8 had arisen or that, although the surveillance was properly authorised, a breach had nevertheless occurred since, for example, the requirements of proportionality under Art 8(2) had not been met. Assuming that the surveillance was not authorised, it would not be unlawful unless existing tortious liability had arisen and/or the public authority in question had incurred liability under s 6 of the HRA for breaching Art 8. In other words, surveillance which incurs no tortious or criminal liability, but only leads to a breach of Art 8, is unlawful only in the sense that the public authority using it (normally, of course, the police) has failed to abide by its duty under s 6 of the HRA. It should be noted that there is no offence of conducting unauthorised surveillance, in contrast to the position as regards unauthorised interception,[368] and, as indicated in the Code on Surveillance and discussed below, surveillance will not be unlawful solely on the ground that authorisation has not been sought. The court, as itself a public authority under s 6 of the HRA, is bound to accept that a remedy must be available for a breach of Art 8. The public authority using it would have to provide such redress, but as explained below, owing to s 65 of the RIPA, this argument would usually be raised in the single tribunal where a complainant is seeking a remedy for breach of Art 8. But, in criminal proceedings, the redress sought could include exclusion of evidence. Thus, the defence could argue either that the evidence had been obtained unlawfully since, for example, the police had committed a trespass in obtaining it *and* had breached Art 8, or that it had been obtained unlawfully due to such a breach alone. In either instance, there might appear to be an argument, which is considered further in Chapter 13, that the evidence obtained should be excluded under s 78 of PACE. However, the courts are likely to continue to be unreceptive to this argument.

---

367 These guidelines were provided in *Davis, Rowe and Johnson* [1993] 1 WLR 613. Now that the use of public interest immunity in that case has been found to breach Art 6 by the Court (*Rowe and Davis v UK* Appl No 28901/95; [1999] Crim LR 410; judgment of the Court of 16/2/00 (2000) 30 EHRR 1) they will have to be re-examined. The domestic courts will have the opportunity of doing so now that Human Rights Act is fully in force. The findings in the same context in *Fitt and Jasper v UK* (1999) EHRLR 430 will be relevant. The Court said that in those instances, the judge had been able to consider the sensitive material in question and therefore was able to conduct a balancing act between fairness to the defence and to the prosecution. On that basis, no breach of Art 6 was found. The *Davis, Rowe and Johnson* guidelines may be compared with those adopted in other countries, particularly those used in Denmark after the *Van Traa Inquiry Report* (an inquiry which is generally viewed as an especially useful guide to the use of such methods in modern policing) into the use of covert methods, including particularly the use of informers and undercover officers. The Danish law adopted in response sought to ensure that the trial judge or defence would not be subject to complete non-disclosure of evidence and of investigative methods.

368 Under RIPA 2000, s 1, it is an offence to intercept communications intentionally and without lawful authority.

The leading case of *Khan (Sultan)*[369] on exclusion of evidence obtained by the unlawful use of a listening device applies, and at present it is clear that the stance taken still prevails in the post-HRA era since it has been re-affirmed by the House of Lords in *AG's Reference (No 3 of 1999)*.[370] In *Khan*, a listening device had been secretly installed on the outside of a house which Khan was visiting. The case against him rested solely on the tape recording obtained. The defence argued, *inter alia*, that the recording was inadmissible as evidence because the police had no statutory authority to place listening devices on private property, that therefore such placement was a trespass, and, further, that admission of the recording would breach Art 8. The House of Lords agreed with the Court of Appeal that the evidence was admissible, relying on the decision in *Sang*[371] to the effect that improperly obtained evidence other than 'involuntary' confessions is admissible in a criminal trial subject to a narrow discretion under s 78 of PACE to exclude it.[372] The decision in *Khan* not to exclude the evidence was found to accord with Art 6 at Strasbourg.[373] A Chamber of the Court found that, at the time, the interference with the Art 8 guarantees had no basis in law and therefore a breach of Art 8 was found. This breach was *not* found to necessitate exclusion of the evidence obtained on the basis that the assessment of evidence is a matter for the national courts, and therefore no breach of Art 6 was found. This issue is discussed further in Chapter 13.[374]

Thus, although arguments may be raised in court that Art 8 has been breached in conducting surveillance, it is unlikely that exclusion of any evidence obtained would follow. So use of this avenue as a means of encouraging the police to respect the Art 8 guarantees has been at present almost entirely closed off.

Civil actions

Covert surveillance conducted without an authorisation is not unlawful on that basis alone. As indicated above, the Code of Practice on Covert Surveillance (2005) made under s 71(3)(a) of the RIPA makes the position explicit in para 2.2 in stating that there is no requirement on the part of a public authority to obtain an authorisation for a covert surveillance operation and makes it clear that the decision not to obtain an authorisation would not, of itself, make an action unlawful, but that liability could arise under the HRA. Intrusive surveillance involving an entry onto property and/or damage to it could be challenged in the ordinary courts since, if unauthorised, its use will amount to a crime or tort. Where directed surveillance involves an entry on to non-residential premises or damage to them such actions would also be available.

Other forms of surveillance may breach Art 8, but will not be trespassory or attract any criminal liability. In such circumstance a complainant might, theoretically, have a

---

369 [1996] 3 All ER 289; (1996) 146 NLJ 1024, HL; [1995] QB 27, CA.
370 [2001] 2 WLR 56.
371 [1980] AC 402; [1979] 2 All ER 1222, HL.
372 See Chapter 13, p 1290.
373 *Khan v UK* Appl No 35394/97 (1999) 27 EHRR CD 58, judgment of the Court (2000) 8 BHRC 310.
374 Pp 1293–95.

remedy under the doctrine of confidence, assuming that some information was obtained and was used in some manner.[375] But in such cases, the state body in question would normally be able to argue that the public interest defence applied.[376] Any court adjudicating on an action in confidence or trespass in this context would be bound by s 6 of the HRA to ensure that the Convention rights were complied with,[377] but the action would be based on the pre-existing common law, rather than on s 7(1)(a).[378] Where surveillance attracts no existing criminal or civil liability, the position is more complex. The bodies or persons authorising and undertaking covert surveillance are all public authorities under s 6 of the HRA and therefore an action for breach of Art 8 could be brought against them under s 7(1)(a) of the HRA[379] where covert surveillance occurred but was not authorised, or improperly authorised, or properly authorised, but nevertheless in breach of Art 8. A s 7(1)(a) action, however, against the bodies most likely to use surveillance, in particular the police,[380] would have to be brought in the tribunal set up under Part IV of the RIPA due to the provision of s 65(2)(a) of the RIPA, which is discussed below. Thus, in most circumstances a tort action in direct reliance on Art 8 would not be open.

It should be noted that persons engaged in all forms of surveillance under Part II are exempted from civil liability under s 27(2) in respect of conduct 'incidental' to authorised conduct and – in an opaquely worded provision – in relation to conduct to which the warrant or authorisation procedure under a 'relevant' Act[381] is inapplicable (not capable of being granted) and where it would not reasonably be expected to have been sought. This appears to cover forms of surveillance engaged in by public authorities which have no statutory basis and which, but for s 27(2), might attract liability under existing torts or under s 7 of the HRA in respect of a breach of Art 8. Since s 27(2) could, potentially, prevent a court from discharging its duty under s 6 of the HRA there is a case for suggesting that courts should restrict its ambit by using s 3 of the HRA to interpret the term 'reasonably' restrictively.

---

375 See Chapter 9, pp 876–920.
376 This defence succeeded in *Hellewell* [1995] 1 WLR 804 in respect of unauthorised police use of a photograph of the defendant, who had been convicted of theft from shops, as part of a shopwatch scheme.
377 See Chapter 4, pp 215–17.
378 The process of infusion of the rights into the common law is leading to the creation of new torts or at least a stretching of the boundaries of the old ones. See the comments of Sedley LJ in *Douglas and Others v Hello!* [2001] 2 WLR 992, and see generally Chapter 9, pp 902–15.
379 Under s 7(1)(a) 'a person who claims that a public authority has acted (or proposes to act) in a way that is made unlawful under s 6(1) may bring proceedings against the authority in the appropriate tribunal . . .'. Under s 6(1) 'It is unlawful for a public authority to act in a way which is incompatible with a Convention right [unless the proviso of s 6(2) applies].
380 Section 65(6) provides: 'for the purposes only of subsection (3)', conduct to which Part II applies, an entry on or interference with property or an interference with wireless telegraphy is not conduct falling within sub-section (5) 'unless it is conduct by or on behalf of a person holding any office, rank or position with (a) any of the intelligence services; (b) any of Her Majesty's forces; (c) any police force; (d) the National Criminal Intelligence Service; (e) the National Crime Squad; or (f) the Commissioners of Customs and Excise. . . .'. (The NCIS and NCS were amalgamated into SOCA by the SOCA 2005.)
381 RIPA 2000; Intelligence Services Act 1994, s 5; Police Act 1997, Part III.

Actions under s 7(1)(a) of the HRA

The public authorities using forms of surveillance and authorising officers within the authorities are all, by definition,[382] subject to the Convention under s 6 of the HRA. The possibility of challenging decisions of such public authorities, as opposed to those of Commissioners, under s 7(1)(a), might appear to be available. However, s 65 of the RIPA stands in the way of Convention-based actions in the ordinary courts. Under s 65(2), the tribunal will be the appropriate forum for the purposes of s 7(1)(a) of the HRA in relation to certain proceedings. These proceedings are indicated in ss 65(3) and (5). In essence, these provisions mean that s 65 stands in the way of challenges to actions of the security and intelligence services, or persons acting on their behalf, based on s 6 of the HRA (since s 7(1)(a) of the HRA is intended to provide for the bringing of proceedings where a public authority has acted unlawfully under s 6). Section 65(5) and (6) also bar the way to actions in the ordinary courts under s 7(1)(a) against the police, intelligence services, Customs and Excise, NCIS and the National Crime Squad (now amalgamated in SOCA) in respect of surveillance under Part II of the RIPA or s 93 of the 1997 Act, which raises Convention issues under s 6 of the HRA. These s 7(1)(a) actions must be brought only in the tribunal.

Judicial review

Scrutiny of the Commissioners' oversight function in the ordinary courts also appears to be precluded. The 1997 Act contains an ouster clause in s 91(10) which is very similar to that contained in the Interception of Communications Act 1985. It provides: 'The decisions of the Chief Commissioner or . . . any other Commissioner (including decisions as to his jurisdiction) shall not be subject to appeal or liable to be questioned in any court'. The inclusion of 'decisions as to his jurisdiction' was, of course, intended to make the Commissioners' decisions unreviewable. This ouster clause was not repealed by the RIPA, but it now no longer relates to the Commissioners' complaints' role, which was removed under s 70(2)(c) of that Act.[383]

Section 65 does not prevent challenges by way of judicial review or civil actions against public authorities other than the police or the intelligence and security services or other bodies listed in s 65(6) relating to surveillance.[384] Also, judicial review of decisions of those bodies listed could be sought without relying on s 7(1)(a) of the HRA. Any possibilities of bringing judicial review against the police or intelligence services which existed in the pre-HRA era still exist, due to s 11 of the HRA, so long as such possibilities do not depend on using s 7(1)(a) of the HRA. The ironic possibility arises, in relation to surveillance, that the development of judicial review taking Art 8 into account, as in the pre-HRA era,[385] might be more far-reaching and of greater significance than such development in reliance on s 7(1)(a), despite the fact that the review would be less intensive.[386]

---

382 Section 81(1) provides that 'public authority' has the meaning given it by the HRA 1998, s 6.
383 Sections 106, 107(6) of Sched 7 to the 1997 Act were repealed under the RIPA 2000.
384 This is of significance where, e.g., a public authority not yet brought within the RIPA 2000, Part II used surveillance without falling within any existing liability, or where this occurred and the public authority, although within the Act, fell outside those listed in s 65(6).
385 See Chapter 3, pp 130–33.
386 See Chapter 4, pp 235–39.

Section 66 leaves open the possibility that the remaining jurisdiction of the ordinary courts in relation to surveillance (and, if necessary, to interception) will be partially ousted, by executive order, in providing: 'An order under section 65(2)(d) allocating proceedings to the Tribunal may (a) provide for the Tribunal to exercise jurisdiction in relation to that matter to the exclusion of the jurisdiction of any court or tribunal; but (b) if it does so provide, must contain provision conferring a power on the Tribunal, in the circumstances provided for in the order, to remit the proceedings to the court or tribunal which would have had jurisdiction apart from the order.' In other words, an avenue to court action would be left open if this course was taken in future.

Conclusions

The upshot, then, is that challenges by way of judicial review or tortious actions remain available against some public authorities, whether or not it is argued that the authority has breached s 6 of the HRA. Actions against the police or intelligence services in relation to surveillance operations, based on ss 6 and 7(1)(a) of the HRA, will have to be brought in the new tribunal only because of s 65 of the RIPA. It is notable that court action was not ruled out expressly under the Security Services Act 1989, the Intelligence Services Act 1994 or the Police Act 1997, although it was – in effect – under s 9 of the 1985 Act. In providing for complaint to be made to the old tribunal, s 5 of the 1989 Act and s 9 of the 1994 Act implied that complaint could not be made to a court. The same could be said of the Commissioner mechanism under the 1997 Act. But the provisions did not expressly exclude the jurisdiction of the courts since otherwise, the agencies would then have been placed, in effect, above the law. Section 65 does not exclude the courts' jurisdiction regarding surveillance by the police and intelligence services except in relation to breach of the Convention rights. Therefore, one purpose of the RIPA is to insulate all surveillance undertaken by the intelligence services, and much of that undertaken by the police, from the effects of the HRA, applied in the ordinary courts, except within prosecutions.

6 The single tribunal

Introduction

This tribunal, set up under s 65 of the RIPA,[387] has taken over from the Interception of Communications Tribunal and the Intelligence and Security Services Tribunals; it has also taken over the complaints role of the Commissioners set up under Part III of the 1997 Act.

---

387 Schedule 3 governs the membership of the single tribunal. Members, who are appointed for five years by the Lord Chancellor on behalf of the Queen, must have held 'high judicial office' or have a 10-year general qualification within the meaning of s 71 of the Courts and Legal Services Act 1990; in Scotland and Northern Ireland they must be practitioners of at least 10 years' standing. Thus, they need not be judges, although the President must be a judge. Its members are remunerated by the Secretary of State, but can be removed from office only on an address to the Queen by both Houses of Parliament under Sched 3, para 1(5). These arrangements afford the tribunal a measure of independence from the executive.

It may be noted initially that in practice, applications to the tribunal are not be frequent since, as noted above, an individual has normally no means of knowing that an interception or surveillance has occurred; in contrast to the position in Germany[388] or Denmark,[389] the police and the other state agencies have no duty to inform him or her of the interception, after it is over. This position is contrary to the recommendation of the Data Protection Working Party for the European Commission which said in May 1999 that a 'person under surveillance [should] be informed of this as soon as possible'.[390] An individual is therefore normally only able to bring complaints or proceedings to the tribunal only if she has become aware of the surveillance due to criminal proceedings. Section 17 of the RIPA will normally prevent this occurring in respect of interception and therefore complaints regarding interception are likely to be very rare. Police officers or other state agents who are aware that improperly authorised or unauthorised interception is occurring have no means of complaining to the tribunal or the Commissioners.[391] Section 4(3) of the Official Secrets Act 1989, as amended by the 2000 Act,[392] is also available to punish such disclosures.

A further limitation is placed on complaints relating to interceptions. Section 67(5) provides that unless the tribunal in the circumstances considers it 'equitable' to do so, such complaints will not be considered if made more than one year after the conduct in question took place. Otherwise, conduct under s 65(5) can be considered whenever it occurred. Thus, pre-commencement surveillance can be brought before the tribunal.

Jurisdiction

Under s 65(2), the tribunal has three main functions and a potential fourth one. First, challenges to surveillance on Convention grounds by certain bodies or to interception by all bodies must be brought within it. In the words of the sub-section, 'it will be the only appropriate tribunal for the purposes of section 7 of the HRA 1998 in relation to any proceedings under sub-section (1)(a) of that section (proceedings for actions incompatible with Convention rights) which fall within sub-section 3 of this section'. Under s 65(3), they are proceedings against any of the intelligence services '. . . or against any other person in respect of any conduct, or proposed conduct, by or on behalf of any of those services' or 'relating to the taking place in any challengeable circumstances of any conduct falling within subsection (5)'.

Section 65(5) applies to 'conduct . . . (whenever it occurred) by or on behalf of any of the intelligence services; in connection with the interception of communications in the course of their transmission by means of a postal service or telecommunication system'; conduct to which . . . Part II applies, any entry on or interference with property

---

388 See *Klass v Federal Republic of Germany* (1978) 2 EHRR 214. Germany's current bugging law contains this requirement.

389 Criminal Procedure Code, para 788.

390 See Statewatch (1999) Vol 9 Nos 3 and 4. The UK is the only member state to have entered a derogation to Principle 2(2) of the Council of Europe Recommendation on the use of data in the police sector R(87)15.

391 Under RIPA 2000, s 19(4), any such disclosure is an offence punishable on indictment by a maximum term of five years' imprisonment: s 19(4)(a).

392 Schedule 4, para 5.

or any interference with wireless telegraphy'. Section 65(6) introduces a significant limitation in providing: 'for the purposes only of subsection (3)', conduct to which Part II applies, an entry on or interference with property or an interference with wireless telegraphy is not conduct falling within sub-section (5) 'unless it is conduct by or on behalf of a person holding any office, rank or position with (a) any of the intelligence services; (b) any of Her Majesty's forces; (c) any police force; (d) the National Criminal Intelligence Service; (e) the National Crime Squad; or (f) the Commissioners of Customs and Excise . . .'. In other words, as indicated above, the intention is that surveillance by these bodies can be challenged only in the tribunal where it is argued that they have breached a Convention right.

Secondly, the tribunal is the appropriate forum for complaints if, under s 65(4), 'it is a complaint by a person who is aggrieved by any conduct falling within subsection (5) which he believes to have taken place in relation to him, to any of his property, to any communications sent by or to him, or intended for him, or to his use of any postal service, telecommunications service or telecommunication system; and to have taken place in challengeable circumstances or to have been carried out by or on behalf of any of the intelligence services'. Sections 65(7) and (8) apply in relation to both ss 65(3) and (4). Section 65(7) defines 'challengeable circumstances' as conduct which '(a) takes place with the authority, or purported authority, of anything falling within subsection (8); or (b) the circumstances are such that (whether or not there is such authority) it would not have been appropriate for the conduct to take place without it, or at least without proper consideration having been given to whether such authority should be sought'.

Thus, in its complaints and 'proceedings' jurisdiction, the tribunal can consider unauthorised interception. In relation to complaints, the term used under s 67(3)(b) is 'investigate the authority' which does not appear to confine the tribunal, bearing in mind the meaning of challengeable circumstances', to merely considering whether the authority (if it exists) was properly given. Section 65(8) covers: interception warrants under the Acts of 1985 or 2000, an authorisation under Part II of the 2000 Act, a permission of the Secretary of State under Sched 2 (relating to powers to obtain data protected by encryption), or an authorisation under s 93 of the Police Act 1997.

Thirdly, the tribunal has jurisdiction (s 65(2)(c)) to determine a reference to them by a person that he has suffered detriment as a consequence 'of any prohibition or restriction' under s 17 (the exclusion of evidence section) on his relying on any matter in, or for the purposes of, civil proceedings. It is notable that no means is provided of seeking redress for detriment arising when evidence is excluded in *criminal* proceedings.[393] Finally, under s 65(2)(d), the Secretary of State can also, by order, allocate other proceedings to the tribunal but a draft of the order must have been approved by a resolution of each House of Parliament.[394]

---

393 See *R v Preston* [1993] 4 All ER 638 (above, p 686) in which the appellants may have suffered detriment due to the exclusion of material derived from phone tapping under the predecessor of s 17, s 9 of the 1985 Act.
394 Section 66(3).

Procedure

The tribunal is modelled on the Special Immigration Appeals Commission (SIAC)[395] which in turn provided the model for the tribunal set up under the Northern Ireland Act 1998.[396] The Investigatory Powers Tribunal Rules[397] came into force on the same date as the HRA – 2 October 2000. Under s 68, the tribunal is entitled to determine its own procedure, subject to these rules. The current rules follow the old practices in various respects. Hearings are secret.[398] The Rules envisage the possibility of an oral hearing, but there is no right to such a hearing.[399] The Rules allow for the possibility of separate oral hearings; the applicant and the representatives of the public authority will not confront each other.[400] Under s 68(6) and (7)(i) 'every person by whom or on whose application there has been granted any authorisation under Part II . . . must disclose or provide to the Tribunal all such documents and information as the tribunal may require [in the exercise *inter alia* of its jurisdiction under s 65(2)(a)]'. But information given at the separate hearing can be withheld from the applicant unless the person providing it consents to its disclosure.[401]

The current tribunal, like the old one, merely reports its conclusion; it cannot report the reason for the decision.[402] If it finds that no warrant or authorisation exists and that apparently no surveillance or interception is occurring, or that proper authorisation occurred, it merely informs the complainant that the complaint has not been upheld. The complainant who suspects, for example, that his or her phone or e-mails are being tapped is then left not knowing whether in fact tapping is occurring. As indicated above, on no occasion so far in the six years of its existence has the Tribunal concluded that there has been a contravention of RIPA or the Human Rights Act 1998. But if the complaint is upheld, the complainant will know that tapping/surveillance was occurring but unauthorised. This is, at least theoretically, an improvement on the old position since previously the fact that a complaint was not upheld could still mean that unauthorised tapping was occurring. For example, on 6 December 1991, Alison Halford complained to the Interception of Communications Tribunal in respect of the suspected tapping of her home and office telephones.[403] From the circumstances, it appeared that tapping was probably occurring. She was informed on 21 February 1992, without any

---

395 Set up under s 1 of the Special Immigration Appeals Act 1997 in response to the findings in *Chahal v UK* (1997) 23 EHRR 413.

396 Under s 90.

397 SI 2000/2665.

398 Rule 9(6): 'The Tribunal's proceedings, including any oral hearings, shall be conducted in private.'

399 Rule 9(2): 'The Tribunal shall be under no duty to hold oral hearings but may do so in accordance with this rule (and not otherwise).' Rule 9(3): 'The Tribunal may hold oral hearings at which the complainant may make representations, give evidence and call witnesses.'

400 Rule 9(4): 'The Tribunal may hold *separate* oral hearings which the person whose conduct is the subject of the complaint, the public authority against whom s 7 proceedings are brought . . . may be required to attend and at which that person or authority may make representations, give evidence and call witnesses' (emphasis added).

401 Under Rule 2, the tribunal may not disclose to the complainant or any other person any information disclosed or provided to the tribunal in the course of [an oral hearing] without the consent of the person who provided it.

402 The 2000 Act, s 68(4). This matter was covered by the 1985 Act, s 7(4)(1) and Sched 1, para 4(2).

403 See the facts of *Halford v UK* [1997] IRLR 471; (1997) 24 EHRR 523, p 1042 above.

reason given, that the complaint had not been upheld: no contravention of ss 2–5 of the Act had been found. It later confirmed by letter that it could not specify whether any interception had in fact taken place. She was left in ignorance as to whether an intercept had indeed been authorised, whether one was in place, although unauthorised, or whether no interception was occurring.[404] Had it been authorised it is inconceivable, bearing in mind the circumstances, for it to have been authorised properly.

In its 'proceedings' under s 65(2)(a), the tribunal uses 'the principles applicable by a court on an application for judicial review'. Under the HRA it therefore must apply the principles a court bound by s 6 of the HRA would apply on such an application. The proportionality requirements under the RIPA should be strictly scrutinised. But one problem is, as Leigh and Lustgarten have argued, that the procedure may be unsuitable as a means of conducting such scrutiny due to its inefficacy in a fact-finding role.[405] Clearly, this problem is likely to be exacerbated by the non-disclosure of relevant information.

So it appears likely that the determinations of the current tribunal will be as secretive as those of the old and the position of the complainant equally weak. Clearly, the difficulty with tribunals of this nature is that they may seek to give the appearance of adversarial proceedings, but the limitations under which they operate, which severely curtail opportunities of challenging evidence, undermine the potential benefits of such proceedings.[406]

Remedies

The remedial powers of the current tribunal are similar to those of the old.[407] Under s 67(7), 'the Tribunal . . . shall have power to make any such award of compensation or other order as they think fit; [subject to the power of the Secretary of State to make rules under section 69(2)(h)] . . . and . . . may make an order quashing or cancelling any warrant or authorisation; and an order requiring the destruction of any records of information which has been obtained in exercise of any power conferred by a warrant or authorisation; or is held by any public authority in relation to any person' (subject to s 69 orders). Thus the award of remedies continues to be discretionary; the successful complainant or applicant could be left remediless. The tribunal does not have the

---

404 Lord Nolan, the previous Commissioner, has defended the failure to inform complainants as to whether an intercept has occurred on this basis: 'If the tribunal were able to tell a complainant that he or she had not been the subject of legitimate interception, silence or any equivocal answer on another occasion might be interpreted as an implication that interception had taken place. Furthermore a positive answer would allow criminals or terrorists to know whether they were subject to interception or not.' (Report of the Commissioner under the Interception of Communications Act 1998, Cm 4364, published June 1999, p 2, para 13 and p 11).

405 See Leigh, I and Lustgarten, L, 'Making rights real: the courts, remedies and the Human Rights Act' (1999) 158 CLJ 509.

406 See Walker, C, *The Prevention of Terrorism*, p 82; he advocates an inquisitorial system for such tribunals; see also White [1999] PL 413, discussing the tribunal set up under the Northern Ireland Act 1998.

407 Under the 1985 Act, s 7(5), the tribunal could order quashing of the warrant, destruction of material obtained and payment of compensation to the victim.

power to make a declaration of incompatibility.[408] If the tribunal finds in favour of an applicant, a report would not automatically go to the Prime Minister under s 68(5); it would do so only if the Secretary of State bore some responsibility in the matter.

Recourse to the courts from the tribunal

At present, the RIPA seeks to make it impossible for a member of the public who is dissatisfied with the outcome of the tribunal procedure to seek a remedy in the courts. The Act, like the 1985, 1989, 1994 and 1997 Acts, contains a post-*Anisminic* ouster clause. Section 67(8) provides: 'Except to such extent as the Secretary of State may by order otherwise provide, determinations, awards, orders and other decisions of the tribunal (including decisions as to whether they have jurisdiction) shall not be subject to appeal or be liable to be questioned in any court.' This leaves open the possibility that a tribunal or other body might be established to hear appeals.[409] Under s 67(9), the Secretary of State is under a duty to establish such a body to hear appeals relating to the exercise of the tribunal's jurisdiction under s 65(2)(c) or (d), but not, significantly, in relation to the broader and much more important jurisdiction under s 65(2)(a) or (b).

The upshot is, at present, that the citizen cannot challenge a finding as to interception rather than surveillance outside the tribunal since both s 17 and s 67(8) stand in the way of so doing. A citizen seeking to challenge a tribunal decision in respect of surveillance would be unaffected by s 17, but would have to seek to circumvent s 67(8).

Under s 3 of the HRA it is conceivable that s 67(8) could be interpreted in an application for leave under Order 53[410] in accordance with the Convention in such a way as to allow review. The argument for seeking to circumvent s 67(8) would depend upon the extent to which the tribunal appeared to meet Convention requirements, considered below. The courts have not so far circumvented such post-*Anisminic*[411] clauses. It could be argued that the wording of s 67(8) cannot be intended to be taken literally. The courts could rely on *Anisminic* itself in seeking to satisfy s 6 of the HRA, in that since the word 'decision' is used in relation to tribunal findings themselves, and in relation to its jurisdiction, the argument is open that any decision tainted by an error of law is a nullity; and therefore the ouster clause cannot bite on it.

Since the tribunal can determine its own jurisdiction under s 67(8), and it is bound by s 6 of the HRA, argument could also be raised before it that, at least in respect of the circumstances of certain claims, it does not provide a fair hearing under Art 6, due *inter alia* to orders made under s 69, and that therefore its duty under s 6 requires it to declare that its jurisdiction does not cover such claims. If the tribunal is unreceptive to such claims, which is, of course, likely, they may eventually have to be raised at Strasbourg.

---

408 See the HRA 1998, s 4(5), discussed in Chapter 4, p 200.
409 Section 67(8) by an Order of the Secretary of State.
410 Of the Rules of the Supreme Court and the Supreme Court Act 1981, s 31.
411 In *Anisminic v Foreign Compensation Commission* [1969] 2 AC 147 the House of Lords refused to accept that the jurisdiction of the courts was entirely ousted on the basis that the Commission had acted outside its powers. Therefore, it had not made a determination; it had made a purported determination – i.e., a nullity. The ouster clause under the RIPA seeks to avoid this possibility, since it provides that the jurisdiction of the tribunal cannot be questioned in any court.

The influence of the HRA

The tribunal is bound by all the rights, including Art 6, under s 6 of the HRA, but Art 6 will apply only if the tribunal hearings are within its field of application. The proceedings or determination of complaints in the tribunal could be viewed as the 'determination of civil rights and obligations' under Art 6(1). The term 'civil' has, however, been taken to mean that these are rights in private rather than public law,[412] although it has been argued that: 'Recent jurisprudence by which more and more rights and obligations have been brought within Art 6, is not easy to explain in terms of any distinction between private and public law which is found in European national law'.[413]

In its proceedings, it will be likely to inquire into breaches of Art 8, which represents a right binding on public authorities, including the agencies, under s 6 of the HRA. At Strasbourg, that in itself would not be sufficient to engage Art 6, while domestically, the guarantees may be viewed as operating in public law only, in which case Art 6 would not apply. On the other hand, certain of the rights claimed are private law rights, since where authorisation is not given, existing tortious liability may arise.[414] The term 'civil' has an autonomous Convention meaning and therefore cannot merely be assigned the meaning of 'private' as understood in UK administrative law. Whether a breach of the RIPA, which gives rise to liability only under Art 8, could be viewed as a matter of private law is debatable, although Strasbourg may be moving towards a position in which 'all those rights which are individual rights under the national legal system and fall into the sphere of general freedom . . . must be seen as civil rights'.[415] Where it could be argued that breach of the RIPA did not give rise to liability under Art 8,[416] which may be the case in relation to some use of covert human sources, this question would be even more problematic and it would appear that Art 6 would not be engaged, although arguably it would where (a) existing tortious liability and breach of a Convention right appeared to arise; and (b) where breach of a right only appeared to arise.[417] SIAC, which resembles this tribunal, has been found to fall within Art 6 on the basis that it is determining civil rights and obligations.[418]

The better view is, it is contended, that the tribunal is bound by Art 6, at least in relation to its 'proceedings' jurisdiction, in which it is acting in a more judicial manner. It has potentially a pivotal role in upholding Convention rights in the face of the most significant assertions of state power. It would therefore be contrary to its role to find that it itself was not bound by the key due process guarantee. From a domestic standpoint, it would be anomalous in the extreme if were not so bound, bearing in mind its role in satisfying s 7(1)(a) of the HRA in respect of the obligations of a wide range of bodies, including, in particular, the police, under the RIPA. Whether it is within the field of application of Art 6 will be a matter which, initially, may be raised before the tribunal

---

412   *Ringeisen v Austria* A 13 (1971), para 94.
413   Harris, O'Boyle, Warbrick, *The European Convention on Human Rights* 1995, pp 174–75.
414   See *Golder v UK* A 18 (1975).
415   *Bentham v UK* B 80 (1983), para 10, dissenting opinions of Mr Melchior and Mr Frowen.
416   See above, pp 1042–46, 1068–75, for discussion as to invasions of privacy which are likely to engage Art 8.
417   But see *Fayed v UK* (1994) 18 EHRR 393, in which it was found that although, strictly speaking, there was no legal basis for the action and so no dispute to trigger Art 6, Art 6 applied to blanket immunities preventing access to a court.
418   See *A and Others*, discussed Chapter 14, pp 1340–41.

itself. If it considers that it is adjudicating on a public law matter, and is therefore outside Art 6, the matter will no doubt be raised at Strasbourg eventually.

Assuming that the tribunal is covered by Art 6(1) or, under the development of the Strasbourg jurisprudence may be found to be so covered in future, it is hard to see that it meets the Art 6 fair hearing requirements, bearing in mind the procedure it may follow, indicated above, since the complainant or applicant may be in such a weak position before it. As Chapter 2 indicated, since Art 6(3) contains *minimum* guarantees, the para 1 protection of a fair hearing goes beyond para 3.[419] In investigating a fair hearing, the domestic authorities are not confined to the para 3 guarantees; they can consider further requirements of fairness. If consideration is given to the procedures in question, it is apparent that, apart from any of the other requirements of fairness, the minimal safeguards of Art 6(3) may not be satisfied. In particular, as indicated above, the power to limit or prevent cross-examination, or exclude the applicant[420] or her legal representative, or limit disclosure of evidence, may not comply with Art 6(1) or (3).[421]

As indicated, the tribunal will apply the principles of judicial review in its adjudications, which will include considering proportionality, since it is bound by s 6 of the HRA, and Art 8(2) requires such consideration. The problem will be, as Chapter 4 indicated, that in order to consider proportionality the tribunal may need to evaluate a number of factual matters. But it is bound, as indicated, by subordinate legislation and may have no discretion as to requiring cross-examination or disclosure of documents. Thus, the procedural limitations under which it operates may place even greater difficulties in its path in considering issues of proportionality than there would be in an ordinary court, in judicial review proceedings. It appears therefore that it operates a very 'light touch' review, based in effect on *Wednesbury* unreasonableness, and so it may fail to satisfy the demands of Art 13, as recently interpreted at Strasbourg;[422] therefore *a fortiori* there is an argument that it does not satisfy Art 6. This will depend on its interpretation of the requirements of judicial review: under the HRA the use of judicial review principles by the tribunal should now include consideration of compliance with the Convention rights and therefore a more intensive review. If, despite the constraints it is under, it operates such review, at least in instances in which national security is not in issue, Art 13 may now be satisfied.[423] Its inability to give reasons or to take a binding decision may not render it ineffective.[424]

---

419 See pp 60–64.
420 See, on this point, *Zana v Turkey* (1997) 27 EHRR 667, in which, in the context of terrorism, the applicant was not allowed to be present at the trial; a breach of Art 6 was found on this basis.
421 See further Chapter 13, pp 1259–60.
422 *Smith and Grady v UK* (2000) 29 EHRR 493. The domestic court found that the continuance of the ban on homosexuals in the armed forces was not beyond the range of responses which was open to a reasonable decision maker. The Strasbourg Court considered that the threshold at which the domestic court could find the policy irrational was set so high that it effectively precluded consideration of the proportionality of the ban with the aim in view. Therefore judicial review was not found to satisfy the requirements of Art 13. The findings in *Smith and Grady v UK* on this point marked a departure from the stance preciously taken: see *Soering v UK* A 161 (1989). See also *Esbester v UK* 18 EHRR CD 72, on this point.
423 See further Chapter 2, pp 106–8 and Chapter 4, p 165.
424 *Esbester v UK* 18 EHRR CD 72.

Following *Tinnelly v UK*,[425] if it is argued that documents or sources cannot be disclosed on grounds of national security or the prevention of crime under Art 8(2), the applicant could argue that the Art 6 requirements override such a claim. The success of such an argument would depend upon the particular circumstances of a claim and in particular the ground under the RIPA in question since, as the Court found in *Tinnelly*, proportionality should be found between the infringement of the rights of the claimant and the aim in question. Where the aim concerns, for example, one of the 'economic' grounds founding directed surveillance under the RIPA, the claim of the state would be less pressing and the question of proportionality should be more intensively scrutinised. If this was impossible due to the procedural constraints, the applicant could claim that the tribunal should consider whether its duty under s 6 of the HRA requires it to disapply the subordinate legislation in question, and conduct, in such circumstances, a more intensive inquiry. This possibility would be open to it since s 6(2)(b) of the HRA does not apply in respect of subordinate legislation, while it cannot be said that s 69 of the RIPA, which only provides that the Secretary of State *may* make the orders in question, requires the tribunal to depart from Art 6.

In respect of the national security ground under the RIPA, the tribunal probably takes the view that it cannot consider the documents in question or other relevant matters in order to make a finding as to proportionality. In *Balfour v Foreign and Commonwealth Office*,[426] the Court found that once an actual or potential risk to national security had been demonstrated by a public interest immunity certificate, the Court should not exercise its right to inspect the documents. This view of national security as the exclusive domain of the executive was not adhered to in the robust approach taken to the concept in the context of deportation by the Special Immigration Appeals Commission (on which the new tribunal is partially modelled) in the case of *Secretary of State for the Home Dept v Rehman*.[427] However, the Court of Appeal overturned their ruling, finding that the threat to national security was for the government to determine and that it should be broadly defined to include the possibility of future threats, including those to the UK's 'allies'. The House of Lords confirmed that finding.[428]

These findings are not, it is argued, fully in accordance with the findings of the Strasbourg Court in *Tinnelly* or in *Chahal v UK*.[429] Both, particularly *Tinnelly*, took the view that the threat to national security should be demonstrated. Where Art 13, as opposed to Art 6, was in question, as in *Chahal*, the requirements thereby placed on the state would be weaker, since Art 13 must be read with Art 8(2).[430] But where Art 6 is engaged, as indicated, the requirements would be stricter. The tribunal may be placed in the difficult position of choosing between the domestic and the Strasbourg jurisprudence as to the stance it should take in respect of assertions of national security considerations. If so, the way would be open, under s 3 of the HRA, to depart from the former.

---

425 (1998) 27 EHRR 249.
426 [1994] 2 All ER 588.
427 [1999] INLR 517.
428 [2001] 3 WLR 877, HL; [2000] 3 All ER 778, CA; for comment, see Ryder [2000] J Civ Lib 358.
429 (1998) 27 EHRR 249 (in the context of Art 13).
430 *Leander v Sweden* (1987) 9 EHRR 433.

As indicated above, it could also be argued before the Tribunal (or, if necessary, at Strasbourg) that it ought to provide an effective remedy under Art 13. It may be noted that in *Khan v UK*[431] the Court found that exclusion of evidence under s 78 of PACE would not provide such a remedy,[432] so it must be provided – in respect of the surveillance of a number of public authorities – only in the tribunal. This is clear since ss 7 and 8 of the HRA are intended to take the place of Art 13 domestically and the tribunal is the 'appropriate forum' for s 7(1)(a) purposes. In *Khan v UK*, which also critiqued police disciplinary procedures, it was found that the procedures failed to meet Art 13 standards due to the influence of the Home Secretary. Although the arrangements for the current tribunal differ,[433] the strong influence of the Home Secretary in determining the procedure to be followed might be said to impair the tribunal's independence.

The tribunal should play a part in providing an aggregate of remedies which, combined, would provide an effective remedy,[434] but the other potential remedies, such as raising complaints with an MP, are too ineffective to make much contribution. In *Harman and Hewitt v UK*,[435] a breach of Art 13 was found on the basis of the lack of an effective remedy. The 1989 Act was precisely intended to address this failure by creating the oversight mechanisms. In *Christie v UK*,[436] the Commission avoided the question whether the Interception of Communications Tribunal had provided an effective remedy since it found that the applicant did not have an 'arguable case' and that therefore Art 13 was inapplicable.[437] However, it found that it did provide such a remedy 'in principle'.[438]

In *Govell v UK*,[439] the use of a bugging device was the subject of an unsuccessful police complaint. The Commission found that the police investigative system did not meet the requisite standards of independence under Art 13 since, *inter alia*, the Home Secretary appointed and remunerated members of the Police Complaints Authority and the Home Secretary had a guiding role in determining the withdrawal of charges. In *Chahal v UK*, the Advisory Panel on deportation decisions was not found to satisfy Art 13 since it failed to offer sufficient safeguards for Art 13 purposes. The Court said that the remedy offered should be 'as effective as it can be' given the need, in the context in question, to rely on secret sources. In relation to the new tribunal, it might be argued that the Orders made by the Secretary of State may reduce its efficacy to the point where it no longer satisfies Art 13. While the tribunal's adjudications may

---

431 (2000) 8 BHRC 310.
432 Paragraph 44.
433 See fn 387.
434 Ibid.
435 Appl No 121175/86; (1992) 14 EHRR 657.
436 Also, in *Christie v UK* 78-A DR E Com HR 119 the Commission found that the Interception of Communications Act 1985, the model for the 1989 and 1994 Acts, met the 'in accordance with the law' requirement of Art 8(2).
437 Similarly, in *Halford v UK* (1997) 24 EHRR 523, in respect of alleged tapping of the applicant's home phone, which was within the 1985 Act, the Court avoided this question in relating to the old tribunal since it found that the applicant did not have an 'arguable case' and that therefore, Art 13 was inapplicable.
438 See also *Esbester v UK* (1993) 1860/91; affirmed in *Matthews v UK* [1997] EHRLR 187.
439 (1997) 4 EHRLR 438.

appear adversarial in a superficial sense, the position of the applicant may be so weakened by the procedural limitations under which it operates that it cannot be said to be effective.

Unless a means of appeal from the tribunal is created in relation to its jurisdiction under s 65(2)(a), there will be no clear independent domestic means of determining whether the tribunal offers an effective remedy and whether it should abide by Art 6, which does not require that a court to which to appeal should be available. But it could be argued that Art 6 itself requires that the question of its own field of application should be able to be raised before an independent body.[440] While the Strasbourg jurisprudence would probably not support such an argument at present, it could be argued – somewhat less boldly – that Art 6 requires that the question whether a particular body provides an effective remedy under Art 13 should be able to be raised before an independent body and not merely in the disputed body itself. In principle, this is a strong argument, bearing in mind the fact that the tribunal is, in most circumstances arising under the Intelligence Services Act 1994, the Police Act 1997 and the RIPA, the only forum in which citizens are able to raise the issue of violation of Art 8 rights.

The mere fact that a body termed a 'Tribunal' has been created should not obscure the possibility that it may have a merely cosmetic effect. Had a body been created which appeared to have even less credibility, such as a Panel of Advisers or Commission, or a body required to accept National Security certificates, the guarantee under Art 6 of access to a court[441] or, under Art 13, of providing an effective remedy, might have been found at Strasbourg to have been violated,[442] and the domestic expectation would have been that this would eventually be the case. But the formal appearance of the current tribunal may be belied by the nature of its proceedings which may mean that, substantively, it is as ineffective as such bodies would have been.

7 The Anti-Terrrorism, Crime and Security Act: acquisition of information

Introduction

The Anti-Terrorism, Crime and Security Act 2001 (ACTSA) introduced certain measures that aid in state surveillance. The ACTSA contains a range of miscellaneous provisions which relate to criminal law and criminal justice matters; they have no direct connection with terrorism and still less with the 9/11 terrorist attacks, although the ACTSA represented the UK response to the attacks. Certain of the provisions introduced build on those introduced under Regulation of Investigatory Powers Act 2000, the Criminal Justice and Police Act 2001 and the Electronic Communications Act 2000. In this class there are powers to obtain disclosure of information in Part 3 ACTSA; and a voluntary Code of Practice on the retention of communications data – websites visited, mobile phone calls made and so on – was introduced by Part 11. As Walker and Akdeniz note, not 'all data of interest [to law enforcement bodies] will be

---

440   See Van Dijk, P and Van Hoof, F, *Theory and Practice of the European Convention on Human Rights*, 1998.
441   Such a guarantee has been implied into Art 6(1): see *Omar v France* (2000) 29 EHRR 210.
442   As in *Tinnelly* (1998) 27 EHRR 249 and *Chahal* (1997) 23 EHRR 413 respectively.

conveniently held by compliant public authorities'.[443] The Code was introduced to seek to ensure that private communications service providers would retain communications data for investigatory purposes. It was drafted by the Home Office and can be used, for example, to order mobile phone companies to retain communications' information relating to their customers for future use by the police and other law enforcement bodies. However, at present compliance with the Code is voluntary. So Parts 3 and 11 may be viewed as having similar aims.[444] If the data is retained access would then have to occur via RIPA.

Part 3: information acquisition

A number of the provisions in this category allow for the enhancement and extension of police powers and are unconnected to terrorism. The Part 3 provisions allow the police and other investigatory bodies to obtain information about citizens from a range of public authorities. In contrast Part 11, discussed below, is intended to allow for information acquisition from private bodies via the Code. Potentially the Part 3 provisions affect a very large number of British citizens because they are not confined to use against those involved in serious crime or suspected terrorists or even to those already suspected of criminal offences. There was, therefore, no justification for including them in a Bill which was presented to Parliament as a response to an emergency. It is clearly unwarranted to use the brief Parliamentary timetable adopted for emergency legislation for provisions which could have been included in ordinary criminal justice legislation. Moreover, they are not subject to sunset clauses. If they were justified after September 11, although they were not previously, one might have considered that a sunset clause was essential since such wide-ranging powers could hardly have been passed, (at least without amendment in the Commons) had they not been viewed as special powers warranted by the exigencies of the situation. They are now likely to remain on the statute book indefinitely and certainly long after the 'emergency' has subsided.

Section 17(2)(a)–(d) is the key provision in providing greatly extended powers of obtaining information from public authorities, which are used mainly by the police. Section 17(2) takes 66 existing statutory disclosure powers, listed in Sched 4, and deems each of them to include a number of further disclosure powers by providing that they:

> shall have effect in relation to the disclosure of information by or on behalf of a public authority as if the purposes for which the disclosure of information is authorised by that provision included each of the following: (a) the purposes of any criminal investigation whatever which is being or may be carried out, whether in the United Kingdom or elsewhere; (b) the purposes of any criminal investigation whatever which has been or may be initiated, whether in the United Kingdom or elsewhere; (c) the purposes of the initiation or bringing to an end of any such investigation or proceedings; (d) the purposes of facilitating a determination of whether any such investigation or proceedings should be initiated or brought to an end.

---

443 See Walker, C and Akdeniz, Y, 'Anti-Terrorism Laws and Data Retention' [2003] 54(2) NILQ 159–82 at p 161.

444 For further discussion see Walker, C and Akdeniz, Y, "Anti-Terrorism Laws and Data Retention" [2003] 54(2) NILQ 159–82.

Section 17(6) provides a saving power for any disclosure power not mentioned in Sched 4. Thus, any public authority in the UK must disclose information covered by the 66 statutory provisions, but for the far wider range of purposes. The term 'public authorities' in this context has the same meaning as under the HRA s 6(3).[445] Therefore it includes private bodies and companies in so far as they have a public function – 'functional' public authorities. In other words, a vast range of bodies is affected. Only 'purely' private bodies are not covered;[446] they are affected instead, as discussed below, by the Code under Part 11 applying to private communications service providers which sets out the guidelines for retaining data beyond the point where it would be needed for their own business purposes. The list of 66 statutes is not exhaustive and can be added to by statutory instrument, under s 17(3), although after amendment of the Bill this power was made subject to the affirmative resolution procedure, under s 17(4).

Section 17(2) is extraordinarily wide in a number of respects. The immense broadening of the existing disclosure powers is not confined under it to the protection of national security or to the fight against terrorism. It is not confined even to the investigation and prevention of serious crime. It extends to any offence whatever and therefore could include private prosecutions. The powers under (c) and (d) in particular are amazingly broad: s 17(2)(c) speaks of 'for the purpose of initiating any investigation', while s 17(2)(d) provides for disclosure at an even earlier stage – before it has been determined that an investigation should be initiated. Therefore the information-sharing requirements can apply even before a suspicion has arisen as to any offence. Section 17(2)(c) and (d) are not qualified by any requirement that there should be certain initial grounds for suspicion.

The Lords put forward an amendment, which was carried, to the effect that whether disclosure was voluntary or was supplied on request it could be provided only where the public authority 'believes or suspects' that the relevant information, 'may relate directly or indirectly to any risk to national security or to a terrorist'. However, this amendment was removed in the Commons and this was eventually accepted in the Lords on the basis that certain concessions, although, as indicated below, quite minor ones, had already been made. A similar amendment was carried in the Lords in relation to s 19 which gave a new, broad power relating to disclosure of information held by revenue departments for the same wide purposes as those in s 17. This amendment was also agreed to and the government again defeated. But again the amendment was removed in the Commons and was not reinstated.

Section 17(5) was included as a Lords' amendment. It demands that the use of such powers must be proportionate to the aim pursued. However, this requirement would in many cases be imposed by Art 8(2)[447] of the Convention under the Human Rights Act

---

445　Section 6(3) provides that 'public authority' includes 'a court or tribunal' and 'any person certain of whose functions are functions of a public nature'.

446　See s 6(5) HRA.

447　Art 8 is discussed at various points in this book and in Chapter 2, pp 69–74. A reminder of its provisions may be convenient at this point; Art 8(1) provides: 'Everyone has the right to respect for his private and family life, his home and his correspondence.' Art 8(2) provides: 'There shall be no interference by a public authority with the exercise of this right except such as is in accordance with the law, and is necessary on a democratic society in the interests of national security, public safety or the economic well-being of the country, for the prevention of disorder or crime, for the protection of health or morals, or for the protection of the rights or freedoms of others.' The requirement that

in any event since Art 8 is binding on all the bodies concerned under s 6 HRA. Some disclosures, however, might not raise Art 8 issues, in which case the proportionality requirement might have some safeguarding impact. Also the legitimate aims under s 17(2)(a)–(d) might be viewed as going beyond the aims of Art 8(2). Thus s 17(5) may deter the use of general fishing expeditions, to an extent. However, given that the aims of s 17(2) are so very broad it would be hard to say whether a disclosure was disproportionate to the aim in question given the uncertainty generated by the wording 'any criminal investigation whatsoever' and the lack of a need for any existing suspicion.

Where requests are made by public authorities or individuals abroad s 18 provides a safeguard of sorts where the legal system, procedures or integrity of the relevant foreign jurisdiction are not comparable to those of the UK and do not provide comparable protection, as it allows for the Secretary of State to give a direction which specifies any overseas proceedings and prohibits the making of a disclosure for the purposes of those proceedings. The Secretary of State cannot give a direction unless 'it would be more appropriate' for the investigation to be carried out by a court or other authority of the UK or of a third country. Thus the section does not indicate the grounds on which a direction would be viewed as needed on the grounds of the appropriateness in question. This opaque section provides for the only safeguard introduced under Part 3 against disclosures abroad which could be to a wide range of regimes. Clearly, the safeguard is also dependent on its actually being exercised by the Home Secretary.[448]

In essence therefore it may be said that in a startling fashion s 17(2) destroys the balance created by a large number of existing carefully considered, and often highly detailed schemes permitting disclosure and preserving confidentiality. Together with s 19 and the associated Part 11, especially ss 102 and 103,[449] it provides a regime allowing the police, the security services and other public authorities to obtain a vast range of personal and other information. The answer of the government to concerns in the Lords and Commons regarding the breadth of the s 17 provisions was to point repeatedly to the provisions of the Human Rights Act as providing a remedy for the citizen.[450]

There is a clear tension between Art 8 and the Part 3 provisions since in a number of instances personal information, including very sensitive information,[451] could be

---

an interference with the Art 8 guarantee should be 'necessary on a democratic society' includes the requirement that it should be proportionate to the legitimate aim pursued.

448 Such disclosures would be open to challenge by way of judicial review or under the Human Rights Act (see below).

449 Part 11 is also concerned with the collection of information and allows for a Code of Practice to be made by the Home Secretary ordering mobile phone companies to retain information for future use. Thus Parts 3 and 11 may be viewed as having similar aims.

450 See, e.g., HL Deb cols 949–72 6 Dec 2001.

451 Section 17(2) overrides certain provisions of the Data Protection Act 1998. The Security Service does not have to comply with the Data Protection Act 1998, even in its criminal function. In relation to personal information, the police do not have to comply with the fair and lawful processing provisions of the first data protection principle, subject access requests, or restrictions on disclosure of personal information, except in relation to "sensitive" data, if to do so would be likely to prejudice the prevention and detection of crime or the apprehension and prosecution of offenders. (These are not blanket exemptions; they should be considered in their application to individual cases, but see the JUSTICE report *Under Surveillance: Covert Policing and Human Rights Standards* (1998) Chapter 4, especially

disclosed.[452] But it is disingenuous to suggest that the citizen can rely on Art 8 as a safeguard since there are both procedural and substantive problems in so doing. There is no mechanism for informing the citizen that disclosure has occurred, and therefore opportunities for raising Art 8 arguments are limited. They would normally have to be raised within a trial where the information disclosed formed part of the evidence against the defendant. However, at present the courts are unlikely to take the view that information obtained in breach of Art 8 is required to be excluded from evidence.[453] The citizen could bring a civil action against the public authority in question, or the investigatory body, under s 7(1)(a) HRA post-trial, relying on Art 8. But the s 17(2) powers are so broad that the body could normally claim that most disclosures satisfied the statutory tests. Thus the plaintiff might have to claim that s 17(2) itself breaches Art 8. Without considering this argument in detail, it clearly seems to be plausible to argue that a power to obtain personal information which is not dependent on showing any initial suspicion relating to the individual in question is disproportionate to the legitimate aim in view – that of preventing crime, under Art 8(2). But, unless a court could find a way of narrowing the provisions of s 17(2)(c) and (d), by relying on the interpretative obligation of s 3(1) HRA,[454] it would merely have to apply the provisions in reliance on its duty under s 6(2) HRA.[455] A court of sufficient authority could issue a declaration of the incompatibility between Art 8 and s 17(2)(c) and (d), under s 4 HRA, but this would not provide the aggrieved citizen with a remedy. In considering compatibility a court should take into account the lack of an effective remedy (as guaranteed under Art 13)[456] for breach of Art 8: since, as indicated, in many instances a citizen would never know that a disclosure had occurred, it is hard to argue that such a remedy is available,[457] meaning that since disclosures may often remain unchallengeable, Art 8 could to a large extent be reduced to a nullity.[458]

at pp 92–95). Where sensitive data is obtained under s 17(2) the exception in respect of such data will not apply.

452   See discussion in Fenwick, H, *Civil Rights: New Labour Freedom and the Human Rights Act*, 2000, Chapter 8, pp 325–31; Chapter 9, pp 364–68.

453   See *Khan v UK* (2000) 8 BHRC 310; *R v Khan* [1997] AC 558; *Attorney General's Reference (No 3 of 1999)* [2001] 2 WLR 56.

454   Section 3 provides that 'so far as it is possible to do so' legislation 'must be read and given effect in a way which is compatible with the Convention rights'.

455   Section 6(2) HRA provides that s 6(1) 'does not apply to an act if (a) as a result of one or more provisions of primary legislation the authority could not have acted differently or in relation to incompatible provisions "the authority was acting so as to give effect to or enforce those provisions'.

456   See further on remedies for breach of the Convention rights and the relevance of Art 13 under the HRA, Chapter 2, pp 106–8 and Chapter 4, p 165.

457   In *Klass v Germany* (1979–80) 2 EHRR 214, in the context of secret surveillance for the purposes of protecting national security, it was found that effective controls ensuring that Art 8 rights were guaranteed were created by means of a scheme in which a citizen could be notified subsequently of the surveillance (para 58). Article 13 was satisfied since the citizen could then seek various remedies (para 71). It may therefore be argued that Arts 8 and 13 may be breached by the use of the Part 3 scheme, albeit allowing for disclosure of personal information as opposed to surveillance and use of information, since no provision for subsequent notification is made. This argument is all the stronger, bearing in mind the use of the scheme not in the context of national security or even serious crime, but before suspicion as to criminal activity has arisen.

458   See *Klass v Germany*, ibid, para 38.

Part 11: retention of communications data by private companies

On 15 March 2006 the European Union formally adopted Directive 2006/24/EC, on 'the retention of data generated or processed in connection with the provision of publicly available electronic communications services or of public communications networks and amending Directive 2002/58/EC'. The Directive requires Member States to ensure that communications providers must retain, for a period of between six months and two years, necessary data as specified in the Directive, *inter alia*: to trace and identify the source of a communication; to trace and identify the destination of a communication; to identify the type of communication; and to identify the communication device. The data is required to be available to competent national authorities in specific cases, 'for the purpose of the investigation, detection and prosecution of serious crime, as defined by each member state in its national law'.

The Directive, as adopted, covers fixed telephony, mobile telephony, internet access, internet email and internet telephony. Member States are required to transpose it into national law within 18 months, and no later than September 2007. However, they may if they wish postpone the application of the Directive to internet access, internet email and internet telephony for a further 18 months after this date. Member States retain the flexibility to go substantially further than the Directive mandates. Subject to notification to the Commission, they may require data to be held longer than the two-year maximum set by the Directive. They retain the freedom under Article 15(1) of the earlier Directive 2002/58/EC to legislate official access to the retained data for purposes beyond those set out in the Data Retention Directive.

As mentioned above, the UK already has an extensive system of data retention, under the voluntary Code agreement made with the industry, but it is not yet on a statutory basis. As discussed, Part 11 of the ACTSA contains a number of sections which deal with the retention of communications data by fixed line and mobile telephone service providers and internet service providers. Communications data includes data which identifies the users of services, data which identifies which services were used and when they were used, and data which identifies who the user contacted. It does not include the content of communications. For example, in the case of a call from a mobile telephone the data to be retained would include data identifying the owner of the phone, who was called, the duration of the call and the approximate locations of both parties. Section 102 of the Act requires the Secretary of State for the Home Office to issue a voluntary code of practice on data retention. A code of practice has been issued and contains the requirements set out below.

The Home Office *Voluntary Code of Practice on Data Retention* requires that subscriber information has a retention period of 12 months. This covers subscriber details relating to the person such as: name, date of birth, installation and billing address, payment methods, account/credit card details. Telephony Data has a retention period of 12 months; this covers all numbers associated with calls. Email Data[459] has a retention period of six months. ISP Data has a retention period of six months. Web

---

459 This covers: log-on (authentication user name, date and time of log-in/log-off, IP address logged-in from); sent email (authentication user name, from/to/cc email addresses, date and time sent); received email (authentication user name, from/to email addresses, date and time received).

Activity Logs have a retention period of four days; this includes IP address used, URL's visited and services. Web browsing information is retained to the extent that only the host machine or domain name (website name) is disclosed.

There are very clear tensions between Art 8 and the Part 11 provisions since in a number of instances personal information, including very sensitive information, can be disclosed. But it is arguable that the citizen cannot rely on Art 8 under the HRA as a safeguard since the bodies in question are not public authorities and so they are not subject to the duty to act in a manner compatible with Convention rights under s 6 HRA. On the other hand, it is arguable that their regulation via a Code of Practice recognised in a statute – the ACTSA – could give them the status of functional public authorities under s 6 HRA in relation to their data retention function, using the analogy of the PCC, which is discussed in Chapter 9.[460] The PCC has a regulatory role in relation to personal data via a voluntary Code which is recognised in a statute – the HRA s 12. The PCC appears to view itself as a public authority for HRA purposes in relation to its policing of the PCC Code.[461] This analogy is uncertain: the PCC is the regulatory body, while the newspapers remain private bodies, albeit regulated indirectly by the PCC Code. In this instance the Communications Service Providers (CSPs) are the private bodies and no regulator stands between them and the Code. It could be argued that since no regulatory body exists and the CSPs are regulated on a voluntary basis directly by the Code, they are in a position more analogous to that of the PCC than that of the newspapers; thus they are private bodies with one public function – the retention of data for state use. It is submitted that this is the better view but this point cannot be determined with certainty at present. When compliance with data retention requirements for law enforcement purposes is placed on a statutory basis in order to comply with EU requirements, the CSPs might more readily be viewed as public authorities unless – which is probable – compliance is enforced via a regulator with functions similar to those of Ofcom when it acts in its privacy-protecting role, discussed in Chapter 9.[462]

The Joint Committee on Human Rights has criticised the Part 11 provision; in its Sixth Report it found: 'we were not satisfied that the arrangements in the draft code would ensure that the interference with rights under ECHR Article 8.1 would be proportionate to legitimate objectives so as to be justifiable under ECHR Article 8.2.'[463] The Newton Committee, after reviewing the Code, considered that: 'it would be beneficial for both users and subjects of the data if retention and access were based on a coherent statutory framework'. It considered that this should be part of mainstream legislation, not special terrorism legislation and that the maximum period of retention should be one year. The one-year period would it was considered, strike a balance between the justifiable need for access to the data when combating terrorism and other serious crimes and the protection of the right to privacy.[464] The Newton Committee also recommended that the whole retention and access regime should be subject to unified oversight by the Information Commissioner. It recommended that

---

460 See in particular pp 846–47.
461 See *R (on the application of Ford) v PCC* [2002] EMLR 5.
462 See pp 840–49.
463 (2004) para 56.
464 Newton Committee Report, ACTSA – Review (2003) HC 100, para 391.

a comprehensive legislative framework, going beyond that currently available in the Regulation of Investigatory Powers Act 2000, should be put in place to govern both retention of and access to communications data. The Joint Committee endorsed the conclusions of the Newton Committee, as being 'likely to allow, for the first time, some confidence that rights under ECHR Article 8 would be properly safeguarded in this field'.[465]

The UK will have to introduce the requisite statutory framework in order to comply with the demands of Directive 2006/24/EC. Placing the current voluntary regime on a statutory basis with penalties for non-compliance has profound implications under Art 8. The indiscriminate mass collection of communications data offends against the core privacy principle that citizens should have notice of the circumstances in which the State may conduct surveillance, so that they can regulate their behavior to avoid unwanted intrusions. It also offends against the principle of informational autonomy discussed in Chapter 9 since citizens cannot choose to avoid disclosure of websites visited or of addresses of emails sent. Clearly, both these principles have to give way to the legitimate aims of prevention of crime and of terrorist activity but under Art 8 the means used should be proportionate to those aims. The data retention requirement could be so extensive and subject to such meagre checks that it would be arguable that it was not in proportion to the law enforcement objectives served and so could not be said to be necessary in a democratic society.[466] The arrangements for the storing and destruction of information will be crucial.

8 Conclusions

The central value which is revealed by consideration of the statutory schemes governing the operation of the intelligence services and the State surveillance arrangements generally is secrecy, in the protection of State interests. The value of individual privacy is, it is argued, consistently and readily overcome, at almost every point in the arrangements at which a choice was made. The HRA had aroused the expectation, not only that a new comprehensive statutory basis for invasion of privacy would be introduced, but that it would be underpinned by Convention principles.[467] While the introduction of such a basis in the RIPA is clearly a significant step forward in terms of protection of individual rights, there is little evidence of commitment to those principles despite the influence of the Convention on its inception. The same may be said of the Intelligence Services Act 1994 and of the Police Act 1997: both were introduced largely to meet the demands of Art 8 and both, it is argued, fail to show the respect for individual privacy which would therefore be expected. Perhaps ironically, the scheme enshrined in PACE 1984 for search and seizure does show such respect, to an extent, although it is only incidental to its traditional concern to protect the interest in property. Perhaps the contrast between PACE and the other statutory schemes considered reflects the lack of

---

465 Ibid para 59.
466 See, e.g., *Klass v Germany* (1978) 2 EHRR 214, *Amann v Switzerland* (2000) ECHR 87, *Rotaru v Romania* (2000) ECHR 192; *Malone v United Kingdom* (1984) 7 EHRR 14, *Kruslin v France* (1990) 12 EHRR 528, *Kopp v Switzerland* (1999) 27 EHRR 91 and *Foxley v United Kingdom* (2000) ECHR 224.
467 This was the expectation of the Justice report, *Under Surveillance*, 1998.

understanding of the value of individual privacy, as opposed to property, which has long influenced the common law and which, despite the reception of Art 8 into domestic law, continues to influence the regulation of secret investigatory powers.

The ability of the ordinary citizen to rely on Art 8 under the HRA in order to protect her privacy from State intrusion is highly circumscribed in a number of respects. A breach of Art 8 in searching for and seizing confidential documents is very unlikely to lead to their exclusion from evidence in court. Where there is doubt as to the standard of scrutiny applied by a magistrate in considering an application for a search warrant, again leading to a breach of Art 8, it is unclear that any redress is likely to be available. Perhaps the most striking feature of the RIPA is the determination evinced under it to prevent citizens invoking Convention rights in the ordinary courts against State bodies in respect of the profound threat to privacy represented by interception and surveillance.[468] The development of Convention jurisprudence in the ordinary courts in relation to such techniques has largely been prevented, before it had a chance to begin. A conflict is therefore revealed, it is contended, between the values underlying the RIPA and those underlying the HRA, despite their introduction by the same government.

The democratic values enshrined in the Convention demand that citizens in the democracy should be able to feel confident that surveillance and interception by the State is undertaken for appropriate ends, by proportionate means and with respect for privacy. The RIPA, like the Security Services Act, the Intelligence Services Act and the Police Act, pays lip service to proportionality while largely emasculating methods of scrutinising it. It is apparent that statutory schemes which hide the operations they empower largely from scrutiny, and which, for the most part, place power in the hands of the executive, while shrouding the citizen's complaints' mechanisms in secrecy, fail to reflect those democratic values.

---

468 For further discussion, see Akdeniz, Y, Taylor, N and Walker, C, 'RIPA (1): State surveillance in the age of information and rights' [2001] Crim LR 73.

Part IV

Personal liberty

Part IV considers the extent to which agents of the state have the power to interfere with individual liberty and freedom of movement. Such interference occurs in the name of the prevention of crime, in order to counter terrorism, and to preserve national security. The driving force behind a number of the very recent measures adopted has been the perceived and actual threat of terrorism, post 9/11 and 7/7. In the case of police powers to stop, arrest and detain, and of special counter-terrorism powers, complex statutory schemes put in place under the previous Conservative governments have been built upon by the current Labour government in creating increasingly illiberal schemes. There remains the possibility that the Human Rights Act (HRA) may prove a corrective to the authoritarian tendency of the statutory schemes in this context.

But at the present time the impact of the HRA appears uncertain, inconsistent and muted. Clear tensions can be discerned between a number of the recent statutes considered in the four following chapters and the Human Rights Act. This is especially true of the Serious and Organised Crime Act 2005, the Terrorism Act 2000, the Prevention of Terrorism Act 2005, the Terrorism Act 2006 and the Criminal Justice and Police Act 2001. The legislation considered in these four chapters has certain hallmarks, all of which are of doubtful legitimacy in Human Rights Act terms. There is a very marked tendency to increase the discretion of the police and of other law enforcement officials, and, as was discussed in Chapter 10, to seek to curb the ability of the ordinary courts to keep a check on the use of that discretion in the interests of protecting individuals from abuse of power. The previous 'balance' struck between state powers and individual rights – often pre-HRA - has been eroded.

As will be discussed, the Anti-Terrorism, Crime and Security Act 2001 Part 4, which allowed for the detention without trial for non-British citizens suspected of terrorism, with appeal to the Special Immigration Appeals Commission (SIAC, discussed in Chapter 14) represented the culmination of the Labour government's tendency to introduce provisions in severe tension with human rights' values. The tension between Part 4 and the European Convention on Human Rights reached the point at which it was only possible to declare the 2001 Bill compatible with the Convention by derogating from Art 5 in respect of Part 4. This detention scheme was abandoned since it was found by the House of Lords to contravene the European Convention on Human Rights, Arts 5 and 14, in the seminal decision in *A and Others v Secretary of State for the Home Dept.*[1]

---

1   (2004) UKHL 56; [2005] 2 AC 68; [2005] 2 WLR 87; [2005] 3 All ER 169.

The derogation was not found to be justified since it went further than demanded by the exigencies of the situation. The Convention has also had an impact on the application of the Prevention of Terrorism Act 2005, as discussed in Chapter 14. Where executive discretion is at stake in certain terrorist-related decisions, the judiciary have, as Chapter 14 suggests, shown a preparedness, at times, to rely on the Human Rights Act to do precisely what s 6 of that Act allows them to do – to find that a breach of the Convention rights by a public authority is unlawful. Thus the HRA has had the effect of curbing the use of the more extreme measures, particularly in the context of terrorism. But in terms of the less dramatic and more commonly used powers – particularly powers used in the context of street policing – it has so far had little impact.

In so far as the ordinary courts post-2000 have had the opportunity to consider executive use of coercive power in the contexts in question, in judicial review proceedings, or in the course of the criminal process, the judiciary has not shown a clear or consistent determination to use the Human Rights Act as a corrective. Thus they have not, for example, as Chapter 13 will argue, shown a willingness to rely on Art 6 to exclude evidence as a form of redress for police misuse of power which has resulted in the production of non-confession evidence. The weakness of the Strasbourg jurisprudence in this respect may have played a part in the adoption of this stance, but the far more likely explanation is that the judges have clung to their traditional common law-based fondness for retaining the maximum discretion for the judiciary.

When the HRA has been invoked to curb the more extreme measures that have been introduced in the terrorism context, the Labour government has been gravely displeased by such uses of the Act which it itself introduced – a displeasure which, it is suggested, underlies some of the provisions of the proposed new counter-Terrorism Bill 2007. Far from sympathising with activist interpretations of the Convention, or even with applications of the plain words of the HRA and the Convention, the government appears, in this crucial context, to want the judges to deliver less rights protection than Strasbourg does.

This Part begins, in Chapter 11, by considering police powers to stop and search, arrest and detain suspects. Chapter 12 examines the rules governing police questioning of suspects. In both Chapters 11 and 12 the differences between the schemes for terrorist and non-terrorist suspects are highlighted. Chapter 13 considers the means of redress available if the police breach the rules already discussed or otherwise abuse their powers in dealing with suspects. Chapter 14 goes on to consider the range of terrorist offences currently available and the use of control orders allowing for interventions to curb the activities of terrorist suspects who have not been convicted of any crime.

Chapter 11

Freedom from arbitrary search, arrest and detention; suspects' rights in criminal investigations

1 Introduction[1]

Crime control and due process

The exercise of police powers such as arrest and detention represents an invasion of personal liberty which is tolerated in the interests of the prevention and detection of crime. However, the interest in personal liberty requires that such powers should be strictly regulated. One way of putting this is to say that due process requirements inevitably place curbs on police powers. Thus, the rights-based due process model seeks to recognise the 'primacy of the individual and the complementary concept of limitation of official power'.[2] It calls for the police to be subject to tightly defined and rigorous control and for clear, legally guaranteed safeguards for suspects, with clear remedies for abuse through the courts.[3] In contrast, the crime control model

---

1 For current comment on PACE and the Terrorism Act 2000, and on the relevant provisions under the Criminal Justice and Public Order Act 1994, see: Ashworth, A, *The Criminal Process*, 3rd edn, 2005; Feldman. D, *Civil Liberties and Human Rights in England and Wales*, 2nd edn, 2002, Chapters 5 and 9; Sanders, A and Young, R, *Criminal Justice*, 3rd edn, 2007; Zander, M, *The Police and Criminal Evidence Act 1984*, 2003; Clark, D, *Bevan and Lidstone's The Investigation of Crime*, 2004. For background reading, see: Hewitt, P, *The Abuse of Power*, 1982, Chapter 3; Lustgarten, L, *The Governance of Police*, 1986, Sweet and Maxwell; Leigh, LH, *Police Powers in England and Wales*, 2nd edn, 1985, Butterworths; Robilliard, J and McEwan, J, *Police Powers and the Individual*, 1986, Blackwell; Benyon, J and Bourn, CJ, *The Police: Powers, Procedures and Proprieties*, 1986, Pergamon; Newburn, T, *Crime and Criminal Justice Policy*, 1995, Longman, Chapter 3; Leishman, F, Loveday, B and Savage, S (eds), *Core Issues in Policing*, 1996, Longman; Morgan, R and Newburn, T, *The Future of Policing*, 1997, OUP. For early comment on the Police and Criminal Evidence Act, see [1985] PL 388; [1985] Crim LR 535. See also: Levenson, H and Fairweather, F, *Police Powers; a Practitioner's Guide*, 1990, Legal Action Group; McConville, M, Sanders, A and Leng, R, *The Case for the Prosecution*, 1991, Routledge; Bailey, SH, Harris, DJ and Jones, BL, *Civil Liberties: Cases and Materials*, 2002, Chapter 2; Reiner, R and Leigh, LH, 'Police powers', in McCrudden, C and Chambers, G (eds), *Individual Rights and the Law in Britain*, 1994, Clarendon; Klug, F, Starmer, K and Weir, S, *The Three Pillars of Liberty*, 1996.

2 Packer, H, *The Limits of the Criminal Sanction*, 1968, Stanford University Press. As Walker puts it: 'The primacy of individual autonomy and rights is central to the due process model', *Miscarriages of Justice*, 1999, p 39.

3 See further Baldwin, R, 'Taking rules to excess: police powers and the Police and Criminal Evidence Bill 1984' in Brenton, M and Jones, C (eds), *The Year Book of Social Policy in Britain 1984–85*, 1985, Routledge, pp 9–29; Jones, P, 'Police powers and political accountability: the Royal Commission on Criminal Procedure'; Hillyard, P, 'From Belfast to Britain: some critical comments on the Royal Commission on Criminal Procedure', both in *Politics and Power*, Vol 4, 1981; Jefferson, T, 'Policing the miners: law, politics and accountability', in Brenton, M and Ungerson, C (eds), *The Year Book of Social Policy in Britain 1985–86*, 1986, pp 265–86.

values a 'quick, accurate and efficient administrative fact-finding role ... over slow, inefficient, and less accurate judicial trials' in order to achieve 'the dominant goal of repressing crime'.[4]

Current analysis of aspects of the criminal justice system continues to rely quite heavily on the two familiar models of crime control and due process.[5] But while a rhetorical commitment to due process is still evident,[6] there is a clear perception that the law does not currently reflect this model. As Sanders and Young put it: 'Police and Court officials need not abuse the law to subvert the principles of justice; they need only use it.'[7] Further, as many scholars have argued, the impact of externally imposed rules on actual police practice is limited and uncertain;[8] in particular, researchers have highlighted the problems of rule-evasion – the avoidance of apparent safeguards through the use of informal practices[9] – and of deterrence.[10] There is general agreement that internal police governance and culture will be highly significant in determining the extent to which suspects' rights are delivered, but it should also be emphasised that that culture is itself likely to be influenced by enhanced possibilities of external review of internal police decisions. There appears to be academic agreement that the relationship between external rules and police culture is a complex one and that rather than tending merely towards straightforward evasion of the legal rules, the institutional culture may encourage the development of strategies intended to adapt and accommodate the rules within the practices it has already fostered.[11] But it is also suggested that enhanced external review of such practices under the Human Rights Act (HRA) may be encouraging a shift from the working rules formulated by the police towards an infusion of the legal rules into their informal counterparts. As Dixon puts it: '[Rule] compliance has to be sought by skilfully blending negotiation and imposition.'[12]

4 Packer (1968).
5 Packer, ibid. e.g., the two models are extensively relied on in Walker, C and Starmer, K (eds), *Miscarriages of Justice*, 1999. For discussion and criticism of the two models, see Sanders and Young, *Criminal Justice*, 2007, Chapter 1, Part 5.
6 See, e.g., *Legislation Against Terrorism: A Consultation Paper*, Cm 4178, 1998, esp para 8 of the Introduction.
7 Sanders and Young, op. cit., fn 1, p 20, 2nd edn, 2000.
8 See: the PSI Report's distinction between Presentational, Inhibitory and Working Rules; Dixon, D, *Law and Policing: Legal Regulation and Police Practices*, 1997, Clarendon.
9 See, e.g., Goldsmith, A, 'Taking police culture seriously: police discretion and the limits of the law' (1990) Policing and Society Vol 1, pp 91–114.
10 There is some evidence that use of exclusion of evidence may encourage police officers to observe suspects' rights. See Orfield, JR, 'The exclusionary rule and deterrence: an empirical study of Chicago narcotics officers' (1987) 54 U Chicago L Rev 1016–69. In the context of PACE, this finding receives some support from research by Sanders, Bridges, Mulvaney and Crozier entitled 'Advice and assistance at police stations', November 1989; it was thought that unlawful denials of legal advice had been discouraged by the ruling in *R v Samuel* [1988] 2 All ER 135. The research found that in 1987, before the ruling, delay was authorised in around 50% of applicable cases; in 1990–91, in only one case out of 10,000. Such evidence cannot, however, be treated as conclusive of the issue; apart from other factors, police officers will be aware that the question of exclusion of evidence is unlikely to arise since the case is unlikely to come to a full trial; even if it does arise, a conviction may still be obtained. Any deterrent effect is therefore likely to be undermined.
11 See Smith, DJ, 'Case construction and the goals of the criminal process' [1997] 37 Br Journal of Criminology 319; Ericson, RV, *Making Crime: A Study of Detective Work*, 1981, University of Toronto Press.
12 In Walker, C and Starmer, K (eds), *Miscarriages of Justice*, 1999, p 67.

The Police and Criminal Evidence Act 1984: context

Before the inception of the Police and Criminal Evidence Act 1984 (PACE), the police had no general and clear powers of arrest, stop and search or entry to premises. They wanted such powers put on a clear statutory basis so that they could exercise them where they felt it was their duty to do so without laying themselves open to the possibility of a civil action. Thus, PACE was introduced in order to provide clear and general police powers, but these were supposed to be balanced by greater safeguards for suspects which took into account the need to ensure that miscarriages of justice, such as that which occurred in the *Confait* case,[13] would not recur. The Royal Commission on Criminal Procedure,[14] whose report influenced PACE, was set up largely in response to the inadequacies of safeguards for suspects which were exposed in the *Confait* report.[15]

The result was a scheme in which the broad discretionary powers granted were to be balanced by two central structuring constraints. First, there were general precedent conditions for the exercise of such powers, the most common and significant being the requirement of reasonable suspicion or belief. Secondly, there was the provision of specific countervailing due process rights, in particular a general right of custodial access to legal advice, in most cases laid down in, or underpinned by, quasi- and non-legal rules – the Codes of Practice and Notes for Guidance made under PACE.[16] Redress for breaches of the due process safeguards was largely to be within the disciplinary rather than the judicial sphere: breach of the Codes at the inception of PACE constituted *automatically* a breach of the police disciplinary Code.[17] That is no longer the case, as discussed below, although breach of the Codes can be taken into account in disciplinary proceedings.

The driving force behind PACE may have been, despite concerns raised by the *Confait* case, much more to do with crime control than with due process, but the scheme adopted under the statute did not lose sight entirely of the reasons for adopting it. Post-PACE, the discovery of a number of miscarriages of justice – the cases of the *Birmingham Six*,[18] the *Guildford Four*,[19] *Judith Ward*,[20] *Stefan Kiszko*,[21] the *Tottenham Three*,[22] the *Maguire Seven*[23] – raised due process concerns again, although in only one of these instances was PACE applicable.[24] After the Birmingham Six were freed

---

13 See Report of the Inquiry by the Hon Sir Henry Fisher, HC 90 of 1977–78.
14 Royal Commission on Criminal Procedure Report, Cmnd 8092, 1981 (RCCP Report).
15 Report of the Inquiry by the Hon Sir Henry Fisher, HC 90 of 1977–78.
16 PACE 1984, s 66, Codes of Practice.
17 Ibid, s 67(8).
18 See *R v McIlkenny and Others* [1992] 2 All ER 417.
19 See May, J (Sir), *Report of the Inquiry into the Circumstances Surrounding the Convictions Arising out of the Bomb Attacks at Guildford and Woolwich in 1974, Final Report,* 1993–94 HC 449, Chapter 17.
20 *R v Ward* (1992) 96 Cr App R 1.
21 (1992) *The Times*, 18 February.
22 (1991) *The Times*, 9 December.
23 See *R v Maguire* [1992] 2 All ER 433.
24 The case of the *Tottenham Three* revealed flaws in the PACE scheme. It predated the introduction of PACE, but PACE was being used on a dry-run basis by the Metropolitan Police at the time. In the case of Winston Silcott, one of the Three, case notes of his confession, supposedly contemporaneous, were found under ESDA to have been tampered with, and his conviction was quashed in 1991; see (1991) *The Times*, 9 December.

in 1992, the Home Secretary announced the setting up of another Royal Commission under Lord Runciman[25] in order to consider further measures which could be introduced, but although there appeared to be a link between the announcement of the Royal Commission and the *Birmingham Six* case owing to proximity in time, the Commission interpreted its remit as not requiring an analysis of the miscarriage of justice in that case. The remit was to examine the efficacy of the criminal justice system in terms of securing the conviction of the guilty and the acquittal of the innocent.[26] Once again, a Royal Commission was seeking to reconcile potentially conflicting aims – concern to protect due process, but also to further crime control. As a number of commentators have observed, however, not only was the former part of this remit largely swallowed up in the latter,[27] it failed to articulate a principled account of investigative procedures.

After the Commission reported, the Major government passed legislation, most notably the Criminal Justice and Public Order Act 1994 (CJPOA), which increased police powers significantly while removing a number of safeguards for suspects. In particular, the 1994 Act curtailed the right of silence, although the Runciman Royal Commission had recommended that the right should be retained since its curtailment might lead to further miscarriages of justice. Thus, there were significant developments in police powers during the Major years and the balance PACE was supposed to strike between such powers and due process was, it will be argued, undermined.

Since the Labour government took office in 1997, there have been, apart from the passing of the HRA, no indications of attempts to break with the criminal justice legislative policies of the Conservative Party. In particular, the Terrorism Act 2000, as amended by the Criminal Justice Act 2003, and then by the Terrorism Act 2006, has increased the period of time for which terrorism suspects can be detained to 28 days. Amendations made to PACE by the Serious and Organised Crime Act 2005 have significantly extended the arrest power. Both before and after the general elections of 2001 and 2005, both major parties were seeking to outdo each other in encouraging and pandering to populist notions of crime control. One especially evident tendency has been the movement away from the need to show reasonable suspicion as a condition precedent for the exercise for police powers. Despite the fact that this condition appeared to offer little restraint in practice to police officers,[28] it may be said that its abandonment in the introduction of recent stop, arrest and detention powers is indicative of a formal acceptance of a less fettered police discretion, as opposed to the discretion developed *de facto* in police practice. Section 44 TA and s 60 CJPOA exemplify this tendency.

---

25 Runciman Report, Cm 2263, 1993, Chapter 1, para 5; Royal Commission on Criminal Procedure chaired by Lord Runciman; it was announced by the Home Secretary on 14 March 1991, HC Deb Vol 187 Col 1109. It reported on 6 July 1993; see (1993) 143 NLJ 933–96 for a summary of its recommendations in respect of police investigations, safeguards for suspects, the right to silence and confession evidence.

26 Effectiveness in securing 'the conviction of those guilty of criminal offences and the acquittal of those who are innocent', Runciman Report, ibid., Chapter 1, para 5.

27 See Sanders, A and Young, R,'The RCCJ' [1994] 14 OJLS 435; Walker, C and Starmer, K (eds), *Miscarriages of Justice*, 1999, especially p 57.

28 See 'Arrest and reasonable suspicion' (1988) 85 Law Soc Gazette, 7 September, p 22, and see below, p 1116.

However, in the HRA the UK has a benchmark by which to measure standards of procedural justice. This chapter will outline the trend away from due process post-PACE, and thus away from the balance PACE originally struck. It will consider the concomitant legislative tendency to render police powers susceptible to subjective exercise, and the *de facto* discretion in respect of the delivery of due process rights which has developed, due at least in part to a largely unmet need for their enforcement. The HRA may be perceived as providing an opportunity to re-infuse due process into criminal procedure. It will be argued, however, that the impact of the HRA has been diluted and unpredictable and that this is due in part to the weakness of the Strasbourg jurisprudence in certain key areas, such as the admissibility of non-confession evidence, or the use of stop and search powers, areas in which the common law traditionally failed to protect due process. Early decisions under the HRA indicate, this chapter and the next will argue, that the inception of the HRA is having little or no impact in such areas. The discussion below, and in Chapters 12 and 13, will demonstrate that there have been some significant post-HRA decisions in this context, but it is fair to say that the inception of the HRA has not had a strong impact. To some extent this is unsurprising since the European Convention on Human Rights creates a floor rather than a ceiling of rights. One would not expect it to have a radical impact in a country like the UK with strong due process traditions. But in certain contexts, particularly where the pressure to discard due process is strongest, as in the treatment of terrorist suspects, or in respect of stop and search without reasonable suspicion, change might have been expected, prompted by the HRA. Clearly, such changes might have had a muted impact in practice, bearing in mind that judicial intervention and formal rules have always had, as indicated above, an uncertain impact on the institutional culture of the criminal justice system.

In this chapter, the powers of the police and the safeguards which restrict the use of police powers to stop, search, arrest, and detain are evaluated with a view to considering how far the suspects' rights granted by PACE have had an impact on police working practice and how far, if at all, changes are occurring in the light of the HRA. A key theme of this chapter and the next concerns the extent to which the 'balance' PACE was supposed to create between suspects' rights and police powers has been eroded, partly due to measures adopted to curb organised crime, and, post-2001, in the wake of increased concern after 9/11 to combat terrorism. It will be argued that one of the problems of introducing special counter-terrorist powers is that they may be used outside the terrorist sphere. This discussion of the current 'balance' between police powers and suspects' rights is followed in Chapter 13 by a consideration of the value of the means of redress available, as affected by the inception of the HRA, if the police fail to comply with the rules.

The structure of the PACE rules

At present, the rules governing the exercise of police powers are largely contained in the scheme created under PACE, as amended, which is made up of rules deriving from the Act itself, from the Codes of Practice made under it, and the Notes for Guidance contained in the Codes. It is also influenced by Home Office circulars. The difference in status between these four levels and the significance of adopting this four-tiered approach is considered below. (It should be emphasised at this point that a number of significant police powers are not contained in PACE, as will be indicated.) The PACE pre-trial scheme must be examined in conjunction with the scheme that was created under the Terrorism Act 2000, as amended, with a view to creating at certain points a lesser level of protection for terrorist suspects.

PACE and the Codes of Practice

Until 2006 there were six Codes of Practice: Code A, covering stop and search procedures, Code B, covering searching of premises, Code C, covering interviewing and conditions of detention, Code D, covering identification methods and Code E, covering tape recording. Code F covering visual recording of interviews was introduced in 2004, a new version coming into force in 2006. Thus, each covers a particular area of PACE, although not all areas were covered: arrest, for example, was, until 2006, governed only by statutory provisions.[29] The Codes have gone through a number of revisions post-PACE, becoming steadily longer and more cumbersome in the process (Code C, for example, now runs to over 80 pages). In 2006 new, revised versions of the existing Codes came into force and the Codes were also added to. A new Code G covering arrest was introduced, as was a special new Code – Code H. It was introduced to govern the rights of terrorist suspects in police questioning and detention, meaning that the provisions of Code C relating to such suspects were removed, reappearing in a revised form in Code H. Thus 2006 saw a very dramatic revision and extension of the Codes.

If safeguards for suspects are taken seriously then why do they largely appear in the Codes rather than in PACE itself? It may be asked why all of the stop and search rules, for example, were not merely made part of the Act. The answer may partly lie in the need for some flexibility in making changes: the Codes are quicker and less cumbersome to amend than statutory provisions. However, it is also probable that the government did not want to create rules which might give rise to liability on the part of the police if they were broken; rules which could operate at a lower level of visibility than statutory ones may have appeared more attractive. It has for some time been apparent that the police powers were contained in PACE, as amended, and other statutes, while suspects' rights were largely contained in the non-statutory Codes. That tendency has only become more marked post-PACE. The proliferation of Code provisions, especially in 2006, has not been accompanied by any determination to deal with their very doubtful legal status.[30] At the same time certain safeguards of particular significance have always remained in the statute, in particular the provisions governing time limits on police detention. It is hard to escape the conclusion that the safeguards surrounding the questioning of suspects, contained mainly in Codes C and H, are viewed as of less significance.

---

29 Report of the Inquiry by the Hon Sir Henry Fisher, HC 90 of 1977–78.
30 In *Delaney* (1989) 88 Cr App R 338; (1988) *The Times*, 20 August, CA, the status of the Codes was considered. It was held that the mere fact that there had been a breach of the Codes of Practice did not of itself mean that evidence had to be rejected. Section 67(11) of the Act provides that '. . . if any provision of such Code appears to the court . . . to be relevant to any question arising in the proceedings, it shall be taken into account in determining that question'.

Section 67(10) of PACE makes clear the intended distinction between Act and Codes in providing that no civil or criminal liability will arise from a breach of the Codes. But the question of civil liability in respect of a breach of PACE, as opposed to the Codes, is not without difficulty. Liability will arise where a police power is needed in order to render an act non-tortious that would otherwise be tortious. For example, an arrest would give rise to liability for false imprisonment if no power to arrest arose. Certain PACE rules have been treated by the courts as mandatory and therefore adherence to them is necessary in order to render the act in question lawful, as will be discussed below. So breach of certain PACE rules will give rise to civil liability because they operate in the context of existing areas of tortious liability, whereas breach of the Codes cannot give rise to liability, even within that context.

This distinction is of significance in relation to the stop and search, arrest and detention provisions of Parts I–IV of PACE,[31] in comparison with the Code provisions in those areas, in Codes A and G. However, this distinction does not seem to have any significance as far as the interviewing provisions of Part V are concerned. The most important statutory safeguard for interviewing, the entitlement to legal advice, has not been affected by the availability of tortious remedies.[32] Thus statutory and Code provisions concerned with safeguards for suspects in police interviewing are in an equally weak position in the sense that a clear remedy is not available if they are breached. The context in which breaches of the interviewing provisions have been considered is that of exclusion of evidence.[33] In that context, the courts have not drawn a clear distinction between the provisions of the Act or of the Codes, except to require that breach of a Code provision should be of a substantial and significant nature[34] if exclusion of evidence is to be considered.

However, a new possibility of affording the Code provisions a status that they currently lack has become apparent as a result of the Strasbourg decision in *Wainwright v UK*,[35] which is fully discussed below. Breach of the Convention rights is a statutory tort under the HRA. If Code provisions designed in effect to prevent a breach of a right are breached, it is more likely, following that decision, that the right itself will be found to be breached, meaning that an action is available against the police, relying on s 7 HRA; damages could be awarded under s 8. This is of significance where the Article – such as Art 5 – operates in the context of an existing tort, since breach of the Code

---

31 In that respect, such claims are significant; e.g. in 1991, the Metropolitan Police faced an increase in claims of 40% over 1990. See HC Deb Vol 193 Col 370w. For discussion of the use of tortious claims in this context, see Chapter 13, pp 1303 *et seq*.

32 The question whether an unlawful denial of access to legal advice amounts to a breach of statutory duty has been considered in an unreported case, 26 October 1985, QB (Rose J), which is cited by Clayton, R and Tomlinson, H in *Civil Actions Against the Police*, 1st edn, 1992, p 359. It was held that the application would be refused even if jurisdiction to make the order sought existed as it would 'cause hindrance to police inquiries'.

33 Breach of a code provision is quite frequently taken into account in determining whether or not a confession should be excluded, usually under PACE, s 78. Breach of a code provision will not lead to automatic exclusion of an interview obtained thereby, but a substantial and significant breach may be the first step on the way to its exclusion (see *Walsh* [1989] Crim LR 822, CA, transcript from LEXIS).

34 *Keenan* [1989] 3 All ER 598, CA.

35 Appl No 12350/04; 26.9.06.

provision alone would not give rise to tortious liability. It is also of particular significance where the Code provision affects matters, such as protecting the privacy and dignity of the detainee, that are designed – in effect – to ensure that Art 8 is not breached since there is no general tort of invasion of privacy. All of these points would also apply to *statutory* provisions which are not underpinned by a tortious remedy if breached.

Notes for Guidance

The Notes for Guidance are contained in the Codes but are not part of them.[36] They were apparently intended, as their name suggests, to be used merely as interpretative provisions and, it appears, to have no legal status at all. However, as will be seen, they contain some very significant provisions, although it is unclear what the consequences of breach of a Note are. Evidence tainted by breach of a Note for Guidance is unlikely to be excluded since, unlike Code provisions, s 67(11) of PACE does not require a court to take the Notes into account in determining any question.[37] However, in *DPP v Blake*,[38] the Divisional Court impliedly accepted that a Note for Guidance should be considered in relation to exclusion of evidence if it can be argued that it merely amplifies a particular Code provision and can therefore be of assistance in determining whether breach of such a provision has occurred. Moreover, certain Notes need not merely be considered in conjunction with the Code paragraph they derive from; the ruling in *DPP v Rouse* and *DPP v Davis*[39] that they can sometimes be used as an aid to the interpretation of Code C as a whole extended their potential impact. Thus, it may be said that the Notes are of a very uncertain legal status but that their importance has been recognised in certain decisions as to admission of evidence. These decisions clearly raise the question why important safeguards were placed in the Notes at all. Thus the courts have partially made up for another deficiency of the Codes.

Home Office circulars

There are a large number of such circulars dealing with disparate subjects relevant to the use of police powers; some of them are intended to work in tandem with a part of PACE as amplifying provisions and some operate in an area uncovered by the other provisions. They are in an even more equivocal legal position than the Notes. Their legal significance derives from their relevance to the obligations arising from the relationship between police forces and the Home Office and it is likely to be in that context rather than in relation to questions of admissibility that they will be considered.[40] Clearly,

---

36 This is provided for in the first paragraph of each Code; see, e.g., Code C, para 1.3.
37 PACE 1984, s 67(11) provides: 'In all criminal and civil proceedings any such code shall be admissible in evidence; and if any provision of such a code appears to the court or tribunal conducting the proceedings to be relevant to any question arising in the proceedings it shall be taken into account in determining that question.'
38 [1989] 1 WLR 432, CA.
39 (1992) Cr App R 185.
40 See *Home Secretary ex p Westminster Press Ltd* (1991) the *Guardian*, 12 February; *Secretary of State for the Home Dept ex p Lancashire Police Authority* (1992) *The Times*, 26 May. They may also be relevant to issues arising under the Police Act 1996, s 89 (formerly the Police Act 1964, s 51). In *Collins and Wilcock* [1984] 3 All ER 374; [1984] 1 WLR 1172, Home Office Circular 109/59 was

argument that a court may be disinclined to consider a Note for Guidance applies *a fortiori* to the circulars.[41] It also seems clear that a decision taken in breach of a circular will not be susceptible to judicial review.[42]

Obstruction or assault on a police officer in the course of his duty

A number of the powers discussed below may be discussed within the contexts of the offences of assault on or obstruction of an officer in the course of his duty. The formal position remains unchanged – police officers have no right to detain and search or question a person in the absence of specific statutory powers allowing them to do so. Of course, society considers it desirable that the police should be able to make contact with citizens in order to make general inquiries without invoking any specific powers; on the other hand, citizens are not lawfully bound to reply to such inquiries. A police officer can ask a citizen to refrain from doing something, but in general, the citizen may refuse if the action is not in itself unlawful. If this were not the case, there would be little need for other specific powers; an officer could, for example, merely ask a person to submit to a search and if he refused, warn him that he could be charged with obstruction. However, some otherwise lawful behaviour, including failure to obey a police officer, may bring a citizen within the ambit of the offence of obstruction of a constable which arises under s 89(2) of the Police Act 1996 (formerly under s 51(3) of the Police Act 1964), and therefore, the way it has been interpreted determines the borderline between legitimate and illegitimate disobedience to police instructions or requests.[43] Section 89(2) creates an area of liability independent of any other substantive offence. Behaviour is criminalised in relation to police officers which would not give rise to criminal liability if directed at any other group of persons. Thus, some contacts between police officer and citizen may result in the creation of liability where, otherwise, none would have existed.[44]

Following *Rice v Connolly*,[45] three tests must be satisfied if liability for this offence is to be made out. First, it must be shown that the constable was in the execution of his or her duty. Actions outside an officer's duty would seem to include any action which is unlawful or contrary to Home Office circulars[46] or the Codes of Practice.

wrongly interpreted by a police officer; her actions in reliance on the incorrect interpretation were held to be outside the execution of her duty. However, the question whether breach of provisions contained in a circular could lead to exclusion of evidence has not yet been determined.

41 This point was made in Wolchover, D and Heaton-Armstrong, A, 'The questioning Code revamped' [1991] Crim LR 232, with reference to the revision of Code C.

42 See *Gillick v West Norfolk and Wisbech AHA* [1986] AC 112, HL (non-statutory administrative guidance by government departments to subordinate authorities is not as a general rule subject to judicial review). Applicability of this rule to circulars directed to the police was confirmed in *Home Secretary ex p Westminster Press Ltd* (1991) the *Guardian*, 12 February.

43 For discussion of the development of this offence, see [1982] PL 558; (1983) MLR 662; [1983] Crim LR 29; [1983] Crim LR 21.

44 See further on this point [1983] Crim LR 21, 36.

45 [1966] 2 QB 414; [1966] All ER 649; [1966] 3 WLR 17, DC.

46 In *Collins v Wilcock* [1984] 3 All ER 374; [1984] 1 WLR 1172 a police officer wrongly interpreted a Home Office circular; her actions in reliance on the incorrect interpretation were held to be outside the execution of her duty.

However, some actions which may be termed unlawful may be found too trivial to take the officer outside the execution of his or her duty. In *Bentley v Brudzinski*[47] an officer laid a hand on the shoulder of the defendant in order to detain him so as to ask further questions. The court found that in trying to prevent the defendant from returning home, the officer was acting outside the execution of his duty, but considered that not all instances in which an officer used some physical restraint would be treated in the same way. Reference was made to *Donelly v Jackman*[48] in which, on very similar facts, it was found that an officer was not outside the execution of his duty. All that can be said, then, is that all the circumstances of the case must be considered in determining whether an officer is within the execution of his duty and that the more significant the restraint used, the more likely it is that the officer will be outside it. Does it follow that any action of an officer which is not unlawful or contrary to official guidance will be within the execution of duty? It was found in *Coffin v Smith*[49] that any action within the officer's duty as a 'keeper of the peace' would be within his or her duty. Thus, an officer does not need to point to a specific requirement to perform a particular duty imposed by superiors, but equally, some actions which are not unlawful would seem to fall outside his duty.

Secondly, it must be shown that the defendant did an act which made it more difficult for the officer to carry out her or his duty. Physically attempting to prevent an arrest, as in *Hills v Ellis*,[50] will satisfy this test. This is not to imply that a physical act must occur, but that the police must actually be impeded in some way. In *Lewis v Cox*[51] a persistent inquiry as to where an arrested friend was being taken was held to amount to obstruction. The defendant opened the door of the police van, clearly preventing it from driving off, in order to make the inquiry after being told to desist. The ruling in *Ricketts v Cox*[52] that a refusal to answer questions accompanied by abuse was obstruction may delineate the lowest level of behaviour which may be termed obstructive. According to *Rice v Connolly*, a refusal to answer questions does not amount to obstruction; therefore, the abuse alone must have constituted the obstruction. This decision, which has been widely criticised,[53] is perhaps hard to reconcile with *Bentley v Brudzinski* and possibly interpreted the meaning of obstruction too widely.

It must, finally, be shown, following *Lewis v Cox*, that the defendant behaved wilfully in the sense that he acted deliberately with the knowledge and intention that he would obstruct the police officer. A defendant may be 'wilful' even though his purpose is to pursue some private objective of his own, rather than to obstruct the officer, so long as his act is deliberate and he realises that it will in fact impede the officer. This

---

47 [1982] Crim LR 825; (1982) *The Times*, 3 and 11 March.
48 (1970) Cr App R 229; [1970] 1 WLR 562.
49 (1980) Cr App R 221.
50 [1983] QB 680; [1983] 1 All ER 667.
51 (1985) Cr App R 1.
52 (1981) Cr App R 298; see commentary by Birch, D, 'Confessions and confusions under the 1984 Act' [1989] Crim LR 95; Smith, JC and Hogan, J, *Criminal Law*, 1988, p 394; Lidstone, K, [1983] Crim LR 29, pp 33–35.
53 See Williams, G *Textbook of Criminal Law*, 1983, Stevens and Sons, p 204; Lidstone, K [1983] Crim LR 29, pp 33–35.

will be the case, according to *Hills v Ellis*, even if the purpose of the defendant is to help the officer.[54]

If a person physically resists an arrest or stop in the belief that it is unlawful, he may incur liability under the offence of assault on a constable in the execution of duty which now arises under s 89(1) of the Police Act 1996. Liability may arise even though the defendant is unaware that the person he is assaulting is a police officer.[55] This is strange, since the only justification for creating an area of liability in addition to common law assault and battery would seem to be that there is greater culpability in striking an officer rather than any other individual owing to the officer's special position as keeper of the peace. However, if the defendant believes that unlawful force is being used against him, he can avail himself of the defence of self-defence, although according to *Albert v Lavin*,[56] the belief in the need to act in self-defence must be based on reasonable grounds. This limitation was not accepted by the Court of Appeal in *Gladstone Williams*:[57] it was found that an honest belief would be sufficient. However, it appears that if the honest belief is arrived at through intoxication, the facts will be considered as an objective observer would have perceived them to be.[58] Apart from the assault, the other elements will be interpreted as for obstruction.

2 Stop and search powers

Introduction[59]

The PACE stop and search powers were meant to maintain a fair balance between the interest of society, as represented by the police, in crime control and national security, and the interest of the citizen in personal liberty. Under the due process model, detention short of arrest – usually, although not invariably, exercised in the form of stop and search powers – should be based on reasonable suspicion relating to the specific actions of an individual. Under the crime control model, such detention is viewed as an investigative tool which should be based on general police experience; inhibitory rules should be kept to a minimum in order to allow police officers to act on instinct; police discretion should be the guiding principle. The use of such powers is currently viewed as a necessary part of effective modern policing. It has been argued that much policing is reactive; it is initiated by civilians[60] and therefore the nature of stop and search powers assumes

---

54 Cf *Wilmott v Atack* [1977] QB 498; [1976] 3 All ER 794.
55 *Forbes* (1865) 10 Cox CC 362; for criticism, see Williams, G *Textbook of Criminal Law*, 1983, p 200.
56 [1982] AC 546; [1981] 3 All ER 878, HL. See (1972) 88 LQR 246 on the use of self-defence in these circumstances.
57 (1983) Cr App R 276; see commentary [1984] Crim LR 164.
58 See *O'Connor* [1991] Crim LR 135.
59 For further comment on PACE and the Terrorism Act 2000, and on the relevant provisions under the Criminal Justice and Public Order Act 1994, see Sanders, A and Young, R, *Criminal Justice*, 3rd edn, 2007, Chapter 2; Ashworth, A, *The Criminal Process*, 3rd edn, 2005; Feldman, D, *Civil Liberties and Human Rights in England and Wales*, 2nd edn, 2002, Chapters 5 and 9; Zander, M, *The Police and Criminal Evidence Act 1984*, 2003; *Home Office Stop and Search Manual*, 2005; Lustgarten, L, 'The future of stop and search' [2003] Crim LR 603.
60 See Shapland, J and Vagg, J, *Policing by the Public*, 1988, Routledge.

less significance, but this argument is open to question.[61] However, at the present time the growth of intelligence-led policing[62] especially in the context of terrorism, has led to a more proactive stance, which is tending to enhance the importance of stop and search powers. The powers represent less of an infringement of liberty than an arrest, but on the other hand their exercise may create a sense of grievance and of violation of personal privacy. Such feelings may contribute to the alienation of the police from the community, leading to a breakdown in law and order expressed in its most extreme form in rioting,[63] and otherwise in a general lack of co-operation with the police, affecting the acquisition of intelligence. Thus, the extensiveness of stop and search powers may tell us something about the extent to which UK society values individual liberty, but it is also clear that this is a complex issue: too great an infringement of liberty may be as likely to result ultimately in less effective crime control as in too great a restriction of police powers.

The use of these powers remains a contentious matter that continues to attract public attention, especially as it has frequently been suggested that they may be used in a discriminatory fashion. While it now appears incontrovertible that racial discrimination affects their use, the extent to which this is the case remains controversial.[64] Their recorded use has more than trebled since PACE came into force in 1986[65] and, as indicated below, a large number of further powers have been introduced in the post-PACE period. One factor influencing the rise in their use may have been the introduction of 'zero tolerance' policies in the mid-1990s. The efficacy of such powers is debatable. Only around 10%–14% of stops led to an arrest and only around 3% to a charge.[66] These figures do not include stops which did not lead to a search, or voluntary stops, and therefore the percentage of stops leading to a charge must be lower than this. There are, of course, other methods of measuring the crime control value of stop and search powers; in particular, they have some value in terms of information-gathering[67] and, more controversially, as a means of asserting police authority on the streets.

This proliferation of usage and of powers post-PACE was not accompanied by a full official review of their crime control value or adverse due process impact[68] until the issues were raised in relation to the *Lawrence* case in the MacPherson Report in 1999.[69] Owing to its remit, they did not form a central focus of the Report; in so far as powers to detain short of arrest were considered, the concern centred on the question of institutionalised racism in relation to their use. The part which such powers might play in miscarriages of justice and their general links with other aspects of policing,

---

61 In 1993–94, 24% of arrests resulted from proactive policing including stopping and searching: Phillips, C and Brown, D, *Home Office Research Study No 185*, 1998. Sanders and Young, op. cit., fn 1, 2000, p 70 argue that in future, stopping and searching may play a greater part in arrests.

62 See Chapter 10, p 1032 *et seq*.

63 See, on this point, Lord Scarman, *The Brixton Disorders*, Cmnd 8427, 1981; McConville, M, 'Search of persons and premises' [1983] Crim LR 604–14.

64 See Sanders, A and Young, R, *Criminal Justice* (2007), Chapter 2.3 and pp 1124–26 below.

65 Home Office Statistical Bulletin 21/93; Statistical Bulletin 27/97; see further Sanders and Young, *Criminal Justice* (2007), pp 98–101.

66 *Home Office Statistical Bulletin 21/93*.

67 *Home Office Stop and Search Manual*, 2005, 28.

68 They were outside the remit of the Runciman Royal Commission.

69 Cm 4262-I. (1999).

especially the interview, has hardly had an airing in recent official reports.[70] As discussed in Chapter 12, the possibility that informal street contacts may influence and structure the formal interview is especially significant in the post-HRA era.[71]

As this chapter will indicate, the grant of further powers post-PACE has not been accompanied by a concomitant strengthening of the protection for the due process rights affecting arrest and detention. One of the key structuring constraints identified above as intended to protect due process under the Police and Criminal Evidence Act 1984 was the requirement of reasonable suspicion. This requirement has been eroded in the post-PACE developments; it has been dropped from the more recently introduced special powers under the CJPOA, and under the Terrorism Act 2000, s 44 it continues to be unnecessary in respect of terrorist suspects. There are now a large number of stop and search powers which are divided into those based on reasonable suspicion and those requiring an authorisation, but without a reasonable suspicion requirement.[72] This distinction is explored further below. One problem has, however, been addressed: until 2003 the prevalence of voluntary searches continued to undermine the reasonable suspicion requirement, and while this problem was recognised post-PACE, no serious attempt was made to address it until revised Code A came into force in 2003.

The PACE stop and search power

There was no general power at common law to detain without the subject's consent in the absence of specific statutory authority.[73] Instead, there was a miscellany of such powers, many of which were superseded by PACE. A large number, however, such as the power to search for firearms under s 47 of the Firearms Act 1968, continued to subsist alongside the PACE power. The Phillips Royal Commission, whose report influenced PACE,[74] recommended the introduction of a new general power, but accepted the need to maintain a balance between the interest of society as represented by the police in crime control, and the interest of the citizen in personal liberty and privacy. This balance was sought to be achieved partly by introducing a reasonable suspicion element into the PACE powers.

Under s 1 of PACE for the first time a general power to stop[75] and search persons (s 1(1)) or vehicles (s 1(2))[76] was conferred on police constables. It arises if the constable

---

70 E.g., the *Consultation Paper on Terrorism*, Cm 4178, 1998, which recommended the retention of counter-terrorist stop and search powers, failed to consider these matters, and made no reference to research it might have been based on.

71 It should be noted that the use of the stop and search powers is not necessarily linked to arrest; arrests may occur for reasons unlinked to the apparent basis for the stop and search: Ayres, M and Murray, L, *Arrests for Recorded Crime 2004/5*, 2005.

72 A non-exhaustive list of current statutory stop and search powers to which Code A applies is given in Annex A to Code A (2006 version).

73 For a full list of the powers arising from 16 statutes, see RCCP Report 1981.

74 Cmnd 8092 (1981).

75 It should be noted that the police do not need to search the suspect once he or she has been stopped; they may decide not to. Nevertheless, reasonable suspicion that stolen goods or articles are being carried must arise before the stop can be made. Under Code A 2.11: 'There is no power to stop or detain a person in order to find grounds for a search.'

76 A power to stop vehicles which is not dependent on reasonable suspicion arises under s 163 of the Road Traffic Act 1988. PACE 1984, s 4 regulates it when it is used as the basis for a general road check.

forms the reasonable suspicion that stolen goods, or prohibited articles (including offensive weapons)[77] will be found by searching the suspect. It may be that the suspect appears to be in innocent possession of the goods or articles; this does not affect the power to stop, although it would affect the power to arrest; in this sense, the power to stop is broader than the arrest power. Section 4 of PACE enables the police to use their powers under the Road Traffic Act 1988 to set up roadblocks and to stop and search any vehicle to see whether it contains a wanted person.

Under s 1(6), if an article is found which appears to be stolen or prohibited, the officer can seize it. The s 1 power may be exercised in any place to which the public, or a section of it, have access (s 1(1)(a)) or in any other place 'to which people have ready access at the time when [the constable] proposes to exercise the power but which is not a dwelling' (s 1(1)(b)). Powers to enter a dwelling arise under ss 17 and 18, but an officer can search a suspect in a garden or yard or other land 'occupied with or used for the purposes of a dwelling' (assuming, of course, that the provision of s 1 as to reasonable suspicion are fulfilled) if it appears that the person does not reside in the dwelling or have the permission of the owner to be there (s 1(4)).

This general power to stop, search and seize is balanced in two ways. First, the concept of reasonable suspicion allows it to be exercised only when quite a high level of suspicion exists. Secondly, under s 2, the police officer must provide the person to be searched with certain information. These requirements are discussed below.

Power to search for drugs

Section 23 of the Misuse of Drugs Act 1971 provides a stop and search power which is very frequently invoked. Under s 23, a constable may stop and search a person whom the constable has reasonable grounds to suspect is in possession of a controlled drug. This power may be exercised anywhere, unlike the power under s 1 of PACE; thus, persons on private premises may be searched once police officers are lawfully on the premises. The provisions as to reasonable suspicion will be interpreted in accordance with Code A. Code A and ss 2 and 3 of PACE apply to this power as they do to all the other statutory stop and search powers unless specific exceptions are made (see below).

Reasonable suspicion

Reasonable suspicion is a flexible, broad and uncertain concept. Code of Practice A on Stop and Search, as revised in 2006,[78] and applying to *all* statutory search powers,

---

77 Under s 1(7), the articles are '(a) offensive weapons or (b) articles (i) made or adapted for use in the course of or in connection with an offence to which this sub-paragraph applies; or (ii) intended by the person having it with him for such use by him or by some other person'. Under s 1(8), the offences to which s 1(7)(b)(i) above applies are: '(a) burglary; (b) theft; (c) offences under s 12 of the Theft Act 1968; (d) offences under s 15 of that Act.' Section 1(8A) applies 'to [any article which falls within] s 139 of the Criminal Justice Act 1988'. Under s 1(9), offensive weapon means 'any article (a) made or adapted for use for causing injury to persons or (b) intended by the person having it with him for such use by him or by some other person.'

78 It was revised in 1991, 1995, 1997, 1999, 2003.

sets out to explain what it means. Paragraphs 2.2–2.11 Code A apply to searches dependent on reasonable suspicion. Currently, para 2.2 of Code A provides that it is not enough for a police officer to have a hunch that a person has committed or is about to commit an offence; there must be a concrete basis for this suspicion which relates to the particular person in question and could be evaluated by an objective observer. Para 2.2 provides:

> There must be an objective basis for that suspicion based on facts, information, and/or intelligence which are relevant to the likelihood of finding an article of a certain kind or, in the case of searches under section 43 of the Terrorism Act 2000, to the likelihood that the person is a terrorist.

Paragraph 2.2 not only explains the objective nature of reasonable suspicion, but forbids stereotyping in arriving at such suspicion:

> a person's race, age, appearance, or the fact that the person is known to have a previous conviction, cannot be used alone or in combination with each other as the reason for searching that person. Reasonable suspicion cannot be based on generalisations or stereotypical images of certain groups or categories of people as more likely to be involved in criminal activity . . .

In particular it provides: 'A person's religion cannot be considered as reasonable grounds for suspicion.' That provision is obviously intended to deter the police from targeting Muslims in the wake of 9/11 and 7/7. Paragraph 2.4 provides:

> . . . reasonable suspicion should normally be linked to accurate and current intelligence or information, such as information describing an article being carried, a suspected offender, or a person who has been seen carrying a type of article known to have been stolen recently from premises in the area. Searches based on accurate and current intelligence or information are more likely to be effective.

Paragraph 2.3 provides:

> Reasonable suspicion can sometimes exist without specific information or intelligence and on the basis of some level of generalisation stemming from the behaviour of a person. For example, if an officer encounters someone on the street at night who is obviously trying to hide something, the officer may (depending on the other surrounding circumstances) base such suspicion on the fact that this kind of behaviour is often linked to stolen or prohibited articles being carried.

Thus, if based on powers requiring reasonable suspicion, the decision to stop and search must – according to Code A – be based on all the facts which bear on the likelihood that an article of a certain kind will be found.

The most significant change brought about when Code A was revised in 1991 was the omission of the requirement that the suspicion should be of the same level as that necessary to effect an arrest.[79] The original intention behind including this provision was to stress the high level of suspicion required before a stop and search could take place; this change, therefore, tended to remove some of that emphasis and could be taken to imply that there are two levels of suspicion, the level required under Code A being the lower. However, although this omission may convey such a message to police officers, it may not make much difference to the way the police actually operate stop and search.

When Code A was revised in 1997,[80] some departure from the 'objective grounds for suspicion' stance was effected, and this was carried through into the current, 2006, version. Paragraph 2.6 allows an officer to take into account information that members of a particular gang habitually carry knives, other weapons or have drugs in their possession; where a person wears an item of clothing or other insignia suggesting that he belongs to such a gang, that may give rise to reasonable suspicion allowing that person to be stopped and searched.

In practice, despite the wordy strictures of Code A, there is little evidence that reasonable suspicion acts as a constraint if police officers wish to stop and search without it.[81] Research in the area suggests that there is a tendency to view reasonable suspicion as a flexible concept which may denote a very low level of suspicion.[82] In 2000 Sanders and Young concluded, having reviewed the relevant research, that 'the legal understanding of reasonable suspicion plays little part in officers' thought processes or decision-making',[83] although they also suggested that PACE may have brought about some change in 'cop culture'; young officers may now be taught to act 'according to the book', as opposed to acting instinctively. In 2006 they concluded that there was some evidence of this, but that the Code A guidance did not have a very significant impact on police behaviour, compared to the influence of established cop culture.[84] 'Reasonable' suspicion, they find, does not connect very strongly with 'police suspicion'.

The case law is extremely meagre and unhelpful, but suggests that a highly imprecise and inconsistent standard is maintained. In *Slade*,[85] the suspect was close to the house of a well-known drug dealer; on noticing the officer, he put his hand in his pocket and smiled. This was found to constitute reasonable suspicion. However, in *Black v DPP*,[86] the fact of visiting a well-known drug dealer was found to be insufficient as the basis for finding reasonable suspicion. In *Francis*[87] the police purported to have reasonable suspicion to stop and search on the basis that the person in question was driving in an area known for drug use, with a passenger. The person had been stopped previously and her passenger at the time had been found to be in possession of drugs. Reasonable suspicion was not found to be established. This handful of cases clearly does very little

---

79 Previously contained in Annex B, para 4 of Code A.
80 SI 1997/1159.
81 See Foster, J, 'Police Cultures' in Newburn, T, (ed) *The Handbook of Policing*, 2003, Willan.
82 See Dixon (1989) 17 Int J Soc Law 185–206.
83 Sanders and Young, op. cit., fn 1, 2nd edn, 2000, p 43.
84 Sanders and Young, op. cit., fn 1, 3rd edn, 2007, pp 71–73.
85 LEXIS CO/1678/96 (1996).
86 (1995) unreported, 11 May.
87 (1992) LEXIS CO/1434/91.

to define the concept of reasonable suspicion, although it could be taken to indicate that extremely vague and broad bases for suspicion will not be sufficient.

Counter-terrorist stop and search powers

Section 44 of the Terrorism Act 2000 (TA) provides a power to stop and search without reasonable suspicion once an authorisation has been given. Section 43 provides a power that, unlike the s 1 PACE power, is not based on reasonable suspicion that a person is carrying an item, but on reasonable suspicion of being a terrorist. These powers are not new; they are based on powers provided under the previous counter-terrorist legislation. The Prevention of Terrorism (Temporary Provisions) Act 1989, as amended (PTA), and the Northern Ireland (Emergency Provisions) Act 1996, as amended (EPA), contained special powers providing for the detaining, questioning and searching of pedestrians and vehicles for articles of use in carrying out acts of terrorism and to prevent terrorist attacks. The powers under ss 43–47 of the TA are based on the PTA and EPA powers and, as Chapter 14 explains, they can potentially be applied to a far wider range of people under s 1 TA owing to the very broad definition of 'terrorism' that s 1 introduced.[88] It may be noted that under s 116(2) of the TA, the powers conferred under the Act to stop persons are deemed to include powers to stop vehicles, and it is an offence to fail to stop a vehicle.

Section 44 – stop and search without reasonable suspicion

The s 44 power has a number of controversial and significant features. Not only does it arise independently of reasonable suspicion relating to objects suspected of being carried, or of reasonable grounds to believe that acts of terrorism may occur in the are covered by the authorisation, but it is an offence in itself to refuse to comply with the search. It is not an offence under PACE to refuse to comply with a s 1 search, or to obstruct it, although to do so would probably amount to the offence of obstructing a constable under s 89(2) of the Police Act 1996.[89] Authorisations apply to a specific area and are for a maximum of 28 days, but that period can be continually renewed. Authorisations can be renewed for a further period or periods of up to 28 days at a time. The authorisation has to stipulate both the area to which it applies and the period, not exceeding 28 days, for which it will remain in force. Under s 44(3) 'an authorisation under sub-section (1) or (2) may be given only if the person giving it considers it expedient for the prevention of acts of terrorism'. The word 'expedient' is obviously significant – it is not necessary to demonstrate that terrorist acts are likely to occur or more likely to occur in the area covered by the authorisation than in other areas. Since the term 'expedient' is used, there is no requirement that the officer granting the authorisation should reasonably believe that it is *necessary* in order to prevent the commission of acts of terrorism. The term clearly connotes a less rigorous requirement.

88 See Chapter 14, pp 1377–81.
89 Reproducing the Police Act 1964, s 51(3).

If such an authorisation is in force, an officer can stop any person or vehicle within the specified locality in order to look for articles which could be used for the commission of acts of terrorism. The area may be very large – it can include the whole of the police area in question, or part of it. The authorisation must be given by a very senior police officer; in London the officer must be of the rank of Commander or above; outside London he or she must be of the rank of Assistant Chief Constable or above. Reproducing ss 13A(4) and 13B(3) PTA, the TA provisions expressly confirm that reasonable suspicion remains irrelevant, once the authorisation is in place. Section 45(1)(a) provides that the powers under s 44 'may be exercised only for the purpose of searching for articles of a kind which could be used in connection with terrorism', but in order to ensure that this is not interpreted as a limiting requirement, s 45(1)(b) provides that the powers 'may be exercised whether or not the constable has grounds for suspecting the presence of articles of that kind'.

One difference between the TA and PTA powers is that vehicle stop and search authorisations, as well as pedestrian ones, will have to be confirmed by the Secretary of State within 48 hours of their being made, or they will cease to have effect. This appears to be a gesture in the direction of due process, since it rectifies the anomaly of the difference between the exercise of the powers in respect of pedestrians and those in respect of vehicles, and provides, at least theoretically, a level of oversight in relation to both.[90] An authorisation confirmed by the Secretary of State, can be renewed at the end of 28 days under s 46(7) which provides: 'An authorisation may be renewed in writing by the person who gave it or by a person who could have given it; and sub-sections (1) to (6) shall apply as if a new authorisation were given on each occasion on which the authorisation is renewed.' Thus, theoretically, authorisations can be continually renewed, depending on the intervention of the Secretary of State. The tendency of this provision may be in effect to leave the authorisation power largely in police hands alone.

If a person fails to stop and submit to a search[91] when asked by a constable acting under s 44 of the TA to do so, or wilfully obstructs the constable in exercising these

---

90 Under the Major government, additional stop and search powers were added to the PTA. Section 81(1) of the CJPOA 1994 amended the PTA by inserting into it s 13A which provided that an officer of the rank of Commander as regards the Metropolitan area or the City of London, or of the rank of Assistant Chief Constable as regards any other police area, could authorise officers to stop and search vehicles and their occupants within a particular locality if he or she considered that it was expedient to do so to prevent acts of terrorism. The PTA was further amended by the Prevention of Terrorism (Additional Powers) Act 1996 to include a number of further stop and search powers. The government considered that introduction of the powers was necessary because of the threat of IRA activity on the British mainland in spring 1996. These included a power under s 1, which inserted s 13B into the PTA, to stop and search citizens in designated areas without reasonable suspicion. The authorisation requirements were the same as those under s 13A, but for the added requirement that the authorisation must be confirmed by the Secretary of State within 48 hours. If it was not so confirmed, it ceased to have effect (s 13A(8)), but if confirmed it remained in force, and subsisted for up to 28 days. Refusing to comply with the search was an offence carrying a penalty higher than those which could be used, if necessary, under the general offence of obstructing a constable. The powers under ss 13A and B formed the basis for the powers now arising under ss 44–46 of the Terrorism Act 2000, which replaced them.

91 The search only authorises a constable to require a person to remove headgear, footwear, outer coat, jacket or gloves (Code A para 4A).

powers, he or she will be liable to a fine of £5,000 or a prison sentence of six months, or both, under s 47. Thus, if someone who is not involved in terrorism resists a search in a designated area, and is, for example, found to be carrying a small amount of cannabis, he or she might in theory face a prison sentence, although the offence committed – possession of cannabis – would not usually lead to the imposition of such a sentence and might well be dealt with by way of caution.

Section 44 is clearly a particularly controversial provision; it has been used to impose an authorisation on the whole of London ever since it came into force. It has already been suggested that the reasonable suspicion requirement of a number of powers, including s 1 PACE, does not have a strong inhibitory effect. However, s 44 provides police officers with an even broader discretion, and clearly there is a danger that it could be used in a racially discriminatory fashion. Sections 44–47 do not spell out what a police officer must have in mind before conducting a search; the power is therefore non-transparent and not based on objectively justifiable criteria. As discussed below, Code A makes certain somewhat contradictory gestures in the direction of curbing the broad discretion provided.

It appears that, at Strasbourg, the short period of detention represented by a stop and search may be sufficient to constitute a deprivation of liberty.[92] However, the decision of the House of Lords in *R (on the application of Gillan) v Commissioner of Police for the Metropolis*[93] indicates that this has not been accepted domestically. The first appellant, Mr Gillan, came to London in September 2003 to protest peacefully against an arms fair being held at the ExCel Centre, Docklands, in east London. He was riding his bicycle near the Centre when he was stopped by two male police officers. They searched him and his rucksack and found nothing incriminating. They gave him a copy of the Stop/Search Form 5090 which recorded that he was stopped and searched under section 44 of the 2000 Act. The search was said to be for 'articles concerned in terrorism'. The whole incident lasted about twenty minutes. The second appellant, Ms Quinton, was an accredited freelance journalist and went to the Centre in September 2003 to film the protests taking place against the arms fair. She was stopped by a female police officer near the Centre and asked to explain why she had appeared out of some bushes. Ms Quinton was wearing a photographer's jacket and carrying a small bag and a video camera. She explained she was a journalist and produced her press passes. The officer searched her, found nothing incriminating, and gave her a copy of Form 5090. Ms Quinton estimated that the search lasted for thirty minutes, the police five.

The appellants argued, *inter alia*, that the stops and searches had constituted a breach of Article 5, Sched 1 HRA. Article 5 provides:

> 1   Everyone has the right to liberty and security of the person. No one shall be deprived of his liberty save in the following cases and in accordance with a procedure prescribed by law: . . . (b) the lawful arrest or detention of a person for non-compliance with the lawful order of a court or in order to secure the fulfilment of any obligation prescribed by law . . .

92 *X v Austria* (1979) 18 DR 154.
93 [2006] UKHL 12.

The other exceptions were deemed not relevant. Lord Bingham, who gave the leading judgment, sought to determine firstly whether the stops and searches were 'a deprivation of liberty' in Art 5(1) terms. He found:

> . . . the clearest exposition of principle by the Strasbourg court is to be found in *Guzzardi v Italy*,[94] an exposition repeatedly cited in later cases. In paragraphs 92–93 the Court observed: '92. The Court recalls that in proclaiming the "right to liberty", paragraph 1 of Article 5 is contemplating the physical liberty of the person; its aim is to ensure that no one should be dispossessed of this liberty in an arbitrary fashion. As was pointed out by those appearing before the Court, the paragraph is not concerned with mere restrictions on liberty of movement; such restrictions are governed by Article 2 of Protocol No 4 which has not been ratified by Italy. In order to determine whether someone has been "deprived of his liberty" within the meaning of Article 5, the starting point must be his concrete situation and account must be taken of a whole range of criteria such as the type, duration, effects and manner of implementation of the measure in question . . . 93. The difference between deprivation of and restriction upon liberty is nonetheless merely one of degree or intensity, and not one of nature or substance.'

Lord Bingham found (in para 25) that there was no deprivation of liberty in Art 5(1) terms:

> It is accordingly clear, as was held in *HL v United Kingdom*,[95] that:
>
> > 'in order to determine whether there has been a deprivation of liberty, the starting-point must be the concrete situation of the individual concerned and account must be taken of a whole range of factors arising in a particular case such as the type, duration, effects and manner of implementation of the measure in question.'
>
> I would accept that when a person is stopped and searched under sections 44–45 the procedure has the features on which the appellants rely. On the other hand, the procedure will ordinarily be relatively brief. The person stopped will not be arrested, handcuffed, confined or removed to any different place. I do not think, in the absence of special circumstances, such a person should be regarded as being detained in the sense of confined or kept in custody, but more properly of being detained in the sense of kept from proceeding or kept waiting. There is no deprivation of liberty. That was regarded by the Court of Appeal as 'the better view' (para 46), and I agree.

These findings leave some leeway, but not very much, for finding that in different circumstances Art 5(1) was engaged. Lord Bingham went on to consider the question whether, had there been a deprivation of liberty, it would have been justified as within Art 5(1)(b). He found that the statutory regime and the authorisation itself were 'prescribed by law' and that:

---

94 (1980) 3 EHRR 333.
95 (2004) 40 EHRR 761, at para 89.

the respondents bring themselves within the exception, for the public are in my opinion subject to a clear obligation not to obstruct a constable exercising a lawful power to stop and search for articles which could be used for terrorism and any detention is in order to secure effective fulfilment of that obligation.

Continual renewal of the authorisation was found acceptable under Art 5 which was thus deemed inapplicable, but even if it had been found to be applicable, the stops and searches would have been justified. This judgment, therefore, found not merely that the stops and searches were justified in Art 5 terms, but gave no encouragement to the raising of Art 5 arguments in relation to stop and search, in future. It is hard to see that he left the question of the engagement of Art 5(1) by stops and searches open since he found that there was no deprivation of liberty in unambiguous terms, but it could be suggested that since the case was considered and determined under Art 5(1)(b), that question could be reraised in future.

Section 43 – stop and search on reasonable suspicion of being a terrorist

Section 43 TA provides:

> A constable may stop and search a person whom he reasonably suspects to be a terrorist to discover whether he has in his possession anything which may constitute evidence that he is a terrorist.

'Being a terrorist' is not in itself an offence under the TA (unless the 'terrorist' group in question is also proscribed), although some, but not all, actions falling within the definition of terrorism in s 1 of the TA are coterminous with existing offences. Therefore, this power is not dependent on suspicion of commission of an offence or of carrying prohibited articles. As indicated above, para 2.2 Code A makes that clear.

Section 15(3) and (4) of the PTA empowered a police officer to stop and search anyone who appeared to him to be liable for arrest under s 14 of the Act and to search him for anything which might confirm the officer's suspicions as to his involvement in terrorism. Under s 14(1)(b), in order to arrest, a constable had to have reasonable grounds for suspecting that a person was 'concerned in the preparation or instigation of acts of terrorism connected with the affairs of Northern Ireland or any other act' of non-domestic terrorism.[96] The s 15 power was partially influenced by the reasonable suspicion requirement. It did not depend on the need to show reasonable suspicion that the suspect was carrying the items which might be searched for, but the officer had to have reasonable grounds for suspecting that the suspect was liable to arrest under s 14. These stop and search powers were reproduced, but broadened, under the Terrorism Act 2000.

Other powers – ports and border controls

There were also powers in s 16 of and para 4(2) of Sched 5 to the PTA, which empowered the police and others to stop, question and search people, vehicles and

---

96 See below, p 1147.

unaccompanied freight, which were about to enter or leave Great Britain or Northern Ireland, to determine whether they had been concerned in the commission, preparation or instigation of acts of terrorism. These powers formed part of the 'ports and border controls' contained in the PTA. They are reproduced in Sched 7 of the TA and again, they are not dependent on showing reasonable suspicion.

Special powers to prevent anticipated local violence

Section 60 of the Criminal Justice and Public Order Act 1994, as amended by s 8 of the Knives Act 1997, provides police officers with a further stop and search power which does not depend on showing reasonable suspicion of particular wrongdoing on the part of an individual. An officer of at least the rank of inspector can authorise the stop and search of any person or vehicle within a particular locality if he or she reasonably believes that incidents involving 'serious violence' may take place in that area and that authorisation is expedient in order to prevent their occurrence. The authorisation may apply to a period not exceeding 24 hours, but it can be renewed for a further 24 hours if such an authorisation is in force. An officer may stop anyone within the specified locality in order to look for offensive weapons or dangerous instruments whether or not there any grounds for suspecting that such articles are being carried. In contrast to s 1 of PACE, failure to stop is an offence under s 60(8).

Section 60 was amended by s 25 of the Crime and Disorder Act 1998 to provide a power under s 60(4A)(a) to demand the removal of a face covering 'if the constable reasonably believes that person is wearing [it] wholly or mainly for the purpose of concealing his identity'. Section 25 also amended s 60 to provide a further, separate, power under s 60(4A)(b) to 'seize any item which the constable reasonably believes any person intends to wear wholly or mainly for that purpose'. This power was revised by s 94 Anti-Terrorism Crime and Security Act 2001 to add a new s 60AA allowing a constable to require a person to remove any item that he reasonably believes the person is wearing wholly or mainly to conceal his identity. The items can also be seized on that basis (s 60AA(2)). This is not, formally, a power to stop and search for face coverings or other items that could be used to conceal identity. The constable must be acting under another power or the person must be carrying the covering (or item which could be used as a covering) openly. It is an arrestable[97] offence under s 60(8)(b) to fail to remove a face covering. These provisions have clear implications for public protest, which are discussed in Chapter 8.[98] While, on their face, they do not create a new power of stop and search, they may do so in practice since, once an authorisation is in force under s 60, a constable does not require reasonable suspicion that dangerous weapons or instruments will be found in order to stop and search. However, the provisions are not covered by Code A.[99]

Section 163 of the Road Traffic Act 1988

A very broad power to stop vehicles arises under s 163 of the Road Traffic Act 1988 (RTA). Its ambit remains unclear. Section 163 provides a constable in uniform with

---

97 The 1998 Act, s 27(1) amends PACE 1984, s 24 for this purpose.
98 See p 673.
99 See *DPP v Avery* [2003] 1 Cr App R 31.

power to stop vehicles, which appears to be unqualified as to purpose[100] and does not depend upon reasonable suspicion. The only limitation is that it must not be used oppressively.[101] If s 163 is of general application, s 1(2) of PACE appears to provide a power to search a vehicle and to detain it for that purpose once it has been stopped under s 163.[102] If s 163 is concerned only with traffic offences, s 1(2) must contain an implied power to stop a vehicle in order to detain it for a search. The Police Reform Act 2002, s 49 provides for a power of arrest for failing to stop.

Use of the counter-terrorist, road traffic and special powers

It is notable that no judicial body is involved in the pre-search supervision of the counter-terrorist and special powers. All of them are subject to executive supervision only, either by the police themselves or, in the case of s 44 TA, by the Home Secretary. These powers discard a key due process safeguard and therefore might be justified only if they are likely to have real value in terms of curbing criminal or terrorist activity. In debate on the 1996 Bill, Michael Howard was asked how many arrests and convictions had followed use of the existing s 13A power to stop and search. In reply, he said that there had been 1,746 stops and 1,695 searches of vehicles, 2,373 searches of persons as occupants of vehicles in the five Metropolitan police areas and 8,142 stops and 6,854 searches of vehicles and 40 searches of persons as occupants of vehicles within the Heathrow perimeter. These had together led to two arrests under the PTA and to 66 other arrests.[103] These figures are clearly telling. They suggest that stopping and searching without reasonable suspicion leads to an extremely low level of arrests and therefore may not be the most effective use of police resources. This very low level of arrests may be compared with the general level flowing from stop and search with reasonable suspicion, which is now around 10%.[104] This figure itself is low (and may not be reliable), but nevertheless suggests that stop and search with reasonable suspicion (even though that concept may be interpreted very flexibly) is more productive on the face of it in crime control terms than stop and search without it. Howard, however, also made the point, although unsupported by specific evidence, that this does not represent the whole picture, since would-be terrorists may be diverted from their activities, information may be gathered and weapons may be found.

The figures given above also suggest that in so far as these powers do have a value, it lies partly in their (albeit low) level of apprehension of persons engaged in non-terrorist offences. If one of the objects of introducing the powers under s 44 TA was in reality to curb drug trafficking, it should have been debated in Parliament on that basis. The 1999 revision of Code A introduced the requirement under para 1.16 that the ss 13A and B powers should 'not be used for stop and search for reasons unconnected with terrorism', and this provision is now contained in para 2.24 (2006 version). Para 2.24 provides:

100 See HC Standing Committee E, Col 339, 13 December 1983.
101 See *Stewart v Crowe* [1999] SLT 899.
102 This would confirm *Lodwick v Sanders* [1985] 1 All ER 577.
103 HC Deb Col 211, 2 April 1996.
104 Wilkins, G and Addicot, C, *Home Office Statistical Bulletin 2/99*, 1999.

When an authorisation under section 44 is given, a constable in uniform may exercise the powers: (a) only for the purpose of searching for articles of a kind which could be used in connection with terrorism; (b) whether or not there are any grounds for suspecting the presence of such articles.

However, as discussed below, this provision is virtually unenforceable. Para 2.26 Code A provides:

> The powers under sections 43 and 44 of the Terrorism Act 2000 allow a constable to search only for articles which could be used for terrorist purposes. However, this would not prevent a search being carried out under other powers if, in the course of exercising these powers, the officer formed reasonable grounds for suspicion.

The provision of para 2.26 means that while the police have not been given a blanket power to search for e.g. drugs without reasonable suspicion, they can in practice now do so, if an authorisation under s 44 is in force. The reasonable suspicion required could presumably be aroused by finding the drug (assuming that it could be found without requiring removal of more than outer clothing), or by efforts of the subject to conceal it.

Section 44 TA, s 60 CJPOA, which may allow near-random stopping once an authorisation is in force, may, as indicated, result not in arrests for terrorist offences or offences of serious violence, but for drug-related or other, more minor offences. It has often been observed that arrests may well be entirely unrelated to the reason for the original encounter with the police. These powers are therefore objectionable in the sense that they have been adopted apparently in response to near-crisis situations, whereas they may be used in situations which would not alone have justified their adoption. Since the wide powers under s 60 of the 1994 Act and s 44 of the Act of 2000 are not subject to limitation flowing from the concept of reasonable suspicion, they represent a departure from the principle that only an individual who has given rise to such suspicion due to his or her actions should suffer the infringement of liberty represented by a stop and search.

Discriminatory use of stop and search powers

All the stop and search powers discussed could be used in a discriminatory fashion, and this is especially true of the powers that do not depend on showing reasonable suspicion. Since all such powers, on their face, allow for stop and search on subjective grounds, they may tend to be used disproportionately against the black community. Post-PACE research has consistently suggested that stop and search powers in general are used in a discriminatory fashion[105] and in response, a rather ambiguous anti-racism

---

105 See Skogan, W, *HO Research Study No 117*, 1990 p 34; *Entry into the Criminal Justice System*, August 1998 and *Statistics on Race and the Criminal Justice System*, December 1998; MacPherson Report, 1999, Cm 4262-I. According to the report, in 1999 blacks were six times more likely than whites to be stopped; in 1998, blacks were five times more likely to be stopped than whites. See: *Home Office Statistics on Race and the Criminal Justice System 2001*, 2001–2; *Home Office Statistics on Race and the Criminal Justice System 2003–2004*, 2005. In 2000–2 stops and searches of Asians

provision was introduced in the 1999 revision of Code A, and carried forward in the 2006 revision. Para 2.25 gives an initial appearance of seeking to address the problem of racist stops in stating provides:

> The selection of persons stopped under section 44 of Terrorism Act 2000 should reflect an objective assessment of the threat posed by the various terrorist groups active in Great Britain. The powers must not be used to stop and search for reasons unconnected with terrorism. Officers must take particular care not to discriminate against members of minority ethnic groups in the exercise of these powers.

But the paragraph continues:

> There may be circumstances, however, where it is appropriate for officers to take account of a person's ethnic origin in selecting persons to be stopped in response to a specific terrorist threat (for example, some international terrorist groups are associated with particular ethnic identities).

This hazily worded provision might be interpreted as legitimising racist stops and as thereby undermining the preceding words. The provision of para 2.25 indicates that in certain circumstances the police can use racial profiling as the basis for the use of the s 44 power.

In 1995, Note 1A of Code A was revised to add the requirement that 'the selection of those questioned or searched is based upon objective factors and not upon personal prejudice'. In the 2006 revision, this requirement is stated more clearly; under para 1.1:

> Powers to stop and search must be used fairly, responsibly, with respect for people being searched and without unlawful discrimination. The Race Relations (Amendment) Act 2000 makes it unlawful for police officers to discriminate on the grounds of race, colour, ethnic origin, nationality or national origins when using their Powers.

Further requirements were added in subsequent revisions of Code A regarding the use of the power under s 60AA CJPOA to provide a power to demand the removal of a face covering. In the 2006 version Note 4 Code A provides:

> Many people customarily cover their heads or faces for religious reasons – for example, Muslim women, Sikh men, Sikh or Hindu women, or Rastarfarian men ... A police officer cannot order the removal of a head or face covering except where there is reason to believe that the item is being worn by the individual wholly or mainly for the purpose of disguising identity.

---

increased by 40% and of black suspects by 30%; the equivalent increase for white suspects was 8%. See further Mooney, J and Young, J, 'Policing Ethnic Minorities' in Marlow and Loveday, *Policing After the Stephen Lawrence Inquiry*, 2000; Waddington, P *et al*., 'In proportion: Race and police Stop and Search' (2004) 44(6) BJ Crim 889.

It also provides that if asking such persons to remove a covering, the officer should permit this to be done out of public view.

Thus, as far as s 163 of the 1988 Act, s 60 of the CJPOA and s 44 of the TA are concerned, these requirements contained in quasi- or non-legal provisions are the only 'safeguards' against a racially or religiously stereotyped or insensitive use of these powers. As discussed below, this problem may be addressed under the HRA, while the amendments made to the Race Relations Act 1976 in 2000 by the Race Relations (Amendment) Act 2000 may have an impact on police practice since, as Chapter 15 explains,[106] discrimination on grounds of race in law enforcement is now covered by the 1976 Act. However, the efficacy of this provision must remain in doubt; it would seem that the plaintiff would face a near-impossible task in raising an inference that a power not based on reasonable suspicion had been used in a racially discriminatory fashion.

Apart from their human rights implications, these powers, especially those not based on reasonable suspicion, may be having a counter-productive effect. They may be aiding in the construction of certain communities as 'suspect communities'. This may tend to inhibit intelligence-gathering among such communities, and may in general promote non-co-operation with the police. The impact of stop and search sweeps on community relations has long been recognised;[107] at present it is a particular problem in the context of terrorism, given that the most effective source of information allowing for the foiling of intended bomb attacks may be the Muslim community itself.[108] The possibility of raising European Convention on Human rights arguments in respect of discriminatory searches is considered below.

Voluntary searches

Until 2003 consensual searches were permissible but the apparently voluntary basis of a large number of searches continued to be questionable.[109] Inconsistency of practice between forces was readily apparent.[110] Although such searches were apparently outlawed in Code A para 1.5 (unchanged in the 2006 version), it is possible that they are still continuing. Persons may be intimidated by police authority and may submit to a search where no power to search in fact exists. Such searches may come to light only if the suspect later raises the argument that the police had no power to search or if the suspect resists and is charged with assaulting an officer in the course of his duty.[111]

---

106 See pp 1508–10.

107 See: Fitzgerald, M et al., *Policing for London* (2002), Willan; Clark, R et al., 'Crime and Police Effectiveness', HO Research Study no 79, 1984; the study looked at the effect of broad stop and search sweeps. See further Sanders and Young, *Criminal Justice*, 2007, pp 107–9.

108 On 10 August 2006, 24 suspects were arrested on suspicion of plotting to blow up planes flying from Britain to the US. The original information about the plan came from the Muslim community in Britain, according to British intelligence officials (see media reports on 11 August 2006, including CNN.com) .

109 Dixon, D, Coleman, C and Bottomley, K, 'Consent and the legal regulation of policing' (1990) 17 JLS 345.

110 Certain forces, such as Bedfordshire, used a separate consent form for voluntary searches, but such practice was by no means universal. See 'Modernising the tactic: improving the use of stop and search', *Policing and Reducing Crime: Briefing Note No 2*, November 1999.

111 See *Osman v Director of Public Prosecutions* (1999) *The Times*, 29 September, judgment of 1 July 1999, in which Sedley LJ indicated that an initial passive response to a search would not entitle officers to assume that the subject was consenting to it.

Code A does not, in general, affect ordinary consensual contact between police officer and citizen; officers can ask members of the public to stop and can ask them questions and, at least theoretically, the citizen can refuse. Prior to 2003 'voluntary' searches were possible. However, the voluntariness of such contacts was frequently doubtful: some people might 'consent' to a search in the sense of offering no resistance to it, owing to uncertainty as to the basis or extent of the police power in question.[112] The search could then be classified as voluntary and subsequently it would be difficult, if not impossible, to determine whether such classification was justifiable. Once a search was so classified, none of the statutory or Code A safeguards had to be observed. Original Code A failed to recognise this problem, although a Home Office circular issued in December 1985[113] did recognise it. When the Codes were revised in 1991, the concerns articulated in the circular were given expression in new Notes for Guidance 1D(b) and 1E which created certain restrictions on voluntary searches. Under Note 1E, persons belonging to three of the vulnerable groups recognised throughout the Codes as requiring special treatment – juveniles, the mentally handicapped or mentally disordered[114] – could not be subject to a voluntary search at all.[115]

In 2003, and now in the 2006 revision of Code A, 'voluntary' stops and searches were forbidden, under para 1.5. This provision appears to solve the problem, but there are loop-holes in it in practice. It appears to apply only to searches and not to stops – thus voluntary stops are still possible, even if they lead to 'consensual' detention for a period of time. This appears to be implicit in para 4.12 Code A which provides:

> When an officer requests a person in a public place to account for themselves, i.e. their actions, behaviour, presence in an area or possession of anything, a record of the encounter must be completed at the time and a copy given to the person who has been questioned. The record must identify the name of the officer who has made the stop and conducted the encounter.

A stop cannot occur in order to find the grounds for a search, under Code A para 2.11, but since this provision is virtually unenforceable, as discussed below, it appears probable that the continued availability of voluntary stops significantly undermines the prohibition on voluntary searches.

---

112 For further discussion of this point, see Dixon et al., 'Consent and the legal regulation of policing' (1990) 17 JLS 245–362.

113 Circular no 88/1985 stated in para 1: 'The co-operation of the citizen should not be taken as implying consent . . . Whilst it is legitimate to invite co-operation from the public in circumstances where there is no power to require it, the subject of a voluntary search should not be left under the impression that a power is being exercised. Voluntary search must not be used as a device for circumventing the safeguards established in Part I of the Act.'

114 See, in particular, Code C, para 3(b), Detained Persons: Special Groups.

115 The prohibition also applied to a range of other persons who were not deemed capable of giving an informed consent to a search, such as the hearing impaired or persons not proficient in English who are also recognised in the Codes as belonging to vulnerable groups. Persons who did not fall within the above groups could be subject to a voluntary search under Note 1D(b) as revised in 1995, but the officer had to 'always make it clear that he is seeking the consent of the person concerned to the search being carried out by telling the person that he need not consent and that without his consent, he will not be searched'.

If a search occurred on an apparently consensual basis where no power arose to search, because reasonable suspicion was required and was not present, para 1.5 would be breached, but no liability could arise in respect of the Code breach. However, if the situation was viewed as one of searching without a power to do so (under e.g. s 1 PACE), which is the better view , then liability might arise, for trespass to the person or – if an item was seized – to goods. However, if a person was asked to turn out his pockets and did so voluntarily without physical contact with the police officers, no liability would arise, unless an item was seized. There would also be the practical difficulty of establishing a breach, bearing in mind the low level of suspicion required. Thus if an item was found and seized during a 'voluntary' search, it could lead to an arrest or conviction on the one hand, while on the other it is unclear that redress would be available in respect of the police action.

If, as discussed above, a 'voluntary' stop occurred, and the suspect's demeanour or behaviour during it gave rise to sufficient reasonable suspicion to allow for a search based on one of the statutory powers, para 2.11 of Code A would be breached, but a power to search under the power in question would arise. (In this context, the deterioration of police/community relations due to the over-use of stop and search against the black or Asian community discussed above should be taken into account, since it is more likely that a suspect from one of those communities might respond to a request to stop in a non-co-operative or belligerent manner, thereby providing the basis for reasonable suspicion to conduct a search.) Therefore it would appear that no civil liability could arise. It is notable that the provisions previously restricting the use of consensual stop and search against certain persons belonging to vulnerable groups – such as the mentally disordered – did not and do not apply to stops. One way of escaping from the conclusion that no liability would arise would be to argue that the reasonable suspicion requirement under the statutory power in question should be interpreted to exclude such suspicion acquired during the course of an apparently consensual stop where, in the circumstances, no true consent was given (in such circumstances an action for false imprisonment would technically speaking arise in respect of the stop itself unless the period of time in question was regarded as too minimal to found such an action, but damages would probably be derisory).[116] It could be argued that the statutory requirement should be interpreted under s 3 HRA, relying on Art 5, to exclude reasonable suspicion formed in those circumstances, since otherwise the search power could be viewed as arbitrary and oppressive. Where the stop appeared to be consensual this point would be debatable. A further possibility would be to reinterpret the tort of false imprisonment under s 6 HRA to encompass such a requirement. Clearly the analysis in *Gillan* creates problems for these arguments since it is not possible to rely on s 3 HRA (or on s 6) if Art 5 is not engaged in the first place. This point is returned to below.

Use of force

The use of force in order to carry out a stop and search is permitted under s 117 of PACE, which provides: 'the officer may use reasonable force, if necessary, in the exercise of the [PACE] power'. The TA provides an equivalent provision in s 114(2).

---

116 See Chapter 13, pp 1303 *et seq.* for discussion of tort damages in respect of police misuse or abuse of power.

But, under Art 3 ECHR, the use of force must be strictly in proportion to the conduct of the detainee; this is discussed further in respect of forcible arrest.[117] Under these provisions, the use of extreme force is permissible if necessitated by the conduct of the detainee, but if the use of such force causes death, it would appear to breach Art 2 which permits the use of lethal force to 'effect an arrest', not to effect a detention short of arrest. However, if the detainee sought to escape after being detained for the purposes of a stop and search, this might fall within the second limb of Art 2(2)(b): 'to prevent the escape of a person lawfully detained'. The lawfulness of the initial detention would then have to be considered, bearing in mind the arguments above.

Special seizure powers

The Criminal Justice and Police Act 2001 (CJP) introduced certain new seizure powers. Under s 51(1) and (2) of the CJP, if an officer already has a power of search he or she can seize property which may not be covered by that power if it is not practicable to ascertain what the item is at the time or if it is attached to something that the officer does have the power to seize. This new provision is significant since *inter alia* it allows the police officers to remove items from persons even where they are not certain that – apart from s 51 – they have the power to do so.

This power is 'balanced' by the provisions of ss 52–61 which provide a number of safeguards. Notice must be given to persons whose property has been seized under s 52, and under s 59 he or she can apply to the 'appropriate judicial authority' for the return of the whole or part of the seized property, on the ground that there was no power to seize it or that excluded or special procedure material or legally privileged material[118] is not comprised in other property as provided for in ss 54 and 55. Under s 60 a duty to secure the property arises which includes the obligation under s 61 to prevent, *inter alia*, copying of it. Special provisions are made for the return of excluded or special procedure material or material covered by legal privilege, which are discussed in Chapter 10.[119] The property can be retained under s 56 if it appears to have been obtained in consequence of the commission of an offence and otherwise it might be lost, damaged, altered or destroyed. The idea behind these powers is to allow the seizure of documents or computer discs which cannot readily be examined on the street. But despite the safeguards introduced, it is not clear that these powers, especially to seize and use legally privileged material, are compatible with the requirements of the Convention under the HRA. For example, arguments could be raised at trial that Art 8 was breached due to the seizure of confidential material; it could be argued that due to the nature of these provisions they should be afforded a strict construction, using s 3 of the HRA if necessary.

Procedural requirements for stop and search powers

Under s 2(1) of PACE, the procedural safeguards it sets out, together with those under s 3, apply to the PACE power and to powers under any other statutory provisions. All

---

117 See p 1163.
118 See Chapter 11, pp 1002–3.
119 See pp 1004–5.

other statutory powers of search are also subject to the same procedural requirements under Code A as those relating to the powers under s 1 of PACE, apart – where relevant – from the Code A provisions relating to reasonable suspicion (Code A, para 2). The special counter-terrorism powers are subject to such requirements, apart from searches carried out for the purposes of examination under Sched 7 to the Terrorism Act 2000 which are covered by a TA Code of Practice.[120]

An element of due process is introduced into all these statutory stop and search powers by the information giving and recording requirements under ss 2 and 3 of PACE and Code of Practice A, paras 3 and 4. Under s 2(3) PACE, the constable must give the suspect certain information before the search begins, including 'his name and the name of the police station to which he is attached; the object of the proposed search; the constable's grounds for proposing to make it'. Under s 3, he or she must make a record of the search, either on the spot if that is practicable or as soon as it is practicable. The subject of the search can obtain a copy of the search record later on from the police station. Code A, para 3.8 also covers the information-giving requirement,[121] and para 4 covers search records. General guidance as to the conduct of the search is contained in Code A, paras 3.1–3.3; they require the officer to complete the search speedily, to minimise embarrassment and to seek co-operation.

The statutory and Code information-giving and record-keeping requirements give the impression of creating due process-based controls since they mean that the citizen can make a complaint and the police station will have a record of the number of stops being carried out. These procedural requirements are supposed to inject some accountability into stopping and searching, but in so far as they rely on Code A, they are effectively virtually unenforceable. The status of the ss 2 and 3 PACE requirements is considered below.

Redress for breaches of the stop and search rules; reliance on Convention arguments

A search would be unlawful if no reasonable suspicion arose in the circumstances – as required by the statutory provision that the police officers purported to be relying on, or if the police purported to act under an authorisation which was not in fact in force. A search would also be unlawful if one of the *mandatory* statutory procedural requirements was not complied with.

The lack of means of creating accountability by enforcing the due process safeguards for searches, especially in respect of CJPOA or TA authorisations, encourages the idea of resort to the HRA. In this context there were grounds for expecting that arguments

---

120 PACE 1984, Code A was applied to the additional PTA powers introduced in 1996. The TA, ss 99 and 101 in respect of Northern Ireland and the new Code introduced under Sched 14, para 6 in respect of the UK generally will apply the TA Codes to the TA powers. Under Sched 14, para 5, 'An officer shall perform functions conferred on him by virtue of this Act in accordance with any relevant code of practice in operation under paragraph 6'. Paragraph 6(1) provides: 'The Secretary of State shall issue codes of practice about the exercise by officers of functions conferred on them by virtue of this Act.'

121 *Inter alia*, the record must include the name, address, date of birth and ethnic origin of the person searched (unless he or she is not willing to disclose the name and address).

raised under the Act might lead to judicial intervention in this largely unregulated area. However, the decision of the House of Lords in *Gillan*[122] has put paid to such expectations in most circumstances, as explained above. But possibilities of raising Convention points in relation to searches remain. For example, as Chapter 13 will argue, Art 6 could be relied upon where it was claimed at trial that a search had not been based on any statutory power, or where breaches of Code A had occurred during the search, including breaches which might also amount to violations of Art 8.[123] Code A, para 3.5 provides safeguards against a search of more than outer clothing which appear to be coterminous with the right to respect for privacy under Art 8. However, Note 7 provides that there is nothing to prevent officers from asking a suspect to remove more than outer clothing in public, on a voluntary basis. This Note is of doubtful compatibility with Art 8, since persons who complied with such a 'request', believing that they had to, would suffer an interference with their Art 8 rights, which would arguably not be in accordance with the law. It could be argued that any evidence obtained in respect of an unlawful search, or one that breached Art 8, should be excluded in order to ensure a fair trial, although as Chapter 13 demonstrates, this argument would be very unlikely to succeed. There would however be a free-standing action in respect of a breach of Art 8 under s 7(1)(a) HRA and damages could be awarded under s 8.

Engagement of Article 5(1)

Article 5 provides a guarantee of 'liberty and security of person'. Following *Gillan* it does not appear to be necessary, except in exceptional circumstances (possibly where a stop and search was particularly prolonged) to show that an exception to Art 5 applies, since Art 5(1) is not, apparently, engaged. However, as discussed above, that question may still be open, especially in circumstances differing from those applicable in *Gillan*.

The reliance in *Gillan* on *Guzzardi* was doubtful, since the question in *Guzzardi* was whether restrictions on freedom of movement were sufficient to amount to deprivation of liberty. *Guzzardi* was detained on an island and therefore had some freedom of movement; the Court thought that his detention was somewhat akin to that experienced by someone in an open prison. In contrast, Gillan and Quinton were completely detained – i.e. they could not move appreciably from the spot on which they were stopped and searched. Had they sought to do so they would probably have been arrested for the offence encapsulated in s 47 – that of failing to stop when ordered to do so. The TA itself does not provide a power of arrest in relation to this specific offence, but that is in any event unnecessary since a power would arise under s 24 PACE, as amended (discussed below). The officer could have arrested, say, Quinton if she had made a move to leave the spot, before actually leaving it, under s 24(1)(c) PACE; if she had succeeded in moving away from the spot she could have been arrested under s 24(1)(d); s 24(5)(e) would also have had to be satisfied, and would have been, on those facts. Thus, Quinton and Gillan's situation was readily distinguishable from that of Guzzardi. The question

---

122 (2006) UKHL 12; [2006] 2 WLR 537.
123 E.g., regarding the requirements as to conduct of the search under Code A, para 3, including requirements as to removal of only outer clothing in public.

in their case was that of *duration of time*, not, on its face, of deprivation of liberty. In common parlance, they had clearly been deprived of liberty in the sense of being unable to move from one spot, whereas Guzzardi was able to move around the island; the question was whether the restraints on his movement amounted to a deprivation of liberty in Art 5 terms. Quinton and Gillan were deprived of liberty in the sense of being unable to move from one place, under threat of arrest. Had they been detained any longer, e.g. for one hour, it would have been difficult to suggest that that was not a deprivation of liberty in Art 5 terms. It is arguable that Art 5 therefore applied. *X v Austria*[124] arguably provided a closer analogy: a man was forcibly compelled to submit to a blood test, and the Strasbourg Court found a deprivation of liberty. Thus Lord Bingham's findings are open to question, although that it is probable that that question will now only be likely to be raised at Strasbourg.

Application of Art 5(1)(b)

Assuming that an exception had to be shown, it probably could be established in most instances. In *Gillan* Lord Bingham found that Art 5(1)(b) would have applied. Deprivation of liberty can occur only on a basis of law and in certain specified circumstances, including, under Art 5(1)(b), the detention of a person in order to secure the fulfilment of any obligation prescribed by law. Article 5(1)(c) provides an exception in respect of the 'lawful detention of a person effected for the purpose of bringing him before the competent legal authority on reasonable suspicion of having committed an offence' but this exception appears to apply to arrest rather than to stop and search. That was the view taken in *Gillan*. Section 1 PACE requires suspicion as to carriage of an article, not as to an offence; it is clearly aimed at gathering evidence of offences and its requirements are not fully coterminous with the relevant range of offences. Carrying certain of the articles which fall within s 1 of PACE is not an offence[125] even if the carrier can be said to 'possess' them, although the officer also requires suspicion as to *mens rea*, while carriage of prohibited articles without sufficient 'possession' will clearly not constitute an offence. Code A, para 2.7 provides that where a police officer has reasonable grounds to suspect that a person is in innocent possession of a stolen or prohibited article, or other item for which he is empowered to search, the power of stop and search exists despite the absence of a power of arrest. That Code provision clearly allows searches that could not be covered by Art 5(1)(c).

Thus Art 5(1)(b) could cover potentially temporary detention for the purposes of a search. The provision under Art 5(1)(b) raises difficulties of interpretation and is clearly not so straightforward as the form of detention permitted under Art 5(1)(c). On its face, its broad wording appears to allow arbitrary detention on a broader basis than that permitted based on the requirements of reasonable suspicion or authorisation which PACE, other statutory powers and the TA depend upon, and without intervention by a court. At first glimpse it gives the impression of representing a scheme which affords less weight to due process than the current domestic one.

---

124 (1979) 18 DR 154.
125 Under s 1(7)(b), such articles could include credit cards or keys.

However, Art 5(1)(b) has received a restrictive interpretation at Strasbourg. In *Lawless*,[126] it was found that a specific and concrete obligation must be identified; once it has been, detention can in principle be used to secure its fulfilment. It is probable that the term 'obligation' could apply to the current statutory provisions – if Art 5(1), exceptionally, was found to be engaged. The requirements are to submit to a search, and, apart from the power under s 163 of the Road Traffic Act, to remain under police detention for the period of time necessary to allow it to be carried out.[127] Following this interpretation, the PACE, CJPOA and TA stop and search provisions are probably compatible with Art 5(1)(b). In *McVeigh, O'Neill and Evans*[128] a requirement to submit to an examination on arrival in the UK was found not to violate Art 5(1)(b) since it was sufficiently specific and concrete, but the Commission emphasised that this was found on the basis that the obligation in question only arose in limited circumstances and had a limited purpose – to combat terrorism. The PACE powers, the Misuse of Drugs Act power and, arguably, the power arising under s 43 of the TA, which is a permanent power, not one adopted temporarily to meet an emergency as in *McVeigh*, could not readily be said to arise in limited circumstances but the obligation would probably be found to arise since they are founded upon a requirement of reasonable suspicion. The CJPOA and other TA powers have more limited purposes in the sense that the place in which they can be exercised is circumscribed either by its nature (as in port or border controls) or by the authorisation given, which is based on the need for special powers. Whether any particular authorisation would be viewed as rendering the obligation in question sufficiently specific would be open to question, depending on the factual situation.[129]

The exercise of the powers under s 60 CJPOA and s 44 TA appears to be compatible with Art 5(1)(b), following *Gillan*. The power under s 163 of the Road Traffic Act also appears to be compatible with Art 5(1)(b) since it is exercised in respect of a specific obligation, as explained in *McVeigh*. The obligation may be viewed as one inherent in the use of a vehicle on the roads. The power probably carries with it, impliedly, the power to detain for a short period.[130] The offence under the RTA of failing to stop would probably be committed if the response to the stop was to brake and pause for an instant before driving on. It appears, after *Gillan* that Art 5 is not normally engaged by the use of this power, but that if it were engaged, it would usually fall within the exception.

---

126 Report of 19 December 1959, B1 (1960–61) p 64; judgment of 1 July 1961, A 3 (1960–61); (1961) 1 EHRR 15.
127 See *McVeigh, O'Neill and Evans* (1981) 5 EHRR 71; the obligation imposed was a requirement to 'submit to examination'. In *Reyntjens v France* Appl No 16810/90 (1992) unreported, the obligation was to submit to an identity check.
128 (1981) 5 EHRR 71.
129 See further Reiner, R and Leigh, I, 'Police powers', in McCrudden and Chambers, op. cit., fn 1, pp 93–94; Klug, Starmer and Weir argue in op. cit., fn 1, that police stop and search powers may breach Art 5: pp 250–51.
130 This may be suggested by the findings in *Lodwick v Sanders* [1985] 1 WLR 382.

General requirements under Art 5

Article 5 also imposes further, general requirements. The detention must not be arbitrary; this is implicit in the requirement of lawfulness.[131] A detention with the real purpose of searching for drugs, which had been authorised under s 44 of the TA in respect of terrorism, might be viewed as arbitrary in the sense that it was not proportionate to the purpose of ensuring the fulfilment of an obligation prescribed by the relevant law[132] – the TA. If such an argument was advanced at Strasbourg, involving, as it does, review of the proportionality of decisions taken by the state authorities, a certain margin of appreciation would be afforded to those authorities in respect of their assessment of the relevant circumstances.[133] But in the domestic courts, under the HRA, this approach would be inappropriate. Applying the notion of a discretionary area of judgment[134] would also arguably be inappropriate, since a search under terrorism legislation, but for a non-terrorist purpose, does not call for deference. However, the argument that the search was arbitrary was not accepted in *Gillan*, even though it appeared to be for a non-terrorism related purpose, on the basis that sufficient safeguards, partly arising from Code A, surround the use of s 44.

Article 13?

If, as argued above, the House of Lords fell into error in *Gillan*, it is possible that an application might be made to Strasbourg, arguing for a breach of both Arts 5 and 13. Article 13 would arguably be breached in circumstances where it would be necessary to establish a breach of Art 5 in order to afford a remedy, as opposed to circumstances where a remedy would be available under trespass to the person or false imprisonment. The use of a 'voluntary' stop to fuel reasonable suspicion in order to search under a statutory power could arguably provide such an instance.

Judicial review

Article 5 arguments might also be raised under s 7(1)(b) HRA in the context of judicial review proceedings. *Gillan* has obviously discouraged argument that Art 5 itself has been breached, but the possibility of arguing that a breach of Art 5 read with Art 14 had occurred might prove more fruitful. In appropriate cases, bearing in mind the recent evidence noted above of a police tendency to show racial bias in decisions to stop and search,[135] violation of Art 5(1) might be found when read with the Art 14 guarantee of freedom from discrimination in the enjoyment of the Convention rights. This might particularly be the case under s 44 TA or s 60 CJPOA, given the very broad, unstructured discretion they hand to the police. The possibility of relying on the HRA is of less significance after the amendments made to the Race Relations Act 1976 in 2000, allowing claimants to bring actions against the police in respect of direct or

131 *Winterwerp v Netherlands* A 33 (1979), para 39.
132 Ibid; *Bouamar v Belgium* A 129 (1988), para 50.
133 Ibid, para 40.
134 See Chapter 4, p 265 *et seq*.
135 See above pp 1124–26.

indirect discrimination in policing decisions, including decisions to stop and search. However, a defendant would also have the option of raising an Art 5 and 14 argument during the criminal process. It could be argued, for example, under Art 6(1) that if Art 14, read with Art 5, had been breached through a discriminatory search (one which would otherwise be lawful as in conformity with, for example, s 60 of the 1994 Act or s 44 of the TA), any products of the search could be excluded from evidence under s 78 of PACE, and in so far as the contact had influenced the subsequent investigation, evidence deriving from it should also be excluded. Such an argument would of course require recognition to be given to possible racial stereotyping behind stop and search decisions.[136] It is argued that despite Lord Bingham's findings in *Gillan*, Art 5 could be engaged by a stop and search that also engaged Art 14 on the basis of extending the ambit of Art 5 where Art 14 was engaged.[137]

In *Gillan* Lord Bingham failed to deal with the question of the possible discriminatory use of the s 44 power, which did not – it appeared – arise in the instant cases. However, Lord Hope of Craighead and Lord Brown of Eaton-under-Heywood considered this issue. Lord Hope said (para 38):

> How does the fact that it is likely to be difficult in practice to detect discriminatory use of the power square with the principle of legal certainty that requires that the use of such powers must be in accordance with the law if they are to be compatible with the Convention rights? And how in practice is discriminatory use of the power to be prevented, given the nature of the terrorist threats that it is designed for?

He elaborated on this point at para 43: 'What then if it is found that the police are using the section 44 power more frequently to stop Asians than other racial groups in the community? Does this amount to direct discrimination contrary to domestic law . . .' He found that the issue could not be overlooked, in view of the concern that the House expressed in *R (European Roma Rights Centre) v Immigration Officer at Prague Airport (United Nations High Commissioner for Refugees intervening)*[138] about the fact that all Roma applicants were being routinely treated, simply because they were Roma, with more suspicion and subjected to more intensive and intrusive questioning than non- Roma. The evidence, he said, showed that the operation that was being conducted in that case was 'inherently and systematically discriminatory and unlawful'.

But Lord Hope managed to distinguish the exercise of the s 44 power from the exercise of the power in the *Roma* case on the following grounds:

> But a decision to use the section 44 power will in practice always be based on more than the mere fact of a person's racial or ethnic origin if it is to be used properly and effectively, especially in places where people are present in large numbers. The selection process will be more precisely targeted, even if in the end

---

136 In the US context, AC Thompson argues that the tendency of the judiciary is to impose neutral explanations on searches (based on the notion of police expertise in spotting criminal possibilities in neutral behaviour) on stop and 'frisk' decisions and to ignore, if possible, any racial element: 'Race and the Fourth Amendment' (1999) 74(4) New York UL Rev 956.

137 See Chapter 15, pp 1483, 1526.

138 [2005] 2 AC 1.

it is based more on a hunch than on something that can be precisely articulated or identified. Age, behaviour and general appearance other than that relating to the person's racial or ethnic background will have a part to play in suggesting that a particular person might possibly have in his possession an article of a kind which could be used in connection with terrorism. An appearance which suggests that the person is of Asian origin may attract the constable's attention in the first place. But a further selection process will have to be undertaken . . .

Therefore he found that the power was not discriminatory, although he did think that it should be used sparingly.[139]

This is questionable. The *Roma* decision might be viewed as relating to behaviour at one end of the spectrum of direct discrimination, while a decision to stop and search based wholly on an Asian person's individual behaviour, such as seeking to conceal an object, might be viewed as at the other. In other words, the first instance would clearly be directly racially discriminatory, the second would not. But the use of the s 44 power under the TA could be viewed as coming somewhere between the two instances since the ethnic origin of persons stopped could be allowed – according to Lord Hope – to play a part in the decision to stop and search. Arguably, that is direct discrimination, albeit of a less overt quality than that at issue in the *Roma* case, since on Lord Hope's analysis, persons could be singled out for law enforcement attention on the basis of their ethnic origin. In practice it would also be very difficult, since no objective criteria are laid down to govern the *other* grounds – apart from discriminatory ones – for selecting persons for stops, to be able to say with certainty that direct discrimination had not occurred. Although this was not Lord Hope's point, if considered under Art 14 (read with Art 5 on the basis of an assumed extended ambit of Art 5(1)), the discriminatory treatment could potentially be justified if proportionate; if considered under the Race Relations Act 1976, as amended, it could not. The discussion in *Gillan* was technically *obiter* since the issue did not arise in the instant case; it is to be hoped that if it is revisited in future, it receives further and stricter scrutiny.

Argument based on the decision of the European Court of Human Rights in *Wainwright v UK*[140] would be relevant in this context. In that instance the Court accepted that the search in question pursued the legitimate aim under Art 8(2) of fighting the drugs problem in the prison. On the other hand, it was not satisfied that the searches were proportionate to that aim in the manner in which they were carried out. It was found that where procedures were laid down for the proper conduct of searches the prison authorities were required to comply strictly with those safeguards and by rigorous precautions protect the dignity of those being searched as far as possible. Failure to do so had meant that the intrusion onto dignity represented by the search could not be viewed as proportionate to the aim pursued. In this context, Code A lays down detailed rules regarding the avoidance of discriminatory searches. The same or similar arguments could be applied in the context of Art 5 read with Art 14, where the Code A rules were not adhered to. Article 14 contains an implied proportionality test;[141] it

139 At para 92.
140 Appl No 12350/04; 26 September 2006.
141 See Chapter 2, p 109.

could be argued that although taking account of a person's race in the manner referred
to by Lord Hope might be justifiable, it would be less likely that it could be justified
if the police had failed to adhere to the Code provisions in conducting searches based,
in effect, on racial profiling.

Tortious remedies

A citizen who submitted to a search where no power arose to search in the circumstances
would have a remedy in trespass to the person. If a search is conducted unlawfully, the
citizen is entitled to resist and to sue for assault. But in many instances, and especially
where a search is conducted under one of the provisions which do not require reasonable
suspicion, the citizen has no means of knowing that the search is unlawful. A citizen
who believed that there could be no grounds for a search and therefore resisted it
would be taking a risk. Resistance to an authorised TA or CJPOA search could incur
criminal liability, not only, in all probability, in respect of obstruction or assault of a
constable,[142] but under the special TA or CJPOA search-related offences as well. Article
5 arguments, possibly combined with Art 14 ones, could be raised under s 7(1)(b) HRA
in the context of a civil action for false imprisonment or trespass to the person. Clearly,
Gillan has not encouraged such argument, but *Gillan* did not rule out the possibility that
in certain circumstances Art 5 could be engaged by a stop and search, or that Art 5 read
with Art 14 would not be breached in certain circumstances by a discriminatory use of
the stop and search power. If Art 5 alone or read with Art 14 was found to be breached,
the options of extending an existing tort in order to cover the instance in question would
arise, or of merely affording a remedy under s 8 HRA. A racially discriminatory stop
and search would also be tortious under the Race Relations Act 1976, as amended.[143] If
there was a doubt as to the ambit of the tort in question, suggesting that in the particular
instance it might be inapplicable, it could be argued that it should be extended to cover
the breach of Art 5 in question.[144] If Code A had been breached during the stop and
search that in itself would not give rise to any civil liability, but the breach could be
relied upon as part of an argument that Art 5 itself had been breached.[145] The use of tort
actions in this context is discussed further in Chapter 13.

There is no provision under the TA, PACE or Code A to the effect that if the *procedural*
requirements are not complied with, the search will be unlawful. As indicated, a number
of due process requirements are contained only in Codes[146] and, therefore, their breach
cannot give rise to civil liability,[147] although breach of certain of the *statutory* procedural

---

142 Offences arising under the Police Act 1996, s 89(1) and (2).
143 See Chapter 15, pp 1509–10.
144 See further on this point Chapter 4, pp 252–56.
145 See further on this point, above, pp 1107–8.
146 Code A made under PACE 1984, s 66 and the TA Code made under the TA, ss 96 and 98 in respect of
     Northern Ireland and the new Code introduced under Sched 14 in respect of the UK. See pp 1106–7
     above.
147 Under PACE 1984, s 67(10). The TA Codes will have the same status as the PACE Codes; under
     Sched 14, para 6(2) 'The failure by an officer to observe a provision of a code shall not of itself make
     him liable to criminal or civil proceedings', but under sub-para (3) 'A code (a) shall be admissible in
     evidence in criminal and civil proceedings, and (b) shall be taken into account by a court or tribunal
     in any case in which it appears to the court or tribunal to be relevant'.

requirements will render searches unlawful, as will breach of the statutory powers. It has been held that a failure to make a written record of the search in breach of s 3 will not render it unlawful,[148] whereas a failure to give the grounds for it will do so, following *Fenelley*[149] and *Samuel v Comr of Police for the Metropolis*,[150] as will a failure to comply with the duties to provide identification under s 2(3), following *Osman v Director of Public Prosecutions.*[151] In *Osman*, proper authorisation had been given for the police to search members of the public entering a park under s 60(4) and 60(5) of the CJPOA 1994. When the defendant was searched, police officers failed to comply with s 2; the search was resisted and the defendant charged with assaulting an officer in the execution of his duty. It was found on appeal that it was plain from the mandatory words of s 2 that any search initiated without prior compliance with the duties set out in s 2 would mean that no officer was actually assaulted in the execution of his duty, since any search of a person might be a trespass requiring proper justification in law; the breach of s 2(3) meant that the search was unlawful and therefore not in the execution of their duty. The facts that the officers were clearly local and that numbers could have been obtained from their uniforms were found to be insufficient to avoid the finding of unlawfulness.[152] The strict interpretation of the information-giving duties evident in *Fenelley* and *Osman* was equally apparent in *Lineham v DPP*[153] in the context of a search of premises.

Exclusion of the products of the search from evidence; trial remedies

The PACE and TA Codes are admissible in evidence.[154] It would be possible for a defendant who claims that a search was conducted improperly or unlawfully to seek the limited form of redress represented by exclusion of evidence which has been obtained after a breach of ss 2 or 3 PACE and/or Code A. A stop and search is most likely to produce physical evidence such as drugs or perhaps a weapon, but the courts are very reluctant to exclude such evidence unless there has been deliberate illegality because it is less likely to be unreliable than confession or identification evidence.[155] Thus, the mechanism of exclusion of evidence as a form of redress for breach of a Code provision, which has operated to underpin Codes C and D, is not as appropriate in relation to Code A, although an effective sanction is clearly needed.

---

148 *Basher v DPP* (1993) unreported, 2 March.
149 [1989] Crim LR 142.
150 (1999) unreported, 3 March.
151 (1999) *The Times*, 29 September, judgment of 1 July 1999.
152 The Crown Court had found that there had been a breach of the 1984 Act, s 2(3)(a), but given the fact that the officers were clearly local police officers policing a local event in broad daylight, as expeditiously as possible, and because numbers could readily be obtained from the officers' uniforms, the breach was not so serious as to render the search unlawful. These findings would clearly have undermined s 2(3).
153 (1999) unreported, judgment of 8 October. Laws LJ found that police officers who conducted a search under PACE 1984, s 18 had not been acting in the execution of their duty because they had failed to inform the appellant so far as possible as to the reason why they intended to search the premises.
154 PACE 1984, s 67(11); TA, Sched 14, para 6(3).
155 See the pre-PACE ruling of the House of Lords in *Fox* [1986] AC 281; see also *Thomas* [1990] Crim LR 269 and *Khan* [1996] 3 All ER 289; cf *Fenelley* [1989] Crim LR 142. See further Chapter 13, pp 1288 *et seq.*

This weakness is further exacerbated in relation to breaches of the Notes for Guidance rather than of Code A itself; and since the Notes do not have the same legal status as Code provisions, they are more likely to be ignored by officers. What would be the position if, for example, a police officer required a Muslim woman to remove a veil in public view in breach of Note for Guidance 4 Code A? A judge might well be minded to view breach of a Note for Guidance as of insufficient significance to lead to exclusion of any identification evidence obtained.

Article 6 arguments would be available where a breach of Art 5 was alleged which might affect the fairness of the trial; they could be raised in respect of admission of evidence obtained after a breach of Art 5, or in respect of an argument for abuse of process; these possibilities are considered further in Chapter 15. Again, *Gillan* has not encouraged such argument, but *Gillan* did not rule out the possibility that in certain circumstances Art 5 could be engaged by a stop and search, or that Art 5 read with Art 14 could be breached in certain circumstances by a discriminatory use of the stop and search power. These arguments could be raised at trial in respect of failing to stop, either under one of the specific offences under the relevant statute or under s 89(1) or (2) of the Police Act 1996. Further possibilities are considered in respect of arrests in breach of Art 5, below.

Disciplinary action

Disciplinary action, the other form of redress for breach of a Code provision, may be even less effective in relation to Code A than Codes C, D and E, which largely govern interrogation and identification, because stop and search powers are exercised away from the police station, at a low level of visibility. Moreover, if a police officer decides that a search can be called voluntary, he need not give his name or number and therefore it will be almost impossible to bring a complaint against him. Thus, it is fair to say that in so far as the balance between police powers and individual rights is supposed to be maintained by the Code A provisions, it is largely dependent on voluntary adherence to them. The police are bound by the Convention rights under s 6 HRA and therefore argument that a right had been breached could be raised in disciplinary proceedings, although it would not be conclusive. This is discussed further in Chapter 13.

3 Powers of arrest

Introduction[156]

Under traditional common law doctrine an arrest occurs at the point when liberty ceases. A person has been arrested when, if he tried to exercise his liberty to go where

---

156 See further: Home Office, *Modernising Police Powers to Meet Community Needs – a consultation paper*, Aug 2004. For current comment on PACE and the Terrorism Act 2000, see Ashworth, A, *The Criminal Process*, 3rd edn, 2005; Feldman, D, *Civil Liberties and Human Rights in England and Wales*, 2nd edn, 2002, Chapters 5 and 9; Sanders, A and Young, R, *Criminal Justice*, 3rd edn, 2007, Chapter 3; Zander, M, *The Police and Criminal Evidence Act 1984*, 2003; Clark, D, *Bevan and Lidstone's The Investigation of Crime*, 2004; Starmer, K and Hopkins, A *Human Rights in the Investigation of Crime* (2007), OUP; Ayres, M, Murray, L and Fiti, R (2003) *Arrests for Notifiable Offences*, Home Office Paper 17/03; Healy, P, 'Investigative Detention in Canada' [2005] Crim LR 98 at p 105.

he wills, he would be prevented from doing so.[157] Some forms of detention are not deprivations of liberty, and so are not arrests, as Lord Bingham sought to indicate in *Gillan*. They are temporary impediments to exercising liberty. But it does not follow that a deprivation of liberty cannot occur outside the context of an arrest. The common law has long recognised that deprivations of liberty short of arrest can lawfully occur (*Albert v Lavin*).[158] This was recently reaffirmed by the House of Lords in *R (on the application of Laporte) (FC) v Chief Constable of Gloucestershire*.[159] It is suggested that, after *Gillan*,[160] and *Laporte* an arrest should no longer be viewed as a factual situation,[161] but as a legal concept.

Arrest may often be the first formal stage in the criminal process. It does not need to be; the process could begin with a consensual interview with the suspect, perhaps in his or her own home, followed by a summons to appear at the magistrates' court. It appears that arrests are sometimes effected unnecessarily; this contention is supported by the pre-PACE variation in practice regarding arrest between police areas,[162] which does not seem to be explicable on the ground of necessity, but seems to be attributable to different policies in the different areas. Any arrest represents a serious curtailment of liberty; therefore, use of the arrest power requires careful regulation. An arrest, in common with the exercise of other police powers, is seen as prima facie illegal, necessitating justification under a specific legal power. If an arrest is effected where no arrest power arises, a civil action for false imprisonment will lie.

Despite the need for clarity and precision, such powers were, until relatively recently, granted piecemeal, with the result that prior to PACE, they were contained in a mass of common law and statutory provisions. No consistent rationale could be discerned for the grant or lack of powers, and there were a number of gaps and anomalies. For example, the Criminal Law Act 1967 gave a power of arrest without warrant where the offence in question arose under statute and carried a sentence of five years. Thus, no power of arrest arose in respect of common law offences carrying such a sentence. This situation was detrimental to civil liberties owing to the uncertainty of the powers, but it may also have been detrimental in crime control terms since officers may have been deterred from effecting an arrest where one was necessary. The powers are now contained largely in PACE, as amended, but common law powers remain, while a number of statutes create a specific power of arrest which often overlaps with the PACE powers. The PACE arrest power is very broad, as explained below. Aside from PACE, a number of very broad and imprecisely defined offences exist to which arrest powers attach,

---

157 See *Shabaan Bin Hussein v Chong Fook Kam* [1970] AC 942 at p 949.
158 [1982] AC 546.
159 [2006] UKHL 55, para 39 CA: *R (on the application of Laporte) v CC of Gloucester Constab* [2004] EWCA Civ 1639. See below for discussion pp 1142–43. The case is fully discussed in Chapter 8, pp 757–63.
160 [2006] UKHL 12.
161 In *Lewis v CC of the South Wales Constab* [1991] 1 All ER 206 the traditional position was re-stated – that arrest is not a legal concept, but a factual situation, at pp 209–10 .
162 E.g., in 1976 in Cleveland, 1% of persons were summonsed for an indictable offence, whereas in Derbyshire, 76% of suspects were, as were 40% of suspects in West Yorkshire and North Wales: Royal Commission Report 1981, Cmnd 8092, para 3.72. See further Bailey, SH and Gunn, MJ, *Smith and Bailey on the Modern English Legal System*, 1991, Sweet and Maxwell, pp 630–32.

such as s 5 Public Order Act 1986[163] or certain terrorism offences;[164] the existence of such offences affords the police a great deal of leeway as to whether or not to arrest. Thus, the clarification of the arrest power that occurred under PACE has not led to any curbing of the ability of the police to interfere with liberty, quite the reverse.

The due process and crime control views of arrest and detention are diametrically opposed. Under the due process model, arrest should be based on strong suspicion that the individual has committed a specific offence, since arrest and subsequent detention represent a severe infringement of individual rights. Under the crime control model, arrest and detention need not be sanctioned merely in relation to specific offences, but should be both an investigative tool and a means of asserting police authority over persons with a criminal record or of doubtful character, with a view to creating a general deterrent effect. Under this model, reasonable suspicion is viewed as a needless irrelevancy, an inhibitory rule standing in the way of an important police function.

The body of research into the use of arrest and detention powers is to an extent conflicting, one school of analysis suggesting that the procedural due process elements which were supposed to create restraints on the powers largely fail to do so in practice in a number of respects.[165] A partially opposed view agrees as to 'the limited effectiveness of PACE's control mechanisms, including routinisation of supervisory controls', but suggests that 'the potential exists for [the PACE reforms] to be given more (or less) substance'.[166] It will be argued below that such potential may be realised under the impact of the HRA, but that its influence will be variable, especially as between the conventional and counter-terrorist schemes. While the conventional scheme shows a formal adherence to due process, which appears to have a subtle impact in practice, especially as regards controls on detention, the counter-terrorist scheme adheres, formally, to a lower standard, thereby providing greater leeway for departure from due process without necessarily breaching the rules.

At common law – power to arrest for breach of peace

PACE has not affected the power to arrest which arises at common law for breach of the peace. Factors present in a situation in which breach of the peace occurs may also give rise to arrest powers under PACE, but may extend further than they do owing to the wide definition of breach of the peace. The leading case is *Howell*,[167] in which it was found that breach of the peace will arise if violence to persons or property, either actual or apprehended, occurs. Threatening words are not in themselves a breach of the peace, but they may lead a police officer to apprehend that a breach will arise. Where a breach of the peace is threatened by some members of a group, the police

---

163 See Chapter 8, pp 781–83.
164 See Chapter 14, pp 1406 *et seq.*
165 See Sanders and Young, *Criminal Justice*, 2007, Chapters 3 and 4; McConville, Sanders and Leng, op. cit., fn 1, esp p 189.
166 Dixon, in Walker and Starmer, *Miscarriages of Justice* (1999), p 67.
167 [1982] QB 416; [1981] 3 All ER 383, CA; for comment, see Williams (1982) 146 JPN 199–200, 217–19.

may be justified in detaining all of them.[168] A police officer or any other person may arrest if a breach of the peace is in being or apprehended,[169] but not when it has been terminated, unless there is reason to believe that it may be renewed.[170] In *Humphries v Connor*,[171] Fitzgerald J summarised a constable's duty as follows:

> With respect to a constable, I agree that his primary duty is to preserve the peace; and he may for that purpose interfere, and, in the case of an affray, arrest the wrongdoer; or, if a breach of the peace is imminent, may, if necessary, arrest those who are about to commit it, if it cannot otherwise be prevented.

A temporary detention effected in order to prevent a breach of the peace need not amount to an arrest. However, in order to effect such detention, short of arrest, a breach of the peace must be imminent in the same way as would be required to justify an arrest. In other words, the requirements are *not* diminished where the action that is taken falls short of an arrest. Lord Bingham so found in *R (on the application of Laporte) (FC) (Original Appellant and Cross-respondent) v Chief Constable of Gloucestershire*:[172]

> . . . there is a power and duty resting on constable and private citizen alike to prevent a breach of the peace which reasonably appears to be about to be committed. That is the test laid down in *Albert v Lavin*,[173] which means what it says. It refers to an event which is imminent, on the point of happening. The test is the same whether the intervention is by arrest or (as in *Humphries v Connor, King v Hodges*[174] and *Albert v Lavin* itself) by action short of arrest. There is nothing in domestic authority to support the proposition that action short of arrest may be taken when a breach of the peace is not so imminent as would be necessary to justify an arrest.

In *Laporte*, in relation to the detention of protesters on a coach which had been turned back by the police from an anti-war demonstration, the Chief Constable did not think a breach of the peace was so imminent as to justify an arrest. Therefore, the House of Lords found, it could not justify a detention short of arrest. Also action is only permitted to prevent a breach of the peace 'by the person arrested',[175] or against 'the

---

168 *Austin v Commissioner of Police of the Metropolis* [2005] HRLR 20. 3,000 people were detained for 7 hours in London during a May Day demonstration; it was held that the actions of the police were lawful on the basis that a breach of the peace was apprehended on the part of some members of the group.

169 Following *Foulkes* [1998] 3 All ER 705, the breach must be imminent.

170 For commentary on this point and on breach of the peace generally, see Williams, G, [1954] Crim LR 578. The view that there is no power to arrest once a breach of the peace is over was put forward in the Commentary on *Podger* [1979] Crim LR 524 and endorsed *obiter* in *Howell* [1982] QB 416; [1981] 3 All ER 383, CA. See Chapter 8, pp 752 *et seq.* for full discussion of the use of breach of the peace.

171 (1864) 17 ICLR 1, 8–9.

172 [2006] UKHL 55, para 39. CA: *R (on the application of Laporte) v CC of Gloucester Constab* [2004] EWCA Civ 1639.

173 [1982] AC 546.

174 [1974] Crim LR 424.

175 *R v Howell*, above, fn 170, at p 426.

person who is . . . threatening to break the peace'.[176] That condition was also unfulfilled in the circumstances in *Laporte* as there was no reason to believe that all the protesters would breach the peace. Thus the detention in *Laporte* was unlawful. *Laporte* is the most recent and authoritative pronouncement on arrest or detention where breach of the peace is apprehended. The decision is discussed further in Chapter 8.[177]

Power of arrest with warrant

This power does not arise under PACE. There are a large number of statutory provisions allowing an arrest warrant to be issued, of which the most significant is that arising under s 1 of the Magistrates' Courts Act 1980.[178] Under this power, a warrant may be issued if a person aged at least 17 is suspected of an offence which is indictable or punishable with imprisonment or of any other offence and no satisfactory address is known allowing a summons to be served. This provision therefore limits the circumstances under which a warrant can be sought as an alternative to using the non-warrant power under PACE and as the police have such broad powers of arrest under PACE, arrest in reliance on a warrant is used even less under PACE than it was previously. The recent amendments to PACE, broadening the power of arrest under s 24, is only likely to enhance this tendency. The result is that judicial supervision of arrests is minimised.[179] This tendency leaves the operation of the arrest power to the discretion of the police and is part of a general move away from the judicial supervision of police powers.

Under PACE: power of arrest without warrant

Prior to PACE, only certain offences were arrestable without a warrant, under the Criminal Law Act 1967. PACE broadened the category of arrestable offences. Originally PACE contained two separate powers of arrest without warrant, one arising under s 24 and the other under s 25. In very broad terms, s 24 provided a power of arrest in respect of more serious offences while s 25 covered *all* offences, however trivial (including, for example, dropping litter) *if* – and this was the important point – certain conditions were satisfied *apart from* suspicion that the offence in question has been committed. Thus, s 25 operated to cover persons suspected of offences falling outside s 24. An 'arrestable offence' was therefore one for which a person could be arrested if the necessary reasonable suspicion was present, without the need to demonstrate that any other ingredients were present in the situation at the time of arrest. But under s 25 non-arrestable offences became arrestable if the s 25 conditions were satisfied. The difference between ss 24 and 25 was quite significant in due process terms: the scheme recognised that providing a power of arrest for all offences, however trivial, was disproportionate to the crime control aim being served. Such a power was reserved therefore for more serious offences; under s 25 it was *also* necessary to satisfy the arrest conditions. Further, once a person had been arrested under s 24, he or she was said to have been arrested for 'an arrestable offence' and this might have an effect on

176 *Albert v Lavin*, above, *per* Lord Diplock, p 565.
177 See pp 757 *et seq*.
178 See [1962] Crim LR 520, p 597 for comment on these powers.
179 See, e.g., *Criminal Statistics*, Cm 2680, 1993, Table 8.2, p 191.

his or her treatment later on. In certain circumstances, suspects in custody for more serious offences could experience a lesser level of safeguards.

However, s 25 was repealed in 2005 by s 110 Serious and Organised Crime Act 2005, and a new s 24 PACE was introduced, making the available arrest powers much broader. Under s 24 a person can now be arrested by a constable on reasonable suspicion of being in the act of committing (s 24)(1)(d)), having committed (s 24)(2)), or being about to commit (s 24)(1)(c)), an offence – any offence. Thus this power now allows an officer to arrest for any offence so long as reasonable suspicion can be shown. A person can also be arrested by a constable if in the act of committing (s 24)(1)(b)), having committed, (s 24)(3)(a)) or being about to commit (s 24)(1)(a)), an offence. In other words, the officer can arrest on a hunch so long as it turns out to be justified. This possibility, which was also available prior to 2005, may tend to undermine the reasonable suspicion requirement since police officers are aware that the likelihood of being called to account for the false arrest is not high. Thus, s 24 originally broadened the category of arrestable offences – those that were arrestable without a warrant. Under the current s 24 the difference between arrestable and non-arrestable offences has been abolished: all offences are arrestable so long as certain other conditions are also satisfied.

This broad power is apparently balanced by a further requirement based on the 'general arrest conditions' from the old s 25, which must also be fulfilled. Therefore, in order to arrest under s 24, two steps must be taken: first, there must be reasonable suspicion relating to the offence in question, unless s 24(1)(b), s 24(3)(a) or s 24(1)(a) applies (the 'hunch' provisions). Second, there must be reasonable grounds for thinking that one of the arrest conditions is satisfied. The need for the officer to have reasonable suspicion relating to the offence in question *and* as to the further requirement (previously – general arrest conditions) was emphasised on appeal in *Edwards v DPP*[180] in relation to s 25, but the decision is applicable to the new s 24.

The further requirements, which are alternatives, are, under s 24(5), to:

(a) to enable the name of the person in question to be ascertained (in the case where the constable does not know and cannot readily ascertain the person's name or where the constable has reasonable grounds for doubting whether a name given by the person as his name is his real name;

(b) correspondingly as regards the person's address;

(c) to prevent the person in question:

   (i) causing physical injury to himself or any other person;
   (ii) suffering physical injury;
   (iii) causing loss of or damage to property;
   (iv) committing an offence against public decency; or
   (v) causing an unlawful obstruction of the highway;

(d) to protect a child or other vulnerable person from the person in question.

Crucially, two new alternative requirements have been added under the new s 24. The police also have the further options of showing that the arrest is needed to allow

180 (1993) 97 Cr App R 301; (1993) *The Times*, 29 March.

the prompt and effective investigation of the suspected offence in question, or to prevent prosecution of the offence from being hindered by the suspect's disappearance (s 24(5)(e) and(f)). These two new reasons were not available under s 25, and greatly broaden the ambit of this new power.

It can be seen that the reasons based on the old conditions divide into two groups: those in which there is or appears to be a failure to furnish a satisfactory name or address, so that the service of a summons later on would be impracticable, and those which concern the immediate need to remove the suspect from the street, which would make it inappropriate to serve a summons later. The inclusion of these provisions implies that the infringement of civil liberties represented by an arrest should be resorted to only where no other alternative exists. The two new reasons, however, make it unnecessary in most instances to rely on these more limiting possibilities. It is highly probable that one of these reasons will be found to be satisfied in relation to most arrests. Thus the police now have the broad power of arrest that would have been viewed as too draconian had it been introduced in 1984. Some attempt at balancing this power with increased safeguards for arrestees was made by the introduction of Code G, the arrest Code, in 2006. For example, s 1.3 Code G demands that the arrest be proportionate to the objectives of the investigation. Section 1 also reminds police that arrest should not be resorted to readily; it should only be used if other means of achieving the objectives of the investigation are not feasible. However, breach of Code G does not give rise to civil liability, and it is probable that its safeguards will have little significant impact on street policing.

An ordinary citizen has more limited powers: he or she can arrest under s 24A[181] in the same way, in respect of indictable offences, with the omission of the possibility of arresting where the offence is about to be committed. The reasons are more limited than under s 24(5). Under s 24A they are:

> to prevent the person in question:
>
> (i)   causing physical injury to himself or any other person;
> (ii) suffering physical injury;
> (iii) causing loss of or damage to property; or
> (iv) making off before a constable can assume responsibility for him.

Although Code G exhorts the police to use arrest as a last resort, in practice arrest under s 24 is likely to be resorted to quite readily, following the practices already established under ss 25 and 24. A key potentially limiting requirement under s 24, as under the previous s 25, is the need to show 'reasonable grounds' for suspicion in relation to the s 24(5) requirements. The phrase suggests that a clear, objective basis for forming the view in question should exist. The decision in *Edwards v DPP*[182] suggests that the courts appreciate the constitutional significance of upholding the requirements under the general arrest conditions. In *Edwards*, an officer arrested the appellant in the course

---

181   Section 24A was inserted by s 111 Serious and Organised Crime Act 2005. If reasonable suspicion exists but the offence has not been committed, the arrest will be unlawful: *Self* [1992] 3 All ER 476.
182   (1993) 97 Cr App R 301; (1993) *The Times*, 29 March.

of a struggle, stating that the arrest was 'for obstruction'. Since no power of arrest arises in respect of obstruction, the arrest must have been under s 25. However, it was found to be necessary to demonstrate that the officer had the general arrest conditions in mind when arresting. This might have been inferred, but the express reference to obstruction was thought to preclude an inference that he had other matters in mind. But where it appears that one of the conditions is contemplated, the reasonable grounds for suspicion do not appear to create an exacting standard. In *G v DPP*[183] a belief that an address was false, based on a general assumption that people who commit offences give false details was accepted as based on reasonable grounds. On this interpretation, the s 24(5) requirements are unlikely to act as curbs on the arrest power: once an offence is suspected, it would seem that one of them would be almost automatically fulfilled. The two new requirements clearly enhance this possibility.

Counter-terrorist powers

There are two powers of arrest under the Terrorism Act 2000.[184] The power of arrest under s 41 TA is first in respect of reasonable suspicion of having committed certain terrorist offences, when read in conjunction with s 40(1)(a).[185] Under s 40(1)(a): 'In this Part a "terrorist" means a person who has committed [certain TA] offences.'[186] This definition is not exclusive; its other part is dependent upon s 40(1)(b). Section 40(1)(b) defines a terrorist as 'a person who is or has been concerned in the preparation or instigation of acts of terrorism'. Thus s 41 read with s 40(1)(b) allows, second, for an arrest, not in respect of a specific offence but on suspicion of 'being a terrorist' in the sense indicated. The broader and more uncertain a power of arrest, the more it may come into tension with Art 5. In considering the exceptional circumstances in which liberty can be taken away under Art 5, the requirements connoted by the general

---

183 [1989] Crim LR 150. For comment, see [1993] Crim LR 567.
184 Originally, under the TA there were further powers of arrest which were repealed. Part II of the EPA contained powers of arrest which were supplementary to those in s 14 of the PTA. They were applicable only in Northern Ireland and went further than those existing in the rest of the UK. Under s 18 of the EPA, a constable could arrest without warrant anyone whom he had reasonable grounds for suspecting of committing, having committed, or being about to commit, a scheduled offence or an offence under the EPA which was not a scheduled offence. Under s 19 of the EPA, a member of the armed forces on duty could arrest and detain a person for up to four hours on suspicion that he had committed, was committing or was about to commit any offence. The soldier was not required to inform the arrested person of the grounds of the arrest; and to effect the arrest he could enter and search any premises without a warrant. These powers were reproduced in ss 82 and 83 of the TA respectively. They continued to apply only in Northern Ireland. The continued absence of the need to give the grounds for arrest clearly raised the possibility that incompatibility with Art 5 will be found. Section 83(2) provided: 'A person making an arrest under this section complies with any rule of law requiring him to state the ground of arrest if he states that he is making the arrest as a member of Her Majesty's forces'. Section 83(6) then appeared to accept that s 83(2) would lead to findings that Art 5(3) has been breached in providing: 'The reference to a rule of law . . . does not include a rule of law which has effect only by virtue of the HRA'. Sections 82 and 83 have been repealed.
185 The power of arrest under s 14 of the PTA had two limbs. The first, s 14(1)(a), empowered a constable to arrest for certain specified offences under the PTA. As these offences were arrestable offences in any event, this power overlapped with that under s 24.
186 This includes offences under any of ss 11, 12, 15–18, 54 and 56–63.

provision that they must have a basis in law under Art 5(1) are also implied into the 'prescribed by law' rubric of each sub-paragraph.[187]

Arrests can obviously be made in respect of the terrorist offences under the Terrorism Act 2000 under s 24 of PACE. But if an arrest is effected under s 41 TA, as opposed to s 24 of PACE, this has an effect on the length of detention, as discussed below. From a constable's point of view it would probably be preferable to arrest under the TA rather than s 24 PACE, since the extra requirement under s 24(5) would not apply.

The ordinary arrest powers under PACE or under the first power of s 41 of the TA, read with s 40(1)(a), would almost certainly cover many arrests which could be undertaken under the second power covered by s 41 and s 40(1)(b) since there are a range of very broad terrorism offences. Police discretion is obviously particularly wide where no reasonable suspicion of any particular offence is necessary in order to arrest. This second power is clearly aimed at allowing arrest as a stage in the investigation, not as the culmination of it, and it may therefore be said to be firmly based on the crime-control model which views the purpose of arrest as a means of furthering general investigative goals. It therefore represents a clear departure from the traditional due process view of arrest taken by Phillips in 1981 as justified only after the investigation has uncovered sufficient evidence. The power was severely criticised when its predecessor was used in the context of Irish terrorism; it has now been transplanted into a different context and afforded a far wider application.

Section 41 TA read with s 40(1)(b) largely reproduces s 14(1)(b) of the Prevention of Terrorism (Temporary Provisions) Act 1989 (PTA)). The government, in its 1998 Consultation Paper on Terrorism,[188] acknowledged the criticisms which s 14(1)(b) had attracted:

> . . . if the police have proper cause to suspect that a person is actively engaged in terrorism, they must have sufficient information to justify an arrest under PACE . . . the absence of any requirement for reasonable suspicion of a specific offence effectively allows the police free rein to arrest whomsoever they wish without necessarily having good reason, including those who should not be arrested at all.[189]

However, the government took the view that although the ordinary powers of arrest are extensive, they are insufficient to deal with the sophisticated evasion techniques of terrorists.[190] This claim might have been applicable to the well-organised Irish groups which caused extensive and severe harm during 'the Troubles'. But in respect of the vast range of groups potentially covered by the current legislation, it is more doubtful, especially bearing in mind the wide range of TA offences, many based, as indicated in Chapter 14, on a minimal *actus reus* and requiring no proof of *mens rea*.

---

187 *Winterwerp v Netherlands* A 33 (1979), para 39.
188 *Legislation Against Terrorism: A Consultation Paper*, Cm 4178, 1998.
189 Ibid, para 7.5.
190 Since they are 'skilled in, and dedicated to, evading detection . . . terrorist crime is often quite different [from serious non-terrorist crime] both in terms of the sophistication of the techniques deployed and the (potential) harm caused': ibid, para 7.8.

The continuation of this power is thus controversial. Under s 14(1)(b), a constable had to have reasonable grounds for suspecting that a person was concerned in the preparation or instigation of acts of terrorism connected with the affairs of Northern Ireland or 'any other act of terrorism except those connected solely with the affairs of the UK or a part of the UK' in order to arrest. Under s 41 TA and s 40(1)(b), the qualifying words are omitted. In other words, the arrest power is now applicable to non-Irish UK domestic groups who can be viewed as terrorist groups, including groups such as environmental activists threatening direct action. As the author suggested in 2000 might occur,[191] there is evidence that the arrest power is being used in respect of groups such as animal rights activists[192] since they fall within the s 1 TA definition. In practice, since s 14(1)(b) did not require suspicion relating to an offence, it was used for investigation, questioning and general intelligence gathering which may be conducted, it has been said, for the purpose of 'isolating and identifying the urban guerrillas and then detaching them from the supportive or ambivalent community'.[193]

Owing to its departure from due process principle in failing to require arrest for a particular offence, the reproduction of s 14(1)(b) of the PTA in ss 41 and 40(1)(b) of the TA rendered the arrest power vulnerable to a challenge under Art 5 of the Convention, which in para 5(1)(c) encapsulates that principle. The test under Art 5(1)(c) relies on reasonable suspicion regarding an offence and therefore calls into question s 41 of the TA, in so far as it relates to suspicion that a person is a terrorist in the sense of (under s 40(1)(b)) being concerned in the commission, preparation, or instigation of an act of terrorism. Section 41 therefore allows for arrest without reasonable suspicion that a particular offence has been committed. The compatibility of s 41 and Art 5(1)(c) depends on the interpretation afforded to *Brogan and Others v UK*.[194] The case concerned the EPA provision which was largely reproduced in s 41, read with s 40(1)(b). The Court applied two tests to the basis for the arrests in finding that the power of arrest was justified within Art 5(1)(c). First, the definition of acts of terrorism was 'well in keeping with the idea of an offence'.[195] Secondly, after arrest, the applicants were asked about specific offences. Thus, 'the Court decided the point on the basis that involvement in "acts of terrorism" indirectly meant the commission of specific criminal offences under Northern Irish law, which would appear to be the better approach on the facts'.[196]

On either test, arrests under s 41 read with s 40(1)(b) might be in a more doubtful position. The definition of terrorism relevant in *Brogan* was identical to the s 20 PTA definition – the use of violence for political ends. The current definition under s 1 of the TA is far wider: it covers the use or threat, 'for the purpose of advancing a political, religious or ideological cause', of action, designed to influence the government or intimidate the public, which involves serious violence against any person or serious damage to property, or is designed to seriously disrupt an electronic system, or endangers life, or creates a serious risk to health or safety. Unlike the previous one, this definition

191 See Fenwick, H, *New Labour, Freedom and the Human Rights Act*, 2000, Chapter 3, pp 79–80.
192 CAMPAC, *Terrorising Minority Communities: anti-terrorism powers, their use and abuse*, 2003.
193 Lowry (1976–77) 8–9 col *Human Rights L Rev* 185, p 210.
194 Judgment of 29 November 1988 (1989) Series A 145-B (1989) 11 EHHR 117.
195 Paragraph 51.
196 Harris, D, O'Boyle, K and Warbrick, C, *Law of The European Convention on Human Rights*, 1995, p 116.

may cover matters, such as threatening to hack into a computer system, or to destroy genetically modified crops, which do not clearly correspond to existing offences and therefore might not be viewed so readily as 'in keeping with the idea of an offence'. The application of the second test would partly depend in practice on the particular instance which arose before a domestic court. If a person was arrested under s 41 as part of an investigation and was not asked about specific offences on arrest, the connection with the basis of the arrest, bearing in mind the width of the s 1 TA definition, might be viewed as too tenuous to be termed an arrest on reasonable suspicion of an offence. Moreover, the purpose of such an arrest would not appear to be in accordance with the Art 5 requirement, since it would not be to 'bring [the suspect] before the competent legal authority'.

This possibility was recognised by Lord Lloyd, whose 1996 Report, prepared for Michael Howard, the then Conservative Home Secretary, underlay the Terrorism Act 2000.[197] He suggested that, in order to circumvent Art 5, a new offence of being concerned in the commission, preparation or instigation of acts of terrorism should be created. Having considered this suggestion, the government at the time rejected it, coming to the view, which is evaluated below, that this arrest power is compatible with Art 5(1)(c).[198] However, Lord Carlile, the government's current independent reviewer of terrorist law and policy, supports the introduction of this offence, and it was recently introduced under the Terrorism Act 2006, ss 1 and 5. Since an arrest can now occur for those offences, which replicate the wording under s 40(1)(b), it will need to be less frequently invoked. Thus arrest for preparatory offences is now possible, ss 41 and 40(1)(a) of the TA, tending to avoid incompatibility with Art 5 since it is less necessary to rely on s 40(1)(b).

Other statutory powers of arrest

If a statute creates any offence, then obviously the arrest power under s 24 is applicable so long as one or more of the requirements under s24(5) is satisfied. Section 11 of the Public Order Act 1986 and s 89 of the Police Act 1996 provide examples of such offences. However, certain statutes expressly create specific powers of arrest which are not dependent on ss 24 or 25, such as ss 12 and 14 of the Public Order Act. In such cases, the procedure under s 28 of PACE (which is discussed below) will still apply.

Reasonable suspicion

Level of suspicion

Apart from the second arrest power under s 41 TA, and the s 24 provisions relating to involvement or attempted involvement in an offence, as opposed to suspected

---

197 Cm 3420.
198 Ibid, para 7.14. A further aspect of s 40 may raise issues under Art 5. Between the First and Second Readings of the Bill, s 40 was subtly changed to include reference to persons concerned in terrorism 'whether before or after the passing of this Act'. Since the definition of terrorism in s 1 is much wider than that previously used in the PTA, s 20, s 40 allows arrest of a person for activity which would not have justified arrest (either under the PTA, s 14(1)(b) or at all) at the time when it was undertaken. The coverage of pre-commencement activity is confirmed in s 40(2).

involvement, the powers discussed depend on the concept of reasonable suspicion relating to an offence. Article 5(1)(c) of the Convention sets out one of the circumstances in which an individual can be detained. It permits the lawful arrest or detention of a person effected for the purpose of bringing him before the competent legal authority on reasonable suspicion of having committed an offence, or where it is reasonably considered that an arrest is necessary to prevent the person in question from committing an offence or fleeing after having done so. In requiring arrest only for specific offences, and not for general crime control purposes, Art 5(1)(c) adheres closely to the due process model of arrest indicated above. Section 24 of PACE (apart from the 'hunch' provisions) and s 41 TA (in so far as it relates to certain specific terrorist offences under s 40(1)(a)) appear prima facie to comply with Art 5(1)(c) owing to their requirements of reasonable suspicion.

The idea behind the concept of reasonable suspicion is that an arrest should take place at quite a late stage in the investigation;[199] this limits the number of arrests and makes it less likely that a person will be wrongfully arrested. It seems likely that it will be interpreted in accordance with the provisions as to reasonable suspicion under Code A although, as will be discussed below, the courts have not relied on Code A in ruling on the lawfulness of arrests. Annex B, para 4 of original Code A stated that the level of suspicion for a stop would be 'no less' than that needed for arrest. Although this provision is omitted from the current revision of Code A, it would seem that in principle, the Code A provisions should be relevant to arrests if the Codes and statute are to be treated as a harmonious whole. Moreover, it would appear strange if a more rigorous test could be applied to the reasonable suspicion necessary to effect a stop than that necessary to effect an arrest. If this is correct, it would seem that certain matters, such as an individual's racial group, could never be factors which could support a finding of reasonable suspicion. It would seem that a future revision of the Codes might usefully state that the concept of reasonable suspicion in Code A applies to arrest as well; if so, it would at least outlaw the use of such factors as the basis of reasonable suspicion.

Code G on arrest has far less to say on the concept of reasonable suspicion than Code A does; what it has to say is only contained in the Notes; under Note 2: 'There must be an objective basis for that suspicion based on facts, information, and/or intelligence which are relevant to the likelihood the offence has been committed and the person to be questioned committed it.' The opening words of this Note echo those of para 2.2 Code A on reasonable suspicion and support the supposition that the two concepts are similar. Of course, the suspicion under Code A relates to carrying an article, whereas under Code G it relates to an offence. These words used in Note 2 largely echo the approach of the European Court of Human Rights in *O'Hara v UK*,[200] discussed below, which represents the most recent and definitive pronouncement on the matter from Strasbourg, and therefore would be expected to determine the nature of this concept in the UK courts, under the HRA.

The objective nature of suspicion required for most arrests, and now reflected in Code G, is echoed in various decisions on the suspicion needed for an arrest. In *Dallison*

---

199 See the Phillips Royal Commission Report, Cmnd 8092 (1981).
200 (2002) 34 EHRR 32.

v Caffrey[201] Lord Diplock said the test was whether 'a reasonable man assumed to know the law and possessed of the information which in fact was possessed by the defendant would believe there were [reasonable grounds]'. Thus, it is not enough for a police officer to have a hunch that a person has committed or is about to commit an offence; there must be a clear basis for this suspicion which relates to the particular person in question and which would also be apparent to an objective observer. If an officer only has a hunch – mere suspicion as opposed to reasonable suspicion – he or she might continue to observe the person in question, but could not arrest until the suspicion had increased and could be termed 'reasonable suspicion'. Clearly, the officer could, however, arrest under the relevant provisions of s 24, if prepared to take the risk that the hunch might turn out to be incorrect.

However, this concept of reasonable suspicion still leaves a great deal of leeway to officers to arrest where suspicion relating to the particular person is at a low level, but they want to further the investigation by gathering information. At present, the courts seem prepared to allow police officers such leeway and it should be noted that PACE endorses a reasonably low level of suspicion owing to the distinction it maintains between belief and suspicion, suspicion probably being the lower standard.[202] The decision in *Ward v Chief Constable of Somerset and Avon Constabulary*[203] suggests that a high level of suspicion is not required, and this can also be said of *Castorina v Chief Constable of Surrey*.[204] Detectives were investigating a burglary of a company's premises and on reasonable grounds came to the conclusion that it was an 'inside job'. The managing director told them that a certain employee had recently been dismissed and that the documents taken would be useful to someone with a grudge. However, she also said that she would not have expected the particular employee to commit a burglary. The detectives then arrested the employee, having found that she had no previous criminal record. She was detained for nearly four hours and then released without charge. She claimed damages for false imprisonment and was awarded £4,500. The judge considered that it was necessary to find that the detectives had had 'an honest belief founded on a reasonable suspicion leading an ordinary cautious man to the conclusion that the person arrested was guilty of the offence'.

However, the Court of Appeal overturned the award on the basis that the test applied by the judge had been too severe. It was held that the question of honest belief was irrelevant; the issue of reasonable suspicion had nothing to do with the officer's subjective state of mind. The question was whether there was reasonable cause to suspect the plaintiff of burglary. Given that certain factors could be identified, including inside knowledge of the company's affairs and the motive of the plaintiff, it appeared that there was sufficient basis for the detectives to have reasonable grounds for suspicion.

---

201 [1964] 3 WLR 385. See also *Shabaan Bin Hussein v Chong Fook Kam* [1970] AC 942, esp at p 948.

202 Section 17(2)(a) requires belief, not suspicion, that a suspect whom an officer is seeking is on premises; similarly, powers of seizure under s 19(2) depend on belief in certain matters. The difference between belief and suspicion and the lesser force of the word 'suspect' was accepted as an important distinction by the House of Lords in *Wills v Bowley* [1983] 1 AC 57, p 103, HL. See also *Johnson v Whitehouse* [1984] RTR 38, which was to the same effect.

203 (1986) *The Times*, 26 June; cf *Monaghan v Corbett* (1983) 147 JP 545, DC (however, although this demonstrated a different approach, the restriction it imposed may not be warranted: see *DPP v Wilson* [1991] Crim LR 441, DC).

204 (1988) 138 NLJ 180, transcript from LEXIS.

Clayton and Tomlinson criticised the decision in these terms: 'if the police are justified in arresting a middle-aged woman of good character on such flimsy grounds without even questioning her as to her alibi or possible motives, then the law provides very scant protection for those suspected of crimes.'[205]

Castorina may be compared with the findings of the Strasbourg Court in *Fox, Campbell and Hartley v UK*.[206] The applicants had been arrested in accordance with s 11 of the Northern Ireland (Emergency Provisions) Act 1978 which required only suspicion, not reasonable suspicion. The only evidence put forward by the government for the presence of reasonable suspicion was that the applicants had convictions for terrorist offences and that when arrested, they were asked about particular terrorist acts. The government said that further evidence could not be disclosed for fear of endangering life. The Court found that although allowance could be made for the difficulties of evidence gathering in an emergency situation, reasonable suspicion which 'arises from facts or information which would satisfy an objective observer that the person concerned may have committed the offence'[207] had not been established. Moreover, 'the exigencies of dealing with terrorist crime cannot justify stretching the notion of reasonableness to the point where the essence of the safeguard secured by Art 5(1)(c) is impaired'.[208] The arrests in question could not, therefore, be justified. In *Murray v UK*[209] this test was viewed as a lower standard for reasonable suspicion, applicable in terrorist cases, but it was again emphasised that an objective standard of reasonable suspicion was required,[210] although the information grounding the suspicion might acceptably remain confidential in the exigencies of a situation such as that pertaining at the time of the arrest in question, in Northern Ireland.[211] It is debatable whether the UK courts are in general applying a test of reasonable suspicion under PACE or the TA which reaches the standards which the European Court had in mind, especially where terrorism is not in question. The departure which the HRA brings about is to encourage stricter judicial scrutiny of decisions to arrest.

The European Court of Human Rights in *O'Hara v UK*[212] commented on the nature of the reasonable suspicion required to satisfy Art 5(1)(c). The Court found that it requires the existence of some facts or information which would satisfy an objective observer that *the person concerned* may have committed the offence. However, the Court also accepted that the reasonable suspicion at the time of arrest need not be of the same level as that necessary to bring a charge.[213] As mentioned above, this statement accords with the test under Code A and that under Code G. Unsurprisingly, it confirms the need for an objective test, but otherwise is generally likely to affect no radical change in the stance of the courts in relation to this concept.

However, the later decision in *Cumming v Chief Constable of Northumbria Police*[214] appears to be out of line with that of the European Court. The five claimants worked

205 (1988) Law Soc Gazette, 7 September, p 26.
206 A 182 (1990); 13 EHRR 157.
207 Ibid, para 32.
208 Ibid, para 32.
209 [1994] EHRR 193.
210 Paragraph 50.
211 Paragraphs 58–59.
212 (2002) 34 EHRR 32.
213 Ibid, paras 34, 36.
214 [2003] EWCA Civ 1844.

for a local authority department concerned with monitoring recordings made by the town's closed circuit television cameras. They were arrested following the discovery of tampering with tapes showing the possible commission of an offence. They had no links with the suspected offender and were all of good character. Their claims for damages for wrongful arrest and false imprisonment were dismissed[215] and they appealed against this finding. The claimants submitted that mere opportunity could not found the requirements of reasonable suspicion under s 24(6) of the Police and Criminal Evidence Act 1984. However, it was found by the Court of Appeal that there was nothing in principle to prevent opportunity from amounting to reasonable grounds. It was also acceptable to arrest more than one person even if only one could have committed the offence (*Hussein v Chong Fook Kam*[216] was relied upon). In the instant case only a small number of people could be clearly identified as the ones with the opportunity of committing an offence. That could in principle afford reasonable grounds for suspecting each of them in the absence of any information enabling further elimination. It was noted that in *Fox, Campbell and Hartley v United Kingdom*[217] the European Court had held that the protection of Art 5 of the Convention was met by the requirement that there be reasonable grounds for an arrest. Therefore, it was found, the Convention did not require the Court to evaluate the exercise of police discretion in any different way from the exercise of any other executive discretion. Thus, the Court of Appeal found that where there were reasonable grounds to suspect that one out of a certain group of people had committed an offence, there could be said to be reasonable grounds for arresting all of them. This decision does not demand that the reasonable suspicion should relate to the specific person arrested, although the test laid down by the Strasbourg Court does make that demand.

Reasonable suspicion and police working rules

As Sanders and Young observe, commenting on *Castorina*, 'The decision gives the police considerable freedom to follow crime control norms, in that it allows them to arrest on little hard evidence'.[218] In practice, the concept of reasonable suspicion is interpreted very flexibly by the police, as it is in respect of stop and search powers. Doubtful grounds often appear to be sufficient to provide reasonable grounds to justify deprivation of liberty. Only in exceptional instances will an officer's use of this power be found to have been wrong. As in this instance the courts tend to be reluctant to interfere with the police interpretation and use of the arrest power. Post-PACE decisions, including this one, leave a great deal of leeway to officers to arrest where suspicion relating to the particular person or persons arrested is at a low level. The conclusion drawn by the Court as to the exercise of police discretion under the Convention does not follow from its findings as regards the exception under Art 5(1)c – which was referred to.

Research into the use of arrest suggests that in practice, the concept of reasonable suspicion is interpreted very flexibly by the police, as it is in respect of stop and search

---

215 By Judge Hewitt, sitting in Newcastle upon Tyne County Court on 27 January 2003.
216 [1970] AC 942.
217 (1990) 13 EHRR 157.
218 Sanders and Young, 2nd edn, 2000, op. cit., fn 1, at p 86.

powers. A wealth of academic research and analysis has established that the need for reasonable suspicion provides little protection against wrongful arrest. Very doubtful grounds often appear to be sufficient to provide reasonable grounds to justify deprivation of liberty. Further, only in exceptional instances will an officer's use of this power be found to have been wrongful; the courts are quite ready to find that these somewhat hazy tests have been satisfied.[219]

Sanders and Young speak of appearing 'suspicious' as being 'a key working rule' in arrests and stops, and observe that association with other criminals is also often the basis for arrest even where the police are 'entirely without reasonable suspicion', since the object is to obtain statements against associates.[220] The courts appear to be reluctant to interfere with the police interpretation and use of the arrest power. The post-PACE decisions discussed leave a great deal of leeway to officers to arrest where suspicion relating to the particular person is at a low level, but they want to further the investigation by gathering information.[221] As a number of commentators have pointed out, arrest became under PACE avowedly no longer the culmination of the investigative process but an integral part of it.[222] The strong evidence founding the charge which used to be obtained, it has been suggested,[223] prior to arrest, thus ensuring that innocent persons were unlikely to be arrested and that the infringement of liberty of a person innocent in the eyes of the law was kept to a minimum, tended after PACE to be found in the form of a confession, after arrest. PACE also confirmed the movement away from judicial supervision of arrest, by means of the warrant procedure, which had already begun.

Arresting officer must form reasonable suspicion

If there is no evidence that the arresting officer thought that an offence had been committed, even if objectively speaking there are reasonable grounds for suspicion, the arrest will be unlawful (*Chapman v DPP*).[224] If the arresting officer considers that there is no possibility that a charge will be brought the arrest will be unlawful since it would not be for a proper purpose: *Plange v Chief Constable of South Humberside Police*.[225] The reasonable suspicion must be formed by the arresting officer himself or herself. In *O'Hara v Chief Constable of the RUC*,[226] a decision on s 12(1) of the Prevention of Terrorism Act 1989, the House of Lords found that a constable could form a suspicion based on what he had been informed of previously as part of a briefing by a superior

---

219   See McConville, Sanders and Leng, op. cit., fn 1; Sanders and Young, op. cit., fn 2, (2007), Chapter 3.4; Ryan, C and Williams, K, 'Police discretion' [1986] Public Law 285, and Clayton and Tomlinson, (1988) Law Society Gazette 7 Sept, p 22.

220   Sanders and Young, op. cit., fn 1 (2007), pp 143–48 esp at 144, based on research undertaken by Leng (Royal Commission on Criminal Justice Research Study No 10), 1993.

221   See *Ward v Chief Constable of Somerset and Avon Constabulary* (1986) *The Times*, 26 June; *Castorina v Chief Constable of Surrey* (1988) NLJ 180, transcript from LEXIS.

222   Sanders and Young, op. cit., fn 1, (2007) at pp 138–150; Ewing, KD and Gearty, CA, *Freedom under Thatcher*, 1989, p 24.

223   Ewing and Gearty, ibid., p 25.

224   (1988) 890 Cr App R 190.

225   (1992) *The Times*, 23 March.

226   [1997] 2 WLR 1; [1997] 1 All ER 129.

officer, or otherwise. The question to be asked was whether a reasonable man would personally have formed the suspicion after receiving the relevant information. It was not enough for the arresting officer to have been instructed by a superior officer to arrest; his own personal knowledge must provide him with the necessary reasonable suspicion. In the instant case, the arresting officer had sufficient personal knowledge of matters, which it was found provided a basis for reasonable suspicion. The House of Lords stated that these findings applied to arrest powers other than the one arising under s 12. The Court of Appeal has found, following *O'Hara*, that reasonable suspicion based on an entry in the police national computer is sufficient.[227] The European Court of Human Rights in *O'Hara v UK*[228] has found that the approach taken in *O'Hara* is in accordance with the demands of Art 5. The Court accepted that the reasonable suspicion must be formed personally by the arresting officer, but could be based on information from other sources.

Arresting on a 'hunch'

As indicated, under s 24 it is not always necessary to show that reasonable suspicion exists. If an offence is *in fact* being committed or has been committed or is about to be committed, a constable can arrest even if he or she is just acting on a hunch which luckily turns out to be justified. Of course, if an officer arrests without reasonable suspicion, he or she is taking a risk. These provisions were included because it might seem strange if a person could found an action for false imprisonment on the basis that although he was committing an offence, he should not have been arrested for it. However, if it cannot be established that the offence was committed or was about to be committed, it is not enough to show that reasonable grounds for suspicion did in fact exist although the officer did not know of them. In *Siddiqui v Swain*[229] the Divisional Court held that the words 'reasonable grounds to suspect' used in s 8(5) of the Road Traffic Act 1972 include the requirement that the officer should *actually* suspect. This approach was also adopted in *Chapman v DPP*.[230] Article 5(1)(c) also calls into question the provision under s 24 of PACE allowing for arrest without reasonable suspicion so long as a 'hunch' turns out to be justified (s 24(4)(a), (5)(a) and (7)(a)). Sanders and Young call this possibility a 'classic crime control norm since the ends are regarded as justifying the means'.[231] Such an arrest would appear to be unlawful under s 6 of the HRA where effected by a police constable since no exception under Art 5 appears to allow for it.

Purpose of the arrest

In *Castorina* Purchas LJ also ruled that once reasonable suspicion arises, officers have discretion as to whether to arrest or do something else, such as making further inquiries,

227 *Hough v Chief Constable of Staffordshire*, 16 January 2001, unreported.
228 (2002) 34 EHRR 32.
229 [1979] RTR 454.
230 (1988) Cr App R 190; [1988] Crim LR 843.
231 Sanders and Young, *Criminal Justice*, 1st edn, 1994, p 76.

but that this discretion can be attacked on *Wednesbury* principles.[232] In making this ruling, Purchas J relied on the ruling of the House of Lords in *Holgate-Mohammed v Duke*.[233] The House of Lords had confirmed that in addition to showing that the relevant statutory conditions are satisfied, the exercise of statutory powers by officers must not offend against *Wednesbury* principles; officers must not take irrelevant factors into account or fail to have regard to relevant ones; an exercise of discretion must not be so unreasonable that no reasonable officer could have exercised it in the manner in question. Thus, an arrest will be found to be unlawful if no reasonable person looking at the circumstances could have considered that an arrest should be effected, if the decision is based on irrelevant considerations and if it is not made in good faith and for a proper purpose.[234]

It was found in *Castorina* that no breach of these principles had occurred and, as reasonable grounds for making the arrest were found, the first instance judge had erred in ruling that further inquiries should have been made before arresting. The need to make further inquiries would be relevant to the first stage – arriving at reasonable suspicion – but not to the second – determining whether to make an arrest. That it must be relevant to the first is axiomatic: an investigation passes through many stages, from the first, in which a vague suspicion relating to a particular person arises, up until the point when that person's guilt is established beyond reasonable doubt. At some point in that process, reasonable suspicion giving rise to a discretion as to whether to effect an arrest arises; thus, there must be a point in the early stages at which it is possible to say that more inquiries should have been made, more evidence gathered, before the arrest could lawfully take place. The courts appear prepared to accept that arrest at quite an early stage in this process may be said to be based on reasonable grounds. The application of *Wednesbury* principles left little leeway for challenge to the decision to arrest, so it may be said that the interest of the citizen in his or her personal liberty was not being accorded sufficient weight under the pre-HRA tests.[235]

Auld LJ in the post-HRA case of *Al Fayed v Commissioner of Police for the Metropolis*[236] reaffirmed that *Castorina* involves asking three questions and that in determining all *Castorina* questions the state of mind is that of the arresting officer, subjective as to the first question, the fact of his suspicion, and objective as to the second and third questions, whether he had reasonable grounds for it and whether he exercised his discretionary power of arrest *Wednesbury* reasonably. It is for the police to establish the first two *Castorina* requirements, namely that an arresting officer suspected that the claimant had committed an arrestable offence and that he had reasonable grounds for his submission.[237] If the police establish those requirements, the arrest is lawful unless the claimant can establish on *Wednesbury* principles that the arresting officer's exercise

---

232 *Associated Provincial Picture Houses Ltd v Wednesbury Corpn* [1948] 1 KB 223; [1948] 2 All ER 680, CA.

233 [1984] 1 AC 437; [1984] 1 All ER 1054, HL.

234 For discussion of police discretion in this respect, see [1986] PL 285.

235 See further as to reasonable grounds for suspicion, Clayton, R and Tomlinson, H, 'Arrest and reasonable suspicion' (1988) Law Soc Gazette, 7 September, p 22; Dixon, D, Bottomley, K and Coleman, C, 'Reality and rules in the construction and regulation of police suspicion' (1989) 17 Int J Soc Law, 185–206; Sanders and Young, *Criminal Justice*, 2007, Chapter 3.4.

236 [2004] EWCA Civ 1579, at para 83.

237 *Holgate Mohammed*, *per* Lord Diplock at p 441F–H, and *Plange*, *per* Parker LJ.

or non-exercise of his power of arrest was unreasonable, the third *Castorina* question.[238] The findings in *Austin and Saxby v Commissioner of Police of the Metropolis*[239] also took account of those issues, as discussed in Chapter 8.[240]

Article 5 considerations are able to limit the application of the broad *Wednesbury* principle.[241] Under the HRA, courts also have to consider whether the Convention rights have been adhered to; it is not enough to ask whether the decision to arrest was reasonable. The *purpose* of the arrest should also be in compliance with Art 5(1)(c), even where reasonable suspicion is established, in that it should be effected in order to 'bring [the suspect] before the competent legal authority', although this does not mean that every arrest must lead to a charge.[242] In the individual circumstances of a case, a breach of Art 5(1)(c) might be found where, although reasonable suspicion was present on the facts, the arrest discretion was not exercised in accordance with Art 5(1)(c) since the purpose of the arrest was in reality for general information-gathering ends. This might occur where, although there were, objectively, reasonable grounds for suspicion, the police had no belief in the guilt of the suspect. In such an instance, the arrest would be unlawful under s 6 of the HRA, not merely *Wednesbury* unreasonable. A breach might also be established where the arrest was unnecessary in order to further the purpose in question. For example, if the suspect was co-operative, there would appear to be no need to arrest her since the purpose under Art 5(1)(c) could be served by interviewing her in her own home. That purpose would not appear to cover an arrest undertaken merely for the purpose of interviewing such a suspect in the police station.[243] It was found, however, in *Chalkley and Jeffries*,[244] that the existence of a collateral motive for an arrest would not necessarily render it unlawful. Under the HRA, a domestic court has to consider whether Art 5 is satisfied by an arrest with a 'mixed' purpose.

Procedural elements of a valid arrest[245]

Informing the arrestee

For an arrest to be made validly, not only must the power of arrest exist, whatever its source, but the procedural elements must be complied with. The fact that a power

---

238 *Holgate-Mohammed, per* Lord Diplock at p 446A–D; *Plange, per* Parker LJ; and Cumming, *per* Latham LJ at para 26.

239 [2005] EWHC 480; [2005] HRLR 20; (2005) 155 NLJ 515, (2005) *The Times* April 14; 23 March 2005, Queen's Bench Division of the High Court.

240 See pp 766–70.

241 See the House of Lords in *R v SSHD ex p Bugdaycay* [1987] AC 514; *R v SSHD ex p Brind* [1991] 1 AC 696, see, e.g., *per* Lord Bridge of Harwich, at pp 748F–747B. See *Cumming*, paras 43 and 44: '. . . it seems to me that it is necessary to bear in mind that the right to liberty under Article 5 was engaged and that any decision to arrest had to take into account the importance of this right even though the Human Rights Act was not in force at the time . . . The court must consider with care whether or not the decision to arrest was one which no police officer, applying his mind to the matter could reasonably take bearing in mind the effect on the appellants' right to liberty'.

242 *K-F v Germany* (1997) 26 EHRR 390.

243 Cf *Holgate-Mohammed v Duke* [1984] AC 437.

244 [1998] 2 All ER 155.

245 The term 'valid arrest' is open to attack on the ground that there can be no such thing as an invalid arrest. However, a valid arrest may be contrasted with a purported arrest and this is the sense in which it is used in this section.

of arrest arises will not alone make the arrest lawful. These elements are of crucial importance owing to the consequences which may flow from a lawful arrest which will not flow from an unlawful one.[246] Such consequences include the right of the officer to use force in effecting it under s 117 of PACE or s 114 of the TA, if necessary, and the loss of liberty inherent in an arrest. If an arrest has not occurred, the citizen is free to go wherever she will and any attempt to prevent her doing so will be unlawful.[247] It is therefore important to convey the fact of the arrest to the arrestee and to mark the point at which the arrest comes into being and general liberty ceases. At common law, there had to be a physical detention or a touching of the arrestee to convey the fact of detention, unless he or she made this unnecessary by submitting to it;[248] the fact of arrest had to be made clear[249] and the reason for it had to be made known.[250] Conveying the fact of the arrest need not involve using words.

But it appears that conveying to the person in question the fact that a deprivation of liberty has occurred need not be taken to imply, necessarily, that an arrest has occurred. This follows from the decision in *Laporte*.[251] An arrest is the lawful apprehension of a person in order to bring him to a police station; a temporary deprivation of liberty, short of arrest, can be for some different purpose, such as transferring the person from one area to another, in order to prevent a breach of the peace. So since it appears that the police have the power at common law to deprive a person of liberty without perpetrating an arrest, it appears that indicating to the person by words or action that a deprivation of liberty has occurred could be interpreted as indicating that either a power of arrest or of a temporary detention is being invoked. It also follows from *Gillan* that it can be indicated to a person that they are not lawfully free to leave the spot for a short period of time, but that they are not under arrest or deprived of liberty. Presumably, in all these instances, since the police are acting within their powers, resistance to the detention would be unlawful. Clearly, the citizen is left in an uncertain position in relation to deprivation of liberty. As discussed below, the *reason* for the arrest has to be conveyed to the person. So it could be argued that an arrest occurs when a deprivation of liberty occurs *and* the reason is given. But even that suggestion does not capture the notion of an arrest, since the reason need only be given if it is practicable to do; also a reason need not be given if the arrest is for breach of the peace rather than an offence.[252]

The common law safeguards have been modified and strengthened by s 28 of PACE, which provides that both the fact of and the reason for the arrest must be made known at the time or as soon as practicable afterwards. However, an ordinary citizen is not

---

246 The question as to the difference between a valid and invalid arrest has been much debated; see Lidstone, KW [1978] Crim LR 332; Clark and Feldman [1979] Crim LR 702; Zander, M (1977) NLJ 352; Smith, JC [1977] Crim LR 293.

247 *Rice v Connolly* [1966] 2 QB 414; *Kenlin v Gardner* [1967] 2 QB 510 (see above, pp 1109–11 in relation to obstruction of or assault on a police officer in the course of his duty).

248 *Hart v Chief Constable of Kent* [1983] RTR 484.

249 *Alderson v Booth* [1969] 3 QB 216.

250 *Christie v Leachinsky* [1947] AC 573; [1947] 1 All ER 567, HL.

251 [2006] UKHL 55.

252 See *Williamson v CC of Great Midlands* [2004] 1 WLR 14; the Court of Appeal stated that it would be good practice for a person in this position to be treated as if subject to the PACE provisions. See also Chapter 8, pp 752 *et seq.*

under this duty if the fact of the arrest and the reason for it are obvious. Conveying the reason for the arrest does not involve using a particular form of words,[253] but it appears that reasonable detail must be given so that the arrestee will be in a position to give a convincing denial and therefore be more speedily released from detention.[254] Given the infringement of liberty represented by an arrest and the need, therefore, to restore liberty as soon as possible, consistent with the needs of the investigation, it is unfortunate that s 28 did not make it clear that a reasonable degree of detail should be given. In *Mullady v DPP*[255] where the arrest reasons were given as 'obstruction', it was held that where the reasons given to a suspect for his arrest are invalid or are the wrong reasons, then the arrest itself is unlawful. 'Obstruction' was not deemed sufficient since it is not an arrestable offence. It was found that where a police officer has given a reason for an arrest, another reason cannot be substituted, whether that involves the substitution of another offence or the inference that s 25(3)(a) of the 1984 Act was satisfied. This finding should also be applied to the conditions now applicable under s 24(5). The reason should be correct (*Wilson v Chief Constable of Lancashire Constabulary*).[256] In *Wilson* the arrestee was not given enough information to enable him to challenge the arrest, rendering the arrest unlawful. Code G makes further provision for informing the arrestee. Under para 2.2 Code G officers need to inform the suspect of the fact of the arrest even if it is obvious. Further, significantly, information as to the relevant circumstances of the arrest relating to *both* elements of s 24 must be given. But if the reason for the arrest was given in terms of the offence arrested for, as appears to be required by s 28, but no reason was given relating to the requirements of s 24(5) as required by Code G, it would appear that the arrest would still be lawful.

Informing promptly

However, the reason for the arrest need only be made known as soon as practicable. The meaning and implications of this provision were considered in *DPP v Hawkins*.[257] A police officer took hold of the defendant to arrest him, but did not give the reason. The youth struggled and was therefore later charged with assaulting an officer in the execution of his duty. The question which arose was whether the officer was in the execution of his duty since he had failed to give the reason for the arrest. If the arrest was thereby rendered invalid, he could not be in the execution of his duty, since it could not include effecting an unlawful arrest. It was determined in the Court of Appeal that the arrest became unlawful when the time came at which it was practicable to inform the defendant of the reason but he was not so informed. This occurred at the police

---

253 The Court of Appeal confirmed this in *Brosch* [1988] Crim LR 743. In *Abassey and Others v Metropolitan Police Comr* [1990] 1 WLR 385, it was found that there was no need for precise or technical language in conveying the reason for the arrest; the question whether the reason had been given was a matter for the jury. See also *Nicholas v Parsonage* [1987] RTR 199.
254 *Murphy v Oxford*, 15 February 1985, unreported, CA. This is out of line with the CA decision in *Abassey* [1990] 1 WLR 385, in which *Murphy* unfortunately was not considered.
255 [1997] COD 422; WL 1103678.
256 (2000) 23 November 2000, unreported.
257 [1988] 1 WLR 1166; [1988] 3 All ER 673, DC; see also *Brosch* [1988] Crim LR 743, CA.

station or perhaps in the police car, but did not occur earlier because of the defendant's behaviour. However, the arrest did not become retrospectively unlawful and therefore did not affect acts done before its unlawfulness came into being, which thus remained acts done in the execution of duty. Thus, the police have a certain leeway as to informing the arrestee; the arrest will not be affected, nor will other acts arising from it, until the time when it would be practicable to inform of the reason for it has come and gone. However, if there was nothing in the behaviour of the arrestee to make informing him or her impracticable, then the arrest will be unlawful from its inception. Following the decision in *Hawkins*, what can be said as to the status of the suspect before the time came and passed at which the requisite words should have been spoken? Presumably he was under arrest at that time. Where the procedural elements are not complied with but no good reason for such failure arises (or if no power to arrest arose in the first place), the arrestee will have grounds for bringing an action for false imprisonment. Moreover, if a false arrest occurs and subsequently physical evidence is discovered or the defendant makes a confession, the defence may argue that the evidence should be excluded owing to the false arrest. This is discussed in Chapter 13.[258]

Some delay in informing of the arrest will not create incompatibility with Art 5(2), which provides that a person must be informed promptly of the reason for arrest, and corresponds to s 28 of PACE. In *Fox, Campbell and Hartley v UK*[259] the applicants, who were arrested on suspicion of terrorist offences, were not informed of the reason for the arrest at the time of it, but were told that they were being arrested under a particular statutory provision. Clearly, this could not convey the reason to them at that time. At a later point, during interrogation, they were asked about specific criminal offences. The European Court of Human Rights found that Art 5(2) was not satisfied at the time of the arrest, but that this breach was healed by the later indications made during interrogation of the offences for which they had been arrested. In *Murray v UK*,[260] soldiers occupied a woman's house, thus clearly taking her into detention, but did not inform her of the fact of arrest for half an hour. The House of Lords had found that the delay in giving the requisite information was acceptable because of the alarm which the fact of arrest, if known, might have aroused in the particular circumstances – the unsettled situation in Northern Ireland.[261] The European Court of Human Rights found no breach of Art 5(2); Mrs Murray was eventually informed during interrogation of the reason for the arrest and, in the circumstances, it was found acceptable to allow an interval of a few hours between the arrest and the point when she was informed of the reason for it. (The claim also made, that Art 8 had been breached, was dismissed. The violation of privacy fell within the exception under Art 8(2) in respect of the prevention of crime and was found to be necessary and proportionate to the aims of that exception.)

The decisions in both *Fox* and *Murray* were influenced by the terrorist context in which they occurred, and provide examples of the Court's tenderness to claims of a threat to national security made by governments of member states. In both, a very

---

258 See pp 1277 *et seq.*
259 (1990) A 182; 13 EHRR 157.
260 *Murray v UK* (1994) 19 EHRR 193.
261 *Murray v Ministry of Defence* [1988] All ER 521, HL; for comment, see Williams (1991) 54 MLR 408.

wide margin of appreciation was allowed. Probably as a result, both were influenced by the crime control consideration of allowing leeway to the police to resort to doubtful practices in relation to terrorist suspects and both exhibit a lack of rigorousness in relation to due process. Such lack of rigour might be acceptable if there was a real connection between a failure to give information to suspects and an advantage to be gained in an emergency situation, since proportionality might be satisfied. However, in Mrs Murray's case, once she was in detention, and her house in effect sealed off from the outside world, it is unclear that telling her of the fact of the arrest could create or exacerbate an unsettled situation. Giving the requisite information would not have raised an alarm which had not already been raised when the soldiers entered the house. Following these judgments it seems that, where special circumstances may be said to obtain, an arrest which does not comply with all the procedural requirements will still be an arrest, for a period of time, as far as all the consequences arising from it are concerned, under Art 5(2).

If the word 'practicable' in s 28 is interpreted in accordance with the interpretation of Art 5(3) in both *Murray* and *Fox* it seems that, depending on the circumstances, a certain amount of leeway is created in respect of informing the arrestee. On somewhat doubtful grounds, the Convention has allowed some departure from the principle that there should be a clear demarcation between the point at which the citizen is at liberty and the point at which her liberty is restrained. Sanders and Young observe, commenting on the House of Lords' decision in *Murray*, 'Even where the legislature, as in s 28 of PACE, appears to be creating strong inhibitory rules, the judiciary still manages to draw their due process sting by rendering them largely presentational'.[262] This might also be said of the decision of the European Court. A domestic court in the post-HRA era might, however, be prepared to take a more activist approach to the application of Art 5(2), especially where a s 41 TA arrest, accompanied by delay in informing of the reason owing (apparently) to the terrorist context, occurred in circumstances which could not be compared in terms of volatility to the situation in Northern Ireland when *Murray* was decided.

Consensual detainment

Apart from situations in which reasonable suspicion relating to an offence arises, there is nothing to prevent a police officer asking any person to come to the police station to answer questions. There is no legal power to do so, but equally, there is no power to prevent such a request being made. The citizen is entitled to ask whether he or she is being arrested and, if not, to refuse. However, if he or she consents, no action for false imprisonment can arise. This creates something of a grey area, since the citizen may not realise that he or she does not need to comply with the request.[263] The government refused to include a provision in PACE requiring the police to inform citizens of the fact that they are not under arrest. However, when a suspect is cautioned he must also be told that he is free to leave if he is not under arrest (para 3.21 Code C). This is repeated in Code G (para 3.2).

---

262 Sanders and Young, *Criminal Justice*, 1st edn, 1994, p 103.
263 See McKenzie, I, Morgan, R and Reiner, R, 'Helping the police with their enquiries' [1990] Crim LR 22.

The requirement under s 29 that volunteers at police stations – those who are not under arrest – should be able to leave at will unless placed under arrest, does not appear to have much impact on police practice since many people may not realise that they can leave. Section 29 is backed up by para 3.2 Code G. However, this provision is less protective than it appears to be at first sight. A person need only be cautioned if there are grounds to suspect her of an offence. But if there are such grounds, she could probably be arrested, depending on the nature of the offence. Thus, para 3.2 would only come into play at the point when arrest could occur. It would only protect due process (assuming that it was adhered to) if it demanded cautioning on the arrival of a volunteer at a police station. Certain provisions included in Code of Practice C (see below) were intended to ensure that volunteers were not disadvantaged in comparison with arrestees.[264] Of course, such provisions do not affect the fact that some 'volunteers' might not have gone to the police station at all had they realised at the outset that they had a choice.

Use of force[265]

The police may use reasonable force so long as they are within one of the powers allowed under the PACE scheme. This is provided for under s 3 of the Criminal Law Act 1967 and s 117 of PACE 1984. Section 3 is in one sense wider than s 117, since it authorises the use of force by any person, although only in relation to making an arrest or preventing crime. The prevention of crime would include resistance to an unlawful arrest. Section 117 only applies to police officers and then only in relation to provisions under PACE which do not provide that the consent of someone other than a constable is required. Section 114 TA provides an equivalent provision in respect of the TA powers. Force may include as a last resort the use of firearms; such use is governed by Home Office guidelines,[266] which provide that firearms should be issued only where there is reason to suppose that a person to be apprehended is so dangerous that he could not be safely restrained otherwise. An oral warning should normally be given unless impracticable before using a firearm.[267] Under the 1967 Act, the force can only be used if it is 'necessary' and the amount of force used must be 'reasonable'. 'Reasonable' is taken to mean 'reasonable in the circumstances'[268] and, therefore, allows extreme force if the suspect is also using or appears to be about to use extreme force.

It may be argued that further guidance as to the meaning of 'reasonable' should be provided in PACE. Section 117 provides that 'the officer may use reasonable force, if necessary, in the exercise of the [PACE] power'. This could be taken to mean that any force used which was not, objectively speaking, absolutely necessary will be unreasonable or it might suggest that any force used which appeared necessary at the

---

264 In particular, Code C, paras 3.15 and 3.16. See Chapter 12, pp 1199–1200 below for further discussion of the position of volunteers.

265 For consideration of the use of force, see [1982] Crim LR 475; *Report of Commissioner of Police of the Metropolis for 1983*, Cmnd 9268; Waddington, PAJ, *The Strong Arm of the Law*, Clarendon, 1991.

266 The guidelines were reviewed in 1987 and reissued: see 109 HC Deb Cols 562–63, 3 February 1987; (1987) 151 JPN 146.

267 For comment on the use of firearms, see [1990] Crim LR 695.

268 See the ruling in *Farrell v Secretary of State for Defence* [1980] 1 All ER 166, HL.

time will be reasonable, but it is likely that the courts will adopt the latter view. As Chapter 2 demonstrated, Art 2 of the European Convention allows the use of even lethal force which is 'absolutely necessary' in order to arrest;[269] therefore, UK law may not be in harmony with the Convention since a 'reasonableness' test is used. The Convention requirements refer to the amount of force to be used, not to the question whether to use any force at all. But the Convention jurisprudence suggests that standards may differ in terms of planning operations[270] and executing them in the immediate situation.[271] Section 117 of PACE and s 114 of the TA allow for the use of 'reasonable force', if necessary, in the exercise of the powers they provide. This wording could be taken to mean that any force used which was not, objectively speaking, necessary would be unreasonable, or it might suggest that any force used which appeared, subjectively, necessary at the time would be reasonable. Article 2 suggests that the latter test should be used.[272] Where lethal force has been used it is arguable that, under s 3 of the HRA, the term 'absolutely' should be implied into the domestic provisions.

4 Detention in police custody

Introduction

Article 5(1) of the Convention provides a right to liberty subject to certain exceptions which must have a basis in law. Not only must an exception apply, but the requirements under Art 5(2), (3) and (4) must also be met. The current domestic arrest and detention scheme for non-terrorist suspects is, as one would expect, largely coterminous, formally speaking, with these provisions, and in some respects may afford a higher – or, at least, clearer – value to due process. But the use of Art 5 as an interpretative tool may lead to a more rigorous judicial approach to the detention scheme. Breaches of Art 5 are most likely to be established in respect of the special counter-terrorist arrest and detention powers available under the Terrorism Act 2000, as amended in 2006. At present detention in police custody for nearly a month is possible.

As discussed in Chapter 13, Art 5 arguments could be raised within the trial process, by means of a civil action or under the police complaints provisions. Judicial review, on Art 5 principles, of decisions within the police complaints process, or in respect of judicial authorisations within the PACE or TA schemes, or of police decisions relating to detentions would also be available under HRA s 7(1).

A procedure prescribed by law

The first and most essential requirement of Art 5 is that a person's detention is in accordance with a procedure prescribed by law. This means that the procedure should be in accordance with national law and with recognised Convention standards, including

---

269 See pp 39 *et seq*.
270 *McCann, Farrell and Savage v UK* (1995) 21 EHRR 97, A 324, Council of Europe Report. For further discussion of this issue, see above, pp 44–45.
271 *Andronicou and Constantinou v Cyprus* (1996) 22 EHRR CD 18.84. See above, p 41.
272 See *Kelly v UK* (1985) 8 EHRR 45.

Convention principles, and should not be not arbitrary.[273] Thus, where one of the Art 5(1) exceptions applies to a person's detention, this requirement will also have to be satisfied. The procedure covers the arrest provisions[274] and the procedure adopted by a court in authorisations of detention.[275] The requirement that the detention should be in accordance with the law was given a robust interpretation based on due process norms in one of the first domestic decisions in the pre-HRA period to place a heavy reliance on Art 5. In *Chief Constable of Kent Constabulary ex p Kent Police Federation Joint Branch Board and Another*,[276] the Court had to consider an application by Kent Police Federation Joint Branch Board, representing all ranks of the Kent Constabulary, for judicial review of the proposal by the Chief Constable of Kent that the conduct of reviews of police detention under s 40(1)(b) of the 1984 Act should be, in the majority of cases, by video link.

Lord Bingham referred to Art 5 and said that, although not yet part of domestic law, it embodied important and basic rights recognised and protected by English law. If citizens were to be deprived of their liberty, such deprivation had to be in accordance with the law. He found that the Court was dealing with an area of extreme sensitivity, namely the circumstances in which, and the conditions on which, a citizen not convicted or even charged with crime might be deprived of his or her liberty. The Act and the Codes giving it effect represented, he said, a complex and careful balance between the obviously important duty of the police to investigate crime and apprehend criminals on the one hand and the rights of the private citizen on the other. Under s 37(5), a written record of the grounds of detention had to be made by the review officer 'in the presence of the person whose detention is under review'. He found that that condition was not met if the review officer was in one place and the person whose detention was under review was in another. Section 37(5) did not refer to physical presence, but 'presence' in ordinary parlance meant physical presence.

Lord Bingham concluded that Parliament had provided for a face-to-face confrontation between the review officer and the suspect and, if important rights enacted to protect the subject were to be modified, it was for Parliament after appropriate consultation so to rule and not for the courts. This decision indicated a determination to give real efficacy to Art 5, where a contrary interpretation, impliedly supported by a guiding note,[277] was readily available. Review by video link would have meant the intrusion of technology, controlled by the police, into the review process, leading arguably to a depersonalised confrontation and possibly to a further impression of tokenism. As discussed below, this decision was then reversed legislatively, but it is indicative of the more rigorous scrutiny that the HRA has instilled into criminal procedure.

---

273 *Winterwerp v Netherlands* A 33 (1979), para 39.
274 *Fox, Campbell and Hartley v UK*, Appl No 182; (1990) 13 EHRR 157.
275 *Weston v UK* 3 EHRR 402; *Van der Leer v Netherlands* A 170-A (1990).
276 (1999) *The Times*, 1 December, judgment 18 November 1999.
277 He found that the provisions of Code C do not provide conclusive support for either construction. Note for guidance 15C (of the revision of the Code at the time) permitted review by telephone so long as the requirements of s 40 were met, but Lord Bingham had difficulty in seeing how a review conducted over the telephone could ever comply with those requirements, as that Note appeared to envisage.

Time limits on detention after arrest under PACE

The position under the law prior to the 1984 Act with regard to detention before charge and committal before a magistrate was very uncertain. It was governed by s 43 of the Magistrates' Courts Act 1980, which allowed the police to detain a person in custody until such time as it was 'practicable' to bring him before a magistrate, in the case of a 'serious' offence. Since a person would be charged before being brought before the magistrate, this meant that the police had to move expeditiously in converting suspicion into evidence justifying a charge.[278] However, the common law had developed to the point when it could be said that detention for the purpose of questioning was recognised.[279] Thus, prior to PACE, the police had no clearly defined power to hold a person for questioning. The detention scheme governed by Part IV of PACE put such a power on a more certain basis in accordance with the Phillips recommendations,[280] that the purpose of the detention is to obtain a confession.[281] This was foreshadowed in the developing common law recognition that detention was for the purpose of questioning.[282]

Phillips did not, however, envisage that the decision to arrest would become, in effect, the decision to detain. This is reflected in the role of the custody officer under s 37 of PACE. Under s 37 the custody officer should decide whether there is sufficient evidence to charge the suspect with the offence at this point. If not, the suspect should be released with or without bail, unless there are reasonable grounds for believing that detention is necessary 'To secure or preserve evidence relating to an offence for which he is under arrest or to obtain such evidence by questioning him.'[283] The second ground is the most frequently used. In theory, the custody officer could refuse to accept the arrestee into detention. In practice this is extremely rare, if not unknown; the custody officer almost always simply rubber-stamps the arresting officer's decision that the suspect should be detained[284] and custody officers appear to disregard the requirement to consider whether the detainee should be charged at the 'booking in' stage.[285] Thus, although s 37(3) appears to protect due process since it provides that the custody officer must be satisfied that there are reasonable grounds for the detention,[286] in practice it does not appear to affect police working practices.

Under s 41, the detention can be for up to 24 hours, but in the case of a person in police custody for a serious arrestable offence (defined in s 116) it can extend to 96 hours. Part IV of PACE does not apply to detention under the Terrorism Act 2000, as amended, (below) or to detention by immigration officers.[287] Under s 42(1), a police

---

278   See *Holmes* [1981] 2 All ER 612; [1981] Crim LR 802.
279   *Holgate-Mohammed v Duke* [1984] AC 437; [1984] 1 All ER 1054, HL.
280   See Phillips Royal Commission, Cmnd 8092 (1981).
281   Part IV, s 37(2).
282   *Mohammed-Holgate v Duke* [1984] QB 209.
283   Section 37(2). See also the reasons for continued detention after charge under s 38.
284   See Dixon, D *et al.*, 'Safeguarding the rights of suspects in police custody', 1 Policing and Society 115, p 130.
285   See Capes, E, 'Detention without Charge' [1999] Crim LR 874.
286   Under s 45A, PACE allows regulation to be made allowing the decision under s 37 to be taken by means of video-conference. This power is not yet in force.
287   PACE 1984, s 51.

officer of the rank of superintendent or above can sanction detention for up to 36 hours if three conditions apply: he or she has reasonable grounds for believing that either the detention is necessary to secure or preserve evidence relating to an offence for which the detainee is under arrest or to obtain such evidence by questioning him; an offence for which the detainee is under arrest is a serious arrestable offence; and the investigation is being conducted diligently and expeditiously. After 36 hours, detention can no longer be authorised by the police alone. Under s 43(1), the application for authorisation must be supported by information and brought before a magistrates' court, which can authorise detention under s 44 for up to 96 hours if the conditions are met as set out above. Detention must be reviewed periodically;[288] in the case of a person who has been arrested and charged, the review must by the custody officer; in the case of a person arrested but not yet charged, by an officer of at least the rank of inspector. The detainee or his solicitor (if available) has the right to make written or oral representations.[289]

Research suggests, however, that these reviews are not treated as genuine investigations into the grounds for continuing the detention, but as routinised procedures requiring a merely formal adherence.[290] Perhaps in recognition of the need for rigour in relation to reviews, a proposal made in 1999 by the Chief Constable of Kent Police that detention review should be by video link in the majority of cases was rejected in judicial review proceedings on the ground, discussed above, that it might undermine the protection for liberty they are intended to offer, taking Art 5 into account.[291]

However, the government then brought forward legislation – s 73 of the Criminal Justice and Police Act 2001 (CJP) – to reverse the effect of this decision. Section 73 inserted ss 40A and 45A into PACE to allow for the use of telephone and video links for reviews of detention. Section 40A allows for review by an officer of at least the rank of inspector by telephone where it is not reasonably practicable for the officer to be present at the station, and where the review is not one authorised to be carried out by video link under s 45A. Section 45A is an enabling section: it allows for the Secretary of State to make regulations to allow an officer to perform functions in relation to detainees when he or she is not present in the station but has access to a video link. The functions include carrying out the function of custody officer under ss 37, 38 and 40 and the carrying out of a review under s 40(1)(b). The function of custody officer can only be carried out by a custody officer at a designated station (s 45A(4)). Clearly, these new provisions in relation to review of detention detract from the face to face confrontation that was originally envisaged by Parliament.

The powers of detention are very significant, but they are intended to embody the principle that a detained person should normally be charged within 24 hours and then either released or brought before a magistrate. They are supposed to be balanced by all the safeguards created by Part V of PACE and Codes of Practice C, E (and F, although visual recording is not a requirement). It may be noted that a person unlawfully detained

288 Under s 40(1)(b).
289 Under s 40(12) and (13).
290 Dixon, D et al., 'Safeguarding the rights of suspects in police custody', 1 Policing and Society 115, pp 130–31.
291 R v Chief Constable of Kent Constabulary ex p Kent Police Federation Joint Branch Board and Another (1999) The Times, 1 December, judgment 18 November 1999.

can apply for a writ of habeas corpus in order to secure release from detention, and this remedy is preserved in s 51(d). Its usefulness in practice is, however, very limited since the courts have developed a practice of adjourning applications for 24 hours in order to allow the police to present their case. Thus, detention can continue for that time allowing the police to carry out questioning or other procedures in the meantime.

Detention under the Terrorism Act 2000, as amended

The detention scheme adopted in respect of terrorist suspects allowed for the suspect to be detained for longer periods than for non-terrorist suspects, and for a lower level of due process safeguards to be applicable during detention.[292] The detention scheme for terrorist suspects has been through a number of revisions, as discussed below, which have been driven on the one hand by due process demands imposed in effect by the European Court of Human Rights and on the other by governmental crime control concerns; it is still under review. Essentially, the period of detention has become incrementally longer, but it is subject to judicial authorisation.

Detention with judicial authorisation

Previously, if a person was arrested under s 14 of the PTA, as opposed to s 24 of PACE, whether the arrest was for an offence or on suspicion of being a terrorist, the detention provisions under PACE did not apply. The arrestee could be detained for up to 48 hours following arrest (s 14(4)) of the PTA) but this period could be extended by the Secretary of State by further periods not exceeding five days in all (s 14(5) of the PTA). Thus, the whole detention could be for seven days and, in contrast to the PACE provisions, the courts were not involved in the authorising process; it occurred at a low level of visibility as an administrative decision.

The similar provision under the PTA 1984 was found to be in breach of Art 5(3) in *Brogan v UK*.[293] Article 5(3) confers a right to be brought promptly before the judicial authorities; in other words, not to be held for long periods without a hearing. It covers both arrest and detention. There will be some allowable delay in both situations; the question is therefore what is meant by 'promptly'. Its meaning was considered in *Brogan* in relation to the arrest and detention of the applicants considered above, arising by virtue of the special powers under s 12 of the PTA. The UK had entered a derogation under Art 15 against the applicability of Art 5(3) to Northern Ireland, but withdrew that derogation in August 1984. Two months later, the *Brogan* case was filed. The applicants complained, *inter alia*, of the length of time they were held in detention without coming before a judge, on the basis that it could not be termed prompt. The Court took into account the need for special measures to combat terrorism; such measures had to be balanced against individual rights. However, it found that detention for four days and six hours was too long on the ground that holding a person for longer than four days without judicial authorisation was a violation of the requirement that persons should be brought promptly before a judicial officer. The Court did not specify how long was

292 See below, Chapter 12, pp 1191 *et seq.* for discussion of such safeguards.
293 Judgment of 29 November 1988; (1989) 11 EHRR 117; A 145.

acceptable; previously, the Commission had seen four days as the limit. The government made no move to comply with this decision; instead, it entered a derogation under Art 15 to Art 5(3).

This derogation was challenged unsuccessfully in *Brannigan and McBride v UK*[294] as invalid. The European Court of Human Rights found that it was justified since the state of public emergency in Northern Ireland warranted exceptional measures. The Court found: 'a wide margin of appreciation [on the question] of the presence of an emergency . . . and on the nature and scope of derogations necessary to avert it [should be allowed]'.[295] Among the government contentions uncritically accepted by the Court was one to the effect that in the particular situation, the judiciary should not be permitted a role in protecting the liberty of detainees. As Judge Walsh pointed out in his dissenting opinion, this was precisely a role which the public would expect a judge to have. *Brannigan* might appear a doubtful decision because the derogation was entered after the decision in *Brogan*, although it might also be said that states should not be encouraged to enter derogations too readily on 'insurance' grounds in order to pre-empt claims. Arguably, although there was a state of emergency in 1989, the UK had chosen not to enter a derogation even though one would have been warranted. Whatever the merits of this argument in the particular situation, it is questionable whether the exigencies of the situation did require detention of six days without recourse to independent review. Possibly it was assumed on insufficient grounds that such review would prejudice the legitimate purpose of the investigation.

The *Brogan* decision clearly presented the government with a difficulty in formulating the Terrorism Act 2000. Although the HRA continued the derogation entered in *Brogan*, under s 14(1)(a) HRA, for a time, it was vulnerable to challenge at Strasbourg at some future point, in the light of the new settlement in Northern Ireland. The government put forward various justifications for producing new terrorist legislation in 2000, but it recognised that it might be in difficulties in arguing that a state of emergency sufficient to support the derogation could be said to exist post-2000.[296] Its solution, in the TA, was to make provision for judicial authorisation of detention, rather than to decrease the length of time during which terrorist suspects could be detained, harmonising it with the PACE period. In deciding on these arrangements, including the retention of the possibility of up to seven days' detention, the government rejected the suggestion of Lord Lloyd that once there was a lasting peace in Northern Ireland, it ought to be possible to reduce the maximum period for which a suspect could be detained under the new legislation to a total of four days – two days on the authority of the police and two days with judicial authorisation.

The maximum period of detention, applicable to a person arrested under s 41 of the TA, was seven days; it was extended to 14 days by amendment to s 41(7) and Sched 8 TA under the Criminal Justice Act 2003, and then, after the July 2005 bombings in London, it was extended again by further amendment under the Terrorism Act 2006, to 28 days. The government sought to extend the period of time to 90 days but was defeated in the House of Commons. At the time of writing the government intends to

294   Series A, 258-B (1993); (1993) 17 EHRR 594.
295   Paragraph 207.
296   See *Legislation Against Terrorism* (1988) Cm 4178, para 8.2.

seek to bring forward the 90-day period once again in a possible new Terrorism Bill 2007 or 2008. Thus terrorism suspects can be held in detention for almost a month, in strong contrast to non-terrorist suspects, who can only be held for 96 hours, even for the most serious offences.

After 48 hours of detention judicial approval is needed. Para 29, Sched 8 TA provides that the detention must be under a warrant issued by a 'judicial authority'.[297] Under para 32, the warrant may be issued if there are reasonable grounds for believing that 'the detention of the person to whom the application relates is necessary to obtain relevant evidence whether by questioning him or otherwise or to preserve relevant evidence'. The detainee or his solicitor has the right to make written or oral representations under para 33(1). Thus, authorisation may not be merely 'on the papers'. Such a possibility might not have satisfied the aim of achieving compliance with Art 5(3), despite the involvement of a judicial figure. Judicial authorisation meant that the derogation was no longer needed, and it was lifted on 19 March 2001.

In requiring judicial authorisation for detention for up to seven days under s 41 and Sched 7 of the TA, the government has sought to ensure that the new detention provisions comply with Art 5(3) as interpreted in *Brogan* and *Brannigan*, meaning that it became possible to withdraw the derogation and, once this was accomplished, the HRA was accordingly amended.[298] One question which will probably be raised eventually in the domestic courts or at Strasbourg will be whether allowing a detention for seven days, even with judicial authorisation, is in accordance with Art 5.

Detention authorised by police alone

The provisions provide for a twin track system of detention, one dependent on the judicial authority and one on the police themselves. The police can detain a person on their own authority for 48 hours under s 41(3) which provides:

> *Subject to* subsections (4) to (7), a person detained under this section shall (unless detained under any other power) be released not later than the end of the period of 48 hours beginning –
>
> (a) with the time of his arrest under this section, or
> (b) if he was being detained under Schedule 7 when he was arrested under this section, with the time when his examination under that Schedule began (emphasis added).

These provisions differ quite significantly from those under the PTA. Section 14(4) of the PTA provided that the 48 hour period is subject *only* to sub-section 5, which allowed for extension of detention by the Secretary of State. Section 41(4)–(7) of the TA appears to

---

297 Paragraph 29(4) provides: 'In this Part "judicial authority" means (a) in England and Wales, the Senior District Judge (Chief Magistrate) or his deputy, or a District Judge (Magistrates' Courts) who is designated for the purpose of this Part by the Lord Chancellor, (b) in Scotland, the sheriff, and (c) in Northern Ireland, a county court judge, or a resident magistrate who is designated for the purpose of this Part by the Lord Chancellor.'

298 See further Chapter 2, p 57.

provide three possibilities of continuing the detention beyond 48 hours, over and above the possibility of extension under judicial authorisation. These possibilities represent, depending on the interpretation they are afforded, quite notable departures from the previous scheme. Section 41(6) provides that if an application for an extension of detention is made, or under s 41(5), it is intended that it will be made, detention can continue while it is pending. This impliedly means that the police can continue to detain for more than 48 hours so long as an application is being made or is about to be made, even if it is subsequently refused. The application need not be made during the 48 hours; under Sched 8, Part III, para 30 it may be made within six hours of the end of that period.

If, for example, towards the end of 54 hours in detention (a possibility under the TA, as indicated above) the police decided to apply for an extension of detention, they would have the power under s 41(5) to continue the detention while the application was being made and then under s 41(6) while the hearing was occurring. This possibility does not appear to accord with *Brogan* and *Brannigan* since there is no possibility of judicial authorisation of detention. Bearing in mind the wide margin of appreciation allowed in *Brannigan*, a domestic court taking a more activist stance might be prepared to find a breach of Art 5(3) in respect of a s 41 detention, depending on its length, in the particular circumstances before it. One clear possibility would be to limit the application of s 41(4) in accordance with the government's intention that the detention regime should comply with Art 5(3) which allowed for the withdrawal of the derogation.

The 48-hour period is also subject to s 41(4), which provides: 'If on a review of a person's detention under Part II of Schedule 8 the review officer does not authorise continued detention, the person shall (unless detained in accordance with sub-sections (5) or (6) or under any other power) be released.' The reviews have to occur every 12 hours. This is not well expressed but is intended to mean that within the 48-hour period the review officer (this must be an officer of at least the rank of superintendent after the first 12 hours) can continue the detention periodically, at 12-hour intervals, so long as the review conditions (which are the same as the warrant conditions) continue to apply. No express time limit is placed on the total period which the review officer can authorise. Clearly, s 41(4) should be interpreted to mean that *within* the 48 hour period there must be periodic reviews (subject to the provisions for delaying reviews); the possibility of providing the police with a new power to extend detention beyond 48 hours under s 41(4) should be rejected, since it seems to be due to ambiguous drafting. It is unlikely that s 41(4) could be interpreted to allow leeway to continue to detain beyond 48 hours, but the provision could be viewed as detracting from the certainty of the 48-hour deadline. The stricter interpretation accords with the government's intention as expressed in the Consultation Paper.[299] If, in practice, s 41(4) was interpreted on occasion to allow some detentions on the authority of the review officer only, beyond 48 hours, such detentions would obviously be more likely than those under the previous provisions to create breaches of Art 5(3).

As part of the port and border controls regime, Sched 5 to the PTA provided a further power of detention in allowing a person to be detained for 12 hours before examination at ports of entry into Britain or Northern Ireland. The period could be extended to 24 hours if the person was suspected of involvement in the commission, preparation or

---

299 *Legislation Against Terrorism* (1988) Cm 4178.

instigation of acts of terrorism. These provisions are partially reproduced in Sched 7 of the TA; they are modified to take account of the abolition of the exclusion power.[300]

Clearly, the PACE and TA detention schemes differ quite radically in due process terms, despite the fact that many of those who will be potentially subject to the new TA scheme are likely to represent a far more divergent group than the previous one which fell within the rubric of 'terrorist'. Even within that previous group, as a number of the most famous miscarriage of justice cases imply, those who were designated terrorist suspects, such as *Judith Ward*,[301] were often remarkably ill-suited to the draconian terrorist regime to which they were subject. The peace process presented an opportunity for the harmonisation of the PACE and counter-terrorist regimes that might have avoided the potential for future miscarriages which, it is suggested, is inherent in the TA scheme, bearing in mind the special propensity evidenced in the cases of the *Birmingham Six*, [302]*Guildford Four*,[303] *Maguire Seven*,[304] *Ward*,[305] and *UDR Four*,[306] of terrorist cases to miscarry.

Treatment in detention

The role of the custody officer

The general use of custody officers provided for under s 36 is a key feature of the scheme for detention, treatment and questioning created under Parts IV and V of PACE. The custody officer's role is to underpin the other safeguards by ensuring that the suspect is treated in accordance with PACE and the Codes and by generally overseeing all aspects of his or her treatment.[307] Use of custody officers was intended to ensure that somebody independent of the investigating officer could keep a check on what was occurring. The scheme was not a new idea; in certain police stations an officer was already fulfilling this role, but PACE clarifies the duties of custody officers and ensures that most stations have one. Thus, best practice was placed on a statutory basis.

However, the efficacy of the custody officer scheme may be called into question. It may not always be in operation: in non-designated police stations, there must simply be someone who can act as custody officer if the need arises and in designated police stations, there need not always be a custody officer on duty. The ruling in *Vince and Another v Chief Constable of Dorset*[308] made it clear that s 36 does not require that a custody officer must always be present. The plaintiffs (acting for members of the joint branch board of the Police Federation of England and Wales of the Dorset Police) sought a declaration that by virtue of s 36(1) of PACE a custody officer should normally be available in a police station. However, it was found that s 36(1) clearly provided that

300 See Chapter 14, p 1406.
301 *Ward* (1992) 98 Cr App R 1.
302 See *McIlkenny and Others* [1992] 2 All ER 417.
303 See May, J, *Report of the Inquiry into the Circumstances surrounding the Convictions Arising out of the Bomb Attacks at Guildford and Woolwich in 1974, Final Report*, 1993–94 HC 449, Chapter 17.
304 See *Maguire* [1992] 2 All ER 433.
305 *Ward* (1992) 98 Cr App R 1.
306 See [1988] 11 NIJB 1.
307 For discussion of judicial interpretation of the PACE provisions, see Feldman, D, [1990] Crim LR 452.
308 (1992) *The Times*, 7 September.

the Chief Constable had a duty to appoint one custody officer for each designated police station and a power to appoint more in his discretion which had to be reasonably exercised. It was found that there had been no breach by the Chief Constable, implying that a decision that a custody officer need not always be on duty is a reasonable one. It may be argued that this case exposes a weakness in one of the central safeguards provided under PACE. This was referred to by Steyn LJ, who commented that the Royal Commission on Criminal Procedure[309] might wish to consider this loophole in the PACE provisions. As indicated above, s 45A of PACE, inserted by s 73 of the CJP 2001, allows for a custody officer at a designated police station to act as a custody officer for the purposes of ss 37, 38 and 40(1)(b) of PACE by video link. Under the Police Reform Act 2002 a number of the police powers exercised in detention may be exercised by civilian detention officers, including powers to search, to take photographs, fingerprints and samples.

The custody officer may not always be able to take a stance independent of that of the investigating officer.[310] This weakness in the scheme arises from the lowly rank of the custody officer; under s 38(3), the officer need only be of the rank of sergeant and may therefore be of a lower rank than the investigating officer, making it very difficult to take an independent line on the treatment of the suspect. If the two disagree, the custody officer must refer up the line of authority (s 39(6)); there is no provision allowing the custody officer to overrule the investigating officer. Thus, there is a danger that the custody officer will merely rubber-stamp the decisions of the investigating officer; whether this occurs in practice may largely depend on the attitude of the superior officers in a particular force to the provisions of the PACE scheme.

Vulnerable groups

Throughout the Codes, including Code H, the Code governing the treatment of terrorist suspects in detention, recognition is given to the special needs of certain vulnerable groups: juveniles, the mentally disordered or handicapped, those not proficient in English, the hearing impaired or the visually handicapped. Juveniles and the mentally handicapped or disordered should be attended by an 'appropriate adult'. The Runciman Royal Commission Report 1993 recommended a review of the role of appropriate adults with a view to considering their training and availability and the criteria employed by the police in order to determine when an adult was needed.[311] In response, the Home Office set up a review group which, in June 1995, made a number of recommendations. They included entitling appropriate adults to a confidential interview with the suspect; defining the role of appropriate adults in Code C; providing guidance for professionals and others likely to act in this role and setting up local appropriate adult panels.[312] The Codes, particularly Codes C and H, now contain more detailed provisions regarding the role of appropriate adults.

---

309 Set up in 1992 after the miscarriage of justice which occurred in the case of the *Birmingham Six*. See p 1103 above.

310 See Sanders and Young, *Criminal Justice* 2007, Chapter 4, pp 168–170.

311 Proposal 72. For further discussion, see Hodgson J [1997] Crim LR 785.

312 The Report is available from the Chairman of the Review Group: Mr Stephen Wells, F2 Division, Home Office.

Under para 1, Code C or Code H the 'appropriate' adult in the case of a juvenile will be the parent or guardian, a social worker or another adult who is not a police officer. The suspect should be informed by the custody officer that the appropriate adult is there to assist and advise him and can be consulted with privately (para 3.18 Code C, para 3.19 Code H). However, research suggests that this requirement is not always observed and that in any event, appropriate adults often seem unclear as to the role they are supposed to play.[313] Under the 2006 version of Code C the estranged parent of a juvenile cannot be the appropriate adult,[314] if the juvenile 'expressly and specifically objects to his presence'. Previously this was possible and, in such instances, the parent was likely to collude with the police or generally show hostility to the juvenile rather than look after his or her interests.[315] This change was originally prompted by the decision in *DPP v Blake*[316] that a confession obtained from a juvenile in the presence of an estranged parent acting as the appropriate adult may be excluded from evidence. Compliance with the provisions of para 11, indicating the respects in which the appropriate adult should look after the interests of the juvenile, could not be ensured if an estranged parent was present.

In the case of a mentally disordered or handicapped detainee, the appropriate adult under para 1 will be a relative, guardian, other person responsible for his or her welfare or an adult who is not a police officer.[317] The custody officer must as soon as practicable inform the appropriate adult of the grounds for the person's detention and ask the adult to come to the police station to see him or her. If a person appears physically or mentally ill, the custody officer ensures that he or she receives appropriate clinical attention, or, in urgent cases, send the person to hospital or call the nearest available medical practitioner.[318]

It will be found, in discussion in Chapter 13 of unreliable confessions, that mentally handicapped or disordered persons are very likely to make an untrue or exaggerated confession and therefore it is particularly important that all the safeguards available should be in place when such a person is interviewed. However, there is provision for urgent interviewing of such persons without the appropriate adult if an officer of the rank of superintendent or above considers that delay will involve an immediate risk of harm to persons or serious loss of or serious damage to, property.[319] The main defect in the provisions relating to the mentally handicapped or disordered is that they rely on the ability of officers who will have had little or no training in the field to make the judgment that a person is mentally disordered.[320] It would seem essential that custody officers at

---

313 Brown, D, Ellis, T and Larcombe, K, *Changing the Code: police detention under the revised PACE Codes of Practice*, 1993, HO Research Study No 129.
314 Note 1B of Codes C and H. The change to Code C was introduced in 1991.
315 See Softley, P, 'Police interrogation: an observational study in four police stations' (1985) Policing Today 119.
316 [1989] 1 WLR 432, CA; this problem also arose recently at first instance in *Morse* [1991] Crim LR 195.
317 Paragraph 1.7; Code H, para 1.13.
318 Code C, para 9.5; Code H, para 9.6.
319 See Codes C and H, para 11.(d).
320 Codes C and H, Annex E, para 1, provide that if an officer 'has any suspicion or is told in good faith that a person of any age, whether or not in custody, may be suffering from medical disorder or is mentally handicapped or cannot understand the significance of questions put to him or his replies, then he shall be treated as a mentally disordered or mentally handicapped person'.

least should have special training in this regard. Various provisions are also available for the protection of members of the other vulnerable groups mentioned. A blind or visually handicapped person must have independent help in reading documentation.[321]

Conditions of detention

Code H, governing the conditions of detention for terrorist suspects, is of particular significance since such suspects may be in detention for up to 28 days. Code H, as opposed to the statutory provisions, governs the physical treatment of terrorist suspects, the provision of medical care and the issue of mental illness. The mental impact of almost a month in custody on the basis of reasonable suspicion only may be very significant. Physical treatment of detainees is governed by paras 8 and 9 of Codes C and H, and it is intended that they should be provided with basic physical care. Paragraphs 8 and 9 embody the principle that the detainee's physical safety should be ensured and his basic physical needs met. Persons detained should be visited every hour but, where possible, juveniles should be visited 'more frequently';[322] those who are drunk should be visited every half hour. The paragraphs do, however, allow more than one detainee to be placed in the same cell if it is impracticable to do otherwise (para 8.1) and although a juvenile must not be placed in a cell with an adult, no clear provision for frequent checks on juveniles in police cells is made. Paragraph 8.2 provides that cells should be adequately heated, cleaned, lit and ventilated and that three meals should be offered in any 24-hour period. A juvenile will only be placed in a police cell if no other secure accommodation is available and the custody officer considers that it is not practicable to supervise him if he is not placed in a cell. No additional restraints should be used within a locked cell unless absolutely necessary and then only suitable handcuffs (para 8.2). Reasonable force may be used if necessary (para 1), by designated persons where a police officer would also have that power. Under para 9, if a person appears mentally or physically ill or injured, or does not respond normally to questions or conversation (other than through drunkenness alone) or otherwise appears to need medical attention, the custody officer must immediately call the police surgeon (or, in urgent cases, send the person to hospital or call the nearest available medical practitioner).

Code H, like Code C, makes reference to allowing outdoor exercise, but the provisions are more detailed, Code H, para 8.7); Code H, unlike Code C, provides for facilities for detainees to conduct religious observance – in para 8.8. Code H also makes some further provision for medical treatment, requiring in para 9.1 that detainees held for more than 96 hours must be visited by a healthcare professional at least once every 24 hours. This provides a further check, over and above the provisions of para 9 for clinical treatment.

Treatment of a detainee can engage Art 3, which provides a guarantee against torture or inhuman or degrading treatment.[323] Article 3 could be engaged due to the conditions of detention or where physical force is used in the course of an arrest and detention.

---

321 Paragraph 3.17; Code H 3.18.
322 Codes C and H, Note 9B.
323 Article 3 treatment may be justifiable where its object is to satisfy the demands of Art 2, the right to life: *Herczegfalvy v Austria* A 244 (1992).

In *Ribbitsch v Austria*[324] the Court said: 'any recourse to physical force which has not been made strictly necessary by his own conduct diminishes human dignity and is in principle an infringement of the right set forth in Article 3.'[325] Force may only be used where it is strictly required to restrain the detainee and the force used must go no further, in terms of causing injury or humiliation, than is strictly necessary to achieve the purpose of restraint. Thus, a strict proportionality test is applied and force outside the limits it sets will infringe Art 3. *A fortiori*, this must be the case under Art 2, where lethal force is used.[326]

Article 3 treatment may arise in respect of a number of other aspects of detention. Failure to obtain medical treatment after a forcible arrest was found to infringe Art 3 in *Hurtado v Switzerland*.[327] In the *Greek* case,[328] the conditions of detention were found to amount to inhuman treatment owing to inadequate food, sleeping arrangements, heating and sanitary facilities combined with overcrowding and inadequate provision for external contacts. It was also found that conduct which grossly humiliates may amount to degrading treatment contrary to Art 3. Such treatment may include racially discriminatory and, probably, sexually discriminatory arrests and treatment in detention;[329] it might be found to fall more readily within Art 3 in a non-terrorist context.[330] Where discrimination is a factor, Art 14 would also be engaged.

The cases of *Tomasi v France*,[331] *Tekin v Turkey*,[332] *Selmouni v France*,[333] and *McGlinchey v UK*[334] make it clear that standards change over time, so that what might be

---

324 (1996) 21 EHRR 573.

325 See p 26. See *Selmouni v France* (2000) 29 EHRR 403 for an example of treatment in police custody found to amount to torture.

326 Article 2 therefore calls into question the recent cases of death caused by restraint during arrest. In 'Deaths in police custody: learning the lessons', Police Research Series Paper 26, 1998, Leigh, Johnson and Ingram found, in section 6, 13 cases of death in which police restraint may have been a factor. They found six cases where restraint may have led to 'postural' or 'positional asphyxia', leading to death. In two others, death was due to a neck-hold; in a further two, to force applied with a baton. They viewed these cases as having implications for training. *The Butler Report*, 1998, also considered a number of death in custody cases. In one of these, that of O'Brien, the arrestee, after being handcuffed, was held face down on the ground by at least four officers, one of whom knelt on his back, and one on his legs. The evidence was conflicting, but his family and a bystander stated that he was saying that he could not breathe. The post mortem found that he had died due to postural asphyxia and he had bruising to his head, shoulders and right arm. See Chapter 13, p 1321 in relation to criticism of decisions of the CPS in relation to this case. It is suggested that, prima facie, the force used went well beyond that which was absolutely necessary, and therefore it was not in accord with Art 2.

327 A 280-A (1994) Com Rep.

328 12 YB 1 (1969) Com Rep.

329 *East African Asians* cases (1973) 3 EHRR 76. See also *Lustig-Prean and Beckett v UK* (1999) 29 EHRR 548, and *Smith and Grady v UK* (2000) 29 EHRR 493, which suggested that grossly humiliating, intrusive interrogation could, if of an extreme and prolonged nature, amount to a breach of Art 3 (discussed below, pp 1207–8).

330 In *McFeeley v UK* (1980) 20 DR 44, intimate body searches in a terrorist context did not give rise to a breach of Art 3, but it has been suggested (see Harris, O'Boyle and Warbrick, Harris, D, O'Boyle, K and Warbrick, C, *Law of The European Convention on Human Rights*, 1995, p 83) that this finding might not apply in a non-terrorist context.

331 (1993) 15 EHRR 1.

332 (2001) 31 EHRR 4.

333 (1999) 29 EHRR 403.

334 (2003) 37 EHRR 41.

viewed as degrading treatment in the past might now be viewed as torture. Ill treatment that might not have been viewed as 'degrading' 20 years ago might now fall within Art 3. The Scottish case of *Napier v Scottish Ministers*[335] accepted that a broader concept of Art 3 treatment should now be adopted. Assuming that the treatment arguably falls within Art 3, the burden of proof on the detainee is affected, following the decisions in *Tomasi v France*[336] and *Aksoy v Turkey*.[337] Once the detainee has shown that he was free of the injury or harm in question before arrest, the state will then bear the burden of providing a plausible explanation for it which is consistent with the evidence. If it does not do so, the domestic court should assume that the injuries in question were caused in the manner alleged by the complainant.

Where Art 3 is inapplicable, since the treatment does not reach the level of severity the Article envisages, a breach of Art 8 might be established in respect of treatment invasive of privacy in police detention. In *Wainwright v Home Office*[338] the House of Lords had to consider whether humiliating treatment of visitors to a prison amounted to a breach of Art 3 or 8. The findings could readily be applied by analogy to detainees in police custody. The applicants, Mary Wainwright and her son, Alan Wainwright, went to visit Ms Wainwright's son, Patrick O'Neill, in prison. Mr Wainwright has cerebral palsy and severe arrested social and intellectual development. They were informed that they would be strip-searched, as there was reason to believe that they were carrying drugs. Leeds Prison has internal rules designed to reduce the embarrassment of strip-searching as far as possible. They are modelled on the code of practice issued to the police. They provide that the search must take place in a completely private room in the presence of two officers of the same sex as the visitor. The visitor is required to expose first the upper half of his body and then the lower but not to stand completely naked. His body (apart from hair, ears and mouth) is not to be touched. Before the search begins, the visitor is asked to sign a consent form which outlines the procedure to be followed. The Wainwrights were told that, if they refused, they would not be allowed to visit Mr O'Neill. Ms Wainwright was subjected to a strip search with visual examination of her vagina and anus. Mr Wainwright was subjected to such a search but his penis was physically examined. Both were very distressed by the searches. The Court of Appeal found that the prison officers had not followed their own rules in conducting the searches. Both the Wainwrights had been asked to uncover all or virtually all of their bodies at the same time; and neither were given the consent form until after the search had been completed; the room used to search Mrs Wainwright was not private because it had an uncurtained window from which someone across the street could have seen her, and one prison officer had touched Alan's penis to lift his foreskin.

The House of Lords proceeded on the basis that the searches took place under statutory authority, and were governed by the internal prison rules in question, but that the rules had not been adhered to, although the prison officers had honestly believed that they were entitled to conduct the searches. Mr Wainwright was awarded damages for

---

335 (2004) UKHRR 881.
336 A 241-A (1992).
337 (1996) 23 EHRR 553. These decisions should also be taken into account where treatment in police custody results in death, engaging Art 2. See Chapter 13, p 1321.
338 (2003) 4 All ER 969.

battery. The HRA was not in force at the time when the facts of *Wainwright* took place, but the House was invited by counsel for the plaintiffs to consider extending the common law of battery or the doctrine in *Wilkinson v Downton*[339] in order to provide a remedy for the breaches of the Convention rights which, counsel argued, had occurred.

On the question of the violation of Arts 3 or 8, Lord Hoffmann, giving the leading judgment, took a restrictive view, at least of the proportionality aspect of Art 8. Article 3, it was found, was not violated by the treatment that they were subjected to. On this point Lord Hoffmann found (para 49):

> I have no doubt that there was no infringement of article 3. The conduct of the searches came nowhere near the degree of humiliation which has been held by the European Court of Human Rights to be degrading treatment in the cases on prison searches to which we were referred: see *Valasinas v Lithuania*[340] (applicant made to strip naked and have his sexual organs touched in front of a woman); *Iwanczuk v Poland*[341] (applicant ordered to strip naked and subjected to humiliating abuse by guards when he tried to exercise his right to vote in facilities provided in prison); *Lorsé v The Netherlands*[342] (applicant strip searched weekly over six years in high security wing without sufficient security justification).

In relation to Art 8 he found (paras 51 and 52):

> Although article 8 guarantees a right of privacy, I do not think that it treats that right as having been invaded and requiring a remedy in damages, irrespective of whether the defendant acted intentionally, negligently or accidentally . . . Article 8 may justify a monetary remedy for an intentional invasion of privacy by a public authority, even if no damage is suffered other than distress for which damages are not ordinarily recoverable. It does not follow that a merely negligent act should, contrary to general principle, give rise to a claim for damages for distress because it affects privacy rather than some other interest like bodily safety: compare *Hicks v Chief Constable of the South Yorkshire Police*.[343] Be that as it may, a finding that there was a breach of article 8 will only demonstrate that there was a gap in the English remedies for invasion of privacy which has since been filled by sections 6 and 7 of the 1998 Act.

Lord Hoffmann also found that there was no general tort of invasion of privacy (at para 32), and that there was no need to adopt one, either by modification of common law doctrines or by accepting a general common law principle that a privacy remedy is required in order to satisfy the demands of Art 8:

> Nor is there anything in the jurisprudence of the European Court of Human Rights which suggests that the adoption of some high level principle of privacy is necessary

339 [1897] 2 QB 57.
340 Appl No 44558/98 (unreported) 24 July 2001.
341 Appl No 25196/94 (unreported) 15 November 2001.
342 Appl No 52750/99 (unreported) 4 February 2003.
343 [1992] 2 All ER 65.

to comply with article 8 of the Convention. The European Court is concerned only with whether English law provides an adequate remedy in a specific case in which it considers that there has been an invasion of privacy contrary to article 8(1) and not justifiable under article 8(2).[344]

Further, there was, he found, no need to modify common law doctrines order to satisfy the demands of Art 8 (para 52):

> . . . a finding that there was a breach of article 8 will only demonstrate that there was a gap in the English remedies for invasion of privacy which has since been filled by sections 6 and 7 of the 1998 Act. It does not require that the courts should provide an alternative remedy which distorts the principles of the common law.

It is notable that Lord Hoffmann did not deal with the question of proportionality in relation to negligent acts of public authorities. The internal rules applicable were designed in effect to prevent a breach of Art 8 if adhered to, in the sense that while strip searches prima facie create a breach of Art 8, the invasion of privacy can (arguably) be justified under Art 8(2) as proportionate to the aim – of preventing drug use in prison – pursued, *if* the search is fully compliant with the rules. Lord Hoffmann did not take that into account. The decision left open the possibility that only deliberate invasions of privacy would require a remedy, although it also found that even in such instances no remedy would be available at common law. However, at Strasbourg it was found that the treatment of the Wainwrights did amount to a breach of Art 8, although not of Art 3, in *Wainwright v UK*.[345]

The European Court of Human Rights took a different view as to the ambit of Art 8 in this context, in *Wainwright v UK*. The treatment, it was found, undoubtedly caused the applicants distress but did not, in the Court's view, reach the minimum level of severity prohibited by Art 3. Rather, the Court found that the case fell within the scope of Art 8.[346] The Court accepted that the search pursued the legitimate aim under Art 8(2) of fighting the drugs problem in the prison. On the other hand, it was not satisfied that the searches were proportionate to that aim in the manner in which they were carried out. Where procedures were laid down for the proper conduct of searches on outsiders to the prison who might very well be innocent of any wrongdoing, the prison authorities, it was found, were required to comply strictly with those safeguards and by rigorous precautions protect the dignity of those being searched as far as possible. The Court found that they did not do so in the applicants' case. Considering that the searches

---

344   He went on to look at the relevant authorities: 'So in *Earl Spencer v United Kingdom* 25 EHRR CD 105 it was satisfied that the action for breach of confidence provided an adequate remedy for the Spencers' complaint and looked no further into the rest of the armoury of remedies available to the victims of other invasions of privacy. Likewise, in *Peck v United Kingdom* (2003) 36 EHRR 41 the court expressed some impatience, at paragraph 103, at being given a *tour d'horizon* of the remedies provided and to be provided by English law to deal with every imaginable kind of invasion of privacy. It was concerned with whether Mr Peck (who had been filmed in embarrassing circumstances by a CCTV camera) had an adequate remedy when the film was widely published by the media. It came to the conclusion that he did not.'

345   Appl No 12350/04, 26 September 2006.

346   See the discussion of Art 8 in Chapter 2, pp 69–71

carried out on the applicants could not be regarded as 'necessary in a democratic society', the Court found that there had been a breach of Art 8.

In relation to *remedies* for breaches of Arts 3 or 8 in police detention, the Strasbourg decision does not add very much to that of the House of Lords as the HRA ss 7 and 8 now provides a remedy since the police are a public authority under s 6 HRA. But, importantly, the Strasbourg decision takes a more expansive view of Art 8-compliant treatment than the House of Lords did. If it is accepted that the findings on Art 8 need not be viewed as part of the ratio of the case in the House of Lords, since Lord Hoffmann appeared to leave the question of a breach of Art 8 open,[347] it would seem that the domestic courts should now apply the interpretation of Art 8 from *Wainwright v UK*.

The Court also observed that, while it was true that the applicants took domestic proceedings seeking damages for the searches and the effects they had had on them, they were unsuccessful, save as regards the instance of battery on Mr Wainwright. As regards the other elements of the strip-searches, the Court observed that the House of Lords found that the negligent action disclosed by the prison officers did not give grounds for any civil liability, in particular as there was no general tort of invasion of privacy. In those circumstances, the Court found that the applicants did not have available to them a means of obtaining redress for the interference with their rights under Art 8. There had therefore also been a violation of Art 13.

The Convention rights only lay down very broad guarantees and only reflect minimum standards. The detailed 'guarantees' of proper conditions of detention is found in Codes C and H. Thus in so far as certain standards for the conditions of detention are expressly stated, domestic law currently reflects the Art 8 or 3 guarantees in non-statutory rules alone. For example, the conduct of intimate searches is governed by s 55 of PACE, but its provisions are fleshed out in Annex A of Codes C and H. Strip-searches, as opposed to intimate searches, are covered only by part B of Annex A to Codes C and H. The use of force to conduct them is authorised by s 117 of PACE.[348] The provisions governing the conditions of detention mentioned in the *Greek* case arise only in Codes C and H, paras 8 and 9. Provisions in Code C and H, para 8 regarding the use of restraints, including handcuffs, in cells can be viewed as intended to ensure that Art 3 is not infringed.

Bearing in mind the quasi-legal status of the Codes, and the lack of a remedy for their breach, their provisions might be afforded, indirectly, a higher status due to their role in upholding the standards demanded by Arts 3 and 8, under ss 2 and 6 of the HRA.[349] The Codes might readily be viewed as analogous to the prison rules, at issue in *Wainwright*, and also of quasi-legal status. The point made by the Strasbourg Court in *Wainwright* to the effect that procedures laid down for the proper conduct of searches should be strictly complied with if no breach of Art 8 was to arise could readily be applied to the Code provisions. Those provisions are there to act as safeguards – in effect – against treatment that might otherwise breach Arts 8 or 3. In other words, they are there to ensure that basic human rights standards are maintained in that detainees

---

347 See Chapter 4, p 197 on the question of conflicts between House of Lords' decisions and subsequent Strasbourg rulings.
348 Clearly, criminal law applicable to indecent assault would not be applicable where the search was properly authorised.
349 See above, pp 1106–7.

are not treated in a disproportionately humiliating fashion, injured or otherwise maltreated in police custody – a matter that is of particular significance in relation to terrorist suspects, bearing in mind the length of time that they may be in detention. If the Code provisions are not complied with, the *Wainwright* decision implies that a breach of Art 3 or 8 might more readily be found under the HRA. Strasbourg was referring to persons probably innocent of any wrong-doing – visitors to a prison. Clearly, the fact of being a suspect in police custody is inherently humiliating and distressing. Thus the status of persons as suspects in police custody would have some impact on the proportionality analysis under Art 8. But since a number of Code H, D and C provisions are clearly in place in order to guard, so far as possible in the context, against invasions of privacy while in police custody, it can be assumed that they should be adhered to if a breach of Art 8 is not to arise.

Remedies under either common law or criminal law would not be applicable in certain instances of treatment non-compliant with the demands of Art 3 or Art 8. This would be the case where there was no physical contact with the detainee, as in the case of Ms Wainwright. Following the *Wainwright* decision, it is clear that there is no common law tortious remedy in respect of certain forms of humiliating privacy-invading treatment imposed upon persons by state agents. If they amount to a breach of Art 8 – or, if severe enough – of Art 3, the remedy will be available under ss 7 and 8 HRA. Sections 7 and 8 HRA therefore, provide guarantees against various forms of maltreatment in police detention, which are not currently duplicated in domestic statutory or common law provisions. In relation to Art 3, however, the guarantees are limited since Art 3 demands that such maltreatment should be of a high level of severity. Article 8 provides a guarantee of much more general application, covering preservation of dignity, so far as possible in this context. In general, in this context the HRA provides a remedy that was previously unavailable. Allegations of ill-treatment in police custody have frequently raised grave concerns;[350] they can now be addressed by the use of Arts 3 or 8 in actions directly against the police under s 7(1)(a) of the HRA.

The Strasbourg decision in *Wainwright* is arguably of great significance where no public authority is involved in perpetrating the Art 8-breaching treatment (even though it was given in the context of maltreatment by a public authority), but that is a matter outside the scope of this chapter.[351] Had Lord Hoffmann taken the path taken (arguably) by the House of Lords in *Campbell*,[352] in accepting an extension of the existing common law to cover the invasion of privacy at issue in *Wainwright* – even if denying the need for a remedy in the instant case – the UK would not have been found to have violated Art 13 as well as Art 8 at Strasbourg. The HRA was not in force at the time when the facts of *Wainwright* occurred. However, Lord Hoffmann could merely have relied on Art 8 as a means of influencing domestic law and extending it to cover the facts before

---

350   See the *Report of the European Committee for the Prevention of Torture and Inhuman or Degrading Treatment or Punishment*, based on a visit carried out from 8 to 17 September 1999. See also the Butler Report, 1998. *Inter alia*, the Report covers the case of Derek Treadaway (pp 37–38). He alleged that he had suffered ill-treatment, possibly amounting to torture, in police custody, and successfully sought judicial review (31 July 1997) of the decision of the CPS not to prosecute the officers involved. For relevant Convention jurisprudence, see above, Chapter 2, pp 45–48.

351   See Chapter 9, pp 817–20.

352   See Chapter 9, pp 911–13.

him, even without the assistance of s 6 HRA. He made it clear that if the HRA had been in force he would not have contemplated the possibility of extending the common law (obviously it would have been unnecessary to do so in relation to the instant case). Clearly, when the House of Lords decided the case they were aware of the findings of Lord Justice Sedley in *Douglas v Hello!*,[353] which were referred to in *Wainwright*, as to the potential effect of the Convention on the common law, albeit under the HRA. *Campbell* and *Douglas* obviously related to deliberate invasions of privacy, *Wainwright* to a negligent invasion. However, Art 8, it is now clear, covers negligent invasions of privacy, according to the findings in *Wainwright v UK*. Lord Hoffmann's judgment missed the point that such invasions still have to satisfy the doctrine of proportionality under Art 8(2). It also missed the point that private actors could subject persons to similar invasions of privacy (e.g. a requirement to submit to a search for drugs on the premises of the company that the employee works for),[354] but that even after the HRA came into force, no remedy would be available in such circumstances.

Searches of detained persons

Detained persons may not automatically be searched, but the power to search arrestees under s 32(1) of PACE is quite wide. It arises under s 32(1) if the suspect has been arrested somewhere other than a police station and a constable has reasonable grounds to suspect that an arrestee has anything on him which might be evidence relating to an offence or might be used to help him escape from custody or that he may present a danger to himself or others. The much wider power arises under s 32(2) and allows search, again on reasonable grounds, for anything which might be evidence of an offence or could help to effect an escape from lawful custody. The nature of the search must relate to the article it is suspected may be found; if it is a large item, the search may not involve more than removal of a coat. Such searching may occur routinely, but it must be possible to point to objectively justified grounds in each case which must not go beyond those specified.[355] A power of search also arises under s 54, as amended, allowing search to ascertain property the detainee has with him or her, which will apply if someone has been arrested at the police station or brought there after being arrested elsewhere. The custody officer must determine whether it is necessary to conduct a search for this purpose.

Intimate searches, bodily samples, swabs and impressions

Under s 55 PACE, an intimate search can only be ordered if an officer of the rank of superintendent or above has reasonable grounds for believing that an article which could cause physical injury to a detained person or others at the police station has been concealed or that the person has concealed a Class A drug which he intends to supply to another or to export. Even if such suspicion arises, the search should not be carried

---

353 See Chapter 9, pp 903–5.
354 This would also be the case in respect of an invasion of privacy during the course of perpetrating criminal actions, such as rape. Obviously, redress would be available under the civil law for battery, but not for invasion of privacy.
355 *Eet* [1983] Crim LR 806.

out unless there is no other means of removing the object. Before it can be carried out, the reasons for undertaking it must be explained to the suspect and a reminder given of the entitlement to legal advice.[356] An intimate search at a police station may only be carried out by a registered medical practitioner or registered nurse unless, under Codes C and H Annex A, the authorising officer considers, in the case of a concealed object which could cause injury, that it is not practicable to wait, in which case a police officer of the same sex as the suspect can carry it out. Under Codes C and H an intimate search at a police station of a juvenile or a mentally disordered or mentally handicapped person must take place only in the presence of the appropriate adult of the same sex, unless the suspect requests otherwise.[357] Codes C and H Annex A provide that an intimate search must be conducted with proper regard to the 'sensitivity and vulnerability' of the suspect. It must take place in a completely private room in the presence of two persons of the same sex as the detainee. A juvenile has the right to have the appropriate adult present unless he or she requests otherwise in the presence of the adult.[358]

Codes C and H Annex A also make provision for strip searches. They must also be conducted with proper regard to the 'sensitivity and vulnerability' of the suspect, must not be used routinely, must take place in a private room and must be conducted by two officers of the same sex as the detainee. The suspect is required to expose first the upper half of his body and then the lower but not normally to stand completely naked. Bodily orifices are not to be touched. Searches should not be carried out routinely, but only if necessary to remove an article that the officer reasonably considers the detainee might have concealed.

Evidence obtained from the suspect himself can identify the suspect as the person who committed the offence in question, or can demonstrate that he is innocent of it. Identification procedures are largely governed by the provisions of Code D which has, as its overall aim, the creation of safeguards against wrongful identification, bearing in mind that mistaken identification can be a very significant cause of wrongful convictions.[359] Code D, together with Codes C and H, Annex A, contains provisions which are intended to safeguard vulnerable groups and to ensure that the invasion of privacy represented by some methods of identification is kept to a minimum consistent with the Code's overall aim. Many of the procedures will only take place with the suspect's consent, although if consent is not forthcoming, this may be used in evidence against him or her.[360] In the case of a mentally handicapped or disordered person, consent given out of the presence of the 'appropriate adult' will not be treated as true consent while the consent of a juvenile alone will not be treated as valid if the adult does not also consent.[361]

---

356 See Codes C and H, para 4.1 and Annex A.
357 Under Annex A, para 5 in the case of a juvenile, the search may take place in the absence of the appropriate adult only if the juvenile signifies in the presence of the appropriate adult that he prefers the search to be done in his absence and the appropriate adult agrees.
358 Codes C and H, Annex A, para 6.
359 The Criminal Law Revision Committee 1972 considered that wrongful identification was the greatest cause of wrongful convictions (para 196).
360 Codes C and H, Annex A, para 2A.
361 Code D, para 2.12.

Bodily samples, swabs and impressions may be taken in respect of recordable offences. The relevant provisions are ss 62 and 63 PACE, as amended, and the Terrorism Act 2000, Sched 8. Intimate samples may be taken if the officer has reasonable grounds to believe that such an impression or sample will tend to confirm or disprove the suspect's involvement in the offence and with the suspect's written consent. But the suspect must be warned that if they refuse without good cause the refusal may be used against them at trial.[362] The suspect must be warned using the warning as set out in Code D, Note 6D. He must also be reminded of his entitlement to have free legal advice and the

---

362 For non-terrorist suspects, s 62 PACE governs the taking of intimate samples and s 63 PACE covers the taking of non-intimate samples. Terrorist suspects are governed by the Terrorism Act 2000, Sched 8, paras 10–13 in respect of intimate and non-intimate samples. See also Code D, para 6. Under s 62 PACE:

(1) Subject to section 63B below an intimate sample may be taken from a person in police detention only –

    (a) if a police officer of at least the rank of inspector authorises it to be taken; and
    (b) if the appropriate consent is given.

(1A) An intimate sample may be taken from a person who is not in police detention but from whom, in the course of the investigation of an offence, two or more non-intimate samples suitable for the same means of analysis have been taken which have proved insufficient –

    (a) if a police officer of at least the rank of inspector authorises it to be taken; and
    (b) if the appropriate consent is given.

(2) An officer may only give an authorisation under subsection (1) or (1A) above if he has reasonable grounds –

    (a) for suspecting the involvement of the person from whom the sample is to be taken in a recordable offence; and
    (b) for believing that the sample will tend to confirm or disprove his involvement.

(3) An officer may give an authorisation under subsection (1) or (1A) above orally or in writing but, if he gives it orally, he shall confirm it in writing as soon as is practicable.
(4) The appropriate consent must be given in writing . . .

   . . .

(9A) In the case of any other form of intimate sample, except in the case of a sample of urine, the sample may be taken from a person only by –

    (a) a registered medical practitioner; or
    (b) a registered health care professional.

(10) Where the appropriate consent to the taking of an intimate sample from a person was refused without good cause, in any proceedings against that person for an offence –

    (a) the court, in determining –

        (i)   whether to commit that person for trial; or
        (ii)   whether there is a case to answer; and

    (aa) a judge, in deciding whether to grant an application made by the accused under paragraph 2 of Schedule 3 to the Crime and Disorder Act 1998 (applications for dismissal); and

    (b) the court or jury, in determining whether that person is guilty of the offence charged, may draw such inferences from the refusal as appear proper.

   . . .

(12) Nothing in this section applies to a person arrested or detained under the terrorism provisions; and subsection (1A) shall not apply where the non-intimate samples mentioned in that subsection were taken under paragraph 10 of Schedule 8 to the Terrorism Act 2000.

reminder must be noted in the custody record. Intimate samples[363] may only be taken under ss 62 PACE, as amended, or under the Terrorism Act 2000, Sched 8 para 12, by a registered medical or dental practitioner or registered nurse, whereas non-intimate samples[364] may be taken by a police officer. They may be taken without consent if an officer of the rank of inspector or above has reasonable They may be taken without consent if an officer of the rank of inspector or above has reasonable grounds for believing that the sample will tend to confirm or disprove his involvement in it.[365]

A person arrested or detained under the terrorism provisions can have intimate samples taken under the Terrorism Act 2000, Schedule para 12 under similar provisions, and a refusal to allow the sample to be taken can be used against the suspect under the Terrorism Act 2000; Schedule para 13.

363 'Blood, semen or any other tissue fluid, urine, saliva or pubic hair or a swab taken from a person's body orifice' (PACE, s 65).

364 Including hair other than pubic hair or a sample taken from a nail or from under a nail or a skin impression (PACE, s 65, as amended by CJPOA 1994, s 80(5)(b)).

365 See PACE s 63, as amended and Code D paras 6.5–6.9. The Terrorism Act 2000 Sched 8 para 10 covers non-intimate samples taken from terrorist suspects. Under s 63:

(1) Except as provided by this section, a non-intimate sample may not be taken from a person without the appropriate consent.

(2) Consent to the taking of a non-intimate sample must be given in writing.

(2A) A non-intimate sample may be taken from a person without the appropriate consent if two conditions are satisfied.

(2B) The first is that the person is in police detention in consequence of his arrest for a recordable offence.

(2C) The second is that –

(a) he has not had a non-intimate sample of the same type and from the same part of the body taken in the course of the investigation of the offence by the police, or

(b) he has had such a sample taken but it proved insufficient.

(3) A non-intimate sample may be taken from a person without the appropriate consent if –

(a) he is being held in custody by the police on the authority of a court; and

(b) an officer of at least the rank of inspector authorises it to be taken without the appropriate consent.

(3A) A non-intimate sample may be taken from a person (whether or not he is in police detention or held in custody by the police on the authority of a court) without the appropriate consent if –

(a) he has been charged with a recordable offence or informed that he will be reported for such an offence; and

(b) either he has not had a non-intimate sample taken from him in the course of the investigation of the offence by the police or he had a non-intimate sample taken from him but either it was not suitable for the same means of analysis or, though so suitable, the sample proved insufficient.

(3B) A non-intimate sample may be taken from a person without the appropriate consent if he has been convicted of a recordable offence.

(3C) A non-intimate sample may also be taken from a person without the appropriate consent if he is a person to whom section 2 of the Criminal Evidence (Amendment) Act 1997 applies (persons detained following acquittal on grounds of insanity or finding of unfitness to plead).

(4)   An officer may only give an authorisation under subsection (3) above if he has reasonable grounds –

  (a) for suspecting the involvement of the person from whom the sample is to be taken in a recordable offence; and

  (b) for believing that the sample will tend to confirm or disprove his involvement ...

(6)   Where (a) an authorisation has been given; and (b) it is proposed that a non-intimate sample shall be taken in pursuance of the authorisation, an officer shall inform the person from whom the sample is to be taken – (i) of the giving of the authorisation; and (ii) of the grounds for giving it.

(7)   The duty imposed by subsection (6)(ii) above includes a duty to state the nature of the offence in which it is suspected that the person from whom the sample is to be taken has been involved.

(8)   If a non-intimate sample is taken from a person by virtue of subsection (3) above –

  (a) the authorisation by virtue of which it was taken; and

  (b) the grounds for giving the authorisation, shall be recorded as soon as is practicable after the sample is taken.

(8A) In a case where by virtue of [subsection (2A), (3A)] [FN1], (3B) or (3C) above a sample is taken from a person without the appropriate consent –

  (a) he shall be told the reason before the sample is taken; and

  (b) the reason shall be recorded as soon as practicable after the sample is taken.

(8B) If a non-intimate sample is taken from a person at a police station, whether with or without the appropriate consent –

  (a) before the sample is taken, an officer shall inform him that it may be the subject of a speculative search; and

  (b) the fact that the person has been informed of this possibility shall be recorded as soon as practicable after the sample has been taken.

(9)   If a non-intimate sample is taken from a person detained at a police station, the matters required to be recorded by subsection (8) or (8A) or (8B) above shall be recorded in his custody record ...

(10) Nothing in this section applies to a person arrested or detained under the terrorism provisions.

(11) Nothing in this section applies to a person arrested under an extradition arrest power.

A person arrested or detained under the terrorism provisions can have non-intimate samples taken under the Terrorism Act 2000, Schedule para 10 under similar provisions.

Chapter 12

Police questioning: safeguards for suspects

I Introduction[1]

In crime control terms, the police interview occupies a central position in the criminal justice system; it represents an effective use of resources, since if a confession becomes available, the criminal process is likely to be accelerated.[2] In particular, since *mens rea* is a requirement of most offences, admissions provide the most readily available means of establishing the state of mind of the suspect at the relevant time. The interview may, in effect, replace the trial, since its results may play a key part in the pre-trial risk-balancing and negotiating process in which the suspect decides whether to plead guilty. Clearly, the stronger the risk of a conviction which would be unaccompanied by a sentence discount, the less likely it is that he or she will plead not guilty.[3] If the suspect has confessed or made some admissions, he may feel that there is no point in pleading not guilty even if the admissions are false, exaggerated or misleading. The interview may also frequently play a part in general criminal intelligence gathering.[4] On their face, the crime control advantages of the interview are readily apparent although, clearly, if an intimidating atmosphere and a lack of due process safeguards lead a suspect to make false admissions that cannot advance crime control ends.

From a due process perspective the police interview is largely unjustifiable, since its *raison d'être* is to secure admissions which probably would not otherwise be secured; it therefore undermines the privilege against self-incrimination. This due process norm traditionally underpinned criminal justice practice,[5] but it was gradually

---

1 For further comment, particularly on the 1984 Act and on the relevant provisions under the Criminal Justice and Public Order Act 1994, as amended, see: Sanders, A and Young, R, *Criminal Justice*, 3rd edn, 2007; Feldman. D, *Civil Liberties and Human Rights in England and Wales*, 2nd edn, 2002, Chapters 5 and 9; Clark, D *Bevan and Lidstone's the Investigation of Crime*, 2004; Levenson, H and Fairweather, F, *Police Powers*, 1990; McConville, M, Sanders, A and Leng, R, *The Case for the Prosecution*, 1991; Bailey, SH, Harris, DJ and Jones, BL, *Civil Liberties: Cases and Materials*, 2002, Chapter 2; Zander, M, *The Police and Criminal Evidence Act 1984*, 2003; Reiner, R and Leigh, LH, 'Police powers', in McCrudden, C and Chambers, G (eds), *Individual Rights and the Law in Britain*, 1994; Klug, F, Starmer, K and Weir, S, *The Three Pillars of Liberty*, 1996.
2 See McConville, M (1993) RCCJ Research Study No 13, 1993; Baldwin, J, 'Police interview techniques; establishing truth of proof' (1993) 33 Br J Criminology 325.
3 See Sanders and Young, *Criminal Justice*, 3rd edn, 2007, Chapter 8, Part 2.
4 Maguire and Morris, RCCJ Research Study No 5, 1992.
5 The 1912 Judges' Rules did not allow police interrogation, although the police could invite and receive voluntary statements.

abandoned until it became accepted in the pre-PACE years that the purpose of the interrogation was to obtain admissions.[6] The precarious position of the interview from this perspective explains, it is suggested, why it seemed necessary, when PACE placed police interrogations on a formal basis, to infuse due process elements into them. Such elements are intended to detract from any impression that the confession is involuntary. The police, however, remain the gatekeepers to these safeguards, which seem to run counter to their crime control concerns, and therefore they may not be observed or, more subtly, the weaknesses and loopholes in the interviewing scheme will be discovered and explored.

PACE strongly reflects this uneasy compromise between crime control and due process: the detainee can be detained for the purposes of obtaining a confession under s 37(2), but a number of safeguards were created which are influenced by due process concerns to lessen the coerciveness of the interview and to ensure its integrity and reliability so that it can be used as evidence. The extensive and complex rules of Code C which appear to surround police interviews with a range of safeguards, afford the interview an appearance of due process. A number of flaws, however, in due process terms, were built into the scheme when it was first introduced. Most significantly, there are no sanctions for breach of the interviewing rules, including those arising under PACE itself, apart from the possibility of disciplinary action.[7] There is uncertainty as to when an exchange with police becomes an interview so as to attract all the safeguards. There is scope for interviewing away from the police station, thereby evading the most significant safeguards, those of access to legal advice and tape recording. Virtually no guidance is given as to the acceptable limits of 'persuasive' interviewing, so long as it is not oppressive. This is particularly a matter of concern in respect of the questioning of terrorist suspects, especially bearing in mind the length of the detention to which they can be subjected – up to 28 days at present. As discussed below, the level of protection for due process is lower at a number of points than for non-terrorist suspects. Code H, which governs their treatment in police questioning, does recognise to an extent that such lengthy detention has particular implications in terms of its mental impact,[8] but, although there are a number of provisions for obtaining medical aid in respect of such suspects, the problem of relying on admissions made after a lengthy period of detention are not, it is argued, afforded sufficient recognition.

The link between due process in the custodial period and at trial is recognised in Art 6, under HRA, Sched 1. As Chapter 13 will demonstrate, arrest and detention and, where relevant, treatment within that period may be considered under Art 6, whether or not a breach of Art 5 or any other Article is established.[9] Under Art 6, the European Court of Human Rights has developed the concept of the fairness of the trial 'as a whole', allowing for consideration of custodial treatment in a broad sense. In *Saidi v France*[10] the Court said that its role was to determine 'whether the

---

6 *Holgate-Mohammed v Duke* [1984] 1 AC 437; [1984] 1 All ER 1054.
7 This possibility became even more remote when PACE, s 67(8), rendering breach of the Codes automatically a breach of the police Disciplinary Code, was repealed in 1994 by the Police and Magistrates' Courts Act 1994, s 37 and Sched 9.
8 See also Chapter 11, p 1174.
9 See pp 1259–62.
10 (1994) 17 EHRR 251.

proceedings in their entirety ... were fair'.[11] In *Barbéra, Messegué and Jabardo*,[12] the trial taken as a whole could not be said to be fair. This was partly due to features of the treatment of the defendants pre-trial, taken cumulatively. They were held for a substantial period of time incommunicado and when they confessed to the police they did not have legal assistance. Nevertheless, their confessions were significant in later questioning by examining judges. The unfair pre-trial treatment clearly had a tendency to render the trial unfair, although it is improbable that such a tendency would have been found without the unfairness at the hearing itself.[13] Nevertheless, the findings in *Barbéra* are significant, since they emphasise the need to consider the whole criminal process, including any custodial period, in determining fairness. It might be appropriate where the pre-trial custodial treatment, including the manner of questioning, had had a cumulatively harsh effect, to stay the prosecution for abuse of process; or exclusion of admissions obtained during, or as a result of, a course of harsh or adverse treatment might be appropriate in order to satisfy Art 6. Civil actions may be brought against the police, including claims for damages in respect of breaches of the rights. These possibilities are discussed further in Chapter 13.[14]

This chapter does not concentrate only on questioning of suspects inside the police station because contact between police and suspect takes place a long time before the police station is reached, and this has been recognised in the provisions of Part V of PACE and Codes of Practice C and H, which govern treatment of suspects and interviewing, but have some application outside as well as inside the police station. It should be noted that many of the key provisions relating to interviewing are contained in Codes C or H rather than in PACE itself. The most crucial events during a person's contact with police will probably be the interviews, and therefore this section will concentrate on the safeguards available which are intended to ensure that interviews are fairly conducted and are properly recorded wherever they take place. This chapter examines the key aspects of the interviewing scheme by considering the points at which the various safeguards must be in place; the conduct of the interview; the means of recording the interview. It then goes on to consider the right of access to legal advice, the curtailed right to silence and its relationship with the legal advice scheme. The effect of flaws in the pre-trial procedures discussed here on the fairness of the trial is considered in Chapter 13.

The PACE Codes and police questioning

Under the pre-PACE rules, safeguards for the interview were governed largely by the Judges' Rules and Administrative Directions to the Police[15] and s 62 of the Criminal Law Act 1977. The latter provided for access to a solicitor (although it was frequently ignored). The former provided, *inter alia*, for the issuing of cautions when a person was charged (not necessarily when he was arrested) and for the exclusion in evidence of statements and confessions which were not 'voluntary' (see below). Under PACE, those

---

11 Paragraph 43.

12 A 14 6(2) (1989).

13 There were 'unexpected changes' in the membership of the court, the hearing was brief; most importantly, there was a failure to adduce and discuss evidence orally in the accused's presence.

14 See pp 1303–10.

15 E.g., Home Office Circular 89/1978, Appendices A and B.

rules were replaced by rules contained either in the Act itself or in Code of Practice C. As discussed below, most of the safeguards related to questioning are contained only in the Codes.

It might be expected that the distribution of the provisions governing the interviewing scheme would give some recognition to theoretical differences in status between PACE, the Codes, the Notes for Guidance and Home Office circulars, the most fundamental provisions being contained in the Act and so on. In fact, this is not the case: although the Act contains the right to legal advice in s 58, and the right to have someone informed of detention in s 56, the other important features of the interviewing scheme, including the right to silence,[16] are governed by non-statutory provisions. Just as it cannot be assumed that in due process terms Code provisions are less weighty than statutory ones, equally the Notes for Guidance and even the Circulars[17] do not invariably contain less crucial provisions than the Codes. In other words, the distribution of provisions between the four tiers does not follow a consistent pattern: the source of a provision has an effect on the likelihood that it will be complied with, but does not necessarily say much about its significance.

The original interviewing scheme under Code C was revised in 1991 and improved by the introduction of tape recording under Code E. That revision, was, it is suggested, concerned wholly with improving the scheme's due process elements, albeit in a manner best described as superficial: the rules became more complex in order to deal with police evasion of them, but their fundamental flaws were hardly addressed. Despite the relationship a number of commentators had observed to exist between coerced confessions and miscarriages of justice,[18] the recommendations made by the 1993 Runciman Royal Commission on Criminal Procedure, which might, minor as they were, have continued the improvements undertaken in 1991, were largely ignored.[19] Under the Major Government, the disciplinary sanction for breaching the Codes was removed under s 37(f) of the Police and Magistrates Court Act 1994, and the right to silence was curtailed under ss 34–37 of the CJPOA 1994. Largely as a consequence of the changes introduced under the CJPOA, the PACE Codes were revised once again in 1995; this revision, unlike the previous one, appeared to have a dual aim: it seemed to be intended to have some weak due process impact in eradicating loopholes, but it also introduced various provisions in order to give effect to the curtailment of the right to silence. These changes indicated a move away from the rather ineffectual attempts previously undertaken to protect the due process elements in the interviewing process.

---

16 As contained in the caution: Code C, para 10.5 (Code H, para 10.4) (and, of course, recognised at common law).

17 E.g., a provision in the 1991 Circular required that where a suspect had changed his mind after requesting legal advice, a note should be made in the custody record of the reason for the change. The provision was presumably included with a view to discouraging police officers from providing misleading information which might induce the suspect to forgo legal advice.

18 See Walker, *Miscarriages of Justice*, 1999, p 54.

19 E.g., the Runciman Report, Chapter 4, para 23 put forward a recommendation to retain the right to silence, in the context of improved safeguards for suspects, taking into account recommendations intended to lead to improvement in the quality of custodial legal advice. The Report made other proposals for improvement of the interviewing scheme including the video taping of a waiver of legal advice (Proposal 57) and a special warning to juries regarding uncorroborated confessions (Chapter 4, paras 56–87).

Codes C and E were issued in revised versions which came into effect in 1999, but no radical change from the 1995 version was made. The opportunity presented by the 1999 revision of taking forward the improvements made in 1991 was therefore lost, as was the possibility of addressing some of the more fundamental flaws of Code C, in the light of the inception of the HRA.

The 2003 version of Code C contained the significant restriction on drawing adverse inference from silence where no opportunity to have access to legal advice had been given, reflecting amendment that had occurred to the CJPOA, as explained below. Code F governing visual recording was introduced in 2004. Code C was revised again in 2006 and Code H, covering questioning of terrorist suspects, was introduced. Codes C and H reflected the 2003 changes, but were there were some further minor changes, discussed below. The failures to provide any sanction for breach of the Codes, to address the uncertainty as to the status of the Notes, which continue to contain significant protections for due process, to reduce the scope for out of station interviews and afford such interviews greater due process protection, or to remove provisions which are arguably not fully in harmony with the Convention rights, were all continued in the 2006 revision. These flaws, and their implications, are discussed at the relevant points, below. The interviewing rules continue to form the most detailed and complex part of the whole scheme, and the tendency for the powers to appear in PACE, while the suspects' rights appear only in the Codes, or in Notes for Guidance, has only become more marked.

Vulnerable groups and police questioning

Throughout Codes C and H, recognition is given to the special needs of certain vulnerable groups in police interviews: juveniles, the mentally disordered or handicapped, those not proficient in English, the hearing impaired or the visually handicapped. Juveniles and the mentally handicapped or disordered should be attended by an 'appropriate adult'. The role of the appropriate adult has received greater recognition in the later versions of Code C. Under Note 1F of Codes C and H, the solicitor should not be the appropriate adult; this provision was included in response to some evidence that the police had been treating the solicitor as the appropriate adult, thereby producing a conflict of interests.[20] It was thought that the roles of legal adviser and appropriate adult differed; the same person could not therefore fulfil both. It should be noted that the juvenile can be interviewed without the presence of an appropriate adult if an officer of the rank of superintendent or above considers that delay will involve an immediate risk of harm to persons or serious loss of or serious damage to property.[21] At various points to be discussed, the particular vulnerability of juveniles is recognised, but although this is to be welcomed, research suggests that the treatment of juveniles, particularly during interviews, is still sometimes unsatisfactory.[22]

---

20 LAG Bulletin, November 1989.

21 See Codes C and H, para 11(d): urgent interviews.

22 Evans, R, 'The conduct of police interviews with juveniles' (1993) Home Office Research Study No 8. On the treatment of juveniles generally, see Dixon, D, 'Juvenile suspects and PACE', in Freestone, D (ed), *Children and the Law*, 1990, Hull University Press, pp 107–29.

The notification of rights must be given in the presence of the adult,[23] which may mean repeating the notification, but if the suspect wants legal advice, this should not be delayed until the adult arrives.[24] The appropriate adult who is present at an interview should be informed that he or she is not expected to act simply as an observer; and also that the purposes of being present are, first, to advise the person being interviewed and to observe whether or not the interview is being conducted properly and fairly and, second, to facilitate communication with the person being interviewed.[25]

It will be found in discussion in Chapter 13 of unreliable confessions, that mentally handicapped or disordered persons are very likely to make an untrue or exaggerated confession and therefore it is particularly important that all the safeguards available should be in place when such a person is interviewed. However, there is provision for urgent interviewing of such persons without the appropriate adult if an officer of the rank of superintendent or above considers that delay will involve an immediate risk of harm to persons or serious loss of or serious damage to, property.[26] A deaf or speech-handicapped person, or someone who has difficulty understanding English, must only be interviewed in the presence of an interpreter,[27] but this may be waived in the case of urgent interviewing under Annex C.

Terrorist suspects

The interviewing scheme had, from its inception, created a twin-track system under PACE, the counter-terrorist legislation and the Codes, that is, one in which terrorist suspects were exposed to a regime adhering to a lower level of due process than that applicable in respect of 'ordinary' suspects. This regime afforded the coercive elements of the scheme greater rein both formally and informally. Most obviously, as explained in Chapter 13, terrorist suspects could be exposed to a much longer period of detention, which allowed greater scope for prolonged pressure during interrogation. The interviewing regime for such suspects was also less protective. The counter-terrorist scheme introduced by the Labour Government under the Terrorism Act 2000 (TA), its Codes of Practice and the 1999 revision of Codes C and E not only confirmed and extended the twin track system, but applied it to a much wider and more diverse range of suspects. The twin-track system has now been placed on a more formal basis, while at the same time the detention period has been extended to 28 days – although clearly most suspects will not stay in detention for all of that period. Code H was introduced in 2006, applying only to terrorist suspects. It covers the questioning and detention of such suspects, while non-terrorist suspects continue to be covered by Code C. The only new concession to due process introduced under the TA is the extension of audio recording, already occurring on a voluntary basis, to interviews with terrorist suspects, as explained below. The acceptance of the primacy of crime control values as underpinning police interviewing, reflected in the changes undertaken in the CJPOA,

---

23 Paragraph 3.17 (Code H, para 3.18).
24 This used not to be the case: Note 3G and Annex E, Note E2. Now Code C, para 6.5A and Code H, para 6.6 imply that it is.
25 See Code C, para 11.17; Code H, para 11.10.
26 See Codes C and H, para 11.(d).
27 Paragraph 13.

marked a turning point in criminal justice policies which was unaffected by the change of government in 1997.

Notification of rights

When the detainee arrives at the police station, he or she will be 'booked in'. The crucial nature of this stage in the proceedings is made clear below in relation to the discussion of the legal advice provisions. Under para 3 of Codes C and H, a person must be informed orally and by written notice of four rights on arrival at the police station after arrest: the right, arising under s 56 of PACE, to have someone informed of his detention;[28] the right to consult a solicitor and the fact that independent legal advice is available free of charge; the right to consult the other Codes of Practice, and the right to silence as embodied in the caution.

2 Police interviews

Interviews may be formal or informal. They may consist of questioning in the street, before arrest. Street interviewing remains at quite a high level,[29] while the key due process safeguards of access to legal advice and audio recording continue to be reserved for formal interviews within the police station. The caution which, as suggested below, serves both crime control and due process purposes, can be, and in most instances should be, used outside as well as inside the police station, with the result that the suspect is warned of the dangers of failing to speak before the key safeguards can be in place. Due process protection outside the police station is minimal; it consists only of contemporaneous note-taking under caution if an interview is occurring or accurate non-contemporaneous note-taking if the exchange is not an interview. Relevant non-interview exchanges with juveniles and mentally disordered persons may be admissible in evidence even though no adult is present.

Not only, therefore, is due process virtually abandoned in relation to out of police station exchanges and interviews, they may also have a structural formative influence on formal interviews and ultimately on the outcome of the process,[30] thereby undermining the protection available for such interviews. Suspects may feel, rightly or wrongly, that they have already prejudiced their position too far during informal exchanges to attempt to retrieve it in a formal taped interview; therefore, any confession made in such an interview – or any ill-considered silence – may not be truly voluntary. Thus, it is extremely important to determine how far the scheme leaves scope for exchanges to occur before the police station is reached.

---

28 Under para 5.1, if the person cannot be contacted, the person in charge of detention or of the investigation has discretion to allow further attempts until the information has been conveyed (see Notes 5C and 5D to Codes C and H). Section 56 PACE is subject to exceptions, similar to those under s 58 in respect of access to legal advice; for those s 58 exceptions, see pp 1216–17 below.

29 See Brown, Ellis and Larcombe, *Home Office Research Study No 129*, 1993; the study showed that questioning or unsolicited comment occurred outside the station in 24% of cases. The Runciman Royal Commission found that around 10% of interviews took place outside the police station: RCCJ Report, Cm 2263, 1993; see also Sanders and Young, *Criminal Justice*, 2007, pp 259–63.

30 See *James* [1996] Crim LR 650.

From both a due process and a crime control perspective, it would not be appropriate to address the leeway in the scheme for informal interviewing by requiring that, where sufficient suspicion is present, suspects should always be arrested and taken to the police station before any exchange occurs. In crime control terms, this might not represent an efficient use of resources since some unnecessary arrests would be made. In due process terms, there are some disadvantages in police station interviewing: the element of detention is coercive and the fact of detention may lead suspects to make admissions in order to leave it. Rather, the due process 'deficit' in street exchanges may be addressed, to an extent, by applying stronger safeguards to such interviewing[31] and, as discussed in Chapter 13, by giving careful consideration, under Art 6, to the admission of such exchanges as evidence.

The most significant safeguards available for interviews under PACE, the TA and Codes C, E and H include contemporaneous noting down of the interview or audio-recording, the ability to verify and sign the notes of the interview as a correct record, the legal advice provisions and, where appropriate, the presence of an adult. One of the most important issues in relation to these safeguards and reflected in the current revision of Code C,[32] is the question when they come into play. There may be a number of stages in a particular investigation beginning with first contact between police and suspect and perhaps ending with the charge. At various points the safeguards mentioned have to come into play and two factors can be identified which decide which safeguards should be in place at a particular time. First, it must be asked whether an exchange between police and suspect can be termed an interview and secondly, whether it took place inside the police station or was lawfully conducted outside it.

Interviews and non-interviews[33]

Code C creates a complex scheme in relation to the difference between interviews and non-interviews, and, to add to the complexity, Code H creates a scheme which differs from it in various significant respects. The correct interpretation of the term 'interview' under the original Code C scheme was highly significant because the relevant safeguards were unavailable unless an exchange[34] between police officer and suspect was designated an interview. The term therefore tended to be given a wide interpretation[35] and eventually the definition given to it by the Court of Appeal in *Matthews*[36] – 'any discussion or talk between suspect and police officer' – brought within its ambit many exchanges far removed from formal interviews. It also covered many interviewees, as it spoke in terms of 'suspects', not arrestees. However, it was qualified by the

---

31 Using hand-held tape recorders and notifying the suspect of the right of access to legal advice as part of the caution.

32 This was also very much an issue in relation to the 1991 and, to an extent, the 1995 revisions.

33 See Fenwick, H, 'Confessions, recording rules and miscarriages of justice' [1993] Crim LR 174–84.

34 'Exchange' will be used throughout this section to denote any verbal interaction between suspect and police officer, including unsolicited admissions.

35 The Court of Appeal in *Absolam* (1989) 88 Cr App R 332 defined it as 'a series of questions directed by the police to a suspect with a view to obtaining admissions'. This definition was quite wide in that it obviously included informal questioning.

36 [1990] Cr App R 43; [1990] Crim LR 190, CA, transcript from LEXIS.

ruling in *Scott*[37] that unsolicited admissions cannot amount to 'interviews' and by the ruling in *Marsh*[38] to the same effect as regards 'genuine requests' from the police for information. In *Marsh*, police officers investigating a burglary suddenly came across wraps of papers and asked the appellant about them; the questions and answers were admissible although no caution had been given because until that point, the officers had had no reason to suspect her of any drug-related offence. The ruling in *Marsh* bears some resemblance to that in *Maguire*[39] which pre-dated *Matthews*. It was determined that questioning an arrestee near the scene of the crime apparently in order to elicit an innocent explanation did not constitute an interview. Thus, the original interpretation of an interview created some leeway – but not much – for gathering (or apparently gathering) admissions in informal situations before any safeguards were in place.

In one respect, distinguishing between interviews and non-interviews is not as crucial under the current scheme as it was previously: under Code C, para 11.13 as revised, any comments relevant to the offence made by a suspected person outside the context of an interview must be accurately recorded[40] and then verified and signed by the suspect. However, making such a distinction is still highly significant, because it remains the first step towards bringing the other safeguards into play. Code H does not contain an equivalent of para 11.13; it merely provides in Note 11 E that significant statements (para 11.4) outside the context of the interview must be 'recorded'.

A definition of the term 'interview' is now contained in Code C, para 11.1A which reads: 'An interview is the questioning of a person regarding his involvement or suspected involvement in a criminal offence or offences which by virtue of para 10.1 of Code C must be carried out under caution.' In contrast, Code H provides in para 11.1: 'An interview is the questioning of a person arrested on suspicion of being a terrorist, which under para 10.1 must be carried out under caution.'

Code C paragraph 10.1 reads:

> A person whom there are grounds to suspect of an offence must be cautioned before any questions about it (or further questions if it is his answers to previous questions which provide the grounds for suspicion) are put to him regarding his involvement or suspected involvement in that offence if his answers or his silence (i.e. failure or refusal to answer a question or to answer satisfactorily) may be given in evidence to a court in a prosecution. He therefore need not be cautioned if questions are put to him for other purposes, for example, solely to establish his identity or his ownership of any vehicle or to obtain any information in accordance with any relevant statutory requirement ... or in furtherance of the proper and effective conduct of a search.

Code H, para 10.1 reads:

---

37 [1991] Crim LR 56, CA. See also *Younis* [1990] Crim LR 425, CA.
38 [1991] Crim LR 455.
39 (1990) 90 Cr App R 115; [1989] Crim LR 815, CA.
40 It may be noted that the weight actually given to this provision may depend on the question of whether its breach may be described as substantial and significant (see below, Chapter 13, p 1280); in this respect it is disturbing to note a first instance decision in which it was found that it should not be so described: *Oransaye* [1993] Crim LR 772.

A person whom there are grounds to suspect of an offence must be cautioned before any questions about an offence, or further questions if the answers provide the grounds for suspicion are put to them, if either the suspect's answers or silence ... may be given in evidence to a court in a prosecution.

The differences between the Code H and C definitions of an interview are considered below. It may be noted that the list of examples of instances under Code C, para 10.1 in which no caution would be necessary is not exhaustive. No such definition appeared in the original Code, but Note 12A read: 'The purpose of any interview is to obtain from the person concerned his explanation of the facts and not necessarily to obtain an admission.' The current definition obviously differs from this considerably and differs even more from the definition of an interview contained in *Matthews*.[41] It echoes the rulings of the Court of Appeal in *Maguire*[42] and *Marsh*[43] in attempting to draw a distinction between questioning a person regarding suspected involvement in an offence and questioning for other purposes. It appears that cautioning would not be required if the information obtained is in fact relevant to the offence, but the questioning was not directed towards uncovering such information. Such an interpretation would be in conformity with the ruling in *Marsh* that the level of suspicion excited in police officers present at the scene determines when an exchange becomes an interview. This approach is readily justifiable. However, para 11.1A combined with para 10.1 does not make it sufficiently clear that where an explanation of the facts does relate to suspected involvement in an offence and is either perceived to do so by the officer concerned or would be by the ordinary reasonable officer,[44] an interview will take place.

Thus, Code C, para 11.1A combined with para 10.1 may on occasion have acted as an invitation to police officers to play down the level of suspicion excited by the circumstances in order to demonstrate that no interview took place. Such tactics would amount to a self-fulfilling prophecy, in the sense that the officer concerned would have an interest in viewing the exchange as a non-interview requiring only accurate rather than contemporaneous recording; such recording would create more scope for giving the exchanges the character of a non-interview, and it would therefore appear for future purposes that a non-interview did indeed take place. The only person able to impede this process would be the suspect, who must be asked to verify and sign the record of the exchanges; it is unlikely, however, that he would appreciate the implications of what had occurred.

Arguably, the Code C, para 11.1A and Code H, para 11.1 tests must be qualified by the ruling of the Court of Appeal in *Weekes*.[45] Once an exchange becomes an interview, that fact will have a retrospective effect on earlier exchanges; if safeguards applicable to an interview are not available in respect of such exchanges, they may be excluded from evidence. It will not be possible to sever them from the 'interview'. This ruling

41 [1990] Crim LR 190.
42 (1990) 90 Cr App R 115; [1989] Crim LR 815.
43 [1991] Crim LR 455.
44 This qualification should, it is argued, be introduced to take account of the situation which arose in *Sparks* [1991] Crim LR 128; the officer who questioned the appellant apparently did not recognise the significance of the admissions made and therefore did not consider it necessary to caution him.
45 [1993] Crim LR 222; (1992) *The Times*, 15 May, CA.

seems to be in conflict with *Marsh*. However, as the *Weekes* ruling concerned a juvenile, it may be confined to such instances.

Where the level of suspicion clearly falls within para 10.1 of both Codes as, of course, it will do after arrest, the use of the term 'questioning' in Code C, para 11.1A, and in Code H, para 11.1, nevertheless impliedly excludes instances where nothing definable as questioning has taken place. This is the correct interpretation where the police have apparently merely recorded what was said, according to the Court of Appeal in *Menard*.[46] Both paragraphs may also exclude chats or discussions between suspect and police officer or statements or commands which happen to elicit an incriminating response.[47] This interpretation seems to lead to a conflict between the definitions of an interview and the ruling from *Matthews*,[48] which could possibly be resolved by arguing that rulings of the Court of Appeal will prevail over a provision contained only in a Code provision.[49] This would be the more satisfactory result, as more likely to curtail opportunities for 'verballing' (concocting admissions). However, a possible response might be that the definition from *Matthews* is now enshrined in para 11.13 and is not therefore inconsistent with para 11.1A. In other words, the *Matthews* definition applies to most exchanges between suspect and police officer, but para 11.1A applies to certain particularly important ones labelled 'interviews'. This interpretation is to an extent supported by the wording of para 11.13: 'a written record shall also be made of any comments made by a suspected person, including unsolicited comments which are outside the context of an interview but which might be relevant to the offence . . .', thus implying that comments relevant to the offence other than unsolicited comments will not invariably be part of an interview. It also receives some support from the ruling in *Williams*,[50] which seems to have accepted impliedly that 'social visits' by police to suspects in the cells involving conversations relevant to the offence in question do not constitute interviews, although they are to be discouraged. This interpretation would mean that a number of exchanges which would previously have been interviews will no longer be so labelled, and this is especially of concern owing to evidence that police officers tend to favour the informal chat in the police station.[51] These comments are also applicable to the scheme under Code H, which also accepts in para 11.4 and Note 11E that significant statements may be made outside the context of an interview

Thus at present certain safeguards are now triggered off only in a confined group of situations in relation to interviews of terrorist and non-terrorist suspects. In *Cox*,[52]

---

46 [1995] Cr App R 306.
47 See *Absolam* (1989) 88 Cr App R 332.
48 If statements or commands eliciting a response from the suspect could be said to fall outside the *Matthews* ([1990] Crim LR 190) definition of an interview, which is unlikely, they could still constitute an interview according to the ruling in *Absolam*, ibid.
49 The Codes of Practice brought in by a resolution of both Houses of Parliament do not have statutory authority. It has, however, been held by the Court of Appeal that they can prevail over rules derived from case law (*McCay* [1990] Crim LR 338), although commentators have thought that the Court of Appeal was mistaken in this view (Birch, D [1990] Crim LR 338 at 340).
50 (1992) *The Times*, 6 February, CA.
51 See Holdaway, S, *Inside the British Police*, 1985, Blackwell; Sanders [1990] Crim LR 494, referring to his research on access to legal advice in police stations (research undertaken by Sanders, Bridges, Mulvaney and Crozier, entitled *Advice and Assistance at Police Stations*, November 1989) found that such practices were still continuing post-PACE.
52 [1993] Crim LR 382; see also *Goddard* [1994] Crim LR 46.

however, the Court of Appeal adopted what might be termed a 'purposive approach' to Note 11A (which previously contained the definition of an interview, under the 1991 revision) in finding that the intention of the 1991 revision was to increase rather than decrease protection for suspects and therefore, Note 11A should be interpreted in the light of previous decisions such as *Matthews* which broadened the definition of an interview. This was followed in *Oransaye*,[53] which suggested that the emphasis should not be placed on the form of the exchange – on whether or not questions were asked – but on whether what was said went to 'the heart of the matter'. If so, the exchange should be termed an interview.[54] But these decisions pre-dated the more recent revisions of the Codes and there is currently little evidence that the courts are taking this approach. In *R v James*,[55] for example, the police questioned the business partner of a man who had disappeared. Initially he was not under suspicion, but during the interview the officers formed the suspicion that James had murdered his partner. No caution was given, and the Court of Appeal held that this was not an interview – despite the fact that James was asked directly whether he had killed his partner – and that therefore it could be admitted in evidence. Had it been found to be an interview it would probably have had to be excluded since the safeguards applicable to an interview were not in place.

Interviews inside and outside the police station

Under s 30 PACE, as amended,[56] the suspect must be taken to the police station as soon as practicable after arrest. Under para 11.1 of Code C and Code H, para 11.2 the suspect should be taken to the station (or a designated place of detention in the case of terrorist suspects) once the decision to arrest has been made, unless certain exceptions apply. As discussed below, these provisions provide scope for informal interviewing outside the place where most of the due process safeguards are available.

Once an exchange could be called an interview, the safeguards applying to it under the original Code C provisions differed quite markedly depending on where it took place. Those available *inside* the police station included contemporaneous recording[57] or tape recording,[58] the ability to read over, verify and sign the notes of the interview as a correct record,[59] notification of legal advice,[60] the right to have advice before questioning[61] and, where appropriate, the presence of an adult.[62] If the interview took

---

53 [1993] Crim LR 772.

54 For discussion of the meaning of 'interview', see Field, S, 'Defining Interviews Under PACE', 1993, 13(2) LS 254.

55 [1996] Crim LR 650.

56 The Criminal Justice Act 2003 insets a new s 30A into s 30, allowing an arrested person to be released on bail at any point before the police station is reached.

57 Original para 11.3 provided that if the interview took place in the police station or at other premises, 'the record must be made during the course of the interview unless in the investigating officer's view this would not be practicable or would interfere with the conduct of the interview'.

58 Under original para 11.3.

59 Under Code E, para 3.

60 Under original para 12.12.

61 Under Codes C and H, para 3.1.

62 The Court of Appeal in *Absolam* (1989) 88 Cr App R 332 determined that no questioning could take place inside the police station before the suspect had been notified of the right to legal advice; answers allegedly made to questions put before such notification were thereby rendered inadmissible.

place on 'other premises', the same safeguards would apply apart from the requirements to *inform*[63] of the right to legal advice and to allow the suspect to verify and sign the record of the interview.

Outside the police station, however, it was only necessary to ensure that an accurate record of the interview was made[64] and, where appropriate, an adult was present.[65] Thus, originally, a minimum level of protection only was available creating scope for impropriety, including fabrication of confessions. In particular, it meant that only the experienced suspect interviewed outside the police station would be aware of the right to legal advice. Thus, however widely the term 'interview' was interpreted, it was of little use to suspects who made (or allegedly made) admissions outside the police station.

The 1991 revision reduced the significance of this factor to some extent. Provision for contemporaneous recording and for giving the suspect the record of the interview to verify and sign was moved out of para 12, applying only to interviews in the police station and into para 11,[66] which is headed 'Interviews general',[67] although this change was made less significant by the provisions of para 11.13. The verifying and signing rules were supplemented in 1995 by the requirement, imposed, however, only in a Note for Guidance, Note 11D (now 11E), that the suspect should declare in his or her own hand on the interview record that it is correct. Such a provision clearly has more value than the requirement only to obtain a signature. Under Code C, para 11.7, the interview must be recorded contemporaneously wherever it takes place, unless this would not be practicable, while it must be offered to the suspect to verify and sign, under Code C, para 11.11. These changes were continued in the 2006 revision; that revision undermines the value of contemporaneous recording to an extent since it allows for an accurate summary rather than a verbatim record. The recording of interviews with terrorism suspects is not covered by Code H; the verifying and recording provisions under the TA Code for detention of terrorist suspects will apply.

However, under the 2006 revision, the unseasoned suspect interviewed outside the police station will still be unaware of the right to legal advice[68] and it is also at present unlikely that the interview would be tape recorded: Code E does not envisage tape recording taking place anywhere but inside the police station.[69] In some circumstances

---

63   Under original para 13.

64   Section 58, governing the right of access to legal advice, is expressed to apply to persons in police detention and para 3.1, governing the right to be notified of the s 58 entitlement was (and is) expressed to apply only to those in the police station. However, volunteers under caution in the police station or on other premises had the right to be informed of the entitlement to legal advice under original para 10.2 – now Code H, para 3.21, Note 1A.

65   Original para 13 did not state expressly that an adult must be present during any interview whether conducted in or out of the police station when a juvenile was interviewed. However, this could be implied; the ruling in *Fogah* [1989] Crim LR 141 confirmed that this was the correct interpretation.

66   Paragraph 11.7; para 11.8 Code H refers to the Code for detention and questioning made under the TA.

67   The Court of Appeal determined in *Brezenau and Francis* [1989] Crim LR 650 that these provisions could only apply inside the police station; departure from the clear words of para 12 was not warranted.

68   This is governed by para 3.1, which is expressed to apply only to persons in the police station.

69   Code E, para 3.1 states: '. . . tape recording shall be used at police stations for any interview . . .'. Some police forces have experimented with hand held tape recorders used outside the police station, but at present this is by no means common practice.

suspects are not, however, be disadvantaged by these differences, thanks to the provisions of para 11.1, introduced by the 1991 revision, which reads: 'Following a decision to arrest a suspect he must not be interviewed about the relevant offence except at a police station [except in certain instances specified in 11.1(a), (b) and (c) which call for urgent interviewing].'

Paragraph 11.1 could merely have read: 'A suspect must not be interviewed about the relevant offence except at a police station . . .'. Clearly, it was designed to allow *some* interviewing outside the police station owing to its requirement of a higher level of suspicion than that denoted by para 11.1A and para 10.1. It implies that a police officer should categorise someone either as possibly involved in an offence or as on the verge of arrest; so long as the first category is applicable, questioning can continue. This category was presumably intended to include persons under caution, because a caution must be given 'when there are grounds to suspect (him) of an offence'.[70] Obviously, these categories tend to merge into each other. However, it is difficult to be certain in retrospect as to which applied, although the police may find it difficult where there are very strong grounds for suspicion to support a claim that interviewing could continue because the decision to arrest had not been taken. However, there appear to be no decisions on this point, and given that para 11.1 was introduced over 15 years ago, it appears that this issue is not being raised, probably because of the ambiguity surrounding the words 'once the decision to arrest has been taken' and due to the breadth of the exceptions allowing for urgent interviewing outside the police station.

It is clear that the problems associated with exchanges between suspect and officer still remain, and it is evident that a significant number of suspects are still interviewed outside the police station.[71] The Runciman Royal Commission proposed that admissions made outside the police station should be seen as needing some form of corroboration such as their acceptance by the suspect on tape at the police station,[72] and this was implemented under the 1995 revision in para 11.2A. However, para 11.2A is omitted from the 2006 version of Code C; it is only necessary for there to be a written record of comments made outside the context of an interview under para 11.13 which the suspect should be shown so that he can verify it. Further, para 11.13 does not provide that admissions or silences made outside the police station will be inadmissible if *not* accepted by the suspect at the police station. Therefore, presumably, if no breaches of Code C have occurred, they would be admissible even though uncorroborated, subject to the possibility of excluding them under s 76 or s 78 of PACE, as discussed in Chapter 13.

Original para 10.2 provided that a volunteer who was questioned under caution on 'other premises' had to be told of his right to legal advice. This placed such persons in a better position than arrestees and, therefore, tended to be evaded by bringing forward the moment of arrest. The current version of Code C removes the special requirement for volunteers, but they should under a Note for Guidance – Note 1A – be allowed access to legal advice when they are in the station. Thus, volunteers under caution outside the police station are disadvantaged because they can be questioned without

---

70 Codes C and H, para 10.1.
71 Brown, Ellis and Larcombe, *Home Office Research Study No 129*. The study showed that questioning and/or unsolicited comments occurred in 24% of cases. Questioning occurred in 10% of cases.
72 Royal Commission Report 1993, Proposal 40.

notification of the right to legal advice, whereas once the decision to arrest has been made, a suspect should not normally be questioned before arrival at the police station, where he will be informed of the right. In other words, in the context of the current provision under para 11.1, the old requirement under para 10.2 would have had some value; had it been retained and extended to all volunteers under caution, it would have removed some of the incentive which now exists to delay, or apparently delay, the decision to arrest in order to interview outside the police station. Clearly, this would have been a radical move, but it might have been welcome as harmonising the position of such suspects with that of arrestees.

Most significantly, since suspects not at the police station can be interviewed, without having had an opportunity to consult a solicitor, they are not protected by the provision of s 34(2A) of the CJPOA: adverse inferences can be drawn if they remain silent. Further, s 34(2A) does not affect the position of suspects who make admissions despite not having had that opportunity. This is because they are technically free to leave and seek legal advice before being arrested. Section 34(2A) only applies inside the police station or other place of detention. But this position is flawed in two respects. First, many suspects may not realise that they could leave, and may reply to questions in the street or police car, before being arrested, without realising that they could have legal advice. Once arrested the person in question is no longer free to leave, but might reply to questions or even volunteer admissions in the police car, on the way to the station, again without realising that he is entitled to have legal advice once the police station is reached. The second situation arguably leads to an infringement of Art 6, even though s 34(2A) appears to condone it – as discussed below.[73]

Where the level of suspicion would obviously justify an arrest, a police officer who is eager to keep a suspect out of the police station for the time being might be able to invoke one of the more broadly worded exceptions allowing urgent interviewing in order to avert certain specified risks. The first exception under para 11.1(a), allowing interviewing to take place at once where delay might lead to interference with evidence, could be interpreted very broadly and could apply whenever there was some likelihood that evidence connected with any offence but not immediately obtainable was in existence. Even if there were no others involved in the offence who had not been apprehended, it could be argued that the evidence was at risk from the moment of arrest because news of the arrest might become known to persons with a motive for concealing it. This argument could also apply to the exception under (c) with the proviso that it will apply to a narrower range of offences. Once an arrest has occurred, the provision of s 30(1) PACE that the suspect must be taken to the police station by the constable as soon as practicable applies. Under s 30(1)), the police can delay doing so if the suspect is needed elsewhere to carry out investigations which it is reasonable to carry out immediately. The key words in s 30 are obviously 'as soon as practicable'. Thus, further leeway for informal interviewing *after* arrest is created.

Once the suspect is inside the police station under arrest or under caution,[74] any interview[75] (using this term to connote an exchange which falls within para 11.1A)

---

73 See pp 1213–14.

74 Under para 3.1 of Code E, once a volunteer becomes a suspect (i.e., at the point when he should be cautioned) the rest of the interview should be tape recorded.

75 Under para 3.1(a), an interview with a person suspected of an offence triable only summarily need not be taped.

should be audio-recorded under Code E, but there is an exception in respect of terrorist suspects, which is considered below. Many of the criticisms advanced above could also be applied under Code H. Under that Code an interview only occurs after the suspect is *arrested*. After that point he should be taken to a place designated for detention under TA, Sched 8, para 1, following Code H, para 11.2, unless one of the urgent interviewing exceptions apply (the exceptions are the same as those under Code C para 11.1). This means that any informal exchanges prior to the point of arrest, which might well be viewed as interviews if covered by Code C, will not count as interviews and therefore will not attract the safeguards. Admissions are made before being cautioned, even if the suspect is being directly questioned about the offence, but is not under arrest, would be admissible in evidence. No contemporaneous recording of such admissions would be necessary so long as a record was made later.

Varying levels of protection for exchanges

It is now possible to identify the points at which the safeguards will be brought to bear and it is apparent not only that there are three levels of protection available, but that they vary as between terrorist and non-terrorist suspects:

(1) Inside or outside the police station, if the exchange cannot be (or at times is not) labelled an 'interview', even though it may be relevant to the offence, it seems that the level of protection provided by Code C, para 11.13 only will apply (for Code H, only the protection of Note 11E). This will be the case even where the suspect is an arrestee or a volunteer under caution.

(2) If an interview of a non-terrorist suspect takes place outside the police station and falls outside the Code C, para 11.1 prohibition and within the leeway created by s 30(1) PACE, the verifying and recording provisions under paras 11.11 and 11.7 will apply, with the proviso that contemporaneous recording is likely to be viewed as impracticable.[76] What is impracticable does not connote something that is extremely difficult, but must involve more than mere inconvenience.[77] Where appropriate, an adult must be present, which probably means that interviews requiring an appropriate adult would have to take place at the station.[78] Notification of the right of access to legal advice will not occur, although adverse inferences could be drawn if the suspect remains silent.

If an interview of a non-terrorist suspect takes place outside the police station and falls outside the Code H, para 11.2 prohibition and within the leeway created by s 30(1) PACE, the verifying and recording provisions under the TA Code for detention of terrorist suspects will apply. Otherwise everything said above as regards interviews outside the station under Code C is applicable. It should be noted in particular that notification of the right of access to legal advice will not occur,

---

76 The mere fact that an interview is conducted in the street may not be enough to support an assertion that it could not be contemporaneously recorded. This seems to follow from the decision in *Fogah* [1989] Crim LR 141.

77 *Parchment* [1989] Crim LR 290. Note-taking while the suspect was dressing and showing the officers round his flat was held to be impracticable.

78 Code C, para 11.15; Code H, para 11.9.

although the suspect is not free to leave since he will be under arrest, and adverse inferences could be drawn under s 34(2A) CJPOA if the suspect remains silent. It is readily arguable, as mentioned above, that this position does not accord with the demands of Art 6.

(3) As far as non-terrorist suspects are concerned, inside the police station, if the person in question is an arrestee or a volunteer under caution[79] and the exchange is an interview, all the available safeguards, including access to legal advice and tape recording, will apply.[80] As far as terrorist suspects are concerned, inside the designated place of detention, if the person in question is an arrestee the exchange will be an interview if the other aspects of para 11.1 apply; therefore all the available safeguards, including access to legal advice, will apply. The provisions as to audio-recording in Code E will not apply (Code E, para 3.2). If the suspect is a volunteer he or she appears to be entitled to have access to legal advice, under Code H, Note 1A, but the exchange will not be an interview and therefore, it appears that the other safeguards, including the presence of an appropriate adult, will not apply. Also, although the suspect can have access to legal advice (albeit only under a Note), he or she does not appear to have a right to have the adviser present when questioned.

Thus, wide but uncertain scope still remains for interviewing outside the police station and for gathering admissions outside the context of an interview. The main objection to this scheme, apart from its complexity,[81] is that the degree of protection available is too dependent on factors irrelevant to the level of suspicion in question. It may be pure chance, or something more sinister, which dictates whether a volunteer under caution is interviewed inside or outside the police station or whether or not an exchange with an arrestee can successfully be characterised or disguised as a non-interview. Bearing in mind that unreliable confessions may be most likely to emerge from informal exchanges, it is argued that the mechanisms triggering off the main safeguards – para 11.1A and para 11.1 – are deficient both in creating large areas of uncertainty as to the level of protection called for at various points and in allowing the minimal level of protection under Code C, para 11.13 to operate in too many contexts. The greater leeway within the Code H scheme for questioning suspects before arrest and therefore outside the context of an interview is a matter of particular concern, given the diversity of terrorist suspects, and the particular propensity of terrorist cases to miscarry.

79 Under para 3.21, which largely reproduces original para 3.9, volunteers under caution have the right to be told that they may obtain legal advice; see Code H, Note 1A. The other important Code C safeguards are contained in paras 11 and 12 and apply to arrestees and volunteers under caution. Under Code E, tape recording must be used for interviews with persons under caution in the police station (E 3.1(a)) – but not for persons suspected of summary offences.

80 Unless under Code E, para 3.3, it would not be reasonably practicable to tape the interview owing to failure of the recording equipment or non-availability of an interview room or recorder. Note 3B of Code E provides that if necessary, an officer must be able to justify the decision not to delay the interview.

81 The need to adopt a commonsense approach to the rules was expressed in *Marsh* [1991] Crim LR 455 by Bingham LJ in relation to the original scheme. However, the current scheme does not lend itself readily to a simple interpretation. See especially the comments of McCullough J in *Cox* [1993] Crim LR 382 regarding Note 11A.

Recording methods

Audio recording

Section 60 of PACE allowed for the issuing of a Code of Practice in connection with tape recording of interviews, and this was accomplished by means of Code of Practice E. Once the non-terrorist suspect is inside the police station under arrest or under caution,[82] any interview (that is, an exchange which falls within para 11.1A of Code C) with a person who has been cautioned in respect of an indictable or 'either way' offence[83] should be audio recorded under Code of Practice E. Initial resistance by the police gave way to a recognition of the advantages of audio recording, which seems to be generally accepted[84] as reflecting a truer picture of an interview than note-taking[85] and, thanks to recent developments, the jury are in one sense even *better* placed than they would have been had they been present at the interview because they may be allowed to take the tape recordings into the jury room[86] to replay as necessary.[87]

However, exchanges may occur between formal interviews, when the tape is switched off, which affect the formal interview and although they should be recorded in writing under para 11.13, the record may not cover everything that was said, and the facts recorded by the police officers may be disputed by the suspects. In other words, leeway for falsely imputing admissions to the suspect is still apparent.[88]

Audio recording was not initially used in terrorist cases, under Code E, para 3.2, or in cases of espionage under s 1 of the Official Secrets Act 1989. This provision was clarified under Note for Guidance 3G of Code E; interviews with those suspected of terrorism solely connected with the affairs of the UK or any part of the UK other than Northern Ireland should be tape-recorded. A written contemporaneous record could still be made of interviews which fell within Code E, para 3.2. This exemption was included because it was feared that the contents of tapes might become available to terrorist organisations. The Home Office reviewed it in 1990,[89] and although it did not introduce mandatory audio recording, police in Britain undertook it in terrorist cases on

---

82 Under para 3.4 of Code E (1999 version), once a volunteer becomes a suspect (i.e., at the point when he should be cautioned) the rest of the interview should be tape recorded.

83 Under para 3.1(a), an interview with a person suspected of an offence triable only summarily need not be audio taped, although under Note 3A it can be recorded at police discretion.

84 See Wills, McLeod and Nash, *The Tape Recording of Police Interviews with Suspects*, 2nd Interim Report, Home Office Research Study No 97, 1988. The study found that police officers and prosecutors generally welcomed taping, since it is a faster recording method and renders them less vulnerable to allegations of 'verballing'.

85 Research conducted by Baldwin and Bedward of the Institute of Judicial Administration, University of Birmingham, on summaries made of tape recorded interviews found that the summaries were often of a very poor quality and presented a distorted picture of what occurred during the interview. However, they also found that the police were aware of this problem and were beginning to address it. See [1991] Crim LR 671.

86 *Emmerson* [1991] Crim LR 194. In *Riaz and Burke* [1991] Crim LR 366, the Court of Appeal held (in instances where the jury had not already heard the tapes) that better practice would be to reassemble the court and play the tapes in open court.

87 This permission was expressed to extend only to those parts of the tapes which had been heard in open court; other material would have to be edited out.

88 See *Dunn* (1990) 91 Cr App Rep 237.

89 HC Deb Vol 168 col 273, 1 March 1990.

a voluntary basis. Since, under s 1 of the TA, terrorism is defined much more widely to include those covered by Note G, and the problem of Irish terrorism has diminished, the obvious step is to make audio recording of interviews with terrorist suspects mandatory. This was accomplished by Sched 7, para 9 to the TA, which provided for the audio recording of any interview by a constable of a person detained under s 41 and Sched 7 to the TA, once a new Code of Practice had been introduced. This step would not have changed current practice, apart from that in Northern Ireland, but it would have afforded formal recognition to this due process safeguard. The current position is that Code E is entirely inapplicable to interviews with terrorist suspects since Note 3G has been removed from the current version. Audio recording is dealt with by a Code of Practice for audio recording of suspects arrested under TA, s 41 or detained under TA, Sched 7, issued by the Secretary of State.[90]

Video recording

The recording of police interviews is one of the most rapidly developing areas of policing. The possibility that the introduction of tape recording,[91] replacing contemporaneous note-taking,[92] would eventually be overtaken by video taping has been under consideration for some time.[93] Video taping of police interviews was until recently at the experimental stage and the Home Office made it clear in 1991 that it supported its introduction[94] as a step in the direction of preventing miscarriages of justice. Section 60 of PACE was amended by s 76 of the Criminal Justice and Police Act 2001 to insert s 60A, which provided the Secretary of State with the power to issue a Code of Practice for the 'visual recording of interviews'. Commentators have given video taped interviews a cautious welcome;[95] criticism has largely been directed towards the difficulty of ensuring

---

90 Schedule 8, para 3(1) and (7) .

91 Governed by Code of Practice E, which came into force on 29 July 1988.

92 Originally governed by Code C, para 11.3 and under revised Code C by para 11.5. Tape recording has not entirely replaced contemporaneous note-taking, first because it does not apply to all interviews (see Code E, para 3) and secondly, because contemporaneous note-taking applies to interviews outside the police station where practicable, whereas tape recording is at present only required inside it (Code E, para 3.1).

93 Video taping of interviews as opposed to audio taping was one of the possibilities considered by the Royal Commission on Criminal Procedure chaired by Lord Runciman. See (1991) 141 NLJ 1512 for a brief interim report by John Baldwin of a study of video taping experiments that took place in four police stations. For some time, the police have been able to video tape a confession if they first obtained the consent of the accused: *Li Shu-Ling* [1989] Crim LR 58, PC. The Runciman Royal Commission proposed that further research into the use of video taping for interviews should be carried out (Proposal 70). However, the Home Office issued a circular on video recording of interviews which advised against moving quickly to introduce video recording owing to the cost of so doing (Circular 6, 1993). Video-taping is still not mandatory but is being used on a voluntary basis; it is now governed by Code F.

94 In response to a request from Sir John Farr MP for video taping of all police interviews in order to prevent miscarriages of justice, John Patten, then Secretary of State for the Home Office, indicated that this course would be considered after the results of a pilot project conducted for the Association of Chief Police Officers in conjunction with the Home Office were known. HC Deb Vol 200 col 391, 5 December 1991.

95 See, e.g., Barnes, M, 'One experience of video recorded interviews' [1993] Crim LR 444.

that they are not subverted by 'informal' contacts between police and suspect,[96] rather than at the quality of the recordings.[97] Arguably, such difficulties are endemic in the interviewing scheme as currently conceived, regardless of the recording technique used. Code F now governs visual recording, but recognises that it is not mandatory.

Interviewing techniques

There seems to be a tendency in some quarters to see developments in recording techniques as going a long way towards solving the problem of unreliable confessions.[98] However, there is a danger that other relevant issues will be obscured. It is important not to over-emphasise the value of recording techniques at the expense of provisions which may have a more direct effect on their reliability. This danger was perhaps most readily apparent in the juxtaposition in the remit of the Royal Commission on Criminal Procedure of the possibility of introducing video taping with that of abolishing the right to silence,[99] and it is instructive to compare the enthusiasm for video-taping of interviews[100] with the decision to abolish the right to silence.[101] Video-taping is to be welcomed, as providing a fuller picture of an interview than audio-recording, and as a means of inhibiting the use of intimidatory tactics, at least in the formal interview, but arguably its value should not be over-stressed. Video-taping might faithfully reflect the interview during which a confession was made,[102] but fail to affect the pressure likely to make it unreliable flowing from the suspect's perception that he must speak. The fact that it was video-taped might give the confession a spurious credibility. This

96 See McConville, M, 'Video taping interrogations: police behaviour on and off camera' [1992] Crim LR 532.

97 However, quality has been questioned: see John Baldwin's interim report of experiments with video taping of interviews, which found that there were fairly serious or very serious problems with video taping in over 20% of the recordings. These included poor picture or sound quality or camera malfunction (see (1991) 141 NLJ 1512).

98 When Kenneth Baker, the then Home Secretary, announced the inception of the Royal Commission on Criminal Procedure, he suggested that recent improvements in the provision for recording of police interviews would prevent miscarriages of justice in future: HC Deb Vol 187 col 1109, 14 March 1991.

99 In announcing the Royal Commission (ibid) the then Home Secretary stated that part of its remit was to consider 'the extent to which the courts might draw proper inferences from any failure (on the part of the suspect) to take advantage of opportunities to state his position', at col 1115. On 5 December 1991, John Patten, then Secretary of State for the Home Office, made it clear that the Royal Commission would be considering video taping of police interviews: HC Deb Vol 200 Col 391, 5 December 1991.

100 See fn 93 and 94, above; see also Campbell, 'Videos of interviews "would help police"' (1991) the *Guardian*, 9 December.

101 The Home Office set up a working group in 1989 to consider the right to silence: see fn 240, after the right had already been modified in Northern Ireland by the Criminal Evidence (Northern Ireland) Order 1988. The group's recommendations assumed that abolition was necessary. For criticism, see Greer, S (1990) 53 MLR 709 and Zuckerman, A, 'Trial By Unfair Means – The Report of the Working Group on the Right to Silence' [1989] Crim LR 855. Kenneth Baker signalled that interest in this possibility was still very much alive when announcing the remit of the Royal Commission on Criminal Procedure, ibid. The Home Secretary announced in October 1993 that the right to silence would be abolished and this was brought about under the Criminal Justice and Public Order Act 1994, ss 34, 36 and 37.

102 But see John Baldwin's findings, (1991) 141 NLJ 1512 for a study of video taping experiments that took place in four police stations.

is not an argument against video taping in general, but against its use as part of the justification for failing to reverse the modification of the right to silence. It might be argued that unreliable confessions would be almost eliminated by the use of such advanced recording techniques, thereby providing a justification for increasing the pressure on the suspect to speak.

Improvement in the recording provisions is not aimed directly at promoting the reliability of a confession, but at allowing a court to consider an accurate record of it and to assess what occurred when it was made. There is clearly a difference between the reliability of admissions and the reliability of the *record* of them.[103] In contrast to the success of the scheme in this direction, there has been little development in the area of provisions able to *affect* what occurred; PACE does not attempt to regulate the conduct of the interview except in so far as such regulation can be implied from the provision of s 76 that confessions obtained by oppression[104] or in circumstances likely to render them unreliable will be inadmissible. Code C of PACE forbids oppressive interviewing in Code C, para 11.5[105] and Code H, para 11.6; some very general guidance as to interviewing mentally disordered or handicapped suspects is given in Codes C and H, Note 11C. No such provision is duplicated in PACE itself although, as indicated in Chapter 15, oppression is defined under s 76(8) PACE as including Art 3 treatment, and under s 76(2)(a) a confession obtained by oppression is subject to an absolute exclusionary rule.

Obviously, the provisions governing detention and the physical comfort of the detainee[106] have relevance in this context; they provide the setting for the interrogation and remove from the situation some of the reasons why a suspect might make an unreliable confession. Provisions relating to medical treatment and to assessing the detainee's mental and physical condition are also relevant,[107] especially in relation to terrorist suspects, who may be detained for up to 28 days. But, once their limits have been set, they cannot influence what occurs next, and it seems that the use of intimidation, haranguing and indirect threats is still quite common, especially in interviews with juveniles.[108] The Runciman Royal Commission proposed that the role of the appropriate adult should be reviewed[109] and that officers should receive training in the role a solicitor would be expected to play,[110] but did not make general proposals

---

103 See the discussion of *Paris* (1993) 97 Cr appl R 99 in Chapter 13, p 1272–73.

104 Misleading statements made during an interview distorting the state of the evidence against the defendant or hectoring and bullying may well lead to exclusion of any confession obtained under either s 76 or s 78. See *Mason* [1987] Crim LR 119; [1987] 3 All ER 481, CA; *Beales* [1991] Crim LR 118; *Blake* [1991] Crim LR 119; *Heron* (1993) unreported, discussed in Chapter 14.

105 Code C, para 11.5 and Code H, para 11.6 provide: 'No police officer may try to obtain answers to questions or to elicit a statement by the use of oppression.'

106 Paragraphs 8 and 9 of Code C and Code H; para 12(a) regulates the physical conditions in the interview room.

107 See Chapter 11, pp 1172–75. See Code H, governing the treatment of terrorist suspects, paras 8 and 9.

108 See Evans, R, 'The Conduct of Police Interviews with Juveniles', *Home Office Research Study No 8*, 1993. See (1994) 144 NLJ 120 and (1994) 144 NLJ 203 for criticism of a variety of interview techniques.

109 Proposal 72.

110 Proposal 64.

as to outlawing or regulating use of certain interviewing techniques.[111] Such proposals would be particularly relevant after the evidence of use of bullying techniques in interrogations which arose from the post-PACE case of *Paris, Abdullah and Miller* (the Cardiff Three).[112] In fact, such techniques may be in the process of being replaced by a more subtle 'investigative approach',[113] but this is no substitute for specific guidance under Code C as to improper techniques. The very significant increase in the period for which terrorism suspects can be detained – currently up to 28 days – makes it even more imperative that consideration should be given to ensuring the reliability of admissions made, especially as terrorist suspects differ from each other so markedly: some may have been trained to withstand interrogation, while others may be completely inexperienced in criminal justice terms.

The lack of provision in PACE and the TA as regards interviewing techniques encourages resort to the HRA. On its face, the Convention does not bear upon this issue, except in so far as Art 3 covers oppressive interviewing. But, as indicated above, the general requirements of fairness under Art 6 will allow consideration of interviewing techniques as part of the fairness of the criminal process as a whole. Arguments could also be raised regarding unethical, intrusive interviewing techniques under Arts 3, 8 and 14.

Articles 3, 8 and 14 might be engaged where the interrogation itself was of an especially intrusive nature, particularly where it could also be said to be discriminatory. Grossly humiliating treatment may breach Art 3, and this might include very intrusive, prolonged questioning. Where such questioning was accompanied by racist, sexist[114] or homophobic abuse, a breach might be found of Art 3 read with Art 14. Article 8 could also be considered where the questioning dealt, for example, with sexual matters. These possibilities were considered in *Lustig-Prean and Beckett v UK* and *Smith and Grady v UK*[115] in the context of an investigation by service police concerning their homosexuality, but by analogy, the findings of the Court would appear to be applicable to police interviewing in certain circumstances. The Court considered the investigations, and in particular the interviews of the applicants, to have been exceptionally intrusive and to constitute especially grave interferences with their private lives, which could not be justified within the meaning of Art 8(2). It considered that treatment grounded upon a predisposed homophobic bias, as in the present case, could, in principle, fall within the scope of Art 3 and that the investigations were undoubtedly distressing and humiliating, but that in the circumstances of the case, the treatment did not reach the minimum level of severity which would bring it within the scope of Art 3. Having found a breach of Art 8, the Court did not go on to consider Art 14 as a separate issue.

The failure to regulate interviewing techniques is a significant gap in the PACE and TA schemes, bearing in mind the established likelihood of a link between coercive

---

111 See Baldwin, J, 'The Royal Commission, Power and Police Interviews' (1993) 143 NLJ 1194 for criticism of the failure of the Royal Commission in this respect. See also Reiner, R, 'The Royal Commission on Criminal Justice (1) Investigative Powers and Safeguards for Suspects' [1993] Crim LR 808.

112 (1993) 97 Cr App R 99.

113 Baldwin notes ((1993) 143 NLJ 1195 and 1197) that 1993 training manuals for police interviewers advocate this approach. It is advocated in the Interviewer's Rule Book.

114 *East African Asians* cases (1973) 3 EHRR 76.

115 (1999) 29 EHRR 548, and (2000) 29 EHRR 493.

questioning and unreliable confessions.[116] Although there has been a movement from such questioning towards so called ethical techniques,[117] it cannot be assumed that interviewing will not at times verge on the oppressive and abusive. Use of Art 8 as in *Lustig-Prean* may encourage a movement towards ethical interviewing and provide an avenue by which to challenge humiliating, discriminatory questioning under the HRA. As discussed above, the Race Relations Act 1976, after amendment in 2000, provides a means of redress in respect of racial abuse or racially discriminatory treatment by police, which will also cover interviewing. But, this possibility does not exist in respect of other forms of discriminatory treatment, including treatment which is gender-related or homophobic.[118]

3 The right of access to legal advice

Introduction

There is general agreement that the most significant protection for due process introduced for the first time by PACE[119] was that of the right of access to legal advice.[120] But this right is far from absolute. It is subject to a number of formal exceptions, which are broader in terrorist cases, and it is dependent on a formal request to exercise it. It is also limited to interviewing in police stations, and may be subverted informally in a variety of ways. Nevertheless its impact in due process terms should not be under-estimated. It has been bolstered by the domestic response to a key decision at Strasbourg, *Murray v UK*.[121] The legislative response to *Murray*, considered below, means that where suspects, including terrorist suspects, are in police detention and have been formally denied access to legal advice, adverse inferences cannot be drawn from silence.

---

116 See Justice, *Unreliable Evidence? Confessions and the Safety of Convictions*, 1994.
117 Home Office Central Planning and Training Unit, The Interviewer's Rule Book, 1992; Home Office Circular 7/1993 'Investigative interviewing'.
118 The Sex Discrimination Act 1975 has not been amended in the same way as the Race Relations Act (under the Race Relations (Amendment) Act 2000) and therefore will not cover the actions of public authorities except in the contexts covered by s 6 of the Act. At present, no statute forbids discriminatory treatment in the criminal justice system on grounds of sexual orientation. Bearing in mind the 'dualist' impact of international law in the UK, this means that Protocol 12 (see Chapter 2, p 106) may not provide a remedy for such treatment domestically, even if it is eventually received into domestic law under the HRA. See further Chapter 15, p 1486.
119 The Criminal Law Act 1977, s 62 declared a narrow entitlement to have one reasonably named person informed of the arrest. It did not provide that the arrestee must be informed of this right, nor did it provide any sanction for non-compliance by a police officer. That statutory form of this right gave it no greater force than the non-statutory Judges' Rules (rules of practice for the guidance of the police: see *Practice Note* [1984] 1 All ER 237; 1 WLR 152). The Judges' Rules upheld the right of the suspect/arrestee in the police station to communicate with/consult a solicitor, but permitted the withholding of such access 'lest unreasonable delay or hindrance is caused to the process of investigation or the administration of justice'. Any officer, in relation to a person detained for any offence, could deny access to legal advice on these broad grounds; see *Lemsatef* [1977] 1 WLR 812; [1977] 2 All ER 835.
120 See, e.g.,Sanders and Young, *Criminal Justice*, 3rd edn, 2007, Chapter 4.5; Dixon, D, *Miscarriages of Justice*, 1999, p 67. The research studies mentioned in this chapter do not question the value of the legal right of access *per se*, although they do question its quality and the responses of the police.
121 (1996) 22 EHRR 29.

Access to legal advice has an impact in upholding due process which encompasses, but goes beyond, advising on making 'no comment' answers. How far it has such an impact in practice is debatable. The impact varies, depending on the contact with the suspect. The Sanders research in 1989 found that telephone advice alone had little impact on suspects: 50% of those who received telephone advice made admissions, as opposed to 59.6% of those who received no advice.[122] The research criticised the great variation in practice between advisers, and considered that too many duty solicitors gave telephone advice only, thereby depriving the client of most of the benefits of legal advice.[123] Subsequent research suggests that in 23% of cases when advice is requested, telephone advice only continues to be given, and only around 12–14% of suspects in police interviews have an adviser present.[124]

The relationship between access to legal advice and the right to silence is complex,[125] particularly in view of the curtailment of the right to silence under ss 34, 36 and 37 of the CJPOA 1994, which is discussed below. The available research lends some support to the following propositions. The suspect will probably be aware, if he has had advice, that he can keep silent and also that this is likely to be a risky course of action. It was, however, clear, even prior to 1994, that advisers did not advise silence routinely.[126] Dixon found in 1991 that solicitors were likely to advise silence at least temporarily if the client was in a confused or emotional state[127] or had been bullied or deceived, or where the police had refused to disclose at least some of the evidence against the client to the adviser.[128]

The legal adviser may help the suspect to maintain silence where advice alone – in the absence of the adviser - might not be enough. It should be recognised, however, that the key question is not whether the presence of a legal adviser means that the detainee remains silent, but whether it means that he or she is unlikely to make an unreliable confession. Further, assuming for the moment an inverse correlation between a legal adviser's presence and an unreliable confession, what contribution to it, if any, is made by the right to silence in its current modified form? Obviously, the detainee will not make such a confession if he remains silent, but that is a highly dubious strategy

---

122 Sanders *et al.*, *Advice and Assistance at Police Stations*, November 1989.

123 The Sanders research, ibid, found that only 50% of solicitors attended the police station: 25% gave advice over the telephone and 25% gave no advice. Even attendances at the police station were not always followed by attendance at the interview. A few solicitors merely put the police case to the suspect (p 150). It appeared that some advisers who did attend the interview disadvantaged the client by seeming to give their imprimatur to improper police behaviour.

124 Brown, *PACE Ten Years On: A Review of the Research*, Home Office Research Study 155, 1997, at pp 94–95.

125 The relationship is a matter of some controversy; the Home Office, *Working Group on the Right to Silence* (C Division, Home Office, London, 13 July 1989; see [1989] Crim LR 855 for comment) considered that there was a causal relationship between legal advice and silence, but this finding has been doubted by Dixon, D, 'Common sense, legal advice and the right to silence' [1991] PL 233, p 251. However, the Sanders research (1989) found that suspects confess less often when they have advice: 35.8% of those whose solicitor was present at the interrogation confessed, as opposed to 59.6% of those who did not receive advice (at p 136). Confirmed by Bucke *et al.*, *The Right of Silence: The Impact of the CJPOA 1994*, Home Office Research Study No 199, 2000.

126 See the research undertaken by Sanders *et al.*, ibid, p 129, which found that out of 24 suspects, only two were advised to remain silent. Dixon's findings, ibid, p 243 were to the same effect.

127 See Dixon, D, ibid, p 244.

128 Ibid, pp 246 and 247.

given that adverse inferences may be drawn against him at trial. In any event, it is an ineffective[129] way of tackling the risk of such confessions; the real concern here is with the question whether the legal adviser will enable the detainee to maintain a selective silence when under pressure from police, or refuse to depart from his version of events at key points in the interview.

Rights of access to legal advice

The right of access to legal advice is really a bundle of rights. Both PACE and the Terrorism Act 2000 entitle a suspect to consult an adviser privately.[130] The statutory entitlement is therefore both to access to legal advice and to the preservation of the confidentiality of solicitor/client consultation,[131] a matter that is also viewed as of great significance at Strasbourg.[132] The access to legal advice is available under a publicly funded scheme;[133] under Codes C and H the suspect is entitled to be informed of this right;[134] given, if necessary, the name of the duty solicitor,[135] and be permitted to have the solicitor present during questioning.[136] The right to have a solicitor present in the interview, available only under Codes C and H, rather than PACE or the TA, is arguably the most significant right.

The right of custodial access to legal advice is also protected by Art 6 of the European Convention on Human Rights, under the HRA. Article 6(3)(c) provides that everyone charged with a criminal offence has the right to defend himself through legal assistance of his own choosing.[137] Access to legal advice in pre-trial questioning, as opposed to such access for the purposes of the trial, is not expressly provided for in Art 6. However, protection for such access has been implied into Art 6(1) and 6(3)(c). Where a violation of Art 6 is claimed in respect of a lack of access to legal advice in pre-trial questioning, a breach of both paras (1) and (3) will be in question. The judgment in *Imbrioscia v Switzerland*[138] suggests that if either the accused or his lawyer requests that the latter should be present in pre-trial questioning, this should be allowed if the answers to questions would be likely to prejudice the defence; it is now clear, as discussed below, that the ruling is applicable to police interviews.

---

129 The Sanders research (1989) found that only 2.4% of suspects exercised their right to silence as against 54.1% who made admissions (the others denied the offence) (1989, p 136).

130 PACE, s 58(1): 'A person in police detention shall be entitled, if he so requests, to consult a solicitor privately at any time.' For TA suspects, this right also arises under the TA, Sched 8, para 7.

131 But see below p 1225 in relation to exceptions to the privacy requirement in relation to terrorism suspects.

132 See below p 1225.

133 See the Legal Aid Act 1988, Sched 6; the Access to Justice Act 1999. Everyone is entitled to free legal advice at the police station from a solicitor whose office is contracted with the Legal Services Commission, whatever their income and capital/savings. The Access to Justice Act provides for payment to franchised firms for most criminal legal aid work, on a fixed fee contract basis.

134 Codes C and H, para 3.1(ii).

135 Codes C and H, Note 6B. The duty solicitor arrangements are governed by the Legal Aid Board Duty Solicitor Arrangements (1994).

136 Code C, para 6.8; Code H, para 6.9.

137 See Chapter 2, pp 65–66.

138 (1993) 17 EHRR 441; A 275 (1993).

Access to legal advice where adverse inferences may be drawn from silence

The Court went further than *Imbrioscia* in *Murray (John) v UK*[139] in finding that Art 6(1) and (3)(c) had been breached by the denial of custodial access to a lawyer for 48 hours, since such access was essential where there was a likelihood that adverse inferences would be drawn from silence. It found that where such inferences could be drawn, Art 6 would normally require that the accused should be allowed to benefit from the assistance of a lawyer in the initial stages of police interrogation, although that right might be subject to restrictions for good cause.

These findings were confirmed in *Averill v UK*.[140] The applicant was denied access to a solicitor during the first 24 hours of interrogation; he was then allowed to consult a solicitor, but the solicitor was not allowed to be present during subsequent interviews. The provisions governing access to a solicitor were contained in s 45 of the EPA 1991. Adverse inferences were drawn from his silence at trial under Art 3 of the Criminal Evidence (Northern Ireland) Order 1988. The Court found that no breach of Art 6(1) had occurred; he had been subject to 'indirect compulsion', due to the probability that adverse inferences would be drawn if he remained silent, but that in itself was not decisive.[141] The drawing of adverse inferences, it was found, did not render the trial unfair since the presence of incriminating fibres found on his clothing called for an explanation from him. Further, the drawing of adverse inferences was only one factor in the finding that the charges were proved. However, the Court did find a breach of Art 6(3)(c) read with Art 6(1) on the basis – which it noted in *Murray* – that, bearing in mind the scheme contained in the 1998 Order, it is of 'paramount importance for the rights of the defence that an accused has access to a lawyer at the initial stages of police interrogation'.[142] This was because, under the scheme, the accused is confronted with a dilemma from the outset. If he remains silent, adverse inferences may be drawn. If he breaks his silence, his defence may be prejudiced. In order to deal with this dilemma, the Court found, legal advice is needed at the initial stages of the interrogation.[143] Thus, a right of access to legal advice in custodial questioning may be implied into Art 6(3)(c) when read with Art 6(1) where the drawing of adverse inferences is a relevant issue.

It appeared from *Murray* and *Averill* that *any* delay in affording the suspect access to legal advice where adverse inferences could be drawn would result in a breach of Art 6, but *Brennan v UK*[144] suggests that the position is less straightforward than that. In *Brennan* the accused had been denied access to legal advice but the denial of access was then lifted, although the accused did not in fact receive legal advice. At that point he made a confession. The European Court found that no adverse inferences had in fact been drawn from his silence at trial, and that he had made the confession at a time when the formal denial of access was no longer operative. Taking those factors into

---

139 (1996) 22 EHRR 29.
140 (2001) 31 EHRR 36; (2000) *The Times*, 20 June. See also *Magee v UK* (2001) 31 EHRR 35; (2000) *The Times*, 20 June.
141 Paragraph 48.
142 Paragraph 59.
143 Paragraph 57.
144 (2002) 34 EHRR 18.

account, no breach of Art 6 was found. *Brennan* therefore creates quite a significant departure from the more strongly due process-based findings in *Murray* and *Averill*.

Brennan implies that a breach of Art 6 cannot be established until the trial; in other words, the question is not whether there was a possibility that adverse inferences would be drawn from silence at a point when the suspect did not have access to legal advice, but whether such inferences were in fact drawn. It is suggested that *Murray* and *Averill* are to be preferred on this point: a domestic trial court should approach the matter from the *Murray* point of view, rather than the *Brennan* one, since it is in a different position from the Strasbourg Court – it obviously cannot consider the proceedings as a whole, including the trial proceedings, in determining whether a breach of Art 6 occurred.

Further, there may be many situations in which an accused is not *formally* denied legal advice, but where adverse inferences could be drawn from silence – a number of such situations are discussed below. It is readily arguable that the suspect could be placed in a dilemma that would require consultation with a legal adviser in such circumstances in order to satisfy the demands of fairness under Art 6. Arguably, *Murray* and *Averill*, but not *Brennan* might support an argument that Art 6 would be breached where a suspect had been affected by police ploys in failing to obtain advice, although he needed advice since he was aware that adverse inferences could be drawn from silence. It should be irrelevant that the suspect himself did not demand legal advice since he did not appreciate its significance at the time. However at present the position cannot be regarded as settled. Thus if the loopholes in the legal advice scheme are explored, with the result that a suspect who wants legal advice does not obtain it, it is at present unclear whether Art 6 demands that adverse inferences should not be drawn from silence or that admissions made should be excluded. These points are explored further below.

Murray required a domestic answer, bearing in mind the curtailment of the right to silence that had occurred under ss 34–37 Criminal Justice and Public Order Act 1994, discussed fully below. Under s 34:

> where . . . evidence is given that the accused . . . (a) on being questioned under caution by a constable trying to discover whether or by whom the offence had been committed, failed to mention any fact relied on in his defence . . . or (b) on being charged . . . or on officially being informed that he might be prosecuted . . . failed to mention any such fact, being a fact which in the circumstances existing at the time the accused could reasonably have been expected to mention when so questioned, charged or informed . . . sub-s (2) below applies.

Under s 34(2)(d), the court or jury 'in determining whether the accused is guilty of the offence charged may draw such inferences as appear proper'. The Code C, para 10.5 caution, introduced in the 2003 version of Code C, reflected this curtailment of the right to silence in warning the suspect that adverse inferences could be drawn. The response to *Murray* was eventually provided by s 58 of the Youth Justice and Criminal Evidence Act 1999 (which came into force in 2003). Section 58 inserted s 34(2A) into the CJPOA to provide essentially that adverse inferences shall not be drawn from a suspect's silence under caution before or after charge at an authorised place of detention if he has not been allowed an *opportunity* to consult a solicitor before that point (emphasis added).

Codes C and H reflect s 34(2A) in the sense that they provide in Annex C that a restriction on drawing adverse inferences applies when the suspect has not had an opportunity to have access to legal advice. The restriction is reflected in the use of the Annex C para 2 caution, encapsulating the traditional right to silence, which must be used where an opportunity to have legal advice has not been given. Thus s 34(2A) CJPOA is likely to encourage the police to afford access to legal advice. To an extent, s 34(2A) and the current version of Code C reflect *Murray* rather than *Brennan*. At the point when the caution is given it is, of course, not possible to know whether or not adverse inferences will in fact be drawn at trial, and yet the suspect has the right to remain silent without risk. This position accords with Art 6, following *Murray*.

The scheme under ss 34, 36 and 37 of the CJPOA is similar to the scheme under the 1988 Order, so the findings in *Murray* and *Averill* appear to cover all police interviews under the Code C para 10.5 caution, since once the caution has been given, it is clear that adverse inferences may be drawn from silence. However, the limitations on access to legal advice and certain of the formal and informal loopholes in the access discussed below arguably may not fully accord with the requirements of Art 6(3)(c) in conjunction with Art 6(1) as interpreted in *Murray* and *Averill*. So if s 34(2A) allows for any departure from *Murray*, or fails to satisfy *Murray* fully, s 3 HRA could be relied upon to improve the scheme by reference to Art 6. The impact of *Murray* could, however, be curtailed in so far as *Brennan* departs from *Murray*. The term 'circumstances' in ss 34, 36 and 37 of the CJPOA could be strictly interpreted to include a failure to have access to legal advice. The phrase 'had not been allowed to consult a solicitor' in s 58 of the Youth Justice and Criminal Evidence Act 1999 could also be construed broadly to cover informal denials or even informal encouragement to forgo advice. This would depend on the domestic interpretation of *Murray*, *Averill* and *Brennan* and on how flexible judges and magistrates are prepared to be in respect of their interpretative obligation under HRA, s 3.

Whether s 34(2A) will encourage adherence to the legal advice provisions in practice will depend on the interpretation of the term given to the provision. Clearly, the term 'opportunity' may be taken to mean that, formally, an opportunity had been offered, but the suspect had not availed himself of it. This would not curb the use of ploys discussed below. Section 34(2A) also excludes questioning under caution at somewhere other than an authorised place of detention. Thus it does not apply to silences occurring in out of police station interviews (which will be prior to the point of notification of the availability of legal advice). The rationale is that in such interviews the suspect who has not been arrested is free to leave and could go to seek legal advice. However, the less experienced suspect may not realise that this is the case. As explained above, Code C allows for informal interviews outside the police station, under caution. Theoretically, then, such an interview, in which a suspect had remained silent and arguably had not had a true opportunity to consult a solicitor, could be adduced in evidence and s 34(2A) would not prevent the drawing of adverse inferences. Such a possibility would not appear to accord fully with the Art 6 jurisprudence since the suspect was confronted with a dilemma once cautioned, but could not avail himself of legal advice. It is suggested that the objections, based on *Murray* and *Averill*, to the drawing of adverse inferences from such silences cannot be fully met by the provision of para 11.4 of Codes C and H to the effect that any significant silence or statement outside the police station should be put to the suspect at the beginning of an interview at the police station. In such out of station interviews, the dilemma mentioned by the Court of Human Rights arises since the suspect should be under caution and therefore formally aware of the dangers of remaining silent. Street interviews or exchanges, of necessity without advice, may have an impact on later interviews even where para 11.2A is adhered to. In the light of these comments, it arguable that the revision of Code C in 2006 or 2003 should have responded to *Murray* by modifying paras 11.1, 11.1A, 11.13 and 3.1 which provide leeway for interviews to occur outside the police station without notification that access to legal advice is available. Thus, at present, it may be argued that the reform effected by s 34(2A) is flawed and incomplete.

On its face, s 34(2A) can have a direct impact only on suspects who have formally been denied an opportunity to have access to legal advice, who then remain silent, are charged and plead not guilty. Nevertheless, it may be having a general effect on police adherence to the legal advice scheme, since the impact it may have in any particular instance will not be apparent at the relevant points in detention. If a suspect has not formally had an 'opportunity' to have access to legal advice he must be cautioned using the terms of the 'old' caution, under Annex C, para 2 since the restriction on drawing adverse inferences from silence applies. But everything depends on the term 'opportunity' and on whether Art 6 only covers formal denials of access to legal advice. If in a sense the suspect appears to have had an opportunity, whereas in fact it has been subverted by police ploys, the caution under Code C, para 10.5 applies, placing the suspect under pressure to speak.

Under the current domestic provisions discussed below there are instances when suspects will be interviewed in the knowledge that adverse inferences may be drawn from silence, but access to legal advice will not be available, although not formally denied. If the suspect stays silent and the case comes to trial he could argue that in accordance with Art 6 no adverse inferences should be drawn from silence. However, as discussed above, the Strasbourg case law does not clearly cover informal subversion of the opportunity to have legal advice. If it is argued that it does, following *Murray* and *Averill*, then finding a breach of Art 6 would depend on determining the genuineness of the opportunity. That would depend on seeking to unravel precisely what had occurred at the police station or earlier in order to determine whether a real opportunity to have advice had been given or not. The findings in *Murray, Averill* and *Brennan* are not confined to a circumstance where the defendant in fact stayed silent. Rather, as the Court implied in *Murray*, it may be that the suspect who fails to remain silent is most in need of legal advice.[145] As Chapter 13 will point out, the Court in *Teixeira de Castro v Portugal*[146] found that certain pre-trial procedures render a fair trial almost impossible and therefore curb the discretion of the Court in its response.[147] This finding was not made in the context of custodial legal advice but, together with the findings in *Murray*, and *Averill* could be applied to s 78 of PACE, in support of an argument that the exclusionary discretion embodied under the section should be used to exclude interviews where no access to legal advice was made available before or during the police interview which is proffered in evidence (possibly even if the lack of access was

---

145 See further on this point Bucke *et al.*, *The Right of Silence: The Impact of the CJPOA 1994*, Home Office Research Study No 199, 2000.
146 (1998) 28 EHHR 101.
147 See, pp 1291–94.

not due to a clear breach of statutory or Code provisions), although the suspect was aware that adverse inferences might be drawn from silence.[148] It would be arguable that such an interview should be excluded from evidence under s 78, following *Murray* and *Averill*, on the basis that otherwise Art 6 would not appear to be satisfied.

An argument similar to this one did not receive much encouragement in one of the early decisions on the Convention, from Scotland.[149] In *Paton v Procurator Fiscal*,[150] the appellant was to be interviewed about attempted theft and at the police station he indicated that he wanted a solicitor to be informed of his detention. When he was interviewed, his solicitor was not present and he was not told that the police had a discretion to allow his solicitor to be present during the interview if he so wished. After caution, the appellant admitted that he was trying to break into the premises in question. When the charges were recited,[151] the appellant said that he had been merely passing by when the police chased him. The appellant argued that Art 6(1) and 6(3)(c) of the Convention had been contravened. The Court took into account the fact that the appellant had not made a request for his solicitor to be present and that neither Scots law nor the Convention required that in all cases a detained person should be afforded the opportunity to have a solicitor present. The Court found that the question whether a fair trial could be achieved depended not simply upon what happened during the preliminary investigation, but on the whole proceedings, and a number of safeguards were accorded to the accused during the investigation and the trial process; on this basis, the appeal was refused and the case was remitted to the sheriff to proceed to trial.

These findings do not appear to encourage the notion that certain rights, such as access to custodial legal advice, are of especial constitutional significance; they encourage a broad brush approach which appears to assume that a breach of suspects' rights may be cured by affording other rights. However, these findings may be based on the lack of a right to have a solicitor present in interviews in Scotland and, it is suggested, on a doubtful, minimalist interpretation of Art 6. It was also decided prior to the changes introduced by s 34(2A). The courts have not yet had a chance to consider whether s 34(2A) should be extended to cover instances in which legal advice has not been afforded although it has not been formally denied, and the suspect has remained silent.

It should finally be noted that neither s 34(2A) nor Art 6 provide a remedy where the suspect who has requested it has not received legal advice, although adverse inferences could be drawn from silence, and the case does not come to trial because he pleads guilty or the case is dropped. This applies to informal denials and also where a suspect has been formally denied legal advice and the 'wrong' caution is used: so he is warned via the caution that adverse inferences will be drawn from silence.

---

148 Under PACE 1984, Code C, this would include all interviews since, as indicated above, under para 11.1.A the definition of an interview is an exchange regarding involvement in criminal activity which is required to be under caution.

149 By virtue of the Scotland Act 1998, s 57(2), a Scottish court is required, *inter alia*, to take into account the various rights enshrined in the Convention. At the time, the Human Rights Act itself was not fully in force in Scotland.

150 Judgment of 24 November 1999 (unreported).

151 He was charged with attempting to break into premises with intent to steal and, in the alternative, that he was found at premises without lawful authority, the inference being that he might commit theft contrary to the Civil Government (Scotland) Act 1982, s 57(1).

Formal exceptions, limitations and informal subversion

The rights of access to legal advice are limited in formal and informal fashion. The formal PACE and TA exceptions are narrowly drawn and, as indicated below, have received a narrow interpretation. This cannot, however, be said of the formal Code C and H exceptions. Further, the factor which previously motivated the police to delay (or refuse) access to legal advice remains unchanged: the suspect still has the right to remain silent and the legal adviser may advise him or her to exercise it in the particular circumstances of the case, despite the risk that adverse inferences may be drawn later at court. Even if the solicitor does not advise silence, the police may think that they are more likely to obtain incriminating admissions from detainees in the absence of a solicitor and therefore at times may deny the access to one envisaged by s 58. Quite a large body of research suggests that the police continue to prefer to interview suspects who have not had advice and without an adviser present.[152] Research confirms that the possibility of formally delaying access to legal advice is almost certainly not as significant as the more informal police influence on the notification and delivery of advice and on securing the presence of the adviser.[153] This may be due in part to the determination shown by the Court of Appeal to protect this due process right by restrictive interpretation of the formal exceptions under s 58(8) of PACE in a key decision.[154] However, there are a number of loopholes in the legal advice scheme which may allow for less formal methods of evading its provisions and it may be that the suspects who are thereby most disadvantaged are those most in need of legal advice. A number of formal and informal methods of evading the scheme are available and the key methods are identified below.

As the discussion below explains, Codes C and H provide that in respect of formal denials the restriction on drawing adverse inferences applies, and the suspect should be cautioned accordingly, under Annex C para 2 of both Codes (the traditional pre-1994 caution). But in respect of other instances in which legal advice is not afforded, the Codes provide expressly or impliedly that the restriction does not apply and therefore the suspect is warned via the caution that if he remains silent adverse inferences may be drawn.

Delaying access – harm-based exceptions

Non-terrorist suspects

The most direct method of delaying legal advice involves invoking one of the s 58(8) PACE exceptions. The exceptions come into operation if the suspect is in police

---

152 The research undertaken by Sanders *et al., Advice and Assistance at Police Stations*, November 1989; Brown, *PACE Ten Years On: A Review of the Research*, Home Office Research Study 155, 1997, p 77.

153 The research undertaken by Sanders *et al.*, ibid, put the figure at around 2%. In comparison, Brown, ibid, found that approximately 35% of suspects may have been influenced against advice by the police. The government's *Consultation Paper on Terrorism* (1998) stated that it was not aware of any formal denial in terrorist cases over the last two years in Britain (para 8.31).

154 *R v Samuel* [1988] 2 All ER 135; [1988] 2 WLR 920.

detention for an indictable offence. It used to be the case that the exceptions applied in respect of 'serious arrestable offences'. The concept of an arrestable offence under s 24 was abolished in 2005 when PACE was amended, so s 58(8) has now broadened to cover indictable offences.[155] Section 58(8) allows an officer of at least the rank of superintendent to authorise delay, in respect of a suspect in detention for an indictable offence. If both these conditions are fulfilled, access, if requested, can be delayed for up to 36 hours. under s 58(8) which provides:

> An officer may only authorise delay where he has reasonable grounds for believing that the exercise of the right . . . (a) will lead to interference with or harm to evidence connected with an indictable offence or interference with or physical injury to other persons; or (b) will lead to the alerting of other persons suspected of having committed such an offence but not yet arrested for it; or (c) will hinder the recovery of any property obtained as a result of such an offence.

Under sub-section (8A), delay can also be authorised:

> where the indictable offence is a drug trafficking offence and the officer has reasonable grounds for believing (a) that the detained person has benefited from drug trafficking and (b) that the recovery of the value of that person's proceeds of drug trafficking will be hindered by the exercise of the right . . .'.

A further exception was added (s 58(8A) and (8B)) relating to confiscation orders under Part 2 of the Proceeds of Crime Act 2002. Delay is permitted where the detainee has benefited from the offence, and it is considered on reasonable grounds that recovery of the benefit would be hindered if the solicitor is contacted.

In other words, the officer must believe on reasonable grounds that exercise of the right at the time when the person in police detention desires to exercise it will lead to the solicitor acting as a channel of communication between the detainee and others – alerting them or hindering the recovery of stolen property or the products of drug trafficking, or the benefits of crime. These exceptions are repeated in Annex B of Code C, which also provides that if the exception is invoked the suspect must be allowed to choose another solicitor.

The leading case determining the scope of the s 58 exceptions is *Samuel*.[156] The appellant was arrested on suspicion of armed robbery and, after questioning at the police station, asked to see a solicitor. The request was refused, apparently on the grounds that other suspects might be warned[157] and that recovery of the outstanding stolen money might thereby be hindered.[158] The appellant subsequently confessed to the robbery and was later convicted. On appeal, the defence argued that the refusal of access was

---

155 A serious arrestable offence was defined in s 116. The amendment was made to s 58(6) by the Serious and Organised Crime Act 2005 Sched 7(3), para 43 (10)(b). The Criminal Justice Act 1988, s 99 extended the exceptions to drug trafficking offences.

156 [1988] QB 615; [1988] 2 All ER 135; [1988] 2 WLR 920, CA.

157 Section 58(8)(b).

158 Section 58(8)(c).

not justifiable under s 58(8) and that therefore, the confession obtained should not have been admitted into evidence as it had been obtained through impropriety. The Court of Appeal considered the use of the word 'will' in s 58(8), which suggests that the police officer must be virtually certain that a solicitor, if contacted, will thereafter either commit a criminal offence or unwittingly pass on a coded message to criminals. It must be asked, first, whether he did believe this and second, whether he believed it on reasonable grounds. The Court considered that only in the remote contingency that evidence could be produced as to the corruption of a particular solicitor would a police officer be able to assert a reasonable belief that a solicitor would commit a criminal offence. They went on to hold that showing a reasonable belief that a solicitor would inadvertently alert other criminals would also be a formidable task; such a belief could only reasonably be held if the suspect in question was a particularly resourceful and sophisticated criminal or if there was evidence that the solicitor sought to be consulted was particularly inexperienced or naïve. It was found that as no evidence as to the naivety or corruption of the solicitor in question had been advanced it could not be accepted that the necessary reasonable belief had existed. The police had made no attempt to consider the real likelihood that the solicitor in question would be utilised in this way; in fact, it was apparent that the true motive behind the denial of access was a desire to gain a further opportunity to break down the detainee's silence. It should be noted that Code C expressly disallows denial of access to a solicitor on the ground that he or she will advise the suspect to remain silent.[159]

This interpretation of s 58(8) greatly narrowed its scope, since it means that the police are no longer able to make a general, unsubstantiated assertion that it was thought that others might be alerted if a solicitor was contacted. The authorising officer has to show, on very specific grounds, why this was thought to be the case. This has meant that the exceptions are very rarely invoked; the change to allow them to operate in respect of indictable offences is unlikely to have any significant impact in encouraging police to invoke them since the central difficulty of showing that a specific solicitor would act dishonestly or naively in the ways indicated still remains. Code C reflects the s 58 exceptions in para 6.6, and they are repeated in Annex B. If an exception is invoked the restriction on drawing adverse inferences applies under CJPOA, s 34(2)(A), and this is stated in Code C, para 6.6(b). The question of exclusion of a confession where an exception is improperly invoked is considered in Chapter 13.[160]

Terrorist suspects

Under the TA 2000, as amended, the access can be delayed for up to 48 hours (see Sched 8, para 8(2)) on the grounds for delay mentioned above, with additional ones relating to terrorism. The right can be delayed if a superintendent reasonably believes that communication with an adviser will lead to interference with the gathering of information about the commission, preparation, or instigation of acts of terrorism or make it more difficult to prevent an act of terrorism or apprehend and prosecute the

159 Codes C and H, Annex B, para 4.
160 See pp 1281–83.

perpetrators of any such act. Delay can be for 48 hours, which is also the period of time for which the suspect can be detained on police authority alone, without recourse to judicial authorisation.[161]

The TA harmonises the arrangements for delay in Northern Ireland with those in England and Wales, in that once access has been granted, it will not then be withheld.[162] The arrangements in Scotland under the TA allow for delay under Sched 8, para 16(7) if, under para 17(3), delay is 'in the interests of the investigation or prevention of crime, or in recovering property criminally obtained, or in confiscating the proceeds of an offence, or of the apprehension, prosecution or conviction of offenders'. In all three jurisdictions, when a review officer authorises continued detention under Sched 8 of the TA he must remind the detainee of his rights to contact a friend or relative and to consult a solicitor[163] and, if applicable, of the fact of their being delayed. The officer must also consider whether the reason or reasons for which the delay was authorised continue to subsist, and if not, he must inform the officer who authorised the delay of his opinion. However, there is no provision allowing the review officer to override the view of the officer who originally authorised delay. The TA provisions largely continue the previous counter-terrorism regime, and therefore do not address the concerns of those who view confessions obtained after 24 hours in detention as inherently fallible,[164] particularly where the detainee has also been held without access to legal advice and incommunicado.[165]

Under this scheme, the power of delay in Scotland is wider and is less dependent than in the other jurisdictions on the interests of preventing or detecting acts of terrorism. This seems to be anomalous given that one of the aims of the TA was to harmonise the position of terrorist suspects throughout the UK. The changes under the TA also provide further grounds for delay in obtaining access to legal advice which apply to a far wider group of persons than those covered previously by the PTA and EPA since, potentially, a far larger group can now be viewed as 'terrorist' suspects.[166] Within that group are persons who signally fail to fit the stereotype of the 'terrorist', and are therefore more in need of legal advice. The wider possibilities of delaying access under the TA in relation to the terrorist, as opposed to the conventional suspect, are therefore open to question under Art 6, as discussed below. Code H reflects the TA exceptions in para 6.7(iii), and they are repeated in Annex B. If an exception is invoked the restriction on drawing adverse inferences applies under CJPOA, s 34(2)(A), and this is stated in Code H in para 6.7(b).

161 See Chapter 11, pp 1169–70.
162 Under the EPA and its Codes, the powers to delay access were broadly the same as under the PTA, but also, once the police had allowed access, further delays could be imposed and there was no right to have advisers present in interviews.
163 Under Sched 8, para 27. These rights arise under paras 6 and 7 of Sched 8.
164 See, e.g., Walker, *Miscarriages of Justice*, 1999, pp 18, 39.
165 See above, p 1188. The exceptions to the right to have someone informed of detention are similar to those allowing delay in providing access to legal advice.
166 See Chapter 14, pp 1377–81.

Further formal exceptions under Codes C and H[167]

Harm-based exceptions

As indicated, para 6.6(b) of both Codes C and H reflects the TA and PACE exceptions to an extent. Those exceptions are repeated word for word in Annex B of both Codes. But the wording of para 6.6 (b) (6.7(b) in Code H) is significantly different and broader. Under para 6.6(b), a power to proceed with the interview, although the suspect has not had advice, arises if an officer of superintendent rank or above has reasonable grounds for believing that delay would: lead to interference with or harm to evidence connected with an offence; lead to interference with or harm to other people or serious loss of or damage to property, or hinder the recovery of property obtained in consequence of the commission of an offence; or lead to the alerting of people suspected of having committed an offence but not yet arrested for it. The para 6.6 provisions are not dependent on the offence in question being an indictable one. These exceptions are significantly broader than those contained in PACE or the TA and repeated in Annex B of both Codes. However, the curbing effect of the *Samuel* argument would still

---

167 Code C, para 6.6 provides: A person who wants legal advice may not be interviewed or continue to be interviewed until he has received such advice unless –

(a) Annex B applies in which case the restriction on drawing adverse inferences from silence (para 10.4) will apply because the person is not allowed an opportunity to consult a solicitor; or

(b) an officer of the rank of superintendent or above has reasonable grounds for believing that–

   (i) the consequent delay would be likely to lead to interference with or harm to evidence connected with an offence or physical harm to other people or serious loss of, or damage to, property; or lead to the alerting of other people suspected of having committed an offence . . . or hinder the recovery of property obtained in consequence of the commission of an offence;

   (ii) where a solicitor, including a duty solicitor, has been contacted and has agreed to attend, awaiting his arrival would cause unreasonable delay to the process of investigation; and in these cases the restriction on drawing adverse inferences from silence (para 10.4) will apply . . .

(c) The solicitor nominated by the person, or selected by him from a list –

   (i) cannot be contacted; or

   (ii) has previously indicated that they do not wish to be contacted; or

   (iii) having been contacted, has declined to attend; and the person has been advised of the Duty Solicitor Scheme but has declined to ask for the duty solicitor. In these circumstances the interview may be started or continued without further delay provided that an officer of the rank of Inspector or above has given agreement for the interview to proceed. In these circumstances the restriction on drawing adverse inferences from silence (para 10.4) will not apply because the person is allowed an opportunity to consult a solicitor.

(d) The person who wanted legal advice changes his mind, in which case the restriction on drawing adverse inferences from silence (para 10.4) will not apply because the person is allowed an opportunity to consult a solicitor. In these circumstances the interview may be started or continued without further delay provided that the person has given his agreement in writing or on tape to being interviewed without receiving legal advice and that an officer of the rank of Inspector or above, having inquired into the suspect's reasons for his change of mind, has given agreement for the interview to proceed in those circumstances. The name of the authorising officer and the reason for the suspect's change of mind should be recorded and repeated on tape at the beginning or re-commencement of interview.

apply: it would still have to be shown that a particular adviser would be likely to act as a channel of communication with others or act dishonestly in some other fashion in relation to the harm envisaged. The restriction on drawing adverse inferences from silence applies if one of these exceptions is invoked.

Unavailability of nominated solicitor or delay

Further powers to delay access and to interview the suspect without his having had legal advice arise under Codes C and H. Code C, para 6.6(b)(ii) provides that the interview can be started although the suspect has not received advice if 'a solicitor has agreed to attend, and awaiting his arrival would cause unreasonable delay to the process of the investigation'. This is repeated in Annex B. Code H contains the same exception in para 6.7. The restriction on drawing adverse inferences from silence applies. But even where the restriction on drawing adverse inferences applies, it is clear that there should be good cause for the delay in obtaining advice, following *Murray*. That requirement may not be satisfied by these grounds for proceeding with the interview, although advice has not been obtained, since the use of the word 'unreasonable' means that the test is broad and imprecise and could offer leeway to the police to invoke it in a wide range of circumstances

Sub-paragraph 6.6(c) Code C and 6.7 (c) Code H provides two further exceptions: that the detainee can be interviewed without legal advice if the nominated solicitor is unavailable and, first, notification of the duty solicitor scheme is given but the duty solicitor is unavailable, or second, he or she is not required. In these instances the restriction on drawing adverse inferences from silence does *not* apply on the basis that the suspect has an opportunity to have advice. The first exception does not, it is argued accord with Art 6 as interpreted in *Murray* and *Averill* since where both the nominated and duty solicitor are unavailable, the suspect cannot be said to have had an opportunity to have legal advice. It is argued that regardless of the provision in Codes C and H para 6 that adverse inferences can be drawn, s 34(2A) CJPOA should be invoked, taking the demands of Art 6 into account, in such circumstances, to provide that adverse inferences cannot be drawn from silence in an interview affected by that exception.

Consent to forgo advice

The detainee who has decided to have advice can nevertheless change his or her mind; this is provided for by sub-para 6.6(d) of both Codes, if the consent is given in writing or on tape and an officer of the rank of inspector or above has inquired into the reason for the change of mind and gives authority for the interview to proceed.[168] However, there is some leeway allowing police officers to engineer a change of heart.

---

168 This provision was originally included in the 1991 Home Office circular. It required a note to be made in the custody record of the reason for the suspect's change of heart and this circular provision, in the form of a requirement to record the reason for the change of mind and repeat it on tape, became part of para 6.5 under the 1995 revision to Code C. (When the revised PACE Codes came into force in April 1991, a Home Office circular was issued in conjunction with them by F2 Division, Home Office.)

No limitations were placed on the reasons for giving such consent, thus creating a serious flaw in the legal advice provisions. In particular, if the consent is based on a police misrepresentation, ought it to be treated as genuine? This question arises in part due to the lack of certainty as to the relationship between sub-para 6.6(d) and (c). For example of a detainee nominates a particular solicitor who turns out to be unavailable, and then consents to go ahead with the interview without advice, he or she should clearly be treated as falling within para (c) as opposed to para (d). The provisions under sub-paras 6.6(c) and (d) appear to be expressed as alternatives, but the drafter's intention must surely have been that the police should not be able to obtain the detainee's consent to be interviewed merely by failing to inform him or her of the duty solicitor scheme.

The first instance decision in *Vernon*[169] suggested that the consent must be genuine; in other words, it must not be based on misleading information given by the police. The defendant consented to be interviewed under the misapprehension that if her own solicitor was unavailable, there was no alternative means of obtaining advice; the confession so obtained was excluded. Andrew J held that as her consent to the interview was given under the misapprehension that otherwise, the interview would be delayed till the morning, this could not be termed true consent: had she known of the availability of the duty solicitor, she would have withheld her consent. Thus, the exception under sub-para 6.3(d) (now para 6.6(d)) was not fulfilled: para 6.3 had been breached. This ruling suggests that although the exceptions under sub-paras 6.6(c) and (d) are expressed disjunctively, they should be read together; if a detainee has fallen within sub-para 6.6(c) by nominating a solicitor and being disappointed, he or she should then be informed of the alternative. It would not seem to accord with the drafter's intention to treat the consent of such a person in the same way as that of a detainee who has decided against having a solicitor at all.

The ruling of the Court of Appeal in *Hughes*,[170] however, suggested that if the police misled the suspect without bad faith, a resultant consent would be treated as genuine. The appellant, disappointed of obtaining advice from his own solicitor, inquired about the duty solicitor scheme but was informed, erroneously (but in good faith), that no solicitor was available. Under this misapprehension, he gave consent to be interviewed and the Court of Appeal took the view that his consent was not thereby vitiated. Sub-paragraphs 6.3(c) and (d) (now 6.6(c) and (d)) were to be treated as alternatives and the fact that the detainee was within (c) did not vitiate his consent under (d). Thus, no breach had occurred. The Court did not advert to the difficulty that there can be no difference in principle between failing to inform a detainee of the scheme and informing him or her of it but stating wrongly that no solicitor is available.

This ruling opens the possibility that the consent given in *Vernon* will in future be treated as true consent. The only distinction between the cases is that in *Hughes*, the misrepresentation was apparently made innocently, while in *Vernon*, the failure to give the information was deliberate: *Vernon* demonstrates a willingness to interpret Code C restrictively against the police if bad faith is demonstrated. The view was taken in *Hughes* that if the misrepresentation had been made negligently or deliberately, a different conclusion would have been reached. This seems to confuse the para 6.3(d)

169 [1988] Crim LR 445.
170 [1988] Crim LR 519, CA, transcript from LEXIS.

issue and the issue of fairness under s 78 (which will be considered fully in Chapter 13);[171] the judgment would have been clearer if the court had considered first, whether a breach of para 6.3 had occurred and, second, whether the breach in the circumstances would have an adverse effect on the fairness of the trial. Innocence or bad faith on the part of the police has been determined to be relevant when considering s 78,[172] but there is nothing in Code C to suggest that these matters are relevant in relation to the narrow question of failure to fulfil a Code provision. Generally, consent to forgo a right should be treated with caution when the parties are on an unequal footing; and the possible unfairness is exacerbated when the party who will obtain an advantage from the consent gives false information in obtaining it. Had the Court of Appeal found itself able to hold that such consent is not true consent, the onus would have been placed on the police to ensure that administrative practice in relation to the duty solicitor scheme was tightened up. As it is, moves towards obtaining consent in similar circumstances may become more marked and it is likely to be the more suggestible detainee who suffers.

As indicated, under the 2006 version of Codes C and H, once the suspect has changed his mind about having advice, the interview can proceed subject to the need to obtain the permission of an officer of the rank of inspector or above. This was the main change from the original Code and was obviously not a full safeguard against the possibility of pressure from the police considered above. The requirement that the inspector inquires into the reason for the change of mind provides, however, a partial safeguard. Inclusion of a provision that a consent based on erroneous information given by the police could not be treated as true consent might have encouraged the police to tighten up administrative practices and perhaps avoided a recurrence of the *Hughes* type of situation. This provision may allow a court to determine whether the consent was based on misleading information, but it leaves open the possibility of treating the consent as valid so long as such information was apparently given in good faith. The restriction on drawing adverse inferences does not apply since the suspect has apparently consented to forego advice.

Debarring solicitors' representatives

As already noted, s 58(1) entitles the detainee to consult a solicitor at any time. This provision does not extend to solicitors' clerks but, under Code C, para 6.12 (previously para 6.9), if the solicitor who has been contacted decides to send a clerk, he or she should be admitted to the police station. After the decision in *Samuel*,[173] access to a solicitor can be delayed only in very specific circumstances. These exceptions do not apply to clerks under both Codes C and H, but, since the decision of the Court of Appeal in *Chief Constable of Avon ex p Robinson*,[174] access to a clerk can be denied in a much wider range of circumstances. The Chief Constable had issued instructions that the character and antecedents of certain unqualified clerks employed by the applicant – a solicitor – were such as to make their presence at police interviews with suspects undesirable.

---

171 See Chapter 13, pp 1277–78.
172 See *Alladice* (1988) 87 Cr App R 380, CA; [1988] Crim LR 608. See Chapter 13, p 1282.
173 [1988] QB 615; [1988] 2 All ER 135; [1988] 2 WLR 920, CA.
174 [1989] All ER 15; [1989] 1 WLR 793.

The Chief Constable left the final decision on access to the officer in question, but gave his opinion that it would only rarely be appropriate to allow these particular clerks access to a suspect. The applicant sought judicial review of the instructions, contending that they were in breach of para 6.9.

The Court of Appeal considered the scope of the express exception to para 6.9: '. . . the clerk shall be admitted unless an officer of the rank of inspector or above considers that such a visit will hinder the investigation of crime'. (Similar wording is now used in para 6.12.) It was held that the investigating officers had been entitled in each instance to invoke the exception because they had known of the criminal activities of the clerks. They had been informed of such activities by the Chief Constable, but he had not imposed a blanket ban on the clerks; the discretion to debar the clerks had been left with the officers concerned. Accordingly, there had been no breach of para 6.9 and the application would therefore be refused. May LJ, in a lengthy *dictum*, also considered that there was an implied requirement under para 6.9 that a clerk be capable of giving advice on behalf of the solicitor and therefore a police officer would be entitled to exclude a clerk if he appeared incapable of giving advice owing to his age, appearance, mental capacity or known background.

The concern as to the possible effects of employing these untrained clerks was understandable, but the result of this decision was to confer a very wide power on the police to exclude clerks, which potentially has unfortunate consequences. If a detainee asks for legal advice and a clerk arrives but is not admitted to the police station on one of the grounds considered above, or if he or she is not allowed to remain in the interview, the police, under Code C, para 6.14, must give the original solicitor the opportunity of making other arrangements. The Code is silent as to what should happen if the solicitor is unable to do so, although under para 6.10, if a solicitor is excluded from the station, the police must give the suspect an opportunity to consult another solicitor. Paragraph 6.12 now provides that para 6.10 applies to clerks and, therefore, in the circumstances described, the police as a last resort presumably ought to inform the detainee of the duty solicitor scheme. It is probably regrettable that the Court of Appeal suggested such wide grounds on which to exclude clerks. If the police take advantage of their width to exclude clerks rather too readily, some detainees may be likely to experience substantial delay in obtaining advice. There is always the danger when advice is delayed that a detainee will succumb to pressure to get the interview over with quickly and will consent to be interviewed without advice.

The 1995 revision addressed this possibility to some extent and the changes appear in the 2006 revision of Code C, and in Code H: para 6.13 restricts the grounds for exclusion as far as clerks or other accredited representatives of solicitors are concerned, since it defines such persons as 'solicitors'. This means that the trainee, clerk or legal executive is 'an accredited or probationary representative included on the register of representatives maintained by the Legal Sevices Commission'. Therefore, the more restrictive provisions relating to exclusion from the interview of solicitors, paras 6.9, 6.10, 6.11 and 6.12, will apply. Under para 6.10, the solicitor may be excluded from the interview if his or her conduct is such that the investigating officer is unable properly to question the suspect. Under para 6.14, an accredited or probationary representative may be excluded from the police station if an officer of the rank of inspector or above considers that the visit would hinder the investigation of crime and directs otherwise. The factors influencing the discretion to exclude such advisers from the police station are set out in paras 6.15, and include taking account of 'any matters set out in any written letter of authorisation provided by the solicitor'. It is unclear that this discretion is markedly narrower than that indicated in *Robinson* and, therefore, it will be hard ever to challenge a decision to exclude such persons, leaving open the possibility that officers may at times exercise this power rather too readily. Once advice is delayed, a detainee may succumb to pressure to forgo it in order to speed matters up. But under para 6.16 the solicitor in question must be notified and given an opportunity to make other arrangements. Under para 6.19 a record must be made if a detainee asks for legal advice and an interview is begun without it, or the solicitor or representative has been required to leave the interview. Nothing is said about applying the restriction on drawing adverse inferences, despite the fact that the detainee may not in fact obtain an opportunity to have legal advice. Again this is an instance in which, it is argued, s 34(2A) should be applied, adopting a broad interpretation based on the Art 6 jurisprudence, so that such inferences should not be drawn.

Disallowing private consultation for terrorist suspects

There is an extra exception in Code H under para 6.5, based on TA, Sched 8, para 9. The detainee can be forbidden a private consultation with the solicitor if an officer of the rank of Commander or Assistant Chief Constable gives authority for this on the basis that otherwise the consequences set out in the TA, Sched 8, paras 8(4) or 8(5) might reasonably be expected to arise. Those are the consequences allowing for delay in access to legal advice. This provision is in doubtful conformity with Art 6 since in a number of cases the Strasbourg Court has stressed the importance of maintaining the confidentiality of solicitor/client consultation (*Brennan v UK*; *S v Switzerland*).[175] In *R (La Rose) v Commissioner of Police of the Metropolis* the applicant was forced to obtain telephone advice using a phone on the custody officer's desk, while other officers were in the room. It appeared that confidentiality may have been impaired and he was inhibited in his consultation with the solicitor as a result. However, the Divisional Court found no breach of his Art 6 rights. Since it was unclear that there was a pressing reason to use a phone in a situation in which the applicant could be over heard, it is likely that the Strasbourg would take a different view. The exception based on TA, Sched 8, para 9 does relate to pressing reasons. But, on *Samuel* lines, and taking account of the Art 6 jurisprudence on confidentiality, it is argued that the police would have to demonstrate that there was some quality about the particular solicitor that would lead him or her to divulge information resulting in one of the harmful consequences envisaged in Sched 8, if the conversation was confidential.

Implied limitations and informal subversion of the rights

Suspects who are thinking of asking for legal advice straight away may still be persuaded out of doing so by various methods and the Sanders research found that such methods – termed 'ploys' – were, unsurprisingly, most successful against the least experienced

175 29 November 1991.

suspects.[176] However, there have been some attempts in the various revisions of Code C to combat the use of such ploys, as discussed below.

Out of station interviews

Interviews outside the police station continue to be unaffected by rights of access to legal advice, in the sense that notification of the right under para 3.1 of Codes C and H is reserved for the police station, thus disadvantaging the inexperienced suspect who is not already aware of it at the point when admissions may be made.[177] The very significant reform of notification of legal advice on caution was omitted from all the Code C revisions, including the 2006 one, despite the fact of curtailment of the right to silence and of the findings discussed at Strasbourg to the effect that questioning accompanied by the risk of drawing adverse inferences from silence without access to legal advice breaches Art 6(1).[178] The restriction on drawing adverse inferences from silence where no opportunity to have access to legal advice has been given (in Codes C and H, Annex C), goes only part of the way to meet those findings, it is argued, since the restriction only applies inside the police station, as considered further below. The lack of notification of legal advice outside the police station, combined with the leeway for interviewing before the police station is reached within Codes C and H, is probably one of the key flaws in the PACE scheme in due process terms.

Subverting notification

It is probably fair to assume, first, that many suspects, including those who are criminally experienced,[179] are aware of the right to legal advice and, second, that the group who are not so aware would tend to include some of the more vulnerable members of society, or first-time suspects. It has already been noted above that there is leeway in the interviewing scheme to allow admissions to be made before notification of advice during 'booking in' at the police station. At the point of notification, the suspect not already aware of the right to advice is in a very vulnerable position since he is dependent for information on the very persons who have an interest in withholding it or misleading him. Research conducted by Sanders has demonstrated that notification can be subverted by various methods, most commonly by ensuring that suspects never really take in what is on offer.[180] When Code C was revised in 1991 and in 1995, this problem was recognised and an attempt was made to address it. The reforms are carried through into the 2006 version and also appear in Code H.

---

176 The take-up rate for advice among suspects with no previous convictions 'declined sharply as more ploys were used'. This was contrasted with the smaller correlation between the use of ploys and take-up rate among all suspects (Sanders, 1989, pp 57 and 61).

177 Softley's research into the issue indicated that when suspects were informed of this right, requests for advice were three times as high as when they were not so informed (Softley, *Police Interrogations*, 1980).

178 Above, p 1211.

179 The Sanders research, above (1989), supports this suggestion; out of 60 suspects who knew that they had a right to legal advice, only 23.3% did not know this before informed of it by the police: p 46.

180 Sanders found that the most popular ploy (used in 42.9% of the instances observed) was to read the rights too quickly or incomprehensibly or incompletely: ibid, p 59.

The requirement of notification under para 3.1 was backed up by a para 6.3 (6.2 in Code H), requiring that police stations display a prominent poster (under Note 6H with ethnic translations if appropriate) advertising the right to have advice. Suspects were supposed to be given a leaflet under original Note 3E explaining the arrangements for obtaining advice, including the fact that it was free, but in practice a number of suspects did not receive it or did not understand it, thereby enabling police officers to mislead them.[181] Currently, under para 3.1(ii), of both Codes C and H the suspect must now be informed that advice is free[182] (although the posters need not carry this information). Further, general discouragement of ploys is articulated in para 6.4, which provides that no attempt should be made to dissuade the suspect from having advice.

However, it must be questioned whether the provision of posters will make much difference. The 'booking in' stage is likely to be one of the more traumatic points in the process, especially for the suspect who is inexperienced or in some other way vulnerable. Whether he is likely to notice and take in a message conveyed in this way, which is not specifically directed at him, is open to question. If he remains silent in the face of a rapid notification, his silence can be taken as a waiver of advice when in actuality it merely denotes incomprehension. The requirement (introduced in 1995) under para 6.5 (6.4 in Code H) that the suspect should be asked his reason for declining legal advice, and that this should be noted on the custody record, may go some way towards ensuring that suspects understand what is on offer and may curb police 'ploys', as may the requirement to point out that the suspect may speak on the telephone with a solicitor. Nevertheless, the possibility of manipulation of the custody record remains, since the whole process of making the record remains in the hands of the custody officer.[183] Research conducted after the 1991 revision of Code C found that a higher proportion of suspects were being informed of the right to legal advice,[184] but that the information was given in a quarter of cases in an unclear or unduly rapid fashion.

Encouragement to defer the decision

If the suspect does take in what is being offered, he may be encouraged not to exercise the right straight away. In fact, the Sanders research suggested that encouraging a suspect to defer the decision to have advice was quite popular.[185] The 1991 revision of Code C did address this problem and again the reforms are carried through into

---

181 This ploy was used in less than 1.5% of the instances observed: ibid, p 59.
182 The research by Brown *et al.* (1997) shows a dramatic improvement in the number of suspects informed that advice is free after the revision of the Codes: 73%, compared with 5%.
183 It has been suggested (by Wolchover and Heaton-Armstrong (1990) 140 NLJ 320–21) that a requirement of an own hand declaration of waiver of advice would have represented an effective means of addressing the problem because it would have forced the custody officer to ensure that the suspect understood what was being offered and would require positive action on the suspect's part to refuse it.
184 Brown, Ellis and Larcombe, *Changing the Code: Police Detention under the revised PACE Codes of Practice* (research conducted for the Royal Commission on Criminal Procedure), 1993, Home Office Research Study 129. It found that 73% of suspects, as opposed to 66% prior to April 1991, received notification.
185 This 'ploy' was used in 8.2% of the cases observed. In a further 1.8% of cases, it was suggested that the suspect waited until after his transfer to another station before having advice and in a further 2.7% of cases that he waited until he got out of the police station; Sanders, 1989, p 59.

the 2006 version of Code C. Paragraph 3.1 Codes C and H now provides that it is a 'continuing right which may be exercised at any stage' and under para 11.2 of both Codes, a suspect must now be reminded of the right before each interview in the police station. Although this change is to be welcomed, it should not obscure the value of having advice before any interviewing at all takes place.[186] It is therefore unfortunate that para 3.1 does not make this clear and could even be said to encourage the suspect to defer the decision. Note 3G seemed designed to dissuade some suspects from deferring it by providing that a request for advice from a mentally disordered or handicapped person or a juvenile should be pursued straight away without waiting for the appropriate adult to arrive. This provision does not appear in the 2006 version of Code C, or in Code H. It appeared to be intended to prevent police officers playing off adult against suspect by telling the suspect to defer making a decision about advice until the adult arrives,[187] and then giving the adult the impression that the juvenile has waived advice or does not need it.[188] It appeared that this provision did not have much impact,[189] which might be because it was contained in a Note and not in the Code itself. Provision aimed at preventing this ploy could have been taken further by including a requirement that even where a suspect had waived advice, suspect and adult should be left alone together for a few minutes after re-notification of the right. Instead, attempts to combat it appear to have been abandoned.

Conclusions; improving the legal advice scheme

Clearly, the curtailment of the right to silence discussed is tending to affect the nature of custodial legal advice. It has affected the role of the legal adviser in the police station; that role was already, it seemed, interpreted in a variety of ways by advisers, but in circumstances where silence would previously have been advised by most of them it seems possible that, at present, it may not be.[190] It appears that the difficulty of advising the client as to when to remain silent and when not to take the risk of so doing may mean that some inexperienced advisers tend to adopt the role of referee or counsellor rather than that of legal adviser. More experienced advisers will, however, be of great value to the client, since they will be able to advise on the risks of staying silent, which may be much greater in response to certain questions than to others.[191] The main studies in this area[192] recognised that interviews may be a means of constructing or creating truth rather

---

186 Sanders found that suspects had often made admissions in the absence of the solicitor and that therefore 'the potential impact of the solicitor was neutralised in advance by the police': ibid, p 143. This finding arose in the context of informal questioning, but could be equally applicable to instances where the suspect defers the decision to have advice.

187 This ploy was used in 5.4% of instances observed: ibid, p 59.

188 This ploy was used in 2.4% of instances observed: ibid, p 59.

189 Brown et al., 1997; apart from this propensity, particular problems were found with the notification of this right to juveniles, with a wide variation in the number of juveniles requesting advice in the different stations: 7% to 58%.

190 See Bucke et al., The Right of Silence: The Impact of the CJPOA 1994, Home Office Research Study No 199, 2000.

191 For further discussion, see Fenwick, H, 'Curtailing the Right to Silence, Access to Legal Advice and Section 78' [1995] Crim LR 132; Jackson, M, 'Interpreting the silence provisions: The Northern Ireland cases' [1995] Crim LR 587.

192 The Sanders research (1989), the Home Office Study by Brown (1997) and the study by Bucke et al. (2000).

than discovering it, but their concern was more with the causal relationship between the presence of a legal adviser and exercise of the right to silence than with the relationship between such presence and the making of an unreliable confession. This issue was touched on in the study by Dixon,[193] which found that legal advisers were more likely to advise silence at least temporarily if the client was in a confused or emotional state[194] or had been bullied or deceived.[195] A further study, conducted for the Royal Commission on Criminal Justice[196] found, not surprisingly, that the relationship between legal advice and the right to silence was affected by the quality of the advice given. The research found that many 'legal advisers' are clerks, secretaries and former police officers with no legal education or training in the provision of custodial legal advice. Such persons, it was found, often had little or no grasp of the case in question and little apparent understanding of the need, at times, for the client to maintain a selective silence. According to the research, 78% of the advisers counselled the client to co-operate with the police. Some recent research echoes these findings as to the quality of advice and suggests that advisers adopt a passive stance in interviews, failing to intervene where intervention is clearly called for.[197] McConville found that the presence of some legal advisers in interviews may have had a detrimental impact on suspects: 'Lacking any clear understanding of their role in the process, some advisers simply become part of the machine which confronts the suspect.'[198] The suggestions that advisers are reluctant to adopt an adversarial stance were given credence by the two post-PACE cases of oppression which arose in respect of tape recorded interviews with an adviser present.[199] The advisers must operate on police territory and may, as Dixon puts it, deal with the resultant pressures by making 'some positive adaptation'.[200] However, more recent research has pointed out that intervention is not called for in around one-quarter of interviews, that advisers usually intervene when it is called for but, in half of such cases, do not do so as often as is needed.[201]

Thus, despite the general perception that legal advice reduces the likelihood that unreliable confessions will be made, the available empirical evidence relating specifically to the issue allows only the tentative suggestion that the adviser may ensure that the client is aware of the right to silence and may sometimes advise that he exercises it, despite the risks, especially where the client does not seem able to cope with the interview.[202] In this context, it is worth bearing in mind that it tends to be a feature

193 See Dixon, D, 'Common sense, legal advice and the right to silence' [1991] PL 233.
194 Ibid, p 244.
195 Ibid, pp 246 and 247.
196 The study by Hodgson and McConville took place over an eight-month period during which the researchers followed suspects and advisers into 180 interrogations; see (1993) 143 NLJ 659.
197 *The Role of Legal Representatives at Police Stations*, HMSO 1992 Research Study No 3, summarised at [1993] Crim LR 161. The approach of the research has been criticised: see Roberts, D, 'Questioning the suspect: the solicitor's role' [1993] Crim LR 368, with reply by Baldwin, p 371.
198 McConville, M and Hodgson, J, *Custodial Legal Advice and the Right to Silence*, Royal Commission Study No 13.
199 *R v Paris* (1993) 97 Cr App R 99; *Heron* (1993) unreported, judgment of Mitchell J, 1 November 1993.
200 Dixon, D, 'Common sense, legal advice and the right to silence' [1991] PL 233 at pp 236–37.
201 Bridges, L and Choongh, S, *Improving Police Station Legal Advice*, 1998, The Law Society.
202 It is worth noting that the Court of Appeal has accepted as a general rule that most suspects, unless clearly experienced and independently minded, are less likely to make any confession in the presence of a solicitor (*Samuel* [1988] 1 QB 615; [1988] 2 All ER 135; [1988] 2 WLR 920, CA; *Dunford* (1990) 140 NLJ 517, CA).

of cases in which a miscarriage of justice has occurred that the confessions were uttered in the absence of a legal adviser.[203] This has not invariably been the case; the confessions gained by oppression in the case of the *Cardiff Three* were obtained in the presence of a solicitor.[204] Of course, if an unreliable confession is made in the presence of a legal adviser, this may say much more about the quality of the advice given than it does about the principle of having legal advice. The presence of a solicitor can affect the reliability of the confession in other ways. The suspect may feel generally reassured by the presence of a person independent of the police who is undaunted by the interview process.

Moreover, the presence of the adviser may sometimes be a potent factor discouraging use of improper tactics,[205] and may help to alter the balance of power between interviewer and interviewee, thus tending to create a climate in which an unreliable confession is less likely to be uttered. Reassurance deriving from the presence of a solicitor is not merely valuable in terms of the reliability of the confession; it may serve to make the whole experience of police detention less traumatic and daunting. In theory, the solicitor will intervene if the interview is conducted in an intimidatory fashion or if other improper tactics are used. Although it seems clear that the quality of legal advice improved over the 1990s, the availability of legal advice may not always have such effects, as indicated above. In other words, the mere fact that a person labelled a 'legal adviser' turns up at the police station and may be present at the interview may have little impact in terms of evening up the balance of power between suspect and police officer. Indeed, the presence of such a person may sometimes be to the disadvantage of the suspect, as it may offer a reassurance which it does not warrant.

The result is that the introduction of provisions aimed at curbing informal subversion are unlikely to have much impact and police working practices of subverting the new provisions themselves will tend to develop. It has been found that 'in around 28% of cases prior to the 1991 revisions but in 35% afterwards suspects may have been influenced against seeking advice by the police'.[206] The percentage of suspects who receive advice remains relatively low and the research suggests that this continues to be due in part to subversion of notification and the responses of the police to requests for advice.[207]

This discussion has suggested that the revisions of Code C in 1991 and 1995 tinkered with the problem of informal subversion of the right, but no radical change

---

203 E.g., the *Confait* case: see the *Report of an Inquiry by the Hon Sir Henry Fisher* (1977) HC 90; the case of the *Birmingham Six* (1991) *The Times*, 28 March; *Silcott* (1991) *The Times*, 8 December.

204 *Paris* (1993) 97 Cr App R 99; [1994] Crim LR 361, CA. This also occurred in *Heron* (1993) unreported, judgment of Mitchell J, 1 November 1993; the judge, Mitchell J, drew attention to the fact that only a legal executive was present during oppressive questioning and said that this was unacceptable.

205 One of the conclusions of the Sanders research (1989), p 150, was that suspects who did not receive advice or whose solicitors did not attend the interrogation would have been greatly assisted had the solicitor been present. Two examples are given, pp 138 and 139, of forceful or threatening questioning which produced a possibly unreliable confession from an easily intimidated suspect in the absence of a solicitor. This finding received some support from Dixon's study (Dixon, D, 'Common sense, legal advice and the right to silence' [1991] PL 233). See also Bucke *et al.*, 2000. See also Sanders and Young, *Criminal Justice*, 3rd edn, 2007, Chapter 4.5 at pp 208–9.

206 Brown *et al.*, 1997.

207 Brown, ibid, pp 94–95; Bucke, 2000.

was undertaken. The 1999 revision signalled an abandonment of attempts to improve the scheme, despite the fact that after 1995, commentators had continued to point out its defects.[208] The two revisions after the coming into force of CJPOA, s 34(2A) included the restriction on drawing adverse inferences from silence where the detainee had not had an opportunity to have access to legal advice. The 2006 revision includes the restriction and the two different cautions, reflecting it. The restriction may have some impact on the legal advice scheme in encouraging police to go further in the direction of offering an opportunity of advice to the suspect. But ploys are unlikely to be fully ruled out, partly because failing to offer such an opportunity will usually have no adverse consequences from a police perspective, as discussed below and in Chapter 15. Otherwise the 2006 revision of Code C merely continued the reforms already in place, without introducing any significant change. The fundamental problem is that the process of delivering advice remains in the hands of a body which has an interest in withholding it, while many suspects continue to need disinterested advice regarding the decision whether to have advice.[209]

Exclusion of admissions obtained after a breach of the legal advice provisions may have encouraged police officers to adhere to the scheme. However, most of the methods of evading the legal advice provisions considered here tend to consist of rule evasion as opposed to rule breaking. Courts tend to prefer the defence to point to a specific breach of a Code provision before deciding whether to invoke s 78 to exclude admissions.[210] However, the disapproval of persuading an inexperienced suspect to forgo advice expressed in *Beycan*[211] suggests that there may be a willingness on the part of the judiciary to consider rule evasion in this context. Where it seems that such evasion has occurred, it could be characterised as general subversion of the legal advice scheme or perhaps as a breach of the para 6.4 provision that no attempt must be made to persuade the suspect to waive advice. There would be scope for such argument where, for example, a suspect who made admissions in an interview after he had waived his entitlement to advice stated that something an officer said (such as an overstatement of the time needed to contact a solicitor) or failed to say to him, persuaded him to the decision not to have advice.

Although para 6.4 seems to be aimed at preventing such improper persuasion at the 'booking in' stage, it might also apply if it appeared that police officers had pressurised or misled a suspect into reversing the decision to have advice. For example, an untrue representation (even though made in good faith) that the duty solicitor was unavailable which had the effect of persuading the detainee to reverse the decision to have advice might be brought within para 6.4. If no reason for such a reversal was recorded, that might lend weight to the argument that the suspect was improperly persuaded to forgo advice. It is clear that although para 6.4 has not so far received much attention, it does open up a number of possibilities.

---

208 See Brown, ibid; Sanders, A, 'Access to justice in the police station: an elusive dream?', in *Access to Justice*, 1996.
209 The Sanders research found that suspects quite often asked officers whether or not they should have advice (1989), p 65.
210 See, e.g., *Keenan* [1989] 3 WLR 1193.
211 [1990] Crim LR 185.

Where access to legal advice has formally been delayed, and the suspect has stayed silent, s 34(2A) will not allow the drawing of adverse inferences. In such an instance, there would be no need to rely at trial or in judicial review proceedings on arguments raised under s 7(1)(b) of the HRA. But as discussed above, there are grounds for delay under Codes C and H, para 6 to which the restriction on drawing adverse inferences is not applicable; in such instances the question whether the suspect had a true opportunity to have advice should be subjected to strict scrutiny in the light of the requirements of Art 6. Equally that question would arise where access to legal advice has been informally delayed. This argument might be raised where a suspect has been influenced by police ploys in failing to obtain advice – whether due to inadequacies in the informing procedure or to direct or more subtle persuasion – and the suspect has stayed silent. This point will be returned to in Chapter 13 when exclusion of evidence as a form of redress for a breach of the Codes or PACE is considered. However, it should be noted here that even if methods of evading the legal advice scheme could be given the character of such a breach, exclusion of evidence would not necessarily follow. Thus, this 'sanction' remains extremely weak and is, of course, inapplicable to a suspect who is improperly denied advice or encouraged to forgo it, but later pleads guilty.

A further significant question is whether Art 6 might be breached where legal advice is not formally denied to the defendant for a period of time, as in *Murray*, although he has not in fact received advice before being interviewed and making admissions. The admission of a subsequent interview might be viewed as affecting the fairness of the trial, following *Murray*. This argument would be strongest where other adverse factors were also present, including a confession made after 24 hours or more in detention, or where the inexperienced, young, emotionally unstable or educationally sub-normal suspect could not be expected to make his or her own assessment as to the value of having legal advice and was therefore very vulnerable to police suggestions. This appears to be a particularly pertinent question in respect of terrorism suspects since they can be held for up to 28 days.

If Art 6 is concerned with the objective reliability of the interview in influencing the integrity and fairness of the trial, it can be argued that, unless the defendant made a clear, positive (albeit possibly misguided) decision not to have custodial advice, the admission into evidence of an interview under caution without such advice, whatever the reason for the failure, might affect the fairness of the trial. It is unclear that the fact that a vulnerable defendant (for example, on the verge of mental handicap) had waived advice or had received brief telephone advice only, would be sufficient where it could be said that the trial, objectively speaking, might be rendered unfair by the admission of the interview. Similar arguments could perhaps also be raised where the adviser attends the station to see a mentally vulnerable suspect or one with a poor command of English, but the advice obtained is clearly inadequate. When the Strasbourg Court spoke of the need for legal advice where adverse inferences were to be drawn from silence, it may be suggested that it had in mind – taking into account the general need for the rights to be genuinely efficacious, not illusory – the notion of sound, adversarial advice.

Various suggestions for reform of the legal advice scheme have already been made above which could bring about significant improvement without necessitating a radical change. There are other possibilities: ploys could be discouraged and untrue allegations by suspects of lack of notification of advice precluded if the 'booking in' stage were video or audio taped.[212] Such an innovation could be used in conjunction with the para 6.4 prohibition of attempts to dissuade the suspect to forgo advice. Inadequate notification of advice could be characterised as an attempt at persuasion to forgo it on the ground that it was intended to and did have that effect. Finally, and very importantly, notification of legal advice could take place on arrest or even on caution, thereby harmonising the position of all suspects. Clearly, such changes would not ensure that all suspects who needed it received advice.

Further, improvement in the quality and delivery of advice can be brought about only by an increase in funding for the scheme. It may be argued that only specially trained solicitors should offer advice, but until better funding is available, solicitors will delegate this function. The Royal Commission, in its 1993 report, proposed that the performance of solicitors should be monitored and that the police should receive training in the role solicitors are expected to play.[213] In a response to the available research and recommendations of the Runciman Royal Commission,[214] the Law Society undertook a programme of training with a view to ensuring that clerks or other non-solicitor advisers are accredited in accordance with the Law Society's scheme for accreditation. Thus, when non-solicitors give advice, they are normally accredited,[215] although it has been pointed out that firms can use untrained paralegals who are not trained and then replace them after six months with another untrained trainee.[216] Under Codes C and H a solicitor includes 'probationary or accredited representatives'. But the quality of advice, although improving, remains variable: around 26% of those giving custodial legal advice are non-solicitors[217] and where an 'own' as opposed to a duty solicitor gives advice, there is no requirement that he or she should have specialist training in this area.

However, it may be that more radical action is necessary to address this problem. There are various possibilities; for example, suspects could routinely be offered the chance at booking in to speak to a duty solicitor on the phone regarding the question of having legal advice. More radically, and expensively, legal advisers (who might be trainee solicitors and should at least have some legal education) could be employed on a temporary basis to attend all interviews in police stations except where the suspect requested his own solicitor or a duty solicitor or specifically required that a legal adviser should not be present. Such advisers could receive some special training concerned specifically with advising the suspect in the police station.[218] Apart from such advisers,

---

212 The suggestion of video taping was made by Fordham J (1991) 141 NLJ 677. He suggested that it could take place by means of a fixed camera focused on the 'booking-in' desk. The Royal Commission Report 1993 also proposed (Proposal 57) that a waiver of advice at this point should be video taped.

213 Proposals 64–69.

214 Runciman Report Recommendations 61–68. In response to the McConville study, reported at (1993) 143 NLJ 659, the Law Society and Legal Aid Board announced that from October 1993, legal aid would not be available for police station work unless advisers had been through a training course and passed a Law Society test. They now have to be accredited; see p 1224 above.

215 See further Cape, E, *Defending Suspects at Police Stations*, 1999, Legal Action Group.

216 Bridges, L and Choongh, S, *Improving Police Station Legal Advice*, 1998.

217 Brown, 1997, p 108. See, e.g., Sanders and Young, *Criminal Justice*, 3rd edn, 2007, Chapter 4.5 at pp 205–12.

218 E.g., the College of Law course: 'Advising the suspect at the police station'.

persons other than solicitors should not attend the suspect during interviews. Arguably, Codes C and H should be revised to allow for notification of advice on caution, to clarify the provisions allowing for delays in access and to require a positive decision to refuse advice. Further moves towards improving the quality of advice may have to be undertaken. Such a scheme would not only address most of the difficulties outlined here, but also the problems caused by the reluctance of solicitors to attend the police station[219] and the variation in the quality of the response of solicitors to the request for advice.[220]

The courts continue to have the opportunity, if they are prepared to take an activist line in giving a broad interpretation to *Murray* and *Averill*, to curb the formally allowed and informally developed police discretion in affording access to legal advice which this part of this chapter has discussed. At present, however, they show little inclination to do so: the high watermark in due process terms represented by the decision in *Samuel* in 1988 has not been revisited in recent decisions in this context, despite the influence of the HRA. This point is explored further below, in relation to the right to silence.

4 The right to silence

Introduction

There is general academic agreement that, as Sanders and Young have put it, 'it is over the right of silence that due process and crime control principles clash most fundamentally'.[221] The right to silence, in the sense of the immunity of an accused person from having adverse inferences drawn from failure to answer questions during police questioning, is central to the due process model. In contrast, adherence to crime control principles logically demands not only that such inferences should be drawn, but that in some or all circumstances, refusal to answer police questions should be an offence in itself, on the ground that innocent persons would not thereby be disadvantaged and the burden on the prosecution would be eased.

Within the due process camp, retention of the right to silence was advocated on the grounds of its value in protecting suspects and also on the basis that it symbolises the presumption of innocence. In the crime control camp abolition was often advocated on the ground that only the guilty have something to hide; the innocent need fear nothing from speaking.[222] But one group of abolitionists departed from a classic crime control stance in arguing for an 'exchange' or trade-off between the PACE suspects' rights and the right to silence.[223] Since the inception of PACE, which adopted the due process stance,[224] there has been a clear movement towards the crime control position, on the

---

219 The Sanders research found that 25.6% of solicitors gave telephone advice only, which was less valuable for the suspect (1989), p 104.
220 The Sanders research found an enormous variation in the quality of service offered in this context, ibid, pp 112–17.
221 *Criminal Justice*, 3rd edn, 2007, p 223.
222 See Greer, S, 'The Right of Silence: A Review of the Current Debate', (1990) 53 MLR 709.
223 See Greer, ibid.
224 The only recognition given to this right in PACE was in Code C, in the wording of the caution, para 10.4.

basis of exchanging enhanced suspects' rights for curtailment of the right to silence. Curtailment of the right was effected under the CJPOA 1994, ss 34–37, but subsequent jurisprudence under Art 6 of the European Convention on Human Rights has led, as will be discussed, to a partial return to the original due process position.

Article 6 of the Convention contrasts with Art 14(3) of the International Covenant on Civil and Political Rights and with Art 34(1) of the South African Bill of Rights in that it does not expressly forbid using compulsion to obtain confessions.[225] The expectation under Art 6(2) that the state bears the burden of establishing guilt impliedly requires that the accused should not be expected to provide involuntary assistance by way of a confession. Thus, the presumption of innocence under Art 6(2) is closely linked to the right to freedom from self-incrimination which the Court has found to be covered by the right to a fair hearing under Art 6(1).[226]

Article 6(2) further impliedly requires that when carrying out their duties, members of a court should not start with the preconceived idea that the accused has committed the offence charged; the burden of proof is on the prosecution, and any doubt should benefit the accused. These matters are at issue when silence under interrogation by law enforcement bodies is penalised by a formal penalty or by drawing adverse inferences from it. The Court has drawn a distinction between these matters, although it recognised in *Murray (John) v UK*[227] that they were not entirely distinct, since adverse inference-drawing is clearly a form of penalty; it was termed 'indirect compulsion'.

Curtailment of the right

The right to silence was abrogated in 1988 in Northern Ireland in terms of allowing adverse inferences to be drawn from silence at trial.[228] But, post-PACE, the right was retained for most suspects, including terrorist suspects, in England and Wales until it was curtailed or undermined, although not abolished, under ss 34, 36 and 37 of the CJPOA 1994. The right, in the sense of an immunity from criminal sanctions due to a refusal to answer questions under suspicion, still exists as far as the majority of suspects are concerned.[229]

The majority of the Runciman Royal Commission agreed with the Phillips Commission in recommending that the right to silence should be retained, although it considered that provision to deal with so called 'ambush' defences (defences sprung on the prosecution at the last minute by a defendant who has hitherto remained silent as to his or her defence) should be introduced.[230] The Commission's recommendation was based not on

---

225 It may be noted that the UN Human Rights Committee has already expressed concerns regarding the compatibility of the CJPOA 1994, ss 34, 36 and 37 with Art 14(3).

226 *Funke v France* (1993) 16 EHRR 297.

227 (1996) 22 EHRR 29. For comment, see Munday, R, 'Inferences from silence and European Human Rights Law' [1996] Crim LR 370.

228 Criminal Evidence (Northern Ireland) Order SI 1988/1987 NI 20 1988.

229 See below pp 1249 *et seq.* for a number of statutory provisions which penalise silence.

230 RCCJ Report p 84, para 2. The proposal found effect in the Criminal Procedure and Investigations Act 1996, which imposes a duty of defence disclosure in most Crown Court cases. Michael Zander, a member of the RCCJ, considered that such disclosure would undermine the presumption of innocence (Zander, RCCJ Report, *A Note of Dissent*, p 22, paras 8 and 11). It may be found that the provisions of the 1996 Act are not fully in compliance with Art 6(2) of the Convention which guarantees the presumption of innocence. See below, pp 1239–41.

a 'symbolic' but an 'instrumental retentionist' approach;[231] it arose from a concern that otherwise, a risk of miscarriages of justice might arise.[232] Given that the Commission was convened in the wake of a number of miscarriages of justice, it might have been expected that the government of the time would give these findings some weight.

The then Home Secretary, however, took what could be termed an exchange abolitionist approach[233] – suspects have greater rights than they did in pre-PACE days and therefore do not need the right to silence. In other words, the right could be curtailed in exchange for the enhanced suspects' rights available under PACE and Codes C and E. Since curtailment of the right was unlikely to have any effect at all on the crime rate, it seems most likely that it was undertaken not in order to gain genuine crime control advantage, but in order to give the impression that such advantage might be gained. The conviction rate was unaffected since the change had an impact only on the small number of criminals who are detected and who would otherwise have remained silent. While it may have had some influence on decisions to plead guilty, its main effect has probably been on that tiny percentage of cases which come to court[234] in which the defendant has remained silent and has pleaded not guilty. The academic consensus is that the advantages in terms of crime control are very doubtful, whereas the risk of miscarriages of justice has been increased.[235] At the same time it was acknowledged, prior to curtailment, that 'the reality of the right to silence is much closer [in practice] to the crime control model than it might first appear',[236] partly due to informal inference drawing by juries and magistrates.[237]

Thus, it is fair to say that prior to the CJPOA changes, the right to silence did not necessarily have a significant impact on the conduct of the interview or ensure that a suspect had a bulwark against giving in to pressure to speak. In fact, few suspects refused to answer questions[238] and, as discussed above, silence was not routinely advised by solicitors. One of the key reasons for retaining the right to silence is that the suspect may be under stress and unable to assess the situation clearly; he or she may have a number of reasons for reluctance to speak, including fear of incriminating another and uncertainty as to the legal significance of various facts. It may also be argued that the right should be reinstated in full in order to guard against the possibility that the suspect will concoct a confession in order to escape the pressure of the interrogation. A juvenile suspect in the *Silcott* case,[239] questioned about the murder of police officer

---

231 See Greer, S, 'The Right of Silence: A Review of the Current Debate' (1990) 53 MLR 709.
232 Runciman, RCCJ Report, p 55.
233 Greer, 1990, p 719.
234 Over 74% of defendants to be tried in magistrates' courts plead guilty; for Crown Court defendants the figure is 61.5%. Crown Prosecution Service Annual Report 04–05. See further Sanders and Young, *Criminal Justice*, 2007, Chapter 8.
235 See Zander, M, *The Police and Criminal Evidence Act 1984*, 1995, pp 303–23 (current edn, 2003); Fenwick, H, 'Curtailing the Right to Silence, Access to Legal Advice and Section 78' [1995] Crim LR 132; Jackson, M, 'Interpreting the silence provisions: The Northern Ireland cases' [1995] Crim LR 587; Pattenden, R, 'Inference from Silence' [1995] Crim LR 602–11.
236 Sanders and Young, *Criminal Justice*, 1994, p 193 (current edn, 2007).
237 Zander and Henderson, *Crown Court Study*, RCCJ Research Study No 19, 1993.
238 See Leng, *The Right to Silence in Police Interrogation*, Home Office Research Study No 10, 1993. Only 4.5% of suspects exercised their right to silence.
239 (1991) *The Times*, 9 December.

Blakelock by a riotous mob, made up a detailed confession based on suggestions put to him by police officers, although it was later found that he could not have been present at the scene. This suspect made the confession despite his right to exercise silence, suggesting that the right to silence alone will not benefit such suggestible detainees. However, as argued above, the right to silence in conjunction with advice from an experienced solicitor would seem to provide a surer safeguard against false confessions than either silence or legal advice alone. In other words, the pressure on the suspect in police interviews was already high prior to curtailment of the right, and did not appear to be compensated for by other factors such as audio-recording and access to legal advice. Thus, the large body of writing on the right to silence generally came down on the side of its retention.[240]

Section 34(1) of the CJPOA 1994 curtailed the 'right to silence' in police interviews; it provides:

> where ... evidence is given that the accused ... (a) on being questioned under caution by a constable trying to discover whether or by whom the offence had been committed, failed to mention any fact relied on in his defence ... or (b) on being charged ... or on officially being informed that he might be prosecuted ... failed to mention any such fact, being a fact which in the circumstances existing at the time the accused could reasonably have been expected to mention when so questioned, charged or informed ... sub-ss (2) below applies.

Under s 34(2)(d), the court or jury 'in determining whether the accused is guilty of the offence charged may draw such inferences as appear proper'. The difference between sub-sections (1)(a) and (1)(b) is of interest. It is notable that sub-section(1)(b) makes no mention of questioning. It implies that an inference of guilt may be drawn from the failure of the accused to volunteer information when charged. Sections 36 and 37 of the 1994 Act provide that adverse inferences may be drawn from a failure to account for possession of substances or objects, or presence at a particular place. Under 38(4), the conviction cannot be based on silence alone; the burden of proof remains throughout on the prosecution to prove its case; in effect, a silence will be only one factor which can be used to make out the case. Under s 34 the prosecution have to identify a fact relied on in his defence which he did not mention under questioning.

Under all these provisions, there is still a right to remain silent so long as the accused is prepared to take the risk that so doing may have an adverse impact on his defence, if the case comes to trial. The caution under Code C, para 10.4 was accordingly revised in 1995 to read: 'You do not have to say anything, but it may harm your defence if you do not mention when questioned something which you later rely on in court. Anything you do say may be given in evidence.' In contrast to the old caution, this one has a dual and contradictory effect: it can no longer be seen simply as a safeguard; it must also be seen as part of the coerciveness inherent in the police interviewing and detention powers. Further special cautions were adopted under

---

240 See *Report of the Home Office Working Group on the Right to Silence*, 1989 (in favour of modification of the right). For criticism of the report, see Zuckerman, (1989) Crim LR 855. For review of the debate, see Greer (1990); Coldrey (1991) 20 Anglo-Am L Rev 27. In favour of modification of the right, see Williams (1987) 137 NLJ 1107; editorial (1988) Police Review, 29 April.

para 10.5A and B of Code C in order to take account, respectively, of the provisions of ss 36 and 37 of the 1994 Act.

It is implicit in all three sections – ss 34, 36, 37 – that inferences may only be drawn if a sound explanation for the silence is not put forward. Although staying silent carries risks, it may be, depending on the circumstances, less risky than making ill-considered admissions since silence, unlike admissions, must be corroborated.[241] However, as the Runciman Commission pointed out, the caution is likely to put most pressure on vulnerable suspects.[242] The suspect most likely to be unable to evaluate the riskiness of silence is precisely the type of suspect who needs the protection originally afforded by the right. Vulnerable persons interviewed outside the police station may be confused by the caution and without the benefit of legal advice may be pressurised into making inaccurate and ill-considered admissions and perhaps into mentioning matters they have not been questioned about.[243] Thus, although it may be argued that in a number of circumstances it may not be 'proper' for a jury to be directed to draw adverse inferences from silence or that it was not reasonable in the circumstances existing at the time to expect the suspect to speak, this will not benefit the suspect who does in fact speak in response to the current caution. Ironically, it is probably the seasoned criminal who understands the operation of s 34 of the CJPOA and may be able to predict that silence may not be a more risky strategy than it was previously, who has not been disadvantaged by the change.[244]

The case law on s 34 of the CJPOA establishes, following *R v Cowan*,[245] that the jury should only consider drawing inferences under s 34 if a prima facie case to answer has been made out by the prosecution. It has also been made clear that where the prosecution do not seek to rely on a silence, the judge should direct the jury positively not to draw inferences.[246] Inferences may only be drawn if a sound explanation for remaining silent is not proffered;[247] it cannot be inferred that the reason for silence was the need to concoct a false explanation if the real and innocent reason for silence is put forward, so long as the reason is plausible. A number of circumstances can be taken into account. In *Argent*,[248] the Court of Appeal found that when considering whether, in the circumstances existing at the time, the defendant could reasonably have been expected to mention the fact he now relies on, the Court should take into account matters such as the defendant's age, health, experience, mental capacity, sobriety, tiredness, personality and legal advice. It is a matter for the jury to resolve whether, bearing these matters in mind, the defendant could have been expected to mention the fact in question, although the judge may give them guidance. Any restrictive impact of these

---

241 CJPOA 1994, s 38(3).
242 RCCJ Report, para 4.50.
243 It was found in *Nicholson* [1999] Crim LR 61 that if the police have not asked about facts, adverse inferences should not be drawn against the defendant if he does not state those facts.
244 See Moston, S and Williamson, T, 'The extent of silence in police stations', in Greer and Morgan (eds), *The Right to Silence Debate*, 1990, Bristol Centre for Criminal Justice.
245 [1996] 1 Cr App R 1.
246 *R v McGarry* [1998] 3 All ER 805.
247 This is implicit in *R v Cowan* [1996] 1 Cr App R 1; see also *R v Argent* [1997] Cr App R 27.
248 [1997] 2 Cr App R 27; (1996) *The Times*, 19 December. See Broome, K, 'An inference of guilt' (1997) 141 SJ 202.

findings is doubtful; in *R v Friend*[249] adverse inferences were drawn under s 35 against a defendant aged 14, with a mental age of nine.

The case law on s 34 CJPOA suggests that the courts are not on the whole taking a restrictive approach. In *Murray v DPP*,[250] which was decided on the 1988 Northern Ireland Order, but is clearly applicable to s 34, the House of Lords found that silence allows the drawing, not only of specific inferences from failure to mention particular facts, but also of the inference that the defendant is guilty. The question of what counts as a 'fact' under s 34 that the defendant did not mention in police questioning but which he could be said to be relying on in his defence has also been given a broad interpretation. The House of Lords found in *Webber*[251] that even if the defendant does not give evidence at trial, he can be said to be relying on a fact when counsel for the defence, acting on his client's instructions, puts a specific and positive case to prosecution witnesses.

The restriction on drawing adverse inferences

Under the Blair Government, the CJPOA provisions were retained, but it was already clear that the curtailment of the right to silence under CJPOA 1994, ss 34, 36 or 37 was in tension with the demands of Art 6 of the European Convention on Human Rights. Depending on the particular circumstances of a case, the curtailment had the potential to lead to a breach of Art 6 on the basis that it infringes the presumption of innocence under Art 6(2) and the right to freedom from self-incrimination.[252] Consideration of the judgments in *Saunders v UK*[253] and *Murray (John) v UK* reveals that it is only where a penalty formally attaches to silence, and the interview may then be used in evidence, that a breach of Art 6 is almost *bound* to be established, but that where adverse inferences can be drawn from the silence at trial, a breach is likely to be established if the suspect has been denied access to legal advice before being questioned under caution. *Saunders v UK* concerned the sanction for refusing to answer questions in serious fraud investigations under s 437 of the Companies Act 1985. Acting under s 437, Inspectors of the Department of Trade and Industry had interviewed Saunders regarding allegations of fraud. He was forced to answer the questions put to him and therefore lost his privilege against self-incrimination, which he argued was unfair and amounted to an abuse of process. The interviews were admitted in evidence under s 431(5) of the Companies Act and he was convicted.[254] The Strasbourg Court found that the applicant's right to freedom from self-incrimination under Art 6(1) had been infringed due to the threatened imposition of a penalty for remaining silent and the subsequent admission of the interviews into evidence. This finding was based on the

---

249 [1997] 1 WLR 1433.
250 [1994] 1 WLR 1.
251 [2004] UKHL 1.
252 See the comments of the Court of Appeal in *Birchall* [1999] Crim LR 311; see also the study by Bucke *et al.*, *The Right of Silence: The impact of the CJPOA 1994*, Home Office Research Study No 199, 2000.
253 (1997) 23 EHRR 313; Appl No 19187/91, Com Rep, paras 69–75.
254 His appeal on grounds of abuse of process and on the basis that the interviews should not have been admitted into evidence under s 78 was rejected: *R v Saunders and Others* [1996] 1 Cr App R 463.

special compulsive regime applicable to Department of Trade and Industry inspections, but the key issue was the use made of the material obtained in court.

The decision in *Murray (John) v UK*[255] may be contrasted with that in *Saunders* since it made it clear that, depending on the circumstances of a case, Art 6 takes a different stance towards imposing a formal penalty on silence and drawing adverse inferences from it. Murray was arrested under the Prevention of Terrorism (Temporary Provisions) Act 1989 and taken to the police station. A detective superintendent, pursuant to the Northern Ireland (Emergency Provisions) Act 1987, decided to delay access to a solicitor for 48 hours. While being interviewed, Murray repeatedly stated that he had 'nothing to say'. After he had seen his solicitor, he stated that he had been advised not to answer the questions. As indicated above, the Criminal Evidence (Northern Ireland) Order 1988 enables a court in any criminal trial to exercise discretion to draw adverse inferences from an accused's failure to mention a fact during police questioning. Such inferences were drawn from Murray's silence in the police interviews once the prosecution had established a prima facie case against him, and he was convicted. The subsequent decisions in *Averill v UK* and *Brennan v UK*[256] were discussed above, and confirmed the finding in Murray, although Brennan took a somewhat more restrictive view of the circumstances in which a breach of Art 6 would arise.

The Strasbourg Court emphasised that its decision in *Murray* was confined to the particular facts of the case in finding that no breach of Art 6(1) or (2) had occurred where adverse inferences had been drawn at trial from the applicant's refusal to give evidence, taking into account the degree of compulsion exerted on the applicant and the weight of the evidence against him. The Court placed emphasis on the fact that he had been able to remain silent; also, given the strength of the evidence against him, the matter of drawing inferences was one of common sense which could not be regarded as unfair.[257] But, crucially, the Court did find that Art 6(1) and (3)(c) had been breached by the denial of custodial access to a lawyer for 48 hours, since it found that such access was essential where there was a likelihood that adverse inferences would be drawn from silence. In effect, therefore, the Court adopted something close to an exchange abolitionist approach.[258] The distinction it drew, impliedly, between direct and indirect compulsion flowing from the risk of adverse inference drawing and criminal penalties respectively was not explicated and rests, it is suggested, on doubtful premises.

The regime under the 1988 Order is, in essentials, the same as that under s 34 of the CJPOA, which therefore became vulnerable to challenge under the HRA. The question of affording access to legal advice before questioning the suspect if adverse inferences might be drawn from silence had to be addressed; this has already been discussed above, and is considered further below. There were other aspects of *Murray*, relating specifically to the privilege against self-incrimination. As indicated, the findings in *Murray* were carefully confined to the particular facts of the case, and therefore must be treated with caution. But it is clear that the right to freedom from self-incrimination cannot be viewed as absolute under Art 6. Drawing adverse inferences from silence in police interviewing does not necessarily breach Art 6(2), but the greater the reliance

255 (1996) 22 EHRR 29.
256 (2002) 34 EHRR 18.
257 Paragraph 54.
258 See Greer, S (1990) 53 MLR 709.

placed on such inferences at the trial, the greater the likelihood that a breach will occur. The Court said that it would be incompatible with Art 6(1) and (2) 'to base a conviction solely or mainly on the accused's silence or refusal to answer questions'. As already noted, under s 38(3) of the CJPOA, a conviction cannot be based 'solely' on silence. Article 6(1) and (2) might therefore be found to be breached in circumstances differing from those applicable in *Murray*, including those in which the evidence against the defendant was less overwhelming. A domestic judge would not satisfy Art 6 if he directed a jury that the drawing of adverse inferences could play a major part in a conviction. Further, in *Murray*, there was no jury: the case was decided by a 'Diplock' court. Therefore, the evidence was weighed up by a professional who had the expertise to determine how much weight to give to aspects of it, including the 'no comment' interviews.

Murray made it clear that drawing adverse inferences from silence when the defendant had not had access to legal advice prior to the failure to reply to questioning will breach Art 6; as indicated above, s 58 of the Youth Justice and Criminal Evidence Act 1999 addressed that finding by inserting s 34(2A) into the CJPOA.[259] The amendments provide that if the defendant was at an authorised place of detention and had not had an opportunity of consulting a solicitor at the time of the failure to mention the fact in question, inferences cannot be drawn. This is a very significant change to the interviewing scheme; a number of the implications of this change were considered above in relation to the custodial right of access to legal advice.[260] Once s 34(2A) came into force in 2003 no adverse inference could be drawn from silence unless the suspect was under caution (s 34(1)(A) of the CJPOA 1994), and he had had the opportunity of having legal advice In that instance under s 34(2A) of the CJPOA, no inferences may be drawn from silence. It is notable that s 34(2A) does not provide that such a silence will be inadmissible. Informal inference drawing, which appeared to occur prior to the introduction of ss 34, 36 and 37 of the CJPOA, could therefore still occur. Further, s 34(2A) of the CJPOA does not cover the defendant who has not had legal advice but makes admissions in response to the new caution or (prima facie) the defendant

---

259 The Criminal Justice and Public Order Act 1994 (CJPOA) now contains 34(2)(A) which provides:

Where the accused was at an authorised place of detention at the time of the failure [to mention any fact relied on in his defence when questioned under caution] subsections (1) and (2) above [allowing adverse inferences to be drawn from the failure to answer] do not apply if he had not been allowed an opportunity to consult a solicitor prior to being questioned, charged or informed as mentioned in subsection (1) above.

(3) In section 36 (effect of accused's failure or refusal to account for objects, substances or marks), after subsection (4) there shall be inserted –

(4A) Where the accused was at an authorised place of detention at the time of the failure or refusal, subsections (1) and (2) above do not apply if he had not been allowed an opportunity to consult a solicitor prior to the request being made.

(4) In section 37 (effect of accused's failure or refusal to account for presence at a particular place), after subsection (3) there shall be inserted –

(3A) Where the accused was at an authorised place of detention at the time of the failure or refusal, subsections (1) and (2) do not apply if he had not been allowed an opportunity to consult a solicitor prior to the request being made.

260 See pp 1211–14.

who fails to obtain advice, although no formal denial of an opportunity to consult a solicitor occurs. These very significant matters are discussed further below.

As a result of this development Code C was amended in 2003 to introduce the possibility of using one of two cautions, and that amendment is carried forward into the 2006 version of Code C, and into Code H. The caution originally introduced in 1995 still applies, reflecting the curtailment of the right to silence. It is used where an opportunity to have access to legal advice has been given or is about to be given, and is in the following terms: '*You do not have to say anything. But it may harm your defence if you do not mention when questioned something which you later rely on in court. Anything you do say may be given in evidence.*'[261] Minor deviations do not constitute a breach of this requirement, provided that the sense of the caution is preserved. The caution must be repeated during the interview if there is any doubt as to whether the detainee realises that it still applies. If a juvenile or a person who is mentally disordered or mentally handicapped is cautioned in the absence of the appropriate adult, the caution must be repeated in the adult's presence.[262] The change to the caution which occurred to reflect s 34 of the CJPOA 1994, discussed further below, means that the suspect is warned that refusing to answer questions may lead to the drawing of adverse inferences in court. Importantly, Codes C and H restrict the circumstances in which inferences can be drawn.

Code C, para 10.11 provides:

> For an inference to be drawn when a suspect fails or refuses to answer a question about one of these matters or to answer it satisfactorily, the suspect must first be told in ordinary language:
>
> (a) what offence is being investigated;
> (b) what fact they are being asked to account for;
> (c) this fact may be due to them taking part in the commission of the offence;
> (d) a court may draw a proper inference if they fail or refuse to account for this fact;
> (e) a record is being made of the interview . . .

Code H para 10.10 is in the same terms. But Code C, and Code H (Annex C) also provide for a restriction on drawing adverse inferences from silence of the suspect. The provisions of ss 34, 36 and 37 of the Criminal Justice and Public Order Act 1994 are made subject to an overriding restriction, following from s 34(2A) which means that a court or jury is not allowed to draw adverse inferences from a person's silence, if the suspect:

> (a) is detained at a police station and before being interviewed . . .
> (i) has asked for legal advice,
> (ii) has not been allowed an opportunity to consult a solicitor . . . and
> (iii) has not changed their mind about wanting legal advice . . . .

This restriction on drawing adverse inferences from silence is reflected in the second, alternative caution in Annex C, para 2. This is the old caution reflecting the full right

261 Code C, para 10.5; Code H, para 10.4.
262 Code H, para 10.11; Code C, para 10.12.

to silence prior to its curtailment: '*You do not have to say anything but anything you do say may be given in evidence.*' The police must use it *within* the police station when it is clear that the suspect has had an *opportunity* to have access to legal advice (emphasis added).[263] These restrictions on this partial restoration of the full right of silence are significant. In particular, the term 'opportunity' should be noted – it is not necessary that the suspect should actually have obtained access to legal advice. This change clearly reflects an exchange abolitionist approach: the suspect is in effect entitled to the full right to silence or to access to legal advice, but not to both. This is objectionable in due process terms since the two entitlements, as discussed above, tend to be most valuable in conjunction with each other.

The position of the suspect may change; he or she may be able to be silent without risk in one interview, but pressurised to speak in a subsequent one. This is provided for in Annex C para 3 of both Codes:

> Whenever the restriction on drawing adverse inferences from silence (para 10.4) either begins to apply or ceases to apply after a caution has already been given, the person shall be re-cautioned in the appropriate terms. The changed position on drawing inferences and the fact that the previous caution no longer applies shall also be explained to him in ordinary language.

The loopholes in the provision for restricting the circumstances in which adverse inferences can be drawn were canvassed above, in relation to rights of access to legal advice. Suffice to say here that the suspect may well be cautioned that such inferences may be drawn in circumstances in which he has had no *true* opportunity to have access to legal advice. Given that the case is unlikely to come to court, the police are unlikely to be called to account, in any sense, in such circumstances, even assuming that what occurred in the police station could be unravelled sufficiently to demonstrate that no such opportunity in fact occurred. The restriction on drawing adverse inferences appears to adhere to the due process demands of Art 6 but, it is argued, falls short of them in practice.

Relying on legal advice in remaining silent

In applying ss 34, 36 and 37 it was noted above that if a sound explanation for remaining silent is given, the jury should be directed that if they accept the explanation they should not draw adverse inferences. (Clearly, they might informally draw them, as they almost certainly did in many instances prior to the 1994 changes.) The explanation often given for remaining silent is that the legal adviser advised silence, or at least a selective silence. This explanation has given rise to a problem that is still bedeviling the UK courts, and it is argued that they still have not dealt with it satisfactorily in Art 6 terms, despite more than one trip to Strasbourg, pre-HRA. From a crime control perspective the concern is that allowing this explanation would drive a coach

---

263 Under Codes C and H, Annex C, para 2: Whenever a requirement to administer a caution arises and at the time it is given the restriction on drawing adverse inferences from silence applies, the caution shall be [in those terms].

and horses through the CJPOA provisions: legal advisers could merely advise silence in almost all circumstances, and so doing would normally preclude the drawing of adverse inferences.

But from a due process perspective, accepting the drawing of adverse inferences when the solicitor has advised silence is equally problematic. The solicitor is there in the police station to represent the interests of his or her client; he or she may consider that the best recourse for the client is silence, if, for example, the client has been pressurised or intimidated, or is unable to cope with the questioning. A number of studies have shown that many suspects may not realise that they are being lead by police into admitting to having the *mens rea* of the offence in question, since, for example, the use of the word 'reckless' might appear to mean colloquially something rather different from its technical, legal, sense.[264] The police may have disclosed only part of their case against the suspect and that part may in itself be misleading.[265] In *Argent* the Court of Appeal rejected the argument that it was reasonable in the circumstances for the suspect to have stayed silent, on legal advice, when the police had not disclosed an outline of their case. So the solicitor, in seeking to further the best interests of the client, is clearly placed in a dilemma: if she advises silence this may turn out to be to the client's disadvantage. So the solicitor may be forced to advise a client to talk against her better judgment, for fear of the penalty attaching to silence later on. The domestic courts have tended to adopt the crime control stance in dealing with this issue.

The decision in *Condron and Another*,[266] in relation to the treatment in court of legal advice to stay silent, was later found at Strasbourg to have led to a breach of Art 6. The appellants were to be questioned by police at the police station on suspicion of being involved in the supply and possession of heroin. The police surgeon found that they were fit to be interviewed, but their solicitor considered that they were unfit, since they were suffering withdrawal symptoms, and so advised them not to answer any questions. They relied on that advice during the interview and remained silent. At trial, the defence involved reliance on facts which had not been mentioned in the course of the interview and thus potentially fell within s 34 of the CJPOA. The judge held a *voir dire* and rejected argument under s 78 that the no comment interview should be excluded as unfair because they were unfit to be interviewed. Argument that it would be improper to allow an inference to be drawn under s 34 because in making no comment they had only followed the *bona fide* advice of their solicitor was also rejected. The interviews were admitted and the prosecution then argued that they could reasonably have been expected to mention at interview the facts they now relied on in their defence; they were cross-examined on their failure to mention such facts. They gave the explanation that they had relied on the solicitor's advice. In summing up, the judge directed the jury that they must determine whether any adverse inferences should be drawn from the failure of the defendants to mention the facts in question during the police interview. The judge did not explain that the inferences could only be drawn if, despite the explanation, the jury concluded that the silence could only sensibly be attributed to the defendants having no satisfactory explanation to give.

264 See McConville, M and Baldwin, J, *Custodial Legal Advice and the Right to Silence*, RCCJ Research Study No 16.
265 See *Rosenberg* (2006) EWCA Crim 6.
266 [1997] 1 Cr App R 185.

Thus, it is possible that the jury may have drawn adverse inferences despite accepting the defendants' explanations.

The appellants were convicted and argued on appeal that the jury should not have been directed that they could draw adverse inferences from the refusal to answer questions since they had followed the advice of their solicitor in so refusing. The Court of Appeal took into account an earlier case, *Cowan and Others*,[267] which concerned the position of defendants failing to testify in court under s 35, and applied the principles enunciated to police questioning. The principles were as follows. A jury cannot infer guilt from silence alone (s 38(3)), so that the jury should only consider drawing inferences if a prima facie case to answer has been made out by the prosecution. Also, the burden of proof remains throughout on the prosecution to prove their case; in effect, a silence will be only one factor which can be used to make out the case. Inferences can be drawn if the only sensible explanation of silence was that the suspect had no explanation, or none that would stand up to cross-examination. The judge's direction was criticised in that it did not make this clear. The Court then considered the procedure to be followed in relation to s 34, where silence is on legal advice. The jury may draw an adverse inference from the failure unless the accused gives the reason for the advice being given. The reason for the advice is legally privileged, since it is part of a communication between solicitor and client, but once the client gives evidence of the nature of the advice, that will probably amount to a waiver of privilege so that the solicitor and/or client can then be asked about the reasons for the advice in court. The Court found that if an accused gives as the reason for not answering questions in a police interview that he has been advised not to do so, this assertion without more will not amount to a sufficient reason for not mentioning relevant matters which may later be relied on in defence. The convictions were upheld on the basis of the overwhelming evidence of drug supply, despite the flaw in the summing up.

It was made clear in *Bowden*[268] that explaining the grounds for the advice will amount to a waiver of legal privilege. Therefore, the prosecution can cross-examine the adviser on what was said to the suspect with a view to discovering discrepancies between the grounds put forward at trial and those discussed in the police station. The effect of these two decisions is to place the defendant and adviser in an invidious position. The adviser may be reluctant to advise silence even where there seem to be good reasons for doing so.[269] If the adviser advises silence, it may well appear to the defendant that that in itself is a sound reason for remaining silent. But that reason will not be accepted by a court. The adviser can either refuse to waive legal privilege and accept that adverse inferences will be drawn from the silence, or he can waive it and hope that the reasons given for the advice will be accepted in order to discourage the drawing of inferences. There may also be other confidential matters which the adviser does not wish to be asked about. It has been pointed out that solicitors may breach their professional Code of Conduct if they act for a client when they may be a material witness in the court case.[270] But if there is an arguably sound reason for advising silence,

---

267 [1996] QB 373; [1995] 4 All ER 939.
268 (1999) *The Times*, 25 February.
269 See, as to the difficulties facing advisers, Cape, E, 'Advising on silence' (1999) LAG, 14 June.
270 Tregilgas-Davey, M, 'Adverse inferences and the no-comment interview' [1997] 141 SJ 500; *The Guide to the Professional Conduct of Solicitors*, 1996, para 21.12.

the jury should be directed, following the findings of the Court of Appeal in *Condron*, that if they view the reason as sound, they should not draw adverse inferences.

It was found at Strasbourg that the applicants in *Condron v UK*[271] had failed to receive a fair trial under Art 6 on the basis that the appeal court should not have found that the conviction was safe, despite the erroneous direction of the judge to the jury. Since the Court could not know what part the drawing of adverse inferences played in the jury's decision, it should have allowed the appeal. That decision impliedly confirms that juries should be directed that they should not draw adverse inferences when silence has been advised in the police interview, except in certain circumstances. The Court found that where a defendant refuses to answer questions on legal advice, the jury should not be directed to draw an adverse inference from the silence unless they were first told that they should only do so if they considered that the silence could only sensibly be attributed to the suspect having no good answer to the questions. The Court was not, however sympathetic towards the dilemma that the applicants and solicitor were placed in (para 60):

> The court would observe at this juncture that the fact that the applicants were subjected to cross-examination on the content of their solicitor's advice cannot be said to raise an issue of fairness under Article 6 of the Convention. They were under no compulsion to disclose the advice given, other than the indirect compulsion to avoid the reason for their silence remaining at the level of a bare explanation. The applicants chose to make the content of their solicitor's advice a live issue as part of their defence.

The indirect compulsion in question was in fact quite significant if they had to demonstrate in the domestic court that their reliance on the advice was reasonable. The decision affects the role of trial judges; it does not give guidance on, *inter alia*, the question when a no comment interview, based on legal advice, should be excluded from evidence. It still leaves advisers in a state of some uncertainty as to when to advise a suspect to remain silent. However, it makes it somewhat easier for the solicitor to advise silence and safer for the client to rely on that advice.

The European Court of Human Rights confirmed its ruling in *Condron* in *Beckles v United Kingdom*.[272] The victim had gone to a flat where he was allegedly robbed by the defendant and others, prevented from leaving, and then thrown out of the window, sustaining very severe injuries. When arrested the defendant said that the victim 'wasn't pushed, he jumped' but, after seeing his solicitor, refused to answer any questions when interviewed. The judge did not direct the jury that they should not draw adverse inferences from the defendant's silence during the interview with the police if they considered that his silence was attributable to legal advice rather than to having no sensible answer to the questions. He was convicted of two counts of robbery, one count of false imprisonment and one count of attempted murder for which he was sentenced to a total of 15 years' imprisonment. The Court found that there had been a violation of Art 6(1) of the European Convention of Human Rights

---

271 [2001] 31 EHRR 1, Appl No 35718/97; [2000] Crim LR 679.
272 (2002) 36 EHRR 162.

as to the trial judge's directions to the jury. The misdirection concerned the instruction to the jury as to their right, under s 34 of the 1994 Act, to draw adverse inferences from the defendant's silence during an interview with police. The Court had found that the jury should have been directed that if they considered that the defendant had genuinely remained silent on legal advice they should consider refusing to draw an adverse inference from his silence.

In *R v Beckles*[273] the applicant appealed on the ground that there had been a misdirection to the jury as to their right, under s 34 of the Criminal Justice and Public Order Act 1994, to draw adverse inferences from the defendant's silence during an interview with police. Lord Woolf found that in a case where a solicitor's advice was relied upon by the defendant in the police interview, the ultimate question for the jury, under s 34, remained whether the facts relied on at the trial were facts which the defendant could reasonably have been expected to mention at interview. If the jury considered that the defendant had genuinely relied on the advice, that was not necessarily the end of the matter. If it was possible to say that the defendant had genuinely acted upon the advice, but had done so because it suited his purpose, that might mean that he had acted unreasonably in not mentioning the facts. The jury had to make a determination on his reasonableness in not mentioning the facts. If they concluded that he had been acting unreasonably they could draw an adverse inference from the failure to mention the facts. The trial judge had not directed the jury to consider the reasonableness or the genuineness of the defendant's reliance on his solicitor's advice as the reason why he did not answer questions in interview. It was found that that misdirection made the defendant's conviction unsafe. The appeal was allowed and a retrial was ordered. Thus Lord Woolf purported to take account of the Strasbourg decision in his findings. However, the emphasis on, in a sense, justifying the silence – even where it was genuinely in reliance on the legal advice – represents some departure from the ECHR decision. *Beckles* is indicative of a Court of Appeal tendency, after *Condron v UK*, to take an unsympathetic stance towards defendants who rely on legal advice in remaining silent.[274]

Since *Beckles* s 34 has remained a difficult and confusing area of law, and the problems are evident in the decision in *R v Bresa*.[275] Here the appellant was suspected of wounding with intent to do grievous bodily harm; he did not have English as his first language, was unfamiliar with the British legal system and was advised to give no comment by his solicitor in the police interview. At court neither he nor the solicitor gave an explanation for the legal advice. He put forward a defence of self defence which he did not mention in the police interviews. In giving a direction to the jury on the effect of s 34 the judge failed to say that to draw adverse inferences the jury had to be *sure* that the defendant had remained silent, not because of the legal advice but because he had no answer to give in the interview. The judge's direction, the Court of Appeal found, tended to undermine the confidentiality of solicitor and client discussions, and did not stress enough that the jury had to consider whether it was reasonable for the defendant to rely on the advice given; the judge had said:

---

273 [2004] EWCA 2766.
274 See *R v Inman* [2002] EWCA 1950; *R v Chenia* [2003] 2 Cr App 6; *R v Hoare and Pierce* [2004] EWCA Crim 784; *R v Howell* [2003] Crim LR 405; *R v Turner* [2004] 1 All ER 1025.
275 [2005] EWCA Crim 1414.

. . . when you are considering whether it was reasonable to expect him to mention [the relevant facts] in interview, and when he says that he didn't do so because he was advised to make no comment, you are entitled to look at that explanation in the knowledge that he has gone no further into why it was that the advice was given.

The Court of Appeal found that the direction was flawed, the conviction therefore unsafe, and ordered a retrial. The Court said the judge should have given a direction in (broadly) the following terms:

If you accept the evidence that he was so advised [to remain silent], this is obviously an important consideration; but it does not automatically prevent you from drawing any conclusion from his silence . . . a person given legal advice has the choice whether to accept or reject it . . . You have no explanation for the advice in this case. It is the defendant's right not to reveal the contents of any advice from his solicitor . . . The question for you is whether the defendant could reasonably have been expected to mention the facts on which he now relies and saying that he had legal advice without more cannot automatically make it reasonable. If, for example, you consider that he had or may have had an answer to give, i.e. that he was acting in self-defence, but genuinely and reasonably relied on the legal advice to remain silent, you should not draw any conclusion against him. But if, for example, you were sure that the defendant remained silent, not because of the legal advice, but because he had not acted in self-defence and that was a matter which he fabricated later, and merely latched on to the legal advice as a convenient shield behind which to hide, you would be entitled to draw a conclusion against him.[276]

It is difficult to see how a jury could be sure that the defendant had genuinely and reasonably relied on the legal advice. A jury might tend to take the 'common sense' view that anyone who in fact had a genuine defence of self defence would mention it at that point, regardless of the legal advice. Jurors might fail to take account of the coerciveness and intimidatory quality of police detention, especially for more vulnerable suspects. The direction in *Bresa* – based on the current JSB Guidelines for such directions – is not of much value in giving a guide to solicitors advising clients in police stations. The problem in essence is that if the solicitor and client do not breach the confidentiality of their consultations, they run the risk that the jury, without an explanation for the reasons behind the legal advice, will assume that the defence was fabricated later and that the advice is merely 'a convenient shield behind which to hide'. At present, therefore, the circumstances in which adverse inference drawing will create a breach of Art 6 still remain somewhat uncertain,[277] except in the instance in which access to legal advice is also denied.

It is clear that affording a suspect an opportunity to have access to legal advice before being questioned under caution is a necessary but not sufficient condition in Art

---

276 At para 49.
277 See further Birch, D, 'Suffering in silence: a cost–benefit analysis of s 34 of the CJPOA' [1999] Crim LR 769; Cape, E, *Defending Suspects at Police Stations*, 4th edn, 2003.

6 terms, for the drawing of adverse inferences, and s 34(2A) caters for that requirement. But, equally clearly, Art 6 will not necessarily be satisfied where adverse inferences are drawn after a defendant has had such access prior to that point and has remained silent. Cases such as *Condron* or *Bowden*, where the defendants had had legal advice and had acted on it in remaining silent, will have to be considered on their particular facts, in relation to the Art 6 requirements. Such cases obviously differ from *Murray* on the issue of the relationship between silence and legal advice. In *Condron* the defendants acted on legal advice in refusing to answer questions; in *Murray* a breach of Art 6(1) was found on the basis of inference-drawing in the absence of legal advice (not on the basis of inference-drawing *per se*). In *Condron*, the fact of having legal advice was not to the defendants' advantage, possibly the reverse, since in a sense they may have been misled into remaining silent. When will a breach of Art 6(1) arise if adverse inferences are drawn in that context – where the apparent explanation for silence was that it was on legal advice, following the domestic decision in *Beckles*? It must be borne in mind that a solicitor in the police station might need to seek to make a determination as to this question, in order to decide whether or not to advise silence.

This might be appropriate if it was unclear whether or not the advice would happen to coincide with the defendant's purpose, and the defendant could not be expected – due to his or her low intelligence, youth or other vulnerability – to decide to whether to speak or remain silent without the advice. It might also be safe to advise silence where the police had disclosed little of the case against the suspect before interviewing him under caution. To hold otherwise might be viewed as undermining the value attached in *Murray* to granting access to legal advice where adverse inferences would be drawn from silence.[278] The principle from *Murray* clearly rests impliedly on the value of such advice, while the domestic decision in *Beckles* accords that value a lesser weight. This is an instance in which the domestic courts are failing to use the HRA in a way which ensures at least as much rights-protection as could be delivered at Strasbourg. Their consistently crime control-based stance has led them to disregard the values associated with the presumption of innocence and the privilege against self incrimination which underpinned the traditional right to silence.

Penalising silence

Prior to the inception of the CJPOA, the right to silence was abolished in certain specific circumstances under a number of provisions which made failing to answer questions an offence. The provisions included: s 172 of the Road Traffic Act 1988, as amended; s 2 of the Criminal Justice Act 1987; ss 177 and 178 of the Financial Services Act 1986; ss 236 and 433 of the Insolvency Act 1986; s 437 of the Companies Act 1985; the Banking Act 1987 and the Friendly Societies Act 1992. These provisions, apart from s 172 of the RTA, were amended in 1999, as explained below. Thus, in a number of specific instances, the right to silence in the sense of penalising silence in criminal investigations had already been eroded until it reached the point where it could be said

---

278 It may be noted that such a finding would involve a departure from the current position under UK law as set out in *Condron* [1997] 1 Cr App R 185 and confirmed in *Bowden* (1999) *The Times*, 25 February.

to have virtually disappeared in those contexts.[279] If, for example, inquiries were made into a failed business, its owner could receive a 's 2 notice' from the Serious Fraud Office issued under the Criminal Justice Act 1987 which meant that a criminal offence would be committed if he or she did not attend for interview and answer questions (*Director of the Serious Fraud Office ex p Smith*).[280] Also, if the company was being investigated, a refusal to answer questions under s 432(2) of the Companies Act 1985 attracted criminal liability.

While the Conservative Governments of 1989–97 were responsible for the shift towards the crime control position which occurred under these provisions and under the CJPOA 1994, the Blair Government was responsible for a further marked shift in that direction. The Terrorism Act 2000 abolished the right to silence – in the sense of making it an offence to refuse to answer questions in defined circumstances – at certain points in the investigation of terrorism cases. The government raised the possibility of creating an offence of refusing to answer questions in the Consultation Paper on Terrorism in 1998. It noted that the recent Criminal Justice (Terrorism and Conspiracy) Act 1998 'extends the provisions by allowing inferences to be drawn in connection with membership of a specified proscribed organisation; but even there that is insufficient in itself to secure a conviction'. The intention was to take this provision further by creating an additional offence of refusing to answer questions, modelled on the power currently given to investigators in a range of cases, such as serious fraud investigations, and customs and licensing inquiries. The government recognised that there were what it termed 'serious ECHR constraints on this option'[281] and that, in order to circumvent these constraints, the resulting evidence, whether answers or silence, could not be used in a subsequent case against the individual concerned. The government clearly had in mind the case of *Saunders v UK*,[282] which is considered below.

These considerations led to the inclusion of paras 13, 14 and 16 in Sched 5 of the 2000 Act. The provisions relate to terrorism generally, not merely to proscription, but their relatively limited nature indicates the influence the Convention has had in tempering legislation in attempts to ensure that it is compatible with the Convention. The government clearly did not wish to risk the political embarrassment which it would have incurred had it included provision allowing coerced statements to be included as evidence, provision which would have necessitated issuing with the Act a statement of incompatibility under s 19 of the HRA.

The provisions as they stand are, however, arguably of doubtful compatibility. The requirements of para 13 represent a further infringement of the rights of the suspect, albeit of a relatively limited nature and subject to judicial authorisation. Under para 13 of Sched 5: 'a constable may apply to a circuit judge for an order . . . requiring any person specified in the order to provide an explanation of any material – (a) seized in pursuance of a warrant under paragraph 1 or 11, or (b) produced or made available to a constable under paragraph 5'. This does not affect material protected by legal privilege, but under para 13(3) a lawyer may be required to provide the name and address of her

279 See *Re London United Investments* [1992] 2 All ER 842; *Ex p Nadir* (1990) *The Times*, 5 November; *Bishopsgate Investment Management Ltd v Maxwell* [1992] 2 All ER 856, CA.

280 [1993] AC 1; [1992] 3 WLR 66; see also *AT & T Istel Ltd v Tulley* [1992] 3 All ER 523, HL.

281 *Legislation Against Terrorism: A Consultation Paper*, Cm 4178, 1998, para 14.3.

282 (1997) 23 EHRR 313. See below, pp 1251–54, and above, p 1239.

client. Under para 13(5), para 10 applies to such orders: they will have effect as if they were orders of the Crown Court. Thus, a person who refused to comply could incur liability for contempt. But any statement obtained cannot be used in evidence except on a prosecution for an offence under para 14. Paragraph 14(1) provides: 'a person commits an offence if, in purported compliance with an order under paragraph 13, he makes a statement which he knows to be false or misleading in a material particular', or recklessly makes such a statement. This offence is punishable by a maximum prison sentence of two years. Paragraph 16 is even more controversial; it provides a further possibility, untrammelled by judicial intervention, of punishing persons for failing to give explanations, or giving misleading ones. Paragraph 16(1) provides: 'if a police officer of at least the rank of superintendent has reasonable grounds for believing that the case is one of great emergency he may by a written notice signed by him require any person specified in the notice to provide an explanation of any material seized in pursuance of an order under paragraph 15.' Under para 16(3), in contrast to para 13, the suspect will commit an offence carrying a maximum prison term of six months if he fails to comply with a notice under the paragraph.

Both paras 13 and 16 allow for the admissibility of coerced statements, although in respect of the para 14 offence only. Thus, courts will have to consider whether admitting such statements in respect of that offence would be compatible with Art 6. Further, the paragraphs do not refer to silences which may be admissible in respect of other offences, or to the use of evidence from the statement against another person. Also, the evidence from any statements made, while not directly available to the court, may nevertheless underpin the other prosecution evidence, thereby arguably undermining the right to freedom from self-incrimination (see above).[283]

The transitional provisions applying to Northern Ireland create a further erosion of the right to silence. Under s 89(2) of the TA it is an offence punishable by a fine not to stop when required to do so by an officer; it is also an offence to refuse to answer a question asked during the stop or to answer it inadequately, failing to answer 'to the best of his knowledge and ability'.

As *Saunders v UK*[284] establishes, the use of formal coercion to obtain statements from persons will clearly be incompatible with Art 6 if the statement is then used against him or her in criminal proceedings. In *R v Staines; R v Morrisey*[285] the Court of Appeal refused, despite the judgment in *Saunders*, to overturn a conviction although the trial judge had refused to exclude evidence under s 78 of PACE obtained in a similar manner to that adopted in *Saunders*. In the post-HRA era, such a response would not appear to satisfy the duty of the court under s 6 of the HRA or the interpretative obligation of the judiciary under s 3. As indicated above, a large number of statutes contain provisions broadly equivalent to the provisions of the Companies Act 1985 which were at issue in *Saunders*. The Attorney General has issued guidance to prosecutors with a view to ensuring that evidence gained under a number of those provisions should not be used in criminal proceedings. This issue may not, therefore, arise at present under certain of these statutory provisions – a significant instance in which primary legislation was

283 See pp 1239–40.
284 (1997) 23 EHRR 313; Appl No 19187/91, Com Rep, paras 69–75.
285 [1997] 2 Cr App R 426.

rendered nugatory even before the HRA was in force. This matter was placed on a statutory basis in s 59 of and Sched 3 to the 1999 Act. Schedule 3 lists the statutory provisions mentioned above,[286] apart from s 172 of the Road Traffic Act 1988, and provides that the coerced statements will be inadmissible.

Nevertheless, certain very significant statutory provisions allowing for coercion, including a number arising under the Terrorism Act 2000, are used in the post-HRA era. Section 172 of the Road Traffic Act 1988 makes it an offence for motorists not to tell police who was driving their vehicle at the time of an alleged offence. The coerced statement can then be used in evidence at trial for the RTA offence in question. The provision clearly contravenes the right against self-incrimination, and this was found to be the case in Scotland in *Stott v Brown*[287] during the period of time when the Convention was in force in Scotland, but not in England.[288] The defendant encountered the police officers after parking her car and was suspected of driving while intoxicated; she was asked under s 172 to reveal the name of the person driving the car at the relevant time. On pain of the penalty under s 172 she did so, revealing that she had been driving, and was convicted of driving while intoxicated, after the coerced statement was admitted into evidence. Her conviction was overturned on appeal owing to the finding that s 172 contravened Art 6. The ruling of the Edinburgh High Court is of interest since the court rendered s 172, effectively, nugatory. This stance was taken on the basis of the requirements of the Scotland Act, which differ from those of s 6 of the HRA since they do not include the possibility envisaged under s 6(2)(b) that the authority was 'acting so as to give effect to or enforce those provisions [of incompatible primary legislation]'.

As Chapter 4 explained, the ruling of the Edinburgh High Court was overturned by the Privy Council: *Brown v Stott*.[289] The Privy Council did not find it necessary to declare that s 172 is incompatible with Art 6(1) or (2). They reached the decision that the two were compatible, despite the findings in *Saunders v UK*, on the basis that the requirements of Art 6 admit of implied restriction. The restriction, Lord Hope said, must have a legitimate aim in the public interest. It was found that this was the case, bearing in mind the need to promote road safety. If so, he went on to ask, 'is there a reasonable relationship of proportionality between the means employed and the aim sought to be realised?'[290] He found that the answer to the question, in terms of limiting the right not to incriminate oneself under Art 6(1), was in the affirmative since the section demands a response to a single question, and does not allow prolonged questioning, as in *Saunders*.

The decision in *Brown* rested on the finding that coercing a statement from the defendant was not a disproportionate response to the legitimate aim of seeking to address the problem of road safety. However, it is arguable that it re-opens the whole question of the compatibility of penalising silence in other contexts. If it can be argued that the requirement of s 172 is in proportion to the problem it seeks to address, it might be argued equally that where the legitimate aim in question is even more pressing,

---

286 See p 1249.
287 2000 SLT 379; see [2000] J CIV LIB 193.
288 The Convention rights were brought into force in Scotland under the Scotland Act 1998, s 57(2).
289 [2001] 2 WLR 817. See Chapter 4, pp 176–77.
290 See above, p 176.

as in the case of combating terrorism, a more intrusive provision, allowing for more prolonged questioning, could be viewed as a proportionate legislative response.

Therefore, it can no longer be said with certainty that the decision in *Saunders v UK* calls into question the provisions allowing a limited use of coerced statements in evidence in terrorist investigations under Sched 5, paras 13 and 16 to the TA. Such statements may be admitted into evidence in order to convict of the offence under para 14 of making a statement which the defendant knows to be false or misleading in a material particular, or as to which he is reckless, in purported compliance with an order under para 13. Clearly, a misleading statement might not be made but for the pressure flowing from the penalties which para 13 and, to a greater extent, para 16, carry. Nevertheless, it is now debatable whether the possibility of admitting the statement is incompatible with the right against self-incrimination.

Further, despite the evident attempt in paras 13 and 16 to achieve Convention compliance, bearing *Saunders* in mind, the possibility of incompatibility remains, taking into account the broader implications of fairness in the trial as a whole under Art 6(1). If someone other than the person who had made the coerced statement was on trial and the prosecution wished to admit the statement in evidence, argument could be raised as to the fairness of so doing, bearing in mind the fact that the statement could not be used against its maker.[291] The issue of the fairness of the trial as a whole[292] could also be raised where the statement had influenced the prosecution or enabled the police to obtain evidence, since it could be argued that the statement had had an indirect impact in undermining the right against self-incrimination. Admittedly, there are precedents in current UK law for basing a prosecution on evidence uncovered in reliance on information from statements which are themselves inadmissible.[293] However, each of those precedents will need to be tested against Art 6 standards, taking into account all the circumstances applicable in an individual case.

The further question is whether Art 6 might be breached in an instance in which a silence in response to the threat of penalties under the paragraphs in question was admitted in respect of one of the other offences under Sched 5, or indeed any other offence. *Brown* and *Saunders* do not expressly address the question whether the admission into evidence of a no-comment interview (as opposed to admissions) in response to formal coercion would breach Art 6. Obviously, a situation can be envisaged in which the accused might decide to risk the imposition of the penalty in question. The prosecution might then put forward the interview in evidence for the purpose of drawing adverse inferences from it. On one view, the case for drawing such inferences might be strengthened on the argument that if the accused is prepared to risk the imposition of the penalty in question, he must have something very significant to hide. But equally, it might be argued that a vulnerable defendant who did not have legal advice (as a result

291   Analogy might be drawn with *Rowe and Davis v UK* (2000) 30 EHRR 1, in which statements made by accomplices were used against the accused, although the statements had been extracted on the basis of promise of immunity from prosecution and financial reward. These matters, which did not come to light at the trial, owing to the use of PII certificates, led the Court to find that the accused had not had a fair trial, in breach of Art 6.

292   The concept of the fairness of the trial taken as a whole was developed in *Barbéra, Messegué and Jabardo*, A 14 6(2) (1989).

293   PACE 1984, s 76(4). Impliedly under the Regulation of Investigatory Powers Act 2000, s 17.

of factors other than its formal denial) had made no comment, perhaps due to fear of retaliation from the real perpetrator of the offence. Such situations appear to fall more within the ruling from *Murray* than within that from *Saunders*; therefore, the factors identified here as relevant to arguments based on *Murray* would be applicable.

Section 89(2) of the TA, applicable only in Northern Ireland, raises similar issues. Section 89(2) provides that it is an offence punishable by a fine to refuse to answer a question asked during a stop or to answer it inadequately, failing to answer 'to the best of his knowledge and ability'. Evidence obtained under s 89 can be used to convict of the s 89 offence itself; further, the TA does not expressly provide that it cannot be used in respect of other TA offences, although in practice it would be unlikely that it would be so used, owing to the incompatibility of so doing with Art 6(1) and (2).

It may be noted that the PACE Code C provisions, paras 10.1 and 10.5C, which envisage the possibility of coercion under the statutory provisions mentioned, and make provision for it, may also be incompatible with Art 6. Paragraph 10.1 provides that there is no need to caution if information is to be obtained under a 'relevant statutory requirement', while para 10.5C provides that the suspect should be informed of the consequences of failing to co-operate in the interview, regardless of the caution, where a statutory requirement to provide information applies and may render him liable to conviction for an offence or arrest. These provisions should therefore have been omitted or modified in the 1999 revision of the Codes. As they stand, the relevant parts of the paragraphs appear to amount to incompatible subordinate legislation which can simply be rendered invalid, if necessary, under the HRA since, although they reflect primary legislation, it cannot be said that such legislation 'prevents the removal of the incompatibility'.[294]

---

294 See HRA 1998, s 3(2)(c).

Chapter 13

Redress for police malpractice

1 Introduction[1]

Chapters 11 and 12 were concerned with the question of the balance to be struck between the exercise of powers by the police in conducting an investigation on the one hand and safeguards for the suspect against abuse of power on the other. As we have seen, the statutory rules, including in particular those under the Police and Criminal Evidence Act 1984 (PACE), the Criminal Justice and Public Order Act 1994 (CJPOA), the Criminal Justice and Police Act 2001 (CJP) and the Terrorism Act 2000 (TA) contain, on the one hand, provisions intended to secure suspects' rights, such as s 58 of PACE and Sched 8, para 7 to the TA, while on the other they create or extend a statutory basis for the exercise of police powers, which frequently enhances those powers.[2] Thus, the rules can be viewed as reflecting the two different models of crime control and due process, and since the approach and aims of those models is conflicting, the statutes in question and their application in practice reflect the resulting inevitable tension. This may be said even of provisions which appear to be intended, fairly obviously, to enhance police powers, such as ss 50 and 51 of the CJP. These provisions provide, as Chapters 11 and 12 indicated, new powers of seizure during searches of people or of premises. But they are 'balanced' by the provisions of ss 52–61 which, while affording the extended powers of retention of the property seized a clear statutory basis, also provide for notice to persons whose property has been seized, and safeguard its use by various provisions.[3] It is not suggested that the balance struck is satisfactory, but it is clear that, although

---

1 Texts referred to below: Ashworth, A, *The Criminal Process*, 3rd edn, 2005; Feldman, D, *Civil Liberties and Human Rights in England and Wales*, 2nd edn, 2002, Chapters 5 and 9; Sanders, A and Young, R, *Criminal Justice*, 3rd edn, 2007, Chapter 12; Zander, M, *The Police and Criminal Evidence Act 1984*, 2003; Clark, D, *Bevan and Lidstone's The Investigation of Crime*, 2004; Clayton, R and Tomlinson, H, *The Law of Human Rights*, 2nd edn, 2006, Chapter 11; See also: Maher, G, *A Theory of Criminal Process*, 2000, Hart; McConville, M, Sanders, A and Leng, R, *The Case for the Prosecution*, 1991; Bailey, SH, Harris, DJ and Jones, BL, *Civil Liberties: Cases and Materials*, 5th edn, 2002, Chapter 2; Reiner, R and Leigh, I, 'Police powers', in McCrudden, C and Chambers, G (eds), *Individual Rights and the Law in Britain*, 1994; Klug, F, Starmer, K and Weir, S, *The Three Pillars of Liberty: Political Rights and Freedoms in the UK*, 1996; Sharpe, S, *Judicial Discretion and Criminal Investigations*, 1998, Sweet and Maxwell; Nobles, R and Schiff, D, 'Due process and Dirty Harry dilemmas: criminal appeals and the Human Rights Act' [2001] 64(6) MLR pp 911–22; Ashworth, A, 'Criminal Justice Reform' [2004] Crim LR 516.
2 Such as PACE 1984, s 24 and TA, s 41.
3 Including the duty to secure the property arising under s 61 by preventing, *inter alia*, copying of it.

these CJP provisions are very much orientated towards crime control, they are limited by provisions reflecting due process concerns. This could also be said to an extent of s 110 of the Serious and Organised Crime and Police Act 2005, which extended the PACE arrest power: it created a safeguard for potential arrestees of a sort in requiring police officers to be satisfied as to the fulfilment of a further requirement (based on the 'arrest conditions' from old s 25 but extending them as discussed below), apart from reasonable suspicion relating to the offence in question, a requirement that was not present under the old s 24 PACE. The PACE Codes, as revised and extended in 2006, contain a wide range of safeguards for suspects.

Thus, the relevant statutory and Code provisions declare that certain standards for the conduct of criminal and terrorist investigations must be maintained; in order to create them a complex, not to say cumbersome, domestic scheme is currently in place, part of it post-dating the Human Rights Act (HRA). It is one that has become incrementally more extensive post-PACE, especially if the Code provisions are taken into account. Under the European Convention on Human Rights, another scheme setting standards for criminal justice is apparent. Clearly, the two schemes are very different. Not only is the domestic scheme far more detailed, but also they have different starting points. One – the domestic scheme – essentially sets out police powers and then provides for restrictions on them, and for safeguards for suspects during their exercise. The other – the Convention – sets out fundamental rights and then, in the case of the right to liberty under Art 5, the guarantees of a fair trial under Art 6 and the right to be free of torture, inhuman or degrading treatment under Art 3, leaves them unqualified or not materially qualified. Only Art 5 could be said to create exceptions which correspond to aspects of domestic police powers. Nevertheless, it can be said at a high level of generality that both schemes set standards for administering criminal justice. As explored in Chapters 11 and 12, the standards of the domestic scheme and those recognised under the Convention are not necessarily the same. Each scheme does two things – it sets certain standards for crime control and for suspects' rights; it then provides that there should be a means of redress if the standards are breached. The domestic scheme goes on to prescribe in more detail the forms of redress that are potentially available, especially in relation to the question of exclusion of evidence. The international scheme provides the basic safeguard that the remedies should be effective.

The HRA brings the two schemes into juxtaposition, or perhaps confrontation, and demands under s 3(1) that, in so far as the domestic scheme is statute or Code-based, it should, if interpretation will so allow, be compatible with the requirements of the other. The HRA also demands, under s 6, that each person or body administering the domestic scheme should, unless primary legislation using very clear words provides otherwise, abide by the Convention rights. The position is complex as regards the fair trial rights under Art 6. Although in practice a court may use the methods available to it to seek to ensure that despite failures to adhere to the rights in the pre-trial period, the proceedings as a whole comply with Art 6, it is arguable that a remedy should still be available in respect of the failures of the police or other public authorities. It is not enough, it is contended, if the police do not adhere to the Convention, but that there is the potential for this then to be 'rectified' in court so that in their entirety the pre-trial and trial process ultimately so adheres. Each actor in it should (since all are public authorities) adhere to Art 6 in their own actions and decisions, bearing in mind that the case may well never come to trial. The basis for the counter-argument is that since Art 6 is concerned with the fairness of the trial, it only makes sense to consider the effect of a failure of such access within the context of the trial. It will be suggested below that this argument is flawed. At present this argument is prevailing and therefore it can be said that even under the HRA there is no effective remedy domestically for breach of certain rights within the criminal justice system. The HRA should provide at least the same protection for rights as Strasbourg would, but it is not clear that Strasbourg has taken the stance that Art 6 rights are free-standing, outside the trial context. This point is pursued below.

It may be said, then, that the HRA provides mechanisms for asking, first, whether the standards expressed by the domestic scheme are in conformity with the Convention rights. This was the question addressed by Chapters 11 and 12. Second, it ensures that the question is asked whether the means of redress provided are in conformity with what the Convention demands in terms of an effective remedy. This question is addressed in this chapter. This latter question has four facets. It asks: (a) if the domestic standards *themselves* are not in conformity, what can be done to rectify that by reliance on the Convention and the HRA; (b) what domestic means of redress are available for breach of the standards set for the criminal justice system and described in Chapters 11 and 12, and do they provide an effective remedy in Convention terms; (c) if the police do not abide by those standards, does the Convention under the HRA add anything to what can be done under the other current domestic provisions to provide redress; (d) is reliance on the Convention rights under the HRA an effective method of providing a remedy in respect of breaches of the standards set by the domestic provisions, including the Code provisions? It will be argued that it is in respect of redress that the domestic scheme is the most lacking but that in both legal and practical terms the HRA can only make up for the deficiency to an extent.

There are a number of domestic methods of providing redress: the police complaints and disciplinary process; prosecutions of the police; civil actions; judicial review of police actions; exclusion of evidence; trial "remedies", including stays for abuse of process, other than exclusion of evidence. The use of judicial review was considered in Chapter 11.[4] The police complaints process and exclusion of evidence have been found to fail to provide an effective remedy for breaches of the Convention rights at Strasbourg[5] and the complaints and disciplinary process has since been reformed. Civil actions (outwith ss 7(1)(a) and 8 HRA) will provide such a remedy, but are not applicable to many breaches of the scheme. Stays for abuse of process are rarely used and would not be used in respect of some breaches of Convention rights – a matter that is explored below. Prosecutions of the police are very rare and can only indirectly protect Convention rights.[6]

Typically, the question of redress may arise as follows: an investigation may not, at certain points, reach the standards set by the statutory scheme and it may at the same time breach one or more of the Convention rights. The police may sometimes feel hampered by all the PACE and Code provisions; they may feel, for example, that they are close to obtaining a confession from a detainee, but that in order to obtain it,

---

4 See in particular pp 1134–37.

5 In *Khan v UK* (2000) 8 BHRC 310, paras 44–47.

6 Since no criminal liability is created under the HRA 1998.

they need to bend or break the interviewing rules. Similarly, police officers may purport to act within a power, such as the power to arrest or search premises, where no power to do so arises. In such circumstances, certain remedies are available: a civil action leading to an award of damages, if successful, or a complaint leading to disciplinary action against the officers involved, if upheld. However, as already noted, civil actions are not available for breach of the Codes and will be inapplicable to some breaches of PACE itself, such as improper denial of access to legal advice. Police disciplinary action is applicable to breaches of both PACE itself and the Codes, but at present it is arguable that, despite reform, it still does not represent an effective remedy. Apart from these two remedies, a further means of redress exists, represented by the use of exclusion of evidence, and it is in this context – as well as in the context of judicial review proceedings – that many breaches of PACE and the Codes have in fact been considered. Therefore, argument raised under s 7(1)(b) of the HRA may often be put forward in respect of exclusion of evidence. But not only is such exclusion irrelevant in the vast majority of cases since the suspect will plead guilty, it cannot be viewed, even where the case does come to trial, as an effective remedy for breaches of the Convention rights, for reasons to be considered below. Possibly, it could be viewed as an effective remedy for breaches of the statutory and Code-based scheme itself.

Thus, ss 7 and 8 HRA fill a clear gap, since a remedy in damages for breach of the Convention rights in the criminal justice system pre-trial is now available. If aspects of the domestic scheme, including Code provisions, are coterminous with the Convention rights, they have now received for the first time a remedial underpinning, where breach of such provisions would not attract a tortious remedy. However, that remedy may not be available in respect of some breaches of Art 6, including failures of access to custodial legal advice, since it appears to be assumed that the remedy would be provided in the trial itself.

The key contention of this chapter is that no sufficient or effective means of redress are available in respect of police abuse of power, although the HRA has enhanced the remedial scheme to an extent. Therefore, the safeguards considered in Chapters 11 and 12 are far from fully underpinned by such a scheme. Clearly, even if such a scheme were available in the form, for example, of a fully independent police disciplinary system, police internal practices and culture would still have an impact on the delivery of the safeguards. But, as Chapters 11 and 12 argued, externally imposed rules can affect that culture.[7] If the enforcement of those rules is weak, as this chapter contends, their impact on institutional practices is bound to be diminished.

This reading of the domestic and Convention provisions addresses significant matters, and is the main concern of this chapter, but alone it would be, it is suggested, inadequate. At the end of the chapter it will be possible to discern that the Convention under the HRA has had at least some impact in terms of reviving and reaffirming a concern for due process which has gradually been eroded in the post-PACE years. In other words, a return to those values expressed quite strongly by PACE and less so in the later legislation might become apparent in the HRA era. But such an account would not be influenced by a victim-oriented or feminist perspective. By concentrating only on due process concerns, such perspectives could be ignored. The implication would

---

7 See above, p 1116 and pp 1153–54, 1186–90.

be that where a choice had to be made legislatively, judicially or executively (and the latter term, of course, includes the police themselves), the demands of due process and crime control would provide the parameters of the debate. But adoption of such a gender-neutral stance would ignore the gendered impact of the decision which would then be made, as well as the impact on victims. Thus, this chapter will argue for a more developed conception of the criminal justice system, one that recognises the values of privacy and equality as well as those of due process.

2 The Human Rights Act and trial remedies

Requirements of Article 6

As Chapter 2 indicated, Art 6 is seen as a central Convention Article which holds a pre-eminent position in the Convention jurisprudence since the right it protects is so fundamentally important in a democratic society.[8] It expresses a 'fundamental principle of the rule of law'[9] and is to be interpreted broadly.[10] The Court has tended to take an increasingly interventionist stance towards the right to a fair trial. Such a stance was evident in *Teixeira v Portugal*,[11] *Van Mechelen v Netherlands*,[12] *Saidi v France*[13] and *Rowe and Davis v UK*[14] although the Court continues to adhere to the principle that the assessment of evidence is for the national court.[15] Apart from the right to be presumed innocent under Art 6(2), the guarantee of the access to legal advice and the other minimal guarantees of para 6(3),[16] the Court has found that a number of rights are implicit in the term a 'fair hearing'.[17] The principle of 'equality of arms' – equality between defence and prosecution – arising from Art 6(1) affects all aspects of a hearing, therefore overlapping with its expression under Art 6(3).[18]

Duties of the courts under the HRA

The domestic courts will, save for the s 6(2) HRA proviso concerning incompatible legislation, fail to satisfy s 6 of the HRA if they act incompatibly with the Convention rights, since they are themselves public authorities. The position appears to be that wherever a court has a discretion in the course of criminal procedure, a decision regarding its use of that discretion will amount to an 'act' within the meaning s 6

---

8 See pp 59 *et seq.*

9 *Salabiaku v France* (1988) 13 EHRR 379.

10 *Delcourt v Belgium* (1970) 1 EHRR 355.

11 (1998) 28 EHHR 101; [1998] Crim LR 751.

12 (1998) 25 EHRR 657.

13 (1994) 17 EHRR 251.

14 (2000) 30 EHRR 1.

15 *Khan v UK* (2000) 8 BHRC 310.

16 See Chapter 2, pp 65–66; Chapter 13, pp 1210–12.

17 For general discussion see Harris, D, O'Boyle, K and Warbrick, C, *Law of The European Convention on Human Rights*, 1995, Chapter 6; Ovey, C, 'The ECHR and the criminal lawyer: an introduction' [1998] Crim LR 4; Clayton and Tomlinson, op. cit., fn 1, Chapter 11.

18 The principle is fully established and long standing in the Art 6 jurisprudence: see *X v FRG* (1963) 6 YB 520, p 574. See further Chapter 2, p 64.

of the HRA.[19] If a court does violate the rights in taking decisions as to, *inter alia*, exclusion of evidence or abuse of process, ss 7 and 8 of the HRA will be relevant. As Chapter 4 explains, s 7 allows a victim of an alleged violation, or proposed violation, of a Convention guarantee to rely on the right in litigation, and to argue in particular that he would be a victim of an unlawful act if the act proposed is undertaken. Section 8 allows courts to grant such remedies as seem to them just and convenient for such violations.

It is not enough for breaches of Art 6 by courts to be remedied through the appeal process. The House of Lords in the leading pre-HRA decision, *R v DPP ex p Kebilene and Others*[20] found in considering Art 6, that the domestic court is not, of necessity, in the same position as the Strasbourg court: 'it was inevitable that the European Court would conduct a retrospective review of [whether a trial was fair or unfair in Art 6(1) terms] in the national court', but that in the domestic court, this matter could be considered before completion of a trial. In other words, the Strasbourg Court could consider the whole pre-trial and trial process and come to a determination as to its fairness under Art 6(1). The domestic court would have to consider, during pre-trial hearings, the trial process, or on appeal, not only whether an actual or potential breach had occurred, but also whether Art 6 would be breached owing to its own regulation of the process.

The defendant might, for example, raise the argument that if the court failed to exclude evidence, Art 6(1) would be breached and that therefore, ss 6,7 and 8 require that the evidence should be excluded in order to avoid the breach. Section 8, as indicated, appears to afford some discretion to a court as to awarding the remedy, but it is almost inconceivable that a court during a trial would accept the argument that it was about to act unlawfully, within s 6, but then, although it found leeway to do so and was not therefore affected by s 6(2), fail to provide a remedy by resiling from the threatened unlawfulness. A court might, of course, find, erroneously, that its particular decision during the criminal procedure would not breach Art 6, in which case the issue would have to be raised on appeal. A court adjudicating on the current grounds for allowing an appeal would itself be bound by s 6, but would theoretically also retain a discretion under s 8 as to the award of a remedy.

In accordance with the Strasbourg jurisprudence and s 6 of the HRA, the appeal court is itself bound by Art 6.[21] The test for criminal appeals from the Crown Court is simply whether the conviction is 'unsafe'.[22] In *Mullen*,[23] the Court of Appeal said that an abuse of process, or, equally, material irregularities at the trial would empower the court to find that a conviction was unsafe. If the Court of Appeal considered that despite a pre-trial breach of the Convention, a conviction was safe, this view could be challenged as itself – in the particular circumstances – contrary to Art 6. If Art 6 was

---

19 This is the stance of the Strasbourg Court: see *Z v Finland* (1997) 25 EHRR 371.
20 [1999] 3 WLR 972.
21 *Delcourt v Belgium* A 11 (1970).
22 The Criminal Appeals Act 1968, s 2(1), as amended by the Criminal Appeals Act 1995. This provision, which allows the conviction to stand despite, e.g., a misdirection of the judge, may require modification owing to the findings of the European Court in *Condron v UK* (2001) 31 EHRR 1; see (2000) J Civ Lib 253.
23 [1999] 2 Cr App R 143.

itself breached owing to the effect of pre-trial improprieties, which were not cured at trial, it is hard to see that the conviction could be regarded as 'safe'.

This was broadly the stance, with a narrow caveat, taken by the Court of Appeal pre-HRA. In *Pearson*,[24] the Court of Appeal said: 'where this court takes the view that an appellant did not receive a fair trial this court would not, save in the most exceptional circumstances, reach the view that the conviction was nevertheless safe'. Now that Art 6 is binding on the Court of Appeal, the exception mentioned ceases to apply since otherwise, that court would be declaring, in effect, its intention to breach the Convention guarantee of a fair trial, contrary to s 6 of the HRA.

Theoretically, a defendant could be convicted after an investigative, pre-trial and trial process which taken as a whole failed to meet Art 6 standards, where the unfairness was due to incompatible domestic legislation. This is allowed for under s 6(2)(b) HRA, as Chapter 4 points out.[25] If so, the conviction would have to stand and therefore, prima facie, there would appear to be no benefit in appealing to a higher court which could issue a declaration of incompatibility. But, there would be an incentive to appeal where there was leeway for the higher court to take a different view on incompatibility by finding a way of reconciling the domestic legislation with Art 6 under s 3 HRA[26] or if there were grounds for expecting the higher court, once it had made the declaration, to award a lower sentence. In practice, however the domestic courts seek to avoid convict and possibly imprisoning a defendant under legislation which breaches the Convention, by declaring an abuse of process.[27]

Pre-HRA, a key question that a number of commentators emphasised was whether the requirement of fairness under Art 6(1) would be likely to add anything to the possibilities of creating police accountability by excluding evidence or staying the proceedings that already existed pre-HRA, domestically.[28] In particular, where the police have not adhered to the statutory safeguards for suspects, it appeared that it might be more likely under the HRA that evidence thereby obtained would be excluded, possibly providing greater protection for suspects. As indicated above, Art 6(1) allows each member state to determine its own rules of evidence. Nevertheless, the admission of evidence obtained in certain ways has been found to infringe Art 6. In these situations, the duty of the court under s 6 of the HRA requires it to exclude the evidence or stay the proceedings. Thus, in certain circumstances, Art 6 may have created greater accountability. Strasbourg has not offered much general guidance as to the use exclusion of evidence or a stay where police impropriety has occurred in order to meet the requirements of Art 6. Article 6 under the HRA has not had a radical impact in terms of trial remedies. As indicated below, the domestic courts are likely to concentrate on the particular facts of each case and, in particular, on the question of the reliability of the evidence, in relation to the question of its exclusion. In contrast, a stay may occasionally be determined upon, even where the evidence may be reliable. Clearly, in the case of very serious malpractice, including breaches of Convention rights, the court would view it as impossible to sustain the view that Art 6 would not

24   (1998) *The Times*, 20 February.
25   See pp 215–16.
26   *Brown v Stott* [2001] 2 WLR 817.
27   See the judgment of Lord Steyn in *Ex p Kebeline* [1999] 4 All ER 801.
28   See, e.g., Clayton and Tomlinson, op. cit., fn 1, 1st edn, p 1465.

be breached if the trial went ahead or if, depending on the circumstances, evidence was not excluded.

3 Exclusion of evidence

Introduction: conflicting values

An example may illustrate the effect of exclusion of evidence. Assume that the police have arrested a man on suspicion of theft. They are fairly certain that he is guilty and think that they have a good chance of getting him to confess. However, he asks for legal advice. The police think that a solicitor may advise him not to answer some questions or may at least help him to withstand certain questioning techniques and so they tell him (untruthfully) that the duty solicitor is unavailable and that they might as well get on with the interview rather than prolong the process. They then question him for four hours without a break. Eventually, he succumbs to the pressure and makes a full confession to theft.

The police have breached PACE and Code C (s 58, para 6.6 and – depending on circumstances and interpretation – para 12.8). Arguably, they have also breached, or potentially breached, a Convention right: Art 6(3)(c).[29] Some meagre methods of redress are potentially available. The suspect can make a complaint. He could seek to bring an action against the police under s 7(1)(a) HRA for the arguable breach of Art 6 – but this method of obtaining redress is very doubtful; no domestic authority supports its availability. But, most significantly, the flawed interrogation may affect the trial; the trial may lead to a conviction and possibly imprisonment. He may decide to plead guilty. But if he pleads not guilty, his counsel may ask the judge at the trial not to admit the confession in evidence on the basis that the interrogation which produced it was conducted unfairly. The trial judge then has the opportunity to ensure that the original abuse of power on the part of the police is unable to affect the fairness of the trial. Unfairness is arguably less likely to occur if the judge refuses to admit the confession in evidence. The judge can hold a *voir dire* (a trial within a trial) by sending out the jury and then hearing defence and prosecution submissions on admitting the confession. If it is not admitted, the jury will never know of its existence and will determine the case on the basis of any other available evidence. The judge is in a difficult position. On the one hand, it is apparent that the police have abused their powers; the judge does not want to condone or appear to condone such behaviour by admitting the evidence gained thereby. On the other, the prosecution case may collapse and a possibly guilty man walk free from the court if the confession is excluded. Assuming that he is guilty, that would be to the detriment of the victim of the theft and to society in general. Also, if the other evidence against the defendant is strong, it could be argued that admission of the confession would have little or no impact on the fairness of the trial since even if it was excluded the defendant would probably be convicted.

If the defendant did commit the theft, it might be said that the end in view – the conviction – justifies the means used to obtain it, but should the judge ignore the fact that the confession might not be before the court at all had the police complied with

29 See Chapter 12, pp 1210 *et seq.*

PACE and Code C? Should the judge merely consider the punishment of one defendant in isolation? If the confession is admitted, the judge is arguably making in effect a public declaration that the courts will not use their powers to uphold standards for police investigations. The result may be that in future, PACE due process standards are not adhered to and that, occasionally, an innocent citizen is convicted after a false confession has been coerced from him. The multiplicity of issues raised by examples of this nature have provoked a long-running debate among academics and lawyers as to the purpose of excluding evidence which has been obtained improperly, and a number of schools of thought have arisen, advocating different principles on which evidence should be excluded. Such principles, it will be argued, are affected by the inception of the HRA.

The crime control position is that evidence should be excluded only if it appears to be unreliable, that is, in the case of a confession, false or inaccurately recorded.[30] Taken to its logical conclusion, this would mean that if a true confession (able to be verified as true) has been extracted by torture, it should nevertheless be admitted. This is argued on the basis that the function of a criminal court is to determine the truth of the charges against the accused, not to inquire into alleged improprieties on the part of the police. It is not equipped to conduct such an inquiry; therefore, if evidence is excluded on the basis that impropriety occurred in the investigation, the reputation of the police officer in question will be damaged after a less than full investigation into his or her conduct. On this argument, the court in admitting evidence obtained by improper methods is not condoning them. It is acknowledging that it is not within its function to inquire into them. Further, it can be argued on principle that even if impropriety did occur in the investigation, which the court could be viewed as disregarding or even condoning, this should not allow a guilty defendant to walk freely from the court due to the impact on society and on the victim. The adverse impact on society is three-fold. First, valuable resources have been wasted since the police and other bodies have processed the defendant through the criminal justice system without having any impact on controlling crime. Second, the defendant may commit further crimes, causing distress and financial loss to the victims and a general rise in insurance premiums. Third, society may lose faith in the criminal justice system if the guilty are not convicted.

It is suggested that in so far as this position reflects the current approach of domestic courts,[31] it has been called into question by the HRA. It implies, *inter alia*, that despite its duty under s 6 HRA, the court could simply ignore a breach of the Convention rights which has occurred in the pre-trial or custodial procedures and which has been instrumental in obtaining evidence. In respect of non-confession evidence, this is the current approach of the domestic courts. There is in fact an argument, considered below, that this position is sustainable to an extent under the HRA, but clearly it has now been placed under pressure.

From a due process stance, it has been argued that a court cannot merely inquire into the truth of the charges against a particular defendant: it must also play a part in

---

30 See Wigmore, JH, *Treatise on Evidence*, 3rd edn, 1940, and Andrews, JA, 'Involuntary Confessions and Illegally Obtained Evidence in Criminal Cases' [1963] Crim LR 15, p 77.
31 See *Chalkley* [1998] 2 Cr App R 79, discussed below, p 1290.

maintaining standards in criminal investigations.[32] The court has one particular part to play in the processing of the defendant through the criminal justice system: it should not play its brief part and ignore what has gone before. If the courts are prepared to accept evidence obtained by improper methods, the police may be encouraged to abuse their powers to the detriment of the citizen. Exclusion of evidence should be used to punish the police by depriving them of the fruits of their impropriety and to deter them from using such practices. This principle – the disciplinary principle – may encompass either a deterrent or a punitive role for exclusion of evidence, although it is recognised that no clear-cut relationship between police behaviour and rejection of evidence should be envisaged.[33] Obviously the defendant may plead guilty so that any punitive or deterrent role is undermined. Since most defendants plead guilty, it may appear to a police officer that there is more to be gained than lost by placing pressure on suspects to make admissions.

The use of exclusion of evidence to punish the police has come to be viewed by most commentators as an inefficient and possibly ineffective means of protecting due process, and this has led Ashworth to suggest a somewhat different principle, which he terms protective.[34] He contends that once a legal system has declared a certain standard for the conduct of investigations, the citizen obtains corresponding rights to be treated in manner that adheres to those standards. If such rights are denied and evidence gained as a result, the court can wipe out the disadvantage to the defendant flowing from the denial by rejecting the evidence in question. If, for example, it appears that the defendant would not have made the confession if the police had afforded him access to legal advice, the judge could recreate the situation for the jury's benefit as it would have been had the access been afforded, by excluding the confession. In the eyes of the jury, the position would be as if the right had never been denied; the judge would therefore have succeeded in protecting the defendant's right of access to legal advice in the interview. It must be pointed out that use of this argument in practice became more problematic when the caution became a warning that silence may be commented on adversely in court. If access to legal advice is not given, it might be argued that such a failure could not be causally related to the confession, since the adviser would have advised the defendant not to risk remaining silent in any event. This point will be returned to below.

An alternative but allied argument, also founded on due process values, may be termed the 'reputation' or 'integrity' principle. It can be argued that admitting the confession causes the trial to appear unfair because the court thereby appears to condone or lend itself to the original unfairness. The imprimatur of the court is necessary in order to allow the impropriety to bear fruit. If the trial is viewed, not as a separate entity, but as the culmination of a process in which the court and the police both play their part as emanations of the state, it can be argued that the court should refuse to lend itself to the unfairness which has gone before in order to ensure that the state does not profit from its own wrong. It cannot wipe out the unfairness, but it can wipe out its consequences, thereby ensuring that the reputation of the criminal justice

---

32　E.g. Cross, R (Sir), *Cross on Evidence*, 5th edn, 1979, Butterworths, pp 318–28.
33　Ibid, p 328.
34　See Ashworth, A, 'Excluding Evidence as Protecting Rights' [1977] Crim LR 723.

system is not tarnished. But it need concern itself with the police unfairness only if that unfairness did have consequences. If it concerned itself with an inconsequential breach, the reputation of the criminal justice system would also suffer since the detriment caused to society in allowing someone who has perpetrated a serious crime to walk free from the court would be perceived as entirely outweighing the detriment to the defendant caused by the breach. Ashworth has found, after surveying the position in a number of jurisdictions, that where the police have breached a Convention right, evidence thereby obtained should be excluded partly to vindicate the right and partly to preserve the integrity of the criminal justice system.[35]

It might appear that the inception of the HRA lends force to arguments based on the protective principle since the citizen obtains rights, not merely as an extrapolation from the standards declared in the statutory scheme, including that under PACE, but also under the Convention, on the basis that is unlawful for the public authority in question – the police – to breach them, under s 6 HRA. It might also be said that by giving further effect to the Convention rights, and placing a duty on the courts to uphold them, the HRA implies that the integrity of the criminal justice system would be compromised where evidence is admitted in breach of a right. However, although there are suggestions from the case law that the approach of the courts in the early post-PACE years was consistent with this argument to an extent, that approach was hardly evident in the immediate pre- HRA period, and the inception of the HRA did not affect that position.

The position in other common law jurisdictions

The US Supreme Court has taken the disciplinary and protective principles into account in determining that evidence obtained by improper methods should be excluded. For example, in *Mapp v Ohio*,[36] the police conducted an illegal search of Mrs Mapp's boarding house and seized certain obscene materials. The Supreme Court held that the evidence obtained in the course of the illegal search was inadmissible. The majority opinion gave two main reasons for reaching this conclusion: first, that the police should be discouraged from conducting illegal searches, and secondly, that the defendant's entitlement to freedom from such search and seizure should be recognised by excluding the evidence obtained thereby. The *Mapp* rule on searches was mirrored by the *Miranda* rule, that improperly obtained confessions would be inadmissible in evidence.[37] However, there has been some retreat recently from *Mapp* and *Miranda*, seen in decisions such as that in *Moran v Burbine*,[38] which have brought America somewhat closer to the position adopted under UK common law.[39]

The argument that evidence should be excluded if obtained through impropriety consisting of a fundamental breach of a constitutionally recognised right, receives

---

35 See Clayton and Tomlinson, op. cit., fn 1, 1st edn, p 1465.
36 (1961) 367 US 643.
37 Deriving from *Miranda v Arizona* (1966) 384 US 436.
38 (1986) 475 US 412.
39 See Stuntz, W, 'The American exclusionary rule and defendants' changing rights' [1989] Crim LR 117.

explicit recognition under the Canadian Charter.[40] This argument was accepted until recently in New Zealand.[41] However, in *R v Shaheed*[42] the Court of Appeal abandoned the established prima facie rule of exclusion for evidence obtained by the police in violation of the New Zealand Bill of Rights Act 1990. A court must now decide if exclusion is a proportionate remedial response to the particular breach of the Bill of Rights that is at issue in the instant case, taking account of a range of factors. In Australia, evidence may be admitted although obtained by trickery and it has been found that the trial may still be viewed as fair.[43] In other words, by making a determination that admission of such evidence does not impair fairness, the finding was avoided that evidence was being admitted in breach of a fundamental right. However, it has been found that evidence obtained by secret recording will be excluded where unfairness has been caused to the accused.[44]

Exclusion of evidence and abuse of process

If malpractice by police or prosecutors reaches a certain level of seriousness, the trial can halted on the basis that to do otherwise would be an abuse of process. The House of Lords found in *Latif*[45] that in considering whether to stay the proceedings for abuse of process, the judge should weigh the public interest in ensuring that those accused of serious crimes are brought to trial against the public interest in avoiding giving the impression, based on classic crime control norms, that courts are prepared to find that the end justifies the means. This balancing of interests may be termed the '*Latif* test'. The stance taken in *Latif* may be compared with that taken in *Mullen*[46] in which the Court of Appeal said: 'the need to discourage [blatant and very serious malpractice] . . . is a matter of public policy to which . . . very considerable weight should be attached'. However, these remarks do not suggest that an absolute test is in contemplation and in so far as there is a difference between the approaches of *Mullen* and *Latif* it is probable that the *Latif* test will prevail, since it derives from a House of Lords decision and is more in harmony with the approach taken to improperly obtained evidence under s 78, as indicated above.

In *Chalkley*,[47] Auld LJ stated that the issue of exclusion of evidence is distinct from the question whether the prosecution should be stayed for abuse of process. He said that while the discretion to declare an abuse of process would be governed

---

40　Section 24(2). In *Feeney* [1997] 2 SCR 13, the Canadian Supreme Court said that admission of evidence obtained through a serious breach of the appellant's Charter rights would be more damaging to the reputation of the criminal justice system than would its exclusion. (See also *Burlingham* [1995] 2 SCR 206.) A more technical breach has not been found, however, to demand exclusion since to do so would cause greater affront to the system than its inclusion: *Belnavis* [1997] 3 SCR 341.

41　*R v Butcher* [1992] 2 NZLR 257; *R v Te Kira* [1993] 3 NZLR 257; *Simpson v AG* [1994] 3 NZLR 703.

42　[2002] 2 NZLR 377 (CA). For discussion, see Mahoney R, 'Abolition of New Zealand's Prima Facie Exclusion Rule' [2003] Crim LR 607.

43　*Ridgeway v the Queen* (1995) 129 ALR 41.

44　*Swaffield, Pavic v R* (1998) 151 ALR 98.

45　[1996] 1 All ER 353.

46　[1999] 2 Cr App R 143, p 157.

47　[1998] 2 Cr App R 79.

by the balancing test referred to above, the discretion under s 78 would be governed almost entirely by the question whether the impropriety of the police or prosecutor had affected the reliability of the evidence. In other words, in exceptional circumstances, the trial might be halted to mark the court's disapproval of pre-trial malpractice; he considered that this would virtually never occur in respect of exclusion of evidence, except in the case of confessions.

The domestic stance

As has been indicated, the question of exclusion of evidence where there has been police breach of statutory or Code standards has been left largely up to the domestic courts by Strasbourg; domestic courts seeking to apply the Strasbourg jurisprudence under s 2 HRA have been given the message, via *Khan*, that no breach of Art 6 will occur if evidence obtained in breach of a Convention right or domestic due process-based rule is admitted. The only exception might arise if the matter could be characterised as one falling within the ruling in *Teixeira*. It may therefore be argued that the domestic courts could look to other jurisdictions for guidance as to the requirements of due process in relation to exclusion of evidence. The counter-arguments are that the HRA does not require them to do so, that other jurisdictions have developed their own rules, in accordance with their own traditions, for the assessment of evidence, as has Britain, and that therefore the domestic common law tradition should prevail in the HRA era. It is suggested that the early HRA cases demonstrate that this is the approach will continue to prevail. Therefore, the discussion below will concentrate on the established domestic position.

The common law pre-PACE went some way towards endorsing the crime control 'reliability' principle. Illegally obtained evidence other than 'involuntary' confessions was admissible in a criminal trial. Involuntary confessions were inadmissible on the ground that if a defendant was in some way induced to confess during a police interrogation, his confession might be unreliable. A confession would be involuntary if it was obtained by oppression[48] or 'by fear of prejudice or hope of advantage exercised or held out by a person in authority'.[49] According to the Court of Appeal in *Isequilla*,[50] 'oppression' denoted some impropriety on the part of the police, but the House of Lords in *Ping Lin*[51] doubted whether such impropriety was necessary if the real issue was the reliability of the confession. Uncertainty as to the need for impropriety on the part of the police and as to the kind of impropriety which could amount to oppression, allowed cases such as the *Confait* case[52] to slip through the net. In that case, three young boys, one of them mentally handicapped, confessed to involvement in a murder they could not have committed after they had been denied both legal advice and the presence of an adult during the police interrogation. The confessions were admitted in evidence and led to the conviction of all three. They were finally exonerated seven years later.

---

48 *Prager* [1972] 1 All ER 1114, CA.
49 *Ibrahim* [1914] AC 599.
50 [1975] All ER 77.
51 [1976] AC 574.
52 See Price, C and Caplan, J, *The Confait Confessions*, 1976, Marion Boyars; Report of the Inquiry by the Hon Sir Henry Fisher, HC 90 (1977–79).

The concept of fear of prejudice or hope of advantage was at one time interpreted strictly against the police and very mild inducements were held to render a confession involuntary. In *Zaveckas*,[53] for example, the Court of Appeal held that a confession had been rendered involuntary because the defendant had asked the police officer whether he could have bail if he made a statement. However, in the case of *Rennie*,[54] Lord Lane held that a confession need not be excluded simply because it had been prompted in part by some hope of advantage. This case paved the way for the relaxation of this rule which can be found in the PACE scheme on exclusion of evidence.

Physical evidence discovered as a result of an inadmissible confession was admissible;[55] the police witness would have to state at the trial that after interviewing the defendant, the evidence in question was discovered – in the hope that the jury would see the connection. Illegally or improperly obtained non-confession evidence, such as fingerprints, was admissible at common law unless the evidence had been tricked out of the detainee,[56] in which case there would be a discretion to exclude it. However, the House of Lords in *Sang*[57] re-affirmed the rule that non-confession evidence, however obtained, is admissible subject to a narrow discretion to exclude it.

Exclusion of evidence was largely placed on a statutory basis under PACE.[58] PACE differentiates between confession and non-confession evidence, reflecting the previous common law stance. PACE contains four separate tests which can be applied to a confession to determine whether it is admissible in evidence. In theory, all four tests could be applied to a particular confession, although in practice it may not be necessary to consider all of them. The four are the 'oppression' test under s 76(2)(a), the 'reliability' test under s 76(2)(b), the 'fairness' test under s 78 and the residual common law discretion to exclude evidence, preserved by s 82(3). It will become apparent that there is a large area of overlap between all four tests. Section 78 could cover unreliable evidence and also evidence obtained by the use of improper methods, whether amounting to oppression or not. Equally, certain types of improper behaviour could be termed oppressive, thus falling within s 76(2)(a), but they could also be viewed as circumstances likely to render a confession unreliable, falling therefore within s 76(2)(b). The courts have gone some of the way towards creating a distinct role for each test, but not all the way.[59] In some circumstances, a confession will obviously fail one of the tests under s 76 and there will be no need to consider the other three. In other circumstances, it may be worth considering all four tests. The scheme in respect of non-confession evidence is less complex: only ss 78 and 82(3) are applicable. Significantly, physical evidence which is discovered as a result of an inadmissible confession will be admissible under s 76(4)(a). In practice, s78 appears to have taken over the role of s82(3), and therefore it is rare for s82(3) to receive separate consideration.

53 (1970) 54 Cr App R 202, CA.
54 [1982] 1 All ER 385, CA.
55 *Sang* [1980] AC 402; [1979] 2 All ER 1222, HL.
56 *Callis v Gunn* [1964] 1 QB 495.
57 [1980] AC 402; [1979] 2 All ER 1222, HL.
58 For general commentary, see Birch, D, 'Confessions and confusions under the 1984 Act' [1989] Crim LR 95; Feldman, D, 'Regulating Treatment of Suspects in Police Stations: Judicial Interpretation of Detention Provisions in the Police and Criminal Evidence Act 1984' [1990] Crim LR 452.
59 See Birch, ibid.

It is important to bear in mind that even if a confession is admitted, the jury may differ from the judge in their evaluation of the circumstances in which it was obtained. The jury may decide that they should not place weight on it due to those circumstances, thereby in effect taking the view that the judge may have erred in deciding to admit it. This rule was reaffirmed in *R v Mushtaq*;[60] it was found:

> The law is clear that where a judge has ruled on a *voir dire* that a confession is admissible the jury is fully entitled to consider all the circumstances surrounding the making of the confession to decide whether they should place any weight on it, and it is the duty of the trial judge to make this plain to them.

Section 76(2)(a) of PACE: the 'oppression' test

Section 76(2)(a) provides that where:

> . . . it is represented to the court that the confession was or may have been obtained by oppression of the person who made it . . . the court shall not allow the confession to be given in evidence against him except in so far as the prosecution proves to the court beyond reasonable doubt that the confession (notwithstanding that it may be true) was not obtained as aforesaid.

This test derives from the rule as it was at common law: if it is put to the court that the confession was or may have been obtained by oppression of the person who made it and the prosecution cannot prove beyond reasonable doubt that the police did not behave oppressively, the confession is inadmissible. The judge has no discretion in the matter. The wording derives from Art 3 of the Convention,[61] but it is not necessary for torture or inhuman or degrading treatment to be present, as discussed below. The idea behind the old common law rule, and now s 76(2)(a), is that threats of violence or other oppressive behaviour are so abhorrent that no further question as to the reliability of a confession obtained by such methods should be asked. But the principle of reliability underlies the rule, as does the principle of voluntariness. In *R v Mushtaq* Lord Hutton said:

> It is clear that there are two principal reasons underlying the rule that a confession obtained by oppression should not be admitted in evidence. One reason, which has long been stated by the judges, is that where a confession is made as a result of oppression it may well be unreliable, because the confession may have been given, not with the intention of telling the truth, but from a desire to escape the oppression imposed on, or the harm threatened to, the suspect. A further reason, stated in more recent years, is that in a civilised society a person should not be compelled to incriminate himself, and a person in custody should not be subjected by the police to illtreatment or improper pressure in order to extract a confession.[62]

---

60 [2005] 1 WLR 1513 at para 3.
61 See Chapter 2 pp 45–50 for the wording of Art 3 and for Strasbourg case law on the meaning of the three terms used in it.
62 [2005] UKHL 25 at para 7. He relied on *Wong Kam-ming v The Queen* [1980] AC 247, 261 and *Lam Chi-ming v The Queen* [1991] 2 AC 212, p 220 E–G.

He found that these principles were in harmony with those accepted under Art 6(1): 'These two reasons also underlie the decision of the European Court of Human Rights in *Saunders v The United Kingdom*.'[63] This rule has the dual function of removing any incentive to the police to behave oppressively, and of protecting the detainee from the consequences of oppressive behaviour if it has occurred.

Under this head, once the defence has advanced a reasonable argument (*Liverpool Juvenile Court ex p R*)[64] that the confession was obtained by oppression, it will not be admitted in evidence unless the prosecution can prove that it was not so obtained. If no reasonable doubt is raised it will be admitted. The reliability of a confession obtained by oppression is irrelevant to the issue of exclusion: it matters not whether the effect of the oppression is to frighten the detainee into telling the truth or alternatively into lying in order to get out of the situation. But it is highly relevant if the confession is admitted. In *R v Mushtaq*[65] the House of Lords had to consider the appropriate direction to a jury, taking account of Art 6(1), where a confession alleged to have been obtained by oppression was admitted in evidence. The question certified by the Court of Appeal was: whether 'in view of article 6 of the Convention for the Protection of Human Rights', a judge 'is required to direct the jury, if they conclude that the alleged confession may have been [obtained by oppression] they must disregard it'. Lord Hutton answered the question posed in the negative because he considered that the defendant's right not to incriminate himself against his will:

> . . . is protected by the judge and his right not to be convicted on the basis of a confession which may be untrue because it may have been obtained by oppression is protected both by the judge and also subsequently by the jury if the judge admits the confession.[66]

Therefore he considered that if a judge directed a jury that, even if they were satisfied that a confession was true, they must exclude it from their consideration if they concluded that it might have been obtained by oppression, then the jury would be usurping the judge's function in determining facts relevant to the question whether it could be taken into account as evidence. But the majority in the House of Lords answered this question in the affirmative. They found that both the judge and the jury are public authorities under s 6 HRA. Therefore it would be unlawful for the judge and jury to act in a way which was incompatible with a defendant's right against self-incrimination as implied into Art 6(1).

The judge had directed the jury that, if they were sure that the appellant's confession was true, they might rely on it even if they considered that it might have been made as a result of oppression.

> Such a direction was an invitation to the jury to act in a way that was incompatible with the appellant's right against self-incrimination under article 6(1). As such, the direction was itself incompatible with that right . . . It follows, both on the basis

63 [2005] UKHL 25 at para 8; (*Saunders* [1996] 23 EHRR 313).
64 [1987] All ER 688.
65 [2005] 1 WLR 1513.
66 [2005] UKHL 25 at para 23.

of section 76(2) when viewed without regard to the Convention and on the basis of the appellant's article 6(1) Convention right against self-incrimination, that the judge misdirected the jury . . .[67]

The Court of Appeal had referred to the last sentence of the judge's direction: 'If, on the other hand, you are sure that it is true you may rely on it, even if it was or may have been made as a result of oppression or other improper circumstances.' The Court found, and the House of Lords agreed, that the jury would have received more assistance if the second part of the sentence had been omitted. Lord Hutton said: 'the words might to some extent deflect the jury from concentrating on the question whether, if there was a reasonable possibility of oppression, it would be safe to rely on the confession as being truthful'.

This situation is not likely to arise frequently since the judge can admit confession evidence only if satisfied beyond a reasonable doubt that it was not obtained by oppression or any other improper means. If there is anything in the evidence that gives rise to a reasonable doubt, the confession must be excluded. So the direction to disregard the confession would only be relevant where, despite the judge's view that, beyond a reasonable doubt, the confession was not obtained by oppression or any other improper means, the jury decided that it was, or might have been, obtained in that way. In the instant case the trial judge had found that the evidence had not been obtained by oppression. Therefore, although the judge's direction had been at fault, the conviction was found to be safe.

The only evidence given in the Act as to the meaning of oppression is the non-exhaustive definition contained in s 76(8): 'In this section "oppression" includes torture, inhuman or degrading treatment and the use or threat of violence (whether or not amounting to torture).' The word 'includes' ought to be given its literal meaning according to the Court of Appeal in *Fulling*.[68] Therefore, it appeared that the concept of oppression might be fairly wide: the question was whether it encompassed the old common law rulings on its width. In *Fulling*, the Court of Appeal held that PACE is a codifying Act and that therefore, a court should examine the statutory language uninfluenced by pre-Act decisions. The Court then proffered its own definition of oppression: '. . . the exercise of authority or power in a burdensome, harsh or wrongful manner; unjust or cruel treatment of subjects, inferiors, etc; the imposition of unreasonable or unjust burdens'. It thought that oppression would almost invariably entail impropriety on the part of the interrogator.

However, the terms 'wrongful' and 'improper' used in this test could potentially cover *any* unlawful action on the part of the police. This could have been taken to mean that any breach of the Act or Codes could constitute oppression. This wide possibility was briefly pursued at first instance in the early post-PACE period,[69] but has been abandoned.[70] The Court of Appeal in *Hughes*[71] held that a denial of legal advice, owing not to bad faith on the part of the police, but to a misunderstanding,

---

67 At paras 53 and 54, *per* Lord Rodger of Earlsferry.
68 [1987] QB 426; [1987] 2 All ER 65, CA.
69 In *Davison* [1988] Crim LR 442.
70 See *Parker* [1995] Crim LR 233.
71 [1988] Crim LR 519.

could not amount to oppression. In *Alladice*[72] the Court of Appeal also took this view in suggesting, *obiter*, that an improper denial of legal advice, if accompanied by bad faith on the part of the police, would certainly amount to 'unfairness' under s 78 and probably also to oppression. In *Beales*,[73] rather heavy-handed questioning accompanied by misleading suggestions, although not on the face of it a very serious impropriety, was termed oppressive because it was obviously employed as a deliberate tactic. In *Paris*,[74] the case of the *Cardiff Three*, confessions made by one of the defendants after some 13 hours of highly pressured and hostile questioning were excluded on the ground of oppression. He was a man of limited intelligence, but the Court of Appeal thought that the questioning would have been oppressive even in relation to a suspect of normal intelligence.

This emphasis on bad faith may be criticised because, from the point of view of the detainee, it matters little if mistreatment occurs because of an administrative mix-up, an innocent misconstruction of powers or malice. Looking to the state of mind of the suspect rather than that of the oppressor would enable account to be taken of the very great difference in impact of certain conduct on a young, inexperienced suspect and on a hardened, sophisticated criminal. However, at present the courts have not shown a desire to import a subjective assessment of oppression into s 76(2)(a), although at common law such an assessment would have been warranted.[75]

On the other hand, it cannot be said that the Court of Appeal has consistently invoked s 76(2)(a) rather than s 78 when the police *have* deliberately misused their powers in obtaining a confession; in *Mason*,[76] for example, a trick played deliberately on the appellant's solicitor led to exclusion of the confession under s 78. In *Blake*,[77] misleading statements made to the detainee, presumably in bad faith, led to exclusion of the confession under s 76(2)(b) or s 78. Thus, apart from the requirement of bad faith, it also seems necessary to show that the improper behaviour has reached a certain level of seriousness in order to show oppression.[78] However, the case law does not yet clearly indicate the level of seriousness needed. All that can be said with some certainty is that the impropriety should be of a serious nature and that bad faith appears to be a necessary, but not sufficient condition for the operation of s 76(2)(a), whereas it will probably automatically render a confession inadmissible under s 78.[79]

So oppression will arise if, first, improper behaviour of a certain level of seriousness has occurred. The behaviour in *Paris* was clearly oppressive; other improper behaviour might fall only just within the category of oppressive behaviour; Second, the behaviour must be perpetrated deliberately. Improper treatment falling outside s 76(8) and of insufficient seriousness to be termed oppressive or oppressive behaviour unaccompanied by bad faith could fall within s 76(2)(b) if the confession was likely to have been

---

72 (1988) 87 Cr App R 380, CA.
73 [1991] Crim LR 118. See, to the same effect, *Heron* (1993) unreported; forceful questioning was accompanied by lies as to the identification evidence.
74 (1993) 97 Cr App R 99; [1994] Crim LR 361, CA.
75 *Priestley* (1966) 50 Cr App R 183, CA.
76 [1987] Crim LR 119; [1987] 3 All ER 481, CA.
77 [1991] All ER 481, CA.
78 See *L* [1994] Crim LR 839.
79 For discussion of the effect of bad faith under s 78, see below, pp 1286–87.

rendered unreliable thereby. The emphasis on bad faith or the lack of it at least gives an indication as to when improper behaviour on the part of the police will lead to automatic exclusion of the confession under s 76(2)(a) and when it will merely suggest the likelihood of unreliability under s 76(2)(b). But, since s 76(2)(a) only operates to exclude confessions obtained as a result of very serious impropriety on the part of the police, meaning that confessions are rarely excluded under the sub-section, its ability to protect due process is limited. However, its impact on due process should not be disregarded. It sets a basic standard for police behaviour, probably deterring police from forms of impropriety still relatively common in some jurisdictions.

Section 76(2)(b): the 'reliability' test

Section 76(2)(b) provides that where a confession was or may have been obtained:

> . . . in consequence of anything said or done which was likely in the circumstances existing at the time, to render unreliable any confession which might be made by him in consequence thereof, the court shall not allow the confession to be given in evidence against him except in so far as the prosecution proves to the court beyond reasonable doubt that the confession (notwithstanding that it may be true) was not obtained as aforesaid.

The 'reliability' test of s 76(2)(b) derives from the rule as stated in *Ibrahim*[80] on inducements to confess. However, as will be seen, it represents a relaxation of that rule as it was applied in *Ibrahim*. It also works certain changes in the emphasis of the test. The test does not reflect the full rigour of the reliability principle, which requires that a confession extracted by torture but determined to be true should be admitted in evidence.[81] Instead it is concerned with objective reliability: the judge must consider the situation at the time the confession was made and ask whether the confession would be *likely* to be unreliable, not whether it *is* unreliable.

It must be borne in mind that if an offer of some kind is made to the detainee in response to an inquiry from him, this will not render the subsequent confession unreliable,[82] thus explicitly rejecting the *Zaveckas* approach. It is not necessary, under this section, to show that there has been any misconduct on the part of the police. In *Harvey*,[83] a mentally ill woman of low intelligence may have been induced to confess to murder by hearing her lover's confession. Her confession was excluded as being likely to be unreliable. In *Harvey*, the 'something said or done' (the first limb of the test under s 76(2)(a)) was the confession of the lover while the 'circumstances' (the second limb) were the defendant's emotional state, low intelligence and mental illness. The 'something said or done' cannot consist of the defendant's own mental or physical state, according to *Goldberg*.[84] In that case, the defendant was a heroin addict who confessed because he was desperate to leave the police station and obtain a 'fix'. The

---

80 [1914] AC 599; see p 1267, above.
81 As advocated by Andrews, op. cit. [1963] Crim LR 15, p 77; see p 1263 above.
82 Code C, para 11.3.
83 [1988] Crim LR 241.
84 [1988] Crim LR 678.

contention of the defence counsel that the defendant's decision to confess prompted by his addiction amounted to 'something said or done' was not accepted by the court. In *Wahab*[85] the defendant tried to negotiate the release of his family from arrest with the police by offering to confess. The police did not make the bargain but he confessed in any event and tried later to have the confession excluded under s 76(2)(b). This was refused partly on the ground that the confession was reliable, but also on the ground that the inducement to confess did not come from the police.

In most instances, then, the 'something said or done' must consist of some impropriety on the part of the police. Having identified such a factor, a court will go on to consider whether any circumstances existed which rendered the impropriety particularly significant. The 'circumstances' could include the particularly vulnerable state of the detainee. In *Mathias*,[86] the defendant was particularly vulnerable because he had not been afforded legal advice although an offer of immunity from prosecution had been made to him. The Court of Appeal held that the offer had placed him in great difficulty and that this was a situation in which the police should have ensured that he had legal advice. From the judgment, it appears that if an inducement to confess is offered to the detainee, the police should ensure that he or she can discuss it with a solicitor, even if the police are entitled to deny access to legal advice, on the ground that the detainee falls within s 58(8) (see above). Thus in such instances s 76(2)(b) may be satisfied since the 'circumstances' will be the lack of legal advice and the 'something said or done', the inducement.

The vulnerability relied upon by the defence as a special circumstance may relate to a physical or mental state. In *Trussler*[87] the defendant, who was a drug addict and had been in custody 18 hours, had been denied legal advice and had not been afforded the rest period guaranteed by Code C, para 12. His confession was excluded as likely to be unreliable. In *Delaney*[88] the defendant was 17, had an IQ of 80 and, according to an educational psychologist, was subject to emotional arousal which would lead him to wish to bring a police interview to an end as quickly as possible. These were circumstances in which it was important to ensure that the interrogation was conducted with all propriety. In fact, the officers offered some inducement to the defendant to confess by playing down the gravity of the offence and by suggesting that if he confessed, he would get the psychiatric help he needed. They also failed to make an accurate, contemporaneous record of the interview in breach of Code C, para 11.3 (version of Code C in force at the time). Failing to make the proper record was of indirect relevance to the question of reliability since it meant that the court could not assess the full extent of the suggestions held out to the defendant. Thus, in the circumstances existing at the time (the mental state of the defendant), the police impropriety did have the special significance necessary under s 76(2)(b). The decision in *Marshall*[89] was to similar effect, although it did not identify a specific breach of Code C: the defendant was on the borderline of sub-normality and therefore, after an interview accompanied by his solicitor, he should not have been re-interviewed unaccompanied about the same matters.

85 [2003] 1 Cr App R 15.
86 (1989) *The Times*, 24 August.
87 [1988] Crim LR 446.
88 (1989) 8 Cr App R 338; (1988) *The Times*, 20 August, CA.
89 (1992) *The Times*, 28 December.

From the above it appears that the 'circumstances existing at the time' may be circumstances created by the police (as in *Mathias*) or may be inherent in the defendant (as in *Delaney*). Impropriety on the part of the police can go to either limb of the test, but a state inherent in the detainee (such as mental illness) can go only to the 'circumstances' limb. Thus, a single breach of the interviewing rules such as a denial of legal advice in ordinary circumstances would not appear, as far as the current interpretation of s 76(2)(b) is concerned, to satisfy both limbs of the test. On the other hand, a doubtful breach or perhaps no breach but, rather, behaviour of doubtful propriety, such as misleading the suspect as to the need to have legal advice, might satisfy the 'something said or done' test where special circumstances were also present.

So far, the courts have considered instances where something is said or done, in particularly significant circumstances, which increases the likelihood that a confession will be unreliable. However, it is arguable that s 76 might exceptionally be applicable where something is said or done which might affect a subsequent confession, but the circumstances are normal. The example was given above of a detainee who was deprived of sleep as a result of an administrative mix-up. Deprivation of sleep would be likely to render a confession unreliable, but which 'circumstances' could be pointed to as existing at the time – as required by the second limb of s 76(2)(b)? The answer could be that the ordinary police methods of interrogation, applied to a detainee who had been deprived of sleep, would amount to 'circumstances' falling within s 76(2)(b). Thus, this would be an impropriety which could go to both limbs of the test. Such instances of breaches of Code C could also fall within s 78, as will be seen below. However, defence counsel would be expected to argue the point first under s 76(2)(b) as the prosecution would then have the onus of proving beyond reasonable doubt that the deprivation of sleep did not take place.

It must now be apparent that s 76(2)(b) could be used to exclude all confessions obtained by oppression. It may then be wondered why s 76(2)(a) exists at all. The principle lying behind the two heads of s 76 appears to be that some types of impropriety on the part of the police are so unacceptable that it would be abhorrent in a court to go on to consider the reliability of a confession gained by such methods. In other words, s 76(2)(a) can speed up a process which could be carried out under s 76(2)(b).

Causation and the two heads of s 76

The words of s 76(2): ' [if] it is represented to the court that the confession was or may have been obtained' by [oppression or by behaviour in circumstances conducive to unreliability] appear to import a causal link between the police behaviour (the 'something said or done' or the oppression) and the confession. (It should be noted that the sections could also apply to persons other than police officers.) Thus, if the police threaten the suspect with violence *after* he has confessed, this will clearly be irrelevant to the obtaining of the confession. However, it is possible that under s 76(2)(a), the causal link will not be much scrutinised so long as the oppression precedes the confession. This receives some support from *dicta* in *Alladice*;[90] the Court of Appeal determined that the improper denial of legal advice had not caused the detainee to confess, but still found that, had it been accompanied by bad faith, exclusion of the confession under

---

90 (1988) 87 Cr App R 380, CA.

s 76 might have been undertaken. The general rule appears, then, to be that where the causal link in question clearly does not exist, s 76(2)(a) cannot be invoked, but in all other instances the fact that the confession was made subsequent to the oppression may be sufficient.

The question of causation under s 76(2)(b) appears, on the face of it, quite complex. From the wording of the sub-section it appears to be necessary to adopt a two stage test, asking first whether something was said or done, likely in the circumstances to render any confession made unreliable – an objective test – and, second, whether that something actually caused the detainee to confess – a subjective test.

The relationship between ss 76 and 78

In general, the s 76 tests for admissibility of confessions could work to the detriment of inexperienced and more vulnerable detainees. In *Canale*,[91] the police breached the recording provisions and allegedly played a trick on the appellant in order to obtain the confession. Ruling that the confession should have been excluded under s 78, the Court of Appeal took into account the fact that the appellant could not be said to be vulnerable or weak-minded; it was therefore thought inappropriate to invoke s 76(2)(b).[92] Thus, the need to identify special factors in the situation in order to invoke either head of s 76 means that breaches of the interviewing rules unaccompanied by any such factor are usually considered under s 78. Furthermore, allegedly fabricated confessions cannot fall within s 76(2) owing to its requirement that something has happened to the defendant which caused *him* to confess; its terms are not therefore fulfilled if the defence alleges that no confession made by the defendant exists.

In practice, confessions are rarely excluded under either head of s 76; this may be in part because the judges strongly wish to retain a discretion as to admissibility. As indicated above, even where a confession is excluded, physical evidence found as a result of information given in it need not be, under s 76(4).[93] Therefore, it may be said that s 76 has had limited impact in upholding due process. This stance has not changed under the HRA – there has been no evidence post-HRA of greater judicial willingness to use the sub-sections. Thus, s 78 has operated as a catch-all section, bringing within its boundaries many confessions which pass the tests contained in either head of s 76.

91 [1990] All ER 187, CA.
92 Section 76(2)(a) was not invoked, although apparently the police deliberately breached the recording provisions. Presumably, breaches of the interviewing rules were not seen as behaviour serious enough to be termed 'oppression'. However, if the defence makes a – contested – allegation that the police made threats or deliberately tricked the detainee into confessing, the prosecution might not be able to prove beyond reasonable doubt that the police had in fact behaved properly owing to the breach of the recording provisions. This alternative line of argument could have been considered in *Canale* [1990] All ER 187, CA.
93 See further Mirfield, P, *Silence, Confessions and Improperly Obtained Evidence*, 1997, Clarendon; Mirfield, P, 'Successive confessions and the poisonous tree' [1996] Crim LR 554; Sharpe, *Judicial Discretion and Criminal Investigation*, 1998.

Section 78: the 'fairness' test[94]

Section 78 provides:

> In any proceedings the court may refuse to allow evidence on which the prosecution proposes to rely to be given if it appears to the court that, having regard to all the circumstances, including the circumstances in which the evidence was obtained, the admission of the evidence would have such an adverse effect on the fairness of the proceedings that the court ought not to admit it.

Section 78 can be invoked to argue for: (a) exclusion of confessions, and is of particular pertinence if they cannot be excluded under s 76 since the behaviour relied upon to argue for exclusion does not satisfy the tests discussed under s 76; (b) exclusion of non-confession evidence, including silences. Section 78 may be invoked where police questioning meets with a no comment response from a defendant. Such a response cannot be considered within s 76 due to the use of the word 'confession' within that section. It would be a very distorted use of statutory language to use the term 'confession' to cover a silence. If a silence is excluded from evidence under s 78, adverse inferences obviously cannot be drawn from it (unless the jury or magistrate becomes aware of it in the course of hearing other evidence) and therefore argument on this issue has arisen, although so far the courts have shown themselves reluctant to exclude no comment interviews.[95] It was argued in Chapter 12 that where access to legal advice has been delayed, and the accused has remained silent in interviews without having had access to legal advice, a breach of Art 6(3)(c) and possibly of Art 6(1) is likely to occur if adverse inferences are then drawn at trial.[96] One method of preventing this, which has not been catered for expressly under domestic law,[97] would be to exclude the interviews. A similar argument can also be put forward where, in the same circumstances, the accused had in fact made admissions in the interviews.

Section 78 confers an exclusionary *discretion* on a judge and appears to have been conceived to cover the very narrow function of the old common law discretion[98] to exclude improperly obtained non-confession evidence. Until the ruling in *Mason*,[99] it was uncertain whether s 78 also covered confessions. Under s 6 HRA domestic courts have a duty to exercise their discretion under s 78 in such a way as to ensure that

---

94 For discussion of the operation of s 78, see Allen, CJW, 'Discretion and Security: excluding evidence under section 78(1) of the Police and Criminal Evidence Act 1984' [1990] 49(1) 80; Gelowitz, M, 'Section 78 of the Police and Criminal Evidence Act 1984: Middle ground or no man's land?' (1990) 106 LQR 327; May [1988] Crim LR 722; Stone, R, 'Exclusion of Evidence under section 78 of the Police and Criminal Evidence Act: Practice and Principles' (1995) 3 Web JCL 1; Sanders and Young, op. cit., fn 1, Chapter 11, Part 5; Choo, AL-T and Nash, S, 'What's the matter with s 78?' [1999] Crim LR 929–40; Hunter, M, 'Judicial Discretion: s78 in practice' (1994 Crim LR 558; Ormerod, D and Birch, D, 'The evolution of the discretionary exclusion of evidence' (2004) Crim LR 767.

95 See *Condron* [1997] 1 WLR 827.

96 See pp 1210–15. This argument is based on *Murray v UK* (1996) 22 EHRR 29, *Averill v UK* (2001) 31 EHRR 35, and *Magee v UK* (2001) 31 EHRR 35.

97 Youth Justice and Criminal Evidence Act 1999, s 58, only provides that in such circumstances adverse inferences may not be drawn.

98 See *Sang* [1980] AC 402; [1979] 2 All ER 1222, HL.

99 [1987] Crim LR 119; [1987] All ER 481, CA.

compliance with Art 6(1) is achieved, but as discussed below, that duty has added little to the approach to s 78 established pre-HRA. The domestic jurisprudence is far more extensive on this matter than that at Strasbourg regarding confessions under Art 6, and, despite the reluctance of the judiciary to lay down guiding principles for the application of s 78, academics in an extensive literature have identified some indications of adherence to such principle.[100] It might have been expected that the effect of Art 6 would be to encourage the articulation of some clearer statements of principle under s 78. But the difficulty of discerning consistency of principle in the decisions under s 78 only became more apparent in the later 1990s and post-HRA.[101]

Section 78 provides a discretion to exclude evidence if admitting it would render the trial unfair. In adopting this formula, it was clear that the government did not wish to import into this country a USA-type exclusionary rule. The Home Secretary informed the House of Commons[102] that the function of exclusion of evidence after police misconduct must not be disciplinary, but must be to safeguard the fairness of the trial. The idea behind this was that non-confession evidence obtained by improper means could still be admitted on the basis that police misconduct could be dealt with by internal disciplinary procedures. Similarly, confessions obtained improperly in circumstances falling outside s 76 could nevertheless be admissible in evidence, with the proviso that the trial should not thereby be rendered unfair. In fact, as will be seen, the courts have managed to create a role for s 78 which, as far as confessions are concerned, is probably rather far removed from the government's original intention. The approach adopted towards confessions tends to reflect to an extent the protective and integrity principles.

It may be noted that s 78 is not explicit as to who bears the burden of proof where a breach of the rules is alleged, but in *Vel v Owen*[103] the Divisional Court ruled that the defence should make good its objection. In *Anderson*,[104] however, the Court said that it was not entirely clear where the burden of proof lay.

Section 78: excluding confessions

Section 78 must be applied in accordance with the courts' duty under Art 6. Article 6(1) is silent as to the admissibility of improperly obtained evidence. The Strasbourg Court has emphasised that the assessment of evidence is for the domestic courts[105] and that Art 6 does not require any particular rules of evidence. Thus, it has allowed the national authorities a wide margin of appreciation in this respect. It was found in an early decision, *Austria v Italy*,[106] that maltreatment with the aim of extracting a confession created a breach of Art 6(2). This argument can be applied where 'compelled' admissions, including those obtained by treatment falling within s 76, and those obtained on pain of a penalty under the TA,[107] while not themselves used in evidence, had led to the

---

100   See: Allen [1990] CLJ 80; Gelowitz (1990) 106 LQR 327; May [1988] Crim LR 722; Stone (1995) 3 Web JCL 1; Sanders and Young, op. cit., fn 1, (2007) Chapter 12, Part 5.
101   See Ormerod, D and Birch, D, 'The evolution of the discretionary exclusion of evidence' (2004) Crim LR 767.
102   1983–84, HC Deb col 1012, 29 October 1984.
103   (1987) JP 510.
104   [1993] Crim LR 447.
105   *Edwards v UK* A 247-B (1992).
106   Appl No 788/60 4 YB 112 (1961).
107   See Chapter 12, pp 1249–54.

uncovering of other evidence. It could be argued, in furtherance of a fair procedure under Art 6, that that other evidence should be excluded under s 78. The question of pressure on the applicant in the interview was taken into account by the Court in reaching its conclusion that Art 6 had been breached in *Saunders v UK*[108] by the admission in evidence of the coerced admissions, and the argument could be extended to encompass other evidence uncovered as a result of such admissions. Clearly, the decision in *Brown v Stott*[109] has, however, weakened this argument to an extent, since the courts in future are likely to consider the legitimate aim of the compulsion and the question whether the compulsion is in proportion to the aim in creating a minimal impact on the accused's Art 6 rights.

The courts have been very reluctant to lay down general rules for the application of s 78,[110] but the attempt will be made here, albeit tentatively, to identify some of the factors which tend to be taken into account in relation to admissions. Non-confession evidence will be considered separately. If it is found that admission of an interview would render the trial unfair, then not only the interview affected, but possibly any interviews subsequent to that one[111] may be excluded from evidence under s 78.

The PACE interviewing scheme, made up to a significant extent of Code-based rules, may be breached or undermined in a variety of ways. There may be a clear failure to put in place one of the safeguards, such as access to legal advice or tape recording. However, it is not always possible to identify such a clear breach of the rules. The failure to do so may have contributed to the decision in *Hughes*:[112] a misrepresentation as regards unavailability of legal advice made to the appellant did not involve a clear breach of a specific Code provision and therefore, may have led to the reluctance to exclude the confession. Similarly, in *Khan*[113] it was found that while s 30(1) of PACE allowed officers to keep a suspect out of the police station for a time in order to make investigations, including a search, questioning during that time should be limited, since otherwise the provisions of the interviewing scheme would be subverted. Some of the questions which had in fact been asked went beyond what was needed for the search; however, it was found, they should not have been excluded, since the matter was 'a question of degree', although officers did not have *carte blanche* to interview suspects in such circumstances.

In contrast to this approach, there has been some willingness at first instance to consider situations where the PACE interviewing scheme seemed to have been infringed, although it was impossible to point to a clear breach.[114] The interviewing scheme lends itself to many methods of infringement, some of which may occur at a low level of visibility, but which may nevertheless be of significance. For example, there may be breach of a rule contained in a non-statutory instrument other than PACE itself or

---

108 (1997) 23 EHRR 313. *Saunders* is discussed in Chapter 12, pp 1251–54.
109 [2001] 2 WLR 817.
110 See the comments of Auld J in *Katz* (1990) 90 Cr App R 456, CA.
111 *Ismail* [1990] Crim LR 109, CA; cf *Gillard and Barrett* (1991) 155 JP Rep 352 and *Y v DPP* [1991] Crim LR 917. Later interviews may be found to have been contaminated by earlier breaches if those breaches are of a fundamental and continuing character and the accused has not had sufficient opportunity of retracting what was said earlier: *Neill* [1994] Crim LR 441, CA.
112 [1988] Crim LR 519. See Chapter 12, p 1222 for discussion of the decision.
113 [1993] Crim LR 54, CA.
114 See, e.g., *Vernon* [1988] Crim LR 445; *Woodall and Others* [1989] Crim LR 288.

Code C;[115] there may be evasion or bending of a rule as opposed to breaking it; there are instances where the interviewing scheme itself leaves it unclear whether or not a particular safeguard should have been in place at a given stage in the process.[116] Clearly, a court may never have an opportunity to hear such argument. Infringement of this type is difficult to detect; for example, a suspect who is persuaded to forgo legal advice at the 'booking in' stage may be unaware that something has occurred to his disadvantage, unlike the suspect who has been straightforwardly refused advice. Even assuming that the suspect pleads not guilty, defence counsel may be reluctant to argue for exclusion of a confession if unable to point to a clear breach of the rules.

In *Keenan*,[117] the Court of Appeal ruled that once a breach of the rules can be identified, it will be asked whether it is substantial or significant. The Court found that a combination of breaches of the recording provisions satisfied this test. In contrast, a breach of para 10.2 requiring a police officer to inform a suspect that he is not under arrest, is free to go and may obtain legal advice, has been held to be insubstantial.[118] This view of para 10.2 also seems to have been implicit in the ruling of the Court of Appeal in *Joseph*,[119] although a breach of para 10.5 governing contemporaneous recording (now para 10.7), in contrast was clearly found to be substantial and significant in order to merit exclusion of the confession. In *Walsh*,[120] the Court of Appeal held that what was significant and substantial would be determined by reference to the nature of the breach except in instances where the police had acted in bad faith: '. . . although bad faith may make substantial or significant that which might not otherwise be so, the contrary does not follow. Breaches which are themselves significant and substantial are not rendered otherwise by the good faith of the officers concerned.'

This test has so far been applied only to Code provisions. It seems likely that breach of rules contained in Notes for Guidance or Home Office circulars would fail it – assuming that a court was prepared to consider such breaches at all. The courts have been reluctant to take such rules into account in the context of exclusion of evidence or, as far as the Notes are concerned, in any other context. This was the approach taken in *DPP v Billington*;[121] the Court of Appeal preferred not to consider Note 6C

---

115 The Notes for Guidance, which are not part of the Codes (see Codes C and H, para 1.3 – the provision to the same effect is the first paragraph of each Code) and therefore may in effect be said to form part of a separate instrument; Home Office Circulars; Force Standing Orders.

116 This may be said in particular of Code C, para 11.1A and para 10.1 which determine when the safeguards surrounding interviews should be in place. See above, pp 1193–97 (discussed in Fenwick, H, 'Confessions, recording rules and miscarriages of justice' [1993] Crim LR 174).

117 [1989] 3 WLR 1193; [1989] All ER 598, CA.

118 *Rajakuruna* [1991] Crim LR 458.

119 [1993] Crim LR 206, CA.

120 [1989] Crim LR 822; (1989) 19 Cr App R 161.

121 (1988) Cr App R 68; [1988] 1 All ER 435. The court had to consider whether a desire to consult a solicitor first could properly found a refusal to furnish a specimen of breath under the Road Traffic Act 1972, s 8(7). Para 6 of Code C provides that a person who has requested legal advice may not be interviewed until he has received it. Note 6C (version of Code C in force at the time; the equivalent provision now appears in para 11.1A) provides that the s 8 procedure does not constitute an interview, but Lloyd LJ preferred not to take it into account while reaching a conclusion which was nevertheless in accordance with it. Thus, the issue which fell to be determined did not concern the question of exclusion of evidence, but has a bearing upon the general question whether courts are prepared to place any reliance upon the Notes.

of Code C despite its relevance to the question before it. However, there are some patchy signs that the judiciary are prepared to react to the Notes differently, perhaps owing to a perception that their legitimacy derives from their substance, as opposed to their source. In *DPP v Blake*[122] the Divisional Court impliedly accepted that a Note for Guidance will be considered if it can be argued that it amplifies a particular Code provision, and can therefore be of assistance in determining whether breach of such a provision has occurred. The question arose whether an estranged parent could be the appropriate adult at the interview of a juvenile under Code C, para 13.1;[123] that provision was interpreted in accordance with Note 13C, which at the time described the adult's expected role,[124] and it was then found that para 13.1 had been breached.[125] A variation on this view of the Notes, which nevertheless supports the argument that they are unlikely to be considered in their own right, was expressed by the Court of Appeal in relation to one of the most significant Notes, Note 11A. It was taken into account on the basis that it could be seen as part of para 11.1 and could thereby acquire the status of a paragraph.[126] (Note – the references to the Code provisions are to the provisions in force at the time.)

Once a court has identified a significant and substantial breach of the interviewing rules, it may then take some account of the *function* of the rule in question. Rules governing access to legal advice and the right to silence provide rights which are valuable in themselves in due process terms; they also tend to place the suspect on a more equal footing with police officers during the interview. These rights are also reflected in the Convention in Art 6(2) and 6(3)(c).[127] An innocent detainee who is confused and upset by the interrogation may be less likely to make false admissions if a legal adviser is present at the interview.[128] In contrast, the verifying and recording rules may be said to be concerned mainly with the evidential integrity of admissions rather than with providing rights valuable in themselves. Categorising the interviewing rules in this way – by means of their dominant function – may be useful as a means of determining the type of unfairness which may flow from their breach. However, occasionally, what may be termed the *subordinate* function of a rule may be relevant to the question of fair treatment, with the result that, for example, a breach of a recording rule could be treated for s 78 purposes in the same way as breach of the legal advice provisions.

In *Samuel*,[129] the Court of Appeal found that the confession should have been excluded under s 78 because it was causally linked to the police impropriety – a failure to allow the appellant access to legal advice. In order to establish this point, the solicitor

---

122 [1989] 1 WLR 432, CA.
123 Now para 11.15 under the 2006 revised Code.
124 This role is now described in para 11.17; this provision has therefore been elevated in status, indicating its importance. The decision in *DPP v Blake* found recognition in Note for Guidance 1B.
125 This decision was followed in the first instance decision of *Morse* [1991] Crim LR 195; see also *DPP v Rouse* and *DPP v Davis* (1992) 94 Cr App R 185.
126 *Cox* (1993) 96 Cr App R 464; [1993] Crim LR 382; (1992) *The Times*, 2 December.
127 See Chapter 12, pp 1210–15, 1235 and 1239–41.
128 As pointed out at a number of points in Chapter 12, the evidence as to the advantage to the detainee of having the adviser present at the interview is of a rather mixed nature; see, e.g., comment on the solicitor's role at [1993] Crim LR 368.
129 [1988] QB 615; [1988] 2 All ER 315; [1988] 2 WLR 920, CA.

in question gave evidence that had he been present, he would have advised his client to remain silent in the last interview, whereas in fact Samuel made damaging admissions in that interview which formed the basis of the case against him. It could not be said with certainty that he would have confessed in any event: he was not, it was determined, a sophisticated criminal who was capable of judging for himself when to speak and when to remain silent. Thus – although this was not made explicit – the Court of Appeal was in effect prepared to make the judgment that a trial would be rendered unfair if a court associated itself with a breach of the PACE interrogation procedure. The Court of Appeal in *Alladice*,[130] also faced with a breach of s 58, accepted that the key factor in exercising discretion under s 78 after a breach of the interviewing rules was the causal relationship between breach and confession (and, it appeared by implication, between breach and fairness at the trial). On the basis of this factor, it was determined that the confession had been rightly admitted despite the breach of s 58 because no causal relationship between the two could be established. This finding was based partly on the defendant's evaluation of the situation (that he only wanted the solicitor to see fair play and did not require legal advice), and partly on the fact that he had exercised his right to silence at certain points. Therefore, it was determined that he would have made the incriminating admissions in any event – even with the benefit of legal advice. Possibly this was surprising in view of the fact that the appellant, as the court itself accepted, was an unsophisticated criminal who did in fact make admissions in the absence of a solicitor which formed the basis of the case against him.[131]

In the early post-PACE years, there was a tendency for judges to move rather rapidly from a finding that the police had breached Code C to a determination that s 78 should be invoked to exclude the confession, without explicitly considering whether a causal relationship between the breach and the confession existed.[132] Such a tendency can be discerned in the case of *Absolam*[133] in which the Court of Appeal, in finding that 'the prosecution would not have been in receipt of these admissions if the appropriate procedures had been followed', seemed to assume that the causal relationship between the impropriety[134] and the admissions did exist. The chain of causation would have been fairly long – had the detainee been informed of his right to legal advice, he would have exercised it; had he exercised it, he would not have made the incriminating admissions – but the Court of Appeal did not make much attempt to scrutinise its links.[135] However,

---

130 (1988) 87 Cr App R 380. The Court of Appeal appeared to have a similar test in mind in relation to a failure to caution in *Weerdesteyn* (1995) 1 Cr App R 405; [1995] Crim LR 239, CA.

131 See also *Dunford* (1990) 91 Cr App R 150; (1990) 140 NLJ 517, CA: the Court of Appeal determined that the criminally experienced appellant had made his own assessment of the situation in deciding to make certain admissions and legal advice would not have affected his decision; the failure to allow legal advice was not therefore causally linked to the confession.

132 See *Williams* [1989] Crim LR 66 and *Mary Quayson* [1989] Crim LR 218.

133 (1989) Cr App R 332.

134 A failure to inform Absolam of his right to legal advice in breach of Code C, para 3.1(ii).

135 Possibly, this may have arisen because the defendant had denied making the admissions in question; the court was therefore placed in the position of accepting the word of the police officer against that of the defendant – precisely the problem which Code C, para 11 was designed to prevent. The Court of Appeal, while speaking in the language of causation, may simply have had a doubt as to whether the admissions were made at all.

in *Walsh*,[136] the Court of Appeal reaffirmed the need to identify the causal relationship between the breach in question and the confession.

Deciding that an impropriety is causally linked to the confession does not of itself explain why admission of the confession will render the trial unfair, although it is perhaps reasonable to conclude that admission of a confession which is not so linked will *not* render the trial unfair. The necessary unfairness must arise through admission of the confession, in other words *after* its admission; the unfairness in the interrogation cannot therefore without more satisfy this requirement; instead, the unfairly obtained confession must be the agent which somehow creates unfairness at the trial. It must be acknowledged that at present the courts have not addressed this question. In *Samuel*, for example, the Court of Appeal merely stated:

> . . . the appellant was denied improperly one of the most important and fundamental rights of the citizen . . . if [the trial judge] had found a breach of s 58 he would have determined that admission of evidence as to the final interview would have 'such an adverse effect on the fairness of the proceedings' that he ought not to admit it.[137]

Broadly, it could be argued that if the court refuses to take the opportunity afforded by s 78 to put right what has occurred earlier in the process, this will give an appearance of unfairness to the trial. This argument is based on the 'protective principle':[138] if admissions gained in consequence of denial of a right (in the broad sense of an entitlement) are excluded, the particular right is being protected in the sense that the defendant is being placed at trial – as far as the jury is concerned – in the position he or she would have been in had the right not been denied. If s 78 is, at least in part, concerned with ensuring fairness to the defence, it is arguable that the court should take the opportunity offered to it of upholding the standards of fairness declared by PACE. However, following an argument based on the reputation or integrity principles, if the police unfairness has had no consequences for the defendant, the court need not exclude the confession since to do so would place him in a more favourable position than he would have been in had the proper standard of fairness been observed.

Admittedly, both these arguments assume that the court will appear to be associating itself unfairly with the prosecution, rather than dealing even-handedly, if it admits the evidence in question and that therefore, the court should refuse to do so. They therefore seem to beg the very question to which s 78 demands an answer. If admitting the confession despite the breach *could* be seen as fair, the court would not be associating itself with unfairness and could not be seen as lacking even-handedness. But bearing in mind the balance PACE is supposed to create between increased police powers and safeguards for suspects, it can perhaps be argued that to accept evidence deriving from an interview in which the police were able to use their powers to the full, but the defendant was unable to take advantage of an important safeguard, would not be perceived by most reasonable people as fair. The findings of the Privy Council

---

136   [1989] Crim LR 822.
137   [1988] 2 WLR 920, p 934.
138   See Ashworth, A [1979] Crim LR 723.

in *Mohammed (Allie) v State*[139] in respect of a denial of custodial access to legal advice adopted this stance: 'The stamp of constitutionality on a citizen's rights is not meaningless: it is clear testimony that added value is attached to the protection of the right ... Not every breach will result in a confession being excluded. But their Lordships make clear that the fact that there has been a breach of a constitutional right is a cogent factor militating in favour of the exclusion of the confession. In this way the constitutional character of the infringed right is respected and accorded a high value ...' This stance receives clear, albeit indirect support from Strasbourg, as will be indicated below.[140]

In this context, the curtailment of the right to silence under the CJPOA, discussed in Chapter 12, is particularly significant. One result of its curtailment appears to be that it is harder to argue that an improper denial of access to legal advice should lead to exclusion of admissions obtained under s 78. This is because the main basis for excluding confessions gained after denial of legal advice has been eroded. Prior to curtailment of the right to silence, the courts had been excluding them mainly on the ground that had the legal adviser been present, he or she would probably have advised the client to remain silent, but if this cannot be contended, the causal relationship between breach and confession is destroyed. How far this is happening depends on the readiness of legal advisers to advise their clients to remain silent in the face of the knowledge that such silence may be commented on in court. At present, it is unclear that legal advisers are less disposed than they were previously to advise silence.[141] However, if such a tendency did become apparent, a number of consequences might follow. The police may have been encouraged to afford access to a legal adviser, but, on the other hand, any disincentive to deny access – the result of such decisions as *Samuel* and *Absolam* – has been undermined. The balance still comes down in favour of discouraging, delaying or denying access.[142]

If, on a *voir dire*, a court has to consider such a denial, it is harder than it was previously to contend confidently that the legal adviser would have advised the client to remain silent; the result is that the courts are finding themselves less able to uphold this particular safeguard for the suspect. Of course it might be said, in the light of a large amount of research,[143] that it was, even prior to the inception of the CJPOA, *already* becoming difficult to contend confidently that a legal adviser would have advised silence, except perhaps in cases where the client was under very obvious pressure.[144] However, that problem can be addressed by means of better training in the provision of custodial legal advice. The effect of curtailment of the right to silence, however, is probably in the long run to undermine one of the props holding up the legal advice scheme.

139 [1999] 2 WLR 552 (Trinidad and Tobago); judgment delivered by Lord Steyn on 8 December 1998.
140 See also Chapter 12, pp 1210–14.
141 See Chapter 12, pp 1229–36.
142 See Chapter 12, pp 1230–33.
143 See, e.g., McConville, M and Hodgson, J, *Custodial Legal Advice and the Right to Silence*, 1993, Royal Commission Study No 16. See further Chapter 12, pp 1228–34.
144 See Dixon's findings in this respect: [1991] PL 233, p 244: '... silence may be advised ... when the suspect is confused or highly emotional ... several solicitors stressed that their clients are under great pressure'.

Breach of rules aimed at ensuring that the record of an interview can be relied on at trial need not be considered under s 78 in terms of their impact on the defendant during the interview. The question is not normally whether the breach of the recording rules placed the defendant at a disadvantage during the interview. Once such a breach, of a substantial nature, has been identified, a court will be likely to react by excluding the confession on the basis that it is impossible to be sure of its reliability,[145] and therefore its prejudicial quality may outweigh its probative value. In other words, a jury may place reliance on an inaccurate record or believe a fabricated confession which clearly has no evidential value at all. An obvious example of such a breach is a failure to make contemporaneous notes of the interview in breach of Code C, para 11.7, allowing a challenge to the interview record by the defence on the basis that the police have fabricated all or part of it. The court then has no means of knowing which version of what was said is true, precisely the situation which Code C was designed to prevent. In such a situation, a judge may well exclude the interview record on the basis that it would be unfair to allow evidence of doubtful reliability to go before the jury. If, however, as in *Dunn*,[146] the defence has an independent witness to what occurred – usually a solicitor or solicitor's clerk – the judge may admit the confession as the defence now has a proper basis from which to challenge the police evidence.

It is fairly clear that allowing a confession which may have been fabricated to go before the jury may render a trial unfair. On the one hand, the jury may rely on a confession which may be entirely untrue, while on the other, if the defendant alleges that the police fabricated the confession, the prosecution can then put his character in issue and the jury may hear of his previous convictions. The jury may then tend to rely on his convictions in deciding that his guilt is established on this occasion. In both circumstances, the defendant is placed at a clear disadvantage.

When a breach of Code C has occurred which casts doubt on the accuracy of the interview record, the defence may not necessarily submit that the police have fabricated admissions; the judge may merely have to determine whether the trial will be rendered unfair if a possibly inaccurate record of an interview is admitted in evidence. There is authority to suggest that a judge in such circumstances will exclude the record,[147] presumably owing to the risk that the jury will rely on fabricated admissions.

As noted above, identifying the dominant function of the interviewing rule in question need not circumscribe the inquiry into the unfairness caused by its breach. Although identifying the dominant function of a rule may simplify this task in most circumstances, it is suggested that a court may sometimes focus on its subordinate function. For example, a breach of the recording provisions would be directly relevant to placing the suspect in a disadvantageous position at interview where there was no dispute between defence and prosecution as to the admissions made (although the defence may be alleging that they are untrue), but there was an allegation that the breach had allowed some impropriety to occur which had pressurised the suspect into making admissions. It may now be impossible to determine whether the defence or prosecution version of events during the interview is correct because of the defective

---

145 See, e.g., *Keenan* [1989] 3 WLR 1193; [1989] 3 All ER 598, CA.
146 (1990) 91 Cr App R 237; [1990] Crim LR 572, CA. See also *Heslop* [1996] Crim LR 730.
147 *Foster* [1987] Crim LR 821; *Keenan* [1989] 3 All ER 598.

record. Equally, access to legal advice can affect the evidential integrity of a confession: the legal adviser can give evidence in court as to what occurred during the interview and, if the interview record is defective, can support the defendant's version of what was said, thus lending support to the argument that the interview should be admitted. Conversely, if in such circumstances legal advice had been improperly denied, but the defendant was able to cope without advice, the unfairness would arise out of the inability of the defence to challenge the defective interview record, rather than due to the adverse effect of lack of advice.[148] In such instances, the subordinate function of the rule should determine the test to be applied. Thus, in the first example given, the only question would be whether the causal relationship between impropriety and confession could be established, assuming that it was impossible to determine the truth or otherwise of the allegation of impropriety.

In the cases considered above, it was not clear that the police had *deliberately* failed to comply with the rules; the failures in question may have arisen out of a mistake as to the application of PACE or Code C or because of an administrative error. It seems that if the police have acted deliberately, the exercise under s 78 will be far less complex. Lord Lane CJ in *Alladice*[149] stated that he would not have hesitated to hold that the confession should have been excluded had it been demonstrated that the police had acted in bad faith in breaching s 58. The lack of emphasis that he thought should in general be placed on the causal relationship in question, if bad faith on the part of the police could be demonstrated, was the most striking feature of this decision. His approach appears to involve asking only whether a breach was accompanied by bad faith. If so, that would appear to be the end of the matter: exclusion of the confession would follow almost automatically. If the breach occurred in good faith, however, a close scrutiny of the causal relationship should follow.

Using the questions of bad faith and causation as alternatives to keep a check on a too ready exclusion of confessions can be criticised because it is hard to see why an instance of bad faith on the part of the police which is not causally linked to the confession should be considered in relation to its admissibility. Deliberate denial of rights certainly gives a greater appearance of unfairness to the interrogation than an innocent denial, but if the detainee is unaffected by it, why should it affect the trial? It cannot be said that the court is associating itself with or condoning the bad faith displayed by the police in the interrogation because the link between the admissions arising and the denial of rights is missing. If, in future, the situation which arose in *Alladice* recurs, but with the added ingredient of bad faith, it is hard to see why the consequences for the future defendant should differ so greatly. The only justification appears to be that the police are 'punished' for their deliberate impropriety, but the disciplinary approach has been explicitly repudiated, in *Delaney*[150] and *Chalkley*,[151] on the basis that it is not part of the proper purpose of a criminal trial to inquire into

---

148 This occurred in *Dunn* (1990) 91 Cr App R 237; [1990] Crim LR 572, CA. Ironically, the confession was admitted into evidence owing to the fact that the defendant's legal adviser had been present and could support his assertion that it had been fabricated; the jury presumably disbelieved her and convicted on that basis.

149 (1988) 87 Cr App R 380.

150 (1989) 88 Cr App R 339; (1988) *The Times*, 20 August, CA.

151 [1998] 2 All ER 155.

wrongdoing on the part of the police. Nevertheless, at present, deliberate breaches of Code C will almost certainly lead to exclusion of evidence under s 78 whether the breaches were linked to the confession or not. The Court of Appeal in *Walsh*[152] confirmed that this was the correct approach and suggested that it would be followed even if the breach was of a trivial nature. In fact, the dearth of cases on this point suggests that courts are reluctant to accept that a breach of PACE may have been perpetrated deliberately by the police; they appear to be satisfied that breaches arise due to administrative errors or incompetence rather than bad faith.

It may be noted that a judge may exceptionally admit the confession after deciding to exclude it because some particular feature of the trial proceedings makes it necessary to do so in order to maintain the balance of fairness between prosecution and defence.[153] In other words, if it was clear that in some way the prosecution is at a disadvantage which could be seen as equal to that experienced by the defendant, the judge might allow the confession to be admitted. This flows from the concern of s 78 with the fairness of the proceedings rather than simply with fairness to the defence. On the other hand, it does not appear that reconsidering the decision to *admit* the confession is covered by s 78 – in the sense of telling the jury to disregard the confession – due to its focus on determining whether to admit the confession (although s 82(3) might be invoked – see below).

Section 78: exclusion of non-confession evidence[154]

The discussion has shown that the courts have continued the common law tradition within the PACE scheme of excluding confessions tainted by impropriety, but they have shown great reluctance to exclude other evidence which is equally tainted. A stay will be used only in relation to certain instances of gross malpractice. The arguments above have concentrated on exclusion of admissions, but non-confession evidence can also be excluded under s 78 (or s 82(3)), although not under s 76. Where non-confession evidence is concerned, the courts have taken a stance which differs strongly from that taken to admissions obtained in police interviews which breach PACE. The general stance taken is that improperly obtained evidence is admissible in a criminal trial subject to a discretion to exclude it. Except in one instance – that of identification evidence – the discretion is viewed as very narrow, although where the impropriety consists of some forms of trickery, it may be wider. This stance has not changed under the HRA. Pre-HRA the courts demonstrated little inclination to take a different stance where the impropriety consisted of a breach of a Convention right,[155] and, following

---

152 [1989] Crim LR 822.
153 See *Allen* [1992] Crim LR 297: having decided to exclude a conversation between police officers and the defendant because of breaches of the recording provisions, the judge reconsidered when the nature of the defence case became apparent; it placed prosecution witnesses at an unfair disadvantage if they were unable to refer to the excluded conversation. Thus, it appears that in such circumstances the original unfairness caused to the defendant may be outweighed by unfairness to the prosecution if the confession is not admitted.
154 For discussion see Gelowitz (1990) 106 LQR 327; Choo, AL-T and Nash, S, 'What's the matter with s 78?' [1999] Crim LR 929–40. Choo (1989) 9(3) LS 261; Allen [1990] CLJ 80; Choo (1993) Journal of Crim Law 195; Sharpe, op. cit., fn 1, (1998) Chapter 2.
155 See the judgment of the House of Lords in *Khan* [1997] AC 558.

the Strasbourg jurisprudence, it is not necessary for that approach to change under the HRA, as discussed below.

Identification evidence

Identification evidence has been seen as particularly vulnerable and may therefore be treated in the same way as a confession obtained in breach of PACE. Arguments can be raised as to the reliability of identification evidence and also as to police impropriety in conducting identification. For example, if no reminder as to the availability of legal advice were given (Code D, para 3.17(ii)) before an identification was arranged, it could be argued that the form of the identification used prejudiced the position of the defendant, who would have asked for a different form had he had advice. It could be argued that no identification would have been made had the other form been used and that therefore, the failure to remind of the right to advice was causally linked to the identification evidence obtained. If some doubt is raised as to the reliability of the identification owing to delay[156] or to a failure to hold an identification parade where one was practicable,[157] the identification evidence is likely to be excluded. However, in the leading decision on identification evidence, *Forbes*,[158] the House of Lords found that despite a breach of Code D, para 2.3, there had been no need to exclude the evidence.

Thus, following this decision, each case must turn on its own facts, except where bad faith is shown in conducting the identification procedure. In such an instance, it seems that the courts will react to it as they would in relation to confessions.[159] It will mean that no causal relationship between the breach and the evidence obtained need be shown and, possibly, that the breach need not be substantial and significant. It may be argued that there is a stronger case than that considered above in relation to confessions for treating bad faith shown during the identification process with particular stringency owing to the appearance of unfairness created to the defendant who may think that there has been collusion between witnesses and the police.

Other non-confession evidence

On due process grounds, the argument accepted in *Samuel*[160] as to the causal relationship between an impropriety and a confession (where bad faith is not shown) should be applied to non-confession evidence, such as a weapon or drugs found on the suspect or his premises during an improper or unlawful search. However, the stance taken by the courts is based on crime control principles. Where non-confession evidence is in question, the discretion under s 78 is applied very narrowly. The first instance decision in *Fennelly*[161] in which a failure to give the reason for a stop and search led to exclusion of the heroin found is out of line with the later decisions. Indeed, even if

---

156   *Quinn* [1990] Crim LR 581, CA; (1990) *The Times*, 31 March.
157   *Ladlow* [1989] Crim LR 219.
158   [2001] Crim LR 649.
159   *Finley* [1993] Crim LR 50, CA.
160   [1988] QB 615.
161   [1989] Crim LR 142.

the principles developed under s 78 with respect to confession evidence were generally applied to other evidence, *Fennelly* would still be a doubtful decision since, on the facts, no causal relationship could exist between the impropriety in question and the evidence obtained.

According to *Thomas*[162] and *Quinn*,[163] physical evidence will be excluded only if obtained with deliberate illegality; the pre-PACE ruling of the House of Lords in *Fox*[164] would also lend support to this contention. In *Fox*, the police made a *bona fide* mistake as to their powers in effecting an unlawful arrest and the House of Lords, in determining that the physical evidence obtained was admissible, considered that the unlawful arrest was merely part of the history of the case and not the concern of the court. This stance is in accord with that taken in *Sang*[165] and confirmed as correct in *Khan (Sultan)*.[166] It appears to be in accord with the general PACE scheme, since evidence obtained as a result of an inadmissible confession will be admissible under s 76(4).

Zander has pointed out,[167] citing, *inter alia, Sharpe v DPP*,[168] that the courts have rejected the 'real' evidence of intoxication in certain drink-driving cases under s 78 owing to the way in which the evidence was obtained, even where bad faith may not have been present. Zander views the Divisional Court decision in *Sharpe*, along with the decisions in cases such as *Samuel* and *Gall*[169] (on identification evidence) as affirming an abandonment of 'the amoral common law tradition of receiving non-confession evidence regardless of how it was obtained'.[170] However, it may now be said with some certainty that the amoral common law tradition has continued and will continue to prevail. The inception of the HRA has not affected this position.

The position as regards unlawfully obtained evidence, which reflects a crime control stance, is as stated by the House of Lords in *Khan (Sultan)*,[171] now the leading case on s 78. It suggests that a narrow exclusionary discretion only is available under s 78, save where a confession may be said to be involuntary (in which case it would be excluded under s 76). A bugging device had been secretly installed on the outside of a house which Khan was visiting. Khan was suspected of involvement in the importation of prohibited drugs and the tape recording obtained from the listening device clearly showed that he was so involved. The case against him rested wholly on the tape recording. The defence argued, first, that the recording was inadmissible as evidence because the police had no statutory authority to place listening devices on private property and that therefore, such placement was a trespass and, further, that admission of the recording would breach Art 8 of the European Convention on Human Rights, which protects the right to privacy. Secondly, it was argued that even if the recording was

162 [1990] Crim LR 269. See, to the same effect, *Wright* [1994] Crim LR 55.
163 [1990] Crim LR 581, CA.
164 [1986] AC 281; see to the same effect *DPP v Wilson* [1991] Crim LR 441. On similar facts, in *Matto v Wolverhampton Crown Court* [1987] RTR 337, physical evidence was excluded since the police had acted with *mala fides*.
165 [1980] AC 402; [1979] 2 All ER 1222, HL.
166 [1997] AC 558; [1996] 3 All ER 289.
167 Zander, op. cit., fn 1, 2nd edn, pp 236–37.
168 (1993) JP 595.
169 (1990) 90 Cr App R 64.
170 Zander, op. cit., fn 1, 2nd edn, p 236.
171 [1996] 3 All ER 289; (1996) 146 NLJ 1024. For comment, see Carter (1997) 113 LQR 468.

admissible, it should be excluded from evidence under s 78 because of the unfairness of admitting the evidence so. It was accepted in the Court of Appeal that trespass to the building had occurred as well as some damage to it and that there had been an invasion of privacy. However, the Court of Appeal found,[172] supporting the trial judge, that these factors were of slight significance and therefore were readily outweighed by the fact that the police had largely complied with the Home Office guidelines and that the offences involved were serious. The court found that since the Convention is not part of UK law, it was of only persuasive assistance.

The House of Lords upheld the Court of Appeal. The Lords relied on the decision in *Sang*[173] to the effect that improperly obtained evidence other than 'involuntary' confessions is admissible in a criminal trial. Involuntary confessions were inadmissible on the ground that if a defendant was in some way induced to confess during a police interrogation, his confession might be unreliable. It was argued for the appellant that the recording fell within the category of involuntary confessions and therefore was outside the rule from *Sang*. The House of Lords disagreed and went on to find that *Sang* would be inapplicable only if there were a right to privacy in UK law and breach of such a right could be treated as a form of impropriety different in kind from that covered by *Sang* and so serious that it would render evidence thereby obtained inadmissible. Neither of these two new principles was accepted; therefore, the recording was admissible.

Should the recording have been excluded under s 78, taking Art 8 into account? The House of Lords found that although a judge in exercising discretion under s 78 might take Art 8 into account; or any relevant foreign law, an apparent breach of Art 8 would not necessarily lead him or her to conclude that the evidence in question should be excluded. The key question would be the effect of the breach upon the fairness of the proceedings. The House of Lords concluded that the circumstances in which the evidence was obtained, even if they involved a breach of Art 8, were not such as to require exclusion of the evidence.

This decision confirms that, apart from admissions falling within s 76 of PACE (which has partly replaced the common law concept of involuntariness), improperly obtained evidence is admissible in criminal trials subject to a discretion to exclude it. Thus, it fails to take a stance which protects due process. The House of Lords was only prepared to find that the Convention would be 'relevant' to the exercise of discretion under s 78 and further found that where a breach of the Convention was found, this would not necessarily lead a judge to conclude that evidence should be excluded. In *Chalkley*,[174] the same stance was taken. The evidence consisted of incriminating statements made by the accused which were secretly recorded by the police. Despite the impropriety of the police actions, it was found that the evidence was rightly admitted. This stance did not change with the inception of the HRA. In *AG's Reference (No 3 of 1999)*,[175] a rape case, DNA evidence against the suspect should have been destroyed but had not been, in breach of s 64 of PACE. The evidence was not admitted under s 78 and the defendant was acquitted. On a reference of the Attorney General, it was found by the House of Lords, following the *Sang* principle, that the evidence could

172 *Khan* [1996] 3 All ER 289; (1996) 146 NLJ 1024, HL; [1995] QB 27, CA.
173 [1980] AC 402; [1979] 2 All ER 1222.
174 [1998] 2 Cr App R 79.
175 [2001] 2 WLR 56.

have been admitted, despite the breach of PACE. It was not found that Art 6 affected the position, since the Court has left the assessment of evidence to the national courts. This stance was affirmed in later decisions.[176]

This current narrow interpretation of s 78 of PACE[177] means that improperly obtained non-confession evidence will rarely be excluded, whether or not the impropriety also amounted to a breach of a Convention right. In other words, the admission of evidence in such circumstances need not amount to a breach of Art 6. The findings in *AG's Reference (No 3 of 1999)*[178] suggest that at present, there is a tendency to reject the possibility of using exclusion of evidence to uphold fundamental rights. This seems to be the case even where such rights are recognised within a statutory scheme; and possibly also where the breach is of a Convention right. In *Schenk v Switzerland*[179] the Strasbourg Court found no breach of Art 6(1) when an illegally obtained incriminating tape recording was admitted in evidence, and made it clear that unlawfully obtained evidence is not necessarily inadmissible. The Court found: 'While Article 6 guarantees the right to a fair trial it does not lay down any rules as to admissibility of evidence as such, which is therefore primarily a matter of regulation under national law'. The test is to ask whether the trial as a whole would be rendered unfair if the 'tainted' evidence was admitted.[180]

In the late 1990s, a change in the Court's stance occurred, although the *principle* deriving from *Schenk* remained unaffected. A much more interventionist approach was adopted in a number of judgments, in particular that in *Teixeira de Castro v Portugal*.[181] The applicant, who had no criminal record and was previously unknown to the police, was introduced by a third party to two undercover police officers who told him that they wished to buy 20 grams of heroin. He bought the drugs on their behalf at a price allowing him to take a profit. He was then tried and convicted on the evidence of the officers of drug dealing and sentenced to six years' imprisonment. The Court found, by 8 votes to 1, that the entrapment by the police officers in order to secure evidence had made a fair trial impossible: 'right from the outset the applicant was definitively deprived of a fair trial.'[182]

In the context of exclusion of evidence, it might have been expected that where the pre-trial impropriety consisted of a fundamental breach of another Convention right, the *Teixeira* approach would have been followed. However, a Chamber of the Court did not adopt this stance in its important decision on admission of non-confession evidence under Art 6 in *Khan v UK*,[183] despite finding a breach of Art 8. A fundamental breach

---

176 See *Button* [2005] Crim LR 571. See further Ormerod, D, 'Trial remedies for Art 8 breaches?' [2003] Crim LR 61.
177 See *Chalkley* [1998] 2 All ER 155; *Khan* [1997] AC 558 and *Shannon* [2001] 1 WLR 51.
178 [2001] 2 WLR 56, p 64, *per* Lord Steyn, and p 65, *per* Lord Cook of Thorndon.
179 (1988) 13 EHRR 242.
180 A 140 (1988), para 46. This test was also used in *Khan v UK* (2000) 8 BHRC 310.
181 (1998) 28 EHRR 101; [1998] Crim LR 751. See also *Van Mechelen v Netherlands* (1998) 25 EHRR 647; the findings of the Commission and Court in *Rowe and Davis* (2000) 30 EHRR 1; *Condron v UK* (2001) 31 EHRR 1.
182 Ibid, para 39.
183 (2000) 8 BHRC 310; Commission decision: (1999) 27 EHRR CD 58.

of Art 8 (secret recording which was not in accordance with the law)[184] had occurred in obtaining the only evidence against the defendant, but, following *Schenk*,[185] no breach of Art 6 was found, owing to the admission of the evidence. The Court said that it was not its role to determine whether unlawfully obtained evidence should be admissible. Thus, the Court appears to adhere to two, partly conflicting views. First, if the pre-trial behaviour is such that the trial is almost bound to be unfair, a breach of Art 6 will be found. The Court has not characterised this issue as one relating to exclusion of evidence; it could relate to abuse of process. Secondly, where pre-trial practices, although consisting of a breach of another Convention right, are viewed as creating less unfairness to the accused, and the question of a breach of Art 6 arises in the form of the question of admissibility, the Court leaves the matter to the national courts. Possibly, the difference between these two positions is justifiable, but the Court has made little attempt to consider such justification. The case of *Khan v UK*[186] therefore can be utilised by the courts to support their stance in relation to non-confession evidence, despite the inception of the HRA.[187]

An argument for exclusion of evidence, taking account of Art 6(1) could also be raised where admitting material deriving from informers, although not illegally obtained, might affect the fairness of the trial,[188] particularly where part of the evidence and/or the identity of the informer was not disclosed to the defence.[189] The rules on disclosure under the Criminal Procedure and Investigations Act 1996 create a regime which allows sensitive material to be withheld by the prosecution so that neither the court nor the defence is aware of its existence.[190] Where this has occurred, argument for exclusion of the material from evidence based on Art 6 demands could be raised at first instance or on appeal, relying on the general requirements of fairness under Art 6(1) and on the 'equality of arms' principle.[191] The domestic courts are expected to test issues of admissibility of evidence and of disclosure more directly against the requirements of Art 6 than has generally occurred at Strasbourg, owing to the effect of the margin of appreciation doctrine.

Thus, it may be said that the common law, post-HRA, continues to adhere to the crime control values implicit in the reliability principle. The domestic decision in *Khan* may be consistent with certain of the decisions on evidence obtained in breach of the interviewing or identification rules since, in such instances, it may be said that

---

184 See Chapter 10, p 1077.
185 (1988) 13 EHRR 242.
186 (2000) 8 BHRC 310.
187 See also *PG v UK* [2002] Crim LR 308.
188 For detailed discussion see Justice, *Under Surveillance: Covert Policing and Human Rights Standards*, 1998, Chapter 2, especially pp 37–51 and Chapter 3, especially pp 70–74.
189 E.g., the evidence might be tainted owing to the motivation of the informer. In *Windisch v Austria* [1990] 13 EHRR 281 the Court said: 'the Convention does not preclude reliance, at the investigation stage, on sources such as anonymous informants. However, the subsequent use of their statements by the trial court to found a conviction is another matter.' But see *Edwards v UK* (1992) 15 EHRR 417 (it was found that the hearing in the CA remedied the failure of disclosure). These issues were, however, raised successfully under Art 6 in *Rowe and Davis v UK* (2000) 30 EHRR 1.
190 For discussion see *Archbold: Criminal Pleading, Practice and Evidence*, 1999, para 12–52.
191 In *Jespers v Belgium*, Appl No 8403/78, 27 DR 61, the Commission found that under Art 6(3), the accused has the right 'to have at his disposal . . . all relevant elements that have been or could have been collected by the relevant authorities'.

the evidence is unreliable.[192] However, *Khan* is not consistent with the decisions on excluding apparently reliable but improperly obtained confession evidence.

Thus, it seems that improperly obtained non-confession evidence, apart from identification evidence, will be admissible subject to a very narrow discretion to exclude it. This stance seems to afford encouragement to police officers to disregard suspects' rights in the pursuit of such evidence and amounts to a declaration by the courts that a conviction may be based on evidence which would not be before a court had police officers not acted unlawfully. In due process terms, a principled justification for creating a distinction between improperly obtained, but probably reliable, confession evidence and improperly obtained physical evidence is not apparent. The due process argument, to the effect that certain types of impropriety should lead almost automatically to exclusion of the evidence affected by them, has so far been rejected. However, the courts have not yet been faced, post-HRA, with non-confession evidence obtained through a breach of a Convention right. There are indications in *Khan* that in such circumstances, it might be excluded, on the basis of the integrity principle.

It is arguable, despite *Khan v UK*, that the stance currently taken towards non-confession evidence, including evidence obtained from informers and from other forms of surveillance, may not fully satisfy Art 6(1). As indicated, under domestic practice, evidence gained through a very serious impropriety, including a breach of a Convention right, is admissible, as is, under s 76(4) of PACE, physical evidence uncovered through an inadmissible confession gained as a result of impropriety, not excluding Art 3 treatment. The discretion to exclude non-confession evidence is very narrow and the impact which s 78 has had in encouraging adherence to due process may be diminishing at the present time. As L-T-Choo observes: 'recent decisions of the Court of Appeal signal a movement away from focusing on the nature of the breach [of PACE or the Codes] and towards an approach which takes the nature of the evidence as its central consideration'.[193] In other words, the movement is away from due process values and towards acceptance of the crime control norm that the end – a conviction – justifies the means. Until fairly recently, there were expectations that such movement could be reversed under Art 6 following an interpretation of the *Teixeira* approach to the effect that some forms of evidence gathering would almost automatically render the trial unfair.

From a due process perspective, such an activist interpretation of Art 6 has been urged, and some commentators have argued for a near-absolute rule requiring exclusion of evidence where it has been obtained in breach of a fundamental constitutional right or where its admission would breach the right to a fair trial.[194] Clearly, it was tempting to argue that Art 6 requires that a court should not merely inquire into the truth of the charges against a defendant: it should also play a part in maintaining standards in criminal investigations, in discouraging police abuse of power and upholding the due process elements within the investigative process which correspond to the rights of the detainee recognised under PACE and the TA.

192 See the comments of the Court of Appeal in *Bray* (1998) 31 July, unreported, to the effect that where the impropriety does not affect the quality of the evidence, it should be admitted.

193 Choo, AL-T and Nash, S, 'What's the matter with s 78?' [1999] Crim LR 929–40.

194 See, e.g., Ashworth, A, 'Article 6 and the fairness of trials' [1999] Crim LR 261, p 271.

Clearly, the requirements placed on the domestic courts depend on the view taken of the meaning of fairness under Art 6. Strasbourg and the domestic courts have united in finding that a breach of another Convention right, perpetrated pre-trial, does not automatically render the trial unfair.[195] Therefore, the fact that such a breach has occurred is part of the history of the case which can be taken into account in considering the proceedings as a whole, but which, except in the case of a breach of Art 3 in order to obtain a confession,[196] is not conclusive of the issue regarding fairness. The same argument applies to findings that flaws in the custodial and investigative procedures, including breaches of the PACE or TA Codes of Practice, not amounting in themselves to breaches of Convention rights, have occurred. They could be addressed, taking account of s 6 HRA, by means of exclusion of evidence or a stay for abuse of process, in order to avoid breaching Art 6(1), but only if it was possible to argue that the trial would otherwise be rendered unfair.

It was found in *Khan* that the admission of evidence obtained in breach of Art 8 did not create a breach of Art 6. It could be argued on a broad view of the decision that *Teixeira de Castro* is apparently out of accord with *Khan* since, in so far as the effect of the impropriety at issue in *Teixeira* might have been cured by exclusion of the evidence, the Court implied that there would be virtually no judicial discretion left to exercise to admit it.

Clearly, this is not the reading of *Teixeira* that the courts are adopting, as indicated above. But it is a possible reading. It is unfortunate that the Court did not address the question whether excluding the evidence obtained by entrapment would have rendered the trial fair. In the particular circumstances, the trial would probably have collapsed and therefore that question was of little import. But presumably, the Court itself wished to characterise the matter as one that did not reach into the question of exclusion of evidence since otherwise, it would have had to take a stance on the question of the assessment of evidence which it prefers to leave to the national court. But since it deliberately avoided the question of exclusion of evidence, it is arguable that in some circumstances the principle from *Teixeira* could be utilised to argue, not for the abandonment of the trial, but for exclusion of the evidence tainted by the unfairness. Moreover, there is a readily apparent argument to the effect that *Khan v UK* does not in fact imply that the failure to exclude evidence obtained in breach of a fundamental right meets nationally accepted standards of procedural justice, since Strasbourg merely decided that the assessment of evidence was for the national court. In other words, it conceded a margin of appreciation to the national court, leaving it free to take a different stance as to the exclusion of improperly obtained evidence.

A robust interpretation of the Art 6 guarantee of fairness, bearing *Teixeira* in mind, would support a requirement that an impropriety or illegality in the custodial or investigative procedures would tend to tip the scales towards exclusion of the evidence obtained as a result, including non-confession evidence.[197] The difference between the

---

195 *Khan* [1997] AC 558 and *Khan v UK* (2000) 8 BHRC 310.
196 Under s 76(2)(a).
197 In this context, the decision of the Court of Appeal in *R v Radak and Others* [1999] 1 Cr App R 187; (1999) *The Times*, 7 October should be noted. The decision related to admission of a written witness statement pursuant to the Criminal Justice Act 1988, ss 23, 25 and 26, and was concerned with prosecution rather than police impropriety. But the decision is of interest since the court relied heavily

positions of the Strasbourg and the national courts would support such an interpretation. In particular, it could be found that breach of the Convention guarantees in the pre-trial procedures would make it probable that the trial would be rendered unfair if evidence deriving from the breach were not excluded.

If this interpretation were to be adopted, which currently appears to be very unlikely, it would mean that in so far as certain of the due process rights enshrined in PACE, the TA and their associated Codes reflect certain of the principles enshrined in Arts 3, 5, 6 or 8, their status might be enhanced. One particular effect would be that the PACE or TA Code provisions in question, as the detailed domestic embodiment of those rights, would be accorded *de facto* a higher value than their legal status would appear to warrant.

Evidence obtained by entrapment or other deceptions[198]

As indicated, *Sang*[199] stated the general rule that improperly obtained evidence other than 'involuntary' confessions is admissible in a criminal trial subject to a very narrow discretion to exclude it. The fact that the police have acted as agents provocateurs, entrapping the defendant into a crime he would not otherwise have committed, was not found in *Sang* to mean that the evidence gained thereby should be excluded. The position as regards tricks or undercover work by police that still prevails was stated by the Court of Appeal in *Smurthwaite*.[200] The mere fact that the evidence has been obtained in the course of an undercover operation, of necessity involving deceit, does not of itself require a judge to exclude it. Everything will depend on the particular circumstances in question. For example, how active or passive was the officer's role in obtaining the evidence? What is the nature of the evidence and is it unassailable? If the officer's role is active, the evidence will be viewed as having been obtained by entrapment or by an agent provocateur and will probably be excluded. *Smurthwaite* suggests that the discretion to exclude 'unfair' evidence is of a somewhat wider scope than that indicated in *Sang*.

However, in the majority of cases, evidence obtained by a deception has been admitted,[201] but where the deception 'creates' the evidence and it is not possible to say that the defendant has applied himself to the ruse, the courts will tend to exclude it.[202] In *Williams and O'Hare v DPP*,[203] police officers set up a 'virtue-testing' operation in order to see who might succumb to temptation. An insecure vehicle apparently loaded

on Art 6(1) and (3)(d) in finding that the judge's discretion under s 26 had been wrongly exercised, since he had failed to safeguard the defendants' rights in accordance with the Art 6 requirements.

198 For discussion, see Sharpe [1994] Crim LR 793; Robertson, Crim LR 805; Heydon [1980] Crim LR 129; Birch, D 'Excluding Evidence from Entrapment: What is a "Fair Cop"?' (1994) 47 *Current Legal Problems* 73; Bradley, CM, *The Failure of the Criminal Procedure Revolution*, 1993, University of Pennsylvania Press; Choo, A L-T, *Abuse of Process and Judicial Stays of Criminal Proceedings*.
199 [1980] AC 402; [1979] All ER 1222, HL.
200 [1994] All ER 898; (1994) 98 Cr App R 437, CA.
201 See, e.g., *Maclean and Kosten* [1993] Crim LR 687; *Gill and Ranuana* [1991] Crim LR 358; *Edwards* [1991] Crim LR 45, CA.
202 See *Colin Stagg* (1994) unreported, but see news items in the *Guardian*, 15 September 1994, and *The Independent*, 15 September 1994; feature in *The Independent on Sunday*, 18 September 1994, p 16; see recent discussion: Cohen, N, *Observer*, 25 June 2006; *H* [1987] Crim LR 47.
203 [1993] Crim LR 775.

with cigarettes was left in a high crime area in order to catch would-be thieves. The resultant evidence was not excluded, since it was not found that it had been obtained by means of entrapment. The stance taken in *Smurthwaite* was confirmed by the House of Lords in *Shannon*[204] although the Lords took, it is suggested, a narrower view of practices amounting to entrapment. Reporters rather than undercover officers carried out a 'sting' operation in which evidence of drug dealing was obtained. Although it was arguable that the accused had, to an extent, been enticed into incriminating himself, the Lords found that the evidence thereby gained could rightly be viewed as admissible. It is suggested below that this stance is not fully in accord with that taken at Strasbourg.

In *Mason*,[205] the defendant had been tricked into confessing to damaging his neighbour's car by the police, who had falsely informed him and his solicitor that his fingerprints had been found on incriminating evidence. The Court of Appeal held that the confession should have been excluded under s 78: the trial judge had erred in omitting to take into account the deception practised on D's solicitor. The court appeared to view the deliberate deception practised by the police as the most significant factor without making it clear why the trial would be rendered unfair by admission of the confession gained thereby. It might have been better to have shown explicitly that the confession should be excluded on the basis that the police had acted improperly in deceiving the solicitor; the deception of the solicitor had resulted in receipt of the confession and the failure to exclude it meant that the court of first instance had, in effect, condoned the impropriety involved.

However, although deliberate impropriety may lead to the exclusion of evidence, it must, of course, be determined whether certain techniques will be designated improper. This issue has arisen particularly in the context of undercover police operations and secretly taped conversations. In *Bailey*,[206] investigating officers and the custody officer put on a charade intended to convince the suspects who had been charged that they did not wish to place them both in the same cell, which was bugged. This fooled the suspects who made incriminating admissions. It was submitted that the admissions should not have been admissible as undermining the spirit of Code C and especially the right to silence, since the men could not have been questioned by police at that point. However, the Court of Appeal rejected this argument on the basis that the evidence was reliable and that the conversation between the suspects could not be equated with a police interview. In other words, although there was a deception, and therefore the police could be viewed as passively recording a conversation that would have occurred anyway, that fact had no influence on the decision.

In *Christou*,[207] undercover police set up a jeweller's shop purporting to be willing to deal in stolen property and transactions with customers were recorded by means of recording equipment hidden in the shop. The police officers engaged in conversation with the defendants who came to sell recently stolen jewellery and asked them questions.

204 [2001] 1 WLR 51.
205 [1987] Crim LR 119; [1987] 3 All ER 481, CA; see also *Woodall and Others* [1989] Crim LR 288 in which the 'trick' consisted of allowing the detainee to think that an off-the-record interview could take place in the police station.
206 (1993) *The Times*, 22 March; [1993] 3 All ER 513.
207 [1992] QB 979; [1992] 4 All ER 559, CA. See also *Williams and O'Hare v DPP* [1993] Crim LR 775; *Smurthwaite* [1994] 1 All ER 898, CA.

They also asked the defendants to sign receipts for the jewellery. The defendants were convicted of handling stolen goods and appealed on the basis that all the evidence against them gained through the undercover operation should have been excluded either at common law under the principles enunciated in *Sang*[208] or under s 78 as obtained by deception: they would not have entered the shop had they known its true nature. This submission was rejected on the basis that the appellants had not been tricked, but had 'voluntarily applied themselves to the trick'; although specific deception had occurred, such as the request to sign the receipts, that was to be treated as part of the general deceit concerning the dishonest jeweller's shop. Therefore, the trick had not resulted in unfairness. The test for unfairness was the same at common law and under s 78.

It was also submitted that the conversations were an interview within the purview of Code of Practice C; the provisions applying to interviews should, therefore, have been followed. This submission was rejected on the basis that the Code provisions were intended to apply only where police officer and suspect were on an unequal footing because the officer was perceived to be in a position of authority. However, this was not to be taken as encouragement to officers to use undercover operations as a method of circumventing the Code provisions. In saying this, the court clearly recognised the danger that this ruling might encourage plain clothes police officers to operate secretly using hidden tape recorders to tape admissions, in preference to arresting openly and administering a caution. However, their remarks left open the possibility that such action, if cleverly enough disguised as a genuinely necessary undercover operation, could lead to circumvention of Code C and consequent erosion of the privilege against self-incrimination.

In *Bryce*,[209] the Court of Appeal was clearly fully alive to this danger. An undercover police officer posed as the buyer of a stolen car and, in conversation with the appellant, asked him questions designed to show that the car in question was stolen. The appellant allegedly gave incriminating replies. He was then arrested, refused to comment during the tape recorded interview, but allegedly made further admissions after the tape recorder had been turned off. He appealed against conviction on the ground that the evidence of the conversations and the interview was inadmissible under s 78. On the issue as to the admissibility of the conversation with the undercover officer, it was determined that the case differed from that of *Christou* on the following grounds: first, the questions asked went directly to the issue of dishonesty and were not necessary to the undercover operation; secondly, the possibility of concoction arose, whereas in *Christou* the conversations were taped. As to the unrecorded interview, the possibility of concoction clearly arose, owing to the suspicious willingness of the appellant to make admissions after refusing to do so during the recorded interview. Therefore, the judge at trial should have exercised discretion to exclude both the conversation and the unrecorded interview. Difficulty will arise after these two cases where it appears possible that a purported undercover operation has been used to circumvent the provisions of Code C, especially the need to caution, but the possibility of concoction does not arise, owing to the use of a hidden tape recorder. A court may have to draw a very fine line between questions asked going directly to the issue of guilt and those touching obliquely on it.

208 [1980] AC 402; [1979] 2 All ER 1222, HL.
209 [1992] 4 All ER 567; (1992) Cr App R 230; (1992) 142 NLJ 1161, CA.

The common theme running through the cases considered is the use of a deception of one sort or another. The courts have had to draw fine lines between degrees of deception in determining whether or not admission of the evidence obtained would render the trial unfair. A rather different stance is taken, as indicated above, towards instances of secret recording in which no positive deception occurs, those in which it may be said that the role of the police is confined only to recording a conversation which would have taken place in any event. In such instances, it cannot be said that the police deception is instrumental in obtaining the evidence except in the hypothetical sense: had the defendant applied his mind to the possibility of secret recording, he might not have made the admissions in question. Passive secret recording may thus be contrasted with instances in which the police, or someone acting on their behalf, have created a situation which makes it likely that admissions will be made where otherwise they would not have been. This distinction may have led the courts to accept evidence derived from secret recordings[210] (except in the case of telephone tapping, where special rules apply)[211] more readily than evidence deriving from a 'positive' deception, since in comparison with other forms of deception, secret recording seems to be at the lower end of the scale. Moreover, although evidence obtained from secret recordings may have the same inculpatory effect as a confession made in police custody, the courts seem to view the two methods of obtaining admissions differently. The tendency, which reflects the reliability principle, is to view secretly recorded evidence as unaffected by the manner of its acquisition, unlike admissions made to the police in an interview conducted in breach of PACE. However, although secret recording may be regarded as less improper than the use of a positive deception, it may involve other forms of impropriety. Thus, in focusing only or mainly on the reliability of evidence obtained, the courts have demonstrated a clear preference for crime control over due process.

As discussed above, *Teixeira de Castro v Portugal*[212] laid down quite a strict test in relation to evidence obtained by entrapment. Where there had been enticement by undercover officers to supply drugs, the applicant was found to have been 'definitively deprived of a fair trial'.[213] The case could be distinguished from *Ludi v Switzerland*,[214] in which no breach of Art 6 was found where a police officer had posed as a buyer in a drug deal which was already under way. The Court, therefore, did not find that undercover work of this type would inevitably affect the fairness of the trial. The test was whether the defendant could be said to be 'predisposed' to commit the offence in question. If so, unfairness would not be established. This test arguably differs slightly from the current one under UK law. As indicated above, if undercover officers give the defendant an *opportunity* to commit the offence where it appears that he would have committed it had the opportunity been offered by someone else, that is not entrapment;

---

210 See, e.g., *Shaukat Ali* (1991) *The Times*, 19 February; *Chief Constable of West Yorkshire Police ex p Govell* (1994) transcript from LEXIS; *Effick* (1992) 95 Cr App R 427, CA; [1994] 3 All ER 458, HL; *Roberts* (1997) 1 Cr App R 217.

211 See *Preston* [1993] 4 All ER 638; (1994) 98 Cr App R 405, HL. See now the scheme under RIPA 2000, s 17; discussed in Chapter 10, pp 1047–52.

212 (1998) 28 EHRR 101; [1998] Crim LR 751. See also *Van Mechelen v Netherlands* (1998) 25 EHRR 647; the findings of the Commission and Court in *Rowe and Davis* (2000) 30 EHRR 1; *Condron v UK* (2001) 31 EHRR 1.

213 Ibid, para 39.

214 (1993) 15 EHRR 173.

but it will amount to entrapment if they impliedly persuade him into it or otherwise can be said to instigate it. It is suggested that while *Smurthwaite*[215] is probably in harmony with the test as laid down by the Court in *Teixeira, Williams and O'Hare v DPP* is not, since it was not certain that the particular offences in question would have been committed without the intervention of those conducting the 'sting'.

However, the first domestic decision to apply *Teixeira, Nottingham CC v Mohammed Amin*,[216] gave it a restrictive interpretation in distinguishing it on somewhat narrow grounds. The respondent, who was driving an unlicensed motor vehicle, responded to a flagging down by two constables posing as members of the public; he took them to their destination, where the fare was paid over. He contended that the constables had not confined themselves to passive investigation but had incited him to commit the offence, thereby rendering the proceedings as a whole unfair. Lord Bingham found that he had not been pressured or incited into committing an offence. The basis on which it was found that flagging him down – a positive action – was not incitement to commit the offence is, it is suggested, unclear. The respondent had turned off his light, thereby indicating that he was not for hire. Similarly, in *Shannon*,[217] the Court of Appeal was unwilling to characterise the behaviour of the reporters as being that of *agents provocateurs*. But it was also found that even if their behaviour had crossed the borderline into that of an agent provocateur, it would not have been viewed as right to disturb the discretion of the judge to admit the evidence.[218] This stance was confirmed in *AG's Reference (No 3 of 2000)*[219] in which, on facts bearing quite a strong resemblance to those of *Teixeira*, it was found that the judge should not have stayed the trial, applying *Teixeira*, on the basis that the defendant had been encouraged to commit the offence in question by the undercover officers. Instead, it was found that the fact of enticement to commit the offence was not enough: a number of questions should have been asked concerning the defendant's freedom of choice and the extent to which he had been pressured into supplying drugs.

Thus, the key question appears to be whether the courts are prepared to express disapproval of certain evidence gathering techniques by excluding the evidence in question, as *Teixeira* arguably appears to require. In *Shannon*, the Court of Appeal appeared to be determined to view *Teixeira* as an abuse of process case rather than as applicable to exclusion of evidence, on the basis that to find otherwise would create a conflict with the finding of the Court in *Schenk*.[220] On this basis, the courts are able to disregard possible conflicts between the domestic basis for excluding evidence obtained by *agent provocateurs* and the Strasbourg basis, as expressed in *Teixeira*. It is suggested that determination to retain and maximise judicial discretion, allowing for the pursuit of crime control aims untrammelled by due process constraints imported from Strasbourg, provides the true reason for taking this view of *Teixeira*.

215 [1994] 1 All ER 898.
216 [2000] 1 WLR 1071; [2000] Crim LR 174.
217 [2001] 1 WLR 51.
218 Ibid, p 73, para 50.
219 [2001] Crim LR 645.
220 (1988) 13 EHRR 242.

Section 82(3): the common law discretion

Section 82(3) provides:

> Nothing in this part of the Act shall prejudice any power of a court to exclude evidence (whether by preventing questions from being put or otherwise) at its discretion.

This provision presumably preserves the whole of the common law discretion to exclude evidence, thanks to inclusion in it of the words 'or otherwise'. In practice, its role as regards exclusion of evidence is likely to be insignificant, owing to the width of s 78. However, a distinct function for s 82(3) was suggested in *Sat-Bhambra*;[221] it was held that ss 76 and 78 only operate before the evidence is led before the jury, but that s 82(3) can be invoked after that point. Similarly, Zander[222] argues that the common law discretion to exclude evidence is covered by both s 78 and s 82(3). Thus at present, s 82(3) may have a significant role to play only in preserving the judicial function of the judge in protecting witnesses or asking the jury to disregard evidence. The judge can at any point direct the jury to disregard evidence which has already been admitted and which may be unreliable.

In *O'Leary*,[223] May CJ expressed the view that s 82(3) rather than s 78 preserves the common law discretion to exclude unreliable evidence (presumably in circumstances falling outside s 76(2)(b)). However, it is hard to see how to separate the questions of the admissibility of unreliable evidence and of unfairness at the trial. Admission of unreliable evidence will always affect the trial. In *Parris*,[224] evidence which may have been fabricated by the police was excluded under s 78, not s 82(3). It appears likely that s 78 will continue to be used as a means of excluding unreliable evidence if s 76(2)(b) cannot be invoked.

Mentally handicapped defendants: special rules

As noted above, the confession of a suspect who is mentally disordered or of low intelligence may be rendered inadmissible under s 76(2)(b) if the interrogation is not conducted with particular propriety.[225] However, special rules will apply in the case of some mentally handicapped defendants. The confession of a mentally retarded defendant must be treated with particular caution. Under s 77, in such an instance, if the confession was not made in the presence of an independent person and if the case depends largely on the confession, the jury must be warned to exercise particular caution before convicting. (This does not apply to the mentally ill, although the Royal Commission has recommended that it should be extended to cover all categories of mentally disordered suspects.)[226]

---

221 (1988) JP Rep 365; (1988) Cr App R 55.
222 Zander, op. cit., fn 1 2nd edn, p 210. Case law has not identified a distinction between the functions of the two sections (see, e.g., *Christou* [1992] 4 All ER 559).
223 [1988] Crim LR 827, CA.
224 (1989) 9 Cr App R 68, CA.
225 See above, p 1274.
226 Report Proposal 85.

In some such instances, s 77 need not be invoked because the judge should withdraw the case from the jury. In *McKenzie*[227] the appellant, who was of subnormal intelligence and had sexual problems, was arrested and questioned about arson offences and about the killing of two elderly women. He made detailed admissions as to the arson offences and the two killings in a series of interviews. He also admitted to ten other killings which he had not committed. He appealed against his conviction for manslaughter and arson and it was held on appeal that where the prosecution case depends wholly on confession evidence, the defendant is significantly mentally handicapped and the confessions are unconvincing, the judge should withdraw the case from the jury. When these three tests were applied in the instant case in respect of the confessions to the killings, it was found that they were satisfied, the third largely by the doubt cast on the appellant's credibility owing to his confessions to killings he could not have committed. However, the first test was not satisfied in respect of the convictions for arson. Those convictions could therefore stand, but those for manslaughter were quashed. These rules are clearly of value as a means of affording protection to a group of persons who are least able to withstand pressure from the police and most likely to make a false confession. However, it is suggested that the second test could usefully be broadened so that it includes all those suffering from significant mental impairment at the time when the offences took place.

Conclusions: moving beyond due process and crime control

It was argued in the Introduction to this chapter that a more developed conception of criminal justice would take into account the interests of victims in dignity and in equality as well as the requirement of fairness to the accused. The issues of exclusion of evidence and of staying the proceedings provide a forum for considering what such a more developed conception might mean. Rape cases in particular highlight the problem of concentrating only on a gender-neutral account of the requirements of fairness to the accused, although the issues they raise also have a wider application.

It could be argued that where evidence which is reliable is crucial to the case, the Convention rights of the victim should be taken into account in making a determination as to its admittance or exclusion. If the accused walks free from court, the victim's life may be profoundly disrupted owing to psychological disturbance, fear, and physical constraints, such as feeling forced to move to a different area. She is likely to be profoundly affected in the free ordering of her life by the knowledge that the rapist is at large. These experiences may occur in any event, but there is a large body of evidence to the effect that the victim's recovery is affected by the conviction of the attacker,[228] while her physical security at the point at which she is psychologically most vulnerable will be affected by the fact that he has been imprisoned. Thus, it is argued that a developed conception of criminal justice would allow such considerations to be taken into account, under the rubrics of Arts 8, 14 and 3. The issue might be put squarely before the court if, for example, a women's campaigning group was allowed

---

227 [1993] 1 WLR 453; (1992) 142 NLJ 1162, CA.
228 See, e.g., Lees, S, *Ruling Passions, Sexual Violence, Reputation and the Law*, 1997, Open University Press; *Sexual Violence: The Reality for Women*, 1999, The Women's Press.

to intervene in order to argue that the courts' duty under s 6 of the HRA required it to take the victims' Convention rights into account.

Similar considerations apply in respect of the victims of many offences. The victim of a serious violent offence may be said to suffer a violation of his or her right to security of the person and possibly to privacy and freedom of movement if an offender is acquitted, not on the basis of doubts about his or her guilt, but as a result of police impropriety. The victim of a racial attack, or the family of the victim, may experience a similar restriction. Article 2 might also be engaged. To take an extreme example: if, in the case of a trial for attempted murder, a court excluded, owing to a serious breach of Art 8, tape recorded evidence linking a defendant with a history of domestic violence to the attempted murder of his wife, the possibility of her subsequent murder could be viewed as engaging the duty of the court under s 6 of the HRA to abide by Art 2.[229]

Such arguments clearly look like crime-control arguments and they may well lead to the same outcome. However, feminist and victim-orientated arguments should not merely be co-opted by advocates of crime control.[230] The difference is that such arguments may be viewed as based on principle, while crime control arguments are purely consequentialist. While the crime control model would not allow for a nuanced, proportionate approach to exclusion of evidence since it would merely ask whether it was reliable, the approach which takes account of the victims' interests can be more nuanced since in some instances, the victims' interests could not be said to be engaged. The question is whether to elevate the concerns of Art 6 above those of Arts 8 or 3 or 14, which are, or may be, it is argued, engaged by the issues in question. Clearly, the court has a public duty to uphold standards of criminal justice which go beyond the interests of the victim.[231] However, strands of Convention jurisprudence are emerging which may allow for those interests to be taken into account in adoption of a nuanced approach.[232] The Convention provides a growing recognition of victims' rights.[233] In particular, there is now a significant body of jurisprudence recognising rights of victims and victims' families within the criminal justice system where the state is the 'attacker'.[234] Thus, there is a case for arguing, under the HRA, that the impact of a decision to exclude evidence or stay the proceedings should be considered from a perspective which is not bounded by Art 6 concerns alone.

While due process demands that improperly obtained evidence should be excluded, that the police officers involved should be disciplined or prosecuted, and, where appropriate, that compensation should be available, it is unclear that it demands, in principle, that a person who is factually guilty of an offence should be acquitted. If evidence is excluded and, as a result, the burden of proof cannot be discharged, acquittal must clearly follow. But methods of escaping from the conflicts of interest indicated

---

229 See *Osman v UK* (2000) 29 EHRR 245, discussed in Chapter 2, pp 41 and 62.

230 For discussion, see Whitty, N, Murphy, T and Livingstone, S, *Civil Liberties Law*, 2000, p 194; Young, J, *The Exclusive Society: Social Exclusion, Crime and Difference in Late Modernity*, 1999, Sage.

231 See Fenwick, H, 'Procedural rights of victims of crime: public or private ordering of the criminal justice process?' (1997) 60 MLR 317–33.

232 See further Chapter 2, pp 41–42.

233 See *X and Y v Netherlands* (1985) 8 EHRR 235.

234 *Kaya v Turkey* (1998-I) ECtHR 297; *Akdivar v Turkey* (1997) 23 EHRR 143; *Mentes v Turkey* (1997) 27 EHRR 595; *Gulec v Turkey* (1999) 28 EHRR 121; *Cetin v Turkey* (unreported); *Tekin v Turkey* RJD 1998-IV 53.

inherent in such exclusion should be sought. Such acquittals uphold the integrity of the criminal justice system since they demonstrate a refusal of the courts to associate themselves with a fundamental breach of rights, but they profoundly fail to address the interests of victims, also recognised at Strasbourg, their relatives, and the general societal interest in the prevention of crime. Moreover, although exclusion of evidence may have symbolic value in terms of integrity, it has not been viewed at Strasbourg as providing an effective remedy for breach of a Convention right,[235] and it clearly can have no impact on the overwhelming majority of cases in which the defendant pleads guilty. Given that, increasingly, the police know that the case is unlikely to come to trial,[236] the deterrent effect of exclusion, such as it is, may be diminishing. Even in cases that do come to trial, exclusion of evidence can have no impact where there is other evidence which can support the conviction. Stays for abuse of process are rarely used and arguably their use is arbitrary; therefore, they are unlikely to have a significant impact on police practice.

These arguments strengthen the case for further, more radical reform of the police complaints and disciplinary system and of CPS decision-making, since so doing would tend to discourage illegality and impropriety and enhance levels of adherence to the PACE rules, including the Code provisions. Arguments for exclusion of evidence on the basis of police impropriety might be raised less frequently. There is a further pragmatic reason for adopting this approach. The judges have made it clear that despite the inception of the HRA, they are wedded to the common law tradition of admitting evidence even if it has been obtained improperly. If anything, decisions such as *Forbes* and *Shannon* suggest that their determination to adhere to this tradition has been *strengthened* by the inception of the HRA. Possibly, this is another example of the common law resisting or subsuming the influence of the Convention. Maintenance of judicial discretion to react to the facts of particular cases remains the overwhelming priority and, in furtherance of this aim, the requirements of Art 6 have been minimised. Given that this clear pattern is now emerging, remedies must be sought elsewhere, while at the same time failures of police accountability should be used to press for organisational reforms.[237] The efficacy of such other remedies is considered below.

4 Tortious remedies[238]

Tort actions

Tort damages will be available as a result of some breaches of PACE, the TA and other relevant statutes. For example, if a police officer arrests a citizen where no reasonable suspicion arises under s 24 PACE, an action for false imprisonment will be available. Equally, such a remedy would be available if the Part IV provisions governing time

---

235 *Khan v UK* (2000) 8 BHRC 310, paras 44–47.
236 See further Sanders and Young, op. cit., fn 1, Chapter 7.
237 See Sanders and Young, op. cit., fn 1, pp 724–30.
238 See Clayton, R and Tomlinson, H, *Civil Actions Against the Police*, 3rd edn, 2003, for examples of recent damages awards. See also Sanders and Young, op. cit., fn 1, Chapter 12, Part 3.

limits on detention were breached[239] or if a detention review failed to occur for a period of time.[240] Trespass to land or to goods will occur if the statutory provisions providing powers to search premises or seize goods are not followed. Malicious prosecution will be available where police have abused their powers in recommending prosecution to the Crown Prosecution Service. Also, one of the ancient 'malicious process torts' may be available where a malicious search or arrest has occurred, although in fact these actions are extremely rare and their continued existence is in doubt.[241] Such actions may not be brought because a claim of false imprisonment is preferred, but there is a distinction between malicious process torts and false imprisonment in that in the former case, but not the latter, all the proper procedural formalities will have been carried out. Actions for malicious prosecution are quite common, but the plaintiff carries quite a heavy burden in the need to prove that there was no reasonable or probable cause for the prosecution.[242] It may be that if the prosecution is brought on competent legal advice, this action will fail, but this is unclear.[243]

Almost the whole of the interviewing scheme, which is contained mainly in Codes C, E and H rather than in PACE or the TA, is unaffected by tortious remedies. Section 67(10) of PACE provides that no civil or criminal liability arises from a breach of the Codes of Practice. The same is true of the TA Codes under Sched 12, para 6 to the TA. This lack of a remedy also extends to some statutory provisions, in particular the most significant statutory interviewing provision, the entitlement to legal advice, arising under both PACE and the TA.[244] There is no tort of denial of access to legal advice; the only possible tortious action would be for breach of statutory duty. It might have been expected that an action for false imprisonment might lie where gross breaches of the questioning provisions had taken place, such as interviewing a person unlawfully held incommunicado: a detention in itself lawful might thereby be rendered unlawful. However, although the ruling in *Middleweek v Chief Constable of Merseyside*[245] gave some encouragement to such argument, it now seems to be ruled out by the decision in *Weldon v Home Office*[246] in the context of lawful detention in a prison. It seems likely, therefore, that access to legal advice, like the rest of the safeguards for interviewing, will continue to be unaffected by the availability of the pre-HRA tortious remedies although, as discussed below, action under s 7(1)(a) of the HRA might be possible.

Where actions in tort *are* available against the police, they may be of particular value owing to the willingness of the courts to accept that exemplary or punitive damages may sometimes be appropriate. Such damages are awarded to punish the defendant and

---

239 E.g., *Edwards v Chief Constable of Avon and Somerset* (1992) 9 March, unreported; the plaintiff was detained for 8 hours, 47 minutes following a lawful arrest. The detention was wrongful because it was 'unnecessary'; compensation was awarded.

240 In *Roberts* [1999] 1 WLR 662 the review took place two hours after it should have done. The Court of Appeal found that Roberts had been falsely imprisoned during those two hours even though it was found that, had the review taken place, he would have remained in detention.

241 See Clayton, R and Tomlinson, H, *Civil Actions Against the Police*, 1st edn, 1987, p 284. For discussion, see Winfield, *History of Conspiracy and Abuse of Legal Process*, 1921.

242 See *Glinskie v McIver* [1962] AC 726.

243 *Abbott v Refuge Assurance Co Ltd* [1962] 1 QB 632.

244 See Chapter 12, p 1210.

245 [1992] AC 179; [1990] 3 WLR 481.

246 [1991] WLR 340, CA.

will be available only in two instances:[247] where there has been 'oppressive, arbitrary or unconstitutional behaviour by the servants of the government' or where the profit accruing to the defendant through his conduct may be greater than the compensation awarded to the plaintiff. Only the first of these two categories will be relevant in actions against the police, and in order that such damages should be available, the term 'servant of the government' has been broadly interpreted to include police officers.[248]

If a civil action is brought against an officer on the basis that he or she has acted *ultra vires* and the officer shows that the statutory conditions for the exercise of power were present, the onus lies on the plaintiff to establish the relevant facts (*Greene v Home Secretary*).[249] In *Holgate-Mohammed v Duke* (1984),[250] the House of Lords confirmed that, in addition to showing that the relevant statutory conditions are satisfied, the exercise of statutory powers by officers must not offend against *Wednesbury* principles; officers must not take irrelevant factors into account or fail to have regard to relevant ones; an exercise of discretion must not be so unreasonable that no reasonable officer could have exercised it in the manner in question. In *Ministry of Defence ex p Smith and Others*,[251] the Court of Appeal affirmed that in judging whether the decision-maker had decided unreasonably, the human rights context was important; the more substantial the interference with human rights, the more the court would require by way of justification before it was satisfied that the decision was reasonable. Under s 6 HRA, the question (which arises under s 7) is whether, in the exercise of discretionary powers, whether or not statute-based, the police breached a Convention right. Section 3 HRA is also relevant. This question is returned to below.

Quantum of damages

Civil actions against the police have in the past attracted high levels of damages. One of the highest awards was made in *White v Metropolitan Police Comr*.[252] Police officers unlawfully entered the home of a middle-aged black couple at night and attacked the plaintiffs. The police then charged both plaintiffs with various offences in order to cover up their own conduct. The plaintiffs were awarded £20,000 exemplary damages each and, respectively, £6,500 and £4,500 aggravated damages. One of the highest awards was made in *Treadaway v Chief Constable of West Midlands*:[253] £50,000, which included £40,000 exemplary damages, was awarded in respect of a serious assault perpetrated in order to obtain a confession. In 1996, a number of very high awards were made against the Metropolitan Police. In *Goswell v Comr of Metropolitan Police*[254] the plaintiff was awarded £120,000 damages for assault, £12,000 for false imprisonment and £170,000

247 This limitation was imposed by the House of Lords in *Rookes v Barnard* [1964] AC 1129, p 1226. Note that the Law Commission, *Consultation Paper on Punitive Damages*, Consultation No 132, 1993, advocates, in its provisional conclusion, retention of such damages, but that they should be placed on a more principled basis.
248 *Broome v Cassell and Co* [1972] AC 1027, at 1088.
249 [1942] AC 284, HL.
250 [1984] AC 437; [1984] 1 All ER 1054, HL.
251 [1996] 1 All ER 257; [1996] ICR 740.
252 (1982) *The Times*, 24 April.
253 (1994) *The Times*, 25 October.
254 (1996) the *Guardian*, 27 April.

exemplary damages for arbitrary and oppressive behaviour. Mr Goswell, who is black, was waiting in his car when a police officer approached. Goswell complained about the lack of police activity over an arson attack on his home. He was handcuffed to and then struck by the officer; the blow left a permanent scar. Goswell was then arrested for assault and threatening behaviour. He was cleared of these charges and then brought the successful civil action.

In *Hsu v Comr of Metropolitan Police*,[255] the plaintiff won £220,000 damages for assault and wrongful arrest at his home. In *Kownacki v Comr of Metropolitan Police*,[256] actions for false imprisonment and malicious prosecution against the Metropolitan Police were successful; 200 police invaded the plaintiff's pub and charged him with supplying cannabis and allowing the premises to be used for drug dealing. When the case came to trial, the prosecution offered no evidence and he was acquitted. As a result, he suffered depression and paranoia, which affected his work. The jury found that the officers had failed to prove that they had seen cannabis being openly smoked and sold on the premises during the surveillance operation; £108,750, including £45,000 of punitive damages, were awarded to reflect the jury's disapproval.

However, these high awards are no longer available. The question of the appropriate level of damages was addressed by the Court of Appeal in *Thompson v Commissioner of Police for the Metropolis*.[257] The Court laid down guidelines for the award of damages which took as a starting-point a basic award of £500 for the first hour of unlawful detention, with decreasing amounts for subsequent hours. It was found that aggravated damages could be awarded where there were special features of the case, such as oppressive or humiliating conduct at the time of arrest. Such damages would start at around £1,000 but would not normally be more than twice the level of the basic damages. Exemplary damages should only be awarded where aggravated and basic damages together would not appear to provide a sufficient punishment. Exemplary damages would be not less than £5,000, but the total figure awarded as exemplary damages would not be expected to amount to more than the basic damages multiplied by three. The overall award should not exceed £50,000. In accordance with these guidelines, the award made in *Hsu* was reduced to £50,000.

The HRA and tortious liability

Sections 6 and 8 of the HRA require the courts to offer a remedy where a public authority violates the Convention rights,[258] unless in so doing it is acting in accordance with incompatible legislation.[259] As Chapter 11 indicated, Arts 3, 5, 8 and 14 potentially cover certain pre-trial rights of suspects, regardless of the trial context. Tortious liability arises and damages can be awarded under s 8 of the HRA if one or more of these Articles is found to have been breached in respect of police treatment of suspects. As indicated, some custodial treatment in breach of these Articles is already tortious

---

255 [1997] 2 All ER 762.
256 (1996) the *Guardian*, 30 April.
257 [1997] 2 All ER 762.
258 Sections 6(1), 7 and 8. For discussion, see Chapter 4, pp 215 *et seq.*, esp 241–47.
259 Section 6(2). Section 3 requires that the legislation should rendered compatible with the Convention rights 'so far as it is possible to do so'.

under domestic law, and civil actions against the police have provided an increasingly significant means of creating some police accountability,[260] but this possibility is clearly of particular significance where domestic law currently fails to provide a tortious remedy in respect of the maltreatment of detainees.

The domestic courts may eventually have to reconsider their current approach to conditions of detention in terms of tortious liability. Prior to the inception of the HRA, so long as existing torts or offences, such as assault, were not committed in detention, it followed from the findings in *Weldon v Home Office*[261] that no means of redress in respect of adverse conditions, other than a complaint, was available. The possible creation of liability[262] under the Convention by means of a creative interpretation of the guarantee under Art 8 not only fills a gap in domestic law, it could in effect extend the Convention rights which, as noted above, do not on their face cover most conditions of detention. Such a course would not necessarily involve departing from the findings in *Weldon v Home Office*, since the liability would be for breach of a Convention right under s 6, using s 7(1)(a) of the HRA, not for false imprisonment. In any event, departure from case law is clearly possible under the HRA, relying on the duty of the court under s 6 and the effect of the Strasbourg jurisprudence under s 2.[263]

The HRA affects existing tort actions in three ways in this context where a tort operates in the same area as a Convention right. First, the powers that the police are relying on in order to prevent civil liability from arising can be interpreted under ss 3 and 6 HRA and the relevant right, more narrowly. Once this has occurred, the action may be found to be tortious, whereas pre-HRA it would have been non-tortious. Thus, where an existing tort action is brought which covers the same ground as a Convention right and relates to the exercise of discretionary powers by the police, it can be argued under s 7(1)(b) that the officer had breached the Convention right in their exercise and had therefore acted unlawfully. This is in essence a question of proportionality in relation to Art 8 or a question of the content and requirements of the right in relation to Arts 2, 3, 5 and 6.[264] Unless s 6(2) HRA applies to a statutory power, the action would succeed if the breach could be established, whether or not the exercise of the power appeared to have a statutory or common law basis. Alternatively, s 3 HRA can be relied on where the power is statute-based in order to show that once the provision in question is interpreted compatibly with the relevant Convention right(s), it does not provide the power to act as the officer did.

Second, the tort action itself should be interpreted compatibly with the Convention rights under s 6 HRA (if it is statute-based, s 3 would also be relevant). It is arguable that it should be aligned with the relevant Convention right, but in any event it should not be interpreted in such a way as to be found to be incompatible with that right.

---

260 See the Home Affairs Committee First Report 1997–98, *Police Disciplinary and Complaints Procedures* printed 16.12.97, which noted (para 32) the 'striking' rise in the cost of civil settlements for the Metropolitan Police, from £0.47m in 1991 to £2.69m in 1996. (This figure may decline owing to the decision in *Thompson*, [1997] 2 All ER 762.) The Police Action Lawyers Group and the Commission For Racial Equality attributed the rise to disillusionment with the complaints process.
261 [1990] 3 All ER 672.
262 Under HRA 1998, ss 6 and 7. The HRA does not allow for the creation of new criminal liability.
263 See, in a different context, *Douglas v Hello!* [2001] 2 WLR 992.
264 See further Chapter 2, p 40 *et seq*.

Third, where a Convention right covers the same ground as a tort action, the plaintiff may claim a cause of action under the tort and also under the right, relying on s 7(1)(a) HRA. So the ambit of the right and the width of any exceptions to it will form part of the judgment; Strasbourg case law and domestic case law on those matters will be taken into account. So where a tort action arises within the area covered by a Convention right, the right, and ss 6 and 7 HRA, have a triple impact. This triple effect is illustrated in the discussion of the following case. It is fully discussed in Chapter 8,[265] but parts of the discussion are highly relevant here so some repetition is unavoidable.

Austin and Saxby v Commissioner of Police of the Metropolis[266] concerned a political demonstration against capitalism and globalisation that was organised in the heart of the West End of London on May Day 2001. The police detained thousands of demonstrators for about seven hours by forming a cordon around them on the grounds of the need to prevent a threatened breach of the peace. The claimants brought a claim for damages, alleging false imprisonment and also deprivation of liberty, contrary to Art 5, European Convention on Human Rights, raising the claim under s 7 HRA. The issues under the tort action and under Art 5 were dealt with separately since, as discussed in Chapter 8, the judge found that different factors were relevant in both claims. The judge accepted that the tort must not be interpreted inconsistently with Art 5, under s 6. Clearly this would mean, under s 6, that a claim could not succeed under Art 5 but fail under the tort, although the converse would be possible. Much of the judgment concerned the extent of the powers to prevent a breach of the peace that the police relied on in order to justify the detention. Those aspects answer to the first aspect of the effect of the HRA on tort actions against the police, and are considered in Chapter 8.

Having considered the ambit of Art 5(1) and the width of the exception under Art 5(1)(c) – the third matter mentioned above – the detention was found to be justified under Art 5(1)(c). So the claims of breach of Art.5 were found to fail in respect of both claimants. It was found, in relation to the claim of false imprisonment, that the claimants had been imprisoned within the cordon, but that the police had a defence of necessity in so trapping them, which defeated the false imprisonment claim. The judge sought to ensure that the tort was interpreted compatibly with Art 5 under s 6 HRA, but as argued in Chapter 8, he fell into error in allowing a broad defence of necessity to operate, which it is argued in that chapter, is not in harmony with the exception under Art 5(1)(c).[267]

As indicated in Chapter 11, a breach of the Code-based safeguards applying to the exercise of a prima facie tortious power will not deprive it of lawful authority owing to the provision against civil liability for such a breach under s 67(10) of PACE and Sched 12, para 6 to the TA. This is also the case, *a fortiori*, where a police action which does not require lawful authority in order to avoid such liability breaches a Code provision. But where provisions of Arts 3, 8, 5 or 14 are coterminous with Code safeguards, liability to pay damages under the HRA for breach of the Convention guarantees might provide the Code provisions with a form of indirect protection, as the more detailed embodiment of the Convention requirements. Chapter 11 identified, at the relevant points, Convention guarantees, including aspects of the Art 3 requirements, which have no domestic statutory basis, but are recognised only in certain Code provisions.[268] The creation of tortious liability indirectly protective of such provisions under the HRA is a very significant matter, since it might lead to a regulation of police interviewing practices and techniques which has been largely absent from UK law.

However, at present it is very doubtful whether Art 6 itself can be viewed as providing free-standing rights. Possible breaches of Art 6 are currently addressed within the criminal process itself. The Strasbourg jurisprudence does not cover instances in which the pre-trial procedure is flawed in a manner which might be viewed, potentially, as infringing the Art 6(1) guarantee of a fair trial, but where no court action in fact occurs. However, given that certain of the rights, and in particular the implied right of access to custodial legal advice under Art 6(3)(c), clearly have value outside the trial context, an action based on s 7(1)(a) or on a breach of the statutory duty under s 58 of PACE, but raising Art (3)(c) arguments under s 7(1)(b), might resolve this issue in favour of the complainant, domestically.

The quantum of damages must be determined in accordance with the provisions of s 8 which include the requirement, under s 8(4) of the HRA, that the court should take into account the principles applied by the European Court of Human Rights in relation to the award of compensation.[269] As indicated in Chapter 4, reliance on such principles means that the level of damages awarded is fairly low;[270] in particular, the Court has not, formally, awarded exemplary or aggravated damages[271] and it is probably the case that exemplary damages are not available under the HRA.[272] But where the applicant has a coterminous tort action, such as false imprisonment, s 8 should not be used to detract from the level of damages which would have been awarded prior to enactment of the HRA.[273] It may be noted that Art 5(5) provides an independent right to compensation if Art 5 is breached, but this does not appear to add anything to the damages already available for false imprisonment.

Conclusions: value of civil actions

The value of civil actions against the police in terms of ensuring police accountability is limited for a variety of reasons.[274] The cost factor will deter most potential plaintiffs from suing the police, especially now that legal aid is unavailable for an increasing

---

268 See esp pp 1171–83.

269 See further Leigh, I and Lustgarten, L, 'Making rights real: the courts, remedies and the Human Rights Act' [1999] CLJ 509; Feldman, D, 'Remedies for violations of human rights under the Human Rights Act' (1998) EHRLR 691; Amos, M, 'Damages for breach of the Human Rights Act' (1999) EHRLR 178.

270 Non-pecuniary damages are likely to be in the range of £10,000–15,000: see *Johnson v UK* (1997) 27 EHRR 296.

271 *B v UK* A 136-D (1988), paras 7–12.

272 See Clayton and Tomlinson, op. cit., fn 1, p 1437.

273 This follows from the HRA 1998, s 11.

274 It may be noted that if a civil action against a police officer is successful, he or she will not be personally liable. The Police Act 1964, s 48, provides that a chief constable will be vicariously liable in respect of torts committed by constables under his direction or control in the performance or purported performance of their functions.

section of the population.[275] There is a strong tendency to settle actions, which means that the police do not admit liability. Even where a civil action is successful, disciplinary charges are unlikely to be brought against the officers concerned. This has been justified by the police in the past on the basis of the differing standards of proof: civil claims need only be proved on the balance of probabilities while, until recently, disciplinary charges had to be proved beyond reasonable doubt. This is no longer the case, as explained below. Therefore, disciplinary action might be expected to follow a successful civil action, although there is no statutory requirement that it must do so, even in particularly serious cases. The high jury awards of damages in 1996 may reflect a growing public perception that the police are insufficiently accountable. If nothing else, a continuing propensity to make such awards might have helped to draw public and parliamentary attention to an unsatisfactory situation. However, the decision of the Court of Appeal in *Thompson* will make this less likely.

The HRA has not affected the quantum of damages or the practical problems of suing the police. There is clearly something anomalous about creating a vast, complex statutory or quasi-legislative edifice (PACE, the TA, the CJP, the Codes) which governs police powers and suspects' rights, but then failing to provide a remedy if those rights are breached, except where that breach is coterminous with an existing area of tortious liability. Thus the HRA can, in theory, have a significant impact in respect of civil liability, since it has created for the first time under ss 7(1)(a) and 8 a remedy in damages where Convention rights are breached in custody by the police, whether or not existing tortious liability would arise. Moreover, the Convention rights now provide the parameters within which discretionary powers must be exercised, under s 6 of the HRA.

5 Complaints against the police and disciplinary action[276]

The current scheme[277]

Background[278]

Clearly, the police complaints and disciplinary system provides a potential method of ensuring that the police adhere to the safeguards created by PACE, as amended, and the

---

275 See *Legal Action*, April 2000, p 34; for discussion, see Hansen, O, 'A future for legal aid?' (1992) 19 JLS 85; see also Sanders and Young, op. cit., fn 1, p 680.

276 See Maguire, M, 'Complaints against the police: the British experience', in Goldsmith, A (ed), *Complaints Against the Police: A Comparative Study*, 1990, Clarendon; Greaves [1985] Crim LR; Khan (1984) 129 SJ 455; Williams [1985] Crim LR 115; Lustgarten, L, *The Governance of Police*, 1986, pp 139–40. The Runciman Commission considered that the existing arrangements probably do not command public confidence: Cm 2263, p 46; Harrison, J, *Police Misconduct: Legal Remedies*, 1987, Legal Action Group; Triennial Review of the PCA 1991–94, HC 396 (1994–95); Home Affairs Committee Fourth Report, HC 179 (1991–92); Sanders, A and Young, R, *Criminal Justice*, 3rd edn, 2007, Chapter 12, Part 4; House of Commons Home Affairs Select Committee, Police Disciplinary and Complaints Procedure, First Report, HC-258-1 (1998).

277 See further R Stone *Civil Liberties and Human Rights*, 6th edn, 2006, Chapter 4.6.3; Complaints Against the Police: A Framework for a New System – available from the Home Office website: www.homeoffice.gov.uk.

278 See further: Goldsmith, AJ, *Complaints Against the Police: The Trend to External* Review, 1991; Goldsmith, AJ, 'Necessary but Not Sufficient: The Role of Public Complaints Procedures in Police Accountability', in Stenning, P C, (ed), *Accountability for Criminal Justice*, 1995, University of Toronto Press,

TA. PACE set up the Police Complaints Authority (PCA) as an independent body with an involvement in the complaints and disciplinary system, replacing the Police Complaints Board (PCB), which was set up under the Police Act 1976.[279] The idea was to afford an appearance of independence to the system. The scheme set up by PACE for dealing with complaints, contained in ss 83–106, was repealed and re-enacted in the Police Act 1996.[280] A new scheme was subsequently introduced under the Police Reform Act 2002. Under s 67(2) of the Police Act 1996, a complaint went in the first instance to the Chief Officer of Police of the force in question, who had to determine by reference to the section whether or not he was the appropriate person to deal with it and whether it, in fact, constituted a complaint about 'the conduct of an officer' and not about 'the direction or control' of a police force.[281] The decision as to the side of the dividing line on which a particular complaint fell was made by the police force complained about. Therefore, at the very outset, 'an issue of independence [arose]'.[282]

A complaint had to be referred to the PCA if it concerned serious misconduct.[283] Under s 75(3) of the 1996 Act, if the Chief Officer determined that the report on the complaints investigation indicated that a criminal offence might have been committed, he had to send a copy of it to the DPP. In addition, there was a discretionary power to refer complaints to the PCA. It did not carry out the investigation itself in such cases, but supervised it and received a report at the end of it under s 72. Thus, its role in relation to complaints was very limited. Independence was lacking in other respects: the remuneration system was under the control of the Home Secretary,[284] and under s 83 of the Police Act 1996, his guiding role was retained. Under s 69(5),[285] a member of the force which was the subject of the complaint could conduct the investigation

The changes to the complaints procedure which occurred in the mid-1990s, partly in response to the Runciman Royal Commission Report, did not involve any radical reform. In particular, they did not include the introduction of a new, independent element into the process. The Police and Magistrates' Courts Act 1994, which was then consolidated in the Police Act 1996, made only limited changes to the functions and powers of the PCA. Under s 37(a) of the 1994 Act, a breach of the PACE Codes became no longer automatically a breach of the Police Discipline Code.[286] This change could be seen merely as legitimising police working practices, since it appeared that very few complaints in respect of breaches of the Codes were made; those that were rarely led to disciplinary proceedings. Unsurprisingly, this trend continued after the 1994 Act came into force.[287] Part IV of the Police Act 1996, which then created

---

pp 110–34; Prenzler, T and Ronken, C, (2001), 'Models of Police Over sight: A Critique', *Policing and Society*, 11/3: pp 151–80.

279 The operation of the PCB did not create confidence in the complaints system: see Brown, *Police Complaints Procedure*, Home Office Research Study No 93, 1987.

280 Which came into force on 1 April 1999, replacing PACE 1984, Part IX.

281 PACE 1984, s 84(4) and (5). The requirement regarding 'the conduct of a police officer' then arose under s 65 of the 1996 Act.

282 Home Affairs Committee First Report (1997–98), para 47.

283 Police Act 1996, s 70, formerly PACE 1984, s 87(4).

284 See PCA Report 1998–99 Appendix C, para 5.

285 Which has replaced PACE 1984, s 105(4).

286 Section 37(a) repealed PACE 1984, s 67(8).

287 E.g., the PCA Report for 1998–99 showed that there were 107 complaints relating to breach of Code A, governing stop and search in the period. One led to disciplinary charges (Table 5, p 13).

the scheme governing complaints and discipline, did not affect this position; it was merely a consolidating, not a reforming, measure.

The 1997 Report of the Select Committee on Home Affairs[288] made a number of recommendations, reflecting a number of the criticisms as to lack of independence, and the Home Secretary, Jack Straw, said that he had accepted the case for speedy reform. But the initial proposals for reform[289] mirrored the moderate changes proposed by the Conservative Government in 1993.[290] Racist language and behaviour is now a breach of the police code of conduct, but it is not yet possible to determine how far reaching such change might be. It might also lead to a breach of the Race Relations Act 1976, as amended.[291]

The PCA in its 1998–99 Report noted that further, more radical changes, in particular the 'use of non-police investigators in exceptional cases', although accepted by the Home Secretary in principle, had been relegated to future legislation. The PCA concluded that there was no prospect of early legislation and mentioned its unsuccessful attempts to make the more non-controversial changes by means of Private Members' Bills.[292]

The House of Commons Home Affairs Committee[293] found 'perhaps the most telling evidence that all is not well ... comes from the opinion of almost all the parties involved';[294] they concluded: 'there is a great deal of justified dissatisfaction with elements of the disciplinary and complaints system.'[295] These criticisms echo those which have, for a number of years, been directed against the whole police disciplinary process, including the hearings, and it is generally agreed that the present system is defective as a means of redress.[296] Maguire and Corbett conducted a review of the operation of the complaints system from 1968 to 1988[297] which found that the majority of complainants were dissatisfied and that the public did not have confidence in the system. The Runciman Commission considered that the existing arrangements probably do not command public confidence.[298]

---

288 HC 258-I (1997–98).
289 HC 683 (1997–98).
290 The government issued a consultation paper in April 1993 which included various proposals, including abolition of the criminal standard of proof in discipline cases and the double jeopardy rule, which meant that criminal proceedings against officers were not followed by disciplinary proceedings. See 143 NLJ 591; in its Triennial Review 1988–91, HC 352, 1991, the PCA also made this proposal. The Labour proposals also addressed the tendency of police officers who are facing disciplinary charges to take extended sick leave and/or early retirement, thereby evading the disciplinary process.
291 See Chapter 15, pp 1508–10.
292 PCA Report (1998–99), p 53.
293 Home Affairs Committee, HC 258-I (1997–98).
294 Paragraph 35.
295 Paragraph 40.
296 See Greaves [1985] Crim LR; Khan (1984) 129 SJ 455; Williams [1985] Crim LR 115; Lustgarten, L, *The Governance of Police*, 1986, pp 139–40; Harrison and Cragg (1993) 143 NLJ 591; Maguire, *A Study of the Police Complaints System*, 1991, Stationery; RCCJ Report, Cm 2263, p 46; Kennedy, H, in Walker, C and Starmer, K (eds), *Miscarriages of Justice: A Review of Justice in Error*, 1999, p 374; Goldsmith, A, *External Review and Self Regulation: Complaints Against the Police – The Trend to External Review*, 1988; Harrison, J and Cuneen, M, *An Independent Police Complaints Commission*, 2000.
297 *A Study of the Police Complaints System*, 1991.
298 RCCJ Report, Cm 2263, p 46.

Prior to the introduction of the Police Reform Act 2002 a strong consensus had emerged that the independent element in the complaints and disciplinary process was too weak and was the key factor in the inefficacy of the system.[299] Maguire and Corbett commented in their 1991 review that an independent system might lead to an improvement in public confidence in the system, although they expressed doubts about its efficacy in other respects.[300] The MacPherson Report recommended that there should be an independent tribunal for serious complaints.[301] Morgan and Newburn found: 'The fact that most complaints . . . continue to be investigated exclusively by the police themselves is almost certainly an important factor in explaining why so few complaints are made compared with the proportion of members of the public who report having felt like making a complaint.'[302] The Police Action Lawyers Group stated: 'the fundamental problem . . . is the lack of independence in the system.'[303] The House of Commons Home Affairs Committee found that the introduction of an independent element is desirable in principle.[304] Doubts were expressed, however, taking into account experience from other jurisdictions, about the efficacy of a completely independent investigatory body,[305] but prior to the issuing of the Consultation Paper in 2000, there appeared to be a degree of consensus regarding the need for a stronger element of independence which could be achieved through the co-operation of police and expert civilian investigators, drawn from the ranks of bodies such as lawyers and customs officials.

The Police Reform Act 2002

In 2000, the government commissioned a feasibility study into the practicality of using independent investigators in exceptional cases,[306] and put proposals to use such investigators to the annual Police Federation Conference in May 2000.[307] The government issued a Consultation Paper *Complaints against the Police* in 2000 which proposed importing greater independence into the system, by means of a new body,

---

299 Sanders and Young, op. cit., fn 1, p 702; Kennedy, H, in Walker, C and Starmer, K (eds), *Miscarriages of Justice: A Review of Justice in Error*, at 374, 1999; Bailey, SH, Harris, DJ and Ormerod, DC, *Bailey, Harris and Jones: Civil Liberties: Cases and Materials*, 5th edn, 2002, Chapter 2 at pp 122–39.

300 *A Study of the Police Complaints System*, 1991.

301 Cm 4262-I, 1999, Recommendation 58.

302 *The Future of Policing*, 1997, p 53; finding based on Skogan, W, *Contacts between Police and Public: Findings from the 1992 British Crime Survey*, HO Research Study No 134, 1994.

303 Home Affairs Committee Report, para 43.

304 Home Affairs Committee, HC 258-I (1997–98), Recommendation 11.

305 See Goldsmith, A, *External Review and Self Regulation: Complaints Against the Police – The Trend to External Review*, 1988; Maguire, M, 'Complaints against the police: the British experience', in Goldsmith, A (ed), *Complaints Against the Police: A Comparative Study*, 1990; Loveday, B, 'Police complaints in the USA' (1988) 4 Policing 172.

306 The study was conducted by the consultants KPMG. They reported on 17 May 2000; their report was accompanied by an independent report by Liberty, recommending the setting up of an independent body to hear police complaints.

307 On 17 May 2000. For comparative discussion of this possibility, see Goldsmith, A and Lewis, C (eds), *Civilian Oversight of Policing*, 2000, Hart.

the Independent Police Complaints Commission,[308] but made it clear that in the vast majority of cases, a full independent investigation would not occur, owing to cost. The Home Office Consultation Paper 2000[309] accepted that the system had failed to win public confidence.

The result of the consultation was the Police Reform Act 2002, Part 2 and Sched 3, which came into force April 2004 and made certain changes to the previous system, intended to increase public confidence in the police and in particular in the complaints system.[310] One of its aims was to make investigations more open, timely, proportionate and fair. Under Sched 3 Police Reform Act 2002, a complaint may be received in the first instance by the Chief Constable, the police authority or the new Independent Police Complaints Commission (IPCC). It must then be determined who is the 'appropriate authority' for the purposes of the investigation (Sched 3, para 1). This will normally be the Chief Constable of the force in question. The Chief Constable then appoints an officer to carry out a formal investigation, unless the complaint can be informally resolved. Therefore, it is still fair to say, despite the reforms, that an issue of independence arises at the beginning of the process.[311] Informal resolution can only occur if the complainant consents and the authority is satisfied that, even if the complaint is proved, no criminal or disciplinary proceedings would be appropriate (Sched 3, para 6).

A complaint must be referred to the IPCC if the alleged misconduct resulted in death or serious injury, (Sched 3, para 6) or where the Secretary of State has provided by regulations that the investigation of the complaint must be supervised by the IPCC (intended to be in the case of more serious misconduct). In addition, there is a discretionary power to refer complaints to the PCA and it can require a complaint to be referred to it. Where a complaint is referred to it the IPCC decides on the procedure (Sched 3, para 15). It can carry out the investigation itself using its own staff where a complaint is referred to it. This is the key difference from the previous scheme. It can also supervise or manage the investigation by the appropriate authority and then receive a report at the end of it. The appropriate authority can also carry out the investigation on behalf of the IPCC. If it appears once an investigation has been completed that a criminal offence may have been committed, the case must be referred to the DPP.

The procedure at the hearing is now governed by the Police (Conduct) Regulations 2004 which repealed the regulations introduced in April 1999.[312] The 1999 Regulations followed up the initial Labour proposals for reform,[313] including in particular abolition of the criminal standard of proof in disciplinary proceedings.[314] The 2004 Regulations do not create radical changes but do improve the position of the complainant to an extent. Under the procedure as governed by the 1999 Regulations, the hearing was private,

308 *Complaints against the Police: A Consultation Paper*, 2000. See proposals: HL Deb, Vol 620, col WA45, 19.12.00.
309 London, Home Office, 2000.
310 For criticism of the new scheme, see Sanders and Young *Criminal Justice*, 3rd edn, 2007, Chapter 12.4.
311 Home Affairs Committee First Report (1997–98), para 47.
312 The Police (Conduct) Regulations 1999. The procedures operated alongside the 1995 ones until March 2000, when the transitional arrangements ended; all cases were then dealt with under the 1999 procedures. The 2004 Regulations are contained in SI 845 and now govern the procedure.
313 HC 683 (1997–98).
314 Op. cit., fn 312, reg 27(3)(b) (previously reg 23(3)).

but the complainant could attend the proceedings although not before his evidence was given.[315] Now he or she can attend for the full hearing but can be excluded on public interest grounds if there are sensitivities regarding the evidence.[316] The hearing is still conducted in private, which does not aid in creating public confidence in the system, but provision is made for it to be conducted in public in exceptional circumstances,[317] and for the participation of the IPCC.[318] The complainant is allowed to cross-examine the officer concerned; cross examination of witnesses generally is not expressly covered.[319]

The key change under the reformed scheme is that the police are for the first time subject to external investigation. Nevertheless, it is probable that in the majority of cases, due to lack of resources, the IPCC's role in relation to the investigation – as opposed to the supervision – of complaints will tend to remain limited. Many complaints will never be referred to the IPCC but will remain in the hands of the police force in question. Thus despite the involvement (albeit limited) of the Independent Police Complaints Commission, introduced by the 2002 Act, with a view to creating a stronger independent element in the system, the complaints procedure is still largely administered by the police themselves. Although the system contains this independent element, a number of problems remain even in relation to those exceptional cases in which independent investigation by civilian investigators occurs. Institutional factors, including obstruction of the system by the police and the possibility that civilian investigators will be affected by police culture, may continue to hamper the system; the success rate may remain low.[320] As Sanders and Young argue, the IPCC is in the same position as the PCA since in general it relies on reports of the facts of a case, compiled by police officers. The police concerned use various techniques to discredit a complaint, constructing the case in a manner that justifies no further action.[321]

Thus, despite evidence of police malpractice from miscarriage of justice cases such as that of the *Birmingham Six*[322] and the subsequent indications discussed above of poor practice and deliberate wrong-doing within the police service, the system for accountability remains, in essentials, the same since the new element of independence is unlikely to have any impact in the majority of instances. As Smith argues, '. . . the complaints reform programme has been driven by the prevailing managerialist orthodoxy and the principal effect of the legislation will be to transfer some responsibilities for the management of police complaints to another public body which will report directly to

---

315 Ibid, reg 25(3).
316 A number of provisions, however, previously allowed for the exclusion of the complainant: under reg 25(5) the complainant could be removed if he interrupted. Now under reg 31 (previously reg 27) he can be excluded if matters arise which it would not be in the public interest to disclose to him.
317 Reg 30(5): Where a case arises from a complaint or conduct matter which has been investigated under para 19 of Sched 3 to the 2002 Act and the Commission considers that because of its gravity or other exceptional circumstances it would be in the public interest to do so, the Commission may, having consulted the appropriate authority, the officer concerned, the complainant and any witnesses, direct that the whole or part of the hearing will be held in public.
318 Reg 25.
319 Ibid, reg 25(4). Now reg 29(5) but this only covers cross examination of the officer concerned.
320 See Harrison, J and Cuneen, M, *An Independent Police Complaints Commission*, 2000; Goldsmith, A and Faran, S, 'Complaints against the police in Canada: a new approach' [1987] Crim LR 615.
321 See Sanders and Young, *Criminal Justice*, 3rd edn, 2007, at p 615.
322 See *R v McIlkenny and Others* [1992] 2 All ER 417.

the Home Secretary'.[323] The system still raises various serious issues under the HRA. It does not generate confidence that it will play a significant part in ensuring that police officers and forces act in compliance with the Convention. In so far as the Convention rights are reflected in the safeguards for suspects contained in PACE, the TA and their associated Codes, it is not fully apparent that it can ensure adherence to them.

Where officers are placed under investigation with a view to disciplinary charges, they may take early retirement or resign on medical grounds. After the MacPherson Report[324] into the *Stephen Lawrence* case, disciplinary charges were recommended against five officers involved. All, however, retired and therefore could not face charges. The Home Office has considered the possibility of disciplinary action up to five years after retirement.[325] In the wake of the MacPherson Report, and with the inception of the new complaints system, racist police behaviour may begin to lead more frequently to disciplinary charges,[326] as well as liability under the Race Relations Act 1976, as amended, although such a trend cannot yet be discerned.[327] There remains a disconnection between successful civil actions against the police and disciplinary action or prosecution.[328] For example, in the *Hsu* case,[329] it was found that Mr Hsu was assaulted, racially abused and falsely arrested. It was accepted that the police officers in question had lied on oath and fabricated note-book entries. Mr Hsu was awarded £200,000 damages (reduced on appeal to £35,000), but no officer was disciplined.[330]

Probability of disciplinary action after a complaint

Under the pre-2004 system, the overwhelming majority of complaints did not result in disciplinary proceedings: as many as 30 per cent of complaints were dealt with by

323 Smith, G, 'Rethinking Police Complaints' Brit J Crminol. (2004) 44, 15–33, at p 28.
324 Cm 4262-I, 1999.
325 MacPherson Report, Recommendations 55–57.
326 E.g., in February 2000 a police officer, PC Hutt, was disciplined and dismissed from the force for oppressive, racist behaviour (news report, 22 February 2000).
327 The 1998–99 Annual Report of the PCA, Table 5: 2,415 complaints concerned assaults; 81 disciplinary charges were preferred. 203 complaints concerned racially discriminatory behaviour; three charges were preferred. There is quite a lot of evidence that stop and search is still carried out in a racially discriminatory fashion: see Chapter 11, p 1125–26.
328 *The Butler Report*, 1998, criticised the CPS for its decision-making in the *Treadaway* case; Derek Treadaway was awarded £50,000 in damages in respect of a serious assault by police officers while he was in custody: *R v DPP ex p Treadaway* (1997) *The Times*, 18 November. The CPS decided not to prosecute the officers. Treadaway successfully sought judicial review of this decision and the case was remitted for re-consideration by the CPS.
329 *Thompson v Comr of Police for the Metropolis, Hsu v Comr of Police for the Metropolis* [1997] 2 All ER 762.
330 See further the Home Affairs Committee First Report (1998), Section B: 'The evidence from civil actions'. A further example, in which the disciplinary sanction was, in effect, rescinded, is provided by *Goswell v Comr of Metropolitan Police* (the *Guardian*, 27 April 1996). The officer who was found in that case to have perpetrated a serious assault, PC Trigg, was dismissed as a result of a complaint from Goswell. In the civil action Goswell had been awarded £120,000 for assault, £12,000 for false imprisonment and £170,000 for arbitrary and oppressive behaviour. Trigg appealed against his dismissal and was reinstated by the Home Secretary, Michael Howard. On the face of it, his reinstatement after it had been proved beyond reasonable doubt (in the disciplinary proceedings) that Trigg had perpetrated the assault in question appeared highly questionable.

informal resolution[331] and 50% of complaints were withdrawn.[332] Clayton and Tomlinson noted that the 16,712 complaints dealt with in 1990 led to 305 criminal or disciplinary charges and advice or admonishment in 573 cases; thus, less than 2% of complaints led to any disciplinary action.[333] The PCA Report of 1995 reported that out of 245 complaints of serious assault by police officers, eight led to disciplinary charges; none led to dismissal of an officer from the service. Out of 6,318 complaints of assaults, disciplinary charges were preferred in 64 cases; none led to dismissal of the officer.[334] The PCA Report of 1998 stated that 141 complaints concerned serious assaults; 8% of those fully investigated led to disciplinary action. A total of 16,550 complaints were received in 1998–99; 317 were fully investigated, a figure of approximately 2%.[335] In 1997, the Home Affairs Committee considered the figures for the outcome of complaints and found that over the previous two years, 2% of all recorded complaints were substantiated following a formal investigation and less than half of 1% of complaints led to disciplinary or criminal charges.[336] The record for 1998–99 suggests that the figures would be approximately the same. In 1999–2000, 8,048 complaints were formally investigated but only 353 officers had disciplinary charges proved against them. The figures were similar in 2000–2001. In 2003–4, 25,376 complaints were made; 961 were substantiated and 89 led to disciplinary action; 867 were deal with by 'other means'. The 'other means' included retirements, and informal admonition.[337] While the figures may be, to an extent, misleading,[338] they strongly suggested that the system was not operating fairly and effectively.

The Independent Police Complaints Commission published statistics for the number of complaints recorded by police in England and Wales, for the year ended 31 March 2005, after the IPCC had been responsible for public complaints and conduct issues since April 2004.[339] A total of 27,909 allegations were recorded in 2004–5. These were dealt with as follows: 50% were dealt with by local resolution (13,936 compared with 8,914 informal resolutions in 2003–4); 20% were dealt with by formal investigation (5,585 compared with 7,761 in 2003–4); 17% by dispensation (4,737 compared with 5,863); and 13% withdrawn (3,651 compared with 2,838). Of those allegations formally investigated, 745 (13%) were substantiated. In 2004–5 a total of 22,898 complaint cases were

---

331 PCA Triennial Review, HC 466 (1985–88), para 1.14, p 8.
332 See Triennial Review of the PCA 1991–94, HC 396, 1994–95; Clayton, R and Tomlinson, H, *Civil Actions Against the Police*, 2nd edn, 1992, p 13.
333 Clayton and Tomlinson, ibid, p 13.
334 See Triennial Review of the PCA 1991–94, HC 396, 1994–95.
335 The 1998–99 Annual Report of the PCA, Table 5: 2,415 complaints concerned assaults; 81 disciplinary charges were preferred; 203 complaints concerned racially discriminatory behaviour; three charges were preferred. The Report does not give the figure for disciplinary action as a percentage of fully investigated complaints.
336 Home Affairs Committee First Report (1997–98), *Police Disciplinary and Complaints Procedures*, printed 16 December 1997, para 27.
337 Home Office Statistical Bulletin 21/01.
338 See Lersch and Mieczkowski (2000) 23(1) Policing. They considered arguments that the numbers of complaints may not be indicative since citizens may under-complain for various reasons, including lack of confidence in the process. They also looked at the possibility of over-complaint.
339 Police Complaints: Statistics for England and Wales 2004/05, Emily Gleeson and Tom Bucke, IPCC Research and Statistics Series: Paper 3. Published by IPCC, London ISBN 0–9552083–1-9 and ISBN 978–0-955–2083–1-7, www.ipcc.gov.uk.

recorded, marking a 44% increase on the previous year. There was a great deal of variation across police forces, with some but not all experiencing very large increases in complaints.

In 2004–5 the IPCC received 768 valid appeals from complainants. Half (49%) were against the non-recording of a complaint, one-third (35%) about the outcome of a supervised or local investigation and 17% about the local resolution process. Nearly half (46%) of the appeals against non-recording were upheld, compared to one-fifth of those against the outcome of an investigation and 13% of those against the local resolution process. In 2004–5 misconduct sanctions were imposed on 1,204 police officers. For 80 of these officers the charges related to a public complaint. A total of 324 officers received sanctions resulting from a misconduct hearing. Of these, a total of 34 officers were dismissed and 57 officers were requested to resign. Since April 1 2004 the IPCC has used its powers to begin 87 independent and 322 managed investigations into the most serious complaints against the police. The IPCC considered that the increase in complaints was due to a number of factors. The Police Reform Act 2002 (PRA Act) widened the categories of complainant and those who could be subject to complaints. More significantly, in preparation for the PRA Act, police forces made improvements in accessibility and recording procedures. Such improvements are likely to have resulted in more people being included in the complaints system who in the past would have had their complaint dealt with informally or who, while aggrieved, would not have presented their complaint.

So once the 2002 Act had been in place for a year, in 2004–5, a total of 22,898 complaints were received; of the allegations formally investigated, 13% were substantiated. Appeals to the IPCC led to misconduct charges against 80 officers. Further charges related to misconduct not the subject of a public complaint. These figures demonstrate that a rise in the number of complaints has occurred and also in the number of substantiated complaints since the inception of the IPCC. But a 13% substantiation rate remains low; a large number are still withdrawn or informally resolved. The difference between the number of complaints and the number substantiated, and between those substantiated and those leading to disciplinary charges, remains dramatic.

The HRA and the police complaints and disciplinary system

The police complaints mechanism potentially provides a means of creating police accountability, both in terms of underpinning the balance apparently struck by PACE, the TA and the Codes between police powers and suspects' rights, and in ensuring compliance with the Convention under the HRA. The bodies administering the mechanism, the Independent Police Complaints Commission (IPCC), Chief Police Officers, and police disciplinary tribunals are all bound by the Convention as public authorities under s 6 of the HRA. They are also in the position of hearing complaints regarding police officers who are themselves so bound. Both aspects should inform their work and could be raised as issues by way of judicial review. Further, the statutory provisions governing police complaints should be interpreted compatibly with the Convention under s 3 of the HRA.

It is possible, although doubtful, that police disciplinary hearings fall within the field of application of Art 6. Under Art 6, the hearing might be viewed, first and foremost, as forming the determination of a 'criminal charge' against the officer concerned, although this is uncertain. Military and prison disciplinary proceedings fall within the term, owing to the severity of the possible penalty, which includes the possibility of imprisonment. The position regarding disciplinary proceedings carrying the possibility of lesser, albeit quite severe, penalties, such as dismissal or the loss of pension rights, is not yet clearly settled, although there are indications that the Court would view proceedings carrying the possibility of lesser penalties as falling outside the meaning of criminal charge.[340] Disciplinary proceedings and hearings might also be viewed as the determination of the 'civil rights and obligations' of the complainant under Art 6(1), since they may frequently involve inquiry into breaches of such rights, including breaches of the Convention itself. The term 'civil' has, however, been taken to mean that these are rights in private rather than public law,[341] although a clear distinction between rights in private as opposed to public law is not apparent in recent Strasbourg jurisprudence. Possibly, complaints proceedings might be found to fall within this term at Strasbourg, or domestically, in future. This view might be encouraged since, as indicated above, the proceedings became more court-like after the 1999 reforms.

On the premise that disciplinary proceedings and the occasional disciplinary hearings ordered by the PCA might be found in future to fall within Art 6, it is arguable that they fail to comply with its requirements since the complainant is in such a weak position in them. They appear to fail to provide a fair hearing for the complainant, bearing in mind the procedure they follow. In investigating a fair hearing, the domestic authorities may take into account the Art 6(3) guarantees even in respect of civil determinations, since they are viewed as minimum guarantees which are covered by the wider para (1) protection of a fair hearing. If consideration is given to the procedures in question it is apparent that, apart from any of the other requirements of fairness, the minimal safeguards of Art 6(3) may not be present, depending on the application of the new regulations in any particular case.[342] The system does not allow for the complainant or her legal representative to attend the full disciplinary proceedings or hearings. The independence and impartiality of the hearing may also be questioned, particularly as the vast majority of hearings are not ordered or supervised by the PCA. No compensation can be awarded to the complainant.

There is also the possibility of considering whether the disciplinary system affords the complainant an effective remedy for breach of his or her Convention rights. This argument could be raised under Art 13 which, while omitted from the rights given further effect under the HRA, may have some effect in domestic law.[343] It is debatable whether the police complaints and discipline process should be seen as being the appropriate forum for s 7(1)(a) HRA purposes, since breach of Convention rights by police officers could be raised in the ordinary courts under that sub-section. But, in any event, the Art 13 issue could be raised in, for example, a challenge to a breach of a Convention right in judicial review proceedings, if the applicant had made an unsuccessful complaint. In *Govell v UK*,[344] the Commission found that the police investigative system did not meet the requisite standards of independence under Art 13 since the Chief Constable

340 See *Demicoli v Malta* A 210 (1991) and *Ravnsborg v Sweden* A 283-B (1994).
341 *Ringeisen v Austria* A 13 (1971), para 94.
342 See further Chapter 2, pp 65–66.
343 See Chapter 4, p 165.
344 (1997) 4 EHRLR 438. See also *Khan v UK* (2000) 8 BHRC 310, paras 45–47.

can appoint a member of the same force to investigate; the Home Secretary appoints and remunerates members of the Police Complaints Authority and has a guiding role in determining the withdrawal of charges. The rules considered in *Govell* were the PACE rules, but the new rules maintain the same system. In *Khan v UK*,[345] the Court also found that the police disciplinary system failed to satisfy Art 13 because of the lack of independence. It is not clear that the 2002 Act has gone far enough to meet the deficiency found in *Khan*.

A further issue may arise in respect of public interest immunity attaching to documents coming into existence during a police complaints investigation. The position of the parties to court actions in relation to disclosure of material relating to a complaint was placed on a more equal basis as a result of *Chief Constable of West Midlands Police ex p Wiley*; *Chief Constable of Nottinghamshire Police ex p Sunderland*.[346] All the parties concerned argued that public interest immunity did not attach, on a class basis, to documents coming into existence during a police complaints investigation. The House of Lords had to consider whether *Neilson v Laugharne*[347] and the decisions following it were wrongly decided. In *Neilson*, Lord Oliver had determined that a class immunity should attach to police complaints documents on the basis that the police complaints procedure would be placed in jeopardy if that was not the case. However, the House of Lords considered that there was insufficient evidence to support Lord Oliver's conclusion as to the need for a new class claim to public interest immunity. Thus, it was found that *Neilson* must be regarded as wrongly decided, but that did not mean that public interest immunity would not attach to police complaints documents: whether it did or not would depend on the nature of the particular document or documents in question. This decision emphasises that a clear case must be made out for use of a broad class claim to public interest immunity. It is in the interests of a fair hearing under Art 6(1) and 6(3)(d), since it goes some way towards ensuring that, in actions against the police, or in prosecutions where previous disciplinary findings may be relevant, both parties have access to the same information. However, it leaves open the possibility of a contents claim or of a class claim in relation to specific groups of documents, although a strong justification would be required to establish such a claim. In *Taylor v Anderton*,[348] the Court of Appeal found that the reports prepared by investigating officers were entitled to class immunity, but that a litigant might nevertheless obtain disclosure of part or all of a report if the judge could be persuaded that the public interest in disclosure outweighed the interest in immunity.

It is debatable whether the current position would satisfy the findings as to the duty of disclosure to the defence in *Rowe and Davis v UK*[349] or in *Tinnelly and McElduff v UK*,[350] depending on the particular circumstances of a case. In *Tinnelly*, the Court found that the use of a conclusive certificate preventing disclosure of the

345 Ibid, paras 44–47; [2000] Crim LR 684.
346 [1995] AC 274; [1994] 3 All ER 420; (1995) 1 Cr App R 342, HL.
347 [1981] QB 736.
348 [1995] All ER 420, CA. See also *Kelly v Comr of Police of the Metropolis* (1997) *The Times*, 20 August in which it was found that PII attaches to certain of the forms which are sent to the CPS by police forces.
349 (2000) 30 EHRR 1; (1998) 25 EHRR CD 118 (admissibility decision).
350 (1998) 27 EHRR 249.

reasons for a decision[351] breached Art 6, since it prevented the tribunal from effectively reviewing the facts. Any judge determining the imposition of a contents immunity, whether in a civil action against the police or in a prosecution, would have to take the jurisprudence regarding the equality of arms provision arising both under Art 6(1) and 6(3) into account, as well as the general requirements of a fair trial. The latter requirement is ultimately the overriding one, since merely placing both parties in an equally disadvantageous position would not necessarily satisfy it.

6 Prosecution of the police

Introduction

Police actions that are unauthorised may create criminal as well as civil liability. For example, the use of force in effecting an unlawful arrest would be an assault. The use of lethal force in such circumstances might give rise to liability for murder or manslaughter. Equally, excessive force used to effect a lawful arrest or to restrain a suspect lawfully detained might give rise to criminal liability. In practice, successful prosecutions of police officers are very rare.[352] A number of high profile cases have failed to lead, ultimately, to successful prosecutions. The Home Affairs Committee noted that no convictions of police officers had arisen from the recent miscarriage of justice cases despite strong evidence of fraud or perjury on the part of some of the officers involved.[353] The number of deaths annually in police custody remains high; between January 1990 and December 1996, 380 such deaths were reported to the Home Office,[354] and the failure of disciplinary charges or prosecutions in relation to complaints arising from such deaths has attracted quite severe criticism.[355] In 1997, the Home Affairs Committee considered evidence from the organisation Inquest which submitted 11 case studies, in certain of which no prosecution or disciplinary action had been taken against officers, despite apparently substantial evidence against them.[356] The Police Reform Act 2002 does not distinguish between complaints of criminal conduct and of unprofessional behaviour (s 12); thus it does not facilitate the use of the criminal process as distinct from the disciplinary one, where a complaint reveals that a criminal act by a police officer may have occurred.

---

351 This was not a PII certificate, which would not be conclusive, but a certificate provided for under the Fair Employment Act 1976 in Northern Ireland.
352 Only about 1.5% of cases concerning the police referred to the DPP are prosecuted. See Hyder, 'Cause for complaint' (1990) *New Statesman and Society*, 12 January.
353 Ibid, para 24.
354 Leigh, Johnson and Ingram, *Deaths in Police Custody*, Police Research Series Paper 26 (1998).
355 See *The Butler Report*, 1998; Kennedy, H, in Walker, C and Starmer, K (eds), *Miscarriages of Justice: A Review of Justice in Error*, 1999, p 374. Note the report in June (1999) LAG 21 regarding the inquest into the death of N Delahunty due to cocaine intoxication aggravated by police restraint. See also November (1999) LAG 6 regarding the acquittal of police officers for the death of a Mr O'Brien in custody after a restraint by a number of police officers. His death was considered in *The Butler Report*, s 6. In s 8, the report criticised the CPS system for considering prosecutions in respect of deaths in custody (including that of O'Brien) as 'inefficient and fundamentally unsound'. See above, Chapter 11, p 1175, fn 326.
356 Ibid, para 25.

Crown Prosecution Service decision-making

The Crown Prosecution Service takes the decision as to prosecution, but their impartiality and independence have been questioned. It appears that the issue of independence arises at every stage in the decision-making process of the CPS in relation to the question whether to prosecute police officers where complaints appear to disclose criminal offences.[357] The CPS is, of course, independent of the police, but 'the issue is whether it exercises this independence properly'.[358] Evidence submitted in 1997 to the Home Affairs Committee regarding the matter indicated a 'lack of willingness' on the part of the CPS and DPP to prosecute. 'There is clearly bias which pervades both the police and the CPS preventing viable prosecutions through nonsensical analysis of evidence.'[359] The issue of the quality of CPS decision-making in this context clearly raises a number of Convention-based arguments.

The *Butler Report* (1998) made a number of recommendations designed to improve the quality of CPS decisions as to prosecution. They included sending every death in custody case for a decision as to whether or not to prosecute to the Assistant Chief Prosecutor and instituting a compulsory training programme for all those employed in central casework at the CPS.[360] The Report also expressed unease with the system whereby the police themselves investigate and report to the CPS on a death in custody. It also suggested that where such a death had occurred and an inquest jury returned a verdict of unlawful killing, the reason for the decision not to prosecute should be given.[361]

Impact of the HRA

No criminal liability is created under the HRA, so that a breach of, for example, Art 3 or 8, non-coterminous with existing offences, could not found a prosecution. But decisions as to prosecutions of the police raise a number of Convention issues which are likely to be addressed in proceedings for judicial review of a decision not to prosecute. The burden of proof would be affected where it was alleged that Art 3 had been breached by custodial maltreatment, or, under Art 2, where a death had occurred in custody. Once it was shown that the detainee was free of the injury in question,[362] or was not already in a life threatening condition, before arrest, the state would bear the burden of exculpating the officers involved. This test appears to differ from that currently used by the CPS, which was criticised in the *Butler Report*.[363] The Butler recommendations, which were largely concerned with procedural matters, including clarification of the system of decision-making in the CPS, did not, it is argued, fully address these Convention matters. Possibly it will become apparent that reforms based on a greater awareness of the demands of the Convention in this context are necessary under the HRA.

---

357 See further Smith, G, 'Police Complaints and Criminal Prosecutions', (2001) *Modern Law Review*, 64/3: 372–92.
358 See Home Affairs Committee First Report (1997–98), para 88.
359 Ibid, para 90.
360 Ibid, pp 53–54.
361 Ibid, p 55.
362 *Tomasi v France* A 241-A (1992). See also Chapter 2, p 48.
363 Ibid.

7 Conclusions

A recurring theme throughout this chapter and Chapters 11 and 12 has concerned the extent to which a 'balance' is struck between suspects' rights and police powers. The dual themes of the need for enhanced police powers but also for the introduction of rules to protect due process, are only clearly evident in the piece of legislation which is still central to police powers – the Police and Criminal Evidence Act 1984. The notion of achieving in PACE what Reiner has called 'a fundamental balance'[364] has some foundation. It may be said that on the face of it, the balance struck by PACE is fairly acceptable, at least in relation to the non-terrorist suspect, despite the increased powers of arrest and stop and search which PACE confers. Concern may be expressed as to the uncertainty of the concept of reasonable suspicion on which these powers depend but, nevertheless, taking PACE and the Codes at face value, a concern to protect the rights of suspects is evident. It is, however, less clear that the later legislation, the Criminal Justice and Public Order Act 1994, the Terrorism Acts 2000 and 2006, and the Criminal Justice and Police Act 2001, reflects such a concern.

The post-PACE legislation, then, has effected continued extensions of police powers, but has brought about only minor increases in safeguards for suspects. Those increases, including the use of judicial authorisation for the lengthy detention of terrorist suspects[365] and the requirement of access to legal advice if adverse inferences are to be drawn from silence,[366] were in effect imposed on the government by decisions of the European Court of Human Rights. The later legislation made no attempt to address one of the central problems inherent in the provision for safeguarding suspects' rights in PACE, the TA and the Codes – the lack of effective sanctions for its breach.

This was a recurring theme in this chapter. It is particularly true of Codes C and H; they create a scheme which seems to make every effort to ensure fair treatment in custody and in the interview, but which operates outside the realm of general legal sanctions since breaches may be remedied (in the accepted sense of that word) only in internal disciplinary proceedings, and only very rarely then. The right to legal advice, although on a statutory basis, is in an equally weak position. The Notes for Guidance, which occupy key points in the interviewing scheme, appear to be intended to have no legal status at all. Since no other effective means is available of ensuring that the rules are adhered to, the courts have stepped into the breach and have developed complex rules for the exclusion of confessions obtained in breach of the interviewing rules. Thus, in effect, exclusion of confession evidence has become one of the main methods of upholding the rights of the suspect while in custody and in the interview.

But the use of exclusion of evidence as a means of redress clearly leads to an ineffective protection for suspects' rights. It can only operate where the case comes to court and the suspect pleads not guilty. Even then it is only likely to occur in relation to admissions and where the breach of the provision in question can be shown to have been substantial and significant. Many Code or statutory provisions relate to physical treatment or to interaction outside the police station and have no obvious linkage with the making of admissions. Where non-confession evidence is obtained in breach of the

---

364 Reiner, R, 'The politics of the Act' [1985] PL 394, p 395.
365 See Chapter 11, pp 1167–69.
366 See Chapter 12, pp 1211–15.

PACE or TA standards, it is highly probable, as *Forbes*[367] and *AG's Reference (No 3 of 1999)*[368] indicated, that the courts will admit it, thereby possibly encouraging laxity in relation to the rules. Thus, the police may still be inclined to break the rules in the hope of obtaining a guilty plea, or merely on the basis that the rules fail to harmonise with police culture. Further, the detrimental impact on the victim and on the criminal justice system, in terms of placing pressure on resources if a case collapses due to exclusion of crucial evidence, renders this method, it is argued, disproportionate in some instances to the aim pursued.

Therefore, since the rules are not underpinned by effective remedies for their breach, many suspects may experience a process, including interviews, that falls below standard apparently set by the TA, PACE and the Codes. If, in particular instances, this does not come to light, a doubtful guilty plea may be accepted, or a false confession may be admitted, leading to a miscarriage of justice, while on the other hand such failures may sometimes mean that reliable confession evidence cannot be accepted in court, although it would have been had the rules been observed. If confession evidence would not have been available but for oppressive questioning, it is argued on the grounds of both protection for suspects and reliability that the energies of the police should have been devoted to uncovering other evidence. Curtailment of the right to silence has merely exacerbated the situation, since it is likely in itself to increase the pressure on the suspect to speak and it has also undermined the safeguard which, it is suggested, has most real value in the interview: the provision of legal advice from an experienced solicitor.

There is the further problem that, as this chapter and Chapter 11 have shown, the Code C, H and statutory safeguards can be evaded by operating entirely outside the PACE and TA schemes, using secret surveillance techniques,[369] as occurred in *Khan*[370] and *Chalkley*,[371] or operating undercover, as in *Amin*.[372] Thus, the safeguards for suspects can be marginalised. While such techniques are effective in crime control terms,[373] the concern must arise that they may be used deliberately in some instances rather than arresting and interviewing a suspect, thereby triggering off all the safeguards. As Chapter 10 explained, such techniques are now regulated by the Police Act 1997 and the Regulation of Investigatory Powers Act 2000 (RIPA). But a breach of either statute does not in itself give rise to liability, unless the action, if unauthorised, would create existing tortious or criminal liability. As seen in *Chalkley*, the courts are not willing to use exclusion of evidence as a means of upholding the integrity of the criminal justice system where such liability could have been incurred in the gathering of evidence. Further, following *Chalkley*, they are unlikely to do so, even under the HRA, where no existing liability could have been incurred, but a breach of Art 8 has been caused. This latter instance is clearly of particular importance, not only because

---

367 [2001] Crim LR 649.
368 [2001] 2 WLR 56.
369 See Ormerod, D and Birch, D, 'The evolution of the discretionary exclusion of evidence' [2004] Crim LR 767.
370 [1996] 3 All ER 289; (1996) 146 NLJ 1024.
371 [1998] 2 Cr App R 79.
372 [2000] 1 WLR 1071; [2000] Crim LR 174.
373 See Chapter 10, pp 1053–54.

it would mean that the courts are prepared to receive evidence obtained in breach of a fundamental human right, but also because no other remedy would be available, apart from the possibility of mounting a challenge to the police operation in the tribunal set up under the RIPA.[374]

Thus, it is fair to conclude that while the PACE and TA schemes themselves have not been upheld where non-confession evidence is obtained, it is also apparent that when the police operate outside those schemes, and act unlawfully, the courts are not prepared to exclude the evidence thereby obtained in order to vindicate the rights violated. As argued above, the use of exclusion of evidence in this fashion can ignore the interests of victims. But to argue for a nuanced approach which would allow consideration of such interests and of due process, depending on the particular circumstances of a case, is to demand a theorised and developed approach which it is currently almost impossible to discern in decision-making processes based largely on crime control values. In other words, the trend away from due process evident in the legislative developments is echoed in the current judicial tendencies. As indicated, the other possible remedies available have had little impact in creating police accountability, either in terms of upholding suspects' rights generally, or in respect of the statutory and Code-based safeguards.

However, the same government that introduced the TA and the CJPOA also introduced the HRA. One might have expected that the HRA would prove to be to an extent a corrective to the dominance of crime control values evident in criminal justice policies and in judicial decisions. In the pre-HRA period and in the period immediately after the HRA came into force, there was a view that the Act might allow for a 'reinvigoration of fundamental values' in the criminal justice system.[375] It appeared possible that the inception of the HRA might herald a return to an emphasis on such values which has not been evident since the early 1990s. These three chapters have sought to suggest that, despite unfavourable statutory provisions, particularly those of the TA, the Convention offers some possibilities of curbing police discretion in the interests of due process values since it does allow domestic judges to look more closely and directly at standards of fairness in the criminal justice system. But this chapter has suggested that a number of the decisions on the Convention in the first seven years of the HRA, in particular *AG's Reference (No 3 of 1999), Gillan, Condron, Brown v Stott*[376] and *Shannon*,[377] do not suggest that such a return is probable, although there have been decisions in the field of stop and search and detention short of arrest that suggest otherwise.[378] Also, where conditions of detention or secret police operations do not infringe existing tortious liability, the HRA provides the only method, under s 7(1)(a), of challenging the police, although, as explained in Chapter 11 in respect of surveillance, such a challenge would have to be brought in the tribunal set up under the RIPA, not in the ordinary courts.

---

374 See Chapter 10, pp 1080 *et seq.*
375 Walker, C, in Walker, C and Starmer, K (eds), *Miscarriages of Justice: A Review of Justice in Error*, 1999, p 62.
376 [2001] 2 WLR 817.
377 [2001] 1 WLR 51.
378 See Chapter 11, pp 1137–38 and Chapter 8, pp 757–62.

It appears likely that the HRA will continue to have a diffuse and patchy effect; it will not have a radical impact on the use of the current repressive legislation or the further powers to be introduced under the Terrorism Act 2007. It may itself be manipulated either by the judiciary or the legislature, in the sense that in court, the Convention rights can be 'read down' in order to preserve the effect of such legislation, while the use of s 19 statements of compatibility may provide such legislation with a spurious appearance of rectitude. MPs may accept that a process of human rights auditing has occurred, allaying concerns about the provisions. A blending of the Convention values with those of the common law is becoming especially apparent in this field, but it is suggested that those of the Convention will only attain an appearance of gaining greater respect owing to the HRA, where they harmonise with values *already* held dear by the common law. It may be said that where the judiciary have traditionally established a firm opposition to due process values, as they have in respect of the admission of improperly obtained non-confession evidence, the HRA is likely to have little impact, although it may do so where they have traditionally been sympathetic to due process, as they have been in relation to the deprivation of liberty in police detention.[379] Possibly the difference of attitude is attributable to a traditional common law acceptance and understanding of certain basic human rights, including the right to liberty, but not of more sophisticated and nebulous ones, such as rights to be free from humiliating treatment or arbitrary invasion of privacy. Thus, both the creation of greater police accountability and the tempering of the effects of repressive legislation that could have occurred under the HRA are likely to continue to be muted and inconsistent.

Nevertheless, the Convention rights set basic standards in this context which are accessible to suspects domestically under the HRA. The possibility that a Convention right such as Art 8 is more likely to be found to be breached if the Code rules relating to it are not adhered to, arising from *Wainwright v UK*,[380] affords the Codes an underpinning they would otherwise lack. The impact of Code rules and the Convention rights on police culture is nebulous but evident: it is no coincidence that the courts must struggle to determine whether instances of maltreatment leading to a confession should be viewed as creating unreliability or as amounting to oppression: cases falling self-evidently within the rubric of 'torture' or 'degrading' treatment are rare.

The legislation discussed in these chapters reflects the change in the political climate that became evident in the mid-1990s. As Dixon puts it, 'The political and professional consensus about the need for criminal justice reform [in the face of discovery of a number of miscarriages of justice] had broken down . . . the new Home Secretary encouraged renewed populist obsession with law and order . . .'[381] At the time, the Conservative Party had a Home Secretary, in Michael Howard, who was perceived in many quarters as long on right-wing law and order rhetoric, and tabloid appeal, but short on measured criminal justice policies.[382] The aims of crime control were furthered, so Howard claimed, by ensuring an enormous increase in the prison population, by

---

379   See *Roberts v Chief Constable of Cheshire* [1999] 1 WLR 662.

380   See Chapter 11, pp 1178–79.

381   In Walker, C and Starmer, K (eds), *Miscarriages of Justice*: *A Review of Justice in Error*, 1999, p 73.

382   Maguire, M, 'The wrong message at the wrong time?' in Morgan, D and Stephenson, G (eds), *Suspicion and Silence*, 1994, Blackstone, p 48.

increasing, on pain of penal sanctions, the number of instances in which the citizen must take orders from the police,[383] and by abolishing or undermining the rights of suspects, in particular the right to silence.[384] The stance taken was well summed up in Howard's own words as seeking to redress 'the balance in our criminal justice system which has tilted much too far in favour of the criminal and away from the protection of the public'.[385]

From the mid-1990s, once Tony Blair became Shadow Prime Minister and Jack Straw Shadow Home Secretary, the Labour Party in opposition adopted a very similar crime control stance to that of the Conservative Party. Since the Labour Government took office in 1997 there have been few indications of attempts to break with the criminal justice legislative policies of the Conservative Party, apart from the very significant passing of the HRA. Post-2000, both major parties were seeking to outdo each other in encouraging and pandering to populist notions of crime control. The attack on the World Trade Centre in New York in September 2001 fostered the production of further counter-terrorist legislation in the UK which has continued the trend away from due process in terrorist investigations. The Terrorism Act 2006 introduced a further police power to detain suspects for up to a month. It is probably safe to predict that the introduction of a new Terrorism Act in 2007 or 2008 is also likely to aid in confirming the continuing devaluation of due process in criminal justice policies. The HRA, Strasbourg decisions such as *Murray* or *Beckles*,[386] and improvement in the police disciplinary system, are, as indicated, having a countering effect. But the impact of the HRA is not of the radical nature sometimes previously predicted.

---

383 In the CJPOA 1994, especially ss 71 and 68.
384 In the CJPOA 1994, ss 34, 36, 37; see Chapter 12, pp 1234–54.
385 HC Deb col 211, 2 April 1996.
386 See Chapter 14, pp 1211–14 and pp 1246–49 for discussion of both decisions.

Anti-terrorism law and human rights

1 Introduction[1]

[This case] calls into question the very existence of an ancient liberty of which this country has until now been very proud: freedom from arbitrary arrest and detention. The power which the Home Secretary seeks to uphold is a power to detain people indefinitely without charge or trial. Nothing could be more antithetical to the instincts and traditions of the people of the United Kingdom.[2]

'It is all too easy for us to respond to terror in a way which undermines commitment to our most deeply held values and convictions, and which cheapens our right to call ourselves a civilized nation.'[3]

---

1 Texts referred to below and background: Fenwick, H, 'The Anti-terrorism, Crime and Security Act 2001' (2002) 65 MLR 724; Feldman, D, 'Human Rights, Terrorism and Risk: the Roles of Politicians and Judges' [2006] PL 364; Dickson, B, 'Law versus terrorism: can law win?' [2005] EHRLR 11; Walker, C, 'The Treatment of Foreign terror suspects' [2007] 70(3) MLR 427; Ramraj, VV, Hor, M and Roach, K (eds) *Global Anti-terrorism Law and Policy*, 2005, CUP; Walker, C, 'Terrorism and criminal justice' [2004] CLR 311; Scraton, P (ed), *Beyond September 11*, 2002, Pluto; Walker, C, 'Terrorism and criminal justice' [2004] CLR 311; Scraton, P (ed), *Beyond September 11*, 2002, Pluto; Alexander, Y and Brenner, EH, *The UK's Legal Responses to Terrorism* 2003, Transnational; Silke, A (ed), *Terrorists, Victims and Society*, 2003, Wiley; Strawson, J (ed), *Law after Ground Zero* 2002, Routledge; Michaelsen, C, 'Derogating from International Human Rights Obligations in the "War Against Terrorism"? – A British–Australian Perspective' [2005] 17 (1–2) Terrorism and Political Violence 131–55; Warbrick, C, 'The principles of the European Convention on Human Rights and the responses of states to terrorism' [2002] *European Human Rights Law Review* 287; Tomkins, A, 'Legislating against terror' [2002] *Public Law* 205; Gearty, C, 'Terrorism and Human Rights' [1999] LS 366; Thomas, PA, 'Emergency and anti-terrorist powers' (2003) 36 *Fordham International Law Journal* 1193; Walker, C, 'Liability For Acts Of Terrorism: United Kingdom Perspective' in *European Centre for Tort and Insurance Law Liability for Acts of Terrorism*, 2004; Sterba, JP, *Terrorism and International Justice*, 2003, OUP; Walker, C, 'Policy Options and Perspectives: British perspectives' in van Leeuwen, M, *Confronting Terrorism*, 2003, Brill; Walker, C, 'Political violence and commercial risk' (2004) 56 *Current Legal Problems* 531; Walker, C, 'Prisoners of "War all the time" ' [2005] *European Human Rights Law Review* 50; Horgan, J and Taylor, M (eds), *The Future of Terrorism*, 2000, Frank Cass; Idriss, MM, 'Religion and the Anti-terrorism, Crime and Security Act 2001' [2002] *Crim. LR* 89; Horgan, J, *The Psychology of Terrorism*, 2005, Frank Cass; Gearty, C, *Terror*, 1991, Faber and Faber.

2 *A and Others v Secretary of State for the Home Dept* [2005] 2 AC 68; [2005] 2 WLR 87; [2005] 3 All ER 169, at para 86, *per* Lord Hoffmann.

3 Cherie Booth, QC (26 July 2005); 19th Sultan Azlan Shah Law Lecture delivered by Cherie Booth in Kuala Lumpur, Malaysia, on 26 July 2005.

9/11 re-shaped the counter-terrorist response in the UK. After 9/11, war on terror was viewed, as 'not a matter of choice but a strategic imperative'.[4] Thus the response has been heavily influenced post-2001 by the government's view of the threat posed by extremist Islamic groups and the fear of suicide-bombing. The counter-terrorist measures adopted post-9/11 and again post-7/7 have tended to be of a proactive as opposed to a reactive nature. In other words, rather than charging persons with terrorist crimes and bringing them to trial, attention has turned to targeting possible terrorist suspects – persons who may in future commit terrorist acts – and curtailing their liberty in order to prevent terrorist activity before it can occur. But proactive measures are clearly more risky and pernicious in human rights terms since they are not subject to the normal due process safeguards created by the criminal justice system, and therefore miscarriages of justice are more likely to occur. This chapter documents the counter-terrorist law and policy of the Labour Government from 2000 to 2007. The following pages evaluate a very wide range of counter-terrorist provisions, including a large number of special terrorism offences and pro-active sanctions applied outside the criminal justice system, and in so doing the three key themes outlined below are explored.

Human rights and counter-terrorist sanctions

A tediously familiar aspect of the counter-terrorist scheme is that it often runs counter to British common law traditions and opposes the values of the European Convention on Human Rights (ECHR).[5] This chapter will seek to demonstrate that the current Labour Government has introduced a new model of counter-terrorist legislation, one that has much more severe human rights implications than that of the 70s, 80s and 90s. The Terrorism Act 2000 remains the central measure within this scheme, but the later additions to its provisions in the Anti-Terrorism, Crime and Security Act 2001 (ATCSA), the Prevention of Terrorism Act 2005 and the Terrorism Act 2006 have tended to increase the tension between the counter-terrorist measures and human rights. The imposition of reverse burdens and presumptions against the defendant, and the use of sanctions imposed on the civil standard of proof or on the basis of reasonable suspicion, eases the task of the prosecution or the Home Secretary in seeking to apply the sanctions, but tends to fail to adhere to Convention and common law values. The more harsh the sanction, in certain instances, the easier it is to apply it. Thus, indefinite detention could from 2001 to 2004 be imposed without trial, under ATCSA 2001, on a burden of proof below the civil standard and without a pre-detention court hearing. The complete banning (proscription) of a terrorist group – which can include an organisation supporting direct action against property abroad in opposition to a despotic regime – can also be accomplished with quite astonishing ease. When over-broad provisions are applied on the basis of a low standard of due process, the human rights traditions of the UK are undermined, possibly with a counter-productive security impact and without a rational security basis. The most obvious example was the use of indefinite detention against non-British suspected terrorists after 9/11; had that legislation still

---

4   Freedman, L (ed), *Superterrorism*, 2002, Blackwell at p 44.
5   See Warbrick, C, 'The principles of the European Convention on Human Rights and the responses of states to terrorism' [2002] *European Human Rights Law Review* 287; Tomkins, A, 'Legislating against terror' [2002] *Public Law* 205.

been in place prior to 7/7 it could not have been used against the suicide bombers, all of whom were British citizens.

If a democracy appears to abandon its democratic ideals too readily, including adherence to human rights and the rule of law, in the face of terrorist activity, it lays itself open to the charge that its attachment to them was always precarious and qualified. In defending the introduction of new counter-terrorism legislation, the Terrorism Act 2000, with immense potential to extend the impact of the previous legislation, Jack Straw, the then Home Secretary, claimed in 1999 that the TA was simply intended to protect democracy, and that extensive measures were needed since 'by its nature terrorism is designed to strike at the heart of our democratic values'.[6] In justifying similar, if far less wide-ranging, extensions of such legislation in the face of high levels of IRA activity during the 1970s and 1980s, Mrs Thatcher famously said in 1988: 'We do sometimes have to sacrifice a little of the freedom we cherish in order to defend ourselves from those whose aim it is to destroy that freedom altogether . . .'

This is a powerful argument, but it must fully confront the question of the extent to which counter-terrorist measures can undermine democracy in seeking to defend it: they may themselves strike at fundamental democratic values if they appear to be disproportionate to the aim of protecting them. As Tony Blair, the then Shadow Home Secretary, observed in 1993: 'if we cravenly accept that any action by the government and entitled "prevention of terrorism" must be supported in its entirety and without question we do not strengthen the fight against terrorism, we weaken it'.[7] If democratic ideals are not to be undermined, counter-terrorist measures should be effective in improving security, have a minimal impact on human rights and avoid counter-productive effects, including alienating 'suspect communities' and thereby increasing the risk from terrorist acts. As J Wadham of *Liberty* has argued: 'Draconian anti-terrorist laws . . . have a far greater impact on human rights than they ever will on crime.'[8]

The counter-terrorist policy of the current Labour Government is not entirely out of kilter with previous policies, relating to IRA violence, as this chapter seeks to make clear. The key difference is that a political settlement appears not to be possible, leading to greater authoritarianism – with no end in sight – and therefore to a stronger appearance of injustice and of human rights abuse. The possibility of suicide bombing is also a relevant factor. Three standard governmental policy responses to terrorism have been identified:[9] a military one, treating the fight against terrorism as a form of warfare; a police-based one, treating it simply as a form of criminal activity, to be detected and then defeated using (perhaps some modified version of) the criminal justice system; and a political one, viewing it as a form of armed rebellion to be resolved through negotiation and the political process.[10] All three responses to terrorism may be evident in any particular instance. The UK Government's response to the Al-Qaeda

---

6 See the *Guardian*, 14 November 1999.

7 Hansard House of Commons 10 March 1993 col 975.

8 See the *Guardian*, 14 November 1999.

9 Whitty, Murphy and Livingstone *Civil Liberties in the Human Rights Act Era*, 2001, at pp 128–29.

10 See Fenwick, H and Phillipson, G, 'Legislative over-breadth, democratic failure and the judicial response: fundamental rights and the UK's anti-terrorist legal policy' in Ramraj, VV, Hor, M and Roach, K, *Global Anti-terrorism Law and Policy*, 2005.

threat has military aspects – the wars in Iraq and Afghanistan – but within the UK itself it is police-based: it has involved a very significant ratcheting up of the state's coercive powers in terms of surveillance, data-sharing, detention and other invasions of personal liberty. The UK Government considers that negotiation with Al-Qaeda or linked groups is not possible, and is reluctant to link the terrorist threat in the UK with the war in Iraq or other aspects of foreign policy. In its public statements it does not therefore focus on negotiations in relation to foreign policy as a means of defusing the terrorist threat in the UK, but largely concentrates instead on counter-terrorist police-based measures. This stance, which differs from that adopted by Spain after the Madrid bombings, meant continuation of a policy of adopting measures in tension with fundamental common law and Convention principles.

Thus, since the response is founded on the view that political negotiation is not possible, the resultant significant rise in the adoption of authoritarian powers has placed a concomitant strain on human rights. The implications of these points were illustrated in the House of Commons debate on the Terrorism Act 2006, which ushered in a range of new offences, including that of glorifying terrorism, an offence at the outer limits of what is acceptable in a society committed to the free speech principle. The principle of the Bill was debated in the House of Commons on October 26. In the opening speech Charles Clarke asserted that the government was not prepared to adopt a change in government policy likely to diminish the significance of the United Kingdom as an Al-Qaeda target:

> Its nihilism means that our societies would cease to be a target only if we were to renounce all the values of freedom and liberty that we have fought to extend over so many years. Our only answer to this threat must be to contest and then to defeat it, and that is why we need this legislation.

From a reactive to a proactive counter-terrorist strategy

This chapter focuses on the central and changing characteristics of the UK's current counter-terrorist response post-2000 and post-2001. Its second notable aspect has been the shift from reactive to proactive measures as an aspect of the 'war on terror' post-9/11. The current Labour Government introduced a new counter-terrorist scheme with the introduction of the Terrorism Act 2000 (TA). A change in policy was encapsulated in the Terrorism Act 2000 in that temporary, graduated measures were replaced with permanent, broadly applied ones, but the 2000 Act relied on a traditional reactive approach, that of seeking to charge terrorist suspects with offences and bring them to trial. This scheme offered quite a strong contrast to the previous one of the 70s, 80s and 90s. The previous UK counter-terrorist scheme – under the Prevention of Terrorism (Temporary Provisions) Act 1989 and the Northern Ireland (Emergency Provisions) Act 1996, as amended — revealed some acceptance of the principle that emergency measures should be adopted only in the face of immediate and severe need. The TA was introduced at a time when terrorist attacks were not of the scale that they had been previously, although the government clearly had an impending threat from extremist Islamic groups in mind. The TA applied all the special terrorism offences to a far wider range of groups than had previously been the case; it was therefore a much less graduated measure than the previous ones.

But the TA, despite its immense and unprecedented scope, was viewed in 2001 by the government as inadequate to address the terrorist threat post-9/11. Following those attacks on Washington and New York, the government introduced the Anti-Terrorism, Crime and Security Act 2001. The ATCSA, controversially, ushered in the proactive measure of detention without trial in Part 4 aimed at suspected international terrorists as a preventive measures, as opposed to seeking to charge such persons with criminal offences under the TA provisions, or with ordinary criminal offences. When the key provisions of Part 4 were declared incompatible with Arts 5 and 14 of the European Convention on Human Rights by the House of Lords in *A and Others v Secretary of State for the Home Dept*,[11] the government accepted that it could no longer sustain the scheme and introduced the Prevention of Terrorism Act 2005. In that Act Parliament repealed the key provisions of Part 4 and introduced a new scheme relying on the use of control orders imposed outside the criminal justice system.

The main change in UK anti-terrorist policy in recent years has been described as being 'the shift to intelligence-based and proactive methods [with] the primary aim of preventing terrorist attacks, rather than responding to events and attempting to solve crimes after they occur'.[12] The control orders scheme represents the current response to the threat to security. It is, like Part 4, proactive rather than reactive – it does not depend on reacting to a terrorist threat after it has manifested itself, but on targeting and controlling the activities of suspected terrorists.

Thus the TA provisions have been added to under the succeeding 2001 and 2005 measures which have been more controversial, since they rely on interfering proactively with the liberty of suspects before any offences have been committed, or where it appears difficult to prove that they have been committed. Broad proactive measures were introduced post-2000, but they were not applied, as they would have been under a more authoritarian regime, to a large number of persons. In a fashion typical of the UK counter-terrorist response (also evident in public order and criminal justice measures), over-broad and arguably counter-productively draconian proactive measures were introduced in 2001 and in 2005, but then they were significantly under-used. They were applied only to a tiny minority of terrorist suspects.

Part 4 ATCSA and the Prevention of Terrorism Act 2005 represented the high water mark of Convention-infringing measures. The Terrorism Act 2006 saw no further introduction of proactive measures, but a return to the reactive TA model, albeit with a further racheting up of state powers. It adds to the very broad panoply of offences already in existence under the 2000 Act and reaffirms the use of a more draconian pre-trial regime for terrorist suspects. It provided for lengthier detention of terrorist suspects, discussed in Chapter 11,[13] introduced new offences of activities preparatory to terrorist acts, and a new offence of indirect encouragement of acts of terrorism, including glorification of terrorism, discussed below. The introduction of the new very

---

11 (2004) UKHL 56; [2005] 2 AC 68; [2005] 2 WLR 87; [2005] 3 All ER 169.
12 Whitty, Livingstone and Murphy, at 143. As Clive Walker puts it, 'The trend [of UK anti-terrorist policy] . . . represents a part of a fundamental switch away from reactive policing of incidents to proactive policing and management of risk': Walker, C, 'Terrorism and Criminal Justice: Past, Present and Future' [2004] Crim LR, May, 311, 314. Walker further cites Ericson, RV and Haggerty, KD, *Policing the Risk Society*, 1997, University of Toronto Press.
13 See pp 1168–69.

broad preparatory offence and the new offence of glorification, although open to criticism in a number of respects, can be seen as expressing some acceptance of the human rights problems that arise when counter-terrorist sanctions such as semi-house arrest are applied without trial and with minimal judicial supervision under control orders.

Symbolic effect of counter-terrorism provisions

One of the most striking aspects of these provisions is their under-use. On their face, due to over-breadth, they apply potentially not only to groups that might be viewed in common parlance as 'freedom fighters' or protest groups rather than 'terrorists', they also apply to a very large number of persons, including ordinary citizens, such as journalists, property agents, accountants, bankers, who have some association with terrorist groups, sometimes unknowingly.[14] In practice the executive does not seek to apply the counter-terrorist sanctions to all the groups or persons that meet the statutory definitions. This is partly due, in relation to supporters of Al-Qaeda, as discussed below, to the difficulty of uncovering evidence and of transforming security and intelligence service material into evidence that could be put forward in a criminal trial. Not only may it genuinely be of a very sensitive nature, involving, *inter alia*, informants whose lives might be put at risk,[15] but the security services may be very reluctant for it to be put forward as evidence for reasons that may not fully relate to genuine concerns of that nature.[16] Such reasons also appear to relate to the continuing refusal to allow intercept material to be put forward as evidence in a criminal trial, discussed in Chapter 10.[17]

But those are not the only reasons for the under-use of the counter-terrorist sanctions, or alternatively for their very existence as additions to the ordinary criminal law. The counter-terrorism provisions documented in this chapter appear to be intended to have an effect that, to an extent, is more symbolic than actual.[18] They are viewed by government as playing an important role in signalling this society's rejection of the message of certain groups – to isolate and marginalise them,[19] to deny them some legitimacy on the basis that they have refused to use democratic methods, resorting instead to the anti-democratic course of creating terror by using violence targeted at civilians.

This can most obviously be said of Al-Qaeda and linked groups. The London bombings of 7/7 constituted an act of aggression opposed to the most basic values of a democracy. But the adoption of over-broad definitions in counter-terrorist law,

---

14 See Walker, C, 'Political violence and commercial risk' (2004) 56 *Current Legal Problems* 531.

15 The questions of sensitivity and disclosure in the criminal trial (including informants), graymail and prosecutorial discretion are addressed in Lustgarten, L and Leigh, I, *In From the Cold: National Security and Parliamentary Democracy*, 1994, Chapter 11.

16 See pp 1466–67 below.

17 See pp 1047–52.

18 See, e.g., Tushnet, M and Yackle, L, 'Symbolic Statutes and Real Laws: The Pathologies of the Antiterrorism and Effective Death Penalty Act and the Prison Litigation Reform Act', *Duke Law Journal*, Vol 47, No 1 (Oct 1997), pp 1–86; Freedman, L, 'The Coming War on Terror' in Freedman, L (ed), *Superterrorism*, 2002.

19 See, in particular pp 1381–82 below.

meaning that sanctions such as proscription are available to marginalise and demonise other more moderate groups, may be having an effect in constructing some national groups as 'suspect communities',[20] thereby playing into the hands of extremist elements and so encouraging the growth of terrorism. If terrorism is defined in an over-broad fashion, and then broadly drawn offences and sanctions are introduced founded on that definition, it appears that no distinction is made between Al-Qaeda and moderate groups prepared to use the democratic process to further their cause The result may be to erode that distinction in reality, arguably aiding Al-Qaeda recruitment, enhancing its support, and making the task of the police and intelligence services more difficult in obtaining information about possible terrorist activity within certain communities.

If the broad definitions and over-broad sanctions in UK counter-terrorist law are taken at face value it can be argued that democratic ideals are being abandoned and that the legitimacy of the UK in terms of the values that it stands for is being undermined. So it is made less easy to place a vision of British values against that of the extremists in terms of winning over hearts and minds. The adoption of over-broad counter-terrorist sanctions on the basis of their symbolic value, but relying on an unspoken traditional British consensus that they will never be fully used, may be a mistaken policy, not least because some religious or ethnic groups were never part of that consensus.

Route-map of this chapter

Chapters 11 and 12 considered the differences between the police powers under the Terrorism Acts 2000 and 2006 applicable to terrorist suspects and to 'ordinary' suspects. Under the PTA and EPA criminal procedure in respect of suspected terrorists differed at significant points from that applicable to 'ordinary' suspects. The provisions regarding stop and search, arrest, detention, police interviewing, which are dealt with in Chapters 11 and 12, created a pre-trial scheme which was of a significantly lower standard in terms of safeguards for suspects, than the ordinary scheme. This was also true of the trial process itself. In effect, a twin-track scheme was created in which lesser standards of criminal justice were maintained in respect of persons suspected of the special terrorist offences. This system is continued under the Terrorism Acts 2000 and 2006, and applied, potentially, to a far wider range of defendants. The special criminal justice regime for terrorists, affording them lesser rights within the criminal justice system than 'ordinary' criminals, can now be applied to members of any group falling within s 1 TA,[21] whether or not the group is proscribed, since arrest under s 41 TA need not be for a specific terrorist offence, as Chapter 11 makes clear.[22]

This chapter charts the change from a broadly reactive approach under the Terrorism Act 2000 to the post-9/11 approach, which placed a greater emphasis on proactive measures, ushered in by the detention without trial measure introduced by the Anti-Terrorism, Crime and Security Act 2001. In the section below, this chapter begins by considering the tension between the terrorism provisions introduced from 2000 to 2007 and the guarantees of the European Convention on Human Rights, received into

---

20 See Ansari, F, *British Anti-Terrorism: A Modern Day Witch-hunt*, October 2005, Islamic Human Rights Commission, www.ihrc.org.uk.
21 See below, pp 1377–78.
22 See further, Chapter 11, 1146–47.

domestic law under the HRA. It is not possible to consider all the instances in which this legislation gives rise to potential conflicts with Convention rights; the focus will be on certain of its key aspects. The specific problems of compatibility between the various provisions and the Convention rights are considered at various points below, but a number of general themes are apparent that are applicable in a range of contexts.

The third part of this chapter is concerned centrally with the provisions of the Terrorism Act 2000. It introduced a new and broad definition of terrorism and used it as the basis for applying a wide range of established terrorist offences. The sanctions it provides depend upon reacting to offences, including preparatory, incitement or 'association' offences, after they have been committed. Not only does it remain the central counter-terrorist measure, providing a definition of terrorism that all the later measures depend upon, it also introduced changes in UK counter-terrorist strategy that had very significant human rights implications. The attention that has been focused upon the controversial post-9/11 and post-7/7 measures should not be allowed to deflect attention away from such implications. Further broad offences were introduced to add to the TA measures, especially under the Terrorism Act 2006. The TA, and the additional offences introduced post-2000, provide a wide range of very broad offences relating to proscription and to terrorism that can be utilised, rather than resorting to sanctions without a criminal trial. On the other hand, as will be discussed, proscription has features not readily associated with traditional criminal justice measures. The fourth part of this chapter concentrates on the emergency detention without trial measures under ATCSA. The fifth considers the control orders regime under the Prevention of Terrorism Act 2005, which replaced Part 4 but are also imposed by executive action. The tensions between the various counter-terrorist provisions, especially the proactive ones, and the European Convention on Human Rights, are explored throughout this chapter.

2 Terrorism and human rights

Introduction

The provisions of the Terrorism Act 2000, the Anti-Terrorism Crime and Security Act 2001 (ATCSA), the Prevention of Terrorism Act 2005 (PTA), and the Terrorism Act 2006 come into conflict in a potentially unjustifiable fashion with a range of Convention rights.[23] Clearly, a number of the provisions under the current counter-terrorism scheme may have been of doubtful compatibility with the Convention when they were only applied in practice pre-2000 to certain Irish terrorist groups. But once they were applied far more widely, the issue of compatibility, on a domestic level under the HRA, became far more problematic. Since they tend to run counter to common law and Convention principle, the judiciary have utilised the Human Rights Act in order to seek to impose Convention-compliance upon them. This enterprise – the imposition of Convention-compliance on a scheme that Parliament had accepted as having already achieved such compliance – was not initially, this chapter will indicate, taken in the post-HRA era

---

23 See Warbrick, C, 'The principles of the European Convention on Human Rights and the responses of states to terrorism' [2002] *European Human Rights Law Review* 287.

with the seriousness that is currently apparent. The decision of the House of Lords in *A and Others v Secretary of State for the Home Dept*[24] in 2004 marked the turning point. The stance taken by Lord Bingham in defence of Convention, international and common law human rights principles in that decision, and in other similarly seminal ones discussed below, has been pivotal.

Before moving on, it is important to bear in mind the Convention exceptions and derogation system, discussed in Chapter 2 and of particular pertinence in this context. If the aim of a terrorist organisation is the destruction of democracy, the application of the Convention rights in relation to it can be circumscribed. Al-Qaeda's aims appear to relate to foreign policy, but it could readily be described as an anti-democratic organisation, opposed to fundamental human rights values. In this context Art 17 may be relevant and has not so far had much impact in judicial decisions. As discussed in Chapter 2, Art 17 provides a general exception where an organisation's aim is the destruction of Convention rights. It provides:

> Nothing in this Convention may be interpreted as implying for any state, group or person any right to engage in any activity or perform any act aimed at the destruction of any of the rights and freedoms set forth herein or at their limitation to a greater extent than is provided for in the Convention.

Thus, Art 17 prevents a person relying on a Convention right where his or her ultimate aim is the destruction or limitation of Convention rights. Article 17, together with the demands of proportionality, may have a role to play in creating greater marginalisation of Al-Qaeda-related groups, in imposing a focus on the counter-terrorist that is not apparent from a face-value reading of its provisions. It may have a part to play in greater differentiation within the counter-terrorist scheme between those organisations that pose a serious and continuing threat to security in the UK, and those which do not, but are covered by it.

In proceedings on the application of the special terrorist provisions the courts must interpret them, under s 3 of the HRA, compatibly with the Convention rights if possible; they must also discharge their duty under s 6 HRA in terms of their application in the particular instance. The approach of the courts towards the counter-terrorist provisions has been and is crucial. Traditionally, since terrorism has been viewed as threatening national security, the courts have adopted a deferential stance.[25] While a far wider range of persons and activities have been designated 'terrorist' under the TA, and a very large number of groups have been proscribed since 2000, it is apparent that the actions of many such persons and groups do not genuinely threaten national security, either because their operations are directed at a regime in another jurisdiction – as in the case of the People's Mujahideen Organisation of Iran, or because the group in question has called a ceasefire, as in the case of the Kurdistan Workers' Party.

---

24 (2004) UKHL 56; [2005] 2 AC 68; [2005] 2 WLR 87; [2005] 3 All ER 169.
25 In *CCSU v Minister for the Civil Service* [1985] AC 374 the House of Lords accepted the government's claim that national security was at risk, without demanding that evidence should be put forward to support it. In the case of *Shafir ur Rehman* (judgment of 24 May 2000) the Court of Appeal accepted that it was for the government alone to determine whether a threat to national security, broadly defined, existed. Thus, pre-HRA the judiciary tended to accept government claims that such a threat is self-evident or must be taken on trust.

The approach taken by the House of Lords pre-HRA in *Ex p Kebilene*[26] to counter-terrorist provisions, particularly the findings of Lord Hope of Craighead, suggested that where national security *is* in issue the judges tend to refuse (overtly) to apply the international margin of appreciation doctrine, and yet may adopt a restrained approach. It was said in *Ex p Kebilene* in the context of the case, which concerned the compatibility of terrorist legislation with Art 6, that a deferential approach could be justified. Under the previous legislation, in the context of Irish terrorism, the courts tended to take an absolutist approach, readily making the assumption that considerations of national security outweighed the individual rights at stake. The post-HRA approach of the courts continues to be affected by the extent to which national security can be said to be at stake but, as discussed below, the courts are more prepared than they were pre-HRA to take a *selectively* deferential approach, an approach which considers how far a particular decision is genuinely within a particular area of constitutional competence. This stance, it will be argued below, was taken by the House of Lords in *A and Others v Secretary of State for the Home Dept.*[27]

The courts are less likely to be deferential where national security is not genuinely at stake, and in any event they appear at present to be taking their role under s 6 HRA very seriously.[28] They are currently showing a greater willingness to take a robust approach to counter-terrorist provisions that, on their face, violate Convention and common law principles. As will be found below, the HRA has been used in some instances in the courts, either to modify the provisions in question under s 3 in order to render them Convention-compliant, or to declare them incompatible with the Convention under s 4. The two key decisions in this respect so far have been those of the House of Lords in *A and Others v Secretary of State for the Home Dept*[29] in which a declaration of incompatibility was made between Part 4 ATCSA 2001 and Arts 5 and 14 ECHR, and *Attorney General's Reference (No 4 of 2002)*[30] in which s 3 HRA was employed in order to impose Art 6-compliance on the offence of belonging to a proscribed organisation under the TA 2000. *Attorney General's Reference (No 4 of 2002)* is of particular significance since it extends to all offences that impose a reversed burden of proof on the defendant, or require him to disprove a significant element of the offence. In *R v Keogh*[31] the Court of Appeal confirmed the broad application of the House of Lords' decision. Those two House of Lords decisions illustrate the impact that the HRA has had – and is still likely to have – on the counter-terrorist scheme. The courts are using the principle of proportionality to force the counter-terrorist scheme into a Convention compliancy that the executive alleged in Parliament had been achieved at the time of passing the provisions in question (s 19(1)(a) HRA), and which Parliament – as a matter of constitutional theory – accepted had been achieved.

---

26 Below. Divisional Court [1999] 3 WLR 175.
27 (2004) UKHL 56; [2005] 2 AC 68; [2005] 2 WLR 87; [2005] 3 All ER 169.
28 See Chapter 4, pp 280–91.
29 (2004) UKHL 56; [2005] 2 AC 68; [2005] 2 WLR 87; [2005] 3 All ER 169.
30 [2004] UKHL 43; [2005] 1 AC 264; [2005] 1 All ER 237. The House of Lords took account of *R v Lambert* [2002] 2 AC 545, HL(E), *R v A* (No 2) [2002] 1 AC 45, HL(E), *R v Johnstone* [2003] 1 WLR 1736, HL(E), *Ghaidan v Godin-Mendoza* [2004] 2 AC 557, HL(E) and *Attorney General's Reference (No 1 of 2004)* [2004] 1 WLR 2111, CA.
31 [2007] All ER (D) 105 (Mar); [2007] EWCA Crim 528, 7 March 2007.

But Parliament has also played a significant part in imposing Convention-compliancy on provisions that were probably non-compliant as originally drafted. The Joint Committee on Human Rights has played an important advisory role in this respect. This was especially the case in relation to the offence of glorification of terrorism introduced under the Terrorism Act 2006. The Joint Committee gave significant advice on its compliance with Art 10, as originally drafted,[32] and the House of Lords introduced a number of significant amendments to the Bill which narrowed down the offence significantly.

But Parliamentary and judicial intervention have not, it will be argued below, fully succeeded in ensuring Convention compliance in respect of all aspects of the current counter-terrorist scheme, including those of proscription under the TA 2000, as amended in 2006, and of control orders under the PTA 2005. These problems of compatibility and the response of the domestic courts are considered in relation to specific provisions below. But a number of general themes cut across a range of provisions, including those introduced in the 2006 Act.

Ambit of the Convention rights interpreted domestically

It may be relevant in a particular instance to seek to rely on an expanded conception of a Convention guarantee; this is not confined to this context, but may be of particular pertinence within it, given Strasbourg's tendency to accord a wide margin of appreciation to the state in cases concerning terrorism where national security may be affected, or where the state puts forward a reasonable case that it may be.[33] It is argued that Lord Bingham relied impliedly on an expanded conception of Art 6(1) in respect of the use of evidence in terrorism cases suspected to derive from the use of torture in other jurisdictions in *A and Others*[34] (the 2005 'third party torture material judgment'), a point that is returned to below.[35]

As discussed in Chapter 4, para 1 of the materially qualified Articles should be interpreted domestically in a way that delivers no more than would be delivered at Strasbourg if the Strasbourg jurisprudence on the point at issue was settled and constant.[36] This was found in *R (on the application of Ullah) v Special Adjudicator*,[37] in the context of s 2 HRA. The domestic courts, in other words, have no mandate to expand the ambit of the qualified rights. Chapter 4 discussed methods of escaping from this stricture – for example, where the jurisprudence can reasonably be viewed as not yet settled.[38] However, while following *Ullah*, Lord Steyn considered in the House of Lords

---

32 See p 1417 below.
33 See, e.g., the discussion of the Strasbourg derogation cases, pp 1425, 1435 below. See also Chapter 4, pp 265–69, 272–73; Chapter 2, pp 37, 110–11.
34 [2005] UKHL 71.
35 See pp 1455–59.
36 See Chapter 4, pp 193–95. The decision leaves open the possibility that domestic cultural traditions could be relevant to the ambit of the absolute or semi-absolute rights since it would seem strange that such traditions could find an entry point due to the qualifications to the rights, but not in relation to the absolute ones. This point may be of pertinence in this context in relation in particular to Art 3.
37 [2004] UKHL 26.
38 See Chapter 4, p 196.

in *Marper*[39] that while Art 8(1) should not be expanded domestically by reference to domestic cultural traditions, including common law conceptions of human rights principle, Art 8(2) could be. Lord Steyn considered that such traditions *would* be relevant in determining whether the *infringement* of the right was justified: 'I do accept that when one moves on to consider the question of objective justification under Article 8(2) the cultural traditions in the United Kingdom are material . . . the same is not true under article 8(1) . . . .'[40]

Arguably, that dicta can equally be applied to Arts 10 and 11, para 2, and to other qualified Convention rights. This is of great significance in this context since at Strasbourg it is normally argument on para 2 that is affected by the concession of a wide margin of appreciation to the state, on national security grounds, leading to outcomes adverse to the claimant. The *ratio* of the decisions in *Ullah* and *Marper* concerned the ambit of Art 8(1); arguably, they leave open the possibility that domestic cultural traditions could be relevant to the ambit of the absolute or semi-absolute rights, since it would seem strange that such traditions could find an entry point due to the qualifications to the rights, but not in relation to the absolute ones. This point may be of pertinence in this context in relation in particular to Art 3.

Fair trial under Article 6(1) – Proceedings before courts outside the criminal justice system

It is convenient to quote Art 6(1), the right to a fair and public hearing, in full here. In the proceedings considered it appears at present that the rest of Art 6 is inapplicable since it only applies in criminal trials. Its application in criminal trials is considered in Chapters 11–13.[41] Article 6(1) states:

> In the determination of his civil rights and obligations or of any criminal charge against him, everyone is entitled to a fair and public hearing within a reasonable time by an independent and impartial tribunal established by law. Judgment shall be pronounced publicly but the press and public may be excluded from all or part of the trial in the interest of morals, public order or national security in a democratic society, where the interest of juveniles or the protection of the private life of the parties so require or to the extent strictly necessary in the opinion of the court in special circumstances where publicity would prejudice the interests of justice.

Field of application of Article 6?

A number of the procedures made available to challenge the imposition of sanctions on persons suspected of terrorist activity, or those belonging to a proscribed organisation, are problematic in terms of their compliance with Art 6(1) – the 'fair trial' Article, discussed at various points in this book.[42] They tend to place the accused person in

---

39 *R (on the application of Marper) v Chief Constable of South Yorkshire* [2004] 1 WLR 2196.
40 Ibid at 27.
41 See in particular pp 1215–20 and 1259–62.
42 See Chapter 2, pp 59–66; Chapter 13, pp 1291–95.

a very weak position in the proceedings and provide a level of scrutiny far short of that available in a criminal trial, despite the fact that sanctions tantamount to those available in the criminal process are being imposed. In a number of respects the judicial supervision involved affords, it will be contended, a somewhat thin veneer of legitimacy to the process, which is arguably not fully in accord with the demands of Art 6.

Clearly, Art 6 applies to the proceedings considered below only if the hearings are within its field of application. The proceedings are those in the Special Immigration Appeals Commission (SIAC), in the Proscribed Organisations Appeals Commission (POAC) and control order proceedings. As can be seen from the opening words of Art 6(1) set out above, it applies only if those procedures are viewed as the 'determination of a criminal charge' or of 'civil rights and obligations'. It might be thought that the proceedings in question *should* be viewed as criminal due to the sanctions that can be imposed, that the values underlying Art 6 would argue against circumventing its fundamental safeguards by such devices as control orders, executive certification of suspects and 'preventive' executive detention, as opposed to charging suspects with offences and prosecuting them. The mere designation of detention or the use of control orders as preventive, allowing the avoidance thereby of the need for a charge or for proof of an offence beyond reasonable doubt – themselves aspects of due process – arguably should not, in accordance with those values, be allowed to obscure the true nature of the situation. In terms of their impact on liberty, the sanctions imposed in control order proceedings can be seen in essence as almost indistinguishable from detention. When obligations are imposed on a suspect under a control order they will be experienced by the controlee as the use of sanctions as punishment. This point is perhaps even clearer in relation to proscription since on their face the proscription provisions criminalise a person who is a member of a proscribed organisation at the time when the organisation is proscribed, even though he or she had no warning that this was about to occur. Thus if POAC refuses to allow de-proscription a number of persons are automatically criminalised. (As discussed below, the House of Lords in 2004 used s 3 HRA to alleviate the problem of compliance with Art 6 which arose from that position.)[43]

However, the orthodox view apparent from the cases discussed below in the context of control order proceedings appears to be that the use of sanctions tantamount to, or almost indistinguishable in their impact from criminal ones, outside the criminal process, is *not* the equivalent of a criminal charge.[44] Clearly, SIAC, the POAC and courts in control order proceedings are not dealing with such a charge as a matter of domestic law, although this in itself does not determine the matter since the term has an autonomous Convention meaning.[45] Their proceedings are in effect determinative of a deprivation of liberty, but it can be argued that the procedure is precisely not the determination of a charge and that if a criminal charge could have been brought it would have been, that the proceedings are in a sense a substitute for a criminal trial. The procedures in question do, however, represent a 'determination of civil rights and obligations'. This view was taken in the Court of Appeal in *Secretary of State v MB*[46]

---

43 See pp 1353, 1391–92.
44 See p 1448 below.
45 See: *Campbell and Fell v UK* A 80 (1984); *Benham v UK* (1996) 22 EHRR 293.
46 [2006] EWHC 1000, [2006] HRLR 29, [2006] 8 CL 108 at para 53.

in relation to proceedings very similar to those of SIAC – control order proceedings. The sanctions supervised by the courts in question, including SIAC, can be viewed, not as punishments in themselves, but as precautionary since no liability is necessarily imposed. In terms of Convention principle, this, it is argued, is a limited but orthodox perspective. It is the one accepted by the executive and Parliament at present. The House of Lords in *A and Others* in 2005 left the question open whether such proceedings should be viewed as criminal or only as civil, attracting a lower level of safeguards.[47]

What is the basis for viewing the procedures in question as representing a 'determination of civil rights and obligations'? Civil rights and obligations are normally viewed as matters – broadly speaking – of private law,[48] not aspects of public law.[49] It is well established at Strasbourg that all the Convention rights are not 'civil rights' for the purposes of Art 6(1)[50] although the 'family' rights under Art 8(1) generally are viewed as 'civil rights'.[51] In *re S and Re W (Care Orders)*[52] Lord Nicholls found:

> Although a right guaranteed by article 8 is not *in itself* a civil right within the meaning of article 6(1), the Human Rights Act has now transformed the position in this country. By virtue of the Human Rights Act article 8 rights are now part of the civil rights of parents and children for the purposes of article 6(1). This is because now, under section 6 of the Act, it is unlawful for a public authority to act inconsistently with article 8.[53]

In other words, Convention rights that would not be viewed as civil rights for Art 6 purposes at Strasbourg (due to the lack of a basis in domestic law) can now be so viewed, as a matter of domestic law, due to s 6 HRA. Clearly, Lord Nicholls was referring to Art 8 rights which might have been viewed as having such a basis anyway, but his point is that since Strasbourg requires a footing for the right in domestic law that footing has been established due to the HRA. As discussed below, the proceedings in question relate to a range of Convention rights and it has been accepted that the domestic consideration of the alleged breach of those rights in control order proceedings does amount to the determination of civil rights and obligations.[54] Since the proceedings are so viewed domestically they must therefore be Art 6 compliant. But only the guarantees of Art 6(1) apply; the other guarantees of Art 6 do not since they are applicable only in criminal matters.[55]

Further, as discussed in Chapter 2, Art 5(4) in any event provides a right to review of detention, whatever the basis of the detention.[56] The detainee must be able to take

---

47 See p 1455 below.
48 At Strasbourg they would be viewed as the determination of 'civil rights and obligations' since these are matters – broadly speaking – of private law: *Ringeisen v Austria* A 13 (1971), para 94.
49 See, e.g., *Agee v UK* No 7729/76, 7DR 164 (1976).
50 *Golder v UK* (1975) 1 EHRR 524.
51 *W v UK* A121 (1987).
52 [2002] UKHL 10.
53 At para 71.
54 See p 1448.
55 The guarantees of Art 6(2) and Art (3) are only applicable where the hearing is the 'determination of a criminal charge'. See Chapter 2, pp 60–61.
56 See p 58.

court proceedings in order to determine whether a detention is unlawful. This is an independent provision: even if it is determined in a particular case by the Commission that the detention was lawful, there could still be a breach of Art 5(4) if no possibility of review of the lawfulness of the detention by the domestic courts arose. It is well established that proceedings for the purposes of satisfying Art 5(4) must satisfy the basic requirements of a fair trial.[57] Art 5(4) is only applicable if the proceedings relate to 'detention'; therefore its applicability would depend on the issue being determined. If, for example, a control order proceeding concerned obligations that affected Art 8 or 10 rights, it would appear that Art 5(4) would be inapplicable, but that Art 6(1) would continue to apply as the proceedings would concern the determination of civil rights.

But it is arguable that the proceedings *should* be viewed as criminal rather than civil. In *Benham v UK*,[58] the leading case at Strasbourg on 'criminal charge', the Court found that although reg 41 of the Community Charge (Administration and Enforcement) Regulations, the legislation in question, clearly did not create a criminal offence in UK law, it should be accounted criminal for Art 6(1) purposes. The proceedings against the applicant (in respect of default on payment of the community charge or poll tax) were brought by the public authorities; the proceedings had some punitive elements and the bringing of them implied fault on the part of the applicant: the magistrates could only exercise their power of committal on a finding of wilful refusal to pay or culpable neglect.[59] Further, the penalty was severe (committal to prison for up to three months).

If *Secretary of State v MB* is appealed, this point is likely to be argued before the House of Lords. Clearly, if control order proceedings were viewed as the 'determination of a criminal charge' that would undermine the ability of the Home Secretary to employ the control order scheme since the greater safeguards under Art 6(2) and (3) would be applicable. However, Art 6(1) and (2) do not require proof beyond reasonable doubt: a wide margin of appreciation has been conceded to national courts in respect of the burden of proof.[60] As a matter of domestic law proceedings viewed as criminal in character would require proof beyond reasonable doubt, but these would be proceedings deemed criminal due to the autonomous Convention meaning of the term 'criminal charge'; therefore the *domestic* requirements of criminal proceedings would not necessarily apply.

If it appeared that greater efforts were being made to bring *prosecutions* against suspected Al-Qaeda supporters, as opposed to deploying control orders, the courts might possibly feel somewhat less impelled to characterise control order proceedings as criminal in nature. In this context it may be noted that in *Secretary of State for the Home Dept v E*,[61] discussed below, it was found that the Home Office had received judgments from Belgium against the applicant in 2006 that might have provided a basis for a prosecution, but the Court found that there had been no review of the possibility of prosecuting E in the light of them. For this reason, it was found, the decision thereafter to maintain E's control order was flawed.

---

57 *Garcia Alva v Germany* (2001) 37 EHRR 335; *R (West) v Parole Board, R (Smith) v Parole Board (No 2)* [2005] UKHL 1, [2005] 1 WLR 350.
58 (1996) 22 EHRR 293.
59 para 56 of the Judgment.
60 See *Austria v Italy* 6 YB 740 at 784 (1963) Com Rep; CM Res DH (63) 3.
61 [2007] EWHC 33 (Admin).

The procedure for the use of closed material and the use of a special advocate

The requirements of fairness, expressed or implied in Art 6(1), including those of equality of arms,[62] are applicable. In these proceedings closed material on which the grounds for the suspicion against the applicant may be wholly or partly based, is withheld from the person controlled or his legal representatives. Limitations on the disclosure of evidence in such proceedings have the potential to breach Art 6(1). In *Balfour v Foreign and Commonwealth Office*[63] the Court found that once an actual or potential risk to national security had been demonstrated by a public interest immunity certificate, the Court should not exercise its right to inspect the documents. This view of national security as the exclusive domain of the executive was not adhered to in the robust approach taken to the concept in the context of deportation by SIAC in the case of *Secretary of State for the Home Dept ex p Rehman.*[64] However, the House of Lords disagreed with their findings, ruling that the threat to national security is a matter for 'executive judgment' which need not be demonstrated to the civil standard of proof.[65] It is argued that these findings were not fully in accordance with the findings of the Strasbourg Court in *Tinnelly v UK*[66] or in *Chahal v UK.*[67] Both, particularly *Tinnelly*, took the view that the threat to national security should be demonstrated. In *Chahal* the Court said that the remedy offered should be 'as effective as it can be' given the need, in the context in question, to rely on secret sources. Clearly, the government in closed hearings before SIAC, the POAC, or in control order proceedings, has an opportunity to demonstrate the threat to national security and to indicate that the statutory requirements in question are satisfied. The problem is that the standard to which it must be established that they are satisfied following the findings on this point in *Rehman* would be viewed at Strasbourg as unacceptably low. Thus the powers to exclude the applicant[68] and his/her legal representative from the proceedings when closed material is examined would not on their face meet the Art 6(1) requirements of fairness.

However, the Special Advocates (SAs) scheme – whereby security-cleared advocates are appointed to represent the applicant – appears to mean that in that respect Art 6 compliance has been achieved, as discussed below. The role of the special advocates is to represent the interests of an organisation or other applicant, but they are not instructed by or responsible to that organisation or person. SAs are selected from advocates with special experience of administrative and public law, but do not at present receive training.

The special advocates see all the closed material. They are not permitted to disclose any part of that material to those whom they represent, so, as Lord Carlile puts it, they

> have the difficult task of being asked by or on behalf of those whose interests they are instructed to serve to present facts or versions of events in relation to

62 See Chapter 2, p 64.
63 [1994] 2 All ER 588.
64 [2000] 3 WLR 1240.
65 Ibid at para 22.
66 (1998) 27 EHRR 249.
67 (1997) 23 EHRR 413 (in the context of Art 13).
68 See on this point, *Zana v Turkey* (1999) 27 EHRR 667, in which, in the context of terrorism, the applicant was not allowed to be present at the trial; a breach of Art 6 was found on this basis.

which there is the strongest contradictory evidence, but evidence which they are not permitted to reveal in any form.[69]

Perhaps more pertinently, that means that although the special advocate is able to cross-examine witnesses on the applicant's behalf, he is denied the full benefit of this right; since he does not know the closed evidence against him, he cannot indicate to counsel the points upon which witnesses should be challenged. The claimants whose interests the SAs represent can, and in practice do, have their own lawyers too, but those lawyers are excluded from closed evidence and closed sessions. So the entitlement of the appellant to his own counsel throughout the proceedings is valueless since that counsel is also prohibited from attending the closed hearings and knowing the closed evidence against the claimant. Lord Steyn said of the SA system in his dissenting judgment in *Roberts v Parole Board*:[70]

It is not to the point to say that the special advocate procedure is 'better than nothing'. Taken as a whole, the procedure completely lacks the essential charac- teristics of a fair hearing. It is important not to pussyfoot about such a fundamental matter: the special advocate procedure undermines the very essence of elementary justice. It involves a phantom hearing only.

The procedure for closed material and the use of a special advocate was designed to accord with the Canadian SA model referred to in *Chahal*, to which the ECtHR gave approval. In *Tinnelly & McElduff v UK*[71] the ECtHR referred to this procedure, as provided for in the Special Immigration Appeals Commission Bill with approval as a method of seeking comply with Art 6 while also complying with the demands of national security.[72] In *R v H*[73] the House of Lords considered Strasbourg jurisprudence, when considering the procedure to be adopted where public interest immunity was claimed in a criminal trial. The House approved, in exceptional circumstances, consideration of evidence by the Court without notice to a defendant and, if necessary, the appointment of special counsel to protect the interests of the defendant. It held, however, that disclosure must be ordered if the effect of non-disclosure would be to render the trial process, viewed as a whole, unfair to the defendant. Lord Bingham, giving the opinion of the House, reviewed the Strasbourg jurisprudence and began by stating:

The problem of reconciling an individual defendant's right to a fair trial with such secrecy as is necessary in a democratic society in the interests of national security or the prevention or investigation of crime is inevitably difficult to resolve in a liberal society governed by the rule of law. It is not surprising that complaints of violation have been made against member states including the United Kingdom, some of which have exposed flaws in or malfunctioning of our domestic procedures. The European Court has however long accepted that some operations must be conducted secretly if they are to be conducted effectively.

---

69 Ibid at 51.
70 [2005] UKHL 45 at para 88.
71 (1999) 27 EHRR 249.
72 See para 52, and para 78.
73 [2004] UKHL 3; [2004] 2 AC 134.

The use of the special advocate procedure has been considered by the domestic courts. In *A v Secretary of State for the Home Dept*[74] Lord Woolf held:

> The proceedings before the Commission involved departures from some of the requirements of article 6. However, having regard to the issues to be inquired into, the proceedings are as fair as could reasonably be achieved. It is true that the detainees and their lawyers do not have the opportunity of examining the closed material. However, the use of separate counsel to act on their behalf in relation to the closed evidence provides a substantial degree of protection. In addition, in deciding upon whether there has been compliance with article 6 it is necessary to look at the proceedings as a whole (including the appeal before this court). When this is done and the exception in relation to national security, referred to in article 6, is given due weight, I am satisfied there is no contravention of that article.

The decision of the Court of Appeal was reversed by the House of Lords, but not in circumstances that affected Lord Woolf's decision on this point. Lord Woolf's decision was approved in *A v Secretary of State for the Home Dept (No 2)*.[75] In *Secretary of State v MB*,[76] as discussed further below, the Court of Appeal also gave approval to the use of Special Advocates and the closed material procedure.[77] In his 2006 Review of the TA[78] Lord Carlile, the government reviewer of the TA, considered that the SA system works rigorously in practice, although he also argued that special training for SAs would be desirable. However, he noted that Amnesty International, Liberty and other such groups

> take a very straightforward view of POAC and its sister organisation the Special Immigration Appeals Commission [SIAC], which dealt amongst other things with the detention provisions now removed from ATCSA 2001. This view is that international and European human rights law do not permit of a jurisdiction in which an individual or organisation is not told the nature of all the evidence to be deployed against them.[79]

'Public' hearing

The hearings in SIAC are not 'public' as required under Art 6(1), but this is justifiable in the interests of national security as Art 6(1) provides, so long as the restriction is proportionate to the legitimate aim pursued. However, arguably proportionality may not be satisfied since even where national security is not in issue – when, for example, the question of Art 3 treatment abroad is being considered – no provision is made for part of the proceedings to be held in public in the sense of admitting journalists to any

74 [2002] EWCA Civ 1202; [2004] QB 335 at para 57.
75 [2004] EWCA Civ 1123; [2005] 1 WLR 414 by Pill LJ at para 51 and Laws LJ at para 235. Once again this decision was reversed by the House of Lords, but not in circumstances which affected the passages in question.
76 [2006] EWHC 1000, [2006] HRLR 29, [2006] 8 CL 108 at paras 85–6; see also para 53.
77 See pp 1450–51.
78 Report on the Operation in 2005 of the Terrorism Act 2000, May 2006, at para 50.
79 Ibid at para 54.

part of them. The POAC sits in public, but is able to hear closed evidence in camera and with the applicant and their representatives excluded. Control order proceedings can be held in private as accepted in *Secretary of State for the Home Dept v E*[80] and in *Secretary of State for the Home Dept v Rideh and J.*[81]

Use of material obtained by third party Article 3 treatment (torture or inhuman or degrading treatment) under Article 6 in non-criminal proceedings?

In *A and Others*,[82] as discussed in detail below,[83] the House of Lords had to consider whether the court could take account of evidence that might have derived from torture perpetrated in another country. The decision is, it is argued, relevant to proceedings not only in SIAC, but also in the POAC and in control order proceedings. In criminal proceedings s 76(2)(a) PACE would apply and the evidence could not be admitted.[84] Lord Bingham, giving the leading judgment in *A and Others*, considered that the issue was one of constitutional principle, and found that evidence obtained by torturing another human being cannot lawfully be admitted against a party to proceedings in a British court, irrespective of where, or by whom, or on whose authority the torture was inflicted.[85] But the most important aspect of the case was that of the burden of proof placed on the Secretary of State where the question is raised whether the material relied on might have been obtained by third party torture.

The majority in the House found that SIAC should not admit the evidence if it concluded on a balance of probabilities that it was obtained by torture. In other words, where SIAC was left in doubt as to whether the evidence was obtained in this way, it should admit it. It was found that it would be unrealistic to expect SIAC to demand that each piece of information should be traced back to its ultimate source and the circumstances in which it was obtained investigated so that it could be proved piece by piece, that it was *not* obtained under torture. Lord Hope, in the majority, considered that the threshold should not be put that high[86] and the majority in the Lords agreed to that test.

Thus, reliance can be placed by the Secretary of State on material obtained by torture if the court cannot determine on the balance of probabilities that it was so obtained. Further, the initial decision by the Secretary of State to impose a control order under PTA 2005 or to proscribe an organisation under TA 2000, as amended in 2006, could be based on material obtained by torture. Further, if material was obtained by the use of inhuman or degrading treatment, but not torture, it could, according to this decision, be admitted and relied on. This appears to be the case even if it was proved by the applicant beyond reasonable doubt that the material was so obtained. If inhuman or degrading treatment was perpetrated by British officials to obtain the material, then

---

80 [2007] EWHC 33 (Admin).
81 [2007] EWHC 804 (Admin).
82 [2005] UKHL 71.
83 See pp 1454–62.
84 See Chapter 13, p 1269.
85 At para 51.
86 At para 119.

clearly the applicant could rely on Art 3 and s 7(1)(a) HRA to bring proceedings against the state. But, it appears, from *A and Others*, that he could not rely on Art 6(1) in arguing that the evidence should not be admitted.

Reversed burdens of proof and the presumption of innocence in Article 6(2)

The right to a fair criminal trial arises under Art 6(1), and the presumption of innocence is guaranteed in Art 6(2). That presumption is an aspect of the right to a fair trial. Article 6(2) provides: 'Everyone charged with a criminal offence shall be presumed innocent until proved guilty according to law.' A number of the offences under the TA 2000, as amended, may be regarded as infringing the presumption of innocence at trial. This may be due to the use of presumptions against the defendant, and/or to the lack of a need to prove *mens rea*. A number of the special offences contain, as discussed below, a 'reversed' *mens rea*: the defendant has the burden of disproving knowledge or intent. Strictly speaking, the burden of proof is unchanged but, clearly, where the prosecution has merely to prove a minimal *actus reus* beyond reasonable doubt, its burden is significantly lowered, while the presumption of innocence is undermined. For example, under s 57 TA an accused who chooses not to give or call evidence may be convicted by virtue of presumptions against him and on reasonable suspicion falling short of proof. Section 58 TA allows an accused who chooses not to give or call evidence to be convicted without any *mens rea* being proved. A number of the offences under the TA, including those contained in ss 11, 12, 13, 18, 19, 56 TA have similar features: there is no need for the prosecution to show *mens rea* and the *actus reus* of these offences tends to be minimal. For example, certain offences rely on a need to prove reasonable suspicion only, regarding the main or only ingredient of the offence; under s 13 TA the *actus reus* can consist of doing something which gives rise to reasonable suspicion that support is being expressed for a proscribed organisation; under s 19 TA the prosecution merely has to prove that the defendant failed to report information. Unwittingly collecting funds that could eventually be used by an organisation within s 1 TA is an offence under s 18, and the main burden of proof is then placing on the defendant to disprove a key element of the offence, under s 18(2). Clearly, the interpretation of these provisions in practice will depend on the attitude of the domestic judiciary. The offences introduced under the TA 2006 of glorifying terrorism (s 1) and of engaging in preparation of terrorist acts (s 5), while very broad, place a conventional burden on the prosecution to prove *mens rea*.[87]

Ex p Kebilene and Others

Since presumptions against the accused and the lack of need to show *mens rea* are features of a number of provisions of the TA 2000;[88] they may therefore undermine the guarantee under Art 6(2). The decisions in the Divisional Court on appeal and in

---

87 See pp 1410, 1418 below.

88 It may be noted that a means of narrowing down the use of presumptions was established in *R v Killen* [1974] NI 220 which held that, under the existing law, although the fact of possession constituted a prima facie case, the guilt of the accused still had to be proved beyond all reasonable doubt.

the House of Lords in *R v DPP ex p Kebilene and Others*[89] provided highly significant indications as to the stance which was likely to be taken regarding the compatibility of Art 6 with such provisions, since they concerned provisions which were then reproduced in the TA. The decision also influenced the drafting of the TA in relation to certain defences in it, as discussed below.

A robust interpretation of Art 6(2) was adopted in the Divisional Court. The first three defendants had been arrested and charged under s 16A of the Prevention of Terrorism Act 1989, as inserted (now encapsulated in s 57 TA). At trial the judge ruled that s 16A is incompatible with Art 6(2). The DPP, when asked to reconsider his consent to the prosecution, appeared before the judge to argue that the ruling was wrong since in his opinion, based on legal advice, the two were compatible. The fourth defendant, Rechachi, was arrested and charged under ss 16A and 16B of the 1989 Act, as inserted. Following the DPP's consent to the institution of proceedings, he was arraigned and pleaded not guilty. The defendants sought judicial review of the DPP's decisions. The Lord Chief Justice found that the crucial question concerned the impact, if any, of the Human Rights Act on the exercise of the DPP's decision to give his consent to prosecute, between its enactment and the bringing into force of its main sections. The decision to give consent was reviewed, taking into account the ruling of the judge as to the incompatibility of s 16A and Art 6(2). The public interest in prosecution was taken into account. One relevant aspect of that interest was whether, if the applicants were convicted, their convictions would be upheld on appeal. If at the time of any appeal, it was found, the main provisions of the Human Rights Act were in force, the applicants would be entitled to rely on ss 7(1)(b) and 22(4) of the Act (affording the Act a measure of retrospectivity when used as a 'shield' against a public authority).[90] The DPP had relied on legal advice to the effect that the provisions in question were not incompatible with Art 6(2). The Court could therefore, properly, consider the soundness of that advice despite the provision of s 29(3) of the Supreme Court Act 1981, which impliedly precludes such review.

The applicants submitted that the presumption of innocence under Art 6(2) was infringed if a legal burden was placed on a defendant to disprove any substantial ingredient of the offence with which he was charged. They argued that ss 16A and B placed such a burden on defendants. The Lord Chief Justice, Lord Bingham, found that both sections undermined the presumption of innocence under Art 6(2) 'in a blatant and obvious way' due to the use of presumptions and the possibility of conviction on reasonable suspicion falling short of proof under s 16A, and the lack of a need to prove *mens rea* under s 16B. Lord Bingham observed: 'Under section 16A a defendant could be convicted even if the jury entertained a reasonable doubt whether he knew that the items were in his premises and whether he had the items for a terrorist purpose.'[91] He pointed out that this conclusion was influenced by the absolute nature of the guarantees under Art 6. Therefore the DPP's continuing decision to proceed with the prosecution of the defendants under ss 16A and 16B was declared to be unlawful. This decision was intended to mean, in effect, that ss 16A and 16B of the 1989 Act should be rendered

---

89 [1999] 4 All ER 801.
90 See Chapter 4, pp 239–40.
91 At p 190H.

nugatory due to the incompatibility found. It was especially of interest for its robust interpretation of the requirements of the presumption of innocence under Art 6(2).

The House of Lords, in a cautious judgment, unanimously overturned the Divisional Court decision, on the narrow ground that under s 29(3) of the Supreme Court Act the DPP's consent to a prosecution is not reviewable, or reviewable only in exceptional cases. The appeals before the House were only by Mr Kebeline and two others; the case against Rechachi had been discontinued. The focus was therefore only on s 16A. On the issue of judicial review Lord Steyn noted that the Divisional Court had accepted that once the HRA was fully in force it would not be possible to apply for judicial review on the ground that a decision to prosecute is in breach of a Convention right. The only available remedies would be in the trial process or on appeal. He found that it would be strange if in the interim period between the enactment of the HRA and the coming into force of its central provisions, defendants in criminal trials were entitled to an additional remedy by way of judicial review. He also found that since reverse legal burden provisions appeared in other legislation in force at the time,[92] the entertaining of such challenges outside the trial and appeal process might seriously disrupt the criminal justice system. In support of this point he also noted that if the Divisional Court's present ruling was correct, it would be possible in other cases, which did not involve reverse legal burden provisions, to challenge decisions to prosecute in judicial review proceedings.

Lord Hope agreed with Lord Steyn as regards the non-availability of judicial review. He went on to consider the view that might be taken of the compatibility of s 16A with Art 6(2). He said:

> I see great force in the Divisional Court's view that on the natural and ordinary interpretation there is repugnancy [in s 16A]. To introduce concepts of reasonable limits, balance or flexibility, as to none of which article 6.2 says anything, may be seen as undermining or marginalising the philosophy embodied in the straightforward provision that everyone charged with a criminal offence shall be presumed innocent until proved guilty according to law.

But he went on to find that s 16A might be compatible with Art 6(2) bearing in mind the 'strong adjuration' of s 3 HRA. He considered that s 3 might require s 16A to be interpreted as imposing on the defendant an evidential, but not a persuasive (or ultimate), burden of proof, although he found that this was 'not the natural and ordinary meaning of section 16A'. It was, however, he found, a *possible* meaning. In so finding he cited Professor Glanville Williams in 'The Logic of "Exceptions"'[93] to the effect

---

92 The Prevention of Corruption Act 1916, s 2; the Sexual Offences Act 1956, s 30(2); the Obscene Publications Act 1959, s 2(5); the Obscene Publications Act 1964, s 1(3); the Misuse of Drugs Act 1971, s 28; the Public Order Act 1986, ss 18(4), 19(2), 20(2), 21(3), 22(3)–(5) and 23(3); the Criminal Justice Act 1988, s 93D(6); the Prevention of Terrorism (Temporary Provisions) Act 1989, ss 10(2)–(3), 11(2), 16A(3), 16B(1) and 17(3)(a) and (3A)(a) (now repealed by the TA 2000); the Official Secrets Act 1989, ss 1(5), 2(3), 3(4) and 4(4)–(5); and the Drug Trafficking Act 1994, ss 53(6) and 58(2)(a). To this list there may be added the Explosive Substances Act 1883, s 4(1): see *R v Fegan* [1972] NI 80; *R v Berry* [1985] AC 246.

93 [1988] CLJ 261, p 265.

that: 'unless the contrary is proved' can be taken, in relation to a defence, to mean 'unless sufficient evidence is given to the contrary'; and that the statute may then be satisfied by 'evidence that, if believed and on the most favourable view, could be taken by a reasonable jury to support the defence'. Lord Hope took *R v Killen*[94] into account in support of the possibility of such an interpretation. It was held in *Killen* that an identical provision in s 7(1) of the Northern Ireland (Emergency Provisions) Act 1973, placing an onus on the accused to disprove his knowledge of possession, should not be used unless, having done so, the court would be left satisfied beyond reasonable doubt of the guilt of the accused.

In other words, Lord Hope considered that the meaning of s 16A could be affected by reading into it an implied meaning under s 3 HRA. But in arriving at the meaning of s 16A he thought that Art 6(2) could be viewed as qualified to an extent despite the fact that the guarantee it enshrines is expressed in absolute terms.[95] He said: 'In this area difficult choices may have to be made by the executive or the legislature between the rights of the individual and the needs of society.' He considered that in interpreting s 16A in the light of Art 6(2) the interests of the individual could be balanced against those of society and that in striking that balance the Convention jurisprudence and that which is to be found from cases decided in other jurisdictions suggest that account might legitimately be taken of the problems which the legislation is designed to address. He looked at the example of *Salabiaku v France*[96] in which it was found that while Art 6(2) 'does not ... regard presumptions of fact or of law provided for in the criminal law with indifference' it permits the operation of such presumptions against the accused so long as the law in question confines such presumptions 'within reasonable limits which take into account the importance of what is at stake and maintain the rights of the defence'.[97] The Court was concerned with an article in the Customs Code dealing with the smuggling of prohibited goods. Where possession of prohibited goods was established, the person was deemed liable for the offence of smuggling. The provision appeared to lay down an irrebuttable presumption; the code did not provide expressly for any defence. But the Court held that there was no failure to comply with Art 6(2), because in practice the courts were careful not to resort automatically to the presumption but exercised their power of assessment in the light of all the evidence. Lord Hope noted that the guidance which was given in *Salabiaku* was applied by the Commission in *H v United Kingdom*,[98] in which the complaint was that the burden on the accused in criminal proceedings to prove insanity on the balance of probabilities

---

94 [1974] NI 220.
95 He recognised the difficulty that Art 6(2) is expressed in unqualified terms: 'It will be easier for such an area of judgment to be recognised where the Convention itself requires a balance to be struck, much less so where the right is stated in terms which are unqualified. It will be easier for it to be recognised where the issues involve questions of social or economic policy, much less so where the rights are of high constitutional importance or are of a kind where the courts are especially well placed to assess the need for protection. But even where the right is stated in terms which are unqualified the courts will need to bear in mind the jurisprudence of the European Court which recognises that due account should be taken of the special nature of terrorist crime and the threat which it poses to a democratic society.' He gave the example of the ruling of the Court in *Murray v United Kingdom* (1994) 19 EHRR 193, 222, para 47.
96 (1988) 13 EHRR 379.
97 At p 388, para 28.
98 Appl No 15023/89.

was contrary to the presumption of innocence and therefore in violation of Art 6(2). He also considered *Bates v United Kingdom*,[99] in which the complaint was that Art 6(2) had been violated by the presumption of fact in s 5(5) of the Dangerous Dogs Act 1991 by which it is to be presumed that the dog is one to which s 1 of that Act applies unless the contrary is shown by the accused. In the *Bates* case the Commission held that s 5(5) fell within reasonable limits, even in the light of what was at stake for the applicant, given the opportunity expressly provided to the defence to rebut the presumption of fact, and that s 5(5) was applied in a manner compatible with the presumption of innocence.

Lord Hope concluded that although Art 6(2) is expressed in absolute terms, it is not regarded as imposing an absolute prohibition on reverse onus clauses, whether they be evidential (presumptions of fact) or persuasive (presumptions of law). Applying an approach which balanced the interests of the individual and society[100] he found:

> It is not immediately obvious that it would be imposing an unreasonable burden on an accused who was in possession of articles from which an inference of involvement in terrorism could be drawn to provide an explanation for his possession of them which would displace that inference.

He left open the question whether s 16A did in fact strike the right balance, but he clearly reached a conclusion which differed sharply from that of Lord Bingham in the Divisional Court in finding that Art 6(2) could be interpreted in such a way as to permit the use of presumptions against the accused.

Lord Hope's approach is open to criticism in two respects. He rejected the use of the doctrine of the margin of appreciation as inapplicable in national courts. But he proceeded to take the outcomes of applications at Strasbourg into account without adverting to the influence the doctrine had had on them. He also took account of s 1 of the Canadian Charter which states that the rights and freedoms it guarantees are 'subject only to such reasonable limits prescribed by law as can be demonstrably justified in a free and democratic society' without adverting to the deliberate omission of such wording from certain Articles of the Convention, including Art 6. In contrast, such wording is clearly reflected in the exceptions of para 2 of Arts 8–11 which allow interferences with the primary rights if, *inter alia*, 'necessary in a democratic society'. The clear implication is that certain of the Articles, including Art 6, do not admit of an interpretation similar to that of s 1 of the Charter. Although the Court in *Salabiaku* accepted that some presumptions against the accused might not infringe Art 6(2), such acceptance appeared to rest partly on the application of the margin of appreciation doctrine, and partly on the finding that in practice the courts were careful not to resort automatically to the presumption, but exercised their power of assessment in the light of all the evidence. Lord Hope's approach would tend to water down the rights enshrined in the Convention, even where they were unqualified. The Lord Chief Justice's approach was more robust than that of Lord Hope and would tend to give the rights full weight and efficacy.

---

99 Appl No 26280/95.
100 With reference to Lord Woolf's findings in *Attorney-General of Hong Kong v Lee Kwong-kut* [1993] AC 951, at pp 970–71.

The post-HRA approach to the Terrorism Act offences

Kebilene is relevant to all those offences under the TA, as amended, that create presumptions against the defendant. A finding that those features are incompatible with Art 6(2) now has to be made during the trial or on appeal, rather than in judicial review proceedings. Lord Steyn's judgment suggests that a finding of an abuse of process might be made at trial even where the primary legislation allowed such an abuse and that if this occurred Parliamentary sovereignty would not be undermined even if, effectively, certain provisions of the 2000 Act were thereby rendered virtually nugatory. It was clear pre-HRA that a number of the TA provisions uncovered by s 118 might have to be reinterpreted under s 3 HRA, to read down legal burdens to evidential ones. On this basis it was apparent that the application of s 6(2)(b) HRA, allowing for the possibility of a prosecution under a provision incompatible with the Convention,[101] could be avoided.

A number of the TA offences considered below infringe the presumption of innocence encapsulated in Art 6(2) since they impose a legal burden on the accused to prove his innocence of blameworthy conduct. In a number of instances the accused may commit a criminal offence without engaging in such conduct – this is particularly true of the proscription provisions discussed below; he is then placed in the position of having to disprove a significant element of the offence. In other instances the provision imposes a reversed *mens rea* on the accused – this is true of a number of possession and preparatory offences. Where this occurs there are at least three different Convention-based arguments that can be employed to ease the burden on the defendant, depending on the offence involved and whether a defence is provided.

First, s 118 TA addresses compatibility with Art 6(2). It appeared that s 118 was a direct response to the views expressed by both the Divisional Court and the House of Lords in *R v Director of Public Prosecutions ex p Kebilene*.[102] Section 118 deals with defences provided to a person charged with certain offences under the Act, applying where it is a defence for a person charged with an offence to prove a particular matter. It provides that certain defences impose only an evidential burden, not a legal burden, on the defendant. Section 118 provides:

(1) Sub-section (2) applies where in accordance with the provisions mentioned in sub-section (5) it is a defence for a person charged with an offence to prove a particular matter.

(2) If the person adduces evidence which is sufficient to raise an issue with respect to the matter the court or jury shall assume that the defence is satisfied unless the prosecution proves beyond reasonable doubt that it is not.

. . .

(5) The provisions in respect of which sub-sections (2) and (4) apply are:

(a) sections 12(4), 39(5)(a) 54, 57, 58, 77 and 103 of this Act . . .

---

101 See Chapter 4, p 216.
102 [2000] Cr App R 275; [2000] 2 AC 326.

This section was enacted in order to deal with the possibility that certain of the statutory provisions providing for such defences would probably constitute an unjustified infringement of a person's rights under Art 6(2) of the Convention in that they infringed the presumption of innocence by imposing the burden of disproving guilt on the defendant. Section 118 appears to mean that s 57 of the 2000 Act (reproducing s 16A) is rendered compatible with Art 6(2).[103] Under s 118(2) if the accused person 'adduces evidence which is sufficient to raise an issue with respect to the matter the court or jury shall assume that the defence is satisfied unless the prosecution proves beyond reasonable doubt that it is not'. But s 118 only deals with certain sections of the Act.[104]

Second, even if the offence in question is not one to which s 118 applies, the House of Lords' decision in *Attorney General's Reference (No 4 of 2002)*,[105] discussed further below, may apply. Lord Bingham took a stance towards Art 6(2) that differed from that of Lord Hope in *Kebilene* since he did not take the course of implying limitations into Art 6(2). He found that a person who had not engaged in any blameworthy conduct could commit an offence under the Act (the case related to s 11(1) TA – the offence of belonging to a banned organisation) and that the presumption of innocence was infringed by requiring him or her to disprove involvement in the organisation at the time in question (s 11(2)). Since the Lords found that this burden placed on the accused impermissibly infringed the presumption of innocence, it was found appropriate, pursuant to s 3 of the 1998 Act, to read down s 11(2) so as to impose on the defendant an evidential burden only, even though that was not Parliament's intention when enacting the sub-section.[106] So Art 6(2) compliance was imposed on the offence of belonging to a proscribed organisation. Obviously this decision only related to one offence. However, as indicated above, a number of offences under the TA follow a similar pattern and are also not covered by s 118.

It was found in *R v Keogh*[107] in the Court of Appeal that *Attorney General's Reference (No 4 of 2002)* extends to other offences that impose in effect a reversed burden of proof on the defendant. In *R v Keogh*[108] the Court of Appeal had to consider the Official Secrets Act 1989, ss 2(3) and 3(4); the provisions, as discussed in Chapter 7,[109] impose a reverse burden according to their natural meaning, namely, that a defendant who was charged under those provisions with making a damaging disclosure had to prove that he had no knowledge or reasonable cause to believe that the disclosure would be damaging. It was found that the Act could operate effectively without the

---

103 *Ex p Kebilene* itself did not provide such guidance. When it came to trial, in February 2000, the prosecution offered no evidence and it was therefore found that there was no case to answer. The prosecution took that course, it appeared, in order to avoid the possibility of having to reveal their sources of information.

104 Sections 12(4), 39(5)(a) 54, 57, 58, 77 and 103.

105 [2004] UKHL 43; [2005] 1 AC 264; [2005] 1 All ER 237. The House of Lords took account of *R v Lambert* [2002] 2 AC 545, HL(E); *R v A (No 2)* [2002] 1 AC 45, HL(E); *R v Johnstone* [2003] 1 WLR 1736, HL(E); *Ghaidan v Godin-Mendoza* [2004] 2 AC 557, HL(E); and *Attorney General's Reference (No 1 of 2004)* [2004] 1 WLR 2111, CA. See pp 1391–92 below.

106 At paras 48–53, 55, 56.

107 [2007] All ER (D) 105 (Mar); [2007] EWCA Crim 528, 7 March 2007.

108 See also Chapter 7, pp. 605–6.

109 See pp 600–2.

imposition of the reverse legal burdens, and that to accord them that meaning would be disproportionate and unjustifiable. If given their natural meaning, those provisions were, it was found, incompatible with art 6 of the Convention, so, following the House of Lords' decision, they should be read down by applying a similar interpretation to that achieved by s 118 of the Terrorism Act 2000, namely, that it was a defence for a defendant to prove a particular matter in that if he adduced evidence which was sufficient to raise an issue with respect to the matter, the court or jury should assume that the defence was satisfied unless the prosecution proved beyond reasonable doubt that it was not. *Keogh* was concerned with a reverse burden – to disprove *mens rea* – while technically *A G's Reference* was not, but with a requirement for a defendant to disprove a significant element of the offence. But it is clear that Art 6(2) applies under s 3 HRA to demand that a reversed burden requiring the defendant to disprove *mens rea*, or a burden placed on the defendant to disprove a significant element of the offence should be read down to an evidential burden only.

Third, if there is no defence on which the *Attorney General's Reference* case argument could bite, it is still arguable that it is relevant where non-blameworthy conduct, or conduct that would not normally be accounted criminal (to use Lord Bingham's words from the House of Lords' decision) is established, but no defence is overtly made available. It would arguably appear anomalous if the fact that Parliament *failed* to provide a defence worsened the position of the defendant. It could be argued that the offence can only be applied in a manner that satisfies the demands of Art 6 and that therefore the defendant must be able to raise Convention points, including Art 6 ones, even where there is no statutory defence. This point was considered in Chapter 8.[110] Where the defendant does raise such points it would appear, following *Attorney General's Reference*, that he would only bear an evidential burden in relation to them.

Freedom of expression, association and assembly under Articles 10 and 11

The Terrorism Act 2000, as amended, together with the Terrorism Act 2006, creates offences and sanctions able to stifle the expression of a range of dissenting groups and outlaw the very existence of many of them. Certain provisions potentially also prevent or curb journalistic investigation of the activities of certain of those groups. Proscription – the banning of groups deemed 'terrorist' clearly strikes at freedom of association as well as freedom of expression, taking account, *inter alia*, of the offences of belonging to a proscribed organisation and the offences relating to meetings where members of such organisations are speaking. The provisions discussed below under the TA making it a criminal offence for proscribed organisations to distribute literature, hold or speak at meetings. The offence of 'glorification' of terrorism under the TA 2006, clearly represents an infringement of freedom of expression, although potentially justifiable. Control orders imposed under the Prevention of Terrorism Act 2005, which impose curfews on suspects and disallow communication with non-approved persons, clearly affect the freedoms of expression, association and assembly.

110 See p 783.

If Arts 10 or 11 are relevant due to the nature of the offence in question (or other Convention Articles, such as Art 1 of the First Protocol where terrorist funding or property is involved) then they can be raised under the argument that the court is under a duty due to s 6 HRA to apply the provisions compatibly with the Convention guarantees,[111] whether a defence is or is not expressly provided. They should not be raised merely as part of a defence – such as a defence of 'reasonable excuse' – since to do so turns those Articles on their heads: under para 2 of each Article it is for the state to prove that the interference with the right is necessary and proportionate, not for the defendant to prove that a Convention guarantee constitutes a defence to a state action.

The ability of the 2000 Act, and the additional offences introduced in 2001 and 2006, to threaten expression and association is in particular the case given that the aims of some of the groups likely to be affected are, broadly speaking, political ones, and so the expression in question may fall into the category of political speech.[112] The high regard in which freedom of speech and of the press, as 'essential foundations of a democratic society'[113] is held by the Strasbourg institutions was discussed in Part II and need not be rehearsed in any detail here. As discussed, it is a marked feature of the Strasbourg Art 10 jurisprudence that clearly political speech receives a particularly high degree of protection. Where national security was raised as an issue in *Observer and Guardian Newspapers v UK*[114] the margin of appreciation conceded was broader but a violation of Art 10 was found. Where the speech directly concerns government actions – such as the war in Iraq – the stance taken is particularly robust, even where issues of national security appear to arise. In *Incal v Turkey*,[115] finding a breach of Art 10, the Court said that 'the limits of permissible criticism are wider with regard to the government than in respect of private citizens', and that the dominant position the government occupies should persuade it to display restraint in resorting to criminal proceedings. The Court found that although the argument had been raised that the measures in question were counter-terrorist, the links of the applicant to terrorism were uncertain.[116] This stance reflects values endemic in the Convention: it is clearly difficult to show that an interference with democracy-supporting speech is 'necessary in a democratic society'.[117]

Determination to protect political expression is readily evident in UK courts, as the introduction to Part II indicated, particularly in cases where journalistic material raises political issues,[118] although deference to widely drafted primary legislation,[119] or

---

111 See Chapter 4, pp 216–17.
112 See Barendt, E, *Freedom of Speech*, 1st edn, 1987, pp 20 and 23 respectively. See Meiklejohn, A, 'The First Amendment is an Absolute' (1961) Sup Ct Rev 245 and *Political Freedom* (1960), esp pp 115–24.
113 *Observer and Guardian v United Kingdom*, judgment of 26 November 1991, Series A, no 216, pp 29–30, para 59.
114 (1991) 14 EHRR 153.
115 (2000) 29 EHRR 449.
116 The conviction of the applicant was found to be disproportionate to the aim of countering terrorism pursued.
117 Article 10(2).
118 *Reynolds v Times Newspapers* [1999] 4 All ER 609; *Derbyshire County Council v Times Newspapers* [1993] AC 534.
119 *Secretary of State for Home Affairs ex p Brind* [1991] 1 AC 696.

governmental arguments from national security,[120] has resulted in the ready upholding of restrictions on directly political speech. Earlier findings to the effect that: 'The media . . . are an essential foundation of any democracy'[121] were reinforced by pronouncements in the House of Lords' decision in *Reynolds*,[122] which afforded an explicit recognition to the duty to inform the people on matters of legitimate public interest.[123]

Since press freedom in relation to political expression has clearly been recognised as having a particularly high value in UK and Convention jurisprudence, and therefore the possible inclusion of journalists in the wide net of counter-terrorist liability discussed below requires a very strong justification, particularly as it potentially extends to a range of groups covering such divergent issues as animal rights, environmental matters, abortion, the national identity of groups such as the Kurds in Turkey, and also militant fundamentalist religious beliefs. It creates dilemmas for journalists that have any association with such groups – by, for example, producing specialist publications aimed at minority groups with some association with a proscribed group. This is true, for example, of publications aimed at the Kurdish minority in the UK who may have some associations with the PKK.[124] *R (on the application of the Kurdistan Workers' Party and Others) v Secretary of State for the Home Dept*,[125] discussed below, illustrated the problem for journalists. The case of *Gillan*, discussed in Chapter 11,[126] demonstrated that provisions aimed at terrorism can readily have an effect on the freedom of expression of those entirely uninvolved in terrorist activity but participating in or reporting on dissent. However, the activities and stance of certain groups, including Al-Qaeda run counter to the justifications for political speech, so the argument from democracy does not apply to them.

While earlier Strasbourg jurisprudence was more protective of state interests,[127] the recent 'association' jurisprudence of the Court is more interventionist. In *Socialist Party and Others v Turkey*[128] the Court allowed only a very narrow margin of appreciation in finding that the dissolution of the Socialist Party of Turkey had breached Art 11. The Court said that democracy demands that diverse political programmes should be debated, 'even those that call into question the way a state is currently organised'. The Court did not accept that the message of the group that a federal system should be put in place which would ensure that Kurds would be put on an equal footing with Turkish citizens generally, amounted to incitement to violence. The dissolution of the party was disproportionate to the aim in view – the preservation of national security. This stance

---

120 *Attorney General v Guardian Newspapers (No 2)* [1990] 1 AC 109.
121 *Francome v Mirror Group Newspapers* [1984] 1 WLR 892, p 898, *per* Sir John Donaldson.
122 *Reynolds v Times Newspapers* HL [1999] 4 All ER 609, judgement of 28 October available from the House of Lords website: www.publications.parliament.uk/pa/ld/ldjudinf.htm.
123 As Lord Nicholls put it: 'freedom to disseminate and receive information on political matters is essential to the proper functioning of the system of parliamentary democracy cherished in this country. This freedom enables those who elect representatives to Parliament to make an informed choice, regarding individuals as well as policies, and those elected to make informed decisions'.
124 See p 1404.
125 [2002] EWHC Admin 644.
126 See pp 1119–21.
127 See *Glasenapp v FRG* A 104 (1986); *Kosiek v FRG* A 105 (1986); *CCSU v UK* (1988) 10 EHRR 269.
128 Judgment of 25 May 1998 (Appl No 20/1997/804/1007); (1999) 27 EHRR 51, paras 41, 47 and 50.

was in accordance with the Convention jurisprudence which has quite consistently recognised the need to protect the interests of minority and excluded groups.[129] Similar findings were made in *Sidiropoulos v Greece*.[130] The Court said that one of the most important aspects of freedom of association was that citizens should be able to form a legal group with the aim of acting collectively in their mutual interest. Similarly, in *Vogt v Germany*[131] the Court held that a woman dismissed from her teaching post due to her membership of an extreme left wing group had suffered a violation of both Arts 10 and 11.

In *United Communist Party of Turkey v Turkey*[132] the United Communist Party of Turkey, TBKP, was formed in 1990. The Constitutional Court made an order dissolving the TBKP, which entailed the liquidation of the party and the transfer of its assets to the Treasury. The order was based on the inclusion in its name of the prohibited word 'communist' and the alleged encouragement of Kurdish separatism. The TBKP and its leaders applied to the Commission, complaining that the dissolution of the party infringed their right to freedom of association as guaranteed by the European Convention on Human Rights 1950, Art 11. It was found that Art 11 was applicable to the present case. It was further found that the exceptions set out in Art 11(2) had to be construed strictly in relation to political parties. In that case, a political party's choice of name was in principle not able justify dissolution in the absence of other relevant and sufficient circumstances, and there was no evidence that the TBKP represented a real threat to Turkish society or the Turkish state. A scrutiny of the TBKP's programme showed that it intended to resolve the Kurdish issue through dialogue. As such, it was penalised solely for exercising freedom of expression. In the circumstances, the drastic measure of the dissolution of the TBKP was disproportionate to the aim pursued and consequently unnecessary in a democratic society. Accordingly, it was found that the measure infringed Art 11.

In relation to certain groups the infringement of Arts 10 and 11 may be proportionate to the aims pursued, but this is not necessarily the case in relation to all such groups, especially those whose 'terrorist' activities only threaten regimes abroad. The 2000 Act also has the potential to threaten rights of assembly and expression of groups only doubtfully viewed in common parlance as 'terrorist', such as animal rights' or environmental activists. Proscription orders are not sought against all the groups that meet the definition of terrorism under s 1 TA; in effect, proportionality is built into the scheme via executive decisions as to which groups to proscribe or prosecute under the general counter-terrorist offences. The proscription or prosecution of members of Al-Qaeda or linked groups can clearly be viewed as proportionate to the aim pursued under Arts 10 and 11, para 2, and quite probably in any event Art 17, providing that the Convention is not to be interpreted so as to imply a right 'for any state, group or

---

129 Such groups have included criminals: *Soering v UK* A 161 (1989); prisoners: *Ireland v UK* A 25 (1978), *Golder v UK* A 18 (1975); racial minorities: *East African Asians* cases 3 EHRR 76 (1973), *Hilton v UK* No 5613/72, 4 DR 177 (1976) (no breach found on facts); sexual minorities: *Dudgeon v UK* A 45 (1981), *B v France* A 232-C (1992); political minorities: *Arrowsmith v UK* No 7050/75, 19 DR 5 (1978); religious minorities: *Kokkinakis v Greece* A 260-A (1993).

130 (Chamber) (1998) available from the Court's website, www.dhcour.coe.fr.

131 (1995) 21 EHRR 205.

132 1998 WL 1043934 (ECHR), 4 BHRC 1; (1998) 26 EHRR 121; [1998] HRCD 247.

person to engage in any activity . . . aimed at the destruction of any of the [Convention rights] or at their limitation to a greater extent than . . . provided for in the Convention', would apply.[133] Al-Qaeda is not seeking to use legitimate democratic means in order to persuade persons of its political agenda, and therefore the invocation on its behalf of Convention rights fundamentally based on democratic values is affected. But, as argued below, certain groups have been proscribed, such as the PKK, where it is arguable that the initial proportionality inquiry carried out in effect by the Home Secretary was defective.

Counter-terrorist provisions, therefore, which potentially extend to domestic protest groups putting forward a wide range of political messages – using that term in the broad sense which Strasbourg has endorsed – interfere with the flow of information and ideas; this can also be said of groups that do not threaten national security in the UK and which could be viewed as 'freedom fighters'. Such provisions therefore come into conflict with the expression, association, and assembly of a very wide and diverse range of groups and persons and therefore call into question their compatibility with democratic values. As discussed in Chapter 8, domestic 'protest' groups that adopt the use of direct action may create the possibilities of disorder, of harm to citizens and damage to property.[134] They may eventually, if sufficiently resourced and well organised, threaten national security. Clearly, the state has a duty to protect citizens from their attentions. The need to give weight to such interests explains the general acceptance of the freedoms of expression, assembly and association as non-absolute rights,[135] even though it may be that direct action and more forceful protest is most likely to bring about change. 'Terrorist'/protest groups that may affect national security in another country but not in the UK may want to use the legitimate outlets of expression and protest to further their cause in the UK. The ordinary criminal law exists, however, in order to punish members of all such groups for specific actions domestically, such as causing criminal damage, while public order law is available to control protests where harm to persons or property is a possibility. It will be argued below that the potentially chilling impact of the counter-terrorist legislation on the freedoms of expression and assembly, and on the right to a fair trial, is disproportionate to the aims pursued and in a number of respects is, therefore, contrary to the claims of the Home Secretary, unnecessary in a democratic society.

Article 3 treatment

Deporting suspected terrorists who could face Article 3 treatment abroad?

The government views itself as confronted by a dilemma in respect of persons who are suspected of being international terrorists but who cannot be extradited, or deported to their country of origin, because there are grounds to think that they would there be subject to torture or inhuman and degrading treatment, since to do so would violate

---

133 See further Chapter 2, p 112.
134 See pp 696–98.
135 See the leading US case, *Hague v Committee for Industrial Organisation* 307 US 496 (1938). For further discussion, see Williams, DGT [1987] Crim LR 167.

Art 3 of the Convention. The decision of the European Court of Human Rights in *Soering v UK*,[136] confirmed in *Chahal v UK*,[137] found that a breach of Art 3 will arise where a country deports a person to another country, knowing that he or she will face a substantial risk of Art 3 treatment in that other country. It should also be noted that the UK has ratified Protocol 6[138] and therefore cannot deport persons to countries where there is a real risk that the death penalty will be imposed.[139]

It is not possible for the government to enter a derogation to Art 3 under Art 15 of the Convention.[140] If this was possible it would have allowed the Home Secretary to deport persons to various countries, regardless of the fact that they might there be subjected to torture or other forms of Art 3 treatment. The Joint Committee on Human Rights at one point appeared to take the view that the government could have escaped from the demands of Art 3 by denouncing the whole Convention[141] and then re-entering it, at the same time entering a reservation to Art 3.[142] However, it is probable that such a reservation would have been viewed as invalid since as a matter of general international law it is accepted that reservations are not permitted to non-derogable Articles.[143] Had the UK sought to take this immensely controversial course, it would almost certainly have been found to be in breach of Art 3 and would also have breached the International Covenant on Civil and Political Rights (ICCPR) which does not allow for derogation from Art 7, which covers Art 3 treatment.[144] It is also a party to the United Nations Convention Against Torture and Other Cruel, Inhuman

---

136 (1989) 11 EHRR 439, paras 90–91.

137 (1996) 23 EHRR 413, para 74.

138 Protocol 6 prohibits the death penalty in time of peace: it was ratified on 27 January 1999.

139 *X v Spain* D R 37 (1984) p93; *Aylor-Davis v France* (1994) 76-A DR 164; *Raidl v Austria* (1995) 82-A DR 134.

140 The guarantee under Art 3 is one of the non-derogable guarantees under Art 15(2).

141 Under Art 58. See 2nd Report of the Joint Committee, para 19.

142 Section 15 HRA provides powers for the Secretary of State to make designated reservations by order. Under Art 57 of the Convention this power can only be exercised at the point of ratification.

143 There is no explicit exclusion of the right to make reservations to Art 3. The matter is one of general international law: reservations may not be made which are incompatible with the object and purpose of a treaty (Vienna Convention, Art 19(c)). There is little doubt that the ECtHR would claim the right to determine this question under the ECHR (see Van Dijk and Van Hoof, *The European Convention on Human Rights: Theory and Practice*, 2nd edn, 1998, pp 774–75 and cf p 776 for the non-derogable provisions). It has not yet had to do so. France has a reservation with respect to Art 15: 17 YB 4 (1974). The general opinion is that this does not give France the right to derogate from a non-derogable provision, nor would it protect France from the jurisdiction of the Court to determine the question. The UN Human Rights Committee (HRC) has taken a strong position against the power of states to make reservations with respect to the non-derogable provisions of the Covenant (General Comment 24) and, in the case of torture, an absolute one, since the HRC says torture is contrary to a peremptory norm of international law. Thus, even if the UK could avoid the Art 3 duty under the ECHR by reservation, it could not do so under the ICCPR, Art 7. Obviously the UK would not be permitted to enter a reservation to the UN Convention Against Torture. It may be noted that the UN Committee Against Torture made a statement directly communicating with the state Parties (22 November 2001, 27th session) reminding them, in the light of the September 11 atrocities, that obligations under the Convention against Torture in Arts 2, 15 and 16 are non-derogable and 'must be observed in all circumstances'.

144 Article 4(2).

or Degrading Treatment or Punishment 1984[145] and the European Convention for the Prevention of Torture and Inhuman and Degrading Treatment or Punishment 1987.[146]

The government is currently seeking to escape from the effects of *Chahal* by two methods. First, it is hoping that *Chahal* can be – in effect – overturned at Strasbourg. The government is seeking to overturn the *Chahal* ruling by supporting Holland in a case being brought by Mohammad Ramzy, an Algerian accused by the Dutch authorities of involvement in Islamic terrorism. Second, it is seeking to conclude agreements with countries to which it could return the suspects in question. The idea is that under the agreement the returnee would not be exposed to Art 3 treatment in the state to which he was returned. After the London transport bombings in July 2005, the Blair Government signed a series of memorandums of understanding with North African and Middle Eastern countries that would allow terrorist suspects who cannot be tried in Britain to be deported. Memoranda have already been agreed with the governments of Jordan and Libya, and negotiations are underway with Algeria and Lebanon.[147] However, SIAC ruled in April 2007 that two alleged Libyan terrorists could not be deported because they were unlikely to get a fair trial in Libya. The decision threatened the agreement between the British and the Libyan Governments.[148] Libya had pledged that no one deported from Britain would be subjected to torture or other unfair treatment. But SIAC found that deporting the two men would violate the European Convention on Human Rights. It also found, on the basis of the closed evidence, that the two men are a danger to Britain. Neither they nor their lawyers were allowed to see the evidence. This ruling clearly jeopardised the current and potential agreements.

There seems to be no possibility of seeking to justify deporting persons at risk of Art 3 treatment abroad on the basis of implying a proportionality test into Art 3. The argument would have been based on a spectrum analysis of Art 3 treatment, allowing for implied exceptions on grounds of government policy in relation to protecting national security. That possibility – in a different context – was contemplated in the findings of the three dissenting judges in the Court of Appeal in *R (Limbuella) v Secretary of State for the Home Dept.*[149] The case did not arise in the context of terrorism, but in that of asylum-seeking. The respondents were all, at the time when their applications were heard in the Administrative Court, asylum seekers. The Secretary of State decided that they did not make their claims for asylum as soon as reasonably practicable after their arrival in the United Kingdom. So they were excluded from conventional support by the National Asylum Support Service under Part VI of the Immigration and Asylum

---

145 (1985) Cmnd 9593; it came into force in 1987 and it was ratified by the UK in December 1988.

146 (1991) Cm 1634; it was ratified by the UK in June 1988. For discussion, see Evans, M and Morgan, R, *Preventing Torture: A Study of the European Convention for the Prevention of Torture*, 1998. The right to freedom from torture or inhuman or degrading treatment or punishment is also recognised in Art 5 of the Universal Declaration on Human Rights and in many jurisdictions: see Clayton and Tomlinson *The Law of Human Rights*, 2000, Chapter 8, esp pp 412–29. Torture is a crime under International Law: see *R v Bow Street Stipendiary Magistrate ex p Pinochet Ugarte (No 3)* [1999] 2 WLR 827.

147 HC 11.1.06 col GC107.

148 See (2007) *The Times* 27 April.

149 House of Lords: [2005] UKHL 66; Court of Appeal: [2004] QB 1440. For discussion of the case, see Warbrick, C, in Fenwick, Masterman and Phillipson (eds), *Judicial Reasoning Under the Human Rights Act*, 2007.

Act 1999 (the 1999 Act) by s 55(1) of the Nationality, Immigration and Asylum Act 2002. The question considered by the House of Lords was whether the Secretary of State was nevertheless obliged by s 55(5)(a) of the 2002 Act to provide support for the respondents under Part VI of the 1999 Act (asylum support) for the purpose of avoiding a breach of Art 3 within the meaning of the HRA. The Court of Appeal and House of Lords dismissed the Secretary of State's appeal against the finding that he was obliged to provide the support in question.

The dissenting judges in the Court of Appeal took the view that it might be possible to justify some forms of Art 3 treatment. They took the view that Art 3 covers degrees of ill-treatment, some of which might be capable of justification. Laws LJ[150] suggested that some acts which exposed the individual to grave suffering from his point of view, might, nevertheless be justified if they arise in the administration or execution of government policy. He subjected Art 3[151] to a spectrum analysis, finding that at one end of the spectrum were acts of violence, including torture, authorised by the state, which are absolutely forbidden. At the other end of the spectrum, he found, a decision in the exercise of lawful policy might expose an individual to a marked degree of suffering due to his particular circumstances, which could be subject to justification. Laws LJ took the view that a decision in relation to policy would be lawful unless the degree of suffering for the individual was so high that the Court was bound to limit its right to implement the policy.

Lord Nicholls, however, found in the House of Lords that an exercise of judgment is required in order to determine whether in any given case the treatment or punishment has attained the necessary degree of severity. He found that at that point it would be open to a court to consider whether, taking all the facts into account, that test had been satisfied. But he found that it would be wrong to lend any encouragement to the idea that the test could be more exacting where the treatment or punishment which would otherwise be found to be inhuman or degrading was the result of what Laws LJ referred to as legitimate government policy. He said that that would be to:

> ... introduce into the absolute prohibition, by the backdoor, considerations of proportionality. They are relevant when an obligation to do something is implied into the Convention. In that case the obligation of the state is not absolute and unqualified. But proportionality, which gives a margin of appreciation to states, has no part to play when conduct for which it is directly responsible results in inhuman or degrading treatment or punishment. The obligation to refrain from such conduct is absolute.[152]

It appears therefore that the key question that arises when deportation to another country is contemplated on the basis that the potential deportee poses a risk to national security is whether the ill-treatment to which he might be exposed crosses the Art 3 threshold.

---

150 [2004] QB 1440, at para 68.
151 Ibid, para 70.
152 At para 55.

Indefinite detention without trial – incompatibility with Article 3?

Part 4 ATCSA allowed for indefinite detention without trial. It was repealed, but the possibility of reinstating detention without trial was retained in the Prevention of Terrorism Act 2005, as discussed below. It would require a derogation from Art 5 to activate the PTA provisions. It is arguable that subjecting a person to such detention in itself breaches Art 3, as considered in *R v Offen*.[153] The detainee's position could remain uncertain for a very long period. It could be argued in such an instance that detention for an indefinite period of time, combined with the psychological damage caused by such uncertainty and by the inability to reach a secure position, could in itself amount to Art 3 treatment. The conditions of detention on the high security wing of Belmarsh prison have been criticised, and in particular the point was made that they were inappropriate in respect of detainees who have suffered severe psychological damage after being tortured abroad.[154]

There is also the possibility that the application of the derogating control orders scheme (if it is deployed) under PTA 2005 could in itself amount to Art 3 treatment where the only means of escape for non-British citizens from indefinite detention without trial in prison conditions[155] would be to accept the risk of Art 3 treatment abroad. Could it be said in itself to amount to Art 3 treatment to confront a person over a long period of time with such a dilemma, causing severe mental distress? In other words, having been detained without trial for, say, three years, such a detainee might feel, with mounting anguish, that she has no real choice but to take that risk, since she sees little prospect of release otherwise. If the deportation or extradition of a person to a country where she is at risk of facing Art 3 treatment is in breach of Art 3, it is arguable that one could say the same, in principle, of forcing a person to choose between indefinite detention without trial and accepting the risk of Art 3 treatment abroad, since the 'choice' is so circumscribed.

The application of Part 4 placed – and was intended to place – some detainees in the position of being forced to choose between two fundamental rights – the rights to liberty and to freedom from torture or inhuman or degrading treatment. It appeared therefore possible to argue that Part 4 was incompatible with Art 3 since it was so deeply opposed to the values it enshrines. However, that argument was not accepted in SIAC or in the Court of Appeal when Part 4 was challenged in *A and Others v Secretary of State for the Home Dept*;[156] as discussed below, Part 4 was repealed due to the finding in the House of Lords that it was incompatible with Arts 5 and 14. However it is possible that this argument may be raised at Strasbourg, or if detention

---

153 [2001] 1 WLR 253, CA.

154 The National Council for the Welfare of Muslim Prisoners visited a detainee, Mahmoud Abu Rideh; his supporters argued that after being tortured in Israel, prison could not provide the quality of care that he needed.

155 The detainees were kept in remand conditions. The National Council for the Welfare of Muslim Prisoners asked for a meeting with the Home Secretary in order to raise concerns regarding the conditions under which the s 23 detainees were kept. They were subject to prolonged periods of solitary confinement (see the *Guardian* 15 April 2002, p 8) in Belmarsh prison's high-security unit and in Highdown prison. It may be noted that the detainees were visited over a period of five days by the Anti-Torture Committee of the Council of Europe: Strasbourg 22 February 2002; the UK has not yet agreed to make its report available to the public.

156 (2004) UKHL 56; [2005] 2 AC 68; [2005] 2 WLR 87; [2005] 3 All ER 169.

without trial is reinstated, under the derogating control orders scheme introduced in 2005, that it might eventually be re-raised domestically.

Government Ministers might seek to counter this argument on the ground that there must come a point at which the responsibility of democratic states for the treatment by some countries of their own citizens should cease and that, moreover, the responsibility of such states for the safety of their own citizens should not be undermined due to the evil propensities of other regimes. A member of a terrorist group at risk of Art 3 treatment might be likely to have the resources and ability to leave such a regime and enter Britain. It might seem anomalous to find that the mere fact of so doing should prevent both his detention and deportation. It was argued, and accepted in the Court of Appeal in *A and Others*, that the possibility of detention rather than deportation to face the risk of Art 3 treatment, represents a compromise designed to *avoid* Art 3 treatment that falls short in itself of such treatment, taking into account the duties of democracies in respect of suspected terrorists and public safety.

Discrimination – Article 14

A number of the powers discussed below can be challenged – and have been challenged – by reading Arts 6, 5, 10, 8 and Art 1, Protocol 1 with Art 14[157] together on the basis that a number of provisions may create discrimination on the basis of race or nationality, direct or (possibly), indirect. (The question of indirect discrimination under Art 14 is examined in Chapter 15.)[158] The discrimination may be justifiable, but only if the demands of proportionality are satisfied; that would mean that there had to be a rational connection between the interference in question and the aim pursued, and that the interference went no further than necessary to achieve that end.[159] The key anti-terrorist measure adopted post-9/11 under Part IV ATCSA allowed non-British suspected international terrorists to be detained without trial. This detention scheme was abandoned since, *inter alia*, it was found by the House of Lords to be discriminatory on the ground of nationality and therefore it contravened the European Convention on Human Rights, Arts 5 and 14, in the seminal decision in *A and Others v Secretary of State for the Home Dept*,[160] discussed below.

3 The Terrorism Acts 2000 and 2006 – extending the ambit of the counter-terrorism scheme

This part of this chapter begins by focusing on the pre-2000 position. It then considers the change from the UK's counter-terrorist response of the 70s, 80s and 90s which occurred under the Labour Government with the introduction of the Terrorism Act 2000 (TA). The TA represented a break with the previous counter-terrorist policy in certain respects, although it appeared to represent merely a rationalisation of the law. The TA proscription provisions are evaluated; then, in looking at the special TA terrorism

---

157 See pp 1431–38. Article 14 provides a guarantee of non-discrimination in the context of the other rights. Even where the other Article would not be breached if read alone, it may be found to be breached when read with Art 14. See Chapter 2, pp 108–9; Chapter 15, pp 1482–86.
158 See p 1483.
159 See Chapter 4, pp 288–90.
160 (2004) UKHL 56; [2005] 2 AC 68; [2005] 2 WLR 87; [2005] 3 All ER 169.

offences it also considers the very important new provisions allowing extensions of the counter-terrorist scheme introduced under the Terrorism Act 2006.

The legal and political background to the Terrorism Act 2000[161]

The recent history of the UK's counter-terrorism legislation – essentially the Prevention of Terrorism (Temporary Provisions) Act 1989 (the 'PTA') and the Northern Ireland (Emergency Provisions) Act 1996 (the 'EPA'), as amended by the Northern Ireland (Emergency Provisions) Act 1998 – revealed some acceptance of the principle that emergency measures should be adopted only in the face of immediate and severe need. When the then Home Secretary Roy Jenkins introduced the first Prevention of Terrorism (Temporary Provisions) Act in 1974, he referred to the powers it granted as 'unprecedented in peacetime' but 'fully justified to meet the clear present danger'. The Act was introduced soon after the Birmingham pub bombings that same year, in which 21 people died and over 180 were injured.

Despite pronouncements such as that of Lord Jenkins, which are scattered across the Parliamentary debates of the 70s, 80s and 90s on extensions of the counter-terrorist legislation, it cannot be said that Parliament demonstrated a genuine commitment to the principle that such legislation must be introduced only to meet a clear and present danger. In the 1990s Parliament quite frequently showed a marked readiness to accept claims that a number of proposed statutory measures would lead to the curbing of terrorist activity. Although such measures were likely to represent an infringement of civil liberties, they did not in general encounter determined criticism from the opposition. For example, the debate in the House of Commons on the Prevention of Terrorism (Additional Powers) Act 1996, which was guillotined, failed to consider in depth either the efficacy of the measure in terms of curbing terrorist activity or its likely impact on civil liberties. The debate provided, in microcosm, a good instance of the debasement and impoverishment of Parliamentary criminal justice debate in the mid-1990s. The Labour Party supported the proposals partly on the narrow ground that they represented only a small increase in the extended police powers to combat terrorism, which were included in the Criminal Justice and Public Order Act 1994, and which were not challenged on grounds of principle at the Committee stage of that Bill.[162] Issues as to the real value of these powers were raised only by certain back benchers due to pressure of time and to the stance of the Labour leadership.

The incremental extension of the Prevention of Terrorism (Temporary Provisions) Act 1989, which was originally intended in 1974 to be a temporary measure, reluctantly adopted as an unpalatable but necessary response to an emergency, is charted below. Many of the measures discussed in this chapter clearly indicate a willingness to abandon the rule of law in the face of terrorism despite uncertainty as to the need to adopt them. The pre-2000 pattern, as this chapter indicates, was one of steady additions to those 'temporary' provisions, meaning, inevitably, that provisions originally viewed as draconian began to look normal and acceptable compared with their successors.

---

161 For further comment, see Brandon, B, 'Terrorism, Human Rights and the Rule of Law: 120 years of the UK's legal response to terrorism' [2004] Crim LR 981.
162 See Straw, J, HC Deb, 2 April 1996 col 221.

Thus, what may be termed the old model for counter-terrorist legislation – temporary, incrementally developed in the face of particular emergencies, with localised effect – could readily be viewed as flawed on the ground that it was deceptive. Also the legislation became more far-reaching as the terrorist activity diminished. As explained below, it was at its most extensive, as a temporary measure, in 1998, although the peace process was in being. Nevertheless, it had not entirely lost touch with the values espoused by Lord Jenkins in 1974, in the sense that additions to the original legislation were relatively minor and usually had at least an apparent justification as a response to a genuine danger. The Criminal Justice (Terrorism and Conspiracy) Act 1998, for example, was passed in the wake of the Omagh bombing, carried out by the splinter-group, the Real IRA, which caused the deaths of some 22 people.

The pre-2000 temporary counter-terrorism legislation

Although the level of Irish terrorist violence was at its highest between 1968 when the Troubles began and the early 70s, extension of the Prevention of Terrorism (Temporary Provisions) Act 1974 and then of the 1989 Act continued to occur over the succeeding 25 years, under Thatcher, Major and Blair. The 1974 Act was passed at time when the level of IRA violence was very high: in 1973 there were 86 explosions; before the Birmingham pub bombs 20 people had been killed in 1974 and over 150 injured. In 1972 103 soldiers and 321 civilians died. The argument in favour of adopting extreme rights-abridging measures looked reasonably plausible in the early 1970s. The Report of Lord Diplock's Commission led to the passage of the EPA. As well as providing special powers for the security forces, the 1973 Act established different arrangements, including mode of trial, for terrorist cases. It was also made subject to annual review and to renewal by Parliamentary debate. Features of the earlier pre- and post-war anti-IRA measures were found in the EPA which provided a model for the 1974 Act and was similarly extended:[163] 'One of [the EPA's] features has been a steady increase in size and scope'.[164] As noted at various points below, the more draconian measures were confined to Northern Ireland. Where the threat was perceived to be most obvious, therefore, the measures were more far-reaching. This is not to suggest that the measures were justified or effective. It has been said: '[the EPA's] real purpose is to placate the electorate, as well as some of the elected, who demand that some steps must be taken by the law to counteract terrorism, regardless of how effective these might prove in practice'.[165]

The original emergency provisions under the 1974 Act had a renewal period of six months. This was soon extended to one year under the Prevention of Terrorism (Temporary Provisions) Act 1976. The Prevention of Terrorism (Temporary Provisions) Act 1984 included 'international terrorism' for the first time among its provisions. It was to be regularly reviewed and was to expire in five years. It was replaced by the Prevention of Terrorism (Temporary Provisions) Act 1989, also subject to annual renewal, but without the five-year time limit. By 2000 the PTA had been in existence

---

163 It was amended in 1975, consolidated in 1978, amended again in 1987 and consolidated with further amendments in 1991 and 1996.
164 Bailey, Harris and Jones *Civil Liberties: Cases and Materials*, 1st edn, 1995 at p 283.
165 Dickson, B, 'Northern Ireland's Emergency legislation' [1992] PL 592, at p 597.

for 11 years and was extended again throughout the 1990s. It was renewed for the last time[166] immediately after the Second Reading on the Terrorism Bill 2000.

Since 1989 additional powers were added by subsequent statutes – the Criminal Justice Act 1993, the Criminal Justice and Public Order Act 1994, the Prevention of Terrorism (Additional Powers) Act 1996 and the Criminal Justice (Terrorism and Conspiracy) Act 1998. The Northern Irish provisions followed a similar pattern, culminating in the passing of the Northern Ireland (Temporary Provisions) Act 1998. Paradoxically, although the level of violence had dropped over the 25 years since the first Act was passed, its pre-2000 successor represented a greatly enlarged version of the first Act. Extension was not discouraged by the cease-fire in September 1994 (which broke down in 1996) or the peace process in 1998. Thus, the notion that only a severe emergency, such as the one which appeared to be in being in 1974, could justify such far-reaching provisions, was gradually abandoned. The reality behind the 'temporary' provisions appeared to be that for much of the twentieth-century UK governments kept emergency legislation on file or in suspension, ready to be brought into law at short notice under a supine Parliament.

This governmental stance persisted, despite the fact that the efficacy of the Prevention of Terrorism Acts remained in doubt. Walker found that the Act was 'largely peripheral in effect'[167] and that the ordinary criminal law was on the whole being used against terrorism. The fact that the level of violence had tended to drop over the 25 years (albeit inconsistently) since 1974 did not appear to be attributable to the operation of the 1974 Act or its successors, but to changes in policy at government level and within the Republican organisations themselves. The level of violence was in fact particularly high in the two years immediately after the 1974 Act was passed. It may therefore be said that Parliament demonstrated, not only that it was willing to move quickly to cut down freedoms in situations perceived as emergencies, but that it then showed little inclination to repeal the measures adopted, preferring instead a process of normalisation, extension and accretion.

The Criminal Justice (Terrorism and Conspiracy) Act 1998

Once the peace process in Northern Ireland was placed on a formal basis under the *British Irish Agreement reached in the multi-party negotiations*[168] the fear became that splinter groups such as the Continuity IRA and the Real IRA, who, for various reasons deplored the abandonment of para-military tactics, would seek to disrupt it. This occurred in the Omagh bombing carried out by the Real IRA, in August 1998. It prompted the introduction in the 1998 Act of new draconian anti-terrorist measures to be inserted into the PTA. The Criminal Justice (Terrorism and Conspiracy) Bill 1998 was rushed through both Houses in two days (in fact, 27 hours) in the wake of the bombing. The argument for the speed was that the powers it contained were needed immediately for operational reasons. The Bill was only published to MPs at 6 pm on the day before the debate. A two-line whip was imposed on Labour MPs and the opposition parties supported the Bill. Nevertheless, a number of MPs opposed it

---

166   Prevention of Terrorism (Temporary Provisions) Act 1989 (Continuance) Order 2000. See HC Debs 15 March 2000 col 474.

167   Walker, C, *The Prevention of Terrorism*, 1986, at p 183.

168   Cm 3883 (1998).

on the basis that even in the face of terrorism the freedom to discuss the legislative response should not be abandoned.[169]

The Act was intended to make it easier to convict members of proscribed groups; it introduced ss 2A and 2B into the PTA for that purpose (discussed below). In fact no immediate action at all was taken in reliance on the powers the Act conferred. After two months the UK Act had still not been used (the equivalent legislation in Northern Ireland had been) although persons had been arrested in respect of the bombing. It appeared that the Act was passed more as a propaganda exercise than because the powers were genuinely needed. The Act ensured 'symmetry' with Ireland since the Dail was passing a similar Act on the same day. It was suggested in Parliament that the Act had in reality been passed in order to win the approval of President Clinton who was visiting Belfast in the same week.[170] Apart from such 'political' motivation, the curtailment of Parliamentary debate and its debatable efficacy in practice, a frequent hallmark of 'emergency' legislation is that other, unrelated controversial provisions which have been awaiting an opportune moment to get onto the statute book are added,[171] and are also able to take advantage of the stifling of Parliamentary debate which occurs in apparent response to the 'emergency'. The Criminal Justice (Terrorism and Conspiracy) Act 1998 exhibited all these characteristics.

The Act brought together two entirely separate and controversial matters – provisions related to proscribed terrorist organisations and to conspiracies. Only the first of these was clearly concerned with the threat and use of violence for political ends (terrorism as defined in the 1989 Act, s 20(1)). Section 5 of the Act added s 1A to the Criminal Law Act 1977, making it a criminal offence to conspire in any act 'or other event' which would also be an offence under the law of a foreign country so long as the offence in question would also be unlawful in the UK.[172] It was not therefore confined to terrorist offences as defined in s 20 of the 1989 Act, although it was introduced in terrorist legislation. The conspiracy can be to commit any offence, however trivial, so long as it is an offence in both Britain and the 'target' country. The s 1A offence opened up the possibility that politically active refugees discussing possible means of overcoming repressive regimes abroad might fall foul of s 5.[173] It was pointed out in Parliament that the provisions could also apply to 'an environmental pressure group organising a peaceful protest in Germany against the dispatch of some toxic material to Britain'.[174] This would be the case, assuming that the protest would be likely to infringe criminal law in both Britain and Germany.

The government considered that sufficient safeguards were introduced in providing that the offence plotted must be a crime in both countries and by requiring that, in most cases, the Attorney General must give his personal consent, having regard to the public interest, for the prosecution. The government stated its belief that:

---

169 See, e.g., comments of Richard Shepherd MP Hansard House of Commons 2nd September 1998 cols 714 and 715.

170 Mr J Sayeed HC Debs 2nd September 1998 col 726.

171 The Bill substantially reproduced provisions in an earlier Bill on conspiracy which the Major Government had been forced to drop in 1996.

172 It may be noted that Crown servants are exempted from these provisions, presumably on the ground that otherwise they would catch some activities of the Security and Intelligence Services.

173 It is ironic to note that plans to assassinate Hitler during World War 2 by, e.g., dissident Germans in England would have been covered by s 5.

174 By Mr Alan Beith, Deputy Leader of the Liberal Democrats, HC Debs 2 Sept 1998 col 735.

these provisions strike the right balance between ensuring it is possible to take decisive action against those plotting terrorist and other criminal acts elsewhere from the UK while building in safeguards . . . these provisions on conspiracy will continue to play an important role in deterring international terrorists from using this country as a base for their operations.[175]

These arguments and those used in Parliament were, however, disingenuous in their indications that the new provisions were necessary in order to curb international terrorism. Section 1A of the 1977 Act made no mention of terrorism and left a disturbingly broad discretion to the Attorney General as to their use against non-terrorist groups.

This Act represented the final extension of the temporary legislation and, in terms of the proscription-related provisions, indicated the willingness of the Labour Government to depart from previously accepted criminal justice standards – a characteristic which found a much fuller expression in the Terrorism Act 2000. The 1998 Act was the fore-runner of the Act of 2000 and in some respects it foreshadowed the developments of that Act since it introduced a far-reaching and controversial change to standards of criminal evidence[176] and brought an unprecedented range of groups within its ambit.

The single, permanent anti-terrorism statute – the Terrorism Act 2000

Key themes

The permanent counter-terrorist scheme created by the TA 2000 under the current Labour Government represented a dramatic break with the values arguably adhered to in relation to the previous scheme – that as emergency legislation the provisions should be temporary and graduated to the level and location of the threat. The peace process in Northern Ireland culminating in the *British Irish Agreement reached in the multi-party negotiations*[177] is still in existence.[178] The process and the Agreement, which included releasing those imprisoned on terrorist charges, recognised that criminalisation of persons engaging in a struggle largely viewed in Republican communities in Northern Ireland as political, was counter-productive. It gave the impression to those communities that no real alternative other than violence was available to them. The Agreement has, to an extent, marginalised those Republican splinter groups which rejected the possibility of a peaceful solution, preferring to continue the use of para-military tactics. By the end of 1999, just before introduction of the TA, some of these groups had also declared a cease-fire, although some remained adamantly opposed to the peace process. As the 1998 Labour Government consultation paper *Legislation Against Terrorism*[179] put it:

175 *Legislation Against Terrorism: a Consultation Paper* Cm 4178, prepared 17 December 1998, at para 4.18.
176 The provisions inserting s 2A into the PTA.
177 Cm 3883 (1998).
178 It may be noted that in November 1999 after Senator Mitchell had negotiated a settlement Sinn Fein announced the beginning of de-commissioning.
179 Home Office and Northern Ireland Office *Legislation against Terrorism. A consultation paper*, Cm 4178, prepared 17 December 1998.

'subsequent progress including elections to the Northern Ireland Assembly mean that the outlook in Northern Ireland is changing, and suggest that the days of widespread violence and terrorism may soon be gone for good'.

Repeal of the Prevention of Terrorism (Temporary Provisions) Act 1979 which, in its original form, was introduced after the IRA pub bombings in Birmingham in 1974, might therefore have been expected. This would probably have been the expectation in 1974. The PTA embodied the paradoxical nature of the measures adopted for use against the IRA over the last 20 years. As Ewing and Gearty have pointed out, it and its predecessors were adopted as emergency anti-terrorist measures, but were then applied as ordinary criminal legislation.[180] Since the 'criminalisation' approach had largely been abandoned, repeal of much of the legislation that accompanied it would have appeared to be appropriate. Since a threat from 'international terrorism' remained, it could have been met by powers graduated to levels of threat. In fact, the counter-terrorism provision post-2000 under the Terrorism Act 2000 is more extensive than in the worst years of Irish terrorist violence. The provisions are, on their face, graduated only in respect of the two different regimes for proscribed and other terrorist groups. This chapter argues that the Labour Government in 2000 showed little recognition of the need to repeal provisions viewed as tolerable only for a short period of time in the face of a pressing emergency, and which were accompanied by a conscious acceptance of an abandonment of democratic ideals.

Ironically, the key development able to temper the excesses of the TA was the Human Rights Act (HRA), although the UK also remained bound by the ECHR at the international level. As the findings of the Divisional Court and House of Lords in *Ex parte Kebilene*[181] (discussed below) indicate, the HRA had already shown its potential in this regard before the TA was introduced. Interestingly, the consultation paper which preceded the legislation[182] appeared to assume that most of its proposals would not lead to conflicts with the Convention, under the HRA. At certain points this issue was explicitly addressed; at others the relevant Convention Articles were simply not mentioned. When the Home Secretary introduced the Terrorism Bill to Parliament in December 1999 he made a declaration of its compatibility with the Convention rights under s 19(1)(a) HRA, but obviously the courts remained at liberty to find incompatibility.[183]

This was an instance in which the courts were clearly going to have the key role to play in tempering the potential of the legislation. This was apparent, bearing in mind the role played by Parliament in debating the Terrorism Bill 2000, which was circumscribed – in civil liberties' terms – due to the very large majority of the Labour Government and the stance of the main opposition party. Parliament had already shown itself willing to pass draconian legislation, the Criminal Justice (Terrorism and Conspiracy) Act 1998, with no significant amendment, although during debate concerns were strongly

---

180 *Freedom under Thatcher*, 1989, p 213.
181 Divisional Court [1999] 3 WLR 372; HL [1999] 4 All ER 801, available from the Lords' website. It may be noted that *Ex p Kebilene* concerned legislation, the Criminal Justice and Public Order Act 1994, s 82, passed under the Major Government. But the provisions at issue have been reproduced in the Act of 2000 in ss 57 and 58 (see below).
182 Cm 4178, prepared 17 December 1998.
183 See further Chapter 4, pp 206–11.

expressed in certain quarters.[184] In debate on the Bill of 2000 the main proposals made by the Conservative opposition were more draconian than those of the government. They included the re-introduction of internment[185] and the extension of detention by executive, not judicial, authorisation.[186] The stance of the courts was also of indirect significance in shaping the response of the executive to the TA powers.

As discussed below, at many points the TA powers leave a very broad and thinly regulated discretion to the executive. The most significant executive decision is that of the Home Secretary in determining whether or not to seek the proscription of a particular group. A further example is provided by the power of the Attorney General to give or withhold consent to prosecutions for the offence of conspiracy in the UK to commit offences abroad. It is to be expected that where the conspirators are seeking to overthrow a dictatorship, the consent would be withheld, even though, technically the offence has been committed. Section 117 TA requires the consent of the DPP or the Attorney General to prosecutions in respect of most offences under the TA 2000. Obviously, the police always have a discretion in determining when to arrest. Lord Carlile, the government reviewer of the TA, said on this point, in his 2006 Review of the TA, having acknowledged that the TA, s 1, while, in his view, 'practical and effective', leaves a lot of discretion to the prosecuting authorities: 'we are entitled to assume that in a democratically accountable system there will be a sensible use of the discretion to prosecute'.[187] It is a hallmark of terrorist legislation that it is often marginalised in favour of the use of ordinary criminal provisions.[188] It was clear from the outset that if, when prosecutions were brought, the judiciary took a robust line as regards ECHR standards, under their ss 3 or 6 HRA duty, it would be possible to address executive failures to achieve full Convention-compliance. As discussed below, the courts have brought a number of provisions of the TA into closer compliance with the ECHR.

Introduction of the Terrorism Act 2000; relationship with the previous scheme

The government published a consultation paper on the future of anti-terrorism laws in December 1998.[189] It was intended to address the question of the rationale of retaining 'emergency' anti-terrorism laws in the face of the peace process[190] and therefore to counter the argument that the current version of the PTA with its various later accretions should be repealed and not replaced. The 1998 Paper was based on a report prepared

---

184 See, e.g., Mr Sayeed: 'The government are used to using their very large majority to bully through inadequate legislation,' (HC Debs 2nd Sept 1998 col 726); Mr McNamara: 'The Bill is dangerous and we have been rushed into it without any proper thought' (HC Debs 2nd Sept 1998 col 786).

185 A new Sched 2 and a new clause which would have effected this was proposed: HC Debs 15 March 2000 cols 331–37. Both were defeated, Labour and Liberal Democrat MPs voting together: HC Debs 15 March 2000 col 347.

186 HC Debs 15 March 2000 col 431.

187 Report on the Operation in 2005 of the Terrorism Act 2000, May 2006, at para 30.

188 See: Walker, C, *The Prevention of Terrorism*, 1986 at p 183.

189 *Legislation against Terrorism. A Consultation Paper*, Cm 4178.

190 See the Introduction to the Paper, and in particular para 6.

by Lord Lloyd of Berwick in 1996.[191] In 1995 Lord Lloyd had been asked by Michael Howard, the then Home Secretary, to consider the future of anti-terrorist legislation on the assumption that a lasting peace was achieved. He recommended in his report that a new permanent anti-terrorist law should replace the temporary provisions. The policy adopted in his report formed the background to the consultation paper and in turn to the Terrorism Bill 2000. Once the Act of 2000 came into force, it repealed the PTA and EPA.[192] The TA has four key hallmarks. It is far more extensive, covering a much wider range of groups; it is permanent; its main provisions apply equally across the UK, although there were special transitional provisions for Northern Ireland, and it retains almost all the draconian special powers and offences adopted under the previous 'temporary' counter-terrorist scheme, while adding new incitement offences.

The justification for the TA provisions was that they were needed post-2000 to combat the threat from three groups. The first of these comprised those Irish splinter groups opposed to the peace process.[193] The second comprised 'international terrorists'. The paper noted that across the world there had been 'a rise in terrorism motivated by religious idealism'.[194] Both these groups were already covered under the existing legislation, although not all the special provisions were applied equally to international terrorism. The threat was apparently mainly from the new, third, group, on which the case for the new legislation appeared mainly to rest. This group comprised of a wide and disparate range of domestic groups other than those connected with Irish terrorism, such as animal rights or environmental activists,[195] and, possibly, anti-abortion groups.[196]

191 Lord Lloyd of Berwick's *Inquiry into legislation against terrorism* (Cm 3420), published in October 1996.

192 As noted below, the PTA was renewed for the last time on 15 March 2000. The EPA was renewed for the last time on 24 August 2000. The special measures it provided for Northern Ireland will be provided in Part VII of the Act of 2000.

193 In the Paper the government found: 'there are small numbers who remain opposed to peace and wedded to violence. So, even though the context is of a general movement towards lasting peace in Northern Ireland, it is too soon to be confident that all terrorism has been abandoned' (ibid, para 2.3).

194 Lord Lloyd's Report drew attention to 'possible future changes in the terrorist threat' and to lives and property in the UK; 'changes which mirror what is happening across the world' (ibid, para 2.4). Examples were given of the rise of 'Islamic extremism' and the use of Sarin nerve gas on the Tokyo underground in 1995 by the Aum Shinrikyo religious cult, which killed 12 people and affected up to 5,500.

195 'The threat from some marginal but extreme elements of the animal rights movement continues to be of more concern to the Government [than Scottish or Welsh nationalist groups].' The Paper noted that animal rights extremists have in the past sent letter bombs to the leaders of major political parties, attacked Bristol University's Senate House with a high explosive bomb, targeted a veterinary surgeon and a psychologist with car bombs and caused millions of pounds worth of damage. 'The shape of new counter-terrorist legislation needs to reflect the possible threat from indigenous groups too' (Chapter 2 of the Paper, at para 2.5). In Chapter 3 of the Paper the concerns regarding these groups are given some further substance. It is noted that in 1997 more than 800 incidents were recorded by the Animal Rights National Index (ARNI) and 'these included attacks on abattoirs, laboratories, breeders, hunts, butchers, chemists, doctors, vets, furriers, restaurants, supermarkets and other shops' which resulted in injuries although not in deaths and in damage done in 1997 estimated at more than 1.8 million (ibid, para 3.10). See also Home Office, Animal Rights Extremism, 2001.

196 The Paper speculated as to the possibility that anti-abortion groups might adopt terrorist methods in the UK: 'In the United States, for example, there is an increasing tendency by individuals and groups to resort to terrorist methods. Some of those opposed to the USA's laws on abortion have bombed clinics and attacked, and, in a number of cases, killed doctors and nursing staff employed by them.

The paper accepted that the level of violence associated with such groups was low compared with the level of IRA violence in the early 1970s. However, it argued that those groups posed a continuing threat and that other single issue groups might be set up and might use violent methods 'to impose their will on the rest of society'.[197] Thus, the paper switched the focus of concern from the need for measures to combat a high and rising level of violence to the need to be ready to combat the possibility of violence in the future. The threat of violence from environmental, animal rights' or anti-abortion activists might have appeared to be a real possibility but it had not, pre-2000, materialised on anything like the scale previously thought of as necessary to justify draconian anti-terrorist laws. Moreover, the ordinary criminal law, including the wide range of public order provisions documented in Chapter 8, was arguably adequate as a response to the activities of such groups. The paper merely provided assertions rather than evidence as to the need for special counter-terrorist measures, as opposed to a more effective use of the existing criminal law. No effort was made to analyse the need for the extension of the special provisions to a very wide range of new groups, including protest groups. The Paper did not appear, for example, to draw on experience from other countries, including European ones, which were equally faced with extremist groups. The problems experienced in the US were mentioned, but the Paper did not examine the efficacy of the means used to combat them.

The conclusion of the government in the consultation paper was that a threat comparable to that existing in 1974 could be discerned: 'In the language of the then Home Secretary introducing the PTA legislation in 1974, the Government believes that there exists now a clear and present terrorist threat to the UK from a number of fronts.'[198] But if those examples of group violence are compared with those available in 1974, it is immediately apparent that they were far more uncertain and speculative. The keynote of the paper was the need to safeguard the UK from future threats from indigenous groups, most of which had not arisen. The unquestioned assumption was that the legislation would aid in countering any future threat before it materialised. No attention was paid in the paper to the possibility of counter-productivity – that the designation of some indigenous groups as terrorist might encourage a growth in extremism within such groups which might as a result perceive themselves as unable to use the normal channels of political campaigning. In comparison with the climate in 1974 or even, to a lesser extent, in 1998, in the wake of the Omagh bombing, the case for the TA based on the threats indicated, was not, it is argued, made out.

The intention was that the Terrorism Act 2000 would be permanent; this had the advantage, as the paper pointed out,[199] of being 'transparent', that is, no pretence was made that the legislation would be repealed. This was a strong argument, given the spurious nature, indicated above, of claims that the previous legislation was temporary and passed only in response to a current emergency. But it abandoned even the pretence that temporary and regrettable emergency measures, involving an ordinarily unacceptable infringement of civil liberties, were in contemplation. The paper noted

---

Although there have been no comparable attacks in the United Kingdom, the possibility remains that some new group or individual could operate in this way in the future' (ibid, para 3.12).
197   Para 3.12.
198   Ibid, at para 2.7.
199   Ibid, at para 2.8.

that the vast majority of criminal law is permanent, implying that this provided a reason for abandoning the temporary nature of the counter-terrorism legislation and thereby blurring past distinctions between criminal law and special measures adopted to meet specific emergencies.

Parliamentary scrutiny of the new legislation was also virtually abandoned, although the government did accept concerns expressed in the Second Reading of the Bill, to the extent of agreeing to an annual report to Parliament.[200] A clause supported by the Liberal Democrats making the legislation renewable was rejected by the government[201] and no provision for the full review of the legislation was included. Therefore it was intended that the permanent powers would receive even less scrutiny than the temporary ones did. The clause was withdrawn after the Home Office Minister had pointed out that the Human Rights Act would provide 'an important new safeguard'.[202] The justification offered for abandoning the review process was that it did not, 'reflect the current reality that such powers are likely to be needed for the foreseeable future'.[203] This bland statement, based on little evidence, failed to take account of the fact that these powers were adopted and extended over a long period of time (apparently) to meet the serious threat posed by a particular group of highly-organised terrorists, the IRA, commanding a range of arms. It also failed to take account of the need for Parliamentary scrutiny to oversee the workings of the powers. It left their use far more overtly in executive as opposed to Parliamentary hands.

If certain of the powers were not used in practice it should have been possible to repeal them, and in fact the powers were strikingly under-used, post-2000; an annual review would have provided a forum for arguing for such repeal. This appeared to be precisely what the government was seeking to avoid, presumably in the interests of avoiding political controversy. While the TA may have greater symbolic than real value, government spokespersons in public statements take the stance that all the powers are genuinely needed, making it difficult to explain why they are under-used. Human rights appeared to be viewed as a commodity which could be afforded value only when convenient. While it may be argued that the previous review process achieved little, it was at least possible, in the post-HRA era, that such a process could have allowed for a stricter scrutiny.

The main provisions of the Terrorism Act 2000 apply equally across the UK. This, on its face, represents a more satisfactory approach than passing more draconian legislation for Northern Ireland, which had in the past been the case, or, in effect, trying out such legislation in Northern Ireland first and then transferring it to the rest of the UK. But once again it eroded the principle that the special powers should be as narrow as possible; although counter-terrorist legislation appeared to have been adopted in Northern Ireland for reasons other than its efficacy in countering terrorism,[204] it is undeniable that the threat of terrorism was greater in Northern Ireland than in the rest of the UK. The universal application of the TA was initially only an aspiration, since under Part VII of the Act it retained for five years a number of differentials between

---

200 See HC Debs 15 March 2000 col 360. This provision is now s 126.
201 See HC Debs 15 March 2000 cols 352–56.
202 See HC Debs 15 March 2000 col 363.
203 Ibid, para 2.8.
204 See: Dickson, B, 'Northern Ireland's Emergency legislation' [1992] PL 592, at p 597.

the powers applicable to Northern Ireland and to Britain.[205] The TA included in Part VII a number of temporary provisions specific to Northern Ireland. The government stated that its objective was: 'progressively to transform the security environment as appropriate, and achieve complete normalisation as part of the implementation of the [Belfast] Agreement as a whole'. Once that was achieved, the government's position was that there would be no need for any temporary Northern Ireland specific powers.[206] The temporary provisions were made subject to annual review and to Parliament's approval of the Home Secretary's orders of renewal.[207]

Extending the definition of 'terrorism' under the Terrorism Act 2000

The definition of 'terrorism' under the TA provides the foundation for a very wide range of broad special terrorism offences in the TA, and for those subsequently introduced under the Anti-Terrorism, Crime and Security Act 2001 and the Terrorism Act 2006. The definition also allows, as discussed below, for the application of special terrorism sanctions under the Prevention of Terrorism Act 2005, not dependent on charging a person with a specific offence and without proof of an offence.

Defining 'terrorism'

The problem of defining terrorism has spawned an extensive literature.[208] One 1988 study identified a total of 109 different definitions in use across the world[209] and the number is far higher today. Attempts to develop a generally accepted legal definition of terrorism have failed. Golder and Williams find:[210] 'Some have likened "the search for the legal definition of terrorism . . . [to] the quest for the Holy Grail". Others, such as Judge Richard Baxter, formerly of the International Court of Justice, writing in 1974, have questioned the utility of a legal definition, stating: "We have cause to regret that a legal concept of terrorism was ever inflicted upon us. The term is imprecise; it is ambiguous; and, above all it serves no operative legal purpose".'[211]

---

205 Under s 112(4) the additional temporary measures for Northern Ireland only were time-limited to 5 years.
206 Ibid, para 1.3.
207 This was promised in the Paper (ibid, para 1.4) and is now contained in s 123(4)(f).
208 See, e.g.: Primoritz, I, 'What is Terrorism?' in Gearty, C (ed)*Terrorism*, 1996, p 130; Butko, T 'Terrorism redefined' (2005) 18 *Peace Review* 145; Donohue, L K, 'Terrorism and the counter-terrorist discourse' in Ramraj, VV, Hor, M and Roach, K, *Global Anti-terrorism Law and Policy*, 2005; Claridge, D, 'State terrorism? Applying a definitional model' (1996) 8 *Terrorism and Political Violence* 47; Levitt, G, 'Is "Terrorism" Worth Defining?' (1986) 13 *Ohio Northern University Law Review* 97; Schmid, A and Jongman, A *Political Terrorism*, 1987, Royal Netherlands Academy of Arts and Sciences; Murphy, JF, 'Defining International Terrorism: A Way Out of the Quagmire' (1989) 19 *Israel Yearbook on Human Rights* 13, 14; Gearty, C, *Terror*, 1991. Levitt, G, 'Is "Terrorism" Worth Defining?' (1986) 13 *Ohio Northern University Law Review* 97.
209 Schmid, AP and Jongman, AJ, *Political Terrorism: A New Guide to Actors, Authors, Concepts, Databases, Theories, and Literature*, 1988, 5.
210 Golder, B and Williams, G, 'What is "Terrorism"? Problems of Legal Definition' [2004] 27(2) *UNSW Law Journal*, Vol 27(2) 271, at p 271.
211 Baxter, RR, 'A Skeptical Look at the Concept of Terrorism' (1974) 7 *Akron Law Review* 380, p 380.

Terrorism was defined in section 20(1) of the Prevention of Terrorism (Temporary Provisions) Act 1989 as 'the use of violence for political ends and includes any use of violence for the purpose of putting the public, or any section of the public in fear'. But this did not mean that the PTA powers applied to all activities which fell within that definition. The special powers conferred applied only to 'terrorism connected with the affairs of Northern Ireland' or (in certain instances) to international terrorism. Non-Irish domestic terrorism, that is, terrorism having its origins in the affairs of any part of the United Kingdom other than Northern Ireland, was excluded from the scope of the Act. The s 20 definition of terrorism was in fact extraordinarily wide and imprecise since the use of the word 'includes' meant that the requirement of putting a section of the public in fear was not an essential ingredient of it. The terms 'violence' and 'political ends' were undefined. Arguably, therefore, 'the use of violence for political ends' could have included some direct action public protest. It is unclear whether s 20 was confined to violence against persons. The definition might therefore have been unworkable in practice had it not been for the qualified application of the powers. Even bearing those qualifications in mind, the definition meant that the special powers could be used against a very wide range of activities so long as a connection with Northern Irish affairs or, even more vaguely (in the case of certain powers), an 'international' aspect, could be found. The definition of terrorism in the EPA was identical to that in s 20 of the PTA. The EPA did not impose any limitations on the kinds of terrorism to which it applied. But there appeared to be official agreement that in practice the powers would only be used to combat Irish terrorism.[212]

In his report Lord Lloyd criticised the definition of terrorism in s 20, and the restrictions imposed throughout that Act limiting the use of the powers to certain terrorist groups. He suggested that there is no difference in principle between the activities of those groups and those of domestic 'terrorist' groups unconnected with Irish affairs.[213] Presumably Lord Lloyd, in using the term 'terrorist' in relation to such groups, was relying on the very wide s 20 definition. This, however, failed to address the possibility that this definition would have been unsatisfactory had it not in practice been unused in determining the application of the special powers. If that definition had been solely relied upon, many groups would have fallen within it and in principle would therefore have been subject to the special powers. This raised the question whether a much narrower definition of terrorism should have been used in the TA to justify the broader use of such powers. The government, in supporting a broad definition in the TA, agreed with Lord Lloyd, arguing that the suffering of the victims would be the same, whether caused by 'a republican or loyalist paramilitary, an international terrorist or an animal rights activist'.[214]

But the argument which seeks to extend the definition of terrorism on the basis that the experience of the victims is the same whether the group in question is officially designated 'terrorist' or not is flawed. The experience of a person who is attacked for

212 Ibid, para 3.2.
213 Ibid, para 3.5.
214 'the methods which ["terrorists"] employ are those in common currency amongst terrorists everywhere – bombs, incendiaries, shootings, arson and so forth. Nor is there any difference in the fear, pain or despair felt by the victims or their families . . . The injuries and the destruction of life and property are the same' (ibid, para 3.6).

motives of jealousy or greed is the same as that of one who is killed due to a political motive. Most grave and prolonged of all may be the suffering of the victim of the sexually motivated killer. On this argument, either all serious crimes against the person should be designated terrorist, or no crimes should be. It has been argued that it is the quality of indiscriminate public violence, causing terror, which is fundamental.[215] On the other hand, the fear experienced by many women of being randomly selected for sexual attack may be of a similar quality, and not all terrorist violence is indiscriminate. The reason for treating so-called terrorist activity differently from 'ordinary' crime is not the suffering of the victim, but the potentially profound effect on the established order which terrorism may have but which ordinary crime (unless it reaches certain levels)[216] does not. Ordinary crime is normally targeted directly at the victim; terrorism targets the victim in order to further a political end. Thus, the definition of terrorism should only encompass groups which use attacks on people in order to serve the end of seeking to overthrow or undermine the established order. There is a further issue – should attacks on property alone, or threats to attack property, fall within the definition of terrorism? It might be argued that if the attack on property is targeted deliberately at the property due to its symbolic nature – destroying a field of GM crops would provide an example – and does not carry an implied threat to life, it should fall outside the definition of terrorism since it is only threats to life, implied or actual, or the taking of life that creates terror. The ordinary criminal law could be used in relation to damaging property.

Proceeding from its doubtful premise, the government found in the consultation paper that the special powers were needed to combat all forms of 'terrorism', indigenous or otherwise, and that therefore the restricting qualifications under the PTA should be abandoned.[217] But it rejected the option of simply adopting the s 20 definition, without any qualification as to the use of the powers. It agreed with Lord Lloyd in finding the definition too wide in that it could cover the use of trivial violence which should be dealt with by the ordinary criminal law, and too narrow because it might not cover adequately the activities of religiously inspired groups.[218] Lord Lloyd recommended that the definition of terrorism used by the FBI in the USA should be adopted. Its definition at the time was: 'the use of serious violence against persons or property, or the threat to use such violence, to intimidate or coerce a government, the public, or any section of the public in order to promote political, social or ideological objectives'.[219] The government, however, rejected this definition as too broad since it included the use of serious violence for 'social' objectives,[220] and too narrow in that it did not

---

215 Primoritz, I, 'What is Terrorism?' in Gearty, C (ed) *Terrorism*, 1996, p 130.
216 Once ordinary crime reaches certain levels it arguably has as de-stabilising an effect on society as terrorism has. For example, in certain parts of the UK ordinary crime has had a very localised profoundly destabilising effect in terms of the encouragement of vigilantism and the infringement and undermining of the enjoyment of the benefits of a civilised society, such as personal security, freedom of movement, privacy etc.
217 Ibid, para 3.13.
218 Ibid, para 3.14.
219 See below fn 223 for the current definition.
220 The latter could, for example, include crimes committed by criminals other than terrorists such as blackmail or extortion for gain (ibid, para 3.16).

cover forms of damage to property.[221] The government stated that its proposed new definition was: 'the use of serious violence against persons or property, or the threat to use such violence, to intimidate or coerce a government, the public, or any section of the public for political, religious or ideological ends'.[222]

The proposed definition was an extraordinarily wide interpretation of 'terrorism'. Clearly, it was intended to include forms of direct action adopted by environmental groups or animal rights' activists. This definition was in some respects wider than that under s 20, since it clearly applied to property as well as persons, and covered serious disruption as well as violence. Its *application* would also have been far wider than the application of the definition under the PTA. It was, however, narrower than that under s 20 in that it made it clear that intimidating or coercing a government, the public, or any section of the public, was an essential ingredient. The definition actually adopted under s 1 of the TA is significantly wider even than the proposed one or that under s 20.

The definition adopted under the Terrorism Act 2000

The very broad definition adopted under s 1 of the Terrorism Act 2000 (TA),[223] as amended by s 34 Terrorism Act 2006, has three main elements. 'Terrorism' means, first, the use or threat of action involving serious violence against any person or serious damage to property, which endangers the life of any person, or 'creates a serious risk to the health or safety of the public or a section of the public, or is designed seriously to interfere with or seriously to disrupt an electronic system'. Second, the use or threat must be for the purpose of advancing a 'political, religious or ideological' cause. Third, the use or threat must be 'designed to influence the government or an international governmental organisation[224] or to intimidate the public or a section of the public'

---

221 It appears not to cover the damage and serious disruption which might result from a terrorist '. . . contaminating a public utility system such as a water or sewage works [or] . . . hacking into some vital computer installation and, without using violence, altering, deleting, or disrupting the data held on it' (ibid, para 3.16).

222 Ibid, para 3.17.

223 Section 1 of the Terrorism Act, as amended, provides in full:

  (1) In this Act 'terrorism' means the use or threat of action where –

   (a) the action falls within sub-section (2),
   (b) the use or threat is designed to influence the government or an international governmental organization or to intimidate the public or a section of the public, and
   (c) the use or threat is made for the purpose of advancing a political, religious or ideological cause.

  (2) Action falls within this sub-section if it –

   (a) involves serious violence against a person,
   (b) involves serious damage to property,
   (c) endangers a person's life, other than that of the person committing the action,
   (d) creates a serious risk to the health or safety of the public or a section of the public, or
   (e) is designed seriously to interfere with or seriously to disrupt an electronic system.'

224 The words 'or an international governmental organisation' were added by the Terrorism Act 2006, s 34.

(s 1(1)(b)). It may be noted that the third element is not needed if firearms or explosives are used.[225] The Act applies *wherever* terrorist action takes place, under s 1(4), not just in the UK. The requirement of a threat to the established order contained in the words: 'to intimidate or coerce a government', the main limiting factor under the proposed definition, was watered down to 'influence'. This definition does not in itself create a criminal offence of 'being a terrorist'. But the key point is that in its potential effect the s 1(1) definition is far wider in practice than s 20 since the TA, unlike the PTA, allows the *definition itself* to determine the application of the special powers. The government assumes that such application will, due to the decisions of police officers, the DPP and CPS, in practice affect only the most extremist groups. But given the lack of effective, independent control over the day-to-day decision-making of such bodies, this is not, it is argued, a satisfactory position in civil liberties' terms. Moreover, government Ministers cannot necessarily be trusted to use the offences and sanctions dependent on the TA definition in a restrained fashion as the proscription decisions taken so far post-2000, and discussed below, indicate.

The definition was attacked in Parliament as creating a 'fatally flawed' Bill. It was also said: '. . . it is utterly perplexing that we should apparently be wedded to a definition that threatens to undermine so sweepingly civil liberties and the credibility of governance itself'.[226] However, the amendments put forward by the Liberal Democrats, which would have narrowed it down, were overwhelmingly defeated, Labour and Conservative MPs (with a few exceptions) voting together.[227] (The limiting words of s 1(1)(b) were added as a Lords' amendment, reluctantly accepted by the government.)

This definition of terrorism is, on its face, sweepingly broad and extraordinarily imprecise. It makes no provision that the action or threat should be criminal; it covers threats to property; it also contains no clause providing exemption for state action. The government reviewer of the terrorism legislation, Lord Carlile, has pointed out, however, that the breadth of the UK definition 'should be placed in the international context. For example, most countries in South Asia define terrorism far more broadly, as well as interpreting their own definitions widely'.[228] Some examples from other countries are illustrative. They indicate that the UK definition, while particularly wide, is not markedly out of line with definitions used in a number of other countries. In some instances this is not surprising since they are modelled on the TA definition. However, many of them were adopted in the face of the heightened threat post-9/11. In Australia, Sched 1 to the Security Legislation Amendment (Terrorism) Act 2002 (Cth) (introduced after September 11), inserted a new definition of 'terrorist act' into the Criminal Code Act 1995 (Cth)33 (Criminal Code), which was clearly modelled on the TA, s 1 defintion. The definition appears in s 100.1 of part 5.3 of the Code and provides:

---

225 See further: Fenwick, H, *Civil Rights: New Labour, Freedom and the Human Rights Act*, 2000, Chapter 3; Walker, C, *A Guide to the Anti-Terrorism Legislation*, 2002, Blackstone; Rowe, JJ, 'The Terrorism Act 2000' [2001] Crim LR 527.

226 Mr Simpson MP, HC Debs 15 March 2000, cols 399 and 394.

227 HC Debs 15 March 2000 col 415.

228 Report on the Operation in 2005 of the Terrorism Act 2000 by Lord Carlile of Berriew QC, at para 29. In 2001 he was appointed as Independent Reviewer of the Terrorism Act 2000. His reports can be found at www.homeoffice.gov.uk.

(1) In this Part: . . . terrorist act means an action or threat of action where:

(a) the action falls within sub-section (2) and does not fall within sub-section (3); and

(b) the action is done or the threat is made with the intention of advancing a political, religious or ideological cause; and

(c) the action is done or the threat is made with the intention of: ii) intimidating the public or a section of the public.

Under (2) the action that falls within that sub-section is defined as in the TA 2000. Israeli law does not address terrorism specifically, but the Israel Prevention of Terrorism Ordinance No 33 of 5708–1948 interprets 'terrorist organisation' as meaning a body of persons 'resorting in its activities to acts of violence calculated to cause death or injury to a person or to threats of such acts of violence'.

Shortly after 9/11, the US Congress passed the Uniting and Strengthening America by Providing Appropriate Tools Required to Intercept and Obstruct Terrorism Act of 2001 (USA Patriot Act), s 802 of which amended the definition of 'domestic terrorism' within Title 18 of the United States Code. Section 2331 of Title 18 now provides:

'(2) the term "international terrorism" means activities that –

(a) involve violent acts or acts dangerous to human life that are a violation of the criminal laws of the United States or of any state, or that would be a criminal violation if committed within the jurisdiction of the United States or of any state;

(b) appear to be intended –

(i) to intimidate or coerce a civilian population;
(ii) to influence the policy of a government by intimidation or coercion; or
(iii) to affect the conduct of a government by mass destruction, assassination, or kidnapping; and

(c) occur primarily outside the territorial jurisdiction of the United States, or transcend national boundaries in terms of the means by which they are accomplished, the persons they appear intended to intimidate or coerce, or the locale in which their perpetrators operate or seek asylum.

. . .

(5) the term "domestic terrorism" means activities that –

(a) involve acts dangerous to human life that are a violation of the criminal laws of the United States or of any state;

(b) appear to be intended –

(i) to intimidate or coerce a civilian population;
(ii) to influence the policy of a government by intimidation or coercion; or
(iii) to affect the conduct of a government by mass destruction, assassination, or kidnapping; and

(c) occur primarily within the territorial jurisdiction of the United States'.

All these definitions are broad in that they cover action against any foreign government, however oppressive; they do not recognise the possibility of the legitimate use of violence by civilians against an invader in an occupied country, and thus label all resistance movements terrorist groups; they potentially cover almost all liberation movements, whether or not fighting against an undemocratic regime which does not respect human rights; they do not distinguish between those aiming only at military targets and those aiming at civilian targets. Thus all of them accept impliedly the grave difficulties of seeking to distinguish between 'terrorists' and 'freedom fighters', and so rely on executive discretion in choosing the targets of the anti-terrorism provisions. Ronald Dworkin described the US definition as a 'new, breathtakingly vague and broad definition of terrorism'.[229] Nevertheless, the US definition is in one respect not as broad as the UK or Australian ones since it does not include threats of action or damage to property or threats to damage property.

The TA definition allowed the activities of a number of groups, including protest groups, previously criminal, to be re-designated – potentially – as terrorist. The response of some groups to their re-designation as terrorist may have exacerbated the threat they pose; extremism may have been encouraged as legitimate avenues of protest in a democracy appeared to close,[230] especially where such groups were also proscribed. If they are not proscribed, groups may be uncertain whether their actions might be labelled terrorist, given the imprecision and breadth of the definition. In fact, as indicated below, only a minority of the groups which potentially fall within s 1(1) have so far been proscribed; broadly speaking the special powers seem to be aimed in practice at proscribed groups only. However, the special powers (apart from those specifically linked to proscription) can potentially be used against any group falling within the broad definition of terrorism.

The definition expressly covers threats of serious disruption or damage to, for example, computer installations or public utilities. The definition is therefore potentially able to catch a number of forms of public protest. Danger to property, violence or a serious risk to safety that can be described as 'ideologically, politically, or religiously motivated' may arise in the context of many demonstrations and other forms of public protest, including some industrial disputes. The government stated in the consultation paper that it had 'no intention of suggesting that matters that can properly be dealt with under normal public order powers should in future be dealt with under counter-terrorist legislation'.[231] But once special arrest and detention powers are handed to the police they can be used, at their discretion, if a particular person or group falls, or appears to fall, within the TA definition.

Some direct action against property by anti-war, animal rights or environmental activists falls within it, on its face. As Chapter 8 points out, some 'direct action' by such groups may be viewed as forms of expression and as having, to varying extents, the same role as political speech.[232] Some direct action, such as the destruction of genetically modified

229 Dworkin, R, 'The Threat to Patriotism' (2002) 49(3) *New York Review of Books* 44.
230 See Ansari, F, *British Anti-Terrorism: A Modern Day Witch-hunt*, October 2005, Islamic Human Rights Commission, www.ihrc.org.uk.
231 Ibid, para 3.18.
232 Such action is likely to be already tortious or criminal but, as Chapter 4 argues, defendants can raise Arts 10 and 11 arguments in defence.

crops, may be intended both to disrupt and to draw attention to a cause. Direct action forms of protest going beyond persuasion may provide a substantive means of engaging in the more *effective* means of communicating with others (since such forms are most likely to attract media attention). To label forms of such action 'terrorist', as, in effect, s 1 TA does, is not only to devalue that term, but also to take a stance towards forms of protest more characteristic of a totalitarian state than of a democracy. It was always unlikely that the TA would be used to a significant extent against protest groups, but it is argued that they should have been expressly exempted. Direct action is already extensively covered by the public order provisions discussed in Chapter 8.

The definition also allowed the previously *non-criminal* actions of a number of persons to be re-designated as terrorist since the special terrorist offences, discussed below, were applied to a wide range of persons, including those who have some contact with persons designated 'terrorist'. Thus, technically speaking, the then Home Secretary was right in stating, as he did, that the definition *itself* did not create any new offences.[233] But it potentially led to the criminalisation of the actions or omissions of a wide range of persons, many of whom did not themselves fall within the definition.

Proscription

Introduction

The government stance is that the proscription – banning – of terrorist organisations contributes towards making the UK a hostile environment for terrorists and sends a clear message to the international community and to UK citizens that the UK absolutely rejects such organisations and any of their claims to legitimacy as opposition groups. Proscription is a strong and far-reaching power since it has the effect of outlawing previously lawful activity without recourse to a court, except retrospectively – after proscription has occurred. The use of proscription means that in effect the definition of terrorism is extended because a range of people become terrorist suspects, or suspects associated with terrorist activity, who do not necessarily fall within the s 1 definition themselves. Proscription under the TA 2000 is a reactive measure in the sense that if criminal sanctions are to be applied a trial must occur, but it is proactive in that the initial decision to proscribe is not taken by a judicial body, but by the Home Secretary with – it is argued – a thin veneer of Parliamentary oversight. As discussed below, it is a criminal offence to belong to, support, glorify or display support for a proscribed organisation; the Terrorism Act 2000 also allows the police to seize all the property of a proscribed organisation. Once a group is proscribed the freedom of speech, assembly and association of its members is severely curtailed, or abrogated entirely, in relation to the political, religious or ideological cause upon which the initial proscription was based. This is also true of supporters of the group who are not members of it. The proscription-related offences and the proceedings allowing for challenge to the proscription decision are also in doubtful compliance with Art 6.

Under s 1 of the PTA, the Secretary of State could by order proscribe any organisation which appeared to him to be concerned in Irish terrorism, or in promoting it or

---

233 See the *Guardian*, 14 November 1999.

encouraging it. No provision was made under the PTA for proscribing international terrorist organisations active in the UK. At the time of the inception of the TA the IRA and INLA were proscribed and these powers were extended to Northern Ireland by virtue of s 28 of the Northern Ireland (Emergency Provisions) Act 1991.[234] Proscription of the IRA was taken to include splinter groups such as the Continuity IRA and the Real IRA. Equivalent provisions in Northern Ireland were set out in ss 30 and 31 of and Sched 2 to the EPA. Twelve organisations, including the IRA, the INLA, the UDA, the UVF, the UFF, the LVF and the Continuity Army Council, were proscribed. 'Organisations' was widely defined as 'any association or combination of persons' (s 1(6) of the PTA). An organisation did not need to engage in terrorism itself; it was enough if it promoted or encouraged it.

Proscription may be seen as providing a legitimate means of expressing outrage at certain activities, thereby tending to prevent illegitimate expressions of public anger. It has been argued that it may discourage supporters of terrorist organisations and may signal political strength.[235] But it has also been contended that these benefits are minimal and that it was 'a cosmetic part of the PTA' which was in fact 'counterproductive as it impedes criminal investigation and political discussion'.[236] Lord Jellicoe's review of the operation of the PTA doubted the value of proscription, considering that its detrimental effects in terms of constraining the free expression of views about Northern Ireland outweighed its benefits.[237] In response, a Home Office circular was issued[238] giving guidance to the police as to the proper use of ss 1 and 2, bearing in mind the possible effect on freedom of expression. There were no convictions for proscription-related offences in Britain between 1990 and 2000, although in the same period 195 convictions were obtained in Northern Ireland. Therefore the need to retain the power to proscribe in relation to Britain under the TA was not made out in relation to Irish terrorism. Clearly, the government wanted to retain it in relation to extremist Islamic groups and other international armed opposition groups.

Walker has argued, in relation to the PTA and EPA provisions, that, prima facie proscription breaches Arts 10 and 11 of the European Convention on Human Rights but that, apart from exceptions contained in those Articles, Art 17 might justify it since it limits Convention guarantees to activity in harmony with its aims, and this could not be said of IRA methods.[239] As discussed above, Art 17 provides that the Convention is not to be interpreted so as to imply a right 'for any state, group or person to engage in any activity . . . aimed at the destruction of any of the [Convention rights] or at their limitation to a greater extent than . . . provided for in the Convention'. This appears to be true of Al-Qaeda and linked groups. But a number of groups might be proscribed under the current provisions, taking s 1 TA into account, which cannot so readily be

---

234 For commentary on the predecessor to the 1991 Act, see *Review of the Operation of the Northern Ireland (Emergency Provisions) Act 1978*, Cmnd 9222; Bonner, D [1984] PL 348.
235 Wilkinson, P, *Terrorism and the Political State*, 1986, Macmillan, p 170.
236 See Walker, C, *The Prevention of Terrorism in British Law*, 2nd edn, 1992, p 64. See also Bonner, D [1989] PL 440.
237 Cmnd 8803, 1983; the review did not, however, recommend deproscription, since it would create public resentment.
238 On 9 August 1983 (*Current Law Statutes* 1984, note to s 1(1)).
239 Walker, C, *The Prevention of Terrorism in British Law* (1992) pp 49–50.

viewed as out of harmony with the aims of the Convention, and therefore the exceptions under the relevant Articles would usually have to be relied on if compatibility between the proscription provisions and the Convention is to be found. But the current reliance on the executive to satisfy the demands of proportionality by showing restraint in taking decisions as to groups to be included in proscription orders put before Parliament can hardly be seen as a satisfactory safeguard.

Proscription under the TA, as amended in 2006

Under the Terrorism Act 2000 the very broad power of proscription, and all the proscription-related offences, were retained, and their impact was greatly extended. The notion of increasing the number of groups to be proscribed lay at the heart of the introduction of the TA. Clearly, it was intended that a range of extremist Islamic groups would be proscribed, some, but not all, linked with Al-Qaeda, and that occurred shortly after the TA came into force. Other international groups have been proscribed, some that do not appear to create a security risk within the UK itself. Amendation under s 22 of the 2006 Act allows the Home Secretary to list names that are used as aliases by proscribed organisations.

Section 3(1) TA provides: 'For the purposes of this Act an organisation is proscribed if it is listed in Schedule 2, or it operates under the same name as an organisation listed in that Schedule.' The power to add to or delete groups from the Schedule is exercised under s 3(3) by the Secretary of State, by order. Under s 3(4) the power may be exercised 'only if he believes that [the organisation] is concerned in terrorism'. Thus no express distinction is created by the TA between organisations falling within s 1 and those which can be proscribed; the power of seeking proscription is left entirely at the Home Secretary's discretion – it is entirely unregulated by the TA itself, though it is subject to the Parliamentary affirmative resolution procedure. This provides the Home Secretary with an extraordinarily wide power, bearing in mind that Parliament has not refused an order on the four occasions that one has been sought since 2000. The consequences of proscription are far more harsh than the consequences flowing from the possibility that a group falls within the s 1 TA definition.

The breadth of the definition of terrorism means that any armed opposition group, or any person or group that supports an armed opposition group in any part of the world, including those who oppose repressive regimes, are 'terrorists'. Section 3 permits the proscription of organisations that would normally not be proscribed in practice,

> including organisations which are fighting against undemocratic and oppressive regimes and, in particular, those which have engaged in lawful armed conflict in the exercise of the internationally recognised right to self-determination of peoples (where the United Kingdom is bound in international law to recognise the right and to refrain from offering material support to states engaged in the suppression of the exercise of the right by military or other coercive means).[240]

---

240 See *R (on the application of the Kurdistan Workers' Party and Others) v Secretary of State for the Home Dept* [2002] EWHC Admin 644, at para 47.

Support has come from the West for a number of organisations that are terrorist under this definition, including UNITA in Angola and the mujahidin in Afghanistan; the West also sought, prior to the Iraq war, to persuade the Shi'a in Iraq to rise against Saddam Hussein. Some of the proscribed groups are from countries where repressive regimes prevent them from exercising democratic rights and provide them with no legitimate means of pursuing their ends. In a number of instances the proscribed organisation would have had no method open to it to seek its objectives peacefully through the political system. This can be said of the Kurds, who are not recognised as a minority in Turkey and are persecuted as terrorists there, and the People's Mujahidin of Iran (Mujahidin e Khalq). In Iran anyone questioning the supremacy of the religious leader can be criminalised; widespread executions and murders against the People's Mujahidin of Iran have been documented.

Significantly, the power of proscription is, on its face, broader even than the ambit of s 1 TA would permit. Groups which do not themselves fall within the s1 definition, but which are in any way 'concerned' in terrorism can be proscribed. The addition of the term 'concerned in terrorism' makes this provision wider than that under the PTA. Parliament's approval is required for additions to, or deletions from, the list, as it was under the PTA provisions.[241] Under s 3(5) a group is 'concerned in terrorism', and so is a candidate for proscription, if it: '(a) commits or participates in acts of terrorism, (b) prepares for terrorism, (c) promotes or encourages terrorism, or (d) is otherwise concerned in terrorism', and now (under the Terrorism Act 2006) if it glorifies it.[242] In other words, the group itself need not have issued threats or taken part in action covered by s 1 TA. Thus, for example, a group verbally supporting on a website the use of threats to property as part of opposition to a despotic regime could theoretically be proscribed.

---

241 Under s 123(4) of the Act of 2000: 'An order or regulations under any of the following provisions shall not be made, subject to sub-section (4), unless a draft has been laid before and approved by resolution of each House of Parliament . . .' The provisions listed include s 3(3). Section 123(5) covers cases of urgency, in which case an order may be made without approval, if so it will lapse after 40 days unless approved.

242 The 2006 Act provided that encouraging terrorism included the 'unlawful glorification' of 'acts of terrorism'. The following words were added by the 2006 Act:

(5A) The cases in which an organisation promotes or encourages terrorism for the purposes of sub-section (5)(c) include any case in which activities of the organisation–

(a) include the unlawful glorification of the commission or preparation (whether in the past, in the future or generally) of acts of terrorism; or

(b) are carried out in a manner that ensures that the organisation is associated with statements containing any such glorification.

(5B) The glorification of any conduct is unlawful for the purposes of sub-section (5A) if there are persons who may become aware of it who could reasonably be expected to infer that what is being glorified, is being glorified as –

(a) conduct that should be emulated in existing circumstances, or

(b) conduct that is illustrative of a type of conduct that should be so emulated.

(5C) In this section –

'glorification' includes any form of praise or celebration, and cognate expressions are to be construed accordingly;

'statement' includes a communication without words consisting of sounds or images or both.

But the lack of information available to Parliament as to the groups to be proscribed means that it has little chance of exercising any genuine control over the executive. Further, when Parliament is asked to approve a proscription order, it is asked to approve or disapprove it in its entirety. Thus if a group such as Al-Qaeda is included – or a similar group – along with groups that could be viewed as 'freedom fighters' and pose no threat to the UK since their concern is with an oppressive regime abroad, Parliament would have to refuse to proscribe Al-Qaeda if it wished to disapprove of proscription of the latter groups. As mentioned above, over the seven years between 2000 and 2007 four proscription orders have been laid before Parliament; none has been refused.

The main objection to proscription is that the key decisions are in executive hands: a person can become subject to a large range of criminal offences on the basis of an executive decision. In effect a person can be criminalised by executive decision alone – with a very thin veneer of Parliamentary or judicial oversight – because if an organisation is proscribed any member of it commits a criminal offence purely by virtue of their status (s 2(1)(a)). Persons receive no warning that the organisation of which they are members is about to be proscribed since the Home Office policy is not to comment on whether or not a particular organisation is being considered for proscription, or to give reasons for an organisation's absence from the list.[243] Persons in that position can only escape conviction in limited circumstances and on the basis of a reversed burden of proof, as discussed below. In effect, they are first criminalised and then the case against them can be inquired into – if they challenge the proscription order. The decision to proscribe is likely to be based on classified material from the UK and foreign intelligence services, along with police, security and legal advice. Where proscription is based on confidential information available to the Home Secretary, it is difficult for organisations to mount effective appeals against it without access to such information. If an organisation is proscribed that appears to be no longer functional in the UK, the mounting of a challenge to the proscription demonstrates that it is no longer defunct and identifies those associated with it. This has security benefits, but it also operates as a significant deterrent to challengers, although they have immunity from prosecution in certain circumstances, as discussed below.

The implicit, tacit assumption on which the legislation rests is that the Secretary of State will not proscribe certain organisations despite the fact that they meet the statutory criteria of ss 1 and 3. Thus, the relationship between the s 1 definition of terrorism and the s 3 proscription power is of interest. The very broad s 1 definition is objectionable

---

243 See, e.g., Parliamentary and Health Service Ombudsman, *Investigations Completed* July 2004–March 2005, Part Two, Home Office, A.26/05. On 17 February 2004 Ms T wrote to the Home Office and, citing the Code of Practice on Access to Government Information (now superseded by the Freedom of Information Act 2000 from 1 January 2005 onwards; see Chapter 7, pp 606 *et seq*), asked what steps the government had taken to proscribe the organisation known as the al-Aqsa Martyrs' Brigade. She also asked why the government had not listed this organisation as a proscribed terrorist group. The Home Office acknowledged the request on 30 March 2004 and replied in full on 27 April 2004. They said that the government's list of proscribed organisations was kept under constant and active review. However, they said that it was their policy not to comment on whether or not a particular organisation was being considered for proscription, or upon the reasons for an organisation's absence from the list. It was found that the Home Office had been justified in refusing to release the information sought by Ms T, under Exemption 1 of the Code – although the Ombudsman was critical of the Home Office's handling of the request.

as discussed, but it was always highly improbable that the Home Secretary would seek to proscribe all, or even the majority, of the groups falling within s 1. Sections 1 and 3 combined are convenient since it maximises executive discretion as to proscription. As political alliances change, the proscription or deproscription of relevant groups can occur, and the lack of information available to Parliament means that no real check on the exercise of that discretion is available. The proscription of a new group in order to placate an ally or cement a new international agreement clearly arises; the possibilities of arbritrariness and injustice are apparent. Clearly, it is difficult, if not impossible, to devise a definition of terrorism that differentiates between good and bad terrorists – between 'terrorists' and 'freedom-fighters'. Proscription provides a somewhat clumsy means of doing so, which in effect trusts the executive to make the differentiation.

Choosing the groups to proscribe

Clearly, the Home Secretary and other relevant members of the executive are bound by s 6 HRA to abide by the Convention. Articles 10 and 11 should therefore be taken into account in taking decisions to add groups to the list of those proscribed under the TA.

Difficult decisions had to be taken concerning the range of 'terrorist' groups (under the s 1 TA definition) chosen initially for proscription. In 2000 under Sched 2 TA the groups listed had already been proscribed under the EPA; they were then proscribed throughout the UK.[244] But a key issue under the TA was whether all or most of the other groups falling within the s 1 definition would eventually be proscribed. There appeared to be three options for the trend of proscription over a period of time – although it is suggested that in reality there were only two.

First the current proscriptions could have been retained, merely adding further Irish splinter groups if necessary. Second, the option was open of proscribing both Irish and international terrorist groups, leaving domestic groups which fell within the s 1 definition unproscribed. Third, the possibility arose of proscribing *all* or most groups falling within the TA definition. So far, unsurprisingly, the government has taken the second option, proscribing over the last seven years a range of international 'terrorist' groups, including a very large number of extremist Islamic groups.[245] The fact that

---

244 The following groups are listed in Sched 2: The Irish Republican Army, Cumann nam Ban, Fianna nah Eireann, The Red Hand Commando, Saor Eire, The Ulster Freedom Fighters, The Ulster Volunteer Force, The Irish National Liberation Army, The Irish People's Liberation Organisation, The Ulster Defence Association, The Loyalist Volunteer Force, The Continuity Army Council, The Orange Volunteers, The Red Hand Defenders.

245 Al-Qaeda itself and its associated groups are of course proscribed, along with a number of other groups not linked to it, including the PKK and various groups associated with Northern Ireland, as indicated above. Under Statutory Instrument 2001 No 1261, The Terrorism Act 2000 Proscribed Organisations (Amendment) Order 2001, the organisations added to Sched 2 to the TA were: Al-Qaeda, Egyptian Islamic Jihad, Al-Gama'at al-Islamiya, Armed Islamic Group (Groupe Islamique Armée) (GIA), Salafist Group for Call and Combat (Groupe Salafiste pour la Prédication et le Combat) (GSPC), Babbar Khalsa, International Sikh Youth Federation, Harakat Mujahideen, Jaish e Mohammed, Lashkar e Tayyaba, Liberation Tigers of Tamil Eelam (LTTE), Hizballah External Security Organisation, Hamas-Izz al-Din al-Qassem Brigades, Palestinian Islamic Jihad – Shaqaqi, Abu Nidal Organisation, Islamic Army of Aden, Mujaheddin e Khalq, Kurdistan Workers' Party (Partiya Karkeren Kurdistan) (PKK), Revolutionary Peoples' Liberation Party-Front (Devrimci Halk Kurtulus Partisi-Cephesi) (DHKP-

a group is about to be added to the list is not made known in advance; there is no consultation with the groups concerned, meaning that a person is suddenly subject to criminal sanctions by virtue of his membership of or support for a newly proscribed group. This may be a desirable stance to take in security terms if the group does pose a threat to the security of the UK, but it has significant Convention implications; this point is returned to below. This position means that groups that fall within s 1 TA but are unproscribed can be dealt with for a time under the general TA provisions, particularly under s 56, the offence of directing a terrorist organisation. But at any point, without warning, the group can be proscribed, meaning that the proscription-based offences can also be utilised.

In considering which international terrorist organisations should be subject to proscription, the Home Secretary takes the following five factors into account: (1) the nature and scale of an organisation's activities; (2) the specific threat that it poses to the UK; (3) the specific threat that it poses to British nationals overseas; (4) the extent of the organisation's presence in the UK; and (5) the need to support other members of the international community in the global fight against terrorism.[246] But despite factor (5), the fact that an organization is added to the European Union's list of recognised terrorist groups or designated by the United States as a 'Foreign Terrorist Organisation' does not necessarily mean that the group will be proscribed as a terrorist organisation by the UK Government.[247] On the other hand, a group may be proscribed in the UK but not in, for example, Germany, meaning that if a member of the group travels to Britain he or she commits a criminal offence as soon as he or she arrives in the UK (this is discussed further below). Quite a large number of groups have been added to the list since the 2000 Act was introduced, and at present 54 organisations are proscribed,[248] of which 14 have their origins in Northern Ireland and/or Ireland, while the rest are international terrorist organisations, within the ss 1 TA definition. No organisations were removed during the period 2002–7.

In terms of doubtful decisions, the example of the PKK comes to mind since it has declared a ceasefire in Turkey. Clearly the ceasefire might break down, but while it is in

---

C), Basque Homeland and Liberty (Euskadi ta Askatasuna) (ETA), 17 November Revolutionary Organisation (N17). The Terrorism Act 2000 Proscribed Organisations (Amendment) Order 2006 (SI 2006/2016) added Al-Ghurabaa, The Saved Sect, Baluchistan Liberation Army, Teyrebaz Azadiye Kurdistan to the list.

246 See HL Debs vol 613 col 252, 16 May 2000; Home Office Press Release, 28 February 2001; these factors have continued to be reiterated: see, e.g., Parliamentary and Health Service Ombudsman, Investigations Completed July 2004–March 2005, Part Two, Home Office, A.26/05; *Home Secretary To Ban Terror Groups*, Home Office Press Release 17 July 2006.

247 E.g. the al-Aqsa Martyrs' Brigade was added to the European Union's list of recognised terrorist groups in June 2002 but was not proscribed in the UK.

248 See fns 244 and 245 above. There have been four proscription orders laid since introduction of the Terrorism Act 2000. The first draft order to proscribe 21 international organisations under the Terrorism Act 2000 was laid before Parliament on 28 February 2001 (Home Office press notice 058/2001). The order came into force on 29 March 2001 (SI 2001/1261). This was followed by a further draft order in October 2002 that sought the proscription of four groups (Home Office press notice 283/2002). That order came into force on 1 November 2002 (SI 2002/2724). The third order, proscribing 15 international groups, was laid before Parliament on 10 October 2005 and came into force on 14 October 2005 (Home Office press notice 147/2005) (SI 2005/2892). A further four new organisations concerned in terrorism were designated to be banned in 2006 (press release 17 June 2006).

existence the case for proscription of the PKK appears not to be strong enough. Lord Carlile in his 2006 Report on the operation of the TA singled out the Iran opposition group commonly known as the PMOI:

> They claim to have disarmed in 2003 to become a political organisation dedicated to the reform of government in Iran. They certainly have significant Parliamentary support across parties at Westminster. I am sure that [the working group existing within the government service at which all the interested parties meet and scrutinise proscriptions] will give serious examination to whether the PMOI really should remain proscribed.[249]

The decision to proscribe a range of international terrorist groups, not all those that fall within the s 1 definition, means that while the members of certain domestic activist or protest groups have, in effect, been re-defined as 'terrorists', the groups remain openly able to engage in various public activities such as advertising for members, fund-raising, holding marches or possibly even putting up members to stand for elections.[250] The government had signalled from the outset that it would begin with the addition of international groups to the proscribed list.[251] Lord Lloyd recommended adoption of the third option. This option would be highly problematic in practical terms and deeply objectionable at the level of principle. The government was apparently attracted to it since it would provide 'a mechanism to signal clearly condemnation of any terrorist organisation whatever its origin and motivation'.[252] It was also clear that the government saw advantages in criminalising fund-raising activity of any kind for a particular group since that would remove the requirement to prove end use of funds. But it recognised the practical problem that the provisions could be circumvented by changing the group's name.

Between 2001 and 2007 the focus of government attention was on the threat posed by groups associated with Al-Qaeda. The proscription of a range of animal rights, anti-abortion, or environmental groups that fall within s 3 TA is not particularly high on the political agenda. If the third option of proscribing such groups was eventually adopted, it is arguable that the list, if it was to have any credibility, would have to be exhaustive: it would clearly be inequitable to proscribe one group falling within the definition while failing to proscribe another which was equally within it. Given its width, the definition potentially covers a vast range of organisations. There would clearly be insuperable practical difficulties in drawing up and then maintaining an

---

249 Report on the Operation in 2005 of the Terrorism Act 2000 by Lord Carlile of Berriew QC, at para 43. In 2001 he was appointed as Independent Reviewer of the Terrorism Act 2000. His reports can be found at www.homeoffice.gov.uk.

250 All these activities might in certain respects fall within the terrorist offences discussed below, but they do not in themselves either constitute offences or lead almost inevitably to liability under the proscription-related offences.

251 The explanatory notes to the Act state: 'The Government is considering which organisations involved in international terrorism might be added to the Schedule'.

252 'The current provisions, under which only Irish terrorist groups can be proscribed, could be construed by some as indicating that the Government does not take other forms of terrorism as seriously. Furthermore a wider provision could deter international groups from establishing themselves in the UK' (the 1998 consultation paper *Legislation on Terrorism*, at para 4.14).

up-to-date list of international and domestic groups to be proscribed. The list would be of immense scope; it would probably include hundreds of names and it would quickly become out of date. Clearly, it might come to appear ludicrously broad and simply unworkable, undermining the credibility of the proscription scheme. Apart from the severe practical problems, s 1 – if fully utilised – is so far out of kilter with Arts 10 and 11 ECHR that challenges relying on those Articles would have a strong chance of success in relation to some groups that could be proscribed. The conflicts created with Arts 10 and 11 would appear to be especially grave and would be politically unpalatable since these groups are driven by ideologies with which some in the UK sympathise, while disapproving of the methods that some of these groups adopt. Once a group is proscribed the freedom of speech, assembly of its members, or supporters, is severely curtailed: it is very difficult or impossible for any speech relating to the cause in question to be promulgated or for any meeting to occur, legally. The freedom of association of the members is completely abrogated.

The government stated in 2000 that it was unlikely to put the third option into practice for some years.[253] In fact it is suggested that the government never seriously intended that all those groups covered by s 1 TA would be proscribed, and it is unlikely that any future UK Government would seek to proscribe the majority of the groups falling within that definition, but in the traditional style of British Governments preferred to adopt very broad provisions with the intention that they would never be fully utilised. At the same time the provisions were of value since they left open the possibility that in extreme and possible future circumstances, such as the mounting of a violent campaign by an anti-abortion activist group in the UK, they could be utilised. The threat of proscription may also be of some value in deterring groups from adopting methods other than recognised democratic ones to push their political agenda.

Proscription-related offences

Belonging to a proscribed organisation

Section 11 of the 2000 Act makes it an offence to belong to a proscribed organisation.[254] Under s 11(1) a person commits an offence if he belongs or professes to belong to a proscribed organisation; a maximum penalty of 10 years' imprisonment is imposed. It is notable that there is no *mens rea* requirement. There is a limited defence under s 11(2):

> it is a defence for a person charged with an offence under sub-section (1) to prove that the organisation was not proscribed on the last (or only) occasion on which he became a member or began to profess to be a member, and that he has not taken part in the activities of the organisation at any time while it was proscribed.

Section 11 in effect comes close to imposing a reverse burden of proof on the defendant once the prosecution has discharged its burden in showing that he was a member

---

253 At the Committee stage in the House of Commons, the government said that in the immediate future it would not add domestic groups to the list; see HC Debs 15 March 2000 col 431.
254 Previously this was provided for under s 2(1)(a) of the PTA.

of a proscribed organisation, even if he was unaware that it had been proscribed (and as indicated above organisations are constantly added to the list of proscribed organisations and the members are given no warning of this beforehand). The burden of proof is then placed on him to prove that it was not proscribed when he was a member under s 11(2). This appears to infringe the presumption of innocence under Art 6(2), discussed above, and in Chapters 2 and 12,[255] since it places a burden on a defendant who has arguably not engaged in any blameworthy conduct to disprove a substantial element of the offence. However, as mentioned in Chapter 4, the UK courts have engaged in 'reading down' under s 3 HRA of legal burdens to evidential ones in order to seek to create compliance with Art 6(2).[256] Thus they have sought to give effect to the fundamental right encapsulated in Art 6(2),[257] and long recognised under common law principle.[258]

This issue was raised in the Court of Appeal in *Attorney General's Reference (No 4 of 2002)*.[259] The Court had to consider the nature of the s 11(2) defence. The defendant, A, was charged, *inter alia*, with offences contrary to s 11(1) TA 2000 of being a member of, and professing to be a member of, a proscribed organisation, Hamas-Izz al-din al Qassem Brigades. The defendant argued that at the time when he became a member, or professed to become a member, of the organisation it had not yet been proscribed (the defence provided by s 11(2)). He said that he had been a member of Hamas from either 1997 or 1998, but that he had left in 1999 because he had discovered that it was involved in the killing of innocent civilians. At trial the prosecution accepted, following *R v Lambert*,[260] that 'A' bore only an evidential burden in relation to the defence under s 11(2). The trial judge concluded that the prosecution had failed to establish to the criminal standard of proof that 'A' had taken part in the activities of the proscribed organisation since proscription, and ruled that there was no case to answer; subsequently a verdict of not guilty was entered in respect of each of the counts. The Attorney General referred two questions for the opinion of the Court of Appeal, namely:

(1) What are the ingredients of an offence contrary to s 11(1) of the Terrorism Act 2000; (2) Does the defence contained in s 11(2) of the Terrorism Act 2000 impose a legal, rather than an evidential burden of proof on an accused and, if so,

---

255 See pp 64–65 and pp 1239–40.
256 See pp 178–79. For further discussion, see: Tadros, V and Tierney, S, 'The Presumption of Innocence and the Human Rights Act' (2004) 67 MLR 402, at p 403; Simester, AP and Sullivan, GR, *Criminal Law: Theory and Doctrine*, 2nd edn, 2004, Hart, esp p 69; Dennis, I, 'Reverse Onuses and the Presumption of Innocence: In Search of Principle' [2005] CLR 901; Dingwall, G, 'Statutory Exceptions, Burdens of Proof and the Human Rights Act 1998' (2002) 65 MLR 40; Ashworth, A, 'Four Threats to the Presumption of Innocence' (2006) 10 *International Journal of Evidence and Proof* 241; Ashworth, A, 'Criminal Justice Reform: Principles, Human Rights and Public Protection' [2004] Crim LR 516.
257 See Chapter 2, pp 64–65.
258 See *Woolmington* [1935] AC 462, pp 481–82. See further Ashworth, A and Blake, M, 'The Presumption of Innocence in English Criminal Law', [1996] CLR 306.
259 2003] EWCA Crim 762; [2003] 3 W.L.R. 1153; [2004] 1 All E.R. 1; [2003] 2 Cr. App. R. 22; [2003] HRLR 15.
260 [2002] 2 AC 545.

is such a legal burden compatible with the European Convention for the Protection of Human Rights and Fundamental Freedoms, and in particular, with Arts 6(2) and 10 of the Convention?

The Court found that the answer to question (1) was that the ingredients of the offence contrary to s 11(1) of the Terrorism Act 2000 were fully set out within that section. Thus the Court found that s 11(2) did not relate to an element of the offence. The Court went on to find that in any event if it did it was compatible with Art 6(2). The answer to question (2) was that the defence in s 11(2) imposed a legal, rather than an evidential, burden of proof on an accused to establish the matters set out in (a) and (b) on the balance of probabilities. This was not, it was found, incompatible with Art 6.2 or with Art 10 of the European Convention for the Protection of Human Rights. Section 11(2), it was found, identified a very specific exception applicable to a limited class of defendants which did not in any way affect the criminal offence fully identified in s 11(1), which defined the elements of the offence. Parliament, it was found, had intended that a person should be guilty of an offence under s 11(1) irrespective of whether or not he had played any active part in the organisation. Section 11(2) therefore, it was determined, did not infringe the presumption of innocence so as to breach Art 6.2.

However, it was found that if that conclusion was wrong, any infringement by way of imposition of a legal burden was justified and proportionate, and that Parliament was entitled to take the view that a legal burden was appropriate. Further, the Court said that it was difficult to see how imposing the legal burden of proof on a defendant charged with an offence under s 11(1) could ever amount to an unjustified and disproportionate interference with his right to freedom of expression so as to breach Art 10, except in circumstances where, in a particular case, a statutory provision such as s 11 might involve a disproportionate infringement of an individual's rights under Art 10 to freedom of expression. Accordingly, the trial judge should not have ruled that there was no case to answer.[261]

However, the House of Lords, by a three to two majority, reversed this decision in the joined cases *Sheldrake v DPP; Attorney General's Reference (No 4 of 2002).*[262] In *Attorney General's Reference (No 4 of 2002)*, Lord Bingham, giving the opinion of the House, found that a person who had not engaged in any blameworthy conduct could come within s 11(1) and that the presumption of innocence was infringed by requiring him or her to disprove involvement in the organization at the time in question. He said that there was a real risk that a person who was innocent of any blameworthy or properly criminal conduct, but who was unable to establish a defence under s 11(2) might fall within s 11(1), thereby resulting in a clear breach of the presumption of innocence and an unfair conviction. He found that, bearing in mind the difficulties a defendant would have in proving the matters contained in s 11(2), and the serious consequences for the defendant in failing to do so, the imposition of a legal burden

---

261   The decisions in *Sheldrake v Director of Public Prosecutors* [2003] EWHC Admin 273, [2003] 2 Cr App R 206, DC, and *R v Lambert* [2001] 2 Cr App R 511; [2002] 2 A C 545, HL, were distinguished.

262   [2004] UKHL 43; [2005] 1 AC 264; [2005] 1 All ER 237. The House of Lords took account of *R v Lambert* [2002] 2 AC 545, HL(E), *R v A (No 2)* [2002] 1 AC 45, HL(E), *R v Johnstone* [2003] 1 WLR 1736, HL(E), *Ghaidan v Godin-Mendoza* [2004] 2 AC 557, HL(E).

upon the defendant was not a proportionate and justifiable legislative response to the threat of terrorism. Further, it was found that while security considerations always carried weight, they did not absolve member states from their duty to ensure that basic standards of fairness were observed; and that since s 11(2) impermissibly infringed the presumption of innocence, it was appropriate, pursuant to s 3 of the 1998 Act, to read down s 11(2) so as to impose on the defendant an evidential burden only, even though that was not Parliament's intention when enacting the sub-section.[263]

Thus the Lords found that s 11(2) imposes an evidential burden only. A majority of the House of Lords relied on s 3 to read the word 'prove' as though it meant 'adduce sufficient evidence to raise an issue in the case'. Thus the Lords ameliorated the difficulty facing defendants in proving their innocence in relation to s 11 and created a compatibility with Art 6(2) that was not previously present. The decision has implications for a number of the offences in the TA and TA 2006, as discussed below.

But it is not a defence to prove that the defendant did not know that the organisation was proscribed or that it was engaged in activities covered by ss 1(1) and 3 of the Act. This was reaffirmed in *R v Hundal (Avtar Singh); R v Dhaliwal (Kesar Singh)*.[264] The defendants appealed against convictions for belonging to a proscribed organisation contrary to TA 2000, s 11(1), and against sentences of 30 months' imprisonment. They had been stopped and searched whilst entering the UK from Germany. The first defendant had been in possession of various documents which had included an International Sikh Youth Federation (ISYF) membership card. They contended that they had been members of the ISYF in Germany but, as far as they were concerned, had not been members when they had entered the UK and had not realised it was a proscribed organisation. The ISYF had been proscribed in the UK since March 2001 under the 2000 Act, but had not been illegal in Germany. The defendants contended that the 2000 Act did not apply as they had joined the ISYF in a country outside the court's jurisdiction. It was held that the 2000 Act was applicable to the circumstances of the instant case. It required that a person in the UK, while in the UK, was a member of a proscribed organisation. Both defendants were members of a proscribed organisation while in the UK. But it was found that the sentences of 30 months' imprisonment were manifestly excessive given that the judge had sentenced on the basis that neither defendant was aware that what they were doing contravened legislation in the UK. The sentences were quashed and sentences of 12 months' imprisonment were substituted.

Symbols of allegiance to a proscribed group; meetings

If proscription is at least partly of symbolic value, as an affirmation of society's rejection of the value of associating with certain groups, then it follows that visible signs of allegiance to those groups will also be banned. Therefore there are a number of further offences relating to badges, symbols and meetings. Under s 12(1) TA it is an offence

---

263 At paras 48–53, 55 and 56.
264 2004 WL 62035 (CA (Crim Div)), [2004] 2 Cr App R 19, [2004] 2 Cr App R (S) 64 (2004), *The Times*, 13 February, 62,035 [2004] EWCA Crim 389.

to solicit support, other than money or other property, for a proscribed organisation.[265] This offence now overlaps with the offence of indirectly (including glorifying) or directly encouraging terrorism under the Terrorism Act 2006. It is also an offence under s 12(2) for a person to arrange, manage or assist in arranging or managing a meeting which he knows is: '(a) to support a proscribed organisation, (b) to further the activities of a proscribed organisation, or (c) to be addressed by a person who belongs or professes to belong to a proscribed organisation'. It is an offence under s 12(3)(a) TA to address such a meeting in order to encourage support for a proscribed organisation or 'further its activities'. These are broadly drawn offences, although they do include a *mens rea* ingredient. Their impact on speech, association and assembly is clearly far-reaching, bearing in mind the wide range of meetings, including very small, informal ones, covered.

The fact that the majority of speakers at a meeting were opposed to the methods or aims of a proscribed group would not affect the liability of the organiser so long as s/he was aware that a speaker was a member, or professed member, of such an organisation, speaking in support of it. A meeting is defined as one at which three or more persons are present and there is no need for it to be open to the public. A narrow defence is provided under s 12(4) in relation to private meetings only if the defendant can show that he had no reasonable cause to believe that the address as mentioned in s 12(2)(c) was to support a proscribed organisation. Section 12(4) is covered by s 118, meaning that if the accused puts forward evidence sufficient to raise a doubt as to whether he or she had no cause to believe that the address would be in support of such an organisation, the court or jury must assume that the defence is satisfied unless the prosecution proves beyond reasonable doubt that it is not. The maximum punishment for this offence is ten years' imprisonment. The problem is that s 12(4) is narrowly drawn; a person who assisted in arranging a public meeting, even if of only three people, not knowing that the member of the proscribed organisation would speak in support of the organisation, would commit an offence.

Restrictions on the use of badges or uniforms as signals of support for certain organisations are intended to have the dual effect of preventing communication – by those means – of the political message associated with the organisation and of tending to minimise the impression that the organisation is supported, thereby denying reassurance to its members, lowering their morale and preventing them from arousing public support. Under s 13 TA it is an offence to 'wear any item which arouses a reasonable apprehension that a person is a member or supporter of a proscribed organisation',[266] and it is an offence to wear an item of clothing, or wear, carry or display an article, 'in such a way or in such circumstances as to arouse reasonable suspicion [that the person in question] is a member or supporter of a proscribed organisation'. Again it is notable that no element of *mens rea* is included. The offence can be established on the basis of proof of reasonable suspicion alone and no defence is provided.

An overlapping offence arises under s 1 of the Public Order Act 1936: it is an offence to wear a uniform signifying association with any political organisation or with the

---

265 Previously this was provided for under s 2(1)(a) PTA.
266 Previously this was provided for under s 3 PTA.

promotion of any political object. Section 1 was invoked in *Whelan v DPP*[267] against leaders of a Provisional Sinn Fein protest march against internment in Northern Ireland, all of whom wore black berets while some wore dark glasses, dark clothing and carried Irish flags. It was found that, first, something must be 'worn' as apparel and second, that it must be a uniform. Something might amount to a uniform if worn by a number of persons in order to signify their association with each other or if commonly used by a certain organisation. By this means, the third requirement that the uniform must signal the wearer's association with a particular political organisation could also be satisfied. Alternatively, it might be satisfied by consideration of the occasion on which the uniform was worn without the need to refer to the past history of the organisation. It was found that the items worn could amount to a uniform; this decision therefore greatly diminished the distinction between this offence and that under the PTA. The justification for retention of the PTA provisions in the TA is therefore doubtful due to the overlap between the two offences.

The decision of the House of Lords in *Attorney General's Reference (No 4 of 2002)*[268] is arguably relevant to a number of these offences since, apart from s 12(4), they are not covered by s 118. But it may be problematic to apply the House of Lords' decision where no defences are available. In that case, as discussed above, Lord Bingham found that a person who had not engaged in any blameworthy conduct could commit an offence under the Act and that the presumption of innocence was infringed by requiring him or her to disprove a significant element of the offence. Since the Lords found that this burden placed on the accused impermissibly infringed the presumption of innocence, they employed s 3 HRA to read down the relevant section so as to impose on the defendant an evidential burden only. A number of these offences allow for the criminalisation of the defendant despite the fact that arguably his or her conduct was not blameworthy.

As discussed, a person who is acc§used of being a member of a proscribed organisation under s 11 has a defence if he can raise the possibility that he was not a member of it at the time when it was proscribed. The burden then passes to the prosecution to prove beyond reasonable doubt that he was a member of it at the relevant time. It is not a defence under s 13 to prove that at the time when the support was accorded to the organisation by the defendant, it was not proscribed, but that requirement could be read into the offence. In order to prevent anomalies arising, s 13 should be interpreted compatibly with s 11; the word 'currently' could be implied into the section before the word 'proscribed'. It is not a defence under either s 11 or s 13 that the defendant did not know that the organisation had been proscribed at the time in question. Thus the defendant under s 13 in that position must seek to disprove that the organisation was proscribed at the time, unless a court was prepared to read the word 'knowingly' into s 13.

A number of objections of principle arise in respect of the application of the proscription-related offences to a wider range of groups. The key objection is that, by making it possible to proscribe a wide range of groups, the legislation potentially

---

267 [1975] QB 864.
268 [2005] 1 AC 264; [2005] 1 All ER 237.

curtails proscription-related activities which previously would not have been conceived of as related to terrorism. Some examples are illustrative of the broad potential of the TA, which however has not been fully exploited. It is an offence to wear a badge expressing support for the PKK or to carry a leaflet which arouses reasonable suspicion that such support was being expressed, and this would be the case even if the leaflet was in fact that of a similar but non-proscribed group. If a person who opposed the use of violence to further the cause of animal rights organised a meeting to express such views in private with two other people, one of whom was a member of a proscribed animal rights group, who spoke in its favour, she could commit an offence carrying a maximum penalty of ten years' imprisonment. A group which did not itself engage in terrorism but which, for example, expressed support during one of its assemblies for the 'serious disruption' of a computer system could be proscribed as falling within the terms of ss 1 and 3 combined. If, during a march, members of a group opposed to the introduction of GM crops wore badges expressing support for a proscribed environmental activist group, they would commit an offence. They would also attract criminal liability if they carried leaflets which aroused reasonable suspicion that such support was being expressed.

These proscription-linked offences strike directly at freedom of political expression, which, as indicated above, is viewed as one of the 'essential foundations of a democratic society', so that exceptions to it 'must be narrowly interpreted and the necessity for any restrictions ... convincingly established'.[269] The use of these offences is prima facie an interference with the guarantee under Art 10 since all, including the wearing of an item, or organising a meeting at which a member of a proscribed organisation is speaking, involve or relate to exercises of expression. Such offences include those of wearing any item that arouses a reasonable apprehension that a person is a member or supporter of a proscribed organisation, of organising a meeting at which a member of a proscribed organisation is speaking, and that of soliciting support for such an organisation. In particular, the provision of s 12 regarding meetings affords very little recognition to the value of peaceful protest and assembly. Strasbourg, as indicated above, affords that value pre-eminence in a democracy.[270] Charging a member of an assembly with one of these offences would clearly, therefore, amount to an interference with the Art 10 guarantee. The domestic court would be expected to observe the same or higher standards than Strasbourg in scrutinising the need for the interference, bearing in mind the narrow margin of appreciation afforded to states in respect of interference with political speech, especially where it concerns criticism directed at the government itself.[271]

Obviously, the view taken of the necessity and proportionality of the interference would depend on the particular circumstances behind the charging of the offence in

---

269 *Observer and Guardian v United Kingdom* judgment of 26 November 1991, Series A no 216, pp 29–30, para 59.

270 See *Ezelin v France* (1991) 14 EHRR 362. On political expression generally, see *Castells v Spain* A 236, p 23, para 43; judgment of 23 April 1992.

271 See *Incal v Turkey* (2000) 29 EHRR 449 and see above, p 1355. See also the discussion of *Marper,* Chapter 4, pp 193–96 in relation to taking a more generous approach than Strasbourg when dealing with para 2 of the materially qualified Articles.

the instance before the court. But to take the example used above of a person making arrangements to meet privately with two others and hearing a member of a proscribed group speak: it might be problematic to find that the necessity for the interference with freedom of expression in a democratic society had been convincingly established. This offence is especially pernicious in terms of freedom of expression since the meeting in question might be entirely peaceful: liability would indirectly relate to the *content* of the speech of at least one of the speakers. Since no defences are provided on which s 3 HRA could bite, a declaration of incompatibility between the relevant section and Arts 10 and 11 might have to be made. However, a court could instead rely on s 6 HRA on the argument that the offence has to be applied in a manner that ensures that the demands of necessity and proportionality are satisfied, an argument that has been used post-HRA in the public protest context, as Chapter 8 notes.[272] Account could be taken of the necessity and proportionality of charging the defendant with a criminal offence in the first place. The threat posed by the prescribed group could be taken into account.

Fund-raising; terrorist property; commercial risks

Further criminal offences, punishable by up to 14 years' imprisonment, exist under s 15 in relation to fund-raising for the purposes of terrorism, under s 16 in relation to the use or possession of money or other property for the purposes of terrorism, under s 17 in relation to arrangements to make money or property available for the purposes of terrorism (funding arrangements), and under s 18 in relation to arrangements facilitating the retention or control of terrorist property by concealment, removal, transfer etc, (money laundering). These offences are not limited to proscribed organisations, but s 14 defines 'terrorist property' as including any resources of a proscribed organisation and, s 1(5) provides that action 'for the purposes of terrorism' includes action taken for the benefit of a proscribed organisation. Pursuant to s 19 it is an offence to fail to disclose any belief or suspicion that another person has committed an offence under any of ss 15–18 if that belief or suspicion is based on information which comes to a person's attention in the course of a trade, profession, business or employment. These offences, affecting businesses, are discussed further below.[273]

Challenges to proscription; deproscription

Under the previous scheme if an organisation was proscribed on insufficient grounds there was little possibility of challenge to the order. There was no right of appeal against proscription, and judicial review, while theoretically available, was likely to create extremely limited scrutiny. In *McEldowney v Forde*[274] an order was made under statutory instrument banning republican clubs or any like organisation, thus potentially outlawing all Nationalist political parties. Nevertheless, the House of Lords preferred

---

272 See pp 783, 797.
273 See pp 1411–15.
274 [1971] AC 632.

not to intervene, Lord Diplock stating that he would do so only if proscription were extended to bodies obviously distanced from Republican views.

The TA set up, under s 5, the Proscribed Organisations Appeal Commission (POAC). It is modelled on the Special Immigration Appeals Commission which also provided the model for the Tribunal set up under the Regulation of Investigatory Powers Act 2000, discussed in Chapter 10.[275] The Commission also appears to have certain parallels with the Security and Intelligence Service Tribunals, also discussed in Chapter 10, which had never upheld a complaint. Rules have been made under s 9 providing that the POAC is the forum in which proceedings under s 7 HRA can be brought.[276]

Under s 4, if an individual is affected by proscription, or an organisation considers that it should not have been proscribed, the first step is to ask the Secretary of State to deproscribe; the Secretary of State is obliged to consider such applications within a period of time specified in the Proscribed Organisations (Applications for Deproscription) Regulations 2001, made under s 4(3). The Regulations lay down the procedure for applications to the Secretary of State and provide, *inter alia*, that he is to determine an application within 90 days from its receipt. Such an application may be made by the organisation itself or by any person affected by the organisation's proscription.

Appeals to the POAC

If the Secretary of State refuses to deproscribe, then the organisation or individual may appeal to the POAC as set out in s 5 and Sched 3.[277] Clause 9 of the original Bill provided that the reference to those principles would allow the appellant to raise points concerning those rights under the European Convention on Human Rights which are 'Convention rights' under the HRA. After amendment this provision was removed, but the Commission in any event has to apply Convention principles as a court would in judicial review proceedings, due to s 6 HRA.[278] Under s 5(3): the Commission must allow an appeal against a refusal to deproscribe an organisation if it 'considers that the decision to refuse was flawed when considered in the light of the principles applicable on an application for judicial review'. The POAC itself, as a public authority, must apply the Convention rights in its adjudications and therefore, in relation to the

---

275 At pp 1080 *et seq.*

276 Under the Proscribed Organisations Appeal Commission (Human Rights Act Proceedings), rr 2001, POAC is the appropriate tribunal for the purposes of s 7 HRA in relation to any proceedings under s 7(1)(a) against the Secretary of State in respect of a refusal by him to exercise his power of deproscription under s 3(3)(b).

277 It may be noted that under s 10 immunity from criminal proceedings is conferred upon a person who seeks deproscription by way of application or appeal under ss 4 or 5, either on behalf of the proscribed organisation or as the person affected. Clearly, otherwise, such a person would be discouraged from pursuing either course, or from instituting proceedings under s 7 of the Human Rights Act, by the risk of prosecution for certain offences, for example the offence of membership of a proscribed organisation. Section 10 provides that evidence of anything done, and any document submitted for these proceedings, cannot be relied on in criminal proceedings for such an offence except as part of the defence case.

278 See Chapter 4, pp 238–39.

question of deproscription, it should take the relevant Convention rights into account. As indicated, the POAC is the appropriate tribunal for s 7(1) HRA purposes under s 9 TA. The rules made by the Lord Chancellor under s 9, providing that proceedings under s 7(1)(a) HRA are to be brought in the POAC, should be interpreted compatibly with the Convention under s 3 HRA.

The procedure before the POAC is far removed from that which would be applicable in an ordinary court in a criminal trial. Under Sched 3, para 5(1) the Lord Chancellor has the power to make rules regulating the exercise of the right of appeal to the Commission and prescribing practice and procedure to be followed in its proceedings. Its members are appointed by the Lord Chancellor; three of them must attend the proceedings and one must be a person who holds or has held high judicial office.[279] Under powers in Sched 3 the Lord Chancellor has the power to make rules providing that proceedings may be determined without an oral hearing in specified circumstances; provision may be made regarding the burden of proof; full particulars of the reasons for proscription or refusal to deproscribe may be withheld from the organisation or applicant concerned; the Commission may exclude persons, including legal representatives, from all or part of the proceedings and permit proceedings for leave to appeal to a court under s 6 to be determined by a single member.

The constitution and procedure of POAC are currently laid down the Proscribed Organisations Appeal Commission (Procedure) rr 2001.[280] Pursuant to TA 2000, Sched 3, para 7, special advocates are appointed by the Law Officers of the Crown 'to represent the interests of an organisation or other applicant in [the] proceedings . . .'. The current rules make provision, *inter alia*, for the appointment of a special advocate to represent the interests of the appellant in the proceedings, in particular in any proceedings from which the appellant and his representative are excluded (r 10). POAC sits in public in Central London, but is able to hear closed evidence in camera and with the applicant and their representatives excluded. POAC considers all the evidence upon which the Secretary of State relies in support of his grounds for opposing the appeal, including evidence that by statute or on general grounds of public interest cannot be disclosed to the appellant or his representative, with the POAC sitting in private for that purpose, and evidence that would not be admissible in a court of law (see rr 21–22). Thus, although the procedure may appear adversarial, its procedural limitations are likely to handicap one side so greatly that the Commission may be unable to discharge its fact-finding role effectively. It may therefore prove ineffective in protecting bodies from unjustified proscription.[281] This procedure is clearly designed to keep de-proscription claims, for the most part, out of the ordinary courts.

Bearing these comments in mind, a further feature of the proceedings is significant. By s 18(1)(f) of the Regulation of Investigatory Powers Act 2000 the normal prohibition on the receipt of evidence based on intercepted communications does not apply to the

---

279 Within the meaning of the Appellate Jurisdiction Act 1876.
280 Made under para 5 of Sch 3.
281 For discussion of the similar limitations in respect of the Tribunal set up under the Regulation of Investigatory Powers Act 2000, see Chapter 10, p 1083–84, 1086–90.

POAC.[282] Thus, the Commission may take its decision on the basis of secret intercept evidence. But such evidence cannot be disclosed to the organisation concerned, its legal representatives or the applicant under para 8(2). Therefore the applicant or the legal representatives would have no means of challenging it or of bringing forward other evidence which might be relevant to it; Art 8 or Art 6 arguments could not be made. An appeal to the RIPA Tribunal could not be mounted, unless on speculative grounds only.[283]

If the Commission finds in favour of an applicant and makes an order to that effect, this has the effect of requiring the Secretary of State either to lay a draft deproscription order before Parliament or to make a deproscription order on the basis of the urgency procedure. Such a finding is to be treated, under s 9(4)(b), as determining that 'an action of the Secretary of State is incompatible with a Convention right'. The powers of POAC and the consequences of its allowing an appeal are set out in s 5(3)–(5).[284] Under s 7, if an appeal to the POAC is successful, and an order has been made deproscribing the organisation, anyone convicted of one of the offences listed in sub-section (1)(c) in respect of the organisation, may appeal against his conviction to the Court of Appeal or Crown Court which must allow the appeal,[285] so long as the offence was committed after the date of the refusal to deproscribe. This provision covers members of the organisation itself, and persons who have been convicted of proscription-related offences at a point after a refusal to de-proscribe, who have already exhausted ordinary avenues of appeal.

If the POAC finds against the applicant, s 6 of the 2000 Act allows a further appeal from its decision to a court, on a point of law, if leave is given by the POAC or where POAC refuses permission the Court of Appeal. The Act does not contain an ouster clause.

Judicial review of POAC decisions or appeals from POAC on points of law

Judicial review can be sought of decisions taken under the TA. The courts are able to apply the Convention rights in judicial review proceedings or on an appeal on a point of law to a court against a refusal to de-proscribe. The procedural rules for appeals from POAC to the Court of Appeal require that the Court of Appeal must secure that information is not disclosed contrary to the interests of national security. This enables

---

282 Previously, under Sched 3, para 8, s 9(1) of the Interception of Communications Act 1985 'shall not apply in relation to (a) proceedings before the Commission, or (b) proceedings arising out of proceedings to which paragraph (a) applies'. For discussion of the equivalent provisions under the Regulation of Investigatory Powers Act 2000, see Chapter 10, pp 1047–51.

283 See Chapter 10, p 1081–82.

284 (4) Where the Commission allows an appeal under this section by or in respect of an organisation, it may make an order under this sub-section. (5) Where an order is made under sub-section (4) the Secretary of State shall as soon as is reasonably practicable– (a) lay before Parliament, in accordance with section 123(4), the draft of an order under section 3(3)(b) removing the organisation from the list in Schedule 2; or (b) make an order removing the organisation from the list in Schedule 2 in pursuance of section 123(5).

285 Under s 7(2), once deproscription has occurred, if the convicted person appeals to the Court of Appeal under s 1 of the Criminal Appeal Act 1968 (appeal against conviction on indictment) 'the court shall allow the appeal'.

the Court of Appeal, like POAC, to exclude any party (other than the Secretary of State) and his representative from the proceedings on the appeal.[286] If a court found in judicial review proceedings that a decision taken under one of the provisions of the TA could not be justified under the relevant Article, it could quash the decision on the basis, as argued in Chapter 4, that it can never be said to be impossible for a person who has a discretion conferred by primary legislation, such as that to proscribe an organisation, to act otherwise.[287] Various Convention points can be raised in these proceedings.

POAC procedure satisfies Arts 6 and 13?

It could be argued that the POAC does not meet the requisite standards of independence under Art 13 or under Art 6(1) since, *inter alia*, the Lord Chancellor appoints its members. Thus it could be considered whether the POAC provides an effective remedy for the citizen. (As regards Art 13 this argument would probably have to be raised at Strasbourg since Art 13 was not included in Sched 1 HRA.)[288] The ability of the Lord Chancellor to regulate its procedure is also relevant. This argument depends on the view taken of the role of the Lord Chancellor, and in particular whether it could be said that in appointing the POAC and regulating it he should be viewed as acting as part of the executive. It is suggested that the appointments procedure for the POAC complies with the Art 6 impartiality and independence requirements in these respects,[289] but that it is debatable whether this is the case in relation to the possibilities provided for under the Act for the determination of its procedure by the Lord Chancellor.[290]

It could also be argued that the POAC fails to comply with the fair trial provisions of Art 6(1) since the applicant may be in such a weak position before it. As discussed above, Art 6 guarantees a fair hearing in the determination of civil rights and obligations or a criminal charge.[291] The Art 6(1) requirements are discussed further in Chapters 2, 12 and 13.[292] It could be argued that the POAC's appeal function should be viewed as the 'determination of a criminal charge' since proscription of an organisation creates the possibility of imposing criminal liability on a range of persons including existing members of the newly-proscribed organisation. However, at present it is assumed that the POAC is determining civil rights and obligations only. It is arguable that the POAC

---

286   The Court of Appeal (Appeals from Proscribed Organisations Appeal Commission) Rules 2002.

287   See pp 215–16.

288   See *Govell v UK* (1997) 4 EHRLR 438, and see Chapter 2 at pp 106–8. It is, however, possible that courts could take Art 13 into account due to the *Pepper v Hart* statement of the Lord Chancellor in Parliament to the effect that although Art 13 was omitted from the rights protected by the HRA, the courts could view acceptance of the need to allow an effective remedy under Art 13 as an aspect of the intention behind the Act. See *Hansard* HL 18 November 1997 col 477, *Hansard* HC 20 May 1998 col 980.

289   See *Campbell and Fell v UK* A 80 (1984).

290   *Sramek v Austria* A 84 (1984). One of the central questions, which cannot yet be answered will be the practice adopted: *Campbell and Fell v UK* A 80 (1984). See also the findings on impartiality in the context of military discipline - *Findlay v UK* (1997) 24 EHRR 221; *Hood v UK*, judgment of 25 February 1997.

291   For further discussion as to the field of application of Art 6, see Chapter 2, pp 60–61.

292   See, in particular, pp 1210–15, 1259–61.

may not provide a fair hearing for the appellant, bearing in mind the procedure which can be followed, described above.

Proscription and the guarantees under Arts 10 and 11

Various features of decisions to proscribe and of the proscription scheme itself raise further Convention issues under Arts 10 and 11, as discussed in the human rights section of this chapter, above. Under the HRA the compatibility of the proscription of a range of groups with Arts 10 and 11 is problematic since the complete outlawing of a group constitutes prima facie a breach of those Articles. In findings as to proscription, therefore, the focus must be on the demands of para 2 of those Articles, unless Art 17 applies.[293] As discussed in Chapter 2, state interference with the Arts 10 and 11 guarantees must be prescribed by law, have a legitimate aim, be necessary in a democratic society and be applied in a non-discriminatory fashion if it is to be justified. It can almost certainly be assumed that the exercise of the proscription power can be viewed domestically as prescribed by law since it is enshrined in primary legislation, and Parliament must approve proscription orders, although the 'quality' of proscription decisions is clearly open to question.[294]

In freedom of expression cases Strasbourg's main concern has unsurprisingly been with the 'necessary in a democratic society' requirement. In *Sidiropoulos v Greece*[295] the Court considered the outlawing in Greece of an association called the Home of Macedonian Civilisation which had been formed in Macedonia. The authorities refused to register it, on the basis that it was viewed as intended to undermine Greece's national integrity, contrary to Greek law, since it intended to publicise the idea that there is a Macedonian minority in Greece. The Court indicated the stance it would take towards the aims of the state authorities – the preservation of national security and the prevention of disorder – in this context. They were found to be legitimate, but the means used to further them – disallowing the registration of the group and therefore outlawing it – was found to be disproportionate to them and therefore unnecessary in a democratic society. Thus, proscription of a particular group, depending on the extent to which there was evidence that it threatened national security and public order, might be found domestically to violate these two Articles. Where, for example, a group presenting no risk to national security in the UK had been proscribed on the basis of its action in seeking to combat an oppressive regime or in providing support for another group operating against such a regime, it could be found that proscription was disproportionate to the aims in view. So far this has not occurred under the TA.

R (on the application of the Kurdistan Workers' Party and others)

The Convention issues raised by proscription are conveniently encapsulated in the following decision. The claim failed, on procedural grounds, but the substantive issues raised on behalf of the three proscribed organisations in question strongly highlighted the

---

293 See Chapter 2, p 112.
294 See Chapter 2, pp 68–69.
295 (57/1997/841/1047) 10 July 1998; available from the Court's website.

flawed nature of the proscription scheme in human rights terms. The case represented an attempt to circumvent the POAC procedure, presumably on the basis that the claimants had doubts as to its efficacy. The claimants clearly preferred to seek judicial review of the proscription decisions instead. In *R (on the application of the Kurdistan Workers' Party and Others) v Secretary of State for the Home Dept, R (on the application of the People's Mojahedin Organisation of Iran and Others) v Secretary of State for the Home Dept, R (on the application of Ahmed) v Secretary of State for the Home Dept,*[296] three organisations sought to challenge the lawfulness of their proscription and the lawfulness of the regime of offences laid down by the 2000 Act. The organisations were the People's Mojahedin Organisation of Iran (the PMOI), the Kurdistan Workers' Party or Partiya Karkeren Kurdistan (the PKK), and Lashkar e Tayyabah (the LeT). Each was proscribed under the Terrorism Act 2000 (Proscribed Organisations) (Amendment) Ord 2001 (the 2001 Order). In each case the Court had to determine whether to grant or refuse permission to apply for judicial review. An application for deproscription of the PMOI was made on behalf of the PMOI and refused by the Secretary of State. The refusal was the subject of an appeal to the POAC, but before the appeal was heard the application for permission to apply for judicial review was lodged. An application for deproscription of the LeT was made and refused; an appeal to the POAC was lodged, as was an application for permission to apply for judicial review. The PKK and the individual claimants in the PKK case did not apply for deproscription but moved straight to their application for permission to apply for judicial review. But an application for deproscription of the PKK was, however, made by the Federation of Kurdish Community Associations in Great Britain and resulted in a decision by the Secretary of State not to deproscribe. There was no appeal against that decision to the POAC. So the judicial review proceedings pre-dated the appeals to the POAC.

The claimants thus sought judicial review of the decision of the Secretary of State to lay the 2001 Order before Parliament, the 2001 Order itself and the provisions of the 2000 Act. They sought declarations to the effect that the inclusion of the organisation in question in the list of proscribed organisations was unlawful; alternatively, they sought a declaration that the relevant provisions of the 2000 Act were incompatible with their Convention rights. They also sought damages pursuant to s 8 of the Human Rights Act, if successful.

The claimants argued that their proscription and the consequential criminal prohibitions under ss 11–19 of the 2000 Act gave rise to a substantial interference with their right to freedom of expression under Art 10 of the Convention, to freedom of association under Art 11 and the enjoyment of property under Art 1 of the First Protocol. The interference with Arts 10 and 11 was, it was argued, especially pernicious since it operated as a prior restraint upon the exercise of their Convention rights. The PMOI argued that its inclusion in a list containing organisations of a wholly different nature, such as Al-Qaeda, gave rise to an interference with its civil right to a good reputation under Art 8, and with the right to the enjoyment of Convention rights without discrimination under Art 14.

296   [2002] EWHC Admin 644.

In his note to Members of Parliament in support of the draft order seeking proscription of the PMOI, the Secretary of State described it as 'an Iranian dissident organisation based in Iraq which claims to be seeking the establishment of a democratic, socialist, Islamic republic in Iran'. The note referred briefly to the organisation's history, stating that the organisation undertakes cross-border attacks into Iran, including terrorist attacks, that it has assassinated senior Iranian officials and launched mortar attacks against government buildings in Tehran and elsewhere, and that in June 2000 the Iranian government claimed to have foiled a plot by the organisation to assassinate a former Iranian foreign minister. The note stated that the organisation had not attacked UK or Western interests and had no acknowledged presence in the UK. In refusing the application to deproscribe the PMOI, the Secretary of State stated:

> In the case of Mujaheddin e Khalq, the Secretary of State believes that the nature and scale of the organisation's activities and the need to support other members of the international community in the global fight against terrorism are relevant . . . the Secretary of State believes that proscription of Mujaheddin e Khalq should continue . . . The Home Secretary stated . . . that he had taken full account of the assertion that Mujaheddin e Khalq is involved in a legitimate struggle against a repressive regime and has no choice but to resort to armed resistance. But he stated that he did not accept any right to resort to acts of terrorism, whatever the motivation.

The PMOI described itself as a broad-based popular resistance movement committed to the establishment of a democratic, secular and pluralist government in Iran which would respect human rights and the internationally recognised norms of state behaviour. It stated that it had sought to achieve its aims through the political system, but it had been denied access to it through brutal suppression at the hands of the Iranian regime. It said that it had therefore been driven to resort to armed struggle in Iran. It was argued on its behalf that the Secretary of State had unfairly discriminated against it by including the PMOI in a list with organisations such as Al-Qaeda. Of the 21 organisations in the list, the PMOI was the only one recognised by the Secretary of State to be democratic in its aims. The list also, it said, excluded many groups that use or threaten violence for political ends. The list, it was argued, was therefore both over-inclusive and under-inclusive. It was argued that it is incumbent on the Secretary of State to provide an objective justification for such differences of treatment. It was also pointed out that MPs, in considering whether to approve the order, were faced with a dilemma either to proscribe Al-Qaeda and all the others in the list or to proscribe none of them.

In the case of the PKK, the Secretary of State had stated that he believed that the nature and scale of the organisation's activities, the specific threat that it posed to UK nationals overseas, the extent of the organisation's presence in the UK, meant that it should not be de-proscribed. The claimants described the PKK as a political party committed to the recognition and establishment of Kurdish identity and the rights of the Kurdish people. They laid emphasis on the PKK's formal abandonment of military action in favour of a non-violent political and democratic agenda in 1999. On behalf of the PKK it was argued that for many persons in the UK the PKK is the sole means of political expression, but that proscription had made it an offence to invite support for the PKK even if it related specifically to its commitment to a policy of non-violence.

Proscription meant that all political debate was suppressed relating to the PKK, and it was pointed out that members of the Kurdish community would commit an offence simply by displaying PKK badges or participating in demonstrations of more than three people. Further, one of the witnesses described her work for Kurdish organisations in the United Kingdom and stated that it would be impossible for those groups to remove the PKK from their contacts or discussions. She also said that proscription of the PKK had a serious effect on her journalistic work as editor of the Kurdistan Report. She stated that she faced the impossible choice of going to the police with knowledge or suspicion of fund-raising activities for the PKK, making her work in the Kurdish community impossible, or committing a crime by failing to do so.

It was argued on behalf of the PKK that although the Secretary of State had notified to Parliament that certain non-statutory factors would be taken into account (namely the nature and scale of the organisation's activities, the specific threat that it poses to the UK, the specific threat that it poses to UK nationals overseas, the extent of the organisation's presence in the UK, and the need to support other members of the international community), they did not amount to adequate or intelligible criteria for the exercise of the very wide discretion provided under s 3 TA. Those criteria provided, it was argued, no basis for determining which of the organisations meeting the statutory tests would be proscribed.[297]

LeT was described by the claimants as a movement committed to the cause of self-determination for the people of Kashmir by means of the holding of a plebiscite as required by UN resolutions. But the Secretary of State's note to Members of Parliament described it as an organisation seeking independence for Kashmir and the creation of an Islamic state using violent means. The note stated that it had a long history of mounting attacks against the Indian security forces in Kashmir, and that it had been blamed for the massacre of 35 Sikhs in Jammu and Kashmir in March 2000, and that more recently it had launched attacks in which several people were killed. On behalf of LeT it was contended that the making of the order was unlawful because it included 21 organisations and Parliament was unable to consider the individual merits of proscribing each organisation; it was unfair because no opportunity was given beforehand to make representations; the order was not 'prescribed by law' because the 2000 Act impermissibly gave complete discretion of the Secretary of State as to which organisations falling within the wide definition should in fact be proscribed. The proscription was not necessary in a democratic society, it was argued, because it amounted to a disproportionate interference with the rights under Arts 10 and 11 of the Convention; finally it was argued that the proscription was discriminatory and therefore in breach of Art 14.

The key issue that the judge had to decide was whether to give permission for judicial review of the decision to proscribe the three organisations, as opposed to insisting that they appeal to the POAC. It was argued on behalf of the Home Secretary that judicial review is a remedy of last resort, and that judicial review is not normally allowed where there is an alternative remedy by way of appeal.[298] In contrast, it was argued on behalf

---

297 At para 48.
298 Counsel for the Home secretary relied on *R v Panel on Take-overs and Mergers, ex p Guinness plc* [1990] QB 146, [1989] 1 All ER 509; *R v Chief Constable of Merseyside Police ex p Calveley* [1986] 1 QB 424, [1986] 1 All ER 257. He also relied, by analogy, on statements in *R v DPP ex p Kebilene*

of the claimants that an alternative procedure should be exhausted first only if it is at least as extensive as judicial review, and that where the suggested alternative forum could not consider the entirety of a complaint which can be raised by way of judicial review, the court should entertain a claim for judicial review.[299]

For a range of reasons the judge decided that the POAC was the appropriate forum within which the claims should be raised. He found that Parliament, although not seeking to exclude the possibility of judicial review, had intended the POAC to be the forum of first resort for the determination of claims relating to the lawfulness of proscription under the 2000 Act. Also the POAC was designated as the appropriate tribunal for the purposes of s 7 of the Human Rights Act in relation to proceedings against the Secretary of State in respect of a refusal to deproscribe. He also noted that it is a specialist tribunal with procedures designed specifically to deal with the determination of claims relating to proscription; in particular he noted that the POAC is expressly excluded from the prohibition on the disclosure of intercepted communications, a very important area of evidence.

Conclusions

After this decision it is clear that the remedy provided by the POAC means that judicial review of the decision to make proscription order is unavailable unless the POAC remedy has already been exhausted. Section 9 appears to be intended as far as possible to keep proceedings based on s 7 HRA largely in the POAC, thereby tending to prevent the ordinary courts from hearing points raised under s 7 HRA. This decision did not address the substantive human rights issues. But the issues raised in the case highlight the deficiencies of the proscription provisions. Clearly, a very wide range of organisations meet the definition under s 1 TA. No check on the decision to proscribe groups falling within that definition is provided in the TA itself. The check on the Secretary of State's discretion provided by Parliament is clearly limited; Parliament in that instance was asked to proscribe all 21 organisations, including Al-Qaeda, or none of them. It therefore could not scrutinise the individual circumstances of each organisation in any detail. Further, it lacked the information to provide any meaningful scrutiny. The Secretary of State argued that the relevant decision to proscribe could be viewed as sufficiently precise and accessible to be seen as prescribed by law for the purposes of Arts 10 and 11, since it was not that of the Secretary of State under s 3 of the 2000 Act, but the decision taken by Parliament in the form of its approval of the order. However, given the limited scrutiny possible in Parliament in the circumstances, it is argued that the decision remained in effect largely in executive hands. The Parliamentary oversight is inadequate, it is contended, to ensure that proportionality is observed by the Home Secretary in taking the initial decision to proscribe a group.

The key point was that the circumstances relied on for the proscription of the claimant organisations were, it is argued, doubtfully able to justify the very serious

---

[2000] 2 AC 326, [1999] 3 WLR 972 and *R (Pretty) v DPP* [2002] 1 All ER 1, [2001] 3 WLR 1598 to the broad effect that satellite litigation by way of judicial review is to be avoided in relation to issues arising in the context of criminal proceedings. He argued that the same principle should apply in relation to issues that have been or could be raised in proceedings before POAC.

299 *R v IRC ex parte Mead* [1993] 1 All ER 772, [1992] STC 482 was relied on.

interferences with the Convention rights of the individual claimants, in particular the chilling effect on free speech. The basis for proscription is in general, it is argued, too imprecise to satisfy the requirement that interferences with the right to freedom of expression and association be both prescribed by law and proportionate. A very wide range of terrorism offences are available in the TA, as discussed below, not dependent on proscription; it may therefore be argued that sufficient curbs are already available to use against a number of the organisations that are already proscribed or against groups that are currently candidates for proscription

Special 'terrorism' offences under the TA; additional offences introduced under the Terrorism Act 2006

Introduction

Virtually all the extensive range of special terrorist offences were retained under the TA, and most of them were applied to the vast range of groups which could, potentially, fall within the s 1 definition.[300] One controversial power, of exclusion, was, however, abolished under the TA. Section 5 of the PTA provided for exclusion from Great Britain, s 6 for exclusion from Northern Ireland and s 7 for exclusion from the whole of the United Kingdom. In effect, these powers meant that Northern Irish citizens could be forced to go back to Northern Ireland; there was little reciprocity in terms of excluding Irish citizens to Britain.[301] These provisions were reviewed by Lord Jellicoe in 1983;[302] he concluded that the exclusion power should be allowed to lapse as soon as circumstances suggested that it was not strictly necessary.[303] The powers were being used with increasing infrequency: there were 248 orders in force in 1982; by the end of 1996 there were 24. In 1997 the Home Secretary considered that they were no longer effective in combating terrorism and revoked the 12 which remained. The exclusion powers were not in force at the time of the inception of the TA. These powers were largely irrelevant in relation to the domestic groups designated as terrorist under s 1 TA and probably largely irrelevant to the small Irish splinter groups, such as the Real IRA. They would have been extremely complex to operate in respect of 'international terrorists'. Thus, even if they had been retained, these powers would probably have remained largely unused under the TA. Nevertheless, their repeal is to be welcomed on the principle that such laws should be repealed rather than left to lie on the statute book, with the possibility that they could be arbitrarily reactivated in future.

The TA provides a very extensive portfolio of counter-terrorist offences since it adopted EPA offences that had previously not been applied in the UK generally. The extensive range of offences of a preparatory nature were added to under ATCSA 2001

---

300 Under Part VII some offences continued to apply only to Irish rather than to international terrorist groups.

301 See Walker, *The Prevention of Terrorism*, 2nd edn, 1992, pp 84–85; only four persons have been excluded to Britain.

302 *Report on the Operation of the Prevention of Terrorism (Temporary Provisions) Act 1978.*

303 Jellicoe (1983): para 200; however the review by Lord Colville recommended on this basis that power to make exclusion orders should be repealed (*Report on the Operation in 1990 of the Prevention of Terrorism Act 1989*).

and the Terrorism Act 2006. The Terrorism Act 2006 introduced in particular two new and very broadly defined offences of preparation of terrorist acts under s 5 and of glorifying terrorism under s 1. The range of offences based on failing to give information or relating to property draw ordinary citizens, including the commercial sector, into the scheme. Clearly, the groups affected by the proscription scheme can also be affected by the general terrorism offences. The very wide range of terrorist offences now available, and their far-reaching impact, highlights the potentially immensely broad scope of s 1 TA, and its partially symbolic rather than actual import. In examining the current incrementally extended range of offences, it must be remembered that they are of course *additional* to the provisions of the ordinary criminal law. Violent terrorist acts infringe a number of criminal law provisions, without the need for recourse to the special terrorism offences. It might be asked, looking over the vast list of provisions, whether special terrorism offences and sanctions have real value given that they are under-used. If one of the 7/7 suicide bombers in London had survived he could have been charged with a number of criminal offences, beginning with murder.

The offences discussed below, which were originally developed in the context of the PTA or EPA, could probably only have been introduced in the context of the threat from Irish terrorism, in some instances, as indicated above, at a time when the number of deaths from bomb attacks had been very high in the preceding years. At the time MP's obviously could not know that in 2000 they would be asked to apply all those offences to a wide range of groups, some of which, in terms of their ability to create a serious threat to life and their willingness to do so, cannot be compared with the IRA. Moreover, certain of these offences appeared only in the EPA, partly on the basis, as indicated above, that the threat was greatest in Northern Ireland and that without some apparently strong justification, they should not be included in the PTA. Unless the Home Secretary proscribes all the groups covered by s 1 TA, including protest groups advocating direct action, the proscription-related offences do not apply to them. But all the special terrorist offences, which have no equivalents in ordinary criminal law, can be applied. The use of the stop and search power under s 44 TA, discussed in Chapter 11, in relation to reporters and protesters, is indicative of the possibility of applying terrorism offences in the public protest context, as was its use against a peace activist attempting an anti-war protest at the Labour Party conference in 2005.[304] A number of the offences create prima facie infringements of certain of the Convention rights, albeit potentially justifiable, most notably Arts 10, 11, 6 and 5, under the HRA.

Directing a terrorist organisation

Section 56 TA 2000 makes it an offence to direct 'at any level' a terrorist organisation. Thus, the leaders, and all with some authority within the vast range of groups within the

---

304 Walter Wolfgang, a well-known peace activist, currently Vice President of the Campaign for Nuclear Disarmament (CND), Vice Chair of Labour CND and a supporter of the Stop the War Coalition, was ejected from the Labour Party conference for protesting against the Iraq war; when he attempted to re-enter the conference later the same day, his pass showed that he had been removed previously, and he was briefly held by police under s 44 of the Terrorism Act.

UK which may fall within the s 1 definition, are liable to a sentence of life imprisonment simply by virtue of their position. It does not appear to cover minor figures in the organisation.[305] The maximum sentence which can be given on conviction for the offence is life imprisonment. The PTA contained no equivalent provision; the offence was only provided in the EPA, in s 29. The term 'directing' was not defined in the EPA, but it clearly had the meaning of taking some authority for actions to be carried out, or playing some part in giving orders in relation to them.[306] The Consultation paper noted that there had only been two convictions for this offence, pointing out that its nature means that it is difficult to get evidence to support a charge; witnesses are particularly reluctant to make statements implicating people who hold positions of authority within terrorist organisations. But where a conviction was obtained, it was thought that it would be 'likely to be of some significance and to have a major impact on the terrorist organisation in question'.[307] Lord Lloyd considered that the offence had been of real value. He recommended that it should be retained in permanent legislation and it should be extended to cover the whole of the United Kingdom and all forms of terrorism. The government agreed with his recommendation,[308] which is fully reflected in s 56 of the TA. This offence has the advantage that it can be used to disrupt groups falling within s 1 TA even though they have not (yet) been proscribed. The police and prosecuting authorities have so far shown discretion in seeking to use this offence, and have not applied it to the leaders of e.g. protest groups advocating direct action, but it is unsatisfactory that the leaders of such groups should be placed in a precarious position in relation to the criminal law, one that is merely dependent on forbearance.

The offence under s 56 of the TA to direct 'at any level' a terrorist organisation is not confined to proscribed groups. If a relatively minor figure in an organisation which met the wide definition of terrorism under s 1, but was within its less serious aspects, was charged with this offence, a court which found that this interference with Art 11 was disproportionate to the aims pursued could interpret the terms used in s 56, especially 'directing' and 'at any level' under s 3 HRA so as to exclude such figures from the ambit of the section. For example, taking the terms together it could be argued that the term 'directing' qualifies 'at any level' so that only figures at the highest level within the *leadership* sector of the organisation are covered.

Preparatory and possession offences

A number of offences introduced under the Terrorism Acts 2000 and 2006, and in the ATCSA cover activities ancillary to terrorism and broadly of a preparatory nature; some are aimed at terrorist conspiracies and at fund-raising and other activities of

---

305 HC Debs vol 187 col 404, 6.3 1991. See Walker, C and Reid, K, 'The Offence of directing Terrorist Organisations' (1993) Crim LR 669 on the previous equivalent offence under the EPA.
306 In the consultation paper the government explained: 'The offence is aimed at the strategists – those who plan campaigns and order them to be carried out, but who do not normally themselves take any part in the detailed planning or execution of the individual attacks which make up the campaign.' (ibid, para 12.9).
307 Ibid, para 12.9.
308 Ibid, para 12.10.

terrorist groups ancillary to acts of terrorism; some are aimed at businesses and ordinary citizens. These offences disrupt terrorist funding activities, and are of value in relation to the threat of suicide bombing since they can allow for the arrest of terrorists at an early planning stage, but a number of them were so broadly drawn as to fail to achieve Convention-compliance.

As mentioned above, a large number of further criminal offences, not limited to proscribed organisations, and punishable by up to 14 years' imprisonment, exist under ss 14–18 in relation to fund-raising for the purposes of terrorism; the use or possession of money or other property for the purposes of terrorism; arrangements to make money or property available for the purposes of terrorism (funding arrangements), and under s 18 in relation to arrangements facilitating the retention or control of terrorist property by concealment, removal, transfer, etc (money laundering). The offences provided under ss 14–18 impose a range of significant responsibilities on members of the public; s 18 is broadly defined and could cover, for example, a property agent collecting rent from premises unaware that the ultimate beneficiary of the profits was a company operating for the benefit of a terrorist organisation. If charged, the statutory defence made available under s 18(2) would place a reverse burden upon him to show 'that he did not know and had no reasonable cause to suspect that the arrangement related to terrorist property'. However, if this occurred, following *Attorney General's Reference (No 4 of 2002)*,[309] discussed above, the burden should be read down under s 3 HRA to an evidential burden only in order to ensure compliance with Art 6(2).

Section 16A(1) of the Prevention of Terrorism Act 1989, as inserted by s 82 of the Criminal Justice and Public Order Act 1994, provides that a person is guilty of an offence if he has an article in his possession in circumstances giving rise to a reasonable suspicion that the article is in his possession for a purpose linked to terrorism. Under s 16A(3) the accused could rebut this presumption of guilt by proving that the article was not in his possession for the purpose mentioned in s 16A(1). Under s 16A(4) if it is proved that the article and the accused were both present on the premises, or that the article is present on premises which he occupies or habitually uses, this may be sufficient evidence of possession, unless he proves that he did not know of its presence or had no control over it. This offence was reproduced in s 57 TA. The 'possession of an article in circumstances which give rise to a reasonable suspicion that [it] is for a purpose connected with the commission, preparation or instigation of an act of terrorism' carries a ten-year jail sentence under s 57. An amendment put forward by the Liberal Democrats, which would have removed the presumption that proof of the presence of the article on the occupier's premises is sufficient to establish the offence, was overwhelmingly defeated by a combination of Labour and Conservative MPs.[310] As discussed above, s 57 only imposes an evidential, not a legal burden, on the defendant, in order to satisfy Art 6(2): s 118 of the Act applies to s 57 and provides that if the defendant adduces evidence which is sufficient to raise an issue with respect to the matter, the court or jury shall assume that the defence is satisfied unless the prosecution proves beyond reasonable doubt that it is not.

309 [2004] UKHL 43; [2005] 1 AC 264; [2005] 1 All ER 237.
310 HC Debs 15 March 2000 col 435.

Section 28 TA 2000 provides for civil forfeiture proceedings in relation to seized cash.[311] Evidence that the cash is terrorist property is required only to the civil standard of proof. Proceedings for a criminal offence are not needed. The provisions do not therefore allow for a *conviction* on the civil standard.[312] The forfeiture provisions under s 28 need to satisfy the requirements of a fair hearing under Art 6.[313] As discussed above, the term 'criminal charge' has an autonomous Convention meaning: *Benham v UK*.[314] It was found that s 41 of the Community Charge (Administration and Enforcement) Regulations, the legislation in question, should be accounted criminal for Art 6(1) purposes. Section 28 has certain features which are comparable to those of s 41; if forfeiture is ordered the implication is that the defendant is concerned in terrorism although the possibility of imprisonment does not arise. Article 6(1) and (2) do not require proof beyond reasonable doubt: a wide margin of appreciation has been conceded to national courts in respect of the burden of proof.[315]

These offences of possession of information or objects were added to under the Terrorism Act 2006 which introduced a range of new offences of 'acts preparatory to terrorism'. The new offences are aimed at those planning acts of terrorism in a manner not already covered by the existing offences. Section 5 prohibits anyone from engaging in any conduct in preparation for an intended act of terrorism. The offence requires intention, but the *actus reus* is exceptionally broad. Under s 5:

(1) A person commits an offence if, with the intention of–

(a) committing acts of terrorism, or

(b) assisting another to commit such acts, he engages in any conduct in preparation for giving effect to his intention.

(2) It is irrelevant for the purposes of sub-section (1) whether the intention and preparations relate to one or more particular acts of terrorism, acts of terrorism of a particular description or acts of terrorism generally.

Under s 5(3) the maximum penalty is life imprisonment. Section 5 is obviously intended to be a catch-all offence able to allow intervention in relation to would-be terrorists at a very early stage, before any conduct linked to the actual preparation of a terrorist act has occurred. For example, visiting a 'jihadist' website could be covered so long as the requisite intention could be shown. This offence overlaps to an extent with the proscription offences, but it obviates the need to show membership of Al-Qaeda or a related organisation.

Section 5 is clearly aimed at criminalising Al-Qaeda supporters largely on the basis of that support, but the person in question must have the intention of committing or

---

311 *Raimondo v Italy* A 21–4 (1994), a decision on similar provisions, suggested that they may be compatible with the Convention on the basis that the aim of such provisions is in the general interest.

312 It may be noted that these provisions reverse the principle put forward in *Webb v Chief Constable of Merseyside Police* [2000] 1 All ER 209 to the effect that the seizure of cash linked, on the civil standard of proof, to drug dealing, was unlawful.

313 Rules were made, under s 31 TA, governing the procedure to be followed.

314 (1996) 22 EHRR 293. See further above, p 1342.

315 See *Austria v Italy* 6 YB 740 at 784 (1963) Com Rep; CM Res DH (63) 3.

assisting in the commission of a 'terrorist' act, although that need not be a specific act. Presumably that term would be defined by reference to s 1 TA. The addition of 'acts of terrorism generally' brings this offence very close to 'thoughtcrime'. Lord Carlile, the government reviewer of the TA, supported the introduction of this offence, allowing for very early intervention in preparatory activity, on the basis that: 'there is clear evidence that such an offence would provide for some cases a way of dealing with suspects more acceptable in perceptual terms than control orders. It is better that sanctions should follow conviction of crime rather than mere administrative decisions'.[316] This is clearly laudable in principle, especially as the control orders scheme, as discussed below, is over-broad in human rights terms but under-inclusive in security terms – since the orders do not at the moment include detention. But as the widest offence introduced so far in the counter-terrorist scheme, it again relies heavily on executive discretion in deploying it.

A number of new offences relating to materials that could be used in an attack were also introduced in the 2006 Act.[317] Section 12 TA 2006 extends the ban on trespassing in specified locations imposed by the Serious and Organised Crime and Police Act 2005, to cover any nuclear site. Section 6 prohibits anyone from training others in terrorist activities, or from receiving training and carries a maximum penalty of ten years' imprisonment. A further new offence of 'terrorist training' was introduced under the 2006 Act to be added to the existing offence under s 54 Terrorism Act 2000; under s 54 those who give or receive training in the making or use of weapons or explosives, or recruit persons for this purpose, are liable to ten years in prison. Section 8 prohibits anyone from being at a place where training is going on (whether in the United Kingdom or abroad), provided the person knew or reasonably believed that training was happening. The offence carries a maximum penalty of ten years' imprisonment. The new offence is much broader in that s 8 makes it an offence merely to be in attendance at any place in the world where such instruction is taking place. Lord Carlile has pointed out that this would leave open the possibility of prosecuting journalists reporting in the public interest from camps of fighting groups revolting against despotic regimes.[318]

Positive obligations to report information[319]

A very wide range of other people, including ordinary citizens, banks and businesses, who are not part of any of the groups covered by s 1 TA, are potentially criminalised under various offences relating to the reporting of information. Section 18 of the PTA controversially made it an offence to fail to report information to the police which might be of material assistance in preventing an act of terrorism or in arresting someone

---

316 Report on the Operation in 2005 of the Terrorism Act 2000, May 2006, at para 33.
317 Section 9 prohibits the making or possession of any radioactive device (i.e. a 'dirty' bomb). The maximum penalty is life imprisonment. Section 10 prohibits using radioactive materials or a radioactive device in a terrorist attack, and the sabotage of nuclear facilities which causes a radioactive leak. The maximum penalty is life imprisonment. Section 11 covers terrorist threats relating to devices, materials or facilities; it prohibits anyone from making threats to demand that they be given radioactive materials. The maximum penalty is life imprisonment.
318 Ibid (2006).
319 See further Walker, C, *The Anti-Terrorism Legislation* (2002), Chapter 3.

carrying out such an act. It applied only to acts of terrorism in Northern Ireland. Lord Lloyd questioned the practical value of this offence and recommended that an offence of this sort should not be included in any permanent legislation.[320] However, the government considered that its existence gave a 'clear signal' to citizens regarding the abhorrence of terrorism, and included it in the Act, in s 19, in a somewhat modified and narrowed form. Suspicions arising in home life are no longer covered, but the offence is nevertheless of extremely wide application.[321] Section 19 goes well beyond requiring banks and other businesses to report any suspicion they might have that someone is laundering terrorist money or committing any of the other terrorist offences in ss 15–18. It applies to all employees or employers and means that if, during the course of their work, a person comes across information about, or becomes suspicious of, someone whom she suspects may be using money or property to contribute to the causes of terrorism, she will commit a criminal offence carrying a maximum penalty of five years' imprisonment if she does not report them.

Section 38B, inserted by s 117 ATCSA, creates a much broader provision: it is based on s 18 PTA and so negates the reform that s 19 TA brought about. It is also broader in *application* than s 18 PTA since it relies on s 1 TA and therefore is applied universally across the UK, rather than only to Northern Ireland. Section 38B makes it an offence, subject to an unexplicated defence of reasonable excuse, for *any* person to fail to disclose to a police officer any information which he knows or believes *might* be of material assistance in preventing an act of terrorism or securing the apprehension or conviction of a person involved in such an act.[322]

---

320 Ibid, para 12.7.
321 Section19(1) provides:

this section applies where a person –

    (a) believes or suspects that another person has committed an offence under any of sections 15 to 18, and

    (b) bases his belief or suspicion on information which comes to his attention in the course of a trade, profession, business or employment.

(2) The person commits an offence if he does not disclose to a constable as soon as is reasonably practicable –

    (a) his belief or suspicion, and

    (b) the information on which it is based'.

Sub-section (5) preserves the exemption in respect of legal advisers' privileged material.
322 Section 38B provides: Information about acts of terrorism

(1) This section applies where a person has information which he knows or believes might be of material assistance –

    (a) in preventing the commission by another person of an act of terrorism, or

    (b) in securing the apprehension, prosecution or conviction of another person, in the United Kingdom, for an offence involving the commission, preparation or instigation of an act of terrorism.

(2) The person commits an offence if he does not disclose the information as soon as reasonably practicable in accordance with sub-section (3) . . .

(4) It is a defence for a person charged with an offence under sub-section (2) to prove that he had a reasonable excuse for not making the disclosure.

ATCSA 2001 also inserted new ss 21A and 21B into TA 2000, placing new responsibilities on the regulated financial sector.[323] This is a stricter duty, applied instead of, rather than in addition to, the duty under s 19. Section 21A provides that if a person believes or suspects or has reasonable grounds for knowing or suspecting that another person has committed an offence under any of ss 15–18, and the basis for the belief or suspicion came to him in the course of a business in the regulated sector, he will commit an offence if he does not disclose the information in question to a constable or nominated officer as soon as is reasonably practicable. Under s 21A(5) he has a defence of reasonable excuse for not disclosing the information or other matter, or he can raise legal professional privilege.

Journalists are among the groups of ordinary citizens affected by these duties of disclosure of information. Sections 19 and 38B potentially curb journalistic investigation into the activities of a very wide range of groups, since journalists are unlikely to be prepared to incur the risk of a lengthy prison sentence. The offence also potentially places journalists investigating, or in some way associated with, the activities of certain groups, such as the PKK or Teyrebaz Azadiye Kurdistan, in a very difficult position, especially where they have contacts within the group. It would appear almost impossible for any investigative journalism to occur in such circumstances, without risk of incurring a five-year prison sentence. The provision requiring the surrender of information might mean that the identity of sources could not be protected. But it is clear that the two offences may be having a strong deterrent effect on investigative journalism in relation to extremist groups. This might have the counter-productive effect of helping to keep the activities of the more secretive of such groups out of the public eye.

These provisions afford very little recognition to the role of the media in investigating matters of public interest and informing the public. Strasbourg, as indicated in Part 2 to this chapter, and in the Introduction to Part II of this book, gives pre-eminence to the role of the press in a democracy.[324] Restrictions placed on the press in performing this vital role have been subjected to the strictest scrutiny.[325] Charging a journalist with these offences would clearly, therefore, amount to an interference with the Art 10 guarantee. The domestic court would be expected to observe the same or (arguably) higher standards than Strasbourg in scrutinising the need for the interference, bearing in mind the narrow margin of appreciation afforded to states in respect of interference with political speech, especially where it concerns criticism directed at the government itself.[326] The Divisional Court in *Ex p Kebilene*[327] (as discussed above) indicated the strictness of the standards which domestic courts are capable of applying, albeit in relation to Art 6(2) rather than Art 10.

323 As defined in new Sched 3A. Supervisory authorities include: the Bank of England; the Financial Services Authority; the Council of Lloyd's; the Director General of Fair Trading; a body which is a designated professional body for the purposes of Part 20 of the Financial Services and Markets Act 2000; The Secretary of State; The Treasury. There are increasing concerns in banks and businesses in the regulated sector about the difficulties of compliance.
324 *Castells v Spain*, judgment of 23 April 1992, Series A no 236, p 23, para 43.
325 *Goodwin v UK* (1996) 22 EHRR 123.
326 *Incal v Turkey* (2000) 29 EHRR 449 (above, p 1355).
327 [1999] 4 All ER 801.

The offence that is now s 38B was one of the most controversial in the PTA, but while it is justifiable in relation to the knowledge of an imminent bomb attack, it clearly appears needlessly draconian when applied – via the s 1 definition of terrorism – to a much greater range of people. Anyone working with someone, such as an anti-Ghadaffi activist who is active abroad in the manner designated terrorist under the TA, or someone whose work happens to bring them into contact in some way with information related to activities linked to terrorism, has been placed in an invidious position. Such people may suffer a conflict of loyalties, especially if they have sympathy with the activities of the group in question, while not wishing to become a member of it. They may also fear reprisal and may therefore be forced to face the dilemma of the choice between risking violence or committing an offence. Section 19, it may be noted, does not necessarily exempt family members from the duty since many small businesses employ other members of the family, including teenagers.

Defences are provided in relation to these offences which – apart from that of s 21A – appear to be aimed, *inter alia*, at journalists. The s 21A defence would be relevant in relation to the presumption of innocence. All three offences provide: 'it is a defence for a person charged with an offence under [the relevant sub-section] to prove that he had a reasonable excuse for not making the disclosure'. Under ss 19 and 38B this defence would allow a journalist to raise Art 10 points under the HRA. The defence of 'reasonable excuse' under ss 19 and 38B could be afforded a wide interpretation in order to protect investigative journalism. Section 21A and ss 19 and 38B all have to be interpreted compatibly with Art 6(2), as discussed above. Section 118 eases the burden of proof on defendants, in accordance with the presumption of innocence under Art 6(2), as discussed above, but it does not cover s 19, or s 38B or s 21A. However, the decision of the House of Lords in *Sheldrake v DPP; Attorney General's Reference (No 4 of 2002)*[328] is relevant. First, it may be noted that requiring a journalist to prove reasonable excuse stands Art 10 on its head since freedom of expression is not viewed as a defence under Art 10; the justification for the interference operates in a sense as a defence negating the potential breach. Second, following the House of Lords' decision the defences in question could be read down so as to impose on the defendant an evidential burden only. The Court of Appeal in *R v Keogh*[329] accepted that the principle from *Attorney General's Reference* must be applied in a wide range of situations. Given the burden that is being placed on groups of citizens, including those working in the financial sector, by these offences, it is arguable that requiring a defendant to prove a defence of reasonable excuse, could be viewed as requiring him to disprove a substantial element of the offence, so as to engage the principle from *Attorney General's Reference.*

A further wide range of citizens and businesses can be criminalised under the provision relating to the collection of information, which is based on s 16B of the PTA. Section 16B made it an offence in England, Wales and Scotland to collect, record or possess any information which might be useful to terrorists; it applied to both Irish and international terrorism. Equivalent provision was made for Northern Ireland in s 33 of the EPA. This offence was designed principally to catch those compiling or possessing

---

328 [2005] 1 AC 264; [2005] 1 All ER 237.
329 [2007] All ER (D) 105 (Mar); [2007] EWCA Crim 528, 7 March 2007.

targeting information. Lord Lloyd found that the police considered the offence to have been particularly useful in Northern Ireland. He recommended its retention, and it is included in s 58(1) which provides: 'A person commits an offence if (a) he collects or makes a record of information of a kind likely to be useful to a person committing or preparing an act of terrorism, or (b) he possesses a document or record containing information of that kind.'

This is another extremely wide offence, particularly since, in common with the one arising under s 56, it lacks any requirement of knowledge regarding the nature of the information, or any requirement that the person intended to use it in order to further the aims of terrorism. It could catch, for example, a journalist, or an accountant who had records of information relating to funding activities of terrorist groups abroad that could be useful to a group within s 1. A defence of proving that 'he had a reasonable excuse for his action or possession' is provided. As discussed above, it was apparent from *R (on the application of the Kurdistan Workers' Party and Others) v Secretary of State for the Home Department*[330] that persons, including journalists, were placed in a difficult position in working for Kurdish organisations in the UK since it was very difficult to ensure that the PKK was excluded from their networks, and journalists who were in possession of information relating to the PKK were placed in an impossible position. The deterrent effect on journalism in such circumstances is clearly severe, especially as the maximum penalty is imprisonment for ten years. Section 58, however only imposes an evidential, not a legal burden, on the defendant, in order to satisfy Art 6(2): s 118 of the Act, as discussed above, applies to s 58 and provides that if the defendant adduces evidence which is sufficient to raise an issue with respect to the matter the court or jury shall assume that the defence is satisfied unless the prosecution proves beyond reasonable doubt that it is not.

Inciting terrorism abroad and encouraging/glorifying terrorism

The TA not only applies the old PTA and EPA offences to a much wider range of groups; it also created new offences of inciting terrorism abroad, which apply under ss 59, 60 and 61 to England and Wales, Northern Ireland and Scotland, respectively. In the consultation paper the government expressed concerns as to the effect on free speech: 'the incitement offence could be difficult in practice to prove and ... the effect of [its creation] could be to constrain freedom of expression. On the other hand ... considerable concern can be caused by ... statements ... encouraging and glorifying acts of terrorism'.[331] The government came down on the side of inclusion of the offence. Under s 59(1) 'A person commits an offence if (a) he incites another person to commit an act of terrorism wholly or partly outside the United Kingdom, and (b) the act would, if committed in England and Wales, constitute one of the offences listed in sub-section (2)'. Under s 59(2) the offences are the more serious offences against the person: murder, an offence under ss 18, 23, 24, 28 or 29 of the Offences against the Person Act 1861 (OAPA) and an offence under s 1(2) of the Criminal Damage Act 1971. Under s 59(3), the penalty for conviction under this section will be the penalty

---

330 [2002] EWHC Admin 644.
331 Ibid, para 4.19.

'to which he would be liable on conviction of the offence listed in sub-section (2) which corresponds to the act which he incites'. Sections 60 and 61 create equivalent provisions relating to Scotland and Northern Ireland.

In defending the introduction of the incitement offence Jack Straw pointed out that existing legislation, which had implemented various international covenants, meant that it was already an offence to incite anyone abroad to hijack an aircraft or to invite someone in Turkey or India to commit murder. Therefore, extending the offence to other countries, such as Japan or Australia, was logical: 'Every terrorist attack represents a violation of our democratic values . . . our response must be sufficiently robust to challenge and defeat these . . . activities. I think we have got the balance right'.[332] This claim was presumably based on the restriction of the offence to incitement to commit the serious offences listed. Nevertheless, it is open to question. It means that a person who encouraged another to assassinate a dictator of an oppressive regime would commit an offence punishable with a mandatory sentence of life imprisonment. The offence might also be committed during a demonstration at which words spoken denouncing such a dictator could be construed as amounting to incitement to assassinate him. Section 59 also creates doubtful distinctions between offences. Sometimes very little separates the person who commits grievous bodily harm (s 18 of the OAPA) from the person who commits serious bodily harm (s 20 OAPA), and this is more clearly the case where the attack need not in fact have been committed. But the s 20 offence is not listed in s 59(2). Therefore, determination that a person is subject to a penalty of a maximum of life imprisonment or to no penalty at all may rest on a very fine distinction.

The incitement provisions under ss 59, 60 and 61 afford very little recognition to the value of protest and assembly. They are unconfined to members of proscribed groups. Taking the example used above of charging the offence in respect of persons at a public meeting denouncing a terrorist dictator, a court which viewed the interference with freedom of expression as, in the circumstances, disproportionate to the aims in view, could take the opportunity of construing the wording of the provisions very strictly. In particular, where there was leeway to do so, on a very strict interpretation of the application of certain of the offences listed in s 59(2), it might be found that incitement merely of lesser, similar, but unlisted offences had occurred.

This incitement offence is aimed at incitement of specific and serious acts of violence. The offence of indirect encouragement of acts of terrorism which includes the glorification of such acts – a much broader offence – was introduced in the Terrorism Act 2006. It is not confined to glorifying acts of terrorist violence that also amount to serious criminal offences, and it does not require *incitement* since it includes the condoning of acts that have already occurred. The Act was drafted in the aftermath of the 7 July 2005 London bombings. On August 5, the Prime Minister made a statement at his regular monthly news conference in relation to the proposed legislation. He said:

> . . . there will be new anti-terrorism legislation in the Autumn. This will include an offence of condoning or glorifying terrorism. The sort of remarks made in recent days should be covered by such laws. But this will also be applied to justifying or glorifying terrorism anywhere, not just in the United Kingdom.

332 J Straw in an article in the *Guardian*, 14 December 1999.

The reference to 'the sort of remarks made in recent days' was generally taken as a reference to Omar Bakri Muhammad who had received a great deal of publicity for his reaction to the London bombing. There had been other statements, made by a number of controversial figures, including Muslim clerics such as Abu Qutada and Abu Hamza al-Masri about the September 11, 2001 attacks and attacks on US and UK forces in Iraq.

The concept of 'glorification' is imprecise; apparently modelled on the Spanish law of 'apologia de terrorismo', it is based on the principle, already established as acceptable in UK law, but not in such a broad fashion, of criminalising persons for what they say rather than what they do. As the Joint Committee on Human Rights put it in its Report on the Terrorism Bill 2006[333] in relation to the two offences – the existing offence of incitement and the new offence of glorification: 'In his view, the law already outlaws incitement to commit a particular terrorist act, such as the statement "Please will you go and blow up a tube train on 7 July in London?" but not a generalised incitement to terrorist acts such as "We encourage everybody to go and blow up tube trains".'[334] The Committee also noted that the offence overlapped with existing criminal offences which had been used in this context,[335] including the very broad offence of soliciting to murder. They noted that in *R v El-Faisal*,[336] for example, in 2004 the Court of Appeal had upheld the convictions of a minister of Islam for soliciting murder under s 4 Offences Against the Person Act 1861 and incitement to racial hatred under the Public Order Act 1986, for having made audio tapes urging Muslims to fight and kill, among others, Jews, Christians, Americans, Hindus and other 'unbelievers'.[337] They also noted that the Muslim cleric Abu Hamza Al-Masri was charged in 2004, with solicitation to murder for soliciting or encouraging others at a public meeting to kill non-believers in the Muslim faith, and with incitement to racial hatred. The Committee considered therefore that the strict necessity for a new offence might be thought to be questionable, but accepted that there was some uncertainty about the scope of the existing offences.

---

333 Report on the Prevention of Terrorism Bill (2005–6) HL Paper 75–1, HC 561–1.
334 Report on the Prevention of Terrorism Bill (2005–6) at para 21.
335 Ibid at paras 23 and 24.
336 [2004] EWCA Crim 456.
337 They noted that in the course of its judgment the Court of Appeal explained the very great width of the offence of soliciting to murder:

26 The offence of soliciting to murder is contained in s 4 of the 1861 Act which states:

'Whosoever shall solicit, encourage, persuade or endeavour to persuade, or shall propose to any person, to murder any other person, whether he be a subject of her Majesty or not, and whether he be within the Queen's dominions or not, shall be guilty of a misdemeanour, and being convicted thereof shall be liable to imprisonment for life.'

27 The scope of the behaviour sufficient to constitute the offence was classically identified as follows in *R v Most* (1881) 7 QBD 244, *per* Huddleston B at 258:

'The largest words possible have been used, "solicit" that is defined to be, to importune, to entreat, to implore, to ask, to attempt to try to obtain; "encourage", which is to intimate, to incite to anything, to give courage to, to inspirit, to embolden, to raise confidence, to make confident; "persuade" which is to bring any particular opinion, to influence by argument or expostulation, to inculcate by argument; "endeavour" and then, as if there might be some class of cases that would not come within those words, the remarkable words are used, "or shall propose to", that is say, make merely a bare proposition, an offer for consideration.'

In its report on the Terrorism Bill 2006 the Joint Committee on Human Rights also expressed strong reservations about both the breadth and vagueness of the provisions as originally drafted.[338] It pointed out that there was no requirement that the maker of the statement had to intend or even be reckless as to whether his statement was likely to be taken as encouragement of inducement to commit acts of terrorism: it sufficed if he had 'reasonable grounds' for so believing. In other words, the offence could be committed, in effect, by negligence. But amendments introduced in the House of Lords curtailed the scope of the offence as originally drafted, so that it could no longer be committed negligently, although it remains a very broad offence.

Section 1(1) prohibits the publishing of:

> a statement that is likely to be understood by some or all of the members of the public to whom it is published as a direct or indirect encouragement or other inducement to them to the commission, preparation or instigation of acts of terrorism or Convention offences.

Statements of indirect encouragement include every statement which glorifies the commission or preparation (whether in the past, in the future or generally) of such acts or offences. But this very broad provision of s 1 is qualified in a number of respects by s 1(2). A person commits an offence under s 1(2)(a) if:

> he publishes a statement to which this section applies or causes another to publish such a statement on his behalf; and

> (b) at the time he does so, he intends the statement to be understood as mentioned in sub-section (1) or is reckless as to whether or not it is likely to be so understood.

> (3) For the purposes of this section the statements that are likely to be understood by members of the public as indirectly encouraging the commission or preparation of acts of terrorism or Convention offences include every statement which –

> (a) glorifies the commission or preparation (whether in the past, in the future or generally) of such acts or offences; and
> (b) is a statement from which those members of the public could reasonably be expected to infer that what is being glorified is being glorified as conduct that should be emulated by them in existing circumstances.

The statement indirectly or directly encouraging terrorism is to be taken as a whole and looked at in the all the circumstances in which it was made (sub-section (4)). It is not necessary to show that anyone was actually 'encouraged or induced' to commit any relevant offence by the statement (sub-section (5)). The words 'by *them* in *existing* circumstances'[339] do narrow the scope of the offence since they require that members

---

338 Report on the Prevention of Terrorism Bill (2005–6) HL Paper 75–1, HC 561–1.
339 The words 'by them' were added by the government by amendment at report stage in the Commons to cl 1(4)(b).

of the audience *themselves* might commit the acts of terrorism. Also they indicate that it would not suffice to show that the acts being glorified are acts that might be committed many years in the future by an audience member. Equally, it must be possible for the audience to emulate such acts in the present context; it is not enough for the speaker to glorify past acts, such as the Crusades. But those limiting words appear only to be intended to apply to indirect encouragement by means of glorification; they do not appear to apply to *other* forms of encouragement, although possibly s 3 HRA could be used to apply them to the offence generally. There is a defence of innocent publication, where the statement is published electronically, a defence intended to benefit those who run websites, on which such statements might be published without their knowledge or consent (sub-section (6)). Section 2 prohibits the dissemination of a publication which is either (a) likely to be understood as directly or indirectly encouraging terrorism, or (b) includes information which is likely to be understood as being useful in the commission or preparation of an act of terrorism. The maximum penalty for both offences is seven years' imprisonment.

The Joint Committee on Human Rights considered that the offence might be compatible with Art 10, under the existing Strasbourg case law. It found that restrictions on *indirect* incitement to commit violent terrorist offences are capable in principle of being compatible with Art 10,[340] provided that they are necessary, defined with sufficient precision to satisfy the requirements of legal certainty, and proportionate to the legitimate aims of national security, public safety, the prevention of crime and the protection of the rights of others.[341] In terms of necessity, whilst the Committee thought that general statements encouraging terrorism might well fall within the existing law on soliciting murder,[342] it accepted that 'there is some uncertainty about the scope of the existing offences'. It found that:

> A clarification of the law is therefore in principle justifiable, even if it overlaps to some extent with other existing offences. We therefore accept, on balance, that the case has been made out by the Government that there is a need for a new, narrowly defined criminal offence of indirect incitement to terrorist acts.[343]

A very significant concern of the Committee was as to the imprecision of the new offence: 'The legal certainty concern is that terms such as glorification, praise and celebration are too vague to form part of a criminal offence which can be committed by speaking.' The Committee pointed out that the Home Secretary rested upon a distinction between: 'encouraging and glorifying on the one hand and explaining or understanding on the other. The last two, he says would not be caught by the new offence, because they do not amount to encouraging, glorifying, praising or celebrating'.[344] The Committee was unconvinced by this reasoning on the basis that no 'bright line' distinction can be drawn consonant with legal certainty, between glorifying and explaining in this context:

---

340 It gave the example of *Hogefeld v Germany*, Appl No 35402/97 (20 January 2000).
341 Report on the Prevention of Terrorism Bill (2005–6) at para 20.
342 Under the Offences Against the Person Act 1861, s 4.
343 Report on the Prevention of Terrorism Bill (2005–6) HL Paper 75–1, HC 561–1, at para 25.
344 Ibid at para 27.

In our view, the difficulty with the Home Secretary's response is that his distinction is not self-executing: the content of comments and remarks will have to be carefully analysed in each case, including the context in which they were spoken, and there will be enormous scope for disagreement between reasonable people as to whether a particular comment is merely an explanation or an expression of understanding or goes further and amounts to encouragement, praise or glorification. The point is made by the vast range of reaction to the comments of both Cherie Booth QC and Jenny Tonge MP about suicide bombers. Some reasonable people thought they fell on one side of the Home Secretary's line, other reasonable people thought they fell on the other.[345]

The Committee also considered that the offence was over-broad. The offence relies on the very broad definition of 'terrorism' in the 2000 Terrorism Act, which is discussed above. As indicated above, the definition under s 1 TA covers the use or threat, 'for the purpose of advancing a political, religious or ideological cause', of action anywhere in the world 'designed to influence a government or to intimidate the public or a section of the public', which involves serious damage to property. Thus the new offence, on its face, covers those who express support for armed resistance in Palestine or Iraq, for example. The new offence makes it criminal to vocalise support for armed opposition to regimes viewed by the speaker and by others in the international community as tyrannous and illegitimate. Since 'terrorist' acts are defined so broadly under s 1 TA, it is not necessary that the acts glorified could threaten life. It includes, on its face, the glorification of threats to damage property abroad in furtherance of the cause of a group fighting to establish a democratic regime in an oppressive state, since that action is covered by s 1 TA. The law is also drafted very broadly to include the 'glorification' of 'acts of terrorism' in the past. It is reasonably clear, however, that although the offence covers such speech, it was not intended for use against those speaking to condone or in defence of actions of groups operating only abroad, such as the PMOI in Iran who are 'terrorists' within s 1 TA, but could probably be regarded as 'freedom fighters'. But obviously it hands a very broad discretion to the executive as to its application.

Intent or recklessness as to the statement being understood by the audience as mentioned in s 1(2) is required for an offence to be committed. Thus, the offence can be committed by means of subjective recklessness or oblique intent. So even if the defendant has no intention of inciting people to support or condone terrorist actions, he/she could still be committing an offence so long as members of the public might reasonably regard it as direct or indirect encouragement, if he adverts to that possibility. It is also possible that the new offence could prove to be discriminatory in its application, raising questions as to its impact under Arts 10 and 14 combined. Arguably, certain statements made by Muslims could be regarded as 'glorification' if addressed to a Muslim audience, but not if addressed to a non-Muslim audience, due to the requirement under s 1(3)(b) that the audience 'could reasonably be expected to infer that what is being glorified is conduct that should be emulated by them in existing circumstances'. It is also possible that prosecutions will be discriminatory in terms of selecting those to be rendered accountable under the new offence. For

345 Ibid at para 28.

example, the Egyptian cleric Sheykh Yusuf al-Qaradawi and Cherie Booth have both publicly stated that they can understand why oppressed Palestinians become human bombers.[346] But it is more probable that Sheykh Qaradawi might be subject to arrest for glorification of terrorism. The over-breadth of this offence opens the door to its use in a discriminatory fashion.

The incitement offence, together with the new offence of indirect encouragement of terrorism, were employed in 2007 as part of a long-term proactive investigation into alleged incitement and radicalisation of Muslims. A number of persons allegedly associated with the extremist Islamic group al-Ghurabaa, including Abu Izadeen, were arrested on grounds of incitement in April 2007. A further three persons stood trial on incitement charges in April 2007.[347]

4 The Anti-Terrorism, Crime and Security Act 2001, Part IV – the detention without trial scheme

Introduction

As part of its legislative response to the attacks on New York and Washington on 11 September 2001 the UK Government took the decision to seek to introduce detention without trial for foreign nationals suspected of being 'international terrorists' who could not be deported. In general, non-British citizens who present a risk to national security can be deported.[348] The government achieved its aim when Parliament passed the Anti-Terrorism, Crime and Security Act 2001 (ATCSA). Part 4 of the Act contained the detention without trial provisions. The claim was made that the controversial measures were necessary to protect our human rights and the democratic way of life: Mr David Blunkett, the Home Secretary, said of the Bill – 'strengthening our democracy and reinforcing our values is as important as the passage of new laws . . . the legislative measures which I have outlined today will protect and enhance our rights, not diminish them . . .'.[349] However, Part 4 of ATCSA created, as the discussion below reveals, an impact on human rights which went well beyond providing a response to September 11.

The detention without trial measure was the subject of stringent criticism before its introduction from various bodies, including the Joint Committee on Human Rights, and that criticism was reiterated in 2003 by the bodies charged with reviewing the scheme.[350] The failure of the government to respond to rights-based criticism of the

---

346 See Islamic Human Rights Commission, *United to Protect our Rights* (Sept 2005), p 5.
347 See the *Guardian* report, 25 April 2007, p 4.
348 See now the Immigration, Asylum and National Security Act 2006 and the Nationality, Immigration and Asylum Act 2002. For comment, see Walker, C, 'The Treatment of Foreign Terror Suspects' (2007) 70(3) MLR 427. The 2006 Act builds in part on the government's proposals in 'Confident Communities in a Secure Britain', the Home Office Strategic Plan, 2004–2008, published in July 2004.
349 HC Debs 15 Oct 2001 col 925.
350 See: the Newton Report 2003 (Privy Council Review Committee) and the Carlile Report 2003 (ATCSA 2001, Part 4, Review by Lord Carlile of Berriew QC Feb 2003) and the Joint Committee on Human Rights (ATCSA Statutory Review and Continuance of Part 4, 6th Report of Session 20034, February 2004).

ATCSA was a continuing theme.[351] Part 4 created conflicts with a number of the guarantees of the European Convention on Human Rights received into domestic law under the Human Rights Act 1998. The Part 4 scheme could not be reconciled with the fundamental guarantee of liberty of the person under Art 5, so the government was forced to derogate from Art 5.

Part 4 was eventually repealed in 2005, as discussed below, after the House of Lords found that it was a disproportionate response to the emergency and conflicted with Arts 5 and 14 of the Convention read together. However, Part 4 is discussed in detail below, partly in order to provide the context and background for the control orders scheme under the Prevention of Terrorism Act 2005, which succeeded it, and partly because it forms part of a very significant chapter in the UK's human rights history.

Introduction of Part 4 ATCSA, and the Derogation Order

The ATCSA builds upon the Terrorism Act 2000 (TA), which as indicated above already provided an extremely extensive range of coercive and investigatory powers. A number of measures were introduced in the ATCSA,[352] some of which were not counter-terrorist measures, but this part of this chapter will focus on Part 4 as the most controversial aspect of the Act. The TA is itself, as discussed, an immensely controversial piece of legislation which was apparently intended, at the time of its inception, to provide a complete package of counter-terrorist measures. The focus of counter-terrorist measures was changing and the TA was intended to provide recognition of the change. In particular, it was intended to broaden the focus of such measures, allowing, *inter alia*, for the effective targeting of terrorist groups motivated by fundamentalist religious ideals. In introducing the ATCSA, however, the government claimed that, despite the range of offences it offered, the TA did not provide it with sufficient powers. It stated that as a response to September 11 it needed a power to detain non-British citizens suspected of international terrorism, without trial. Thus, before the TA had been in force for one year, it came to be viewed as inadequate.

The problem faced by the government after September 11 was presented to Parliament and a number of Parliamentary committees[353] in the following terms: a dilemma had arisen in respect of persons suspected of being international terrorists but who could not be placed on trial due to the sensitivity of the evidence and the high standard of proof, and could not be extradited, or deported to their country of origin, or another country, because there were grounds to think that they would there be subject to torture or inhuman and degrading treatment, in breach of Art 3 of the European Convention. However, characterising the problem in this fashion ignored the fact that the security

---

351 See: *Counter-Terrorism Powers: Reconciling Security and Liberty in an Open Society, A Discussion Paper*, Cm 6147, presented to Parliament by the Secretary of State for the Home Department (25 February 2004), David Blunkett. The government refused to accept the validity of the criticisms: 'The Government believes that these powers continue to be an essential part of our defences against attack.'

352 See: Fenwick, H, 'The Anti-Terrorism, Crime and Security Act 2001: A proportionate response to September 11' [2002] 65 MLR 724–62; Walker, C and Akdeniz, Y, 'Anti-Terrorism laws and data retention: war is over?' (2003) 54 *Northern Ireland Legal Quarterly* 159.

353 Home Affairs Select Committee, *The Anti-Terrorism, Crime and Security Bill* (HC (2001–2) 351, 10 November 2001), First Report.

problem was created by British extremist Muslims linked to Al-Qaeda, as well as non-British citizens.

The dilemma arose due to the decision of the European Court of Human Rights in *Chahal v UK*,[354] in which it found that a breach of Art 3 will arise where a country deports a person to another country, knowing that he or she will face a substantial risk of Art 3 treatment in that other country.[355] Mr Chahal was an Indian citizen who had been granted indefinite leave to remain in the UK but his activities as a Sikh separatist brought him to the notice of the authorities; the Home Secretary at the time decided that he should be deported because his continued presence was not conducive to the public good for reasons of a political nature, namely the international fight against terrorism. He resisted deportation on the ground (among others) that, if returned to India, he faced a real risk of death, or of torture in custody contrary to Art 3 of the European Convention which provides that 'No one shall be subjected to torture or to inhuman or degrading treatment or punishment.'

Before the European Court the United Kingdom contended that the effect of Art 3 should be qualified in a case where a state sought to deport a non-national on grounds of national security. The Court, affirming a unanimous decision of the Commission, rejected that argument. It said:[356]

> Article 3 enshrines one of the most fundamental values of democratic society. The Court is well aware of the immense difficulties faced by states in modern times in protecting their communities from terrorist violence. However, even in these circumstances, the Convention prohibits in absolute terms torture or inhuman or degrading treatment or punishment, irrespective of the victim's conduct. Unlike most of the substantive clauses of the convention and of Protocols Nos. 1 and 4, Article 3 makes no provision for exceptions and no derogation from it is permissible under Article 15 even in the event of a public emergency threatening the life of the nation.
>
> The prohibition provided by Article 3 against ill-treatment is equally absolute in expulsion cases. Thus, whenever substantial grounds have been shown for believing that an individual would face a real risk of being subjected to treatment contrary to Article 3 if removed to another state, the responsibility of the Contracting state to safeguard him or her against such treatment is engaged in the event of expulsion. In these circumstances, the activities of the individual in question, however undesirable or dangerous, cannot be a material consideration. The protection afforded by Article 3 is thus wider than that provided by Articles 32 and 33 of the United Nations 1951 Convention on the Status of Refugees.

The Court went on to consider whether Mr Chahal's detention, which had lasted for a number of years, had exceeded the period permissible under Art 5(1)(f). The Court, differing from the unanimous decision of the Commission, held that it had not. But it reasserted[357] that 'any deprivation of liberty under Article 5(1)(f) is justified only

---

354 (1996) 23 EHRR 413.
355 Ibid at para 74.
356 Ibid, in paras 79–80 of its judgment.
357 At para 113.

for as long as deportation proceedings are in progress'. In a case like Mr Chahal's, where deportation proceedings were precluded by Art 3, Art 5(1)(f) would not sanction detention because the non-national would not be 'a person against whom action is being taken with a view to deportation'. A person who commits a serious crime under the criminal law of this country may of course, whether a national or a non-national, be charged, tried and, if convicted, imprisoned. But a non-national who faces the prospect of torture or inhuman treatment if returned to his own country, and who cannot be deported to any third country, and is not charged with any crime, may not under Art 5(1)(f) of the Convention and Sched 3 to the Immigration Act 1971 be detained here even if judged to be a threat to national security.

Thus Art 3 imposes an absolute obligation on signatory states not to deport persons where they are at risk of Art 3 treatment in the receiving country[358] As a matter of domestic law, it is clear that the power to detain persons prior to deportation under the Immigration Act 1971, Sched 3, para 1 is limited to such time as is reasonable to allow the process of deportation to be carried out, and that deportation should follow promptly after the making of the order: *R v Governor of Durham prison ex p Singh*.[359] Thus the available powers of detention prior to deportation did not provide the government with a solution since the suspected terrorists in question could not be deported within a reasonable time, or, in some instances, at all.

The government's preferred solution to the dilemma was to introduce detention without trial for suspected terrorists even where they could not be deported. But it considered that the new provisions would be incompatible with Art 5(1) of the European Convention on Human Rights, which protects the right to liberty and security of the person, afforded further effect in domestic law under the HRA. Although there is an exception under Art 5(1)(f) allowing for detention of 'a person against whom action is being taken with a view to deportation or extradition', it was clear, following *Chahal*, that it would not cover the lengthy detentions envisaged during which deportation proceedings would not be in being.[360]

Therefore, in order to introduce the new provisions it was necessary to derogate from Art 5(1). The derogation was made by giving notice to the Secretary-General of the Council of Europe under Art 15(3) of the Convention. As discussed in Chapter 2, Art 15 provides that 'in time of war or other public emergency threatening the life of the nation' any of the contracting parties may take measures derogating from its obligations under the Convention, 'provided that such measures are not inconsistent with its other obligations under international law'. No derogation from Arts 3, 4(1), 7 or 2 (except in respect of deaths resulting from lawful acts of war) can be made under Art 15.[361] Before giving notice to the Secretary-General the government made an

---

358 Further, the UK has ratified Protocol 6 of the Convention and therefore cannot deport persons to countries where there is a real risk that the death penalty will be imposed. See *X v Spain*, DR 37 (1984) p 93; *Aylor-Davis v France* (1994) 76-A DR 164; *Raidl v Austria* (1995) 82-A DR 134. Protocol 6 prohibits the death penalty in time of peace: it was ratified by the UK on 27 January 1999.

359 [1984] 1 WLR 704.

360 At para 113. In order to detain, deportation proceedings should be in being and it should be clear that they are being prosecuted with due diligence.

361 See Chapter 2, pp 110–11.

order under s 14 HRA, the Human Rights Act (Designated Derogation) Order 2001[362] setting out the derogation from Art 5(1). The derogation itself was expressed to subsist until it was withdrawn, but for HRA purposes it was to cease to have effect after five years unless its extension was approved by the positive resolution procedure in both Houses of Parliament.[363] The schedule to the Derogation Order, which took the form of a draft letter to the Secretary-General, pointed out that the UN Security Council recognised the September 11 attacks as a threat to international security and required states in Resolution 1373 to take measures to prevent terrorist attacks, which would include denying a safe haven to those who plan, support or commit such acts. The schedule argued that on this basis there was a domestic public emergency, which was especially present since there were foreign nationals in the UK who threatened its national security. Therefore, it argued, the measures in Part 4 of ATCSA were clearly and strictly required by the very grave nature of the situation. The government also derogated from Art 9 of the International Covenant on Civil and Political Rights as a further method of safeguarding the new measures from challenge.[364]

The European Court of Human Rights has never found that a claim for a derogation is unjustified on the basis that such a state of emergency does not exist. In *Lawless v Ireland*[365] the Court considered whether Ireland was justified in entering a derogation under Art 15 to Art 5. It found that any terrorist threat must affect the whole population, must be in being or be imminent, and must have produced a situation in which the usual law enforcement mechanisms are unable to function. It found that these conditions were satisfied in 1957 due to the existence of a 'secret army' operating in Ireland and in the UK and because of the alarming rise in terrorist activities in the previous year.[366] The introduction of special powers in Ireland, including internment, in 1971 was found to be justified by an upsurge in terrorist activity together with serious and prolonged rioting.[367]

It may be noted that, as discussed above,[368] a broad view was taken by the House of Lords in *Secretary of State for the Home Dept v Rehman*[369] of the meaning of a threat to national security; it was found that such a threat should be broadly defined to include the possibility of future threats, including those to the UK's allies. In introducing the ATCSA the Home Secretary said that the government held secret information suggesting that members of some international terrorist groups are currently in Britain.[370] The government took the view that, taking into account the September 11 atrocities and

---

362   SI 2001/3644. It was laid before Parliament on 12 November 2001, coming into effect on the following day. It designated the proposed derogation as one that was to have immediate effect.

363   Section 16 HRA.

364   Under Art 4(1) of the Covenant: see *UK Derogation under the ICCPR*, 18 Dec 2001. See further, Michaelsen, C, 'Derogating from International Human Rights Obligations in the "War Against Terrorism"? – A British–Australian Perspective' [2005] 17 (1–2) Terrorism and Political Violence 131–55.

365   A 3 (1961).

366   Ibid, para 28.

367   *Ireland v UK* A 25 (1978), para 23.

368   See above p 1343.

369   [1999] INLR 517 (SIAC); [2000] 3 All ER 778, CA; [2001] 3 WLR 877, HL.

370   See HC Debs 15 Oct 2001 col 924; evidence of the Home Secretary given to the Joint Committee on Human Rights, Second Report, Questions 3–7 and 9.

Britain's support for America, a state of public emergency affecting the life of the nation could be said to exist. The Joint Committee on Human Rights, however, expressed concern in its second report about the lack of specificity in the reasons given for taking this view.[371] It examined the Home Secretary in oral evidence on the reasons for thinking that a state of emergency existed differing from that facing the country when the TA 2000 was enacted; he replied that the current threat was greater than that posed by the IRA since the 1970s because the terrorists in question were thought to have access to weapons of mass destruction.[372] The Committee found that there might be evidence of a state of public emergency but that no evidence of it had been disclosed by the Home Secretary.

The Part 4 detention provisions

Detention under Part 4 ATCSA depended on certification by the Home Secretary as – in effect – a substitute for a trial. Under s 21(1) the Home Secretary could issue a certificate in respect of a person on the basis of (a) a reasonable belief that the person's presence in the UK was a 'risk to national security' and (b) reasonable suspicion that he or she was a terrorist. It may be noted that as a result of the decision in *Rehman v Secretary of State for the Home Dept*[373] the Home Secretary was accorded, as discussed below, a broad latitude in determining when a risk to national security arises.

Under s 21(2) ATCSA a 'terrorist' was a person who was or had been 'concerned in the commission, preparation or instigation of acts of international terrorism' or was (b) a member of or belonged to an international terrorist group or (c) had 'links' with such a group. Under s 21(4) such links would exist only if the person supported or assisted the international terrorist group. 'Terrorism' was afforded the meaning given to it in s 1(1) of the TA.[374] Thus the TA and ATCSA had to be read together. The detention provisions in the 2001 Act clearly did not apply to all those persons who fell within the definition in s 1(1) TA; the power to detain only applied to 'suspected international terrorists' who were non-British citizens. Under s 21(5) ATCSA a 'suspected international terrorist' was a person who fell within the definition of terrorism in s 1 of the TA 2000 and who had been certified under s 21(1).

It was crucial that the definition of a 'suspected international terrorist' should be precise since such a person could be subject to lengthy – perhaps indefinite – detention without trial. But, as indicated above, the definition of 'terrorism' under s 1 TA, on which it was centrally based, is itself immensely broad and imprecise. No full definition of an 'international' terrorist was contained in the Act, but s 21(3) provided that an international terrorist group 'is a group subject to the control or influence of persons outside the UK' and 'the Home Secretary suspects' (not qualified by 'reasonably') 'that it is concerned in the commission, preparation and instigation of acts of terrorism'. Further, a person could be termed a 'suspected international terrorist' on the basis that he or she had 'links' with an international terrorist group.

---

371 Ibid, at para 29.
372 Second report and oral evidence appended to the report, Questions 3–7 and 9 (para 29).
373 [2001] 3 WLR 877.
374 Section 21(5).

The power of certification could be exercised in respect of persons who, under s 22, could be subject to various immigration controls,[375] thus excluding British citizens from the scheme, however far they posed a risk to national security. Under s 23(1) persons falling within s 21 could be:

> detained under a provision specified in sub-section (2) despite the fact that his removal or departure from the UK is prevented (whether temporarily or indefinitely) by (a) a point of law which wholly or partly relates to an international agreement or (b) a practical consideration.

Section 23(2) referred to Sched 2, para 16 of the 1971 Act (detention of persons liable to examination or removal) and Sched 3 para 2 of that Act (detention pending deportation). No definition or explanation of the terms used in s 23(1) was offered. Provision under (a) had to be taken to relate to Art 3 and Protocol 6 of the European Convention on Human Rights, while the 'practical consideration' covered, *inter alia*, a failure to identify a country which would take the person.

As the Joint Committee on Human Rights pointed out, the Part 4 provisions went beyond answering to the dilemma the government claimed to be addressing.[376] The scheme covered, on its face, a range of persons unconnected with Al-Qaeda – the terrorist group which was almost certainly responsible for the September 11 attacks. It appeared to cover those who posed a threat only to other countries, such as Tamil Tigers, and also those who merely had 'links' with such groups. In theory, the scheme could have covered a Kurd who supported the PKK and had come to Britain to hand out leaflets about them, or a non-British citizen fund-raising in support of a non-proscribed activist environmental group advocating direct action abroad. In fact the first of these persons could have been arrested and charged with one of the proscription-linked offences under the TA.[377] The second arguably would not have committed any existing offence. Therefore, disturbingly enough, ss 21 and 23 not only allowed for the detention of those who – apparently – could not be brought to trial due to the sensitivity of the evidence, but also of those who could not have been brought to trial in any event.

Even accepting the necessity of introducing detention without trial, the separate question arose of the proportionality between the emergency situation and the detention scheme in Part 4 remains.[378] Bearing in mind the doubts that have been expressed as to the existence of a public emergency, it is fair to argue that if one existed it appeared to be one that only marginally fell within that term. Therefore, it is suggested, the government should have viewed itself as circumscribed in its choice of the measures

---

375 In terms of: a refusal of leave to enter or remain, or a variation of a limited leave to enter or remain in the UK under ss 3–3B Immigration Act 1971 or to a recommendation to deport under s 3(6) of that Act, or a decision to deport or an order to deport under s 5(1), refusal to revoke a deportation order, a cancellation of leave to remain, a direction of removal under paras 8–10 or 12–14 of that Act or a direction of removal under s 10 of the Immigration and Asylum Act 1999 or the giving of a notice of a decision to deport under the 1999 Act.

376 Fifth Report of the Joint Committee on Human Rights (2001), para 6.

377 Section 12(1) TA would provide the obvious one.

378 The tests of *both* necessity and proportionality must be satisfied: *Lawless v Ireland* A 3 (1961); *De Becker v Belgium* B4 (1962), at para 271.

to be taken. Among the possible measures which could have been adopted the less repressive ones should have been chosen. The choice in fact made failed, it is argued, to satisfy the requirements of proportionality due to the use of extraordinarily broad definitions, of 'terrorism', and of national security, on which the power of certification depended. As indicated above, the scheme was over-inclusive since it covered persons who were suspected of being part of or linked to international terrorist organisations but who had no links with Al-Qaeda. The 'emergency' was apparently imminent due to the September 11 attacks. Therefore a measure allowing for the detention without trial of those who were unconnected in any way to those involved in the attacks appeared to be disproportionate to the demands of the post-September 11 situation. But it was also under-inclusive: it could not have covered the 7/7 London suicide bombers since they were British citizens.

A number of qualifying provisions that would have improved this scheme in human rights terms were notable by their absence. For example, it was not necessary prior to certification[379] for the Home Secretary to receive an assessment from legal advisers regarding the feasibility of bringing any of the potential detainees to trial rather than relying on this scheme. Nor was it necessary for an interim assessment to be made on the basis that fresh evidence had been obtained while the detainee was in detention, rendering a prosecution feasible. The significance of this omission was highlighted in the case of *Abu Qatada and Secretary of State for the Home Dept*:[380] SIAC found that the evidence against Qatada was very strong[381] and the extensive evidence against him was reviewed. Clearly, the question why Qatada could not be prosecuted under one of the TA offences arose. The offence under s 59(1) TA, for example, might well have been applicable. Obviously some of the evidence would have been difficult to present in court, but Special Immigration Appeals Commission (SIAC)'s judgment gave the impression that sufficient evidence existed that could have been presented in a trial, probably with safeguards such as anonymity for certain witnesses.

There was no express provision allowing for the release of the detainee if, for example, the group to which he allegedly belonged, or had links to, renounced terrorist activity. No particular conditions of detention were prescribed, and bearing in mind that it was in effect indefinite, the detainees were under a particular mental stress. It may be noted that in April 2004 SIAC ordered the release to house arrest of one of the detainees on the basis of the grave deterioration of his mental condition. Another detainee who was released[382] told the press that a number of the detainees became mentally ill as a result of their detention. The detainees were subject to the same conditions as remand prisoners in general – albeit in high security detention applicable to category A prisoners – although the mental stress that they were under differed greatly from that of a remand prisoner who could expect to be detained for a relatively short period of time. There was no express provision placing an obligation on the Home

---

379 If this procedure had been instituted the person in question could have been detained under the Part 4 power or remanded in custody while the necessity of certification as opposed to trial was being assessed.
380 File No SC15/2002.
381 Ibid, at para 9.
382 See *M v Secretary of State for the Home Dept* [2004] EWCA Civ 324.

Secretary to receive independent and continuing assessments of the degree to which a particular detainee was at risk of Art 3 treatment if deported.[383]

Sections 21–23, on their face, discriminated against non-nationals since only such persons were targeted for detention – and detention that could be very lengthy. Further, they lost, in effect, the right to a trial before the possibility of being detained could arise. British citizens who fell within the definition of 'suspected international terrorists' still had to be brought to trial (probably under one of the TA offences) before the possibility of detention could arise. Due process was entirely discarded by allowing for the detention without trial of such persons. The level of suspicion was – of necessity – well below the 'beyond reasonable doubt' standard, and since the necessary 'evidence' for the formation of the suspicion was not subjected to the check of a trial process, the risk that miscarriages of justice could occur was very high: had the scheme not been abandoned, some persons might have been wrongfully detained for a number of years. Since a power of *indefinite* detention was in effect provided, the need for such a check was especially apparent. It should be noted that possible limits on a power providing for 'indefinite detention' were apparent, but there was little reason to expect that they would lead to the ending of the detention. The detention powers in Part 4 were to expire on 10 November 2006.[384] Detention was therefore limited initially to a little less than five years for those arrested immediately after the Act was passed in December 2001. However, it appeared that the government's intention was to introduce legislation to Parliament in order to retain these powers, once they lapsed, assuming that the current 'emergency' was considered to be ongoing at that point.[385] Part 4 also had to be renewed by order, subject to Parliamentary approval, every 15 months.[386] In human rights terms this scheme was objectionable in a number of respects, and those objections were considered by the House of Lords in 2004, as discussed below, in the context of the European Convention on Human Rights.

The role of the Special Immigration Appeals Commission

The Special Immigration Appeals Commission (SIAC), established under s 1 of the Special Immigration Appeals Commission Act 1997 (SIACA), played a crucial role in this scheme since in most instances it represented the only means of challenging the decision to detain. Under s 21(8) ATCSA the Secretary of State's decision in connection with certification could only be questioned under ss 25 or 26, which dealt with challenges to the certificate or reviews of it by SIAC. There were two methods of judicial control enshrined in Part 4. Under s 25 a detainee could appeal to SIAC which had the power to cancel the certificate of the Home Secretary if it found that there were no reasonable grounds for a belief or suspicion of the kind referred to in

---

383 There was no *express* provision allowing persons at risk of Art 3 treatment abroad to leave if they were prepared to take the risk of that treatment. There was no express provision requiring that detainees must be deported or removed, if they wished to be, when and if a safe third country could be found, or indeed imposing any duty at all regarding the possibility of finding a safe third country.

384 Section 29(7). However, new legislation would probably have been introduced giving the same powers.

385 See: *Counter-Terrorism Powers: Reconciling Security and Liberty in an Open Society, A Discussion Paper*, Cm 6147.

386 Sub-section 29(1)–(6),

s 21(1)(a) or (b), or that for 'some other reason' the certificate should not have been issued. The Commission could allow the appeal and cancel the certificate, but the Home Secretary could then issue a further certificate under s 27(9). There was also a distinct power of review of the certificate, which was not instigated by the applicant and which had to occur in SIAC.

The procedure in SIAC is governed by SIAC's Rules of Procedure, as amended.[387] The rules allow for hearings in the absence of the person bringing the proceedings and his or her legal representative. In such instances a special advocate (SA) will be appointed who has had security clearance. The procedure is divided between closed and open sessions. Under s 5(3)(b) SIACA and Rules of Procedure, r 19, the appellant and his or her advocate are excluded from the closed sessions. The SA can attend the closed sessions; the benefit of these closed sessions is that the government can put forward the facts on which it bases its case. However, it means that the applicant cannot know all or much of the basis of the case against him and therefore cannot challenge it. He may not even be allowed to see a summary of the case. He cannot instruct the SA. Clearly, the position of the applicant is weak before SIAC. The extent to which the evidence can genuinely be tested is questionable. As C White put it in relation to this type of tribunal: it 'attempts to create an adversarial forum where one of the parties is severely hampered in presenting his or her case'.[388] This was of particular concern in relation to Part 4 since it allowed for a power of indefinite detention, demanding greater judicial scrutiny of the basis for the suspicion.

However, in the case of *M v Secretary of State for the Home Dept*[389] the SAs were able to mount an effective challenge in the closed sessions to the evidence that M had links to Al-Qaeda. As a result, SIAC decided that reasonable suspicion was not established, and the Court of Appeal upheld this ruling. This instance indicated that the SIAC procedure had some efficacy as a means of testing the basis of the certification. Nevertheless, the SIAC procedure was defective in human rights terms since the detainee was in such a vulnerable position before it, compared to the position of a defendant in a criminal trial. The question of the compliance of such proceedings with Art 6 is considered below in relation to control order proceedings. But control orders obligations do not at present include detention, so the SIAC proceedings in relation to Part 4 raised greater concerns.

The challenge to the derogation and the Part 4 scheme in A and Others[390]

The detention powers were used immediately to detain 11 persons in Belmarsh Prison in London. Two of them stated that they were prepared to leave the country and did

---

387   SI 1998/1881, amended by SI 2000/1849.

388   For discussion, see White, C, 'Security Vetting, Discrimination and the Right to a Fair Trial' [1999] PL 406–18, at p 413. See also Walker, C, *The Prevention of Terrorism* (1986) p 82; he advocated an inquisitorial system for such tribunals.

389   See *M v Secretary of State for the Home Dept*, SIAC – SC/15/2002; CA 2004 EWCA Civ 324.

390   For comment on *A and Others*, see: '*A v Secretary of State for the Home Department* Introduction' [2005] 68(4) MLR 654; Hickman, T, 'Between Human Rights and the Rule of Law: Indefinite Detention and the Derogation Model of Constitutionalism' (2005) 68(4) MLR 655–68; Hiebert, J, 'Parliamentary Review of Terrorism Measures' (2005) 68(4) MLR 676–80.

so.[391] A further five persons were later detained. In the 11 cases determined by SIAC following appeal against certification, the Home Secretary's decision to certify was upheld in all but one of them; the Court of Appeal agreed with SIAC's decision in all instances.[392] The result was therefore that one detainee was released, while the powers were still in force, on the ground that the evidence against him did not satisfy the 'reasonable suspicion' test of s 21 and he was released on bail, on strict conditions, in April 2004. One of the detainees was transferred to Broadmoor Hospital on grounds of mental illness in July 2002. The Home Secretary revoked his certification of another in September 2004, and he was released without conditions.

The decision in *A and Others v Secretary of State for the Home Dept*[393] eventually led to the abandonment of the scheme after it was declared incompatible with Arts 5 and 14 under s 4 HRA by the House of Lords in 2004. The detainees began their challenge to the designated derogation in SIAC, under s 30 ATCSA.[394] They also challenged the detention scheme in relation to the Convention rights scheduled in the HRA. SIAC had to consider first whether there had been compliance with the requirements for derogation, meaning that it had to examine the demands of Art 15. Article 15(1) provides:

> In time of war or other public emergency threatening the life of the nation any High Contracting Party may take measures derogating from its obligations under this Convention to the extent strictly required by the exigencies of the situation, provided that such measures are not inconsistent with its other obligations under international law.

The government had not claimed that this was a time of war, and therefore the first question which the Commission had to consider was whether there was a public emergency threatening the life of the nation, within the meaning of Art 15.

Following *Rehman*, it was always likely that SIAC would accept a broad interpretation of a state of emergency. In making its assessment as to the actual existence of the state of emergency it seemed possible that SIAC might apply a somewhat stricter standard of review than that at Strasbourg since as a domestic court it does not concede a margin of appreciation to the national authorities. However, it accepted that the executive had a discretionary area of judgment[395] in determining whether a public emergency existed.[396] SIAC took the view that it was acting in accordance with the Strasbourg jurisprudence in examining the closed material on which the assertion of an emergency was based, but it also found that in the context in question – that of national security – it had to decide 'whether the decision that there was such an emergency as justified derogation was one which was reasonable on all the material or . . . one that he was entitled to

391 See the *Guardian*, 15 April 2002.
392 See *M v Secretary of State for the Home Dept* SIAC – SC/15/2002; CA 2004 EWCA Civ 324.
393 (2004) UKHL 56; [2005] 2 AC 68; [2005] 2 WLR 87; [2005] 3 All ER 169.
394 *A and Others v Secretary of State for the Home Dept*, determination: 30 July 2002, unreported.
395 See: *R v DPP ex p Kebeline* [1999] 3 WLR 372; *Secretary of State for the Home Dept ex p Rehman* [2001] 3 WLR 877.
396 At para 15 of the SIAC judgment.

reach'.[397] This standard of scrutiny appeared to resemble the *Wednesbury* approach and therefore, it is argued, was too low.[398] Having adopted this approach, SIAC accepted the existence of an emergency within the terms of Art 15 due to the fact that 'the UK is a prime target, second only to the US[399] .... an emergency can exist and can ... be imminent if there is an intention and a capacity to carry out serious terrorist violence even if nothing has yet been done ....'.[400]

In determining the issues of necessity and proportionality SIAC relied on the relevant Strasbourg jurisprudence in considering the necessity of introducing the Part 4 detention scheme, bearing in mind the other available measures which had not themselves necessitated derogation.[401] SIAC found that so long as the detention scheme fell within the range of reasonable legislative responses it should not be viewed as over-broad merely because other alternatives were available. It went on to consider the key issue of over-inclusiveness and found that account should be taken of the potential effect of s 3(1) HRA (providing that legislation should be rendered compatible with the Convention rights if at all possible) and the power of SIAC to set aside the certificate under s 25(2)(b) ATCSA. Section 3(1) could be used, it was found, to narrow down the provisions of ss 21–23 and, moreover, if the powers were exercised against a person unconnected with Al-Qaeda that would provide a basis for setting aside the certificate under s 25(2)(b). Thus the detention scheme was found to satisfy this test.

The key argument put before SIAC was that the scheme was racially discriminatory and therefore breached Art 14 which provides: 'The enjoyment of the rights and freedoms set forth in this Convention shall be secured without discrimination on any ground such as sex, race .... national or social origin, association with a national minority . . .' As discussed in Chapter 2, Art 14 is parasitic on another Article: it is not free-standing. But, as both SIAC and the Court of Appeal agreed, the derogation did not prevent consideration of Art 14 in relation to Art 5 since Art 14 itself had not been derogated from. It had been established in *Ireland v UK* that a successful derogation from another Article does not mean that it is unnecessary to consider whether unlawful discrimination has occurred in the context of that other Article. The fact that a violation of Art 5(1) itself could not be established does not affect this analysis: in *Abdulaziz v UK*[402] it was found that even where no violation of the other Article was established that did not preclude finding of a violation of Art 14.

In general, as discussed in Chapter 15, a breach of Art 14 can be established where other persons in an analogous position enjoy differential treatment (in relation to another Convention guarantee) and there is no objective and reasonable justification for the distinction.[403] In the domestic courts it has been found under Art 14 that there will be an objective justification for different treatment where it pursues a legitimate aim and

---

397   Para 21.
398   This point was raised on behalf of the applicants in the Court of Appeal; the Court considered that these words merely meant that SIAC recognised that it must afford a reasonably wide margin of discretion (para 59, CA).
399   At para 35.
400   At para 24.
401   See: *Lawless v Ireland* A 3 (1961), at para 36; *Ireland v UK* A 35 (1978), at para 212.
402   (1985) 7 EHRR 471.
403   *Stubbings v UK* (1996) 23 EHRR 213. See Chapter 15, p 1483.

the treatment bears a reasonable relationship or proportionality with the aim sought to be realised.[404] SIAC found that since a number of British nationals would fall within the definition of a 'suspected international terrorist' under s 21 ATCSA, but could not be subject to detention under Part 4, the detention scheme created discrimination on grounds of nationality. A breach of Art 14 was therefore established. SIAC proceeded to quash the derogation order and made a declaration of incompatibility (under s 4 HRA) between s 23 ATCSA and Art 14 read with Art 5. This was clearly a highly significant finding. It meant that a key aspect of the UK's response to September 11 was deeply flawed since it had failed to comply with the fundamental principle of non-discrimination.

SIAC's decisions were then appealed to the Court of Appeal.[405] When the Court of Appeal[406] considered the case, it also accepted the existence of an emergency in Art 15 terms. As indicated, the second question to be asked under Art 15 is whether the derogation applies 'only to the extent strictly required by the exigencies of the situation'. The Court of Appeal agreed with SIAC in accepting that the measures taken were strictly required in the circumstances, taking into account the limited class of foreign nationals at which they were aimed. The judges found that it was well established that in some circumstances, particularly in times of emergency, states may distinguish between nationals and non-nationals.

Lord Woolf considered that s 3(1) HRA need not be used to narrow down the detention provisions: he said that they would have to be read narrowly in any event so as to ensure that they were covered by the derogation order, since otherwise they would conflict with Art 5. However, this point appeared to ignore the fact that primary legislation incompatible with a Convention right remains valid under s 3(2) HRA, and that s 3(1) is the mechanism to be used to seek to ensure that incompatibility does not arise. On the basis that the provisions would in any event have to be read narrowly, Lord Woolf accepted the government's undertaking that the detention power would only be used in relation to the emergency which was the subject of the derogation.[407] This was a very significant reading down of the statute and imposed a proportionality on the scheme which was not originally present since after the Court of Appeal findings it appeared that only members of Al-Qaeda, or those with links to Al-Qaeda, could legitimately be detained.

The Court of Appeal agreed with SIAC that the derogation did not prevent consideration of Art 14. However, the Court of Appeal disagreed with SIAC's conclusion that the scheme was discriminatory. The Court, unanimously, 'reached a different conclusion on the basis that British nationals are not in an analogous situation to foreign nationals who currently cannot be deported because of fears for their safety".[408] Lord Woolf CJ said that he reached this conclusion partly on the basis of the tension between Arts 14 and 15.[409] Article 15, as indicated above, debars the taking of action

---

404 *Michalak v London Borough of Wandsworth* [2002] EWCA Civ 271 at para 20.
405 *A, X and Y and Others v Secretary of State for the Home Dept* [2002] EWCA Civ 1502; [2003] 1 All ER 816. At that point 13 people were detained.
406 [2003] 1 All ER 816.
407 CA [2002] EWCA Civ 1502, at para 42.
408 See para 56.
409 At para 45.

to meet the emergency that is more than is strictly necessary. The Home Secretary had come to the conclusion that it was only necessary to take action in respect of non-national suspected terrorists and that was a conclusion, it was found, that should be treated deferentially by the courts. Action taken also against *national* suspected terrorists might have been more effective but could not, it was found, be viewed as strictly necessary in Art 15 terms, bearing in mind the Home Secretary's decision. The basis for singling out non-national suspected terrorists – that they, unlike nationals, are liable to be deported, even if, perforce, there is a delay before deportation can occur, was, in Lord Woolf's view, rational. Thus, the different treatment could be justified since it had a reasonable relationship or proportionality with the aim – of meeting the emergency – sought to be realised.

In any event, Lord Woolf found, and the other members of the Court of Appeal agreed, that the comparators – nationals who were suspected terrorists – were not in an analogous position to non-national suspected terrorists since they would have a right of abode, while the non-nationals merely had a contingent right not to be removed (due to the risk of Art 3 treatment abroad, or where no country could be identified that was prepared to accept them). Lord Woolf in the Court of Appeal took the view as indicated that the 'tension' between Arts 14 and 15 aided him in reaching this conclusion. He considered that targeting all 'suspected international terrorists' would have created a greater invasion of human rights than the Part 4 scheme created since the rights of nationals would also have been invaded. Thus, the appeal from SIAC's decision was allowed. The use of nationality as the determinant of the reach of the scheme was found to be non-discriminatory.

These findings missed the point that a much more narrowly targeted scheme – aimed, *on its face*, only at Al-Qaeda members or supporters – national and non-national – would have created a much more confined invasion. The choice to target instead the much wider group, based on the necessarily unconnected factor of nationality – since Al-Qaeda is a group defined by ideology, not nationality – was very difficult to defend in terms of rationality. The Court of Appeal succeeded in accepting the government defence only by adopting a strikingly deferential stance towards the Home Secretary's contention that an emergency created by Al-Qaeda would be most effectively addressed by targeting persons on the ground of nationality rather than on that of involvement in Al-Qaeda.[410] Clearly, a scheme that had included British citizens would have been viewed as more draconian since they could not be deported and so would not have been able to leave detention for an indefinite period. However, almost all the suspects who were detained could not in any event leave detention, for fear of Art 3 treatment abroad, and therefore that distinction was not of great significance in practice.

The House of Lords considered the scheme in December 2004. In argument before the House, *Liberty* made written and oral submissions in support of the appellants, as it had done in the courts below. Amnesty International also made written submissions in support of the appellants. Lord Bingham, giving the opinion of the majority of the House, noted that in Resolution 1271 adopted on 24 January 2002,[411] the Parliamentary

---

410 See para 40 of the judgment.
411 At para 9.

Assembly of the Council of Europe resolved that: 'In their fight against terrorism, Council of Europe members should not provide for any derogations to the European Convention on Human Rights.' Lord Bingham found that it had not been shown that SIAC or the Court of Appeal had misdirected themselves on the question whether a state of emergency was in being. He noted that SIAC had considered a body of closed material, but that in any event the view that it accepted was one that it could have reached on the open evidence in the case.

Lord Bingham went on to review the Strasbourg authorities in relation to the question whether an emergency was in being as required by Art 15.[412] He relied in particular on *Lawless v Ireland (No 3)*[413] in which grave loss of life caused by terrorism had not occurred, so the threat to security was implied. He noted that it had never been disavowed and that the House was required by s 2(1) HRA to take it into account. He said that the decision might be explained as showing the breadth of the margin of appreciation accorded by the Court to national authorities. But he found that if it was open to the Irish Government in *Lawless* to conclude that there was a public emergency threatening the life of the Irish nation, then the British Government could not be faulted for reaching that conclusion in the much more dangerous situation which arose after September 11. Thirdly, as discussed further in Chapter 4, he accepted that great weight should be given to the judgment of the Home Secretary, his colleagues and Parliament on the question of an emergency, because they were called on to exercise a pre-eminently political judgment.[414]

The majority of the Lords agreed (Lord Hoffmann dissenting on this point), and so did conclude that it was open to the government to find that there was a state of emergency within the terms of Art 15; that was viewed by the majority as a largely political judgment. Taking into account the breadth of the definition of an emergency under Art 15, and the fact that the domestic courts had to assess, on the basis of very sensitive intelligence, not an overt but a covert, implicit and speculatively imminent state of emergency, it was unsurprising that they concluded that one was in existence in the UK

The second question to be asked under Art 15 is whether the derogation applies 'only to the extent strictly required by the exigencies of the situation'. That was a more problematic issue. The Joint Committee on Human Rights had concluded that even if the requisite state of emergency existed, it doubted whether the measures in the Bill could be said to be strictly required, bearing in mind the array of measures already available to be used against terrorism, and the fact that no other European country had derogated from Art 5.[415] Other legal opinion on this issue was quite firmly to the

---

412 At para 28. He said: 'The European Court decisions in *Ireland v United Kingdom* (1978) 2 EHRR 25; *Brannigan and McBride v United Kingdom* (1993) 17 EHRR 539; *Aksoy v Turkey* (1996) 23 EHRR 553 and *Marshall v United Kingdom* (10 July 2001, Appl No 41571/98) seem to me to be, with respect, clearly right. In each case the member state had actually experienced widespread loss of life caused by an armed body dedicated to destroying the territorial integrity of the state. To hold that the Art 15 test was not satisfied in such circumstances, if a response beyond that provided by the ordinary course of law was required, would have been perverse.'

413 (1961) 1 EHRR 15.

414 At para 29. See Chapter 4, pp 282–83.

415 Second Report, para 30.

effect that the detention scheme was unjustified on the basis that it went further than was required by the exigencies of the situation.[416]

The Lords were prepared to adopt a strict scrutiny of the measures taken and so accepted, as discussed in Chapter 4, that a strict proportionality test should be adopted.[417] Lord Bingham said:

> the appellants are in my opinion entitled to invite the courts to review, on proportionality grounds, the Derogation Order and the compatibility with the Convention of section 23 and the courts are not effectively precluded by any doctrine of deference from scrutinising the issues raised.[418]

On the question of proportionality under Art 15 – that the measures went no further than required by the exigencies of the situation – the Lords made the point that ss 21 and 23 ATCSA did not rationally address the threat to the security of the United Kingdom presented by Al-Qaeda terrorists and their supporters because (a) they did not address the threat presented by UK nationals, (b) they permitted foreign nationals suspected of being Al-Qaeda terrorists or their supporters to pursue their activities abroad if there was any country to which they were able to go, and (c) the sections permitted, on their face, the certification and detention of persons who were not suspected of presenting any threat to the security of the United Kingdom as Al-Qaeda terrorists or supporters.

Further, they found that if the threat presented to the security of the United Kingdom by UK nationals suspected of being Al-Qaeda terrorists, or their supporters, could be addressed without infringing their right to personal liberty, it had not been shown why similar measures could not adequately address the threat presented by foreign nationals. So the Part 4 measures allowed both for the detention of those presenting no direct threat to the United Kingdom and for the non-detention or the release of those who – allegedly – did. The House of Lords accepted that such a 'paradoxical conclusion was hard to reconcile with the strict exigencies of the situation'. The key problem, they found, was that the choice of an immigration measure to address a security problem had had the inevitable result of failing adequately to address that problem. The Lords found the conclusion that the derogation order and s 23 were, in Convention terms, disproportionate to the aims pursued, to be irresistible.

The Lords then turned to the question of discrimination under Art 14. The UK had not derogated from Art 14 of the European Convention (or from Art 26 of the ICCPR, which corresponds to it). The Attorney General did not submit in the House of Lords that there had been an implied derogation from Art 14. The appellants argued that in providing for the detention of suspected international terrorists who were not UK nationals, but not for the detention of suspected international terrorists who were

---

416 David Pannick wrote a legal Opinion for *Liberty*; David Anderson QC and Jemima Stratford wrote one for the group JUSTICE on this issue (Memorandum from Justice). Both came to the conclusion, on different grounds, that the derogation was unjustified. The Opinion for JUSTICE considered that Part 4 went beyond what was strictly required by the exigencies of the situation in covering a wide range of suspected international terrorists.

417 See pp 287–90.

418 At para 42.

UK nationals, s 23 unlawfully discriminated against them as non-UK nationals in breach of Art 14.

Lord Bingham found that the question to be asked under Art 14 was whether persons in an analogous or relevantly similar situation enjoyed preferential treatment, without reasonable or objective justification for the distinction, and whether and to what extent differences in otherwise similar situations would justify a different treatment in law.[419] He relied in particular on *R (S) v Chief Constable of the South Yorkshire Police*[420] from which he considered that the questions to be asked were:

(1) Do the facts fall within the ambit of one or more of the Convention rights? (2) Was there a difference in treatment in respect of that right between the complainant and others put forward for comparison? (3) If so, was the difference in treatment on one or more of the proscribed grounds under article 14? (4) Were those others in an analogous situation? (5) Was the difference in treatment objectively justifiable in the sense that it had a legitimate aim and bore a reasonable relationship of proportionality to that aim?

The facts were found to fall within Art 5; difference of treatment had been accorded to the applicants and their comparators since the applicants had been detained; the treatment related to an impliedly proscribed ground – that of nationality. The appellants' chosen comparators were suspected international terrorists who were UK nationals. The appellants pointed out that they shared with this group the important characteristics (a) of being suspected international terrorists and (b) of being irremovable from the United Kingdom (due to the effect of *Chahal*). The Lords accepted this. Suspected international terrorists who are UK nationals were, it was found, in a situation analogous with the appellants because, in the present context, they shared the most relevant characteristics of the appellants.

The measure taken might have been reasonable and justified in an immigration context, but not in a security one since the threat came from both nationals and non-nationals; the Court of Appeal had erred in its findings on this point since it had accepted a differentiation based on the use of an immigration measure when the whole issue was the appropriateness of using that measure. Lord Bingham found on this point:

Article 15 requires any derogating measures to go no further than is strictly required by the exigencies of the situation and the prohibition of discrimination on grounds of nationality or immigration status has not been the subject of derogation. Article 14 remains in full force. Any discriminatory measure inevitably affects a smaller

---

419   At para 50. Lord Bingham relied on: *Stubbings v United Kingdom* (1996) 23 EHRR 213, para 70. He said that the parties were agreed that in domestic law, seeking to give effect to the Convention, the correct approach was to pose the questions formulated by Grosz, Beatson and Duffy, *Human Rights: The 1998 Act and the European Convention* (2000), para C14–08, substantially adopted by Brooke LJ in *Wandsworth London Borough Council v Michalak* [2002] EWCA Civ 271, [2003] 1 WLR 617, para 20, and refined in the later cases of *R (Carson) v Secretary of State for Work and Pensions* [2002] EWHC 978 (Admin), [2002] 3 All ER 994, para 52, [2003] EWCA Civ 797, [2003] 3 All ER 577, paras 56–61, *Ghaidan v Godin-Mendoza* [2004] UKHL 30, [2004] 3 WLR 113, paras 133–34.
420   [2004] UKHL 39, [2004] 1 WLR 2196 para 42.

rather than a larger group, but cannot be justified on the ground that more people would be adversely affected if the measure were applied generally. What has to be justified is not the measure in issue but the difference in treatment between one person or group and another. What cannot be justified here is the decision to detain one group of suspected international terrorists, defined by nationality or immigration status, and not another. To do so was a violation of article 14. It was also a violation of article 26 of the ICCPR and so inconsistent with the United Kingdom's other obligations under international law within the meaning of article 15 of the European Convention.[421]

So since the different treatment could not be justified, the scheme was found to violate Arts 14 and 5 read together on the basis of differentiating between groups of suspected international terrorists on the basis of nationality – this was found to be the key weakness of the scheme. The derogation order was quashed and a declaration of incompatibility between Arts 14 and 5 and s 23 was made. Since, in contrast with the position in Canada,[422] under the HRA judges cannot strike down provisions that conflict with fundamental rights, the detainees remained in Belmarsh while the government decided how to respond to the decision, and the new legislation was prepared. But as discussed in Chapter 4, declarations of incompatibility place a lot of pressure on the government to respond, under s 10 HRA.[423] This is especially the case when, as in this instance, a declaration is made by a unanimous nine-member House of Lords. The government accepted that it could no longer sustain the scheme. It could theoretically have continued it in the face of an admitted violation of Art 5 (since the derogation order had been quashed) and of Art 5 and 14 read together – but it bowed to the pressure and accepted that Part 4 must be repealed. It was replaced by the control orders scheme, discussed below.

5 The Prevention of Terrorism Act 2005 – control orders

Introduction

Control orders were introduced under the Prevention of Terrorism Act 2005 (PTA) as a replacement for the abandoned and repealed Part 4 ATCSA scheme. The PTA, ss 1–9

---

421 At para 68.

422 In a similar decision, *Charkaouri v Canada*, 24 February 2007, Canada's Supreme Court unanimously struck down the use of secret testimony to imprison and deport foreigners as possible terrorist suspects, ruling that the procedures violated Canada's Charter of Rights and Freedoms. The six men were detained without trail under a 'security certificate'. Two are now being held in a special prison, three are free on bond and a fourth has been ordered released on bond. The Court however suspended its ruling for a year. The ruling has been hailed as a victory for civil rights as an aspect of dismantling what has been termed 'Canada's Guantanamo North'. Thus, although the Canadian Supreme Court can strike down statutory provisions, unlike the House of Lords, the detainees in the UK reached a position of legal certainty earlier.

423 See pp 202–3.

is subject to annual renewal, by order,[424] and the sections have been renewed since 2005 on a yearly basis.[425] The scheme draws a fundamental distinction between derogating and non-derogating orders. Non-derogating orders, imposing obligations short of detention, such as curfews, semi-house arrest and tagging, were considered not to breach Art 5, and therefore no derogation order was thought to be needed. The non-derogating control orders scheme thus appeared to be less invasive of human rights than Part 4. At their most stringent, however, control orders can allow for detention without trial (either full house arrest or in prison) and would require a derogation; they are termed derogating control orders. However, the current lack of a derogation should not be viewed, as the discussion below reveals, as signalling that the current non-derogating orders applied under the 2005 Act are compatible with the European Convention on Human Rights, Art 5.

The PTA, like the ATCSA Part 4, creates a scheme operating on a low standard of proof as regards non-derogating control orders – reasonable suspicion. No criminal trial, or indeed civil action, is needed in order to subject an individual to the sanctions represented by the non-derogating orders. The subjection of persons to control orders broadens the definition of terrorism in effect since it places a number of persons in the position of being terrorist suspects and makes them subject to a range of sanctions – via control orders – despite the fact that they may not themselves fall within the s 1 TA definition since they have not themselves taken part in terrorist activity, and that only a very low level of proof is needed that they are in any way associated with terrorism. Therefore miscarriages of justice may occur. The 2005 measures thus remain controversial in human rights terms, since, like Part 4 ATCSA, they rely on interfering proactively with the liberty of suspects before any offences have been committed, or where it appears difficult to prove that they have been committed.

A control order can be viewed as a last resort measure, necessary to address the threat from an individual where prosecution is not possible and, in the case of a foreign national, where it is not possible to deport him or her due to the UK's international human rights obligations (in particular, where there is a real risk of torture in the receiving country). Before making, or applying for the making of, a control order, a duty is placed on the Secretary of State under s 8(2) PTA to consult the chief officer of the police force as to whether there is evidence available that could realistically be used for the purposes of a prosecution of the individual for an offence relating to

---

424 Under s 13(2) PTA The Secretary of State may, by order made by statutory instrument –

(a) repeal sections 1 to 9;

(b) at any time revive those sections for a period not exceeding one year; or

(c) provide that those–

(i) are not to expire at the time when they would otherwise expire under sub-section (1) or in accordance with an order under this sub-section; but (ii) are to continue in force after that time for a period not exceeding one year.

425 On 1 February 2007 the Home Secretary laid before both Houses the draft Prevention of Terrorism Act 2005 (Continuance in force of sections 1 to 9) Order 2007, along with an Explanatory Memorandum ('EM').

terrorism.[426] Under s 8(4) it is the duty of the chief officer to ensure that investigation of the individual's conduct with a view to his prosecution for an offence relating to terrorism is kept under review during the period that the order is in force against the individual. But, despite the provision of s 8 PTA, the possibility arises that the scheme is being used in *preference* to prosecuting where, especially under a proscription offence or ss 1 or 5 of the 2006 Act, a prosecution might have been feasible. The stated intention is that the police and the Control Order Review Group (CORG) keep the issue of prosecution in control order cases under continuous review. However, the judgment of the High Court in the case of *E* (below) demonstrated that this process of internal review is inadequate. Mr Justice Beatson said in his judgment, 'a process which simply relied on the chief officer of the Police force or the Police officer present at the relevant meeting of CORG to bring matters forward is insufficient'.[427]

In a fashion typical of the UK counter-terrorist response the scheme is over-broad in human rights terms and arguably counter-productive in security terms. But the control orders scheme has not been applied, as it would have been under a more authoritarian regime, to a large number of persons. It has been applied only to a tiny minority of terrorist suspects. Control orders were sought against the ten people who had been detained under the 2001 Act in March 2005. The orders of eight of the ten were revoked in August 2005 and they were then either detained pending deportation, on bail pending deportation, or they then left the country. There are currently 15 control orders made by the Secretary of State in operation. Nine of these are in respect of foreign nationals; the other six are in respect of British citizens.

The control orders scheme

Section 1(1) PTA defines a 'control order': 'In this Act "control order" means an order against an individual that imposes obligations on him for purposes connected with protecting members of the public from a risk of terrorism.' The orders can be applied to British and non-British suspects alike. As indicated, the PTA scheme creates derogating and non-derogating orders. The derogating orders can create sanctions that include detention without trial. A derogating obligation is an obligation placed on an individual

---

426 Section 8 Criminal investigations after making of control order:

(1) This section applies where it appears to the Secretary of State –

    (a) that the involvement in terrorism-related activity of which an individual is suspected may have involved the commission of an offence relating to terrorism; and

    (b) that the commission of that offence is being or would fall to be investigated by a police force.

(2) Before making, or applying for the making of, a control order against the individual, the Secretary of State must consult the chief officer of the police force about whether there is evidence available that could realistically be used for the purposes of a prosecution of the individual for an offence relating to terrorism.

(3) If a control order is made against the individual the Secretary of State must inform the chief officer of the police force that the control order has been made and that sub-section (4) applies.

(4) It shall then be the duty of the chief officer to secure that the investigation of the individual's conduct with a view to his prosecution for an offence relating to terrorism is kept under review throughout the period during which the control order has effect.

427 [2007] EWHC 33 (Admin) para 292.

which is incompatible with his right to liberty under Art 5 of the European Convention on Human Rights, but which falls within the ambit of an order designating a derogation from the Convention pursuant to s 14(1) of the Human Rights Act. The other type of control order – a non-derogating order – is one which is judged by the Secretary of State not to be incompatible with the suspect's rights under Art 5.

Thus, control orders theoretically fall into the categories of derogating control orders and non-derogating ones; the distinction between derogating ones and non-derogating is not made in the Act – a non-derogating order is merely defined as one made by the Secretary of State, rather than a court. This is an important distinction; it is not necessarily clear which orders would require a derogation. If on legal advice the Secretary of State made a control order, and it was found later on appeal against it that it in fact required a derogation and so should have been made by a court, the person concerned would nevertheless been subject to the order in breach of Art 5 for a period of time. This situation has arisen in the United Kingdom, as discussed below.

Under s 1(3) a control order made against an individual can impose *any* obligations that the Secretary of State or the court considers necessary for purposes connected with preventing or restricting involvement by that individual in terrorism-related activity. This is in itself a very broad term that is afforded a very wide definition in s 1(9) as any one or more of the following:

(a) the commission, preparation or instigation of acts of terrorism;
(b) conduct which facilitates the commission, preparation or instigation of such acts, or which is intended to do so;
(c) conduct which gives encouragement to the commission, preparation or instigation of such acts, or which is intended to do so;
(d) conduct which gives support or assistance to individuals who are known or believed to be involved in terrorism-related activity; and for the purposes of this sub-section it is immaterial whether the acts of terrorism in question are specific acts of terrorism or acts of terrorism generally.

These measures can be applied to any individual, irrespective of nationality, and whatever the nature of the terrorist activity.

Control orders are preventative. They place one or more obligations upon an individual in order to prevent, restrict or disrupt involvement in terrorism-related activity. A range of obligations can be imposed to address the risk viewed as posed by the individual concerned, including an 18-hour curfew, restrictions on the use of communication equipment; restrictions on the people that the individual can associate with; travel restrictions; electronic tagging; the suspect's house can be subject to a search at any time; communication with any person may be disallowed unless approved; prohibitions are placed on electronic communication.

The nature of the obligations imposed by the orders means that other Convention Articles apart from Art 5 are also clearly implicated, in particular Arts 8, 10 and 11 – since privacy, communication and association are affected. Obviously, para 2 of those Articles could be invoked, but the interference would only be justified if the order satisfied the demands of necessity and proportionality in those paragraphs.[428] The extent of the interference created by a number of the orders might make that difficult.

---

428 See discussion of Art 10 in Chapter 2, pp 92–96.

Non-derogating control orders

The crucial distinction between derogating and non-derogating orders is that the latter are made initially by the Secretary of State who obtains, as explained below, permission from the court, without notice to the controlee. The Secretary of State is also given power to revoke or modify such an order. Under s 2 PTA the Home Secretary can make a control order that imposes non-derogating obligations (obligations that apparently do not require a derogation from Art 5, guaranteeing the fundamental right to liberty, or from any other Convention guarantee)[429] if he has reasonable grounds for suspecting that an individual is or has been involved in 'terrorist-related activity' (s 1(9)). As indicated above this is a very broad concept. It means that the person in question has engaged in some activity of a facilitative or supportive nature in relation to a group that itself falls within s 1 TA. It does not demand that the individual himself or herself falls within s 1. It could include, for example, writing a letter expressing approval of the aims of a group falling within s 1 TA operating abroad. Section 2(4) provides that a non-derogating control order has effect for 12 months and may be renewed on one or more occasion. Sub-section 1(9) provides:

> It shall be immaterial, for the purposes of determining what obligations may be imposed by a control order made by the Secretary of State, whether the involvement in terrorism-related activity to be prevented or restricted by the obligations is connected with matters to which the Secretary of State's grounds for suspicion relate.

Section 7 provides that a controlled person can apply to have a non-derogating control order revoked or modified if he considers that there has been a change of circumstances affecting the order.

Derogating orders

Section 4 provides that in the case of an order imposing derogating obligations, the order must be made by the *court* on an application by the Secretary of State, as discussed below. Section 7 makes provision permitting the Secretary of State or the controlled person to apply to the court for the revocation or modification of a derogating control order. Section 4(8) provides that a derogating control order ceases to have effect after six months, unless renewed.

Derogating orders – in particular imposing house arrest or detention – are viewed as incompatible with the right to liberty, and possibly also with other Articles, and so would require at the least a derogation from Art 5. A derogation has not yet been sought to allow for the reintroduction of detention without trial, but given the ruling of the House of Lords in *A and Others* that a state of emergency was in being in 2004, and taking account of the London bombing in 2005, the courts would probably accept that a state of emergency is still in being. Thus a derogating order, if sought, would not be struck down on that basis, but there would still be a problem in demonstrating

---

429 See discussion of Art 5 in Chapter 2, pp 51–59.

proportionality. If house arrest, or detention in prison was imposed, the impact of the derogating control orders on liberty would still have to be proportionate to the exigencies of the security situation under Art 15 ECHR.[430] The decision of the House of Lords in *A and Others*, above, indicates that the courts would be unlikely to accept that such control orders could be justified since the detention imposed would presumably be, in effect, indefinite and the evidence would not have been tested to a high standard or proof.

The term 'terrorist-related activity' is even broader than the terms used in Part 4 ATCSA; therefore someone could be detained on a very flimsy basis. No mention is made of Al-Qaeda, but it can be assumed that if derogating control orders are imposed, once a derogation order has been sought, they could be applied only to Al-Qaeda members or supporters, or linked groups, since otherwise the demands of proportionality in Art 15 could not be met, as demonstrated in the Court of Appeal judgment on Part 4 ATCSA in *A and Others*. If they were applied only to such persons, British and non-British citizens alike, they would be afforded a rational connection with the basis for seeking the derogation. On the other hand, the PTA, like Part 4, taken at face value, is over-broad in allowing for the detention of persons who have no connection with the current emergency.

The scheme applies to British and non-British citizens alike and so does not create discrimination on grounds of nationality, but that would not necessarily mean that it was found to be proportionate to the aims pursued. The fact that at the present time, and for the past two years, control orders, not including detention, are being used could arguably be taken to imply that the more draconian measure of detention is not needed since the security situation is currently being addressed without resorting to detention without trial. Further, the 'state of emergency' assessment would clearly be open to future revision if Al-Qaeda's operational effectiveness appeared to diminish, and if that occurred it would also affect the assessment of proportionality. In this respect it should be noted that in its notification of derogation from Art 15, in relation to Part 4 ATCSA, the UK Government pledged that the derogation would be withdrawn as soon as it was no longer necessary. No derogation has now been in place for over two years.

At the present time, as discussed below, non-derogating orders are being applied that have been found by the courts to breach Art 5 due to their cumulative effect on liberty. The introduction of derogating control orders, as opposed to orders breaching Art 5, but purporting to be non-derogating, would place the obligation to ensure proportionality on a clearer legal basis under Art 15, taking s 3 HRA into account. It would also allow the order to receive a higher level of judicial scrutiny. It would therefore be preferable in one sense since the government would have to be open about its intention to breach Art 5, and would have to justify the derogation. But the objections of principle on human rights grounds discussed would still remain since the PTA derogating orders scheme has many of the hallmarks of the Part 4 scheme.

---

430 Art 15 provides: '(1) In time of war or other public emergency threatening the life of the nation any High Contracting Party may take measures derogating from its obligations under this Convention to the extent strictly required by the exigencies of the situation, provided that such measures are not inconsistent with its other obligations under international law . . .'

Role of the court in making a derogating order

The role of the court in respect of a derogating control order is set out in s 4. This order is made, not by the Secretary of State, but by the court on an application by the Secretary of State. That application is made at a preliminary hearing, which may be heard in the absence of, and without notice to, the suspect. Section 4(3) provides:

> At the preliminary hearing, the court may make a control order against the individual in question if it appears to the court –
>
> (a) that there is material which (if not disproved) is capable of being relied on by the court as establishing that the individual is or has been involved in terrorism-related activity;
>
> (b) that there are reasonable grounds for believing that the imposition of obligations on that individual is necessary for purposes connected with protecting members of the public from a risk of terrorism;
>
> (c) that the risk arises out of, or is associated with, a public emergency in respect of which there is a designated derogation from the whole or a part of Article 5 of the Human Rights Convention; and
>
> (d) that the obligations that there are reasonable grounds for believing should be imposed on the individual are or include derogating obligations of a description set out for the purposes of the designated derogation in the designation order.

The preliminary hearing is followed by a full hearing at which the court may confirm, modify or revoke the order. Section 4(7) provides:

> At the full hearing, the court may confirm the control order (with or without modifications) only if –
>
> (a) it is satisfied, on the balance of probabilities, that the controlled person is an individual who is or has been involved in terrorism-related activity;
>
> (b) it considers that the imposition of obligations on the controlled person is necessary for purposes connected with protecting members of the public from a risk of terrorism;
>
> (c) it appears to the court that the risk is one arising out of, or is associated with, a public emergency in respect of which there is a designated derogation from the whole or a part of Article 5 of the Human Rights Convention; and
>
> (d) the obligations to be imposed by the order or (as the case may be) by the order as modified are or include derogating obligations of a description set out for the purposes of the designated derogation in the designation order.

Thus indefinite detention could be imposed on the civil standard, if a derogation was in place, and the derogation was in accord with the demands of Art 15. This scheme is an improvement on Part 4 since court approval of the order is needed and the standard of proof is higher. But the proceedings described below fall far short, in terms of due process, of a criminal trial. So the safeguard of the court hearing may not be sufficient to guard against miscarriages of justice.

Court supervision of non-derogating control orders

Permission is needed by a court to make a non-derogating order, under s 3(1) PTA, unless the order is urgent or the person was detained under Part 4. If an order is made without the court's permission, the Secretary of State must immediately (within seven days) apply to the court, and the function of the court on the application is to consider whether the decision of the Secretary of State to make the order that he did was obviously flawed (s 3(3)). Section 3(2) of the PTA makes provision for permission by the court when the control order made against the respondent is made with permission. Section 11(2) PTA provides that, 'The court is the appropriate tribunal for the purposes of s 7 of the Human Rights Act 1998 in relation to proceedings all or any part of which call a control order decision or derogation matter into question.'

Under s 3(2) when the Secretary of State makes an application for permission to make a non-derogating control order against an individual,

(a) the function of the court is to consider whether the Secretary of State's decision that there are grounds to make that order is obviously flawed;

(b) the court may give that permission unless it determines that the decision is obviously flawed; and

(c) if it gives permission, the court must give directions for a hearing in relation to the order as soon as reasonably practicable after it is made.

The permission proceedings can occur, under s 3(5):

(a) in the absence of the individual in question;

(b) without his having been notified of the application or reference; and

(c) without his having been given an opportunity (if he was aware of the application or reference) of making an representations to the court; but this section is not to be construed as limiting the matters about which rules of court may be made in relation to the consideration of such an application or reference.

Since the court can only refuse permission when the decision is 'obviously flawed', it is unlikely at that stage that permission will be withheld. Under s 3(6), if the court determines that the decision of the Secretary of State to make a non-derogating control order against the controlled person was obviously flawed, it must quash the order. If it determines that that decision was not obviously flawed, but that a decision of the Secretary of State to impose a particular obligation by that order was obviously flawed, it must quash that obligation but confirm the order. The use of the term 'obviously flawed' makes it unlikely that a control order would be refused at the permission stage.

Once the order is confirmed a hearing must be ordered (s 3(2)) by the court giving permission (s 3(10)). At the hearing under s 3(10) the function of the court is to determine whether any of the following decisions of the Secretary of State was flawed '(a) his decision that the requirements of section 2(1)(a) and (b) were satisfied for the making of the order; and (b) his decisions on the imposition of each of the obligations imposed by the order'.

In making these determinations the court must apply the principles applicable on an application for judicial review (s 3(11)). So s 3(10) requires the court, when performing this function, to consider two questions - whether the decision of the Secretary of State in relation to the making of the control order was flawed *and* whether the decision to impose particular obligations was flawed. As discussed in Part 2 of this chapter, the court is required to follow a special procedure, involving closed material and the use of a special advocate (SA),[431] that is very similar to the procedure applicable to proceedings before the Special Immigration Appeals Commission (SIAC).[432]

The special rules are contained in Part 76 of the CPR.[433] Under them, the Secretary of State must apply to the court for permission to withhold the closed material from

---

431 The schedule to the Act enables special rules of court to be made in respect of control order proceedings. Paragraph 4(3) states that such rules must secure –

   (a) that in control order proceedings and relevant appeal proceedings the Secretary of State is required (subject to rules made under the following paragraphs) to disclose all relevant material;

   (b) that the Secretary of State has the opportunity to make an application to the relevant court for permission not to disclose relevant material otherwise than to that court and persons appointed under paragraph 7;

   (c) that such an application is always considered in the absence of every relevant party to the proceedings and of his legal representative (if he has one);

   (d) that the relevant court is required to give permission for material not to be disclosed where it considers that the disclosure of the material would be contrary to the public interest;

   (e) that, where permission is given by the relevant court not to disclose material, it must consider requiring the Secretary of State to provide the relevant party and his legal representative (if he has one) with a summary of the material;

   (f) that the relevant court is required to ensure that such a summary does not contain information or other material the disclosure of which would be contrary to the public interest;

   (g) that provision satisfying the requirements of sub-paragraph (4) applies where the Secretary of State does not have the relevant court's permission to withhold relevant material from a relevant party to the proceedings or his legal representative (if he has one), or is required to provide a summary of such material to that party or his legal representative.

   (4) The provision that satisfies the requirements of this sub-paragraph is provision which, in a case where the Secretary of State elects not to disclose the relevant material or (as the case may be) not to provide the summary, authorises the relevant court –

   (a) if it considers that the relevant material or anything that is required to be summarised might be of assistance to a relevant party in relation to a matter under consideration by that court; and

   (b) in any other case, to ensure that the Secretary of State does not rely in the proceedings on the material or (as the case may be) on what is required to be summarised.

432 See pp 1429–30 above.

433 The special rules contained in Part 76 of the CPR, r 76.2 require the court to give effect to the overriding objective in such a way as to 'ensure that information is not disclosed contrary to the public interest'. For the purposes of Part 76, the public interest is defined by Rule 76.1(4): '. . . disclosure is made contrary to the public interest if it is made contrary to the interests of national security, the international relations of the United Kingdom, the detection and prevention of crime, or in any other circumstances where disclosure is likely to harm the public interest.' Rule 76.22 enables the court to conduct hearings in private and to exclude the controlee and his representatives from all or part of the hearing. Rule 76.24 describes the functions of the Special Advocate. Rule 76.26 modifies the general rules of evidence and enables the court to 'receive evidence that would not but for this rule be admissible in a court of law': see r 76.26(4). Rules 76.28 and 76.29 set out the procedure for dealing with closed material. Rule 76.29(6) states that: 'Where the court gives permission to the Secretary of State to withhold closed material, the court must – (a) consider whether to direct the

the person controlled or his legal representatives, and file a statement explaining his reasons for withholding that material. The closed material is then considered by the SA. If the SA challenges the need to withhold all or any of the closed material, the court must arrange the hearing to determine the issue (r 76.29), unless the Secretary of State and SA agree that the court may decide the issue without a hearing. Evidence can be received that would not normally be admissible in a court of law.

These provisions provide, on their face, only a thin veneer of judicial supervision. The level of supervision and its compliance with Art 6(1) was considered in *Secretary of State v MB*.[434] The Secretary of State had applied to the court without notice to MB under s 3(1)(a) PTA for permission to make a non-derogating control order against him. Ouseley J had granted that permission under s 3(2)(b) PTA, subject to some minor amendments that he required by way of clarification. A range of obligations were imposed by the order, including restrictions on residence and movement. MB had to surrender his passport and submit to searches of his home.[435]

Judge Sullivan found, under s 3(10) PTA, in relation to a non-derogating control order made under s 2(1) of the Act, that the procedures in s 3 of the Act relating to the supervision by the court of non-derogating control orders made by the Secretary of State were incompatible with the respondents' right to a fair hearing under Art 6(1). He therefore made a declaration of the incompatibility under s 4(2) HRA 1998, but decided under section 3(13) of the Act that the control order was to continue in force.

Secretary of State to serve a summary of that material on the relevant party or his legal representative; but (b) ensure that no such summary contains information or other material the disclosure of which would be contrary to the public interest.'

434 [2006] EWHC 1000, [2006] HRLR 29, [2006] 8 CL 108.
435 The order stated:

(1) You will reside at [address given] ('the residence') and shall give the Home Office at least seven days' prior notice of any change of residence.

(2) You shall report in person to your local police station (the location of which will be notified in writing to you at the imposition of this order) each day at a time to be notified in writing by your contact officer, details to be provided in writing upon service of the order.

(3) You must surrender your passport, identity card or any other travel document to a police officer or persons authorised by the Secretary of State within 24 hours. You shall not apply for or have in your possession any passport, identity card, travel document(s) or travel ticket which would enable you to travel outside the UK.

(4) You must not leave the UK.

(5) You are prohibited from entering or being present at any of the following:-

(a) any airport or sea port;
(b) any part of a railway station that provides access to an international rail service.

(6) You must permit entry to police officers and persons authorised by the Secretary of State, on production of identification, at any time to verify your presence at the residence and/or to ensure that you can comply with and are complying with the obligations imposed by the control order. Such monitoring may include but is not limited to:

(a) a search of the residence;
(b) removal of any item to ensure compliance with the remainder of the obligations in these orders; and
(c) the taking of your photograph.

In the Court of Appeal[436] the Secretary of State appealed against the decision that the procedures in s 3 PTA, relating to the supervision by the Court of non-derogating control orders made by the Secretary of State, were incompatible with the rights of the respondent to a fair hearing under the HRA, Sched 1, Part I, Art 6(1), on the basis that the decision of the Home Secretary could only be quashed if it was obviously flawed. It was accepted by both sides that the control order interfered with MB's civil rights and that, if the PTA was to comply with the European Convention on Human Rights, it had to be possible for MB to challenge the validity of the control order by legal proceedings which satisfied the requirements of Art 6 of the Convention.

It was clear to the Court that the justification for the obligations imposed on MB lay in the closed material. The SA did not challenge the Secretary of State's application to withhold the closed material, so there was no need for a hearing under r 76.29. The SA also agreed with counsel for the Secretary of State, that it would not be possible to serve a summary of the closed material on MB or his legal advisers which would not contain information or other material the disclosure of which would be contrary to the public interest. So MB was not provided with a summary of the material disclosing the basis of the case against him. The Court said that it was arguable that, by giving a remedy in civil proceedings for infringement of the Convention rights, the HRA had converted those rights into civil rights, so that Art 6 applied to them, but in any event it was clear that the control order adversely affected MB's civil rights, and therefore that the proceedings involved the determination of his civil rights and obligations so as to engage Art 6(1).[437]

The Court found that s 11(2) had to be interpreted, so far as possible, in a manner which was compatible with the Convention rights under s 3 HRA. It was found that s 11(2) required the court, in so far as it was able, to give effect to MB's Convention rights having regard to the state of affairs that existed at the time that the court reached its decision. It was further found that s 3(10) could not be read so as to restrict the court, when addressing a human rights issue, to a consideration of whether, when he made his initial decision, the Secretary of State had reasonable grounds for doing so.

Sullivan J had considered that Art 6 required that the court should carry out a 'full merits review' of the justification for the control order and its terms. On his reading of s 3(10) that was not possible. But the Court of Appeal did not consider that the terms of s 3(10), when read in the light of s 11(2), restricted the court to a standard of review falling short of that required to satisfy Art 6. The Court found that it had all the powers it required, including the power to hear oral evidence and to order cross-examination of witnesses, to enable it to substitute its own judgment for that of the decision maker, if that was what Art 6 required. The Court noted that s 3 HRA requires that s 3(10) and s 11(2) of the PTA be interpreted, if possible, in a manner that enables the court to carry out a review of the Secretary of State's decision that complies with the requirements of Art 6. So far as the standard of review is concerned, the Court saw no difficulty in reading those sections so as to produce that result.[438]

---

436 [2006] EWCA Civ 1140; (2006) 156 NLJ 1288; (2006) 150 SJLB 1055.
437 See pp 1339–42 above.
438 At para 48.

It was not necessary, it was found, in order to determine the appeal, for the Court to express a view as to the standard of review required when considering the decisions of the Secretary of State when making a non-derogating control order. Nevertheless, since the matter had been debated before the Court at length, the Court decided that it should not be left unresolved. Sullivan J had held that he was bound by the decision of the Court of Appeal in *A v Secretary of State for the Home Department*[439] to hold that proceedings under s 3 PTA did not amount to the determination of a criminal charge for the purposes of Art 6. He held, however, that they came as close to this as it was possible to be. Counsel for MB argued that the judge was right to hold that they came very close to being criminal proceedings, and reserved the right to argue that they were criminal proceedings if the case went to the House of Lords. In this approach he was supported by JUSTICE, who intervened by written submissions which 'reserved' the question of whether control order proceedings are criminal proceedings under Art 6. The Court of Appeal stated their view, however, that the proceedings under s 3 PTA did not involve the determination of a criminal charge.

The Court said that it is a pre-condition to the making of a control order under s 3 that there must be reasonable suspicion that the controlled person has been engaged in terrorism-related activity, and that the obligations that may be imposed under a non-derogating control order, while falling short of infringing Art 5 of the Convention, nonetheless could impact severely on both civil and Convention rights. It was argued on behalf of the appellant that, in the light of these factors, the Art 6 requirement of a trial before 'an independent and impartial tribunal established by law' could only be satisfied if the court made its own independent assessment of whether the requirements for imposing the control order were satisfied. This was the approach adopted by s 4 in relation to a derogating control order, and a similar approach, it was argued on behalf of MB, was required in respect of the court's role under s 3. It was argued on the other hand, on behalf of the Secretary of State that his decision was essentially an executive one governed by public law, and that Art 6 was only engaged because the decision incidentally had the effect of determining civil rights. The Secretary of State, it was argued, was the decision maker, and the role of the court was merely to review the legality of his decision, according him a substantial measure of discretion, having regard to the fact that the subject matter of the decision was national security.

The Court noted that s 3(10)(a) PTA requires the court to consider whether the decision of the Secretary of State that there were reasonable grounds for suspecting that the subject of the order was involved in terrorism-related activity was flawed. It pointed out that involvement in terrorist-related activity, as defined by s 1(9) PTA, is likely to constitute a serious criminal offence, although it will not necessarily do so. That suggested, it was found, that when reviewing a decision by the Secretary of State to make a control order, the court must make up its own mind as to whether there were reasonable grounds for the necessary suspicion. The Court found that whether there are reasonable grounds for suspicion is an objective question of fact and it was not possible to see how the court could review the decision of the Secretary of State without itself deciding whether the facts relied upon by the Secretary of State amounted to reasonable grounds for suspecting that the subject of the control order was or had been involved in terrorism-related activity.

439 [2004] EWCA Civ 324; [2004] QB 335.

However, the Court thought that somewhat different considerations would apply in respect of the second element in the Secretary of State's decision. Section 3(10) requires the court to review the decision of the Secretary of State that it was necessary, for purposes connected with protecting the public from a risk of terrorism, to make the control order. The Court noted that whether it was necessary to impose any particular obligation on an individual in order to protect the public from the risk of terrorism involved the customary test of proportionality. The Court held that a degree of deference had to be paid to the decisions taken by the Secretary of State.[440] However, the Court found that there would be scope for the court to give intense scrutiny to the necessity for each of the obligations imposed on an individual under a control order, and that it must do so; some obligations could be particularly onerous or intrusive and, in such cases, the court, it found, should explore alternative means of achieving the same result.

The Court also considered the standard of proof involved, and found that considering whether reasonable suspicion of involvement in terrorist-related activities was established would involve considering a matrix of alleged facts, some of which were clear beyond reasonable doubt, some of which could be established on the balance of probability and some that were based only on circumstances giving rise to suspicion. The task of the Court, it was found, was to consider whether that matrix amounted to reasonable grounds for suspicion, and that exercise differed from that of deciding whether a fact has been established according to a specified standard of proof. It was, the Court said, the procedure for determining whether reasonable grounds for suspicion were in existence that had to be fair if Art 6 was to be satisfied.

The Court said that the impact of the provisions in the PTA for the use of closed material was the aspect of the case that was of particular concern since to deny to a party to legal proceedings the right to know the details of the case against him was, on the face of it, fundamentally at odds with the requirements of a fair trial. However, the Court noted that both Strasbourg and domestic authorities had accepted that there were circumstances where the use of closed material was permissible.[441] The Court

---

440 At para 64 the Court said: 'it is appropriate to accord such deference in matters relating to state security has long been recognised, both by the courts of this country and by the Strasbourg court, see for instance: *Secretary of State for the Home Dept v Rehman* [2001]UKHL 47; [2003] AC 153; *The Republic of Ireland v The United Kingdom* (1978) 2 EHRR 25'.

441 At paras 71–73 the Court said: 'In *Chahal v UK* (1996) 23 EHRR 413 at para 131, in the context of Arts 5(4) and 13, the ECtHR observed: "The Court recognises that the use of confidential material may be unavoidable where national security is at stake. This does not mean, however, that the national authorities can be free from effective control by the domestic courts whenever they choose to assert that national security and terrorism are involved. The Court attaches significance to the fact that, as the intervenors pointed out in connection with Article 13, in Canada a more effective form of judicial control has been developed in cases of this type . . . The confidentiality of security material is maintained by requiring such evidence to be examined in the absence of both the applicant and his or her representative. However, in those circumstances, their place is taken by a security-cleared counsel instructed by the court, who cross-examines the witnesses and generally assists the court to test the strength of the state's case. A summary of the evidence obtained by this procedure, with necessary deletions, is given to the applicant."' The Court noted that 'the procedure for closed material and the use of a special advocate was designed to accord with the model referred to in *Chahal*, which the ECtHR appeared to have approved. In *Tinnely & McElduff v UK* (1999) 27 EHRR 249, this time when considering whether there had been compliance with Article 6, the ECtHR referred to this procedure, as provided for in the Special Immigration Appeals Commission Bill (see paragraph 52).'

found therefore that the Strasbourg court had accepted that there could be circumstances where material evidence need not be disclosed in order to satisfy the requirements of Art 6 or Art 13. The Court also accepted that it was bound by the same finding of the Court of Appeal. The Court went on to find that while reliance on closed material was permissible, this could only be on the basis that appropriate safeguards against the prejudice that this may cause to the controlled person are in place. The provisions of the PTA for the use of a special advocate, and of the rules of court made pursuant to para 4 of the Schedule to the PTA, were found to constitute appropriate safeguards.[442] Article 6 of the Convention would not, it was found, automatically require disclosure of the evidence of the grounds for suspicion. It was found that Judge Sullivan had erred in holding that the provisions for review by the court of the making of a non-derogating control order by the Secretary of State did not comply with the requirements of Art 6. Therefore the appeal was allowed so that the validity of the order could be reconsidered, adopting an approach in accordance with the judgment.

Incompatibility of the non-derogating control orders regime with Article 5?

The package of measures applied to persons subject to control under non-derogating orders is so stringent that the Parliamentary Joint Committee on Human Rights considers that the orders breach the fundamental right to liberty under Art 5 ECHR. This has now been found to be the case in the Court of Appeal. The issue was raised in *Secretary of State for the Home Dept v JJ, KK, GG, HH, NN, LL*.[443] Judge Sullivan found in the High Court that the restrictions were 'the antithesis of liberty and equivalent to imprisonment'. He said 'Their [the suspects'] liberty to live a normal life within their residences is so curtailed as to be non-existent for all practical purposes.' He found:

> . . . a basic distinction is to be drawn between mere restrictions on liberty of movement and the deprivation of liberty. The former are governed by Article 2 of Protocol no 4 and do not amount to a breach of Article 5. This has been repeatedly spelt out by the European Court of Human Rights in cases such as *Guzzardi v Italy*.[444] Secondly, the distinction is one merely of degree or intensity of restrictions, not of nature or substance. Thirdly, the court must start with the concrete or actual situation of the individual concerned and take account of a range of criteria, such as the type, duration, effects and manner of implementation of the measure in question. Fourthly, account must be taken of the cumulative effect of the various restrictions. All these principles flow from the cases cited above.[445]

Relying on *Guzzardi*, he found that the control orders breached Art 5(1) ECHR. The Court found as a preliminary issue that the obligations imposed by those orders were

---

442 At para 86.
443 [2006] EWHC 1623 (Admin), High Court of Justice Queen's Bench Division Administrative Court, 28th June, 2006.
444 [1980] 3 EHRR 333. He also cited: *Ashingdane v United Kingdom* [1985] 7 EHRR 528 and *HM v Switzerland* [26 February 2002] Appl No. 39187/98.
445 At para 35 of the judgment.

so severe that they amounted to deprivation of liberty contrary to Sched 1, Part I, Art 5 of the 1998 Act. He found that they were in effect derogating control orders, that the Secretary of State had no power to make, not non-derogating ones. Therefore the government should have sought a derogation from Art 5(1). As it had not, the orders were incompatible with Art 5. The judge quashed the orders, holding that s 3(12) of the 2005 Act gave him power to do so, as the orders were made without jurisdiction and were nullities

The Court of Appeal upheld this finding.[446] The Secretary of State appealed on the issue of whether the judge was correct to hold that the obligations imposed by the orders amounted to a deprivation of liberty contrary to Sched 1, Part I, Art 5 of the 1998 Act and, if so, whether it was appropriate to quash the orders rather than to quash or modify the obligations. The Court noted that the appellants were obliged to remain within their residences, which in each case consisted of a one-bedroom flat, at all times save for a period of six hours. Visitors had to provide their names, addresses, dates of birth, and photo identification to the Home Office. Their residences were subject to spot searches by police and, when permitted to leave their homes, they were restricted to confined urban areas. The Court found that Judge Sullivan's decision that the cumulative effect of the orders amounted to a deprivation of liberty contrary to Sched 1, Part I, Art 5 of the 1998 Act was correct.

It was found that he had properly taken as his starting point the physical restriction of confining the appellants for 18 hours a day to small flats. He had then taken into account a range of other material factors that interfered with their normal lives, including the effect of the physical restraints in the context of the restrictions that applied when they were allowed to leave their residences. After that, he had considered the extent to which those restrictions would prevent an individual from pursuing the life of his choice, taking account of *Guzzardi*.[447] It was found that he had been right to quash the orders rather than to modify them. It was found that it was questionable whether the provisions of s 3(10) and 3(12) of the 2005 Act were designed to deal with a challenge to a control order on the ground that it was *ultra vires* by virtue of infringing Sched 1, Part I, Art 5(1) of the 1998 Act. However, it was found that the judge was correct to conclude that he had jurisdiction to quash the orders.

A similar conclusion was reached in *Secretary of State for the Home Dept v E*[448] in which the *JJ* judgment was followed. In 2005 the Home Secretary made a control order against E under powers in the Prevention of Terrorism Act 2005 (the PTA). The order required E to reside at a particular address and to remain within the residence between 7 pm and 7 am, prohibited unauthorised visitors to the residence or prearranged meetings elsewhere, and prohibited him from having a mobile telephone, or equipment capable of connecting to the internet.

The High Court heard evidence both in an open hearing and a closed one. It concluded that in the light of the material considered in the open hearing, in particular references

---

446 The Court of Appeal confirmed Judge Sullivan's findings as to the breach of Art 5 on 1 August 2006, *Secretary of State for the Home Dept v JJ* (2006) EWCA 1141; (2006) HRLR 38; [2006] 3 WLR 866.

447 *Guzzardi v Italy* (A/39) (1981) 3 EHRR 333.

448 [2007] EWHC 33 (Admin).

to E and his activities in judgments of the Belgian courts, the Secretary of State had reasonable grounds for suspecting that E was a senior terrorist recruiter and facilitator with a wide range of contacts, and had been involved in terrorism-related activity.

The Court found that the cumulative effect of the curfew and the other obligations in the control order, in particular the requirement that all visitors to E's home and all pre-arranged meetings by him outside his home be approved in advance, deprived E of his liberty in breach of Art 5 of the Convention. E's 12-hour curfew was a major restriction on his liberty of movement, but did not *in itself*, it was found, constitute a deprivation of his liberty. In looking at the cumulative effect of the restrictions in the control order, the Court followed the approach of the Court of Appeal in *Home Office v JJ and Others*. On behalf of E and his family it was argued that the decisions to make and to maintain the control order were flawed on a number of other grounds. The Court found that the provisions in the PTA empowering the making of control orders did not violate the ECHR's requirement of 'legal certainty'. It was also found that in making the control order the Home Secretary had not breached his statutory duty under s 8 PTA to consult the police about the possibility of prosecuting E for terrorist offences.

The Home Office had received the Belgian judgments by January 2006 and had put them into the open evidence in September 2006, but the Court found that there had been no review of the possibility of prosecuting E in the light of them. For this reason, the decision thereafter to maintain E's control order was flawed. It was found that the Home Secretary was sufficiently informed about E's mental health and the health of his family and the impact of the obligations on them. The cumulative impact of the obligations on E's children was not found to violate or risk violating the children's rights under Art 3 ECHR. Initially there were delays in responding to requests for authorisations and variations to the control order by E and his family. However the Home Office on the whole responded to the requests without undue delay. The Home Office did not invite E and his family to make representations about the control order and the individual obligations after it was made in 2005 and before it was renewed in 2006. However, their solicitors made representations to the Home Office throughout the period of the control order. In view of the Court's decision on Art 5, and the failure to revisit the possibility of prosecuting E for terrorist offences in the light of the Belgian judgments, it was not necessary to decide whether in these circumstances the failure to invite E to make representations justified quashing the control order.

The Court found that since the PTA does not empower the Home Secretary to make a control order which has the effect of depriving a person of his liberty, the Court must quash the control order under the power given to it by s 3(12)(a) PTA. It would, Judge Beatson said, also have quashed the control order because of the failure to review the possibility of prosecuting E in the light of the Belgian judgments.

The same conclusion was reached in the High Court in *Secretary of State for the Home Dept v Rideh and J*.[449] It was found that Parliament, in passing the PTA, had decided that the Secretary of State should not have power to make a control order that had the effect of depriving a person of his liberty in breach of Art 5 of the

449 [2007] EWHC 804 (Admin).

Convention. It was found that the cumulative effect of the control order made against the respondent had deprived him of his liberty. Therefore the Secretary of State had had no power to make the order, and, following the findings of the Court of Appeal in *JJ and Others*,[450] the proper course was found therefore to be to quash the control order under the powers in s 3(12) (a) of the Act.

Use of evidence obtained by torture?

Introduction

The evidence on which the decision to impose a control order is based could arise from a number of sources. In *A and Others v Secretary of State for the Home Dept (No 2)*[451] (the 2005 'foreign torture material' judgment) the House of Lords had to consider whether, in deciding to impose detention under Part 4, the court could take account of evidence that might have derived from torture perpetrated in another country. Although Part 4 has been repealed, the decision is, it is argued, relevant to the decision to impose a control order, although the Lords did not expressly apply it to control order proceedings. But it can be assumed that the ruling applies in derogating and non-derogating control order proceedings since the proceedings are very similar in form to those in SIAC at issue in the Lords' judgment, and, following the Court of Appeal decision in *MB*, are deciding similar issues.

Clearly, SIAC, the courts in control order proceedings, and the Secretary of State are public authorities within the meaning of s 6 HRA, so they must not act incompatibly with a Convention right. The rights particularly at issue are: Art 3, which guarantees the absolute, non-derogable right not to be subjected to torture or to inhuman or degrading treatment,[452] Art 6(1) and Art 5(4). Article 5(4) is relevant if infringement of Art 5 is in issue, as it is in derogating control order proceedings, and as it has been found to be in non-derogating control order proceedings. Lord Hoffmann found in *Montgomery v HM Advocate, Coulter v HM Advocate*:[453]

> an accused who is convicted on evidence obtained from him by torture has not had a fair trial. But the breach of article 6(1) lies not in the use of torture (which is, separately, a breach of article 3) but in the reception of the evidence by the court for the purposes of determining the charge. If the evidence had been rejected, there would still have been a breach of article 3 but no breach of article 6(1).

---

450 [2006] 3 WLR 866 at para 27.
451 [2005] UKHL 71. For comment, see Rasiah, N, '*A v Secretary of State for the Home Department (No 2)*: Occupying the Moral High Ground?' (2006) 69(6) MLR 995–1005.
452 Lord Bingham noted that *Soering v United Kingdom* (1989) 11 EHRR 439, para 88 enshrined 'one of the fundamental values of the democratic societies making up the Council of Europe' and that the European Court had used such language on many occasions (*Aydin v Turkey* (1997) 25 EHRR 251, para 81).
453 [2003] 1 AC 641, p 649.

The admissibility of 'foreign torture evidence'

The specific question before the Lords was whether the Special Immigration Appeals Commission (SIAC), a superior court of record established by statute, when hearing an appeal under s 25 of the Anti-Terrorism, Crime and Security Act 2001 by a person certified and detained under ss 21 and 23 of that Act, could receive evidence which has or may have been procured by torture inflicted, in order to obtain evidence, by officials of a foreign state without the complicity of the British authorities? The Secretary of State agreed that such evidence could not be received in any case where the torture had been inflicted by or with the complicity of the British authorities. He also stated that it was not his intention to rely on, or present to SIAC or to the Administrative Court in relation to control orders, evidence which he knew or believed to have been obtained by a third country by torture.

The appellants argued that the common law forbids the admission of evidence obtained by the use of torture, and that it does so whether the product is a confession by a suspect or a defendant, and irrespective of where, by whom or on whose authority the torture was inflicted. They also argued for that conclusion under the European Convention. Lord Bingham, giving the opinion of the House, noted that different views had been expressed previously on whether, for the purposes of Art 6, the proceedings before SIAC should be regarded as civil or criminal. The parties agreed not to pursue that point since their challenge to their detention pursuant to the Secretary of State's certification fell within Art 5(4). That provision entitles anyone deprived of his liberty by arrest or detention to take proceedings by which the lawfulness of his detention shall be decided speedily by a court and his release ordered if the detention is not lawful. As the Lords noted, it is well established that such proceedings must satisfy the basic requirements of a fair trial.[454]

Lord Bingham noted that the European Court of Human Rights had consistently declined to articulate evidential rules to be applied in all member states, and had preferred to leave such rules to be governed by national law.[455] But he also noted that the Court had insisted on its responsibility to ensure that the proceedings, viewed overall on the particular facts, had been fair, and it had recognised that the way in which evidence has been obtained or used might be such as to render the proceedings unfair.[456]

The appellants also relied on the well-established principle that the words of a UK statute, passed after the date of a Treaty and dealing with the same subject-matter, must be construed, if they are reasonably capable of bearing such a meaning, as intended to carry out the Treaty obligation, and not to be inconsistent with it.[457] Further, as Lord Bingham noted, the duty of the courts under s 6 HRA is not to act incompatibly with a Convention right. He found that, to the extent that development of the common

---

454 *Garcia Alva v Germany* (2001) 37 EHRR 335; *R (West) v Parole Board, R (Smith) v Parole Board (No 2)* [2005] UKHL 1; [2005] 1 WLR 350.

455 *Schenk v Switzerland* (1988) 13 EHRR 242, para 46; *Ferrantelli and Santangelo v Italy* (1996) 23 EHRR 288, para 48; *Khan v United Kingdom* (2000) 31 EHRR 1016, para 34. This point is discussed further in Chapter 13, pp 1291–92.

456 He relied on *Saunders v United Kingdom* (1996) 23 EHRR 313, a case of compulsory questioning, and in *Teixeira de Castro v Portugal* (1998) 28 EHRR 101, para 39, a case of entrapment.

457 *Garland v British Rail Engineering Ltd* [1983] 2 AC 751, 771.

law is called for, such development should ordinarily be in harmony with the UK's international obligations.[458] The appellants argued that the European Convention is not to be interpreted in a vacuum, but by taking account of other international obligations to which member states are subject, as the European Court of Human Rights has in practice done.[459] They pointed out that the prohibition of torture enjoys the highest normative force recognised by international law.

The prohibition requires states not merely to refrain from authorising or conniving at torture but also to suppress and discourage the practice of torture and not to condone it. They pointed out that Art 15 of the Torture Convention[460] requires the exclusion of statements made as a result of torture as evidence in any proceedings.[461] It was pointed out that the rationale of the exclusionary rule in Art 15 lay not only in the general unreliability of evidence procured by torture, but also in its offensiveness to civilised values and its degrading effect on the administration of justice. The applicants also argued that on that basis measures directed to counter the grave dangers of international terrorism could not be permitted to undermine the international prohibition of torture. Lord Bingham accepted that the *jus cogens erga omnes* nature of the prohibition of torture requires member states to do more than just eschew the practice of torture.[462] He relied on *Kuwait Airways Corporation v Iraqi Airways Co (Nos 4 and 5)*,[463] in which the House of Lords refused recognition to conduct which represented a serious breach of international law.

Lord Bingham found that Art 15 of the Torture Convention could not be read, as counsel for the Secretary of State had submitted, as intended to apply only in criminal proceedings. He also found that it did not apply only where the state in whose jurisdiction the proceedings are held had inflicted or been complicit in the torture.[464] He noted that the European Court of Human Rights had emphasised that Art 3 of the European Convention is an absolute prohibition, not derogable in any circumstances, including in

---

458 At para 27.

459 Lord Bingham noted that the Court had in its decisions invoked a wide range of international instruments, including the United Nations Convention on the Rights of the Child 1989 and the Beijing Rules (*V v United Kingdom* (1999) 30 EHRR 121, paras 76–77), the Council of Europe Standard Minimum Rules for the Treatment of Prisoners (*S v Switzerland* (1991) 14 EHRR 670, para 48) and the 1975 Declaration (*Ireland v United Kingdom* (1978) 2 EHRR 25, para 167). Lord Bingham said that, pertinently to the appeals, the Court had repeatedly invoked the provisions of the Torture Convention: see, for example, *Aydin v Turkey* (1997) 25 EHRR 251, para 103; *Selmouni v France* (1999) 29 EHRR 403, para 97.

460 The Convention against Torture and Other Cruel, Inhuman or Degrading Treatment or Punishment which was adopted by the United Nations General Assembly on 10 December 1984 and entered into force on 26 June 1987. But state torture was already an international crime; Lord Browne-Wilkinson pointed this out in *R v Bow Street Metropolitan Stipendiary Magistrate, ex p Pinochet Ugarte (No 3)* [2000] 1 AC 147, p 198G.

461 It provides that any statement which is established to have been made as a result of torture or other cruel, inhuman or degrading treatment or punishment may not be invoked as evidence against the person concerned or against any other person in any proceedings. Each state Party shall ensure that any statement which is established to have been made as a result of torture shall not be invoked as evidence in any proceedings, except against a person accused of torture as evidence that the statement was made.

462 At para 34.

463 [2002] UKHL 19, [2002] 2 AC 883, paras 29, 117.

464 At para 35.

the context of terrorism.[465] He pointed out that that the Torture Convention, including Art 15, enjoys the same absolute quality.

The Secretary of State based his case in essence on the statutory scheme established by Part 4 of the 2001 Act. He relied on the appellants' acceptance that he was able, when forming the reasonable belief and suspicion required for certification under s 21, and when acting on that belief in terms of ordering arrest, search or detention of a suspect, to act on information which had or might have been obtained by torture inflicted in a foreign country, without British complicity. That acceptance, he submitted, supported the important and practical need for the security services and the Secretary of State to obtain intelligence and evidence from foreign official sources, some of which (in the less progressive countries) might dry up if their means of obtaining intelligence and evidence were the subject of intrusive inquiry. But, he argued, it would create a mismatch which Parliament could not have intended if the Secretary of State were able to rely on material at the certification stage which SIAC could not later receive. He argued that that would emasculate the statutory scheme, specifically designed to enable SIAC to see all relevant material, including ordinarily inadmissible material obtained on warranted intercepts. This position, it was pointed out on his behalf, was reflected in r 44(3) of the rules applicable to proceedings in SIAC, which dispenses with all rules of evidence, including any that might otherwise preclude admission of evidence obtained by torture in the circumstances indicated.

Lord Bingham accepted that the Secretary of State would not act unlawfully in relation to certifying, arresting, searching and detaining suspects on the strength of what he termed 'foreign torture evidence'. He considered that it was questionable whether he would act unlawfully if he based similar action on intelligence obtained by officially authorised British torture. In such circumstances there would obviously have been a breach of Art 3 by the state, but there would not be a breach of Art 5(4) or 6 in accepting the evidence in non-criminal proceedings. In such a circumstance the Secretary of State had accepted that such evidence would be inadmissible before SIAC. Lord Bingham pointed out that that position indicated that there is no correspondence between the material on which the Secretary of State may act and that which is admissible in legal proceedings.[466] He noted that this position arose whenever the Secretary of State (or any other public official) relied on information which the rules of public interest immunity prevented him adducing in evidence.[467] He pointed out that that situation comes about in respect of executive action based on a warranted interception where there is no dispensation permitting evidence to be given. He said that the position could be seen as anomalous, but that it sprang from the tension between practical common sense and the need to protect the individual from unfair incrimination.

---

465 He noted that in *Chahal v United Kingdom* (1996) 23 EHRR 413, para 79, it ruled: 'Article 3 enshrines one of the most fundamental values of democratic society. The Court is well aware of the immense difficulties faced by states in modern times in protecting their communities from terrorist violence. However, even in these circumstances, the Convention prohibits in absolute terms torture or inhuman or degrading treatment or punishment, irrespective of the victim's conduct. Unlike most of the substantive clauses of the Convention and of Protocols Nos. 1 and 4, Article 3 makes no provision for exceptions and no derogation from it is permissible under Article 15 even in the event of a public emergency threatening the life of the nation.'

466 See paras 47 and 48.

467 He relied on *Makanjuola v Comr of Police of the Metropolis* [1992] 3 All ER 617, p 623e–j; *R v Chief Constable of West Midlands Police ex p Wiley* [1995] 1 AC 274, pp 295F–297C.

Lord Bingham accepted that Parliament could pass a statute forcing SIAC to accept torture evidence, but he said that the English common law had regarded torture and its fruits with abhorrence for over 500 years, and that that abhorrence was now shared by over 140 countries which had acceded to the Torture Convention. He said that he was:

> startled, even a little dismayed, at the suggestion (and the acceptance by the Court of Appeal majority) that this deeply-rooted tradition and an international obligation solemnly and explicitly undertaken can be overridden by a statute [ATCSA] and a procedural rule which make no mention of torture at all.[468]

He said that the matter is governed by the principle of legality as explained by Lord Hoffmann in *R v Secretary of State for the Home Dept, ex p Simms*:[469]

> Parliamentary sovereignty means that Parliament can, if it chooses, legislate contrary to fundamental principles of human rights. The Human Rights Act 1998 will not detract from this power. The constraints upon its exercise by Parliament are ultimately political, not legal. But the principle of legality means that Parliament must squarely confront what it is doing and accept the political cost. Fundamental rights cannot be overridden by general or ambiguous words. This is because there is too great a risk that the full implications of their unqualified meaning may have passed unnoticed in the democratic process. In the absence of express language or necessary implication to the contrary, the courts therefore presume that even the most general words were intended to be subject to the basic rights of the individual. In this way the courts of the United Kingdom, though acknowledging the sovereignty of Parliament, apply principles of constitutionality little different from those which exist in countries where the power of the legislature is expressly limited by a constitutional document.

Lord Bingham's conclusion on the key point was that:

> It trivialises the issue before the House to treat it as an argument about the law of evidence. The issue is one of constitutional principle, whether evidence obtained by torturing another human being may lawfully be admitted against a party to proceedings in a British court, irrespective of where, or by whom, or on whose authority the torture was inflicted. To that question I would give a very clear negative answer.[470]

He accepted the broad thrust of the appellants' argument on the common law. He said that the principles of the common law, standing alone, 'compel the exclusion of third party torture evidence as unreliable, unfair, offensive to ordinary standards of humanity and decency and incompatible with the principles which should animate a

---

468   At para 51.
469   [2000] 2 AC 115, p 131.
470   At para 51.

tribunal seeking to administer justice'. He further found that effect must also be given to the European Convention, which itself takes account of the near-universal consensus embodied in the Torture Convention.

He went on to find that the principle he had enunciated did *not* apply to material obtained by means of inhuman and degrading treatment; he said that the authorities on the Torture Convention did not justify the assimilation of those two kinds of abusive conduct, since special rules were applicable to torture, and should continue to be. But he noted that the standard of what amounts to torture is not immutable. In other words, treatment regarded in the past as 'inhuman' might, as standards change, now be regarded as 'torture'.[471]

The burden of proof in relation to 'foreign torture evidence'

The other Law Lords agreed with Lord Bingham as to the non-admissibility of third party torture evidence in court proceedings. However, the majority in the Lords disagreed with Lord Bingham as to the burden of proof placed on the Secretary of State when he presented material to SIAC which could have been derived from torture. Lord Bingham said that the appellant must ordinarily, by himself or his special advocate, advance some plausible reason why evidence might have been procured by torture. That could be done, he said, by showing that evidence has, or probably has, come from one of those countries widely known or believed to practise torture. Once that plausible reason had been given, he found, or where SIAC with its knowledge and expertise in this field knows or suspects that evidence might have come from such a country, SIAC should then make such inquiry as to enable it to form a fair judgment whether the evidence had, or whether there was a real risk that it might have been, obtained by torture or not. He said that if SIAC was unable to conclude that no real risk that the evidence had been obtained by torture was apparent, it should refuse to admit the evidence.

The majority in the Lords agreed that a conventional approach to the burden of proof would be inappropriate in the context of SIAC proceedings. The detainee could not be expected to prove anything since he was denied access to so much of the information that was to be used against him. Lord Hope said that he could merely raise the issue by asking that the point be considered by SIAC; he could point to the fact that the information which was to be used against him may have come from one of the many countries around the world that are alleged to practise torture.[472] SIAC would then have to look at the facts in detail and decide whether there were reasonable grounds to suspect that torture was used in the individual case under scrutiny. He found that SIAC should not admit the evidence if it concluded on the balance of probabilities that it was obtained by torture. In other words, where SIAC was left in doubt as to whether the evidence was obtained in this way, it should admit it. He said that it would be unrealistic to expect SIAC to demand that each piece of information should be traced back to its ultimate source, and the circumstances in which it was obtained investigated so that it could be proved piece by piece, that it was *not* obtained under torture. He

---

471 He noted that this point was made by the European Court in *Selmouni v France* (1999) 29 EHRR 403, paras 99–101. See also Chapter 11, pp 1174–76 on this point.
472 At para 116.

considered that the threshold should not be put that high,[473] and the majority in the Lords agreed as to that test.

The minority judges in the House of Lords wanted a more stringent test – that the Home Secretary should have to prove on the balance of probabilities that the evidence was not obtained by torture. Lord Bingham said of the decision of the majority as to the burden of proof: 'I regret that the House should lend its authority to a test which will undermine the practical efficacy of the Torture Convention and deny detainees the standard of fairness to which they are entitled under article 5(4) or 6(1) of the European Convention.'[474] Lord Nicholls said that placing on the detainee a burden of proof which, for reasons beyond his control, he can seldom discharge was to pay lip-service to the principle that courts will not admit evidence procured by torture.[475]

Impact of the HRA on the control orders scheme: future directions?

The courts, in the decisions considered on the control orders scheme, have sought to impose a Convention-compliance on it that it failed to achieve when the PTA passed through Parliament, despite the fact that the PTA was declared compatible with the Convention, and no derogation was sought from Art 5. The decision in *JJ* made it clear to the government that the current control order regime creates an invasion of Art 5. The declaration of compatibility made under s 4 HRA in relation to Art 5 in *JJ* requires modification of the current obligations imposed by non-derogating control orders. The government therefore has to accept that modifications to the package of obligations imposed, affording the suspect a greater degree of liberty, have to be made. The non-derogating control orders regime can continue to be used but, unless a derogation from Art 5 is sought, a less stringent regime has to be imposed on individuals, one that imposes restraints on freedom of movement, but does not go so far in doing so that it breaches the right to liberty under Art 5. It is notable that in *E* the 12-hour curfew imposed was, not found *in itself* to constitute a deprivation of his liberty. It was the cumulative effect of the restrictions that led to a breach of Art 5. In order to answer to the decision in *E* the government also has to make greater efforts to seek to prosecute suspects rather than imposing control orders since if that does not occur further orders may be quashed. As discussed above, the broad offences of ss 1 and 5 TA 2006 provide a further opportunity of doing so.

Further challenges to the scheme on human rights grounds are probable. If the Secretary of State wishes to continue to impose the package of obligations so far imposed it will now require a derogation from Art 5, unless *JJ* is successfully appealed to the House of Lords by the Secretary of State. That would mean that the procedure to be used for the imposition of derogating control orders would have to be used. Also, as discussed above, if a derogation is sought from Art 5 in order to employ control orders allowing for the imposition of obligations that have been found to breach Art 5, the impact of the orders on liberty would still have to be proportionate to the exigencies of the security situation under Art 15 ECHR.

---

473 At para 119.
474 At para 62.
475 At para 80.

In *MB* the Court of Appeal improved the procedure for reviewing the making of a non-derogating control order to an extent, by adopting a purposive interpretation of the PTA, taking the fair trial right under Art 6[476] into account. Following this decision, it is clear that the procedure adopted in control proceedings must adhere to Art 6; the court itself must consider whether there were reasonable grounds for suspicion; that exercise must now differ from that of deciding whether a fact had been established according to a specified standard of proof. The procedure for determining whether reasonable grounds for suspicion existed must be fair if Sched 1, Part I, Art 6 to the 1998 Act is to be satisfied. This decision has built in a greater safeguard against unfair proceedings and against miscarriages of justice than was present under the PTA as interpreted without reference to s 3 HRA. However, fundamental problems remain: the court merely has to consider whether reasonable suspicion could be arrived at on the basis of the relevant material. That means that control orders can be imposed on a standard of proof below the civil standard; that is a low standard to apply, bearing in mind the impact on the controlee of control orders. Further, depending on the circumstances of the case, the control order decision can be affirmed although the applicant has not been made aware even of a summary of the case against him.

As discussed above, judicial supervision of control orders occurs by applying judicial review principles in the control order proceedings. After the decision of the Court of Appeal in *Secretary of State for the Home Dept v MB*[477] – which was handed down after the House of Lords judgment in the 'torture evidence' case – it was made clear that in order to comply with Art 6 the court has to consider whether there were reasonable grounds for suspicion as the basis for imposing the order. That means that the court has to inquire into the evidence relied on by the Home Secretary, and so appears to mean that if the claimant raises the possibility that the material relied upon was obtained by torture, the court should inquire into the matter. However, as the Lords determined, it appears that if the court is left in doubt as to this issue, so that if it is not satisfied on the balance of probabilities that the material was obtained by torture, it can receive the evidence in question and take account of it in finding that reasonable suspicion was arrived at.

This means that the evidence on which the decision to impose a control order is based could still include evidence obtained by torture, so long as the inquiries that the court is capable of making are unlikely to demonstrate to that standard of proof that the evidence was so obtained. The Home Secretary does not have to prove on the balance of probabilities that the evidence was not obtained by torture before relying on it. If, for example, the evidence emanated from Guantanemo Bay in which the use of various techniques amounting to torture has been documented, then it is possible that a court would take the view that there was a reasonable basis for suspecting that it might have been obtained by torture. However, it is probable that the test laid down in the Lords would not be satisfied without further inquiries which the court in control order proceedings would be very ill-equipped to make. The court could consider the evidence available in the closed sessions, but if it merely left open the possibility that torture had been used, it would not appear that the court could be satisfied on

---

476 See the discussion of Art 6 in Chapter 2, pp 59–66.
477 [2006] EWCA Civ 1140; (2006) 156 NLJ 1288; (2006) 150 SJLB 1055.

the balance of probabilities that it had been. The court would be in an even more difficult position if the material was obtained from a source which merely refused to state whether torture could have been used; it would appear in that instance that the evidence could be used.

In other words, the prohibition on the use of material obtained by third party torture could be viewed as close to a merely paper guarantee. Inhuman or degrading treatment is not covered by the House of Lords ruling; therefore it seems that evidence obtained by those methods can be accepted. Section 76(2)(a) PACE, discussed in Chapter 13, demands that the prosecution should prove beyond reasonable doubt that the evidence was not obtained by the use of 'oppression', which includes Art 3 treatment but is not confined to it. However, s 76(2)(a) would not be applicable to the proceedings in question since they are not viewed at present as the determination of a criminal charge for Art 6 purposes. (Possibly, although this would create an anomalous two-tier system of criminal proceedings, s 76(2)(a) could be viewed as inapplicable even if the proceedings were characterised as criminal ones under Art 6(1) on the basis that the designation was based on the autonomous Convention meaning of 'criminal charge'.) This also means that if evidence may have been obtained by inhuman or degrading treatment as opposed to torture and there is a doubt as to the method that was used (torture or lesser abusive treatment) the evidence can be accepted. Thus, in relation to methods of obtaining evidence, those subject to control orders are placed in a doubly invidious position in due process terms. The evidence only has to be sufficient to found reasonable suspicion, and it can be obtained by methods which would render it inadmissible in a criminal trial.

6 Conclusions

As this chapter has demonstrated, the terrorist attacks of 9/11 and of 7/7 in London immediately placed the Labour Government's commitment to the Human Rights Act under great pressure. It appeared initially probable that as an aspect of counter-terrorist policy they would exploit the leeway created by the HRA for introducing legislation incompatible with the Convention. However, even during a 'war on terror' that Britain had not 'won' after six years, the Labour Government did *not* take that route in introducing counter-terrorist measures; after 9/11 they continued to rely on the Convention qualifications to the rights, based on proportionality, and on employing derogations, rather than the escape routes available under the HRA, via the use of rights-infringing primary legislation. Their stance, which reflects the international obligations that the UK is under regardless of the HRA, reveals the cynicism of Conservative plans to repeal the Human Rights Act, a measure highly likely to be passed off in parts of the media as an aid to anti-terrorist strategy. David Cameron is of course aware of the UK's obligations under the Convention at the international level,[478] but, as the Conservative Party may recognise, the less responsible sections of the media are likely to gloss over that point. Since the case for the HRA has not fully been made to the British public, and certain sections of the media have deliberately presented the public with a partial

478 Discussed in Chapter 2.

and distorted view of the Act,[479] the difference between the obligations under HRA and those under the Convention has hardly entered the public consciousness.

This chapter has charted a dramatic change from the old model for counter-terrorist laws – a reactive model used in the TA 2000 – to the new, proactive model, introduced under the Labour Government in the ATCSA Part 4 and now in the PTA 2005. The Terrorism Act 2000, despite the breadth of many of the offences that it introduced – in terms of their application to a wide range of groups – was largely a reactive measure. In other words, it relied on charging persons with offences and seeking to bring them to trial. Although in that sense it appears less pernicious in human rights terms than the measures that succeeded it, post-9/11, introduced under Part 4 ATCSA and under the PTA 2005, it must not be forgotten that its very broad definition of terrorism lies at the heart of the proactive measures introduced by its successors, and that it represented at the time one of the most significant extensions of 'emergency' legislation over the last 30 years.

The TA's introduction in the absence of any 'clear and present' danger evident in 2000 may be said to provide a signal example of a failure of democracy to protect civil liberties. The legislation is remarkable in its abandonment of all the features which sought to make the original PTA and EPA legislation appear tolerable: its limited application, its temporary nature, annual review and scrutiny of the continuing threat. Paradoxically, it affords the legislation all the hallmarks of ordinary criminal law while continuing to justify its draconian nature on the basis of the special need to combat terrorism. In this sense it is contradictory and possibly counter-productive: the more that terrorism becomes indistinguishable from ordinary criminal activity, the less the term 'terrorist' is likely to appear to justify special measures. The failure to include safeguards, such as renewal, in the legislation comes to seem even more indefensible. Such safeguards may have been weak and hypocritical, but they showed some symbolic attachment to a notion of respect for the rule of law.

The pre-2000 legislation relied on actual terrorist activity to justify the adoption of draconian laws, on incremental development and a nuanced approach. In other words, particular temporary measures were adopted for periods of time and on a localised basis, to answer to particular threats. Graduation was, in a sense, achieved since where the threat was perceived to be most severe, more severe measures were adopted to meet it. Had the TA introduced greater graduation, depending on different offences and levels of threat, together with a more specific and limited definition of terrorism, its permanent nature might have been less objectionable. But it adhered to an absolutist approach in failing to introduce express graduation while abandoning each of the features of the previous counter-terrorist scheme. It is more coherent and bold than the previous legislation; it has spurned the hypocrisy of the past which pretended that these measures were temporary. But, it is argued, its adoption showed an even greater degree of cynical opportunism than that which has such a marked pedigree in the long history of counter-terrorist measures. The government seemed to fail to understand that the reluctance to take each step reflected some adherence to democratic principle and explained *why* the previous legislation was piecemeal, anomalous, incremental and localised. In so far as the TA allows for greater breadth and unpredictability in the application of the terrorist offences, the Human

---

479 See Chapter 4, pp 162–63.

Rights Act had to be looked to, to seek to prevent the departures from the rule of law it threatened, and which Parliament was unable or unwilling to prevent.[480]

The argument that proscription and the TA generally are needed since they marginalise some groups from mainstream society represents a limited perspective. It fails to consider what part the TA and other legislation plays in discouraging some dissident groups, more moderate than Al-Qaeda, from seeking to employ the democratic process to express dissent. Removing democratic rights such as free expression from certain groups on the ground that they are (a) opposed to democracy and (b) are uninterested in using democratic means, fails to ask the question as to what part removing their ability to use that process plays – what effect it has on encouraging extremism and hence terrorist activity. Trusting the executive to address the demands of proportionality – which is what the current counter-terrorist scheme does in terms of proscription decisions, and the initial step in imposing control orders, unless the decision is 'obviously flawed' – is unsatisfactory in human rights terms. At the extremes so far proportionality has been observed; for example, animal rights or environmental groups have not yet been proscribed. However, this may merely reflect a perception that to proscribe them could appear to make a mockery of the proscription process, since once proscribed their members probably would not be prosecuted for the proscription-based offences. Police resources would be stretched too thinly if serious attempts were made to apply the proscription-based offences to members of such groups. But certain groups, such as the PKK or PMOI, which do not appear to represent a threat to security in the UK, have been proscribed. Proscription of such groups is unlikely to attract any adverse attention in the mainstream media, and may indeed be welcomed in it. It means that the effect of the relevance of proscription as a negotiating weapon in diplomatic machinations is felt by vulnerable members of weak and already marginalised groups, as exemplified in the *Kurdistan* proscription case discussed above, and in relation to the Sikh youths coming to the UK from Germany where ISYF is not proscribed. The relevance of all this to security in the UK is tenuous at best and probably counter-productive to it.

As this chapter has demonstrated, the HRA has had a significant impact in terms of tempering the effects of the TA. *Ex p Kebilene* affected the drafting of the TA, and *Attorney General's Reference (No 4 of 2002)*[481] completed the process of imposing Art 6 compliance on the provisions. But the effect of the HRA on other aspects of the over-broad application of the TA provisions has been limited, partly because the TA offences have been under-used. Further, the substantive issue in the *Kurdistan* proscription case has not yet been considered in the courts. The Human Rights Act has had very little impact on curbing the use of anti-terrorism provisions in the context of public protest. This is partly because little opportunity for it to do so has arisen. When the opportunity did arise, in *R (on the application of Gillan) v Comr of Metropolitan Police*[482] in relation

---

480 At a number of points in the debate on the Second Reading of the Bill in the Commons MPs noted that it did not appear to be compatible with the Convention: 'we are continuously finding as we go through the Bill provisions that seem contrary to the spirit and precise provisions of the Convention and of the decisions of the Court' (HC Debs 15 March 2000 col 432). Nevertheless, all amendments which might have removed incompatibilities were overwhelmingly defeated due to the government's very large majority and the determination of the Conservative opposition to appear to be 'tougher on terrorism' than the Labour Party.

481 [2004] UKHL 43; [2005] 1 AC 264; [2005] 1 All ER 237.

482 [2006] UKHL 12.

to the key TA stop and search measure, it was not taken, as Chapter 8 demonstrates. The use of anti-terrorism powers against climate change protesters at Heathrow – as currently planned by the Metropolitan police in August 2007 – may provide the courts with a further opportunity. However, the HRA has had, as discussed, a significant impact in imposing compliance with Art 6 on the TA.

The courts have also taken a firm stance in relation to the proactive measures introduced post-2000. Part 4 ATCSA was modified due to court intervention on human rights grounds, and then finally abandoned after the Lords' decision in *A and others*. The control orders scheme under the 2005 Act seems to be following a similar path, in the sense that the HRA is being used in order to seek to impose Convention-compliance upon it, although since it is a more nuanced scheme it can be modified rather than entirely abandoned.[483] The use of control orders, rather than charging suspects with offences actually committed, is a logical conclusion of the proactive approach: as discussed, persons may suffer interferences with their liberty, private life, association and communication, not because of what they have actually done, but for fear of what they might do, based upon suspicion of their involvement with Al-Qaeda generally.

The use of proactive rather than reactive measures appears, on its face, to represent the most effective strategy in relation to the threat of suicide bombing, and the attacks in London on 7/7 and in the US on 9/11 were of course carried out by suicide bombers. Those who *plan* to die in carrying out attacks self-evidently cannot be 'punished' after the event and are unlikely to be deterred by the threat of conviction and imprisonment. However, preventive measures are only of utility in relation to those likely to carry out suicide bombings if they are *effective* in targeting the right people; over-broad preventive measures, including the control orders discussed in this chapter, may have counter-productive effects in encouraging persons to contemplate engaging in suicide bomb attacks. It should also be noted that the imprisonment of those engaged in planning and preparation for such attacks, for example, on conviction for proscription-based offences, for conspiracy, or under the broad preparatory offences available, would assist in preventing them.

Post-2000 it became incrementally easier in the UK to fall within the legal category of a 'terrorist suspect; attention has turned to adopting broad definitions of such suspects, facilitating the application of sanctions outside the criminal process. Counter-terrorist law and policy has concentrated on widening the legal net so that greater numbers of persons can potentially be viewed as terrorist suspects, partly by adopting definitions of 'terrorist activity' that in effect broaden the basic definition of terrorism under the TA and partly by lowering the standard of proof needed in order to apply counter-terrorist sanctions to suspects. The current dramatically broad construction of the 'terrorist suspect' depends on *both* legal developments, taken together, in contradistinction to the broadening of the definitions of terrorist offences, which is simultaneously occurring in the TA 2006. But the range of special counter terrorist and proscription offences, as well as the proactive measures of executive detention and control orders, have been under-utilised. The attempt has not been made to apply all the terrorism offences and sanctions to the wide range of groups and persons that s 1 TA potentially covers. The counter-terrorist

---

483 At present the government is consulting on security with the intention of publishing a national security strategy in autumn 2007, which may include a proposal for a derogation from Art 5 (see fn 487 below). The current scheme is not effective in security terms: so far five suspects under control orders have absconded.

provisions create an appearance of extreme authoritarianism which is not in general borne out by the reality. The greatest concern is to seek to apply them to groups linked to Al-Qaeda, that do threaten national security. But only a tiny handful of persons were subjected to the detention without trial scheme under ATCSA, and less than 20 people are currently subject to control orders under PTA. In certain instances the ordinary criminal law has been employed against terrorist attacks rather than the special counter-terrorism provisions. In particular, those conspiring with the 7/7 bombers were charged in 2007 and convicted of an offence in a criminal law statute passed in 1883.[484]

The government in 2005 stated that it intended to bring forward a terrorism consolidation Bill in 2007, which would create an opportunity to amend the control orders provisions. However, that Bill has not made an appearance, and as the Joint Committee on Human Rights pointed out in 2007 it now seems, from the comments of the Minister during the renewal debate in the Commons, that there is no guarantee that this consolidation bill will appear before the next annual renewal of the control orders scheme. That means that Parliament has been denied an opportunity to debate that scheme in full, taking account of the findings that a number of the orders breach Art 5.[485] The problem remains that the control order regime is being operated in practice in breach of the right to liberty in Art 5, because the control orders which are being imposed are so restrictive as to amount to a deprivation of liberty, which is unlawful in the absence of a derogation from Art 5.[486] In July 2007 Prime Minister Gordon Brown made a Commons statement on security.[487] The government intends to bring forward a new counter-terrorism bill in autumn 2007. The intention is, after consultation, that it should include plans to extend detention without charge, possibly to 56 days, to allow suspects to be questioned after they have been officially charged, and to allow for the admission in evidence of material deriving from phone intercepts. The possibility of derogating from parts of the ECHR has also been raised. The government can expect support from the Liberal Democrats and the Conservatives on questioning subjects after they have been officially charged, and on phone-tapping evidence. But the opposition has made it clear that unless they hear the evidence to support extending the limit on detention without charge, the government will be defeated again on that issue.[488] The position on control orders in future remains undetermined, but no proposal to abandon the control orders scheme was made in the Commons statement.

---

484 The charge against them alleged that between November 1, 2004 and June 29, 2005, they 'unlawfully and maliciously' conspired with the four 7/7 bombers – Mohammed Sidique Khan, Shezhad Tanweer, Jermaine Lindsay and Hasib Hussein – to cause 'by explosive substance explosions on the transport for London system and/or tourist attractions in London in a nature likely to endanger life or cause serious injury to property'. The alleged offence is contrary to s 3(1)(a) of the Explosive Substances Act 1883. See *The Telegraph*, 6 April 2007. The conspirators, with two acquittals, were convicted on 1 May 2007.

485 JCHR 8th Report Session 2009–7, 28 March 2007. The JCHR pointed out in its report that the unsatisfactory nature of a debate on an affirmative order was 'graphically illustrated in the renewal debate in the Commons when the Minister was unable to reply to an important question about whether any of the charges pending for breach of control orders related to the three individuals who had been subject to control orders for the longest time' para 15. The debate was only for one and a half hours. See fn 494 for the current proposals for the Counter-terror Bill 2007.

486 Ibid at para 18.

487 Prime Ministers' Commons Statement on Security 25 July 2007.

488 See news reports, including Guardian Unlimited 7 June 2007.

The question arises, and must be in the minds of judges – are control orders being used (as detention might have been under Part 4 ATCSA)[489] where a prosecution could succeed instead under the criminal law or under one of the many broad offences of the Terrorism Acts of 2000 and 2006?[490] If so, is this at least partly due to a lack of devotion of resources to the issue of bringing a prosecution and to a preference for controlling an individual's movements on the basis of a very low standard of proof because that avoids the difficulties of persuading the security services that it is possible to use some sensitive material as evidence, with appropriate safeguards, in a criminal trial? The campaigning group Justice argued in 2007 that greater effort could be devoted to seeking to bring prosecutions under the ordinary criminal law or the special terrorism offences. So doing could include relaxing the ban on the use of intercept material as evidence,[491] and making greater efforts to turn security material into evidence. While the impact of relaxing the ban on use of intercept material as evidence should not be exaggerated, it may be noted that virtually all other countries have dropped their bans, indicating that any value they had is outweighed by the value of using such material in criminal trials.

Future strands of counter-terrorism policy seem likely to continue to come into conflict with the European Convention on Human Rights, although the government seems to be adopting a more nuanced approach in response to the human rights embarrassment it suffered as a result of the House of Lords' decision in *A and Others*. The government continues to explore the possibility of introducing very broad anti-terrorist offences, the latest exemplars being those introduced in the 2006 Act. It continues to see the control orders scheme as a central part of its counter-terrorist strategy. As discussed above, it is seeking at the time of writing to 'overturn' the decision in *Chahal* in the European Court of Human Rights, meaning that it could deport persons creating a security risk abroad, despite the risk that they would there be subject to Art 3 treatment. Some attention has already turned to relying on closed evidence, in SIAC and in control order hearings, but so far such measures have not been adopted within the *mainstream* criminal justice system as a means of watering down criminal trials.

At present, as this chapter has shown, two parallel schemes are operating in Britain in respect of the counter-terrorist response: the use of control orders based on certification by the Home Secretary for a tiny group of suspected terrorists, and a reactive scheme based on a range of very broad special terrorism offences, but dependent on trial and conviction, for all suspected terrorists. The creation of the two schemes reveals a clear disjunction of aim between the creation of ever-broader substantive offences and the due process demands of criminal trials. Ironically, the special terrorist offences appear to be viewed by the government as ineffective in relation to some of those who pose the greatest security threat. The introduction of control orders amounts to an admission of the failure of the criminal law to deal with this threat. So far the government has not sought to introduce modifications to the criminal trial itself[492] – such as allowing

---

489 See p 1428 above.
490 See further on this point the Draft Prevention of Terrorism Act 2005 (Continuance in Force of Sections 1 to 9) Order 2007 JUSTICE Briefing for House of Commons Debate February 2007 at paras 5–8.
491 See Chapter 10, pp 1047–52. See also fn 494 below.
492 Apart from the introduction, in places, of reverse burdens of proof, as in s 57 TA – see pp 1353–54 above. The key proposals from the Newton Committee had that objective in mind: they were intended

the use of intercept material in evidence – with a view to bringing those subject to control orders, and other suspects, to trial. There seems to be a continuing reluctance to use security material as evidence in a criminal trial – arguably evident in the *E* case – partly explaining the reliance on proactive measures outside the criminal justice system, currently non-derogating control orders. So, despite the introduction of new offences under the TA 2006, there seems to be little prospect of a significant increase in the use of the criminal justice process and no prospect of a *political* solution to the current situation. Thus the executive will probably continue to rely on the use of interventions outside that process, and the courts' deployment of the Human Rights Act, will continue to play a key role in creating a Convention-compliant balance between rights and security.

This chapter has sought to argue that there is a dissonance between the vast array of counter-terrorist provisions it has discussed, and the preservation of the security of the UK. The passing of two very broad anti-terrorism statutes – TA 2000 and ATCSA – did not prevent the worst terrorist atrocity in Britain in recent years – the London bombings in 2005. This chapter is arguing for a narrower targeting of the provisions – at Al-Qaeda and linked groups, and for greater efforts to prosecute their members and supporters employing, *inter alia*, the new offences under the TA 2006. The use of control orders, which at present do not include detention, not only runs counter to a number of Convention principles, it is ineffective in security terms.[493] The use of the principle of proportionality by the courts has created, and has the potential to continue to create, a narrow focus for the counter-terrorist scheme that brings it to bear on targets that genuinely threaten security. There is an argument for encapsulating that principle in a future consolidating counter-terrorist statute itself, rather than relying on the courts to impose proportionality on its provisions under s 3 HRA.[494]

to allow for the use of the special terrorism and proscription offences in prosecutions against members or supporters of Al-Qaeda. But under current proposals intercept material may be made admissible in evidence (see fn 487).

493 As Justice pointed out in 2007 in its Draft Prevention of Terrorism Act 2005 (Continuance in Force of Sections 1 to 9) Order 2007 JUSTICE Briefing for House of Commons Debate February 2007, the recent abscondment of two individuals subject to control orders – one from a psychiatric hospital and one from a mosque – raises serious questions about the use of control orders.

494 However, current proposals for a 2007 Counter-terror Bill indicate that no such provision will be made. It does not appear that the new Bill will be a consolidating measure. Nor will it radically change the current scheme, including the control orders scheme. Instead, under current proposals (see Government discussion document 7 June 2007) it will introduce a package of further counter-terrorist measures, including: powers to stop and question suspects; extension of the detention period in police custody beyond 28 days, possibly to 56 days; the use of intercept material as evidence.

Part V

Equality and theories of anti-discrimination laws

One of the main themes in human rights jurisprudence concerns the duty of states to treat citizens with equal concern and respect. This does not mean that no differentiation between citizens should occur, but that inequality of treatment should not be based on factors which do not justify it. Thus, discrimination may be defined as morally unjustifiable as opposed to justifiable differentiation.[1] It may be said that the latter occurs when a difference in treatment is accorded owing to behaviour which is the result of voluntary choice, the former when it is based on an attribute over which the individual has no control, such as sex or skin colour. Thus, in a society that allows or imposes discrimination in this sense, the groups affected will be entirely frustrated in pursuing their objectives in all areas of life because the disadvantage they are under cannot be removed. These statements alone, however, are inadequate as failing to deal with behaviour which may in a sense be the result of voluntary choice, but might also be said to be determined by social conditioning. Further, they do not explain whether differentiation would be justified if based on behaviour to which a person is morally committed owing to her membership of a certain group. Thus, it should also be argued that morally unjustifiable differentiation would also occur, at least presumptively, if different treatment was based on behaviour over which the individual had little real choice, or where it would be morally unjustifiable to force the individual to choose between adherence to a particular group, and disadvantage. Finally, this argument should encompass the notion that the physical attribute or behaviour in question may, exceptionally, be objectively relevant to the differential treatment and thereby could justify it. As Chapter 15 will demonstrate, anti-discrimination schemes tend to begin by outlawing discrimination on the basis of sex, race or skin colour. They then move on to a more developed conception of equality, which understands that discrimination can also occurs on the basis of a number of other factors, including sexual orientation, transsexuality, religion or disability.

Once factors that do not justify differentiation are identified, the state can be said to be under a duty to ensure that unequal treatment on the basis of such factors does not occur, at least in spheres under its control. However, at different times, and according to different schools of thought, the scope of the duty varies. Under early classic liberal rights theory, the state came under a duty to ensure that no formal discriminatory mechanisms were in place, but once that was done, it was thought that individuals would

---

1 See Wallman, S, 'Difference, differentiation, discrimination', 5 New Community 1.

have equal freedom to exercise their talents.[2] However, this theory came to encompass the notion of state intervention in order to ensure that some individuals did not prevent others from exercising their talents. This is the dominant theory underpinning the UK legislative policy on equality: it assumes that once people have equal freedoms, they will have equal opportunities and thus all that is needed is to ensure such freedoms. Some egalitarians would go further, insisting that persons should be placed in a similar position, even if in order to do so they are treated unequally. Some forms of liberal thought[3] would now also support treating persons unequally in order to ensure equality of opportunity. However, broadly, liberals view equality as formal, while egalitarians, including socialists or communitarians, view it as substantive. Formal equality[4] (or treating like as like) is the limitation placed upon equality legislation by liberalism; its drawback is that it puts the protection of such legislation beyond the reach of those who are differently situated.[5] For example, if women's domestic and parental roles[6] tend to differ from those of men, even though that position is changing, and those roles interfere with women's role as (cost efficient) workers, in a formal equality model, which takes the male as the norm and assumes that a woman is like a man, the employer may justifiably treat women differently. Similarly, if some persons from minority groups are educationally or socially disadvantaged, their difference of situation cannot be addressed by means of legislation based on a formal equality model.

This argument does not imply that the imposition of formal equality has *no* impact on the distribution of social benefits. In particular, formal equality affects the market by inducing it not to act in an arbitrary and ultimately inefficient fashion. Formal equality, if fully established, disallows the individual biases of employers to feed into the market,[7] and may therefore promote genuine competition based on individual merit, thereby preventing the unwarranted under- or over-advantaging of certain groups. Perpetuation of an unequal pay policy may not seem to lead clearly and immediately to an inefficient operation of the market. If a certain group can be treated disadvantageously in terms of pay, this may appear in some respects to benefit the market, since the availability of cheap labour may lead to increased productivity and market expansion. Nevertheless, unequal pay may eventually distort the operation of market forces, creating dysfunction in the market, since certain professions and certain specialities within professions may

---

2   See Mill, JS, *On the Subjection of Women*, 2nd edn, 1869.

3   See Raz, J, *The Morality of Freedom*, 1986, Clarendon; Dworkin, R, *Taking Rights Seriously*, 1978, p 272.

4   Under classic liberalism as expressed by Mill, op. cit., fn 2.

5   Several feminist writers have pointed out that the principal limitation of the formal equality principle is that it assumes that the male is the norm. MacKinnon puts it particularly aptly, 'Why should you have to be the same as a man to get what a man gets simply because he is one?' See MacKinnon, C, 'Difference and dominance: on sex discrimination', in Bartlett, K and Kennedy, R (eds), *Feminist Legal Theory*, 1991; see also MacKinnon, C, 'Reflections on sex equality under law' (1991) 100 Yale LJ 1286–93.

6   Matters belonging to the 'private' sphere, in a liberal conception. Mill's view, as expressed in op. cit., fn 2, was that formal equality operates in certain 'public' spheres, such as franchise, employment and education.

7   This argument is put forward by Weiler in 'The wages of sex: the uses and limits of comparable worth' (1986) 99 Harv L Rev 1728, p 1762: '. . . real world labour markets leave a good deal of leeway for countless managerial judgments about how to classify, value and pay certain jobs in comparison to others.'

be shunned by advantaged groups because of the low pay they offer, with the result once again that genuine competition is not fostered within them.

Thus, it may be argued that formal equality 'perfects' the market: rather than allowing bias to benefit certain individuals at the expense of others, it forces the market to treat every employee or would-be employee as an autonomous individual having made a free choice as regards position in the market. Further, it can force the market to treat each individual as an equivalent 'unit of production'.[8] Beyond that it will not go, and therefore it is not ultimately gravely disruptive of market forces. Once a formal equality regime is established and internalised by the market, market forces can have free rein.

Substantive equality, on the other hand, demands not merely that persons should be judged on individual merit, but that the real situation of many women and/or members of minority groups which may tend to place them in a weaker position in the market should be addressed by a variety of means, including anti-discrimination legislation. Proponents of this argument recognise that the achievement of substantive equality involves more than a few discrimination claims. Such claims can only have limited impact in bringing about social change; far reaching structural changes can be achieved only as a result of government policy and changed social expectations. Nevertheless, under a substantive equality model, equality legislation would attempt to reflect and further the societal movement towards equality which is taking place in the member states of the EU. Thus, legislation enshrining anti-discrimination measures may move beyond seeking to ensure formal equality and may encompass a more sophisticated notion of equality, requiring understanding of the differential impact of certain measures on certain groups, and of the value of positive action.

From inequality to neutrality, from formal to substantive equality

During the twentieth and twenty-first centuries in Western democracies, it has been possible to discern a pattern in the landscape of 'equality' law. There has been a clear movement, reflected in the law, towards acceptance of the equal treatment of persons, and towards a more developed conception of equality, and away from the acceptance of unjustifiable differentiation, which reflects to an extent the different theories considered above. In the first phase such differentiation, based on particular protected grounds expressly enshrined in the law, is gradually removed; in the second, there may be a hiatus during which the law is neutral and there is freedom to discriminate; in the third, the law may be used to try expressly to prevent discrimination, or at least certain aspects of it, on such grounds. In the fourth, a more developed conception of equality may become apparent – the aim will be to achieve equality of outcome: in this phase, the law will tend to *permit* discrimination – termed positive or affirmative action – on the ground that it is morally justified as a temporary measure intended to combat the effects of previous discrimination.

---

8   In other words, formal equality requires in general that one employee should not be perceived as more expensive than another and therefore the market need not accommodate the cost of individuals who are given unnecessary special protection such as, e.g., barring women from night work during pregnancy.

However, although this general pattern can usually be identified, it may well be that particular aspects of the 'first phase' discrimination which, for various reasons – usually associated with the most conservative bastions in society such as religion or the armed forces – are especially resistant to change, are still in existence during the third phase. Such aspects will still tend to follow the general trend, but more slowly, and will themselves almost certainly move eventually from one phase to another.[9] In other words, some specific inequalities may still be enshrined in law in the third or fourth phases. Moreover, *within* each phase there may be movement; in the first, legislation may enshrine gross and absolute inequality, which gradually gives place to a lesser and more pragmatic inequality. An example is afforded by the legal regulation of sexual acts between consenting males: until 1967 these were merely forbidden, on the ground that sexual satisfaction gained in this manner was seen as inimical to the moral basis of society. The removal of this barrier but the initial fixing of the age of consent for male homosexuals at 21, and then at 18, suggested a retreat from an absolutist position, but a disinclination, until the age of consent was equalised in 2003, to carry through such a retreat fully.

Since slavery was abolished at the beginning of the nineteenth century, generalised racial inequality has never been enshrined in law in the UK in the way that sexual inequality has been until relatively recently. People from certain ethnic backgrounds have not been prevented from voting, from holding civic office, from owning property or from forming contracts. The legal scheme which until quite recently governed sexual inequality in the UK would probably find parallels in terms of *racial* inequality only under regimes such as that in South Africa during the apartheid years.

The movement towards equality on the grounds of sexual orientation is currently poised between the second and third phases, although a very few instances of legally enshrined inequality remain. For example, same sex couples can register a civil partnership under the Civil Partnership Act 2004, but they cannot marry.[10] In the UK, it is clear that its full entry into the third phase is imminent; it seems highly probable that it will do so in 2007 or 2008. Prior to 2003, when the first dedicated measure combating sexual orientation was put in place, the signs that such a measure would be adopted were already apparent: the existence of pressure groups operating within the UK and abroad; and official recognition afforded to such groups in some other Western democracies coupled with instances in which their policies had been afforded a degree of legal recognition.[11] Moreover, instruments which are capable of affecting law and policy in the UK already enshrined guarantees of freedom from discrimination on this ground, including the European Convention on Human Rights and the International Convention on Civil and Political Rights. Recently, more far-reaching European legal

9   An example is afforded by the exclusion of women from the Anglican priesthood, an instance of 'first phase' discrimination which survived until 1994. 'First phase' discrimination in this context, although almost squeezed out of existence, will subsist: under the current arrangements, women priests cannot become bishops, although this appears to be about to change.

10   Although little turns on the legal distinction between marriage and civil partnership. The Act led to amendment of many areas of discrimination, such as property transfer on death, intestacy laws, enduring power of attorney and hospital access.

11   E.g., prior to the lifting of the ban on homosexuals serving in the armed forces in the UK, the armed forces in Belgium, Denmark, The Netherlands and Spain were all open to homosexuals. See further *Homosexuality: A Community Issue*, 1993, a report compiled by the European Human Rights Foundation.

instruments have been introduced, at international level, which already have and address discrimination on this ground domestically. Arguments in favour of discrimination on the ground of sexual orientation in various spheres such as housing may now be viewed as rooted only in prejudice: the social need to retain such discrimination is not apparent.[12] Prior to 2003, such prejudice was allowed relatively free rein and therefore could affect every area of life, from employment to expressions of sexuality, and since the UK until 2004 did not, in general, recognise same-sex partners, they suffered in comparison with heterosexual couples in relation to immigration, pensions and inheritance rights.[13]

Anti-assimilationism

Although this chapter concentrates on the extent to which the law has influenced equality of opportunity, it does not imply that all members of the groups in question will necessarily *want* the opportunity to adopt the way of life of the dominant group. Some women and some members of ethnic minorities believe that true equality means accepting and respecting different values rather than trying to extinguish them.[14] The notion of 'assimilationism' has come particularly under attack[15] in various writings on feminist legal theory, which have advocated the 'feminism of difference' and rejected the rights analysis of the liberal feminist.[16] Of course, there is a crucial difference here between the assertion of the values of groups of persons belonging to ethnic minorities and those of women, in that women will be committed to an enormous and disparate range of values and will therefore behave as differently from each other as men do.[17] However, assuming for the purposes of the argument that a body of values of a more nurturing, caring, conscience-based kind can be associated with women, just as certain values and beliefs can be associated with groups such as Sikhs or Muslims, it could be argued that such values are not necessarily opposed in their entirety to those of

---

12 Some Conservative opinion takes the view that homosexuality is a form of immorality which should be suppressed in order to uphold the moral bonds which keep society together. This view may derive from that expressed by Lord Devlin (*The Maccabaean Lecture, The Enforcement of Morals*, 1959, reprinted in 1965). It seems likely that this body of opinion would not support legislation aimed at preventing discrimination in, e.g., employment on grounds of sexual orientation. For discussion of Lord Devlin's view see Chapter 5, p 269.

13 See below, pp 1513 *et seq.*

14 E.g., MacKinnon, C, 'Toward feminist jurisprudence', 34 Stanford L Rev; Littleton, CA, 'Reconstructing sexual equality', in Bartlett, op. cit., fn 5.

15 See Gilligan, C, *In A Different Voice: Psychological Theory and Women's Development*, 1982, Harvard University Press. It should be noted that the 'feminism of difference' has itself come under attack from postmodern feminists as impoverished and limited in its assumption that there is essential commonality between all women. See Cain, P, 'Feminist jurisprudence: grounding the theories', in Bartlett and Kennedy, op. cit., fn 5, pp 265–68.

16 'Feminist rights analysis generally pretends that there are no differences between men and women and attempts to advance women by giving them the rights men have': Olsen, F, 'Statutory rape: a feminist critique of rights analysis', in Bartlett and Kennedy, op. cit., fn 5, p 312.

17 The argument that women can and should be viewed as a homogeneous group has been put by Martha Minow: 'cognitively we need simplifying categories and the unifying category of "woman" helps to organise experience even at the cost of denying some of it' (Minow, M, 'Feminist reason: getting it and losing it', 38 J Legal Educ 47, p 51).

the dominant group and, in any event, need not be rejected in seeking to overcome disadvantage. In suggesting this, the danger should be borne in mind that extreme forms of 'celebration of difference' may be merely another route to economic and political subjugation; history does not afford many examples of groups who overcame disadvantage by rejoicing in their rejection of the whole body of values which originally placed them in that position. In any event, despite a difference of emphasis, there is a measure of harmony between moderate anti-assimilationist theory and liberal rights theory as regards the need to protect people from discrimination on unjustifiable grounds by outlawing sex- and race-based disadvantages, so that women or members of ethnic minorities can choose whether or how far to accept – while perhaps working to modify – the lifestyle associated with the dominant group.

Discrimination and the law

This part begins, in the second section of Chapter 15, by considering and evaluating the domestic and European legislation aimed specifically at preventing discrimination based on certain protected grounds including those of race, sex and disability. The anti-discrimination scheme adopted in respect of disability is compared with those applicable to discrimination on grounds of sex or race. The chapter considers the means used in the legislation of distinguishing between relevant and irrelevant factors founding differentiation, since only the former provide a morally justifiable basis for different treatment. The legal means of ensuring that such distinctions can be made can then be contrasted with the failure so far to ensure that homosexuality *per se* is not regarded by the law as an irrelevant factor on which to base differentiation in such spheres as employment, housing and education.

Broadly, the legislation embodies two methods of challenging direct discrimination and discriminatory practices: under the first, the 'individual' method, the responsibility lies mainly with the victim of discrimination to bring an action against the discriminator, while under the second, termed the 'administrative' method, an institution or body uses various methods of seeking to ensure that discrimination is prevented. Chapter 15 moves on to consider the efficacy of the current legal model in practice.

The main emphasis of Chapter 15 will be on the tensions placed on the interpretation of the legislation, not only as claimants have sought to use it to do more than merely bring about formal equality, but also as they have sought to bring further grounds within the category of those that are protected. It will be apparent that a number of further grounds have received protection – the anti-discrimination schemes, both domestic and European, have widened their scope and are currently under pressure to widen still further. The potential of the Human Rights Act (HRA) to influence the domestic scheme in both respects is quite a significant theme, although, owing to the influence of EU law, the HRA is likely to have less influence in this context than in others considered by this book.

The anti-discrimination legislation focuses on certain specific and limited areas of activity, in particular that of employment. However, the use of anti-discrimination laws may be inefficacious in addressing specific life-style matters, such as employment detriment flowing from pregnancy. Therefore, laws other than dedicated anti-discrimination statutes are also considered subsisting alongside and providing an alternative to use of the specific anti-discrimination laws. Many aspects of discrimination on grounds of race were, in a very significant reform, brought within the race discrimination scheme by its amendment in 2000, and in 2007 the scheme relating to gender discrimination will follow suit. The extent to which the anti-discrimination schemes stand in the way of positive action designed to allow for equality of outcome will form an important theme.

Chapter 15

Anti-discrimination legislation

1 Introduction[1]

This chapter covers a vast, complex range of legislation aimed at curbing discrimination and promoting equality. But one of its key themes will be that the formal equality model on which most of this legislation is based is deeply flawed and may be standing in the way of achieving equality of outcome. Forty years ago, in the UK, protection from discrimination was only offered under the Race Relations Act 1976 and the Sex Discrimination Act 1975. Disability as a protected ground was included over ten years ago, and subsequently the grounds on which discrimination is prohibited have greatly increased: new protected grounds were added, including sexual orientation, age, religion and belief. The full list of protected grounds now includes: race, nationality, national origins, colour, gender, disability, gender reassignment, marital status, pregnancy, sexual orientation, age, religion and belief. So a range of statutes and regulations have been introduced, and amended, since 1975 when the Sex Discrimination Act was introduced, providing comprehensive protection from discrimination for the first time in UK law. In contrast to other areas of civil liberties and human rights considered in this book,

---

1 Texts referred to below: Clayton, R and Tomlinson, H, *The Law of Human Rights*, 2006, Chapter 17; Connolly, M, *Discrimination Law*, 2006, Sweet and Maxwell; Feldman, D, *Civil Liberties* 2nd edn, 2002, Chapter 3, (esp 3.4); Fredman, S, *Discrimination Law*, 2002, Clarendon; Connolly, M, *Townshend-Smith on Discrimination Law: Text, Cases and Materials*, 2nd edn, 2004, Routledge; EOC's *Submission to the Discrimination Law Review*, 2006; McColgan, A, *Discrimination Law: Text, Cases and Materials*, 2000, Hart; Ewing, K, Bradley, A and McColgan, A, *Labour Law: Text and Materials*, 2001, Hart; Hepple, B, Coussey, M and Choudhury, T, *Equality: A New Framework – The Independent Review of the Enforcement of UK Anti-Discrimination Legislation*, 2000, Hart; Fredman, S, *The Future of Equality in Britain*, EOC Working Paper No 5, 2002; Baker, A, *The Enjoyment of Rights and Freedoms: a New Conception of the Ambit under Article 14 ECHR* (2006) 69 MLR 714; Baker, A, 'Comparison Tainted by Justification: Against a "Compendious Question"' 2006 PL 476; Dine, J and Watt, B (eds), *Discrimination Law*, 1996, Longman; Palmer, *Discrimination at Work*, 3rd edn, 1996, Legal Action Group; McCrudden, C (ed), *Anti-Discrimination Law*, 1991, Dartmouth; Hepple, B and Szyszczak, E (eds), *Discrimination and the Limits of the Law*, 1992, Continuum; Collins, H, 'Discrimination, Equality and Social Inclusion' (2003) 66 MLR 16; Fredman, S, 'Equality: A New generation?' [2001] 30(2) ILJ 145–68; Johnes, G, Career Interruptions and Labour Market Outcomes (2006) EOC Paper No 45; von Prondzynski, F and Richards, W, 'Tackling indirect discrimination' [1995] PL 117; Gardner, J, 'Discrimination as injustice' (1996) 16(3) OJLS 353; Livingstone, S, 'Article 14 and the prevention of discrimination in the ECHR' (1997) EHRLR 25; Ewing, KD, 'The HRA and labour law' (1998) 27 ILJ 275; Deakin, S and Morris, J, *Labour Law*, 2nd edn, 1998, Butterworths, Chapter 6; Bindman, *Discrimination Law*, 2000; Gregory, J, *Sex, Race and the Law: Legislating for Equality*, 1987, Sage.

such as free speech, the common law had completely failed to provide protection in this area. The judicial culture that lay behind the failure of the common law to create tortious protection from discrimination is now, it is argued, evident in the strong judicial stance taken against affirmative action.[2]

The legislative schemes prohibiting discrimination all follow the same model. They set out the protected ground and define the forms of discrimination covered and the method of establishing discrimination. They then set out the contexts in which discrimination will be unlawful, provide defences, exclusions, procedures and remedies. Certain of the schemes, but not all, also set up an administrative body – a watchdog body that can aid aggrieved individuals and has a separate role in challenging discrimination. All the schemes concentrate heavily on the tort model – an individualistic remedial model – that is, one that relies on the aggrieved individual seeking a remedy. They are largely based on formal equality, on comparing like with like – meaning that the schemes are, apart from that relating to disability, symmetrical. In other words, they apply equally to members of the 'victim' group and the 'non-victim' group. For example, the Sexual Orientation Regulations were clearly aimed at employment disadvantage suffered by gays, but apply equally to homosexuals and heterosexuals. The Sex Discrimination Act was aimed at adverse treatment of women, but applies equally to women and men, and men have quite frequently taken advantage of it. The victim of discrimination must find an individual from a group without their regulated characteristic, and in a like situation, as a comparator. This symmetrical approach has created grave difficulties, especially in relation to pregnancy and harassment, since it is difficult to find a male equivalent of a pregnant or harassed woman, and this approach has meant that employers can argue that men and women are equally subjected to sexist taunts or adverse treatment for sickness (seeing pregnancy as an illness), and therefore women are not being discriminated against. Moreover, the formal equality model in the UK continues to bar the way to affirmative action. The use of this model in respect of the various protected grounds also means, depending on trade union involvement, or the involvement of the watchdog body, that a member of an already weak and disadvantaged group may find that their disadvantage is exacerbated by the burdensome process of bringing an action.[3]

But the similarity between the schemes must not be pressed too far – they are far from identical. It is clear that at present certain of the protected grounds are 'poor relations'. As Fredman puts it: 'a hierarchy of protection [is] established in the EU, with race given the widest reach, and disability, age, religion and sexual orientation the narrowest'.[4] There are significant differences between the current anti-discrimination schemes which highlight the weaknesses of some of them. Inequalities are created in the protection offered even in relation to the well-established grounds of race and gender. The schemes only apply arbitrarily to certain protected grounds. Protection from discrimination on the ground of sexual orientation is not covered in all the contexts in which discrimination on grounds of race or sex are covered. Previously no protection was available on this ground and so attempts were made through the courts to obtain it, using non-dedicated provisions, and may still be made, which were intended to extend the protection into contexts uncovered by the provisions. The protection on the

2 See below pp 1574–5.
3 See, especially, pp 1529–30, 1562–63, below.
4 Fredman, S, 'Equality: A New generation?' [2001] 30(2) ILJ 145–68 at p 145.

ground of race is at present stronger, in a number of respects, than that on the ground of sex – although this is about to change. Since much of the legislation is EU-driven, the strongest protection is available in areas of EU competence. The net result is that a mass of complex and, in some respects, unsatisfactory law has gathered around certain protected grounds, while the protection offered varies between them. In respect of the newly protected grounds the protection is based, or partly based, on secondary legislation only, although bolstered by the doctrine of the supremacy of EU law, and is in many ways less extensive.

The current schemes are complex, tortuous and formalistic. The various anti-discrimination measures provide a protection against discrimination which has often been found to be patchy, inconsistent and ineffective.[5] At the same time it has also often been said that there is 'too much law' in this area. In the UK, there are three sources of the law in this context – domestic dedicated anti-discrimination statutes and regulations, the legislation of the European Union, and that of the European Convention on Human Rights which operates at the international level and domestically through the Human Rights Act. A further reason for the over-abundance of law is that a struggle is evident at every point in the schemes to take account of the needs of employers and others, bearing in mind that the private sector is affected, while affording recognition to the detriment that discrimination creates. Thus, measures have been carefully tempered by exception clauses, which have then in turn gathered complex legal accretions. In other words, there are strong indications, especially in the sexual orientation scheme, of reluctant and timid reform. Nowhere is such reluctance more evident, it will be argued, than in relation to the nature of the remedies and their delivery.

Nevertheless, this complex web of law acts as a symbolic affirmation of society's disapproval of discrimination, and arguably provides a focus for challenge that fuels determination to seek further change rather than distracting attention away from more fruitful avenues. It is important to remember when confronting a mass of very technical and complex legislation that it deals with the fundamental concept of equality: the technicality should not be allowed to obscure the end that is sought. But key themes of the chapter will be: that institutional change is more effective than placing the onus on the individual to seek change; that providing rights, such as flexible parental leave for both partners, may be more valuable than providing a remedy after a wrong has occurred; and that providing remedies for *harms*, such as the stress caused by harassment at work, may well be more valuable than asking an individual to demonstrate that unequal treatment has occurred.

This subject is vast and in a book of this length selectivity is necessary; this chapter will concentrate on anti-discrimination measures aimed at curbing discrimination on grounds of race, gender and sexual orientation. An overview only of the provisions relating to gender reassignment, pregnancy, marital status is offered. The disability provisions are looked at in somewhat more detail since there are certain significant characteristics unique to that scheme that single it out from all the others. Those protected grounds are chosen since, broadly speaking, the model used is similar in relation to the other protected grounds – age, religion and belief. They also illustrate the very significant changes that have occurred, driven by EU law. But while similarities

---

5 See the criticisms in Hepple, Coussey and Choudhury, op. cit., fn 1.

in the legal tests and procedures are found using these examples, they also highlight the failure so far of equality legislation to provide equal protection from discrimination on the various protected grounds. This failure is highlighted with especial starkness when the strongest provisions – those available in respect of race – are compared with some of the weakest – those available in respect of discrimination on grounds of sexual orientation.

The chapter begins by indicating the sources of anti-discrimination law in the UK. It then moves on to consider the background to and ambit of the relevant statutes and regulations. It proceeds to take a closer look at certain of the protected grounds – race, gender, sexual orientation, disability, under the heads of: direct discrimination, indirect discrimination, lawful discrimination, harassment and victimisation, positive action, remedies and enforcement. Finally it turns to considering the work of the equality Commissions. The chapter ends with consideration of the future – of moving away from the formal equality model, and indeed away from anti-discrimination legislation, in favour of addressing specific problems and harms, towards a new conception of equality.

2 Sources of anti-discrimination law

In the UK there are three strands of law, deriving from the domestic schemes, the legislation of the European Union, and from the European Convention on Human Rights. The Human Rights Act (HRA) has complicated the issue since it has introduced a form of anti-discrimination law into domestic law – Article 14 – but has given it a lesser status than EU law. At the same time, at the international and domestic level, the Convention is a source of general principles for EU law.

European Union law

Anti-discrimination law in the UK cannot be studied without taking into account European Union law, which has been a highly significant influence. EU law has led to the introduction of provisions prohibiting discrimination outside the established areas of gender and race. Treaty Articles have both direct and horizontal effect and, therefore, Art 141 EC Treaty, which provides for equal pay for equal work without discrimination on grounds of sex, can be enforced in domestic courts against private and state bodies through the vehicle of the Equal Pay Act (below).[6] In other words, the provisions of the Act can be ignored or twisted out of their natural meaning in order to give effect to Art 141.[7] Directives, in contrast, only have vertical effect; they can, if sufficiently precise, clear and unconditional, be enforced against state bodies – emanations of the state.[8] Also, they can have indirect horizontal effect against private bodies through interpretation.[9] They can also by this means have indirect vertical effect (the interpretative obligation can be employed in an action in reliance on the domestic implementing legislation where the respondent is a state body).

6 See *Biggs v Somerset CC* [1996] IRLR 203.
7 See *Worringham v Lloyds Bank plc* Case C-69/80 [1981] ECR 767; for the CA decision, see [1982] IRLR 84.
8 See *Francovich v Italy* [1992] 21 IRLR 84; [1991] ECR I-5357; [1995] ICR 722.
9 Through s 2(4) of the European Communities Act 1972.

Sex discrimination law was until recently the only area directly affected. Article 119 of the Treaty of Rome, which was signed by Britain in 1973, governed the principle of equal pay for equal work. It is now Art 141 of the EC Treaty. It is amplified by the Equal Pay Directive 75/117, while the Equal Treatment Directive 76/207 and the Pregnancy Directive 92/85 govern other aspects of sexual discrimination. The Burden of Proof Directive affected the anti-sex discrimination scheme, as indicated below. Until 2003 domestic race discrimination provisions were influenced indirectly but they were then expressly covered by the Race Directive.[10]

There have been a number of further very significant developments, widening and deepening the protection from discrimination.[11] The Race Directive, extending beyond the employment field, which was implemented in 2003, brought race discrimination within the direct coverage of EC law for the first time. Article 39 EC Treaty covers nationality discrimination in employment. The very significant Framework Directive on equal opportunities in employment, adopted, like the Race Directive, under Art 13 of the EC Treaty,[12] allowed for the extension of anti-discrimination measures into the new areas of discrimination on grounds of sexual orientation, age, religion and belief. The Framework Directive also improved the protection offered by the Sex Discrimination Act. Development in this area continues apace. The Equal Treatment in Goods and Services Directive[13] extends Community discrimination law to the fields of supply of goods and services. Council Directive 2006/54/EC, described as a Directive 'on the implementation of the principle of equal opportunities and equal treatment of men and women in matters of employment and occupation', consolidates a number of previous Directives in this area, notably, the Directive 76/207/EEC.[14] The new Directive has to be implemented by member states by 15 August 2008.

Thus, there was clear pressure emanating from the EU to develop a broader and stronger anti-discrimination programme domestically. The largely EU-driven reforms are having two effects. First, the depth and impact of the current established domestic provisions relating to discrimination on grounds of sex, gender reassignment, race and disability, has been strengthened. Second, the anti-discrimination programme has broadened so that discrimination on new bases, in particular that of sexual orientation, but also that of transsexuality *per se*, is recognised within the law as unjustifiable.

---

10 Dir 2000/43/EC; Com 2000 328 (01), adopted in June 2000 by the Council of Ministers. The 'Race Directive' came into force on 19 July 2000 and was implemented by member states within three years of this date (for comment, see Lord Lester of Herne Hill QC, 'New European equality measures' [2000] PL 562).

11 For discussion, see Lord Lester of Herne Hill QC, ibid.

12 For discussion of Art 13, which was added by the Amsterdam Treaty, see Bell [1999] 6 Maastricht J of European and Comp Law 5.

13 Dir 2004/113/EC, due in force by 21 December 2007.

14 The consolidated Directives are: No 75/117 on equal pay for men and women; No 76/207 on equal treatment for men and women relating to access to employment; No 2002/73, amending Directive No 76/207, on equal treatment for men and women relating to employment, vocational training and promotion and working conditions; No 86/378 on equal treatment for men and women in occupational social security schemes; No 96/97, amending Directive No 86/378, on the implementation of the principle of equal treatment for men and women in occupational social security schemes; No 97/80 on the burden of proof in cases of discrimination based on sex; No 98/52 on the extension of Directive No 97/80 to the UK.

The commitment of the EU to equality currently receives its most broad and dramatic expression in The Charter of Fundamental Rights, which provides in Art 21(1):

> Any discrimination based on any ground such as sex, race, colour, ethnic or social origin, genetic features, language, religion or belief, political or any other opinion, membership of a national minority, property, birth, disability, age or sexual orientation shall be prohibited.

This is the broadest anti-discrimination measure in EU law in that it refers to a range of protected grounds and is not confined to the sphere of employment. It was to become part of the EU Constitution, but in 2005 the referenda in both France and the Netherlands rejected adoption of the Constitution. At present it is merely waiting in the wings, but it can be referred to in the European Court of Justice, so it may be viewed as having some impact on the development of EU law; it is an indication of the extent to which the concept of equality lies at the heart of the EU. Institutional change is also ongoing; in 2003, the European Council of Ministers agreed to create a new Fundamental Rights Agency (FRA) for the European Union, which will be broadly similar in remit, although by no means identical, to the new Commission for Equality and Human Rights in the UK, set up in 2007. The FRA's remit will cover all areas of equality, except gender, which is to be covered by a separate institute.

Domestic Anti-Discrimination Legislation – overview

There is a bewildering amount of dedicated domestic legislation in this area and it is rapidly, albeit incrementally, increasing, so an overview is of use. The HRA also makes an important contribution in this field which is considered below. As discussed below, the provisions were broadened in scope and new protected grounds were added under the impetus of EU law. The provisions are enumerated in the order in which they were introduced. The Sex Discrimination Act 1975 (SDA), as amended a number of times,[15] and most recently in 2005, covers discrimination on a number of protected grounds: sex, pregnancy, marital status and gender reassignment. The Equal Pay Act 1970 (EPA), as amended, covers sex discrimination in pay. The Sex Discrimination (Amendment) Regulations 2003 and the Employment (Equality) Sex Discrimination Regulations 2005 were also introduced into domestic law to implement the relevant aspects of the Framework Directive.[16] The Race Relations Act 1976, (RRA) as amended, covers discrimination on grounds of race, nationality, colour, ethnicity, national origins. The Disability Discrimination Act 1995 (DDA), as amended, covers discrimination on grounds of disability. The employment provisions in the 1995 Act were amended in 2003[17] and again in 2005 under the Disability Discrimination Act 2005. Thus, various, mainly EU driven, amendments were made to the SDA, RRA and DDA, since they were introduced

---

15 See SI 2001/2660, the Sex Discrimination (Indirect Discrimination and Burden of Proof) Regulations 2001, in force from 12 October 2001. For discussion, see Guild (2000) 29 ILJ 416.

16 Dir 2000/78/EC. Adopted under Art 13 of the Treaty Establishing the European Community (TEC).

17 By the Disability Discrimination Act (Amendment Regulations) 2003, passed in response to the Framework Directive.

which had the effect of both widening and strengthening the protection offered.[18] All these statutes cover discrimination in the contexts of employment, education, housing, the provision of goods and services, but not all the protected grounds are covered within all of these contexts, as explained below.

A number of new protected grounds – sexual orientation, age, religion and belief, had to be recognised in domestic law in order to implement European Council Directive 2000/78/EC (the Framework Directive). The Employment Equality (Sexual Orientation) Regulations 2003 cover discrimination on grounds of sexual orientation, but only in the context of employment. Part 3 of the Equality Act 2006 provides a power to extend the coverage of the regulations into other fields, and in January 2007 the Sexual Orientation (Goods and Services) Regulations were passed by Parliament to apply in Northern Ireland. The equivalent regulations for Britain are expected to be introduced into Parliament in 2007.[19] The Employment Equality (Religion or Belief) Regulations 2003 cover discrimination on grounds of religion or belief, but only in the context of employment. However, Part 2 of the Equality Act 2006 extended the coverage to premises, education, the provision of goods, facilities and services. The Employment Equality (Age) Regulations 2006,[20] creating protection for discrimination on grounds of age in employment, came into force in 2006.

The Equality Act 2006, as indicated, is *not* a comprehensive equality statute, bringing all anti-discrimination provisions together in one statute, and eliminating the gaps and anomalies in the protection. However, it improved the protection for discrimination based on religion and provided powers to improve it for discrimination based on sexual orientation. It also set up the new Commission for Equality and Human Rights (CEHR). A comprehensive, all encompassing Single Equality Act which would streamline all these equality provisions, is in contemplation at the present time.[21]

The Human Rights Act and the European Convention on Human Rights

The EU provisions are in many respects more valuable than the guarantee of freedom from discrimination under Art 14 of the European Convention, partly because they may override domestic statutory provisions in domestic courts,[22] and partly because, as Chapter 2 explained, Art 14 only covers areas falling within the scope of the other

---

18 Directive 97/80, the Burden of Proof Directive, implemented in the Sex Discrimination (Indirect Discrimination and Burden of Proof) Regulations 2001 (SI 2001/2660), affected the anti-sex discrimination scheme as did the Framework Directive on equal opportunities in employment.

19 In order to implement the Equal Treatment in Goods and Services Directive.

20 SI 2006/1036.

21 See www.womenandequalityunit.gov.uk/dlr.

22 In general, EU directives are enforceable in national courts only against the state or against bodies under the control of the state (*Foster v British Gas plc* [1990] 3 All ER 897) but not against private bodies. However, it was found in *Francovich v Italy* [1992] 21 IRLR 84; [1991] ECR I-5357; [1995] ICR 722 that an individual who suffers loss at the hands of a private body owing to the state's failure to undertake full implementation of a directive may have a claim against the state. See further Ellis, E, *European Community Sex Equality Law*, 2nd edn, 1998, Clarendon, Chapter 4. For discussion of the influence of EU equality laws, see McCrudden (1993) 13 OJLS 320; Ellis [1994] 31 CMLR 43.

Articles,[23] although the other Article may be viewed as having an extended ambit where Art 14 is also argued.[24] This limitation was highlighted in *Botta v Italy*.[25] The European Court of Human Rights considered a claim that the lack of disabled facilities at a seaside resort violated the applicant's right to equal enjoyment of his right to respect for private life under Art 8 read together with Art 14. The claim was rejected on the basis that 'social' rights, such as the participation of disabled people in recreational facilities, fall outside Art 8. Therefore, Art 14 did not apply. If, even on an extended view of the ambit of a Convention right, it would still be very difficult to show that any right applied, Art 14 cannot be employed.

Even where Art 14 may apply, Strasbourg has often been reluctant to afford it separate consideration, if a breach of another Convention right is established.[26] Where Art 14 has been considered, it has been afforded a narrow interpretation by the Commission. For example, in *Stedman v UK*[27] a requirement to work on a Sunday led to the dismissal of the applicant, who had religious objections to Sunday working. It was found by the Commission that a general requirement that has a disproportionate impact on one group is not discriminatory. This decision suggests that Art 14 does not recognise indirect discrimination, although it is not conclusive of that matter,[28] and also that, as Ewing puts it, 'the Convention rights can be qualified by contract'.[29] This is far from meaning, however, that Art 14 is of limited value in this area.

The Court tends to adhere to a more developed conception of discrimination and has departed, as it has done in some other contexts, from the stance taken by the Commission. In *Schuler-Zgraggen v Switzerland*[30] the Court said: 'the advancement of the equality of the sexes is today a major goal in the member states of the Council of Europe and very weighty reasons would have to be put forward before such a difference of treatment [as occurred in the instant case] could be regarded as compatible with the Convention.'[31] The Court has recognised that positive discrimination may be appropriate in some circumstances; it has said that the guarantee under Art 14 will be violated where persons in analogous situations are treated differently where there is no objective and reasonable justification, but also where states without such justification fail to treat differently persons whose situations are significantly different.[32]

Further, Art 14 covers discrimination on a wide range of bases and therefore, combined with Art 8 or, in some circumstances, a range of the Articles, in particular Arts 5, 6, 10 or 11, it can be used to address discrimination that is currently outside the

23 See Chapter 2, p 108.
24 See Baker, A, 'The Enjoyment of Rights and Freedoms: A New Conception of the "Ambit" under Article 14 ECHR' [2006] 89 MLR 714; 'Article 14 ECHR: A Protector, Not a Prosecutor' in Fenwick, H, Phillipson, G and Masterman, R (eds), *Judicial Reasoning and the Human Rights Act 1998*, 2007.
25 (1998) 26 EHRR 241.
26 See *Dudgeon v UK* (1982) 4 EHRR 149, para 69; discussed in Chapter 2, pp 81–82.
27 (1997) 23 EHRR CD 168.
28 It should be compared with *Thlimmenos v Greece*, Judgment of 6 April 2000 which could be viewed as opening the door to recognition of indirect discrimination.
29 Ewing, op. cit., fn 1, p 288.
30 (1993) 16 EHRR 405, para 22; see also *Van Raalte v Netherlands* (1997) 24 EHRR 503, para 39.
31 See further Livingstone, op. cit., fn 1; Ewing, op. cit., fn 1, p 288; Clayton and Tomlinson, op. cit., fn 1, Chapter 17.
32 *Thlimmenos v Greece*, judgment of 6 April 2000.

EC or domestic anti-discrimination schemes. For example, it can be used to attack discrimination on the grounds of sexual orientation or of religion, in contexts that are not covered under the domestic schemes discussed below, or under the current EU schemes.[33] It can also, very significantly, fill gaps in those schemes even within the contexts they do cover. But the HRA itself curbs the effect of the Convention since it only binds public authorities under s 6. Since it currently appears that the HRA does not create direct horizontal effect,[34] its impact in this area is subject to certain limitations.

If a standard public authority, or a functional public authority acting in its public function, discriminates in a manner that could be addressed by Art 8 in conjunction with Art 14, or Art 8 alone, a free-standing action could be brought against it under s 7(1)(a) HRA, although not in an Employment Tribunal (ET) which has no jurisdiction to hear such claims. If a discriminatory measure is contained in a statute, s 3 HRA and Arts 8 (or another relevant Article) and 14 can be brought to bear upon the offending provision. Section 3 can apply to the statutory anti-discrimination measures, including the SDA and RRA, if it appears that there is a potential gap in the provisions where, under Arts 14 and 8 combined, a remedy would be available. As discussed below, this may open the possibility of bringing some forms of discrimination within the Sex Discrimination Act that are not currently covered by it. The problem is that the statutory scheme is limited to discrimination on certain grounds and it may not be possible to interpret the provisions widely enough to cover other forms of discrimination. But by this route, it is possible that gaps in the statutory schemes, including the scheme relating to disability, could be narrowed. Section 3 and Art 14 (so long as another Article is relevant) can also have an effect on any relevant statutory provision, such as the provisions affecting unfair dismissal,[35] meaning that Art 14's anti-discrimination protection has a very wide-ranging potential, on both neutral and overtly discriminatory provisions. Since this area of law is largely (although not wholly) covered by statute, Arts 8 and 14 combined can have quite a wide ranging indirect horizontal effect. A number of discrimination claims are, however, brought in Employment Tribunals, and an ET's powers to give effect to Convention rights are limited in a number of significant respects, even beyond the limitations already imposed by the HRA. Apart from its inability to hear s 7(1)(a) HRA claims, ETs and the Employment Appeal Tribunal (EAT) have no power to

---

33 See Chapter 2, pp 108–9.
34 See Chapter 4, pp 250–56 and Chapter 9, pp 824–26, 902–15.
35 See *X v Y* [2004] IRLR 471; ICR 1634 in which the Employment Appeals Tribunal (EAT) laid out the way that Art 14 could affect unfair dismissal and other statutory claims in Tribunals. It is not possible to bring a claim for 'breach of Convention rights' in the ET under s 7(1)(a) HRA, but a claimant can argue that the HRA requires that UK legislation be interpreted in a particular way so as not to breach her Convention rights. This approach was taken in *X v Y* and in *Pay v Lancashire Probation Service* [2004] IRLR 129. In both instances claimants were dismissed due to their activities outside work. Each claimant claimed that such a dismissal was necessarily unfair under the Employment Rights Act 1996 (ERA), because it involved an infringement of their right to respect for their private life under Art 8 and their right of freedom of expression under Art 10. The dismissal in each case was found to be fair on the facts of the case, but the EAT in *Pay* and the Court of Appeal in *X v Y* agreed that when deciding whether an employer has acted reasonably in dismissing an employee, the ET should interpret the words 'reasonably or unreasonably' in s 98(4) of the ERA as meaning 'reasonably or unreasonably having regard to the applicant's Convention rights'. In *X v Y* the Court of Appeal said that the effect of this was that it would not normally be fair for an employer to dismiss an employee for a reason which was an unjustified interference with the employee's private life.

make a declaration of incompatibility.[36] This limitation means on occasion that an ET cannot provide a remedy to a claimant even where it has found that an individual's Convention rights have been infringed. It can merely refer the matter to the Court of Appeal, which does have the power to make a declaration of incompatibility.[37] An ET is also in the same position as are courts in general under the HRA in that if a provision in domestic legislation is found to be incompatible with Convention rights, it has no power to disapply the incompatible provision, and has to give effect to it as it stands. This contrasts with the position in cases where domestic law is incompatible with an European Directive or EC Treaty, where the ET can disapply the domestic law.

Where a provision in itself appears to be compatible with the relevant Convention Article(s) that of course does not exhaust the duty of the court/tribunal in relation to the Convention, due to s 6 HRA. When a court or tribunal is applying statutory provisions, including anti-discrimination statutes, in relation to, for example, an employment matter, it must abide by its duty under s 6 HRA, which means *applying* the provision compatibly with Art 14 (assuming that another Convention right touches on the matter at hand).

Thus, unless the courts eventually take the view that they themselves, as public bodies, must seek to ensure that an applicant obtains his or her Convention rights – which they are unlikely to do – the anti-discrimination provisions of Arts 14 and another Article (usually Art 8) combined are not directly justiciable against private bodies, except as a matter of interpretation or application where a statute applies and s 3 or s 6 HRA – or both – have an impact. It is hard to see that indirect horizontal effect could be created by seeking to develop the existing common law under the impetus of s 6 of the HRA[38] since the common law has failed so far to develop any anti-discrimination remedies. Thus, the potential of Art 14 domestically is doubly limited – first by its own inherent limitation, since it is non-free standing, and second by the lack of direct horizontal effect under the HRA. In general, therefore, it is not expected that at present the impact of the HRA in this context will be very great, although in respect of certain current areas in which discrimination can occur unchecked it may be of great value, while it may also be valuable in extending the meaning of statutory provisions, by considering the effect of Arts 8 and 14 read together. This is an instance therefore in which EU law is of far more significance than the ECHR in the private sector due to the lack of private common law on which the Convention can bite via s 6 HRA.

---

36 As Chapter 4 pointed out, only those courts listed in s 4(5) HRA (the High Court, Court of Appeal and House of Lords, and the High Court of Justiciary and Court of Session in Scotland) can make such a declaration.

37 In e.g. *Whittaker v P&M Watson Haulage* (EAT 157/01, unreported) both the ET and EAT held that the exclusion then in place in the Disability Discrimination Act 1995 for employers with less than 15 employees was incompatible with Art 6 of the ECHR because it contravened Mr Whittaker's right to have his claim regarding his civil rights heard. However, the EAT could not provide Mr Whittaker with a remedy, because it was not possible to interpret the DDA compatibly with his Convention rights, so it had to apply the DDA as drafted. It could not make a declaration of the incompatibility. All it could do was to refer the matter to the Court of Appeal, which did have the power to make a declaration of incompatibility.

38 As occurred in *Douglas v Hello!* [2001] 2 WLR 992; see Chapter 9, pp 903–5, and Chapter 4, p 252; *Campbell* – see Chapter 4, pp 253–55, and Chapter 9, pp 826, 911–13.

Where another Article and Art 14 combined cover the same area as EU provisions, they can be used as a source of general principles for the interpretation of the EU law, under Art 6 of the Treaty of Rome (now Art 13, as amended by the Amsterdam Treaty). The EU provisions can override domestic law and, therefore, by this means those Convention Articles could be given, in a sense, further effect than the HRA allows them. Thus, for example, an applicant bringing an action against a private body and seeking to rely on the Sex Discrimination Act in respect of discrimination on grounds of gender reassignment in a context excluded from the Act, could begin by arguing that s 3 of the HRA should be used to broaden the meaning of the Act in reliance on Arts 8 and 14. If this failed, on the basis that such an interpretation would amount to legislating, the applicant could rely on s 2(4) of the European Communities Act 1972[39] in arguing that the interpretation in question should be adopted in order to satisfy the demands of the Equal Treatment Directive or any other relevant Directive.[40] At that stage, in order to determine the requirements of the Directive, Strasbourg jurisprudence on Arts 8 and 14 could re-enter the argument. This possibility could be even more significant in relation to the domestic measures that have been adopted in response to the Framework and Race Directives.

As Chapter 2 explained, Protocol 12 provides a free-standing right to freedom from discrimination.[41] Protocol 12 is evidence of a clear recognition of the weakness of the anti-discrimination measure under Art 14 of the Convention, and its existence may be prompting the European Court of Human Rights to move away from its previous stance under Art 14 in favour of a more developed and determined position on anti-discrimination under that Article, even prior to the ratification of Protocol 12. If Protocol 12 is eventually ratified by the UK and then included in Sched 1 to the HRA, it will have a far reaching impact in this context, since a free-standing right to non-discrimination on a wide range of grounds, including those of sexual orientation or religion, would then be created, which would have direct effect as against public authorities. It might also have an impact on the currently protected grounds since it could be relied upon in an attempt to extend or fill gaps in the legislation. Thus, it would create new rights against public authorities and, possibly, via statute, against both public and private bodies. At present, Protocol 12 has not been ratified and the government is opposed to ratification.

3 Domestic anti-discrimination measures

Discrimination on grounds of sex[42]

At common law and under statute, women were historically subject to a number of legal disabilities, but the end of the 19th and the beginning of the twentieth century saw

---

39 See Chapter 3, p 152.

40 See pp 1504–5, below.

41 See p 106 for further discussion, see Khaliq, V, 'Protocol 12 to the ECHR: a step forward or a step too far?' [2001] PL 457.

42 Texts referred to: Deakin and Morris, op. cit., fn 1, Chapter 6; von Prondzynski and Richards, op. cit., fn 1; Connolly, M, op. cit., fn 1; Barnard, C and Hepple, B, 'Substantive equality' (2000) 59(3) CLJ 562; Hepple, Coussey and Choudhury, op. cit., fn 1; Clayton and Tomlinson, op. cit., fn 1, Chapter 17; McColgan, op. cit., fn 1; Honeyball, *Sex, Employment and the Law*, 1991, Blackwell; McCrudden, op. cit., fn 1; Rhode, D, *Justice and Gender: Sex Discrimination and the Law*, 1989; Fenwick, H and Hervey, T,

the gradual removal of such disabilities by statute. Women obtained the right to sign contracts, to own property irrespective of their marital status, to vote and to stand for Parliament. The Sex Disqualification (Removal) Act 1919 removed any disqualification by way of sex or marriage for those who wished to exercise a public function, hold a civil or judicial office, enter any civil profession or vocation or be admitted to any incorporated society. However, the marriage bar continued to operate in many jobs until the Second World War.[43] Once these disabilities had been removed there was opposition to further legislation.[44] It was thought that the barriers preventing women entering public life were down and therefore further measures were unnecessary. However, the fact that women were, for the first time, able to enter the public domain did not mean that they were accepted there. Theoretically, women had the same opportunities as men but, in practice, since there were no formal barriers to discrimination by employers and others, these practices continued. It may be assumed that this was due in part to prejudice and in part to the operation of the market which had no interest in ensuring better treatment for a group of employees who could traditionally be treated badly. Employers openly paid the 'women's' rate for the job,[45] a lower rate than that for men, and openly refused to appoint women above a certain level or to do certain jobs.[46] Under the common law, it was immaterial that the grounds for such decisions might be capricious or reprehensible.

The view taken in the 1974 White Paper on Sex Discrimination preceding the 1975 Act was that women were being held back in employment and other fields because they were not being judged on their individual merits, but on the basis of a general presumption of inferiority. It was apparent that the common law was not going to bring about change, partly because the judiciary saw the creation of a comprehensive anti-discrimination code as the province of Parliament but also because, even in the 1970s, sympathy with discriminatory practices was evident among certain judges. In *Morris v Duke-Cohen*,[47] for example, a judge was prepared to find a solicitor negligent

'Sex equality in the Single Market: new directions for the European Court of Justice' [1995] 32 CMLR 443–70; Hervey, T, *Justifications for Sex Discrimination in Employment*, 1993, Butterworths; Ellis, 'The definition of discrimination in EC sex equality law' (1994) 19 EL Rev 563; Millar and Phillips, 'Evaluating anti-discrimination legislation in the UK: some issues and approaches' (1983) 11 Int J Soc Law 417; McGinley, 'Judicial approaches to sex discrimination in US and UK – a comparative study' (1986) 59 MLR 413, p 415; on pregnancy, see Conaghan (1993) 20 JLS 71. Current reading: Fredman, S, *Women and the Law*, 1997, Clarendon, esp Chapters 5, 7, 9; McGlynn, C, 'Reclaiming a feminist vision: the reconciliation of paid work and family life in EU law and policy' (2001) 7 Columbia Journal of European Law 241; Atkins and Hoggett, *Women and the Law*, 1984, Blackwell, pp 1–63 for background; Pannick, D, *Sex Discrimination Law*, 1985, Clarendon; Bourne, C and Whitmore, J, *Anti-discrimination Law in Britain*, 3rd edn, 1996, Sweet and Maxwell; Fuller, A, Unwin, Lorna and Beck, V, (2005) *Employers, young people and gender segregation*. Equal Opportunities Commission Working Paper Series No 28, Manchester: EOC

43 The 1919 Act was found to mean only that the employers must lift restrictions on women; it did not prevent particular employers imposing restrictions on women and it gave rise to no right of litigation: see *Price v Rhondda Urban Council* [1923] 2 Ch 372.

44 Atkins and Hoggett *Women and the Law*, 1984 note the lack of Parliamentary concern about women at work and failure to debate the problem, p 19.

45 In 1970, women's average pay was 63.1% that of men (EOC, Annual Report 1988, p 45).

46 The study by National Segregation 1979 showed that by 1971, over half of all men were in occupations where they outnumbered women by at least 9 to 1 and 77% worked in occupations which were at least 70% male.

47 (1975) 120 SJ 826.

for taking advice from a wife when a husband was available, on the basis that a sensible wife would expect her husband to make the major decisions.

Formal and substantive equality

The Sex Discrimination Act 1975 affords recognition to two competing views as to the most effective means of securing equality: the so called formal equality approach and the substantive equality or pluralist approach.[48] The former, which, as mentioned above, is based on classic liberalism and is the dominant approach, assumes that in a just society, the sex of a person would carry no expectations with it; it would be as irrelevant as their eye colour. It takes the view that women and men are equally able to take advantage of opportunities and that therefore, if a similarly situated man would also have been treated adversely, no discrimination has occurred. Thus, once specific instances of differential treatment based on sex are prevented or addressed, under this approach women would no longer be viewed as placed at a disadvantage.

The formal equality approach has some strong advantages which should not be forgotten. It is intuitively appealing – in the sense that it is self-evidently 'fair' to treat like as like rather than favouring males. If pre-SDA women were treated on the basis of an unfounded assumption of inferiority, conversely men were treated on the basis of an unfounded assumption of superiority. Thus it appears, up to a point, to promote competition: in effect, positive action in favour of men meant that they were insulated from competition with women. In fact, positive action in favour of men took the form of reverse discrimination: however high the claims of the woman candidate for, for example, higher education, based on merit, they were irrelevant since they would always be displaced by the claims of a male, even if wholly inferior in terms of merit. In higher education, for example, during the nineteenth century and part of the 20th, men obtained places in Universities in competition only with other men. This was also the case in respect of almost all professions. In other words, men obtained preferential treatment based purely on gender and not on merit – they were protected from competition. The current situation in which men, at least in respect of education and the lower reaches of all professions – except the armed services and some religious orders – are in effect forced by the SDA to compete on equal terms with women, aids in ensuring that the better candidate is chosen rather than the male candidate. Private clubs, certain sporting associations, the armed services (in terms of restrictions relating to direct combat) and the Catholic Church enjoy the dubious distinction of continuing to discriminate.

But the formal equality approach has limitations since it only inquires into equal treatment of those in like situations. The substantive equality approach, on the other hand, which was imported from the US,[49] takes a number of factors, such as past discrimination or social conditioning, into account and asks whether policies and practices which are neutral on their face actually have an adverse impact on women owing to factors which particularly affect them. It accepts that there may be differences between the situations of men and women, but holds that penalties should not inevitably

---

48 See Gardner (1989) 9 OJLS 1 and Brest (1976) 90 Harv LR 1 on the different philosophies apparent in the legislation.

49 For a comparative discussion of the approaches to UK and US discrimination, see McGinley, op. cit., fn 59.

attach to the recognition of those differences. This approach derives from the Supreme Court decision in *Griggs v Duke Power Company*;[50] when the defendant company administered an aptitude test to all job applicants it was shown that significantly fewer blacks than whites passed the test and that the skills examined by the test were not particularly relevant to the jobs applied for. In these circumstances, it was held that the test was discriminatory.[51] This latter approach is given some recognition in the SDA within the concept of indirect discrimination.

In the context of sex discrimination, the use of aptitude or other tests would be unlikely to disadvantage women. But past discriminatory practices – although their effects are becoming less apparent – might do so.[52] Most significantly, the effect of child-caring responsibilities tend to do so: for example, currently more women than men are single parents. Further, as discussed below, although this is changing rapidly, men have not fully accepted an equal share of child-care responsibilities,[53] and parental leave is still not equally available to both men and women, although the Work and Families Act 2006 will bring about some improvements in that position.[54] Discrimination based purely on *gender* appears to be dying out gradually; once women entered education and the professions on equal terms with men, directly discriminatory arguments that women were unsuitable for certain jobs, or could not perform at the same level as boys in certain subjects were abandoned;[55] indeed, in education the problem of under-performance of boys compared to girls is a constant feature of educational debate. As indicated below, discrimination against women now relates far more to pregnancy and childcare, and to unconscious or conscious stereotyping relating to maternity, than to gender *per se*.[56] But when employment detriment based on maternity arises it is more effectively addressed as a free-standing harm, rather than as discrimination. This point gives rise to consideration of the statutory protections for maternity, outside the SDA. Although indirect discrimination is an aspect of substantive equality, its recognition in the SDA relies only on addressing inequality of treatment; it does not ensure equality of outcome.

Child care responsibilities and flexible working

A number of measures emanating from the EU have had some effect on the work/life balance, including the Working Time Directive,[57] which was implemented in the Working Time Regulations 1998.[58] But it is generally accepted that while the regulations have had some impact on the long hours culture of the UK,[59] it has not been of a radical

---

50 (1971) 401 US 424.

51 For further discussion in the US context see Wilborn, 'The disparate impact model of discrimination: theory and limits' (1985) 34 American University L Rev 799.

52 See *Steel v Post Office* [1977] IRLR 288.

53 See Johnes, G, *Career Interruptions and Labour Market Outcomes* (2006) EOC Paper No 45.

54 See p 1492 below.

55 The discussion of indirect discrimination on grounds of sex (see pp 1539–44) indicates that current discrimination tends to relate to maternity, not to gender *per se*.

56 Miller, L, Neathey, F, Pollard, E and Hill, D, (2004) *Occupational segregation, gender gaps and skill gaps*. Equal Opportunities Commission Working Paper Series No 15, Manchester: EOC.

57 Directive 93/104/EC.

58 SI 1998/1833.

59 See the TUC Report, March 2001 'Burnout Britain' factsheet, www.tuc.org.uk.

nature, partly because of the possibilities of opting out of the provisions.[60] The Part-Time Workers Directive[61] was implemented in the Part-Time Workers (Prevention of Less Favourable Treatment) Regulations 2000.[62] The regulations prohibit discrimination against part-time workers. But the employee must point to a comparator under the regulations, although possibly to a hypothetical comparator under the Directive, and must show that he or she has been treated unfavourably in comparison with a comparable employee working full-time, on the ground of part-time working. The unfavourable treatment can be justified. Thus, the scheme was always likely to be limited in its effects; it was estimated that, owing to the need to find an appropriate comparator, it was likely to affect only about 7% of UK part-time workers.[63] The regulations do not provide a right to work part-time or to work flexible hours to accommodate caring responsibilities, or to job-share. In order for employees to seek to assert such rights, they must use, as indicated above, the difficult route provided by the SDA.

Thus, although social patterns are changing,[64] and men increasingly have responsibilities as carers, the current gendered divide in caring responsibilities[65] has not elicited a legislative response that fully recognises that divide, thus sometimes forcing women into a dependency on men or on the state which may result in a blighting of their lives and those of their children.[66] As Johnes has found, such dependency is linked to educational levels;[67] those already in the weaker positions in the labour market[68] tend to weaken their positions further by leaving it for periods of time. Child-rearers and other carers with relatively high levels of education are more likely to continue working full-time, and unlikely to leave labour market employment altogether. Conversely, those with

---

60 See further Ewing, Bradley and McColgan, op. cit., fn 1, Chapter 4, pp 411–13.

61 Directive 96/34/EC.

62 SI 2000/1551.

63 Government's Regulatory Impact Assessment.

64 See Chartered Institute of Personnel and Development (2004) *Flexible working and paternity leave.* Available at: http://www.cipd.co.uk/NR/rdonlyres/AE77D6F3–99DA-4845-A0B6-FE027C466C01/0/paternity1004.pdf; Weiss, C.R. (2001) 'On flexibility', *Journal of Economic Behavior and Organisation*, 46: 347–56.

65 See Brewer, M and Paull, G, *Newborns and new schools: critical times in women's employment*, 2006, Research Report No 308 London: Department for Work and Pensions; Henz, U, 'The effects of informal care on paid-work participation in Great Britain: a lifecourse perspective', (2004) *Ageing and Society*, 24: 851–80; Henz, U, 'Informal caregiving at working age: effects of job characteristics and family configuration', (2006) *Journal of Marriage and Family*, forthcoming; Maher, J and Green, H, *Carers 2000*, 2002, Norwich: Office for National Statistics.

66 See Cabinet Office Briefing: *Women's Incomes Over the Lifetime and Women and Men in the UK: Facts and Figures* (www.women.unit.gov.uk/publications.htm); Darton, D and Hurrell, K, *People working part-time below their potential*, 2005, Equal Opportunities Commission; *Free to choose: tackling gender barriers to better jobs; Greater expectations*, (2005) Equal Opportunities Commission; Grant, L, Yeandle, S and Buckner, L, *Working below potential: women and part-time work*, 2005, Equal Opportunities Commission Working Paper Series No 19 Sigle-Rushton, W and Perrons, D, *Employment transitions over the life cycle: a statistical analysis*, 2006, Equal Opportunities Commission Working Paper Series No 46, Manchester: EOC. Walling, A, 'Families and work', Labour Market Trends, 2005 July: pp 275–83.

67 See Johnes, G, *Career Interruptions and Labour Market Outcomes* (2006) EOC Paper No 45.

68 See: (2005) *Part-time is no crime - so why the penalty?*, Equal Opportunities Commission; Francesconi, M and Gosling, A, *Career paths of part-time workers*, 2005, Equal Opportunities Commission Working Paper Series No. 19; Manning, A and Petrongolo, B, *The part-time pay penalty*, 2004.

relatively low levels of education are less likely to continue working full-time, and are more likely to leave labour market employment. Some 61% of women who are educated to A-level or above standard remain in full-time work a year after childbirth, but only 46% of those who are less highly educated do so.[69] At the same time the proportion of women who, following childbirth, ceased to be employed in the labour market has been steadily declining in the 1990s and post-2000. In 1992–97, 32% of such women who were previously working full-time were not working in the labour market in the following year. By 1998–2003, this proportion had fallen to 19%.[70]

Use of the indirect discrimination route under the SDA in efforts to seek flexible working in order to stay within the labour market and avert the adverse possibilities associated with leaving it, is, as discussed below, burdensome and fraught with pitfalls, but it has been eased somewhat by the importation of the more generous test considered below. Nevertheless, this avoids the question whether use of the SDA can ever be very effective in enhancing the ability of parents to avoid disadvantage in the labour market. The EOC has argued that employment laws (such as flexible working regulations, maternity and paternity leave provisions) that are currently outside the scope of the equality enactments could be brought within the currently proposed Single Equality Act.[71] That would aid in dealing with the complexity and overlap of the current laws. But more importantly it would recognise that arguing for flexible working or maternity rights through the vehicle of equality law – at least on the SDA model – is ineffective and may aid in creating disadvantage.

Pregnancy and parental rights

Rights to leave or pay based on pregnancy and maternity have developed in a manner that takes them a long way from sex discrimination law, but it is convenient to discuss them at this point. In discussing pregnancy and maternity, it must be borne in mind that the legislation relating to maternity leave enshrines straightforward direct discrimination on grounds of sex since it differentiates between women and men in a manner that may disadvantage both. Parental leave was available in most of the EU member states[72] prior to the implementation of the Parental Leave Directive, implemented by the Parental Leave and Maternity etc Regulations.[73] The regulations allowed for three months' unpaid leave for any person having responsibility for a child until it is five. This is in addition to maternity leave provision. Section 57A of the ERA also allowed for reasonable time off for carers. The take up of parental leave was clearly likely to be low since it is unpaid, while take up under s 57A was likely to be slow. As indicated above, under s 99 of the Employment Rights Act 1996 (ERA) a woman is protected from dismissal on grounds of pregnancy and under s 71 of the ERA, as amended, all

---

69 See Johnes, G, *Career Interruptions and Labour Market Outcomes* (2006) EOC Paper No 45; Gregg, P, Gutierrez-Domenech, M and Waldfogel, J *The employment of married mothers in Great Britain: 1974–2000*, 2003, Centre for Market and Public Organisation Working Paper 03/078, University of Bristol.

70 Ibid.

71 See EOC's *Submission to the Discrimination Law Review* (2006).

72 For details see McColgan, op. cit., fn 1, pp 378–79.

73 The Parental Leave and Maternity etc Regulations 1999 (SI 1999/3312).

women have automatic rights to maternity leave. If a woman has one year's continuous service, she has a right to an additional period of leave.[74] Compensation under the ERA is much lower than that available under the SDA.

The Work and Families Act 2006, which came into force in April 2007, creates new rights to more maternity and paternity leave and pay. Under the Act working parents will be entitled to: nine months statutory maternity pay, statutory adoption pay and maternity allowance (and it is intended that this be increased to a year's paid leave). There will be a new right to an additional period of paternity leave for fathers, which will be introduced alongside the extension of statutory maternity pay, adoption pay and maternity allowance to 12 months. This will enable them to benefit from leave and statutory pay if the mother returns to work after six months but before the end of her maternity leave period. 'Keeping in Touch' days will be introduced so that a woman on maternity leave can go into work for a few days, without losing her right to maternity leave or a week's statutory pay. But it is notable that the statute still determines which member of the couple will take advantage of which package, meaning that the couple cannot decide for themselves, depending on their individual employment circumstances, how they would prefer to divide up the package.

A preferable approach would be to offer a more generous parental leave entitlement to parents rather than giving preference to mothers, to be divided between the partners as they saw fit. The five-year cut-off point under s 57A is also very grudging. At present, women are doubly disadvantaged: on becoming parents they have in effect no choice but to be the partner taking the longer period of leave, whether they would prefer to be that partner or not. Employers may therefore view them as less reliable or less committed owing to this fact. Even women who do not wish to have children may experience discrimination on this ground since, at the point of appointment to a post, the possibility that they may have children and therefore take leave may be covertly, even unconsciously, held against them. At present, as indicated by the provision for parental leave, recognition, of a slow and reluctant nature, of the responsibilities of fathers is occurring.[75] When flexible working hours were introduced as a right[76] they were applicable to both parents. Employees who meet certain eligibility criteria have a right to request flexible working. The right is set out in s 80F ERA, as amended by the Employment Act 2002. It does not detract from the existing rights to work flexibly protected under the SDA, in the sense that in dealing with requests for flexible working, indirect discrimination is more likely to occur.

74 ERA, s 73 and the Parental Leave and Maternity etc. Regulations 1999, regs 5 and 7. Previously, she had a right to return to work within 29 weeks of the birth under the Employment Protection Consolidation Act 1978, s 39(1)(b). For further discussion of the current position see McColgan, A, 'Family friendly frolics' (2000) 29 ILJ 125.

75 Note: the proposals under the Green Paper on Parental Rights 2001 which proposed the introduction of paid paternity leave and 26 weeks' adoptive leave were limited to parents of disabled children and adoptive parents. The government opposed paid parental leave. But see now the Work and Families Act 2006.

76 The proposals under the Green Paper on Parental Rights 2001 included the possibility of an entitlement to reduced hours working for both parents. See below, pp 1543–44 for discussion of some of the current measures relating to the work/life balance.

Without further change in this direction the problems associated with the legally enshrined expectation that some women will damage their career for their home life,[77] while some men will conversely damage their home life to further their career, will continue. These include the likelihood that some women will forgo or delay having children, and that some of those who do have children may suffer employment detriment, including periods without work, leading to poverty and insecurity for themselves and their children, and severely affecting them after they reach pensionable age.[78] At present, some employers recognise that many employees have children and that seeking to enable them to continue at work without suffering stress is good practice that makes business sense, since skills and training are not lost to the company and productivity is enhanced.[79] A company which could only or mainly rely on those without parental responsibilities would clearly be impoverished in terms of the pool of talent it could count on. But the stance of the current government in seeking to enhance opportunities to achieve work/family balance, while showing greater imagination and far-sightedness than the previous one, has so far been hesitant and reluctant. The case for a much stronger SDA and/or for measures generally aiding parents does not rest only on enhancing opportunities for women. The economic case for making stronger and faster progress towards sex equality is clear. The Women and Work Commission has found that the pay and productivity gap costs the UK £23 billion each year. The *Equalities Review Interim Report* indicates that the 'employment penalty' (i.e. the difference caused by a particular characteristic), for women with children, whilst falling dramatically, is '*still by far the largest of all employment penalties recorded*'.[80] The review reports that single mothers and partnered mothers with children under 11 face the largest employment penalty in the workforce, followed by Pakistani and Bangladeshi women.[81] As the review notes, women in the workforce provide a huge opportunity for Britain to improve its competitiveness and productivity, particularly given their high educational standard. The questions of flexible working and support for parents are considered further below, in relation to indirect discrimination on grounds of sex.

Equal pay and sex discrimination

The Equal Pay Act 1970 (EPA) governs the contractual aspects of a woman's employment. It is anomalous in that it is separate from the SDA; there is no good reason for having two separate instruments and it merely introduces further complexity and technicality into an already complex scheme. The Act received the royal assent in 1970, but it did not come into force until 1975; the idea was that employers would voluntarily remove sexual discrimination in pay. In fact, as the TUC warned the government would occur,

77 See, for discussion, Smeaton, D, 'Work return rates after childbirth in the UK', *Women, Employment and Society*, (2006) 20, 1: 5–25; Smeaton, D and Marsh, A, *Maternity and paternity rights and benefits: survey of employees 2005*, (2006) Employment Relations Research Series No 50, London: Department of Trade and Industry.

78 See TUC Submissions to the House of Commons Social Security Committee, June 1999 (see TUC website: www.tuc.org.uk); Jacobs, S, (1999) 'Trends in women's career patterns and in gender occupational mobility in Britain', *Gender, Work and Organization*, 6: pp 32–46.

79 See (2005) *Britain's hidden brain drain*. Manchester: Equal Opportunities Commission.

80 The Equalities Review: Interim Report for Consultation, p 55.

81 Ibid p 58.

employers moved women off the 'women's grade' on to the lowest grades with a view to minimising their statutory obligations and made sure that men and women were not working on comparable jobs.

The aim of the Act is to prevent discrimination as regards terms and conditions of employment between men and women and, to this end, it employs the device of an equality clause. If certain conditions are satisfied, the terms of the woman's contract are deemed to include such a clause. Under the original provisions, the equality clause only operated in two circumstances: that the woman was employed on like work with men in the same employment under s 1(2)(a) or on work rated by a job evaluation scheme as equivalent to that of a man in the same employment under s 1(2)(b). The latter provision was not of much value as it was voluntary and it was, therefore, left to the woman to persuade her employer to undertake such a scheme. In practice, this meant that women were left with the like work provisions. Owing to sexual segregation in the job market, women were concentrated in certain occupations, such as cleaning or cooking, and were unable to point to a man doing like work even where he was in the same employment.

Thus, the Act had little impact on women's lower pay since it could only be used against the most gross forms of pay discrimination. However, in 1982 the European Commission brought an action against the United Kingdom (*Commission of European Communities v UK*)[82] on the basis that the UK was in breach of its obligations under the Equal Pay Directive owing to the narrow application of the equality clause. In response, the UK Government was forced to amend the 1970 Act in order to include the possibility of making an equal value claim. It did so very reluctantly and this was reflected in the response. The amendment (s 1(2)(c)) was effected by statutory instrument, thereby curtailing debate on the new provisions, and the new regulations were intended to operate only as a last resort: the other two possibilities had to be tried first. Moreover, an attempt was made to widen the defences available to employers by using a different wording for equal value claims.

Choice of comparator

The first step under the Act is for the woman to choose a comparator. This might have caused difficulty where the woman was employed doing like work with a few men but wanted to compare herself with a man doing work of equal value; however, the issue was resolved in favour of claimants by the House of Lords in *Pickstone v Freemans*.[83] Mrs Pickstone and other warehouse operatives were paid less than male warehouse checkers, but a man was employed as an operative. The defendants therefore argued that the claim was barred owing to the wording of s 1(2)(c): '. . . where a woman is employed on work which, *not being work to which (a) or (b) applies*, is "of equal value"' (emphasis added). Paragraph (a) did apply because one man was employed doing the same work and therefore it could be argued that a like work claim arose, but not an equal value one. The House of Lords considered that allowing this argument to succeed would mean that Parliament had failed once again to implement its obligations

---

82   [1982] ICR 578; [1982] 3 CMLR 284.
83   [1988] AC 66; [1988] 2 All ER 803; for comment, see: (1988) 51 MLR 221; [1988] PL 483.

under Art 119 and it could not have intended such a failure. In such circumstances, any interpretation should take into account the terms in which the amending regulations were presented to Parliament; in other words, a purposive approach should be adopted. Using this approach, the defendants' argument could be rejected on the basis that the claimant should be able to choose her comparator, rather than allowing the employer to impose one on her. This ruling put an end to what has been termed the 'token man loophole':[84] had it gone the other way, employers might have been encouraged to employ one man alongside a large number of women in order to bar equal value claims.

'Same employment'

Once a claimant has chosen a comparator, it must be shown that they are in the same employment. The meaning of this provision was considered by the House of Lords in *Leverton v Clwyd CC*.[85] A nursery nurse who wished to compare her pay with that of clerical staff was not employed in the same establishment as they were. Under s 1(6), 'the same employment' is defined as meaning at the same establishment or by the same employer and that the same conditions of employment are observed. The claimant and comparators were employed by the same employer and, although there were some differences in the individual terms of employment, it was still possible for the House of Lords to find on a broad view of the agreement governing the terms of employment of claimant and comparator that they were sufficiently similar to satisfy the s 1(6) test.

Clearly, it would be possible to frame legislation allowing equal value claims so that it would operate in one of three circumstances: it could apply to all employees who could point to any other employee, wherever employed, doing work of equal value; it could apply to employees employed by the same employer governed by roughly similar terms of service – the position taken under the UK legislation – or it could apply to employees working under the same roof as their comparators. In making it clear that a broad middle way is open to such claims, the House of Lords gave encouragement to them and followed a policy which seemed to be in tune with that underlying the legislation.

However, it is worth considering the advantages of the first and least restrictive method which was omitted from the legislation in order to minimise disruption to existing pay structures. If, in principle, a person doing work of equal value to that of another worker should be paid an equal wage, if the inequality is attributable to sex discrimination, then it ought to be immaterial that the two workers are employed by two different employers. It might be said that an employer cannot be expected to take responsibility for the wage policies of other concerns, but can only be expected to remove pay discrimination within the sphere he or she is able to affect. However, on a broader view, it might be argued that an employer has a duty to ensure that his or her own concern is not operating a discriminatory wage scheme whatever the basis of comparison. In closing off that broad possibility, the legislation leaves intact the grossest pay disparities arising from establishments with low paid all-female workforces,

---

84 See Napier, B, 'Julie Hayward and the continuing saga of equal value' (1998) 138 NLJ 341.
85 [1989] 2 WLR 47; [1989] 1 WLR 65, HL.

because they cannot point to a male comparator. This aspect of the legislation may even encourage sexual segregation in employment because if no male is employed (other than those prepared to work for the same low wages as the women) – at least in any post conceivably comparable with that of the majority of the workforce – equal value claims are precluded. The result in some occupations may be the encouragement of a low paid all-female workforce overseen by a few men in managerial positions.[86]

The term-by-term approach

Assuming that a claimant can point to a comparator in the same employment, the industrial tribunal will appoint an independent expert in order to determine whether the two jobs are of equal value under such heads as responsibility, skill, effort, qualifications and length of training. The expert's report is not conclusive of the issue, but the tribunal is unlikely to reject it. If the jobs are of equal value, then a term of the claimant's contract which is less favourable than a term of her comparator's will be compared. It is now clear after the ruling of the House of Lords in *Hayward v Cammell Laird*[87] that the term by term approach – as opposed to consideration of the contract as a whole – is correct. The defendants had resisted the plaintiff's claim on the ground that her contract and that of the male comparators must each be looked at as a whole, in which case her perks – such as free lunches and two additional days' holiday – equalled the £25 per week extra which the men received. The House of Lords found that the word 'term' in s 1(2) was to be given its natural and ordinary meaning as a distinct part of a contract and, therefore, it was necessary to look at one term of the claimant's contract; if there was a similar provision in the comparator's contract which was found after they had been compared to be less favourable to the woman than the term in the comparator's, then the equality clause would operate to make that term equally favourable to her.

Obviously, this ruling prevented employers claiming that fringe benefits equalled pay. Such a claim might have been advantageous to an employer who might be able to provide a benefit at little real cost, such as free meals for a cook. Moreover, previously, employers might have provided a 'protective package' for female employees which included less pay but more time off or more sick benefits. All women, whether desirous of such a package or not, would receive it whether or not they would have preferred to be paid more. Employers, however, feared that the *Hayward* ruling would lead to 'leap frogging'; women would receive the male higher pay; the men would then claim the women's old fringe benefits and all employees would level up to the detriment of the company, which would be faced with a great increase in costs. However, employers may be able to avoid this by gradually modifying practices on pay and fringe benefits. There would also be the possibility – mentioned only as *dicta* in *Hayward* – that certain fringe benefits might be used to found a defence to an equal value claim (see below).

---

86 Walby, S and Olsen, W, *The impact of women's position in the labour market on pay and implications for UK productivity*, 2002, London: Department of Trade and Industry, Women and Equality Unit.
87 [1988] WLR 265; [1988] 2 All ER 803; for comment, see Ellis (1988) 51 MLR 781; Napier, 'Julie Hayward and the continuing saga of equal pay' (1998) 138 NLJ 341.

The 'material factor' defence

Even if a woman is able to show that she is doing like work, work rated as equivalent or work of equal value to that of her comparator, the claim will fail if a s 1(3) defence operates:

> ... an equality clause shall not operate in relation to a variation between the woman's contract and the man's contract if the employer proves that the variation is genuinely due to a material factor which is not the difference of sex and that factor:
>
> (a) in the case of an equality clause falling within subsection (2)(a) or (b) above, must be a material difference between the woman's case and the man's; and
> (b) in the case of an equality clause falling within subsection (2)(c) above, may be such a material difference.

This is known as the 'material factor' defence. The difference in wording for equal value claims was intended to mean that a 'material factor' could be interpreted more widely in such claims. In fact, as will be seen, the width of the interpretation given to the defence in all three types of claim means that this possibility is of less significance than was expected. The defence will operate if a material difference between the cases of the woman and the man can be identified which is not the difference of sex – such as additional payment for the geographical difference in the location of two parts of the same concern. As the 1970 Act must be construed in harmony with the SDA, the variation in pay must be genuinely due to the factor in question; otherwise it may be discriminatory. Therefore, in *Shields v E Coomes*,[88] the difference in pay was apparently due to the protective function exercised by the male employees in a betting shop. However, not all the men discharged such a function, but all received the higher pay and, therefore, allowing the protective function to operate as a material factor would have been directly discriminatory because a woman who exercised no protective function would not receive the higher pay, while a man in the same position would.

In *Leverton v Clwyd CC*[89] the House of Lords found that different hours and holidays could amount to a material factor under s 1(3) if pay could be broken down into a notional hourly income. If, once this was done, the pay of claimant and comparator were found to be equal, the claim would fail on the basis that the difference in salaries was due to the difference in hours and not to the difference of sex. This point was touched on *obiter* in *Hayward*, but in *Leverton* it was made clear that a s 1(3) defence might be available where a man and a woman had different contractual packages so long as the packages did not contain any element of direct or indirect discrimination. It may be noted that more than one material factor may be identified; if so, it is not necessary for the employer to establish the proportion which each factor contributes to the difference in pay.[90]

---

88 [1978] WLR 1408, CA.
89 [1989] WLR 47.
90 *Calder v Rowntree Macintosh Ltd* [1993] IRLR 27.

The most far-reaching and controversial argument under s 1(3) has been termed the 'market forces argument',[91] since it allows the employer to argue that because the market may favour some employees more than others, they must be paid more, and that to fail to do so would be to disrupt normal market forces.[92] In other words, if a woman is willing to work for less than a man, this provides a reason for paying her less. The early cases rejected this argument;[93] in *Jenkins v Kinsgate*,[94] for example, a part-time worker was paid at a different hourly rate from the full-time workers. The employer tried to use the s 1(3) defence in answer to her claim for equal hourly pay in arguing that part-time workers have less bargaining power and therefore the market demanded that he should pay full-time workers more. The argument was that this was a genuine difference between the two cases which was not sex-related; any part-time worker, male or female, would have been paid less. However, the part-timers were all female and so the practice had a disparate impact on women. Construing the EPA in accordance with the SDA, the EAT concluded that a practice which had a disparate impact on women could not sustain a s 1(3) defence, as to allow it to do so would be indirectly discriminatory.

However, this approach was not followed in *Rainey v Greater Glasgow Health Board*,[95] which concerned a comparison between female and male prosthetists working in the NHS. The men were receiving higher pay, but the defendants argued that this was due to the need to attract them from the private sector in order to set up the prosthetist service. This argument entailed consideration not just of factors relating to the personal attributes of the claimant and comparator, such as length of experience, but also the difference in their individual positions in the market. In other words, it widened what could be considered as a material factor. The relevant circumstances were that those from the private sector had to be paid above the normal rate to attract them. However, the House of Lords held that although taking this into account as a material factor was acceptable, it must be objectively justified – no element of discrimination must have crept into the circumstances. In order to ensure this, the House of Lords used the same test as for justification under indirect discrimination – the *Bilka* test laid down by the European Court of Justice.[96] Here, the objective was setting up the NHS prosthetist service which entailed attracting sufficient experienced prosthetists. The means chosen involved attracting persons from the private sector which involved paying them more. It was accepted that this was both appropriate and necessary. So the material factor passed the *Bilka* test and further, because this was a like work case, the factor had

91 Townshend-Smith, *Sex Discrimination in Employment* 1989, p 175.
92 The US doctrine of 'comparable worth' has also been attacked as disruptive of market forces: see, e.g., Weiler, P, 'The wages of sex: the uses and limits of comparable worth' (1986) 99 Harv L Rev 1728.
93 *Clay Cross v Fletcher* [1978] 1 WLR 1429; [1979] 1 All ER 474.
94 [1981] IRLR 388, p 390.
95 [1987] AC 224; [1987] 1 All ER 65; [1986] 3 WLR 1017, HL. It may be that the reasoning in *Rainey* will be applied only where indirect discrimination can be identified affecting the factor in question: *Strathclyde Regional Council v Wallace* [1996] IRLR 672, noted (1997) 26(2) ILJ 171. If this is correct, the factor need not be objectively justified: it need only be genuinely necessary and material, i.e., relevant. One problem with this approach is that it may lead to failures to recognise the existence of indirect discrimination affecting material factors.
96 In *Bilka-Kaufhaus GmbH v Weber von Hartz* [1986] IRLR 317; [1986] CMLR 701. See above, pp 1540–41.

to be a difference between comparator and claimant. The difference was that she was from the public sector, while he was from the private sector.

Thus, this ruling broadened what could be termed a material factor and allowed market forces to defeat equal pay claims so long as no indirect discrimination was shown. Clearly, the danger of the market forces argument is that employers will often argue that business will suffer if a group of women are paid more. What are sometimes termed 'women's jobs' have traditionally been undervalued by the market; the equal pay legislation was specifically aimed at breaking down traditional pay hierarchies and, therefore, this argument, if allowed too wide a scope, could completely undermine it. However, the *Rainey* ruling does appear to an extent to be trying to keep the argument in check in finding that only in objectively justified circumstances should more be paid to a certain group; this is not the same as allowing the market generally to set the rate. The effect of this argument was further curbed in *Benveniste v University of Southampton*;[97] it was found that although particular constraints might affect pay and might lead to a pay differential between a man and a woman, they could do so only while the constraint was in operation. Once it had ceased to apply, the lower pay should be raised to the level it would have been at had it not been affected by the constraint.

A variation on the market forces argument was put forward in *Enderby v Frenchay*.[98] Speech therapists wished to compare their pay with that of clinical psychologists and pharmacists who were paid at much higher rates. The employers denied that the work of the two groups was of equal value, but argued that in any event, a material factor justified the difference: it had emerged as a result of different pay negotiations and, moreover, the pharmacists were in demand in the private sector and this had influenced pay. The employers further argued that the speech therapists could not assert that the material factor was tainted by indirect discrimination without first showing that a condition had been applied to employees which had an adverse impact on women. The employer thus had two arguments: first, no condition could be identified which had been applied; secondly, if it had been, it could be justified by the factors mentioned: the separate pay processes in conjunction with market forces.

The claimant, however, argued that the salaries of the therapists were low because the profession was predominantly female and that whether a condition could be identified or not was immaterial: in practice, one type of work was largely done by women and another largely by men and, although of equal value, the men's work attracted a higher salary. These factors, it was claimed, gave rise to a presumption of discrimination which could not be objectively justified because the reason for the difference was that the profession in question was staffed by women. This argument, if accepted, would have distinguished the claim from that in *Rainey*.

The EAT found for the employers, ruling that the pay was the result of different bargaining processes which, looked at separately, were not indirectly discriminatory. Therefore, a material factor could be identified which was influenced by market forces. Further, even if the factor identified did not justify all of the difference in pay, that did not matter because it was impossible to say how much was needed above normal

---

97 [1989] IRLR 122.
98 [1994] 1 All ER 495; [1993] ECR I-5535, ECJ; [1992] IRLR 15, CA.

rates to attract and retain certain staff. It was clear that the case raised difficult issues, and so at the Court of Appeal stage three questions were referred to the European Court of Justice:

> (1) If there is a difference in pay between two jobs assumed to be of equal value, of which one is carried out almost exclusively by women and the other predominantly by men, must the difference be objectively justified by the employer? Does this mean that all the steps needed to show indirect discrimination should be taken, including identifying a particular barrier?
>
> (2) Are separate bargaining processes a sufficient justification for a variation in pay if they are not internally discriminatory?
>
> (3) If there is a need to pay men more to attract them, but only part of the difference in pay is for that purpose, then does that justify all of the difference?

The first question relates to the determination of a prima facie case of indirect sex discrimination; is it necessary to be able to identify a 'barrier' or 'condition' which it is more difficult for women to meet than men (or vice versa) in order to show indirect discrimination? The second and third questions relate to justifications for indirect discrimination. First, is the use of separate sex-neutral collective bargaining systems sufficient justification for indirect sex discrimination? Secondly, will the more favourable market position of certain employees justify unequal pay? In other words, can the overt operation of market forces justify indirect sex discrimination?

Assuming that the jobs compared were of equal value, the Court of Justice held,[99] reiterating the well established principle of reversal of the burden of proof in indirect sex discrimination cases (citing Case C-33/89 *Kowalska v Freie und Hansestadt Hamburg*[100] and Case C-184/89 *Nimz v Freie und Hansestadt Hamburg*[101] concerning measures distinguishing between employees on the basis of their hours of work, including equal pay cases) that '. . . it is for the employer to prove that his practice in the matter of wages is not discriminatory, if a female worker establishes, in relation to a relatively large number of employees, that the average pay for women is less than that for men'.

Applying these rulings by analogy to this equal value claim, the Court concluded that there is a prima facie case of sex discrimination, where the pay of speech therapists is significantly lower than that of clinical psychologists and pharmacists and speech therapists are almost exclusively women. The 'factual' considerations as to whether the jobs are indeed of equal value and whether the statistics adduced support the required disparities are questions for the national court. At this point, the burden of objective justification shifts to the employer.

The Court replied in the negative to the question whether separate collective bargaining processes, which are each, in themselves, non-discriminatory, constitute sufficient objective justification for the differences in pay. The fact that the different wages are reached by separate processes of collective bargaining does not of itself

---

99   *Enderby v Frenchay* [1994] 1 All ER 495; [1993] ECR I-5535, ECJ; [1992] IRLR 15, CA.
100   [1990] ECR I-2591.
101   [1991] ECR I-297.

justify the discrimination, since it is a merely descriptive explanation. It fails to explain why one process produced a more favourable result for the employees than the other. Moreover, allowing that justification would enable employers to circumvent the principle of equal pay very readily by using such separate processes.

In contrast to its answer to the second question, the Court accepted 'the state of the employment market' in its answer to the third as a possible justification for indirect discrimination. The market forces concerned here were the shortage of candidates for the more highly paid job and the consequent need to offer higher pay in that job in order to attract candidates. The Court repeated that it is the duty of the national courts to decide 'questions of fact' such as this and reiterated from its previous case law[102] some forms of 'needs of the employer' which may constitute justification for indirect sex discrimination.[103]

While the questions referred to the ECJ were unanswered, the issue raised in (2) was resolved in *Barber and Others v NCR (Manufacturing) Ltd*[104] using a completely different approach from that of the EAT in *Enderby*, and one which seems to be more in harmony with the policy of the Act and with the *Bilka* test. Indirect clerical workers, who were mainly women, wanted to claim equal pay with direct clerical workers who were mainly men (the women's work was 'indirect' as not directly related to shop floor production). The direct workers negotiated a new agreement regarding hours and moved to a shorter week. Thus, the hourly rates of the two groups now differed although it had been the same. The EAT considered whether the employer had established that because the difference arose from different collective bargaining agreements untainted internally by discrimination this could found a s 1(3) defence. In putting forward this argument, the employers had relied on *Enderby* where the EAT had held that this was possible. The EAT said that the correct question to be asked must first be identified. It could be asked whether the cause of the variation in pay was free from sex discrimination, or it could be asked whether the variation was itself genuinely due to a material factor other than the difference of sex. The second question was the right one because the cause – separate collective bargaining processes – might be free from discrimination, but the result might not be. In this instance, the evidence showed why the difference had been arrived at, but did not show any objective factor which justified it. Thus, there was a pay difference which was not based on a material factor. The equality clause therefore operated, meaning that although the claimants did not obtain the same pay as the comparators because of the difference in hours, the hourly rates were equalised. The EAT considered that it did not need to refer to the ECJ or await the decision in *Enderby*, since the proper result could be arrived at under domestic law.

This ruling was foreshadowed in *Handels-og Kontorfunktionaerernes Forbund i Danmark v Dansk Arbejdsgiverforening* (the *Danfoss* case),[105] which was a Danish reference to the ECJ. The Court did not need to consider the question as to the relevance

---

102 Case 170/84 *Bilka* [1986] ECR 1607, Case C-184/89 *Nimz v Freie und Hansestadt Hamburg* [1991] ECR I-297 and Case 109/88 *Danfoss* [1989] ECR 3199; [1989] IRLR 532.
103 In 1997, the government conceded the equal value issue and settled the claim: see April 1997 IRLB No 567.
104 [1993] IRLR 95. Cf the decision in *British Coal Corporation v Smith* [1993] IRLR 308.
105 [1989] ECR 3199; [1989] IRLR 532.

of two separate collective agreements, one for women, one for men, but when the Advocate General addressed this point he determined that the existence of such agreements would not exclude the operation of the Equal Pay Directive although it would not inevitably be unlawful to have two separate agreements; it would be the manner of the agreements which would be relevant.

This approach should prevail, it is submitted, because merely to ask whether arriving at two levels of pay was due to the operation of two different bargaining processes would be to obscure the discriminatory nature of the result.[106] It is necessary to look behind the bargaining processes and to ask why one was able to arrive at a more favourable result. This might be because unions have traditionally been more effectual in obtaining better pay for men than for women and in itself this may be due to the fact that men's work has traditionally been valued more highly by the market than women's. Thus, to use different agreements as a material factor in themselves would be to cloak the discriminatory forces which lie behind them.

The main issue in the *Danfoss* case arose because the Danfoss Company paid the same basic wage to all employees, but also an individual supplement based on factors such as mobility and training. The result was that a somewhat lower average wage was paid to women and it was therefore claimed that the system was discriminatory. The Court determined that because the system lacked transparency, once a woman had shown that the average wage of women and men differed, the burden of proof would shift to the employer to prove that the wage practice was not discriminatory. It would have been unfair to expect the woman to prove that the system was discriminatory since she would not have been able to work out which factors had been taken into account. The Court considered that even if the application of criteria such as the need to be mobile worked to the detriment of women, the employer could still use them in relation to specific tasks entrusted to the employee so long as the *Bilka* test was satisfied.

Conclusions

The *Enderby* approach in the European Court of Justice obviously eases the task of the claimant in showing that a material factor is tainted with indirect discrimination in order to shift the onus onto the employer and determines that asking an employee to identify a specific requirement or condition where it is alleged that a material factor is so tainted is misconceived. Sometimes, it may be possible to identify a condition such as a need to be mobile in order to attract higher pay. However, and this seems to be the basis of the decision in *Enderby*, in many instances it may not be possible to identify any such condition with sufficient specificity. Instead, it would seem that where two jobs are of equal value, but that held by the woman attracts lower pay, the suggestion is that the market has allowed differentiation because of the traditional expectation that a woman would not be the breadwinner and would therefore work for less.[107]

---

106 For comment on this issue, see 'Equal value claims and sex bias in collective bargaining' (1991) 20 ILJ 163; see, also (1989) 18 ILJ 63.

107 See Olsen, W and Walby, S, *Modelling gender pay gaps*, 2005, Equal Opportunities Commission Working Paper Series No 17, Manchester: EOC.

Thus, the 'condition' which has been applied, in a general sense, is for a woman to work in a traditionally 'male' occupation, such as lorry driving, rather than in one of a traditionally 'female' nature, such as cooking, in order to obtain the higher pay. Obviously, some women can do so, but such a requirement hits disproportionately at women since, in practice, they will be less likely to enter the 'male' occupation owing to tradition, discrimination against them – perceived and real – in such occupations and social conditioning. Identifying such a 'condition' should suffice to raise an inference of indirect discrimination which, of course, would be open theoretically to rebuttal by an objective justification. To go further as the EAT appeared to do in *Enderby* and require identification of some specific condition which the particular employer has imposed is to misunderstand the nature of equal pay claims and the scheme of the Act which is predicated on the assumption that it is not pure coincidence that some jobs done predominantly by women are paid less than those done predominantly by men. In other words, the 'condition' should be assumed to apply to a largely female profession; the question is whether the difference in pay can be justified and it may be argued that where a particular occupation is staffed predominantly by women and is of equal value to one staffed predominantly by men but there is a wide disparity in pay, it would be hard for the employer, if not impossible, to show that the difference arose from anything other than the mere fact that one occupation was female dominated. In any event, it is clear that the fact of separate bargaining processes merely amounts to a smokescreen obscuring the traditional operation of market forces founding the difference in pay and therefore clearly should not be able to justify it, given that the legislation was introduced in order to interfere with, rather than bow to, market forces.

The material factor defence could potentially be seen as operating at three different levels of generality. First, it might only arise where a difference in the 'personal equation' of the man and the woman, such as length of experience or qualifications, could be identified. This was the approach rejected in *Rainey*. Second, a factor might be identified going beyond the personal equation of the complainant, but still amounting to a non-sex-based difference between her and her comparator. At the present time this is the predominant approach. The most significant factor of this type and the one most likely to undermine the equal pay scheme is the 'market forces' factor, which received some endorsement from the ECJ in *Enderby*. This factor is, however, subject to a rigorous application of the *Bilka* test; it does not mean that the laws of supply and demand can simply determine the rates of pay in question. Nevertheless, adoption of this approach may tend to undermine the aim of the Act as removing pay discrimination. Third – and this defence would be available only in respect of equal value claims because of the wider wording applicable – there might be scope for a number of market-based arguments not based on a difference between the man's and the woman's case, such as using the leap frogging argument from *Hayward* as being in itself a material factor, although arising only from the general operation of the concern in question. This possibility has not yet been put forward; it would, of course, be out of harmony with the policy of the Act and arguably could not be termed an 'objectively justified reason' under the *Bilka* test. The complexities of the second approach, which the courts are currently trying to get to grips with, illustrate the difficulty adverted to at the beginning of this chapter of ensuring that only morally justifiable differentiation occurs.

The Sex Discrimination Act

Introduction

The two methods of securing equality embodied in the SDA – the individual approach and the general administrative approach under the keeping of a watchdog body – need not entirely be considered in isolation from each other. The weakness of the first is that specific instances of discrimination may be addressed only if the individual concerned is prepared to take on the burden of a legal action. Such an approach is clearly only capable of bringing about slow and piecemeal change, especially as the two parties concerned – usually the woman and her employer – are clearly not confronting each other on equal terms; the lack of legal aid exacerbates this situation. However, apart from bringing about general change by addressing itself to institutionalised discrimination, the administrative body created by the legislation can aid the individual and on occasion can undertake an investigation triggered off by an individual action.

Protected grounds

The Sex Discrimination Act 1975 (SDA), as amended, covers discrimination on a number of protected grounds: sex, pregnancy or maternity leave, marital status and gender reassignment. Section 3 covers discrimination on the grounds of marital status, but in this instance the comparison is between a single person and a married person of the same sex. The protection on grounds of sex applies equally to men. The provision against marital discrimination is more circumscribed: it is confined to the employment field only and discrimination on the grounds of divorce or of being unmarried is not covered.

Section 2A, which now prohibits discrimination on grounds of gender reassignment, is even more circumscribed; it only covers direct (not indirect) discrimination in employment and training and in relation to barristers (in Scotland, advocates). The prohibition of discrimination on grounds of gender reassignment arose from the findings of the ECJ in Case 13/14 *P v S and Cornwall CC*.[108] P had been dismissed from her employment on the ground that she was a transsexual. Her application under the SDA failed as it was found that transsexuals were outside the terms of the Act. It was argued in the European Court of Justice that her case fell within the Equal Treatment Directive. The decision of the European Court of Human Rights in *Rees v UK*[109] was relied upon by the European Court of Justice in deciding that transsexuals fall within the Directive. This was found on the basis that the Directive is simply the expression of the principle of equality, which is one of the fundamental principles of European Union law. It was found that where a person is dismissed on the basis that they have undergone or are about to undergo gender reassignment, he or she is being discriminated against in comparison with persons of the sex to which he or she was deemed to belong before undergoing gender reassignment. This ruling was given domestic effect in the Sex Discrimination (Gender Reassignment) Regulations 1999, which brought direct discrimination on grounds of gender reassignment within the SDA 1975 by introducing

---

108 Judgment of 30 April 1996; [1996] ECR I-2143; [1996] IRLR 347.
109 (1986) 9 EHRR 56.

s 2A.[110] However, the domestic implementation may be inadequate. In particular, the exclusion of indirect discrimination may mean that s 2A does not do enough to comply with the Equal Treatment Directive.

As indicated above, an argument that the provisions of the SDA should be extended by purposive interpretation in order to comply with the EU Directives could be strengthened by taking account both of s 3 of the HRA and of the general requirement under EC law to use the Convention as a source of general principle. Further, since Directives have vertical effect, they can, if sufficiently precise, clear and unconditional, be enforced against state bodies – emanations of the state. Thus, for example, if necessary, a claim for indirect discrimination on the ground of gender reassignment could be brought against such a body relying only on the Directive.

Contexts

Pay-related discrimination on the ground of gender reassignment is dealt with under the SDA, although such discrimination on grounds of sex is dealt with in the EPA. In other words, the SDA covers only the non-pay-related aspects of employment discrimination on grounds of sex – the pay-related aspects fall within the EPA. As will be seen, this separation has added to the complexity of the substantive law, although the two statutes are intended to work together as a complete code. The EOC has recommended that equal pay and sex discrimination provisions should be combined in one statute, but this has not been implemented.[111] The Act does not make discrimination on the protected grounds generally illegal; it only outlaws it in the contexts in which it operates. Thus, a two-stage approach has been created; first, discrimination on one of the grounds must be shown, and second, that it occurred within one of the contexts covered by the Act. The contexts are: employment (s 6), education (s 22), housing, and the provision of goods and services (s 29). Section 29 was found to have a narrow application to public bodies by the House of Lords in *Amin*.[112] A number of public functions, including policing decisions, were excluded.

The specific protection for pregnancy and maternity leave was introduced in 2005, in response to the Framework Directive, via Regulations, as indicated above, in a new s 3A SDA. Crucially, it does not depend on showing a comparison with a man. The comparison is with a non-pregnant woman. Section 3A(1) provides:

> In any circumstances relevant for the purposes of a provision to which this subsection applies, a person discriminates against a woman if
>
> (a) at a time in a protected period, and on the ground of the woman's pregnancy, the person treats her less favourably than he would treat her had she not become pregnant; or

110 SI 1999/1102; see the Government's Consultation Paper *Legislation Regarding Discrimination on Grounds of Transsexualism in Employment*; for discussion see McColgan, op. cit., fn 1, pp 382–86 and see further Griffiths, E, (1999) J Civ Lib, July, p 230.
111 See further p 1602 below.
112 [1983] 2 AC 818 HL. The decision partly relied on interpreting RRA 1976, s 75 as intended to limit the application of the Act in respect of public authorities.

(b) on the ground that the woman is exercising or seeking to exercise, or has exercised or sought to exercise, a statutory right to maternity leave, the person treats her less favourably than he would treat her if she were neither exercising nor seeking to exercise, and had neither exercised nor sought to exercise, such a right.[113]

Section 3A goes on to define the 'protected period'. It may be noted that if the special protection under s 3A does not apply, for example because discrimination appears to be related to pregnancy but is outside the protected period,[114] the provisions outlawing discrimination on grounds of sex would have to be relied on in seeking to challenge the discrimination. Section 3A is an extremely significant provision since discrimination against women often tends to be pregnancy-related and, as discussed below, women experienced difficulties in using sex discrimination legislation to combat pregnancy discrimination.

---

113 Section 3A further provides:

(2) In any circumstances relevant for the purposes of a provision to which this subsection applies, a person discriminates against a woman if, on the ground that section 72(1) of the Employment Rights Act 1996 (compulsory maternity leave) has to be complied with in respect of the woman, he treats her less favourably than he would treat her if that provision did not have to be complied with in respect of her.

(3) For the purposes of subsection (1) –

(a) in relation to a woman, a protected period begins each time she becomes pregnant, and the protected period associated with any particular pregnancy of hers ends in accordance with the following rules –

(i) if she is entitled to ordinary but not additional maternity leave in connection with the pregnancy, the protected period ends at the end of her period of ordinary maternity leave connected with the pregnancy or, if earlier, when she returns to work after the end of her pregnancy;

(ii) if she is entitled to ordinary and additional maternity leave in connection with the pregnancy, the protected period ends at the end of her period of additional maternity leave connected with the pregnancy or, if earlier, when she returns to work after the end of her pregnancy;

(iii) if she is not entitled to ordinary maternity leave in respect of the pregnancy, the protected period ends at the end of the 2 weeks beginning with the end of the pregnancy;

(b) where a person's treatment of a woman is on grounds of illness suffered by the woman as a consequence of a pregnancy of hers, that treatment is to be taken to be on the ground of the pregnancy;

(c) a 'statutory right to maternity leave' means a right conferred by section 71(1) or 73(1) of the Employment Rights Act 1996 (ordinary and additional maternity leave).

(4) In subsection (3) 'ordinary maternity leave' and 'additional maternity leave' shall be construed in accordance with sections 71 and 73 of the Employment Rights Act 1996.

(5) Subsections (1) and (2) apply to –

(a) any provision of Part 2,

(b) sections 35A and 35B, and

(c) any other provision of Part 3, so far as it applies to vocational training.

114 See on this: Adams, L, McAndrew, F and Winterbotham, M, *Pregnancy discrimination at work: a survey of women*, 2005, Equal Opportunities Commission Working Paper Series No 24, Manchester: EOC.

Discrimination on grounds of race[115]

It was apparent that the common law would not provide a sufficient remedy for racial discrimination. For example, in *Constantine v Imperial Hotels*[116] nominal damages only were awarded in respect of clear racial discrimination although the applicant had attempted to claim exemplary damages. However, the discriminatory effect of a contract or covenant could be taken into account by a court as a matter of public policy in reaching a decision,[117] while discriminatory words contained in a trust might, under certain circumstances, be struck out, although the courts have tended to be reluctant to do this.[118] The discriminatory nature of foreign legislation might also be considered in determining its impact,[119] and this possibility still exists, although it is not of great significance. There seemed to be a clear need for further measures and therefore the first Race Relations Act (RRA) was passed in 1965, although it was soon superseded by the 1968 Act and then by the 1976 Act. The 1976 Act is much more far-reaching than its predecessors; under the 1968 Act, an individual had to complain to the Race Relations Board rather than take the complaint to court. The 1976 Act was modelled on the SDA; it makes discrimination a statutory tort, follows the same pattern as regards direct and indirect discrimination and sets up the Commission for Racial Equality with a similar role to the Equal Opportunities Commission,[120] set up under the 1975 Act. It also operated initially in the same contexts and uses the same terms as the SDA; therefore, decisions under one of the two statutes affect the other. The Act provides a remedy for direct or indirect discrimination on the grounds of colour, race, nationality or ethnic or national origins.

Meaning of racial group

The applicant must show that the group falls within the definition of racial grounds in s 3(1) of the Act which covers 'colour, nationality, ethnic or national origins' and a racial group is defined by reference to the same. Employment of the concept of 'ethnic origins' widens the meaning of 'racial grounds' and means that some religious groups may fall within it even though discrimination on the grounds of religion is not expressly

---

115 Texts referred to in this section: Clayton and Tomlinson, op. cit., fn 1, Chapter 17; McColgan, op. cit., fn 1; Bailey, SH, Harris, DJ and Jones, BL, *Civil Liberties: Cases and Materials*, op. cit., fn 1, Chapter 10; Lustgarten, L, *The Legal Control of Racial Discrimination*, 1980, Macmillan; Gregory, op. cit., fn 1; Bourne, C and Whitmore, J, *Race and Sex Discrimination*, 1993; Feldman, op. cit., fn 1, esp pp 133–78; Lustgarten, L, 'Racial inequality and the limits of law' (1986) 49 MLR 68–85; Bindman, G, 'Reforming the Race Relations Act' (1985) 135 NLJ 1136–38 and 1167–69; Deakin and Morris, op. cit., fn 1, Chapter 6; von Prondzynski and Richards, op. cit., fn 1; Barnard and Hepple, 'Substantive Equality' [2000] 59(3) CLJ 562; Hepple, Coussey and Choudhury, op. cit., fn 1; Millar and Phillips, [1983] 11 Int Journal Soc Law 417.
116 [1944] KB 693.
117 On public policy at common law, see Cretney (1968) 118 NLJ 1094; Garner (1972) 35 MLR 478.
118 *Re Lysaght* [1966] Ch 191 (in order to qualify for a scholarship under the trust a student had to be male, British and could not be Catholic or Jewish; this was not found contrary to public policy, but as the college which was to be a trustee refused to discriminate on religious grounds, those words were struck out); for comment see (1966) 82 LQR 10.
119 See *Oppenheimer v Cattermole* [1975] 2 WLR 347.
120 See below, pp 1594 and 1597–1600 for consideration of the role of both bodies.

covered. The leading case on the meaning of 'racial group' is *Mandla v Dowell Lee*.[121] The House of Lords had to consider whether Sikhs constituted an ethnic group and defined the term 'ethnic group' as one having a long shared history and a cultural tradition of its own, often, but not necessarily, associated with religious observances. On that definition Sikhs were a racial group and fell within s 3(1). This does not mean that a purely religious group will fall within s 3(1).

Using this definition it was found in *CRE v Dutton*[122] that gypsies, who have a shared history going back 700 years, may be termed a racial group and the definition was considered further in *Dawkins v Department of Environment*[123] in relation to the claim that Rastafarians constitute a racial group. It was found that the group in question must regard itself and be regarded by others as a distinct community by virtue of certain characteristics. The two essential characteristics were: a long shared history of which the group was conscious, and a cultural tradition of its own including family and social customs. Lord Fraser considered that there could be other relevant, but not essential characteristics such as a common geographical origin, a common language, literature and religion. It was found that Rastafarians did have a strong cultural tradition which included a distinctive form of music and a distinctive hair style. However, the shared history of Rastafarians as a separate group only went back 60 years; it was not enough for them to look back to a time when they, in common with other Africans, were taken to the Caribbean. That was not sufficient to mark them out as a separate group since it was an experience shared with other Afro-Caribbeans. It appears, then, that this first step is complex and, it might seem, not entirely free from ambiguity. The exclusion of religious groups such as Muslims from the scope of the legislation was problematic, but they could now take advantage of the Employment Equality (Religion or Belief) Regulations.[124] Also religious groups may possibly fall within the indirect discrimination provisions as indicated below.

Contexts covered by the RRA

The discrimination must occur within the areas covered by the Act: employment, education, housing or the provision of goods and services. Section 20 of the RRA, which covers the provision of goods and services, was found to have a narrow application to public functions owing to the decision in *Amin*.[125] Thus, areas of governmental activity were excluded from the ambit of the Act. The prison service was not covered, nor were a number of police activities such as exercising stop and search powers or investigating offences. Thus the RRA, like the SDA, had an inconsistent and arbitrary application to the police. Until its amendment in 2000, the RRA could not be used to challenge allegedly discriminatory practices in the criminal justice system except in the

---

121 [1983] All ER 1062; [1983] 2 AC 548; for comment, see Beynon and Love (1984) 100 LQR 120; McKenna (1983) 46 MLR 759; Robilliard [1983] PL 348; Pagone (1984) 43 CLJ 218.
122 [1989] WLR 17; [1989] 1 All ER 306, CA. See also *Souster v BBC Scotland* [2001] IRLR 150.
123 [1993] ICR 517; for comment, see Parpworth (1993) 143 NLJ 610.
124 It should be noted that religious discrimination in employment could give rise to liability in Northern Ireland under the Fair Employment (NI) Act 1976.
125 [1983] 2 AC 818 HL. The decision partly relied on interpreting RRA 1976, s 75 as intended to limit the application of the Act in respect of public authorities.

spheres it covered, including employment. Thus, for example, racial discrimination in a prison resulting in refusal of employment would be covered,[126] but other discriminatory practices within the criminal justice system, such as racially discriminatory arrests or stops and searches, fell outside the Act.

However, the decision in *Farah v Comr of Police of the Metropolis*[127] made it clear that racial bias in policing decisions will fall within the Act although, importantly, it did not create vicarious liability in respect of such decisions. Farah, a Somali citizen and refugee who was 17 at the time, was attacked by a group of white teenagers who set a dog on her and injured her. She summoned police help by telephone; when the police arrived, they made no attempt to arrest her attackers, but arrested her and charged her with affray, assault and causing unnecessary suffering to a dog. No evidence was offered when she appeared to answer the charges, and she was acquitted. She brought an action for damages against the Commissioner of Police of the Metropolis, alleging false imprisonment, assault and battery and malicious prosecution. She included in the statement of claim an allegation that the conduct of the police officers amounted to unlawful racial discrimination. Judge Harris refused to strike out the allegation of racial discrimination. He also allowed her to amend that part of her claim, so that she alleged that the officers were acting as the Commissioner's agents and had discriminated against her on grounds of race in both failing to afford her the protection which would have been afforded to white victims of crime and in bringing the proceedings against her. The commissioner appealed against the refusal to strike out the allegation of racial discrimination.

The Court of Appeal found that two important issues fell to be determined. First, whether a police officer came within s 20 of the RRA 1976, which prohibits racial discrimination in the provision of services and, secondly, if he did, whether his Chief Officer of Police would be answerable in law for any breaches of the Act he might have committed. The court held that an officer providing protection to a citizen was providing a service within the section. Policy reasons against such a conclusion, including the possibility that the police would have to face numerous claims of race discrimination, were rejected as outweighed by the need to provide a remedy for a citizen who had suffered discrimination in a situation where she was in dire need of protection. Moreover, nothing in the Act made police officers immune from claims of racial discrimination. However, the Court found that the Commissioner was not vicariously liable for the acts of the officers. Section 53 appeared to deny vicarious liability, except in so far as provided for by the Act. Her claim against the individual officers for discrimination was out of time. The appeal was allowed and therefore her claim of discrimination had to be struck from the statement of claim. This decision was to be welcomed as making it clear that the possibility of compensation for racially discriminatory police actions and decisions was available. However, it also hedged this possibility around with restrictions, since it denied the possibility of vicarious liability.

However, after amendment by the Race Relations (Amendment) Act 2000 (which inserted s 19B into the 1976 Act), discrimination (direct or indirect) by a public authority

---

126 RRA 1976, Part II; in *Alexander v Home Office* [1988] 1 WLR 968, CA (the plaintiff, a prisoner, was refused work in prison kitchen owing to racial stereotyping).
127 [1997] 1 All ER 289.

in carrying out its functions is brought within the ambit of the Act. This amendment of the RRA was effected to implement Recommendation No 11 of the MacPherson Report into the death of Stephen Lawrence,[128] after the MacPherson inquiry found 'institutional racism' in the Metropolitan Police, which had resulted in significant failures in the investigation of his death at the hands of racists. The term 'public authority' is to be interpreted consistently (although not identically) with the interpretation afforded to the same term under the HRA.[129] Law enforcement by public authorities is now brought within the statutory framework for the prohibition of discrimination, thus closing the gap that was dramatically and disturbingly highlighted by the Stephen Lawrence case. Thus, the actions of the police in investigating crime are now covered by the RRA, as are other functions of public authorities. Section 4 of the 2000 Act inserts ss 76A and B into the RRA, providing that chief officers of police will be vicariously liable for the actions of their officers. However, there are still exceptions to the coverage of the Act, created by the amendments. Section 19D exempts 'any act done for the purpose of making a decision about instituting criminal proceedings'. This formulation leaves open the possibility that acts remote from that decision, including the uncovering of evidence, are covered by the RRA.

SDA and RRA – differences

The amendments to the RRA now represent one of a number of important differences between the statutory scheme covering discrimination on grounds of sex and that covering the ground of race. The RRA creates the most comprehensive domestic scheme that this chapter considers: the provisions under the RRA outlawing discrimination in private clubs of 25 members or more, segregation and 'transferred discrimination' – discrimination on the grounds of another's race – have no counterparts under the SDA. The 'functions of a public authority' head is not yet replicated in the SDA, although it will be in 2007.[130] Employment covers 'pay' in the RRA, thus ensuring a less complex scheme than that applying in respect of sex discrimination claims.

The influence of the EU has been until recently less important in the context of race discrimination, although rulings of the European Court of Justice and of the domestic courts taking EU provisions into account affected concepts under the RRA. It should be noted that even prior to the introduction of the Race Directive 2003, the EU did not ignore race discrimination and had passed a number of resolutions and declarations giving guidance to member states,[131] but its influence in this area, although beginning to develop, remained until 2003 at a much earlier stage than its influence on sex discrimination. Aside from EU provisions, the UK is a party to a number of international declarations on race discrimination and xenophobia which, although not

---

128 Cm 4262-I. For discussion of the amendments, see O'Cinneide, C, 'The Race Relations (Amendment) Act 2000' [2001] PL 220.

129 See Chapter 4, pp 216 et seq.

130 See pp 1577–79 below.

131 See Resolutions, Reports and Declarations of the Council of the EC: Resolution of 16 July 1985 (OJ C186 26.7.85, p 3); Declaration of 11 June 1986 (OJ C158 25.6.86, p 1); Resolution of 24 May 1988 (OJ C177 6.7.88, p 5); Council Decision 88/348/EEC (OJ L158 25.6.88); Eurigenis Report 1991. For criticism of the EU stance on racism, see Bindman (1994) 144 NLJ 352; see also Lester, 'New European Equality Measures' [2000] PL 562.

part of UK law, may influence it.[132] As indicated above, the Race Directive brought race discrimination directly within the ambit of EU law. Its domestic implementation made a number of changes to the 1976 Act, as discussed below.

Discrimination on grounds of disability

Introduction[133]

The Disability Discrimination Act 1995 (DDA), as amended, is modelled to an extent on the SDA and RRA schemes; the DDA adopted the concepts of direct discrimination and victimisation used in the SDA and RRA and a body was set up to promote and monitor the scheme, although it initially had only an advisory role. But the DDA scheme differs in some important respects from the earlier schemes. In general, it is narrower in scope than the earlier legislation, in terms both of its application and of the forms of discrimination covered. Originally, the Act only applied to employers who employ more than 20 people. It is now applicable to those employing more than 15 (s 7(1)).[134] Thus, many small businesses will still fall outside its scope. Most significantly, the Act does not import the concept of indirect discrimination in its full sense, although, as indicated below, the concept of direct discrimination is broader than that used in the SDA and RRA. Also, direct discrimination can be justified; this is understandable, within limits, in this context. Unlike the provisions against race and sex discrimination, the Act is incomplete – it relies on being fleshed out by non-statutory rules.[135] Under one of the more significant SIs, tribunals are bound to take into account the Disability Discrimination Code of Practice, which came into force in December 1996.[136]

The Act does not adopt the symmetrical, formal equality approach of the other statutes or regulations: it does not take the stance that a disabled person is asking for equal treatment with an able-bodied person; she is asking for *different* treatment in order to put her in the same position as an able-bodied person. For example, a person who needs to use a wheel chair is asking for equal access to the work place – probably via a lift – not an equal right to use the stairs. So the formal equality approach plays a minor part in the Act. The key concepts under it are those of disability-related discrimination and the duty of reasonable adjustment.

A medical model

The Act adopts what may be termed a 'medical' as opposed to a 'social' model of discrimination. Under a medical model, the impairment is located in the person in

---

132 European Convention on Human Rights, Arts 3 and 14; International Labour Organisation; International Covenant on Civil and Political Rights; the International Covenant on Economic, Social and Cultural Rights, para 2; International Convention on the Elimination of All Forms of Racial Discrimination.

133 Texts referred to: McColgan, op. cit., fn 1, Chapter 8; 'Interpreting the Disability Discrimination Act (1998) 80 EOR 14; M Connolly op. cit., fn 1; Doyle, B, 'Enabling legislation or dissembling law? The DDA 1995' (2001) 64 MLR 7; *Butterworth's Discrimination Law Handbook*, 2000; Clayton and Tomlinson, op. cit., fn 1, pp 1230–33.

134 By 2004, this figure is to be reduced to apply to employers who employ more than two employees.

135 See SI 1996/1996; SI 1996/2793; SI 1996/1836.

136 Under SI 1996/1996.

question; he or she must claim to be significantly impaired in his or her ability to perform certain tasks in order to come within the scope of the legislation. Under a social model, the impairment depends on the attitudes of others. The medical model on which the DDA is based includes the concept of reasonable adjustment – that is, of placing a duty on the employer or other party to take reasonable steps in order to allow the disabled person to perform their duties despite their disability. Under provisions based on either model the arrangements for, for example, access to buildings could create discrimination against disabled people. Under either a medical or a social model, a person who has, for example, muscular dystrophy and has as a result significant mobility difficulties might well have no difficulty in performing a managerial job which depends on skills unrelated to mobility, so long as no obstacles are placed in her way in the form, for example, of steps which make it difficult for her to enter her own workplace. If a lift or other means of access were provided, she would not be impaired in her ability to perform the job. Thus, the impact of her disability would be determined by factors such as the willingness of the management to install a lift, rather than by the inherent nature of her disability.

But provisions based on a social model of disability can cover a wider range of circumstances than provisions based on the medical model. For example, a person might suffer discrimination due to a *perception* that he or she is disabled. An employer might perceive, for example, that a person with a cleft lip was mentally disordered. In fact the person's ability to perform a job would not be affected by the disfigurement, but he or she might nevertheless suffer discrimination based on social attitudes. Thus the DDA cannot address all disability-linked discrimination.

The Act creates complex definitions as to those who are covered by it. Under s 1(1) the person concerned must have 'a physical or mental impairment which has a substantial and long-term adverse effect on his ability to carry out normal day-to-day activities'. The definition includes within its scope progressive diseases such as multiple sclerosis or forms of dystrophy which may not currently be of great significance in terms of impairment, but are likely to become so. The DDA also covers those who have had a disability in the past, whether or not they have recovered (s 2(1)). Thus a three-stage approach has been created; first it must be shown that the applicant is 'disabled' within the definition, then discrimination must be shown, and then that it falls within one of the contexts covered by the Act, as amended. Further, as discussed below,[137] a duty of adjustment is placed on various bodies under the Act.

Field of application

The DDA 1995, as amended, does not make discrimination on the ground of disability generally illegal; as with the sex and race legislation, it only outlaws it in the contexts in which it operates: employment (Part II), disposal of premises (s 22) and the provision of goods and services (s 19). The Act was also amended and extended by the Special Education Needs and Disability Act 2001 to place duties on schools and on the providers of post-16 education and related services. The Act applies to all employers who have 15 or more employees, but it excludes a number of occupations, including the police,

137 See pp 1550–54.

firefighters, barristers, prison officers, the armed forces, and those working on ships or aircraft.[138] Unlike the provisions in respect of employment, which do not apply at present to businesses with fewer than 15 staff, the service provisions apply across the board. These provisions require traders not to refuse service to disabled people or to offer an inferior service. The Special Educational Needs and Disability Act 2001, which adds s 28A to the DDA, covering schools, and s 28R covering further and higher education, leaves the full field of application to orders made by the Secretary of State in respect of coverage of certain educational institutions under s 28R(6)(c) and in respect of the services covered within schools under s 28A(3). Further amendments were made by the DDA 2005, extending the Act's coverage in most areas.

The employment-related provisions came into force in December 1996. The first part of Part III of the Act, the provision of access to goods, facilities and services, also came into force in December 1996. The second part of Part III of the Act, the duty to make reasonable adjustments in the context of the provision of access to goods, facilities and services, did not come into force until 1 October 1999. The third stage of Part III came into force in 2004[139] and requires traders to make physical alterations to premises to facilitate equal service, typically by installing lifts or ramps. The provisions regarding education came into force in 2002.[140]

Discrimination on grounds of sexual orientation

Introduction[141]

Until 2003 a person who was refused promotion or dismissed from a job on grounds of sexual orientation, was in the same position as a woman so treated would have been before 1975, in the sense that no anti-discrimination legislation specifically covered his or her situation. Indeed, far from seeking to outlaw discrimination on this ground, certain legal provisions discussed below implied that until recently such discrimination was approved of by the law and therefore by society. However, the situation has changed, partly as a result of the election of the Labour Government in 1997, meaning that

138 See below for consideration of certain exclusions.
139 SI 2001/2030, Art 3(a).
140 See Special Educational Needs and Disability Act 2001
141 Texts referred to: M Connolly (2006), op. cit., fn 1; E Heinze, *Sexual Orientation: A Human Right: An Essay on International Human Rights Law*, 1995, Martinus Nijhoff; Wintemute, R, 'Recognising new kinds of direct sex discrimination: transsexualism, sexual orientation and dress codes' (1997) 60(3) MLR 334; Bamforth, *Sexuality, Morals and Justice*, 1997, Continuum; Skidmore (1997) 26(1) ILJ 51;. For discussion from a non-liberal standpoint, see Stychin, C, *Law's Desire: Sexuality and the Limits of Justice*, 1995, Routledge. See also: Rubin, G, 'Section 146 of the Criminal Justice and Public Order Act 1994 and the decriminalisation of homosexual acts in the armed forces' [1996] Crim LR 393; Smith, AM, *New Rights Discourses on Race and Sexuality*,1994, CUP; Duffy, P, 'A case for equality' (1998) EHRLR 134; Wintemute, R, 'Lesbian and gay inequality 2000: the potential of the HRA and the need for an Equality Act 2002' (2000) 6 EHRLR 603; Hewitt, P, *The Abuse of Power*, 1982, Chapter 9; Wintemute, R, *Sexual Orientation and Human Rights: The US Constitution, the ECHR and the Canadian Charter*, 1995; Hervey, T and O'Keeffe, D (eds), *Sex Equality Law in the European Union*, 1996, Chancery, Chapter 17; Wilkinson, B, 'Moving towards equality: homosexual law reform in Ireland' (1994) 45 NILQ 252; Wilets, *The Human Rights of Sexual Minorities*, 1996, Continuum; Pannick, D, 'Homosexuals, transsexuals and the law' [1983] PL 279; Crane, P, *Gays and the Law*, 1982, Pluto.

a greater willingness to introduce anti-sexual orientation discrimination legislation became apparent, but most importantly due to developments in EU law.

Prior to 2003 there was clearly a growing recognition in Europe that discrimination on grounds of sexual orientation amounted to a general problem which should be addressed. A report compiled for the Commission of the European Communities in May 1993[142] on discrimination against homosexuals found that the UK was one of the worst offenders and was one of only four member states which provided no legal protection against discrimination. The report also criticised the Commission, which had argued that homosexuality is a matter to be left to individual governments. The Report recommended that human rights for homosexuals should be enshrined in European Community law.

The EOC, in the wake of the *Lustig-Prean* case,[143] proposed that there should be a statutory provision outlawing discrimination in employment and other fields on the ground of sexual orientation. The Labour Government, however, responded only by introducing an unenforceable Code of Practice covering such discrimination.[144] A Code of Practice was clearly unlikely to have much influence. It could not outlaw discrimination on grounds of sexual orientation and was likely to be ignored by many employers. The very fact that a Code rather than a statute was introduced signalled to employers and others that this was not a significant matter.

The Employment Equality (Sexual Orientation) Regulations 2003 were inroduced in response to the Framework Directive; until that point no specific protection from discrimination on this ground was offered in UK law. At present a person who is treated detrimentally in terms of housing or in educational provision outside the educational contexts covered by the regulations, or is adversely treated on the ground of sexual orientation in terms of access to goods and services, will find that no dedicated anti-discrimination legislation specifically covers his or her situation, although this situation should change later in 2007. New regulations are to be introduced in 2007, extending the protection offered from discrimination on this ground into the field of goods and services. Thus the unprotected area is incrementally diminishing.

Thus some protection is available, but the protection is clearly inadequate when compared with that available in respect of race or sex discrimination. Owing to the current gap in the law, leaving discrimination on this ground in certain contexts to go relatively unchecked, the HRA and European Convention on Human Rights may be looked to as a method of providing some protection for the right to freedom from discrimination of homosexuals.[145] At the present time, certain legal provisions, discussed below, appear to imply that discrimination on this ground is still, in certain spheres of activity, approved of by the law and therefore by society. Articles 8 and 14 of the Convention are the Articles most likely to be utilised to fill the gaps in the current law. Indeed, the HRA and Convention offer a protection from sexual orientation discrimination that is almost certainly broader than that which they offer to persons affected by discrimination on grounds of sex, outside the contexts covered by the SDA.

---

142 By Peter Ashman, Director of the Independent European Human Rights Foundation.
143 See pp 1520–21 below.
144 In February 2000, the government asked the EOC to draw up a Code governing this area: *Daily Telegraph*, 18 February 2000.
145 See Wintemute, R, 'Recognising new kinds of direct sex discrimination: transsexualism, sexual orientation and dress codes' (1997) 60(3) MLR 334.

Comprehensive anti-discrimination legislation, reaching into the contexts uncovered by the current regulations, is still clearly needed. It would have a dual function. It would offer a remedy which is only currently available in the spheres of employment and vocational training. Secondly, it would affirm symbolically the abhorrence of society for homophobic attitudes and behaviour in the key contexts. It would be likely, eventually, to have the effect of indicating to persons inclined to homophobic views that those views are as unacceptable in society as racist or sexist ones.

EU provisions

Article 6a of the Amsterdam Treaty, signed by the member states on 19 June 1997, provided that the Council could adopt provisions intended to combat discrimination on grounds of sexual orientation. The pressure coming from Europe, within the EC and Convention systems, for the introduction of measures to combat discrimination on this ground found realistion within European Council Directive 2000/78/EC, the Framework Directive,[146] on equal opportunities in employment which, *inter alia*, required the extension of anti-discrimination measures to cover the ground of sexual orientation. The Employment Equality (Sexual Orientation) Regulations 2003 Regulations introduced in order to implement the Framework Directive now cover discrimination on grounds of sexual orientation, but only in the context of employment. Part 3 of the Equality Act 2006 provides a power to extend the coverage of the regulations into other fields and in January 2007 the Sexual Orientation (Goods and Services) Regulations were passed by Parliament to apply in Northern Ireland. The equivalent regulations for Britain are expected to be introduced into Parliament in 2007, so the current gap in the law is expected to be merely temporary. If the domestic implementation of the Directive is inadequate in providing full protection for persons discriminated against on grounds of sexual orientation in employment or vocational training, it could be challenged in the ECJ. Its adequacy is considered below.

The Sex Discrimination Act

There have been various attempts to bring homosexuals within the SDA. Although it is no longer necessary to seek to do this in the context of employment or vocational training, it would be worth trying to show that the SDA applied to sexual orientation discrimination in the other contexts it covers. Prior to the inception of the HRA, it became clear that a homosexual applicant could not fall within the SDA unless he or she could show that someone of the opposite sex would have been treated more favourably. In other words, where a lesbian woman or gay man would be subjected to equal and unfavourable treatment, no action would lie[147] since it was found that s 1 of the SDA is concerned with grounds of sex, not sexual orientation. In the UK courts it was also found in 1996 that applicants treated unfavourably because of their sexual orientation are not covered by the Equal Treatment Directive.

---

146 Adopted under the Treaty Establishing the European Community (TEC), Art 13.
147 *Smith v Gardner Merchant* [1996] ICR 790; [1996] IRLR 342, noted [1996] 67 EOR 48.

However, in 1997, it appeared that the weak position of homosexuals who are dismissed from employment or otherwise detrimentally treated might be about to change under the influence of EU law. In Case 13/14 *P v S and Cornwall CC*,[148] P was dismissed from her employment on the ground that she was a transsexual. Her application under the SDA 1975 failed as it was found that transsexuals were outside the terms of the Act. As indicated above, it was found that her case fell within the Equal Treatment Directive on the basis that the Directive is simply the expression of the principle of equality, which is one of the fundamental principles of European Union law. Once it was found that transsexuals were within the Directive, it appeared probable that it would also cover homosexuals. The words 'on grounds of sex' within the Directive could be found to relate, *inter alia*, to the sex of the partner. Thus, where a woman was in a partnership with a man, she would not be likely to experience adverse treatment on that ground. But where a woman was or was potentially in partnership with a woman, she might experience discrimination on that ground. In that respect, discrimination 'on grounds of sex' could include discrimination on grounds of sexual orientation. In other words, if discrimination occurs due to the fact that a person's partner is or is potentially of the 'wrong' gender, the Directive could, in principle, cover such a situation.

This argument was considered in *Secretary of State for Defence ex p Perkins*,[149] which concerned the ban on homosexuals in the armed services, and it was determined that, owing to the *P v S* decision, the case must be referred to the ECJ. In Case 249/96, *Grant v South West Trains Ltd*,[150] it was argued that a refusal to allow a lesbian partner the same employment perks as those which would be allowed to a heterosexual partner is discrimination contrary to the Directive and Art 119 (as it was). The Advocate General gave his Opinion that discrimination contrary to the Equal Pay Directive and Art 119 had occurred. However, the Court failed to decide in the same way, taking the view that discrimination on grounds of sexual orientation is not covered, with the result that lesbians and homosexuals were unable to claim in the domestic courts any pay or fringe benefits currently only available to heterosexuals. Thus, the Court refused to take this step forward in terms of outlawing discrimination on grounds of sexual orientation. In *Grant*, EU law stepped out of harmony with ECHR law, as interpreted in *Lustig-Prean v UK* and *Smith and Grady v UK*. The most pressing need at that time was then to outlaw discrimination on grounds of sexual orientation within decisions as to dismissal and appointment. When provision was made in that sphere it still meant that the argument rejected in *Perkins* could be raised in the contexts in which protection was not available, where they were covered by the SDA.

Smith v Gardner Merchant[151] followed *Grant*; the Court of Appeal found that a male homosexual could bring a claim under the SDA, but only if he could show that a female homosexual would have been treated more favourably. In other words, the claim would have to be based on grounds of gender and not on grounds of sexual orientation. However, it appeared possible, once the HRA was in force, that a different interpretation of the SDA could be adopted, and that it would be possible to find that discrimination on grounds of sexual orientation can be covered. This interpretation

148   Judgment of 30 April 1996; [1996] ECR I-2143; [1996] IRLR 347.
149   [1997] IRLR 297.
150   [1998] IRLR 206.
151   [1998] 3 All ER 852.

was adopted in *MacDonald v MOD*,[152] a Scottish case relying on the Convention. It was found that a creative interpretation of s 1 of the SDA on the lines indicated above, referring to the gender of a partner, would allow sexual orientation to fall within the Act. This decision was, however, overturned by the Court of Sessions, which followed *Smith v Gardner Merchant*.

In *Secretary of State for Defence v Scotland; Pearce v Mayfield Secondary School Governing Body* the House of Lords considered the joined cases of *Pearce* and of *McDonald* since they raised the same issue: could sexual orientation discrimination fall within the SDA? The House of Lords held that in these cases the Sex Discrimination Act 1975 does not protect persons from discrimination on the grounds of sexuality. They also overturned the previous decision of the EAT in *Burton v De Vere Hotels Ltd*,[153] discussed below, and concluded that sexual harassment is not unlawful discrimination in itself but requires a comparison with how a comparator of the opposite sex was or would have been treated. Mr Macdonald had been discharged from the RAF after having admitted to being gay. Ms Pearce was a teacher at Mayfield Secondary School. She came out as a lesbian and then suffered homophobic abuse by pupils at the school, including the use of words such as 'dyke', 'lesbian shit', 'lemon', 'lezzie' or 'lez'. Ms Pearce was driven to resign from her job as a teacher after this vicious campaign of anti-lesbian abuse from pupils. She claimed sex discrimination, arguing that the school had failed to take effective action to protect her from homophobic harassment. An employment tribunal (ET) dismissed her claim. It found that the detrimental treatment was on grounds of sexual orientation rather than sex and that there could only be discrimination if a hypothetical male homosexual teacher would have been treated differently from Ms Pearce; there was no evidence that this was the case. In other words, a homosexual male teacher would have been treated equally badly.

Both cases predated implementation of the Human Rights Act 1998, which therefore could not directly assist them in obtaining redress. The new Employment Equality (Sexual Orientation) Regulations 2003 had not come into force. As a result, both applicants had to seek to rely on the SDA to obtain a remedy. Both applicants conceded that the words 'on the grounds of sex' in the SDA do not include 'on the grounds of sexual orientation'. Both applicants broadly advanced the same argument before the House of Lords. Their case was that Mr Macdonald was discharged from the RAF for being attracted to men. A woman in the same circumstances would not be discharged for being attracted to men. A female comparator would therefore be treated more favourably because she is a woman and not a man. The fact that Mr Macdonald was gay and the comparator was a heterosexual was not it was argued a relevant factor in making the like-for-like comparison.

The House of Lords found that in the context of s 1 SDA 'sex' means gender and does not include sexual orientation. Thus harassment on the grounds of sexual orientation does not of itself amount to discrimination on the grounds of sex for the purposes of the SDA. Ms Pearce had argued that the appropriate comparator for establishing whether she had been less favourably treated under the SDA was a heterosexual man. He would also have been attracted to women, but would not have been treated in the same way

---

152 [2001] 1 All ER 620. On appeal: 2001 SLT 819. HL decision in *McDonald v MOD; Pearce v Mayfield School*: [2003] IRLR 512.
153 [1996] IRLR 596.

as her. In other words, she was arguing that the potential partner's gender could be the determining factor; the discrimination was on grounds of gender because had Ms Pearce been male and attracted to women she would not have suffered the abuse.

However, the Lords disagreed. In their view this was not comparing 'like with like', as required by s 5(3) SDA. They considered that the appropriate comparison was with a homosexual man. Since Ms Pearce had accepted that the pupils would have pursued a similar campaign of harassment against a homosexual teacher, she could not establish that she had been treated 'less favourably' on the ground of her sex. Ms Pearce also argued that the use of words such as 'lezzie' amounted to 'gender-specific' harassment. This, it was submitted, was capable of amounting to less favourable treatment on the ground of her sex without the need to identify a male comparator. The Lords disagreed. The House of Lords found that, if the treatment is gender specific, it will suggest that the reason for the harassment is the woman's gender but it would not dispense with the need for the ET to be satisfied that the reason why she was being harassed was her sex. In Ms Pearce's case, it was clear that it was her sexual orientation, not her gender, which was the reason for the abuse she suffered.

The House of Lords conclusively rejected this argument. It found that the sexual orientation of the applicants was a relevant factor that had to be taken into account in making a like-for-like comparison. In the above examples, the reason for the treatment was the sexual orientation. For Mr Macdonald, therefore, his female comparator also had to be gay, otherwise the comparison would not involve comparing like with like. A gay male applicant must show that he had been treated less favourably than a lesbian comparator. That it was found was not the evidence in the instant case which was to the effect – in relation to Mr McDonald – that a gay female would also have been discharged. The situation was the same, in reverse, for Ms Pearce. The case could therefore not succeed. The House of Lords was influenced by the finding, already considered, that sexual orientation discrimination is not covered by the Equal Treatment Directive.

At present, there seems to be a possibility of bringing about change in the contexts currently uncovered by the 2003 Regulations – housing, provision of goods and services, aspects of education. A court might take the view that since the *MacDonald; Pearce* case was not decided under the HRA, a different approach could be adopted, using s 3 of the HRA to interpret s 1 of the SDA purposively in order to give effect to the protection for sexual orientation within Art 8, relying on *Lustig-Prean v UK* and *Smith and Grady v UK* (discussed below). In taking this radical approach, such a court could find support from the House of Lords' decision in *R v A*[154] in which the Lords went so far as to read words into a statute in order to achieve a result that they viewed as in compliance with Art 6 of the Convention.

Employing the HRA against sexual orientation discrimination

The HRA is significant in this field in three respects. First a free-standing action could be brought under it, relying on s 7(1(a)), against a public authority – but not a private body – allegedly discriminating on this ground. Second, any body, including private bodies allegedly discriminating on this ground in reliance on legislative provisions in,

---

154 See Chapter 4, pp 174–76.

for example, housing could find that the use of s 3 HRA means that the discrimination is outlawed. Third, the reach of the Sexual Orientation Regulations could be broadened by reliance on ss 3 and 6 HRA. So long as either s 3 or s 6 HRA (or both) were applicable, a person discriminated against on grounds of sexual orientation could seek to rely on Art 8, either read with Art 14 or on its own. Article 14 only operates in conjunction with another Convention Article. But even where that other Article is not itself breached, a breach might be found when it is read with Art 14.

But if the regulations are inapplicable, the alleged discriminator is not a public authority, and no statutory provision (other than – arguably – the SDA) covers the alleged discrimination, the Human Rights Act can be of no assistance, even though at Strasbourg a remedy would be available, relying on Arts 14 and 8 combined. The only way of finding a remedy domestically in that circumstance would be to seek to rely on the SDA, probably bolstered by use of s 3 HRA. But arguments in reliance on the SDA have met with no success so far. As Chapter 2 explained, Protocol 12 provides a free-standing right to freedom from discrimination.[155] However, as indicated above, the domestic response to Protocol 12 is at present not very favourable. As will be indicated, the HRA provides the best possibility of providing protection from discrimination on this ground in a number of these fields, where a public authority has some responsibility for the discrimination in question.[156] The discussion below considers the provisions that can be utilised to seek to provide protection from discrimination on this ground in the various fields that would normally appear in anti-discrimination legislation, other than employment and vocational training.

The guarantee of freedom from discrimination under Art 14 of the Convention, received into domestic law under the HRA, covers discrimination on grounds of sexual orientation through its use of the words 'without discrimination on any ground such as . . .'.[157] Therefore, a number of possibilities are open. As indicated above and in Chapter 2, Art 14 only operates in conjunction with another Convention Article. But even where that other Article is not itself breached, a breach may be found when it is read with Art 14.

Prior to the inception of the HRA, judicial review provided a means of challenging decisions or policies having a discriminatory effect, but until the HRA came into force, the threshold for challenge was set so high that it provided an ineffective remedy. This was made clear in the case discussed below. In the UK until recently, homosexuals were barred from the merchant navy and the armed forces, where homosexual acts were classed as 'disgraceful conduct',[158] although the armed forces in Belgium, Denmark, France, The Netherlands and Spain are all open to homosexuals. The legality of the policy of the Ministry of Defence in maintaining the ban was challenged in *Ministry of*

---

155 See Chapter 2, p 106; for further discussion on Protocol 12, see Khaliq [2001] PL 457.

156 See Wintemute, R, 'Recognising new kinds of direct sex discrimination: transsexualism, sexual orientation and dress codes' (1997) 60(3) MLR 334.

157 *Salgueiro da Silva Monta v Portugal* [2001] 1 FCR 653. In *Dudgeon* (1982) 4 EHRR 149 the Court of Human Rights was asked to consider the application of Art 14 read in conjunction with Art 8. It appeared to assume that Art 14 did cover discrimination on this ground, although it found that it did not need to consider the application of Art 14 in the instant case since a breach of Art 8 had been found.

158 See the Army Act 1955, s 66; the Sexual Offences Act 1967, ss 1(5) and 2.

Defence ex p Smith and Others.[159] The applicants, homosexuals who had been dismissed owing to the existence of the ban, applied for review of the policy. Their application was dismissed at first instance in the Divisional Court and the applicants appealed.

Rejecting the argument of the MOD that it had no jurisdiction to review the legality of the policy in question, the Court applied the usual *Wednesbury* principles. This meant that it could not interfere with the exercise of an administrative discretion save where it was satisfied that the decision was unreasonable in the sense that it was beyond the range of responses open to a reasonable decision maker. But, in judging whether the decision maker had exceeded that margin of appreciation, the human rights context was important: '. . . the more substantial the interference with human rights, the more the Court will require by way of justification before it will be satisfied that the decision was reasonable.'[160] Applying such principles and taking into account the support of the policy in both Houses of Parliament, it could not be said that the policy crossed the threshold of irrationality, although it was criticised.

In *Lustig-Prean v UK*[161] and *Smith and Grady v UK*[162] the European Court of Human Rights found that the applicants had been subjected to treatment in breach of Art 8 when they were dismissed from the armed services on grounds of their sexual orientation. It may be noted that previously the Commission had rejected a challenge to the provision relating to the army as inadmissible on the argument that there is a special need to prevent disorder in the armed forces.[163] However, the Court found that the ban infringed Art 8 and Art 13; its absolute nature meant that it could not be viewed as being in proportion to a legitimate aim. Not only the ban itself, but also the intrusive questioning of the applicants after their homosexuality was suspected, was found to constitute an interference with the respect for their private life under Art 8. The applicants also argued that Art 3 had been infringed but, although the Court considered that this was a possibility in respect of discrimination on grounds of sexual orientation, it did not consider that the strict Art 3 test had been met in the circumstances of the case. As a result of this ruling, discharges from the armed services on grounds of sexual orientation have now ceased.

The ruling in *Lustig-Prean* has further implications. It could be utilised under the HRA relying on Arts 8 and 14 within the context of employment or vocational training as an *alternative* to relying on the 2003 Regulations. Or it could be relied upon outside the contexts covered by the regulations. Under the HRA, a public authority which detrimentally treated a homosexual on grounds of sexual orientation outside those contexts – for example, in housing – could be challenged in the courts under ss 6 and 7(1)(a) of the Act, relying on Art 8. Where a private body was the employer, the applicant could rely on s 3 of the HRA in seeking to persuade a tribunal to afford an interpretation to statutory provisions which would prevent the discrimination from

---

159 [1996] 1 All ER 257; [1996] ICR 740. Noted: Skidmore, P (1995) 24 ILJ 363; (1996) 25 ILJ 63. For discussion, see Skidmore, P, 'Sex, Gender and Comparators in Employment Discrimination' (1997) 26(1) ILJ 51; see also: Rubin, G, 'Section 146 of the Criminal Justice and Public Order Act 1994 and the decriminalisation of homosexual acts in the armed forces' [1996] Crim LR 393.
160 Ibid, p 263.
161 (1999) 29 EHRR 548; (1999) 7 BHRC 65.
162 (2000) 29 EHRR 493.
163 *B v UK* 34 D & R (1983); (1983) 6 EHRR 354.

occurring. This possibility would, of course, also be available in proceedings against a public authority. But the ruling of the Court in *Lustig-Prean* could only be relied upon under s 2 HRA when seeking review of a decision or policy of a public authority which was discriminatory on grounds of sexual orientation. If the UK fails to introduce anti-discrimination legislation in the contexts uncovered by the regulations, s 7(1)(a) of the HRA provides an important substitute means of obtaining a remedy, at least where the other party is a public authority. This route could be not be used in respect of discriminatory actions outside the employment or vocational training context by private bodies where no statutory provision was relevant.

Despite that important limitation, the potential of the HRA in this area has not yet been realised. So long as the alleged discriminator is a public authority under s 6 of the HRA, there are a number of other possibilities, not all of which depend on using Art 8 (which has already shown its potential in this area read alone), but there might also be instances in which, although an invasion of privacy grounded on homosexuality fell within one of the exceptions, it could nevertheless be established taking Art 14 into account owing to its discriminatory nature. It could range far outside the contexts covered by the discussion above and far beyond the contexts covered by the SDA or RRA. Article 6 might be used where a homosexual was refused a hearing in, for example, a child care or adoption case where a heterosexual would not have been so refused. Article 10 read in conjunction with Art 14 might offer protection to expressions of the homosexual way of life such as the wearing of badges or even some physical gestures.[164] In *Salgueiro da Silva Mouta v Portugal*[165] the Court relied on Art 14 in finding that a breach had occurred where a parent was denied contact with his child on the ground of sexual orientation. The anomalies thereby created are part of the argument that the government must move to introduce the regulations covering goods and services promptly. However, that would still leave aspects of the context of education uncovered.

Sexual orientation discrimination in employment

Pre-2003 provision against unfair dismissal

Prior to 2003, if a lesbian or homosexual had been employed for at least two years before dismissal, the provisions against unfair dismissal under the Employment Rights Act 1996 (previously contained in the Employment Protection (Consolidation) Act 1978) could offer some protection, although a dismissal would be fair if it is for 'some other substantial reason of a kind to justify dismissal', provided that the employer had acted

---

164 In *Masterson v Holden* [1986] 3 All ER 39; [1986] 1 WLR 1017 the Divisional Court found that magistrates were entitled to view the behaviour of two homosexuals in kissing and cuddling as insulting for the purposes of the Metropolitan Police Act 1839, s 54(13). This approach might also be taken under the Public Order Act 1986, s 5, but such a wide interpretation of 'insulting' could allow many restrictions on the public expression of homosexuality, which might be in breach of Art 10, either read alone or in conjunction with Art 14. It appears that Art 10 does not cover homosexual intercourse *per se*, but may cover the physical as well as verbal expression of homosexual love: *X v UK* (1981) 3 EHRR 63.

165 [2001] 1 FCR 653, judgment of 21 December 1999.

reasonably. Where dismissal was on grounds of sexual orientation, a wide interpretation was given to the meaning of 'reasonable' in the older decisions. In *Saunders v Scottish National Camps*,[166] the applicant, who was employed as a maintenance handyman at a boys' camp, was dismissed on the grounds of homosexuality although his duties did not ordinarily bring him into contact with the boys. His dismissal was nevertheless held to be fair on the ground that many other employers would have responded in the same way. The decision is clearly open to attack on the ground that even when his duties brought him into contact with the boys, there would have been no more reason to believe that they would have been in danger from him than would girls from a male heterosexual. Similarly, it has been found that the dismissal of a homosexual from GCHQ as a threat to national security was not unreasonable, despite the fact that he had been open about his homosexuality and therefore could not be blackmailed.[167]

In the late 1990s, there was some recognition that discrimination on grounds of sex orientation was unacceptable. In *O'Connor v Euromoney Publications Inc*[168] the defendants admitted that O'Connor had been subjected to 'unacceptable and offensive' comments and had been discriminated against on the ground of his sexual orientation. He had also been dismissed from his job with the company. The respondents apologised and, in an out of court settlement, paid a large sum of damages in respect of the dismissal.

The Employment Equality (Sexual Orientation) Regulations 2003

There is now a new specific provision against discrimination on this ground. Discrimination on grounds of sexual orientation in employment and vocational training was covered from December 2003 by the Employment Equality (Sexual Orientation) Regulations 2003 implementing European Council Directive 2000/78/EC (the Framework Directive). The Equality Act 2006 s 81 provided the power to make the Sexual Orientation Regulations. The regulations cover discrimination against heterosexuals, bisexuals and homosexuals. Regulation 2(1) provides: 'In these Regulations, "sexual orientation" means a sexual orientation towards – (a) persons of the same sex; (b) persons of the opposite sex; or (c) persons of the same sex and of the opposite sex.'

The regulations cover discrimination on grounds of sexual orientation in employment and vocational training, and discrimination by way of victimisation or harassment on grounds of sexual orientation. A range of forms of employment detriment, including dismissal, are covered, as is adverse treatment on this ground in relation to vocational training.[169] The new Regulations are considered in more detail below.

---

166 (1981) EAT 7/80, judgment delivered 14 April 1980, for criticism, see quoted comments of Levin in Beer *et al.*, *Gay Workers, Trade Unions and the Law*, 1981, National Council for Civil Liberties, p 27. See, to similar effect, *Boychuk v Symons Holdings Ltd* [1977] IRLR 395, but cf *Bell v Devon and Cornwall Police Authority* [1978] IRLR 283, McColgan, op. cit., fn 1, Chapter 6, pp 387–97.

167 *Director of GCHQ ex p Hodges* (1988) COD 123; (1988) *The Times*, 26 July.

168 (1999) the *Guardian*, 6 June.

169 Regulation 6 of SI 2003 No 1661 provides :

(1) It is unlawful for an employer, in relation to employment by him at an establishment in Great Britain, to discriminate against a person –

(a) in the arrangements he makes for the purpose of determining to whom he should offer employment;

Clearly, merely offering a remedy where discrimination has occurred is only part of the answer to the problems caused where persons discriminate on this ground. Many homosexuals 'choose' discrimination-avoidance or harassment-avoidance by concealing their homosexuality. It has been found in a survey of 2,000 lesbians and gay men at work that 56% concealed their sexuality in all jobs and 33% concealed it in some.[170] A number of surveys have found evidence of widespread discrimination against persons on grounds of sexual orientation and a high incidence of harassment.[171] Offering a remedy in such instances must be a last resort and one that many persons would be unwilling to take. The discussion above as to claims based on the other protected grounds has sought to indicate that seeking to address discrimination through legal claims is fraught with difficulties and may leave a vulnerable person in a more vulnerable position.

Sexual orientation discrimination in education

The 2003 Regulations cover aspects of sexual orientation discrimination in higher and further education,[172] but do not cover schools. Discrimination against homosexuals

> (b) in the terms on which he offers that person employment; or
> (c) by refusing to offer, or deliberately not offering, him employment.
>
> (2) It is unlawful for an employer, in relation to a person whom he employs at an establishment in Great Britain, to discriminate against that person –
>
> (a) in the terms of employment which he affords him;
> (b) in the opportunities which he affords him for promotion, a transfer, training, or receiving any other benefit;
> (c) by refusing to afford him, or deliberately not affording him, any such opportunity; or
> (d) by dismissing him, or subjecting him to any other detriment.
>
> (3) It is unlawful for an employer, in relation to employment by him at an establishment in Great Britain, to subject to harassment a person whom he employs or who has applied to him for employment.
> (4) Paragraph (2) does not apply to benefits of any description if the employer is concerned with the provision (for payment or not) of benefits of that description to the public, or to a section of the public which includes the employee in question, unless –
>
> (a) that provision differs in a material respect from the provision of the benefits by the employer to his employees; or
> (b) the provision of the benefits to the employee in question is regulated by his contract of employment; or
> (c) the benefits relate to training.
>
> (5) In paragraph (2)(d) reference to the dismissal of a person from employment includes reference –
>
> (a) to the termination of that person's employment by the expiration of any period (including a period expiring by reference to an event or circumstance), not being a termination immediately after which the employment is renewed on the same terms; and
> (b) to the termination of that person's employment by any act of his (including the giving of notice) in circumstances such that he is entitled to terminate it without notice by reason of the conduct of the employer.

170 See Palmer, *A Survey of Lesbians and Gay Men at Work*, 1993.
171 'Equality for lesbians and gay men in the work place' (1997) Equal Opportunities Review 20.
172 Regulation 20(1): It is unlawful, in relation to an educational establishment to which this regulation applies, for the governing body of that establishment to discriminate against a person –
>
> (a) in the terms on which it offers to admit him to the establishment as a student;
> (b) by refusing or deliberately not accepting an application for his admission to the establishment as student; or

in the field of education was enshrined in s 2A of the Local Government Act 1986, inserted by s 28 of the Local Government Act 1988 and amended by s 104 of the Local Government Act 2000; it prohibited the deliberate promotion of homosexuality by local authorities or the teaching of 'the acceptability of homosexuality as a pretended family relationship'. Thus, local authorities could still fund certain groups so long as this was aimed at benefiting the group rather than at promoting homosexuality. Robertson argued that s 28 did not have a significant effect in schools, as local authorities do not directly control the curriculum[173] (and this is particularly the case under local management of schools). However, s 28 served to ratify and legitimise intolerance of homosexuals in education and outside it. In opposition, the Labour Party pledged to abolish s 28 and in government it brought forward a Bill in order to do so in 2000. The Scottish Parliament repealed 's 28' as far as Scotland is concerned under ss 25–26 of the Ethical Standards in Public Life (Scotland) Act 2000. The Labour Party's original Bill was defeated in the House of Lords, but the intention of the government continued to be to repeal s 28. This was eventually achieved by s 122 of the Local Government Act 2003. The Act repealed s 2A of the 1986 Act when it came into force.

A person discriminated against in the field of education, such as a pupil forced – in effect – to leave a school or other institution not covered by the regulations owing to homophobic bullying which appeared to be condoned by the authorities, could consider bringing an action in negligence against the institution in question or the education authority. But he or she could also bring an action under s 7(1)(a) of the HRA, relying on Arts 8 and 14, so long as the institution was a public authority. In relation to teaching Art 2 of the First Protocol might be used to argue that education in accordance with one's own philosophical convictions must include the need to allow some teaching about the homosexual way of life.

Sexual orientation discrimination in housing provision

Housing legislation tends to enshrine and rely on a limited notion of the 'family', and therefore it has led to discrimination against homosexuals living in a settled partnership.

    (c) where he is a student of the establishment –

        (i) in the way it affords him access to any benefits,

        (ii) by refusing or deliberately not affording him access to them, or (iii) by excluding him from the establishment or subjecting him to any other detriment.

(2) It is unlawful, in relation to an educational establishment to which this regulation applies, for the governing body of that establishment to subject to harassment a person who is a student at the establishment, or who has applied for admission to the establishment as a student.

(3) Paragraph (1) does not apply if the discrimination only concerns training which would help fit a person for employment which, by virtue of regulation 7 (exception for genuine occupational requirement etc), the employer could lawfully refuse to offer the person in question.

(4) This regulation applies to the following educational establishments in England and Wales, namely –

    (a) an institution within the further education sector (within the meaning of section 91(3) of the Further and Higher Education Act 1992);

    (b) a university;

    (c) an institution, other than a university, within the higher education sector (within the meaning of section 91(5) of the Further and Higher Education Act 1992).

173 Robertson, G, *Freedom, the Individual and the Law*, 7th edn, 1993, p 382.

In *Fitzpatrick v Sterling Housing Association*[174] the Court of Appeal had to consider whether the homosexual partner of a deceased tenant could take over the tenancy under the Rent Act 1977, which limited such succession to persons who had lived with the original tenant 'as wife or husband' or were a member of his 'family'. The Court, by a majority, found that the term 'family' was to be construed in the conventional sense, bearing prevailing social attitudes in mind. It was found that a 'family' was an entity which consisted of 'persons of the opposite sex cohabiting as man and wife'. Ward LJ, dissenting, pointed out that a number of other European countries had begun to allow same-sex couples to enter into property agreements on the same basis as unmarried heterosexual couples and that the US Supreme Court had recently found that a family should include 'two adult lifetime partners whose relationship is long term and characterised by an emotional and financial commitment and interdependence'. He found that 'the trend is to shift the focus ... from structure and components to function and appearance'. In other words, if a group acts as society expects a family to act, it is a family. He found that the exclusion of same-sex couples from the protection of the Rent Act which would follow from the preferred interpretation of the majority amounted to an assertion by society that their relationships are judged to be 'less worthy of respect, concern and consideration than the relationship between members of the opposite sex'.

On appeal, a bare majority of the House of Lords, in a landmark decision,[175] found that the term 'family' could be taken to include a cohabiting couple of the same sex. If it could be taken to include a cohabiting heterosexual couple, it was found that the term could be taken to include a homosexual one since, in principle, it was the bond and commitment between the two persons, not their sexual orientation, which was significant. The Lords did not consider, however, that a person could live with another of the same sex as his 'husband or wife'.

But in *Ghaidan v Godin-Mendoza*[176] the Court of Appeal took a step further. On the death of a protected tenant of a dwelling-house his or her surviving spouse, if then living in the house, becomes a statutory tenant by succession. But a person who was living with the original tenant 'as his or her wife or husband' is treated as the spouse of the original tenant so also succeeds to the tenancy.[177] The Court of Appeal found that Sched 1, para 2 of the 1977 Act infringed Art 14. That breach could be remedied by way of s 3 HRA by construing the words 'as his or her wife or husband' in Sched 1, para 2 as if they meant 'as if they were his or her wife or husband'. In reaching this decision the Court found that Art 14 would be engaged even where there was 'the most tenuous link with another provision in the Convention' (*Petrovic v Austria*).[178] It considered that the positive obligation on the part of the state to promote the values that Art 8 protected was wide enough to bring legislation that affected the home within the ambit of Art 8. *Marckx v Belgium*[179] was applied and *Michalak v Wandsworth LBC*[180]

---

174 [1998] 2 WLR 225.
175 [1999] 3 WLR 1113.
176 [2003] 2 WLR 478; [2002] 4 All ER 1162.
177 Rent Act 1977, Sched 1, para 2(2).
178 (20458/92) (2001) 33 EHRR 14.
179 (A/31) (1979–80) 2 EHRR 330.
180 [2002] EWCA Civ 271.

was followed. The facts of the applicant's case did therefore fall within the ambit of Art 8 as that Article was understood for the purposes of Art 14(1). The House of Lords in *Ghaidan v Godin-Mendoza*[181] used s 3 HRA to interpret the statute to avoid the discrimination against homosexuals. This meant not merely changing the meaning given to certain words, but the addition of (a few) words that were not included in the provision. The claim was that the inapplicability of this inheritance right to stable homosexual couples violated Art 8 read with Art 14.[182] The House of Lords managed to find that the words 'living with the tenant as his or her wife or husband' could be interpreted as meaning: 'living with the tenant, as *if they were* his or her wife or husband'.

Ghaidan is one of the most creative decisions under the HRA and demonstrates what can be done in this field – not only in relation to housing provision, but in other contexts too, if a statutory provision creates discrimination on this ground. Assuming that the protection against discrimination is extended into the housing context in 2007, as the government plans, there will be no need to rely on s 3 HRA and Arts 8 and 14 in relation to housing provision generally.[183] But in relation to specific statutory provisions such as the one at issue in *Ghaidan* it might appear at first sight that it would still be necessary to do so since the proposed Sexual Orientation (Goods and Services) regulations are secondary legislation. However, although they are secondary legislation, they will be enacted to give effect to an EU Directive which is directly effective – the Framework Directive – and therefore the supremacy of EU law doctrine applies and, depending on interpretation, including the possibility of employing s 3 HRA, the offending statutory provision might have to be disapplied, as in *Factortame*. This argument rests on the assumption that the new 2007 Regulations would cover a *Ghaidan* type of situation; they may not do so. If not, the Directive itself, if sufficiently precise, could be relied upon against emanations of the state or, alternatively, the new Commission for Human Rights and Equality could seek judicial review of the 2007 Regulations on the basis of inadequate implementation of the Directive.

4 Direct discrimination on grounds of sex, marital status, gender reassignment, race, disability, sexual orientation

As discussed above, the legislation, apart from the DDA, recognises two types of discrimination – direct and indirect. It is worth noting that it is important to plead the right type of discrimination at the outset or to plead both in the alternative. *Ali v*

---

181 [2004] 2 AC 557 (HL). The case concerned the re-interpretation of a statute so as to give members of homosexual couples the same rights to succeed to tenancies upon the death of their partner as were enjoyed by heterosexual couples.

182 The right to non-discrimination in the exercise of Convention rights.

183 The Regulations currently covering Northern Ireland cover disposal or management of premises; under reg 6(1) 'It is unlawful for a person with power to dispose of any premises to discriminate against another –

   (a)   in the terms on which he offers him those premises; or
   (b)   by refusing his application for those premises; or
   (c)   in his treatment of him in relation to any list of persons in need of premises of that description.

Office for National Statistics[184] was brought as a case of direct discrimination The Court of Appeal, in a narrow and technical interpretation of the provisions, placed a strong emphasis on pleading the right type of discrimination claimed (direct or indirect) at an early stage decision. In this case Mr Ali claimed that he was racially discriminated against when applying for two different jobs at the Office for National Statistics. In his original application, he asked the tribunal to consider whether he had been victimised or discriminated against on racial grounds contrary to the 1976 RRA. He won a claim of direct discrimination, but when this was overturned on appeal, the Employment Appeals Tribunal (EAT) sent the case back to the tribunal to be reheard. Mr Ali then tried to amend his claim to include indirect as well as direct discrimination. However, the tribunal decided that, even though his original claim referred to racial discrimination in general, this amounted to a new claim, which was being brought out of time. The tribunal noted that direct discrimination and indirect discrimination are two different types of unlawful acts and, therefore, a person who alleged in his original application to the tribunal that he had been directly discriminated against must seek permission to amend his or her claim inside the time limit, to include a claim of indirect discrimination.

Sex discrimination

The concept of direct discrimination on grounds of sex governed by s 1(1)(a) of the Sex Discrimination Act 1975 embodies the formal equality approach. It involves showing that the applicant has been less favourably treated than a man has been or would be treated. There is little guidance in the Act as to the basis for comparison; s 5(3) merely provides that there must be no material difference between the situations of the man and the woman. Thus, the comparison is between a woman and a comparable man. It should be noted that it is possible for the applicant to compare herself with a hypothetical man; the issue is not whether a man or a woman receives a benefit, but whether the woman would have been better treated if she had been a man.

The test can be broken down into three stages. First, the woman must show that there has been differentiation in the treatment afforded to herself and a man (or a hypothetical man). Motive is irrelevant; the question at this stage is merely whether a woman has been treated one way and a man another. Second, she must show that her treatment has been less favourable and third, following the ruling of the House of Lords in *James v Eastleigh BC*,[185] that there is a causal relationship between her sex and the treatment; in other words that but for her sex, she would have been treated as favourably as a man was or would have been (see also *Glasgow CC v Zafar*).[186] Following *Birmingham CC ex p EOC*[187] it is not necessary to show that the less favourable treatment is accorded through an intention to discriminate: motive is irrelevant.

---

184 (2005) unreported.
185 [1990] AC 751; [1990] 2 All ER 607; [1989] IRLR 318; [1989] 3 WLR 122; the 'but for' test applied in *James* was put forward by Lord Goff in the House of Lords in *Birmingham CC ex p EOC* (1989) 18 ILJ 247; for comment, see Ellis (1989) 52 MLR 710.
186 [1998] ICR 120.
187 [1989] AC 1155; [1989] 1 All ER 769.

Proving direct discrimination

The plaintiff bore the burden of showing that the differential treatment was on grounds of sex and not for some neutral reason. She was always likely to find difficulty in discharging this burden of proof, as the ruling in *Saunders v Richmond-upon-Thames LBC*[188] suggests. The applicant applied for a job as a golf professional and was asked questions at the interview which were prima facie discriminatory. She was asked, for example, whether she thought she would be able to control unruly male players and whether she considered the job unglamorous. She was not appointed, although she was somewhat better qualified than the man who was. The EAT held that had her qualifications been substantially better than those of the appointee, that would have raised a prima facie inference of discrimination which the employer would have had to rebut by giving a satisfactory explanation. It was found that the nature of the questions, taking all the circumstances into account, did not of themselves raise a sufficient inference.

In *Khanna v MOD*[189] it was found that the evidential burden would shift only when the evidence was all on one side, but this was clarified by the finding in *Dornan v Belfast CC*[190] that once the woman has raised a prima facie inference of discrimination, the burden would shift to the employer to show that the differentiation occurred on non-discriminatory grounds. In other words, although the plaintiff began the case bearing the burden of proof, it might shift to the defendant once a certain stage was reached. Thus, the formal burden of proof remained on the plaintiff, but once it appeared that a minimum threshold of proof of discrimination is established, the burden shifted to the defendant. Now, under amendments to the Act introduced by the EU-driven Sex Discrimination (Indirect Discrimination and Burden of Proof) Regulations 2001 the complainant need not prove her case, merely the facts of the case, from which the court of tribunal should draw inferences of discrimination if the employer does not provide a satisfactory explanation.[191] This shift in the burden of proof only applies, however, in employment cases.[192] In *Igen v Wong*[193] and in *Chamberlain and Emezie v Emokpae* and *Webster v Brunel University*[194] the Court of Appeal introduced new guidelines on the burden of proof in discrimination claims, which are set out below.[195]

In order to raise a prima facie case of direct discrimination it is not enough to show that a member of a protected group was treated unfavourably. In *University of Huddersfield v Wolff*[196] a female lecturer was rejected for promotion in favour of a male colleague. She complained of direct sex discrimination. Those facts alone were not found to be enough to raise a prima facie case and transfer the burden of proof to the University.

188 [1978] IRLR 362.
189 [1981] ICR 653, EAT.
190 [1990] IRLR 179. See, further, [1990] IRLR 161.
191 The Regulations came into force on 12 October 2001.
192 See SDA 63A and 66A.
193 [2005] ICR 931, para 76.
194 8 February 2004, unreported.
195 See pp 1586–87.
196 [2004] ICR 828.

Discrimination on grounds of maternity and child care

As discussed above, adverse treatment on grounds of pregnancy and maternity leave is no longer treated as discrimination but as a wrong in itself under the SDA, after changes introduced in 2005. Section 3A, as indicated above, now covers certain forms of detrimental action based on pregnancy and maternity leave. However, some detrimental treatment on grounds of maternity not covered by s 3A may still need to be argued as direct sex discrimination. In other words, if the discriminatory action appears to be based on pregnancy or child birth but is not covered by s 3A, the sex discrimination provisions may need to be relied upon, so the case law below is still relevant. It also demonstrates why it was necessary to introduce s 3A.

The problem that s 3A sets out to solve is that is very difficult to conceptualise pregnancy discrimination as sex discrimination due to the need for a male comparator. Detrimental action on the ground of maternity might appear to be discriminatory on grounds of sex since only women can be pregnant, but the wording of s 1(1) does not allow such action to fall readily within the scope of direct discrimination because in making the comparison between a woman and a man it is required under s 5(3) that 'the relevant circumstances in the one case are the same or not materially different in the other'. Dismissal on grounds of pregnancy was covered by s 60 of the Employment Protection (Consolidation) Act 1978, which provided that if a woman were dismissed because she was pregnant then the dismissal was automatically unfair, but in order to rely on this an employee had to have been employed for two years; where this was not the case, the employee had to seek to show that the 1975 Act applied. Pregnancy dismissals were regulated from October 1994 by ss 23–25 of and Scheds 2 and 3 to the Trade Union Reform and Employment Rights Act (TURERA) 1993,[197] and then by s 99 of the Employment Rights Act 1996. Under s 99, such dismissal was unfair from the date on which employment begins. Further, under s 47C of the 1996 Act, as amended by the Employment Relations Act 1999, an employee has the right not to be subjected to a detriment done for a prescribed reason. Such reason is prescribed by regulations made by the Secretary of State and relates to pregnancy, maternity, childbirth, and maternity leave. Section 3A can also be relied on if the dismissal occurs within the protected period and is based on pregnancy or maternity leave.

Since pregnancy dismissals were therefore only recently addressed under other legislation, applicants sought to rely on the SDA.[198] The decisions discussed below could now be relied upon in an action in which it was argued that *other* employment discrimination based on maternity had arisen which also fell outside s 3A. Section 47 of the 1996 Act would provide a further possible argument in such circumstances. A pregnancy dismissal was at issue in *Turley v Allders*;[199] since the applicant did not have the requisite period of continuous employment, she sought to rely on the SDA. The EAT held that there was no male equivalent to a pregnant woman and therefore, as no comparison could be made, the action must fail. However, a method of making

---

197 The TURERA sections mentioned implemented the EC Pregnancy Directive 92/85.
198 See Fredman, S, 'A difference with distinction: pregnancy and parenthood re-assessed' (1994) 110 LQR 106.
199 [1980] ICR 66.

the comparison was found in a later EAT decision, *Hayes v Malleable WMC*;[200] it was found that it could be made between a pregnant woman and a man with a long-term health problem. Thus, it would be direct discrimination if a woman was dismissed on grounds of pregnancy where a man needing the same period of absence through illness would not have been dismissed. This analogy was not well received;[201] it has been pointed out that pregnancy is a healthy, normal state, not an illness;[202] moreover, it may be planned, unlike an unexpected illness, and in any event there will normally be far more notice before the absence takes place than there would be in a case of illness. Commentators have found the comparison between a pregnant woman and a diseased man inherently distasteful. It is also, most pertinently, highly disadvantageous to women, a very high percentage of whom may become pregnant at some time during their working life and in particular between the ages of 20 and 35 (the time when women are most likely to become pregnant), while the percentage of men likely to take around two or more months off work during those years owing to an illness or accident is clearly likely to be far lower.

The *Hayes* approach was abandoned after certain decisions of the European Court of Justice. In *Dekker v VJV Centrum*[203] the Court found that a woman who was not appointed to a post because she was pregnant at the time of the interview, although she was considered to be the best candidate, was the victim of direct discrimination. *Webb v Emo Air Cargo (UK) Ltd*[204] concerned the dismissal of the claimant after it was found that she was pregnant. She had been recruited to replace an employee going on maternity leave, but had then discovered herself to be pregnant and therefore (it seemed) unavailable for duties in the period required. The question was whether her dismissal constituted direct discrimination within the terms of s 1(1)(a) of the Sex Discrimination Act 1975, in the light of Community law. The Court of Appeal continued the *Hayes* approach in determining that if a man with a medical condition as nearly comparable as possible (with the same practical effect upon availability to do the job) with pregnancy would also have been dismissed, then the dismissal of the woman was not sex discrimination. Thus, the plaintiff who was, owing to pregnancy, unavailable for duties in the period required, could be dismissed without infringing the SDA because a diseased man who was similarly unavailable at the relevant time would also have been dismissed. The argument was therefore rejected that since only a woman can be pregnant, it followed that a woman who is dismissed for any reason related to her pregnancy is dismissed because of her sex and thus discriminated against. The House of Lords favoured the approach of the Court of Appeal, but since it considered that the relevant rulings of the European Court of Justice did not indicate clearly whether the dismissal would be regarded as based on pregnancy or on unavailability at the relevant time, it referred the following question to the Court:

---

200 [1985] ICR 703. See also *Brown v Rentokil Ltd* [1992] IRLR 302; *Shomer v B and R Residential Lettings Ltd* [1992] IRLR 317. It may be noted that dismissal on grounds of pregnancy seems to be increasing. The EOC cited a number of such instances in its 1991 report.

201 See *Proposals of the Equal Opportunities Commission: Equal Treatment for Men and Women*, 1988, Chapter 2.

202 Lacey (1987) 14 JLS 411, p 417.

203 [1991] IRLR 27; [1990] ECR I-3941.

204 [1993] 1 WLR 49, HL; [1992] 1 CMLR 793, CA.

Is it discrimination on grounds of sex contrary to the Equal Treatment Directive for an employer to dismiss a female employee:

(a) whom it engaged for the specific purpose of replacing another female employee during the latter's forthcoming maternity leave,

(b) when very shortly after appointment the employer discovers that the appellant herself will be absent on maternity leave during the maternity period of the other employee and the employer dismisses her because it needs the jobholder to be at work during that period, and

(c) had the employer known of the pregnancy of the appellant at the date of appointment she would not have been appointed, and

(d) the employer would similarly have dismissed a male employee engaged for this purpose who required leave of absence at the relevant time for medical or other reasons?

The European Court of Justice found that the plaintiff should not be compared with a man unavailable for work for medical or other reasons, since pregnancy is not in any way comparable with pathological conditions. The Court then found that, since the plaintiff had been employed permanently, her dismissal could not be justified on the ground of inability to fulfil a fundamental condition of her employment contract because her inability to perform the work was purely temporary. In other words, it could not be said that she had been taken on solely to cover a maternity leave. The Court further found that the protection of Community law for pregnant women could not be dependent on the question whether the woman's presence at work during the maternity leave period is essential to the undertaking in which she is employed. Thus, dismissal of the plaintiff clearly constituted sex discrimination, contrary to the Equal Treatment Directive. (When the House of Lords reconsidered the case in the light of these findings, it allowed the appeal and remitted the case to the IT to consider the award of compensation to the applicant (*Webb (No 2)*).[205]

In a similar decision, *Habermann-Beltermann*,[206] rather than relying directly upon unavailability, the employer sought to rely upon the statutory exclusion (with criminal sanctions)[207] of pregnant women from night work, which 'caused' Habermann-Beltermann's temporary unavailability for work. The Court's decision that the statute could not justify Habermann-Beltermann's dismissal, or the termination of her contract, reflects a refusal to focus upon a male norm or to pander to the argument that the continuation of the employment relationship in such circumstances produces undue financial burdens upon the employer.[208] However, in both *Habermann-Beltermann* and *Webb*, the Court refused to confront clearly the question whether any adverse treatment of women connected with pregnancy amounts to sex discrimination. In both judgments, the crucial fact upon which the Court relied was that the employment contracts in

---

205 [1994] QB 718; [1994] 4 All ER 115; [1994] 3 WLR 941. *Webb* was applied in *O'Neill* (1996) *The Times*, 7 June in relation to a pregnancy dismissal. Following *Webb*, the dismissal was found to be unlawful.

206 [1994] ECR I-1657.

207 The German *Mütterschutzgesetz* (MSchG), para 8(1), which prohibits the employment of pregnant or breast-feeding women on night work.

208 See the Opinion of the Advocate General, para 16.

question were of a permanent and not a fixed term nature. The decision of the Court in both cases was based upon the mismatch between the period for which the employee would be unavailable and the period for which she had been employed (indefinitely). This was a very significant development from the stark statement of principle in *Dekker*. The court's conclusion that the termination of Habermann-Beltermann's contract was not 'on the ground of pregnancy' but by reason of the statutory provision in the MSchG, opens the door to a narrower interpretation of the *Dekker* ruling than that ruling seemed at first to promise.[209] The result was that the Court, unlike the Advocate General,[210] was able to avoid making explicit the point that a justification based on availability, with reference to market cost to the employer, would be by definition excluded in a case of direct discrimination on grounds of pregnancy, thereby, by implication, leaving it open in future cases.

Likewise, the ruling in *Webb* is not ultimately fully supportive of substantive equality since it leaves open the possibility of an apparently neutral explanation for pregnancy dismissals: that a pregnant woman recruited on a temporary basis may justifiably be dismissed if unable through unavailability to fulfil the purpose for which she was recruited. The argument is therefore left open that if a temporarily employed man or hypothetical man would have been dismissed, if unable through unavailability to satisfy a purpose for which he was employed, a woman so unavailable through pregnancy, who has been dismissed, has not been discriminated against. Therefore, by the recruitment of temporary staff, the employer can safeguard its market position. Elements of the ruling, however, suggest a desire to go further and it is in this sense internally inconsistent: it asserts that in general, to dismiss a pregnant woman through unavailability at a time when she is essential to a purpose of the undertaking can never be justifiable, but it leaves open the possibility that the employer can do just that so long as she was recruited on a temporary basis specifically for that purpose.

Thus, both judgments impliedly accepted that adverse treatment flowing from pregnancy is susceptible to justification. Therefore, an employer may be able to contend successfully that not only market costs associated with unavailability, but also other costs arising from pregnancy,[211] not the pregnancy itself, were the 'cause' of the dismissal of a pregnant woman. It is even possible that such an argument could be used in relation to a *permanently* employed woman, since the Court's mismatch argument is not so readily applicable to a justification based on the other costs associated with pregnancy. This is not to contend that the Court would necessarily accept such assertions by employers, merely to note that, in principle, the judgments leave open these possibilities. The effect of the judgments may be to disadvantage women doubly: they may have to take the risk that they will have no remedy if employed on a temporary basis, but dismissed

---

209 This part of *Habermann-Beltermann* is similar to the Court's ruling in *Hertz* that dismissal through absences caused by illness, where those absences arise outside the protected period of maternity leave, is permissible, even where the illness is pregnancy-related. See Shaw, J, 'Pregnancy discrimination in sex discrimination' (1991) 16 EL Rev 313–20.

210 Opinion of the Advocate General, para 16.

211 E.g., adjustment of working conditions, time off for ante-natal examinations, removal of hazardous substances from the working environment or other measures of special protection for pregnant workers required, e.g., by the Pregnancy and Maternity Directive, Council Directive 92/85/EEC.

for reasons connected with pregnancy,[212] and they may tend to find that they are more likely to be offered temporary contracts, thereby undermining their bargaining power in the market still further.

In both judgments, the Court could have rejected a formal equality interpretation of the legislation in favour of completely excluding the use of unavailability through pregnancy or the cost of pregnancy as a justification,[213] thereby affording recognition to the real situation of women. In support of this, it should be pointed out that the real situation of women which may mean that they are unavailable for work for a period is only biologically determined in so far as the bearing of children is concerned; in terms of caring for children, it is legally and socially determined. The legal and social factors in question which found the perception that pregnancy, maternity leave and child care are to be viewed as one single indivisible burden to be shouldered by women alone, arise, it is submitted, from a sexually stereotyped view of the child care responsibilities of males and females. Thus, unavailability for work arising, or apparently arising,[214] from pregnancy, maternity leave and child care is not a sex-neutral justification for adverse treatment.

At the least, the Court could have achieved a compromise somewhat more satisfactory in terms of promotion of substantive equality than the one it does achieve, by framing its judgment in terms of the proportion of the period for which the woman was employed during which she would be unavailable. Thus, a woman employed, for example, on a temporary three-year contract in order to fulfill a particular purpose who would be unavailable for three months on maternity leave and therefore unable to fulfill it would be said nevertheless to be available for a substantial part of the period. Instead, the Court chose to confine its ruling to those employed for an indefinite period.

Section 3A uses the phrase 'on the ground of pregnancy'. Detrimental action *related to* pregnancy but not viewed by domestic courts as *on grounds of* pregnancy other than dismissal (such as demotion or failure to appoint or to promote) and so not covered by s 3A will fall within the *Webb* approach, and it is therefore unfortunate that the European Court of Justice failed to rule clearly that such action would be direct sex discrimination. A possible approach would be to treat detrimental action on grounds of pregnancy as indirect rather than direct discrimination on the ground that a condition is being applied to all employees not to need certain periods of time off work. As argued above, this is very likely to have an adverse impact on women and arguably cannot be justified using the current tests for justification (see below). This is not to suggest that this would be a satisfactory approach: the use of equality law in relation to pregnancy is flawed since it relies on comparisons with men rather than

212 So long as the context allows the dismissal to be characterisable as owing to unavailability and therefore inability to satisfy a particular purpose.

213 The argument for so doing was put succinctly by Stevens J in a dissenting US judgment: commenting on a rule allowing adverse treatment of women for reasons connected with pregnancy, he said: 'By definition such a rule discriminates on grounds of sex, for it is the capacity to become pregnant which primarily differentiates the female from the male.' *General Electric Co v Gilbert* (1976) 429 US 126, pp 161–62.

214 It appeared that no attempt was made to ascertain the period for which the plaintiff would actually be unavailable. See *Webb v EMO Air Cargo* [1992] 4 All ER 929, HL, p 932, *per* Lord Keith. It is not mandatory that employees should be absent from work for the whole period of maternity leave or that, during maternity leave, they should be out of communication with the workplace.

simply acknowledging, as pregnancy-related legislation does, that proper provision for maternity is good employment practice. As will be seen below, there have been a number of instances in which women, especially single parents, have been forced to address the issue of flexible working – in the sense of working hours that fit in with child care – by seeking to use the concept of indirect discrimination. In many ways this attempt has highlighted the problem of using this concept in the way that the early (and, to an extent, also the later) decisions on pregnancy-as-direct-sex-discrimination did.

Discrimination on grounds of marital status

The concept of direct discrimination on grounds of marital status is governed by s 3(1)(a) of the SDA 1975. Under s 3(1)(a), the applicant must show that he or she has been less favourably treated on grounds of marital status than a single person of the same sex has been or would be treated. There is little guidance in the Act as to the method of making the comparison; s 5(3) merely provides that there must be no material difference between the situations of an unmarried and a married person. As with discrimination on grounds of sex, it is possible for the applicant to compare him or herself with a hypothetical single person. The test can be broken down into three stages. First, the married person must show that there has been differentiation in the treatment afforded to him or herself and a single person (or a hypothetical single person). Motive is irrelevant. Second, he or she must show that the treatment has been less favourable and, third, following the ruling of the House of Lords in *James v Eastleigh BC*,[215] that there is a causal relationship between his or her marital status and the treatment; in other words that but for her marital status, she would have been treated as favourably as a single person was or would have been. The plaintiff bears the burden of showing that the differential treatment was on grounds of marital status and not for some neutral reason.

Discrimination on grounds of gender reassignment

Under s 2A(1) of the SDA 'person A discriminates against another person B if he treats B less favourably than he treats or would treat other persons, and does so on the ground that B intends to undergo, is undergoing, or has undergone gender reassignment'. This provision is based on the models already considered relating to discrimination on grounds of sex and marital status. Thus, the same steps must be taken and the plaintiff bears the burden of showing that the differential treatment was on grounds of gender reassignment. It must be pointed out that s 2A does not prohibit discrimination on grounds of transsexuality in a general sense,[216] and that therefore there is a significant gap in the legislation which possibly could be filled by the use of purposive interpretation, as discussed above.[217]

---

215 [1990] AC 751; [1990] 2 All ER 607; [1989] IRLR 318; [1989] 3 WLR 122; the 'but for' test applied in James was put forward by Lord Goff in the House of Lords in *Birmingham CC ex p EOC* (1989) 18 ILJ 247; for comment, see Ellis, (1989) 52 MLR 710.
216 See *Bavin v The NHS Trust Pensions Agency and Secretary of State for Health* [1999] ICR 1192.
217 See pp 1479–86.

Race discrimination

Direct discrimination arises under s 1(1)(a) of the RRA and the test to be applied mirrors that under the SDA, except that the unfavourable treatment in question must be on 'racial grounds'. This means that discrimination on the grounds of someone else's race is covered (transferred discrimination).[218] For example, if a waitress disobeyed an instruction to serve whites only and was dismissed for serving black customers, that would be discrimination on racial grounds.[219]

A decision made on racial grounds means that the alleged discriminator made a decision influenced by racial prejudice, but according to the ruling in *CRE ex p Westminster Council*,[220] this does not mean that the discriminator must have a racial motive. The council wanted to employ a black man as a refuse collector, but withdrew the offer after pressure from the all-white work force. The Commission for Racial Equality (CRE) initiated a formal investigation and served a non-discrimination notice on the council. The council challenged the service of the notice by means of judicial review and sought certiorari on the basis that the CRE's findings were perverse – a finding that the CRE could not reasonably make. However, it was held that the decision was made on racial grounds, although it was found that the employer was not motivated by racial prejudice, but by the desire to avoid industrial unrest. Nevertheless, that was irrelevant; the decision was influenced by racial prejudice, although it was not the prejudice of the respondent.

Segregation

Under s 1(2) of the Act it will be direct discrimination to maintain separate facilities for members of different races, even though they are equal in quality. However, if segregation grows up because of practices in the workforce, the employer will not come under an obligation to prevent it according to the ruling in *Pel Ltd v Modgill*[221] although this seems to be in conflict with s 32 of the Act which provides that an employer will be liable for acts done by employees in the course of employment unless he or she has taken reasonable steps to prevent such acts. It would seem that the employer should come under some obligation to prevent segregation even if he or she did not instigate it. Moreover, even if segregation in itself is not unlawful, it may be that once a black/white divide in the workforce is established, a practice of treating the black group differently may develop, which will raise an irresistible inference of direct discrimination even though such treatment might not raise such an inference if applied to an individual black worker.[222]

---

218 It was confirmed in *Showboat Entertainment Centre v Owens* [1984] 1 WLR 384 that dismissal for refusal to obey an unlawful discriminatory instruction would fall within s 1(1)(a). See, to the same effect, *Zarczynska v Levy* [1979] 1 WLR 125.
219 See *Zarczynska v Levy* [1979] 1 WLR 125.
220 [1984] IRLR 230, QBD.
221 [1980] IRLR 142.
222 See John Haggas plc (1993) the *Guardian*, 29 May: different, less favourable treatment of the black group was found to be direct discrimination.

Proving direct discrimination

Often, the hardest task in a direct discrimination case, as discussed in relation to sex discrimination, will be proving that the unfavourable treatment was on grounds of race. The decision in *Dornan*[223] applies in race discrimination cases and means that once an inference has been raised that discrimination has occurred, the burden of proof will shift to the employer to prove that the decision in question was made on other grounds. In the areas of EU competence, as discussed above, a shifting burden of proof now applies.[224] The decision in *Igen* v *Wong*, a direct discrimination case on grounds of sex, now provides the guidelines to be applied, which are set out below.[225]

Raising the requisite inference may involve obtaining statistical material from the employer. In *West Midlands Passenger Transport Executive v Jaquant Singh*[226] the applicant, who believed that he had been racially discriminated against in being refused promotion, wanted an order of discovery in respect of specific material held by his employers indicating the number of whites and non-whites appointed to senior posts. He claimed that if he were able to obtain access to the material, he would be able to invite an inference of direct racial discrimination. The employers resisted discovery. The Court of Appeal held that discovery would be ordered only where it could be termed necessary, but that it could be so termed since the employee had to establish a discernible pattern of treatment towards his racial group and there was no other way of raising the necessary inference. A tribunal can draw an inference of discrimination from an employer's nonexistent or evasive reply to a race relations questionnaire (the statutory RR65 form). The decision of the EAT in *Dattani v Chief Constable of West Mercia Police*[227] established that the same inference can be drawn from replies made outside the statutory procedure; for example, in the employer's notice of appearance.

Disability discrimination

The concept of direct discrimination within the DDA 1995, as amended in 2004,[228] only operates within the field of employment; it involves showing, under s 3A(5), that the applicant has been less favourably treated on the ground of her disability than a person would be or has been treated 'not having that particular disability whose relevant circumstances, including his abilities, are the same as or not materially different from those of the disabled person'. The phrase 'on the ground of' rather than 'related to' makes this a narrow definition: it is aimed at facially clear discriminatory practices. The test is seeking to draw a distinction between the disability and its consequences; it is aimed in particular at stereotyping. So, for example, if an employer refused a job as a taxi driver to a person who could not drive safely due to muscular dystrophy the relevant comparator would be a person without dystrophy who could not drive safely. So the reason for refusing the job to the applicant would be that the person could

---

223 [1990] IRLR 179. See above, p 1528.
224 See RRA, ss 54A and 57ZA.
225 See pp 1586–87.
226 [1988] WLR 730.
227 2005, unreported.
228 By the Disability Discrimination (Amendment) Regulations 2003 passed in response to the Framework Directive. Further amendments were made to the employment provisions by the DDA 2005.

not drive safely, and not due to her disability. If on the other hand the applicant had diabetes which did not affect her driving the relevant comparator would be someone with a similar ability to drive. If the employer decided not to short-list the applicant on the ground of her diabetes without considering its lack of impact on her ability to drive, she would have suffered direct discrimination on grounds of disability, assuming that the employer would have offered the job to the comparator.

The test can be broken down into four stages. First, the applicant must show that she is disabled within the meaning of the Act. Second, she must show that there has been differentiation in the treatment afforded to herself and a non-disabled person (or a hypothetical person) with similar relevant abilities. Third, she must show that her treatment has been less favourable. Fourth, the applicant can rely on the ruling of the House of Lords in *James v Eastleigh BC*,[229] the sex discrimination case mentioned above, in showing that there is a causal relationship between her disability and the treatment; in other words that 'but for' her disability she would have been treated as favourably as a non-disabled person with similar abilities was or would have been. Following *Birmingham CC ex p EOC*,[230] it is not necessary to show that the less favourable treatment is accorded by an intention to discriminate: motive is irrelevant. There is no provision allowing the alleged discriminator to seek to justify the treatment.

The plaintiff bears the burden of showing that the differential treatment is on grounds of disability and not for some neutral reason. Discharging this burden of proof may be problematic, although it may sometimes be clearly apparent that the employment detriment was on grounds of disability, and attention will shift to considering whether the disability fell within the Act. The shifting burden of proof applies in disability discrimination cases and means that once an inference has been raised that discrimination has occurred, the burden of proof will shift to the employer to prove that the decision in question was made on other grounds[231] and the guidelines from *Wong*, above, will apply.

Direct discrimination on grounds of sexual orientation

The Sexual Orientation Regulations cover, under reg 6, a number of forms of employment detriment. In relation to such detriment, such as a failure to promote, the applicant must show, under reg 3, that he or she has been treated less favourably on the ground of sexual orientation than other persons. Regulation 3(1) provides: 'For the purposes of these Regulations, a person ("A") discriminates against another person ("B") if – (a) on grounds of sexual orientation, A treats B less favourably than he treats or would treat other persons . . .'

Thus, as in relation to the other protected grounds, motive is irrelevant; it is not necessary to show that the employer is motivated by homophobia. The first question to be asked is merely whether the applicant has been treated in a particular way and other persons have between treated more favourably. Then, following the ruling of

---

229 [1990] AC 751; [1990] 2 All ER 607; [1989] IRLR 318; [1989] 3 WLR 122; the 'but for' test applied in *James* was put forward by Lord Goff in the House of Lords in *Birmingham CC ex p EOC* [1989] 18 ILJ 247; for comment, see Ellis, (1989) 52 MLR 710.
230 [1989] AC 1155; [1989] 1 All ER 769.
231 DDA, s 17A(1C) and s 25(9).

the House of Lords in *James v Eastleigh BC*[232] (see also *Glasgow CC v Zafar*)[233] the applicant must show that there is a causal relationship between her sexual orientation and the treatment; in other words that but for her sexual orientation, she would have been treated as favourably as other persons are or would have been treated. The burden of proof will shift to the employer in the same way as for direct discrimination cases on the other protected grounds. [234]

5 Indirect discrimination on grounds of sex, race or sexual orientation; disability-related discrimination

Sex discrimination

The concept of indirect discrimination was imported into the SDA under s 1(1)(b) with a view to outlawing practices which, while neutral on their face as between men and women, have a disproportionately adverse impact on women.[235] It was intended to outlaw not only isolated acts of discrimination, but also institutionalised discrimination. This reflects the substantive equality approach; it takes account, for example, of past discrimination against women. In asking not whether a woman can, in theory, comply with a condition, but whether she can do so in practice, it broadens the area of morally unjustifiable differentiation. Indirect discrimination was defined under s 1(1)(b) which imported a somewhat opaque and tortuous test into the Act. When the SDA was amended in response to the Burden of Proof Directive, (implemented in SI 2001/2660) and again in 2005[236] a more generous version of indirect discrimination was imported into it under a new s 1(2), but only applying in the sphere of employment, although it is due to be extended into the other contexts by the end of 2007.[237] Thus the SDA now recognises two concepts of indirect discrimination, under s 1(1)(b) and under s 1(2). The case law established under s 1(1)(b) will be relevant to an extent under s 1(2).

The definition of indirect discrimination under s 1(1)(b)

There are four stages in operating this concept. The case law was developed in the employment context, but it will now be applied as far as possible to s 1(2) or to indirect discrimination in the other contexts covered by the Act – the residual areas. First, it must be shown that a condition has been applied to the applicant. It might be

---

232 [1990] AC 751; [1990] 2 All ER 607; [1989] IRLR 318; [1989] 3 WLR 122; the 'but for' test applied in James was put forward by Lord Goff in the House of Lords in *Birmingham CC ex p EOC* (1989) 18 ILJ 247; for comment, see Ellis (1989) 52 MLR 710.
233 [1998] ICR 120.
234 Regs 29 and 32.
235 See Byre, A, *Indirect Discrimination*, 1987, Equal Opportunities Commission; McGinley, G, 'Judicial approaches to sex discrimination in US and UK – a comparative study' (1986) 49 MLR 413, pp 427–35; Hunter, R, *Indirect Discrimination in the Workplace*, 1992, William Gaunt and Sons; von Prondzynski and Richards, op. cit., fn 1; Gardner, J, 'Discrimination as injustice' (1996) 16(3) OJLS 353; Townshend-Smith, R, 'Justifying indirect discrimination in English and American law: how stringent should the test be?' (1995) 1 Int Journal of Discrimination and the Law 103.
236 By Art 2 Equal Treatment (Amendment) Directive 2002/73/EC.
237 By the General Sex Equality Directive 2004/113/EC.

to be of a certain seniority, height or type of experience. Second, it must be shown that the condition is one which will have a disproportionate impact on women; in other words, considerably fewer women than men will be able to comply with it. For example, fewer women than men might have a certain type of experience owing to a now outlawed system of keeping women at a certain level and thereby preventing them gaining the experience in question. Third, once the claimant has proved these two requirements, the burden of proof shifts to the employer to show that the condition is justifiable regardless of sex. For example, there are fewer women engineering graduates than men; therefore, a requirement that applicants have a degree in engineering hits disproportionately at women. However, the employer will normally be able to show that a degree in engineering is genuinely needed for the job. Fourthly, if the employer cannot show that the requirement is genuinely needed for the job, the woman must show that it is to her detriment because she cannot comply with it. This requirement was included because it was thought necessary that the woman should be the victim rather than allowing anyone to bring a claim in respect of a discriminatory practice operating at her place of employment.

Two early decisions made clear the grounds for including this second type of discrimination in the Act and demonstrated the way in which it would operate. The case of *Steel v Post Office*,[238] which concerned the allocation of postal walks to postmen or women, illustrated the operation of the four stages. Certain walks were more in demand than others and the walks were allocated on the basis of the seniority of the employee. Ms Steel made a bid for a walk, but lost it to a younger man. She had worked for the Post Office much longer than he had, but she had only been accepted into the permanent grade in 1975 when the SDA came into force. Before 1975, the Post Office had directly discriminated against women by refusing to allow them to enter the permanent grade. Ms Steel's seniority had been calculated from that point. The practice in question was interpreted as a 'requirement', thereby widening the meaning of the term. It had a disparate impact on women because fewer of them could comply with it than men because of the past discrimination and the requirement as to seniority could not otherwise be justified. 'Justified' was strictly interpreted as meaning 'necessary'. Finally, the requirement was clearly to her detriment, as she could not comply with it.

The application of the phrase 'can comply' was considered in *Price v Civil Service Commission*.[239] The Civil Service had a rule that applicants had to be under 28. Mrs Price, who was 35, applied but was rejected and claimed sex discrimination. It was found that owing to the prevailing social conditions, more men than women could comply with the requirement because at the time, there was a general expectation that women would rear a family and so would be less likely to be available in the job market at that age than men. However, women could theoretically comply with a requirement to be 28 and available in the job market; they could choose not to have children. The words 'can comply' were interpreted to mean that in practice, fewer women could comply with the condition. The Court also considered the means of identifying a group of men and women to be looked at in order to see whether fewer women could comply with

238 [1977] IRLR 288.
239 [1977] 1 WLR 1417.

the condition. It found that the group to be considered would be the pool of men and women with the relevant qualifications; it would not include the whole population.[240] The applicant's case, therefore, passed all four tests and succeeded, with the result that the Civil Service altered the age bar.

The main difficulties in the operation of indirect discrimination have arisen in three areas: the finding of a disparate impact, involving identification of the correct 'pool', the meaning of justifiability and the determination as to the meaning of 'a requirement or condition'. Cases on establishing disparate impact are discussed below since the same issues now arise under s 1(2)(b).

The meaning of 'justifiable' has undergone considerable change since the ruling in *Ojutiku v Manpower Services Commission*[241] in which, departing from the *Steel* interpretation, it was held to mean 'reasons which would appear sound to right thinking people'. This obviously widened its meaning and would have allowed a great many practices to be justified, greatly undermining s 1(1)(b). However, in *Clarke v Eley IMI Kynoch Ltd*,[242] its meaning was somewhat narrowed. The company had a policy of always selecting part time workers for redundancy first, regardless of their length of service, although for full time workers a 'last in, first out' system was in operation. Therefore, the requirement to work full time so as not to be made redundant hit disproportionately at women, as more women than men worked part time. The employer argued that the practice could be justified because it was long standing and the workforce liked it, but it was found that this was not sufficient to render it 'justifiable', and the claimant therefore succeeded. This was clearly in accord with the policy of including indirect discrimination in the statutory scheme in order to outlaw long-standing discriminatory practices.

The test for the meaning of justifiable[243] was more precisely defined by the European Court in *Bilka-Kaufhaus GmbH v Weber von Hartz*.[244] Under this test, conditions creating disparate impact will be justifiable if they amount to a means chosen for achieving an objective which correspond to a real need on the part of the undertaking, are appropriate to that end and necessary to that end. So this test would be fulfilled if, for example, an undertaking had a real need to increase its scientific expertise in a certain area. The means used to do so would have to be appropriate, such as asking that applicants have a degree in a certain science. If other means of increasing its expertise were not available, it would be seen as necessary to impose the condition that applicants have a science degree. This approach was taken in *Hampson v Dept of Education and Science*,[245] and means that s 1(1)(b) has been brought broadly into line with the 'material difference' defence under s 1(3) of the Equal Pay Act 1970.

---

240 See *Jones v Manchester University* (1993) *The Times*, 12 January, CA, which reaffirmed this approach to the 'pool', holding that the applicant could not redefine its parameters, which would be fixed by the relevant advertisement.

241 [1982] ICR 661; [1982] IRLR 418.

242 [1983] ICR 703.

243 For discussion of the test, see Leigh, I, 'Of Racial Groups and Non-Groups' (1986) 49 MLR 235.

244 [1986] IRLR 317; [1986] CMLR 701; see also *Rinner-Kuhn v FWW Spezial-Gebäudereinigung* [1989] IRLR 493.

245 [1991] 1 AC 171; [1990] 2 All ER 513, HL; on the Court of Appeal decision, see Bourn, C, Collins, HG and Freedland, MR, 'The Defence of Justifiability' (1989) 18 ILJ 170; Napier, B, 'Statutory Interpretation and Indirect Discrimination in the Court of Appeal' (1989) 48 CLJ 187.

The *Bilka* decision narrowed the defence available to employers, but the findings in *Perera v Civil Service Commission*[246] (a race discrimination case) mean that a number of requirements or conditions creating disparate impact will fall outside the Act and will obviously not require application of the *Bilka* test because they will not support an indirect discrimination claim at all. It was held in *Perera* that a condition must amount to an *absolute* bar in order to be termed a requirement or condition. If the employer has only taken the factor into account as one among others, it will not fall within s 1(1)(b). This is very restrictive, as non-absolute criteria could clearly be used and could have an adverse impact on an applicant. For example, an unjustifiable height bar might normally be operated, but the employer might be prepared on occasion to consider people under it. Nevertheless, the bar could have a significantly adverse effect on women. Thus, the development of indirect discrimination has been constrained and the EOC has therefore argued for reform of the meaning of the term 'condition'.[247] The decision in *Perera* may be out of accord with the ruling of the European Court of Justice in *Enderby v Frenchay*,[248] which is discussed below. In *Falkirk Council v Whyte*,[249] the decision was found to be out of accord with the purposive approach to legislation that implements a Directive, which has been adopted in a number of equal pay cases. It was found that the term 'a requirement or condition' should not be afforded a restrictive interpretation; the proper test, it was said, was to ask whether the 'factor' hindered women as opposed to men in the particular context.

The definition of indirect discrimination under s 1(2)(b)

In the field of employment only the difficulty of using s 1(1)(b) was eased slightly when the new definition of indirect discrimination was imported under s 1(2). Indirect discrimination arises if under s 1(2)(b) if:

[the employer] applies to her a provision, criterion or practice which he applies or would apply equally to a man, but—

(i)   which puts or would put women at a particular disadvantage when compared with men,
(ii) which puts her at that disadvantage, and
(iii) which he cannot show to be a proportionate means of achieving a legitimate aim.

A similar definition was also imported in relation to marital status.[250] The test under s 1(2)(b) uses the broader term 'practice' as opposed to 'requirement or condition' in

---

246 [1983] ICR 428; [1983] IRLR 166.
247 See Proposals of the EOC: Equal Treatment for Men and Women, p 9.
248 [1994] 1 All ER 495; [1993] ECR I-5535, ECJ; [1992] IRLR 15, CA.
249 [1997] IRLR 560.
250 Under s 3(1) (definition of indirect discrimination against married people in the field of employment) indirect discrimination arises if '(b) [the employer] applies to that person a provision, criterion or practice which he applies or would apply equally to an unmarried person, but – (i) which puts or would put married persons at a particular disadvantage when compared with unmarried persons of the same sex, (ii) which puts that person at that disadvantage, and (iii) which he cannot show to be a proportionate means of achieving a legitimate aim.'

response to the Burden of Proof Directive, (implemented in SI 2001/2660) since the terms used are 'provision, criterion or practice', which appear to cover non-absolute criteria. It also overtly imports a test of proportionality into the 'justifiability' stage. The most difficult step tends to be proving that women are more disadvantaged by the practice than men – that it creates disparate impact. The case law previously established under s 1(1)(b) remains relevant to this issue. The current position as regards disparate impact may be summed up in the following manner, which is based on the ruling of Mustill LJ in *Jones v Chief Adjudication Officer*:[251]

(a) identify the criterion for selection (the condition);
(b) identify the relevant population, the 'pool', comprising all those who satisfy the other criteria for selection and ignoring the allegedly discriminatory condition;
(c) divide the relevant population into groups representing, first, those who satisfy the allegedly discriminatory criterion and secondly, those who do not;
(d) ascertain what are the actual male/female balances in the two groups;
(e) if women are found to be under-represented in the first group, it is proved that the criterion creates disparate impact.

Following *Jones* the pool consists of a group of persons in the same situation as the applicant in terms of satisfying the requirements for the post apart from the challenged condition – which should be ignored in determining the pool. But a recent House of Lords decision has thrown this analysis into jeopardy. In *Rutherford v Secretary of State for Trade and Industry (No 2)*[252] the applicant, a man, was dismissed at the age of 67; under s 109 ERA 1996 those over 65 cannot claim unfair dismissal. The applicant claimed that this created indirect discrimination against men, contrary to EC law. He argued that men had a greater tendency to work beyond 65 and that therefore the condition adversely affected men. The pool he argued for consisted in effect of the entire workforce and the condition was to be under 65. On that basis there was some disparate impact on men, but the minority did not find that the impact was significant enough. But the majority in the Lords compared all men and women in the work force over 65 in finding that the disputed provision had no disparate impact on men – it affected men and women equally. Their approach was one that *included* the challenged condition in determining the makeup of the pool. This appears to be the wrong approach, but arguably *Rutherford* can be confined to its own facts: on the face of it it was difficult to equate an age limit with a condition that could be applied more generally, such as the condition considered in *Seymour-Smith*, below. Also *Rutherford* was decided under s 1(1)(b), meaning that a 'requirement or condition' had to be identified. It can probably be distinguished on that basis when considered in relation to the more generous wording of s 1(2).

Assuming that the disputed condition can be ignored, thereafter choosing the appropriate 'pool' is crucial to the plaintiff's chances of success. The tribunal may decide that she has chosen the wrong pool and that therefore, the statistical evidence

251 (1990) EOR 1991.
252 [2006] UKHL 19.

she has prepared showing disparate impact relates to the wrong groups of persons.[253] However, a more relaxed approach was evident in *London Underground v Edwards (No 2)*[254] (discussed further below) in which the Court of Appeal accepted that the tribunal could take into account the common knowledge that there are more female than male lone parents. Once the calculation has been completed, it will be possible to determine the proportions of women and of men affected by the disputed requirement. But it must be found that the proportion of women who can comply is 'considerably smaller' than the equivalent proportion of men.

In *Secretary of State for Employment ex p Seymour-Smith and Perez*[255] a challenge was mounted against the increases in the qualifying period for redundancy from one to two years in 1985. It was argued that a considerably smaller proportion of women than of men could comply with it and that therefore, it breached the Equal Treatment Directive. In 1985, 77.4% of men and 68.9% of women fulfilled the condition. On a reference to the ECJ, it was found that such figures would not reveal that a considerably smaller proportion of women than men could fulfil the requirement. However, the ECJ also pointed out that a less than considerable differential, which persisted over a long period, could satisfy the requirement of indirect discrimination. The House of Lords considered the position as at 1991, not 1985, since both parties accepted that 1991 was the relevant date. Looking at the years between 1985 and 1991, there was a constant disparity between men and women: the ratio of men to women who qualified was 10:9. Given the persistence of this disparity it could not, it was found, be brushed aside as inconsiderable, bearing in mind the context of equality of treatment.

It is clear from this decision that determining the relevant proportions of men and women who can comply with a condition is not necessarily a straightforward matter that can be resolved by a 'snap-shot' approach. Further guidance was given in *Barry v Midland Bank*,[256] in which it was found that since the smaller the disadvantaged group in proportionate terms, the narrower the differential, a better guide may be to consider expressing the proportions as ratios of each other. Lord Nicholls explained that therefore, in a workforce of 10,000 employers of which 10% work part time, where 90% of the part timers are women, a requirement that disadvantages part timers will disadvantage 0.2% of males and 1.8% of women. Those proportions would not appear to satisfy the 'considerably smaller' requirement. But if the proportions are expressed as ratios of each other it will be found that the ratio of women who cannot comply compared to that of men who cannot is 9:1.

Work/life balance

One of the key issues in relation to indirect discrimination on grounds of sex that has arisen over the last 15 years is that of flexible working. The term 'flexible' can be used in two senses. First, it can relate to the need of parents or other carers to work hours which do not impinge too greatly on their caring responsibilities – a matter forming one aspect of the 'work/life' balance. Second, it can refer to the preference of some

253 See *Pearse v City of Bradford MC* [1988] IRLR 379.
254 [1998] IRLR 364.
255 [2000] IRLR 263, HL.
256 [1999] 1 WLR 1465.

employers to demand that employees work hours which suit the changing needs of the business or concern in question. These matters are increasingly becoming the subject of indirect discrimination claims.

In *London Underground v Edwards (No 2)*[257] the plaintiff, a woman train driver, brought an indirect discrimination claim after the employer imposed shift changes in accordance with its new business plan. She could not comply with the changed shifts because of her responsibilities as a single parent. It was found that out of the pool of train drivers there were 2,000 men, all of whom could comply with the new shift arrangements. There was a component of only 21 women in the pool. Out of that number, one woman – the applicant – could not comply. Thus, 95.2% of women could comply and 100% of men could comply. In determining that a 'considerably' smaller proportion of women could comply, the Court of Appeal took into account the small number of women in the pool, suggesting that women already found it hard to comply with the requirements of the job. Further, if one more woman had been unable to comply, that would have had a significant effect on the proportion of women who could not comply, whereas if one man had not been able to comply, that would have had little effect on the male figures. On the issue of justification, the Court of Appeal found that employers should recognise the need to take a reasonably flexible attitude to accommodating the needs of their employees. They considered that London Underground could have quite readily accommodated the needs of a good employee (she had worked for them for 10 years and there had been no complaints about her work) which would not have been damaging to their business plan.

A different attitude was evident in *Clymo v Wandsworth LBC*[258] which concerned the employee's need to adopt a different pattern of working. The plaintiff had returned to work after childbirth and found she could not comply with a requirement to work full time; she wished to work part time. The EAT found that no *requirement* to work full time had been applied. In any event, it was found, she could comply with it – she merely had to make a choice between her childcare responsibilities and full time working. This was a very technical approach to the statute, which gave priority to the employer's autonomy in choosing to impose full time working rather than to the employee's choices. It appears to be out of accord with the approach taken in *Edwards* and that taken in other, later decisions,[259] although it cannot be assumed that it has been entirely discarded. Possibly it can be distinguished as decided under s 1(1)(b) and relying on the word 'requirement'.

Race discrimination

When the RRA was amended in 2003 in response to the requirements of the Race Directive a more generous version of indirect discrimination was imported into it under a new s 1(1A), but only applying in the areas of EU competence – in respect of race, ethnic or national origins, not colour or nationality. But the new definition operated in *all* spheres, not just that of employment. In the context of race discrimination

---

257 [1998] IRLR 364.
258 [1989] ICR 250.
259 See *Zurich Insurance Co v Gulson* [1998] IRLR 118.

the more favourable scheme is not applicable, even in the employment context, in relation to nationality or colour. Thus the RRA now recognises two concepts of indirect discrimination, under s 1(1)(b) and under s 1(1A). The case law established under s 1(1)(b) will be relevant to an extent under s 1(1A). Also if discrimination on grounds of colour or nationality is alleged, the old, less generous concept of indirect discrimination under s 1(1)(b) should be used. The discussion begins with the more generous conception of indirect discrimination, which will be used in most instances.

Indirect discrimination under s 1(1A)

A person discriminates against another if

> ... he applies to that other a provision, criterion or practice which he applies or would apply equally to persons not of the same race or ethnic or national origins as that other, but –
>
> (i)   which puts or would put persons of the same race or ethnic or national origins as that other at a particular disadvantage when compared with other persons,
> (ii) which puts that other at a disadvantage, and
> (iii) which he cannot show to be a proportionate means of achieving a legitimate aim.

This definition of indirect discrimination is more generous than the old one in a number of respects, which were discussed above in relation to the similar definition under the SDA. The first step in a case of indirect discrimination on racial grounds is for the applicant to define to which racial group he or she belongs. For example, an individual could be defined as non-British, non-white, Asian or a sub-group of Asian. The choice of group is important, since discrimination affects racial groups differently. For example, a requirement to be clean-shaven might discriminate against Sikhs, but might not affect West Indians. Therefore, if in such circumstances the applicant chose 'non-white' as his group, the claim would fail. However, if he chose Sikh and non-Sikh, it would be more likely to succeed. The applicant should argue all possible groups in the alternative but clearly, if possible, he or she should seek to come within s 1(1A) rather than s 1(1)(b).

The next step is to identify a provision or practice. Once the Race Directive was implemented, it became clear that indirect discrimination could be found to exist where a non-absolute requirement was applied to the applicant. The Directive used the same wording – 'a provision, criterion or practice' – as that adopted in the Burden of Proof Directive.[260] Thus informal practices and discriminatory preferences can still count as "practices". The choice of pool, the determinations as to disparate impact and as to proportionality will be made in the same way as for indirect sex discrimination.

Indirect discrimination under s 1(1)(b)

The tests to be applied in the residual areas to establish indirect discrimination under s 1(1)(b) of the 1976 Act are identical to those arising under the Sex Discrimination

---

260 See above, pp 1541–42.

Act, apart from the need to show that the requirement or condition which has been applied adversely affects persons of a particular racial group.

The next step under s 1(1)(b), according to *Perera v Civil Service Commission*,[261] is for the applicant to show that an *absolute* condition has been applied to him or her. In *Perera* this concerned a requirement that a candidate for the Civil Service had a good command of English. This requirement was sometimes waived; it was determined that it could not, therefore, amount to a 'requirement or condition' for indirect discrimination purposes. As noted above in relation to indirect sexual discrimination, this decision placed a brake on claims of indirect discrimination[262] although that approach was being criticised even prior to implementation of the Burden of Proof Directive. It was pointed out in *Meer v Tower Hamlets*[263] by Balcombe LJ in the Court of Appeal that it allows discriminatory preferences free rein, as long as they are not expressed as absolute requirements. In that case, a candidate who had previous experience working in the local authority was preferred although such experience was not absolutely required, and this had a tendency to debar non-British applicants. The Commission for Racial Equality recommended that this interpretation should be abandoned so that non-absolute criteria can be considered[264] and under the changes introduced in response to the Race Directive indirect discrimination can be found to exist where a non-absolute requirement is applied to the applicant. However, this problem still subsists where s 1(1)(b) applies.

If a condition can be identified, the applicant must show that a 'considerably smaller proportion of his or her group can comply with it', and the approach adopted in sex discrimination cases, discussed above, will be used, although where indirect discrimination is based on nationality and affects an EC national it will be sufficient to establish a risk that the group of workers in question is unable to comply with the requirement.[265] This approach would obviate the need to produce statistical evidence proving the effect of the requirement in practice. This approach would not apply in other instances of indirect discrimination, but it may be introduced under the Race Discrimination Directive, which requires the applicant to show that the provision or practice in issue 'would put persons of a racial or ethnic group at a *particular disadvantage* compared with other persons' (emphasis added). That approach may appear to allow for consideration of a risk of inability to comply, although the use of the word 'would' as opposed to 'could' does not make this interpretation certain.

Once the applicant has established a prima facie case of indirect discrimination, the burden of proof shifts to the employer to show that the requirement or condition is justifiable.[266] In *Ojutiku v Manpower Services Commission*[267] two African students obtained places on a polytechnic management course, but were refused grants by the Manpower Services Commission since they lacked industrial experience. They claimed that this requirement was indirectly discriminatory as it was more difficult for African

---

261 [1983] ICR 428; [1983] IRLR 166.
262 For criticism of the decision, see Mead, G, 'Intentions, Conditions and Pools of Comparison' (1989) 18 ILJ 59.
263 [1988] IRLR 399, p 403.
264 CRE, *Second Review of the Race Relations Act*, 1991.
265 *O'Flynn v Adjudication Officer* Case C-237/94 [1996] All ER (EC) 541.
266 For discussion of the justification defence, see Lustgarten, L (1983) 133 NLJ 1057 and (1984) 134 NLJ 9.
267 [1982] IRLR 418.

applicants to show that they had previous management experience. However, the claim failed on the basis that the requirement could be justified. The test for justification was determined to be somewhat short of 'necessary', connoting a belief which would be justifiable if held on reasonable grounds, and this was reiterated in *Singh v British Railway Engineers*.[268] The applicant, who wore a turban in accordance with his religious beliefs, could not comply with a requirement to wear protective headgear and therefore had to take a less well-paid job. It was found that while the requirement did have an adverse impact it was justifiable, partly because the other employees would resent exceptions being made. However, the term 'justifiable' is now to be interpreted in accordance with the *Bilka* test,[269] which is applicable in sex discrimination cases and should therefore, by extension, apply to the equivalent provision under the RRA according to *Hampson v DES*.[270] This accords with the ruling in *Rainey v Greater Glasgow Health Board*[271] that the *Bilka* test would be applicable in sex discrimination and equal pay cases in respect of the grounds on which differential treatment could be justified. At the time this was an important instance of the indirect influence of EU law on national provisions against racial discrimination.

The Commission for Racial Equality had, for a number of years, criticised the interpretation of indirect discrimination and proposed a new definition: any practice or policy which is continued or allowed should be unlawful if it has a significant adverse impact on a particular racial group and is not necessary. It has further proposed that significant adverse impact should mean a 20% difference in impact between groups.[272] These proposals were, broadly, encapsulated in the Race Directive, which, as discussed, was implemented in 2003. However, the less generous elements of indirect discrimination on grounds of race are still relevant in the residual area that s 1(1)(b) continues to affect.

Discrimination relating to disability

As indicated above, the DDA does not cover indirect discrimination; apart from direct discrimination, discrimination relating to disability can occur if unfavourable treatment is imposed which relates to the disabled person's disability or if the duty to make reasonable adjustment is not complied with by the provider of services or education, or the employer. These two possibilities are considered in turn below. The majority of cases are brought under the disability-related discrimination head, and the duty of reasonable adjustment is then of relevance as explained below in relation to the justification defence, although it is also, as indicated, a separate cause of action.

Disability-related discrimination

The requirements regarding unfavourable treatment which relate to the disabled person's disability under s 3A(1) DDA bear some resemblance to the indirect discrimination

---

268 [1986] ICR 22.
269 Above, p 1540.
270 [1991] 1 AC 171; [1990] 2 All ER 513, HL.
271 [1986] 3 WLR 1017, HL.
272 See the CRE Consultative Paper, *Second Review of the Race Relations Act 1976*, 1991. The 20% notion derives from US civil rights law.

provisions relating to the other protected grounds discussed. Section 3A(1) provides that a person discriminates against a disabled person if '(a) for a reason which relates to the disabled person's disability he treats him less favourably than he treats or would treat others to whom that reason does not or would not apply; and (b) he cannot show that the treatment in question is justified'. The idea is to outlaw practices which, while appearing neutral on their face as between disabled and non-disabled people, place some disabled people at a substantial disadvantage for a reason related to their disability. The test under the DDA is similar to that of the RRA or SDA in that the less favourable treatment can be justified. This is inevitable, since otherwise a mentally handicapped person with severe learning difficulties could win an action under the DDA in respect of failure to appoint her to, for example, a post as a teacher on the basis that a requirement to have certain educational qualifications placed her at a disadvantage. Under s 3A(3) of the DDA, the adverse treatment is justified only if the reason for it is material to the circumstances of the case and is substantial.

No guidance is given in the Act as to the basis for making a comparison between the two persons. It should be noted that it is possible for the applicant to compare herself with a hypothetical person; the issue is not whether a disabled or non-disabled person receives a benefit, but whether the disabled person would have been treated more favourably if she had not been disabled. The test can be broken down into five stages. First, the applicant must show that she is disabled within the meaning of the Act. Then she must show that treatment has been applied that relates to her disability. Third, she must show that the treatment has had a less favourable impact. The treatment must create differentiation between the disabled person and a non-disabled person (or a hypothetical person). Fourth, the applicant can rely on the ruling of the House of Lords in *James v Eastleigh BC*,[273] the sex discrimination case mentioned above, in showing that there is a causal relationship between her disability and the treatment; in other words that but for her disability she would have been treated as favourably as the comparator, a non-disabled person, was or would have been. Following *Birmingham CC ex p EOC*[274] it is not necessary to show that the less favourable treatment is accorded by an intention to discriminate: motive is irrelevant. Fifth, the alleged discriminator can seek to justify the treatment.

It is important for the tribunal to choose the right comparator. The correct test was set out in *Cosgrove v Caesar and Howie*.[275] Ms Cosgrove was dismissed after she had been off work for one year with depression. The employer argued that it would have dismissed any worker who had been absent for one year and therefore it had not treated the applicant less favourably. However, the dismissal was *related* to her disability; the correct comparator was, the EAT held, a person who had not been off work for one year. The plaintiff bears the burden of proving facts from which the tribunal could conclude in the absence of an adequate explanation that the respondent committed an act of discrimination against the complainant.[276] It may sometimes be clearly apparent

---

273 [1990] AC 751; [1990] 2 All ER 607; [1989] IRLR 318; [1989] 3 WLR 122; the 'but for' test applied in James was put forward by Lord Goff in the House of Lords in *Birmingham CC ex p EOC* [1989] 18 ILJ 247; for comment, see Ellis (1989) 52 MLR 710.
274 [1989] AC 1155; [1989] 1 All ER 769.
275 [2001] IRLR 653. This finding followed *Clark* [1999] ICR 951.
276 DDA s17A(1)(c), s 25(9). This is the same formula as is used in the other statutes or Regulations.

that the employment detriment was on grounds of disability, in which case attention will shift to considering whether the disability fell within the Act and whether the detriment can be justified.

In relation to educational provision post-16, wording similar to that used in respect of employment is used in order to comply with the Framework Directive; the changes came into force in 2006. Wording similar to that of s 5(3) is used in s 28B(7) in relation to schools, but less favourable treatment can also be justified if it is the result of a 'permitted form of selection' as defined in s 28B(6). Essentially, this means that where a school operates a form of selection, either as a private school or under the relevant legislation (on grounds of ability or special aptitude), that may justifiably preclude the admission of a disabled pupil.

The test for justification in respect of the provision of goods and services differs from the key test in relation to employment or education. It consists of a list of instances in which the unfavourable treatment will be justified, under s 20(4). They include two specified conditions for all services. The first is that the treatment is necessary in order not to endanger health or safety; the second is capacity to contract. There are three additional specified conditions for services to the public only: that the treatment is necessary since otherwise the service could not be provided to members of the public generally; that the inferior treatment is necessary in order to provide the service at all; third that it may be acceptable for there to be a difference in the cost of providing the service to the disabled person and to members of the public.

The test under s 5(3) (and the equivalent tests in relation to education) bears at first glimpse some similarity to the need to show justification for an indirectly discriminatory requirement under s 1(1)(b) of the SDA or RRA. But it is not as strict a test as that of objective justification laid down in *Bilka-Kaufhaus GmbH v Weber von Hartz*,[277] which is discussed below. Under the *Bilka* test, conditions creating disparate impact will be justifiable if they amount to a means chosen for achieving an objective which correspond to a real need on the part of the undertaking, are appropriate to that end and are necessary to that end. It was found that the DDA test differed from that in *Bilka*, and the difference between the tests was made clear, by the EAT in *Baynton v Saurus*.[278] It was determined that the individual circumstances in question must relate to both employer and employee and that a balancing of those circumstances can be carried out. In *Heinz v Kendrick*,[279] the EAT followed *Baynton*, but made it clear that once the test was satisfied, the disadvantage must be justified, even though this meant that justification could readily be found. It criticised the lowness of the threshold, but considered that Parliament alone could remedy it.

In *Jones v Post Office*[280] Arden LJ said *obiter* that the term 'substantial' in s 5(3) of the DDA means that the reason given by the employer (or educational institution) must carry real weight, but this does not mean that the employer must take into account all the latest research on the subject. The Court of Appeal in that case gave further elucidation. It was found that the reason given by the employer (or other) must

277 [1986] IRLR 317; [1986] CMLR 701.
278 [1999] IRLR 604.
279 [2000] IRLR 141.
280 [2001] IRLR 384; [2001] ICR 805.

fall within the band of reasonable responses of a reasonable employer.[281] Thus, the burden placed by the justification test on the employer in this context is lighter than in respect of the other protected grounds in relation to indirect discrimination. So long as the employer has made a properly conducted risk assessment and then acts within the band of responses open to the reasonable employer, the unfavourable treatment can be justified. If no attempt at reasonable adjustment – discussed below – has been made, the treatment cannot be justified. But it could be justified if reasonable adjustment has been attempted and has failed.

The duty to make reasonable adjustment

Employment

The duty will be discussed mainly within the employment context, although it also applies with some modifications within the other contexts covered by the DDA, as amended.[282] The duty is placed on employers, on providers of services and on providers of education at all levels. As indicated, the DDA does not cover indirect discrimination, but the duty of reasonable adjustment bears some resemblance to the indirect discrimination provisions discussed. It also represents a form of positive action, since the duty creates obligations to take positive steps to seek to remedy certain disadvantages that disabled persons might be under. The idea is to outlaw practices which, while neutral on their face as between disabled and non-disabled people, place some disabled people at a substantial disadvantage.

Previously, under s 5, the DDA would be breached if the employer failed to comply with a duty of reasonable adjustment and could not show that the failure to comply was justified. Section 5(5) of the DDA previously provided that if an employer was under a duty to make reasonable adjustment under s 6, but failed without justification to make any such adjustment, his treatment of that person could not be justified, unless it would have been justified even if he had complied with the duty. This requirement was reiterated, with examples in the applicable Code.[283] This meant, for example, that a requirement to drive on a daily basis in a job description or advertisement might be subject to the duty; it would not affect some disabled people, but would probably discourage a candidate with epilepsy. Assuming that the employer had failed to make any such adjustment, the question would then be first whether that failure was justified and, secondly, whether, once it was justified, or even if it was unjustified, the requirement to drive would have been justifiable even after the adjustment was made. In the circumstances, it might be possible to make adjustment by organising another person to drive the disabled person or by enabling her to use public transport. If such adjustment was not possible, or would have placed an unreasonable burden on the employer, it would be justifiable not to make it. Alternatively, it might be possible to make some such adjustment which the employer refused to make, such as employing a person to drive the disabled person part of the week. In either circumstance, if the

---

281 That test was also accepted as the proper one in *Foley v Post Office* [2000] ICR 1283.
282 See s 21; SI 2001/2030, Art 3(a); SI 2005/3258; SI 2005 No 2774, Art 4; ss 24A–24L; ss 28A–28Q.
283 Paragraph 4.7.

requirement to drive a car on a daily basis was found to be essential to the job, the less favourable treatment – not offering the job – would not breach the Act.

Section 6 provided that if arrangements made by the employer or physical features of the employer's premises 'place the disabled person at a substantial disadvantage in comparison with persons who are not disabled, it is the duty of the employer to take such steps as it is reasonable in the circumstances of the case for him to take to prevent the arrangements or feature having that effect'. Under s 6(3), a non-exhaustive list of examples of adjustments was given. Such adjustment could include, for example, making adjustments to premises, making alterations to working procedures or hours, allowing absence for rehabilitation, assessment or treatment. In practice, such adjustments might mean providing Braille keyboards, installing ramps or lifts, or sanitary facilities with disabled access. In *Morse v Wiltshire CC*[284] it was made clear that the duty of the employer involves the taking of a number of sequential steps. It must first be asked whether there is a duty to adjust. Secondly, it must be considered whether the employer has taken reasonable steps to make the adjustment, and thirdly, whether any failure to take the steps can be justified.

However, under changes introduced in 2004, the employer is under an enhanced duty to make reasonable adjustment. The scope of the duty was widened as of 1 October 2004 by the Disability Discrimination Act 1995 (Amendment) Regulations 2003. These changes were introduced to give effect to the disability provisions of the 'Framework Directive' (Directive 2000/78/EC Establishing a General Framework for Equal Treatment in Employment and Occupation). The basic duty to make adjustments is now set out in s 4A(1) of the DDA which provides:

Where –

(a) a provision, criterion or practice applied by or on behalf of an employer, or
(b) any physical feature of premises occupied by the employer,

places the disabled person concerned at a substantial disadvantage in comparison with persons who are not disabled, it is the duty of the employer to take such steps as it is reasonable, in all the circumstances of the case, for him to have to take in order to prevent the provision, criterion or practice, or feature, having that effect.

Thus, the duty now applies to any 'provision, criterion or practice' applied by or on behalf of an employer; the previous confusing justification defence has been removed, and the burden of proof has been altered to make it more favourable to the applicant. A failure to comply with the duty to make reasonable adjustments is a separate act of discrimination under s 3A(2) of the Act; it is actionable without the need to show discrimination due to less favourable treatment for a reason related to disability. The Court of Appeal has found that where there are claims of both discrimination for a reason relating to disability and discrimination by failure to comply with the duty to make reasonable adjustments, the latter claim should be considered first.[285] This is

284 [1998] ICR 1023; [1998] IRLR 352.
285 *Collins v Royal National Theatre Board Ltd* [2004] IRLR 395, para 24; *Murphy v Slough BC* [2005] ICR 721, paras 38–9; the decision approved *Paul v National Probation Service* [2004] IRLR 190 EAT para 20, and *Smith v Churchills Stairlifts plc* [2006] IRLR para 15.

because, under s 3A(6), less favourable treatment for a reason related to disability cannot be justified if there has been a failure to comply with the duty to make reasonable adjustments unless it would have been justified even if the employer had complied with that duty. So s 3A(6) bars any defence of justification which depends directly or indirectly on a breach of the duty to make reasonable adjustments.

The duty only arises if the employer has knowledge of the disability of the complainant. Under s 4A(3) no duty is imposed on an employer who does not know, and could not reasonably be expected to know that the person concerned has a disability and is likely to be placed at a substantial disadvantage. In relation to job applicants or potential applicants, the employer must also know that the person concerned is, or may be, an applicant.

The proper approach to the duty once it arises was set out in *Nottinghamshire CC v Meikle*[286] by the Court of Appeal. The applicant was a teacher whose sight had deteriorated. She requested various adjustments, including the enlargement of documents, an increase in non-contact time during the day so that she could do her teaching preparation in daylight, and adjustments to her timetable to give her more time to move between classrooms. None of these adjustments were made. She was absent from work with eye strain. Her sick pay was halved under the employer's policy, which was to reduce sick pay after an absence of over 100 days. An employment tribunal held that there had been a failure to make reasonable adjustments, but the halving of the sick pay was justified. The Court of Appeal held that the proper approach was to ask whether the employer had shown that, if all reasonable adjustments had been made, she would still have been absent for over 100 days. The employer had not argued this, and the medical evidence suggested that if they had done so, such an argument would have failed.

Once the duty arises, the employer must take 'such steps as it is reasonable, in all the circumstances of the case, for him to have to take' in order to prevent the substantial disadvantage. Section 18B(1) gives a non-exhaustive list of factors to which regard should be had in determining whether it is reasonable for a person to take a particular measure of adjustment:

(a) the extent to which taking the step would prevent the effect in relation to which the duty is imposed;
(b) the extent to which it is practicable for him to take the step;
(c) the financial and other costs which would be incurred by him in taking the step and the extent to which it would disrupt any of his activities;
(d) the extent of his financial or other resources;
(e) the availability to him of financial or other assistance with respect to taking the step;
(f) the nature of his activities and the size of his undertaking;
(g) where the step would be taken in relation to a private household, the extent to which taking it would–

   i   disrupt that household, or
   ii disturb any person residing there.

286 [2004] IRLR 703, at paras 40–53.

Section 18B(2) gives examples of steps an employer may need to take in order to comply with a duty to make reasonable adjustments:

(a) making adjustments to premises;
(b) allocating some of the disabled person's duties to another person;
(c) transferring him to fill another vacancy;
(d) altering his hours of working or training;
(e) assigning him to a different place of work or training;
(f) allowing him to be absent during working or training hours for rehabilitation, assessment or treatment;
(g) giving, or arranging for, training or mentoring (whether for the disabled person or any other person);
(h) acquiring or modifying equipment;
(i) modifying instructions or reference manuals;
(j) modifying procedures for testing or assessment;
(k) providing a reader or interpreter;
(l) providing supervision or other support.

In *Archibald v Fife Council*[287] the House of Lords gave an indication of the extent of the duty. The applicant was employed by the Council as a road-sweeper. A complication during minor surgery left her almost unable to walk; so she was unable to fulfill the duties of her job. The Council arranged for her to attend computer and administration skills, and automatically short-listed her for office-based jobs. She applied for over 100 of these, but, because they were at a slightly higher grade than her manual worker's job as a road-sweeper, the Council's policy required her to undertake competitive interviews. She was unsuccessful in all her applications, and put this down to her industrial background. Having exhausted all possibilities, the Council dismissed her. In an appeal brought by the Disability Rights Commission (DRC) the House of Lords held that the duty to take reasonable steps could potentially encompass transferring the applicant to a slightly higher grade without a competitive interview; while it was accepted that the Council's policy in asking for an interview, was relevant, it might also be reasonable for an employer to have to take the difficulties faced by an employee transferring from an industrial background into office work into account.

Provision of goods and services

In comparison with employment claims, those in respect of goods and services got off to a slow start after the inception of the DDA.[288] A duty of adjustment also arises under s 19 in relation to the provision of goods and services. The reach of s 19 was widened when private clubs were included under s 21F, inserted by s 12 DDA 2005.

---

287 [2004] IRLR 651.
288 In 1998, the Institute of Employment Studies (IES) carried out a major survey looking at how the DDA was working and its effectiveness. This report entitled 'Monitoring the Disability Discrimination Act 1995' was published in 1999 and revealed that, between 2 December 1996 and 9 July 1998, only nine DDA goods, facilities, services and premises cases were lodged in the county court. This was compared to 2,456 cases which had been lodged in employment tribunals.

Section 21B outlaws discrimination in a class of public authority functions not already covered.[289] Under s 19, a service provider discriminates under the Act if he refuses to provide to the disabled person a service he provides to other members of the public. Section 21 provides that if the service provider has a practice that makes it impossible or unreasonably difficult for disabled persons to make use of a service which he provides to other members of the public, it is the duty of the provider to take such steps as it is reasonable in the circumstances of the case for him to take to prevent the practice having that effect. This means adjustment to current means of service provision, including provision of auxiliary aids and availability of alternative means of delivering a service. Unlike the provisions in respect of employment, which do not apply to businesses with fewer than 15 staff, the service provisions apply across the board. However, this requirement is qualified by the need to make only 'reasonable' adaptation. Thus, for example, a large restaurant chain might be expected to provide menus in Braille, but a small high-street café might satisfy this requirement by having a waiter read out the menu.

Thus, the DDA will also be breached if the provider of services fails to comply with the duty of reasonable adjustment, depending on what is reasonable in the circumstances. A shop owner who refused to allow guide dogs on the premises would breach the DDA, although she could refuse to allow all other animals to enter. The duty might also mean that a café should display a price list in large type, an estate agent or bank might need to install an induction loop for those with impaired hearing. It might mean merely ensuring that a member of staff was available to open a door to a disabled person or to retrieve articles from high shelves.

There is quite a lot of evidence suggesting that these requirements have not been brought to the attention of service providers. The Chairman of the National Disability Council, the official advisory body on disability (now replaced by the Disability Rights Commission),[290] has expressed concern that many businesses, especially small ones, were not aware of the requirements of the Act.[291] For example, a survey commissioned by the Guide Dogs for the Blind Association found in October 2001 that thousands of pubs and restaurants continue to refuse to accept guide dogs; only two respondents to the survey of 500 publicans and restaurateurs said that they were aware of the law.[292] Companies such as large supermarket operators are aware of the law, but tend to under-enforce it. For example, supermarkets provide disabled parking, but clearly prefer to use persuasive ('talking' spaces) rather than coercive means (wheel clamps) to prevent non-disabled drivers using the disabled spaces.

Education

Sections 28C and 28T the DDA, as amended by the 2001 Act, are breached if the provider of education in question fails to comply with a duty of reasonable adjustment and he cannot show that the failure to comply is justified. Sections 28C and T provide that if arrangements made by the provider for admission to the institution in question

---

289   SI 2005/2774, Art 4.
290   See below, p 1593.
291   See the *Guardian*, 29 September 1999.
292   See the *Guardian*, 3 October 2001.

and in relation to the services provided 'place the disabled person at a substantial disadvantage in comparison with persons who are not disabled', it is the duty of the provider to take such steps as it is reasonable for it to have to take to prevent that effect from occurring. The steps that should be taken do not require schools, under s 28C(2), to alter or remove a physical feature or provide auxiliary aids or services; the precise steps to be taken in schools are determined by regulations made under s 28C(3). Examples of adjustments that can be made in schools include timetabling lessons on the ground floor if there is no lift and bringing library books to a disabled pupil if the library is inaccessible.[293] The duties placed on higher and further educational institutions by the 2001 Act, while closing a significant gap in the DDA provision, were of quite a qualified and indeterminate kind. In this respect the 2001 Act continued the stance adopted by the DDA itself. But the provision for Higher or Further education must accord with the Framework Directive since it covers vocational training as well as employment, so the current, post-2006, provision is very similar to the existing employment provision. The provision for further educational institutions resembles that for schools. Their duty of reasonable adjustment includes a duty to provide auxiliary aids.[294] In determining the steps to be taken the institution must, under s 28T(2), have regard to the code of practice issued under s 53A of the DDA.

Discrimination on grounds of sexual orientation

The Sexual Orientation Regulations 2003 import the concept of indirect discrimination in employment (under reg 3(1)(b)), which provides that such discrimination arises if:

> A applies to B a provision, criterion or practice which he applies or would apply equally to persons not of the same sexual orientation as B, but –
>
> (i)   which puts or would put persons of the same sexual orientation as B at a particular disadvantage when compared with other persons,
> (ii) which puts B at that disadvantage, and
> (iii) which A cannot show to be a proportionate means of achieving a legitimate aim.
>
> (2) A comparison of B's case with that of another person under paragraph (1) must be such that the relevant circumstances in the one case are the same, or not materially different, in the other.

Thus reg 3(1)(b) outlaws practices which, while neutral on their face, have a disproportionately adverse impact on persons due to their sexual orientation. Making allowance for indirect discrimination means that the regulations cover not only isolated acts of discrimination, but also institutionalised discrimination. This reflects the pluralist approach; it takes account, for example, of endemic practices of discriminating on this ground in, for example, certain police forces. In asking not whether a person can, in theory, comply with a condition, but whether he or she can do so in practice, it broadens the area of morally unjustifiable differentiation.

---

293 Standing Committee B Fourth Sitting col 151, 29 March 2001.
294 Section 28S.

There are four stages in operating this concept. First, it must be shown that a condition has been applied to the applicant. Second, it must be shown that the condition is one which puts or would put persons of the same sexual orientation as the applicant 'at a particular disadvantage when compared with other persons'. The term 'particular disadvantage' will now have to be interpreted as cases arise. It may be taken to mean that considerably fewer persons of a particular sexual orientation are able to comply with the condition than other persons. Third, the claimant must show that the condition puts him or her at a particular disadvantage; in other words the claimant must be a 'victim' due to the application of the condition: test cases cannot therefore be brought by pressure groups such as *Stonewall*. Once the claimant has proved these three requirements, the burden of proof shifts to the employer to show if possible that the condition is a 'proportionate means of achieving a legitimate aim'. The decisions under the race and sex provisions as to indirect discrimination can be applied in this context since the key tests are the same.

6 Victimisation and harassment: sex, race, disability, sexual orientation

Harassment

Introduction

Under the SDA and RRA as originally introduced victims of harassment had to fashion their claims as discrimination claims. This meant that claims might well fail on technicalities. Now as a result of European Directives, free-standing harassment claims can be brought without the need to prove discrimination. This is now the case in respect of all the protected grounds discussed in this section. Under the amendments to the SDA, the RRA, the DDA and under the Sexual Orientation Regulations, it is clear that behaviour that can reasonably be viewed as humiliating or degrading will not necessarily also amount to discrimination: all will depend on the specific circumstances.

Harassment as discrimination[295]

Prior to reforms introduced as a result of the European Directives, it was clear under the SDA and RRA that if the employer subjected the applicant to employment detriment arising from harassment, such as a transfer from one establishment to another, this would be direct discrimination.[296] Moreover, sexual or racial harassment appeared arguably to be a detriment in itself[297] if it was discriminatory under s 6(6)(b) SDA or s 4 RRA which speak of 'or subjecting [the employee] to any other detriment', even though it did not lead to other unfavourable action, so long as some employment disadvantage

---

295 See generally Hadjifotiou, H, *Women and Harassment at Work*, 1983, Pluto; MacKinnon, C, *Sexual Harassment of Working Women*, 1979, Yale University Press; Mullender, R, 'Racial harassment, sexual harassment and the expressive function of law (1998) 61 MLR 236.
296 *Porcelli v Strathclyde Regional Council* [1986] ICR 564.
297 Although see (1985) 101 LQR 471 on this point.

arises. In *De Souza v Automobile Association*[298] the Court of Appeal found that racial abuse in itself is not enough to cause an employee detriment within the meaning of s 4 of the RRA. The Court had to find that by reason of the act complained of, a reasonable worker would or might take the view that he had thereby been disadvantaged in the circumstances in which he had thereafter to work. Such disadvantage was interpreted quite broadly. In *Hereford and Worcester CC v Clayton*,[299] firefighters were informed of the 'bad news: the new firefighter is a woman'. This was found to be a sexist insult capable of detrimental consequences. It sent the wrong signal to the firefighters and might have been likely to cause victimisation. This was less favourable treatment on the grounds of sex and amounted to unlawful sex discrimination. The decisions as to what amounted to humiliating behaviour were made in the employment field, but were applicable to the fields of education and housing. For example, under s 17 of the RRA, which provided that discrimination by bodies in charge of educational establishments may occur if a person is subjected 'to any other detriment', an action could have been successful against school administrators who failed to prevent racial harassment of a pupil.

The problem inherent in viewing harassment as discrimination is that the judicial inquiry necessarily focuses on the question of *equal* treatment rather than on the nature of the treatment. In other words, where a man or other comparator was or would also have been subjected to the behaviour in question, experienced by the applicant as humiliating or degrading, the claim may fail.[300] This problem was illustrated by the findings in *Stewart v Cleveland Guest Ltd*.[301] The claim was brought by a woman who had been subjected to a display of sexually explicit pictures of women in the workplace. She had also been subjected to sexual assault and to sexual harassment at work, although these incidents were not included in her claim. She had eventually got the pictures removed, when her union intervened, but the management had allowed the workers to know who was to blame for their removal, and she had felt unable to return to the workplace. The tribunal found that the display was sexually neutral (despite the fact that the pictures were only of women and women were in the minority in the workplace), although it also found that her objections to the pictures were reasonable. It reached the decision to dismiss her claim on the basis that other women in the workplace did not object and, therefore, it could be said that, objectively, the pictures were not offensive or created humiliating conditions of work. However, taking into account all the circumstances of the case, it could be argued that there was sufficient evidence that the pictures were, objectively, offensive and degrading and that the other women had been, as was argued, desensitised by the male-oriented general ethos. The EAT upheld the tribunal, but left open the possibility that apparently neutral general treatment which had a particular impact on women could be viewed as discrimination.

298 [1986] ICR 514.
299 (1996) *The Times*, 8 October.
300 For criticism of this approach, which compares it with the evolving stance in US law away from the requirement to prove differential treatment and towards emphasis on the question whether there had been creation of a hostile working environment, see Dine, J and Watt, B, 'Sexual harassment: moving away from discrimination' (1995) 58 MLR 343.
301 [1996] ICR 535.

However, in a later decision, *Sidhu v Aerospace Composite Technology Ltd*,[302] a different approach was taken. The plaintiff had been subject to racial abuse and an assault. He and the racist workmates were dismissed because of his violent reaction to the assault. The racist element in it was disregarded by the employers in taking the decision to dismiss him. It was found in the EAT that to disregard this element was a 'race-specific' decision having a 'race-specific' effect. The nature and effect of the decision was found to amount to treatment on racial grounds amounting in itself to racial discrimination under s 1(1)(a) of the RRA, and it was not found necessary to consider whether a person of a different racial group or a white person would have been treated differently. Clearly, the claim might have failed had the employer been allowed to rely on the argument that a white person who had reacted to a racist assault in the same way would have been treated in the same way. Thus, it appeared that two different approaches were emerging.

However, in *Secretary of State for Defence v Scotland; Pearce v Mayfield Secondary School Governing Body*, which is discussed above, the House of Lords considered the joined cases of *Pearce* and of *McDonald* since they raised the question whether sexual orientation discrimination fall within the SDA. The House of Lords overturned the previous decision of the EAT in *Burton v De Vere Hotels Ltd*,[303] discussed further below, and concluded that sexual harassment is not unlawful discrimination in itself but requires a comparison with how a comparator of the opposite sex was or would have been treated. In *Pearce* a male homosexual, it was found, would have been treated equally badly and therefore the SDA could not be employed since it is based on formal equality – equal treatment for persons in a like position. The decision illustrates the limitations of the formal equality position.

Free standing harassment claims on the protected grounds

Prior to the reforms considered below the European Commission had defined sexual harassment as 'conduct of a sexual nature or other conduct based on sex affecting the dignity of men and women at work'.[304] In other words, it was not defined as discrimination but as a discrete wrong. The definition proffered clearly covered verbal or physical conduct. The Commission published a Code of Practice[305] on sexual harassment based on the definition above, which was supported by the Council of Ministers,[306] giving guidance to employees and employers and stating that harassment 'pollutes the working environment and can have a devastating effect upon the health, confidence, morale and performance of those affected by it'.[307] The Commission recommended that

---

302 [1999] IRLR 683.
303 [1996] IRLR 596.
304 OJ C157/2. See Employment Law Review for 1992, below.
305 Commission Recommendation of 27 November 1991 on the Protection of the Dignity of Men and Women at Work OJ L49 3, 1992. This followed a report by Rubenstein, M, *The Dignity of Women at Work: A Report on the Problem of Sexual Harassment in the Member States of the European Communities*, 1987. See above, fn 322. For criticism of the Code, see (1993) 143 NLJ 1473.
306 In a Declaration (see (1992) 217 European Industrial Relations Review 21; see also Rubenstein, M (1992) 21 ILJ 70).
307 See OJ 4.2.1992.

the Code should be adopted by member states,[308] which should also take other action to address this problem, but the UK Government did not show any inclination to respond. However, industrial tribunals faced with an allegation of sexual harassment as a form of direct discrimination had regard to the guidance offered by the Code.[309]

In response to the relevant EU Directives, harassment on all the main protected grounds is no longer treated as discrimination. The Race Discrimination Directive[310] defined harassment as behaviour that creates an 'intimidating, hostile, degrading or offensive, humiliating or offensive environment' and has the purpose or the effect of violating a person's dignity. This definition of harassment was imported into the RRA via s 3A and is included in the SDA under s 4A.[311] It is also adopted under the DDA[312] and the Sexual Orientation Regulations.

The definition of 'harassment' on grounds of sexual orientation is echoed in the other provisions. Under reg 5(1) of the regulations:

> For the purposes of these Regulations, a person ('A') subjects another person ('B') to harassment where, on grounds of sexual orientation, A engages in unwanted conduct which has the purpose or effect of
>
> (a) violating B's dignity; or
> (b) creating an intimidating, hostile, degrading, humiliating or offensive environment for B.
>
> (2) Conduct shall be regarded as having the effect specified in paragraph (1)(a) or (b) only if, having regard to all the circumstances, including in particular the perception of B, it should reasonably be considered as having that effect.

The issues considered below arise in respect of all the key protected grounds.

It is clear that the harasser need not appreciate the effect of his or her behaviour and need not have intended it to cause humiliation. Under the previous case law there was some uncertainty as to whether 'detriment' should be interpreted subjectively or objectively and a tendency to adopt the latter approach where the applicant was perceived as particularly sensitive[313] and the former where he or she was thought to be more robust.[314] This approach arguably rendered the previous test for harassment under-inclusive. The current harassment provisions seem to encapsulate a mixed approach; a mainly objective test is used, involving asking whether the offending behaviour had reached a level at which reasonable people would term it humiliating. This stems from *Driskel*[315] in which, however, it was also said that the tribunal should consider the victim's subjective perception of the conduct. The explanatory memoranda

---

308 Commission Recommendation of 27 November 1991.
309 *Wadman v Carpenter Farrer Partnership* (1993) *The Times*, 31 May, EAT.
310 Directive 2000/43/EC.
311 In force from October 2005.
312 Section 16A.
313 *Wileman v Minilec Engineering Ltd* [1988] ICR 318; for criticism see Gay (1990) 19 ILJ 35, who considered this ruling to be an 'example of judicial insensitivity'.
314 *Snowball v Gardner Merchant* [1987] ICR 719.
315 [2000] IRLR 151.

accompanying the new amendments and regulations stated that the *Driskel* approach was encapsulated in the new provisions.[316]

A range of forms of behaviour can amount to harassment. The harassment does not have to be direct and it can emanate from employees, and not from the employer. Certain recent cases are considered below in which, apart from one, it was not necessary to prove discrimination. The first case to be brought under the Sexual Orientation Regulations for discrimination on the grounds of sexual orientation was a harassment case, *Whitfield v Cleanaway UK*.[317] Mr Whitfield, a gay office manager, stated that he had been subject to homophobic abuse. This abuse included name-calling and taunting. He resigned from his job and brought a claim for constructive dismissal and harassment due to his sexual orientation. He was successful in his claim and the ET awarded him £35,000.

In *Whitfield* the employee was the direct recipient of homophobic abuse. In the case of *Whitehead v Brighton Marine Palace and Pier Company Ltd*[318] Mr Whitehead raised a grievance at work regarding his manager's attitude towards him. Mr Whitehead was absent from work due to sickness shortly after raising the grievance. On returning from his sick leave he was informed by a colleague that his manager had referred to him in a particularly offensive and homophobic manner. He had not heard his manager make this comment, but he resigned and successfully brought a claim in the ET for harassment due to his sexual orientation.

In a sex discrimination case (under the previous provisions), *Moonsar v Fiveways Express Transport Ltd*,[319] the EAT held that it was sex discrimination, in these circumstances, for a man to download porn at work. Ms Moonsar brought a claim for sex discrimination on the grounds that male members of staff downloaded pornographic images onto screens in a room where she was working, on three different occasions. The material was not circulated directly to her, but she knew what was going on; she made no complaint at the time because she wanted to keep her job. The tribunal decided that this could not amount to sex discrimination because she had not been shown the images and had not made any complaint about the men viewing them. Ms Moonsar argued that in claims of sex discrimination the tribunal was legally obliged (under s 63 of the Sex Discrimination Act and the decision in *Barton v Investec*)[320] to look for any evidence from which it could conclude that there had been sex discrimination. If they decided there was, then the burden of proof passed to the employer to prove that he or she did not discriminate.

Ms Moonsar argued that the facts of the case could easily have amounted to sexual harassment, whether or not the images were circulated to her. It was clear that the men's behaviour amounted to an affront to her dignity. The tribunal had even made a finding that she found their behaviour unacceptable. The logic of that finding meant that she had suffered a 'detriment' or disadvantage. She also argued that her failure to complain was not relevant in assessing whether she had suffered a detriment. She

---

316   See, e.g., the pre-consultation Explanatory Notes to the Regulations on Sexual Orientation.
317   4 February 2005, unreported.
318   Case 3102595/04 on 18th April 2005.
319   27 September 2004.
320   [2003] ICR 1205.

relied on the EAT's decision in *Driskel v Peninsula Business Services Ltd*[321] to support her point that the men's behaviour was so obviously detrimental to her that it was 'of no significance' that she had not complained. The EAT accepted this argument. It said that, viewed objectively, the men's behaviour could be regarded as degrading or offensive to a woman. It was, therefore, potentially less favourable treatment. The burden should then have shifted to the employers to show that there was not less favourable treatment – they had not done so. The EAT said it had to substitute a finding that there was sexual discrimination in this case. Under the current free-standing provisions provisions it would not be necessary to show that there was less favourable treatment. The findings are still of value as giving an indication as to the type of behaviour that would be viewed as an affront to dignity.

In *Empower Scotland Ltd v Khan*[322] the links between racial and religious discrimination, especially in relation to Muslims, were illustrated. The EAT upheld a claim of harassment brought by an employee of *Ethnic Minorities Participating On Wider Economic Responsibilities (Empower) Scotland* against a colleague. Mr Khan, a Muslim of Pakistani origin, claimed that Mr Singh, an Indian Sikh, had made sweeping statements, such as, 'you Pakistanis are all the same', and 'you Muslims are all troublemakers'. The judge said that, 'given that 90 per cent of Pakistanis are Muslim, and given that the maker of the statement considers that all Muslims are troublemakers, it follows that a Pakistani who is a Muslim is a troublemaker'. The EAT dismissed the employers' appeal, saying that there was 'a sound basis' for the tribunal's finding that the claimant was abused on grounds of his Pakistani national origin.

An issue may arise as to the employer's responsibility for the harassment. Section 41(1) of the SDA states that an act done by an employee in the course of employment shall be treated as done by the employer as well as by him or her, whether or not it was done with the employer's knowledge or approval. There are equivalent provisions in s 32 of the RRA and s 58 of the DDA. In respect of the previous position a harassment claim on the protected grounds could be brought where the employer had made little or no effort to curb the harassment.[323] These decisions appear now to be applicable to free-standing harassment claims. In *Tower Boot Co v Jones*,[324] the Court of Appeal adopted a purposive approach to the legislation in finding that employers must take steps to make themselves aware of harassment in the workplace and must take further steps to prevent it. It was not sufficient for employers simply to argue that the harassment did not take place in the course of employment:[325] this would create an obvious anomaly, since gross harassment (which occurred in *Jones*) could never be said to take place in the course of employment.

The decision reaffirmed a broad liability of employers for racial abuse, and in *Burton and Another v De Vere Hotels*[326] it was found that the employer will be liable if it allows employees to be subject to racial abuse where it could have been prevented, even if the abuser is not an employee. The case of *Burton v De Vere Hotels Ltd* was

321 [2000] IRLR 151.
322 2005, unreported, noted in the CRE's 2005 Annual Report.
323 See *Enterprise Glass Co Ltd v Miles* [1990] Ind Relations Review and Report 412–15C.
324 [1997] ICR 254; [1997] IRLR 168.
325 This had been accepted by the EAT: see [1995] IRLR 529.
326 (1996) *The Times*, 3 October.

often relied upon by applicants in harassment cases, such as Ms Pearce, where the harasser was not an employee of the applicant's employer. Instead, for example, they may be an external third party. The usual vicarious liability provisions of the Sex Discrimination and Race Relations Acts do not apply because the applicant and harasser are not employed by the same employer. Thus, unless the applicant's employer could be fixed with liability, the applicant would be without a remedy. In the *Burton* case, the hotel owner, who employed the black female applicant waitresses, was held liable for the racist offence caused by the jokes of Bernard Manning who had been engaged to entertain the guests in the hotel restaurant. In adopting a purposive interpretation that emphasised the need to protect employees in these circumstances, the EAT in *Burton* concluded that the issue that had to be determined was whether the incidents were 'sufficiently under the control of the employer so that he could, by the application of good employment practice, have prevented the harassment'. By this route, applicants harassed by third parties could normally obtain redress against their own employers where they argued that the employer could have controlled the situation but failed to do so. On this principle, an action might be brought successfully where the employer did not know of the harassment but should have known, thus placing a duty upon employers to be aware of what is occurring in the workplace.[327]

However, in *Secretary of State for Defence v Scotland*; *Pearce v Mayfield Secondary School Governing Body*,[328] which is discussed above, the House of Lords overturned the previous decision of the EAT in *Burton v De Vere Hotels Ltd*. In *Pearce* the homophobic abuse had come from pupils, not from employees. Ms Pearce had argued that the school, although not the employer of the pupils, was liable for failing to control their conduct. Her claim was against the school as her employer. But the campaign of abuse mounted against her was a campaign by pupils of the school, not by members of the school staff. So the Lords found that Ms Pearce was not assisted by s 41(1) SDA. It was argued that nevertheless the school could and should have taken steps to shield Ms Pearce, and its failure to do so constituted sex discrimination.

The Lords found that the *Burton* decision had treated an employer's inadvertent failure to take such steps as discrimination even though the failure had nothing to do with the sex or race of the employees. It was found that in this crucially important respect the decision had given insufficient heed to the statutory discrimination provisions. An essential element of 'direct' sex discrimination by an employer is that, on the grounds of sex, the employer treats the employee less favourably than he treats or would treat an employee of the opposite sex. Similarly with 'direct' racial discrimination: the 'less favourable treatment' comparison is an essential ingredient of the statutory wrong: see s 1(1)(a) RRA. Unless the employer's conduct satisfies this 'less favourable treatment' test, the employer is not guilty of direct sex or racial discrimination. In making this comparison acts of persons for whose conduct an employer is vicariously responsible are to be attributed to the employer. It is otherwise in respect of acts of third parties for whose conduct the employer is not vicariously liable. It was found that the harassment in *Burton* was committed by third parties for whose conduct the employer was not vicariously responsible. The Lords concluded that racial discrimination on the part of

---

327 This has been accepted in the US: *Continental Can Co v Minn* 297 NW 2d 241.
328 [2003] IRLR 512.

the employer had not arisen.[329] This decision turned on the need to show discrimination, which is no longer necessary under the free-standing harassment provisions. However, it does not determine whether harassment by third parties in the work place could be viewed in similar circumstances as sufficiently under the employer's control so as to render the employer liable in respect of it.

Victimisation

Protection against discrimination is insufficient; the legislation needs to protect persons from recrimination if they take action under it. Under the relevant statutes, victimisation occurs when a discriminator treats a person less favourably for taking action or aiding in an action under the RRA, SDA, EPA, DDA or Sexual Orientation Regulations – for doing a 'protected act'.[330] The provisions under s 2 of the RRA and s 55 of the DDA are almost identical to the equivalent 'victimisation' provisions under s 4 of the SDA and similar to those under reg 4 of the Sexual Orientation Regulations, and have the same aim – to deter employers and others from dismissing or treating adversely someone who undertakes a 'protected act' or aids another in doing so.

In order to determine whether the unfavourable treatment is linked to the protected act, it is necessary to ask whether the claimant would have been subjected to the treatment but for performing the protected act. In order to decide this question, it must be asked how a comparable person would have been treated. According to the findings in *Aziz v Trinity St Taxis*[331] the comparison must be between a person who has done the act and a person who has not, not between a person who has done the act and a person who has taken action under other legislation. This stance was confirmed by the Court of Appeal in *Brown v TNT Express Worldwide (UK) Ltd*[332] and by the House of Lords in *Chief Constable of West Yorkshire Police v Khan*.[333]

Following *Aziz v Trinity St Taxis*[334] there has to be a clear causal relationship between the action brought and the unfavourable treatment. Aziz, a taxi driver and a member of Trinity Street Taxis (TST), thought that TST were unfairly treating him and made a tape recording of a conversation to prove it. He took his claim of race discrimination to an industrial tribunal, but it failed. He was then expelled from TST and claimed victimisation. The Court of Appeal considered the question of causation: had TST treated him less favourably by reason of what he had done in making the tapes with a view to bringing a race discrimination case, or had it expelled him because of the breach of trust involved in making the tapes? It was found that the necessary causal relationship was not established; it was not apparent that TST were influenced in their decision to expel him by the fact that the tapes were made in order to bring a race relations case; they would have expelled him anyway because of the breach of trust.

---

329 The similar case of *Go Kidz Go Ltd v Bourdouane*, unreported, Employment Appeal Tribunal, 10 September 1996, was also stated to be wrongly decided. *Burton* is reported: [1996] IRLR 596.
330 For discussion of the victimisation provisions, see Ellis, E and Miller, CJ, 'The victimisation of anti-discrimination complainants' [1992] PL 80.
331 [1988] WLR 79; [1988] 2 All ER 860.
332 [2001] ICR 182.
333 (2001) *The Times*, 16 October, HL; [2000] IRLR 324; [2000] ICR 1169, CA.
334 [1988] WLR 79; [1988] 2 All ER 860.

This was a fine distinction to make and it is arguable that once a plaintiff has shown that unfavourable treatment has prima facie some causal relationship with a protected act, some causal potency, the burden of proof should shift to the employer to show that it was entirely unrelated to that act.

Under s 4(1) of the SDA, less favourable treatment of someone because she has done a 'protected act' – brought an action or intends to do so or has assisted in such action under the 1975 Act or the EPA – amounts to victimisation. The usefulness of this provision has been diminished owing to the need to show that the unfavourable treatment is solely due to the protected act and not in part for some other reason.[335] It may often be hard to prove that this is the case and this is particularly unfortunate owing to evidence which is beginning to emerge in both race and sex discrimination cases that in respect of certain professions, including in particular the police, those in authority are becoming more likely to respond to a protected act by bringing disciplinary proceedings which might not otherwise have been undertaken. This occurred when Alison Halford brought discrimination proceedings against, *inter alia*, Merseyside Police Authority and was probably a factor in her decision to settle the discrimination claim rather than pursue it to a conclusion.[336] A further barrier to victimisation claims was identified in *Wales v Comr of Police for the Metropolis*;[337] it was found that unless the first action complained of amounts to actionable discrimination (the action would have succeeded had it been brought), further unfavourable acts occurring owing to the complaint do not fall within s 4(1). This decision may be incorrect and the decision of the Court of Appeal in *Tower Boot Co v Jones*[338] may ameliorate its impact (since many victimisation claims could be brought as harassment claims), but it does narrow down one avenue leading to possible redress.

Under the DDA, victimisation occurs when a discriminator treats a person, disabled or non-disabled, less favourably for complaining that the DDA has been breached or aiding in that complaint. Following *Aziz v Trinity St Taxis*,[339] there has to be a clear causal relationship between the action brought and the unfavourable treatment. In relation to sexual orientation, victimisation, defined in reg 4, occurs where a person receives less favourable treatment than others by reason of the fact that he has brought (or given evidence in) proceedings, made an allegation or otherwise done anything under or by reference to the regulations.

The approach in victimisation cases may, however, change somewhat as a result of the findings of the House of Lords in *Nagarajan v London Regional Transport*.[340] The Lords found that the alleged discriminator need not have the protected act consciously in mind; all it is necessary to show is that an important or significant cause of the less favourable treatment is the fact that he or she had knowledge of the fact

---

335 *Aziz v Trinity St Taxis* [1988] 2 All ER 860, CA.

336 A similar conclusion was reached in a race discrimination case which was settled in May 1993. Joginder Singh Prem claimed that Nottinghamshire Police had discriminated against him in failing to promote him. They responded by bringing disciplinary charges which were later dismissed. He was awarded a payment of £20,000 in respect of the discrimination and an ex gratia payment of £5,000 in respect of the victimisation, although it was denied. See (1993) the *Guardian*, 5 May.

337 [1995] IRLR 531. For discussion, see (1997) 26(2) ILJ 158.

338 [1997] ICR 254; [1997] IRLR 168. See above, p 1561.

339 [1988] WLR 79; [1988] 2 All ER 860.

340 [1999] 4 All ER 65; [1999] 3 WLR 425.

that the applicant had done a protected act. Such a formulation of the test, which echoes the test under s 1(1)(1)(a) of the RRA and SDA, might have led to a different result in *Aziz* since it could have been argued that the employer had the protected act subconsciously in mind. At the least, it makes it clear that the alleged discriminator need not have a conscious motive connected with the relevant legislation and that there may be more than one cause of the unfavourable treatment. Thus, this decision and that in *Aziz* regarding the choice of comparator afforded greater force to the anti-victimisation provisions of the RRA, which also extends to the equivalent provisions of the SDA and DDA. The question to be asked, following *Nagarajan*, was: can a causal connection between the protected act and the unfavourable treatment be established?

However, the decision of the House of Lords in *Chief Constable of West Yorkshire Police v Khan*[341] signalled, to an extent, a change of direction which may detract from the impact of *Nagarajan*. The Lords found that where a person who has made a claim to a tribunal alleging discrimination subsequently applies for another job, it is not victimisation for the current employer to refuse to provide a reference, citing the claim as the reason. The Chief Constable of Khan's force had stated in response to the reference request that he could not comment as to the reference for fear of prejudicing his own case before the tribunal. The Lords reached their conclusion on the ground that although Khan had been unfavourably treated by comparison with other employees who had not done a protected act (in respect of such persons, the reference would have been sent), the treatment was not by reason of his having done the protected act; it was due to the existence of the proceedings which made it reasonable for the Chief Constable to seek to preserve his position. The proper question to be asked was not merely 'But for the protected act would the adverse treatment have occurred?', but to inquire into the motivation of the alleged discriminator. In this instance, the motive concerned the need to preserve his position in relation to the legal claim; he did not, according to the House of Lords, act as he did in refusing to give the reference for the reason that Khan had done a protected act. So the simple 'but for' test established in *Nagarajan* was rejected.

The problem with this approach is that it means that initiating a protected act is likely or bound to set in motion a chain of events, allowing an alleged discriminator to claim that it was one of those events, not the act itself, which led to the unfavourable treatment. If the focus of the inquiry is on the motivation of the alleged discriminator and not on the causal relationship between the unfavourable treatment and the protected act, the claim of victimisation may fail where the alleged discriminator can plausibly (and even with factual correctness) argue that he or she was motivated by one of the events set in motion by the doing of the protected act, not the act itself. In relation to this point it can be argued that two persons may be placed in a very difficult position by reason of the doing of the protected act – the alleged discriminator and the alleged victim. In the instant case, the Chief Constable might have prejudiced his position by writing the reference. Equally, Khan may have been adversely affected by the fact that it was not written. He did have an interview for the other post, but was eventually rejected. It is impossible to say whether the rejection was due at least in part to the lack of a reference and to the fact that he was known to be bringing a discrimination

341 (2001) *The Times*, 16 October, HL; [2000] IRLR 324; [2000] ICR 1169, CA.

claim. Therefore, there is a choice in such instances before the courts. Should the position of the alleged discriminator or that of the alleged victim be protected? If a test of a straightforward causal relationship is used, the latter is likely to be protected. If a subjective test is used, the position of the former will be protected. The policy of the legislation appears to be to protect the position of the latter and, therefore, a causal relationship test should have been used.

But in future a person who has brought a discrimination claim will have to suffer the detriment of knowing that while the claim is pending, he or she is in difficulties in applying for another post, thus possibly missing significant opportunities and also being forced to stay in the same workplace in which he has made the claim, which may well be very unpleasant. Thus, the decision of the House of Lords allows a person who has done a protected act to suffer some detriment which is causally linked to the doing of the act. The decision may deter some claimants, precisely the outcome that the legislation appeared to be designed to prevent. In the instant case, it would not have seemed too onerous to expect the police force in question to have put a procedure in place designed to cope with this very situation, such as devolving the writing of the reference to a person not directly implicated in the discrimination claim. If that had any effect on the position of the Chief Constable in relation to the claim, that might be viewed as an inevitable consequence of seeking to protect the position of persons who undertake protected acts. In any event, it is hard to see that it would have such an effect since the person writing the reference would presumably rely on personnel records in order to do so which presumably would be disclosed in any event to the tribunal hearing the claim.

Derbyshire v St Helen's Met BC[342] followed *Khan* in finding that although the treatment of persons who had brought an equal pay claim was less favourable, and the less favourable treatment was causally linked to the claim, the employer had acted 'honestly and reasonably' in trying to settle the proceedings. The net result of the decision in *Khan* is to allow some detrimental action against persons who have done protected acts.

Flawed as the provisions protecting from victimisation are, it should be pointed out that they do not appear to cover the employee who is victimised for taking *any* form of legal action against a colleague; nor do they apply to post-employment victimisation.[343] Thus, where a police officer brought an allegation of rape and buggery against a colleague in respect of an alleged off-duty attack, her subsequent vicious and prolonged victimisation at work could not, it was found, be addressed under the anti-victimisation provisions of the SDA,[344] although it might be said that a clearer example of gross discrimination on grounds of sex could hardly be found. She was, for example, threatened with violence by her chief superintendent, forced to undergo psychological analysis, advised to leave the force, harassed, and denied time off work.

This might be an instance in which action under the HRA would provide an alternative possibility. Indeed, the HRA may provide the possibility of curbing victimisation in relation to the taking of legal action in situations ranging far outside the employment

342 [2006] ICR 90.
343 *Adekeye v Post Office (No 2)* [1997] IRLR 105.
344 *Waters v Comr of Police of the Metropolis* [1997] IRLR 589. Arguably, she could now rely on s 7(1)(a) HRA and Art 8 (or 3) as an alternative possibility.

context, although, due to s 6, not where the responsibility lies with a private body. Where an applicant has been victimised in a work-related situation, or indeed in any situation for which a public authority has responsibility, such as in an educational institution, as a result of instigating legal action, whether against a colleague or the employer, or perhaps against any person or body, it would be arguable that Art 6 has been breached on the basis that the victimisation is intended to force her to drop the action, thus impairing her exercise of her Art 6 rights.[345]

It could also be argued that where a person has been victimised post-employment on the basis of taking action under the RRA, SDA, DDA, or Sexual Orientation Regulations, or any protected ground, on the basis of alleged employment detriment under other legislation or on other unprotected grounds, Arts 6 and 14 could be engaged.[346] The same argument could be made on any protected ground within Art 14, including on the grounds of race, sex or disability, outside the contexts and/or grounds covered by the anti-discrimination legislation. Where victimisation reaches the level of viciousness found in the instance given above, an action based on Art 3 or Art 8[347] could be brought. In all these instances, assuming that the body responsible, directly or indirectly, for the victimisation, was a public authority, the action could be brought directly against it under s 7(1)(a) of the HRA. This is clearly a very significant possibility, and since one might have expected the courts, under the impetus of the HRA, to seek to prevent victimisation by private bodies with a view to punishing persons for or preventing them from taking legal action, it is at least possible that eventually a right to take legal action free from victimisation will be discovered to exist arising from common law principle.[348]

7 Lawful discrimination

Exclusions from the Sex Discrimination Act

A large number of exclusions were embodied in the Sex Discrimination Act and therefore discrimination in such circumstances was lawful under domestic legislation.[349] Certain occupations were excluded under s 19, which covers employment for the purpose of organised religion, and s 21, which covers mine workers. The armed forces were also

---

345 See the general discussion of Art 6 in Chapter 2, pp 63–64.

346 On the basis that Art 14 encompasses a number of protected grounds in a non-exhaustive list; see Chapter 2, p 108.

347 Arguably, the treatment to which the woman police officer was subjected could be viewed as analogous to that suffered by the applicants in *Lustig-Prean v UK* (1999) 7 BHRC 65; *Smith and Grady v UK* (2000) 29 EHRR 493. Indeed, it is suggested that it might, unlike the treatment in those instances, fall within the boundaries of Art 3.

348 There are recent indications that the common law is showing a robustness in providing for protection against discrimination which was not previously evident: see *Matadeen and Another v Pointu and Others, Minister of Education and Science and Another* [1999] 1 AC 98, but there would be the grave problem of finding an existing cause of action. The alternative is that direct horizontal effect will at some future point be found to arise under the HRA on the basis that a court is a public authority under s 6; see Chapter 4, pp 216, 255–56.

349 See further, for discussion of the original provisions: Pannick, D, *Sexual Discrimination Law* 1985, pp 255–70; McColgan, op. cit., fn 1, Chapter 6, pp 346–54.

excluded under s 85(4), but this exclusion was abolished under ss 21–28 of the Armed
Forces Act 1996. Acts safeguarding national security were exempted (s 52), as were
acts done under statutory authority (s 7 and s 51) for the protection of women. This
last provision means that the 1975 Act is of lower status than other statutes, since it is
unable to prevail over other statutory provisions relating to the protection of women even
though they were passed before it. Thus, statutes intended to enshrine discrimination in
their provisions for such protection are not affected by the 1975 Act;[350] this exception
is permitted under Art 2(7) Equal Treatment Directive. These exceptions have tended
to be narrowed down owing to the impact of the Equal Treatment Directive (ETD).
For discussion of lawful discrimination under EU law, see below.[351]

A general exception to provisions against discrimination in the employment field
also arises where sex can be said to be a genuine occupational qualification (GOQ)
under one of the s 7 provisions.[352] Until 2005 Art 2(2) of the ETD provided a general
exception where the employment activities 'by reason of their nature or the context in
which they are carried out, the sex of the worker constitutes a determining factor'. After
amendment, Art 2(6) operates only where sex constitutes 'a genuine and determining
occupational requirement provided that the objective is legitimate and the requirement is
proportionate'.[353] All exceptions in domestic law must comply with these requirements;
so the GOQs under s 7 SDA must be read subject to them. The s 7 GOQs arise in a
number of contexts, including those where the job appears to call for a man for reasons
of physiology (excluding physical strength or stamina)[354] under s 7(2)(a), or for reasons
of authenticity in respect of plays or other entertainment, or to preserve decency or
privacy under s 7(2)(b), or where the job involves dealings with other countries where
women are less likely to be able to carry them out effectively because of the customs of
that other country, under s 7(2)(g). MacKinnon has argued that these exceptions are too
broad as extending some way beyond biological differences and accepting differential
treatment based solely on social categorisation.[355] On this basis, it is arguable that they
are due to be overhauled and narrowed down, particularly the last-mentioned, on the
ground that the UK should not bow to discriminatory practices in other countries. The
new limiting provisions under the ETD, as amended, mean that significant narrowing
down could occur, in accordance with the demands of proportionality.

The existing GOQs under s 7 of the SDA are also applied under s 7A in respect of
discrimination on grounds of gender reassignment. Further GOQs are applied under
s 7B where (a) the job involves the likelihood of performing intimate physical searches
pursuant to statutory powers, or (b) living in a private home where objection might
reasonably be taken to allowing the person in question 'the degree of physical or
social contact with a person living in the home' or 'knowledge of intimate details of

---

350   Section 51 was substituted by the Employment Act 1989, s 3, which is of narrower scope. For discussion
      of provisions intended to protect women, especially in relation to reproductive risks, see Kennedy
      (1986) 14 IJSL 393.
351   See pp 1579–86. See, particularly, the discussion of *Johnston v Chief Constable of the RUC* [1986]
      ECR 1651.
352   For analysis of s 7, see Pannick, D (1984) OJLS 198.
353   Equal Treatment (Amendment) Dir 2002/73/EC.
354   For criticism of this provision see Pannick, *Sex Discrimination Law* 1985, p 238.
355   MacKinnon, C, *Sexual Harassment of Working Women*, 1979, pp 121 and 180.

the person's life'; or (c) it is necessary to live on premises provided by the employer since it is impracticable for the holder of the job to live elsewhere and objection could be taken to the job holder sharing accommodation with persons of either sex while undergoing gender reassignment; or (d) the job holder provides personal services to vulnerable individuals and the employer reasonably believes that they cannot be effectively provided by a person while undergoing gender reassignment. The GOQs under ss 7A and 7B do not apply to persons whose gender reassignment is complete and who have obtained a gender recognition certificate under the Gender Recognition Act 2004. It is arguable that the width of these GOQs means that the SDA is not in compliance with the Equal Treatment Directive, in which case, as argued above, the Directive itself could be relied upon or a purposive approach could be adopted to the SDA. As a last resort, the HRA could be relied upon if the action was against a public authority, using ss 6, 7(1)(a) and relying on Art 8.[356]

Exclusions from the Race Relations Act

The RRA cannot affect discrimination which falls outside its scope. Previously it could not affect discrimination enshrined in other statutes, even those which predated it (s 41(1))[357] but this exception now only applies to the residual areas.[358] The RRA cannot affect discrimination occurring within the scope of a specific exception.[359] In respect of discrimination outside its scope this includes not only racist behaviour falling outside the contexts covered by the Act, but also such behaviour occurring within those contexts but unable to find a legal niche within them owing to the particular wording of the Act. For example, it was found in *De Souza v AA*[360] that racial insults, as such, do not amount to 'unfavourable treatment' within employment.

Alternatively, one of the exceptions may apply. Exceptions in respect of small premises or partnerships with less than six partners are provided by s 10 and s 32, but now only apply in the residual areas. Under s 75, restrictions on employment in Crown Service are permissible, although the government has accepted that this provision should be narrowed down.[361] Section 42 provides that nothing in the RRA 'shall render unlawful an act done for the purpose of safeguarding national security'. Prior to the passing of the Race Relations (Amendment) Act 2000, s 69(2)(b) provided for the use of ministerial certificates as conclusive evidence that acts or arrangements specified were done for that purpose. Section 7 of the 2000 Act amends s 42 to add the words 'if the doing of the act was justified for that purpose', and repeals s 69(2)(b).

---

356 See further on this point above, in relation to discrimination on grounds of sexual orientation; pp 1483–86.
357 The scope of s 41 was narrowed by the House of Lords in *Hampson v DES* [1990] 2 All ER 513 to cover only acts done in necessary performance of an express statutory obligation, not acts done in the exercise of a discretion conferred by the statute.
358 Section 41(1A).
359 For discussion, see McColgan, op. cit., fn 1, Chapter 7, pp 433–45.
360 [1986] ICR 514; for comment, see Carty (1986) 49 MLR 653; see also *Khan v GMC* (1993) *The Times*, 29 March.
361 Government Response to the CRE's Reform of the RRA 1976 (1998); available at http://195.44.11.137/coi/coipress.nsf.

The Act employs the concept of a genuine occupational qualification (GOQ) under s 5, but the GOQs are of much narrower scope than those arising under the 1975 Act. They come down to two. First, that for reasons of authenticity, a person of a particular racial group must be employed. This might cover plays and restaurants or clubs with a particular national theme. Second, the services being provided are aimed at persons of a specific racial group and can most effectively be provided by persons of that same racial group. In *Lambeth BC v CRE* [362] it was determined that this requirement would be interpreted restrictively: a managerial position which involved little contact with the public would not fulfil it. A new s 4A RRA was included in 2003 in response to the Race Directive, providing that a difference of treatment related to racial or ethnic origin is not discrimination where by reason of the particular occupational activities carried out, or the context in which they are carried out, such a characteristic constitutes a genuine and determining occupational requirement, provided that the objective is legitimate and the requirement is proportionate. Section 4A operates in the areas of EU competence, so it appears that s 5 operates in the residual areas.

Exceptions to the Sexual Orientation Regulations

The regulations are qualified since being of a particular sexual orientation can be 'a genuine and determining occupational requirement', although it must also be 'proportionate to apply that requirement in the particular case'.[363] There is a general exception in reg 7(2):

> This paragraph applies where, having regard to the nature of the employment or the context in which it is carried out –
>
> (a) being of a particular sexual orientation is a genuine and determining occupational requirement;
> (b) it is proportionate to apply that requirement in the particular case; and
> (c) either –
>
>> (i) the person to whom that requirement is applied does not meet it, or
>> (ii) the employer is not satisfied, and in all the circumstances it is reasonable for him not to be satisfied, that that person meets it, and this paragraph applies whether or not the employment is for purposes of an organised religion.

The organised religion exception applies under reg 7(3):

> This paragraph applies where –
>
> (a) the employment is for purposes of an organised religion;

---

362 [1990] IRLR 231, CA.
363 Section 7(1) provides: 'In relation to discrimination falling within regulation 3 (discrimination on grounds of sexual orientation) (a) regulation 6(1)(a) or (c) does not apply to any employment; (b) regulation 6(2)(b) or (c) does not apply to promotion or transfer to, or training for, any employment; and (c) regulation 6(2)(d) does not apply to dismissal from any employment, where paragraph (2) or (3) applies.'

(b) the employer applies a requirement related to sexual orientation –

    (i) so as to comply with the doctrines of the religion, or

    (ii) because of the nature of the employment and the context in which it is carried out, so as to avoid conflicting with the strongly held religious convictions of a significant number of the religion's followers; and

(c) either –

    (i) the person to whom that requirement is applied does not meet it, or

    (ii) the employer is not satisfied, and in all the circumstances it is reasonable for him not to be satisfied, that that person meets it.

The wording of reg 7(3)(c)(ii) means that discrimination can occur, not only on the basis of the applicant's sexual orientation, but on the basis of his or her reasonably *perceived* orientation. It was found in *AMICUS v Secretary of State for Trade and Industry*[364] that this phrase is compatible with the Framework Directive.

Religious organisations, such as Church of England or Catholic schools, might seek to rely on reg 7(3), which, if broadly interpreted, could allow many such organisations to discriminate openly on this ground. Such organisations can discriminate if, *inter alia*, the employer is on reasonable grounds not satisfied that the applicant meets a requirement to be of a particular sexual orientation. This creates, on its face, a number of possible avenues to discrimination; under one of them it means that if the employer considers on reasonable grounds that an applicant is gay, although he or she has not stated that this is the case, and that employing a gay person will conflict with religious convictions of a number of followers of the religion, the employer can openly discriminate. It is not necessary from the wording of the regulation for the requirements of proportionality to be satisfied.

However, in applying this exception an interpretation of it could arguably be adopted under s 3(1) HRA which affords it a narrow scope. The key phrase 'for purposes of an organised religion' could be afforded a narrow interpretation so that the exception only covered employment, such as the employment of priests, which is clearly for the purposes of organised religion. It could be argued that, for example, the employment of a gay teacher in a Catholic school was not linked strongly to 'that purpose'. Or it could be argued that the sexual orientation of a teacher was irrelevant to teaching or leading children in prayer in assemblies, and that nothing in the 'doctrines of the religion' demanded a particular sexual orientation when conducting assemblies or teaching, even if the religion could be viewed as condemning sexual relations between same-sex couples.

It is notable that there is no requirement of proportionality in reg 7(3), although one is included in reg 7(2). It can be argued that one must be read into it in order to comply with the Directive which does not include the exception under reg 7(3) and only allows for a 'genuine occupational requirement' (GOR) defence if the requirements of proportionality are satisfied. As a further possible argument Art 8(2) imports a requirement of proportionality. Thus it may be argued that such a requirement should be read into reg 7(3) via Art 8 (probably read with Art 14) and s 3 HRA. The employment context is not one to which Art 8 is obviously applicable. But a *Dudgeon* and *Smith and Grady* argument could be employed in order to bring sexual orientation discrimination in this context within Art 8, read with Art 14. The argument would be that unless reg 7(3) is read generously, teachers and others working in or for religious organisations might be forced to hide their sexuality in order to avoid employment detriment. They could be faced with a choice of concealing their sexuality, even living a celibate life, or facing such detriment. The measures they might have to adopt could be viewed as a continuing invasion of their private lives.

The exceptions under reg 7(2) and (3) were challenged by a group of unions in *AMICUS v Secretary of State for Trade and Industry*,[365] arguing that due to the exceptions the new rules outlawing discrimination on the basis of sexual orientation were defective. The unions argued that various exemptions in the Employment Equality (Sexual Orientation) Regulations 2003 were incompatible with the obligations imposed on the UK by the EC Equal Treatment Framework Directive 2000, and conflicted with provisions of the European Convention on Human Rights. The High Court rejected the challenge but found that the scope of the 'organised religion' exception is very limited. It was also found that the GOR in reg 7(3) for 'organised religion' should be given a narrow interpretation. The judge considered that, for example, it was unlikely to apply to a teacher in a faith school. This narrow approach is likely to be persuasive for tribunals interpreting the application of the exemption. The High Court found that although reg 7(2) does not state explicitly that a GOR must pursue a 'legitimate objective' as required by the Directive, that concept is implicit and tribunals should interpret the regulation accordingly. The unions were given leave to appeal.

Regulation 24 provides an exception in respect of national security. In the public authority context this raises a number of possibilities. For example, a large number of posts in the Home Civil Service[366] are subject to positive vetting (PV). In 1982, the Security Commission recommended[367] that male homosexuality should be dealt with on a case-by-case basis in relation to PV clearance, but that it should be refused if the individual's practice of his homosexuality placed any doubt upon his discretion or reliability. PV clearance for the Diplomatic Service or armed forces was automatically refused. If security clearance for any governmental post was refused on the ground of sexual orientation, a challenge could be mounted relying on the regulations and arguing for a narrow interpretation of reg 24 in reliance on the Directive or on s 3 HRA. The question would be whether national security was genuinely at stake in such an instance

8 Positive action: sex, race, disability, sexual orientation

Theoretical basis[368]

A significant divergence within equality theory lies between belief in equality of outcome and belief in equal treatment. The two views diverge in the sense that achieving an

---

365 [2004] EWHC 860.

366 In 1982, PV covered 68,000 posts (Cmnd 8540, p 5).

367 Cmnd 8540, 1982.

368 For general discussion, see Edwards, J, *Positive Discrimination: Social Justice, and Social Policy*, 1987, Routledge; Sacks, V, 'Tackling discrimination positively in Britain', and Parekh, B, 'The case for positive discrimination', in Hepple and Szyszczak, op. cit., fn 1.

equal outcome may mean treating persons unequally for a time, as opposed to treating them equally even if that produces unequal results. Nevertheless, it may be argued that such divergence is to an extent more apparent than real, since the underlying aim of providing equal treatment may be to ensure, ultimately, an equal outcome. The conflict between ensuring equality of treatment and furthering equality of outcome by means of positive action is essentially founded on the perception that such action means treating two likes unalike and thereby creating a denial of formal equality. In espousing a very significant principle, equal treatment of two likes or formal equality has a clear, simple and, to an extent, warranted appeal. But positive action cannot be accommodated within a formal equality model, since such a model only permits unlike (and, presumptively, unfavourable) treatment if difference is identified. In terms of pure theory, positive action has no place within a formal equality model, either as an aspect of the equality principle or as an exception to it. In practice, an unsatisfactory compromise may be reached whereby positive action is viewed as an exception to the equality principle. Once that principle has been abandoned, unequal treatment may be meted out.

But, apart from the conceptual incoherence of this position, it is suggested that it is unsatisfactory in that it does not readily provide a means of recognising the convergence between equality of outcome and of treatment which is not apparent within the other exceptions to the equality principle. However, it is possible to escape from the constraints of formal equality by adopting a substantive as opposed to a formal equality model. Substantive equality recognises that men and women, whites and blacks, straights and gays may be differently situated, but seeks to prevent both perpetuation of such difference and disadvantage flowing from it. In particular, substantive equality recognises that merely treating like as like, while ignoring the context within which such treatment is meted out, fails to understand the disadvantages certain groups may be under because of past discrimination, social attitudes and unequal distribution of social benefits. One factor both springing from and underpinning such a situation appears to be a lack of women or blacks in more advantageous and influential employment. Thus, use of positive action may be accommodated within a substantive equality model, since an outcome which both countered prior disadvantage and tended to change the context within which women or members of ethnic minorities take part in employment would be in accordance with such a model.

Forms of positive action and their recognition in national law

Four types of positive action may be identified:[369]

(1) reverse discrimination, which in its most absolute form would mean favourable treatment of a woman or a member of an ethnic minority on the ground of gender or race despite inferior qualification for a job or an inferior claim (in terms of criteria other than race or gender) to a facility such as housing;

(2) affirmative action – adopting a presumption in favour of appointing a candidate from the under-represented group if his or her qualifications are equal to those of a person from the non-disadvantaged group; once threshold equality is established,

---

369 For discussion of forms of positive action, see McCrudden (1986) 15 ILJ 219.

the member of the under-represented group is appointed; often takes the form of a quota system which is abandoned when proportionate representation is reached;
(3) preferential training opportunities – action to promote opportunities for members of the disadvantaged group in order to ensure that its members are in a strong position to compete for employment;
(4) inclusionary employment policies: adoption of equal opportunities policies particularly affecting advertising and recruiting – outreach programmes; regular reviews of employment policies.

All the provisions against discrimination on the protected grounds are based on the formal equality model. The dominance of this model in UK anti-discrimination law, in the established and the most recently introduced provisions, means that the first two forms of positive action are unlawful since they amount to direct discrimination. The symmetrical approach favoured in all the legislation, apart from the DDA, whereby straights and gays, men and women, blacks and whites can equally take advantage of the relevant legislation, means that it is not possible to favour the 'victim' group at which the relevant legislation was in reality aimed.

At present, there is virtually no scope for positive action in the first two forms under the SDA, RRA or Sexual Orientation Regulations, while scope for the third and fourth forms is extremely limited. Apart from one exception, the first two forms of positive action, above, are unlawful under the wording of s 1(1) of both statutes. Even guidance reminding selectors of equal opportunities policies but requiring them to select candidates on merit appears to be outlawed. In *ACAS v Taylor* [370] a majority of females were selected for interview for senior ACAS posts. Guidance had been given to the effect that more needed to be done to 'ensure the reality of the claim that ACAS is an equal opportunities employer . . . All staff should be considered on their merits . . .'. Mr Taylor, one of the candidates, was found to have suffered direct discrimination on the basis that the guidance could have influenced selectors in favour of positive action. The limits of the RRA were illustrated in *Lambeth LBC v CRE* [371] in which it was found that positive action to benefit racial groups was forbidden by the RRA. [372]

The limitations of the SDA in this respect due to its adherence to the formal equality model were tellingly illustrated in one context – the crucial one of Parliamentary representation. The current Labour Government wanted to create all-women short-lists in order to address the gross under-representation of women in Parliament; it wanted to go further than merely setting non-statutory, voluntary goals. When it did so the policy was challenged successfully by two male candidates as direct discrimination under the SDA in *Jepson and Dyas-Elliott v Labour Party.* [373] It was found that the use of all-women short-lists created unlawful discrimination against men. The government had to bring forward legislation in order to reverse this decision – the Sex Discrimination (Election Candidates) Act 2001. The legislation amended the SDA by including s 42A to allow for all-women short lists in order to increase the representation of women in

---

370 EAT/788/97.
371 [1990] ICR 768.
372 See also *Riyat v London Borough of Brent* (1983) (cited in IDS *Employment Law Handbook* 28, 1984, p 57); it was held that discrimination in favour of black job applicants was unlawful.
373 [1996] IRLR 116.

Parliament to a ratio of 50:50 women MPs. So a small exception to the formal equality model has been created under the SDA – but only in the context of elections. This was especially necessary due to past historical discrimination against women in terms of being able to stand for Parliament which means that the preponderance of men in Parliament – which creates a male-dominated environment – is based not on merit but on that historical legacy. The exception to the SDA would allow for the creation of all-women short-lists by the other two main parties. The Conservative Party, although very concerned at the gross under-representation of women in its group of MPs, has made no proposal likely to have any significant impact in changing the representation, while the Liberal Democrats voted against introducing all-women short-lists in their Autumn 2001 conference. They are therefore likely to remain in the same position as the Conservative Party in this respect.

The EOC argued in 2006 that some employers want to take positive action but find themselves prevented by the law from doing so. It considered that the Discrimination Law Review[374] should look at the case for extending the current positive action provisions so that 'employers are empowered, and in certain circumstances, might even be required, to take positive action to redress disadvantages faced by certain groups where it would be proportionate to do so'. In certain sectors there is 'a real desire to redress gender imbalance in the workforce, such as in the uniformed services, and there is concern that the SDA does not allow them to go far enough in their efforts to recruit and retain under-represented groups'.[375] The EOC considers that the positive action provisions in the SDA are little known and little understood. Since the provisions are narrowly drawn and complex they tend to act as a disincentive to employers since they fear that they may incur liability in putting them into practice.

The DDA does not take a symmetrical approach – those without disabilities cannot invoke it. So positive action is possible under the DDA and the duty of reasonable adjustment discussed above can be viewed as a form of positive action. However, s 7 Local Government Act requires that candidates be appointed on merit, so posts it covers cannot be offered only to disabled people on a quota basis.

Training and outreach policies

Acts done to meet the special needs of certain racial groups (such as by the provision of English language classes) in regard to education, welfare and training are permissible under the RRA, but such provision can only be made available where there are no, or very few, members of the group in question doing that work in the UK at the time.[376] Also, under s 37 of the RRA, employers can encourage applications from members of particular racial groups which are under-represented in the workforce. Similarly, s 48 SDA covers giving training to existing workers in order to take up particular work where they are under-represented in those jobs. Section 47(3) of the SDA permits the restriction of access to training facilities to those 'in special need of training by reason of the period for which they have been discharging domestic

---

374 The consultation process behind the Single Equality Act.
375 EOC (2006) op. cit., fn 1, paras 42, 43.
376 RRA 1976, ss 35–38.

or family responsibilities'. It should be noted that employers and others are under no duty to make such provision.

Thus, employers can pursue equal opportunities policies such as stating in job advertisements that applications from certain groups will be welcomed, but in general cannot appoint an equally well-qualified member of an ethnic minority or woman on a quota basis in preference to a white male in order to address under-representation of black people or women caused by past discrimination. Nor can they import a general presumption, subject to exceptions, that a woman or member of an ethnic minority with equal qualifications to those of other candidates should be appointed.

The position is the same under the Sexual Orientation Regulations which provide in reg 26(1):

> Nothing in Part II or III shall render unlawful any act done in or in connection with –
>
> (a) affording persons of a particular sexual orientation access to facilities for training which would help fit them for particular work; or
> (b) encouraging persons of a particular sexual orientation to take advantage of opportunities for doing particular work, where it reasonably appears to the person doing the act that it prevents or compensates for disadvantages linked to sexual orientation suffered by persons of that sexual orientation doing that work or likely to take up that work.

A particular type of positive action known as 'contract compliance', which fell within the third and fourth forms of action identified above and had the potential to produce quite far reaching beneficial effects, was outlawed by the then Conservative Government.[377] Under this method, organs of the state such as local authorities produced a 'check list' of equal opportunities policies and asked the companies with which it was thinking of dealing to show evidence of compliance with such policies. If the company could not show in response that certain procedures were in place intended to combat racism or sexism, it lost business.[378]

Duties of Public Bodies – inclusionary employment policies and promotion of equality

The government has not committed itself to the establishment of quotas on the lines of that considered in *Marschall*, below; it has instead preferred an approach relying on 'goals and timetables'. In July 1998, a target of a 50:50 male/female appointment ratio for men and women in public life, based on merit, was established.[379] In its White Paper *Modernising Government* it committed itself to a pro rata representation of ethnic minority groups in public appointments and to targets of 35% women in the

---

377 Under the Local Government Act 1988, s 17; for criticism, see Townshend-Smith, R, *Sex Discrimination in Employment*, 1989, pp 237–38.
378 The 1988 Act, s 18. Parliament, however, left intact a limited power to vet potential contractors as regards their race relations record.
379 Press release of a speech by Joan Ruddock, *Minister for Women*, at a TUC Conference, 9 July 1999 – www.dss.gov.uk/hq/press/1998/july98/186.htm.

top 3,000 Civil Service posts and 25% in the top 600. It also committed itself to a target of 3.2% of ethnic minority post-holders in the top 3,000 posts and stated that an equivalent target would be set for disabled persons. In 2005 it launched *Improving Opportunity, Strengthening Society* (IOSS), the government's strategy to increase racial equality and community cohesion.[380]

The RRA, after amendment by the Race Relations (Amendment) Act 2000 (which inserted s 71 into the 1976 Act), places a general duty on public authorities to 'eliminate unlawful racial discrimination' and to 'promote equality of opportunity and good relations between persons of different racial groups',[381] also referred to as the race equality duty. The aim was to help them to provide fair and accessible services, and to improve equal opportunities in employment. The race equality duty requires public authorities to pay 'due regard' to the need to eliminate unlawful racial discrimination and to promote equality of opportunity and good race relations. A similar duty is being introduced in 2007 relating to gender[382] and was introduced for disability in 2006.[383] As part of the race equality duty, most public authorities have to carry out race equality impact assessments (REIAs), to consider the likely effects a policy or legislative proposal might have on people from different racial groups and to aid in helping public authorities to develop sound policies promoting racial equality. In 2005 the CRE monitored the performance of Whitehall departments in carrying out REIAs on new policies, and requested copies of their REIAs for specific policies. As a result of intervention by the CRE, the Department of Health announced in 2005 that it was delaying the passage of the Mental Health Bill, partly so that a full REIA could be carried out.

This general duty under the RRA is supported by specific duties set out in subordinate legislation and those specific duties are enforceable by the CRE. The specific duties allow for positive action of types (3) and (4), indicated above. Guidance is offered by Codes of Practice promulgated by the CRE under s 71C. Thus some authorities are also bound by specific duties; for example, they must publish a race equality scheme (or race equality policy, in the case of schools and further and higher education institutions), listing the functions they have identified as being relevant to race equality, and describing their arrangements for meeting the duty. The CRE can seek to enforce the specific duties by issuing a compliance notice under s 71D. It can require the person in question to comply with the specific duty and can also require the person to furnish

380 Home Office, 2005. See also: *Race Equality in Public Services*; it brings together race equality performance data for key public service areas and provides the statistical background to the IOSS strategy, and covers Public Service Agreement targets to tackle inequalities in public services; *Summary of Responses to Strength in Diversity: towards a community cohesion and race equality strategy*, setting out responses to the consultation in 2004; see also Home Office documents, including: *Overarching Home Office Race Equality Scheme and The Core (non-IND) Home Office Associate Race Equality Scheme*, setting out how the Home Office will meet the duties set out in the Race Relations (Amendment) Act 2000 and associated secondary legislation; *Race Equality – the Home Secretary's Employment Targets*, detailing progress against the targets set in 1999 to measure the recruitment, retention and career progression of minority ethnic staff in the Department and its agencies; *The Home Office Diversity & Equal Opportunities Report 2003/2004*, the findings from a range of diversity monitoring processes to provide a comprehensive picture of the diversity of Home Office staff. See also CRE Annual Report for 2005 (published 2006).
381 For discussion see O'Cinneide, C [2001] PL 220.
382 SI 2006/1082, Art 4.
383 SI 2005/1676; 2005/2774, Arts 3 and 4.

the CRE with information in order to verify that the duty has been complied with. A court order can be obtained under s 71E to force the public authority to furnish the information and to comply with any requirement of the notice. The CRE has developed compliance procedures; it issues a warning letter to authorities indicating how their race equality scheme, policy, and/or employment arrangements may be non-compliant, and gives them the opportunity to rectify any deficiencies. If it receives a satisfactory response, no further action is taken. If not, a compliance notice may be served on the authority. The CRE considers that this process works well.[384]

This means that around 43,000 public authorities have a statutory duty to promote race equality. In 2005, in line with its commitments under IOSS the CRE launched *Promoting Good Race Relations: A guide for public authorities* in order to aid authorities in meeting this duty. Inspection, audit and guidance Inspectorates, such as the Audit Commission and the Office for Standards in Education (Ofsted), are not only bound by the race equality duty, but are also responsible for making sure that other public authorities are meeting it.[385] The CRE works closely with inspectorates, seeking to encourage them to include racial equality as part of their standards and inspection processes, to carry out reviews of racial equality, to develop comprehensive race equality schemes, and to share their information with the CRE. In 2005 public authorities in England and Wales listed under Schedule 1A of the Act had to review their list of functions, policies and proposed policies in line with the government's commitments under *Improving Opportunity, Strengthening Society* (IOSS), the government's strategy to increase racial equality and community cohesion.[386] The CRE works closely with public sector inspectorates and service providers to help them meet the race equality duty. During 2005, according to the 2005 CRE Report, all the key inspectorates revised or developed their methodologies, indicators or guidance.

Apart from the possibility of judicial review, the failure to comply with the s 71 duty may have legal implications if proceedings are brought for discrimination by individuals. In *Elias v Secretary of State for Defence*[387] it was found that a compensation scheme had resulted in indirect discrimination on grounds of national origins. The Court also found that the MoD had not carried out a race equality impact assessment. There had been no careful attempt to assess whether the scheme raised issues relevant to racial equality, although the possibility was raised; nor was any attempt made to assess the extent of any adverse impact, or to find ways of eliminating or minimising such impact. The MoD accepted the need to review the scheme. Both sides decided to appeal on the indirect discrimination element of the judgment, so the scope of any necessary review will not be clear until all legal proceedings have been concluded.

---

384 It notes in its 2005 Annual Report, Part 4: 'In 2005, we dealt with 13 cases under section 71D of the Race Relations Act. We sent formal warning letters to all 13 authorities and served compliance notices on two of them, both schools, when they failed to provide a satisfactory response within the required timescale. In the first case, the school produced a revised, compliant policy; the second case remained ongoing at the end of 2005. Of the remaining 11 cases, one authority responded satisfactorily and 10 cases were ongoing. In addition, as a precursor to the use of our compliance procedures, we issued 33 letters to Whitehall departments and inspectorates regarding their performance in respect of the race equality duty.'
385 CRE Annual Report for 2005 (published 2006).
386 CRE Annual Report for 2005 (published 2006).
387 2005, unreported, noted by CRE, ibid.

As indicated above, the Gender Equality Duty will also be imposed on public authorities from April 2007 onwards. It will apply to all public authorities and some public service providers from the private and voluntary sectors. It is probably the most significant change in sex equality legislation for 30 years. When it comes into force in April 2007, public authorities will have to take action to eliminate sex discrimination and harassment and to promote equality for women and men. Instead of depending on individuals making complaints about sex discrimination, the duty gives public authorities legal responsibility for demonstrating that they treat women and men fairly in policy-making, services and employment. The Equal Opportunities Commission and, in future, the Commission for Equality and Human Rights will be able to enforce the duty in the courts as the CRE does in respect of the race equality duty.

Affirmative action favouring women under EU law

The discussion below considers the position of affirmative action under the Equal Treatment Directive, concentrating on the irony of viewing such action as a derogation from the equality principle, and therefore in the same position as action taken to 'protect' women in employment – action which frequently in practice works to their detriment. Given the recent increase in the use of positive action within some member states of the Community and the acceptance of the need for such action by the European Council and Parliament (see Council Recommendation 84/635 EEC, below, and para 26 of the Advocate General's Opinion in *Kalanke* below) and in much of the relevant literature[388] the decision in Case 450/93 *Kalanke v Freie Hansestadt Bremen*[389] was highly significant in terms of its ability to affect an emerging tendency.

Within the Equal Treatment Directive positive action is viewed, under Art 2(4), as a derogation from the equal treatment principle which must, it seems, be looked at in the same light as the other derogations from that principle under Art 2(2) and (3). The exception under Art 2(2) is applicable to occupations in which the sex of the worker is a determining factor; Art 2(3) covers the provision of special protective measures for women, particularly those relating to pregnancy and maternity. The conceptual similarity between the derogations was confirmed and made explicit by the Advocate General and, to a lesser extent, by the Court of Justice in *Kalanke*; the decisions in Case 318/86 *Commission v France*[390] and Case 222/84 *Johnston v Chief Constable of the RUC*[391] on Art 2(3) and (4) are therefore relevant for comparative purposes.

The decision in Case 318/86 *Commission v France* concerned in part a quota system used to allot only 10–30% of posts to women in the French national police and prison service, regardless of their performance in the recruitment competition. The system was therefore intended to ensure that men overwhelmingly outnumbered women in these services. The French Government sought to justify this policy within Art 2(2) on the ground that appointing an 'excessive proportion of women' would 'seriously damage the credibility' of the police corps since it would have difficulty in maintaining public order. The Court of Justice found that certain activities within the police service could

---

388 See, e.g., Morris G and Deakin, S, *Labour Law*, 1995, Chapter 6, p 589.
389 [1995] IRLR 660. For discussion see Shiek, D (1996) 25 ILJ 239.
390 [1989] 3 CMLR 663; [1988] ECR 3559.
391 [1986] ECR 1651.

properly be performed by men only, but that this could not provide justification for a system of recruitment which left it unclear whether the quotas operating for each sex actually corresponded to the specific activities for which the sex of the person in question constituted a determining factor. The lack of transparency – the fact that no objective criteria determining the quotas laid down were available – made it impossible to verify such correspondence. This part of the Court's decision, therefore, left open the possibility of allocating men and women to different specific activities and thereby excluding women from certain areas of employment on grounds which, it would appear, were in themselves non-transparent, since the assumption that women police officers would be unable to carry out effectively activities intended to maintain public order was in itself untested. In effect, one non-transparent factor – the system of recruitment – cloaked another; the first such factor was rejected, but the second accepted. The other part of the decision concerned direct discrimination within the system of promotion to the post of head warder within the French prison corps. The Court found that 'having regard to the need to provide opportunities for promotion within the corps of warders' (p 3580, para 17) justification for the discrimination could be found. This finding was made despite acceptance by the Court that sex was not a determining factor for the appointment of governors owing to the administrative nature of the job.

A similar position was taken in Case 222/84 *Johnston v Chief Constable of the RUC* in which the Court found that Art 2(2) might in principle allow a wide derogation from the principle of equal treatment since 'in a situation characterised by serious internal disturbances the carrying of firearms by policewomen [in the Royal Ulster Constabulary (RUC)] might create additional risks of their being assassinated and might therefore be contrary to the requirements of public safety' (para 16). Thus, the sex of the worker could be a 'determining factor' in making appointments to posts which necessitated carrying arms. However, the national court might only rely on this derogation if it ensured compliance with the proportionality rule. It was for the national court to determine whether proportionality had been observed and therefore the Court did not give an opinion on the matter (para 9). In contrast to this stance, the Court took a narrow view of Art 2(3), finding that it would not allow a reduction of the rights of women on the basis of a need for protection 'whose origin is socio-cultural or even political' (p 1659, para 8). It thereby created an appearance of accepting substantive equality arguments, but abandoned them in favour of focusing on special female vulnerability in relation to Art 2(2), readily accepting the assumption that women were more at risk than men and that women police officers could therefore be confined to other duties of a narrower, family-oriented nature. In a manner recalling the position taken in *Commission v France*, the Court did not appear to recognise that there was a contradiction in rejecting a potential basis for derogation on the ground that it was founded on socio-cultural considerations, but opening the way to acceptance of another which appeared to be equally open to such criticism.

The decision in *Kalanke v Freie Hansestadt Bremen* concerned a quota system which was in a sense the converse of that in question in *Commission v France* in that it ensured positive action in favour of women. In the German public services, an appointing procedure had been adopted whereby women with the same qualifications as men had to be given automatic priority in sectors in which they were under-represented. In evaluating qualifications family, work, social commitment or unpaid activity could be taken into account if relevant to the performance of the duties in question.

Under-representation was deemed to exist when women did not make up at least half the staff in the individual pay brackets in the relevant personnel group or in the function levels provided for in the organisation chart. Mr Kalanke was not approved for promotion under this procedure and sought a ruling from the *Bundesarbeitsgericht* that the quota system was incompatible with the German basic law and the German civil code. The *Bundesarbeitsgericht* considered that no such incompatibility arose since the system only favoured women where candidates of both sexes were equally qualified and, further, that the quota system was interpreted in accordance with German basic law which meant that although in principle priority in promotions should be given to women, exceptions must be made in appropriate cases. However, since the national court was uncertain whether the system was in accord with the Equal Treatment Directive, it referred to the European Court of Justice questions relating to the scope of the derogations permitted to the principle of equal treatment under the Directive.

The Court found that the quota system created direct discrimination within Art 2(1) but that it might be permissible under Art 2(4), basing this finding on the ruling from *Commission v France* cited by the Advocate General (para 18). It approved the finding of the Council in the third recital in the preamble to Recommendation 84/635/ EEC of 13 December 1984 in relation to positive action (OJ 1984 L331, p 34) that 'existing legal provisions on equal treatment ... are inadequate for the elimination of all existing inequalities unless parallel action is taken by government ... and other bodies ... to counteract the prejudicial effects on women in employment which arise from social attitudes, behaviour and structures' (para 20). It then went on to find, citing *Johnston*, that derogations from the equality principle must be narrowly construed and that national rules which guarantee women 'unconditional priority' go beyond promoting equal opportunities and overstep the limits of the exception in Art 2(4). Although the Court found that Art 2(4) permits 'national measures relating to access to employment, including promotion, which give a specific advantage to women with a view to improving their ability to compete on the labour market' (para 19), it did not find that the promotion scheme at issue fell within the exception. This conclusion was apparently founded on the distinction it drew between equality of opportunity and equality of outcome in finding that the quota system 'substitutes for equality of opportunity the result which is only to be arrived at by providing such equality of opportunity'. It therefore found that national rules of the type in question are precluded by Art 2(1) and (4).

As this ruling and the Opinion of the Advocate General make clear, the Equal Treatment Directive encapsulates a view of equality under Art 2(1) which impliedly finds inequality of outcome acceptable so long as equal treatment is accorded. Positive action aimed at reducing such inequality must be seen as an exception to the equal treatment principle: the relationship between the two can be viewed only in negative terms under Art 2(4). The Directive therefore creates a conceptual separation between positive action and the equality principle which necessitates characterising such action as direct discrimination that may be susceptible to justification only within the specified exception.[392] There is therefore, it seems, no room for an argument from principle in

---

392   See Ellis, E, 'The definition of discrimination in European Community sex equality law' (1994) 19 EL Rev 563–80, pp 567–68; Hepple, B, 'Can direct discrimination be justified?' (1994) 55 EOR 48.

favour of equality of outcome as an aspect of the equality principle encapsulated under the Directive. (It may be noted that this stance is out of accord with the UN Convention on the Elimination of All Forms of Discrimination Against Women 1979 Art 4(1), which provides that 'the adoption of temporary special measures aimed at accelerating *de facto* equality between men and women shall not be considered discrimination'.)

As the Advocate General observed, the stance of the Directive under Art 2(1) reflects a formal equality position. A formal equality model only permits unlike (and, presumptively, unfavourable) treatment if difference is identified. Nevertheless, as the Advocate General pointed out, positive action may be viewed as furthering substantive as opposed to formal equality. However, the Advocate General appeared to view substantive equality measures as confined to those which would allow individual women to compete with men on a formal equality basis. He did not appear to recognise that furtherance of substantive equality demands that the context within which such competition takes place must change. As MacKinnon has argued,[393] substantive equality recognises that the context within which women take part in employment may place them under a disadvantage owing to past discrimination, social attitudes and a gendered social situation. Positive action may be viewed not as compensating women for historical disadvantage, but as an effective means of allowing its effects to be more rapidly overcome in future. In finding that the quota system could not fall within Art 2(4), the Court and the Advocate General failed to give weight to the substantive equality argument that the social context within which women undertake employment, which is influenced by the imbalance between women and men in senior or more influential posts, tends to perpetuate inequality. Although the Court found that certain measures giving a specific advantage to women would be permissible within Art 2(4), it considered that measures used to address such an imbalance could not be seen as a means of creating a reduction in the 'actual instances of inequality which may exist in the reality of social life'. The position adopted appeared to be contradictory since it accepted that ensuring equality of 'starting points' would not lead to achieving substantive equality and yet viewed substantive equality as the ultimate objective of providing equal opportunities (para 14).

The Opinion of the Advocate General and the judgment of the Court also reveal, it is suggested, a contradiction in the application of the proportionality principle. The Court, unlike the Advocate General, did not expressly apply that principle in finding that the limits of Art 2(4) had been overstepped. However, that finding in itself involved, it is suggested, *application* of the proportionality principle: the quota system appeared to fall within the Court's interpretation of Art 2(4) but created, in the view of the Court, too great an offence to the equality principle owing to its unconditional nature. In *Johnston*, in contrast, the Court found that the national court might only rely on the derogation under Art 2(2) if it ensured compliance with the proportionality rule, but that ensuring such compliance was a matter for the national court to decide and therefore the Court did not give an opinion on the matter (para 9). However, it also found that in determining the scope of the derogation, proportionality must be observed (para 38), implying that making such a determination would not be a matter solely within the jurisdiction of the

---

393 MacKinnon, C, *Towards a Feminist Theory of the State*, 1989, Harvard University Press; 'Reflections on sex equality under law' (1991) 100 Yale LJ 1281.

national court. Comparing the findings within these two lines of case law, it is suggested that the point at which the Court of Justice accepts that the principle of proportionality allows a derogation to apply, thereby leaving the determination as to compliance with proportionality in the particular instance to the national court, is unclear; the two exercises of jurisdiction are in danger of being unclearly demarcated, laying the Court open to the charge that the principle is being used to excuse either intervention or failure to intervene in national policies in a non-transparent and subjective fashion.

If the findings in *Kalanke* and *Johnston* are inconsistent as regards the demarcation between the point at which proportionality becomes a matter for the national court and the point at which it remains a matter for the Court of Justice, it is suggested that the use made of the proportionality principle in *Kalanke* to find that the derogation under Art 2(4) did not apply is also incompatible with the view taken in *Johnston* that proportionality would be sufficiently adhered to in allowing the policy in question to fall within the Art 2(2) derogation. This may also be said, it is suggested, of the ruling in *Commission v France* in so far as aspects of the systems at issue in that case were found to fall within Art 2(2). It is contended that it would have been open to the Court in *Kalanke*, basing itself on the previous line of case law, to find that proportionality would be sufficiently observed in bringing the quota system within the scope of the derogation and, further, that the case for so doing was stronger than in either of the other two instances. This is contended taking into account the extent to which the policies at issue in *Johnston* and *Commission v France* created inequality of treatment, and the extent to which they were found to be subject to justification

The German quota system was dependent on equality of qualifications and, according to the national court, would not be rigidly adhered to. In contrast, the policy considered in Johnston operated on the same basis as reverse discrimination since it was unable to take account of the fact that the qualifications of women applicants might be superior to those of male applicants. That policy created a greater affront to the equality principle than the German system in that it aimed at creating a complete imbalance between men and women in the body of police in question, thereby ensuring inequality of treatment and of outcome, whereas under the German system it seemed probable that ensuring equality of outcome would have led eventually to equality of treatment, once the imbalance in certain sectors of the German Civil Service had been corrected. Moreover, in contrast to the position in Johnston and in relation to the post of governor under the French system, the German quota rules did not preclude applications from men for the posts in question.

The justification underpinning the French public service quota system arose from the view that disorder would be less readily contained if an imbalance between men and women in the police service was not maintained, basing this view on an untested assumption regarding the possibility that the presence of a certain number of female police officers might detrimentally affect the power of the police to control disorder. This assumption was accepted by the Commission (p 3581, para 23) and the Court in relation to specific activities, but it is suggested that the means adopted were not clearly an appropriate means of achieving the end in question or necessary to that end (the test for proportionality from *Johnston*, para 38). The same criticism may be levelled, it is submitted, at the justification advanced to defend the UK policy for the RUC, namely that reserving posts exclusively for men would ensure that persons in those posts would be subject to a lesser risk of assassination. In contrast, it is suggested that adoption of positive action in *Kalanke* would have been likely to contribute to achieving the desired outcome: as the Advocate General accepted, the imposition of quotas 'is an instrument which is certainly suitable for bringing about a quantitative increase in female employment' (para 9).

It is further suggested that if one applies the 'very logic underlying the derogations', which according to the Advocate General is aimed at 'ensuring the efficacy of the principle of equal treatment' (para 17) to the German quota system, it may be found to cause less affront to that principle than the systems at issue in the other two rulings. As argued above, the German system was in accordance with substantive equality in that it sought to achieve an outcome which would counter past disadvantage and it recognised the real and gendered situation in which women take part in employment. In contrast, it is suggested that in both *Johnston* and *Commission v France* the Court allowed the national authorities some discretion as to permitted exceptions from the equality principle on grounds which failed to further either formal or substantive equality. Thus, acceptance of positive action could have been seen merely as a means of moving more speedily towards a desired outcome and therefore, in contrast to the position taken in both the previous decisions, the offence to the equality principle could have been viewed as less significant. By this means, the Court could have recognised the distinction between the exception under Art 2(4) and the other two exceptions. Once the offence to the equality principle created by the German quota system is balanced, as indicated here, against the underlying justifications for it, it is suggested that scope can be created for finding that Art 2(4) was applicable.

However, in Case C-409/95 *Marschall v Land Nordrhein-Westfalen*[394] the Court found that a quota system allowing affirmative action was lawful on the basis that it was conditional (para 33 of the judgment). The Court said (para 29) 'even where male and female candidates are equally qualified males tend to be promoted . . . particularly because of prejudices and stereotypes concerning the role and capacities of women in working life . . .'. So a rule can fall within Art 2(4) if it counteracts the prejudicial effect on women of those prejudices (para 31). But since it is a derogation, it must be strictly construed, and so it must contain a proviso (as did the scheme at issue) allowing men to be promoted or employed if special circumstances apply (paras 32 and 33). In taking this stance, the Court appears to have adopted the course the Court left open to it (as argued above) in *Kalanke*. Similarly, in *Badek and Others v Landesanwalt bein Staatgerichtshof des Landes Hessen*[395] the Court found that the ETD does not preclude a rule applying in public service sectors where women are under-represented which gives priority to women where male and female candidates are equally qualified, so long as an objective assessment of the candidates is carried out which takes account of their specific personal situations. A scheme established in Sweden in response to under-representation of women in the Swedish University sector at Professorial level breached this principle since it did not contain a saving clause and did open the possibility of using reverse discrimination. The ECJ found that it breached the Directive in *Abrahamsson and Anderson v Fogelqvist*.[396]

---

394 [1995] IRLR 39, Judgment of 11 November 1997.
395 Case C-158/97 [2000] All ER (EC) 289.
396 Case C-407/98 [2000] IRLR 732.

Article 141 of the Treaty, as amended by the Amsterdam Treaty, replaced Art 119, which provided for equal pay for work of equal value. Article 141 makes the same provision, but para 3 empowers the Council to adopt measures to ensure the application of the principle of equal opportunities and equal treatment including (emphasis added) the equal pay principle. Thus, measures may be adopted going beyond the provision of equal pay. Paragraph 4 provides:

> . . . the principle of equal treatment shall not prevent any member state from maintaining or adopting measures providing for specific advantages in order to make it easier for the under-represented sex to pursue a vocational activity or to prevent or compensate for disadvantages in their professional careers.

This wording differs from that used in Art 2(4) of the Equal Treatment Directive since, *inter alia*, the word 'opportunities' which was central to the findings in *Kalanke* is not used: it speaks instead of making it easier for the under-represented sex to pursue a 'vocational activity' or preventing or compensating for disadvantages in professional careers. But the term 'specific advantages' is reminiscent of the terms used by the Advocates General in *Kalanke* and *Marschall*, and may imply that covert disadvantages are outside the scope of the provisions. Indeed, the paragraph could be interpreted simply as seeking to ensure equality of starting points in the manner of para 2(4) as interpreted in these two instances. But it seems to have been adopted in response to *Kalanke*, and wording which is deliberately different from that used in Art 2(4) has been used. Thus, Art 141 appears to be in accordance with the findings of the Court in *Marschall* and may even go beyond them. The Framework Directive and Race Directive restate this formula.

Thus, forms of positive action, in the sense in which that term is usually understood, are lawful in the Community so long as provisos apply. Positive action in the form of training opportunities may also be lawful within Art 2(4), but since, in referring to the areas covered in Art 1(1), Art 2(4) covers training in apparent contradistinction to access to employment and promotion, it would appear that measures going beyond allowing special training opportunities should be covered. The Advocate General mentioned positive action in the form of the development of child care structures, but this begs the question why such measures should be viewed as positive action, as opposed to being offered to all carers of children, men and women. Offering such measures only to women reinforces the perception not only that they are more expensive employees, but also that they should shoulder the main burden of responsibility in caring for children.

The main barrier to acceptance of positive action within the Equal Treatment Directive is created by its restrictive approach, which allows such action to be scrutinised only as an exception to the equality principle. Nevertheless, adoption of a broad approach to Art 2(4), similar to that taken in relation to Art 2(2) in *Johnston* and *Commission v France*, allowed the accommodation within the Directive of forms of positive action in *Marschall*. Such an approach can be justified in relation to Art 2(4), although not in relation to Art 2(2), on the basis that it provides a means of recognising the limitations of the formal equality approach.

9 Remedial action: efficacy of the individual method

Remedies

The remedial aspect of the individual method under the anti-discrimination schemes has been perceived as one of its main weaknesses.[397] The various remedies available in discrimination cases (apart from an award of equal pay) have generally been perceived as inadequate, although that position has improved.[398] The means of enforcing them and of addressing their wider implications has also been criticised.[399] The EOC finds: 'Even where discrimination is proven, remedies do little to tackle the systemic problems that give rise to the case in the first place'.[400]

As discussed above, since discrimination is a civil wrong the burden of proof is on the plaintiff to prove the case on the balance of probabilities. However, the burden of proof in either employment tribunals or in county courts is eased in the areas falling within EU competence. This covers discrimination in employment on grounds of sex[401] and sexual orientation.[402] It covers discrimination in all contexts, including employment, on grounds of race or national or ethnic origins.[403] In *Igen v Wong*[404] and in *Chamberlain and Emezie v Emokpae* and *Webster v Brunel University*[405] the Court of Appeal introduced new guidelines on the burden of proof in discrimination claims – which are applicable to all the protected grounds in the fields of EU competence. The guidelines run as follows:

1   Pursuant to s 63A of the SDA, it is for the claimant who complains of sex discrimination to prove on the balance of probabilities facts from which the tribunal could conclude, in the absence of an adequate explanation, that the respondent has committed an act of discrimination against the claimant which is unlawful by virtue of Part II or which by virtue of s 41 or s 42 of the SDA is to be treated as having been committed against the claimant. These are referred to below as 'such facts'.
2   If the claimant does not prove such facts he or she will fail.
3   It is important to bear in mind in deciding whether the claimant has proved such facts that it is unusual to find direct evidence of sex discrimination. Few employers would be prepared to admit such discrimination, even to themselves. In some cases the discrimination will not be an intention but merely based on the assumption that 'he or she would not have fitted in'.

---

397   See Lustgarten, L, *The Legal Control of Racial Discrimination*, 1980, pp 225–28; Cotterrell, R, 'The Impact of Sex Discrimination Legislation' [1981] PL 469, p 475; McColgan, op. cit., fn 1, Chapter 5, pp 280–88.
398   See Connolly, M, *Discrimination Law* (2006) at pp 396–7.
399   See Bourne and Whitmore op. cit., fn 1 at 263–4. 54. In the EOC's *Submission to the Discrimination Law Review* (2006) it urged the DLR to review current provisions for enforcement of awards where the discriminator fails to pay compensation awarded as the present system is unwieldy" (para 54).
400   EOC's Submission to the Discrimination Law Review (2006).
401   SDA s 63A and s 66A.
402   SI 2003 No 1661, regs 29 and 32.
403   RRA ss 4A and 57ZA.
404   [2005] ICR 931, para 76.
405   8 February 2004, unreported.

4   In deciding whether the claimant has proved such facts, it is important to remember that the outcome at this stage of the analysis by the tribunal will therefore usually depend on what inferences it is proper to draw from the primary facts found by the tribunal.

5   It is important to note the word 'could' in s 63A(2). At this stage the tribunal does not have to reach a definitive determination that such facts would lead it to the conclusion that there was an act of unlawful discrimination. At this stage a tribunal is looking at the primary facts before it to see what inferences of secondary fact could be drawn from them.

6   In considering what inferences or conclusions can be drawn from the primary facts, the tribunal must assume that there is no adequate explanation for those facts.

7   These inferences can include, in appropriate cases, any inferences that it is just and equitable to draw in accordance with s 74(2)(b) of the SDA from an evasive or equivocal reply to a questionnaire or any other questions that fall within s 74(2) of the SDA.

8   Likewise, the tribunal must decide whether any provision of any relevant code of practice is relevant and if so, take it into account in determining, such facts pursuant to s 56A(10) of the SDA. This means that inferences may also be drawn from any failure to comply with any relevant code of practice.

9   Where the claimant has proved facts from which conclusions could be drawn that the respondent has treated the claimant less favourably on the ground of sex, then the burden of proof moves to the respondent.

10 It is then for the respondent to prove that he did not commit, or as the case may be, is not to be treated as having committed, that act.

11 To discharge that burden it is necessary for the respondent to prove, on the balance of probabilities, that the treatment was in no sense whatsoever on the grounds of sex, since 'no discrimination whatsoever' is compatible with the Burden of Proof Directive.

12 That requires a tribunal to assess not merely whether the respondent has proved an explanation for the facts from which such inferences can be drawn, but further that it is adequate to discharge the burden of proof on the balance of probabilities that sex was not a ground for the treatment in question.

13 Since the facts necessary to prove an explanation would normally be in the possession of the respondent, a tribunal would normally expect cogent evidence to discharge that burden of proof. In particular, the tribunal will need to examine carefully explanations for failure to deal with the questionnaire procedure and/or code of practice.

To sum up, based on *Igen v Wong*, the claimant first has to prove, on the balance of probabilities, facts from which the tribunal could conclude, in the absence of an adequate explanation, that the respondent has committed an unlawful act of discrimination. At this stage, a tribunal should consider what inferences could be drawn from these facts. It must *assume* at this point that there is no adequate explanation for them. It should not take the employer's explanation into account at this stage. So it draws inferences, at this point, regardless of the explanation. Second, if the claimant has proved facts from which conclusions could be drawn that the respondent has treated the claimant less favourably, then the burden of proof moves to the respondent. Third, the respondent must prove, on the balance of probabilities, that the treatment was not on the grounds of race, sex, disability, religion or belief or sexual orientation.

Under the RRA, SDA, DDA and Sexual Orientation Regulations a tribunal can award a declaration which simply states the rights of the applicant and the respect in which the employer has breached the law. It can also award an action recommendation which will be intended to reduce the effect of the discrimination.[406] However, the EAT in *British Gas plc v Sharma*[407] held that this could not include a recommendation that the applicant be promoted to the next suitable vacancy since this would amount to positive discrimination. It has, however, been pointed out that this would merely be putting the person in the position he or she should have been in rather than giving them a special preference.[408]

The most important remedy is the award of compensation;[409] it is determined on the same basis as in other tort cases. In relation to damages the RRA and SDA originally provided that in the context of indirect discrimination 'no award of damages shall be made if the respondent proves that the requirement or condition was not applied with the intention of treating the claimant unfavourably'.[410] No compensation was therefore payable in respect of indirect discrimination unless it was shown that there was an intention to discriminate; this exclusion from the compensation scheme was much criticised[411] and appeared to contravene European law.[412] The EOC had recommended that the distinction between indirect and direct discrimination as regards compensation should be abolished. Thus, where a person had acted in an indirectly discriminatory fashion, although unmotivated by sexism, compensation would still be payable. This is desirable because there is some evidence that some employers have deliberately failed to conduct a review of working practices so as to be able to put forward a convincing

---

406 E.g. under the Sexual Orientation Regulations, reg 30(1): Where an employment tribunal finds that a complaint presented to it under regulation 28 is well-founded, the tribunal shall make such of the following as it considers just and equitable –

(a) an order declaring the rights of the complainant and the respondent in relation to the act to which the complaint relates . . .

(c) a recommendation that the respondent take within a specified period action appearing to the tribunal to be practicable for the purpose of obviating or reducing the adverse effect on the complainant of any act of discrimination or harassment to which the complaint relates.

407 [1991] ICR 19; [1991] IRLR 101.

408 See Rubenstein [1991] IRLR 99.

409 E.g. under Sexual Orientation Regulations, reg 30(1): Where an employment tribunal finds that a complaint presented to it under regulation 28 is well-founded, the tribunal shall make such of the following as it considers just and equitable . . .

(b) an order requiring the respondent to pay to the complainant compensation of an amount corresponding to any damages he could have been ordered by a county court or by a sheriff court to pay to the complainant if the complaint had fallen to be dealt with under regulation 31 (jurisdiction of county and sheriff courts);

(c) a recommendation that the respondent take within a specified period action appearing to the tribunal to be practicable for the purpose of obviating or reducing the adverse effect on the complainant of any act of discrimination or harassment to which the complaint relates. See also SDA ss 65(1)(b), 66(1); RRA ss 56(1)(b), 57(1); DDA s 17A(3).

410 SDA, s 66(3), RRA, s 57(3).

411 See, e.g., Townshend-Smith, *Sex Discrimination in Employment* 1989, p 206.

412 In *Von Colson v Land Nordrhein-Westfalen* [1984] ECR 1891 the Court held that any sanction must have a real deterrent effect. See also *Marshall (No 2)* [1993] QB 126.

argument that they did not appreciate the discriminatory affect of certain practices. When it became clear that this limitation was not in accordance with EU law, it was reformulated, although it still applies outside the areas of EU competence.[413]

Damages will be awarded for pecuniary loss and injury to feelings; the claimant as in other tort cases is under a duty to mitigate his or her loss. Previously it appeared that exemplary damages were not available but, as discussed below, it is now clear that that is not the case. Awards in the early years of the SDA and RRA tended to be low,[414] but they rose somewhat after the decision in *Noone*[415] in which a consultant who was not appointed on grounds of race was awarded £3,000 for injury to feelings. In *Alexander*, some guidance as to awarding compensation for injury to feelings was given by May LJ: '. . . awards should not be minimal because this would tend to trivialise or diminish respect for the public policy to which the Act gives effect. On the other hand . . . awards should be restrained'.

He considered that they should not be set at the same level as damages for defamation and awarded £500 for injured feelings owing to racial discrimination.[416] The legislation placed an upper limit on awards which was equivalent to that payable under the compensatory award for unfair dismissal. However, the upper limit on damages in respect of sex discrimination was challenged before the European Court of Justice in *Marshall (No 2)*.[417] The ECJ found that the award of compensation in sex discrimination cases brought against organs of the state should be set at a level which would allow the loss sustained to be made good in full. Thus, the Court found that the fixing of an upper limit of this nature was contrary to the principle underlying the Equal Treatment Directive since it was not consistent with the principle of ensuring real equality of opportunity. In response to this decision, the upper limits for compensation under the SDA and RRA were abolished.[418] It seems fairly clear that awards made at the levels mentioned prior to the *Marshall (No 2)* decision were unlikely to deter employers from discrimination or to affect deeply rooted discriminatory ideologies in institutions.

The result has been a dramatic increase in the size of awards. For example, in *Johnson v HM Prison Service and Others*,[419] an award of £28,500 was upheld on appeal. It was found that the award was not excessive in the circumstances; severe victimisation on racial grounds had occurred. It may be noted that this was at the time the highest

413 SDA, s 65(1B) provides that for cases of unintentional indirect discrimination compensation would be awarded when it was 'just and equitable' to do so *and* the tribunal is satisfied that the power to make a declaration and a recommendation are not in themselves an adequate remedy in the circumstances. The original restriction remains for county court hearings. The formula without the second restriction is used for the Sexual Orientation Regulations in relation to indirect discrimination in reg 30(2); the RRA indirect discrimination cases in the area of competence of the Race Directive use the same formula, but for cases outside that competence – cases relating to colour or nationality – the original restriction applies.
414 Gregory notes that in 40% of cases, the award was less than £200 and in only 29% did it exceed £1,000 (Gregory, op. cit., fn 1, pp 80–81).
415 [1988] ICR 813; [1988] 83 IRLR 195.
416 [1988] 1 WLR 968, CA.
417 [1993] QB 126; [1993] 3 WLR 1054; [1993] 4 All ER 586; [1993] IRLR 445, ECJ; [1994] 1 All ER 736, HL.
418 SI 1993/2798; Race Relations Remedies Act 1994.
419 (1996) *The Times*, 31 December. In a race discrimination case, *Virdi v MPS* (see (2001) the *Guardian*, 14 February) Virdi received £350,000 compensation.

UK award made in a racial harassment case. The question of exemplary damages remained problematic until recently. The significance of an award of exemplary damages – which is designed to punish the respondent – is that the award is, in addition to the compensation, designed to compensate the applicant for his or her losses. The EU Directives indicate that exemplary damages should be available since they take the stance that the remedy of compensation should both effective and dissuasive.[420] Until the case of *Kuddus v Chief Constable of Leicester Constabulary*,[421] tribunals were bound by earlier cases that had ruled that exemplary damages could not be awarded for torts (such as sex, race and disability discrimination which are statutory torts) for which exemplary damages had not been awarded prior to 1964. As none of the anti-discrimination legislation was in force in 1964, the argument was that exemplary damages could not be awarded against discriminators. In *Kuddus* the House of Lords considered that the award of exemplary damages depended on the conduct of the public authority rather than on the cause of action. It appeared that the House of Lords' judgment in *Kuddus* had opened the door to exemplary damages in discrimination claims.

It was also finally made clear that exemplary damages are available in *Julie Bower v Cheapside (SSL) Ltd (formerly Schroder Securities Ltd) ET*,[422] although they were not awarded; nevertheless, a very high award was made. The case was brought by Julie Bower and funded by the EOC. She claimed sex discrimination, equal pay and unfair dismissal against her former employer – a large City institution. It was made clear that tribunals can award compensation to an applicant in order to punish the respondent in two situations. First, this would arise where there had been oppressive, arbitrary or unconstitutional actions by servants of the government (this would include, for example, local authorities and the police). Second, it would arise where the respondent's conduct had been calculated by him to make a profit for himself which might well exceed the compensation payable to the applicant. Such an award would be made in order to drive home the message to the respondent that wrongdoing does not pay. It was found that it would extend to circumstances where the respondent commits a tort deliberately in order to obtain an advantage which would outweigh any compensatory damages likely to be obtained by the victim. It would apply where it appeared that a defendant had cynically calculated that the money to be made out of his wrongdoing would probably exceed the damages to be awarded. The award was not intended to be limited to precise mathematical calculations; it was made clear that the important and necessary element in the second category is that the defendant did direct his mind to the material advantage to be gained by committing the tort and came to the conclusion that it was worth the risk of having to compensate the plaintiff if he or she should bring an action. In this instance the tribunal ultimately decided that the bank's conduct did not quite fall into the second category since it did not appear that it was calculating to make a profit by its conduct. The eventual award was the largest award made for sex discrimination compensation of close to £1.5 million. The case exposed discriminatory City employment practices via the proceedings of the ET.

The principles set out in this decision as regards exemplary damages remain unchallenged as the respondent withdrew its appeal to the EAT. There will be many

---

420 See, e.g., 2000/78/EC, Art 17.
421 [2002] 2 AC 122.
422 2002, unreported.

other cases which will follow this one where exemplary damages are now likely to be awarded. It is argued that in accordance with EU law the dissuasive element in exemplary damages should outweigh the profit element. It is suggested that if a respondent deliberately commits a tort on the basis that advantage – not necessarily *material* advantage – might be gained, considering that the outcome, if the victim brought proceedings, would probably be neutral in monetary terms, that should be sufficient. Thus, even where it appeared that the concern in question had not expected to make a profit, or had not set out to make one, an award of exemplary damages should be made in order to dissuade concerns from tortious behaviour. This argument would also support the awards of such damages even where the concern expected to make a net *loss* in monetary terms since the perceived advantage of, for example, dismissing one person in order to replace them, might not be quantifiable in monetary terms.

It is fairly common for the defendant to fail to comply with the award[423] and, if so, the applicant must return to court in order to enforce it. If an action recommendation has not been complied with, the tribunal will award compensation, but only if compensation could have been awarded at the original hearing. Previously this was unlikely to be the case in an indirect discrimination claim, no remedy was available, except to apply to the CRE or the EOC alleging persistent discrimination. This is still the case outside the areas of EU competence.

Success rate of applications

The individual method appears to have had so far only limited success in bringing about change.[424] In an early study, Gregory noted that in 1976, only 40% of applications in respect of sex discrimination were heard and 10% were successful, while in the same year 45% of applications in respect of race discrimination were heard and 3.4% were successful.[425] The number of applications began to decline from 1976 onwards, although it rose again in the 1990s.[426] Possibly, the decline may have occurred because the success rate was so low that applicants were deterred from bringing a claim in the first place. In other words, the number of applications may have been self-limiting: only the very determined applicants would pursue cases all the way to a hearing. Of course, the decline in the rate of applications may have been partly attributable to the initial rush to attack very blatant examples of sexism and racism, which died away as employers and others began to ensure that policies enshrining such values were either abolished or made less overt.

Less than half of the applications are heard; there appears to be a strong tendency to give up a claim half way through. There may be a number of reasons why cases are not brought, why they are abandoned and why the success rate is so low. Obviously, the applicant is in a very vulnerable position; the position of the parties is usually unequal,

---

423 Leonard, A, *Judging Inequality*, 1987, Civil Liberties Trust, found that almost 50% of applicants reported delay in getting the employer to pay the compensation (pp 27–29).
424 See Hepple, B, Coussey, M and Choudhury, T, *Equality: A New Framework—The Independent Review of the Enforcement of UK Anti-Discrimination Legislation*, 2000.
425 Gregory, op. cit., fn 1, pp 87–88.
426 *The Equality Challenge*, EOC Annual Report for 1991; it showed an increase of 40% in applications in that year.

especially if an applicant is bringing the claim against his or her employer. The applicant may be afraid of being labelled a troublemaker, perhaps of being dismissed or pressured into resigning, despite the victimisation provisions of the relevant legislation, or of losing promotion prospects.[427] There may be pressure, not only on the applicant to withdraw, but also on any workmates who have consented to act as witnesses in the claim and they may withdraw their consent to act. The weakness of the remedies may have discouraged claims in the past. The extreme complexity and technicality of the substantive law may also act as a deterrent. It may do so in any event, but coupled with the lack of legal aid,[428] the task facing the applicant may appear to be overwhelming.

These two factors are exacerbated by and also contribute to the lack of experience tribunal members have of discrimination cases. The applicant may be aided by the EOC or the CRE or the DRC. In 2005, for example, the CRE dealt with over 1,000 complaints of racial discrimination. Individuals were also helped by the local racial equality organisations that the CRE funded, devoting £3.3 million to them.[429] However, the EOC and CRE have to refuse the majority of applications owing to their lack of funds.[430]

The lack of legal aid may have had an impact on the quality of decision-making in ETs, and it appears possible that employers' lawyers may have been able to manipulate the members of the tribunal because of their lack of experience in the area. Thus, a vicious circle is arguably set up. The tribunals need more experience in these cases, but do not receive it because of the factors mentioned here; when a tribunal does hear such a case, there may be flaws in its handling of it, thereby having some effect in terms of deterring future applicants and ensuring that tribunals do not gain more

427 The EOC finds (EOC, 2006, op. cit., fn 1): 'Currently, all claimants who wish to make a claim to the Employment Tribunal must pursue the proceedings in their own name. This makes some individuals feel unable to pursue a claim themselves for fear of victimisation, as has been found to be a significant problem in the EOC's general formal investigation into pregnancy discrimination. The EOC is of the view that if CEHR, trade unions, etc were permitted to take representative actions this problem would be alleviated' (para 96).

428 EOC (2006) para 55: the EOC recommends that the DLR consider extension of legal aid to employment tribunals to improve access to justice.

429 CRE Annual Report for 2005 (published 2006).

430 For example, in 2005, the CRE received 1,028 applications for assistance. This represented an increase of 85% on applications received in 2004. Almost two-thirds of applications for assistance were from men. Of the 477 applications from Black applicants, 214 came from Black Africans (up 95% on 2004), and 213 from Black Caribbean applicants (up 157% on the previous year). The number of applicants from Asians – mainly Indians (88) and Pakistanis (85) – rose from 166 (or 30% of the total) in 2004 to 196 (or 19% of the total) in 2005; however, as a proportion of the total number of applications in 2005, this represented a fall of around 38%. In 2005, 503 applicants were given full advice and assistance, while 10 were offered advice and assistance limited to conciliation (see Table 2). Three applicants (one Black African, one Black Caribbean and one White) received full CRE representation. At the end of the reporting period, two of these remained pending, awaiting a hearing, and negotiations were under way for settling the third. Just over half (52%) of the applications for assistance received in 2005 were related to employment. Most applications (53%) came from the public sector, with the largest number (158), as 2004, coming from the courts, police, prison and probation services). Three cases were settled by CRE legal affairs officers in 2005, for a total amount of £4,300. (Ibid – figures from Table 4 of the Report.)

experience.[431] In recognition of this problem the CRE has proposed that there should be a discrimination division of industrial tribunals dealing only with discrimination claims.[432] Such tribunals would be able to gather expertise in such cases and could be equipped with powers to order higher levels of compensation. It would be possible for legal aid to be made available in this specialist division even though it remained unavailable in respect of other tribunal cases. However, this proposal has not been implemented.

10 The Commission for Racial Equality; the Equal Opportunities Commission; the Disability Rights Commission; the new Commission for Equality and Human Rights

Introduction

Apart from the individual method of bringing about change, the RRA and SDA also contain an administrative method, which was included with the aim of relieving the burden on individual applicants.[433] The Disability Discrimination Commission introduced under the DDA represented a much weaker form of administrative method since the Commission had an advisory capacity only. It did not have the power to issue a non-discrimination notice in respect of discriminatory practices. However, the Disability Rights Commission Act (DRCA) 1999 brought counter-disability discrimination powers in this respect into line with those under the RRA and SDA, by creating the Disability Rights Commission (DRC) while effecting certain improvements. The Special Educational Needs and Disability Discrimination Act 2001 amended the DDA to extend the role of the DRC to discrimination in education.

The administrative method represents a more coherent and effective approach than the piecemeal method of bringing individual cases. The aim is to bring about general changes in discriminatory practices rather than waiting for an individual to take on the risk and the burden of bringing a case. Both the CRE and the EOC have three main powers. They can assist and advise claimants, they can issue Codes of Practice[434] and they can conduct formal investigations or general investigations and issue a non-discrimination notice in respect of discriminatory practices. The RRA, after amendment by the Race

---

431 For early comment on sex discrimination claims, see Leonard, *Judging Inequality*, 1987; on race claims, see Lustgarten (1986), 49 MLR 68–85. See, too, generally, Honeyball, *Sex, Employment and the Law*, Chapter 1 and McColgan, op. cit., fn 1, Chapter 5.

432 Review of the Race Relations Act 1976: Proposals for Change, Proposal 10.

433 For discussion of the role of these two bodies in their relatively early years, see Lustgarten, L, 'The CRE under attack' [1982] PL 229; Lacey, 'A change in the right direction? The CRE's consultative document' [1984] PL 186; Lustgarten (1983),133 NLJ 1057. For the EOC, see Sacks, V, 'The EOC – 10 years on' (1986) 49 MLR 560.

434 E.g. the current CRE statutory code of practice on racial equality in employment came into effect in 2006. The revised code gives employers, trade unions, recruitment agencies, professional organisations and individual workers in Britain practical guidance on how to avoid unlawful racial discrimination and harassment in employment. It outlines employers' legal responsibilities under the Race Relations Act, and recommends procedures and practices intended to ensure equal treatment. The revised code was launched in November 2005, giving employers enough time to adopt the policies and systems they would need before it came into effect on 6 April 2006.

Relations (Amendment) Act 2000 (which inserted s 71 into the 1976 Act), provided new powers for the CRE, as indicated above. It can seek to enforce specific duties on public authorities intended to create equality of opportunity for persons of different racial groups by means of a compliance notice backed up by a court order. Its general duty, extended to further functions by the Race Relations (Amendment) Act 2000, to 'eliminate unlawful racial discrimination' in public authorities was not backed up by any new powers, but is subject to the powers discussed below.

The Commissions are non-departmental public bodies established by statute. The Secretary of State for the Home Department appoints the members of the Commissions and, with the endorsement of the Prime Minister, the chairpersons. The Secretary of State is answerable to Parliament for the Commissions, and is responsible for making financial provision for their needs; received as grant-in-aid from the Home Office, the CRE received £19.100 million in 2005–6.[435] The Commissions employ permanent staff; the CRE currently has 195 staff.

Investigative and remedial powers

An investigation into apparently discriminatory practices where there may be no known victim who wants, or is prepared, to bring a claim might arise because the company or institution had effectively deterred certain people from coming forward with applications for a job. In such circumstances, if indications of discrimination became apparent – if, for example, it seemed that very few of a certain group were employed – then first a formal investigation (ss 48–50 of the RRA) would be conducted. This decision might be taken if, for example, the workforce was only 1% black although the company was in a racially mixed area in which the black group comprised about 30% of the population. It might be found that the recruiting policy was indirectly discriminatory; for example, it might largely be by word of mouth and therefore the existing workforce might tend to reproduce itself. If discriminatory practices were found, a non-discrimination notice would be issued and the CRE might apply for an injunction to enforce it under s 62(1).

However, the CRE had the use of its power to issue a non-discrimination notice curbed by the House of Lords' decision in *CRE ex p Prestige Group plc*.[436] It was found that the CRE was not entitled to investigate a named person or company unless it already had a strong reason to believe that discrimination had occurred. This meant that where such suspicion did not exist, the CRE could embark on a general investigation only, meaning that it could not subpoena evidence or issue a non-discrimination notice. Thus, the CRE and the EOC are now confined to a more reactive approach; they can only react to very blatant forms of discrimination rather than investigating the more subtle and insidious instances of discrimination, which may be the more pernicious.

---

435   The Commission received £19.100 million in grant-in-aid in the year ended 31 March 2006 (£17.361 million in 2004–5), consisting of £18.664 million for revenue expenditure and £436 thousand for capital expenditure. Net operating expenditure during the year ended 31 March 2006 amounted to £19.531 million resulting in a retained surplus in the income and expenditure account for the year of £166,000 (figures from 2005 Annual Report).

436   [1984] 1 WLR 335; [1984] ICR 473.

After this decision, the CRE had to abandon a number of investigations which it had already begun and those formal investigations that it or the EOC did undertake took much longer.[437] There has, therefore, been a tendency for subtle institutionalised racism or sexism to continue unchecked,[438] although more blatant racism, such as the phrase 'no blacks' – which used to appear in advertisements – has now disappeared.

The DRC has powers similar to those of the other two bodies, but s 3 of the DRCA appears to have been included with a view to curbing or excluding a *Prestige* interpretation of the provisions. Nevertheless, it is unclear that the wording will prevent emasculation of the provisions by the judiciary.[439] Under s 53A of the DDA, as amended by s 36 of the 2001 Act, the DRC can issue Codes of Practice giving guidance to employers, service providers, educational bodies and others as to the avoidance of discrimination on grounds of disability.

The new Commission for Equality and Human Rights

Introduction

Both the CRE and EOC, over the 40 years of their existence, have put forward various proposals for reform which would strengthen the individual method of challenging discriminatory practices by allowing it to a greater extent to work in tandem with the general, administrative method. They have also made proposals for reform which would strengthen the administrative method[440] and allow it to work more closely in harmony with the individual method. The CRE wants to try to narrow the gap between individual cases and what can be achieved by a formal investigation and has proposed that in order to do this, it should be able to join in the individual's case as a party to the action so as to draw attention to the likelihood of further discrimination occurring. Thus, the individual would receive the remedy, but the general effect of discrimination in the defendant body would be addressed by issuing a non-discrimination notice at the same time. This might be supported on the ground that if one individual brings a successful case against an employer, it is probable that discrimination in that concern is quite widespread. In particular, both the EOC and the CRE have proposed that legislation should be passed to reverse the *Prestige* decision as they consider that they need to be able to launch investigations into a named person or company even when there is no initial strong evidence of discrimination.[441] A process of reform is currently under way, but questions must be raised as to the extent that it addresses the concerns expressed over the last 40 years in the annual reports of both the EOC and CRE.

437 See Sacks, [1986] 49 MLR 560.
438 For criticism of *Prestige*, see Ellis and Appleby (1984) 100 LQR 349; [1984] PL 236.
439 For discussion, see McColgan, op. cit., fn 1, pp 307–9.
440 See the two CRE reviews of the 1976 Act, 1985 and 1991. See the EOC document, *Equal Treatment for Men and Women: Strengthening the Acts*, 1988.
441 See the reviews of the Race Relations Act by the CRE – reform proposals of 1992 and 1998 and the EOC 1988 proposals.

A single Commission

In 2003 Patricia Hewitt and Lord Falconer announced the inception of a new Commission for Equality and Human Rights (CEHR) to combat discrimination. The White Paper on the Commission was published in 2004.[442] The CEHR was set up under Part 3 Equality Act 2006. It will take responsibility for the new laws on discrimination on a range of grounds including the established ones. Thus for the first time there will be an institution which has as part of its remit the responsibility for aiding the combating of discrimination on the ground of sexual orientation and promoting non-discriminatory policies on this ground. The inception of the Commission also has of course enormous implications for human rights and equality generally. The CEHR will bring together the work of the three existing equality Commissions as well as taking on new responsibilities in relation to the Human Rights Act and new grounds of discrimination.

At present no administrative 'watchdog' body such as the EOC has the responsibility for overseeing the use of the new Sexual Orientation Regulations and supporting persons bringing actions. The CEHR will absorb the Equal Opportunities Commission and the Disability Rights Commission by the end of 2007, while it will absorb the Commission for Racial Equality in 2009. The inception of the Commission thus has significant implications for the protection of human rights and the promotion of equality. The Commission will not have the distinctive remit that the separate Commissions currently have. The CRE is concerned that there is no obligation for the CEHR to consider every application for assistance from individuals who think that they might have been discriminated against, and that race might be diluted in a single equality organisation. During 2005 racial equality councils and national ethnic minority networks made the case for a statutory race committee, similar to the disability committee that had been agreed, with powers to dispense grants for local racial equality work. The CEHR also stressed that it was vital that local expertise, built up over the past 30 years through a network of racial equality councils, should not be lost when setting up the CEHR.[443] In 2005 the CRE took the view that a new organisation should be set up, in addition to the CEHR, to continue the CRE's work building good community relations, following closure of the CRE in 2009.[444]

The government's intention is that the CEHR will build on the work of the existing equality commissions, and will 'promote equality, human rights and cohesion as core values for a fair Society'. It will inherit the Commission for Racial Equality's responsibilities for promoting good race relations between different communities. The government has stated that the CEHR's powers will 'fully match those of the existing Commissions but with increased breadth and flexibility where needed, for example in updated inquiry and investigation powers'.[445] It is intended that it will monitor and to seek to improve compliance with the Race Relations (Amendment) Act public authority duty.

442 See the White Paper *Fairness for All* (2004) Cm 6185, paras 3.35 and 3.36.
443 CRE Annual Report for 2005 (published 2006), Introduction.
444 Ibid.
445 See IOSS 2005, para 50.

Like the CRE and the EOC, the CEHR will have three main powers. It will be able to assist and advise claimants, issue Codes of Practice[446] and conduct formal investigations or general investigations and issue a non-discrimination notice in respect of discriminatory practices. In each of these instances its remit will cover all the protected grounds. So it will issue Codes of Practice covering new protected grounds under s 14.[447]

This does not however give any information as to the probable budget of the new body; for example will it be at least as great, eventually, as the budgets of the three current Commissions combined? It should be much greater since the new Commission will have to accept a range of new responsibilities.

Investigatory powers

The new Commission has two investigatory powers under the 2006 Act. It can launch 'Inquiries' and 'Investigations'. Investigations are more serious matters since they can have legal consequences. Inquiries can be conducted in the general pursuit of its duties but if during the Inquiry the Commission suspects that an unlawful act has been committed it must stop the Inquiry and launch an Investigation. Under s 20 of the 2006 Act the formal investigative power is in essentials the same as the powers previously afforded to the EOC and CRE, discussed above. The suspicion triggering the investigation can arise during the course of an Inquiry.

The CEHR power to carry out general inquiries is intended to mean that it can promote improved practice in response to particular areas of concern and can focus on specific sectors. Its power to conduct general inquiries will extend to the discrimination, equal opportunities, good relations and human rights parts of its remit. The CEHR will not have additional enforcement powers relating to human rights legislation on the (doubtful) basis that legal aid is available.[448]

---

446 E.g. the current CRE statutory Code of Practice on racial equality in employment came into effect in 2006. The revised code gives employers, trade unions, recruitment agencies, professional organisations and individual workers in Britain practical guidance on how to avoid unlawful racial discrimination and harassment in employment. It outlines employers' legal responsibilities under the Race Relations Act, and recommends procedures and practices intended to ensure equal treatment. The revised code was launched in November 2005, giving employers enough time to adopt the policies and systems they would need before it came into effect on 6 April 2006.

447 Section 14(1): The Commission may issue a code of practice in connection with a matter addressed by any of the following –

(a) the Equal Pay Act 1970 (c 41),

(b) Parts 2 to 4 and section 76A of the Sex Discrimination Act 1975 (c 65) or an order under section 76B or 76C of that Act,

(c) Parts 2 to 4 and section 71 of the Race Relations Act 1976 (c 74),

(d) Parts 2 to 4 and 5A of the Disability Discrimination Act 1995 (c 50) except for sections 28D and 28E (accessibility in schools),

(e) Part 2 of this Act,

(f) regulations under Part 3 of this Act,

(g) Parts 2 and 3 of the Employment Equality (Sexual Orientation) Regulations 2003 (SI 2003/1661), and

(h) Parts 2 and 3 of the Employment Equality (Religion or Belief) Regulations 2003 (SI 2003/1660).

448 White Paper (2004), para 4.2.

This general inquiries model has been developed to build on the model established for the existing Commissions. There are many examples of inquiries, including those given in the White Paper: the CRE's 2003 investigation into race equality in prisons, and into police forces in 2005, the DRC's 2002 investigation into the accessibility of websites for disabled people, and the EOC's 2003 inquiries into pregnancy dismissal and occupational segregation in apprenticeships. The CEHR's powers will have a much broader base, allowing it to look at issues that might affect two or more protected groups, as well as focusing on one equality strand when appropriate. In order to ensure that it can obtain sufficient information to conduct a thorough and useful investigation, the CEHR will be able as a last resort to apply to the Secretary of State for permission to compel third parties to provide certain information relevant to the inquiry.[449]

It will be able to initiate these inquiries either independently or at the request of the Secretary of State. It will have to publish terms of reference before launching an inquiry, and will publish reports at the end of the process, which could include recommendations for changes to policies, practices or legislation. General inquiries will not be able to target individual bodies. This last limitation indicates that the *Prestige* limitation still applies.

Aiding claimants

The CEHR's powers to aid individuals are similar to those of the existing Commissions, described above. The EOC takes the view that its powers should be extended further. It argues that the law would be more effective for all involved if the CEHR (and other representative groups) was able to take representative actions on behalf of individuals. It considers that CEHR should be empowered to institute proceedings in its own name in relation to discriminatory practices.[450] It has been argued, on the other hand, that that the CEHR should provide support for smaller claims as a separate service from the championing of landmark causes.[451]

Judicial review

The EOC and CRE were able to bring about general changes in discriminatory practices by seeking a direct change in domestic law in reliance on European Union law. In *Secretary of State for Employment ex p EOC*[452] it was found that the EOC can seek a declaration in judicial review proceedings to the effect that primary UK legislation is not in accord with EU equality legislation. Certain provisions of the Employment Protection (Consolidation) Act 1978 governed the right not to be unfairly dismissed, compensation for unfair dismissal and the right to statutory redundancy pay. These rights did not apply to workers who worked less than the specified number of hours

---

449 White Paper, paras 4.4–4.6.
450 EOC's Submission to the Discrimination Law Review (2006), paras 48, 49.
451 Baker, A, 'A Tale of Two Projects: Emerging Tension between Public and Private Aspects of Employment Discrimination Law' 21 *International Journal of Comparative Labour Law and Industrial Relations* 591 (2005).
452 [1994] All ER 910; [1994] ICR 317.

a week. The Equal Opportunities Commission considered that since the majority of those working for less than the specified number of hours were women, the provisions operated to the disadvantage or women and were therefore discriminatory. The EOC accordingly wrote to the Secretary of State for Employment expressing this view and arguing that since the provisions in question were indirectly discriminatory, they were in breach of EU law.

The Secretary of State replied by letter that the conditions excluding part-timers from the rights in question were justifiable and therefore not indirectly discriminatory. The EOC applied for judicial review of the Secretary of State's refusal to accept that the UK was in breach of its obligations under EC law. The application was amended to bring in an individual, Mrs Day, who worked part-time and who had been made redundant by her employers. It was found that Mrs Day's claim was a private law claim which could not be advanced against the Secretary of State, who was not her employer and was not liable to meet the claim if it was successful.

The Secretary of State further argued that the EOC had no *locus standi* to bring the proceedings. However, the House of Lords found that since the EOC had a duty under s 53(1) SDA to work for the elimination of discrimination, it was within its remit to try to secure a change in the provisions under consideration and therefore the EOC had a sufficient interest to bring the proceedings and hence *locus standi*. The Secretary of State also argued that no decision or justiciable issue susceptible of judicial review existed. However, the House of Lords found that although the letter itself was not a decision, the provisions themselves could be challenged in judicial review proceedings. In other words, the real question was whether judicial review was available for the purpose of securing a declaration that certain UK primary legislation was incompatible with EU law and, following *Secretary of State for Transport ex p Factortame*, it would appear that judicial review was so available.

As regards the substantive issue – whether the provisions in question, while admittedly discriminatory, could be justified – the House of Lords thought that in certain special circumstances an employer might be justified in differentiating between full and part-time workers to the disadvantage of the latter, but that such differentiation, employed nationwide, could not be justified. Thus the EOC, but not an individual applicant, was entitled to bring judicial review proceedings in order to secure a declaration that UK law was incompatible with EU law. Declarations were made that the conditions set out in the provisions in question were indeed incompatible with EU law.

This was a very far-reaching decision: it means that where UK legislation is incompatible with EU law, a declaration can be obtained to that effect far more rapidly than if it was necessary to wait for an individual affected to bring a case against the particular person or body who was acting within the terms of the UK legislation in question. The decision itself did not directly have an effect on race discrimination, but it opened the possibility that the CEHR will be able to challenge other provisions of UK law in relation to the various EU Directives, including in particular the Framework and Race Directives. As discussed above, the Sexual Orientation Regulations have already been challenged by way of judicial review by a group of unions. Even where challenges fail, the resulting judgments provide useful guidance to tribunals and courts on the interpretation of provisions introduced into UK law in order to implement EU law. But, as discussed in Chapter 4, the CEHR will not be able to use judicial review in relation to the human rights part of its remit, unless EU law applies.

Advisory role

The CEHR will have an advisory role in relation to individuals and pressure or community groups. Under s 13 of the 2006 Act, which covers its advisory role, it will:

(a) publish or otherwise disseminate ideas or information;
(b) undertake research;
(c) provide education or training;
(d) give advice or guidance (whether about the effect or operation of an enactment or otherwise) . . .

The CEHR will also act in an advisory capacity in relation to proposed legislation[453] under s 12. It is intended that it should give Ministers advice or make proposals on any aspect of current or proposed law that relates to any part of its remit. This would enable the CEHR, for example, to advise that a particular feature of a proposed piece of employment legislation could result in indirect discrimination against women, or would cause particular difficulties for disabled people. Its role in this respect will not be confined simply to discrimination legislation and related good practice. It is intended that it should give advice on good practice in relation to the protected groups including the practical application of any law that impacts on their equal opportunities or on the treatment of disabled people.

11 Conclusions

This chapter has charted a period of immense change in anti-discrimination provision. The provisions have both broadened and strengthened, although many areas of weakness remain. There is a lot of government rhetoric, but there has been a very clear reluctance to do anything that was not forced through by EU law. IOSS, for example, appears to be merely descriptive and rhetorical.

This chapter has noted a number of instances of delayed and reluctant implementation of EU law; it was unclear why, for example, exemplary damages were apparently unavailable in discrimination cases, until recently. The recent changes made only in the areas of EU competence, such as the importation of a more generous concept of indirect discrimination, have made the law extremely complex and difficult to use, as well as creating a number of indefensible anomalies.

The reluctance to introduce legislative change is matched by the failure to increase funding. Again there has been a lot of rhetoric, but no acceptance that legal aid should be available for discrimination cases, and compensation for unintentional indirect discrimination had to be forced into domestic legislation; obviously the RRA or SDA could have been amended at any time to effect this change. Owing to their levels of funding, both the CRE and EOC have had to refuse many applications from individuals asking for help in bringing cases; such under-funding suggests that there is at present a lack of genuine commitment in the government to ending discriminatory practices. There has also been no acceptance of anything but the most limited forms of positive action. No advantage has been taken – except in relation to elections – of the possibility of

453 See the White Paper *Fairness for All* (2004) Cm 6185, paras 3.35 and 3.36.

using positive action presented by EU law. The advantage of positive action is that it can drive change in even the most resistant areas of public and private life. It can create opportunities in itself; for example, if a person is promoted to one post via a positive action scheme that person then acquires an opportunity to apply for posts at the next level up which might not otherwise have been open to them. Women and members of ethnic minorities can provide a role model for younger colleagues in terms of demonstrating what can be achieved and in creating critical mass.

It seems reasonably clear from the discussion above that institutional change is more effective than placing the onus on individuals to seek redress once they have already been wronged. Therefore it is unfortunate that this chapter has had to focus mainly on the individual method. Where trade unions or the EOC, CRE or DRC have aided the individual applicant victories through the courts have been valuable in bringing about change. But there is still a mismatch between what the CRE, EOC and DRC (and, in future, the CEHR) can do and the use of the individual method. If an individual does win a case, indicating that discriminatory practices in a particular institution may be occurring, there is no clear means by which the relevant watchdog body can take follow-up action. The EOC has said of the 'institutional change' approach: 'It achieves that change in approach in the public sector, placing responsibility with organisations rather than individuals. We believe that this approach should form an intrinsic part of the vision for the future of equality law.' However, this argument is not suggesting that the individual method has become redundant. It is important that it exists, as a potential avenue of legal challenge, deterring employers and others from discrimination, especially if exemplary damages are sought, but also it represents the main means of forcing change in the private sector. Public authorities have little choice but to comply with initiatives such as that represented by the public authority duty to abide by gender and race principles. It is clear that private sector change has mainly come about via the impact of EU law, and even then change has been slow and reluctant.

The chapter is entitled 'anti-discrimination law', but in fact it is about a lot of law that is not based on the concept of discrimination; the concept of having to demonstrate disadvantage under a formal equality model is becoming out of date. Ironically it can disadvantage the disadvantaged groups in trying to demonstrate it, and in many circumstances demonstrating lack of equal treatment does not aid the disadvantaged person; the most obvious example is harassment, and the law has now recognised the limitation of basing anti-harassment laws on discrimination. Current discrimination laws also create a barrier to the use of affirmative action.

The EOC argued in 2006:

> Although the Sex Discrimination Act and Equal Pay Act have been vitally important, they are now 30 years old and their limitations are clear. The EOC's work – such as our recent investigation into pregnancy discrimination – shows that our existing laws with their onus for action by individuals are not working well for either individuals or employers. Employees are frequently unable to take action or suffer from doing so. The current laws were framed when the world of work was very different from today. At the present time women form nearly half the workforce and the norm is to combine a parenting role with work. Part-time working is now common. New fathers are today much more likely to be active carers of their children. Now that fathers are taking on greater childcare roles, and the gender

balance between carers is more evenly split, sex discrimination law needs to catch up with the changes to women's and men's daily lives.[454]

These social changes have meant that the concept of indirect discrimination is becoming out of date; as fathers take on caring roles it is more difficult to show that women are placed at a particular disadvantage if flexible working is denied to them or child care responsibilities ignored. Ironically, successful social change, partly driven by anti-discrimination law, is meaning that specifically anti-discrimination law is becoming redundant. This is evident in relation to disability, where the formal equality model is clearly inappropriate, and in relation to harassment and positive action, across all the protected grounds.

Forty years on from the time when the first major pieces of anti-discrimination legislation were introduced, at a time when the reach of equality law is about to become wider than ever before, it is pertinent to look towards a new concept of equality. Fredman argues:

> . . . the new concept of equality cannot function solely within the traditional structure of anti-discrimination law, which assumes that discrimination consists of individual acts of prejudice, perpetrated against individual victims, to be remedied by litigation in court to produce compensation for the victim. Societal discrimination extends well beyond the individual acts of prejudice. This means that the duty should not be confined to compensating identified victims. It should extend to the restructuring of institutions. Integral to the new vision therefore is the positive duty to promote equality, through such strategies as mainstreaming and positive action.[455]

In a similar spirit the EOC has agreed a set of principles that its Commissioners believe should underpin a new unified Single Equality Act.[456] Although developed in the context of sex discrimination law, they can be applied to all the protected grounds. These are that the legislation should be outcome-focused: the purpose of the unified Equality Act is to promote substantive equality and to eliminate systemic as well as individualised discrimination. There should be equality amongst the different strands of discrimination law affecting the different protected grounds; the anti-discrimination provisions should be harmonised up to the highest standard to give all protected persons equally comprehensive rights. The SEA should promote respect for equal dignity and worth for each individual, recognising that substantive equality is fundamental to personal development, to economic growth and to a successful, cohesive society, and set standards which are clear, intelligible and consistent. The law should place the onus for achieving equality and eliminating discrimination primarily with political, economic and social institutions: it should require them to act and facilitate efforts to do so effectively. The law should be capable of being effectively and efficiently enforced when necessary, with accessible, effective and timely means of securing redress for individuals and, where appropriate, groups of individuals. The law should also be

454 EOC's Submission to the Discrimination Law Review (2006).
455 Paragraph 2.3, *The Future of Equality in Britain*, Fredman, S, EOC Working Paper No 5, 2002.
456 EOC's Submission to the Discrimination Law Review (2006).

inclusive; it should provide opportunities for individuals and communities to engage in the process of change and participate in decisions that affect their own lives.

Anti-discrimination law is about to enter a new era from 2007 onwards with the advent of the CEHR, protection for persons on a much wider range of protected grounds and in a wider range of contexts. The Single Equality Act is in the offing. But the extent of real change will partly depend on the extent to which the principles put forward receive recognition in the new legislation, and on acceptance of the need in some contexts to move beyond anti-discrimination law.

Index

Abortion, and right to life, 80, 285
Abuse of process, 1266–67
Access to a court, under ECHR, 62–63
Access to information *see* Freedom of
    Information Act
Access to information, prior to Freedom of
    Information Act 2000, 626–28
Access to legal advice, 1208–34
    Codes C and H, formal exceptions under,
        1220–25
    consent to forgo advice, 1221–23
    debarring solicitors' representatives, 1223–25
    delaying access, 1216–19
    encouragement to defer decision, 1227–28
    formal exceptions, limitations and informal
        subversion, 1216
    harm-based exemptions, 1220–21
    implied limitations and informal subversion
        of rights, 1225–28
    improving legal advice scheme, 1228–34
    non-terrorist suspects, 1216–18
    out of station interviews, 1226
    rights of access, 1210
    silence, adverse inferences drawn from,
        1211–15
    solicitors, unavailability or delay, 1221
    subverting notification, 1226–28
    terrorist suspects, 1218–19
        disallowing private consultation, 1225
Accountability, of police, 1007–10, 1261–65,
    1303–27
    see also Evidence, exclusion of
Activism
    domestic application of Arts 10 and 11,
        695–96
    Human Rights Act, under, 278–91
Actus reus
    contempt *see Actus reus*, contempt
    offences under Official Secrets Act *see*
        Official secrecy
    offences under Terrorism Act 2000 *see*
        counter-terrorism

Actus reus, contempt
    common law, 334, 335, 337
    prejudgment test, 336
    protection of justice as continuing process,
        396
    Spycatcher litigation, 372, 373, 375
    statutory test for, 339–56
Admissibility of applications to European
    Court of Human Rights, 27–31
    complaints, 28–35
    European Commission of Human Rights,
        23, 24
Admissibility of evidence *see* exclusion of
    evidence
    torture, evidence obtained by, 1269–73,
        1455–59
Adverse inferences, drawn from silence,
    1211–15
    restriction on drawing, 1239–43
Advertising, political, 209
Advertising Standards Authority (ASA), 574,
    576, 577
Affirmative action *see* Positive discrimination
Affray, 799–800
Age of consent, homosexuals, 82, 1472
AIDS/HIV, fear of, 83, 84
Aliens, 55, 111–12
Allen, Graham, 145
Al-Qaeda, 289, 1330–34
    see also Counter-terrorism
    ATCSA (Anti-Terrorism, Crime and Security
        Act) 2001 (Part 4), 1434, 1436
    derogating orders, and, 1443
    human rights and counter-terrorist sanctions,
        1330–31
    proscription, and, 1388
    related groups, 1336
    terrorism offences, and, 1410–11
American Cyanamid case, implications for
    media freedom, 378
American Declaration of Independence, 8
Anarchy, State and Utopia (Nozick), 6

Anti-assimilationism and discrimination law,
1473–74
Anti-discrimination law, 1474–75,
1476–1576
see also Discrimination
administrative method of combatting,
1593–94
harassment *see* Harassment
individual applications, efficacy, 1586–93
success rate of applications, 1591–93
investigative and remedial powers, of
"watchdog" bodies, 1594–95
remedies, 1586–91
sources of
domestic legislation, 1481–82
EU law, 1479–81
HRA and ECHR, 1482–86
Anti-social behaviour and public protest, 480,
870–73
see also Public disorder and anti-social
behaviour, criminalising
Anti-Terrorism, Crime and Security Act
(ATCSA) 2001, 1090–97, 1421–38
see also Counter-terrorism
communications data, retention of by private
companies, 1095–97
declarations of compatibility, and, 211
detention without trial scheme (Part 4), 288,
1421–38
challenges to derogation, case law,
1430–38
derogation orders, 1424–26
introduction of Part 4, 1422–26
provisions, 1426–29
information acquisition, 1091–94
Anti-terrorism law *see* Counter-terrorism
Appeals, under FoI - time limits on applying
for information, 653
Arrest
arrestee, informing, 1157–61
reason for arrest, 56–57, 1159–61
breach of the peace, common law,
1141–43
consensual detainment, 1161–62
counter-terrorism, 1146–49
detention following arrest
time limits, 1165–67
force, use of, 1162–63
'hunch', relying on, 1155
informing promptly of, 56–57, 1159–61
powers of, 1139–63
public protest and, 676
statutory, 1149
purpose of, 1155–57
reasonable suspicion, 1149–57
arresting officer, formed by, 1154–55

level of, 1149–53
police working rules, and, 1153–54
reason for, promptly informing of, 56–57,
1159–61
valid, procedural elements, 1157–61
without warrants, 1143–46
with warrants, 1143
ASA (Advertising Standards Authority), 574,
576, 577
Assembly *see* Freedom of protest and
assembly
Association *see* Freedom of association
Australia, Security Service, 118
Autonomy of individual
bodily integrity, and, 74–80
informational autonomy 804–7
moral, 301–2, 455
sexual, 80–85

Bad faith, and exclusion of evidence, 1272,
1286
Bail
breach of the peace, 774
no absolute right to, 58
Banning orders and public protest
assemblies, 709–20
Jones & Lloyd v DPP, 711–20
marches, 707–9
BBC *see* British Broadcasting
Corporation
BBFC (British Board of Film Classification),
551–71
BCC (Broadcasting Complaints Commission),
839
Bentham, Jeremy, 7, 8, 146
Bias
independent and impartial tribunal, need for,
63, 1090
racial, 1509
Bill of Rights debate, 140–52, 156, 298
adoption of Bills of Rights worldwide, 115
American Bill of Rights, 167
central arguments, 145–52
Conservative Governments, and, 116, 298
'controversy' thesis, 149
domestic judiciary, readiness to use rights-
based reasoning, 151–52
ECHR, possible models for protection of,
152–56
"modern British Bill of Rights", replacing
HRA?, 156, 298
morality, and, 461–62
New Zealand Bill of Rights, 170, 173
notwithstanding clause, 147, 154, 170
political history, of Bill of Rights debate,
pre-HRA, 116, 141–45

Conservative Party, 116, 142–43
  Labour position, 119, 144–45, 150
  Liberals and Liberal Democrats, 119,
    143–44
  UK, and, 115, 140–151
  unelected judges, ceding power to, 147–51
Binding over, 750, 751
  see also Breach of the peace
Blasphemy law
  domestic approaches to, 491–97
  margin of appreciation doctrine, and, 38
  Strasbourg stance on, 487–91
  Visions of Ecstasy video, 490, 491
BNP (British National Party), 499
Bodily integrity, 74–80
  parental rights, 75
  physical punishment, 74–75
  privacy rights, 76
  sexual autonomy, 80–85
  state agents, intrusion by, 75
Border controls, 1121–22
Breach of confidence, 876–910, 915–20
  see also Confidentiality
  official secrecy, and, 616–17
  personal information, protection, 877, 878
Breach of "privacy", 911–15
Breach of the peace, 751, 752–80
  see also Binding over
  arrest, powers of, 1141–43
  bail conditions, 774
  contra bono mores power, 751–52
  Human Rights Act, impact of, 774–80
  immediacy, 754–71
  provoking, 771–74
Bringing Rights Home (Green Paper), 291
British Board of Film Classification (BBFC),
    551–71
British Broadcasting Corporation (BBC)
  see also Television
  Ofcom regime, and, 520–30
  privacy, and, 841–43
  Programme Content standards, 521
  public authority status, 233, 234, 235, 530
  Royal Charter, 519, 521
British National Party (BNP), 499
Broadcasting Complaints Commission (BCC),
    839
Broadcasting regulation, 509–50, 839–46
  see also Films, Internet, Television
  Communications Act 2003, 512–50, 839–46
    Ofcom regime, and BBC, 520–30, 841–43
    statutory regime, 519–20
    Television Without Frontiers Directive,
      and, 513
  content regulation, offence avoidance,
    515–19

basic regulatory regime, 518–19
  Human Rights Act and the Pro-Life Alliance
    decision, 268, 276, 280, 530–45
  market-based 'deregulation', in UK, 512–15
  OFCOM, and see OFCOM
  political advertising, 209
  Pro-Life Alliance decision, 268, 276, 280,
    530–45
  public authority/private body distinction,
    233–35, 530–33
  satellite broadcasting, EU-based, 545–49
  successful challenges to current regime,
    544–45
Buggery, 81–82, 83
Bugging devices, 1056–63
Burden of proof
  anti-terrorism legislation, and, 1352–54, 1443
  'foreign torture evidence', 1459
  official secrecy, and, 605–6
  reversed, and presumption of innocence,
    1347–54
  sex discrimination, indirect, in, 1500
Butler Report (1998), and CPS decision
    making, 1322

Canadian Charter of Rights and Freedoms
    1982, 147, 261, 262, 320, 1266
Canadian Security Intelligence Service, 1018
CAP (British Code of Advertising, Sales
    Promotion and Direct Marketing) Code,
    576, 577
Capital punishment see Death penalty
Care homes, as public authorities, 223–27,
    228
Cash for Honours inquiry 2007, 915
Causation
  evidence, exclusion of, (PACE), 1275–76
CEHR see Commission for Equality and
    Human Rights
Censorship
  British Board of Film Classification (BBFC),
    552–53
  films, 262, 550–71
  pornography, 305, 456–61
Charges see Criminal charges
Charter '88 Group, 140
Children and young persons
  child care responsibilities, and sex
    discrimination, 1489–91
  detention of minors, 54, 58
  ECHR court jurisdiction
    case law, 861–65
    effect of Human Rights Act, 858–60
    pre-HRA inherent jurisdiction, 855–58
  juveniles, in criminal proceedings, 854–55
  pornographic material, protection from, 548

private hearings, statutory restrictions on
    identification, 853
reporting restrictions, 392–93
wardship proceedings, 391
Church of England
    Parochial Church Councils, and, 220
    protection of religious organisations, and,
        211–12, 846–47
Civil actions
    police malpractice, and, 1303–10
    state surveillance, and, 1077–78
Civil liberties, pre-HRA, 124–27
    administrative law, outside
        case law, 125–26
    and civil and political rights, 5
    civil rights distinguished from, 14–16
    democratic process, as guardian of, 116–22
    ECHR, influence prior to HRA 1998,
        134–37
    government secrecy and executive
        discretion, 117–18
    judicial review, pre-HRA, and, 127–33
    opposition complicity in curtailing, 118–20
    protection, methods of
        democratic process, 116–22
        rules and judicial interpretation, 122–34
    residual, 122–24
    rules and judicial interpretation, 122–34
Civil rights
    civil liberties distinguished from, 14–16
    Convention meaning, 61
    family rights as, 1341
CJPOA see Criminal Justice and Public Order
        Act 1994
Closed circuit television, 1068
CLS (Critical Legal Studies), 9–10
Codes of Practice see PACE codes and
        Freedom of Information
Commission for Equality and Human Rights,
        293–95, 1595–1600
    advisory role, 1600
    aiding claimants, 1598
    establishment, 293
    judicial review, and, 1598–99
    powers, 294
        investigatory, 1597–98
    as single Commission, 1596–97
Commission for Racial Equality, 1507,
        1577–78, 1593–95
Commission of Human Rights see European
        Commission of Human Rights
Committee of Ministers
    complaints, 32
    European Commission, and, 21, 22
    Protocol 14 reforms, and, 35
    Reports to, 32

role, 25, 26
    supervision of Court judgments by, 34–35
Common law
    breach of the peace, powers of arrest, and,
        1141–43
    contempt, pre -1981 domestic provision,
        334–37
    ECHR, domestic impact on, pre-HRA, 137
    Human Rights Act 1998 (s 2), and, 198
    Human Rights Act 1998, impact of, 252–56
        see also Private life, right to respect for
    powers of entry and search, 1000
Communications, interception of, 1032–52
    in accordance with law, 1043–44
    Commissioner, role, 1039–40
    court proceedings, raising ECHR issues in,
        1047–52
    Human Rights Act, impact of, 1042–52
    lawful interception, without warrant,
        1037–38
    legitimate aims, and necessity in democratic
        society, 1044–46
    obligations of oversight bodies, 1047
    parliamentary oversight, 1041
    primary rights, interference with, 1042
    Regulation of Investigatory Powers Act 2000
        (Part I), 1034–41
    tribunal system, reform, 1040–41
    unauthorised interceptions, 1038–39
    use of intercepted material, 1038
    warrants for, 1034–37, 1047
Communitarians, 9
Community, concept of, 728
Compensation
    liberty and security of person, right to, 59
    public authorities, remedies against, 242–47
Competing rights, 13, 943–81
Complaints and security and intelligence
        services, powers, 1022–24
Complaints, police (against), 1310–21
    background, 1310–13
    Complaints against the Police (Consultation
        Paper), 1313
    current scheme, 1310–16
    disciplinary action, probability of, 1316–18
    HRA, and, 1318–21
    Police Reform Act 2002, 1313–16
Complaints to European Court of Human
        Rights
    fast track procedure, 28
    individual applications, 26–27
        procedure, 27–35
    inter-State applications, 26
Complaints to Ombudsman, 628
Computer misuse and personal information,
        923–24

Confessions
  evidence, exclusion of, 1278–87
  non-confession evidence, 1287–1300
Confidentiality, 876–910, 915–20
  see also Breach of confidence
  breach of privacy, 911–15
  confidential official information, emanating
      from other state, 601
  discarding need for confidential relationship,
      896–902
  Human Rights Act, and, 902–15
  surveillance, and, 1064–65
Conservative Party
  Bill of Rights debate, and, 116, 142–43, 298
Contempt of court, 316–450
  see also Contempt of Court Act 1981;
      Prejudicing proceedings
  actus reus see Actus reus, contempt
  administration of justice, and media freedom,
      322–28
  European Convention on Human Rights
      balance between Arts 6 and 10, 328–30
      domestic impact, and HRA, 330–34
  'ignorance' defence, 361
  impediment or prejudice to legal
      proceedings, 339–57
  journalistic material, seizure of, 440–50
      HRA implications, 445–48
      Official Secrets Act 1989, 444–45
      PACE, 440–42
      requirements to provide information,
          442–44
  jury deliberations, disclosure, 398–408
  justice, protection as continuing process,
      394–98
  media, and see Media: contempt, liability for
  mens rea, 372, 373, 374, 380, 394
  neutralising model, 319
  penal legislation, and, freedom from
      retrospective effect, 67
  Phillimore Committee, 337
  prior restraints, restricting reports of court
      proceedings, 383–94
  protection of sources, 408–50
      Contempt of Court Act 1981, 410–18
      Norwich Pharmacol jurisdiction, 410
      post-HRA jurisprudence, 419–39
  protective model, and, 319
  public affairs/public interest, 357–61
  publicity, types, 345
  real risk of prejudice, 368
  'rights of others' exception, 333, 334
  scandalising the court, 394, 396
  serious prejudice/impediment to justice,
      publication creating substantial risk,
      339–56

Human Rights Act, 350–52, 354–56
  Strasbourg stance, 321–30
  strict liability, and publications prejudicing
      proceedings, 319–62, 381
      common law, pre -1981, 334–37
      Strasbourg stance, on, 321–30
  sub judice period, 335, 338
Contempt of Court Act 1981
  see also Contempt
  'active' proceedings, 338–39
  common law, and, 380–81
  evaluation of, 381–82
  Human Rights Act 1998, and, 330, 331
  'ignorance' defence (s 3), 361
  public affairs/public interest, 357–61
  publications falling within Section 1,
      337–38
  rebalancing of, 361–62
  reform of s 5, 359–61
  Section 5 (public affairs discussion
      prejudicing legal proceedings)
      interpretation of, 357–61
      reform, 359–61
  serious prejudice/impediment to justice,
      publication creating substantial risk,
      339–56
      HRA reform, case law, 354–56
      key factors, in determining, 341–50
      post-HRA era, use of s 2(2), 350–52
      threshold created by s 2(2) test,
          352–54
  sources, protection of (s 10), 410–18
Contra bono mores power
  freedom of protest and assembly, 751–52
  statutory indecency, 480
Control orders, 1438–68
  derogating, 1441–42
  Human Rights Act, impact of, 1460–62
  non-derogating, 1442
      court supervision, 1445–51
      incompatibility with Art 5, 1451–54
  scheme, 1440–43
Convention rights, 45–50
  see also European Convention on Human
      Rights (ECHR)
  anti-terrorism law, and, domestic
      interpretation of, 1338–39
  compatibility of new Bills with, 206–11
  destruction of (Art 17), 112
  discrimination, prohibition of (Art 14),
      108–9
      see also Anti-discrimination law;
          Discrimination
  fair hearing, right to (Art 6) see Fair trials
  family life, right to respect for, 87–89
      see also Private life, right to respect for

freedom of assembly (Art 11) *see* Freedom
    of protest and assembly
freedom of association (Art 11) *see* Freedom
    of protest and assembly
freedom of expression (Art 10) *see*
    Freedom of expression
freedom of thought, conscience and religion
    (Art 9), 91
groups, claiming, 18–19
inhuman or degrading treatment, freedom
    from (Art 3), 45–50
liberty and security of person, right to (Art
    5), 51–59
life, right to (Art 2), 39–45
marriage and founding of families, right to
    (Art 12), 102–4
privacy, right to respect for (Art 8) *see*
    Private life, right to respect for
retrospective penal legislation, freedom
    from (Art 7), 66–69
Corporal punishment
    bodily integrity, interference with, 74–75
Correspondence
    prisoners', 90–91
Council of Europe
    Committee of Ministers, and, 25
    European Convention drafted by, 17
    Parliamentary Assembly, 20
Counter-terrorism
    see also Terrorism; Terrorism Act 2000;
        Terrorist suspects
    arrest, powers of, 1146–49
    Criminal Justice (Terrorism and
        Conspiracy) Act 1998, 1366–68
    human rights and counter-terrorist
        sanctions, 1329–31
    pre-2000 temporary counter-terrorism
        legislation, 1365–66
    reactive to proactive strategy, 1331–33
    stop and search, 1117–22
    symbolic effect of counter-terrorism
        provision, 1333–34
    Terrorism Acts, 1363–1421
Court of Human Rights *see* European Court
    of Human Rights
CPS (Crown Prosecution Service)
    police, prosecution of, 1322
CRA (Constitutional Reform Act) 2005
    judiciary, reform, 257
Crime control
    due process, and, 1101–2
    evidence, exclusion of, 1301–3
    'reliability' principle, 1267
Criminal cases and the ECHR
    cross-examination, 66
    innocence, presumption of, 64–65

'regulatory' offences, 61
time, facilities and legal representation,
    65–66
Criminal charge, Convention meaning of, 60,
    1339–42
Criminal Justice and Public Order Act 1994
    (CJPOA)
    Human Rights Act, impact on, 743–50
    trespass
    s 69 directions, and, 741–43
Criminal proceedings
    see also Criminal charge, Due process
    juveniles in, reporting restrictions,
        854–55
    surveillance, and, 1075–77
    web-based pornography, and, 582–87
Critical Legal Studies (CLS), 9–10
Cross-examination, and right to a fair hearing
    under ECHR, 66
    see also Fair trials/hearings
Crown Prosecution Service (CPS)
    police, prosecution of, 1322
Custody *see* Detention

Damages
    Court of Human Rights on, 242, 243,
        246
        non-pecuniary damage, 245
    Human Rights Act, under, 242–47
    police malpractice, and, 1305–6
    "privacy" breach - sanctions, 982–83
Data protection
    Computer Misuse Act 1990, 923–24
    control over personal information, 921–22,
        927–30
    data controllers, obligations, 929–30
    Data Protection Act 1998 (DPA), 926–37
        background/context, 921–24
        Human Rights Act 1998, and, 936–37
        manually held personal information prior
            to, 924–26
        media, use against, 933–35
        regime created by, 922–23
    Data Protection Commissioner, 935–36
    Data Protection Principles, 928–29
    data subjects, 922
    data users, 922, 923
    manually held personal information, prior
        to DPA 1998, 924–26
    media, impact on, 930–35
        conditions, 931–32
        DPA, use against media, 933–35
        enforcement, 935–36
        HRA and DPA, 936–37
        media exemptions, 932–33
        obligations of data controllers, 929–30

personal data, defined, 927
  regime created by DPA 1984, 922–33
Data Protection Act 1998 (DPA), 926–29
  see also Data protection
  background/context, 921–24
  Human Rights Act 1998, and, 936–37
  manually held personal information prior
      to, 924–26
  media, use against, 933–35
  regime created by, 922–23
Data Protection Registry, 923
D (Defence) notice system, 624
Deception
  evidence, exclusion, and, 1295–99
Declarations of incompatibility
  under Human Rights Act 1998 (s 4),
      199–204, 214
Defamation
  malicious falsehood, 873–74
Deference
  Human Rights Act, under, 265–91
  media regulation, and, 849–51
Democracy
  civil liberties, democratic process as
      guardian of, 116–22
  justice, non-arbitrary nature, and, 317
  margin of appreciation, and, 38
  "necessity in democratic society", 72, 94,
      1044–46
  origins of rights, and, 7
  participation in, and freedom of expression,
      303–5
  peaceful assemblies, and, 666
Demonstrations in vicinity of Parliament,
      730–33
  see also Public protest
Department of Constitutional Affairs
  Human Rights Division, 215
  Review of the Implementation of the Human
      Rights Act, 162
Deportation
  detention of deportees, 55
  terrorist suspects, 1358–61
Derogating control orders, 1442–43
  detention without trial (anti-terrorism), and,
      1424–26
  role of court in making, 1444
Derogations, 1424–26
Detention
  aliens, of, 55
  conditions of, 75–76
  consensual detainment, 1161–62
  conviction, following, 53
  deportees, of, 55
  discretionary life sentences, and, 58
  following arrest under ECHR, 54

  to fulfil an obligation, 53
  indefinite, without trial
      anti-terrorism legislation, 1362–63
  minors, 54, 58
  non-criminals, for protection of society, 55
  policy custody, in see Police custody,
      detention in
  position of detainees, 48
  review of, 58–59
Dicey, AV, on civil liberties, 122–23, 124, 158
  freedom of expression, and, 313
  Human Rights Act 1998, and, 160
Direct action and domestic application of Arts
      10 and 11, 696–98
Direct discrimination, 1526–38
  disability discrimination, 1536–37
  racial discrimination, 1535–36
  sex discrimination, 1527–34
      gender reassignment, 1534
      marital status, 1534
      maternity/child care grounds, 1529–34
      proving direct discrimination, 1528
  sexual orientation, 1537–38
Directorate of Judicial Offices for England and
      Wales (DJO), 258
Disability discrimination
  direct, 1536–37
  Disability Discrimination Commission, 1593
  disability-related, 1547–50
  duty to make reasonable adjustment
      employment, 1550–53
      goods and services provision, 1553–54
  education, 1554–55
  field of application, 1512–13
  indirect, 1547–55
  medical model, 1511–12
Disciplinary action
  criminal law, and, 60
  police malpractice, and, 1310–21
      HRA, and, 1318–21
      probability of action following complaint,
          1316–18
  stop and search powers, and, 1139
Discrimination
  see also Anti-discrimination law; Disability
      discrimination; Equal pay; Positive
      discrimination; Racial discrimination;
      Sex discrimination; Sexual orientation
      discrimination
  direct, 1526–38
      maternity/child care grounds, 1529–34
      proving, 1528
      racial discrimination, 1535–36
      sex discrimination, 1527–34
  disability see Disability discrimination
  harassment as, 1556–58

indirect
  disability discrimination, 1547–55
  racial discrimination, 1544–47
  sex discrimination, 1538–44
  sexual orientation, 1555–56
lawful, 1567–72
positive action *see* Positive discrimination
prohibition of, as primary right, 108–9
racial *see* Racial discrimination
religious, 507
remedies for, 1588–90
sex *see* Sex discrimination
sexual orientation *see* Sexual orientation:
    discrimination on grounds of
stop and search powers, and, 1124–26
suicide, and, 78
terrorism, and, 1363
unjustifiable, 109
victimisation, 1563–67
DJO (Directorate of Judicial Offices for
    England and Wales), 258
Double effect doctrine, and murder, 77
DPA (Data Protection Act) 1998 *see* Data
    Protection Act 1998 (DPA)
Drittwirkung phenomenon, 29
Due process, 51–56, 1083–90, 1339–54; *see
    also* fair trials/hearings
  crime control, and, 1101–2
  evidence, exclusion of, 1301–3
Dworkin, Ronald
  nature of rights, 5, 7, 11, 12, 13, 14,
    15
  on pornography, 455, 457

Ecclesiastical courts, and blasphemous libel,
    484
ECHR (European Convention of Human
    Rights) *see* European Convention on
    Human Rights (ECHR)
Education discrimination
  see also Racial discrimination; Sex
    discrimination
  disability, 1554–55
  sexual orientation, 1523–24
Effective remedies, right to, 106–8
Egalitarianism, and utilitarianism, 7
Emergencies
  see also Derogations
  anti-terrorist laws, 1370
  arrest, promptly informing of reason for,
    56–57
  margin of appreciation doctrine, and, 36, 37
  restriction of rights and freedoms, 110–11
Employment discrimination, 1553–54
  see also Equal pay
  disability, 1550–53

sex discrimination, 1495–96
sexual orientation
Employment Equality (Sexual Orientation)
    Regulations 2003, 1522–23
unfair dismissal, pre-2003 provision,
    1521–22
Enforcement of FoI legislation
  applying for information, and time limits,
    651–53
  appeals, 653
  basic mechanism, 651–53
Entrapment/deception
  evidence, exclusion of, 1295–99
Equal Opportunities Commission, 1507,
    1593–1600
Equal pay
  Bilka test, 1498, 1503, 1549
  comparator, choice of, 1494–95
  Equal Pay Amendment Regulations, 174
  market forces argument, 1498, 1499
  'material factor' defence, 1497–1502
  'same employment', 1495–96
  sex discrimination, 1493–1503
  term by term approach, 1496
Equalities Review Interim Report, 1493
Equality
  see also Discrimination
  anti-discrimination laws, and, 1469–75
  formal and substantive, sex discrimination,
    1488–89
  phases, of, 1471–73
Equal treatment *see* Discrimination; Equal Pay
Equal Treatment Directive, and Sex
    Discrimination Act, 1515
EU (European Union)
  see also Council of Europe; ECHR
    (European Commission of Human
    Rights); Social Charter 1961
  discrimination law, 1479–81
  Fundamental Rights Agency, 1481
  influence of law, 138–40
  satellite television, 545–49
  sexual orientation discrimination, provisions
    against, 1515
  women, affirmative action favouring,
    1579–85
European Commission of Human Rights
  admissibility, role in, 23, 24
  European Court compared, 24–25
    see also European Court of Human Rights
  origins of, 21–22
  previous role, 22–23
European Convention for the Prevention of
    Torture and Inhuman and Degrading
    Treatment or Punishment 1987, 45,
    1360

European Convention on Human Rights
    (ECHR), 17–114
  see also Human Rights Act 1998 (HRA)
  anti-discrimination law, 1482–86
  Bill of Rights debate, 140
  binding nature of rights, 215–16
  breach of rights, as 'constitutional tort', 238
  children and young persons, reporting
      restrictions
    case law, 861–65
    effect of Human Rights Act, 858–60
    pre-HRA inherent jurisdiction, 855–58
  choice of rights, under HRA, 165–66
  communications, interception, and, 1047–52
  compatibility of new Bills with, 206–11
  complaints, individual applications, 27
  contempt, publications prejudicing
      proceedings
    balance between Arts 6 and 10, 328–30
    domestic impact of Convention, on,
        330–34
  criticisms of, 167–68
  declarations as to compatibility of new Bills
      with, 206–11
  declarations of incompatibility, 199–204, 214
  deficiencies and limitations, 166–69
  destruction of Convention rights, 112
  domestic impact
    HRA, and, 330–34
    prior to HRA, 136–37
  enforcement machinery, 21
  evaluation, 112–14
  freedom of expression and information,
      625–26
    see also Freedom of information
    domestic application of Art 10, 690–701
  freedom of protest and assembly
    domestic application of Art 11, 690–701
    public protest, right to make, 681–83
  international level, impact at, 159
  margin of appreciation doctrine, 36–39
  Member States, change in laws and
      practices, 113
  origins of, 17
  possible models for protection of, 152–56
  primary rights, additional guarantees, 106–9
  Protocols, 19, 104–6
    Art 2, 105
    Art 3, 105–6
    Protocol 14 reforms, 35
  public authorities
    and binding effect of rights against,
        215–16
    invoking rights against, 235–37
  Public Order Act 1986 (ss 12–14A), and,
      724–26
  public protest, right to make
    freedom of assembly (Art 11), 681–83
    protest as expression (Art 10), 684–85
  security and intelligence services, powers,
      1025–30
  statements of compatibility, 207
  stop and search powers
    Article 13, and, 1134
    Article 5, and, 1131–34
  substantive rights and freedoms *see*
      Convention rights
  supervisory procedure, 20–39
  and torture, freedom from (Art 3) *see*
      Torture
European Court of Human Rights, 23–25
  abortion, and, 80
  blasphemy, stance on, 487–91
  case load, 35
  Chambers, 25, 28, 33
  complaints *see* Complaints
  Court Registry, 28
  damages awards, 242, 243, 246
    non-pecuniary damage, 245
  explicit expression, stance on, 462
  friendly settlements, 18, 24
    examination of complaint applications,
        31–32
  impact of jurisprudence, 19–20
  individual applications *see* Individual
      applications
  judgments, 32–34
    supervision by Committee of Ministers,
        34–35
  legal status of jurisprudence, 192–96
  margin of appreciation doctrine, 36–39, 113,
      332
  membership terms, 24
  obscene publications and protection of
      morals, stance on, 467–68, 475
  origins of, 21
  personal information, protection, stance on,
      813–24
  persuasive/consensus-based approach, 18
  purpose of Convention, 278
  restitutio in integrum principle, 245
  speech and privacy claims, balancing (HRA),
      stance on, 943–50
  supervisory procedure of Convention, 23–25
  on 'victims', stance, 235, 236
European Social Charter 1961, 19
Euthanasia, and right to life, 76–77
Evidence
  confessions, excluding, 1278–87
  exclusion *see* Evidence, exclusion
  identification, 1288
  torture, obtained by, 1454–62

admissibility of, 1455–59
burden of proof, 1459–60
Evidence, exclusion of
abuse of process, 1266–67
causation, 1275–76
common law discretion, 1300
common law jurisdictions, other, 1265–66
confessions, 1278–87
conflicting values, 1262–65
crime control, 1301–3
domestic stance, 1267–69
due process, and, 1301–3
entrapment/deception, 1295–99
'fairness' test, 1277–99
identification evidence, 1288
Latif test, 1266
mentally handicapped defendants, 1300–1301
non-confession evidence, 1287–1300
'oppression' test (PACE), 1269–73
Police and Criminal Evidence Act (PACE)
    1984
  causation, 1275–76
  'fairness' test, 1277–99
  'oppression' test, 1269–73
  'reliability' test, 1267, 1269, 1273–75
police malpractice, and, 1262–1303
'reliability' test (PACE), 1267, 1269,
    1273–75
search products, and, 1138–39
Exhaustion of remedies, complaints under
    ECHR, 30–31
Expulsion *see* Deportation

Fair trials/hearings
access to a court, 62–63
Convention rights, 59–66
criminal justice system, proceedings outside
  closed material, procedure for use,
      1343–45
  field of application of Art 6, 1339–42
  'public' hearing, 1345–46
  special advocate, use, 1343–45
  third party, material obtained by Art 3
      treatment, 1346–47
cross-examination, 66
field of application of Art 6, 60–61,
    1339–42
freedom of expression, and, 362
hearing within reasonable time, 63–64
implied rights under Art 6, 64
independent and impartial tribunal, 63, 323
innocence, presumption of in criminal cases,
    64–65
  see also Burden of proof
meaning of 'fair hearing' under Art 6,
    64

police malpractice, and, 1259
public hearings, 383
reporting restrictions, and, 852
time, facilities and legal representation, in
    criminal cases under Art 6, 65–66
Family life, right to respect for
  see also Private life, right to respect for
concept of family life, 87–89
home, respect for, 89–90
Fast track procedure under s 10 HRA
amendments to legislation, 205
complaints, 28
declarations of incompatibility, 202
Fawcett Society, 260
Feminism, and pornography, 456–61
Films, 550–87
age restrictions, 553–60
British Board of Film Classification
    (BBFC), 551–71
censorship, 262, 550–71
classification and censorship systems,
    552–53
Human Rights Act, impact, 566–70
pornographic *see* Pornography
theatrical release, 560–62
Videoworks, statutory regulation, 562–66
Flexible working, 1489–91
Force, use of
arrest, powers of, 1162–63
life, right to, 43–44
stop and search, 1128–29
Forced labour, freedom from, 50–51
Foreign and Commonwealth Office, Legal
    Advisers Department, 24
Forfeiture, obscene material, 474–75
Franks Committee, official secrecy, 595
Freedom of assembly *see* Freedom of protest
    and assembly
Freedom of association
  see also Freedom of protest and assembly
anti-terrorism legislation, and, 1354–58
Convention rights, and, 97–102
ILO Committee, 37
non-union associations, 97–98
trade unions, 98–102
Freedom of expression, 92–96, 299–315
anti-terrorism law, and, 1354–58
democracy, participation in, 303–5
domestic application of Art 10, 690–701
  activism, 695–96
  direct action, 696–98
  minimalism, 690–95
  positive obligations, 699–700
  procedural problems, 700–701
efficacy of speech, 318
fair trial rights, and, 362

free speech protection, practical implications, 311–15
information, receiving/imparting, 93
justifications for, 300–311
   recognition in Strasbourg and UK jurisprudence, 309–11
market freedom, and, 308–9
moral autonomy, and, 301–2
neutrality of content, 307
primary right, scope of, 92–94
protest as expression, 684–85
restrictions on
   blasphemy see Blasphemy
   broadcasting see Broadcasting regulation
   contempt, and restraining freedom of expression see Contempt
   content and form-based interferences, 306–8
   defamation see Defamation
   exceptions under Art 10, 94–96
   market freedom and creative freedom, 308–9
   offensiveness see Offensive material
   US model, 308, 309
self-fulfilment, and, 305–6
speech and privacy claims, balancing (HRA)
   developing jurisprudence on clashing rights, 943–50
   domestic approaches, 950–81
   examples of outcomes, 970–81
   factors weighing on either side of balance, 968–70
   free speech theories, and privacy, 939–43
   mutually supporting guarantees, Articles 8 and 10 as, 960–62
   parallel analysis or 'ultimate balancing act', 958–59
   underlying rationales of Articles, values, 965–68
truth, and, 302–3
utilitarianism, and, 8
Freedom of information
see also Official secrecy
applying for information, and time limits, 650–53
   enforcement mechanism, 651–53
Commissioner's decision, ministerial veto, 654–54
Freedom of Information Act 2000, 630–57
   exemptions under, 634–50
   fundamentals of freedom of information, 631–50
   proposals to restrict use of, 655–57
   rights granted by, 634
   rights prior to, 626–28

scope of, 632–33
government secrecy and executive discretion, 117
principles, and ECHR Art 10, 625–26
publication schemes, 654
Public Records Acts, 629
Freedom of protest and assembly, 659–802
see also Freedom of association
affray, 799–800
anti-terrorism law, and, 1354–58
assemblies
   banning orders, 709–20
   Convention rights, and, 96–97
banning orders
   assemblies, 709–20
   Jones & Lloyd v DPP, 711–20
   marches, 707–9
binding over, 750, 751
breach of the peace see Breach of the peace
Convention rights, and, 96–102
demonstrations in vicinity of Parliament, 730–33
direct action, 666, 667
domestic application of Art 11
   activism, 695–96
   direct action, 696–98
   minimalism, 690–95
   positive obligations, 699–700
   procedural problems, 700–701
forms of protest, 666–67
highway obstruction see Highway obstruction
justifications for interferences with primary rights, 685–89
legal responses to protest, 668–80
meetings and marches, legal regulation see Marches; Meetings
physical obstruction or interference, 667
private premises, meetings on, 675–77
public disorder see Public disorder and anti-social behaviour, criminalising
public order law
   development of, 668–72
   nature, of, 672–75
public protest, rights to make under ECHR, 680–90
   freedom of assembly (Art 11), 681–83
   protest as expression (Art 10), 684–85
rights to assemble and to protest, 678–701
riots, 667–68, 799–800
traditional legal recognition of freedom of assembly, 678–80
trespass see Trespass
underlying justifications, 663–68
violent disorder, 799–800
Freedom of religion see Religion

Gagging injunctions and writs, 335, 619
Gender reassignment *see* Transsexuals
Glorification of terrorism, 1415–21
Griffiths, John, 259
Guarantees of:
    fair trials, 60
    mutually supporting, Arts 8 and 10 as,
        960–62
Gypsies, and respect for home, 89–90

Hague, William, 143
Harassment
    civil liability, and, 870–71
    discrimination, as, 1556–58
    free standing claims, on protected grounds,
        1558–63
    new privacy tort, and, 870–73
        offences and civil liability, 870–71
    press intrusion, 871
        press intrusion, use against, 871
    Protection from Harassment Act 1997
        publication of information causing
            distress, 871–72
        similar offences, 872
    publication of information causing distress,
        as, 871–72
    public disorder and anti-social behaviour,
        criminalising, 787–95
Hate speech *see* Racial hatred, incitement to;
    Religious hatred
Hattersley, Roy, 144, 145
Hearings
    see also Fair trials/hearings
    fair *see* Fair trials
    promptness, 57–58
    within reasonable time, 63–64
Her Majesty's pleasure, detention of young
    offenders at, 58
Highway obstruction, 734–37
    Human Rights Act, impact, on, 735–37
    interpretation prior to Human Rights Act,
        734–35
Hohfield, Wesley,14–16
Holocaust, 306
Home, respect for, 89–90
Home Office Affairs Committee, police
    prosecution, 1321
Home Office circulars (PACE), 1108–9
Homosexuals *see* Sexual orientation
Horizontal effect
    see also Private life, right to respect for
    direct, 255
    Human Rights Act 1998, 250–56, 911–15
    indirect, 251–56, 911–15
    private life, right to respect for, 815,
        824–28

House of Lords
    civil liberties, and, protection of, 120–21
Housing, sexual orientation discrimination in,
    190, 1524–26
Howard, Michael, 119, 120
HRA (Human Rights Act) 1998 *see* Human
    Rights Act 1998 (HRA)
HRU (Human Rights Unit), 215
Human Rights Act 1998 (HRA), 157–298,
    1062
    activism, under, 278–91
    anti-discrimination law, and, 1482–86
    blasphemy, domestic approach, 491–97
    breach of the peace, and, 774–80
    choice of rights, under, 165–69
    common law, and s 2, 198
    common law, and, 251–56, 911–15
    communications, interception, and,
        1042–52
    contempt
        ECHR, and, 330–34
        post-HRA jurisprudence on, 419–39
    control orders, and, 1448–54, 1460–62
    Criminal Justice and Public Order Act
        1994, impact on, 743–50
    data protection, and, 936–37
    discretionary areas of judgment, deference
        and proportionality, 265–91
    domestic precedents, ECHR conflict with,
        197
    European Convention on Human Rights
        see also European Convention of Human
            Rights
        contempt, and, 330–34
        deficiencies and limitations of, 166–69
        influence prior to HRA 1998, 134–37
    film regulation, and, 566–70
    flaws in post-HRA judicial reasoning,
        429–39
    horizontal effect, 250–56, 911–15
    incompatibility, declarations of (s 4),
        199–204, 214
    interpretative obligation (section 3), 169,
        171–91
        compatibility issues, 185, 186
        current approach, 183–86
        effect of s 2, 191–99
        resource allocation issues, 185
        social policy issues, 185
        subject-matter of provision, 185
        techniques adopted, 174–83
    journalistic material, seizure, and,
        445–48
    judges, role under, 192–96
    jurisprudence, legal status, and role of
        judges, 192–96

media
    protecting, 212–13
    regulation, and, 846–51
minimalist approach, 196, 269–78
new Bills, declarations as to compatibility
    with Convention rights, 206–11
Northern Ireland Assembly, and, 213
obscene publications, and protection of
    morals, and, 475–76
offensive material, and protection of morals
    exceptions
    indecency, 480–84
    obscene publications, 475–76
personal information, 813–30, 911–15
    'horizontal effect' of Art 8, 824–28
    Strasbourg jurisprudence, 813–24, 829–30
police malpractice, and
    complaints and disciplinary action,
        1318–21
    prosecution of police, 1322
    tortious liability, 1306–9
powers of entry and search, and, 1007–10
prejudicing proceedings, and
    serious prejudice/impediment to justice,
        publication creating substantial risk,
        350–52, 354–56
primary and secondary legislation, meaning,
    199
private bodies, 249–50
Pro-Life Alliance decision, and broadcasting
    regulation, 268, 276, 280, 530–45
public authorities, 215–49
    Convention rights against, invoking,
        235–37
    private bodies, and, 216–18
Public Order Act 1986 (ss 12–14A), and
    ECHR jurisprudence, 724–26
    HRA mechanisms, 720–24
    radical approach, 726–30
racial hatred, incitement to, and, 500–501
religious organisations, protecting, 211–12
remedial process (s 10), 204–6
reporting restrictions, and, 865–66
Review of the Implementation of the
    Human Rights Act (Department of
    Constitutional Affairs), 162
rights protected under, 165–66
riots, violent disorder and affray, 800
Scottish Parliament, and, 213
scrutiny of workings of, 291–95
security and intelligence services, powers,
    and, 1024–32
sexual orientation, discrimination on grounds
    of, and, 1518–21
single tribunal under RIPA, and, 1086–90
speech and privacy claims, balancing, under

developing jurisprudence on clashing
    rights, 943–50
domestic approaches, 950–81
examples of outcomes, 970–81
factors weighing on either side of balance,
    968–70
free speech theories, and privacy,
    939–43
mutually supporting guarantees,
    Articles 8 and 10 as, 960–62
parallel analysis or 'ultimate balancing
    act', 958–59
underlying rationales of Articles, values,
    965–68
surveillance by state, and see Surveillance
Welsh Assembly, and, 213
Human Rights Commission see European
    Commission of Human Rights
Human Rights Convention see European
    Convention on Human Rights (ECHR)
Human Rights Unit (HRU), 215
Hunt, Murray, 292
Hurd, Douglas, 595–96
Hutton Report, and BBC Charter, 521

ICRA (Internet Content Rating Association),
    581
Identification evidence, 1288
ILO (International Labour Organisation)
    Committee on Freedom of Association, 37
Immunities, as rights, 15
    see also Public interest immunity
Impartiality
    see also Bias
    defined, 321
    independent and impartial tribunal, need for,
        63
Incompatibility, declarations of
    Human Rights Act 1998 (s 4), 199–204,
        214
Indecency
    common law offences, 481–84
    meaning of, 476–77
    sexual behaviour, 82–83
    statutory, 476
    HRA and protection of morals exception,
        480–84
Independent and impartial tribunal, fair trials,
    63, 323
    see also Fair trials/hearings
Independent Police Complaints Commission
    (IPCC), 1314, 1315, 1317, 1318
Indirect discrimination, 1490, 1538–56
    definition, statutory, 1538–43
    disability discrimination, 1547–55
    racial discrimination, 1544–47

sex discrimination, 1538–44
    work/life balance, 1543–44
sexual orientation, 1555–56
Individual applications to ECHR
    see also Complaints
    admissibility of, determination, 28–35
    Court, judgment of, 19, 32–34
    examination of, and friendly settlement,
        31–32
    increase in numbers of, 20
    pre-complaints procedure, 27–28
    procedure, 27–35
    registration of, 28
Informational autonomy
    moral, 301–2, 455
    sexual, 80–85
Inhuman or degrading treatment, freedom from,
        45–50, 1174–81
    see also Torture
    anti-terrorism legislation, and Article 3
        treatment
        deporting suspects facing potential
            Art 3 treatment abroad, 1358–61
        indefinite detention without trial, 1362–63
        third party material, obtained by, 1346–47
    bodily integrity, interference with, 75
    Convention rights, and, 45–50
    'degrading treatment', 47
    exceptions, lack of, 46
    Soering principle, 49, 50
    State responsibility for, 46
    violation of Art 3, 48, 49
Injunctions
    ex parte and inter partes, 618
    gagging, 619
    interim, 374, 375, 983–90
    media, impact on, 212–13
    privacy sanctions, 983–90
Innocence, presumption of see Presumption of
        innocence
Integrity see Bodily integrity and autonomy
Intelligence and Security Committee, 1011,
        1014–15
Intelligence services see Security and
        intelligence services
Interception of communications, 1032–52
    see also Telephone tapping
    in accordance with law, 1043–44
    Commissioner, role, 1039–40
    court proceedings, raising ECHR issues in,
        1047–52
    Human Rights Act, impact of, 1042–52
    lawful interception, without warrant,
        1037–38
    legitimate aims, and necessity in democratic
        society, 1044–46

obligations of oversight bodies, 1047
parliamentary oversight, 1041
primary rights, interference with, 1042
Regulation of Investigatory Powers Act 2000
    (Part I), 1034–41
tribunal system, reform, 1040–41
unauthorised interceptions, 1038–39
use of intercepted material, 1038
warrants for, 1034–37, 1047
International Covenant on Civil and Political
        Rights
    Article 3, 1359
    European Convention, and, 17, 21
    religious hatred, 501
International Convenant on Economic, Social
        and Cultural Rights, 19
International Labour Organisation see ILO
    (International Labour Organisation)
Internet, 571–87
    criminal law, applying to web-based material,
        582–87
    regulation, 574–78
        voluntary, 578–82
Internet Content Rating Association (ICRA),
        581
Internet Service Provider Associations (ISPAs),
        578
Interpretation see Statutory interpretation
Inter-State applications, complaints, 26
Interviews see Police questioning
IPCC (Independent Police Complaints
        Commission), 1314, 1315, 1317, 1318
IRA (Irish Republican Army), 1366
Iraq war, Britain's entry into, 672
Islam
    blasphemy, 487
    racial hatred, 499
    religious hatred, 506, 508
ISPAs (Internet Service Provider Associations),
        578

JAC (Judicial Appointments Commission)
    judiciary, reform, 257, 258
JACO (Judicial Appointments and Conduct
        Ombudsman), 258
JCHR (Joint Parliamentary Committee on
        Human Rights), 292, 293
    see also Joint Committee on Human Rights
Jenkins, Roy, 144
Joint Committee on Human Rights
    Article 3, stance on, 1359
    Protocol 14 reforms, 35
    Protocols, ratification, 19
    public authorities, stance on, 232
    terrorist offences, stance on, 1419
Journalistic material, seizure of, 440–50

HRA implications, and, 445–48
Official Secrets Act 1989, 444–45
PACE (Police and Criminal Evidence Act)
    1984, 440–42
Production Orders, terrorism legislation,
    442–44
Judges
    see also Judiciary
    judcial supremacism controversy, 260
    male, 260
    power of, 190
    role, 192–96
        under HRA, 265–91
    unelected, 147–51
Judgments of European Court of Human
    Rights
    Committee of Ministers, supervision by,
        34–35
    discretionary areas of judgment, HRA, and,
        265–91
    individual applications, complaints, 32–34
Judicial Appointments and Conduct
    Ombudsman (JACO), 258
Judicial Appointments Commission (JAC)
    judiciary, reform, 257, 258
Judicial review
    civil liberties, protection, and, 127–33
    Commission for Equality and Human Rights,
        and, 1598–99
    POAC decisions, 1399–1405
    stop and search, and, 1134–37
    surveillance, and, 1079–80
Judiciary
    see also Judges; Statutory
        interpretation
    Canada, lessons from, 261–63
    composition and independence, reform,
        257–61
    free speech, threats to, stance, 303–4
    Human Rights Act, stance in adjudicating,
        256–91
    interpretative obligation, 191
    margin of appreciation, domestic approaches
        to, 263–65
    rights-based reasoning, readiness to use,
        151–52
    sex discrimination, and, 261
    unelected judges, and Bill of Rights debate,
        147–51
Juries, disclosure of deliberations, 398–408
Jurisdiction
    Norwich Pharmacol, 410
    reporting restrictions, children, 855–65
    single tribunal, and, 1081–82

Kurdistan Workers' Party, 1336, 1402

Labour Party
    Bill of Rights debate, and, 119, 144–45, 150
Lashkar e Tayabah (LeT), 1402
Law Commission
    on blasphemous and seditious libel, 486
    on privacy invasions, 809
Laws, Sir John, 129–32, 267
Legal advice
    access to *see* Access to legal advice
    improving scheme, 1228–34
    relying on, in remaining silent, 1243–54
Legal positivism, 8, 10
Legal privilege, material covered by, 1002–3
Legal representation
    see also Access to legal advice; Solicitors
Legislation Against Terrorism, *see* terrorism
Libel
    see also Defamation; Seditious libel
    blasphemous and seditious, 484–87
    writ for, 335
Liberals and Liberal Democrats
    Bill of Rights debate, and, 119, 143–44
Liberty and security of person, right to, 51–59
    see also Arrest
    arrest, promptly informing reason for, 56–57
    compensation, and, 59
    detention *see* Detention; Police custody,
        detention in
    judicial hearing, promptness, 57–58
    safeguards, 55–56
Liberty (pressure group), 168, 232
Life, right to, 39–45
    abortion, 80, 285
    'absolutely necessary' test, 44, 45
    euthanasia, 76–77
    exceptions, 43–45
    scope of right, 40–43
    suicide, 76, 78–79, 80
Locke, John, 6

MacPherson Report
    police malpractice, 1316
    public interest, 641
    racial discrimination, 1510
    stop and search, 1112
Make Poverty History (pressure group), 209
Malicious falsehood, 873–74
Manifesto for Human Rights (manifesto), 168
Marches, 701–33
    see also Meetings and marches, legal
        regulation
    assemblies, 709–20
    banning orders, 707–9
    conditions, imposing on, 704–7
        Public Order Act 1986, 704–7
    Human Rights Act, impact, and, 720–30

processions, advance notice of, 702–4
triggers for imposing conditions on, 704
Margin of appreciation doctrine, 36–39, 262
  arrest, promptly informing of reason for,
      and, 56
  blasphemy, and, 491
  common standards, notion, 38
  domestic approaches to, 263–65
  emergencies, 36, 37
  European Convention on Human Rights, and,
      36–39, 113
  European Court of Human Rights, and, 36,
      113, 332
  judiciary, stance on, 257
  minimalist approach under HRA, 270
  penal legislation, freedom from retrospective
      effect, and, 68
  proportionality, and, 69
  proscription orders, and, 548
  protests, and, 686
  Protocols to Convention, and, 104
  sexual autonomy, and, 82, 84
Marital status, sex discrimination, 1534
Market freedom and freedom of expression,
    308–9
Marriage and founding of families, right to
    (Art 12), 102–4
  transsexuals, 87
Marxism, 9
'Material factor' defence, equal pay, 1497–1502
Media
  see also Broadcasting; Journalists;
      Prejudicing proceedings; Press;
      Reporting restrictions
  American Cyanamid case, implications, 378
  contempt, liability for, 319
      see also Contempt; Contempt of Court Act
      1981; Prejudicing proceedings
  court order, frustrating, 368–69
  data protection, impact on, 930–35
      conditions, 931–32
      enforcement, 935–36
      HRA and DPA, 936–37
      legislation, 933–35
      media exemptions, 932–33
  freedom of, and administration of justice,
      322–28
      'balancing of competing interests', 327
  protecting, 212–13
  regulation, and HRA
      deference, 849–51
      ECHR rights, impact, 847–49
      PCC, marginalisation, 846–47
Meetings
  see also Assemblies
  conditions, imposed on, 704–7

Human Rights Act, impact of, 720–30
legal regulation, 701–33
offences, proscription-related, 1392–96
on private premises, 675–77
processions, advance notice, 702–4
triggers for imposing conditions on, 704
Mens rea
  see also Burden of proof
  burden of proof, reversed
      presumption of innocence, 1347
  contempt, 372, 373, 374, 380, 394
  official secrecy, 603, 604, 614
  public disorder and anti-social behaviour,
      relevance, 787
Mentally handicapped defendants
  evidence, exclusion of, 1300–1301
  medical evidence, 55
MI5, MI6, 118
  see also Security and Intelligence services
  functions, 1013
Mill, John Stuart, 8, 302
Minimalism in judicial reasoning
  domestic application of Arts 10 and 11,
      690–95
  Human Rights Act, under, 269–78
Minority rights, 7
Moral autonomy, and freedom of expression,
    301–2
Moral rights, legal rights distinguished, 10–11
Morals, protection of
  statutory indecency, 480–84
  statutory obscenity, 475–76

National security
  see also Counter-terrorism; Security and
      intelligence services
  detention of non-criminals for protection of
      society, 55
  margin of appreciation, and, 37
Natural law, 10–11
Natural rights, 8
New Charter (pamphlet), 142
Newspapers see Press
New Zealand
  Bill of Rights, 170, 173
  rule of construction, under, 174
Nilsen, Denis, 162
9/11 Attacks see September 11 attacks
Non Departmental Public Body (NDPB), 257
Northern Ireland
  Art 5, applicability to, 57
  Assembly, and Human Rights Act, 213
  British Irish Agreement reached in the multi-
      party negotiations 1998, 1366, 1368
  Continuity IRA, 1366
  homosexual activity, in, 81–82

Omagh bombing 1998, 1366
Orange Parades in, 663
Real IRA, 1366
Norwich Pharmacol jurisdiction
   sources, protection of, 410
Notes for Guidance (PACE), 1108
Notwithstanding clause, Bill of Rights debate,
   147, 154, 170
Nozick, Robert, 6
Nuremberg trials, and natural law, 10

Obscene publications
   common law offence, 481–84
   forfeiture proceedings, 474–75
   freedom of expression, restrictions/exceptions
      under Art 10, 94–95, 464–68
   mailing of, 479
   public good defence, 472–74
   statutory obscenity, 468–72
      'deprave and corrupt' test, 470–73, 526
      HRA and protection of morals exception,
         464–68, 475–76
OFCOM, 519–30, 831, 840–49
   BBC, and, 520–30, 840–43
   Broadcasting Code, 521, 524–30
   privacy regime, 840–44
   Code, 844–46
Offensive material
   broadcasting regulation, 522–24
   forfeiture proceedings, for obscence material,
      474–75
   indecency
      common law offence, 481–84
      meaning of, 476–77
      statutory, 476, 480–84
   legal responses to explicit expression,
      461–84
   obscene publications, 468–72
      common law offence, 481–84
      'deprave and corrupt' test, 470–73, 526
   pornography, 453–61
      conservative position, 454
      liberal position, 455–56
      pro-censorship feminist position, 456–61
   public displays of, 476
   public good defence, 472–74
   specific offences, variety of, 477–80
   statutory obscenity
      HRA and protection of morals exception,
         475–76
   Strasbourg stance on, 463–67
      applying Strasbourg jurisprudence under
         HRA, 467–68
Official secrecy, 590–658, 637
   see also Freedom of information; Public
      interest immunity

breach of confidence, 616–17
Code of Practice on Access to Government
   Information, 645
confidential information, emanating from
   other State, 601
exemptions from FoI, statutory
   categories, 637
   class, 639–41
   expiry of certain, 649–50
   harm-based, 647–50
   public interest test, not subject to, 647–48
Franks Committee, 595
harm-based exemptions under FoI
   not subject to public interest test, 647–48
   subject to public interest test, 648–49
harm test under FoI, 603, 605, 610, 613, 637
'interests of State', 594
international relations, 601
journalistic material, seizure, 444–45
Katharine Gunn affair 2003, 615–16
MacPherson Report, 641
Official Secrets Act 1911, 592–95
Official Secrets Act 1989, 595–616
   criminal liability for disclosing
      information, 596–605
   defences, 605–12
   journalistic material, seizure, 444–45
   Shayler litigation, 597, 606–16
public interest under FoI, 638
   class exemptions not subject to, 638–41,
      639–41
   class exemptions subject to, 641–47
   definitions, 638
   harm-based exemptions not subject to,
      647–48
   harm-based exemptions subject to, 648–49
Scott Report, 593
Shayler litigation, 597, 606–16
Spycatcher litigation, 618–24
   see also Spycatcher litigation
   case law subsequent to, 623–24
telephone tapping, 594–95
Ombudsman *see* Parliamentary Commissioner
   for Administration
On Liberty (J S Mill), 302
Open justice principle, 316–30
   prohibiting reporting of information, 390–94
   public hearings, 383
Oppression test
   evidence, exclusion of, 1269–73

PACE (Police and Criminal Evidence Act) 1984
   see Police and Criminal Evidence Act
      1984 (PACE)
Paramountcy principle, reporting restrictions,
   and, 855–61

Parental Leave Directive, and sex discrimination, 1491
Parental rights, 1491–93
Parliament, demonstrations in vicinity of, 730–33
Parliamentary sovereignty *see* Sovereignty of Parliament
Parochial church councils *see* PCCs (parochial church councils)
Partiya Karkeren Kurdistan (PKK), 1402, 1403, 1404
Part-time workers, discrimination against, 1490
Party Election Broadcasts (PEBs), 533, 539, 544
Party Political Broadcasts (PPBs), 533
PCCs (parochial church councils)
  marginalisation, 846–47
  as public authorities, 220, 225
Peace, breach of *see* Breach of the peace
PEBs (Party Election Broadcasts), 533, 539, 544
Penal legislation, freedom from retrospective effect, 66–69
  general restriction on rights and freedoms, 68–69
People's Mujahideen Organisation (PMOI), Iran, 1336, 1402, 1403
Persistent vegetative state, 76–77
Personal files, security and intelligence services, 1020–21
Personal information, 809–992
  see also Broadcasting regulation; Data protection; Private life, right to respect for
  definition of 'private' information, 879–86
  Human Rights Act, protection under, 813–30
    'horizontal effect' of Art 8, 252–56, 815, 824–28
  intimate, 928
  new privacy doctrine, liability for disclosing information under, 876–920
  privacy of, 73–74, 805–7, 809–30, 876–920
  public domain, 886–95
    information already known to some, 887–91
    information obtained in public places, 891–94
  sensitive, 928
  Strasbourg jurisprudence, 813–24
    judicial responses to, 829–30
PHA (Protection from Harassment Act) 1997
  civil liability, 870–71
  press intrusion, 871
  publication of information causing distress, 871–72
  similar offences, 872
Phillimore Committee, on contempt, 337

Physical punishment
  bodily integrity, interference with, 74–75
PKK (Partiya Karkeren Kurdistan), 1402, 1403, 1404
PMOI (People's Mujahideen Organisation), 1336, 1402, 1403
POAC (Proscribed Organisations Appeal Commission), 1340, 1397–99, 1400–1
  appeals from, 1399–1405
  appeals to, 1397–99
  judicial review of decisions, 1399–1405
  procedure, and Arts 6 and 13, 1400–1401
  Special Immigration Appeals Commission, and, 1397
Police
  see also Arrest; Detention; Police and Criminal Evidence Act 1984 (PACE); Police custody, detention in; Police malpractice, redress for; Police questioning; Powers of entry and search; Searches; Seizure
  accountability, 1007–10, 1261–65, 1303–7
  consensual detainment, 1161–62
  entry, powers of *see* Powers of entry and search
  obstructing or assaulting in course of duty, 1109–11
Police and Criminal Evidence Act 1984 (PACE)
  arrest, powers of (without warrant), 1143–46
  Codes of Practice, 1106–8
    access to legal advice, exceptions (Codes C and H), 1220–25
    breaches (Code B), 1007–8
    breaches (Code C), 1285
    police questioning (Codes C and H), 1188–90
    procedural safeguards (Code B), 1005–7
  context of, 1103–5
  democratic process, and, 119
  detention after arrest, time limits, 1165–67
  entry without warrant, 996–97
  evidence, exclusion of, 1267–1300
    causation, 1275–76
    'fairness' test, 1277–99
    'oppression' test, 1269–73
    'reliability' test, 1267, 1269, 1273–75
  Home Office circulars, 1108–9
  interviewing scheme, 1186–1254, 1279
    see also Police interviews
  journalistic material, seizure of, 440–42
  Notes for Guidance, 1108
  Royal Commission on Criminal Procedure, 1103
  rules structure, 1105–9
  stop and search powers, 1113–14
Police custody, detention in, 1163–84

authorised by police alone, 1169–71
conditions of detention, 1174–81
custody officer, role, 1171–72
judicial authorisation, 1167–69
law, procedure prescribed by, 1163–64
samples, swabs and impressions, taken
    during, 1183–84
searches of detained persons
    intimate, 1181–82
    strip, 1182
Terrorism Act 2000, 1167
time limits on, following arrest, 1165–67
treatment, 1171–84
vulnerable groups, 1172–74
Police interviews, 1192–1208
    see also Police questioning
inside and outside police station,
    1197–1201
non-interviews, 1193–97
outside station, 1226
techniques, 1205–8
varying levels of protection for exchanges,
    1201–2
Police malpractice, 1255–1327
background, 1310–13
complaints against police
    current scheme, 1310–16
    disciplinary action, probability, 1316–18
    HRA, and, 1318–21
    Police Reform Act 2002, 1313–16
court duties under s 6 HRA, and,
    1259–62
Crown Prosecution Service decision
    making, 1322
evidence, exclusion of *see* Evidence,
    exclusion
Human Rights Act
    Article 6 requirements, 1259
    impact of, 1322
    trial remedies, 1259–62
miscarriage of justice cases, 1315
prosecution of police, 1321–22
Select Committee on Home Affairs, Report,
    1312
tortious remedies
    civil actions, value of, 1309–10
    HRA and tortious liability, 1306–9
    quantum of damages, 1305–6
    tort actions, 1303–5
Police questioning, 1186–1254
    see also Police interviews
notification of rights, 1192
PACE Codes, 1188–90
recording methods, 1203–8
    audio recording, 1203–4
    video recording, 1204–5

terrorist suspects, 1191–92
vulnerable groups, 1190–91
Political liberalism, 5
The Politics of the Judiciary (Griffiths), 259
Pornography
censorship, 305, 456–61
conservative position, 454
hardcore, 460, 463, 479, 524
    satellite television, 546
law, and, 453–61
liberal position on, 455–56
pro-censorship feminist position, 456–61
violent, 459
Ports and border controls, 1121–22
Positive discrimination
forms, 1573–74
    recognition in national law, 1574–75
public bodies, duties, 1576–79
theoretical basis, 1572–73
training and outreach policies, 1575–76
women, affirmative action favouring (EU
    law), 1579–85
Positive obligations
domestic application of Arts 8, 10 and 11,
    70–71, 699–700, 814–28
Powers of entry and search, 995–1010
Article 8, reliance on, 1008–10
common law, 1000
entry without warrant, 996–98
freedom assembly, and, 676–77
Human Rights Act, impact of, 1007–10
Police Act 1997, 998
search warrants, 998–1000
Terrorism Act 2000, 997
Preference maximisation, 7
Preference utilitarianism, 148
Pregnancy and parental rights, 1491–93, 1532
Prejudgment test, contempt, 336
Prejudicing proceedings
    see also Contempt
'active' proceedings, 338–39
administration of justice, and media
    freedom, 322–28
common law, 363–81
    Contempt of Court Act 1981, and,
        380–81
    imminence, 365–67
    intention to prejudice administration of
        justice, 363–65
    pre-1981, 334–37
Contempt of Court Act 1981, 337–62
    common law, and, 380–81
    'ignorance' defence, 361
    prejudice or impediment, 357–61
    public affairs, discussion of (s 5),
        357–61

rebalancing, 361–62
serious prejudice/impediment to justice,
    publication creating substantial risk,
    339–56
European Convention on Human Rights
    Articles 6 and 10, 328–30
    domestic impact, 330–34
impediment or prejudice to legal proceedings
    and s 5, 357–61
intentional prejudice, 363–83
intention and imminence, 365–67
postponing reporting to avoid risk of
    prejudice, 384–89
public affairs/public interest, 357–61
Punch, critique of, 375–79
real risk of prejudice, 368
    frustrating action against media body,
        369–80
    methods of fulfilling test, 367–69
Spycatcher litigation, 369–75
    abolition of doctrine?, 379–80
Strasbourg stance, 321–30
strict liability, 319–62, 381
substantial risk of serious prejudice or
    impediment to justice, publications
    creating, 339–56
    HRA reform, case law, 354–56
    key factors, 341–50
    post-HRA era, 350–52
    threshold created by s 2(2) test, 352–54
Press
    freedom of, 319
    Press Complaints Commission *see* Press
        Complaints Commission
    Press Council, 832
    Protection from Harassment Act 1997, and,
        871
    self-regulation, 832–39
Press Commission Code
    sources, protection of, and, 409
Press Complaints Commission, 831
    Code of Practice
        policing, 833–38
        privacy provisions, interpretation, 836–37
        provisions, 834–36
        sanctions, 837–38
    marginalisation of, 846–47
    status as public authority, 212, 836, 848–51
Pressure groups, and declarations of
    compatibility under HRA, 209
Presumption of innocence
    burden of proof
        post-HRA approach, terrorism offences,
            1352–54
        reversed, case law, 605–6, 1347–51
    fair hearing, right to, 64–65

Primary rights under ECHR
    see also European Convention on Human
        Rights (ECHR); Human Rights Act
        1998 (HRA)
    additional guarantees, 106–8
    interference with
        communications, interception, and, 1042
        public protest, and, 685–89
Prior restraints
    see also Censorship; Injunctions
    court reports, restricting, 383–94
Prisoners' rights
    see also Detention
    compensation, 59
    correspondence, 90–91
    discretionary life sentences, and review of
        detention, 58
    prison service, and, 218
    Secretary of State, role in sentencing, 177
Privacy *see* Horizontal effect; Private life, right
    to respect for
Private bodies, 249–50
    public authorities, and, 216–18
Private life, right to respect for, 69–91
    see also Surveillance; Personal information;
        Powers of entry and search; Security
        and intelligence services
    bodily integrity and autonomy, 74–80
    breach of privacy, 911–15
    confidentiality obligation *see* Confidentiality
    defamation and malicious falsehood, 873–74
    disclosure of personal information *see*
        Personal information
    domestic protection, 807–8, 824–30,
        863–64
    entry and search powers, reliance on Art 8,
        1008–10
    exceptions and justification under Art 8, 72
    harassment *see* Harassment
    mutually supporting guarantees, Arts 8 and
        10 as, 960–62
    new "privacy" tort
        civil and criminal liability, invasion of
            privacy, 866–70, 911–15
        harassment, alarm or distress and anti-
            social behaviour, 863, 870–73
        proposals for, 867–70
    personal autonomy, 76
    private life, concept of respect for, under Art
        8, 73–87
    public interest defence, 915–20
    reasoning process, parallel analysis,
        structure, 962–81
    remedies, 981–90
        damages and accounts of profit, 982–83
        interim injunctions, 983–90

reporting restrictions *see* Reporting
    restrictions
sexual autonomy, 80–85
sexual identity, 85–87
speech and privacy claims, balancing
    (HRA), 937–81
    developing jurisprudence on clashing
        rights, 943–50
    domestic approaches, 950–81
    examples of outcomes, 970–81
    factors weighing on either side of
        balance, 968–70
    free speech theories, and privacy,
        939–43
    parallel analysis or 'ultimate balancing
        act', 958–59
    reasonableness test, 937
    underlying rationales of Articles, values,
        965–68
telephone tapping, 73, 1032–52
theoretical considerations, 804–7
unauthorised use of information, detriment
    arising from, 920
waiver in confidence cases, 918–20
Processions, advance notice of, 702–4
Pro-Life Alliance decision, and broadcasting
    regulation, 268, 276, 280, 530–45
Proportionality, 265–91, 964
    activism, and, 285, 287, 289
    anti-discrimination legislation, and, 1459
    anti-terrorism measures, and, 1436
    arrest, promptly informing of reason for, 57
    civil liberties, protection of, and, 129
    contempt, and, 374
    discretionary areas of judgment, Human
        Rights Act and, 268, 269–91
    life, right to, and, 45
    margin of appreciation, and, 69, 265–66,
        271–74
    media and administration of justice, 324
        interference with legitimate aims, 326
    privacy, and, 964–68
    protests, and, 686, 688
Proscription, 1381–1406
    see also Counter-terrorism; POAC
        (Proscribed Organisations Appeal
        Commission); Terrorism; Terrorism Act
        2000; Terrorist suspects
    Articles 10 and 11, relevance of guarantees
        under, 1354–58, 1389–96, 1401
    challenges to, 1396–97
    choice of groups to proscribe, 1386–89
    commercial risks, 1396
    deproscription, 1397
    fund-raising, 1396
    margin of appreciation, and, 548

offences, proscription-related, 1389–96
    belonging to proscribed organisation,
        1389–92
    meetings, 1392–96
    symbols of allegiance to proscribed group,
        1392–96
    Terrorism Act 2000, as amended in 2006,
        and, 1383–86
    terrorist property, 1396
Protection from Harassment Act 1997 *see* PHA
    (Protection from Harassment Act) 1997
Protests *see* Freedom of protest and assembly
Public authorities
    BBC as, 530
    broadcasting regulation, 530–33
    categories, 217–18
    core and functional status, tests determining,
        219–29
    European Convention on Human Rights, and,
        binding effect of rights under, 215–16
        invoking rights against public authorities,
            235–37
    function, and SDA, 1510
    housing associations, 221
    Human Rights Act 1998
        position under, 215–49
        Section 7(1), relying on, 237–39
        Sections 3 and 6, relationship between,
            216
    'hybrid' status, 220
    private care homes, 223–27, 228
    public function tests, critiquing, 229–32
    reforms possible, 247–49
    remedies, 241–47
    retrospectivity, 239–40
    specific bodies, categorising, 233–35
    standard and functional, 216–29
    time limits, 240–41
    victims, 235–37
Public disorder and anti-social behaviour,
    criminalising
    see also Public protest and the Public Order
        Act 1986 (POA)
    harassment, 787–95
    private common law remedies, 798–99
    public nuisance, 798
    reasonableness defences, 796–97
    threats, abuse and insults, 781–87
Public good defence, obscene material, 472–74
Public interest defence in confidence, 915–20
Public interest in FoI
    see also Public interest immunity
    categories of exemptions in FoI, 637
        class, 639–47
        harm-based, 647–50
    class exemptions not subject to, 639–41

class exemptions subject to, 641–47
harm-based exemptions not subject to, 647–48
harm-based exemptions subject to, 648–49
official secrecy, and, 641–50
   definitions of 'public interest', 638
Publicity
'generic', 'threshold' or prejudicial, 345
Public nuisance, 798
Public Order Act 1986 *see* Public protest and the Public Order Act 1986 (POA)
Public order law
   see also Freedom of protest and assembly; Public protest and the Public Order Act 1986 (POA)
   development, 668–72
   nature, 672–75
Public/private divide
   see also Private life, right to respect for
   broadcasting regulation, 530–33
   Human Rights Act 1998
      private bodies, 249–50
      public authorities, 216–18
Public processions
   advance notice of, 702–4
Public protest and the Public Order Act 1986 (POA), 1340
   Human Rights Act, impact on Sections 12–14A, 720–30
      ECHR jurisprudence, 724–26
      radical approach, 726–30
   Section 11 - notification, 702–4
   Section 12 power, 704–6
      liability under, 707
   Section 14 power, 706–7
      liability under, 707
   serious offences, 799–800
Public protest under ECHR
   see also Freedom of protest and assembly; Public protest and the Public Order Act 1986
   freedom of assembly (Art 11), 681–83
   justifications for interferences with primary rights, 685–89
   protest as expression (Art 10), 684–85

Questioning of suspects *see* Police questioning

Race discrimination and the Race Relations Act 1976 (RRA), 1507–11
   see also Commision for Racial Equality; Discrimination
   Commission for Equality and Human Rights, 1595–1600
   Commission for Racial Equality, 1593–95
   common law right to non-discrimination, lack of, 1507
   contexts covered by RRA, 1508–10
   direct, 1535–36
   equal pay, 1510
   exclusions from RRA, 1569–70
   formal and substantive equality, 1489
   indirect, 1544–47
   positive action, 1575–79
   protected grounds, 1507–8
   remedies for, 1588–90
   SDA compared with, 1510–11
   success rate of applications, 1591–93
Race Relations Board, 1507
Racial discrimination, 1507–11
   direct, 1535–36
      proving, 1536
   indirect, 1544–47
   Race Relations Act 1976, 1507
      contexts covered, 1508–10
      SDA compared with, 1510–11
   racial group, meaning of, 1507–8
   segregation, 1535
Racial hatred, incitement to, 497–500
   see also Religious hatred
   domestic provisions, 497–500
   Human Rights Act, impact on, 500–501
Rape, within marriage, 67
Rawls, John
   nature of rights, and, 5, 6, 7, 8, 12
Reasonableness
   see also Reasonable suspicion; *Wednesbury* reasonableness
   detention on remand, and, 57
   public disorder and anti-social behaviour, criminalising, 796–97
Reasonable suspicion
   see also Detention; Stop and search
   arrest, powers of *see* Arrest: reasonable suspicion
   detention following arrest, 54
   stop and search with, 1114–17
   stop and search without, 1117–21
   telephone tapping, and, 73
   terrorism, and, 54, 1121–22
Refugees *see* Asylum *seekers*
Regulation of Investigatory Powers Act 2000 *see* RIPA (Regulation of Investigatory Powers Act) 2000
Religion
   see also Blasphemy
   discrimination, 507
   freedom of thought, conscience and religion (Art 9), 91
   margin of appreciation, and, 38
   religous organisations, protecting, 211–12

Religious hatred
  see also Racial hatred, incitement to
  incitement to, 501–9
Remand, continued detention on, 57–58, 59
Remedies
  see also Compensation; Effective remedies,
      right to; Exhaustion of local remedies
  damages and accounts of profit in "privacy"
      cases, 982–83
  domestic, exhaustion of, 30–31
  Human Rights Act, under, 241–47
  interim injunctions, 983–90
  private common law, 798–99
  public authorities, against, 241–47
  right to, before national authority, 106–8
  Single Tribunal under RIPA, and, 1084–85
  tortious *see* Tortious remedies
Reporting restrictions, 390, 851–66
  see also Contempt; Injunctions
  anonymity preservation, 391, 393
  children and young persons
      ECHR jurisdiction, 855–65
      juveniles, in criminal proceedings, 854–55
      private hearings, 853
  Human Rights Act, impact on, 865–66
  postponing reporting to avoid risk of
      prejudice, 384–89
  prior restraints, and contempt, 383–94
  prohibiting reporting of information, 390–94
  sexual offences, victims, 393, 851–52
  trial-related (adults), 852
Reputation principle
  police malpractice, and, 1264
Restitutio in integrum principle
  European Court of Human Rights, 245
Restriction of rights and freedoms
  see also European Convention on Human
      Rights
  aliens, political activities, 111–12
  freedom of expression
      blasphemy, 487
      broadcasting, 509–50
      content and form-based interferences,
          306–8
      market freedom and creative freedom,
          308–9
      offensive material *see* Offensive material;
          Pornography
      racial hatred, 497–501
      religious hatred, 501–9
      restriction and exceptions, 94–96
      US model, 308, 309
  general, freedom from retrospective penal
      legislation, 68–69
  margin of appreciation, and, 37–39
  public emergency, and, 110–11

reporting restrictions *see* Reporting
      restrictions
  reservation, making (Art 57), 112
  system of restrictions, under ECHR, general,
      110
Retrospectivity
  criminalisation of Nazi crimes, 11
  penal legislation, 66–69
      general restriction on rights and freedoms,
          68–69
  public authorities, and, 239–40
*Review of the Implementation of the
      Human Rights Act* (Department of
      Constitutional Affairs), 162
Rights
  see also European Convention on Human
      Rights; International Covenant on Civil
      and Political Rights
  competing, 13, 943–81
  immunities as, 15
  implied, right to fair trial, 64
  infringement of, 13, 15
  liberal conception of, opposition to, 8–10
  meaning of, 10–16
  moral and legal distinguished, 10–11
  natural, 8
  origins of, 6–10
  overriding, 12, 13
  penumbra, 13
  risk to society, and, 14
  'trump' status, 12
  US Constitution, 15
  weak, in UK, 15
Right to life *see* Life, right to
Right to silence *see* Silence, right to
Riots, 667–68, 799–800
  see also Public order
RIPA (Regulation of Investigatory Powers Act)
      2000, 1034–68
  Code of Practice on Covert Surveillance,
      1066–68
  communications, interception, 1034–41
  surveillance, 1058–68
Road traffic accidents, stop and search powers,
      1122–24
Royal Commission on Criminal Procedure,
      1103, 1205
RRA (Race Relations Act) 1976 *see* Race
      discrimination and the Race Relations
      Act 1976 (RRA)
Rule utilitarianism, 8

Samples, swabs and impressions
  detention in police custody, 1183–84
Satanic Verses, and blasphemy, 487
Satellite television, EU-based, 545–49

Scandalising the court, contempt, 394–98
Schools, physical punishment in, 74–75
Scottish Parliament, and Human Rights Act
    1998, 213
Scott Report, official secrecy, 593
SDA (Sex Discrimination Act) 1975 *see* Sex
    Discrimination Act 1975 (SDA)
Searches
    see also Stop and search
    detained persons, of, 1181–84
    entry and search powers, 995–1010
    intimate, 1181–82
    samples, swabs and impressions, 1183–84
    strip, 1182
    Terrorism Act 2000, and, 997
    voluntary, 1000–1, 1126–28
    warrants, 998–1000
Secret Intelligence Service, 1010
Security *see* Liberty and security of person,
        right to; National security; Security and
        intelligence services
Security and intelligence services, powers,
        1010–32
    agencies, framework for, 1013–14
    complaints against, 1022–24
    European Convention requirements,
        1025–30
    Human Rights Act, impact of, 1024–32
        using HRA, in practice, 1030–32
    Intelligence and Security Committee, 1011,
        1014–15
    personal files, 1020–21
    warrant procedure, 1016–19
Segregation, racial discrimination, 1535
Seizure
    Criminal Justice and Police Act 2001, power
        under, 1003–5
    excluded/special procedure material,
        1002–3
    journalistic material
        HRA implications, 445–48
        Official Secrets Act 1989, 444–45
        PACE (Police and Criminal Evidence Act)
            1984, 440–42
        Production Orders, terrorism legislation,
            442–44
    legal privilege, material covered by, 1002–3
    power of, 1001–3
    special powers, 1129
September 11 attacks
    see also Counter-terrorism; Terrorism
    freedom of protest and assembly, and, 672
    Human Rights Act 1998, and, 164
Serious and Organised Crime Agency (SOCA),
        1013
Servitude, freedom from, 50–51

Sex discrimination, 1486–1506
    child care responsibilities, 1489–91
    Convention rights, 108–9
    direct, 1527–34
    equal pay *see* Equal pay
    flexible working, 1489–91
    formal and substantive equality, 1488–89
    gender reassignment, 1534
    indirect, 1538–44
    judiciary, and, 261
    marital status, 1534
    maternity/child care grounds, 1529–34
    part-time workers, 1490
    pregnancy and parental rights, 1491–93
    Sex Discrimination Act 1975
        see also Sex discrimination
        contexts, 1505–6
        protected grounds, 1504–5
    White Paper 1974, 1487
    Work and Families Act 2006, 1492
    work/life balance, 1543–44
Sex Discrimination Act 1975 (SDA)
    contexts, 1505–6
    exclusions from, 1567–69
    protected grounds, 1504–5
    RRA compared with, 1510–11
    sexual orientation, 1515–18
Sexual autonomy
    private life, right to respect for, 80–85
Sexual identity
    private life, right to respect for, 85–87
Sexual offences, victims, 393, 839, 851–52
    see also Rape, within marriage
Sexual orientation, 1569–70
    discrimination on grounds of, 1513–26
        direct discrimination, 1537–38
        education, 1523–24
        employment, 1521–23
        EU provisions, 1515
        housing provision, 190, 1524–26
        Human Rights Act 1998, and, 1518–21
        Sex Discrimination Act 1975, 1515–18
    Employment Equality (Sexual Orientation)
        Regulations 2003, 1522–23
        exceptions to, 1570–72
    equality on grounds of, 1472–73
    homosexuals, 81–82
        age of consent, 82, 1472
        AIDS/HIV, fear of, 83, 84
        concealing of sexual orientation, 1523
        interference with private life, 81–82
        Rent Act, and, 188
        sado-masochism, and, 83
    nature of rights, and, 7–8
Shayler litigation
    official secrecy, 597, 606–16

SIAC (Special Immigration Appeals
    Commission) *see* Special Immigration
    Appeals Commission
Silence
    adverse inferences drawn from, 1211–15
        restriction on drawing, 1239–43
    penalising, 1249–54
    relying on legal advice in remaining silent,
        1243–54
    right to, 1234–54
        curtailment of right, 1235–39
Slavery
    abolition, 1472
    freedom from, 50–51
Smith, John, 145
SOCA (Serious and Organised Crime Agency),
    1013
Social Charter 1961, 19
Social contract, hypothetical vs actual, 7
Society, risk to
    strength of rights, and, 14
Soham murders 2002, 344
Solicitors
    see also Access to legal advice
    debarring representatives, 1223–25
    unavailability or delay, 1221
Sovereignty of Parliament, 186, 280
Sovereignty of Parliament and Human Rights
    Act, 171, 186, 280
Special Advocates (SA) scheme, 1343, 1344
Special Immigration Appeals Commission
    anti-terrorism law, and, 1340, 1429–30
    burden of proof, 'foreign torture evidence',
        1459
    POAC, and, 1397
    role, 1429–30
    Single Tribunal, and, 1083
Speech *see* Freedom of expression
Spycatcher litigation, 369–75
    abolition of doctrine?, 379–80
    case law subsequent to, 623–24
    official secrecy, 618–24
    Punch, critique, 375–79
Statements of compatibility under HRA,
    206–11
    see also Human Rights Act 1998 (HRA)
State security *see* National security
Statutory interpretation
    arrest, powers of, and, 1149
    ECHR, domestic impact pre-HRA, and,
        136–37
    indecency, 476
        HRA and protection of morals exception,
            480–84
    obscenity, 468–72
        'deprave and corrupt' test, 470–73, 526

HRA and protection of morals exception,
    475–76
offensive material
    indecency, 476, 480–84
    obscene publications, 468–72, 475–76
    specific offences, variety of, 477–80
Stop and search, 1111–39
    see also Arrest; Searches
    breaches of rules, redress, 1130–31
    counter-terrorism, 1117, 1123–24
    disciplinary action, 1139
    discriminatory use of powers, 1124–26
    drugs, searching for, 1114
    European Convention on Human Rights, and
        Article 5, 1131–34
        Article 13, 1134
    exclusion of products of search from
        evidence, 1138–39
    force, use of, 1128–29
    judicial review, 1134–37
    PACE powers, 1113–14
    ports and border controls, 1121–22
    procedural requirements, 1129–30
    reasonable suspicion, 1114–17
        of being terrorist, 1121–22
        without, 1117–21
    remedies
        tortious, 1137–38
        trial, 1139
    road traffic accident powers, 1122–24
    seizure powers, special, 1129
    special powers, 1123–24
    tortious remedies, 1137–38
    violence, anticipated
        special powers to prevent, 1122
Straw, Jack, 119, 145, 210
Strict liability
    see also Contempt
    prejudicing proceedings, and, 319–62, 381
Sub judice period, contempt, 335, 338
Suicide
    assisted, 78–79, 80
    bodily integrity, and, 76
Surveillance, 1053–80
    see also Interception of communications;
        Telephone tapping
    in accordance with law, 1071–73
    Article 8, interference with guarantees,
        1068–71
    authorisation procedure, Police Act 1997,
        1056–58
    civil actions, and, 1077–78
    closed circuit television, 1068
    Commissioners
        duties, 1075
        oversight role, 1065

confidential information, 1064–65
criminal proceedings, 1075–77
directed, 1017, 1062–63
Human Rights Act 1998, and, 1068–75
  actions under s 7(1)(a), 1079
  using, 1075–80
intrusive, 1017, 1060–62
judicial review, and, 1079–80
legitimate aims, 1073
necessity in democratic society, 1074–75
Police Act 1997, and, 1056–58
public telecommunications system,
  meaning, 1034
Regulation of Investigatory Powers Act
  2000 (Part II), 1058–68
RIPA Code of Practice on Covert
  Surveillance, 1066–68

TA (Terrorism Act) 2000 see Terrorism Act
  2000 (TA)
Telephone tapping, 1032–52
evidence, exclusion of, 1298
official secrecy, 594–95
privacy rights, 73
surveillance, 1061
Television
see also Broadcasting regulation; Films
BBC and Ofcom regime, 520–30
closed circuit, 1068
ITC Code, 524, 525, 527
public authorities, and, 233
satellite, 545–49
Television Without Frontiers Directive, 513,
  514, 517
Terrorism
see also Al-Qaeda terrorists; Counter-
  terrorism; September 11 attacks;
  Terrorist suspects
Anti-Terrorism, Crime and Security Act see
  Anti-Terrorism, Crime and Security
  Act (ATCSA) 2001
Article 3 treatment (ECHR)
  deporting suspects facing potential
    treatment abroad, 1358–61
  indefinite detention without trial,
    1362–63
  third party material, obtained by, 1346–47
Birmingham pub bombings 1974, 118
Control orders, 1438–62
see also Control orders
Convention rights, domestic interpretation,
  and, 1338–39
counter-terrorism see Counter-terrorism
court proceedings outside criminal justice
  system, and
see also Fair trials/hearings

closed material, procedure for use,
  1343–45
field of application, 1339–42
'public' hearing, 1345–46
special advocate, use, 1343–45
third party, material obtained by
  Article 3 treatment, 1346–47
definitions, 1148
extending under 2000 Act, 1374–81
directing a terrorist organisation, 1407–8
'domestic', meaning, 1379
encouraging/glorifying, 1415–21
  intent or recklessness, 1420
freedom of expression, association and
  assembly, 1354–58
human rights, and, 1335–63
  Article 3 treatment (ECHR), 1346–47,
    1358–63
  burdens of proof (reversed) and
    presumption of innocence, 1347–54
  Convention rights, interpreted
    domestically, 1338–39
  discrimination (Art 14), 1363
  fair trials, 1339–47
inciting abroad, 1415–21
'international', meaning, 1379
London bombings 2005, 344, 672, 1360,
  1416
positive obligations to report information,
  1411–15
preparatory and possession offences,
  1408–11
presumption of innocence, and burdens of
  proof (reversed)
  case law, 1347–51
  post-HRA approach, terrorism offences,
    1352–54
Prevention of Terrorism Act 2005, and
  control orders, 1438–62
Proscribed Organisation Appeal
  Commission see POAC (Proscribed
  Organisations Appeal
  Commission)
reasonable suspicion, 54, 1121–22
special offences, 1406–21
Terrorism Act 2000 (TA)
see also Terrorism; Terrorist suspects
definition of terrorism, extending, 1374–81
detention in police custody, 1167
key themes, 1368–70
legal and political background, 1364–68
pre-2000 temporary counter-terrorism
  legislation, 1365–66
previous measures, 1370–74
proscription see Proscription
search powers, 997

stop and search, without reasonable
suspicion, 1117–21
Terrorism Act 2006
additional offences introduced by, 1407,
1408, 1411
'war on' terrorism, 164
weapons of mass destruction (WMD), 409
Terrorist suspects
see also Terrorism
access to legal advice
delaying, 1218–19
disallowing private consultation, 1225
deporting, facing potential Art 3 treatment
abroad, 1358–61
police questioning, 1191–92
reasonable suspicion of being terrorist,
1121–22
Thatcherism, and civil liberties, 117, 158, 159,
160
A Theory of Justice (Rawls), 6
Threats, criminalising use of, 781–87
Time limits
detention following arrest, 1165–67
information, applying for under FoI, 650–53
enforcement, 651–53
public authorities, Convention rights against,
240–41
Tomlinson, Richard, 1012
Tortious remedies
civil actions, value, 1309–10
Human Rights Act, and tortious liability,
1306–9
police malpractice, and, 1303–10
quantum of damages, 1305–6
stop and search, 1137–38
tort actions, 1303–5
Torture
see also Inhuman or degrading treatment,
freedom from
anti-terrorism legislation, and Art 3
treatment
deporting suspects facing potential
treatment abroad, 1358–61
indefinite detention without trial, 1362–63
third party material, 1346–47
as crime under international law, 45–46
freedom from, as Convention right (Art 3),
45–50
non-derogability of right to freedom from, 12
Trade unions
freedom of association, 98–102
Transsexuals
privacy rights, 85–87
sex discrimination, 1504, 1534
Trespass
aggravated, 738–41

criminalising, 733, 737–50
Criminal Justice and Public Order Act 1994
s 69 directions, 741–43
mass, 737–38
privacy, right to respect for, 874–75
simple, 737
Trials see Fair trials/hearings
Tribunals
see also Independent and impartial tribunal
communications, interception, 1040–41
single, under RIPA, 1080–90
HRA, influence on, 1086–90
jurisdiction, 1081–82
procedure, 1083–85
recourse to courts from, 1085

Unfair dismissal, pre-2003 provision, 1521–22
United Nations Convention Against Torture
and Other Cruel, Inhuman or Degrading
Treatment or Punishment 1984, 45,
1359–60
United Nations Covenant on Civil and Political
Rights
complaints, and, 29
United Nations Declaration of Human Rights
European Convention based on, 17
United States
Constitution, 15
First Amendment, 311–12, 320, 456
freedom of expression, restrictions on, 308,
309
quasi-public forums, 749
Use of force see Force, use of
Utilitarianism
nature of rights, and, 7, 8–9
preference, 148

VAC (Video Appeals Committee), 552
Vagrants, 55
Victimisation, 1563–67
Victims, under HRA, 235–37
Video Appeals Committee (VAC), 552
Videoworks, statutory regulation of, 550–60,
562–66
Violence
see also Public order
anticipated, special powers to prevent,
1122
freedom of protest and assembly, 666,
667
group, 667
violent disorder, 799–800
Visions of Ecstasy video, and blasphemy,
490, 491
Void dire (trial within a trial)
evidence, exclusion, 1262, 1284

Vulnerable groups
    detention in police custody, 1172–74
    police questioning, 1190–91

Warrants
    arrest, powers of *see* under Arrest
    communications, interception, 1034–37
      without warrants, 1037–38
    entry without, 996–98
    procedure, 1016–19
    search, 998–1000
Wednesbury reasonableness
    activism, and, 285, 288
    Human Rights Act 1998, and, 276
    judicial review, 128–29
    limitations, 133
Welsh Assembly, and Human Rights Act, 213

Whitehouse, Mary, 454
Williams Committee on Obscenity and Film
    Censorship, 455, 570
Witnesses
    anonymity of, 391
    cross-examination, 66
Women and Work Commission, 1493
Working Time Directive/Regulations
    sex discrimination, 1489
World Administrative Radio Conference 1977,
    546
World Trade Centre attacks *see* September 11
    attacks
Writs, 335, 619

Young persons *see* Children and young
    people